# THE LAW OF CONTRACT

Fifteenth Edition

# THE LAW OF CONTRACT

Fifteenth Edition

**EDWIN PEEL, BCL, MA**
*Professor of Law*
*Clarendon Harris Fellow in Law, Keble College, Oxford*
*Barrister, One Essex Court*



SWEET & MAXWELL THOMSON REUTERS

First Edition 1962
Second Edition 1966
Third Edition 1970
Fourth Edition 1975
Fifth Edition 1979
Sixth Edition 1983
Seventh Edition 1987
Eighth Edition 1991
Ninth Edition 1995
Tenth Edition 1999
Eleventh Edition 2003
Twelfth Edition 2007
Reprinted 2010
Thirteenth Edition 2011
Fourteenth Edition 2015
Fifteenth Edition 2020

Published in 2020 by Thomson Reuters, trading as Sweet & Maxwell. Thomson Reuters is registered in England & Wales, Company No.1679046. Registered Office and address for service: 5 Canada Square, Canary Wharf, London, E14 5AQ.

For further information on our products and services, visit *www.sweetandmaxwell.co.uk*

Typeset by Letterpart Limited, Caterham on the Hill, Surrey, CR3 5XL.

Printed and bound in Great Britain by CPI Group (UK) Ltd, Croydon, CR0 4YY.

No natural forests were destroyed to make this product: only farmed timber was used and re-planted.

A CIP catalogue record of this book is available from the British Library.

Extracts from various cases are reproduced with the kind permission of the ICLR.

An extract from A. Burrows, *A Restatement of the English Law of Contract* (Oxford: Oxford Publishing Limited (Academic), 2016) is reproduced with permission of the Licensor through PLSclear.

ISBN: 978-0-414-07071-4

## Acknowledgments

Grateful acknowledgment is made to the following authors and publishers for permission to quote and reproduce material from their works:

— The Incorporated Council of Law Reporting for England and Wales (I.C.L.R.).
— An extract from A. Burrows, *A Restatement of the English Law of Contract* (Oxford: Oxford Publishing Limited (Academic), 2016) is reproduced with permission of the Licensor through PLSclear.

While every care has been taken to establish and acknowledge copyright, and contact the copyright owners, the publishers tender their apologies for any accidental infringement. They would be pleased to come to a suitable arrangement with the rightful owners in each case.

# Professor Sir Guenter Treitel

## QC, DCL, FBA

## 26 October 1928–14 June 2019

It was with great sadness that I learned of the death of my colleague and mentor while working on this latest edition. The first edition was published in 1962 and Guenter Treitel was responsible for 11 editions in total, before putting down his pen (and it was a pen) in 2003. For as long as future editions are my responsibility, this book will continue to be known simply as "*Treitel*". In a world now somewhat obsessed by brand recognition, it is clear from any conversations with fellow academics, practitioners and judges that Guenter's "brand" is highly valued, though I am fairly certain that he would have objected to such terminology. This short tribute is a purely personal recollection of my association with Guenter. For a fuller account of his remarkable life, readers are referred to his obituary in *The Times* (*https://www.thetimes.co.uk/article/professor-sir-guenter-treitel-qc-obituary-79hzl3s0p*) and to the recording of his address to the Oxford University Chabad Society in 2012 on his early life in Germany and England as a child refugee on the Kindertransport (*https://vimeo.com/48474737*). The latter is a compelling piece of oral history and perfectly captures my urbane, modest and gentle former colleague.

Apart from sitting in his lectures as an undergraduate, my association with Guenter began when he invited me to All Souls and asked me to consider whether I would succeed him as the author of the book for which he was most well-known. I have Guenter's long-time friend and colleague Francis Reynolds to thank for the suggestion that I might be suited to the task. I take this opportunity to record my inestimable thanks to him for this and for his role as another of my mentors over many years. The answer was obvious, but was confirmed over lunch at Guenter's house with him and his wife Phyllis. This will live long in the memory for the sight of this giant of the legal academic world on his hands and knees entertaining my very small children. Since that occasion, we would meet, usually over lunch at All Souls or Keble and sometimes followed by a stroll through the grounds of his beloved Magdalen, invariably to discuss the merits or demerits of some recent leading case, but also, from time to time, the merits (only merits) of Jane Austen's novels. I never had the courage to admit that I had not quite found the time to read them all. What marked out any conversation with Guenter was his careful and precise use of language and I very much hope that this is still as evident in this edition of his book, as it is in the editions for which he was responsible.

There are two anecdotes which, to me, capture the way Guenter was so expert at ensuring the precision to which I have just referred, while at the same time balancing it with kindness, civility and good humour. When he handed over this book, he made clear that it was now mine to do with as I saw fit, but that he was happy to be consulted, if I would find it helpful. On submitting the manuscript for the first edition under my hand, I sent Guenter a draft of the preface in which I explained the changes I had made which were not simply the result of further development of the law. I still have a copy of the letter in reply in his customarily neat handwriting, in the first paragraph of which he wrote that he detected an apologetic tone in my covering letter, but assured me that this was unnecessary because changes were important to keep the book "alive". The second, rather longer, paragraph begins: "That said…".

The second anecdote also stems from the same edition. I was horrified to discover a rather prominent typographical error on the title page which was also repeated in the heading to the preface and informed Guenter with some trepidation. He replied immediately by telephone (itself an unusual event) and told me not to concern myself, but to take a copy of the fourth edition off my shelf and look at the title page. It needed Guenter to point out to me that he was described as "All Souls Reader in English". Given his love of Jane Austen's novels, I suspect he may not have been too disappointed with that. At our next meeting, he asked if I had also noticed that there was a five year interval between the third and fourth editions, whereas four years had been customary. He explained that, on receiving the proofs for the fourth edition, he discovered that the text had been sabotaged (apparently by a disgruntled employee of the printer) by converting any appearance of the word "lawful" to "unlawful", "legal" to "illegal", and vice versa; and by inserting or removing the word "not". Some delay was therefore inevitable while Guenter worked on detecting and making the necessary changes. Without wishing to alarm current readers, he told me, with an evident twinkle in his eye, that he thought he might have found them all by the time he handed over the book to me.

Oxford<br>1 October 2019

## Preface to the Fifteenth Edition

In the preface to the 14th edition of this book, it was noted that the courts had been relatively quiet and the more significant developments had been the result of legislation. In the four and a half years since then, it is quite the reverse. Indeed, such has been the extent of the development of the law of contract in the courts that the need to account for it has delayed the publication of this edition until a little later than originally planned. An attempt has been made to state the law as at 30 September 2019.

If one starts nonetheless with legislation, the principal development is that legislation which was referred to in the last edition, but which had not yet come into force, has now done so: the Insurance Act 2015 and the Consumer Rights Act 2015 (the "CRA"). The relevant provisions of the Insurance Act are dealt with primarily in Ch.9. The CRA has a much wider application. It was dealt with in the last edition in a separate chapter on the basis that it remained necessary in the rest of the book to give an account of what was still the current law at the time of publication. Any reader who would like an account of the effect of the CRA as a whole on the law of contract is referred to that separate chapter. While contracts may still come before the courts which were entered into before the CRA came into force (1 October 2015), in this edition each of the chapters affected by it (principally Chs 7, 18, 20 and 21) attempts to state the law as affected by the CRA and no separate chapter is included. So far as any secondary legislation is concerned, a note may be made of the Business Contract Terms (Assignment of Receivables) Regulations 2018 which are dealt with in Ch.15. The potential effect of the UK's possible withdrawal from the EU is dealt with only briefly in Ch.1; in part because it may not happen, but also because the effect on the substantive law of contract as applied in the courts of England and Wales will be very limited.

When one turns to the courts, there has been significant development at the highest level. At a time when it is more often pre-occupied with aspects of public law, it is doubtful whether the Supreme Court (and the House of Lords before it) has, in the period between editions of this book, decided quite as many cases with a bearing on the law of contract as it has done on this occasion. In chapter order, the more significant decisions which have resulted in substantial reorganisation or rewriting are noted herein.

The decision of the Court in *Rock Advertising Ltd v MWB Business Exchange Centres Ltd* might be seen as something of a missed opportunity. One of the grounds for appeal raised the question of whether part payment of a pre-existing debt can suffice as consideration in support of a binding variation of the contract under which it is due. The Court acknowledged that the decision of the House of Lords in *Foakes v Beer* that it cannot, even where it confers a "practical benefit", is "probably ripe" for re-examination. However, it was unnecessary to decide the point (which merited consideration before an enlarged panel) because the appeal had already been disposed of by a rather dogmatic decision that a contract which contains a clause requiring certain formalities to be observed for its variation cannot, in any circumstances, be varied without complying with the formalities laid down. The proposition that any injustice to which this may give rise is better dealt with by the doctrine of estoppel seems very likely to be tested in subsequent cases. This development is considered in Ch.4.

In *Arnold v Britton* and *Wood v Capita Insurance Services Ltd* the Court has, according to Lord Sumption, "sounded the retreat" from the approach to interpretation advocated by Lord Hoffmann in cases like *Investors Compensation Scheme v West Bromwich Building Society* and *Chartbrook Ltd v Persimmon Homes Ltd*, but in Ch.6, where these decisions are considered, a preference is expressed for Lord Justice Beatson's description of an "adjustment of emphasis". A similar "retreat" is evident in the decision in *Marks & Spencer Plc v BNP Paribas Securities Services Trust Co (Jersey) Ltd* on the tests for implying a term "in fact", also considered in Ch.6.

Perhaps the most significant decision of the Court in the period since the last edition is *Patel v Mirza* in which the majority of a nine member panel held that the "reliance rule", as laid down by the House of Lords in *Tinsley v Milligan* to determine the effect of illegality on a claim of civil liability, should no longer be followed. Instead, the majority preferred a test which asks whether to enforce the claim "would be harmful to the integrity of the legal system", a question which is answered by taking into account a "range of factors": the underlying purpose of the prohibition which has been transgressed and whether that purpose will be enhanced by denial of the claim; any other relevant public policy on which the denial of the claim may have an impact; and whether denial of the claim would be a proportionate response to the illegality, bearing in mind that punishment is a matter for the criminal courts. This has elements of the approach which was advocated in earlier editions of this book and is welcomed, notwithstanding the forceful criticism of the minority that it amounts to the introduction of an unwarranted and uncertain exercise in judicial discretion. The decision is reflected in a substantially rewritten section of Ch.11 on the effects of illegality. In the same chapter, an account is given of the decision in *Tillman v Egon Zehnder Ltd* on the circumstances in which a restrictive covenant may be severed to avoid a finding that it is in restraint of trade, where the Court found it necessary to overrule the decision of the Court of Appeal in *Attwood v Lamont*.

In conjoined appeals in *Cavendish Square Holding BV v El Makdessi* and *ParkingEye Ltd v Beavis* a submission that the rule against penalties should be abolished was rejected but, acknowledging the anomalous nature of the rule, the Court advocated a broader approach, and one which it seems is intended to make it less likely (it was never common) for a clause to be unenforceable as a penalty, particularly in a commercial contract. This development is reflected in Ch.20 on Damages which also takes account of a triumvirate of decisions on "mitigation in fact" (*Lowick Rose v Swynson Ltd, Tiuta International Ltd v De Villiers Surveyors*

*Ltd* and *The New Flamenco*), as well as the latest application of the *SAAMCO* principle in *BPE v Hughes-Holland*, and the relevance of post-breach events in *Bunge SA v Nidera BV*. The decision in *Lowick Rose v Swynson Ltd* is also significant for the observations of the Court on the recovery of damages for third party loss (Ch.14). The most significant decision on damages may be that reached by the Court in *Morris-Garner v One Step (Support) Ltd* on the availability of "negotiating damages".

Other decisions of the Supreme Court which may be more briefly noted are: *Wells v Devani* (certainty and implied terms (Ch.2)); *BNY Mellon Corporate Trustee Services Ltd v LBG Capital No.1 Plc* (interpretation (Ch.6)); *Hayward v Zurich Insurance Co Plc* (the test of inducement for fraudulent misrepresentation (Ch.9)); *Bailey v Angove's Pty Ltd* (irrevocable agency (Ch.16)); and *The Res Cogitans* (obiter comments on the availability of the action for the price in contracts for the sale of goods and the effect of the Sale of Goods Act 1979 s.49(1) (Ch.21)).

In the Court of Appeal, the most important development is probably the decision of the Court in *FSHC Group Holdings Ltd v Glas Trust Corp Ltd* on the requirements of rectification for "common mistake". Lord Hoffmann's obiter dictum in *Chartbrook Ltd v Persimmon Homes Ltd* in favour of an objective interpretation of the parties "common intention" prior to execution of the written contract is no longer to be followed. Instead, the written contract will only be rectified if it departs from the subjective common intention of the parties (save where the prior common intention is already a binding contract). This is a difficult area, not least because it raises fundamental questions about the extent to which an objective, or a subjective, approach should be taken to the formation of the parties' agreement, but the decision in *FSHC* is likely to be welcomed by the majority of the large number of commentators and judges (writing extra-judicially) who had commented on this area since the decision in *Chartbrook*. It is considered in Ch.8. Other significant decisions of the Court of Appeal to highlight are: *Transocean Drilling UK Ltd v Providence Resources Plc* and *Nobahar-Cookson v The Hut Group Ltd* (*contra proferentem* (Ch.7)); *Goodlife Foods Ltd v Hall Fire Protection Ltd* (incorporation and the test of reasonableness under the Unfair Contract Terms Act 1977 (Ch.7)); *First Tower Trustees Ltd v CDS (Superstores International) Ltd* ("no representation" and "non-reliance" clauses (Ch.9)); *Salt v Stratstone Specialist Ltd* (damages in lieu of rescission for misrepresentation (Ch.9)); *BV Nederlandse Industrie Van Eiprodukten v Rembrandt Enterprises* (fraudulent misrepresentation (Ch.9) and damages for third party loss (Ch.14)); *MSC Mediterranean Shipping Co SA v Cottonex Anstalt* ("automatic" termination for repudiatory breach (Ch.18)); *Classic Maritime Inc v Limbungan Makmur SDN BHD* (*force majeure* (Ch.19)); *Wellesley Partners LLP v Withers LLP* (remoteness in cases of "concurrent liability" for breach of contract and tort (Ch.20)); and *Triple Point Technology Inc v PTT Public Co Ltd* (liquidated damages (Ch.20)).

In the High Court, a number of decisions have grappled with a burgeoning law of "good faith". In particular, whether a term requiring performance in "good faith" is implied "in law" or "in fact" (e.g. *Sheikh Tahnoon Bin Saeed Bin Shakhboot Al Nehayan v Kent, Bates v Post Office* and *UTB LLC v Sheffield*

*United Ltd* (Ch.6)), and whether the exercise of contractual discretion engages the so-called "*Braganza* duty" (e.g. *Watson v Watchfinder.Co.UK Ltd, Shurbanova v Forex Capital Markets Ltd* and *Faieta v ICAP Management Services Ltd* (Ch.6)). The decision in *Canary Wharf (BP4) T1 Ltd v European Medicines Agency* provides a comparatively rare opportunity to revisit a plea of frustration of purpose (as well as frustration for supervening illegality), on this occasion in the context of the UK's potential withdrawal from the EU (Ch.19), while *Phones 4U Ltd v EE Ltd* addresses the inter-relationship between different rights of termination and the recovery of damages for "loss of bargain" (Ch.18). Finally, *Blue v Ashley* provides an entertaining illustration of the principle that an intention to create legal relations must be assessed objectively and in context; in a pub to be precise (Ch.2).

I welcome the opportunity to place on record my thanks to the Warden and Fellows of Keble College for a period of leave to assist in the writing of this edition and the Oxford Law Faculty for providing the support and infrastructure which helped to make it possible, not least the provision of the IT services which are now so indispensable. My thanks also to Maria Zhang who spent a week of work experience with me as a research assistant, sourcing statutory material. I have continued to benefit from discussions about the development of the law with a number of colleagues; in particular, Adrian Briggs, Andrew Dickinson, Andrew Burrows, James Goudkamp, Donal Nolan, Kelry Loi, Laurence Rabinowitz, Ian Glick, Steven Elliott, Andrew Summers, Paul Davies, Adam Kramer, William Day and Carmine Conte. The Senior Publishing Editor, Nicola Thurlow, has seen through the work on this edition, as she has done on all four editions for which I have been responsible and was kind enough to extend the deadline for submission of the text to the maximum extent possible. This was further assisted by Lesley Davis who dealt patiently with my queries and amendments at the proofs stage.

My greatest thanks, as ever, go to my wife Helen and our children Emily and Charlotte, for their unending patience, love and support. Emily and Charlotte were born around the time I first started my association with this book and now they are fast approaching adulthood: "*Tempus fugit*", as my late mother was fond of saying and to whom this edition is dedicated.

Edwin Peel

Oxford, 1 October 2019

The cover image is a painting of the coronation of Edward VII. The cancellation of the original ceremony because of the King's illness led to several cases on mistake or frustration of purpose which are considered in Chs 8 and 19.

# TABLE OF CONTENTS

## 5. FORM



## 6. THE CONTENTS OF A CONTRACT



## 7. EXEMPTION CLAUSES AND UNFAIR TERMS

## 15. ASSIGNMENT

## 22. RESTITUTION

# TABLE OF CASES

# TABLE OF STATUTES

# TABLE OF STATUTORY INSTRUMENTS

# TABLE OF EUROPEAN LEGISLATION

CHAPTER 1

# INTRODUCTION

**Contract as enforceable agreement.** A contract is an agreement giving rise to obligations which are enforced or recognised by law. The factor which distinguishes contractual from other legal obligations is that they are based on the agreement of the contracting parties. This proposition remains generally true, even though it is subject to a number of important qualifications. 1–001

**The objective principle.**[1] The first such qualification is that the law is often concerned with the objective appearance, rather than with the actual fact, of agreement: a person is bound "whatever [his] real intention may be", if "a reasonable man would believe that he was assenting to the terms proposed by the other party and that other party upon that belief enters into a contract with him".[2] This objective principle is based on the needs of commercial convenience. Considerable uncertainty would result if A, after inducing B reasonably to believe that he (A) had agreed to certain terms, could then escape liability merely by showing that he had no "real intention" to enter into that agreement. The principle is an important one; but it would be wrong to say that the law of contract has no concern at all with actual agreement. This would put too much emphasis on the exceptional situation; for in most cases, the appearance corresponds with the fact of agreement. And the principle is not purely objective: A is not bound merely because "a reasonable man would believe that he was assenting to the terms proposed by the other party". In particular, there will be no contract if (in spite of the objective appearance of agreement) B *actually knows* that A in fact has *no* intention to contract with him, or to contract on the terms alleged.[3] 1–002

A subjective element thus qualifies the objective principle; and this follows from the purpose of that principle, which is to protect B from the prejudice which he might suffer as a result of relying on a false appearance of agreement. There is clearly no need in this way to protect a party who knows that the objective appearance does not correspond with reality. It also follows from the purpose of the objective principle that it will not apply where A's apparent assent is based on a mistake induced by B's negligence.[4] More generally, it may be said that the objective principle applies only where serious inconvenience would be caused by allowing a party to rely on his "real intention". In the interests of convenience the

---

[1] Friedmann 119 L.Q.R. 68.

[2] *Smith v Hughes* (1871) L.R. 6 Q.B. 597 at 607; see para.8–047; Howarth 100 L.Q.R. 265; Vorster 103 L.Q.R. 274; Howarth 103 L.Q.R. 527.

[3] e.g. paras 2–002–2–003, 8–054. Whether, in such a case, there is a contract on the terms which A intends is more difficult: see below, para.8–092.

[4] e.g. para 8–056; cf. *Norwich Union Fire Insurance Society Ltd v Price* [1934] A.C. 455 at 463.

law may sometimes hold that there is a contract although there was not even the objective appearance of an agreement.[5] It does not follow that the law is not concerned with any sort of agreement at all: to allege that this was the position "would introduce into the law of contract a novel heresy".[6]

1–003 **Standards of behaviour imposed on the parties.** The idea that contractual obligations are based on agreement must, secondly, be qualified because contracting parties are normally expected to observe certain standards of behaviour. These are the result of terms implied by law[7] into certain types of contract, for example, into contracts for the sale of goods or of employment. The parties may be able to vary or exclude some such terms by contrary agreement; but unless they do so they are bound by many duties to which they have not expressly agreed and of which they may have never thought. Agreement is not the *sole* factor which determines the legal effects of a contract once it is shown to exist. But it remains an important factor. For example, the intention of the parties (objectively ascertained) determines whether a statement made at the time of contracting has contractual force or is a mere representation[8]; and it determines whether a term which is not expressly stated in the contract should be implied in fact, i.e. because the parties must have intended to incorporate it.[9]

It has been suggested that in such cases the courts only *say* that the intention of the parties is the determining factor, but really apply rules based on various considerations of policy unconnected with that intention.[10] Such an argument can, perhaps, be based on the history of the doctrine of frustration, under which contracting parties may be discharged from liability by supervening events,[11] e.g. where such events make performance impossible. The doctrine was at one time justified by saying that the parties had impliedly agreed to be discharged in such circumstances; but many lawyers now prefer to say that the parties are discharged by operation of law, whether they would have agreed to discharge or not. This may be true; but the intention of the parties cannot for that reason be wholly disregarded. Before holding that parties are discharged, the court must find out what they contracted about: they may have deliberately taken the risk of supervening impossibility. The court must decide whether the parties contracted about a certainty or about a possibility; and it does so by ascertaining, as best it can, their intentions in the matter.

1–004 **A standard of good faith?** A more recent controversy is the extent to which the parties, in the *performance* of the contract, are required to adhere to a standard of "good faith".[12] No such general standard is imposed by law in contracts

---

[5] See para.2–056.
[6] *The Hannah Blumenthal* [1983] 1 A.C. 854 at 916–917.
[7] See para.6–067 and following.
[8] See para.9–056.
[9] See para.6–051.
[10] See, e.g. Atiyah, *An Introduction to the Law of Contract*, 5th edn (Oxford University Press, 1995), pp.20–21.
[11] See Ch.19.
[12] An agreement to negotiate in good faith, without more, remains unenforceable: para.2–100.

generally,[13] though many of the interventions of law referred to below may be said to have an underpinning of "good faith". It has, however, been said that there is "no difficulty, in implying such a duty in any ordinary commercial contract based on the presumed intention of the parties."[14] Since the methodology is that of implying a term in fact,[15] this development is considered in more detail in a later chapter.[16] It may only be noted here that, even if such a term is implied, it begs the question of what is meant by "good faith". It must be an ordinary incident of any contract (i.e. a term implied by law) that the parties will perform their obligations honestly but it has been said that "good faith" may extend "beyond" honesty and require that the parties will perform in a way which is "commercially acceptable".[17] This of course rather begs the question, in turn, of what is meant by "commercially acceptable". It is ultimately a process of construction of the contract which is therefore "sensitive to context",[18] but a key feature of the "context" is the adherence of English law to the principle of freedom of contract and the normal requirement that the parties, if they wish to protect their interests, should do so expressly.[19]

**The scope of freedom of contract.** The idea that contractual obligations are based on agreement must, thirdly, be qualified in relation to the scope of the principle of freedom of contract.[20] In the nineteenth century, judges took the view that persons of full capacity should in general be allowed to make what contracts they liked: the law only interfered on fairly specific grounds such as misrepresentation, undue influence or illegality.[21] It did not interfere merely because one party was economically more powerful than the other and so able to drive a hard bargain. This attitude became particularly important when the courts recognised the validity of standard form contracts[22] drawn up by one party on terms designed to protect its interests at the expense of those of the other. This practice of contracting on standard terms is now very common; and it is arguable that a customer who contracts on such standard terms has them imposed on him, and does not really "agree" to them at all. This argument is particularly strong where standard terms are used by a monopoly supplier, or where all suppliers in a particular field use the same standard terms. The customer's only choice may then be one of accepting those terms or doing without the goods or services in question; and often he cannot in practice do without. On the other hand, exact 1–005

[13] *Yam Seng Pte Ltd v International Trade Corp Ltd* [2013] EWHC 111 (QB); [2013] 1 Lloyd's Rep. 526 at [131]. It has long been recognised that a duty of good faith is implied by law as an incident of certain categories of contract, e.g. employment contracts (see para.6–067).

[14] *Yam Seng Pte Ltd v International Trade Corp Ltd* [2013] EWHC 111 (QB); [2013] 1 Lloyd's Rep. 526 at [131].

[15] Though there is some doubt about this: see para.6–076.

[16] See para.6–051.

[17] *Yam Seng Pte Ltd v International Trade Corp Ltd* [2013] EWHC 111 (QB); [2013] 1 Lloyd's Rep. 526 at [138].

[18] *Mid Essex Hospital Services NHS Trust v Compass Group UK and Ireland Ltd* [2013] EWCA Civ 200; [2013] B.L.R. 265 at [150] (Beatson LJ).

[19] *Mid Essex Hospital Services NHS Trust v Compass Group UK and Ireland Ltd* [2013] EWCA Civ 200; [2013] B.L.R. 265 at [105] (Jackson LJ).

[20] For an historical account, see Atiyah, *The Rise and Fall of Freedom of Contract* (1995).

[21] See Chs 9–11.

[22] See Ch.7.

equality of bargaining power is probably rare; and there can be much dispute as to the precise degree of pressure which makes the difference between consent reluctantly given and a state of mind which cannot properly be described as consent at all. The amount of pressure which can be brought to bear on the customer does not depend solely on the respective wealth and power of the parties, but also on market conditions. In a buyer's market, an insistent private customer may be able to induce a normally powerful supplier to modify his standard terms, rather than lose a sale; while in a seller's market a customer may be ready to agree to any terms which the seller puts forward, or be willing to take his chance on the contents of any document put forward by the seller. A person may also agree to contract on a set of terms although he does not know in detail what they provide, e.g. where parties contract on terms settled by a trade association, or where a person takes employment on terms negotiated between employers and a trade union.[23] In such cases the parties would not deny that they *had* agreed to the terms, whatever they might be.

1–006 **Legislative interventions.** Important inroads on the principle of freedom of contract have been made by legislation passed to redress some real or supposed imbalance of bargaining power. For example, the contents of many contracts of employment are now regulated in some detail by legislation. Under other statutes, terms are compulsorily implied into contracts and cannot be excluded by contrary agreement;[24] and legislation has further entrenched many of the rights and remedies conferred on "consumers" when contracting with "traders".[25] In all these cases the main relationship between the parties is still based on agreement, but many of the obligations arising out of it are imposed or regulated by law.

1–007 **Doubtful cases.** There are cases in which the law plays so large, and the agreement of parties so small, a part that it becomes doubtful whether the relationship can still be called contractual. The agreement of the parties may create a status, such as marriage, the main legal incidents of which are fixed by law and cannot be varied by the parties at all.[26] Sometimes, the terms on which a person is employed (especially in the public service) are governed in part by legislation; and in one such case it was said that a claim under the "statutory scheme of employment"[27] could not "be dealt with as though it were an ordinary master and servant claim in which the rights of the parties were regulated solely by contract".[28]

1–008 **Freedom not to contract.** In the cases so far considered the parties are free to decide whether or not to enter into the relationship (though the law may fix some or all of its incidents); but there are other cases in which the law to some extent restricts even this freedom. A person may be forbidden to refuse to contract by

---

[23] See para.6–007.
[24] e.g. Equality Act 2010 ss.66, 144; cf. National Minimum Wage Act 1998 s.49.
[25] See Ch.7.
[26] The parties "contract into the package which the law of the land lays down": *Radmacher v Granatino* [2010] UKSC 42; [2011] 1 A.C. 534 at [132].
[27] *Barber v Manchester Regional Hospital Board* [1958] 1 W.L.R. 181 at 196.
[28] *Barber v Manchester Regional Hospital Board* [1958] 1 W.L.R. 181.

legislation aimed to prevent discrimination on grounds of age, disability, gender reassignment, marriage and civil partnership, pregnancy and maternity, race, religion or belief, sex or sexual orientation.[29] It is also unlawful to refuse a person employment "because he is, or is not, a member of a trade union".[30] In these cases a relationship which results from some degree of legal compulsion may nevertheless be regarded as contractual, because the parties still have considerable freedom to regulate its incidents. But there are other cases in which a relationship created by legal compulsion is clearly not contractual. A person whose property is compulsorily acquired against his will does not make a contract with the acquiring authority even though he receives compensation;[31] a patient who is treated in a hospital under the National Health Service is not considered to make a contract with the hospital authority;[32] nor does one to whom medicines are supplied under the Service make a contract to buy them, even if he pays a prescription charge.[33]

**Two key questions: agreement and enforceability.** In spite of the above qualifications, it remains broadly true that the law of contract is concerned with the circumstances in which agreements are legally binding. Thus it deals mainly with the two questions of agreement and legal effects or enforceability. The rules relating to offer and acceptance,[34] for instance, deal with the process of reaching agreement. Those relating to consideration and contractual intention[35] concern the requirements which must normally be satisfied before an agreement will be legally enforced; while the rules relating to misrepresentation, duress, undue influence and illegality[36] deal with the effect of special factors on account of which the law may refuse to enforce agreements which would, apart from such factors, be binding. The rules which limit the contractual capacity of certain individuals[37] are based partly on the view that certain classes of persons cannot form the requisite contractual intention, and partly on the view that it is undesirable to enforce agreements against them. The rules relating to mistake are based partly on the view that there is no agreement when the parties are at cross-purposes on a fundamental point,[38] and partly on the view that an agreement has no legal effect if both parties were under a fundamental mistake as 1–009

[29] See, generally, the Equality Act 2010.

[30] Trade Union and Labour Relations (Consolidation) Act 1992 s.137(1)(a); cf. Trade Union and Labour Relations (Consolidation) Act 1992 s.138(1)(a); under s.140 the remedy (in the last resort) is by way of compensation; cf. Human Rights Act 1998 s.1 and Sch.1 Pt I art.11.

[31] See *Sovmots Investments Ltd v S of S for the Environment* [1977] Q.B. 411 at 443; affirmed [1979] A.C. 144 without reference to this point. If a price is agreed after notice to treat, there is said to be a "statutory contract": *Munton v GLC* [1976] 1 W.L.R. 649. Even where this is not the case, the transaction may be regarded as a contract for the purpose of a particular statute: *Ridge Nominees v IRC* [1962] Ch. 376.

[32] *Allen v Bloomsbury Health Authority* [1993] 1 All E.R. 651.

[33] See *Pfizer Corp v Ministry of Health* [1965] A.C. 512; *Appleby v Sleep* [1968] 1 W.L.R. 948; *Re Medicaments Reference* [1970] 1 W.L.R. 1339.

[34] See Ch.2.

[35] See Chs 3, 4.

[36] See Chs 9–11.

[37] See Ch.12.

[38] See Ch.8, para.8–034 and following.

to the subject-matter.[39] The rules relating to the contents of a contract, performance, breach and frustration[40] are again partly based on the agreement between the parties, and partly on rules of law which determine the precise legal effect of that agreement.

1–010 **Other topics.** If the bulk of the law of contract is concerned with the questions of agreement and legal enforceability, a number of other topics also call for discussion. Thus the rules relating to plurality, third parties, assignment and agency[41] determine who is bound by, and entitled to the benefit of, a contract. The rules relating to remedies[42] assume the existence of an enforceable agreement, and deal with the methods of, and limits on, enforcement. These are in principle determined by law. Thus the agreement of the parties does not determine whether a contract is to be enforced specifically, or only by an award of damages; though the agreement may be relevant in determining the precise amount of damages which will be awarded for a breach of contract.

1–011 **Remedies: protection of the "expectation" or "performance" interest.** Remedies for breach of contract are discussed in Chs 20 and 21; but one fundamental point relating to them must be made at this stage. Such remedies might attempt to do one of two things. First, they might attempt to put the injured party into the position in which he would have been if the contract *had never been made*. This would require the party in breach to restore anything that he had received under the contract, and also to compensate the injured party for any loss that he had suffered by acting in reliance on the contract. Such remedies are said to protect the injured party's *restitution* and *reliance* interests.[43] But remedies for breach of contract go beyond the pursuit of these objectives. Their distinguishing feature is that they seek to put the injured party into the position in which he would have been if the contract *had been performed.*[44] If, for example, a seller agrees to sell goods for less than they are worth, and then fails to deliver them, he must compensate the buyer for not having received goods which are worth more than he had agreed to pay for them. Conversely, if a buyer contracts to buy goods for more than they are worth, and then fails to pay for them, he is liable for the agreed price[45]: it is quite immaterial that the value of the goods with which the seller has parted was lower than that price. What the law does in these cases is to protect the injured party's "expectation" or "performance" interest.[46] Sometimes it does so directly, by actually ordering the party in breach to perform his part of the contract.[47] Sometimes it does so indirectly by ordering him to pay the injured party damages for loss of his bargain.

[39] See Ch.8, para.8–002 and following.
[40] See Chs 6, 17, 18, 19.
[41] See Chs 13–16.
[42] See Chs 20–21.
[43] See para.20–029 and following.
[44] See para.20–024 and following.
[45] Assuming that the conditions stated at paras 21–005–21–015 are satisfied.
[46] See para.20–024 and following.
[47] See para.21–018 and following.

The result of awarding damages on this basis is to compensate the injured party, not because he is worse off than he was before the contract was made, but because the other party has failed to make him better off.[48] The law of contract takes this position in response to the needs of commercial certainty. The protection of the expectation interest promotes stability and furthers one of the central purposes of the law of contract in providing the legal framework required for commercial relations.

**Relationship with EU law.** The account which is given in this book is an account of the English law of contract, but the content of that law is, in some respects, EU law, as a result of its implementation in accordance with the Treaty obligations of the UK. There have also been a number of projects aimed at developing common principles of European contract law,[49] but thus far they have resulted only in the adoption of an optional instrument.[50] **1–012**

**Brexit.** At the time of writing, it is yet to be determined if, and on what terms, the UK will leave the EU following the result of the "Brexit" referendum held on 23 June 2016 and the text of this edition is written on the basis that the UK remains a member of the EU. If Brexit goes ahead, it will have little impact on substantive English contract law. Under the European Union (Withdrawal) Act 2018, the European Communities Act 1972 will be repealed on "exit day". However, any "EU-derived domestic legislation…continues to have effect in domestic law on and after exit day",[51] and any "direct EU legislation, so far as operative immediately before exit day, forms part of domestic law on or after exit day".[52] The effect of these provisions is to preserve as purely domestic law, which may subsequently be amended as such, secondary legislation which has been enacted under the 1972 Act, such as the Regulations dealing with Commercial Agents,[53] and directly applicable EU Regulations some of which may affect contract law.[54] Any UK primary legislation which has been passed to implement the UK's obligations under EU law is also preserved.[55] By far the most important example of such legislation for contract law is the Consumer Rights Act 2015 which is referred to at various points in this book.[56] So far as the interpretation of any such instruments are concerned, any case law of the European Court of Justice before "exit day" continues to be applicable, but may be departed from by the Supreme **1–013**

---

[48] *South Australian Asset Management Corp v York Montague Ltd* [1997] A.C. 191 at 216.

[49] See, e.g. Lando and Beale, *Principles of European Contract Law Parts I and II*; Study Group on a European Civil Code; and Research Group on EC Private Law (Acquis Group), *Principles, Definitions and Model Rules of European Private Law: Draft Common Frame of Reference*; Whittaker (2007) European Review of Contract Law 381; Whittaker (2009) 125 L.Q.R. 616; Jansen & Zimmerman [2010] C.L.J. 98; Whittaker 2011/3 *European Review of Contract Law* 1.

[50] Proposal for a *Regulation on a Common European Sales Law* Com (2011) 635 final; Whittaker (2012) 75 M.L.R. 578.

[51] 2018 Act s.2(1).

[52] 2018 Act s.3(1).

[53] See para.16–014.

[54] No such Regulations are covered in this book given its concern with substantive contract law, but see, e.g. the Rome I Regulation which determines the law applicable to contractual obligations: Regulation 593/2008.

[55] 2018 Act s.2(2).

[56] Most notably, in Ch.7.

Court, applying "the same test as it would apply in deciding whether to depart from its own case law."[57] The courts "may have regard" to case law of the European Court after exit day.[58]

[57] 2018 Act s.6(5).
[58] 2018 Act s.6(2).

CHAPTER 2

# AGREEMENT



The first requisite of a contract is that the parties should have reached agreement. **2–001**
Generally speaking, an agreement is made when one party accepts an offer made

by the other. Further requirements are that the agreement must be certain and final; and special problems arise from conditional agreements.

## 1. OFFER

### (a) Offer defined

2–002 **The objective test.** An offer is an expression of willingness to contract on specified terms, made with the intention that it is to become binding as soon as it is accepted by the person to whom it is addressed.[1] Under the objective test of agreement,[2] an apparent intention to be bound may suffice, i.e. the alleged offeror (A) may be bound if his words or conduct[3] are such as to induce a reasonable person to believe that he intends to be bound, even though in fact he has no such intention.[4] For example, if A offers to sell a book to B for £10 and B accepts the offer, A cannot escape liability merely by showing that his actual intention was to offer the book to B for £20, or that he intended the offer to relate to a book different from that specified in the offer.[5]

2–003 **The offeree's state of mind.** Whether A is actually bound by an acceptance of his apparent offer depends on the state of mind of the alleged offeree (B); to this extent, the test is not purely objective.[6] With regard to B's state of mind, there are three possibilities. First, B actually believes that A intends to be bound: here the objective test is satisfied so that B can hold A to his apparent offer even though A did not, subjectively, have the requisite intention.[7] The general view is that there is no further requirement that A must also be aware of B's state of mind.[8] Secondly, B knows that, in spite of the objective appearance, A does not have the requisite intention: here A is not bound; the objective test does not apply in favour of B as he knows the truth about A's actual intention.[9] Thirdly, B has simply not

---

[1] e.g. *Storer v Manchester CC* [1974] 1 W.L.R. 1403; *Air Transworld Ltd v Bombardier Inc* [2012] EWHC 243; [2012] 1 Lloyd's Rep. 349 at [75]. Contrast *Crest Nicholson (Londinium) Ltd v Akaria Investments Ltd* [2010] EWCA Civ 1331.

[2] See para.1–002; *RTS Flexible Systems Ltd v Molkerei Alois Müller GmbH & Co KG* [2010] UKSC 14; [2010] 1 W.L.R. 753.

[3] For offers made by conduct, see para.2-004; *The Aramis* [1989] 1 Lloyd's Rep. 213 (where the objective test was not satisfied); *G Percy Trentham Ltd v Archital Luxfer Ltd* [1993] 1 Lloyd's Rep. 25 at 27.

[4] *Maple Leaf Macro Volatility Master Fund v Rouvroy* [2009] EWCA Civ 1334; [2010] 2 All E.R. (Comm) 788 at [10], [17].

[5] cf. *Centrovincial Estates Plc v Merchant Investors Assurance Co Ltd* [1983] Com. L.R. 158; *Whittaker v Campbell* [1984] Q.B. 318 at 327; *OT Africa Line Ltd v Vickers Plc* [1996] 1 Lloyd's Rep. 700 at 702.

[6] *The Hannah Blumenthal* [1983] 1 A.C. 854 at 924.

[7] *The Splendid Sun* [1981] 1 Q.B. 694; as explained in *The Hannah Blumenthal* [1983] 1 A.C. 854; *The Multibank Holsatia* [1988] 2 Lloyd's Rep. 486 at 493.

[8] The suggestion that A must be aware of B's state of mind was made by Lord Diplock in *The Hannah Blumenthal* [1983] 1 A.C. 854 at 916 but Lord Brightman's contrary view, expressed in [1983] 1 A.C. 854 at 924 has been generally preferred: see *The Multibank Holsatia* [1988] 2 Lloyd's Rep. 486 at 492.

[9] See above, para.1–002; *Ignazio Messina & Co v Polskie Linie Oceaniczne* [1995] 2 Lloyd's Rep. 566 at 571; *OT Africa Line Ltd v Vickers Plc* [1996] 1 Lloyd's Rep. 700 at 703; *Attrill v Dresdner*

formed any view about A's intention, so that B neither believes that A has the requisite intention nor knows that A does not have this intention: this situation has given rise to a conflict of judicial opinion. One view is that A is not bound: in other words, the objective test is satisfied only if A's conduct is such as to induce a reasonable person to believe that A had the requisite intention *and* if B actually held that belief.[10] The opposing view is that (in our third situation) A is bound: in other words, the objective test is satisfied if A's words or conduct would induce a reasonable person to believe that A had the requisite intention, so long as B does not actually know that A does *not* have any such intention.[11] This latter view no doubt facilitates proof of agreement, but it is hard to see why B should be protected in the situation to which it refers. Where B has no positive belief in A's (apparent) intention to be bound, he cannot be prejudiced by acting in reliance on it; and the purpose of the objective test is simply to protect B from the risk of suffering such prejudice.[12] The test embodies a principle of convenience; it is not based on any inherent superiority of objective over subjective criteria. It is therefore submitted that the objective test should not apply to our third situation since in it B's state of mind is such that there is no risk of his suffering any prejudice as a result of the objective appearance of A's intention.[13]

**An offer may be made expressly or by conduct.** An offer may be addressed either to an individual, or to a group of persons, or to the world at large; and it may be made expressly or by conduct.[14] 2–004

**Inactivity as an offer by conduct.** A number of cases raise the further question whether the "conduct" from which an offer may be inferred can take the form of inactivity. The issue in these cases was whether an agreement to submit a dispute to arbitration could be said to have been "abandoned" where, over a long period of time, neither party had taken any steps in the arbitration proceedings.[15] Such a question could also arise in the context of the alleged abandonment of some other 2–005

*Kleinwort Ltd* [2013] EWCA Civ 394; [2013] 3 All E.R. 607 at [86]; and see the authorities cited in fn.11. Whether B should be bound to the terms intended by A is more difficult: see para.8–072.

[10] *The Hannah Blumenthal* [1983] 1 A.C. 854 as interpreted in *The Leonidas D* [1985] 1 W.L.R. 925; Beatson 102 L.Q.R. 19; Atiyah 102 L.Q.R. 392; *The Agrabele* [1987] 2 Lloyd's Rep. 223, especially at 235; cf. *Cie Française d'Importation SA v Deutsche Continental Handelsgesellschaft* [1985] 2 Lloyd's Rep. 592 at 597; *Amherst v James Walker Goldsmith and Silversmith Ltd* [1983] Ch. 305.

[11] *The Golden Bear* [1987] 1 Lloyd's Rep. 330 at 341 (doubted on another point at para.2–044); this view was approved in *The Antclizo* [1987] 2 Lloyd's Rep. 130 at 143 but doubted in [1987] 2 Lloyd's Rep. 130 at 147; affirmed [1988] 1 W.L.R. 603 without reference to the point; *The Multibank Holsatia* [1988] 2 Lloyd's Rep. 486 at 492 ("at least did not conflict with [B's] subjective understanding"); *The Maritime Winner* [1989] 2 Lloyd's Rep. 506 at 515.

[12] See para.1–002.

[13] *Maple Leaf Macro Volatility Master Fund v Rouvroy* [2009] EWHC 257 (Comm); [2009] 1 Lloyd's Rep. 475 at [228]; affirmed [2009] EWCA Civ 1334; [2010] 2 All E.R. (Comm) 788 without consideration of this point, but see at [17]; cf. *Novus Aviation Ltd v Alubaf Arab International Bank BSC* [2016] EWHC 1575 (Comm); [2017] 1 B.C.L.C. 414 at [54]–[59].

[14] *Hart v Mills* (1846) 15 L.J. Ex. 200; para.2–018; cf. *Steven v Bromley & Son* [1919] 2 K.B. 722; *The Saronikos* [1986] 2 Lloyd's Rep. 277; *Glencore Energy UK Ltd v OMV Supply & Trading Ltd* [2018] EWHC 895 (Comm); [2018] 2 Lloyd's Rep. 223.

[15] The arbitrators have a statutory power to dismiss claims for want of prosecution (Arbitration Act 1996 s.41(3)), but that power may be excluded by agreement (Arbitration Act 1996 s.41(2)).

type of right or remedy.[16] The arbitration cases indicate that, when inactivity is combined with other circumstances (such as destruction of relevant files),[17] it may, on the objective test, amount to an offer of abandonment, even though those other circumstances would not, of themselves, constitute evidence from which an offer could be inferred. But when inactivity stands alone, it is unlikely[18] to have this effect, for it is equivocal and explicable on other grounds, such as inertia or forgetfulness, or the simple tactical consideration that the party alleged to have made the offer does not wish to re-activate his opponent's counter claims.[19] Consequently, it will not normally suffice to induce a reasonable person in the position of the other party to believe that an offer is being made[20]; and the mere fact that the other party nevertheless had this belief cannot suffice to turn the former party's inactivity into such an offer.[21]

### (b) Offer distinguished from invitation to treat

2–006 **A test of intention.** When parties negotiate with a view to making a contract, many preliminary communications may pass between them before a definite offer is made. One party may simply respond to a request for information (e.g. by stating the price at which he might be prepared to sell a house),[22] or he may make such a request (e.g. where he asks a prospective supplier whether he can supply goods suitable for his purpose).[23] That party is then said to make an "invitation to treat": he does not make an offer but invites the other party to do so.[24] The question whether a statement is an offer or an invitation to treat depends primarily on the intention with which it was made. It follows from the nature of an offer as described above[25] that a statement is not an offer if it in terms negatives the maker's intention to be bound on acceptance: for example, if it

16 cf. *Amherst Ltd v James Walker Goldsmith & Silversmith Ltd* [1983] Ch. 305; *Collin v Duke of Westminster* [1985] Q.B. 581; *MSC Mediterranean Shipping Co SA v BRE Metro Ltd* [1985] 2 Lloyd's Rep. 239.

17 *The Splendid Sun* [1981] Q.B. 694, as explained in *The Hannah Blumenthal* [1983] 1 A.C. 854 (though this explanation was doubted in *Cie Française d'Importation SA v Deutsche Conti Handelsgesellschaft* [1985] 2 Lloyd's Rep. 592 at 599); *Tracomin SA v Anton C Nielsen* [1984] 2 Lloyd's Rep. 195; *The Multibamk Holsatia* [1988] 2 Lloyd's Rep. 486; for the question whether such an offer can be *accepted* by inactivity, see para.2–044.

18 *Unisys International Services Ltd v Eastern Counties Newspapers Group Ltd* [1991] 1 Lloyd's Rep. 538 at 553; cf. *The Boucraa* [1994] 1 A.C. 486 at 521, describing the "abandonment" approach as "largely useless in practice".

19 *Unisys International Services Ltd v Eastern Counties Newspapers Group Ltd* [1991] 1 Lloyd's Rep. 538 at 553.

20 *The Leonidas D* [1985] 1 W.L.R. 925; *Cie Française d'Importation etc. SA v Deutsche Conti Handelsgesellschaft* [1985] 2 Lloyd's Rep. 592; *The Antclizo* [1988] 1 W.L.R. 603; contra, *The Golden Bear* [1987] 1 Lloyd's Rep. 330; see also para.2–048.

21 *The Antclizo* [1988] 1 W.L.R. 603; Davenport 104 L.Q.R. 493.

22 *Harvey v Facey* [1893] A.C. 552; *Gibson v Manchester CC* [1979] 1 W.L.R. 294; cf. *The Barranduna* [1985] 2 Lloyd's Rep. 419; *Michael Gerson (Leasing) Ltd v Wilkinson* [2000] Q.B. 514 at 530.

23 *Interfoto Picture Library Ltd v Stiletto Visual Programmes Ltd* [1989] Q.B. 433 at 436.

24 *Photolibrary Group Ltd v Burda Senator Verlag GmbH* [2008] EWHC 1343 (QB); [2008] 2 All E.R. (Comm) 811 at [63]–[64] where, because of a course of dealing between the parties, either analysis was "viable".

25 See para.2–002, fn.1.

expressly provides that he is *not* to be bound merely by the other party's notification of assent, but only when he himself has signed the document in which the statement is contained.[26] Apart from this type of case, the wording is not conclusive. A statement may be an invitation to treat, although it contains the word "offer"[27]; as, for example, in *Datec Electronic Holdings Ltd v United Parcels Service Ltd*[28] where an "offer" of carriage subject to certain restrictions was regarded as an invitation to treat. Had it been regarded as an offer in the strict sense, there would have been no contract when the shipper tendered goods that did not comply with the restrictions. The correct analysis was that the shipper made the offer which was accepted by conduct by the carrier and the non-conformity of the goods affected the nature of the contractual regime, e.g. the carrier was entitled to refuse to collect the goods, or to suspend carriage, neither of which it did prior to the loss of the goods. Conversely, a statement may be an offer although it is expressed to be an "acceptance",[29] or requests the person to whom it is addressed to *make* an "offer".[30]

**Prima facie rules of law.** The distinction between an offer and an invitation to treat is often hard to draw as it depends on the elusive criterion of intention. But there are certain stereotyped situations in which the distinction is determined, at least prima facie, by rules of law. It may be possible to displace these rules by evidence of contrary intention, but in the absence of such evidence they will determine the distinction between offer and invitation to treat, and they will do so without reference to the intention (actual or even objectively ascertained) of the maker of the statement. The most commonly encountered examples are discussed in the following paragraphs. 2–007

**Auction sales.** At an auction sale, the general rule is that the offer is made by the bidder and accepted by the auctioneer when he signifies his acceptance in the customary manner, e.g. by fall of the hammer.[31] Before acceptance the bidder may withdraw his bid and the auctioneer may withdraw the goods. It seems, moreover, that the offer made by each bidder lapses[32] as soon as a higher bid is made. Thus if a higher bid is made and withdrawn the auctioneer can no longer accept the next highest. 2–008

When property is put up for auction subject to a reserve price, there is no contract if the auctioneer by mistake purports to accept a bid lower than the reserve price.[33] Where the auction is without reserve, there is no contract *of sale* between the highest bidder and the *owner* of the property if the auctioneer refuses to accept the highest bid. But it has been held that the *auctioneer* is in such a case liable on a separate, or collateral, contract between him and the highest bidder

[26] *Financings Ltd v Stimson* [1962] 1 W.L.R. 1184.
[27] *Spencer v Harding* (1870) L.R. 5 C.P. 561; *Clifton v Palumbo* [1944] 2 All E.R. 497.
[28] [2007] UKHL 23; [2007] 1 W.L.R. 1325.
[29] *Bigg v Boyd Gibbins Ltd* [1971] 1 W.L.R. 913.
[30] *Harvela Investments Ltd v Royal Trust Co of Canada (CI) Ltd* [1986] A.C. 207.
[31] Sale of Goods Act 1979 s.57(2); *British Car Auctions Ltd v Wright* [1972] 1 W.L.R. 1519.
[32] See para.2–063.
[33] *McManus v Fortescue* [1907] 2 K.B. 1.

that the sale will be without reserve.[34] Although a mere advertisement of an auction is not an offer to hold it,[35] the actual request for bids seems to be an offer by the auctioneer that he will on the owner's behalf accept the highest bid; and this offer is accepted by the bidding.[36]

2–009 **Shop display.** The general rule is that a display of price-marked goods in a shop window[37] or on the shelves of a self-service shop[38] is not an offer to sell goods but is an invitation to a customer to make an offer to buy which the retailer may accept or reject. Similar principles would seem to apply where a supplier of goods or services indicates their availability on a website: that is, the offer would seem to come from the customer (e.g. when he clicks the appropriate "button") and it is then open to the supplier to accept or reject that offer.[39] There is judicial support for the view that an indication of the price at which petrol is to be sold at a filling station is likewise an invitation to treat,[40] the offer to buy being made by the customer and accepted by the seller's conduct in putting the petrol into the tank,[41] but in the now more common situation in which the station operates a self-service system, it seems more likely that the seller is making an offer which is accepted by the customer when he fills up his tank.[42]

The general rule relating to shop and similar displays is well established, but the reasons given for it are not entirely convincing. One argument is that if the display were regarded as an offer, the retailer might be exposed to many actions for damages if more customers purported to accept than his stock could satisfy.[43] But such an offer could be construed as one which automatically expired when the retailer's stock was exhausted: this would probably be in keeping with the common expectation of both retailer and customer. It has also been said that, if a display in a self-service shop were an offer, the undesirable result would follow that the customer would be bound to buy as soon as he picked up the goods to examine them.[44] But if the display were an offer, it could be argued that there was no acceptance until the customer did some less equivocal act, such as presenting the goods for payment.[45]

It may be asked whether the general rule might sometimes cause injustice. Customers may be induced by a window display to believe that they will be able

---

[34] *Warlow v Harrison* (1859) 1 E. & E. 309; cf. *Barry v Davies* [2001] 1 W.L.R. 1962. *Contra*, *Fenwick v Macdonald Fraser & Co Ltd* (1904) 6 F. (Ct. of Sess.) 850.

[35] *Harris v Nickerson* (1873) L.R. 8 Q.B. 286.

[36] The question whether there is any consideration for the auctioneer's undertaking is discussed para.3–164.

[37] *Timothy v Simpson* (1834) 6 C. & P. 499; *Fisher v Bell* [1961] 1 Q.B. 394; contrast *Wiles v Maddison* [1943] 1 All E.R. 315 at 317.

[38] *Pharmaceutical Society of Great Britain v Boots Cash Chemists Ltd* [1952] 2 Q.B. 795; [1953] 1 Q.B. 401; cf. *Lacis v Cashmarts Ltd* [1969] 2 Q.B. 400; *Davies v Leighton* [1978] Crim. L.R. 575.

[39] See para.2–016 for what *constitutes* an acceptance, and para.2–035, fn.191 for the *time* of acceptance, in such cases.

[40] *Esso Petroleum v Commissioners of Customs & Excise* [1976] 1 W.L.R. 1 at 5, 6, 11; *Richardson v Worrall* [1985] S.T.C. 693 at 717.

[41] *Re Charge Card Services* [1989] Ch. 497 at 512.

[42] cf. para.2–011, fn.57.

[43] *Esso Petroleum v Commissioners of Customs & Excise* [1976] 1 W.L.R. 1 at 11.

[44] *Pharmaceutical Society of Great Britain v Boots Cash Chemists Ltd* [1952] 2 Q.B. 795 at 802.

[45] See *Lasky v Economic Grocery Stores* 65 N.E. 2d 305. (1946).

to buy goods at exceptionally low prices and to wait outside the shop for many hours in reliance on that belief. Is it right to allow the retailer to go back on such a statement at the very moment when the customer demands the goods? It seems that the special terms of a display, or the circumstances in which it is made, may be evidence of intention to be bound and so displace the prima facie rule that the display is not an offer: thus in one case a notice in a shop window stating that "We will beat any TV … price by £20 on the spot" was described as "a continuing offer".[46] The customer might, indeed, still lose his bargain since the offer could be withdrawn at any time before it was accepted;[47] but if it is so withdrawn the person displaying the notice may incur criminal liability under legislation passed for the protection of consumers.[48]

**Advertisements of unilateral contracts.** Advertisements of rewards for the return of lost or stolen property, or for information leading to the arrest or conviction of the perpetrator of a crime,[49] are invariably treated as offers: the intention to be bound is inferred from the fact that no further bargaining is expected to result from them. The same is true of other advertisements of *unilateral* contracts.[50] Thus in *Carlill v Carbolic Smoke Ball Co*,[51] an advertisement promising to pay £100 to any user of a carbolic smoke ball who caught influenza was held to be an offer. The intention to be bound[52] was made particularly clear by the statement that the advertisers had deposited £1,000 in their bank "shewing our sincerity". A case nearer the borderline was *Bowerman v Association of British Travel Agents Ltd*[53] where a package holiday had been booked with a tour operator who was a member of the defendant association (ABTA). A notice displayed on the tour operator's premises stated, inter alia, that in the event of the financial failure of an ABTA member before commencement of the holiday, "ABTA arranges for you to be reimbursed the money you have paid for your holiday". A majority of the Court of Appeal held that these words constituted an offer from ABTA since, on the objective test,[54] they would reasonably be regarded as such by a member of the public booking a holiday with an ABTA member. 2–010

**Advertisements of bilateral contracts.** Such advertisements are not usually held to be offers since they often lead to further bargaining, and since the advertiser may legitimately wish, before becoming bound, to assure himself that the other party is able to perform his part of any contract which may result. Thus a 2–011

---

[46] *R. v Warwickshire CC Ex p. Johnson* [1993] A.C. 583 at 588.
[47] See para.2–059.
[48] Consumer Protection from Unfair Trading Regulations 2008 (SI 2008/1277) reg.3(4)(d), Sch.1 para.6. For any civil liability, under the 2008 Regulations, see paras 9–002, 10–051.
[49] e.g. *Gibbons v Proctor* (1891) 64 L.T. 594; *Williams v Carwardine* (1833) 5 C. & P. 566; 4 B. & Ad. 621; para.2–049.
[50] See para.2–052, for the meaning of "unilateral contracts".
[51] [1893] 1 Q.B. 256.
[52] Contrast *Lambert v Lewis* [1982] A.C. 225 at 262 (Stephenson LJ); affirmed [1982] A.C. 271 without reference to this point.
[53] [1996] C.L.C. 451.
[54] See para.2–002.

newspaper advertisement that goods are for sale is not an offer[55] and the circulation of a price-list by a wine merchant is only an invitation to treat.[56] On the other hand, a notice at the entrance to an automatic car park may be an offer which can be accepted by driving in[57] and a display of deck chairs for *hire* has been held to be an offer.[58] No useful purpose is served by attempting to reconcile all the cases on this subject, since the question is one of intention in each case.[59]

2–012 **Timetables and passenger tickets.** There is a remarkable diversity of views on the question just when a contract is made between a carrier and an intending passenger. It has been said that rail carriers make offers by issuing advertisements stating the times at and conditions under which trains would run;[60] and that a road carrier makes offers to intending passengers by the act of running buses.[61] Such offers could be accepted by an indication on the part of the passenger that he wished to travel, e.g. by applying for a ticket or getting on the bus. Another view is that the carrier makes the offer at a later stage, by issuing the ticket; and that this offer is accepted by the passenger's retention of the ticket without objection,[62] or (even later) by claiming the accommodation offered in the ticket.[63] On this view the passenger makes no more than an invitation to treat when he asks for the ticket to be issued to him; and the offer contained in the ticket may be made to, and accepted by, the passenger even though the fare is paid by a third party (e.g. the passenger's employer).[64] Where the booking is made in advance, through a travel agent, yet a third view has been expressed: that the contract is concluded when the carrier indicates, even before issuing the ticket, that he "accepts" the booking[65] or when he issues the ticket.[66] On this view, it is the passenger who makes the offer. The authorities yield no single rule: one can only say that the exact time of contracting depends in each case on the wording of the relevant document and on the circumstances in which it was issued.

2–013 **Tenders.** At common law, a statement that goods are to be sold by tender is not normally an offer, so that the person making the statement is not bound to sell to

---

[55] *Partridge v Crittenden* [1968] 1 W.L.R. 1204; cf. *Rooke v Dawson* [1895] 1 Ch. 480.
[56] *Grainger & Sons v Gough* [1896] A.C. 325; quaere whether a price-list sent on request to a single customer could be an offer.
[57] *Thornton v Shoe Lane Parking Ltd* [1971] 2 Q.B. 163 at 169.
[58] *Chapelton v Barry Urban DC* [1940] 1 K.B. 532.
[59] Contrast *Harvey v Facey* [1893] A.C. 552 with *Philip & Co v Knoblauch,* 1907 S.C. 994.
[60] *Denton v GN Ry* (1856) 5 E. & B. 860; *Thompson v LM&S Ry* [1930] 1 K.B. 41 at 47.
[61] *Wilkie v LPTB* [1947] 1 All E.R. 258 at 259.
[62] *Thornton v Shoe Lane Parking Ltd* [1971] 2 Q.B. 163 at 169; *Cockerton v Naviera Aznar SA* [1960] 2 Lloyd's Rep. 450. Such acceptance would be by conduct rather than by silence: cf. para.2–048.
[63] *MacRobertson-Miller Airline Service v Commissioner of State Taxation* (1975) 8 A.L.R. 131; the principle resembles that stated in *Heskell v Continental Express Ltd* [1950] 1 All E.R. 1033 at 1037 in relation to carriage of goods by sea.
[64] *Hobbs v L&SW Ry* (1875) L.R. 10 Q.B. 111 at 119; as explained in *MacRobertson-Miller Airline Service v Commissioner of State Taxation* (1975) 8 A.L.R. 131 at 147.
[65] *The Eagle* [1977] 2 Lloyd's Rep. 70; *Oceanic Sun Line Special Shipping Co v Fay* (1988) 165 C.L.R. 97; cf.*The Anwar al Sabar* [1980] 2 Lloyd's Rep. 261 at 263 (carriage of goods by sea).
[66] *The Mikhail Lermontov* [1991] 2 Lloyd's Rep. 155 at 159; reversed on other grounds: *Baltic Shipping Co v Dillon* (1993) 176 C.L.R. 344.

the person making the highest tender.[67] Similarly a statement inviting tenders for the supply of goods or for the execution of works is not normally an offer.[68] The offer comes from the person who submits the tender and there is no contract until the person asking for the tenders accepts[69] one of them. The preparation of a tender may involve considerable expense; but the tenderer normally incurs this at his own risk. The position is different where the person who invites the tenders states in the invitation that he binds himself to accept the highest offer to buy[70] (or, as the case may be, the lowest offer to sell or to provide the specified services).[71] In such cases, the invitation may be regarded *either* as itself an offer *or* as an invitation to submit offers coupled with an undertaking to accept the highest (or, as the case may be, the lowest) offer; and the contract is concluded as soon as the highest offer to buy (or lowest offer to sell, etc.) is communicated.[72] There is also an intermediate possibility. This is illustrated by a case[73] in which an invitation to submit tenders was sent by a local authority to seven selected parties; the invitation stated that tenders submitted after a specified deadline would not be considered. It was held that the authority was contractually bound *to consider* (though not to accept)[74] a tender submitted before the deadline.

The common law position stated above is in some situations modified by legislation, for example by regulations[75] which give effect to EC Council Directives, the object of which is to prevent discrimination in the award of major contracts for public works, supplies and services in one Member State against nationals of another Member State. These regulations restrict the freedom of the body seeking tenders to decide which tender it will accept and provide a remedy in damages for a person who has made a tender and is prejudiced by breach of the rules.

**Sales of shares.** A company which, in commercial language,[76] makes an "offer to the public", asking them to subscribe for shares in it, does not in law offer to sell the shares. It invites members of the public to apply for them, reserving the right to decide how many (if any) to allot to each applicant.[77] But where a company makes a "rights" issue of shares to its existing shareholders, entitling each shareholder to buy a number of new shares in proportion to the shares he already holds, the letter informing the shareholder of his rights is regarded as an offer.[78] 2–014

67 *Spencer v Harding* (1870) L.R. 5 C.P. 561.

68 *Spencer v Harding* (1870) L.R. 5 C.P. 561 at 564.

69 See para.2–022.

70 *Spencer v Harding* (1870) L.R. 5 C.P. 561 at 563.

71 See *William Lacey (Hounslow) Ltd v Davis* [1957] 1 W.L.R. 932 at 939.

72 *Harvela Investments Ltd v Royal Trust of Canada (CI) Ltd* [1986] A.C. 207 at 224–225.

73 *Blackpool and Fylde Aero Club Ltd v Blackpool BC* [1990] 1 W.L.R. 1195. No decision was reached on the quantum of damages: as to this, see para.20–062.

74 cf. *Fairclough Building v Port Talbot BC* (1992) 62 B.L.R. 82.

75 Public Contracts Regulations 2015 (SI 2015/12) (see *Brent LBC v Risk Management Partners Ltd* [2011] UKSC 7; [2011] 2 W.L.R. 166, decided under the previous Regulations (SI 2006/5); Utilities Contracts Regulations 2016 (SI 2016/274).

76 And in the terminology of Companies Act 2006 ss.755, 756 and of Financial Services and Markets Act 2000 s.102B.

77 e.g. *Harris' Case* (1872) L.R. 7 Ch. App. 587; *National Westminster Bank Plc v IRC* [1995] 1 A.C. 119 at 126; cf. *Wallace's Case* [1900] 2 Ch. 671; *Rust v Abbey Life Ins Co* [1979] 2 Lloyd's Rep. 335.

78 *Jackson v Turquand* (1869) L.R. 4 H.L. 305.

This letter will set out the precise rights of each shareholder, thus showing an intention on the part of the company to be bound, if the shareholder takes up his rights.

### (c) Where and when an offer takes effect

2–015 In one sense an offer cannot take effect until it is received, for until the offeree knows about it he can take no action in reliance on it. But for the purpose of determining whether a contract can be sued on in a particular court it has been held that an offer sent through the post was made *where* it was posted.[79] The question *when* such an offer was made may also arise for the purpose of determining whether the offer has expired by lapse of time[80] before it was accepted. In *Adams v Lindsell*[81] an offer to sell wool was made by a letter which was misdirected. The letter reached the offerees two days late; and they immediately posted an acceptance which was held binding because the delay arose "entirely from the mistake of the [offerors]".[82] From this emphasis on the offerors' fault, it seems that the decision might have gone the other way if the delay had been due to some other factor, e.g. to an accident in the post. In such a case the time for acceptance probably runs from the moment at which the letter would, but for such accident, have reached the offeree's address. Even where the delay is due to the offeror's fault, the offer may have lapsed before its receipt by the offeree. Obviously, the offer could not be accepted if it reached the offeree only after the date expressly specified in it as the last date for acceptance. The position is probably the same where it is clear to the offeree that there has been such a long delay in the transmission of the offer as to make it obvious to the offeree that the offer was "stale" when it reached him.

## 2. ACCEPTANCE

### (a) Acceptance defined

2–016 **An objective test.** An acceptance is a final and unqualified expression of assent to the terms of an offer. The objective test of agreement applies to an acceptance no less than to an offer.[83] On this test, the mere acknowledgment that an offer has been received would not be an acceptance; nor would a person to whom an offer to sell goods had been made accept it merely by replying that it was his "intention to place an order"[84] or by asking for an invoice.[85] But an "acknowledgment" may by its express terms or, in a particular context by implication, contain a statement that the sender agreed to the terms of the offer and that he was therefore accepting

[79] *Taylor v Jones* (1871) 1 C.P.D. 87.
[80] See para.2–065.
[81] (1818) 1 B. & Ald. 681.
[82] *Adams v Lindsell* (1818) 1 B. & Ald. 681 at 683.
[83] See para.2–002; *Inland Revenue Commissioners v Fry* [2001] S.T.C. 1715 at [6], [7]; *University of Edinburgh v Onifade,* 2005 S.L.T. (Sh Ct) 63 at [6].
[84] *OTM Ltd v Hydranautics* [1981] 2 Lloyd's Rep. 211 at 214.
[85] *Michael Gerson (Leasing) Ltd v Wilkinson* [2000] Q.B. 514 at 530.

it: this might, for example, be the effect of an "acknowledgment" of a customer's order in website trading. Where the offer makes alternative proposals, the reply must make it clear to which of them the assent is directed. In one case an offer to build a freight terminal was made by a tender quoting in the alternative a fixed price and a price varying with the cost of labour and materials. The offeree purported to accept "your tender" and it was held that there was no contract as there was no way of telling which price term had been accepted.[86]

**Continuing negotiations.** When parties carry on lengthy negotiations, it may be hard to say exactly when an offer has been made and accepted. As negotiations progress, each party may make concessions or new demands and the parties may in the end dispute whether they had ever agreed at all. The court must then look at the whole correspondence and decide whether, on its true construction, the parties had agreed to the same terms.[87] If so, there is a contract even though both parties, or one of them, had reservations not expressed in the correspondence.[88] In *Allianz Insurance Co (Egypt) v Aigaion Insurance Co SA*[89] an insurance slip was emailed by the reinsured without a warranty that the parties had previously agreed, but the appearance of "finality" in the reinsurer's emailed reply meant that it took effect as an acceptance and there was a contract which omitted the warranty.[90] **2–017**

The court will be particularly anxious to conclude that there was a contract where the performance which was the subject-matter of the negotiations has actually been rendered. In one such case, a building sub-contract was held to have come into existence (even though the parties had not yet reached agreement when the contractor began the work) as during its progress outstanding matters were resolved by further negotiations.[91] The contract may then be given retrospective effect so as to cover acts done before the final agreement was reached.[92] Performance of the work is not however decisive and each case depends upon its own facts.[93] Furthermore, in the absence of an enforceable contract, performance may give rise to a restitutionary claim for the value of the goods supplied or the work done.[94]

Businessmen do not, any more than the courts, find it easy to say precisely when they have reached agreement, and may continue to negotiate after they appear to have agreed to the same terms. The court will then look at the entire course of the negotiations to decide whether an apparently unqualified acceptance

---

[86] *Peter Lind & Co Ltd v Mersey Docks & Harbour Board* [1972] 2 Lloyd's Rep. 234.

[87] See, e.g. *Glencore Energy Ltd v Cirrus Oil Services Ltd* [2014] EWHC 87 (Comm); [2014] 2 Lloyd's Rep. 1.

[88] *Kennedy v Lee* (1817) 3 Mer. 441; cf. *Cie de Commerce v Parkinson Stove Co* [1953] 2 Lloyd's Rep. 487; *Thorensen Car Ferries Ltd v Weymouth Portland BC* [1977] 2 Lloyd's Rep. 614; *The Bay Ridge* [1999] 2 All E.R. (Comm) 306.

[89] [2008] EWCA Civ 1455; [2008] 2 C.L.C. 1013.

[90] Quaere why there had been no plea of rectification (see para.8–063 and following): [2008] EWCA Civ 1455; [2008] 2 C.L.C. 1013 at [37].

[91] *G Percy Trentham Ltd v Archital Luxfer Ltd* [1993] 1 Lloyd's Rep. 25; cf. *RTS Flexible Systems Ltd v Molkerei Alois Müller GmbH & Co KG* [2010] UKSC 14; [2010] 1 W.L.R. 753.

[92] *G Percy Trentham Ltd v Archital Luxfer Ltd* [1993] 1 Lloyd's Rep. 25 at 27; *Twintec Ltd v Volkerfitzpatrick Ltd* [2014] EWHC 10 (TCC); [2014] B.L.R. 150.

[93] *RTS Flexible Systems Ltd v Molkerei Alois Müller GmbH & Co KG* [2010] UKSC 14; [2010] 1 W.L.R. 753 at [54]; *CRS GT Ltd v McLaren Automotive Ltd* [2018] EWHC 3209 (Comm).

[94] See para.22–031

did in fact conclude the agreement.[95] If it did, the fact that the parties continued negotiations after this point will not normally affect the existence of the contract;[96] it will do so only if the continuation of the negotiations can be construed as an agreement to rescind the contract. A fortiori, the binding force of an oral contract is not affected or altered merely by the fact that, after its conclusion, one party sends to the other a document containing terms significantly different from those which had been orally agreed.[97]

2–018 **Acceptance by conduct.** An offer may be accepted by conduct, e.g. by supplying or despatching goods in response to an offer to buy them,[98] or by beginning to render services in response to an offer in the form of a request for them.[99] Similarly, an offer to supply goods (made by sending them to the offeree) can be accepted by using them.[100] The conduct of the offeree must be "unequivocal"[101] and indicate that he did the act with the intention (ascertained in accordance with the objective principle[102]) of accepting the offer.[103] Thus a buyer's taking delivery of goods after the conclusion of an oral contract of sale will not amount to his acceptance of written terms which differ significantly from those orally agreed and which are sent to him by the seller after the making of that contract but before taking delivery.[104] That conduct is referable to the oral contract rather than to the attempted later variation. Nor is a company's offer to insure a car accepted by taking the car out on the road, if there is evidence that the driver intended to insure with another company.[105]

---

95 *Hussey v Horne-Payne* (1878) 4 App. Cas. 311; *British Guiana Credit Corp v Da Silva* [1965] 1 W.L.R. 248; *Container Transport International Inc v Oceanus Mutual etc Association* [1984] 1 Lloyd's Rep. 476; *Pagnan SpA v Feed Products Ltd* [1987] 2 Lloyd's Rep. 601 at 619; *Ignazio Messina & Co v Polskie Linie Oceaniczne* [1995] 2 Lloyd's Rep. 566; *Global Asset Capital Inc v Aabar Block S.A.R.L.* [2017] EWCA Civ 37; [2017] 4 W.L.R. 163.

96 *Perry v Suffields Ltd* [1916] 2 Ch. 187; *Davies v Sweet* [1962] 2 Q.B. 300; *Cranleigh Precision Engineering Ltd v Bryant* [1965] 1 W.L.R. 1293; *Maple Leaf Macro Volatility Master Fund v Rouvroy* [2009] EWHC 257 (Comm); [2009] 1 Lloyd's Rep. 475 at [230]; affirmed [2009] EWCA Civ 1334; [2010] 2 All E.R. (Comm) 788, without reference to this point; cf. *Virulite LLC v Virulite Distribution Ltd* [2014] EWHC 366 (QB) at [74].

97 *Jayaar Impex Ltd v Toaken Group Ltd* [1996] 2 Lloyd's Rep. 437.

98 *Harvey v Johnston* (1848) 6 C.B. 295 at 305; cf. *Steven v Bromley & Son* [1919] 2 K.B. 722 at 728; *Interfoto Picture Library Ltd v Stiletto Visual Programmes Ltd* [1989] Q.B. 433 at 436; *Re Charge Card Services* [1989] Ch. 497 at 512.

99 *The Kurnia Dewi* [1997] 1 Lloyd's Rep. 533; *Datec Electronic Holdings Ltd v United Parcels Service Ltd* [2007] UKHL 23; [2007] 1 W.L.R. 1325: para.2–006; *Reveille Independent LLC v Anotech International (UK) Ltd* [2016] EWCA Civ 443; 166 Con L.R. 79.

100 *Weatherby v Banham* (1832) 5 C. & P. 228; or even by using part of the goods: cf. *Hart v Mills* (1846) 15 L.J. Ex. 200.

101 *Aroca Seiquer & Asociados v Adams* [2018] EWCA Civ 1589; [2018] P.N.L.R. 32 at [33]; *Arcadis Consulting (UK) Ltd v AMEC (BCS) Ltd* [2018] EWCA Civ 2222; [2019] B.L.R. 27 at [91]–[93] (offeree need not use the word "accept").

102 See para.2–002.

103 *Brogden v Metropolitan Ry* (1877) 2 App. Cas. 666; *Reveille Independent LLC v Anotech International (UK) Ltd* [2016] EWCA Civ 443; 166 Con L.R. 79 at [40]; *Novus Aviation Ltd v Alubaf Arab International Bank BSC* [2016] EWHC 1575 (Comm); [2017] 1 B.C.L.C. 414 at [103]. In the context of employment contracts, see: *Abrahall v Nottingham CC* [2018] EWCA Civ 796; [2018] I.R.L.R. 628.

104 *Jayaar Impex Ltd v Toaken Group Ltd* [1992] 2 Lloyd's Rep. 437.

105 *Taylor v Allon* [1966] 1 Q.B. 304.

Where it is alleged that an offer has been made, or accepted, by conduct it is often hard to say exactly what terms have been agreed. The difficulty may be so great as to lead to the conclusion that no agreement was reached at all.[106] But the court has considerable power to resolve uncertainties. If the offer is silent as to the rate of payment the court may imply a term that a reasonable amount should be paid.[107] Or the court may import into the contract the terms of another contract between the parties, or of a draft agreement between them,[108] or even of a contract between one of them and a third party.[109]

**Acceptance must be unqualified.** A communication may fail to take effect as an acceptance because it attempts to vary the terms of the offer. Thus an offer to sell 1,200 tons of iron is not accepted by a reply asking for 800 tons;[110] an offer to pay a *fixed* price for building work is not accepted by a promise to do the work for a *variable* price;[111] an offer to *supply* goods is not accepted by an "order" for their "supply and installation".[112] Nor, generally, is an offer accepted by a reply which varies one of its other terms (e.g. that specifying the time of performance),[113] or by a reply which is intended to introduce an entirely new term.[114] Such replies are not acceptances but counter-offers[115] which the original offeror can accept or reject. 2–019

The requirement that the acceptance must be unqualified does not, however, mean that there must be precise *verbal* correspondence between offer and acceptance.[116] An acceptance could be effective even though it departed from the wording of the offer by making express some term which the law would in any case imply.[117] And a reply which adds some new provision by way of indulgence to the offeror (e.g. one allowing him to postpone payment) may be an acceptance. Conversely, an acceptance in which the acceptor asks for extra time to pay may

---

[106] *Capital Finance Co Ltd v Bray* [1964] 1 W.L.R. 323.

[107] Sale of Goods Act 1979 s.8(2); Supply of Goods and Services Act 1982 s.15(1); cf. *Steven v Bromley & Son* [1919] 2 K.B. 722; para.2–087.

[108] e.g. *Brogden v Metropolitan Ry* (1877) 2 App. Cas. 666; contrast *D&M Trailers (Halifax) Ltd v Stirling* [1978] R.T.R. 468; *Jayaar Impex Ltd v Toaken Ltd* [1996] 2 Lloyd's Rep. 437.

[109] e.g. *Pyrene Co Ltd v Scindia Navigation Co Ltd* [1954] 2 Q.B. 402; see para.14–080; cf. *AstraZeneca UK Ltd v Albemarle International Corp* [2011] EWHC 1574 (Comm); [2011] 2 C.L.C. 252; para.2–096.

[110] *Tinn v Hoffmann & Co* (1873) 29 L.T. 271; cf. *Jordan v Norton* (1838) 4 M. & W. 155; *Harrison v Battye* [1975] 1 W.L.R. 58.

[111] *North West Leicestershire DC v East Midlands Housing Association* [1981] 1 W.L.R. 1396.

[112] *Butler Machine Tool Co Ltd v Ex-Cell-O Corp (England) Ltd* [1979] 1 W.L.R. 401.

[113] *Butler Machine Tool Co Ltd v Ex-Cell-O Corp (England) Ltd* [1979] 1 W.L.R. 401; *North West Leicestershire DC v East Midlands Housing Association* [1981] 1 W.L.R. 1396; cf. *Brinkibon Ltd v Stahag Stahl und Stahlwarenhandelsgesellschaft mbH* [1983] 2 A.C. 34.

[114] *Jackson v Turquand* (1869) L.R. 4 H.L. 305; *Bircham & Co Nominees (No.2) Ltd v Worrell Holdings Ltd* [2001] EWCA Civ 725; (2001) 82 P. & C.R. 427 at [11]. Statements which are *not* intended to add new terms do not vitiate the acceptance: *Simpson v Hughes* (1897) 66 L.J.Ch. 334; *Butler Machine Tool Co Ltd v Ex-Cell-O Corp (England) Ltd* [1979] 1 W.L.R. 401.

[115] *Jones v Daniel* [1894] 2 Ch. 332; *Von Hatzfeld-Wildenburg v Alexander* [1912] 1 Ch. 284; *Lark v Outhwaite* [1991] 2 Lloyd's Rep. 132 at 139; *Beazley Underwriting Ltd v Travelers Companies Inc* [2011] EWHC 1520 (Comm); [2012] 1 All E.R. (Comm) 1241 at [184].

[116] *Midgulf International Ltd v Group Chimique Tunisien* [2010] EWCA Civ 66; [2010] 2 Lloyd's Rep. 543 at [45].

[117] *Lark v Outhwaite* [1991] 2 Lloyd's Rep. 132 at 139.

be effective, so long as he makes it clear that he is prepared to perform in accordance with the terms of the offer even if his request is refused. The question is whether what has been introduced would have been regarded by a reasonable offeror as introducing a new term into the bargain rather than acceptance of the offer.[118] It is also possible for a communication which introduces a new term to amount at the same time to a firm acceptance and also to a further offer relating to the same subject-matter but emanating from the original offeree.[119] In such a case, there will be a contract on the terms of the original offer, but none on the terms of the new offer unless that is, in turn, accepted.[120]

After parties have reached agreement, the offer and acceptance may be set out in formal documents. The purpose of such documents may be merely to record the agreed terms;[121] and where one of the documents performs this function accurately while the other fails to do so, the discrepancy between them will not prevent the formation of a contract. In such a case, the court can rectify[122] the document which fails to record the agreed terms, and a contract will be on those terms.[123]

2–020 **The battle of forms.** The prevalent use of printed contract forms by one or both parties has given rise to problems with regard to the rule that the acceptance must correspond to the offer. Two situations call for discussion.

First, A may make an offer to B by asking for a supply of goods or services. B may reply that he is willing to supply the goods or services on B's terms. Prima facie, B's statement is a counter-offer which A is free to accept or reject, and he may accept it by accepting the goods or services. If he does so, there is a contract between A and B which is governed by B's terms.[124]

Secondly, *each* party may purport to contract with reference to his own set of standard terms and these terms may conflict. In *BRS v Arthur V Crutchley Ltd*[125] the claimants delivered a consignment of whisky to the defendants for storage. Their driver handed the defendants a delivery note purporting to incorporate the claimants' "conditions of carriage". The note was stamped by the defendants: "Received under [the defendants'] conditions". It was held that this amounted to a counter-offer which the claimants had accepted by handing over the goods, and the contract therefore incorporated the defendants' and not the claimants' conditions.

---

118 *G Percy Trentham Ltd v Archital Luxfer Ltd* [1993] 1 Lloyd's Rep. 25 at 28; *Maple Leaf Macro Volatility Master Fund v Rouvroy* [2009] EWHC 257 (Comm); [2009] 1 Lloyd's Rep. 475 at [247]; affirmed [2009] EWCA Civ 1334; [2010] 2 All E.R. (Comm) 788; *Midgulf International Ltd v Group Chimique Tunisien* [2010] EWCA Civ 66; [2010] 2 Lloyd's Rep. 543 at [45].

119 *AB v CD Ltd* [2013] EWHC 1376; [2013] B.L.R. 435 at [28].

120 *The Master Stelios* [1983] 1 Lloyd's Rep. 356.

121 e.g. *OTM Ltd v Hydranautics* [1981] 2 Lloyd's Rep. 211 at 215; cf. para.2–091.

122 See para.8–063.

123 *Domb v Isoz* [1980] Ch. 548.

124 A may challenge the incorporation of B's terms on grounds which are considered below: para.6–004 and following.

125 [1968] 1 W.L.R. 811; cf. *OTM Ltd v Hydranautics* [1981] 2 Lloyd's Rep. 211; *Muirhead v Industrial Tank Specialities Ltd* [1986] Q.B. 507 at 530; *Claxton Engineering Services Ltd v TXM Olaj-és Gázkutató Kft* [2010] EWHC 2567 (Comm); [2011] 1 Lloyd's Rep. 252.

**The "last shot" doctrine.** The decision in *Crutchley* gave some support to the so-called "last shot" doctrine: i.e. to the view that, where conflicting communications are exchanged, each is a counter-offer so that if a contract results at all (e.g. from an acceptance by conduct) it must be on the terms of the final document in the series leading to the conclusion of the contract.[126] But this view requires some modification in the light of *Butler Machine Tool Co Ltd v Ex-Cell-O Corp (England) Ltd*.[127] In that case sellers offered to supply a machine for a specified sum. The offer was expressed to be subject to certain terms and conditions, including a "price-escalation clause", by which the amount payable by the buyers was to depend on "prices ruling upon date of delivery". In reply, the buyers placed an order for the machine on a form setting out their own terms and conditions, which differed from those of the sellers in containing no price-escalation clause and in various other respects.[128] It also contained a tear-off slip to be signed by the sellers and returned to the buyers, stating that the sellers accepted the order "on the terms and conditions stated therein". The sellers did so sign the slip and returned it with a letter saying that they were "entering" the order "in accordance with" their offer. This communication from the sellers was held to be an acceptance of the buyers' counter-offer[129] so that the resulting contract was on the buyers' terms, and the sellers were not entitled to the benefit of the price-escalation clause. The sellers' reply to the buyers' order did not prevail (though it was the "last shot" in the series) because the reference in it to the original offer was not made for the purpose of reiterating all the terms of that offer, but only for the purpose of identifying the subject-matter.[130] It would, however, have been possible for the sellers to have turned their final communication into a counter-offer by explicitly referring in it, not only to the subject-matter of the original offer, but also to all its other terms. In that case no contract would have been concluded, since the buyers had made it clear before the machine was delivered that they did not agree to the "price-escalation" clause.[131] 2–021

Thus it is possible by careful draftsmanship to avoid losing the battle of forms, but not (if the other party is equally careful) to win it. In the *Butler Machine Tool* case, for example, the sellers' conditions included one by which their terms were to "prevail over any terms and conditions in Buyer's order"; but this failed (in

---

[126] As in *Zambia Steel & Building Supplies Ltd v James Clark & Eaton Ltd* [1986] 2 Lloyd's Rep. 225.

[127] [1979] 1 W.L.R. 401, especially at 405; Adams 95 L.Q.R. 481; Rawlings 42 M.L.R. 715. See also *Tekdata Interconnections Ltd v Amphenol* [2009] EWCA Civ 1209; [2010] 1 Lloyd's Rep. 357 where the Court of Appeal acknowledged that the multiple relationships established in a long-term supply chain might indicate that the parties did not intend to contract on the terms found to apply as a consequence of the "battle of the forms" rules, but held that this was not made out on the facts of the case; cf. *Trebor Bassett Holdings Ltd v ADT Fire & Security Plc* [2011] EWHC 1936 (TCC); [2011] B.L.R. 661; *Transformers & Rectifiers Ltd v Needs Ltd* [2015] EWHC 269 (TCC); [2015] T.C.L.R. 2.

[128] See para.2–019, fnn.112 and 113.

[129] *Butler Machine Tool Co Ltd v Ex-Cell-O Corp (England) Ltd* [1979] 1 W.L.R. 401 (Lawton and Buckley LJJ); Lord Denning MR also uses this analysis, but prefers the alternative approach of considering "the documents … as a whole": see at 405 and cf. para.2–076.

[130] cf. *Allianz Insurance Co (Egypt) v Aigaion Insurance Co SA* [2008] EWCA Civ 1455; [2008] 2 C.L.C. 1013.

[131] *Butler Machine Tool Co Ltd v Ex-Cell-O Corp (England) Ltd* [1979] 1 W.L.R. 401 at 406 (Lawton LJ).

consequence of the terms of the buyers' counter-offer) to produce the effect desired by the sellers.[132] The most that the draftsman can be certain of achieving is the stalemate situation in which there is no contract at all, or no contract on either parties' terms.[133] Such a conclusion will often be inconvenient,[134] though where the goods are nevertheless delivered it may lead to a liability on the part of the buyers to pay a reasonable price.[135]

2–022 **Acceptance of tenders.** The submission of a tender normally amounts to an offer,[136] and the effect of an "acceptance" of the tender depends on the interpretation of the documents. Where, for example, a tender is submitted for the construction of a building, acceptance will normally create a binding contract unless it is expressly stipulated that there is to be no contract until certain formal documents have been executed.[137] But where a tender is made for an indefinite amount, e.g. for the supply of "such quantities (not exceeding 1,000 tons) as you may order" the person to whom the tender is submitted does not incur any liability merely by "accepting" it. He becomes liable only when he places an order for the goods;[138] and he is not bound to place any order at all (unless he has expressly or by necessary implication[139] indicated in his invitation for tenders that he would do so).[140] Once an order has been placed, the party who has submitted the tender is bound to fulfil it.[141] Whether he can withdraw before an order has been placed, or avoid liability with regard to future orders, depends on the interpretation of the tender. If it merely means "I will supply such quantities as you may order" he can withdraw before a definite order is placed.[142] But he will not be entitled to withdraw if the tender means "I hereby bind myself to execute any orders which you may place", and if there is some consideration for this undertaking.[143]

2–023 **Acceptance by tender.** An invitation for tenders may, exceptionally, amount to an offer, e.g. where the person issuing the invitation binds himself to accept the highest tender to buy (or the lowest tender to sell).[144] The acceptance then takes the form of the submission of a tender; but difficulties can arise where several tenders are made and one (or more) of them takes the form of a so-called

[132] cf. *Commercial Management (Investments) Ltd v Mitchell Design & Construct Ltd* [2016] EWHC 76 (TCC); 164 Con L.R. 139.

[133] *GHSP Inc v AB Electronic Ltd* [2010] EWHC 1828 (Comm); cf. *Matter of Doughboy Industries Inc* 233 N.Y.S. 2d. 488 at 490 (1962): "The buyer and seller accomplished a legal equivalent to the irresistible force colliding with the immoveable object".

[134] It seems to have been rejected for this reason in *Johnson Matthey Bankers Ltd v State Trading Corp of India* [1984] 1 Lloyd's Rep. 427.

[135] cf. *Peter Lind & Co Ltd v Mersey Docks & Harbour Board* [1972] 2 Lloyd's Rep. 234.

[136] See para.2–013.

[137] See para.2–091.

[138] *Percival v London CC Asylum Committee* (1918) 87 L.J.K.B. 677.

[139] e.g. *Sylvan Crest Sand & Gravel Co v US Trust Co of Canada (CI) Ltd* US, 150 F. 2d. 642 (1945).

[140] cf. *Harvela Investments Ltd v Royal* [1986] A.C. 207.

[141] *Great Northern Ry v Witham* (1873) L.R. 9 C.P. 16.

[142] *Great Northern Ry v Witham* (1873) L.R. 9 C.P. 16 at 19.

[143] *Percival v London County Council Asylum Committee* (1918) 87 L.J.K.B. 677; cf. *Miller v FA Sadd & Son Ltd* [1981] 3 All E.R. 265; para.3–162.

[144] See para.2–013.

"referential bid". In *Harvela Investments Ltd v Royal Trust Co of Canada (CI) Ltd*[145] an invitation for the submission of "offers" to buy shares was addressed to two persons; it stated that the prospective sellers bound themselves to accept the "highest offer". One of the persons to whom the invitation was addressed made a bid of a fixed sum while the other submitted a "referential bid" undertaking to pay either a fixed sum or a specified amount in excess of the bid made by the other, whichever was the higher amount. It was held that this "referential bid" was ineffective and that the submission of the other bid had concluded the contract. The House of Lords stressed that the bids were, by the terms of the invitation, to be confidential, so that neither bidder would know the amount bid by the other. In these circumstances the object of the invitation, which was to ascertain the highest amount which each of the persons to whom it was addressed was willing to pay, would have been defeated by allowing it to be accepted by a "referential bid".

## (b) Communication of acceptance

### *(i) General rule*

**Acceptance must be communicated to the offeror.** The general rule is that an acceptance has no effect until it is communicated to the offeror.[146] One reason for this rule is the difficulty of proving an uncommunicated decision to accept, but this is not the sole reason for the rule, which applies even where the fact of acceptance could be proved with perfect certainty.[147] The main reason for the rule is that it could cause hardship to an offeror if he were bound without knowing that his offer had been accepted. It follows that there can be a contract if the offeror knows of the acceptance although it was not brought to his notice *by the offeree*.[148] However, there will be no contract if the communication is made by a third party without the authority of the offeree in circumstances indicating that the offeree's decision to accept was not yet regarded by him as irrevocable.[149] For an acceptance to be "communicated" it must normally be brought to the notice of the offeror. Thus if an oral acceptance is "drowned by an aircraft flying overhead" or is spoken into a telephone after the line has gone dead, or is so indistinct that the offeror does not hear it, there is no contract.[150] The requirement of "communication" may, however, sometimes be satisfied even though the acceptance has not actually come to the notice of the offeror: e.g. where a written notice of acceptance is left at his address.[151] 2–024

---

145 [1986] A.C. 207.

146 *M'Iver v Richardson* (1813) 1 M. & S. 557; *Ex p. Stark* [1897] 1 Ch. 575; *Holwell Securities Ltd v Hughes* [1974] 1 W.L.R. 155 at 157; *The Leonidas D* [1985] 1 W.L.R. 925 at 937.

147 *Kennedy v Thomassen* [1929] 1 Ch. 426; *Brogden v Metropolitan Ry* (1877) 2 App. Cas. 666 at 692.

148 *Bloxham's Case* (1864) 33 Beav. 529; (1864) 4 D.J. & S. 447; *Levita's Case* (1867) L.R. 3 Ch. App. 36.

149 This seems to be the best explanation of *Powell v Lee* (1908) 99 L.T. 284.

150 *Entores Ltd v Miles Far East Corp* [1955] 2 Q.B. 327 at 332.

151 cf. para.2–059.

### (ii) *Exceptional cases*

2–025 In a number of cases, contrary to the general rule, an acceptance is, or may be, effective although it is not communicated to the offeror.

2–026 **Communication to offeror's agent.** The effect of giving an acceptance to the agent of the offeror depends on the nature of the agent's authority.[152] If the agent has authority to *receive* the acceptance, it takes effect as soon as it is communicated to him, e.g. if acceptance of an offer made by a company is communicated to its managing director. But if the agent is only authorised to *transmit* the acceptance to the offeror, it may not take effect until the offeror receives it, e.g. if a written acceptance is given to a messenger.

2–027 **Offeror's fault.** An offeror may be precluded from denying that he received the acceptance if "it is his own fault that he did not get it", e.g. "if the listener on the telephone does not catch the words of acceptance, but nevertheless does not … ask for them to be repeated"[153]; or if the acceptance is sent during business hours by telex but is simply not read by anyone in the offeror's office when it is there transcribed on his machine.[154] If such a message is received out of business hours, it probably takes effect at the beginning of the next business day.[155]

2–028 **Communication waived by the terms of the offer.** An offer may expressly or impliedly waive the requirement that acceptance must be communicated.[156] This is often the case where an offer invites acceptance by conduct. Thus where an offer to sell goods is made by sending them to the offeree, it may be accepted by simply using them without communicating this fact to the offeror.[157] Similarly, it seems that, where an offer to buy goods is made by asking the seller to supply them, it may be accepted by simply despatching the goods to the buyer.[158] And a tenant can accept an offer of a new tenancy by simply staying on the premises.[159]

2–029 **Unilateral contracts.** Communication of acceptance is scarcely ever required in the case of an offer of a unilateral contract.[160] Thus in *Carlill v Carbolic Smoke Ball Co*,[161] the court rejected the argument that the claimant should have notified the defendants of her acceptance of their offer before starting to use the smoke

---

[152] *Henthorn v Fraser* [1892] 2 Ch. 27 at 33.
[153] *Entores Ltd v Miles Far East Corp* [1955] 2 Q.B. 327 at 333.
[154] cf. *The Brimnes* [1975] Q.B. 929.
[155] *The Pamela* [1995] 2 Lloyd's Rep. 249 at 252; *The Petr Schmidt* [1998] 2 Lloyd's Rep. 1.
[156] *Argo Fund Ltd v Essar Steel Ltd* [2005] EWHC 600 (Comm); [2005] 2 Lloyd's Rep. 203 at [53]; affirmed [2006] EWCA Civ 241; [2006] 2 Lloyd's Rep. 134, without reference to this point; *Attrill v Dresdner Kleinwort Ltd* [2013] EWCA Civ 394; [2013] I.R.L.R. 548 at [98].
[157] *Weatherby v Banham* (1832) 5 C. & P. 228; cf. *Minories Finance Ltd v Afribank Nigeria Ltd* [1995] 1 Lloyd's Rep. 134 at 140.
[158] cf. American Uniform Commercial Code (U.C.C.) s.2–206(1)(b); *The Kurnia Dewi* [1997] 1 Lloyd's Rep. 553 at 559.
[159] *Roberts v Hayward* (1828) 3 C. & P. 432; but not if the tenant disclaims the intention to accept: *Glossop v Ashley* [1921] 2 K.B. 451.
[160] For the meaning of "unilateral contract," see para.2–052.
[161] [1893] 1 Q.B. 256; see para.2–010.

ball. Similarly, where a reward is offered for the return of lost property the finder need not notify the owner in advance of his acceptance: he can accept by finding and returning the thing; and once he has found it the owner probably cannot withdraw.[162] Again, the contract which arises[163] between a bank which has issued a credit card to one of its customers and the retailer to whom the customer presents the card has been described as unilateral,[164] so that the bank's offer can be accepted by the retailer's dealing with the customer even before that acceptance is communicated to the bank.[165]

### *(iii) Acceptance by post*

There are many possible solutions to the problem: when does a posted acceptance take effect? Such an acceptance could take effect when it is actually communicated to the offeror, when it arrives at his address, when it should, in the ordinary course of post, have reached him, or when it is posted. As the following discussion will show, each of these solutions is open to objections on the grounds of convenience or justice.[166] This is particularly true where the acceptance is lost or delayed in the post.[167] 2–030

**The posting rule.** What is usually[168] called the general rule is that a postal acceptance takes effect when the letter of acceptance is posted.[169] For this purpose a letter is posted when it is in the control of the Post Office,[170] or of one of its employees authorised to receive letters: handing a letter to a postman authorised to *deliver* letters is not posting.[171] 2–031

**Reasons for the posting rule.** Various reasons for the rule have been suggested. One is that the offeror must be considered as making the offer all the time that his offer is in the post, and that therefore the agreement between the parties is complete as soon as the acceptance is posted.[172] But this does not explain why posting has any significance at all: any other proof of intention to accept would equally well show that the parties were in agreement. Another suggested reason for the rule is that the Post Office is the common agent of both parties, and that 2–032

---

[162] See paras 2–054–2–058.
[163] See para.3–024.
[164] *First Sport Ltd v Barclays Bank Plc* [1993] 1 W.L.R. 1229 at 1234.
[165] *First Sport Ltd v Barclays Bank Plc* [1993] 1 W.L.R. 1229 at 1234–1235.
[166] In *Conductive Interjet Technology Ltd v Uni-Pixel Displays Inc* [2013] EWHC 2968 (Ch); [2014] F.S.R. 22, the court found, for the purpose of permission to serve the claim form out of the jurisdiction, that there was a "good arguable case" that the contract was made *in both* of the countries from which the parties had sent and received copies.
[167] See, e.g. after fn.176.
[168] But see para.2–036.
[169] *Henthorn v Fraser* [1892] 2 Ch. 27 33; *Adams v Lindsell* (1818) 1 B. & Ald. 681; cf. *Bruner v Moore* [1904] 1 Ch. 305 (telegram); *Stevenson Jacques & Co v McLean* (1880) 5 Q.B.D. 346; *Cowan v O'Connor* (1888) 20 Q.B.D. 640 (place of acceptance).
[170] *Brinkibon Ltd v Stahag Stahl und Stahlwarenhandelsgesellschaft mbH* [1983] 2 A.C. 34 at 41; the "Post Office" here refers to the provider of the universal postal service under Postal Services Act 2011, by whatever name that provider may from time to time be known.
[171] *Re London & Northern Bank* [1900] 1 Ch. 220.
[172] *Henthorn v Fraser* [1892] 2 Ch. 27 at 31.

communication to this agent immediately completes the contract.[173] But the contents of a sealed letter cannot realistically be said to have been communicated to the Post Office, which in any case is at most an agent to *transmit* the acceptance, and not to *receive* it.[174] It has also been suggested that the rule minimises difficulties of proof in that it is easier to prove that a letter has been posted than that it has been received. But this depends in each case on the efficiency with which the parties keep records of incoming and outgoing letters.[175]

The rule is in truth an arbitrary one, little better or worse than its competitors.[176] When negotiations are conducted by post, one of the parties may be prejudiced if a posted acceptance is lost or delayed; for the offeree may believe that there is a contract and the offeror that there is none, and each may act in reliance on his belief. The posting rule favours the offeree, and is sometimes justified on the ground that an offeror who chooses to start negotiations by post takes the risk of delay and accidents in the post; or on the ground that the offeror can protect himself by expressly stipulating that he is not to be bound until actual receipt of the acceptance.[177] Neither justification is wholly satisfactory, for the negotiations may have been started by the offeree;[178] and the offer may be made on a form provided by the offeree,[179] in which case he, and not the offeror, will for practical purposes be in control of its terms. The rule does, however, serve a possibly useful function in limiting the offeror's power to withdraw his offer at will:[180] it makes a posted acceptance binding although that acceptance only reaches the offeror after a previously posted withdrawal reaches the offeree.[181]

2–033 **Must be reasonable to use post.** The posting rule only applies when it is reasonable to use the post as a means of communicating acceptance. Generally an offer made in a letter sent by post may be so accepted; but it may be reasonable to accept by post even though the offer was not sent in this way. In *Henthorn v Fraser*[182] the mere fact that the parties lived at a distance justified acceptance by post of an oral offer. It would not normally be reasonable to reply by a posted

[173] *Household etc Insurance Co Ltd v Grant* (1879) 4 Ex. D. 216 at 220.

[174] *Henthorn v Fraser* [1892] 2 Ch. 27 at 33; See para.2–026.

[175] See Winfield 55 L.Q.R. 509.

[176] In *Four Seasons Holdings Inc v Brownlie* [2017] UKSC 80; [2018] 1 W.L.R. 192 Lord Sumption (at [16]) described it as a rule of "pragmatic convenience" which provides "a perfectly serviceable test for determining whether a contract has been concluded *at all*" (emphasis added), but which is less satisfactory for determining *when* or *where* a contract was made; cf. *Newcastle upon Tyne Hospitals NHS Foundation Trust v Haywood* [2018] UKSC 22; [2018] 1 W.L.R. 2073 (notice of termination of employment contract only effective when received and read, or ought reasonably to have been read).

[177] *Household etc Insurance Co Ltd v Grant* (1879) 4 Ex. D. 216 at 223.

[178] It is often hard to tell which party is offeror and which is offeree, especially if the final offer was a counter-offer (see para.2–019).

[179] See para.2–043.

[180] See para.2–059. In countries in which the acceptance is only effective when communicated a similar result is often reached by legally limiting the offeror's power to withdraw his offer.

[181] See para.2–059.

[182] [1892] 2 Ch. 27.

letter to an offer made by telex,[183] email or telephone. Nor would it be reasonable to accept by post if the acceptor knew that the postal service was disrupted.[184]

**Terms of the offer.** The posting rule can be excluded by the terms of the offer. This may be so even though the offer does not expressly provide when the acceptance is to take effect. In *Holwell Securities Ltd v Hughes*[185] an offer to sell a house was made in the form of an option expressed "to be exercisable by notice in writing to the Intending Vendor … ". Such a notice was posted but did not arrive. It was held that there was no contract of sale as the terms of the offer, on their true construction, required the acceptance to be actually communicated. **2–034**

**Instantaneous and electronic communications.**[186] The posting rule does not apply to acceptances made by some instantaneous mode of communication, e.g. by telephone or by telex.[187] Such acceptances are therefore governed by the general rule that they must have been communicated to the offeror.[188] The reason why the rule does not apply in such cases is that the acceptor will often know at once that his attempt to communicate was unsuccessful,[189] so that it is up to him to make a proper communication. But a person who accepts by letter which goes astray may not know of the loss or delay until it is too late to make another communication. Fax messages seem to occupy an intermediate position. The sender will usually know at once if his message has not been received at all, and where this is the position the message should not amount to an effective acceptance. But if the message is received in such a form that it is wholly or partly illegible, the sender is unlikely to know this at once, and it is suggested an acceptance sent by fax might well be effective in such circumstances.[190] Communication by fax must now be very rare, but the same principles should apply to other forms of electronic communication such as email[191] or website **2–035**

183 cf. *Quenerduaine v Cole* (1883) 32 W.R. 185 (telegram).

184 *Bal v Van Staden* [1902] T.S. 128.

185 [1974] 1 W.L.R. 155; cf. *New Hart Builders Ltd v Brindley* [1975] Ch. 342.

186 Nolan, in Burrows and Peel (eds), *Contract Formation and Parties* (Oxford: Oxford University Press, 2010).

187 *Entores Ltd v Miles Far East Corp* [1955] 2 Q.B. 327; *Brinkibon Ltd v Stahag Stahl und Stahlwarenhandelsgesellschaft mbH* [1983] 2 A.C. 34; cf. *Gill & Duffus Landauer Ltd v London Export Corp GmbH* [1982] 2 Lloyd's Rep. 627.

188 See para.2–024; the exceptions set out in paras 2–026–2–028 may also apply, but not the exception in the form of the posting rule.

189 See *Entores Ltd v Miles Far East Corp* [1955] 2 Q.B. 327 at 333; and *Brinkibon Ltd v Stahag Stahl und Stahlwarenhandelsgesellschaft mbH* [1983] 2 A.C. 34 at 43; *Greenclose Ltd v National Westminster Bank Plc* [2014] EWHC 1156 (Ch); [2014] 2 Lloyd's Rep. 169 at [140].

190 In *JSC Zestafoni Nikoladze Ferroalloy Plant v Ronly Holdings Ltd* [2004] EWHC 245 (Comm); [2004] 2 Lloyd's Rep. 335 at [75] a fax was regarded as a form of instantaneous communication; the issue was *where* acceptance had taken effect, not *whether* it had done so, and there was no consideration of the latter of the two situations considered in the text.

191 *The Eastern Navigator* [2005] EWHC 3020 (Comm); [2006] 1 Lloyd's Rep. 537 at [29]–[31]; *Greenclose Ltd v National Westminster Bank Plc* [2014] EWHC 1156 (Ch); [2014] 2 Lloyd's Rep. 169 at [138] ("a form of near-instantaneous communication"). For various possible times at which an email can be said to have been *received*, see the *Greenclose* case at [132] ("a recipe for argument"); the present question is whether such a message may be effective *before* it is received.

trading:[192] here again the effects of unsuccessful attempts to communicate should depend on whether the sender of the message knows (or has the means of knowing) at once of any failure in communication.

2–036 **Applications of the posting rule.** Discussions of this subject sometimes start by stating the "general rule" that an acceptance takes effect when posted, and then proceed to deduce various "consequences" from this rule. In fact few, if any, judges or writers have been prepared to follow all these deductions to their logical conclusions; and it would be more accurate to admit that there is no single or universal rule which determines the effect of a posted acceptance.[193] The effect of such an acceptance has to be considered *as against* various competing factors, such as withdrawal of the offer, loss or delay of the acceptance, subsequent revocation of the acceptance, previous rejection of the offer and so forth. Obviously, a rule laid down in a case concerning the effect of a posted acceptance as against a withdrawal of the offer is no real guide to the solution of the problem whether such an acceptance is effective as against a subsequent revocation of the acceptance. The English cases in fact only support three "consequences" of the posting rule. The first, and probably the most important,[194] is that a posted acceptance prevails over a previously posted withdrawal of the offer which had not yet reached the offeree when the acceptance was posted.[195] A second, and more controversial,[196] application of the rule is that an acceptance takes effect on posting even though it never reaches the offeror because it is lost through an accident in the post,[197] and the same rule probably applies where the acceptance is merely delayed through such an accident.[198] Thirdly, the contract is taken to have been made at the *time* of posting so as to take priority over another contract affecting the subject-matter made after the original acceptance had been posted but before it had reached the offeror.[199] Whether a posted acceptance should take effect against *other* competing factors is a question of policy and convenience.[200]

---

[192] Clicking "I accept" on a website button may satisfy the requirement of *signature* (*Bassano v Toft* [2014] EWHC 377 (QB) at [43] and [44]; Law Com No.386 at 3; see para.5–030), but this does not determine whether it is an offer or an acceptance, or specify *when* it takes effect. The Electronic Commerce (EC Directive) Regulations 2002 (SI 2002/2013) reg.11(2)(a) states that "the order and the acknowledgement of receipt will be deemed to be received when the parties to whom they are addressed are able to access them"; but this form of words does not of itself answer the question whether the contract may not be concluded even before that time.

[193] See Evans 15 I.C.L.Q. 553.

[194] See para.2–032 text to fn.181.

[195] *Harris' Case* (1872) L.R. 7 Ch. App. 587; *Byrne & Co v Leon van Tienhoven* (1880) 5 C.P.D. 344; *Henthorn v Fraser* [1892] 2 Ch. 27; *Re London & Northern Bank* [1900] 1 Ch. 220.

[196] See para.2–030.

[197] *Household etc Insurance v Grant* (1879) 4 Ex. D. 216; overruling *British and American Telegraph Co v Colson* (1871) L.R. 6 Ex. 108.

[198] See *Dunlop v Higgins* (1848) 1 H.L.C. 381, which would probably be followed in England though it is expressly restricted (at 402) to Scots law.

[199] *Potter v Sanders* (1846) 6 Hare 1.

[200] *Brinkibon Ltd v Stahag Stahl und Stahlwarenhandelsgesellschaft mbH* [1983] 2 A.C. 34 at 41; *Gill & Duffus Landauer Ltd v London Export Corp GmbH* [1982] 2 Lloyd's Rep. 627 at 631.

The posting rule will not apply where it would lead to "manifest inconvenience and absurdity".[201] Its scope is determined by practical considerations rather than by "deductions" from a "general" rule.

**Misdirected acceptance.** A letter of acceptance may be lost or delayed because it bears a wrong, or an incomplete, address. Normally, such misdirection will be due to the carelessness of the offeree and the posting rule should not apply to such cases.[202] Even if an offeror can be said to take the risk of accidents in the post, it would be unreasonable to impose on him the further risk of the offeree's carelessness. It does not follow that a misdirected acceptance should necessarily take effect when received. For such a rule may actually favour the careless acceptor, e.g. when an offer is made to sell "at the market price prevailing when this offer is accepted," and the market falls after the misdirected acceptance has been posted. Moreover, the misdirection may be due to the fault of the offeror himself,[203] e.g. if he makes the offer in a letter on which his own address is incompletely or illegibly written, or if he uses an out-of-date letter-head.[204] The better rule, therefore, seems to be that a misdirected acceptance takes effect (if at all) at the time which is least favourable to the party responsible for the misdirection.[205] **2–037**

**Garbled messages.** A message may be garbled as a result of some inaccuracy in transmission for which the sender is not responsible. This problem used to arise in the case of telegraphed messages and could still arise from the use of now more common modes of communication: e.g. where an electronic message was corrupted in transmission without any fault on the part of the sender. The discussion of garbled telegraphic messages in (and arising from) the older authorities may provide some guidance to the solution of such problems. In one such case, it was held that an offeror was not bound by a telegraphed offer which was garbled so as to indicate that he was placing an order for a different quantity of goods from that which he wished to buy.[206] But there is no English authority on the question whether an offeror would be bound where it was the acceptance rather than the offer which was garbled in this way. It is submitted that if the offeree sends a message of acceptance in words corresponding to the offer, then (so long as it was reasonable for the offeree to accept in this way), the offeror would be bound by the acceptance and would not be entitled to treat it as a counter-offer. If an offeror takes the risk of such accidents in the post as loss or delay, he should similarly take the risk of errors in the transmission of a message; for in each case the offeree will have no means of knowing that something has gone wrong until it is too late to make another, proper, communication.[207] **2–038**

---

201 *Holwell Securities Ltd v Hughes* [1974] 1 W.L.R. 157 at 161.

202 *LJ Korbetis v Transgrain Shipping BV* [2005] EWHC 1345 (QB).

203 Fault of one party may not be the effective cause of the misdirection if the resulting error is obvious to the other party.

204 cf. *Townsend's Case* (1871) L.R. 13 Eq. 148.

205 *LJ Korbetis v Transgrain Shipping BV* [2005] EWHC 1345 (QB) at [15].

206 *Henkel v Pape* (1870) L.R. 6 Ex. 7.

207 cf. para.2–032.

2–039 **Revocation of posted acceptance.** An offeree may, after posting an acceptance, attempt to revoke it by a later communication which reaches the offeror before, or at the same time as, the acceptance. There is no English authority on the effectiveness of such a revocation. One view is that the revocation has no effect, since, once a contract has been concluded by posting of the acceptance, it cannot be dissolved by the unilateral act of one party.[208] But this argument has little to commend it if (as has been suggested above) it is undesirable to resolve what are really issues of policy by making "logical" deductions from some "general" rule as to the effect of posted acceptances. As a matter of policy, the issue is whether the offeror would be unjustly prejudiced by allowing the offeree to rely on the subsequent revocation. On the one hand, it can be argued that the offeror cannot be prejudiced by such revocation as he had no right to have his offer accepted and as he cannot have relied on its having been accepted before he knew of the acceptance. Against this, it can be argued that, once the acceptance has been posted, the offeror can no longer withdraw his offer,[209] and that reciprocity demands that the offeree should likewise be held to his acceptance. For if the offeree could revoke the acceptance he would be able, without risk to himself, to speculate at the expense of the offeror.[210] He could post his acceptance early in the morning of a working day and could, if the market moved against him, revoke his acceptance the same afternoon, while the offeror had no similar freedom of action. It has been suggested[211] that the offeror should take this risk just as much as he takes the risk of loss or delay; but here again it is submitted that while the offeror may take the risk of accidents in the post, he should not have to take risks due entirely to the conduct of the offeree.

So far, it has been assumed that it is in the offeror's interest to uphold the contract. But to hold the acceptance binding as soon as it was posted, in spite of an overtaking communication purporting to revoke it, might cause hardship to the *offeror*. This is particularly true where he had acted in reliance on the revocation. Suppose that A offers to sell B a car. After posting a letter of acceptance, B sends an overtaking email, telling A to ignore that letter. On receipt of the email, A sells the car to C. Could B change his mind yet again, and claim damages from A? There are several ways of avoiding such an unjust result. The first is to say that there had once been a contract but that it was later rescinded by mutual consent: B's email was an offer to release A, which A accepted by conduct; communication of such acceptance could be deemed to have been waived. The second is to regard B's email as a repudiation amounting to a breach of contract; and to say that, by "accepting" the breach, A has put an end to his obligations

---

[208] Turpin [1975] C.L.J. 25; Hudson 82. L.Q.R. 169.

[209] See para.2–032.

[210] cf. *LJ Korbetis v Transgrain Shipping BV* [2005] EWHC 1345 (QB) at [11], dealing with a similar possible outcome in the case of a misdirected acceptance.

[211] Hudson 82 L.Q.R. 169, who also argues that the offeror can protect himself by stipulating that he is not to be bound till the acceptance reaches him, or that the offeree is to be bound as soon as he posts the acceptance.

under the contract.[212] This analysis is preferable from A's point of view if the sale to C is for a lower price than that to B, for it would enable A to claim the difference from B as damages.[213]

**Consumer's right to cancel distance contracts.** While not strictly a matter of revoking an acceptance, it should be noted that a contract made by (for example) exchange of letters, faxes or emails or by website trading may fall within the definition of a "distance contract" under the Consumer Contracts (Information, Cancellation and Additional Charges) Regulations 2013.[214] The Regulations do not specify when such a contract is made; but if it has been made, they give the consumer the right to cancel it[215] by notice within a cancellation period specified in the Regulations.[216] Cancellation "ends the obligations of the parties to perform the contract",[217] but the parties come under obligations which are intended to restore any benefits received under the contract, e.g. reimbursement of any payment, return of goods, etc.[218] The effect of the exercise of the right to cancel is therefore not the same as the effect of saying that no contract has been concluded by (e.g.) exchange of letters under the common law rules of offer and acceptance discussed above; on the contrary, the very concept of the consumer's "right to cancel" is based on the assumption that, as a matter of common law, a contract has come into existence. 2–040

### (c) Prescribed method of acceptance

**Offeror not generally bound by another method.** Where an offer states that it can only be accepted in a specified way,[219] the offeror is not, in general, bound unless acceptance is made in that way. Thus if the offeror asks for the acceptance to be sent to a particular place an acceptance sent elsewhere will not bind him;[220] nor, if he asks for an acceptance in writing, will he be bound by one that is oral.[221] The rule is particularly strict where the offer is contained in an option.[222] The offeror will, however, be bound if he acquiesces in the different mode of acceptance and so waives the stipulated mode. Alternatively, a contract may be concluded if the purported acceptance (which is ineffective as such for failure to comply with the stipulated method) can be regarded as a counter-offer and if that counter-offer is then accepted by the counter-offeree.[223] Since such acceptance 2–041

---

[212] See para.18–016.

[213] See para.17–079 and following; cf. *Kinch v Bullard* [1999] 1 W.L.R. 423 where the withdrawal held ineffective against the addressee was said (at 430–431) to be effective against the sender.

[214] SI 2013/3134 reg.5

[215] Regulation 29(1). The same right also applies to "off-premises contracts" (reg.5); it is subject to the limits set out in reg.28.

[216] Regulation 30.

[217] Regulation 33(1)(a).

[218] Regulations 34–36.

[219] *Mulcaire v News Group Newspapers Ltd* [2011] EWHC 3469 (Ch); [2012] Ch. 435 at [11].

[220] *Frank v Knight* (1937) O.Q.P.D. 113; cf. *Eliason v Henshaw* (1819) 4 Wheat. 225.

[221] *Financings Ltd v Stimson* [1962] 1 W.L.R. 1184 at 1186. Contrast *Hitchens v General Guarantee Corp* [2001] EWCA Civ 359; *The Times*, 13 March 2001.

[222] *Holwell Securities Ltd v Hughes* [1974] 1 W.L.R. 157.

[223] *Wettern Electric Ltd v Welsh Development Agency* [1983] Q.B. 796.

may be effected by conduct,[224] the contract may be concluded without any further communication between the parties after the original, ineffective, acceptance.

2–042 **Equally effective alternative method.** Where the offeror prescribes a method of acceptance, he usually does so with some particular object in view, e.g. to secure a speedy acceptance, or one which will prevent disputes from arising as to the terms of the agreement. An acceptance which accomplishes that object just as well as, or better than, the stipulated method may, by way of exception to the general rule, bind the offeror.[225] For the purpose of this exception, it must first be determined what object the offeror had in view. If he says "reply by letter sent by return of post" this may simply mean "reply quickly": the words may "fix the time for acceptance and not the manner of accepting."[226] If so, a reply by email would suffice. But such a reply would not suffice if the offer meant "reply quickly and by letter, I do not like emails as they are often obscure".

2–043 **Prescribed method waived.** An offeror can waive any requirement as to the form of acceptance if the stipulation as to form is solely for its benefit.[227] But if the stipulation is for the benefit of both parties it must be clear that both parties have waived the stipulation.[228] Stipulations as to the mode of acceptance may also be made for the protection and benefit of the *offeree*, e.g. where a customer submits a proposal to enter into a hire-purchase agreement; or where an offer is made on a form of tender provided by the offeree. If the offeree accepts in some other way, this will often be evidence that he has waived the stipulation; and it is submitted that the acceptance ought to be treated as effective unless it can be shown that failure to use the stipulated mode has prejudiced the offeror.[229]

### (d) Acceptance by silence

2–044 **Offeree generally not bound.** An offer may specify, not that it *must*, but that it *may*, be accepted in a particular way. In cases of this kind, particular difficulty arises from provisions to the effect that the offeree may accept by silence. As a general rule, an offeree who simply does nothing on receipt of an offer which

[224] As in *Wettern Electric Ltd v Welsh Development Agency* [1983] Q.B. 796; provided, however, that such conduct is accompanied by the requisite contractual intention: see *Harvela Investments Ltd v Royal Trust Co of Canada (CI) Ltd* [1986] A.C. 207; and para.4–003.

[225] *Manchester Diocesan Council for Education v Commercial and General Investments Ltd* [1970] 1 W.L.R. 242.

[226] *Tinn v Hoffmann & Co* (1873) 29 L.T. 271 at 278; *Manchester Diocesan Council for Education v Commercial & General Investments Ltd* [1970] 1 W.L.R. 242; cf. *Edmund Murray v PSB Foundations* (1992) 33 Con L.R. 1.

[227] *MSM Consulting Ltd v Tanzania* [2009] EWHC 121 (QB); 123 Con L.R. 154 at [120]; *A Ltd v B Ltd* [2015] EWHC 137 (Comm) at [29].

[228] *MSM Consulting Ltd v Tanzania* [2009] EWHC 121 (QB); 123 Con L.R. 154 at [120]; cf. *The Botnica* [2006] EWHC 1360 (Comm); [2007] 1 Lloyd's Rep. 37.

[229] See *Robophone Facilities v Blank* [1966] 1 W.L.R. 1423; *Carlyle Finance Ltd v Pallas Industrial Finance Ltd* [1999] 1 All E.R. (Comm) 659 at 670 (approving reasoning identical with that in the text above); cf. *Manchester Diocesan Council for Education v Commercial and General Investments Ltd* [1970] 1 W.L.R. 242. From this point of view, these cases are, it is submitted, to be preferred to *Financings Ltd v Stimson* [1962] 1 W.L.R. 1184.

states that it may be accepted by silence is not bound. In *Felthouse v Bindley*[230] an uncle offered to buy his nephew's horse by a letter in which he said: "If I hear no more about him, I shall consider the horse mine." Later, the horse was, by mistake, included in an auction sale of the nephew's property. The uncle sued the auctioneer for damages for the conversion of the horse. It was held that, at the time of the auction, there was no contract for the sale of the horse to the uncle because: "The uncle had no right to impose upon the nephew the sale of his horse … unless he chose to comply with the condition of writing to repudiate the offer …".[231] The reason for the rule is that it is, in general, undesirable to impose the trouble and expense of rejecting an offer on an offeree who does not wish to accept it.[232]

The question whether silence can amount to an acceptance binding the offeree has also arisen in the cases, already discussed, in which the issue was whether an agreement to abandon an earlier agreement to submit a claim to arbitration could be inferred from inactivity, in the form of long delay in prosecuting the claim.[233] In these cases, it had been held that, even if one party's inactivity could be regarded as an offer to abandon the arbitration, the mere silence or inactivity[234] of the other did not normally amount to an acceptance. For one thing, such inactivity was often[235] equivocal,[236] being explicable on other grounds (such as forgetfulness). For another, acceptance could not, as a matter of law, be inferred from silence alone[237] "save in the most exceptional circumstances".[238]

**Offeree exceptionally bound?** As the above reference to "exceptional circumstances" suggests, there may be exceptions to the general rule that an offeree is not bound by silence. If the offer has been solicited by the offeree, the argument that he should not be put to the trouble of rejecting it loses much of its force,[239] especially if the offer is made on a form provided by the offeree[240] and that form stipulates that silence may amount to acceptance.[241] Again, if there is a course of dealing between the parties, the offeror may be led to suppose that 2–045

[230] (1862) 11 C.B. (N.S.) 869; affirmed (1863) New Rep. 401; Miller 35 M.L.R. 489; cf. *Financial Techniques* (*Planning Services*) *v Hughes* [1981] I.R.L.R. 32 at 35.

[231] *Felthouse v Bindley* (1862) 11 C.B. (N.S.) 869 at 875.

[232] The evidence in *Felthouse v Bindley* that the nephew did in fact wish to sell the horse to the uncle means that the actual decision is hard to support, but this is no criticism of the general rule laid down.

[233] See para.2–005.

[234] For acceptance by silence *and conduct*, see para.2–048.

[235] But not always: see fn.243.

[236] e.g. *Jayaar Impex Ltd v Toaken Group Ltd* [1996] 2 Lloyd's Rep. 437 at 445.

[237] *The Leonidas D* [1985] 1 W.L.R. 925 at 927; *Rafsanjan Pistachio Producers Co-operative v Bank Leumi (UK) Plc* [1992] 1 Lloyd's Rep. 513 at 542.

[238] *The Leonidas D* [1985] 1 W.L.R. 925 at 927; *Vitol SA v Norelf Ltd* [1996] A.C. 800 at 812. Such "exceptional circumstances" may be illustrated by *The Splendid Sun* [1981] Q.B. 694 (where acceptance may have been by conduct: para.2–048) though this case is hard to reconcile with *The Leonidas D*; cf. *Cie Française d'Importation v Deutsche Continental Handelsgesellschaft* [1985] 2 Lloyd's Rep. 592 at 598. *The Golden Bear* [1987] 1 Lloyd's Rep. 330 is hard to reconcile with these cases and was apparently doubted in *The Antclizo* [1987] 2 Lloyd's Rep. 130 at 147 (affirmed [1988] 1 W.L.R. 603).

[239] cf. *Rust v Abbey Life Ins Co* [1979] 2 Lloyd's Rep. 335.

[240] cf. para.2–043.

[241] As in *Alexander Hamilton Institute v Jones*, 234 Ill. App. (1924).

silence amounts to acceptance: e.g. where a retailer's offers to buy goods from a wholesaler have in the past been accepted as a matter of course by the despatch of the goods in question.[242] In such a case it may not be unreasonable to require the offeree to give notice of his rejection of the offer, especially if the offeror, in reliance on his belief that the goods would be delivered in the usual way, had forborne from seeking an alternative supply. On a somewhat similar principle, one party's wrongful repudiation of a contract may be accepted by the other party's failure to take such further steps in the performance of that contract as he would have been expected to take, if he were treating the contract as still in force.[243]

There may also be "an express undertaking or implied obligation to speak"[244] arising out of the course of negotiations between the parties, e.g. "where the offeree himself indicates that an offer is to be taken as accepted if he does not indicate the contrary by an ascertainable time",[245] particularly if the parties are "sorting out details against the background of a concluded contract."[246] Failure to perform such an "obligation to speak" could enable the *offeror* to treat that failure as an acceptance by silence. But it is not normally open to the *offeree* to treat his own silence (in breach of his "duty to speak") as an acceptance.[247] This course would be open to him only in situations such as that in *Felthouse v Bindley*,[248] in which the offeror had indicated (usually in the terms of the offer) that he would treat silence as an acceptance.

There is also the possibility that silence may constitute an acceptance by virtue of the custom of the trade or business in question.[249]

2–046 **Alternative liability of the offeree.** Even where silence of the offeree does not amount to an acceptance, it is arguable that he might be liable on a different basis. In *Spiro v Lintern* it was said that:

> "If A sees B acting in the mistaken belief that A is under some binding obligation to him and in a manner consistent only with such an obligation, which would be to B's disadvantage if A were thereafter to deny the obligation, A is under a duty to B to disclose the non-existence of the supposed obligation."[250]

Although this statement was made with reference to wholly different circumstances,[251] it could also be applied to certain cases in which an offeror had, to the

[242] As in *Cole-McIntyre-Norfleet Co v Holloway,* 141 Tenn. 679; 214 S.W. 87 (1919).
[243] *Vitol SA v Norelf Ltd* [1996] A.C. 800; see para.18–012.
[244] *The Agrabele* [1985] 2 Lloyd's Rep. 496 at 509 (Evans J, whose statement of the relevant legal principles was approved on appeal, though the actual decision was reversed on the facts: [1987] 2 Lloyd's Rep. 223 at 225). The case would now be governed by Arbitration Act 1996 s.41(3): see para.2–005.
[245] *Re Selectmove* [1995] 1 W.L.R. 474 at 478 (where the point was left open).
[246] *The Harriette N* [2008] EWHC 2257 (Comm); [2008] 2 Lloyd's Rep. 685 at [70]; citing *Pagnan SpA v Feed Products Ltd* [1987] 2 Lloyd's Rep. 601 at 614.
[247] *Yona International Ltd v La Réunion Française* [1996] 2 Lloyd's Rep. 84 at 110.
[248] See para.2–044, further discussed below.
[249] *Minories Finance Ltd v Afribank Nigeria Ltd* [1995] 1 Lloyd's Rep. 134.
[250] *Spiro v Lintern* [1973] 1 W.L.R. 1002 at 1011.
[251] See para.16–033.

offeree's knowledge,[252] acted in reliance on the belief that his offer had been accepted by silence. The liability of the offeree would then be based on a kind of estoppel.[253] The application of this doctrine to cases of alleged acceptance by silence gives rise to the difficulty that an estoppel can only arise out of a "clear and unequivocal"[254] representation, and that such a representation cannot generally be inferred from mere inactivity.[255] But this general rule does not preclude the application of the doctrine of estoppel to exceptional cases of the kind here under discussion, in which there are special circumstances which give rise to a "duty to speak", and in which it would be unconscionable for the party under that duty to deny that a contract had come into existence.[256]

If the offeror, to the offeree's knowledge, actually performs in accordance with his offer and so confers a benefit on the offeree, the solution in this type of case may be to make the offeree restore the benefit rather than to hold him to an obligation to perform his part of a contract to which he had never agreed.[257]

**Offeror bound?** There is some authority for saying that the offeror cannot, any more than the offeree, be bound where the offeree simply remains silent in response to the offer,[258] and the case is not one of the exceptional ones discussed above[259] in which an offer can be accepted by silence. But the object of the general rule laid down in *Felthouse v Bindley*[260] is to protect *the offeree* from having to incur the trouble and expense of rejecting the offer so as to avoid being bound. No such argument can normally be advanced for protecting the offeror. He may indeed be left in doubt on the question whether his offer has been accepted; but this is not a matter about which he can legitimately complain where he has drawn up his offer in terms which permit (and even encourage) acceptance by silence.[261] Thus the uncle in *Felthouse v Bindley* might have been bound if the nephew had resolved to accept the offer and had, in reliance on its terms, forborne from attempting to dispose of the horse elsewhere. This possibility has been judicially doubted,[262] but in the case in which the doubt was raised it was not an express term of the offer that silence would be regarded as acceptance. 2–047

[252] See *Yona International Ltd v La Réunion Française* [1996] 2 Lloyd's Rep. 84 at 107 (where this requirement was not satisfied).

[253] See paras 3–090, 9–190; cf. (in another context) *The Stolt Loyalty* [1993] 2 Lloyd's Rep. 281 at 289–291; affirmed [1995] 1 Lloyd's Rep. 598, without reference to this point. The case would not be one of estoppel by convention (para.3–094), for such estoppel is based on an *agreed* assumption of fact, while in cases of the present kind the question is whether there was any agreement.

[254] See paras 3–081, 9–190.

[255] See para.3–082.

[256] cf. *AC Yule & Son Ltd v Speedwell Roofing & Cladding Ltd* [2007] EWHC 1360 (TCC); [2007] B.L.R. 499 (obligation to respond to adjudicator's requests under the Housing Grants, Construction and Regeneration Act 1996 Pt II).

[257] Burrows, *The Law of Restitution*, 3rd edn (2010), pp.334–339.

[258] *Fairline Shipping Corp v Adamson* [1975] Q.B. 180 at 189.

[259] At para.2–045.

[260] See para.2–044.

[261] This reasoning would not apply where the terms of the offer had been drawn up by the *offeree*: cf. para.2–043.

[262] *Fairline Shipping Corp v Adamson* [1975] Q.B. 180 at 189.

Where the offeror has expressly formulated his offer in such terms, it is submitted that the offeree's silence in response to the offer should be capable of binding the offeror.

It is settled that a creditor can accept his debtor's offer to give additional security for a debt by simply forbearing to sue for the debt.[263] If such forbearance can be regarded as silence, this rule supports the view that acceptance by silence can bind the offeror. Another possible explanation of the rule is that a creditor who forbears accepts by conduct[264] rather than by silence.

2–048 **Silence and conduct.** In *Roberts v Hayward*[265] a tenant accepted his landlord's offer of a new tenancy at an increased rent by simply staying on the premises. It was held that he had accepted the landlord's offer by silence; but it seems better to say that he accepted by conduct and that the landlord waived notice of acceptance.[266] Similarly an offer made *to* a landowner to occupy land under a licence containing specified terms may be accepted by the landowner's permitting the offeror to occupy the land.[267] An offeree is not, for the present purpose, "silent" merely because his acceptance is not expressed in words.[268] The possibility of acceptance by conduct is, yet again, illustrated by the arbitration cases already mentioned,[269] according to which, an offer of abandonment can be accepted by reacting to it, not merely by inactivity,[270] but also by some further conduct: e.g. by closing or disposing of relevant files.[271] It also appears to be accepted that, in context, "conduct can take the form of forbearance".[272]

In *Rust v Abbey Life Ins Co*[273] the claimant applied and paid for a "property bond" which was allocated to her on the terms of the defendants' usual policy of insurance. After having retained this document for some seven months, she claimed the return of her payment, alleging that no contract had been concluded. The claim was rejected on the ground that her application was an offer which had been accepted by issue of the policy. But it was further held that, even if the policy constituted a counter-offer, this counter-offer had been accepted by "the conduct of the [claimant] in doing and saying nothing for seven months …".[274] Thus mere inaction was said to be sufficient to constitute acceptance; and it seems to have amounted to no more than silence in spite of having been described as "conduct". The conclusion that it amounted to acceptance can, however, be justified in the circumstances. The negotiations had been started by the

---

263 See para.3–040.
264 See para.2–018.
265 (1828) 3 C. & P. 432.
266 cf. para.2–028.
267 *Wettern Electric Ltd v Welsh Development Agency* [1983] Q.B. 796.
268 *Aspinall's Club Ltd v Al Zayat* [2007] EWCA Civ 1001 at [30].
269 See para.2–044.
270 cf. *Collin v Duke of Westminster* [1985] Q.B. 581.
271 See *The Splendid Sun* [1981] Q.B. 694 at 712, 713 ("closed their files"); cf. at 706 ("did so act"); *The Multibank Holsatia* [1988] 2 Lloyd's Rep. 486 at 493 (where the offeree had destroyed relevant files, so that the case was not one of mere inaction).
272 *Vis Trading v Nazarov* [2014] EWCA Civ 313 at [40].
273 [1979] 2 Lloyd's Rep. 335.
274 *Rust v Abbey Life Ins Co* [1979] 2 Lloyd's Rep. 335; affirming [1978] 2 Lloyd's Rep. 386 at 393.

claimant[275] (the counter-offeree), and in view of this fact it was reasonable for the defendants to infer from her long silence that she had accepted the terms of the policy which had been sent to her and which she must be "taken to have examined".[276] The case thus falls within one of the suggested exceptions[277] to the general rule that an offeree is not bound by silence.

### (e) Acceptance in ignorance of offer

**Generally ineffective.** The general view is that acceptance in ignorance of an offer cannot create a contract since the parties must *reach* agreement: it is not enough that their wishes happen to coincide: the act or promise constituting the acceptance must be "given in exchange for the offer".[278] The same reasoning applies where a person once knew of the offer but had at the time of the alleged acceptance forgotten it.[279] On this basis, a person who gives information for which a reward has been offered cannot claim the reward unless at the time of giving it he knew of the offer of reward. The English case of *Gibbons v Proctor*[280] is sometimes thought to support the contrary view, but can be explained on the ground that the claimant did know of the offer of reward by the time the information was given on his behalf to the person named in the advertisement. 2–049

In the "reward case", it is hard to see what prejudice the offeror would suffer if he had to pay the reward to someone who had complied with the terms of the offer without being aware of it.[281] The reasons for holding that there is no contract in such a case seem to be largely doctrinal; but more practical difficulties can arise where the acts alleged to amount to an acceptance can not only confer rights on the actor, but also deprive him of rights[282] or impose duties on him. This last possibility may be illustrated by reference to *Upton Rural DC v Powell*[283] where the defendant, whose house was on fire, telephoned the Upton police and asked for "the fire brigade". He was entitled to the service of the Pershore fire brigade free of charge as he lived in its district; but the police called the Upton fire brigade, in the belief that the defendant lived in that district. The latter fire brigade for a time shared this belief and thought "that they were rendering gratuitous services in their own area". It was held that the defendant was contractually bound to pay for these services. But even if the defendant's telephone call was an offer, it is hard to see how the Upton brigade's services,

---

[275] cf. para.2–039; and *Vitol SA v Norelf Ltd* [1996] A.C. 800; para.2–045.

[276] Contrast *Yona International Ltd v La Réunion Française* [1996] 2 Lloyd's Rep. 84 at 110; *Cooper v National Westminster Bank Plc* [2009] EWHC 3035 (QB); [2010] 1 Lloyd's Rep. 490.

[277] See para.2–045.

[278] *R. v Clarke* (1927) 40 C.L.R. 227 at 233; *Tracomin SA v Anton C Nielsen* [1984] 2 Lloyd's Rep. 195 at 203; *Lark v Outhwaite* [1991] 2 Lloyd's Rep. 132 at 140.

[279] *R. v Clarke* (1927) 40 C.L.R. 227 at 233 at 241.

[280] (1891) 64 L.T. 594, sub nom. *Gibson v Proctor* 55 J.P. 616. See Hudson 84 L.Q.R. 513.

[281] The possibility of acceptance without being aware of the offer, in the case of a unilateral contract, was left open in *The Jag Ravi* [2011] EWHC 1372 (Comm); [2011] 2 Lloyd's Rep. 309 at [48]; affirmed [2012] EWCA Civ 180; [2012] 1 Lloyd's Rep. 637, though on the basis that no contract was concluded: see para.14–103.

[282] e.g. *Tracomin SA v Anton C Nielsen* [1984] 2 Lloyd's Rep. 195 at 203.

[283] *Upton Rural DC v Powell* [1942] 1 All E.R. 220; Mitchell 12 J.C.L. 78.

given with no thought of reward, could be an acceptance. It would have been better to give the claimants a restitutionary remedy than to hold that there was a contract.[284] The case was concerned only with the rights of the fire brigade, but the fire brigade could also have owed more extensive duties as contractors than as volunteers. It may well be hard to subject a person who reasonably thinks that he is a volunteer to the more stringent duties of a contractor.[285]

2–050 **Cross-offers.** The requirement that the offeree must know of the offer at the time of the alleged acceptance also accounts for the rule that there is no contract if two persons make identical cross-offers, neither party knowing of the other's offer when he makes his own, e.g. if A writes to B offering to sell B his car for £5,000 and B simultaneously writes to A offering to buy the car for £5,000. If no further communication took place in such a case, the parties might well be in doubt as to whether there was indeed a contract between them; and the view that "cross offers are not an acceptance of each other"[286] can be supported on the ground that it tends to promote certainty.

2–051 **Relevance of motive for acceptance.** A person who knows of the offer may do the act required for acceptance with some motive other than that of accepting the offer. In *Williams v Carwardine*[287] the defendant offered a reward of £20 to anyone who gave information leading to the conviction of the murderers of Walter Carwardine. The claimant knew of the offer, and, thinking that she had not long to live, signed a "voluntary statement to ease my conscience, and in hopes of forgiveness hereafter". This statement resulted in the conviction of the murderers. It was held that the claimant had brought herself within the terms of the offer and was entitled to the reward. Patteson J said: "We cannot go into the (claimant's) motives".[288] Similarly, in *Carlill v Carbolic Smoke Ball Co*[289] the claimant recovered the £100, although her predominant motive in using the smoke ball was (presumably) to avoid catching influenza. But in the Australian case of *R. v Clarke*[290] a reward had been offered for information leading to the arrest and conviction of the murderers of two police officers. Clarke, who knew of the offer and was himself suspected of the crime, gave such information. He admitted that he had done so to clear himself of the charge, and with no thought of claiming the reward. His claim for the reward failed as he had not given the information "in exchange for the offer".[291] It seems that an act which is *wholly* motivated by factors other than the existence of the offer cannot amount to an acceptance,[292]

[284] cf. Burrows, *The Law of Restitution* (2010), pp.241–242; *The Sibohelle* [2011] EWHC 1150 (Comm); [2011] 2 Lloyd's Rep. 220 at [44].
[285] cf. *BSC v Cleveland Bridge & Engineering Co Ltd* [1984] 1 All E.R. 504 at 510; *Air Transworld Ltd v Bombardier Inc* [2012] EWHC 243; [2012] 1 Lloyd's Rep. 349 at [75].
[286] *Tinn v Hoffmann & Co* (1873) 29 L.T. 271 at 278.
[287] (1833) 5 C. & P. 566; 4 B. & Ad. 621; it must be assumed that the claimant knew of the offer: *Carlill v Carbolic Smoke Ball Co Ltd* [1892] 2 Q.B. at 489, fn.2.
[288] *Williams v Carwardine,* 4 B. & Ad. 621 at 623.
[289] [1893] 1 Q.B. 256, para.2–010.
[290] *R. v Clarke* (1927) 40 C.L.R. 227.
[291] *R. v Clarke* (1927) 40 C.L.R. 227 at 233.
[292] *Lark v Outhwaite* [1991] 2 Lloyd's Rep. 132 at 140.

but if the existence of the offer plays some part, however small, in inducing a person to do the required act, there is a valid acceptance of the offer.

### (f) Acceptance in unilateral contracts

An offer of a unilateral contract is made when one party promises to pay the other a sum of money[293] if the other will do (or forbear from doing) something without making any promise to that effect: e.g. when one person promises to pay another £100 if he will walk from London to York,[294] or give up smoking for a year.[295] The contract which arises in these cases is called "unilateral" because it arises without the offeree's having made any counter-promise to perform the required act or forbearance; it is contrasted with a bilateral contract, in which each party undertakes an obligation and in which acceptance, as a general rule, takes the form of a communication by the offeree of his counter-promise. The distinction between the two types of contract sometimes gives rise to difficulty,[296] because a contract may be in its inception unilateral, but become bilateral in the course of its performance.[297] For example, A may promise to pay B £1,000 for some service (such as repainting A's house) which B does not promise to render. Here B would not be liable if he did nothing; but once he began the work (e.g. by stripping off the old paint) he might be held to have impliedly promised[298] to complete it, so that at this stage the contract would become bilateral[299] and both parties would be bound by it. 2–052

**General rules as to acceptance.** Once a promise is classified as an offer of a unilateral contract, a number of rules apply to the acceptance of such an offer. First, the offer can be accepted by fully performing the required act or forbearance.[300] Secondly, there is no need to give advance notice of acceptance to the offeror.[301] And thirdly, the offer can, like all other offers, be withdrawn before it has been accepted. But there is much dispute as to the exact stage at which the offer is "accepted" so as to deprive the offeror of the power of withdrawal. 2–053

---

[293] Or to do some other act, or to forbear from doing something. In the text we shall deal only with the most common case of a promise to pay money.

[294] An old example: *Rogers v Snow* (1573) Dalison 94; cf. *Great Northern Ry v Witham* (1873) L.R. 9 C.P. 16 at 19.

[295] cf. *Hamer v Sidway,* 124 N.Y. 538 (1881).

[296] See generally Llewellyn 48 Yale L.J. 1, 799.

[297] cf. *The Eurymedon* [1975] A.C. 154 at 167–168 ("a bargain initially unilateral but capable of becoming mutual"): see further para.14–069.

[298] According to a dictum in *Little v Courage Ltd* (1995) 70 P. & C.R. 469 at 475, terms which impose legal obligations cannot be implied into a unilateral contract; but this view would not preclude such a contract from becoming bilateral after it had originally come into existence. See further para.6–061.

[299] See *The Unique Mariner* [1979] 2 Lloyd's Rep. 37 at 51–52; *The Kurnia Dewi* [1997] 1 Lloyd's Rep. 553 at 559; contrast *BSC v Cleveland Bridge & Engineering Co Ltd* [1984] 1 All E.R. 504 at 510–511 where such an implied promise was negatived by the fact that the terms of a bilateral contract were still under negotiation and were never agreed.

[300] See *Daulia Ltd v Four Millbank Nominees Ltd* [1978] Ch. 231 at 238; cf. *Harvela Investments Ltd v Royal Trust of Canada (CI) Ltd* [1986] A.C. 207 at 224.

[301] *Carlill v Carbolic Smoke Ball Co* [1893] 1 Q.B. 256; *Bowerman v Association of British Travel Agents* [1995] N.L.J. 1815.

2–054 **Acceptance by part performance.** It is probable that the offer can be accepted *only* by some performance and not by a counter-promise to walk to York, or to give up smoking; for such a counter-promise would not be what the offeror had bargained for. Thus the offeror could still withdraw after such a counter-promise had been made. It is less clear whether the offeror can still withdraw after the offeree has *partly* performed the required act or forbearance, e.g. if he has walked half way to York or refrained from smoking for six months. The first problem (which will be discussed here) is whether the offeree has at this stage accepted the offer; the second (to be discussed in Ch.3)[302] is whether he has provided consideration for the offeror's promise.

According to one view, there is no contract until the required act or forbearance has been completed, and this is said to give effect to the intention of the parties, each of whom intends, until then, to reserve a *locus poenitentiae*.[303] But in most cases[304] it is unlikely that the offeree intends to expose himself to the risk of withdrawal when he has partly performed and is willing and able[305] to complete performance for the sake of securing the promised benefit. The general view is that it would cause hardship to the offeree to allow the offeror to withdraw in such a case; and most writers try to find some reason for saying that part-performance prevents the offeror from withdrawing the offer. One possibility is to say that the offeror makes two offers: (1) the principal offer; and (2) a collateral one to keep the principal offer open once performance has begun; this latter offer is accepted by beginning to perform.[306] But this analysis is artificial: it is more realistic to say that the principal offer itself is accepted by beginning to perform.[307] Acceptance is no more (or less) than an unqualified expression of assent to the terms of the offer by words or conduct and the question whether an inference of such assent can be drawn from part-performance is simply one of fact. The sight of a man walking northwards from London may or may not suggest that he does so in response to an offer to pay him £100 if he reaches York, but, if his conduct does clearly suggest this, there is no theoretical difficulty in saying that he has accepted the offer. Factual difficulties might, of course, arise in distinguishing between commencement of performance and mere preparation to perform. Thus it is probable that an offer of a reward for the return of lost property could still be withdrawn after someone had spent time looking for the property without success, but not after he had actually found it and was in the process of returning it to the owner.

---

[302] See para.3–160.

[303] Wormser in *Selected Readings on the Law of Contracts from American and English Legal Periodicals* (MacMillan Co, 1931), p.307; but for the same writer's later views see 3 Jl. Leg. Educ. 146.

[304] For a possible exception, see para.2–057.

[305] It is assumed that performance remains within the offeree's power. If not, the offeror can withdraw: see *Morrison SS Co v The Crown* (1924) 20 Lloyd's Law Rep.283.

[306] McGoveney in *Selected Readings on the Law of Contracts from American and English Legal Periodicals* (1931), p.300.

[307] Pollock, *Principles of Contract*, 13th edn (Stevens & Sons, 1950), p.19; Ballantine, *Selected Readings*, p.312.

Support for the above view is provided by *Errington v Errington*[308] where a father bought a house subject to a mortgage, allowed his son and daughter-in-law to live in it, and told them that, if they paid the mortgage instalments, the house would be theirs when the mortgage was paid off. The couple started to live in the house and paid some of the mortgage instalments; but they did not bind themselves to go on making the payments. It was held that this arrangement amounted to a contract which could not, after the father's death, be revoked by his personal representatives. Denning LJ said:

> "The father's promise was a unilateral contract—a promise of the house in return for their act of paying the instalments. It could not be revoked by him once the couple entered on performance of the act, but it would cease to bind him if they left it incomplete and unperformed, which they have not done."[309]

**Continuing guarantees.** The view that part-performance of a unilateral contract can amount to an acceptance is further supported by the law relating to continuing guarantees. These may be divisible, where each advance constitutes a separate transaction; or indivisible, e.g. where, on A's admission to an association, B guarantees all liabilities that A may incur as a member of the association.[310] If the guarantee is divisible, it can be revoked at any time with regard to future advances;[311] but an indivisible guarantee cannot be revoked after the creditor has begun to act on it by giving credit to the principal debtor.[312] This rule applies even though the contract of guarantee is unilateral in the sense that the creditor has not made any promise to the guarantor (in return for the guarantee) to give credit to the debtor. 2–055

**Bankers' irrevocable credits.** This subject is more fully explained in Ch.3.[313] Here it need only be said that the essence of the system is that a bank, on the instruction of its customer (usually a buyer of goods) notifies a third person (usually the seller) that it has opened an irrevocable credit in his favour, promising to pay him a stipulated sum if he will present certain specified documents to the bank. The general view is that the bank cannot revoke the promise once it has been notified to the seller; and, as the seller makes no promise *to the bank*, this result is sometimes explained in terms of a unilateral contract between these parties. In most cases there will be some act of part-performance by the seller, e.g. in shipping the goods so as to procure the required documents. But the bank's promise is regarded as binding as soon as it is 2–056

308 [1952] 1 K.B. 290. The reasoning of this case was doubted, but not on this point, in *National Provincial Bank Ltd v Ainsworth* [1965] A.C. 1175 at 1239–1240, 1251–1252.

309 *Errington v Errington* [1952] 1 K.B. 290 at 295; cf. *Soulsbury v Soulsbury* [2007] EWCA Civ 969; [2008] 2 W.L.R. 834 at [50] (where performance had been completed); *Schweppe v Harper* [2008] EWCA Civ 442; [2008] B.P.I.R. 1090 at [46]: "Where there is an offer to pay for the performance of a certain task, part performance can produce a contract under which that offer cannot be withdrawn" (Waller LJ, dissenting).

310 As in *Lloyd's v Harper* (1880) 16 Ch D. 290.

311 As in *Offord v Davies* (1862) 12 C.B.N.S. 748.

312 *Lloyd's v Harper* (1880) 16 Ch D. 290.

313 See para.3–161.

notified to the seller, i.e. before he has done any act in response to it. The binding force of such irrevocable credits is not, therefore, easily explicable in terms of acceptance of an offer.

2–057 **Estate agents' contracts.** Where an estate agent is engaged to negotiate the sale of a house, it is arguable that his client's promise to pay a commission on sale gives rise to a unilateral contract, for in one case of this kind it was said that "No obligation is imposed on the agent to do anything."[314] It is settled that the client (the offeror) can, without liability, revoke his instructions before a claim to commission has accrued, in spite of the fact that the agent (the offeree) has made considerable efforts to find a purchaser.[315] Hence these cases could be said to support the view that an offer of a unilateral contract can be withdrawn after part-performance by the offeree. But the better explanation is that this is one of the exceptional cases in which, on the true construction of the offer, a *locus poenitentiae* is reserved to the client even after part-performance by the agent. This view is supported by the fact that the right to revoke instructions exists even where the contract is bilateral because the agent has, expressly or by implication, made some promise: e.g. one to use his best endeavours to effect a sale[316] or one to bear advertising expenses.[317] Such promises have been found to exist where the agent has been appointed "sole agent", but in practice they are commonly made by other agents as well. A "sole agent" is entitled to damages if the client sells through another agent,[318] but not if he simply revokes his instructions or sells "privately", without the help of any agent at all.[319] These rules apply irrespective of the unilateral or bilateral nature of the contract; so that the estate agency cases shed little, if any, light on the question of acceptance by part-performance of unilateral contracts.

2–058 **Extent of recovery.** Where a unilateral contract takes the shape of a promise to pay a sum of money, it is generally assumed that the promisee must either get nothing or the full sum. But this seems unnecessarily inflexible. If the promisee has walked half way to York before the offer is withdrawn, it is arguable that he should desist and recover damages.[320] This may take the form of a discounted payment of the sum promised to reflect the fact that he may not have completed performance.[321]

---

[314] *Luxor (Eastbourne) Ltd v Cooper* [1941] A.C. 108 at 124. In fact the agent often does undertake to do something; see fnn.316, 317.

[315] See para.16–101.

[316] *Christopher v Essig* [1958] W.N. 461; *John McCann & Co v Pow* [1974] 1 W.L.R. 1643 at 1647.

[317] cf. *Bentall Horsley & Baldry v Vicary* [1931] 1 K.B. 253.

[318] *Hampton & Sons Ltd v George* [1939] 3 All E.R. 627; *Christopher v Essig* [1958] W.N. 461; para.16–104.

[319] See para.16–104.

[320] Unless the promisee has a "substantial or legitimate interest" in going on, this may be the law under the principles laid down in *White & Carter (Councils) Ltd v McGregor* [1962] A.C. 413; para.21–013.

[321] *Schweppe v Harper* [2008] EWCA Civ 442; [2008] B.P.I.R. 1090 at [53] (Waller LJ, dissenting).

## 3. TERMINATION OF OFFER

### (a) Withdrawal

**Communication to offeree generally required.** As a general rule, an offer can be withdrawn at any time before it is accepted.[322] It is not withdrawn merely by acting inconsistently with it, e.g. by disposing of the subject-matter.[323] Notice of the withdrawal must be given and must actually reach the offeree,[324] or an agent of the offeree with authority to receive notification of withdrawal:[325] mere posting will not suffice. In *Byrne & Co v Leon van Tienhoven*[326] an offer to sell tinplates was posted in Cardiff on 1 October and reached the offerees in New York on 11 October, and they immediately accepted it by a telegram which they confirmed by a letter of 15 October. Meanwhile, the offerors had on 8 October posted a letter withdrawing their offer, but that letter of withdrawal did not reach the offerees until 20 October. It was held that there was a contract since the withdrawal had not been communicated when the offer was accepted. Thus there was a contract in spite of the fact that the parties were demonstrably not in agreement, for when the offerees first knew of the offer, the offerors had already ceased to intend to deal with the offerees. The rule is based on convenience; for no one could rely on a postal offer if it could be withdrawn by a letter already posted but not yet received. **2–059**

**Communication need not come from offeror.** Although withdrawal must be communicated to the offeree, it need not be communicated by the offeror. It is sufficient if the offeree knows from any reliable source that the offeror no longer intends to contract with him. Thus in *Dickinson v Dodds*[327] it was held that an offer to sell land could not be accepted after the offeror had, to the offeree's knowledge, decided to sell the land to a third party. The decision is based on the fact that there is in such a case no agreement between the parties. But this would be equally true if the offeree did not know of the withdrawal at all when he accepted the offer: yet in that case there is normally[328] a contract.[329] The rule that communication of withdrawal need not come from the offeror can be a regrettable source of uncertainty. It puts on the offeree the possibly difficult task of deciding whether his source of information is reliable, and it may also make it **2–060**

[322] *Routledge v Grant* (1828) 4 Bing 653; *Offord v Davies* (1862) 12 C.B.N.S. 748; *Scammell v Dicker* [2001] 1 W.L.R. 631; *Bircham & Co Nominees (No.2) v Worrell Holdings* [2001] EWCA Civ 775; (2001) 82 P. & C.R. 472 at [24], [35].

[323] *Adams v Lindsell* (1818) 1 B. & Ald. 681; *Stevenson, Jacques & Co v McLean* (1880) 5 Q.B.D. 346.

[324] An initial offer may be withdrawn by making a further offer depending on the nature of the two offers and the circumstances in which they were made: *Pickfords Ltd v Celestica Ltd* [2003] EWCA Civ 1741 at [17].

[325] *Financing Ltd v Stimson* [1962] 1 W.L.R. 1184; *CF Asset Finance Ltd v Okonji* [2014] EWCA Civ 870; [2014] E.C.C. 23.

[326] (1880) 5 C.P.D. 344. Under Consumer Credit Act 1974 s.69(1)(ii) and (7) posting is, exceptionally, sufficient (as is "transmission" of an electronic communication).

[327] (1876) 2 Ch D. 463; cf. *Cartwright v Hoogstoel* (1911) 105 L.T. 628.

[328] i.e. subject to the exceptions stated in the following paragraph.

[329] *Byrne & Co v Leon van Tienhoven* (1880) 5 C.P.D. 344, fn.326.

hard for him to tell exactly when the offer was withdrawn. In *Dickinson v Dodds*, for example, it is not clear whether this occurred when the offeree realised that the defendant had: (a) sold the land to the third party; or (b) begun to negotiate with the third party; or (c) simply decided not to sell to the claimant. Certainty would be promoted if the rule were that the withdrawal must be communicated by the offeror, as well as to the offeree.

2–061 **Exceptions.** The general rule that the withdrawal must be "brought to the mind of"[330] the offeree is subject to a number of exceptions. First, the requirement cannot be taken quite literally where an offer is made to a company whose mail is received, opened and sorted in different offices and then distributed to be dealt with in various departments. Is a letter withdrawing such an offer communicated when it is received, or when it is opened, or when it is actually read by the responsible officer?[331] In the interests of certainty it would probably be held that communication took place when the letter was "opened in the ordinary course of business or would have been so opened if the ordinary course was followed."[332] Secondly (as the concluding words of the passage just quoted suggest) the general rule may be displaced by the conduct of the offeree. A withdrawal which had reached the offeree would be effective even though he had simply failed to read it after it had reached him: this would be the position where a withdrawal by fax or email reached the offeree's office during business hours[333] even though it was not actually read by the offeree or by any of his staff till the next day.[334] Of course the withdrawal would not be effective in such a case if it had been sent to the offeree at a time when he and all responsible members of his staff were, to the offeror's knowledge, away on holiday or on other business.[335] A third exception to the requirement that a withdrawal must be actually communicated relates to offers made to the public, e.g. of rewards for information leading to the arrest of the perpetrator of a crime. As it is impossible for the offeror to ensure that the notice of withdrawal comes to the attention of everyone who knew of the offer, it seems to be enough for him to take reasonable steps to bring the withdrawal to the attention of such persons, even though it does not in fact come to the attention of them all.[336]

---

330 *Henthorn v Fraser* [1892] 2 Ch. 27 at 32.

331 cf. *Curtice v London Bank* [1908] 1 K.B. 291 at 300–301 (notice to countermand a cheque).

332 *Eaglehill Ltd v J Needham (Builders) Ltd* [1973] A.C. 992 at 1011, discussing notice of dishonour of a cheque; *The Pamela* [1995] 2 Lloyd's Rep. 249 at 252; cf. *The Pendrecht* [1980] 2 Lloyd's Rep. 56 at 66 (telex notice of arbitration); *The Eastern Navigator* [2005] EWHC 3020 (Comm); [2006] 1 Lloyd's Rep. 537 (email notice of arbitration).

333 For the effect of such messages when sent *out* of business hours, see para.2–027. But see the comment in fn.335.

334 *The Brimnes* [1975] Q.B. 929 (notice withdrawing ship from charterparty); cf. *Newcastle upon Tyne Hospitals NHS Foundation Trust v Haywood* [2018] EKSC 22; [2018] 1 W.L.R. 2073 (notice of termination of employment contract only effective when received and read or ought reasonably to have been read).

335 cf. *Brinkibon Ltd v Stahag Stahl und Stahlwarenhandelsgesellschaft mbH* [1983] 2 A.C. 34 at 42 (communication of acceptance). Quaere how strictly such a principle should be applied now when so many communications are by email and the proliferation of remote devices for their transmission has blurred the line between "business" and "non-business" hours.

336 *Shuey v US* 92 U.S. 73 (1875).

**Revival of a withdrawn offer.** An attempt to accept an offer which has been withdrawn is ineffective as an acceptance, but it may amount to a new offer on the same terms as the withdrawn offer which can be accepted by the conduct of the original offeror.[337] **2–062**

## (b) Rejection

**An offer is terminated by rejection.** [338] An attempt to accept an offer on new terms, not contained in the offer, may be a rejection of the offer accompanied by a counter-offer.[339] An offeree who makes such an attempt cannot later accept the original offer.[340] A communication from the offeree *may* be construed as a counter-offer (and hence as a rejection) even though it takes the form of a question as to the offeror's willingness to vary the terms of the offer.[341] But such a communication is not *necessarily* a counter-offer: it may be a mere inquiry[342] or request for information made without any intention of rejecting the terms of the offer. Whether the communication is a counter-offer or a request for information depends on the intention, objectively ascertained,[343] with which it was made. If, for example, an offer is made to sell a house at a specified price, an inquiry whether the intending vendor is prepared to reduce the price will not amount to a rejection if the inquiry is "merely exploratory."[344] **2–063**

**Rejection must be communicated to offeror.** It seems that a rejection has no effect unless it is actually communicated to the offeror. There is no ground of convenience for holding that it should take effect when posted. The offeree will not act in reliance on it as he derives no rights or liabilities from it; and the offeror will not know that he is free from the offer until the rejection is actually communicated to him. Hence, if a letter of rejection is overtaken by an acceptance sent by email there should be a contract, provided that the offeree has made his final intention clear to the offeror. But once the rejection had reached the offeror he should not be bound by an acceptance posted after the rejection and also reaching the offeror after the rejection. To hold the offeror bound,[345] merely because the acceptance was *posted* before the rejection had reached him, could expose him to hardship, particularly when he had acted on the rejection, e.g. by disposing elsewhere of the subject-matter. If the offeree has posted a rejection **2–064**

---

[337] *Pickfords Ltd v Celestica Ltd* [2003] EWCA Civ 1741 at [26].
[338] *Tinn v Hoffmann & Co* (1873) 29 L.T. 271 at 278.
[339] See para.2–020.
[340] *Hyde v Wrench* (1840) 3 Beav. 334; cf. *Mulcaire v News Group Newspapers Ltd* [2011] EWHC 3469 (Ch); [2012] Ch. 435 where the offeree's response was "collateral" and did not amount to a rejection of the offer. The common law principle in *Hyde v Wrench* does not apply to an offer under CPR 36: *Gibbon v Manchester CC* [2010] EWCA Civ 726; [2010] W.L.R. 2081; cf. *DB Bank Ltd v Jacobs Solicitors* [2016] EWHC 1614 (Ch); [2016] 2 W.L.R. 184.
[341] See the treatment in *Tinn v Hoffman* (1873) 29 L.T. 271 at 278 of the claimant's letter of 27 November.
[342] *Stevenson Jacques & Co v Maclean* (1880) 5 Q.B.D. 346 at 349.
[343] See para.2–002.
[344] *Gibson v Manchester CC* [1979] 1 W.L.R. 294 at 302.
[345] Under the "posting rule", para.2–031.

and then wishes, after all, to accept the offer, he should ensure that his subsequently-posted acceptance actually comes to the notice of the offeror before the latter receives the rejection.

## (c) Lapse of time

2–065 An offer which is expressly stated to last for a fixed time cannot be accepted after that time; and an offer which stipulates for acceptance "by return" (of post) must normally[346] be accepted either by a return postal communication or by some other, no less expeditious method. An offer which contains no express provision limiting its duration terminates after lapse of a reasonable time.[347] What is a reasonable time depends on such circumstances as the nature of the subject-matter and the means used to communicate the offer. Thus an offer to sell a perishable thing, or one whose price is liable to sudden fluctuations, would determine after a short time. The same is true of an offer made by telegram[348] or by some other, at least equally speedy, means of communication such as email.

2–066 **Extension of reasonable time.** The period that would normally constitute a reasonable time for acceptance may be extended if the conduct of the offeree within that period indicates an intention to accept and this is known to the offeror. Such conduct would often of itself amount to acceptance, but this possibility may be ruled out by the terms of the offer, which may require the acceptance to be by written notice sent to a specified address.[349] In such a case the offeree's conduct, though it could not *amount* to an acceptance, could nevertheless prolong the time for giving a proper notice of acceptance. For the offeree's conduct to have this effect, it must be known to the offeror; for if this were not the case the offeror might reasonably suppose that the offer had not been accepted within the normal period of time, and act in reliance on that belief: e.g. by disposing elsewhere of the subject-matter.

## (d) Occurrence of condition

2–067 An offer which expressly provides that it is to terminate on the occurrence of some condition cannot be accepted after that condition has occurred; and such a provision may also be implied. If an offer to buy or hire-purchase goods is made after the offeror has examined them, it may be an implied term of the offer that they should at the time of acceptance still be in substantially the same state as that in which they were when the offer was made. Such an offer cannot be accepted

---

346 See para.2–041.

347 *Ramsgate Victoria Hotel Co Ltd v Montefiore* (1866) L.R. 1 Ex. 109; *Cemco Leasing SpA v Rediffusion Ltd* [1987] F.T.L.R. 201; *L.J. Korbetis v Transgrain Shipping BV* [2005] EWHC 1345 (QB).

348 *Quenerduaine v Cole* (1883) 32 W.R. 185.

349 As in *Manchester Diocesan Council for Education v Commercial and General Investments Ltd* [1970] 1 W.L.R. 241.

after the goods have been seriously damaged.[350] On the same principle, it is submitted that the offer which is made by bidding at an auction by implication provides that it is to lapse as soon as a higher bid is made.[351]

## (e) Death

One possible view is that the death of either party terminates the offer, as the parties can no longer reach agreement.[352] But there may be a contract in spite of a demonstrable lack of agreement if to hold the contrary would cause serious inconvenience.[353] In accordance with this principle, it is submitted that the death of either party should not of itself terminate the offer except in the case of such "personal" contracts as are discharged by the death of either party.[354] **2–068**

**Death of offeror.** The effect of the death of the offeror has been considered in a number of cases concerning continuing guarantees. In general, a continuing guarantee, e.g. of a bank overdraft, is divisible:[355] it is a continuing offer by the guarantor, accepted from time to time as the banker makes loans to his customer. Each loan is a separate acceptance, turning the offer pro tanto into a binding contract. It seems that such a guarantee is not terminated merely by the death of the guarantor.[356] But it is terminated if the bank knows that the guarantor has died and that his personal representatives have no power under his will to continue the guarantee;[357] or if for some other reason it is inequitable for the bank to charge the guarantor's estate.[358] If the guarantee expressly provides that it can be terminated only by notice given by the guarantor *or his personal representatives*, the death of the guarantor, even if known to the bank, will not terminate the guarantee: express notice must be given.[359] **2–069**

**Death of offeree.** Two cases have some bearing on the effect of the death of the offeree. In *Reynolds v Atherton*[360] an offer to sell shares was made in 1911 "to the directors of" a company. An attempt to accept the offer was made in 1919 by the survivors of the persons who were directors in 1911 and by the personal representatives of those who had since died. The purported acceptance was held to be ineffective; and Warrington LJ said obiter that an offer "made to a living person who ceases to be a living person before the offer is accepted … is no **2–070**

---

[350] *Financings Ltd v Stimson* [1962] 1 W.L.R. 1184; cf. *Canning v Farquhar* (1885) 16 Q.B.D. 722; *Looker v Law Union & Rock Ins Co Ltd* [1928] 1 K.B. 554

[351] See para.2–008.

[352] *Dickinson v Dodds* (1876) 2 Ch D. 463 at 475.

[353] See para.2–059.

[354] e.g. contracts of employment or agency: para.16–122. In such cases the legal effects of saying that the offer was terminated, so that there was never any contract, is likely to differ from those of saying that there had been a contract which had been discharged, e.g. Law Reform (Frustrated Contracts) Act 1943 could apply to the latter, but not to the former, situation.

[355] See para.2–055.

[356] *Bradbury v Morgan* (1862) 1 H. & C. 249; *Coulthart v Clementson* (1879) 5 Q.B.D. 42 at 46.

[357] *Coulthart v Clementson* (1879) 5 Q.B.D. 42.

[358] *Harriss v Fawcett* (1873) L.R. 8 Ch. App. 866.

[359] *Re Silvester* [1895] 1 Ch. 573.

[360] (1921) 125 L.T. 690; affirmed (1922) 127 L.T. 189.

longer an offer at all". The actual ground for the decision, however, was that the offer had, on its true construction, been made to the directors of the company for the time being, and not to those who happened to hold office in 1911. In *Kennedy v Thomassen*[361] an offer to buy annuities was accepted by the solicitors of the annuitant after she had, without the solicitors' knowledge, died. This acceptance was held to be ineffective on the grounds that the solicitors' authority was terminated by their client's death and that the acceptance was made under a mistake.[362] Neither case supports the view that an offer can never be accepted after the offeree's death. It is submitted that, where an offer related to a contract which was not "personal",[363] it might, on its true construction, be held to have been made to the offeree or to his executors, and that such an offer could be accepted after the death of the original offeree.

### (f) Supervening incapacity

2–071 **Mental incapacity.** If an offeror subsequently lacked mental capacity he would not be bound by an acceptance made after this fact had become known to the offeree, or after the offeror's property had been made subject to the control of the court. But the other party would be bound; and an offer made to a person who later lacked mental capacity could be accepted so as to bind the other party. These rules can readily be deduced from the law as to contracts with persons who lack mental capacity.[364]

2–072 **Companies governed by the Companies Act 2006.** Such a company may lose its capacity to do an act by altering its articles of association.[365] The general rule is that acts done by the company can no longer be called into question on the ground that the company lacked capacity to do them by reason of anything in its constitution;[366] and that, in favour of a person dealing with the company in good faith, the power of the board of directors to bind the company, or to authorise others to do so, is deemed to be free of any limitation under the company's constitution.[367] But a member of the company may bring proceedings to restrain the doing of acts beyond the powers of the directors, except where such acts are done in fulfilment of legal obligations arising from previous acts of the company.[368] The effect of these provisions must be considered on offers made *to* and *by* the company.

2–073 **Company as offeree.** A company may receive an offer to enter into a contract and then alter its articles of association so as to deprive itself of the capacity to

[361] [1929] 1 Ch. 426.
[362] cf. para.8–008.
[363] See fn.354.
[364] See para.12–053 and following.
[365] See para.12–069.
[366] Companies Act 2006 s.39(1) (for companies which are charities: ss.39(2), 42); para.12–070, fn.216.
[367] Companies Act 2006 s.40(1) (for companies which are charities: ss.40(6), 42); and transactions with directors and their associates: ss.40(6), 41; para.12–071.
[368] Companies Act 2006 s.40(4).

enter into that contract. If it nevertheless accepts the offer, the acceptance is effective in favour of a person who deals with the company in good faith; but before the company has accepted the offer, the directors can be restrained from doing so in proceedings brought by one of its members.

**Company as offeror.** A company may make an offer to enter into a contract and then alter its articles of association so as to deprive itself of the capacity to enter into that contract. An acceptance of that offer is nevertheless effective in favour of a person dealing with the company in good faith; but it is not entirely clear whether in this situation a member of the company could take proceedings to prevent the conclusion of the contract by the directors. Such proceedings lie only to restrain "the doing of an act"[369] by the directors and since the relevant act (i.e. the making of the offer) would already have been done when the company still had capacity to do it, there seems to be nothing for the member to restrain, unless holding the offer open could be described as a continuing act. **2–074**

Of course, the company itself could normally withdraw the offer and would be likely to do so in pursuance of the policy which had led it to change its articles of association. But this possibility would not be open to the company where it had bound itself not to withdraw the offer, i.e. where it had granted a legally enforceable option;[370] and in such a case a member could not take proceedings to prevent the conclusion of the contract since such proceedings cannot be taken "in respect of an act to be done in fulfilment of a legal obligation arising from a previous act of the company":[371] i.e. from the grant of the option.

**Other corporations.**[372] Companies may also be incorporated by Royal Charter or by special legislation. Charter corporations have the legal capacity of a natural person so that an alteration of the charter would not affect the validity of an offer or acceptance made by the corporation.[373] The legal capacity of corporations incorporated by special statute is governed by the statute, and acts not within that capacity are ultra vires[374] and void. An alteration of the statute could therefore prevent the company from accepting an offer made to it, and from being bound by the acceptance of an offer made by it, where the offer was made before the alteration came into effect. In practice, the problem is likely to be dealt with in the statute which changes the capacity of the corporation. **2–075**

369 Companies Act 2006 s.40(4).
370 For legally enforceable options, see para.3–160.
371 Companies Act 2006 s.40(4).
372 Problems of the kind here under discussion cannot arise with regard to limited liability partnerships incorporated under the Limited Liability Partnerships Act 2000 as they have "unlimited capacity" (s.1(3)).
373 See para.12–065; but members of a corporation could bring proceedings to restrain the conclusion of the contract: para.12–065.
374 See para.12–074.

## 4. SPECIAL CASES

2–076 In some situations already discussed, the analysis of agreement into offer and acceptance gives rise to considerable difficulty,[375] and in others, to be discussed in this section, such analysis is impossible or highly artificial.[376] For this reason, it has been suggested that the analysis is "out of date"[377] and that "you should look at the correspondence as a whole and at the conduct of the parties and see therefrom whether the parties have come to an agreement".[378] The objection to this view, however, is that it provides too little guidance for the courts (or for the legal advisers of the parties) in determining whether agreement has been reached. For this reason, the situations to be discussed below are best regarded as exceptions[379] to a general requirement of offer and acceptance. This approach is supported by cases in which it has been held that there was no contract precisely because there was no offer and acceptance;[380] and by those in which the terms of a contract have been held to depend on the analysis of the negotiation into offer, counter-offer and acceptance.[381] That said, the offer and acceptance analysis does not require "rigorous compliance" and the "the court will, if appropriate, assess a person's conduct over a period and decide whether its cumulative effect is that he has evinced an intention to make the contract."[382]

2–077 **Multipartite agreements.** In *The Satanita*[383] the claimant and the defendant entered their yachts for a regatta. Each signed a letter, addressed to the secretary of the club which organised the regatta, undertaking to obey certain rules during the race. It was held that there was a contract between all the competitors on the terms of the undertaking, though it is not clear whether the contract was made when the competitors entered their yachts or when they actually began to race. In either event, it is difficult to analyse the transaction into offer and acceptance.[384]

---

375 See paras 2–007, 2–017, 2–020.

376 *Gibson v Manchester CC* [1978] 1 W.L.R. 520 at 523; reversed [1979] 1 W.L.R. 294; cf. *The Eurymedon* [1975] A.C. 154 at 167.

377 *Butler Machine Tool Co Ltd v Ex-Cell-O Corp (England) Ltd* [1979] 1 W.L.R. 401 at 404; cf. *Interfoto Picture Library Ltd v Stiletto Visual Programmes Ltd* [1989] Ch. 433 at 443.

378 *Gibson v Manchester CC* [1978] 1 W.L.R. 520 at 523; reversed [1979] 1 W.L.R. 294; cf. *Finmoon Ltd v Baltic Reefer Management Ltd* [2012] EWHC 920; [2012] 2 Lloyd's Rep. 388 at [22].

379 *Gibson v Manchester CC* [1979] 1 W.L.R. 294 at 297; *G Percy Trentham v Archital Luxfer Ltd* [1993] 1 Lloyd's Rep. 25 at 27, 29–30; *Tekdata Interconnections Ltd v Amphenol* [2009] EWCA Civ 1209; [2010] 1 Lloyd's Rep. 357 at [25].

380 *The Kapetan Markos NL (No.2)* [1987] 2 Lloyd's Rep. 323 at 331 ("What was the mechanism for offer and acceptance?"); cf. *The Good Helmsman* [1981] 1 Lloyd's Rep. 377 at 409; *The Aramis* [1989] 1 Lloyd's Rep. 213; Treitel [1989] L.M.C.L.Q. 162. The "offer and acceptance" analysis was also regarded as decisive in many of the arbitration cases discussed at para.2–005, though it was viewed with scepticism in *The Multibank Holsatia* [1988] 2 Lloyd's Rep. 486 at 491; and in *The Maritime Winner* [1989] 2 Lloyd's Rep. 506 at 515.

381 e.g. the "battle of forms" cases discussed at paras 2–020–2–021.

382 *Maple Leaf Macro Volatility Master Fund v Rouvroy* [2009] EWHC 257 (Comm); [2009] 1 Lloyd's Rep. 475 at [242]; affirmed [2009] EWCA Civ 1334; [2010] 2 All E.R. (Comm) 788; cf. *Premier Paper Group Ltd v Buchanan McPherson Ltd* [2018] EWCA Civ 15 at [29]; *Anchor 2020 Ltd v Midas Construction Ltd* [2019] EWHC 435 (TCC); 184 Con L.R. 215 at [91].

383 [1895] P. 248; affirmed sub nom. *Clarke v Dunraven* [1897] A.C. 59; Phillips 92 L.Q.R. 499.

384 cf. *Kingscroft Ins Co Ltd v Nissan Fire and Marine Ins Co Ltd* [2000] 1 All E.R. (Comm) 272 at 291.

If the contract was made when the yachts were entered, one would have to say that the entry of the first competitor was an offer and that the entry of the next was an acceptance of that offer and (simultaneously) an offer to yet later competitors; but this view is artificial and unworkable even in theory unless each competitor knew of the existence of previous ones. It would also lead to the conclusion that entries which were put in the post together were cross-offers and thus not binding on each other.[385] If the contract was made when the race began, then it seems that each competitor simultaneously agreed to terms proposed by the officers of the club, and not that each proposed an identical set of terms amounting at the same time to an offer to the others and to an acceptance of the offers at that instant made by them. Even if the second view of the facts could be taken, the "offers" and "acceptances" would all occur at the same moment. Thus they would be cross-offers and would not create a contract. The competitors, no doubt, reached agreement, but they did not do so by a process which can be analysed into offer and acceptance. Similar reasoning would seem to apply to the contract which governs the legal relations between members of an unincorporated association.[386]

The above discussion is based on the assumption that all the parties to the alleged multilateral contract were willing to agree to the same terms. Where one of the negotiating parties had refused to accept one of the terms of the proposed contract, no multilateral contract would arise between that party and any of the others, unless the others agreed to be bound to that party on terms excluding the one rejected by him.[387]

**Reference to third party.** Where two negotiating parties reach deadlock, they may ask a third party to break it. If both simultaneously assent to a solution proposed by him, there is a contract, but it is again impossible to say which party has made the offer and which the acceptance.[388] The same is true where the parties negotiate through a single broker who eventually obtains their consent to the same terms.[389] **2–078**

## 5. CERTAINTY

An agreement is not a binding contract if it lacks certainty, either because it is too vague or because it is obviously incomplete. The role of the courts is to enforce the agreement made by the parties; it is not to make an agreement for them.[390] **2–079**

[385] See para.2–050.
[386] See *Artistic Upholstery Ltd v Art Forma (Furniture) Ltd* [1999] 4 All E.R. 277 at 285; though breach of the rules by one member may not, on their true construction, be actionable in damages at the suit of another: *Anderton v Rowland, The Times*, 5 November 1999.
[387] *Azov Shipping Co v Baltic Shipping Co* [1999] 2 Lloyd's Rep. 159 at 165.
[388] Pollock, *Principles of Contract* (1950), p.5.
[389] *Pagnan SpA v Feed Products Ltd* [1987] 2 Lloyd's Rep. 601 at 616.
[390] Fridman 76 L.Q.R. 521.

## (a) Vagueness

2–080 **Agreements too vague to enforce.** An agreement may be so vague that no definite meaning can be given to it without adding new terms. Thus in *G Scammell & Nephew Ltd v Ouston*[391] the House of Lords held that an agreement to buy goods "on hire-purchase" was too vague to be enforced, since there were many kinds of hire-purchase agreements in widely different terms, so that it was impossible to say on which terms the parties intended to contract. Similarly, agreements "subject to war clause",[392] "subject to strike and lockout clause",[393] and "subject to force majeure conditions"[394] have been held too vague, there being no evidence in any of the cases of a customary or usual form of such clauses or conditions.[395] Similar reasoning has sometimes been applied where agreements were made subject to the "satisfaction" of one party.[396] The problems arising from such provisions are discussed later in this chapter.[397] But the courts do not expect commercial documents to be drafted with strict precision, and will, particularly if the parties have acted on an agreement,[398] do their best to avoid striking it down on the ground that it is too vague.[399]

2–081 **Custom and trade usage.** Apparent vagueness can be resolved by custom. Thus a contract to load coal at Grimsby "on the terms of the usual colliery guarantee" was upheld on proof of the terms usually contained in such guarantees at Grimsby.[400] It has similarly been held that an undertaking to grant a lease of a shop "in prime position" was not too uncertain to be enforced since the phrase was commonly used by persons dealing with shop property, so that its meaning could be determined by expert evidence.[401] And courts often enforce commercial contracts expressed in abbreviations whose meaning is certain and notorious.

---

391 [1941] A.C. 251.

392 *Bishop & Baxter Ltd v Anglo-Eastern Trading Co* [1944] K.B. 12.

393 *Love & Stewart Ltd v S Instone & Co* (1917) 33 T.L.R. 475.

394 *British Electrical Industries Ltd v Patley Pressings Ltd* [1953] 1 W.L.R. 280.

395 For further illustrations, see para.2–081.

396 *Stabilad Ltd v Stephens & Carter Ltd (No.2)* [1999] 2 All E.R. (Comm) 651 at 659.

397 See para.2–110.

398 *Brown v Gould* [1972] Ch. 53 at 57–58; *Tito v Waddell* (*No.2*) [1977] Ch. 106 at 314; *Sudbrook Trading Estate Ltd v Eggleton* [1983] 1 A.C. 444; *The Mercedes Envoy* [1995] 2 Lloyd's Rep. 559 at 564.

399 "Void for uncertainty is a last resort conclusion": *Shaw v Lighthousexpress Ltd* [2010] EWCA Civ 161 at [21]. See also: *Nea Agrex SA v Baltic Shipping Co Ltd* [1976] Q.B. 933 at 943 ("a counsel of despair"); *Deutsche Schachtbau-und-Tiefbohrgesellschaft mbH v Ras Al Khaimah National Oil Co* [1990] 1 A.C. 295 at 306; reversed on other grounds: [1990] 1 A.C. 295 at 329 and following; *Scammell v Dicker* [2005] EWCA Civ 405; [2005] 3 All E.R. 838 at [31]; *Schweppe v Harper* [2008] EWCA Civ 442; [2008] B.P.I.R. 1090 at [75], [82]; *Durham Tees Valley Airport Ltd v Bmibaby Ltd* [2010] EWCA Civ 485; [2011] 1 Lloyd's Rep. 68; *Openwork Ltd v Forte* [2018] EWCA Civ 783 at [25]; *Wells v Devani* [2019] UKSC 4; [2019] 2 W.L.R. 617 at [18].

400 *Shamrock SS Co v Storey & Co* (1899) 81 L.T. 413; cf. *Hart v Hart* (1881) 18 Ch D. 670; *Baynham v Philips Electronics (UK) Ltd, The Times*, 19 July 1995.

401 *Ashburn Anstalt v Arnold* [1989] Ch. 1 at 27; overruled on another ground in *Prudential Assurance Co Ltd v London Residuary Body* [1992] A.C. 386.

**Reasonableness.** In *Hillas & Co Ltd v Arcos Ltd*,[402] an agreement for the sale of timber "of fair specification", was made between persons well acquainted with the timber trade. The agreement was upheld as the standard of reasonableness could be applied to make the otherwise vague phrase certain since the words of the contract imported some objective standard for assessing the quality of the goods to be supplied. In *Attrill v Dresdner Kleinwort Ltd*[403] the promise of a "guaranteed" bonus pool was not too uncertain to amount to a variation of a contract of employment notwithstanding that certain matters were left open, e.g. whether the bonus was to be paid in the form of cash or shares; such matters could be resolved by dealing with the fund "in the usual way".[404] These cases should be contrasted with one in which a supplier of clothing to a retail chain alleged that there was an implied contract between them not to terminate their long-standing relationship except on reasonable notice. One ground for rejecting the claim was that there were "no objective criteria by which the court could assess what would be reasonable either as to quantity or price."[405] 2–082

**Duty to resolve uncertainty.** An agreement containing a vague phrase may be binding because one party is under a duty to resolve the uncertainty. In one case an agreement to sell goods provided for delivery "free on board … good Danish port". It was held that the agreement was not too vague: it amounted to a good contract under which the buyer was bound to select the port of shipment.[406] 2–083

**Meaningless and self-contradictory phrases.** The court will make considerable efforts to give meaning to an apparently meaningless phrase;[407] but, even where these efforts fail, the presence of such phrases does not necessarily vitiate the agreement. In *Nicolene Ltd v Simmonds*[408] steel bars were bought on terms which were certain except for a clause that the sale was subject to "the usual conditions of acceptance". There being no such usual conditions, it was held that the phrase was meaningless, but that this did not vitiate the whole contract: the words were severable and could be ignored. A self-contradictory clause can be treated in the 2–084

---

[402] (1932) 147 L.T. 503 (and see para.2–097); *Sweet & Maxwell Ltd v Universal News Services Ltd* [1964] 2 Q.B. 699; cf. *Greater London Council v Connolly* [1970] 2 Q.B. 100; *Scammell v Dicker* [2005] EWCA Civ 405; [2005] 3 All E.R. 838; *Bear Stearns Bank Plc v Forum Global Equity Ltd* [2007] EWHC 1576 (Comm) at [64]; *Furmans Electrical Contractors Ltd v Elecref Ltd* [2009] EWCA Civ 170; [2009] T.C.L.R. 6 at [33].

[403] [2013] EWCA Civ 394; [2013] 3 All E.R. 607.

[404] *Attrill v Dresdner Kleinwort Ltd* [2013] EWCA Civ 394; [2013] 3 All E.R. 607 at [60].

[405] *Baird Textile Holdings Ltd v Marks & Spencer Plc* [2001] EWCA Civ 274; [2002] 1 All E.R. (Comm) 737 at [30]; cf. *Schweppe v Harper* [2008] EWCA Civ 442; [2008] B.P.I.R. 1090 at [72] ("reasonable finance" too uncertain).

[406] *David T Boyd & Co v Louis Louca* [1973] 1 Lloyd's Rep. 209; cf. *Siew Soon Wah v Yong Tong Hong* [1973] A.C. 831; *Pagnan SpA v Feed Products Ltd* [1987] 2 Lloyd's Rep. 601; *Bulk Trading Co Ltd v Zenziper Grains and Feedstuffs* [2001] 1 Lloyd's Rep. 357 (seller's duty to specify place of delivery under f.o.t. contract). Contrast *Mehboob Travel Ltd v Pakistan Inernational Airlines Corp* [2013] EWHC 2120 (QB) at [57].

[407] *The Tropwind* [1982] 1 Lloyd's Rep. 232.

[408] [1953] 1 Q.B. 543; discussed in *Heisler v Anglo-Dal Ltd* [1954] 1 W.L.R. 1273; cf. *Slater v Raw*, *The Times*, 15 October 1977; *The Scaptrade* [1981] 2 Lloyd's Rep. 425 at 432; affirmed without reference to this point [1983] 2 A.C. 694.

same way.[409] Thus where an arbitration clause provided for arbitration of "any dispute" in London and of "any other dispute" in Moscow the court disregarded the clause and determined the dispute itself.[410] Such cases show that the question whether a meaningless phrase vitiates the contract, or can be ignored, depends on the importance which the parties may be considered to have attached to it. If it is simply verbiage, not intended to add anything to an otherwise complete agreement, or if it relates to a matter of relatively minor importance, it can be ignored. But if the parties intend it to govern some vital aspect of their relationship, its vagueness will vitiate the entire agreement.

## (b) Incompleteness

2–085 Our principal concern in this part is with the effect of the parties' failure to have agreed on all of the terms of the contract, but this cannot be considered entirely separately from the question of whether the parties had the necessary intention to be bound.[411] For example, the court may conclude that the parties did not intend to be bound until some further term or terms had been agreed,[412] and this is the reasoning employed in a number of the decisions considered below. In other cases, it may be that the parties intended to be bound notwithstanding that there were further terms to be agreed and the courts will enforce their agreement unless the failure to have agreed the outstanding terms "renders the contract as a whole unworkable or void for uncertainty".[413] This is a conclusion which the courts are reluctant to reach, particularly if the parties have acted upon the agreement.[414] The parties need not have agreed every detail of their agreement,[415] but must have agreed the terms which "the law requires as essential for the formation of legally binding relations".[416]

### *(i) Agreement in principle only*[417]

2–086 **No contract if agreement incomplete in important respect.** Parties may reach agreement on essential matters of principle, but leave important points unsettled,

---

[409] *Scammell v Dicker* [2005] EWCA Civ 405; [2005] 3 All E.R. 838 at [31].

[410] *ERJ Lovelock v Exportles* [1968] 1 Lloyd's Rep. 163; cf. *The Star Texas* [1993] 2 Lloyd's Rep. 445.

[411] *Dhanani v Crasnianski* [2011] EWHC 926 (Comm); [2011] 2 All E.R. (Comm) 799 at [75]. On intention generally, see Ch.4.

[412] *Pagnan SpA v Feed Products Ltd* [1987] 2 Lloyd's Rep. 601 at 619 (see the third of the principles stated by Lloyd LJ); cf. *Macinnes v Gross* [2017] EWHC 46 (QB).

[413] *Pagnan SpA v Feed Products Ltd* [1987] 2 Lloyd's Rep. 601 at 619 (Principle (5)); *Barbudev v Eurocom Cable Management Eood* [2012] EWCA Civ 548; [2012] 2 All E.R. (Comm) 963 at [32].

[414] *Maple Leaf Macro Volatility Master Fund v Rouvroy* [2009] EWHC 257 (Comm); [2009] 1 Lloyd's Rep. 475 at [235] (affirmed [2009] EWCA Civ 1334; [2010] 2 All E.R. (Comm) 788).

[415] If they have, they may nonetheless still not intend to be bound until some further step is taken, such as the formal execution of the contract: see para.4–011.

[416] *RTS Flexible Systems Ltd v Molkerei Alois Müller GmbH* [2010] UKSC 14; [2010] 1 W.L.R. 753 at [45]; *Bear Stearns Bank Plc v Forum Global Equity Ltd* [2007] EWHC 1576 at [155].

[417] Lücke 3 Adelaide L. Rev. 46.

so that their agreement is incomplete.[418] There is, for example, no contract if an agreement for a lease fails to specify the date on which the term is to commence,[419] or if an option for shipbuilding contracts does not include delivery dates for the vessels because they have not yet been "mutually agreed".[420] Similarly, an agreement for the sale of land by instalments is not a binding contract if it provides for conveyance of "a proportionate part" as each instalment of the price is paid but fails to specify which part was to be conveyed on each payment.[421]

**Not all details necessarily required.** On the other hand, the agreement does not have to be worked out in meticulous detail.[422] Under the Sale of Goods Act 1979, an agreement for the sale of goods may be binding as soon as the parties have agreed to buy and sell, where the remaining details can be determined by the standard of reasonableness or by law.[423] Even failure to fix the price is not necessarily fatal in such a case. Section 8(2) of the Act provides that, if no price is determined by the contract, a reasonable price must be paid. This, and other similar statutory provisions,[424] assume that the agreement amounts to a contract in spite of its failure to fix the price or remuneration. The very fact that the parties have not reached agreement on this vital point may indicate that there is *no* contract, e.g. because the price or remuneration is to be fixed by further agreement.[425] In such a case, the statutory provisions for payment of a reasonable sum do not apply. There may, however, be a claim for payment of such a sum at common law: e.g. where work is done in the belief that there was a contract or in the expectation that the negotiations between the parties would result in the conclusion of a contract.[426] Such liability arises in restitution, in spite of the fact that there was *no* contract. It follows that the party doing the work, though he is entitled to a reasonable sum, is not liable in damages, e.g. for failing to do the work within a reasonable time.[427] 2–087

Even an agreement for the sale of land dealing only with the barest essentials may be regarded as complete if that was the clear intention of the parties. Thus in

[418] *Bols Distilleries BV v Superior Yacht Services Ltd* [2006] UKPC 45; [2007] 1 W.L.R. 12; *Cobbe v Yeoman's Row Management Ltd* [2008] UKHL 55; [2008] 1 W.L.R. 1752 (para.3–129); *Whittle Movers Ltd v Hollywood Express Ltd* [2009] EWCA Civ 1189; [2009] 2 C.L.C. 771 at [14].

[419] *Harvey v Pratt* [1965] 1 W.L.R. 1025.

[420] *Teekay Tankers Ltd v STX Offshore & Shipbuilding Co Ltd* [2017] EWHC 253; [2017] 1 Lloyd's Rep. 387.

[421] *Bushwall Properties Ltd v Vortex Properties Ltd* [1976] 1 W.L.R. 591; cf. *Hadley v Kemp* [1999] E.M.L.R. 589 at 628; *London & Regional Investments Ltd v TBI Plc Belfast International Airport Ltd* [2002] EWCA Civ 355.

[422] *First Energy (UK) Ltd v Hungarian International Bank Ltd* [1993] 2 Lloyd's Rep. 195 at 205; *Bear Stearns Bank Plc v Forum Global Equity Ltd* [2007] EWHC 1576 (Comm).

[423] *Hughes v Pendragon Sabre Ltd* [2016] EWCA Civ 18; [2016] 1 Lloyd's Rep. 311.

[424] Supply of Goods and Services Act 1982 s.15(1); Consumer Rights Act 2015 s.51(2); cf. at common law, *Way v Latilla* [1937] 3 All E.R. 759; *The Tropwind* [1982] 1 Lloyd's Rep. 232; *Furmans Electrical Contractors Ltd v Elecref Ltd* [2009] EWCA Civ 170; [2009] T.C.L.R 6 at [32].

[425] e.g. *May & Butcher v R.* [1934] 2 K.B. 17n.; *Courtney & Fairbairn Ltd v Tolaini Bros (Hotels) Ltd* [1975] 1 W.L.R. 297; *Chamberlain v Boodle & King* [1982] 1 W.L.R. 1443n; *Russell Bros (Paddington) Ltd v John Elliott Management Ltd* (1995) 11 Const. L.J. 377.

[426] See para.22–031.

[427] *BSC v Cleveland Bridge & Engineering Co Ltd* [1984] 1 All E.R. 504.

*Perry v Suffields Ltd*[428] an offer to sell a public house with vacant possession for £7,000 was accepted without qualification. It was held that there was a binding contract, in spite of the fact that many important points such as the date of completion[429] and the question of paying a deposit, were left open.[430] In another case[431] a buyer and seller of corn feed pellets had reached agreement on the "cardinal terms of the deal: product, price, quantity, period of shipment, range of loading ports and governing contract terms".[432] The agreement was held to have contractual force even though the parties had not yet reached agreement on a number of other important points, such as the loading port,[433] the rate of loading and certain payments (other than the price) which might in certain events become due under the contract. In these cases, the courts took the view that the parties intended to be bound at once in spite of the fact that further significant terms were to be agreed later[434]; and that even their failure to reach such agreement would not invalidate the contract unless without such agreement the contract was unworkable or too uncertain[435] to be enforced.

**2–088** **Implied terms.** Any incompleteness in an agreement which renders it too uncertain to enforce may be remedied by an implied term,[436] provided the test for such implication is met.[437] In *Wells v Devani*[438] an estate agent had agreed to sell a property on behalf of the defendant owner for a commission of 2 per cent. The parties had not, however, agreed the event upon which the commission was payable: finding a willing purchaser, exchange of contracts, completion, etc.[439] The Supreme Court held that, in the absence of any express agreement, it would be naturally understood as a matter of *interpretation* that the agent was engaged on the "usual terms" under which payment would become due on completion from the proceeds of sale.[440] If necessary, the same result could have been reached by implying a term that commission was payable upon completion. The Court of Appeal had ruled out this possibility on the basis that no terms can be implied until the court is first satisfied that there was a legally binding bargain.[441] The Supreme Court did not agree with such a "far-reaching proposition".[442] The case upon which the Court of Appeal had relied demonstrated only that an

428 [1916] 2 Ch. 187; *Elias v George Sahely & Co (Barbados) Ltd* [1982] 3 All E.R. 801.
429 cf. *Storer v Manchester CC* [1974] 1 W.L.R. 1403.
430 For the resolution of such points, see para.2–092.
431 *Pagnan SpA v Feed Products Ltd* [1987] 2 Lloyd's Rep. 601.
432 *Pagnan SpA v Feed Products Ltd* [1987] 2 Lloyd's Rep. 601 at 611.
433 cf. para.2–083, fn.406.
434 cf. *RTS Flexible Systems Ltd v Molkerei Alois Müller GbmH* [2010] UKSC 14; [2010] 1 W.L.R. 753 at [45]; *Attrill v Dresdner Kleinwort Ltd* [2013] EWCA Civ 394; [2013] 3 All E.R. 607 at [60]; *Proton Energy Group SA v Orlen Lietuva* [2013] EWHC 2872 (Comm); [2014] 1 Lloyd's Rep. 100.
435 See para.2–080.
436 *F.&.G. Sykes (Wessex) Ltd v Fine Fare Ltd* [1967] 1 Lloyd's Rep. 53.
437 See para.6–051.
438 [2019] UKSC 4; [2019] 2 W.L.R. 617.
439 See para.16–101.
440 cf. *Fowler v Bratt* [1950] K.B. 96; *Dennis Reed Ltd v Goody* [1950] 2 Q.B. 277; *Midgley Estates v Hand* [1952] 2 Q.B. 432.
441 Based on the comments of Lord Roskill in *Scancarriers A/S v Aotearoa International Ltd* [1985] 2 Lloyd's Rep. 419 at 422.
442 *Wells v Devani* [2019] UKSC 4; [2019] 2 W.L.R. 617 at [33].

agreement may be so vague and incomplete that the parties cannot have intended it to be legally binding so that "nothing can be done to render it enforceable".[443] As a counter example Lord Kitchin referred to an agreement under which the parties have made no express provision as to price where it "may be appropriate to imply a term that, in default of agreement, a reasonable price must be paid".[444]

**Further agreement needed for continued operation of contract.** A distinction must be drawn between cases in which agreement on such matters as the price is required for the making, and those in which it is required for the *continued operation*, of a contract. The latter possibility is illustrated by a case[445] in which an agreement for the supply of services for 10 years fixed the fee to be paid only for the first two years. On the parties' failure to fix the fee in later years, it was held that they had intended to enter into a 10-year contract and that a term was to be implied into that contract for payment of a reasonable fee in those later years. **2–089**

### (ii) *Agreements "subject to contract"*

An agreement may be made "subject to contract". Such an agreement is incomplete until the details of a formal contract have been settled and approved by the parties.[446] But even when the terms of the formal contract have been agreed, there is no binding contract until the parties have gone through the procedure necessary to indicate that the agreement is no longer "subject to contract", e.g. in contracts for the sale of land by private treaty, when there has been an "exchange of contracts".[447] Before the "exchange", there is no uncertainty as to the terms of the agreement, but there is no contract because neither party intends to be legally bound until the "exchange of contracts" takes place. Since the principal effect of the stipulation that an agreement is "subject to contract" is to negate the intention of the parties to be bound, it is dealt with in further detail in Ch.4.[448] **2–090**

### (iii) *Execution of formal document required*

One possible effect of a stipulation that an agreement is to be embodied in a formal written document is that the agreement is regarded by the parties as **2–091**

[443] In reality the communication between the parties in the *Scancarriers* case amounted to no more than a quote.

[444] *Wells v Devani* [2019] UKSC 4; [2019] 2 W.L.R. 617 at [33]; cf. Sale of Goods Act 1979 s.8(2) referred to in para.2–087 which does not refer to the requirement to pay a reasonable price as an "implied term".

[445] *Mamidoil-Jetoil Arab Petroleum Co SA v Okta Crude Oil Refinery AD* [2001] EWCA Civ 406; [2001] 2 Lloyd's Rep. 76. For further proceedings arising out of the same contract, see [2003] 1 Lloyd's Rep. 1; para.2–097.

[446] *Winn v Bull* (1877) 7 Ch D. 29. cf. *The Junior K* [1988] 2 Lloyd's Rep. 583; *Drake & Scull Engineering Ltd v Higgs & Hill (Northern) Ltd* (1995) 11 Const. L.J. 214; *Regalian Properties Plc v London Dockland Development Corp* [1995] 1 W.L.R. 212; contrast *Prudential Assurance Co Ltd v Mount Eden Land Co Ltd* [1997] 1 E.G.L.R. 37 (consent to alterations given by landlord "subject to licence" held effective as the consent was a unilateral act, so that no question of agreement arose).

[447] See para.4–012.

[448] See para.4–011 and following.

incomplete, or as not intended to be legally binding,[449] until the terms of the formal document are agreed and the document is duly executed in accordance with the terms of the preliminary agreement (e.g. by signature).[450] A second possibility is that such a document is intended only as a solemn record of an already complete and binding agreement:[451] for example, a contract of insurance is generally regarded as complete as soon as the insurer initials a slip setting out the main terms of the contract, even though the execution of a formal policy is contemplated.[452] The question whether an agreement which expressly requires the execution of a formal document is incomplete depends on the purpose of the requirement in each case;[453] and there is no point multiplying examples.[454]

Even where, under the principles here stated, the agreement has no contractual force, a party to it may be liable on other grounds: e.g. in unjust enrichment,[455] or under a separate preliminary contract coming into existence when one party begins to render services requested by the other and entitling the former to a reasonable remuneration for those services;[456] or under a constructive trust.[457]

---

[449] *BSC v Cleveland Bridge & Engineering Co Ltd* [1984] 1 All E.R. 504; *Ignazio Messina Co v Polskie Linie Oceaniczne* [1995] 2 Lloyd's Rep. 566; *Petromec Inc v Petroleo Brasileiro SA Petrobas* [2005] EWCA Civ 891; [2006] 1 Lloyd's Rep. 161 at [74]–[77]; *Diamond Build Ltd v Clapham Park Homes Ltd* [2008] EWHC 1439 (TCC); 119 Con L.R. 32 (where the parties remained bound only by a letter of intent as a result).

[450] *Okura & Co Ltd v Navara Shipping Corp SA* [1982] 2 Lloyd's Rep. 537; cf. *New England Reinsurance Corp v Messoghios Insurance Co SA* [1992] 2 Lloyd's Rep. 251; *Thoresen & Co (Bangkok) Ltd v Fathom Marine Co* [2004] EWHC 167; [2004] 1 Lloyd's Rep. 622; *Investec Bank (UK) Ltd v Zulman* [2010] EWCA Civ 536; *Grant v Bragg* [2009] EWCA Civ 1228; [2010] 1 All E.R. (Comm) 1166; *Whittle Movers Ltd v Hollywood Express Ltd* [2009] EWCA Civ 1189; [2009] 2 C.L.C. 771.

[451] *Rossiter v Miller* (1878) 3 App. Cas. 1124; cf. *Filby v Hounsell* [1896] 2 Ch. 737; *Branca v Cobarro* [1947] K.B. 854; *E R Ives Investment Ltd v High* [1967] 2 Q.B. 379; *The Blankenstein* [1985] 1 W.L.R. 435; *Jayaar Impex Ltd v Toaken Group Ltd* [1996] 2 Lloyd's Rep. 437; *Harvey Shopfitters Ltd v ADI Ltd* [2003] EWCA Civ 1752; [2004] 2 All E.R. 982; *Bryen & Langley Ltd v Boston* [2005] EWCA Civ 973; [2005] C.I.L.L. 2261; *Maple Leaf Macro Volatility Master Fund v Rouvroy* [2009] EWCA Civ 1334; [2010] 2 All E.R. (Comm) 788 at [16]; *Edge Tools and Equipment Ltd v Greatstar Europe Ltd* [2018] EWHC 170 (QB).

[452] *Ionides v Pacific Insurance Co* (1871) L.R. 6 Q.B. 674 at 684; *General Reinsurance Corp v Forsakringsaktiebolaget Fennia Patria* [1983] Q.B. 856; *Youell v Bland Welch & Co Ltd* [1992] 2 Lloyd's Rep. 127 at 140–141; *HIH Casualty & General Insurance Ltd v New Hampshire Insurance* [2001] EWCA Civ 735; [2001] 2 Lloyd's Rep. 161 at [86]–[87].

[453] *Von Hatzfeldt-Wildenburg v Alexander* [1912] 1 Ch. 284 at 288–289; *Immingham Storage Co Ltd v Clear Plc* [2011] EWCA Civ 89; 135 Con L.R. 224; *CRS GT Ltd v McLaren Automotive Ltd* [2018] EWHC 3209 (Comm).

[454] For an extensive survey of the authorities and the considerations to be derived from them, see *Benourad v Compass Group Plc* [2010] EWHC 1882 (QB) at [106].

[455] *Rotam Agrochemical Co Ltd v GAT Microencapsulation* GmbH [2018] EWHC 2765 (Comm); see para.22–031.

[456] *The Kurnia Dewi* [1997] 1 Lloyd's Rep. 553; cf. *Galliard Homes Ltd v Jarvis Interiors* [2000] C.L.C. 411, where the incomplete agreement expressly provided for such a remuneration in the events which happened.

[457] *Banner Homes Ltd v Luff Development Ltd* [2000] Ch. 372 (party to joint venture agreement, which lacked contractual force, acquiring proposed subject-matter for himself); contrast *London & Regional Investments Ltd v TBI Plc Belfast International Airport Ltd* [2002] EWCA Civ 355 (where such an agreement was expressly "subject to contract": see para.4–011 and following).

### (iv) Terms left open

Parties may be reluctant to commit themselves to a rigid long-term contract, particularly when prices and other factors affecting performance are likely to fluctuate. They therefore attempt sometimes to introduce an element of flexibility into the agreement; a number of devices which have been used for this purpose call for discussion. 2–092

**Terms "to be agreed".** One possibility is to provide that certain matters (such as prices, quantities or delivery dates) are to be agreed later, or from time to time. The question whether the resulting agreement is a binding contract then depends primarily on the intention of the parties; and inferences as to this intention may be drawn both from the importance of the matter left over for further agreement, and from the extent to which the parties have acted on the agreement. 2–093

**Agreements found to be unenforceable.** Sometimes such agreements have no contractual force. In *May & Butcher v R.*[458] an agreement for the sale of tentage provided that the price, dates of payment and manner of delivery should be agreed from time to time. The House of Lords held that the agreement was incomplete as it left vital matters still to be settled. Had the agreement simply been silent on these points, they could perhaps have been settled in accordance with the provisions of the Sale of Goods Act 1979;[459] or by the standard of reasonableness;[460] but the parties showed that this was not their intention by providing that such points were to be settled by further agreement between them. It has similarly been held that a lease at "a rent to be agreed" was not a binding contract.[461] In these cases, the most natural inference to be drawn from the fact that the parties left such an important matter as the price to be settled by further agreement was that they did not intend to be bound until they had agreed on the price. Even where the points left outstanding are of relatively minor importance, there will be no contract if it appears from the words used or other circumstances that the parties did not intend to be bound until agreement on these points had been reached.[462] A fortiori they are not bound by a term requiring outstanding points to be agreed if that term forms part of an agreement which itself is not binding because it was made without any intention of entering into contractual relations.[463] 2–094

---

[458] [1934] 2 K.B. 17n.; cf. *British Homophone Ltd v Kunz* (1935) 152 L.T. 589; *The Shamah* [1981] 1 Lloyd's Rep. 40 at 83; *The Gudermes* [1985] 2 Lloyd's Rep. 623; *Grow With Us Ltd v Green Thumb (UK) Ltd* [2006] EWCA Civ 1201 at [29], where it was found there was not even an *agreement* to agree.

[459] See para.2–087.

[460] cf. *Mamidoil-Jetoil Greek Petroleum SA v Okta Crude Oil Refinery AD* [2001] EWCA Civ 406; [2001] 2 Lloyd's Rep. 76, especially at [73].

[461] *King's Motors (Oxford) Ltd v Lax* [1970] 1 W.L.R. 426; cf. *King v King* (1981) 41 P. & C.R. 311 (rent review clause).

[462] *The Gladys* [1994] 2 Lloyd's Rep. 402; *Ignazio Messina & Co v Polskie Linie Oceaniczne* [1995] 2 Lloyd's Rep. 566.

[463] *Orion Insurance Plc v Sphere Drake Insurance Plc* [1992] 1 Lloyd's Rep. 239.

2–095 **Agreements found to be enforceable.** Where it can be inferred that the parties intended to be bound immediately, in spite of the provision requiring further agreement, a binding contract can be created at once;[464] for the courts are "reluctant to hold void for uncertainty any provision that was intended to have legal effect".[465] This judicial attitude is illustrated by *Foley v Classique Coaches Ltd*.[466] The claimant owned a petrol-filling station and adjoining land. He sold the land to the defendants on condition that they should enter into an agreement to buy petrol for the purpose of their motor-coach business exclusively from him. This agreement was duly executed, but the defendants broke it, and argued that it was incomplete because it provided that the petrol should be bought "at a price agreed by the parties from time to time". The Court of Appeal rejected this argument and held that, in default of agreement, a reasonable price must be paid.[467] *May & Butcher v R.*[468] was distinguished on a number of grounds: the agreement in *Foley*'s case was contained in a stamped document; it was believed by both parties to be binding and had been acted upon for a number of years; it contained an arbitration clause in a somewhat unusual form which was construed to apply "to any failure to agree as to the price";[469] and it formed part of a larger bargain under which the defendants had acquired the land at a price which was no doubt fixed on the assumption that they would be bound to buy all their petrol from the claimant.[470] While none of these factors in itself is conclusive,[471] their cumulative effect seems to be sufficient to distinguish the two cases.[472]

Thus an agreement is not incomplete *merely* because it calls for some further agreement between the parties:

> "Even if certain terms of economic or other significance to the parties have not been finalised, an objective appraisal of their words and conduct may lead to the conclusion that they did not intend agreement of such terms to be a pre-condition to a concluded and legally binding agreement."[473]

---

[464] *Pagnan SpA v Feed Products Ltd* [1987] 2 Lloyd's Rep. 601.

[465] *Brown v Gould* [1972] Ch. 53 at 57–58; cf. *Smith v Morgan* [1971] 1 W.L.R. 803 at 807; *Snelling v John G Snelling Ltd* [1973] 1 Q.B. 87 at 93; *Queensland Electricity Generating Board v New Hope Colliery Pty Ltd* [1989] 1 Lloyd's Rep. 205 at 210.

[466] [1934] 2 K.B. 1.

[467] cf. *British Bank for Foreign Trade v Novinex* [1949] 1 K.B. 623; *Beer v Bowden* [1981] 1 W.L.R. 522; *The Tropwind* [1982] 1 Lloyd's Rep. 232 at 236; *Mamidoil-Jetoil Greek Petroleum SA v Okta Crude Oil Refinery AD* [2001] EWCA Civ 406; [2001] 2 Lloyd's Rep. 76; *MRI Trading AG v Erdenet Mining Corp LLC* [2013] EWCA Civ 156; [2013] 1 Lloyd's Rep. 638.

[468] See at fn.458.

[469] *Foley v Classique Coaches Ltd* [1934] 2 K.B. 1 at 10; the clause covered disputes as to "the *subject matter or* construction of this agreement," while the arbitration clause in *May & Butcher v R.* covered "disputes with reference to or arising out of this agreement." For the distinction between the two forms of clause, see *Heyman v Darwins* [1942] A.C. 356 at 382, 392; cf. also *Queensland Electricity Generating Board v New Hope Collieries Pty Ltd* [1989] 1 Lloyd's Rep. 205.

[470] Scrutton LJ said [1934] 2 K.B. 1 at 7 that he was glad to decide in favour of the claimant "because I do not regard the [defendants'] contention as an honest one".

[471] R.S.T.C. 49 L.Q.R. 316.

[472] *Foley*'s case was approved by the House of Lords in *G Scammell & Nephew Ltd v Ouston* [1941] A.C. 251.

[473] *RTS Flexible Systems Ltd v Molkerei Alois Müller GmbH & Co KG* [2010] UKSC 14; [2010] 1 W.L.R. 753 at [45] (Lord Clarke).

Even the parties' later failure to agree on the matters left outstanding will vitiate the contract only if it makes the agreement "unworkable or void for uncertainty."[474] Often, the failure will not have this effect, for it may be possible to resolve the uncertainty in one of the ways already discussed, e.g. by applying the standard of reasonableness;[475] or by imposing on one party the duty to resolve the uncertainty;[476] or by regarding the matter to be negotiated as of such subsidiary importance[477] as not to negative the intention of the parties to be bound by the more significant terms to which they have agreed.[478] There can be no doubt as to the commercial convenience of this approach. Commercial agreements are often intended to be binding in principle even though the parties are not at the time able or willing to settle all the details. For example, contracts of insurance may be made "at a premium to be arranged" when immediate cover is required but there is no time to go into all the details at once: such agreements are perfectly valid and a reasonable premium must be paid.[479] All this is not to say that the courts will hold parties bound when they have not yet reached substantial agreement;[480] but once they have reached such agreement it is not necessarily fatal that some points (even important ones) remain to be settled by further negotiation.

**Options and rights of pre-emption.** An option to purchase land "at a price to be agreed" is not a binding contract;[481] but such an option must be distinguished from a "right of pre-emption" by which a landowner agrees to give the purchaser the right to buy "at a figure to be agreed" should the landowner wish to sell.[482] An *option* has at least some of the characteristics of an offer[483] in that it can become a contract of sale when the purchaser accepts it by exercising the option; and it cannot have this effect where it fails to specify the price. A *right of pre-emption* is not itself an offer[484] but an undertaking to make an offer in certain specified future circumstances. An agreement conferring such a right is therefore not void **2–096**

474 *Pagnan SpA v Feed Products Ltd* [1987] 2 Lloyd's Rep. 601 at 619; *Bear Stearns Bank Plc v Forum Global Equity Ltd* [2007] EWHC 1576 (Comm) at [155].

475 See para.2–082; *Associated British Ports v Tata Steel UK Ltd* [2017] EWHC 694 (Ch); [2017] 2 Lloyd's Rep. 11.

476 See para.2–083, fn.406; *Pagnan SpA v Feed Products Ltd* [1987] 2 Lloyd's Rep. 601.

477 Though this point is not decisive: see para.2–094, fn.462.

478 *Nelson v Stewart* (1991) S.L.R. 523.

479 *Gliksten & Son Ltd v State Assurance Co* (1922) 10 Ll.L. Rep. 604; cf. Marine Insurance Act 1906 s.31(2); contrast *American Airline Inc v Hope* [1973] 1 Lloyd's Rep. 233; affirmed [1974] 2 Lloyd's Rep. 301 ("at an additional premium *and geographical area* to be agreed").

480 See *Shackleford's Case* (1866) L.R. 1 Ch. App. 567; *Loftus v Roberts* (1902) 18 T.L.R. 532; *The Intra Transporter* [1986] 2 Lloyd's Rep. 132; *Pagnan SpA v Granaria BV* [1986] 2 Lloyd's Rep. 547; *Alfred McAlpine Construction Ltd v Panatown Ltd* [2001] EWCA Civ 485; (2001) 67 Con L.R. 224 at [35].

481 See *Brown v Gould* [1972] Ch. 52 (where, however, the option was binding for the reason stated below, fn.488); cf. *Teekay Tankers Ltd v STX Offshore & Shipbuilding Co Ltd* [2017] EWHC 253; [2017] 1 Lloyd's Rep. 387 (delivery dates to be agreed in option for shipbuilding contracts).

482 *Pritchard v Briggs* [1980] Ch. 339.

483 See para.3–162; *Bircham & Co Nominees (No.2) Ltd v Worrell Holdings Ltd* [2001] EWCA Civ 775; (2001) P. & C.R. 427 at [41].

484 *Bircham & Co Nominees (No.2) Ltd v Worrell Holdings Ltd* [2001] EWCA Civ 775; (2001) P. & C.R. 427 at [16], [23]; *Tiffany Investments Ltd v Bircham & Co Nominees (No.2) Ltd* [2003] EWCA Civ 1759; [2004] 2 P. & C.R. 10.

for uncertainty merely because it fails to specify the price. It obliges the landowner to offer the land to the purchaser at the price at which he is prepared to sell; and if the purchaser accepts that offer there is no uncertainty as to price.[485] This is so even though the parties have described the right as an "option" when its true legal nature is that of a right of pre-emption.[486] Where a third party has offered terms which the grantor of the right of pre-emption is minded to accept, the right of pre-emption is observed by first affording to the grantee the opportunity to match the third party's offer.[487]

2–097 **Criteria specified in the agreement.** An agreement may fail to specify matters such as price or quality but lay down *criteria* for determining those matters. For example, in *Hillas & Co Ltd v Arcos Ltd*[488] an option to buy timber was held binding even though it did not specify the price, since it provided for the price to be calculated by reference to an official price list. Even a provision that hire under a charterparty was in specified events to be "equitably decreased by an amount to be mutually agreed" has been held sufficiently certain to be enforced: it was said that "equitably" meant "fairly and reasonably"[489] and that a "purely objective standard has been prescribed."[490] Where, on the other hand, an agreement provided for payment of a fixed percentage of the "open market value" of shares in a *private* company, it was held that these words did not provide a sufficiently precise criterion since there was more than one formula for calculating the market value of shares in such a company.[491]

2–098 **Machinery specified in the agreement.** Alternatively, the agreement may provide *machinery* for resolving matters originally left open. Perhaps the most striking illustration of this possibility is provided by cases in which such matters are to be resolved by the decision of one party, but clear words are required to achieve that result[492] and the power which is conferred is limited by an implied term that it must not be exercised "dishonestly, for an improper purpose,

---

[485] *Smith v Morgan* [1971] 1 W.L.R. 803; cf. *Snelling v John G Snelling* [1973] 1 Q.B. 87 at 93; *Miller v Lakefield Estates Ltd* [1988] 1 E.G.L.R. 212 (where some doubts were expressed about *Smith v Morgan*).

[486] See *Fraser v Thames Television Ltd* [1984] Q.B. 44.

[487] *AstraZeneca UK Ltd v Albemarle International Corp* [2011] EWHC 1574 (Comm); [2011] 2 C.L.C. 252.

[488] (1932) 147 L.T. 503; cf. *Miller v FA Sadd & Son Ltd* [1981] 3 All E.R. 265; *Mamidoil-Jetoil Greek Petroleum Co SA v Okta Crude Oil Refinery AD* [2003] 1 Lloyd's Rep. 1 at [161]–[165]; *Brown v Gould* [1972] Ch. 53 (option to renew a lease "at a rent to be fixed having regard to the market value of the premises"); *Yedina v Yedin* [2017] EWHC 3319 (Ch) at [288] (payment of "reasonable maintenance" enforceable).

[489] *The Didymi* [1988] 2 Lloyd's Rep. 108 at 116, 118.

[490] *The Didymi* [1988] 2 Lloyd's Rep. 108 at 117. Contrast *Willis Management (Isle of Man) Ltd v Cable & Wireless Plc* [2005] EWCA Civ 806; [2005] 2 Lloyd's Rep. 597 (parties agreed that one would take a "fair" share of losses incurred by the other, but the evidence indicated that the parties meant fair share *to be agreed*).

[491] *Gillatt v Sky Television Ltd (Formerly Sky Television Plc)* [2000] 1 All E.R. (Comm) 461.

[492] *Lombard Tricity Finance Ltd v Paton* [1989] 1 All E.R. 918; *Esso Petroleum Co v Addison* [2003] EWHC 1730 (Comm); *West Sussex CC v Amberley UK Ltd* [2011] EWCA Civ 11.

capriciously or arbitrarily";[493] a standard which it has been said should be equated to the test of "*Wednesbury*" reasonableness applied to the review of the exercise of executive power.[494] Similarly, an arbitration clause can validly provide for the arbitration to take place at one of two or more places to be selected by one of the parties.[495] Agreements are a fortiori not incomplete merely because they provide that outstanding points shall be determined by arbitration,[496] or by the courts,[497] or by the valuation of a third party.[498] The Sale of Goods Act 1979 provides that if the third party "cannot or does not make the valuation, the agreement is avoided";[499] but an agreement is not necessarily ineffective merely because the agreed machinery fails to work. In *Sudbrook Trading Estate Ltd v Eggleton*[500] a lease gave the tenant the option to purchase the premises "at such price as may be agreed upon by two Valuers, one to be nominated by" each party. The landlord having refused to appoint a valuer, the House of Lords held that the option did not fail for uncertainty. It amounted, on its true construction, to an agreement to sell at a reasonable price to be determined by the valuers; and the stipulation that each party should nominate one of the valuers was merely "subsidiary and inessential".[501] So long as the agreed machinery (which fails to operate) is of this character,[502] the court can substitute other machinery: e.g. it can itself fix the price with the aid of expert evidence. This is so not only where the agreed machinery fails because of one party's refusal to operate it,[503] but also where it fails for some other reason, such as the refusal of a designated valuer to make the valuation.[504]

---

[493] *The Product Star (No.2)* [1993] 1 Lloyd's Rep. 397; *Paragon Finance Ltd v Nash* [2001] EWCA Civ 1466; [2001] 2 All E.R. (Comm) 1025 at [36]; cf. *Lymington Marina Ltd v Macnamara* [2007] EWCA Civ; [2007] N.P.C. 27; *Socimer International Bank Ltd v Standard Bank London Ltd* [2008] EWCA Civ 116; [2008] 1 Lloyd's Rep. 558 at [110]. Contrast *GX Networks Ltd v Greenland* [2010] EWCA Civ 784; [2010] I.R.L.R. 991 (discretion to be exercised "by exception only"); *Attrill v Dresdner Kleinwort Ltd* [2013] EWCA Civ 394; [2013] 3 All E.R. 607 at [57].

[494] *Braganza v BP Shipping Ltd* [2015] UKSC 17; [2015] 1 W.L.R. 1661 at [103].

[495] *The Star Texas* [1993] 2 Lloyd's Rep. 445.

[496] *Arcos Ltd v Aronson* (1930) 36 Lloyd's Law Rep.108; cf. *Thomas Bates & Son Ltd v Wyndham's (Lingerie) Ltd* [1981] 1 W.L.R. 505, where a lease was rectified (para.8–076) to include such a clause; *Queensland Electricity Generating Board v New Hope Collieries Pty Ltd* [1989] 1 Lloyd's Rep. 205.

[497] *Alstom Signalling Ltd v Jarvis Facilities Ltd* [2004] EWHC 1232 (TCC); 95 Con L.R. 55.

[498] As in *Heathrow Airport Ltd v Thames Water Utilities Ltd* [2009] EWCA Civ 992.

[499] Sale of Goods Act 1979 s.9(1); cf. *Pym v Campbell* (1856) 6 E. & B. 370.

[500] [1983] 1 A.C. 444.

[501] *Re Malpass (Deceased)* [1985] Ch. 42 at 50; *Tito v Waddell (No.2)* [1977] Ch. 106 at 314; *The Didymi* [1988] 2 Lloyd's Rep. 108 at 115.

[502] i.e. not if it is "an integral and essential part of the definition of the payments to be made": *Gillatt v Sky Television Ltd (Formerly Sky Television Plc)* [2000] 1 All E.R. (Comm) 461 at 479; cf. *Manchester Ship Canal Co Ltd v Environment Agency* [2017] EWHC 1340 (QB).

[503] As in *Sudbrook Trading Estate Ltd v Eggleton* [1983] 1 A.C. 444; cf. *Cream Holdings Ltd v Davenport* [2011] EWCA Civ 1287; [2012] 1 B.C.L.C. 365 (term implied that the transferor of shares under a right of pre-emption would co-operate with the appointment of a valuer and not unreasonably refuse to agree the terms of engagement).

[504] As in *Re Malpas (Deceased)* [1985] Ch. 42.

### (v) *Facts to be ascertained*

2–099 An agreement is not ineffective on the ground of uncertainty merely because the facts on which its operation depend are not known when it is made: the requirement of certainty is satisfied if those facts become ascertainable and are ascertained (without the need for further negotiation) after the making of the agreement.[505]

### (vi) *Agreement to negotiate*[506]

2–100 In some cases of incomplete agreements it is said that there is an agreement to agree,[507] or an agreement to negotiate. It is necessary at the outset to stress that, even if such an agreement is enforceable, it must be distinguished from the ultimate contract which the parties were hoping to agree, or to negotiate; it is a form of preliminary contract. For example, if the parties have entered into an agreement to negotiate the sale of a business and it is alleged that one party, in breach, has failed to negotiate, it does not follow that, even if they had negotiated (i.e. if the contract had been performed), the parties would have concluded the sale of the business. For this reason, it has been acknowledged that "damages for breach of such an obligation could be problematical".[508] This is not a problem which the courts have been called upon to resolve[509] because, in fact, an agreement to agree or an agreement to negotiate is unenforceable.[510] Either the ultimate contract is itself enforceable, because any uncertainty over the outstanding terms can be resolved (e.g. by resort to objective criteria,[511] or to objective machinery[512]), or it is not. In this sense, to conclude that the parties have concluded no more than an agreement to agree, or an agreement to negotiate, is to conclude that it has not been possible to resolve the uncertainty and there is no enforceable contract, or obligation between them.[513]

---

505 *Welsh Development Agency v Export Finance Ltd* [1992] B.C.L.C. 148.

506 Peel in Burrows and Peel (eds), *Contract Formation and Parties* (2010); Berg 119 L.Q.R. 357; Hoskins 130 L.Q.R. 131; Trakman & Sharma [2014] C.L.J. 598.

507 For the position where this expression refers to an agreement to execute a formal document incorporating terms on which the parties have previously agreed, see para.2–091.

508 *Jet2.Com Ltd v Blackpool Airport Ltd* [2012] EWCA Civ 417; 142 Con L.R. 1 at [65]. Damages might be awarded on the basis of a "loss of chance": *Petromec Inc v Petroleo Brasileiro SA Petrobas* [2005] EWCA Civ 891; [2006] 1 Lloyd's Rep. 161 at [118]; *Walford v Miles* (1991) 62 P & CR 410 at 423 (Bingham LJ (dissenting)); cf. *Jones v Ricoh UK Ltd* [2010] EWHC 1743 (Ch) at [77]–[78]. See, generally, para.20–062.

509 A "loss of chance" approach was adopted in the context of breach of an agreement *not to* negotiate with a third party in *Dandara Holdings Ltd v Co-operative Retail Services Ltd* [2004] EWHC 1476 (Ch) (no damages awarded).

510 See para.2–101.

511 See para.2–098.

512 See para.2–097.

513 *Dhanani v Crasnianski* [2011] EWHC 926 (Comm); [2011] 2 All E.R. (Comm) 799 at [95]; *Mehboob Travel Ltd v Pakistan International Airlines Corp* [2013] EWHC 2120 (QB) at [36].

**Agreement to negotiate is unenforceable.** In spite of occasional dicta to the contrary,[514] it has been held that an agreement to negotiate is not a contract "because it is too uncertain to have any binding force."[515] Such an agreement is no more enforceable if it is couched in terms of an obligation to negotiate in good faith. The leading case in this regard is *Walford v Miles*[516] in which the vendors agreed not to negotiate with any third party (a "lock-out" agreement) during negotiations for the sale of a business. This agreement lacked certainty because it failed to specify any time limit;[517] and the House of Lords unanimously rejected the argument that it could be made certain by implying a term which required the vendors to continue to negotiate in good faith with the purchasers for so long as the vendors continued to desire to sell, since such a term was itself too uncertain to be enforced. The uncertainty lay in the fact that the alleged duty was "inherently inconsistent with the position of a negotiating party"[518] who must normally[519] be free to advance his own interests during the negotiations. The point is well illustrated by the facts of *Walford v Miles* itself, where the defendants had agreed subject to contract to sell a property to the purchasers for £2 million and had ("in breach" of the ineffective "lock-out" agreement) sold it to a third party for exactly that sum, and the purchasers then claimed damages of £1 million on the basis that the property was (by reason of facts known to them but not the defendants) worth £3 million. If a duty to negotiate in good faith exists, it must be equally incumbent on both parties, so that it can hardly require a vendor to agree to sell a valuable property for only two-thirds of its true value when the facts affecting that value are known to the purchaser and not disclosed (as good faith would seem to require) to the vendor. The actual result in *Walford v Miles* (in which the purchasers recovered the sum of £700 in respect of their wasted expenses as damages for misrepresentation,[520] but not the £1 million which they claimed as damages for breach of contract)[521] seems, with respect, to be entirely 2–101

[514] *Chillingworth v Esche* [1924] 1 Ch. 97 at 113; *Hillas & Co Ltd v Arcos Ltd* (1932) 147 L.T. 503 at 515.

[515] *Courtney & Fairbairn Ltd v Tolaini Bros (Hotels) Ltd* [1975] 1 W.L.R. 297 at 301; cf. *Von Hatzfeldt-Wildenburg v Alexander* [1912] 1 Ch. 284 at 249; *Mallozzi v Carapelli SpA* [1976] 1 Lloyd's Rep. 407; *The Scaptrade* [1981] 2 Lloyd's Rep. 425 at 432 (affirmed without reference to this point [1983] 2 A.C. 694); *Mamidoil-Jetoil Greek Petroleum SA v Okta Crude Oil Refining AD* [2001] EWCA Civ 406; [2001] 2 Lloyd's Rep. 76 at [53], [59].

[516] [1992] 2 A.C. 128; Neill 108 L.Q.R. 405; Mills & Loveridge [2011] L.M.C.L.Q. 528.

[517] A "lock out" agreement is enforceable where a time limit is agreed: *Pitt v PHH Asset Management Ltd* [1994] 1 W.L.R. 327. Further, such an agreement is not uncertain if a temporal limit can be implied which is not tied to the parties' obligation to negotiate: *Compere Associates Ltd v Halsey* [2004] EWHC 1317 (Ch); cf. *JSD Corporation Pte Ltd v Al Waha Capital PJSC* [2009] EWHC 3376 (Ch).

[518] *Walford v Miles* [1992] 2 A.C. 128 at 138; cf. *Surrey CC v Bredero Homes Ltd* [1993] 1 W.L.R. 1361 at 1368; *Baird Textile Holdings Ltd v Marks and Spencer Plc* [2001] EWCA Civ 274; [2002] 1 All E.R. (Comm) 737 at [68].

[519] For an exception, see *Re Debtors (Nos 4449 and 4450 of 1998)* [1999] 1 All E.R. (Comm) 149 at 158 (Lloyd's bound to negotiate in good faith with its names as it was "performing functions in the public interest within a statutory framework"). See further: para.2–103.

[520] See *Walford v Miles* [1992] 2 A.C. 128 at 136. In some circumstances, a quantum meruit may be awarded to reflect the value of work done by the claimant before negotiations have broken down: *Cobbe v Yeoman's Row Management Ltd* [2008] UKHL 55; [2008] 1 W.L.R. 1752; para.22–031.

[521] See *Walford v Miles* [1992] 2 A.C. 128 at 135.

appropriate on the facts, especially because the vendors reasonably believed themselves to be protected from liability in the principal negotiation by the phrase "subject to contract".

2–102 **Criticism and scope.** In *Walford v Miles* the House of Lords rejected the solution of an *implied* obligation to negotiate in good faith but it has been suggested that a different approach might be taken in relation to an *express* agreement to negotiate in good faith.[522] However, subsequent cases have also ruled that an express agreement to agree, or to negotiate in good faith, is unenforceable[523] and the same result has been reached where the parties have agreed to agree, or negotiate with a third party;[524] where they have agreed to use their best or reasonable endeavours[525] to agree, or negotiate an agreement;[526] and where they have entered into such an agreement as a condition precedent.[527] Nevertheless, the "blanket unenforceability" of a provision to which the parties have expressly agreed and by which they intended to be bound is a result which the courts will strive to avoid.[528] It should be stressed that, when the courts have avoided this result, the conclusion which is in fact reached is that the "ultimate" contract between the parties was itself certain and enforceable, e.g. because any failure to agree by the parties could be resolved by objective criteria or machinery, or because the terms upon which the parties have failed to agree were not essential to the enforceability of the contract.[529] As stated at the outset, an agreement to agree, or an agreement to negotiate, is itself unenforceable.

---

[522] See, in particular, the *obiter dictum* of Longmore LJ in *Petromec Inc v Petroleo Brasileiro SA Petrobas* [2005] EWCA Civ 891; [2006] 1 Lloyd's Rep. 161 at [121]; *Knatchbull-Hugessen v SISU Capital Ltd* [2014] EWHC 1194 (QB) at [23]. See also Lord Steyn, writing extra-judicially: 113 L.Q.R. 433 at 439.

[523] *Barbudev v Eurocom Cable Management Eood* [2012] EWCA Civ 548; [2012] 2 All E.R. (Comm) 963; *DS Rendite Fonds NR v Titan Maritime SA Panama* [2015] EWHC 2488 (Comm) at [15].

[524] *Shaker v Vistajet Group Holding SA* [2012] EWHC 1329 (Comm); [2012] 2 Lloyd's Rep. 93; *Dany Lions Ltd v Bristol Cars Ltd* [2014] EWHC 817 (QB); [2014] 2 All E.R. (Comm) 403. Contrast *Astor Management AG v Atalaya Mining Plc* [2017] EWHC 425 (Comm); [2017] 1 Lloyd's Rep. 476 at [64] (upheld on appeal without consideration of this issue: [2018] EWCA Civ 2407; [2019] 1 B.C.L.C. 409).

[525] On the meaning of "best" and "reasonable" endeavours, see: *Sheffield District Railway Co v Great Central Railway Co* (1911) 27 T.L.R. 471; *IBM United Kingdom Ltd v Rockware Glass Ltd* [1980] F.S.R. 335 at 339, 343; *Yewbelle Ltd v London Green Developments* Ltd [2007] EWCA Civ 475; [2007] 23 E.G. 164; *Rhodia International Holdings Ltd v Huntsman International LLC* [2007] EWHC 292 (Comm); [2007] 2 Lloyd's Rep. 325 at [33]–[35]; *Sidhu v Sandhu* [2010] EWCA Civ 531 at [16]; *Jet2.Com Ltd v Blackpool Airport Ltd* [2012] EWCA Civ 417; 142 Con L.R. 1.

[526] *Little v Courage* (1995) 70 P. & C.R. 469 at 475; *Phillips Petroleum Co UK Ltd v Enron Europe Ltd* (1997) C.L.C. 329 (Potter LJ); *London & Regional Investments Ltd v TBI Plc Belfast International Airport Ltd* [2002] EWCA Civ 355 at [39]; *Multiplex Constructions UK Ltd v Cleveland Bridge UK Ltd* [2006] EWHC 1341 (TCC); affirmed [2007] EWCA Civ 443, without reference to this point; cf. *Morris v Swanton Care & Community Ltd* [2018] EWCA Civ 2763 at [32].

[527] *Shaker v Vistajet Group Holding SA* [2012] EWHC 1329 (Comm); [2012] 2 Lloyd's Rep. 93.

[528] *Petromec Inc v Petroleo Brasileiro SA Petrobas* [2005] EWCA Civ 891; [2006] 1 Lloyd's Rep. 161.

[529] *Jet2.Com Ltd v Blackpool Airport Ltd* [2012] EWCA Civ 417; 142 Con L.R. 1 at [59] (Lewison LJ dissenting); *Shaker v Vistajet Group Holding SA* [2012] EWHC 1329 (Comm); [2012] 2 Lloyd's Rep. 93 at [17].

**Exceptions?** In a number of cases, the parties have agreed to dispute resolution clauses which, for example, allow for arbitration but only after certain steps have been taken to resolve the dispute. Such clauses have also been held to be unenforceable if, because of a lack of certainty, they amount to no more than an agreement to agree, or to negotiate a settlement.[530] In *Emirates Trading Agency LLC v Prime Mineral Exports Private Ltd*[531] the parties agreed to arbitration but only after seeking to resolve the dispute or claim "by friendly discussion". Teare J held such a provision to amount to an agreement to seek to resolve the dispute "in good faith", but also went on to regard it as an enforceable condition precedent to the jurisdiction of the tribunal (one which had been met on the facts). His decision is not easy to reconcile with the earlier authorities. He was influenced by the "public interest" in seeking to give effect, in particular, to dispute resolution clauses.[532] 2–103

Where the parties have reached agreement on all essential points, but have left other points open, it has been held that the courts may then imply a term that they are to negotiate in good faith so as to settle the outstanding details which are to be incorporated in the formal document setting out the full terms of the contract between them.[533] Whether such a term is any more enforceable than other agreements to negotiate is open to debate and the better analysis may be that the outstanding details are simply not essential to the enforceability of the contract which the parties have entered into, or may be resolved by resort to objective criteria.[534]

## 6. Conditional Agreements

### (a) Classification

**Different meanings of "condition".** An agreement is conditional if its operation depends on an event which is not certain to occur. Discussions of this topic are made difficult by the fact that in the law of contract "condition" is "a chameleon-like word which takes on its meaning from its surroundings."[535] At 2–104

[530] *Itex Shipping v China Ocean Shipping* [1989] 2 Lloyd's Rep. 522; *Cable & Wireless Plc v IBM United Kingdom Ltd* [2002] EWHC 2059 (Comm); [2003] B.L.R. 89; *Sulamérica CIA Nacional de Seguros SA v Enesa Engenharia SA* [2012] EWCA Civ 638; [2013] 1 W.L.R. 102; *Wah v Grant Thornton International Ltd* [2012] EWHC 3198 (Ch); [2013] 1 Lloyd's Rep. 11.

[531] [2014] EWHC 2104 (Comm); [2014] 2 Lloyd's Rep. 457.

[532] cf. *United Group Rail Services v Rail Corp New South Wales* (2009) 127 Con L.R. 202.

[533] *Donwin Productions Ltd v EMI Films Ltd*, *The Times*, 9 March 1984 (not cited in *Walford v Miles* [1992] 2 A.C. 128).

[534] *Wah v Grant Thornton International Ltd* [2012] EWHC 3198 (Ch); [2013] 1 Lloyd's Rep. 11 at [57]. In *Petromec Inc v Petroleo Brasileiro SA Petrobas* [2005] EWCA Civ 891; [2006] 1 Lloyd's Rep. 161 the parties expressly agreed to negotiate the "reasonable cost" of an upgrade to a vessel. There may be no uncertainty in agreeing "cost", or a "fair price"; the courts can make a finding as to what that might be, in the absence of the parties' agreement (see para.2–097). But Longmore LJ also thought that the court could make a finding as to an element of "uplift" by way of profit on the basis of the obligation to negotiate in good faith; cf. *Butters v BBC Worldwide Ltd* [2009] EWHC 1954 (Comm) at [148]–[151], affirmed [2009] EWCA Civ 1160; [2010] Ch. 347 without reference to this point; *Gold Group Properties Ltd v BDW Trading Ltd* [2010] EWHC 1632 (TCC) at [87].

[535] *The Varenna* [1984] Q.B. 599 at 618.

this stage, we are concerned with only one of these meanings; but to clear the ground it is necessary to draw a number of preliminary distinctions.

2–105 **Promissory and contingent conditions.** The word "condition" may refer either to an *event*, or to a *term* of a contract (as in the phrase "conditions of sale"). Where "condition" refers to an event, that event may be either an occurrence which neither party undertakes to bring about, or the performance by one party of his undertaking. The first possibility is illustrated by a contract by which A is to work for B, and B is to pay A £50, "if it rains tomorrow". Here the obligations of both parties are contingent on the happening of the specified event which may therefore be described as a *contingent* condition. The second possibility is illustrated by the ordinary case in which A agrees to work for B at a weekly wage payable at the end of the week. Here the contract is immediately binding on both parties, but B is not liable to pay until A has performed his promise to work. Such performance is a condition of B's liability, and, as A has promised to render it, the condition may be described as *promissory*.[536] In this chapter our concern is with contingent conditions;[537] promissory conditions will be discussed in Chs 17 and 18.[538]

Contingent conditions may be precedent or subsequent. A condition is precedent if it provides that the contract is not to be binding until the specified event occurs. It is subsequent if it provides that a previously binding contract is to determine on the occurrence of the event: e.g. where A contracts to pay an allowance to B until B marries.[539]

## (b) Degrees of obligation

2–106 **No duty to render principal performance.** Where an agreement is subject to a contingent condition precedent, there is, before the occurrence of the condition, no duty on either party to render the principal performance promised by him: e.g. a seller is not bound to deliver and a buyer is not bound to pay. Nor, in such a case, does either party undertake that the condition will occur. But an agreement subject to such a condition may impose some degree of obligation on the parties or on one of them. Whether it has this effect, and if so what degree of obligation is imposed, depends on the true construction of the term specifying the condition.[540]

536 *Total Gas Marketing Ltd v Arco British Ltd* [1998] 2 Lloyd's Rep. 209 at 215, 218; *UR Power GmbH v Kuok Oils and Grains Pte Ltd* [2009] EWHC 1940 (Comm); [2009] 2 Lloyd's Rep. 495 at [14]–[15].

537 The "event" which is made a contingent condition precedent may be the fulfilment of a promissory obligation, e.g. in a compromise agreement, the employee's warranty that he has not committed a repudiatory breach of the employment contract: *Collidge v Freeport Plc* [2008] EWCA Civ 485; [2008] I.R.L.R. 697.

538 See paras 17–015—17–018, 18–042—18–066.

539 cf. *Brown v Knowsley BC* [1986] I.R.L.R. 102; *Jameson v CEGB* [2000] 1 A.C. 455 at 477.

540 *The MV Pacific Champ* [2013] EWHC 470 (Comm); [2013] 2 Lloyd's Rep. 320 at [68]. For special difficulties where the condition precedent is implied, see *Bentworth Finance Ltd v Lubert* [1968] 1 Q.B. 680; Carnegie, 31 M.L.R. 78.

**Parties free to withdraw.** One possibility is that, before the event occurs, each party is free to withdraw from the agreement. In *Pym v Campbell*[541] an agreement for the sale of a patent was executed, but the parties at the same time agreed that it should not "be the agreement" unless a third party approved of the invention. He did not approve, and it was held that the buyer was not liable for refusing to perform. The written agreement was "not an agreement at all".[542] If this is taken literally, either party could have withdrawn even before the third party had given his opinion. 2–107

**Parties cannot withdraw.** A second possibility is that, before the event occurs, the main obligations have not accrued; but that, so long as the event can still occur, one (or both) of the parties cannot withdraw. Thus in *Smith v Butler*[543] A bought land from B on condition that a loan to B (secured by a mortgage on the premises) would be transferred to A.[544] It was held that A could not withdraw before the time fixed for completion: he was bound to wait until then to see whether B could arrange the transfer. However, if it becomes clear that the condition has not occurred, or that it can no longer occur, within the time specified in the contract,[545] the parties will be under no further obligations under the contract.[546] In such a case, the effect of the non-occurrence of the condition is that the parties are "no longer bound"[547] by the contract, or that the contract is "discharged."[548] What the parties have called a "condition precedent" can thus operate as, or have the effect of, a condition subsequent.[549] 2–108

**Parties must not prevent occurrence of condition.** A third possibility is that, before the event occurs, the main obligations have not accrued; but that in the meantime neither party must do anything to prevent the occurrence of the event. Thus in *Mackay v Dick*[550] an excavating machine was sold on condition that it could excavate at a specified rate on the buyer's property. The buyer's refusal to provide facilities for a proper trial was held to be a breach. Similarly, the seller would have been in breach, had he refused to subject the machine to a proper test. 2–109

---

541 (1856) 6 E. & B. 370.

542 *Pym v Campbell* (1856) 6 E. & B. 370 at 374.

543 [1900] 1 Q.B. 694; cf. *Felixstowe Dock & Ry Co v British Transport Docks Bd* [1976] 2 Lloyd's Rep. 656; *Alan Estates Ltd v WG Stores Ltd* [1982] Ch. 511 at 520.

544 On agreements "subject to finance" see Coote 40 Conv. (N.S.) 37; Furmston 3 O.J.L.S. 438; discussing *Meehan v Jones* (1982) 149 C.L.R. 571.

545 If no time is specified, the court will ordinarily imply a "reasonable time": *Beazley Underwriting Ltd v Travelers Companies Inc* [2011] EWHC 1520 (Comm); [2012] 1 All E.R. (Comm) 1241 at [185].

546 *North Sea Energy Holdings NV v Petroleum Authority of Thailand* [1997] 2 Lloyd's Rep. 418 at 428–429; affirmed on other grounds [1999] 1 Lloyd's Rep. 483.

547 *Total Gas Marketing Ltd v Arco British Land Ltd* [1998] 2 Lloyd's Rep. 209 at 215.

548 *Total Gas Marketing Ltd v Arco British Land Ltd* [1998] 2 Lloyd's Rep. 209 at 218.

549 *Total Gas Marketing Ltd v Arco British Land Ltd* [1998] 2 Lloyd's Rep. 209 at 221, 224.

550 (1881) 6 App. Cas. 251; cf. *Shipping Corp of India v Naviera Letasa* [1976] 1 Lloyd's Rep. 132; *CIA Barca de Panama SA v George Wimpey & Co Ltd* [1980] 1 Lloyd's Rep. 598; *Cream Holdings Ltd v Davenport* [2011] EWCA Civ 1287; [2012] B.C.L.C. 365. Contrast *North Sea Energy Holdings NV v Petroleum Authority of Thailand* [1999] 1 Lloyd's Rep. 483 (duty to co-operate in bringing about the event negatived by terms of the contract).

The same principle is illustrated by a case[551] in which a professional footballer was transferred for a fee, part of which was to be paid only after he had scored 20 goals. Before he had done so, the new club dropped him from their first team, and they were held to be in breach as they had not given the player a reasonable opportunity to score the 20 goals.

The duty not to prevent the occurrence of the condition has been explained as resting on an implied term and this explanation limits the scope of the duty in a number of ways. For example, the implied term may only be to the effect that a party will not *prevent* fulfilment of the condition, so that he is not in breach simply by doing nothing;[552] or that he will not *deliberately* prevent the occurrence of the condition;[553] or (even more narrowly) that he will not *wrongfully* do so.[554] The latter type of implication may allow a party to engage in certain kinds of deliberate prevention but not in others: e.g. it may allow a company which has promised an employee the opportunity of earning a bonus to deprive him of that opportunity by going out of business, but not by simply dismissing him, before the bonus has become due.[555]

2–110 **Approval of one party.** The sort of implied term referred to in the previous paragraph can be excluded by an express contrary provision;[556] in particular, by a provision making the operation of a contract dependent on the "satisfaction" of one party with the subject-matter or other aspects relating to the other's performance.[557] Thus it has been held that there was no contract where a house was bought "subject to satisfactory mortgage";[558] and where a boat was bought "subject to satisfactory survey"[559] it was held that the buyer was not bound if he expressed his dissatisfaction,[560] in spite of the fact that such expression was a deliberate act on his part which prevented the occurrence of the condition. The same is true where goods are bought on approval and the buyer does not approve them,[561] and where an offer of employment is made "subject to satisfactory references," and the prospective employer does not regard the references as satisfactory.[562] There is some apparent conflict in the authorities on the question whether the law imposes any restriction on the freedom of action of the party on whose satisfaction the operation of the contract depends. In one case[563] a proposed royalty agreement relating to the use by a manufacturer of an invention

---

551 *Bournemouth & Boscombe Athletic FC v Manchester United FC*, *The Times*, 22 May 1980. cf. *CEL Group Ltd v Nedlloyd Lines UK Ltd* [2003] EWCA Civ 1716; [2004] 1 Lloyd's Rep. 381 at [21]–[22]; *Luxor (Eastbourne) Ltd v Cooper* [1940] A.C. 108, para.16–101.

552 *Taylor v Rive Droite Music Ltd* [2005] EWCA Civ 1300; [2006] E.M.L.R. 4 at [160].

553 See *Blake & Co v Sohn* [1969] 1 W.L.R. 1412.

554 See *Thompson v ASDA-MFI Group Plc* [1988] Ch. 241.

555 Example based on *Thompson v ASDA-MFI Group Plc* [1988] Ch. 241; and para.16–101.

556 See *Micklefield v SAC Technology Ltd* [1990] 1 W.L.R. 1002.

557 *Schweppe v Harper* [2008] EWCA Civ 442; [2008] B.P.I.R. 1090 at [70].

558 *Lee-Parker v Izett (No.2)* [1975] 1 W.L.R. 775.

559 *Astra Trust Ltd v Adams & Williams* [1969] 1 Lloyd's Rep. 81; doubted in *The Merak* [1976] 2 Lloyd's Rep. 250 at 254; and in *Ee v Kakar* (1979) 40 P. & C.R. 223.

560 But if the buyer declared his satisfaction the seller would be bound even though the survey was not objectively satisfactory: *Graham v Pitkin* [1992] 1 W.L.R. 403 at 405.

561 cf. Sale of Goods Act 1979 s.18, r.4.

562 *Wishart v National Association of Citizens' Advice Bureaux* [1990] I.C.R. 794.

563 *Stabilad Ltd v Stephens & Carter (No.2)* [1999] 2 All E.R. (Comm) 651.

was "subject to detailed evaluation of production and marketing feasibility" by the manufacturer. It was held that his discretion whether to enter into the contract was "unfettered by any obligation to act reasonably or in good faith"[564] and that, as his satisfaction had not been communicated[565] to the other party, the agreement had not acquired contractual force. On the other hand, where a ship was sold "subject to satisfactory completion of two trial voyages" it was said that such a stipulation was to be construed as "subject to bona fides".[566] The distinction between the two lines of cases turns, ultimately, on the construction of the agreement.[567] It has also been held that the party on whose satisfaction the operation of the contract depends must at least provide facilities for, or not impede, the inspection referred to in the agreement.[568] Of course if the result of the inspection is unsatisfactory, the principal obligation of the contract will not take effect.[569]

**One party under duty to use reasonable efforts.** A fourth possibility is that, before the event occurs, the main obligations have not accrued but that one of the parties undertakes to use reasonable efforts to bring the event about (without absolutely undertaking that his efforts will succeed).[570] This construction was applied, for instance, where land was sold subject to the condition that the purchaser should obtain planning permission to use the land as a transport depot: he was bound to make reasonable efforts to obtain the permission, but he was free from liability when those efforts failed.[571] Similarly, where goods are sold "subject to export (or import) licence", the party whose duty it is to obtain the licence[572] does not prima facie promise absolutely that a licence will be obtained,[573] but only undertakes to make reasonable efforts to that end.[574] The principal obligations to buy and sell will not take effect if no licence is **2–111**

564 *Stabilad Ltd v Stephens & Carter (No.2)* [1999] 2 All E.R. (Comm) 651 at 662.

565 For the requirement of communication, see *Stabilad Ltd v Stephens & Carter (No.2)* [1999] 2 All E.R. (Comm) 651 at 660; the requirement may be satisfied by conduct from which satisfaction can be inferred, e.g. where a buyer of goods on approval retains them without notifying rejection for more than the stipulated or a reasonable time: Sale of Goods Act 1979 s.18, r.4(b).

566 *The John S Darbyshire* [1977] 2 Lloyd's Rep. 457 at 464; cf. *BV Oliehandel Jongkind v Coastal International Ltd* [1983] 2 Lloyd's Rep. 463; contrast *The Junior K* [1988] 2 Lloyd's Rep. 583 at 589 (where the words were held to negative contractual intention); *Novus Aviation Ltd v Alubaf Arab International Bank BSC* [2016] EWHC 1575 (Comm); [2017] 1 B.C.L.C. 414 at [64]. See also *El Awadi v Bank of Credit & Commerce International SA* [1990] 1 Q.B. 606 at 619; and in an analogous context, *The Product Star (No.2)* [1993] 1 Lloyd's Rep. 397 at 404 (para.2–098, text to fn.493).

567 *Schweppe v Harper* [2008] EWCA Civ 442; [2008] B.P.I.R. 1090 at [71]; *Novus Aviation Ltd v Alubaf Arab International Bank BSC* [2016] EWHC 1575 (Comm); [2017] 1 B.C.L.C. 414 at [66].

568 *The Merak* [1976] 2 Lloyd's Rep. 250; cf. *Ee v Kakar* (1979) 40 P. & C.R. 223.

569 As in *The John S Darbyshire* [1977] 2 Lloyd's Rep. 457.

570 See the discussion in para.2–114 of the decision in *Astor Management AG v Atalaya Mining Plc* [2018] EWCA Civ 2407; [2019] 1 B.C.L.C. 409 where one party was required to use "all reasonable endeavours".

571 *Hargreaves Transport Ltd v Lynch* [1969] 1 W.L.R. 215 (condition not satisfied); *Richard West & Partners (Inverness) Ltd v Dick* [1969] 2 Ch. 424 (similar condition satisfied); contrast *Tesco Stores Ltd v Gibson* (1970) 214 E.G. 835 (no obligation on purchaser to apply for planning permission).

572 As to which party has this duty, see *HO Brandt & Co v HN Morris & Co* [1917] 2 K.B. 784; *AV Pound & Co v MW Hardy & Co* [1956] A.C. 588.

573 The prima facie rule may be excluded by express words which do, on their true construction, impose an absolute duty; e.g. *Peter Cassidy Seed Co Ltd v Osuustukkukauppa* [1957] 1 W.L.R. 273; *C*

obtained;[575] but if the party who should have made reasonable efforts has failed to do so he will be liable in damages,[576] unless he can show that any such efforts, which he should have made would (if made) have necessarily been unsuccessful.[577]

2–112 **Effect of failure to perform.** It will be seen that in cases falling within the second, third and fourth categories discussed above, a distinction must be drawn between two types of obligation: the principal obligation of each party (e.g. to buy and sell) and a subsidiary obligation, i.e. one not to withdraw, not to prevent occurrence of the condition, or to make reasonable efforts to bring it about. One view is that the party who fails to perform the subsidiary obligation is to be treated as if the condition had occurred; and that he is then liable on the principal obligation. Thus in *Mackay v Dick*[578] the buyer was held liable *for the price*; but there was no discussion as to the remedy. In principle it seems wrong to hold him so liable, for such a result ignores the possibility that the machine might have failed to come up to the standard required by the contract, even if proper facilities for trial had been provided. It is submitted that the correct result in cases of this kind is to award *damages* for breach of the subsidiary obligation: in assessing such damages, the court can take into account the possibility that the condition might not have occurred, even if there had been no such breach.[579] To hold the party in breach liable for the full performance promised by him, on the fiction that the condition had occurred, seems to introduce into this branch of the law a punitive element that is inappropriate to a contractual action.[580] More recent authorities rightly hold that such a doctrine of "fictional fulfilment" of a condition does not form part of English law.[581]

2–113 **Conditions for the benefit of one party.** Where a condition is inserted entirely for the benefit of one party, that party may waive the condition.[582] He can then

---

*Czarnikow Ltd v Centrala Handlu Zagranicznego "Rolimpex"* [1979] A.C. 351 at 371; *Pagnan SpA v Tradax Ocean Transport SA* [1987] 3 All E.R. 565; Yates and Carter 1 J.C.L. 57.

[574] *Re Anglo-Russian Merchant Traders and John Batt & Co (London) Ltd* [1917] 2 K.B. 679; *Coloniale Import-Export v Loumidis & Sons* [1978] 2 Lloyd's Rep. 560; *Gamerco SA v ICM Fair Warning (Agency) Ltd* [1995] 1 W.L.R. 1226 at 1231. Where the contract is expressly subject to the approval of a public authority, there may not even be a duty to make reasonable efforts to secure that approval: see *Gyllenhammar Partners International v Sour Brodegradevna Industria* [1989] 2 Lloyd's Rep. 403.

[575] *Charles H Windschuegl Ltd v Alexander Pickering & Co Ltd* (1950) 84 Lloyd's Rep. 89 at 92–93; *Brauer & Co (Great Britain) Ltd v James Clark (Brush Materials) Ltd* [1952] 2 All E.R. 497 at 501.

[576] e.g. *Malik v Central European Trading Agency* [1974] 1 Lloyd's Rep. 279; *Agroexport v Cie. Européenne de Céréales* [1974] 1 Lloyd's Rep. 499.

[577] *Overseas Buyers Ltd v Granadex SA* [1980] 2 Lloyd's Rep. 608 at 612.

[578] (1881) 6 App. Cas. 251; para.2–109.

[579] *Bournemouth & Boscombe Athletic FC v Manchester United FC, The Times*, 22 May 1980; cf. *The Blankenstein* [1985] 1 W.L.R. 435 (para.18–023); *Alpha Trading Ltd v Dunshaw-Patten Ltd* [1981] Q.B. 290; *George Moundreas & Co SA v Navimpex Centrala Navala* [1985] 2 Lloyd's Rep. 515.

[580] cf. para.20–022.

[581] *Thompson v ASDA-MFI Group Plc* [1988] Ch. 241 at 266 (where the condition was said at 251 to be subsequent); *Little v Courage Ltd* (1995) 70 P. & C.R. 469 at 474.

[582] *Irwin v Wilson* [2011] EWHC 326 (Ch).

sue[583] and be sued[584] on the contract as if the condition had occurred. Obviously this rule does not apply to cases falling within the first of the categories discussed above, in which there is no contract at all before the condition occurs.

**Condition may cease to apply.** In light of subsequent events, a condition precedent may no longer apply, or cease to have effect. Whether it does so depends on the construction of the contract. In *Astor Management AG v Atalaya Mining Plc*[585] payment of the price for the sale of a copper mine was deferred and became payable when two conditions had been fulfilled: governmental authorisation to restart mining activities and the securing of a debt facility by the buyer to allow for such activities to begin. The authorisation was granted, but the buyer raised the necessary funds as equity finance, rather than as debt. The court held that, while the first condition might have ceased to apply if, for example, the need for authorisation was dispensed with by the local government, the second did not.[586] The parties had deliberately chosen to require that finance was raised by the buyer as debt and not in the form of equity, not least because part of the consideration for the seller was the receipt of shares in the buyer and the value of those shares would be reduced if the buyer raised equity finance.[587] To guard against the risk that the buyer might choose not to raise debt, it was required to use "all reasonable endeavours" to secure a debt facility, though it was found not to have breached that obligation because equity finance was the only form of funding that was reasonably available.[588] The unsatisfactory outcome that the buyer might avoid paying much of the price for a mine that was now profitable was avoided on the basis that it was only the provision for *deferred* payment which was not enforceable. The price itself was still due and became payable under other provisions of the contract. **2–114**

[583] *Wood Preservation Ltd v Prior* [1969] 1 W.L.R. 1077; contrast *Heron Garages Properties Ltd v Moss* [1974] 1 W.L.R. 148.

[584] *McKillop v McMullan* [1979] N.I. 85.

[585] [2018] EWCA Civ 2407; [2019] 1 B.C.L.C. 409.

[586] *Astor Management AG v Atalaya Mining Plc* [2018] EWCA Civ 2407; [2019] 1 B.C.L.C. 409 at [33].

[587] As indeed occurred, reducing the seller's shareholding in the buyer from 16 per cent to less than 1 per cent.

[588] There was no appeal on this issue from the decision below: [2017] EWHC 425 (Comm); [2017] 1 Lloyd's Rep. 476.

CHAPTER 3

# CONSIDERATION[1]



[1] Shatwell 1 Sydney L.R. 289; Sutton, *Consideration Reconsidered* (1974); Chen-Wishart (2013) 13 O.U.C.L.J. 209.

## 1. INTRODUCTION

### (a) General

3–001 **General rule.** In English law, a promise is not, as a general rule, binding as a contract unless it is either made in a deed[2] or supported by some "consideration". The purpose of the requirement of consideration is to put some legal limits on the enforceability of agreements even where they are intended to be legally binding[3] and are not vitiated by some factor such as mistake, misrepresentation, duress or illegality.[4] The existence of such limits is not a peculiarity of English law, e.g. in some civil law countries certain promises which in England are not binding for "want of consideration" cannot be enforced unless they are made in some special form, e.g. by a notarised writing. The view was, indeed, put forward at one time that consideration was only evidence of the intention of the parties to be bound, and that (at any rate in the case of certain commercial contracts), such evidence could equally well be furnished by writing.[5] But the view that agreements (other than those contained in deeds) were binding without consideration merely because they were in writing was rejected in England over 200 years ago,[6] though it has been revived as a proposal for law reform.[7] The present position therefore is that English law limits the enforceability of agreements (not in deeds) by reference to a complex and multifarious body of rules known as "the doctrine of consideration".

---

[2] See para.3–172.
[3] See Ch.4.
[4] See Chs 8–11.
[5] *Pillans v Van Mierop* (1765) 3 Burr. 1663.
[6] *Rann v Hughes* (1778) 7 T.R. 350n.; 4 Bro. P.C. 27.
[7] See para.3–177.

**Doctrine based on reciprocity.** This doctrine is based on the idea of reciprocity: "something of value in the eye of the law"[8] must be given for a promise in order to make it enforceable as a contract. An informal gratuitous promise therefore does not amount to a contract.[9] A person or body to whom a promise of a gift is made from purely sentimental or charitable motives gives nothing for the promise; and the claims of such a promisee are less compelling than those of a person who has given (or promised) some return for the promise.[10] The invalidity of informal gratuitous promises of this kind can also be supported on the ground that their enforcement could prejudice third parties such as creditors of the promisor.[11] Such promises, too, may be rashly made;[12] and the requirements of executing a deed or giving value provide at least some protection against this danger. 3–002

**Promises struck down for want of consideration.** The doctrine of consideration has, however, also struck at many promises which were not "gratuitous" in any ordinary or commercial sense. These applications of the doctrine were brought within its scope by stressing that consideration had to be not merely "something of value", but "something of value *in the eye of the law*".[13] The law in certain cases refused to recognise the "value" of acts or promises which might well be regarded as valuable by a layman. This refusal was based on many disparate policies; so that "promises without consideration" included many different kinds of transactions which, at first sight, had little in common. It is this fact which is the cause of the very great complexity of the doctrine; and which has also led to its occasional unwarranted extensions and hence to demands for reform of the law.[14] 3–003

## (b) Definitions

**Benefit and detriment.** The traditional definition of consideration concentrates on the requirement that "something of value" must be given and accordingly states that consideration is either some detriment to the promisee (in that he may give value) or some benefit to the promisor (in that he may receive value).[15] Usually, this detriment and benefit are merely the same thing looked at from different points of view. Thus payment by a buyer is consideration for the seller's promise to deliver and can be described as a detriment to the buyer or as a benefit 3–004

---

[8] *Thomas v Thomas* (1842) 2 Q.B. 851 at 859.

[9] *Re Hudson* (1885) 54 L.J. Ch. 811; *Williams v Roffey Bros & Nicholls (Contractors) Ltd* [1991] 1 Q.B. 1 at 19.

[10] cf. Eisenberg 47 U. of Chi. L. Rev. 1; 85 Cal. L. Rev. 821; Chen-Wishart (2013) 13 O.U.C.L.J. 209.

[11] *Eastwood v Kenyon* (1840) 11 A. & E. 438 at 451.

[12] *Beaton v McDivitt* (1988) 13 N.S.W.L.R. 162 at 170. It is often easier to promise to make a gift than actually to make one.

[13] See fn.8; para.3–006.

[14] See para.3–177.

[15] *Currie v Misa* (1875) L.R. 10 Ex. 153 at 162. See also *Cooke v Oxley* (1790) 3 T.R. 653 at 654; *Bainbridge v Firmstone* (1838) 8 A. & E. 743 at 744; *Thomas v Thomas* (1842) 2 Q.B. 851 at 859; *Bolton v Madden* (1873) L.R. 9 Q.B. 55 at 56; *Gore v Van der Lann* [1967] 2 Q.B. 31 at 42; *Midland Bank & Trust Co Ltd v Green* [1981] A.C. 513 at 531; *Modahl v British Athletics Federation Ltd* [2001] EWCA Civ 1447; [2002] 1 W.L.R. 1192 at [50]; cf. [2002] 1 W.L.R. 1192 at [103].

to the seller; and conversely delivery by a seller is consideration for the buyer's promise to pay and can be described either as a detriment to the seller or as a benefit to the buyer. These statements relate to the consideration *for the promise of each party* looked at separately. For example, the seller suffers a "detriment" when he delivers the goods and this enables him to enforce the buyer's promise to pay the price. It is quite irrelevant that the seller has made a good bargain and so gets a benefit from the performance of the contract. What the law is concerned with is the consideration *for a promise*—not the consideration *for a contract*.

3–005 **Either benefit or detriment sufficient.** Under the traditional definition it is sufficient if there is either a detriment to the promisee or a benefit to the promisor. Thus detriment to the promisee suffices even though the promisor does not benefit,[16] e.g. where A guarantees B's bank overdraft and the promisee bank suffers detriment by advancing money to B, then A is bound by his promise, even though he gets no benefit from the advance to B. The detriment must, however, have been a "requested" detriment, or incurred "in exchange" for the promise.[17] It is not sufficient that the promisee has relied on the promise to his detriment, though this may have other legal effects, i.e. other than the enforcement of the promise.[18] One view is that "[d]etriment to the promisee is of the essence of the doctrine, and benefit to the promisor is, when it exists, merely an accident".[19] But the view that benefit to the promisor is, on its own, sufficient to satisfy the requirement of consideration is supported by a number of cases[20] in which promises were enforced on the ground that such a benefit had been conferred, even though there was no apparent detriment to the promisee.

3–006 **Benefit and detriment may be factual or legal.** The traditional definition of consideration lacks precision because the key notions of "benefit" and "detriment" are used in at least two senses. They may refer, first, to any act[21] which is of some value, or, secondly, only to acts, the performance of which is not already legally due from the promisee. In the first sense, there is consideration if a benefit or detriment is *in fact* obtained or suffered. When the words are used in the second sense this factual benefit or detriment is disregarded, and a notion of what may be called legal benefit or detriment is substituted. Under this notion, the promisee may provide consideration by doing anything that he was not legally bound to do, whether or not it actually occasions a detriment to him or confers a benefit on the promisor; while conversely, he may provide no consideration by doing only what he was legally bound to do, however much this may in fact occasion a detriment to him or confer a benefit on the promisor. The English courts have not consistently adopted either of these senses of the words "benefit" and "detriment." In some of the situations to be

---

[16] *O'Sullivan v Management Agency & Music Ltd* [1985] Q.B. 428 at 459; *Re Dale* [1994] Ch. 31 at 38; cf. *Gill & Duffus SA v Rionda Futures Ltd* [1994] 2 Lloyd's Rep. 67 at 82.

[17] See paras 3–010, 3–011.

[18] See para.3–012.

[19] Holdsworth, *A History of English Law,* Vol.8 (1937), p.11.

[20] e.g. paras 3–025, 3–043 and following, 3–107, 3–111.

[21] Or forbearance, or promise to do or to forbear. For the sake of simplicity references in the text are confined to the doing of an act.

discussed in this chapter, factual benefit is stressed[22] even though legal detriment may also have been present; while in others the absence of a legal detriment or benefit has in the past been regarded as decisive.[23] More recent authority[24] regards factual benefit to the promisor as sufficient in one such situation, even in the absence of a legal benefit to him or of a legal detriment to the promisee and it is possible (though far from certain) that this approach may spread to at least some[25] of the situations in which the courts have in the past insisted on legal benefit or detriment.

**Other definitions.** The traditional definition of consideration in terms of benefit and detriment is sometimes regarded as unsatisfactory. One cause of dissatisfaction is that it is thought to be wrong to talk of benefit and detriment when both parties expect to, and actually may, benefit from the contract. But this reasoning falls, with respect, into the error of treating the subject-matter of the definition as the consideration *for a contract*,[26] when the definition is actually concerned with the consideration *for a promise*.[27] Another cause of dissatisfaction is the artificial reasoning that is sometimes necessary to accommodate decided cases within the traditional definition. Sir Frederick Pollock has, accordingly, described consideration as simply "the price for which the promise is bought".[28] This statement has been approved in the House of Lords[29]; but if it is to be regarded as a definition of consideration it is defective in being so vague as to give no help in determining whether consideration exists on a given set of facts. A view which also leads to uncertainty is that consideration "*means* a reason for the enforcement of promises"[30]—that reason being simply "the justice of the case".[31] But "the justice of the case" is in almost all the decided cases highly debatable, so that the suggested definition provides no basis for formulating a coherent legal doctrine. A modification of the suggested definition, describing consideration as "a reason for the recognition of an obligation",[32] is open to the same objection. Of course the traditional definition does not provide complete (or even a very high degree of) certainty. But it does state the doctrine in a way which gives some basis for predicting the course of future decisions; and it has more support in the authorities than any other definition. For these reasons it will be used in this chapter. 3–007

[22] e.g. in *Bolton v Madden* (1873) L.R. 9 Q.B. 55, para.3–025.
[23] e.g. in some of the existing duty cases discussed at para.3–048.
[24] *Williams v Roffey Bros & Nicholls (Contractors) Ltd* [1991] 1 Q.B. 1, para.3–050.
[25] e.g. to the variation cases discussed at paras 3–062–3–065; but probably not to the forbearance to sue cases discussed at paras 3–066–3–068.
[26] There are traces of this approach in *Williams v Roffey Bros & Nicholls (Contractors) Ltd* [1991] 1 Q.B. 1 at 23: "If both parties benefit from an agreement it is not necessary that each also suffered a detriment."
[27] See para.3–004.
[28] *Principles of Contract*, 13th edn (1950), p.133.
[29] *Dunlop Pneumatic Tyre Co Ltd v Selfridge Ltd* [1915] A.C. 847 at 855.
[30] Atiyah, *Consideration in Contracts: A Fundamental Restatement* (1971), p.60; cf. Llewellyn (1931) 40 Yale L.J. 704, 741. For criticism of Atiyah's views, see Treitel 50 A.L.J. 439.
[31] Atiyah, *Consideration in Contracts: A Fundamental Restatement* (1971), pp.52, 58.
[32] Atiyah, *Essays on Contract* (1990), pp.179, 183.

3–008 **Mutual promises.** So far we have discussed performance by one party as consideration for the promise of the other, e.g. payment by a buyer as the consideration for the seller's promise to deliver, or delivery by a seller as consideration for the buyer's promise to pay. It is, however, also well settled that mutual promises can be consideration for each other. Hence if a seller promises to deliver goods in six months' time and the buyer to pay for them on delivery, there is an immediately binding contract from which neither party can withdraw, though, of course, performance cannot be claimed till the appointed time. Implied, no less than express, promises can constitute consideration for each other.[33]

Some difficulty has been felt in explaining the rule that mutual promises can be consideration for each other. At first sight, it might seem that the mere giving of a promise was not a detriment, nor its receipt a benefit, so as to make the counter-promise binding. It will not do to say that the person making the promise suffers a detriment because he is legally bound to perform it; for if this assumption is made about one of the promises, it must also be made of the other, so that the "explanation" assumes the very point in issue. Probably the reason for the rule is simpler. A person who makes a commercial promise expects to have to perform it (and is in fact under considerable pressure to do so). Correspondingly, one who receives such a promise expects it to be kept. These expectations, which can exist even where the promise is not legally enforceable,[34] are based on commercial morality, and can properly be called a detriment and a benefit; hence they satisfy the requirement of consideration in the case of mutual promises. But there must, at least, be a counter-promise from the promisee: "A promise does not become contractually binding simply because the making of the promise is potentially advantageous to the promisor".[35]

As a general rule a promise is regarded as consideration for a counter-promise only if its performance would also have been so regarded.[36] It follows that a mere promise to accept a gift cannot be consideration for the promise to make it. Similarly, we shall see that a debtor who actually pays part of a debt does not thereby provide consideration for the creditor's promise to release the balance[37] and the position is exactly the same if the debtor *promises* part-payment in return for the creditor's counter-promise to accept the part-payment in full settlement.

3–009 **Invented consideration.** Normally, a party enters into a contract with a view to obtaining the consideration provided by the other, e.g. the buyer wants the goods and the seller the price. In the US it has been said that this is essential, and that "Nothing is consideration that is not regarded as such by both parties."[38] But English courts do not insist on this requirement and often regard an act or

---

[33] *The Aramis* [1989] 1 Lloyd's Rep. 213 at 225. But a mere proposal falling short of a promise does not suffice: *The Kaliningrad and Nadezhda Krupskaya* [1997] 2 Lloyd's Rep. 35 at 39.
[34] cf. *Lipkin Gorman v Karpnale Ltd* [1991] 2 A.C. 548 at 581.
[35] *Ashia Centur v Barker Gillette LLP* [2011] EWHC 148 (QB) at [20].
[36] *Thorp v Thorp* (1702) 12 Mod. 445 at 449; *Re Dale* [1994] Ch. 31 at 38.
[37] See para.3–102.
[38] *Philpot v Gruninger* (1872) 14 Wall 570 at 577; Restatement, Contracts, para.75(1); Restatement 2d, Contracts, para.71(1) and (2). Restatement 2d, Contracts, para.72 also supports the converse proposition, namely that anything is consideration if it is bargained for, even if there is no element of

forbearance as the consideration for a promise even though it may not have been the object of the promisor to secure it,[39] or the promisee may not have consciously realised that he was giving what was, in fact, consideration.[40] They may also regard the possibility of some prejudice to the promisee as a detriment without regard to the question whether it has in fact been suffered.[41] These practices may be called "inventing consideration", and the temptation to adopt one or the other of them is particularly strong when the act or forbearance which was actually bargained for cannot be regarded as consideration for some reason which is thought to be technical and without merit. In such cases the practice of inventing consideration may help to make the operation of the doctrine of consideration more acceptable; but the practice may also be criticised[42] on the ground that it gives the courts a wide discretion to hold promises binding (or not) as they please. Thus the argument that the promisee *might* have suffered prejudice by acting in reliance on a promise is in some cases made a basis of decision,[43] while in others precisely the same argument is rejected.[44] The courts have not been very consistent in the exercise of this discretion and its existence is a source of considerable uncertainty in this branch of the law.

**Motive and consideration.** In *Thomas v Thomas*[45] a testator shortly before his death expressed a desire that his widow should during her life have the house in which he lived, or £100. After his death, his executors "in consideration of such desire" promised to convey the house to the widow during her life or for so long as she should continue a widow, "provided nevertheless and it is hereby further agreed" that she should pay £1 per annum towards the ground rent, and keep the house in repair. In an action by the widow for breach of this promise, the consideration for it was stated to be the widow's promise to pay and repair. An objection that the declaration omitted to state part of the consideration, namely the testator's desire, was rejected. Patteson J said: "Motive is not the same thing with consideration. Consideration means something which is of value in the eye of the law, moving from the [claimant]."[46] This remark should not be misunderstood: a common motive for making a promise is the desire to obtain the consideration; and an act or forbearance on the part of the promisee may fail to constitute consideration precisely because it was not the promisor's motive to **3–010**

benefit or detriment; but this is subject to important exceptions, especially where what is bargained for is the performance of an existing duty or the settlement of an invalid claim: paras 73, 74; as to these topics, see paras 3–036–3–039, 3–043–3–055.

[39] See, e.g. paras 3–031–3–032, 3–165–3–167; cf. *Pollway Ltd v Abdullah* [1974] 1 W.L.R. 493; Zuckerman 38 M.L.R. 384; Thornely [1975] C.L.J. 26; *The Alev* [1989] 2 Lloyd's Rep. 138 at 147.

[40] *Pitts v Jones* [2007] EWCA Civ 1301; [2008] Q.B. 76.

[41] e.g. fn.43.

[42] Holmes, *The Common Law*, p.292. In the US there is less need to invent consideration because of the existence of a broad doctrine of promissory estoppel: see para.3–093.

[43] *Shadwell v Shadwell* (1860) 9 C.B. (N.S.) 159 at 174: the consideration was said by Erle CJ to consist of the possibility that the promisor "may have made a most material change in his position ...".

[44] In *Offord v Davies* (1862) 12 C.B. (N.S.) 748: the argument of counsel (at 750) that "the plaintiff might have altered his position in consequence of the guarantee" was rejected, Erle CJ being again a member of the court.

[45] (1842) 2 Q.B. 851.

[46] *Thomas v Thomas* (1842) 2 Q.B. 851 at 859; cf. *Hadley v Kemp* [1999] E.M.L.R. 589 at 625.

secure it, e.g. where A promises to give B £1,000 and B thereupon buys a diamond ring. What Patteson J meant was that a motive for promising does not amount to consideration unless two further conditions are satisfied, viz: (i) that the thing secured in exchange for the promise is "of some value in the eye of the law",[47] and (ii) that it moves from the promisee;[48] Consideration and motive are not opposites; the former concept is a subdivision of the latter. The consideration for a promise is (unless it is nominal or invented)[49] always a motive for promising; but a motive for making a promise is not necessarily consideration for it in law. Thus the testator's desire in *Thomas v Thomas* was a motive for the executors' promise, but not part of the consideration for it. The widow's promise to pay and repair was another motive for the executors' promise and did constitute the consideration.

3–011 **Consideration and condition.** *Thomas v Thomas* also illustrates the difference between consideration and condition:[50] the claimant's remaining a widow was not part of the consideration but a condition of her entitlement to enforce the executors' promise. Similarly, in *Carlill v Carbolic Smoke Ball Co*[51] the claimant provided consideration for the defendants' promise by using the smoke-ball; but her catching influenza was only a condition of her entitlement to enforce that promise. In these cases, the promisee can be said to have performed the condition, but such performance was not requested by the promisor.[52] Where the promisee's performance of the condition is (or can reasonably be regarded as having been) so requested, it can constitute consideration,[53] e.g. where A promised B to convey a plot of land to B if B built a house on it, B could enforce the promise after he had built the house.[54]

3–012 **Limited effects of promises without consideration.** A promise that is not supported by consideration may nevertheless give rise to certain legal effects. In particular, English law places certain restrictions on the revocability of a promise where the promisee has acted on it in a way that the promisor could have anticipated but had not requested; and it may give a remedy against a promisor who would be unjustly enriched if he were allowed freely to revoke his promise after such action in reliance on it by the promisee. These limited legal effects of promises without consideration will be discussed later in this chapter:[55] here it is only necessary to emphasise that they do not give such promises the full consequences of binding contracts. Thus the restrictions on their revocability may

[47] See paras 3–027–3–055.
[48] See below, paras 3–023–3–026.
[49] See para.3–009, para.3–014. In *Thomas v Thomas* (1842) 2 Q.B. 851 the consideration may not have been adequate, but it was not nominal: cf. para.3–015; and *Westminster CC v Duke of Westminster* [1991] 4 All E.R. 136 at 146 (reversed in part on other grounds (1992) 24 H.L.R. 572).
[50] i.e. a contingent condition: see para.2–105.
[51] [1893] 1 Q.B. 256; para.2–010.
[52] cf. *Dickinson v Abel* [1969] 1 W.L.R. 295.
[53] cf. *Ellis v Chief Adjudication Officer* [1998] 1 F.L.R. 184.
[54] See *Raffaele v Raffaele* [1962] W.A.R. 29; Allan, 79 L.Q.R. 239; cf. *Re Soames* (1897) 13 T.L.R. 439; *Errington v Errington* [1952] 1 K.B. 290 (para.2–054); *The Castle Alpha* [1989] 2 Lloyd's Rep. 383 at 387.
[55] See paras 3–076–3–093, 3–113–3–154.

be only temporary[56] and breach of the promise may not entitle the injured party to the full loss of bargain damages normally awarded for breach of contract,[57] or may not entitle him to them as of right.[58] Only a promise supported by consideration (or one made in a deed) has these full contractual effects. The limited effects of promises without consideration may therefore have mitigated some of the rigours of the strict doctrine; but they have not eliminated consideration as an essential requirement of a binding contract.[59]

## 2. ADEQUACY

### (a) Consideration need not be adequate

Under the doctrine of consideration, a promise has no contractual force unless *some* value has been given for it. But the courts do not, in general, ask whether adequate value has been given,[60] or whether the agreement is harsh or one-sided.[61] The reason for this is not that the courts *cannot* value the promise of each party: they have to do just this when assessing damages.[62] It is rather that they *should not* interfere with the bargain actually made by the parties. The fact that a person pays "too much" or "too little" for a thing may be evidence of fraud or mistake, or induce the court to imply a term as to the quality of the subject-matter or be relevant to the question whether a contract has been frustrated.[63] But it does not of itself affect the validity of the contract. This state of the law sometimes causes dissatisfaction, e.g. when it is said that "excessive" prices are charged for goods or services or accommodation. Such problems are, however, more appropriately dealt with by special legislation or by administrative measures than by the ordinary process of civil litigation. The courts are not well equipped to develop a system of price-control, and their refusal, as a general rule, to concern themselves with the adequacy of consideration is a reflection of this fact. At the same time, the general rule is subject to a number of exceptions, to be discussed later in this book.[64] These indicate that the courts are (even where the legislature has not intervened) by no means insensitive to the problem of unequal bargains; but in none of them is a promise held invalid *merely* because adequate value for it has not been given. Some additional factor is required to bring a case within one of the exceptions, e.g. the existence of a relationship in which one 3–013

---

[56] See paras 3–086, 3–115–3–117, 3–137–3–139.

[57] See Ch.20.

[58] See para.3–145.

[59] See para.3–088.

[60] *Haigh v Brooks* (1840) 10 A. & E. 309 at 320; *Wild v Tucker* [1914] 3 K.B. 36 at 39; cf. *Langdale v Danby* [1982] 1 W.L.R. 1123; *Brady v Brady* [1989] A.C. 755 at 775; Barton, 103 L.Q.R. 118.

[61] *Gaumont-British Pictures Corp v Alexander* [1936] 2 All E.R. 1686; *Midland Bank & Trust Co Ltd v Green* [1981] A.C. 513 at 532. cf. para.10–046, fn.246.

[62] See para.20–023 and following.

[63] e.g. in the coronation cases, paras 19–042–19–044.

[64] See paras 10–046–10–048, 11–130, 21–034; Waddams 39 M.L.R. 393; Tiplady 46 M.L.R. 601.

party is able to take an unfair advantage of the other. The general rule remains that "no bargain will be upset which is the result of the ordinary interplay of forces".[65]

## (b) Nominal consideration

3–014 **Sufficiency of nominal consideration.** The rule that consideration need not be adequate makes it possible to evade the doctrine of consideration, in the sense that a gratuitous promise can be made binding by means of a nominal consideration, e.g. £1 for the promise of valuable property, or a peppercorn for a substantial sum of money. Such cases are merely extreme applications of the rule that the courts will not judge the adequacy of consideration.[66] If, however, it appears on the face of the agreement that the consideration must as a matter of arithmetic be worth less than the performance of the counter-promise, there would seem to be no contract, e.g. if A promised to pay B £100 in return for £1 to be simultaneously paid by B. It is assumed in the example that both sums are simply to be paid in legal tender. An agreement to exchange a specific coin or coins of a particular description for a sum of money greater than their face value (e.g. 20 shilling pieces bearing the date 1900 for £100) would be a good contract. The same would be true of an agreement to pay a sum in one currency in exchange for one payable in another, and of an agreement to pay a larger sum tomorrow in exchange for a smaller sum paid today.

Where an agreement is legally binding on the ground that it is supported by nominal consideration, the doctrine of consideration does not serve its main purpose, of distinguishing between gratuitous and onerous promises. But the law has no settled policy against enforcing all gratuitous promises. It refuses to enforce only *informal* gratuitous promises; and the deliberate use of a nominal consideration can be regarded as a form to make a gratuitous promise binding. In some cases it may, indeed, be undesirable to give nominal consideration the same legal effect as substantial consideration; but these cases are best dealt with by special rules.[67] Such rules are particularly necessary where the promise can cause prejudice to third parties.[68]

3–015 **Nominal consideration distinguished from inadequate consideration.** It is not normally necessary to distinguish between "nominal" and "inadequate" consideration, since both equally suffice to make a promise binding. The need to draw

[65] *Lloyds Bank Ltd v Bundy* [1975] Q.B. 326 at 336 (Lord Denning MR).

[66] Atiyah, *Essays on Contract* (1990), p.194 argues that there is no logical connection between the two rules, relying on the fact that many of the US courts recognise the principle that consideration need not be adequate, while rejecting the device of nominal consideration. The answer to this argument lies in Holmes' aphorism (*The Common Law*, p.1) that "the life of the law has not been logic: it has been experience": American courts which reject the device of nominal consideration do so on policy grounds which have nothing to do with logic.

[67] Thus a nominal consideration was disregarded in *Milroy v Lord* (1862) 4 D.F. & J. 264, discussed at para.15–029 and for the purposes of the Law of Property Act 1925, "'valuable consideration' … does not include a nominal consideration in money"; s.205(1)(xxi).

[68] See, e.g. Insolvency Act 1986 ss.238, 339, 423.

the distinction may, however, arise in some of the exceptional cases[69] in which the law treats promises or transfers supported only by nominal consideration differently from those supported by consideration which is substantial or "valuable" (even though it may be inadequate).

One view is that a nominal consideration is one which is of only token value,[70] while an inadequate consideration is one which has substantial value even though it is manifestly less than that of the performance promised or rendered in return. A second view is that"'[n]ominal consideration' and a 'nominal sum' appear … , as terms of art, to refer to a sum or consideration which can be mentioned as consideration but is not necessarily paid."[71]This was the view of Lord Wilberforce in *Midland Bank & Trust Co Ltd v Green*,[72] where a husband sold a farm, said to be worth £40,000, to his wife for £500. It was held that the wife was, for the purposes of the Land Charges Act 1925 s.13(2), a "purchaser for money or money's worth" so that the sale to her prevailed over an unregistered option to purchase the land, which had been granted to one of the couple's sons. It was not necessary to decide whether the consideration for the sale was nominal but Lord Wilberforce said that he would have had "great difficulty" in so holding; and that "[t]o equate 'nominal' with 'inadequate' or even 'grossly inadequate' consideration would embark the law on inquiries which I cannot think were ever intended by Parliament",[73] i.e. inquiries into the adequacy of the price. On the facts of the case the £500 was in fact paid and was more than a mere token, so that the consideration was not nominal on either of the two views stated above. But if the stated consideration had been only £1, or a peppercorn, it is submitted that it would have been nominal even if it had been paid, or delivered, in accordance with the intention of the parties. So to hold would not lead to enquiries as to the adequacy of consideration; for the distinction between a consideration that is a mere token and one that is inadequate (or even grossly inadequate) is, it is submitted, clear as a matter of common sense. Thus where the question was whether a lease amounted to a "disposition … for a nominal consideration"[74] it was said that "[a]ny substantial value—that is, a value of more than, say, £5 … will prevent [the] disposition from being for a nominal consideration".[75] Such an approach gives rise to no more difficulty than the concept of a consideration which is "mentioned as a consideration but … not necessarily paid". That test would presumably make the question whether consideration was nominal turn on the intention of the parties; and, in the present context, this would be an even more elusive than usual criterion, since no guidance could be obtained from the terms of the contract, those terms being, in cases of this kind, often deliberately drafted so as to conceal the true nature of the transaction.

[69] See at fn.68.

[70] This seems to be the sense in which 10s. was described as "nominal" consideration (for the assignment of a debt) in *Turner v Forwood* [1951] 1 All E.R. 746.

[71] *Midland Bank & Trust Co Ltd v Green* [1981] A.C. 513 at 532.

[72] [1981] A.C. 513.

[73] *Midland Bank & Trust Co Ltd v Green* [1981] A.C. 513 at 532.

[74] Within Law of Property Act 1925 s.84(7).

[75] *Westminster CC v Duke of Westminster* [1991] 4 All E.R. 136 at 146, reversed in part on another ground (1992) 24 H.L.R. 572.

### (c) Attitude of equity

3–016 Equity recognised the general rule that the validity of a contract could not be challenged merely on the ground of inadequacy of consideration.[76] But it sometimes refused specific performance, or set a contract aside, or even reopened it (i.e. varied its terms) on the ground that adequate value had not been given to a party who was thought to need special protection.[77] Equity also refuses to aid a "volunteer"—i.e. a person who has given no substantial consideration but can nonetheless enforce a promise at law because it was made in a deed or supported by nominal consideration.[78] It was evidently thought that even such formal gratuitous promises did not deserve the same degree of enforcement as those for which substantial value had been given, and so the equitable remedy of specific performance is not available in respect of such a promise.[79]

## 3. PAST CONSIDERATION

3–017 **General rule.** The consideration for a promise must be given in return for the promise. If A makes a present of a car to B and a year later B promises to pay A £500 there is no consideration for B's promise as A did not give B the car in return for it. This reasoning often applies where there is an interval of time between an act and the promise said to have been given in return for it. The alleged consideration is then said to be "past consideration" and therefore bad.[80] Thus if a thing is guaranteed *after* it has been sold there is no consideration for the guarantee.[81] Similarly, a promise to pay a sum of money may be made to an employee after his retirement or to an agent after the termination of the agency. If the sole consideration for the promise is the service previously rendered by the employee or agent under the terminated contract, it will be a past consideration so that the promise will not be contractually binding.[82] It will be so binding only if some consideration, other than the past service, has been provided by the promisee. Such other consideration may consist in his giving up rights which are outstanding (or are in good faith believed to be outstanding) under the original contract,[83] or in his promising or accomplishing some other act or forbearance not due from him under the original contract, e.g. in his validly promising not to compete with the promisor.[84]

3–018 **When consideration is past.** In determining whether consideration is past, the court is not, it is submitted, bound to apply a strictly chronological test. If the

[76] See, e.g. *Cheale v Kenward* (1858) 3 D. & J. 27; *Townend v Toker* (1866) L.R. 1 Ch. App. 446.
[77] *Tennent v Tennents* (1870) L.R. 2 Sc. & Div. 6 at 9; paras 10–046–10–048, 21–034.
[78] *Jefferys v Jefferys* (1841) Cr. & Ph. 138.
[79] See para.21–052.
[80] *Dent v Bennett* (1839) 4 My. & Cr. 269; *Eastwood v Kenyon* (1840) 11 A. & E. 438.
[81] *Thorner v Field* (1612) 1 Bulst.120; *Roscorla v Thomas* (1842) 3 Q.B. 234.
[82] cf. *Simpson v John Reynolds* [1975] 1 W.L.R. 617; *Murray v Goodhews* [1978] 1 W.L.R. 489.
[83] e.g. *Bell v Lever Bros Ltd* [1932] A.C. 161 (where the value of the rights given up in return for the payment was uncertain in amount since it included not only future salary but also possible future commission).
[84] cf. *Wyatt v Kreglinger and Fernau* [1933] 1 K.B. 793.

consideration and the promise are substantially one transaction, the exact order in which these events occur is not decisive.[85] A manufacturer's "guarantee" may be given to a customer after he has bought the goods. But the consideration for the guarantee would not be past if the sale and the giving of the "guarantee" were in substance a single transaction,[86] as they would be if the customer at the time of the sale thought that he was buying a guaranteed product.[87] The question whether consideration is past is one of fact: the wording of the agreement is not decisive. Thus in *Re McArdle*[88] a promise made "in consideration of your carrying out" certain work was held to be gratuitous as the work had already been done. Conversely, a promise made "in consideration of your having today advanced … £750" has been held binding on proof that the advance was made at the same time as the promise.[89]

**Past consideration as good consideration.** A past act can be consideration for a promise if three conditions are satisfied: the act must have been done at the request of the promisor;[90] it must have been understood that payment would be made; and the payment, if it had been promised in advance, must have been legally recoverable.[91] In such a case the promisee is, quite apart from the subsequent promise, entitled to a reasonable sum for his services by way of a quantum meruit. The promise can be regarded either as fixing the amount of that sum[92] or as being given in consideration of the promisee's releasing his claim for such a payment. On the other hand, a past service which was not done at the request of the promisor, or one for which payment was not expected, or one for which payment, though expected, is not legally recoverable, is no consideration for a subsequent promise to pay for it.[93] 3–019

The consideration for a promise by A can consist not only of a past *act* done by B at A's request, but also of an earlier *promise* made by B at A's request. Thus in *Pao On v Lau Yiu Long*[94] the claimants had promised the defendants that for one year they would not sell certain shares in a company of which the defendants were the principal shareholders. This promise had been made at the request of the defendants, who were anxious to prevent the value of their own holding from being depressed by a sudden sale of the claimants' shares. Later, the defendants

[85] *Thornton v Jenkyns* (1840) 1 Man. & G. 166; *Tanner v Moore* (1846) 9 Q.B. 1; *Lictor Anstalt v Mir Steel UK Ltd* [2014] EWHC 3316 (Ch) at [223]; *Marsden v Barclays Bank Plc* [2016] EWHC 1601 (QB); [2016] 2 Lloyd's Rep. 420 at [31].

[86] cf. *Classic Maritime Inc v Lion Diversified Holdings Berhad* [2009] EWHC 1142 (Comm); [2010] 1 Lloyd's Rep. 59.

[87] Where the guarantee is a "consumer guarantee" within the Consumer Rights Act 2015 s.30 it binds the guarantor by force of this legislation without the need for the consumer to prove consideration. Curiously, s.30 applies only to the supply of goods and not, for example, digital content which is also covered by the 2015 Act and in relation to which guarantees may be supplied.

[88] [1951] Ch. 669.

[89] *Goldshede v Swan* (1847) 1 Ex. 154. The burden of proving that the consideration was not past is on the person seeking to enforce the promise: *Savage v Uwechia* [1961] 1 W.L.R. 455.

[90] *Southwark LBC v Logan* (1996) 8 Admin. L.R. 315.

[91] *Re Casey's Patents* [1892] 1 Ch. 104 at 115–116; cf. *Lampleigh v Brathwaite* (1615) Hob. 105.

[92] *Kennedy v Broun* (1863) 13 C.B. (N.S.) 677 at 740; *Rondel v Worsley* [1969] 1 A.C. 191 at 236, 278, 287.

[93] *Kennedy v Broun* (1863) 13 C.B. (N.S.) 677 at 740; *Rondel v Worsley* [1969] 1 A.C. 191.

[94] [1980] A.C. 614.

gave the claimants a guarantee in which they promised to indemnify the claimants against any loss which they might suffer if, during the year, the shares fell in value.[95] The Privy Council rejected the argument that the consideration for the guarantee was past.[96] The claimants' promise not to sell the shares was good consideration for the guarantee; for although that promise had been made before the guarantee was given, it had been made at the defendants' request and on the understanding that the claimants were, in return for making it, to receive some form of protection against the risk (to which the promise exposed them) of a fall in the value of those shares.

3–020 **Antecedent debt.** In a number of cases it has been held that the mere existence of an antecedent debt does not constitute "value" for a *transfer* by the debtor as it amounts only to past consideration.[97] These cases are not directly concerned with the question whether such an antecedent debt can constitute consideration for a later *promise* by the debtor, e.g. for one to pay higher interest or to pay early. But they may, by analogy, support the view that, where the only possible consideration for such a promise is an antecedent debt owed by the promisor to the promisee, then such consideration is past, so that the promise is not contractually binding.[98] In practice, however, the creditor (i.e. the promisee) will often provide consideration for such a promise by forbearing, on the strength of it, to sue for the debt.[99]

3–021 **Moral obligation.** It is clear that the moral obligation to perform a promise, once made, cannot provide consideration for it, since this would "annihilate the necessity for any consideration at all."[100] Nor is consideration provided by any antecedent moral obligation. Thus in *Eastwood v Kenyon*[101] the guardian of a young girl had raised a loan to pay for her maintenance and education, and to improve her estate. After she had come of age and married, her husband promised the guardian to pay the amount of the loan. The court dismissed the guardian's action on this promise; the mere existence of the antecedent moral obligation to reimburse the guardian did not amount to consideration for the husband's promise.[102]

---

[95] This guarantee replaced an earlier agreement which was less favourable to the claimants.

[96] For the further argument that the consideration was no more than the promise to perform an existing contractual duty, see para.3–055.

[97] *Roger v Comptoir d'Escompte de Paris* (1869) L.R. 2 C.P. 393; *Re Barker's Estate* (1875) 44 L.J. Ch. 487; *Wigan v English & Scottish Law Life Assurance Society* [1909] 1 Ch. 291.

[98] e.g. *Hopkinson v Logan* (1839) 5 M. & W. 241 (promise fixing date of payment).

[99] See para.3–072.

[100] *Eastwood v Kenyon* (1840) 11 A. & E. 438 at 450.

[101] (1840) 11 A. & E. 438.

[102] A number of earlier cases supported the theory that an antecedent "moral" obligation would suffice where it was derived from a previous obligation of the promisor which was not enforceable because it suffered from a specific legal defect. *Eastwood v Kenyon* did not purport to overrule the "moral obligation" theory in this narrow sense and it has been applied since (*Roscorla v Thomas* (1842) 3 Q.B. 234 at 237; *Flight v Reed* (1863) 1 H. & C. 703 (mentioned with approval by Scrutton LJ in *J Evans & Co v Heathcote* [1918] 1 K.B. 418 at 437)), but its scope has been restricted and the label has become unfashionable.

**Statutory exceptions.** There are two exceptions to the rule that past consideration is no consideration. First, an "antecedent debt or liability" is good consideration for a bill of exchange.[103] Secondly, the Limitation Act 1980[104] provides that, where a debtor in a writing signed by him[105] "acknowledges" a debt, it shall be deemed to have accrued on and not before the date of the acknowledgment. An "acknowledgment" need not take the form of a promise[106]; but if it does take this form the promise can extend the period of limitation even though the only consideration for it was the antecedent debt, and thus past. Further acknowledgments made within such an extended period or periods have the same effect.[107] But once the debt has become statute-barred the right to sue for it cannot be revived by any subsequent acknowledgment:[108] to this extent, the old "moral obligation" theory as applied to statute-barred debts[109] has been reversed. 3–022

## 4. CONSIDERATION MUST MOVE FROM THE PROMISEE

**Promisee must provide consideration.** The rule that consideration must "move from the promisee"[110] means that a person to whom a promise was made can enforce it only if he himself provided the consideration for it. He has no such right if the consideration moved from a third party. Thus if A promises B to pay £10,000 to B if C will paint A's house, and C does so, B cannot enforce A's promise (unless, of course, B had procured, or undertaken to procure, C to do the work). The promisee need not, however, provide the whole consideration for the promise: thus he can enforce a promise, the consideration for which was provided partly by himself and partly by his agent or partner or by some other co-promisee.[111] 3–023

[103] Bills of Exchange Act 1882 s.27(1)(b). Such consideration is not necessarily past: it might consist of forbearance of the creditor to sue for the debt or in his treating the bill as conditional payment: see *Currie v Misa* (1875) L.R. 10 Ex. 153 and cf. para.3–034.

[104] Limitation Act 1980 s.29(5).

[105] Limitation Act 1980 s.30(1).

[106] *Lia Oil SA v ERG Petroli* [2007] EWHC 505 (Comm); [2007] 2 Lloyd's Rep. 509. An admission of liability suffices: *Surrendra Overseas Ltd v Government of Sri Lanka* [1977] 1 W.L.R. 565; *Bradford & Bingley Plc v Rashid* [2006] UKHL 37; [2006] 1 W.L.R. 2066; cf. *Re Overmark Smith Warden Ltd* [1982] 1 W.L.R. 1195. Contrast: *Revenue & Customs Commissioners v Benchdollar* [2009] EWHC 1310 (Ch); [2010] 1 All E.R. 174 (denial of liability no acknowledgement); cf. *Phillips & Co v Bath Housing Co-operative Ltd* [2012] EWCA Civ 1591; [2013] 2 All E.R. 475 (letter questioning amount held to be an acknowledgement).

[107] Limitation Act 1980 s.29(7).

[108] Limitation Act 1980 s.29(7).

[109] *Hyeling v Hastings* (1699) 1 Ld. Raym. 389.

[110] *Barber v Fox* (1682) 2 Wms. Saund. 134, n.(e); *Thomas v Thomas* (1842) 2 Q.B. 851 at 859; *Tweddle v Atkinson* (1861) 1 B. & S. 393 at 398, 399; cf. *Dickinson v Abel* [1969] 1 W.L.R. 295.

[111] *Jones v Robinson* (1847) 1 Ex. 454; *Fleming v Bank of New Zealand* [1900] A.C. 577. For the position where the whole consideration is provided by a co-promisee, see para.13–038.

3–024 **Consideration need not move to promisor.** While consideration must move from the promisee, it need not move to the promisor.[112] It follows that the requirement of consideration may be satisfied where the promisee suffers some detriment at the promisor's request, but confers no corresponding benefit on the promisor. Thus the promisee may provide consideration by giving up a job[113] or the tenancy of a flat,[114] even though no direct benefit results to the promisor from these acts. Consideration may also move from the promisee without moving to the promisor where the promisee at the promisor's request confers a benefit on a third party, e.g. by entering into a contract with the third party.[115] This possibility is illustrated by the case in which goods are bought and paid for by the use of a debit card or credit card. The issuer of the card makes a promise to the supplier of the goods that the supplier will be paid; and the supplier provides consideration for this promise by supplying the goods to the customer.[116] In the case of the credit card transaction, there is also consideration in the shape of the discount allowed by the supplier of the goods to the issuer of the card: this is both a detriment to the supplier and a benefit to the issuer.[117]

3–025 **Benefit to promisor sufficient.** The requirement that consideration must move from the promisee at first sight supports the view that the essence of consideration is detriment to the promisee. But the requirement may be satisfied, even though the promisee in fact suffers no detriment, if he confers a benefit on the promisor, or on a third party at the promisor's request. This possibility is illustrated by *Edmonds v Lawson*,[118] where the relationship between a pupil barrister and the members of the chambers at which she had accepted an offer of pupillage was held to be contractual even though she paid no pupillage fee. The requirement of consideration was satisfied in that her (and other pupils') agreement to accept pupillage "provide[d] a pool of selected candidates who can be expected to compete with each other for recruitment as tenants",[119] and in that "chambers may see an advantage in developing close relationships with pupils who plan to practise as employed barristers or overseas".[120] Both these factors stress the benefit to the promisors (the members of the chambers), moving from the promisee (the pupil barrister) even though no detriment was suffered by her.

The view that consideration can move from the promisee though he in fact suffers no detriment is supported by two further rules to be discussed later in this

[112] *Re Wyvern Developments Ltd* [1974] 1 W.L.R. 1097; cf. *Barclays Bank Plc v Weeks, Legg & Dean* [1998] 3 All E.R. 213 at 220–221; *Hunt v Optima (Cambridge) Ltd* [2014] EWCA Civ 714; [2014] B.L.R. 613 at [81].

[113] *Jones v Padavatton* [1969] 1 W.L.R. 628.

[114] *Tanner v Tanner* [1975] 1 W.L.R. 1346; contrast *Horrocks v Forray* [1976] 1 W.L.R. 230; *Coombes v Smith* [1986] 1 W.L.R. 808.

[115] See *International Petroleum Refining Supply Ltd v Caleb Brett & Son Ltd* [1980] 1 Lloyd's Rep. 569 at 594 (where the promisor benefited indirectly since promisor and third party were associated companies); cf. also *The Chemical Venture* [1993] 1 Lloyd's Rep. 509 at 522.

[116] See *R. v Lambie* [1982] A.C. 449; *Re Charge Card Services Ltd* [1987] Ch. 150; affirmed [1989] Ch. 497.

[117] *Customs & Excise Commissioners v Diner's Club Ltd* [1989] 1 W.L.R. 1196 at 1207.

[118] [2000] Q.B. 501; cf. *Horton v Higham* [2004] EWCA Civ 941; [2004] 3 All E.R. 863 at [21]; *Bolton v Madden* (1873) L.R. 9 Q.B. 55.

[119] *Edmunds v Lawson* [2000] Q.B. 501 at 515.

[120] *Edmunds v Lawson* [2000] Q.B. 501 at 515.

chapter. The first is that performance of an existing contractual duty (or a promise to perform such a duty) can constitute consideration if it benefits the promisor:[121] this benefit "moves" from the promisee in that it is conferred by him, even though it may cause him no detriment[122] in the sense that he was already bound to do the acts in question. The second is that a composition agreement between a debtor and his creditors is binding because it benefits the creditors;[123] and this benefit can be said to "move" from the debtor in that his co-operation is essential to the making and performance of the composition agreement. It could be said that the debtor suffers a legal detriment by signing the agreement when he is not bound to do so. But the rule is not based on this invented consideration.[124] It is based on benefit to the promisors.[125]

**Contracts (Rights of Third Parties) Act 1999.** Under this Act, a term in a contract between A (the promisor) and B (the promisee) is, in specified conditions, enforceable by a third party, C, against A. The Act is more fully discussed in Ch.14;[126] the only points to be made here are that C is not prevented from enforcing the term by the fact that no consideration for A's promise moved from him,[127] and that C's right to enforce that promise can be described as a quasi-exception to the rule that consideration must move from the promisee.[128] It is not a true exception to the rule since in the case put the promisee is B, who must provide consideration for A's promise. 3–026

## 5. CONSIDERATION MUST BE OF SOME VALUE

### (a) Must be of economic value

An act, forbearance or promise will amount to consideration only if the law recognises that it has some economic value. It may have such value even though the value cannot be precisely quantified. But "natural affection of itself is not a sufficient consideration",[129] and the same is true of other merely sentimental motives for promising. This is the reason why in *Thomas v Thomas*[130] the desire of the testator that his widow should live in his house was not part of the consideration for the executors' promise that she might do so. Similar reasoning may also explain the decision in *White v Bluett*[131] that a son had not provided 3–027

[121] See paras 3–049, 3–054–3–055.
[122] *Williams v Roffey Bros & Nicholls (Contractors) Ltd* [1991] 1 Q.B. 1 at 16.
[123] See para.3–111.
[124] See para.3–009. The creditors do not bargain for the debtor's signature but for a dividend. If the debtor's signature were the consideration it could equally well be so regarded in a composition with a single creditor, but this would be contrary to *Foakes v Beer* (1884) 9 App. Cas. 605; para.3–100.
[125] See para.3–102.
[126] See para.14–099 and following.
[127] Law Com. No.242 (on which the Act is based), para.6.8.
[128] See para.14–109.
[129] *Bret v JS* (1600) Cro. Eliz. 756; *Mansukhani v Sharkey* [1992] 2 E.G.L.R. 105.
[130] (1842) 2 Q.B. 851; para.3–011.
[131] (1853) 23 L.J. Ex. 36.

consideration (for his father's promise not to sue him on a promissory note) by promising not to bore his father with complaints.

### (b) Illusory consideration

3–028 **Promise impossible to perform.** A promise may appear to be made for some consideration which is illusory and which must therefore be disregarded. One such situation can arise when the alleged consideration consists of a promise, the performance of which is, to the knowledge of both parties, impossible. For example, a promise by A to pay B £100 in return for B's promise to let A have all the wine in B's cellar would probably be regarded as a gratuitous promise if, when the promise was made, both A and B knew[132] that there was no wine in the cellar. The position would be different if B's promise were to deliver the *future* contents of the cellar. In that case, A would be buying the chance of the cellar's containing wine;[133] and the value of that chance would be illusory only if the question whether any wine was to be put into the cellar had been left entirely to B's discretion.[134]

3–029 **Promisee would have accomplished act or forbearance in any event.** A second situation in which consideration would be illusory is where the promisee would have accomplished the act or forbearance anyway, even if the promise had not been made. This will be the position if A promises B, who has religious objections to smoking, £5 if he will not smoke for a week. Since "it is no consideration to refrain from a course of conduct which it was never intended to pursue",[135] such a promise would not be legally binding. But where the promise provided *an* inducement for the act or forbearance, the requirement of consideration would be satisfied even though there were also other inducements operating on the mind of the promisee.[136] It seems that the burden of proving that the requested act or forbearance would have been accomplished, even if the promise had not been made, is on the promisor.[137]

3–030 **Promise of performance at the discretion of the promisor.**[138] Consideration would again be illusory where it was alleged to consist of a promise the terms of

---

132 There could be a good contract if the parties were in doubt on this point: see *Smith v Harrison* (1857) 26 L.J. Ch. 412.

133 cf. *Brady v Brady* [1989] A.C. 755 at 774 ("at the date of the promise").

134 See at fn.139.

135 *Arrale v Costain Civil Engineering Ltd* [1976] 1 Lloyd's Rep. 98 at 106; cf. *Colchester BC v Smith* [1991] Ch. 448 at 489; affirmed on other grounds [1992] Ch. 421; *Birmingham CC v Forde* [2009] EWHC 12 (QB); [2009] 1 W.L.R. 2732 at [96].

136 *Brikom Investments Ltd v Carr* [1979] Q.B. 467 at 490.

137 *Well Barn Farming Ltd v Backhouse* [2005] EWHC 1520 (Ch); [2005] 3 E.G.L.R. 109 at [47]; cf. the analogous rule in cases of "proprietary estoppel" (para.3–135): *Greasley v Cook* [1980] 1 W.L.R. 1306; and misrepresentation (para.9–030): *Smith v Chadwick* (1884) 9 App. Cas. 187 at 196.

138 "Promisor" here refers to the person making the promise which is claimed to amount to consideration, though he is the promisee so far as the enforcement of the counter-promise, for which he is said to have provided consideration, is concerned.

which left performance entirely to the discretion of the promisor.[139] A person does not provide consideration by promising to do something "if I feel like it", or "unless I change my mind"; and the same principle may apply in analogous cases.[140] Thus a promise may be illusory if it is accompanied by a clause effectively excluding all liability of the promisor for breach.[141] And a promise to buy "so much coal as I may decide to order" would be an illusory consideration for the seller's counter-promise to deliver, which could therefore not be enforced.[142] On the other hand, if the promise were to buy "so much of the coal *that I require* as I may order from you", the court could give reality to the promise by implying a term into it to the effect that at least a reasonable part of any requirements which the promisor actually turned out to have must be ordered from the promisee. Equally a buyer would provide consideration by promising to buy from the seller "*all* the coal I require"; for in such a case, even if the buyer does not promise to have any requirements, he does at least give a definite undertaking not to deal with anybody else.[143] Similarly, a promise which is subject to cancellation by A may nevertheless constitute consideration for a counter-promise from B where A's power to cancel is limited by the express terms of the promise, e.g. where it can be exercised only within a specified time. Such a limitation on the power to cancel may also be implied, so that (e.g.) A could not cancel after B had begun to perform his counter-promise. A's promise would then constitute consideration, so that B would be liable if he failed to complete the performance. Finally, the objection that a promise amounts only to illusory consideration on the grounds here discussed can be removed if the promise is performed: such actual performance can constitute consideration even though the person who has rendered it was not legally obliged to render it.[144]

### (c) Trivial acts or objects

**Acts of very small value.** Since consideration need not be adequate, acts or omissions of very small value can be consideration.[145] Thus it has been said that the act of executing a deed could be consideration for a promise to pay money 3–031

[139] *Stabilad Ltd v Stephens & Carter Ltd (No.2)* [1999] 2 All E.R. (Comm) 651 at 659. Such promises may also give rise to problems of contractual intention: see para.4–023.

[140] In *Spreadex Ltd v Cochrane* [2012] EWHC 2190 (Comm); [2012] Info T.L.R. 1 the provision of an online interactive platform for the placing of bets did not amount to consideration where the betting company reserved an absolute discretion to refuse to accept part or all of any bet.

[141] See para.7–026.

[142] See *Wickham & Burton Coal Co v Farmer's Lumber Co* 189, 179 N.W. 417 (1923); for an exception, see *Citadel Ins Co v Atlantic Union Ins Co* [1982] 2 Lloyd's Rep. 543; para.3–163.

[143] The validity of "requirement" contracts is assumed in such cases as *Metropolitan Electric Supply Co v Ginder* [1901] 2 Ch. 799; and *Dominion Coal Co Ltd v Dominion Steel & Iron Co Ltd* [1909] A.C. 293. Similarly, a contract by a manufacturer to sell his entire output to a particular buyer is binding even though he does not bind himself to have any output: see, e.g. *Donnell v Bennett* (1883) 22 Ch D. 835; Howard 2 U. of Tas. L.R. 446; Adams 94 L.Q.R. 73. For the possible illegality of such promises, see para.11–143 and following.

[144] *Cambridge Nutrition Ltd v BBC* [1990] 3 All E.R. 523 at 538; *Stabilad Ltd v Stephens & Carter Ltd (No.2)* [1999] 2 All E.R. (Comm) 651 at 660.

[145] *Gilbert v Ruddeard* (1608) 3 Dy. 272b (n); cf. *Denton v GN Ry* (1856) 5 E. & B. 860.

although the deed was void;[146] that to show a person a document was consideration;[147] that the grant of permission to cut back undergrowth was consideration for the grant of a licence to occupy land;[148] and that the mere act of conducting negotiations can satisfy the requirement of consideration, even though that act does not commit the promisee to bringing the negotiations to a successful conclusion.[149]

3–032 **Objects of trifling value.** On the same principle, objects of trifling value can constitute consideration. In *Chappell & Co Ltd v Nestlé Co Ltd*,[150] chocolate manufacturers sold gramophone records for 1s. 6d. plus three wrappers of their 6d. bars of chocolate. It was held that the delivery of the wrappers formed part of the consideration, though the wrappers were of little value and were in fact thrown away. If the delivery of the wrappers formed part of the consideration it could, presumably, have formed the whole of the consideration, so that a promise to deliver records for wrappers alone would have been binding.[151]

### (d) Gift of onerous property

3–033 A promise to give away onerous property is binding if the donee promises in return to discharge obligations attached to it. Thus a promise to give away a leasehold house is binding if the donee promises to perform the donor's covenants under the lease, e.g. to repair, to insure and to pay rent;[152] a promise to give away a freehold house is binding if the donee promises to pay outstanding mortgage instalments or other charges;[153] and a promise to give away partly paid-up shares in a company is binding if the donee promises to pay further calls which may be made on the shares.[154]

---

146 *Westlake v Adams* (1858) 5 C.B. (N.S.) 248.

147 *Sturlyn v Albany* (1587) Cro. Eliz. 67; *March v Culpepper* (1628) Cro. Car. 70. Contrast *Re Charge Card Services Ltd* [1987] Ch. 150 at 164; affirmed [1989] Ch. 497 (production of charge card and signature of voucher not the consideration for a supply of goods, evidently because such "consideration" would be blatantly "invented": para.3–009).

148 *Well Barn Farming Ltd v Backhouse* [2005] EWHC 1520 (Ch); [2005] 3 E.G.L.R. 109 at [45].

149 *Sepong Engineering Construction Co v Formula One Management Ltd* [2000] 1 Lloyd's Rep. 602 at 611; but damages for breach of the resulting contract would probably be no more than nominal: cf. para.20–062.

150 [1960] A.C. 87.

151 Contrast *Lipkin Gorman v Karpnale Ltd* [1991] 2 A.C. 548 (gaming chips issued by a gambling club not consideration for the stolen money paid for them, but the context was not the enforcement of a promise; rather, whether the victim of the theft could recover the money from the club).

152 *Price v Jenkins* (1877) 5 Ch D. 619; *Westminster CC v Duke of Westminster* [1991] 4 All E.R. 136; reversed in part on other grounds (1992) 24 H.L.R. 572.

153 *Merritt v Merritt* [1970] 1 W.L.R. 1121.

154 *Cheale v Kenward* (1858) 3 D. & J. 27.

## (e) Compromise and forbearance to sue[155]

### (i) Valid claims

**Promise to release a valid claim is good consideration.**[156] A promise not to enforce a valid claim is clearly good consideration for a promise given in return.[157] If, for example, A is injured by the admitted negligence of B, they can validly compromise the claim, A's promise not to sue B constituting the consideration for B's promise to pay the agreed compensation. Similarly, a creditor to whom a sum of money has become due may promise to give the debtor extra time to pay in return for the debtor's promise to pay higher interest or to give additional security. In such a case there is good consideration for the debtor's promise: he benefits by getting extra time to pay, while the creditor suffers a detriment in that he is, for a time, kept out of his money.[158] There is such benefit to the debtor and detriment to the creditor even if the creditor promises to forbear for only a limited time; and if no time is specified, the court will infer that he undertook to forbear for a reasonable time.[159] 3–034

**Promise to abandon a defence, or a remedy.** The principles just stated apply, not only to a promise not to enforce a claim, but also to a promise to abandon a defence;[160] and to a promise to abandon a particular remedy, e.g. to one to abandon arbitration proceedings.[161] 3–035

### (ii) Invalid and doubtful claims

**Claims known to be invalid.** It used to be thought that a promise by A not to enforce a claim which was invalid was no consideration for a promise given by B in return, since B, if he was not liable, did not benefit from A's promise not to sue him, while A lost nothing by giving up a worthless right.[162] This reasoning still 3–036

[155] This part is not concerned with the settlement of legal proceedings under CPR Pt 36. Such agreements are sui generis and need not have contractual force, though in the vast majority of cases they will also amount to contracts (*Orton v Collins* [2007] EWHC 803 (Ch); [2007] 1 W.L.R. 2953 at [60]) for the reasons which are explained in this part.

[156] We are concerned here only with the question of consideration, but the court may protect the party granting the release on other grounds, e.g. by asking whether the compromise was intended to release all claims: see, e.g. *Bank of Credit and Commerce International SA v Ali* [2001] UKHL 8; [2002] 1 A.C. 251.

[157] e.g. *Greene v Church Commissioners for England* [1974] Ch. 467; *The Attika Hope* [1988] 1 Lloyd's Rep. 439 at 442 (forbearance to sue third party).

[158] *Crowther v Farrer* (1850) 15 Q.B. 677.

[159] *Payne v Wilson* (1827) 7 B. & C. 423; *Oldershaw v King* (1857) 2 H. & N. 517.

[160] See *Banque de l'Indochine v J H Rayner (Mincing Lane) Ltd* [1983] Q.B. 711; *Simantob v Shavleyan* [2019] EWCA Civ 1105.

[161] *The Leonidas D* [1985] 1 W.L.R. 925 at 933, where there was no such abandonment: see para.2–005.

[162] *Jones v Ashburnham* (1804) 4 East 455.

applies where the sole[163] consideration provided by A is his forbearance to enforce a claim which is clearly invalid and which he either knows to be invalid or does not believe to be valid.[164]

3–037 **Doubtful claims.** Where the claim is doubtful in law, a promise to abandon it involves the possibility of detriment to the potential claimant and of benefit to the other party. Such a promise is therefore good consideration for a counter-promise given by the latter party, e.g. for one to pay a sum of money to the party promising to abandon the claim.[165]

3–038 **Claims wrongly believed to be valid.** A promise by A to abandon a claim is also good consideration for a counter-promise made by B, even though A's claim is clearly bad in law, if it is believed by A to be a valid one.[166] One reason which has been given for this rule is that otherwise "in no case of a doubtful claim could a compromise be enforced";[167] but this does not explain why the rule applies where A's claim is not merely "doubtful" but clearly bad. Another suggested reason for the rule is that A suffers detriment because "he gives up what he believes to be a right of action";[168] but, in general, consideration must be something of value, not something believed to be of value. In fact A would be worse off, if he did not forbear, for he would lose his action and the costs. A further suggestion is that A suffers detriment in that it becomes more difficult to get up his case, the longer he waits;[169] this is a possible detriment (even though his action is bound to fail) as the failure may be more expensive than it would have been, had he sued promptly. A may also suffer detriment if as a result of the agreement he loses the right to sue a third party who is liable on the original cause of action.[170] A's forbearance can also be said to confer a benefit on B since "instead of being annoyed with an action, he [B] escapes from the vexations incident to it".[171] There is some difficulty in relying on this benefit as the consideration for B's counter-promise, since it may also exist where A's claim is known to be bad, in

---

[163] The position is different where there is also other consideration: *The Siboen and The Sibotre* [1976] 1 Lloyd's Rep. 293 at 334.

[164] This seems to be the basis of the observation made by Lord Saville in *Borrelli v Ting* [2010] UKPC 21; [2010] Bus. L.R. 1718 at [41].

[165] *Haigh v Brooks* (1839) 10 A. & E. 309; cf. *Colchester BC v Smith* [1992] Ch. 421; *Colonia Versicherung AG v Amoco Oil Co* [1995] 1 Lloyd's Rep. 570 at 577; affirmed [1997] 1 Lloyd's Rep. 261, without reference to this point. See also *North Shore Ventures Ltd v Anstead Holdings Inc* [2011] EWCA Civ 230; [2011] 3 W.L.R. 628 at [42], [58].

[166] *Cook v Wright* (1861) 1 B. & S. 559; *Callisher v Bischoffsheim* (1870) L.R. 5 Q.B. 449; *Holsworthy Urban DC v Holsworthy Rural DC* [1907] 2 Ch. 62; cf. *Horton v Horton* [1961] 1 Q.B. 215; *Freedman v Union Group Plc* [1997] E.G.C.S. 28; *Simantob v Shavleyan* [2019] EWCA Civ 1105.

[167] *Callisher v Bischoffsheim* (1870) L.R. 5 Q.B. 449 at 451.

[168] *Callisher v Bischoffsheim* (1870) L.R. 5 Q.B. 449 at 452.

[169] *Cook v Wright* (1861) 1 B. & S. 559 at 569.

[170] *Cook v Wright* (1861) 1 B. & S. 559 at 569–570.

[171] *Callisher v Bischoffsheim* (1870) L.R. 5 Q.B. 449 at 452; cf. *Pitt v PHH Asset Management Ltd* [1994] 1 W.L.R. 327 at 332, but in this case it is not clear that the party forbearing in fact believed in the validity of his claim. See also *Mousaka Inc v Goldon Seagull Maritime Inc* [2002] 1 Lloyd's Rep. 797 at [14] ("commercial benefit").

which case the compromise is not binding.[172] Perhaps this last rule is based on public policy rather than on want of consideration. As Tindal CJ said in *Wade v Simeon*:[173]

> "It is almost *contra bonos mores* and certainly contrary to the principles of natural justice that a man should institute proceedings against another when he is conscious that he has no good cause of action".

If compromises of such claims were upheld, improper pressure might be brought to bear on persons who "owed" void debts.

The rule that a promise by A to abandon a claim which is clearly bad, but believed to be valid, is good consideration for a counter-promise from B is subject to a number of safeguards.[174] There must be a "reasonable claim",[175] (i.e. one made on reasonable grounds) and A must honestly believe that his claim had at any rate a fair chance of success.[176] And he must show that he seriously intended to enforce the claim.[177]

The cases in the present group all concern claims the validity of which was doubtful in law. It seems that the same rules apply where the claim was doubtful because of a dispute about the facts. A settlement based on a simple *mistake* of fact made by both parties might be void for mistake.[178] But it will not be void on this ground where both parties knowingly take the risk that the actual facts may turn out to be different from the facts as they were supposed to be. This element of risk is always present when parties negotiate a settlement on disputed facts.

**Executed compromises.** The preceding discussion is concerned with the enforceability of an agreement to compromise a claim. Different problems can arise after such an agreement has been *performed*, generally by payment of the amount which one party has agreed to pay under the compromise. Even if, under the rules discussed above, there was no consideration for that party's promise, he will not be entitled to the return of the payment if it was made "to close the transaction":[179] in such a case the payment is treated as if it were an executed gift.[180] To give rise to a claim for repayment, it will be necessary to establish other circumstances than lack of consideration, e.g. that the payment was made under duress.[181] **3–039**

---

172 See fn.164.

173 *Wade v Simeon* (1846) 2 C.B. 548 at 564; cf. *Edwards v Baugh* (1843) 11 M. & W. 641 at 646.

174 It is not entirely clear whether the validity of a compromise is subject to any duty to disclose facts which would enable B to resist the claim: see para.9–176.

175 *Cook v Wright* (1861) 1 B. & S. 559 at 569.

176 *Callisher v Bishchoffsheim* (1870) L.R. 5 Q.B. 449 at 452.

177 *Cook v Wright* (1861) 1 B. & S. 559 at 569; *The Proodos C* [1980] 2 Lloyd's Rep. 287 at 392.

178 e.g. *Gloyne v Richardson* [2001] EWCA Civ 716; [2001] 2 B.C.L.C. 669 at [39]; see Ch.8; Andrews [1989] L.M.C.L.Q. 431; *Grains & Fourrages SA v Huyton* [1997] 1 Lloyd's Rep. 628.

179 *Woolwich Equitable BS v IRC (No.2)* [1993] A.C. 70 at 165.

180 *Woolwich Equitable BS v IRC (No.2)* [1993] A.C. 70; citing *Maskell v Horner* [1915] 3 K.B. 106 at 120.

181 See para.10–002 and following.

### (iii) *Actual forbearance*

3–040 **As evidence of an implied promise to forbear.** A person may forbear from enforcing a claim without expressly promising to do so. The question then arises whether this actual forbearance is consideration for some promise or act of the other party, for example for a promise by him to give security, or for giving the security. Sometimes actual forbearance may be evidence of an implied promise to forbear.[182] Thus the acceptance of a cheque in payment of a debt may be evidence of a promise not to sue the debtor so long as the cheque is not dishonoured, or at least for a reasonable time.[183]

3–041 **Where there is no promise to forbear.** Even where no promise to forbear (express or implied) has been made, an actual forbearance may constitute consideration. In *Alliance Bank v Broom*[184] the defendant owed £22,000 to his bank, which pressed him to give some security. He promised to do so, but the bank made no counter-promise not to sue him. It was held that there was consideration for the defendant's promise as the bank had given, and the defendant received, "some degree of forbearance".[185] On the other hand, in *Miles v New Zealand Alford Estate Co*[186] a company had bought land and then became dissatisfied with the purchase. The vendor later promised to make certain payments to the company, and it was alleged that the consideration for this promise was the company's forbearance to take proceedings to rescind the contract. A majority of the Court of Appeal held that there was no consideration for the vendor's promise as no proceedings to rescind were ever intended; and Cotton LJ added that "it must be shown that there was something which would bind the company not to institute proceedings".[187] Bowen LJ dissented from this proposition,[188] relying on *Alliance Bank v Broom*; but it may be possible to reconcile the cases by reference to the types of claim forborne. A bank to which £22,000 is owed is virtually certain to take steps to enforce its claim, but a dissatisfied purchaser of land is much less certain to take proceedings for rescission. It may, therefore, be reasonable to say that an actual forbearance can amount to consideration in relation to the former type of claim, but that a promise to forbear is necessary where it is problematical whether the claim will ever be enforced at all. A promise to forbear is also, of course, necessary where that is what the debtor bargains for.

Where the consideration consists of a *promise* to forbear which specifies no time the creditor must forbear for a reasonable time.[189] There is no such

[182] *Re Wyvern Developments Ltd* [1974] 1 W.L.R. 1097; *Thornton Springer v NEM Insurance Co Ltd* [2000] 2 All E.R. 489 at 516.

[183] *Baker v Walker* (1845) 14 M. & W. 465; *Elkington v Cooke-Hill* (1914) 30 T.L.R. 670.

[184] (1864) 2 Dr. & Sm. 289; cf. also *Brikom Investments Ltd v Carr* [1979] Q.B. 467 at 490.

[185] *Alliance Bank v Broom* (1864) 2 Dr. & Sm. 289 at 292.

[186] (1886) 32 Ch D. 267; cf. *Hunter v Bradford Property Trust Ltd,* 1970 S.L.T. 173.

[187] *Miles v New Zealand Alford Estate Co* (1886) 32 Ch D. 267 at 285.

[188] *Miles v New Zealand Alford Estate Co* (1886) 32 Ch D. 267 at 291; his view was approved by Lord Macnaghten in *Fullerton v Provincial Bank of Ireland* [1903] A.C. 309 at 314.

[189] See para.3–034.

requirement where the consideration consists of *actual forbearance*: here it is enough that the debtor had "a certain amount of forbearance".[190]

**The promise to be enforced must have been induced by the forbearance.** A forbearance amounts to consideration only for a promise or performance that is induced by it. In *Wigan v English & Scottish Law Life Assurance Society*[191] a debtor executed a mortgage of an insurance policy in favour of his creditor. It was held that the creditor, who knew nothing of the mortgage, had not provided consideration for it merely by having forborne to sue for his antecedent debt. But Parker J added[192] that the creditor would have provided consideration if he had been told of the mortgage and if, "on the strength of" it, he had actually forborne to sue for the debt. The crucial question, therefore, is whether the creditor has forborne "on the strength of" the debtor's act or promise. He will clearly have done so where the debtor has *expressly* requested the forbearance[193] but in *Alliance Bank v Broom*[194] the bank's forbearance was held to constitute consideration even though the defendant had not expressly requested it. The case has been explained on the ground that the debtor had impliedly requested forbearance.[195] But where the forbearance is not requested either expressly or by implication, it is no consideration. In *Combe v Combe*[196] a husband during divorce proceedings promised to pay his wife an annual allowance. In an action to enforce this promise, the wife argued, inter alia, that she had given consideration for it by forbearing to apply to the court for a maintenance order. But her argument was rejected as she had not forborne at the husband's request.[197] 3–042

### (f) Performance of existing duty[198]

Much difficulty arises in determining whether a person who does, or promises to do, what he was already under a legal duty to do thereby provides consideration for a promise made to him. As he was already legally bound to do the act, he suffers no legal detriment.[199] But he may suffer a factual detriment if he actually does the act: this may be more troublesome to him than to pay damages. The promisor may also get a factual benefit, as damages might not fully compensate him for the loss which he would suffer if the duty were broken. Denning LJ has therefore said that the performance of an existing duty, or the promise to perform 3–043

[190] *Alliance Bank v Broom* (1864) 2 Dr. & Sm. 289 at 292; *R. v HM Attorney General for England and Wales* [2003] UKPC 22; [2003] E.M.L.R. 24 at [31]–[32].
[191] [1909] 1 Ch. 291: cf. para.3–020.
[192] *Wigan v English & Scottish Law Life Assurance Society* [1909] 1 Ch. 291 at 298.
[193] *Crears v Hunter* (1887) 19 Q.B.D. 341 at 344.
[194] (1864) 2 Dr. & Sm. 289.
[195] *Fullerton v Provincial Bank of Ireland* [1903] A.C. 309 at 313; *Banque Cantonale de Geneve v Sanomi* [2016] EWHC 3353 (Comm) at [60]–[63].
[196] [1951] 2 K.B. 215.
[197] Quaere whether such a request should not have been implied.
[198] Davis 6 C.L.J. 202; Reynolds and Treitel 7 Malaya Law Rev. 1; Aivazian, Trebilcock & Penny 22 Osgoode Hall L.J. 173; Hooley [1991] J.B.L. 195; Halson 107 L.Q.R. 649.
[199] See para.3–006.

it, was of itself good consideration.[200] This radical view has not been accepted;[201] but the requirement of consideration in this group of cases has been mitigated by recognising that it can be satisfied where the promisee has conferred a factual (as opposed to a legal) benefit on the promisor.[202]

### *(i) Duty imposed by law*

3–044 **Some promises unenforceable on grounds of public policy.** One group of cases denies the enforceability of a promise made in return for the promise to perform, or the performance of, a duty imposed by law (as opposed to one imposed by contract). Thus a public officer cannot enforce a promise to pay him money for doing his duty as such,[203] and generally a person does not provide consideration by forbearing to engage in a course of conduct that is criminal.[204] Enforcement of such promises would tend to encourage an undesirable form of extortion; and it is this ground of public policy, rather than want of consideration, that accounts for most of the authorities in this group.

3–045 **Performance of the duty as consideration.** Promises to pay rewards for information that might lead to the arrest of a felon were often enforced[205] though, till 1968, a person who had such information was bound to communicate it to the police, and indeed committed an offence[206] if he failed to do so. Public policy was not offended by the enforcement of such promises, as they might induce people to look for the information and so promote the interests of justice. These cases show that an act may constitute consideration even though there is a public duty to do it. The contrary view is, indeed, supported by *Collins v Godefroy*[207] where an attorney who had been subpoenaed to give evidence was promised a guinea a day for attendance. This was held to be "a promise without consideration" as he was already bound to attend. But the reasoning is hard to reconcile with the reward cases just mentioned; and the actual decision has long ceased to represent the practice in such cases.[208] A subpoena must be accompanied by a tender of "conduct money";[209] this includes the reasonable expenses of attending the trial, and, in certain cases, compensation for loss of

---

200 *Ward v Byham* [1956] 1 W.L.R. 496 at 498; *Williams v Williams* [1957] 1 W.L.R. 148 at 151.

201 Though see the view expressed by David Donaldson QC, sitting as a Deputy High Court Judge, in *Adam Opel GmbH v Mitras Automotive (UK) Ltd* [2008] EWHC 3205 (QB); [2018] C.I.L.L. 2561 at [42].

202 See paras 3–049, 3–054–3–055.

203 *Wathen v Sandys* (1811) 2 Camp. 640; *Morris v Burdett* (1808) 1 Camp. 218; *Bilke v Havelock* (1813) 3 Camp. 374; *Morgan v Palmer* (1825) 2 B. & C. 729 at 736.

204 *Brown v Brine* (1875) L.R. 1 Ex.D.5 (forbearance to commit criminal libel).

205 *England v Davidson* (1840) 11 A. & E. 856; *Neville v Kelly* (1862) 12 C.B. (N.S) 740; *Bent v Wakefield and Barnsley Union Bank* (1878) 4 C.P.D. 1.

206 i.e. misprision of felony: *Sykes v DPP* [1962] A.C. 528. This offence was abolished by Criminal Law Act 1967 s.1, and replaced with the offence of concealing a relevant offence created by s.5(1) of that Act: para.11–046.

207 (1831) 1 B. & Ad. 950; cf. *Thorensen Car Ferries Ltd v Weymouth Portland BC* [1977] 2 Lloyd's Rep. 614 at 619.

208 *Re Working Men's Mutual Society* (1882) 21 Ch D. 831; *Chamberlain v Stoneham* (1889) 24 Q.B.D. 113.

209 Senior Courts Act 1981 s.36(4).

time. Expert witnesses can validly contract for payment;[210] and it seems that all witnesses who attend in a professional capacity, whether they are strictly expert witnesses or not, are entitled to compensation for loss of time.

**Other consideration.** A person can provide consideration by doing, or promising, *more* than he is by law obliged to do. Thus in *Glasbrook Bros Ltd v Glamorgan CC*[211] mine-owners who feared violence from strikers asked, and promised to pay, for a greater degree of police protection than the police reasonably thought necessary. It was held that the police authority had provided consideration for this promise by giving the extra protection, and that accordingly the promise was enforceable. The position in cases of this kind is now regulated by statute. Section 25(1) of the Police Act 1996 provides that payment can be claimed for "special police services" rendered at the "request" of the person requiring them. Such a request can be implied from conduct, e.g. where a person organises an event which cannot safely take place without such special services. On this reasoning, a football club has been held liable to a police authority for the cost of policing matches played on its ground.[212] Such liability arises irrespective of contract.[213] **3–046**

In *Ward v Byham*[214] the father of an illegitimate child promised to pay her mother £1 per week "providing you can prove that [the child] is well looked after and happy, and also that she is allowed to decide for herself whether or not she wishes to come and live with you". The mother began to look after the child, and it was held that she could enforce the father's promise although she was under a statutory duty to maintain the child. One basis of the decision is that the mother had provided consideration by showing that she had made the child happy, etc.: in this way she can be said to have done more than she was required by law to do, and to have conferred a factual benefit on the father or on the child,[215] even though she may not have suffered any detriment.[216] But if a son's promise not to bore his father is not good consideration,[217] it is hard to see why a mother's promise to make her child happy should stand on a different footing. There is, with respect, force in Denning LJ's view, that the mother provided consideration

---

210 *Goulden v White Barca* [2000] 1 W.L.R. 167.

211 [1925] A.C. 270; cf. *Thorensen Car Ferries v Weymouth Portland BC* [1977] 2 Lloyd's Rep. 614 at 619 (A's promise to make use of B's services for which he was under a legal duty to pay held to constitute consideration for B's counter-promise).

212 *Harris v Sheffield United FC Ltd* [1988] Q.B. 77. Contrast *Reading Festival Ltd v West Yorkshire Police Authority* [2006] EWCA Civ 524; [2006] L.L.R. 583 where a music festival was organised in such a way that the organisers had not made a "request" for the "special services" said to have been provided by the police; cf. *Chief Constable of Greater Manchester v Wigan Athletic Football Club* [2008] EWCA 1449; [2009] 1 W.L.R. 1580; *Leeds United Football Club v Chief Constable of West Yorkshire* [2013] EWCA Civ 115; [2014] Q.B. 168.

213 This submission is retained notwithstanding the observations of Scott-Baker LJ, in the *Reading Festival* case at [50] that: "it is very difficult to see how s.25(1) can operate absent a contract". Since the police have a discretion over how they provide the services requested (*Reading Festival* case at [21]), the most that can be said is that there must be an agreement "in broad terms" (*Reading Festival* case at [21]).

214 [1956] 1 W.L.R. 496.

215 Consideration need not move to the promisor (the father); para.3–024.

216 *Williams v Roffey Bros & Nicholls (Contractors) Ltd* [1991] 1 Q.B. 1 at 13.

217 *White v Bluett* (1853) 23 L.J. Ex. 36; para.3–027.

by merely performing her legal duty to support the child. There was certainly no ground of public policy for refusing to enforce the promise.

### *(ii) Duty imposed by contract with promisor*

3–047 When A was bound by contract with B to do, or to forbear from doing, something, the law at one time took the view that A's performance of that duty (or his promise to perform it) was no consideration for a new promise by B. Later authority has qualified that view but the extent of the qualification remains uncertain.[218]

3–048 **Cases in which there was no consideration.** The view that there was no consideration for B's new promise was first established in cases in which seamen who had bound themselves to serve for a voyage were promised higher wages by the masters of their ships if they performed their duty by working the ships home. It was held that these promises were not binding. Originally this conclusion was based on the ground of public policy that the enforcement of such promises might lead the men to refuse to perform their original contracts unless they were promised extra pay.[219] But according to one of the reports of *Stilk v Myrick*[220] such reasoning was doubted in that case, where the claim for extra pay was instead rejected on the ground that the men had provided no consideration by doing only what they were already bound to do; and this is the explanation of such cases which is now commonly accepted.[221] On the same principle, a promise to pay an extra charge for the carriage of goods to the agreed destination cannot be enforced by the carrier;[222] and a debtor's promise to pay in stated instalments a debt that is already due is no consideration for the creditor's promise not to take bankruptcy proceedings in respect of the debt.[223]

The public policy explanation of the rule, stated above, was always open to the objection that it was based on a danger that was not more than hypothetical: in the cases on seamen's wages, for example, there was no evidence of any refusal on the men's part to perform their original contracts. Even where there is such evidence, the argument is much reduced in importance now that the law has come to recognise that such a refusal may amount to economic duress.[224] Where the refusal *does* amount to duress, a promise induced by it can be avoided (and

---

[218] *WRN Ltd v Ayris* [2008] EWHC 1080 (QB); [2008] I.R.L.R. 889 at [46] (still referring to the fact that it is "well-established that such (i.e. a promise to perform an existing contract) will not, in law, constitute consideration").

[219] *Harris v Watson* (1791) Peake 102; cf. *Scotson v Pegg* (1861) 6 H. & N. 295 at 299.

[220] That in (1809) 2 Camp. 317; the other report, in 6 Esp. 129, does not mention consideration and makes the decision turn on public policy. Both grounds are stated in *Harris v Carter* (1854) 3 E. & B. 559.

[221] *Swain v West (Butchers) Ltd* [1936] 1 All E.R. 224; *The Atlantic Baron* [1979] Q.B. 705 at 712; *Pao On v Lau Yiu Long* [1980] A.C. 614 at 633; *Sybron Corp v Rochem Ltd* [1984] Ch. 112 at 129; *The Alev* [1989] 1 Lloyd's Rep. 138 at 147.

[222] *The Proodos C* [1980] 2 Lloyd's Rep. 390; cf. *Atlas Express Ltd v Kafco (Importers and Distributors) Ltd* [1989] Q.B. 833.

[223] *Vanbergen v St Edmund's Properties Ltd* [1933] 2 K.B. 223. On the enforceability of other arrangements for the payment of existing debts, see para.3–102 and following.

[224] See para.10–007.

money paid in pursuance of it be recovered back) on that ground.[225] This is true even where the promise *is* supported by consideration: for example, because the promisee has undertaken, not merely to perform his duties under the original contract, but also to render some additional performance.[226] If, on the other hand, the promisee's refusal to perform the original contract does *not* amount to duress, it has been held that the promise cannot be impugned merely on the ground that the refusal amounted to an abuse by the promisee of a dominant bargaining position.[227] To allow a promise to be invalidated on this ground alone would introduce an intermediate category of promises unfairly obtained; and this would (in the words of Lord Scarman) "be unhelpful because it would render the law uncertain".[228]

The now more generally held view is that the new promises in the present group of cases are unenforceable for want of consideration; and the reason for this view seems to have been that the promisee suffered no legal detriment[229] in performing what was already due from him, nor did the promisor receive any legal benefit in receiving what was already due to him.[230] But this reasoning takes no account of the fact that the promisee may in fact suffer a detriment: for example, the wages that a seaman could earn elsewhere may exceed those that he would earn under the original contract together with the damages that he would have to pay for breaking it. Conversely, the promisor may in fact benefit from the actual performance of what was legally due to him: in *Stilk v Myrick* the master got his ship home and this may well have been worth more to him than any damages that he could have recovered from the crew.

**Factual benefit to promisor.** The foregoing discussion shows that a new promise by B in consideration of A's performing his duty to B under an earlier contract between them is not necessarily obtained by duress; and that A's performance of the duty may in fact benefit B. Where both these conditions are satisfied, it has been held that A can enforce B's new promise. 3–049

**Williams v Roffey Bros.** In *Williams v Roffey Bros & Nicholls (Contractors) Ltd*[231] B had engaged A as carpentry sub-contractor, for the purpose of performing a contract between B and X to refurbish a number of flats. The amount payable by B to A under the subcontract was £20,000 but B later promised to make extra payments to A, who undertook no additional obligation in 3–050

[225] As in *The Universe Sentinel* [1983] 1 A.C. 366; *B & S Contracts & Designs v Victor Green Publications* [1984] I.C.R. 419; *Atlas Express Ltd v Kafco (Importers and Distributors) Ltd* [1989] Q.B. 833; para.10–009.

[226] e.g. *The Atlantic Baron* [1979] Q.B. 705; fn.263; *The Alev* [1989] 1 Lloyd's Rep. 138.

[227] *Pao On v Lau Yiu Long* [1980] A.C. 614 at 632.

[228] *Pao On v Lau Yiu Long* [1980] A.C. 614 at 634. This statement was made in a case involving three parties, but it is of general application: *Williams v Roffey Bros & Nicholls (Contractors) Ltd* [1991] 1 Q.B. 1 at 15.

[229] See para.3–004.

[230] *Technip-Coflexip SA v Tube Tech International Ltd* [2005] EWCA Civ 1369; 106 Con L.R. 32 at [64].

[231] [1991] 1 Q.B. 1; Adams and Brownsword 53 M.L.R. 536; Hird and Blair [1996] J.B.L. 254.

return.[232] B made this new promise because B's own surveyor recognised that the originally agreed sum of £20,000 was too low, and because B feared that A (who was in financial difficulties) would not be able to complete his work on time, and so expose B to penalties for delay under his contract with X. It was held that B's promise to make the extra payments to A was supported by consideration in the shape of the "practical benefits"[233] obtained by B from A's performance of his duties under the original contract between them.[234] Since no allegation of duress on A's part had been made by B, the new promise by B to pay extra could not be avoided on this ground. There had been no threat by A to break his original contract; indeed, the initiative for the agreement containing the promise of extra pay seems to have come from B.

3–051 **Reconciling the cases.** The element of factual benefit which was stressed in the *Williams* case has also been regarded as consideration where a person performs (or promises to perform) a contractual duty owed to a third party;[235] and the *Williams* case is to be welcomed in bringing the two-party cases in line with those involving three parties.[236] But it is by no means clear how the case is, from this point of view, to be reconciled with *Stilk v Myrick* and with the line of more recent decisions which have followed that case.[237] As has been suggested above, the master in *Stilk v Myrick* also obtained a factual benefit (in getting his ship home); and such a factual benefit will very often be obtained by B where he secures actual performance from A (as opposed to having to sue him for non-performance of the original contract).

In the *Williams* case, *Stilk v Myrick* was not overruled; indeed Purchas LJ described it as a "pillar stone of the law of contract".[238] But he added that the case

---

[232] The payments under the original contract were found to be due in unspecified instalments while those under the new promise were due as each flat was completed, but no attempt was made to argue that this change in the times when payment was due might have been to A's disadvantage and therefore provided consideration. There is perhaps a hint to this effect in Russell LJ's judgment at 19. Similar reasoning is one basis of *Anangel Atlas Compania Naviera SA v Ishikawajima-Harima Heavy Industries Co Ltd (No.2)* [1990] 2 Lloyd's Rep. 526.

[233] *Williams v Roffey Bros & Nicholls (Contractors) Ltd* [1991] 1 Q.B. 1 at 11; cf. at 19, 23. See also *Simon Container Machinery Ltd v Emba Machinery AB* [1998] 2 Lloyd's Rep. 428 at 435; *Horwood v Land of Leather Ltd* [2010] EWHC 546 (Comm); [2010] 1 C.L.C. 423 at [41]. In *Attrill v Dresdner Kleinwort Ltd* [2013] EWCA Civ 394; [2013] 3 All E.R. 607 at [95] employees remaining in post seems to have been regarded as consideration for the promise of a guaranteed bonus; there is no reference to this as a "practical benefit" and if the employees were promising to forego, or foregoing, a right of termination they may have bestowed a legal benefit on the employer.

[234] In fact, B did not secure the whole of this benefit, but this was because B's wrongful failure to make the extra payments justified A's refusal to continue with the work.

[235] See paras 3–053–3–055.

[236] In *Stilk v Myrick* (1809) 2 Camp. 317; 6 Esp. 129, at para.3–048 the distinction was ignored: no one even asked whether the original contract was with the promisor (the master) or with a third party (the shipowner). It is clear from the report in Espinasse that the action was brought against the master; cf. also *Turner v Owen* (1862) 3 F. & F. 176; *B & S Contracts & Designs v Victor Green Publications Ltd* [1984] I.C.R. 419.

[237] See para.3–048. See also *South Caribbean Trading Ltd v Trafigura Beheer BV* [2004] EWHC 2676; [2005] 1 Lloyd's Rep. 128 at [107], where Colman J (obiter) would not have followed the *Williams* case, but for the fact it was binding on him.

[238] *Williams v Roffey Bros & Nicholls (Contractors) Ltd* [1991] 1 Q.B. 1 at 20.

might be differently decided today;[239] while Glidewell LJ said that the present decision did not "contravene" but did "refine and limit"[240] the principle of the earlier case; and Russell LJ said that the "rigid approach" to consideration in *Stilk v Myrick* was "no longer necessary or desirable."[241] The conclusion which may tentatively be drawn from these statements is that the factual benefit to B in securing A's performance of the earlier contract will normally suffice to constitute consideration. The insistence in the earlier cases on the stricter requirement of legal benefit or detriment is no longer justified (if it ever was) by the need to protect B from the undue pressure that A might exert by refusing to perform his original contract; for this need can now be met by the expanding concept of duress. This provides a more satisfactory solution of the present problem since it invalidates promises only where actual duress is established.[242] Where this is not the case, and the promisee has in fact conferred a benefit on the promisor by performing the original contract, then the requirement of consideration is satisfied and there seems to be no good reason for refusing to enforce the new promise.

Nor is it obvious how the decision in the *Williams* case can be reconciled with the earlier decision of the House of Lords in *Foakes v Beer*[243] to reject practical benefit as sufficient for consideration.[244] That decision was reached in the context of part payment of a debt,[245] i.e. a case of accepting less (*Foakes*) rather than promising more (*Williams*). In *Rock Advertising Ltd v MWB Business Exchange Centres Ltd* Lord Sumption acknowledged that there were "arguable points of distinction", but described those arguments as "somewhat forced".[246]

**Other consideration.** The promisee may provide other consideration for the new promise by doing, or promising to do, more than he was bound by the original contract to do.[247] Thus a seaman is entitled to extra wages if, during the voyage, he is promoted and so undertakes additional duties.[248] The same principle was applied where shipbuilders claimed an increase in the agreed price for a supertanker on the ground that the currency in which that price was to be paid had 3–052

[239] *Williams v Roffey Bros & Nicholls (Contractors) Ltd* [1991] 1 Q.B. 1 at 21. But he was not prepared to accept *Watkins v Carrig* 21 A 2d. 591 (1941), where a contractor who had agreed to do excavating work unexpectedly struck hard rock and was held entitled to enforce a promise to pay nine times the originally agreed sum. That case was said not to represent English law in *The Atlantic Baron* [1979] Q.B. 705 at 714, cf. also *Finland SS Co Ltd v Felixstowe Dock Ry Co* [1980] 2 Lloyd's Rep. 390.

[240] *Williams v Roffey Bros & Nicholls (Contractors) Ltd* [1991] 1 Q.B. 1 at 16.

[241] *Williams v Roffey Bros & Nicholls (Contractors) Ltd* [1991] 1 Q.B. 1 at 18.

[242] *Adam Opel GmbH v Mitras Automotive (UK) Ltd* [2008] EWHC 3205 (QB); [2088] C.I.L.L. 2561 at [42]. Colman J's view in *South Caribbean Trading Ltd v Trafigura Beheer BV* [2004] EWHC 2676 (Comm); [2005] 1 Lloyd's Rep. 128 at [109] that duress "precludes" reliance on any factual benefit is, with respect, open to doubt. Whether there has been any consideration and whether the resulting contract is voidable for duress are quite separate issues; to run them together runs the risk of confusing the issues, as in *Stilk v Myrick*.

[243] *Foakes v Beer* (1884) 9 App. Cas. 605.

[244] It appears that the decision in *Foakes v Beer* was not cited in argument in the *Williams* case.

[245] See para.3–102.

[246] *Rock Advertising Ltd v MWB Business Exchange Centres Ltd* [2018] UKSC 24; [2019] A.C. 119 at [18].

[247] *Horwood v Land of Leather Ltd* [2010] EWHC 546 (Comm); [2010] 1 C.L.C. 423 at [39]–[40].

[248] *Hanson v Royden* (1867) L.R. 3 C.P. 47.

been devalued. The contract required the builders to give a performance guarantee, and it was held that they had provided consideration for the prospective owners' promise to pay the price increase by making a corresponding increase in their performance guarantee.[249]

The promisee similarly provides other consideration where, before the new promise is made, circumstances arise which justify his refusal to perform the original contract. Thus the crew of a ship may be justified in refusing to complete a voyage because so many of their fellows have deserted that completion will involve hazards of a kind not originally contemplated. If they are induced to go on by a promise of extra pay, they do something which they were not bound to do, and can recover the extra pay.[250] The same principle applies where the contract is determined by notice or by mutual consent. Thus a promise to pay an employee higher wages after he has lawfully determined his contract by notice is binding. Or the parties might agree to rescind the contract and substitute a new one, at a higher rate of pay; though such a transaction might be hard to distinguish from a simple promise to pay higher wages for continuing to work under the original contract.[251] If the original contract is void, voidable or unenforceable, performance of the work specified would, it seems, be consideration for a promise of extra pay; and if the original contract was in fact good but was believed to be defective, then the new promise might be binding on the analogy of the rule that forbearance to litigate an invalid claim may amount to consideration.[252] A final possibility is that the contract may provide, expressly or by implication, for revision of pay scales from time to time; and in such a case an agreement to pay higher (or to accept lower) wages would clearly be binding.[253]

### *(iii) Duty imposed by contract with a third party*

3–053 Two problems arise under this heading. The first is whether, if A is under a contractual duty to B, the *performance* of this duty can constitute consideration for a promise made to A by C. The second is whether A's *promise* to perform his contractual duty to B can constitute consideration for a counter-promise made to A by C.[254]

3–054 **Performance of the duty.** The view that performance of a contractual duty owed to a third party can constitute consideration for a promise is supported by *The*

[249] *The Atlantic Baron* [1979] Q.B. 705; Coote [1980] C.L.J. 40; Adams 42 M.L.R. 557; cf. *Birmingham CC v Forde* [2009] EWHC 12 (QB); [2009] 1 W.L.R. 2732 at [83].

[250] *Hartley v Ponsonby* (1857) 7 E. & B. 872; *O'Neil v Armstrong, Mitchell & Co* [1895] 2 Q.B. 418; *Palace Shipping Co v Caine* [1907] A.C. 386; *Liston v SS Carpathian (Owners)* [1915] 2 K.B. 42.

[251] cf. paras 3–062, 5–033.

[252] See paras 3–036–3–038; *E. Hulton & Co v Chadwick Taylor Ltd* (1918) 34 T.L.R. 230 at 231.

[253] e.g. *Pepper & Hope v Daish* [1980] I.R.L.R. 13; cf. *Lombard Tricity Finance Ltd v Paton* [1989] 1 All E.R. 98 (credit agreement providing for increases in interest rates to be made by lender).

[254] There is no doubt that C's promise to perform a duty owed by B to A (or the performance of such a promise) can constitute consideration for a promise (express or implied) by A to C: see, e.g. *Brandt v Liverpool SN Co* [1924] 1 K.B. 575; *The Aramis* [1989] 1 Lloyd's Rep. 213 at 225 (where C's claim failed for want of contractual intention: para.4–027).

*Eurymedon*.[255] A (a firm of stevedores) had unloaded goods from B's ship. Some of these belonged to C who, for present purposes,[256] may be taken to have promised A not to sue him for damaging the goods. It was held that A had provided consideration for this promise by unloading the goods even if he was already bound[257] by a contract with B to unload them.

**Promise to perform the duty.** It was at one time thought that a mere promise to perform a contractual duty owed to a third party could not constitute consideration. Thus in *Jones v Waite*[258] it was said that a promise by A to C that A will pay a debt owed by A to B is no consideration for a promise made by C to A. This view seems to be based on the idea that A suffers no (legal) detriment by promising to pay a debt that he was already bound to pay; nor did it appear that C gained any benefit as a result of the promise. It is, however, possible for C to gain such a benefit:[259] for example, where C promises A some benefit in return for A's promise not to carry out his intention of breaking a contract with B, a company in which C has an interest. This was the position in *Pao On v Lau Yiu Long*[260] where A, having entered into a contract with a company (B), refused to perform it unless C, who were shareholders in the company, guaranteed A against loss which might be incurred as a result of the performance of one of the terms of that contract. The guarantee was given in consideration of A's promise to perform their contractual obligations to the company; and was held binding[261] on the ground that "A promise to perform, or the performance of, a pre-existing contractual obligation to a third party can be valid consideration".[262] This view seems, with respect, to be preferable to that expressed in *Jones v Waite*; for the guarantee was certainly not gratuitous in a commercial sense. 3–055

It will, of course, be open to the promisor to avoid liability if he can show that the promisee's refusal to perform the contract with the third party amounted to duress[263] not merely with regard to the third party, but also with regard to the promisor himself.

---

[255] [1975] A.C. 154; followed in *The New York Star* [1981] 1 W.L.R. 138; and *The Antwerpen* [1994] 1 Lloyd's Rep. 213; cf. *The Mahkutai* [1996] A.C. 650 at 664; *The Bulk Chile* [2013] EWCA Civ 184; [2013] 1 W.L.R. 3440 at [34]. The earlier decision in *Shadwell v Shadwell* (1860) 9 C.B. (N.S.) 159 also lends support, but the reasoning employed is not wholly conclusive.

[256] For a discussion of this point, see paras 14–068–14–076.

[257] A question may arise as to whether A has indeed performed or begun to perform his contract with B: *The Rigoletto* [2000] 2 Lloyd's Rep. 532 at 542–545.

[258] (1839) 5 Bing. N.C. 341, 351; affirmed on another ground (1842) 9 Cl. & F. 107.

[259] This seems to be acknowledged in *Aviva Life & Pensions UK Ltd v Strand Street Properties Ltd* [2010] EWCA Civ 444, in the opening lines of [50] but it is not explained precisely what was the benefit to the promisee.

[260] [1980] A.C. 614.

[261] For rejection of the argument that the consideration was past, see para.3–019.

[262] *Pao On v Lau Yiu Long* [1980] A.C. 614 at 632; cf. *Scotson v Pegg* (1861) 6 H. & N. 295 at 301; *The Eurymedon* [1975] A.C. 154 at 183.

[263] See para.3–048.

## 6. RESCISSION AND VARIATION

3–056 A contract may be rescinded or varied by subsequent agreement. The object of rescission is to release the parties from the contract, while that of variation is to alter some term of the contract. Such subsequent agreements give rise to problems of consideration, which will be discussed here, and to problems of form, to be discussed in Ch.5. One aspect of the consideration problem has already been dealt with in our discussion of the question whether the performance by A of his obligations under the old contract could be consideration for a new promise from B.[264] Our present problem is whether there is consideration for a promise by B to accept in discharge of A's obligations some performance *other* than that originally undertaken by A, or to grant A a total release from the contract. Even if there is no such consideration B's subsequent promise may, nevertheless, have some limited legal effect either as a waiver or in equity.[265]

### (a) Rescission

3–057 **Where both parties have outstanding rights.** An agreement to rescind a contract will generate its own consideration whenever each party has outstanding rights under the contract against the other. This is most obviously true where the contract is wholly executory and neither party is in breach.[266] Thus a contract for the sale of goods to be delivered and paid for on a future day can be rescinded by mutual consent at any time before the day fixed for performance. A contract can similarly be rescinded by agreement after both parties have broken it.[267] And a partly executed contract can be rescinded by agreement so long as there are outstanding obligations on both sides: thus a lease for seven years can be rescinded by mutual consent after it has run for three years. In all these cases there is consideration for the rescission in that each party promises to give up his rights against the other under the original contract.[268] It is, of course, essential, that *each* party should make such a promise.[269] If only one party does so, the other making no counter-promise, the former party's promise will be "entirely unilateral and unsupported by any consideration".[270]

3–058 **Where one party has outstanding rights.** An agreement to rescind a contract may also fail to generate its own consideration (and so lack contractual force) where only one party has outstanding rights under the contract. This will often be the position where the contract has been wholly executed by that party. Suppose that goods are sold and delivered but not paid for, and the parties then agree to "rescind" the contract. If the agreement means that the buyer is to return the goods and to be released from his liability to pay the price, there is good

264 See paras 3–047–3–055.

265 See paras 3–066–3–093; 3–113–3–120.

266 *Foster v Dawber* (1851) Ex. 839 at 850; cf. *The Trado* [1982] 1 Lloyd's Rep. 157.

267 e.g. *Morris v Baron & Co* [1918] A.C. 1.

268 cf. *Argo Fund Ltd v Essar Steel Ltd* [2005] EWHC 600 (Comm); [2005] 2 Lloyd's Rep. 203 at [51]; affirmed on other grounds [2006] EWCA Civ 241; [2006] 2 Lloyd's Rep. 134.

269 *Ogilvy & Mather Ltd v Silverado Blue Ltd* [2007] EWHC 1285 (QB) at [21].

270 *Collin v Duke of Westminster* [1985] Q.B. 581 at 598.

consideration for the promise of each party. But if it simply means that the buyer is not to pay the price, it is a gratuitous promise by the seller.[271] Conversely, goods may be sold, delivered and paid for, but turn out to be defective. Here an agreement to "rescind" would be a gratuitous promise if it simply released the seller from his liability under the original contract for the defects. This is what is meant by the statement that rescission after breach requires separate consideration.[272]

That statement must, however, be qualified where the contract is a continuing one, such as one to deliver goods by instalments. An agreement to "rescind" such a contract after one defective instalment had been delivered and paid for would not be a gratuitous release of the seller from his liability for the defects, for he would be giving up his rights to have future instalments accepted and paid for. It is only where the defect is of such a kind as to give the buyer the right as a matter of law to treat the contract as repudiated[273] that the seller may be said to give up nothing in return for the buyer's promise not to sue for the defect. Even in such a case, however, this result would not necessarily follow; for so long as the seller in good faith believed that the contract remained binding he would provide consideration by forbearing to enforce it.[274]

**The need for separate consideration: "accord and satisfaction".** Where the rescinding agreement does not generate its own consideration, it must be supported by separate consideration: there must, in technical language, be not only accord but also satisfaction. Thus a buyer of goods may agree to release a seller who has become liable in damages for non-delivery, if the seller will pay him £50. The agreement to release the seller is the accord; payment of the £50 is the satisfaction.[275] On payment of the £50, the seller is released from his liability in damages. 3–059

**Executory accord.** It was formerly said that an executory accord, i.e. one which had not yet been followed by satisfaction, had no effect: that it neither released the party in breach nor gave the other party any new right of action.[276] But it is settled that an executory accord can be enforced by the party to whom the satisfaction was offered,[277] and it may release the party by whom it was offered if that party's *promise* to perform his part of the accord has, on the true construction of the accord, been accepted by the injured party in discharge of his original cause of action.[278] Even where the injured party has not accepted the wrongdoer's 3–060

---

[271] *Commissioner of Stamp Duties v Bone* [1977] A.C. 511 at 519.

[272] *Atlantic Shipping & Trading Ltd v Louis Dreyfus & Co* [1922] 2 A.C. 250 at 262.

[273] See Ch.18.

[274] See paras 3–036–3–038.

[275] *British-Russian Gazette Ltd v Associated Newspapers Ltd* [1933] 2 K.B. 616 at 643. Mere acceptance of a cheque sent in full settlement is not conclusive evidence of such an agreement: *Stour Valley Builders v Stuart, The Times*, 23 February 1993, following *Day v McLea* [1889] 2 Q.B. 610; *Inland Revenue Commissioners v Fry* [2001] S.T.C. 1715 at [12]. See also *Clarke v Nationwide BS* (1998) 76 P. & C.R. D5 (acceptance of cheque sent "as a gesture of goodwill" not an accord).

[276] *Bayley v Homan* (1837) 3 Bing. N.C. 915; cf. *Morris v Baron & Co* [1918] A.C. 1 at 36.

[277] *Henderson v Stobart* (1850) 5 Ex. 99.

[278] *Elton Cop Dyeing Co v Broadbent & Son Ltd* (1919) 89 L.J.K.B. 186; cf. *Cartwright v Cooke* (1832) 3 B. & Ad. 701; *Crowther v Farrer* (1850) 15 Q.B. 677.

promise in settlement of the cause of action, a question can arise as to the time at which the accord takes effect. In the absence of an express provision in it on the point, the accord releases the original cause of action at the time of the accord,[279] subject only to the implied condition subsequent[280] that it will be retrospectively avoided on the wrongdoer's failure to perform it in accordance with its terms. On such failure, the original liability will therefore revive. The parties may, of course, also agree to make performance of the accord a condition precedent to discharge. If they do so, the party originally in breach will not be discharged by the accord so long as it remains executory; he will be discharged only on giving the agreed satisfaction.[281]

3–061 **Accord without satisfaction.** There is one long-established exception to the rule that accord without satisfaction does not discharge a contract after breach. If the holder of a bill of exchange or promissory note at or after its maturity absolutely, unconditionally and in writing renounces his rights against any person liable on the bill or note, the latter is discharged.[282] The exception provides a comparatively simple way of evading the general rule: the creditor can take a bill or note in satisfaction of the debt and then renounce it.

## (b) Variation

3–062 **Variation amounting to rescission.** A variation of a contract may amount to a rescission of the old contract followed by the making of a new one relating to the same subject-matter. The question whether there is consideration for the rescission then depends on the principles just discussed.[283] If there is consideration for the rescission there is also consideration for the new promises. "The same consideration which existed for the old agreement is imported into the new agreement, which is substituted for it."[284]

3–063 **Variation benefiting either party.** The parties may agree to vary their contract in a way that can benefit either party. Such a variation again normally generates its own consideration. This is the position if a lease is varied by altering the date on which notice of termination can be given;[285] or if a contract of sale is varied by altering the agreed delivery date,[286] or the currency in which payment is to be made.[287] In the latter case, it would make no difference that the new currency was

---

[279] *Jameson v CEGB* [2000] 1 A.C. 455 at 477, where the original liability arose in tort; and see para.13–015.

[280] *Jameson v CEGB* [2000] 1 A.C. 455 at 477; for the distinction between conditions precedent and subsequent, see para.2–105.

[281] cf. *Johnson v Davies* [1999] Ch. 117 at 128 (a case, not of accord and satisfaction at common law, but of a "voluntary arrangement" under the Insolvency Act 1986 Pt VIII).

[282] Bills of Exchange Act 1882 s.62.

[283] See paras 3–057–3–061.

[284] *Stead v Dawber* (1839) 10 A. & E. 57 at 66.

[285] *Fenner v Blake* [1900] 1 Q.B. 427.

[286] *South Caribbean Trading Ltd v Trafigura Beheer BV* [2004] EWHC 2676 (Comm); [2005] 1 Lloyd's Rep. 128.

[287] *WJ Alan & Co Ltd v El Nasr Export & Import Co* [1972] 2 Q.B. 189; *Woodhouse AC Israel Cocoa Ltd SA v Nigerian Produce Marketing Co* [1972] A.C. 741 at 757.

later devalued in relation to the old, for at the time of the variation it could not be certain how the two currencies would move in relation to each other: hence either party *might* benefit from the variation. If a variation is, taken as a whole, capable of benefiting either party, the requirement of consideration will be satisfied even though a particular term of the variation is for the sole benefit of one.[288] A variation does not, however, generate its own consideration if, though capable of benefiting either party, it is in fact made wholly for the benefit of one. For example, a variation as to the place at which a debt is to be paid may benefit either party and thus provide consideration for a promise by the creditor to accept part payment in full settlement. But it will not have this effect if it is introduced solely for the benefit of the debtor.[289] Similarly, an agreement to reduce the quantity of goods to be delivered and paid for under a contract for the sale of goods may benefit either party; but if it is made purely for the seller's convenience it will not be consideration for the buyer's promise to accept the smaller quantity; nor conversely.[290]

**Variation benefiting one party.** The parties may agree to vary the contract in a way that can confer a legal benefit[291] on only one party. In some situations, it is settled that such a variation does not generate its own consideration: thus a promise by a creditor to accept part payment of a debt in full settlement is not binding unless it is supported by some separate consideration.[292] Such separate consideration could be provided by some further variation which may benefit the creditor: for example, by a debtor's promise to make the part payment *before* the day when the debt becomes due.[293] In other situations, it is arguable[294] that the variation may be supported by consideration if, though capable of conferring a legal benefit on only one party, it can also confer a factual benefit[295] on the other, e.g. where a buyer's promise to pay more than the originally agreed price secures eventual delivery when strict insistence on the original contract would have led to nothing but litigation. 3–064

**Variation before contract concluded.** There is the apparently paradoxical possibility that the parties may agree to vary a contract even before that contract has been concluded. This may be the position where A and B negotiate on the basis of formal documents and A represents that the proposed contract will be on terms less favourable to himself than those set out in the documents. If the documents are nevertheless executed without alteration, the representation may then be enforceable as a collateral contract. The consideration for the promise contained in A's representation is provided by B when he executes the documents 3–065

---

[288] *Ficom SA v Sociedad Cadex Ltda* [1980] 2 Lloyd's Rep. 118 at 132.

[289] *Vanbergen v St Edmund's Properties Ltd* [1933] 2 K.B. 233; cf. *Continental Grain Export Corp v STM Grain Ltd* [1979] 2 Lloyd's Rep. 460 at 476.

[290] *Vanbergen v St Edmund's Properties Ltd* [1933] 2 K.B. 233.

[291] See para.3–006.

[292] See para.3–102.

[293] See para.3–107.

[294] On the analogy of the reasoning of *Williams v Roffey Bros & Nicholls (Contractors) Ltd* [1991] 1 Q.B. 1, para.3–050.

[295] See para.3–006.

(and so enters into the principal contract) at the request of A and in reliance on the representation. In *Brikom Investments Ltd v Carr*[296] landlords of blocks of flats negotiated with their tenants for the sale of long leases of the flats on terms requiring the tenants to contribute to the cost of (inter alia) roof maintenance. At the time of the negotiations, the roof was in need of repairs, and the landlords promised to execute these "at our own cost". It was held that one of the tenants had provided consideration for this promise by executing the agreement for the lease, and the lease itself; and that the promise was accordingly binding as a collateral contract.[297] It followed that the landlords could not enforce the term in the lease under which the tenant would (but for the collateral contract) have been liable to contribute to the cost of the roof repairs.[298] Greater difficulty would have arisen if the tenant had already executed the documents *before* the landlord's promise had been made, for in that case the execution of the documents would have been past consideration.[299] The tenants could, however, have succeeded, even in such a case, on an alternative ground. The landlords had been guilty of unreasonable delay in executing the repairs, and the tenants would, by forbearing to take proceedings in respect of that breach,[300] have provided consideration for the landlords' promise to bear the cost of the repairs.

### (c) Waiver[301]

#### *(i) At common law*

3–066 Where a party promises to relinquish some or all of his rights under a contract, he is sometimes said to have "waived" those rights. Unfortunately, however, "the word 'waiver' … covers a variety of situations different in their legal nature …".[302] Of the many senses in which it is used, three are relevant to the present discussion.[303]

3–067 **To mean rescission.** Sometimes "waiver" means total rescission of the contract: "The waiver spoken of in the case is an entire abandonment and dissolution of the contract."[304] This usage assumes that the rescission is supported by consideration.[305] It has been judicially criticised so far as it refers to a purported release

---

296 [1979] Q.B. 467.

297 cf. *Business Environment Bow Lane Ltd v Deanwater Estates* [2007] EWCA Civ 622; [2007] 32 E.G. 90, where no collateral contract was found to exist.

298 This was agreed by all members of the Court of Appeal. For other grounds for the decision, see paras 3–112, 3–117.

299 See para.3–017.

300 See *Brikom Investments Ltd v Carr* [1979] Q.B. 467 at 490; cf. para.3–040. Delay in executing the repairs was a breach irrespective of the question of who was to pay for them.

301 Cheshire and Fifoot 63 L.Q.R. 283; Stoljar 35 Can. Bar. Rev. 485; Dugdale and Yates 39 M.L.R. 681; Phipps 123 L.Q.R. 286; Wilken and Ghaly, *The Law of Waiver Variation and Estoppel*, 3rd edn (2012).

302 *The Laconia* [1977] A.C. 850 at 871; cf. *The Kanchenjunga* [1990] 1 Lloyd's Rep. 391 at 397; *The Happy Day* [2002] EWCA Civ 1068; [2002] 2 Lloyd's Rep. 487 at [64].

303 For further senses, see para.18–089 and following.

304 *Price v Dyer* (1810) 17 Ves. 356 at 364.

305 See para.3–057.

without consideration. "To say that a claim is to be waived is incorrect. If a right has accrued, it must be released or discharged by deed or upon consideration."[306]

**To mean variation.** Sometimes, "waiver" refers to a variation which is supported by consideration and is therefore binding as a contract.[307] It is also used to refer to a variation which, though supported by consideration, is for some other reason *not* contractually binding. This usage occurs in the context of the rule that a contract which is required to be in, or evidenced in, writing can be rescinded but not varied orally.[308] In such cases, the ineffective oral variation is sometimes referred to as a "waiver", so as to contrast it with an effective rescission followed by the making of a substituted contract on new terms: 3–068

> "There was no fresh agreement ... which can be regarded as having been substituted for the original written contract. There was nothing more than a waiver by the defendants of a delivery by the plaintiff in [the originally stipulated month]".[309]

**To mean forbearance.** A variation may not be contractually binding for want of consideration or of contractual intention, or because it fails to comply with a legal requirement that it must be in, or evidenced in, writing.[310] It may nevertheless have certain limited legal effects, which are sometimes said to arise because one party has "waived" his rights. To distinguish such arrangements from contractually binding variations, they will here be referred to as "forbearances".[311] Their effects are as follows. 3–069

**Party requesting forbearance.** The party requesting the forbearance cannot refuse to accept the varied performance. Thus, if a seller at the request of the buyer delivers late, the buyer cannot refuse to accept on the ground that delivery was made after the time specified in the original contract.[312] 3–070

**Varied performance made and accepted.** If the varied performance is actually made and accepted, neither party can claim damages on the ground that performance was not in accordance with the original contract. Thus, in the above example the seller who delivers late, or the buyer who takes delivery late, is not liable in damages. But if the contract is not performed at all, the damages are assessed on the footing that the breach took place at the end of the extended period.[313] 3–071

---

306 *Atlantic Shipping & Trading Co Ltd v Louis Dreyfus & Co* [1922] 2 A.C. 250 at 262; cf. *The Ion* [1980] 2 Lloyd's Rep. 245 at 249.

307 Semble, this is the sense in which the word is used by Roskill and Cumming-Bruce LJJ in *Brikom Investments Ltd v Carr* [1979] Q.B. 467 at 488, 491; for the consideration for the "waiver", see para.3–065; cf. *Shamsher Jute Mills Ltd v Sethia (London) Ltd* [1987] 2 Lloyd's Rep. 388 at 392; *Royal Boskalis Westminster NV v Mountain* [1997] 2 All E.R. 929, where the "waiver", i.e. variation, was not binding because it was vitiated by duress and illegality.

308 See paras 5–034—5–037.

309 *Hickman v Haynes* (1875) L.R. 10 C.P. 598 at 604.

310 See paras 5–034—5–037.

311 cf. *The Kanchenjunga* [1990] 1 Lloyd's Rep. 391 at 397.

312 *Hickman v Haynes* (1875) L.R. 10 C.P. 598; *Levey & Co v Goldberg* [1922] 1 K.B. 688; cf. *British and Beningtons Ltd v NW Cachar Tea Co* [1923] A.C. 48.

313 *Ogle v Vane* (1868) L.R. 3 Q.B. 272.

3–072 **Party granting forbearance.** The cases that give rise to the greatest difficulty are those in which the party *granting* the forbearance refuses to perform, or to accept performance, in accordance with it. Suppose, for example, that a buyer agrees, at the seller's request, to accept late delivery. The buyer cannot then claim damages for the seller's failure to deliver within the contract period;[314] but a further set of problems can arise if, after expiry of that period but within the extended period, the seller tenders delivery, and the buyer refuses to accept it. One possible view is that the seller cannot derive rights from a forbearance which is not binding as a contract, and that therefore he is not entitled to damages for the buyer's refusal to take delivery within the extended, but outside the original, contract period. A claim for such damages was accordingly rejected in *Plevins v Downing*,[315] where the agreement to extend the delivery dates had no contractual force since it was oral when it should, as the law then stood, have been evidenced in writing and since it was probably unsupported by consideration, having been made at the request, and for the sole benefit, of the seller.[316]

But in many cases the party for whose benefit the forbearance was granted was allowed to enforce the contract in accordance with the new terms. In *Hartley v Hymans*[317] a buyer of cotton agreed to allow the seller to make late delivery. It was held that he was liable in damages for peremptorily refusing to take delivery after the period originally specified in the contract had expired. Similarly, a party may acquiesce in a method of payment other than that specified in the contract so as to indicate that the new method is to become the "accepted method."[318] He cannot then refuse to perform his part simply because the other party has not performed his obligation to pay strictly in accordance with the terms originally agreed;[319] nor can he peremptorily require performance strictly in accordance with those terms.[320] In these cases it is sometimes said that there is no variation of the contract, but only a variation of the mode of performance; or that there is no variation, but only a waiver[321] in the sense of forbearance.

3–073 **Forbearance distinguished from variation supported by consideration.** Such a forbearance differs from a variation which is supported by consideration in that it does not *irrevocably* alter the rights of the parties under the original contract. The party granting the forbearance *can generally retract it*, provided that he gives reasonable notice of his intention to do so to the party for whose benefit it was

314 cf. *The Kanchenjunga* [1989] 1 Lloyd's Rep. 354 at 358; affirmed [1990] 1 Lloyd's Rep. 391.

315 (1876) 1 C.P.D. 220.

316 See para.3–063.

317 [1920] 3 K.B. 475; cf. *Tyers v Rosedale & Ferryhill Iron Co* (1875) L.R. 10 Ex. 195; *Besseler Waechter Glover & Co v South Derwent Coal Ltd* [1938] 1 K.B. 408; and see *Leather Cloth Co v Hieronimus* (1874–75) L.R. 10 Q.B. 140 (variation of route of shipment).

318 *The Scaptrade* [1981] 2 Lloyd's Rep. 425 at 431 (where this requirement was not satisfied); affirmed [1983] 2 A.C. 694, without reference to this point; *Hazel v Akhtar* [2001] EWCA Civ 1883, *The Times*, 7 January 2002 (landlord tolerating habitually late payment of rent).

319 *Panoutsos v Raymond Hadley Corp of NY* [1917] 2 K.B. 473; *Tankexpress A/S v Cie Financière Belge des Petroles, SA* [1949] A.C. 76; *Plasticmoda Soc v Davidsons (Manchester) Ltd* [1952] 1 Lloyd's Rep. 527.

320 *Mitas v Hymans* [1951] 2 T.L.R. 1215.

321 e.g. in *Plevins v Downing* (1876) 1 C.P.D. 220 at 225; *Besseler Waechter Glover & Co v South Derwent Coal Co Ltd* [1938] 1 K.B. 408 at 416; *The Kanchenjunga* [1990] 1 Lloyd's Rep. 391 at 397–398.

granted.[322] Thus, in *Charles Rickards Ltd v Oppenhaim*[323] a contract for the sale of a car provided for delivery on March 20. The car was not delivered on that day but the buyer continued to press for delivery and finally told the seller on June 29 that he must have the car by July 25 at the latest. It was held that the buyer could not have refused peremptorily to accept the car merely because the original delivery date had gone by, as he had continued to press for delivery; but that he could refuse on the seller's failure to comply with a notice to deliver within a reasonable time. Here the notice did give the seller a reasonable time to deliver, so that the buyer was justified in refusing to take the car after July 25. A fortiori, the buyer could have refused to take delivery if the original delivery date had been extended only for a fixed time and if delivery had not been made by the end of that time.[324]

**Forbearance made irrevocable by subsequent events.** A forbearance may, however, become irrevocable as a result of subsequent events: for example if a buyer indicates that he is willing to accept goods of a different quality from those contracted for, and the seller, in reliance on that assurance, so conducts himself as to put it out of his power to supply goods of the contract quality within the contract period.[325] 3–074

**Distinction dependent upon the "intention" of the parties.** The distinction between a forbearance and a variation is sometimes said to depend on the intention of the parties:[326] a statement is a forbearance if the party making it intends to reserve a power to retract; but a variation if he intends permanently to abandon his rights under the contract. The courts were, however, anxious to avoid the unjust effects of the rules as to variations that were not contractually binding for lack of consideration or failure to comply with formal requirements. Hence they often interpreted a subsequent agreement as a forbearance, so as to give it at least some legal effects. 3–075

### *(ii) In equity*[327]

**The shortcomings of forbearance.** The common law rules as to waiver in the sense of forbearance are defective in two ways. First, they rest on the tenuous distinction between forbearance and variation, which can be deduced from the judgments, but does not provide any very solid basis for distinguishing between 3–076

---

[322] *Banning v Wright* [1972] 1 W.L.R. 972 at 981; *Ficom SA v Sociedad Cadex Ltd* [1980] 2 Lloyd's Rep. 118 at 131; *Bremer Handelsgesellschaft mbH v Raiffeisen Hauptgenossenschaft EG* [1982] 1 Lloyd's Rep. 599; *MWB Business Exchange Centres Ltd v Rock Advertising Ltd* [2016] EWCA Civ 553; [2017] Q.B. 604 at [64] (appeal allowed on another ground: [2018] UKSC 24; [2019] A.C. 119).

[323] [1950] 1 K.B. 616; cf. *Bird v Hildage* [1948] 1 K.B. 91; *State Trading Corp of India v Cie Française d'Importation et de Distribution* [1983] 2 Lloyd's Rep. 679 at 681.

[324] cf. *Nichimen Corp v Gatoil Overseas Inc* [1987] 2 Lloyd's Rep. 46, where similar fixed term extensions were granted by a seller.

[325] *Toepfer v Warinco AG* [1978] 2 Lloyd's Rep. 569 at 576; *The Bunga Saga Lima* [2005] EWHC 244 (Comm); [2005] 2 Lloyd's Rep. 1 at [31].

[326] *Stead v Dawber* (1839) 10 A. & E. 57 at 64.

[327] Denning 15 M.L.R. 1; Wilson 67 L.Q.R. 330; Sheridan 15 M.L.R. 325; Gordon [1963] C.L.J. 222; Wilson [1965] C.L.J. 93; Thompson [1983] C.L.J. 257; Spence, *Protecting Reliance*.

the actual decisions. It is hard to see, for instance, why the buyer in *Plevins v Downing*[328] was allowed to reject late delivery, while the buyer in *Hartley v Hymans*[329] was not allowed to do so. Secondly, the common law rules produced the paradoxical result that, the more a party purported to bind himself by a subsequent agreement, the less he was likely to be bound. An attempt permanently to renounce a right would be a variation, and ineffective for want of writing or consideration. But an attempt to suspend a right would be effective, to a limited extent, as a forbearance.

3–077 **Equity's solution: "equitable", or "promissory" estoppel.** Equity devised a more satisfactory approach to the problem by concentrating, not on the intention of the party granting the forbearance, but on the conduct of that party and on its effect on the position of the other party. The leading case is *Hughes v Metropolitan Ry*,[330] where a landlord had given his tenant notice requiring him to do repairs within six months. During the six months he began to negotiate with the tenant for the purchase of his lease. When the negotiations broke down, he immediately claimed to forfeit the lease on the ground that the tenant had not done the repairs. The claim was rejected, Lord Cairns saying that if one party leads the other:

> "to suppose that the strict rights arising under the contract will not be enforced, or will be kept in suspense or held in abeyance, the person who otherwise might have enforced those rights will not be allowed to enforce them where it would be inequitable having regard to the dealings which have thus taken place between the parties".[331]

The landlord had by his conduct led the tenant to suppose that during the negotiations he would not enforce his right to forfeit. Hence he could not forfeit immediately the negotiations broke down: he had to give the tenant a reasonable time from that date to do the repairs. This equitable doctrine can now be applied to arrangements which might formerly have been regarded as variations ineffective at common law for want of consideration.[332] For reasons to be discussed later in this chapter[333] the doctrine is often (if somewhat misleadingly) referred to as "equitable" or "promissory" estoppel.

3–078 **Relationships within the doctrine.** The rights which promissory estoppel prevents a promisor or representor from enforcing normally arise out of a contract between him and the other party. But the doctrine can also apply where the relationship giving rise to rights and duties is non-contractual, e.g. to prevent

[328] (1876) 1 C.P.D. 220; para.3–072.
[329] [1920] 3 K.B. 475; para.3–072.
[330] (1877) 2 App. Cas. 439.
[331] *Hughes v Metropolitan Ry* (1877) 2 App. Cas. 439 at 448. cf. *Smith v Lawson* (1998) 75 P. & C.R. 466, para.3–090.
[332] e.g. *Charles Rickards Ltd v Oppenhaim* [1950] K.B. 616 (where both common law and equitable principles were applied).
[333] See para.3–090.

the enforcement of a liability imposed by statute;[334] or to prevent a man from ejecting a woman, with whom he had been cohabiting, from the family home.[335]

**The need for a pre-existing legal relationship.** It has been suggested that promissory estoppel can apply even where, before the making of the promise or representation, there is no legal relationship of any kind between the parties;[336] or where there is only a putative contract between them, e.g. where the promisee is induced to believe that a contract into which he had undoubtedly entered was between him and the promisor, when in fact it was between the promisee and another person.[337] But it is submitted that these suggestions mistake the nature of the doctrine, which is to restrict the enforcement by the promisor of *previously existing* rights against the promisee. Such rights can arise only out of a legal relationship existing between these parties before the making of the promise or representation. To apply the doctrine where there was no such relationship would contravene the rule (to be discussed below) that the doctrine creates no new rights.[338] **3–079**

**Summary of the requirements to be met.** In addition to the need for a pre-existing legal relationship, the operation of promissory estoppel is subject to the requirements set out in the paragraphs below.[339] In summary: (i) there must be a clear promise or representation by one party; (ii) the promisee must have relied upon the promise; and (iii) it must be inequitable for the promisor to go back on the promise. The burden of proving the necessary facts is on the promisee.[340] **3–080**

**A "clear" or "unequivocal" promise or representation.** There must be a promise (or an assurance or representation in the nature of a promise)[341] which is intended to affect the legal relationship between the parties[342] and which indicates that the promisor will not insist on his strict legal rights,[343] arising out of that relationship, against the promisee. Here, as elsewhere,[344] the law applies an objective test. It is enough if the promise induces the promisee reasonably to **3–081**

---

[334] *Durham Fancy Goods Ltd v Michael Jackson (Fancy Goods) Ltd* [1968] 2 Q.B. 839. Contrast *Evans v Amicus Healthcare Ltd* [2004] EWCA Civ 727; [2005] Fam. 1 at [120].

[335] *Maharaj v Chand* [1986] A.C. 898.

[336] See *Evenden v Guildford City FC* [1975] Q.B. 917 at 924, 926; cf. in Australia, *Waltons Stores (Interstate) Ltd v Maher* (1988) 164 C.L.R. 387; para.3–093.

[337] *The Henrik Sif* [1982] 1 Lloyd's Rep. 456 at 466; the actual decision can perhaps be explained as one of liability for actionable non-disclosure: para.9–180.

[338] See para.3–088; *Baird Textile Holdings Ltd v Marks & Spencer Plc* [2001] EWCA Civ 274; [2002] 1 All E.R. (Comm) 737 at [89] apparently doubting some of the reasoning in *The Henrik Sif* above.

[339] See paras 3–081–3–085.

[340] *Habib Bank Ltd v Tufail* [2006] EWCA Civ 374 at [21]; cf. proprietary estoppel: para.3–135.

[341] *James v Heim Galleries* (1980) 256 E.G. 819 at 821; *Collin v Duke of Westminster* [1985] Q.B. 581 at 595.

[342] *Spence v Shell* (1980) 256 E.G. 55 at 63; *Central London Property Trust Ltd v High Trees House Ltd* [1947] K.B. 130 at 134; *Baird Textile Holdings Ltd v Marks & Spencer Plc* [2001] EWCA Civ 274; [2002] 1 All E.R. (Comm) 737 at [94].

[343] Or that he will not rely on an available defence: cf. paras 3–088, 9–191.

[344] See paras 1–002, 2–002.

believe that the other party will not insist on his strict legal rights.[345] A mere threat to do something is not sufficient, nor, probably, is a representation or promise by a person that he *will* enforce a legal right: thus the doctrine does not apply where A tells B that he will exercise his right to cancel a contract between them unless by a specified date B has paid sums due under the contract to A.[346]

The promise or representation must be "clear" or "unequivocal," or "precise and unambiguous."[347] This requirement seems to have originated in the law relating to estoppel by representation[348] and it is now frequently stated in relation to "promissory estoppel."[349] It does not mean that the promise or representation must be express:[350] in *Hughes v Metropolitan Ry*[351] itself the landlord made no express promise that he would not enforce his right to forfeit the lease; but an implication of such a promise fairly arose from the course of the negotiations between the parties. There is some support for the view that the promise must have the same degree of certainty as would be needed to give it contractual effect if it were supported by consideration.[352] Thus if the statement could not have contractual effect because it was too vague,[353] or if it was insufficiently precise to amount to an offer,[354] or if it does not amount to an unqualified acceptance,[355] it will not bring the equitable doctrine into operation.[356]

The purpose of the requirement that the promise or representation must be "clear" or "unequivocal" is to prevent a party from losing his legal rights merely because he has granted some indulgence by failing throughout to insist on strict performance of a contract[357]; or because he has offered some concession in the course of negotiations for the settlement of a dispute arising out of the contract[358]

---

[345] *Bremer Handelsgesellschaft mbH v Vanden Avenne-Izegem PVBA* [1978] 2 Lloyd's Rep. 109 at 126; *Bremer Handelsgesellschaft mbH v Mackprang Jr* [1979] 1 Lloyd's Rep. 221 (both these cases concerned "waiver").

[346] *Drexel Burnham Lambert International NV v El Nasr* [1986] 1 Lloyd's Rep. 356.

[347] It has been said that it is sufficient if "the corpus of the representation should partake of that requirement": *ING Bank NV v Ros Roca SA* [2011] EWCA Civ 353; [2012] 1 W.L.R. 472 at [100].

[348] *Low v Bouverie* [1891] 3 Ch. 82 at 106; *Woodhouse AC Israel Cocoa Ltd SA v Nigerian Produce Marketing Co Ltd* [1972] A.C. 741; *The Shackleford* [1978] 2 Lloyd's Rep. 155 at 159; para.9–190.

[349] *BP Exploration Co (Libya) Ltd v Hunt (No.2)* [1979] 1 W.L.R. 783 at 812; affirmed [1983] 2 A.C. 352, without reference to this point; *The Post Chaser* [1981] 2 Lloyd's Rep. 695 at 700; *The Scaptrade* [1983] Q.B. 529 at 534–535; affirmed [1983] A.C. 694, without reference to this point; *Goldworthy v Brickell* [1987] Ch. 378 at 410; *The Zenovia* [2009] EWHC 739 (Comm); [2009] 2 Lloyd's Rep. 139 at [29]–[34]; *Kim v Chasewood Park Residents Ltd* [2013] EWCA Civ 239; [2013] H.L.R. 24.

[350] *Spence v Shell* (1980) 256 E.G. 55 at 63.

[351] (1877) 2 App. Cas. 439; cf. *The Post Chaser* [1981] 2 Lloyd's Rep. 695 at 700.

[352] *The Winson* [1980] 2 Lloyd's Rep. 213 at 222; reversed on other grounds [1982] A.C. 939; *Baird Textile Holdings Ltd v Marks & Spencer* [2001] EWCA Civ 274; [2002] 1 All E.R. (Comm) 737 at [38], [54]; cf. para.2–079 for the requirement of certainty.

[353] See para.2–080.

[354] See para.2–002.

[355] *Azov Shipping Co v Baltic Shipping Co* [1999] 2 Lloyd's Rep. 159 at 173 (a case of estoppel by representation: see para.9–190). For the requirement of an "unqualified" acceptance, see para.2–019.

[356] *The Winson* [1980] 2 Lloyd's Rep. 213 at 223; reversed on other grounds [1982] A.C. 939.

[357] *The Scaptrade* [1981] 2 Lloyd's Rep. 425 at 431; [1983] Q.B. 529 at 535; affirmed [1983] 2 A.C. 694; cf. *Bremer Handelsgesellschaft mbH v Bunge Corp* [1983] 1 Lloyd's Rep. 476. And see the comment of Longmore LJ in *Collier v P & M.J. Wright (Holdings ) Ltd* [2007] EWCA Civ 1329; [2008] 1 W.L.R. 643 at [48] (considered at para.3–117).

[358] cf. *London & Clydebank Properties v HM Investment Co* [1993] E.G.C.S. 63.

or merely because he has declared his willingness to continue such negotiations.[359] Thus the requirement was not satisfied where one of the parties to such negotiations throughout insisted on strict compliance with the terms of the contract.[360] Nor was it satisfied where he accepted less than that to which he was entitled but did so subject to an express reservation of his rights.[361] Failure, in the course of negotiations of this kind, to object to a defect or deficiency in performance is likewise insufficient if the injured party did not know and could not reasonably have known of it[362] or if full performance remained possible and continued to be demanded by that party.[363] On the other hand, failure to object to a known defect or deficiency within a reasonable time of its discovery[364] may be regarded as an unequivocal indication of the injured party's intention not to insist on his strict legal rights.[365] The position seems to be the same where the defect or deficiency, though not actually known to the injured party, was obvious or could have been discovered by him, if he had taken reasonable steps.[366] But where more than one matter is in dispute between the parties, "emphatic reliance upon some important disputed point does not by itself … imply any unequivocal representation that compliance with other parts of the bargain is thereby waived".[367]

**Silence and inaction.** Although a promise or representation may be made by conduct, mere inactivity will not normally suffice for the present purpose since "it is difficult to imagine how silence and inaction can be anything but equivocal".[368] Unless the law took this view, mere failure to assert a contractual right could lead to its loss; and the courts have on a number of occasions rejected this clearly undesirable conclusion. Thus it has been held that there is "no ground **3–082**

[359] *Seechurn v Ace Insurance SA* [2002] EWCA Civ 67; [2002] 2 Lloyd's Rep. 390, especially at [55].

[360] *V Berg & Son Ltd v Vanden Avenne-Izegem PVBA* [1977] 1 Lloyd's Rep. 500; cf. *Edm J M Mertens & Co PVBA v Veevoeder Import Export Vimex BV* [1979] 2 Lloyd's Rep. 372.

[361] *Finagrain SA Geneva v P. Kruse Hamburg* [1976] 2 Lloyd's Rep. 508; cf. *Cook Industries Inc v Meunerie Liègeois SA* [1981] 1 Lloyd's Rep. 359 at 368; *Peter Cremer v Granaria BV* [1981] 2 Lloyd's Rep. 583; cf. *The Winson* [1980] 2 Lloyd's Rep. 213 (as to which see fn.356).

[362] *Avimex SA v Dewulf & Cie* [1979] 2 Lloyd's Rep. 57.

[363] *The Mihalios Xilas* [1979] W.L.R. 1018; *The Post Chaser* [1981] 2 Lloyd's Rep. 695 at 700.

[364] See *The Laconia* [1977] A.C. 850 (where retention of an under-payment accepted without authority by the payee's bank was held not to amount to a waiver); *The Superhulls Cover Case (No.2)* [1990] 2 Lloyd's Rep. 431 (where the deficiency was not known).

[365] e.g. *Bremer Handelsgesellschaft mbH v Vanden Avenne-Izegem PVBA* [1978] 2 Lloyd's Rep. 109; *Hazel v Akhtar* [2001] EWCA Civ 1883; [2002] P. & C.R. 17; *Argo Systems FZE v Liberty Insurance (PTE)* [2011] EWHC 301 (Comm); [2011] 2 Lloyd's Rep. 61.

[366] See *Bremer Handelsgesellschaft mbH v C. Mackprang Jr* [1979] 1 Lloyd's Rep. 221, where there was a division of opinion on the point in the Court of Appeal. Contrast, for a different type of waiver, para.18–089.

[367] *The Athos* [1983] 1 Lloyd's Rep. 127 at 135; *Rafsanjan Pistachio Producers Co-operative v Bank Leumi (UK) Plc* [1992] 1 Lloyd's Rep. 513 at 542.

[368] *The Leonidas D* [1985] 1 W.L.R. 925 at 937; cf. *Cook Industries v Tradax Export SA* [1983] 1 Lloyd's Rep. 327 at 332; affirmed [1985] 2 Lloyd's Rep. 454; *The August P Leonhardt* [1985] 2 Lloyd's Rep. 28 at 33; *The Superhulls Cover Case (No.2)* [1990] 2 Lloyd's Rep. 431 at 452; and see para.2–005.

for saying that mere delay, however lengthy, destroys the contractual right"[369]; and that the mere failure to prosecute a claim regarded by both parties as hopeless did not amount to a promise to abandon it.[370] The only circumstances in which "silence and inaction" can have this effect are the exceptional ones (discussed elsewhere in this book)[371] in which the law imposes a duty to disclose facts or to clarify a legal relationship and the party under the duty fails to perform it.[372]

3–083 **Reliance upon the representation.** The requirement of reliance means that the promise or representation must in some way have influenced the conduct of the party to whom it was made. Although the promise need not form the sole inducement,[373] it must (it is submitted) be *some* inducement. Hence the requirement would not be satisfied if it could be shown that the other party's conduct was not influenced by the promise at all,[374] so that he was not in any way prejudiced by it.[375] But if this is a matter of "mere speculation",[376] or if the promise or representation "was one of the factors ... relied upon",[377] it would form a sufficient inducement. In other words, where the promisee has, after the promise, conducted himself in the way intended by the promisor, it will be up to the promisor to establish that the conduct was not induced by the promise.[378]

3–084 **Detrimental reliance?** There is sometimes said to be a further requirement, namely that the promisee must have suffered some "detriment" in reliance on the promise.[379] This may mean that the promisee must have done something which he was not previously bound to do and as a result have suffered loss, e.g. by incurring expenditure in reliance on the promise. The alleged requirement of

---

369 *Amherst v James Walker Goldsmith & Silversmith Ltd* [1983] Ch. 305 at 315; cf. in another context, *The Nai Genova* [1984] 1 Lloyd's Rep. 353 at 365.

370 *Collin v Duke of Westminster* [1985] Q.B. 581.

371 See para.9–157 and following, para.2–048; *Petrotrade Inc v Stinnes Handel GmbH* [1995] 1 Lloyd's Rep. 142 at 151, where the statement that there may be a representation by "conduct (including silence)" refers to the exceptional situations described in the text above; cf. *MIOM 1 Ltd v Sea Echo ENE (No.2)* [2011] EWHC 2715 (Admlty); [2012] 1 Lloyd's Rep. 140; *Costain Ltd v Tarmac Holdings Ltd* [2017] EWHC 319 (TCC); [2017] 1 Lloyd's Rep. 331 at [102].

372 cf. *ING Bank NV v Ros Roca SA* [2011] EWCA Civ 353; [2012] 1 W.L.R. 472 in which the comments of Rix LJ that there may be a "duty to speak" should be seen in the context of what was, if anything, an estoppel by convention, notwithstanding his preference for viewing it as promissory estoppel: para.3–095.

373 cf. para.9–032.

374 See *Raiffeisen Hauptgenossenschaft v Louis Dreyfus & Co* [1981] 1 Lloyd's Rep. 345 at 352; *The Scaptrade* [1983] Q.B. 529 at 536; affirmed [1983] 2 A.C. 694, without reference to this point; *Lark v Outhwaite* [1991] 2 Lloyd's Rep. 132 at 142; *The Nerarno* [1996] 1 Lloyd's Rep. 1. In *Kim v Chasewood Park Residents Ltd* [2013] EWCA Civ 239; [2013] H.L.R. 24 the promisee was found to have relied on "a different promise from the one which was in fact made" (at [38]–[39]).

375 *Ets Soules & Cie v International Trade Development Co Ltd* [1980] 1 Lloyd's Rep. 129; *The Multibank Holsatia* [1988] 2 Lloyd's Rep. 486 at 493.

376 *Brikom Investments Ltd v Carr* [1979] Q.B. 467 at 482.

377 *Brikom Investments Ltd v Carr* [1979] Q.B. 467 at 490 (Cumming-Bruce LJ, whose decision was based on the different ground discussed at para.3–065); cf. *Steria Ltd v Hutchinson* [2006] EWCA Civ 1551; [2007] I.C.R. 445 at [117] ("a significant factor").

378 cf. the similar rule in cases of "proprietary estoppel" stated at para.3–135.

379 e.g. *Fontana NV v Mautner* (1979) 254 E.G. 199; *Meng Long Development Pte Ltd v Jip Hong Trading Co Pte Ltd* [1985] A.C. 511 at 524; cf. Wilson 67 L.Q.R. 344.

"detriment" in this sense is based on the analogy of estoppel by representation.[380] But that analogy is (as we shall see)[381] inexact; and promissory estoppel can clearly operate even though there is no "detriment" in this sense.[382] It is enough if the promisee has altered his position in reliance on the promise so that it would be inequitable to allow the promisor to act inconsistently with it.[383] Thus the requirement can be satisfied if the promisee has forborne from taking steps to safeguard his legal position (as in *Hughes v Metropolitan Ry*[384] itself); or if he has performed or made efforts to perform the original obligation as altered by the promise (e.g. where a seller who has been promised extra time for delivery continues to make efforts to perform after the originally agreed delivery date has gone by).

**Inequitable to go back on the representation.** It must be "inequitable" for the promisor to go back on the promise. This requirement cannot be defined with anything approaching precision, but the underlying idea is that the promisee must have acted in reliance on the promise in one of the ways just described, so that he can no longer be restored to the position in which he was before he took such action.[385] If the promisee can be restored to that position, it will not be inequitable for the promisor to go back on the promise.[386] In one case[387] the promisor re-asserted his strict legal rights only two days after the promise had been made. It was held that this was not "inequitable", since the promisee had not, in this short period, suffered any prejudice: he could be, and was, restored to exactly the position in which he had been before the promise was made. Sometimes, moreover, extraneous circumstances will justify the promisor in going back on the promise without notice. In *Williams v Stern*[388] the claimant gave the defendant a bill of sale of furniture as security for a loan; the bill entitled the defendant to seize the furniture if the claimant defaulted in paying instalments due under it. When the fourteenth instalment became due, the claimant asked for extra time, and the defendant said that he "would not look to a week". Three days later he seized the furniture because he had heard that the claimant's landlord intended to distrain it for arrears of rent. It was held that the defendant's seizure was justified. There was no consideration for his promise to give time, nor did *Hughes v Metropolitan Ry*[389] apply. Brett LJ said: 3–085

[380] See para.9–190; *Carr v L & NW Ry* (1875) L.R. 10 C.P. 310 at 317.
[381] See para.3–090.
[382] *WJ Alan & Co Ltd v El Nasr Export & Import Co* [1972] 2 Q.B. 189 at 213.
[383] *The Post Chaser* [1981] 2 Lloyd's Rep. 695 at 701; *The Superhulls Cover Case (No.2)* [1990] 2 Lloyd's Rep. 431 at 454; *Steria Ltd v Hutchinson* [2006] EWCA Civ 1551; [2007] I.C.R. 445 at [73], but contrast [95]; *Virulite LLC v Virulite Distribution Ltd* [2014] EWHC 366 (QB) at [121]; cf. *Seechurn v Ace Insurance SA* [2002] EWCA Civ 67; [2002] 2 Lloyd's Rep. 390 at [25], leaving open the question whether further "detriment" is required.
[384] (1877) 2 App. Cas. 439; para.3–077.
[385] *Maharaj v Chand* [1986] A.C. 898; *The Bunga Saga Lima* [2005] EWHC 244; [2005] 2 Lloyd's Rep. 1 at [31].
[386] See, e.g. *Kim v Chasewood Park Residents Ltd* [2013] EWCA Civ 239; [2013] H.L.R. 24 at [42], though this was not regarded as essential to the outcome on the facts of the case (at [45]).
[387] *The Post Chaser* [1981] 2 Lloyd's Rep. 693; cf. *Bremer Handelsgesellschaft mbH v Bunge Corp* [1983] 1 Lloyd's Rep. 476 at 484.
[388] (1879) 5 Q.B.D. 409.
[389] (1877) 2 App. Cas. 439; para.3–077.

> "Has there been any misconduct on the part of the defendant? I think not: it appears that a distress by the (claimant's) landlord was threatened; and under those circumstances I do not blame the defendant for changing his mind."[390]

His conduct was not "inequitable". It may not be inequitable for the promisor to go back on the promise if it was obtained by the unjustifiable conduct of the promisee.[391]

3–086 **Effect generally suspensory.** The equitable doctrine of promissory estoppel, like the common law doctrine of waiver,[392] does not extinguish, but only suspends, rights. In *Hughes v Metropolitan Ry* the landlord was not forever prevented from enforcing the covenant: he could have enforced it on giving reasonable notice requiring the tenant to do the repairs.[393] This aspect of promissory estoppel was stressed in *Tool Metal Manufacturing Co Ltd v Tungsten Electric Co Ltd,*[394] where a licence for the use of a patent provided that the licensees should pay "compensation" if they manufactured more than a stated number of articles incorporating the patent. In 1942 the owners of the patent agreed to suspend the obligation to pay "compensation" until a new agreement was made. They later gave notice to end the suspension. It was held that they were once again entitled to the payments after the expiry of a reasonable time from the giving of notice. The reason for this rule is that, in equity, the effect of the representation is to give the court a discretion to do what is equitable in all the circumstances;[395] and in the cases just discussed it would not be equitable (or in accordance with the intention of the parties) wholly to extinguish the representor's (or promisor's) rights. In *Hughes v Metropolitan Ry* the representation was in the nature of an "open-ended forbearance"; where the representation has defined the duration of its application,[396] it has been said to be "less than self-evident that it is equitable to revoke the representation part-way through its defined duration".[397] Thus, where the promisor represented that a payment which was due under the contract did not need to be made until the approval of a third party had been obtained and there had been substantial reliance on that representation by the promisee, it was inequitable of the promisor to insist on payment before approval was obtained.[398]

---

[390] *Williams v Stern* (1879) 5 Q.B.D. 409 at 413; cf. also *Southwark LBC v Logan* (1996) 8 Admin. L.R. 315.

[391] *South Caribbean Trading Ltd v Trafigura Beheer BV* [2004] EWHC 2676; [2005] 1 Lloyd's Rep. 128. See also, *D & C Builders v Rees* [1966] 2 Q.B. 617 at 626; *Tonkin v UK Insurance Ltd* [2006] EWHC 1120 (TCC); 107 Con L.R. 107 at [206].

[392] i.e. in the sense of forbearance, para.3–069.

[393] No reference to this point was made in *Smith v Lawson* (1998) 75 P. & C.R. 446 (para.3–089), probably because no attempt was made by the promisor to give notice of any intention to resume his strict legal rights.

[394] [1955] 1 W.L.R. 761; cf. *Banning v Wright* [1972] 1 W.L.R. 972 at 981; *The Post Chaser* [1981] 2 Lloyd's Rep. 695 at 701; *The Kanchenjunga* [1990] 1 Lloyd's Rep 391 at 399; *Hazel v Akhtar* [2001] EWCA Civ 1883; [2002] P. & C.R. 17 at [43].

[395] *Roebuck v Mungovin* [1994] 2 A.C. 224 at 235.

[396] As in *Central London Property Trust Ltd v High Trees House Ltd* [1947] K.B. 130; para.3–114.

[397] *Virulite LLC v Virulite Distribution Ltd* [2014] EWHC 366 (QB); [2015] 1 All E.R. (Comm) 204 at [141].

[398] *Virulite LLC v Virulite Distribution Ltd* [2014] EWHC 366 (QB); [2015] 1 All E.R. (Comm) 204.

**Extinctive effect brought about by subsequent events.** Subsequent events may, in exceptional circumstances, give promissory estoppel an extinctive effect. They can, most obviously, lead to this result where they make it impossible for the promisee to perform his original obligation. In *Birmingham & District Land Co v L & NW Ry*[399] a building lease bound the tenant to build by 1885. The lessor agreed to suspend this obligation; but in 1886, while the suspension was still in force, the land was compulsorily acquired by a railway company, so that performance of the tenant's obligation became impossible. The tenant recovered statutory compensation from the railway company on the footing that the building lease was still binding; but clearly his obligation to build was wholly extinguished. Even where performance of the original obligation has not become literally impossible, promissory estoppel may sometimes have an extinctive effect. For example, in *Ogilvy v Hope-Davies*[400] a vendor of land indicated on August 15 that he would not insist on the contractual completion date of 30 August. It was held that no question of reinstating the contractual completion date could arise "because the time was far too short".[401] Promissory estoppel has an extinctive effect in such cases because subsequent events, or the passage of time, though not making performance of the original obligation impossible, have made it highly inequitable to require such performance even after reasonable notice.[402] 3–087

**"Promissory estoppel" creates no new rights.** Promissory estoppel prevents the enforcement of existing rights, but it does not create entirely new rights or extend the scope of existing ones. This was decided in *Combe v Combe*,[403] where a husband during divorce proceedings promised to pay £100 per annum to his wife who, in reliance on this promise, forbore from applying to the court for maintenance. This forbearance did not constitute consideration for the husband's promise.[404] It was held that promissory estoppel did not entitle the wife to recover the promised payments; nor is there any support in English cases for the view that it could create a cause of action in the narrower sense of "limiting recovery to reliance loss".[405] 3–088

The view that the equitable doctrine gave rise to no new rights came to be associated with its description as a kind of estoppel and hence with the rule, established in relation to another kind of estoppel (known as "estoppel by

---

[399] (1888) 40 Ch D. 268. cf. *Durham Fancy Goods Ltd v Michael Jackson (Fancy Goods) Ltd* [1968] 2 Q.B. 839.

[400] [1976] 1 All E.R. 683; *The Ion* [1980] 2 Lloyd's Rep. 245; *Voest Alpine Intertrading GmbH v Chevron International Oil Co* [1987] 2 Lloyd's Rep. 547 at 560.

[401] *Ogilvy v Hope-Davies* [1976] 1 All E.R. 683 at 696.

[402] See *Maharaj v Chand* [1986] A.C. 898; cf. *WJ Alan & Co Ltd v El Nasr Export & Import Co* [1972] Q.B. 189 (where the actual decision was that there was a variation supported by consideration: para.3–063); *The Bunga Saga Lima* [2005] EWHC 244 (Comm); [2005] 2 Lloyd's Rep. 1 at [31].

[403] [1951] 2 K.B. 215. The point had been foreshadowed in *Central London Property Trust Ltd v High Trees House Ltd* [1947] K.B. 130 at 134.

[404] See para.3–042.

[405] *Baird Textile Holdings Ltd v Marks & Spencer Plc* [2001] EWCA Civ 274; [2002] 1 All E.R. (Comm) 737 at [99]; for the difficulty of distinguishing in that case between reliance and expectation loss, see [2002] 1 All E.R. (Comm) 737 at [81], [82]; for the distinctn general, see below, paras 20–024–20–031.

representation"),[406] that "you cannot found a cause of action on an estoppel".[407] It will be submitted below[408] that the analogy between the two kinds of estoppel is (to say the least) imperfect and that it does not satisfactorily account for the rule that "promissory estoppel" gives rise to no new rights. The more plausible explanation for this restriction on the scope of the equitable doctrine is that the restriction is needed to prevent promissory estoppel from coming into collision with the rules which lay down the requirements for the creation of a binding contract. The significant point in the present context is that the restriction preserves consistency between promissory estoppel and the rule that a promise is not binding as a contract unless it is supported by consideration or made in a deed.[409] *Combe v Combe* has likewise been relied on in support of the view that promissory estoppel could not give rise to a cause of action on a promise which lacked contractual force for want, not of consideration, but of certainty and contractual intention.[410]

The view that promissory estoppel does not create new causes of action seems to have been doubted[411] or ignored[412] by dicta in later cases; but the promises in these cases created new rights on the orthodox ground that they were supported by consideration.[413] *Combe v Combe* therefore still stands as the leading English[414] authority for the proposition that promissory estoppel creates no new rights and this proposition has been reaffirmed in a number of later cases.[415]

It appears to follow from this proposition that promissory estoppel would not enable employees in a case like *Stilk v Myrick*[416] to recover the extra pay which they had been promised. It could, indeed, be argued[417] that in such a case the cause of action was the original contract of employment and that the subsequent

---

406 See para.9–190.

407 *Low v Bouverie* [1891] 3 Ch. 82 at 101; cf. at 105; para.9–190.

408 See para.3–090.

409 This appears to be the point that Denning LJ had in mind in *Combe v Combe* [1951] 2 K.B. 215 at 219 when he said that he did not want the equitable principle to be "stretched too far lest it be endangered"; cf. *Brikom Investments Ltd v Carr* [1979] Q.B. 467 at 486; *Tool Metal Manufacturing Co Ltd v Tungsten Electric Co Ltd* [1955] 1 W.L.R. 761 at 764; contrast *Vaughan v Vaughan* [1953] Q.B. 762 at 768; Denning 15 M.L.R. 1.

410 *Baird Textile Holdings Ltd v Marks & Spencer Plc* [2001] EWCA Civ 274; [2002] 1 All E.R. (Comm) 737 where *Combe v Combe* is cited at [34], and [87] in support of the view stated in the text above; though an alternative explanation for the result in the *Baird* case may be that, in the absence of certainty or contractual intention, the requirements for the operation of the equitable doctrine are simply not satisfied (para.3–081), so that no question can arise as to its effects.

411 *Re Wyvern Developments Ltd* [1974] 1 W.L.R. 1097 at 1104–1105; Atiyah 38 M.L.R. 65 and see Allan 79 L.Q.R. 238. The point was left open in *The Henrik Sif* [1982] 1 Lloyd's Rep. 456 at 466–468 (as to which see fn.337).

412 *Evenden v Guildford City FC* [1975] Q.B. 917 at 924, 926; Napier [1976] C.L.J. 38; and see next note.

413 e.g. *Secretary of State for Employment v Globe Elastic Thread Co Ltd* [1980] A.C. 506; overruling *Evenden v Guildford City FC* [1975] Q.B. 917. Lord Wilberforce remarked at 518 that "To convert this [contract] into an estoppel is to turn the doctrine of promissory estoppel … upside down."

414 For other jurisdictions, see para.3–093.

415 *Argy Trading Development Co Ltd v Lapid Developments Ltd* [1977] 1 W.L.R. 444 at 457; *The Proodos C* [1980] 2 Lloyd's Rep. 390 at 394; *Brikom Investments Ltd v Seaford* [1981] 1 W.L.R. 863; cf. *Taylor Fashions Ltd v Liverpool Victoria Trustees Co Ltd* [1982] Q.B. 133 at 152; *Baird Textile Holdings Ltd v Marks & Spencer Plc* [2001] EWCA Civ 274; [2002] 1 All E.R. (Comm) 737.

416 (1809) 2 Camp. 317; 6 Esp. 129; para.3–048.

417 See *Hiscox v Outhwaite (No.3)* [1991] 2 Lloyd's Rep. 524 at 535.

agreement fell within the principle stated by Denning LJ in *Combe v Combe* that consideration was not necessary for the "modification or discharge"[418] of a contract where the conditions required for the operation of the equitable doctrine were otherwise satisfied. This argument may derive some judicial support from a dictum that promissory estoppel "may enlarge the effect of an agreement";[419] for this could mean that a promise of extra pay on facts such as those of *Stilk v Myrick* could create a cause of action even though it was not supported by consideration. This view is, however, hard to reconcile with the treatment of *Stilk v Myrick* in *Williams v Roffey Bros*[420] and with the fact that the decision in the latter case was based, not on estoppel,[421] but on the ground that the promise of extra pay there was supported by consideration. It is submitted that, when in *Combe v Combe* Denning LJ used the phrase "modification or discharge" he had in mind a modification which *reduced* a party's obligations.[422] To apply it to a case in which it had the effect of *increasing* them necessarily amounts to giving the other party a new cause of action on a promise for which he has not provided any consideration; and *Combe v Combe* decides that this is not the effect of the equitable doctrine here under discussion.[423] A cause of action on a promise unsupported by consideration could, however, arise under other equitable doctrines, e.g. under the doctrine of "proprietary estoppel" to be discussed later in this chapter.[424]

**"Shield" and not a "sword".** The essentially defensive nature of promissory estoppel is sometimes expressed by saying that it operates as a shield and not as a sword.[425] In other words, its normal effect is merely to protect the promisee against enforcement of the original obligation. But the metaphor is apt to mislead,[426] for promissory estoppel can assist a claimant no less than a defendant. For example, a creditor may threaten to seize property on which a debt is secured, after having indicated that he would not insist on punctual payment. In such a case the debtor will, if the requirements of promissory estoppel are satisfied, be able to restrain the creditor's threatened seizure by injunction.[427] **3–089**

Promissory estoppel can also assist the promisee as claimant in that it may prevent the promisor from relying on a defence[428] which would, but for the

[418] *Combe v Combe* [1951] 2 K.B. 215 at 219.

[419] *Baird Textile Holdings Ltd v Marks & Spencer Plc* [2001] EWCA Civ 274; [2002] 1 All E.R. (Comm) 737 at [88].

[420] [1991] 1 Q.B. 1; para.3–050.

[421] Though there are references to estoppel in the *Williams* case [1991] 1 Q.B. 1 at 13 ("not yet fully developed") and 17–18.

[422] As in *Central London Property Trust Ltd v High Trees House Ltd* [1947] K.B. 130; para.3–114, this being the case under discussion in *Combe v Combe* [1951] 2 K.B. 215 at 219.

[423] *The Proodos C* [1980] 2 Lloyd's Rep. 390.

[424] See para.3–120 and following, especially para.3–151.

[425] *Combe v Combe* [1951] 2 K.B. 215 at 224; *Lark v Outhwaite* [1991] 2 Lloyd's Rep. 132 at 142.

[426] *Azov Shipping Co v Baltic Shipping Co* [1999] 2 Lloyd's Rep. 159 at 175 ("largely inaccurate"); *Baird Textile Holdings Ltd v Marks & Spencer Plc* [2001] EWCA Civ 274; [2001] 1 All E.R. (Comm) 737 at [52] ("misleading aphorism").

[427] Such a claim would have succeeded in *Williams v Stern* (1879) 5 Q.B.D. 409 (para.3–085), if the creditor's conduct had been "inequitable."

[428] Promissory estoppel may also, somewhat paradoxically, deprive a promisee of a defence: *Smith v Lawson* (1998) 75 P. & C.R. 466.

promise, have been available to him, e.g. the defence that a claim which the promisee has made against him is time-barred,[429] or that the claim has been satisfied.[430] In such cases, the doctrine will, once again, enable the promisee to win an action which, but for the doctrine, he would have lost. But the promisee's cause of action will have arisen independently of the promise which brought the equitable doctrine into operation: the effect of the doctrine is merely to prevent the promisor from relying on some circumstance which would, if the promise had not been made, *have destroyed the promisee's original cause of action*. This situation must be distinguished from that in which the promisor's "defence" is that (apart from the promise) the promisee's alleged *cause of action never existed at all*. It is submitted that promissory estoppel should not prevent the promisor from relying on a "defence" of this kind. If promissory estoppel were allowed to operate in this way, it would give the promisee a new cause of action based on the promise, even though the promise was not supported by consideration; and such a result would be inconsistent with the essentially defensive nature of the doctrine.[431]

3–090 **Analogy with estoppel by representation.** Promissory estoppel has certain features in common with the doctrine of estoppel by representation.[432] Each is based on a representation followed by reliance on the part of the representee, and each is defensive in nature in that neither is capable in itself of giving rise to new rights. But there are also important differences between them. These differences are reflected in the statement of Millett LJ that the attempt to demonstrate that all estoppel are "governed by the same principle[433] [has] never won general acceptance".[434]

The various kinds of estoppel discussed in this chapter[435] are linked only by the broadest of general principles: that a person's taking of inconsistent positions is in some situations to be discouraged by law; in this sense it can be said that "unconscionability … provides the link between them".[436] But they nevertheless have "separate requirements and different terrains of application"[437] and therefore

[429] See *The Ion* [1980] 2 Lloyd's Rep. 245; *Hazel v Akhtar* [2002] EWCA Civ 1883; *The Times*, 7 January 2002 at [25]. *Commonwealth of Australia v Verwayen* (1990) 170 C.L.R. 394 (discussed by Spence 107 L.Q.R. 221) can be explained on this ground: see *Baird Textile Holdings Ltd v Marks & Spencer Plc* [2001] EWCA Civ 274; [2001] 1 All E.R. (Comm) 737 at [98].

[430] cf. para.9–190.

[431] cf. the criticism (para.3–079) of *The Henrik Sif* [1982] 1 Lloyd's Rep. 456.

[432] See para.9–190.

[433] The reference seems to be to Lord Denning MR's statement in *Amalgamated Investment & Property Co Ltd v Texas Commerce International Bank Ltd* [1982] 2 Q.B. 73 at 122 ("one general principle shorn of limitations") which is cited with apparent approval by Lord Bingham in *Johnson v Gore Wood & Co* [2002] 2 A.C. 1 at 33.

[434] *First National Bank Plc v Thompson* [1996] Ch. 231 at 236; cf. *The Indian Endurance (No.2)* [1998] A.C. 878 at 913.

[435] i.e. estoppel by representation (see also para.9–190), promissory estoppel (discussed here), estoppel by convention (paras 3–094 and following) and proprietary estoppel (para.3–120 and following).

[436] *Johnson v Gore Wood & Co* [2002] 2 A.C. 1 at 41.

[437] *The Indian Endurance (No.2)* [1998] A.C. 878 at 914; cf. *Donegal International Ltd v Zambia* [2007] EWHC 197 (Comm); [2007] 1 Lloyd's Rep. 397 at [495].

"cannot be accommodated within a single formula".[438] An important difference between the two types of estoppel at this stage under discussion relates to the nature of the representations required to bring them into operation. A representation of *intention* or a *promise* suffices for the purpose of promissory estoppel.[439] Estoppel by representation, on the other hand, cannot be based on a representation of intention, but only on one of *existing fact*.[440] There are, moreover, other significant differences between the two doctrines. Promissory estoppel may operate even though there is no such "detriment" as is required to bring the doctrine of estoppel by representation into play.[441] And the effect of promissory estoppel is only to suspend rights,[442] while estoppel by representation, where it operates, has a permanent effect. There is, finally, a difference in the legal nature of the two doctrines. Estoppel by representation prevents a party from establishing *facts*: i.e. from alleging that the facts represented by him are untrue, even where that is actually the case.[443] Promissory estoppel, by contrast, has nothing to do with proof of facts; it is concerned with the *legal effects* of a promise. There was, for example, no dispute about facts in *Hughes v Metropolitan Ry*:[444] the issue was not whether the repairs had been done or whether the landlord had promised or represented that he would not forfeit the lease; it was simply whether he was (to some extent, at least) bound by that promise.

**Analogy with waiver.** The characteristics just described indicate that promissory estoppel is not truly analogous with estoppel by representation. As Denning J (a leading proponent of the modern equitable doctrine) has pointed out, the authorities which support it "although they are said to be cases of estoppel, are not really such".[445] Promissory estoppel has closer affinities with the common law rules of waiver in the sense of forbearance:[446] both are based on promises, or representations of intention; both are suspensive (rather than extinctive) in effect and both are concerned with the legal effects of promises rather than with proof **3–091**

[438] *Johnson v Gore Wood & Co* [2002] 2 A.C. 1 at 41; cf. *Prime Sight Ltd v Lavarello* [2013] UKPC 22; [2014] 2 W.L.R. 84 at [30]. See also, *Steria Ltd v Hutchinson* [2006] EWCA Civ 1551; [2007] I.C.R. 445 at [92] (Neuberger LJ).

[439] e.g. *Woodhouse AC Israel Cocoa Ltd v Nigerian Produce Marketing Co Ltd* [1972] A.C. 741 at 758; *The Post Chaser* [1981] 2 Lloyd's Rep. 695 at 700; *The Kanchenjunga* [1990] 1 Lloyd's Rep. 391 at 398; *Roebuck v Mungovin* [1994] 2 A.C. 224 at 235.

[440] *Jorden v Money* (1854) 5 H.L.C. 185 (Jackson 81 L.Q.R. 84; Halliwell 5 L.S. 15); *Argy Trading Development Co Ltd v Lapid Development Ltd* [1977] 1 W.L.R. 444 at 450; *TCB Ltd v Gray* [1986] Ch. 621 at 634; affirmed [1987] Ch. 458; *Roebuck v Mungovin* [1994] 2 A.C. 224 at 235. "Fact" is used here in contradistinction to a promise of future conduct; in *Steria Ltd v Hutchinson* [2006] EWCA Civ 1551; [2007] I.C.R. 445 at [89] Neuberger LJ thought it "realistic" not to suggest that a claim would fail if the representation was one of law: see further para.3–096

[441] See para.3–084.

[442] See para.3–086.

[443] This point accounts for the rule that estoppel by representation does not give rise to a cause of action. The rule that promissory estoppel does not give rise to a cause of action is based on different grounds explained at para.3–088.

[444] (1877) 2 App. Cas. 439; para.3–077; similarly, in *Central London Property Trust Ltd v High Trees House Ltd* [1947] K.B. 130 (para.3–114).

[445] *Central London Property Trust Ltd v High Trees House Ltd* [1947] K.B. 130 at 134; para.3–114.

[446] *Woodhouse AC Israel Cocoa Ltd v Nigerian Produce Marketing Co Ltd* [1972] A.C. 741 at 762.

of disputed facts. The main difference between them is that the equitable doctrine avoids the difficulties encountered at common law in distinguishing between a variation and a forbearance.[447] In later cases "waiver" and "promissory estoppel" (or the rule in *Hughes v Metropolitan Ry*) are treated as substantially similar doctrines.[448] The two expressions have been judicially described as "two ways of saying exactly the same thing";[449] and, although the use of terminology has not been wholly consistent,[450] the courts often use the two expressions interchangeably when discussing situations in which it is alleged that one party has indicated that he will not enforce his strict legal rights against the other.

3–092 **Distinguished from promises supported by consideration.** Under promissory estoppel, certain limited effects are given to a promise without consideration. But it is nevertheless in the interests of the promisee to show, if he can, that he did provide consideration so that the promise amounted to a contractually binding variation. Such proof will free him from the many rules that restrict the scope of the equitable doctrine: he need not then show that he has "relied" on the promise, or that it would be "inequitable" for the other party to go back on it; the variation will permanently affect the rights of the promisor and not merely suspend them (unless it is expressed so as to have only a temporary effect); and a contractual variation can not only reduce or extinguish existing rights, but also create new ones. Where parties agree to modify an existing contract, the equitable doctrine of promissory estoppel (and its common law counterpart of waiver) may have reduced, but they have by no means eliminated the practical importance of the doctrine of consideration.

3–093 **Other jurisdictions.** The English view that the doctrine of promissory estoppel gives rise to no cause of action has not been followed in other common law jurisdictions. In the US, a similar doctrine has long been regarded as being capable of creating new rights, though both the existence and the content of the resulting rights are matters for the discretion of the courts.[451] A line of Australian cases likewise supports the view that promises or representations which, for want of consideration or of contractual intention, lack contractual force, may nevertheless be enforceable as if they were binding contracts.

The leading Australian case is *Waltons Stores (Interstate) Ltd v Maher*,[452] where A, a prospective lessor of business premises, did demolition and building work on the premises while the agreement for the lease lacked contractual force

[447] See paras 3–072–3–075.

[448] *Finagrain SA Geneva v P Kruse Hamburg* [1976] 2 Lloyd's Rep. 508 at 534; *Brikom Investments Ltd v Carr* [1979] Q.B. 467 at 488, 489, 490; *BICC Ltd v Burndy Corp* [1985] Ch. 232 at 253; *The Chemical Venture* [1993] 1 Lloyd's Rep. 509 at 521.

[449] *Prosper Homes v Hambro's Bank Executor & Trustee Co* (1979) 39 P. & C.R. 395 at 401; *The Nerarno* [1996] 1 Lloyd's Rep. 1 at 6.

[450] For suggestions that "waiver" may be distinguishable from the equitable doctrine, see *WJ Alan & Co Ltd v El Nasr Export Co* [1972] 2 Q.B. 189 at 212; *The Ion* [1980] 2 Lloyd's Rep. 245 at 249–250; *Brikom Investments Ltd v Carr* [1979] Q.B. 467 at 485, 489 (perhaps because there the "waiver" amounted to a variation supported by consideration).

[451] Restatement, Contracts §90 and Restatement 2d, Contracts §90.

[452] (1988) 164 C.L.R. 387; Duthie 104 L.Q.R. 362; Sutton 1 J.C.L. 205.

because it was still subject to contract;[453] he had done so to meet the prospective lessee's (B's) requirements and on the assumption, of which B must have known, that a binding contract would come into existence. B withdrew from the agreement (relying on his solicitor's advice that he was not bound by it); and it was held that he was estopped from denying that a contract had come into existence and that the agreement for the lease was therefore specifically enforceable against him.[454] The reasoning of the High Court is complex, but the basis of the decision appears to be that B had knowingly induced A to believe that a binding contract would come into existence by exchange of contracts[455] and to act in reasonable reliance on that belief.

In English law, such reliance is, in appropriate circumstances, capable of giving rise to a variety of remedies, even where the promise or representation which induces it lacks contractual force. Sometimes the remedy may be the enforcement of the promise according to its terms, as in cases of proprietary estoppel (to be discussed later in this chapter);[456] sometimes it may be an award of the reasonable value of work done in the belief that a contract had, or would, come into existence.[457] Neither of these remedies would have been available in the *Waltons Stores* case since proprietary estoppel does not arise where work is done on the promisee's (rather than on the promisor's) land[458] and a claim for the reasonable value of the claimant's work is not available where he is aware of the fact that no binding agreement has come into existence and so takes the risk that the negotiations may fail.[459] Even where the second of these objections can be overcome (e.g. on the ground that the work was done at the request of the promisor or as a result of his assurance that an exchange of contracts would take place) it does not follow that the appropriate remedy is enforcement of the contract in its terms: if the basis of the Australian doctrine is reliance induced by the promisor, compensation for reliance loss would appear to be the more appropriate remedy.[460] The Australian doctrine also gives rise to the difficulty that there appears to be no clear limits to its scope and this lack of clarity is a source of uncertainty. The doctrine is, moreover, hard to reconcile with a number of fundamental principles of English law, such as the non-enforceability of informal gratuitous promises (even if relied on)[461] and the rule that there is no

---

[453] See para.2–090.

[454] The remedy awarded was damages in lieu of specific performance.

[455] For this requirement, see para.4–011.

[456] e.g. in *Dillwyn v Llewelyn* (1862) 4 D.F. & G. 517; para.3–132.

[457] e.g. in *William Lacey (Hounslow) Ltd v Davis* [1957] 1 W.L.R. 932; *Countrywide Communications Ltd v ICL Pathway Ltd* [2000] C.L.C. 325; *Cobbe v Yeoman's Row Management Ltd* [2008] UKHL 55; [2008] 1 W.L.R. 1752; cf. para.22–031.

[458] See para.3–130.

[459] *Regalian Properties Plc v London Dockland Development Corp* [1995] 1 W.L.R. 212; quaere whether this is still the case after the decision of the House of Lords in *Cobbe v Yeoman's Row Management Ltd* [2008] UKHL 55; [2008] 1 W.L.R. 1752; para.3–129.

[460] In *Waltons Stores* the enforcement of the contract is explained as the minimum equity needed to protect the claimant's reliance, whereas only consideration can guarantee such enforcement; cf. *Commonwealth of Australia v Verwayen* (1990) 179 C.L.R. 394 at 501: "Often the only way to prevent the promisee suffering detriment will be to enforce the promise". But in *Giumelli v Giumelli* (1999) 196 C.L.R. 101 the High Court of Australia expressly rejected the argument that relief should be limited to the reversal of the detriment suffered by the claimant.

[461] See para.3–003.

right to damages for a wholly innocent non-contractual misrepresentation.[462] While on the facts of some of the cases in which the Australian doctrine has been applied the same conclusions would probably be reached in English law on other grounds,[463] the broad doctrine remains, in the present context, inconsistent with the view that the English doctrine of promissory estoppel does not give rise to a cause of action in the sense of entitling the promisee to enforce a promise in its terms, even though it was unsupported by consideration. It is true that other forms of estoppel, such as proprietary estoppel, may produce this result; but the scope of that doctrine is limited in many important ways.[464]

3–094 **Estoppel by convention.** Estoppel by convention may arise where both parties to a transaction "act on an assumed state of facts or law,[465] the assumption being either shared by both or made by one and acquiesced in by the other".[466] The parties are then precluded from denying the truth of that assumption, if it would be unjust or unconscionable to allow them (or one of them) to go back on it.[467] This is perhaps most likely to be the case where the party alleging estoppel has relied on the common assumption to his detriment, but this not an "exhaustive requirement"; it is enough that the party in question has been "materially influenced".[468] The passage of time on its own is unlikely to give rise to the requirement of unconscionability.[469]

Such an estoppel differs from estoppel by representation and from promissory estoppel in that it does not depend on any "clear and unequivocal" *representation* or *promise* by the party alleged to be estopped.[470] It can arise where the assumption was based on a mistake spontaneously made by the party relying on it,[471] and acquiesced in by the other party. Acquiescence may be established by silence in circumstances where there is a duty to speak.[472] Such a duty may arise where "a reasonable man would expect the person against whom the estoppel is raised, acting honestly and responsibly, to bring the true facts to the attention of the other party known by him to be under a mistake as to their respective rights

---

462 e.g. *Oscar Chess Ltd v Williams* [1957] 1 W.L.R. 370; para.9–089.

463 See, e.g. *Commonwealth of Australia v Verwayen* (1990) 179 C.L.R. 394, which could be explained in English law on the ground stated in fn.429.

464 e.g. by the requirements that the promisee must believe that legal rights have been, or will be, created in his favour, and that these are rights in or over the promisor's land: see para.3–130.

465 See para.3–096.

466 *The Indian Endurance (No.2)* [1998] A.C. 878 at 913; for qualification of this formulation, see *The Vistafjord* [1988] 2 Lloyd's Rep. 343 at 351; and see *Shearson Lehman Hutton Inc v Maclaine Watson & Co Ltd* [1989] 2 Lloyd's Rep. 570 at 596; *ING Bank NV v Ros Roca SA* [2011] EWCA Civ 353; [2012] 1 W.L.R. 472 at [61]–[65].

467 *The Vistafjord* [1988] 2 Lloyd's Rep. 343 at 352; *Hiscox v Outhwaite* [1992] 1 A.C. 562; affirmed on other grounds [1992] 1 A.C. 562 at 585; *The Indian Endurance (No.2)* [1998] A.C. 878 at 913.

468 *Amalgamated Investment & Property Co Ltd v Texas Commerce International Bank Ltd* [1982] Q.B. 84 at 104; *Mears Ltd v Shoreline Housing Partnership Ltd* [2015] EWHC 1396 (TCC); 160 Con L.R. 157 at [49]; *Stevensdrake Ltd v Hunt* [2017] EWCA 1173; [2017] B.C.C. 611 at [125].

469 *First National Trustco (UK) Ltd v Page* [2019] EWHC 1187 (Ch) at [125].

470 *Troop v Gibson* (1986) 277 E.G. 1134; *Baird Textile Holdings Ltd v Marks & Spencer Plc* [2001] EWCA Civ 274; [2002] 1 All E.R. (Comm) 737 at [84].

471 The relevant "mistake" may be as to whether there is agreement on the assumed matter: *Starbev GP Ltd v Interbrew Central European Holdings BV* [2014] EWHC 1311 (Comm) at [138].

472 *The Lutetian* [1982] 2 Lloyd's Rep. 140 at 158. "Mere silence" will not suffice: *HIH Casualty & General Insurance Ltd v Axa Corporate Solutions* [2002] EWCA Civ 1253 at [32].

and obligations".[473] However it may arise, the common assumption of the parties, objectively assessed,[474] must itself be "unambiguous and unequivocal".[475]

**The need for a shared assumption.** Because it requires both parties to have conducted themselves on the basis of a shared assumption, it is not enough for estoppel by convention that "each of two parties acts on an assumption not communicated to the other",[476] or for there to be a mere "coincidence of view".[477] The necessary communication or manifestation of assent which has "crossed the line"[478] may be effected by the conduct of one party, known to the other,[479] and may be effected via a third party,[480] provided it is sufficient for the court to conclude that the party to be estopped "may properly be said to have assumed some element of responsibility for" the common assumption.[481] This is largely a question of fact.[482] 3–095

No estoppel by convention arose where each party spontaneously made a different mistake and there was no subsequent conduct by the party alleged to be estopped from which any acquiescence in the other party's mistaken assumption could be inferred.[483] Nor can a party (A) invoke such an estoppel to prevent the other (B) from denying facts alleged to have been agreed between A and B if A has later withdrawn from that agreement; for in the light of A's withdrawal it is no longer unjust to allow B to rely on the true state of affairs.[484] And the necessary shared assumption cannot be implied from the conduct of the parties if that is ruled out by the terms of the contract, e.g. there is no room to argue that estoppel by convention prevents the parties from disputing the validity of sums paid under invoice where the contract expressly states that such payment is not binding. That would only be possible if the party alleging estoppel by convention was also able

---

[473] *The Lutetian* [1982] 2 Lloyd's Rep. 140 at 157; *ING Bank NV v Ros Roca SA* [2011] EWCA Civ 353; [2012] 1 W.L.R. 472 at [93]–[94]. On what it means to be "acting honestly" for these purposes, see the somewhat circular definition of Blair J in *Starbev GP Ltd v Interbrew Central European Holdings BV* [2014] EWHC 1311 (Comm) at [133].

[474] *ING Bank NV v Ros Roca SA* [2011] EWCA Civ 353; [2012] 1 W.L.R. 472 at [84].

[475] *Smithkline Beecham Plc v Apotex Europe Ltd* [2006] EWCA Civ 658; [2007] Ch. 71 at [102]; cf. *Commercial Union Assurance Plc v Sun Alliance Assurance Group Plc* [1992] 1 Lloyd's Rep. 475 at 481. Contrast *ING Bank NV v Ros Roca SA* [2011] EWCA Civ 353; [2012] 1 W.L.R. 472 at [64] where this requirement is doubted.

[476] *The Captain Gregos (No.2)* [1990] 2 Lloyd's Rep. 395 at 405, following *The August P Leonhardt* [1985] 2 Lloyd's Rep. 28 at 35; *Hiscox v Outhwaite (No.3)* [1991] 2 Lloyd's Rep. 524 at 533; *The Indian Endurance (No.2)* [1998] A.C. 878 at 913.

[477] *Blindley Heath Investments Ltd v Bass* [2015] EWCA Civ 1023; [2017] Ch. 389 at [92].

[478] *Blindley Heath Investments Ltd v Bass* [2015] EWCA Civ 1023; [2017] Ch. 389 at [93].

[479] As in *The Vistafjord* [1988] 2 Lloyd's Rep. 343 at 351.

[480] *WS Tankship II BV v Kwangju Bank Ltd* [2011] EWHC 3013 (Comm); [2012] C.I.L.L. 3155 at [183].

[481] *Revenue & Customs Commissioners v Benchdollar* [2009] EWHC 1310 (Ch); [2010] 1 All E.R. 174.

[482] *Blindley Heath Investments Ltd v Bass* [2015] EWCA Civ 1023; [2017] Ch 389 at [93].

[483] *The August P Leonhardt* [1985] 2 Lloyd's Rep. 28.

[484] *Gloyne v Richardson* [2001] EWCA Civ 716; [2001] 2 B.C.L.C. 669 at [41]; cf. *Zvi Construction Co LLC v Notre Dame University (USA) in England* [2016] EWHC 1924 (TCC); [2016] B.L.R. 604 at [64].

to argue that the contractual term in question had been validly modified, or the other party was estopped from relying on it under promissory estoppel.[485]

3–096 **Assumptions of law?** It is often said that the assumption giving rise to an estoppel by convention can be one of "fact or law".[486] The point of reference to "law" in this formulation appears to be to include within the scope of the doctrine assumptions about the interpretation of a contract;[487] for, since the interpretation of a contract is often said to be a matter of "law",[488] all such assumptions would be excluded from the scope of the doctrine (and its scope be unduly narrowed) if it did not include at least an assumption of this kind. The question whether estoppel by convention could be based on assumptions of "law" in a wider sense was the subject of conflicting views in *Johnson v Gore-Wood & Co.*[489] In that case a company had brought a claim for professional negligence against a firm of solicitors who were told that a further claim based on the same negligence would be made against them by the company's managing director. The company's claim was settled on terms which limited some of the director's personal claims against the solicitor and when the director later brought other claims against the solicitors, it was held that this was not an abuse of process. Lord Bingham based this conclusion in part on estoppel by convention: in his view, the terms of the settlement were based on the common assumption that it would not be an abuse of process for the director to pursue the claims which he had in fact brought; and it would be unfair to allow the solicitors to go back on this assumption. All the members of the House of Lords agreed with Lord Bingham's conclusion that there was no abuse of process; but Lord Goff was "reluctant to proceed on estoppel by convention"[490] as the common assumption was in his view one of law, a type of assumption which in his view did not give rise to this form of estoppel.

Support for the view that estoppel by convention can be based on a common assumption of law is admittedly based only on dicta;[491] but it is arguable that those dicta gain support from cases concerned with mistakes (and possibly misrepresentations) of law. In these fields, the distinction between matters of "law" and of "fact" proved hard to draw and appears to have been rejected.[492] On the other hand, the extension of estoppel by convention to *all* common assumptions of "law" could undermine the security of commercial transactions

---

485 *HSM Offshore BV v Aker Offshore Partner Ltd* [2017] EWHC 2979 (TCC); 175 Con L.R. 155.

486 *Amalgamated Investment & Property Co Ltd v Texas Commerce International Bank Ltd* [1982] Q.B. 84 at 122, 126; *The Vistafjord* [1988] 2 Lloyd's Rep. 343 at 351; *Shearson Lehman Hutton Inc v Maclaine Watson & Co Ltd* [1989] 2 Lloyd's Rep. 570 at 596; *The Indian Endurance (No.2)* [1988] A.C. 878 at 913.

487 Such an assumption could also be called one of "private right" and hence of fact: *André & Cie SA v Ets Michel Blanc & Fils* [1979] 2 Lloyd's Rep. 427 at 431, 432.

488 *Carmichael v National Power Plc* [1999] 1 W.L.R. 2042 at 2049.

489 [2002] 2 A.C. 1.

490 *Johnson v Gore-Wood & Co* [2002] 2 A.C. 1 at 40.

491 See fn.486.

492 Certainly, in the case of mistake (see para.8–023), and possibly, in the case of misrepresentation (see para.9–020). In *Steria Ltd v Hutchinson* [2006] EWCA Civ 1551; [2007] I.C.R. 445 at [89], in the context of estoppel by representation, Neuberger LJ thought it "realistic" not to suggest that a claim would fail if the representation was one of law.

by allowing a party to resist enforcement merely on account of an assumption as to the *legal effect* of a contract, the terms or meaning of which were not in dispute; and this is a type of assumption which, on the authorities, does not give rise to such an estoppel.[493]

**Invalidity of assumed term.** A party is not liable on the basis of estoppel by convention where the alleged agreement would, if concluded, have been ineffective for want of contractual intention[494] (where necessary[495]), or on account of a formal defect[496] (other than a minor one[497]), or where the term in respect of which such an estoppel is alleged to operate would, if actually incorporated in the contract, have been invalid.[498] Nor does such an estoppel prevent a party from relying on the true legal effect (as opposed to the meaning[499]) of an admitted contract merely because the parties have entered into it under a mistaken view as to that effect.[500] **3–097**

**Estoppel by convention in practice.**[501] Estoppel by convention was discussed in *Amalgamated Investment & Property Co Ltd v Texas Commerce International Bank Ltd*,[502] where A had negotiated with the X Bank for a loan to B (one of A's subsidiaries). It was agreed that the loan was to be secured by a mortgage and also by a guarantee from A. In the guarantee, A promised the X Bank, in consideration of the Bank's giving credit to B, to "pay you … all moneys … due … *to you*" from B. This was an inappropriate form of words since the loan to B was made, not directly by the X Bank, but by one of its subsidiaries, the Y Bank, with money provided by the X Bank: hence, if the guarantee were read literally, it would not apply to the loan since no money was due from B to the X Bank. The Court of Appeal, however, took the view that this literal interpretation would defeat the intention of the parties, and held that the guarantee applied to the loan made by the Y Bank.[503] But even if the guarantee did not, on its true construction, produce this result, A was estopped from denying that the guarantee covered the **3–098**

[493] See para.3–097.
[494] *Orion Insurance Plc v Sphere Drake Insurance* [1992] 1 Lloyd's Rep. 239.
[495] *Revenue & Customs Commissioners v Benchdollar* [2009] EWHC 1310 (Ch); [2010] 1 All E.R. 174 at [52] (estoppel arising out of non-contractual dealings).
[496] *Yaxley v Gotts* [2000] Ch. 162 at 182. See para.5–012.
[497] cf. *Shah v Shah* [2001] EWCA Civ 527; [2002] Q.B. 35 at [31] (deed signed but not in presence of attesting witness); contrast at [28] (deed not signed at all). The case was one of estoppel by representation.
[498] See *Keen v Holland* [1984] 1 W.L.R. 251; *Godden v Merthyr Tydfil Housing Association* (1997) 74 P. & C.R. D1; contrast *The Amazonia* [1990] 1 Lloyd's Rep. 238 (illegality under foreign law).
[499] See para.3–096.
[500] *Keen v Holland* [1984] 1 W.L.R. 251; cf. *The Nile Rhapsody* [1992] 2 Lloyd's Rep. 399 at 408; affirmed on another ground [1994] 1 Lloyd's Rep. 382.
[501] Estoppel by convention is often concerned with post-contractual "assumptions", but it may also be applied to pre-contractual "assumptions": *Chartbrook Ltd v Persimmon Homes Ltd* [2009] UKHL 38; [2009] A.C. 1101 at [46]. This is most likely to arise where the submission is that a particular clause or expression has an agreed or mutually understood meaning and, in that situation, it may also be possible to invoked the doctrine of rectification (see para.8–063): *Dubai Islamic Bank PJSC v PSI Energy Holding Co BSC* [2011] EWHC 2718 (Comm) at [72].
[502] [1982] Q.B. 84.
[503] cf. on the issue of interpretation, *TCB Ltd v Gray* [1987] Ch. 458; *Bank of Scotland v Wright* [1990] B.C.C. 663.

loan by the Y Bank, since, when negotiating the loan, A and the X Bank had assumed that the guarantee did cover it; and since the X Bank continued subsequently to act on that assumption[504] in granting various indulgences to A in respect of the loan to B and of another loan made directly by the X Bank to A. It made no difference that the assumption was not induced by any representation made by A but originated in the X Bank's own mistake: the estoppel was not one by representation but by convention.[505]

3–099 **Effect of estoppel by convention.** The effect of this form of estoppel is to preclude a party from denying the agreed or common assumption of fact or as to the meaning of a document[506] or (at least to the extent suggested above)[507] of law. One such assumption may be that a particular promise has been made.[508] Thus it is possible to describe the result in the *Amalgamated Investment & Property* case by saying that A was estopped from denying that it had promised the X Bank to repay any sum left unpaid by B to the Y Bank. But, although estoppel by convention may thus take effect in relation to a promise, it is quite different in its legal nature from promissory estoppel. In cases of promissory estoppel, the promisor or representor is not estopped from denying that the promise or representation *has been made*: on the contrary, this must be proved to establish that kind of estoppel, which is concerned with the *legal effects* of a promise that has been shown to exist. Where, on the other hand, the requirements of estoppel by convention are satisfied, then this type of estoppel operates to prevent a party from denying that the assumed promise *has been made*, or that a promise contains the assumed term: it does not specify the *legal effects* of the assumed promise or term. In the *Amalgamated Investment & Property* case, once A was estopped from denying the *existence* of the promise described above, no question arose as to its legal *validity*. There could be no doubt that that promise was supported by consideration:[509] this was provided by the X Bank in making funds available to the Y Bank to enable it to make a loan to B, and in inducing the Y Bank to make that loan. Where the assumed promise is one that would, if actually made, have been unsupported by consideration, both types of estoppel can, however, operate in the same case: estoppel by convention to establish the existence of the promise, and promissory estoppel to determine its legal effect.[510]

3–100 **Whether estoppel by convention can create new rights.** We have seen that promissory estoppel does not "create new causes of action where none existed

---

[504] Contrast *Crédit Suisse v Borough Council of Allerdale* [1996] 2 Lloyd's Rep. 315 at 367, where this requirement was not satisfied as the conduct of the party alleged to be estopped had not "influenced the mind" of the other party; affirmed on other grounds [1997] Q.B. 362.

[505] cf. *The Leila* [1985] 2 Lloyd's Rep. 172; *The Vistafjord* [1988] 2 Lloyd's Rep. 343.

[506] *Amalgamated Investment & Property Co Ltd (In Liquidation) v Texas Commerce International Bank Ltd* [1982] Q.B. 84 at 126, 130.

[507] See para.3–096.

[508] Such an assumption is one of fact (and not as to the future). For the effect of an entire agreement clause, see para.4-009.

[509] This was also true in *The Vistafjord* [1988] 2 Lloyd's Rep. 343; cf. *Mears Ltd v Shoreline Housing Partnership Ltd* [2013] EWCA Civ 639; 148 Con L.R. 221 at [23]; *Rivertrade Ltd v EMG Finance Ltd* [2015] EWCA Civ 1295; [2016] 2 B.C.L.C. 226.

[510] e.g. (apparently) *Troop v Gibson* (1986) 277 E.G. 1134.

before";[511] and the same principle applies to estoppel by representation.[512] Estoppel by convention resembles estoppel by representation in that it can prevent a party from denying existing *facts*, and one would therefore expect estoppel by convention to operate only where its effect was defensive in substance. The question whether estoppel by convention is so limited was discussed in the *Amalgamated Investment & Property* case where Lord Denning MR expressed the principle in such a way as to enable it to give rise to a cause of action:[513] but he was alone in stating the principle so broadly.[514] In *The Vistafjord*[515] the estoppel operated defensively and, while this factor was not stressed in the judgments, there is no suggestion in them that in this respect estoppel by convention differs from estoppel by representation. It is indeed possible for estoppel by convention (as it is for promissory estoppel[516] and estoppel by representation) to deprive the defendant of a *defence* and so to enable the claimant to win an action which otherwise he would have lost:[517] but even in such cases the estoppel does not create the cause of action, for the *facts giving rise to* the cause of action exist independently of the estoppel.[518] Further, as we have seen when discussing the *Amalgamated Investment & Property* case,[519] where an agreement is supported by consideration the effect of estoppel by convention may be to "enlarge the effect" of that agreement by "binding the parties to an interpretation which would not otherwise be correct".[520] The cause of action in such a case is not *founded* on the estoppel, but without being able to *rely* on the estoppel it "would necessarily have failed".[521] No other authority squarely supports the view that estoppel by convention can, of itself, create a new cause of action; and the present position seems to be that it cannot, any more than promissory estoppel or estoppel by representation, produce this effect.[522]

---

[511] *Combe v Combe* [1951] 2 K.B. 215 at 219; para.3–088.

[512] See para.3–090; para.9–190.

[513] *Amalgamated Investment & Property Co Ltd (In Liquidation) v Texas Commerce International Bank Ltd* [1982] Q.B. 84 at 122. A similar view may be hinted at in *Williams v Roffey Bros & Nicholls (Contractors) Ltd* [1991] 1 Q.B. 1 at 17–18.

[514] *Keen v Holland* [1984] 1 W.L.R. 251 at 261–262.

[515] [1988] 2 Lloyd's Rep. 343.

[516] See para.3–089.

[517] e.g. *The Amazonia* [1990] 1 Lloyd's Rep. 238; *Revenue & Customs Commissioners v Benchdollar* [2009] EWHC 1310 (Ch); [2010] 1 All E.R. 174. Semble this is subject to the limitation discussed with regard to promissory estoppel at para.3–088.

[518] cf. *Cheverny Consulting Ltd v Whitehead Mann Ltd* [2007] EWHC 3130 (Ch) at [108]; *Johnson v Gore Wood & Co* [2002] 2 A.C. 1 (para.3–096) where the cause of action was based on negligence but the estoppel helped to dispose of the defendants' objection that the action to enforce that claim was an abuse of process.

[519] See para.3–099, especially text to fn.509.

[520] *De Tchihatchef v Salerni Coupling Ltd* [1932] 1 Ch. 330; *Amalgamated Investment and Property Co Ltd v Texas Commerce International Bank Ltd* [1982] 1 Q.B. 84 at 106; *Rivertrade Ltd v EMG Finance Ltd* [2015] EWCA Civ 1295; [2016] 2 B.C.L.C. 226 at [48]; *Chen v Ng* [2017] UKPC 27 at [33].

[521] *Amalgamated Investment & Property Co Ltd (In Liquidation) v Texas Commerce International Bank Ltd* [1982] Q.B. 84 at 131–132.

[522] *Baird Textile Holdings Ltd v Marks & Spencer Plc* [2001] EWCA Civ 274; [2002] 1 All E.R. (Comm) 73; *White v Riverside Housing Association Ltd* [2005] EWCA Civ 1385; [2006] H.L.R. 15 (though this limit on the estoppel was noted with "regret" by Sir Peter Gibson and Auld LJ); *Smithkline Beecham Plc v Apotex Europe Ltd* [2006] EWCA Civ 658; [2007] Ch. 71 at [112];

3–101 **Whether estoppel by convention can operate prospectively.** It has been said that once the common assumption which forms the basis of estoppel by convention is revealed to be erroneous the estoppel "will not apply to future dealings".[523] The parties are, however, entitled to a reasonable time to react to the discovery of the true state of affairs.[524] What constitutes a reasonable time will be determined by the need to avoid the unconscionable consequences which is the basis of the estoppel itself. Further, where the common assumption is made prior to the contract and it is entered into on that basis, the estoppel will operate throughout the period of the contract.[525] The "fundamental principle" is that the estoppel will be effective, and remain effective, where it would be unjust or unconscionable to allow one party to resile from the assumption.[526]

## (d) Part payment of a debt

### (i) *General rule*

3–102 **Part payment of a debt is no consideration.** The general rule of common law is that a creditor is not bound by an undertaking to accept part payment in full settlement of a debt. An accrued debt can be discharged only by "accord and satisfaction".[527] A promise by the debtor to pay part of the debt provides no consideration for the accord, as it is merely a promise to perform part of an existing duty owed to the creditor. And the actual part payment is no satisfaction under the rule in *Pinnel's Case* that "Payment of a lesser sum on the day in satisfaction of a greater sum cannot be any satisfaction for the whole."[528] This rule was approved by the House of Lords in *Foakes v Beer*.[529] Mrs Beer had obtained a judgment against Dr Foakes for £2,090 19s. Sixteen months later Dr Foakes asked for time to pay. Thereupon the parties entered into a written agreement[530] under which Mrs Beer undertook not to take "any proceedings whatsoever" on the judgment, in consideration of an immediate payment by Dr Foakes of £500 and on condition[531] of his paying specified instalments "until the whole of the said sum of £2,090 19s. shall have been paid and satisfied". Some

*Transgrain Shipping BV v Deiulemar Shipping SpA* [2014] EWHC 4202 (Comm); [2015] 1 Lloyd's Rep. 461 at [39]; Contrast dicta in *Thornton Springer v NEM Insurance Co Ltd* [2000] 2 All E.R. 489 at 516–518.

[523] *Hiscox v Outhwaite* [1992] A.C. 562 at 575 (Lord Donaldson MR); affirmed *Hiscox v Outhwaite* [1992] A.C. 562 at 585 on other grounds; *Phillip Collins Ltd v Davis* [2000] 3 All E.R. 808 at 823.

[524] *Hillingdon LBC v ARC Ltd* [2000] EWCA Civ 191; [2001] C.P. Rep 33 at [64]; *Revenue & Customs Commissioners v Benchdollar* [2009] EWHC 1310 (Ch); [2010] 1 All E.R. 174.

[525] *The Vistafjord* [1988] 2 Lloyd's Rep. 343; *Centrica Plc v Premier Power Ltd* [2006] EWHC 3068 (Comm) at [136].

[526] *Troop v Gibson* [1986] EGLR 1; *Centrica Plc v Premier Power Ltd* [2006] EWHC 3068 (Comm) at [137]; *Sainsbury's Supermarkets Ltd v Bristol Rovers (1883) Ltd* [2016] EWCA Civ 160 at [92].

[527] See para.3–059.

[528] *Pinnel's Case* (1602) 5 Co Rep. 117a; *McManus v Bark* (1870) L.R. 5 Ex. 65; *Underwood v Underwood* [1894] P. 204; *Tilney Engineering v Admos Knitting Machinery* [1987] 2 C.L. 21; *Re Broderick* (1986) 6 N.I.J.B. 36.

[529] (1884) 9 App. Cas. 605; Dixon, *Jesting Pilate* (William S. Hein & Co, 1996), pp.159–165.

[530] Drawn up by Dr Foakes' solicitor: (1884) 9 App. Cas. 625.

[531] Dr Foakes made no promise to pay the instalments.

five years later, when Dr Foakes had paid £2,090 19s., Mrs Beer claimed £360 for interest on the judgment debt. The House of Lords upheld her claim, and the actual decision does not appear to be unjust; for it seems that Mrs Beer intended only to give Dr Foakes time to pay, and not to forgive interest.[532]

**Criticism.** The rule in *Pinnel's Case* may sometimes have served the useful purpose of protecting a creditor against a debtor who had too ruthlessly exploited the tactical advantage of being a potential defendant in litigation.[533] For example, in *D & C Builders Ltd v Rees*[534] the claimants had done building work for the defendant and had presented an account of which some £482 was outstanding. Six months after payment had first been demanded, the defendant's wife (acting on his behalf) offered the claimants £300 in full settlement. They accepted this offer as they were in desperate straits financially; and there was some evidence that the defendant's wife knew this.[535] It was held that the claimants were entitled to the balance; and a majority[536] of the Court of Appeal based their decision on the rule in *Pinnel's Case*. On the other hand, it is arguable that the function of protecting the creditor in such a situation is now satisfactorily performed by the expanding concept of economic duress,[537] while the rule in *Pinnel's Case* is open to two main objections. 3–103

First, it applies to all agreements to accept part payment of debts in full settlement, even though some such agreements are perfectly fair and reasonable transactions.[538] Secondly, as Lord Blackburn said in *Foakes v Beer*, part payment is often in fact more beneficial to the creditor than strict insistence on his full legal rights.[539] A factual benefit[540] of a similar kind has been accepted as sufficient consideration for a promise to make an extra payment for the performance of an existing contractual duty owed by the promisee to the promisor;[541] and the law would be more consistent, as well as more satisfactory in its practical operation, if it adopted the same approach to cases of part payment of a debt. Agreements of the kind here under discussion would then be binding unless they had been made under duress. But the rule in *Foakes v Beer* is open to challenge only in the Supreme Court,[542] which makes it a little unfortunate that

[532] Lords Fitzgerald and Watson thought that the agreement did not, on its true construction, cover interest. Lords Selborne and Blackburn sympathised with this view but felt unable to adopt it as the operative part of the document was too "clear" to be controlled by the recitals.

[533] As Dr Foakes appears to have done. Kelly 27 M.L.R. 540 argues that there is consideration in giving up this advantage, as there is in the compromise of a disputed claim. This may be so, but a compromise is only binding if there is a bona fide dispute as to liability (para.3–036) and there was no such dispute in *Foakes v Beer*.

[534] [1966] 2 Q.B. 617; Chorley 29 M.L.R. 165; Cornish 29 M.L.R. 428.

[535] *D&C Builders v Rees* [1966] 2 Q.B. 617 at 622.

[536] Lord Denning MR based his decision on a different ground: see para.3–119.

[537] cf. para.3–050 and para.10–007.

[538] e.g. on the facts of *Central London Property Trust Ltd v High Trees House Ltd* [1947] K.B. 130; para.3–114.

[539] *Foakes v Beer* (1884) 9 App. Cas. 605 at 617–620.

[540] See para.3–006.

[541] *Williams v Roffey Bros & Nicholls (Contractors) Ltd* [1991] 1 Q.B. 1; para.3–050.

[542] *Re Selectmove Ltd* [1995] 1 W.L.R. 474; Peel 110 L.Q.R. 353; *Collier v P & MJ Wright (Holdings ) Ltd* [2007] EWCA Civ 1329; [2008] 1 W.L.R. 643; *Birmingham CC v Forde* [2009] EWHC 12 (QB); [2009] 1 W.L.R. 2732 at [89].

the opportunity for re-examination was declined in *Rock Advertising Ltd v MWB Business Exchange Centres Ltd*, particularly as the rule was described as "probably ripe" for such re-examination.[543] In the meantime, its operation is mitigated by limitations on its scope at common law and by evasions of it in equity.

### (ii) Common law limitations

3–104 **Disputed claims.** The general rule does not apply where the creditor's claim (or its amount) is disputed in good faith.[544] In such cases, the value of the claim is doubtful and the debtor accordingly provides consideration by paying something, even though it is less than the amount claimed. It makes no difference that the amount paid is small in relation to the amount claimed, or that the creditor has a good chance of succeeding on the claim; for the law will not generally investigate the adequacy of consideration.[545] Where the defendant admits liability for less than the amount claimed, payment of the smaller sum is no consideration for the claimant's promise to accept that payment in full settlement of the larger claim. The rule in *Foakes v Beer* applies since, once a binding admission has been made to pay the smaller sum, the payment of it amounts to no more than the performance of what, at that stage, is legally due from the defendant.[546]

3–105 **Unliquidated claims.** The general rule applies only if the original claim is also a "liquidated" one, i.e. a claim for a fixed sum of money, such as one for money lent or for the agreed price of goods[547] or services. It does not apply to "unliquidated" claims[548] such as claims for damages or for a reasonable remuneration (where none is fixed by the contract). In such cases, the claim is of uncertain value; and even if the overwhelming probability is that it is worth more than the sum paid, the possibility that it may be worth less suffices to satisfy the requirement of consideration. An originally unliquidated claim may later become liquidated by act of the parties. For example, in *D & C Builders v Rees*[549] it does not seem that the contract fixed the price of the work to be done by the claimants.

---

543 *Rock Advertising Ltd v MWB Business Exchange Centres Ltd* [2018] UKSC 24; [2019] A.C. 119 at [18]. The opportunity was declined on the basis that, the appeal having been allowed on other grounds (see para.4-016), any decision would only have been obiter dictum and any re-examination was better undertaken by an enlarged panel of the Court.

544 *Cooper v Parker* (1885) 15 C.B. 822; *Re Warren* (1884) 53 L.J. Ch. 1016; *Anangel Atlas Compania Naviera SA v Ishikawajima Harima Heavy Industries Co Ltd (No.2)* [1990] 2 Lloyd's Rep. 526 at 544; for other consideration in this case, see [1990] 2 Lloyd's Rep. 526 at 545; and para.3–108; *Huyton SA v Peter Cremer GmbH* [1999] 1 Lloyd's Rep. 620 at 629.

545 See para.3–013. But the fact that the sum received is much smaller than that claimed may be evidence that the recipient has not accepted it in full settlement: *Rustenburg Platinum Mines Ltd v Pan Am* [1979] 1 Lloyd's Rep. 19.

546 *Ferguson v Davies* [1997] 1 All E.R. 315 (Henry LJ); Evans LJ's judgment is based on the ground that, as a matter of construction, the claimant had not accepted the smaller sum in full settlement. Aldous LJ agreed with both the other judgments.

547 A claim may be "liquidated" even though it is disputed and even though the dispute relates to its amount, e.g. where it is for the price of goods and the buyer alleges short delivery: *The New Vanguard* [1994] 1 W.L.R. 1634.

548 *Wilkinson v Byers* (1834) 1 A. & E. 106; *Ibberson v Neck* (1886) 2 T.L.R. 427.

549 [1966] 2 Q.B. 617; para.3–103.

When they presented their account they had only an unliquidated claim (for a reasonable remuneration); and if at this stage they had accepted £300 in full settlement they would not have been protected by the rule in *Foakes v Beer*. That rule only became applicable because the defendant had, by retaining the account without protest, impliedly agreed that it correctly stated the sum due, and so turned the claim into a liquidated one.

**Partly liquidated claims.** A creditor may have two claims against the same debtor, one of them liquidated and the other unliquidated; or a single claim which is partly liquidated and partly unliquidated. A promise by the creditor to release the *whole* claim will not be binding if the debtor pays no more than the liquidated amount and if his liability to pay this amount is undisputed. For example, in *Arrale v Costain Civil Engineering Ltd*[550] an employee was injured at work. Legislation in force at the place of work gave him an undisputed right against the employers to a fixed lump sum of £490 and it was assumed that he also had a common law right to sue the employers in tort for unliquidated damages.[551] It was held that any promise[552] which he might have made not to pursue the common law claim was not made binding by the employers' payment of the £490. They had not provided any consideration for such a promise since, in making that payment, they merely did what they were already bound to do.[553] 3–106

**Variations in debtor's performance.** Consideration for a creditor's promise to accept part payment in full settlement can be provided by the debtor's doing an act that he was not previously bound by the contract to do.[554] For example, payment of a smaller sum at the creditor's request before the due day is good consideration for a promise to forego the balance, since it is a benefit to the creditor to receive (and a corresponding detriment to the debtor to make) such early payment.[555] Similarly, where payment of a smaller sum is made at the creditor's request at a place different from that originally fixed for payment,[556] or in a different currency.[557] Again, payment of a smaller sum accompanied at the creditor's request by the delivery of a chattel is good consideration for a promise to forego the balance: "The gift of a horse, hawk or robe, etc., in satisfaction is good. For it shall be intended that a horse, hawk or robe, etc., might be more beneficial than the money …".[558] 3–107

**Other benefit to creditor.** We have seen that a promise to pay a supplier of services more than the agreed sum for performing his part of the contract can be 3–108

[550] [1976] 1 Lloyd's Rep. 98; cf. *Rustenburg Platinum Mines Ltd v Pan Am* [1979] 1 Lloyd's Rep. 19 at 24.
[551] cf. para.6–068.
[552] Lord Denning MR and Stephenson LJ took the view that no such promise had been made.
[553] Stephenson and Geoffrey Lane LJJ. Lord Denning MR based his decision on a different ground: para.3–119.
[554] e.g. *Re William Porter & Co* [1937] 2 All E.R. 361: *Ledingham v Bermejo Estancia Co Ltd* [1947] 2 All E.R. 748.
[555] *Pinnel's Case* (1602) 5 Co. Rep. 117a.
[556] *Pinnel's Case* (1602) 5 Co. Rep. 117a.
[557] cf. para.3–063.
[558] *Pinnel's Case* (1602) 5 Co. Rep. 117a.

supported by consideration in the form of a benefit in fact obtained by the other party as a result of his obtaining the promised performance.[559] Conversely, a promise by the supplier to accept less than the agreed sum may be supported by a similar consideration. The mere receipt of the smaller sum cannot, indeed, constitute the consideration: that possibility is precluded by *Foakes v Beer*.[560] But the provision of some additional benefit beyond payment of the smaller sum may satisfy the requirement of consideration. This possibility is illustrated by the *Anangel Atlas* case,[561] where a shipbuilder's promise to reduce the price which the buyers had agreed to pay was held to have been supported by consideration, and one way in which the buyers had provided consideration was by accepting delivery on the day fixed for such acceptance. Even if the buyers were already bound to take delivery on that day, they had conferred a benefit on the shipbuilder by so doing since they were "core customers"[562] and their refusal to take delivery might have led other actual or potential customers to cancel (or not to place) orders.

A similar argument succeeded in the Court of Appeal in *MWB Business Exchange Centres Ltd v Rock Advertising Ltd*, where the licensor of premises had agreed to defer the payment of arrears by the licensee. This was said to confer a "practical benefit" which "went beyond the advantage of receiving a prompt payment of a part of the arrears and a promise that it would be paid the balance".[563] The additional practical benefit was the continuing occupation of the licensee and the avoidance of an empty property which it was said "may have significant commercial consequences" for the licensor.[564] Since the licensor had exercised its right to lock the licensee out of the premises under the terms of the license, this finding of additional practical benefit is perhaps open to doubt. In the Supreme Court, where it was not necessary to decide the issue of consideration because the appeal was allowed on another ground, Lord Sumption referred to arguable but "somewhat forced" arguments to distinguish *Foakes v Beer*.[565]

3–109 **Forbearance to enforce cross-claim.** The debtor may have a cross-claim against the creditor; and forbearance to enforce such a claim can constitute consideration for the creditor's promise to accept part payment in full settlement. For example, where a landlord promises to accept part payment of rent in full settlement, the

[559] *Williams v Roffey Bros & Nicholls (Contractors) Ltd* [1991] 1 Q.B. 1; para.3–050.

[560] (1884) 9 App. Cas. 605; para.3–102; *Collier v P & MJ Wright (Holdings) Ltd* [2007] EWCA Civ 1329; [2008] 1 W.L.R. 643.

[561] *Anangel Atlas Compania Naviera SA v Ishikawajima-Harima Heavy Industries Co Ltd (No.2)* [1990] 2 Lloyd's Rep. 526. For other consideration in that case, in the form of reducing "a previously ill-defined understanding" to "precise terms," and so settling a potential dispute, see [1990] 2 Lloyd's Rep. 526 at 544.

[562] *Anangel Atlas Compania Naviera SA v Ishikawajima-Harima Heavy Industries Co Ltd (No.2)* [1990] 2 Lloyd's Rep. 526 at 544.

[563] *MWB Business Exchange Centres Ltd v Rock Advertising Ltd* [2016] EWCA Civ 553; [2017] Q.B. 604 at [48] (appeal allowed on another ground: [2018] UKSC 24; [2019] A.C. 119).

[564] *MWB Business Exchange Centres Ltd v Rock Advertising Ltd* [2016] EWCA Civ 553; [2017] Q.B. 604 at [72].

[565] *Rock Advertising Ltd v MWB Business Exchange Centres Ltd* [2018] UKSC 24; [2019] A.C. 119 at [18]; see para.4-016.

tenant may provide consideration for this promise by forbearing to sue the landlord for breach of the latter's obligation to keep the premises in repair.[566]

**Part payment by third party.** Part payment by a third party, if accepted by the creditor in full settlement of the debtor's liability,[567] is a good defence to a later action by the creditor against the debtor for the balance.[568] It is generally agreed that this rule does not depend on any contract between debtor and creditor, so that it can apply even though no promise was made to the debtor and no consideration moved from him. The rule has therefore been explained on other grounds. One such ground is that it would be a fraud on the third party to allow the creditor to sue the debtor for the balance of the debt.[569] The difficulty with this reasoning is that the mere breach of a promise does not usually amount to fraud at common law; it only has this effect if the promisor had no intention of performing the promise when he made it.[570] A second reason for the rule is that the court will not help the creditor to break his contract with the third party by allowing him to recover the balance of the debt from the debtor. On the contrary, it has been held that where A (the creditor) contracts with B (the third party) not to sue C (the debtor), and A nevertheless does sue C, B can intervene so as to obtain a stay of the action.[571] A third explanation is suggested by *Hirachand Punamchand v Temple*,[572] where the defendant was indebted to the claimant on a promissory note. The claimant accepted a smaller sum from the defendant's father in full settlement. It was held that he could not later sue the defendant for the balance of the debt, because the promissory note was extinct: the position was the same as if the note had been cancelled.[573] This reasoning again does not depend on any contract between the claimant and the defendant, for the cancellation of a promissory note can release a person liable on it irrespective of contract and without consideration.[574] Under the Contracts (Rights of Third Parties) Act 1999, the debtor may also, if the requirements of the Act are satisfied,[575] be able to take the benefit of any term in the contract between the creditor and the person making the payment which may exclude the debtor's liability for the balance; and he will be able to do so without having to show that he provided any consideration for the creditor's promise to accept the part payment in full settlement.[576] 3–110

**Composition agreements.** A debtor who cannot pay all his creditors in full may be able to induce them to agree with himself and each other to accept a dividend 3–111

---

566 *Brikom Investments Ltd v Carr* [1979] Q.B. 467; as explained para.3–065.
567 See para.17–007 for this requirement.
568 *Welby v Drake* (1825) 1 C. & P. 557; *Cook v Lister* (1863) 13 C.B. (N.S.) 543 at 595.
569 See the authorities cited in fn.568.
570 See para.9–017.
571 *Snelling v John G Snelling Ltd* [1973] 1 Q.B. 87; distinguishing *Gore v Van der Lann* [1967] 2 Q.B. 31, where no promise was made not to sue C; cf. *South West Trains Ltd v Wightman*, *The Times*, 14 January 1998.
572 [1911] 2 K.B. 330.
573 At 336; cf. in the case of joint debts, the reasoning of *Johnson v Davies* [1999] Ch. 117 at 130.
574 See para.3–061.
575 See para.14–099 and following.
576 See para.3–026 and para.14–109. For the purposes of the Act, it is the debtor who is the "third party".

in full settlement of their claims.[577] A creditor who has accepted a dividend under such an agreement cannot sue the debtor for the balance of his original demand.[578] If the debtor fails to pay the agreed dividend, the original debt revives.[579]

One reason why such composition agreements are binding is again said to be that a creditor who sued for the balance of his debt would commit a fraud on the others.[580] On this view it is unnecessary to look for any consideration moving from the debtor. Alternatively, there is consideration for the creditors' promise to forgo the balance since each creditor benefits from the arrangement: he is certain to get some payment, while in the scramble for priority which would take place if there were no composition agreement he might get nothing at all.[581]

3–112 **Collateral contract.** An agreement to accept part payment of a debt in full settlement may take effect as a collateral contract if the requirements of contractual intention and consideration are satisfied. This was the position in *Brikom Investments Ltd v Carr*[582] where a tenant's liability to contribute to the maintenance costs of a block of flats was held to have been reduced by a collateral contract under which the landlord undertook to execute certain roof repairs at his own expense.[583] The landlord's claim for contribution in this case was probably unliquidated; but the principle seems to be equally applicable where a creditor enters into a collateral contract to accept part payment in full settlement of a liquidated claim.

### (iii) *Equitable evasion*

3–113 The common law limitations can (with one exception[584]) be explained on the ground that there was, in the situations covered by them, some consideration for the creditor's promise to accept the part payment in full settlement. They assume the continued existence of the general, if often inconvenient, rule that, in the absence of such consideration, the creditor's promise was not binding. Equity has gone further in attempting to evade that rule even where there was no consideration for the creditor's promise.

3–114 **Promissory estoppel.** Under the equitable doctrine recognised in *Hughes v Metropolitan Ry*[585] a promise by a contracting party not to enforce his legal rights has (even where it is not supported by consideration) at least a limited effect in

---

577 Insolvency Act 1986 Pts I and VIII.

578 *Good v Cheesman* (1831) 2 B. & Ad. 328; *Boyd v Hind* (1857) 1 H. & N. 938; the bare agreement to pay a dividend may operate as satisfaction, if the parties so intend: *Bradley v Gregory* (1810) 2 Camp. 383.

579 *Evans v Powis* (1847) 1 Ex. 601.

580 *Wood v Roberts* (1818) 2 Stark. 417; *Cook v Lister* (1863) 13 C.B.(N.S.) 543 at 595.

581 *Good v Cheesman* (1831) 2 B. & Ad. 328 at 334; *Garrard v Woolner* (1832) 8 Bing. 258 at 265.

582 [1979] Q.B. 467; cf. *Business Environment Bow Lane Ltd v Deanwater Estates* [2007] EWCA Civ 622; [2007] 32 E.G. 90.

583 For the consideration supporting this promise, see para.3–065; for other grounds for the decision, see para.3–117.

584 i.e. cases of part payment by a third party: para.3–110.

585 (1877) 2 App. Cas. 439; para.3–077.

equity. Before 1946, this doctrine had not been applied where a creditor's promise to accept part payment of a debt in full settlement was not supported by any consideration moving from the debtor. Such an extension of the rule seemed to be barred by *Foakes v Beer*.[586] The possibility of making the extension was, however, suggested in *Central London Property Trust Ltd v High Trees House Ltd*.[587] In 1937 a block of flats had been let to the defendants for 99 years at a rent of £2,500 per annum. In 1940 the landlords agreed to reduce the annual rent to £1,250 as many of the flats were unlet because of war time conditions. After the end of the war, the landlords demanded the full rent for the last two quarters of 1945 and Denning J upheld their claim on the ground that, as a matter of construction, the 1940 agreement was intended to apply only while the war time conditions lasted. But he also said that the landlords would have been precluded by the equitable doctrine from suing for the full rent for the period which *was* covered by the 1940 agreement. He added: "The logical consequence no doubt is that a promise to accept a smaller sum, if acted upon, is binding notwithstanding the absence of consideration."[588] The requirements and effects of the equitable doctrine which is now referred to as "promissory estoppel" have already been discussed.[589] Three points give rise to particular difficulty in its application to cases of part payment of a debt.

**Effect generally suspensory.** The first difficulty is to reconcile the remarks of Denning J in the *High Trees* case with *Foakes v Beer*.[590] If the claimant in *Foakes v Beer* could go back on her promise not to ask for interest, why could not the landlords in the *High Trees* case go back on their promise not to ask for the full rent in, say, 1941, when war time difficulties of letting still prevailed? One possibility is to say that "that aspect was not considered in *Foakes v Beer*"[591] which was decided without reference to equity, and is therefore "no longer valid";[592] but this is unsatisfactory, as the rule that part payment of a debt was no discharge was clearly recognised in equity.[593] Another possibility, and one which does less violence to the authorities, is to say that the creditor's right to the balance of his debt is not extinguished but only suspended.[594] This is generally the sole consequence of promissory estoppel and in the present context it would give effect to the intention of the parties where the purpose of the arrangements **3–115**

---

[586] (1884) 9 App. Cas. 605; para.3–102.

[587] [1947] K.B. 130; Denning 15 M.L.R. 1; Wilson 67 L.Q.R. 330; Sheridan 15 M.L.R. 325; Bennion 16 M.L.R. 441; Guest 30 A.L.J. 187; Turner 1 N.Z.U.L.R. 185; Campbell 1 N.Z.U.L.R. 232.

[588] *Central London Property Trust Ltd v High Trees House Ltd* [1947] K.B. 130 at 134; cf. *Combe v Combe* [1951] 2 K.B. 215 at 220.

[589] See paras 3–077–3–093.

[590] (1884) 9 App. Cas.605; para.3–102.

[591] *Central London Property Trust Ltd v High Trees House Ltd* [1947] K.B. 130 at 146. The argument, with respect, lacks plausibility since *Hughes v Metropolitan Ry* (1877) 2 App. Cas. 439 had been decided only seven years before *Foakes v Beer* and Lords Selborne and Blackburn heard the appeals in both cases.

[592] *Arrale v Costain Civil Engineering Ltd* [1976] 1 Lloyd's Rep. 98 at 102.

[593] *Bidder v Bridges* (1887) 37 Ch D. 406; *Re Warren* (1884) 53 L.J. Ch. 1016.

[594] *Ajayi v RT Briscoe (Nig) Ltd* [1964] 1 W.L.R. 1326 at 1330; cf. *Re Venning* [1947] W.N. 196; Gordon [1963] C.L.J. 222, arguing that the equitable principle is limited to relief against forfeiture. But see Wilson [1965] C.L.J. 93.

was to give the debtor extra time to pay,[595] rather than to extinguish part of the debt. Of course, where the intention is to extinguish, and not merely to suspend, the creditor's right to the balance, the suggestion that the creditor is permanently bound by his promise not to sue for the balance[596] may seem to be an attractive one.[597] But such an extension of promissory estoppel would require the overruling of *Foakes v Beer*. It is, no doubt, with such difficulties in mind that Lord Hailsham LC said that the *High Trees* principle "may need to be reviewed and reduced to a coherent body of doctrine by the courts".[598]

3–116 **Effect on periodic payments.** For the present the better view is that the principle only suspends rights; but the meaning of this statement is not entirely clear where the debtor is under a continuing obligation to make a series of payments, e.g. of rent under a lease (as in the *High Trees* case), or of royalties under a licence to use a patent,[599] or of instalments under a hire-purchase agreement.[600] In such cases the statement may mean one of two things: first, that the creditor is entitled to payment in full only of amounts which fall due *after* the expiry of reasonable notice of the retraction of his promise;[601] or, secondly, that he is then entitled, not only to future payments in full, but also to the unpaid balance of *past* ones. Of course the second of these views might sometimes be at variance with the intention of the parties at the time of the promise.[602] On the other hand it is hard to see why a debtor whose liability accrues from time to time should, for the present purpose, be in a more favourable position than one whose liability is to pay a single lump sum; nor is it clear which of the two views should apply where a debtor who owed a lump sum undertook to pay it off in instalments and the

---

595 e.g. in *Ajayi v RT Briscoe (Nig) Ltd* [1964] 1 W.L.R. 1326. This seems also to have been the position in *Foakes v Beer* (1884) 9 App. Cas. 605.

596 Originally made by Lord Denning in *Central London Property Trust Ltd v High Trees House Ltd* [1947] K.B. 130 at 134; and repeated by him in *D & C Builders Ltd v Rees* [1966] 2 Q.B. 617 at 624; cf. *WJ Alan & Co Ltd v El Nasr Export & Import Co* [1972] 2 Q.B. 189 at 213; and [1972] 2 Q.B. 189 at 218, 220; but in that case there was consideration: para.3–063.

597 Provided that there was no duress: cf. para.3–049.

598 *Woodhouse AC Israel Cocoa Ltd v Nigerian Produce Marketing Co Ltd* [1972] A.C. 741 at 758; cf. *Baird Textile Holdings Ltd v Marks & Spencer Plc* [2001] EWCA Civ 274; [2002] 1 All E.R. (Comm) 737 at [48] ("not yet fully developed").

599 As in *Tool Metal Manufacturing Co Ltd v Tungsten Electric Co Ltd* [1955] 1 W.L.R. 761; para.3–086.

600 As in *Ajayi v RT Briscoe (Nig) Ltd* [1964] 1 W.L.R. 1326.

601 *Banning v Wright* [1972] 1 W.L.R. 972 at 981; cf. *WJ Alan & Co Ltd v El Nasr Export & Import Co* [1972] 2 Q.B. 189 at 213. This view is apparently regarded as correct in *Tool Metal Manufacturing Co Ltd v Tungsten Electric Co Ltd* [1955] 1 W.L.R. 761; but the case is not conclusive as the liability of the licensee to make the payments during the suspension period was not directly considered by the House of Lords.

602 This would be so in cases like the *High Trees* and *Tool Metal* cases—but not in a case like *Ajayi v RT Briscoe (Nig) Ltd* [1964] 1 W.L.R. 1326 as the promise there "was not intended to be irrevocable": *Meng Long Development Pte Ltd v Jip Hong Trading Pte Ltd* [1985] A.C. 511 at 524. See *Virulite LLC v Virulite Distribution Ltd* [2014] EWHC 366 (QB); [2015] 1 Lloyd's Rep. 461 at [125]: "there is scope for confusion in the use of the terms 'suspensory' and 'extinguishing' … since a representation may be revocable, and in that sense suspensory, while effectively extinguishing the representor's right to rely upon his contractual rights during the period of suspension"; *JT Sydenham & Co Ltd v Enichem Elastometers Ltd* [1989] 1 E.G.L.R. 257 at 260 (discussed by Cartwright [1990] C.L.J. 13) purports to give the "estoppel" an extinctive effect; but the amount of rent due in that case was in dispute, so that the actual decision is explicable on the ground stated at para.3–104.

creditor first made, and then gave reasonable notice revoking, a promise to accept reduced instalments. In such a case, it is at least arguable that the intention of the creditor is only to give extra time for payment. Hence the total debt remains due, and the only effect of the promise is to extend the period over which it is to be repaid.[603]

**Exceptional cases where creditor's rights extinguished.** There may, however, be exceptional cases where the creditor's right is wholly extinguished: "all will depend on the circumstances".[604] We have seen that a forbearance cannot be retracted where subsequent events, or the passage of time, make it highly inequitable[605] to require performance of the original obligation, even after reasonable notice. This principle could be applied to cases of the present kind, so that the creditor's right to the balance might be extinguished if, in reliance on that promise, the debtor had undertaken new commitments in relation to the subject-matter, e.g. if the tenant in the *High Trees* case had used the rebate to modernise the flats.[606] 3–117

The creditor's right was also held to have been wholly extinguished in *Brikom Investments Ltd v Carr*.[607] In that case, long leases of flats provided that the tenants should pay (inter alia) contributions in respect of certain expenses incurred by the landlords on repairs. During negotiations leading to the execution of the leases, the landlords had promised to put the roof into repair "at our own cost". This was held to amount to a collateral contract[608] with one of the original tenants, precluding the landlords from enforcing against her the provision in the lease requiring her to contribute to the cost of the roof repairs. It was further held that claims for contributions to the cost of those repairs could not be made against assignees and sub-assignees of original tenants, even though there were no collateral contracts with these persons. Lord Denning MR based this conclusion on the *High Trees* principle which, in his view, was available not only between the original parties, but also in favour of, and against, their assigns.[609] The extinctive effect of the principle in these circumstances can perhaps be supported on the ground that the original tenants, the assignees and the sub-assignees had all, in reliance on the landlord's promise, undertaken fresh commitments by entering into long leases of the flats. Alternatively, the case can be treated, not as one of "promissory estoppel",[610] but as one of "waiver".[611] The latter expression here seems to refer to a variation supported by consideration;[612] for the consideration provided by the tenants[613] could equally support the landlords'

---

[603] *Hardwick v Johnson* [1978] 1 W.L.R. 683 (where the creditor was said at 699 to have agreed to "postpone" the debtor's obligation to pay instalments).

[604] *MWB Business Exchange Centres Ltd v Rock Advertising Ltd* [2016] EWCA Civ 553; [2017] Q.B. 604 at [61] (appeal allowed on another ground: [2018] UKSC 24; [2019] A.C. 119).

[605] See para.3–087.

[606] cf. Mitchell 2 Univ. of Western Australia Annual Law Review 245, 251.

[607] [1979] Q.B. 467.

[608] See para.3–065.

[609] *Brikom Investments Ltd v Carr* [1979] Q.B. 467 at 484–485.

[610] *Brikom Investments Ltd v Carr* [1979] Q.B. 467 at 485, 491.

[611] *Brikom Investments Ltd v Carr* [1979] Q.B. 467 at 488, 490.

[612] cf. para.3–063.

[613] See para.3–065.

promise whether that promise was regarded as a collateral contract[614] or as a variation of the principal contract itself. On this interpretation of the case, it is possible to account for the extinctive effect of the landlord's promise even on the liability of the assignees and sub-assignees. The variation was supported by consideration and so extinguished the liability of the original tenants to contribute to the cost of the repairs in question; and once it had been so extinguished it was not revived on assignment of the leases.

In *Collier v P & MJ Wright (Holdings) Ltd*[615] it was alleged[616] that the defendant had promised the claimant that if he paid one-third of a debt for which the claimant and his two partners were jointly and severally liable, the defendant would not pursue the claimant for the balance. The claimant paid the one-third share. The Court of Appeal held that he had a sufficiently real prospect of relying on promissory estoppel to defeat the defendant's claim for the balance that it should set aside a statutory demand and allow the matter to proceed to trial. After reviewing the cases, most notably the *High Trees* case and *D & C Builders Ltd v Rees*,[617] Arden LJ summed up her conclusion as follows:[618]

> "The facts of this case demonstrate that, if (1) a debtor offers to pay part only of the amount he owes; (2) the creditor voluntarily accepts that offer, and (3) in reliance on the creditor's acceptance the debtor pays that part of the amount he owes in full, the creditor will, by virtue of the doctrine of promissory estoppel, be bound to accept that sum in full and final satisfaction of the whole debt. For him to resile will of itself be inequitable. In addition, in these circumstances, the promissory estoppel has the effect of extinguishing the creditor's right to the balance of the debt. This part of our law originated in the brilliant obiter dictum of Denning J, as he was, in the *High Trees* case. To a significant degree it achieves in practical terms the recommendation of the Law Revision Committee chaired by Lord Wright MR in 1937."

A notable feature of this statement of principle is that there is nothing exceptional, beyond the actual payment of part of the debt,[619] which would seem to merit giving to the defendant's promise an extinctive effect. Such a result may well achieve the recommendation of the Law Revision Committee,[620] but it is also inconsistent with *Foakes v Beer*. If that ruling is no longer to prevail, it would be preferable if that was achieved by a ruling of the Supreme Court, or by

---

614 See para.3–065.

615 [2007] EWCA Civ 1329; [2008] 1 W.L.R. 643.

616 Longmore LJ thought ([2007] EWCA Civ 1329; [2008] 1 W.L.R. 643 at [45]) that it was only just arguable that the statements made by the defendant amounted to a promise of permanent surrender of the right to the balance of the debt. He noted that, if Lord Denning's dictum was to be applied more widely it is "all the more important that agreements which are said to forego a creditor's rights on a permanent basis should not be too benevolently construed" (at [48]).

617 [1966] 2 Q.B. 617; para.3–119.

618 *Collier v P & MJ Wright (Holdings) Ltd* [2007] EWCA Civ 1329; [2008] 1 W.L.R. 643 at [42].

619 This requirement has led to the suggestion that the decision in *Collier v Wright* as well as other cases relying on factual benefit (e.g. *Williams v Roffey Bros & Nicholls (Contractors) Ltd* [1991] 1 Q.B. 1) might be better analysed as turning on the creation of a unilateral contract: Chen-Wishart in Burrows & Peel (eds), *Contract Formation and Parties* (2010); cf. *MWB Business Exchange Centres Ltd v Rock Advertising Ltd* [2016] EWCA Civ 553; [2017] Q.B. 604 at [49], [67], [90] (appeal allowed on a different ground: [2018] UKSC 24; [2019] A.C. 119).

620 Sixth Interim Report on the Statute of Frauds and the Doctrine of Consideration, Cmnd. 5449. The Committee also recommended that the full debt could be discharged by a promise to pay the lesser sum but that if the new agreement was not performed, the original debt revived (para.35).

legislation, at the earliest opportunity and along the lines suggested above, rather than an equitable evasion of uncertain scope.

**The requirement of reliance.** One difficulty which has been felt about the *High Trees* case is that a tenant who is bound to pay £2,500 per annum for 99 years suffers no "detriment", in the sense in which that word is used in the law of estoppel,[621] by paying half that rent for part of the period. Ingenious attempts have been made to find some "detriment" in the case;[622] but Lord Denning himself has said extra judicially that there was none.[623] Nor is the requirement mentioned in the *High Trees* case itself, or in later statements of the principle.[624] And if such "detriment" is not necessary for the purpose of the rule in *Hughes v Metropolitan Ry*[625] it is hard to see why it should be necessary for the purpose of its offshoot, the *High Trees* rule. All that is necessary is that the tenant should have acted in reliance on the promise in such a way as to make it inequitable for the landlord to act inconsistently with it. This requirement was satisfied on the facts of the *High Trees* case, no less than on those of *Hughes v Metropolitan Ry*. 3–118

**Must be inequitable to demand the original debt.** When the debtor makes the part payment in reliance on the creditor's promise, it becomes prima facie "inequitable" for the creditor peremptorily to go back on his promise.[626] But other circumstances may indicate that it would not be "inequitable" for the creditor to reassert his claim for the full amount:[627] this would, for example, be the position where the debtor had failed to perform his promise to pay the smaller amount.[628] It has been suggested that another such circumstance may be the conduct of the debtor in obtaining the promise. Thus in *D & C Builders Ltd v Rees*[629] Lord Denning MR held that the *High Trees* principle did not apply because the builders' promise to accept £300 in full settlement of their claim for £482 had been obtained by taking undue advantage of their desperate financial position. The difficulty with this reasoning is that most debtors who offer part payment in full settlement try to exert some form of "pressure" against their creditors. The law now recognises that it is possible for such pressure to amount to duress;[630] and where it has this effect the promise should clearly not bring the *High Trees* principle into operation. Where, on the other hand, there is no duress, the operation of the *High Trees* principle should not be excluded merely because it could be said that the creditor's promise had, in some sense, been "improperly 3–119

[621] cf. para.3–084.
[622] e.g. Wilson 67 L.Q.R. 330, 344.
[623] 15 M.L.R. 1, 6–8.
[624] e.g. in *Combe v Combe* [1951] 2 K.B. 215 at 220. See also para.3–085 and following.
[625] See para.3–085.
[626] See the passage quoted from Arden LJ in *Collier v P & MJ Wright (Holdings ) Ltd* [2007] EWCA Civ 1329; [2008] 1 W.L.R. 643 at [42].
[627] cf. para.3–085.
[628] cf. *Re Selectmove* [1995] 1 W.L.R. 474 at 481, where the debtor's promise was not to pay less but to pay late; and see *Burrows v Brent LBC* [1996] 1 W.L.R. 1448, where the decision was based on lack of contractual intention so that neither consideration nor the equitable doctrine was discussed.
[629] [1966] 2 Q.B. 617; Winder 82 L.Q.R. 165; para.3–103; cf. *Arrale v Costain Civil Engineering Ltd* [1976] 1 Lloyd's Rep. 98 at 102.
[630] See paras 3–049–3–050; para.10–007.

obtained." Such an intermediate category between promises obtained by duress and those not so obtained should, here as elsewhere,[631] be rejected as "unhelpful because it would make the law uncertain".[632]

## 7. PROPRIETARY ESTOPPEL

3–120 Proprietary estoppel is said to arise in certain situations in which a person has done acts in reliance on the belief that he has, or that he will acquire, rights in or over another's land. Usually, but not invariably, these acts consist of erecting buildings on, or making other improvements to, the land in question. Where the requirements of proprietary estoppel are satisfied, the landowner is precluded from denying the existence of the rights in question, and may indeed be compelled to grant them. Because the estoppel precludes him from denying the existence of rights in property, it has come to be known as "proprietary estoppel". It is distinct[633] from promissory estoppel, both in the conditions which must be satisfied before it comes into operation and in its effects. But under both doctrines some legal effects are given to promises which are not contractually binding for want of consideration; and it is this aspect[634] of proprietary estoppel which calls for discussion in the present chapter.

### (a) Nature and scope of the doctrine

3–121 Proprietary estoppel operates in a variety of cases so disparate that it has been described as "an amalgam of doubtful utility."[635] The cases can be divided broadly into two categories.

3–122 **Cases of acquiescence.** In the first group of cases, one person acts under a mistake as to the existence or as to the extent of his rights in or over another's land. Even though the landowner did not induce the mistake, he might be prevented from taking advantage of it, particularly if he "stood by" knowing of the mistake, or actively encouraged the mistaken party to act in reliance on his mistaken belief.[636] These cases of so-called "acquiescence"[637] do not raise any questions as to the enforceability of promises and therefore do not call for further discussion in this chapter.

---

631 See para.3–055.

632 *Pao On v Lau Yiu Long* [1980] A.C. 614 at 634; cf. *Huyton SA v Peter Cremer GmbH* [1999] 1 Lloyd's Rep 620, where the requirement of consideration was satisfied (para.3–104) but there was no duress (para.10–008).

633 See para.3–149.

634 For wider discussion, see McFarlane, *The Law of Proprietary Estoppel* (2014).

635 *Amalgamated Investment & Property Co Ltd v Texas Commerce International Bank Ltd* [1982] Q.B. 84 at 103.

636 *Willmott v Barber* (1880) 15 Ch D. 96; cf. *Taylor Fashions Ltd v Liverpool Victoria Trustees Co Ltd* [1982] Q.B. 133; *Blue Haven Enterprises Ltd v Tully* [2006] UKPC 17.

637 *Willmott v Barber* (1880) 15 Ch D. 96 at 105.

**Cases of encouragement.** In the second group of cases, there is not merely "acquiescence" by the landowner, but "encouragement":[638] that is, conduct by the landowner, or a representation by him, from which a promise to the other party (the promisee) can be inferred[639] to the effect that the promisee has a legally enforceable[640] interest in the land or that one will be created in his favour. If the other party acts in reliance on such a promise, the question will arise to what extent the promise can be enforced, even though it may not be supported by consideration, or fail to satisfy the other requirements (such as those of certainty or form)[641] of a binding contract. 3–123

**Cases explained by unjust enrichment.** In some cases, the promisee's reliance takes the form of his making improvements to the promisor's land.[642] The most obvious explanation of such cases is that in them the landowner would be unjustly enriched if he were allowed to disregard his promise and to take back the land after he had induced the promisee to make improvements to it. This explanation is, perhaps, reflected in statements found in some cases that the liability is based on "an implied or constructive trust."[643] But the discussion which follows will show that the doctrine can apply even where there is no enrichment of the kind just described, or indeed of any kind at all.[644] Unjust enrichment therefore cannot provide a complete explanation of the doctrine. 3–124

**Cases explained by contract.** In other cases the rights of a person who had expended money on the property of another have been explained as being based on contract;[645] and often such an explanation was sufficiently plausible to make reliance on a doctrine of proprietary estoppel unnecessary.[646] A unilateral contract to transfer an interest in land has been held to arise out of a promise to make the transfer if the promisee would pay instalments due under a mortgage on the house[647]; it can equally arise out of a promise to make the transfer if the promisee 3–125

---

638 *Ramsden v Dyson* (1866) L.R. 1 H.L. 129 at 170. Contrast *Attorney General of Hong Kong v Humphreys Estate (Queen's Gardens)* [1987] A.C. 114, where there was no encouragement.

639 See *Lloyds Bank Plc v Rosset* [1991] 1 A.C. 107; *Keelwalk Properties Ltd v Waller* [2002] EWCA Civ 1076; (2002) 33 E.G. 95 at [63] (where this requirement was not satisfied); cf. *Kim v Chasewood Park Residents Ltd* [2013] EWCA Civ 239; [2013] H.L.R. 24.

640 See *Coombes v Smith* [1986] 1 W.L.R. 808 (where there was no belief in the existence of a legally enforceable right); cf. *Brinnand v Ewens* (1987) 19 H.L.R. 415.

641 See, e.g. fn.643.

642 See para.3–132.

643 *Sen v Headley* [1991] Ch. 425 at 440; *Cobbe v Yeoman's Row Management Ltd* [2008] UKHL 55; [2008] 1 W.L.R. 1752 (Lord Scott).

644 *Canadian Pacific Railway v The King* [1931] A.C. 414; *Armstrong v Sheppard & Short* [1959] 2 Q.B. 384.

645 e.g. *Plimmer v Mayor of Wellington* (1884) 9 App. Cas. 699; as explained in *Canadian Pacific Railway v The King* [1931] A.C. 414 at 428; *Eves v Eves* [1975] 1 W.L.R. 1338; *Tanner v Tanner* [1975] 1 W.L.R. 1346; cf. *Re Sharpe* [1980] 1 W.L.R. 219 at 224; and see *ER Ives Investment Ltd v High* [1967] 2 Q.B. 379 (where there was a contract between the defendant and the claimant's predecessor in title).

646 See *Lloyds Bank Plc v Carrick* [1996] 4 All E.R. 632; *Oxley v Hiscock* [2004] EWCA Civ 546; [2005] Fam. 211 at [35]. Contrast *Yaxley v Gotts* [2000] Ch. 162 at 179, where there was no such contract but, at most, an agreement lacking contractual force.

647 *Errington v Errington* [1952] 1 Q.B. 290; see para.2–054.

will make improvements to the land, or indeed do any other act.[648] But not all cases of proprietary estoppel can be explained as depending on contract.[649] Promises in cases of this kind are often made in a family context, without contractual intention, or the promise may lack consideration because the party relying on the estoppel made no counter-promise and so incurred no obligation, and the arrangement was not one in which it would be in accordance with the intention of the parties to treat it as a unilateral contract.[650] The terms of the alleged contract may also be too vague to satisfy the requirement of certainty,[651] or there may have been a failure to comply with the stringent formal requirements for the making of contracts for the disposition of interests in land.[652]

### (b) Requirements

3–126 **Summary.** The doctrine of proprietary estoppel is based on three main elements: "a representation or assurance made to the claimant; reliance on it by the claimant, and detriment to the claimant in consequence of his (reasonable) reliance."[653] These requirements are considered in more detail below, but while they are considered separately for ease of analysis it is important to bear in mind that proprietary estoppel "cannot be treated as subdivided into three or four watertight compartments".[654] Each of the requirements may, to some extent, influence the other and reliance and detriment, in particular, are often intertwined: "In the end the court must look at the matter in the round."[655]

#### (i) *Representation or assurance*

3–127 **Kinds of promises capable of giving rise to a proprietary estoppel.** A promise may give rise to a proprietary estoppel even though it is not express but is implied, e.g. from the fact that the parties acted on the common assumption that one of them was to have the right to reside on the other's property.[656] The promise must be of such a kind that it is reasonable for the promisee to rely on it

[648] e.g. *Tanner v Tanner* [1975] 1 W.L.R. 1346.
[649] cf. *Beaton v McDivitt* (1988) 13 N.S.W. L.R. 162 at 170–171.
[650] *JT Developments v Quinn* (1991) 62 P. & C.R. 33.
[651] See para.2–079. See *Gillett v Holt* [2001] Ch. 210 at 230; *Banner Homes Group Plc v Luff Developments Ltd* [2000] Ch. 372; *Jennings v Rice* [2002] EWCA Civ 159; [2003] 1 F.C.R. 501 at [10], [49], [50]; *Crabb v Arun DC* [1976] Ch. 179; Atiyah 92 L.Q.R. 174; Millett 92 L.Q.R. 342.
[652] Law of Property (Miscellaneous Provisions) Act 1989 s.2(1)–(3): see para.5–009. Previously the contract could be made informally, but Law of Property Act 1925 s.40 (now repealed) had required either a note or memorandum in writing as evidence of the contract, or "part performance" of the contract. The latter requirement could be satisfied by the conduct of the promisee giving rise to proprietary estoppel; cf. the reference to "part performance" in *Dillwyn v Llewelyn* (1862) 4 D.F. & G. 517 at 521.
[653] *Thorner v Major* [2009] UKHL 18; [2009] 1 W.L.R. 776 at [29].
[654] *Gillett v Holt* [2001] Ch. 210 at 228.
[655] *Gillett v Holt* [2001] Ch. 210 at 228.
[656] e.g. *Re Sharpe* [1980] 1 W.L.R. 219.

and the promisor must have intended the promisee would so rely on it;[657] and it must induce the promisee to believe that a legal right has been, or will be, created in his favour; though there is no further requirement that this belief must be legally well founded.[658]

**The representation or assurance must be "clear enough".** It seems that the representation or assurance relied upon need not be "clear and unequivocal" in the sense in which that requirement is understood for promissory estoppel, or estoppel by representation.[659] Given the various, and in particular the non-commercial, contexts in which proprietary estoppel can arise, it has been stated that the relevant assurance must be "clear enough".[660] This appears to mean an assurance which in all the circumstances "one might reasonably expect to be relied upon by the person to whom it was made."[661] For example, in *Thorner v Major*[662] the claimant did substantial work on the promisor's farm and was found to have done so on the basis of the promisor's assurance that he would inherit "the farm".[663] That assurance was not derived from any express representation, but was "a matter of implication and inference from indirect statements and conduct".[664] It also seems that an assurance may be "clear enough" even if it is ambiguous. If the requirements for proprietary estoppel are otherwise satisfied, the fact that the assurance may have more than one possible meaning should not deprive the claimant of relief, but such relief may be based on the interpretation of the assurance which is least beneficial to the claimant.[665] 3–128

**Representation or promise of a "certain interest in land".** There can normally be no belief on the part of the promisee that a legal right has been, or will be, created in his favour, and hence no proprietary estoppel, if the promise expressly disclaims legal effect,. For example in *Attorney General of Hong Kong v Humphreys Estates (Queen's Gardens)*[666] it was held that no proprietary estoppel arose out of an agreement for the transfer of a number of flats "subject to 3–129

[657] *Gillett v Holt* [2001] Ch. 210 at 228. It seems that, as is the case with the promisee's reliance, the intention of the promisor is assessed objectively: *Thorner v Major* [2009] UKHL 18; [2009] 1 W.L.R. 776 at [78].
[658] *Gillett v Holt* [2001] Ch. 210 at 229.
[659] See para.3–081. This seems to be what is required by Lord Scott in *Cobbe v Yeoman's Row Management Ltd* [2008] UKHL 55; [2008] 1 W.L.R. 1752, a view which is consistent with his narrow view of the scope of proprietary estoppel: fn.674.
[660] *Thorner v Major* [2009] UKHL 18; [2009] 1 W.L.R. 776 at [56] (Lord Walker, who acknowledged the "question-begging formulation"). See also Lord Rodger at [26], Lord Neuberger at [84].
[661] *Walton v Walton* unreported 14 April 1994 at [16] (Hoffmann LJ).
[662] [2009] UKHL 18; [2009] 1 W.L.R. 776.
[663] On the identity of "the farm", see para.3–134.
[664] *Thorner v Major* [2008] EWCA Civ 732 at [65] (Lloyd LJ). Both parties were described as "taciturn and undemonstrative" ([2008] UKHL 55; [2008] 1 W.L.R. 1752 at [59]), which seems to have added weight to the few words and gestures which did pass between them.
[665] *Thorner v Major* [2009] UKHL 18; [2009] 1 W.L.R. 776 at [86] (Lord Neuberger).
[666] [1987] 1 A.C. 114; the case was said in *Waltons Stores (Interstate) Ltd v Maher* (1988) 164 C.L.R. 387 at 404 to be "not a case of proprietary estoppel" but (apparently) one of promissory estoppel; cf. *Saloman v Akiens* [1993] 1 E.G.L.R. 10; *Secretary of State for Transport v Christos* [2003] EWCA Civ 1073; [2004] 1 P. & C.R. 17; *Gonthier v Orange Contract Scaffolding Ltd* [2003] EWCA Civ 873; *Spring Finance Ltd v HS Real Co LLC* [2011] EWHC 57 (Comm) at [57].

contract", it being well known that the effect of these words was to negative the intention to be legally bound.[667] The promisee may have formed "the confident and not unreasonable hope"[668] that the promise would not be withdrawn; but no *belief* to this effect had been encouraged[669] by the promisor or relied on by the promisee.[670]

Such reasoning is not confined to cases where the parties have expressly agreed "subject to contract". In *Cobbe v Yeoman's Row Management Ltd*,[671] the parties had reached an agreement "in principle" that if the claimant obtained planning permission for land owned by the defendant, the defendant would sell the land to the claimant for development for an upfront price and a share of the proceeds of sale of the developed land. The claimant did the work necessary and obtained the permission, but the defendant insisted on re-opening the terms of the agreement. The House of Lords held that, even if the defendant had behaved unconscionably,[672] the claimant had not satisfied the requirements for proprietary estoppel (nor a constructive trust).[673] As Lord Scott explained,[674] the reason why, in a "subject to contract" case, a proprietary estoppel cannot arise is because the expectation of the claimant is speculative; similarly, in *Cobbe* the claimant's expectation was "always speculative"[675] because he knew that his agreement with the claimant was not legally enforceable, either for lack of certainty because key terms were still to be negotiated,[676] or because of non-compliance with the formalities required for contracts for an interest in land.[677] The claimant lacked the expectation of a "certain interest in land",[678] or as Lord Walker put it,

---

[667] See para.4–011.

[668] *Attorney General of Hong Kong v Humphreys Estates (Queen's Gardens)* [1987] 1 A.C. 114 at 124.

[669] cf. para.3–123; *Brinnand v Ewens* (1987) 19 H.L.R. 415.

[670] *Haq v Island Homes Housing Association* [2011] EWCA Civ 805; [2011] 2 P. & C.R. 17 ("subject to contract" not waived on the facts; see para. 4–013); *Crossco No.4 Unlimited v Jolan Ltd* [2011] EWCA Civ 1619; [2012] 2 All E.R. 754 at [133].

[671] [2008] UKHL 55; [2008] 1 W.L.R. 1752; Getzler 125 L.Q.R. 196.

[672] Lord Scott described the defendant's behaviour as "unconscionable" ([2008] UKHL 55; [2008] 1 W.L.R. 1752 at [36]). Lord Walker described it as "unattractive", but not "unconscionable" (at [92]).

[673] He was, however, entitled to a quantum meruit for the value of the services he had rendered: [2008] UKHL 55; [2008] 1 W.L.R. 1752 at [42]; cf. *Walsh v Singh* [2009] EWHC 3219 (Ch); [2010] 1 F.L.R. 1658 at [65]; para.22–031.

[674] *Cobbe v Yeoman's Row Management Ltd* [2008] UKHL 55; [2008] 1 W.L.R. 1752 at [25]. The result in *Cobbe* is entirely consistent with the reasoning employed in the *Humphreys Estates* case and with the requirements for proprietary estoppel as previously understood, but Lord Scott also took a very narrow view of the doctrine, seeing it as only operating to bar the defendant from asserting some fact (or mixed matters of fact and law) that would stand in the way of a right claimed by the claimant. This view, which equates proprietary estoppel with estoppel by representation and denies its operation as an independent source of rights, was not shared by the other members of the House of Lords in *Cobbe* and is implicitly rejected by the reasoning of the majority of the Law Lords in *Thorner v Major* (in which Lord Scott preferred an analysis based on constructive trust): McFarlane and Robertson 125 L.Q.R. 535.

[675] *Cobbe v Yeoman's Row Management Ltd* [2008] UKHL 55; [2008] 1 W.L.R. 1752 at [27].

[676] cf. *Kirker v Ridley* unreported 17 December 2008 Ch D.

[677] See para.5–009.

[678] *Taylor Fashions Ltd v Liverpool Victoria Trustees Co Ltd* [1982] Q.B. 133 at 144 (Oliver J). The necessary certainty is as to the nature of the interest in the land; there need not be certainty as to the precise extent of the property which is the subject of the estoppel: *Thorner v Major* [2009] UKHL 18; [2009] 1 W.L.R. 776 at [94], [98] (Lord Neuberger). See para.3–134.

"conscious reliance on honour alone will not give rise to an estoppel".[679] At one point, Lord Walker stated that the claimant must believe that the assurance was "binding and irrevocable",[680] a requirement that would deprive proprietary estoppel of much of its utility, but it seems clear from the immediately following decision of the House of Lords that a proprietary estoppel did arise in *Thorner v Major*[681] that this requirement is not to be understood literally; rather it emphasises that it is not enough to "hope, or even to have a confident expectation, that the person who has given assurances will do the proper thing."[682]

The different outcomes in *Cobbe* and *Thorner v Major* may be explained in large part by the different contexts in which any assurance was said to have been given;[683] in particular, as a sophisticated commercial property developer the claimant in *Cobbe* knew that there was no legally binding contract and he took the risk that the defendant might exercise the option she had of re-opening the terms of the agreement in principle.[684] But the context—commercial or non-commercial—is not decisive. Thus, where a landowner promised her part-time gardener to leave him her house in her will but told him "not to count his chickens before they were hatched," it was held that no proprietary estoppel arose when, after having made a will in his favour, she then revoked it and made another leaving the property to someone else: in these circumstances it was not unconscionable for the landowner to revoke the promise.[685]

The position is the same where the promise, even though it does not in terms reserve a power of revocation, is in its nature revocable and this is a matter of common knowledge so that the promisee must have been aware of the risk of its being revoked. This will often be the position where the promise is one to make a will in favour of the promisee; but it does not follow as a matter of law that such a promise cannot give rise to proprietary estoppel. In *Gillett v Holt*[686] the claimant had worked for nearly 40 years in the defendant's farming business in reliance on the defendant's frequently repeated promises to leave him the bulk of his estate, and had in various other ways relied on those promises. It was held that the promises were "more than a statement of revocable intention",[687] and that they were capable of giving rise, and did give rise, to a proprietary estoppel.

**Proprietary estoppel normally confined to rights in or over the property of the promisor.** As a general rule, the rights about which the promisee has been assured must be rights in or over the property of the promisor.[688] A representation 3–130

679 *Cobbe v Yeoman's Row Management Ltd* [2008] UKHL 55; [2008] 1 W.L.R. 1752 at [81].
680 *Cobbe v Yeoman's Row Management Ltd* [2008] UKHL 55; [2008] 1 W.L.R. 1752 at [66].
681 *Thorner v Major* [2009] UKHL 18; [2009] 1 W.L.R. 776.
682 *Cobbe v Yeoman's Row Management Ltd* [2008] UKHL 55; [2008] 1 W.L.R. 1752 at [65]; McFarlane and Robertson 125 L.Q.R. 535.
683 See Lord Walker in *Cobbe v Yeoman's Row Management Ltd* [2008] UKHL 55; [2008] 1 W.L.R. 1752 at [68]. See further *Herbert v Doyle* [2010] EWCA Civ 1095; [2011] 1 E.G.L.R. 119; *Burton v Liden* [2016] EWCA Civ 275; [2017] F.L.R. 310 at [24] ("Context is 'hugely important'").
684 But not the risk of not even being paid for his services: fn.673.
685 *Taylor v Dickens* [1998] F.L.R. 806, as explained in *Gillett v Holt* [2001] Ch. 210 at 227.
686 [2001] Ch. 210.
687 *Gillett v Holt* [2001] Ch. 210 at 228.
688 *Newport CC v Charles* [2008] EWCA 1541; [2009] 1 W.L.R. 1884.

by a planning authority to the effect that a landowner does not need permission to carry out development on his *own* land is not capable of giving rise to a proprietary estoppel.[689] The promisor may, however, make two promises, of which the first relates to the promisor's land while the second relates to that of the promisee; and the two promises may be so closely linked as to form in substance a single transaction. If the doctrine of proprietary estoppel applies to that transaction as a whole, then it can provide the promisee with a remedy in respect of the second promise even though that promise, standing alone, could not have given rise to proprietary estoppel because it related only to the promisee's land. In one case,[690] for example, A promised B: (1) to sell blackacre to B to enable B to build on it; and (2) to buy whiteacre from B so that B could pay for the building operations on blackacre. B carried out the building work envisaged in the first of A's promises and it was held that the doctrine of proprietary estoppel provided B with a remedy in respect of the second promise (which had no contractual force), even though that promise related only to B's land. But it was recognised that the doctrine could not have applied to the second promise if it had stood alone and not formed part of a transaction also relating to A's land.[691] It could not, for example, have applied if A had simply made a non-contractual promise to B to buy whiteacre from B, knowing that B intended to use the proceeds of the sale to buy shares from C, and if B had then entered into a contract to that effect with C.

Similarly, the doctrine normally applies to promises to *grant* rights in land *to* the promisee;[692] it only applies to promises to *acquire* such rights *from* him where they are inextricably linked with promises of the former kind.

It has been said there is no reason why the doctrine should not apply to a case where the promisee is alleged to have committed an act of nuisance by interfering with a right of way over his own lands owned by the promisor.[693] Thus, where the promisee did so on the basis of the promisor's representation that he had no objection to such interference, proprietary estoppel applied to prevent the promisor from asserting his "property rights" in the form of the right of way over the promisee's land.[694]

3–131 **Property other than land.** The question whether a promise can give rise to a proprietary estoppel where its subject-matter is property of some kind other than land remains an open one.[695] In *Cobbe v Yeoman's Row Management Ltd* Lord Scott stated that it was "in principle, equally available in relation to chattels or

[689] *Western Fish Products Ltd v Penwith DC* [1981] 2 All E.R. 204 (decided in 1978); cf. *Lloyd's Bank Plc v Carrick* [1996] 4 All E.R. 632 (fn.646).

[690] *Salvation Army Trustee Co v West Yorks Metropolitan CC* (1981) 41 P. & C.R. 179.

[691] *Salvation Army Trustee Co v West Yorks Metropolitan CC* (1981) 41 P. & C.R. 179 at 191. The case was approved but distinguished in *Attorney General of Hong Kong v Humphreys Estate (Queen's Gardens)* [1987] A.C. 114 at 126–127.

[692] For the possibility that the doctrine may prevent A from asserting rights in B's property against C, a purchaser of that property: see *J S Bloor (Measham) Ltd v Calcott (No.2)* (2002) 9 E.G. 222.

[693] *Lester v Woodgate* [2010] EWCA Civ 199; [2010] 2 P. & C.R. 21 at [3].

[694] *Lester v Woodgate* [2010] EWCA Civ 199; [2010] 2 P. & C.R. 21.

[695] *Baird Textile Holdings Ltd v Marks & Spencer Plc* [2001] EWCA Civ 274; [2001] 1 All E.R. (Comm) 737 at [34]–[35], [54], [97]; *Strover v Strover* [2005] EWHC 860; [2005] W.T.L.R. 1245 (proprietary estoppel applied in relation to a life insurance policy, in a case of "acquiescence"); *Fisher v Brooker* [2009] UKHL 41, [2009] 1 W.L.R. 1764 (copyright, but also a case of "acquiescence").

choses in action".[696] Even if the doctrine is extended to such promises, its scope will in one respect remain narrower than that of so-called promissory estoppel:[697] the promise must relate to the acquisition of an interest in the property which is the subject-matter of the promise. It is not enough that the promise should in some other way relate to property, e.g. the doctrine of proprietary estoppel would not apply on the facts of *Central London Property Trust v High Trees House Ltd*.[698]

### *(ii) Reliance*

**Expenditure on another's land.** In *Dillwyn v Llewelyn*[699] a father executed a memorandum "presenting" a named estate to his son "for the purpose of furnishing himself with a dwelling house". The son spent £14,000 in building a house on the land; and it was held (after the father's death) that he was entitled to have the fee simple of the estate conveyed to him. Many later cases similarly give some degree of legal enforceability to a promise by a landowner in reliance on which the promisee has spent money on making improvements to the promisor's land.[700] For example, where A built a bungalow on B's land in reliance on B's promise that A could stay there for the rest of his life;[701] where A spent money on extending or improving B's house in reliance on a similar promise by B;[702] and where, in reliance on such a promise, A actually did the work of improvement him- or herself.[703] 3–132

**Other acts done in reliance on the promise.** Improvement to the promisor's land is not a necessary condition for the operation of proprietary estoppel. The doctrine can apply also where the promisee has conferred some other benefit on the promisor[704] and even where no benefit at all is received by the promisor. The doctrine operated in the absence of any expenditure on the promisor's land in *Crabb v Arun DC*.[705] In that case A (a local authority) by its conduct represented to B that B had a right of way from his land over adjoining land owned by A. In 3–133

---

696 *Cobbe v Yeoman's Row Management Ltd* [2008] UKHL 55; [2008] 1 W.L.R. 1752 at [14]; cf. *Kirker v Ridley* unreported 17 December 2008 Ch D (shares); *Motivate Publishing FZ LLV v Hello Ltd* [2015] EWHC 1554 (Ch) (intellectual property).

697 See paras 3–076–3–092.

698 [1947] K.B. 130; para.3–114; cf. *MWB Business Exchange Centres Ltd v Rock Advertising Ltd* [2016] EWCA Civ 553; [2017] Q.B. 604 at [65] (appeal allowed on another ground: [2018] UKSC 24; [2019] A.C. 119).

699 (1862) 4 D.F. & G. 517; Allan 79 L.Q.R. 238.

700 *Voyce v Voyce* (1991) 62 P. & C.R. 290.

701 *Inwards v Baker* [1965] 2 Q.B. 29.

702 *Hussey v Palmer* [1972] 1 W.L.R. 1286; *Pascoe v Turner* [1979] 1 W.L.R. 431.

703 *Eves v Eves* [1975] 1 W.L.R. 1338.

704 e.g. *Greasley v Cooke* [1980] 1 W.L.R. 1306; *Jennings v Rice* [2002] EWCA Civ 159; [2003] 1 F.C.R. 501 (para.3–145); cf. *Plimmer v Mayor of Wellington* (1884) 9 App. Cas. 699; and *ER Ives Investment Ltd v High* [1967] 2 Q.B. 379 (where the landowner benefited from improvements to his land but also—and more significantly—in other ways); *Grant v Edwards* [1986] Ch. 638 at 657; *Stallion v Albert Stallion Holdings (Great Britain) Ltd* [2009] EWHC 1950 (Ch); [2010] 2 F.L.R. 78; Contrast *Howard v Jones* (1988) 19 Fam. L. 231 (contribution to running cost of another property insufficient).

705 [1976] Ch. 179.

reliance on that representation, B sold part of his own land, so that the only access from the remainder to the nearest public highway was by means of the right of way across A's land. It was held that B had a right to cross A's land for the purpose of access to his retained land. Detrimental reliance by the promisee here gave rise to a proprietary estoppel even though no benefit was conferred on the promisor.[706]

3–134 **Whether reliance must relate to specific property.** The authorities are divided on the question whether, to give rise to a proprietary estoppel, the reliance must relate to identifiable property. According to one case, the promisee's conduct must relate to "some specific asset" in which an interest is claimed; so that proprietary estoppel did not arise merely because B rendered services to A in the expectation of receiving some indeterminate benefit under A's will.[707] But in another case reliance on a similar expectation (induced by A's promise) was held sufficient even though it did not relate to any "particular property".[708] The latter case can perhaps be explained on the ground that the promise did to some extent identify the property.[709] It is submitted that the view that the promise must relate to identified or identifiable property[710] is to be preferred;[711] for, without some such limitation on its scope, the doctrine of proprietary estoppel could extend to any promise on which the promisee had relied to his detriment. Such a very broad doctrine would be fundamentally inconsistent with the doctrine of consideration[712] and, indeed, with the rule that the doctrine of *promissory* estoppel gives rise to no new rights.[713] While the property in question must be identified, or identifiable, the "precise extent of the property" need not be "strictly defined in every case".[714] Thus, in *Thorner v Major*, considered above, the claimant was given the assurance that he would inherit the farm "as it existed from time to time".[715] Lord Neuberger drew an analogy with a floating charge: "the property the subject of the equity could be conceptually identified from the moment the equity came into existence, but its precise extent fell to be determined when the equity crystallised, namely on (the promisor's) death."[716]

3–135 **Burden of proof.** Where a promise has been made which is capable of inducing reliance, and which is in fact followed by such reliance, the question may arise whether the promise actually did induce the reliance. It seems that the burden on this issue is on the promisor: that is, it is up to the promisor, in order to escape

[706] cf. *Hammersmith & Fulham BC v Top Shop Centres Ltd* [1990] Ch. 237.

[707] *Layton v Martin* [1986] 2 F.L.R. 277.

[708] *Re Basham* [1986] 1 W.L.R. 1498 at 1508.

[709] By referring to the promisor's cottage. In *Gillett v Holt* [2001] Ch. 210 the property was likewise identified, if not very precisely; cf. *Jennings v Rice* [2002] EWCA Civ 159; [2003] 1 F.C.R. 501 at [50], where the promise again related in part to the promisor's house.

[710] See, e.g. *Herbert v Doyle* [2010] EWCA Civ 1095; [2011] 1 E.G.L.R. 119; *Suggitt v Suggitt* [2012] EWCA Civ 1140; [2012] W.T.L.R. 1607.

[711] *Thorner v Major* [2009] UKHL 18; [2009] 1 W.L.R. 776 at [61] (Lord Walker).

[712] See, e.g. para.3–001.

[713] See para.3–088.

[714] *Thorner v Major* [2009] UKHL 18; [2009] 1 W.L.R. 776 at [98] (Lord Neuberger).

[715] *Thorner v Major* [2009] UKHL 18; [2009] 1 W.L.R. 776 at [95] (Lord Neuberger).

[716] *Thorner v Major* [2009] UKHL 18; [2009] 1 W.L.R. 776 at [95].

liability, to show that the promisee would have done the acts in question anyway, even if the promise had not been made.[717] The position appears to be different where a proprietary estoppel arises because both parties have acted under a mistake as to their rights in the land.[718] Here it seems to be up to the party relying on the proprietary estoppel to show that his conduct in relation to the property was in fact induced by his belief that he had an interest in it.[719] A further distinction between the two categories of case is that in cases of encouragement the promisor does not need to know precisely what the person encouraged may have actually done in reliance on the encouragement.[720]

### *(iii) Detriment*

The promisee must have relied on the promise or representation to his detriment.[721] The requirement has been doubted,[722] but in the absence of any such reliance it is hard to see why failure to perform a merely gratuitous promise should be regarded as giving rise to any legal liability. The element of detrimental reliance is necessary to satisfy "the essential test of unconscionability"[723] on which the operation of proprietary estoppel depends; and the existence of the requirement is further supported by the rules (to be discussed below) as to the revocability of the promise.[724] The detriment must be "substantial", i.e. such as to make it "unjust or inequitable to allow the assurance to be disregarded";[725] and the question whether it has this character is to be judged "as at the moment when the person who has given the assurance seeks to go back on it".[726] Where the promisee's reliance on the promise results in both a benefit and a detriment, they must be weighed together; if the detriment is not outweighed by any benefit, a proprietary estoppel will still arise.[727] Whether there has been detrimental **3–136**

[717] *Greasley v Cooke* [1980] 1 W.L.R. 1306; cf. *Grant v Edwards* [1986] Ch. 638; *Re Basham* [1986] 1 W.L.R. 1498; *Hammersmith & Fulham BC v Top Shop Centres Ltd* [1990] Ch. 237; *Thompson v Foy* [2009] EWHC 1076 (Ch); [2010] 1 P. & C.R. 16. But see the doubts expressed by Neuberger LJ in *Steria Ltd v Hutchinson* [2006] EWCA Civ 1551; [2007] I.C.R. 445 at [131].

[718] See para.3–122.

[719] *Taylor Fashions Ltd v Liverpool Victoria Trustees Co Ltd* [1982] Q.B. 133; cf. *Coombes v Smith* [1986] 1 W.L.R. 808.

[720] *Crabb v Arun DC* [1976] Ch. 179 at 189, 191; *Taylor Fashions Ltd v Liverpool Victoria Trustees Co Ltd* [1982] Q.B. 133 at 151; *Thorner v Major* [2009] UKHL 18; [2009] 1 W.L.R. 776 at [5]; *Joyce v Epsom and Ewell BC* [2012] EWCA Civ 1398; [2013] 1 E.G.L.R. 21 at [39].

[721] *Greasley v Cooke* [1980] 1 W.L.R. 1306; *Taylor Fashions Ltd v Liverpool Victoria Trustees Co Ltd* [1982] Q.B. 133; *Grant v Edwards* [1986] Ch. 638 at 657; cf. *Lloyds Bank Plc v Rosset* [1991] 1 A.C. 107 at 132; *Henry v Henry* [2010] UKPC 3; [2010] 1 All E.R. 988. The fact that there was no such reliance was one reason why the claim based on proprietary estoppel failed in *Attorney General of Hong Kong v Humphreys Estate (Queen's Gardens)* [1987] A.C. 114; and in *Jennings v Rice* [2002] EWCA Civ 159; [2003] 1 F.C.R. 501 at [21], [49].

[722] By Lord Denning MR in *Greasley v Cooke* [1980] 1 W.L.R. 1306 at 1311.

[723] *Gillett v Holt* [2001] Ch. 210 at 232; *Jennings v Rice* [2002] EWCA Civ 159; [2003] 1 F.C.R. 501 at [21], [49]; *Fisher v Brooker* [2009] UKHL 41; [2009] 1 W.L.R. 1764 at [63].

[724] See para.3–137.

[725] *Gillett v Holt* [2001] Ch. 210 at 232.

[726] *Gillett v Holt* [2001] Ch. 210 at 232.

[727] *Henry v Henry* [2010] UKPC 3; [2010] 1 All E.R. 988; cf. *Fisher v Brooker* [2009] UKHL 41; [2009] 1 W.L.R. 1764; *Creasey v Sole* [2013] EWHC 1410 (Ch); [2013] W.T.L.R. 931 at [111].

reliance sufficient to confer an "equity" on the promisee is "an evaluative judgment on the facts, which normally lies within the exclusive province of the trial judge".[728]

## (c) Effects of the doctrine

### (i) Revocability

3–137 **Revocability under the terms of the promise.** Proprietary estoppel will not arise at all where the promise to confer a benefit on the promisee is revocable in the sense that it reserves a power to the promisor wholly to deprive the promisee of that benefit.[729] But even where the promise does not allow the promisor to do this, and so is capable of giving rise to a proprietary estoppel, the extent of the promisee's rights under the estoppel may be limited by terms of the promise giving the promisor a power of putting an end to those rights. Thus if the landowner promises to allow the promisee to stay on the land "until I decide to sell", then the promisee cannot, merely by spending money on improvements to the land, acquire any right to stay there for a longer period.[730]

3–138 **Promise revoked before acted upon by promisee.** Even where the promise is not expressed to be revocable, it can be revoked before the promisee has acted on it. Thus in *Dillwyn v Llewelyn*[731] the father could have revoked his promise before the son had started to build on the land[732] and in *Crabb v Arun DC*[733] the promise to grant a right of way could have been revoked before the promisee had, by selling off part of his land, made it impossible for himself to obtain access to the retained land except by means of the promised right of way. In this respect proprietary estoppel resembles so-called promissory estoppel (under which promises are similarly revocable)[734] and differs from contractually binding promises which are not revocable unless they expressly or impliedly so provide.

3–139 **Promise revoked after acted upon by promisee.** The cases of proprietary estoppel assume that once the promisee has acted on the representation, he cannot be restored to his original position. Where he has made improvements to land, this will generally be the case. Where a restoration of the status quo is physically possible, it seems that a promise giving rise to a proprietary estoppel could be revoked even after the promisee had acted on it, provided that the promisor in fact restored the promisee to the position in which he was before he had acted in reliance on the promise. A promise which has given rise to proprietary estoppel

[728] *Davies v Davies* [2014] EWCA Civ 568; [2014] Fam. Law 1252 at [33]. An appeal court will only interfere with the judge's assessment if it is perverse or clearly wrong: *Suggitt v Suggitt* [2012] EWCA Civ 1140; [2012] W.T.L.R. 1607 at [37].

[729] See para.3–127.

[730] *E & L Berg Homes v Grey* (1979) 253 E.G. 473.

[731] (1862) D.F. & G. 517; para.3–132.

[732] cf. *Pascoe v Turner* [1979] 1 W.L.R. 431 at 435.

[733] [1976] Ch. 179; para.3–133; cf. *Thorner v Major* [2009] UKHL 18; [2009] 1 W.L.R. 776 at [20].

[734] See para.3–086.

may also be none the less revocable, because the court considers it appropriate in this way to limit the effects to be given to the promise.[735]

### *(ii) Operation of proprietary estoppel*

Where the conditions required to give rise to a proprietary estoppel have been satisfied, the effect of the doctrine is said to be to confer an "equity" on the promisee. Two further questions then arise: namely, what is the extent of that "equity", and what are the remedies for its enforcement?[736] In practice, these questions tend to merge into each other; but an attempt to deal with them in turn will be made in the following discussion. **3–140**

**Extent of the equity.** At one extreme, the promisee may be entitled to conveyance of the fee simple in the property which is the subject-matter of the promise, as in *Dillwyn v Llewelyn*.[737] On the other hand, in *Inwards v Baker*,[738] where a son had also built a house for himself at his father's suggestion on the latter's land, the result of the estoppel was only to entitle the son to occupy the house for life. Similar results were reached in a number of later cases in which the promisee made improvements to the promisor's property (or otherwise acted to his detriment) in reliance on a promise, or common understanding, that the promisee would be entitled to reside there for as long as he or she wished to do so;[739] or for some shorter period, e.g. until her children had left school;[740] or that a lease of the premises, to which the promise related, would be granted to him;[741] or that he would be entitled to a charge over the property.[742] *Dillwyn v Llewelyn* can be reconciled with these cases by reference to the terms of the respective promises, which may be expressed either as an outright gift of the property or merely as an assurance that the promisee would be entitled to reside in the property for the specified period. Another way of giving effect to a promise of the latter kind is by the grant of a long, non-assignable lease at a nominal rent, on terms that ensured that the right of occupation was personal to the promisee.[743] In other cases, not concerned with rights of personal occupation but with the right to keep and use structures on the promisor's land, the promisee has been held entitled only to a revocable licence.[744] **3–141**

[735] See fn.744.
[736] *Crabb v Arun DC* [1976] Ch. 179 at 193 (Scarman LJ).
[737] (1862) D.F. & G. 517; *Durant v Heritage* [1994] E.G.C.S. 134; or, in the exceptional cases discussed at fnn.690 and 692, to orders enforcing the promises made in those cases.
[738] [1965] 2 Q.B. 29; Maudsley 81 L.Q.R. 183.
[739] *Jones v Jones* [1977] 1 W.L.R. 438; *Re Sharpe* [1980] 1 W.L.R. 219; *Greasley v Cooke* [1980] 1 W.L.R. 1306.
[740] *Tanner v Tanner* [1975] 1 W.L.R. 1346 (where there was a contract: cf. above, para.3–125); *Yaxley v Gotts* [2000] Ch. 162 (where the remedy was based on constructive trust).
[741] *JT Developments v Quinn* (1991) 62 P. & C.R. 33.
[742] *McGuane v Welch* [2008] EWCA Civ 785; [2008] 2 P. & C. R. 24 at [47].
[743] *Griffiths v Williams* [1978] E.G. Digest of Cases 919; cf. *Jones v Jones* [1977] 1 W.L.R. 438.
[744] *Canadian Pacific Railway v The King* [1931] A.C. 414; *Armstrong v Sheppard & Short* [1959] Q.B. 384.

3–142 **Equity binding on third party donee or purchaser.** Where the circumstances are such as to give rise to an estoppel against the landowner, the estoppel is equally available against a third party who claims later to have obtained title to the land by way of gift from the landowner.[745] It may also be available against a third party who has purchased the property with the requisite degree of notice.[746]

3–143 **The estoppel may operate conditionally.** The estoppel may operate conditionally where the promisee has acted in reliance on the promise but the terms of the promise show that the promisor did not intend to give up his title gratuitously. This was the position in *Lim Teng Huan v Ang Swee Chuan*[747] where A built a house on land jointly owned by him and L, who had agreed that he was to have no title to the house and would exchange his share in the land for other land. The arrangement had no contractual force as the other land was not identified with sufficient certainty; and it was held that L was estopped from asserting title to the house but that he was entitled to be compensated for the loss of his share in the land. In *Thorner v Major*[748] the farm was awarded to the claimant subject to his indemnifying the promisor's personal representatives against the payment of inheritance tax related to the farm.[749]

3–144 **Rights of access.** Where the promise is one to allow the promisee access to his own land over that of the promisor, the effect of the proprietary estoppel will be to entitle the promisee to an easement or licence on terms.[750] Such terms, if not agreed between the parties, may be imposed by the court: they can specify the extent of the permitted user[751] as well as any payment that the promisee may be required to make for the exercise of the right.[752] However, an order for such payment was held not to be appropriate in one case, because the promisor had already obtained other benefits under the agreement.[753] It may also be inappropriate for other reasons, as the following discussion of the promisee's remedy will show.

3–145 **Remedy: a flexible, principled approach.**[754] The remedy in cases of proprietary estoppel is "extremely flexible", its object being "to do what is equitable in all the circumstances".[755] Although the court thus has a considerable discretion with regard to the remedy in cases of proprietary estoppel, that discretion is not a "completely unfettered"[756] one and a "principled approach"[757] must be taken to

---

745 *Voyce v Voyce* (1991) 62 P. & C.R. 290; *Clark v Clark* [2006] EWHC 275; [2006] 1 F.C.R. 421.

746 *Henry v Henry* [2010] UKPC 3; [2010] 1 All E.R. 988.

747 [1991] 1 W.L.R. 113.

748 [2009] UKHL 18; [2009] 1 W.L.R. 776; see para.3-128.

749 cf. *Bradbury v Taylor* [2012] EWCA Civ 1208; [2013] W.T.L.R. 29.

750 *ER Ives Investment Ltd v High* [1967] 2 Q.B. 379; *Crabb v Arun DC* [1976] Ch. 179.

751 See, e.g. *Joyce v Epsom and Ewell BC* [2012] EWCA Civ 1398; [2013] 1 E.G.L.R. 21.

752 *Crabb v Arun DC* [1976] Ch. 179 at 199.

753 *ER Ives Investment Ltd v High* [1967] 2 Q.B. 379.

754 Gardner 115 L.Q.R. 438; 122 L.Q.R. 492; Robertson [2008] Conv. 295; McFarlane and Sales 131 L.Q.R. 610.

755 *Roebuck v Mungovin* [1994] 2 A.C. 224 at 235; cf. the remedy granted in *Gillett v Holt* [2001] Ch. 210.

756 *Jennings v Rice* [2002] EWCA Civ 159; [2003] 1 F.C.R. 501 at [43].

its exercise. In giving effect to the "equity" account must be taken, not only of the claimant's expectations, "but also of the extent of his detrimental reliance";[758] and "there must be proportionality between the expectation and the detriment".[759] For the purpose of achieving such "proportionality" regard must be had to the degree of precision of the promise giving rise to the expectation. Where this amounts to an assurance that an interest in specific property will be transferred in return for specified acts, then an order for the specific enforcement of that promise (once the acts have been done) may be the appropriate remedy.[760] On the other hand, the terms of the promise may be less precise, amounting only to an assurance that some indeterminate benefit will be conferred on the promisee, so that the expectations reasonably arising from it are, at least objectively, uncertain. If so, the court will not give effect in full to expectations which the promisee may in fact have formed if they are "uncertain or extravagant or out of all proportion to the detriment which the claimant has suffered".[761] In such cases, compensation in money is likely to be the more appropriate remedy. That compensation must be proportionate to the detriment, but need not be its precise equivalent:[762] the fact that the detriment was incurred in response to a promise indicating (though in vague terms) some higher level of recompense is also to be taken into account.

The balancing of such factors is illustrated by *Jennings v Rice*[763] where the claimant had worked as gardener-handyman for an elderly widow for some 17 years without pay and had also provided personal care for her in the years of increasing frailty towards the end of her life. He had done so in response to her statements that "he would be alright" and that "all this will be yours one day". The latter statement referred to her house and its contents, valued on her death at £435,000 out of a total estate of £1.285 million. The Court of Appeal upheld an award of £200,000 as being properly proportionate to the detriment suffered by the claimant in reliance on the assurances given to him.[764] Where the estoppel is based on a finding that the detriment suffered by the promisee outweighed any benefit,[765] the benefit received may nonetheless be reflected in the award of less than the full expectation created by the promise.[766]

The inherent flexibility of proprietary estoppel is also capable of dealing with any changes to the property in question which may have occurred between the time that the promise was made and the time when it is to take effect, e.g. upon

---

757 *Jennings v Rice* [2002] EWCA Civ 159; [2003] 1 F.C.R. 501 at [43].

758 *Jennings v Rice* [2002] EWCA Civ 159; [2003] 1 F.C.R. 501 at [49].

759 *Jennings v Rice* [2002] EWCA Civ 159; [2003] 1 F.C.R. 501 at [36]; cf. at [56]; *Fisher v Brooker* [2009] UKHL 41; [2009] 1 W.L.R. 1764 at [11].

760 *Jennings v Rice* [2002] EWCA Civ 159; [2003] 1 F.C.R. 501 at [45].

761 *Jennings v Rice* [2002] EWCA Civ 159; [2003] 1 F.C.R. 501 at [50].

762 *Jennings v Rice* [2002] EWCA Civ 159; [2003] 1 F.C.R. 501 at [51].

763 [2002] EWCA Civ 159; [2003] 1 F.C.R. 501; cf. *Evans v HSBC Trust Co (UK) Ltd* [2005] W.T.L.R. 1299; [2006] 1 F.C.R. 421; *Suggitt v Suggitt* [2012] EWCA Civ 1140; [2012] W.T.L.R. 1607; *Bradbury v Taylor* [2012] EWCA Civ 1208; [2013] W.T.L.R. 29; *Davies v Davies* [2016] EWCA Civ 463; [2017] 1 F.L.R. 1286; *Moore v Moore* [2018] EWCA Civ 2669; [2019] 1 F.L.R. 1237.

764 cf. *Munt v Beasley* [2006] EWCA Civ 370 at [45].

765 See para.3–136.

766 *Henry v Henry* [2010] UKPC 3; [2010] 1 All E.R. 988.

the promisor's death. In *Thorner v Major*,[767] the effect of such changes was that the farm had increased slightly in size, but conversely it may have been necessary for the promisor to sell half the farm to fund his care into old age.[768] Such changes, and the reasons for them, can be taken into account in the remedy to be awarded.

3–146 **The conduct of the promisor.** Apart from the terms of the promise and the extent of the promisee's reliance on them, the court may also take into account the conduct of the promisor after the facts giving rise to the estoppel. Thus, in *Crabb v Arun DC*[769] the defendants acted without warning in blocking the claimants' access to his land. In view of this "high-handedness"[770] and the resulting loss to the claimant, he was not required to make the payment that would otherwise have been a condition of the exercise of the right of way. Similarly, in *Pascoe v Turner*[771] a proprietary estoppel arose when a man told a woman with whom he had formerly cohabited that the house in which they had lived was hers, and she later spent some £230 of her limited resources on repairs and improvements to it. The Court of Appeal relied on the man's "ruthlessness"[772] in seeking to evict the promisee as a ground for ordering him to convey the fee simple to her. The submission that she should have no more than an irrevocable licence to occupy the house was rejected since this would not protect her against a bona fide purchaser from the promisor. The result seems, with respect, unduly punitive; and intermediate possibilities (such as granting the promisee a long lease)[773] were not put before the court.

3–147 **Rights of occupation, or compensation?** *Pascoe v Turner* illustrates the possibility that the grant of an irrevocable licence to remain on the property may constitute an unsatisfactory remedy because it will not adequately secure the promisee's possession. It may also be unsatisfactory on account of its inflexibility: thus in *Inwards v Baker*[774] the remedy would have been of no use to the promisee, had he wanted to move elsewhere; nor would his dependants have had any remedy had he died shortly after completing the house. In such cases, a remedy by way of compensation in money would be more satisfactory for the promisee; and it would also have the advantage for the promisor that dealing with the property would not be impeded for an indefinite time.[775] Such a remedy was

767 [2009] UKHL 18; [2009] 1 W.L.R. 776; see para.3-128.
768 *Thorner v Major* [2009] UKHL 18; [2009] 1 W.L.R. 776 at [19], [65].
769 [1976] Ch. 179.
770 *Crabb v Arun DC* [1976] Ch. 179 at 199; cf. at 189.
771 [1979] 1 W.L.R. 431; Sufrin 42 M.L.R. 574.
772 *Pascoe v Turner* [1979] 1 W.L.R. 431 at 439; cf. the reference in *Gillett v Holt* [2001] Ch. 210 at 235 to the promisee's "bitter humiliation" on being summarily dismissed and made the subject of a police investigation for allegations of dishonesty which the promisor made no attempt to justify at the trial of the civil action.
773 As in *Griffiths v Williams* [1978] E.G. Digest of Cases 919.
774 [1965] 2 Q.B. 29.
775 cf. criticisms of the law by Browne-Wilkinson J in *Re Sharpe* [1980] 1 W.L.R. 219 at 226.

granted in *Dodsworth v Dodsworth*[776] where the promisees spent £700 on improvements to the promisor's bungalow in reliance on an implied promise (not intended to have contractual force) that they could live there as if it were their home. The Court of Appeal held that to give the promisees a right of occupation for an indefinite time would confer on them a greater interest than had been contemplated by the parties; and that the most appropriate remedy was to repay them their outlay on improvements. Compensation in money will also be the more appropriate remedy where, as a practical matter, the promise which gives rise to the estoppel cannot be specifically enforced, e.g. where its performance would involve occupation of premises by, and co-operation between, members of a family who later quarrel,[777] or between a couple whose relationship has broken down.[778] Where there is evidence that the improved property has increased in value by reason of market fluctuations, it is submitted that the amount recoverable by the promisee should be increased correspondingly; conversely it should be reduced where the market value of the property has declined.[779]

In *Dodsworth v Dodsworth*[780] the court awarded compensation even though, when the action was brought, the promisee was still in possession of the improved property. More commonly this form of remedy is granted where the promisee is no longer in possession, having either left voluntarily[781] or been lawfully ejected as a result of legal proceedings.[782] Where the promisee has been wrongly ordered to give up possession, compensation in money is similarly available,[783] though in such a case the court may alternatively order the promisee to be put back into possession of the premises.[784] The compensation has been assessed in a variety of ways: at the cost of improvements made with the promisee's money;[785] at a proportionate interest in the property;[786] or at the reasonable value of the right of occupation, based (presumably) on the cost to the promisee of equivalent alternative accommodation.[787] The flexibility of the remedy also enables the court to combine monetary compensation with specific relief, e.g. in *Gillett v Holt*[788] the promisee was awarded part of the property to which the promise referred, together with a cash payment to compensate him for his exclusion from the farming business on that property.

**Balance of hardship.** The court may, finally, deny the promisee a remedy where, on balance, greater hardship would be produced by giving effect to the promise **3–148**

[776] [1973] E.G. Digest of Cases 233; cf. *Campbell v Griffin* [2001] EWCA Civ 990; [2001] W.T.L.R. 981; *Jennings v Rice* [2002] EWCA Civ 159; [2003] 1 F.C.R. 501; *Evans v HSBC Trust Co (UK) Ltd* [2005] W.T.L.R. 1299.

[777] *Burrows and Burrows v Sharp* (1991) 23 H.L.R. 82; cf. *Baker v Baker* (1993) 25 H.L.R. 408 (where the action was for damages).

[778] *Clough v Kelly* (1996) 72 P. & C.R. D22.

[779] cf. *Cheese v Thomas* [1994] 1 W.L.R. 129, a case of undue influence.

[780] [1973] E.G. Digest of Cases 233.

[781] As in *Hussey v Palmer* [1972] 1 W.L.R. 1286; and *Eves v Eves* [1975] 1 W.L.R. 1338.

[782] As in *Plimmer v Mayor of Wellington* (1884) 9 App. Cas. 699.

[783] *Tanner v Tanner* [1975] 1 W.L.R. 1346 (where there was a contract).

[784] *Tanner v Tanner* [1975] 1 W.L.R. 1346.

[785] *Hussey v Palmer* [1972] 1 W.L.R. 1286; *Burrows and Burrows v Sharp* (1991) 23 H.L.R. 82.

[786] *Eves v Eves* [1975] 1 W.L.R. 1338.

[787] *Tanner v Tanner* [1975] 1 W.L.R. 1346; *Baker v Baker* (1993) 25 H.L.R. 408.

[788] [2001] Ch. 210.

than by allowing the promisor to go back on it, including any hardship which would be done to third parties.[789] This was the position in *Sledmore v Dalby*,[790] where the promisee had contributed to major improvements to the property but at the time of the proceedings had already enjoyed 20 years' rent-free occupation and was gainfully employed, while the promisor was a widow living on social security benefits. The promisee's claim to be entitled to a licence for life to stay in the house was in these circumstances rejected and the promisor was held entitled to possession.

### *(iii) Proprietary and promissory estoppels contrasted*[791]

3–149 **Common features.** Proprietary and promissory estoppels have a number of points in common. Both can arise from promises;[792] consideration is not, while action in reliance is, a necessary condition for their operation;[793] and both are, within limits, revocable.[794] But there are also important differences between the two doctrines.[795]

3–150 **Proprietary estoppel narrower than promissory estoppel.** The scope of proprietary estoppel is in two respects narrower than that of promissory estoppel. First, proprietary estoppel is restricted to promises relating to property (generally the land) of another. Promissory estoppel may, on the other hand, arise (if other necessary conditions are satisfied)[796] out of *any* promise that strict legal rights will not be enforced: there is no need for those rights to relate to land or other property. Secondly, proprietary estoppel requires the promisee to have acted to his detriment,[797] while promissory estoppel may operate even though the promisee merely performs a pre-existing duty and so suffers no detriment in the sense of doing something that he was not previously bound to do.[798] This difference between the two doctrines follows from the fact that promissory estoppel is (unlike proprietary estoppel) concerned only with the variation or abandonment of rights arising out of a pre-existing legal relationship between promisor and promisee.

---

789 See, e.g. *Suggitt v Suggitt* [2011] EWHC 903 (Ch); [2011] 2 F.L.R. 875 at [65]; affirmed [2012] EWCA Civ 1140; [2012] W.T.L.R. 1607; *Evans v HSBC Trust Co (UK) Ltd* [2005] W.T.L.R. 1299.
790 (1996) 72 P. & C.R. 196; cf. *Henry v Henry* [2010] UKPC 3; [2010] 1 All E.R. 988.
791 Evans [1988] Conv. 346.
792 See paras 3–081, 3–090, 3–114, 3–123.
793 See paras 3–083, 3–114, 3–136.
794 See paras 3–086, 3–115, 3–137.
795 In *Cobbe v Yeoman's Row Management Ltd* [2008] UKHL 55; [2008] 1 W.L.R. 1752 Lord Scott (at [14]) described proprietary estoppel as a "sub-species" of promissory estoppel, a view which may be thought consistent with his very narrow conception of proprietary estoppel: see above, fn.674. In *Thorner v Major* [2009] UKHL 18; [2009] 1 W.L.R. 776, Lord Walker (at [67]) had "some difficulty" with Lord Scott's observation, a view which may, in turn, be consistent with his implicit rejection of Lord Scott's narrow conception.
796 See paras 3–081–3–085, 3–112–3–119.
797 See para.3–136.
798 See para.3–084.

**Proprietary estoppel wider than promissory estoppel.** On the other hand, the scope of proprietary estoppel is in two respects wider than that of promissory estoppel. First, promissory estoppel arises only out of a representation or promise that is "clear" or "precise and unambiguous".[799] Proprietary estoppel, on the other hand, can arise where there is no actual promise at all:[800] e.g. in cases of "acquiescence" where one party makes improvements to another's land under a mistake[801] and the other either knows of the mistake[802] or seeks to take unconscionable advantage of it.[803] Even in cases of "encouragement" the requirement of a "clear" representation may not be the same as the requirement for promissory estoppel.[804] **3–151**

**Proprietary estoppel can give rise to a cause of action.** Secondly (and more significantly), while promissory estoppel is essentially defensive in nature,[805] proprietary estoppel can give rise to a cause of action.[806] The promisee is not merely entitled to raise the estoppel as a defence to an action of trespass or to a claim for possession: the court can make an order for the land to be conveyed to him,[807] or for compensation,[808] or for such other remedy as appropriate.[809] Although the authorities support this second distinction between the two kinds of estoppel, they do not make any attempt to explain or justify it. It is submitted that the explanation is in part historical and terminological. Proprietary estoppel was originally explained in terms of *acquiescence*[810] or *encouragement*.[811] Hence no conflict with the requirement that *promises* must be supported by consideration was perceived; or where it was perceived the facts were said to give rise to a contract.[812] Promissory estoppel, on the other hand, dealt principally with the renegotiation of contracts; it obviously depended on giving binding effect to promises, and it did so in the context of releases and variations, in which the common law requirement of consideration had long been established.[813] The rule that promissory estoppel gives rise to no cause of action was evolved to prevent what would otherwise be an obvious conflict between the doctrines of promissory estoppel and consideration. In cases of proprietary estoppel there was no such conflict where liability was based on "acquiescence"; and where it was based on "encouragement" the conflict, though sometimes real enough, was at least less **3–152**

799 See para.3–081.

800 *Thorner v Major* [2009] UKHL 18; [2009] 1 W.L.R. 776: "the classic example of proprietary estoppel is based on silence and inaction" (Lord Neuberger (at [84]); cf. Lord Walker at [54]–[55]).

801 See paras 3–122.

802 *Willmott v Barber* (1880) 15 Ch D. 96 at 105 (the claim in that case failed as the party against whom it was made did not know of the extent of his own rights or of the other party's mistake).

803 *Taylor Fashions Ltd v Liverpool Victoria Trustees Co Ltd* [1982] Q.B. 133.

804 See para.3–128.

805 See paras 3–086–3–088.

806 *Crabb v Arun DC* [1976] Ch. 179 at 187; *Taylor Fashions Ltd v Liverpool Victoria Trustees Co Ltd* [1982] Q.B. 133 at 148; *Thorner v Major* [2009] UKHL 18; [2009] 1 W.L.R. 776 at [61].

807 e.g. *Dillwyn v Llewelyn* (1862) 4 D.F. & G. 517.

808 e.g. *Eves v Eves* [1975] 1 W.L.R. 1338.

809 See paras 3–145–3–148.

810 *Willmott v Barber* (1880) 15 Ch D. 96 at 105.

811 *Ramsden v Dyson* (1866) L.R. 1 H.L. 129 at 170.

812 *Dillwyn v Llewelyn* (1862) 4 D.F. & G. 517 at 522; paras 3–132–3–133.

813 See paras 3–056—3–065.

obvious. There are, moreover, two aspects of proprietary estoppel which help to justify the distinction. These are that the acts done by the promisee are not ones which he was under any previous legal obligation to perform; and that generally their effect would be to unjustly enrich the promisor if he were allowed to go back on his promise.[814] In these respects, the facts on which proprietary estoppel is based provide more compelling grounds for relief than those commonly found in cases of promissory estoppel.

3–153 **Common basis: unconscionability.** While the two doctrines are in these respects distinct it can also be argued that they have a common basis, namely that it would be unconscionable for the promisor to go back on his promise after the promisee has acted on it; and that the precise labels to be attached to them are "immaterial".[815] It is perhaps for these reasons that the distinction between the two kinds of estoppel was described as "not … helpful" by Scarman LJ in *Crabb v Arun DC*.[816] That decision was, in a later case, said to illustrate "the virtual equation of promissory estoppel and proprietary estoppel",[817] perhaps because it extended the operation of proprietary estoppel beyond the situations originally within its scope, namely those in which the promisor would be unjustly enriched by the work done by the promisee on the land unless some legal effect were given to the promise. Nevertheless it is submitted that the doctrines are distinct in the respects stated above.[818] Attempts to unite them by posing "simply" the question whether it would be "unconscionable"[819] for the promisor to go back on his promise are, for reasons given earlier in this chapter,[820] unhelpful;[821] and they are also open to the objection that they provide no basis on which a legal doctrine capable of yielding predictable results can be developed.

### (iv) *Proprietary estoppel and contract contrasted*

3–154 We have seen that some cases which have been said to support the doctrine of proprietary estoppel can be explained on the alternative basis that there was a contract between the parties.[822] But this explanation will not cover all the cases; for proprietary estoppel can operate even though the conditions required for the creation of a contract are not satisfied. The need to discuss the doctrine in this chapter arises precisely because a promise can give rise to a proprietary estoppel

---

[814] See the reference to the landowner's "profit" in *Ramsden v Dyson* (1866) L.R. 1 H.L. 129 at 141 and cf. para.3–133.

[815] *Taylor Fashions Ltd v Liverpool Victoria Trustees Co Ltd* [1982] Q.B. 133 at 153, where, however, a distinction is also drawn between "promissory estoppel" and the principle in *Ramsden v Dyson* (1866) L.R. 1 H.L. 129 (i.e. proprietary estoppel).

[816] [1976] Ch. 179 at 193.

[817] *Taylor Fashions Ltd v Liverpool Victoria Trustees Co Ltd* [1982] Q.B. 133 at 153; cf. also fn.719.

[818] At fnn.805–814.

[819] *Taylor Fashions Ltd v Liverpool Victoria Trustees Co Ltd* [1982] Q.B. 133 at 155; cf. *Amalgamated Investment & Property Co Ltd v Texas Commerce International Bank Ltd* [1982] Q.B. 84 at 104, 122.

[820] See para.3–090.

[821] *Haslemere Estates Ltd v Baker* [1982] 1 W.L.R. 1109 at 1119; cf. *Cobbe v Yeoman's Row Management Ltd* [2008] UKHL 55; [2008] 1 W.L.R. 1752 at [28], [46].

[822] See para.3–133.

even though it is not supported by consideration; and a promise can also give rise to such an estoppel even though it cannot take effect as a contract because it is not sufficiently certain or because it fails to comply with formal requirements. Moreover, the effect of a proprietary estoppel differs from that of a contract. Sometimes, indeed, the result of a proprietary estoppel is to give effect to the promise in the terms in which it was made;[823] but such a result does not follow as of right. We have seen that the promisee's rights may depend, not only on the terms of the promise and on the extent to which he has acted on it, but also on the subsequent conduct of the promisor.[824] The rights arising under a binding contract are fixed at its formation and not subject to such variation in the light of the court's approval or disapproval of the subsequent conduct of one of the parties. For this reason, and because proprietary estoppel may be revocable,[825] it will generally be more advantageous to a party to show the existence of a binding contract (if he can) than to rely on a proprietary estoppel.

## 8. SPECIAL CASES

### (a) Defective promises[826]

Mutual promises are generally consideration for each other,[827] but difficulty is sometimes felt in treating one promise as consideration for another if the first promise suffered from some defect by reason of which it was not legally binding. The law on this topic is based more on expediency than on any supposedly logical deductions which might be drawn from the doctrine of consideration. The question whether a defective promise can constitute consideration for a counter-promise depends on the policy of the rule of law making the former promise defective. 3–155

**Policy considerations.** One group of cases concerns contracts made between persons, one of whom lacks contractual capacity.[828] A minor can enforce a promise made to him under such a contract, even though the only consideration for that promise is his own promise, which does not bind him by reason of his minority.[829] The same rule applies to contracts with persons who lack mental capacity.[830] The reason for these rules is that it is the policy of the law to protect the person under the incapacity, and not the other party, who is therefore not allowed to rely on that incapacity. A contrasting group of cases concerns promises which are illegal. Obviously the illegal promise cannot be enforced; and if both promises are illegal the consequence that neither can be enforced follows from the policy of the invalidating rule rather than from the fact that an illegal promise 3–156

[823] e.g. *Dillwyn v Llewelyn* (1862) 4 D.F. & G. 517.
[824] See para.3–153.
[825] See para.3–137.
[826] Treitel 77 L.Q.R. 83.
[827] See para.3–008.
[828] See Ch.12.
[829] *Holt v Ward Clarencieux* (1732) 2 Stra. 937.
[830] See para.12–053 and following.

cannot constitute consideration.[831] But in some cases of illegal contracts the illegality affects the promise or promises of only one party: this is, for example, often the position where the contract is in restraint of trade. In such a case, the party who makes the illegal promise cannot enforce the counter-promise (e.g. to pay a sum of money) if the illegal promise constitutes the sole consideration for the counter-promise.[832] Indeed, the position is the same if the illegal promise is the *main* consideration for the counter-promise, even though there was also some other consideration for it.[833] The reason for this rule lies in the policy of the law to discourage illegal bargains.

3–157 **Performance of defective promise.** Where a defective *promise* does not amount to consideration its *performance* can nevertheless sometimes provide consideration for the counter-promise. For example, a mere promise to negotiate has no contractual force[834] and so cannot constitute consideration for a counter-promise; but actually carrying on the negotiations can satisfy the requirement of consideration.[835] A similar principle accounts for the rule that a victim of misrepresentation, duress or undue influence can sue but not be sued: by suing, he affirms the contract, makes his own promise binding on himself, and so supplies consideration for the other party's promise. But where the promise of one party is illegal, even its performance does not entitle that party to enforce the counter-promise,[836] for the law must not give him any incentive to perform the illegal promise.

3–158 **Promise defective by statute.** Where a promise is defective by statute, the terms of the statute may solve the problem whether the person giving the defective promise can sue on the counter-promise.[837] Thus a party who gives a promise which is defective under s.4 of the Statute of Frauds 1677, or under s.34 of the Matrimonial Causes Act 1973, may, in spite of not being bound by that promise, be entitled to enforce the counter-promise;[838] and this may be so even though for other purposes (such as the validity of a disposition) a promise, precisely because it is defective by statute, does amount to consideration.[839] Where a statute invalidates a promise but does not provide for the effect of its invalidity on the other party's promise, it seems that the invalid promise is not good

[831] As suggested in *Nerot v Wallace* (1789) 3 T.R. 17 at 23.
[832] e.g. *Wyatt v Kreglinger & Fernau* [1933] 1 K.B. 793.
[833] See *Goodinson v Goodinson* [1954] 2 Q.B. 118; the actual decision is obsolete in view of Matrimonial Causes Act 1973 s.34.
[834] See para.2–100.
[835] *Sepong Engineering Construction Co Ltd v Formula One Management Ltd* [2000] 1 Lloyd's Rep. 602 at 611, where it was also said that damages for breach of the resulting contract would be no more than nominal: para.20–062.
[836] e.g. *Wyatt v Kreglinger & Fernall* [1933] 1 K.B. 793.
[837] See *Laythoarp v Bryant* (1836) 2 Bing. N.C. 735.
[838] See paras 5–027, 11–048.
[839] *Re Kumar* [1993] 1 W.L.R. 224, where a void promise was held not to constitute consideration for the purpose of protecting third parties under Insolvency Act 1986 s.339.

consideration;[840] but, unless the promise is illegal, the party giving it can sue on the counter-promise if he actually performs his own promise.[841]

**Both promises defective by statute.** A statute may also invalidate *both* promises: this was formerly the position with regard to wagering contracts which were "null and void" under s.18 of the Gaming Act 1845.[842] Performance of one such promise clearly would not make the other enforceable;[843] but the question whether performance of the void promise could constitute consideration might also arise in another context, e.g. in the context of the question whether the performance amounted to consideration for the purpose of a rule of law by which a transfer or disposition of property was effective only if made for valuable consideration. This was the question which arose in *Lipkin Gorman v Karpnale Ltd*,[844] where stolen money was used by the thief for gambling at a club of which he was a member, and it was held that the club had not received the money for valuable consideration so as to be entitled, as against the owner of the money, to retain it. We have already noted that the club did not provide consideration for the payment by exchanging the money for gaming chips.[845] The present point is that the club did not provide consideration for the payments made to it by the member by allowing him to gamble and promising to pay, or actually paying him, the amount of any bets which he had won. The club's *promise* to pay did not amount to consideration since it was, at that time, void under s.18 of the 1845 Act. 3–159

### (b) Unilateral contracts[846]

In the case of a unilateral contract the promisee clearly provides consideration if he completes the required act or forbearance (such as walking to York or not smoking for a year).[847] This amounts in law to a detriment to the promisee; and the promisor may also obtain a benefit, e.g. where he promises a reward for the return of lost property and it is actually returned to him. But it has been suggested that if the promisee has begun, but not yet completed, the required act or forbearance the promisor can still withdraw. At this stage, there is said to be no consideration for the promise, since the promisee is not bound to complete performance.[848] But it may in law be detriment to walk part of the way to York, or to forbear from smoking for part of the year. Questions of fact may, indeed, arise in determining whether performance has actually begun, particularly where the 3–160

[840] *Clayton v Jennings* (1760) 2 W. Bl. 706.
[841] This, it is submitted, is the best justification for *Rajbenback v Mamon* [1955] 1 Q.B. 283; see 77 L.Q.R. 95. For another view, see Unger 19 M.L.R. 99.
[842] Repealed by s.334 of the Gambling Act 2005.
[843] cf. at fn.832.
[844] [1991] 2 A.C. 548.
[845] See para.3–032, fn.151.
[846] See para.2–052 and following.
[847] See para.2–053; *Marshall v N M Financial Management Ltd* [1997] 1 W.L.R. 1527 at 1533. For controversy whether the act must be "requested" by the promisor in cases of unilateral contracts, see A.L.G. 67 L.Q.R. 456; Smith 69 L.Q.R. 99; A.L.G. 69 L.Q.R. 106.
[848] Wormser in *Selected Readings on the Law of Contracts*, p.307; but for the same writer's later views, see 3 Jl. Leg. Educ. 146.

stipulated performance was a forbearance; but if an actual forbearance *to sue* can constitute good consideration,[849] it must in principle be possible to tell when a forbearance has begun. Thus commencement of performance (whether of an act or of a forbearance) may provide consideration for the promise and so deprive the promisor of the power to withdraw it. Of course, the promisor's liability to pay the amount promised (e.g. the £100 for walking to York) does not accrue before the promisee has fully performed the required act or forbearance. The present point is merely that, after part performance by the promisee, the promisor cannot withdraw his promise with impunity.[850]

It has been suggested that a unilateral contract may be made as soon as the offer is received by the offeree;[851] and this could be interpreted to mean that the contract was binding even before the offeree had acted on the offer in any way. But at this stage the offeree has clearly not provided any consideration, and in the case in which the suggestion was made no problem of consideration arose as the offeree had completed the required act[852] before any attempt to withdraw the offer was made. Except in the case of bankers' irrevocable credits (to be discussed below), the better view is that an offer of a unilateral contract is not binding on receipt, but only when the offeree has begun to render the required performance.

### (c) Bankers' irrevocable credits

**3–161** Contracts for the international sale of goods often provide for payment by irrevocable credit.[853] The buyer instructs his bank to open an irrevocable credit in favour of the seller; and the bank then notifies the seller that such a credit has been opened in his favour, and that he will be paid, usually when he tenders specified shipping documents to the bank. The general view is that the bank is bound by this arrangement and is not entitled to withdraw simply because the shipping documents have not yet been tendered.[854] But it is very doubtful whether at this stage there is any consideration, moving from the seller, for the bank's promise to him.[855] If (as seems probable) this view also represents the law, it is best regarded as an exception to the doctrine of consideration.[856]

---

849 See para.3–040.

850 *Schweppe v Harper* [2008] EWCA Civ 442; [2008] B.P.I.R 1090 at [42].

851 *Harvela Investments Ltd v Royal Trust Co of Canada (CI) Ltd* [1986] 1 A.C. 207 at 224 ("when the invitation was received").

852 By submitting the requested bid: cf. para.2–022.

853 See generally *Guaranty Trust Co of NY v Hannay* [1918] 2 K.B. 623 at 659.

854 *WJ Alan & Co Ltd v El Nasr Export & Import Co* [1972] 2 Q.B. 189 at 208; cf. [1972] 2 Q.B. 189 at 218; *Trendtex Trading Corp v Central Bank of Nigeria* [1977] Q.B. 529 at 551; *The American Accord* [1983] 1 A.C. 168 at 183.

855 cf. *Raiffeisen Zentralbank Osterreich Attorney General v China Marine Bunker (Petrochina) Co Ltd* [2006] EWHC 212; [2006] All E.R. (D) 37 at [31] (collecting bank entitled to sue buyer under irrevocable payment undertaking: consideration from the bank "may be said to be provided by the recognised financial role of the bank in the transaction in making funds available").

856 cf. in the US, U.C.C. ss.5–105.

## (d) Firm offers

**Revocable unless supported by consideration.** A "firm" offer is one containing a promise not to revoke it for a specified time. Such a promise is not binding unless the offeree has provided some consideration for it. Thus in *Dickinson v Dodds*[857] it was held that an offer to sell land "to be left over until Friday" could be withdrawn on Thursday. Consideration for such a promise is most obviously provided if the offeree pays (or promises to pay) a sum of money for it and so buys an option.[858] It may also be provided by some other promise, e.g. in the case of an offer to sell a house, the offeree may provide consideration for the offeror's promise to hold the offer open, by promising to apply for a mortgage on the house; and, in the case of an offer to buy shares, the offeree may provide consideration for the offeror's promise not to revoke the offer for a specified time, by promising not to dispose of those shares elsewhere during that time. 3–162

The performance of the offeree's promises in such cases could likewise provide consideration for the offeror's promise to keep the offer open. In one case a vendor of land entered into a so-called "lock-out" agreement[859] by which he promised a prospective purchaser not to consider other offers if that purchaser would exchange contracts within two weeks; and it was said that "the promise by the [purchaser] to get on by limiting himself to just two weeks"[860] constituted consideration for the vendor's promise not to consider other offers. Such a "lock out" promise is not strictly a firm offer since it does not prevent the vendor from deciding not to sell at all; but the reasoning quoted above could apply to the case of a firm offer. On the facts of the case from which it is taken, the reasoning gives rise to some difficulty since it does not appear that the purchaser there made any *promise* to exchange contracts within two weeks. It seems more plausible to say that the vendor's promise had become binding as a unilateral contract under which the purchaser had provided consideration by actually making efforts to meet the deadline, even though he had not promised to do so.

Similar reasoning can apply if a seller of land promises to keep an offer open for a month, asking the buyer during that period to raise the necessary money. If the buyer makes efforts to that end (without actually promising to do so) it is arguable that he has by part performance accepted the seller's offer of a unilateral

[857] (1876) 2 Ch D. 463; cf. *Routledge v Grant* (1828) 4 Bing. 653; *Head v Diggon* (1828) 3 M. & Ry. 97.

[858] The legal characteristics of such an option have been variously described: (1) as a contract: *Greene v Church Commissioners for England* [1974] Ch. 467 at 476, 478; though not one of sale: *Chippenham Golf Club v North Wilts Rural DC* (1992) 64 P. & C.R. 527; (2) as a transaction which, even though it is not a contract, gives rise to an interest in property: *Re Button's Lease* [1964] Ch. 263 at 270–271; *Armstrong & Holmes Ltd v Holmes* [1994] 1 All E.R. 826; (3) as a unilateral contract: *United Scientific Holdings Ltd v Burnley BC* [1978] A.C. 904 at 945; *Little v Courage Ltd* (1995) 70 P. & C.R. 469 at 474; (4) as a conditional contract: *Bircham & Co Nominees (No.2) Ltd v Worrell Holdings Ltd* [2001] EWCA Civ 773; (2001) 82 P. & C.R. 427 at [45]; (5) as "an irrevocable offer which only matures into a bilateral contract upon its due exercise": *Re Gray* [2004] EWHC 1538 (Ch); [2005] 1 W.L.R. 815 at [25]; and (6) as being sui generis: *Spiro v Glencrown Properties* [1991] Ch. 537 at 544. See Mowbray 74 L.Q.R. 242; Lücke 3 Adelaide L. Rev. 200.

[859] See para.4–015.

[860] *Pitt v PHH Asset Management Ltd* [1994] 1 W.L.R. 327 at 332; for other consideration in this case, see para.3–038; *Tye v House* [1997] 2 E.G.L.R. 171.

contract to keep the principal offer open. On the other hand promissory estoppel[861] will not avail the offeree since it does not create new causes of action where none existed before.[862] Nor does it seem likely that an offeree who suffers loss as a result of the withdrawal of the offer will be able to claim damages in tort[863] for misrepresentation.[864]

3–163 **Criticism.** The rule in *Dickinson v Dodds* can lead to inconvenience, so much so that there are some situations in which it has been said that "the market would disdain"[865] to take the point that there was no consideration for a promise to keep an offer open. In the case of certain international sales, the rule is rejected by the Vienna Convention on Contracts for the International Sale of Goods.[866] It is also subject to a common law exception in the law of insurance where an underwriter who initials a slip under an "open cover" arrangement is regarded as making a "standing offer" which the insured can accept from time to time by making "declarations" under it. The underwriter's commitment is regarded as binding even though there is no consideration for his implied promise not to revoke the "standing offer".[867] But even with these mitigations, the rule can still cause hardship to an offeree who has acted in reliance on the assurance that the offer will be kept open for a stated time. Such hardship can, for example, arise where a builder submits a tender in reliance on offers from sub-contractors, expressed to remain "firm" for a fixed period, and those offers are withdrawn within that period but after his tender has been accepted. On the other hand, the rule does sometimes provide necessary protection for the offeror, e.g. when an offer is made by a customer on a form provided by a supplier and expressed to be irrevocable; or when the period of irrevocability is not specified so that the offeror is left subject to an indefinite obligation without acquiring any corresponding right. Any further development of the law on the point will require a balancing of these conflicting factors.[868]

---

861 See para.3–077 and following.

862 See para.3–088.

863 cf. *Holman Construction Ltd v Delta Timber Co Ltd* [1972] N.Z.L.R. 1081; and see *Blackpool and Fylde Aero Club Ltd v Blackpool BC* [1990] 1 W.L.R. 1195 at 1202.

864 i.e. under *Hedley Byrne & Co Ltd v Heller & Partners Ltd* [1964] A.C. 465; para.9–042.

865 *Jaglom v Excess Insurance Co Ltd* [1972] 2 Q.B. 250 at 258; cf. *County Ltd v Girozentrale Securities* [1996] 3 All E.R. 834 at 837. For the view that the statement in *Jaglom*'s case was not an offer, but an acceptance (and binding as such), see *General Reinsurance Corp v Forsakringsaktiebolaget Fennia Patria* [1983] Q.B. 856 at 863–864.

866 Article 16(2); cf. U.C.C. s.2–205, limiting the period of irrevocability to three months on the theory that unlimited irrevocability could unreasonably prejudice the offeror.

867 *Citadel Insurance Co v Atlantic Union Insurance Co* [1982] 2 Lloyd's Rep. 543 at 546. Contrast *Beazley Underwriting Ltd v Travelers Companies Inc* [2011] EWHC 1520 (Comm); [2012] Lloyd's Rep. I.R. 78 at [173] ("preliminary" slips).

868 See Law Commission, Working Paper No.60 (1975).

### (e) Auction sales without reserve[869]

Where goods are put up for auction without reserve, there is no contract *of sale* if the auctioneer refuses to knock the goods down to the highest bidder; but the auctioneer is liable to the highest bidder on a separate promise that the sale will be without reserve.[870] It is arguable that there is no consideration for this promise as the highest bidder is not bound by his unaccepted bid.[871] But it has been held that the bidder suffers a detriment by bidding on the strength of the promise, for he runs the risk of being bound by a contract of sale;[872] and the auctioneer benefits as the bidding is driven up.[873] Hence there is consideration for the separate promise, and it makes no difference to the auctioneer's liability *on this promise* that he would not be liable if he did not put the goods up for sale at all (since an advertisement of an auction is not an offer to hold it)[874] or that there was no contract *of sale* because of his refusal to accept the highest bid.[875] **3–164**

### (f) Novation of partnership debts

When the composition of a partnership changes, it is usual to arrange that liability for the debts owed by the existing partners should be transferred by novation[876] to the new partners. Two situations may be considered. **3–165**

**Retirement and admission of new partner.** A and B are in partnership; A retires and C is admitted as a new partner; it is agreed between A, B and C, and the creditors of the old firm of A and B, that A shall cease to be liable for the firm's debts, and that C shall undertake such liability. The result is that the creditors can sue C[877] and can no longer sue A. They provide consideration for C's promise to pay by abandoning their claim against A; and A provides consideration for their promise to release him by procuring a substitute debtor, C. **3–166**

**Retirement without admission of new partner.** A and B are in partnership; A retires; it is agreed between A, B and the creditors of the firm that A shall cease to be liable and that B shall be solely liable. It seems that the creditors cannot sue A, but it is hard to see what consideration moves from him. In one case it was said that there was consideration in that a remedy against a single debtor might be **3–167**

[869] See also para.2–008.

[870] *Warlow v Harrison* (1859) 1 E. & E. 309; approved in *Harris v Nickerson* (1873) L.R. 8 Q.B. 286 at 288; *Johnston v Boyes* [1899] 2 Ch. 73 at 77.

[871] For discussion of this point, see Slade 68 L.Q.R. 238; Gower 68 L.Q.R. 457; Slade 69 L.Q.R. 21.

[872] An "invented" consideration: see para.3–009.

[873] *Barry v Davies* [2000] 1 W.L.R. 1962 at 1967.

[874] *Harris v Nickerson* (1873) L.R. 8 Q.B. 286; para.2–008.

[875] See para.2–008.

[876] See para.15–003; cf. Partnership Act 1890 s.17(3).

[877] cf. *Re Burton Marsden Douglas* [2004] EWHC 593; [2004] 3 All E.R. 2322 where two new partners could not be sued because there had been no agreement to novate and no consideration from the creditor since there was no promise to release the original partner.

easier to enforce than one against several, all of whom are solvent;[878] thus the creditors benefit by the release of A. This is a possible, if invented[879] consideration.[880]

### (g) Gratuitous bailments

3–168 **Bailment for the benefit of the bailee.** A gratuitous bailment may be for the benefit of either the bailee or the bailor. The first possibility is illustrated by *Bainbridge v Firmstone*[881] where the defendant asked for, and received, permission from the claimant to weigh two boilers belonging to the claimant. In performing this operation, the defendant damaged the boilers; and he was held liable for breach of his promise to return them in good condition. The court rejected the argument that, as the defendant was not paid to weigh, or look after, the boilers, there was no consideration for his promise. Patteson J said: "I suppose the defendant thought he had some benefit; at any rate there is a detriment to the (claimant) from his parting with the possession for even so short a time."[882] It is more doubtful whether there would be any consideration moving from the defendant for any promise by the claimant to allow the defendant to have possession of the boilers. A mere promise by the defendant to return the boilers might not suffice as it would only be a promise to perform a duty imposed by law on all bailees; but a promise to repair the boilers or to improve them in some way would probably be regarded as consideration moving from the defendant.[883]

3–169 **Bailment for the benefit of the bailor.** The second possibility arises where A undertakes the safekeeping of B's chattel without reward. Here B's parting with the possession is hardly a detriment to him; and A's duty to look after the thing[884] does not arise out of a contractual promise made by him but is imposed by the general law. It follows that A's *only* duty is that imposed by the law.[885] Thus A is under no obligation before he actually receives the thing; and if he promised to do anything which went beyond the duty imposed by law (e.g. to keep the thing in repair) he would be bound by this promise only if B had provided some consideration for it apart from the delivery of the chattel.[886] To constitute such consideration, it is not necessary to show that A profited from the transaction;

[878] *Lyth v Ault* (1852) 7 Ex. 669; *Thompson v Percival* (1834) 5 B. & Ad. 925 is based on reasoning which is obsolete after *D & C Builders Ltd v Rees* [1967] 2 Q.B. 617.
[879] See para.3–009.
[880] cf. *Re Burton Marsden Douglas* [2004] EWHC 593 (Ch), [2004] 3 All E.R. 222 (no novation where A incurred a debt as an individual and then went into partnership with B and C).
[881] (1838) 8 A. & E. 743.
[882] *Bainbridge v Firmstone* (1838) 8 A. & E. 743 at 744.
[883] cf. *Verrall v Farnes* [1966] 1 W.L.R. 1254, a case relating to land; followed in *Mitton v Farrow* (1980) 255 E.G. 449.
[884] For this duty see *Coggs v Bernard* (1703) 2 Ld.Raym. 909; *Mitchell v Ealing LBC* [1979] Q.B. 1; *Port Swettenham Authority v T W Wu & Co* [1979] A.C. 580 at 590.
[885] *Morris v CW Martin Ltd* [1966] 1 Q.B. 716 at 731.
[886] cf. *Charnock v Liverpool Corp* [1968] 1 W.L.R. 1498; para.14–007. The scope of A's duty imposed by law may nonetheless take into account "promises" which are made, e.g. as to the mode of safekeeping: *Yearworth v North Bristol NHS Trust* [2009] EWCA Civ 37; [2010] Q.B. 1.

thus it is enough if B reimburses (or promises to reimburse) any expenses that A has incurred for the purpose of performing his promise.[887]

### (h) Gratuitous services

**No liability in contract.** Normally, a promise to render services without reward is not binding contractually as no consideration for it is provided by the promisee. For example, where A gratuitously promises B to insure B's property but fails to do so, A is not liable to B for breach of contract if the property is lost or damaged.[888] It may sometimes be possible to find consideration in an indirect benefit which the promisor obtains from the arrangement, e.g. in the form of favourable publicity.[889] **3–170**

**Liability in tort.** Even where the promise is not supported by consideration, the promisor may be liable in tort for negligence if he renders the gratuitous services but does so without due care and so causes loss. A banker who gives a negligent credit reference may be liable on this ground even though he makes no charge to the person to whom the information is given.[890] Similarly, where A gratuitously promised B to insure B's property and did so negligently, so that the policy did not cover the loss which occurred, A was held liable to B in tort.[891] In one case, a person was even held liable in tort for negligently giving free advice to a friend in connection with the purchase of a second-hand car which turned out to be seriously defective.[892] **3–171**

In the cases just considered, the defendant was guilty of the negligent *performance* of a gratuitous service. In tort there is generally no liability for *non-performance*, i.e. "for pure omission",[893] but where there has been an "assumption of responsibility" by the defendant upon which the claimant has relied,[894] a duty of care may be owed and it has been said that such liability covers "acts of omission, as well as acts of commission".[895] While therefore it has been said that to impose liability in tort for simply doing nothing after having

---

[887] *CCC Films (London) Ltd v Impact Quadrant Films Ltd* [1985] Q.B. 16 at 27.

[888] *Argy Trading & Development Co Ltd v Lapid Developments Ltd* [1977] 1 W.L.R. 444.

[889] cf. *De la Bere v Pearson* [1908] 1 K.B. 280 at 287.

[890] See *Hedley Byrne & Co Ltd v Heller & Partners Ltd* [1964] A.C. 465; cf. para.9–042.

[891] *Wilkinson v Coverdale* (1793) 1 Esp. 75.

[892] *Chaudhry v Prabhakar* [1989] 1 W.L.R. 29 where the defendant conceded that he owed a duty of care to the claimant and two members of the Court of Appeal seem to have regarded this concession as correct; Brown [1989] L.M.C.L.Q. 148. Contrast *Henderson v Merrett Syndicates Ltd* [1995] 2 A.C. 145 at 181, suggesting that there may be no liability in respect of services rendered on "an informal occasion."

[893] *Outram v Academy Plastics Ltd* [2001] I.C.R. 367 at 372.

[894] See para.9–046.

[895] *White v Jones* [1995] 2 A.C. 207 at 268, 295 (where the solicitor was under a duty to act under his contract with the testator: see para.14–057); *Lennon v Metropolitan Police Commissioner* [2004] EWCA Civ 130; [2004] 1 W.L.R. 2594 at [21]. Quaere whether the wrongful conduct in *Lennon* was one of "omission", or "commission"; cf. *Van Oppen v Clerk to the Bedford Charity Trustees* [1990] 1 W.L.R. 235 at 260.

promised to render services gratuitously "would be inconsistent with fundamental principle",[896] it seems that, in some cases, such a promise may be enforceable in negligence.

## 9. PROMISES IN DEEDS

3–172 **Requirements for a deed.** Consideration is not necessary for the validity of a promise in a deed.[897] The binding force of such a promise does not depend on contract at all. Thus, it can take effect although the person in whose favour it was made did not know of it.[898] To take effect as a deed, an instrument must make it clear on its face that it is intended to be a deed and must be validly executed as such.[899] At common law, execution of an instrument as a deed had to be under seal, but in many cases the requirement of sealing has been abolished by legislation. Sealing is no longer necessary in the case of an instrument executed as a deed by an individual.[900] To be validly executed as a deed, such an instrument[901] must be signed[902] by or at the direction of the person making it in the presence of one attesting witness if it is signed by that person or of two such witnesses if it is signed at his direction;[903] and it must also be delivered.[904] Sealing is also no longer necessary for the execution of a deed by a company incorporated under the Companies Acts: a document signed by two "authorized signatories",[905] or by a director of the company in the presence of a witness who attests the signature has the same effect as if executed under the common seal of the company;[906] and (even if the company has no common seal)[907] a document executed by the company which makes it clear on its face that it is intended to be

---

[896] *The Zephyr* [1985] 2 Lloyd's Rep. 529 at 538; cf. *Burgess v Lejonvarn* [2017] EWCA Civ 254; [2017] B.L.R. 277 at [88].

[897] Though see the reference to the "presumed consideration imported by the deed" in Consumer Rights Act 2015, s.3(3)(d).

[898] *Hall v Palmer* (1844) 3 Hare 532; *Macedo v Stroud* [1922] 2 A.C. 330.

[899] Law of Property (Miscellaneous Provisions) Act 1989 s.1(2). The requirement to make clear the intention to create a deed is separate from the requirement of valid execution: *HSBC Trust Co (UK) Ltd v Quinn* [2007] EWHC 1543 (Ch) at [51]; *Katara Hospitality v Guez* [2018] EWHC 3063 (Comm).

[900] 1989 Act s.1(1)(b).

[901] On what is, and is not, permissible to produce the instrument in accordance with the requirements in s.1(3), see *R. (on the application of Mercury Tax Group Ltd) v Revenue and Customs Commissioners* [2008] EWHC 2721; [2009] S.T.C. 743 at [40].

[902] Making one's mark suffices: Law of Property (Miscellaneous Provisions) Act 1989 s.1(4).

[903] Law of Property (Miscellaneous Provisions) Act 1989 s.1(3)(a). In *Shah v Shah* [2001] EWCA Civ 527; [2001] 4 All E.R. 138 it was held that, though the requirement of signing was "fundamental" (at [28]), the requirement of the attesting witness' presence at the time of the signature was not; and that the maker of the instrument could be estopped from denying that the latter requirement was satisfied where, by delivering the instrument, he had unambiguously represented that the instrument had been validly executed.

[904] Law of Property (Miscellaneous Provisions) Act 1989 s.1(3)(b); see para.3-174.

[905] As defined by Companies Act 2006 s.44(3).

[906] Companies Act 2006 s.44(4). This provision can apply where a document purporting to be sealed is not properly sealed: *OTV Birwelco Ltd v Technical & General Guarantee Co* [2002] EWHC 2240 (TCC); [2002] 4 All E.R. 668 at [70]; cf. *Redcard Ltd v Williams* [2011] EWCA Civ 466; [2011] All E.R. 444.

[907] Companies Act 2006 s.45(1).

a deed has effect upon delivery as a deed.[908] Under the system of electronic conveyancing made possible by the Land Registration Act 2002, certain electronic documents relating to the transfer of interests in land[909] are to be regarded as deeds "for the purposes of any enactment".[910]

**Sealing.** The common law requirement of sealing, where it is still required, has been laxly interpreted. There need be no actual seal: it is enough if the document indicates where the seal is meant to be, and is signed with the intention of executing it as a deed.[911] **3–173**

**Delivery.** Delivery does not mean transfer of possession, but conduct indicating that the person who has executed the deed intends to be bound by it.[912] Delivery can be effected by giving the deed to the beneficiary, or to a third person to hold for him, but it is perfectly possible for the grantor to "deliver" the deed and yet keep possession of it.[913] In the case of both a corporation aggregate[914] and a company incorporated under the Companies Act 2006,[915] a document is presumed to be delivered upon its being executed,[916] unless a contrary intention appears. **3–174**

**Delivered as an escrow.** A document may be executed as a deed and delivered with the intention that it is to take effect only on the occurrence of some condition. The document is then said to be delivered as an escrow.[917] It will become effective as a deed only if the condition occurs; though it may then relate back to the date of the original delivery. For example, if the document is a lease, rent under it is payable from that date, unless the document specifies some other date.[918] Even before the occurrence of the condition, the document has some legal effect; it cannot be revoked by the grantor so long as it remains possible for the condition to occur.[919] The document will, however, cease to have this effect if the condition fails to occur within the time specified for its occurrence by the document.[920] Where no such time is specified, a term is likely to be implied that the condition must be fulfilled within a reasonable time.[921] **3–175**

[908] Companies Act 2006 s.46(1).

[909] See para.5–009.

[910] Land Registration Act 2002 s.91(5).

[911] *First National Securities Ltd v Jones* [1978] Ch. 109. Contrast *TCB Ltd v Gray* [1987] Ch. 458; *Rushingdale SA v Byblos Bank SAL* 1985 P.C.C. 342.

[912] *Xenos v Wickham* (1866) L.R. 2 H.L. 296; cf. *Beesly v Hallwood Estates Ltd* [1960] 1 W.L.R. 549 at 562; affirmed [1961] Ch. 105; *Vincent v Premo Enterprises (Voucher Sales) Ltd* [1969] 2 Q.B. 609; *Bibby Financial Services Ltd v Magson* [2011] EWHC 2495 (QB).

[913] *Doe v Knight* (1826) 5 B. & C. 671.

[914] Law of Property Act 1925 s.74(A)(2).

[915] Companies Act 2006 s.46(2).

[916] The requirements for valid execution still differ as between the two: para.3–172.

[917] See, e.g. *Davy Offshore Ltd v Emerald Field Contracting Ltd* [1992] 2 Lloyd's Rep. 142 at 155.

[918] *Alan Estates Ltd v WG Stores Ltd* [1982] Ch. 511.

[919] *Alan Estates Ltd v WG Stores Ltd* [1982] Ch. 511 at 520–521 and 527 rejecting a dictum in *Terrapin International Investments v IRC* [1976] 1 W.L.R. 665 at 669 that before the condition is fulfilled the escrow has "no effect whatsoever"; cf. para.2–107.

[920] *Glessing v Green* [1975] 1 W.L.R. 863.

[921] *Alan Estates Ltd v WG Stores Ltd* [1982] Ch. 511 at 520.

It is sometimes difficult to distinguish between a deed which has not been delivered at all and one which has been delivered as an escrow.[922] The distinction depends on the intention of the grantor. If he reserves an overriding power to recall the deed at his discretion, it is not delivered as an escrow but is simply an undelivered deed.[923]

## 10. PROPOSALS FOR REFORM

3–176 **Criticism.**[924] The doctrine of consideration has attracted much criticism on general and on particular grounds. It has been said that the doctrine is an historical accident; that foreign systems do without it; and that it can easily be evaded, e.g. by the device of nominal consideration.[925] But these criticisms fail to come to grips with the fundamental question: whether it is desirable to enforce informal gratuitous promises. So long as the rights and interests of third parties are adequately protected,[926] the enforcement of such promises may do no harm. On the other hand, English law does recognise, in the deed, a perfectly safe and relatively simple means of making gratuitous promises binding. Many such promises are in fact made by deed for tax purposes; and for this reason the legal enforceability of promises to give money to charitable institutions presents no serious problem in England.[927] Moreover, the small amount of extra effort, which the execution of a deed requires the promisor to make, may be a useful safeguard against rash promises.[928] The availability of the deed does not solve the problem of action in reliance on an *informal* gratuitous promise; but where there is such action the court may be able to invent consideration, or to give at least some effect to the promise under the doctrine of waiver or in equity.[929]

The doctrine can also cause inconvenience where the law for some reason treats a promise as not being supported by consideration even though the parties reasonably regard it as having been made for value.[930] This is particularly true in the existing duty cases, and in the cases on part payment of a debt. In those cases the doctrine of consideration may indeed at one time have performed a useful function in protecting a promisor against undue pressure or other undesirable conduct on the part of the promisee.[931] But this function is now more

[922] See *Vincent v Premo Enterprises (Voucher Sales) Ltd* [1969] 2 Q.B. 609; *Kingston v Ambrian Investments Ltd* [1975] 1 W.L.R. 161.

[923] *Windsor Refrigerator Co Ltd v Branch Nominees Ltd* [1961] Ch. 88 at 102; actual decision reversed on other grounds [1961] Ch. 375; cf. *Silver Queen Maritime Ltd v Persia Petroleum Services Plc* [2010] EWHC 2867 (QB).

[924] *Gay Choon Ing v Loh Sze Ti Terence Peter* [2009] 2 S.L.R. 332 at [92]–[118].

[925] See para.3–014.

[926] cf. para.3–013; *Eastwood v Kenyon* (1840) 11 A. & E. 438 at 450; and *Horrocks v Forray* [1976] 1 W.L.R. 230 (where a finding that there was no consideration helped to protect the creditors of the alleged promisor).

[927] There appear to be only two reported cases in which such claims failed for want of consideration; *Re Hudson* (1885) 54 L.J. Ch. 811; and *Re Cory* (1912) 29 T.L.R. 18.

[928] cf. para.5–002.

[929] See paras 3–009, 3–076–3–092, 3–113–3–119.

[930] e.g. paras 3–043–3–052, 3–102–3–103.

[931] See paras 3–044, 3–102.

satisfactorily provided by the expanding notion of duress,[932] and the authorities have recognised this point, by holding that the requirement of consideration can be satisfied by the performance of, or the promise to perform, an existing duty, even if it causes no legal detriment to the promisee, so long as it results in a factual benefit to the promisor.[933] On the other hand, the function of the doctrine in providing protection against the different risk of being bound by rashly made gratuitous promises remains an important one and must be taken into account in formulating proposals for reform.

**Proposals for reform.**[934] A number of such proposals were made in 1937 by the Law Revision Committee.[935] Detailed discussion of these proposals no longer seems to be appropriate since some of them have been overtaken by later developments in the law[936] and since proposals for reform, if now revived, would no doubt differ substantially from those made in 1937. Two central questions remain: first, whether the law should protect the promisor and third parties by retaining restrictions on the enforceability of gratuitous promises; and secondly, to what extent the law should protect a promisee who has reasonably acted in reliance on a promise which is not supported by consideration. So far as the second question is concerned, the present law amounts to a compromise solution,[937] giving the promisee *some* remedy on the ground of such reliance. This compromise could be carried further[938] by providing that the promisee, while not necessarily entitled in full to the promised performance,[939] should at least be compensated to the extent to which he has been prejudiced as a result of his reliance on the promise.[940] **3–177**

---

[932] See para.3–048, para.10–007.

[933] *Pao On v Lau Yiu Long* [1980] A.C. 614; para.3–055; *Williams v Roffey Bros & Nicholls (Contractors) Ltd* [1991] 1 Q.B. 1; para.3–050.

[934] Chen-Wishart, in *Contract in Commercial Law*, Degeling, Edelman & Goudkamp (eds.) (2016).

[935] Law Revision Committee, *6th Interim Report* (1937), Cmnd.5449; Hamson 54 L.Q.R. 233; Hays 41 Col. L. Rev. 849; Chloros 17 I.C.L.Q. 137; Beatson [1992] C.L.P. 1.

[936] e.g. in the cases on existing duties as consideration, on promissory estoppel and on proprietary estoppel.

[937] See paras 3–076–3–154.

[938] e.g. by allowing "promissory estoppel" (para.3–090) to give rise to a cause of action or by extending the categories of cases covered by proprietary estoppel (para.3–120).

[939] The qualification would not preclude such enforcement at the discretion of the court, as at present in cases of proprietary estoppel: para.3–145.

[940] cf. para.3–093, and Restatements, Contracts, §90. Restatement 2d, Contracts, §90 imposes somewhat less stringent conditions and concludes: "The remedy … may be limited as justice requires."

CHAPTER 4

# CONTRACTUAL INTENTION



An agreement, though supported by consideration, is not binding as a contract if it was made without any intention of creating legal relations. As noted in Ch.2, in some cases the question of whether the parties had an intention to be bound may overlap with the question of whether they had reached agreement. For example, the court may conclude that they did not intend to be bound because they had yet to reach agreement on all the terms, or all the essential terms, of the contract.[1] But it is clear that intention is a separate requirement which must be met in all cases, including those where the parties have reached agreement. This is most obviously illustrated by cases in which the parties have expressly indicated that they do not intend to be bound until some further step has been taken, or some further procedure followed, e.g. where they reach agreement “subject to contract”.[2] **4–001**

[1] See para.2–085. The vagueness of any agreement reached may also negative intention: para.2–080; para.4–033.

[2] See para.4–011.

## 1. PROOF OF INTENTION

4–002 **Objective test.** The test of contractual intention is normally an objective one[3] so that where, for example, an agreement for the sale of a house is not made "subject to contract",[4] both parties are likely to be bound even though one of them subjectively believed that he would not be bound till the usual exchange of contracts had taken place.[5] But the objective test is here (as elsewhere)[6] subject to the limitation that it does not apply in favour of a party who knows the truth. Thus in the example just given the party who did not intend to be bound would not be bound if his state of mind was actually known to the other party.[7] Nor could a party who did not in fact intend to be bound invoke the objective test so as to hold the other party to the contract:[8] to apply that test in such a case would pervert its purpose, which is to protect a party who has relied on the objective appearance of consent from the prejudice which he would suffer if the other party could escape liability on the ground that he had no real intention to be bound. A purposive approach to the objective test was taken in *Attrill v Dresdner Kleinwort Ltd*[9] in which an employer promised a "guaranteed" bonus pool to employees. The employer argued that the promise was unenforceable because there was no intention to create legal relations. Certain background evidence which reinforced that, on an objective assessment, the promise was intended to be binding was held to be admissible, even if it was not known to the employees. Elias LJ stated[10]:

> "An offeror should not be allowed to assert that there was no intention to create legal relations and at the same time seek to take advantage of a rule designed to benefit the offeree in order to conceal from the courts evidence which is inconsistent with his assertion."

In a subsequent case, however, it has been stressed that this observation, as well as being obiter,[11] was made in the context of a unilateral offer against the backdrop of an existing contractual relationship.[12] In the more "straightforward

---

3 See paras 1–002, 2–002; *RTS Flexible Systems Ltd v Molkerei Alois Müller GmbH & Co KG* [2010] UKSC 14; [2010] 1 W.L.R. 753 at [45]; *Baird Textile Holdings Ltd v Marks & Spencer Plc* [2001] EWCA Civ 274; [2002] 1 All E.R. (Comm) 737; *Maple Leaf Macro Volatility Master Fund v Rouvroy* [2009] EWCA Civ 1334; [2010] 2 All E.R. (Comm) 788 at [17]; *Barbudev v Eurocom Cable Management Eood* [2012] EWCA Civ 548; [2012] 2 All ER (Comm) 963 at [30]; *Novus Aviation Ltd v Alubaf Arab International Bank BSC* [2016] EWHC 1575 (Comm); [2017] 1 B.C.L.C. 414 at [54]–[59]; *New Media Holding Co LLC v Kuznetsov* [2016] EWHC 360 (QB).

4 See para.4–011.

5 *Tweddell v Henderson* [1975] 1 W.L.R. 1496; *Storer v Manchester CC* [1974] 1 W.L.R. 1403 at 1408.

6 See para.2–003.

7 *Pateman v Pay* (1974) 263 E.G. 467.

8 *Lark v Outhwaite* [1991] 2 Lloyd's Rep. 132 at 141.

9 [2013] EWCA Civ 394; [2013] 3 All E.R. 607.

10 *Attrill v Dresdner Kleinwort Ltd* [2013] EWCA Civ 394; [2013] 3 All E.R. 607 at [87].

11 The court found that the evidence in question was, in fact, known to the employees.

12 A point emphasised by Elias LJ himself: [2013] EWCA Civ 394; [2013] 3 All E.R. 607 at [89].

situation" of two parties negotiating a contract by an exchange of correspondence, there is no basis for derogating from the ordinary rule under which the parties' communications are to be objectively construed.[13]

**Burden of proof.** The question of contractual intention is, in the last resort, one of fact.[14] In deciding it, a distinction must be drawn between implied and express agreements.[15] **4–003**

**Implied agreements.** Claims based on implied agreements are approached on the basis that "contracts are not lightly to be implied" and that the court must therefore be able "to conclude with confidence that … the parties intended to create contractual relations".[16] The burden of proof on this issue is on the proponent of the implied contract, and in a number of cases claims or defences based on implied contracts have been rejected precisely on the ground that contractual intention had not been shown by that party to exist.[17] **4–004**

**Express agreements.** Where a claim is based on a proved or admitted express agreement, including the introduction of an express term into a pre-existing contract,[18] the courts do not require, in addition, proof that parties to an ordinary commercial relationship[19] actually intended to be bound. On the contrary, the onus of proving that there was no such intention "is on the party who asserts that no legal effect was intended, and the onus is a heavy one".[20] In deciding whether the onus has been discharged, the courts will be influenced by the importance of the agreement to the parties, the context in which it was reached,[21] and by the fact that one of them has acted in reliance on it.[22] Contractual intention is not **4–005**

---

[13] *Rosalina Investments Ltd v New Balance Athletic Shoes (UK) Ltd* [2018] EWHC 1014 (QB) at [41].

[14] See *Zakhem International Construction Ltd v Nippon Kohan KK* [1987] 2 Lloyd's Rep. 596.

[15] For judicial recognition of the distinction, see *Baird Textile Holdings Ltd v Marks & Spencer Plc* [2001] EWCA Civ 274; [2002] 1 All E.R. (Comm) 737 at [61]; *Modahl v British Athletics Federation Ltd* [2001] EWCA Civ 1447; [2002] 1 W.L.R. 1477 at [102]; *In the matter of MF Global UK Ltd* [2016] EWCA Civ 569; [2016] Pens. L.R. 225 at [36].

[16] *Blackpool and Fylde Aero Club v Blackpool BC* [1990] 1 W.L.R. 1195 at 1202; cf. *Baird Textile Holdings Ltd v Marks & Spencer Plc* [2001] EWCA Civ 274; [2002] 1 All E.R. (Comm) 737 at [20], [21], [30], [62]; *Alstom Transport v Tilson* [2010] EWCA Civ 1308; [2011] I.R.L.R. 169; *In the matter of MF Global UK Ltd* [2016] EWCA Civ 569; [2016] Pens. L.R. 225 at [36].

[17] *The Aramis* [1989] 1 Lloyd's Rep. 213. See also: *Whittle Movers Ltd v Hollywood Express Ltd* [2009] EWCA Civ 1189; [2009] 2 C.L.C. 771; *JD Cleverly Ltd v Family Finance Ltd* [2010] EWCA Civ 1477; [2011] R.T.R. 22; cf. *Goshawk Dedicated Ltd v Tyser & Co Ltd* [2006] EWCA Civ 54; [2006] 1 Lloyd's Rep. 566 at [66].

[18] *Attrill v Dresdner Kleinwort Ltd* [2013] EWCA Civ 394; [2013] 3 All E.R. 607; cf. *Judge v Crown Leisure Ltd* [2005] EWCA Civ; [2005] I.R.L.R. 823 at [23].

[19] For social or domestic arrangements, see paras 4–019–4–022.

[20] *Edwards v Skyways Ltd* [1964] 1 W.L.R. 349 at 355; cf. *The Zephyr* [1985] 2 Lloyd's Rep. 529 at 537 (disapproving [1984] 1 Lloyd's Rep. 58 at 63–64); *Yani Haryanto v ED & F Man (Sugar) Ltd* [1986] 2 Lloyd's Rep. 44; *Orion Ins Co Plc v Sphere Drake Ins Plc* [1992] 1 Lloyd's Rep. 239 at 263; *Mamidoil-Jetoil Greek Petroleum Co SA v Okta Oil Refinery AD* [2002] EWHC 2210 (Comm); [2003] 1 Lloyd's Rep. 1 at [159].

[21] *Blue v Ashley* [2017] EWHC 1928 (Comm), discussed at para 4–028.

[22] See para.4–022; *Kingswood Estate Co Ltd v Anderson* [1963] 2 Q.B. 169; *Maple Leaf Macro Volatility Master Fund v Rouvroy* [2009] EWCA Civ 1334; [2010] 2 All E.R. (Comm) 788 at [21].

negatived merely by the fact that the parties were companies in the same group and that the terms of their agreement "might not in practice be strictly enforced between them".[23]

## 2. ILLUSTRATIONS

### (a) Mere puffs

4–006 A statement inducing a contract may be so vague, or so clearly one of opinion, that the law refuses to give it any contractual effect.[24] Even a statement that is perfectly precise may nevertheless not be binding if the court considers that it was not seriously meant.[25] In *Lambert v Lewis*[26] a manufacturer stated in promotional literature that his product was "foolproof" and that it "required no maintenance". These statements did not give rise to a contract between the manufacturer and a dealer (who had bought the product from an intermediary) as they were "not intended to be, nor were they, acted on as being express warranties".[27]

### (b) Other statements inducing a contract

4–007 **Representation or term?** A statement inducing a person to enter into a contract may be *either* "mere representation" *or* a term of the contract. The distinction between these categories turns on the intention with which the statement was made.[28] In most cases on this subject the question is merely as to the *contents* of a contract which is proved or admitted to exist. But sometimes the test of intention determines the very existence of the contract itself. This happens when a statement inducing a principal contract for some reason cannot take effect as one of its terms, but only as a collateral contract.[29] In *Heilbut, Symons & Co v Buckleton*[30] the claimant said to the defendants' manager that he understood the defendants to be "bringing out a rubber company." The manager replied that they were, on the strength of which statement the claimant applied for, and was allotted, shares in the company. It turned out not to be a rubber company. The claimant alleged that the defendants had warranted that it was a rubber company, but it was held that nothing said by the defendants' manager was intended to have

---

[23] *The Marine Star (No.2)* [1994] 2 Lloyd's Rep. 629 at 632; reversed on other grounds [1996] 2 Lloyd's Rep. 383; cf. *In the matter of MF Global UK Ltd* [2016] EWCA Civ 569.

[24] See paras 9–013–9–014.

[25] *Weeks v Tybald* (1605) Noy 11; cf. *Dalrymple v Dalrymple* (1811) 2 Hag.Con. 54 at 105.

[26] [1982] A.C. 225.

[27] *Lambert v Lewis* [1982] A.C. 225 at 262; contrast *Carlill v Carbolic Smoke Ball Co Ltd* [1893] 1 Q.B. 256; and *Bowerman v Association of British Travel Agents* [1995] N.L.J. 1815; para.2–010.

[28] See para.9–056 and following; but, where applicable, see the Consumer Rights Act 2015 s.50(1).

[29] See paras 5–010, 6–038, 9–063, 14–006–14–008. Under Consumer Rights Act 2015 s.30 a "consumer guarantee" given on the sale or supply of goods to a consumer "takes effect … as a contractual obligation owed by the guarantor" and seems to do so by force of the Act, without regard to the issue of contractual intention.

[30] [1913] A.C. 30; *IBA v EMI Electronics Ltd* (1980) 14 Build. L.R. 1; cf. *Strover v Harrington* [1988] Ch. 390 at 410.

contractual effect: "Not only the terms of such contracts, but the existence of an *animus contrahendi* on the part of all the parties to them must be clearly shewn".[31]

### (c) Intention expressly negatived

An agreement has no contractual force if it expressly negatives the intention to be legally bound.[32] It is a question of construction whether a particular provision has this effect.[33] **4–008**

#### (i) *Entire agreement clauses*

We noted above that whether a pre-contractual statement becomes a term of the contract depends on the intention of the parties.[34] It follows that a statement made in the course of negotiations will not take effect as a term in the main contract or as a collateral contract where the terms of the main contract show that the parties did not intend the statement to have such effect. For example, where the main contract contains an "entire agreement" clause under which the parties agree that statements made in the course of negotiations are to "have no contractual force" unless they are expressly included as terms of the contract.[35] **4–009**

The effect of an entire agreement clause was considered, indirectly, by the Supreme Court in *Rock Advertising Ltd v MWB Business Exchange Centres Ltd*[36] in the context of a "no oral modification clause".[37] According to Lord Sumption, the "true position" is that if a collateral agreement is capable of operating as an "independent agreement … supported by its own consideration" then "most"[38] entire agreement clauses will not prevent its enforcement.[39] But if it is relied

---

[31] *Heilbut Symons & Co v Buckleton* [1913] A.C. 30 at 47; *The Kapetan Markos NL (No.2)* [1987] 2 Lloyd's Rep. 323 at 332.

[32] e.g. *Broadwick Financial Services Ltd v Spencer* [2002] EWCA Civ 35; [2002] 1 All E.R. (Comm) 446 at [27].

[33] *R. v Lord Chancellor's Departments Ex p. Nangle* [1991] I.C.R. 743.

[34] See para.4–007.

[35] *Inntrepreneur Pub Co (GL) v East Crown Ltd* [2000] 2 Lloyd's Rep. 611 at 614; *White v Bristol Rugby Club Ltd* [2002] I.R.L.R. 204; *Cheverny Consulting Ltd v Whitehead Mann Ltd* [2005] EWHC 243; [2006] EWCA Civ 1303 (for further proceedings, see [2007] EWHC 3130 (Comm)); *Ravennavi SpA v New Century Shipbuilding Co Ltd* [2007] EWCA Civ 58; [2007] 2 Lloyd's Rep. 24; *Business Environment Bow Lane Ltd v Deanwater Estates* [2007] EWCA Civ 622; [2007] 32 E.G. 90; *North Eastern Properties Ltd v Coleman* [2010] EWCA Civ 274; [2010] 1 W.L.R. 2715; *Ryanair Ltd v SR Technics Ireland Ltd* [2007] EWHC 3089 (QB); *Matchbet Ltd v Openbet Retail Ltd* [2013] EWHC 3067 (Ch) at [112]; *Mileform Ltd v Interserve Security Ltd* [2013] EWHC 3386 (QB) at [93]–[101]; *Adibe v National Westminster Bank Plc* [2017] EWHC 1655 (Ch) at [29]; *ZCCM Investments Holdings Plc v Konkola Copper Mines Plc* [2017] EWHC 3288 (Comm) at [21].

[36] [2018] UKSC 24; [2019] A.C. 119.

[37] See para.4–016.

[38] Presumably it depends on the precise wording.

[39] The following are cited in support: *Business Environment Bow Lane Ltd v Deanwater Estates* [2007] EWCA Civ 622; [2007] 32 E.G. 90 at [43]; *North Eastern Properties Ltd v Coleman* [2010] EWCA Civ 274; [2010] 1 W.L.R. 2715 at [57], [82]–[83]; see para.5–010, n.51.

upon as "modifying" the main agreement, the courts will enforce the entire agreement clause by declining to give effect to the collateral agreement.[40]

An entire agreement clause may also preclude estoppel by convention[41] where the estoppel involves the assertion of an additional contractual term,[42] but not it seems where it prevents a party from enforcing an existing contract term in a way contrary to the parties' shared understanding.[43] Nor does it preclude reliance on the parties' "understanding" for the purpose of proprietary estoppel.[44]

### *(ii) Honour clauses*

4–010 In *Rose & Frank Co v JR Crompton & Bros Ltd*[45] an agency agreement provided:

> "This arrangement is not entered into, nor is this memorandum written, as a formal or legal agreement, and shall not be subject to legal jurisdiction in the Law Courts … but is only a definite expression and record of the purpose and intention of the … parties concerned, to which they each honourably pledge themselves … ."

These words were held to negative contractual intention, so that the agreement did not amount to a legally binding contract. On the other hand, contractual intention was not negatived where an arbitration clause in a reinsurance contract provided that "this treaty shall be interpreted as an honourable engagement rather than as a legal obligation … ". The contract as a whole was clearly intended to be legally binding and the purpose of the words quoted was merely to free the arbitrator "to some extent from strict legal rules"[46] in interpreting the agreement.

### *(iii) "Subject to contract"*

4–011 An agreement may be made "subject to contract", either expressly,[47] or by implication.[48] Such an agreement is incomplete until the details of a formal

---

[40] Lord Briggs was not persuaded by the analogy between an entire agreement clause and a no oral modification clause, but made no comment about Lord Sumption's assessment of the effect of the former.

[41] See para.3–094 and following.

[42] *S.E.R.E Holdings Ltd v Volkswagen Group United Kingdom Ltd* [2004] EWHC 1551 at [25]–[26].

[43] *Dubai Islamic Bank PJSC v PSI Energy Holding Co BSC* [2011] EWHC 2718 (Comm) at [83]; cf. *Mears Ltd v Shoreline Housing Partnership Ltd* [2015] EWHC 1396 (TCC); 160 Con L.R. 157 (where there was no overt discussion of this point). The reasoning in the *Dubai Islamic* case is based on an analogy with rectification which is not precluded by an entire agreement clause: *JJ Huber Ltd v The Private DIY Company Ltd* 70 P. & C.R. 33; *Surgicraft Ltd v Paradigm Biovices Inc* [2010] EWHC 1291 (Ch). For the effect of such a clause on any implied term, see para.6–063.

[44] *Lloyd v MGL (Rugby) Ltd* [2007] EWCA Civ 153; (2007) 22 E.G. 162. For proprietary estoppel, see para.3–120 and folllowing.

[45] [1925] A.C. 445; *County Ltd v Girozentrale Securities* [1996] 3 All E.R. 834.

[46] *Home Insurance Co v Administratia Asigurarilor* [1983] 2 Lloyd's Rep. 674 at 677; cf. *Overseas Union Ins Ltd v International Ins Ltd* [1988] 2 Lloyd's Rep. 65; *Home & Overseas Ins Co Ltd v Mentor Ins (UK) Ltd* [1989] 1 Lloyd's Rep. 473.

[47] Without needing to use the words "subject to contract" as such: *RTS Flexible Systems Ltd v Molkerei Alois Müller GmbH & Co KG* [2010] UKSC 14; [2010] 1 W.L.R. 753.

[48] *Cheverny Consulting Ltd v Whitehead Mann Ltd* [2006] EWCA Civ 1303 at [45]; *Moria v Bednash* [2011] EWHC 839 (Ch); *Rosalina Investments Ltd v New Balance Athletic Shoes (UK) Ltd* [2018] EWHC 1014 (QB).

contract have been settled and approved by the parties.[49] But even when the terms of the formal contract have been agreed, there is no binding contract until the parties have gone through the procedure necessary to indicate that the agreement is no longer "subject to contract",[50] e.g. in contracts for the sale of land by private treaty,[51] when there has been an "exchange of contracts".[52] Before the "exchange", there is no uncertainty as to the terms of the agreement, but there is no contract because neither party intends to be legally bound until the "exchange of contracts" takes place.

**Contracts for the sale of land.** Contracts for the sale of land must satisfy certain formal requirements. Each party must sign a document containing all the terms which have been expressly agreed[53]; and the requirement of exchange traditionally refers to the handing over by each party to the other of one of these documents, or to their despatch by post; if the latter method is adopted, the process is completed on the receipt of the second of the posted documents.[54] This state of the law, which enables either party with impunity to go back on a concluded agreement prior to exchange, has been described as "a social and moral blot on the law"[55]; and the courts have been prepared to mitigate the strictness of the requirement of "exchange of contracts". Thus, it has been held that the exchange may be effected by telephone or telex[56]; that certain technical slips in the process may be disregarded[57]; that exchange is not necessary where the parties use the same solicitor[58]; and that where the two parts do not match precisely there may nevertheless be a contract, the discrepancy being remedied by rectification.[59] **4–012**

In "a very strong and exceptional context"[60] the court may infer that the parties intended to be legally bound when executing the original document, even though it is expressed to be "subject to contract". This was held to be the position where a document containing these words laid down an elaborate timetable, imposed a duty on the purchaser to approve the draft contract (subject only to reasonable amendments) and required him then to exchange contracts.[61] The

[49] See para.2–090.

[50] *Rose & Frank Co v JR Crompton & Bros Ltd* [1923] 2 K.B. 261 at 294.

[51] Such agreements are usually made "subject to contract", but not always: *Storer v Manchester CC* [1974] 1 W.L.R. 1403.

[52] *Eccles v Bryant & Pollock* [1948] Ch. 93; cf. *Chillingworth v Esche* [1924] 1 Ch. 97; *Raingold v Bromley* [1931] 2 Ch. 307; *Bolton MBC v Torkington* [2003] EWCA Civ 1634; [2004] Ch. 66 at [53]; *Taylor v Burton* [2015] EWCA Civ 142.

[53] Law of Property (Miscellaneous Provisions) Act 1989 s.2(1), (3). See para.5–009.

[54] *Commission for the New Towns v Cooper (Great Britain) Ltd* [1995] Ch. 259 at 285, 289; cf. [1995] Ch. 259 at 293, 295.

[55] *Cohen v Nessdale* [1981] 3 All E.R. 118 at 128 (affirmed [1982] 2 All E.R. 97); cf. Law Com. No.65.

[56] *Domb v Isoz* [1980] Ch. 548.

[57] *Harrison v Battye* [1975] 1 W.L.R. 58.

[58] *Smith v Mansi* [1963] 1 W.L.R. 26; exchange is also unnecessary in the case of a deed, which takes effect as soon as it has been duly executed (paras 3–172–3–174): *Vincent v Premo Enterprises Ltd* [1969] 2 Q.B. 609; *D'Silva v Lister House Development Ltd* [1971] Ch. 17.

[59] *Sindel v Georgio* (1984) 1454 C.L.R. 661; for rectification see para.8–063 and following.

[60] *Alpenstow Ltd v Regalian Properties Ltd* [1985] 1 W.L.R. 721 at 730; Harpum [1986] C.L.J. 356.

[61] *Alpenstow Ltd v Regalian Properties Ltd* [1985] 1 W.L.R. 721 at 730.

words "subject to contract" were taken merely to mean that the parties had not yet settled all the details of the transaction and therefore not to negative the intention to be bound.

Agreements for the sale of land by auction or by tender are not normally made "subject to contract". The intention of the parties in such cases is to enter into a binding contract as soon as an offer to buy has been accepted. In one case[62] of a sale by tender, the words "subject to contract" were, by a clerical error, typed on one of the contractual documents. In these circumstances,[63] the words were held to be meaningless, so that there was a binding contract.[64]

4–013 **Waiving "subject to contract".** The parties may also create a binding contract by a subsequent agreement to remove the "subject to contract" requirement, thus indicating their intention henceforth to be legally bound.[65] The court will "not lightly so hold"[66] and any such agreement to waive the procedure required must be unequivocal, but it need not be express if it can be inferred from communications between the parties and the conduct of one party known to the other.[67] In *RTS Flexible Systems Ltd v Molkerei Alois Müller GmbH & Co KG*[68] the parties negotiated a contract for the installation of a packaging line on the basis of certain terms, one of which stated that the contract "shall not become effective until each party has executed a counterpart and exchanged it with the other." No execution or exchange had taken place, but the Supreme Court found that the parties were nonetheless bound. The "striking features" of the case were that essentially all the terms had been agreed,[69] substantial works had been carried out[70] and the agreement was "varied" in important respects.

---

[62] *Michael Richard Properties Ltd v St Saviour's Parish* [1975] 3 All E.R. 416; Emery [1976] C.L.J. 28.

[63] See also *Munton v GLC* [1976] 1 W.L.R. 649.

[64] *Westway Homes v Moore* (1991) 63 P. & C.R. 480.

[65] *Law v Jones* [1974] Ch. 112, as explained in *Daulia v Four Millbank Nominees* [1978] Ch. 231 at 250; *Cohen v Nessdale* [1981] 3 All E.R. 118 at 127; [1982] 2 All E.R. 97 at 104; see also *Tiverton Estates Ltd v Wearwell* [1975] Ch. 146. In the context of settlement agreements, see: *Jirehouse Capital v Beller* [2009] EWHC 2538 (Ch); cf. *Morgan Walker Solicitors LLP v Zurich Professional and Financial Lines* [2010] EWHC 1532 (Ch).

[66] *RTS Flexible Systems Ltd v Molkerei Alois Müller GmbH & Co KG* [2010] UKSC 14; [2010] 1 W.L.R. 753 at [56].

[67] *RTS Flexible Systems Ltd v Molkerei Alois Müller GmbH & Co KG* [2010] UKSC 14; [2010] 1 W.L.R. 753 at [67]; cf. *Reveille Independent LLC v Anotech International (UK) Ltd* [2016] EWCA Civ 443; 166 Con L.R. 79; *Global Asset Capital Inc v Aabar Block S.A.R.L.* [2017] EWCA Civ 37; [2017] 4 W.L.R. 163; *Anchor 2020 Ltd v Midas Construction Ltd* [2019] EWHC 435 (TCC); 184 Con L.R. 215. The process of waiver "must itself require agreement, so it has to be bilateral, and not unilateral": *Haq v Island Homes Housing Association* [2011] EWCA Civ 805; [2011] 2 P. & C.R. 17 at [72].

[68] [2010] UKSC 14; [2010] 1 W.L.R. 753.

[69] The Supreme Court found that the parties were bound to the terms which had been agreed. The trial judge had found there was a simple contract for a price and no more ([2008] EWHC 1087 (TCC)); the Court of Appeal had found that there was no contract at all ([2009] EWCA Civ 26; [2009] B.L.R. 181).

[70] Initially under a letter of intent, but the parties agreed that that had expired; cf. *Diamond Build Ltd v Clapham Park Homes Ltd* [2008] EWHC 1439 (TCC); 119 Con L.R. 32 where the parties' failure to execute the required formal contract meant that they continued to be bound by the terms of a letter of intent: see para.4–024.

**Liability on other grounds.** Subsequent conduct may also give rise to liability on other grounds: where one party to the agreement encourages the other to believe that he will not withdraw, and the other acts to his detriment in reliance on that belief, the former may be liable on the basis of "proprietary estoppel".[71] If no contract is formed, but one party has done work which has benefited the other, a quantum meruit may be awarded to the party which has done the work.[72] 4–014

**Collateral contract.** A party's freedom to withdraw from an agreement "subject to contract" may be restricted by a collateral contract. For example, a vendor who has agreed to sell land "subject to contract" may, either at the same time or subsequently, undertake not to negotiate for the sale of the land with a third party. Such a collateral agreement (sometimes called a "lock-out" agreement) must satisfy the requirement of certainty[73] and in *Walford v Miles*[74] it was held that this requirement had not been satisfied where the agreement failed to specify the time for which the vendor's freedom to negotiate with third parties was to be restricted. But in a later case[75] it was held that a vendor's promise not to negotiate with third parties *for two weeks* was sufficient to satisfy the requirement of certainty and so to give rise to a collateral contract. 4–015

### *(iv) "No oral modification" clauses*

**Clauses prohibiting informal variation.** A contract may contain a term stipulating that it can only be modified or varied in a particular form, e.g. in writing and signed by a duly authorised signatory of the parties in question: a "no oral modification clause". In a series of decisions, in many of which the issue was obiter, the courts held that the contract could still be varied without complying with the agreed procedure provided it was the intention of the parties not to require such compliance.[76] If there was anything to question in such decisions, it was that the courts were perhaps a little too easily persuaded that such an intention must follow from any informal variation. In *Rock Advertising Ltd v MWB Business Exchange Centres Ltd*,[77] however, a majority of the Supreme Court went to the other extreme by ruling that a contract containing such a term can only be modified if the agreed procedure is followed. With respect, the 4–016

---

71 See the discussion at para.3–129 of *Attorney General of Hong Kong v Humphreys Estate (Queen's Gardens)* [1987] A.C. 114; cf. *Cobbe v Yeoman's Row Management Ltd* [2008] UKHL 55; [2008] 1 W.L.R. 1752 at [25]–[26].

72 See para.2–021; para.22–031.

73 See para.2–079.

74 *Walford v Miles* [1992] 2 A.C. 128. See further para.2–101.

75 *Pitt v PHH Asset Management Ltd* [1994] 1 W.L.R. 327; cf. *Tye v House* [1997] 2 E.G.L.R. 171; *JSD Corp Pte Ltd v Al Waha Capital PJSC* [2009] EWHC 3376 (Ch).

76 See, e.g. *Westbrook Resources Ltd v Globe Metallurgical Inc* [2009] EWCA Civ 310; [2009] 2 Lloyd's Rep. 224 at [13]; *World Online Telecom Ltd v I-Way Ltd* [2002] EWCA Civ 413 at [9]; *Energy Venture Partners Ltd v Malabu Oil and Gas Ltd* [2013] EWHC 2118 (Comm) at [273]–[274]; *Virulite LLC v Virulite Distribution Ltd* [2014] EWHC 366 (QB); [2015] 1 All E.R. (Comm) 204 at [60]; *Globe Motors Inc v TRW Lucas Varity Electric Steering Ltd* [2014] EWHC 3718 (Comm) at [487]; [2016] EWCA Civ 396; 168 Con L.R. 59. Contrast *United Bank Ltd v Asif* 11 February 2000 CA.

77 [2018] UKSC 24; [2019] A.C. 119; *Great Dunmow Estates Ltd v Crest Nicholson Operations Ltd* [2019] EWCA Civ 1683 at [24]; O'Sullivan 135 L.Q.R. 1.

reasoning of Lord Sumption, which departs from that adopted in other common law jurisdictions,[78] is open to question. He drew an analogy with statutory requirements of form, such as those applied to contracts for the disposition of an interest in land,[79] to conclude that there "is no principled reason why the parties should not adopt the same principle by agreement". Indeed, there is no reason why they should not, but it is precisely because they adopt it "*by agreement*" in a contract which otherwise has no mandatory requirement of form that they should also be free to depart from it by such an agreement,[80] provided their intention to do so is clearly established, either expressly or by necessary implication.[81] This was the approach taken by Lord Briggs which is to be preferred.

4–017 **A role for estoppel.** As it is, the approach of the majority in the *Rock Advertising* case increases the risk of the parties acting on an unenforceable informal variation. Any potential for injustice in this regard is to be met by the law of estoppel under which a party may be precluded from relying on the no oral modification clause "to the extent that the other party has relied (or reasonably relied)" on his conduct.[82] But, by analogy with the position taken in relation to guarantees,[83] the scope for estoppel is not to be drawn broadly. According to Lord Sumption:

> "(i) there would have to be some words or conduct unequivocally representing that the variation was valid notwithstanding its informality; and (ii) something more would be required for this purpose than the informal promise itself."[84]

As Lord Briggs acknowledged, when put in these terms, any estoppel and his proposal that the courts should allow for the waiver of the no oral modification clause by necessary implication "are likely to go hand in hand", but there is an important difference in practice. If the no oral modification clause is waived, the modification of the contract is valid and effective unless and until there is a further valid and effective modification. But any estoppel which will have to be resorted to as a consequence of the decision of the majority can only be invoked

[78] See, e.g. Australia: *Liebe v Molloy* (1906) 4 C.L.R. 347; *Commonwealth v Crothall Hospital Services (Aust) Ltd* (1981) 54 F.L.R. 439 at 447; *GEC Marconi Systems Pty Ltd v BHP Information Technology Pty Ltd* (2003) 128 F.C.R. 1. And in Canada: *Shelanu Inc v Print Three Franchising Corp* (2003) 226 D.L.R. (4th) 577 at [54].

[79] See para.5–009.

[80] *Rock Advertising Ltd v MWB Business Exchange Centres Ltd* [2018] UKSC 24; [2019] A.C. 119 at [26] (Lord Briggs). Lord Briggs was not persuaded by the analogy drawn by Lord Sumption with entire agreement clauses (see para.4–009) and preferred the analogy with "subject to contract" clauses: see para.4–013.

[81] *Rock Advertising Ltd v MWB Business Exchange Centres Ltd* [2018] UKSC 24; [2019] A.C. 119 at [29]–[30] (Lord Briggs). At one point Lord Sumption appears to elide two quite different questions, namely *can* the parties informally modify the contract (including the no oral modification clause) and *have* they agreed to do so: see at [15].

[82] *Rock Advertising Ltd v MWB Business Exchange Centres Ltd* [2018] UKSC 24; [2019] A.C. 119 at [16] (Lord Sumption).

[83] See para.5–028.

[84] *Rock Advertising Ltd v MWB Business Exchange Centres Ltd* [2018] UKSC 24; [2019] A.C. 119 at [16] (Lord Sumption). This test was not met in *UK Learning Academy Ltd v Sec. of State for Education* [2018] EWHC 2915 (Comm) where no variation was found to have been agreed in any event.

*to the extent that* the other party has relied on the informal variation.[85] This implies that, for example, the variation may be revoked upon giving reasonable notice, if no further prejudice or detriment will be suffered by the other party. That may introduce some uncertainty when the principal basis for the decision of the majority was said to be the "advantage of certainty".[86]

### (v) *Other phrases*

The words "ex gratia" in a promise to make a payment to a dismissed employee have been held not to negative contractual intention: they merely mean that the employers did not admit any pre-existing liability to make the payment.[87] Contractual intention was likewise not negatived where a shipowner, during negotiations for a charterparty said: "we are fixed in good faith".[88] If these words had any effect, they amounted merely to a "collateral understanding"[89] that account should be taken of damage to the vessel, of which both shipowner and charterer were aware. 4–018

## (d) Social and domestic arrangements

**Social arrangements.** Many social arrangements do not amount to contracts because they are not intended to be legally binding. "The ordinary example is where two parties agree to take a walk together, or where there is an offer and an acceptance of hospitality."[90] Similarly it has been held that the winner of a competition held by a golf club could not sue for his prize where "no one concerned with that competition ever intended that there should be any legal results flowing from the conditions posted and the acceptance by the competitor of those conditions"[91]; that the rules of a competition organised by a "jalopy club" for charitable purposes did not have contractual force[92]; that "car pool" and similar arrangements between friends or neighbours did not amount to contracts even though one party contributed to the running costs of the other's vehicle[93]; that an agreement between members of a group of friends relating to musical performances by the group was not intended to have contractual effect[94]; and that 4–019

---

[85] See text to n.82.

[86] *Rock Advertising Ltd v MWB Business Exchange Centres Ltd* [2018] UKSC 24; [2019] A.C. 119 at [16] (Lord Sumption).

[87] *Edwards v Skyways Ltd* [1964] 1 W.L.R. 349.

[88] *The Mercedes Envoy* [1995] 2 Lloyd's Rep. 559.

[89] *The Mercedes Envoy* [1995] 2 Lloyd's Rep. 559 at 612.

[90] *Balfour v Balfour* [1919] 2 K.B. 571 at 578; *Rose & Frank Co v J R Crompton & Bros Ltd* [1923] 2 K.B. 261 at 293; *Wyatt v Kreglinger & Fernau* [1933] 1 K.B. 793 at 806.

[91] *Lens v Devonshire Club*, *The Times*, 4 December 1914; referred to in *Wyatt*'s case, above, from which the quotation in the text is taken.

[92] *White v Blackmore* [1972] 2 Q.B. 651.

[93] *Coward v MIB* [1963] 1 Q.B. 259; overruled, but not on the issue of contractual intention, in *Albert v MIB* [1972] A.C. 301; *Buckpitt v Oates* [1968] 1 All E.R. 1145.

[94] *Hadley v Kemp* [1999] E.M.L.R. 589 at 623.

the provision of free residential accommodation for close friends did not amount to a contract as it was an act of bounty, done without any intention to enter into legal relations.[95]

4–020 **Domestic arrangements.** For the same reason, many domestic arrangements lack contractual force. In *Balfour v Balfour*[96] a husband who worked abroad promised to pay an allowance of £30 per month to his wife, who had to stay in England on medical grounds. The wife's attempt to enforce this promise by action failed for two reasons: she had not provided any consideration, and the parties did not intend the arrangement to be legally binding. On the second ground alone, most domestic arrangements between husband and wife are not contracts. Atkin LJ said:

> "Those agreements, or many of them, do not result in contracts at all … even though there may be what as between other parties would constitute consideration for the agreement … They are not contracts … because the parties did not intend that they should be attended by legal consequences."[97]

It has been said that the facts of *Balfour v Balfour* "stretched that doctrine to its limits";[98] but the doctrine itself has not been judicially questioned and the cases provide many other instances of its application.[99] It does not of course prevent a husband from making a binding contract with his wife[100]: he can be her tenant;[101] and binding separation agreements are often made when husband and wife agree to live apart.[102] More generally, it has been stated that "there is nothing to stop a husband and wife from making legally binding arrangements, whether by contract or settlement, to regulate their property and affairs",[103] as opposed to agreements for "housekeeping or personal allowances" of the type exemplified by *Balfour v Balfour.*

4–021 **Parents and children.** Such issues of contractual intention can also arise between parents and children. An informal promise by a parent to pay a child an allowance during study is not normally a contract, though it may become one, if, for example, it is part of a bargain made to induce the child to give up some occupation so as to enter on some particular course of study.[104] Similarly, where a mother bought a house as a residence for her son and daughter-in-law on the

---

[95] *Heslop v Burns* [1974] 1 W.L.R. 1241.

[96] [1919] 2 K.B. 571; Hedley 5 O.J.L.S. 391.

[97] *Balfour v Balfour* [1919] 2 K.B. 571 at 627.

[98] *Pettitt v Pettitt* [1970] A.C. 777 at 816.

[99] e.g. *Gage v King* [1961] 1 Q.B. 188; *Spellman v Spellman* [1961] 1 W.L.R. 921; cf. *Lloyds Bank Plc v Rosset* [1991] 1 A.C. 107.

[100] *Synge v Synge* [1894] 1 Q.B. 466; cf. *Jennings v Brown* (1842) 9 M. & W. 496.

[101] *Pearce v Merriman* [1904] 1 K.B. 80; contrast *Morris v Tarrant* [1971] 2 Q.B. 143.

[102] e.g. *Merrit v Merrit* [1970] 1 W.L.R. 1211; *Tanner v Tanner* [1975] 1 W.L.R. 1346; cf. paras 11–048–11–050.

[103] *Radmacher v Granatino* [2010] UKSC 42; [2011] A.C. 534 at [142] (Baroness Hale, said in the context of a pre-nuptial agreement where the principal issue was whether its enforcement would be contrary to public policy: para.11–049).

[104] See *Jones v Padavatton* [1969] 1 W.L.R. 328 at 333; cf. *Shadwell v Shadwell* (1860) 9 C.B. N.S. 159.

terms that they should pay her £7 per week to pay off the purchase price, this was held to amount to a contractual licence which the mother could not revoke so long as either of the young couple kept up the payments.[105] Conversely, it has been held that the gift of a flat by a mother to her daughter on condition that the daughter should look after the mother there did not amount to a contract because it was not intended to have contractual force.[106]

**Persons sharing a common household.** The principle of *Balfour v Balfour* can also apply where persons other than husband and wife share a common household. While that household is an ongoing concern, many arrangements will be made about running it from day to day, and it is unlikely that these will be intended to be legally binding. But this may not be true of the financial terms which form the basis on which the household was established. In one case a young couple were induced to sell their house, and move in with their elderly relations, by the latter's promise to leave them a share of the proposed joint home. The argument that this promise was not intended to be legally binding was rejected as the young couple would not have taken the important step of selling their own house on the faith of a merely social arrangement.[107] In another case of this kind,[108] the fact that the promisee had helped to improve the property was relied on to support the conclusion that an express or implied promise, giving her an interest in the property, had contractual force. Formal requirements for contracts for the disposition of interests in land[109] make it unlikely that such an arrangement could now take effect as such a contract, but legal effect could be given to it by holding that it had taken effect by way of constructive trust.[110] **4–022**

In view of the informality of many house-sharing arrangements, it may be hard in a particular case to say just what obligation is created. In *Hussey v Palmer*[111] the claimant spent £600 on having a room added to her son-in-law's house, on the understanding that she could live there for the rest of her life. When she left voluntarily, about a year later, it was held that there was no contract *of loan* in respect of the £600[112] but there probably was a contract to allow her to live in the room for the rest of her life.

An agreement between persons who share a common household may have nothing to do with the management of the household. In *Simpkins v Pays*[113] three ladies who lived in the same house took part in a fashion competition run by a

[105] *Hardwick v Johnson* [1978] 1 W.L.R. 683 (Roskill and Browne LJJ); Lord Denning MR thought that there was no contract but reached the same conclusion on other grounds; cf. *Collier v Hollinshead* (1984) 272 E.G. 941.

[106] *Ellis v Chief Adjudication Officer* [1998] 1 F.L.R. 184 at 188.

[107] *Parker v Clark* [1960] 1 W.L.R. 286; cf. *Schaefer v Schuhmann* [1972] 1 W.L.R. 1286; Lee 88 L.Q.R. 320; *Tanner v Tanner* [1975] 1 W.L.R. 1346. Contrast *Horrocks v Forray* [1976] 1 W.L.R. 320; and *Coombes v Smith* [1986] 1 W.L.R. 808.

[108] *Eves v Eves* [1975] 1 W.L.R. 1338 at 1345 (Browne LJ and Brightman J).

[109] Law of Property (Miscellaneous Provisions) Act 1989 s.2; para.5–009.

[110] The formal requirements imposed by the 1989 Act (fn.109) do not apply to "the creation or operation of … constructive trusts": s.2(5); para.5–012.

[111] [1972] 1 W.L.R. 1286.

[112] But she recovered the £600 on equitable grounds; cf. *Re Sharpe* [1980] 1 W.L.R. 219.

[113] [1955] 1 W.L.R. 975.

newspaper, agreeing to pool their entries and to share the prize which any entry might win; and the agreement to share was held to be legally binding.

### (e) Agreements giving wide discretion to one party

4–023 Contractual intention may be negatived where the terms of a promise leave its performance entirely to the discretion of the promisor. In *Taylor v Brewer*[114] the claimant agreed to do work for a committee who resolved that he should receive "such remuneration … as should be deemed right." His claim for a reasonable remuneration for work done failed: the promise to pay was "merely an engagement of honour".[115] This case is now more often distinguished than followed,[116] but its reasoning would still be followed if the wording made it clear that the promise was not intended to be legally binding.[117] A fortiori, there is no contract where performance by *each* party was left to that party's discretion.[118] Where, however, an agreement is clearly intended to have contractual effect, there is judicial support for the view that a discretion conferred by it on one party is subject to an implied term that it will not be exercised "dishonestly, for an improper purpose, capriciously or arbitrarily".[119]

Performance at the discretion of the promisor should not be confused with the need for the promisor to co-operate in order for performance (which is due) to take place. The promisor can "not set up its own unwillingness to co-operate as a reason for inferring that there was no intention to create legal relations".[120]

### (f) Letters of intent or of comfort

4–024 An issue of contractual intention may arise where parties in the course of negotiations exchange "letters of intent" or where one party gives to the other a "letter of comfort".[121] The terms of such documents may negative contractual intention.[122] This was, for example, held to be the case where a company had issued a "letter of comfort" to a lender in respect of a loan to one of its subsidiaries.[123] The letter stated that "it is our policy that [the subsidiary] is at all

---

114 (1813) 1 M. & S. 290; cf. *Shallcross v Wright* (1850) 12 Beav. 558; *Robinson v Commissioners of Customs & Excise*, *The Times*, 28 April 2000.

115 *Taylor v Brewer* (1813) 1 M. & S. 290 at 291.

116 See para.16–097; cf. *Re Brand Estates* [1936] 3 All E.R. 374.

117 cf. *Re Richmond Gate Property Co Ltd* [1965] 1 W.L.R. 335; para.16–098.

118 *Carmichael v National Power Plc* [1999] 1 W.L.R. 2042; cf. *Prater v Cornwall CC* [2006] EWCA Civ 102; [2006] I.C.R. 731 (no contract in discretionary "arrangement" for referral of pupils for teaching, but each referral accepted constituted a contract).

119 See para.2–098, and the cases cited in fn.493.

120 *Attrill v Dresdner Kleinwort Ltd* [2013] EWCA Civ 394; [2013] 3 All E.R. 607 at [94].

121 *Associated British Ports v Ferryways NV* [2009] EWCA Civ 189; [2009] 1 Lloyd's Rep. 595: while the label used by the parties is "not necessarily determinative" (at [24]), "a document expressed to be a letter of comfort will usually not give rise to legal obligations" (at [27]).

122 *Snelling v John G Snelling Ltd* [1973] Q.B. 87; cf. *Montreal Gas Co v Vesey* [1900] A.C. 595; *BSC v Cleveland Bridge & Engineering Ltd* [1984] 1 All E.R. 504; *Monk Construction v Norwich Union Life Assurance Society* (1992) 62 B.L.R. 107.

123 *Kleinwort Benson Ltd v Malaysian Mining Corp* [1989] 1 W.L.R. 379; Reynolds 104 L.Q.R. 353; Davenport [1988] L.M.C.L.Q. 290.

times in a position to meet its liabilities in respect of the loan." This was interpreted to be no more than a statement of the company's present policy: it was not an undertaking that the policy would not be changed, since neither party had intended the statement to take effect as a contractual promise. The expectations generated by industry practice might also lead equivocal language reasonably to be understood only as a non-binding statement of intent.[124] On the other hand, where the language of such a document does not in terms negative contractual intention, it is open to the courts to hold the parties bound by the document; and they will, in particular, be inclined to do so where the parties have acted on the document for a long period of time or have expended considerable sums of money in reliance on it.[125] The fact that the parties envisage that the letter is to be superseded by a later, more formal, contractual document does not, of itself, prevent it from taking effect as a contract.[126]

## (g) Collective agreements

Agreements as to rates of wages and conditions of work are commonly reached **4–025** after collective bargaining between trade unions and employers or associations of employers. The general common law view was that such collective agreements were prima facie not intended to be legally binding[127] as between the trade unions and the employers. The Trade Union and Labour Relations (Consolidation) Act 1992 goes further in providing that a collective agreement[128] is "*conclusively* presumed not to have been intended by the parties to be a legally enforceable contract" unless it is in writing and expressly provides the contrary (in which case the agreement is conclusively presumed to have been intended by the parties to be a legally enforceable contract).[129] The parties can also validly provide for part of a written collective agreement to be a legally enforceable contract, in which event the remainder shall be presumed not to have been intended to be such a contract.[130] To displace the presumption that a collective agreement is not intended to be a legally binding contract, the agreement must provide that it was intended to be *legally* binding. The presumption is not displaced by a statement that the parties shall be "bound" by the agreement, for this may mean that they are to be bound in honour only.[131] It is unusual to find provisions in a collective agreement expressing an intention that all or any part of the agreement itself is intended to be a legally enforceable contract.[132] More commonly, the question is

---

[124] *Novus Aviation Ltd v Alubaf Arab International Bank BSC* [2016] EWHC 1575 (Comm); [2017] 1 B.C.L.C. 414 at [51], where there was no ambiguity in a commitment letter found to be binding.

[125] cf. *Turriff Construction Ltd v Regalia Knitting Mills* (1971) 22 E.G. 169; *Wilson Smithett & Cape (Sugar) Ltd v Bangladesh Sugar and Food Industries Ltd* [1986] 1 Lloyd's Rep. 378; *Chemco Leasing SpA v Rediffusion* [1987] 1 F.T.L.R. 201.

[126] See para.2–091; *Diamond Build Ltd v Clapham Park Homes Ltd* [2008] EWHC 1439 (TCC); 119 Con L.R. 32.

[127] *Ford Motor Co Ltd v AEF* [1969] 1 W.L.R. 339.

[128] As defined by s.178(1) and (2) of the 1992 Act.

[129] Trade Union and Labour Relations (Consolidation) Act 1992 s.179(1) and (2); *The Universe Sentinel* [1983] A.C. 366 at 380; cf. *Cheall v APEX* [1983] 1 A.C. 180 at 189.

[130] Trade Union and Labour Relations (Consolidation) Act 1992 s.179(3).

[131] *NCB v NUM* [1986] I.C.R. 736.

[132] *Commission of the European Communities v United Kingdom* [1984] I.C.R. 192 at 195.

whether its terms (or any of them) have become incorporated into a contract of employment between employer and employee so as to be legally enforceable between them.[133]

### (h) Other cases

4–026 The cases in which there may be no intention to create legal relations cannot be exhaustively classified. Contractual intention may be negatived by many factors other than those listed above, e.g. by evidence that "the agreement was a goodwill agreement … made without any intention of creating legal relations";[134] that it was a sham, made with "no intention … to create legal relations";[135] and that the parties had not yet completed the contractual negotiations.[136] Where a landlord had agreed not to enforce an order for possession against a tenant who had fallen into arrears with her rent, it was held that the parties "plainly did not intend"[137] the agreement to have contractual force, but intended it merely to turn the tenant into a "tolerated trespasser".[138]

4–027 **Intention negatived by pre-existing rights and obligations.** A number of cases support the view that an arrangement which was believed simply to give effect to pre-existing rights was not a contract because the parties had no intention to enter into a *new* contract.[139] This may be true even where the contract giving rise to those rights had been discharged, so long as the parties believed that it was still in existence.[140] But contractual intention is not negatived where the conduct of the parties to an earlier contract makes it clear that they intended not merely to give effect to that contract but also to enter into a new contract containing additional terms.[141] Nor is contractual intention necessarily negatived where the conduct of only *one* party to the alleged new contract consisted of his performance of an earlier contract between him and a third party.[142]

---

[133] See para.6–081.

[134] *Orion Ins Co Plc v Sphere Drake Ins Plc* [1990] 1 Lloyd's Rep. 465 at 505; affirmed [1992] 1 Lloyd's Rep. 239; cf. *County Ltd v Girozentrale Securities* [1996] 3 All E.R. 834 at 837; *Clarke v Nationwide Building Society* (1998) 76 P. & C.R. D5.

[135] *The Ocean Enterprise* [1997] 1 Lloyd's Rep. 449 at 484; *Hitch v Stokes* [2001] EWCA Civ 63; [2001] S.T.C. 214; cf. *Autoclenz Ltd v Belcher* [2011] UKSC 41; [2011] 4 All E.R. at 745 where the issue was the *nature* of the relationship created (employment contract or contract for services).

[136] *The Bay Ridge* [1999] 2 All E.R. (Comm) 306 at 329.

[137] *Burrows v Brent LBC* [1996] 1 W.L.R. 1448 at 1454; cf. *Stirling v Leadenhall Residential 2 Ltd* [2001] EWCA Civ 1011; [2002] 1 W.L.R. 499.

[138] *Burrows v Brent LBC* [1996] 1 W.L.R. 1448 at 1455.

[139] *Beesly v Hallwood Estates Ltd* [1960] 1 W.L.R. 549 at 558; affirmed on other grounds [1961] Ch. 105; cf. *Harvela Investments Ltd v Royal Trust Co of Canada (CI) Ltd* [1986] A.C. 207. See also *The Aramis* [1989] 1 Lloyd's Rep. 213; Treitel [1989] L.M.C.L.Q. 162; *JLT Specialty v Craven* [2018] EWCA Civ 2487 at [16].

[140] *GF Sharp & Co v McMillan* [1998] I.R.L.R. 632.

[141] *The Amazonia* [1990] 1 Lloyd's Rep. 238 at 241–242; cf. *Stirling v Leadenhall Residential 2 Ltd* [2001] EWCA Civ 1011; [2002] 1 W.L.R. 499.

[142] *Pyrene v Scindia Navigation Co Ltd* [1954] 2 Q.B. 402; *The Eurymedon* [1975] A.C. 514; cf. *Halifax Building Society v Edell* [1992] Ch. 436; *Elite Property Holdings Ltd v Barclays Bank Plc* [2018] EWCA Civ 1688; [2018] 2 B.C.L.C. 460.

**Intention negatived by context.** The context in which an agreement is made may negative contractual intention.[143] For example, we have seen that where an express agreement is reached between parties to an ordinary commercial relationship there is a strong presumption that the parties intended to be legally bound.[144] But where the owner of a business was alleged to have reached an agreement with a consultant that he would pay him a bonus if he could "get" the share price of the business to £8 per share,[145] any such agreement was not legally binding given that it was reached in a pub, in the context of a jovial conversation after the consumption of alcohol. As the judge found: "no reasonable person present in the Horse & Groom on 24 January 2013 would have thought that the offer to pay Mr Blue £15 million was serious and was intended to create a contract".[146] Mr Blue failed in his attempt to demonstrate that, for the owner of the business, this was normal practice and therefore still an ordinary commercial relationship. **4–028**

**Multi-party contracts.** Where A and B on the one part purport to contract with C, but B is not bound, A will not be bound if it was his intention only to be bound *if B was bound*. Many of the cases in this context have arisen in the context of guarantees,[147] but not all. In *Marlbray Ltd v Laditi*[148] A purported to execute a contract for the purchase of a flat with C on behalf of himself and his wife (B). A had no authority to execute the contract on B's behalf and nor did B ratify the contract.[149] The contract was nevertheless binding on A alone.[150] He may subjectively have intended only to proceed with the purchase with B, but there was nothing to support such a finding on an objective analysis. **4–029**

**Church appointments.** It had been held that the appointment of a minister of a church did not give rise to a contract as the relationship was not one "in which the parties intended to create legal relations between themselves so as to make the agreement ... enforceable in the courts".[151] But it is now recognised "that employment arrangements between a church and its ministers should not lightly be taken as intended to have no legal effect and, in consequence, its ministers **4–030**

---

[143] *Rederiaktiebolaget Amphitrite v R.* [1921] 2 K.B. 500 at 503.

[144] See para.4-005.

[145] The agreement was also too vague to be enforceable, a factor which also pointed to a lack of intention to be bound: see para.4–033.

[146] *Blue v Ashley* [2017] EWHC 1928 (Comm) at [142].

[147] See *Hansard v Lethbridge*; (1892) 8 T.L.R. 346; *James Graham & Co (Timber Ltd) v Southgate Sands* [1986] 1 Q.B. 80; *Byblos Bank Sal v Al-Khudhairy* [1987] B.C.L.C. 232; *TCB Ltd v Gray* [1988] 1 All E.R 108; *Capital Bank Cashflow Finance Ltd v Southall* [2004] EWCA Civ 817; *Harvey v Dunbar Assets Plc* [2013] EWCA Civ 952; [2013] B.I.P.R. 722; *Katara Hospitality v Guez* [2018] EWHC 3063 (Comm).

[148] [2016] EWCA Civ 476; [2016] 1 W.L.R. 5147.

[149] See para.16–049.

[150] The contract made clear that the obligations of A and B were joint *and several* so that A could be sued on his several obligation: see para.13–003.

[151] *President of the Methodist Conference v Parfitt* [1984] Q.B. 368 at 378.

denied this protection."[152] Whether there is a contract therefore depends on the facts of each individual case and there is no presumption that the parties did not intend to create a legal relationship.[153]

4–031 **Crown appointments.** At one time, it was thought that the relationship between the Crown and one of its civil servants was not contractual because the Crown did not, when the relationship was entered into, have the necessary contractual intention.[154] But in one of the cases which supported that view it was said that there was evidence that the Crown was reconsidering its position on the point;[155] and it has been held[156] that the requirement of contractual intention was satisfied in spite of the fact that the terms of appointment stated that "a civil servant does not have a contract of employment" but rather "a letter of appointment". These words were not sufficient to turn a relationship which, apart from them, had all the characteristics of a contract into one which was binding in honour only.

4–032 **Police appointments.** It has been said that a police constable is a person who "holds an office and is not therefore strictly an employee";[157] and that there is "no contract between a police officer and a chief constable".[158] But it does not follow that the relationship is binding in honour only: the resulting relationship is "closely analogous to a contract of employment"[159] so that duties analogous to those arising out of such a contract may be owed to the constable.

4–033 **Intention negatived by vagueness.** The use of deliberately vague language was held to negative contractual intention where a property developer reached an "understanding" with a firm of solicitors to employ them in connection with a proposed development, but neither side entered into a definite commitment.[160] The assumption was that the parties had reached agreement, and it was the lack of contractual intention which prevented that agreement from having legal effect. Vagueness may also be a ground for concluding that the parties had never reached

---

152 *Percy v Board of National Mission of Scotland* [2005] UKHL 73; [2006] 2 A.C. 28 at [26].

153 *New Testament Church of God v Stewart* [2007] EWCA Civ 1044; [2008] I.R.L.R. 134; *President of the Methodist Conference v Preston* [2011] EWCA Civ 1581; [2012] 2 W.L.R. 1119 (reversed in the Supreme Court [2013] UKSC 29; [2013] 2 A.C. 163 on the basis that, in the particular circumstances of that case, there was no contractual intention); cf. *Sharpe v Bishop of Worcester* [2015] EWCA Civ 399; [2015] I.R.L.R. 663.

154 See *R. v Civil Service Appeal Board Ex p. Bruce* [1988] I.C.R. 649; affirmed on other grounds [1989] I.C.R. 171; *McLaren v Home Office* [1990] I.C.R. 824.

155 *R. v Civil Service Appeal Board Ex p. Bruce* [1988] I.C.R. 649 at 659.

156 *R. v Lord Chancellor's Department Ex p. Nangle* [1991] I.C.R. 743; cf. Trade Unions and Labour Relations (Consolidation) Act 1992 ss.62(7), 245: "deemed [for certain purposes] to constitute a contract".

157 *White v Chief Constable of the South Yorkshire Police* [1999] A.C. 455 at 481.

158 *White v Chief Constable of the South Yorkshire Police* [1999] A.C. 455 at 497. Nor is there between a GP and a Health Authority: *Essex Strategic HA v David-John* [2004] I.C.R. 112.

159 *White v Chief Constable of the South Yorkshire Police* [1999] A.C. 455 at 497; see also *Waters v Commissioner of Police to the Metropolis* [2000] 1 W.L.R. 1607 at 1616.

160 *JH Milner & Son v Percy Bilton Ltd* [1966] 1 W.L.R. 1582; cf. *Baird Textile Holdings Ltd v Marks & Spencer Plc* [2001] EWCA Civ 274; [2002] 1 All E.R. (Comm) 737 at [10], [46], [47], [73], [76]. See also: *Vaughan v Vaughan* [1953] 1 Q.B. 762 at 765; *Blue v Ashley* [2017] EWHC 1928 (Comm) at [97]; cf. *Jones v Padavatton* [1969] 1 W.L.R. 328; *Windeler v Whitehall* [1990] 2 F.L.R. 505.

agreement at all.[161] This issue is separate from that of contractual intention, which strictly speaking concerns only the *effect* of an agreement which is first shown to exist. But the two issues are related in that a lack of certainty which might be resolved for the purposes of finding agreement, e.g. by resort to a standard of reasonableness,[162] may nonetheless confirm "the absence of any clear evidence of an intention to create legal relations".[163]

**Statements made in jest or anger.** The fact that a statement was made in jest or anger may also negative contractual intention.[164] Thus in *Licenses Ins Corp v Lawson*[165] the defendant was a director of two companies, A and B. The former company held shares in the latter and resolved, in the defendant's absence, to sell them. At a later meeting this resolution was rescinded after a heated discussion during which the defendant said that he would make good any loss which A might suffer if it kept the shares in B. It was held that the defendant was not liable on this undertaking. Nobody at the meeting regarded it as a contract; it was not recorded as such in the minute book; and the defendant's fellow-directors at most thought that he was bound in honour. **4–034**

**Free travel pass.** There are conflicting decisions on the question whether the issue and acceptance of a free travel pass amounts to a contract. In *Wilkie v LPTB*[166] it was held that such a pass issued by a transport undertaking to one of its own employees did not amount to a contract. But the contrary conclusion was reached in *Gore v Van der Lann*[167] where the pass was issued to an old age pensioner. This conclusion was based on the ground that an application for the pass had been made on a form couched in contractual language; and *Wilkie*'s case was distinguished on the ground that the pass there was issued to the employee "as a matter of course ... as one of the privileges attaching to his employment".[168] But as the pass in *Gore*'s case was issued expressly on the "understanding" that it constituted only a licence subject to conditions the distinction seems, with respect, to be a tenuous one. **4–035**

**Difficult cases.** *Esso Petroleum Ltd v Commissioners of Customs and Excise*[169] is the first of two difficult cases in which there was a difference of opinion on the issue of contractual intention. Esso supplied garages with tokens called "World Cup coins", instructing them to give away one coin with every four gallons of petrol sold. The scheme was advertised by Esso and also on posters displayed by the garages. By a majority of four to one, the House of Lords held that there was no "sale" of the coins; but the majority was equally divided on the question **4–036**

[161] See para.2–080.
[162] See para.2–097.
[163] *Baird Textile Holdings Ltd v Marks & Spencer Plc* [2001] EWCA Civ 274; [2002] 1 All E.R. (Comm) 737 at [30]; *In the matter of MF Global UK Ltd* [2016] EWCA Civ 569 at [44].
[164] For "jest", see the discussion of *Blue v Ashley*, para.4–028.
[165] (1896) 12 T.L.R. 501.
[166] [1947] 1 All E.R. 258.
[167] [1967] 2 Q.B. 31.
[168] *Gore v Van der Lann* [1967] 2 Q.B. 31 at 41.
[169] [1976] 1 W.L.R. 1; Atiyah 39 M.L.R. 335.

whether there was any contract at all with regard to the coins. Those who thought that there was a contract relied on the incidence of the burden of proof, and on the point that "Esso envisaged a bargain of some sort between the garage proprietor and the motorist".[170] But this point relates rather to the intention of Esso than to that of the alleged contracting parties. With regard to *their* intention, it is submitted that the more realistic view is that contractual intention was negatived by the language of the advertisements (in which the coins were said to be "going free"), and by the minimal value of the coins.

A second difficult case is *J Evans & Son* (*Portsmouth*) *Ltd v Andrea Merzario Ltd.*[171] The representative of a firm of forwarding agents told a customer, with whom the firm had long dealt, that henceforth his goods would be packed in containers and assured him that these would be carried *under* deck. About a year later, such a container was carried *on* deck and lost. At first instance,[172] Kerr J held that the promise was not intended to be legally binding since it was made in the course of a courtesy call, not related to any particular transaction, and indefinite with regard to its future duration. The Court of Appeal, however, held[173] that the promise did have contractual force, relying principally on the importance attached by the customer to the carriage of his goods under deck, and on the fact that he would not have agreed to the new mode of carriage but for the promise. The case is no doubt a borderline one, but it is submitted that Kerr J's view accords more closely with the objective test of contractual intention. In most cases, that test prevents the *promisor* from relying on his subjective intention not to enter into a contractual undertaking. But it should equally prevent the *promisee's* subjective intention (if not known to the promisor) from being decisive. The Court of Appeal appears with respect to have attached too much weight to the customer's subjective state of mind, and too little weight to the circumstances in which the promise was made.

---

170 *Esso Petroleum Ltd v Commissioners of Customs and Excise* [1976] 1 W.L.R. 1 at 6.

171 [1976] 1 W.L.R. 1078; cf. *El Awadi v Bank of Credit and Commerce International* [1990] 1 Q.B. 606 at 617.

172 *J Evans & Son (Portsmouth) Ltd v Andrea Merzario Ltd* [1975] 1 Lloyd's Rep. 162.

173 *J Evans & Son (Portsmouth) Ltd v Andrea Merzario Ltd* [1976] 1 W.L.R. 1078.

CHAPTER 5

# FORM



## 1. GENERAL RULE

A legal system is said to require that a contract shall be made in a certain form if it lays down the manner in which the conclusion of the contract must be marked or recorded. In modern legal systems, such formal requirements generally consist of writing, sometimes with additional requirements, e.g. those of a deed or (in some countries) of authentication by a notary. 5–001

**Form as a necessary requirement.** Form may be *sufficient* to make a promise binding, as we have seen in discussing the effect of a gratuitous promise made in a deed.[1] It has even been said that consideration is a form,[2] but in this chapter we shall discuss cases in which form is a *necessary* requirement which must be satisfied before the contract is fully effective, notwithstanding there is agreement, consideration and contractual intention. Such a requirement may serve one or more of several purposes. First, it promotes certainty, as it is usually relatively easy to tell whether the required form has been used. A requirement of writing also simplifies the problem of ascertaining the contents of the agreement. Secondly, form has a cautionary effect: a person may hesitate longer before executing a deed than he would before making an oral promise. Thirdly, form has a protective function: it is used to protect the weaker party to a contractual relationship by ensuring that he is provided with a written record of the terms of 5–002

[1] See para.3–172.

[2] Holmes, *The Common Law*, p.273: "Consideration is a form as much as a seal." See also Fuller 41 Col. L. Rev. 799; cf. *The Alev* [1989] 1 Lloyd's Rep. 138 at 147.

the contract.[3] Both the second and the third purposes of form are illustrated by the elaborate formal requirements that protect a debtor under certain consumer credit agreements.[4] It is scarcely fanciful to suggest that these requirements fulfil in a modern context some of the functions formerly performed by use of the seal.

5–003 **General rule: no formality required.** Form has the disadvantage that it is time-consuming and clumsy and that it is a source of technical pitfalls. Even the relatively simple requirement of writing is open to these objections and has therefore been regarded as inconvenient from a commercial point of view. The general rule is that contracts can be made quite informally.[5]

## 2. STATUTORY EXCEPTIONS

5–004 The exceptions to the general rule that no formality is required now all depend on legislation dealing with specific types of contracts. Some such contracts must be made by deed, some must be in writing, and others must be evidenced by a note or memorandum in writing. No attempt can be made in this book to give a complete list of these exceptions. A few illustrations must suffice; after these have been discussed, an attempt will be made to consider the impact of contracting by electronic means.

### (a) Contracts which must be made by deed

5–005 **Lease for more than three years.** A lease for more than three years must be made by deed.[6] If it is not so made, it is "void for the purpose of creating a legal estate".[7] But it operates in equity as an agreement for a lease,[8] which can be specifically enforced if it complies with the formal requirements (to be discussed below)[9] for contracts for the disposition of interests in land.[10] Thus between the parties to the lease lack of a deed is not fatal. But, unless the tenant has registered the lease as a land-charge or, in the case of registered land, is in actual occupation, he can be turned out by a third party to whom the landlord has sold the land.[11]

---

[3] See, e.g. Employment Rights Act 1996 ss.1, 2–4; Landlord and Tenant Act 1985 s.4.

[4] Consumer Credit (Agreements) Regulations (SI 1983/1553).

[5] *Beckham v Drake* (1841) 9 M. & W. 79 at 92.

[6] Law of Property Act 1925 ss.52, 54(2).

[7] Law of Property Act 1925 s.52.

[8] *Walsh v Lonsdale* (1882) 21 Ch D. 9.

[9] See para.5–009.

[10] See, e.g. *Hardy v Haselden* [2011] EWCA Civ 1387; [2011] N.P.C. 122 (where the alleged agreement was neither enforceable as a lease, nor as a contract).

[11] At present under Law of Property Act 1925 s.199(1)(i); Land Registration Act 2002 Sch.3 para.2.

## (b) Contracts which must be in writing

### (i) *Bills of exchange, etc.*

Under nineteenth-century legislation, contracts which must be in writing include bills of exchange, promissory notes[12] and bills of sale.[13] A bill of sale is void unless it is in writing in the statutory form.[14] But if the sort of promise which is normally contained in a bill of exchange or promissory note is made orally, it can result in a perfectly valid contract. The contract is not invalid[15] but will not have the legal and commercial characteristics[16] of a bill or note. 5–006

### (ii) *Consumer credit agreements*

Under the Consumer Credit Act 1974, regulated consumer credit agreements, and certain other agreements[17] are "not properly executed"[18] unless certain formalities are complied with. A regulated consumer credit agreement is one by which a creditor provides an individual debtor with credit[19] of any amount.[20] Both parties must sign a document in the form prescribed by regulations.[21] This must legibly set out all the express terms of the contract[22] and contain a notice of the debtor's statutory right to cancel during the "cooling off" period (where this applies),[23] as well as certain other information.[24] A copy must also be given to the debtor.[25] 5–007

**Effect of non-compliance.** An agreement which is not properly executed can be enforced *against the debtor* "on an order of the court only".[26] In the absence of such an order, no restitutionary remedy is available against the borrower at common law since the award of such a remedy to the lender would be inconsistent with the legislative scheme that, in the case of an improperly executed document, "subject to the enforcement powers of the court, the debtor should not have to pay".[27] An application for an enforcement order shall be dismissed only if the court considers it just to do so.[28] In this regard, the court has a wide discretion. It can take into account the prejudice caused to the debtor and 5–008

[12] Bills of Exchange Act 1882 ss.3(1), 17(2).

[13] Bills of Sale Act 1878 (Amendment) Act 1882.

[14] Bills of Sale Act 1878 (Amendment) Act 1882.

[15] *Hitchens v General Guarantee Corp* [2001] EWCA Civ 359; *The Times* 13 March 2001.

[16] See paras 15–046–15–049.

[17] Such as consumer hire agreements (s.15) and security instruments (s.105).

[18] Consumer Credit Act 1974 s.61(1).

[19] As defined by s.9.

[20] Consumer Credit Act 1974 s.8(1).

[21] Consumer Credit Act 1974 s.61(1)(a); for exceptions, see s.74; cf. para.5–002.

[22] Consumer Credit Act 1974 s.61(1)(b) and (c).

[23] Consumer Credit Act 1974 s.64(5); for "cooling off" periods, see para.10–049.

[24] Consumer Credit Act 1974 s.55(1).

[25] Consumer Credit Act 1974 ss.62, 63.

[26] Consumer Credit Act 1974 s.65(1). The defective agreement is thus unenforceable only and not void: *R. v Modupe* [1991] C.C.L.R. 29.

[27] *Dimond v Lovell* [2002] 1 A.C. 384 at 398.

[28] Consumer Credit Act 1974 s.127(1).

the degree of culpability of the creditor;[29] order enforcement conditionally or subject to variations;[30] or reduce the amount payable by the debtor.[31] This flexible approach, together with the repeal of provisions which had completely prevented the grant of an order for certain formal defects, goes far to meet the objection that formal requirements can give rise to unmeritorious defences based on technical slips.

### *(iii) Contracts for the sale or disposition of an interest in land*

5–009 **Requirements.** Under s.2 of the Law of Property (Miscellaneous Provisions) Act 1989, most contracts for[32] the sale or disposition of an interest in land[33] must be "made in writing".[34] All the terms expressly agreed by the parties must be incorporated in the document[35] (or in each document, where contracts are exchanged).[36] The terms may be incorporated either by being set out in the document, or by reference.[37] The document (or documents) must also be signed "by or on behalf of"[38] each party[39] to the contract. It has, thus far,[40] been unnecessary to amend the 1989 Act to keep pace with advances in technology and more modern methods of communication.[41] For example, the relevant document,

---

[29] Consumer Credit Act 1974 s.127(1)(i).

[30] Consumer Credit Act 1974 s.127(1)(ii).

[31] Consumer Credit Act 1974 s.127(2); *National Guardian Mortgage Corp v Wilks* [1993] C.C.L.R. 1.

[32] i.e. for future disposition and not a contract *of* immediate disposition: see para.5–013.

[33] As defined in Law of Property (Miscellaneous Provisions) Act 1989 s.2(6). A "lock-out" agreement is not within the section: *Pitt v PHH Asset Management Ltd* [1993] 1 W.L.R. 327 (contrast *Lane v Robinson* [2010] EWCA Civ 384 at [11]). Nor is a compromise agreement which merely "relates" to the sale of land: *Nweze v Nwoko* [2004] EWCA Civ 379; [2004] 2 P. & C.R. 33; or trivial dispositions of land pursuant to a boundary demarcation agreement: *Joyce v Rigolli* [2004] EWCA Civ 79; [2004] All E.R. (D) 203; cf. *Nata Lee Ltd v Abid* [2014] EWCA Civ 1652; [2015] 2 P. & C.R. 3; or a settlement under CPR Pt 36 which requires the sale or other disposition of an interest in land: *Orton v Collins* [2007] EWHC 803 (Ch); [2007] 1 W.L.R. 2953. But see also *Kilcarne Holdings Ltd v Targetfollow* [2004] EWHC 2547; [2005] 2 P. & C.R. 8 at [203] (a contract for the sale of land cannot escape s.2 "merely because it is wrapped up in an alleged partnership" (affirmed [2005] EWCA Civ 1355, without consideration of this point)).

[34] Law of Property (Miscellaneous Provisions) Act 1989 s.2(1).

[35] *Firstpost Homes Ltd v Johnson* [1995] 1 W.L.R. 1567.

[36] Law of Property (Miscellaneous Provisions) Act 1989 s.2(1); *Commission for the New Towns v Cooper (Great Britain) Ltd* [1995] Ch. 259 at 285, 293.

[37] Law of Property (Miscellaneous Provisions) Act 1989 s.2(2); *Courtney v Corp Ltd* [2006] EWCA Civ 518; cf. *Record v Bell* [1991] 1 W.L.R. 853, fn.55.

[38] *Braymist v Wise Finance Co Ltd* [2002] EWCA Civ 127; [2002] 2 All E.R. 333 (signature by agent); cf. *Marlbray Ltd v Laditi* [2016] EWCA Civ 476; [2016] 1 W.L.R. 5147 (agent alone bound by the contract as principal). See further: *McLaughlin v Duffill* [2008] EWCA Civ 1627; [2010] Ch. 1.

[39] Law of Property (Miscellaneous Provisions) Act 1989 s.2(3). An option to purchase is within the section, but the notice exercising it is not, and so does not have to be signed by the vendor: *Spiro v Glencrown Properties Ltd* [1991] Ch. 537; cf. *MP Kemp Ltd v Bullen Developments Ltd* [2014] EWHC 2009 (Ch).

[40] See para.5–030.

[41] A system of electronic conveyancing which is allowed for in Pt 8 of the Land Registration Act 2002 has not as yet been developed.

or documents, can take the form of a chain of emails[42] and the document is signed whenever it is endorsed by the "signer" in a way which is intended to provide authentication. Thus, an automatic signature at the end of an email which is created by the signer having previously set up his signature in this way will suffice.[43] It had previously been held that "signed" should be given the meaning which "the ordinary man would understand it to have", but this no longer requires that the parties must write their own names with their own hands upon the document.[44] In addition to an automatically generated signature in an email, the requirement that the document must have been signed does not rule out the use of a signature writing machine.[45] It has been held that it is not satisfied (as it was under earlier legislation superseded by s.2 of the 1989 Act)[46] by merely typing a party's name and address on the document,[47] but it is enough that a party has "written" his initials, provided it is clear that he intended to authenticate all the terms.[48] The requirement of writing does not apply to short leases for less than three years, to sales at public auctions or to transactions in certain forms of investment securities (e.g. unit trust investing in land).[49]

**Failure to include all terms.** Where the document fails to include *all* the terms on which the parties are alleged to have orally agreed, a number of possibilities call for discussion. If the failure was due to the parties' having *deliberately* omitted the term from the written document, then it will not be a term expressly agreed so as to form part of the contract, so that its omission will not affect the validity of the contract as set out in the document.[50] This might be achieved by an appropriately drafted entire agreement clause.[51] If the failure was due to a mistake in recording those terms,[52] it may be possible to rectify the document,[53] i.e. to bring it into line with what was actually agreed.[54] If the failure is due to some other cause, it is sometimes possible to treat the omitted term as a separate or "collateral" contract, independent of the (main) contract set out in the document,[55] which will then satisfy the requirements of s.2. The omitted term cannot, however, be so treated if it is intended to form part of the main contract:[56] 5–010

[42] *Neocleous v Rees* [2019] EWHC 2462 (Ch); cf. *Re Stealth Construction Ltd* [2012] 1 B.C.L.C. 297 at [44].
[43] *Neocleous v Rees* [2019] EWHC 2462 (Ch).
[44] cf. *Firstpost Homes Ltd v Johnson* [1995] 1 W.L.R. 1567 at 1576.
[45] *Ramsay v Love* [2015] EWHC 65 (Ch) at [7].
[46] i.e. Law of Property Act 1925 s.40.
[47] *Firstpost Homes Ltd v Johnson* [1995] 1 W.L.R. 1567.
[48] *Newell v Tarrant* [2004] EWHC 772.
[49] Law of Property (Miscellaneous Provisions) Act 1989 s.2(5).
[50] *Grossman v Hooper* [2001] EWCA Civ 615; [2001] 2 E.G.L.R. 82.
[51] *North Eastern Properties Ltd v Coleman* [2010] EWCA Civ 277; [2010] 1 W.L.R. 2715.
[52] But not if it was the result of an express agreement to omit the terms: *Oun v Ahmad* [2008] EWHC 545 (Ch); [2008] 13 E.G. 149; cf. *Helden v Strathmore Ltd* [2011] EWCA Civ 542; [2011] Bus L.R. 1592 at [29]; *Francis v F. Berndes Ltd* [2011] EWHC 3377 (Ch) at [43].
[53] Law of Property (Miscellaneous Provisions) Act 1989 s.2(4); *Robert Leonard (Developments) Ltd v Wright* [1994] N.P.C. 49.
[54] See *Commission for the New Towns v Cooper (GB) Ltd* [1995] Ch. 259. For rectification, see para.8–063 and following.
[55] e.g. *Record v Bell* [1991] 1 W.L.R. 853.
[56] *Grossman v Hooper* [2001] EWCA Civ 615; [2001] 2 E.G.L.R. 82 at [21].

e.g. if it is so "interwoven with the substance of the transaction"[57] as to form an essential part of it; for to treat a document as sufficient even though it omitted such a term would be inconsistent with the statutory requirement that the document must incorporate all the expressly agreed terms. It seems that a term can for the present purpose be treated as a collateral contract only if it was intended to take effect as an independent contract, separate from that set out in the document. If it can be so treated, two consequences follow. First, a document which omits the term can nevertheless satisfy the statutory requirement of incorporating *all* the express terms of the main contract. Secondly, the collateral contract is binding, even if oral, so long as it is not itself one which is required to be in writing.[58]

5–011 **Effect of non-compliance.** The effect of the requirement that it must be "made in writing" is that a contract for the sale or other disposition of an interest in land does not come into existence if the parties fail to comply with the statutory formal requirements. This could cause hardship where one party has partly performed[59] such a contract, or otherwise acted in reliance on it, e.g. by making improvements to the land in question. But such hardship can be avoided by other judicially developed doctrines, such as proprietary estoppel or constructive trust.[60] Where payment has been made under a contract which does not exist for failure to comply with the requirements of s.2 of the 1989 Act, restitution of the payment will normally be ordered unless payment was also made for other benefits which have still been conferred on the payor.[61]

5–012 **Proprietary estoppel and constructive trust.** Under these doctrines, the court may make an order for the transfer of the land to the party who has acted in reliance on the contract.[62] But the remedy is limited in various ways[63] and does not necessarily lead to enforcement of the contract as such.[64] Thus, while they may play a role similar to that of "part performance",[65] the position of the party who has acted in reliance on the defective contract is now less favourable than it was before the 1989 Act.[66] Section 2(5) of the 1989 Act states only that nothing in s.2 "affects the creation or operation of resulting, implied or constructive trusts". This has led to the view that a "mere estoppel" unassociated with a

[57] *Preece v Lewis* (1963) 186 E.G. 113, decided under Law of Property Act 1925 s.40 but, *semble*, equally applicable under Law of Property (Miscellaneous Provisions) Act 1989 s.2(1); see also Law Com. No.164, paras 5.7, 5.8.

[58] *Record v Bell* [1991] 1 W.L.R. 853; *Business Environment Bow Lane Ltd v Deanwater Estates* [2007] EWCA Civ 622; [2007] 32 E.G. 90.

[59] For the position in relation to fully performed contracts, see para.5–013.

[60] See para.5–012.

[61] *Sharma v Simposh* [2011] EWCA Civ 1383; [2013] Ch. 23; *Marlbray Ltd v Laditi* [2016] EWCA Civ 476; [2016] 1 W.L.R. 5147; cf. *Singh v Sanghera* [2013] EWHC 956 (Ch) (restitution ordered on both sides)

[62] See para.3–141.

[63] See para.3–141; cf. also para.3–145.

[64] See para.3–154.

[65] *Kinane v Mackie-Conteh* [2005] EWCA Civ 45; [2005] 6 E.G. 140 at [32].

[66] Under Law of Property Act 1925 s.40 (now repealed) failure to comply with the statutory requirement of written evidence only made the contract unenforceable; and "part performance" (para.5–028) enabled the party so performing to enforce the contract.

constructive trust cannot be relied upon.[67] The preferable view, it is submitted, is that the saving provision in s.2(5) should not be so limited, since it was the retention of the very flexibility of proprietary estoppel which was contemplated.[68] It should therefore depend upon the facts of the particular case whether the proprietary estoppel in question would offend the policy underlying the Act.[69]

**Contracts fully performed.** Section 2 of the 1989 Act applies to a contract *for* the disposition of a future interest in land, but not to a contract *of* immediate disposition or an actual disposition.[70] Accordingly, a party who wishes to take the point that the contract is void has to do so before it has been fully performed since "an actual transfer, conveyance or assignment, an actual lease, or an actual mortgage are not within the scope of section 2 at all".[71] A wider proposition said to be derived from a dictum of Scott LJ in *Tootal Clothing v Guinea Properties Management*[72] that s.2 is inapplicable once all the "land elements" of the contract have been fully performed,[73] so that the non-land elements of what remains an executory contract can be enforced, was rejected by the Court of Appeal in *Keay v Morris Homes (West Midlands) Ltd*.[74] **5–013**

## (c) Contracts which must be evidenced in writing

### *(i) In general*

Some statutes do not require contracts to be *made* in writing, but only to be *evidenced* by a written document. A contract of marine insurance, for example, is "inadmissible in evidence" unless it is embodied in a marine policy signed by the insurer.[75] This is not a requirement of the making or validity of such a contract: it is enough if the policy is executed *after* the making of the contract. Other statutory provisions are less exacting; they are satisfied if there is merely a "note or memorandum" in writing. The Statute of Frauds 1677 applied this requirement **5–014**

[67] *Kinane v Mackie-Conteh* [2005] EWCA Civ 45; [2005] 6 E.G. 140 at [45]–[46] (Neuberger LJ; contrast Arden LJ at [28]); *Cobbe v Yeoman's Row Management Ltd* [2008] UKHL 55; [2008] 1 W.L.R. 1752 at [29] (Lord Scott); cf. *Thorner v Major* [2009] UKHL 18; [2009] 1 W.L.R. 776 at [99] (Lord Neuberger); *Lancashire Mortgage Corp Ltd v Scottish and Newcastle Plc* [2007] EWCA Civ 684 at [55]; *Herbert v Doyle* [2010] EWCA Civ 1095; [2011] 1 EG.L.R. 119 at [57]; *Crossco No.4 Unlimited v Jolan Ltd* [2011] EWCA Civ 1619; [2011] 2 All E.R. 745 at [107]; *Matchmove Ltd v Dowding* [2016] EWCA Civ 1233; [2017] 1 W.L.R. 749 at [28].

[68] Law Com. No.164, paras 4.3, 5.4 and 5.5; *Yaxley v Gotts* [2000] Ch. 162 at 182; *Whittaker v Kinnear* [2011] EWHC 1479 (Ch) at [30].

[69] *Yaxley v Gotts* [2000] Ch. 162 at 174, 182. Other forms of estoppel are likely to fail: *Yaxley v Gotts* [2000] Ch. 162 at 174, 182; *Eyestorm Ltd v Hoptonacre Homes Ltd* [2007] EWCA Civ 1366 at [51]; *Dudley Muslim Association v Dudley MBC* [2015] EWCA Civ 1123; [2016] 1 P. & C.R. 10 at [33]; *Farrar v Miller* [2018] EWCA Civ 172 at [55]–[63]; *Kensington Mortgage Co Ltd v Mallon* [2019] EWHC 2512 (Ch); cf. the position in relation to guarantees: para.5–028.

[70] *McLaughlin v Duffill* [2008] EWCA Civ 1627; [2010] Ch. 1 at [20]; *Rollerteam Ltd v Riley* [2016] EWCA Civ 1291; [2017] Ch. 109.

[71] *Helden v Strathmore Ltd* [2011] EWCA Civ 542; [2011] Bus L.R. 1592 at [27].

[72] (1992) 64 P. & C.R. 452 at [5].

[73] *Kilcarne Holdings Ltd v Targetfollow* [2004] EWHC 2547; [2005] 2 P & C.R. 8 at [198].

[74] [2012] EWCA Civ 900; [2012] 1 W.L.R. 2855 at [46] (Rimer LJ).

[75] Marine Insurance Act 1906 ss.22 and 24.

to six classes of contracts. Its object was to prevent fraudulent claims based on perjured evidence; but it sometimes gave rise to technical defences which had little merit, so that it was restrictively interpreted by the courts. This process can be illustrated by reference to contracts of guarantee, the only type of contract to which the formal requirements imposed by the Statute still apply.

### (ii) *Contracts of guarantee*

5–015 **Statute of Frauds 1677 section 4.** In its current form s.4 of the Statute of Frauds 1677 provides:

> "No action shall be brought whereby to charge the Defendant upon any special promise to answer for the debt default or miscarriage of another person unless the Agreement upon which such Action shall be brought or some Memorandum or Note thereof shall be in Writing and signed by the party to be charged therewith or some other person thereunto by him lawfully authorised".

This provision applies whether the liability guaranteed is contractual or tortious.[76] It applies only where the defendant's promise to pay the debt is made to the creditor. It does not apply where that promise is made to the debtor.[77] In addition, it does not apply in the cases discussed in paras 5–016 to 5–018.

5–016 **Guarantee or indemnity?** The Statute applies to a guarantee, but not to an indemnity (including an "on demand guarantee"[78]). A guarantee is a promise to pay another's debt if he fails to pay.[79] An indemnity is a promise to indemnify the creditor against loss arising out of the principal contract.[80] In the case of a guarantee the liability of the principal debtor is primary and that of the guarantor only secondary; thus, if for some reason the principal debtor is not liable, the guarantor is not liable either. A promise to indemnify creates primary liability which arises even though the promisee has no enforceable rights under the principal contract.[81]

It follows from its nature that there can be no guarantee if there never was a principal debtor, e.g. if A promises to pay B for doing work for C, which C has not ordered so that C is not liable to pay B for it.[82] Nor is a contract a guarantee if there once was a principal debtor, but if the whole object of the new contract is that his liability should cease and the liability of the new promisor be substituted for it. Thus, a promise by a father to pay his son's creditor, if the creditor will release the son, is an indemnity.[83] But a promise may be an indemnity in spite of the fact that there is a principal debtor whose liability continues. This is the

---

[76] *Kirkham v Marter* (1819) 2 B. & Ald. 613.

[77] *Eastwood v Kenyon* (1840) 11 A. & E. 438.

[78] *WS Tankship II BV v Kwangju Bank Ltd* [2011] EWHC 3103 (Comm); [2011] C.I.L.L. 3155 at [151].

[79] *Lep Air Services v Rolloswin Investments Ltd* [1973] A.C. 331.

[80] *Birkmyr v Darnell* (1704) 1 Salk. 27; *Argo Caribbean Group v Lewis* [1976] 2 Lloyd's Rep. 289; cf. para.9–172.

[81] *Yeoman Credit Ltd v Latter* [1961] 1 W.L.R. 828.

[82] *Lakeman v Mountstephen* (1874) L.R. 7 H.L. 17.

[83] *Goodman v Chase* (1818) 1 B. & Ald. 297.

position if the person making the promise undertakes not merely to pay if the principal debtor fails to do so, but "to put the [creditor] in funds in any event".[84]

It can hardly be said that there is less danger of perjury in the case of an indemnity than in the case of a guarantee. The distinction between them has accordingly been criticised for having "raised many hair-splitting distinctions of exactly that kind which bring the law into hatred, ridicule and contempt by the public".[85] It can only be explained historically as a device for restricting the scope of the Statute of Frauds.

**Guarantee part of larger transaction.** The Statute applies to a guarantee which stands alone but not to one which is part of a larger transaction. It did not, for example, apply where the defendant introduced clients to a firm of stockbrokers on the terms that he was to receive half the commissions earned, and to pay half the losses incurred, by the stockbrokers on transactions with such clients.[86] The promise to pay losses was enforceable, though oral, as it formed part of a larger transaction in which the defendant was interested otherwise than as guarantor. Similarly, the guarantee given by a *del credere* agent is not within the Statute. Such an agent guarantees the solvency of the third party with whom his principal makes a contract: that is, he promises the principal to pay if the third party does not. The main object of a *del credere* agency is to enable the principal to sell and the agent to earn his commission: "Though it may terminate in a liability to pay the debt of another, that is not the immediate object for which the consideration is given."[87] On the wording of the Statute, it is hard to justify the special treatment of these cases. Perhaps it could be said that such promises are more likely to be made than purely disinterested guarantees: hence there is less danger of perjury. **5–017**

**Protection of property.** A guarantee is not within the Statute if it is given to protect some proprietary interest of the guarantor. Thus A may buy goods from B which are held by C as security for a debt owed by B to C. If A induces C to deliver the goods to him by promising to pay B's debt in case B does not pay it, A's promise is not within the Statute.[88] The main object of A's promise is said to be to protect his own property and not to guarantee B's debt. This rule may again be justified on the ground that such promises are more likely to be made than purely disinterested guarantees. But if this is so, it is hard to see why the rule is restricted to cases in which the interest is strictly proprietary. The rule has, for example, been held not to apply where the guarantee was given to protect the assets of a company in which the guarantor was a substantial shareholder or **5–018**

---

[84] *Guild & Co v Conrad* [1894] 2 Q.B. 885 at 892; cf. *Thomas v Cook* (1828) 8 B. & C. 728; *Wildes v Dudlow* (1874) L.R. 19 Eq. 198; *Re Hoyle* [1893] 1 Ch. 84.

[85] *Yeoman Credit Ltd v Latter* [1961] 1 W.L.R. 828 at 835; cf. *Associated British Ports v Ferryways NV* [2009] EWCA Civ 189; [2009] 1 Lloyd's Rep. 595 at [1] (an "old chestnut" which is "technical and inconvenient").

[86] *Sutton & Co v Grey* [1894] 1 Q.B. 285. cf. *Pitts v Jones* [2007] EWCA Civ 1301; [2008] Q.B. 76.

[87] *Couturier v Hastie* (1852) 8 Ex. 40 at 56, reversed on another point: (1856) 5 H.L.C. 673; para.8–009.

[88] *Fitzgerald v Dressler* (1859) 7 C.B. (N.S.) 374.

debenture holder.[89] It was said that to enforce an oral guarantee in such a case would amount to repealing the Statute.[90] But this is also true where the interest protected is a strictly proprietary one.

5–019 **Criticism.** So many subtle distinctions have been drawn to whittle away the application of the Statute to contracts of guarantee that it seems a pity that this part of the Statute has not been replaced by legislation which more effectively furthers its purpose of protecting guarantors. The requirement of written evidence is scarcely an effective means of providing such protection, since it can be satisfied by a standard form of guarantee drafted by a bank to protect its own interests rather than those of the guarantor.[91] Even if the requirement of written evidence did protect the guarantor, it would not do so very effectively, for it can fairly easily be evaded by drawing up the contract as one of indemnity.

5–020 **Type of evidence required.** Contracts within the Statute of Frauds must be evidenced by a signed note or memorandum in writing. The exact nature of the evidence required was not specified by the Statute, but the following rules were later laid down by Parliament and by the courts. Many of the relevant cases concern contracts to which the Statute no longer applies; but the principles to be derived from them still apply, where appropriate, to contracts of guarantee.

5–021 **Parties.** The memorandum must identify the parties by naming or describing them,[92] and state the capacity in which they contract.[93]

5–022 **Consideration.** The memorandum of guarantee need not state the consideration for the guarantee.[94]

5–023 **Terms.** The memorandum must contain all the material terms of the contract.[95] There is some authority for the view that if a term has been omitted from the memorandum the claimant may waive the term if it is solely for his benefit and not of major importance, and enforce the contract without the term.[96] Conversely, if the omitted term is for the benefit of the defendant, the claimant may be able to enforce the contract on agreeing to perform it.[97]

---

89 *Harburg India Rubber Comb Co v Martin* [1902] 1 K.B. 778; *Davys v Buswell* [1913] 2 K.B. 47; *The Anemone* [1987] 1 Lloyd's Rep. 547.

90 *Harburg India Rubber Comb Co v Martin* [1902] 1 K.B. 778 at 787.

91 In relation to regulated agreements, statutory protection is provided by Consumer Credit Act 1974 Pt VIII and s.127: para.5–007.

92 *Re Lindrea* (1913) 109 L.T. 623 (first name sufficient); *Carr v Lynch* [1900] 1 Ch. 613 (description by pronoun sufficient) cf. *Williams v Jordan* (1877) 6 Ch D. 517 ("Sir" not sufficient); *UCB Corporate Services Ltd v Clyde & Co* [2000] 2 All E.R. (Comm) 257 where the guarantor was not named or otherwise identified.

93 *Vandenbergh v Spooner* (1866) L.R. 1 Ex. 316; *Newell v Radford* (1867) L.R. 3 C.P. 52; *Dewar v Mintoft* [1912] 2 K.B. 373.

94 Mercantile Law Amendment Act 1856 s.3.

95 *Hawkins v Price* [1947] Ch. 645; cf. *Marshall v Berridge* (1881) 19 Ch D. 233; *MP Services v Lawyer* (1996) P. & C.R. D49.

96 *North v Loomes* [1919] 1 Ch. 378; *Beckett v Nurse* [1948] 1 K.B. 535.

97 *Martin v Pycroft* (1852) 2 D.M. & G. 785; *Scott v Bradley* [1971] Ch. 850 (refusing to follow *Burgess v Cox* [1951] Ch. 383 on this point).

**Signature.** The memorandum must be signed by the party to be charged or by his agent lawfully authorised to sign for him. The requirement that the memorandum must be "signed" is liberally interpreted. A party need not sign his full name: initials will do.[98] The signature may be printed,[99] and may be in any part of the document, not necessarily at the bottom.[100] It may be put on the document before the contract was made so long as it is "recognised" at the time of contracting. Thus, a form printed before the contract is made and bearing one party's name is "signed" by that party if he at the time of contracting submits it to the other party for signature: he thereby "recognises" his own "signature".[101] These rules are lax, but a document is not signed by a party merely because his name occurs somewhere within it: the signature must authenticate the whole document. Thus if a memorandum is headed "Articles of Agreement between A & B" and concludes "As witness our hands … " the parties must actually subscribe: the mention of their names at the beginning is clearly not intended as a signature.[102] Similarly, where the terms of a guarantee are set out in an email, the memorandum thereby created[103] is not "signed" if the guarantor's name appears only in the address box and was added by the internet service provider.[104] The implication is that it is "signed" if the name is set out in the text of the email since it can then be taken as intended to give authenticity to the document.[105] A party is not considered to have signed a document merely because he adds his signature to it as witness to the signature of the other party.[106] The writing need be signed only by "the party to be charged". Thus, the contract can be enforced against a party who has signed by one who has not.[107] 5–024

**Memorandum need not be prepared as such.** The memorandum need not be prepared for the purpose of satisfying the statutory requirements of written evidence. A writing which comes into existence before an action is brought[108] on the contract will suffice so long as it acknowledges or recognises the existence of 5–025

[98] *Chichester v Cobb* (1866) 14 L.T. 433; *Hill v Hill* [1947] Ch. 231 at 240.

[99] *Schneider v Norris* (1814) 2 M. & S. 286; cf. *Godwin v Francis* (1870) L.R. 5 C.P. 295 (telegram).

[100] *Ogilvie v Foljambe* (1817) 3 Mer. 53; *Durrell v Evans* (1862) 1 H. & C. 174; *Evans v Hoare* [1892] 1 Q.B. 593.

[101] *Schneider v Norris* (1814) 2 M. & S. 286; *Evans v Hoare* [1892] 1 Q.B. 593; *Leeman v Stocks* [1951] Ch. 941.

[102] *Hubert v Treherne* (1842) 3 Man. & G. 743.

[103] See text to fn.115.

[104] *Pereira Fernandes SA v Mehta* [2006] EWHC 813; [2006] 1 W.L.R. 1543; cf. *Lindsay v O'Loughnane* [2010] EWHC 529; [2012] B.C.C. 153 at [95].

[105] *Golden Ocean Group Ltd v Salgaocar Mining Industries PVT* [2011] EWHC 56 (Comm); [2011] 1 W.L.R. 2575 at [104] (affirmed [2012] EWCA Civ 265; [2012] 1 W.L.R. 3674, without discussion of this point). In *WS Tankship II BV v Kwangju Bank Ltd* [2011] EWHC 3103 (Comm); [2011] C.I.L.L. 3155 the court appears to have regarded it as sufficient that the guarantor's name was added automatically by the SWIFT messaging system used by banks (at [155]) and see the reference to "authentication by sending" (at [154]).

[106] *Gosbell v Archer* (1835) 1 A. & E. 500.

[107] *Laythoarp v Bryant* (1836) 2 Bing. N.C. 735; cf. *The Maria D* [1992] 1 A.C. 21 (signature by agent sufficient although he was not liable on the main contract); as to specific performance, see para.21–035.

[108] See *Lucas v Dixon* (1889) 22 Q.B.D. 357; *Farr Smith & Co v Messers* [1928] 1 K.B. 397.

the contract.[109] Thus an offer signed by one party and orally accepted by the other,[110] a recital or disposition in a will,[111] a letter written by one of the parties to his own agent[112] and pleadings in a previous action between different parties[113] have been held sufficient. A letter repudiating liability is a sufficient memorandum if it admits the terms of the contract but denies the construction put upon them by the other party; but not if it denies that a contract was ever made on the terms alleged.[114] Where the essential terms of a guarantee are set out in an email and the offer contained therein is accepted orally, the email constitutes a sufficient note or memorandum in writing for the purpose of the 1677 Act.[115]

5–026 **Joinder of documents?** Earlier cases had established that where no single document fully records the transaction it may be possible to produce a sufficient memorandum by joining together two or more documents. Joinder is, in the first place, possible where one document expressly or impliedly *refers* to another transaction. If that transaction is also recorded in a document, and that document was in existence when the first was signed[116] the two documents can be joined.[117] Joinder may be effected via an intermediate document, e.g. where the first sets out the terms of the guarantee, the second referred to those terms and the third (which is signed by the guarantor) refers to the second.[118] Even where there is no express reference in one document to the other, they can be joined if, on placing them side by side, it becomes obvious without the aid of oral evidence that they are connected.[119] It seems that the original and the photocopy of a document (one signed by one party and the other by the other) could be joined on this ground.[120] But if the document signed by the defendant contains no reference to another document or transaction, and if the connection between the two documents can be established only by oral evidence, joinder is not permitted.[121]

These earlier authorities, and the propositions for which they stand, must now be considered in the light of the decision of the Court of Appeal in *Golden Ocean*

---

[109] *Tweddell v Henderson* [1975] 1 W.L.R. 1496.

[110] *Reuss v Picksley* (1866) L.R. 1 Ex. 342; *Lever v Koffler* [1901] 1 Ch. 543; *Parker v Clark* [1960] 1 W.L.R. 286; cf. *Pereira Fernandes SA v Mehta* [2006] EWHC 813; [2006] 1 W.L.R. 1543.

[111] *Re Hoyle* [1893] 1 Ch. 84; *Schaefer v Schuhmann* [1972] A.C. 572; contrast *Maddison v Alderson* (1883) 8 App. Cas. 467.

[112] *Gibson v Holland* (1865) L.R. 1 C.P. 1.

[113] *Grindell v Bass* [1920] 2 Ch. 487. The position is probably different where reliance is placed on pleadings in an earlier action between the *same* parties; *Hardy v Elphick* [1974] Ch. 65.

[114] See *Buxton v Rust* (1872) L.R. 7 Ex. 279; *Thirkell v Cambi* [1919] 2 K.B. 591; cf. *Dobell v Hutchison* (1835) 3 A. & E. 355.

[115] *J Pereira Fernandes SA v Mehta* [2006] EWHC 813 (Ch); [2006] 1 W.L.R. 1543.

[116] For recognition of, and an exception to, this requirement, see *Re Danish Bacon Co Ltd v Staff Pension Fund* [1971] 1 W.L.R. 248, a case arising under Law of Property Act 1925 s.53(1)(c).

[117] *Long v Millar* (1879) 4 C.P.D. 450; cf. *Reading Trust Ltd v Spero* [1930] 1 K.B. 492; *Holiday Credit Ltd v Erol* [1977] 1 W.L.R. 704; *Elias v George Sahely & Co (Barbados) Ltd* [1983] 1 A.C. 646, where joinder is said at 655 to be possible even though the second document has no contractual force.

[118] *Moat Financial Services v Wilkinson* [2005] EWCA Civ 1253.

[119] *Sheers v Thimbleby* (1879) 13 T.L.R. 451; cf. *Burgess v Cox* [1951] Ch. 383.

[120] *Stokes v Whicher* [1920] 1 Ch. 411 at 419 (top and carbon copies).

[121] *Timmins v Moreland Street Property Co* [1958] Ch. 110; cf. *Boydell v Drummond* (1809) 11 East 192; contrast *Stokes v Whicher* [1920] 1 Ch. 411.

*Group Ltd v Salgaocar Mining Industries PVT*[122] and the view expressed therein that the statute should "be construed in a manner which accommodates accepted contemporary business practice".[123] Adopting this approach, the Court found that there was no "limitation upon the number of documents in which the writing is to be found"[124] and it was satisfied, on the facts of the case, by a "sequence of negotiating emails or other documents of the sort which is commonplace in ship chartering and ship sale and purchase".[125] It was only necessary for the Court to establish that this point was sufficiently arguable for the purpose of service of the claim form out of the jurisdiction, but stressed that this decision was "not simply 'well arguable' but also correct".[126] That said, the Court also cautioned that: "Whether the pattern of contract negotiation and formation habitually adopted in other areas of commercial life presents difficulty in adoption of the same approach must await examination when the problem arises".[127]

**Effect of non-compliance.** Failure to comply with the requirements just described does not make the contract void, but only unenforceable.[128] The contract can be *made* orally, but it can be enforced by action only if a note or memorandum of it exists, signed by the party against whom enforcement is sought. As the contract is not void, money paid or property transferred under it cannot be recovered merely because the contract is not evidenced in writing.[129] For example, a guarantor could not recover from the creditor money which he had paid or property which he had deposited under a guarantee of which there was no sufficient note or memorandum. Similarly, a security given for the guarantor's performance would not be void merely because the guarantee was unenforceable: thus, an action could be brought on a cheque given to the creditor in payment of sums due from the debtor.[130] **5–027**

**Equitable evasion.** When contracts for the sale or other disposition of land were merely required to be *evidenced* in writing, equity would allow the contract to be enforced by a party who had wholly or partly performed on the strength of it, in spite of the lack of a proper note or memorandum. The requirement that such contracts must now be *made* in writing rules out the doctrine of part performance, since there can be no part performance of a non-existent contract.[131] The same doctrine is very unlikely to apply to a guarantee even though it is only required to **5–028**

[122] [2012] EWCA Civ 265; [2012] 1 W.L.R. 3674.
[123] *Golden Ocean Group Ltd v Salgaocar Mining Industries PVT* [2012] EWCA Civ 265; [2012] 1 W.L.R. 3674 at [22].
[124] *Golden Ocean Group Ltd v Salgaocar Mining Industries PVT* [2012] EWCA Civ 265; [2012] 1 W.L.R. 3674 at [21].
[125] *Golden Ocean Group Ltd v Salgaocar Mining Industries PVT* [2012] EWCA Civ 265; [2012] 1 W.L.R. 3674 at [22].
[126] *Golden Ocean Group Ltd v Salgaocar Mining Industries PVT* [2012] EWCA Civ 265; [2012] 1 W.L.R. 3674 at [29].
[127] *Golden Ocean Group Ltd v Salgaocar Mining Industries PVT* [2012] EWCA Civ 265; [2012] 1 W.L.R. 3674 at [22].
[128] *Leroux v Brown* (1852) 12 C.B. 801; *Elias v George Sahely & Co (Barbados) Ltd* [1983] 1 A.C. 646 at 650.
[129] *Thomas v Brown* (1876) 1 Q.B.D. 714.
[130] *Low v Fry* (1935) 152 L.T. 585.
[131] Notwithstanding a dictum to the contrary in *Singh v Beggs* (1996) 71 P. & C.R. 120 at 122.

be *evidenced* in writing,[132] since it is restricted to contracts which are specifically enforceable which, barring unusual circumstances, is not the case with a guarantee.[133] In addition, any part performance by the creditor is likely to be referable to his contract with the debtor, rather than the guarantee.[134]

In *Actionstrength Ltd v International Glass Engineering SpA*[135] the House of Lords did not rule out that the estoppel principle which underpins the doctrine of part performance might nonetheless be applied to contracts of guarantee.[136] If, however, as in that case, the estoppel is said to be based merely on the features which attend the giving of every guarantee, i.e. a representation in the form of the oral guarantee and reliance in the form of the creditor's indulgence of the debtor, the guarantor cannot be prevented from invoking the statute: "To admit an estoppel on these grounds would be to repeal the Statute."[137] "Something more" is required,[138] but this may render the scope for estoppel somewhat redundant. If the guarantor is required to represent expressly, or by necessary implication, that it will not invoke the Statute, the parties are perhaps sufficiently aware of its requirements to ensure that they are met.

A contract of guarantee may be the subject of rectification[139] and there is no limit as such to the terms which may be rectified, but it has been said that the court may need to consider the extrinsic evidence that is presented to it for these purposes with particular care, since to do otherwise risks undermining the protection that the statute was intended to confer.[140]

### (d) Formal requirements and electronic documents

5–029 Problems may arise in determining whether the formal requirement of "writing", or of a "document", or of a "signature" are satisfied in the case of contracts made electronically.

5–030 **Common law.** We have already seen that the requirements of "writing", or of a "document" can be met by forms of electronic communication such as a chain of emails, or trading on a website.[141] The requirement of "signature" can likewise be

---

132 The point was left open in *The Anemone* [1987] 1 Lloyd's Rep. 546 at 557.

133 *Actionstrength Ltd v International Glass Engineering SpA* [2003] UKHL 17; [2003] 2 A.C. 541.

134 *Actionstrength Ltd v International Glass Engineering SpA* [2003] UKHL 17; [2003] 2 A.C. 541 at [48].

135 [2003] UKHL 17; [2003] 2 A.C. 541.

136 cf. *Kok Hoony v Leong Cheong Kweng Mines Ltd* [1964] A.C. 993 at 1015.

137 *Actionstrength Ltd v International Glass Engineering SpA* [2003] UKHL 17; [2003] 2 A.C. 541 at [26].

138 *Actionstrength Ltd v International Glass Engineering SpA* [2003] UKHL 17; [2003] 2 A.C. 541 at [35]; cf. *Fairstate Ltd v General Enterprise and Management Ltd* [2010] EWHC 3072 (QB); 133 Con L.R. 112 at [97]; *Ennis Property Finance Ltd v Thompson* [2018] EWHC 1929 (Ch).

139 See para.8–063 and following.

140 *Fairstate Ltd v General Enterprise and Management Ltd* [2010] EWHC 3072 (QB); 133 Con L.R. 112.

141 See paras 5–009, 5-026; cf. *Victor Chandler International v Customs & Excise Commissioners* [2000] 1 W.L.R. 1296 where it was held that electronically stored information can, in law, constitute a "document".

satisfied in the case of electronic documents, e.g. by a digital signature,[142] by typing a name into an electronic document[143] or even by clicking on a website button.[144] Whether the requirement is actually so satisfied depends in these cases on the common law test of whether the act in question was done with the intention of authenticating the electronic document.

**Statute.** Under s.7 of the Electronic Communications Act 2000, "electronic signatures" are admissible in evidence; but this provision does not specify the *effect* of such signatures, which continues to depend on the common law "authentication" test stated above. Section 8 of the 2000 Act also empowers the appropriate Minister by order to modify existing legislation (such as the legislation discussed in this chapter) so as to authorise the use of electronic communications for the purpose of (inter alia) "the doing of anything which under … such [legislation] is required to be or may be authorised by a person's signature or seal, or is required to be delivered as a deed or witnessed."[145] The Law Commission has (with respect) rightly advised that, since electronic communications will in most cases be capable of satisfying the requirements of writing and signature, legislation of the kind envisaged by s.8 "is not only unnecessary but risky".[146] In a subsequent report, it has again made no formal recommendation for legislative reform.[147] **5–031**

Article 9 of the Directive of the European Parliament and Council on Electronic Commerce[148] (the Electronic Commerce Directive 2000) obliges Member States to:

> "ensure that their legal system allows contracts to be concluded by electronic means"

and that

> "the legal requirements applicable to the contractual process neither create obstacles for the use of electronic contracts nor result in such contracts being deprived of their legal effectiveness on account of their having been made by electronic means".[149]

Legislation to implement art.9 will not be necessary[150] where present formal requirements of writing and signature can (as will commonly be the case) be satisfied by electronic means; the need for it is likely to arise where statutory requirements can be satisfied only by the use of paper documents, e.g. where legislation requires one party to send specified contractual particulars to the other

---

[142] See para.5–009.
[143] See para.5–026.
[144] *Bassano v Toft* [2014] EWHC 377 at [42]–[44].
[145] Electronic Communications Act 2000 s.8(2)(c).
[146] Law Commission, *Electronic Commerce: Formal Requirements in Commercial Contracts* (December 2001) para.3.43.
[147] Law Com. No.386, *Electronic execution of documents*. The report does, however, set out an "option" for the introduction of a "more general legislative statement" and recommends the formation of an industry working group to consider "non-legal issues": para.4.2
[148] Directive 2000/31.
[149] Directive 2000/31 art.9.1.
[150] Parts of Directive 2000/31 (but not art.9) are implemented by the Electronic Commerce (EC Directive) Regulations 2002 (SI 2002/2013).

by post.[151] The obligations imposed by art.9 are, moreover, subject to a number of exceptions, the most important of which, in the present context, relate to: (1) "contracts that create or transfer rights in real estate, except for rental rights";[152] and (2) "contracts of suretyship granted on collateral securities furnished by persons acting outside their trade, business or profession".[153]

## 3. FORMAL REQUIREMENTS FOR RESCISSION AND VARIATION

5–032 So far this chapter has dealt with formal requirements for the making, proof or enforceability of a contract. It is finally necessary to consider the impact of form where a contract which complies with such a requirement, or which is (though it is not required to be) made by deed or in writing, is rescinded or varied by subsequent agreement of the parties. Our present concern is with formal requirements for such agreements. They also give rise to problems of consideration, which have been discussed in Ch.3.[154]

### (a) Rescission

5–033 The general principle is that formal requirements which apply to the making of a contract do not apply to its rescission by mutual consent. For example, a contract of guarantee can be rescinded orally;[155] and the same appears to be true of a contract for the disposition of an interest in land.[156] Somewhat greater difficulty arises where the rescinding agreement is itself a contract which is subject to formal requirements. Suppose, for example, that A in writing guarantees X's debt to B and that the guarantee is later rescinded by an oral agreement by which A guarantees Y's debt to B instead. The oral agreement is a valid contract[157] so that the guarantee of X's debt may be rescinded,[158] but B cannot enforce[159] the guarantee of Y's debt since that guarantee is not evidenced in writing. The position is less certain where the original contract is one which must be *made* (and not merely evidenced) in writing and where the rescinding agreement is also such a contract, e.g. where both agreements are contracts for the disposition of an interest in land and the first does, but the second does not, comply with the

[151] This was previously the requirement under Consumer Credit Act 1974 ss.63(3), 64(2), which now refer to sending by an "appropriate method": inserted by Consumer Credit Act 1974 (Electronic Communications) Order 2004 (SI 2004/3236) which also inserts s.176A setting out the requirements for electronic transmission of documents.

[152] Directive 2000/31 art.9.2(a).

[153] Directive 2000/31 art.9.2(c). Article 9.2(b) also allows Member States to retain requirements of notarial attestation for contracts within the Directive: cf. Recital 36 and art.6.5(d).

[154] See paras 3–056–3–065.

[155] *Close Bros Ltd v Pearce* [2011] EWHC 298 (QB); cf. *Morris v Baron & Co* [1918] A.C. 1.

[156] Law of Property (Miscellaneous Provisions) Act 1989 s.2(1) (para.5–009) provides that such a contract shall be "*made* in writing" and says nothing about how it can be *unmade*; cf. *McCausland v Duncan Lawrie Ltd* [1997] 1 W.L.R. 38 at 48 ("rescission ... may well be capable of being done otherwise than in writing").

[157] See para.5–027.

[158] The guarantee of X's debt may not be rescinded for other reasons, e.g. because rescission was conditional on A providing an enforceable guarantee of Y's debt.

[159] See *Morris v Baron & Co* [1918] A.C. 1; *Goman v Salisbury* (1648) 1 Vern. 240.

formalities required for the making of such contracts.[160] The second agreement is not itself a valid contract to make the new disposition; and one possible view is that that agreement, not having been properly "made",[161] is totally ineffective and so cannot operate even to rescind the first. An alternative (and, it is submitted, a preferable) view is that the second agreement is merely ineffective as a contract for the disposition of an interest in land. On this view, it can nevertheless amount to an agreement, supported by good consideration,[162] to rescind the first contract.[163] Hence the first contract is rescinded but the second is not binding. At common law, a deed could only be rescinded by deed, but this rule did not apply in equity, which now prevails.[164]

## (b) Variation

Difficult problems used to frequently arise out of oral variations of contracts which had to be evidenced in writing. Many of the cases concerned contracts which no longer need to be so evidenced, or which must now be made in writing;[165] but the rules laid down in them continue to apply to contracts which still have to be in, or evidenced in, writing.[166] 5–034

**Oral variation unenforceable.** An oral variation of a contract which had to be evidenced in writing could be regarded as a rescission of the old contract, followed by the making of a new one affecting the same subject-matter. If so, the old contract was effectively rescinded, but the new one could not be enforced for want of writing.[167] Alternatively, it could be said that the parties had simply tried to vary a term of, or to add one to, the original contract. If so, the original contract remained in force, but the variation, being oral, could not be enforced by action.[168] In this sense, a contract which had to be *evidenced in writing* could not be varied orally. For example, a written guarantee may provide that the guarantor is to be liable only if the creditor gives him notice of the debtor's default within one week of its occurrence. If the guarantor then says orally that he will not insist on this requirement, that oral variation does not have contractual force.[169] The position is the same where a contract which must be *made* in writing is varied in a way that does not satisfy the statutory formal requirements, e.g. where a contract for the sale of land[170] which was made in a document signed by both parties is varied in a material respect by an exchange of letters each of which is 5–035

[160] See fn.156.
[161] Law of Property (Miscellaneous Provisions) Act 1989 s.2(1).
[162] See para.3–062.
[163] The mere rescission of a contract for the disposition of an interest in land does not itself appear to amount to a "disposition": Law of Property (Miscellaneous Provisions) Act 1989 s.2(6).
[164] *Berry v Berry* [1929] 2 K.B. 316 at 319; para.5–037.
[165] Law of Property (Miscellaneous Provisions) Act 1989 s.2(1).
[166] See paras 5–006–5–028.
[167] *Morris v Baron & Co* [1918] A.C. 1; *Tyers v Rosedale & Ferryhill Iron Co Ltd* (1875) L.R. 10 Ex. 195.
[168] But it may provide a defence: *Re a Debtor (No.517 of 1991)*, *The Times*, 25 November 1991.
[169] Example based on *Goss v Nugent* (1835) 5 B. & Ad. 58, where the contract was one for the disposition of an interest in land which then required only to be evidenced (not made) in writing.
[170] Law of Property (Miscellaneous Provisions) Act 1989 s.2; para.5–009.

signed by only one party. In one case[171] such a variation substituted an earlier completion date for that specified in the original contract; and it was held that the vendor could not insist on the earlier date.

5–036 **Variation or rescission of original agreement?** In the above examples, the result would have been the same if the subsequent oral agreement had been regarded as a rescission: the guarantor or purchaser would not have been *liable* on the original contract because it was rescinded, nor under the new agreement because it was oral. But the distinction between (on the one hand) a rescission followed by a new agreement and (on the other) a variation would have been crucial if an attempt had been made, not to enforce the subsequent agreement, but to assert rights under the original one.[172] Had the subsequent agreement been a rescission, such an attempt would have failed. Had it been a variation, the attempt would prima facie have succeeded since the original agreement would have remained in force,[173] and the subsequent oral agreement would not have been effective to vary it, though it might have had some effect as a waiver (in the sense of forbearance), or in equity,[174] if the necessary requirements[175] for invoking these doctrines were satisfied.[176]

Whether a subsequent agreement is a rescission or a variation depends on the extent to which it departs from the original contract. It is a rescission if it alters the original contract in some essential way; but if it does not go "to the very root of the original contract"[177] it is only a variation. The distinction is one of degree. In *Morris v Baron & Co*[178] a dispute arising out of a contract for the sale of goods (which then had to be evidenced in writing) was orally compromised: it was agreed that the buyer should have extra time to pay and that he should have an option whether he would take the goods not yet delivered. This compromise was held to be a rescission as it dealt with an essential matter, the quantity of goods to be delivered. On the other hand, alterations in the place and time of delivery have been held to be variations only, so that the original contracts could still be enforced.[179]

---

[171] *McCausland v Duncan Lawrie Ltd* [1997] 1 W.L.R. 38. See also: *Eyestorm Ltd v Hoptonacre Homes Ltd* [2007] EWCA Civ 1366; *MP Kemp Ltd v Bullen Developments Ltd* [2014] EWHC 2009 (Ch) (variation of price); cf. *Courtney v Corp Ltd* [2006] EWCA Civ 518 at [12]–[14] (s.2 does not apply to an agreement by a party to waive a term inserted for his benefit).

[172] e.g. if in *Goss v Nugent* (1835) 5 B. & Ad. 58 the *purchaser* had been suing to enforce the original contract.

[173] *Robinson v Page* (1826) 3 Russ. 114; *Tyers v Rosedale & Ferryhill Iron Co Ltd* (1875) L.R. 10 Ex. 195.

[174] See para.3–066 and following.

[175] See paras 3–080–3–085.

[176] *McCausland v Duncan Lawrie Ltd* [1997] 1 W.L.R. 38 at 49–50.

[177] *British and Beningtons Ltd v NW Cachar Tea Co* [1923] A.C. 48 at 68.

[178] [1918] A.C. 1: criticised as introducing a "formalistic approach", best confined to questions of form, in *Samuel v Wadlow* [2007] EWCA Civ 155 at [46].

[179] e.g. *British and Beningtons Ltd v NW Cachar Tea Co* [1923] A.C. 48; *Hickman v Haynes* (1875) L.R. 10 C.P. 598; *The Arawa* [1980] 2 Lloyd's Rep. 135; cf. *United Dominions Corp* (*Jamaica*) *Ltd v Shoucair* [1969] 1 A.C. 340 (temporary variation in rate of interest held not to amount to rescission of a mortgage).

**Contracts made by deed.** At common law a deed could not be varied except by another deed; but this rule did not apply in equity which now prevails.[180] Later cases apply the rule in equity even where the original contract was by law required to be made by deed.[181] These decisions are hard to reconcile with the reasoning of the cases which hold that a contract required to be evidenced or made in writing cannot be varied orally.[182] They are best explained on the ground that, though the variations were not contractually binding, they nevertheless had a limited effect under the rules of waiver in the sense of forbearance,[183] or in equity.[184] 5–037

**Informal variation of contracts in writing but not as required by law.** The foregoing discussion concerns contracts which are subject to some formal requirement imposed by law. If, however, a contract which is not subject to any such legal requirement merely happens to have been executed in writing or by deed, it can be varied informally. 5–038

[180] *Berry v Berry* [1929] 2 KB 316.

[181] *Plymouth Corp v Harvey* [1971] 1 W.L.R. 549 (lease for seven years); and possibly *Mitas v Hyams* [1951] 2 T.L.R. 1215 (where the length of the lease is not stated).

[182] See para.5–036.

[183] See para.3–069.

[184] See para.3–076 and following.

## CHAPTER 6

# THE CONTENTS OF A CONTRACT



The contents of a contract depend primarily on the words used by the parties in entering into the contract: these make up its express terms. A contract may, in addition, contain terms which are not expressly stated, but which are implied, either because that is found to be the intention of the parties, or by operation of law, or by custom or usage. **6–001**

## 1. EXPRESS TERMS

The ascertainment of the express terms of a contract terms raises in the first place a pure question of fact: what did the parties say, or agree to be bound by, either orally or in writing? Particular problems can arise where there is little or no discussion of the terms, but they are nonetheless said to be "incorporated" in the contract.[1] Where the express terms are found in several documents, the courts may have to resolve a conflict, or apparent conflict, between them[2] and further problems of ascertaining or proving express terms can arise in relation to the evidence which the courts can take into account if the contract is, or appears to **6–002**

[1] See para.6–004 and following.
[2] See para.6–017 and following.

have been, reduced to writing.[3] Once this question of fact has been determined, a further question can arise as to the meaning of the words used.[4]

6–003 **Representation or term?** In determining the express terms of the contract, one question which may arise is whether a representation made during the negotiations was also intended as a term of the contract. This question is addressed primarily in Ch.9.[5]

## (a) Incorporation of terms into the contract[6]

### *(i) Signature*

6–004 **The signature rule.** A person who signs a contractual document is bound by its terms. In *L'Estrange v F Graucob Ltd*[7] the owner of a café bought an automatic cigarette vending machine. She signed, but did not read, a sales agreement which contained an exemption clause "in regrettably small print".[8] It was held that she was bound by the clause, so that she could not rely on defects in the machine, either as a defence to a claim for part of the price, or as entitling her to damages. It would have made no difference had she been a foreigner who could not read English.[9] A party is, however, bound by terms of which he was unaware only if the document which he has signed was one which could reasonably have been expected to contain contractual terms. Where, for example, a hirer of machinery together with a driver had signed weekly time-sheets, it was held that he was not bound by terms printed on these sheets since their purpose was merely to record the hours worked and not to vary the terms of the earlier oral contract of hire.[10]

6–005 **"Onerous or unusual terms."** We shall see below that, if a term is "onerous or unusual", special steps may need to have been taken for it to have been incorporated by notice.[11] The courts appear to be divided over the question of whether even such a term is always incorporated by signature. In some, it has been held that a signature binds the signer, without exception.[12] In others, it has

[3] See para.6–021 and following.
[4] See para.6–040 and following.
[5] See para.9–056 and following. See also the discussion of entire agreement clauses in para.4–009.
[6] Many of the cases which are referred to in this part were concerned with the incorporation of one particular type of term, namely an exemption clause by reference to which a party seeks to exclude or restrict its liability. The principles of incorporation for which they stand are nonetheless applicable to any term. For certain particular rules applicable to exemption clauses, see Ch.7.
[7] [1934] 2 K.B. 394; *Levison v Patent Steam Cleaning Co Ltd* [1978] Q.B. 69; for criticism, see *McCutcheon v David MacBrayne Ltd* [1964] 1 W.L.R. 125 at 133; cf. Spencer [1973] C.L.J. 104.
[8] *L'Estrange v F Graucob Ltd* [1934] 2 K.B. 394 at 405.
[9] *The Luna* [1920] P. 22; cf. *Barclays Bank Plc v Schwartz*, *The Times*, 2 August 1995.
[10] *Grogan v Robin Meredith Plant Hire*, *The Times*, 20 February 1996; cf. at fn.23.
[11] See para.6–012.
[12] *Bates v Post Office* [2019] EWHC 606 (QB) at [1055]; cf. *Amiri Flight Authority v BAE Systems Plc* [2003] EWCA Civ 1447; [2003] 2 Lloyd's Rep. 767 at [16].

been suggested that "in some extreme circumstances even signature might not be enough" unless, in addition, steps were taken[13] to draw the attention of the signer to the term in question.[14]

**Exceptions.** A party will not be bound by its signature if it was obtained by a misrepresentation of the other party.[15] In *Curtis v Chemical Cleaning & Dyeing Co Ltd*,[16] the claimant took a dress to the defendants to be cleaned. She signed a receipt after being told that it exempted the defendants only from liability for certain specified kinds of damage, when it actually exempted them for liability "for any damage, however arising". It was held that the defendants could not rely on the clause as they had induced the claimant to sign the receipt by misrepresenting its contents.[17] Denning LJ said[18] that mere failure to draw attention to the existence or extent of the exemption clause might in some circumstances amount to misrepresentation, but it has subsequently been said that the principle in the *Curtis* case requires a positive representation that the claimant "need not bother to read the documents".[19] The signer might also be able to rely on the doctrine of *non est factum* but if this applies there is no contract at all.[20] 6–006

## *(ii) Notice*

If terms are set out, or referred to,[21] in a document which is simply handed by one party to the other, or displayed where the contract is made, they will be incorporated in the contract only if the latter party either knew that the document contained (or was likely to contain) such terms,[22] or if reasonable notice of their existence is given to that party. Whether such notice has been given depends on all the circumstances, but the following factors have been taken into account by the courts. 6–007

**Nature of the document.** A term is not incorporated in the contract if the document in which it is set out (or referred to) is not intended to have contractual 6–008

[13] i.e. in accordance with the requirements stated at para.6–012.

[14] *Ocean Chemical Transport Inc v Exnor Craggs Ltd* [2000] 1 Lloyd's Rep. 446 at 454. But see the doubts expressed in *HIH Casualty & General Insurance Ltd v New Hampshire Insurance Co* [2001] EWCA Civ 735; [2001] 2 Lloyds Rep.161 at [209]; *Do-Buy 95 Ltd v National Westminster Bank Plc* [2010] EWHC 2862 (QB) at [91]; *Dawson v Bell* [2016] EWCA Civ 96; [2016] 2 B.C.L.C. 59; *Cargill International Trading Pte Ltd v Uttam Galva Steels Ltd* [2019] EWHC 476 (Comm) at [87]–[88].

[15] *L'Estrange v F Graucob Ltd* [1934] 2 K.B. 394 at 403.

[16] [1951] 1 K.B. 805; cf. *Horry v Tate & Lyle Refineries Ltd* [1982] 2 Lloyd's Rep. 416 at 422.

[17] The decision is said to rest on a finding that the clause had not been incorporated into the contract: *Axa Sun Life Services Plc v Campbell Martin Ltd* [2011] EWCA Civ 133; [2011] 2 Lloyd's Rep. 1 at [105] (Rix LJ, doubting the reasons given by Denning LJ).

[18] *Curtis v Chemical Cleaning & Dyeing Co Ltd* [1951] 1 K.B. 805 at 809.

[19] *Peekay Intermark Ltd v ANZ Banking Group Ltd* [2006] EWCA Civ 386; [2006] 2 Lloyd's Rep. 511 at [47].

[20] See para.8–086.

[21] cf. para.6–010; para.6–017.

[22] *Lacey's Footwear (Wholesale) Ltd v Bowler Insurance Ltd* [1997] 2 Lloyd's Rep. 369 at 378.

force, e.g. if the document is a mere receipt for payment.[23] On the other hand, the mere fact that a document is called a "receipt" will not prevent it from having contractual effect.[24] A document will have such effect if the party to whom it was handed knew that it was intended to be a contractual document or if it was handed to him in such circumstances as to give him reasonable notice of the fact that it contained contractual terms.[25] It will also be contractual if it is obvious to a reasonable person that it must have been intended to have this effect. This will be the case if the document is of a kind that generally contains contractual terms.[26] Whether a document falls into this class depends on current commercial practice, which may vary from time to time.[27]

6–009 **Degree of notice.** The party relying on the term need not show that he actually brought it to the notice of the other party, but only that he took reasonable steps to do so. The test is whether the former party took such steps[28]—not whether the latter should, in the exercise of reasonable caution, have discovered or read the term.[29] Where the term is printed on a ticket, it is not enough to show that the party to whom it was handed knew that there was writing on the ticket,[30] for the writing might not have been intended to have contractual effect. Nor is one party's reference in a telephone conversation to his own standard terms sufficient notice of those terms if the other party has no knowledge or means of knowledge of them.[31] The question whether the adequate degree of notice has been given turns principally on two factors: the steps taken to give notice and the nature of the terms.

6–010 **Incorporation by reference.**[32] Where the notice is contained in a contractual document it is normally sufficient for the term to be prominently set out or referred to on the face of the document. In *Thompson v LM & S Ry*[33] the claimant asked her niece to buy a railway excursion ticket for her. The ticket (which cost 2s. 7d.) had on its face the words "see back" and on the back a statement that it was issued subject to the conditions set out in the company's timetables, which could be bought for 6d. These conditions included an exemption clause. The claimant could not read the words on the ticket as she was illiterate; and the jury found that the defendants had not taken reasonable steps to bring the conditions

---

[23] *Chapelton v Barry Urban DC* [1940] 1 K.B. 532; cf. *The Eagle* [1977] 2 Lloyd's Rep. 70; Clarke [1978] C.L.J. 22.

[24] *Harling v Eddy* [1951] 2 K.B. 739 at 746; *Parker v South Eastern Ry* (1877) 2 C.P.D. 416.

[25] *Watkins v Rymill* (1883) 10 Q.B.D. 178.

[26] *Nunan v Southern Ry* [1923] 2 K.B. 703 at 707; *Thompson v London, Midland & Scottish Ry* [1930] 1 K.B. 41 at 46.

[27] Contrast *Parker v South Eastern Ry* (1877) 2 C.P.D. 416 at 424; with *Alexander v Railway Executive* [1951] 2 K.B. 882 at 886.

[28] *Parker v South Eastern Ry* (1877) 2 C.P.D. 416 at 424; cf. *Burnett v Westminster Bank Ltd* [1966] 1 Q.B. 742.

[29] *Parker v South Eastern Ry* (1877) 2 C.P.D. 416.

[30] This was the majority view in *Parker v South Eastern Ry* (1877) 2 C.P.D. 416. Bramwell LJ dissented on this point.

[31] *Jayaar Impex Ltd v Toaken Group Ltd* [1996] 2 Lloyd's Rep. 437.

[32] See further, paras 6–010–6–013.

[33] [1930] 1 K.B. 41; cf. *Hood v Anchor Line* [1918] A.C. 837; *O'Brien v MGN Ltd* [2001] EWCA Civ 1279; [2002] C.L.C. 33.

to the claimant's notice. But the Court of Appeal held that there was no evidence to support this finding as the notice was clear and the ticket was a common form contractual document. Hence the exemption clause was held to be incorporated in the contract. The case is an extreme one since the timetable cost nearly a fifth of the fare paid by the claimant and was evidently a volume of some size, the exemption clause being set out on its 552nd page.[34] The likelihood of its being bought (let alone read) by an excursion passenger was, to say the least, remote; and it seems probable that the steps taken to incorporate the clause would not now be regarded as sufficient.[35] The principle that a term can be incorporated by reference[36] nevertheless seems to be a sound one.[37] Many common contractual documents would become impossibly bulky if that principle were to be rejected.

On the other hand, the clause is unlikely to be incorporated if there are no words on the face of the document drawing attention to it,[38] or if words on the front of the document refer to terms on the back but the back is blank (only the front having been transmitted by fax),[39] or if the words are made illegible by a date stamp,[40] or if the term is buried in a mass of advertisements.[41]

**Relevance of any disability of the party said to be bound.** In *Thompson*'s case, the illiteracy of the claimant was treated as immaterial; but the position would probably be different where the party relying on the clause knew or should have known of the other party's disability. In an earlier case[42] some reliance was placed on the fact that the other party was a steerage passenger and so could not have been expected to read clauses in small print. Extra steps may therefore have to be taken to bring the notice home to a person suffering from a *known* disability, e.g. translating it to a party who is known not to understand the language in which it is expressed, if such a step is reasonably practicable.[43] A person trying to incorporate the terms of a document should, however, beware of translating only part of it; for by doing this he may suggest that the rest is of no importance and so be unable to rely on it.[44] **6–011**

[34] *Thompson v LM & S Ry* [1930] 1 K.B. 41 at 46.

[35] cf. *The Mikhail Lermontov* [1990] 1 Lloyd's Rep. 579 at 594; affirmed [1991] 2 Lloyd's Rep. 155 though reversed on other grounds: sub nom. *Baltic Shipping Co v Dillon* (1993) 176 C.L.R. 344.

[36] cf. *Smith v South Wales Switchgear Ltd* [1978] 1 W.L.R. 165 (indemnity clause).

[37] *Sumukan Ltd v Commonwealth Secretariat* [2006] EWHC 304; [2006] 2 Lloyd's Rep. 53; *Impala Warehousing and Logistics (Shanghai) Co Ltd v Wanxiang Resources (Singapore) Pte Ltd* [2015] EWHC 25 (Comm) at [16] (reference to terms on a website); cf. *Transformers & Rectifiers Ltd v Needs Ltd* [2015] EWHC 269 (TCC); [2015] B.L.R. 336 and the requirement (at [50]) of having to send a copy of the terms themselves if "non-standard".

[38] *Henderson v Stevenson* (1875) L.R. 2 Sc. & Div. 470; *Richardson, Spence & Co v Rowntree* [1894] A.C. 217. As to the form of words needed on the face of the document, compare *J Murphy & Sons Ltd v Johnston Precast Ltd* [2008] EWHC 3024 (TCC) with *Rooney v CSE Bournemouth Ltd* [2010] EWCA Civ 1364.

[39] *Poseidon Freight Forwarding Co Ltd v Davies Turner Southern Ltd* [1996] 2 Lloyd's Rep. 388; cf. *J Murphy & Sons Ltd v Johnston Precast Ltd* [2008] EWHC 3024 (TCC).

[40] *Sugar v London, Midland & Scottish Ry* [1941] 1 All E.R. 172.

[41] *Stephen v International Sleeping Car Co Ltd* (1903) 19 T.L.R. 620.

[42] *Richardson, Spence & Co v Rowntree* [1894] A.C. 217.

[43] *Geier v Kujawa, Weston & Warne Bros Transport* [1970] 1 Lloyd's Rep. 364.

[44] *H Glynn (Covent Garden) Ltd v Wittleder* [1959] 2 Lloyd's Rep. 409.

6–012 **"Onerous or unusual" clauses.** The more unusual or unexpected a particular term is, the higher will be the degree of notice required to incorporate it. If the term is of such a nature that the party adversely affected would not normally expect it, then the other party will not be able to incorporate it by simply handing over or displaying a document containing the term. He must go further and "make it conspicuous"[45] or take other special steps to draw attention to it. For example, a person who drives his car into a car park might expect to find in his contract a term excluding the proprietor's liability for loss of or damage to the car. But in *Thornton v Shoe Lane Parking Ltd*[46] the car park ticket referred to a term purporting to exclude liability for *personal injury*.[47] It was held that adequate notice of this term had not been given, even though the steps taken by the proprietor might have been sufficient to incorporate the more usual terms excluding or limiting liability for property damage. As Denning LJ had said in an earlier case: "Some clauses I have seen would need to be printed in red ink on the face of the document with a red hand pointing to it before the notice could be held to be sufficient."[48]

Such reasoning also forms one basis of *Interfoto Picture Library Ltd v Stiletto Visual Programmes Ltd*.[49] In that case, the defendants (an advertising agency) had hired photographic transparencies from the claimants under a contract allegedly incorporating the terms of the claimants' delivery note, which had been sent with the goods. One of these terms purported to make the defendants liable for a "holding charge" of £5 per day (an unusually high rate)[50] for each transparency retained for more than 14 days. In holding that the defendants were not liable to pay this charge, both members of the Court of Appeal regarded it as crucial that the claimants had failed to take reasonable steps to bring the term to the attention of the defendants. But while Dillon LJ drew from this failure the orthodox conclusion that the term had not been incorporated in the contract,[51] it is less clear exactly why Bingham LJ regarded the failure as vital. It seems that he so regarded it (even on the assumption that the terms of the delivery note *had* been incorporated into the contract), because, on account of the failure, it would not be "fair to hold [the defendants] bound by the condition in question".[52] He went on to suggest that "this may yield a result not very different from the civil law principle of good faith, at any rate so far as the formation of the contract is

---

[45] *Crooks v Allen* (1870) 5 Q.B.D. 38 at 40.

[46] [1971] 2 Q.B. 163; cf. *The Eagle* [1977] 2 Lloyd's Rep. 70; *AEG UK Ltd v Logic Resource Ltd* [1996] C.L.C. 265; *Goodlife Foods Ltd v Hall Fire Protection Ltd* [2018] EWCA Civ 1371; 178 Con L.R. 1 at [35] (doubting the relevance to the issue of incorporation that an onerous clause might be unreasonable under the Unfair Contract Terms Act 1977: see para.7–039 and following); Chandler and Holland 104 L.Q.R. 359; Macdonald [1988] J.B.L. 375 and 8 *Legal Studies* 48.

[47] Where the injury is caused *by negligence* such a provision is now ineffective: paras 7–048, 7–098.

[48] *J Spurling Ltd v Bradshaw* [1956] 1 W.L.R. 461 at 466. Contrast *Ocean Chemical Transport Inc v Exnor Cragg Ltd* [2000] 1 Lloyd's Rep. 446 at 454 ("neither onerous nor unusual"); *O'Brien v MGN Ltd* [2001] EWCA Civ 1279; [2002] C.L.C. 33 at [21] (term not "onerous or outlandish").

[49] [1989] Q.B. 433.

[50] *Interfoto Picture Library Ltd v Stiletto Visual Programmes Ltd* [1989] Q.B. 433 at 436: the "normal" rate would have been £3.50 per transparency per week.

[51] *Interfoto Picture Library Ltd v Stiletto Visual Programmes Ltd* [1989] Q.B. 433 at 439.

[52] *Interfoto Picture Library Ltd v Stiletto Visual Programmes Ltd* [1989] Q.B. 433 at 445; cf. *Timeload Ltd v British Telecommunications Plc* [1995] E.M.L.R. 459 at 468; contrast *Nutting v Baldwin* [1995] 1 W.L.R. 201 at 211, where the term was "neither onerous nor unusual".

concerned".[53] The reference here to "formation" seems to indicate that Bingham LJ was, after all, concerned with the incorporation of the clause and perhaps intended to make the point that "this unreasonable and extortionate clause"[54] was not incorporated *merely* because the formal requirements of offer and acceptance had been satisfied:[55] there must, in addition, be "fair" notice, and the degree of notice required increases with the unusualness or unreasonableness of the clause.[56]

**Time of notice.** The steps required to give notice of a term must be taken before or at the time of contracting, unless it is possible to argue for a variation of the contract. In *Olley v Marlborough Court*[57] the claimant booked a room in the defendants' hotel. She later saw a notice in her bedroom exempting the defendants from liability for articles lost or stolen unless handed to the management for safe custody. It was held that, as the contract had been made at the reception desk when the defendants agreed to accept the claimant as a guest and as the notice in the bedroom could not have been seen by the claimant until later, its terms were not incorporated in the contract. **6–013**

**Course of dealing.** Parties may for some time have dealt with each other on terms that were usually incorporated by signature or notice. On the occasion in question, however, the usual document may by some oversight not have been handed over or signed at the time of contracting; and the question then arises whether the usual terms are nevertheless incorporated in that particular transaction. A negative answer to this question was suggested by Lord Devlin in *McCutcheon v David MacBrayne Ltd* where he said: "Previous dealings are relevant only if they prove knowledge of the terms, actual and not constructive, and consent to them."[58] However, this view is inconsistent with at least one earlier case.[59] Furthermore, a course of dealing is simply an alternative basis upon which a party may meet the requirement of having given reasonable *notice* and for that it is not necessary that the other party should have discovered or read the term in question.[60] Accordingly, the House of Lords has held that if there has been a regular and consistent course of dealing on a set of terms then those terms may apply to a particular transaction even though in relation to it the usual steps to incorporate the terms have not been taken.[61] The terms will not apply if the **6–014**

---

[53] *Interfoto Picture Library Ltd v Stiletto Visual Programmes Ltd* [1989] Q.B. 433 at 445; cf. *Laceys Footwear (Wholesale) Ltd v Bowler International Ltd* [1997] 2 Lloyd's Rep. 369 at 384.

[54] *Interfoto Picture Library Ltd v Stiletto Visual Programmes Ltd* [1989] Q.B. 433 at 445.

[55] cf. para.2–076.

[56] cf. para.6–005, text to fn.14.

[57] [1949] 1 K.B. 532; cf. *Thornton v Shoe Lane Parking Ltd* [1971] 2 Q.B. 163; *The Eagle* [1977] 2 Lloyd's Rep. 70.

[58] [1964] 1 W.L.R. 125 at 134 (emphasis added).

[59] *J Spurling Ltd v Bradshaw* [1956] 1 W.L.R. 461.

[60] See para.6-009.

[61] *Hardwick Game Farm v Suffolk Agricultural, etc. Association* [1969] 2 A.C. 31 at 90, 104, 105, 113, 130; and see *SIAT di dal Ferro v Tradax Overseas SA* [1978] 2 Lloyd's Rep. 470, affirmed [1980] 1 Lloyd's Rep. 53; *George Mitchell (Chesterhall) Ltd v Finney Lock Seeds Ltd* [1983] Q.B. 284 at 295, affirmed [1983] 2 A.C. 803, without reference to this point; *Circle Freight International Ltd v Mideast & Gulf Exports Ltd* [1988] 2 Lloyd's Rep. 427.

course of dealing falls short of having given reasonable notice: if the transaction in question was not part of a consistent course of dealing[62]; if the transactions were spread over a long period of time and their number was so small that they could not be said to give rise to a course of dealing;[63] if the steps necessary to incorporate the clause had never been taken at any stage of the dealings between the parties;[64] or if the terms of each transaction in the series had been separately negotiated and expressly agreed between the parties.[65]

6–015 **Attempt to alter terms after a course of dealing.** The fact that there has been a long course of dealing may also be relevant to the degree of notice required when the party claiming the benefit of a term seeks to alter it to his own advantage. As the other party is reasonably entitled to assume that the course of dealing is continuing on the accustomed terms, it seems that special steps would have to be taken to draw his attention to any such alteration.[66]

6–016 **Trade custom.** The course of dealing referred to above is one between the parties to the contract.[67] A term may also be implied into a contract because of a general course of dealing amounting to a trade custom or usage.[68] Such an implication can arise even though the parties to the particular contract in question have not previously dealt with each other. In practice, incorporation may be the result of a combination of trade custom and course of dealing.[69]

## (b) Joinder of documents

6–017 **Incorporation by express reference.** As we have seen, the terms of a contract may be contained in more than one document.[70] One of these may expressly refer to another, e.g. where a contract is made subject to standard terms settled by a

---

[62] *McCutcheon v David MacBrayne Ltd* [1964] 1 W.L.R. 125 can be explained on the ground that the parties contracted sometimes on one set of terms and sometimes on another; cf. *Mendelssohn v Normand Ltd* [1970] 1 Q.B. 177; *Transformers & Rectifiers Ltd v Needs Ltd* [2015] EWHC 269 (TCC); [2015] B.L.R. 336.

[63] On this question, contrast *Hollier v Rambler Motors (AMC) Ltd* [1972] 2 Q.B. 71 (three or four transactions in five years) and *Metaalhandel JA Magnum BV v Ardfields Transport Ltd* [1988] 1 Lloyd's Rep. 197 at 203 ("isolated affairs") with *Hardwick Game Farm v Suffolk Agricultural, etc. Association* [1969] 2 A.C. 31 (three or four contracts a month for three years); cf. *Balmoral Group Ltd v Borealis (UK) Ltd* [2006] EWHC 2228 (Comm); *Capes (Hatherden) Ltd v Western Arable Services Ltd* [2009] EWHC 3065 (QB); [2010] 1 Lloyd's Rep. 477.

[64] *Smith v Taylor* [1966] 2 Lloyd's Rep. 231.

[65] *Johnson Matthey Bankers Ltd v State Trading Corp of India* [1984] 1 Lloyd's Rep. 427 at 433.

[66] See *Pancommerce Co SA v Veecheema BV* [1983] 2 Lloyd's Rep. 304 at 305 ("in bold type"); and contrast *Burnett v Westminster Bank Ltd* [1966] 1 Q.B. 742 with *Re Bond Worth Ltd* [1980] Ch. 228.

[67] Or between one of them and a group of companies to which the other belongs, as in *SIAT di dal Ferro v Tradax Overseas SA* [1978] 2 Lloyd's Rep. 470; affirmed [1980] 1 Lloyd's Rep. 53; and in *The Raphael* [1982] 2 Lloyd's Rep. 42.

[68] *British Crane Hire Corp Ltd v Ipswich Plant Hire Ltd* [1975] Q.B. 303; para.6–082; cf. *Smith v South Wales Switchgear Ltd* [1978] 1 W.L.R. 165; *Matrix Europe Ltd v Uniserve Holdings Ltd* [2009] EWHC 919 (Comm).

[69] See, e.g. *The Havprins* [1983] 2 Lloyd's Rep. 356 at 362 (three transactions in five years sufficient, but incorporation was "not by course of dealing alone")

[70] See para.6–010.

trade association. Those terms are then incorporated by reference into the contract; if there are several editions of the standard terms, the contract is prima facie taken to refer to the most recent edition.[71] It may also incorporate amendments validly made by the association.[72]

**Inconsistent terms.** The parties may purport to incorporate one document in another by express reference, not realising that the terms of the two documents conflict. Where there is an inconsistency between negotiated terms and incorporated standard terms, it is the former which will prevail,[73] subject to any overriding provision in the standard terms.[74] It has been said that the inconsistency must be "clear and direct".[75] It is not enough if one term "qualifies or modifies" the effect of another[76] and the court should ask whether a "reasonable commercial construction of the whole [contract] can reconcile two provisions (whether typed or printed)."[77] In *Pagnan SpA v Tradax Ocean Transportation SA*[78] the special conditions in the contract were said to "prevail in so far as they may be inconsistent" with the printed clauses of a standard form (GAFTA 119) which was incorporated into the contract. The special conditions required the sellers "to provide for export certificate", whereas one of the terms of GAFTA 119 provided that "in case of prohibition of export (etc.) … this contract or any unfulfilled portion thereof shall be cancelled." It was held that the two terms could be reconciled on the basis that the sellers were to provide for the export certificate, but, in case of prohibition of export by the government, the unfulfilled portion of the contract was to be cancelled. This did not deprive the special condition of effect. If the certificate was not provided for as a result of oversight, or error, or possibly simply because the authorities failed to issue it, the sellers would have been liable. 6–018

**Determining whether there is any inconsistency.** The decision in the *Pagnan* case may be contrasted with the subsequent decision in *Alexander v West Bromwich Mortgage Co Ltd*.[79] The claimant borrower took out a mortgage with the defendant lender which consisted of the "Offer of Loan" and the "Mortgage Conditions". The latter expressly incorporated the former and stated that in the event of any inconsistency "the terms in the Offer of Loan will prevail". In the Offer the interest rate was fixed for an initial period and thereafter at a variable 6–019

[71] *Smith v South Wales Switchgear Ltd* [1978] 1 W.L.R. 165.

[72] *Shearson Lehman Hutton Inc v Maclaine Watson & Co* [1989] 2 Lloyd's Rep. 570 at 589; cf. *The Marinor* [1996] 1 Lloyd's Rep. 301.

[73] *Adamastos Shipping Co v Anglo-Saxon Petroleum* [1959] A.C. 133; *The Leonidas* [2001] 1 Lloyd's Rep. 533 at 536; *The Starsin* [2003] UKHL 12; [2004] 1 A.C. 715.

[74] *Northwest Regional Metropolitan Hospital Board v TA Bickerton & Sons Ltd* [1970] 1 W.L.R. 607 at 617; *Fenice Investments Inc v Jerram Falkus Construction Ltd* [2009] EWHC 3272 (TCC); 128 Con L.R. 124.

[75] *The Eternity* [2008] EWHC 2480 (Comm); [2009] 1 Lloyds Rep. 107 at 113.

[76] *Pagnan SpA v Tradax Ocean Transportation SA* [1987] 2 Lloyd's Rep. 342 at 350.

[77] *The Leonidas* [2001] 1 Lloyd's Rep. 533 at 536.

[78] [1987] 2 Lloyd's Rep. 342; cf. *The Leonidas* [2001] 1 Lloyd's Rep. 533; *The Lowlands Orchid* [2009] EWHC 2883 (Comm); [2010] 1 Lloyd's Rep 317; *Public Company Rise v Nibulon SA* [2015] EWHC 684 (Comm); [2015] 2 Lloyd's Rep. 108; *MT Højgaard A/S v E.ON Climate & Renewables UK Robin Rigg East Ltd* [2017] UKSC 59; 173 Con L.R. 1.

[79] [2016] EWCA Civ 496; [2017] 1 All E.R. 942.

rate of 1.99 per cent above the Bank of England base rate. A term in the Mortgage Conditions entitled the lender to vary the interest rate specified in the Offer except during the period when the fixed rate applied. At the end of the fixed rate period, the lender increased the variable rate to 3.99 per cent above the base rate, but the Court of Appeal held that it was not entitled to do so because the term relied upon was inconsistent with the rate in the Offer which prevailed. Since the two documents were clearly meant to be read together, there was in one sense no inconsistency: the variable rate was 1.99 per cent over base rate, or whatever the lender decided. Hamblen LJ rejected such an approach on the basis that the court had to start first with the Offer (as the negotiated terms) and, if one did that, the reasonable borrower would understand that it was being offered a rate which would only change if there was a variation in the base rate. The term in the Mortgage Conditions allowing for a completely different method of variation was therefore clearly inconsistent with the "main purpose or object of the contract."[80] If the lender wanted to preserve the power to vary the rate, it was necessary to have made that clear in the Offer itself.[81]

6–020 **Incorporation without express reference.** A contract may be contained in several documents even though one does not expressly refer to the other. Suppose, for example, that a series of dealings takes place under a "master contract", a separate document being executed each time an individual contract is made. All these contracts may be subject to the master contract, even though they do not refer to it.[82] Similarly, a policy of insurance can be read together with the rules of the mutual insurance society which had issued it,[83] although the policy does not expressly refer to the rules;[84] and a contract to purchase securities may be held to incorporate the terms of a prospectus on the faith of which they were bought.[85] A chain of emails may also be read together even if a later email does not expressly refer back to the earlier emails.[86] Such incorporation without express reference appears to depend on the intention of the parties, determined in accordance with the objective test of agreement.[87]

[80] *Glynn v Margetson & Co* [1893] A.C. 351 at 357; see further para.7–026.
[81] *Alexander v West Bromwich Mortgage Co Ltd* [2016] EWCA Civ 496; [2017] 1 All E.R. 942 at [92].
[82] *Panorama Developments (Guildford) Ltd v Fidelis Furnishing Fabrics Ltd* [1971] 2 Q.B. 711.
[83] *Edwards v Aberayron Insurance Society Ltd* (1876) 1 Q.B.D. 563.
[84] For difficulties relating to joinder where contracts have to be evidenced in writing, see para.5–026.
[85] *Jacobs v Batavia & General Plantations Trust Ltd* [1924] 1 Ch. 287; affirmed [1924] 2 Ch. 329; another possible explanation of the case is that there was a collateral contract: para.6–038.
[86] *Golden Ocean Group Ltd v Salgaocar Mining Industries PVT* [2012] EWCA Civ 265; [2012] 1 W.L.R. 3674.
[87] For a statutory instance of incorporation regardless of the intention of the parties, see Consumer Rights Act 2015 s.50(1) (information about the trader or service under a contract for services).

### (c) The parol evidence rule

#### (i) *Statement of the rule*

The parol evidence rule states that evidence cannot be admitted (or, even if admitted, cannot be used) to add to, vary or contradict a written instrument.[88] In relation to contracts, the rule means that, where a contract has been reduced to writing, neither party can rely on extrinsic evidence of terms alleged to have been agreed, i.e. on evidence not contained in the document. Although the rule is generally stated as applying to *parol* evidence, it applies just as much to other forms of extrinsic evidence. Of course, if a contractual document incorporates another document by reference, evidence of the second document is admissible, but the rule prevents a party from relying on evidence that is extrinsic to both documents.[89] 6–021

There are obvious grounds of convenience for the application of the parol evidence rule to contracts: certainty is promoted by holding that parties who have reduced a contract to writing should be bound by the writing and by the writing alone.[90] On the other hand, the parol evidence rule will commonly be invoked where a dispute arises after the time of contracting as to what was actually said at that time; and in such cases one of the parties could feel aggrieved if evidence on the point was excluded merely because the disputed term was not set out in the contractual document.[91] Evidence extrinsic to the document is therefore admitted in a number of situations (to be discussed below) which amount either to exceptions or which fall outside the scope of the rule.

#### (ii) *Cases in which extrinsic evidence is admissible*

**Written agreement not the whole agreement.** When a contract is reduced to writing, there is a presumption that the writing was intended to include all the terms of the contract;[92] but this presumption is rebuttable.[93] If the written document was not intended to set out all the terms on which the parties had actually agreed, extrinsic evidence is admissible. It seems that a document which is intended simply to form a record of a previously concluded contract will prima facie be a mere memorandum;[94] while a document the execution of which marks 6–022

---

[88] *Jacobs v Batavia & General Plantations Trust Ltd* [1924] 1 Ch. 287 at 295; *Rabin v Gerson Berger Association Ltd* [1986] 1 W.L.R. 526 at 531, 537; *Orion Ins Co v Sphere Drake Ins Plc* [1992] 1 Lloyd's Rep. 239 at 273.

[89] *Jacobs v Batavia & General Plantations Trust Ltd* [1924] 1 Ch. 287.

[90] *Rabin v Gerson Berger Association Ltd* [1986] 1 W.L.R. 526 at 534, 537; *AIB Group Plc v Martin* [2001] UKHL 63; [2002] 1 W.L.R. 94 at [4].

[91] Contrast *AIB Group Plc v Martin* [2001] UKHL 63; [2002] 1 W.L.R. 94 at [4] with [44] on the question whether this was the position in that case.

[92] *Glencore Agriculture BV v Navig8 Chemicals Pool Inc* [2018] EWCA Civ 1901; [2018] 2 Lloyd's Rep. 374 at [23] ("strong" presumption in the case of an indemnity).

[93] *Gillespie Bros & Co v Cheney, Eggar & Co* [1896] 2 Q.B. 59 at 62.

[94] e.g. *Allen v Pink* (1838) 4 M. & W. 140; cf. *J Evans & Son (Portsmouth) Ltd v Andrea Merzario* [1976] 1 W.L.R. 1078 at 1083; *The Riza and Sun* [1997] 2 Lloyd's Rep. 314 at 319–320.

the actual conclusion of a contract is more likely to be taken to contain all the terms of the contract.[95] The inclusion of an "entire agreement" clause attempts to put the matter beyond doubt.[96]

It has been argued that the right of a party to rely on extrinsic evidence in the present group of cases turns the parol evidence rule (as applied to contracts) into "no more than a circular statement".[97] For if the rule applies only where the written document is intended to contain *all* the terms of the contract, evidence of other terms would be useless even if admitted (since they would not form part of the contract); while the rule never prevents a party from relying on evidence of terms which *were* intended to be part of the contract. Accordingly, on this view, no injustice is caused by the operation of the rule.[98] There is much force in this view in cases in which, at the time of contracting, both parties actually shared a common intention with regard to the term in question. But in most cases in which the rule is invoked this is not the position: the dispute arises precisely because the parties had different intentions, and one alleges, while the other denies, that terms not set out in the document were intended to form part of the contract. In such cases, the court will attach importance to the appearance of the document: if it *looks* like a complete contract to one of the parties taking a reasonable view of it, then the rule will prevent the other party from relying on extrinsic evidence to show that the contract also contained other terms.[99]

This result has been described as being simply an application of the objective test of agreement;[100] but, even if it can be so regarded, it is such a common and frequently recurring application of this test as to amount to an independent rule. In cases of the present kind, moreover, the law goes beyond the normal objective test. That test normally requires the party relying on it to prove that he reasonably believed that the other party was contracting on the terms alleged.[101] Where a document *looks* like a complete contract, the party relying on it does not have to prove that he had such a belief: he can rely on a presumption to that effect which it is up to the other party to rebut.[102] As laymen are known to attach greater importance than the law does to writing in a contractual context, it will be hard for the party relying on extrinsic evidence to rebut the presumption that the written document was an exclusive record of the terms agreed. Moreover, the objective test normally prevents a party from relying on his "private but uncommunicated intention as to what was to be agreed".[103] The presumption which applies in the case of an apparently complete contractual document goes

[95] *Hutton v Watling* [1948] Ch. 398 at 404.

[96] See para.4–009; *JN Hipwell & Son v Szurek* [2018] EWCA Civ 674; [2018] L. & T.R. 15 at [20].

[97] Law Commission, *Report on The Parol Evidence Rule* (1986), Law Com. No.154, para.2.7; Marston [1986] C.L.J. 192; *Prince Jefri Bolkiah v Brunei Darussalam* [2007] UKPC 63 at [47].

[98] Law Commission, *Report on The Parol Evidence Rule*, para.2.7; and see also para.1.7. See, to similar effect, the willingness of the courts to allow in terms notwithstanding the inclusion of an entire agreement clause: *Cheverny Consulting Ltd v Whitehead Mann Ltd* [2005] EWHC 2431; [2006] EWCA Civ 1303.

[99] Wedderburn [1959] C.L.J. 58, 62.

[100] Law Commission, *Report on The Parol Evidence Rule*, paras 2.14, 2.17; cf. *National Westminster Bank Plc v Binney* [2011] EWHC 694 (QB) at [14].

[101] See paras 1–002, 2–002.

[102] See fn.93.

[103] Law Commission, *Report on The Parol Evidence Rule*, para.2.14; cf. para.4–002.

beyond this: it prevents a party from relying on evidence of intention that was not "private and uncommunicated" at all, but simply not recorded in the document.

For these reasons, it is submitted that the admissibility of extrinsic evidence, where it is proved that the document was not in fact intended to contain all the terms of the contract, does not turn the rule into a merely "circular statement".[104] Whether it also supports the conclusion that the rule is not one that "could lead to evidence being unjustly excluded"[105] is perhaps more doubtful. The primary purpose of the rule, like that of the objective test of agreement, is to promote certainty, sometimes even at the expense of justice.[106] Where the parties have brought into being an apparently complete contractual document, the rejection of evidence of extrinsic terms that were actually agreed may cause injustice to the party relying on those terms, while the reception of such evidence may cause injustice to the other party, if he reasonably believed that the document formed an exclusive record of the contract.[107] The question is which, on balance, is the greater injustice. Where the evidence is rejected because the party relying on it cannot overcome the presumption arising from the fact that the document *looks* like a complete contract, the greater injustice would appear to lie in the exclusion of the evidence; for the presumption seems to be based on the nature and form of the document, rather than on any actual belief of the party relying on it, that it formed an exclusive record of the contract.[108]

**Validity of the contract.** The rule prevents a party from relying on extrinsic evidence only as to the *contents* of the contract, and not as to its *validity*. Such evidence can therefore be used to establish the presence or absence of consideration or of contractual intention,[109] or some invalidating cause such as incapacity, misrepresentation, mistake[110] or *non est factum*.[111] Evidence has similarly been held admissible to show that provisions in an agreement purporting to be a licence to occupy a room (as opposed to a lease of it) were a "mere sham"[112] in that they had failed to state the parties' true intention and had been inserted simply in an attempt to evade the Rent Act. **6–023**

**Terms implied by law.** The rule prevents a party from relying on extrinsic evidence only as to the express terms of the contract. Where the contract is silent **6–024**

[104] cf. the authorities cited in fn.88.

[105] Law Commission, *Report on The Parol Evidence Rule*, para.2.7.

[106] *AIB Group Plc v Martin* [2001] UKHL 63; [2002] 1 W.L.R. 94 at [4].

[107] For the rejection of evidence in such circumstances, see *Hutton v Watling* [1948] Ch. 398 at 404; cf. *Rabin v Gerson Berger Association Ltd* [1986] 1 W.L.R. 526.

[108] The Law Commission had, before publishing Report No.154, provisionally recommended the abolition of the rule: Law Commission Working Paper No.76 (1976).

[109] *Clever v Kirkman* (1876) 33 L.T. 672; *Kleinwort Benson Ltd v Malaysian Mining Corp* [1989] 1 W.L.R. 379 at 392; *Carmichael v National Power Plc* [1999] 1 W.L.R. 2042; *Ove Arup & Partners International Ltd v Mirant Asia-Pacific (Hong Kong) Construction Ltd* [2003] EWCA Civ 1729; [2004] B.L.R. 75.

[110] *Campbell Discount Co v Gall* [1961] 1 Q.B. 431.

[111] *Roe v R A Naylor Ltd* (1918) 87 L.J.K.B. 958 at 964; para.8–086.

[112] *AG Securities v Vaughan* [1990] 1 A.C. 417 at 469, 475; cf. *Chase Manhattan Equities Ltd v Goodman* [1991] B.C.L.C. 897.

on a matter on which a term is normally implied by law,[113] parol evidence may be given to support, or to rebut, the usual implication. Thus a buyer of coal can show that he made known to the seller the particular purpose for which he required the coal, so as to raise the implication that he relied on the seller's skill and judgment.[114] Conversely, a person who takes out a policy of marine insurance can show that the insurer knew the ship to be unseaworthy, and so negative the usual implied warranty of seaworthiness.[115]

6–025 **Oral warranties and representations.** Where parties enter into a written contract, the rule would prima facie prevent either party from relying on evidence of oral undertakings or representations as to the subject-matter of the contract; but this application of the rule is subject to two qualifications. First, an oral undertaking may take effect as a "collateral contract".[116] Secondly, an oral statement of fact may operate as a misrepresentation in spite of its purported incorporation into the contract as a warranty;[117] and where this is the case, the oral statement can be used as evidence, not of the contents of the contract, but of an invalidating cause.

6–026 **Operation of the contract.** Extrinsic evidence can be used to show that the contract does not yet operate, or that it has ceased to operate. Thus in *Pym v Campbell*[118] a written agreement for the sale of a patent was drawn up, and evidence was admitted of an oral stipulation that the agreement should not *become operative* until a third party had approved of the invention. It seems from the reasoning of the court that evidence of an oral stipulation that the agreement should *cease to bind* if the third party disapproved of the invention would not have been admissible. On the other hand, evidence is admissible to show that a written contract has been varied or rescinded.[119] It is not easy to deduce from the purpose of the parol evidence rule why evidence should be admissible in the first and third, but not in the second of these cases.

6–027 **Evidence as to the parties.** Extrinsic evidence can be used to identify the parties[120] and to show in what capacities the parties contracted.[121] Where a person contracts ostensibly as principal, evidence is admissible to prove that he really

[113] See para.6–067.
[114] *Gillespie Bros & Co v Cheney, Eggar & Co* [1896] 2 Q.B. 59.
[115] *Burges v Wickham* (1863) 3 B. & S. 669.
[116] See para.6–038.
[117] Misrepresentation Act 1967 s.1(a); para.9–108; cf. para.9–011.
[118] (1856) 6 E. & B. 370.
[119] *Morris v Baron & Co* [1918] A.C. 1; *Goss v Nugent* (1833) 5 B. & Ad. 58 at 65.
[120] *Gastronome (UK) Ltd v Anglo-Dutch Meats (UK) Ltd* [2006] EWCA Civ 1233; [2006] 2 Lloyd's Rep 587 at [16]–[17]; *Hamid v Francis Bradshaw Partnership* [2013] EWCA Civ 470; [2013] B.L.R. 447 at [57]; cf. *Shogun Finance v Hudson* [2003] UKHL 62; [2004] 1 A.C. 919; discussed at para.8–041; *Aspen Underwriting Ltd v Credit Europe Bank NV* [2018] EWCA Civ 2590; [2019] 1 Lloyd's Rep. 221 at [49].
[121] *Newell v Radford* (1867) L.R. 3 C.P. 52; cf. *The Riza and Sun* [1997] 2 Lloyd's Rep. 314 at 320; *Manches LLP v Freer* [2006] EWHC 991 at [12].

acted as another's agent so as to entitle the latter to sue[122] unless such evidence contradicts the express description of the agent in the contract.[123] As the ostensible contracting party is in such cases personally liable even if he acted as agent, the evidence would not normally relieve him from liability.[124]

**Defence to specific performance.** Failure to perform an oral promise may be available as a defence when the party who made it claims specific performance of the written agreement.[125] Alternatively, in such a case, the court may have discretion to order specific performance on the terms that the claimant performs the oral undertaking.[126] Where, as in the authorities which support these propositions, the contract was one for the disposition of an interest in land, it now generally has to be made in writing by incorporating *all* its express terms in a contractual document.[127] Failure to incorporate the oral promise would therefore prevent the contract from coming into existence,[128] and would lead to the dismissal of a claim (whether for specific performance or for damages) on that ground, unless the promise could be said to take effect only as a collateral contract.[129] But the reasoning of the older authorities would still apply where specific performance was sought of a contract which was in fact in writing, even though there was no legal requirement to this effect. **6–028**

**As an aid to interpretation.** It has been said that where the words of the contract are "clear", extrinsic evidence cannot be used to explain their meaning,[130] unless they have a special meaning by custom.[131] Extrinsic evidence could, on the other hand, be used to explain words or phrases which are ambiguous,[132] or which, if taken literally, make no sense,[133] or conflict with others in the same document,[134] as well as technical terms. This restricted approach to the admissibility of extrinsic evidence must now be reassessed in light of the second of the principles of interpretation "re-stated" by Lord Hoffmann in the *ICS* case.[135] Subject to the first of the exceptions to be mentioned below, he was of the view that the **6–029**

---

[122] *Humfrey v Dale* (1857) 7 E. & B. 266; affirmed (1858) E.B. & E. 1004; *Internaut Shipping GmbH v Fercometal SARL* [2003] EWCA Civ 812; [2003] 2 Lloyd's Rep. 430 at [56] (evidence to show no agency); cf. *Hamid v Francis Bradshaw Partnership* [2013] EWCA Civ 470; [2013] B.L.R. 447.

[123] See para.16–067.

[124] But see *Wake v Harrop* (1861) 6 H. & N. 768; affirmed 1 H. & C. 202; cf. *Sun Alliance Pensions Life & Investment Services Ltd v RJL* [1991] 2 Lloyd's Rep. 410.

[125] *Martin v Pycroft* (1852) 2 D.M. & G. 785, 795; cf. *Scott v Bradley* [1971] Ch. 850.

[126] See *London & Birmingham Ry v Winter* (1840) Cr. & Ph. 57.

[127] Law of Property (Miscellaneous Provisions) Act 1989 s.2(1); para.5–009.

[128] See para.5–009.

[129] See para.5–009; para.6–038.

[130] *Bank of New Zealand v Simpson* [1900] A.C. 182 at 189.

[131] See para.6–035.

[132] *Bank of New Zealand v Simpson* [1900] A.C. 182; cf. *Pao On v Lau Yiu Long* [1980] A.C. 614 at 631; *Forsikringsaktieselskapet Vesta v Butcher* [1989] A.C. 852 at 909–910; *Shearson Lehman Hutton Inc v Maclaine Watson & Co Ltd* [1989] 2 Lloyd's Rep. 570 at 591.

[133] *The Sounion* [1987] 1 Lloyd's Rep. 230.

[134] e.g. *Mannai Investment Co Ltd v Eagle Star Life Assurance Co* [1997] A.C. 749; *BOC Group Plc v Centeon LLC* [1999] 1 All E.R. (Comm) 970 at 979.

[135] *Investors Compensation Scheme Ltd v West Bromwich Building Society* [1998] 1 W.L.R. 896; discussed at para.6–041 and following.

"background" against which the meaning of a document should be ascertained includes "absolutely anything"[136] which would have affected the way the language used would have been understood by a reasonable person. Furthermore, there is no prior requirement that the language used should have been ambiguous.[137] Rather than regarding extrinsic evidence as generally inadmissible, subject to exceptions under which it is admissible, the present approach appears to be to regard it as generally admissible, subject only to exceptions under which it is inadmissible: "The exclusion of background material from the process of interpretation should be the exception rather than the rule".[138] An entire agreement clause does not preclude the admission of evidence which is otherwise admissible as an aid to interpretation.[139]

6–030 **Pre-contractual negotiations.**[140] The first of the exceptions referred to by Lord Hoffmann is described as "the previous negotiations of the parties and their declarations of subjective intent".[141] Given the objective nature of the process of interpretation, the exclusion of the parties' declarations of subjective intent is entirely understandable.[142] The exclusion more generally of evidence of the pre-contractual negotiations has been the subject of criticism[143] and it is argued that the more relevant question is the *weight* to be given to such evidence rather than its *admissibility*.[144] Nonetheless, this exception was upheld by the House of Lords in *Chartbrook Ltd v Persimmon Homes Ltd*[145] on pragmatic grounds. Since, in most cases, evidence of the pre-contractual negotiations would be irrelevant or carry little weight,[146] it would create greater uncertainty and add to the cost of advice, litigation or arbitration to admit it in every case in the hope of finding something relevant. Lord Hoffmann also acknowledged that its admission could prejudice third parties, such as assignees, who would not have taken part in the negotiations (though, as he also pointed out, they may not be familiar with the "background" to the contract, which is admissible).[147] There is no further bar to admission where the contract takes the form of a settlement agreement and the

[136] i.e. anything relevant: see para.6–043.

[137] See para.6–043.

[138] *Cherry Tree Investments Ltd v Landmain Ltd* [2012] EWCA Civ 736; [2013] 2 W.L.R. 481 at [37].

[139] *John v Price Waterhouse* [2002] EWCA Civ 899 at [67]; *Barclays Bank plc v Unicredit Bank AG* [2014] EWCA Civ 302 at [27]; *NHS Commissioning Board v Vasant* [2019] EWCA Civ 1245 at [46]–[47].

[140] Mitchell 26 J.C.L. 134.

[141] *Investors Compensation Scheme Ltd v West Bromwich Building Society ICS* [1998] 1 W.L.R. 896 at 913.

[142] What is excluded is "subjective intention about what the contract in question means", not "a statement of what one party intends *to do* outside the contract and after it has been executed": *Kason Kek-Gardner Ltd v Process Components Ltd* [2017] EWCA Civ 2132 at [16] (emphasis added).

[143] McMeel 119 L.Q.R. 272; Nicholls 121 L.Q.R. 577; McLauchlan (2009) 31 *Sydney Law Review* 5.

[144] McKendrick in Worthington (ed.) *Commercial Law and Commercial Practice* (2003); *Proforce Recruit Ltd v The Rugby Group Ltd* [2006] EWCA Civ 69 at [33]–[36]; Berg 122 L.Q.R. 354.

[145] [2009] UKHL 38; [2009] A.C. 1101; McLauchlan [2011] L.M.C.L.Q. 30.

[146] Because it would mainly attest to the parties' desires or aspirations, rather than what they had agreed.

[147] *Chartbrook Ltd v Persimmon Homes Ltd* [2009] UKHL 38; [2009] A.C. 1101 at [40].

negotiations were conducted "without predjudice"; the rules applicable to contracts generally apply and no more.[148]

The exclusion of the previous negotiations of the parties is, in part, based on the difficulty the courts would face in distinguishing between evidence that would assist in determining the intention of the parties, objectively ascertained, and evidence of their declarations of subjective intent.[149] But by continuing to exclude such evidence altogether, the courts have to grapple with other, and possibly equally, difficult distinctions. For example, in the *Chartbrook* case Lord Hoffmann acknowledged that evidence of previous negotiations may be admitted to "establish that a fact which may be relevant as background was known to the parties".[150] The continued exclusion of previous negotiations is also difficult given the requirement to interpret the language used in light of the "commercial purpose"[151] of the contract in question. It seems that it is necessary to "distinguish between admissible background evidence relating to the nature and object of the contractual venture and inadmissible evidence of the terms for which each party was contending in the course of negotiations."[152] This may be a particularly difficult distinction to draw.[153] Lord Hoffmann was of the opinion that the risk of any injustice in holding the parties to a contract which they did not intend, had their intention been objectively assessed with the benefit of evidence of previous negotiations, should be met by admitting such evidence for the purpose of rectification,[154] or estoppel by convention.[155]

**Deleted words.** The submission that the pre-contractual negotiations of the parties should be more a question of weight rather than admissibility would appear to have prevailed where such evidence takes the form of deletions from an earlier draft of the contract.[156] While the position remains uncertain,[157] in the most recent consideration of this issue, Briggs LJ formulated the following principle: " … if the fact of deletion shows what it is the parties agreed that they **6–031**

[148] *Oceanbulk Shipping & Trading SA v TMT Asia Ltd* [2010] UKSC 44; [2010] 3 W.L.R. 1424.

[149] Such evidence is obviously irrelevant: *Prenn v Simmonds* [1971] 1 W.L.R. 1381 at 1385; *Pritchard v Briggs* [1980] Ch. 338.

[150] *Chartbrook Ltd v Persimmon Homes Ltd* [2009] UKHL 38; [2009] A.C. 1101 at [42]. Expert evidence may be admitted to establish what the parties knew or believed at the time of the contract: *Pink Floyd Music Ltd v EMI Records Ltd* [2010] EWCA Civ 1429; [2011] 1 W.L.R. 770.

[151] *Reardon Smith Line Ltd v Yngvar Hansen-Tangen* [1976] 1 W.L.R. 989 at 995–996.

[152] *The Tychi (No.2)* [2001] 2 Lloyd's Rep 403 at [29]; cf. *IRC v Raphael* [1935] A.C. 96 at 142; *Prenn v Simmonds* [1971] 1 W.L.R. 1382 at 1385; *Youell v Bland Welch & Co Ltd* [1992] 2 Lloyd's Rep. 127 at 133; *Merthyr (South Wales) Ltd v Merthyr Tydfil County Borough Council* [2019] EWCA Civ 526; [2019] J.P.L. 989.

[153] *Excelsior Group Productions Ltd v Yorkshire Television Ltd* [2009] EWHC 1751 (Comm) at [24] ("a line so fine it almost vanishes").

[154] See para.8–063 and following. Whether its admission for the purposes of rectification would be any less prejudicial to an assignee is open to question: Berg 124 L.Q.R. 6; para.8–082.

[155] See para.3–094 and following.

[156] For deletions from a prior *contract*, see para.6–032.

[157] For a more detailed account of the authorities, see Lewison, *The Interpretation of Contracts* (6th edn), para.3.04.

did not agree and there is ambiguity in the words that remain, then the deleted provision may be an aid to construction, albeit one that must be used with care."[158]

6–032 **Prior contracts.** Evidence of a prior *contract* between the parties may be admissible as an aid to interpretation as part of the "background" of the contract in issue,[159] though if that later contract was intended to supersede the prior one, then evidence of the prior contract is either inadmissible[160] or, even if admissible, "of little relevance".[161] Where the prior contract is admitted to draw comparison with a subsequent and similar contract in which certain words which appeared in the prior contract have been deleted, some caution is required in determining what assistance this may provide in interpreting the subsequent contract.[162]

6–033 **"Private dictionary".** Evidence of pre-contractual negotiations is admissible as an aid to interpretation under the "private dictionary principle", i.e. to show that the parties placed on certain words or phrases in their contract an unconventional meaning, or gave meaning to a phrase that has no conventional meaning,[163] "especially where the expression in question is used in a particular sector of economic activity".[164] This does not apply in a case where the court has to decide between two perfectly conventional meanings. If evidence of negotiations was admissible to aid the court's choice in such a case, it would negate the exclusionary rule itself.[165]

6–034 **Subsequent conduct.** A second exception to the admissibility of extrinsic evidence as an aid to interpretation is that evidence of the *conduct* of the parties *after* the making of the contract will not be admitted. If such evidence were admitted, it might follow "that a contract meant one thing the day it was signed but, by reason of subsequent events, meant something different a month or a year

[158] *Narandas-Girdhar v Bradstock* [2016] EWCA Civ 88; [2016] 1 W.L.R. 2366 at [20]; cf. *Bou-Simon v BGC Brokers LP* [2018] EWCA Civ 1525; 179 Con L.R. 32 at [27]–[32], [35]–[36] (an implied term case: see para.6–062).

[159] *Egan v Static Control Components (Europe) Ltd* [2004] EWCA Civ 392; [2004] 2 Lloyd's Rep. 429 at [35]; *KPMG v Network Rail Infrastructure Ltd* [2007] EWCA Civ 363; [2007] Bus L.R. 1336; cf. *HIH Casualty & General Insurance Ltd v New Hampshire Insurance Co* [2001] 2 All E.R. (Comm) 39; [2001] EWCA Civ 735 at [83]; *St Ivel Ltd v Wincanton Group Ltd* [2008] EWCA Civ 1286.

[160] *Youell v Bland Welch & Co Ltd* [1992] 2 Lloyd's Rep. 127 at 141.

[161] *HIH Casualty & General Insurance Ltd v New Hampshire Insurance Co* [2001] 2 All E.R. (Comm) 39; [2001] EWCA Civ 735 at [83].

[162] *Health & Case Management Ltd v Physiotherapy Network Ltd* [2018] EWHC 869 (QB) at [71]–[73].

[163] *Proforce Recruit Ltd v The Rugby Group Ltd* [2006] EWCA Civ 69, for further proceedings, see: [2007] EWHC 1621 (QB); cf. *The Pacific Colocotronis* [1981] 2 Lloyd's Rep. 40; *Jones v Bright Capital Ltd* [2006] EWHC 3151 (Ch); [2007] Pens L.R. 31.

[164] *NHS Commissioning Board v Vasant* [2019] EWCA Civ 1245 at [42].

[165] See Lord Hoffmann's criticism of *The Karen Oltmann* [1976] 2 Lloyd's Rep. 708 in *Chartbrook Ltd v Persimmon Homes Ltd* [2009] UKHL 38; [2009] A.C. 1101 at [47].

later".[166] It may be admissible to show whether there was a contract[167] and what the terms of the contract were,[168] or that the written terms were a "mere sham",[169] or that the contract had been varied by subsequent agreement,[170] or to raise an estoppel[171]; or in support of a claim for rectification,[172] but it cannot be used to elucidate the original meaning of the contract.[173]

**To prove custom.** Evidence of custom is admissible "to annex incidents to written contracts[174] in matters with respect to which they are silent".[175] It is generally said that the evidence can be used to add to, but not to contradict, the written contract.[176] Thus, the evidence cannot be used where the custom, if actually written into the contract, would make it "insensible or inconsistent".[177] For example, where a bill of lading provided for "freight payable in London" this was held to be inconsistent with a custom that it was payable *in advance* in London.[178] But where a bill of lading provided for freight at a specified rate, evidence of a customary deduction of interest was held merely to add to the contract since the discount was calculated on the contract rate of freight.[179] In such borderline cases, the distinction between customs which add to and those which contradict the written contract is largely one of emphasis. Custom can also be used as an aid to interpretation.[180] For this purpose, evidence of custom is **6–035**

166 *James Miller & Partners v Whitworth Street Estates (Manchester) Ltd* [1970] A.C. 583 at 603, 606; *Wickman Ltd v Schuler AG* [1974] A.C. 325; cf. *Houlder Bros & Co Ltd v Commissioners of Public Works* [1908] A.C. 276 at 285.

167 *E.D. & F. Man Commodity Advisers Ltd v Fluxo-Cane Overseas Ltd* [2009] EWCA Civ 406 at [20]–[21]; cf. *Gibbs v Lakeside Developments Ltd* [2016] EWHC 2203 (Ch); *Global Asset Capital Inc v Aabar Block S.A.R.L.* [2017] EWCA Civ 37; [2017] 4 W.L.R. 163; *CRS GT Ltd v McLaren Automotive Ltd* [2018] EWHC 3209 (Comm) at [128]. Contrast *Newbury v Sun Microsystems* [2013] EWHC 2180 (QB) at [27]; *Kyte v Revenue & Cutsoms Commissioners* [2018] EWHC 1146 (Ch) at [15].

168 *Ferguson v Dawson & Partners (Contractors) Ltd* [1976] 1 W.L.R. 1213; *Carmichael v National Power Plc* [1999] 1 W.L.R. 2042 at 2050–2051; cf. para.6–022.

169 See fn.112.

170 *McCausland v Duncan Lawrie Ltd* [1997] 1 W.L.R. 38 at 49.

171 *James Miller & Partners Ltd v Whitworth Street Estates (Manchester) Ltd* [1970] A.C. 583 at 611, 615; cf. *Amalgamated Investment & Property Co Ltd v Texas Commerce International Bank Ltd* [1982] Q.B. 84 at 119; para.3–094.

172 See para.8–066.

173 For criticism, see fn.143.

174 Including those made by deed: *Wigglesworth v Dallison* (1779) 1 Doug. 201.

175 *Hutton v Warren* (1836) 1 M. & W. 466 at 475. For terms that may be *implied* by custom, see para.6–080.

176 *Phillips v Syndicate 992 Gunner* [2003] EWHC 48; [2004] Lloyd's Rep I.R. 426 at [25].

177 *Humfrey v Dale* 7 E. & B. 266, 275: affirmed (1858) E.B. & E. 1004; *Palgrave Brown & Son Ltd v SS Turid (Owners)* [1922] 1 A.C. 397; cf. *Mowbray Robinson & Co v Rosser* (1922) 91 L.J.K.B. 524.

178 *Krall v Burnett* (1877) 25 W.R. 305; advance freight would be payable even though the ship failed to reach the contractual destination: para.19–118.

179 *Brown v Byrne* (1854) 3 E. & B. 703.

180 e.g. *Norden Steam Co v Dempsey* (1876) 1 C.P.D. 654; Evidence of "market practice" may be admitted by way of expert evidence: *Crema v Cenkos Securities Plc* [2010] EWCA Civ 1444; [2011] 1 W.L.R. 2066.

admissible even though it contradicts the ordinary meaning of the words used in the contract, e.g. to show that "1,000 rabbits" meant "1,200 rabbits."[181]

6–036 **To identify the subject-matter.** Extrinsic evidence is admissible to identify the subject-matter of a contract, e.g. to show that "your wool" meant not only wool produced by the claimant but also wool produced on a neighbouring farm.[182] Similarly, such evidence is admissible to define the extent of a party's obligations under a contract, e.g. to show that a contract to pump oil out of a stranded tanker obliged the party rendering the service to take away only so much oil as was necessary to avert the risk of pollution;[183] or to show whether a guarantee related to one debt only or was a continuing one;[184] or to which of a number of transactions a guarantee related.[185]

6–037 **Rectification.** A document may be meant to record a previous agreement, but fail accurately to do so. Such a document can sometimes be rectified, i.e. brought into line with the previous agreement.[186] When this is done evidence of the previous agreement must inevitably be admitted, including evidence arising in the course of the pre-contractual negotiations, and evidence of subsequent conduct if it helps to ascertain the parties' intention at the time when the document is executed.[187] This does not mean that a party can claim rectification merely by alleging that terms which were in fact agreed were not incorporated in the document. The remedy of rectification is based on a *mistake* in the recording of a previous agreement.[188] In most of the cases in which the parol evidence rule is invoked the parties make no such mistake: they know perfectly well that the extrinsic term is not incorporated in the document, so that rectification is not available.

6–038 **Collateral contracts.** Even where extrinsic evidence cannot be used to vary, add to or contradict the terms of a written agreement, it may be possible to show that the parties made two contracts, the main written contract and a "collateral contract". In *Mann v Nunn*[189] the claimant orally agreed to take a lease of the defendant's premises if the defendant would first do certain repairs. A written agreement was later executed, but did not refer to the defendant's promise to do the repairs. The claimant was nonetheless able to enforce this promise. "The parol agreement neither alters nor adds to the written one, but is an independent

---

181 *Smith v Wilson* (1832) 3 B. & Ad. 728.

182 *Macdonald v Longbottom* (1859) 1 E. & E. 977; cf. *Compagnie Noga d'Importation et d'Exportation SA v Abacha (No.4)* [2003] EWCA Civ 1100; [2003] 2 All E.R. (Comm) 915; *Kason Kek-Gardner Ltd v Process Components Ltd* [2017] EWCA Civ 2132 at [21].

183 *The Pacific Colocotronis* [1981] 2 Lloyd's Rep. 40; cf. *Essex CC v Ellam* [1989] 2 All E.R. 494 (evidence admissible as to legal nature of payments made under covenant).

184 *Heffield v Meadows* (1869) L.R. 4 C.P. 595.

185 *Perrylease Ltd v Imecar Ltd* [1988] 1 W.L.R. 463.

186 See para.8–063 and following.

187 *Equity Syndicate Management Ltd v Glaxosmithkline Plc* [2015] EWHC 2163 (Comm) at [26]; *Saga Group Ltd v Paul* [2016] EWHC 2344 (Ch); [2017] 4 W.L.R. 12 at [43].

188 See para.8–063; cf. *Rabin v Gerson Berger Association Ltd* [1986] 1 W.L.R. 526 at 534; *The Riza and Sun* [1997] 2 Lloyd's Rep. 314 at 320.

189 (1874) 30 L.T. 526; cf. *Walker Property Investments (Brighton) Ltd v Walker* (1947) 177 L.T. 204.

agreement."[190] Thus evidence is admissible if it proves an "independent agreement"; but it is often hard to say whether the evidence has this effect or whether it varies, or adds to, the terms of the main contract. The test seems to be whether the evidence relates to a term which would go to the essence of the whole transaction: if so, it cannot be regarded as evidence of a collateral contract and will be inadmissible.[191]

In *Mann v Nunn* the executed lease contained no provisions as to putting the premises in repair, so that the landlord's promise merely *added* to it. According to two later cases, evidence of a collateral contract is inadmissible if it *varies* or *contradicts* a term actually set out in the main written contract. In the first,[192] a lease of a furnished house specified the furniture to be included. Evidence of a collateral agreement, made before the lease, to put in more furniture, was held inadmissible. In the second,[193] rent under a lease was payable quarterly in advance. Evidence of a collateral agreement allowing the tenant (in effect) to pay the rent in arrear was similarly held inadmissible. On the other hand, in *City & Westminster Properties (1934) Ltd v Mudd*[194] a lease contained a covenant to use the premises for business purposes only. The tenant had been induced to sign it by an oral assurance that the lessors would not object to his continuing to reside on the premises (as he had done in the past). In spite of the fact that this assurance contradicted the lease, evidence of it was held admissible to prove a collateral contract. The case is hard to distinguish from the cases discussed above,[195] but since evidence of a collateral contract is meant to give effect to an independent agreement, there is no compelling reason why this agreement should not contradict the written document.

It can be argued that the collateral contract device largely destroys the parol evidence rule, especially if *Mudd*'s case is right. Some limitations on this device are imposed by the requirements that a statement operates as a collateral contract only if intended to be legally binding and supported by separate consideration.[196] Such consideration will often be provided by the promisee's act of entering into the main contract.[197] But this act could not be consideration for the collateral promise if that promise was made *after* the conclusion of the main contract; for in that case the consideration would be past and hence of no effect in law.[198]

---

[190] *Mann v Nunn* (1874) 30 L.T. 526 at 527. For other requirements of collateral contracts, see paras 4–015, 5–010, 9–063–9–065.

[191] e.g. *The Nile Rhapsody* [1992] 2 Lloyd's Rep. 399 at 407; affirmed [1994] 1 Lloyd's Rep. 382; cf. in the context of formal requirements para.5–010.

[192] *Angell v Duke* (1875) 32 L.T. 320.

[193] *Henderson v Arthur* [1907] 1 K.B. 10.

[194] [1959] Ch. 129; cf. *Couchman v Hill* [1947] K.B. 554, where one reason for the decision was that the oral warranty was a collateral contract; and *Brikom Investments Ltd v Carr* [1979] Q.B. 467 (para.3–065), where no point as to admissibility of evidence seems to have been taken.

[195] The fact that the tenant actually *refused* to sign the lease until he was given the oral assurance may distinguish *Mudd*'s case from *Angell v Duke* (1875) 32 L.T. 320 and *Henderson v Arthur* [1907] 1 K.B. 10.

[196] See para.3–065; para.9–065.

[197] e.g. in *City of Westminster Properties (1934) Ltd v Mudd* [1959] Ch. 129.

[198] See para.3–017.

6–039 **Consideration.** In *Turner v Forwood*[199] a person assigned a debt due to him from a company to one of its directors by a deed stated to have been made for a nominal consideration. It was held that evidence was admissible to show that there was a substantial consideration for the assignment.[200] This evidence did not really contradict the deed as the nominal consideration was mentioned only as a matter of form.[201] Where an agreement states a substantial consideration, evidence of *additional* consideration is also admissible, so long as it does not contradict that stated in the written agreement.[202]

## (d) Interpretation[203]

6–040 Lord Goff has noted that it is neither "easy", nor "helpful" to consider cases on the interpretation of contracts, since they depend so much on the particular words of the contract[204] and, one might add, the "background" against or "context" in which they were used.[205] It is nevertheless possible to give some indication of the general principles[206] and the broad approach of the courts, which has altered over time.

6–041 **The basic principle.** In *Investors Compensation Scheme Ltd v West Bromwich Building Society* Lord Hoffmann summarised the approach of the courts to the interpretation of contracts in five principles.[207] The first of those principles he stated as follows:

> "Interpretation is the ascertainment of the meaning which the document would convey to a reasonable person having all the knowledge which would reasonably have been available to the parties in the situation in which they were at the time of the contract."[208]

In *The Starsin* Lord Hoffmann refined this basic principle so as to refer to the:

---

199 [1951] 1 All E.R. 746.

200 cf. para.3–015.

201 i.e. to avoid the implication of a use.

202 *Pao On v Lau Yiu Long* [1980] A.C. 614 at 631.

203 Lewison, *The Interpretation of Contracts*, 6th edn (2017); McMeel, *The Construction of Contracts: Interpretation, Implication, and Rectification*, 3rd edn (2017); Calnan, *Principles of Contractual Interpretation*, 2nd edn (2017); Staughton [1999] C.L.J. 303; McLauchlan (2000) 19 N.Z.U.L.R. 147; McMeel 119 L.Q.R. 272; Nicholls 121 L.Q.R. 577; Berg 122 L.Q.R. 354; Spigelman 81 A.L.J. 322; Grabiner 128 L.Q.R. 41; McLauchlan [2017] L.M.C.L.Q. 506.

204 [1984] L.M.C.L.Q. 382 at 385.

205 See para.6–043.

206 Particular aspects of interpretation are considered elsewhere, e.g. the admissibility of extrinsic evidence as an aid to interpretation (see para.6–029) and the rules relating to the interpretation of exemption clauses (see para.7–008 and following).

207 *Investors Compensation Scheme Ltd v West Bromwich Building Society* [1998] 1 W.L.R. 896 at 912–913. While his summary has been described as a "re-statement", Lord Hoffmann was of the view that a "fundamental change" had already overtaken this branch of the law as a result of a number of earlier cases; in particular: *Prenn v Simmonds* [1971] 1 W.L.R. 1382 at 1384–1386; and *Reardon Smith Line Ltd v Yngvar Hansen-Tangen* [1976] 1 W.L.R. 989.

208 *Investors Compensation Scheme Ltd v West Bromwich Building Society ICS* [1998] 1 W.L.R. 896 at 912.

"reasonable person having all the background knowledge which is reasonably available to the *person or class of persons to whom the document is addressed.*"[209]

Thus, in *The Starsin* the contractual document in question was a bill of lading and it was appropriate to ask what meaning it would have conveyed to the merchants or bankers to whom it was addressed and who would rely on it in their dealings.[210] More generally, in the commercial context, the approach taken is "that a business sense will be given to business documents"[211] and where the contract incorporates standard terms they should be given a consistent meaning in "all [cases] in which the events [that] have given rise to the dispute do not differ from one another in some relevant respect."[212] The courts will assume that the parties intended to use words which have a special or peculiar meaning in a trade in that way.[213]

**An objective approach.** It is clear from the basic principle that the document[214] setting out the parties' agreement is interpreted objectively; it is not a question of what one party actually intended, or what the other party actually understood to have been intended, but rather what a reasonable person in the position of the parties[215] would have understood the words to mean. The same approach is taken to the interpretation of a unilateral contractual notice.[216] At the outset, it is important to stress that the perception of the reasonable person is something quite different from the search for a reasonable outcome. As Lord Hoffmann has explained, writing extra-judicially: **6–042**

"It is important to note that 'the reasonable person' is the notional audience, not the notional parties. The reasonable audience will expect parties to a legal document to have said something which, against the available background, makes rational sense, but will not

[209] *Homburg Houtimport BV v Agrosin Private Ltd (The Starsin)* [2003] UKHL 12; [2004] 1 A.C. 715 at [73] (emphasis added).

[210] Lord Steyn emphasised that the bill should be read in the way in which a reasonable person "versed in the shipping trade" would read it: [2004] 1 A.C. 715 at [45].

[211] *Glynn v Margetson & Co* [1893] A.C. 351 at 359; approved by Lord Bingham in *The Starsin* [2003] UKHL 12; [2004] 1 A.C. 715 at [10]; *Mannai Investment Co Ltd v Eagle Star Life Assurance Co Ltd* [1997] A.C. 749 at 771.

[212] *The Nema* [1982] A.C. 724 at 737; cf. *Lomas v JFB Firth Rixson* [2010] EWHC 3372 (Ch); [2011] 2 B.C.L.C 120 at [53]; *LSREF III Wight Ltd v Millvalley Ltd* [2016] EWHC 466 (Comm); 165 Con L.R. 58 at [42]; *Lehman Brothers International (Europe) v Exxonmobil Financial Services BV* [2016 [EWHC 2699 (Comm); [2016] 2 C.L.C. 578 at [103]; Taylor [2017] L.M.C.L.Q. 261.

[213] *Myers v Saarl* (1860) 3 El. & El. 306; *Crema v Cenkos Securities Plc* [2010] EWCA Civ 1444; [2011] 1 W.L.R. 2066 at [43]; *Gard Marine v Tunnicliffe* [2011] EWHC 1658 (Comm); [2012] Lloyd's Rep I.R. 1 at [38]. This is not to be confused with the "private dictionary" principle referred to above, para.6–033.

[214] The vast majority of the cases, and all those considered in this part, have been concerned with the interpretation of written contracts, but there is nothing to suggest that a different approach is taken to the interpretation of oral contracts.

[215] Depending on the nature of the contract, it may be appropriate to assume that the parties (and therefore the reasonable person in the position of the parties) "would have had advice from reasonably sophisticated and informed advisers": *BNY Mellon Corporate Trustee Services Ltd v LBG Capital No.1 Plc* [2016] UKSC 29; [2016] 2 Lloyd's Rep. 119 at [33].

[216] *Mannai Investment Co Ltd v Eagle Star Life Assurance Co Ltd* [1997] A.C. 749; *Stobart Group Ltd v Stobart* [2019] EWCA Civ 1376.

> necessarily expect them to have been reasonable in the sense of being fair to each other. It does not matter whether that meaning would have been in some commercial sense 'reasonable' or not."[217]

That this is the correct approach to interpretation is generally accepted,[218] but what is more contentious is how the objective meaning is to be arrived at; in particular, to what extent does it depend simply on the words in the document, or the context in which they were used?[219]

6–043 **A "unitary exercise".** The knowledge reasonably available to the parties at the time of the contract is sometimes referred to as the "background", or "the matrix of facts",[220] or the "context".[221] In the second of his principles set out in the *ICS* case, Lord Hoffmann explained that:

> "Subject to the requirement that it should have been reasonably available to the parties[222] and to the exception to be mentioned next, it includes absolutely anything which would have affected the way in which the language of the document would have been understood by a reasonable man."[223]

The exception to which Lord Hoffmann refers is the non-admissibility of the "previous negotiations of the parties and their declarations of subjective intent."[224] This is dealt with above.[225] In *BCCI v Ali*[226] Lord Hoffmann felt it necessary to stress both that the "background" only includes "absolutely anything" which a reasonable person would have regarded as *relevant* and that the "primary source for understanding what the parties meant is their language interpreted in accordance with conventional usage".[227] But it is not a case of first interpreting the wording of the contract alone and only considering the background if there should be any uncertainty as to its meaning. In *Rainy Sky SA v Kookmin Bank* it was acknowledged by the Supreme Court that interpretation is a "unitary exercise", i.e. the court from the outset considers both the language of the contract and the context in which it was used.[228] That said, with certain types

[217] Hoffmann 134 L.Q.R. 553 at 569.

[218] *Spencer v Sec. of State for Defence* [2012] EWHC 120 (Ch); [2012] L. & T.R. 21 at [62] (" … how could it be otherwise? It would be impossible for the court to construe contracts by reference to the subjective intentions of the parties, when by the time every case came to be decided, the competing parties would be swearing blind that they had subjectively "intended" the meaning for which they were now contending").

[219] See para.6–044.

[220] *Prenn v Simmonds* [1971] 1 W.L.R. 1382 at 1384 (Lord Wilberforce).

[221] It can be informed by the recitals to the contract: *Blackpool Football Club v JSC Baltic International Bank* [2018] EWCA Civ 732.

[222] i.e. *both* (or all) parties: *Arnold v Britton* [2015] UKSC 36; [2015] A.C. 1619 at [35]; *Kason Kek-Gardner Ltd v Process Components Ltd* [2017] EWCA Civ 2132 at [16].

[223] *Investors Compensation Scheme Ltd v West Bromwich Building Society* [1998] 1 W.L.R. 896 at 912–913.

[224] *Investors Compensation Scheme Ltd v West Bromwich Building Society* [1998] 1 W.L.R. 896 at 913.

[225] See paras 6–031—6–032, 6–034.

[226] [2001] UKHL 8; [2002] 1 A.C. 251.

[227] *BCCI v Ali* [2001] UKHL 8; [2002] 1 A.C. 251 at [39].

[228] *Rainy Sky SA v Kookmin Bank* [2011] UKSC 50; [2011] 1 W.L.R. 2900 at [21]; cf. *Bright Asset Ltd v Lewis* [2011] EWCA Civ 122 at [28] ("The interpretative exercise is the single exercise taking

of contract, such as a security deed which is intended to secure a variety of creditors holding different instruments, issued at different times and in different circumstances, the wording is paramount and the background is only relevant "in the most generalised way".[229] The unitary exercise involves an "iterative process" by which each suggested interpretation is checked against the provisions of the contract and its commercial consequences are investigated.[230] As stated by Lord Hodge in *Wood v Capita Insurance Services Ltd*[231]:

> " ... once one has read the language in dispute and the relevant parts of the contract that provide its context, it does not matter whether the more detailed analysis commences with the factual background and the implications of rival constructions or a close examination of the relevant language in the contract, so long as the court balances the indications given by each."

**"Literalism" and "contextualism".** What continues to be the subject of debate is how the courts should strike the "balance" referred to in the dictum of Lord Hodge above. He stressed that interpretation "is not a literalist exercise focused solely on a parsing of the wording of the particular clause"[232]: rather "the court must consider the contract as a whole and, depending on the nature, formality and quality of drafting of the contract, give more or less weight to elements of the wider context in reaching its view as to that objective meaning."[233] Aside from the rejection of an entirely literal approach, this still leaves the question of the relative weight to be given to what is sometimes referred to as the "dictionary" or "natural and ordinary meaning" (the "literal meaning") and the "contextual meaning", to the extent that they may appear to differ. **6–044**

**The primacy of the language of the contract.** In striking the balance between "literalism" (or "textualism") and "contextualism", recent decisions of the Supreme Court have considered it necessary to further stress the primacy of the language of the contract.[234] As Lord Neuberger put it in *Arnold v Britton*: **6–045**

---

into account the factual matrix"); *Napier Park European Credit Opportunities Fund Ltd v Harbourmaster Pro-Rata CLO BV* [2014] EWCA Civ 984 at [36]. This is not a new idea: see *Arbuthnot v Fagan* [1995] C.L.C. 1396 at 1400 ("a composite exercise, neither uncompromisingly literal or unswervingly purposive").

[229] *Re Sigma Finance Corp* [2009] UKSC 2; [2010] 1 All E.R. 571 at [37]; cf. *BNY Mellon Corporate Trustee Services Ltd v LBG Capital No.1 Plc* [2016] UKSC 29; [2016] 2 Lloyd's Rep. 119 at [31]; *Netherlands v Deutsche Bank AG* [2019] EWCA Civ 771 at [49].

[230] *Re Sigma Finance Corp* [2009] UKSC 2; [2010] 1 All E.R. 571 at [12]; *Arnold v Britton* [2015] UKSC 36; [2015] A.C. 1619 at [77].

[231] [2017] UKSC 24; [2017] A.C. 1173 at [12]. In practice, the "starting point is the 'natural and ordinary meaning' of the contractual language": *Spirit Energy Resources Ltd v Marathon Oil (UK) LLC* [2019] EWCA Civ 11 at [35].

[232] A literal approach is said to be exemplified by the observations of Cozens Hardy MR in *Lovell and Christmas Ltd v Wall* (1911) 104 L.T. 85. See also *Shore v Wilson* (1842) 9 Cl. & Fin. 355 at 365; and Lord Steyn's example of an entirely literal approach taken from *The Works of William Paley* in *Sirius International Ins Co v FAI General Ins Ltd* [2004] UKHL 54; [2004] 1 W.L.R. 3251 at [19]; cf. *Charter Reinsurance Co Ltd v Fagan* [1997] A.C. 313 at 326 and 350; *Prenn v Simmonds* [1971] 1 W.L.R. 1382 at 1384 (Lord Wilberforce: "there is no need to appeal here to any modern, anti-literal, tendencies, for Lord Blackburn's well-known judgment in *River Wear Commissioners v Adamson* (1877) 2 App. Cas. 743, 763 provides ample warrant for a liberal approach").

[233] *Wood v Capita Insurance Services Ltd* [2017] UKSC 24; [2017] A.C. 1173 at [10].

[234] A certain primacy is not new: see text to fn.227.

> "the reliance placed in some cases on commercial common sense and surrounding circumstances … should not be invoked to undervalue the importance of the language of the provision which is to be construed." [235]

His concern was to ensure that the courts do no more than address any deficiency in the drafting of the contract and do not attempt to redress what either is, or may have become, a bad bargain. *Arnold v Britton* may be taken as a case in point,[236] where the service charge in a lease for a chalet in a caravan park was expressed in the following terms[237]:

> "To pay to the Lessor without any deductions in addition to the said rent as a proportionate part of the expenses and outgoings incurred by the Lessor in the repair maintenance renewal and renewal of the facilities of the Estate and the provision of services hereinafter set out the yearly sum of Ninety Pounds and Value Added tax (if any) for the first Year of the term hereby granted increasing thereafter by Ten Pounds per hundred for every subsequent year or part thereof."

The lessor claimed that this required the lessee to pay the fixed sum of £90 with an annual uplift of 10 per cent on a compounded basis. The lessee claimed that it required the payment of the lessee's share ("proportionate part") of the costs referred to, where the reference to the fixed sum represented a cap on such liability. It is hard to dispute that the lessor's interpretation produced an unreasonable outcome in that, by the time of the litigation between the parties, some service charges amounted to £2,500 and, by the end of the term in 2072, some would exceed £500,000. This was the consequence of fluctuations in the rate of inflation which stood at or above 10 per cent at the time the leases were entered into in the 1970s and early 1980s, but which has been significantly lower for the vast majority of the time since. But the effect of the service charge was clear "as a matter of language"[238] and, even allowing for wider arguments of commerciality, it was precisely this historical context which led to the conclusion of the majority[239] that, at the time the leases were entered into, the parties intended that the fixed sum should be paid with the annual uplift.[240] Put in the terms of an earlier decision of the Court of Appeal, the lease in *Arnold v Britton* was a contract which "will work perfectly sensibly in the context in which it was made, but it contains a flaw in that it does not provide for all eventualities."[241] Put even more simply, it is an example of a contract which had become a bad bargain.

---

235 *Arnold v Britton* [2015] UKSC 36; [2015] A.C. 1619 at [17]; cf. *Prophet Plc v Huggett* [2014] EWCA Civ 1013; [2014] I.R.L.R. at [797].

236 cf. *Teva Pharma – Produtos Farmaceuticos LDA v Astrazeneca Produtos Farmaceuticos LAD* [2017] EWCA Civ 2135; *NHS Commissioning Board v Silovsky* [2017] EWCA Civ 1389; (2018) 159 B.M.L.R. 92.

237 There were a number of leases to be interpreted and the service charge was not expressed in identical terms in all of them, but the differences were not found to be material.

238 *Arnold v Britton* [2015] UKSC 36; [2015] A.C. 1619 at [35].

239 Lord Carnwath dissented.

240 The parties took a gamble on inflation, but it was a "bilateral gamble": *Arnold v Britton* [2015] UKSC 36; [2015] A.C. 1619 at [36].

241 *ING Bank NV v Ros Roca SA* [2011] EWCA Civ 353; [2012] 1 W.L.R. 472 at [110].

**The quality of the drafting.** As noted by Lord Hodge above,[242] in determining the weight to be given to the "wider context", including arguments about which of any rival interpretations make the greater commercial or business sense, the quality of the drafting is a material factor.[243] As Lord Neuberger explained in *Arnold v Britton*, the worse the drafting "the more ready the court can properly be to depart from [the] natural meaning".[244] But how does the court determine if it is the drafting which has gone astray? **6–046**

For example, in *Rainy Sky SA v Kookmin Bank*[245] the claimant buyers were entitled to a refund under a shipbuilding contract if the contract was terminated, or there was an "insolvency event" in relation to the builder. They claimed a refund for an insolvency event and sought recovery from the defendant bank under a guarantee given in support of the refund obligation of the builder. One paragraph in the guarantee referred to "all such sums due to [the claimant] under the Contract", but another referred only to the buyers' entitlement to a refund on "termination" and did not refer to an insolvency event. The defendant argued that the guarantee therefore only extended to a refund payable on termination. Lord Clarke acknowledged that if "the parties have used unambiguous language, the court must apply it",[246] notwithstanding that it may produce what seems a commercially improbable result.[247] But the apparent inconsistency between the two paragraphs created some doubt and "if there are two possible constructions, the court is entitled to prefer the construction which is consistent with business common sense and to reject the other."[248] In preferring the buyers' interpretation that the guarantee was not confined to a refund on termination, Lord Clarke placed emphasis on the paragraph which referred in general terms to "all such sums due" and held that it made no commercial sense for the parties to have agreed that the buyers would not be able to call on the guarantee on the happening of the event, namely the insolvency of the builder, which would be most likely to require the first class security intended to be provided by a guarantee.[249] But as Patten LJ put it in the Court of Appeal, which had found for the bank[250]: "... merely to say that no credible commercial reason has been advanced for the limited scope of the bond does, in my view, put us in real danger

[242] See text to fn.233.

[243] *National Bank of Kazakhstan v Bank of New York Mellon* [2018] EWCA Civ 1390; [2018] 2 C.L.C. 103 at [39]; cf. *Thorney Park Golf Ltd v Myers Catering Ltd* [2015] EWCA Civ 19.

[244] *Arnold v Britton* [2015] UKSC 36; [2015] A.C. 1619 at [18]; cf. *Hopkinson v Towergate Financial (Group) Ltd* [2018] EWCA Civ 2744.

[245] [2011] UKSC 50; [2011] 1 W.L.R. 2900.

[246] Presumably subject to the principles which are discussed in the next paragraph: *Sugarman v CJS Investments LLP* [2014] EWCA Civ 1239; [2015] 1 B.C.L.C. 1 at [43].

[247] *Rainy Sky SA v Kookmin Bank* [2011] UKSC 50; [2011] 1 W.L.R. 2900 at [23]; cf. *Co-operative Wholesale Society Ltd v National Westminster Bank Plc* [1995] 1 E.G.L.R. 97 at 98.

[248] *Rainy Sky SA v Kookmin Bank* [2011] UKSC 50; [2011] 1 W.L.R. 2900 at [21]; *HHY Luxembourg SARL v Barclays Plc* [2010] EWCA Civ 1248; [2011] 1 B.C.L.C. 336 at [25]–[26].

[249] This, of course, requires some explanation for the paragraph which had omitted any reference to an insolvency event. The buyers submitted that it was merely a "preamble": *Rainy Sky v Kookmin Bank* [2011] UKSC 50; [2011] 1 W.L.R. 2900 at [3].

[250] By majority; Tuckey LJ dissented.

of substituting our own judgment of the commerciality of the transaction for that of those who were actually party to it."[251]

6–047 **The correction of mistakes.** In the *Rainy Sky* case the court sought to resolve an apparent ambiguity in the language of the contract by reference to the wider context and considerations of commercial sense. In some cases, however, the courts have gone further by invoking the fourth and fifth of the principles summarised by Lord Hoffmann in the *ICS* case. Under the fourth principle:

> "The background may not merely enable the reasonable man to choose between the possible meaning of words which are ambiguous but even (as occasionally happens in ordinary life) to conclude that the parties must, for whatever reason, have used the wrong words or syntax, or that something must have gone wrong with the language."[252]

The fifth principle merely reinforces this:

> " ... if one would nevertheless conclude from the background that something must have gone wrong with the language, the law does not require judges to attribute to the parties an intention which they plainly could not have had."[253]

As Lord Hoffmann emphasised, the power of the courts to make corrections as a matter of interpretation is not one to be lightly invoked since one does "not easily accept that people have made linguistic mistakes, particularly in formal documents".[254] What is required is that it should be clear both that an error has been made and what a reasonable person would have understood the parties to have meant.[255] It has been said that the correction of drafting errors by way of interpretation, as opposed to rectification,[256] may not be appropriate for "negotiable and registrable contracts or public documents", i.e. contracts which are later read and relied upon by third parties.[257]

6–048 **Chartbrook v Persimmon Homes.** Perhaps the leading example in practice of Lord Hoffmann's fourth and fifth principles is the decision of the House of Lords

---

[251] [2010] EWCA Civ 582; [2011] 1 Lloyd's Rep. 233 at [51], a view which echoes that of Lord Lloyd in the *ICS* case, fn.258 and of Lord Walker in *In re Sigma Finance Corp* [2009] UKSC 2; [2010] 1 All E.R. 571 at [44]. Writing extra-judicially, Lord Sumption has described the reasoning of the Supreme Court in the *Rainy Sky* case as overriding, rather than understanding, the language of the contract: (2016–2017) 8 *UK Supreme Court Yearbook* 74 at 82.

[252] *Investors Compensation Scheme Ltd v West Bromwich Building Society ICS* [1998] 1 W.L.R. 896 at 913.

[253] *Investors Compensation Scheme Ltd v West Bromwich Building Society ICS* [1998] 1 W.L.R. 896 at 913.

[254] *Investors Compensation Scheme Ltd v West Bromwich Building Society ICS* [1998] 1 W.L.R. 896 at 913.

[255] *Chartbrook Ltd v Persimmon Homes Ltd* [2009] UKHL 38; [2009] A.C. 1101 at [25]; cf. *East v Pantiles (Plant Hire)* [1982] 2 E.G.L.R. 111 at 112; *Littman v Aspen Oil (Broking) Ltd* [2005] EWCA Civ 1579; [2006] 2 P. & C.R. 2.

[256] See below, para.8–063.

[257] *Cherry Tree Investments Ltd v Landmain Ltd* [2012] EWCA Civ 736; [2013] 2 W.L.R. 481 (registered land charge); contrast *Caresse Navigation Ltd v Office National de Electricite* [2013] EWHC 3081 (Comm); [2014] 1 Lloyd's Rep. 337 where the "obvious mistake" principle was applied to a bill of lading.

in *Chartbrook Ltd v Persimmon Homes Ltd*.[258] It appears to have become something of a test case for determining whether the more recent decisions of the Supreme Court in *Arnold v Britton* and *Wood v Capita Insurance Services Ltd*, and the emphasis given therein to the primacy of the language of the contract, should be seen as a change in approach. For example, in *Arnold v Britton* Lord Neuberger referred specifically to the reasoning in the *Chartbrook* case when emphasising that commercial common sense should not be invoked to undervalue the importance of the language of the contract[259] and, writing extra-judicially, Lord Sumption has referred to it as an example of case law which "involves treating the background circumstances as an alternative guide to the parties' intentions instead of a means of interpreting their language".[260]

In the *Chartbrook* case, the claimant owned land which it licensed to the defendant builder for the development and sale of flats. The price to be paid by the defendant to the claimant was the aggregate of the land value and an "Additional Residential Payment" (ARP) which depended on the final sale price achieved for each flat. The land value was a guaranteed sum of £53,438 per flat and the ARP was defined in the contract as "23.4% of the price achieved [for each flat] in excess of [the guaranteed sum]". As a matter of conventional syntax, the meaning of this provision was clear and unambiguous. It entitled the claimant to 23.4 per cent of any price achieved for a flat in excess of £53,438. The defendant submitted that this was not what the parties meant. Rather, the claimant was supposed to receive as an additional payment "*the amount by which* 23.4% of the price achieved [for each flat] *is* in excess of [the guaranteed sum]." On that basis, an additional payment was only due if the sale price for a flat exceeded £228,000. This result could only be reached by the insertion of the italicised words into the definition of the ARP and this was the decision of the House of Lords.

According to Lord Hoffmann, there were several reasons why this was a case where it was clear that something had "gone wrong with the language" and clear "what a reasonable person would have understood the parties to have meant". First, both the admissible background and the contract as a whole indicated that the ARP was a contingent payment intended to deal with the possibility that the flats might sell for a higher price than the parties anticipated when agreeing the guaranteed sum for the land value. For example, another provision in the contract referred to "the date of payment *if any*" of the ARP (emphasis added). On the claimant's literal interpretation of the ARP there was "virtually no element of

[258] [2009] UKHL 38; [2009] A.C. 1101. The decision in the *ICS* case itself is a further example, in which a majority held that "any claim (whether sounding in rescission for undue influence or otherwise)" should, in context, be read to mean "any claim sounding in rescission (whether for undue influence or otherwise)". Lord Lloyd dissented, on the basis that this amounted to impermissible "creative interpretation": [1998] 1 W.L.R. 896 at 904. See also *Mannai Investment Co Ltd v Eagle Star Life Assurance Co Ltd* [1997] A.C. 749. Contrast *Bashir v Ali* [2011] EWCA Civ 707; [2011] 2 P. & C.R. 12; *McKillen v Misland (Cyprus) Investments Ltd* [2012] EWCA Civ 179; [2012] B.C.C. 575.

[259] See above, text to fn.235.

[260] (2016–2017) 8 *UK Supreme Court Yearbook* 74 at 81. In the same lecture, immediately after considering both *Chartbrook* and the *Rainy Sky* case, Lord Sumption observed that "some, perhaps most of these cases might have been decided the same way on more traditional principles of construction" (at 82). The decision in *Chartbrook* might have been reached as a matter of rectification (though that is not free from difficulty: see below, para.8–069), but it is hard to see how it could have been reached as a matter of construction other than on the basis explained by Lord Hoffmann.

contingency at all" if an additional payment was due for any sale price in excess of £53,438.[261] Indeed, on that basis the claimant would receive a "guaranteed" sum of around £4.5m and an "additional" payment of around £4.5m. Secondly, the contract was entered into at a time of rising prices, but of course they might have fallen, in which case a sale price in excess of £53,438 would still represent a contingency. However, as Lord Hoffmann explained, even if the parties had intended to allow for the unlikely assumption of a catastrophic fall in the market on what rational basis would they have agreed a figure as precise as £53,438 to deal with such a contingency? It was clear that that figure "must have been intended to function as a minimum land value, not a minimum sale price."[262]

6–049 **The current approach.** Notwithstanding the primacy now to be given to the language of the contract, it is clear that where there is an obvious deficiency in the drafting, there is still room for the correction of mistakes as a matter of interpretation.[263] Whether the courts would still go as far as the House of Lords in the *Chartbrook* case is more debatable. However, it is submitted, with respect, that the apparent attempt to "sound the retreat"[264] from Lord Hoffmann's approach may be misconceived. Properly understood, that approach is still to be commended. There are three key points to such a proper understanding. First, the object of interpreting a contract is, with one important exception, no different to the object of interpreting language in general, namely to ascertain what the speaker meant by the words used.[265] Secondly, the important exception is that contracts, especially written contracts, are usually drafted by lawyers who may be expected to have chosen the language which is intended to express what the parties meant with care. Accordingly, the courts should start with a "strong presumption" that a contract does not contain any linguistic mistakes;[266] cases such as the *Chartbrook* case are rare, but even lawyers make mistakes. Thirdly, the court must be satisfied that the relevant mistake is a mistake in the language and not in the "failure to anticipate its consequences",[267] i.e. a case of bad drafting, rather than a bad bargain.[268] The touchstone is that the admissible background must lead to the conclusion that the literal interpretation is irrational

[261] *Chartbrook Ltd v Persimmon Homes Ltd* [2009] UKHL 38; [2009] A.C. 1101 at [18].
[262] *Chartbrook Ltd v Persimmon Homes Ltd* [2009] UKHL 38; [2009] A.C. 1101 at [19].
[263] See, e.g. *BNY Mellon Corporate Trustee Services Ltd v LBG Capital No.1 Plc* [2016] UKSC 29; [2016] 2 Lloyd's Rep. 119; *Hopkinson v Towergate Financial (Group) Ltd* [2018] EWCA Civ 2744; *R & S Pilling v UK Insurance Ltd* [2019] UKSC 16; [2019] 2 W.L.R. 1015; *Vitol E&P Ltd v New Age (African Global Energy) Ltd* [2018] EWHC 1580 (Comm) (rogue comma).
[264] Sumption (2016–2017) 8 *UK Supreme Court Yearbook* 74 at 86.
[265] *Investors Compensation Scheme Ltd v West Bromwich Building Society ICS* [1998] 1 W.L.R. 896 at 912; Hoffmann 134 L.Q.R. 553.
[266] See text to fn.254; Hoffmann 134 L.Q.R. 553 at 559–560. This presumption is reinforced by the restrictions on the admissible evidence which the court may take into account (see above, para.6–030).
[267] *ING Bank NV v Ros Roca SA* [2011] EWCA Civ 353; [2012] 1 W.L.R. 472 at [24]; *Trillium (Prime) Property GP Ltd v Elmfield Road Ltd* [2018] EWCA Civ 1556 at [15].
[268] cf. *Ardagh Group SA v Pillar Property Group Ltd* [2013] EWCA Civ 900; [2014] S.T.C. 26 at [66] (Underhill LJ: "parties not uncommonly make contracts which work out expensively for them in particular situations for which they have failed to provide. This is a very long way from the sort of case considered in *Chartbrook*").

and not just unreasonable.[269] If these considerations are borne in mind, there may not in fact be a great deal of difference in the recent approach of the courts in emphasising the primacy of the language of the contract.[270] It may be most correct to say that there has been an "adjustment of emphasis"[271] which appears to advocate a more, if not entirely, literal approach.[272]

## 2. IMPLIED TERMS

Though it remains a matter of debate, implied terms may be divided into three main groups. The first consists of terms implied in fact, that is, terms which were not expressly set out in the contract, but which it is found that the parties must have intended to include. The second consists of terms imported by operation of law. The third consists of terms implied by custom. As well as addressing these three main groups of implied terms, separate consideration will be given to a relatively recent development in the form of an implied obligation of good faith. 6–050

### (a) Terms implied in fact[273]

#### *(i) The general approach*

**A question of interpretation?** As will be seen below, the courts have developed a number of tests, and take into account a number of factors, to determine whether a term of the contract may be implied in fact, i.e. if necessary to give effect to the intention of the parties. That the process involved is one of giving effect to the intention of the parties means that there has always been a certain affinity between this form of implication and the interpretation of the express terms to which the parties have agreed.[274] In *Attorney General of Belize v Belize Telecom Ltd*[275] Lord Hoffmann, giving the Opinion of the Judicial Committee of the Privy Council, went perhaps a little further. He referred to the tests, or factors, 6–051

[269] Hoffmann 134 L.Q.R. 553 at 570.

[270] *Wood v Capita Insurance Services Ltd* [2017] UKSC 24; [2017] A.C. 1173 at [14] (Lord Hodge: "On the approach to contractual interpretation, *Rainy Sky* and *Arnold* were saying the same thing.")

[271] *Globe Motors Inc v TRW Lucas Varity Electric Steering Ltd* [2016] EWCA Civ 396; 168 Con L.R. 59 at [58].

[272] Fort a retreat too far into literalism, see *Grimes v Essex Farmers & Union Hunt Trustees* [2017] EWCA Civ 361; [2017] L. & T.R. 28.

[273] Kramer [2004] C.L.J. 384.

[274] *Trollope & Colls Ltd v North West Metropolitan Regional Hospital Board* [1973] 1 W.L.R. 601, 609; *Luxor (Eastbourne) Ltd v Cooper* [1941] A.C. 108 at 130 (Lord Wright: "what is in question in all these cases is the interpretation of a particular contract"); *Equitable Life Assurance Society v Hyman* [2002] 1 A.C. 408 at 459; *Clin v Walter Lilly & Co Ltd* [2018] EWCA Civ 490; [2018] B.L.R. 321 at [25]. And see the earlier observation of Lord Hoffmann in *Banque Bruxelles Lambert SA v Eagle Star Insurance Co Ltd* [1997] A.C. 191 at 212E that the process of implication "is one of construction of the agreement as a whole in its commercial setting".

[275] [2009] UKPC 10; [2009] 1 W.L.R. 1988; Davies [2010] L.M.C.L.Q. 140; Macdonald 26 J.C.L. 97; McCaughran [2011] C.L.J. 607; Hooley [2014] C.L.J. 315; McClauchlan [2014] L.M.C.L.Q. 203.

which the courts have employed to determine whether a term should be implied in fact, as summarised by Lord Simon in *BP Refinery (Westernport) Pty Ltd v Shire of Hastings*[276]:

> "(1) it must be reasonable and equitable;[277] (2) it must be necessary to give business efficacy to the contract, so that no term will be implied if the contract is effective without it;[278] (3) it must be so obvious that 'it goes without saying';[279] (4) it must be capable of clear expression;[280] (5) it must not contradict any express term of the contract.[281]"

Each of these tests, or factors, will be considered in further detail below, but Lord Hoffmann stressed that they are not a series of "independent tests" each of which have to be surmounted; rather they are:

> "a collection of different ways in which judges have tried to express the central idea that the proposed implied term must spell out what the contract actually means, or in which they have explained why they did not think that it did so".[282]

In his opinion there is "only one question": if the implied term is included "is that what the instrument,[283] read as a whole against the relevant background, would reasonably be understood to mean?"[284]

6–052 **A strict test.** The "one question" formulated by Lord Hoffmann was clearly intended to emphasise that when it comes to the implication of a term in fact it is, *like* interpretation, the process of elucidating what is meant by the "speaker", i.e. in this context what is meant by the parties to the contract.[285] In the same way that, in the ordinary use of language, something can be implied without being said,[286] so too in the making of a contract. In this sense: "the implication of the term is not an addition to the instrument. It only spells out what the instrument means."[287] However, at no point in his Opinion in the *Belize* case did Lord Hoffmann suggest that the process of implication is the *same* as the process of interpretation, not least because, especially if lawyers are involved, the strong presumption is now not just that the parties will have chosen the language of the

---

276 (1978) 52 A.L.J.R. 20 at 26, 60 PC. Lord Simon acknowledged that these tests "may overlap": see further para.6–060.

277 See para.6–062.

278 See para.6–057.

279 See para.6–055.

280 See para.6–064.

281 See para.6–063.

282 *Attorney General of Belize v Belize Telecom Ltd* [2009] UKPC 10; [2009] 1 W.L.R. 1988 at [27].

283 The instrument in the *Belize* case was the articles of association of a company, but it is clear that Lord Hoffmann intended the approach advocated to apply to any written instrument, including a contract.

284 *Attorney General of Belize v Belize Telecom Ltd* [2009] UKPC 10; [2009] 1 W.L.R. 1988 at [21].

285 It is said to have imposed a "superstructure of interpretation" on the conditions necessary for the implication of terms: *Groveholt Ltd v Hughes* [2010] EWCA Civ 538 at [45].

286 See Lord Hoffmann's own example, writing extra-judicially, of the offer of a lift to a rugby match: Hoffmann 134 L.Q.R. 553 at 557. The express offer may only be of a lift *to* the match, but the background and the reasonable expectations of the parties obviously imply that it is also the offer of a *return* after the match.

287 *Attorney General of Belize v Belize Telecom Ltd* [2009] UKPC 10; [2009] 1 W.L.R. 1988 at [18].

contract with care (interpretation[288]), but the yet stronger presumption that they will have addressed all aspects of the contract about which they had formed an intention. Lord Hoffmann himself stressed that, if the contract does not expressly provide for what is to happen when some event occurs, the "most usual inference in such a case is that nothing is to happen" and "[i]f the event has caused loss to one or other of the parties, the loss lies where it falls".[289] As Lord Bingham MR has stated, in this respect there remains a fundamental difference between interpretation and the implication of terms in fact[290]:

> "The courts' usual role in contractual interpretation is, by resolving ambiguities or reconciling apparent inconsistencies, to attribute the true meaning to the language in which the parties themselves have expressed their contract. The implication of contract terms involves *a different and altogether more ambitious undertaking*: the interpolation of terms to deal with matters for which, ex hypothesi, the parties themselves have made no provision. It is because the implication of terms is potentially so intrusive that the law imposes strict constraints on the exercise of this extraordinary power."

**A separate test.** Notwithstanding the stress laid by Lord Hoffmann on the strictness of the test for implying a term in fact, or that he emphasised that it is not sufficient to imply a term that it would lead to a more reasonable result,[291] the Supreme Court has considered it necessary to "sound the retreat"[292] in relation to terms implied in fact, in the same way that it has sounded the retreat in relation to interpretation.[293] It did so in *Marks & Spencer Plc v BNP Paribas Securities Services Trust Co (Jersey) Ltd* in which Lord Neuberger concluded that Lord Hoffmann's observations in the *Belize* case "should henceforth be treated as characteristically inspired discussion rather than authoritative guidance on the law of implied terms."[294] The decision in the *Marks & Spencer* case itself is considered below.[295] Suffice it to say here, the perception of the Court appears to have been that Lord Hoffmann had blurred the lines between interpretation and implication[296] with the attendant risk that the strictness of the test for the latter might not be observed and the courts might be persuaded too easily to imply a **6–053**

---

[288] See para.6–049.

[289] *Attorney General of Belize v Belize Telecom Ltd* [2009] UKPC 10; [2009] 1 W.L.R. 1988 at [27]. For a clear illustration of this, see *Estafnous v London & Leeds Business Centres Ltd* [2011] EWCA Civ 1157.

[290] *Philips Electronique Grand Public SA v BSkyB Ltd* [1995] E.M.L.R. 472 at 480 (emphasis added); cf. *Legal & General Assurance Society Ltd v Expeditors International (UK) Ltd* [2007] EWCA Civ 7; (2007) 5 E.G. 307 at [47].

[291] *Attorney General of Belize v Belize Telecom Ltd* [2009] UKPC 10; [2009] 1 W.L.R. 1988 at [17].

[292] This is the term deployed by Lord Sumption, writing extra-judicially: (2016–2017) 8 *UK Supreme Court Yearbook* 74 at 86.

[293] See para.6–049.

[294] *Marks & Spencer Plc v BNP Paribas Securities Services Trust Co (Jersey) Ltd* [2015] UKSC 72; [2016] A.C. 742 at [31]; Peel 132 L.Q.R. 531. Ironically, one of the criticisms is that what Lord Hoffmann said in the *Belize* case is "open to more than one interpretation" (at [31]). It may be that others have placed an interpretation on it which is "wrong in law" (at [31]) but there is much to be said for the view of Lord Carnwath that "properly understood … it is a valuable and illuminating synthesis of the factors which should guide the court" (at [74]); cf. para.6–059.

[295] See para.6–059. See also: *Ali v Petroleum Co of Trinidad and Tobago* [2017] UKPC 2; [2017] I.C.R. 531 at [5].

[296] *Marks & Spencer Plc v BNP Paribas Securities Services Trust Co (Jersey) Ltd* [2015] UKSC 72; [2016] A.C. 742 at [27].

term, not only where it is necessary, but also where it might only be reasonable to do so.[297] The retreat is implemented by stressing that "construing the words used and implying additional words are different processes governed by different rules."[298] In practice, this appears to mean two things. First, that the express terms of the contract must be interpreted before the court considers any question of implication.[299] Secondly, when it comes to implication, the tests of obviousness or necessity referred to below[300] are to be applied without the gloss of Lord Hoffmann's "one question".[301]

6–054 **An objective test.** It is important to stress the limited nature of the retreat which was sounded in the *Marks & Spencer* case. Most significantly, the implication of a term in fact remains a process of discerning the intention of the parties, but, as with interpretation, such intention is established on an objective basis. If the hypothetical question is: did the parties intend to include the term alleged, one is "not strictly concerned with the hypothetical answer of the actual parties, but with that of notional reasonable people in the position of the parties at the time at which they were contracting".[302]

### *(ii) Tests*

6–055 **Officious bystander.** One test for the implication of a term in fact is the "officious bystander" test derived from the judgment of Scrutton LJ in *Reigate v Union Manufacturing Co (Ramsbottom) Ltd*.[303] As MacKinnon LJ put it in *Shirlaw v Southern Foundries (1926) Ltd*:

> "*Prima facie* that which in any contract is left to be implied and need not be expressed is something so obvious that it goes without saying; so that, if while the parties were making their bargain, an officious bystander were to suggest some express provision for it in the agreement, they would testily suppress him with a common 'Oh, of course!'"[304]

---

[297] Sumption (2016–2017) 8 *UK Supreme Court Yearbook* 74.

[298] *Marks & Spencer Plc v BNP Paribas Securities Services Trust Co (Jersey) Ltd* [2015] UKSC 72; [2016] A.C. 742 at [27]; cf. *Trump International Golf Club Scotland Ltd v Scottish Minister* [2015] UKSC 74; [2016] 1 W.L.R. 85 at [35].

[299] *Marks & Spencer Plc v BNP Paribas Securities Services Trust Co (Jersey) Ltd* [2015] UKSC 72; [2016] A.C. 742 at [28]; *Impact Funding Solutions Ltd v Barrington Support Services Ltd* [2016] UKSC 57; [2017] A.C. 73 at [31].

[300] See paras 6–055—6058.

[301] It is noticeable that in the subsequent Opinion given by the Privy Council in *Hallman Holding Ltd v Webster* [2016] UKPC 3 any reference to *Belize Telecom* is singularly absent from the list of cases which Lord Hodge cited (at [14]) as the "more recent judicial pronouncements" on implied terms, notwithstanding that the *Belize* case had, as predicted, been much referred to by the lower courts: *The Reborn* [2009] EWCA Civ 531; [2009] 2 Lloyd's Rep. 639 at [8].

[302] *Marks & Spencer Plc v BNP Paribas Securities Services Trust Co (Jersey) Ltd* [2015] UKSC 72; [2016] A.C. 742 at [21].

[303] [1918] 1 K.B. 592 at 605.

[304] *Shirlaw v Southern Foundries (1926) Ltd* [1939] 2 K.B. 206 at 227; affirmed [1940] A.C. 701); cf. *Comptoir Commercial Anversois v Power, Son & Co* [1920] 1 K.B. 868 at 899–900.

For example, in one case[305] a vendor of land undertook that, if he later sold certain adjoining land, he would give the purchaser the "first refusal" of it. A term was implied to prevent the vendor from defeating the purchaser's expectation by disposing of the land to a third party by way of gift.

**The state of knowledge of the parties.** As noted above, the process of implication is an objective one; it "is not critically dependent on proof of an actual intention of the parties."[306] But just as the state of *knowledge* of the parties may be relevant to the background for the purpose of interpretation,[307] it is also relevant to implication in fact.[308] In *KC Sethia (1944) Ltd v Partabmull Rameshwar*[309] sellers of Indian jute to Italian buyers could not perform their contract because they failed to obtain a quota for shipment to Italy. They argued that the contract was impliedly "subject to quota", and one reason why the argument was rejected was that the buyers (and therefore any reasonable person in the position of the buyers) did not know that the sellers had no quota for Italy. Similarly, the reasonable person will not conclude that the parties would obviously have agreed to the proposed term if, at the time of the contract, it is clear that each of them was aware that that it was something about which they had divergent views.[310] For example, in *Luxor (Eastbourne) Ltd v Cooper*[311] the defendant had employed an estate agent to sell two cinemas and promised to pay him a commission "on completion of sale". Before the agent had effected a sale, the defendant sold the cinemas himself. It was held that no term could be implied to the effect that the defendant should not (except for good cause) refuse to sell to a person introduced by the agent. While Viscount Simon stated that he was not satisfied that "the vendor would acquiesce",[312] his conclusion is consistent with the objective nature of the test for implication since he later stated that "upon the true construction" of the contract, the agent took the risk of the defendant not being willing to conclude the sale with the person introduced by the agent.[313] As Lord Wright explained: "what it is sought to imply is based on an intention *imputed* to the parties *from their actual circumstances*."[314] 6–056

[305] *Gardner v Coutts & Co* [1968] 1 W.L.R. 173; cf. *Bournemouth & Boscombe Athletic FC v Manchester United FC, The Times*, 22 May 1980; *Fraser v Thames Television Ltd* [1984] Q.B. 44 at 57; *Independiente Ltd v Music Trading Online (HK) Ltd* [2007] EWCA Civ 111; [2008] 1 W.L.R. 608.

[306] *Equitable Life Assurance Society v Hyman* [2002] 1 A.C. 408 at 459: approved in *Marks & Spencer Plc v BNP Paribas Securities Services Trust Co (Jersey) Ltd* [2015] UKSC 72; [2016] A.C. 742 at [21]; cf. *BP Refinery (Westernport) Pty Ltd v Shire of Hastings* (1978) 52 A.L.J.R. 20 at 26, PC.

[307] See text to fn.150.

[308] *McCutcheon v David MacBrayne Ltd* [1964] 1 W.L.R. 125 at 128, 134; cf. *Spring v NASDS* [1956] 1 W.L.R. 585 at 599; *Wilson v Best Travel* [1993] 3 All E.R. 353.

[309] [1950] 1 All E.R. 51; affirmed [1951] 2 Lloyd's Rep. 89.

[310] *Attica Sea Carriers Corp v Ferrostaal Poseidon Bulk Reederei GmbH* [1976] 1 Lloyd's Rep. 250; *Frobisher (Second Investments) Ltd v Kiloran Trust Co Ltd* [1980] 1 W.L.R. 425; *Nutting v Baldwin* [1995] 1 W.L.R. 201 at 211.

[311] [1941] A.C. 108; cf. *Shell UK Ltd v Lostock Garage Ltd* [1976] 1 W.L.R. 1187; Russell 40 M.L.R. 582; *Lonrho v Shell Petroleum Co* [1981] Com. L.R. 74; affirmed [1981] 2 All E.R. 456, without reference to the point; *The Good Luck* [1989] 2 Lloyd's Rep. 238 at 273 (reversed on other grounds [1992] 1 A.C. 233); *The Gudermes* [1993] 1 Lloyd's Rep. 311 at 323.

[312] *Luxor (Eastbourne) Ltd v Cooper* [1941] A.C. 108 at 117.

[313] *Luxor (Eastbourne) Ltd v Cooper* [1941] A.C. 108 at 118.

[314] *Luxor (Eastbourne) Ltd v Cooper* [1941] A.C. 108 at 137 (emphasis added).

6–057 **Necessary for "business efficacy".** A second test for the implication of a term in fact referred to by Lord Wright in the *Luxor* case is that it should be "necessary to give the transaction such business efficacy as the parties must have intended".[315] It is sometimes also said that all implied terms are subject to a requirement of "necessity",[316] as if that were an additional requirement, but in the present context "necessity" seems to be no more than a part of the "business efficacy" test[317] or, if preferred, the "business necessity" test.[318] The necessity required is "necessity for the business efficacy of *the contract*; not some wider business purpose of a contracting party."[319]

6–058 **Illustrations.** In *The Moorcock*[320] the defendants owned a wharf and made a contract to allow the claimants to unload their ship at the wharf. The ship was damaged by settling at low water on a ridge of hard ground. It was held that the defendants were liable for this damage as they were in breach of an implied term that they would take reasonable care to see that the berth was safe. Bowen LJ said:

> "In business transactions such as this, what the law desires to effect by the implication is to give such business efficacy to the transaction as must have been intended at all events by both parties who are businessmen."[321]

As Lord Hoffmann stated in the *Belize* case, there is a danger in detaching the phrase "necessary to give business efficacy" from the process of construction of the instrument: the contract "may work perfectly well in the sense that both parties can perform their express obligations, but the consequences would contradict what a reasonable person would understand the contract to mean".[322] For example, in *The Reborn*[323] the parties entered into a voyage charterparty with a named loading port under the express terms of which the owner warranted that the vessel would comply with all "restrictions" of the port.[324] The hull of the vessel was penetrated by a hidden underwater projection and it was claimed by the owner that there was an implied warranty on the part of the charterer to nominate a safe berth, so that it was the charterer who was liable for damage done to the vessel. The Court of Appeal held that no such term was implied, in part by posing the question: "is the proposed implied term necessary to make the contract

315 *Luxor (Eastbourne) Ltd v Cooper* [1941] A.C. 108 at 137.

316 *Luxor (Eastbourne) Ltd v Cooper* [1941] A.C. 108 at 125; *Hughes v Greenwich LBC* [1994] A.C. 170 at 179; *Baker v Black Sea & Baltic Ins Co Ltd* [1998] 1 W.L.R. 974 at 980 (but see [1998] 1 W.L.R. 974 at 978).

317 *Reigate v Union Manufacturing Co (Ramsbottom) Ltd* [1918] 1 K.B. 592 at 605; *Trollope & Colls Ltd v North West Metropolitan Regional Hospital Board* [1973] 1 W.L.R. 601 at 609; *Concord Trust v The Law Debenture Trust Corp* [2005] UKHL 27; [2005] 1 W.L.R. 1591 at [37].

318 *Marks & Spencer Plc v BNP Paribas Securities Services Trust Co (Jersey) Ltd* [2015] UKSC 72; [2016] A.C. 742 at [21]; cf. *Friends Provident Life Office v Hillier Parker May & Rowden* [1995] 4 All E.R. 260 at 279.

319 *Kason Kek-Gardner Ltd v Process Components Ltd* [2017] EWCA Civ 2132 at [55].

320 (1889) 14 P.D. 64.

321 *The Moorcock* (1889) 14 P.D. 64 at 68 (emphasis added).

322 *Attorney General of Belize v Belize Telecom Ltd* [2009] UKPC 10; [2009] 1 W.L.R. 1988 at [23].

323 [2009] EWCA Civ 531; [2009] 2 Lloyd's Rep. 639.

324 i.e. risks arising from the specifications and restrictions of the berth, but not "hidden dangers".

work?"[325] But that question on its own is inconclusive. The contract could "work" either by leaving the loss with the owner, if there was no implied term, or by imposing liability on the charterer, if there was an implied term. By contrast, if one posed the question of what the charterparty was reasonably understood to mean when read against the relevant background, as the Court of Appeal also did,[326] i.e. whether the charterers had obviously agreed to take the risk of hidden dangers in the berth, the answer to that was "no". The implied term contended for was not necessary "to give effect to the reasonable expectations of the parties",[327] or to make the contract "work in the way the parties would reasonably have expected it to work."[328]

**The Marks & Spencer case.** Notwithstanding the "retreat" from some of what Lord Hoffmann had to say in the *Belize* case, a similar point may be made in relation to the *Marks & Spencer* case, where the claimant, as lessee, exercised its right to break a lease on a particular date. In order to do so, it had to pay a premium and ensure that it was not in arrears with the rent. As rent was paid quarterly in advance and was due only one month before the break date, the claimant had paid rent for two months after the break when it would not be in possession. The claimant sought recovery of the rent for the two months on the basis of an implied term, there being no express provision to deal with the situation. **6–059**

According to Lord Neuberger there was a "powerful case" for such implication.[329] For example, because the break date was dependent on the date on which the head-landlord gave its consent to the grant of an earlier lease, the parties had agreed the break terms not knowing whether the break dates would be shortly after, before, or on, a quarter day. As Lord Neuberger observed: "This supports the notion that they are unlikely to have intended that the apportioned rent was … to be retained by the landlords as part of the compensation for the tenant's operation of the break clause."[330] In addition, the claimant could also point to a term in the lease under which rent was to be "paid yearly and *proportionately for any part of a year* by equal instalments in advance".[331] It was common ground that the effect of these words was that if the parties knew in advance when the lease would come to an end (e.g. at the end of the term), then the claimant was only obliged to pay rent in advance for the part of the quarter when it would be in possession. In the case of a break, the parties would have been in this position if the claimant had paid the break premium before the previous quarter day and not after, as it had done. This allowed for the submission

---

[325] *The Reborn* [2009] EWCA Civ 531; [2009] 2 Lloyd's Rep. 639 at [18].
[326] *The Reborn* [2009] EWCA Civ 531; [2009] 2 Lloyd's Rep. 639 at [45].
[327] *Equitable Life Assurance Society v Hyman* [2002] 1 A.C. 408 at 459 (Lord Steyn).
[328] *Equitas Insurance Ltd v Municipal Mutual Insurance Ltd* [2019] EWCA Civ 718; [2019] 3 W.L.R. 613 at [150].
[329] *Marks & Spencer Plc v BNP Paribas Securities Services Trust Co (Jersey) Ltd* [2015] UKSC 72; [2016] A.C. 742 at [37].
[330] *Marks & Spencer Plc v BNP Paribas Securities Services Trust Co (Jersey) Ltd* [2015] UKSC 72; [2016] A.C. 742 at [34].
[331] Emphasis added.

that the claimant should be in the same position whether it paid the premium before the quarter day, or after as it was entitled to do.[332]

The Supreme Court held, nonetheless, that there was no implied term entitling the claimant to a refund. The factors referred to above were met by two principal considerations. First, the fact that the lease was a very detailed document entered into by substantial and experienced parties, aided in their negotiations by expert legal advice, was a highly relevant factor.[333] Since the lease made provision for a large number of contingencies, but not the contingency which had emerged, this reinforced the default position that when the contract is silent, the loss lies where it falls.[334] Secondly, the "surrounding circumstances known to both parties at the time of the contract"[335] included the general law on the apportionment of rent. It is well established that rent, whether payable in arrears or in advance, is not apportionable in time at common law; and nor is rent payable in advance apportionable under s.2 of the Apportionment Act 1870.[336] Against such a "long and clearly established" position in law, it would be wrong, save in a "very clear case" to attribute to the parties a contrary intention.[337]

One can debate whether the Court reached the right conclusion,[338] but of greater interest is that it was a result reached on the basis that the implied term was not necessary for business efficacy. This still leaves the difficulty identified by Lord Hoffmann in the *Belize* case that this is a rather question-begging test. The lease in the *Marks & Spencer* case was "efficacious" whether the term was implied or not. This is, in effect, conceded by Lord Neuberger who, in his summary of the law, acknowledged that "necessity for business efficacy involves a value judgment … the test is not one of absolute necessity".[339] He suggested that it may be more helpful to ask whether the contract would "lack commercial, or practical coherence" without the implied term,[340] but this appears equally question-begging.[341] Ultimately, the court has to make a choice and there is still

---

332 *Marks & Spencer Plc v BNP Paribas Securities Services Trust Co (Jersey) Ltd* [2015] UKSC 72; [2016] A.C. 742 at [35].

333 This obviously mirrors the "quality of the drafting" factor which is taken into account in interpretation: see para.6–044.

334 *Marks & Spencer Plc v BNP Paribas Securities Services Trust Co (Jersey) Ltd* [2015] UKSC 72; [2016] A.C. 742 at [40].

335 *Marks & Spencer Plc v BNP Paribas Securities Services Trust Co (Jersey) Ltd* [2015] UKSC 72; [2016] A.C. 742 at [27].

336 *Ellis v Rowbotham* [1900] 1 Q.B. 740. One might question the further reference made to cases involving forfeiture (see e.g. *Canas Property Co Ltd v KL Television Services Ltd* [1970] 2 Q.B. 433; [1970] 2 W.L.R. 1133) given that the present case was concerned with the effects of a consensual break clause. For further consideration of the 1870 Act, see para.17–047.

337 *Marks & Spencer Plc v BNP Paribas Securities Services Trust Co (Jersey) Ltd* [2015] UKSC 72; [2016] A.C. 742 at [50].

338 As Rix LJ has acknowledged, "Lord Mansfield is supposed to have said, in effect, that it is easier for a judge to get the answer right than it is for him to give sound reasons for his correct answer. In a sense, this is one of those areas of the law which puts me in mind of that dictum": *The Reborn* [2009] EWCA Civ 531; [2009] 2 Lloyd's Rep. 538 at [47].

339 *Marks & Spencer Plc v BNP Paribas Securities Services Trust Co (Jersey) Ltd* [2015] UKSC 72; [2016] A.C. 742 at [21].

340 *Marks & Spencer Plc v BNP Paribas Securities Services Trust Co (Jersey) Ltd* [2015] UKSC 72; [2016] A.C. 742 at [21].

341 If one emphasises the concept of "practical coherence", it may be that the significance of the *Marks & Spencer* case is to stress the need for an absurd, or irrational, or capricious result before a

much to be said for Lord Hoffmann's view that to imply a term or not is dictated by what the contract would reasonably be understood to mean.

**Relationship between the two tests.** In the *Marks & Spencer* case Lord Neuberger accepted that the tests of business necessity and obviousness "can be alternatives in the sense that only one of them needs to be satisfied",[342] although it will be a rare case where one is satisfied but not the other.[343] He understood Lord Hoffmann to have suggested the same in the *Belize* case,[344] but this was very much on the basis of the latter's view that that they are merely different ways in which the courts establish, or express their conclusion as to, what the contract would reasonably be understood to mean. 6–060

**Unilateral contracts.** It has been said that it is "impossible to imply terms ( … which impose legal obligations) … into a unilateral contract";[345] for, where such an implied term would impose obligations on both parties,[346] it would destroy the unilateral nature of the contract. But it is not obvious why such reasoning should preclude the implication of a term which imposed an obligation only on the *promisor*. Nor does the reasoning exclude the possibility of implying a term which imposed an obligation on the *promisee* in cases (of the kind discussed in Ch.2)[347] in which an originally unilateral contract becomes bilateral in the course of its performance.[348] 6–061

### *(iii) Factors to be taken into account*

**Reasonableness.** As noted above, the term to be implied "must be reasonable and equitable",[349] but reasonableness alone will not suffice.[350] The courts "will not … 6–062

term should be implied, in contradistinction to a test of reasonableness, but we have seen that Lord Hoffmann rejected reasonableness alone as sufficient and in the *Marks & Spencer* case Lord Neuberger conceded that not to imply the term produced a "capricious" result (at [49], [51]). Hence, the court is still left with the choice referred to at the end of para.6–059.

342 *Marks & Spencer Plc v BNP Paribas Securities Services Trust Co (Jersey) Ltd* [2015] UKSC 72; [2016] A.C. 742 at [21]. For the view that both tests must be satisfied, see: *Stubbs v Trower Still and King* [1987] I.R.L.R. 321 at 324; *McAuley v Bristol CC* [1992] Q.B. 134 at 147. For the view that it is sufficient to satisfy either test, see: *The Manifest Lipkowy* [1989] 2 Lloyd's Rep. 138 at 143 and 144; cf. *The Kurnia Dewi* [1997] 1 Lloyd's Rep. 553 at 559; *Clarion Ltd v National Provident Association* [2000] 1 W.L.R. 1888 at 1896; *Greene Wood & McLean LLP v Templeton Insurance Ltd* [2009] EWCA Civ 65; [2009] 1 W.L.R. 2013 at [15].

343 In the *BP Refinery* case referred to above (fn.276), Lord Simon acknowledged that the tests he referred to "may overlap"; cf. *Lymington Marina Ltd v Macnamara* [2007] EWCA Civ 151; [2007] 2 All E.R. Comm 285 at [37], [44]; *Adler v Ananhall Advisory & Consultancy Services Ltd* [2009] EWCA Civ 586; [2009] N.P.C. 80.

344 *Attorney General of Belize v Belize Telecom Ltd* [2009] UKPC 10; [2009] 1 W.L.R. 1988 at [27].

345 *Little v Courage Ltd* (1995) 70 P. & C.R. 469 at 474.

346 The only term which, in *Little v Courage Ltd*, the court was prepared to imply did not impose any obligation on either party: see para.18–084.

347 See para.2–052.

348 *Wells v Devani* [2019] UKSC 4; [2019] 2 W.L.R. 617 at [36].

349 See text to n.277; *Young & Marten Ltd v McManus Childs Ltd* [1969] 1 A.C. 454 at 465; *Liverpool CC v Irwin* [1977] A.C. 239 at 262.

350 *Reigate v Union Manufacturing Co (Ramsbottom) Ltd* [1918] 1 K.B. 592 at 605; *Liverpool CC v Irwin* [1977] A.C. 239 at 266: "The touchstone is always necessity and not merely reasonableness";

improve the contract which the parties have made for themselves, however desirable the improvement might be".[351] The decision of the Court of Appeal in *Bou-Simon v BGC Brokers LP*[352] provides a good illustration. The defendant was employed by the claimant partnership and entered into an agreement that, upon becoming a partner, he would be advanced a loan which he was required to repay out of partnership distributions. A provision in the agreement stated that, if he "cease[d] to be a partner", any sum outstanding under the loan would only be written off if he had served at least four years of his employment contract. The defendant left the claimant's employment before four years had passed and with the loan outstanding, but the provision dealing with this did not apply because the claimant had never in fact become a partner. On that basis, the loan was advanced to him in error and there may well have been a claim in restitution, but the claim for its recovery was made under the loan agreement. This claim succeeded before the trial judge on the basis of an implied term which stated simply that the loan would be repayable if the defendant failed to serve for four years, i.e. with no reference to his status as a partner. This decision was overturned because the term had been implied on the erroneous basis that it reflected "the merits of the situation as they now appear".[353] As Asplin LJ explained:

> "It is not appropriate to apply hindsight and to seek to imply a term in a commercial contract merely because it appears to be fair or because one considers that the parties would have agreed it if it had been suggested to them."[354]

It was not necessary to imply a term for repayment to deal with circumstances not just "omitted" but which were "outwith the scope of the agreement altogether."[355]

6–063 **Conflict with express terms.** It follows from the nature of the process of implication in fact that a term cannot be implied if it conflicts with the express terms of the contract.[356] As we have seen,[357] the courts are also reluctant to imply

cf. Lord Simonds' warning in *Scruttons Ltd v Midland Silicones Ltd* [1962] A.C. 446 at 467 that the process of implication is one "against the abuse of which the courts must keep constant guard"; *Attorney General of Belize v Belize Telecom Ltd* [2009] UKPC 10; [2009] 1 W.L.R. 1988 at [17]; *The Reborn* [2009] EWCA Civ 531; [2009] 2 Lloyd's Rep. 538 at [15]; *Marks & Spencer Plc v BNP Paribas Securities Services Trust Co (Jersey) Ltd* [2015] UKSC 72; [2016] A.C. 742 at [21].

351 *Trollope & Colls Ltd v NW Metropolitan Hospital Board* [1973] 1 W.L.R. 601 at 609; cf. *Philips Electronique Grand Public SA v British Sky Broadcasting Ltd* [1995] 1 E.M.L.R. 472; *Johnson v Davies* [1999] Ch.117 at 128.

352 [2018] EWCA Civ 1525; 179 Con L.R. 32.

353 *Bou-Simon v BGC Brokers LP* [2018] EWCA Civ 1525; 179 Con L.R. 32 at [12].

354 *Bou-Simon v BGC Brokers LP* [2018] EWCA Civ 1525; 179 Con L.R. 32 at [12], echoing the earlier comment to similar effect by Lord Bingham MR in *Philips Electronique Grand Public SA v BSkyB Ltd* [1995] E.M.L.R. 472 at 482.

355 *Bou-Simon v BGC Brokers LP* [2018] EWCA Civ 1525; 179 Con L.R. 32 at [18].

356 *Duke of Westminster v Guild* [1985] Q.B. 688 at 700; cf. *Johnstone v Bloomsbury Health Authority* [1992] Q.B. 333 (Leggatt LJ and Browne-Wilkinson VC); *Johnson v Unisys Ltd* [2001] UKHL 13; [2003] 1 A.C. 518 at [37]; *Lancore Services Ltd v Barclays Bank Plc* [2010] EWCA Civ 752; [2010] 1 All E.R. 763 at [28]; *Irish Bank Resolution Corp Ltd v Camden Market Holdings Corp* [2017] EWCA Civ 7 at [39] ("in substance inconsistent with"); *Merthyr (South Wales) Ltd v Merthyr Tydfil County Borough Council* [2019] EWCA Civ 526 at [28]; *Stevensdrake Ltd v Hunt* [2017] EWCA 1173; [2017] B.C.C. 611.

357 See above, text to fn.333.

a term "where the parties have entered into a carefully drafted written contract containing detailed terms agreed between them",[358] particularly where it is essential that contracts of a particular type "should operate in accordance with the terms which appear on their face", e.g. the financial undertakings used in connection with international commerce.[359] That said, if the tests for implication in fact have been met, the term is "intrinsic" to the agreement and is not excluded by an entire agreement clause;[360] it seems that an "express specific exclusion" is required.[361]

**Vagueness.** The implied term must not be too vague,[362] and it must be possible to formulate its content with "adequate precision".[363] 6–064

### *(iv) Examples*

As will be seen below, the defining feature of terms implied in law is that they are implied into all contracts of a particular type. By contrast, terms are implied in fact on the basis of the circumstances of individual contracts. Nevertheless, the same, or similar, circumstances may be repeated and it is on this basis that there is some value in noting some of the leading examples of terms which may be implied in fact, bearing in mind that it does not follow that the courts will always imply the terms in question just because the case before them shares the same broad features.[364] Thus, the courts may imply a term that the parties will "co-operate" to ensure performance where they have agreed that "something shall be done which cannot effectively be done unless both concur in doing it";[365] 6–065

---

358 *Shell UK Ltd v Lostock Garage Ltd* [1976] 1 W.L.R. 1187 at 1200; *Duke of Westminster v Guild* [1985] Q.B. 688; *BDW Trading Ltd v JM Rowe Investments Ltd* [2011] EWCA Civ 548 at [39]; *UTB LLC v Sheffield United Ltd* [2019] EWHC 2322 (Ch) at [206] (no room for implied obligation of good faith; see para.6-076). Contrast *Associated Japanese Bank (International) v Crédit du Nord SA* [1989] 1 W.L.R. 255.

359 *Uzinterimpex JSC v Standard Bank Plc* [2008] EWCA Civ 819; [2008] 2 Lloyd's Rep. 456 at [23].

360 *Axa Sun Life Services Plc v Campbell Martin Ltd* [2011] EWCA Civ 133; [2011] 2 Lloyd's Rep. 1 at [41]; *Great Elephant Corp v Trafigura Beheeer BV* [2012] EWHC 1745 (Comm); [2012] 2 Lloyd's Rep. 503 at [90]; *Kason Kek-Gardner Ltd v Process Components Ltd* [2017] EWCA Civ 2132 at [54]; *JN Hipwell & Son v Szurek* [2018] EWCA Civ 674; [2018] L. & T.R. 15 at [27].

361 *Axa Sun Life Services Plc v Campbell Martin Ltd* [2011] EWCA Civ 133; [2011] 2 Lloyd's Rep. 1 at [41]; cf. *Federal Republic of Nigeria v JP Morgan Chase Bank NA* [2019] EWHC 347 (Comm) at [37] ("an entire agreement clause may or may not exclude an implied term"); affirmed [2019] EWCA Civ 1641.

362 *Shell UK Ltd v Lostock Garage Ltd* [1976] 1 W.L.R. 1187; cf. *Paul Smith Ltd v H & S International Holdings Inc* [1991] 2 Lloyd's Rep. 127 at 131; *Walford v Miles* [1992] 2 A.C. 128 (para.2–100); *Socimer International Bank Ltd v Standard Bank London Ltd* [2008] EWCA Civ 116; [2008] 1 Lloyd's Rep. 558 at [110].

363 *Luxor (Eastbourne) Ltd v Cooper* [1941] A.C. 108 at 117; *BP Refinery (Westernport) Pty Ltd v Shire of Hastings* (1978) 52 A.L.J.R. 20, PC; *Consolidated Finance Ltd v McCluskey* [2012] EWCA Civ 1325; [2012] C.T.L.C. 133; *Ukraine v Law Debenture Trust Corp Plc* [2018] EWCA Civ 2026; [2019] 2 W.L.R. 655 at [212].

364 *Ashmore v Corp of Lloyd's (No.2)* [1992] 2 Lloyd's Rep. 620 at 631.

365 *Mackay v Dick* (1881) 6 App. Cas. 251 at 263; *Luxor (Eastbourne) Ltd v Cooper* [1941] A.C. 108 at 117; *General Trading Co (Holdings) Ltd v Richmond Corp Ltd* [2008] EWHC 1479; [2008] 2 Lloyd's Rep. 475 at [87]; *Ukraine v Law Debenture Trust Corp Plc* [2018] EWCA Civ 2026; [2019] 2 W.L.R. 655 at [207] ("there is no general rule").

similarly, that one party will not do anything "of his own motion" to put an end to any state of circumstances on which the performance of the contract depends.[366] Where the contract confers rights on one party subject to the consent of other, the court may imply a term that such consent must not be withheld arbitrarily or unreasonably,[367] and where a contract is subject to a condition precedent, a term may be implied that neither party must do anything to prevent the occurrence of the event,[368] or that one party must use reasonable efforts to bring the event about.[369]

It is clear that contracts with commission agents "do not follow a single pattern"[370] and the courts have refused to imply a term that the principal would not, by going out of business, deprive the agent of a chance of earning his commission.[371] On the other hand, where a seller's agent had negotiated a sale of particular goods, a term was implied that the seller would not, by breaking that contract of sale, deprive the agent of his right to commission.[372] This implied term made the seller liable to the agent only if he broke one particular contract of sale, without otherwise restricting his freedom to go out of business.

6–066 **Obligation to perform in good faith.** A relatively recent development is the recognition by the courts of an implied duty of good faith. It seems that this obligation is only owed, if at all, as a term implied in fact, but since such a term appears to be confined to contracts of a certain type, ie "relational contracts", it is considered in more detail below after an assessment of terms implied in law.

## (b) Terms implied in law[373]

6–067 Many of the obligations arising out of particular types of contracts are, at any rate presumptively, determined by rules of law; and some such obligations are said to be the result of implied terms.[374]

[366] Though such a term may be regarded as one imposed by operation of law: see para.6–072.

[367] *Eastleigh BC v Town Quay Developments Ltd* [2009] EWCA Civ 1391; [2010] 2 P. & C.R. 2; cf. *Lymington Marina Ltd v Macnamara* [2007] EWCA Civ 151; [2007] N.P.C. 27. See further the cases discussed at para.2–098, fn.493.

[368] See para.2–109.

[369] See para.2–111.

[370] *Luxor (Eastbourne) Ltd v Cooper* [1941] A.C. 108 at 119.

[371] *Rhodes v Forwood* (1876) 1 App. Cas. 256; cf. *Hamlyn & Co v Wood* [1891] 2 Q.B. 488; *Sun Alliance Pensions Life & Investment Services Ltd v RJL* [1991] 2 Lloyd's Rep. 410. Contrast cases in which the principal has *expressly* promised to stay in business: *Reigate v Union Manufacturing Co (Ramsbottom) Ltd* [1918] 1 K.B. 592; cf. *Ogdens Ltd v Nelson* [1905] A.C. 109.

[372] *Alpha Trading Ltd v Dunshaw-Patten* [1981] Q.B. 290; para.16–104; cf. *C Christo & Co Ltd v Marathon Advisory Service Ltd* [2015] EWHC 1971 (QB). Contrast *The Manifest Lipkowy* [1989] 2 Lloyd's Rep. 138.

[373] Peden 117 L.Q.R. 190; Phang [1993] J.B.L. 242; [1994] J.B.L. 255. Detailed discussion of the terms implied by law into particular types of contracts will be found in specialist works on such contracts. But points of general interest arise out of the distinction between terms implied in fact and terms implied in law, and out of the legal nature of terms of the latter kind. These points are considered in this part.

[374] *Clarion Ltd v National Provident Association* [2000] 1 W.L.R. 1888 at 1897.

**Common law.** In a contract of employment the employee impliedly undertakes that he is reasonably skilled,[375] that he will faithfully serve his employer[376] and not act against the employer's interests,[377] and that he will indemnify his employer against liabilities incurred by the employer as a result of his wrongful acts.[378] The employer, for his part, impliedly undertakes that he will not require the employee to do any unlawful act,[379] that he will provide safe premises,[380] that he will take reasonable care not to endanger the employee's health,[381] and that he will not without reasonable cause conduct himself so as to destroy or seriously damage the relationship of trust and confidence between himself and the employee.[382] Similarly, a party instructed to act in a professional capacity assumes an obligation to exercise the skill and care which is to be expected of a reasonably competent member of the profession; he does not normally impliedly guarantee a specified result.[383] In some cases, however, the particular circumstances may show that, in addition, a warranty has been given in relation to some part of the service provided.[384] A term implied in law can generally[385] be excluded by a contrary agreement,[386] but this may require "clear wording".[387] **6–068**

**Statute.** Many terms which are implied in law have been put into statutory form. For example, a number of important terms implied into contracts for the sale of goods are stated in ss.12–15 of the Sale of Goods Act 1979,[388] and similar terms are implied by statute into hire-purchase agreements,[389] other contracts for the supply of goods[390] and contracts for the supply of services.[391] The power to exclude these terms is now severely restricted by legislation.[392] **6–069**

**Terms implied in law distinguished from terms implied in fact.** The implication of a term in fact is based on the inference that the parties intended (in the objective sense[393]) to incorporate the term into their contract,[394] but no such **6–070**

---

[375] *Harmer v Cornelius* (1858) 5 C.B. (N.S.) 236.

[376] *Hivac Ltd v Park Royal Scientific Instruments Ltd* [1946] Ch. 169; cf. *Faccenda Chicken Ltd v Fowler* [1987] Ch. 117.

[377] *Wessex Dairies Ltd v Smith* [1935] 2 K.B. 80; *Sanders v Parry* [1967] 1 W.L.R. 753.

[378] *Lister v Romford Ice & Cold Storage Co Ltd* [1957] A.C. 555; para.6–072.

[379] *Gregory v Ford* [1951] 1 All E.R. 121.

[380] *Matthews v Kuwait Bechtel Corp* [1959] 2 Q.B. 57.

[381] *Johnstone v Bloomsbury Area Health Authority* [1992] 2 Q.B. 333.

[382] *Malik v BCCI* [1998] A.C. 20.

[383] See, e.g. in the context of surgery: *Eyre v Measday* [1986] 1 All E.R. 488; *Thake v Maurice* [1986] Q.B. 644; para.17–069.

[384] *Platform Funding Ltd v Bank of Scotland Plc* [2008] EWCA Civ 930; [2009] 2 W.L.R. 1016.

[385] i.e. subject to exceptions such as those discussed at paras 7–049–7–050, 7–058—7–059.

[386] e.g. *The Berge Sund* [1993] 2 Lloyd's Rep. 453; *The Spiros C* [2000] 2 Lloyd's Rep. 319 at 335.

[387] *Federal Republic of Nigeria v JP Morgan Chase Bank NA* [2019] EWHC 347 (Comm) at [37]; affirmed [2019] EWCA Civ 1641 (see text to fn.478); cf. *NHS Commissioning Board v Vasant* [2019] EWCA Civ 1245 at [51].

[388] cf. Consumer Rights Act 2015 ss.9–14, but such terms are not "implied": see text to n.410.

[389] Supply of Goods (Implied Terms) Act 1973 ss.8–11.

[390] Supply of Goods and Services Act 1982 ss.2–5, 7–10.

[391] Supply of Goods and Services Act 1982 ss.13–14.

[392] See para.7–049 and following.

[393] See para.6–051.

inference is necessary for the implication of a term in law.[395] The question whether any, and if so what, term is to be implied at common law often turns on distinctions which are so subtle that they can scarcely be based on the intention of the parties, even on an objective basis.[396] Whether any, and if so what, term should be implied in law is often decided exclusively by the citation of earlier cases.[397] This is done to determine an issue of "pure law"[398] and not to ascertain the intention of the parties.

6–071 **A test of policy and not of necessity.** The implication of a term in law is simply a way of specifying some of the duties which prima facie arise out of certain types of contracts, or, as it has been put, "legal incidents of those ... kinds of contractual relationship".[399] In deciding whether to imply a term in law, the courts are guided by general policy considerations affecting the type of contract in question;[400] and to this extent considerations of reasonableness and fairness may enter into the implication of such terms.[401] It has been suggested that, even in this type of case, the test of implication is "necessity, not reasonableness".[402] If appropriate at all,[403] necessity in this context has a different shade of meaning from that which it has in formulations of the business efficacy test.[404] The House of Lords has distinguished "between the search for an implied term *necessary* to give business efficacy to a particular contract and the search, based on wider considerations, for a term which the law will imply as a *necessary* incident of a definable category of contractual relationship".[405] In accordance with this test, it has for example been held that it was an implied term in a contract of employment that the employer should inform the employees of steps which they

---

[394] This is true though the implication of even such terms may be a question of "law" in the sense of an *inference* based on primary facts: see *O'Brien v Associated Fire Alarms* [1968] 1 W.L.R. 1916.

[395] *McAuley v Bristol CC* [1992] Q.B. 134 at 147; *Scally v Southern Health & Social Services Board* [1992] 1 A.C. 294 at 307; *Timeload Ltd v British Telecommunications Plc* [1995] E.M.L.R. 459 at 467; *Equitable Life Assurance Society v Hyman* [2002] 1 A.C. 408 at 459.

[396] See, e.g. the contrast between *Young & Marten Ltd v McManus Childs Ltd* [1969] 1 A.C. 454; and *Gloucestershire CC v Richardson* [1969] 1 A.C. 480.

[397] e.g. *Yeoman Credit Ltd v Apps* [1962] 2 Q.B. 508.

[398] *Malik v BCCI* [1998] A.C. 20 at 46.

[399] *Mears v Safecar Securities Ltd* [1983] Q.B. 54 at 78; cf. *Liverpool C v Irwin* [1977] A.C. 239; *Johnstone v Bloomsbury Health Authority* [1992] Q.B. 333 at 343; *Jameson v CEGB (Central Electricity Generating Board) (No.1)* [2000] 1 A.C. 455 at 477–478.

[400] *The Star Texas* [1993] 2 Lloyd's Rep. 445; *Crossley v Faithful & Gould Holdings* Ltd [2004] EWCA Civ 293; [2004] I.R.L.R. 377 at [36].

[401] *Crossley v Faithful & Gould Holdings* Ltd [2004] EWCA Civ 293; [2004] I.R.L.R. 377; cf. *Re Charge Card Services Ltd* [1989] Ch. 497 at 513; *Galaxy Energy International Ltd v Bayoil SA* [2001] 1 Lloyd's Rep. 512 at [27]; *Haywood v Newcastle upon Tyne Hospitals NHS Foundation Trust* [2018] UKSC 22; [2018] 1 W.L.R. 2073 at [32]; *James-Bowen v Commissioner of Police of the Metropolis* [2018] UKSC 40; [2018] 1 W.L.R. 4021 at [20]–[21].

[402] *Scally v Southern Health and Social Services Board* [1992] 1 A.C. 294 at 307; cf. *Tai Hing Cotton Mill Ltd v Liu Chong Hing Bank Ltd* [1986] A.C. 80 at 104–105: *Spring v Guardian Insurance Plc* [1995] 2 A.C. 296 at 339, 354; *Reid v Rush & Tompkins Group Plc* [1990] 1 W.L.R. 212 at 220.

[403] *Timeload Ltd v British Telecommunications Ltd* [1995] E.M.L.R. 459 at 467.

[404] *Baker v Black Sea & Baltic General Insurance Co* [1998] 1 W.L.R. 974 at 980.

[405] *Scally v Southern Health & Social Services Board* [1992] 1 A.C. 294 at 307 (emphasis added); *Malik v BCCI* [1998] A.C. 20 at 45.

were entitled to take to enhance their pension rights.[406] Such an implication was not necessary to give business efficacy to any individual employment contract, but it was a necessary aspect of employment relationships of the type before the court.[407] It is submitted that such decisions are clearly based on considerations of "justice and policy"[408] and there is much to be said for abandoning "the elusive concept of necessity".[409]

**Imposition of a legal duty.** In many cases of the kind under consideration, the same process can with equal plausibility be described either as the implication of a term in law or as the imposition of a legal duty. In this respect it is noticeable that the Consumer Rights Act 2015 abandons the terminology of "implied" terms and refers instead to terms "to be treated as included".[410] In one case concerning a landlord's duty to repair the outside of the premises the court indiscriminately refers to an "implied term" and to an "implied obligation"[411] which must be "imposed on"[412] the landlord. Where a term is imposed in law, the two processes are, as a practical matter, indistinguishable. It is, for example, commonly said that a landlord *impliedly covenants* that his tenant shall have quiet possession, and that the tenant is under an *obligation* not to commit waste. One could just as well say that the landlord was under an obligation to let the tenant have quiet possession, and that the tenant impliedly covenanted not to commit waste. Again, it is said that if a party enters into an arrangement which can take effect only if a given state of circumstances continues, he impliedly promises not to put an end to it.[413] But in a case in which this rule was applied, Lord Atkin said: **6–072**

> "Personally, I should not so much base the law on an implied term, as on a positive rule of the law of contract that conduct of either promisor or promisee which can be said to amount to himself 'of his motion' bringing about the impossibility of performance is in itself a breach."[414]

This point would not be worth stressing[415] if the true nature of the inquiry before the court were not sometimes obscured by the use of the expression "implied

[406] *Scally v Southern Health and Social Services Board* [1992] 1 A.C. 294; cf. *Corsham v Police & Crime Commissioner for Essex* [2019] EWHC 1776 (Ch).

[407] It is not an implied term of *any* contract of employment that the employer will take reasonable care for the economic well-being of his employee, whatever form that might take: *Crossley v Faithful & Gould Holdings* Ltd [2004] EWCA Civ 293; [2004] I.R.L.R. 377.

[408] *The Star Texas* [1993] 2 Lloyd's Rep. 445 at 491.

[409] *Crossley v Faithful & Gould Holdings* Ltd [2004] EWCA Civ 293; [2004] I.R.L.R. 377 at [36], though Dyson LJ more cautiously suggested it is better to "focus" on policy rather than necessity.

[410] See ss.9(1), 10(3), 11(1), 12(2), 13(2), 14(2).

[411] *Barrett v Lounava (1982) Ltd* [1990] 1 Q.B. 348 at 359; cf. *Scally v Southern Health & Social Services Board* [1992] 1 A.C. 294 at 307B ("terms which the law will imply"), 307D ("necessary … to imply an obligation").

[412] *Barrett v Lounava (1982) Ltd* [1990] 1 Q.B. 348 at 358; cf. *Spring v Guardian Ins Plc* [1995] 2 A.C. 296 at 353 ("imposing a duty").

[413] *Stirling v Maitland* (1864) 5 B. & S. 840; *CEL Group Ltd v Nedlloyd Lines UK* Ltd [2003] EWCA Civ 1716; [2004] 1 Lloyd's Rep. 381 at [11].

[414] *Southern Foundries (1926) Ltd v Shirlaw* [1940] A.C. 701 at 717; cf. *Spring v Guardian Ins* [1995] 2 A.C. 296 at 320.

[415] As it was not in *Duval v 11-13 Randolph Crescent Ltd* [2018] EWCA Civ 2298; [2019] 2 W.L.R. 761 at [24].

term" to refer to the imposition of a legal duty, and by the failure to distinguish between terms implied in fact and terms implied in law. In *Lister v Romford Ice and Cold Storage Co Ltd*[416] a lorry driver injured a third party by negligent driving in the course of his employment. The third party recovered damages from the employers, who obtained judgment for an indemnity from the driver on the ground that he had broken the implied term in the contract of employment to drive with proper care.[417] The driver in turn argued that the contract also contained an implied promise by the employers. This was formulated in various ways: as a promise to indemnify the driver against liability to third parties if the employers were insured, or if they were required by law to be insured, or if they ought as reasonable and prudent persons to have been insured. The House of Lords, by a majority, held that no such term could be implied. Some of the reasons given by the majority are reasons against the implication of a term *in fact.* The implication was not "precise and obvious";[418] it was not necessary to give business efficacy to the contract;[419] and it was not clear that both parties, as reasonable persons, would have agreed to it.[420] But many terms implied *in law* would fail to pass these tests. Whether such terms should be implied is not a question of intention, but one of policy: "*Should* one imply [the alleged] term … ?"[421] In fact the House of Lords in *Lister*'s case was, to a large extent, concerned with considerations of policy. The argument that seems to have weighed most heavily with the majority was that it would be undesirable to allow a driver to recover an indemnity from his employer as he might then drive less carefully. Considerations of this kind always influence the implication of terms in law; but they have nothing to do with the intention of the parties, and hence with the implication of terms in fact.

The distinction between the two types of implication is clearly drawn in the later case of *Reid v Rush & Tompkins Group Plc*,[422] where an employee was injured, while working abroad, as a result of the fault of a third party who could not be traced. He argued that his contract of employment contained an implied term obliging his employers to warn him to insure against such risks; but the argument was rejected on two separate grounds. First, no such term *could* be implied in fact since it would not have been agreed by the parties. And secondly, no such term *should* be implied in law by the court as the exact scope of such an implication raised issues of policy which could be resolved only by the

[416] [1957] A.C. 555.
[417] Employers' insurers have agreed not to make such claims against employees, so that the decision has little practical effect.
[418] *Lister v Romford Ice and Cold Storage Co Ltd* [1957] A.C. 555 at 574.
[419] *Lister v Romford Ice and Cold Storage Co Ltd* [1957] A.C. 555 at 583.
[420] *Lister v Romford Ice and Cold Storage Co Ltd* [1957] A.C. 555 at 578.
[421] *Rockeagle Ltd v Alsop Wilkinson* [1992] Ch. 47 at 51.
[422] [1990] 1 W.L.R. 212.

legislature.[423] It is, conversely, possible for both tests to support the conclusion that a term should be implied,[424] in which case the implication can be said to arise both in fact and in law.

There are, however, also cases in which, though no term can be implied in fact, it may be desirable to attach certain "legal incidents"[425] to a contract, or, in other words, to impose a legal duty. This point has sometimes been overlooked,[426] so that it was occasionally held that no terms *should* be implied in law merely because none *could* be implied in fact. But such reasoning would now be inconsistent with *Liverpool CC v Irwin*.[427] The House of Lords there held that it was an implied term of a lease of a maisonette in a Council block that the landlord should take reasonable care to keep the common parts of the block in a reasonable state of repair. The term was clearly not implied in fact: the "officious bystander" test was not satisfied;[428] nor was the implication necessary to give business efficacy to the contract.[429] The implication arose because the nature of the relationship made it desirable to place some obligation on the landlord as to the maintenance of the common parts of the premises. It amounted to the imposition of a legal duty, in spite of the fact that no term could be implied in fact.[430]

### (c) Doubtful cases

Sometimes it is not clear whether a particular term is implied in fact or in law. 6–073

**Party relying on his own breach.**[431] It has been said that in the absence of a contrary intention "it is to be presumed that it was not the intention of the parties that either party should be entitled to rely upon his own breaches of his primary obligations as bringing the contract to an end",[432] or to obtain some benefit under it. In the case in which this dictum appears it is referred to as "the well-known 6–074

---

[423] The decision in this case has to some extent been overtaken by subsequent decisions (such as *Scally v Southern Health and Social Services Board* [1992] 1 A.C. 294) in which the courts have, in certain restricted circumstances, implied a term whose effect is to impose a duty on the employer to safeguard his employee's economic interests: *Crossley v Faithful & Gould Holdings* Ltd [2004] EWCA Civ 293; [2004] I.R.L.R. 377 at [46].

[424] See *The Island Archon* [1994] 2 Lloyd's Rep. 227 at 237; cf. *St Albans City and District Council v International Computers Ltd* [1996] 4 All E.R. 481.

[425] See fn.399.

[426] e.g. in *Abbott v Sullivan* [1952] 1 K.B. 189 where, it is submitted, a term might well have been implied in law (though on the principle stated at fn.310, none could be implied in fact). *The Aramis* [1989] 1 Lloyd's Rep. 213 is open to criticism on similar grounds: see Treitel [1989] L.M.C.L.Q. 162; cf. *John v Rees* [1970] Ch. 345 where a term was implied in law.

[427] [1977] A.C. 239; *Duke of Westminster v Guild* [1985] Q.B. 688 at 697–698; *Sim v Rotherham MBC* [1987] Ch. 216 at 245.

[428] *Liverpool CC v Irwin* [1977] A.C. 239 at 283–290. This was also the position in *Barrett v Lounava (1982) Ltd* [1990] 1 Q.B. 348 (where a term was nevertheless implied in law).

[429] *Liverpool CC v Irwin* [1977] A.C. 239 at 255.

[430] cf. *McAuley v Bristol CC* [1992] Q.B. 134.

[431] See also the analogous rule that that one party will not do anything "of his own motion" to put an end to any state of circumstances on which the performance of the contract depends: fn.366 and fn.413.

[432] *Cheall v APEX* [1983] 2 A.C. 180 at 189; para.18–005

rule of construction" which, in the light of the *Belize Telecom* case, may suggest that it should be viewed as a term implied in fact,[433] but it also appears to have the "status of a rule of law which is imposed upon the parties to a contract almost regardless of what they have agreed".[434] In practice, it is probably something of a hybrid in that it "can be excluded or modified by the terms of the contract and … its scope in any particular case will depend upon the construction of the relevant agreement".[435]

6–075 **Obligation to perform in good faith.**[436] A duty of good faith is implied by law as an incident of certain categories of contract, e.g. contracts of employment and contracts between partners or others whose relationship is characterised as fiduciary. In *Yam Seng Pte Ltd v International Trade Corp Ltd*[437] Leggatt J doubted that English law had reached the stage where it was ready to recognise a requirement of good faith as a duty implied by law into all commercial contracts,[438] but he held that[439]:

> "Nevertheless, there seems to me to be no difficulty, following the established methodology of English law for the implication of terms in fact, in implying such a duty in any ordinary commercial contract based on the presumed intention of the parties".

6–076 **A duty implied in law, or in fact?** While it is clearly stated above that the test to be met is that for the implication of a term *in fact*, what makes this a doubtful case so far as ordinary commercial contracts are concerned is the further recognition that such a term may be implied into a certain *type* of contract, sometimes referred to as a "relational" contract.[440] This is defined as a contract which requires "a high degree of communication, co-operation and predictable performance based on mutual trust and confidence" and which involves "expectations of loyalty".[441] Leggatt J gave as examples "some joint venture agreements, franchise agreements and long term distributorship agreements"; and as a counter-example which would not amount to a "relational" contract, "a

---

433 In *BDW Trading Ltd v JM Rowe Investments Ltd* [2011] EWCA Civ 548 at [34] Patten LJ refers to "the implication of a term embodying the own wrong principle" and also prays in aid the principles set out by Lord Hoffmann in *Attorney General of Belize v Belize Telecom Ltd* [2009] UKPC 10; [2009] 1 W.L.R. 1988; cf. *Extra MSA Services Cobham Ltd v Accor UK Economy Hotels Ltd* [2011] EWHC 775 (Ch).

434 *BDW Trading Ltd v JM Rowe Investments Ltd* [2011] EWCA Civ 548 at [31].

435 *BDW Trading Ltd v JM Rowe Investments Ltd* [2011] EWCA Civ 548 at [31].

436 Campbell 77 M.L.R. 475.

437 [2013] EWHC 111 (QB); [2013] 1 Lloyd's Rep. 526; Whittaker 129 L.Q.R. 463.

438 The general rule in commercial contracts is that "if the parties wish to impose such a duty they must do so expressly": *Mid Essex Hospital Services NHS Trust v Compass Group UK and Ireland Ltd* [2013] EWCA Civ 200; [2013] B.L.R. 265 at [105].

439 *Yam Seng Pte Ltd v International Trade Corp Ltd* [2013] EWHC 111 (QB); [2013] 1 Lloyd's Rep. 526 at [131].

440 In the *Yam Seng* case Leggatt discussed the concept of a relational contract only in the context of obligations of disclosure ([2013] EWHC 111 (QB); [2013] 1 Lloyd's Rep. 526 at [142]), but in subsequent cases, including the further decision of Leggatt LJ in the *Tahnoon* case (see n.446), it has been identified as a more general consideration.

441 *Yam Seng Pte Ltd v International Trade Corp Ltd* [2013] EWHC 111 (QB); [2013] 1 Lloyd's Rep. 526 at [142]; cf. *Bates v Post Office* [2019] EWHC 606 (QB) at [725].

simple exchange".[442] The reference to "some" joint venture agreements clearly indicates that not every such agreement will amount to a relational contract. What is less clear is whether, once an agreement is recognised as a relational contract, that is sufficient for the duty of good faith to be implied. That begins to look more like the methodology for terms implied in law,[443] but to say that the agreement amounts to a relational contract may simply represent the conclusion that, in relation to *the particular contract* before the court, the test for a term implied in fact has been met. Alternatively, even if an agreement is identified as a relational contract, this may simply be a factor to take into account in deciding whether the test for implication in fact has been met.[444] This appears to have been what Leggatt J meant given the emphasis placed on the methodology of implication in fact in the *Yam Seng* case and his reference to the concept of a relational contract as part of a wider discussion of the relevant background against which a contract may have been made.[445] This discussion took place in the context of Lord Hoffmann's approach to both interpretation and terms implied in fact, from which, as we have seen, there has been something of a retreat,[446] but Leggatt LJ appears to adopt the same approach in a more recent case, decided after the decisions in which the "retreat" has been sounded.[447] However, in that case he would have reached the same conclusion "by applying the test … for the implication of a term in law, on the basis that the nature of the contract as a relational contract implicitly requires (in the absence of a contrary indication) treating it as involving an obligation of good faith."[448]

In a number of cases in which the courts have declined to imply a duty of good faith, they have done so with little or no reference to the concept of a relational contract, but nonetheless on the basis that the test for a term implied in fact had not been met.[449] In cases in which such a duty has been implied, the agreement in question has been identified as a relational contract, but again seemingly on the basis that this allowed for the conclusion that the test for a term implied in fact

---

[442] *Yam Seng Pte Ltd v International Trade Corp Ltd* [2013] EWHC 111 (QB); [2013] 1 Lloyd's Rep. 526 at [142].

[443] It is not "a special rule of interpretation for this category of contract": *Globe Motors Inc v TRW Lucas Varity Electric Steering Ltd* [2016] EWCA Civ 396; 168 Con L.R. 59 at [67].

[444] *Monde Petroleum SA v Westernzagros Ltd* [2016] EWHC 1472; [2016] 2 Lloyd's Rep. 229 at [250] ("the mere fact that a contract is a long-term or relational one is not, *of itself*, sufficient" (emphasis added)); *UTB LLC v Sheffield United Ltd* [2019] EWHC 2322 (Ch) at [203].

[445] *Yam Seng Pte Ltd v International Trade Corp Ltd* [2013] EWHC 111 (QB); [2013] 1 Lloyd's Rep. 526 at [133] and following.

[446] See para.6–049.

[447] *Sheikh Tahnoon Bin Saeed Bin Shakhboot Al Nehayan v Kent* [2018] EWHC 333 (Comm); [2018] 1 C.L.C. 216, especially at [174].

[448] *Sheikh Tahnoon Bin Saeed Bin Shakhboot Al Nehayan v Kent* [2018] EWHC 333 (Comm); [2018] 1 C.L.C. 216 at [174].

[449] *TSG Building Services Plc v South Anglia Housing Ltd* [2013] EWHC 1151 (TCC); [2013] B.L.R. 484; *Hamsard 3147 Ltd v Boots UK Ltd* [2013] EWHC 3251 (Pat); *Greenclose Ltd v National Westminster Bank Plc* [2014] EWHC 1156 (Ch); [2014] 2 Lloyd's Rep. 169; *Carewatch Care Services Ltd v Focus Caring Services Ltd* [2014] EWHC 2313 (Ch); *Acer Investment Management Ltd v Mansion Group Ltd* [2014] EWHC 3011 (QB); *National Private Air Transport Services Co v Windrose Aviation Co* [2016] EWHC 2144 (Comm) at [133]–[136]; cf. *General Nutrition Investment Co Ltd v Holland & Barrett International Ltd* [2017] EWHC 746 (Ch) at [321].

had been met,[450] though not without a degree of ambiguity which perhaps follows from Leggatt LJ's suggestion above that the same result might be reached on the basis of a term implied in fact, or in law.[451]

6–077 **What does "good faith" require?** If such a duty of good faith is implied, what does it require of the party or parties by whom it is owed? According to Leggatt J, it is context specific and has an objective meaning,[452] but that still leaves the question of its particular content.[453] It has been held to extend beyond the "core requirement" of honesty and includes "fidelity to the parties' bargain"[454] and the need to avoid "commercially unacceptable" conduct.[455] A similar interpretation has been given to express contractual duties of good faith,[456] but the concept of "commercially unacceptable" conduct is uncertain[457] and a party wishing to restrain or compel any particular conduct would be advised to include an express term to that effect.[458] As it is, more concrete aspects of the duty of good faith may include a limited duty of disclosure,[459] the duty of "co-operation" in performance,[460] a duty not unreasonably to withhold consent where it is required,[461] and the duty, to be discussed below, of exercising any contractual

---

450 *Bristol Groundschool Ltd v Intelligent Data Capture Ltd* [2014] EWHC 2145 (Ch) at [196]; cf. *D&G Cars Ltd v Essex Police Authority* [2015] EWHC 226 (QB) where the *Yam Seng* methodology led to the finding of an implied term of "honesty and integrity".

451 See *Bates v Post Office* [2019] EWHC 606 (QB) at [743] where Fraser J draws a distinction between terms "consequential upon" the finding of a relational contract and terms implied because necessary for business efficacy (17 terms were implied as part of "good faith" and three directly under the "business efficacy" test).

452 *Yam Seng Pte Ltd v International Trade Corp Ltd* [2013] EWHC 111 (QB); [2013] 1 Lloyd's Rep. 526 at [144].

453 *Sheikh Tahnoon Bin Saeed Bin Shakhboot Al Nehayan v Kent* [2018] EWHC 333 (Comm) at [175] ("perhaps impossible to spell out an exhaustive description of what this obligation involved").

454 *Yam Seng Pte Ltd v International Trade Corp Ltd* [2013] EWHC 111 (QB); [2013] 1 Lloyd's Rep. 526 at [139].

455 *Yam Seng Pte Ltd v International Trade Corp Ltd* [2013] EWHC 111 (QB); [2013] 1 Lloyd's Rep. 526 at [138]; *Bristol Groundschool Ltd v Intelligent Data Capture Ltd* [2014] EWHC 2145 (Ch) at [196].

456 *Berkeley Community Villages Ltd v Pullen* [2007] EWHC 1330 (Ch); [2007] 3 E.G.L.R. 101; *CPC Group Ltd v Qatari Diar Real Estate Investment Co* [2010] EWHC 1535 (Ch); [2010] N.P.C. 74; *Health & Case Management Ltd v Physiotherapy Netwrork Ltd* [2018] EWHC 869 (QB). The courts have tended to interpret the *scope* of such provisions narrowly: *Mid Essex Hospital Services NHS Trust v Compass Group UK and Ireland Ltd* [2013] EWCA Civ 200; [2013] B.L.R. 265; *Sainsbury's Supermarkets Ltd v Bristol Rovers (1883) Ltd* [2016] EWCA Civ 160; *VR Global Partners LP v Exotix Partners LLP* [2017] EWHC 2620 (Comm) at [36].

457 Quaere therefore whether "good faith" meets the criterion that the implied term should be capable of clear expression: see para.6–064.

458 cf. *Bates v Post Office* [2019] EWHC 606 (QB), fn.451.

459 *Yam Seng Pte Ltd v International Trade Corp Ltd* [2013] EWHC 111 (QB); [2013] 1 Lloyd's Rep. 526 at [142]; *Sheikh Tahnoon Bin Saeed Bin Shakhboot Al Nehayan v Kent* [2018] EWHC 333 (Comm); [2018] 1 C.L.C. 216 at [176]; see para.9–181.

460 *Yam Seng Pte Ltd v International Trade Corp Ltd* [2013] EWHC 111 (QB); [2013] 1 Lloyd's Rep. 526 at [145]; see para.6–065.

461 *Yam Seng Pte Ltd v International Trade Corp Ltd* [2013] EWHC 111 (QB); [2013] 1 Lloyd's Rep. 526 at [145]; see para.6–065.

discretion in good faith.[462] It "does not involve the court in imposing its view of what is substantively fair on the parties."[463]

**Obligation to exercise contractual discretion in good faith.** A more limited duty of "good faith" may be implied to constrain the exercise of discretion conferred on one party to the contract; namely that it should not be exercised arbitrarily, capriciously, irrationally, or for an improper purpose.[464] In *Braganza v BP Shipping Ltd*[465] the Supreme Court acknowledged that this equates to the test of "*Wednesbury* reasonableness" which is applied to the review of the exercise of public law powers. That test applies both to the "decision-making process" and the "outcome",[466] the latter of which requires only a rational decision, not a reasonable one, i.e. a decision which is not so unreasonable that no reasonable decision-maker could have reached it.[467] A rational decision is one which may still allow the party in question to "have regard to its own commercial interests".[468] This more limited obligation of good faith is also regarded as a term implied in fact when it is necessary to make the contract "work in the way the parties would reasonably have expected it to work."[469] While it therefore depends on the particular circumstances of the contract in question, a number of decisions have established that an element of choice for one party under the contract does not always engage the sort of discretion required. For example, it is not implied where one party is deciding whether or not to exercise an "absolute contractual right",[470] such as a remedial right to terminate the contract,[471] or rescind for misrepresentation.[472] It has been said that it is only necessary where the actions of **6–078**

[462] *Yam Seng Pte Ltd v International Trade Corp Ltd* [2013] EWHC 111 (QB); [2013] 1 Lloyd's Rep. 526 at [145]; see para.6–078.

[463] *Yam Seng Pte Ltd v International Trade Corp Ltd* [2013] EWHC 111 (QB); [2013] 1 Lloyd's Rep. 526 at [150].

[464] See, e.g. *The Product Star (No.2)* [1993] 1 Lloyd's Rep. 397; *Cantor Fitzgerald International v Horkulak* [2004] EWCA Civ 1287; [2005] I.C.R. 402; *Socimer International Bank Ltd v Standard Bank London Ltd* [2008] EWCA Civ 116; [2008] 1 Lloyd's Rep 558.

[465] [2015] UKSC 17; [2015] 1 W.L.R. 1661.

[466] *Braganza v BP Shipping Ltd* [2015] UKSC 17; [2015] 1 W.L.R. 1661 at [103]; cf. *Patural v DB Services (UK) Ltd* [2015] EWHC 3659 (QB); [2016] I.R.L.R. 286 at [61] (sounding "a note of caution"). As to the burden of proof, see: the *Braganza* case at [37]; *Hills v Niksun* [2016] EWCA Civ 115; [2016] I.R.L.R. 715.

[467] On the difference between rationality and reasonableness, see: *Hayes v Willoughby* [2013] UKSC 17; [2013] 1 W.L.R. 935 at [14]; cf. *Faieta v ICAP Management Services Ltd* [2017] EWHC 2995 (QB); [2018] I.R.L.R. 227 at [28] (the test of irrationality sets a "high hurdle": at [40]).

[468] *Lehman Brothers International (Europe) v Exxonmobil Financial Services BV* [2016 [EWHC 2699 (Comm); [2016] 2 C.L.C. 578 at [287].

[469] *Equitas Insurance Ltd v Municipal Mutual Insurance Ltd* [2019] EWCA Civ 718; [2019] 3 W.L.R. 613 at [150]; cf. *Socimer International Bank Ltd v Standard Bank London Ltd* [2008] EWCA Civ 116; [2008] 1 Lloyd's Rep 551 ("a standard term"); *Watson v Watchfinder.Co.Uk Ltd* [2017] EWHC 1275 (Comm); [2017] Bus L.R. 1309 at [102] ("whether as a matter of construction or the implication of a term").

[470] *Mid Essex Hospital Services NHS Trust v Compass Group UK & Ireland Ltd* [2013] EWCA Civ 200; [2013] B.L.R. 265 at [91]; *Brogden v Investec Bank Plc* [2016] EWCA Civ 1031; [2017] I.R.L.R. 90 at [20].

[471] *Lomas v JFB Firth Rixson Inc* [2012] EWCA Civ 419; [2012] 2 Lloyd's Rep. 548 at [46]; *Monde Petroleum SA v Westernzagros Ltd* [2016] EWHC 1472; [2016] 2 Lloyd's Rep. 229. Contrast *Bates v Post Office* [2019] EWHC 606 (QB) at [899].

[472] *Shurbanova v Forex Capital Markets Ltd* [2017] EWHC 2133 (QB) at [93].

one party involve "making an assessment or choosing from a range of options, taking into account the interests of both parties".[473]

6–079 **Can the implied duty of good faith be excluded?** Whether it is implied in law or in fact, it must follow that any implied duty of good faith can be excluded by the express terms of the contract[474] and this is acknowledged "in principle" by Leggatt J in the *Yam Seng* case. The reason for the hesitation in a conclusion reached only in principle is that "in practice it is hardly conceivable that contracting parties would attempt expressly to exclude the core requirement to act honestly."[475] If they did, it seems very likely that any such exclusion would be void or unenforceable by analogy with the rule that a party cannot exclude liability for his own fraud.[476] But what of any attempt to exclude the duty of good faith beyond the core requirement of honesty? In one case concerned with the implied duty of good faith in the exercise of discretion, it was said that such a term is extremely difficult to exclude, but not "utterly impossible".[477] This may also depend on whether the term is implied in fact, or in law since it has been said that "a term implied by law, at common law or by statute, as opposed to some terms implied by fact or by custom, confers a particularly valuable right so that it is unlikely that a party has agreed to give up that right other than by clear wording."[478]

## (d) Terms implied by custom or trade usage

6–080 **Custom.** We have seen that evidence of custom is admissible to add to, but not to contradict, a *written* contract.[479] Further, *any* contract (whether written or not) may be deemed to incorporate any relevant and notorious[480] custom of the market, trade or locality in which it is made,[481] unless the custom is inconsistent with the express (or necessarily implied) terms, or with the nature, of the

[473] *Mid Essex Hospital Services NHS Trust v Compass Group UK and Ireland Ltd* [2013] EWCA Civ 200; [2013] B.L.R. 265 at [83].

[474] See text to fn.356; and text to fn.386.

[475] *Yam Seng Pte Ltd v International Trade Corp Ltd* [2013] EWHC 111 (QB); [2013] 1 Lloyd's Rep. 526 at [149].

[476] See para.7–034.

[477] *Mid Essex Hospital Services NHS Trust v Compass Group UK and Ireland Ltd* [2013] EWCA Civ 200; [2013] B.L.R. 265 at [83] in which an express term in the nature of an entire agreement clause was held not to be effective; cf. *British Telecommunications plc v Telefónica O2 UK Ltd* [2014] UKSC 42; [2014] Bus L.R. 765 at [37] ("very clear language to the contrary").

[478] *Federal Republic of Nigeria v JP Morgan Chase Bank NA* [2019] EWHC 347 (Comm) at [37]; affirmed [2019] EWCA Civ 1641.

[479] See para.6–035.

[480] See *Turner v Royal Bank of Scotland* [1999] 2 All E.R. (Comm) 664, where this requirement was not satisfied; cf. *Lehman Brothers International (Europe) v Exotix Partners LLP* [2019] EWHC 2380 (Ch) at [167].

[481] At the date it was made: see *Phillips v Syndicate 992 Gunner* [2003] EWHC 1084; [2004] Lloyd's Rep I.R. 426 at [24].

contract.[482] In cases of such inconsistency the custom is said to be "unreasonable", and binds a party only if he knew of it. A custom which is "reasonable" binds both parties, whether they knew of it or not.[483] It is sometimes said that the incorporation of custom into a contract is based on the presumed intention of the parties,[484] but the question whether a custom binds depends on whether it is "reasonable", and this question can give rise to complex issues of law and fact which are more akin to the process of implication in law.[485]

**Collective agreements.** The terms of collective agreements between trade unions and employers may be incorporated in the employment contracts of individual employees by express reference,[486] or by being acted on over a period of time.[487] Between employer and union, such agreements normally have no contractual force because they are not intended to be legally binding.[488] But when their terms are incorporated in individual contracts of employment, those terms can, if so intended,[489] become legally binding between employer and employee.[490] It has, moreover, been suggested that the terms of collective agreements may be incorporated in contracts of employment as "crystallised custom".[491] The "custom" may be incorporated even in contracts with employees who are not members of the union which has negotiated the agreement, so long as there is some evidence of intention to incorporate it.[492] Once the terms of the collective agreement have been incorporated in the contract of employment, the employee can enforce rights under that contract, even after the collective agreement itself has, as between the union and the employer, been brought to an end.[493] **6–081**

**Trade usage.** Terms may also be implied by trade usage.[494] For example, where the owner of a crane hired it out to a contractor who was also engaged in the same business, it was held that the hirer was bound by the owner's usual terms though **6–082**

---

482 Such inconsistency was one ground why the alleged custom was not incorporated in the contract in *Danowski v Henry Moore Foundation* [1996] E.M.L.R. 364. An appropriately drafted entire agreement clause may exclude an implied term based on custom or usage: *The Helene Knutsen* [2003] EWHC 1964; [2003] 2 Lloyd's Rep. 686.

483 *Reynolds v Smith* (1893) 9 T.L.R. 494; for other illustrations, see para.16–023.

484 e.g. in *Produce Brokers Co Ltd v Olympia Oil & Cake Co Ltd* [1916] 1 A.C. 314 at 324; cf. *Garratt v Mirror Group Newspapers Ltd* [2011] EWCA Civ 425; [2011] I.C.R. 880 at [45]–[46].

485 cf. *The Maira (No.3)* [1990] 1 A.C. 637 at 681.

486 *Hooker v Lange, Bell & Co* [1937] 4 L.J.N.C.C.R. 199; *Camden Exhibition & Display Ltd v Lynott* [1966] 1 Q.B. 555.

487 *NCB v Galley* [1958] 1 W.L.R. 16.

488 See para.4–025.

489 *NCB v NUM* [1986] I.C.R. 736; *Kaur v MG Rover Group Ltd* [2004] EWCA Civ 1507; [2005] I.R.L.R. 40; *Malone v British Airways Plc* [2010] EWCA Civ 1225; [2011] I.C.R. 125; *George v Ministry of Justice* [2013] EWCA Civ 324.

490 *Robertson v British Gas Corp* [1983] I.C.R. 351; *Alexander v Standard Telephone and Cables Ltd* [1990] I.C.R. 291 at 303 (where the intention was later found to have been negatived: see [1991] I.R.L.R. 286); *Keeley v Fosroc International Ltd* [2006] EWCA Civ 1277; [2006] I.R.L.R. 961; *Sparks v Department of Transport* [2016] EWCA Civ 360; [2016] I.C.R. 695.

491 Kahn-Freund in Flanders & Clegg (eds), *The System of Industrial Relations in Great Britain* (1954), Ch.2, p.58.

492 *Young v Canadian Northern Ry* [1931] A.C. 83.

493 *Gibbons v Associated British Ports Authority* [1985] I.R.L.R. 376.

494 See *Baker v Black Sea & Baltic General Ins Co Ltd* [1998] 2 All E.R. 833 for proof of such usage.

these were not actually communicated at the time of contracting.[495] They were, however, based on a model supplied by a trade association; and references in the judgment to the fact that they were reasonable and prevalent in the trade[496] suggest that they were incorporated on a principle similar to that which applies to customary terms.

[495] *British Crane Hire Corp Ltd v Ipswich Plant Hire Ltd* [1975] Q.B. 303; *Harlow & Jones Ltd v American Express Bank Ltd* [1990] 2 Lloyd's Rep. 343.

[496] *British Crane Hire Corp Ltd v Ipswich Plant Hire Ltd* [1975] Q.B. 303 at 311, 313; contrast *Salsi v Jetspeed* [1977] 2 Lloyd's Rep. 57 (where there was no evidence of usage).

## CHAPTER 7

# EXEMPTION CLAUSES AND UNFAIR TERMS[1]



This chapter is concerned with contracts which are otherwise valid and unenforceable,[2] but in which particular terms are unenforceable because they are "unfair". In the case of consumer contracts, the test laid down by statute for terms which are not wholly ineffective is indeed one of "fairness". In the case of non-consumer contracts, the test is one of reasonableness. There are other instances where a term of a contract may be void or unenforceable for reasons **7–001**

[1] Coote, *Exception Clauses* (1964).

[2] The terms of a contract may be "unenforceable" because the contract as a whole is set aside for some "vitiating factor", such as misrepresentation or duress: see Chs 9 and 10.

which may, broadly speaking, be concerned with "fairness", e.g. because enforcement would be contrary to public policy. Such instances are dealt with elsewhere.[3]

7–002 **Standard form contracts.** Many of the cases considered in this chapter are concerned with contracts made in "standard form". Contractual terms are often set out in standard forms which are used for all contracts of the same kind, and are only varied so far as the circumstances of each contract require. Such terms may be settled by a trade association for use by its members for contracting with each other or with members of the outside public. One object of these standard forms is simply to save time. They can be used to determine in advance who is to bear the expense of insuring against contractual risks;[4] and they also facilitate the quotation of differential rates, e.g. where a carrier's form provides for goods to be carried either at his or at the customer's risk, and the charge is adjusted accordingly. Between commercial parties bargaining at arm's length such uses of standard forms can be perfectly legitimate;[5] and this may be true even where the party to whom the standard terms are presented is a private consumer who has or is likely to have insured against the loss which has occurred. But a less defensible object of the use of standard terms has been the exploitation or abuse of the superior bargaining power of commercial suppliers when contracting with such consumers. The supplier can draft the standard terms in ways highly favourable to himself, both by means of clauses which exclude or limit his liability for failure to perform or for defective performance, and by provisions which confer rights on him under the contract.

7–003 **Development of the law.** In cases concerning exemption clauses, the courts were to some extent able to redress the balance in favour of parties prejudicially affected by standard form contracts; but they were less inclined to do so where standard terms conferred rights on the supplier. In both fields, legislative intervention has become increasingly important, some of it intended to implement EU legislation aimed at harmonising the level of protection for consumers. The most important legislative provisions are contained in the Unfair Contract Terms Act 1977[6] and the Consumer Rights Act 2015.[7] The 1977 Act applies to non-consumer contracts and is confined to exemption clauses or notices, broadly defined.[8] It makes some terms or notices wholly ineffective[9] and subjects others to a requirement of reasonableness.[10] The 2015 Act applies to

[3] See, e.g. Ch.11 (illegality and public policy); paras 20–136-20–176 (penalty clauses and relief against forfeiture).

[4] See *Photo Production Ltd v Securicor Transport Ltd* [1980] A.C. 827 at 843, 851; cf. *A Schroeder Music Publishing Co Ltd v Macaulay* [1974] 1 W.L.R. 308 at 316.

[5] See *Photo Production Ltd v Securicor Transport Ltd* [1980] A.C. 827 at 851; *Ailsa Craig Fishing Co Ltd v Malvern Fishing Co Ltd* [1983] 1 W.L.R. 964 at 966.

[6] See para.7–039 and following.

[7] See para.7–086 and following.

[8] See paras 7–043–7–046.

[9] See paras 7–047–7–050.

[10] See paras 7–051–7–060.

consumer contracts[11] (and some consumer notices) and, with limited exceptions,[12] applies to any terms. It makes some terms wholly non-binding,[13] while others are not binding if they fail a test of fairness.[14] In a significant number of cases, however, contracts are not affected by these legislative provisions and continue to be governed only by rules of common law. These rules therefore still call for discussion, even though many of the cases from which they are derived would now be differently decided under the legislative provisions just referred to, or under other legislation to be described later in this chapter.[15] For the most part, the common law rules are concerned with the efficacy of exemption clauses; but it will be necessary also to consider the common law approach to other types of terms.

**The control of terms in non-standard form** Some of the controls on the use of exemption clauses and other unfair terms which are considered in this chapter are not confined to standard form contracts.[16] They may be applied even to fully negotiated terms, including terms agreed by two commercial parties. Where they do apply, the fact that the terms have been negotiated or that the parties are of equal bargaining power may be a factor to take into account in determining their enforceability, e.g. where the issue is the reasonableness of a term under the 1977 Act. **7–004**

## 1. COMMON LAW

**Incorporation and construction.** At common law, a court may not enforce a term either because it has not been incorporated into the contract, or because, as a matter of construction (interpretation), it does not apply to the situation at hand. Incorporation and construction in general have been considered in Ch.6. In this part we shall consider, in particular, the construction of exemption clauses and analogous terms, such as indemnity clauses. **7–005**

**Substantive control.** It is not inconsistent with the principle of freedom of contract for the courts to determine whether a term is part of the contract (incorporation) and what it means (construction). If these requirements are met, it is inconsistent with that principle for the courts to refuse to enforce the term. There are, however, a few instances in which, even at common law, some terms are unenforceable on substantive grounds.[17] **7–006**

[11] See paras 7–088—7–091.
[12] See paras 7–119–7–120.
[13] See paras 7–094–7–099.
[14] See paras 7–100–7–107.
[15] See paras 7–129–7–132.
[16] One of the changes introduced by the Consumer Rights Act 2015 is that the test of fairness is no longer confined to terms which have not been individually negotiated, which was the position under the Regulations which are replaced by Pt 2 of the 2015 Act: see para.7–087.
[17] See paras 7–033–7–037.

**7–007** **Third parties.** The question whether exemption clauses can protect or prejudice third parties is discussed in Ch.14.[18]

## (a) Construction

**7–008** Under this heading we shall first discuss the general principle that exemption clauses are construed *contra proferentem*, before considering the construction of exemption clauses in certain commonly occurring situations, e.g. where one party has sought to protect himself from liability for a particularly serious breach, or for negligence.

### (i) *Contra proferentem*[19]

**7–009** **Statement of the rule.** *Contra proferentem* may be used to describe what, in fact, are two rules of construction. The first is that, in case of doubt, wording in a contract is to be construed against a party who seeks to rely on it in order to exclude or limit a legal liability which arises by operation of law, such as liability for negligence or the liability to pay damages for breach.[20] The second is that: "again in case of doubt, wording is to be construed against the party who proposed it for inclusion in the contract".[21] The first rule applies because of the nature of the clause.[22] The second rule applies if one party can be identified as the *proferens*, i.e. the party who "prepared the clause, or … for whose benefit the clause operates".[23] In practice, both rules will often apply to an exemption clause, but the first rule alone will suffice. As Briggs LJ has put it:

> "… the underlying rationale for the principle that, if necessary to resolve ambiguity, exclusion clauses should be narrowly construed has nothing to do with the identification of the *proferens*, either of the document as a whole or of the clause in question. Nor is it a principle derived from an identification of the person seeking to rely upon it. Ambiguity in an exclusion clause may have to be resolved by a narrow construction because an exclusion clause cuts down or detracts from the ambit of some important obligation in a contract, or a remedy conferred by the general law such as (in the present case) an obligation to give effect to a contractual warranty by paying compensation for breach of it. The parties are not lightly to be taken to have intended to cut down the remedies which the law provides for breach of important contractual obligations without using clear words having that effect."[24]

[18] See para.14–063 and following.

[19] Peel, in Burrows & Peel (eds), *Contract Terms* (2007); Tofaris [2019] L.M.C.L.Q. 270.

[20] *Photo Production Ltd v Securicor Transport Ltd* [1980] A.C. 827 at 850.

[21] *Youell v Bland Welch & Co Ltd* [1992] 2 Lloyd's Rep. 127 at 134; cf. *Pera Shipping Corp v Petroship SA* [1984] 2 Lloyd's Rep. 363 at 365.

[22] *Impact Funding Solutions Ltd v Barrington Support Services Ltd* [2016] UKSC 57; [2017] A.C. 73 at [7].

[23] *Hut Group Ltd v Nobahar-Cookson* [2016] EWCA Civ 128; [2016] 1 C.L.C. 573 at [14]. For the view that it is not enough that the relevant clause was put forward *on behalf* of one of the parties; it must be shown that it was put forward for his *benefit*, see: *Royal and Sun Alliance Ins Plc v Dornoch Ltd* [2004] EWHC 803; [2004] Lloyd's Rep I.R. 815 at [82]; affirmed [2005] EWCA Civ 238.

[24] *Hut Group Ltd v Nobahar-Cookson* [2016] EWCA Civ 128; [2016] 1 C.L.C. 573 at [18], citing *Gilbert-Ash (Northern) Ltd v Modern Engineering (Bristol) Ltd* [1974] A.C. 689 at 717, but contrast: *Transocean Drilling UK Ltd v Providence Resources Plc* [2016] EWCA Civ 372; [2016] 2 Lloyd's Rep. 51 at [21].

Both rules are said to apply when there is ambiguity in the wording of the clause in question. That is certainly true of the second rule. It is a rule of "last resort"[25] and "can only apply if a document, properly interpreted, admits of doubt."[26] The same is not necessarily true of the first rule. As will be seen in some of the examples considered below, the wording of such a clause may appear unambiguous on its face. It is only when one considers the obligation which it is claimed to diminish or exclude that there may be thought to be some doubt as to the intention of the parties.[27] An alternative explanation of the first rule may therefore be that *any* exemption clause falls to be construed *contra proferentem*, but if it is nonetheless unambiguously worded, its meaning may be clear.[28] Normally, however, the court will express its conclusion in terms that the *contra proferentem* rule does *not apply* if the clause has a clear meaning: "The contra proferentem rule may still be useful to resolve cases of genuine ambiguity, but ought not to be taken as the starting point".[29] It is with the first rule that the remainder of this part is principally concerned.

**Does the rule still apply?** In his re-statement of the principles of interpretation in the *ICS* case, Lord Hoffmann commented that "almost all the old intellectual baggage of 'legal' interpretation had been discarded".[30] His further comments in a later case[31] may indicate that one example of "legal interpretation" which he had in mind was *contra proferentem*.[32] What he may have been referring to was the particularly strained approach to the interpretation of exemption clauses, intended to protect consumers, which was rejected after the passing of the Unfair Contract Terms Act 1977.[33] What is clear is that cases decided since the *ICS* case 7–010

[25] *The Olympic Brilliance* [1982] 2 Lloyd's Rep 205 at 208; *McGeown v Direct Travel Insurance* [2003] EWCA Civ 1606; *Pilkington UK Ltd v CGU Ins Plc* [2004] EWCA Civ 23; [2004] B.L.R. 97 at [53]; *K/S Victoria Street v House of Fraser (Stores Management) Ltd* [2011] EWCA Civ 904; [2012] Ch. 497 at [68] ("rarely if ever of any assistance"); *BNY Mellon Corporate Trustee Services Ltd v LBG Capital No.1 Plc* [2016] UKSC 29; [2016] 2 Lloyd's Rep. 119 at [53] ("almost an admission of defeat").

[26] *Static Control Components (Europe) Ltd v Egan* [2004] EWCA Civ 392; [2004] 2 Lloyd's Rep 429 at [37]; *Cattles Plc v Welcome Financial Services Ltd* [2010] EWCA Civ 599; [2010] 2 Lloyd's Rep. 514 at [43], [48].

[27] See *Kudos Catering (UK) Ltd v Manchester Central Convention Complex Ltd* [2013] EWCA Civ 38; [2013] 2 Lloyd's Rep. 270 and Tomlinson LJ's reference to "apparently clear words" (at [22]).

[28] See *Frans Maas (UK) Ltd v Samsung Electronics (UK) Ltd* [2004] EWHC 1502; [2004] 2 Lloyd's Rep 251, where Gross J appeared to see no contradiction in his interpretation of a limitation clause by starting with the *contra proferentem* rule (at [138]) and concluding that the "language" of the clause was "clear" (at [141]); cf. *Scottish Power UK Plc v BP Exploration Operating Co Ltd* [2016] EWCA Civ 1043 at [29] ("if the answer *becomes* clear") (emphasis added)).

[29] *Taberna Europe CDO II Plc v Selskabet* [2016] EWCA Civ 1262; [2017] Q.B. 633 at [23]; cf. *Price Waterhouse v University of Keele* [2004] EWCA Civ 583; [2004] P.N.L.R. 43 at [26] (Arden LJ), but contrast at [35] (Buxton LJ).

[30] *Investors Compensation Scheme Ltd v West Bromwich Building Society* [1998] 1 W.L.R. 896 at 912.

[31] *Bank of Credit and Commerce International SA v Ali* [2001] UKHL 8; [2002] 1 A.C. 251.

[32] cf. *Tradigrain SA v Intertek Testing Services Canada Ltd* [2007] EWCA Civ 154 at [46].

[33] See below, paras 7–039—7–085. If only because of the doctrine of precedent, some examples of this particularly strained approach continue to survive, e.g. that liability for breach of the implied conditions under the Sale of Goods Act 1979 can only be excluded by an express reference to "conditions" or terms "which must necessarily be taken to refer to" conditions: *The Mercini Lady*

have continued to apply the *contra proferentem* rule.[34] Indeed, it has been referred to as the "dominant principle" in the interpretation of "clauses by which a party seeks to relieve itself from legal liability."[35] Nonetheless, it may to some extent be subsumed within the general principles of interpretation, in the sense that it is merely "helpful guidance on the proper approach to interpretation".[36] Seen within the context of interpretation generally, *contra proferentem* is a question of emphasis: "the degree of strictness appropriate to be applied" will depend upon the extent to which the exemption clause in question involves "departure from the implied obligations".[37] The extent of the departure may be determined by the exemption clause itself operating from a common starting point, e.g. a clause which merely seeks to limit liability will be construed less strictly than one which purports to exclude it altogether.[38] Alternatively, the extent of the departure may be determined by how far the same clause has to go from each starting point, e.g. whether it is relied upon to exclude or limit liability for breach of contract, or negligence,[39] or fraud.[40] Yet more recent case law has renewed the debate about whether *contra proferentem* should be applied to exemption clauses, in particular where the parties are of equal bargaining power and the clause is of mutual benefit.[41] It is submitted that, properly understood, this does not amount to the outright rejection of *contra proferentem*, but rather an acknowledgement that it is not to be applied "mechanistically" and that it is unnecessary to resort to it if, in context, the intention of the parties is clear.[42]

7–011 **The meaning of "consequential loss".** The approach of the courts to the meaning of "consequential loss" may be seen as an example of *contra proferentem*. In a series of rulings,[43] some of which post-date Lord Hoffmann's

---

[2010] EWCA Civ 1145; [2011] 1 Lloyd's Rep. 142; applying *Wallis, Son & Wells v Pratt & Haynes* [1911] A.C. 394; *Henry Kendall & Sons v William Lillico & Sons* [1969] 2 A.C. 31; cf. *Air Transworld Ltd v Bombardier Inc* [2012] EWHC 243 (Comm); [2012] 1 Lloyd's Rep. 349.

[34] Some of them feature in the examples below. See also: *The Starsin* [2003] UKHL 12; [2004] 1 A.C. 715 at [144]; *Dairy Containers Ltd v Tasman Orient Line CV* [2004] UKPC 22; [2005] 1 W.L.R. 215 at [12].

[35] *William Hare Ltd v Shepherd Construction Ltd* [2010] EWCA Civ 283; 130 Con L.R. 1 at [18].

[36] *HIH Casualty & General Ins Ltd v Chase Manhattan Bank* [2003] UKHL 6; [2003] 2 Lloyd's Rep 61 at [11] (Lord Bingham, said in the context of the "*Canada Steamship* rules" which are considered at para.7–028).

[37] *Photo Production Ltd v Securicor Transport Ltd* [1980] A.C. 827 at 850; *Whitecap Leisure Ltd v John H Rundle Ltd* [2008] EWCA Civ 429; [2008] 2 Lloyd's Rep. 216 at [20].

[38] See para.7–012.

[39] See para.7–028.

[40] See para.7–034.

[41] *Transocean Drilling UK Ltd v Providence Resources Plc* [2016] EWCA Civ 372; [2016] 2 Lloyd's Rep. 51 at [20]; *Motortrak Ltd v FCA Australia Pty Ltd* [2018] EWHC 990 (Comm) at [112]; Peel 133 L.Q.R. 7; *Federal Republic of Nigeria v JP Morgan Chase Bank NA* [2019] EWHC 347 (Comm) at [34]; affirmed [2019] EWCA Civ 1641.

[42] *Hut Group Ltd v Nobahar-Cookson* [2016] EWCA Civ 128; [2016] 1 C.L.C. 573 at [19]; *Transocean Drilling UK Ltd v Providence Resources Plc* [2016] EWCA Civ 372; [2016] 2 Lloyd's Rep. 51 at [28]; *JP Morgan Chase Bank NA v Federal Republic of Nigeria* [2019] EWCA Civ 1641 at [63]; cf. *Bates v Post Office* [2019] EWHC 606 (QB) at [638] where it is respectfully submitted Fraser J goes too far and, as a result, does not ask the operative question, i.e. whether there is any ambiguity.

[43] See, e.g. *Millar's Machinery Co Ltd v David Way & Son* (1935) 40 Comm. Cas. 204; *Saint Line Ltd v Richardsons Westgarth Ltd* [1940] 2 KB 99; *Croudace Construction Ltd v Cawood's Concrete*

restatement of the principles of interpretation in the *ICS* case,[44] the courts have held that, in the context of an exemption clause, "consequential loss" (or "indirect or consequential loss") normally refers to losses which would be recoverable only under the "second limb" of the test for remoteness laid down in *Hadley v Baxendale*.[45] It is an interpretation which is not free from difficulty,[46] and it departs from the meaning usually given to "consequential loss" in the law of damages generally.[47] Such a departure is perhaps best explained by the *contra proferentem* rule. If the meaning which is given to "consequential loss" in the law of damages generally was applied to the interpretation of exemption clauses, it may then include, for example, all lost profits, as opposed to lost profits falling within the "second limb". But if that is the intention of the parties, it is easy to use a form of words which leave no room for doubt. If the reason why a simpler and more obvious form of words is not used is because, as one suspects, the other party may not agree to it, this rather proves the point: it must be clear that the parties really intended to forego that to which they would otherwise be entitled.

**Clauses limiting liability.** Although the *contra proferentem* rule applies to all exemption clauses, the courts do not apply it with the same rigour to clauses which merely limit liability as they do to those which purport to exclude it.[48] While it is thought to be "inherently improbable" that the injured party will agree to a total exclusion of the other party's liability, "there is no such high degree of improbability that he would agree to a limitation of … liability."[49] **7–012**

*Products Ltd* [1978] 2 Lloyd's Rep 55; *British Sugar Plc v NEI Power Projects Ltd* (1998) 87 B.L.R. 42; *Deepak v ICI* [1999] 1 Lloyd's Rep 387; *BHP Petroleum Ltd v British Steel Plc* [1999] 2 Lloyd's Rep. 583; affirmed in part, [2000] 2 Lloyd's Rep. 277; *Watford Electronics Ltd v Sanderson CFL Ltd* [2001] EWCA Civ 317; [2001] B.L.R. 218; *GB Gas Holdings Ltd v Accenture (UK) Ltd* [2010] EWCA Civ 912; and the additional cases referred to in fn.46 below.

44 But note the reservation of Lord Hoffmann himself as to the correctness of the interpretation in these cases: *Caledonia North Sea Ltd v BT Plc* [2002] UKHL 4; [2002] 1 Lloyd's Rep 553 at [100]; cf. *Transocean Drilling UK Ltd v Providence Resources Plc* [2016] EWCA Civ 372; [2016] 2 Lloyd's Rep. 51 at [15].

45 See para.20–128. In context, a wider meaning may be given which would also include losses falling within the first limb: *Star Polaris LLC v HHIC-PHIL INC* [2016] EWHC 2941 (Comm); [2017] 1 Lloyd's Rep. 203.

46 *BHP Petroleum Ltd v British Steel Plc* [1999] 2 Lloyd's Rep. 583 at 597–600; affirmed in part [2000] 2 Lloyd's Rep. 277. And see the difference of opinion between Rix J in the *BHP* case and Andrew Smith J in *Ease Faith Ltd v Leonis Marine Management Ltd* [2006] EWHC 232; [2006] 1 Lloyd's Rep. 673 on the effect of words such as "or *any other* indirect or consequential (loss)"; cf. *Ferryways NV v Associated British Ports* [2008] 1 Lloyd's Rep. 639; *BSkyB Ltd v HP Enterprise Services UK Ltd* [2010] EWHC 86 (TCC); *Proton Energy Group SA v Orlen Lietuva* [2013] EWHC 2872 (Comm); [2014] 1 Lloyd's Rep. 100; *Glencore Energy UK Ltd v Cirrus Oil Services Ltd* [2014] EWHC 87 (Comm); [2014] 2 Lloyd's Rep. 1 at [96]–[98]; *Polypearl Ltd v E.On Energy Solutions Ltd* [2014] EWHC 3045 (QB).

47 *McGregor on Damages*, 20th edn (2017), para.3–012 which criticises the approach taken in the cases discussed in the text: paras 3–014–3–016.

48 *Ailsa Craig Fishing Co v Malvern Fishing Co Ltd* [1983] 1 W.L.R. 964; Palmer 45 M.L.R. 327; *George Mitchell (Chesterhall) Ltd v Finney Lock Seeds Ltd* [1983] 2 A.C. 803 at 814; cf. *McGee Group Ltd v Galliford Try Building Ltd* [2017] EWHC 87 (TCC); 170 Con L.R. 203.

49 *Ailsa Craig Fishing Co v Malvern Fishing Co Ltd* [1983] 1 W.L.R. 964 at 970.

7–013 **Liquidated damages.** Exclusion and limitation clauses must be distinguished from clauses that fix damages in advance,[50] e.g. a demurrage clause under which a charterer is required to pay a sum for each day he detains the ship for loading or unloading beyond the time allowed under the charterparty. In the *Suisse Atlantique* case[51] demurrage was fixed at $1,000 per day and one ground for the decision that it was enforceable, even though its *effect* was to limit the liability of the charterer, was that the *purpose* of the demurrage clause was not to limit damages but rather to fix in advance the damages payable in the event of certain breaches.[52] Under a limitation clause the owners would have recovered such loss as they could prove, with an upper limit of $1,000 per day. Under the demurrage clause they were entitled to $1,000 per day even if they could not prove any loss at all, or only a smaller loss. In the circumstances, the clause operated to limit the liability of the charterers; but it differed from a limitation clause in that it was capable of benefiting either party. Therefore, there was less need to apply strict rules of construction to it.

7–014 **"Duty defining" clauses.** Clauses which assume that there has been a breach and exclude or limit liability may be distinguished from those which define a contracting party's duty.[53] For example, a building contract may provide for completion by a fixed date and contain an "exception" for delays caused by strikes. This may only be another way of saying that the builder will complete by the agreed date, if strikes do not prevent him from doing so: he is under no higher duty.[54] In these cases, if delay has been caused, failure to complete on the fixed date is not a breach at all.[55] On the other hand, a clause which provided that a builder was not to be liable for loss or damage due to his defective workmanship would be an exemption clause, for it would be absurd to suppose that a building contract should impose no duty at all with respect to the standard of workmanship.[56] This is all the more obvious where the clause only limits, and does not wholly exclude, liability. While *contra proferentem* applies to exemption clauses,[57] it has been said that it does not apply to clauses which merely define the duties of a contracting party,[58] e.g. an exception in an insurance policy which determines the extent of the cover.[59] In borderline cases the distinction between the two types of clauses will not be easy to draw;[60] but one important test is

---

[50] See para.20–135 and following.

[51] *Suisse Atlantique Société d'Armement SA v NV Rotterdamsche Kolen Centrale* [1967] 1 A.C. 361.

[52] *Suisse Atlantique Société d'Armement SA v NV Rotterdamsche Kolen Centrale* [1967] 1 A.C. 361 at 395, 421, 435–436.

[53] See *The London Lion* [1980] 2 Lloyd's Rep. 456 at 468; *The Saudi Prince* [1988] 1 Lloyd's Rep. 1.

[54] Semble, the position is the same under Unfair Contract Terms Act 1977 s.3(2)(b)(i). See further, para.7–056.

[55] *The Angelia* [1973] 1 W.L.R. 210 at 230, disapproved, but on another point, in *The Nema* [1982] A.C. 724; para.19–071.

[56] cf. in another context, *The Union Amsterdam* [1982] 2 Lloyd's Rep. 432 at 436.

[57] Subject to the debate referred to above, para.7–010

[58] *The Angelia* [1973] 1 W.L.R. 210 at 231; *Kenyon Son & Craven Ltd v Baxter Hoare & Co* [1971] 1 W.L.R. 519 at 522; cf. *The Gudermes* [1993] 1 Lloyd's Rep. 311 at 328.

[59] *Impact Funding Solutions Ltd v Barrington Support Services Ltd* [2016] UKSC 57; [2017] A.C. 73 at [7]; cf. *Crowden v QBE Insurance (Europe) Ltd* [2017] EWHC 2597 (Comm); [2017] 2 C.L.C. 444.

[60] It is a question of "substance" rather than "form": see, e.g. para.9–139. See generally, Coote, *Exception Clauses* (1964).

whether the events in which a clause is expressed to operate are beyond the control of the party relying on it. If they are, the clause is likely to be regarded as a provision defining the contractual duty rather than as an exemption clause.[61]

**The rule applied in favour of the wrongdoer.** The *contra proferentem* rule is intended to protect the injured party but it may sometimes paradoxically have the opposite effect. For example, where an exemption clause is subject to a legislative requirement of reasonableness, it may, on a narrow construction of its words, satisfy that requirement while, on a wider construction it would not have done so. If the narrow construction suffices to protect the alleged wrongdoer, it will be in his interest to rely on that construction to prevent the clause from being struck down for unreasonableness.[62] 7–015

### *(ii) Burden of proof*

**General rule.** As a general rule, the burden of proving that a claim falls within the scope of an exemption clause falls on the party who seeks to rely upon it.[63] An exemption clause may be held not to cover certain serious breaches[64] and it may be alleged that the loss which has been suffered is due to such a breach. The question then arises whether it is up to the claimant to show that the breach which has occurred was of this kind or whether it is up to the defendant to show that the loss was not due to a breach of this kind (but to one that is covered by the clause). This question has arisen in a number of cases in which goods were lost by a bailee to whom they had been entrusted for storage, carriage or cleaning. On the one hand, it can be argued that the bailee should not have the burden of proving that the loss was not due to the serious breach alleged, as it is notoriously difficult to prove a negative. On the other hand, the bailee will generally be in a better position than the bailor to know how the goods were lost and the bailor should not have the burden of proving facts peculiarly accessible to the other party. After some conflict in the authorities, the latter argument has prevailed, so that the burden is on the bailee to show that the breach was not so serious as to fall outside the scope of the exemption clause.[65] 7–016

**Exception.** The cases just discussed all concern breaches by bailees of their duty with regard to the safekeeping of the goods. They do not necessarily apply where the breach consists of delay in performance and is alleged to be serious because 7–017

---

[61] *The Angelia* [1973] 1 W.L.R. 210 at 231; contrast *Blackburn v Liverpool, etc. SN Co* [1902] 1 K.B. 290 ("exception" expressly including negligence).

[62] As in *Watford Electronics Ltd v Sanderson Ltd* [2001] EWCA Civ 317; [2001] B.L.R. 143.

[63] *The Glendarroch* [1894] P. 226 at 231; *Pegler Ltd v Wang (UK) Ltd* [2000] B.L.R. 218 at 227.

[64] See para.7–020 and following.

[65] *Levison v Patent Steam Cleaning Co Ltd* [1978] Q.B. 68. See also *J Spurling Ltd v Bradshaw* [1956] 1 W.L.R. 461 at 466, 470; and cf. *United Fresh Meat Co Ltd v Charterhouse Cold Storage Ltd* [1974] 2 Lloyd's Rep. 286 (deterioration of goods in a warehouse). The normal rule as to burden of proof in such cases may be reversed by the terms of the contract: see *Thames Tideway Properties Ltd v Serfaty* [1999] 2 Lloyd's Rep. 110, but such a term may be subject to statutory control: see paras 7–043, 7–092.

of its *consequences*.[66] In such cases it is probably the claimant who has the burden of proving that the delay is so serious as not to be covered by the clause. This is consistent with the principle of the bailment cases; for the consequences of the breach on the claimant's position would be a matter peculiarly within *his* (rather than the defendant's) knowledge.

### *(iii) Fundamental breach*

7–018 **The rise and fall of the doctrine of fundamental breach.**[67] Prior to the Unfair Contract Terms Act 1977, the decisions of the courts contained examples of particularly strained construction of an exemption clause in favour of the claimant, principally in an attempt to produce a degree of consumer protection. In some cases, where there was no room even for a strained approach, the courts appeared to go further and introduce a substantive rule that no exemption clause, however worded, could be relied upon to escape a particularly serious breach of contract—often referred to as "fundamental breach".[68] In the *Suisse Atlantique* case,[69] the House of Lords had denied the existence of such a rule but did so in language which suggested that it was significant that the claimant had affirmed the contract.[70] This left room for a further argument that, where the claimant accepted the breach and terminated,[71] the contract itself came to an end and, with it, the exemption clause relied upon by the defendant.[72] This fallacious argument, and any suggestion of the existence of a substantive rule, was finally laid to rest by the House of Lords in *Photo Production Ltd v Securicor Transport Ltd*.[73] Lord Diplock confirmed[74] that the effect of electing to terminate a contract for breach is not to bring *the contract* to an end. The parties are released from performance of any future "primary" obligations,[75] but the contract itself continues, including any exemption clause. Whether the clause applies to the "secondary" obligation of the party in breach to provide a remedy is purely a matter of construction.[76] Unfortunately, the language of "fundamental breach" still persists and is

---

[66] e.g. in cases like *Suisse Atlantique Société d'Armement SA v NV Rotterdamsche Kolen Centrale* [1967] 1 A.C. 361; para.7–013.

[67] Grunfeld 24 M.L.R. 62; Guest 77 L.Q.R. 98; Reynolds 79 L.Q.R. 534; Devlin [1966] C.L.J. 192.

[68] See, e.g. *Karsales (Harrow) Ltd v Wallis* [1956] 1 W.L.R. 936; *Yeoman Credit Ltd v Apps* [1962] 2 Q.B. 508; *Charterhouse Credit Co Ltd v Tolly* [1963] 2 Q.B. 683.

[69] *Suisse Atlantique Société d'Armement Maritime SA v NV Rotterdamsche Kolen Centrale* [1967] 1 A.C. 361.

[70] For the principles of "affirmation", see para.18–089.

[71] See Ch.18.

[72] See, e.g. *Harbutts "Plasticine" Ltd v Wayne Tank Co Ltd* [1970] 1 Q.B. 447; *Kenyon Son and Craven Ltd v Baxter Hoare & Co Ltd* [1971] 1 W.L.R. 519; *Levison v Patent Steam Cleaning Co Ltd* [1978] Q.B. 69.

[73] [1980] A.C. 827; Guest 96 L.Q.R. 342; Sealy [1980] C.L.J. 252; Nicol & Rawlings 43 M.L.R. 567. See para.7–027. See also *George Mitchell (Chesterhall) Ltd v Finney Lock Seeds Ltd* [1983] 2 A.C. 803 at 813.

[74] The true effect of termination of a contract for breach had previously been clearly and accurately summarised by Lord Porter in *Heyman v Darwins Ltd* [1942] A.C. 356; para.18–016.

[75] i.e. those obligations which would have accrued *after* the date of termination; para.18–016.

[76] See para.7–020 and following.

sometimes used to refer to a repudiatory breach,[77] or a serious breach which is not covered as a matter of construction,[78] but there is no longer any substantive rule of the type just described.

**Fundamental terms.** In addition to the concept of "fundamental breach", statements can also be found in earlier cases in support of the existence of a category of "fundamental terms".[79] To the extent that this was just a way of describing terms the breach of which would always be so serious that an exemption clause would have no application,[80] it does not survive the rejection of the doctrine of fundamental breach by the House of Lords. As will be seen below, *as a matter of construction*, where a serious breach has been committed the courts will look closely at the wording of any exemption clause to determine whether it was the intention of the parties to have excluded or limited liability, even in the circumstances of such a breach. The importance of the term broken will be *a* factor in assessing the seriousness of the breach and the likelihood that the parties intended to include it within the scope of the relevant exemption clause. Since, however, each case will depend on its own particular circumstances, it is submitted, with respect,[81] that there is nothing to be gained by any longer seeking to identify a category of fundamental terms. 7–019

### *(iv) Seriousness of breach*

**Seriousness of breach as a matter of construction.** Although the doctrine of fundamental breach may have been abrogated, it is still the case, *as a matter of construction* that the more serious the breach the more closely the courts will look to determine if it was the intention of the parties to exclude or restrict liability. It is submitted that this is simply the application of *contra proferentem* to the interpretation of exemption clauses: "the degree of strictness appropriate to be applied to their construction may properly depend upon *the extent to which* they involve departure from the implied obligations."[82] Thus, general words which at first sight appear to cover even the most serious breach may not be interpreted in this sense, if to give them this effect "would lead to an absurdity, or because it would defeat the main object of the contract or perhaps for some other reason".[83] 7–020

---

[77] See Ch.18.

[78] See para.7–020.

[79] *Smeaton Hanscomb & Co Ltd v Sassoon I Setty & Co (No.1)* [1953] 1 W.L.R. 1468 at 1470; *RW Green Ltd v Cade Bros Farms* [1978] 1 Lloyd's Rep. 602.

[80] *Karsales (Harrow) Ltd v Wallis* [1956] 1 W.L.R. 936 at 943.

[81] This is a departure from the view expressed up until the 11th edition of this book, and see: Treitel, *Some Landmarks of Twentieth Century Contract Law* (2002), Ch.3; cf. *China Shipbuilding Corp v Nippon Yusen Kabukishi Kaisha* [2000] 1 Lloyd's Rep. 367 at 376.

[82] *Photo Production Ltd v Securicor Transport Ltd* [1980] A.C. 827 at 850 (Lord Diplock (emphasis added)).

[83] *Suisse Atlantique Société d'Armement Maritime SA v NV Rotterdamsche Kolen Centrale* [1967] 1 A.C. 361 at 398; para.7–026.

For example, a carrier who had undertaken to deliver goods to one person could not rely on such general words if he deliberately delivered the goods to another person, or threw them into the sea.[84]

That this is, however, only a matter of construction is confirmed by the decisions of the House of Lords in the two cases which heralded the demise of the doctrine of fundamental breach. In the *Suisse Atlantique*[85] case, the liability of charterers for delays was limited to $1,000 per day by a demurrage clause even though it was accepted[86] that the delays which had taken place were so long as to amount to a "fundamental breach".[87] In the *Photo Production*[88] case a security firm which had been engaged to safeguard a factory was protected by an exemption clause which was "clearly and fairly susceptible of one meaning only",[89] even though the firm's breach resulted in the total destruction of the factory by fire. Similarly, in the *Ailsa Craig*[90] case, a security firm was protected by a clause limiting its liability to £1,000, even though the firm had committed a "total" breach of its undertaking to provide a continuous security service for fishing boats, leading to a loss valued at £55,000. As the potential loss which might be caused by the breach was very great in proportion to the sums that could be charged for the service, and as the loss suffered was likely to have been covered by insurance, it was not inherently improbable that the owners of the boats should have agreed to the limitation of liability.

What follows is merely an indication of the sort of considerations which the courts may take into account when construing an exemption clause; in particular, where the breach may be regarded as a serious one. While it will be evident that the court's reluctance to construe a clause so as to apply to a particular breach will, in general, be directly proportioned to the gravity of that breach, each case turns on its own circumstances, including the precise form of words used by the parties.

7–021 **The status of earlier authorities on fundamental breach.** In the course of the developments which led to the rejection of fundamental breach as a substantive rule, the House of Lords overruled a small number of cases that were consistent

[84] *Sze Hai Tong Bank Ltd v Rambler Cycle Co Ltd* [1959] A.C. 576 at 587; cf. in a different context, *Kenyon Son & Craven Ltd v Baxter Hoare & Co Ltd* [1971] 1 W.L.R. 519 (warehouseman's "gross and culpable" failure to take care to prevent damage to nuts covered by an exemption clause, but Donaldson J said (at 532) that the clause would not have protected him if he had stored the nuts in the open or in an area which was prohibited by the contract); *Mediterranean Shipping Co SA v Trafigura Beheer BV* [2007] EWCA Civ 794; [2007] 2 Lloyd's Rep. 622 at [30]–[32].

[85] *Suisse Atlantique Société d'Armement Maritime SA v NV Rotterdamsche Kolen Centrale* [1967] 1 A.C. 371; Drake 30 M.L.R. 531; Fridman 7 Alberta L.Rev. 281; Treitel 29 M.L.R. 546.

[86] *Suisse Atlantique Société d'Armement Maritime SA v NV Rotterdamsche Kolen Centrale* [1967] 1 A.C. 371 at 419, 430.

[87] *Suisse Atlantique Société d'Armement Maritime SA v NV Rotterdamsche Kolen Centrale* [1967] 1 A.C. 371 at 433.

[88] *Photo Production Ltd v Securicor Transport Ltd* [1980] A.C. 827; para.7–027.

[89] *Photo Production Ltd v Securicor Transport Ltd* [1980] A.C. 827 at 851; *Swiss Bank Corp v Brink's-Mat Ltd* [1986] 2 Lloyd's Rep. 79 at 92.

[90] *Ailsa Craig Fishing Co Ltd v Malvern Fishing Co Ltd* [1983] 1 W.L.R. 964; Palmer 45 M.L.R. 322.

only with the substantive doctrine;[91] but it did not cast doubt on many other decisions in which the seriousness of the breach had been a ground for holding that an exemption clause afforded no protection. It seems that these earlier cases are to be reinterpreted rather than rejected or ignored. In support of this view, it can be said that some of the earlier judgments explicitly proceeded on the basis that the rule applied was one of construction,[92] while others, though originally based on the substantive doctrine, were later explained as illustrations of the rule of construction,[93] or on other special grounds.[94] Consequently, some of them feature below as illustrations of the courts' approach to the construction of exemption clauses in cases of serious breach.

**Non-performance and defective performance: "peas and beans".** If, as a matter of construction, a clause only exempts the defendant from liability for "defective" performance, it will not protect him if, in fact, he is guilty of "non-performance". For example, if the defendant agrees to supply peas, but sends beans instead, he cannot rely upon a clause which protects him from liability for "defective" peas, because what he has delivered are not peas at all.[95] This approach first requires the courts to establish precisely what it is for which the parties have contracted. In *George Mitchell (Chesterhall) Ltd v Finney Lock Seeds*, the defendant agreed to supply the claimant with winter cabbage seed, but mistakenly supplied autumn cabbage seed instead. The defendant relied upon an exemption clause which limited its liability for defective "seeds". Parker J[96] and a majority of the Court of Appeal[97] held that the defendant was unable to rely on the clause. It began by referring to the "seeds or plants sold or *agreed to be sold* by us"[98] and it was held that any other reference to "seeds" should be construed accordingly. On that basis, the defendant had agreed to supply winter cabbage seed and had only limited its liability for the supply of defective winter cabbage seed. The delivery of autumn cabbage seed amounted to non-performance and was not affected by the clause. The House of Lords,[99] and Lord Denning in the Court of Appeal,[100] rejected this construction and held that the defendant had simply agreed to supply "seed". Accordingly, the supply of autumn cabbage seed 7–022

[91] i.e. *Charterhouse Credit Co Ltd v Tolly* [1963] 2 Q.B. 683 ("though the result might have been reached on construction of the contract": *Photo Production Ltd v Securicor Transport Ltd* [1980] A.C. 827 at 845); *Harbutt's "Plasticine" Ltd v Wayne Tank Co Ltd* [1970] 1 Q.B. 477.

[92] *Gibaud v GE Ry* [1921] 2 K.B. 426: see *Suisse Atlantique Société d'Armement Maritime SA v NV Rotterdamsche Kolen Centrale* [1967] 1 A.C. 361 at 412; and see the judgment of Pearson LJ in *UGS Finance Ltd v National Mortgage Bank of Greece* [1964] 1 Lloyd's Rep. 446 at 453.

[93] e.g. *Levison v Patent Steam Cleaning Co* [1978] Q.B. 69: see *Photo Production Ltd v Securicor Transport Ltd* [1980] A.C. 827 at 845, 846; and cf. *Charterhouse Credit Co Ltd v Tolly* [1963] 2 Q.B. 683; see fn.91.

[94] i.e. the deviation cases: see para.7–036.

[95] *Chanter v Hopkins* (1834) 4 M. & W. 399 at 404; *Nicol v Godts* (1854) 10 Ex. 191; *Pinnock Bros v Lewis & Peat Ltd* [1923] 1 K.B. 690; *Smeaton Hanscomb & Co Ltd v Sassoon I Setty & Co (No.1)* [1953] 1 W.L.R. 1468 at 1470; *Yeoman Credit v Apps* [1962] 2 Q.B. 508; Unger [1957] J.B.L. 30.

[96] *George Mitchell (Chesterhall) Ltd v Finney Lock Seeds* [1981] 1 Lloyd's Rep. 476 at 480.

[97] *George Mitchell (Chesterhall) Ltd v Finney Lock Seeds* [1983] Q.B. 284 at 305.

[98] Emphasis added.

[99] *George Mitchell (Chesterhall) Ltd v Finney Lock Seeds* [1983] 2 A.C. 803; Clarke [1983] C.L.J. 32; Adams 46 M.L.R. 147.

[100] *George Mitchell (Chesterhall) Ltd v Finney Lock Seeds* [1983] Q.B. 284 at 296.

fell within the clause, but it would not have applied if the defendant had supplied something which did not amount to seeds at all. There is no doubt that Lord Denning and the House of Lords were encouraged to reject what might be viewed as the strained construction of the majority in the Court of Appeal, since they were able to decide that the clause was, in any event, ineffective because it was unreasonable under s.55 of Sale of Goods Act 1893[101] (a forerunner of the Unfair Contract Terms Act 1977). According to Lord Bridge, the adoption of such a "strained construction" would come "dangerously near to reintroducing by the back door the doctrine of 'fundamental breach' which this House in the *Photo Production* case had so forcibly evicted from the front."[102]

7–023 **Manner of breach.** The courts are reluctant to construe exemption clauses so as to apply to acts amounting to a deliberate disregard of the main purpose of the contract. They assume that "the parties never contemplated that such a breach should be excused or limited."[103] In accordance with this assumption, it has been held that a tug-owner could not rely on a clause which protected him from liability for "omission" and "default," where he had deliberately abandoned the tow;[104] and that a carrier of goods by sea could not rely on a clause, which protected him from liability after the goods were "discharged", where he had delivered the goods to a person who, as the carrier knew, had no authority to receive them.[105] The former substantive doctrine of fundamental breach was often invoked in cases in which a bailee of goods had delivered them to the wrong person. It was held that exemption clauses did not apply where the misdelivery was deliberate[106] or reckless,[107] but could apply where it was merely negligent.[108] Thus the manner of breach was the crucial point, since the term was broken and the consequences of the breach were (in these misdelivery cases) always the same: because of delivery to the wrong person, the goods were lost to the owner.

The cases in which the decisive factor was the manner of breach gave rise to much difficulty. For one thing, a "deliberate" breach is hard to define.[109] For another, it was puzzlingly held that a deliberate misdelivery by an employee did not deprive the employer of the protection of an exemption clause where the

---

101 As amended by Supply of Goods (Implied Terms) Act 1973.

102 *George Mitchell (Chesterhall) Ltd v Finney Lock Seeds* [1983] 2 A.C. 803 at 813.

103 *Suisse Atlantique Société d'Armement Maritime SA v NV Rotterdamsche Kolen Centrale* [1967] 1 A.C. 361 at 435; cf. at 394, 397.

104 *The Cap Palos* [1921] P. 458; cf. *A Turtle Offshore SA v Superior Trading Inc* [2008] EWHC 3034; [2009] 1 Lloyd's Rep. 177. These decisions are better explained as examples of the main purpose rule: para.7–026.

105 *Sze Hai Tong Bank Ltd v Rambler Cycle Co Ltd* [1959] A.C. 576; *The Ines* [1995] 2 Lloyd's Rep. 144 at 152; *Motis Exports Ltd v Dampskibsselskapet AF 1912* [2000] 1 Lloyd's Rep. 211.

106 *Alexander v Railway Executive* [1951] 2 K.B. 882.

107 *J Spurling Ltd v Bradshaw* [1956] 1 W.L.R. 461 at 466; cf. *United Fresh Meat Co Ltd v Charterhouse Cold Storage Ltd* [1974] 2 Lloyd's Rep. 286 at 291.

108 *Hollins v J Davy Ltd* [1963] 1 Q.B. 844; Guest 26 M.L.R. 301; cf. *The New York Star* [1981] 1 W.L.R. 138.

109 Probably it meant delivery "to someone known to have no right" to the goods: *Hollins v J Davy Ltd* [1963] 1 Q.B. 844 at 856.

employee had acted with the intention of defrauding his employer.[110] The need for "reconciling" the cases has largely disappeared now that each must be explained as turning on the construction of the clause in question. The fact that the breach was deliberate may be a ground[111] for holding that the clause was not intended to cover the breach; but it would no longer be a decisive ground. Thus an exemption clause may apply to a breach in spite of the fact that it is deliberate if it is of only trivial importance: "for example, a deliberate delay of one day in unloading."[112] This may be so even where a deliberate but trivial breach gives rise to unexpectedly serious consequences.[113] It has been said that where a breach is from the outset both deliberate and repudiatory there is a "strong presumption" that it is not intended to be covered and only the most explicit form of wording may suffice to exclude liability,[114] but this has been criticised as "heterodox" and "regressive" and not properly to "represent the current state of English law".[115]

**Express proviso for certain types of conduct.** The parties may, of course, expressly agree that any exclusion or limitation of liability does not extend to certain degrees of fault, e.g. "fraud",[116] "wilful misconduct",[117] "deliberate default",[118] or "gross negligence".[119] In one case, the parties expressly agreed that a limitation of liability did not apply to "negligence" which had the potential to deprive the clause of much if its utility. The Court of Appeal held that "negligence" referred only to claims in the "freestanding tort of negligence" and not to any conduct which also amounted to a breach of the contractor's contractual duty of care.[120] **7–024**

---

[110] *John Carter (Fine Worsteds) Ltd v Hanson Haulage (Leeds) Ltd* [1965] 2 Q.B. 495—a case to be "treated with caution": *W & J Lane v Spratt* [1970] 1 All E.R. 162 at 172; cf. also *Levison v Patent Steam Carpet Cleaning Co Ltd* [1978] Q.B. 82.

[111] e.g. *The Cap Palos* [1921] P. 458; *Sze Hai Tong Bank Ltd v Rambler Cycle Co Ltd* [1959] A.C. 576; see fn.104.

[112] *Suisse Atlantique Société d'Armement Maritime SA v NV Rotterdamsche Kolen Centrale* [1967] 1 A.C. 361 at 435.

[113] e.g. *Photo Production Ltd v Securicor Transport Ltd* [1980] A.C. 827 at 840: see para.7–027.

[114] *Internet Broadcasting Corp Ltd v MAR LLC* [2009] EWHC 84 (Ch); [2009] 2 Lloyd's Rep. 295.

[115] *AstraZeneca UK Ltd v Albemarle International Corp* [2011] EWHC 1574 (Comm); [2011] 2 C.L.C. 252 at [301]; cf. *Kudos Catering (UK) Ltd v Manchester Central Convention Complex Ltd* [2013] EWCA Civ 38; [2013] 2 Lloyd's Rep. 270 at [28].

[116] *Interactive E-Solutions JLT v O3B Africa Ltd* [2018] EWCA Civ 62; [2018] B.L.R. 167.

[117] *National Semiconductors (UK) Ltd v UPS Ltd* [1996] 2 Lloyd's Rep. 212 at 214; *De Beers UK Ltd v Atos Origin IT Services UK Ltd* [2010] EWHC 3276 (TCC); [2011] B.L.R. 274 at [206], citing Romer J in *Re City Equitable Fire Insurance Co Ltd* [1925] 1 Ch. 407; *Alpstream AG v PK Airfinance Sarl* [2015] EWCA Civ 1318; [2016] 1 C.L.C. 135 at [270].

[118] *De Beers UK Ltd v Atos Origin IT Services UK Ltd* [2010] EWHC 3276 (TCC); [2011] B.L.R. 274 at [206]; cf. *Mutual Energy Ltd v Starr Underwriting Agents Ltd* [2016] EWHC 590 (TCC); [2016] B.L.R. 312.

[119] As to the meaning of which, see *Camarata Property Inc v Credit Suisse Securities (Europe) Ltd* [2011] EWHC 479 (Comm); [2011] 1 C.L.C. 267 at [161]; citing *The Hellespont Ardent* [1997] 2 Lloyd's Rep. 547 at 586; cf. *Winnetka Trading Corp v Julius Baer International Ltd* [2011] EWHC 2030 (Ch); [2012] 1 B.C.L.C. 588 at [16].

[120] *Triple Point Technology Inc v PTT Public Co Ltd* [2019] EWCA Civ 230; [2019] 1 W.L.R. 3549. The only example given of liability in the "freestanding tort of negligence" was of personal injury caused by the contractor to one of the employer's employees, but a claim by the employee would not have been subject to the limitation of liability in the contract between the employer and the contractor in any event.

7–025 **Consequences of breach.** A breach may be serious by reason of its practical consequences. Failure to perform at the agreed time is always a breach of the same term; but an exemption clause may be construed so as to cover only slight delays and not those that are so prolonged as to cause serious prejudice to the injured party.[121] Again, goods supplied under a contract of sale or hire-purchase may not be fit for the particular purpose for which the customer has acquired them and in a number of cases it has been held that the supplier was not protected by an exemption clause because the defect was so serious as to make the thing practically useless for the customer's purposes.[122] The same result was reached where the proprietor of a parking garage had undertaken to keep a car which had been parked there locked, but left it unlocked, so that the customer's luggage was stolen.[123]

7–026 **Main "purpose" or "object" of the contract.** If the literal effect of a clause is to exempt one party from liability for *any* breach, this would seem to be inconsistent with the main purpose of the contract and may negate the idea that the parties were in a contractual relationship in the first place.[124] Since, by their conduct, it may be clear that the parties intended to create a legal relationship, the court will give the clause a restricted meaning.[125] In *The TFL Prosperity*[126] the claimant charterer suffered a financial loss because the defendant owner's ship was unable to carry the required load, in breach of warranty. The defendant sought to rely on an exemption clause, the potential effect of which was summed up by Lord Roskill as follows:

> "the charter virtually ceases to be a contract … and becomes no more than a statement of intent by the owners in return for which the charterers are obliged to pay large sums of hire, though if the owners fail to carry out their promises as to description or delivery, [the charterers] are entitled to nothing in lieu."[127]

[121] See, e.g. *Bontex Knitting Works Ltd v St John's Garage* [1943] 2 All E.R. 690; [1944] 1 All E.R. 381; *Suisse Atlantique Société d'Armement Maritime SA v NV Rotterdamsche Kolen Centrale* [1967] 1 A.C. 361; cf. *Brandt v Liverpool, etc. SN Co Ltd* [1924] 1 K.B. 575 at 597, 601.

[122] *Yeoman Credit Ltd v Apps* [1962] 2 Q.B. 508; *Farnsworth Finance Facilities Ltd v Attryde* [1970] 1 W.L.R. 1053.

[123] *Mendelssohn v Normand Ltd* [1970] 1 Q.B. 177; Treitel 32 M.L.R. 685.

[124] *Suisse Atlantique Société d'Armement Maritime SA v NV Rotterdamsche Kolen Centrale* [1967] 1 A.C. 361 at 432; cf. *Firestone Tyre & Rubber Co Ltd v Vokins & Co Ltd* [1951] 1 Lloyd's Rep. 32 at 39: "It is illusory to say—'we promise to do a thing but we are not liable if we do not do it.'"

[125] *Suisse Atlantique Société d'Armement Maritime SA v NV Rotterdamsche Kolen Centrale* [1967] 1 A.C. 361 at 432; *The Cap Palos* [1921] P. 458; *Sze Hai Tong Bank Ltd v Rambler Cycle Co Ltd* [1959] A.C. 576; *Glynn v Margetson & Co* [1893] A.C. 351; *J Evans & Son (Portsmouth) Ltd v Andrea Merzario Ltd* [1976] 1 W.L.R. 1078; *Mitsubishi Corp v Eastwind Transport Ltd* [2004] EWHC 2924; [2005] 1 Lloyd's Rep. 383; *A Turtle Offshore SA v Superior Trading Inc* [2008] EWHC 3034; [2009] 1 Lloyd's Rep. 177.

[126] [1984] 1 W.L.R. 48.

[127] *The TFL Prosperity* [1984] 1 W.L.R. 48 at 58–59; cf. *AstraZeneca UK Ltd v Albemarle International Corp* [2011] EWHC 1574 (Comm); [2011] 2 C.L.C. 252 at [313]; *Kudos Catering (UK) Ltd v Manchester Central Convention Complex Ltd* [2013] EWCA Civ 38; [2013] 2 Lloyd's Rep. 270 at [19].

He rejected that construction on the ground that it did not accord with "the true common intention of the parties".[128] The obvious danger with any approach which relies upon an inherent limitation upon the wording employed by the parties is that it comes close to the reintroduction of a substantive rule that the parties cannot agree to exempt liability for serious (i.e. fundamental) breach.[129] Thus, when it has been said that an exemption clause "cannot be taken to refer" to "total breach",[130] the best interpretation is, perhaps, that the courts will "lean against"[131] such an outcome, while not wholly ruling out the possibility of its being achieved by sufficiently clear words.[132] This also explains why it has been referred to as a principle of "last resort" which applies only where the effect of the clause is "to relieve one party from *all* liability for breach of *any* of the obligations which he has purported to undertake".[133]

**Effect of termination.**[134] It is clear from the decision in the *Suisse Atlantique* case, where the shipowners were found to have affirmed the charterparty,[135] that affirmation after a serious breach does not affect the operation of an exemption clause which is expressed so as to exclude or restrict only *the right to damages* for that breach:[136] that right continues, after affirmation, to depend on the construction of the clause. The position was formerly thought to be different if the injured party did not affirm the contract but terminated it on account of the serious breach. It was argued that, by terminating, the injured party could bring the whole contract to an end; and that in this way he could get rid of an exemption clause even though the clause, on its true construction, excluded or restricted his right to damages for the breach.[137] But this view was rejected in 7–027

[128] *The TFL Prosperity* [1984] 1 W.L.R. 48 at 58. In fact, the defendant was unable to rely on the exemption clause on the narrower ground that references to "loss" in the exemption clause referred only to physical damage to goods and not the purely financial loss which the charterer had suffered through the carrying of a smaller load than anticipated; cf. *The Chanda* [1989] 2 Lloyd's Rep. 494.

[129] See *George Mitchell (Chesterhall) Ltd v Finney Lock Seeds* [1983] 2 A.C. 803 at 814 (Lord Bridge).

[130] *Suisse Atlantique Société d'Armement Maritime SA v NV Rotterdamsche Kolen Centrale* [1967] 1 A.C. 361 at 432.

[131] *Motis Exports Ltd v Dampskibsselskapet AF 1912* [2000] 1 Lloyd's Rep. 211 at 216.

[132] *The Cap Palos* [1921] P. 458 at 471–472; *Motis Exports Ltd v Dampskibsselskapet AF 1912* [2000] 1 Lloyd's Rep. 211 at 217. See also: *The Kapitan Petko Voivoda* [2003] EWCA Civ 451; [2003] 2 Lloyd's Rep. 1 at [23], [29].

[133] *Transocean Drilling UK Ltd v Providence Resources Plc* [2016] EWCA Civ 372; [2016] 2 Lloyd's Rep. 51 at [27] (emphasis added); *Great North Eastern Railway Ltd v Avon Insurance Plc* [2001] EWCA Civ 780; [2001] Lloyd's Rep. I.R. 793; *Motortrak Ltd v FCA Australia Pty Ltd* [2018] EWHC 990 (Comm) at [129]; cf. *Fujitsu Services Ltd v IBM United Kingdom Ltd* [2014] EWHC 752 (TCC); 153 Con L.R. 203 at [61] leaving open whether the "statement of intent" rule can be applied to a particular part of the contract.

[134] For the requirements and effects of termination and affirmation generally, see Ch.18.

[135] *Suisse Atlantique Société d'Armement Maritime SA v NV Rotterdamsche Kolen Centrale* [1967] 1 A.C. 361 at 395, 398, 409, 410, 437.

[136] This view is also supported by *Chandris v Isbrandtsen-Moller Inc* [1951] 2 K.B. 240; reversed on another ground [1951] 1 K.B. at 256. For the apparently contrary decision in *Charterhouse Credit Ltd v Tolly* [1963] 2 Q.B. 683, see fn.91.

[137] e.g. *Harbutt's "Plasticine" Ltd v Wayne Tank Co Ltd* [1970] 1 Q.B. 447; overruled in *Photo Production Ltd v Securicor Transport Ltd* [1980] A.C. 827.

*Photo Production Ltd v Securicor Transport Ltd*,[138] where defendants had agreed to provide a "night patrol service" for the claimants' factory for a weekly charge of £8 15s. One of their employees started a small fire which got out of control so that the factory, worth £650,000, was destroyed. The contract contained an exemption clause which, on its true construction, applied to this breach, in spite of the seriousness of its effects. The House of Lords held that the claimants could not get rid of the clause by electing to terminate the contract; for to allow their claim on this ground would have amounted to a reintroduction of the "substantive doctrine" after its rejection in the *Suisse Atlantique* case. The effect of the claimants' election to terminate was to put an end to obligations of further performance *after* that election.[139] But it did not operate retrospectively so as to deprive the defendants of the protection of the clause with respect to loss suffered *before* that election had been made.

Where a party exercises his right to terminate for breach, he may, however, be prima facie entitled to damages not only in respect of past loss but also in respect of prospective loss, i.e. loss which he will suffer after termination, as a result of the other party's wrongful repudiation.[140] Suppose, for example, that in the *Suisse Atlantique* case the shipowners had justifiably terminated when only half the period of the charter had expired, and that they had found alternative employment for the ship for the rest of that period. They would then, but for any exemption clauses, have been entitled to damages in respect of: (i) detention of the ship before termination; and (ii) loss suffered thereafter if the alternative employment of the ship was less profitable than that under the original contract. When Lord Reid said that the shipowners would have been entitled to damages over and above the agreed demurrage if, instead of affirming the charterparty, they had justifiably terminated it,[141] he was (it is submitted) referring to this prospective loss. This assumes that the demurrage clause did not cover this type of loss, but only damages for detention under the first head.[142] If an exemption clause on its true construction did cover prospective loss under the second head, it is submitted that the injured party could not, by simply terminating the contract on account of the breach, get rid of the clause so as to recover full damages in respect of loss of this kind. To allow him to do so would not, indeed, infringe the general principle that termination for breach has no retrospective effect on the operation of exemption clauses; but it would be inconsistent with the rejection of the substantive doctrine of fundamental breach. This submission is supported by a dictum of Lord Diplock in the *Photo Production* case that liability for such loss can be "excluded or modified by express words".[143]

---

[138] [1980] A.C. 827; Guest 96 L.Q.R. 324; Sealy [1980] C.L.J. 252; Palmer and Yates [1981] C.L.J. 108; Nicol and Rawlings 43 M.L.R. 567.

[139] *Photo Production Ltd v Securicor Transport Ltd* [1980] A.C. 827 at 844–845, 849–850.

[140] See para.18–022.

[141] *Suisse Atlantique Société d'Armement Maritime SA v NV Rotterdamsche Kolen Centrale* [1967] 1 A.C. 361 at 398; cf. at 419 and 437.

[142] See further: *A/S Reidar v Arcos* [1927] 1 K.B. 352; *Chandris v Isbrandtsen-Moller* [1951] 1 K.B. 240 at 248–255; *The Bonde* [1991] 1 Lloyd's Rep. 136 at 139–142; Gay [2004] L.M.C.L.Q. 72.

[143] *Photo Production Ltd v Securicor Transport Ltd* [1980] A.C. 827 at 849; cf. *Shared Network Services Ltd v Nextiraone UK Ltd* [2011] EWHC 3845 (Comm) at [14].

### (v) *Negligence and intentional wrongs*

**Clear words needed: the "*Canada Steamship*" rules.** Legislation has severely restricted the effectiveness of clauses purporting to exempt a party from liability for negligence.[144] But even where it remains possible to exclude liability for negligence, "clear words" must be used for this purpose, since the courts regard it as "inherently improbable that one party to a contract should intend to absolve the other party from the consequence of his own negligence".[145] The requirement is most obviously satisfied where the exemption clause expressly refers to negligence: i.e. uses the word "negligence",[146] or some synonym for it.[147] It *may* be satisfied, even though there is no such express reference to negligence, if the words are nevertheless wide enough to cover negligence, e.g. if the clause exempts a party from "all liability whatsoever".[148] But whether such general words *actually are* effective to exclude liability for negligence may depend on a further distinction: namely that between cases in which, but for the clause, the party relying on it may be liable irrespective of negligence, and those in which his only possible liability is for negligence.[149] The requirements to be met are sometimes referred to as the "*Canada Steamship* rules" after a case of the same name.[150] They are also applied to indemnity clauses[151] and it has been suggested that they are "now more relevant to indemnity clauses than to exemption clauses".[152] **7–028**

**Party liable irrespective of negligence** If there is a realistic possibility (as opposed to a merely fanciful one)[153] that a party can be made liable irrespective of negligence, an exemption clause in general terms will not normally be construed so as to cover liability for negligence.[154] For example, a common **7–029**

---

[144] See paras 7–048, 7–098.

[145] *Gillespie Bros Ltd v Roy Bowles Transport Ltd* [1973] Q.B. 400 at 419; cf. *Sonat Offshore SA v Amerada Hess Development Ltd* [1988] 1 Lloyd's Rep. 145 at 157.

[146] e.g. *Spriggs v Sotheby Parke Bernet & Co* [1986] 1 Lloyd's Rep. 487; *Henderson v Merrett Syndicates Ltd* [1995] 2 A.C. 145 at 183; *Monarch Airlines Ltd v Luton Airport* [1998] 1 Lloyd's Rep. 403.

[147] *Canada SS Lines Ltd v The King* [1952] A.C. 192 at 208.

[148] *Canada SS Lines Ltd v The King* [1952] A.C. 192 at 208; such general words do not amount to an *express* reference to negligence: see *Smith v South Wales Switchgear Ltd* [1978] W.L.R. 165 at 173; and *Smith v UMB Chrysler (Scotland)* 1978 S.C. (H.L.) 1 at 12; disapproving dicta in *Gillespie v Roy Bowles Transport Ltd* [1973] Q.B. 400 at 420, 421; *The Raphael* [1982] 2 Lloyd's Rep. 42; cf. *Brown v Drake International Ltd* [2004] EWCA Civ 1629 at [21] which must be open to doubt.

[149] *Canada SS Lines Ltd v The King* [1952] A.C. 192 at 208.

[150] *Canada SS Lines Ltd v The King* [1952] A.C. 192. For a helpful summary of the "rules", see: *Capita (Banstead 2011) Ltd v RFIB Group Ltd* [2015] EWCA Civ 1310; [2016] Q.B. 835 at [16].

[151] *Smith v South Wales Switchgear Ltd* [1978] 1 W.L.R. 165.

[152] *Persimmon Homes Ltd v Ove Arup & Partners Ltd* [2017] EWCA Civ 373; [2017] B.L.R. 417 at [56].

[153] See *Hair & Skin Trading Co Ltd v Norman Airfreight Carriers Ltd* [1974] 1 Lloyd's Rep. 442; *Smith v South Wales Switchgear Ltd* [1978] 1 W.L.R. 165 at 178; *The Raphael* [1982] 2 Lloyd's Rep. 42.

[154] *Canada SS Lines Ltd v The King* [1952] A.C. 192, especially at 208; *White v J Warwick & Co Ltd* [1953] 1 W.L.R. 1285; Gower 17 M.L.R. 155; cf. *EE Caledonia Ltd v Orbit Valve Co Europe* [1994] 1 W.L.R. 221; *Casson v Ostley PJ Ltd* [2002] 18 Const. L.J. 145; *The Socol 3* [2010] EWHC 777 (Comm); [2010] 2 Lloyd's Rep. 221.

carrier of goods is strictly liable if they are lost or damaged.[155] A clause exempting him from liability "for loss or damage"[156] would be construed to refer to his strict liability only. The position is the same where it is doubtful in law whether the party relying on the clause is liable irrespective of negligence: here again a clause which does not refer to negligence will not prima facie be construed to exempt him from liability for negligence.[157] But in all the situations just described it is not absolutely necessary to refer expressly to negligence; for the rule is one of construction only and "should not be applied rigidly or mechanically so as to defeat [the] intentions [of the parties]".[158] Thus, in the *HIH* case,[159] a clause in an insurance policy excluded the insurer's right to avoid the policy for "any" misrepresentation or non-disclosure by an agent of the insured. Such general wording could have been confined to the right to avoid for innocent misrepresentation, or non-disclosure, but it was clear from all the circumstances that the intention of the parties was to "distance" the insured from any misconduct of the agent,[160] including negligence.[161] It was stressed that the "*Canada Steamship* rules" are not rules as such, but rather "helpful guidance" on the proper approach to interpretation.[162]

7–030 **Clauses limiting liability.** The fact that the clause only *limits* (and does not wholly *exclude*) liability may also be relevant. Thus a seller is strictly liable for defects in goods; so that prima facie general words would not exclude liability for defects due to his negligence. But where a seller of seeds undertook to replace defective seeds or to refund the price paid for them, it was held that a clause excluding "all [further] liability" did, as a matter of construction, apply where the

[155] A common carrier accepts for carriage the goods of all comers on a given route, subject to capacity limits. It is now "an almost extinct category": *Volcafe Ltd v Compania Sud Americana de Vapores SA* [2018] UKSC 61; [2019] A.C. 358 at [9].

[156] See *Rutter v Palmer* [1922] 2 K.B. 87; cf. *The Fantasy* [1991] 2 Lloyd's Rep. 391; affirmed [1992] 1 Lloyd's Rep. 235, without reference to this point.

[157] *The Emmanuel C* [1983] 1 Lloyd's Rep. 310; *The Oceanic Amity* [1984] 2 All E.R. 140 at 151.

[158] *The Golden Leader* [1980] 2 Lloyd's Rep. 573 at 574; cf. *Shell UK Ltd v Total UK Ltd* [2010] EWCA Civ 180; [2010] 3 W.L.R. 1192 at [12]–[16].

[159] *HIH Casualty & General Ins v Chase Manhattan Bank* [2003] UKHL 6; [2003] 2 Lloyd's Rep 61. See also: *Joseph Travers & Sons Ltd v Cooper* [1915] K.B. 73; cf. *A E Farr Ltd v Admiralty* [1953] 1 W.L.R. 965; *Trident Turboprop (Dublin) Ltd v First Flight Couriers Ltd* [2008] EWHC 1686 (Comm); [2009] 2 Lloyd's Rep. 581; affirmed [2009] EWCA Civ 290; [2010] Q.B. 86 without reference to this point; *Robinson v PE Jones (Contractors) Ltd* [2011] EWCA Civ 9; [2012] Q.B. 44 at [85].

[160] The policy was for film insurance and the insured, a syndicate of banks financing the film production, was "not in the usual position of an insured" (at [48]), being in no better a position than the insurer to estimate the risk.

[161] So far as "pure non-disclosure" was concerned (i.e. non-disclosure not amounting to an implicit misrepresentation) the House of Lords, unlike the Court of Appeal ([2001] EWCA Civ 1250; [2001] 2 Lloyd's Rep. 483), did not rely on the "unitary and absolute" nature of the duty of disclosure which makes no distinction between the ways in which it may be broken, i.e. innocently, negligently, or fraudulently; there "is no reason why the parties should not make such distinctions in a contractual provision which limits its scope": at [74].

[162] *HIH Casualty & General Ins v Chase Manhattan Bank* [2003] UKHL 6; [2003] 2 Lloyd's Rep 61 at [11]; cf. *Greenwich Millennium Village Ltd v Essex Services Group Plc* [2014] EWCA Civ 960; [2014] 1 W.L.R. 3517 at [91] (but see the distinction drawn in that case between "passive negligence", which may be covered by general words, and "active negligence", which may not).

seller was negligent in supplying seeds which were defective. One reason given for this conclusion was that the rules limiting the scope of exemption clauses in cases of negligent breach "cannot be applied in their full rigour to limitation clauses".[163]

**Party liable only for negligence.** Where a contracting party is liable only for negligence, the rule of construction discussed above obviously does not apply. It follows that in such cases an exemption clause in general terms (i.e. one not specifically referring to negligence) *can* cover negligence.[164] It used, moreover, to be thought that, in cases of this kind, a clause in general terms necessarily *did* cover negligence, since "it would otherwise lack subject-matter":[165] it would have no effect if it did not exclude the only liability which the defendant could incur. But this reasoning no longer prevails. Even where the defendant's only liability is for negligence, the clause must make it clear that *liability* is to be excluded. It may do so by general words not containing any express reference to negligence,[166] but this is not necessarily the case. For example, in *Hollier v Rambler Motors* (*AMC*) *Ltd*[167] a customer's car had been left with the defendants for repair and was damaged in a fire caused by their negligence. It was held that they could not rely on a provision that they were "not responsible for damage caused by fire to customer's cars on the premises". This was so even though they were liable for such damage only if the fire was due to their negligence: the provision merely operated as a warning to the customer that the garage proprietors were not liable for loss caused by a fire which was *not* due to their negligence. Obviously, a clause cannot be construed merely as such a warning if it expressly exempts a party from liability for negligence.[168] 7–031

Even where a defendant is liable only for negligence and clearly intends to exclude that liability, general words may fail to protect him. In *Re Polemis*[169] a clause in a charterparty provided that liability for fire should be *mutually* excepted, i.e. that neither shipowner nor charterer should be liable for fire. The

[163] *George Mitchell (Chesterhall) Ltd v Finney Lock Seeds Ltd* [1983] 2 A.C. 803 at 814; cf. *Tradigrain SA v Intertek Testing Services Canada Ltd* [2007] EWCA Civ 154; [2007] 1 C.L.C. 188 at [49].

[164] e.g. *White v Blackmore* [1972] 2 Q.B. 651; *Rutter v Palmer* [1922] 2 K.B. 87; cf. *Levison v Patent Steam Carpet Cleaning Co Ltd* [1978] Q.B. 69 at 83–84; *BHP Petroleum Ltd v British Steel Ltd* [2000] 2 Lloyd's Rep. 277 (where the duties of the party in breach were partly strict and partly duties of diligence); *Co-operative Retail Services Ltd v Taylor Young Partnerships Ltd* [2002] UKHL 17; [2002] 1 W.L.R. 1419 at [42]–[44]; *Persimmon Homes Ltd v Ove Arup & Partners Ltd* [2017] EWCA Civ 373; [2017] B.L.R. 417 (indemnity clause).

[165] *Alderslade v Hendon Laundry* [1945] K.B. 189 at 192; cf. *Gibaud v Great Eastern Ry* [1921] 2 K.B. 426; *The Ballyalton* [1961] 1 W.L.R. 929.

[166] *Alderslade v Hendon Laundry Ltd* [1945] K.B. 189; as explained in *Hollier v Rambler Motors* (*AMC*) *Ltd* [1972] 2 Q.B. 71. For a similar interpretation of indemnity clauses, see *Gillespie Bros & Co Ltd v Roy Bowles Transport Ltd* [1973] Q.B. 400; *Arthur White* (*Contractors*) *Ltd v Tarmac Civil Engineering Ltd* [1967] 1 W.L.R. 1506; and *Thompson v T Lohan* (*Plant Hire*) *Ltd* [1987] 1 W.L.R. 649; cf. *The Super Servant Two* [1990] 1 Lloyd's Rep. 1 at 8 (similar construction of cancellation clause).

[167] [1972] 2 Q.B. 71; cf. *Olley v Marlborough Court* [1949] 1 K.B. 532.

[168] *Spriggs v Sotheby Parke Bernet & Co* [1986] 1 Lloyd's Rep. 487.

[169] [1921] 3 K.B. 560.

shipowner was a common carrier and therefore liable without negligence.[170] Thus, the clause would not exempt him from liability for negligence, but only from strict liability. In view of this, it was held that the clause did not exempt the charterer from liability for negligence either, although he was liable only for negligence.

7–032 **Liability based on intentional wrongs.**[171] The "*Canada Steamship* rules" may also be applied to a clause which purports to exclude or indemnify liability based on intentional wrongdoing, e.g. under the so-called "economic torts", but it has again been stressed in this context that it is ultimately a question of the proper construction of the clause in question. For example, in *Mir Steel UK Ltd v Morris*[172] the rules were considered in relation to an indemnity against "any claim" which was held to cover potential liability for inducing a breach of contract, or unlawful means conspiracy, notwithstanding that other forms of liability might have been incurred.

## (b) Substantive control

7–033 The English common law does not, as a general rule, control the *substance* of the clause; it does not impose any further requirement that contracts must be reasonable or that contractual rights must be exercised reasonably.[173] The rejection by the courts of the substantive doctrine of fundamental breach[174] can be said to support this general common law rule. It was also rejected because it did not distinguish between contracts where some form of further protection might be justified and those where it was not, based on the bargaining power of the parties.[175] This was left to the intervention of Parliament, as we shall see below. However, there are, or may be, some surviving substantive rules of common law under which an exemption clause is regarded as unenforceable.

7–034 **Fraud.** A party cannot contract that he shall not be liable for his own fraud.[176] It remains an open question whether this rule of law, which is based on public policy, extends to the fraud of an agent.[177] There is some support for the view that

---

[170] See text to fn.155.

[171] Liability in fraud is discussed below: see para.7–034.

[172] [2012] EWCA Civ 1397; [2013] 2 B.C.L.C. 76.

[173] See, e.g. *Margaronis Navigation Agency Ltd v Henry W Peabody of London Ltd* [1965] 1 Q.B. 300; *Innisfail Laundry v Dawe* (1963) 107 S.J. 437; for exceptions, see para.4–023 and paras 20–173–20–174; and cf. *Paula Lee Ltd v Robert Zehil & Co Ltd* [1983] 2 All E.R. 390; *Walkinshaw v Diniz* [2001] 1 Lloyd's Rep. 632 at 649; affirmed [2002] 2 Lloyd's Rep. 165.

[174] See para.7–018.

[175] *Suisse Atlantique Société d'Armement Maritime SA v NV Rotterdamsche Kolen Centrale* [1967] 1 A.C. 361 at 406.

[176] *HIH Casualty & General Ins v Chase Manhattan Bank* [2003] UKHL 6; [2003] 2 Lloyd's Rep. 61; *S Pearson & Son Ltd v Dublin Corp* [1907] A.C. 351 at 353, 362; *Skipskreditforeningen v Emperor Navigation* [1998] 1 Lloyd's Rep. 67 at 76; cf. *Garden Neptune Shipping Ltd v Occidental Worldwide Investment Corp* [1990] 1 Lloyd's Rep. 330 at 335.

[177] *HIH Casualty & General Ins v Chase Manhattan Bank* [2003] UKHL 6; [2003] 2 Lloyd's Rep. 61. Of the majority in the *HIH*, case only Lord Hobhouse held that it does so extend (a view endorsed by Handley 119 L.Q.R. 537); cf. Lord Scott (dissenting) at [122].

it may be possible to exclude liability for the fraud of an agent in the *performance* of the contract, but not in its *making*.[178] That there is no direct authority on the point is probably explained by the fact that, as a matter of construction, the intention to exclude such liability "must be expressed in clear and unmistakeable terms on the face of the contract"; general words will not suffice.[179] It is unlikely that the parties will agree to a term which excludes liability for the fraud of an agent with sufficient clarity to raise the issue whether it should be lawful to do so.[180]

**Breach of fiduciary duty.** The promoter of a company is under a fiduciary duty to the company not to make a profit out of the promotion without disclosing it to the company. He cannot contract out of this duty.[181] It is submitted that any contract term by which a person who was under a fiduciary duty attempted to exempt himself from liability for a deliberate breach of that duty would be similarly ineffective.[182] **7–035**

**Deviation and analogous rules.** In a contract for the carriage of goods by sea, the benefit of an exemption clause is normally lost by a carrier who has deviated,[183] i.e. departed from the agreed or usual route without justification.[184] The same is true where a warehouseman has stored the goods in a place other than that agreed[185]; and where a bailee such as a cleaner or carrier has in the course of unauthorised subcontracting parted with the possession of goods entrusted to him.[186] On the other hand, such a person will not lose the protection of an exemption clause merely because he has broken some other term such as a **7–036**

---

178 *HIH Casualty & General Ins v Chase Manhattan Bank* [2003] UKHL 6; [2003] 2 Lloyd's Rep. 61 at [77]. See also *Tullis v Jacson* [1892] 3 Ch. 441, which was criticised in *Czarnikow v Roth, Schmidt & Co* [1922] 2 K.B. 478 at 488.

179 *HIH Casualty & General Ins v Chase Manhattan Bank* [2003] UKHL 6; [2003] 2 Lloyd's Rep. 61 at [16]. General words may suffice for fraud in the *performance* of the contract by an agent or employee: *Frans Maas (UK) Ltd v Samsung Electronics (UK) Ltd* [2004] EWHC 1502; [2004] 2 Lloyd's Rep. 251 at [152] ("liability howsoever arising" held to limit liability for employee's wilful default).

180 *HIH Casualty & General Ins v Chase Manhattan Bank* [2003] UKHL 6; [2003] 2 Lloyd's Rep. 61 at [81].

181 *Gluckstein v Barnes* [1900] A.C. 240.

182 Contrast *Bogg v Raper, The Times*, 22 April 1998. See also: *Armitage v Nurse* [1998] Ch. 241; *Spread Trustee Co Ltd v Hutcheson* [2011] UKPC 13; [2012] 2 A.C. 194 (liability of trustee for *gross negligence* excluded); *Barnsley v Noble* [2016] EWCA Civ 799; [2017] Ch. 191; McCormack [1998] Conv. 100.

183 *Joseph Thorley Ltd v Orchis SS Co Ltd* [1907] 1 K.B. 660; *Stag Line Ltd v Foscolo, Mango & Co Ltd* [1932] A.C. 328. A strict approach is taken to the interpretation of any clause in the contract said to confer a liberty to deviate: *Glynn v Margetson & Co* [1893] A.C. 351; cf. *GH Renton & Co v Palmyra Trading Corp of Panama* [1957] A.C. 149.

184 See *Kish v Taylor* [1912] A.C. 604 at 617; Carriage of Goods by Sea Act 1971 Sch. art.IV 4: deviation may be justified for the purpose of saving life or property at sea, or if it is "reasonable".

185 *Woolf v Collis Removal Services* [1948] 1 K.B. 11 at 15; cf. *The OOCL Bravery* [2000] 1 Lloyd's Rep. 394 at 401 (parking container lorry in street instead of in secured depot).

186 *Davies v Collins* [1945] 1 All E.R. 247; *Garnham, Harris & Elton Ltd v Alfred W Ellis (Transport) Ltd* [1967] 1 W.L.R. 940.

carrier's undertaking to supply a seaworthy ship[187]; or a warehouseman's undertaking to exercise reasonable care in looking after the goods.[188] The reason for the distinction is sometimes said to be that the terms as to the route and as to the place where the goods are to be stored are fundamental,[189] while the other terms mentioned are not. Thus, in the deviation cases, the courts are not concerned with the effect of the breach: *any* departure from the agreed route "however for practical purposes irrelevant"[190] normally deprives the shipowner of the benefit of the exemption clause. Furthermore, the deviation cases appear to represent an exception to the general rule that termination does not retrospectively deprive a party of the benefit of exemption clauses. It is commonly held that the carrier is deprived of the benefit of exemption clauses in respect of loss which has occurred before the owner of the goods elected to terminate the contract.[191] One possible explanation for this state of the law is that it follows from the special considerations which affect deviation. One reason for classifying deviation as a breach of a "fundamental term" is that it deprives the cargo-owner of his insurance cover[192]; and since it so deprives him automatically and "as from the time of the deviation",[193] the same reasoning would seem to support the view that deviation deprives the carrier of the benefit of exemption clauses in the contract of carriage from the same time and with the same retrospective effect.

The special rule as to the effects of deviation has been criticised.[194] It appears to be a surviving remnant of the discredited doctrine of fundamental breach[195] and the preferable view is that it should be "assimilated into the ordinary law of contract".[196] On that basis, the question of whether an exemption clause applies and, if so, from when, should be decided simply as a matter of the proper construction of the clause in question. This view is supported by developments in

[187] *The Europa* [1908] P. 84; *Kish v Taylor* [1912] A.C. 604. If the unseaworthiness *causes* the loss, the carrier cannot rely on the exceptions provided under Carriage of Goods by Sea Act 1971: see *Maxine Footwear Ltd v Canadian Government Merchant Marine Ltd* [1959] A.C. 589; but he can rely on the *limitation* so provided: *The Happy Ranger* [2002] EWCA Civ 694; [2002] 2 Lloyd's Rep. 357 at [38].

[188] *J Spurling Ltd v Bradshaw* [1956] 1 W.L.R. 461; *Kenyon Son & Craven Ltd v Baxter Hoare & Co Ltd* [1971] 1 W.L.R. 519.

[189] See *Smeaton Hanscomb & Co v Sassoon I Setty* [1953] 1 W.L.R. 1468 at 1470, describing deviation as a breach of a fundamental term.

[190] *Suisse Atlantique Société d'Armement Maritime SA v NV Rotterdamsche Kolen Centrale* [1967] 1 A.C. 361 at 423, e.g. it is irrelevant that the deviation did not cause, or increase the risk of, loss: *Joseph Thorley Ltd v Orchis SS Co Ltd* [1907] 1 K.B. 660; *James Morrison & Co v Shaw, Savill & Albion Co Ltd* [1916] 2 K.B. 783.

[191] See the authorities cited at fnn.183, 185.

[192] *Hain SS Co v Tate & Lyle Ltd* (1936) 41 Com. Cas. 350 at 354. In fact the goods-owner may not suffer the hardship on which the rule is based, since his insurance policy may provide that he is to be "held covered" in case of deviation at a premium to be arranged: see *State Trading Corp of India v S M Golodetz Ltd* [1989] 2 Lloyd's Rep. 277 at 289.

[193] Marine Insurance Act 1906 s.46(1); *The Good Luck* [1992] A.C. 233; para.18–008 (dealing with the corresponding wording in s.33(3)).

[194] *Farr v Hain SS Co* (*The Tregenna*) 121 F 2d. 940 at 944 (1941). This case arose from the same facts as *Hain SS Co v Tate & Lyle Ltd*, above; cf. Reynolds, *Butterworth Lectures* 1990–91, pp.29–52.

[195] See para.7–018

[196] *The Antares (Nos 1 and 2)* [1987] 1 Lloyd's Rep. 424 at 430; *The Kapitan Petko Voivoda* [2003] EWCA Civ 451; [2003] 2 Lloyd's Rep. 1 at [14]; *Dera Commercial Estate v Derya Inc* [2018] EWHC 1673 (Comm); [2019] 1 Lloyd's Rep. 57 at [107].

relation to stowage on deck which has been equated with deviation. In *The Kapitan Petko Voivoda*,[197] the question of whether a carrier which was guilty of unauthorised deck stowage could rely on the package limitation laid down in the Hague Rules was regarded purely as a question of construction. Since the relevant limitation was expressed to apply "in any event",[198] the carrier was entitled to rely upon it.[199] Given the analogy between the substantive rule of deviation and the doctrine of fundamental breach, it may be argued that the decisions upon which it is based[200] have been impliedly overruled by the decisions of the House of Lords in the *Suisse Atlantique* case[201] and the *Photo Production* case.[202] This submission has been rejected[203] and for now it seems that it is a rule which, on account of its historical and commercial background, must be treated as sui generis.[204]

**Unreasonableness.** It is sometimes said that exemption clauses may be held invalid on the ground that they are "unreasonable in themselves or irrelevant to the main purpose of the contract"[205] or "so unreasonable that no-one could contemplate that they exist".[206] Unreasonableness of the latter kind can certainly be relevant to the process of incorporation of a clause in a contract, in the sense that the degree of notice required for this purpose increases in proportion to the unusualness of the clause.[207] Some dicta go further and suggest that even a properly incorporated clause can be unenforceable at common law on the ground of unreasonableness[208] or unfairness.[209] But no decision squarely supports this view,[210] and the existence of the legislative requirements now applied to **7–037**

[197] *The Kapitan Petko Voivoda* [2003] EWCA Civ 451; [2003] 2 Lloyd's Rep. 1.

[198] Article IV(5). The same wording is included in the limitation provided by the Hague-Visby Rules art.IV(5).

[199] The earlier decision in *The Chanda* [1989] 2 Lloyd's Rep. 494 was overruled. See also: *The Antares (No.2)* [1987] 1 Lloyd's Rep. 424; *The Pembroke* [1995] 2 Lloyd's Rep. 290 (*The Chanda* followed in New Zealand); *The Happy Ranger* [2002] EWCA Civ 694; [2002] 2 Lloyd's Rep. 357; cf. *Dera Commercial Estate v Derya Inc* [2018] EWHC 1673 (Comm); [2019] 1 Lloyd's Rep. 57 at [111] (one year time bar (obiter)).

[200] *Stag Line Ltd v Foscolo, Mango & Co Ltd* [1932] A.C. 328; *Hain SS Co v Tate & Lyle Ltd* (1936) 41 Com. Cas. 350.

[201] *Suisse Atlantique Société d'Armement Maritime SA v NV Rotterdamsche Kolen Centrale* [1967] 1 A.C. 361; para.7–020.

[202] *Photo Production Ltd v Securicor Transport Ltd* [1980] A.C. 827; para.7–027.

[203] *Dera Commercial Estate v Derya Inc* [2018] EWHC 1673 (Comm); [2019] 1 Lloyd's Rep. 57 at [113].

[204] *Photo Production Ltd v Securicor Transport Ltd* [1980] A.C. 827 at 845, per Lord Wilberforce.

[205] *Watkins v Rymill* (1883) 10 Q.B.D. 178 at 189.

[206] *Thompson v London, Midland & Scottish Ry* [1930] 1 K.B. 41 at 56.

[207] See para.6–012.

[208] See, e.g. Lord Denning MR in *Thornton v Shoe Lane Parking Ltd* [1971] 2 Q.B. 163 at 170; *Levison v Patent Steam Carpet Cleaning Co Ltd* [1978] Q.B. 68 at 69.

[209] *Laceys (Wholesale) Footwear Ltd v Bowler International Ltd* [1997] 2 Lloyd's Rep. 369 at 384–385 (Brooke LJ); the majority based their decision on the construction of the clause.

[210] It is rejected in other dicta: *Van Toll v South Eastern Ry* (1862) 12 C.B.N.S. 75 at 85; *Grand Trunk Ry of Canada v Robinson* [1915] A.C. 740 at 747; *Ludditt v Ginger Coote Airways Ltd* [1947] A.C. 233 at 242.

exemption clauses has reduced both the need for, and the likelihood of, the recognition of unreasonableness or unfairness as grounds for the invalidity of exemption clauses at common law.

### (c) Other common law limitations

7–038 **Collateral contract.** An exemption clause in a document with reference to which the parties contract can be overridden by an express inconsistent undertaking given at or before the time of contracting. Thus a buyer of goods by auction can recover damages for breach of an oral undertaking given at the time of sale although the printed conditions of sale exempt the seller from all liability for defects.[211] To bring this rule into operation, there must be an "express specific oral promise"[212] which is inconsistent with the exemption clause and which takes effect as a collateral contract.[213] A party is not prevented from relying on a clause merely because no reference was made to it at the time of contracting, so that (in this sense) it can be said to be inconsistent with the terms expressly agreed. Where a series of contracts is made under a master agreement, an obligation imposed by that agreement may similarly override an exemption clause contained in a written document evidencing the terms of the particular contract in question.[214]

## 2. UNFAIR CONTRACT TERMS ACT 1977[215]

7–039 The Unfair Contract Terms Act 1977 ("UCTA") deals almost exclusively with exemption clauses in contracts.[216] It makes some such clauses ineffective in all circumstances and others ineffective unless they comply with a requirement of reasonableness.

---

[211] *Couchman v Hill* [1947] K.B. 554; *Harling v Eddy* [1951] 2 K.B. 739; cf. *Brikom Investments Ltd v Carr* [1979] Q.B. 467 at 480; *Hughes v Pendragon Sabre Ltd* [2016] EWCA Civ 18; [2016] 1 Lloyd's Rep 311 at [34].

[212] *George Mitchell (Chesterhall) Ltd v Finney Lock Seeds Ltd* [1983] Q.B. 284 at 309; affirmed [1983] 2 A.C. 803, without reference to this point.

[213] For the requirements of which, see paras 3–065, 6–038, 9–063.

[214] *Gallaher v BRS Ltd and Containerway & Roadferry* [1974] 2 Lloyd's Rep. 440; *J Evans & Son (Portsmouth) Ltd v Andrea Merzario* [1976] 1 W.L.R. 1078; cf. *Mendelssohn v Normand Ltd* [1970] 1 Q.B. 177.

[215] Coote (1978) 41 M.L.R. 312; Sealy [1978] C.L.J. 15; Reynolds [1978] 1 L.M.C.L.Q. 201; Adams and Brownsword 104 L.Q.R. 94. What follows is concerned with the 1977 Act as amended by the Consumer Rights Act 2015 which applies to contracts entered into on or after 1 October 2015: SI 2015/1630. For contracts made before that date, see the previous edition of this book.

[216] UCTA also deals with certain notices not having contractual effect, e.g. in s.2. Attempts by such notices to exclude or restrict tort liability are beyond the scope of this book.

## (a) Scope[217]

**"Business liability".** With one limited exception,[218] the controls on the enforceability of exemption clauses in UCTA apply only to "business liability". Under s.1(3) "business liability" is defined as "liability for breach of obligations or duties arising: (a) from things done or to be done by a person in the course of a business (whether his own business or another's); or (b) from the occupation of premises used for business purposes of the occupier".[219] Such a person will in the following discussion be called B. 7–040

**"In the course of a business".** For the purpose of UCTA, "business" includes a profession and activities of government departments or local or public authorities.[220] There is no direct authority on the meaning of "in the course of a business" under s.1(3), but the same wording appeared in s.12 as part of the definition of "dealing as consumer".[221] Since the concept of "dealing as consumer" is now redundant under UCTA,[222] s.12 has been repealed, but the cases decided under that section may still be relevant in determining "business liability" under s.1(3). In the cases decided under s.12 it was held that a contract is made "in the course of" a business only if it is "integral" to that business or, if not integral, it nevertheless forms part of the regular course of dealing of that business.[223] That may be contrasted with the more literal interpretation given to the phrase "in the course of a business" in s.14(2) of the Sale of Goods Act 1979 under which an irregular and non-integral sale is covered provided it was sufficiently part of the business of the party in question and not a purely private sale.[224] It is submitted that, with the repeal of s.12, the opportunity should be taken by the courts to adopt a consistent approach and, when the issue arises directly under s.1(3), the interpretation relied upon under s.14(2) of the Sale of Goods Act should prevail.[225] 7–041

---

[217] The issues which are discussed in this part concern the general scope of UCTA. Certain specific situations and types of contract are also excluded from its scope, but they are more easily explained below (see paras 7–119–7–122) after consideration of the Act in general.

[218] Section 6(4); see below, para.7–049. But see also s.8 which amends s.3 of the Misrepresentation Act 1967: para.9–132.

[219] UCTA s.1(3). Liability to persons gaining access to premises for recreational or educational purposes is excepted, in certain circumstances.

[220] UCTA s.14.

[221] Under s.12(1) it was a question of whether a party "*makes the contract* in the course of a business", whereas s.1(3) refers more generally to "obligations or duties arising: (a) from *things done or to be done by a person* in the course of a business". As far as contractual liability is concerned, the relevant thing done must be the making (and performance) of the contract, but "things done" is also wide enough to cover, for example, liability in negligence which might be excluded by a non-contractual notice, to which UCTA will also apply if it is a "business liability".

[222] See para.7–042.

[223] *R & B Customs Brokers Ltd v United Dominions Trust Ltd* [1988] 1 W.L.R. 321; *Feldaroll Foundry Plc v Hermes Leasing (London) Ltd* [2004] EWCA Civ 747; *Air Transworld Ltd v Bombardier Inc* [2012] EWHC 243 (Comm); [2012] 1 Lloyd's Rep. 349.

[224] *Stevenson v Rogers* [1999] Q.B. 1028; cf. *GE Capital Bank Ltd v Rushton* [2005] EWCA Civ 1556; [2006] 1 W.L.R. 899 (whether purchaser "carries on business" for the purpose of s.27(2) of the Hire Purchase Act 1964).

[225] cf. the definitions given to "trader" and "consumer" under the Consumer Rights Act 2015: see paras 7–090—7–091.

7–042 **Non-consumer contracts.** Section 12 of UCTA was repealed because a contract made between a "trader" and a "consumer" ("a consumer contract"), which might previously have fallen within UCTA, is now governed solely by the Consumer Rights Act 2015. The relevant parts of the 2015 Act with which this chapter is concerned apply only to consumer contracts (and some consumer notices), so defined, and in some circumstances only when it is the trader who supplies the consumer with goods, digital content, or services; not vice versa.[226] They do not apply to a contract made between parties neither of whom is a consumer, nor a contract made between two consumers, nor in relation to some provisions of the 2015 Act in the unlikely event that a consumer supplies a trader with goods, digital content, or services. However, not all such contracts fall within UCTA. Save for the limited exception already referred to,[227] the requirement of a "business liability"[228] means that UCTA is confined to contracts between parties neither of whom is a consumer.

7–043 **Types of clause covered.** They key sections of UCTA limit the effectiveness of clauses that "exclude or restrict" liability.[229] To the same extent these sections also prevent a party from doing certain analogous things: making liability or its enforcement subject to "restrictive or onerous conditions",[230] e.g. imposing a short time-limit within which claims must be brought;[231] excluding or restricting a particular right or remedy, or subjecting a person to any prejudice in consequence of pursuing a right or remedy,[232] e.g. excluding the right of set-off;[233] and excluding or restricting rules of evidence or procedure.[234]

7–044 **A test of substance.** Other clauses which do not in terms exclude or restrict liability may nevertheless have this effect in substance. For example, a provision in a contract between X and Y that Y will indemnify X for any liability which X may incur to Y is in substance a clause excluding X's liability to Y and will be treated as such for the purposes of UCTA.[235] A clause requiring an employee to work such long hours as would lead to injury to his health could likewise be regarded as one which exempted the employer from liability which, but for the

---

[226] Such as the provisions found in Pt 1 of the 2015 Act, namely ss.1–57: ss.1(1), 1(3).

[227] UCTA s.6(4); see para.7–049.

[228] See para.7–040.

[229] See, e.g. ss.2–3 and 6–7.

[230] UCTA s.13(1)(a).

[231] e.g. *Granville Oil & Chemicals Ltd v Davis Turner & Co Ltd* [2003] EWCA Civ 570; [2003] 2 Lloyd's Rep. 356.

[232] UCTA s.13(1)(b).

[233] *Stewart Gill Ltd v Horatio Myer & Co Ltd* [1992] Q.B. 600; *Esso Petroleum Ltd v Milton* [1997] 1 W.L.R. 938; *Schenkers Ltd v Overland Shoes Ltd* [1998] 1 Lloyd's Rep. 499; *Axa Sun Life Services Plc v Campbell Martin Ltd* [2011] EWCA Civ 133; [2011] 2 Lloyd's Rep. 1; cf. *BOC Group Plc v Centeon Plc* [1999] 1 All E.R. (Comm) 970.

[234] UCTA s.13(1)(c).

[235] *Phillips Products Ltd v Hyland* [1987] 1 W.L.R. 659 ("no mystique" about exclusion clauses; "look at the effect of the term … at its substance"). An indemnity against X's liability to a third party is now no longer regulated by UCTA since the control of such a clause was confined to what is now regarded as a consumer contract falling within the Consumer Rights Act 2015; s.4 of UCTA is accordingly repealed.

clause, he would incur in respect of the injury.[236] On the other hand, a valid agreed damages clause[237] is probably not subject to UCTA, for such a clause may extend as well as restrict liability. An agreement in writing to submit present or future differences to arbitration is not to be treated as excluding or restricting liability.[238]

**Excluding or restricting duties.** In two cases, UCTA explicitly[239] prevents a party from excluding or restricting *duties* (as opposed to *liabilities*): namely where a provision purports to exclude: (i) the duty of care giving rise to liability in negligence;[240] or (ii) the duties arising out of terms implied by statute in contracts for the supply of goods.[241] Thus a provision purporting to exclude or restrict a seller's duty as to the fitness of goods for a particular purpose would only be effective to the extent permitted by UCTA.[242] **7–045**

At common law a distinction is sometimes drawn between clauses which exclude or restrict liability and those which prevent it from arising[243] and in some cases this distinction is no doubt relevant for the purposes of UCTA. For example, if a seller of goods expressly warned the buyer *not* to use goods for a specified purpose, any implied term of fitness for that particular purpose would be negatived, and the warning would not be subject to UCTA.[244] But to give such effect to all provisions which might at common law prevent liability from arising would, it has been said, "emasculate"[245] UCTA. In *Smith v Eric S Bush*[246] the House of Lords has therefore held that a clause purporting to exclude responsibility for negligence on the part of the valuer of a house was subject to the test of reasonableness under UCTA. The decision was based on s.13(1), by which a term purporting to exclude the duty of care giving rise to liability in negligence is to be treated as a term excluding or restricting liability. In order to determine whether such a duty existed, the court must disregard the term purporting to exclude it, and ask itself whether, but for the existence of the term, there would have been such a duty; if so, the effectiveness of the term is then subject to the restrictions imposed by UCTA.[247] *Smith v Eric S Bush* deals only with clauses purporting to exclude the duty of care giving rise to liability in negligence. It seems that the "but for" test there formulated would not apply to

[236] *Johnstone v Bloomsbury Health Authority* [1992] Q.B. 333.

[237] See para.7–013; para.20–135.

[238] UCTA s.13(2). A jurisdiction agreement may fall within s.13(1)(a) (making enforcement subject to "restrictive or onerous conditions"): *Snookes v Jani-King (GB) Ltd* [2006] EWHC 289; [2006] I.L.Pr. 19.

[239] The practical effect of s.3(2)(b)(i) (para.7–056) may also be to prevent a party from excluding or restricting duties which were "reasonably expected".

[240] See the reference to s.2 in s.13(1).

[241] See the reference to ss.6 and 7 in s.13(1).

[242] See s.6(1A).

[243] cf. para.7–014.

[244] *Wormell v RHM Agriculture (East) Ltd* [1987] 1 W.L.R. 1091; cf. *Harlingdon & Leinster Enterprises Ltd v Christopher Hull Fine Art Ltd* [1990] 1 All E.R. 737 at 753, and the examples given at para.7–014.

[245] *Smith v Eric S Bush* [1990] 1 A.C. 831 at 848.

[246] [1990] 1 A.C. 831; cf. *Davies v Parry* [1988] 1 E.G.L.R. 147.

[247] The possible application of s.13(1) would appear to have been overlooked in *Galliford Try Infrastructure Ltd v Mott Macdonald Ltd* [2008] EWHC 1570 (TCC); 120 Con L.R. 1 at [332].

the sale of goods case referred to above. In order to determine for what "particular purpose" goods had been bought, a warning such as the one given in that case would, it is submitted, have to be taken into account. However, it seems likely that the courts will also "look behind" certain other clauses which are similarly being used in an obvious attempt to evade UCTA.[248]

7–046 **Non-contractual notices.** In relation to liability in negligence, UCTA also applies to non-contractual notices which purport to exclude or restrict liability.[249]

### (b) Wholly ineffective terms and notices

7–047 In the following cases, terms or notices which attempt to exclude or restrict liability[250] are wholly ineffective under UCTA.

7–048 **Negligence liability: death or personal injury.** Under s.2(1) B[251] cannot by any contract term or notice exclude or restrict[252] his liability for death or personal injury[253] resulting from negligence to persons generally or any particular person.[254] "Negligence" includes "the breach of any obligation, arising from the express or implied terms of a contract, to take reasonable care or exercise reasonable skill in the performance of the contract".[255] Section 2(1) does not apply where death or personal injury results from a breach of contract or duty which can be, and is, committed without negligence, e.g. where a seller supplies defective goods to a buyer, where a producer incurs "product liability" in respect of defective products, or where a person who does work for the provision of a dwelling fits defective components.[256] Clauses purporting to exclude liability for such breaches may, however, be ineffective under other provisions of UCTA,[257] or under other Acts.[258]

7–049 **Sale of goods and hire-purchase.** Section 6(1) provides that liability for breach of the undertakings as to title implied by statute[259] into contracts for the sale or hire-purchase of goods cannot be excluded or restricted by reference to any contract term. As a general principle the only types of terms to which UCTA applies are those purporting to exclude or restrict "business liability".[260] Section

---

248 cf. paras 9–139–9–140.
249 See paras 7–048, 7–052.
250 In the extended sense described in para.7–043.
251 See para.7–040
252 *Phillips Products Ltd v Hyland* [1987] 1 W.L.R. 659, fn.235, where the effect in substance of the indemnity clause was to exclude liability in negligence; cf. *Thompson v T Lohan (Plant Hire) Ltd* [1987] 1 W.L.R. 649.
253 As defined by s.14.
254 Section 2(1) does not apply to a term in a consumer contract, or a consumer notice (s.2(4)), but see the corresponding provision in the Consumer Rights Act 2015 s.65: para.7–098.
255 UCTA s.1(1)(a).
256 For strict liability in such cases, see para.17–066.
257 e.g. ss.6, 7.
258 Defective Premises Act 1972 s.1(1) and s.6(3); Consumer Protection Act 1987 ss.5 and 7(1).
259 By Sale of Goods Act 1979 s.12 and Supply of Goods (Implied Terms) Act 1973 s.8.
260 See para.7–040.

6(4), however, provides that the liabilities referred to "in this section" are not only "business liabilities ... but include those arising under any contract of sale of goods or hire-purchase agreement". It follows that a private (non-business) seller cannot exclude or restrict liability for breach of the implied undertakings as to title.

**Other contracts for the supply of goods.** Section 7 deals with contracts for the supply of goods other than contracts of sale and hire-purchase, e.g. contracts of exchange, pledge or hire. So far as B's[261] liability for breach of the implied terms as to title in such contracts[262] is concerned, a distinction must be drawn. Such liability cannot be excluded or restricted by reference to any contract term where the contract is one by which he transfers or agrees to transfer the property in the goods to another:[263] this rule would, for example, apply to a contract of exchange. But where the contract is not one by which property is transferred or to be transferred (e.g. where it is one of pledge or hire) attempts by B to exclude or restrict such liability are subject only to the test of reasonableness.[264] 7–050

### (c) Terms and notices subject to the requirement of reasonableness[265]

In the following cases, exemption clauses are, under UCTA, subject to the requirement of reasonableness. 7–051

**Negligence liability: harm other than death or personal injury.** By s.2(2) the requirement of reasonableness applies to a contract term or notice[266] by which B[267] seeks to exclude or restrict[268] his liability for negligence[269] giving rise to loss or damage other than death or personal injury.[270] The meaning of "negligence" has been considered above, in relation to liability for personal injury or death.[271] 7–052

**Contractual liability.** Terms which purport to exclude or restrict B's[272] liability for breach of contract, or exclude or restrict the level of performance which may be expected of B are regulated by s.3 of UCTA. There is however a limit to the 7–053

---

[261] See para.7–040.
[262] Supply of Goods and Services Act 1982 s.2.
[263] UCTA s.7(3A).
[264] UCTA s.7(4).
[265] Brown and Chandler 109 L.Q.R. 41.
[266] A trustee exemption clause is neither a term nor a notice and is not, therefore, subject to s.2(2), nor to UCTA generally: *Baker v JE Clark & Co* [2006] EWCA Civ 464; [2006] Pens L.R. 131.
[267] See para.7–040.
[268] See fn.250.
[269] As defined by s.1(1).
[270] Section 2(2) does not apply to a term in a consumer contract, or a consumer notice (s.2(4)), but see the Consumer Rights Act 2015 s.62: para.7–108.
[271] See para.7–048.
[272] See para.7–040.

scope of s.3,[273] and some uncertainty as to the type of term to which it extends so far as B's level of performance is concerned.[274]

7–054 **Written standard terms of business.** Section 3 applies to a contract made on B's "written standard terms of business".[275] The burden of proving this requirement is on the party relying on the Act.[276] There is no statutory definition of "written standard terms of business". In almost every contract there will be some negotiation, about the subject matter and the price if nothing else, but if other terms are introduced by B in standard form and are not the subject of negotiation, or are left "effectively untouched", it is likely that the contract has been made on B's written standard terms.[277] It is not essential that B has previously used the same terms on numerous occasions, but it may be necessary in some cases to establish by discovery whether a "one-off" contract is, in fact, simply one party's standard terms of business.[278] It is, inevitably, a question of degree and there is some evidence that the courts take into account the underlying mischief towards which the reference to "standard" terms is aimed, i.e. the relative bargaining power of the parties.[279] Where B makes use of a standard form drafted by a trade association or similar body, the terms of that form are B's "standard terms" only if he "invariably or at least usually" contracted on those terms.[280] An employee does not deal on the employer's written standard terms of business, in relation to terms which regulate the work he does for the employer, and the payment he receives for it.[281]

---

[273] See para.7–054.

[274] See paras 7–056–7–057.

[275] If the contract is a consumer contract, s.3 does not apply, but see the Consumer Rights Act 2015 s.62: para.7–108. For an exception to the requirement that, between parties acting in the course of a business, the contract must be on written standard terms, see Late Payment of Commercial Debts (Interest) Act 1998 s.14(2); para.20–068.

[276] *African Export-Import Bank v Shebah Exploration & Production Co Ltd* [2017] EWCA Civ 845; [2018] 1 W.L.R. 487 at [18]. If, however, the reasonableness test applies, the burden of proving that the term is reasonable is on B: see para.7–062.

[277] *St Alban's City and District Council v International Computers Ltd* [1995] F.S.R. 686 at 706; cf. *Pegler v Wang (UK) Ltd* [2000] B.L.R. 218; *Hadley Design Associates Ltd v Westminster London Borough Council* [2003] All E.R. (D.) 164; *Ferryways NV v ABP* [2008] EWHC 225 (Comm); [2008] 1 Lloyd's Rep. 639 at [92]; *Yuanda (UK) Co Ltd v WW Gear Construction Ltd* [2010] EWHC 720 (TCC); [2010] B.L.R. 435 at [20]–[21]; *Commercial Management (Investments) Ltd v Mitchell Design & Construct Ltd* [2016] EWHC 76 (TCC); 164 Con L.R. 139 at [61]–[73]; *African Export-Import Bank v Shebah Exploration & Production Co Ltd* [2017] EWCA Civ 845; [2018] 1 W.L.R. 487 at [35].

[278] *Oval (717) Ltd v Aegon Insurance (UK) Ltd* (1997) 54 Con L.R. 74; *The Chester Grosvenor Hotel Company Ltd v Alfred McAlpine Management Ltd* (1991) 56 B.L.R. 115; *South West Water Services Ltd v ICL* [1999] B.L.R. 420.

[279] *Salvage Association v CAP Financial Services* [1995] F.S.R. 654 at 672.

[280] *British Fermentation Products Ltd v Compair Reavell Ltd* [1999] 2 All E.R. (Comm) 389 at [46]; approved in *African Export-Import Bank v Shebah Exploration & Production Co Ltd* [2017] EWCA Civ 845; [2018] 1 W.L.R. 487 at [20].

[281] *Commerzbank AG v Keen* [2006] EWCA Civ 1536; [2007] I.C.R. 623 (leaving open that there may be some terms which are covered, i.e. where the employee is the recipient of the goods or services which are the business of the employer).

**Excluding or restricting liability for breach of contract.** If s.3 applies, B[282] cannot by reference to any contract term exclude or restrict[283] any liability in respect of his own breach,[284] except in so far as the term satisfies the requirement of reasonableness.[285] 7–055

**Rendering performance different from that reasonably expected.** Section 3(2)(b)(i) also applies the test of reasonableness to any term by reference to which B[286] claims "to be entitled .... to render a contractual performance substantially different from that which was reasonably expected of him".[287] It has been held that a clause giving a lender power to vary interest rates did not fall within s.3(2)(b)(i) since the exercise of that power was not a "contractual performance."[288] Where a term in a contract for services entitles the provider to change those services, the questions what the recipient reasonably expected and whether the change is substantial can obviously give rise to difficult questions of fact and degree.[289] It seems that s.3(2)(b)(i) could apply to provisions in a contract between a carrier and a tour operator purporting to entitle the carrier to change the advertised route, accommodation or means of transport.[290] B could not rely on the provision even though he was not actually obliged to render the performance expected: the criterion is the reasonable expectation of the other party, not the obligation of B under the contract. There would, however, be no such reasonable expectation where the contract made it clear that, while B would endeavour to provide a particular service, he also reserved the right to substitute a reasonable alternative.[291] Section 3(2)(b)(i) may also apply to an "entire agreement" clause.[292] 7–056

---

[282] See para.7–040.

[283] In the extended sense discussed in para.7–043.

[284] Breach of the terms implied by legislation into contracts for the sale or supply of goods is dealt with separately: see paras 7–048—7–049, 7–058—7–059.

[285] UCTA s.3(2)(a).

[286] See para.7–040.

[287] In addition to the cases cited below, see also: *Brigden v American Express Bank* [2000] I.R.L.R. 94; *Peninsula Business Services Ltd v Sweeney* [2004] I.R.L.R. 49; *City Index Ltd v Stevenson* 6 November 2001; *Durabella Ltd v J Jarvis & Sons Ltd* 83 Con L.R. 145; *Lalji v Post Office Ltd* [2003] EWCA Civ 1873; *Rolls Royce Power Engineering Plc v Ricardo Consulting Engineers Ltd* [2003] EWHC 2871 (TCC); [2004] 2 All E.R. (Comm) 129 at [75]–[76]; *Bates v Post Office* [2019] EWHC 606 (QB) at [1081]–[1082].

[288] *Paragon Finance Ltd v Nash* [2001] EWCA Civ 1466; [2002] 1 W.L.R. 685 at [75].

[289] Contrast *Timeload Ltd v British Telecommunications Plc* [1995] E.M.L.R. 459 with *Zockoll Group Ltd v Mercury Communications Ltd (No.2)* [1999] E.M.L.R. 385.

[290] e.g. it would apply to a situation such as that which arose in *Anglo-Continental Holidays Ltd v Typaldos Lines (London) Ltd* [1967] 2 Lloyd's Rep. 61. A contract of this kind between the tour operator and consumer would be governed by Package Travel and Linked Travel Arrangements Regulations 2018 (SI 2018/634). Under reg.11, where the "organiser" is "constrained" to alter "the main characteristics of the travel services", the "traveller" is entitled to cancel the contract. For the relationship between such legislation and the Consumer Rights Act 2015, see para.7–120.

[291] *Duffy v Newcastle United Football Club Ltd, The Times*, 7 July 2000.

[292] *Axa Sun Life Services Plc v Campbell Martin Ltd* [2011] EWCA Civ 133; [2011] 2 Lloyd's Rep. 1 at [50]; cf. *SAM Business Systems Ltd v Hedley & Co* [2002] EWHC 2733 (TCC); [2003] 1 All E.R. (Comm) 465 at [62].

7–057 **Rendering no performance at all.** Under s.3(2)(b)(ii) B[293] cannot by reference to any contract term "claim to be entitled … in respect of the whole or any part of his contractual obligation to render no performance at all". This provision, like s.3(2)(b)(i), is not free from difficulty. The criterion is not (as it is under s.3(2)(b)(i)) what the other party reasonably expects: it is the obligation undertaken by B. If the "contract term" gives B a totally free discretion whether to perform or not, there might be no "contractual obligation" on B at all; and in such a case the requirement of reasonableness need not be satisfied. Section 3(2)(b)(ii) would also not apply to a clause defining B's duty[294] in such a way that in the circumstances which have occurred no duty arose; e.g. where B promised to perform "subject to strikes" and strikes have prevented performance.

In a number of other situations, the scope of s.3(2)(b)(ii) is harder to determine. A contract may provide that B is entitled to cancel it by giving notice, or on the occurrence of specified events, e.g. on the other party's failure to perform (whether or not it amounts to a breach) or on some other event, such as the other party's death.[295] Or it may require B to perform only when the other party's performance has been rendered in full, or when some prescribed part of the performance has been rendered.[296] For example, a building contract may provide that nothing is to be paid till the work is completed, or that instalments of the price are to be paid only when specific parts of the work have been done. Such provisions might at first sight appear to be literally within s.3(2)(b)(ii); but it does not seem to have been the purpose of that enactment to alter the law as to cancellation clauses of the kind mentioned above,[297] or as to the effect of the other party's breach on the obligations of B. It is submitted that the scope of the enactment must be narrowed by a restrictive interpretation of the opening words of s.3(2), according to which B cannot do the three things specified in the subsection "by reference to any contract term". These words should be taken to mean "by reference *only* to such a term"—not by reference to it combined with other circumstances justifying B's refusal, such as a failure by the other party to perform his part.[298]

7–058 **Supply of goods: correspondence with description, quality, fitness for purpose, etc.** By s.6(1A), the requirement of reasonableness applies to a term in a contract for the sale or hire-purchase of goods purporting to exclude or restrict liability for breach of the statutorily implied terms[299] as to correspondence of the goods with description or sample, or as to their quality or fitness for a particular purpose.[300] As we have seen, s.6 is not confined to "business liability", so a

---

[293] See para.7–040.

[294] See para.7–045; s.3 is *not* referred to in s.13(1).

[295] See para.18–067.

[296] See paras 17–031—17–040.

[297] The view that s.3(2)(b)(ii) does not apply to such cancellation clauses is supported by *Paragon Finance Ltd v Nash* [2001] EWCA Civ 1466; [2002] 1 W.L.R. 685 at [76]–[77]; the question was left open in *Timeload Ltd v British Telecommunications Plc* [1995] E.M.L.R. 459 at 468; cf. *Hadley Design Associates v Westminster CC* [2003] EWHC 1617; [2004] T.C.L.R. 1.

[298] For the position under the Consumer Rights Act 2015 Sch.2 Pt.1 para.18, see para.7–116.

[299] Sale of Goods Act 1979 ss.13–15: Supply of Goods (Implied Terms) Act 1973 ss.9–11.

[300] This provision does not apply where the buyer or hirer is a consumer (s.6(5)), but see the provisions applicable under the Consumer Rights Act 2015 s.31: para.7–094.

private (non-business) seller might also have to satisfy the requirement of reasonableness. However, in some cases, the statutorily implied terms only arise at all where the supplier acts in the course of a business. This is true of the implied terms as to satisfactory quality and fitness for a particular purpose.[301] A similar rule is laid down by s.7(1A) with regard to terms in other contracts for the supply of goods (such as contracts of hire or exchange) purporting to exclude liability for breach of similar terms implied by law in such contracts.[302]

**Supply of goods: ownership or possession.** We have seen that B cannot exclude or restrict his liability for breach of the implied terms as to title in contracts of sale and hire-purchase, and in certain other contracts under which he transfers or agrees to transfer the property in goods[303] (such as contracts of exchange). In contracts for the transfer or supply of goods which fall outside this group, s.7(4) applies the requirement of reasonableness to terms by which B seeks to exclude or restrict such liability: this would, for example, be the position in contracts of pledge,[304] or hire. As s.7 applies only to "business liability",[305] a private supplier's right to exclude or restrict liability in respect of defects of title in contracts of this kind is in no way affected by UCTA. This is also true where a private supplier enters into a contract (other than one of sale or hire-purchase) by which he transfers or agrees to transfer the property in goods, e.g. where the contract is one of exchange.[306] Where, on the other hand, the contract is one of sale or hire-purchase, a term by which even a private supplier seeks to exclude or restrict liability for breach of the implied undertakings as to title is simply ineffective,[307] without regard to its reasonableness. **7–059**

**Misrepresentation.** Section 8 of UCTA[308] amends s.3 of the Misrepresentation Act 1967 and terms excluding or restricting liability for pre-contractual misrepresentation are now subject to the requirement of reasonableness as defined by UCTA.[309] The requirement is not restricted to "business liability" and is further discussed in Ch.9.[310] **7–060**

---

301 Sale of Goods Act 1979 s.14(2); Supply of Goods (Implied Terms) Act 1973 s.10(2) and (3) (for goods supplied to a non-consumer); Where the supply is to a consumer, the same terms are implied (or "treated as included") under the Consumer Rights Act 2015, but only as against a "trader": see para.6–072.

302 This provision does not apply where the person supplied is a consumer (s.7(4A)), but see the provisions applicable under the Consumer Rights Act 2015 s.31: below, para.7–094.

303 See paras 7–049–7–050.

304 See Supply of Goods and Services Act 1982 s.1(2)(e).

305 UCTA s.1(3); see para.7–040.

306 The restriction on the effectiveness of terms excluding liability for breach of the implied terms as to title in such contracts is imposed by s.7(3A) which, like the rest of s.7 only applies to "business liability": s.1(3); see para.7–040.

307 UCTA s.6(1); para.7–049.

308 UCTA s.8.

309 Section 3 of the 1967 Act does not apply to a term in a consumer contract (s.3(2)), but see the Consumer Rights Act 2015 s.62: para.7–108.

310 See para.9–132.

## (d) The test of reasonableness

**7–061** A judicially administered requirement of reasonableness is open to the objection that it is a source of uncertainty.[311] To meet this objection, UCTA lays down a number of rules and guidelines.[312] The vast majority of reported cases in which the reasonableness test has been applied have been concerned with contracts between two businesses and, after the Consumer Rights Act 2015, UCTA is almost exclusively confined to such contracts.[313] In such cases there is an evident judicial awareness that a finding of unreasonableness should not lightly be reached, given the interference with freedom of contract and the parties' allocation of risk.[314] As stated by Chadwick LJ[315]:

> "Where experienced businessmen representing substantial companies of equal bargaining power negotiate an agreement, they may be taken to have had regard to the matters known to them. They should, in my view, be taken to be the best judge of the commercial fairness of the agreement which they have made; including the fairness of each of the terms in that agreement. They should be taken to be the best judge on the question whether the terms of the agreement are reasonable. The court should not assume that either is likely to commit his company to an agreement which he thinks is unfair, or which he thinks includes unreasonable terms. Unless satisfied that one party has, in effect, taken unfair advantage of the other – or that a term is so unreasonable that it cannot properly have been understood or considered – the court should not interfere."[316]

The reference to one party taking "unfair advantage of the other" is to some extent borne out by the cases, in that those few in which the relevant term has been found to be unreasonable might best be explained on the basis that there was no conscious and deliberate allocation of risk, i.e. there was an element of "unfair surprise".[317] It has been argued that this should be the principal criterion for a finding of unreasonableness under UCTA.[318]

**7–062** **Burden of proof.** Where the requirement of reasonableness applies, the burden of proving (and of pleading[319]) that it is satisfied lies on the party claiming that it is met.[320]

---

311 Treitel, *Doctrine and Discretion in the Law of Contract* (1981), pp.13–19.

312 See paras 7–062–7–065.

313 See para.7–042.

314 The courts have occasionally felt it appropriate to make a finding of reasonableness even in support of an application for summary judgment: *Macquarie International Investments Ltd v Glencore UK Ltd* [2008] EWHC 2716 (Comm); [2008] 2 B.C.L.C. 565.

315 Echoing the sentiments expressed by Lord Diplock at the outset of UCTA: *Photo Production Ltd v Securicor Transport Ltd* [1980] A.C. 827 at 851.

316 *Watford Electronics Ltd v Sanderson Ltd* [2001] EWCA Civ 317; [2001] B.L.R. 143 at [55]. See also: *Granville Oil & Chemicals Ltd v Davis Turner & Co Ltd* [2003] EWCA Civ 570; [2003] 2 Lloyd's Rep. 356 at [31]; *Goodlife Foods Ltd v Hall Fire Protection Ltd* [2018] EWCA Civ 1371; [2018] B.L.R. 491 at [88]–[93] rejecting a submission that Chadwick LJ's observations should be confined to terms which have been the subject of detailed negotiations.

317 See, e.g. *Britvic Soft Drinks Ltd v Messer UK Ltd* [2002] EWCA Civ 548; [2002] 2 Lloyd's Rep. 368; *Bacardi Martini Beverages Ltd v Thomas Hardy Packaging Ltd* [2002] EWCA Civ 549; [2002] 2 Lloyd's Rep. 379.

318 See Beale in Burrows & Peel (eds), *Contract Terms* (2007).

319 *Sheffield v Pickfords Ltd* [1997] C.L.C. 648.

320 UCTA s.11(5).

**Time for determining reasonableness.** The question whether a contract term satisfies the requirement of reasonableness is determined by reference to the time at which the contract was made.[321] If the term was a fair and reasonable one to be included having regard to the circumstances which were or should reasonably have been known to or in the contemplation of the parties at that time, its effectiveness will not be impaired by subsequent events. 7–063

**Resources and insurance.** Section 11(4) of UCTA lays down two guidelines for determining the reasonableness of provisions limiting a person's liability to a specific sum of money. In those circumstances, regard is to be had to: (a) the resources which that person could expect to be available to him for the purpose of meeting the liability; and (b) how far it was open to him to cover himself by insurance.[322] Under the second of these guidelines, a clause limiting the liability of a manufacturer for defects would not be reasonable if he could have insured against the liability without materially raising the price of his product (particularly if it would have been difficult or virtually impossible for the customer to have insured against the loss),[323] or if he actually had so insured.[324] On the other hand, a clause limiting the liability of a person engaged in the storage or carriage of goods would be reasonable if he had little knowledge of the nature or value of the goods, and if the goods could be more cheaply insured by their owner than by the bailee.[325] In applying the second guideline, the court considers the *availability* of insurance to the defendant, rather than his *actual* insurance position.[326] It may sometimes appear as if it is the actual insurance position of the parties which has been taken into account, but this may be explained as the best evidence of what was available.[327] The two guidelines stated in s.11(4) do not contain an exhaustive list of factors to be taken into 7–064

[321] UCTA s.11(1). In the case of a non-contractual notice (para.7–046) the relevant time is the time when the liability arose or, but for the notice, would have arisen: s.11(3): see *Monarch Airlines Ltd v London Luton Airport* [1998] 1 Lloyd's Rep. 403.

[322] UCTA s.11(4). The subsection is in terms applicable only to terms which *limit* (as opposed to those which wholly *exclude*) liability: *The Flamar Pride* [1990] 1 Lloyd's Rep. 434 at 438; but the guidelines in question can be applied by analogy to clauses of the latter kind: see para.7–066.

[323] *Salvage Association v CAP Services* [1995] F.S.R. 654.

[324] *George Mitchell (Chesterhall) Ltd v Finney Lock Seeds Ltd* [1983] A.C. 803 at 817, decided under earlier and now superseded legislation not containing this guideline; *St Albans City and District Council v International Computers Ltd* [1995] F.S.R. 686, reversed but not on the application of the reasonableness test: [1996] 4 All E.R. 481.

[325] *Singer (UK) Ltd v Tees & Hartlepool Port Authority* [1988] 2 Lloyd's Rep. 164; cf. *Goodlife Foods Ltd v Hall Fire Protection Ltd* [2018] EWCA Civ 1371; [2018] B.L.R. 491 at [77] (insurance "a critical factor": at [83]).

[326] *Singer (UK) Ltd v Tees & Hartlepool Port Authority* [1988] 2 Lloyd's Rep. 164 at 169; *The Flamar Pride* [1990] 1 Lloyd's Rep. 434 at 439; *Monarch Airlines Ltd v London Luton Airport* [1998] 1 Lloyd's Rep. 403 at 413.

[327] *Balmoral Group Ltd v Borealis (UK) Ltd* [2006] EWHC 1900 (Comm); [2006] 2 Lloyd's Rep. 629 at [422]; cf. *St Albans City and District Council v International Computers Ltd* [1995] F.S.R. 686. Quaere the approach taken in *Trustees of Ampleforth Abbey Trust v Turner & Townsend Management Ltd* [2012] EWHC 2137 (TCC); 144 Con L.R. 115.

account in deciding whether a limitation clause satisfies a reasonableness test. A negative answer to this question may, for example, be given because of the "insufficient clarity"[328] of the clause.

7–065 **Schedule 2 guidelines.** Where a term in a contract for the supply of goods is subject to the requirement of reasonableness under ss.6 or 7,[329] UCTA provides five further guidelines in Sch.2:[330] the strength of the bargaining positions of the parties relative to each other;[331] whether the customer received an inducement to agree to the term (e.g. in the form of a lower price) or could have bought elsewhere without being subjected to a similar term;[332] the customer's knowledge or means of knowledge of the existence and extent of the terms;[333] where the term excludes or restricts liability if some condition is not complied with, whether it was reasonable at the time of the contract to expect that compliance with that condition would be practicable;[334] and whether the goods were manufactured, processed or adapted to the special order of the customer. Under these guidelines, the fact that the contract was in a standard form settled after negotiations between trade associations to which both parties belonged is relevant to the issue of reasonableness; for it helps to show that its terms were "not imposed by the strong upon the weak".[335] A fortiori, terms are unlikely to be struck down for unreasonableness under UCTA where the contract in which they are contained was made between commercial companies "of equal bargaining power"[336] after negotiations in which each party had made concessions to the other.[337] But where a term has *not* been the subject of negotiation, it may be struck down, even in a contract between such parties, if its effect is to "contradict

---

328 *Overseas Medical Supplier Ltd v Orient Transport Services Ltd* [1999] 2 Lloyd's Rep. 273 at 280.

329 See paras 7–058—7–059.

330 UCTA s.11(2).

331 See, e.g. *Bates v Post Office* [2019] EWHC 606 (QB) at [1097] and following.

332 See *Balmoral Group Ltd v Borealis (UK) Ltd* [2006] EWHC 1900 (Comm); [2006] 2 Lloyd's Rep. 629 at [423]. Contrast *Goodlife Foods Ltd v Hall Fire Protection Ltd* [2018] EWCA Civ 1371; [2018] B.L.R. 491 at [73], where the court also took into account (at [79]) that B also offered alternative terms at a different price.

333 The question whether a term has been incorporated in the contract is, however, a separate question, as is recognised by the concluding words of s.11(2): see paras 6–004—6–016.

334 See *Commercial Management (Investments) Ltd v Mitchell Design & Construct Ltd* [2016] EWHC 76 (TCC); 164 Con L.R. 139.

335 *RW Green Ltd v Cade Bros Farms Ltd* [1978] 1 Lloyd's Rep. 602 at 607; *Granville Oil & Chemicals Ltd v Davis Turner & Co Ltd* [2003] EWCA Civ 570; [2003] 2 Lloyd's Rep. 356; contrast *George Mitchell (Chesterhall) Ltd v Finney Lock Seeds Ltd* where the conditions were not negotiated by the National Farmers Union but simply introduced by seed merchants without objection from farmers: see [1983] 2 A.C. 803 at 817, but even where terms are produced by one of the parties, and not by a trade association, some weight may still be given to the fact they are "normal in the trade": *Expo Fabrics UK Ltd v Naughty Clothing Co Ltd* [2003] EWCA Civ 1165 at [27].

336 *Watford Electronics Ltd v Sanderson Ltd* [2001] EWCA Civ 317; [2001] B.L.R. 143 at [55]; *Granville Oil & Chemicals Ltd v Davis Turner & Co Ltd* [2003] EWCA Civ 570; [2003] 2 Lloyd's Rep. 356 at [31].

337 *Watford Electronics Ltd v Sanderson Ltd* [2001] EWCA Civ 317; *Axa Sun Life Services Plc v Campbell Martin Ltd* [2011] EWCA Civ 133; [2011] 2 Lloyd's Rep. 1.

a fundamental assumption that all parties have made in this respect",[338] e.g. where a seller of ingredients to a manufacturer of beverages supplied a defective ingredient which made the resulting product unsaleable.

**Statutory guidelines applied by analogy.** These statutory guidelines no doubt help to reduce the uncertainty to which the requirement of reasonableness gives rise; but the restrictions on their scope are hard to understand. It is not easy to see why the strength of the bargaining positions of the parties is relevant only in contracts for the supply of goods; nor why the five guidelines[339] which can apply where a seller delivers goods of the wrong *quality*[340] do not also apply where he delivers goods of the wrong *quantity*.[341] The courts have remedied this defect in the wording of UCTA by treating the guidelines referred to in paras 7–064—7–065 as being of general application, so that they may be applied by analogy to other types of contracts and other types of clauses.[342] 7–066

**Other factors.** Even in relation to the situations covered by them, the statutory guidelines are by no means exhaustive; indeed it has been said that it is "impossible to draw up an exhaustive list of factors to be taken into account when a judge is faced with this very difficult question".[343] In *Smith v Eric S Bush*[344] the House of Lords held that a term purporting to exclude the liability in negligence of surveyors (engaged by a building society) to buyers of dwelling houses did not satisfy the reasonableness test. The principal factors leading to this conclusion were that there was no equality of bargaining power, that the houses were of modest value so that it was not reasonable to expect the buyers to commission their own structural survey, and that the surveyors could easily have insured against the risk without unduly increasing their charges.[345] On the other hand, a disclaimer might be reasonable if the task undertaken had been one of great difficulty and complexity; if the value of the subject-matter had been very high, so that insurance against professional liability would have been very expensive or impossible to obtain;[346] or if it would have been reasonable for the injured party to have taken steps to discover the truth. Thus the requirement of reasonableness was held to have been satisfied where an estate agent disclaimed liability in 7–067

[338] *Britvic Soft Drinks Ltd v Messer UK Ltd* [2002] EWCA Civ 548; [2002] 2 Lloyd's Rep. 368 at [26]; *Bacardi Martini Beverages Ltd v Thomas Hardy Packaging Ltd* [2002] EWCA Civ 549; [2002] 2 Lloyd's Rep. 379 at [26].

[339] See para.7–065.

[340] UCTA s.6(1A): see para.7–058.

[341] If s.3 applies: see para.7–053.

[342] *Singer (UK) Ltd v Tees & Hartlepool Port Authority* [1988] 2 Lloyd's Rep. 164 at 169; *The Flamar Pride* [1990] 1 Lloyd's Rep. 434 at 439; *Overseas Medical Supplies Ltd v Orient Transport Services Ltd* [1999] 2 Lloyd's Rep. 273 at 276–277; *West v Ian Finlay & Associates* [2014] EWCA Civ 316; [2014] B.L.R. 214 at [65]; cf. *Overland Shoes Ltd v Schenkers Ltd* [1998] 1 Lloyd's Rep. at [498].

[343] *Smith v Eric S Bush* [1990] 1 A.C. 831 at 858.

[344] [1990] 1 A.C. 831; Kaye 52 M.L.R. 841; for other factors relevant to the issue of reasonableness, see *George Mitchell (Chesterhall) Ltd v Finney Lock Seeds Ltd* [1983] 2 A.C. 803, decided under an earlier (now superseded) statutory reasonableness test; *Overseas Medical Supplies Ltd v Orient Transport Services Ltd* [1999] 2 Lloyd's Rep. 273 at 280.

[345] *Smith v Eric S Bush* [1990] 1 A.C. 831 at 851–854, 858–859.

[346] *Smith v Eric S Bush* [1990] 1 A.C. 831 at 859.

respect of representations as to area made to the prospective purchaser who later contracted to buy the property in question for £875,000:[347] in such a transaction the purchaser could be expected to make his own investigations before exchanging contracts. The availability to the *other* party of an opportunity of discovering the defect in respect of which he is seeking to exclude liability can likewise be relevant to the issue of reasonableness. Thus where the seller of a car was a company which had been brought into the transaction purely to provide finance, it was said that the test of reasonableness would have been satisfied (if applicable) because the company had never seen the car.[348]

7–068 **Nature of decision on reasonableness.** A decision on the issue of reasonableness is not merely an exercise of judicial discretion;[349] for it involves the application of statutory and judge-made guidelines. Nevertheless, in the *George Mitchell* case Lord Bridge described such a decision as one on which there "will sometimes be room for a legitimate difference of judicial opinion"; and as one with which an appellate court should not interfere "unless satisfied that it proceeded on some erroneous principle or was plainly and obviously wrong".[350] These remarks are intended to restrict, but not to rule out, the possibility of successful appeals on the issue of reasonableness. An appeal may, for example, succeed where the trial judge has held the clause to be unreasonable by attributing to it a wider meaning than that which, in the view of the appellate court, it could, on its true construction, bear.[351]

7–069 **"Severability" under the reasonableness test.** A term which fails the test of reasonableness is ineffective and it is clear that the court has no power to modify it so as to make it reasonable, e.g. by allowing a limitation of liability where the contract had provided for total exclusion,[352] or by striking out an unreasonably low limitation in the contract and substituting a higher one that the court regards as reasonable. What is much less clear is the extent to which a court may sever a term, by deleting or ignoring such parts of the clause that are automatically ineffective, or unreasonable, if what remains would be effective. There are two aspects of UCTA which may suggest that this should be possible. First, the Act does not invalidate contractual provisions as such: it simply says that specified

[347] *McCullagh v Lane Fox & Partners Ltd* [1996] 1 E.G.L.R. 35.

[348] *R & B Customs Brokers Ltd v United Dominions Trust Ltd* [1988] 1 W.L.R. 321 at 332. But contrast *Lease Management Services v Purnell Secretarial Services* [1994] Tr. L.R. 337; *Sovereign Finance v Silver Crest Furniture* [1997] C.C.L.R. 76; *Danka Rentals Ltd v Xi Software Ltd* [1998] 17 Tr. L.R. 74.

[349] *George Mitchell (Chesterhall) Ltd v Finney Lock Seeds Ltd* [1983] 2 A.C. 803 at 816; cf. *Comemsco Ltd v Contrapol* (unrep.), referred to by Kerr LJ in [1983] Q.B. 284 at 315.

[350] *George Mitchell (Chesterhall) Ltd v Finney Lock Seeds Ltd* [1983] 2 A.C. 803 at 810; *Phillips Products Ltd v Hyland* [1987] 1 W.L.R. 659 at 669; *St Albans City & District Council v International Computers Ltd* [1996] 4 All E.R. 481; *Schenkers Ltd v Overland Shoes Ltd* [1998] 1 Lloyd's Rep. 499; *Overseas Medical Supplies Ltd v Orient Transport Services Ltd* [1999] 2 Lloyd's Rep. 273 at 276. For a case where the Court of Appeal indicated that it might have found a term to be reasonable, but the finding of unreasonableness was nonetheless upheld, see *Cleaver v Schyde Investments Ltd* [2011] EWCA Civ 929; [2011] 2 P & C.R. 21.

[351] *Watford Electronics Ltd v Sanderson Ltd* [2001] EWCA Civ 317; [2001] B.L.R. 143.

[352] *George Mitchell (Chesterhall) Ltd v Finney Lock Seeds Ltd* [1983] 2 A.C. 803 at 816; cf. *Esso Petroleum Ltd v Milton* [1997] 1 W.L.R. 938.

liabilities cannot be excluded or restricted "by reference" to them. Secondly, where the test of reasonableness applies, a term is ineffective "except in so far as"[353] it satisfies the requirement of reasonableness. The words "in so far as" would seem to allow the court to hold one part of a term effective and another ineffective. That has not always proved to be the case and it is not easy to reconcile the decisions reached by the courts.

**One term, or several?** As a preliminary point, to the extent that it is the term which is rendered ineffective, the court has to decide whether it is dealing with one term, or several. This is not determined solely as a matter of drafting since otherwise the application of UCTA would depend on the "adventitious consideration" of whether a clause had been divided into its component parts, or expressed as one.[354] Thus, in a number of cases where the contract on its face contained one compendious term, the courts have held that in fact it amounted to a number of different terms, e.g. where one clause contained both an exclusion of certain types of liability and a limitation on any remaining liability.[355] As Rix LJ observed: "It is true that clause 23 was not divided up into separate sub-clauses in the way that … I have treated it by introducing the numbers (1), (2), (3) and (4) … Nevertheless, it is plain that clause 23(4) is *independent* of clause 23(3)."[356] The willingness of the court to recognise that what may appear to be one term is in fact a number of terms, some of which may be effective under UCTA while others are not, amounts to a severance of sorts.[357] But what is the position if the court decides that it is dealing with just one term? 7–070

**One term which is in part wholly ineffective and in part subject to the test of reasonableness.** In *Trolex Products Ltd v Merrol Fire Protection Engineers Ltd*[358] Staughton LJ proceeded on the basis that one term of the contract purported to exclude liability for personal injury, which was wholly ineffective, and to exclude liability for other loss or damage, which was subject to the test of reasonableness, but nonetheless reasonable standing on its own.[359] He had no doubt that severance was permissible in these circumstances and held that "if part of a term is ineffective by reason of section 2(1),[360] the remainder can 7–071

[353] UCTA ss.2(2), 3(2), 6(1A), 7(1A) and 7(4).

[354] *Trolex Products Ltd v Merrol Fire Protection Engineers Ltd* unreported 20 November 1991 CA Nourse LJ.

[355] *Regus (UK) Ltd v Epcot Solutions Ltd* [2008] EWCA Civ 361; [2009] 1 All E.R. (Comm) 586. See also: *Trolex Products Ltd v Merrol Fire Protection Engineers Ltd* unreported 20 November 1991 CA (Nourse LJ; cf. Staughton LJ para.7–071); *Watford Electronics Ltd v Sanderson Ltd* [2001] EWCA Civ 317; [2001] B.L.R. 143; *J Murphy & Sons Ltd v Johnston Precast Ltd* [2008] EWHC 3024 (TCC) at [137]. Contrast *Lobster Group Ltd v Heidelberg Graphic Equipment Ltd* [2009] EWHC 1919 (TCC) at [131], where it must be assumed the different parts of the clause were not sufficiently "independent".

[356] *Regus (UK) Ltd v Epcot Solutions Ltd* [2008] EWCA Civ 361; [2009] 1 All E.R. (Comm) 586 at [46] (emphasis added).

[357] *Regus (UK) Ltd v Epcot Solutions Ltd* [2008] EWCA Civ 361; [2009] 1 All E.R. (Comm) 586 at [45] (Rix LJ: "… it is now conceded that clause 23(3) could be *severed* so as to leave clause 23(4) intact" (emphasis added).

[358] unreported 20 November 1991 CA.

[359] cf. para.7–070.

[360] See para.7–048.

nevertheless be upheld as reasonable." An alternative explanation for the decision in the *Trolex* case is that the term in question amounted to several terms. This was the view of Nourse LJ, but, if it was one term, he agreed with Staughton LJ.[361] The decision in the *Trolex* case is not easy to reconcile with the decision in *Witter Ltd v TBP Industries Ltd*[362] where it was held that a term which excluded liability for *any* pre-contractual misrepresentation was unreasonable and ineffective,[363] even if it was only relied upon to exclude liability for non-fraudulent misrepresentation,[364] because it purported also to exclude liability for fraud, i.e. a different liability which cannot be excluded at all.[365] If the issue is approached strictly as a matter of severance, the two decisions might be distinguished on the basis that, in the *Trolex* case, it was a question of excising the reference to personal injury, whereas in the *Witter* case the problem arose because of the broad reference to "any misrepresentation",[366] which could only be remedied by the addition of a reference to non-fraudulent misrepresentation. While it is not possible to read such a term as amounting to several terms, i.e. one excluding liability for fraudulent misrepresentation and another excluding liability for non-fraudulent misrepresentation, it may nonetheless be effective by finding that, as a matter of construction, the general wording employed by the parties was not intended to exclude liability for fraud at all.[367] In practice, and no doubt as a consequence of the decision in the *Witter* case, the parties themselves will usually ensure that this is the case by *expressly* agreeing that liability in fraud is not excluded.[368]

7–072 **One term which is subject only to the test of reasonableness.** In the *Trolex* case Staughton LJ observed that "[t]he wider question, whether one can sever words when only reasonableness is in issue, does not arise" and he expressed no opinion upon it. This was the issue in *Stewart Gill Ltd v Horatio Myer & Co Ltd*[369] in which a clause excluded a customer's right to withhold payment of any amount due from him to a supplier by reason of "any payment credit set off [or] counterclaim". It was held that it was unreasonable to exclude his right to rely on payment already made, or any credit and that, as a consequence, the clause as a

[361] See also *Goodlife Foods Ltd v Hall Fire Protection Ltd* [2017] EWHC 767 (TCC); [2017] B.L.R. 389; affirmed without reference to this point: [2018] EWCA Civ 1371; [2018] B.L.R. 491.
[362] [1996] 2 All E.R. 573; para.9–150.
[363] Under s.3 of Misrepresentation Act 1967 which applies the test of reasonableness as set out in s.11(1) of UCTA 1977: see para.7–060.
[364] e.g. under s.2(1) of the Misrepresentation Act 1967, or in negligence: see para.9–042 and following.
[365] In the case of fraud, as a matter of the common law: see para.7–034.
[366] cf. "any breach": see *George Mitchell (Chesterhall) Ltd v Finney Lock Seeds Ltd* [1983] Q.B. 284 at 303, 309 decided under an earlier and now superseded statutory requirement of reasonableness and affirmed without reference to this point in [1983] 2 A.C. 803.
[367] *Zanzibar v British Aerospace (Lancaster House) Ltd* [2001] 1 W.L.R. 2333; *Regus (UK) Ltd v Epcot Solutions Ltd* [2008] EWCA Civ 361; [2009] 1 All E.R. (Comm) 586; para.9–150.
[368] See para.7–024.
[369] [1992] Q.B. 600; Hedley [1992] C.L.J. 418; Peel 56 M.L.R. 98; cf. *Skipskreditforeningen v Emperor Navigation* [1998] 1 Lloyd's Rep. 67 at 75 (but see Mance J: "The court should not be too ready to focus on remote possibilities or to accept arguments that a clause fails the test [of reasonableness] by reference to relatively uncommon or unlikely situations"); *Deutsche Bank (Suisse) SA v Khan* [2013] EWHC 482 (Comm) at [326].

whole was unreasonable. The references to "payment" or "credit" could not be severed so as to confine the clause to excluding the right of set-off based on a breach of contract by the supplier. It was said that to do this would be inconsistent with the wording of s.11(1) of UCTA, under which the requirement of reasonableness "is that the *term* shall have been a fair and reasonable one to be included having regard to the circumstances which were, or ought reasonably to have been, known to or in the contemplation of the parties when the contract was made."[370] This decision is not easy to reconcile with an earlier case where a clause in a contract for the sale of goods imposed a short time-limit on all claims and also limited the seller's liability to the amount of the contract price. It was held that the first part of the clause was reasonable, and the second unreasonable,[371] but the seller could rely on the first part. It may be distinguished on the basis that the court was willing to regard the clause in question as amounting to two separate terms.[372] If the main reason for the decision in the *Stewart Gill* case is the need to assess the reasonableness of the term as a whole at the time of the contract, it is difficult to see why this does not also apply to a case like *Trolex* where part of the term is wholly ineffective. As it is, the decision in the *Stewart Gill* case means that, rather than rely on the courts to do so after the event, the drafter of a contract should take into account the "adventitious consideration" of using several terms, rather than one.

### (e) Restrictions on evasion

**Secondary contract.** A term restricting or excluding liability may be contained, not in the principal contract itself, but in another (secondary) contract. To meet the possibility that this would allow for the evasion of UCTA, s.10 provides that: **7–073**

> "A person is not bound by any contract term prejudicing or taking away rights of his which arise under, or in connection with the performance of, another contract,[373] so far as those rights extend to the enforcement of another's liability which this Part of this Act [374] prevents[375] that other from excluding or restricting."

Unfortunately, the terminology of s.10 differs from that used elsewhere in UCTA, and this fact gives rise to a number of difficulties of interpretation.

**"Prejudicing or taking away rights".** Section 10 refers to a contract term "prejudicing or taking away rights", not to one "excluding or restricting liability". **7–074**

---

[370] Emphasis added.

[371] *RW Green Ltd v Cade Bros Farms* [1978] 1 Lloyd's Rep. 602, decided under s.55 of Sale of Goods Act 1893 (now superseded) under which a term was "enforceable ... to the extent that" it satisfied the requirement of reasonableness.

[372] See para.7–070.

[373] Section 10 does not apply where a contract between A and B takes away A's right to sue a third party, C, *in tort*, since A's right against C does not arise "under ... another contract": *The Chevalier Roze* [1983] 2 Lloyd's Rep. 438 at 422.

[374] i.e. Pt I, which extends to England and Wales and to Northern Ireland.

[375] i.e. (*Semble*) not only by making it totally ineffective but also by subjecting it to the requirement of reasonableness.

The statutory explanation of the latter phrase[376] therefore does not apply to s.10. In particular, it is by no means clear whether the section would cover a secondary contract excluding a particular *remedy,* or one imposing onerous conditions (such as short time-limits) on the enforcement of a liability; or whether it would apply to a subsequent agreement to submit disputes under the original contract to arbitration.[377]

7–075 **Interaction with s.3.** The exact scope of s.10 is also in doubt in relation to contracts on written standard terms. Section 3(2) applies the requirement of reasonableness to terms in such contracts which: (a) exclude or restrict liability for breach; or (b) purport to entitle a party to render a performance substantially different from that reasonably expected of him, or to render no performance at all.[378] Clearly, a secondary contract seeking to achieve result (a) is within s.10 and thus ineffective. But is the same true of a secondary contract seeking to achieve result (b)? The concluding words of s.10 give rise to a difficulty because the rights affected by the secondary contract must "extend to the enforcement of another's *liability* which … this Act prevents the other from excluding or restricting". Section 3(2) appears to contrast terms *excluding or restricting liability* with terms purporting to *entitle a party to render a performance substantially different*, etc. It is at least doubtful whether s.10 is apt to cover a secondary agreement having the latter effect.

7–076 **Settlement of disputes.** Section 10 does not apply to a contract by which the parties to an earlier contract, containing terms which would be subject to UCTA, reach a settlement of disputes which have arisen between them under the original contract. The argument that such a settlement is a secondary contract within s.10 has been rejected on the ground that there was no hint in the legislative history that the section was intended to strike at such genuine out of court settlements.[379] On the contrary, the legislative history indicates that, in using the phrase "another's liability", s.10 refers to the liability of a third party,[380] so that the section "does not apply where the parties to both contracts are the same".[381] The point of the section is to deal with the case in which a contract between X and Y provides that Y is not to exercise rights against Z under a separate contract between Y and Z. The latter contract may not contain any exemption clause but be of such a kind that, if it did contain such a clause, that clause would be subject to UCTA. At common law, Z could not as a general rule rely on the clause in the contract between X and Y as he was not a party to it;[382] and the statutory right to rely on it, which Z may have under the Contracts (Rights of Third Parties) Act

---

376 UCTA s.13(1), para.7–043.

377 See s.13(2) which, unlike s.10, uses the standard terminology of UCTA—"excluding or restricting liability".

378 See paras 7–055–7–057.

379 *Tudor Grange Holdings Ltd v Citibank NA* [1992] Ch. 53 at 65–67; Brown 108 L.Q.R. 233; Cumberbatch 55 M.L.R. 866.

380 *Hansard*, HL Vol.385, cols 57–59, 511–514 (1977).

381 *Tudor Grange Holdings Ltd v Citibank NA* [1992] Ch. 53 at 66.

382 See para.14–064.

1999, will be of no avail to him where the clause is ineffective under UCTA.[383] The purpose of s.10 of UCTA is to prevent X from enforcing against Y a clause in the contract between X and Y which provides that Y is not to sue Z under the contract between Y and Z and which would have been ineffective under UCTA if it had been contained in the contract between Y and Z. Even apart from s.10 such a proceeding might not be open to X unless X could show that he had a sufficient interest[384] in Z's immunity from being sued by Y. The view that s.10 does not apply where the parties to both contracts are the same (even though it is acknowledged that the words of the section are capable of covering such a case)[385] has also been supported by the argument that, between the parties to the original contract, s.10 would be unnecessary since the secondary contract, no less than the original one, would be subject to the requirement of reasonableness under ss.2 and 3 of UCTA.[386]

**Renegotiated contracts.** The view that s.10 does not apply where the parties to both contracts are the same would also help to solve the problem of the renegotiation of a contract before any dispute under it has arisen. A contract may, for example, contain a term limiting the liability of a party to it, and that term may be subject to, and satisfy, the requirement of reasonableness. The parties may later agree on a lower limit of liability which would also (had it been originally incorporated in the contract) have satisfied that requirement. If that later agreement were within s.10, it would be totally ineffective and incapable of being validated by being shown to be reasonable. This—surely undesirable—result can be avoided by arguing *either* that s.10 does not apply between the parties to the original contract *or* that the later agreement is a variation of the original contract, so that the terms of that later agreement do not prejudice rights which "arise under *another* contract." The new limit of the defaulting party's liability would thus be subject to the same requirement of reasonableness as the term which originally limited that liability. 7–077

**Choice of law clauses.** A second possible way of evading UCTA is to provide that a contract which would otherwise be subject to its provisions shall be governed by the law of a foreign country (which imposes no such restriction on the effectiveness of contract terms). By s.27(2), UCTA applies, even though the contract contains such a clause, where the clause appears to the court to have been "imposed" wholly or mainly to evade UCTA. The effect of this provision is to confer on the controls in UCTA the status of mandatory rules. These are recognised and given effect by an EC Regulation on the law applicable to contractual obligations ("Rome I").[387] 7–078

---

[383] See para.14–125.
[384] See para.14–022.
[385] *Tudor Grange Holdings Ltd v Citibank NA* [1992] Ch. 53 at 66.
[386] *Tudor Grange Holdings Ltd v Citibank NA* [1992] Ch. 53 at 67.
[387] Regulation 593/2008.

### (f) Situations not covered by UCTA[388]

7–079 **Cases not within the scope of UCTA.** As we have seen,[389] contract terms excluding or restricting the liability of a person not acting in the course of a business are generally unaffected by UCTA. It only limits such a person's right to exclude or restrict certain liabilities arising out of contracts for the sale and hire-purchase of goods[390] and for misrepresentation.[391] Even terms excluding or restricting business liability may be outside the scope of UCTA: this is the position where a contract between B1 and B2, not made on written standard terms of business,[392] excludes or restricts a liability other than one for breach of the implied terms in contracts for the supply of goods dealt with in ss.6 and 7 of UCTA,[393] or breach of a contractual duty of care.[394] For example, a clause by which B1 excluded or limited liability to B2 for delay in delivering goods, or for short delivery or for an express undertaking as to quality going beyond those implied by law, would not be affected by UCTA, if the contract is not made on B1's written standard terms of business.

7–080 **Excepted types of contract: Insurance, land, intellectual property, companies and securities.** The principal group of contracts excepted[395] from some of the provisions of UCTA is listed in Sch.1. Paragraph 1 of the Schedule lists a number of contracts to which ss.2 and 3 do not apply. In the excepted cases, contract terms[396] excluding or restricting liability for negligence, and provisions in written standard terms of business excluding or restricting liability for breach of contract are not subject to the provisions of those sections. The contracts within para.1 of the Schedule are contracts of insurance and any contract "so far as it relates to": the creation, transfer or termination of an interest in land or in any patent, trade mark, copyright or other intellectual property; the formation, dissolution or constitution of a company or the rights or obligations of its members; and the creation or transfer of securities or any right or interest in securities. Contracts of insurance are *wholly* excepted, but a contract falling within the other categories is only excepted "*so far as* it relates to" the matter specified.[397] Where a contract relates to such matters and also to others, the specified sections are excluded with regard to the former, e.g. they do not apply to a share option[398] contained in a

[388] In addition to those set out in the text, Sch.1 para.5 excepts from s.2(1) of UCTA the validity of a discharge and indemnity given on or in connection with an award of compensation for pneumoconiosis.

[389] See para.7–040.

[390] UCTA s.6(1), (1A) and (4); paras 7–049—7–050, 7–058—7–059.

[391] UCTA s.8; paras 9–132—9–148.

[392] See s.3(1); para.7–054.

[393] See paras 7–049—7–050, 7–058—7–059.

[394] UCTA ss.1(1)(a), 2; see paras 7–048, 7–052.

[395] By s.1(2).

[396] Section 2 also deals with certain non-contractual notices, but the wording of s.1(2) ("in relation to contracts") indicates that the exclusions in Sch.1 only apply to contract terms.

[397] *Salvage Association v CAP Financial Services* [1995] F.S.R. 654 (s.2 applicable to a clause in a software licence limiting liability for breach of the implied term that the software would be developed with reasonable skill and care).

[398] *Micklefield v SAC Technology* [1990] 1 W.L.R. 1002.

contract of employment.[399] In the case of a contract for the transfer of an interest in land, it has been held that a clause in a lease by which rent was payable "without any deduction or set-off whatsoever" was excepted from ss.2 and 3 since the tenant's covenant to pay rent was "an integral part of the creation of the interest in land".[400] This reasoning gives some support to the view that provisions in the lease which do not "relate to" the transfer would not be so excepted.

**Marine salvage or towage, charterparties and carriage of goods by sea.** Paragraph 2 of the Schedule lists three contracts: contracts of marine salvage or towage, charterparties of ships or hovercraft, and contracts for the carriage of goods by ship or hovercraft.[401] These contracts are subject to s.2(1), which provides that B[402] cannot by any contract term exclude or restrict his liability for death or personal injury resulting from negligence. But they are excepted from the remainder of s.2, as well as from s.3. Since some contracts within this group may involve the hire of a chattel[403] they are also excepted from s.7 which limits the extent to which liability for breach of certain implied terms in such contracts can be excluded or restricted.[404] Paragraph 3 of the Schedule deals with the case where goods are carried by ship or hovercraft under a contract which either specifies that means of carriage only for part of the journey[405] or makes no provision for the means of carriage. Such contracts may not be contracts *for* the carriage of goods by ship or hovercraft, but are nevertheless excepted from the operation of ss.2(2) and 3 in the same way as such contracts. 7–081

**Employment.** By para.4 of the Schedule, ss.2(1) and (2) do not apply to contracts of employment "except in favour of the employee". The liability of the employee for negligence can therefore be restricted or excluded; but the employer cannot exclude or restrict such liability as against the employee. Since s.2 applies only to "business liability" the need for para.4 may not at first sight be apparent. But "business liability" includes liability for breach of a duty arising from things done in the course of *another* person's business so that liability incurred by an employee (whether to his employer or to a third party) can be a "business liability". Moreover, "business" includes a profession[406] so that an employee who in the course of his employment exercises a profession could incur a "business liability" which, but for para.4, would attract the operation of s.2(1) and (2). 7–082

[399] As to which see Sch.1 para.4. For the restricted application of UCTA to employment contracts generally, see para.7–054, fn.281.

[400] *Electricity Supply Nominees Ltd v IAF Group Ltd* [1993] 1 W.L.R. 1059 at 1063; cf. *Unchained Growth III Plc v Granby Village (Manchester) Management Co* [2000] 1 W.L.R. 739; *Connaught Restaurants Ltd v Indoor Leisure Ltd* [1994] 1 W.L.R. 501 where no attempt was made to rely on UCTA, perhaps because the conditions for the applicability of s.3 (para.7–054) were not satisfied.

[401] See, e.g. *The European Enterprise* [1989] 2 Lloyd's Rep. 185. Certain contracts for the carriage of goods by sea also come within the excepting provisions of s.29; para.7–084.

[402] See para.7–048.

[403] e.g. a demise charterparty.

[404] See paras 7–050, 7–058—7–059.

[405] This situation commonly arises where the goods are carried in a container from one inland destination to another in an overseas country.

[406] UCTA s.14.

7–083 **Contracts for the international supply of goods.** In such contracts,[407] none of the limits "imposed by this Act" on contract terms which "exclude or restrict liability" apply.[408] It seems that this includes the limits contained in s.3 of the Misrepresentation Act 1967.[409] Under s.3 of UCTA the requirement of reasonableness also applies to terms which do not "exclude or restrict" liability; e.g. it applies to terms entitling a party to render a performance substantially different from that reasonably expected of him, or to render no performance at all.[410] Where such terms or clauses are contained in a contract for the international supply of goods, the requirement of reasonableness does not apply.[411]

7–084 **Contractual provisions authorised or required under legislation or international agreements.** An increasingly common technique for controlling exemption clauses (and other contract terms) is found in international conventions, for example those regulating the international carriage of goods and passengers. Many such conventions have been given the force of law by statute.[412] These conventions often lay down a limitation of liability and then provide that any attempt at further reduction in the contract is void. This position is preserved by UCTA.[413]

7–085 **Choice of law clauses.** UCTA is intended to deal with contracts having some substantial connection with some part of the UK. A contract may be governed by English law though its connection with England is tenuous (or even non-existent) because it contains an express term that it is to be governed by English law. Section 27(1) accordingly provides that ss.2–7 do not apply where a contract is governed by the law of a part of the UK only by choice of the parties and would apart from that choice have been governed by the law of some country outside the UK.[414] The point is of considerable commercial importance as contracts having no substantial connection with England are quite commonly made subject to English law by choice of the parties.[415]

---

407 As defined by s.26(3) and (4); see *Ocean Chemical Transport Inc v Exnor Craggs* [2000] 1 Lloyd's Rep. 446 at 451; *Amiri Flight Authority v BAE Systems Plc* [2003] EWCA Civ 1447; [2003] 2 Lloyd's Rep. 767; *Balmoral Group Ltd v Borealis (UK) Ltd* [2006] EWHC 1900 (Comm); [2006] 2 Lloyd's Rep. 269 at [436]–[450]; *Trident Turboprop (Dublin) Ltd v First Flight Couriers Ltd* [2009] EWCA Civ 290; [2010] Q.B. 86; *Air Transworld Ltd v Bombardier Inc* [2012] EWHC 243 (Comm); [2012] 1 Lloyd's Rep. 349.

408 UCTA s.26(1).

409 *Trident Turboprop (Dublin) Ltd v First Flight Couriers Ltd* [2009] EWCA Civ 290; [2010] Q.B. 86.

410 See above, paras 7–056–7–057.

411 UCTA s.26(2).

412 e.g. Carriage of Goods by Sea Act 1971 Sch. arts III. 8 and IV. 5.

413 UCTA s.29.

414 As, for example, in *Air Transworld Ltd v Bombardier Inc* [2012] EWHC 243 (Comm); [2012] 1 Lloyd's Rep. 349; cf. *Deutsche Bank (Suisse) SA v Khan* [2013] EWHC 482 (Comm).

415 See *Skipskreditforeningen v Emperor Navigation* [1998] 1 Lloyd's Rep. 67 at 78.

## 3. CONSUMER RIGHTS ACT 2015

The Consumer Rights Act 2015 ("CRA") applies to consumer contracts[416] entered into on or after 1 October 2015.[417] With certain key exceptions,[418] it applies to any term of such a contract, some of which are rendered wholly ineffective,[419] while others may be subject to a test of fairness.[420] The CRA replaces the Unfair Terms in Consumer Contracts Regulations 1999 (the 1999 Regulations) and makes amendments to other legislation, including the Unfair Contract Terms Act 1977 ("UCTA"), which now applies only to certain "non-consumer contracts".[421] Part 2 of the CRA, and the 1999 Regulations before it, implement an EC Council Directive[422] which is intended to promote the harmonisation of the laws of Member States so as to ensure that contracts with consumers do not include terms which are unfair to the consumer.[423] This chapter is concerned only with those aspects of the CRA which control the enforceability of unfair terms, including exemption clauses. Other aspects of the CRA which confer rights and remedies on consumers are dealt with in other chapters.[424] **7–086**

**Changes introduced by the CRA.** At the outset, for readers who may already be familiar with the 1999 Regulations,[425] it is helpful to summarise the changes which are introduced by the CRA.[426] The principal changes are as follows: (i) whereas there was some overlap between the 1999 Regulations and UCTA, there is no overlap between the CRA and UCTA. The CRA applies to consumer contracts,[427] while terms in contracts which do not amount to consumer contracts are controlled, if at all, by UCTA;[428] (ii) the substitution of "trader" for a "seller or supplier";[429] (iii) a slight change to the definition of "consumer";[430] (iv) the test of fairness is not confined to terms which have not been individually **7–087**

[416] See paras 7–088—7–091.

[417] For contracts entered into before that date, see the last edition.

[418] See paras 7–101; 7–119–7–120.

[419] See paras 7–094, 7–099.

[420] See paras 7–100—7–118.

[421] See para.7–042.

[422] Directive 93/13. See Brandner and Ulmer (1991) 29 C.M.L.R. 647; Collins (1994) 14 O.J.L.S. 229. As with other implementing legislation, the English courts are required to interpret the relevant parts of the 2015 Act "as far as possible, in the light of the wording and the purpose of the directive": *Marleasing SA v La Comercial Internacional de Alimentacion SA* (C-106/89) [1990] E.C.R. I-04135 at [8]. To the extent that the CRA provides protection beyond that required under Directive 93/13, this is permitted on the basis that the Directive is aimed at "minimum harmonisation"; cf. *Caja de Ahorros y Monte de Piedad de Madrid v Asociación de Usuarios de Servicios Bancarios (Ausbanc)* (484/08) [2010] E.C.R. I-04785.

[423] Directive 93/13 Recital 4. Part 2 of the CRA also partly implements Directive 2011/83/EU but that is principally implemented by the Consumer Contracts (Information, Cancellation and Additional Charges) Regulations 2013 (SI 2013/3134).

[424] See Chs 6, 18, 20.

[425] For an assessment of the 1999 Regulations themselves, see the previous edition at paras 7–093–7–122.

[426] The amendments made to the Unfair Contract Terms Act are reflected in Pt 2 of this chapter.

[427] See paras 7–088, 7–091.

[428] See para.7–042.

[429] See para.7–090.

[430] See para.7–091.

negotiated;[431] and may also be applied to consumer notices;[432] (v) the addition of an express requirement that terms as to subject matter and price must be "transparent and prominent" before they are excluded from the assessment of fairness;[433] (vi) the addition of three further terms to the indicative list of unfair terms;[434] and (vii) the addition of a provision that terms on the indicative list cannot be excluded from the assessment of fairness.[435]

### (a) Scope[436]

7–088 **CRA Part 1: exemption clauses.** Part 1 of the CRA contains provisions which control the enforceability of certain exemption clauses. It applies to a contract between a trader and a consumer for the trader (but not the consumer) to supply goods, digital content or services. The definition of "trader" and "consumer" is dealt with below. "Goods" means any tangible moveable items,[437] but that includes water, gas and electricity only if they are put up for supply in a limited volume or set quantity.[438] "Digital content" means data which are produced and supplied in digital form. A service is not defined for the purpose of the CRA, but the chapter in Pt 1 dealing with services does not apply to a contract of employment or apprenticeship.[439] In some cases, a contract may be for more than one of goods, digital content, or services ("a mixed contract") in which case each of the relevant chapters in Pt 1 may apply.[440]

7–089 **CRA Part 2: other terms.** Part 2 of the CRA applies to a contract between a trader and a consumer.[441] With the principal exception of a contract of employment or apprenticeship,[442] there is no further limit in Pt 2 to the types of contract which are covered.[443] There is no requirement in Pt 2 (unlike Pt 1) that the trader must be the supplier (of goods, services etc.).[444]

---

431 See para.7–100.
432 See para.7–093
433 See para.7–104.
434 See para.7–118.
435 See para.7–107.
436 The issues which are discussed in this part concern the general scope of the CRA. Certain specific situations and types of contract are also excluded from its scope, but they are more easily explained below (see paras 7–119–7–120) after consideration of the CRA in general. Note also the exclusion of certain terms from the test of fairness: see paras 7–121—7–122.
437 CRA s.2(8).
438 e.g. a gas cylinder, a bottle of water, a battery.
439 CRA s.48(2).
440 CRA s.1(4), (5).
441 CRA s.61(1).
442 CRA s.61(2), see also para.7–122.
443 There was some uncertainty as to the scope of the 1999 Regulations in this regard: see *R. (on the application of Khatun) v Newham LBC* [2004] EWCA Civ 55; [2005] Q.B. 37. The European Court of Justice has confirmed that Directive 93/13 applies to all types of consumer contract, save those expressly excluded: *Brusse v Jahani BV* (C-488/11) [2013] 3 C.M.L.R. 45.
444 It seems that the 1999 Regulations, which Pt 2 replaces, applied where it was the consumer who was the "supplier", e.g. as a guarantor: *Barclays Bank Plc v Kufner* [2008] EWHC 2319 (Comm); [2009] 1 All E.R. (Comm) 1 at [29]; *Royal Bank of Scotland v Chandra* [2010] EWHC 105 (Ch);

**"Trader".** A "trader" means a person acting for purposes relating to that person's trade, business,[445] craft or profession, whether acting personally or through another person acting in the trader's name or on the trader's behalf.[446] "A person" for the purpose of this definition is not confined to a natural person (or persons) but can also include companies, charities and arms of government.[447] "Business" includes the activities of any government department or local or public authority.[448] **7–090**

**"Consumer".** A "consumer" means an individual acting for purposes that are wholly or mainly outside that individual's trade, business,[449] craft or profession.[450] A consumer can only be a natural person and this is also true for those provisions of the CRA which replace provisions in UCTA under which it had been possible for a company to "deal as consumer".[451] The reference to "wholly and mainly" did not appear in the 1999 Regulations. The Explanatory Notes to the CRA provide the following examples:[452] (i) a person who buys a kettle for their home, but who also uses it on the one day a week when they work from home would still be a consumer; and (ii) a sole trader operating from a private dwelling who buys a printer and uses it 95 per cent of the time for the purposes of the business is not likely to be held to be a consumer. It is not difficult to imagine other situations where the answer will be less obvious.[453] It has been held that a person may still be a consumer for the purposes of the 1999 Regulations, which Pt 2 of the CRA replaces, even if the contract is of considerable value, e.g. in one **7–091**

---

[2010] 1 Lloyd's Rep. 677 at [102], not following *Manches LLP v Freer* [2006] EWHC 991; *Williamson v Bank of Scotland* [2006] EWHC 1289 (Ch); [2006] B.P.I.R. 1085.

445 The test of "relating to" his business etc. appears closer to the test applied in *Stevenson v Rogers* [1999] Q.B. 1028, para.7–041.

446 CRA s.2(2); cf. *BKK Mobil Oil Körperschaft des öffentlichen Rechts v Zentrale zur Bekämpfung unlauteren Wettbewerbs eV* (C-59/12) EU:C:2013:634; [2014] 2 C.M.L.R. 1 at [32]–[33] on the interpretation of the similar definition of "trader" in the Directive which is implemented by the Consumer Protection from Unfair Trading Regulations 2008 (SI 2008/1277).

447 Explanatory Notes, para.35.

448 CRA s.2(7); cf. *R. (on the application of Khatun) v Newham LBC* [2004] EWCA Civ 55; [2005] Q.B. 37 (decided under the 1999 Regulations).

449 See text to fn.448.

450 CRA s.2(3). For cases decided under the 1999 Regulations, see: *Office of Fair Trading v Foxtons Ltd* [2009] EWHC 1681 (Ch); [2009] 29 E.G. 98 at [28]; *Barclays Bank Plc v Kufner* [2008] EWHC 2319 (Comm); [2009] 1 All E.R. (Comm) 1; *Turner & Co (GB) Ltd v Abi* [2010] EWHC 2078 (QB); [2011] 1 C.M.L.R. 17; *Overy v PayPal (Europe) Ltd* [2012] EWHC 2659 (QB); [2013] Bus L.R. D1; *Ashfaq v International Insurance Co of Hannover Plc* [2017] EWCA Civ 357; [2017] H.L.R. 29; In *Evans v Cherry Tree Financial Ltd* [2008] EWCA Civ 331; [2008] C.T.L.C. 117, in the context of a loan agreement, it was conceded that if *any* of the purposes for which the claimant borrowed the money were outside his trade or business, he was a consumer. See also: *RTA (Business Consultants) Ltd v Bracewell* [2015] EWHC 630 (QB); [2015] Bus L.R. 800, decided under the Cancellation of Contracts made in a Consumer's Home or Place of Work etc. Regulations 2008 (now superseded by the Consumer Contracts (Information, Cancellation and Additional Charges) Regulations 2013 (SI 2013/3134)).

451 *R & B Customs Brokers Ltd v United Dominions Trust Ltd* [1988] 1 W.L.R. 321.

452 Explanatory Notes, para.31.

453 cf. the approach of the European Court of Justice to a "mixed purpose" contract in the context of other European instruments, e.g. *Gruber v Bay Wa AG* (C-464/01) [2005] E.C.R. I-439.

case, to a contract to acquire foreign currency worth $7 million.[454] A trader who claims that an individual is not a consumer has the burden of proving it.[455]

7–092 **Types of clause covered.** Some sections of Pt 1 limit the effectiveness of clauses that "exclude or restrict the trader's liability".[456] To the same extent these sections also prevent the trader from doing certain analogous things: excluding or restricting a particular right or remedy;[457] making such a right or remedy or its enforcement subject to "a restrictive or onerous condition":[458] putting any person at a disadvantage as a result of pursuing a right or remedy;[459] e.g. imposing a shorter time-limit than would otherwise apply to any enforcement; or excluding or restricting rules of evidence or procedure.[460] The reference to "excluding or restricting" liability in the same sections includes "preventing an obligation or duty arising or limiting its effect".[461] The scope of this extended meaning of excluding or restricting liability is likely to give rise to the same difficulties as the corresponding provisions under UCTA which are discussed above.[462] It may also be assumed that, in identifying a clause which excludes or restricts liability, the same test of substance will be applied as under UCTA, e.g. an indemnity clause under which the consumer agrees to indemnify the trader against any liability of the trader to the consumer will be treated as an exclusion of the trader's liability.[463] An agreement in writing to submit present or future differences to arbitration is not to be regarded as excluding or restricting any liability.[464]

7–093 **Non-contractual notices.** Part 2 of the CRA applies not only to terms in a consumer contract, but also to a "consumer notice",[465] i.e. "a notice[466] to the extent that it (a) relates to rights or obligations as between a trader and a consumer, or (b) purports to exclude or restrict a trader's liability to a consumer."[467]

[454] *Standard Bank of London Ltd v Apostolakis* [2000] I.L. Pr. 766. The result and approach of Longmore J is questioned in *Maple Leaf Macro Volatility Master Fund v Rouvroy* [2009] EWHC 257 (Comm); [2009] 1 Lloyd's Rep. 475 at [208], [270]; affirmed [2009] EWCA Civ 1334; [2010] 2 All E.R. (Comm) 788 without reference to this point.

[455] CRA s.76(3).

[456] CRA ss.31, 47, 57; see paras 7–094–7–096.

[457] CRA ss.31(2)(a), 47(2)(a), 57(4)(a).

[458] CRA ss.31(2)(b), 47(2)(b), 57(4)(b).

[459] CRA ss.31(2)(c), 47(2)(c), 57(4)(c).

[460] CRA ss.31(2)(d), 47(2)(d), 57(4)(d).

[461] CRA ss.31(3), 47(3), 57(5).

[462] See paras 7–043, 7–045.

[463] See para.7–044.

[464] CRA ss.31(4), 47(4), 57(6).

[465] CRA s.61(7).

[466] A notice includes "an announcement, whether or not in writing, and any other communication or purported communication": s.61(8).

[467] CRA s.61(4).

## (b) Wholly ineffective terms and notices

**Supply of goods.** A term of a contract to supply goods[468] is not binding on the consumer to the extent that it would exclude or restrict the trader's liability[469] under the following provisions of the CRA:[470] (i) s.9 (goods to be of satisfactory quality); (ii) s.10 (goods to be reasonably fit for any purpose made known); (iii) s.11 (compliance with description); (iv) s.12 (certain pre-contract information treated as included as a term); (v) s.13 (compliance with sample); (vi) s.14 (compliance with model); (vii) s.15 (liability for incorrect installation in a "mixed contract" for supply and installation); (viii) s.16 (liability for non-conforming digital content in a "mixed contract" for the supply of goods and digital content); (ix) s.17 (trader's right to supply the goods); (x) s.28 (non- or late delivery of goods); and (xi) s.29 (passing of risk). An agreement under which the consumer's short-term right to reject would be lost before the time limit allowed has passed is also not binding on the consumer.[471] 7–094

**Supply of digital content.** A term of a contract to supply digital content[472] is not binding on the consumer to the extent that it would exclude or restrict the trader's liability[473] under the following provisions of the CRA:[474] (i) s.34 (digital content to be of satisfactory quality); (ii) s.35 (digital content to be reasonably fit for any purpose made known); (iii) s.36 (compliance with description); (iv) s.37 (certain pre-contract information treated as included as a term); and (v) s.41 (trader's right to supply the digital content). This list does not include liability for damage done to a device or other digital content, but any exclusion or restriction of such liability may be subject to the test of fairness.[475] 7–095

**Supply of services: liability which cannot be excluded.** A term of a contract to supply services[476] is not binding on the consumer to the extent that it would exclude the trader's liability[477] under the following provisions of the CRA: (i) s.49 (service to be performed with reasonable care and skill);[478] and (ii) s.50 (information about the trader or service made binding).[479] 7–096

---

468 i.e. a sales contract (s.5), a contract for the hire of goods (s.6), a hire-purchase agreement (s.7) and a contract for the transfer of goods (s.8). See further the provisions in ss.3(3), (5).

469 In the extended sense referred to para.7–092.

470 CRA s.31(1).

471 CRA s.22(2).

472 As defined by s.33.

473 In the extended sense referred to para.7–092.

474 CRA s.47(1).

475 CRA s.47(6).

476 As defined by s.48.

477 In the extended sense referred to para.7–092.

478 CRA s.57(1). This provides greater protection to the consumer than the equivalent provision under UCTA which previously would have applied to a consumer (s.2) under which, in the case of loss or damage other than death or personal injury, the trader's exclusion of liability for failure to perform with reasonable care and skill is subject to the test of reasonableness (s.2(2)), rather than wholly ineffective: see para.7–052.

479 CRA s.57(2).

7–097 **Supply of services: liability which cannot be restricted.** A term of a contract to supply services[480] is also not binding on the consumer to the extent that it would restrict the trader's liability[481] under the following provisions of the CRA:[482] (i) s.49 (service to be performed with reasonable care and skill); (ii) s.50 (information about the trader or service made binding); (iii) s.51 (payment of a reasonable price), if applicable; and (iv) s.52 (performance within a reasonable time), if applicable. In all such cases, the term is not binding only if it would prevent the consumer in an appropriate case from recovering the price paid or the value of any other consideration, i.e. the trader cannot limit its liability to less than the contract price. If it would not prevent the consumer from doing so, the term in question may still be challenged under the test of fairness.[483]

7–098 **Negligence liability: personal injury or death.** Under s.65(1) a trader cannot either by a term of a consumer contract or by a consumer notice[484] exclude or restrict liability for death or personal injury[485] resulting from negligence. "Negligence" for this purpose means the breach of:[486] (i) any obligation to take reasonable care or exercise reasonable skill in the performance of a contract where the obligation arises from an express or an implied term of the contract; (ii) a common law duty to take reasonable care or exercise reasonable skill; or (iii) the common duty of care imposed by the Occupiers' Liability Act 1957. It is immaterial whether the breach of any of the obligations just listed was inadvertent or intentional, or whether liability for it arose directly or vicariously.[487] Section 65 does not apply to the following types of contract: (i) an insurance contract;[488] or (ii) any contract so far as it relates to the creation or transfer of an interest in land.[489] It also does not apply to the liability of an occupier of premises to a person who obtains access to the premises for recreational purposes if the person suffers loss or damage because of the dangerous state of the premises and allowing the person access for those purposes is not within the purposes of the occupier's trade, business, craft or profession.[490] Section 65 does not affect the validity of any discharge or indemnity given as part of a settlement under which compensation is paid.[491]

7–099 **Terms conclusively unfair.** Some terms are subject to the test of fairness,[492] but "must be regarded as unfair" if they have certain effects and are, in that sense, wholly ineffective. This is true of any term which has the effect that the consumer

---

480 As defined by s.48.
481 In the extended sense referred to para.7–092.
482 CRA s.57(3).
483 CRA s.57(3); see para.7–100 and following.
484 See para.7–093
485 "Personal injury" includes any disease and any impairment of physical or mental condition: s.65(3).
486 CRA s.65(4).
487 CRA s.65(5).
488 Section 66(1)(a), including "a contract to pay an annuity on a human life".
489 Section 66(1)(b). For discussion of an equivalent provision under UCTA, see para.7–080.
490 Section 66(4). For discussion of an equivalent provision under UCTA, see para.7–041, fn.219.
491 CRA s.66(2).
492 See para.7–100 and following.

bears the burden of proof with respect to compliance by a distance supplier[493] or an intermediary[494] with an obligation under any enactment or rule implementing the Distance Marketing Directive.[495]

### (c) Terms and notices subject to the requirement of fairness

Subject to the restriction which is dealt with in the next paragraph, and to the exclusion of certain specific contracts and terms altogether,[496] the test of fairness potentially applies to any term in a consumer contract[497] and any consumer notice.[498] Unlike the 1999 Regulations, the application of the test of fairness is not confined to a term which "has not been individually negotiated".[499] Any term or notice which is in any event wholly non-binding under the provisions just considered[500] is not affected by the test of fairness.[501] 7–100

**Exclusion of "main subject-matter" and "adequacy of price".**[502] Section 64(1) provides that: 7–101

> "A term of a consumer contract may not be assessed for fairness under section 62 to the extent that (a) it specifies the main subject matter of the contract, or (b) the assessment is of the appropriateness of the price payable under the contract by comparison with the goods, digital content or services supplied under it."

It replaces a similarly worded provision in the 1999 Regulations (reg.6(2)) under which the test of fairness did not apply to "the definition of the main subject-matter of the contract", or "the adequacy of the price or remuneration, as against the goods or services supplied".[503] The exclusion from the test of fairness referred to in s.64(1) only applies if the term is "transparent and prominent".[504]

Section 64(1) may be compared with a number of common law principles discussed elsewhere in this book. The most important of these principles is that the court will not, as a general rule, investigate the adequacy of consideration.[505] Similarly, a term is not unfair for the purposes of the CRA merely because it fixes a price or remuneration which may be regarded as "excessive" by the application of some objective standard of valuation.[506] Conversely, the CRA leaves it open to the parties to define the subject-matter of the contract: in this respect, they

[493] As defined by s.63(7).
[494] As defined by s.63(7).
[495] Directive 2002/65: s.63(6).
[496] See paras 7–119—7–122.
[497] See paras 7–088—7–091.
[498] See para.7–093.
[499] 1999 Regulations reg.5(1).
[500] See paras 7–094—7–098.
[501] CRA s.62(8).
[502] Brandner and Ulmer (1991) 29 C.M.L.R. 647.
[503] A further group of terms excluded from control on the principle of s.64(1) consists of terms in insurance contracts which "clearly define or circumscribe the insured risk and the insurer's liability": Directive 93/13 Recital 19.
[504] CRA s.64(2); see para.7–104.
[505] See para.3–013.
[506] cf. para.10–054.

resemble the common law rules discussed earlier in this chapter, under which there would be no breach at all, even though the subject-matter was in some objective sense defective, if what was supplied was what the parties had contracted about. For example, in the case of the hostess who asked a supplier to "send me peas or if you haven't got peas send me beans, but for heaven's sake send something",[507] the term allowing the supplier to make such a choice would not appear to fall within the CRA.[508]

7–102 **"Core" and "ancillary" provisions.** Section 64(1) is of crucial importance in recognising the parties' freedom of contract with respect to the essential features of their bargain. Part 2 of the CRA is no more intended than the 1999 Regulations to provide a regime of (fair) price control. However, the courts must be wary of giving too wide a scope to s.64(1) since the effect of doing so would be to except too great a range of contract terms from the test of fairness such that the object of that test would be "plainly frustrated".[509] A term which specifies payments to be made by the consumer is not necessarily one which relates to "the appropriateness of the price payable" within s.64(1)(b). The point may be illustrated by reference to a consumer credit agreement and the decision of the House of Lords in *Director General of Fair Trading v First National Bank Plc*,[510] decided under an earlier version of the 1999 Regulations under which the test of fairness did not apply to the "adequacy of the price or remuneration".[511] While a term specifying the rate of interest would no doubt fall within these words, the House of Lords held that they did not cover a term requiring the borrower to pay interest on outstanding amounts, even after judgment had been given against him for the principal sum, since this term was "ancillary"[512] to his principal obligation (it was not a "core provision"). The term was therefore subject to the test of fairness, though it was found not to be unfair, for the reasons which are explained below.[513]

The requirement of considering the appropriateness of the price payable "by comparison with" the subject-matter of the contract could similarly restrict the concept of a "core provision" and hence of s.64(1). The point may be illustrated by reference to the case in which a contract for the hire of goods for a fixed period provides that the hirer is to pay a "holding charge" if he retains the goods after the end of the stipulated period.[514] Although such a provision could be described as the "price" of an option to extend the period of hire,[515] it could also

---

507 See para.7–022.

508 The term would not be even prima facie unfair as one enabling the seller unilaterally to alter the characteristics of the product to be provided (within Sch.2 Pt 1 para.13; see para.7–114) since this product was defined by the contract not as "peas" but as "peas or beans or something".

509 *Director General of Fair Trading v First National Bank Plc* [2001] UKHL 52; [2002] 1 A.C. 481 at [12]; cf. at [34].

510 [2001] UKHL 52; [2002] 1 A.C. 481; Macdonald (2002) 65 M.L.R. 763; Whittaker (2004) ZEuP 75.

511 Unfair Terms in Consumer Contracts Regulations 1994 (SI 1994/3159) reg.3(2)(b).

512 *Director General of Fair Trading v First National Bank Plc* [2001] UKHL 52; [2002] 1 A.C. 481 at [12].

513 See para.7–110.

514 See *Interfoto Picture Library Ltd v Stiletto Visual Programmes Ltd* [1989] Q.B. 433; para.6–012.

515 cf. para.20–141.

be regarded as "ancillary"[516] to the main object of the contract; or as fixing the "price", not of what was to be supplied, but of the option described above.[517] The provision would then be subject to the test of fairness and, if the charge were unusually high, the term requiring it to be paid could be regarded as "unfair". Indeed, the example comes very close to one of the illustrations given in Sch.2 of prima facie unfair terms.[518]

**Bank charges case.** While accepting that reg.6(2) (and therefore now s.64(1)) should be construed restrictively, in *Office of Fair Trading v Abbey National Plc*[519] the Supreme Court did not think that the distinction between the "core bargain" and "ancillary provisions" should be pressed too far. In particular, it rejected the view of the courts below[520] that the distinction between the two should be determined from the perspective of the typical consumer.[521] In that case, a challenge was made to the fairness of the terms under which banks had charged a customer for services provided when the customer's account exceeded an authorised borrowing limit. The Court of Appeal had held that such charges were not part of the price for the services provided because they would not have been viewed by the typical customer as part of the "core bargain". To draw an analogy with the example given in the preceding paragraph, from the typical customer's perspective the main object of the contract with the bank was to run an account in credit for which the price was the foregoing of interest on the sums in the account, or the payment of a low rate of interest; the charges levied on unauthorised borrowing were the "price" for the option of the services provided when the account was overdrawn. That view was rejected on the basis that it departed from the "natural"[522] or "objective"[523] meaning of the text of reg.6(2). Viewed objectively, what the banks provided was a package of services, including unauthorised borrowing, for which a price was payable. It was irrelevant that the charges for services provided when an account exceeded its authorised borrowing limit were contingent and might not ever *be paid* by the majority of customers. 7–103

In reaching its decision, the Supreme Court did not cast any doubt on the correctness of the decision of the House of Lords in the *First National Bank*

[516] See at fn.511.

[517] cf. *Bairstow Eves London Central Ltd v Darlingtons* [2004] EWHC 263; [2004] 2 E.G.L.R. 25 (term allowing for estate agent's commission of 1.5 per cent if payment made early, or of 3 per cent plus interest if payment made late held not to fall within reg.6(2)).

[518] Sch.2 Pt.1 para.15.

[519] [2009] UKSC 6; [2010] 1 A.C. 696; Whittaker 74 M.L.R. 106; Chen-Wishart 126 L.Q.R. 157.

[520] *Office of Fair Trading v Abbey National Plc* [2008] EWHC 875 (Comm); [2008] 2 All E.R. (Comm) 625 (Andrew Smith J); [2009] EWCA Civ 116; [2009] 2 W.L.R. 1286 (the decision of the Court of Appeal was followed by Mann J in *Office of Fair Trading v Foxtons Ltd* [2009] EWHC 1681 (Ch); [2009] 29 E.G. 98).

[521] In *Kásler v OTP Jelzálogbank Zrt* (C-26/13) EU:C:2014:282; [2014] W.L.R. (D) 180 the European Court of Justice also declined to adopt the perspective of the average consumer (in the interpretation of art.4(2) of the Directive) but endorsed the distinction between "essential obligations" and those which are "ancillary" which is to be drawn "having regard to the nature, general scheme and the stipulations of [the contract] and its legal and factual context" (at [51]).

[522] *Office of Fair Trading v Abbey National Plc* [2009] UKSC 6; [2010] 1 A.C. 696 at [45].

[523] *Office of Fair Trading v Abbey National Plc* [2009] UKSC 6; [2010] 1 A.C. 696 at [113].

case.[524] It seems that it can be distinguished on the basis that it concerned a "default" provision.[525] This seems to introduce into the scope of reg.6(2) the same sort of limit which determines the scope of the rule against penalties, i.e. that it only applies to terms requiring payment to be made upon breach of the contract and not to terms where no breach is involved, e.g. price variation clauses.[526] But this limit to the scope of the rule against penalties is vulnerable to manipulation by a skilled draftsman and it has been said that the courts will be alive to the possibility of a disguised penalty clause.[527] A similar sentiment can be detected in the view of the Court of Appeal in the *Abbey National* case that the banks' charges were "*akin* to default charges".[528] That view was rejected by the Supreme Court[529] and it is this which explains the decision to allow the banks' appeal. Nonetheless, the distinction between default provisions, or those which are "akin to default", and those which are genuinely part of the "price" may be no easier to draw than (or very different from) the distinction between "core" and "ancillary" provisions.

7–104 **Core terms must be transparent and prominent.** Under reg.6(2) of the 1999 Regulations the exclusion of "core terms" from the test of fairness only applied if the term in question was in "plain intelligible language". It was acknowledged in the *Abbey National* case that this requirement was assessed from the perspective of the typical consumer,[530] but since it had been found that it was met,[531] there could be no challenge to the fairness of the terms, at least on grounds of the appropriateness of the amount of the charges themselves.[532] In a subsequent

---

[524] See para.7–102. Nor that of Gross J in *Bairstow Eves London Central Ltd v Darlingtons* [2004] EWHC 263; [2004] 2 E.G.L.R. 25: fn.516.

[525] *Office of Fair Trading v Abbey National Plc* [2009] UKSC 6; [2010] 1 A.C. 696 at [32], [43], [102], [113] (and see *Director General of Fair Trading v First National Bank Plc* [2001] UKHL 52; [2002] 1 A.C. 481 at [12] (Lord Bingham), [34] (Lord Steyn).

[526] See para.20–142. In this sense, the material decision in the bank charges case may have been that of Andrew Smith J at first instance ([2008] EWHC 875 (Comm); [2008] 2 All ER (Comm) 625, from which there was no appeal), who found that the rule against penalties did not apply because there was no breach by a customer who exceeded the authorised borrowing limit; note the observation by counsel for the banks which is picked up by Lord Phillips: [2009] UKSC 6; [2010] 1 A.C. 696 at [83].

[527] Most notably by Bingham LJ in *Interfoto Picture Library Ltd v Stiletto Visual Programmes Ltd* [1989] Q.B. 433 (see below, para.20–142) and it is Lord Bingham in the *First National Bank* case who draws the distinction between "core provisions" and "ancillary provisions".

[528] *Office of Fair Trading v Abbey National Plc* [2009] EWCA Civ 116; [2009] 2 W.L.R. 1286 at [107] (emphasis added).

[529] "When the relevant facts are viewed as a whole, it seems clear that the Relevant Charges are not concealed default charges designed to discourage customers from overdrawing on their accounts without prior arrangement", [2009] UKSC 6; [2010] 1 A.C. 696 at [88] (Lord Phillips); cf. *Office of Fair Trading v Ashbourne Management Services Ltd* [2011] EWHC 1237 (Ch); [2011] E.C.C. 31 at [152].

[530] *Office of Fair Trading v Abbey National Plc* [2009] UKSC 6; [2010] 1 A.C. 696 at [103], [109].

[531] At first instance by Andrew Smith J, save in "relatively minor respects": [2008] EWHC 875 (Comm); [2008] 2 All ER (Comm) 625) (at [293]). There was no appeal from his finding in this regard.

[532] This is on the basis that what is excluded by reg.6(2)(b) is any assessment of a price term for fairness by reference to its adequacy as payment for the goods or services provided in exchange and not any assessment of the term itself on other grounds. The distinction between "excluded assessment" and "excluded term" which was drawn by Andrew Smith J at first instance was accepted by both parties in the appeal courts. It has been criticised (Whittaker 74 M.L.R. 1.), but was

decision of the European Court of Justice, the perspective of the average consumer was endorsed for the proviso that the term in question must be in "plain and intelligible language", but it was also explained that this is not merely a question of the terms "being formally and grammatically intelligible".[533] It also imports an element of "transparency" such that "the consumer is in a position to evaluate, on the basis of clear, intelligible criteria, the economic consequences for him" of the term in question.[534] This would appear to be reflected in an amendment introduced in s.64 of the CRA under which a term, even as to "matter" or "price", is not excluded from the test of fairness unless it is "transparent and prominent".[535]

**Transparency.** A term is "transparent" if it is "expressed in plain and intelligible language and (in the case of a written term) is legible".[536] Hence an obscurely expressed price term which entitled the trader to make additions to a price prominently stated elsewhere in the contractual document could, by reason of its obscurity, be an "unfair" term.[537] **7–105**

**Prominence.** A term is "prominent" if it is "brought to the consumer's attention in such a way that an average consumer would be aware of the term."[538] An "average consumer" is one who is "reasonably well-informed, observant and circumspect". It is this express requirement of prominence which represents the amendment introduced by s.64. It would appear to bring the CRA in line with the interpretation of the underlying Directive by the European Court of Justice[539] and to allow a consumer to challenge terms relating to the price or defining the subject matter on grounds of "unfair surprise".[540] **7–106**

**Prima facie unfair terms.** The exclusion from the test of fairness in s.64 does not apply to any term in the indicative list of terms which may be regarded as unfair.[541] **7–107**

acknowledged by the European Court of Justice in *Kásler v OTP Jelzálogbank Zrt* (C-26/13) EU:C:2014:282; [2014] W.L.R. (D) 180 at [54] (in the interpretation of art.4(2) of the Directive); cf. *Casehub Ltd v Wolf Cola Ltd* [2017] EWHC 1169 (Ch), applying s.64(1)(b) of the CRA.

533 *Kásler v OTP Jelzálogbank Zrt* (C-26/13) EU:C:2014:282; [2014] W.L.R. (D) 180 at [71].

534 *Kásler v OTP Jelzálogbank Zrt* (C-26/13) EU:C:2014:282; [2014] W.L.R. (D) 180 at [71]. Quaere whether some of the terms in the bank charges case might have been challenged on this basis. This may be a better explanation for the decision in *Office of Fair Trading v Ashbourne Management Services Ltd* [2011] EWHC 1237 (Ch); [2011] E.C.C. 31 which was reached on the basis of the "excluded assessment" approach referred to above, fn.531.

535 CRA s.64(2).

536 CRA s.64(3).

537 cf. *Financial Services Authority v Asset L.I. Inc* [2013] EWHC 178 (Ch); [2013] 2 B.C.L.C. 480 at [132].

538 CRA s.64(4).

539 See text to fn.533.

540 cf. para.7–111 and the requirement of prominence as part of the test of "good faith".

541 CRA s.64(6); see para.7–113 and following.

## (d) The test of unfairness

7–108 **The test.** Under s.62(4) "[a] term is unfair if, contrary to the requirement of good faith, it causes a significant imbalance in the parties' rights and obligations under the contract to the detriment of the consumer."[542] This is the same test applied under the 1999 Regulations and it may be assumed that earlier decisions of the English courts and the European Court of Justice will continue to be authoritative as to its meaning. The "twin requirements"[543] of "contrary to good faith"[544] and "significant imbalance"[545] are separate requirements, both of which must be met.[546]

7–109 **Burden of proof.** As with the 1999 Regulations, and the Directive, the CRA is silent as to the burden of proof in meeting the test of fairness.[547] The court must consider the fairness of a term even if none of the parties raises it,[548] provided the court has before it sufficient legal and factual material to enable it to do so.[549]

7–110 **Significant imbalance.** In the *First National Bank* case Lord Bingham stated that[550]:

> "The requirement of significant imbalance is met if a term is so weighted in favour of the supplier[551] as to tilt the parties' rights and obligations under the contract significantly in his favour. This may be by the granting to the supplier of a beneficial option or discretion or power, or by the imposing on the consumer of a disadvantageous burden or risk or duty."

The emphasis is on the "substantive fairness of the contract",[552] but the proposition that "significant imbalance" is concerned with "substantive fairness" and "good faith" with "procedural fairness", and any distinction between the two, should not be over-stated: "there is a large area of overlap between the concepts

---

542 The same test applies to a consumer notice: s.62(6).

543 *Director General of Fair Trading v First National Bank Plc* [2001] UKHL 52; [2002] 1 A.C. 481 at [12]; cf. [2002] 1 A.C. 481 at [36] (Lord Steyn).

544 See para.7–111.

545 See para.7–110.

546 *Director General of Fair Trading v First National Bank Plc* [2001] UKHL 52; [2002] 1 A.C. 481 at [17], [36]; *Bryen & Langley Ltd v Boston* [2005] EWCA Civ 973; [2005] C.I.L.L. 2261 at [44]; *UK Housing Alliance Ltd v Francis* [2010] EWCA Civ 117; [2010] 3 All E.R. 519 at [21]–[22]; *West v Ian Finlay & Associates* [2014] EWCA Civ 316; [2014] B.L.R. 214 at [46]; cf. *Munkenbeck & Marshall v Harold* [2005] EWHC 356 (TCC) at [15] where it appears that the finding of unfairness was based on significant imbalance alone; and see the doubt expressed in *Maple Leaf Macro Volatility Master Fund v Rouvroy* [2009] EWHC 257 (Comm); [2009] 1 Lloyd's Rep. 475 at [273] (affirmed without reference to this point [2009] EWCA Civ 1334; [2010] 2 All E.R. (Comm) 788).

547 One view is that there should be no burden of proof and what is called for is a "neutral assessment" by the court: *Chitty on Contracts*, 33rd edn, para.38-393.

548 CRA s.71(2).

549 CRA s.71(3); cf. *Océano Grupo Editorial SA v Murciano* (C-240/98) [2000] E.C.R. I-4941; *Pannon GSM Zrt v Erzsébet Sustikné Győrfi* (C-243/08) [2009] E.C.R. I-4713 at [32].

550 *Director General of Fair Trading v First National Bank Plc* [2001] UKHL 52; [2002] 1 A.C. 481 at [17].

551 Now "trader": see para.7–090.

552 Collins 14 O.J.L.S. 229 at 249.

of good faith and significant imbalance."[553] In the *First National Bank* case itself, it was held that there was no significant imbalance in the term requiring the borrower to pay interest on outstanding amounts, even after judgment had been given against him for the principal sum.[554] Neither party could have supposed that the bank would willingly forgo any part of its principal or interest and the borrower's obligation to repay the principal in full with interest was very clearly and unambiguously expressed in the conditions of contract; the absence of such a term would have unbalanced the contract to the detriment of the lender.[555] The obligation to pay interest after judgment could catch out borrowers who failed to appreciate its significance when they agreed to pay the judgment debt over a period of time by instalments. Any "unfairness" in this respect was the result not of the term in question, but of borrowers not being aware of the statutory procedures available under which they might apply for the underlying agreement to be amended, including the obligation to pay post-judgment interest, at least in relation to "regulated agreements".[556]

The European Court of Justice has said that one factor to take into account in assessing for "significant imbalance" is whether the consumer is in a less favourable position than he would have been on the basis of the default rules of national law which would apply in the absence of the parties' agreement.[557] This was taken into account in *ParkingEye Ltd v Beavis*[558] where consumers were made subject to a charge of £85 for parking if they exceeded a two-hour limit.[559] In the absence of the term imposing the charge, the consumer would only have been liable in tort to the landowner for trespass (and not to the company operating the car park on behalf of the landowner) and such liability would have been limited to the occupation value of the parking space.[560] To that extent there was an imbalance in the parties' rights,[561] but the term was not unfair in any event because it did not arise contrary to the requirement of good faith.[562]

553 *Director General of Fair Trading v First National Bank Plc* [2001] UKHL 52; [2002] 1 A.C. 481 at [37]; cf. *West v Ian Finlay & Associates* [2014] EWCA Civ 316; [2014] B.L.R. 214 at [47].

554 cf. *Spreadex Ltd v Cochrane* [2012] EWHC 1290 (Comm); [2012] Info T.L.R. 1; *Du Plessis v Fontgary Leisure Parks Ltd* [2012] EWCA Civ 409 (term allowing caravan pitch fee to be reviewed and increased); *Parker v National Farmers Union Mutual Insurance Society Ltd* [2012] EWHC 2156 (Comm); [2013] Lloyd's Rep. I.R. 253; *Abbott v RCI Europe* [2016] EWHC 2602 (Ch).

555 *Director General of Fair Trading v First National Bank Plc* [2001] UKHL 52; [2002] 1 A.C. 481 at [20].

556 Consumer Credit Act 1974 ss.129, 136.

557 *Aziz v Caixa d'Estalvis de Catalunya, Tarragona I* (C-415/11) EU:C:2013:164; [2013] 3 C.M.L.R. 5; cf. *Constructora Principado SA v Menéndez Álvarez* (C-226/12) EU:C:2014:10.

558 [2015] UKSC 67; [2016] A.C. 1172.

559 The charge was held not to amount to an unenforceable penalty under the common law rule against penalties: see para.20–161.

560 See para.20–161.

561 *ParkingEye Ltd v Beavis* [2015] UKSC 67; [2016] A.C. 1172 at [107] (Lord Sumption and Lord Neuberger); cf. Lord Toulson (dissenting) (at [307]) who regarded it as a significant imbalance (contrast Lord Mance (at [212])).

562 See text to fn.576.

7–111 **Good faith.** The requirement of good faith has been described in the *First National Bank* case as "one of fair and open dealing".[563] Openness here refers to the way in which terms are set out: they must be "expressed fully, clearly and legibly, containing no concealed pitfalls or traps"[564] and giving due "prominence to terms which might operate disadvantageously to the customer".[565] Fairness requires the trader not:

> "whether deliberately or unconsciously, [to] take advantage of the consumer's necessity, indigence, lack of experience, unfamiliarity with the subject-matter of the contract, [or] weak bargaining position. Good faith in this context looks to … good standards of commercial morality and practice. Regulation 4(1)[566] lays down a composite test, covering both the making and the substance of the contract, and must be applied bearing clearly in mind the objective which the Regulations [now CRA] are designed to promote."[567]

The Directive which is implemented by the CRA lists, among factors relevant to good faith, "the strength of the bargaining positions of the parties,[568] whether the consumer had an inducement to agree to the term and whether the goods or services were supplied to the special order of the consumer".[569] It is probably impossible, and inappropriate,[570] to achieve greater precision in formulating such an essentially flexible requirement,[571] particularly as the Directive also refers to an "overall evaluation of the different interests involved", but the Court of Justice has said that the national court should take into account "whether the seller or supplier,[572] dealing fairly and equitably with the consumer, could reasonably assume that the consumer would have agreed to such a term in individual contract

---

[563] *Director General of Fair Trading v First National Bank Plc* [2001] UKHL 52; [2002] 1 A.C. 481 at [17].

[564] *Director General of Fair Trading v First National Bank Plc* [2001] UKHL 52; [2002] 1 A.C. 481 at [17]; cf. *West v Ian Finlay & Associates* [2014] EWCA Civ 316; [2014] B.L.R. 214 at [56] ("some concern" about the drafting of a net contribution clause, but ultimately held not to be unfair when taking into account all the circumstances including the equal bargaining position of the parties).

[565] *Director General of Fair Trading v First National Bank Plc* [2001] UKHL 52; [2002] 1 A.C. 481 at [17].

[566] Now s.62(4).

[567] *Director General of Fair Trading v First National Bank Plc* [2001] UKHL 52; [2002] 1 A.C. 481 at [17]; *Bryen & Langley Ltd v Boston* [2005] EWCA Civ 973; [2005] C.I.L.L. 2261 at [46]; *UK Housing Alliance Ltd v Francis* [2010] EWCA Civ 117; [2010] 3 All E.R. 519 at [28]; *Turner & Co (GB) Ltd v Abi* [2010] EWHC 2078 (QB); [2011] 1 C.M.L.R. 17 at [45].

[568] See, in this respect: *Deutsche Bank (Suisse) SA v Khan* [2013] EWHC 482 (Comm) at [380]; [2013] EWHC 482; *West v Ian Finlay & Associates* [2014] EWCA Civ 316; [2014] B.L.R. 214 at [60]; contrast *Harrison v Shepherd Homes Ltd* [2011] EWHC 1811 (TCC); (2011) Const. L.J. 709 at [113].

[569] Directive 93/13 Recital (16). These guidelines were formerly contained in Sch.2 to the 1994 Regulations (above, fn.511) but they are not reproduced in the 1999 Regulations, nor the CRA. They are clearly applicable: *UK Housing Alliance Ltd v Francis* [2010] EWCA Civ 117; [2010] 3 All E.R. 519 at [22].

[570] *Director General of Fair Trading v First National Bank Plc* [2001] UKHL 52; [2002] 1 A.C. 481 at [45] (Lord Hope); *Domsalla v Dyason* [2007] EWHC 1174 (TCC); 112 Con L.R. 95 at [78]; *Maple Leaf Macro Volatility Master Fund v Rouvroy* [2009] EWHC 257 (Comm); [2009] 1 Lloyd's Rep. 475 at [272]–[275].

[571] *West v Ian Finlay & Associates* [2014] EWCA Civ 316; [2014] B.L.R. 214 at [45] (requires the assessment of "all possibly relevant considerations").

[572] Now "trader"; see para.7–090.

negotiations".[573] This test was found to have been met by a majority of the Supreme Court in the *ParkingEye* case referred to above. The charge "underpinned a business model which enabled members of the public to park free of charge for two hours" and "it was fundamental to the contractual relationship ... whose whole object was the efficient management of the car park".[574] Whether the consumer would have agreed to the charge is determined objectively and, in the view of the majority, a reasonable user would have agreed to it had it been the subject of individual negotiation,[575] given the benefit of free parking which it supported and the fact that the charge was not unreasonable.[576]

**Factors to be taken into account.** Section 62(5) directs the court to take into account or to refer to a number of factors in assessing the fairness of a term.[577] One such factor is "the nature of the subject matter of the contract"[578] so that, for example, a term which was not fair in a contract for the sale of new goods might be fair if the goods were sold as being second hand. The court is also directed to refer "to all the circumstances existing when the term was agreed":[579] here the fact that the consumer had examined goods before deciding to buy them would be relevant; and in a contract for the supply of services it would be relevant that, when the contract was made, the consumer was in a position to appreciate the risk that the services might fail to achieve the desired purpose. It is significant that the CRA refers at this point to the time of the conclusion of the contract, thus supporting the view that the issue of fairness (like that of reasonableness under the Unfair Contract Terms Act 1977) is to be determined by reference to the time of contracting.[580] Finally, the court is directed to take into account "all of the other terms of the contract or of any other contract on which it depends".[581] The point here is that a term which might, standing alone, appear to be unfair could be fair having regard to the structure or system of rights and immunities created by the contract as a whole. It might, for example, be fair for a trader who undertook liabilities beyond those imposed under a particular type of contract at common 7–112

[573] *Aziz v Caixa d'Estalvis de Catalunya, Tarragona I* (C-415/11) EU:C:2013:164; [2013] 3 C.M.L.R. 5 at [69]; cf. *Director General of Fair Trading v First National Bank Plc* [2001] UKHL 52; [2002] 1 A.C. 481 at [54] (Lord Millett).

[574] *ParkingEye Ltd v Beavis* [2015] UKSC 67; [2016] A.C. 1172 at [107]. This approach, which took into account the "legitimate interest" of the parties, was said to represent an "interest of exactly the kind envisaged" by the Advocate General when addressing the test of good faith in the *Aziz* case, fn.573.

[575] The *ParkingEye* case was decided under the 1999 Regulations which only applied at all to terms which had not been individually negotiated. That requirement is no longer necessary under the CRA (see para.7–100), but this does not detract from the utility of the test referred to in the *Aziz* case, where applicable.

[576] *ParkingEye Ltd v Beavis* [2015] UKSC 67; [2016] A.C. 1172 at [109], [209]; cf. Lord Toulson (dissenting, at [310]–[315]).

[577] A similar set of factors are relevant to the fairness of a notice: s.62(7) The main difference is one of timing, i.e. "all the circumstances existing when the rights or obligations to which it relates arose": s.62(7)(b).

[578] CRA s.62(5)(a).

[579] CRA s.62(5)(b).

[580] *UK Housing Alliance Ltd v Francis* [2010] EWCA Civ 117; [2010] 3 All E.R. 519 at [27]; see above, para.7–063.

[581] CRA s.62(5). See *Domsalla v Dyason* [2007] EWHC 1174 (TCC); 112 Con L.R. 95 at [77].

law to require notice of claims in respect of such liabilities to be given within a period shorter than the normal period of limitation for claims of the kind in question. The words "or of any other contract on which it depends" would apply similar reasoning to the case in which the particular contract in question was made under a "master contract" governing a series of transactions between the parties.

### (e) Terms which may be regarded as unfair

7–113 Schedule 2 to the CRA contains a list of terms "that *may* be regarded as unfair".[582] It is "indicative and non-exhaustive",[583] so that, on the one hand, a term is not unfair merely because it is of a type included in the list; and, on the other hand, a term may be unfair even though it does not fall within, or closely resemble, any such type of term. This list in effect provides further guidelines and it will be convenient to refer to terms included in the list as "prima facie unfair terms". Some of the terms listed in Pt 1 of Sch.2 are qualified by those which are referred to in Pt 2 of Sch.2, in relation to, e.g. the supply of financial services,[584] or contracts for the sale of securities, foreign currency, etc.[585] But while the terms in Pt 2 of Sch.2 are not regarded as part of the indicative list of unfair terms, they may nonetheless still be assessed for fairness unless they fall within one of the exclusions from that assessment.[586] There is little to be gained from simply reproducing the list, but some indication of their scope and nature is provided by considering them in the categories which follow.

7–114 **Terms which would also amount to exemption clauses within UCTA.**[587] Some of the prima facie unfair terms listed in Sch.2 would also be classified as exemption clauses within UCTA, if applicable. Like UCTA, Sch.2 distinguishes between clauses which exclude or limit liability for death or personal injury and other clauses excluding or limiting rights: any term of the former kind is prima facie unfair,[588] while in the case of a term of the latter kind there is the additional requirement that it must "inappropriately" exclude or limit the consumer's rights.[589] The list in Sch.2 also includes terms "limiting" the trader's obligation to respect commitments undertaken by his agents:[590] such a term would clearly be regarded as an exemption clause under UCTA. Other types of terms listed in Sch.2 which might be governed by UCTA, if applicable, are clauses entitling the trader to dissolve the contract at his discretion where the same facility is not

---

582 CRA s.63(1) (emphasis added).

583 CRA s.63(1).

584 CRA Sch.2 Pt 2 paras 21–22.

585 CRA Sch.2 Pt 2 para.24.

586 See para.7–101.

587 Before the CRA came into force, such terms might be assessed under both the 1999 Regulations and UCTA. Now, where the CRA applies, it alone governs the enforceability of the terms which follow.

588 CRA Sch.2 Pt 1 para.1. This does not include a term which is of no effect by virtue of s.65 (exclusion for negligence liability): see para.7–098.

589 CRA Sch.2 Pt 1 para.2.

590 CRA Sch.2 Pt 1 para.17.

granted to the consumer,[591] to terminate a contract of indeterminate duration without reasonable notice (except on serious grounds),[592] to alter the terms of the contract unilaterally without a valid reason which is specified in the contract,[593] to alter unilaterally without a valid reason any characteristic of the product or service to be provided,[594] or providing for the price of goods to be determined at the time of delivery or allowing a trader to increase their price.[595]

**Arbitration and adjudication clauses.** Terms "excluding or hindering"[596] the consumer's right to take legal action or exercise any other legal remedy are included in the list of prima facie unfair terms.[597] In this context, the list refers, in particular, to terms "requiring the consumer to take disputes exclusively to arbitration not covered by legal provisions."[598] At first sight, this goes beyond UCTA, which, while recognising that a term excluding or restricting a remedy may be an exemption clause,[599] expressly excepts arbitration agreements from this category.[600] The reference to arbitration clauses in Sch.2 is, however, restricted by the words "not covered by legal provisions" and the purpose of this restriction may be to narrow the category of prima facie unfair arbitration clauses to those in which the parties have agreed to exclude the powers of the courts to control the arbitrator's decision. In English law, the effectiveness of such a stipulation is subject to limitations which, in the case of a "domestic arbitration agreement", make the stipulation ineffective if it is contained in the original contract between the trader and the consumer.[601] **7–115**

**Terms not amounting to exemption clauses.** Schedule 2 also refers to many varieties of terms which would not be regarded as exemption clauses under UCTA or at common law, and it is this aspect of the Schedule which is significant in indicating the potentially wide scope of Pt 2 of the CRA. The list in Sch.2 in particular includes many types of terms which confer rights (other than rights of cancellation) on the trader. Some such clauses might, indeed, be ineffective at common law on grounds discussed elsewhere in this book. For example, the list **7–116**

[591] CRA Sch.2 Pt 1 para.7; cf. UCTA s.3(2)(b)(ii).

[592] CRA Sch.2 Pt 1 para.8, subject to Sch.2 Pt 2 paras 21 and 24; cf. UCTA s.3(2)(b)(ii).

[593] CRA Sch.2 Pt 1 para.11, subject to Sch.2 Pt 2 paras 22–24; cf. UCTA s.3(2)(b)(i).

[594] CRA Sch.2 Pt 1 para.13; cf. UCTA s.3(2)(b)(i).

[595] CRA Sch.2 Pt 1 para 15, subject to Sch2 Pt 2 paras 22–24; cf. UCTA s.3(2)(b)(i). See *RWE Vertrieb AG v Verbraucherzentrale Nordrhein-Westfalen eV* (C-92/11) EU:C:2013:180; *Du Plessis v Fontgary Leisure Parks Ltd* [2012] EWCA Civ 409.

[596] CRA Sch.2 Pt 1 para.20.

[597] For the application of the 1999 Regulations to adjudication clauses in construction contracts: see *Picardi v Cuniberti* [2002] EWHC 2923; *Zealander v Laing Homes Ltd* (2003) 19 Const. L.J. 350; *Bryen & Langley Ltd v Boston* [2005] EWCA Civ 973; [2005] C.I.L.L. 2261.

[598] CRA Sch.2 Pt 1 para.20. The Arbitration Act 1996 s.91 and the Unfair Arbitration Agreements (Specified Amounts) Order 1999 (SI 1999/2167), makes any arbitration agreement with a consumer unfair where less than £5,000 is claimed. For agreements not deemed unfair under these provisions, but assessed for fairness under the 1999 Regulations, see: *Heifer International Inc v Christiansen* [2007] EWHC 3015 (TCC); [2008] 2 All E.R. (Comm) 831; *Mylcrist Builders Ltd v Buck* [2008] EWHC 2172 (TCC); [2008] B.L.R. 611.

[599] UCTA s.13(1)(b).

[600] UCTA s.13(2).

[601] Arbitration Act 1996 s.87; para.11–050.

includes a term requiring the consumer, when in breach, to pay a disproportionately high sum in compensation.[602] At common law, such a term may be invalid as a penalty.[603] The same might be true of terms entitling the trader to forfeit a deposit paid by the consumer.[604]

7–117 **Terms not subject to any other form of legal control.** A significant number of prima facie unfair terms listed in Sch.2 are, however, of a kind that has not, apart from the CRA, and the 1999 Regulations before that, been subjected to legal control, at least as a matter of general principle, either at common law or by legislation (other than legislation applying to specific types of contract). One type of term within this group is automatically extending a contract of fixed duration unless the consumer gives notice to terminate it, where the time for giving such notice is unreasonably early.[605] In contracts outside the scope of the CRA, there appears to be no ground on which the validity of such a term could be called into question. Another type of prima facie unfair term is that obliging the consumer to fulfil all his obligations where the trader does not perform his.[606] A clause excluding the consumer's right of set-off would no doubt be regarded as an exemption clause for the purposes of UCTA;[607] but the same would not be true of a clause which so defined the consumer's obligation that he had *no* right of set-off but only a cross-claim for damages in respect of the other party's default.[608] Again, a term is prima facie invalid within Sch.2 if it gives the trader "the possibility of transferring his rights and obligations under the contract where this may reduce the guarantees for the consumer, without the consumer's agreement".[609] At common law the trader could not strictly transfer his obligations, though he might arrange for them to be vicariously performed,[610] and he could certainly transfer his rights by assignment;[611] and these powers would not seem at common law to be limited by the possibility that this would impair the consumer's guarantees. A term expressly limiting the effectiveness of guarantees given by the trader would no doubt be subject to control as an exemption clause, but that is not the type of term here under consideration. Yet another prima facie invalid term is one which has the object or effect of "irrevocably binding the consumer to terms with which the consumer had no real opportunity of becoming acquainted before the conclusion of the contract".[612] This may already represent the common law position with regard to the incorporation of standard terms by notice;[613] but at first sight it differs strikingly from the common law rule governing the incorporation of such terms by signature. The latter common law

[602] CRA Sch.2 Pt 1 para.6.

[603] See para.20–135. But see: *Munkenbeck & Marshall v Harold* [2005] EWHC 356 (TCC) (term not a penalty, but found to be unfair).

[604] CRA Sch.2 Pt 1 para.4; see para.20–147.

[605] CRA Sch.2 Pt 1 para.9.

[606] CRA Sch.2 Pt 1 para.18.

[607] See para.7–043.

[608] See para.17–019.

[609] CRA Sch.2 Pt1 para.19.

[610] See para.17–008.

[611] See Ch.15.

[612] CRA Sch.2 Pt 1 para.10.

[613] See paras 6–007–6–016.

rule is, however, concerned with the effect of *signature*,[614] rather than with *terms specifying that effect*. If a consumer signed a document containing a term incorporating by reference conditions set out in another document, then *that term* could be prima facie unfair under the CRA if the other document was not readily accessible to the consumer.

**Terms added to the list in Pt 2 of the CRA.** In comparison with the 1999 Regulations, which Pt 2 of the CRA replaces, three new types of term are added to the list of those which may be regarded as unfair: a term which has the object or effect of requiring that, where the consumer decides not to conclude or perform the contract, the consumer must pay the trader a disproportionately high sum in compensation for services which have not been supplied;[615] a term which has the object or effect of permitting the trader to determine the characteristics of the subject matter of the contract after the consumer has become bound by it;[616] and a term which has the object or effect of giving the trader the discretion to decide the price payable under the contract after the consumer has become bound by it, where no price or method of determining the price is agreed when the consumer becomes bound.[617] 7–118

## (f) Excluded terms

**Mandatory statutory or regulatory provisions.** Part 2 of the CRA does not apply to terms or notices to the extent that they reflect "mandatory statutory or regulatory provisions".[618] The effect of these words is that Pt 2 does not apply to terms which a contract is by other legislation required to contain.[619] Since the rationale for this exclusion is that the legislature may be presumed to have struck a balance between the rights and obligations of the parties to the contract affected,[620] it applies only where the content of the term is prescribed by legislation. It does not apply where, for example, terms which have been previously agreed by the parties are automatically reproduced or extended by 7–119

---

614 See para.6–004.

615 CRA Sch.2 Pt 1 para.5. The list in the 1999 Regulations was confined to a term under which a disproportionately high sum was paid if the consumer "fails to fulfil his obligation" (Sch.2 para.1(e)). The same term is listed by the CRA (Sch.2 Pt 1 para.6) and the addition of para.5 appears to be designed to catch "disguised penalties", i.e. where the consumer exercises an option to cancel but at a high price: see para.20–142.

616 CRA Sch.2 Pt 1 para.12.

617 CRA Sch.2 Pt 1 para.14.

618 CRA s.73(1)(a).

619 e.g. para.7–132. This will cover terms implied by statute. So far as terms implied at common law are concerned, since they must be reasonable it is hard to see how they could ever be found to be unfair, but the view had been expressed that the 1999 Regulations did not apply at all to such terms: *Office of Fair Trading v Abbey National Plc* [2008] EWHC 875 (Comm); [2008] 2 All E.R. (Comm) 625 at [102]; *Baybut v Eccle Riggs Country Park Ltd*, *The Times*, 13 November 2006; nor to an express term which "simply mirrored" an otherwise applicable common law rule: *Direct Line Insurance Plc v Fox* [2009] EWHC 386 (QB); [2009] 1 All E.R. (Comm) 1017 at [50].

620 *RWE Vertrieb AG v Verbraucherzentrale Nordrhein-Westfalen eV* (C-92/11) EU:C:2013:180; [2013] 3 C.M.L.R. 10 at [28].

legislation.[621] Further, the use of the word "mandatory"[622] appears to mean that this exception does not extend to provisions which are merely authorised but not required by other legislation; though the fact that they are so authorised would no doubt be taken into account in determining whether they were "unfair". For example, the Consumer Credit Act 1974 at least by implication authorises a term in a regulated hire-purchase agreement requiring the hirer on exercising his right to cancel to make a minimum payment not exceeding one half of the hire-purchase price.[623] If that sum is excessive, the hirer can seek relief by way of reduction of the minimum payment under the 1974 Act;[624] and an undesirable conflict would be created between that Act and Pt 2 of the CRA if, under the CRA, such a term were held to be "unfair" (and so not binding at all on the hirer).

7–120 **International conventions.** Part 2 also does not apply to terms or notices to the extent that they reflect "the provisions or principles of an international convention to which the United Kingdom or the EU is a party".[625]

## (g) Excluded contracts

7–121 **Employment contracts.** Neither Pt 1,[626] nor Pt 2,[627] of the CRA applies to a contract of employment or apprenticeship.

7–122 **Other excluded contracts.** The Directive which Pt 2 of the CRA is intended to implement excludes a number of other contracts: "contracts relating to succession rights"; "any contract relating to rights under family law"; "contracts relating to the incorporation and organisation of companies or partnership agreements".[628] These exceptions are unlikely to be of great practical importance in English law, which seems to provide no examples of such contracts being made between a trader and a consumer. The Directive finally excludes "contracts relating to the incorporation and organisation of companies or partnership agreements".[629]

## (h) Drafting and interpretation

7–123 **Requirement of transparency.** A trader must ensure that any written term of a consumer contract, or a consumer notice in writing, is transparent.[630] A consumer term,[631] or a consumer notice,[632] is transparent if it is expressed in plain and

[621] *Jones v Roundlistic Ltd* [2018] EWCA Civ 2284; [2019] L & T.R. 6 (decided under the 1999 Regulations).
[622] See at fn.618.
[623] CRA s.100(1).
[624] CRA s.100(3); para.20–144.
[625] CRA s.73(1)(b).
[626] CRA s.48(2).
[627] CRA s.61(2).
[628] Directive 93/13 Recital 10.
[629] Directive 93/13 Recital 10.
[630] CRA s.68(1).
[631] CRA s.64(3).
[632] CRA s.68(2).

intelligible language and it is legible.[633] Failure to express a written term "in plain, intelligible language" does not of itself make the term even prima facie unfair, but there is no reason why this is not a factor which the court might take into account.

**Interpretation.** If a term in a consumer contract, or a consumer notice, could have different meanings, "the meaning that is most favourable to the consumer is to prevail".[634] This is an obvious statutory application of the principle of *contra proferentem*,[635] applied in favour of the consumer. No doubt this will most commonly apply to terms which are not drafted in plain, intelligible language; but it does not appear to be restricted to such terms. Language which is plain and intelligible may nevertheless be ambiguous; the fascination of oracular statements lies precisely in the fact that they combine these qualities. 7–124

## (i) Effects of unfairness

**Unfair term or notice not binding on consumer.** Under s.62(1) an unfair term or notice is not binding on the consumer,[636] but this does not prevent the consumer from relying on the term or notice if the consumer chooses to do so.[637] If the term is one excluding or limiting the liability of the trader, or the rights of the consumer,[638] the latter will be able to enforce those rights as if the term had not been included in the contract. If the unfair term is one conferring rights on the trader (such as one extending a contract of fixed duration without giving the consumer a reasonable opportunity of cancelling it)[639] these rights will not arise. If effect has been given to such rights, s.62(1) may require those effects to be undone, e.g. where the term was unfair because it permitted the trader to retain sums paid by the consumer,[640] any such sums, if paid, would have to be restored.[641] 7–125

**Rest of contract generally unaffected.** In general, the fact that the unfair term does not bind the consumer does not affect the binding force, even on the consumer, of the rest of the contract, e.g. the fact that he is not bound by an exemption clause does not relieve him from liability for the price (though such liability may be reduced to the extent that a breach covered by the ineffective clause has caused him loss). The point is put beyond doubt by s.67, which provides that "the contract continues, so far as practicable, to have effect in every other respect." The inclusion of "so far as practicable" acknowledges that 7–126

[633] The assessment of whether a term is in "plain, intelligible language" is to be made from the perspective of the average consumer: see text to fn.533.
[634] CRA s.69(1). This does not apply to the interpretation of a term or notice in proceedings on an application for an injunction by a regulator under Sch.3: see para.7–131.
[635] See para.7–009.
[636] CRA s.62(1).
[637] CRA s.62(3); cf. *Pannon GSM Zrt v Erzsébet Sustikné Győrfi* (C-243/08) [2009] E.C.R. I-4713.
[638] Under CRA Sch.2 Pt 1 paras 1 and 2.
[639] Under CRA Sch.2 Pt 1 para.9.
[640] Under CRA Sch.2 Pt 1 para.6.
[641] *Chesterton Global Ltd v Finney* unreported 30 April 2010 Lambeth County Ct.

sometimes an invalid term goes so much to the heart of the contract that the effect of its not being binding on the consumer is likely to be that the consumer is not bound by the contract at all. This would, for example, be the position where the term was unfair because it irrevocably bound the consumer to terms with which he "had no real opportunity of becoming acquainted before the conclusion of the contract".[642] If that term was not binding on the consumer, it would seem to follow that the terms to which it referred[643] were not binding on him either; and if those terms contained the whole or the essential part of the contract he would not be bound by any part of that contract. The other party would, however, be so bound if the consumer wished to enforce the contract: the argument that the consumer had provided no consideration because his own promises were not binding would probably be rejected on the ground that it was not the policy of Pt 2 of the CRA to protect the other party.[644]

The question whether a term goes so much to the heart of the contract that the effect of its not being binding on the consumer is to relieve him of all obligations under the contract is obviously in borderline cases one of degree. The point may be illustrated by reference to a term which is prima facie unfair because it provides for the price of goods to be determined at the time of delivery without giving the consumer the right to cancel if that price is "too high in relation to the price agreed [if any?] when the contract was concluded".[645] One possible consequence of the consumer's taking the point that the term is not binding is that the contract contains no price term and is therefore not binding on him at all; another is that the contract contains no price term but remains in being as one under which a reasonable price must be paid;[646] and a third is that the contract remains in being as one under which the originally agreed price (if any) must be paid. No doubt the result will depend on the exact wording of the price term; but, subject to this point, it is submitted that the "reasonable price" solution will normally achieve the most satisfactory balance between the interests of the parties.[647]

## (j) Restrictions on evasion

7–127 **Secondary contracts.** Section 72 of the CRA contains a similar provision to that found in UCTA[648] to counter the evasion of the protections and controls in the Act by the simple device of using a second contract. A curious feature of this provision, however, is that it only extends the reach of the protections and controls in Pt 2 of the CRA,[649] while some of the controls and protections are found in Pt 1, e.g. provisions under which certain exemption clauses are wholly

[642] See CRA Sch.2 Pt 1 para.10.
[643] See para.7–117.
[644] See para.3–156.
[645] See CRA Sch.2 Pt.1 para.15.
[646] See *Kásler v OTP Jelzálogbank Zrt* (C-26/13) EU:C:2014:282; [2014] W.L.R. (D) 180 at [80].
[647] A reasonable price may be payable under other provisions of the CRA: e.g. s.51.
[648] UCTA s.10. The slightly different wording of s.72 of the CRA appears intended to meet some of the difficulty which is created by the interpretation of the wording of s.10 of UCTA: see para.7–073.
[649] CRA s.72(2).

ineffective.[650] Since the equivalent provision in UCTA applies to the Act as a whole,[651] this is one respect in which consumers may now be less protected than they were when UCTA also applied to consumer contracts.[652]

The effect of s.72 is that if a term of a contract ("the secondary contract") reduces the rights or remedies or increases the obligations of a person under another contract ("the main contract"), the term is subject to the provisions of Pt 2 that would apply if it were in the main contract.[653] It does not matter whether the parties to the secondary contract are the same as the parties to the main contract[654] (e.g. where T1 enters into the main contract with C and T2 enters into the secondary contract), or whether the secondary contract is a consumer contract[655] (e.g. where the main contract is between a trader and a consumer, but the secondary contract is between two consumers). Section 72 does not apply if the secondary contract is a settlement of a claim arising under the main contract.[656]

**Choice of law.** Section 74 of the CRA is intended to ensure that the trader cannot evade Pt 2 by choosing another law to govern the contract. Thus, if the law of a country or territory other than an EEA state is chosen by the parties to apply to a consumer contract, but the contract has a close connection with the UK, Pt 2 will apply despite that choice.[657] Once again, this only extends the reach of the protections and controls in Pt 2 of the CRA, and not those in Pt 1.[658] In any event (e.g. where the law applicable has not been chosen or the law of an EEA state is chosen), the consumer may be entitled to rely on the provisions set out in Pt 2 on the basis that they are "mandatory rules".[659] A term which chooses the law of the state where the trader is established is unfair in so far as it misleads the consumer into believing that only the law chosen applies without making him aware that he may have the benefit of mandatory provisions that are applicable notwithstanding the choice of law.[660] **7–128**

650 CRA ss.31, 47 and 57: see paras 7–094—7–095.

651 Strictly speaking, s.10 of UCTA applies only to Pt 1 of that Act, but that deals with the law applicable to England and Wales (Pt II applies to Scotland) and includes both provisions rendering certain clauses wholly ineffective and subjecting others to the test of reasonableness.

652 If the relevant provisions of Pt 1 do not apply to the secondary contract so that they are not wholly ineffective, the terms of that contract may then be subject to the test of fairness under s.62(1). That section is said not to "affect the operation of" ss.31, 47 and 57, but their operation cannot be affected if they do not apply at all.

653 CRA s.72(2).

654 CRA s.72(3)(a).

655 CRA s.72(3)(b).

656 CRA s.72(4).

657 CRA s.74(1).

658 See para.7–127.

659 CRA s.74(2).

660 *Verein für Konsumenteninformation v Amazon EU Sàrl* (C-191/15) EU:C:2016:612; [2017] Q.B. 252.

## 4. OTHER LEGISLATIVE TECHNIQUES

7–129 The most important legislative limitations on the effectiveness of exemption clauses and unfair terms are those contained in UCTA and in the CRA. In both, the technique of control is to deprive certain exemption clauses and unfair terms of their legal force and this is true of other legislation which is beyond the scope of this book.[661] Simply to deprive a term of legal validity might be a wholly ineffective means of control, particularly in consumer contracts. If, for example, a contract contained an invalid exemption clause the consumer might believe that he was bound by it and so not pursue his claim. Even if he did make a claim, the trader might settle it so as to avoid a judicial declaration of invalidity, and then continue to use the clause. To remedy this situation other legislative techniques have been devised.

7–130 **Supervised bargaining.** This technique requires the bargain to be made under the supervision of the court or some administrative body. For example, the Landlord and Tenant Act 1985 provides that in certain leases covenants by the landlord to repair are implied.[662] These can be excluded but only by a court order made with the consent of both parties.[663] The court's supervision ensures that no unfair advantage is taken of the tenant.

7–131 **Administrative control.** This technique involves the intervention of a public authority with powers to enforce certain legislation. It is a technique used by the CRA which empowers certain "regulators" to take action against the use of terms and notices which are considered unfair. It goes further than the 1999 Regulations which it replaces by extending that power[664] to cover terms and notices which are not transparent[665] and terms which would exclude or restrict the liability of the trader under a contract for the supply of goods,[666] digital content[667] and services,[668] or the liability of the trader for death or personal injury resulting from negligence.[669] The principal regulator is the Competition and Markets Authority ("CMA") which, along with the other bodies listed as regulators,[670] may consider a "relevant complaint" about a term or notice.[671] The regulator may apply to the court for an injunction to restrain the use of the term,[672] and may do so whether or not it has received a relevant complaint.[673] The court may grant the injunction on

[661] See, e.g. Carriage of Goods by Sea Act 1971 Sch.1, art.III(8); Public Passenger Vehicles Act 1981 s.29; Consumer Protection Act 1987 s.7; Road Traffic Act 1988 s.149.
[662] CRA s.11.
[663] Landlord and Tenant Act 1985 s.12.
[664] See Sch.3 para.3.
[665] CRA s.68; para.7–123.
[666] CRA s.31; para.7–094.
[667] CRA s.47; para.7–095.
[668] CRA s.57; paras 7–096-7–097.
[669] CRA s.65; para.7–098.
[670] CRA Sch3 para.8. Such other bodies must notify the CMA if they intend to consider a complaint: Sch.3 para.2(2).
[671] CRA Sch.3 para.2(1).
[672] A regulator other than the CMA must first notify the CMA: Sch.3 para.4.
[673] CRA Sch.3 paras 3(1), (6).

such conditions and against such of the respondents to the application as it thinks appropriate.[674] The injunction may include provision not only about the term or notice to which the application relates, but also any term or notice of a similar kind or with a similar effect.[675] If a regulator considers a relevant complaint, but decides not to make an application for an injunction, it must give reasons for its decision to the person who made the complaint.[676] The CMA may also collate and if appropriate make public information about actions taken against certain terms and notices and issue guidance.[677]

The CMA (and most of the other regulators) also has considerable investigatory powers[678] and it is envisaged that they may obtain undertakings from or on behalf of any person as to the continued use of terms or notices which it considers to be unfair in consumer contracts.[679] This continues the aim of promoting negotiations between, on the one hand, the regulators, and, on the other, traders or their trade associations. The CRA also makes amendments to Pt 8 of the Enterprise Act 2002, under which the CMA and other bodies are given powers to enforce certain consumer legislation.[680]

**Prescribing the contents of a contract.** This is another common method of controlling contracts of a particular type. It is well illustrated by the elaborate system of legislative control which exists in relation to regulated consumer credit agreements. To a considerable extent, the contents of such agreements are prescribed by the Consumer Credit Act 1974 and by delegated legislation:[681] the debtor is given a cooling-off period;[682] the creditor's power to terminate on the death of the debtor is restricted[683] and he can terminate for default only after giving a notice calling on the debtor to make good the default;[684] the debtor has the right to make early payment and thereby to earn certain rebates;[685] and in the case of a regulated hire-purchase agreement he can terminate in certain circumstances on making prescribed payments.[686] Any term in such an agreement is void to the extent of its inconsistency with any such legislative provision for the protection of the debtor.[687] A number of other types of contracts are subject to similar detailed legislative control. **7–132**

674 CRA Sch.3 para.5(1).
675 CRA Sch.3 para.5(3).
676 CRA Sch.3 para.2(3).
677 CRA Sch.3 para.7.
678 See CRA Sch.5.
679 CRA Sch.3 para.6.
680 CRA Sch.5, Sch.6 paras 67–81, Sch.7.
681 See para.5–007.
682 CRA s.67.
683 CRA s.86.
684 CRA s.87.
685 CRA ss. 94, 95.
686 CRA ss.99, 100.
687 CRA s.173. See *Wilson v Robertsons (London) Ltd* [2005] EWHC 1425; [2006] 1 W.L.R. 1248.

## CHAPTER 8

# MISTAKE[1]



[1] Cartwright, *Misrepresentation, Mistake and Non-Disclosure*, 5th edn (2019); MacMillan, *Mistakes in Contract Law* (2010); Lawson 52 L.Q.R. 79; Tylor 11 M.L.R. 257; Wade 7 C.L.J. 361; Grunfeld 13 M.L.R. 50; 15 M.L.R. 297; Cheshire 60 L.Q.R. 175; Slade 70 L.Q.R. 385; Atiyah 73 L.Q.R. 340; Atiyah and Bennion 24 M.L.R. 421; Shatwell 33 Can. Bar Rev. 164; Bamford 72 S.A.L.J. 166, 282; Stoljar 28 M.L.R. 265; Cartwright 103 L.Q.R. 594; Smith 110 L.Q.R. 400; Morgan [2018] C.L.J. 559; other articles dealing specifically with mistakes as to identity are cited at fn.178.

## 1. INTRODUCTION

8–001 In *Bell v Lever Bros Ltd*,[2] Lord Atkin said: "If mistake operates at all, it operates so as to negative or in some cases to nullify consent." Mistake *negatives* consent where it puts the parties at cross-purposes so as to prevent them from reaching agreement, e.g. because they intend to contract about different things. The cases in this category are often referred to as cases of "unilateral mistake", though in a few cases it is not possible to say which of the parties is the "mistaken" party.[3] Mistake *nullifies* consent where the parties reach an agreement which is based on a fundamental mistaken assumption made by both of them, e.g. where a contract is made to paint a portrait of someone who, unknown to either party, has just died. The cases in this category are often referred to as cases of "common mistake".[4] At law, the effect of a mistake is to make a contract void;[5] but this rule is confined within very narrow limits. It is thought to be in the interests of commercial convenience that, in general, apparent contracts should be enforced. Equity sometimes gives relief for mistakes which have no effect at common law; but the scope of such relief is restricted.[6]

The effects of unilateral mistake go to the question of whether the parties have reached agreement and may be analysed as part of the rules on offer and acceptance.[7] The effects of common mistake go to the question of whether a legally enforceable contract has been formed where the parties have reached agreement, but have done so on the basis of a shared false premise, and share some similarities with frustration.[8] In some respects, therefore, unilateral mistake and common mistake are not that closely related to each other and might have been assessed separately in other parts of this book. They are assessed here because the cases raising the issues considered in this chapter are most naturally regarded as cases of "mistake" and it is preferable to begin by considering them from that perspective.

In this chapter we shall also deal with two other instances of "mistake". The first is where one of the parties submits that a written version of the contract does not accurately reflect the agreement of the parties and a claim is made to have the written instrument rectified so that it is in accordance with their agreement.[9] The second is where one of the parties asks not to be bound by a written instrument which they have signed in the mistaken belief as to its true nature.[10]

---

2 [1932] A.C. 161 at 217.

3 See para.8–045.

4 They are also sometimes referred to as cases of "mutual mistake", but this is liable to confuse them with a particular category of unilateral mistake which is also referred to as mutual mistake, or mutual misunderstanding: see para.8–045.

5 *Associated Japanese Bank (International) Ltd v Crédit du Nord SA* [1989] 1 W.L.R. 255 at 268.

6 See para.8–030.

7 See para.8–058.

8 Though those similarities should not be pressed too far: see para.19–132.

9 See paras 8–063—8–085.

10 See paras 8–086—8–094.

# 2. COMMON MISTAKE

## (a) Common law

### (i) *In general*

**When is a common mistake "fundamental"?** In some cases, the courts have held that a contract entered into between the parties on the basis of a shared mistaken assumption is void. The conclusion reached in such cases is that the extreme injustice of holding the parties (or one of them[11]) to the contract outweighs the general principle that apparent contracts should be enforced.[12] But the circumstances must be "wholly exceptional and contracts which have been found to be void for mistake are few and far between."[13] Accordingly, a contract will only be void for a "fundamental" mistake and two broad approaches have been taken to identify such a mistake. The first is to ask whether there was an implied term that the validity of the contract depended on the existence of the state of affairs assumed to exist.[14] At one time, the implied term theory was also used to explain the closely related doctrine of frustration,[15] but it fell out of favour and it has also been rejected as the best explanation of cases where the contract is void for common mistake. Instead, but still pursuing the analogy with frustration: 8–002

> "the avoidance of a contract on the ground of common mistake results from a rule of law under which, if it transpires that one or both of the parties have agreed to do something which it is impossible to perform, no obligation arises out of that agreement."[16]

The test of "impossible to perform" should not be taken too literally.[17] It is sufficient that the mistake has rendered the subject-matter of the contract "radically and essentially different" from the subject-matter which the parties

[11] The mistake must have been shared but, when discovered, it will usually be to the advantage of one of the parties who will seek to enforce the contract.

[12] A further injustice can result in that any loss incurred by the parties in attempting to perform the contract before the mistake comes to light is left to lie where it falls. It is left to the law of unjust enrichment to curb the worst excesses of this potential situation. There is no equivalent of the Law Reform (Frustrated Contracts) Act 1943: below, paras 19–103, 19–110.

[13] *Dana Gas PJSC v Dana Gas Sukuk Ltd* [2017] EWHC 2928 (Comm); [2018] 1 Lloyd's Rep. 177 at [57].

[14] Smith 110 L.Q.R. 400, 401. cf. Morgan [2018] C.L.J. 559.

[15] See para.19–124.

[16] *The Great Peace* [2002] EWCA Civ 1407; [2003] Q.B. 679 at [73]; *Chancery Client Partners Ltd v MRC 957 Ltd* [2016] EWHC 2142 (Ch) at [37]; *National Private Air Transport Co v Kaki* [2017] EWHC 1496 (Comm) at [25].

[17] *Apvodedo NV v Collins* [2008] EWHC 775 (Ch) at [46].

believed to exist.[18] By "subject-matter" is meant the "nature, content and/or effect of the contract as a whole" and not just one particular element of the contract.[19]

8–003 **Whether performance is "impossible".** The test of whether performance of the contract is "impossible" depends upon first determining precisely what it is that the parties agreed would constitute performance.[20] For example, in *Griffith v Brymer*[21] a contract was made for the hire of a room on 26 June 1902, the day fixed for the coronation of King Edward VII, for the purpose of viewing the coronation procession. At the time the contract was made, but unknown to the parties, the decision to postpone the coronation had already been taken.[22] If the contract was merely for the hire of the room on 26 June, performance was perfectly possible. If, however, the contract was for the hire of the room on 26 June *to view the coronation procession*, performance was impossible. The contract in this case was, in fact, held void. In many cases, in determining what it is that the parties agreed, it will not be possible to rely solely upon the express provisions of the contract, since they may very well be silent about a situation which neither of the parties had foreseen.[23] It is also necessary to consider "any implications that may arise out of the surrounding circumstances".[24] The parties in *Griffith v Brymer* did not spell out in the contract that the booking was for the purpose of viewing the coronation procession, but in all the circumstances this was found to be the true nature of the "contractual adventure".

8–004 **Whether one party has taken responsibility for the mistake.** The process of determining precisely what it is that the parties have agreed is a question of the proper construction of the contract.[25] The answer to that question may be that, while performance is impossible, one of the parties had taken responsibility for the existence of the assumed state of affairs.[26] Indeed, the "reason why pleas of mistake seldom succeed is that the risk of a mistake is usually allocated by the

---

[18] *Kyle Bay Ltd v Underwriters Subscribing Under Policy No.019057/08/01* [2007] EWCA Civ 57; [2007] 1 C.L.C. 164 at [25]; *Associated Japanese Bank (International) Ltd v Crédit du Nord SA* [1989] 1 W.L.R. 255 at 268F.

[19] *Triple Seven MSN 27251 Ltd v Azman Air Services Ltd* [2018] EWHC 1348 (Comm); [2018] 4 W.L.R. 97 at [62].

[20] *Apvodedo NV v Collins* [2008] EWHC 775 (Ch) at [45].

[21] (1903) 19 T.L.R. 434; cf. para.19–042.

[22] cf. similar cases in frustration where the contract was made before the decision to postpone: see para.19–043.

[23] One exception is a "lost or not lost" clause which may be found in a contract of marine insurance. The effect of this is that both parties are bound although the thing insured had (unknown to them) perished at the time of the contract; cf. Marine Insurance Act 1906 Sch.1 r.1.

[24] *The Great Peace* [2002] EWCA Civ 1407; [2003] Q.B. 679 at [74].

[25] In this context "construction" is a broader process than merely the "interpretation" of any written instrument: see text to fn.24.

[26] *Butters v BBC Worldwide Ltd* [2009] EWHC 1954 (Ch); [2009] B.P.I.R. 1315 at [68]–[69]; *Dany Lions Ltd v Bristol Cars Ltd* [2013] EWHC 2997 (QB); [2014] 1 Lloyd's Rep. 281; *Triple Seven MSN 27251 Ltd v Azman Air Services Ltd* [2018] EWHC 1348 (Comm); [2018] 4 W.L.R. 97 at [91].

contract to one of the parties."[27] This was the position in *McRae v Commonwealth Disposals Commission*,[28] where the defendants purported to sell the wreck of an oil tanker, said to be lying on the Journmand Reef and to contain oil. The claimants sent out an expedition to salvage the tanker but found that there was not and never had been any such tanker. The High Court of Australia held that the defendants had impliedly undertaken that there was a tanker there;[29] and that, being in breach of this undertaking, they were liable in damages.

In other cases, the construction of the contract will lead to the conclusion that one party has taken the risk of the mistake, but without making them liable for breach of contract, as in *McRae*. Instead, the contract remains valid and the party in question is simply required to perform it in a way which is disadvantageous.[30] For example, in one case the tenant of a coal mine agreed to raise a minimum quantity of coal and to pay a minimum rent *in any event*. He was held liable to pay this rent, though there was not so much coal in the mine, because the parties had appreciated the risk and had thrown it on the tenant.[31] Indeed, in all cases where the contract remains valid and performable, the risk of the mistake is, in effect, allocated to one of the parties. In the leading case of *Bell v Lever Bros*,[32] which is discussed below,[33] the decision that the settlement with the directors was not void for mistake had the effect of throwing on the company the risk of the mistaken assumption that the directors had enforceable service contracts.

**Whether mistake was the fault of one of the parties.** A party may be liable, even where he did not expressly or impliedly take the risk of the mistake, if he was at fault in inducing the mistake in the mind of the other party.[34] This was a further ground for the decision in *McRae*'s case,[35] where it was said that a party could not rely on a mistake consisting "of a belief which is … entertained without any reasonable ground, and … deliberately induced by him in the mind of the other party."[36] In most cases, the answer to the question whether the mistake was the fault of one of the parties will be the same as the answer to the question whether one party has taken responsibility for the mistake.[37] 8–005

---

[27] *Dana Gas PJSC v Dana Gas Sukuk Ltd* [2017] EWHC 2928 (Comm); [2018] 1 Lloyd's Rep. 177 at [64]; *Co-operative Bank Plc v Hayes Freehold Ltd* [2017] EWHC 1820 (Ch) at [143]; *Natixis SA v Marex Financial* [2019] EWHC 2549 (Comm); [2019] 2 Lloyd's Rep. 431 at [185].

[28] (1951) 84 C.L.R. 377; and see para.20–029.

[29] cf. the explanation of *McRae's* case in *The Great Peace* [2002] EWCA Civ 1407; [2003] Q.B. 679 at [76]–[77].

[30] *Standard Chartered Bank v Banque Marocaine du Commerce Exterieur* [2006] EWHC 413 (Ch); *Dana Gas PJSC v Dana Gas Sukuk Ltd* [2017] EWHC 2928 (Comm); [2018] 1 Lloyd's Rep. 177.

[31] *Bute v Thompson* (1844) 13 M. & W. 487; cf. *Clifford v Watts* (1870) L.R. 5 C.P. 577.

[32] [1932] A.C. 161.

[33] See para.8–018.

[34] On the question of the scope of this requirement, see *Natixis SA v Marex Financial* [2019] EWHC 2549 (Comm); [2019] 2 Lloyd's rep. 431 at [211].

[35] *McRae v Commonwealth Disposals Commission* (1951) 84 C.L.R. 377.

[36] *McRae v Commonwealth Disposals Commission* (1951) 84 C.L.R. 377 at 408; cf. *The Great Peace* [2002] EWCA Civ 1407; [2003] Q.B. 679 at [76]–[77]. In *Associated Japanese Bank (International) Ltd v Crédit du Nord SA* [1989] 1 W.L.R. 255 at 268 Steyn J carries the principle further by omitting the second requirement (i.e. that of inducement) stated in the passage quoted from *McRae's* case.

[37] *The Great Peace* [2002] EWCA Civ 1407; [2003] Q.B. 679 at [84]. One party may rely simply on the fault of the other in cases where his concern is to show only that he should not be bound, e.g. if the

8–006 **The limits of "construction".** The decision in *McRae*, above, is explained on the basis of an implied term; in that case an implied warranty as to the existence of the tanker. The implied term theory which has been used to explain when a contract may be void[38] takes this process of construction one stage further, in cases where responsibility for the mistake is allocated to neither of the parties, by implying a term that the validity of the contract depends on the existence of the state of affairs assumed to exist, i.e. an implied condition precedent.[39] However, the approach advocated in *The Great Peace*[40] confines the process of construction to determining what it is the parties have agreed,[41] including whether they have allocated responsibility for the mistake to one party or the other.[42] Thereafter, and in the absence of any such allocation of responsibility, it is a question of whether the mistake has rendered performance "impossible". This is simply a different way of reaching the same result and whether one technique or the other is preferred should not affect the outcome in any case.[43] That it may have done so in some cases seems to have been due to the application of a separate doctrine of common mistake in equity (now rejected after *The Great Peace*[44]) which failed to take into account the proper construction of the contract.[45]

8–007 **Summary of requirements for common mistake.** In *The Great Peace*[46] the Court of Appeal summed up the elements which must be present before a contract is void for common mistake as follows:[47] (i) there must be a common assumption as to the existence of a state of affairs; (ii) there must be no warranty by either party that that state of affairs exists;[48] (iii) the non-existence of the state of affairs must not be attributable to the fault of either party;[49] (iv) the non-existence of the state of affairs must render performance of the contract impossible:[50] and (v) the state of affairs may be the existence, or a vital attribute, of the consideration to be provided or circumstances which must subsist if performance of the contractual adventure is to be possible.

---

Commission had sought payment from the salvors in *McRae v Commonwealth Disposals Commission* (1951) 84 C.L.R. 377, but not that the other party should be held liable in damages.

38 See para.8–002.

39 Used in the sense of a contingent condition: see para.2–105.

40 [2002] EWCA Civ 1407; [2003] Q.B. 679.

41 As in *Griffith v Brymer* (1903) 19 T.L.R. 434; para.8–003.

42 As in *McRae v Commonwealth Disposals Commission* (1951) 84 C.L.R. 377; para.8–004.

43 Smith 110 L.Q.R. 400; cf. *Associated Japanese Bank (International) Ltd v Crédit du Nord SA* [1989] 1 W.L.R. 255 where Steyn J applied the implied term theory to find that the contract was void, but then also went on to ask if the mistake was fundamental; it is perhaps not surprising that he reached the same conclusion that the contract was void; cf. *Graves v Graves* [2007] EWCA Civ 660; [2008] H.L.R. 10, where the court found it "not necessary" to consider whether the contract was void for mistake.

44 See para.8–030.

45 See, e.g. *Grist v Bailey* [1967] Ch. 532; *Laurence v Lexcourt Holdings Ltd* [1978] 1 W.L.R. 1128, both of which were doubted in *William Sindall Plc v Cambridgeshire CC* [1994] 1 W.L.R. 1016 at 1035 on the ground that the risk of the mistake had been allocated by the contract.

46 [2002] EWCA Civ 1407; [2003] Q.B. 679 at [76].

47 This is an adaptation of the elements identified by Lord Alverstone CJ in *Blakeley v Muller & Co* (1903) 19 T.L.R. 186 as necessary for a contract to be discharged for frustration.

48 See para.8–004.

49 See para.8–005.

50 See para.8–006.

In the last of these elements the Court of Appeal gives some indication of the difficulty of applying this test to different types of mistake and it is to the types of mistake which may be relied upon that we must now turn. In one sense the only type of mistake which is "fundamental", or makes performance impossible, is a mistake as to the existence of the subject-matter,[51] e.g. in *Griffiths v Brymer*[52] the "subject-matter" of the contract was identified as "a room to view the coronation procession". In the sections which follow, the types of mistake which have been considered by the courts are organised *factually*, but the issue in each case was whether, *legally*, they amounted to a mistake as to the existence of the subject-matter of the contract.

### (ii) *Mistake as to the existence of the subject-matter*

Performance is impossible, and the contract void, where both parties are mistaken as to the existence of the subject-matter. Thus it has been held that a separation deed between a man and a woman, who mistakenly thought that they were married to each other, was void, because it purported to deal with a marriage which did not exist;[53] and that a contract to buy an annuity was void where, at the time of the contract, the annuitant had died, so that the annuity no longer existed.[54] 8–008

**Sale of goods.** Contracts for the sale of non-existent goods illustrate the same point, but give rise to further difficulties. In *Couturier v Hastie*[55] a contract was made for the sale of a cargo of corn with payment due on the handing over of the shipping documents. Before the contract was made, the cargo had, unknown to the parties, become overheated and been sold at Tunis to prevent further deterioration. The seller argued that the buyer was nevertheless liable for the price: what he had bought was an interest in a maritime adventure, or such rights as the seller had under the shipping documents, against which payment was to be made.[56] But the House of Lords rejected this argument and held that the buyer was not liable. Lord Cranworth LC said: 8–009

> "The whole question turns upon the construction of the contract … Looking to the contract…alone it appears to me clearly that what the parties contemplated … was that there was an existing something to be sold and bought."[57]

The contract was for the sale of existing goods—not for the sale of the goods *or* the documents representing them. A similar issue may arise in relation to an

---

[51] *Perpetual Trustee Co Ltd v BNY Corporate Trustee Services Ltd* [2009] EWCA Civ 1160; [2010] Ch. 347 at [108]; *Lehman Brothers International (Europe) v Exotix Partners LLP* [2019] EWHC 2380 (Ch) at [195].

[52] See para.8–003.

[53] *Galloway v Galloway* (1914) 30 T.L.R. 531.

[54] *Strickland v Turner* (1852) 7 Ex. 208.

[55] (1856) 5 H.L.C. 673; Atiyah 73 L.Q.R. 487.

[56] This would normally have satisfied the buyer, as he could have claimed the insurance money. But if the contract was indeed void the buyer would not have acquired any rights by virtue of it under the "shipping documents," including the insurance policy.

[57] *Couturier v Hastie* (1856) 5 H.L.C. 673 at 681.

accessory contract. In *Associated Japanese Bank (International) Ltd v Crédit du Nord SA*[58] a guarantee of the lease of certain machinery was found to contain an express or implied undertaking in favour of the guarantor that the machinery was in existence; and as the machinery did not exist the guarantor was not liable.

In each of these cases the non-existence of the underlying subject-matter merely absolved the party prejudiced by that fact from liability, but it may as a matter of construction also impose a liability on the other party, as in *McRae*.[59] Thus there may be a good contract about a non-existent subject-matter if on the true construction of the contract the risk of non-existence is thrown on one party.[60] In *Couturier v Hastie* the risk was not thrown on the buyer: he was not liable for the price. It is more doubtful whether the risk was thrown on the seller, i.e. whether the buyer could have claimed damages for non-delivery. In *McRae*'s case the court thought that prima facie the seller in *Couturier v Hastie* had promised that the goods were in existence:[61] on this view, the contract in that case was not void and the seller could have been held liable on it. But in *Barrow, Lane & Ballard Ltd v Phillips & Co Ltd*,[62] Wright J said:

> "Where a contract relates to specific goods which do not exist, the case is not to be treated as one in which the seller warrants the existence of those specific goods, but as one in which there has been failure of consideration and mistake."

The English courts would probably adopt this approach. Prima facie a seller would not be held to undertake that the goods existed, any more than the buyer would bind himself to pay for them in any event. Thus, neither party is bound and the contract can properly be called void. This explains why the contract in *Couturier v Hastie* has long been regarded as void for mistake, although the words "void" and "mistake" do not occur in any of the judgments.

8–010 **Sale of Goods Act 1979 s.6.** In *McRae*'s case the tanker never existed; in *Couturier v Hastie* the goods originally existed but had, before the contract was made, "perished" as a commercial entity. This distinction, unimportant in principle, gives rise to difficulty because s.6 of the Sale of Goods Act 1979 provides that: "Where there is a contract for the sale of specific goods, and the goods without the knowledge of the seller have perished at the time when the contract is made, the contract is void." At first sight this section prevents the buyer from recovering damages even though the seller has expressly guaranteed that the goods exist, and the seller from recovering the price or damages even though the buyer has expressly promised to pay whether or not the goods exist. The problem may be of more theoretical than practical interest, for it does not seem that contracts on such terms are at all common. In practice the more important question is whether s.6 would apply where the contract was *either* a sale of alternatives (e.g. of the goods *or* the shipping documents representing

[58] [1989] 1 W.L.R. 255; para.8–019.

[59] See para.8–004.

[60] cf. *Kalsep Ltd v X-Flow BV*, *The Times*, 3 May 2001.

[61] *McRae v Commonwealth Disposals Commission* (1951) 84 C.L.R. 377 at 407.

[62] *Barrow, Lane & Ballard Ltd v Phillips & Co Ltd* [1929] 1 K.B. 574 at 582; para.8–022; cf. *Bell v Lever Bros* [1932] A.C. 161 at 217 (Lord Atkin: "void if in fact the article had perished before the date of the sale").

them)[63] *or* simply one of the documents. Probably s.6 would not apply as such transactions would, in the events which had happened, be sales of things in action and not of goods at all.[64]

If the parties are conscious of a doubt as to the existence of the goods, and one of them expressly undertakes to bear the risk that they may not exist, there seems to be no strong reason against upholding the contract. But in view of s.6 some ingenuity is required to reach this result. One possible argument is that s.6 is only a rule of construction which can be ousted by proof of contrary intention.[65] But many other sections of the Act expressly provide that they are subject to contrary agreement and there is no such provision in s.6. Another possibility is to say that the main contract is void but that the seller can be held liable on a collateral contract that the goods do exist. But if nothing had been done under the main contract it would be hard to find any consideration for the seller's promise under the collateral contract. It is just possible that such consideration could be found in the buyer's act of purporting to enter into the main contract, especially if it involved the execution of a document.[66] There is even more difficulty in seeing how the buyer's promise to pay can be expressed as a collateral contract, for it seems to be merely a reiteration of his principal obligation under the main contract. It is finally possible that a seller who warrants that goods exist may be liable in damages for negligent misrepresentation;[67] but the damages on such a claim would be differently assessed from those for breach of contract,[68] and the claim would fail if the seller was wholly innocent.[69]

### *(iii) Mistake as to the identity of the subject-matter*

Such a mistake usually arises where one party intends to deal with one thing and the other with a different thing, i.e. in cases of "unilateral mistake".[70] A case of common mistake which makes performance impossible could arise if *both* parties thought that they were dealing with one thing when they were in fact dealing with **8–011**

[63] But for this possibility, *Couturier v Hastie* would scarcely have reached the House of Lords. There does not seem to be any English case in which the court was called upon to consider a simple sale of goods "lost or not lost" at the time of the contract unless the buyer was entitled under the contract to documents giving him rights against the carrier or insurer in respect of the loss of the goods in certain events.

[64] See the definition of "goods" given in s.61(1) of Sale of Goods Act 1979. The normal contract for the sale of goods on c.i.f. terms is not regarded as a sale of documents but as a sale of goods to be performed by the delivery of documents: see *Arnhold Karberg & Co v Blythe, Green Jourdain & Co* [1916] 1 K.B. 495 at 510, 514. *Couturier v Hastie* provides an early illustration of a c.i.f. contract.

[65] Atiyah 73 L.Q.R. 340.

[66] cf. para.3–029. Such a consideration would be blatantly invented (para.3–009).

[67] At common law, if there was a "special relationship" (para.9–43); and possibly under s.2(1) of the Misrepresentation Act 1967 (para.9–049). But that subsection only applies "Where a person has entered into a contract ... " and it is not clear whether these words cover the case where the "contract" is wholly void.

[68] See para.9–073; cf. the damages recovered in *McRae v Commonwealth Disposals Commission* (1951) 84 C.L.R. 377 (para.20–029).

[69] See paras 9–087, 9–089–9–092.

[70] See paras 8–045–8–046.

another.[71] Mistake as to a fundamental quality of the subject-matter may sometimes be regarded as affecting the identity of the subject-matter; this possibility is discussed below.[72]

### *(iv) Mistake as to the possibility of performing the contract*

8–012 **Physical impossibility.** In *Sheikh Bros Ltd v Ochsner*[73] a contract was made for the exploitation of sisal, growing on land belonging to A. The contract provided that B was to cut and process the sisal and to deliver an average of 50 tons of sisal fibre per month to A. It was held that the contract was void because (contrary to the parties' belief) the land was not capable of producing 50 tons of fibre per month.

8–013 **Legal impossibility.** A contract may be void if it provides for something to be done which cannot, as a matter of law, be done. For example, a person cannot acquire property which he already owns, and Lords Atkin and Wright have said that, if he purports to do so in the mistaken belief that the property belongs to the other contracting party, the contract is void.[74] On the other hand, a contract is not void merely because it purports to dispose of property which belongs to a third party,[75] for in such a case the vendor might be able to acquire the property and then make a proper transfer.

One special case of legal impossibility is illegality. A contract involving the commission of a crime is often illegal.[76] The contract may be illegal even though both parties believe it to be lawful, so that in a sense they were under a mistake as to the legal possibility of performing it. Persons may, moreover, agree to do what is the actus reus of crime, but may not commit a crime if they do the act because they lack mens rea. Such an agreement might not be illegal, but would probably be void for legal impossibility.

8–014 **Commercial impossibility.** In *Griffith v Brymer*,[77] considered above,[78] performance may have been physically and legally possible, but its commercial object

---

[71] cf. *Diamond v British Columbia Thoroughbred Breeders' Society* (1966) 52 D.L.R. (2d) 146, where two horses at an auction were confused by the auctioneer and by the bidders; but the court held that the difference was one of quality only: sed quaere. See also *Grains & Fourrages SA v Huyton* [1997] 1 Lloyd's Rep. 628.

[72] See para.8–015 and following.

[73] [1957] A.C. 136.

[74] *Bell v Lever Bros Ltd* [1932] A.C. 161 at 218; *Norwich Union Fire Ins Society Ltd v Price* [1934] A.C. 455 at 463. The proposition supported by these dicta remains valid even though, to the extent that they are based on *Cooper v Phibbs* (1867) L.R. 2 H.L. 149, they may involve a misinterpretation of that case: see Matthews 105 L.Q.R. 599. For the view that the contract in that case should now be regarded as void, see also *The Great Peace* [2002] EWCA Civ 1407; [2003] Q.B. 679 at [126]–[128] (though it may not have been so regarded at the time: see [2003] Q.B. 679 at [110]).

[75] *Bell v Lever Bros Ltd* [1932] A.C. 161; *Clare v Lamb* (1875) L.R. 10 C.P. 334.

[76] See below, para.11–011 and following.

[77] (1903) 19 T.L.R. 434.

[78] See para.8–003.

was defeated. It could also be said that the parties had made a mistake about a quality of the subject-matter. On this view, the present status of the decision[79] depends on the discussion that follows.

### (v) *Mistake as to quality*

**Whether sale by description.** Where the subject-matter of the contract lacks some quality which it is believed to have, the first question is whether the quality forms part of the contractual description of the thing. If it does and "the article does not answer the description of that which is sold",[80] the contract is valid and the party who gave the description is in breach.[81] **8–015**

**Contract generally valid.** If there is no contractual misdescription, the general rule is that mistake as to quality does not make performance impossible and the contract remains valid. This is so whether the mistake prejudices the buyer (so that he pays "too much") or the seller (so that he charges "too little"). In *Scott v Littledale*[82] a contract for the sale of tea was held valid in spite of a mistake as to its quality and hence as to its value. The same rule applies where the mistake affects, not the value of the subject-matter, but its utility. In *The Great Peace*[83] a ship had been chartered for a minimum period of five days to provide escort services to another ship which was in distress at sea, in the mistaken belief, apparently shared by charterer and shipowner,[84] that the chartered ship was "in close proximity" to the one in distress or that the former was "the closest vessel" to the latter.[85] This mistake did not make the contract void since the chartered ship could, in spite of it, have reached the scene of the casualty to "provide several days of escort service".[86] This conclusion was supported by the fact that the charterers themselves did not seek to cancel the contract immediately on discovery of the truth, but only when a third ship came on the scene (which happened also to be under charter to the charterers) and was able to provide the escort services. **8–016**

**Contract sometimes void.** It does not follow from these illustrations of the general rule that a mistake as to quality can never make a contract void at law. In **8–017**

---

[79] The case is cited with apparent approval in *The Great Peace* [2002] EWCA Civ 1407; [2003] Q.B. 679 at [67].

[80] *Gompertz v Bartlett* (1853) 2 E. & B. 849 at 853; cf. *Gurney v Womersley* (1854) 4 E. & B. 133. Contrast *Harlingdon and Leinster Enterprises Ltd v Christopher Hull Fine Art Ltd* [1991] 1 Q.B. 564.

[81] *Gompertz v Bartlett* (1853) 2 E. & B. 849; Sale of Goods Act 1979 s.13; Consumer Rights Act 2015 ss.11, 36.

[82] (1858) 8 E. & B. 815; cf. *Pope & Pearson v Buenos Ayres New Gas Co* (1892) 8 T.L.R. 758; *William Sindall Plc v Cambridgeshire CC* [1994] 1 W.L.R. 1016.

[83] [2002] EWCA Civ 1407; [2003] Q.B. 679; cf. *Harrison & Jones v Bunten & Lancaster* [1953] 1 Q.B. 646.

[84] See *The Great Peace* [2002] EWCA Civ 1407; [2003] Q.B. 679 at [162].

[85] *The Great Peace* [2002] EWCA Civ 1407; [2003] Q.B. 679 at [8], [9]. The two ships were believed to have been 35 miles apart when, in fact, the distance between them was 410 miles.

[86] *The Great Peace* [2002] EWCA Civ 1407; [2003] Q.B. 679 at [165].

*Kennedy v Panama, etc. Royal Mail Co*,[87] the claimant applied for shares in a company on the faith of an untrue statement (made in good faith) that the company had secured a contract to carry mail for the New Zealand Government. The shares were allotted to him, and the actual decision was that the resulting contract between him and the company was valid.[88] But in reaching this conclusion Blackburn J referred to the Roman doctrine of *error in substantia*, by which mistakes as to quality may make a contract void if they relate to the "substance" of the subject-matter, e.g. to the metal of which a thing is made.[89] He added that:

> "the principle of our law is the same as that of the civil law; and the difficulty in every case is to determine whether the mistake or misapprehension is as to the substance of the whole consideration, going, as it were, to the root of the matter, or only to some point, even though a material point, an error as to which does not affect the substance of the whole consideration".[90]

This principle did not help the claimant as he got the very shares he bargained for and as his mistake did not affect the substance of the whole transaction. But it may be possible[91] to infer from Blackburn J's approval of the Roman texts that, in his view, mistake as to quality could in some cases make a contract void in English law.

8–018 **Bell v Lever Bros.** Whether this view is correct depends on the decision of the House of Lords in *Bell v Lever Bros Ltd*.[92] Bell and Snelling had agreed with Lever Bros to serve for five years as chairman and vice-chairman of a company controlled by Lever Bros. Before the end of this period Lever Bros wished to terminate these service contracts, and the parties entered into compensation agreements under which Bell and Snelling received between them £50,000 for loss of office. Lever Bros then discovered that Bell and Snelling had broken their service contracts in a way which would have justified their summary dismissal without compensation.[93] It was found that Bell and Snelling had forgotten about these breaches of the service contracts when the compensation agreements were made, so that they were not guilty of fraudulent concealment.[94] The remaining issue was whether the compensation agreements were void for mistake, so as to entitle Lever Bros to recover the £50,000 which they had paid under those agreements.[95] They had made the compensation agreements in the belief that the service contracts still bound them when in fact they were terminable. They had paid £50,000 to get rid of Bell and Snelling, when they might have got rid of them for nothing. Wright J and a unanimous Court of Appeal held that the

---

[87] (1867) L.R. 2 Q.B. 580. Contrast *Emmerson's Case* (1866) L.R. 1 Ch. App. 433 (where special statutory provisions affected the result).

[88] There being then no remedy for innocent misrepresentation at common law: paras 9–089, 9–094.

[89] Lawson 52 L.Q.R. 79; De Zulueta, The Roman Law of Sale, p.26. The Romans did not call such an error one of "quality" but an English lawyer could so describe it.

[90] *Kennedy v Panama, etc. Royal Mail Co* (1867) L.R. 2 Q.B. 580 at 588.

[91] The point is not clear: see *The Great Peace* [2002] EWCA Civ 1407; [2003] Q.B. 679 at [59].

[92] [1932] A.C. 161; MacMillan 119 L.Q.R. 625.

[93] See para.16–110; the harshness of this rule may account for the eventual decision in the case; cf. Treitel 104 L.Q.R. 501 at 505.

[94] Nor were they under any duty to disclose their breaches of duty: cf. para.9–180.

[95] See para.22–021.

compensation agreements were void as Lever Bros had made them under a fundamental mistake. But the House of Lords, by a narrow majority, reversed this decision. The mistake related only to a quality of the service contracts (which were the subject-matter of the compensation agreements), and was not fundamental. Lord Atkin said: "The contract released is the identical contract in both cases,[96] and the party paying for release gets exactly what he bargained for".[97] Lord Thankerton stressed that mistake even as to a fundamental quality was of no effect unless it related to some assumption which *both* parties regarded as essential. In his view there was nothing to show that Bell and Snelling regarded the binding force of the service contracts as vital: only Lever Bros did so.[98]

The mistake in this case gave rise to a belief that subject-matter which was actually worthless had a value of £50,000. It might be thought that if such a mistake is not fundamental, no mistake as to quality can ever have this effect; but once one accepts the principle that a mere mistake as to value is not fundamental, the size of that difference cannot be decisive. *Bell v Lever Bros Ltd* has indeed been described as "a quite exceptional case";[99] and dicta in it do recognise that some mistakes as to quality may be fundamental. Lord Atkin said that mistake as to quality "will not affect assent unless it is the mistake of both parties, and is as to the existence of some quality which makes the thing without the quality essentially different from the thing as it was believed to be".[100] Lord Thankerton said that a mistake as to subject-matter must relate to "something which both must necessarily have accepted in their minds as an essential and integral element of the subject-matter".[101]

**Quality mistakes affecting the subject-matter.** These are stringent requirements, which make the common law doctrine of mistake "markedly narrower in scope than the civilian doctrine"[102] referred to by Blackburn J in the dictum cited above.[103] It follows that generally a mistake as to quality will not make a contract void. According to Lord Atkin, it would not have this effect if a man bought a horse mistakenly believed to be sound; if he bought a dwelling-house mistakenly believed to be inhabitable; if he bought a garage on a road which was about to be starved of all traffic by the construction of a by-pass; and (most difficult of all): "A buys a picture from B; both A and B believe it to be the work of an old master and a high price is paid. It turns out to be a modern copy. A has no remedy in the 8–019

[96] i.e. whether the service contracts were binding on Lever Bros or terminable by them; cf. *Robert A Munro & Co Ltd v Meyer* [1930] 2 K.B. 312.
[97] *Bell v Lever Bros Ltd* [1932] A.C. 161 at 223. It was particularly important for Lever Bros to get rid of Bell and Snelling by 1 May 1929, but this fact is not stressed in the speeches of Lords Atkin and Thankerton.
[98] *Bell v Lever Bros Ltd* [1932] A.C. 161 at 235.
[99] *Associated Japanese Bank (International) Ltd v Crédit du Nord SA* [1989] 1 W.L.R. 255 at 267.
[100] *Bell v Lever Bros Ltd* [1932] A.C. 161 at 218.
[101] *Bell v Lever Bros Ltd* [1932] A.C. 161 at 256.
[102] *Associated Japanese Bank (International) Ltd v Crédit du Nord SA* [1989] 1 W.L.R. 255 at 268; approved in *The Great Peace* [2002] EWCA Civ 1407; [2003] Q.B. 679 at [90]–[91].
[103] See at fn.90.

absence of representation or warranty",[104] i.e. the contract is valid. The same view was taken in *Leaf v International Galleries*,[105] where it was said[106] that a contract for the sale of a picture would not be void if the parties mistakenly believed that it was by Constable. Similarly it was held in *Solle v Butcher*[107] that a lease was not void because the parties mistakenly believed the premises to be free from rent control; and in *Oscar Chess Ltd v Williams* it was said that a contract for the sale of a car would not be void because the parties made a mistake as to its age, so that the buyer paid more than he would have done, had he known the truth.[108]

According to other dicta and decisions a mistake as to quality can sometimes make a contract void.[109] For example, it has been said that a contract for the sale of land believed to be freehold could be avoided if it turned out to be leasehold.[110] In *Bell v Lever Bros Ltd* Greer LJ said in the Court of Appeal that a contract for the sale of a horse, believed to be a racehorse, would be void if it turned out to be a carthorse:[111] it may be significant that Lord Atkin, in his example of the *unsound* horse,[112] did not contradict this suggestion. Similarly, in *Scott v Coulson*[113] a policy on the life of one Death was sold for £460 on the assumption that Death was alive. The price paid was therefore fixed in relation to the surrender value of the policy. In fact Death was dead, so that the policy had matured and was worth £777. The vendor successfully claimed to have the contract set aside and Vaughan Williams LJ said[114] that it was void at law. Again, in the *Associated Japanese Bank*[115] case payments to be made by the lessee under a purported sale and lease-back of machinery were guaranteed by the defendant. In fact no such machinery existed, so that the lease was voidable for fraud; and it was said that the guarantee was void for mistake. And in *Nicholson & Venn v Smith-Marriott*[116] the defendants put up for auction table napkins "with the crest of Charles I and the authentic property of that monarch". On the faith of this

[104] *Bell v Lever Bros Ltd* [1932] A.C. 161 at 224. Contrast *Smith v Zimbalist* 2 Cal. App. 2d 234; 38 P.2d 170 (1934) (violins mistakenly believed to be by Stradivarius and Guarnerius: held buyer not liable for the price on grounds of mistake and breach of warranty).
[105] [1950] 2 K.B. 86.
[106] *Leaf v International Galleries* [1950] 2 K.B. 86 at 89; para.8–020; cf. *Harlingdon and Leinster Enterprise Ltd v Christopher Hull Fine Art Ltd* [1991] 1 Q.B. 564, where the buyer's claim (which failed) was based solely on breach; no attempt was made to base it on mistake as to the authenticity of the picture.
[107] [1950] 1 K.B. 671; cf. *Magee v Pennine Ins Co Ltd* [1969] 2 Q.B. 507; 85 L.Q.R. 454; Harris 32 M.L.R. 688. For the relief given in these two cases on equitable grounds see para.8–028.
[108] *Oscar Chess Ltd v Williams* [1957] 1 W.L.R. 370 at 373; cf. *F E Rose (London) Ltd v W H Pim Jnr & Co Ltd* [1953] 2 Q.B. 450 at 459.
[109] In addition to those referred to in the text, see: *Nutt v Read* (2000) 32 H.L.R. 761.
[110] *Durham v Legard* (1835) 34 Beav. 611 at 613, possibly expressing a purely equitable view.
[111] *Bell v Lever Bros Ltd* [1931] 1 K.B. 557 at 597; cf. *Naughton v O'Callaghan* [1990] 3 All E.R. 191 (horse sold by auction with a false pedigree said to be "a different animal altogether" (at 197) but it was not suggested that the contract was void).
[112] *Bell v Lever Bros Ltd* [1932] A.C. 161 at 224; fn.104.
[113] [1903] 2 Ch. 249.
[114] *Scott v Coulson* [1903] 2 Ch. 249 at 252; cf. *Gloyne v Richardson* [2001] EWCA Civ 716; [2001] B.C.L.C. 669 at [41] (agreement made in mistaken belief that option had been exercised).
[115] *Associated Japanese Bank (International) Ltd v Crédit du Nord SA* [1989] 1 W.L.R. 255; Treitel 104 L.Q.R. 501; Cartwright [1988] L.M.C.L.Q. 300.
[116] (1947) 177 L.T. 189.

description the lot was bought for £787 10s., but the napkins were Georgian and worth £105 only. The buyer recovered damages for breach of contract but Hallett J also said that the contract might have been treated *by the buyer*[117] as void for mistake. The transaction could be regarded in two ways. The parties may have intended to buy and sell antique table linen: in this case a mistake as to its exact age, provenance or value would not be fundamental; performance would not have been "impossible". Alternatively, the parties may have intended to buy and sell a Carolean relic; in this case their mistake would be fundamental; performance would be impossible and the contract would be void. This is just another example of the need, first, to identify precisely what was the subject-matter of the contract.

**A general principle?** The cases and examples concerning mistakes as to quality cannot be perfectly reconciled; but there is a principle which runs through them. A thing has many qualities. A car may be black, old, fast and so forth. For any particular purpose one or more of these qualities may be uppermost in the minds of the persons dealing with the thing. Some particular quality may be so important to them that they actually use it to *identify* the thing. If the thing lacks that quality, it is suggested that the parties have made a fundamental mistake, even though they have not mistaken one thing for another, or made a mistake as to the existence of the thing, as such. The matter may be tested by imagining that one can ask the parties, immediately after they made the contract, what its subject-matter was. If, in spite of the mistake, they would give the right answer the contract is valid at law. Thus in *Bell v Lever Bros Ltd*, the parties would have said, quite rightly: "We are contracting about a service agreement". In *Nicholson & Venn v Smith-Marriott* they might have said, rightly, "We are contracting about antique table linen", in which case the contract would be valid; or they might have said, wrongly, "We are contracting about a Carolean relic", in which case the contract would be void. 8–020

This suggested test for determining whether a mistake is fundamental presupposes that both parties would give the same answer to the question "what are you contracting about?" If they would give different answers, the mistake, whatever else its effect may be, will not *nullify* consent. A seller may intend to sell antique table linen and the buyer to buy a Carolean relic. If the parties are thus at cross-purposes consent may be *negatived*. The question whether the buyer could rely on the mistake as making the contract void at law would then depend on factors discussed later in this chapter.[118]

**Difficult cases.** Most of the cases and illustrations given above can be explained in accordance with the principle just suggested, but three of them give rise to particular difficulty. The first is *Scott v Coulson*,[119] where the subject-matter of the contract would no doubt have been described as "an insurance policy" so that the contract ought to have been valid at law. The view that the contract was void is also very hard to reconcile[120] with *Bell v Lever Bros Ltd*. If the difference 8–021

[117] See para.8–009.
[118] See para.8–034 and following.
[119] [1903] 2 Ch. 249; see para.8–018.
[120] *The Great Peace* [2002] EWCA Civ 1407; [2003] Q.B. 679 at [87].

between a binding and a terminable contract is not fundamental, why is there a fundamental difference between a contingent and an accrued debt?[121]

A second source of difficulty is that the contract of guarantee in the *Associated Japanese Bank* case was held to be *void*. The subject-matter of that contract was not the machinery, but the lease *of* the machinery, and this contract was not void but only voidable for fraud. Yet the compensation agreements in *Bell v Lever Bros Ltd* were held *valid* even though their subject-matter, too, consisted of the earlier service contracts which were also terminable but not void. One possible way of distinguishing the cases is to say that the lease in the *Associated Japanese Bank* case was voidable for fraud, so that it was liable to be rescinded ab initio,[122] while the factor vitiating the service agreements in *Bell v Lever Bros Ltd* was breach, which entitled the employers to terminate them by dismissing the employees, but not with retrospective effect:[123] hence the mistake in the former case could be said to be more serious than that in the latter case. Another is that in the *Associated Japanese Bank* case the guarantee was part of a composite transaction intended to raise money on the security of the alleged machinery, so that "the analogy of the classic *res extincta* cases … [was] fairly close".[124] Hence the crucial fact was that guarantor and lessor both mistakenly believed that *the machinery* existed: this was more important than their state of mind as to the legal effect of the fraud on *the lease*.

The third source of difficulty is Lord Atkin's example of a modern copy bought for a high price in the belief that it is an old master, supported by dicta in *Leaf v International Galleries*.[125] The assumption behind these statements seems to be that the parties would identify the subject-matter simply as "a picture"; but this seems to be a questionable assumption. Suppose that A has just paid B £10 million for what both believe to be a painting by Rembrandt. If A were asked "what have you just bought?" he would almost certainly reply "a Rembrandt"—not "a picture." With the greatest respect, this type of case stands on a different level from Lord Atkin's other examples.[126] Nor are the dicta in *Leaf v International Galleries* conclusive, for the buyer there sought only to rescind the contract for misrepresentation and did not claim that it was void for mistake.[127] It is submitted that, on the bare facts given by Lord Atkin, the contract should be held void. Of course, in practice the facts of cases of this kind are likely to be more complex. On the one hand, it may be a term of the contract that the picture is authentic, in which case the seller is liable for breach of contract[128] so that no

---

121 In *Bell v Lever Bros Ltd* [1932] A.C. 161 at 236 Lord Thankerton regards the contract in *Scott v Coulson* as one for the sale of a non-existent subject-matter.

122 See para.9–093 and following.

123 See paras 18–016–18–017; cf. para.7–027.

124 *Associated Japanese Bank (International) Ltd v Crédit du Nord SA* [1989] 1 W.L.R. 255 at 269.

125 [1950] 2 K.B. 86; cf. also *Hindle v Brown* (1907) 98 L.T. 44, where only misrepresentation was discussed.

126 See para.8–019. The answer to the question "what have you just bought?" would in those cases be: "a horse", "a house", and "a garage."

127 Nor did he claim damages for breach of warranty, though Denning and Jenkins LJJ thought that this remedy was open to him; cf. *Harlingdon and Leinster Enterprises Ltd v Christopher Hull Fine Art Ltd* [1991] 1 Q.B. 564 at 578, stating that, at least between art dealers, the principle of caveat emptor applied.

128 As in *Peco Arts Inc v Hazlitt Gallery Ltd* [1983] 1 W.L.R. 1315.

question of mistake will arise. On the other hand, a picture may be sold speculatively, in which case the contract will be valid and the seller will not be in breach, even though the buyer's belief in the authenticity of the picture turns out to be incorrect. Between these extremes lies the large group of cases in which both parties may believe the picture to be authentic but in which there can be no certainty on the point; scholarly or expert opinion as to the authenticity of a picture may vary from time to time.[129] In cases within this group, it has been held that the seller does not impliedly undertake that the picture is genuine (at least where the sale is by one dealer to another, and the seller indicates that he is not an expert on the work of the artist in question);[130] and it is submitted that the element of uncertainty would make it equally inappropriate to regard such a case as one in which the contract was void for mistake.

### *(vi) Mistake as to quantity*

Mistake as to quantity may be capable of invalidating a contract at law. In *Cox v Prentice*[131] a silver bar was sold under a mistake as to its weight. The buyer (who was the party prejudiced by the mistake) obtained a verdict for damages for the difference in value between the weight of the bar as it was, and as it was believed to be. The court added that the buyer could have recovered the price he paid for the bar, which may suggest that he had the option of treating the contract as void for mistake. Similarly, Lord Atkin in *Bell v Lever Bros Ltd* said: "I agree that an agreement to take an assignment of a lease for five years is not the same thing as to take an assignment of a lease for three years, still less a term for a few months,"[132] though it is not clear from the context whether Lord Atkin thought that such a mistake could make a contract void. And in *Barrow, Lane & Ballard Ltd v Phillips & Co Ltd*[133] a contract for the sale of an "indivisible parcel" of 700 bags of nuts was held to be void because, unknown to the parties, only 591 bags were in existence. 8–022

### *(vii) Mistake of law*

**Contract may be void for mistake of law.** At common law, the traditional view was that a mistake could affect the validity of a contract only if it was one of "fact" as opposed to one of "law". That view was rejected by the Court of Appeal in *Brennan v Bolt Burdon.*[134] In that case litigation was settled after a ruling that the claim form had been served out of time. The mistaken assumption of the parties to the settlement agreement was that, on the basis of the law as it then stood, this ruling could not be successfully challenged. Shortly afterwards, the 8–023

---

[129] See *Firestone & Parson Inc v Union League of Philadelphia* 672 F. Supp. 819 (1987); affirmed 833 F. 2d. 304; cf. *Luxmoore-May v Messenger May Baverstock* [1990] 1 W.L.R. 1009 at 1028; *Thomson v Christie Manson & Woods Ltd* [2005] EWCA Civ 555; [2005] P.N.L.R. 38.

[130] *Harlingdon and Leinster Enterprises Ltd v Christopher Hull Fine Art Ltd* [1991] 1 Q.B. 564.

[131] (1815) 3 M. & S. 344; cf. *Devaux v Connolly* (1849) 8 C.B. 640 at 659.

[132] *Bell v Lever Bros Ltd* [1932] A.C. 161 at 223.

[133] [1929] 1 K.B. 574.

[134] [2004] EWCA Civ 1017; [2005] Q.B. 303.

Court of Appeal[135] reversed the earlier decision upon which the ruling had been based. The issue to which this gave rise was whether the settlement was void by reason of the parties' common mistake of law. The earlier decision of the House of Lords in *Kleinwort Benson Ltd v Lincoln CC*[136] had removed the bar preventing recovery of payments made under a mistake of law, the mistake there being the belief that contracts under which moneys had been paid to local authorities were valid when they were later ruled to be void because the authorities concerned had gone beyond their powers.[137] According to Kay LJ in *Brennan v Bolt Burdon*, it could not be doubted that the effect of the decision in the *Kleinwort Benson* case "now permeates the law of contract",[138] a view which was shared by the other members of the court.[139] It is now possible therefore for a contract to be void for a common mistake of law.[140] This decision is to be welcomed, if only because the distinction between mistakes of fact and mistakes of law was not always easy to draw[141] or to justify.[142] However, it raises the difficult question of *when* a contract will be void for a mistake of law.

8–024 **The nature of a mistake of law.** The principal difficulty faced by the House of Lords in deciding whether to remove the mistake of law bar in *Kleinwort Benson v Lincoln CC* was how to deal with the effect of "changes" in the law; in particular where the law as it is understood at the relevant time is held to be otherwise by a later decision of the courts. The majority accepted the "declaratory theory" under which the later decision does not change the law, but merely declares what it has always been.[143] The effect is that where parties act on the basis that the law is X, including when it has been declared to be X by an earlier judicial decision, they will be found to have been mistaken if the law is later declared to be Y. In *Kleinwort Benson v Lincoln CC* the House of Lords was concerned with the effect of such a "retrospective" mistake[144] on the security of payments. In *Brennan v Bolt Burdon*, the Court of Appeal was concerned with its effect on the certainty of contract.

---

135 *Anderton v Clwyd CC* [2002] EWCA Civ 933; [2002] 3 All E.R. 813.
136 [1999] 2 A.C. 349; para.22–025.
137 *Hazell v Hammersmith and Fulham LBC* [1992] 2 A.C. 1.
138 *Brennan v Bolt Burdon* [2004] EWCA Civ 1017; [2005] Q.B. 303 at [10]. Contrast *S v S* [2002] EWHC 223; [2003] Fam. 1 at [70].
139 Contrast *BP v Aon Ltd* [2006] EWHC 424 (Comm); [2006] 1 C.L.C. 881 at [274]: "substantial area of doubt" whether the *Kleinwort Benson* decision applies to a contract entered into under a mistake of law. The decision in the *Brennan* case is not referred to in the judgment of Colman J.
140 *Graves v Graves* [2007] EWCA Civ 660; [2008] H.L.R. 10 at [32].
141 See *Friends Provident Life Office v Hilliers Parker May & Rowden* [1997] Q.B. 85.
142 cf. *Avon CC v Howlett* [1983] 1 W.L.R. 605 at 620; *Woolwich Equitable Building Society v IRC (No.2)* [1993] A.C. 70 at 154, 199.
143 Finnis 115 L.Q.R. 170. See Beatson, in Burrows & Rodger (eds), *Mapping the Law: Essays in Memory of Peter Birks* (2006) and the comments, in response, of Lord Hoffmann in *Deutsche Morgan Grenfell Group Plc v IRC* [2006] UKHL 49; [2007] 1 A.C. 558 at [23].
144 A change in legislation will only have this effect where the legislation itself is intended to apply retrospectively—a rare occurrence—and even then, two of the Law Lords in the majority in *Kleinwort Benson Ltd v Lincoln CC* [1999] 2 A.C. 349 (Lord Goff, at 381; Lord Hope, at 410) did not think it would lead to a finding of mistake based on the earlier legislation.

**Contracts of compromise.** The settlement in *Brennan v Bolt Burdon* amounted to a compromise of extant litigation, enshrined in a consent order.[145] All three members of the Court of Appeal indicated that there may have been a very short answer to the appeal if it had been argued that, as a matter of public policy, a compromise of extant litigation should never be vitiated for mistake[146] because of the need for finality.[147] As it was, the case was decided on the basis that a compromise *may* be vitiated by a common mistake of law. The Court of Appeal found that the earlier decision supporting the ruling that the claim form was served out of time was open to challenge, even if an opinion had been obtained that it would be difficult. It ought also to have been known that an appeal from that very decision was shortly to be heard. This fell short of the unequivocal but mistaken view of the law in *Kleinwort Benson v Lincoln CC*. As a result, the compromise was not, in fact, void for mistake. **8–025**

**Other contracts.** The likely impact of the decision in *Brennan v Bolt Burdon* for contracts generally is a little difficult to assess because the observations made by the Court of Appeal were so obviously made in the context of a contract of compromise. For example, a certain emphasis was placed on the observation of Lord Hope in *Kleinwort Benson* that "a state of doubt is different from that of mistake".[148] This should not be applied too literally since, even in cases of the most fundamental mistake of fact, there can always be said to have been an element of doubt about the assumptions made by the parties. What matters is the degree of doubt and whether this can be taken to imply that the risk of the mistake had been allocated by the contract.[149] In other words, the mistake of law bar having been lifted, future cases should be decided simply by applying the tests hitherto applied to mistakes of fact.[150] As Sedley LJ observed[151] those tests may have to be adapted a little before the effect of a mistake of law "can be **8–026**

[145] Orders made by consent have the effect of contracts: *Huddersfield Banking Co Ltd v Henry Lister & Son Ltd* [1895] 2 Ch. 273; *Allcard v Walker* [1896] 2 Ch. 369 (order set aside in equity, on terms, for a mistake of law). But a "consent" order may be merely one to which a party submits without objection in which case it does not have the effect of a contract: *Siebe Gorman & Co Ltd v Pneupac Ltd* [1982] 1 W.L.R. 185; and in matrimonial proceedings consent orders are not now regarded as contracts: *Thwaite v Thwaite* [1982] Fam. 1; *Jenkins v Livesey* [1985] A.C. 424.

[146] Kay LJ expressed the rule in terms of vitiation by a subsequent judicial decision, but the policy of finality should exclude vitiation for any mistake, whether of law, or fact.

[147] *Brennan v Bolt Burdon* [2004] EWCA Civ 1017; [2005] Q.B. 303 at [23], [31], [62]; cf. *BCCI v Ali* [2002] 1 A.C. 251 which concerned a general release of a prospective dispute. The case was argued on the basis of construction and the finding of the majority was that an employee had not given up a claim of which he could not have been aware; cf. *Brazier v News Group Newspapers Ltd* [2015] EWHC 125 (Ch); affirmed [2016] EWCA Civ 79. The principal "mistake", if *BCCI v Ali* is considered in such terms, was a mistake of fact, i.e. as to the corrupt way in which the employers had been running the business (though that may only have been a unilateral mistake of the employee); this only became significant as a matter of law when the House of Lords later recognised the availability of damages for the "stigma" of having worked for such an employer: *Malik v BCCI* [1998] A.C. 20. See para.20–097.

[148] *Kleinwort Benson v Lincoln CC* [1999] 2 A.C. 349 at 410B; *In the matter of Kaupthing Singer & Friedlander Ltd* [2010] EWCA Civ 561; [2010] 2 B.C.L.C. 259 at [90].

[149] *Deutsche Morgan Grenfell Group Plc v IRC* [2006] UKHL 49; [2007] 1 A.C. 558 at [22] (Lord Hoffmann); cf. Lord Simon Brown, at [175].

[150] See para.8–007.

[151] *Brennan v Bolt Burdon* [2004] EWCA Civ 1017; [2005] Q.B. 303 at [59].

equiparated with the impossibility of a contractual venture". In *Brennan v Bolt Burdon*, the answer was clearly that the risk of the mistake had been allocated to the claimant, or was the fault of those advising her, so that she was left with a valid, but disadvantageous, contract. That will be the usual outcome in contracts of compromise of whatever hue.[152] For other contracts it may be found that the effect of the mistake is to make performance of the contract something fundamentally different from that which the parties had contemplated, in circumstances where the risk of the mistake had not been allocated to one of them.[153] In such cases the contract will be void for a mistake of law.

### (b) Equity

#### (i) General

8–027 The extent to which it is necessary to take account of a different approach in equity to the effect of a common mistake has been greatly reduced as a result of two developments. First, the Court of Appeal has held that there is no separate doctrine of common mistake in equity under which a contract might be rescinded in circumstances where it is valid at law.[154] Secondly, the lifting of the bar on mistakes of law[155] means that it is no longer necessary to take account of cases in which relief had been given in equity for certain types of mistake which would not have affected the validity of the contract under the common law as it then stood because they were mistakes of law.[156] It is still possible for equity to give relief by refusing specific performance of a contract entered into on the basis of a common mistake which is not sufficient to make the contract void at common law, but this form of relief is largely confined to cases of unilateral mistake.[157] The other form of equitable relief still available, rectification, is specifically concerned with mistakes in reducing the parties' agreement to writing and is considered separately.[158]

#### (ii) No separate doctrine of common mistake in equity

8–028 **The separate doctrine.** A line of twentieth-century cases supported the view that a contract could be rescinded (on terms, if appropriate) on the ground that it was made under a mistake, even though the mistake was not fundamental in the narrow common law sense and so did not affect the validity of the contract at law. The leading case was *Solle v Butcher*[159] where a flat had been let for £250 per annum, both parties mistakenly believing that it was free from rent control, when

[152] See *Kyle Bay Ltd v Underwriters Subscribing Under Policy No.019057/08/01* [2007] EWCA Civ 57; [2007] Lloyd's Rep. I.R. 460.
[153] e.g. the sort of mistake made in *Kleinwort Benson v Lincoln CC* itself, where it was not necessary to rely on a mistake of law to set aside the contract; it was void simply because it was ultra vires.
[154] *The Great Peace* [2002] EWCA Civ 1407; [2003] Q.B. 679. See para.8–030.
[155] See para.8–023.
[156] e.g. *Allcard v Walker* [1896] 2 Ch. 369. See the 11th edn, pp.314–316.
[157] See para.8–032, 8–060.
[158] See para.8–063 and following.
[159] [1950] 1 K.B. 671.

in fact it was subject to the Rent Acts and to a standard rent of £140 per annum. Had the landlord realised this, he could, before granting the lease, have increased the rent to about £250 per annum, on account of the work done by him to the flat; but he had no right to make such an increase during the currency of a lease already granted. The tenant claimed a declaration that the standard rent was £140 per annum and repayment of the excess; the landlord claimed rescission of the lease. It was held that the lease could be rescinded, though it was valid at law. As it would have caused considerable hardship to the tenant to turn him out of the flat, the court gave him the option of staying on if he paid the standard rent plus the amount by which the landlord could have increased it, had he been aware of the true position when he granted the lease.

**Criticism.** In the 50 years after *Solle v Butcher*, the equitable power to rescind contracts for mistakes which did not invalidate them at law was exercised in a number of first instance and Court of Appeal decisions.[160] In one of these cases[161] Winn LJ dissented on the ground that the majority view (that the contract should be rescinded) was inconsistent with the refusal of the House of Lords in *Bell v Lever Bros Ltd*[162] to grant relief for mistake; and no satisfactory way was ever found of explaining the relationship between that leading case and the equitable jurisdiction to rescind.[163] One view was that the equitable jurisdiction could have been exercised in *Bell v Lever Bros Ltd* if an attempt had been made to invoke it; but some of the relevant equity cases were cited to,[164] and equitable principles were discussed by, the House of Lords.[165] A second view was that the exercise of the equitable jurisdiction depended on relative degrees of "fault" so that rescission would not be ordered in favour of a party who was himself at fault,[166] while conversely it could be ordered against one who had acted improperly in inducing the mistake,[167] or whose insistence on his legal rights after becoming aware of the mistake was unconscientious.[168] The difficulty with this view was that, since there was no definition of "fault" for this purpose, it did little to clarify the scope of the jurisdiction. A third view was that the common law rules laid down in *Bell v Lever Bros Ltd* determined the rights of the parties, while the equitable jurisdiction entitled the court to vary these at its discretion, so that 8–029

[160] See, e.g. *Laurence v Lexcourt Holdings Ltd* [1978] 1 W.L.R. 1128; *Grist v Bailey* [1967] Ch. 532 (both of which were doubted in *William Sindall Plc v Cambridgeshire CC* [1994] 1 W.L.R. 1016 at 1035); *Magee v Pennine Ins Co Ltd* [1969] 2 Q.B. 507.
[161] *Magee v Pennine Ins Co Ltd* [1969] 2 Q.B. 507.
[162] [1932] A.C. 161; para.8–018.
[163] A.L.G. 66 L.Q.R. 169; Atiyah & Bennion 24 M.L.R. 421 at 439.
[164] e.g. *Paget v Marshall* (1884) 28 Ch D. 255; cf. *Associated Japanese Bank International Ltd v Crédit du Nord SA* [1989] 1 W.L.R. 255 at 256.
[165] See the discussion in *Bell v Lever Bros Ltd* [1932] A.C. 161 of *Cooper v Phibbs* (1872) L.R. 2 H.L. 149; and the discussion of the latter case in *The Great Peace* [2002] EWCA Civ 1407; [2003] Q.B. 679 at [100] and following.
[166] *Solle v Butcher* [1950] 1 K.B. 671 at 693; cf. *Laurence v Lexcourt Holdings Ltd* [1978] 1 W.L.R. 1128; *Associated Japanese Bank International Ltd v Crédit du Nord SA* [1989] 1 W.L.R. 255 at 270.
[167] e.g. *Cocking v Pratt* (1749) 1 Ves. Sen. 400; *Torrance v Bolton* (1872) L.R. 8 Ch. App. 118; cf. *Beauchamp v Winn* (1873) L.R. 6 H.L. 223 at 233.
[168] e.g. *Hitchcock v Giddings* (1817) 4 Price 135; but see *Riverlate Properties Ltd v Paul* [1975] Ch. 133 at 140–141.

equity "supplemented"[169] the common law; but the difficulty with this view lay in the failure of the relevant cases to formulate any principles governing the equitable discretion.

8–030 **Abolition of the equitable doctrine** At one time it seemed that, in spite of the criticisms summarised in the preceding paragraph, the courts had accepted the existence of the equitable jurisdiction, though without giving any clear answer to the question just when a contract which was valid at law could be rescinded in equity. The issue arose again in *The Great Peace*[170] where, as will be recalled, it was held that a charterparty was not void at law[171] by reason of a mistake as to the "proximity" of the chartered ship to the vessel to which she was to render escort services. The Court of Appeal further held that there was no power to rescind the charterparty in equity. It did so on the ground that *Solle v Butcher* was inconsistent with *Bell v Lever Bros Ltd*[172] and that there was, therefore, no equitable power to rescind a contract which, in spite of the mistake, was "valid and enforceable on ordinary principles of contract law".[173] Only by taking this view could "coherence … be restored to this area of our law" which had been thrown into "confusion" by *Solle v Butcher* and later cases which had exercised the jurisdiction to rescind.[174]

8–031 **Assessment of the current position.** To the extent that equity had allowed rescission for mistakes which do not make a contract void at law, it sacrificed the requirement of certainty which is emphasised by the common law. It may be, however, that the need for certainty is over-stated.[175] This is suggested by the fact that the American rules on this subject are much closer to those of English equity than to those of the English common law,[176] and do not seem to have caused widespread inconvenience. Nor has such inconvenience resulted from the rule that a contract can be set aside for even a wholly innocent misrepresentation.[177] Yet from the representor's point of view this rule creates almost as much uncertainty as would a broad doctrine of mistake. In *The Great Peace* Lord Phillips MR merely hinted that there is "scope for legislation to give greater flexibility to our law of mistake than the common law allows".[178] Two further possibilities cannot be ruled out. The first is that the Supreme Court might yet disagree with the Court of Appeal on the issue of discretionary relief for

---

169 *Associated Japanese Bank (International) Ltd v Crédit du Nord SA* [1989] 1 W.L.R. 255 at 267.
170 [2002] EWCA Civ 1407; [2003] Q.B. 679.
171 See para.8–016.
172 *The Great Peace* [2002] EWCA Civ 1407; [2003] Q.B. 679 at [157], [160].
173 *The Great Peace* [2002] EWCA Civ 1407; [2003] Q.B. 679 at [161].
174 *The Great Peace* [2002] EWCA Civ 1407; [2003] Q.B. 679 at [157].
175 What lies at the heart of the reasoning in *The Great Peace* is the need for doctrinal consistency, rather than any attempt to evaluate past exercises of the equitable jurisdiction on their merits.
176 Restatement 2d, Contracts, paras 152, 153.
177 See para.9–095.
178 *The Great Peace* [2002] EWCA Civ 1407; [2003] Q.B. 679 at [161]. His reference to the analogy of the Law Reform (Frustrated Contracts) Act 1943 is puzzling since that Act deals with the consequences of discharge for frustration and says nothing about *when* a contract is discharged for frustration. There may be scope for something similar to the 1943 Act to deal with the consequences of a finding that a contract is void for mistake (see para.19–133), but that was not the issue Lord Phillips was addressing.

mistake,[179] and the second (no doubt more remote) one is that the Supreme Court might even review the narrowness of the scope of mistake at common law as laid down in *Bell v Lever Bros Ltd*.[180] With regard to *The Great Peace* itself, it may be relevant to note that the question of equitable relief arose in the context of a charterparty, that this is a type of contract in which certainty (which would be subverted by the exercise of a discretion to rescind) is of paramount importance, and that on the facts there was said to be "no injustice in the result".[181]

### (iii) *Refusal of specific performance*

A mistake which is not sufficient to make a contract void at common law may be used as a defence to an action for specific performance.[182] Most of the cases in which specific performance has been refused have been concerned with unilateral mistake,[183] but one possible effect of the decision in *The Great Peace* may be to lead to more widespread use of this form of relief in cases of common mistake, where appropriate.[184] Since it leaves the contract enforceable at law,[185] it does not seriously prejudice the interests of certainty. **8–032**

**No relief for mistake as to expectation.** Equity may grant relief for a mistake which is not fundamental in the narrow common law sense, but not for a mistake "which related to the expectation of the parties".[186] This is illustrated by *Amalgamated Investment & Property Co Ltd v John Walker & Sons Ltd*[187] where a contract was made for the sale of a London warehouse which the purchaser (to the vendor's knowledge) intended to redevelop. Before the contract was made, a government official had decided that the warehouse ought to be listed as a building of special architectural or historic interest. But the actual listing took place only after the conclusion of the contract; its effect was to make it harder to obtain permission to redevelop. If such permission were refused the value of the property would be reduced by some £1,500,000 below the contract price of £1,710,000. The Court of Appeal held that equity could not intervene, whether by **8–033**

---

[179] In *Pitt v Holt* [2013] UKSC 26; [2013] 2 W.L.R. 1200 at [115] the Supreme Court accepted, obiter, that *The Great Peace* had effectively overruled *Solle v Butcher*.

[180] [1932] A.C. 161; cf. Treitel 104 L.Q.R. 501 at 505.

[181] *The Great Peace* [2002] EWCA Civ 1407; [2003] Q.B. 679 at [166]. The outcome was that the owners recovered five days' hire even though the charterers had cancelled only about two hours after the chartered ship had changed course towards the stricken vessel: see [15], [21].

[182] Specific performance will clearly be refused where the contract is void at law, e.g. where a person contracts to buy his own property: *Jones v Clifford* (1876) 3 Ch D. 779.

[183] See para.8–060.

[184] *Heath v Heath* [2009] EWHC 1908 (Ch); [2010] F.L.R. 610 at [26], where the mistake was induced by the party seeking specific performance and was "practically indistinguishable" from misrepresentation. Earlier cases in which equitable relief was given by way of (or amounting to) rescission may still serve to illustrate the types of mistake for which relief will be given by way of refusing specific performance, e.g. *Hitchcock v Giddings* (1817) 4 Price 135; *Colyer v Clay* (1843) 7 Beav. 188; *Cocking v Pratt* (1750) 1 Ves. Snr. 400 (better viewed as a case of undue influence: see para.10–024, fn.121); *Re Garnett* (1885) 31 Ch D. 1.

[185] By way of an action for damages.

[186] *Amalgamated Investment & Property Co Ltd v Walker & Sons Ltd* [1977] 1 W.L.R. 164 at 172.

[187] [1977] 1 W.L.R. 164; Brownsword 40 M.L.R. 467.

rescission or by refusal of specific performance,[188] merely because the purchaser mistakenly believed that the property was "suitable for and capable of being developed".[189] No doubt the official's decision, if known, would have affected the negotiations; but that decision did not amount to a listing, and therefore did not affect the quality of the subject-matter at the time of contracting. It only affected the extent of the risk that permission to redevelop might be refused—a risk which would have existed, though to a lesser extent, quite apart from any question of listing. It follows, a fortiori, that relief will not be given for a mistake which relates neither to subject-matter nor to the terms of contract, but only to "the commercial advantage which the contract gave"[190] to the mistaken party.

## 3. UNILATERAL MISTAKE

8–034 Mistake *negatives* consent where the parties are so much at cross-purposes that they do not reach agreement. This may happen where one party is mistaken about the identity of the other, where one party intends to deal with one thing and the other with something different, or where one party intends to deal on one set of terms and the other on a different set of terms. A mistake as to the other party or as to the subject-matter of the contract has no effect unless it is "fundamental", but this alone does not make a contract void. The mistake must also induce the contract, and be "operative". In many cases, the last requirement will not be satisfied, so that there will often be a contract in spite of the fact that the consent of one of the parties was negatived.

### (a) Types of mistake

#### *(i) Mistake as to the person*[191]

8–035 **The context in which mistaken identity will usually arise.** It will be seen that in the vast majority of the cases which follow, the dispute was between two innocent parties. A seller is induced to sell his goods to a buyer, on credit, in the belief that the buyer is someone, or something, else.[192] Before the buyer has paid for the goods, he sells them on to a sub-buyer for full value. When the seller discovers that he is not going to be paid and the goods are now in the possession of the sub-buyer, he may bring an action in conversion against the sub-buyer. The outcome of this claim will turn on which of the seller or sub-buyer has the better title to the goods. This, in turn, will depend on the effect on the first contract of the seller's "mistake" when selling to the intermediate buyer. Where, as is usually the case, the seller's mistake was induced by the fraudulent misrepresentation of the buyer, the contract will be voidable. If the seller has not taken steps to set aside the contract before the goods are sold to the sub-buyer, title will pass to the

[188] Rescission is now ruled out by the development described at para.8–030.

[189] *Amalgamated Investment & Property Co Ltd v Walker & Sons Ltd* [1977] 1 W.L.R. 164 at 171.

[190] *Clarion Ltd v National Provident Association* [2000] 1 W.L.R. 1888 at 1905.

[191] Goodhart 57 L.Q.R. 228; Williams 23 Can.Bar Rev. 271 at 380; Wilson 17 M.L.R. 515; Unger 18 M.L.R. 259; Smith & Thomas 20 M.L.R. 38; MacMillan [2005] C.L.J. 711.

[192] Whether "some*one*" or "some*thing*" makes all the difference: see para.8–037.

sub-buyer, assuming he has bought them in good faith;[193] in particular, in this context, without notice of the fraud. If the seller is to prevail, he must prove that the contract with the buyer was not merely voidable, but was void. He may do this by proving that he did not intend to sell to the buyer at all, i.e. that he made a fundamental mistake as to the identity of the party to whom he was selling.[194] If the initial contract of sale is void, no title will pass to the buyer, nor to the sub-buyer as a result, in accordance with the general rule of *nemo dat quod non habet*.[195] A recommendation by the Law Reform Committee to reverse this result so as to protect the sub-buyer[196] has not been implemented by legislation and it has been left to the courts to determine whether and when, in this type of case, a contract is void, or voidable.[197] Some cases may perhaps be explained quite simply on the basis of the court's preference for one innocent party over another.[198]

**Fundamental mistake of identity.** A mistake as to the person is fundamental, so that consent is negatived, if one party is mistaken as to the *identity* of the other. In **8–036**
*Cundy v Lindsay*[199] the claimants received an order for handkerchiefs from a dishonest person called Blenkarn, who gave his address as 37, Wood Street, Cheapside. He signed his name to make it look like "Blenkiron & Co", a respectable firm known by reputation to the claimants and carrying on business at 123, Wood Street. The claimants sent the goods to "Blenkiron & Co, 37, Wood Street," where Blenkarn took possession of them. He did not pay for the goods and he later sold them to the defendants. It was held that there was no contract between the claimants and Blenkarn, as the claimants did not intend to deal with him but with someone else. Thus no property in the handkerchiefs passed to Blenkarn,[200] so that he could pass none to the defendants, who were accordingly liable for conversion.

**Mistake as to attribute.** By contrast, a mistake by one party as to an *attribute* of **8–037**
the other will not as a general rule put the parties so seriously at cross-purposes as to negative consent. In *King's Norton Metal Co Ltd v Edridge, Merrett & Co Ltd*[201] the claimants received an order for wire from "Hallam & Co" which was made on the letter-head to appear as a substantial firm having a large factory in Sheffield and depôts in various other places. In fact "Hallam & Co" consisted solely of an impecunious rogue called Wallis. The claimants sent the goods to "Hallam & Co" on credit. Wallis took possession of them, failed to pay, and sold

---

[193] See para.9–124.

[194] He must also show that the mistake induced the contract (para.8–048) and that it was "operative" (para.8–051), both of which will almost certainly be satisfied in this type of case.

[195] "No one gives who possesses not".

[196] 12th Report Cmnd.2958 (1966), para.15.

[197] Or entirely valid, in the rare case where the mistake is not fundamental and has not been induced by a misrepresentation.

[198] *Ingram v Little* [1961] 1 Q.B. 31 would seem to be a prime example and, as a consequence, its authority is in serious doubt after the decision in *Shogun Finance Ltd v Hudson* [2003] UKHL 62; [2004] 1 A.C. 919: see para.8–038.

[199] (1878) 3 App. Cas. 459; cf. *Baillie's Case* [1898] 1 Ch. 110.

[200] cf. para.8–035.

[201] (1897) 14 T.L.R. 98.

them to the defendants. It was held that the claimants had contracted with "the writer of the letters".[202] Thus property in the goods passed to Wallis, so that he could pass it to the defendants, who were accordingly not liable for conversion. As Wallis and "Hallam & Co" were one and the same person, the claimants had not made any mistake as to the identity, but only one as to the credit-worthiness, of the other contracting party, whom they identified as the writer of the letter. The essential point is that "Hallam & Co" *was* Wallis, just as much as "Currer Bell"[203] *was* Charlotte Brontë.

8–038 **Determining whether mistake is one of identity or attribute.** In cases involving mistake as to the person, it may be difficult to say precisely what mistake has been made: i.e. whether B thought that A was C, as opposed to merely making a mistake about A's credit-worthiness. In other cases, it may be clear what mistake has been made, but disputed whether it should be described as one of identity or attribute. It is submitted that the test formulated for the purpose of defining fundamental mistakes as to the subject-matter in cases of common mistake[204] should also (with appropriate modifications) be applied in the present context. A person may be identified by reference to one of his attributes. If a mistake is made as to that attribute,[205] there can be said to be a mistake as to identity. It is supported by a dictum of Greene LJ in *Craven-Ellis v Canons Ltd*,[206] where a director's service agreement was held "void ab initio" as neither he nor those who appointed him had the necessary qualification shares. One reason for this conclusion was that the agreement was made "under a mistake as to the present existence of an essential fact recognised by the law as the foundation of the contract".[207] Other hypothetical cases can be imagined which would come within the same principle. A college may hold a private dance and intend to sell tickets only to past or present members. In such a case, for the purpose of the contract to sell a ticket, the identifying attribute of an applicant might be his or her membership of the college, while more generally such membership would be a mere attribute.

The principle, then, is that a mistake as to *the* attribute by which a person is identified for the purpose of the contract entered into is in law regarded as a mistake of identity. But one attribute on which the mistaken party cannot in law rely for this purpose is that of the credit-worthiness of the other party.[208] In deciding whether the other party is credit-worthy, the mistaken party takes a business risk. It would be undesirable to allow an error of judgment on such a point to negative consent. In applying this principle, the law makes certain prima facie assumptions about the way in which a person is identified, two of which now fall to be considered.

---

202 *King's Norton Metal Co Ltd v Edridge, Merrett & Co Ltd* (1897) 14 T.L.R. 98 at 99.

203 The pseudonym under which Charlotte Brontë wrote *Jane Eyre*.

204 See para.8–020.

205 *Contrast Sunderland Association FC v Uruguay Montevideo FC* [2001] 2 All E.R. (Comm) 828 at 830 (mistake as to the division in which a football club competed not one of identity).

206 [1936] 2 K.B. 403.

207 *Craven-Ellis v Canons Ltd* [1936] 2 K.B. 403 at 413.

208 e.g. *King's Norton Metal Co Ltd v Edridge Merrett & Co* (1897) 14 T.L.R. 98; para.8–037.

**Mistake made "face to face".** The difficulty of deciding whether the mistake is one of attribute or of identity is particularly acute where the parties who are alleged to have contracted have come physically face to face. In *Phillips v Brooks Ltd*,[209] a rogue called North entered a shop and asked to see pearls and rings. He selected (inter alia) a ring worth £450, produced a chequebook, claimed to be Sir George Bullough (a wealthy man known by name to the shopkeeper) and gave Sir George's address. The shopkeeper checked this address in a directory, and then allowed North to take away the ring in exchange for a cheque, which was dishonoured. North later pledged the ring with the defendant. The shopkeeper claimed that there was never any contract between him and North, so that the latter had no title to the ring which he could pass to the defendant. But Horridge J held that the shopkeeper had "contracted to sell and deliver [the ring] to the person who came into his shop … who obtained the sale and delivery by means of the false pretence that he was Sir George Bullough".[210] The shopkeeper's mistake was not one of identity: "His intention was to sell to the person present and identified by sight and hearing."[211] The same result was reached in *Lewis v Averay*,[212] where a person had advertised his car for sale and was visited by a rogue who falsely claimed to be a well-known actor called Richard Greene. By this pretence the rogue induced the seller to sell the car to him on credit and to let him take it away in exchange for a cheque, which was dishonoured. The seller claimed the car from the defendant, who had bought it in good faith from the rogue; but the claim failed as the contract between the seller and the rogue was not void for mistake. The presumption that the seller intended to contract with the person physically before him had not been overcome:[213] his mistake was not one of identity but as to the credit-worthiness of the other party.[214] 8–039

**Rebutting the presumption in "face to face" cases.** The presumption that the seller intends to contract with the person before him is clearly a strong one,[215] but it does not follow from *Phillips v Brooks* or *Lewis v Averay* that there can be no fundamental mistake as to the person merely because the parties alleged to have contracted were in each other's presence. There may be such a mistake where A induces B to deal with him by pretending to act as agent for C, while in fact intending to contract on his own behalf.[216] In such a case it could be said that there was no mistake as to the identity of A, but rather one as to the capacity in which he purported to contract.[217] Beyond the example of agency, however, it is 8–040

---

[209] [1919] 2 K.B. 243; cf. *Dennant v Skinner* [1948] 2 K.B. 164.
[210] *Phillips v Brooks Ltd* [1919] 2 K.B. 243 at 246.
[211] *Phillips v Brooks Ltd* [1919] 2 K.B. 243 at 247.
[212] [1972] 1 Q.B. 198; A.L.G. 88 L.Q.R. 161; Turpin [1972] C.L.J. 19.
[213] *Lewis v Averay* [1972] 1 Q.B. 198 at 208, 209.
[214] *Lewis v Averay* [1972] 1 Q.B. 198 at 209.
[215] In *Shogun Finance Ltd v Hudson* [2003] UKHL 62; [2004] 1 A.C. 919, considered at para.8–041, Lord Millett (at [67]) went so far as to suggest that it is more like a rule of law; cf. Lord Walker (at [187]) for whom it remained a presumption, exceptions to which would be rare.
[216] *Hardman v Booth* (1863) 1 H. & C. 803; cf. *Higgons v Burton* (1857) 26 L.J. Ex. 342. Contrast *Citibank NA v Brown Shipley & Co Ltd* [1991] 2 All E.R. 690 (identity of person acting as mere messenger not fundamental).
[217] This may be the only explanation of Lord Haldane's remark in *Lake v Simmons* [1927] A.C. 487 that there was no contract when a jeweller gave possession of a necklace on approval to a woman

difficult to see the exceptional circumstances which would allow the presumption to be rebutted.[218] In *Ingram v Little*[219] the owners of a car had advertised it for sale and been visited by a rogue who falsely claimed to be "P.G.M. Hutchinson of Stanstead House, Stanstead Road, Caterham." They agreed to sell the car to him on credit, but only after one of them had checked in a telephone directory that there was a person of that name living at that address. The rogue later sold the car to the defendants from whom the owners claimed it when the rogue's cheque was dishonoured. A majority of the Court of Appeal upheld the claim on the ground that the owners had intended to deal with the Hutchinson of Stanstead House and not with the person before them *as such*. The case was doubted in *Lewis v Averay*,[220] and by members of both the majority and the minority in *Shogun Finance Ltd v Hudson*,[221] and it should, with respect, be regarded as wrongly decided.

8–041 **Contracts made in writing.** Where a contract is in writing, the parties to that contract are prima facie the persons described as such in the writing. This view was endorsed in *Shogun Finance Ltd v Hudson*[222] in which the House of Lords reviewed the leading cases on the effect of a mistake as to the person. A rogue obtained possession of a car by pretending to be Mr Durlabh Patel, producing a driving licence in Mr Patel's name and forging his signature to a hire-purchase agreement purporting to be between the claimant finance company selling the car and Mr Patel. The rogue then sold the car to the defendant who bought it in good faith and for full value. All of their Lordships agreed that the validity of the hire-purchase agreement depended on the intention of the claimant, objectively ascertained, i.e. on the basis that the "hirer" made the offer by completing the application form, whose offer did the claimant purport to accept: the rogue's or Mr Patel's?[223] For the majority, in cases where a "contract" is in writing this is simply a question of construction which, "making appropriate use of extrinsic evidence,[224] will normally enable the court to reach a firm conclusion as to the

---

called Esmé Ellison having been told by her that she was married to one Van der Borgh. In *Shogun Finance Ltd v Hudson* [2003] UKHL 62; [2004] 1 A.C. 919 Lord Phillips (at [141]) found his approach inconsistent with *Phillips v Brooks Ltd* [1919] 2 K.B. 243; cf. *Ingram v Little* [1961] 1 Q.B. 31 at 50, 66.

[218] *Shogun Finance Ltd v Hudson* [2003] UKHL 62; [2004] 1 A.C. 919 at [37] (Lord Nicholls).

[219] [1961] 1 Q.B. 31.

[220] [1972] 1 Q.B. 198 at 206, 208 (Megaw LJ).

[221] [2003] UKHL 62; [2004] 1 A.C. 919 at [87] (Lord Millett); at [185] (Lord Walker): considered at para.8–041.

[222] [2003] UKHL 62; [2004] 1 A.C. 919; Elliott [2004] J.B.L. 381; Phang, Lee and Koh [2004] C.L.J. 24; Scott [2004] L.M.C.L.Q. 292; McLauchlan [2005] J.C.L. 1; cf. *The Sibohelle* [2011] EWHC 1150 (Comm); [2011] 2 Lloyd's Rep. 220.

[223] Clearly, there could be no contract with Mr Patel since he had not given the rogue authority to make the contract on his behalf.

[224] Lord Hobhouse applied the parol evidence rule to exclude any evidence which sought to contradict that Mr Patel was the contracting party, and Lord Phillips' approval (at [155]) of the use of the rule in *Young v Schuler* 11 Q.B.D. 651 at 654–655 implies that this is how one should understand his reference to the "appropriate use of extrinsic evidence". But since the issue in *Shogun* was one of contract formation, this application of the rule is open to doubt: *The Starsin* [2003] UKHL 12; [2004] 1 A.C. 715 at [175] (Lord Millett); McLauchlan 121 L.Q.R. 9; Stevens, in Burrows & Peel (eds), *Contract Terms* (2007).

person with whom a party intends to contract."[225] In some cases, it may be found that the party named is a mere alias for the rogue, as in the *King's Norton* case,[226] but where the putative agreement refers to an "unequivocally identifiable" individual, as in *Cundy v Lindsay*,[227] this precludes any other finding; the process of construction leads "inexorably" to the conclusion that the person with whom it was intended to contract was the person thus described.[228] In *Shogun Finance Ltd v Hudson*, the application form filled in by the rogue and accepted by the claimant fell into this category. Accordingly, the rogue was not a party to the agreement, so that the defendant acquired no title to the car.[229]

At the very least then, when the named party is "unequivocally identifiable" there is a strong presumption that the other party intended to contract with the named party and with no one else. As with the presumption in the "face-to-face" cases, it is difficult to see the exceptional circumstances which would allow this presumption to be rebutted,[230] agency apart.[231] The consequence is that most cases will be conclusively determined, and with very different outcomes, on the basis of what may be fine distinctions as to the type of contract involved, i.e. whether "face to face" or "in writing". This will, in turn, depend on what particular form of deception was practised by the rogue involved.[232]

**Criticism.** For the minority in *Shogun Finance Ltd v Hudson* the law in this area had developed in an unacceptable way and, for a number of reasons, their preference was to apply the presumption applicable to face-to-face dealings more generally, i.e. it is presumed that the seller intended to sell his goods to the person *with whom he was dealing*.[233] First, to say that with written contracts it is simply **8–042**

---

[225] *Shogun Finance Ltd v Hudson* [2003] UKHL 62; [2004] 1 A.C. 919 at [154] (Lord Phillips) (emphasis added).

[226] See para.8–037.

[227] See para.8–036, though it may be noted that the rogue did not give the correct address for Blenkiron & Co.

[228] *Shogun Finance Ltd v Hudson* [2003] UKHL 62; [2004] 1 A.C. 919 at [161] (Lord Phillips).

[229] Under Hire-Purchase Act 1964 s.27.

[230] One possible example (hinted at by Lord Phillips (*Shogun Finance Ltd v Hudson* [2003] UKHL 62; [2004] 1 A.C. 919 at [166]) and Lord Walker (at [192])) might have been *Hector v Lyons* (1989) 58 P. & C.R. 156 where a father conducted negotiations for the purchase of a house, and, when these were successfully concluded, instructed his solicitors to draw up the contract in the name of his son (who was a minor) as purchaser. The decision not to award the father specific performance is readily understandable on the basis of ample evidence that he did not come to court with "clean hands" (see para.21–035), but the conclusion that there was no contract at all with the father does perhaps support the view that such cases are based on the parol evidence rule, or something similar to it, i.e. the non-admissibility of evidence to contradict the written contract, which named the son as purchaser. See also: *Dumford Trading AG v OAO Atlantrybflot* [2005] EWCA Civ 24; [2005] 1 Lloyd's Rep. 289 at [37].

[231] *Doncaster MBC v Racing (UK) Ltd* [2005] EWCA Civ 999; *The Sibohelle* [2011] EWHC 1150 (Comm); [2011] 2 Lloyd's Rep. 220; cf. *Young v Schuler* 11 Q.B.D. 651 (where the issue was reversed: did the agent also sign as principal?); cf. para.16–065.

[232] See para.8–043.

[233] *Shogun Finance Ltd v Hudson* [2003] UKHL 62; [2004] 1 A.C. 919 at [28] (Lord Nicholls); at [81] (Lord Millett). Lord Nicholls (at [36]) thought it not easy to think of practical circumstances where "once in point", the presumption would be displaced: *Boulton v Jones* (1857) 2 H. & N. 564 (para.8–049) might be thought to represent an exception, but it is perhaps better explained as a case

a matter of construction "begs the crucial question":[234] to whom was the offer made, or, as in *Shogun*, to whom was the acceptance directed? Secondly, in cases said to involve a mistake of identity, the identity of the other party is usually incidental;[235] the seller sold to the rogue Hallam in the *King's Norton* case in the mistaken belief that he was credit-worthy, but the seller only sold to the rogue in *Cundy* in the mistaken belief that he was Blenkiron and was, *therefore*, credit-worthy, just as the seller did in the face-to-face cases of *Lewis v Averay* and *Phillips v Brooks*. In each case, the mistake made by the seller may explain *why* he sold to the party with whom he was dealing but does not negate his intention to sell *to that person*, i.e. the rogue. Thirdly, as a matter of legal policy the loss is more appropriately borne by the person who takes the risk in parting with his goods on credit.[236] Finally, it is difficult to see how, as has been suggested,[237] the rogue in these cases could have been sued by the seller under what is a supposedly non-existent contract.[238] This is a formidable array of argument. As it is, unless the Supreme Court is persuaded to re-visit this issue, the law can only be rescued from what Lord Nicholls regarded as its "unsatisfactory and unprincipled state" by the intervention of Parliament.[239]

8–043 **Whether the contract is "in writing".** Such is the almost conclusive nature of the presumptions at work in this area, it is crucial to the outcome of any given case which of them applies, e.g. whether the contract is "in writing" so as to attract the presumption upheld by the majority in the *Shogun* case. There are indications from the majority that this category is to be construed narrowly.[240] According to Lord Phillips it should be confined to dealings which are "exclusively conducted in writing".[241] Where there is "*some* form of personal contact",[242] the presumption in the "face-to-face" cases should be applied.[243] Similarly, Lord Walker thought that the presumption in the "face-to-face" cases was not applicable where the "*only* contract[244] was by written communication sent by post or by e-mail".[245] They would probably therefore agree with Lord

where the buyer intended to buy from the person "with whom he was dealing" and this pointed to the named party Brocklehurst and not Boulton, to whom Brocklehurst had transferred his business earlier the same day.

234 *Shogun Finance Ltd v Hudson* [2003] UKHL 62; [2004] 1 A.C. 919 at [30] (Lord Nicholls); at [103] (Lord Millett).

235 *Shogun Finance Ltd v Hudson* [2003] UKHL 62; [2004] 1 A.C. 919 at [35] (Lord Nicholls).

236 *Shogun Finance Ltd v Hudson* [2003] UKHL 62; [2004] 1 A.C. 919 at [35] (Lord Nicholls); at [82] (Lord Millett).

237 See para.8–057.

238 *Shogun Finance Ltd v Hudson* [2003] UKHL 62; [2004] 1 A.C. 919 at [93] (Lord Millett).

239 Possibly by reconsidering the proposals for reform in the 12th Report of the Law Reform Committee (1966), Cmnd.2958, para.15.

240 Perhaps, in part, to allay the concerns of the minority about "fine" and "unprincipled" distinctions.

241 *Shogun Finance Ltd v Hudson* [2003] UKHL 62; [2004] 1 A.C. 919 at [170].

242 *Shogun Finance Ltd v Hudson* [2003] UKHL 62; [2004] 1 A.C. 919 at [170] (emphasis added).

243 There was considerable personal contact in *Hector v Lyons* (1989) 58 P. & C.R. 156, fn.230, a case which is relied on by the majority to support the presumption for contracts made in writing. This may explain why the decision in that case is queried: *Shogun Finance Ltd v Hudson* [2003] UKHL 62; [2004] 1 A.C. 919 at [166] (Lord Phillips), and at [192] (Lord Walker).

244 Perhaps this should read "contact".

245 *Shogun Finance Ltd v Hudson* [2003] UKHL 62; [2004] 1 A.C. 919 at [188].

Nicholls' observation that, if some form of writing had been introduced in *Phillips v Brooks,*[246] such as an invoice or receipt made out in favour of Sir George Bullough, it would "be neither here nor there"[247] and amount to no more than "stark contemporary confirmation that the misrepresentation was made and that the seller believed it".[248] By contrast, in *Cundy v Lindsay*[249] the rogue sent a written order to the seller which simply despatched the goods to the address supplied. There will, inevitably, be more difficult cases. In *Shogun* itself, the hire purchase application form was faxed to the finance house which never met the rogue, but there were telephone communications between the finance house and the dealer making the car available, creating the prospect that it was a face-to-face case if the dealer was acting as agent of the finance house,[250] which clearly he was not.[251] When a fraudster purchases goods over the counter of a shop with the aid of a stolen credit card, it seems that the "face-to-face" presumption must apply, but if he does so over the internet by giving the details from a stolen card, that would seem closer, by analogy, to Lord Walker's example of communication only by email, so as to attract the presumption that the seller only intended to sell to the cardholder.

**Undisclosed principals.** A person who knows that another is unwilling to contract with him may employ an agent to make the contract without disclosing the existence of the principal. In some such cases the undisclosed principal is not allowed to intervene and take the benefit of the contract. But the contract is not void since the agent can (fraud apart) enforce it. These cases are discussed in Ch.16.[252] **8–044**

### *(ii) Mistake as to the subject-matter*

**Subject-matter mistakes.** Consent is negatived if one party intends to deal with one thing, and the other with a different one. This principle may have been applied in *Raffles v Wichelhaus*,[253] where a seller of cotton "to arrive *ex Peerless* from Bombay" tendered cotton from a ship called *Peerless* which had sailed from Bombay in December. The buyer refused to accept the goods, alleging that he had intended to buy the cotton shipped on another *Peerless* which had sailed from Bombay in October: thus it was argued that there was no agreement between the parties. On a claim by the seller, judgment was given for the buyer but, as no reasons were stated, it is hard to tell whether the ground of decision was that there **8–045**

---

246 See para.8–039.

247 According to Lord Phillips in *Shogun Finance Ltd v Hudson* [2003] UKHL 62; [2004] 1 A.C. 919 at [176], the written agreement would have been "no more than peripheral to the dealings".

248 *Shogun Finance Ltd v Hudson* [2003] UKHL 62; [2004] 1 A.C. 919 at [25].

249 See para.8–036.

250 Described by Lord Nicholls (*Shogun Finance Ltd v Hudson* [2003] UKHL 62; [2004] 1 A.C. 919 at [41]) as a "singularly sterile argument" which only served to underline the "practical absurdity" of the distinctions in play.

251 For the reasons explained by Lord Hobhouse: *Shogun Finance Ltd v Hudson* [2003] UKHL 62; [2004] 1 A.C. 919 at [51].

252 See paras 16–065–16–070.

253 (1864) 2 H. & C. 906.

was *no* contract,[254] or that there *was* a contract to deliver cotton from the October *Peerless* which could not be performed by delivering cotton from the December *Peerless*.[255]

Consent was clearly negatived in *Falck v Williams*.[256] A and B were negotiating about two charterparties: one to carry shale from Sydney to Barcelona, and one to carry copra from Fiji to Barcelona. B's agent sent a coded telegram intending to confirm the copra charter, but the telegram was ambiguous and was understood by A to refer to the shale charter. It was held that there was no contract. Similarly, consent is negatived if a buyer at an auction thinks that the lot for which he is bidding consists of hemp when it consists of hemp and tow.[257]

8–046 **Quality mistakes.** On the other hand, consent is not generally negatived by a mere mistake as to quality: thus it was held in *Smith v Hughes*[258] that if a person buys oats, thinking that they are old, from a seller who knows that they are new, there is a good contract. Similarly, a contract for the sale of goods is not void merely because the seller, under a mistake as to the quality of the goods, charges a lower price than he would have done, had he known the truth.[259] In such cases, the parties are at cross-purposes, but not to such an extent that they are not in agreement at all. A mistake as to quality can negative consent only if it is a mistake as to a fundamental quality by which the thing is identified.[260]

### (iii) *Mistake as to the terms of the contract*

8–047 Consent is negatived if the parties intend to contract on different terms, e.g. if A sells goods to B for so many "pounds" intended by A to mean sterling and by B to mean a different currency;[261] or if A intends to sell hare skins at a fixed price per piece when B intends to buy at the same price per pound, there being about three pieces to the pound.[262] Mistakes as to the person and mistakes as to the subject-matter negative consent only if they are fundamental. There seems to be no such requirement where the mistake is as to the terms of the contract. A sale of oats is not void merely because they are believed by one party to be old but known by the other to be new. The mistake is as to a quality of the subject-matter and is not fundamental.[263] But according to *Smith v Hughes*[264] a sale of oats

---

[254] *Smith v Hughes* (1871) L.R. 6 Q.B. 597 at 609; *OT Africa Line Ltd v Vickers Plc* [1996] 1 Lloyd's Rep. 700 at 703. There was no allegation that the seller intended to deal with the cargo of the December rather than the October Peerless. The case was decided on a demurrer so that the facts were never proved.

[255] *Van Praagh v Everidge* [1902] 2 Ch. 266 at 269. On this view the buyer could have got damages for the seller's failure to deliver cotton from the October Peerless.

[256] [1900] A.C. 176.

[257] *Scriven Bros & Co v Hindley & Co* [1913] 3 K.B. 564.

[258] (1871) L.R. 6 Q.B. 597.

[259] *Dip Kaur v Chief Constable of Hampshire* [1981] 1 W.L.R. 578.

[260] As defined at para.8–020.

[261] See *Woodhouse AC Israel Cocoa Ltd v Nigerian Produce Marketing Co* [1972] A.C. 741 at 768; cf. *Felthouse v Bindley* (1862) 11 C.B. (N.S.) 869 ("30" intended to mean pounds by buyer but guineas by seller); *Smidt v Tiden* (1874) L.R. 9 Q.B. 446.

[262] *Hartog v Colin & Shields* [1939] 3 All E.R. 566.

[263] See after fn.257.

believed by the buyer to be *warranted* to be old and not intended by the seller to be so warranted may be void for mistake. The mistake is as to a term of the contract and negatives consent although the term relates to a quality of the subject-matter which is not fundamental. This distinction seems to be generally accepted, but the reason for it is not easy to see. If a quality is not fundamental, a mistake as to its existence does not destroy consent. Why should consent be destroyed by mistake as to a warranty of that same quality? Is it really true, in the latter case, that the parties have not agreed at all?[265] An alternative explanation for this aspect of *Smith v Hughes* will be put forward later in this chapter.[266]

## (b) Mistake must induce the contract

A mistake negatives consent only if it induced the mistaken party to enter into the contract. If that party takes the risk that the facts are not as he supposed them to be,[267] or if he is simply indifferent as to the matter to which the mistake relates, the validity of the contract is not affected. **8–048**

**Mistake as to the person.** In *Mackie v European Assurance Society*[268] the claimant took out an insurance policy through an agent, believing that the agent was acting for one company when in fact he was acting for another. It was held that the policy with the latter company was not void for mistake. The claimant's intention "was not to remain uninsured for one hour and in what office it was a secondary consideration, provided it would meet its engagements and was able to do so".[269] This case should be contrasted with *Boulton v Jones*.[270] Boulton had just bought a shop from one Brocklehurst when the defendant sent his servant to the shop with an order, addressed to Brocklehurst, for a quantity of pipe hose. Boulton supplied the goods, no doubt thinking that the defendant did not care from whom he obtained them. The defendant was apparently satisfied with the goods and used them. He had clearly made a fundamental mistake, in that he thought he was dealing with Brocklehurst when he dealt with Boulton. Ordinarily, that mistake would have had no effect, since it would not matter to the defendant whether the goods were supplied by Boulton or by Brocklehurst. But Brocklehurst owed money to the defendant, who had intended to set off this debt against the price of the goods. He could thus show that it was important for him to contract with Brocklehurst rather than with Boulton. It was therefore held that there was no contract so that the defendant was not liable for the price of the goods.[271] To have held him liable would have been unjust as it would have **8–049**

---

264 (1871) L.R. 6 Q.B. 597; cf. *London Holeproof Hosiery Co Ltd v Padmore* (1928) 44 T.L.R. 499; *Sullivan v Constable* (1932) 49 T.L.R. 369.

265 *The Harriette N* [2008] EWHC 2257; [2008] 2 Lloyd's Rep. 685 at [87].

266 See para.8–055.

267 *Wales v Wadham* [1977] 1 W.L.R. 199 at 220; (approved on the issue of mistake in *Jenkins v Livesey* [1985] A.C. 424); cf. paras 8–004, 8–010.

268 (1869) 21 L.T. 102; cf. *Fellowes v Gwydyr* (1829) 1 Russ. & My. 83.

269 *Mackie v European Assurance Society* (1869) 21 L.T. 102 at 105.

270 (1857) 2 H. & N. 564; L.J. Ex. 117; 6 W.R. 107.

271 cf. *Westminster CC v Reema Construction (No.2)* (1992) 24 Con L.R. 26 (no liability of successor in business under contract with predecessor).

deprived him of the benefit of his set-off against Brocklehurst. But the result of holding him not liable was almost equally unjust. The defendant got the goods for nothing but retained his right to sue Brocklehurst for the amount which the latter owed him. It seems that on such facts the defendant should be under some liability for unjust enrichment.[272]

8–050 **Other types of mistake.** The requirement that the mistake must induce the contract applies not only to mistake as to the person but also to other types of mistake. If in *Raffles v Wichelhaus*[273] both ships had sailed from Bombay on the same day and had arrived at the same time, it might not have mattered to the buyer which cargo he got. In that case he could not have escaped liability by saying that he intended to buy the cargo in the one ship while the seller intended to sell the cargo in the other.[274]

## (c) When mistake is operative

### *(i) Contract generally valid*

8–051 **Contract generally valid under the objective principle.** A mistake which negatives consent does not necessarily make the contract void. On the contrary, the general rule is that a party is bound, in spite of his mistake: this follows from the objective principle,[275] under which one party (A) is often bound if his words or conduct are such as to induce the other party (B) reasonably to believe that A was assenting to the terms proposed by B.[276]

The operation of the objective principle is most easily illustrated by the case of a person who by mistake bids for the wrong lot at an auction. Although the parties may not be ad idem,[277] (as they intended to deal with different things), the bidder is prevented by the objective principle from relying on the mistake and so from saying that the contract is void.[278] The same principle applies to mistakes as to the person[279] and as to the terms of the contract. Thus a seller who, as a result of some miscalculation, offers goods at a price lower than that which he would have asked but for the mistake cannot, after the offer has been accepted, generally rely on the mistake to make the contract void.[280] Similarly, where a landlord as a result of a clerical error offers to grant a tenancy at a rent of £1,000 per month, he cannot, after the offer has been accepted, escape from the transaction merely by

[272] cf. para.22–034; Burrows, *The Law of Restitution*, 3rd edn (2010), pp.387–388.
[273] (1864) 2 H. & C. 906; para.8–045.
[274] cf. *Ind's Case* (1872) L.R. 7 Ch. App. 485 (validity of share transfer not affected by which shares the transferee gets, so long as he gets the quantity contracted for).
[275] See paras 1–002, 2–002.
[276] *Smith v Hughes* (1871) L.R. 6 Q.B. 597, 607; *OT Africa Line Ltd v Vickers Plc* [1996] 1 Lloyd's Rep. 700.
[277] *Van Praagh v Everidge* [1903] 1 Ch. 434.
[278] *Robinson, Fisher & Harding v Behar* [1927] 1 K.B. 513.
[279] *Cornish v Abington* (1859) 4 H. & N. 549; *Re Reed* (1876) 3 Ch D. 123, so far as contra, seems wrong.
[280] This would have been the position in *Hartog v Colin & Shields* [1939] 3 All E.R. 566 (para.8–057) if the court had not taken the view that the claimant must have known of the defendant's mistake.

showing that his real intention was to make the offer at a rent of £2,000 per month.[281] The position is the same where a person signs a document under some other mistake about its terms or legal effects: he cannot, in general, say that the contract is void because of his mistake.[282]

### *(ii) Cases in which mistake is "operative"*

The effect of applying the objective principle is that a contract may be valid in spite of the existence of a mistake by one of the parties, so that it is unnecessary to go into the difficult question whether the mistake is fundamental. That question need only be answered in the following situations, in which the mistake may be said to be "operative". **8–052**

**Ambiguity.** There may be such ambiguity in the circumstances that a reasonable person could not draw any relevant inference from them at all. In *Raffles v Wichelhaus*[283] a reasonable person could not have deduced with which cargo the parties intended to deal. Similarly, if parties stipulate for the payment of freight "per charterparty" but there are two charterparties in the case, providing for payment of different rates of freight, the reasonable person cannot put any definite interpretation on the promises.[284] In these cases, therefore, the mistake is operative and makes the contract void. **8–053**

**Mistake known to non-mistaken party.** The objective principle applies where A's words or conduct induce B reasonably to believe that A is contracting with him; but it does not apply where B actually knows that (in spite of the objective appearance) A has no such intention.[285] It follows that the objective principle will not apply, and that the mistake will be operative, if A's mistake is known to B. This is the reason why the contract in *Cundy v Lindsay*[286] was void. The claimants may have behaved so as to induce a reasonable person to believe that they were dealing with Blenkarn, but the mistake was operative as Blenkarn knew that they had no such intention. The case would have been different if Blenkarn had written to the claimants in good faith and they had misread his signature for "Blenkiron & Co." In such a case, the claimants could not have relied on their mistake, had they simply sent the goods to Blenkarn's address, unless it had been clear to Blenkarn from the contractual documents that they did not intend to deal with him but with Blenkiron & Co.[287] **8–054**

In *Boulton v Jones*[288] the defendant's order was addressed to Brocklehurst, so that Boulton knew it was not meant for him. It is not clear whether he also knew

---

281 *Centrovincial Estates Plc v Merchant Investors Assurance Co Ltd* [1983] Com. L.R. 158.

282 *Blay v Pollard & Morris* [1930] 1 K.B. 628.

283 (1864) 2 H. & C. 906; para.8–045 ("a case of latent ambiguity": *The Great Peace* [2002] EWCA Civ 1407; [2003] Q.B. 679 at [29]); cf. *Hickman v Berens* [1895] 2 Ch. 638; *NBTY Europe Ltd v Nutricia International BV* [2005] EWHC 734; [2005] 2 Lloyd's Rep. 350.

284 *Smidt v Tiden* (1874) L.R. 9 Q.B. 446.

285 See paras 1–002, 2–003.

286 (1878) 3 App. Cas. 459; para.8–036.

287 cf. *The Unique Mariner* [1978] 1 Lloyd's Rep. 438 at 451–452.

288 (1857) 2 H. & N. 564; L.J. Ex. 117; 6 W.R. 107; para.8–049.

*why* the order was not meant for him, i.e. whether he knew that Brocklehurst owed money to Jones. Probably such knowledge is not essential to make the contract void. A person who accepts an offer knowing that it is addressed to another must take the risk that the mistake may turn out to be material.

There is no clear authority on the question of whether a mistake is operative where it ought to have been known to the non-mistaken party,[289] but there is obviously a fine line between a finding that it *ought* to have been known and that it *must* have been known, which was sufficient in *Hartog v Colin & Shields*.[290]

8–055 **Smith v Hughes.** The rule that a mistake of one party is operative if known to the other is further illustrated by *Smith v Hughes*.[291] Oats were bought by sample, the buyer thinking that they were old when, in fact, they were new. He refused to accept them, as he had no use for new oats. In an action for the price, the trial judge told the jury to find for the buyer: (1) if the word "old" had been used in the negotiations, i.e. if the oats had been *expressly described* as old; or (2) if "the [seller] believed the [buyer] to believe, or to be under the impression, that he was *contracting for the purchase of old oats*". The jury found for the buyer, but did not say which of these two questions they had answered in his favour. If they thought that the word "old" had been used, their verdict was clearly correct. But they might have based their verdict on their answer to the second question, so that the court had to decide whether this question was correctly formulated.

If the buyer's mistake had been *as to the subject-matter*, it could not in law negative consent at all because it was not fundamental; it was only a mistake as to quality.[292] The seller's knowledge of the buyer's mistake would not alter this.[293] But if the mistake had been *as to the terms of the contract* it could negative consent.[294] There would have been such a mistake if the buyer believed that the seller had *warranted* the oats to be old, while the seller intended to sell without warranty. Prima facie this mistake would not be operative: the objective principle would apply, the buyer having behaved so as to induce the seller reasonably to believe that the buyer was buying oats of the same quality as those in the sample. The mistake would be operative only if the seller knew of the buyer's mistake, i.e. if he knew that the buyer believed he was buying the oats with a warranty that they were old.[295] Thus if the buyer thought the oats *were old* there was a good contract even if the seller knew of this mistake; but if the buyer thought the oats were *warranted to be old* and the seller knew of this, quite different, mistake the contract was void. The court ordered a new trial because the direction to the jury did not clearly distinguish between the two mistakes which the buyer might have made.

---

[289] See *Centrovincial Estates Plc v Merchant Investors Assurance Co Ltd* [1983] Com. L.R. 158; *OT Africa Line Ltd v Vickers Plc* [1996] 1 Lloyd's Rep. 700

[290] [1939] 3 All E.R. 566; para.8–057; cf. *Chwee Kin Keong v Digilandmall.com Pte Ltd* [2005] SGCA 2; [2005] 1 S.L.R. 502 Singapore CA.

[291] (1871) L.R. 6 Q.B. 597.

[292] See para.8–046.

[293] cf. *The Harriette N* [2008] EWHC 2257 (Comm); [2008] 2 Lloyd's Rep. 685.

[294] See para.8–047.

[295] cf. *Hartog v Colin & Shields* [1939] 3 All E.R. 566 (para.8–057).

It has been suggested above[296] that it is hard to see why a mistake as to a warranty of quality should negative consent when a mistake as to the existence of the quality itself does not have this effect. The distinction is based on *Smith v Hughes*; and it is submitted that if the buyer did believe the oats to have been warranted old, and the seller knew this, the buyer could have been absolved from liability on an alternative ground. In such a case it could be said that there *was* a contract under which the seller was bound by the warranty that the oats were old, because he had behaved so as to induce the buyer reasonably to believe that he was contracting on those terms.[297] Breach of the warranty that the oats were old could have justified the buyer's refusal to accept new oats.[298]

**Mistake negligently induced.** A mistake is operative where one party has negligently led the other to make it.[299] In *Scriven Bros v Hindley & Co*[300] the defendant at an auction bid for two lots believing that both were lots of hemp, whereas one was a lot of hemp and tow. Normally, he could not have relied on this mistake,[301] but he was able to do so in this case because the mistake was caused by the misleading nature of the catalogue and by the conduct of one of the seller's servants. This principle is distinct from that which applies in cases of ambiguity.[302] Where a mistake is negligently induced, the circumstances need not be so perfectly ambiguous as to make each party's view of the contract equally tenable. If auction particulars are so obscure as to lead a purchaser to make a mistake, the mistake will be operative even though the particulars, properly interpreted, can only bear the meaning intended by the vendor.[303] **8–056**

### *(iii) Mistake may operate against one party only*

If A's mistake is deliberately induced by B, then A can treat the contract as void, but it does not follow that B can do so. It seems probable that in *Cundy v Lindsay* Blenkarn could have been sued for the price of the handkerchiefs.[304] The same may be true even where B does not in any way bring about A's mistake. In *Hartog v Colin & Shields*[305] the defendants intended to offer hare skins for sale at a stated price "per piece", but inadvertently offered to sell at that price "per pound". A **8–057**

---

[296] See para.8–047.

[297] This is the argument of counsel for the buyer as reported in 40 L.J.Q.B. at 223. But in the Law Reports, counsel is reported as saying: "The parties were not ad idem" (at 600); cf. para.8–058.

[298] It is true that under Sale of Goods Act 1979 s.11 refusal to accept is (as a general rule) justified only by a breach of condition and not by one of warranty (para.18–043 and following). But in 1871 these words were probably not used in their present sense: see para.18–045; cf. *Hardwick Game Farm v Suffolk Agricultural, etc. Association* [1969] 2 A.C. 31 at 83.

[299] In *Deutsche Bank (Suisse) SA v Khan* [2013] EWHC 482 (Comm) at [268] Hamblen J doubts the existence of such a principle, though he describes it in terms of inducement per se rather than negligent inducement.

[300] [1913] 3 K.B. 564.

[301] See para.8–051; cf. *Lloyds Bank v Waterhouse* [1993] 2 F.L.R. 97 at 123.

[302] See para.8–053.

[303] cf. *Swaisland v Dearsley* (1861) Beav. 430, in equity, but *Scriven Bros & Co v Hindley & Co* [1913] 3 K.B. 564 shows that the common law is the same.

[304] So in the agency situation discussed at para.8–040, the agent might have been liable: cf. *Bell v Balls* [1897] 1 Ch. 663 at 669.

[305] [1939] 3 All E.R. 566.

pound contained, on average, three pieces. The claimant purported to accept this offer. It was held that there was "no contract"[306] as the claimant must have known of the defendants' mistake in expressing their offer. But it is possible that the defendants could have held the claimant liable on his acceptance at the price per pound if a fall in the market had made them wish to do so.[307]

### (d) Theoretical basis

8–058 **The offer and acceptance theory.** It has been suggested[308] that the cases discussed in this section do not depend on mistake at all, but on the rule that there is no contract if offer and acceptance do not correspond. If, for example, contract notes are exchanged by which A agrees to sell "St. Petersburgh clean hemp ex *Annetta*" but B agrees to buy "Riga Rhine hemp ex *Annetta*",[309] then it is as plausible to say that there is no contract because offer and acceptance do not correspond as it is to say that there is no contract because the parties intended to deal with different things.[310] But there are also difficulties in the way of this "offer and acceptance" theory.[311] It clearly does not mean that there is a good contract merely because the express words of the offer correspond with those of the acceptance. In *Raffles v Wichelhaus*,[312] there was, so far as appears from the report, no lack of verbal correspondence between offer and acceptance, and yet (on one view of the case) there was no contract.

Another version of the same theory is that the full terms of the offer, as intended by the offeror, must correspond with the full terms of the acceptance, as intended by the offeree. But on this view it is hard to see why some discrepancies prevent the formation of a contract, while others do not. Two cases may be contrasted. In the first, A intends to sell oats which are new; B intends to buy oats which are old. In the second, A intends to sell cotton ex *Peerless* (December); B intends to buy cotton ex *Peerless* (October). The contract in the first case is expressed to be for "oats" and in the second for "cotton ex *Peerless*". In both cases offer and acceptance correspond verbally. In neither case would they correspond if each party expressed his full intention. Yet in the first case there is a good contract, while in the second there is none. This version of the "offer and acceptance" theory makes no allowance for the crucial distinction between mistakes which are fundamental and those which are not.

306 *Hartog v Colin & Shields* [1939] 3 All E.R. 566 at 567.

307 Quaere whether, in a case where B knows of A's mistake, there is a contract on the terms actually intended by A, i.e. in *Hartog v Colin & Shields* at the price "per piece". For the position in relation to a written contract, see para.8–072.

308 Slade 70 L.Q.R. 385; Shatwell 33 Can. Bar Rev. 164; Atiyah 2 Ottawa L. Rev. 337, esp. at pp. 344–350 and *Essays on Contract*, pp.253–260; Smith 110 L.Q.R. 400; cf. *Whittaker v Campbell* [1984] Q.B. 319 at 327—but in that case the mistake was as to attribute only, and so not fundamental: see [1984] Q.B. 319 at 329.

309 As in *Thornton v Kempster* (1814) 5 Taunt. 786.

310 cf. *The Harriette N* [2008] EWHC 2257; [2008] 2 Lloyd's Rep. 685 at [87] (Aikens J: "Some of the cases talk of such a contract being void, but I think it is clearer to say that there never was a contract at all").

311 cf. Devlin LJ (dissenting) in *Ingram v Little* [1961] 1 Q.B. 31.

312 (1864) 2 H. & C. 906; para.8–045.

A third version of the theory is that the required correspondence is between offer and acceptance *as interpreted by the court*. On this view *Raffles v Wichelhaus* can be explained on the ground that offer and acceptance were so ambiguous that the court could not, in the context, determine their meaning at all. But this version of the theory makes it hard to explain the distinction drawn in *Smith v Hughes* between a mistake as to the age of the oats and a mistake as to a warranty as to their age; and, more generally, to say why offer and acceptance should have been held to correspond in some of the cases discussed in this section, but not in others. It seems that this version of the "offer and acceptance" theory still raises the same difficulties as those which arise under the doctrine of mistake. If the offer and acceptance correspond verbally, the court is unlikely to hold that they do not correspond on their true construction unless the parties are very seriously at cross-purposes; and such a process of construction would not appear to differ substantially from the application of the principle of fundamental mistake.

## (e) Equity

The common law of unilateral mistake can be a source of hardship. A contract may be valid, in spite of the existence of a fundamental mistake, because of the objective principle, or the mistake may be a significant one, but not of the "fundamental type". Here the mistaken party can suffer hardship through being held to a contract which he did not intend to make, though this hardship must be weighed against that which the other party might suffer if the contract were held invalid.[313] Conversely, an innocent third party may suffer hardship where the contract is void, as in *Shogun Finance v Hudson*.[314] Equity provides no relief against the hardship to third parties that can arise when the contract is void at law,[315] and deals only to a limited extent with the hardship which the mistaken party can suffer when the contract is valid. 8–059

**Refusal of specific performance.** Specific performance will clearly be refused where the contract is *void* at law, e.g. where one party, to the knowledge of the other, makes a mistake as to the terms of the contract;[316] or as to its binding force.[317] Specific performance may be refused where the contract is *valid* at law because the mistake is not fundamental,[318] or not operative.[319] Thus in *Day v* 8–060

313 The other party can, however, invoke the objective principle even though he has not suffered any detriment by relying on the appearance of agreement induced by the conduct of the mistaken party: para.8–051.

314 [2003] UKHL 62; [2004] 1 A.C. 919; para.8–041.

315 cf. a number of statements by Lord Denning to the effect that the contract in cases such as *Cundy v Lindsay* (1878) 3 App. Cas. 459 would be voidable in equity: *Solle v Butcher* [1950] 1 K.B. 671 at 692; *Lewis v Averay* [1972] 1 Q.B. 198 at 207. The attraction of this view is that it would enable the court in such cases to protect innocent third parties. But Lord Denning has also said that there was "no contract at all" in *Cundy v Lindsay* (*Gallie v Lee* [1969] 2 Ch. 17 at 33; affirmed [1971] A.C. 1004)); and this view is certainly more consistent with the decision; cf. para.8–062.

316 *Webster v Cecil* (1861) 30 Beav. 62. It seems reasonable to deduce from the report that the claimant knew of the defendant's mistake; but this fact is not actually stated.

317 *Pateman v Pay* (1974) 232 E.G. 457.

318 e.g. *Jones v Rimmer* (1880) 14 Ch D. 588.

*Wells*[320] the defendant instructed an auctioneer to sell cottages thinking that he had told the auctioneer to put a reserve price on them. The auctioneer sold without reserve, at a lower price, and it was held that the defendant could not be compelled to perform specifically.

In exercising its discretion, the court must weigh the hardship of granting the remedy against the uncertainty caused by refusing it. Two cases may be contrasted. In *Malins v Freeman*[321] the defendant at an auction bid for one lot under the mistaken impression that he was bidding for another. Although he was clearly liable at law,[322] it was held that specific performance should not be ordered against him. But in *Tamplin v James*[323] the defendant at an auction bid for an inn and a shop mistakenly believing that the lot included a certain garden. The Court of Appeal ordered specific performance, stressing the uncertainty which would result from allowing the defendant to rely on his own mistake. James LJ said that a defendant could rely on a mistake to which the claimant had not contributed only "where a hardship amounting to injustice would have been inflicted upon him by holding him to his bargain, and it was unreasonable to hold him to it".[324] The two cases may be reconciled by saying that it is a "hardship amounting to injustice" to force a person to take one property when he thinks he has bought another, but not to force a person to take a property which is less extensive than he thought.

Since the object of refusing specific performance is to avoid hardship to the party prejudiced by the mistake, it follows that, where the contract is valid at law, only that party can rely on the mistake. Thus if A thinks that he is buying more than B intends to sell, A can specifically enforce the contract for the smaller quantity intended by B.[325] But where the contract is void at law, neither party can specifically enforce it[326] unless the circumstances are such that, even at law, one party, but not the other, can rely on the mistake.[327]

8–061 **Specific performance on terms.** Equity can take a middle course between refusing specific performance and granting it in spite of the mistake: it can, where the contract is valid at law, grant specific performance on terms. Thus in *Baskcomb v Beckwith*[328] an estate was sold in lots, on the terms that the purchaser of each lot should covenant not to build a public house on it. The vendor kept one of the lots himself, and proposed to build a public house there, but the plan of the lots did not make this clear. It was held that the vendor could specifically enforce the contract but only if he covenanted not to build a public house on the land retained by him. Similarly, equity can order specific performance with

[319] *Manser v Back* (1848) 6 Hare 43; see para.8–051.

[320] (1861) 30 Beav. 220; cf. *Wood v Scarth* (1855) 2 K. & J. 33.

[321] (1837) 2 Keen 25.

[322] See para.8–051.

[323] (1880) 15 Ch D. 215; cf. *Calverley v Williams* (1790) 1 Ves. Jun. 209.

[324] *Tamplin v James* (1880) 15 Ch D. 215 at 221; cf. *Manser v Back* (1848) 6 Hare 433; *Stewart v Kennedy* (1890) 15 App. Cas. 75 at 105.

[325] *Preston v Luck* (1884) 27 Ch D. 497.

[326] *Higginson v Clowes* (1808) 15 Ves. 516 (vendor's claim); *Clowes v Higginson* (1813) 1 Ves & B. 524 (purchaser's claim).

[327] See para.8–057.

[328] (1869) L.R. 8 Eq. 100.

compensation, i.e. abatement or increase of the purchase price, where the value of the property sold is less or greater than supposed because of some misdescription of the property.[329]

**No rescission in equity.** Where a contract is valid because the mistake of one of the parties is not operative, equity may refuse specific performance against the mistaken party, but it will not rescind[330] and so deprive the other party of his remedy at law on the contract; for to take this step would subvert the certainty which the objective principle is intended to promote. Accordingly, equity will, in general, follow the common law rule that a mistake is not operative if the mistaken party, A, has so conducted himself as to induce the other party, B, reasonably to believe that A has agreed to the terms proposed by B. In particular, a person cannot have a contract set aside because of a mistake which he made because he failed to act with due diligence.[331] **8–062**

## 4. RECTIFICATION

### (a) In general

Contracting parties may execute a document purporting to contain the terms previously agreed between them. If, as a result of a mistake, the document fails to contain all those terms, or contains different terms, the court may rectify it by ordering its wording to be changed so as to bring it into line with the earlier agreement;[332] alternatively, the court may treat the document as having been so rectified without making a formal order for its rectification.[333] Having been developed in equity, rectification is a discretionary remedy.[334] It is available where there has been a mistake, not in the *making*, but in the *recording*, of a contract: "Courts of equity do not rectify contracts; they may and do rectify instruments."[335] Rectification can be ordered although the contract is one which must be in, or evidenced in, writing.[336] The requirements to be met differ according to whether the mistake in the recording of the contract in the written instrument is made by both parties,[337] or only by one.[338] **8–063**

[329] See Harpum [1981] C.L.J. 47.

[330] *The Harriette N* [2008] EWHC 2257; [2008] 2 Lloyd's Rep. 685 at [105] disagreeing with *Huyton SA v Distribuidora Internacional de Productos Agricolas SA* [2002] EWHC 2088 (Comm); [2003] 2 Lloyd's Rep. 780 at [455].

[331] *Attorney General v Tomline* (1877) 7 Ch D. 388; *Soper v Arnold* (1877) 37 Ch D. 96; 14 App. Cas. 429; cf. *The Harriette N* [2008] EWHC 2257 (Comm); [2008] 2 Lloyd's Rep. 685. For the common law position, cf. para.8–004.

[332] *Murray v Parker* (1854) 19 Beav. 305; *The Rhodian River* [1984] 1 Lloyd's Rep. 373.

[333] *The Nile Rhapsody* [1994] 1 Lloyd's Rep. 382; *OTV Birwelco Ltd v Technical & General Guarantee Co Ltd* [2002] EWHC 2240 (TCC); [2002] 4 All E.R. 668 at [39].

[334] *Re Butlin's Settlement Trusts* [1976] Ch. 251 at 263.

[335] *Mackenzie v Coulson* (1869) L.R. 8 Eq. 369 at 375; *The Olympic Pride* [1980] 2 Lloyd's Rep. 67 at 72.

[336] *Olley v Fisher* (1886) 34 Ch D. 367; *Johnson v Bragge* [1901] 1 Ch. 28; *USA v Motor Trucks Ltd* [1924] A.C. 196; *May v Platt* [1900] 1 Ch. 616, if contra, is not law: *Craddock Bros v Hunt* [1923] 2 Ch. 136; Law Com. No.164, paras 5, 6.

[337] See para.8–067.

8–064 **Types of mistake rectified.** Rectification is most frequently ordered where the terms of a document do not correspond with those of the agreement between the parties, e.g. where the rent is misstated in a lease, or the area of land to be conveyed is misstated in a conveyance.[339] It has been suggested that rectification cannot be ordered to insert a term which has been omitted,[340] but there seems to be no basis for this restriction. Indeed, it has been said that this is precisely when rectification may be more appropriate than the correction of such an error by way of interpretation,[341] which is discussed next. Rectification is also available where a person who intends to sign a document in one capacity does so in another, e.g. where the name of a person to whom a bill of exchange is meant to be payable is put in as drawer instead of as payee.[342] The court may also rectify a document executed under a mistake as to its meaning or legal effect;[343] but such a mistake will not be a ground for rectification if the true legal effect of the document was fully explained to the party claiming to have made the mistake,[344] or if the mistake is not as to the legal effect of the document but to its consequences.[345] Rectification may be ordered to correct a mistake in a unilateral document, such as a settlement,[346] a notice of severance of a joint tenancy,[347] and a disclosure letter intended to qualify the warranties given in a share purchase agreement.[348]

8–065 **Correction of obvious mistakes by way of interpretation.** As noted above, an obvious drafting mistake may be corrected as a matter of interpretation if it is clear both that an error has been made and what a reasonable person would have understood the parties to have meant.[349] If the interpretation claim succeeds,

---

338 See para.8–076.

339 e.g. *Beale v Kyte* [1907] 1 Ch. 564; *Blacklocks v JB Developments (Godalming) Ltd* [1982] Ch. 183.

340 *OMV Supply and Trading AG v Kazmunaygaz Trading AG* [2014] EWHC 1372 (Comm) at [74].

341 *Cherry Tree Investments Ltd v Landmain Ltd* [2012] EWCA Civ 736; [2013] 2 W.L.R. 481 at [132] (Lewison LJ).

342 *Druiff v Parker* (1868) L.R. 5 Eq. 131; cf. *Co-operative Bank Plc v Tipper* [1996] 4 All E.R. 366 (guarantor's name mistakenly inserted as borrower's).

343 *Re Colebrook's Conveyances* [1972] 1 W.L.R. 1379; cf. *Jervis v Howle & Talke Colliery Ltd* [1937] Ch. 67; following *Burroughes v Abbott* [1922] 1 Ch. 86; *Re Butlin's Settlement Trusts* [1976] Ch. 251. No claim for rectification was made in *Keen v Holland* [1984] 1 W.L.R. 251 (where a mistake as to legal effect was held not sufficient to give rise to an estoppel by convention: para.3–100).

344 *Constantinidi v Ralli* [1953] Ch. 427.

345 *AMP (UK) Plc v Barker* [2001] Pens. L.R. 77 at [70]; *Allnutt v Wilding* [2007] EWCA Civ 412; [2007] W.T.L.R. 941.

346 *Re Butlin's Settlement Trusts* [1976] Ch. 251.

347 *Lee v Lee* [2018] EWHC 149 (Ch).

348 *Persimmon Homes Ltd v Hillier* [2019] EWCA Civ 800.

349 *East v Pantiles (Plant Hire)* [1982] 2 E.G.L.R. 111 at 112; *Littman v Aspen Oil (Broking) Ltd* [2005] EWCA Civ 1579; [2006] 2 P. & C.R. 2. The mistake "on the face" may emerge only when the document is read with regard to the "background or context": *Chartbrook Ltd v Persimmon Homes Ltd* [2009] UKHL 38; [2009] 1 A.C. 1101 at [24]. See para.6–047. For cases of "misnomer", see: *Nittan UK Ltd v Solent Steel Fabrications Ltd* [1981] 1 Lloyd's Rep. 633; *Dumford Trading AG v OAO Atlantrybflot* [2005] EWCA Civ 24; [2005] 1 Lloyd's Rep. 289; *Gastronome (UK) Ltd v Anglo-Dutch Meats (UK) Ltd* [2006] EWCA Civ 1233; [2006] 2 Lloyd's Rep. 587; *Liberty Mercian Ltd v Cuddy Civil Engineering Ltd* [2013] EWHC 2688 (TCC); [2014] B.L.R. 179.

rectification is strictly unnecessary[350] though it may be convenient, e.g. if the contract is likely to come into the hands of a third party. If it fails, rectification may still be available.[351] It has been suggested that the approach which the courts had been taking to the correction of mistakes as a matter of interpretation in cases like *Chartbrook Ltd v Persimmon Homes Ltd*[352] left little or no room for the doctrine of rectification.[353] That is an overstatement since not every error in drafting will reveal itself in a reading of the contract against the admissible background,[354] whereas a feature of rectification is that it allows the courts to go beyond the evidence which is admissible in an interpretation claim.[355] Further, there "will also be cases in which it is obvious that something has gone wrong with the language but no way of discovering from the admissible background what it was actually intended to mean. Here again, the remedy, if any, would lie only in rectification."[356] That said, if the current approach of the courts is to adopt a "more" literal approach to interpretation,[357] the need for a party to resort to rectification, if available, may have increased.

**Clear evidence needed.** The court may admit extrinsic evidence, including evidence of the parties' pre-contractual negotiations in support of a claim for rectification,[358] but it has to guard against two dangers. The first is that the remedy may result in imposing on a party terms to which he might not in fact have agreed.[359] The second is that the "certainty and ready enforceability [of written agreements] would be hindered by constant attempts to cloud the issue by reference to pre-contract negotiations".[360] For these reasons, the burden of proof falls on the party seeking rectification. The standard of proof is the civil standard of balance of probability,[361] but rectification will be ordered only if there is strong and convincing evidence that the document failed accurately to record the intention of the parties.[362] The court is, in particular, reluctant to rectify a contract 8–066

[350] cf. *Mangistaumunaigaz Oil Production Association v United World Trade Inc* [1995] 1 Lloyd's Rep. 617; *Alliance v Tishby* [2011] EWHC 1015 (Ch) at [42]. In *Woodford Land Ltd v Persimmon Homes Ltd* [2011] EWHC 984 (Ch) this produced a rather odd result.

[351] *QRS Sciences Ltd v BTG International Ltd* [2005] EWHC 670 (Ch); [2005] F.S.R. 43; *LSREF III Wight Ltd v Millvalley Ltd* [2016] EWHC 466 (Comm); 165 Con L.R. 58; cf. *Cherry Tree Investments Ltd v Landmain Ltd* [2012] EWCA Civ 736; [2013] 2 W.L.R. 481, where no claim for rectification was in fact brought.

[352] [2009] UKHL 38; [2009] A.C. 1101. See para.6–048.

[353] Burrows in Burrows & Peel (eds), *Contract Terms* (2007); Buxton [2010] C.L.J. 253; Sumption (2016–2017) 8 UK Supreme Court Yearbook 74 at 86. Contrast *Cherry Tree Investments Ltd v Landmain Ltd* [2012] EWCA Civ 736; [2013] 2 W.L.R. 481 at [98], [120].

[354] Hoffmann 134 L.Q.R. 553 at 572.

[355] See para.6–037.

[356] Hoffmann 134 L.Q.R. 553 at 573.

[357] See para.6–049.

[358] See para.6–037.

[359] See further, para.8–077.

[360] *The Olympic Pride* [1980] 2 Lloyd's Rep. 67 at 73.

[361] *Joscelyne v Nissen* [1970] 2 Q.B. 86 at 98; *The Nai Genova* [1984] 1 Lloyd's Rep. 353 at 359.

[362] *Joscelyne v Nissen* [1970] 2 Q.B. 86 ("convincing proof"); *The Olympic Pride* [1980] 2 Lloyd's Rep. 67 at 73 ("high degree of conviction"); *Thomas Bates & Son Ltd v Wyndham's (Lingerie) Ltd* [1981] 1 W.L.R. 505 at 521; *Tartsinis v Navona Management Co* [2015] EWHC 57 (Comm) at [85].

solely on the oral evidence of the party claiming rectification,[363] but there is no absolute rule against rectification on such evidence.[364] An entire agreement clause in the executed document does not preclude a claim in rectification, though it may be a factor to be taken into account for the purpose of common mistake rectification.[365]

### (i) *Common mistake*[366]

8–067 **Summary requirements.** The requirements for rectification of a written instrument on the grounds of common mistake have been summarised as follows[367]:

> "(1) the parties had a common continuing intention, whether or not amounting to an agreement,[368] in respect of a particular matter in the instrument to be rectified; (2) there was an outward expression of accord;[369] (3) the intention continued at the time of the execution of the instrument sought to be rectified;[370] (4) by mistake, the instrument did not reflect that common intention.[371]"

Each of these requirements is considered in further detail below. If they are met, the written instrument will be rectified in such a way as to reflect the parties' common intention. It is not necessary to have formulated the words by which such intention is to be given effect: "Rectification does not fail merely because there is more than one way to give effect to the common intention."[372]

8–068 **A common intention.** The court can rectify a document which was preceded by a concluded agreement or a "continuing common intention"[373] even though there was no prior binding contract;[374] for example, because the prior agreement was

---

[363] *Tucker v Bennett* (1887) 38 Ch D. 1; *Fredensen v Rothschild* [1941] 1 All E.R. 430; *Thomas Bates & Son Ltd v Wyndham's (Lingerie) Ltd* [1981] 1 W.L.R. 505 at 514, 521.

[364] *Cook v Fearn* (1878) 48 L.J. Ch. 63.

[365] *JJ Huber Ltd v The Private DIY Company Ltd* (1995) 70 P. & C.R. 33 (unilateral mistake); *Surgicraft Ltd v Paradigm Biovices Inc* [2010] EWHC 1291 (Ch); *Dubai Islamic Bank PJSC v PSI Energy Holding Co BSC* [2011] EWHC 2718 (Comm) at [83]; *DS-Rendite-Fonds NR.106 VLCC Titan Glory GmbH & Co v Titan Maritime SA* [2013] EWHC 3492 (Comm) at [48]; *LSREF III Wight Ltd v Millvalley Ltd* [2016] EWHC 466 (Comm); 165 Con L.R. 58 at [122]; *Milton Keynes BC v Viridor (Community Recycling MK) Ltd* [2017] EWHC 239 (TCC); [2017] B.L.R. 216 at [77]–[78].

[366] Smith 123 L.Q.R. 116.

[367] *Swainland Builders Ltd v Freehold Properties Ltd* [2002] 2 E.G.L.R. 71 at [33]; cited with approval in *Chartbrook Ltd v Persimmon Homes Ltd* [2009] UKHL 38; [2009] 1 A.C. 1101 at [48].

[368] See paras 8–068–8–072.

[369] See para.8–073.

[370] See para.8–074.

[371] See para.8–075.

[372] *FSHC Group Holding Ltd v Barclays Bank Plc* [2018] EWHC 1558 (Ch) at [43]; affirmed [2019] EWCA Civ 1361; cf. *Equity Syndicate Management Ltd v Glaxosmithkline Plc* [2015] EWHC 2163 (Comm) at [27].

[373] *The Olympic Pride* [1980] 2 Lloyd's Rep. 67 at 72; *Grand Metropolitan Plc v William Hill Group Plc* [1997] 1 B.C.L.C. 390; *Swainland Builders Ltd v Freehold Properties Ltd* [2002] 2 E.G.L.R. 71 at [33].

[374] For the now rejected contrary view, see *Mackenzie v Coulson* (1869) L.R. 8 Eq. 369 at 375.

binding in honour only. In *Joscelyne v Nissen*[375] an agreement for the transfer of a business and premises was negotiated between a father and daughter, it being understood that the father should continue to live in the premises and that the daughter should pay his gas and electricity bills. No provision for such payments was made in the formal contract finally executed. Rectification was ordered even though, before execution of the document, the agreement between the parties had no contractual force. It was enough that there was "some outward expression of accord"[376] and that this was "adhered to in intention by the parties to the subsequent written contract".[377] The common intention must be that of the parties to the written instrument, including any intention which may be attributed to them, as for example where trustees had authorised a beneficiary to negotiate the terms of a share purchase agreement and had instructed their solicitors to produce a written contract that contained those terms.[378]

**An objective common intention?** In *Chartbrook v Persimmon Homes Ltd* Lord Hoffmann held that the test for determining whether the parties had a prior common intention at variance with the written instrument is an objective one,[379] but evidence of subjective intention is admissible, and may be significant, where the alleged prior consensus is based wholly or in part on oral exchanges or conduct. In such a case the subjective understanding of the parties throws light on what they are likely to have said to one another in objective communications "crossing the line".[380] His view in this respect was obiter because the contract in question was corrected as a matter of interpretation, but the significance in practice of an objective test is apparent from the facts of the case. The question for the court was the sum to be awarded to the claimant landowner by way of an additional payment from the defendant builder after the development and sale of flats on the claimant's land. The House of Lords departed from the literal interpretation of the provision which defined the payment due,[381] but had it adhered to the literal interpretation, the defendant had an alternative claim in rectification. This was based primarily on a letter sent by the defendant to the claimant which was not admissible in the interpretation claim as it formed part of the pre-contractual negotiations.[382] The trial judge had found that the letter did **8–069**

---

[375] [1970] 2 Q.B. 86; Bromley 87 L.Q.R. 532; cf. *Wilson v Wilson* [1969] 1 W.L.R. 1470; *Michael Richards Properties v St Saviour's Parish* [1975] 3 All E.R. 416 at 423; *The Olympic Pride* [1980] 2 Lloyd's Rep. 67 at 72.

[376] See para.8–073.

[377] *Joscelyne v Nissen* [1970] 2 Q.B. 86 at 99; *Shipley Urban DC v Bradford Corp* [1936] Ch. 375 at 396.

[378] *Hawksford Trustees Jersey Ltd v Stella Global UK Ltd* [2012] EWCA Civ 55; [2012] 2 All E.R. (Comm) 748; cf. *Murray Holdings Ltd v Oscatello Investments Ltd* [2018] EWHC 162 (Ch) at [198].

[379] *Chartbrook v Persimmon Homes Ltd* [2009] UKHL 38; [2009] 1 A.C. 1101 at [60]; cf. *Dunlop Haywards (DHL) Ltd v Erinaceous Insurance Services Ltd* [2009] EWCA Civ 354; [2009] Lloyds Rep. I.R. 464 at [66]. Earlier authorities had seemed to endorse a subjective approach: see, e.g. *IRC v Raphael* [1935] A.C. 96, 143 ("real intention"); *The Nai Genova* [1984] 1 Lloyd's Rep. 353 at 359; *Munt v Beasley* [2006] EWCA Civ 370 at [36].

[380] *Chartbrook v Persimmon Homes Ltd* [2009] UKHL 38; [2009] 1 A.C. 1101 at [64]–[65].

[381] See para.6–048.

[382] Having been admitted for the rectification claim, the letter had to be discounted for the interpretation claim, but Baroness Hale candidly admitted that she would not have found it "quite so easy" to agree with the conclusion reached as a matter of interpretation had the court not been aware

not suffice as evidence of a common intention at variance with the contract later executed because he accepted the evidence of the two principals of the claimant that they honestly understood the definition in the letter in a way which was consistent with the definition on the literal interpretation of the contract. There was no common subjective intention which was not accurately recorded in the contract because the claimant and the defendant read the letter differently. However, on the basis of the objective approach taken by Lord Hoffmann, the findings of the trial judge did not rule out rectification because it would have been clear to a "reasonable person who read [the letter] in the light of the background known to the parties" that the parties had agreed to a definition of the additional payment due which was different to that included in the contract.[383]

8–070 **Criticism of the objective test of common intention.** The other members of the House of Lords in the *Chartbrook* case expressed their agreement with Lord Hoffmann's endorsement of an objective approach to the prior common intention of the parties. Notwithstanding it was reached on an obiter basis, it was followed on subsequent decisions,[384] but not without some expression of doubt which, it is submitted, is well founded.[385] While an objective approach is taken to the formation of the parties' agreement, we have already seen that this is not to the exclusion of the parties' subjective intentions. B is entitled to hold A to an agreement which A did not intend to make if that is how the agreement would appear to a reasonable person in B's position; it would be both unjust, and render agreements too uncertain, if A could escape on the basis of his subjective intention.[386] But if B knew of A's intention, it would now be unjust for B to rely on the objective approach.[387] When seen in this context, there is perhaps an obvious rationale for rectification if it is based on the subjective intention of the parties: it would be unjust to hold the parties to the written instrument and the objective manifestation of their agreement set out therein if it does not accurately reflect their shared subjective intention (rectification for common mistake), or if it fails to record the intention of one party and the other is seeking unfairly to take

of the agreement which the parties had reached during the negotiations: [2009] UKHL 38; [2009] 1 A.C. 1101 at [99]. She conceded this as part of the debate about whether to admit evidence of the pre-contractual negotiations in an interpretation claim: see para.6–030.

383 *Chartbrook v Persimmon Homes Ltd* [2009] UKHL 38; [2009] 1 A.C. 1101 at [54].

384 See, e.g. *Daventry DC v Daventry & District Housing Association Ltd* [2011] EWCA Civ 1153; [2012] 1 W.L.R. 1333; *Scottish Widows v BGC International* [2012] EWCA Civ 607; 142 Con L.R. 27; *UBS AG v Kommunale Wasserwerke Leipzig GmbH* [2014] EWHC 3615 (Comm); *Tartsinis v Navona Management Co* [2015] EWHC 57 (Comm).

385 See e.g. *Bashir v Ali* [2010] EWHC 2320 (Ch) at [53] (reversed on different grounds without consideration of rectification: [2011] EWCA Civ 707; [2011] 2 P. & C.R. 12); *Crossco No.4 Unlimited v Jolan Ltd* [2011] EWHC 803 (Ch); [2011] N.P.C. 38 at [253]; *Daventry DC v Daventry & District Housing Association Ltd* [2011] EWCA Civ 1153; [2012] 1 W.L.R. 1333 at [176] (Toulson LJ) and at [195]–[196] (Lord Neuberger MR); *Tartsinis v Navona Management Co* [2015] EWHC 57 (Comm) at [90]–[93]; *LSREF III Wight Ltd v Millvalley Ltd* [2016] EWHC 466 (Comm); 165 Con L.R. 58 at [70]; *AML Global Ltd v Exxonmobil Petroleum & Chemical BVBA* [2018] EWHC 3321 (TCC) at [43]; McLauchlan 126 L.Q.R. 8; Ruddell [2014] L.M.C.L.Q. 48; Davies 75 M.L.R. 412; 75 C.L.J. 62; Nugee (2012) 26 *Trust Law International* 76.

386 See para.2–002.

387 See para.2–003, para.8–051.

advantage of that mistake (rectification for unilateral mistake).[388] By contrast, there is no obvious rationale for preferring to hold the parties to one objectively manifested agreement (their prior and possibly non-binding common intention) over another (the binding written instrument).[389] The significant feature of a claim for rectification is that the court starts with a binding written contract, the objective meaning of which one party wishes to depart from.

**A dual approach.** The doubts just expressed about an objective approach to the common intention of the parties were acknowledged by the Court of Appeal in *FSHC Group Holding Ltd v Barclays Bank Plc*.[390] Leggatt LJ found that such an approach was inconsistent with previous authority (in particular, a previous decision of the majority of the Court of Appeal[391]) and, on the basis that Lord Hoffmann's comments in the *Chartbrook* case were obiter dictum, it was held they did not represent the state of the law and should no longer be followed. The fact that, in most cases,[392] the requirement of a subjective consensus will make it more difficult to obtain rectification was regarded as a benefit in policy terms: **8–071**

> "… the fact that a 'subjective consensus' is harder to prove than an 'objective consensus' is not an objection to adopting a subjective test for rectification but a positive merit of such a test. As a matter of policy, rectification should be difficult to prove."[393]

However, Leggatt LJ explained that a subjective approach is only required where rectification is sought on the basis of a prior *non-binding* common intention. Where the parties have already entered into a binding agreement which is subsequently reduced into writing, then an objective approach should be taken. The justification for rectification in the two situations is said to be quite different. In the latter:

> "… if parties make a binding agreement to execute a document containing particular terms but instead execute a document containing different terms, the court may specifically enforce the agreement by rectifying the document; and … in such a case, the terms of the contract to which the subsequent document is made to conform must be objectively determined in the same way as any other contract."[394]

In the former situation, where the parties have a prior non-binding common intention, the justification for rectification is:

> "not to be found in the principle that agreements (as objectively determined) must be kept. It lies elsewhere. It rests on the equitable doctrine that a party will not be allowed to enforce the terms of a written contract, objectively ascertained, when to do so is against conscience

---

[388] See para.8–076.

[389] *Britoil Plc v Hunt Overseas Oil Inc* [1994] C.L.C. 567 at 573 (Hobhouse LJ); *Daventry DC v Daventry & District Housing Association Ltd* [2011] EWCA Civ 1153; [2012] 1 W.L.R. 1333 at [176] (Toulson LJ); *Tartsinis v Navona Management Co* [2015] EWHC 57 (Comm) at [92]–[93].

[390] [2019] EWCA Civ 1361.

[391] *Britoil Plc v Hunt Overseas Oil Inc* [1994] C.L.C. 567 (Lord Hoffmann dissenting).

[392] In the *FSHC* case itself it was the party resisting rectification which advocated an objective approach on the basis that, subjectively, there was a clear consensus at variance with the written instrument, but the Court found that, even on an objective approach, this was also the case.

[393] *FSHC Group Holding Ltd v Barclays Bank Plc* [2019] EWCA Civ 1361 at [174].

[394] *FSHC Group Holding Ltd v Barclays Bank Plc* [2019] EWCA Civ 1361 at [141].

> because it is inconsistent with what both parties in fact intended (and mutually understood each other to intend) those terms to be when the document was executed."[395]

In practice, this is the situation which will most commonly be encountered by the courts and, after *FSHC*, a subjective approach is taken to determine the common intention of the parties.

8–072 **A remaining difficulty?** The distinction between a binding and a non-binding common intention is drawn in the *FSHC* case in part to explain the decision in *FE Rose (London) Ltd v W H Pim, Jnr & Co Ltd*,[396] which is considered below. One difficulty with such a dual approach is that, if the written binding contract must give way to a prior non-binding subjective consensus, why is that not also the case for an earlier binding contract which is then reduced to writing? If that earlier contract is only to be determined objectively, then some odd results are possible. This can be demonstrated by comparing two examples.

In the first example, the parties execute a written contract which, as objectively interpreted, amounts to "X". The previous negotiations of the parties indicate that there was no binding contract until the parties executed the written instrument but that they both subjectively intended "Y" and shared that intention. Let us assume that this subjective consensus is primarily embodied in a letter exchanged by the parties.[397] After the *FSHC* case the written contract will be rectified to "Y".

In the second example, the only difference is that the agreement as embodied in the letter is regarded as binding and the subsequent written instrument is only intended to formalise that earlier contract. According to the *FSHC* case, rectification of the written instrument will now depend on the objective interpretation of the letter, and any other communications which make up the earlier binding agreement. If, objectively interpreted, it amounts to "X", then the written instrument will not be rectified, but what if it can be shown that both parties' subjectively intended "Y" (and shared that intention) and their "mistake" was in the drafting of the letter, which mistake was then simply reproduced in the written instrument? That may seem just as compelling a case for rectification as the first example. It may seem odder still if the letter, as objectively interpreted, amounted to "Y", but the parties subjectively intended "X". In such a case, it seems that the written instrument which says "X" and which is what the parties actually intended would now be rectified so that it amounted to "Y". What these examples may illustrate is that the true basis for rectification for common mistake is simply to bring the written instrument in line with the parties' agreement, but where the parties have the same shared subjective intention, whether or not they have reached the stage of a binding contract, it is this which represents their agreement and not the objective appearance,[398] provided it continues until the time of execution of the written instrument.

---

395 *FSHC Group Holding Ltd v Barclays Bank Plc* [2019] EWCA Civ 1361 at [146].

396 [1953] 2 Q.B. 450; cf. *George Cohen Sons & Co Ltd v Docks and Inland Waterways Executive* (1950) 84 Ll. L. Rep. 97.

397 cf. the *Chartbook* case, which is discussed at para.8–069.

398 See para.1–002; Cartwright, *Misrepresentation, Mistake & Non-Disclosure*, 5th edn (2019), 13-40.

**An outward expression of accord.** It has been said that the need for an "outward expression of accord" should be seen "more as an evidential factor, rather than a strict legal requirement in all cases of rectification."[399] But this view was rejected in the *FSHC* case on the basis that it is "fundamental that contractual rights and obligations should be based on mutual assent which the parties have manifested to each other and not on uncommunicated intentions which happen, without the parties knowing it, to coincide."[400] What this requirement emphasises is that what is needed is a *shared* intention[401]: 8–073

> "It would be capricious if a contractual document could be reformed to reflect the private intention of a party just because, although unknown to that party at the time, it turns out that the other party had a similar intention."[402]

It does not require that the term in question must have been expressly mentioned; the shared understanding may be "tacit",[403] while bearing in mind that clear evidence is needed for rectification.[404]

**A continuing intention.** The common intention of the parties must continue until the time that the written instrument is executed. If the parties have changed their common intention and that changed intention is accurately reflected in the written instrument, there is no basis for rectification; a document cannot be rectified to bring it into line with mere steps in the antecedent negotiations.[405] As explained by Toulson LJ in *Daventry DC v Daventry & District Housing Association Ltd*[406] this can raise a potential conundrum because it must be rare for a written agreement to be executed without some approval of its form at some point in time before the moment of execution. Does the drawing up of a draft for approval which is at variance to any earlier common intention amount to a change of intention, or the first sign of the mistaken recording of that prior intention? The solution of Toulson LJ to this conundrum was to ask "whether on a fair view there was a renegotiation of the prior agreement or a mistake".[407] As the reference to a "fair view" indicates, this amounts to an objective test, but the search for a "renegotiation" requires the court to consider the actions and conduct of both 8–074

[399] *Munt v Beasley* [2006] EWCA Civ 370 at [36]; cf. *JIS (1974) Ltd v MCP Investment Nominees Ltd* [2003] EWCA Civ 721 at [34]; *DS-Rendite-Fonds NR.106 VLCC Titan Glory GmbH & Co v Titan Maritime SA* [2013] EWHC 3492 (Comm) at [47]. An uncommunicated subjective intention is sufficient in the case of a voluntary settlement: *Day v Day* [2013] EWCA Civ 280; [2013] 3 W.L.R. 556 at [48].

[400] *FSHC Group Holding Ltd v Barclays Bank Plc* [2019] EWCA Civ 1361 at [77].

[401] The relevant intentions cannot be "locked separately in the breast of each party": *Joscelyne v Nissen* [1970] 2 Q.B. 86 at 97.

[402] *Tartsinis v Navona Management Co* [2015] EWHC 57 (Comm) at [88] (Leggatt J).

[403] *FSHC Group Holding Ltd v Barclays Bank Plc* [2019] EWCA Civ 1361 at [81], [84] ("so obvious as to go without saying"); cf. *Caraman, Rowley & May v Aperghis* (1923) 17 Ll. L. Rep. 183; *Saga Group Ltd v Paul* [2016] EWHC 2344 (Ch); [2017] 4 W.L.R. 12 at [54]; *Industrial Acoustics Co Ltd v Crowhurst* [2012] EWHC 1614; [2012] Pens. L.R. at [45].

[404] See para.8–066.

[405] *Lovell & Christmas Ltd v Wall* (1911) 104 L.T. 85 at 88; *The Aktor* [2008] EWHC 1330 (Comm); [2008] 2 Lloyd's Rep. 246 at [60].

[406] [2011] EWCA Civ 1153; [2012] 1 W.L.R. 1333 at [158]–[159].

[407] *Daventry DC v Daventry & District Housing Association Ltd* [2011] EWCA Civ 1153; [2012] 1 W.L.R. 1333 at [160].

parties. Lord Neuberger MR and Etherton LJ preferred a test which looks only to the conduct of the party who appears to depart from the prior accord: "whether objectively, prior to the execution of the contract, [B] communicated to [A] that it intended to contract on a different basis".[408] In light of the decision in the *FSHC* case, an objective approach to the question of a *continuing* common intention is no longer appropriate,[409] but the conundrum referred to above remains. On the assumption that an earlier shared subjective intention at variance with the written contract has been proven, it will be for the party resisting rectification to prove it was changed, including the requirement of an outward expression of accord.[410]

8–075 **Rose v Pim.** In *FE Rose (London) Ltd v WH Pim Jnr & Co Ltd*[411] the claimants had received an order from a customer for "Moroccan horsebeans described here as feveroles" and asked the defendants (their suppliers) what "feveroles" were. The defendants replied that feveroles were just horsebeans and orally agreed to sell "horsebeans" to the claimants. When this contract was reduced to writing, the goods were again described as "horsebeans". In fact there were three types of Moroccan horsebeans: feves, feveroles and fevettes. The defendants supplied feves, which were less valuable than feveroles. It was held that the written contract could not be rectified by inserting "feveroles" after "horsebeans", as it accurately recorded the previous oral agreement.[412] As noted above, the case may be explained on the basis that the parties had already entered into a binding agreement before reducing it to writing and, in such a situation, an objective approach is taken.[413] But, as above, there is room to question this approach and the decision reached. If, in establishing the prior agreement of the parties, one takes into account the subjective intention of the parties, the case is one in which they used the word "horsebeans" as their own private label for "feveroles"[414] and subsequent decisions have confirmed that rectification is an available remedy where parties have used the words intended, but have been mistaken as to their meaning.[415] That would be irrelevant if, as was said in *Joscelyne v Nissen*, the parties' misapprehension was "locked separately in the breast of each" of them, so that there was no outward expression of accord.[416] But as Leggatt LJ commented in the *FSHC* case, that suggestion is difficult to follow given that the

---

[408] *Daventry DC v Daventry & District Housing Association Ltd* [2011] EWCA Civ 1153; [2012] 1 W.L.R. 1333 at [91] (Etherton LJ); at [207] (Lord Neuberger MR). They differed in their application of this test to the facts of the case which were unusual to say the least; cf. *Liberty Mercian Ltd v Cuddy Civil Engineering Ltd* [2013] EWHC 2688 (TCC); [2014] B.L.R. 179 at [129].

[409] See para.8–071. An objective approach is taken where there is already a binding contract, but, by definition, there can be no room for a change of intention in such a case.

[410] See para.8–073.

[411] [1953] 2 Q.B. 450; cf. *The Ypatia Halloussi* [1985] 2 Lloyd's Rep. 364 at 371.

[412] The contract was not void for mistake: para.8–016. Nor could the claimants rescind for misrepresentation as they had resold the horsebeans: cf. para.9–114, but they might now be able to claim damages under Misrepresentation Act 1967 s.2(1) (para.9–049). They might also (as Denning LJ suggested) be able to claim damages for breach of a collateral warranty, if the necessary animus contrahendi on the part of the seller could be shown (paras 9–063–9–065).

[413] See para.8–071. The case was decided before *Joscelyne v Nissen* had confirmed that a non-binding common intention would suffice.

[414] *FSHC Group Holding Ltd v Barclays Bank Plc* [2019] EWCA Civ 1361 at [70].

[415] *Re Butlin's Settlement Trusts* [1976] Ch. 251; see para.8–064.

[416] *Joscelyne v Nissen* [1970] 2 Q.B. 86 at 97.

claimants' understanding was derived from communication with the defendants' representative.[417] He agreed with Lewison LJ, writing extra-judicially,[418] that the best justification for the refusal to grant rectification was that the contract between the claimants and the defendants was part of a chain of contracts involving third parties so that, as Denning LJ observed in *Rose v Pim* itself, "it would not be fair to rectify one of the contracts without rectifying all three, which is obviously impossible".[419]

### *(ii) Unilateral mistake*

**Requirement of unconscionable conduct.** Where only one party makes a mistake in the recording of a contract, the relevant document may be rectified if, in addition, the non-mistaken party was guilty of fraud,[420] or misrepresentation,[421] or the requirements for an estoppel have been met.[422] Rectification will also be ordered if the non-mistaken party knew of the mistake and did not draw it to the attention of the mistaken party.[423] As Leggatt LJ explained in the *FSHC* case when considering the relationship between rectification for common mistake and rectification for unilateral mistake: 8–076

> "In the case of common mistake it is inequitable for a party to the contract to seek to apply the contract inconsistently with what that party knew to be the common intention of the parties when the written contract was executed. The doctrine of unilateral mistake extends this principle to the situation where a party seeks to apply the contract inconsistently with what that party knew the other party believed to be the common intention of the parties when the written contract was executed."[424]

For these purposes, knowledge refers not only to actual knowledge, but also includes wilfully shutting one's eyes to an obvious mistake, or wilfully and recklessly failing to make such inquiries as an honest and reasonable man would make.[425] In *Daventry DC v Daventry & District Housing Association Ltd* Toulson LJ was not sure that the test "should be so rigid",[426] but at present it is not

[417] *FSHC Group Holding Ltd v Barclays Bank Plc* [2019] EWCA Civ 1361 at [70].
[418] Jonathan Brock Memorial Lecture, 21 May 2008.
[419] *FE Rose (London) Ltd v WH Pim Jnr & Co Ltd* [1953] 2 Q.B. 450 at 462. For the effect of third party rights, see para.8–082.
[420] *Blay v Pollard & Morris* [1930] 1 K.B. 628 at 633.
[421] *Wimpey (UK) Ltd v VI Construction Ltd* [2005] EWCA Civ 77; [2005] B.L.R. 135 at [54].
[422] *A Roberts & Co Ltd v Leicestershire CC* [1961] Ch. 555; *The Nai Genova* [1984] 1 Lloyd's Rep. 353 at 363.
[423] *A Roberts & Co Ltd v Leicestershire CC* [1961] Ch. 555; *Commission for the New Towns v Cooper (Great Britain) Ltd* [1995] Ch. 259; *Thomas Bates & Son Ltd v Wyndham's (Lingerie) Ltd* [1981] 1 W.L.R. 505; *Wimpey (UK) Ltd v VI Construction Ltd* [2005] EWCA Civ 77; [2005] B.L.R. 135; *Yedina v Yedin* [2017] EWHC 3319 (Ch) at [293].
[424] *FSHC Group Holding Ltd v Barclays Bank Plc* [2019] EWCA Civ 1361 at [105].
[425] *Thomas Bates & Son Ltd v Wyndham's (Lingerie) Ltd* [1981] 1 W.L.R. 505; *Wimpey (UK) Ltd v VI Construction Ltd* [2005] EWCA Civ 77; [2005] B.L.R. 135, based on the analysis of various forms of knowledge made by Peter Gibson J in *Baden v Société Générale pour Favoriser le Développement du Commerce et de l'Industrie en France SA* (Note) [1993] 1 W.L.R. 509.
[426] *Daventry DC v Daventry & District Housing Association Ltd* [2011] EWCA Civ 1153; [2012] 1 W.L.R. 1333 at [184].

sufficient that a reasonable person in the position of the non-mistaken party would have been aware of the mistake.[427]

It has been said that the non-mistaken party must have been guilty of "sharp practice",[428] but the preferable view is that his conduct must be such as to make it inequitable that he should be allowed to object to the rectification of the document.[429] Other forms of unconscionable conduct may therefore suffice,[430] e.g. it is not enough that the non-mistaken party merely suspects that a mistake has been made,[431] but if he intended the other party to be mistaken as to the meaning or effect of the document and prevented him from discovering the mistake by making "false and misleading statements" during the negotiations, then rectification may be ordered.[432]

8–077 **No antecedent agreement necessary?** Unlike rectification for common mistake, there is no requirement to establish that there was an antecedent agreement or common intention of the parties about the clause to be rectified.[433] It has been described as a "drastic" remedy[434] since it imposes on the non-mistaken party "a contract which he did not, and did not intend to, make".[435] As we saw earlier, where no written instrument is involved which might be rectified, there may be *no contract* if one party knows of the other's mistake, but not necessarily a contract on the mistaken party's terms.[436] That outcome is nevertheless acknowledged in *Littman v Aspen Oil (Broking) Ltd*[437] where a landlord put forward a break clause for inclusion in a lease to which the tenant would have objected, but because it included the word "landlord" where "tenant" had obviously been meant, and therefore did not affect the tenant as worded, no objection was raised. There was no common intention because of the other aspects of the clause to which the tenant would not have assented if "tenant" had been correctly used, but had it been necessary[438] the court would have rectified the clause by substituting "tenant" for "landlord". According to Jacob LJ, in reality the tenant's conduct (because he knew of the mistake) "amounted to an agreement—*by accepting the clause knowing what the other side thought it meant*, he was accepting just that and equity should not allow him to resile".[439]

---

[427] cf. McLauchlan 124 L.Q.R. 608; 130 L.Q.R. 83; Burrows in Burrows & Peel (eds), *Contract Terms* (2007).

[428] *Riverlate Properties Ltd v Paul* [1975] Ch. 133 at 140.

[429] *Thomas Bates & Son Ltd v Wyndham's (Lingerie) Ltd* [1981] 1 W.L.R. 505 at 515.

[430] As well as the situations referred to in the text, rectification may be ordered if there was "undue influence or a fiduciary relationship between the parties": *The Nai Genova* [1984] 1 Lloyd's Rep. 353 at 365.

[431] *The Ypatia Halcoussi* [1985] 2 Lloyd's Rep. 364 at 371.

[432] *Commission for the New Towns v Cooper (Great Britain) Ltd* [1995] Ch. 259 at 280; *Hurst Stores and Interiors Ltd v ML Europe Property Ltd* [2004] EWCA Civ 490; [2004] B.L.R. 249 at [19].

[433] *Littman v Aspen Oil (Broking) Ltd* [2005] EWCA Civ 1579; [2006] 2 P. & C.R. 2.

[434] *The Nai Genova* [1984] 1 Lloyd's Rep. 353 at 360 (Slade LJ).

[435] *Wimpey (UK) Ltd v VI Construction Ltd* [2005] EWCA Civ 77; [2005] B.L.R. 135 at [75].

[436] See para.8–005 and the example of *Hartog v Colin & Shields* [1939] 3 All E.R. 566.

[437] [2005] EWCA Civ 1579; [2006] 2 P. & C.R. 2.

[438] The clause was amended as a matter of interpretation under the "obvious mistake" principle: see para.6–047.

[439] *Littman v Aspen Oil (Broking) Ltd* [2006] 2 P. & C.R. 2 at [24] (emphasis added); McLauchlan 124 L.Q.R. 608.

### (iii) Potential limitations on the remedy

**Executed contracts.** Although the contrary has been suggested[440] execution (i.e. performance) of a contract is no bar to rectification. Thus leases and conveyances can be rectified on the ground that they are inconsistent with the contracts which preceded them.[441] Any other view would conflict with the whole concept of rectification, for the formal document which it is sought to rectify often *is* the execution of the prior contract. **8–078**

**No issue between the parties.** In *Whiteside v Whiteside*[442] the court refused to rectify a covenant so as to achieve the tax advantage which the covenantor had intended (but failed) to secure, partly because there was no evidence of the common intention of the parties,[443] and partly because there was no issue between them: the covenantor went on paying the covenantee (his wife) as if the covenant had been rectified. But such an issue can be manufactured by simply refusing to make a single payment. If the document in fact fails to express the intention of the parties, rectification can be ordered even though there is no dispute between them inter se, but only one between them and the Revenue authorities.[444] **8–079**

**Restitutio in integrum impossible.** The impossibility of restoring the parties to the position in which they were before the contract is, in general, no bar to rectification. For example, a marriage settlement can be rectified after the marriage has taken place.[445] **8–080**

**Laches or acquiescence.** A claim for rectification may be barred by lapse of time, or laches.[446] It has been said to be well established that the doctrine of laches "does not come into play before the person against whom it is raised as a defence has discovered the material facts", i.e. the mistake.[447] That would seem to rule out the time when the contract was made if the mistake was not immediately discovered on execution,[448] but what of the time when it should by the exercise of reasonable diligence have been discovered? The latter view **8–081**

---

[440] e.g. in *May v Platt* [1900] 1 Ch. 616; criticised in *Thompson v Hickman* [1907] 1 Ch. 550.

[441] e.g. *Murray v Parker* (1854) 19 Beav. 305; *Cowen v Truefitt Ltd* [1899] 2 Ch. 309; *Stait v Fenner* [1912] 2 Ch. 504.

[442] [1950] Ch. 65; cf. *Rabin v Gerson Berger Assocation Ltd* [1986] 1 W.L.R. 526 at 534 (where no claim for rectification was made).

[443] cf. *Van der Linde v Van der Linde* [1947] Ch. 306.

[444] *Re Colebrook's Conveyances* [1972] 1 W.L.R. 1379; cf. *Re Slocock's Will Trusts* [1979] 1 All E.R. 359; *Lake v Lake* [1989] S.T.C. 865.

[445] *Cook v Fearn* (1878) 48 L.J. Ch. 63; *Johnson v Bragge* [1901] 1 Ch. 28.

[446] *Lindsay Petroleum Co v Hurd* (1873) 5 A.C. 221; *KPMG v Network Rail Infrastructure Ltd* [2006] EWHC 67 (Ch) at [197]; (reversed without consideration of this issue: [2007] EWCA Civ 363; [2007] Bus L.R. 1336); *Ahmad v Secret Garden (Cheshire) Ltd* [2013] EWCA Civ 1005; [2013] 3 E.G.L.R. 42 at [56] ("inordinate delay" necessary); *Milton Keynes BC v Viridor (Community Recycling MK) Ltd* [2017] EWHC 239 (TCC); [2017] B.L.R. 216.

[447] *KPMG v Network Rail Infrastructure Ltd* [2006] EWHC 67 (Ch) at [197]; cf. *Beale v Kyte* [1907] 1 Ch. 564.

[448] cf. *Bloomer v Spittle* (1872) L.R. 13 Eq. 427.

probably applies in cases of innocent misrepresentation[449]; and there seems to be no good reason for applying a different rule where rectification is claimed. A claim for rectification may also be barred by the defence of acquiescence.[450]

8–082 **Third party rights.** The right to claim rectification, like other equitable rights, can be asserted against a purchaser with notice of the mistake,[451] but not against a bona fide purchaser for value without notice, at least in circumstances where the third party has acquired a proprietary interest in the subject-matter, e.g. a tenant cannot claim rectification of the tenancy agreement against any bona fide purchaser of the reversion.[452] In the case of purely contractual rights, an assignee takes "subject to equities"[453] and that may include the equity of rectification even as against an assignee without notice.[454]

8–083 **After judgment.** A claim for rectification is barred by a judgment in proceedings in which the issue of rectification could have been (though it was not) raised.[455] But judgment in proceedings in which the question of rectification could *not* have been raised is no bar to a later claim for rectification.[456]

8–084 **Assignment.** It has been suggested that, even where a contracting party can claim rectification, a person to whom he assigns his rights cannot do so.[457] The basis for this suggestion seems to be that in such circumstances rectification might produce an undeserved windfall for the assignee.

8–085 **Instruments which cannot be rectified.** The articles of association of a company cannot be rectified once they have been registered, even if they contain a simple clerical error.[458] To allow rectification would cut across the scheme laid down by the Companies Acts for the registration and alteration of such documents. In *Phillipson v Kerry*[459] it was held that a deed poll cannot be rectified, though, if executed under a mistake, it can be set aside. One possible reason for this rule, given in the judgment, is that a voluntary gift cannot be rectified. But as it is now clear that a voluntary deed inter partes can be

449 See para.9–130.

450 *Milton Keynes BC v Viridor (Community Recycling MK) Ltd* [2017] EWHC 239 (TCC); [2017] B.L.R. 216.

451 *Craddock Bros v Hunt* [1923] 2 Ch. 136; *Blacklocks v JB Developments (Godalming) Ltd* [1982] Ch. 183.

452 *Smith v Jones* [1954] 1 W.L.R. 1089; cf. *Garrard v Frankel* (1862) 30 Beav. 445.

453 See para.15–037.

454 Berg 124 L.Q.R. 6 at 12, commenting on the decision at first instance in *Chartbrook Ltd v Persimmon Homes Ltd* [2007] EWHC 409; (2007) 11 EG 160; affirmed: [2009] UKHL 38; [2009] 1 A.C. 1101); see para.6–030, fn.154. For the right to rectify of the assignee, see para.8–084.

455 *Caird v Moss* (1886) 33 Ch D. 22.

456 *Crane v Hegeman-Harris Co Inc* [1939] 4 All E.R. 68.

457 *Napier v Williams* [1911] 1 Ch. 361; the actual decision would now be different because of Law of Property Act 1925 s.82. Where the assignment forms part of a conveyance, the assignee can claim rectification by virtue of Law of Property Act 1925 s.63(1): *Boots the Chemist v Street* (1983) 268 E.G. 817; *Berkeley Leisure Group Ltd v Williamson* [1996] E.G.C.S. 18.

458 *Scott v Frank F Scott (London) Ltd* [1904] Ch. 794.

459 (1863) 32 Beav. 628.

rectified,[460] there does not seem to be any convincing reason for the rule. The court cannot rectify a settlement which is binding, not as a contract, but by virtue of a court order.[461] If a mistake is made in drawing up such an order, it is more appropriate to ask the court which made the order to vary it than to ask another court to rectify it.

## 5. DOCUMENTS MISTAKENLY SIGNED

### (a) Development

**Recognition of non est factum.** As a general rule, a person is bound by his signature to a document whether he reads it or understands it, or not.[462] But at the end of the sixteenth century an exception to this rule was established. It was held in *Thoroughgood's Case*[463] that if a person who could not read executed a deed after it had been incorrectly read over to him, he was not bound by it. He could plead *non est factum*: it is not my deed. 8–086

**Extension of the doctrine.** In the nineteenth century, it was settled that this doctrine was no longer confined to persons who were unable to read. The reason for this extension of the doctrine was the insistence on the requirement of *consensus ad idem* in contract. A person who signed a document without being aware of its nature was not bound because "the mind of the signer did not accompany the signature".[464] But if too wide a scope were given to this reasoning, it could lead to results that were inconsistent with the objective principle[465] and with the general common law requirement that a mistake must be fundamental if it is to negative consent.[466] 8–087

As we have seen, the objective principle does not operate in favour of a person who *knows* of the mistake of the signer;[467] and if that person has induced the mistake by some misrepresentation about the document which is alleged to contain the contract between him and the signer, then the signer will be entitled to avoid the contract on that ground.[468] Often, however, the document purports to be a contract between the signer and someone other than the fraudulent party. For example, A may induce B to sign a guarantee of A's bank overdraft by representing that it is an insurance proposal. Here the document is an apparent contract, not between A and B, but between B and *the bank*, which may reasonably believe that B has assented to the terms of the document. As the bank

[460] *Bonhote v Henderson* [1895] 1 Ch. 742; *Re Butlin's Settlement Trusts* [1976] Ch. 251; *Re Slocock's Will Trusts* [1979] 1 All E.R. 359.
[461] *Mills v Fox* (1887) 37 Ch D. 153.
[462] See para.6–004.
[463] (1584) 2 Co. Rep. 9a; cf. *Hitchman v Avery* (1892) 8 T.L.R. 698; *Lloyds Bank Plc v Waterhouse* [1993] 2 F.L.R. 97 at 108.
[464] *Foster v Mackinnon* (1869) L.R. 4 C.P. 704 at 711.
[465] See para.8–051.
[466] See para.8–034, but see para.8–047.
[467] See para.8–054.
[468] See para.9–099; *Lloyds Bank Plc v Waterhouse* [1993] 2 F.L.R. 97 at 111.

is not responsible for the fraud of A, B's only hope is to plead *non est factum*;[469] but the success of the plea would deprive the bank of the protection of the objective principle.

Even if the document is an apparent contract only between A and B, the latter may still try to invoke the doctrine of *non est factum* because it may provide a better remedy for him than rescission on the ground of A's fraud. This will be the position where B has under the contract parted with property and an innocent third party has later acquired an interest in that property for value.[470] If the doctrine of *non est factum* applies, the contract will be void so that B will be entitled to the return of the property; while if the contract is only voidable for A's fraud the third party will be protected. In cases of mistaken identity, the courts have in many cases protected such innocent third parties by a strict insistence on the requirement that the mistake must be fundamental;[471] and a similar requirement has restricted the scope of the *non est factum* defence.[472]

### (b) Scope of the doctrine

8–088 **Persons to whom the plea is available.** The nineteenth-century extension of the doctrine to persons who could read has been called "one of the less happy developments in our law"[473] and it has been suggested that the doctrine should not apply in favour of such persons if they were of full age and capacity.[474] But this very narrow view has not prevailed. In *Gallie v Lee* Lord Reid said that the doctrine may apply to "those who are permanently or temporarily unable through no fault of their own to have without explanation any real understanding of the purport of a particular document, whether that be from defective education, illness or innate incapacity",[475] and to these must be added persons who have been tricked into signing the document.[476] The doctrine may thus apply not only to the blind or illiterate but also to persons who are senile, of very low intelligence or ignorant of the language in which the document is expressed. But it will not normally protect literate persons of full capacity.[477]

8–089 **Serious mistake required.** In their desire to restrict the scope of the doctrine, the courts have insisted that the plea of *non est factum* is available only where the mistake of the signer was a serious one. Formerly, they gave effect to this policy by drawing a distinction between the "character"[478] of a document and its "contents".[479] But in *Gallie v Lee*[480] the House of Lords rejected this distinction

---

469 Unless he can fix the bank with the fraud, or other wrongdoing of A: see para.10–041.

470 As in *Gallie v Lee* [1971] A.C. 1004; para.8–090.

471 See para.8–035 and following.

472 *Norwich and Peterborough BS v Steed (No.2)* [1993] 1 All E.R. 330 at 337.

473 *Gallie v Lee* [1969] 2 Ch. 17 at 43 (Salmon LJ).

474 *Gallie v Lee* [1969] 2 Ch. 17 at 36–37.

475 *Gallie v Lee* [1971] A.C. 1004 at 1016.

476 *Gallie v Lee* [1971] A.C. 1004 at 1025; *Trustees of Beardsley Theobalds Retirement Benefit Scheme v Yardley* [2011] EWHC 1380 (QB).

477 *Gallie v Lee* [1971] A.C. 1004 at 1016, 1025.

478 e.g. *Foster v Mackinnon* (1869) L.R. C.P. 704.

479 e.g. *Howatson v Webb* [1907] 1 Ch. 537; affirmed [1908] 1 Ch. 1.

as unworkable,[481] and put in its place the requirement that the difference between the document as it was and as it was believed to be must be radical or substantial or fundamental.[482] Under this test, the seriousness of the mistake is to be judged by "difference in practical result" rather than by "difference in legal character".[483]

**Gallie v Lee.** The facts of *Gallie v Lee* were that a widow of 78 wanted to help her nephew Parkin to raise money on the security of her leasehold house, provided that she could continue to live there rent free for the rest of her life. Parkin did not want the loan to be in his own name, or to become owner of the house as he feared that this would enable his wife (from whom he was separated) to enforce her claim for maintenance against him. He therefore arranged that the money should be raised through an intermediary called Lee on a mortgage of the house; and as a first step in this scheme a document was prepared which was in fact an assignment on sale of the lease to Lee for £3,000. The widow did not read this document as her glasses were broken, but she signed it after being told by Lee that it was a deed of gift to Parkin (who witnessed the document). Lee mortgaged the house to a building society, but did not pay over the money so raised either to Parkin or to the widow. It was held that the widow was not protected by the doctrine of *non est factum* as her mistake was not sufficiently serious. She believed that the document would enable her nephew to raise money on the security of the house, and the document was in fact designed to achieve this purpose, though by a different process from that contemplated by her.[484] 8–090

**Mistake as to identity.** We have seen that consent may be negatived, so as to make a contract void, where A deals with B in the mistaken belief that B is C.[485] But if A signs a document expressed to be in favour of B, the defence of *non est factum* is not open to A merely because A thought that the party named in the document was C. Thus in *Gallie v Lee*[486] the defence failed even though the widow thought that she was making a gift to Parkin when in fact she was making a conveyance to Lee. The reason for this rule may be that the mistaken party can discover the mistake by reading the document. 8–091

**Ignorance.** The plea of *non est factum* is not normally open to a person who is merely ignorant of (as opposed to mistaken about) what he is signing,[487] e.g. to 8–092

480 [1971] A.C. 1004.

481 *Muskham Finance Ltd v Howard* [1963] 1 Q.B. 904 is, for example, hard to reconcile with *Howatson v Webb* [1907] 1 Ch. 537. See also *Gallie v Lee* [1969] 2 Ch. 17 at 31–32 (Lord Denning MR).

482 *Gallie v Lee* [1971] A.C. 1004 at 1017, 1019, 1021, 1026, 1034.

483 *Gallie v Lee* [1971] A.C. 1004 at 1017.

484 cf. *Mercantile Credit Ltd v Hamblin* [1965] 2 Q.B. 242; *Avon Finance Co v Bridger* [1985] 2 All E.R. 281. For a difference of judicial opinion on a similar point, see *Lloyds Bank Plc v Waterhouse* [1993] 2 F.L.R. 97. And see an apparent difference of opinion between Patten LJ and Lord Dyson MR in *CF Asset Finance Ltd v Okonji* [2014] EWCA Civ 870; [2014] E.C.C. 23.

485 e.g. *Cundy v Lindsay* (1873) 3 App. Cas. 459; *Shogun Finance v Hudson* [2003] UKHL 62; [2004] 1 A.C. 919; paras 8–036, 8–041.

486 [1971] A.C. 1004; cf. *Howatson v Webb* [1907] 1 Ch. 535; affirmed [1908] 1 Ch. 1. For discussion of the mistaken identity point, see *Gallie v Lee* [1969] 2 Ch. 17 at 44.

487 *Norwich and Peterborough BS v Steed (No.2)* [1993] 1 All E.R. 330 at 338–339.

one who signs a document in the belief that it is "only a form" without having any precise idea as to its nature.[488] Similarly, in *Gillman v Gillman*[489] a wife, shortly before her husband left her, signed a document which was in fact a separation deed. She did not know this when she signed it, but neither had she any definite idea as to what it was that she was signing. It was held that she was bound by the deed.

8–093 **Mistake as to capacity.** The rule just stated is subject to an exception where a person signs a document under a mistaken belief as to the capacity in which he signs. Thus in *Lewis v Clay*[490] the defendant was induced to sign two promissory notes by the fraudulent representation that his signature was required as a witness and that the documents were of a private nature. The plea of *non est factum* succeeded even though the defendant could not say precisely what type of document he thought he had signed.

8–094 **Carelessness.** Carelessness of the signer excludes the doctrine of *non est factum*. This was a second ground for the decision in *Gallie v Lee*:[491] the widow could not rely on the doctrine as she had been careless in signing the document without reading it.[492] For the same reason, a person cannot rely on the doctrine if he signs a document containing blanks which are later filled in otherwise than in accordance with his instructions.[493] In this context, the standard of care cannot be that of the reasonable person, for such a person will not normally be able to rely on the doctrine of *non est factum* at all.[494] One has to assume that the person relying on the doctrine falls within the class of persons to whom it is available, and then to ask whether that person took such care as one so disadvantaged could have been expected to take. In *Gallie v Lee* itself, this test was not satisfied; for, although the widow could not be expected to follow the intricacies of conveyancing, she could at least be expected to make sure that the person named in the document as transferee was the person intended by her. It does not follow that failure to read the document will exclude the plea of *non est factum* in all cases: the plea might, for example, still be available if reading the document would not have revealed its true character to a person of the signer's limited capabilities.[495]

---

[488] *Hunter v Walters* (1871) L.R. 7 Ch. App. 75; cf. *National Provincial Bank of England v Jackson* (1886) 33 Ch D. 1.

[489] (1946) 174 L.T. 272; cf. *Mercantile Credit Co Ltd v Hamblin* [1965] 2 Q.B. 242 (but in that case the signer escaped liability on another ground).

[490] (1897) 67 L.J.Q.B. 224.

[491] [1971] A.C. 1004; overruling *Carlisle & Cumberland Banking Co v Bragg* [1911] 1 K.B. 489. See also *Lewis v Clay* (1897) 67 L.J.Q.B. 224 at 226; *Howatson v Webb* [1908] 1 Ch. 1; *Avon Finance Co v Bridger* [1985] 2 All E.R. 281.

[492] cf. *Yedina v Yedin* [2017] EWHC 3319 (Ch) at [262].

[493] *United Dominion's Trust Ltd v Western* [1976] Q.B. 513; cf. *CF Asset Finance Ltd v Okonji* [2014] EWCA Civ 870; [2014] E.C.C. 23.

[494] See para.8–088.

[495] *Gallie v Lee* [1971] A.C. 1004 at 1023; cf. *Lloyds Bank Plc v Waterhouse* [1993] 2 F.L.R. 97.

CHAPTER 9

# MISREPRESENTATION[1]



[1] Cartwright, *Misrepresentation, Mistake and Non-Disclosure*, 5th edn (2019).

9–001 Our concern in this chapter is with the remedies available to a person who has been induced to enter into a contract by a statement which is misleading. These remedies are available only if the statement is of a kind which the law recognises as giving rise to liability, and if certain general conditions of liability are satisfied. The representee may then be able to claim damages or to rescind the contract or to do both these things. Similar remedies may also in certain cases be available where there has been mere non-disclosure of material facts, as opposed to active misrepresentation.

9–002 **Claims available to consumers.** The Unfair Commercial Practices Directive[2] which is implemented by the Consumer Protection from Unfair Trading Regulations 2008[3] and the Business Protection from Misleading Marketing Regulations 2008,[4] includes, among the specific prohibitions, the provision of "false information",[5] or the omission of "material information".[6] The Directive itself operates "without prejudice to contract law, and, in particular, the rules on the validity, formation and effect of a contract".[7] However, as a result of amendments to the Consumer Protection from Unfair Trading Regulations 2008[8] (the 2008 Regulations) remedies are now provided to "consumers"[9] who have entered into a contract with a "trader"[10] for the sale or supply of a product[11] by the trader, or for the sale of goods to a trader, or who have made a payment to a trader as a result of "prohibited practice" amounting to "misleading action"[12] (but

[2] Directive 2005/29 [2005] O.J. L149/22; Twigg-Fleisner 121 L.Q.R. 386.
[3] SI 2008/1277.
[4] SI 2008/1276.
[5] Unfair Commercial Practices Directive art.6.
[6] Unfair Commercial Practices Directive art.7.
[7] Unfair Commercial Practices Directive art.3(2).
[8] Consumer Protection (Amendment) Regulations 2014 (SI 2014/870). The amended 2008 Regulations apply to contracts entered into, or payments made, on or after 1 October 2014.
[9] As defined in reg.2(1) in a way which is very similar to the definition under the Consumer Rights Act 2015 s.2(3): para.7–091.
[10] As defined in reg.2(1) in a way which is very similar to the definition under the Consumer Rights Act 2015 s.2(3): para.7–090.
[11] For limitations on the meaning of "product", see reg.27C (immoveable property), reg.27D (financial services).
[12] This is extensively defined in reg.5.

not "misleading omissions")[13] or "aggressive practice".[14] The requirement that a trader or someone for whom the trader is made responsible[15] must have engaged in a "commercial *practice*" that amounts to misleading action does not rule out a single instance of misrepresentation.[16] The prohibited practice must have been "a significant factor" in the consumer's decision to enter into the contract or make the payment.[17]

**Consumer rights of redress.** The new forms of redress potentially available to consumers include the right to "unwind" the contract and claim a refund[18] (which is very similar in process to rescission of the contract for misrepresentation),[19] the right to a discount[20] and the right to claim damages.[21] The latter remedy not only includes "financial loss" but also damages for "alarm, distress or physical inconvenience or discomfort" caused by the prohibited practice.[22] In both cases the loss must have been reasonably foreseeable at the time of the prohibited practice.[23] The consumer's right to damages is subject to the trader's defence of "reasonable precautions" and "due diligence".[24] Damages for financial loss are not awarded "in respect of the difference between the market price of a product and the amount payable for it under a contract."[25] On the assumption that the "market price" refers to the actual market price (and not the market price if the representation were true), this excludes the primary loss which may be recoverable in an action for misrepresentation.[26] It seems that this form of loss is meant to be covered by the award of a discount. This is determined by the seriousness of the prohibited practice and is confined to fixed reductions, e.g. 25 per cent, or 50 per cent and so on,[27] but if the price paid exceeds £5000 the relevant discount is the percentage difference between the market price of the product and the amount payable for it under the contract, if there is clear evidence of that difference.[28] 9–003

**Effect on the law of misrepresentation.** For the most part, the law which is set out in the rest of this chapter is unaffected by this development since nothing in 9–004

[13] 2008 Regulations regs 27A–27B.
[14] 2008 Regulations reg.7. "Aggressive practice" is more akin to duress and undue influence: see para.10–051.
[15] 2008 Regulations reg.27A(4).
[16] cf. *R v X Ltd* [2013] EWCA Crim 818; [2013] C.T.L.C. 145.
[17] 2008 Regulations reg.27A(6).
[18] 2008 Regulations regs 27E–27H. The right to unwind exists for 90 days from the date when the consumer enters the contract or the "relevant day" (as defined: reg.27E(4)) whichever is the later: reg.27E(1). There is no right to unwind if the right to a discount has been exercised: reg.27E(10).
[19] See para.9–093.
[20] 2008 Regulations reg.27I. A scale of discounts is applied depending upon the level of seriousness of the prohibited practice.
[21] 2008 Regulations reg.27J.
[22] 2008 Regulations reg.27J(1)(b).
[23] 2008 Regulations reg.27J(4).
[24] 2008 Regulations reg.27J(5).
[25] 2008 Regulations reg.27J(1)(a),(3).
[26] See para.9–073.
[27] 2008 Regulations reg.27I.
[28] 2008 Regulations reg.27I(5)–(7).

the amendments made to the 2008 Regulations "affects the ability of a consumer to make a claim under a rule of law or equity, or under an enactment, in respect of conduct constituting a prohibited practice".[29] However, a consumer may not recover compensation under both the 2008 Regulations and another rule of law or equity or an enactment.[30] Further, a specific amendment is made to s.2 of the Misrepresentation Act 1967 which means that any right to damages thereunder is not available to a consumer who has rights of redress under the 2008 Regulations.[31]

## 1. GENERAL CONDITIONS OF LIABILITY

9–005 Where a representation does not have contractual force, it will give rise to the remedies discussed in parts 2 and 3 of this chapter only if it is a false statement of fact or law which is material and which the representee has relied upon.

### (a) False statement of fact or law

9–006 **General rule.** The general rule is that no relief will be given for a misrepresentation as such unless it is a false representation of existing fact or, it now seems, of law.[32] A representation may be express or implied.[33]

9–007 **Objective meaning given to representations.** Whether any and, if so, what representation has been made is to be "judged objectively according to the impact that whatever is said may be expected to have on a reasonable representee in the position and with the known characteristics of the actual representee."[34] In the case of an express representation, "the court has to understand what a reasonable person would have understood from the words used in the context in which they were used."[35] In the case of an implied representation, the court has to "consider what a reasonable person would have inferred was being implicitly represented by the representor's words and conduct in their context."[36] The same objective approach is taken to determine the falsity of any statement. It will be treated as true if it is substantially correct and the difference between what is represented

[29] 2008 Regulations reg.27L(1).

[30] 2008 Regulations reg.27L(2).

[31] SI 2014/870 reg.5 (subject to the qualification which is referred to below): see para.9–051, fn.275.

[32] See para.9–020.

[33] See para.9–008.

[34] *MCI WorldCom International Inc v Primus Telecommunications Inc* [2004] EWCA Civ 957 at [30]; [2004] 2 All E.R. (Comm) 833; cf. *Springwell Navigation Corp v JP Morgan Chase Bank* [2010] EWCA Civ 1221; [2010] 2 C.L.C. 705 at [121].

[35] *IFE Fund SA v Goldman Sachs International* [2006] EWHC 2887 (Comm); [2007] 1 Lloyd's Rep. 264 at [50]; affirmed [2007] EWCA Civ 811; [2007] 2 Lloyd's Rep. 449; cf. *Raiffeisen Zentralbank Österreich AG v Royal Bank of Scotland Plc* [2010] EWHC 1392 (Comm); [2011] 1 Lloyd's Rep. 123 at [82].

[36] *IFE Fund SA v Goldman Sachs International* [2006] EWHC 2887 (Comm); [2007] 1 Lloyd's Rep. 264 at [50].

and what is actually correct would not have been likely to induce a reasonable person in the position of the claimant to enter into the contract.[37]

**Representations implied by conduct.** A representation may be implied by the conduct of the defendant[38] and, if he fails to correct any implication, he cannot rely on the general rule that there is no duty of disclosure.[39] Active concealment of a defect amounts to misrepresentation[40]; and even conduct falling short of this may suffice.[41] In *Property Alliance Group Ltd v Royal Bank of Scotland*[42] a bank was found to have made implied representations about LIBOR (an inter-bank lending rate) and its role in the setting of the rate merely on the basis that it had proposed LIBOR as the rate applicable to the transactions which it had entered into with the claimants. The Court of Appeal approved as a "helpful test" in such cases: 9–008

> "whether a reasonable representee would naturally assume that the true state of facts did not exist and that, if it did, he would necessarily have been informed of it"[43]

but not to the extent of watering down the requirement that "there must be clear words or clear conduct of the representor from which the relevant representation can be implied."[44]

**The relevance of any terms on which the parties have supplied information.** The terms, if any, upon which the parties have exchanged information will be a material factor in determining whether any implied representation has been made.[45] Thus, in *IFE Fund SA v Goldman Sachs International*[46] the defendant arranger of a syndicated loan supplied to the claimant, as a potential lender, pre-acquisition reports on the target company which had been purchased but failed to pass on post-acquisition reports which it was claimed cast doubt on the 9–009

[37] *Avon Ins Plc v Swire Fraser Ltd* [2000] 1 All E.R. (Comm) 573 at [17]; cf. *Raiffeisen Zentralbank Österreich AG v Royal Bank of Scotland Plc* [2010] EWHC 1392 (Comm); [2011] 1 Lloyd's Rep. 123 at [149]. This is consistent with the test for materiality: para.9–023.

[38] *Bodger v Nicholls* (1873) 28 L.T. 441 at 445; *Curtis v Chemical Cleaning & Dyeing Co Ltd* [1951] 1 K.B. 805 at 808; *Geest Plc v Fyffes Plc* [1999] 1 All E.R. (Comm) 672 at 686.

[39] *Walters v Morgan* (1861) 3 D.F. & J. 718 at 723; *Spice Girls Ltd v Aprilia World Service BV* [2002] EWCA Civ 15; [2002] E.M.L.R. 27 at [61]–[63].

[40] *Schneider v Heath* (1813) 3 Camp. 506; *Sybron Corp v Rochem Ltd* [1984] Ch. 112 at 130 ("covering up and deliberately concealing"); *Gordon v Selico Ltd* (1986) 278 E.G. 53.

[41] There is, however, no misrepresentation in tacitly acquiescing in another's self-deception: *Donegal International Ltd v Zambia* [2007] EWHC 197 (Comm); [2007] 1 Lloyd's Rep. 397 at [465].

[42] [2018] EWCA Civ 355; [2018] 1 W.L.R. 3529; cf. *Graiseley Properties Ltd v Barclays Bank Plc* [2013] EWCA Civ 1372.

[43] *Property Alliance Group Ltd v Royal Bank of Scotland* [2018] EWCA Civ 355; [2018] 1 W.L.R. 3529 at [132]; echoing the test of Colman J. in *Geest Plc v Fyffes Plc* [1999] 1 All E.R. (Comm) 672 at 683.

[44] *Property Alliance Group Ltd v Royal Bank of Scotland* [2018] EWCA Civ 355; [2018] 1 W.L.R. 3529 at [132].

[45] *Raiffeisen Zentralbank Österreich AG v Royal Bank of Scotland Plc* [2010] EWHC 1392 (Comm); [2011] 1 Lloyd's Rep. 123 at [97]; *Aquila WSA Aviation Opportunities II Ltd v Inur Air Tasmiacilik AS* [2018] EWHC 519 (Comm) at [107]. See further, para.9–141.

[46] [2006] EWHC 2887 (Comm); [2007] 1 Lloyd's Rep. 264; affirmed [2007] EWCA Civ 811; [2007] 2 Lloyd's Rep. 449.

reliability of the earlier reports. It did so pursuant to an information memorandum in which it was stated that no representation, express or implied, was made as to the "accuracy or completeness" of the information supplied[47] or that the information supplied "will be updated." The claimants argued that still left room for an implied and continuing representation that the defendant knew nothing which showed that the information which had been supplied was *or might be* materially incorrect. According to Toulson J this went too far and would "open up wide and uncertain territory".[48] The only implied representation was that in supplying the information the defendant was acting in good faith, i.e. it did not actually know of anything which made the information given misleading.[49] The claimant in the *IFE* case was a sophisticated commercial entity. In light of the statement above that the courts will take into account the known characteristics of the actual representee,[50] a consumer who is told that no representations are being made to him may be treated differently.[51]

9–010 **Statements made by another and passed on by the representor.** In the *IFE* case above[52] the court was concerned with the representations which were impliedly made in circumstances where the representor passed on information or statements provided by another. In *Webster v Liddington*[53] Jackson LJ provided a non-exhaustive list of the potential implications to be drawn from such a situation in the following terms:[54] (i) the representor may warrant that the information is correct and therefore assume contractual liability[55]; (ii) the representor may adopt the information as his own, thereby taking on such responsibility as he would have if he were the maker of the statement; (iii) the representor may represent only that he believes, on reasonable grounds, the information supplied to be correct,[56] or (iv) the representor may simply pass on the information as material coming from another, about which the representor has no knowledge or belief.[57] In the case of (iv) the representor has no responsibility for the accuracy of the information beyond the ordinary duties of honesty and good faith.[58] Which of these implications, or any others, is to be drawn will depend on the objective test referred to above.[59] In *Webster v Liddington* itself, the representors were clinicians who passed on to the representees brochures provided by the manufacturers of certain beauty products which contained false statements about

[47] The principal significance of this type of provision is the effect that it can have on *excluding* liability for representations that *have been made*: see para.9–141.

[48] *IFE Fund SA v Goldman Sachs International* [2006] EWHC 2887 (Comm); [2007] 1 Lloyd's Rep. 264 at [58].

[49] *IFE Fund SA v Goldman Sachs International* [2006] EWHC 2887 (Comm); [2007] 1 Lloyd's Rep. 264 at [60].

[50] See para.9–007.

[51] *Raiffeisen Zentralbank Österreich AG v Royal Bank of Scotland Plc* [2010] EWHC 1392 (Comm); [2011] 1 Lloyd's Rep. 123 at [81]. See also the discussion of the *Webster* case in the next paragraph.

[52] See para.9–009.

[53] [2014] EWCA Civ 560; [2014] P.N.L.R. 26.

[54] *Webster v Liddington* [2014] EWCA Civ 560; [2014] P.N.L.R. 26 at [46].

[55] See para.9–056.

[56] See, e.g. *Foodco UK LLP v Henry Boot Developments Ltd* [2010] EWHC 358 (Ch).

[57] *Rehman v Santander UK Plc* [2018] EWHC 748 (QB) at [37].

[58] See, e.g. the *IFE* case discussed in para.9–009.

[59] See para.9–007.

the products which were then used on the representees.[60] Given the "stark imbalance of knowledge" between the representors as qualified clinicians, and the representees, as consumers, and the absence of any disclaimer, the Court of Appeal held that the false statements had been adopted by the representors as their own representations, i.e. implication (ii).[61]

**Representations set out in the contract.**[62] In some cases, the representations which the representee claims to have relied upon to enter the contract are set out in the contract itself. If such representations are made for the first time in the contract, it is difficult to see how they can be said to have been relied on as *pre-contractual* representations which induced the very contract in which they are to be found. This would rule out at least some claims for misrepresentation, e.g. a claim under s.2(1) of the Misrepresentation Act 1967.[63] A representation may amount to both a contractual and a pre-contractual representation as, for example, where it appears in earlier drafts of the contract which are considered by the parties during negotiations.[64] However, where the statements relied upon by the representee are set out in the draft contract only as part of any warranties to be given, they may not amount to representations at all. As it has been put: "if a contractual provision states only that a party gives a warranty, that party does not by concluding the contract make any statement to the counterparty that might found a misrepresentation claim."[65] In such circumstances, the draft contract indicates only what the party in question is willing to *warrant* if the contract is entered to. **9–011**

**Ambiguous representation.** A statement may be intended by the representor to bear a meaning which is true, but be so obscure that the representee understands it in another sense, in which it is untrue. In such a case the representor is not liable if his interpretation is the correct one[66]; and even if the court holds that the representee's interpretation was the correct one, the representor is not guilty of fraud.[67] This is so in spite of the fact that the representor's interpretation was an **9–012**

[60] No claim was brought against the manufacturers because they had gone into administration.

[61] *Webster v Liddington* [2014] EWCA Civ 560; [2014] P.N.L.R. 26 at [51]–[52].

[62] The incorporation of a representation as a term of the contract does not preclude a claim in misrepresentation, including the right to rescind: see para.9–108. In this paragraph we are concerned with the question of whether the claimant can point to any pre-contractual representation at all.

[63] *Senate Electrical Wholesalers Ltd v STC Submarine Systems Ltd* unreported 26 May 1994; *Leofelis SA v Lonsdale Sports Ltd* [2008] EWCA Civ 640; [2008] E.T.M.R. 63 at [141]; see para.9–050.

[64] *Eurovideo Bildprogramm GmbH v Pulse Entertainment Ltd* [2002] EWCA Civ 1235 at [20]; *Bikam OOD v Adria Cable S.a.r.l.* [2012] EWHC 621 (Comm) at [27].

[65] *Idemitsu Kosan Co Ltd v Sumitomo Corp* [2016] EWHC 1909 (Comm); [2016] 2 C.L.C. 297 at [20]; cf. *Sycamore Bidco Ltd v Breslin* [2012] EWHC 3443 (Ch) at [209]. Contrast *Invertec Ltd v De Mol Holding BV* [2009] EWHC 2471 (Ch); *Avrora Fine Arts Investment Ltd v Christie Manson & Woods Ltd* [2012] EWHC 2198 (Ch); [2012] P.N.L.R. 35; *Greenridge Luton One Ltd v Kempton Investments Ltd* [2016] EWHC 91.

[66] *McInerny v Lloyds Bank Ltd* [1974] 1 Lloyd's Rep. 246 at 254. Contrast *Spice Girls Ltd v Aprilia World Service BV* [2002] EWCA Civ 15; [2002] E.M.L.R. 27 at [67], where there was held to be no ambiguity in the representation.

[67] *Akerhielm v De Mare* [1959] A.C. 789; *Gross v Lewis Hillman Ltd* [1970] Ch. 445; *Leni Gas and Oil Investments Ltd v Malta Oil Pty Ltd* [2014] EWHC 893 (Comm) at [7]; and cf. para.9–162.

unreasonable one, so long as he honestly believed in it.[68] A fortiori the representee has no remedy in deceit if the representation is ambiguous and he did not in fact understand it in a different sense from that intended by the representor.[69] A representor is guilty of fraud if he makes an ambiguous statement intending it to bear a meaning which is to his knowledge untrue,[70] and if the statement is reasonably understood in that sense by the representee. In such a case it is no defence for the representor to show that, on its true construction, the statement bore a meaning that was in fact true.[71]

9–013 **Mere puffs.** Mere puffs are statements which are so vague that they have no effect at law or in equity. To describe land as "fertile and improvable" is mere sales talk which affords no ground for relief.[72] But there is liability for more precise claims, e.g. that use of a carbolic smoke-ball will give immunity from influenza.[73] The distinction is between indiscriminate praise, and specific promises or assertions of verifiable facts.

9–014 **Statements of opinion or belief.** Even where a statement is not so vague as to be a mere puff, it may nevertheless have no legal effect because it is not a positive assertion that the fact stated is true, but only a statement of the maker's opinion or belief.[74] Assertions that an anchorage was safe and that a piece of land had the capacity to support 2,000 sheep have been held to be of this character;[75] for in each case, the party making the statement had (as the other party knew) no personal knowledge of the facts on which it was based: it was understood that he could only state his belief.

9–015 **Statements of opinion amounting to implied statements of fact.** A statement may, in terms, be one of opinion or belief, but by implication involve a statement of fact: "All depends upon the particular statement in its particular context",[76] including the terms, if any, under which it has been provided.[77] Thus, an incorrect forecast may amount to a misrepresentation, not because the forecast is incorrect, but because of the implied, but false, statement that reasonable care has been taken in making it.[78] It is also a misrepresentation of fact for a person to say that he holds an opinion which he does not hold, e.g. to say that he thinks a picture is

[68] See para.9–039.
[69] *Smith v Chadwick* (1884) 9 App. Cas. 187.
[70] *Henry Ansbacher & Co Ltd v Binks Stern*, *The Times*, 26 June 1997.
[71] *The Siboen and the Sibotre* [1976] 1 Lloyd's Rep. 293 at 318.
[72] *Dimmock v Hallett* (1866) L.R. 2 Ch. App. 21; cf. para.4–006.
[73] *Carlill v Carbolic Smoke Ball Co* [1893] 1 Q.B. 256.
[74] Or a contention, or statement of position, e.g. as to the meaning of a prior contract between parties: *Kyle Bay Ltd v Underwriters Subscribing Under Policy No.019057/08/01* [2007] EWCA Civ 57 at [29]–[37]; cf. *Royal Bank of Scotland v Chandra* [2011] EWCA Civ 192; [2011] N.P.C. 26 at [39] (no misrepresentation in an "over-optimistic" forecast).
[75] *Anderson v Pacific Fire & Marine Ins Co* (1872) L.R. 7 C.P. 65; *Bissett v Wilkinson* [1927] A.C. 177.
[76] *Jaffray v Society of Lloyds* [2002] EWCA Civ 1101 at [59]; *Foodco UK LLP v Henry Boot Developments Ltd* [2010] EWHC 358 (Ch) at [197].
[77] See para.9–009.
[78] *Foodco UK LLP v Henry Boot Developments Ltd* [2010] EWHC 358 (Ch) at [207].

a Rembrandt when he thinks it is a copy.[79] If that party has or professes to have some special knowledge or skill as to the matter stated, the statement is also likely to be treated as one of fact.[80] And if the facts on which an opinion is based are particularly within the knowledge of the person stating the opinion, he may be taken to have represented that those facts exist. For example, where the vendor of a house describes it as "let to a most desirable tenant", when the tenant has for long been in arrears with his rent, he misrepresents a fact, "for he impliedly states that he knows facts which justify his opinion".[81] The same principle applies where a person honestly makes a statement of belief but fails to check the facts on which it appears to be based, when he could easily have done so and therefore impliedly represents that he had reasonable grounds for his opinion.[82] A statement that the representor had been informed of a particular fact has also been held to be a representation, not merely that the representor had been so informed, but that the fact existed.[83]

**Representations as to the future.** A representation as to the future does not, of itself, give rise to any cause of action[84] unless it is binding as a contract. Thus, if A induces B to lend him money by representing that he will not borrow from anybody else, and then does borrow elsewhere, he is not liable to B unless the representation is a term of the contract of loan or amounts to a collateral contract.[85] **9–016**

**Statement of present intention as a statement of fact.** A person who promises to do something may simply be making a statement as to his future conduct; if so, he does not misrepresent a fact merely because he fails to do what he said he would do.[86] But he may also be making a statement of his present intention; if so, he does misrepresent a fact if, when he made the statement, he had no such intention. The courts tend to construe statements as to the future in the second of these two ways in order to protect the interests of persons deceived by them. In *Edgington v Fitzmaurice*[87] the directors of a company procured a loan of money to their company by representing that the money would be used to improve the **9–017**

---

79 *Jendwine v Slade* (1797) 2 Esp. 571 at 573; *Brown v Raphael* [1958] Ch. 636 at 641; contrast *Harlingdon and Leinster Enterprises Ltd v Christopher Hull Fine Art Ltd* [1991] 1 Q.B. 564.

80 e.g. *Esso Petroleum Co Ltd v Mardon* [1976] Q.B. 801; para.9–048; *Thomas Witter Ltd v TBP Industries Ltd* [1996] 2 All E.R. 573 at 594–595.

81 *Smith v Land & House Property Corp* (1884) 28 Ch D. 7 at 15.

82 *Brown v Raphael* [1958] Ch. 636; *Thomson v Christie Manson & Woods Ltd* [2004] EWHC 1101 (QB); [2004] P.N.L.R. 42 at [199] (decision reversed [2005] EWCA Civ 555; [2005] P.N.L.R. 38, without reference to this point)); *Avrora Fine Arts Investment Ltd v Christie Manson & Woods Ltd* [2012] EWHC 2198 (Ch); [2012] P.N.L.R. 35. Contrast *Humming Bird Motors v Hobbs* [1986] R.T.R. 276; *William Sindall Plc v Cambridgeshire CC* [1994] 1 W.L.R. 1016.

83 *Sirius International Ins Corp v Oriental Assurance Corp* [1999] 1 All E.R. (Comm) 699; presumably the latter representation arose by implication from the former.

84 It may be a ground for refusing specific performance: para.21–033. It may also, in combination with other circumstances, give rise to a proprietary estoppel: see para.3–120 and following.

85 cf. *Ex p. Burrell* (1876) 1 Ch D. 537 at 552; *Strachan & Henshaw Ltd v Stein Industrie (UK) Ltd (No.2)* (1998) 87 B.L.R. 52.

86 *The Seaflower* [2000] 2 Lloyd's Rep. 37 at 42; but the eventual outcome was that the representee was entitled to terminate *for breach*: *The Seaflower* [2001] 1 Lloyd's Rep. 341; para.18–055.

87 (1885) 29 Ch D. 459.

company's buildings and to expand its business. In fact, the directors intended to use the money to pay off the company's existing debts. They were held liable to the lender in deceit. Bowen LJ said:

> "There must be a mis-statement of an existing fact; but the state of a man's mind is as much a fact as the state of his digestion ... A misrepresentation as to the state of a man's mind is, therefore, a mis-statement of fact".[88]

9–018 **Statement of present expectation or belief as a statement of fact.** The principle stated above is not restricted to statements of intention. A person may misrepresent a fact if he states an *expectation* or a *belief* which he does not hold as to some future event. A statement of expectation or belief may also be held to contain an implied assertion that the representor had reasonable grounds for making it. For example, a shipowner who in a charterparty says that his ship is "expected ready to load" at a particular port on or about a specified date impliedly represents that he honestly holds that belief, and that he does so on reasonable grounds. If he has no reasonable grounds for holding the belief, he misrepresents a fact.[89] Under the Insurance Act 2015[90] the insured has a "duty of fair presentation" which is satisfied if "every material representation as to a matter of expectation or belief is made in good faith".[91] If the insurance amounts to a consumer insurance contract, it is subject to the Consumer Insurance (Disclosure and Representations) Act 2012 under which the consumer has a duty to take reasonable care not to make a misrepresentation to the insurer.[92] There is no reference in the 2012 Act to the consumer's "expectations" or "belief", but a misrepresentation made dishonestly is always to be taken as showing lack of reasonable care.[93]

9–019 **Statement of intention coupled with statement of fact.** A statement of intention may also be coupled with an *express* statement of existing fact. Thus, a statement by A that he *had* sold flour and *would* pay over the proceeds to B is a misrepresentation of fact if A had made no such sale.[94]

9–020 **Statements of law.** The traditional view, at common law, was that no right to rescind nor any right to damages could be based on a misrepresentation of law, and the same was probably true of claims for damages under the Misrepresentation Act 1967.[95] In equity, too, a money claim could not be based on a

[88] *Edgington v Fitzmaurice* (1885) 29 Ch D. 459 at 482; cf. *Smith Kline & French Laboratories Ltd v Long* [1988] 1 W.L.R. 1; *Kleinwort Benson Ltd v Malaysian Mining Corp* [1989] 1 W.L.R. 379 at 396; *East v Maurer* [1991] 1 W.L.R. 461 at 463; *Tudor Grange Holdings Ltd v Citibank NA* [1992] Ch. 53 at 67–68; *Inter Export LLC v Townley* [2018] EWCA Civ 2068 at [34].

[89] *The Mihalis Angelos* [1971] 1 Q.B. 164 at 194, 205; *Foodco UK LLP v Henry Boot Developments Ltd* [2010] EWHC 358 (Ch) at [207].

[90] The 2015 Act applies to contracts made on or after 12 August 2016, replacing similar but not identical provisions in the Marine Insurance Act 1906.

[91] 2015 Act s.3(3)(c).

[92] 2015 Act s.2(2).

[93] 2015 Act s.3(5).

[94] *Babcock v Lawson* (1880) 5 Q.B.D. 284; cf. *Ismail v Polish Ocean Lines Ltd* [1976] Q.B. 893.

[95] *André & Cie SA v Ets Michel Blanc & Fils* [1979] 2 Lloyd's Rep. 427 at 432, 434–435.

misrepresentation of law,[96] though it was more doubtful whether it was a ground for rescission in equity.[97] It has been said that a *wilful* misrepresentation of law was ground for equitable relief.[98] And equity gave relief for misrepresentation as to private rights,[99] whether or not these were rightly called misrepresentation of fact. In *Kleinwort Benson Ltd v Lincoln CC*[100] the House of Lords removed the bar preventing recovery of payments made under a *mistake* of law. This has led the Court of Appeal to remove the bar which prevents a mistake of law from rendering a contract void[101] and, in so doing, the view was expressed that the effect of the decision in the *Kleinwort Benson* case "now permeates the law of contract".[102] Furthermore, in *Pankhania v Hackney LBC*,[103] it was held that the "misrepresentation of law" rule "has not survived" the decision in the *Kleinwort Benson* case. A degree of caution is perhaps still needed before it can finally be concluded that the distinction between fact and law is no longer relevant to misrepresentation. It is submitted, however, that the decision in *Pankhania* is very likely to be followed by the higher courts when the opportunity arises. The distinction between representations of fact and representations of law was sometimes hard to draw and its effects were hard to justify,[104] and a person who has acted to his prejudice in reliance on a misrepresentation of law has at least as strong a claim for relief as one who is entitled to relief because he has spontaneously made a mistake of law.

**Representation made by another.** As a general rule the representation must have been made by the party against whom relief is sought, or by his agent. In some cases relief may be available even where the representation was made by another party who was not acting as agent, e.g. where A, by a misrepresentation addressed to B, induces B to guarantee A's overdraft with the C bank. The bank's ability to enforce such a transaction depends on whether it is "put on enquiry"[105] as to the circumstances in which it was concluded. Since in most of the recent cases of this kind the alleged vitiating factor has been undue influence (sometimes together with misrepresentation),[106] a full discussion of the effect of such factors on the rights of the third party will be found in Ch.10.[107] 9–021

**Non-disclosure amounting to representation.** As a general rule, a person who is about to enter into a contract is under no duty to disclose material facts known to 9–022

[96] See *Rashdall v Ford* (1866) L.R. 2 Eq. 750; *Eaglesfield v Londonderry* (1876) 4 Ch D. 693.

[97] e.g. in *Wauton v Coppard* [1899] 1 Ch. 92; and *Mackenzie v Royal Bank of Canada* [1934] A.C. 468. But in each of these cases the representation was held to be one of fact.

[98] *West London Commercial Bank v Kitson* (1884) 13 Q.B.D. 360 at 362–363.

[99] *André & Cie SA v Ets Michel Blanc & Fils* [1979] 2 Lloyd's Rep. 427 at 431, 432.

[100] [1999] 2 A.C. 349; para.22–025.

[101] *Brennan v Bolt Burdon* [2004] EWCA Civ 1017; [2005] Q.B. 303; para.8–023.

[102] *Brennan v Bolt Burdon* [2004] EWCA Civ 1017; [2005] Q.B. 303 at [10].

[103] [2002] EWHC 2441 (Ch) at [57].

[104] See *André & Cie SA v Ets Michel Blanc* [1997] 2 Lloyd's Rep. 427 at 431; *Brikom Investments Ltd v Seaford* [1981] 1 W.L.R. 863 at 869; cf. *Amalgamated Investment & Property Co Ltd v Texas Commerce International Bank Ltd* [1982] Q.B. 84 at 122.

[105] *Royal Bank of Scotland v Etridge (No.2)* [2001] UKHL 44; [2002] 2 A.C. 773 at [44].

[106] The same test applies to both: *Annulment Funding Company Ltd v Cowey* [2010] EWCA Civ 711; [2010] B.P.I.R. 1304 at [64].

[107] See paras 10–039–10–045.

him but not to the other party. There are a number of exceptions to this rule and in relation to some the true nature of the non-disclosure is that a representation can be inferred from conduct,[108] or from the surrounding circumstances, e.g. where a representation is falsified by later events,[109] or where a statement is literally true but misleading,[110] or where disclosure is required by custom.[111] They are dealt with in more detail below along with other exceptions to the general rule.[112]

## (b) Materiality

9–023 **When is a representation material?** A representation is "material" if it would affect the judgment of a reasonable person in deciding whether, or on what terms, to enter into the contract; or one that would induce him to enter into the contract without making such inquiries as he would otherwise make.[113] Thus in a contract of insurance it is material that the subject-matter has been grossly overvalued,[114] or that a previous proposal for insuring it has been declined;[115] and in a contract for a loan of money it is material that the lender is a notoriously ruthless money-lender.[116] Conversely, a representation as to the identity of the purchaser may be material where the vendor is willing to sell to X but not to Y. In such a case the vendor can rescind if the purchaser knows that the representation is material, even though he does not know why it is so regarded by the vendor.[117] A misrepresentation may be material although the representor in good faith thinks that it is not material.[118] Under the Insurance Act 2015 the insured party has a duty to make a "fair presentation of the risk" which includes the requirement that any "material representation" is substantially correct.[119] A representation is "material" if it would "influence the judgment of a prudent insurer in determining whether to take the risk and, if so, on what terms".[120] If the insurance amounts to a consumer insurance contract, it is subject to the Consumer Insurance (Disclosure and Representations) Act 2012 which does not refer to the concept of "materiality".

---

[108] See para.9–008.
[109] See para.9–159.
[110] See para.9–162.
[111] See para.9–163.
[112] See para.9–157 and following.
[113] *Traill v Baring* (1864) 4 D.J. & S. 318 at 326; *Whurr v Devenish* (1904) 20 T.L.R. 385; cf. *Raiffeisen Zentralbank Österreich AG v Royal Bank of Scotland Plc* [2010] EWHC 1392 (Comm); [2011] 1 Lloyd's Rep. 123 at [149]; *Industrial Properties Ltd v A E I Ltd* [1977] Q.B. 580 at 597, 601; *Highland Ins Co v Continental Ins Co* [1987] 1 Lloyd's Rep. 109; *Pan Atlantic Ins Co Ltd v Pine Top Ins Co Ltd* [1995] 2 A.C. 501.
[114] *Ionides v Pender* (1874) L.R. 9 Q.B. 531.
[115] *Locker & Woolf Ltd v W Australian Insurance Co Ltd* [1936] 1 K.B. 408.
[116] *Gordon v Street* [1899] 2 Q.B. 641.
[117] *Lonrho Plc v Fayed (No.2)* [1992] 1 W.L.R. 1 at 5–6.
[118] *Lindenau v Desborough* (1828) 8 B. & C. 586; *Joel v Law Union & Crown Ins Co* [1908] 2 K.B. 863 at 883.
[119] 2015 Act s.3(3)(c).
[120] 2015 Act s.7(3).

**Does the representation have to be a material one?** There is no doubt that the representee must have relied on the representation and, if it is material, this raises a presumption of reliance.[121] There is some debate about whether the representation must have been a material one, i.e. whether the representee is entitled to relief where he relies on a representation which is not material. It is submitted that, as a general rule, a misrepresentation has no legal effect unless it is material,[122] but given the exceptions to this general rule, it is only in the most exceptional case that the requirement of reliance will have been met, but not materiality. 9–024

**Exceptions: fraud and express contractual provision.** There are two exceptions to the requirement of materiality. First, a person who has successfully perpetrated a fraud cannot be heard to say that the representation which he used to achieve this end was immaterial.[123] Secondly, every representation is material if the contract so provides. In a policy of insurance, such "basis of the contract clauses"[124] are now ineffective.[125] 9–025

**Requirement of materiality doubted.** As noted above, the requirement of materiality has been doubted,[126] but it is consistent with the objective assessment of whether any representation has been made and its falsity.[127] In evaluating any doubts about a requirement of materiality a distinction should, it is submitted, be drawn between two reasons why the misrepresentation would not affect the judgment of a reasonable person. This may be the position either because of the *circumstances in which the representation was made*, or because of its *contents*. The first possibility is illustrated by *Museprime Properties Ltd v Adhill Properties Ltd*,[128] where a purchaser by auction of commercial property was allowed to rescind for a representation by the auctioneer that higher rents could still be negotiated, when in fact the rents had been fixed for the next rent review period. The court held that it was sufficient for the purchaser to show that his bid had actually been affected by the representation: he did not have to show that a reasonable bidder would have allowed it to affect his bid. The representation could certainly have affected the value of the property and was in this sense material. The only sense in which it was not material was that the representee had 9–026

---

[121] See para.9–030.

[122] *McDowell v Fraser* (1779) 1 Dougl. 247 at 248 (Lord Mansfield); *Lonrho Plc v Fayed* (*No*.2) [1992] 1 W.L.R. 1 at 6.

[123] *Smith v Kay* (1859) 7 H.L.C. 750; cf. *Rafsanjan Pistachio Producers Co-operative v Bank Leumi (UK) Plc* [1992] 1 Lloyd's Rep. 514 at 542; *Dadourian Group International Inc v Simms* [2009] EWCA Civ 169; [2009] 1 Lloyd's Rep. 601 at [101]. A dictum in *Downs v Chappell* [1997] 1 W.L.R. 345 at 351 applies the requirement of materiality even in a case of fraud (cf. *Bonham-Carter v Situ Ventures Ltd* [2012] EWHC 3589 (Ch)), but is obiter since it was not there suggested that the representation was not material.

[124] See, e.g. *Andersen v Fitzgerald* (1853) 4 H.L.C. 484.

[125] Consumer Insurance (Disclosure and Representations) Act 2012 ss.6, 10; Insurance Act 2015 ss.9, 16(1); see para.9–171.

[126] See, e.g. *Chitty on Contracts*, 33rd edn, para.7-042; cf. *MCI WorldCom International Inc v Primus Telecommunications Plc* [2004] EWCA Civ 957; [2004] 2 All E.R. (Comm) 833 at [31] (doubts expressed in previous edition of *Chitty* said to "put the position too cautiously").

[127] See para.9–007.

[128] [1990] 2 E.G.L.R. 196.

(and did not take) the opportunity of discovering the truth; but even though a reasonable person might have made use of such an opportunity, it is settled that a representee's failure to do so is no bar to relief for misrepresentation.[129] The case is, in other words, concerned with the question whether the representee could be taken to have *relied* on the representation (or had been *induced* by it to enter it into the contract); and this is distinct from the question of materiality.[130] The second of the two possibilities mentioned above arises where the matter misrepresented is not "material" because it had little (or only a trivial) effect on the value of the subject-matter. What is an "immaterial" representation (in this sense) can be illustrated by supposing that the auctioneer in the *Museprime* case had represented the tenant to be 40 years old when actually he was 39 or 41, that this representation had (for some reason) been a factor inducing the representee's successful bid, and that its falsity had caused no, or no substantial, loss to the representee. If the representor has made such a representation in good faith it is hard to see why a representee should be entitled to any relief when, by definition, the representation would not have influenced a reasonable person. Damages would be no more than nominal, and a claim to rescind for such a misrepresentation has been rejected as totally unmeritorious.[131]

### (c) Reliance

9–027 While the requirement discussed in this part is most often referred to as "reliance", i.e. the representee must have relied on the representation, or "inducement", i.e. the representee must have been induced by the representation to act as he did, what we are in fact concerned with is a question of causation. Our primary concern is with the necessary causal link between the representation and the representee's decision to enter into the contract with the representor.[132] Reliance must be distinguished from materiality. Whether a representation is material depends, in general,[133] on the significance which a reasonable person would have attached to it. Whether the representee has relied on the representation depends on his actual state of mind.[134] There is still a degree of uncertainty about what constitutes reliance and whether it differs depending upon the nature of the remedy sought (damages or rescission) or the nature of the misrepresentation (fraudulent or non-fraudulent). It is tentatively submitted that the more relevant distinction is one between the *test* of reliance, or inducement, and *proof* that it has been met.

9–028 **The test: "but for" causation.** Various formulations have been used for the test of reliance, or inducement, e.g. that the representation must have been an

[129] See para.9–033 where this settled position is nonetheless called into question.

[130] *The Mercandian Continent* [2001] EWCA Civ 1275; [2001] 2 Lloyd's Rep. 563 at [26].

[131] *Industrial Properties Ltd v A E I Ltd* [1977] Q.B. 580; *Re a Company (No.001946 of 1991) Ex p. Fin Soft Holdings SA* [1991] B.C.L.C. 737 at 748.

[132] For some claims, such as a claim in negligence at common law (see para.9–042), the claimant may have been induced to act in other ways which have led to loss.

[133] See para.9–023.

[134] *Versloot Dredging BV v HDI Gerling Industrie Versicherung AG* [2016] UKSC 45; [2017] A.C. 1 at [32].

"effective cause",[135] a "material inducement",[136] "materially contributed",[137] or played a "real and substantial part".[138] It is respectfully submitted that the test to be met is the normal "but for" requirement of causation,[139] i.e. in the present context, had the representation not been made to him, the representee would not have entered into the contract at all, or would not have done so on the same terms.[140] Some cases appear to support the proposition that if the representee enters into the contract after a fraudulent misrepresentation has been made to him, it is no bar to a claim for rescission[141] that he would have acted in the same way even if the misrepresentation had not been made, provided it had some influence, i.e. it was still *a* reason for his decision.[142] This might be justified as one of a number of harsher rules applied in an attempt to deter fraud,[143] but it may be doubted whether, even as against a defendant who is guilty of fraud, it is appropriate to modify the requirement of causation.[144] Nor is the apparent distinction between rescission and damages easy to justify, given that in most cases the representee's loss flows from the decision to enter the contract, e.g. payment of the price, or a higher price than would otherwise have been paid, and its recovery (excluding any consequential loss) is the monetary equivalent of rescission.[145] It is therefore submitted that no distinction should be drawn based on the remedy sought and that the distinction between fraudulent and

[135] *Assicurazioni Generali SpA v Arab Insurance Group* [2002] EWCA Civ 1642; [2003] 1 W.L.R. 577 at [59].

[136] *Spice Girls Ltd v Aprilia World Service BV* [2002] EWCA Civ 15; [2002] E.M.L.R. 27 at [68]–[72].

[137] *Edgington v Fitzmaurice* (1882) 29 Ch. D 459 at 482.

[138] *JEB Fasteners Ltd v Marks Bloom & Co* [1983] 1 All E.R. 583 at 590; *Dadourian Group International Inc v Simms* [2009] EWCA Civ 169; [2009] 1 Lloyd's Rep. 601 at [100].

[139] Contrast Handley 131 L.Q.R. 274.

[140] *Smith v Kay* (1859) 7 H.L.C. 750 at 776; *Nash v Calthorpe* [1905] 2 Ch. 237 at 245; *Assicurazioni Generali SpA v Arab Insurance Group* [2002] EWCA Civ 1642; [2003] 1 W.L.R. 577 at [59]; *Cassa di Risparmio Della Repubblica di San Marino SpA v Barclays Bank Ltd* [2011] EWHC 484 (Comm); [2011] 1 C.L.C. 701 at [233]; *Raiffeisen Zentralbank Österreich AG v Royal Bank of Scotland Plc* [2010] EWHC 1392 (Comm); [2011] 1 Lloyd's Rep. 123 at [171]–[172] (Christopher Clarke J who regarded this as consistent with the decision of the House of Lords in *Pan Atlantic Ins Co Ltd v Pine Top Ins Co Ltd* [1995] 2 A.C. 501 which was an application to marine insurance of the common law as to inducement); Consumer Insurance (Disclosure and Representations) Act 2012 s.4(1)(b); Insurance Act 2015 s.8(1).

[141] A claim for damages will not succeed unless the claimant can show that the loss in question was caused by the fraud: *Smith New Court Securities Ltd v Scrimgeour Vickers (Asset Management) Ltd* [1997] A.C. 254 at 284; *Barings Plc v Coopers & Lybrand* [2002] EWHC 461 (Ch); [2002] 2 B.C.L.C. 410 at [127]–[130]; cf. *South Australia Asset Management Corp v York Montague Ltd* [1997] A.C. 191 at 216. See para.9–080 text to fn.407.

[142] *Barton v Armstrong* [1976] A.C. 104 (a case of duress to the person: para.10–005) in which an analogy is drawn with fraudulent misrepresentation, based on *Reynell v Sprye* (1852) 1 De G.M. & G. 660 at 678; cf. *UCB Corporate Services Ltd v Williams* [2002] EWCA Civ 555; [2002] 3 F.C.R. 448 at [86], [89] (a case of actual undue influence, which is regarded as a "species of fraud").

[143] See further paras 9–080, 9–129.

[144] *Smith New Court Securities Ltd v Scrimgeour Vickers (Asset Management) Ltd* [1997] A.C. 254 at 267 (Lord Browne-Wilkinson); cf at 285 (Lord Steyn: mitigation (itself an aspect of causation (see para.20–104)) "has no special features in the context of deceit").

[145] See para.9–073.

non-fraudulent misrepresentation should only be relevant to *proving* that the "but for" test has been met.[146] As stated by Lord Sumption in the context of the "fraudulent claims rule" in insurance[147]:

> "In the law of deceit, it is fundamental that the representee must have acted on the misrepresentation. If he would have done the same thing even in the absence of the misrepresentation, a claim based on it will fail. The same applies in a claim to rescind a contract for misrepresentation, fraudulent or otherwise."[148]

9–029 **The relevant counterfactual.** Before turning to the question of proof, there is also some uncertainty about the appropriate counterfactual for the purpose of the "but for" test as applied to claims for misrepresentation.[149] In particular, is the relevant question: what would the representee have done if there had been no representation at all; or what would the representee have done if he had been told the truth? In many cases this will produce the same answer,[150] but it is submitted that, rather than a general rule in favour of "no representation",[151] it is unnecessary to ask anything other than what the position would have been if the (mis)representation had not been made. The answer to that question will depend on the circumstances of the case. In some cases, the defendant would have made no representation at all, e.g. where the misrepresentation was entirely voluntary and unsolicited; in others, the defendant would still have made a representation which, for the purpose of the "but for" test, must be assumed to have been true, e.g. where the representation is made in response to a question asked by the representee, or where the representor was bound to make a representation.[152]

9–030 **Proving reliance.** The burden of proving reliance lies with the representee. The fact that a representation is material, i.e. that it would have induced a reasonable person to enter the contract,[153] gives rise to no "inference of law" that the representation was relied on.[154] It does however lead to an "inference of fact" so that the evidential burden shifts to the representor to prove that the representee would have entered into the contract (or entered into it on the same terms) even if

---

[146] *Pan Atlantic Ins Co Ltd v Pine Top Ins Co Ltd* [1995] 2 A.C. 501 at 542: "In the general law it is beyond doubt that even a fraudulent misrepresentation must be shown to have induced the contract before the promisor has a right to avoid, although the task of proof may be made more easy by a presumption of inducement." (Lord Mustill.)

[147] See para.9–187.

[148] *Versloot Dredging BV v HDI Gerling Industrie Versicherung AG* [2016] UKSC 45; [2017] A.C. 1.

[149] I gratefully acknowledge the insights on this issue obtained by my supervision of the research of Dr Niranjan Venkatesan.

[150] See *Raiffeisen Zentralbank Österreich AG v Royal Bank of Scotland Plc* [2010] EWHC 1392 (Comm); [2011] 1 Lloyd's Rep. 123 at [174]–[191] in which Christopher Clarke J offers the most thorough analysis of this issue.

[151] *Bristol and West Building Society v Mothew* [1998] Ch. 1; cf. *Bank of Tokyo-Mitsubishi UFJ Ltd v Baskan Gida Sanayi Ve Pazarlama AS* [2009] EWHC 1276 (Ch) at [1005].

[152] e.g. the statements which are required to be made in a bill of lading. On this basis, the suggestion of an alternative cause of action in misrepresentation by Kerr LJ in *Procter & Gamble Philippine Manufacturing Corp v Kurt A Becher* [1988] 2 Lloyd's Rep. 21 is perhaps open to doubt.

[153] See para.9–023.

[154] *Smith v Land & House Property Corp* (1884) 28 Ch D. 7 at 16; cf. *JEB Fasteners Ltd v Marks Bloom & Co* [1983] 1 All E.R. 583; affirming [1981] 3 All E.R. 289.

there had been no misrepresentation.[155] It has been said that the inference of fact is "particularly" strong in a case of fraud,[156] and it is in this respect that a distinction might most appropriately be drawn between fraudulent and non-fraudulent misrepresentation.

In *BV Nederlandse Industrie Van Eiproduktien v Rembrandt Enterprises*[157] the defendant was guilty of a fraudulent misrepresentation about the additional costs required to meet US regulations for egg production and the question was whether this induced the claimant's agreement to an increase in the price.[158] In answer to a question about what he would have done if there had been no misrepresentation, the claimant's chief executive replied: "I don't know. It's hypothetical. I can't answer." As Longmore LJ explained, that made this a clear case where the incidence of the burden of proof was important, but as he stressed, it was also important to know *what* has to be proved by the party who has the onus of proof.[159] He accepted that, in cases of non-fraudulent misrepresentation, it appears to be settled that the "but for" test must be met, but acknowledged that the test in fraud is "still controversial" given that some decisions provide support for the view that it is sufficient that the representee "might" have acted differently. For Longmore LJ the onus of proof was nonetheless the key to the case.[160] Given the "particularly strong" inference in cases of fraud, it did not matter that the claimant's own evidence established only that he "might" still have agreed to the price if the misrepresentation had not been made. The court would not interfere with the trial judge's finding that the evidence overall did not have "sufficient clarity and cogency to persuade him that [the claimant's chief executive] *would have agreed to the requested price increase, even if the representation had not been made*."[161] The emphasised words are consistent with a "but for" test which the representor had failed to show had not been met. Of course, the effect of a particularly strong inference of fact is that, in practice, the representee may indeed succeed in a claim for fraudulent misrepresentation where the most that can be said on the basis of *his* evidence is that he *might* have acted differently, not that he would have acted differently.

---

155 *Smith v Chadwick* (1884) 9 App. Cas. 187 at 196; *Barton v County NatWest Ltd* [1999] Lloyd's Rep. Banking 408 at [58]; *Dadourian Group International Inc v Simms* [2009] EWCA Civ 169; [2009] 1 Lloyd's Rep. 601 at [100]; *BV Nederlandse Industrie Van Eiproduktien v Rembrandt Enterprises* [2019] EWCA Civ 596 at [25].

156 *Ross River Ltd v Cambridge City Football Club* [2007] EWHC 2115 (Ch); 117 Con L.R. 129 at [241]; cf. *Hayward v Zurich Insurance Co Plc* [2016] UKSC 48; [2017] A.C. 142 at [37] ("very difficult to rebut the presumption").

157 [2019] EWCA Civ 596; [2019] 3 W.L.R. 1113.

158 The effect of the finding that it did was that the contract at the increased price was rescinded, but the claimant was still liable under the original contract when it refused to accept and pay for the egg products: see para.14–040.

159 *BV Nederlandse Industrie Van Eiproduktien v Rembrandt Enterprises* [2019] EWCA Civ 596; [2019] 3 W.L.R. 1113 at [14].

160 See Longmore LJ's comment at [38] about *Barton v Armstrong*, fn.142: "This is perhaps less controversial than it sounds, since the factual presumption … in *Smith v Chadwick* is another way of expressing the same concept."

161 *BV Nederlandse Industrie Van Eiproduktien v Rembrandt Enterprises* [2019] EWCA Civ 596; [2019] 3 W.L.R. 1113 at [49] (emphasis added).

9–031 **A question of fact.** Given the requirement of reliance, the representee cannot rescind, or claim damages, for misrepresentation if it is proved that he would have entered into the contract in any event,[162] if the representation did not come to his notice,[163] if the representation was made only after he had entered into the contract,[164] or if he relied on his own information.[165] Ordinarily, the requirement of reliance will also not have been met if it is proved that the representee knew the representation was false,[166] or if he took a deliberate risk as to the truth of the matter stated.[167] But this is not necessarily the case. In *Hayward v Zurich Insurance Co Plc*[168] an insurer settled a claim for personal injury against their insured after having reduced the claim because of evidence that it had been exaggerated by the defendant (the claimant in the personal injury action). Later, the insurer discovered further evidence which established that the claim was altogether bogus and sought to have the settlement rescinded on grounds of fraudulent misrepresentation. The Court of Appeal held that the insurer had not been induced to enter into the settlement agreement by any misrepresentation of the defendant, in circumstances where it could not establish that it believed the representations made to be true. The insurer was aware, from the evidence it already had, that the representations may not have been true but accepted that risk by entering into the contract. The insurer's appeal was allowed. As Lord Clarke explained, "inducement and causation are questions of fact"[169] and therefore dependent upon the context. In context, a representation may still have caused the representee to act in a way in which it would not otherwise have done even if he was aware that the representation might not be true. The insurers did not know that what was left of the personal injury claim was based on misrepresentation (or could not be sure of proving this) and had to take into account the risk that the court hearing the claim might believe the defendant.[170] They were therefore induced to enter into a settlement they would not have entered into had they known the true position, or been certain of proving it. Lord Clarke did not rule out that reliance might have been established even in circumstances where the insurers knew that the claimant's representations were false, e.g. because they

---

[162] *JEB Fasteners Ltd v Marks Bloom & Co* [1983] 1 All E.R. 583; affirming [1981] 3 All E.R. 289.

[163] *Ex p. Biggs* (1859) 28 L.J.Ch. 50. It need not come to his attention personally; the automatic processing of a statement by a computer may suffice: *Renault UK Ltd v Fleetpro Technical Services Ltd* [2007] EWHC 2541 (QB).

[164] *Hunt v Optima (Cambridge) Ltd* [2014] EWCA Civ 714; [2014] B.L.R. 613.

[165] *Jennings v Broughton* (1854) 5 D.M. & G. 126; cf. *The Morning Watch* [1990] 1 Lloyd's Rep. 547 at 556.

[166] *Cooper v Tamms* [1988] 1 E.G.L.R. 257; *Eurocopy v Teesdale* [1992] B.C.L.C. 1067; *Rushmer v Smith* [2009] EWHC 94 at [65]–[66]. For the position where the truth is known to the representee's agent, see: *Bawden v London Assurance* [1892] 2 Q.B. 534; *Strover v Harrington* [1988] Ch. 390; contrast *El Ajou v Dollar Holdings Plc* [1994] 2 All E.R. 685 at 689, 702–705; *Wells v Smith* [1914] 3 K.B. 722; *Group Josi Re v Wallbrook Ins Co Ltd* [1996] 1 W.L.R. 1152; *Renault UK Ltd v Fleetpro Technical Services Ltd* [2007] EWHC 2541 (QB).

[167] *Kyle Bay Ltd v Underwriters Subscribing Under Policy No.019057/08/01* [2007] EWCA Civ 57; [2007] 1 C.L.C. 164 at [42], where, however, the circumstances of the case were regarded as "very unusual".

[168] [2016] UKSC 48; [2017] A.C. 142.

[169] *Hayward v Zurich Insurance Co Plc* [2016] UKSC 48; [2017] A.C. 142 at [23]; cf. at [68] (Lord Toulson).

[170] *Hayward v Zurich Insurance Co Plc* [2016] UKSC 48; [2017] A.C. 142 at [32].

still faced the difficulty of proving this before the court hearing the personal injury claim.[171] This is more difficult and it has been suggested that the better explanation for such a case is that the innocent party is not misled, but is subject to duress.[172]

What had concerned Briggs LJ in the Court of Appeal was that:

> "If the mere making of a misstatement rather than belief in its truth is to be a sufficient influencing factor, then there is no telling in what contractual contexts it may be applied, with debilitating effects upon contractual force and certainty."[173]

What appears to have been particularly significant in the context of the *Hayward* case was the absence of, or the restricted, choice facing the insurers. As the trial judge had observed: "This situation is quite different from a proposed purchase, where if in doubt one can simply walk away". In that rather more typical scenario, there is much to be said for the view of Briggs LJ and, in a subsequent case of this sort, it was held that the representee was not induced by representations he knew to be false. The *Hayward* case was distinguished by Nugee J on the basis that "the claims put forward by Mr. Hayward were not just lies told to Zurich; *they were also lies told to the Court*."[174]

**Other inducements.** It is no bar to relief that the claimant entered into the 9–032
contract on the basis of a number of inducements, including misrepresentation. In *Edgington v Fitzmaurice*[175] a lender was induced to lend money to a company by: (i) the misrepresentations which have already been discussed:[176] and (ii) his mistaken belief that he would have a charge on the assets of the company. He was entitled to damages for deceit[177] even though he admitted that he would not have lent the money had he not held this mistaken belief. But if two statements are made to a person, one true and one untrue, and he relies exclusively on the true one, he has no right to relief. In *Heilbut, Symons & Co v Buckleton*[178] a person bought shares in a company after being told: (i) that it was a rubber company (which was untrue); and (ii) that the defendants were "bringing it out" (which was true). One reason given by Lord Atkinson for dismissing the buyer's claim for damages was that he had relied on the second statement to the exclusion of the first.

**Opportunity to find out the truth.** A person who tests the accuracy of the 9–033
representation can be said to rely on his own judgment, rather than on the

[171] *Hayward v Zurich Insurance Co Plc* [2016] UKSC 48; [2017] A.C. 142 at [44]–[45].

[172] Loi [2017] J.B.L. 598.

[173] *Hayward v Zurich Insurance Co Plc* [2015] EWCA Civ 327; [2015] 1 C.L.C. 581 at [35].

[174] *Holyoake v Candy* [2017] EWHC 3397 (Ch) at [392] (emphasis added).

[175] (1885) 29 Ch D. 459; *The Siboen and the Sibotre* [1976] 1 Lloyd's Rep. 293 at 324; *BP Operating Co Ltd v Chevron Transport (Scotland)* [2001] UKHL 50; [2001] 3 W.L.R. 949 at [105]; *Spice Girls Ltd v Aprilia World Service BV* [2002] EWCA Civ 15; [2002] E.M.L.R. 27 at [70]; *UCB Corporate Services Ltd v Williams* [2002] EWCA Civ 555; [2002] 3 F.C.R. 448.

[176] See para.9–017.

[177] See *Standard Chartered Bank v Pakistan National Shipping Co* [2002] UKHL 43; [2003] 1 A.C. 959 at [17] for the view that this rule "probably applies only to fraudulent misrepresentation".

[178] [1913] A.C. 30; para.4–005.

representation,[179] but a person may still be entitled to relief even though he had, but did not take, the opportunity to test its accuracy.[180] This rule is most frequently applied to cases of fraud,[181] but in *Redgrave v Hurd*[182] it was held that such an opportunity to discover the truth was no bar to relief even where the misrepresentation was innocent. In *Peekay Intermark Ltd v ANZ Banking Group Ltd*,[183] in the context of a claim under s.2(1) of the Misrepresentation Act 1967,[184] Moore-Bick LJ also concluded that, once a misrepresentation has been made, "it is not enough to show that the claimant *could have* discovered the truth, but that he *did* discover it".[185] That statement is not easy to reconcile with the decision in the *Peekay* case[186] where the misrepresentation was said to have been corrected "by the express terms of the very contract to which the claimant put his signature", but which he failed to read.[187] One explanation is that the principle in *Redgrave v Hurd* only applies once it is clear that a misrepresentation *has been made* and the decision in *Peekay* amounts to a finding that no misrepresentation was made in the first place. The claimant chose to rely on the "rough and ready" representation made to him by an employee of the defendant about the nature of the investment to be made rather than the contractual documentation which "contained the only formal description he would receive" of the true nature of the investment.[188] On the basis of "the totality of the discussion and the documents provided"[189] no misrepresentation was made which induced the claimant to enter into the contract.

---

[179] *Clarke v Mackintosh* (1862) 4 Giff. 134; *Redgrave v Hurd* (1881) 20 Ch D. 1 at 14; discussing *Attwood v Small* (1838) 6 Cl. & F. 232; *McInerny v Lloyds Bank Ltd* [1974] 1 Lloyd's Rep. 246 at 254.

[180] *Dobell v Stevens* (1825) 3 B. & C. 623; *Reynell v Sprye* (1852) 1 D.M. & G. 660; *Redgrave v Hurd* (1881) 20 Ch D. 1; *Smith v Land & House Property Corp* (1884) 28 Ch D. 7; *Aaron's Reefs Ltd v Twiss* [1896] A.C. 273; cf. *Rignal Developments Ltd v Halil* [1988] Ch. 190 at 199, *aliter*, if a person reads a document revealing the truth, but simply fails to understand it: *Ex p. Briggs* (1866) L.R. 1 Eq. 483.

[181] e.g. *Gordon v Selico Ltd* (1986) 278 E.G. 53 at 61; *Strover v Harrington* [1988] Ch. 390 at 410; cf. *Commission for the New Towns v Cooper (Great Britain) Ltd* [1995] Ch. 259 at 282.

[182] (1881) 20 Ch D. 1; *Laurence v Lexcourt Holdings Ltd* [1978] 1 W.L.R. 1128.

[183] [2006] EWCA Civ 386; [2006] 2 Lloyd's Rep. 511; cf. *Assicurazioni Generali SpA v Arab Ins Group* [2002] EWCA Civ 1642; [2003] 1 All E.R. (Comm) 140; *Flack v Pattinson* [2002] EWCA Civ 1862; [2002] All E.R. (D.) 31 (Dec).

[184] See para.9–049.

[185] *Peekay Intermark Ltd v ANZ Banking Group Ltd* [2006] EWCA Civ 386; [2006] 2 Lloyd's Rep. 511 at [40]. The burden of establishing the correction or withdrawal of a misrepresentation rests on the misrepresentor and the correction must be sufficiently clear in all the circumstances of the case: *Arnison v Smith* (1889) 41 Ch D. 348 at 370, 373; *Mortgage Express v Countrywide Surveyors Ltd* [2016] EWHC 224 (Ch) at [194].

[186] Nor the decision in *Reinhard v Ondra LLP* [2015] EWHC 1869 (Ch); [2016] 2 B.C.L.C. 571 which was said to be "on all fours" with the *Peekay* case; cf. *Banks and Clients Plc v King* [2017] EWHC 3099 (Comm); [2018] B.P.I.R. 333 at [50].

[187] *Peekay Intermark Ltd v ANZ Banking Group Ltd* [2006] EWCA Civ 386; [2006] 2 Lloyd's Rep. 511 at [40].

[188] *Peekay Intermark Ltd v ANZ Banking Group Ltd* [2006] EWCA Civ 386; [2006] 2 Lloyd's Rep. 511 at [52].

[189] This is how it is put by Warren J in *Reinhard v Ondra LLP* [2015] EWHC 1869 (Ch); [2016] 2 B.C.L.C. 571 at [116].

An alternative explanation for the decision in the *Peekay* case is that the principle in *Redgrave v Hurd* should be confined to fraudulent misrepresentation.[190] Support for this can be derived from the decision in *Smith v Eric S Bush.*[191] The claimants in that case had bought a house with the aid of a mortgage, relying on a valuation which had been negligently conducted by a surveyor engaged by the lender. Their claim against the surveyor succeeded in spite of the fact that they might have discovered the truth if they had conducted their own independent survey; for it was neither reasonable to expect them to take this step, nor likely that they would do so, since the house in question was one of modest value. But the House of Lords indicated[192] that the position might be different on the purchase of commercial or industrial premises, or even of residential property of high value. In response to this explanation, it has been suggested that the principle in *Redgrave v Hurd* should continue to apply to claims for rescission even in cases other than fraud, on the basis that the misrepresentor should not retain the advantage of the contract entered into, notwithstanding the carelessness of the representee, and that the observations of the House of Lords in *Smith v Eric S Bush* should be confined to claims for damages against a third party representor.[193]

**Contributory negligence.** The carelessness of the representee in unreasonably failing to take the opportunity to find out the truth may be a ground for reducing damages for negligent misrepresentation, or under the Misrepresentation Act 1967,[194] under the Law Reform (Contributory Negligence) Act 1945. Contributory negligence is not available as a defence to fraudulent misrepresentation[195] and nor would the 1945 Act affect any right to rescind for misrepresentation. 9–034

**Representation addressed to another.** A person may rely on a representation even though it was not made directly to him, e.g. where A makes a representation to B which later comes to the notice of C and induces C to contract with A. If A intended to bring about this result he is liable to C.[196] It is sometimes said more generally that the representor must have intended the representee to act on the representation, but this is usually only a "live issue" in the present context, i.e. where it is said that the representation was not addressed to the claimant or to a 9–035

[190] cf. *Archer v Brown* [1985] Q.B. 401 at 416 (doubting *Redgrave v Hurd* on another point).

[191] [1990] 1 A.C. 831. And see the analogous approach taken in the context of an agent's apparent authority: para.16–030.

[192] *Smith v Eric S Bush* [1990] 1 A.C. 831 at 854, 872 (dealing with the issue of reasonableness under Unfair Contract Terms Act 1977).

[193] *Chitty on Contracts,* 33rd edn (2018), paras 7-044–7-045.

[194] *Gran Gelato Ltd v Richcliff (Group) Ltd* [1992] Ch. 560 at 573–574; cf. *Taberna Europe CDO II Plc v Selskabet* [2016] EWCA Civ 1262; [2017] Q.B. 633.

[195] *Alliance & Leicester BS v Edgestop* [1993] 1 W.L.R. 1462; *Standard Chartered Bank v Pakistan National Shipping Co* [2002] UKHL 43; [2003] 1 A.C. 959.

[196] *Pilmore v Hood* (1838) 5 Bing. N.C. 97; cf. *Tackey v McBain* [1912] A.C. 186; *Standard Chartered Bank v Pakistan National Shipping Corp* [1995] 2 Lloyd's Rep. 365 at 378; *Possfund Custodian Trustees Ltd v Diamond* [1996] 1 W.L.R. 1351; *Taberna Europe CDO II Plc v Selskabet* [2016] EWCA Civ 1262; [2017] Q.B. 633. Contrast *Peek v Gurney* (1873) L.R. 6. H.L. 377 (but see Financial Services and Markets Act 2000 s.90).

class of persons of whom the claimant was one, or if the representation was not intended to be acted on for the purpose of transaction into which the claimant entered.[197]

C need not be in existence at the time of the representation to B if it has a continuing effect and it was relied upon by C, once in existence, to enter into the contract.[198] In *Cramaso LLP v Ogilvie-Grant*[199] a misrepresentation was initially made by A to B, an individual, about the grouse population on a moor which A proposed to let. B then incorporated a limited liability partnership, C, to enter into the lease. C was entitled to set aside the contract and claim damages on the basis of A's misrepresentation.

A representation made by A to B may also make A liable to C where it was reasonable for A to anticipate that the representation would be passed on to C and that C would act on it in some way other than by entering into a contract with A.[200] This possibility is illustrated by cases such as *Smith v Eric S Bush*,[201] where a representation in a report as to the value or condition of a house was made by A to B, was then passed on by B to C, and induced C to buy the house from X. Where the contract induced by the misrepresentation is not made between A and C, it may be difficult to determine whether A owed any duty of care to C. This question is discussed later in this chapter.[202] The present point is simply that the requirement of reliance on the representation may be satisfied even though the representation is not made directly by the representor to the representee.

Where A by misrepresentation induces B to buy something from him, he will not be liable to C merely because B repeats the misrepresentation when later reselling the subject-matter to C. In one such case it was held that the misrepresentation was "spent"[203] when the contract was made between A and B, so that C could not rely on it against A. C might, however, be able to do so if he could show that A knew that B intended to resell and was likely to repeat the misrepresentation on the occasion of the sale to C.[204]

## 2. DAMAGES FOR MISREPRESENTATION

9–036 We now turn to the remedies available for an actionable misrepresentation. This part is concerned with the grounds on which damages can be recovered. We shall first consider the requirements for liability on each ground and then the basis

[197] *Raiffeisen Zentralbank Österreich AG v Royal Bank of Scotland Plc* [2010] EWHC 1392 (Comm); [2011] 1 Lloyd's Rep. 123 at [226].

[198] See para.9–159.

[199] [2014] UKSC 9; [2014] 2 W.L.R. 317.

[200] But not in the absence of such circumstances: *The Zephyr* [1985] 2 Lloyd's Rep. 529 at 539; cf. *Goodwill v British Pregnancy Advisory Service* [1996] 1 W.L.R. 1397.

[201] [1990] 1 A.C. 831; *Yianni v Edwin Evans & Sons* [1982] Q.B. 438.

[202] See para.9–042 and following.

[203] *Gross v Lewis Hillman Ltd* [1970] Ch. 445 at 461.

[204] *Gross v Lewis Hillman Ltd* [1970] Ch. 445 at 461; *The Sennar (No.2)* [1985] 1 W.L.R. 490; cf. *OMV Petrom SA v Glencore International SG* [2015] EWHC 666 (Comm); affirmed without consideration of this point: [2016] EWCA Civ 778; [2016] 2 Lloyd's Rep. 432. In *Clef Aquitaine SARL v Laporte Materials (Barrow) Ltd* [2001] Q.B. 485, where the subject-matter was transferred by B to C by novation. A was a necessary party to this transaction (para.15–003) and knew that his representation would be passed on by B to C, those entities being under the same control.

upon which damages are assessed, including the rules of remoteness which are applied. Where the claimant has relied on the misrepresentation to enter into a contract with the representor, he may also be entitled to rescission of the contract. This remedy is dealt with in the next part of this chapter.

## (a) Liability

**When damages may be awarded.** Damages may be awarded if the representor was guilty of fraud,[205] or negligence,[206] or if he fails to meet the test laid down in s.2(1) of the Misrepresentation Act 1967,[207] or if the representation has become a term of the contract so that the representor is guilty of breach of contract.[208] If the misrepresentation was entirely "innocent" and has not become a term of the contract, the representor has no liability in damages, unless rescission is available and the court exercises its discretion to award damages in lieu of rescission.[209] **9–037**

### *(i) Fraud*

At common law a person who suffers loss as a result of acting in reliance on a fraudulent statement can recover damages in an action of deceit.[210] He can generally do this whether he rescinds the contract or not[211] though he cannot pursue both remedies if this results in his recovering twice over for the same loss.[212] **9–038**

**The fraudulent state of mind.** In *Derry v Peek*[213] the House of Lords held that a statement is fraudulent only if made: (i) with knowledge of its falsity;[214] or (ii) without belief in its truth;[215] or (iii) recklessly,[216] not caring whether it is true or **9–039**

---

[205] See paras 9–038–9–041.
[206] See paras 9–042–9–048.
[207] See paras 9–049–9–055.
[208] See paras 9–056–9–065.
[209] See paras 9–066–9–071.
[210] It is doubtful whether the remedy of an account of profits is available: *Murad v Al-Saraj* [2005] EWCA Civ 959; [2005] W.T.L.R. 1573; *Renault UK Ltd v Fleetpro Technical Services Ltd* [2007] EWHC 2541 (QB) at [152]–[158].
[211] *Newbigging v Adam* (1886) 34 Ch D. 582 at 592; *Archer v Brown* [1985] Q.B. 401 at 415; *Tang Man Sit v Capacious Investments Ltd* [1996] A.C. 514 at 521; *Soden v British & Commonwealth Holdings Plc* [1998] A.C. 298 at 327.
[212] *Archer v Brown* [1985] Q.B. 401 at 415.
[213] (1889) 14 App. Cas. 337 (actual decision was reversed by Directors Liability Act 1890; see now Financial Services and Markets Act 2000 s.90); *The Kriti Palm* [2006] EWCA Civ 1601; [2007] 1 Lloyd's Rep. 555 at [256]–[258].
[214] Including knowingly failing to correct a representation which has become false: *Fitzroy Robinson Ltd v Mentmore Towers Ltd* [2009] EWHC 1552 (TCC); [2009] B.L.R. 555; para.9–159.
[215] Quaere whether this state of mind is sufficient for the personal liability of a mere employee of a company acting under the instructions of a director: *GE Commerce Finance Ltd v Gee* [2005] EWHC 2056 (QB); [2006] 1 Lloyd's Rep. 337 at [111].
[216] Recklessness goes beyond mere carelessness: *The Kriti Palm* [2006] EWCA Civ 1601; [2007] 1 Lloyd's Rep. 555 at [257].

false. Fraud is a serious charge which must be clearly and distinctly proved.[217] Further, "where a defendant has been acquitted of fraud in a court of first instance the decision in his favour should not be displaced on appeal except on the clearest grounds".[218] A person who negligently makes a false statement will now often be liable in damages, but it may still be important that he is not guilty of fraud at common law: damages for fraud may not be the same as damages for negligence;[219] and liability for fraud cannot be excluded,[220] whereas liability in negligence can be, subject to statutory control.[221]

9–040 **Motive irrelevant.** It must be shown that the representor intended the representee to rely on the false statement,[222] but a statement may be fraudulent although it was made without bad motive and without intention to cause loss: an "intention to deceive" suffices even though there is no "intention to defraud".[223] Thus in *Polhill v Walter*[224] an agent purported to accept a bill of exchange on behalf of his principal, knowing that he had no authority to do so but believing that his principal would ratify. He was held liable in deceit. This case should be contrasted with *Angus v Clifford*.[225] The directors of a company which had bought a gold mine issued a prospectus containing extracts from an engineer's report said to have been "prepared for the directors". It had in fact been prepared for the sellers of the mine. The directors knew this, but were held not liable for fraud as they did not at the time of issuing the prospectus appreciate the importance of the words "prepared for the directors". Thus, it seems that a person is not guilty of fraud if he knows that his statement is false but does not appreciate its materiality.[226]

9–041 **Principal and agent.** Responsibility for a statement may be divided between principal and agent or between several agents of the same principal. If an agent within the scope of his authority makes a statement which he knows to be false,

217 *The Kriti Palm* [2006] EWCA Civ 1601; [2007] 1 Lloyd's Rep. 555 at [259]; *Dadourian Group International Inc v Simms* [2009] EWCA Civ 169; [2009] 1 Lloyd's Rep. 601 at [31]–[32].

218 *Akerhielm v De Mare* [1959] A.C. 789 at 806; *Foster v Action Aviation Ltd* [2014] EWCA Civ 1368 at [31].

219 See para.9–080.

220 See para.7–034.

221 See paras 9–132, 9–143.

222 See para.9–035; *Abu Dhabi Investment Co Ltd v H Clarkson & Co* [2008] EWCA Civ 699 at [33]; *Clef Aquitaine Sarl v Laporte Materials (Barrow) Ltd* [2001] 1 Q.B. 488 at 503, 506, 513.

223 *Standard Chartered Bank v Pakistan National Shipping Corp* [1995] 2 Lloyd's Rep. 365 at 375; see further [1998] 1 Lloyd's Rep. 656; *Standard Chartered Bank v Pakistan National Shipping Co (No.2)* [2000] 1 Lloyd's Rep. 218 at 221, 224 (reversed on another point [2002] UKHL 43; [2003] 1 A.C. 959).

224 (1832) 3 B. & Ad. 114; cf. *Edgington v Fitzmaurice* (1885) 29 Ch D. 459 at 481; *Watts v Spence* [1976] Ch. 165 at 176 (where fraud was not alleged).

225 [1891] 2 Ch. 449.

226 But such failure may give rise to liability in negligence (not recognised at the time of *Angus v Clifford*): *Bank of Tokyo-Mitsubishi UFJ Ltd v Baskan Gida Sanayi Ve Pazarlama AS* [2009] EWHC 1276 (Ch) at [1002].

the principal is liable for the fraud of the agent;[227] the agent is also liable for his own fraud.[228] If the agent who made the statement did not know that it was false, but the principal, or another agent did know this, the principal is in general not liable for fraud.[229] The mens rea required for fraud cannot be established by adding together the states of mind of several persons, each of whom is innocent. But if the principal or the second agent stood by, knowing that the representation was being made and that it was false, the principal would be guilty of fraud or liable for the fraud of the second agent.[230] In such a case the principal or second agent has mens rea, though he made no representation. The same rule should apply where the representation is innocently made by the principal, and the agent, acting within his authority, stands by knowing that the representation is going to be made and that it is false.[231]

### *(ii) Negligence at common law*

The principal concern of this chapter is with a misrepresentation which induces the claimant to contract *with the representor*. In such cases, a claim for damages under s.2(1) of the Misrepresentation Act 1967 is the more likely cause of action.[232] A claim in negligence at common law is more likely to be made where the representor has induced the claimant to act to his detriment in ways other than by contracting with the representor, e.g. by contracting with a third party.[233] But a claim in negligence is also potentially available between contracting parties.[234] Since the law of negligence is beyond the scope of this book, what follows therefore is only an outline account of negligent misrepresentation. **9–042**

**Establishing a duty of care.** A misrepresentation is negligent if it is made carelessly and in breach of a duty owed by the representor to the representee to take reasonable care that the representation is accurate. It used to be thought that such a duty could arise only where the relationship between representor and representee arose out of a pre-existing contract between them, or where it was "fiduciary",[235] but this narrow view was rejected in *Hedley Byrne & Co Ltd v* **9–043**

---

[227] *S Pearson & Son Ltd v Dublin Corp* [1907] A.C. 351; *Briess v Woolley* [1954] A.C. 333; cf. *Man Nutzfahrzeuge AG v Freightliner Ltd* [2005] EWHC 2347; *Clapp v Enron (Thrace) Exploration & Production BV* [2005] EWCA Civ 1511; [2006] 1 C.L.C. 94 at [29].

[228] *Standard Chartered Bank v Pakistan National Shipping Co* [2002] UKHL 43; [2003] 1 A.C. 959; *Renault UK Ltd v Fleetpro Technical Services Ltd* [2007] EWHC 2541 (QB). But see the doubts expressed by Tugenhadt J in *GE Commercial Finance Ltd v Gee* [2005] EWHC 2056 (QB); [2006] 1 Lloyd's Rep. 337 at [103]–[104].

[229] *Cornfoot v Fowke* (1840) 6 M. & W. 358; *Gordon Hill Trust Ltd v Segall* [1941] 2 All E.R. 379; *Armstrong v Strain* [1952] 1 K.B. 232; Devlin 53 L.Q.R. 344; Gower 15 M.L.R. 232.

[230] *London County Freehold v Berkeley Property Co Ltd* [1936] 2 All E.R. 1039; *The Siboen and the Sibotre* [1976] 1 Lloyd's Rep. 293 at 321.

[231] Whether the *principal* could be made liable for fraud in such circumstances will depend on the rules for the attribution to one person of the state of mind of another: *Man Nutzfahrzeuge AG v Freightliner Ltd* [2005] EWHC 2347 (no attribution where the agent was neither a director, nor an employee of the defendant company).

[232] See para.9–049 and following.

[233] No claim is available under s.2(1) of the 1967 Act in such circumstances: see para.9–050.

[234] See para.9–048.

[235] *Nocton v Ashburton* [1914] A.C. 932.

*Heller & Partners Ltd.*[236] The claimants in that case suffered loss as a result of having given credit to a firm called Easipower Ltd, in reliance on a reference carelessly given by Easipower's bank, who knew of the purpose for which the reference was required. The actual decision was that the bank was not liable because the reference had been given "without responsibility".[237] If there had been no such disclaimer, the House of Lords made it clear that the bank would have owed to the claimants a duty to take reasonable care in the making of the statements contained in the reference. A duty of the kind just described can arise if there is a "special relationship" between the parties and two tests have been formulated to determine if it exists.[238]

9–044 **The "threefold test".** Under this test, a duty of care may be owed when three conditions are satisfied: it must be reasonably foreseeable by the representor that the representee will rely on the statement; there must be sufficient "proximity" between the parties; and it must be fair just and reasonable for the law to impose the duty.[239] It is obvious that these requirements are closely related, so much so that it has been said that they are "at least in most cases, merely facets of the same thing".[240] In the context of misrepresentation, foreseeable and reasonable reliance by the representee on the representor's statement or advice is the single most important requirement.[241] But while it is a necessary condition of liability in tort for misrepresentation inducing a contract,[242] it is not a sufficient one. Thus, a purely social relationship will not normally suffice to give rise to a duty, so that no action normally lies at common law where a person suffers loss as a result of acting on careless friendly advice,[243] even if it is given by a professional person.[244] In such a case, it would not normally be just and reasonable to impose a duty.

On the other hand, there was a "special relationship" between the claimants and the bank in *Hedley Byrne*'s case,[245] and it is clear from dicta in that case,

236 [1964] A.C. 465.

237 Such a provision would now be subject to the requirement of reasonableness by virtue of the Unfair Contract Terms Act 1977 ss.2(1) and 13(1): see *Smith v Eric S Bush* [1990] 1 A.C. 831 at 875–876; para.7–045.

238 In addition to the two tests referred to below, in *Customs and Excise Commissioners* [2006] UKHL 28; [2007] 1 A.C. 181 at [4] Lord Bingham also commended an "incremental" approach based on established categories of negligence.

239 *Smith v Eric S Bush* [1990] 1 A.C. 831 at 865; *Caparo Industries Plc v Dickman* [1990] 2 A.C. 605 at 617–618; cf. *Yuen Kun Yeu v Attorney General of Hong Kong* [1988] A.C. 175.

240 *Caparo Industries Plc v Dickman* [1900] 2 A.C. 605 at 632.

241 *Murphy v Brentwood DC* [1991] 1 A.C. 398 at 480, 486–487; *Steel v NRAM Ltd* [2018] UKSC 13; [2018] 1 W.L.R. 1190.

242 Though not of liability for negligence arising in other ways: see *White v Jones* [1995] 2 A.C. 207 at 268, 275; *Spring v Guardian Royal Insurance Plc* [1995] 2 A.C. 296 at 344.

243 *Hedley Byrne & Co Ltd v Heller & Partners Ltd* [1964] A.C. 465 at 482; see [1964] A.C. 465 at 531 for possible exceptions. In *Chaudhry v Prabhakar* [1989] 1 W.L.R. 29 (para.3–171) the existence of a duty was conceded; this concession was approved by two members of the court, who, however, also recognised (at 36 and 34) that advice given in "family, domestic or social relationships" would not normally be actionable.

244 *Mutual Life and Citizens' Assurance Co Ltd v Evatt* [1971] A.C. 793 at 806. Contrast *Burgess v Lejonvarn* [2017] EWCA Civ 254; [2017] B.L.R. 277 where an architect provided her services for free but "the context was a professional one. It was not informal or social" (at [86]).

245 *Hedley Byrne & Co Ltd v Heller & Partners Ltd* [1964] A.C. 465 at 494, 502, 538, 539.

from earlier decisions which were overruled[246] or rehabilitated[247] by it, and from later cases, that a duty of care will often arise where the representor makes the representation while acting in some professional capacity. If he makes the representation to his own client, his duty of care with respect to its accuracy will generally be imposed by his contract with that client,[248] though a duty of care imposed by the general law (and giving rise to liability in tort) may exist side by side with such a contractual duty.[249] The more important point to be made here is that such a duty of care may also arise under the law of tort even though there is *no* contract between representor and representee. Thus, the duty may be owed by professionals such as accountants[250] and surveyors and valuers[251] even to persons other than their immediate clients who rely on their statements, where the conditions (stated above) which give rise to a duty of care are satisfied.

**Representations made for a particular purpose.** A duty is more likely to arise in cases of this kind where the statement was made for the purpose of the transaction which it induced than where it was not so made. There was accordingly sufficient proximity between a surveyor and the prospective purchaser of a house, where the surveyor had been commissioned by a building society to report on the value of that house, knowing that his report would be passed on to the purchaser, where it was so passed on, and the house was bought in reliance on it.[252] Similarly, an accountant's report on the financial state of a company can give rise to liability to an intending lender to, or investor in, the company if it was made for the purpose of providing such a person with the information on which his decision whether to make the loan or investment is likely to be, and is in fact, based.[253] But the position is different where auditors are appointed by a company to enable the company to perform its statutory obligation to produce audited annual accounts. In such a case there is no sufficient proximity between those auditors and prospective lenders to, or investors in, the company, or even between the auditors and shareholders in the company who, in reliance on the accounts, buy additional shares.[254] The reason why no duty is owed to these persons is that the audited accounts are produced **9–045**

[246] *Candler v Crane, Christmas & Co* [1951] 2 K.B. 164.

[247] *Cann v Willson* (1883) 39 Ch D. 39.

[248] See para.17–067.

[249] cf. *Henderson v Merrett Syndicates Ltd* [1995] 2 A.C. 145 (a case of negligently rendered *services* rather than negligent *statements*); see para.14–056.

[250] See generally *Jackson & Powell on Professional Liability*, 8th edn (2017), Ch.17.

[251] See generally *Jackson & Powell on Professional Liability*, 8th edn (2017), Ch.10.

[252] e.g. *Smith v Eric S Bush* [1990] 1 A.C. 831. No duty where the purchaser buys a residential house as part of a buy-to-let scheme: *Scullion v Bank of Scotland Plc* [2011] EWCA Civ 693; [2011] 1 W.L.R. 3212.

[253] *Caparo Industries Plc v Dickman* [1990] 2 A.C. 605 at 625, 647–648; *Morgan Crucible Co Plc v Hill Samuel Bank Ltd* [1991] 1 All E.R. 148; *Barings Plc v Coopers & Lybrand* [1997] 1 B.C.L.C. 427; *Law Society v KPMG Peat Marwick* [2000] 1 W.L.R. 1921; *So v HSBC* [2009] EWCA Civ 296; [2009] C.L.C. 503; cf. *Playboy Club London Ltd v Banca Nazionale del Lavoro SpA* [2018] UKSC 43; [2018] 1 W.L.R. 4041. Contrast *James McNaughton Paper Group v Hicks Anderson & Co* [1991] 1 All E.R. 134.

[254] e.g. *Al Saudi Banque v Clark Pixley* [1990] Ch. 313; *Caparo Industries Plc v Dickman* [1990] 2 A.C. 605; Fleming 106 L.Q.R. 349; *The Morning Watch* [1990] 1 Lloyd's Rep. 547. Contrast *Law Society v KPMG Peat Marwick* [2000] 1 W.L.R. 1921.

simply for the purpose of satisfying the statutory obligation described above, and not to induce the transactions in question. The same principle may limit the *scope* of the duty to the particular transaction for the purpose of which the statement was made. Thus, where auditors employed by a company produced accounts which, as they knew, were to determine the price at which the claimants were to acquire a substantial shareholding in the company, the auditors were held to owe a duty to the claimants in respect of that purchase but not in respect of loans of money made to the company, nor in respect of a further purchase of shares in the company made by the claimants over three years after the original transaction.[255]

9–046 **"Assumption of responsibility".** A second test which may be used to determine whether a special relationship exists, and which now applies more generally in the law of negligence, is to ask whether the defendant "assumed responsibility for what he said and did vis-à-vis the claimant, or is to be treated by the law as having done so".[256] As is clear from this dictum of Lord Bingham the test of assumption of responsibility is applied objectively; it is not a case of what the defendant intended but, "as in the case of contractual liability", what would reasonably be inferred from his conduct against the background of the circumstances of the case.[257] As far as the relationship with the threefold test is concerned, it seems that an assumption of responsibility is to be regarded as a sufficient, but not a necessary, condition of liability: if it is satisfied, it is unnecessary to ask whether it would be fair, just and reasonable to impose liability; if not, further consideration is called for under the threefold test.[258] As for the tests themselves, there is candid recognition that they are of doubtful utility.[259] While decisions have been reached by applying one test or the other, of far greater relevance has been the circumstances of the case and the relationship between the parties in the context of their legal and factual situation.[260] Two factors of particular relevance are the purpose for which any representations were

[255] *Galoo Ltd v Bright Grahame Murray* [1994] 1 W.L.R. 1360; cf. in relation to false statements in a company prospectus, *Al Nakib Investments (Jersey) Ltd v Longcroft* [1990] 1 W.L.R. 1390; contrast *Possfund Custodian Trustees Ltd v Diamond* [1996] 1 W.L.R. 1351, where it was arguable such statements were intended to induce "after-market" purchases. These cases concerned common law liability, as opposed to liability under the statutory provisions now contained in Financial Services and Markets Act 2000 ss.90, 90A.

[256] *Customs and Excise Commissioners v Barclays Bank Plc* [2006] UKHL 28; [2007] 1 A.C. 181 at [4] (Lord Bingham). See earlier: *Hedley Byrne & Co Ltd v Heller & Partners Ltd* [1964] A.C. 494 at 529; *Henderson v Merrett Syndicates Ltd* [1995] 2 A.C. 145 at 180, 181, 205; *White v Jones* [1995] 2 A.C. 207 at 256, 268–269; *Spring v Guardian Ins Plc* [1995] 2 A.C. 296 at 324.

[257] *Customs and Excise Commissioners v Barclays Bank Plc* [2006] UKHL 28; [2007] 1 A.C. 181 at [35] (Lord Hoffmann).

[258] *Customs and Excise Commissioners v Barclays Bank Plc* [2006] UKHL 28; [2007] 1 A.C. 181 at [4], [35]; *Henderson v Merrett Syndicates Ltd* [1995] 2 A.C. 145 at 181; *Burgess v Lejonvarn* [2017] EWCA Civ 254; [2017] B.L.R. 277 at [64].

[259] *Customs and Excise Commissioners v Barclays Bank Plc* [2006] UKHL 28; [2007] 1 A.C. 181 at [36]; *Caparo v Dickman* [1990] 2 A.C. 617 at 628; *Merrett v Babb* [2001] EWCA Civ 214; [2001] Q.B. 1174 at [41]; *Natixis SA v Marex Financial* [2019] EWHC 2549 (Comm) at [307].

[260] *Precis (521) v William Mercer Ltd* [2005] EWCA Civ 114; [2005] P.N.L.R. 28.

made,[261] and whether to impose liability in negligence would unduly interfere with any contractual arrangements made by the parties.[262]

**Professional skill.** One feature of the relationships discussed above, in which the representor was held to owe a duty of care, was that he made the statement in the exercise of some professional skill. The absence of this factor was held to negative liability in *Mutual Life and Citizen's Ins Co Ltd v Evatt*,[263] where a company carelessly gave misleading information about an associated company to a prospective investor in the latter company. As a result the investor suffered loss, but the majority of the Privy Council held that the first company was not liable in negligence as it was not and did not purport to be engaged in the business of giving skilled advice on investments.[264] The majority regarded this as an essential ingredient of liability;[265] but the prevailing view is that, so long as the other conditions of liability are satisfied, the representor may be liable even though he was not in the business of giving advice[266] and even though the representee did not seek his advice (but only asked for information).[267] 9–047

**Commercial relationships.** A duty of care may exist at common law even in a purely commercial relationship, such as that of buyer and seller or landlord and tenant. For example, in *Esso Petroleum Co Ltd v Mardon*[268] a tenant was induced to take a lease of a petrol station from an oil company by a statement made by an experienced salesman on the company's behalf, as to the potential future turnover of the premises. As the tenant had relied on the salesman's superior knowledge and experience, it was held that the company was under a duty of care at common law. On the other hand, there are many commercial relationships in which each party consciously relies on his own skill or judgment,[269] or where it is reasonable for the representor to assume that the representee will be advised by his own 9–048

[261] See para.9–045.

[262] See discussion at para.14–050 and following.

[263] [1971] A.C. 793; A.L.G. 87 L.Q.R. 147; Rickford 34 M.L.R. 328.

[264] *Mutual Life and Citizen's Ins Co Ltd v Evatt* [1971] A.C. 793 at 809.

[265] *Mutual Life and Citizen's Ins Co Ltd v Evatt* [1971] A.C. 793 at 805, 809.

[266] The views of the minority in *Evatt*'s case were preferred to those of the majority by Ormrod LJ in *Esso Petroleum Co Ltd v Mardon* [1976] Q.B. 801 at 827 and by Lord Denning MR (dissenting); and Shaw LJ in *Howard Marine & Dredging Co Ltd v A Ogden & Sons (Excavations) Ltd* [1978] Q.B. 574 at 591, 600. The point was left open in *Caparo Industries Plc v Dickman* [1990] 2 A.C. 605 at 637, but the case is viewed with some scepticism in *Spring v Guardian Insurance Plc* [1995] 2 A.C. 296 at 320.

[267] *Box v Midland Bank Ltd* [1979] 2 Lloyd's Rep. 391. Contrast *Royal Bank Trust Co (Trinidad) v John Robert Pampellone* [1987] 1 Lloyd's Rep. 218; *Civic Structures v Clark Quinney & Co* [1991] 2 E.G.L.R. 165: no liability for merely *passing on* information.

[268] [1976] Q.B. 801; cf. dicta in *Hedley Byrne & Co Ltd v Heller & Partners Ltd* [1964] A.C. 465 at 486, 514, 528–529; *Gran Gelato Ltd v Richcliff (Group) Ltd* [1992] Ch. 560 (claim against first defendant); *McCullagh v Lane Fox & Partners* [1996] 1 E.G.L.R. 35 at 42.

[269] *Oleificio Zucchi SA v Northern Sales Ltd* [1965] 2 Lloyd's Rep. 496 at 519; cf. *Amalgamated Metal Trading Ltd v DTI, The Times*, 21 March 1989.

experts.[270] In such cases there would be no duty of care at common law; though, even in the absence of a "special relationship", there can be liability in damages under the Misrepresentation Act.[271]

### (iii) Misrepresentation Act 1967 s.2(1)

**9–049** Section 2(1) of the Misrepresentation Act 1967 creates a statutory liability for misrepresentation. It provides:

> "Where a person has entered into a contract after a misrepresentation has been made to him by another party thereto and as a result thereof he has suffered loss, then, if the person making the misrepresentation would be liable to damages in respect thereof had the misrepresentation been made fraudulently, that person shall be so liable notwithstanding that the misrepresentation was not made fraudulently, unless he proves that he had reasonable ground to believe and did believe up to the time the contract was made that the facts represented were true".

**9–050** **Scope.** Unlike negligence at common law, it is not necessary under s.2(1) to ask whether there was a "special relationship", giving rise to a duty of care, between the parties. It is enough if the representation is made by one contracting party to the other, but the representor can escape liability by proving that his belief in the truth of the facts stated was not formed carelessly. Liability under the subsection is in this respect "essentially founded on negligence".[272] There are two situations in which s.2(1) does not apply, though there may be liability in negligence at common law: namely, where (as in the *Hedley Byrne*[273] case) the representation is made by a stranger to the contract; and where the negotiations between representor and representee do not reach the stage of a concluded contract. The first restriction follows from the requirement that the representee must have been induced by the misrepresentation of the representor to contract *with the representor*.[274]

**9–051** **Claims by consumers.** The scope of s.2(1) is now further restricted by an amendment under which s.2 as a whole "does not entitle a person to be paid damages in respect of a misrepresentation if the person has a right to redress under Part 4A of the Consumer Protection from Unfair Trading Regulations 2008 … in respect of the conduct constituting the misrepresentation".[275] A consumer's "right to redress" under the 2008 Regulations is dealt with above.[276]

---

270 *McInerny v Lloyds Bank Ltd* [1974] 1 Lloyd's Rep. 246.

271 1967 Act s.2(1); on the facts of *Esso Petroleum Co Ltd v Mardon* [1976] Q.B. 801, there would now be liability under this provision.

272 *Gran Gelato Ltd v Richcliff Group Ltd* [1992] Ch. 560 at 573; cf. *South Australia Asset Management Corp v York Montague Ltd* [1997] A.C. 191 at 216.

273 See para.9–043; *Kleinwort Benson Ltd v Malaysian Mining Corp* [1989] 1 W.L.R. 379 at 386.

274 *Taberna Europe CDO II Plc v Selskabet* [2016] EWCA Civ 1262; [2017] Q.B. 633; cf. *The Skopas* [1983] 1 W.L.R. 857; *William Sindall Plc v Cambridgeshire CC* [1994] 1 W.L.R. 1016 at 1037.

275 1967 Act s.2(4), which is inserted by the Consumer Protection (Amendment) Regulations 2014 (SI 2014/870) reg.5. Section 2(4) does not prevent a debtor from bringing a claim under s.75(1) of the Consumer Credit Act 1974 against a creditor under a debtor-creditor-supplier agreement based on the misrepresentation of the supplier: s.2(5).

276 See para.9–002.

**Burden of proof.** At common law, the representee must prove negligence, while under s.2(1) the representor is liable "unless he proves that he had reasonable ground to believe and did believe up to the time the contract was made that the facts represented were true". The difficulty of discharging this burden is illustrated by *Howard Marine & Dredging Co Ltd v A Ogden & Sons (Excavations) Ltd*[277] in which, during negotiations for the hire of barges, the owner's agent mis-stated their deadweight capacity, relying on an erroneous statement in Lloyd's Register. It was held that the burden had not been discharged since the owner could have discovered the true state of affairs by looking at documents in his possession. But where the representor had no such means of discovering the truth, the burden would probably be discharged if he could show that he was himself the victim of an earlier fraud and that he had innocently repeated a representation previously made to him,[278] or that he had reasonably relied on an expert's report on the point in question,[279] or that he had made due enquiries before making the statement.[280] Section 2(1) requires him to prove only that he had reasonable ground for his belief, so that his actual means of knowledge are relevant: accordingly, a layman may succeed in discharging the burden where an expert would fail. 9–052

**Agents.** Under s.2(1), a contracting party can be held liable for a representation made on his behalf by his agent.[281] But the agent himself is not liable under the subsection,[282] though he will be liable in negligence at common law if the representee can establish that there was a "special relationship" between himself and the agent, and that the agent was in breach of the resulting duty of care. The agent would not be so liable where the only special relationship was between his *principal* and the representee.[283] 9–053

**The fiction of fraud.** Section 2(1) has the effect of imposing liability in damages for careless misrepresentation; but instead of simply providing that the representor shall be liable in damages it says that he shall be so liable if he "would be liable to damages … had the misrepresentation been made fraudulently". This fiction of fraud seems to be quite unnecessary; and it may lead the courts to extend to cases within s.2(1) rules which have been developed in the context of fraudulent misrepresentation and which are wholly inappropriate where there is no actual fraud. In the parliamentary debates on the Act, Lord Reid suggested that the effect of the fiction might be to apply to the new cause of action the extended period of limitation which applies where an action is "based upon"[284] fraud. But he added that this result would be "rather unreasonable"[285] 9–054

[277] [1978] Q.B. 574; cf. *Walker v Boyle* [1982] 1 W.L.R. 495 at 509.
[278] As in *Oscar Chess Ltd v Williams* [1957] 1 W.L.R. 370; para.9–060; cf. *Humming Bird Motors v Hobbs* [1986] R.T.R. 276; para.9–062.
[279] *Cooper v Tamms* [1988] 1 E.G.L.R. 257.
[280] *William Sindall Plc v Cambridgeshire CC* [1994] 1 W.L.R. 1016.
[281] *Gosling v Anderson* (1972) 223 E.G. 1743; *Howard Marine & Dredging Co Ltd v A Ogden & Sons (Excavations) Ltd* [1978] Q.B. 574.
[282] *The Skopas* [1983] 1 W.L.R. 857.
[283] *Williams v Natural Life Health Foods Ltd* [1998] 1 W.L.R. 835; *J Jarvis & Sons Ltd v Castle Wharf Development Ltd* [2001] EWCA Civ 19; [2001] Lloyd's Rep. P.N. 308.
[284] See now Limitation Act 1980 s.32(1).

and it has been held that the fiction of fraud would not be applied to this situation.[286] Further support for the view that the fiction is not to be literally applied is provided by a case in which the Court of Appeal has held[287] that a principal may be liable under the subsection for his agent's misrepresentation even though there is no such shared responsibility for the statement as is required to make the principal liable in cases of fraud.[288] It is to be hoped that the courts will similarly reject certain other consequences[289] which could be deduced from the fiction of fraud. One of these consequences, namely the damages recoverable, is discussed below.[290]

9–055 **Effect of affirmation.** The right to *rescind* a contract for misrepresentation can be lost by affirmation;[291] but affirmation does not deprive the representee of his right to damages under s.2(1). Such damages can therefore in principle be recovered if, after having entered into the contract, the representee discovers the truth and nevertheless performs the contract.[292] Of course the right to damages may be limited in such cases, e.g. if the matter to which the misrepresentation relates was so serious that the representee's performance with knowledge of the truth amounts to failure by him to mitigate his loss.[293]

### *(iv) Contractual statements*

9–056 So far, in this section, we have assumed that the misrepresentation induces the representee to enter into the contract, but that it has not become a term of the contract or otherwise acquired contractual force. The nature of the term in question will usually be a warranty (or guarantee) as to the truth of the representation.[294] If the misrepresentation does have such contractual force, the representee is entitled to recover damages for breach of contract. He may also be entitled to terminate the contract for breach,[295] or rescind for misrepresentation.

---

285 Lord Reid 274 H.L. 936.

286 *Garden Neptune Shipping Ltd v Occidental Worldwide Investment Corp* [1990] 1 Lloyd's Rep. 330 at 335; cf. (in another context) *Mander v Evans* [2001] 1 W.L.R. 2378.

287 *Gosling v Anderson* (1972) 223 E.G. 1743.

288 See para.9–041.

289 e.g. the rule that a fraudulent statement need not be material (above, para.9–025), and the rule that a person cannot exclude liability for his own fraud (para.7–034): see *Garden Neptune Shipping Ltd v Occidental Worldwide Investment Corp* [1990] 1 Lloyd's Rep. 330. On the other hand the rule that a representation as to a third person's credit must be in writing to give rise to liability under Statute of Frauds Amendment Act 1828, s.6 applies only to *fraudulent* misrepresentation: *Banbury v Bank of Montreal* [1918] A.C. 626; *Contex Drouzhba Ltd v Wiseman* [2007] EWCA Civ 1201; [2008] 1 B.C.L.C. 631; and in *The Pacific Colocotronis* [1984] Q.B. 713 at 718–719 it seems to have been thought that the fiction of fraud applied in this context, for it was "common ground" that the requirement of writing equally applied for the purpose of an action under Misrepresentation Act 1967 s.2(1).

290 See para.9–082.

291 See para.9–125.

292 *Production Technology Consultants v Bartlett* [1986] 1 E.G.L.R. 82; cf. at common law *Arnison v Smith* (1889) 41 Ch D. 348.

293 See para.20–105.

294 But see para.9–075.

295 See Ch.18.

The relation between these various rights will be considered below;[296] our only concern here is with the right to damages. This differs in two ways from the right to damages previously considered in this section: it can arise without fraud or negligence, and it is governed by different rules as to the assessment of damages and remoteness.[297] It also differs in a number of ways from the power of the court to award damages in lieu of rescission, which will be considered below.[298] That power is discretionary, while damages for breach of contract can be recovered as of right. For all these reasons it is still necessary to distinguish between contractual statements and "mere" representations inducing a contract.[299]

**Statements made in the contract.** Where a contract is in writing, a descriptive statement may actually be made in the contractual document. Such a statement will clearly be a contractual term if it is said to be the basis of the contract.[300] Subject to such express provisions, the question whether the statement is a term or a mere representation is one of construction.[301] The same is true where the statement is contained in a written offer, the acceptance of which concludes the contract.[302] Where a descriptive statement is contained in a contractual document it may be a term even though it did not induce the party complaining of its untruth to enter into the contract,[303] and, indeed, even though he was at the time of contracting unaware of its existence.[304] 9–057

**Statements made in pre-contractual negotiations.** Often a statement inducing a contract will not be set out in the contractual document, but will be made during the negotiations leading up to the contract. Under several provisions of the Consumer Rights Act 2015 certain pre-contract information is automatically treated as included as a term of the contract,[305] but normally the question whether such a statement is a mere representation or a term of the contract depends on the intention with which the statement was made,[306] objectively ascertained.[307] It is impossible to lay down any strict rules for determining when the intention to treat the statement as a term can be said to exist. But a number of guiding principles can be deduced from the cases. 9–058

[296] See paras 9–073–9–076, 9–109.
[297] See paras 9–073–9–082.
[298] See paras 9–066–9–071.
[299] Atiyah 1971 Alberta L. Rev. 347; and *Essays on Contract* (1990), p.275.
[300] e.g. *London Assurance v Mansel* (1879) 11 Ch D. 363.
[301] *Behn v Burness* (1863) 1 B. & S. 751 at 754 (statement in charterparty as to position of ship).
[302] *The Larissa* [1983] 2 Lloyd's Rep. 325 at 330.
[303] Though reliance may be relevant in determining whether the statement was intended as a term: *Harlingdon & Leinster Enterprises Ltd v Christopher Hull Fine Art Ltd* [1991] 1 Q.B. 564 at 574, 579, 584.
[304] cf. para.6–004: the principle of incorporation by signature can here work *in favour* of the signer.
[305] See, e.g. ss.12(2), 37(2), 50(1).
[306] *Howard Marine & Dredging Co Ltd v A Ogden & Son (Excavations) Ltd* [1978] Q.B. 574 at 595.
[307] See paras 1–002, 2–002, 4–002, 6–042.

9–059 **Verification.** A statement is unlikely to be a term of the contract if the person making it expressly asks the other party to verify its truth. In *Ecay v Godfrey*[308] the seller of a boat said that it was sound but advised the buyer to have it surveyed. This advice negatived any intention to warrant the soundness of the boat. The same principle applies where the circumstances are such that the person to whom the statement was made would normally be expected to verify it. This is the reason traditionally given for the view that statements made by sellers of houses in pre-contract negotiations do not normally have contractual force: the buyer is expected to rely on a survey, commissioned by himself or his building society,[309] for information with regard to the state of the premises.[310]

On the other hand, a statement is likely to be a term of the contract if it is intended to prevent the other party from finding out the truth, has this effect, and induces him to contract in reliance on it. This was, for example, said to be the position[311] where a buyer of a horse was about to examine it but was induced to buy without examination by the seller's statement that "You need not look for anything; the horse is perfectly sound. If there was anything the matter with the horse I should tell you". An earlier case,[312] in which a similar statement by a seller was held not to have contractual force, turns on the special facts that the sale was at Tattersall's and that sales there were known by both parties to be without warranty unless the contrary was expressly stated in the catalogue.

9–060 **Importance of the representation.** A statement is likely to be a term of the contract where its importance is such that, if it had not been made, the representee would not have entered into the contract at all.[313] Such a statement can be a term of the contract even though it conflicts with a previous written statement. Thus, in *Couchman v Hill*[314] a heifer was put up for auction under printed conditions of sale which provided that no warranty was given. A bidder asked whether the heifer was in calf, adding that, if she were, he would not bid. He bought the heifer after being assured that she was not in calf, and it was held that this assurance was a term of the contract. On the other hand, in *Oscar Chess Ltd v Williams*,[315] where the defendant sold a car for £280 honestly describing it as a 1948 Morris 10 when it was in fact a 1939 model worth £175, the statement that the car was a 1948 model was held not to be a term of the contract. If in this case, the buyers had known the truth, they might still have bought the car (though for less money)[316] but if the buyer in *Couchman v Hill* had known the truth, he would not have bought at all.

[308] (1947) 80 Ll. L.R. 286; cf. *Mahon v Ainscough* [1952] 1 All E.R. 337; *Eustace v Kempe-Roberts* [1964] C.L.Y. 3280.
[309] *Smith v Eric S Bush* [1990] 1 A.C. 831; para.9–033.
[310] See *Longman v Blount* (1896) 12 T.L.R. 520; cf. *Terence Ltd v Nelson* (1937) 157 L.T. 254.
[311] *Schwawel v Reade* [1913] 2 I.R. 64 HL.
[312] *Hopkins v Tanqueray* (1854) 15 C.B. 130.
[313] *Bannerman v White* (1861) 10 C.B. (N.S.) 844.
[314] [1947] K.B. 554. Alternatively, the statement was said to be a collateral contract: para.9–063; see also *Otto v Bolton* [1936] 2 K.B. 46.
[315] [1957] 1 W.L.R. 370.
[316] cf. *Moore v Khan Ghauri* [1991] 2 E.G.L.R. 9.

**Relative expertise and knowledge of the parties.** The question whether a statement is a contractual term or a mere representation may turn on the relative abilities of the parties to ascertain the truth of what was stated.[317] In *Oscar Chess Ltd v Williams* the seller was a private person to whom the car had been previously sold as a 1948 model, with a forged logbook. The main reason why his statement as to the age of the car was not a term of the contract was that he had no special knowledge as to the age of the car, while the buyers were car dealers, and so in at least as good a position as the seller to know whether the statement was true.[318] The case may be contrasted with *Dick Bentley Productions Ltd v Harold Smith (Motors) Ltd*[319] where a dealer sold a Bentley car, representing that it had only done 20,000 miles since being fitted with a replacement engine, when in fact it had done nearly 100,000 miles since then. He was clearly in a better position than the buyer to know whether the representation was true, and it was held to be a warranty. Salmon LJ based this conclusion on the orthodox test of contractual intention,[320] while Lord Denning MR took a different view. He held that any inducing representation was prima facie a warranty, though the representor could "rebut this inference if he can show that it really was an innocent misrepresentation, in that he was in fact innocent of fault in making it, and that it would not be reasonable for him in the circumstances to be bound by it".[321] The view that an inducing misrepresentation has contractual force unless the representor can disprove "fault" is hard to reconcile with cases in which representors have escaped liability for breach of contract without having disproved "fault"; and in some of these the representors were clearly careless.[322] The representor will often be careless where he is in a better position than the representee to know the truth, but *Gilchester Properties Ltd v Gomm*[323] shows that this fact is not, for the present purpose, decisive.[324] In that case, a statement by the vendor of a block of flats as to the rent at which the flats were let was held to have no contractual force, though obviously the vendor was in a better position than the purchaser to know the truth. Of course, a representor who is guilty of "fault" may be liable for damages in tort at common law or under the Misrepresentation Act;[325] but such liability may differ in extent from liability for breach of contract.[326] **9–061**

[317] cf. *Esso Petroleum Co Ltd v Mardon* [1976] Q.B. 801, where this test was applied to determine the existence of a collateral contract (para.9–063).

[318] cf. *Routledge v McKay* [1954] 1 W.L.R. 615; *Hummingbird Motors v Hobbs* [1986] R.T.R. 276 (para.9–062), where the seller was not a dealer, though he occasionally sold cars; and see *Harrison v Knowles & Foster* [1918] 1 K.B. 608. Contrast *Beale v Taylor* [1967] 1 W.L.R. 1193; this case is hard to reconcile with *Oscar Chess Ltd v Williams* [1957] 1 W.L.R. 370 which was not cited to the court.

[319] [1965] 1 W.L.R. 623.

[320] *Dick Bentley Productions Ltd v Harold Smith (Motors) Ltd* [1965] 1 W.L.R. 623 at 629.

[321] *Dick Bentley Productions Ltd v Harold Smith (Motors) Ltd* [1965] 1 W.L.R. 623 at 627–628. Contrast his dissenting judgment in *Howard Marine & Dredging Co Ltd v A Ogden & Son (Excavations) Ltd* [1978] Q.B. 574 at 591, applying the test of whether the statement was "intended to be binding".

[322] e.g. *Redgrave v Hurd* (1881) 20 Ch D. 1; para.9–033.

[323] [1948] 1 All E.R. 493.

[324] See criticisms in *Heilbut, Symons & Co v Buckleton* [1913] A.C. 30 at 50 of *De Lassalle v Guildford* [1901] 2 K.B. 215 on this point.

[325] See paras 9–042–9–055.

[326] See paras 9–073–9–082; the claim in the *Dick Bentley* case was limited to £400.

9–062 **Statements of opinion.** Statements of opinion which are so vague that they cannot be verified are mere puffs and have no legal effect.[327] But a statement which is one of opinion in the sense that it states a fact which is difficult, but not impossible, to verify may be a term of the contract. In *Jendwine v Slade*[328] Lord Kenyon held that statements that two pictures were respectively by Claude Lorrain and Teniers were not warranties: the authenticity of pictures painted "some centuries back" could only be a matter of opinion. But later cases show that this is not an inflexible rule. In *Power v Barham*[329] it was held that a statement that certain pictures were by Canaletto could be a warranty, *Jendwine v Slade* being distinguished on the ground that Canaletto was "not a very old painter".[330] Similarly, in *Leaf v International Galleries*[331] the Court of Appeal indicated that a representation made in 1945 that a picture was a Constable could be a warranty; though the position will be different where the seller of a picture makes an attribution but expressly disclaims expert knowledge.[332] Nor will a statement be a warranty as to a quality if the statement is *expressly* one of opinion or belief. Thus, where the seller of a car said that, to the best of his knowledge and belief, the odometer reading was correct, it was held that he had not given a warranty of such correctness, and that he was not liable merely because, unknown to him, the odometer had been tampered with before he had acquired the car.[333]

9–063 **Collateral contract.** It may not be possible for a statement made during the negotiations leading up to the contract to take effect as one of its terms. The contract may be in writing, so that extrinsic evidence cannot be used to add to it, or to vary it;[334] or the statement may be oral and the contract one which the law requires to be in, or evidenced in, writing.[335] In such cases[336] the oral statement may nevertheless be enforceable as a "collateral contract". There are then two contracts between the parties: the main (written) contract and the collateral (oral) contract, both relating to the same subject-matter. In *De Lassalle v Guildford*[337] the intending lessee of a house refused to execute the lease unless the landlord first assured him that the drains were in good order. The landlord gave this assurance, which was not incorporated in the lease. He was nonetheless held liable, when the drains were found to be defective, for breach of a collateral contract. The statement made on behalf of the landlord in *Esso Petroleum Co Ltd v Mardon*[338] was similarly held to amount to a collateral contract.

[327] See para.9–013.
[328] (1797) 2 Esp. 571; cf. *Gee v Lucas* (1867) 16 L.T. 357.
[329] (1836) 4 A. & E. 473.
[330] *Power v Barham* (1836) 4 A. & E. 473 at 476. He had died in 1768.
[331] [1950] 2 K.B. 86. Quaere, however, whether there was such a warranty; para.8–021, fn.127.
[332] *Harlingdon and Leinster Enterprises Ltd v Christopher Hull Fine Art Ltd* [1991] 1 Q.B. 564.
[333] *Humming Bird Motors v Hobbs* [1986] R.T.R. 276. Liability in negligence was also excluded; and the seller had not misrepresented his knowledge or belief: cf. para.9–018.
[334] See para.6–021 and following, especially para.6–038.
[335] *Angell v Duke* (1875) L.R. 10 Q.B. 174; *Hill v Harris* [1965] 2 Q.B. 601; Law Com. No.164, paras 5.7–5.8; paras 5–006–5–014.
[336] See *J Evans & Son (Portsmouth) Ltd v Andrew Merzario Ltd* [1976] 1 W.L.R. 1078 at 1083.
[337] [1901] 2 K.B. 215.
[338] [1976] Q.B. 801; para.9–048.

**A test of intention.** A statement can, it seems, take effect as a collateral contract only if two conditions are satisfied. First, it must have been intended to have contractual effect; and secondly, there must be some indication that the parties intended it to take effect as a collateral contract and not simply as a term in the main contract. These requirements have already been discussed[339] and it will suffice here to recall the statement of principle by Lord Moulton in *Heilbut, Symons & Co v Buckleton*[340]: 9–064

> "There may be a contract the consideration for which is the making of some other contract ... Such collateral contracts, the sole effect of which is to vary or add to the terms of the principal contract, are therefore viewed with suspicion by the law ... Not only the terms of such contracts but the existence of an *animus contrahendi* on the part of all the parties to them must be clearly shown".[341]

It follows that statements made during negotiations leading up to the contract will not amount to a collateral contract if the main contract provides that they are *not* to have this effect.[342] Contractual intention may also be negatived by the fact that there was a considerable interval of time between the making of the statement alleged to constitute the collateral contract and the conclusion of the main contract.[343]

**Consideration.** In one respect a person who relies on a statement as a collateral contract is at first sight in a worse position than one who relies on it as a term of the main contract. Since a collateral contract exists apart from the main contract, it must be supported by *separate* consideration. This requirement is usually satisfied by entering into the main contract, so that the only cases in which this analysis could give rise to difficulty are those in which the party relying on the collateral contract is already bound to enter into the main contract, e.g. where a lease is executed in performance of an agreement to enter into it.[344] Even in such cases, however, the act of entering into the main contract (i.e. the execution of the lease) may constitute consideration for the collateral contract if that act in fact conferred a benefit on the other party.[345] 9–065

### (v) *Damages in lieu of rescission*

**Misrepresentation Act 1967 s.2(2).** Before the Misrepresentation Act, damages could not be awarded for a wholly innocent misrepresentation (i.e. for one that was neither fraudulent nor negligent)[346] if it did not have contractual force.[347] The principal remedy for innocent misrepresentation was rescission, though when 9–066

---

339 See paras 5–010, 6–038.

340 [1913] A.C. 30 at 47; para.4–007; *IBA v EMI (Electronics) Ltd* (1980) 14 B.L.R. 1 (para.14–008).

341 cf. *Hill v Harris* [1965] 2 Q.B. 601.

342 *Inntrepreneur Pub Co (GL) v East Crown Ltd* [2000] 2 Lloyd's Rep. 611 at 614 ("entire agreement" clause). Contrast *Cheverny Consulting Ltd v Whitehead Mann Ltd* [2005] EWHC 2431 (for further proceedings, see [2006] EWCA Civ 1303).

343 *Inntrepreneur Pub Co (GL) v East Crown Ltd* [2000] 2 Lloyd's Rep. 611 at 617 (five years).

344 See the discussion of *Brikom Investments Ltd v Carr* [1979] Q.B. 467; para.3–065.

345 *Williams v Roffey Bros & Nicholls (Contractors) Ltd* [1991] 1 Q.B. 1; para.3–050.

346 See paras 9–038, 9–042.

347 *Redgrave v Hurd* (1881) 20 Ch D. 1; *Archer v Brown* [1985] Q.B. 401 at 416; cf. para.9–033.

a contract was rescinded, the court could make some form of monetary adjustment by granting an "indemnity".[348] This position was unsatisfactory since, in cases of wholly innocent misrepresentation, the entire transaction would have to be set aside (even though the misrepresentation related to a matter of relatively minor importance), if any remedy at all were to be given to the representee. Section 2(2) of the Misrepresentation Act partly cures this defect by giving the court a discretionary power to declare the contract subsisting and to award damages in lieu of rescission. It provides:

> "Where a person has entered into a contract after a misrepresentation has been made to him otherwise than fraudulently,[349] and he would be entitled, by reason of the misrepresentation, to rescind the contract, then, if it is claimed, in any proceedings arising out of the contract, that the contract ought to be or has been rescinded, the court or arbitrator may declare the contract subsisting and award damages in lieu of rescission, if of opinion that it would be equitable to do so, having regard to the nature of the misrepresentation and the loss that would be caused by it if the contract were upheld, as well as to the loss that rescission would cause to the other party".

9–067 **Discretionary award.** The power to uphold the contract and to award damages in lieu of rescission is discretionary: neither party has a right to require its exercise. The concluding words of the subsection specify the factors which the court is to consider in deciding whether to exercise the power. It seems that the court can balance the interests of the parties in on the one hand seeking and on the other resisting rescission. The court is likely to confine the representee to damages in lieu if the representation related to a relatively minor[350] matter and if the representor was not guilty of fault,[351] though it may also do so even if the representation is just short of fraudulent, or if the loss caused to the representee by rescission would grossly exceed the loss caused to the representor by upholding the contract.[352] On the other hand, the "policing function"[353] of the remedy of rescission may also be taken into account: this was the ground on which the court refused to uphold a contract of reinsurance which had been induced by a broker's material misrepresentation.[354]

9–068 **In lieu of rescission.** Damages under the subsection can be awarded only "in lieu of rescission", so that the representee cannot rescind *and* claim such damages.[355] If he rescinds on account of a wholly innocent misrepresentation[356] which has no contractual force,[357] any claim for monetary compensation will continue to be

---

348 See paras 9–090–9–091.

349 i.e. it is not confined to wholly innocent misrepresentation.

350 *William Sindall Plc v Cambridgeshire CC* [1994] 1 W.L.R. 1016 at 1036, 1043.

351 See *The Lucy* [1983] 1 Lloyd's Rep. 188 at 202.

352 *UCB Corporate Services v Thomason* [2005] EWCA Civ 225; [2005] 1 All E.R. (Comm) 601 (where fraud was not pleaded, but the representations were described as "multiple, intentional … and fundamental").

353 *Highlands Ins Co v Continental Ins Co* [1987] 1 Lloyd's Rep. 109 at 118.

354 *Highlands Ins Co v Continental Ins Co* [1987] 1 Lloyd's Rep. 109 at 118; cf. *TSB v Camfield* [1995] 1 W.L.R. 430 at 439.

355 *Highlands Ins Co v Continental Ins Co* [1987] 1 Lloyd's Rep. 109 at 118; cf. *TSB v Camfield* [1995] 1 W.L.R. 430 at 439.

356 See at fn.346.

357 For "incorporated misrepresentations" see paras 9–070, 9–108.

governed by the principles which determine the extent of an indemnity.[358] The misrepresentee can, however, still rescind *and* claim damages for fraud, since fraudulent misrepresentation is expressly excepted from the subsection; and there is nothing in the subsection to prevent him from rescinding *and* claiming damages for negligence at common law or under s.2(1).

**The need for a subsisting right to rescind.** A further consequence of the rule that damages under the subsection are "in lieu of rescission" is more controversial. Such damages are available where a person "would be entitled, by reason of the misrepresentation, to rescind the contract". It is not clear from these words whether the court can award damages if the representee once had the right to rescind, but has lost it under one of the bars to rescission to be discussed below.[359] Conflicting views on the point had been expressed in decisions at first instance,[360] but in *Salt v Stratstone Specialist Ltd*[361] the Court of Appeal held that the power to award damages "*in lieu* of rescission" carried the implication that rescission must still have been available at the time the representee claims to have rescinded the contract. Although rescission was still available and was, in fact, ordered in the *Salt* case, this decision must be taken to have settled the point unless and until it is considered by the Supreme Court. While the interpretation of the Court of Appeal seems most consistent with the ordinary meaning of the wording of s.2(2), as a matter of policy it is hard to see why the factors which bar the right to rescind should limit the discretion to award damages. The intervention of third party rights, for instance, may make it highly inappropriate to rescind the contract,[362] but it does not follow that it should prevent the court from awarding monetary compensation to the representee.[363] And if the right to rescind is lost because it is not possible to make counter-restitution through no fault of the representee, an award of damages in lieu may also be regarded as appropriate. Since damages may still be awarded if s.2(1) applies, or negligent misrepresentation is proved, it is only in a case of wholly innocent misrepresentation where the right to rescind has been lost that there is the risk of what might be thought an unjust outcome for the representee. **9–069**

**Incorporated misrepresentation.** A representation originally made to induce a contract may become a term of the contract by being subsequently incorporated in it; and this does not affect the right to rescind for misrepresentation.[364] In such cases the representee is entitled as of right to damages *for breach of contract*;[365] and this right is not subject to the discretion of the court. **9–070**

[358] See paras 9–090–9–091.
[359] See paras 9–110–9–131.
[360] For decisions that damages may still be awarded, see: *Thomas Witter Ltd v TBP Industries Ltd* [1996] 2 All E.R. 573 at 589–590. Contrast: *Zanzibar v British Aerospace (Lancaster House) Ltd* [2001] 1 W.L.R. 2333; *Floods of Queensferry Ltd v Shand Construction Ltd (No.3)* [2000] B.L.R. 81 at 93; *Pankhania v Hackney LBC* [2002] EWHC 2441 (Ch) at [76].
[361] [2015] EWCA Civ 745; [2015] 2 C.L.C. 206.
[362] See para.9–124. The third party cannot invoke s.2(2): see *TSB Bank Plc v Camfield* [1995] 1 W.L.R. 430.
[363] See *Thomas Witter Ltd v TBP Industries Ltd* [1996] 2 All E.R. 573 at 589–590.
[364] See para.9–108.
[365] See para.20–002.

9–071 **Claims by consumers.** As noted above, a consumer with a right to redress under the Consumer Protection from Unfair Trading Regulations 2008 is not entitled to damages under s.2 of the Misrepresentation Act in respect of the conduct constituting the misrepresentation.[366] Since this does not affect the right to rescind, the court still has a discretion to refuse rescission, but since it could no longer award damages in lieu even if it was otherwise inclined to do so, it is unlikely to so refuse.

## (b) Measure

9–072 Where a representee claims damages, questions may arise as to the basis of assessment and remoteness. These questions are discussed generally in Ch.20,[367] but some special factors relating to misrepresentation must be considered here.

### (i) *Basis of assessment*

9–073 **Tort and contract distinguished.**[368] Liability for misrepresentation may arise in tort (where the representation is made fraudulently or negligently) or in contract (where the representation has contractual force). This distinction affects the assessment of damages in the most common case of misrepresentation: namely, where a seller represents that the subject-matter of a contract has a quality which in fact it lacks. The general principle is that in tort the claimant is entitled to such damages as will put him into the position in which he would have been if the tort had not been committed; while in contract he is entitled to be put into the position in which he would have been if the contract had been performed.[369] It is thought to follow that in tort the claimant is entitled to be put into the position in which he would have been if the representation *had not been made*, while in contract he is entitled to be put into the position in which he would have been if the representation *had been true*.[370] If the representation induces the claimant to buy something which, but for the misrepresentation, he would not have bought at all, it follows that the damages in tort are prima facie the amount by which the actual value of the thing bought is less than *the price* paid for it.[371] In contract, on the other hand, the damages are prima facie the amount by which the actual value of the thing bought is less than *the value which it would have had if the representation had been true*;[372] and this value is not relevant to the assessment of

[366] Section 2(4); see para.9–051.
[367] See para.20–040 and following.
[368] Treitel 32 M.L.R. 556.
[369] See para.20–024.
[370] *Smith Kline French Laboratories Ltd v Long* [1989] 1 W.L.R. 1 at 6; *East v Maurer* [1991] 1 W.L.R. 461 at 464, 467, 468; *Gran Gelato Ltd v Richcliff (Group) Ltd* [1992] Ch. 570 at 575; *South Australia Asset Management Corp v York Montague Ltd* [1997] A.C. 191 at 216.
[371] This rule is stated in many cases: see, e.g. *Peek v Derry* (1887) 37 Ch D. 541 at 578 (reversed on liability 14 App. Cas. 337); *Twycross v Grant* (1877) 2 C.P.D. 496 at 504; *Smith v Eric S Bush* [1990] 1 A.C. 831 at 851.
[372] See, e.g. Sale of Goods Act 1979 s.53(3); an alternative measure is the cost of making the defect good (para.20–042).

damages in tort.[373] If the claimant has made a bad bargain, i.e. the value of the thing bought is less than the price paid even if the representation had been true, the claimant will do better under the tortious measure and, if he has a cause of action in both tort and contract, he may choose whichever is the more beneficial remedy.[374]

**Misrepresentation Act 1967 s.2(1).** The generally held view is that damages under s.2(1) of the 1967 Act are "the same as in an action of deceit",[375] i.e. that they are to be assessed on a tortious basis. It is submitted that this is correct since the reference to fraud in s.2(1) indicates that the statutory cause of action is tortious in nature and, as already noted, liability under s.2(1) is "essentially founded on negligence".[376] Accordingly, the tortious basis of assessment applies where the representee has received something which lacked a quality that it was represented to have. 9–074

**Breach of contractual duty of care.** A representation may have contractual force, but the contract may be to the effect, not that the representation is true, but that the representor has taken due care in making it. This was the position in *Esso Petroleum Co Ltd v Mardon*[377] where a tenant was induced to take a lease of a petrol station by a statement made on behalf of the landlord that the future annual turnover could be estimated at 200,000 gallons. The estimate had been carelessly made and the actual turnover was much lower. The landlord was held liable both for negligence at common law and for breach of collateral warranty.[378] But even on the latter basis the tenant did not recover damages for loss of his bargain[379] (i.e. for loss of the profit that he would have made if the turnover had been 200,000 gallons); for the warranty was not that 200,000 gallons would be sold but only that the estimate had been prepared with due care.[380] 9–075

**Loss of opportunity.** In tort, the claimant cannot recover damages for loss of bargain, i.e. he cannot normally recover any element of lost profit. But as the Court of Appeal recognised in *East v Maurer,*[381] he may be entitled to damages 9–076

[373] *Smith New Court Securities Ltd v Scrimgeour Vickers (Asset Management) Ltd* [1997] A.C. 254 at 267 (Lord Browne-Wilkinson) and 283 (Lord Steyn) disapproving *Downs v Chappell* [1997] 1 W.L.R. 426 at 444 on this point; see also *South Australia Asset Management Corp v York Montague Ltd* [1997] A.C. 191 at 215–216 (Lord Hoffmann) expressing no concluded view on the point.

[374] *Wemyss v Karim* [2016] EWCA Civ 27 at [40].

[375] See, e.g. *André &Cie SA v Ets Michel Blanc & Fils* [1977] 2 Lloyd's Rep. 166 at 181; affirmed [1979] 2 Lloyd's Rep. 427, without reference to this point); *Archer v Brown* [1985] Q.B. 401 at 426–427 (denying an item of loss of bargain damages); contrast *Davis & Co (Wines) Ltd v Afa Minerva (EMI) Ltd* [1974] 2 Lloyd's Rep. 27 at 32; Cartwright [1987] Conv. 423.

[376] See text to fn.272.

[377] [1976] Q.B. 801.

[378] See paras 9–048, 9–063.

[379] *Esso Petroleum Co Ltd v Mardon* [1976] Q.B. 801 at 820.

[380] cf. *Lion Nathan v CC Bottlers Ltd* [1996] 1 W.L.R. 1438 (warranty that achievable *profits* had been "calculated in good faith and on a proper basis"); *Wemyss v Karim* [2016] EWCA Civ 27 at [27].

[381] [1991] 1 W.L.R. 461; para.20–024. See also: *4 Eng Ltd v Harper* [2008] EWHC 915 (Ch); [2009] Ch. 91 where damages were discounted to reflect the fact that the owner of the alternative business may not have agreed to sell; *Khakshouri v Jimenez* [2017] EWHC 3392 where the main issue was thought to be the date of assessment: see para.9–083.

for loss of the chance of making profits out of *another* business in which he would have invested, had he not been induced by the misrepresentation to enter into the contract with the defendant. When one takes into account damages for this sort of "loss of opportunity" the distinction between the bases of assessment in tort and contract can be hard to draw. In *Clef Aquitaine Sarl v Laporte Materials (Barrow) Ltd*[382] the claimant was induced by fraudulent misrepresentation to purchase the defendant's product at a higher price than he would have, as part of a 20-year distribution agreement. The claimant still sold the product to customers at a profit, but claimed that, if it had not been for the defendant's misrepresentation, he would have been able to sell at an even higher profit and this difference in profit was recoverable in a claim for misrepresentation. The Court of Appeal found that the difference in profit levels was recoverable, though on slightly differing grounds. According to Simon Brown LJ it was appropriate to extend the loss of opportunity reasoning employed in the earlier case of *East v Maurer* by awarding as damages the *higher* profits which the claimant would have generated under the contract he would have made with the defendant (and not a third party) had the truth been known. According to Ward LJ it was possible to employ the conventional measure of the difference between the price paid and the actual value. Where, as here, there was no market, the actual value was the price which the claimant would have paid had the true state of affairs been known.[383] The fact that the claimant was still able to sell the goods for a sum in excess of that value was disregarded since it was concerned with events occurring after the date of the transaction.[384]

Whichever approach is adopted, it is submitted that the decisions in both *East v Maurer* and the *Clef Aquitaine* case are correct.[385] They are consistent with the aim, in tort, of putting the claimant into the position in which he would have been if the tort had not been committed, i.e. as if the misrepresentation had not been made. Indeed, in another case of fraudulent misrepresentation the principle applied in *East v Maurer* was taken further to allow the claimant to recover not only the profits he would have made under an alternative investment, but also the further profits he would have made from re-investing those profits up until the date of trial (the "profits on profits").[386] It was however emphasised that there was clear evidence of the claimant's remarkable track record as a successful investor.[387] Furthermore, the duty to mitigate may require the claimant to borrow the money lost so as to make the alternative investment and, if so, damages will

---

[382] [2001] Q.B. 488.

[383] Based on the principles expounded by Devlin J in the context of the sale of defective goods: *Biggin & Co Ltd v Permanite Ltd* [1951] 1 K.B. 422 at 437–440. See para.20–050 and following.

[384] *Jamal v Moolla Dawood Sons & Co* [1916] 1 A.C. 175. For the significance of the date of transaction, see para.9–083; cf. para.20–110.

[385] Both are cases of fraud. In principle, the same "loss of opportunity" claim may be made in negligence (and under s.2(1) of Misrepresentation Act 1967, especially if the "fiction of fraud" is applied in full: see para.9–082), but where the loss in question is a consequential loss (as it was in *East v Maurer*) the opportunity said to have been lost may be considered too remote. There is no limit of remoteness in a case of fraud: para.9–080.

[386] *Parabola Investments Ltd v Browallia Cal Ltd* [2010] EWCA Civ 486; [2010] 3 W.L.R. 1266.

[387] *Parabola Investments Ltd v Browallia Cal Ltd* [2010] EWCA Civ 486; [2010] 3 W.L.R. 1266 at [57].

be limited to the cost of borrowing.[388] By parity of reasoning with the cases in which the claimant has recovered the profits he would have made in an alternative transaction if there had been no misrepresentation, it has been held that the court must also take into account losses that would have been incurred.[389]

**Claims by sellers.** In the cases so far discussed, the misrepresentations were made *by* the seller and affected the price paid by the buyer. They may also be made *to* the seller and affect his willingness to contract with a particular buyer. The position of the seller will normally be that, but for the misrepresentation, he would not have entered into the contract to sell to the buyer. In such a case, he should not normally be entitled to the contract price, which would be consistent with the contractual measure of damages, unless in selling to the buyer he lost the opportunity to sell to another buyer[390] and the contact price is the best evidence of the price at which he may have sold to that other buyer. In one case, a seller was induced to sell a cargo of sunflower oil to a company by the fraudulent misrepresentation of the defendant that the company was able to pay. This amounted to a continuing representation[391] which was still being relied upon by the seller when he allowed the oil to be dispatched. In those circumstances, the seller could not use the oil to fulfil another contract and was therefore entitled to its market value.[392] In such a case, the contract price may be the best evidence of the market value. More difficult is the case where manufacturers of pharmaceuticals were induced to sell tablets to a company by the defendant's representation that the company intended to resell them in Central Africa; in fact they were resold in Holland. If there had been no misrepresentation, the sellers would not have sold to the company; but that sale did not affect their capacity to supply other customers and it was conceded that it could be assumed that the tablets had cost nothing to produce. Nevertheless, this was also held to be a case where the proper way of putting the sellers into the position in which they would have been, if the representation had not been made, was to ensure that they received the market value of the tablets, by analogy with the assessment of damages for conversion. As this value was not shown to exceed the contract price, the defendant was liable for no more than the contract price, less that part of it which had already been paid by the company.[393] 9–077

**Valuation by third party.** There is, finally, the possibility that a misrepresentation relating to the value of the subject-matter may be made by a third party. For example, A may lend money to B on the security of B's property in reliance on a valuation of that property negligently made by C. Here the damages for which C is liable to A are based, not on the interest which B should have paid on the loan, 9–078

[388] *Parabola Investments Ltd v Browallia Cal Ltd* [2010] EWCA Civ 486; [2010] 3 W.L.R. 1266 at [58].

[389] *Yam Seng Pte Ltd v International Trade Corp Ltd* [2013] EWHC 111 (QB); [2013] 1 Lloyd's Rep. 526 at [217].

[390] See para.9–076.

[391] See para.9–159. In this case, the continuing representation was false at all times.

[392] *Inter Export LLC v Townley* [2018] EWCA Civ 2068.

[393] *Smith Kline & French Laboratories Ltd v Long* [1989] 1 W.L.R. 1. For criticism of the decision, see *Burrows, Remedies for Torts and Breach of Contract*, 4th edn (2019) at 224–225.

but on the position in which A would have been if C had made the valuation with due care.[394] If on that assumption A would not have made the loan to B, he can recover from C not only loss of principal[395] but also damages for loss of use of the money: i.e. what he would have earned by putting the money on deposit elsewhere, or by using it to enter into other transactions.[396] But C is not liable for any interest above normal market rates which B may have undertaken to pay to A.[397] This is so whether A's claim is brought in contract[398] or in tort since C in such case undertakes only to make the valuation with due care: he makes no promise or representation that B will perform his contractual obligations to A.[399]

### *(ii) Remoteness*

**9–079** The fact that the subject-matter lacks a quality which it was represented to have may, apart from affecting its value, also cause the representee to suffer consequential loss. For example, where diseased cows are sold under representations of soundness and infect the buyer's other animals, he may be able to recover for the loss of those animals;[400] and where a business is sold under misrepresentations as to its profitability the buyer may be able to recover damages for losses suffered in the course of running the business.[401] Consequential losses can, however, be recovered only if they are not too remote.[402]

**9–080** **Fraud.** The rules as to remoteness are more favourable to the claimant in actions of deceit. Lord Denning MR has said that:

> "In fraud ... [t]he defendant is bound to make reparation for all the actual damage directly flowing from the fraudulent inducement ... It does not lie in the mouth of the fraudulent person to say that they could not reasonably have been foreseen".[403]

A number of later dicta in the House of Lords similarly regard foreseeability as irrelevant in actions for deceit.[404] The defendant will however be liable only for all loss "directly flowing" from the fraudulent inducement, e.g. he will not be

[394] Not on the position in which A would have been had C's valuation been correct: cf. at fn.380.

[395] This is subject to the limits on his recovery which may be applied as a result of *South Australia Asset Management Corp v York Montague Ltd* [1997] A.C. 191, discussed at paras 20–025–20–027.

[396] *First National Commercial Bank Plc v Humberts* [1995] 2 All E.R. 673 at 677.

[397] *Swingcastle Ltd v Gibson* [1991] 2 A.C. 223.

[398] See paras 20–025–20–027, for the scope of C's duty where this arises under a contract between A and C.

[399] *Swingcastle v Gibson* [1991] 2 A.C. 223 at 238. For the time at which the loss is suffered, see *First National Commercial Bank Plc v Humberts* [1995] 2 All E.R. 673.

[400] *Mullett v Mason* (1866) L.R. 1 C.P. 559 (fraud); *Smith v Green* (1875) 1 C.P.D. 92 (breach of contract).

[401] *Doyle v Olby (Ironmongers) Ltd* [1969] 2 Q.B. 158; Treitel 32 M.L.R. 556; *Man Nutzfahrzeuge AG v Freightliner Ltd* [2005] EWHC 2347 (Comm); cf. *Naughton v O'Callaghan* [1990] 3 All E.R. 191.

[402] See paras 20–119—20–134.

[403] *Doyle v Olby (Ironmongers) Ltd* [1969] 2 Q.B. 158 at 167.

[404] *Smith New Court Securities Ltd v Scrimgeour Vickers (Asset Management) Ltd* [1997] A.C. 254 at 265, 267, 269; cf. also *South Australia Asset Management Corp v York Montague Ltd* [1997] A.C. 191 at 215; *Kuwait Airways Corp v Iraqi Airways Corp* [2002] UKHL 19; [2002] 2 A.C. 883 at [100].

liable for loss which may be due to the claimant's own unreasonable actions.[405] Thus, the requirements of causation (and mitigation) apply, but there is no additional requirement of foreseeability;[406] dicta which appear to suggest that *some* test of remoteness applies even in fraud should be understood to refer to the requirement of causation.[407]

**Negligence.** In an action based on negligent misrepresentation at common law, the loss must be reasonably foreseeable, that being the general rule applied in actions for negligence.[408] This rule may be less favourable to the claimant than the rule in fraud but it is more favourable than the rule in a contractual action.[409] **9–081**

**Misrepresentation Act 1967 s.2(1).** Where the action is brought under s.2(1) of the Misrepresentation Act, one possible view is that the fraud rule applies by virtue of the fiction of fraud.[410] Support for this view is provided by *Royscot Trust Ltd v Rogerson*,[411] where a car-dealer induced a finance company to enter into a hire-purchase agreement by misrepresenting the amount of the deposit paid by the customer, who later defaulted and sold the car to a third party who obtained good title to the car. The dealer was held liable to the finance company under s.2(1) for the balance due under the agreement on the ground that "the plain words"[412] of the subsection required the court to apply the fraud rule, under which the dealer was liable for "all the losses" suffered by the finance company "even if those losses were unforeseeable".[413] Later discussions of the *Royscot* case in the House of Lords somewhat pointedly refrain from expressing any concluded view as to its correctness;[414] and in one of these discussions the question whether the fraud rule should be applied to cases of "innocent misrepresentation under the Misrepresentation Act 1967"[415] is expressly left open by Lord Browne-Wilkinson. It is submitted that the words of the subsection are not so "plain"[416] as to compel the court to apply the fraud rule in the present **9–082**

[405] *Doyle v Olby (Ironmongers) Ltd* [1969] 2 Q.B. 158 at 171.

[406] *Downs v Chappell* [1997] 1 W.L.R. 426 at 434.

[407] *Doyle v Olby (Ironmongers) Ltd* [1969] 2 Q.B. 158 at 169; *Royscot Trust Ltd v Rogerson* [1991] 2 Q.B. 297 at 307; *Smith New Court Securities Ltd v Scrimgeour Vickers (Asset Management) Ltd* [1997] A.C. 254 at 285; cf. *Man Nutzfahrzeuge AG v Freightliner Ltd* [2005] EWHC 2347 at [213].

[408] *The Wagon Mound* [1961] A.C. 388; cf. *Esso Petroleum Co Ltd v Mardon* [1976] Q.B. 801 at 822.

[409] See *The Heron II* [1969] 1 A.C. 350; paras 20–122 and 20–133.

[410] See para.9–054.

[411] [1991] 2 Q.B. 297; Hooley 107 L.Q.R. 547; cf. *William Sindall Plc v Cambridgeshire CC* [1994] 1 W.L.R. 1016 at 1037, 1043.

[412] *Royscot Trust Ltd v Rogerson* [1991] 2 Q.B. 297 at 306; cf. at 309.

[413] *Royscot Trust Ltd v Rogerson* [1991] 2 Q.B. 297 at 307.

[414] *Smith New Court Securities Ltd v Scrimgeour Vickers (Asset Management) Ltd* [1997] A.C. 254 at 267, 283; *South Australia Asset Management Corp v York Montague Ltd* [1997] A.C. 191 at 216. See also: *Avon Ins Plc v Swire Fraser Ltd* [2000] 1 All E.R. (Comm) 573 at 576; *Raiffeisen Zentralbank Österreich AG v Royal Bank of Scotland Plc* [2010] EWHC 1392 (Comm); [2011] 1 Lloyd's Rep. 123 at [386].

[415] *Smith New Court Securities Ltd v Scrimgeour Vickers (Asset Management) Ltd* [1997] A.C. 254 at 267; the reference seems from the context to be to s.2(1).

[416] *Smith New Court Securities Ltd v Scrimgeour Vickers (Asset Management) Ltd* [1997] A.C. 254 at 283, referring to "the rather loose wording" of the 1967 Act.

context. We have seen that there are other contexts[417] in which the courts have not given a similar literal effect to the fiction of fraud, which could be interpreted to refer to the *existence* of liability, rather than to its extent. This view derives some support from the legislative history of the subsection.[418] It can also be supported on the policy ground that the severity of a rule which is justified in cases of actual fraud will often be inappropriate where the defendant is merely negligent.[419]

### *(iii) Fluctuations in value*

9–083 **Date of transaction rule.** Some of the earlier cases which had established the principle that damages in tort for misrepresentation were based on the difference between the price paid by the injured party and the actual value of the subject-matter[420] also supported the so-called "date of transaction"[421] rule, by which for this purpose the relevant value of the subject-matter was its value at the time of its acquisition.[422] Thus, if the claimant had been induced by fraud to pay £15 each for shares which at that time were worth no more than £10, the defendant was liable for £5 per share, but not for further loss suffered by reason of any later fall in the market value of the shares. As with the so-called "date of breach" rule, which is applied to damages for breach of contract, the principle which explains the date of transaction rule, and the "exceptions" to it, is the claimant's duty to mitigate.[423] In the example just considered, the further loss is irrecoverable because the claimant's retention of the shares on a falling market amounts to a failure on his part to take reasonable steps to mitigate his loss.[424]

9–084 **"Exceptions".** While the "date of transaction" rule continues to be recognised as the general rule,[425] it follows that its inflexible application could lead to injustice where the claimant has acted reasonably in retaining the subject-matter after that date. The courts have therefore recognised "exceptions" to the general rule where the assumptions on which it is based are not in fact true. This may be so for a variety of reasons:[426] the subject-matter may suffer from some hidden flaw, not

417 See para.9–054.

418 See para.9–054.

419 *Yam Seng Pte Ltd v International Trade Corp Ltd* [2013] EWHC 111 (QB); [2013] 1 Lloyd's Rep. 526 at [206]; cf. *Shepheard v Broome* [1904] A.C. 342 at 345, 346.

420 See para.9–073.

421 *Smith New Court Securities Ltd v Scrimgeour Vickers (Asset Management) Ltd* [1997] A.C. 254 at 283.

422 e.g. *Twycross v Grant* (1877) 2 C.P.D. 469; *Peek v Derry* (1887) 37 Ch D. 541; *McConnell v Wright* [1903] 1 Ch. 546.

423 See para.20–076.

424 cf. see para.20–106 (mitigation by means of a substitute transaction).

425 *Smith New Court Securities Ltd v Scrimgeour Vickers (Asset Management) Ltd* [1997] A.C. 254 at 267, 284; cf. *OMV Petrom SA v Glencore International AG* [2016] EWCA Civ 778; [2016] 2 Lloyd's Rep. 432 (for criticism of this decision on the facts, see Summers and Kramer 133 L.Q.R. 41).

426 The instances provided by Lord Browne-Wilkinson, in *Smith New Court Securities Ltd v Scrimgeour Vickers (Asset Management) Ltd* [1997] A.C. 254 at 267, were described by him as "illustrative rather than exclusive": *Parabola Investments Ltd v Browallia Cal Ltd* [2010] EWCA Civ 486; [2010] 3 W.L.R. 1266 at [34].

known to the market,[427] so that its market value at the time of the transaction does not reflect its true value:[428] or the claimant may "by reason of the fraud, [be] locked into the property":[429] or the decline in value may have taken place before the claimant discovered the truth, so that the misrepresentation "continued to operate … so as to induce the (claimant) to retain"[430] the subject-matter. In such cases, damages will be based on the difference between the price which the claimant paid for the subject-matter and *either* the proceeds of his actual disposal of it,[431] *or* the proceeds which would have been realised by an earlier disposal of it which he should, acting reasonably, have made.[432] In a case of the latter kind, he will be compensated for loss due to the fall in the value of the subject-matter up to the time when it was reasonable for such a disposal to have been made, but not for loss due to any further fall in its market value after that time.[433]

**Negligence.** When the general "date of transaction" rule was first developed, liability in damages for misrepresentation existed only in cases of fraud,[434] and that rule must therefore have been restricted to such cases. More recent cases which have established "exceptions" to the general rule have likewise been cases in which the purchase of assets was induced by fraud; and they do not necessarily settle the question of how damages are to be assessed where the inducing representation is merely negligent.[435] There is however no doubt that the general rule applies to such cases, as do the exceptions to it. The rule is applied on the presumption that it gives effect to the overriding compensatory rule,[436] i.e. that it fulfils the aim of putting the claimant in the same position as if there had been no tort (in this case, misrepresentation). The overriding compensatory rule must itself take account of the requirements of causation and mitigation.[437] Where the normal operation of these requirements indicates that the date of transaction rule will under-compensate,[438] or over-compensate[439] it is not applied. **9–085**

---

427 *Smith New Court Securities Ltd v Scrimgeour Vickers (Asset Management) Ltd* [1997] A.C. 254 at 267 ("pregnant with disaster").

428 This is in fact no more than an application of the general rule. What it is really concerned with is the correct method of valuation as at the transaction date.

429 *Smith New Court Securities Ltd v Scrimgeour Vickers (Asset Management) Ltd* [1997] A.C. 254 at 267 (Lord Browne-Wilkinson); *Standard Chartered Bank v Pakistan National Shipping Co (No.3)* [2001] EWCA Civ 55; [2001] 1 All E.R. (Comm) 822 at [37].

430 *Smith New Court Securities Ltd v Scrimgeour Vickers (Asset Management) Ltd* [1997] A.C. 254 at 267; *Man Nutzfahrzeuge AG v Freightliner Ltd* [2005] EWHC 2347.

431 As in *Smith New Court Securities Ltd v Scrimgeour Vickers (Asset Management) Ltd* [1997] A.C. 254.

432 *Downs v Chappell* [1997] 1 W.L.R. 426.

433 *Downs v Chappell* [1997] 1 W.L.R. 426.

434 See para.9–038.

435 In *Thomson v Christie Manson & Woods Ltd* [2005] EWCA Civ 555; [2005] P.N.L.R. 38 at [138] May LJ emphasised that "(this) is not a fraud" case, but found that the "exceptions" laid down in the *Smith New Court* case did not apply in any event.

436 *Smith New Court Securities Ltd v Scrimgeour Vickers (Asset Management) Ltd* [1997] A.C. 254 at 284B; *County Personnel (Employment) Agency Ltd v Alan Pulver & Co* [1987] 1 W.L.R. 916 at 925–926; *Potts v Miller* 64 C.L.R. 282 at 299.

437 It is, with respect, not correct to say that "the transaction date … avoids any question of causation": *Smith New Court Securities Ltd v Scrimgeour Vickers (Asset Management) Ltd* [1997] A.C. 254 at 266C–266F (Lord Browne-Wilkinson).

438 As in the cases considered in para.9–084.

Support for the submission that the date of transaction rule and its exceptions applies equally to claims in negligence can be derived from *Downs v Chappell.*[440] In that case, the representee alleged fraud against the seller of a business but only negligence against his accountants, and *both* these defendants were held liable for an amount by which the value of the business had fallen by reason of a general market decline between the time of the sale induced by the misrepresentation and the time when the representee, acting reasonably, should have disposed of the business. If *Downs v Chappell* does not provide direct authority it is because the accountants were "recklessly negligent";[441] and recklessness suffices to give rise to liability in deceit even though it does not amount to actual dishonesty.[442]

9–086 **Misrepresentation Act 1967 s.2(1).** It is also submitted that the date of transaction rule and the "exceptions" to it apply to claims under s.2(1) of the 1967 Act. Support for this submission can be derived from *Pankhania v Hackney LBC*[443] where the issue was whether the "normal measure" produced by the date of transaction rule would over-compensate the claimant when compared to the level of recovery if the principles of causation and mitigation were applied in the ordinary way.

### (iv) *Misrepresentation Act 1967 s.2(2)*

9–087 **Basis of assessment.** Under s.2(2) "damages" may be awarded in lieu of rescission even if the misrepresentation is wholly innocent[444] and even though it has no contractual force. There is, therefore, no reason for regarding these damages as being either tortious or contractual. They are really sui generis, and s.2(2) gives no clue as to the basis of assessment. The legislative history gives some slight support to the view that the contractual basis was not to be applied;[445] and indeed it seems unreasonable to make a person who has not guaranteed the truth of his representations liable as if he had. On the other hand, a person should not actually profit from even a wholly innocent non-contractual misrepresentation; and accordingly he should be liable for the amount by which the actual

[439] *Pankhania v Hackney LBC* [2004] EWHC 323 (Ch); [2004] 1 E.G.L.R. 135 (where it was not found to result in over-compensation); para.9–086.

[440] [1997] 1 W.L.R. 426. Further support may be derived from *Naughton v O'Callaghan* [1990] 3 All E.R. 191; the case is a difficult one and is probably best explained on the basis that the market value on acquisition did not reflect the true value: see above, fn.428.

[441] *Downs v Chappell* [1997] 1 W.L.R. 426 at 431, 445.

[442] See para.9–039.

[443] [2004] EWHC 323 (Ch); [2004] 1 E.G.L.R. 135. The application of the rule and its "exceptions" could be explained by the fiction of fraud but, as submitted at para.9–054, this should not be applied literally.

[444] i.e. even though it is neither fraudulent nor negligent and even though the representor has discharged the burden of proof under s.2(1).

[445] At one stage an amendment was introduced to apply the contractual basis to actions under s.2(2): Standing Committee G, 23 February 1966. But it was withdrawn without discussion.

value of what he has transferred is less than the price received by him.[446] That is, in effect, the monetary equivalent of rescission.[447]

**Remoteness.** So far as remoteness is concerned, it is submitted that an award of damages in lieu of rescission should not extend to consequential loss at all, though it has been assumed that it does.[448] The basis for this submission is that rescission itself confers no entitlement to consequential loss,[449] so why should an award of damages *as an alternative* confer any such entitlement? Damages under s.2(2) should be limited to the monetary equivalent of rescission.[450] If the misrepresentation is negligent or there is liability under s.2(1)[451] then the claimant may also claim damages in the ordinary way and such damages may extend to consequential loss,[452] but there is no basis for their award for a wholly innocent misrepresentation. This submission can perhaps be supported by reference to s.2(3) which provides that damages may be awarded under s.2(2) against a person who is also liable under s.2(1), "but where he is so liable any award under the said subsection (2) shall be taken into account in assessing his liability under the said subsection (1)". It can be inferred from these words that damages under s.2(2) are meant to be less than damages under s.2(1) and, if the court has already awarded damages under s.2(2), any damages awarded under s.2(1) should be confined to consequential loss. That said, for s.2(2) to be invoked by the court the claimant must have sought rescission, in which case any claim for damages under s.2(1) should have been confined to consequential loss in any event, unless sought as an alternative to rescission. 9–088

A further possible explanation for the wording of s.2(3) is that consequential loss is available under s.2(2), but whereas remoteness is governed by the fraud rule under s.2(1),[453] under s.2(2) damages are limited by the contract[454] rule, which is more restrictive even than that applicable in tort to cases of negligence.[455] Dicta which support this view of the damages recoverable under s.2(2)[456] do not, however, rule out the possibility that such damages may be *less*

[446] In *UCB Corporate Services v Thomason* [2005] EWCA Civ 225; [2005] 1 All E.R. (Comm) 601 the court declined to rescind an agreement waiving the representee's entitlement under a guarantee; damages in lieu were confined to the extent that the representee was worse off as a result of the misrepresentation, rather than the sum due under the guarantee, because there was no evidence that the representee would have recovered any more than the sum paid under the waiver agreement even if it had known the truth.

[447] See Birks [1997] R.L.R. 72 for the argument that it is intended to reverse any unjust enrichment.

[448] *Davis & Co (Wines) Ltd v Afa-Minerva (EMI) Ltd* [1974] 2 Lloyd's Rep. 27; *William Sindall v Cambridgeshire CC* [1994] 1 W.L.R. 1016 at 1044.

[449] An indemnity, which may be awarded as part of rescission, is not an award of damages for consequential loss: see para.9–090.

[450] See para.9–087.

[451] If the misrepresentation is fraudulent, s.2(2) does not apply: see above, para.9–066.

[452] See *Thomas Witter Ltd v TBP Industries Ltd* [1996] 2 All E.R. 573 at 591.

[453] Though this in itself is controversial: see above, para.9–082.

[454] But see text to fn.445.

[455] See para.20–133.

[456] *William Sindall v Cambridgeshire CC* [1994] 1 W.L.R. 1016 at 1038, 1044.

than those recoverable in contract,[457] and they could be less if, under the subsection, consequential loss were not recoverable at all.

### (v) *Limit of the right to damages*

9–089 **Cases in which damages cannot be recovered as of right: innocent misrepresentation.** Although the availability of damages for misrepresentation has been greatly extended by the recognition of negligent misrepresentation at common law and the Misrepresentation Act, there is still no *right* to damages for a wholly innocent misrepresentation which has no contractual force. In the case of such a misrepresentation, the court has a discretionary power to award damages in lieu of rescission;[458] but it cannot rescind the contract, or regard it as rescinded *and* award damages. If the representee wishes to rescind for a wholly innocent non-contractual misrepresentation, and if the court does not think it equitable to declare the contract subsisting and award damages in lieu of rescission, the old rule that damages cannot be recovered for innocent misrepresentation[459] will continue to apply. In such a case the representee may, however, have a remedy by way of an indemnity.

9–090 **Indemnity.** In rescinding a contract, equity will so far as possible order each party to restore benefits received under the contract from the other.[460] In the simplest case, the seller will have to restore the price and the buyer the thing sold. It is sometimes necessary, as part of the process of rescission, to go further and to order one party to "restore" a benefit not received directly by him. Suppose, for example, that a buyer rescinds after having, under the terms of the contract, paid the price to a third party. There is little doubt that in such a case rescission would entitle the buyer to recover the money so paid from the seller. Any question between the seller and third party would not concern the buyer.

On the same principle, the buyer can sometimes recover an "indemnity" in respect of certain expenses; while other expenses are regarded as damages and may therefore be irrecoverable in cases of wholly innocent non-contractual misrepresentation. The distinction can be illustrated by reference to *Whittington v Seale-Hayne*.[461] A tenant had taken a lease of premises for the purpose of breeding poultry; he had done so in reliance on a representation that the premises were in good sanitary condition. In fact the water supply was poisoned so that the tenant's manager became ill and most of the birds died. The landlord submitted to rescission and agreed to repay £20 in respect of rent and rates paid, and repairs done, by the tenant under the lease. On the other hand, claims for loss of profits and loss of stock were disallowed as they were clearly claims for damages. Further claims for removal expenses[462] and medical expenses were rejected on the same ground: they were not claims for an indemnity, since such claims could

[457] *William Sindall v Cambridgeshire CC* [1994] 1 W.L.R. 1016, above, at 1038 ("not necessary … to discuss the circumstances in which they may be less").
[458] See para.9–066.
[459] See para.9–066.
[460] See para.9–119.
[461] (1900) 82 L.T. 49; 16 T.L.R. 181; 44 S.J. 229.
[462] On this point, cf. *Redgrave v Hurd* (1881) 20 Ch D. 1.

be allowed only in respect of expenses incurred in discharging obligations *created* by the contract.[463] The important distinction is that between the money spent on rates and repairs on the one hand, and the removal and medical expenses on the other. It is that the lease obliged the tenant to pay rates and to do repairs, but not to move in and employ a manager. The tenant's undertaking to pay rates and to do repairs was really *part of the price* for the lease of the premises. If the lease had provided that the landlord should do these things, he would no doubt have charged a higher rent, which he would clearly have had to restore. He was under a similar liability in respect of part of the price not paid directly to him, or not paid in cash. The tenant's removal and medical expenses could not be regarded in this way. On the facts of the case a claim for damages under s.2(1) of the Misrepresentation Act would now almost certainly succeed;[464] but if the defendant could discharge the burden of proof under that subsection[465] the representee would still be restricted to a claim for an indemnity. He could not rescind *and* get damages under s.2(2) of the Act.[466]

**Indemnity and damages.** The distinction between indemnity and damages, it is submitted, is that stated in the preceding paragraph, but there is thought to be some conflict of opinion on the point in *Newbigging v Adam*.[467] The representee was induced by the defendants' fraud to enter into a partnership with them and another person. On rescinding the contract of partnership he was clearly entitled to get back the money which he had paid for his share. The Court of Appeal held that he was also entitled to be indemnified against his liability to pay debts incurred by the partnership.[468] The crucial point is that it is a term of a contract of partnership, or a legal incident of it, that each partner is liable for the partnership debts. Hence any partner who pays such debts performs an obligation *under that contract*, though it is also true that the debts arise under another contract (i.e. that with the creditor of the partnership). Accordingly Cotton LJ said that the representee was entitled to an indemnity "against the obligations which he has *contracted under the contract which is set aside*".[469] Bowen LJ similarly said that he was entitled to be restored to his original position "so far as regards the rights and obligations *created by the contract into which he has been induced to enter*".[470] Only Fry LJ appears to state a broader view when he says that the representee is entitled to an indemnity not only against obligations "created by" the contract but also against such "obligations *entered into under the contract* as are within the reasonable expectation of the parties to the contract".[471] What seems to have troubled Fry LJ is that the *debts of the partnership* were not "created by" the contract of partnership. But the representee's *liability to* 9–091

[463] For a possible extension of the right to necessary maintenance costs, see *Lagunas Nitrate Co v Lagunas Syndicate* [1899] 2 Ch. 392.

[464] See para.9–049.

[465] See para.9–052.

[466] See para.9–068.

[467] (1886) 34 Ch D. 582.

[468] In the House of Lords it was held that the question of indemnity did not arise because the debt in question was not enforceable against the firm: *Adam v Newbigging* (1888) 13 App. Cas. 308.

[469] *Newbigging v Adam* (1886) 34 Ch. 582 at 589 (emphasis added).

[470] *Newbigging v Adam* (1886) 34 Ch. 582 at 592–593 (emphasis added).

[471] *Newbigging v Adam* (1886) 34 Ch. 582 at 596 (emphasis added).

*contribute to the payment of those debts* clearly was "created by" or "contracted under" that contract. In the context of *Newbigging v Adam*, it is submitted that Fry LJ's statement does not conflict with the distinction drawn above between indemnity and damages. The point can be illustrated by supposing that the tenant in *Whittington v Seale-Hayne*[472] had employed a builder to do the repairs and a furniture remover to move in his furniture. The debt to the builder would not of course have been "created by" the lease, but the tenant's obligation to repair was so created, thus entitling him to an indemnity against the cost of its performance: this would amount, prima facie, to the sum due to the builder. The debt to the furniture remover would simply have been incurred *in reliance* on the lease: it would obviously not have been "created by" the lease; nor even would it have been "entered into under" the lease within Fry LJ's formulation.

9–092 **No indemnity if right to rescind is barred.** The grant of an indemnity amounts only to "working out the proper result of setting aside a contract in consequence of misrepresentation".[473] It is ancillary to rescission. It follows that, if the right to rescind is barred, the court cannot grant an indemnity unless the representor consents to rescission.[474] As we have seen,[475] where the right to rescind is barred the court also has no power to award damages in lieu of rescission. On this basis the victim of a wholly innocent misrepresentation will be left, in such a case, without any remedy.

## 3. RESCISSION

### (a) Introduction

9–093 It is difficult to understand the authorities on this subject without referring to the difference between the rules of common law and equity before the Judicature Acts 1873–1875.

9–094 **Common law.** At common law the general rule was that a contract could be rescinded *for misrepresentation* only on the ground of fraud; but this requirement of fraud was subject to several qualifications. If an innocent misrepresentation became a term of the contract, it might give rise to a right to "rescind" the contract *for breach*.[476] If it led to a fundamental *mistake* it might make the contract void so that each party could, on returning what he had got under the contract, recover back what he had given. This was sometimes called

[472] See para.9–090.
[473] *Newbigging v Adam* (1886) 34 Ch. 582 at 589.
[474] As in *Whittington v Seale-Hayne* (1900) 16 T.L.R. 181, where the right to rescind was probably barred by the execution of the lease; see now para.9–111.
[475] See para.9–068.
[476] See para.18–030 and following.

"rescinding" the contract, though strictly there was no need to rescind since the contract was void ab initio.[477] Rescission was also available at common law in certain cases of non-disclosure.[478]

**Equity.** In equity, on the other hand, there was a general rule that a contract could be rescinded for "innocent misrepresentation".[479] This phrase covered every misrepresentation which was not fraudulent. Now that the equitable rule prevails, the distinction between rescission at common law and in equity is of small (if any) importance; but the fact that the distinction once existed may account for some of the surviving differences between rescission for fraudulent and for "innocent" misrepresentation. 9–095

**Various meanings of "rescission".** Bowen LJ once said that "A fallacy may possibly lurk in the use of the word 'rescission'";[480] and it is a great pity that subsequent lawmakers have not taken this observation to heart. The Misrepresentation Act, in particular, uses the expressions "rescind", "rescinded" and "rescission" without attempting to define them. They have in the past been used in a number of senses, and it is impossible to say that one of these rather than another is the "correct" one: "there is no primary meaning".[481] The following distinctions, in particular, are relevant in this chapter. 9–096

**Rescission for misrepresentation and "rescission" for breach.** Where a misrepresentation is not a term of the contract, the process which may be referred to as "rescission for misrepresentation" amounts to setting the contract aside for all purposes,[482] so as to restore, as far as possible, the state of things which existed before the contract. Where, on the other hand, a misrepresentation has become a term of the contract[483] the victim of the misrepresentation may seek "rescission for breach", and in some cases this may also result in a restoration of the state of things which existed before the contract.[484] But there is a crucial difference between the two processes.[485] Rescission for misrepresentation involves an allegation that there was a defect in the *formation* of the contract; and if this allegation is substantiated it follows that the contract is avoided ab initio. "Rescission" for breach, on the other hand, involves an allegation that there was a defect in the *performance* of the contract; and the existence of such a defect does not lead to the conclusion that the contract should be treated as if it had never 9–097

[477] See *Kennedy v Panama, etc. Royal Mail Co Ltd* (1867) L.R. 2 Q.B. 580 at 587, stating the common law position before the Judicature Acts.

[478] See para.9–183; see, e.g. *Ionides v Pender* (1874) L.R. 9 Q.B. 531.

[479] See *Redgrave v Hurd* (1881) 20 Ch D. 1.

[480] *Mersey Steel and Iron Co v Naylor Benzon & Co* (1882) 9 Q.B.D. 648 at 671.

[481] *Buckland v Farmar & Moody* [1979] 1 W.L.R. 221 at 232.

[482] *The Kanchenjunga* [1990] 1 Lloyd's Rep. 391 at 398 ("wipe it out altogether"); cf. *TSB Bank Plc v Camfield* [1995] 1 W.L.R. 430 (no partial rescission); contrast *Bank Melli Iran v Samadi-Rad* [1995] 1 F.C.R. 465.

[483] See para.9–108.

[484] See para.22–012.

[485] *Johnson v Agnew* [1980] A.C. 367 at 392–393; cf. *Eagle Star Ins Co Ltd v Provincial Ins Plc* [1994] 1 A.C. 130 at 140; and, in cases of non-disclosure, *The Star Sea* [2001] UKHL 1; [2003] 1 A.C. 469 at [52].

existed. It follows that a party who "rescinds" for breach can also claim damages for breach of the contract;[486] while one who rescinds for misrepresentation has, by treating the contract as if it never existed, prima facie lost the right to claim damages for its breach.[487] If such a conclusion were to cause hardship to the representee the court could exercise its discretion under s.2(2) of the Misrepresentation Act to declare the contract subsisting.[488] Since at least some of the potential for confusion between these two quite different processes may arise from referring to them both as "rescission", this book throughout now refers instead to "termination" for breach.[489]

9–098 **Rescinding and pleading misrepresentation as a defence.** A party who "rescinds" a contract may take active steps to this end, e.g. by seeking the cancellation of the contract, or a declaration of its invalidity, or the return of money or property with which he has parted under the contract, on restoring what he obtained under it. Alternatively, he may simply rely on the misrepresentation as a defence to an action on the contract; and this process is not necessarily governed by the same rules as the active process of rescission.[490]

## (b) Rescission for misrepresentation

### *(i) Contract voidable*

9–099 The general rule is that misrepresentation makes the contract voidable at the option of the representee.[491] In *Redgrave v Hurd*,[492] for instance, the defendant was induced to buy a solicitor's house and practice by an innocent misrepresentation as to the value of the practice. It was held that he could rescind the contract and so get back the deposit he had paid.

9–100 **Effect on property rights.** As misrepresentation makes a contract voidable, but not void,[493] this has important effects on property rights in the subject-matter,[494] both as between the parties and between one of them and a third party. When the contract is one involving the transfer of property in its subject-matter, then between the parties such property is transferred to the representor to the extent that the representee intended it to be so transferred;[495] and if the entire property

[486] See para.18–022.

[487] cf. the rule that a party cannot rescind in part while affirming some particular term of the contract: para.9–127.

[488] See para.9–066. See further para.9–109.

[489] See para.18–001.

[490] See paras 9–104–9–106.

[491] *Clough v L & NW Ry* (1871) L.R. 7 Ex. 26 at 34; *Urquhart v Macpherson* (1878) 3 App. Cas. 831 at 838; cf. *Whittaker v Campbell* [1984] Q.B. 319; *Killick v Roberts* [1991] 1 W.L.R. 1146.

[492] (1881) 20 Ch D. 1.

[493] See the authorities cited in fn.498; for a contrary dictum, see *Pilgram v Rice-Smith* [1977] 1 W.L.R. 671 at 675; Phillips 93 L.Q.R. 497; *Lonrho Plc v Fayed (No.2)* [1992] 1 W.L.R. 1 at 7.

[494] *Lonrho Plc v Fayed (No.2)* [1992] 1 W.L.R. 1.

[495] See *Collings v Lee* [2001] 2 All E.R. 332 (legal title, but not equitable interest, transferred by house-owners to their agent who had fraudulently claimed to have found a purchaser for the house).

has been so transferred, then it remains in the representor until rescission.[496] So far as third parties are concerned, we have seen that if a person obtains goods under a contract which is void for mistake, property in the goods may not pass to him so that the goods can be recovered by the owner from a third person into whose hands they have come.[497] But if a person obtains goods under a contract which is only voidable for misrepresentation, a voidable title passes to him and the former owner's right to avoid it is lost when an innocent third party for value acquires an interest in the goods.[498]

**Effect on assignment.** The position of the third party in such cases should be contrasted with that of a third party to whom a chose in action[499] is assigned. The assignee takes "subject to equities"[500] and one such "equity" is the possibility of rescission for misrepresentation. Thus if A induces B to sell him a gold watch on credit by some fraud (not giving rise to a fundamental mistake) and pledges the watch to C, C's right to retain the watch is not affected by A's fraud, provided C took the pledge in good faith. But if A by fraud induces B to buy a worthless watch, said to be of gold, and assigns the benefit of B's promise to pay for it to C as security for a loan, C's right to sue B is affected by A's fraud, even if he took the assignment in good faith. It looks at first sight strange that the third party's position should depend on whether the fraudulent person was buyer or seller. One reason for treating the two cases differently may be that the law gives greater protection to proprietary than to contractual rights; and this distinction could be justified by saying that the assignee of a chose in action takes a greater business risk than the pledgee of a chattel. 9–101

**Consumer insurance contracts.** The right to rescind a "consumer insurance contract"[501] for misrepresentation is modified by the Consumer Insurance (Disclosure and Representations) Act 2012.[502] The insurer may avoid the contract if the consumer is guilty of a "qualifying misrepresentation"[503] which was "deliberate or reckless"[504] and, in such circumstances, the insurer need not return any premiums paid by the consumer except to the extent that it would be unfair to the consumer to retain them.[505] Where the consumer is guilty of "careless" misrepresentation,[506] the insurer may avoid the contract if it would not have 9–102

---

[496] Before rescission, the representor therefore does not hold the property as trustee for the injured party: *Bristol & West BS v Mothew* [1998] Ch. 1 at 22–23.

[497] e.g. *Shogun Finance Ltd v Hudson* [2003] UKHL 62; [2004] 1 A.C. 919; para.8–041.

[498] *White v Garden* (1851) 10 C.B. 919; *Stevenson v Newnham* (1853) 13 C.B. 285; the third party must give value: *Scholefield v Templer* (1859) 4 D. & J. 429; and see generally para.8–035 and following.

[499] For the meaning of "chose in action", see para.15–002.

[500] See para.15–037; cf. Marine Insurance Act 1906 s.50(2); *William Pickersgill & Sons Ltd v London & Provincial Marine, etc. Ins Co Ltd* [1912] 3 K.B. 614 (non-disclosure).

[501] As defined in s.1.

[502] For the position where the insurer relies on misrepresentation as a defence to claims made under the contract by the consumer, see para.9–107.

[503] A misrepresentation which, if it had not been made, the insurer would not have entered into the contract, or would have done so only on different terms: s.4(1)(b).

[504] As defined in s.5.

[505] 2012 Act Sch.1 para.2

[506] See para.9–166.

entered into the contract on any terms had the consumer complied with his obligation to take reasonable care not to make a misrepresentation, but must return the premiums paid.[507] Where the insurer would have entered the contract on different terms, or would have charged a higher premium, it may "terminate" the contract by giving reasonable notice to the consumer, or it may give notice to the consumer that it intends to treat the contract as having been entered on those different terms, or that it will exercise its right to reduce the amount paid on any claim.[508] Upon receipt of such notice the consumer has the option of terminating the contract upon reasonable notice.[509] If either party terminates the contract the insurer must refund any premiums paid for the terminated cover in respect of the balance of the period.[510] "Termination" in the circumstances just described does not affect the treatment of any claim arising under the contract in the period before termination.[511] The insurer has no right to avoid the contract for innocent misrepresentation.[512]

9–103 **Non-consumer insurance contracts.** Under the Insurance Act 2015, [513] if the insured commits a "qualifying breach"[514] of the duty to make a fair presentation of the risk which is "deliberate or reckless",[515] the insurer may avoid the contract and refuse all claims and need not return any of the premiums paid.[516] In the case of any other qualifying breach the insurer may avoid the contract only if it would not have entered into the contract on any terms and must return the premiums paid.[517] Where the insurer would have entered the contract on different terms, there is no right to avoid the contract but the insurer may, if it so requires, treat the contract as if it had been entered into on those different terms.[518] In addition, if the insurer would have charged a higher premium, the insurer may reduce proportionately the amount to be paid on a claim.[519] The insurer does not have a right to "terminate" the contract for the future of the type conferred under a consumer insurance contract.[520]

### *(ii) Mode of rescission*

9–104 **Legal proceedings not always necessary.** A contract may be rescinded by bringing legal proceedings, or simply by giving notice to the other party. In the

[507] 2012 Act Sch.1 para.9(2).
[508] 2012 Act Sch.1 para.9(4). The insurer may not terminate the contract if it is wholly or mainly one of life insurance: para.9(5).
[509] 2012 Act Sch.1 para.9(6).
[510] 2012 Act Sch.1 para.9(7).
[511] 2012 Act Sch.1 para.9(8); see para.9–107.
[512] 2012 Act s.4(3).
[513] The relevant provisions came into force on 12 August 2016.
[514] i.e. one but for which the insurer would not have entered into the contract, or would have done so only on different terms: s.8(1).
[515] See para.9–023; para.9–167.
[516] 2012 Act Sch.1 para.2.
[517] 2012 Act Sch.1 para.4.
[518] 2012 Act Sch.1 para.5.
[519] 2012 Act Sch.1 para.6
[520] See para.9–102.

latter case, legal proceedings may still be necessary to work out the consequences of rescission. This is most obviously true where, as a result of rescission, a sum of money becomes due to the representee and the representor refuses to pay it. It may also be desirable to have a court order stating that a formal transaction (such as a lease or a transfer of shares) has been or ought to be set aside. Even in such a case rescission is the act of the representee and not that of the court, so that the time at which it takes effect is when the representee gives the notice or commences legal proceedings—not the time of the court's order.[521] In other cases, unless required by statute, no legal proceedings are necessary to give effect to the consequences of rescission.[522] Thus, where goods have been obtained by fraud, rescission can be effected by simply taking them back.[523]

**Notice to the representor not always necessary.** All these modes of rescission involve some degree of notice to the representor; but it has been held that this is not always necessary. In *Car & Universal Finance Co Ltd v Caldwell*[524] the owner of a car was induced by fraud to sell it to a rogue who absconded and could not be traced. On discovering the fraud, the owner notified the police and the Automobile Association and asked them for help in recovering the car. It was held that these acts were enough to rescind the contract, so that an innocent third party who later bought the car got no title to it. It would no doubt be hard on the owner to hold that he could only rescind by communicating with the rogue, for this would deprive him of the right to rescind whenever the rogue disappears. But the actual decision is equally hard on the third party;[525] and the Law Reform Committee has recommended that it should be reversed.[526] It applies only where the representor has disappeared or for some other reason cannot be reached.[527] **9–105**

The general principles governing the mode of rescission apply whether the representation is fraudulent, negligent or innocent. But in *Caldwell's* case the Court of Appeal left open the question whether the rule there laid down applies where the misrepresentation is not fraudulent. The question is perhaps academic since negligent representors are not likely to go into hiding; but it is submitted that the rule can be justified, if at all, only by the strong need to protect victims of fraud and that it should not be applied in cases of negligent or wholly innocent misrepresentation. It is also questionable whether the rule that a contract can be rescinded by simply taking back goods delivered under it should be applied except in cases of fraud.

[521] *Reese Silver Mining Co v Smith* (1869) L.R. 4 H.L. 64.

[522] e.g. Housing Act 1985 s.82.

[523] *Re Eastgate* [1905] 1 K.B. 465, doubted but *semble* not on this point in *Re Goldcorp Exchange Ltd* [1995] 1 A.C. 74 at 103.

[524] [1965] 1 Q.B. 525.

[525] Such a third party may, in appropriate circumstances, be protected by s.25 of the Sale of Goods Act 1979: *Newtons of Wembley Ltd v Williams* [1965] 1 Q.B. 560.

[526] 12th Report (1996), Cmnd.2958, para.16.

[527] *Empresa Cubana de Fletes v Lagonisi Shipping Co Ltd* [1971] 1 Q.B. 488 at 505 (actual decision overruled in *The Laconia* [1977] A.C. 850).

### (iii) *Misrepresentation as a defence*

9–106 The operation of misrepresentation as a defence to an action to enforce the contract is illustrated by further reference to *Redgrave v Hurd*.[528] The purchaser there successfully relied on the misrepresentations as to the value of the practice by way of defence to the vendor's claim for specific performance. Since this process of pleading misrepresentation as a defence is a form of "rescission"[529] it is, in general, subject to the requirement that the representee must return what he got under the contract.[530] But this requirement does not always apply where the representor is guilty of actual fraud. For example, where a ship was insured after she had, to the knowledge of the assured, been lost, it was held that the insurer could repudiate liability under the policy on the ground of fraud, and also keep the premiums.[531] The result is to leave the insurer with a windfall; but the rule may perhaps be justified by the strong need to discourage fraud.[532] Even this justification is, however, hard to square with the further rule that, if the insurer takes the initiative by suing for rescission, he does have to return the premiums.[533] This is also the position where he relies on a negligent or wholly innocent misrepresentation as a defence;[534] unless the policy provides for forfeiture of premiums if *any* false statement is made in the proposal form.[535]

A further situation in which a person can plead fraud as a defence without restoring what he has obtained under the contract is illustrated by *Berg v Sadler & Moore*.[536] The claimant was a retail tobacconist, and knew that the defendants (who were wholesalers) would not supply him as he had been put on a stop-list for price-cutting. He therefore sent one Reece to the defendants to buy cigarettes, ostensibly in his own name. Reece paid with money supplied by the claimant but when the defendants discovered the true facts they refused to deliver the

[528] (1881) 20 Ch D. 1.

[529] See para.9–098.

[530] See para.9–097; para.9–114.

[531] *Feise v Parkinson* (1812) 4 Taunt. 639 at 641; *Anderson v Thornton* (1853) 8 Exch. 425 at 428. Contra, *Fowkes v Manchester, etc. Assurance* (1863) 3 B. & S. 917 at 929, but the corresponding passages in 11 W.R. 622 at 623 and 8 L.T. 309 at 311 suggest that Blackburn J had no intention of departing from the earlier authorities just cited. See also Marine Insurance Act 1906 s.84(1) and (3), restating the common law rule, but these provisions are modified by the provisions of the Consumer Insurance (Disclosure and Representations) Act 2012 (Sch.1 para.17) and the Insurance Act 2015 (Sch.1 para.12) discussed at paras 9–102, 9–103.

[532] If the assured could recover back the premiums, the only risk to which he would be exposed under the civil law would be that of not being able to sue on the policy; and where he had already lost the property this would be no risk at all.

[533] *Barker v Walters* (1844) 8 Beav. 92 at 96; *London Assurance v Mansel* (1879) 11 Ch D. 363; cf. *The Litsian Pride* [1985] 1 Lloyd's Rep. 437 at 515. Quaere whether an insurer who only claims a *declaration* that he is entitled to avoid the policy on the ground of fraud (as in *Fire, etc., Insurance v Greene* [1964] 2 Q.B. 687) must return the premiums. There is nothing to suggest that this curious anomaly should be perpetuated under the statutory regimes referred to in fn.531 and discussed in paras 9–102, 9–103.

[534] *Feise v Parkinson* (1812) 4 Taunt.639; *Anderson v Thornton* (1853) 8 Exch. 425.

[535] *Kumar v Life Ins Corp of India* [1974] 1 Lloyd's Rep. 147. Such a provision is not binding on the consumer under a consumer insurance contract: Consumer Insurance (Disclosure and Representations) Act 2012 s.10. It is binding on the insured under a non-consumer insurance contract only if it meets the requirement of transparency: Insurance Act 2015 s.16(2).

[536] [1937] 2 K.B. 158; Treitel in *Essays in Memory of Sir Rupert Cross*, pp.107–108.

cigarettes or to pay back the price. It was held that the claimant was not entitled to the return of the price, so that (as in the insurance cases discussed above) the defendants were left with a windfall. The court justified this result on the ground that the claimant had been engaged in an attempt to perpetrate a *criminal* fraud; and the rule seems to be based on the supposed need to deter such fraud,[537] though it is far from clear why adequate deterrence is not provided by the criminal law itself.[538] The rule would probably not apply where the fraud was not criminal, e.g. where a statement was made with knowledge of its falsity but without dishonest intent.[539] The rule should certainly not apply where the misrepresentation was only negligent or where it was innocent.

**Consumer insurance contracts.**[540] The circumstances in which an insurer may "avoid" a consumer insurance contract have been noted above[541] and, where this right is available, it may also be exercised in the same way as a defence to a claim made under the contract by the consumer.[542] If the insurer exercises the right to "terminate" the contract, this does not affect any claim under the contract in the period before termination.[543] Such termination only has a prospective effect, but the insurer is entitled to deal with the claim on the basis of the different terms upon which it would have entered into the contract,[544] or by reducing the claim proportionately if it would have charged a higher premium.[545] **9–107**

### (c) Incorporated misrepresentation

**Right to rescind for misrepresentation survives incorporation.** Section 1(a) of the Misrepresentation Act 1967 provides that a person who has entered into a contract after a misrepresentation has been made to him shall be entitled to rescind notwithstanding that "the misrepresentation has become a term of the contract" if he would otherwise be entitled to rescind without alleging fraud. The right to rescind therefore survives when a statement of fact is made to induce a contract and later becomes one of its terms. **9–108**

**Effect of rescission for misrepresentation on damages for breach.** Section 1(a) does not take away any remedies for breach of contract, which in some cases may **9–109**

[537] *South Australia Asset Management Corp v York Montague Ltd* [1997] A.C. 191 at 215; *Smith New Court Securities Ltd v Scrimgoeour Vickers (Asset Management) Ltd* [1997] A.C. 254 at 279.

[538] It has been pointed out (*Chitty on Contracts,* 33rd edn, para.7-118 at fn.557) that *Berg v Sadler & Moore* [1937] 2 K.B. 158 is contrary to dicta of the Exchequer Chamber in *Clough v L. & N.W. Ry.* (1871) L.R. 7 Ex. 26 at 37 which appear not to have been cited and that the refusal of the claim for return of the money may be better explained on the basis of illegality: para.11–089.

[539] See *Polhill v Walter* (1832) 3 B. & Ad. 114; para.9–038.

[540] Under the Insurance Act 2015, which regulates non-consumer insurance contracts, no distinction is drawn between "claims" and the "contract for the future" (as in the 2012 Act). The insurer may exercise what right to avoid that it has (see para.9–103) either by way of defence or by suing to avoid the contract.

[541] See para.9–102.

[542] 2012 Act Sch.1 paras 2, 9(2).

[543] 2012 Act Sch.1 para.9(8).

[544] 2012 Act Sch.1 para.6.

[545] 2012 Act Sch.1 para.7.

be confined to a right to damages and, in others, may give rise to a right to damages and also to a right to terminate.[546] Where an incorporated misrepresentation gives rise to both these rights, they can presumably still be exercised independently of s.1 and the right to terminate for breach is probably unaffected by s.2(2), since that deals only with the case of a person "who is entitled, *by reason of the misrepresentation* to rescind the contract".[547] Where the incorporated misrepresentation gives rise only to a right to damages for breach, the representee can ignore his right to rescind and claim such damages. But he cannot claim such damages if he does "rescind", as he is allowed to, under s.1(a).[548] This might cause hardship where a representee has rescinded out of court (e.g. by returning defective goods) but the court could probably come to his rescue by declaring the contract subsisting under s.2(2) of the Act. It is true that damages in lieu of rescission under that subsection may be less than damages for breach of contract;[549] but one effect of declaring the contract subsisting might be to revive the right to damages for breach of contract, i.e. for the untruth of the incorporated misrepresentation.

## 4. LIMITS TO THE RIGHT TO RESCIND

9–110 The right to rescind a contract may be barred by a number of factors. Before these are considered, two points must be made with regard to the effects of the Misrepresentation Act 1967.

### (a) Effects of Misrepresentation Act 1967

9–111 **Execution of contract no bar to rescission.** First, the Act has abrogated one restriction on the right to rescind. Before the Act, it had been held that certain contracts could not be rescinded for innocent misrepresentation after they had been "executed" (i.e. performed). This rule applied, in particular, where a contract for the disposition of an interest in land was performed by execution of the conveyance or lease;[550] and where a contract for the sale of shares was performed by transfer of the shares.[551] Many applications of the rule were hard to justify, and its scope was uncertain. It was reversed by s.1(b) of the Act, which provides that a person who would otherwise be entitled to rescind a contract for misrepresentation without alleging fraud[552] shall be so entitled notwithstanding that "the contract has been performed". The buyer of a house can therefore rescind for misrepresentation even after conveyance and even though the misrepresentation was wholly innocent.

[546] See para.9–097; para.18–030 and following.
[547] See para.9–066.
[548] See para.9–097.
[549] See para.9–087.
[550] *Angel v Jay* [1911] 1 K.B. 666 (lease).
[551] *Seddon v North Eastern Salt Co* [1905] 1 Ch. 326.
[552] The rule that an executed contract could not be rescinded never applied to cases of fraudulent misrepresentation, so that it was not necessary to change the law in such cases.

**Discretion of court under s.2(2).** Secondly, the right to rescind a contract for misrepresentation is now subject to the discretion of the court under s.2(2) of the Act.[553] In the case just put, of a house-purchaser claiming rescission for wholly innocent misrepresentation, the court might prefer to declare the contract subsisting and to award damages in lieu of rescission. For if (as would often be the case) the vendor had used the purchase-money to buy another house, rescission might cause him severe hardship. This would be a factor which the court could take into account under s.2(2), so that rescission would probably be allowed only where the buyer had suffered serious prejudice as a result of the misrepresentation. Section 2(2) may, similarly, operate in cases which are not precisely covered by the bars to rescission but in which the court nevertheless considers that damages would be a more appropriate remedy than rescission. It is, however, still necessary to define the bars to rescission because if one of them has arisen the court has *no* discretion to allow rescission and cannot award damages under s.2(2) either.[554] 9–112

## (b) Bars to rescission

**Burden of proof.** If it is established that the representee has the right to rescind, the burden of proving that it is precluded by one of the bars which follow lies on the representor.[555] In *Salt v Stratstone Specialist Ltd*[556] the Court of Appeal held that it was no bar to the rescission of a contract for the sale of a car that the representee had had the car for two years during which time it had depreciated and the representee had driven it for about 15,000 miles. The representor could be compensated for such matters and the question of whether this would fail to achieve "practical justice"[557] was something for the representor to "assert and prove".[558] The representee was entitled to rescind in the absence of such evidence and nor was this any basis for the court to award damages in lieu of rescission under s.2(2) of the Misrepresentation Act.[559] 9–113

### (i) *Restitution impossible*

Normally, a party who wishes to rescind a contract for misrepresentation is required to restore to the other any benefits which he has obtained under the contract, e.g. a buyer who wants to rescind with a view to getting back the price must give back the goods. If the benefit obtained is a sum of money[560] there is never any difficulty in complying with this requirement: the representee restores 9–114

---

[553] See para.9–066.
[554] See para.9–069.
[555] *Erlanger v New Sombrero Phosphate Co* (1878) 3 App. Cas. 1218 at 1283.
[556] [2015] EWCA Civ 745; [2015] 2 C.L.C. 206.
[557] See para.9–119.
[558] *Salt v Stratstone Specialist Ltd* [2015] EWCA Civ 745; [2015] 2 C.L.C. 206 at [30].
[559] See para.9–066.
[560] Or the release of an obligation to pay money, as in *The Siboen and the Sibotre* [1976] 1 Lloyd's Rep. 293; see especially at 337.

an equivalent sum. Where he has obtained a benefit other than money, he may for some reason be unable to restore it; and this inability will sometimes bar the right to rescind.

9–115 **Changes made by representee.** Where a contract of sale has been induced by a misrepresentation of the seller, the buyer may lose the right to rescind if he has so changed the subject-matter that he can no longer restore what he obtained under the contract, e.g. the buyer of an animal who has slaughtered it cannot rescind on returning the corpse.[561] Similarly, the purchaser of a business cannot get back his purchase-money after carrying on the business for four months and disposing of some of its assets,[562] or after changing a partnership into a limited company;[563] nor can the purchaser of a mine rescind after he has worked it out.[564] On the same principle a person cannot rescind after he has disposed of the subject-matter of the contract unless, perhaps, he has been able to get back that subject-matter or its substantial equivalent.[565]

9–116 **Other deterioration or decline in value.** In the cases discussed above, deterioration or decline in value barred the right to rescind because it was due to the acts of the representee. Where it is due to other causes, different rules apply. The right to rescind is clearly not barred where the subject-matter deteriorates precisely because it lacks a quality that it was represented to possess. Thus a person who is induced to enter into a partnership by a misrepresentation as to its solvency can still rescind after the bankruptcy of the firm.[566] The position is the same where the deterioration or decline in value is not related to the misrepresentation but is due to some external cause.[567] In *Armstrong v Jackson*[568] a broker purported to buy shares for a client, but in fact sold his own shares to the client. Five years later, when the shares had fallen in value from nearly £3 to 5s., it was held that the client could rescind on account of the broker's breach of duty.[569] He still had the identical shares and was able to return them, together with the dividends he had received. McCardie J said:

---

561 *Clarke v Dickson* (1858) E.B. & E. 148 at 155.

562 *Sheffield Nickel Co Ltd v Unwin* (1877) 2 Q.B.D. 215; cf. *Thomas Witter Ltd v TBP Industries Ltd* [1996] 2 All E.R. 573 at 588.

563 *Clarke v Dickson* (1858) E.B. & E. 148; quaere whether this is per se decisive; *Western Bank of Scotland v Addie* (1867) L.R. 1 Sc. & Div. 145 at 159.

564 *Clarke v Dickson* (1858) E.B. & E. 148; *Lagunas Nitrate Co v Lagunas Syndicate* [1899] 2 Ch. 392.

565 e.g. where a buyer of shares has sold them but can reacquire an equivalent quantity in the market. In *Smith New Court Securities Ltd v Scrimgeour Vickers (Asset Management) Ltd* the Court of Appeal seems to have taken the view that the buyer could not rescind in such a case: [1994] 1 W.L.R. 1271 at 1280; but on appeal Lord Browne-Wilkinson said that the law on the point would have to be "closely looked at hereafter": [1997] A.C. 254 at 264.

566 *Adam v Newbigging* (1886) 34 Ch D. 582; (1888) 13 App. Cas. 308.

567 *Salt v Stratstone Specialist Ltd* [2015] EWCA Civ 745; [2015] 2 C.L.C. 206 (depreciation in value of car).

568 [1917] 2 K.B. 822.

569 See para.16–109.

> "It is only … where the (claimant) has sustained loss by the inferiority of the subject-matter or a substantial fall in its value that he will desire to exert his power of rescission … If mere deterioration of the subject-matter negatived the right to rescind, the doctrine of rescission would become a vain thing".[570]

Similarly, a contractual right to reject is not lost simply because the subject-matter deteriorates without the fault of the party claiming to reject.[571] It is submitted that these rules also apply where the buyer is induced to buy by a misrepresentation which has been incorporated in the contract.[572]

**Changes made by representor.** Where the misrepresentation is that of the seller, the question is whether the buyer (i.e. the representee) can rescind even though he cannot restore the subject-matter in its original state. A sale may also be induced by a misrepresentation on the part of the buyer, e.g. as to his solvency or as to the value of the subject-matter. The question then arises whether the seller's right to rescind is affected by some dealing with the subject-matter by the buyer (who in such a case is the representor). Obviously, the right may be so affected in a practical sense where the buyer consumes the property or so alters it that the seller has no interest in getting it back. As a matter of law, however, a buyer who is guilty of fraud cannot rely on his own dealings[573] with the subject-matter as a bar to the seller's right to rescind. In *Spence v Crawford*[574] A was induced by the fraud of B to enter into a contract by which: (i) A sold to B shares in a company; and (ii) B undertook to relieve A of his liability under a guarantee of the company's bank overdraft, and to procure the release of securities deposited by A with the bank. A duly transferred the shares, while B relieved A of his liability to the bank and freed the securities by giving his own personal guarantee to the bank. The constitution of the company was later altered and some of the shares in it were sold. It was held that this dealing with the shares did not bar A's right to rescind. The question whether it would have had this effect if B's misrepresentation had been innocent was left open.[575] 9–117

**Benefit to representee.** The mere fact that the representee has received a benefit under the contract does not bar his right to rescind, if the representor has not been put to any expense in conferring that benefit. Thus in *Spence v Crawford* the fact that B had relieved A of his liability to the bank and freed his securities did not bar A's right to rescind. B was not put to any expense *by merely giving* the guarantee to the bank, nor was he ever asked to pay anything under it, as the company prospered. We shall see that B did suffer some loss as a result of giving his guarantee, but this did not bar A's claim to rescind as he was able to make allowance for it.[576] 9–118

---

[570] *Armstrong v Jackson* [1917] 2 K.B. 822 at 829.
[571] *Head v Tattersall* (1871) L.R. Ex. 7.
[572] cf. *Long v Lloyd* [1958] 1 W.L.R. 753 at 760.
[573] Nor on the other party's dealings at his request: cf. *Hulton v Hulton* [1917] 1 K.B. 813 (destruction of letters).
[574] [1939] 3 All E.R. 271.
[575] *Spence v Crawford* [1939] 3 All E.R. 271 at 281. The effect of negligence in such a situation is also unclear.
[576] See para.9–119.

Conversely, if no benefit has been received by the representee, the right to rescind is not lost *merely* because the representor has acted on the contract to his prejudice. In *Mackenzie v Royal Bank of Canada*[577] a wife was induced by misrepresentation to deposit share certificates with a bank as security for the overdraft of a company controlled by her husband. She was able to rescind although the bank had, after the deposit, advanced further money to the company, for she had received no benefit from this payment. It is sometimes said that the object of rescission is to restore the parties to the situation in which they would have been if the contract had never been made,[578] but in the light of *Mackenzie's* case such statements are not quite accurate. The essential point is that the representee should not be unjustly enriched at the representor's expense;[579] that the representor should not be prejudiced is a secondary consideration.[580]

9–119 **Precise restitution not necessary.** The general rule requiring restoration of what had been obtained under the contract was very strictly applied at common law where a person sought the return of his money on termination for breach,[581] but a more flexible rule was developed by equity in cases of misrepresentation.[582] A representee who is able to make substantial, though not precise, restitution can rescind if he returns the subject-matter of the contract in its altered state, accounts for any profits derived from it and makes allowance for deterioration caused by his dealing with it.[583] Thus a person who has gone into possession under a contract to buy, or take a lease of, land can rescind[584] on terms of paying rent for the period of his occupation.[585] The court can also set off benefits received by one party against those received by the other.[586] Similarly, in *Erlanger v New Sombrero Phosphate Co*[587] a company bought and worked a phosphate mine, but did not so work it out as to make restitution utterly impossible. It was held that the company could rescind the sale for breach of fiduciary duty by one of its promoters on terms of returning the mine and accounting for the profits of working it. Lord Blackburn said that equity could:

[577] [1934] A.C. 468; cf. *TSB Bank v Camfield* [1995] 1 W.L.R. 430.
[578] e.g. *Gillett v Peppercorne* (1840) 3 Beav. 78 at 81.
[579] *Bouygues Offshore v Ultisol Transport Contractors* [1996] 2 Lloyd's Rep. 153 at 159.
[580] *Halpern v Halpern* [2007] EWCA Civ 291; [2008] Q.B. 195 at [74]; *Salt v Stratstone Specialist Ltd* [2015] EWCA Civ 745; [2015] 2 C.L.C. 206 at [28].
[581] *Hunt v Silk* (1804) 5 East 449; *Blackburn v Smith* (1848) 2 Ex. 783; para.22–013.
[582] cf. *Halpern v Halpern (No.2)* [2007] EWCA Civ 291; [2008] Q.B. 195 (a case of duress); para.10–013.
[583] *Salt v Stratstone Specialist Ltd* [2015] EWCA Civ 745; [2015] 2 C.L.C. 206.
[584] *Redgrave v Hurd* (1881) 20 Ch D. 1.
[585] *Hulton v Hulton* [1917] 1 K.B. 813 at 826. It seems that no such terms were imposed in *Redgrave v Hurd* (1881) 20 Ch D. 1, where the buyer got back the whole of his deposit in spite of having been in possession for a short time.
[586] *Hulton v Hulton* [1917] 1 K.B. 813.
[587] (1878) 3 App. Cas. 1218; cf. *The Lucy* [1983] 1 Lloyd's Rep. 188 at 202.

> "take account of profits and make allowance for deterioration. And I think the practice has always been for a court of equity to give this relief whenever, by the exercise of its powers, it can do what is practically just, though it cannot restore the parties precisely to the state they were in before the contract".[588]

These powers of adjustment are normally exercised where the representee is a buyer who claims back his money. They may also be available in the converse case where the representee is a seller who claims back his property, as in *Spence v Crawford*.[589] The fraudulent buyer in that case had performed his contractual undertaking to relieve the seller of certain obligations to a bank. He was asked by the bank to sell some stock to maintain his liquidity, and the sale resulted in a loss to him of £1,000. The final order made in that case was that the seller should recover back his shares plus the dividends received by the buyer; but that he should repay the purchase price plus interest, and make allowance in respect of part[590] of the £1,000 lost by the buyer on the sale of his stock.

**Nature of subject-matter.** Restitution by the representee may be possible but the court may be unwilling to order it on account of the nature of the property. This was the position in *The Siben*[591] where a contract for the sale of property included an escort agency, the employees of which provided "sexual favours" for its clients. The sale had been induced by the vendor's fraudulent misrepresentations unrelated to this point; and a claim to rescind the contract was rejected on the ground that the court should not "make an order which would in principle have the effect of transferring an illegal business from one party to another".[592] This reasoning is not easy to reconcile with the principle that rescission is the act of the representee, not that of the court;[593] and the return of the illegal business would, moreover, be merely a condition of any judgment which might have been given for the return of the price, so that there would have been no need to make an actual order for the return of that business. **9–120**

**Improvements in the subject-matter.** Two problems arise where dealings with the subject-matter have not decreased its value, but have improved it. The first is whether such dealings bar the right to rescind; the second is what allowance (if any) is to be awarded in respect of the improvements. **9–121**

**Improvements made by the representee.** One illustration of this possibility is provided by *Boyd & Forrest v Glasgow & SW Ry*[594] Contractors alleged that they had been induced to enter into a contract to build a railway by misrepresentations as to the strata. After the railway had been built, they claimed to rescind, with a **9–122**

[588] *Erlanger v New Sombrero Phosphate Co* (1878) 3 App. Cas. 1218 at 1278–1279; approved in *Guiness Plc v Saunders* [1990] 2 A.C. 663 at 698, but distinguished as the agreement in the latter case was not voidable but void.

[589] [1939] 3 All E.R. 271; para.9–117.

[590] This seems to have been a compromise, adopted to avoid the need to take complicated cross-accounts.

[591] [1996] 1 Lloyd's Rep. 35; for further proceedings see [1996] 2 Lloyd's Rep. 667.

[592] *The Siben* [1996] 1 Lloyd's Rep. 35 at 62.

[593] See para.9–104.

[594] 1915 S.C. (H.L.) 20.

view to recovering a quantum meruit (exceeding the contract price) for the cost of the work. The claim failed on a number of grounds, one of which was that the right to rescind was barred since it was no longer possible to restore the railway company to its original position. This is an unusual application of the requirement of restoration, which normally prevents the representee from rescinding unless he can *give back* benefits that he has *received*. In this case, the requirement prevented rescission because the representee could not *take back* benefits that he had *conferred*.[595] The decision can be explained on the ground that it was not practicable to restore the parties to their pre-contract position, so that "rescission" made no practical sense. The more convenient remedy is damages and on such facts this would now generally be available under s.2(1) of the Misrepresentation Act.[596]

A second, and perhaps more common, illustration of this situation is provided by the case of a person who is induced by misrepresentation to buy something which he improves before discovering the truth. In such a case, the improvements probably do not bar the right to rescind; and their cost can often be claimed as damages.[597] Where the representation is wholly innocent and the contract has been rescinded, there will be no such claim;[598] but the representee might be able to set off the cost of the improvements against his liability[599] to make allowance for benefits received by him under the contract.[600]

9–123 **Improvements made by the representor.** In *Spence v Crawford*[601] the fraudulent buyer was granted an allowance in respect of his loss on sale of stock. This loss did not produce any directly corresponding increase in the value of what he had bought; and it was incurred in consequence of something that he was *obliged* under the contract to do. It does not follow from the decision that a buyer who obtains property by misrepresentation can, if the seller claims rescission, insist on an allowance for improvements which he has made *without* being contractually bound to do so. It can be argued on the one hand that the seller would get a windfall if he did not have to pay anything for the improvements;[602] and on the other that he should not be forced to pay for improvements (which he may not want or be able to afford) as a condition of getting back his property. The better view, probably, is that if the seller claims rescission, he should have to make some allowance (based on increase in value rather than the cost of work to the buyer).[603] If the seller is unwilling or unable to pay the allowance he can generally fall back on his alternative remedy of damages.[604]

595 For the suggestion that, in such cases, the representee may be able to "waive restitution due to him", see *Bouygues Offshore v Ultisol Transport Contractors* [1996] 2 Lloyd's Rep. 153 at 159.
596 See para.9–049.
597 See para.9–079 and following.
598 See para.9–089 and following.
599 See para.9–119.
600 cf. *Cooper v Phibbs* (1867) L.R. 2 H.L. 149.
601 [1939] 3 All E.R. 271; paras 9–117, 9–119.
602 e.g. *Williams v Logue* 122 So. 490 (1929).
603 cf. *Walker v Galt* 171 F. 2d 613 (1948); *Cheese v Thomas* [1994] 1 W.L.R. 129 at 137.
604 See para.9–036 and following.

### (ii) *Third party rights*

As we have seen, the right to rescind a contract may be barred by the intervention of third party rights. For example, a person who has been induced by fraud to sell goods cannot rescind after the goods have been bought by an innocent third party, that is, by one without notice of the fraud.[605] **9–124**

### (iii) *Affirmation*

**No rescission if contract affirmed.** A contract cannot be rescinded for misrepresentation if the representee expressly or by conduct affirms it after discovering the truth, i.e. with knowledge of the facts and of his right to rescind.[606] To hear rumours that the representation may be untrue is not, for this purpose, discovery of the truth.[607] But if the representee knows all the facts from which a reasonable person would deduce the truth, he may be taken to know it.[608] Thus a person who is induced by misrepresentation to buy goods cannot rescind if, after discovering the truth, he uses them;[609] a person who is induced by misrepresentation to subscribe for shares in a company cannot rescind if, after discovering the truth, he accepts dividends, votes at meetings or tries to sell the shares;[610] a person who is induced by misrepresentation to take a lease cannot rescind if, after discovering the truth, he stays on and pays rent;[611] a fortiori a mining lease cannot be rescinded if, after discovering the truth, the lessee continues to work the mine.[612] Use of the subject-matter for the sole purpose of testing the accuracy of the representation does not, however, amount to affirmation;[613] nor its use for a short time while awaiting the representor's response to an allegation of misrepresentation.[614] **9–125**

**Affirmation inferred from failure to rescind.** Affirmation may be inferred even from failure to rescind, e.g. where a person wishes to rescind an allotment of shares in a company on the ground of misrepresentation. Such a person is not **9–126**

[605] See para.9–100; and see para.10–040; cf. *Society of Lloyds v Lyon*, *The Times*, 11 August 1997.

[606] *Habib Bank Ltd v Tufail* [2006] EWCA Civ 374 at [20] ("undoubtedly the law that knowledge of the right to rescind is essential"); *Donegal International Ltd v Zambia* [2007] EWHC 197; [2007] 1 Lloyd's Rep. 397 at [467]; cf. the loss of the right to terminate *for breach*: para.18–100. Where the representee does not have the requisite knowledge, he may lose the right to rescind by promissory estoppel, but only if the representor can demonstrate the necessary reliance: *Habib Bank Ltd v Tufail* [2006] EWCA Civ 374; cf. para.3–083, 18–092, 18–104.

[607] *Central Ry of Venezuela v Kisch* (1867) L.R. 2 H.L. 99.

[608] *Scholey v Central Ry of Venezuela* (1870) L.R. 9 Eq. 266n.; *Long v Lloyd* [1958] 1 W.L.R. 753 at 760.

[609] *United Shoe Machinery Co of Canada v Brunet* [1909] A.C. 330; cf. *Long v Lloyd* [1958] 1 W.L.R. 753; *Skipskreditforeningen v Emperor Navigation* [1998] 1 Lloyd's Rep. 67 at 73–74.

[610] *Western Bank of Scotland v Addie* (1867) L.R. 1 Sc. & Div. 145; *Scholey v Central Ry of Venezuela* (1870) L.R. 9 Eq. 266n.; *Ex p. Briggs* (1866) L.R. 1 Eq. 483.

[611] *Kennard v Ashman* (1894) 10 T.L.R. 213.

[612] *Vigers v Pike* (1842) 8 Cl. & F. 562.

[613] *Long v Lloyd* [1958] 1 W.L.R. 753 (first trip); cf. *Lindsay Petroleum Co v Hurd* (1874) L.R. 5 P.C. 221 (sinking exploratory well no bar to rescission).

[614] *Edwards v Ashik* [2014] EWHC 2454 (Ch) (a case of fraud).

allowed to wait and see whether the company will prosper: he must not only tell the company that he rescinds but must also take steps to remove his name from the register of shareholders.[615]

9–127 **No partial rescission.** On a principle analogous to affirmation[616] a person cannot set aside one term of a contract on the ground of misrepresentation while affirming the rest. For example, a person who has been induced to enter into an agreement to take a lease by a misrepresentation relating to one of its terms cannot repudiate that term while affirming the rest of the lease.[617] Similarly, an insurance company can rescind a policy for non-disclosure, but it cannot repudiate a particular claim while purporting to recognise that the policy is still in force.[618] Nor is it open to the court at the request of the representor to restrict rescission to the part of the contract to which the representation relates. If, for example, a guarantee is procured by a representation that it relates only to future debts, when in fact it relates to past and future debts, then the guarantee cannot be rescinded with regard to the past, but upheld with regard to the future debts: such a course would amount to remaking, not to rescinding the contract.[619]

9–128 **Effect of affirmation on a claim for damages** The primary effect of affirmation is that the representee will have lost the right to rescind the contract. But if the representee then claims damages to put him in the same position as if no misrepresentation had been made, that may produce a result which is the monetary equivalent of rescission, e.g. if A is induced by B's misrepresentation to pay £100 for goods which are, in fact, worth £70, the result of rescinding the contract is that A will recover the price and return the goods, i.e. he will be better off by £30. If he has affirmed the contract he must keep the goods and cannot recover the price, but an award of damages would result in him receiving the difference between the price paid and the actual value of the goods,[620] i.e. he will be better off by £30. On this basis, it may be that affirmation should also act as a bar to damages which are "equivalent to the benefit (A) would have received from avoidance."[621] Affirmation would not affect any claim for consequential loss.

### *(iv) Lapse of time*

9–129 **Fraud.** In cases of fraud (or breach of fiduciary duty) lapse of time does not itself bar rescission. It is only evidence of affirmation.[622] This view is supported by the

[615] *First National Reinsurance Co Ltd v Greenfield* [1921] 2 K.B. 260; for a qualification of this principle, see *Pawle's Case* (1869) L.R. 4 Ch. App. 487.
[616] *Urquhart v Macpherson* (1878) 3 App. Cas. 831.
[617] *Inntrepreneur Pub Co v Sweeney* [2002] EWHC 1060 (Ch); [2002] E.G.L.R. 132.
[618] *West v National Motors & Accident Ins Union Ltd* [1955] 1 W.L.R. 343.
[619] *TSB Plc v Camfield* [1995] 1 W.L.R. 430; citing *Barclays Bank Plc v O'Brien* [1994] 1 A.C. 180 at 199; *De Molestina v Ponton* [2002] 1 Lloyd's Rep. 271 at 286–288.
[620] See para.9–073.
[621] *Argo Systems FZE v Liberty Insurance (PTE)* [2011] EWHC 301 (Comm); [2011] 2 Lloyd's Rep. 61 at [46].
[622] *Clough v LNW Ry* (1871) L.R. 7 Ex. 26, 35; cf. (in cases of breach) para.18–100.

rule that time begins to run only from the discovery of the truth;[623] and by the rule that time spent in negotiations to settle the dispute does not bar rescission.[624]

**Innocent and negligent misrepresentation.** In *Leaf v International Galleries*[625] the claimant was induced to buy a picture by the innocent misrepresentation that it was "by J. Constable".[626] Five years later he sought to rescind but it was held that his right to do so was barred by lapse of time. As rescission was sought promptly on discovery of the truth, the lapse of time was not evidence of affirmation, so that, even in the absence of such evidence, lapse of time is a bar to the right to rescind for *innocent* misrepresentation. The length of time required for this purpose seems to be such "that it would be inequitable in all the circumstances to grant rescission".[627] In *Salt v Stratstone Specialist Ltd*[628] a period of two years from the purchase of a car to the date when the purchaser discovered the misrepresentation was not sufficient to bar rescission merely for lapse of time. 9–130

**Loss of the right to rescind by "acceptance"?** In *Leaf v International Galleries* Denning LJ said:[629] 9–131

> "An innocent misrepresentation is much less potent than a breach of condition; and a claim to rescission for innocent misrepresentation must at any rate be barred when the right to reject for breach of condition is barred".

In a non-consumer contract the right to reject for breach of condition[630] is barred by (inter alia) "acceptance", and this takes place: (a) when the buyer intimates that he accepts the goods; (b) when the goods have been delivered to him and he does any act inconsistent with the ownership of the seller; or (c) when after lapse of a reasonable time he retains the goods without intimating that he has rejected them.[631] In the first two cases, the buyer is not deemed to have accepted the goods until he has had a reasonable opportunity of examining them, and in the third the question whether he has had such an opportunity is material in determining whether a reasonable time has elapsed.[632] But in all three cases it is the opportunity of discovering the defect, rather than its actual discovery, which is the crucial factor, so that a buyer may "accept" without discovering the truth, and a literal reading of Denning LJ's dictum would suggest that acceptance will always deprive him of the right to rescind for innocent misrepresentation. But it is submitted that the dictum must be read, according to its context, to refer to cases

---

[623] *Gillett v Peppercorne* (1840) 3 Beav. 78; *Armstrong v Jackson* [1917] 2 K.B. 822; *Aaron's Reefs Ltd v Twiss* [1896] A.C. 273 at 287.
[624] *Erlanger v New Sombrero Phosphate Co* (1878) 3 App. Cas. 1218 at 1252.
[625] [1950] 2 K.B. 86.
[626] See para.8–019.
[627] *Salt v Stratstone Specialist Ltd* [2015] EWCA Civ 745; [2015] 2 C.L.C. 206 at [43]. As Roth J observes, this is "in essence the principle of laches".
[628] [2015] EWCA Civ 745; [2015] 2 C.L.C. 206.
[629] [1950] 2 K.B. 86 at 90.
[630] See para.18–106.
[631] Sale of Goods Act 1979 s.35(1) and (2). For consumer contracts, see para.18–062.
[632] Sale of Goods Act 1979 s.35(4) and (5).

in which a claim to rescission is resisted on the ground of lapse of time. In other words, it means only that, where lapse of time amounts to acceptance, then it may also bar the right to rescind for misrepresentation. If the buyer, in ignorance of the true facts, "accepts" in some other way he may nevertheless be able to rescind for misrepresentation; and he may, by virtue of s.1(a) of the Misrepresentation Act, be able to do this even where the misrepresentation had been incorporated in the contract. Even where lapse of time is in issue, in *Salt v Stratstone Specialist Ltd* Longmore LJ noted that *Leaf v International Galleries* was decided before the Misrepresentation Act was passed and "it must be doubtful … whether it is still good law that a representor should be in no worse position than if the representation had become a term of the contract."[633] In the same case, Roth J noted that the right to reject under a consumer contract is more complex as a result of the Consumer Rights Act 2015[634] and, as a result, it will "no longer be possible to align the equitable right to rescind for pre-contractual misrepresentation with the statutory scheme governing contractual rights."[635]

## 5. EXCLUDING LIABILITY FOR MISREPRESENTATION

9–132 The common law starts with the principle that contract terms which exclude liability for misrepresentation are valid. Their effectiveness may be limited by the general rules relating to exemption clauses, discussed elsewhere in this book,[636] e.g. liability in fraud cannot be excluded.[637] In addition, s.3(1) of the Misrepresentation Act 1967 provides:

> "If a contract contains a term which would exclude or restrict (*a*) any liability to which a party to a contract may be subject by reason of any misrepresentation made by him before the contract was made; or (*b*) any remedy available to another party to the contract by reason of such a misrepresentation, that term shall be of no effect except in so far as it satisfies the requirement of reasonableness as stated in section 11(1) of the Unfair Contract Terms Act 1977; and it is for those claiming that the term satisfies that requirement to show that it does".

### (a) Scope of the Misrepresentation Act 1967 s.3(1)

9–133 **Claims by consumers.** Section 3 of the Misrepresentation Act does not apply to a "consumer contract",[638] but clauses in such contracts which exclude or restrict liability for misrepresentation are subject to a test of fairness under the Consumer Rights Act 2015.[639]

9–134 **Non-contractual notices.** Section 3(1) applies only to contract terms. It does not apply to non-contractual notices which are ineffective if they seek to exclude

633 *Salt v Stratstone Specialist Ltd* [2015] EWCA Civ 745; [2015] 2 C.L.C. 206 at [34].
634 See para.18–062.
635 *Salt v Stratstone Specialist Ltd* [2015] EWCA Civ 745; [2015] 2 C.L.C. 206 at [49].
636 See Ch.7.
637 See para.7–034.
638 See para.7–042.
639 1967 Act s.3(2). See para.7–108.

liability for pre-contractual misrepresentations which have been made,[640] but they can be relied upon by a party to limit the scope of its representations, or determine whether any representations were made, or relied upon.[641]

**Excluding or restricting liabilities or remedies.** Section 3(1) covers not only clauses excluding or limiting a party's liability but also certain analogous terms, e.g. clauses which impose a short time-limit within which claims must be brought, or which exclude a particular remedy (such as rescission or set-off)[642] without affecting another (such as damages).[643] On the other hand, it probably does not cover a valid agreed damages clause, since this might in some circumstances extend rather than restrict liability.[644] The section applies to terms excluding or restricting "*any* remedy". This phrase obviously covers the normal remedies of damages and rescission and has been held to cover a clause under which the representee gives up "any rights" as a result of any misrepresentation.[645] It probably also covers terms restricting or excluding the right to plead misrepresentation as a defence,[646] for this could be described as a "remedy" in a broad sense. Similarly, a term excluding or restricting the right to retake goods obtained by fraud[647] would be within the section. **9–135**

**"No representation" or "non-reliance" clauses.**[648] Some terms purport not to exclude or restrict liability, or any remedy, as such, but rather to prevent liability from arising. The most common instance of this type of provision is a clause in which the parties agree, or acknowledge[649] that no representations have been made, or that they have not relied on any representations that have been made, either at all or save for those that are set out in the contract. The effect of such **9–136**

---

640 i.e. liability of the sort which may arise under s.2(1) of the Misrepresentation Act: see para.9–049. Non-contractual notices may be effective to exclude liability in claims for negligent misrepresentation at common law (see para.9–042) as is acknowledged by s.2 of the Unfair Contract Terms Act which applies to both contract terms and non-contractual notices: *Taberna Europe CDO II Plc v Selskabet* [2016] EWCA Civ 1262; [2017] Q.B. 633 at [18].

641 *IFE Fund SA v Goldman Sachs International* [2006] EWHC 2887 (Comm); [2007] 1 Lloyd's Rep. 264 at [65]; affirmed [2007] EWCA Civ 811; [2007] 2 Lloyd's Rep. 449 without further reference to this point; *Taberna Europe CDO II Plc v Selskabet* [2016] EWCA Civ 1262; [2017] Q.B. 633 at [20]; see para.9–009.

642 *Skipskreditforeningen v Emperor Navigation* [1998] 1 Lloyd's Rep. 67 at 74.

643 cf. para.7–043 for a similar definition in s.13 of Unfair Contract Terms Act 1977. That definition only applies in terms for the purposes of Pt I of the 1977 Act, which is not considered to include (though it amends) s.3 of the Misrepresentation Act 1967: see s.11(1) of the 1977 Act. An arbitration clause is excluded from the definition in s.13 of the 1977 Act, but may be covered by s.3 of the Misrepresentation Act.

644 cf. para.7–044.

645 *Trident Turboprop (Dublin) Ltd v First Flight Couriers Ltd* [2008] EWHC 1686 (Comm); [2008] 2 Lloyd's Rep. 581; affirmed without reference to this point: [2009] EWCA Civ 290; [2009] 3 W.L.R. 361.

646 See para.9–106.

647 See para.9–104.

648 Trukhtanov 125 L.Q.R. 648.

649 Whether it is a case of "agree", "acknowledge" or "represent" has been said not to be significant: *Springwell Navigation Corp v JP Morgan Chase Bank* [2010] EWCA Civ 1221; [2010] 2 C.L.C. 705 at [170]; but see *First Tower Trustees Ltd v CDS (Superstores) International Ltd* [2018] EWCA Civ 1396; [2019] 1 W.L.R. 637 at [94].

provisions has been considered in rather a large number of cases.[650] The position which appears to have been reached[651] may be reduced to the following propositions.

9–137 **Estoppel.** The effect of the type of provision under consideration may be to create an estoppel preventing the representee from basing his claim on the representation in question, because he is estopped from claiming either that a representation was made, or that he relied on it. In the case of estoppel by representation, the representor is required to show that he relied on the representee's counter-representation, in the form of the "no representation", or "non-reliance" clause,[652] and he will not be able to do so if it is clear that he did make a representation and it was intended that the representee should rely upon it.[653] However, the courts have recognised that such clauses may also result in a "contractual estoppel",[654] in relation to which it seems that the only requirement is that the clause is appropriately drafted[655] and has contractual force. There is no requirement of reliance by the representor,[656] nor any need to show, as is required for estoppel by convention,[657] that it would be unconscionable for the representee to resile from his own representation that no representation was made to him or that he did not rely on any that was made.[658] Furthermore, it is no bar to a finding of contractual estoppel that it is invoked to deny past facts,[659] i.e. where a

650 In addition to those cited below, see inter alia: *Camarata Property Inc v Credit Suisse Securities (Europe) Ltd* [2011] EWHC 479 (Comm); [2011] 1 C.L.C. 627; *Bank Leumi (UK) Plc v Wachner* [2011] EWHC 656 (Comm); [2011] 1 C.L.C. 454; *Cassa di Risparmio Della Repubblica di San Marino SpA v Barclays Bank Ltd* [2011] EWHC 484 (Comm); [2011] 1 C.L.C. 701.

651 *First Tower Trustees Ltd v CDS (Superstores) International Ltd* [2018] EWCA Civ 1396; [2019] 1 W.L.R. 637 at [89] (whether s.3 applies to such clauses "has been the subject of uncertainty and … confusion").

652 *Lowe v Lombank* [1960] 1 W.L.R. 196; *Watford Electronics Ltd v Sanderson CFL Ltd* [2001] EWCA Civ 317; [2001] B.L.R. 143 at [39]–[40].

653 *Quest 4 Finance Ltd v Maxfield* [2007] EWHC 2313; [2007] 2 C.L.C. 706.

654 *Peekay Intermark Ltd v ANZ Banking Group Ltd* [2006] EWCA Civ 386; [2006] 2 Lloyd's Rep. 511; *Raiffeisen Zentralbank Österreich AG v Royal Bank of Scotland Plc* [2010] EWHC 1392 (Comm); [2011] 1 Lloyd's Rep. 123; *Springwell Navigation Corp v JP Morgan Chase Bank* [2010] EWCA Civ 1221; [2010] 2 C.L.C. 705. For criticism of the concept of "contractual estoppel" see McMeel [2011] L.M.C.L.Q. 185; cf. Loi [2015] L.M.C.L.Q. 346; Braithwaite 132 L.Q.R. 120.

655 It must of course take effect *as a contract*, but this may be assumed if the clause is set out in what is a binding contract.

656 The basis of the "estoppel" is agreement, not reliance: *Springwell Navigation Corp v JP Morgan Chase Bank* [2010] EWCA Civ 1221; [2010] 2 C.L.C. 705 at [144].

657 See para.3–094.

658 *Springwell Navigation Corp v JP Morgan Chase Bank* [2010] EWCA Civ 1221; [2010] 2 C.L.C. 705 at [177].

659 *Springwell Navigation Corp v JP Morgan Chase Bank* [2010] EWCA Civ 1221; [2010] 2 C.L.C. 705 at [144].

representation was made and was relied upon.[660] As a matter of contract "the parties can bind themselves at common law to a fictional state of affairs".[661]

**Drafting.** It has been noted above that in order to provide the basis for contractual estoppel, the term in question must have been appropriately drafted. It must make clear that any representations that may have been made are "withdrawn, overridden or of no legal effect so far as any liability for misrepresentation may be concerned".[662] It is not sufficient to point to wording that may be typical of an entire agreement clause that any representations made shall not take effect *as terms of the contract*; it is necessary to convey the parties' agreement that they shall not take effect *as representations*.[663] In one case, an entire agreement clause failed in this requirement because there was "no language to the effect that the parties were agreed that no representations had been made or relied upon".[664] 9–138

**An exclusion clause "in substance".** Whether by way of estoppel by representation or contractual estoppel, a "no representation" or "non-reliance" clause may prevent the representee from seeking relief for misrepresentation. So far as the application of s.3(1) of the Misrepresentation Act 1967 is concerned, a potential problem arises in that the wording of the section is limited to terms which "exclude or restrict" liability or any remedy and, strictly speaking, terms of the type under consideration do not exclude or restrict any anterior liability; they prevent it from arising in the first place. Given the ease with which this might allow a party to draft around s.3(1),[665] the courts have said that it is a question of "substance, and not form" whether a term amounts to an exclusion or restriction of liability for the purpose of applying the reasonableness test set out therein.[666] 9–139

**Exclusionary or evidential?** The test of substance requires the court to distinguish between two situations.[667] First, where the term in question is relevant 9–140

660 Comments from Diplock J in *Lowe v Lombank* [1960] 1 W.L.R. 196 in apparent support of such a submission have been found either to be not on point: *Springwell Navigation Corp v JP Morgan Chase Bank* [2010] EWCA Civ 1221; [2010] 2 C.L.C. 705 at [150], or, to the extent necessary, wrong: *Raiffeisen Zentralbank Österreich AG v Royal Bank of Scotland Plc* [2010] EWHC 1392 (Comm); [2011] 1 Lloyd's Rep. 123 at [255].

661 *First Tower Trustees Ltd v CDS (Superstores) International Ltd* [2018] EWCA Civ 1396; [2019] 1 W.L.R. 637 at [47].

662 *BSkyB Ltd v HP Enterprise Services UK Ltd* [2010] EWHC 86 (TCC); [2010] B.L.R. 267 at [382].

663 *BSkyB Ltd v HP Enterprise Services UK Ltd* [2010] EWHC 86 (TCC); [2010] B.L.R. 267; cf. *Deepak v ICI* [1999] 1 Lloyd's Rep. 387; *Mears Ltd v Shoreline Housing Partnership Ltd* [2013] EWCA Civ 639; 148 Con L.R. 221 at [16]–[17].

664 *Axa Sun Life Services Plc v Campbell Martin Ltd* [2011] EWCA Civ 133; [2011] 2 Lloyd's Rep. 1 at [92]; cf. *Al Hasawi v Nottingham Forest Football Club Ltd* [2018] EWHC 2884 (Ch).

665 See, especially, the colourful view of Scarman LJ in *Cremdean Properties v Nash* (1977) 244 E.G. 547 at 550; cf. *First Tower Trustees Ltd v CDS (Superstores) International Ltd* [2018] EWCA Civ 1396; [2019] 1 W.L.R. 637 at [51], [99].

666 See, e.g. *Raiffeisen Zentralbank Österreich AG v Royal Bank of Scotland Plc* [2010] EWHC 1392 (Comm); [2011] 1 Lloyd's Rep. 123 at [310].

667 One way of capturing the distinction which follows is to ask if the term in question purports to "re-write history": *Raiffeisen Zentralbank Österreich AG v Royal Bank of Scotland Plc* [2010] EWHC 1392 (Comm); [2011] 1 Lloyd's Rep. 123 at [314].

to establishing whether a representation was in fact made at all, or was relied upon. This may be referred to as its evidential role. Where the term is relevant in this sense only as part of the "factual investigation", it does not amount, in substance, to an exclusion clause. In the second situation, where it is clear that, as a matter of fact, representations were made and relied upon and the term in question is invoked to defeat the claim that would otherwise be available to the representee, on the basis of an estoppel, it is treated in substance as an exclusion clause falling within s.3.[668] As has been said by Moore-Bick LJ: "Section 3 is concerned with attempts to exclude liability after the event. It is not concerned with the question whether there has actually been a misrepresentation."[669]

9–141 **A question of timing?** In drawing the distinction just referred to, an important factor will be the point in time at which the "no representation" or "non-reliance" clause is agreed. If it is agreed before the parties exchange information in order to regulate their future relationship, then it may have an evidential role; as for example where the parties enter into a confidentiality agreement,[670] or information memorandum.[671] As Leggatt LJ acknowledged in *First Tower Trustees Ltd v CDS (Superstores) International Ltd*, in a case of that kind "there may be a question as to whether, in the light of the term, a particular communication would reasonably be understood to be making a representation of fact [and] [t]he existence of such a term may also be relevant in determining whether the party to whom the communication was addressed did in fact rely on any such representation".[672] Even in such a case, however, if on the facts a claim for misrepresentation is made out, any further reliance on the term to create an estoppel will be regarded as an attempt to exclude liability.[673] The position is said to be "simpler" where the "no representation" or "non-reliance" clause is retrospective in its intended effect because it appears only in the contract which is

---

[668] *First Tower Trustees Ltd v CDS (Superstores) International Ltd* [2018] EWCA Civ 1396; [2019] 1 W.L.R. 637; disapproving *Sears v Minco Plc* [2016] EWHC 433 (Ch) at [80]; and *Thornbridge v Barclays Bank Plc* [2015] EWHC 3430 (QB) at [111]–[112]; cf. *IFE Fund SA v Goldman Sachs International* [2006] EWHC 2887 (Comm); [2007] 1 Lloyd's Rep. 264; affirmed [2007] EWCA Civ 811; [2007] 2 Lloyd's Rep. 449; *Trident Turboprop (Dublin) Ltd v First Flight Couriers Ltd* [2008] EWHC 1686 (Comm); [2008] 2 Lloyd's Rep. 581 (in which Aikens J applies a "but for" test reminiscent of that used in *Smith v Eric S Bush* [1990] 1 A.C. 831 (para.7–045)) affirmed [2009] EWCA Civ 290; [2009] 3 W.L.R. 361; *Raiffeisen Zentralbank Österreich AG v Royal Bank of Scotland Plc* [2010] EWHC 1392 (Comm); [2011] 1 Lloyd's Rep. 123 at [310]–[316]; *Springwell Navigation Corp v JP Morgan Chase Bank* [2010] EWCA Civ 1221; [2010] 2 C.L.C. 705 at [180]. A statement can take effect as a misrepresentation in spite of the fact that it is made in a document expressly warning the representee to make his own enquiries into its accuracy: *Walker v Boyle* [1982] 1 W.L.R. 495; cf. *South Western General Property Co Ltd v Marton* (1982) 263 E.G. 1090.

[669] *Taberna Europe CDO II Plc v Selskabet* [2016] EWCA Civ 1262; [2017] Q.B. 633 at [20].

[670] See, e.g. *Raiffeisen Zentralbank Österreich AG v Royal Bank of Scotland Plc* [2010] EWHC 1392 (Comm); [2011] 1 Lloyd's Rep. 123.

[671] See, e.g. *IFE Fund SA v Goldman Sachs International* [2006] EWHC 2887 (Comm); [2007] 1 Lloyd's Rep. 264; affirmed [2007] EWCA Civ 811; [2007] 2 Lloyd's Rep. 449.

[672] *First Tower Trustees Ltd v CDS (Superstores) International Ltd* [2018] EWCA Civ 1396; [2019] 1 W.L.R. 637 at [106].

[673] *First Tower Trustees Ltd v CDS (Superstores) International Ltd* [2018] EWCA Civ 1396; [2019] 1 W.L.R. 637 at [107].

induced by the alleged misrepresentation.[674] In such a case, the term is not relevant to the "factual investigation" and is only relevant to found a defence, based on the estoppel, which excludes liability and therefore falls within s.3.[675]

**Other terms preventing liability from arising.** In a similar vein to "no representation" or "non-reliance clauses", a clause in an auctioneer's catalogue might provide that all representations in it are statements of opinion only. If the court, on applying the tests stated earlier in this chapter,[676] concludes that a representation in the catalogue would, but for the clause, be one of fact, it may hold that the clause falls within s.3(1). By contrast, it seems that s.3(1) would not apply to a term in a contract made through an agent negativing his ostensible authority to make representations as to the subject-matter.[677] 9–142

**Negligent misrepresentation.** Section 3(1) applies only to provisions excluding or restricting the liability of a "party to a contract", and the subsequent words of the section show that this means *the* contract induced by the misrepresentation. The section therefore would not apply to disclaimers of liability in cases such as *Hedley Byrne & Co Ltd v Heller & Partners Ltd*[678] and *Smith v Eric S Bush*[679] since the contracts induced by the misrepresentations in those cases were not made with the representor but with a third person. Such disclaimers of liability for negligence in giving advice may, however, be subject to the test of reasonableness under s.2(2) of the Unfair Contract Terms Act 1977. As will be seen below,[680] the scope of that test is, in several ways, narrower than that of s.3(1) of the Misrepresentation Act 1967, but the issue just encountered under that section can also arise. For, while s.2(2) is subject to s.13(1) of the 1977 Act which extends it to any term which excludes or restricts the "relevant obligation or duty",[681] that still leaves the question of whether a term excludes or restricts a duty or simply establishes what that duty is in the first place, i.e. determines the scope or "basis" of the contract.[682] 9–143

**Misrepresentation and breach of contract.** Where a misrepresentation has been made, s.3(1) clearly applies to terms excluding or restricting liability for mere misrepresentations.[683] It equally clearly does not apply to terms which exclude or restrict liability only for breaches of pure promises (as opposed to statements of 9–144

---

[674] Quaere the effect of provision of a draft contract containing a "no representation" clause or "non-reliance" clause before information is exchanged, where such clauses may operate as non-contractual notices: see para.9–134.

[675] *First Tower Trustees Ltd v CDS (Superstores) International Ltd* [2018] EWCA Civ 1396; [2019] 1 W.L.R. 637 at [109].

[676] See para.9–015.

[677] See *Overbrooke Estates Ltd v Glencombe Properties Ltd* [1974] 1 W.L.R. 1335; Coote [1975] C.L.J. 17; the amendments to s.3 made by Unfair Contract Terms Act 1977 s.8(1) appear not to affect the point; cf. *Museprime Properties Ltd v Adhill Properties Ltd* [1990] 2 E.G.L.R. 196 at 200.

[678] [1964] A.C. 465; para.9–042.

[679] *Smith v Eric S Bush* [1990] 1 A.C. 831; para.7–045.

[680] See para.9–144.

[681] See para.7–045.

[682] See, e.g. *Crestsign Ltd v National Westminster Bank Plc* [2014] EWHC 3043 (Ch) at [119]; *Thornbridge v Barclays Bank Plc* [2015] EWHC 3430 (QB).

[683] For the possible application of the section to cases of non-disclosure, see para.9–188.

fact) or for breaches of implied terms not dependent on statements of fact. Terms which exclude or restrict liability only for such breaches may be subject to the test of reasonableness under the Unfair Contract Terms Act 1977.[684] But the scope of the test under that Act is limited:[685] it does not, for example, generally apply where the party relying on the clause has made the contract otherwise than in the course of a business, nor does it apply to certain specified contracts, such as contracts for the sale of land.[686] The scope of s.3 of the Misrepresentation Act is not so limited; and the difference in the scope of the two Acts gives rise to two problems.[687] In discussing these, we shall assume that the case is one in which the reasonableness test under the 1977 Act does not apply.

9–145 **Incorporated misrepresentation.** Where a misrepresentation is incorporated in the contract, the right to rescind for misrepresentation is preserved by s.1(a), and a term purporting to exclude or restrict that right would be within s.3(1). But a term may purport to exclude or restrict liabilities or remedies available only because the representation has been incorporated in the contract, e.g. it may provide that the representee is to recover no more than out-of-pocket expenses and is not to have damages for loss of his bargain.[688] It seems that such a term would not be within s.3(1), for the liability which it purported to exclude would arise, not by reason of the *making* of the representation, but by reason of its *incorporation* into the contract. This conclusion is, however, subject to the point next to be discussed.

9–146 **Provision applicable to misrepresentation and breach.** A single term may exclude liability for misrepresentation *and* for breach of contract. A clause excluding liability "for all defects" would have this effect where some defects were merely represented not to exist while others amounted to breaches of contract. Section 3(1) provides that where a term would exclude or restrict any liability for misrepresentation "*that term* shall be of no effect except in so far as" the test of reasonableness is satisfied. It seems to follow that the *whole* term may be subject to the reasonableness test and not only the part of it which excludes liability for misrepresentation, unless that part is severable,[689] in which case the reasonableness of the part relating to breach would, if it fell within relevant provisions of the Unfair Contract Terms Act 1977,[690] have to be determined under that Act. An unseverable term excluding liability for "misrepresentation" generally could be ineffective (if unreasonable)[691] to exclude contractual liability for an incorporated misrepresentation.[692]

684 See para.7–039 and following.
685 See paras 7–079–7–085.
686 See para.7–080.
687 Under the Consumer Rights Act 2015 the same test of fairness, with the same scope for application, is applied to all of the types of clauses discussed in the paragraphs following when included in a "consumer contract": see para.7–100.
688 cf. paras 9–073–9–078.
689 cf. paras 7–069–7–072; para.9–150.
690 See paras 7–051–7–060.
691 See para.9–150.
692 *Skipskreditforeningen v Emperor Navigation* [1998] 1 Lloyd's Rep. 67 at 75 in which Mance J expressed doubt as to the correctness of the rule of "non-severance"; see para.7–069, and para.9–150.

**Misrepresentation in the performance of the contract.** Section 3(1) applies to terms excluding or restricting liability for misrepresentations made before the conclusion of the contract. It does not apply to terms excluding or restricting liability for misrepresentations made in the course of *performing* a contract. However, in general[693] such liability is likely to be incurred only by a person who acts in the course of a business and is negligent, e.g. by a negligent surveyor or valuer. In such a case, a term excluding or restricting liability is subject to the test of reasonableness under the Unfair Contract Terms Act 1977.[694] If the representation was fraudulent, a clause excluding liability for it is void at common law.[695] **9–147**

**International supply contracts.** Section 3(1) does not apply if the contract is an international supply contract within the meaning of s.26 of the Unfair Contract Terms Act.[696] **9–148**

## (b) The reasonableness test

**Guidelines.** Section 3(1) of the Misrepresentation Act applies "the test of reasonableness as stated in s.11(1) of the Unfair Contract Terms Act 1977" to terms falling within its scope. Section 11(1) of the 1977 Act provides that, in order to determine whether the test of reasonableness is satisfied, regard is to be had to the circumstances which were, or ought reasonably to have been, known to or in the contemplation of the parties at the time of contracting. This rule is expressly stated in s.11(1) to apply for the purposes of s.3(1) of the Misrepresentation Act 1967. The 1977 Act also lays down guidelines for determining reasonableness; these take effect under s.11(2) and (4) of that Act.[697] At first sight, none of these guidelines apply for the purpose of s.3(1) of the Misrepresentation Act, since s.3(1) of that Act refers only to s.11(1) of the 1977 Act, while s.11(2) of that Act contains no words that could be taken to refer to s.3(1) of the 1967 Act. However, the guidelines contained in s.11(4) are there said to apply where "the question arises (under this *or any other* Act) whether the term … satisfies the test of reasonableness". In view of the italicised words, those guidelines[698] are, it is submitted, applicable for the purpose of s.3(1) of the Misrepresentation Act. Even the guidelines referred to in s.11(2) apply by analogy to contracts which are not literally within the wording of the subsection[699]; and they could by a process of further analogous extension be applied to cases in which the reasonableness test applies by virtue only of s.3(1) of the 1967 Act. The statutory guidelines are, moreover, not exhaustive for the **9–149**

693 For an exception, see *Chaudhry v Prabhakar* [1989] 1 W.L.R. 29.
694 i.e. s.2(2); para.7–052.
695 See para.7–034.
696 *Trident Turboprop (Dublin) Ltd v First Flight Couriers Ltd* [2009] EWCA Civ 290; [2009] 3 W.L.R. 361.
697 See paras 7–064–7–065.
698 See para.7–064.
699 See para.7–065.

purpose of s.3(1): in this respect their position under this section is indistinguishable from that under the 1977 Act.[700]

9–150 **Severability.** A term which purports to exclude liability for "misrepresentation" or for "any misrepresentation" may be taken to extend to liability for fraudulent misrepresentation, which cannot be excluded as a matter of common law.[701] Since the test of reasonableness is applied to the whole of a term which falls within its scope,[702] it would seem that such a term, if interpreted so as to exclude liability in fraud cannot be enforced, even if it is not being relied upon to exclude such liability.[703] An alternative and, it is submitted, preferable view is that, as a matter of interpretation, when a term purporting to exclude liability refers simply to "misrepresentation" the parties cannot have intended to exclude liability in fraud in the absence of an express provision to this effect.[704]

9–151 **Application of the test.** The reasonableness test has been applied most commonly in connection with "no representation" and "non-reliance" clauses", which are often found to be reasonable in the type of commercial contracts in which they are usually included.[705] In leases or contracts for the sale of land, clauses excluding or restricting liability for misrepresentation have occasionally been found to be unreasonable,[706] even in contracts between commercial parties.[707]

## 6. NON-DISCLOSURE

### (a) General rule

9–152 **No duty of disclosure.** As a general rule, a person who is about to enter into a contract is under no duty to disclose material facts known to him but not to the other party.[708] Thus it has been held that a landlord is not liable in deceit if before letting his house he fails to tell the tenant that it is in a ruinous condition.[709]

---

700 See para.7–066.

701 See para.7–034.

702 See para.9–146.

703 *Thomas Witter Ltd v TBP Industries Ltd* [1996] 2 All E.R. 573 at 598; *South West Water Services Ltd v International Computers Ltd* [1999] B.L.R. 420.

704 *Zanzibar v British Aerospace (Lancaster House) Ltd* [2001] 1 W.L.R. 2333; *Six Continents Hotels Inc v Event Hotels GmbH* [2006] EWHC 2317 (QB) at [53]; *Raiffeisen Zentralbank Österreich AG v Royal Bank of Scotland Plc* [2010] EWHC 1392 (Comm); [2011] 1 Lloyd's Rep. 123 at [325].

705 See, e.g. *Springwell Navigation Corp v JP Morgan Chase Bank* [2010] EWCA Civ 1221; [2010] 2 C.L.C. 705; cf. *National Westminster Bank Plc v Utrecht-America Finance Co* [2001] EWCA Civ 658; [2001] 3 All E.R. 733 at [6]–[61]; *Lloyd v Browning* [2013] EWCA Civ 1637; [2014] 1 P & C.R. 11.

706 *Walker v Boyle* [1982] 1 W.L.R. 495 (residential purchase).

707 *Cleaver v Schyde Investments Ltd* [2011] EWCA Civ 929; [2011] 2 P & C.R. 21; *First Tower Trustees Ltd v CDS (Superstores) International Ltd* [2018] EWCA Civ 1396; [2019] 1 W.L.R. 637.

708 *Norwich Union Life Ins Co Ltd v Qureshi* [1999] 2 All E.R. (Comm) 707 at 717; cf. *The Unique Mariner* [1978] 1 Lloyd's Rep. 438 at 449; *Lloyds Bank v Egremont* [1990] 2 F.L.R. 351.

709 *Keates v Cadogan* (1851) 10 C.B. 591.

Sometimes the rule may appear to operate harshly; but if a general duty of disclosure did exist it would be very hard to say exactly what must be disclosed in any particular case.

**Representation by conduct.** As we have seen, a representation may be implied by the conduct of the defendant,[710] in which case the defendant is liable for misrepresentation and not for non-disclosure. 9–153

**Latent defects known to the seller.** It has been said that a person must disclose latent defects in the subject-matter of the contract which are known to him.[711] But cases which may appear to support this view are also best explained on the ground of active misrepresentation[712] by words or by conduct and the preferable view is that English law does not recognise any general duty to disclose known latent defects. In *Ward v Hobbs*[713] pigs were taken to Newbury market and sold there "with all faults". The seller knew that the pigs were diseased but he did not disclose this fact to the buyer. It was held that the buyer had no remedy as there was no general duty to disclose known latent defects and any representation which might be inferred from the seller's conduct in taking the pigs to market was negatived by the words "with all faults". These words might, on such facts, now protect the seller only if they satisfied the legislative requirements of reasonableness or fairness.[714] Moreover, if the thing sold suffers from a latent defect of which the seller knows, and if that defect causes injury to the buyer, or harm to other property belonging to him, then the seller's failure to warn the buyer of the defect may make him liable in negligence; and it has been suggested that *Ward v Hobbs* may require reconsideration in the light of this possibility.[715] But there is generally no such liability where the defect caused no loss to the buyer except in making the thing sold less valuable than he had supposed it to be.[716] Cases of this kind continue to be governed by the general rule that there is no duty of disclosure. 9–154

**Sale of land.** The general rule has been applied where land sold was subject to a latent physical defect;[717] and it has similarly been held that a vendor of a leasehold interest was not bound to disclose the fact that the organisation to which the premises were let had only a limited "life".[718] There is some support 9–155

---

[710] See para.9–008.

[711] *Horsfall v Thomas* (1862) 1 H. & C. 90 at 100.

[712] e.g. *Hill v Gray* (1816) 1 Stark. 434; as explained in *Keates v Cadogan* (1851) 10 C.B. at 600.

[713] (1878) 4 App. Cas. 13; cf. *Bodger v Nicholls* (1873) 28 L.T. 441, discussed at para.9–008.

[714] See paras 7–052, 9–132 and following.

[715] *Hurley v Dyke* [1979] R.T.R. 265 at 303. For a similar duty to disclose one's own *breach* where it may lead to danger, see para.9–180.

[716] cf. para.14–050. There is no such liability in tort even where (exceptionally) there *is* a duty of disclosure because the contract is uberrimae fidei (para.9–164): *Banque Keyser Ullmann SA v Skandia (UK) Ins Co Ltd* [1990] 1 Q.B. 665 at 798–800; [1991] 2 A.C. 249 at 282 (where the decision was affirmed on other grounds).

[717] *Shepherd v Croft* [1911] 1 Ch. 521.

[718] *Safehaven Investments Ltd v Springbok Ltd* (1996) 71 P. & C.R. 59.

for the view that on a sale of land latent defects of title must be disclosed[719] but even here it seems that there is no general duty of disclosure, and that an undisclosed defect of this kind is a ground for relief only if it is unusual,[720] or if it leads to a breach of contract[721] or to an operative mistake.[722] It can also, if known to the vendor, prevent him from relying on a term of the contract under which the purchaser is deemed to have made enquiries relating to the matter in question and to have knowledge of it.[723]

9–156 **Latent qualities known to the buyer.** The general rule that there is no duty of disclosure also applies where the buyer knows (but the seller does not) of some latent quality which makes the subject-matter of the contract *more* valuable. Thus a contract for the sale of land is binding even though the buyer, but not the seller, knew that it contained valuable minerals.[724]

## (b) Exceptions

9–157 **Extent of duty of disclosure.** There are many important exceptions to the rule that there is no liability for non-disclosure. In these exceptional cases, a person is, in general, bound to disclose only facts which he knew (or which he would have known if he had not "wilfully shut his eyes" to them).[725] A person may, however, be under a duty to disclose facts which, though not known to him, were known to his agent, if that knowledge had been acquired within the scope of the agent's authority and if it was the agent's duty to communicate it to the principal.[726] He may also be under a duty to disclose facts which he ought to have known, if there is a "special relationship" between the parties within *Hedley Byrne & Co Ltd v Heller & Partners Ltd*.[727]

9–158 **A continuing duty.** Where a duty of disclosure exists, it generally continues until the contract becomes legally binding.[728] But where a contract is regarded as binding as a matter of business the duty to disclose may cease at that point even

---

[719] *Selkirk v Romar Investments Ltd* [1963] 1 W.L.R. 1415 at 1423; *Faruqi v English Real Estates* [1979] 1 W.L.R. 963; *William Sindall Plc v Cambridgeshire CC* [1994] 1 W.L.R. 1016 at 1023.

[720] *Molyneux v Hawtrey* [1903] 2 K.B. 487; cf. *Celsteel Ltd v Alton House Holdings Ltd (No.2)* [1986] 1 All E.R. 598 at 607 (not reported on this point in [1986] 1 W.L.R. 666).

[721] e.g. *Flight v Booth* (1834) 1 Bing. N.C. 370; *Peyman v Lanjani* [1985] Ch. 457 at 496. Certain covenants for title are implied under Law of Property (Miscellaneous Provisions) Act 1994 Pt I.

[722] See para.8–051.

[723] *Rignall Developments Ltd v Halil* [1988] Ch. 190.

[724] *Smith v Hughes* (1871) L.R. 6 Q.B. 587 at 604; quaere whether the contract would be specifically enforced: para.21–035; cf. also *Phillips v Homfray* (1871) L.R. 7 Ch. App. 770.

[725] *Blackburn, Low & Co v Vigors* (1887) 12 App. Cas. 531; *Economides v Commercial Union Assurance Co Plc* [1998] Q.B. 587 at 602; cf. *William Sindall Plc v Cambridgeshire CC* [1994] 1 W.L.R. 1016 (where the contract expressly restricted the duty in this way).

[726] *Proudfoot v Montefiore* (1867) L.R. 2 Q.B. 511; *Joel v Law Union and Crown Ins Co* [1908] 2 K.B. 863.

[727] [1964] A.C. 465; para.9–043.

[728] *Container Transport International Inc v Oceanus Mutual, etc., Association* [1984] 1 Lloyd's Rep. 476 at 486; disapproved on another point in *Pan Atlantic Ins Co v Pine Top Incs Co* [1995] 2 A.C. 501 (para.9–168; para.9–028).

though the contract is not yet binding in law. Thus in contracts of insurance[729] the duty ceases when the insurer initials a slip saying that he will accept the risk, even where there is no legally binding contract until a policy is executed.[730] Conversely, the duty may in a sense continue even after the conclusion of the contract. For example, a person who takes a fidelity bond for the honesty of one of his servants is under a continuing duty to disclose to the surety any acts of dishonesty on the part of the servant;[731] and the express or implied terms of a contract may impose a contractual duty of disclosure to be further discussed below.[732] Once the parties become engaged in hostile litigation, however, any continuing duties of disclosure are superseded by the rules of procedure which govern such litigation.[733] Failure to perform a continuing (post-contractual) duty of disclosure does not, moreover, vitiate the *formation* of the contract but amounts to a *breach* of one of its express or implied terms;[734] and this distinction has significant effects, to be discussed below,[735] on the remedies for this type of non-disclosure.

### (i) *Representation falsified by later events*

**Duty to correct representation later made false.** A person may have to disclose material facts which come to his notice[736] before the conclusion of a contract if they falsify a representation previously made[737] by him.[738] In *With v O'Flanagan*[739] negotiations for the sale of a medical practice were begun in January, when the practice was said to be worth £2,000. A contract of sale was made on 1 May, by which time the practice had become worthless because of the intervening illness of the vendor. The contract was set aside on the ground that the vendor ought to have communicated this change of circumstances to the purchasers. But there would probably be no need to disclose minor variations in the income of the practice.[740] And there are obvious limitations on the scope of 9–159

729 See para.9–165.

730 *Cory v Patton* (1872) L.R. 7 Q.B. 304; *Citadel Ins Co v Atlantic Union Ins Co* [1982] 2 Lloyd's Rep. 543 at 548.

731 *Phillips v Foxall* (1872) L.R. 7 Q.B. 666; cf. *Roadworks (1952) Ltd v Charman* [1994] 2 Lloyd's Rep. 99 at 107–108.

732 See para.9–180.

733 *The Star Sea* [2001] UKHL 1; [2003] 1 A.C. 469 at [73]–[78]; *Agapitos v Agnew* [2002] EWCA Civ 247; [2003] Q.B. 556 at [52].

734 cf. para.9–097.

735 See para.9–187.

736 Or, which, if there is a "special relationship", should have come to his notice, had he exercised reasonable care: see para.9–043.

737 For this requirement, see *English v Dedham Vale Properties Ltd* [1978] 1 W.L.R. 93 at 104.

738 The obligation to correct any falsehood applies only to the representor: *The Kriti Palm* [2006] EWCA Civ 1601; [2007] 1 Lloyd's Rep. 555 at [296].

739 [1936] Ch. 575; cf. *Traill v Baring* (1864) 4 D.J. & S. 318; *Brownlie v Campbell* (1880) 5 App. Cas. 925 at 950; *Zamir v S of S for the Home Dept* [1980] A.C. 730 at 750; *Spice Girls Ltd v Aprilia World Service BV* [2002] EWCA Civ 15; [2002] E.M.L.R. 27 at [51], [58]; *Foodco UK LLP v Henry Boot Developments Ltd* [2010] EWHC 358 (Ch) at [214]; *Fitzroy Robinson Ltd v Mentmore Towers Ltd* [2009] EWHC 1552 (TCC); [2009] B.L.R. 555; *Cramaso LLP v Viscount Reidhaven's Trustees* [2014] UKSC 9; [2014] 2 W.L.R. 317; *Inter Export LLC v Townley* [2018] EWCA Civ 2068.

740 For the possible application of the Misrepresentation Act 1967, see para.9–188.

any duty of disclosure which may arise from a statement such as one as to a person's financial position, which can influence a series of transactions extending, perhaps, over many years. A time must come when the representation loses its force and the representee begins to rely rather on his own judgment.[741]

9–160 **Change of mind.** There are conflicting decisions on the question whether a duty of disclosure arises where during negotiations a party makes a representation as to his present intention but changes his mind before the conclusion of the contract. In *Traill v Baring*[742] an insurance company made a proposal for reinsurance to a second company, stating that it would retain part of the risk. This was its intention when it made the representation but before the proposal was accepted it disposed of that part of the risk. It was held that the "change of intention"[743] of the first company should have been disclosed to the second company. On the other hand, in *Wales v Wadham*[744] a husband who had left his wife made her an offer of financial provision after she had declared her intention of not remarrying. She accepted the offer after having decided to marry again. If the husband had known this, he would have made a lower offer; but it was held that the wife was not bound to disclose her change of mind. The duty of disclosing changed circumstances was said only to apply where the original representation was one of *fact*: not where it was one of *intention*.[745] The view that the wife was not bound to disclose her decision to remarry was disapproved by the House of Lords in *Jenkins v Livesey*,[746] but only on the ground that the agreement for financial provision had been embodied in a consent order made in matrimonial proceedings; and that parties seeking such an order were, by statute,[747] under a duty to make full and frank disclosure to the court which made the order. So far as common law liability was concerned, *Wales v Wadham* was approved, though without any reference to *Traill v Baring*. It may be possible to reconcile these two decisions by saying that in *Traill v Baring* the first company had, before acceptance of its offer, not merely changed its mind but acted accordingly, while the wife in *Wales v Wadham* had not actually remarried when she accepted the husband's offer; or by saying that the wife's statement in the latter case was as to an intention so intrinsically likely to be changed that the husband should not have relied on the statement. Subject to these possible distinctions, it is submitted that the principle in *Traill v Baring* is to be preferred; for, in cases of this kind, what was originally a misrepresentation of intention becomes by the time of contracting one of fact, viz. as to the representor's state of mind at that time.[748] And there is no difficulty in specifying exactly what should be disclosed, so that the reason for the general rule against imposing a duty of disclosure does not apply.

---

741 cf. *Argy Trading Development Co Ltd v Lapid Developments Ltd* [1977] 1 W.L.R. 444 at 461–462; *Limit (No.2) Ltd v Axa Versicherung AG* [2008] EWCA Civ 1231; [2008] 2 C.L.C. 673 at [26].

742 (1864) 4 D.J. & S. 318.

743 *Traill v Baring* (1864) 4 D.J. & S. 318 at 326, 330.

744 [1977] 1 W.L.R. 199.

745 *Wales v Wadham* [1977] 1 W.L.R. 199 at 211.

746 [1985] A.C. 424.

747 Matrimonial Causes Act 1973 ss.23–25.

748 See para.9–017.

**Consumer insurance contract.** Under s.2(3) of the Consumer Insurance (Disclosure and Representations) Act 2012 "a failure by the consumer to comply with the insurer's request to confirm or amend particulars previously given is capable of being a misrepresentation" for the purposes of the Act, whether or not it would be apart from s.2(3). **9–161**

### (ii) *Statement literally true, but misleading*

A person is guilty of misrepresentation, though all the facts stated by him are true, if his statement is misleading as a whole because it does not refer to other facts affecting the weight of those stated. In *Notts Patent Brick and Tile Co v Butler*[749] a purchaser of land asked the vendor's solicitor whether the land was subject to restrictive covenants. The solicitor replied that he was not aware of any, but failed to add that this was because he had not troubled to read the relevant documents. The solicitor's reply, though literally true, amounted to a misrepresentation entitling the purchaser to rescind. The duty of disclosure in cases of this kind is narrower than that which exists in contracts uberrimae fidei, which are discussed below.[750] The maker of a statement which is literally true but on the whole misleading is required to disclose only such facts as affect the weight of those stated[751]; he need not disclose further facts merely because they might reasonably be regarded by the representee as material.[752] **9–162**

### (iii) *Custom*

In *Jones v Bowden*[753] pimento was sold after having been damaged by sea water. It was usual in the trade, when pimento had been so damaged, to declare this, but the seller failed to make such a declaration. He was held liable in deceit as, in view of the custom, his silence amounted to misrepresentation. **9–163**

### (iv) *Contracts uberrimae fidei*

There is a duty to disclose material facts in contracts uberrimae fidei (i.e. of "utmost good faith"), in which one party is in a particularly strong position, and the other in a particularly weak one, to know the material facts. **9–164**

**Insurance.** For many years, the principal example of contracts uberrimae fidei has been insurance contracts: **9–165**

749 (1886) 16 Q.B.D. 778; cf. *R. v Kylsant* [1932] 1 K.B. 442; *Faruqi v English Real Estates* [1979] 1 W.L.R. 963; *The Lucy* [1983] 1 Lloyd's Rep. 188; *Cemp Properties (UK) Ltd v Dentsply Research & Development Corp* [1991] 2 E.G.L.R. 197; *Wemyss v Karim* [2016] EWCA Civ 27 at [38].

750 See paras 9–164–9–173.

751 See the common law position with regard to company prospectuses, as stated in *New Brunswick and Canada Ry v Muggeridge* (1860) 1 Dr. & Sm. 363 at 381; approved in *Central Ry of Venezuela v Kisch* (1867) L.R. 2. H.L. 99; cf. *Oakes v Turquand* (1867) L.R. 2 H.L. 325. For statutory duties of disclosure in such cases, see para.9–178.

752 *Aaron's Reefs Ltd v Twiss* [1896] A.C. 273 at 287.

753 (1813) 4 Taunt. 847.

> "It has been for centuries in England the law in connection with insurance of all sorts, marine, fire, life, guarantee and every kind of policy, that, as the underwriter knows nothing and the man who comes to him to ask him to insure knows everything, it is the duty of the assured … to make a full disclosure to the underwriters, without being asked, of all the material circumstances".[754]

However, some important changes to the law have been made in relation to consumer insurance contracts by the Consumer Insurance (Disclosure and Representations) Act 2012 and in relation to non-consumer insurance contracts by the Insurance Act 2015.

9–166 **Consumer insurance contracts.**[755] Under the Consumer Insurance (Disclosure and Representations) Act 2012, the duty of disclosure no longer applies to a "consumer insurance contract".[756] Instead, the insured is only under an obligation to take reasonable care[757] not to make a misrepresentation to the insurer.[758] It was the intention of the Law Commission that "misrepresentation" should be interpreted according to common law principles,[759] but a failure by the consumer to comply with the insurer's request to confirm or amend particulars previously given is capable of being a misrepresentation.[760] The remedies for breach of this duty have been dealt with above.[761]

9–167 **Non-consumer insurance contracts.** The Insurance Act 2015 Act applies to contracts made on or after 12 August 2016[762] and, since it only modifies the application and effect of the requirement of the duty of utmost good faith, it is necessary first to begin with an account of the law as it applies to contracts made before that date before considering the changes introduced by the 2015 Act.

9–168 **The pre-2015 Act duty of disclosure: requirements.** Under the former duty of disclosure, the assured must disclose all such facts as a prudent insurer would take into account in deciding whether or at what premium or on what conditions he would take the risk.[763] A fact may be material even though its disclosure would not necessarily have an effect on the decision whether to take the risk, or at what premium;[764] but as for misrepresentation generally[765] the non-disclosure

---

754 *Rozanes v Bowen* (1928) 32 Ll. L.R. 98 at 102.

755 The 2012 Act applies to contracts made on or after 6 August 2013: SI 2013/450.

756 As defined by s.1.

757 As determined in accordance with s.3: "A misrepresentation made dishonestly is always to be taken as showing a lack of reasonable care" (s.3(5)).

758 2012 Act s.2(2), (4).

759 Law Com No. 319, para.4.7.

760 2012 Act s.2(3).

761 See para.9–102.

762 2015 Act s.23(2).

763 *Lambert v Co-operative Ins Society Ltd* [1975] 2 Lloyd's Rep. 485; Marine Insurance Act 1906 s.18(2) (repealed by the Insurance Act 2015 s.21(2)); *Woolcott v Sun Alliance, etc., Ins Ltd* [1978] 1 W.L.R. 493 at 498; *Woolcott v Excess Ins Co Ltd* [1979] 1 Lloyd's Rep. 231; [1979] 2 Lloyd's Rep. 210. For criticism see *Pan Atlantic Ins Co Ltd v Pine Top Ins Co* [1995] 1 A.C. 501 at 528.

764 *Pan Atlantic Ins Co Ltd v Pine Top Ins Co* [1995] 1 A.C. 501; *Aneco Reinsurance Underwriting v Johnson & Higgins* [1998] 1 Lloyd's Rep. 565 at 589.

765 See para.9–023.

must have induced the contract.[766] A policy of marine insurance can therefore be avoided if the assured conceals the real value of the cargo.[767] A policy can also be avoided on the ground of non-disclosure of facts material to the risk[768] by the insurer,[769] e.g. if he accepts a premium for insuring a voyage which he knows to have been safely accomplished. The assured need not disclose facts which the insurer himself knows or ought to know,[770] facts which diminish the risk, facts which both parties have equal means of knowing, "general topics of speculation",[771] and facts the disclosure of which is waived by the insurer.[772]

**The pre-2015 Act duty of disclosure: nature of the duty.** In *William Pickersgill & Sons Ltd v London, etc. Insurance Co*[773] Hamilton J said: **9–169**

> "The rule imposing an obligation to disclose upon the intending assured does not rest upon a general principle of common law, but arises out of an implied condition, contained in the contract itself, precedent to the liability of the underwriter to pay".

One possible interpretation of this dictum is that, in contracts of insurance, there is a *contractual* duty of disclosure based on an implied term in the contract. This duty, being mutual,[774] would rest on the underwriter no less than on the insured; and failure to perform it would amount to a breach of contract, giving rise to a right, not only to terminate the contract, but also to recover damages for its breach. But the prevailing view is that the duty "derives from a rule of law, not from the parties' agreement",[775] and that the "condition precedent" to which it gives rise is contingent only and not promissory.[776] That is, the party who fails to make the disclosure required of him cannot enforce the contract, but is not, merely on account of the non-disclosure, liable in damages for breach of the contract.[777] Nor does the non-disclosure give the other party a right to claim

---

766 *Pan Atlantic Ins Co Ltd v Pine Top Ins Co* [1995] 1 A.C. 501 at 517–518, 549, 570, 571; *Aneco Reinsurance Underwriting v Johnson & Higgins* [1998] 1 Lloyd's Rep. 565 at 589.

767 *Hood v West End Motor Car Packing Co* [1917] 2 K.B. 38.

768 *Banque Keyser Ullmann SA v Skandia (UK) Ins Co Ltd* [1991] 2 A.C. 249.

769 *Carter v Boehm* (1766) 3 Burr. 1905 at 1909; and Marine Insurance Act 1906 s.17 ("either party") (now modified by the Insurance Act 2015 s.14(3)). No such duty is owed to, or by, an assignee of the policy: *The Good Luck* [1989] 2 Lloyd's Rep. 238 (reversed on other grounds [1992] 1 A.C. 233) or by a third party entitled to the benefit of the policy under the principle stated at para.14–143: *Sumitomo Bank Ltd v Banque Bruxelles Lambert SA* [1997] 1 Lloyd's Rep. 487.

770 Not facts coming to the notice of his agent while acting in fraud of the principal: *PCW Syndicates v PCW Reinsurers* [1996] 1 W.L.R. 1136.

771 *Carter v Boehm* (1766) 3 Burr. 1905 at 1910.

772 *Roberts v Plaisted* [1989] 2 Lloyd's Rep. 341; "waiver" here refers to failure to enquire into circumstances material to the risk when a reasonable insurer would make such enquiries: see *Container Transport International v Oceanus Mutual, etc., Association* [1984] 1 Lloyd's Rep. 476; *WISE Ltd (Underwriting Agency) Ltd v Grupo Nacional Provincial SA* [2004] EWCA Civ 962; [2004] 2 Lloyd's Rep. 483.

773 [1912] 3 K.B. 614 at 621.

774 See para.9–168.

775 *The Star Sea* [2001] UKHL 1; [2003] 1 A.C. 469 at [46]; *Banque Keyser Ullmann SA v Skandia (UK) Ins Ltd* [1988] 2 Lloyd's Rep. 513 at 549; affirmed [1991] 2 A.C. 249.

776 See para.2–105 for the distinction between contingent and promissory conditions.

777 *Banque Keyser Ullmann SA v Skandia (UK) Ins Co Ltd* [1990] 1 Q.B. 665 at 779–781; approved on this point [1991] 2 A.C. 249 at 288, where the case was affirmed on other grounds; cf. *The Good*

damages in tort for negligence, or fraud.[778] It has been said that the effect of allowing such a claim would be to undermine the general common law principle that there is no duty of disclosure in the negotiations leading to the conclusion of a contract.[779] That general principle is attenuated in insurance contracts only to the extent that the law provides a remedy by way of rescission for non-disclosure of material facts.

9–170 **The effect of the 2015 Act.** Under the Insurance Act 2015[780] non-consumer insurance contracts continue to be based on the utmost good faith,[781] but the application and effects of this requirement are modified.[782] So far as any duty of disclosure is concerned, the changes are not, in substance, that significant. As part of the duty of "fair presentation of the risk"[783] the insured is required to disclose, in a manner which would be reasonably clear and accessible to a prudent insurer,[784] the following:[785] (i) every material circumstance which the insured knows or ought to know; (ii) failing that, disclosure which gives the insurer sufficient information to put a prudent insurer on notice that it needs to make further enquiries for the purpose of revealing those material circumstances.[786] A circumstance[787] is "material" if it would influence the judgement of a prudent insurer in determining whether to take the risk and, if so, on what terms.[788] In the absence of enquiry, the insured is not required to disclose a circumstance if:[789] (i) it diminishes the risk; (ii) the insurer knows it; (iii) the insurer ought to know it; (iv) the insurer is presumed to know it; or (v) it is something as to which the insurer waives information. There are elaborate provisions for determining the "knowledge" of the insured and the insurer where relevant to the provisions just set out.[790] The remedies for breach of the duty of fair presentation of the risk have been dealt with above.[791]

*Luck* [1990] 1 Q.B. 818 at 888; reversed on other grounds [1992] 1 A.C. 233; Clarke [1989] C.L.J. 363; Davenport [1989] L.M.C.L.Q. 251; *Agnew v Landsförsäkringsbolagens AB* [2001] A.C. 223 at 246.

[778] *HIH Casualty & General Ins v Chase Manhattan Bank* [2003] UKHL 6; [2003] 2 Lloyd's Rep. 61 at [23], [75]: see fn.847.

[779] *Banque Keyser Ullmann SA v Skandia (UK) Ins Co Ltd* [1990] 1 Q.B. 665 at 801–802, as to which see fn.777.

[780] See Law Com. No.353.

[781] See, e.g. s.17 of the Marine Insurance Act 1906 which is only partially repealed and continues to state that: "A contract of marine insurance is a contract based upon the utmost good faith".

[782] See, e.g. the wording repealed in s.17 of the Marine Insurance Act 1906; and see s.14(1) of the 2015 Act.

[783] 2015 Act s.3(1).

[784] 2015 Act s.3(3)(b).

[785] 2015 Act s.3(4).

[786] Said to reflect the approach taken by the courts in, e.g. *Container Transport International Inc v Oceanus Mutual, etc., Association* [1984] 1 Lloyd's Rep. 476 (Explanatory Notes to the 2015 Act).

[787] A "circumstance" includes any communication made to, or information received by, the insured: s.7(2).

[788] 2015 Act s.7(3); and see the examples given in s.7(4).

[789] 2015 Act s.3(5).

[790] See 2015 Act ss.4–6.

[791] See para.9–103.

**Basis clauses.** The duty of disclosure gives a generous measure of protection to insurers, but they often add that the accuracy and completeness of the answers given by the assured to questions in the proposal form shall be the basis of the contract. The result is that quite unimportant misstatements or failure to disclose some quite trivial matter can vitiate a policy.[792] This position has drawn strong judicial criticism[793] and the courts do their best to protect policyholders by construing basis clauses strictly against insurers.[794] Under the legislation referred to above, such clauses are no longer effective in a consumer insurance contract[795] or a non-consumer insurance contract.[796] 9–171

**Insurance distinguished from suretyship or guarantee.** A contract of insurance must be distinguished from a contract of suretyship or guarantee, since it is disputed whether the latter type of contract is uberrimae fidei.[797] A promise to pay another person's debt if he fails to pay it is normally a contract of guarantee, but it is possible to insure against non-payment of a debt, or against some other breach of contract. In *Seaton v Heath*[798] A guaranteed a loan of £15,000 made by B to X. B then obtained a promise from C "in consideration of a premium of 50s. per cent" to "guarantee" A's solvency. The contract between B and C was held to be one of insurance. But in *Trade Indemnity Co Ltd v Workington Harbour Board*[799] A agreed to build a dock for B. C gave B a "guarantee" of £50,000 that A would complete the work, and it was held that this was not a contract of insurance. The distinction between the two types of contract is that a guarantor is usually provided by the debtor,[800] while an insurer is usually sought out by the creditor. Thus the creditworthiness of the debtor is a matter about which a guarantor is likely to know at least as much as the creditor;[801] while an insurer is likely to know less about it than the creditor, having probably had no previous dealings with the debtor. Hence a higher duty of disclosure is owed to the insurer.[802] 9–172

**Other contracts: family arrangements.** There is a duty to make full disclosure in certain family arrangements, e.g. in agreements between members of a family for settling disputes as to the family property. Thus parties to an agreement for the 9–173

792 *Dawsons Ltd v Bonnin* [1922] 2 A.C. 413.
793 *Joel v Law Union & Crown Ins Co* [1908] 2 K.B. 863 at 885; cf. *The Star Sea* [2001] UKHL 1; [2003] 1 A.C. 469 at [50].
794 *Joel v Law Union & Crown Ins Co* [1908] 2 K.B. 863.
795 Consumer Insurance (Disclosure and Representations) Act 2012 s.6(2).
796 Insurance Act 2015 Act s.9(2).
797 See para.9–174.
798 [1899] 1 Q.B. 782; reversed on another ground [1900] A.C. 135.
799 [1937] A.C. 1; *Trafalgar House Construction (Regions) Ltd v General Surety & Guarantee Co Ltd* [1996] A.C. 199.
800 *The Zuhal K* [1987] 1 Lloyd's Rep. 151 at 155.
801 e.g. where the debtor is a company and the guarantor is one of its directors.
802 cf. *Re Denton's Estate* [1904] 2 Ch. 178 at 188.

division of the property of a deceased member of the family must disclose to each other all facts known to them which bear on their rights to the estate, or on its value.[803]

### *(v) Contracts in which there is a limited duty of disclosure*

9–174 **Suretyship or guarantee.** Contracts of suretyship or guarantee are sometimes said to be uberrimae fidei;[804] but the better view is that they do not fall into this category.[805] The creditor is bound only to disclose unusual circumstances, which the surety would not commonly expect;[806] and even this obligation does not apply to the beneficiary under a demand guarantee.[807] An employer who takes a fidelity bond, by which the honesty of one of his employees is guaranteed, is under a somewhat higher duty: he must disclose to the surety any acts of dishonesty by the employee of which he has notice;[808] even if such acts occur after the execution of the bond.

9–175 **Sale of land.** Contracts for the sale of land are not uberrimae fidei,[809] so that there is in general no duty on a seller of land to disclose latent physical defects, but there may be a duty to disclose *unusual* defects of title which a reasonably prudent purchaser could not be expected to discover.[810]

9–176 **Compromises and releases.** It has been said that parties negotiating a contractual compromise of a disputed claim do not in general owe each other duties to disclose information relating to the claim,[811] but there are dicta which may suggest otherwise.[812] In the context of a release, failure by one party to disclose

---

[803] *Greenwood v Greenwood* (1863) 1 D.J. & S. 28; cf. *Tennent v Tennents* (1870) L.R. 2 Sc. & Div. 6. Contrast *Wales v Wadham* [1977] 1 W.L.R. 199 at 218; *Crowden v Aldridge* [1993] 1 W.L.R. 433 at 442–443.

[804] *Railton v Matthews* (1844) 10 Cl. & F. 934, 943; *March Cabaret Club & Casino Ltd v London Assurance* [1975] 1 Lloyd's Rep. 169 at 175; *Wales v Wadham* [1977] 1 W.L.R. 199 at 214.

[805] *Davies v London & Provincial Marine Ins Co* (1878) 8 Ch D. 469 at 475; *LGOC Ltd v Holloway* [1912] 2 K.B. 72 at 81, 83; *Royal Bank of Scotland v Etridge (No.2)* [2001] UKHL 44; [2002] 2 A.C. 773 at [114]. The point was left open in *Mackenzie v Royal Bank of Canada* [1934] A.C. 468 at 475; and in *Trade Indemnity Co Ltd v Workington Harbour & Dock Board* [1937] A.C. 1 at 18.

[806] *National Provincial Bank of England Ltd v Glanusk* [1913] 3 K.B. 335 at 338; *Cooper v National Provincial Bank* [1946] K.B. 1 at 7; *Levett v Barclays Bank Plc* [1995] 1 W.L.R. 1260; *Estate of Imorette Palmer v Cornerstone Investments and Finance Co* [2007] UKPC 49 at [40]–[41]; *North Shore Ventures Ltd v Anstead Holdings Inc* [2011] EWCA Civ 230; [2011] 3 W.L.R. 628.

[807] *WS Tankship II BV v Kwangju Bank Ltd* [2011] EWHC 3103 (Comm); [2011] C.I.L.L. 3155 at [149].

[808] *LGOC Ltd v Holloway* [1912] 2 K.B. 72.

[809] *Safehaven Investments Ltd v Springbok Ltd* (1996) 71 P. & C.R. 59 at 66.

[810] See para.9–154.

[811] Cartwright, *Misrepresentation, Mistake and Non-Disclosure*, 5th edn (2019), para.17.33, citing *Turner v Green*; and see *Silver Queen Maritime Ltd v Persia Petroleum Services Ltd* [2010] EWHC 2867 (QB) at [130].

[812] *Colchester BC v Smith* [1992] Ch. 421 at 435 ("without concealment of essential information"); cf. *Miles v New Zealand Alford Estate Co* (1886) 32 Ch D. 267 at 284.

that the other party had or might have a claim of which the latter party was ignorant may be a ground on which the latter party can set the release aside.[813]

### (vi) *Fiduciary relationship*

A duty of disclosure may arise from the relationship of the parties. There is clearly such a duty where the relationship is one to which the equitable doctrine of undue influence applies.[814] The duty in such cases is indeed not discharged by mere disclosure; more stringent conditions must be satisfied before a person who is under the duty can take the benefit of a transaction with the person to whom the duty is owed.[815] But there are other cases in which a person is under a fiduciary duty which he can discharge merely by making full disclosure. This is the position between principal and agent,[816] partners,[817] and between a company and its promoters.[818] A company promoter owes no such common law duty to persons who subscribe for shares in the company on the faith of a prospectus or listing particulars issued by him,[819] but he does owe them an extensive statutory duty of disclosure.[820] **9–177**

### (vii) *Legislation*

Duties of disclosure can of course be imposed by legislation.[821] For example, under the Financial Services and Markets Act 2000, extensive duties of disclosure are imposed on persons who apply for an official listing of securities on the Stock Exchange, and on those who issue a prospectus inviting subscriptions for unlisted securities,[822] and in relation to information which is required in order to comply with the Transparency Obligations Directive.[823] **9–178**

Under the Consumer Credit Act 1974 the courts have wide powers to re-open a credit agreement if the relationship between the creditor and the debtor is unfair because of certain factors one of which is "any other thing done (or not done) by, or on behalf of, the creditor (either before or after the making of the agreement or any related agreement)".[824] In *Plevin v Paragon Personal Finance Ltd*[825] the Supreme Court held that a credit agreement amounted to an unfair relationship

---

813 *Bank of Credit and Commerce International SA v Ali* [2001] UKHL 8; [2002] 1 A.C. 251; para.3–035.

814 See para.10–015 and following.

815 See para.10–030.

816 e.g. *Armstrong v Jackson* [1917] 2 K.B. 822.

817 The duty extends to persons negotiating their entry into partnership: *Simms v Conlon* [2006] EWCA Civ 1749; [2008] 1 W.L.R. 484 at [128].

818 *Erlanger v New Sombrero Phosphate Co* (1879) 3 App. Cas. 1218.

819 *Heyman v European Central Ry* (1868) L.R. 7 Eq. 154.

820 See para.9–178. Breach of this duty gives rise to a right to damages against those responsible for the prospectus, but not to a right to rescind an allotment of shares: *Re South of England Natural Gas Co* [1911] 1 Ch. 573. This position seems to be unaffected by Financial Services and Markets Act 2000 s.90.

821 See para.9–170 for the insured's duty of disclosure under a non-consumer insurance contract.

822 FSMA 2000 ss.80, 87A–87B.

823 FSMA 2000 s.90A.

824 Consumer Credit Act 1974 s.140(A)(1)(c). See generally: para.10–050.

825 [2014] UKSC 61; [2014] 1 W.L.R. 4222.

solely[826] on the basis that the creditor had failed to disclose the very high commission it was to receive for having sold the debtor payment protection insurance.

### *(viii) Duty to clarify legal relationship*

**9–179** A duty of disclosure may arise where A sees B acting in reliance on a view of a legal relationship between them which is to A's knowledge false.[827] In the authorities which support the existence of such a duty, the effect of its breach has simply been to give rise to an estoppel;[828] but it is conceivable that such a breach might also invalidate a contract.

### *(ix) Duty of disclosure in performance of contract*

**9–180** So far, our main concern has been with the exceptional cases in which a duty of disclosure may exist in the negotiations leading to the conclusion of a contract. The further question is whether a duty of disclosure can arise in the *performance* of an already concluded contract. At common law, there is no general duty of disclosure in cases of this kind, e.g. a bank which has entered into a contract to provide banking services is under no duty to disclose to its customer (A) that it has made later contracts with other customers for the provision of substantially similar services on terms more favourable to the customers than those of its contract with A.[829] But there are many situations (which may be regarded as exceptions to the general principle) in which such a duty of disclosure does arise.[830] For example, an employee may be bound to disclose breaches of duty of fellow-employees who have defrauded the employer;[831] though he is not normally bound to disclose his own breaches of duty,[832] unless the terms of his contract so require,[833] let alone his intention to commit breaches of duty in the future.[834] A contracting party may, however, be under a duty to disclose his own breaches of the contract on the ground that they may lead to danger of physical injury to persons or to property.[835] A professional person may be under certain duties of disclosure towards the person who has engaged his services; but again

---

826 *Plevin v Paragon Personal Finance Ltd* [2014] UKSC 61; [2014] 1 W.L.R. 4222 at [41].

827 *Bell v Marsh* [1903] 1 Ch. 528 at 541; *Spiro v Lintern* [1973] 1 W.L.R. 1002 at 1010–1011, quoted at para.2–046; *The Henrik Sif* [1982] 1 Lloyd's Rep. 456; *ING Bank NV v Ros Roca* SA [2011] EWCA Civ 353; [2012] 1 W.L.R. 472 at [87]–[96]. Contrast *The Tatra* [1990] 2 Lloyd's Rep. 51 (where A had no such knowledge); *Rafsanjan Pistachio Producers Co-operative v Bank Leumi (UK) Plc* [1991] 1 Lloyd's Rep. 513 at 542.

828 See para.9–190; cf. also the cases of "estoppel by convention" discussed at para.3–094.

829 *Suriya & Douglas v Midland Bank Plc* [1999] 1 All E.R. (Comm) 612.

830 *The Star Sea* [2001] UKHL 1; [2003] 1 A.C. 469 at [50].

831 *Sybron Corp v Rochem Ltd* [1984] Ch. 112 at 126–127, 129; Kerr LJ treated the case as one of "covering up and deliberately concealing": [1984] Ch. 112 at 130.

832 *Bell v Lever Bros* [1932] A.C. 161; *Nottingham University v Fischel* [2000] I.C.R. 1462; cf. *Fassihi v Item Software (UK) Ltd* [2004] EWCA Civ 1244; [2004] I.R.L.R. 928; *Brandeaux Advisers Ltd v Chadwick* [2010] EWHC 3241 (QB); [2011] I.R.L.R. 224 at [47]; *GHLM Trading Ltd v Maroo* [2012] EWHC 61 (Ch); [2012] 2 B.C.L.C 369 at [193] (fiduciary obligation to report).

833 *Customer Systems Plc v Ranson* [2012] EWCA Civ 841; [2012] I.R.L.R. 769 at [55].

834 *Horcal v Gatland* [1984] I.R.L.R. 288; cf. *Balston v Headline Filters* [1990] F.S.R. 385.

835 *The Zinnia* [1984] 2 Lloyd's Rep. 211 at 218.

these duties arise out of the contract (or relationship giving rise to liability in tort)[836] between them: their performance is not a prerequisite for its creation.

**Good faith.** In *Yam Seng Pte Ltd v International Trade Corp Ltd* Leggatt J described as "arguably … too simplistic" the "dichotomy" between fiduciary relationships "in which the parties owe onerous obligations of disclosure to each other, and other contractual relationships in which no duty of disclosure is supposed to operate".[837] He suggested that, as part of an implied obligation of good faith,[838] a positive obligation of disclosure might be owed in a "relational contract" such as the distribution agreement with which he was concerned.[839] It was unnecessary to decide the point, but subsequent cases have recognised a limited duty of disclosure as part of an implied obligation of good faith in the performance of the contract.[840] **9–181**

**Vitiation of a second contract.** Sometimes, failure to perform a duty of disclosure imposed by one contract may vitiate a second contract between the same parties. In one case it was held that an employee's failure to perform his duty under his contract of employment to disclose frauds being perpetrated by his subordinates on his employers entitled the employers to rescind an arrangement with the employee under which he had obtained considerable benefits on "early retirement".[841] Similarly, it has been suggested that, where a bank lends money on a mortgage to one of its customers, it is under a duty "to proffer to her some adequate explanation of the nature and effect of the document which she had come to sign".[842] **9–182**

[836] Cases in which solicitors acting both for mortgage lender and borrowers were held liable to the lender for failing to disclose facts coming to their notice in the course of the transaction fall into the present category: see, e.g. *Bristol & West Building Society v May, May & Merrimans* [1996] 2 All E.R. 801; *Mortgage Express Ltd v Bowerman* [1996] 2 All E.R. 836; contrast *National Home Loans Corp v Giffen Couch & Archer* [1997] 3 All E.R. 808 (where no duty of disclosure arose).

[837] *Yam Seng Pte Ltd v International Trade Corp Ltd* [2013] EWHC 111 (QB); [2013] 1 Lloyd's Rep. 526 at [142]–[143].

[838] See para.6–075.

[839] cf. *Ross River Ltd v Cambridge City Football Club Ltd* [2007] EWHC 2115 (Ch); [2008] 1 All E.R. 1004 at [197] where Briggs J referred to an obligation of good faith, falling short of a "strict duty of disclosure".

[840] *Sheikh Tahnoon Bin Saeed Bin Shakhboot Al Nehayan v Kent* [2018] EWHC 333 (Comm); [2018] 1 C.L.C. 216 at [176]; *Bates v Post Office* [2019] EWHC 606 (QB) at [1746].

[841] *Sybron Corp v Rochem Ltd* [1984] Ch. 112; Honeyball [1983] C.L.J. 218.

[842] *Cornish v Midland Bank Plc* [1985] 3 All E.R. 513 at 523, where the bank was found to be guilty of active misrepresentation. Contrast *Barclays Bank Plc v Khaira, The Times*, 19 December 1991 (no such duty owed to a person who was not a customer of the bank).

### (c) Effects of non-disclosure

#### (i) In general

9–183 In discussing the effects of non-disclosure two preliminary distinctions must be drawn. The first relates to what may be called the nature of the non-disclosure; the second relates to the time when the facts which were not disclosed should have been disclosed.

9–184 **Nature of non-disclosure.** Cases of liability for non-disclosure can be divided into two kinds. First, there are cases in which no misrepresentation has been made in so many words, but one can be inferred from conduct or from the surrounding circumstances, e.g. where a representation is falsified by later events, or where a statement is literally true but misleading, or where disclosure is required by custom.[843] Secondly, there are cases of what may be called "pure" non-disclosure, in which no such inference can be drawn, but the law nevertheless gives a remedy for non-disclosure, e.g. in contracts of insurance, or by statute.[844]

9–185 **Non-disclosure amounting to misrepresentation.** In the first of the above groups of cases, non-disclosure can give rise to the same remedies as active misrepresentation, that is, to a right to rescind the contract (in the sense of setting it aside ab initio for all purposes[845]) and to a common law right to damages for deceit, or for negligence (but not for breach of the rescinded contract).

9–186 **"Pure" non-disclosure.** The position is more complex in the second group of cases, i.e. in those of "pure" non-disclosure. We have seen that failure to perform the duty of disclosure in contracts uberrimae fidei gives rise to a right to rescind,[846] but not to one to damages either for breach of contract, or for negligence, or fraud.[847] Conversely, breach of the statutory duty of disclosure imposed on persons issuing a company prospectus has been held to give rise to a right to damages, but not to one to rescind.[848] General statements about the effects of "pure" non-disclosure are best avoided: the effects depend on the purpose of the rule of law by which the duty of disclosure is imposed.

[843] See paras 9–159–9–163.

[844] See paras 9–165, 9–178.

[845] See para.9–100; *The Grecia Express* [2002] 2 Lloyd's Rep. 88 at 127–128.

[846] See para.9–169; subject now, in the case of insurance contracts, to the modifications introduced by the Insurance Act 2015: see para.9–170.

[847] See para.9–169. Statements to the effect that a fraudulent non-disclosure may give rise to a claim in damages must be treated with care: see, e.g. *Simms v Conlon* [2006] EWCA Civ 1749; [2008] 1 W.L.R. 484 at [130]. Non-disclosure does not "as such" give rise to a claim for damages: *HIH Casualty & General Ins v Chase Manhattan Bank* [2003] UKHL 6; [2003] 2 Lloyd's Rep. 61 at [75]; but a fraudulent breach of the duty to disclose may also, in the circumstances, lead to a finding of fraudulent misrepresentation: "it cannot be easy to conceal material facts in the course of negotiating insurance contracts … without falsifying something which has been expressly or impliedly stated": [2003] 2 Lloyd's Rep. 61 at [71]; cf. *The Star Sea* [2001] UKHL 1; [2003] 1 A.C. 469 at [46]; Cartwright in Burrows and Peel (eds), *Contract Formation and Parties* (2010).

[848] See fn.820.

**Pre- and post-contract non-disclosure.** The remedy of rescission for non-disclosure, in the sense of setting the contract aside ab initio, sometimes operates harshly, e.g. where this remedy is available to an insurer in respect of non-disclosure by the insured which may be quite innocent, though changes have been introduced by the Insurance Act 2015 which are intended to remedy this.[849] Even before those changes were introduced, the courts mitigated the severity of the remedy by distinguishing between cases in which the non-disclosure occurred before, and induced the formation of, the contract, and those in which it occurred after the contract had been made and amounted to a breach of one of its terms.[850] Rescission ab initio (as for misrepresentation) is available (if at all) only in cases of the former kind. Where the non-disclosure is post-contractual and amounts to a breach of the contract, the drastic effects of rescission ab initio would be "disproportionate" and "penal";[851] and the injured party's remedies in respect of it depend on the rules relating to the effects of breach,[852] to be discussed later in this book.[853] These remedies are in one respect more extensive than those for pre-contractual non-disclosure: termination for breach does not deprive the injured party of the right to damages for breach of the contract.[854] On the other hand, while the effect of rescission for pre-contractual non-disclosure is to "wipe [the contract] out altogether",[855] with retrospective effect, termination for breach operates only with *prospective* effect;[856] and the remedy is, as a general rule,[857] available only in respect of a breach which causes serious prejudice to the injured party.[858] The rule that post-contractual non-disclosure has no retrospective effect is, however, subject to an exception in cases of fraud: if an insured person makes a fraudulent claim,[859] the insurer is entitled to reject not only that claim but also any lesser claim which the insured might honestly have made.[860] The exception has been explained on the ground that, if it did not exist, the insured would have nothing to lose (though he would incur the risk of a criminal penalty[861]) by putting forward a fraudulent claim.[862] 9–187

[849] See para.9–103.
[850] See para.9–180.
[851] *The Star Sea* [2001] UKHL 1; [2003] 1 A.C. 469 at [51].
[852] *The Star Sea* [2001] UKHL 1; [2003] 1 A.C. 469 at [50], [52].
[853] See para.18–005 and following.
[854] See para.18–022.
[855] *The Kanchenjunga* [1990] 1 Lloyd's Rep. 391 at 398; para.9–097.
[856] See para.18–017; *The Star Sea* [2001] UKHL 1; [2003] 1 A.C. 469 at [50].
[857] See para.18–041 and following for exceptions.
[858] See para.18–032; *The Mercandian Continent* [2001] EWCA Civ 1275; [2001] 2 Lloyd's Rep. 563 at [14].
[859] i.e. one the *validity* of which depends on the false statement or failure to disclose: *Versloot Dredging BV v HDI Gerling Industrie Versicherung AG* [2016] UKSC 45; [2017] A.C. 1; cf. *The Mercandian Continent* [2001] EWCA Civ 1275; [2001] 2 Lloyd's Rep. 563.
[860] *The Star Sea* [2001] UKHL 1; [2003] 1 A.C. 469 at [62]; *Axa General Ins v Gottlieb* [2005] EWCA Civ 112; [2005] 1 C.L.C. 62 (interim payments already made are also recoverable).
[861] cf. para.9–106.
[862] *The Star Sea* [2001] UKHL 1; [2003] 1 A.C. 469 at [62]. This remedy of the insurer is preserved under the Insurance Act 2015 s.12(1).

### *(ii) Effects of Misrepresentation Act 1967*

9–188 **"Pure" non-disclosure.** The Misrepresentation Act 1967 repeatedly uses the expression "misrepresentation made". This refers primarily to active misrepresentation and not to "pure" non-disclosure,[863] as described above. The Act therefore does not impose liability for such non-disclosure where none existed before.[864] Nor does it affect any liability for, or defence based on, such non-disclosure which did exist before the Act. It follows that liability in damages for "pure" non-disclosure could not arise under s.2(1); that the court has no discretion in cases of such non-disclosure to award damages in lieu of rescission under s.2(2); and that a term whose sole effect was to exclude or restrict liability for such non-disclosure is not affected by s.3(1).

9–189 **Non-disclosure amounting to misrepresentation.** On the other hand, the distinction between cases of "pure" non-disclosure, and those in which a misrepresentation, though not made in so many words, can be inferred from conduct, probably applies for the purposes of the Act. It is submitted that the Act would apply to cases of the latter kind,[865] e.g. where a representation had been made by conduct,[866] and where a representation had been made which was literally true but misleading because it was obscure or only told part of the truth.[867] The Act would also apply where the representation was true when it was made but was falsified by later events.[868] Section 2(1) in particular might be thought to apply to such a case as it requires the representor to show that he believed "up to the time the contract was made that the facts represented were true". It could be said that there was no "misrepresentation made" if the facts originally stated were then true; but the answer to this point is that the representation can be treated as a continuing one and that it would become a *mis*representation when the falsifying event occurred. Section 3(1) could also apply to a term which by general words excluded liability for all non-disclosure, since such words could cover cases in which a representation was inferred from conduct or the surrounding circumstances. In one case[869] a term containing such general words was assumed to be covered by s.3(1) but was held to satisfy the requirement of reasonableness. The question whether the section would apply to a term excluding liability only for "pure" non-disclosure was not discussed.

---

863 *HIH Casualty & General Ins v Chase Manhattan Bank* [2001] EWCA Civ 1250; [2001] 2 Lloyd's Rep. 483 at [51]; affirmed in part, [2003] UKHL 6; [2003] 2 Lloyd's Rep. 61. The 1967 Act has not altered the common law meaning of "misrepresentation": *André & Cie SA v Ets Michel Blanc & Fils* [1979] 2 Lloyd's Rep. 427 at 435.

864 *Banque Keyser Ullmann SA v Skandia (UK) Ins Co Ltd* [1990] 1 Q.B. 665 at 789–790; affirmed [1991] 2 A.C. 249; Cartwright in Burrows and Peel (eds), *Contract Formation and Parties* (2010).

865 See Hudson 85 L.Q.R. 524.

866 See para.9–153.

867 See para.9–162.

868 See para.9–159.

869 *National Westminster Bank v Utrecht-American Finance Co* [2001] EWCA Civ 658; [2001] 3 All E.R. 733 at [59].

## 7. MISREPRESENTATION AND ESTOPPEL

**Estoppel as defence.** Under the doctrine of estoppel by representation,[870] a person who makes a precise and unambiguous[871] representation[872] of fact[873] may be prevented from denying the truth of the statement if the person to whom it was made was intended to act on it, and did act on it to his detriment.[874] It is generally said that the doctrine does not give rise to a cause of action[875] but only to a defence. Thus if A agrees to let a house to B, representing that the drains are sound when they are not, B cannot rely on the doctrine of estoppel to found a claim for damages against A.[876] But the doctrine could provide B with a defence, e.g. if A, immediately after the execution of the lease, brought an action for breach of covenant to repair.[877] Such a defence would be available even though B had affirmed (and not rescinded) the lease. 9–190

**Estoppel to remove a defence.** In addition to providing a defence to the representee, estoppel may remove one that would otherwise be available to the representor. Thus it may help a claimant no less than a defendant.[878] In *Burrowes v Lock*[879] a beneficiary under a trust fund proposed to assign his share for value to a prospective lender, who, before advancing any money, asked the trustee whether the beneficiary had previously encumbered his share. The trustee replied that there was no encumbrance, having forgotten that 10 years earlier the beneficiary had in fact encumbered his share. It was held that the trustee was estopped from denying the truth of his statement. Thus he was liable to pay the assigned share to the assignee, free from the earlier encumbrance. The assignee here had an independent cause of action against the trustee based on the assignment; and the trustee was, by his representation, deprived of the defence that he was already bound to pay part of the fund to the previous encumbrancer. Similarly, a warehouseman may make a contractual promise to deliver goods out of his warehouse; and if the promise is coupled with an untrue statement about the goods (e.g. that they are in good condition, or in the warehouse, when they are not), he may be estopped from denying the truth of the statement.[880] The cause of action is based on the contractual promise, and the effect of the estoppel is simply 9–191

---

[870] In this chapter our only concern is with this kind of estoppel. For promissory estoppel, estoppel by convention and proprietary estoppel, see paras 3–076–3–099, 3–120–3–154.
[871] See para.3–081.
[872] Non-disclosure or inaction will not normally suffice: see para.3–082.
[873] As distinct from one of law: see *Territorial & Auxiliary Forces Association v Nichols* [1949] 1 K.B. 35; *The Argo Hellas* [1984] 1 Lloyd's Rep. 296 at 304; (but see para.9–020); and from a representation as to the future (or a promise): see paras 3–092, 9–016.
[874] See para.3–090.
[875] *Low v Bouverie* [1891] 3 Ch. 82; *The Anemone* [1987] 1 Lloyd's Rep. 546 at 557.
[876] Of course, there might be a claim for damages under one of the five heads discussed at paras 9–037–9–071.
[877] cf. *Oades v Spafford* [1949] 1 K.B. 74.
[878] e.g. *Cotterell v Leeds Day* [2001] W.T.L.R. 435; *Shah v Shah* [2001] EWCA Civ 537; [2002] Q.B. 35 at [31]; *Aker Oil & Gas Technology UK Plc v Sovereign Corporate Ltd* [2002] C.L.C. 557; Jackson 81 L.Q.R. 223; cf. para.3–089.
[879] (1805) 10 Ves. 470; as explained in *Low v Bouverie* [1891] 3 Ch. 82.
[880] See *Coventry Shepherd & Co v GE Ry* (1883) 11 Q.B.D. 76; cf. *Alicia Hosiery Ltd v Brown Shipley & Co Ltd* [1970] 1 Q.B. 195, 206.

to remove a defence.[881] And a person who has entered into a voidable contract may indicate that he is not going to exercise his power to avoid it. The effect of such a representation will be that he is bound by the contract without any power of avoidance;[882] and this result may be explained on the ground of either affirmation or estoppel. If the second explanation is adopted, it is again not the estoppel, but the contract, which constitutes the cause of action: the effect of the estoppel is simply to remove the power of avoidance.

881 e.g. *European Asian Bank v Punjab & Sind Bank* [1983] 2 All E.R. 508; *The Uhenbels* [1986] 2 Lloyd's Rep. 294 at 300.
882 *Janred Properties Ltd v Ente Nazionale Italiano per il Turismo* [1989] 2 All E.R. 444.

CHAPTER 10

# DURESS, UNDUE INFLUENCE AND UNCONSCIONABLE BARGAINS



The consent of a contracting party may have been obtained by some form of pressure which the law regards as improper. The victim of such pressure may be entitled to relief under the common law of duress, and under the equitable rules of undue influence. In some circumstances he may be protected against an "unconscionable bargain". He is also protected by certain special statutory provisions. 10–001

## 1. DURESS

### (a) In general

**Illegitimate pressure.** A contract is voidable at common law if it was made under duress. At one time the common law concept of duress was a very narrow one. It was restricted to actual or threatened physical violence to the person. This view was open to the objection that it failed to give due weight to the coercive 10–002 effect of other illegitimate conduct or threats.[1] It was therefore rejected in *The Siboen and the Sibotre*[2] by Kerr J and his views have been accepted in later cases. It is now a question of whether the threat, whatever its nature, amounts to "illegitimate pressure". A threat may be express or implied[3] and it may be illegitimate either because what is threatened is a legal wrong, or because the threat itself is wrongful (as in the case of the blackmailer's threat to disclose his victim's conduct to third parties),[4] or because it is contrary to public policy,[5] or because it amounts to "unconscionable conduct".[6] The terminology of a "threat" is employed because most of the cases involve a threat of future conduct, but the illegitimate pressure may be based on actual conduct, albeit in such cases it is probably the implicit threat of the same conduct in the future which is material. For example, in *Borrelli v Ting*[7] the Privy Council laid stress on the actual conduct of the defendant in obstructing the liquidators of a company, but the pressure lay in the implicit threat to maintain that obstruction.

10–003 **Causation.** Whether illegitimate pressure actually gives rise to duress must then be considered by reference to its causal effect in each case. It has been said that it must have brought about a "coercion of the will, which vitiates consent".[8] If this is interpreted to mean the absence of consent, it is open to criticism.[9] In cases of duress, it is not that consent is negatived, but that it has been improperly obtained.[10] In practice, the cases divide into three categories of duress: duress of the person, duress of goods and "economic duress". These categories are relevant not only for ease of exposition, but also because the requirements may vary between them; in particular, the necessary causal link may differ depending upon the type of illegitimate pressure involved.[11]

10–004 **Burden of proof.** The burden of proving that a contract was procured by duress falls on the party seeking relief,[12] but it has been suggested that it may be reversed in cases of duress of the person.[13]

---

[1] Equity's solution was to set aside the contract on the grounds of undue influence. Many of the cases in which it did so would, and should, now be regarded as cases of duress: see para.10–019.

[2] [1976] 1 Lloyd's Rep. 293; Beatson 92 L.Q.R. 496.

[3] *Woolwich Equitable BS v IRC (No.2)* [1993] A.C. 70 at 165.

[4] *Thorne v Motor Trade Association* [1937] A.C. 797 at 806; *The Universe Sentinel* [1983] 1 A.C. 366 at 401. See further, para.10–009.

[5] *The Evia Luck* (*No.2*) [1990] 1 Lloyd's Rep. 319 at 329; affirmed [1992] 2 A.C. 152 (where the illegitimacy of the threat was no longer in dispute); cf. *The Evia Luck* [1986] 2 Lloyd's Rep. 165 at 178.

[6] *Borrelli v Ting* [2010] UKPC 21; [2010] Bus. L.R. 1718.

[7] [2010] UKPC 21; [2010] Bus. L.R. 1718.

[8] *Pao On v Lau Yiu Long* [1980] A.C. 614 at 636; cf. *The Atlantic Baron* [1979] Q.B. 705; *The Proodos C* [1980] 2 Lloyd's Rep. 390 at 393; Coote [1980] C.L.J. 40.

[9] Atiyah 98 L.Q.R. 197; *Crescendo Management Pty Ltd v Westpac Banking Corp* (1989–1990) 19 N.S.W.L.R. 40; *The Evia Luck (No.2)* [1992] 2 A.C. 152 at 166.

[10] *The Universe Sentinel* [1983] 1 A.C. 366 at 384, 400; *Huyton SA v Peter Cremer GmbH* [1999] 1 Lloyd's Rep. 620 at 638 (will "deflected"); [1999] 1 Lloyd's Rep. 620 at 642.

[11] See para.10–005.

[12] *Huyton SA v Peter Cremer GmbH* [1999] 1 Lloyd's Rep. 620 at 639.

[13] See para.10–005.

### (b) Duress of the person

Duress of the person involves actual or threatened physical violence, or unlawful constraint.[14] It will normally be directed at the person of the contracting party, but it also includes threats directed at employees for whom he is responsible.[15] In *Barton v Armstrong*,[16] the Privy Council drew an analogy with fraudulent misrepresentation and held that it is not necessary to show that the threat was the sole inducement of the contract, or that it would not have been entered "but for" the threat. It is enough that it was "a reason" or "present in the claimant's mind" and once the threat has been established, the burden is on the defendant to prove that it "contributed nothing" to the decision to enter the contract.[17] Still pursuing the analogy with fraudulent misrepresentation,[18] it is submitted that the "but for" test must be satisfied in all cases of duress and the legal burden lies on the claimant. If, however, a threat to the person is established the "inference of fact" is that the contract was the result of duress and the evidential burden shifts to the defendant to prove that the claimant would have entered into the contract if there had been no threat. Such is the seriousness of the threat in a case of duress to the person, the defendant may be unable to discharge this burden unless the court is satisfied that it played no part at all in the claimant's decision.[19] **10–005**

### (c) Duress of goods

The view that unlawful violence to the person was necessary to constitute duress had led in a number of nineteenth-century cases to the conclusion that a contract could not be invalidated by "duress of goods". This meant that an agreement to pay money for the release of goods unlawfully detained, or to prevent their unlawful seizure, was valid.[20] But it had also been held that money which had actually been paid for such a purpose could be recovered.[21] The authorities now support the view that the "duress of goods" cases are governed by the modern, flexible, test of duress, so that the question in each case is whether there has in fact been illegitimate pressure with the necessary causal effect and that this test governs both the validity of the contract and the right to recover money paid **10–006**

---

[14] *Cumming v Ince* (1847) 11 Q.B. 112 at 120; the violence threatened had to be unlawful: *Biffin v Bignell* (1862) 7 H. & N. 877; *Smith v Monteith* (1844) 13 M. & W. 427; cf. *Latter v Bradell* (1880) 50 L.J.C.P. 166; (1881) 50 L.J.Q.B. 448. It may extend to the threat of requiring conduct contrary to one party's religious belief: *Halpern v Halpern* [2006] EWHC 603 (Comm); [2006] 2 Lloyd's Rep. 83 at [87]; appeal allowed in part [2007] EWCA Civ 291; [2008] Q.B. 195.

[15] cf. *Gulf Azov Shipping Co Ltd v Idisi* [2001] 1 Lloyd's Rep.727.

[16] [1976] A.C. 104.

[17] *Barton v Armstrong* [1976] A.C. 104 at 120.

[18] See para.9–030.

[19] *Sheikh Tahnoon Bin Saeed Bin Shakhboot Al Nehayan v Kent* [2018] EWHC 333 (Comm); [2018] 1 C.L.C. 216 at [233]: "the grave nature of such wrongdoing justifies setting a low threshold for *inferring* that a threat of violence has adversely affected the claimant" (Leggatt LJ, emphasis added). A finding of fraudulent misrepresentation has been said to raise a "particularly strong" presumption of reliance, i.e. causation: see para.9–030.

[20] *Skeate v Beale* (1841) 11 A. & E. 983.

[21] *Astley v Reynolds* (1731) 2 Str. 915; *Maskell v Horner* [1915] 3 K.B. 106; cf. Beatson [1974] C.L.J. 97.

under it.[22] Duress of goods may now be seen as a particular instance of the broader concept of economic duress,[23] so that the test is the same for both. It is considered in the next paragraph.

### (d) Economic duress

10–007 In *The Evia Luck*[24] Lord Goff held that:

> "it is now accepted that economic pressure may be sufficient to amount to duress … provided at least that the economic pressure may be characterised as illegitimate and has constituted a significant cause inducing the [claimant] to enter into the relevant contract."[25]

While not confined to one particular type of economic pressure, the most common instance of economic duress is the threat by one party to break a contract unless the other party agrees to its variation, or compromise.[26] Such a variation or compromise may be unenforceable for want of consideration, but recent developments mean that is less likely[27] and, if consideration is proved, the question then is whether the varied contract, or compromise, is voidable for duress.

10–008 **Illegitimate pressure and causation.** The aim of the courts is to distinguish between agreements which are the result of mere "commercial pressure",[28] and those which are the consequence of unfair exploitation. This is not an easy distinction to apply in practice[29] and it is, perhaps, for this reason that the passage from Lord Goff has been said to "leave room for flexibility in the characterisation of illegitimate pressure and of the relevant causal link".[30] Thus, some cases in which duress has not been established may be best explained on the basis that the threat to break the original contract was not illegitimate in the circumstances,[31] while in others the illegitimate pressure created by the threat may not have

---

[22] *The Universe Sentinel* [1983] 1 A.C. 366; cf. *The Atlantic Baron* [1979] Q.B. 705 (where the claim there failed on the ground of affirmation); *The Alev* [1989] 1 Lloyd's Rep. 138.

[23] See: *The Alev* [1989] 1 Lloyd's Rep. 138; *The Olib* [1991] 2 Lloyd's Rep. 108; *Alf Vaughan & Co Ltd v Royscot Trust Ltd* [1999] 1 All E.R. (Comm) 856.

[24] [1992] 2 A.C. 152 at 165.

[25] See also: *The Universe Sentinel* [1983] 1 A.C. 366 at 400; *R. v HM Attorney General for England and Wales* [2003] UKPC 22; [2003] E.M.L.R. 24 at [15].

[26] It is sometimes said that an agreement cannot be set aside if it is "in submission to an honest claim" (*Maskell v Horner* [1915] 3 K.B. 106) but this should not be interpreted to mean that "a compromise" *cannot* be set aside for duress; it depends upon whether it was made "voluntarily to close the transaction", or "under compulsion of urgent and compelling necessity" (*Maskell v Horner* [1915] 3 K.B. 106 at 118).

[27] See para.3–050; *Williams v Roffey Bros & Nicholls (Contractors) Ltd* [1991] 1 Q.B. 1; *Adam Opel GmbH v Mitras Automotive (UK) Ltd* [2007] EWHC 3205 (QB); [2008] C.I.L.L. 2561.

[28] *The Siboen and the Sibotre* [1976] 1 Lloyd's Rep. 293 at 336.

[29] *Adam Opel GmbH v Mitras Automotive (UK) Ltd* [2007] EWHC 3205 (QB); [2008] C.I.L.L. 2561 at [26] ("involves at least some element of value judgment").

[30] *Huyton SA v Peter Cremer GmbH* [1999] 1 Lloyd's Rep. 620 at 637.

[31] *Huyton SA v Peter Cremer GmbH* [1999] 1 Lloyd's Rep. 620 at 637; *DSND Subsea Ltd v Petroleum Geo-Services ASA* [2000] B.L.R. 530 at [134]; *Pao On v Lau Yiu Long* [1980] A.C. 614; and see text to fn.40.

amounted to "a significant cause"[32] of the decision to enter into the further, or varied, contract. Indeed, the two factors may also be said to be interdependent in the sense that the more illegitimate the pressure the lower the causal threshold. This may explain why, for duress of the person, it has been said that it need only be proved that the threat was "a reason" for entering into the contract,[33] whereas for economic duress the "minimum" requirement is to satisfy the "but for" test, i.e. that but for the illegitimate pressure the agreement would not have been made at all or on the terms it was made.[34]

**The availability of an alternative course of action.** In assessing whether causation is established, the court will take into account[35] what courses of action (other than submission to the threat) were reasonably available to that person,[36] e.g. whether it would have been reasonable for him to have resisted the threatened wrong by taking legal proceedings.[37] An evidential role may also be given to the degree of protest by the party claiming duress, though this may not be given much weight depending on the circumstances.[38] 10–009

**Legitimacy and lawfulness.** It has been suggested above that some cases in which economic duress was not established are best explained on the basis that an unlawful threat to break an existing contract was not illegitimate in the circumstances,[39] i.e. that the lawfulness of the pressure brought to bear on a party is not necessarily coterminous with its legitimacy.[40] This submission is not free from difficulty since detaching these two concepts requires the courts to rely on an alternative test for legitimacy, such as bad faith,[41] or unconscionability,[42] which is less certain.[43] But it is supported by observations of the courts about the converse situation where the action threatened may be lawful, but nonetheless regarded as illegitimate. In *CTN Cash & Carry Ltd v Gallaher Ltd*[44] Steyn LJ did 10–010

---

[32] *The Evia Luck (No.2)* [1992] 2 A.C. 152 at 165.

[33] *Barton v Armstrong* [1976] A.C. 104; para.10–005.

[34] *Huyton SA v Peter Cremer GmbH* [1999] 1 Lloyd's Rep. 620 at 636; *Kolmar Group AG v Traxpo Enterprises Pvt Ltd* [2010] EWHC 113 (Comm); [2010] 2 Lloyd's Rep. 653 at [92]; [2018] 1 C.L.C. 216; *Sheikh Tahnoon Bin Saeed Bin Shakhboot Al Nehayan v Kent* [2018] EWHC 333 (Comm); [2018] 1 C.L.C. 216 at [190].

[35] i.e. as a matter of evidence, not an "inflexible third ingredient" in addition to illegitimate pressure and causation: *Huyton SA v Peter Cremer GmbH* [1999] 1 Lloyd's Rep. 620 at 638; *Sheikh Tahnoon Bin Saeed Bin Shakhboot Al Nehayan v Kent* [2018] EWHC 333 (Comm); [2018] 1 C.L.C. 216 at [191].

[36] *The Universe Sentinel* [1983] 1 A.C. 366 at 400; *B & S Contracts and Designs Ltd v Victor Green Publications Ltd* [1984] I.C.R. 419 at 426, 428; *Huyton SA v Peter Cremer GmbH* [1999] 1 Lloyd's Rep. 620 at 638; *Kolmar Group AG v Traxpo Enterprises Pvt Ltd* [2010] EWHC 113 (Comm); [2010] 2 Lloyd's Rep. 653 at [92], [95].

[37] e.g. *Hennessy v Craigmyle & Co* [1986] I.C.R. 461; cf. *Adam Opel GmbH v Mitras Automotive (UK)* Ltd [2007] EWHC 3205 (QB); [2008] C.I.L.L. 2561; *Astley v Reynolds* (1731) 2 Stra. 915 at 916.

[38] *Pao On v Lau Yiu Long* [1980] A.C. 614; *Maskell v Horner* [1915] 3 K.B. 106 at 120.

[39] See text to fn.31.

[40] Birks, *An Introduction to the Law of Restitution* (1989), p.183.

[41] *DSND Subsea Ltd v Petroleum Geo-Services ASA* [2000] B.L.R. 530 at [131].

[42] *Huyton SA v Peter Cremer GmbH* [1999] 1 Lloyd's Rep. 620 at 637–638.

[43] Davies & Day 134 L.Q.R. 5.

[44] [1994] 4 All E.R. 714.

not rule out the possibility of "lawful act duress" (e.g. in the form of a threat not to enter into a future contract) and one can also point to the example of the blackmailer's threat to disclose his victim's conduct to third parties.[45] Beyond this well-established example, however, the difficulty which remains is how to determine when the threat of lawful action may be regarded as illegitimate. In *Times Travel (UK) Ltd v Pakistan International Airlines Corp* the Court of Appeal regarded the nature of the demand as the key to "lawful act duress".[46] According to David Richards LJ, the *CTN* case established that:

> "where A uses lawful pressure to induce B to concede a demand to which A does not bona fide believe itself to be entitled, B's agreement is voidable on grounds of economic duress."[47]

A's belief does not have to be based on reasonable grounds, provided it is genuinely held.[48] Thus, in the *Times Travel* case an airline was not guilty of duress when, in the context of a dispute over commission payable to a travel agent, it threatened to terminate the existing contract, as it was entitled to do, unless the agent entered into a new contract under which it waived any claim to the disputed commission. There was no finding that the airline lacked a genuine belief in its right to reject the claim to the commission and the agent was not entitled to set aside the new contract for duress.[49]

10–011 **Past unlawful conduct.** The decision in the *Times Travel* case may be contrasted with the decision in *Progress Bulk Carriers Ltd v Tube City IMS LLC*.[50] In that case, the appellant shipowners had been guilty of past unlawful conduct when they committed a repudiatory breach of a charter with the respondents by fixing the vessel in question to another charterer. They offered a substitute vessel at a reduced freight rate but only if the respondents entered into a settlement agreement under which they waived any claims under the original charter. Cooke J upheld the decision of the arbitrators (by majority) that the shipowners had been guilty of illegitimate pressure amounting to duress. Their repudiatory breach was

---

45 See text to fn.4.

46 *Times Travel (UK) Ltd v Pakistan International Airlines Corp* [2019] EWCA Civ 828; [2019] 3 W.L.R. 445 at [69].

47 *Times Travel (UK) Ltd v Pakistan International Airlines Corp* [2019] EWCA Civ 828; [2019] 3 W.L.R. 445 at [62].

48 *Times Travel (UK) Ltd v Pakistan International Airlines Corp* [2019] EWCA Civ 828; [2019] 3 W.L.R. 445 at [105]; cf. *Holyoake v Candy* [2017] EWHC 3397 (Ch) at [236]; *Flying Music Co Ltd v Theater Entertainment SA* [2017] EWHC 3192 (QB) at [87]. Contrast *Sheikh Tahnoon Bin Saeed Bin Shakhboot Al Nehayan v Kent* [2018] EWHC 333 (Comm); [2018] 1 C.L.C. 216 at [188]. In *Al Nehayan* itself duress was established, in part, because of a finding of threats of violence. Threats of unjustified litigation were also regarded as "illegitimate" but were not part of the pleaded case: at [213]. Other threats not to enter into a contract unless "unwarranted demands" were met were found to amount to blackmail, although Leggatt LJ did not think that a finding of illegitimate pressure depended upon that: at [227].

49 In both the *CTN* case and the *Times Travel* case the pressure exerted on B arose as a result of a monopoly of supply enjoyed by A, but, as David Richards LJ commented ([2019] EWCA Civ 828; [2019] 3 W.L.R. 445 at [107]): "the common law has always rejected the use, or abuse, of a monopoly position as a ground for setting aside a contract, leaving it to be regulated by statute"; cf. at [117].

50 [2012] EWHC 273 (Comm); [2012] 1 Lloyd's Rep. 501.

"the root cause of the problem"[51] and their subsequent conduct was designed to take advantage of the position created by that unlawfulness by putting the respondents in a position where they had no option but to accept the settlement agreement in order to avoid further huge losses on a sale contract.[52] The correctness of the decision in the *Progress Bulk* case is not disputed in the *Times Travel* case. It can be explained on the basis that the appellants' demands were not made in good faith.[53]

**Third party duress.** It will be seen below that where A exerts undue influence on B which results in B entering into a transaction with C, B may be entitled to relief against C if C was "put on enquiry" as to this risk[54] and there is no reason why the principles applied, and considerations taken into account, to determine whether C is put on enquiry should not also apply where A is guilty of duress.[55] Where A acts as C's agent, C may be vicariously liable for A's duress.[56] **10–012**

## (e) Remedies

**Rescission.** A contract which has been made under duress is voidable.[57] The right to rescind it is subject to the usual bars against relief: affirmation,[58] lapse of time, intervention of third party rights, and, it seems, the impossibility of making counter-restitution.[59] In many cases, the contract obtained by duress is a variation of an earlier contract. It is only the varied contract which may be rescinded, leaving the parties to their respective entitlements under the original contract. **10–013**

**Damages?** According to Lord Diplock, duress is not a tort per se for which damages may be awarded,[60] but in the same case Lord Scarman held that it "is actionable as a tort, if it causes damage or loss".[61] These differing views may be **10–014**

[51] *Progress Bulk Carriers Ltd v Tube City IMS LLC* [2012] EWHC 273 (Comm); [2012] 1 Lloyd's Rep. 501 at [39].
[52] *Progress Bulk Carriers Ltd v Tube City IMS LLC* [2012] EWHC 273 (Comm); [2012] 1 Lloyd's Rep. 501 at [42].
[53] This is implicit in the comments of David Richards LJ in the *Times Travel* case: [2019] EWCA Civ 828 at [73].
[54] See para.10–042.
[55] cf. *Halpern v Halpern* [2006] EWHC 603 (Comm); [2006] 2 Lloyd's Rep. 83 at [96]; appeal allowed in part [2007] EWCA Civ 291; [2008] Q.B. 195.
[56] *Sheikh Tahnoon Bin Saeed Bin Shakhboot Al Nehayan v Kent* [2018] EWHC 333 (Comm); [2018] 1 C.L.C. 216 at [216].
[57] *Pao On v Lau Yiu Long* [1980] A.C. 614 at 634; *The Universe Sentinel* [1983] 1 A.C. 366 at 383, 400; *The Evia Luck (No.2)* [1992] 2 A.C. 152 at 168.
[58] *The Atlantic Baron* [1979] Q.B. 705; *DSND Subsea Ltd v Petroleum Geo-Services* ASA [2000] B.L.R. 530; *Antonio v Antonio* [2010] EWHC 1199 (QB) at [74]; *Borrelli v Ting* [2010] UKPC 21; [2010] Bus. L.R. 1718 at [37]; *Sheikh Tahnoon Bin Saeed Bin Shakhboot Al Nehayan v Kent* [2018] EWHC 333 (Comm); [2018] 1 C.L.C. 216 at [218].
[59] *Halpern v Halpern* [2007] EWCA Civ 291; [2008] Q.B. 195 at [74]–[75]; *Borrelli v Ting* [2010] UKPC 21; [2010] Bus. L.R. 1718 at [38].
[60] *The Universe Sentinel* [1983] 1 A.C. 366 at 385. Lord Diplock's views on this issue are cited with apparent approval in *The Evia Luck (No.2)* [1992] 2 A.C. 152 at 166–167.
[61] *The Universe Sentinel* [1983] 1 A.C. 366 at 400. In *R. v HM Attorney General for England and Wales* [2003] UKPC 22 at [15] Lord Hoffmann refers to the "wrong of duress".

reconciled on the basis that they both require the duress to take the form of a *separate* tort before damages may be awarded, but Lord Scarman's view may reflect the fact that the sort of threatened conduct which amounts to duress will often also amount to the tort of intimidation.[62] The prevailing view is that conduct amounting to duress "will not *necessarily* give rise to liability in tort"[63] and therefore to a remedy in damages.

## 2. UNDUE INFLUENCE[64]

10–015 A transaction can be set aside in equity if, because it has been procured by undue influence exerted by one party (A) on the other (B), it cannot "fairly be treated as the expression of [B's] free will."[65] Relief can be given on the ground of undue influence even though the person to whom the gift or promise was made obtained no personal benefit from it. Thus the rule applies where the head of a religious order uses a gift wholly for the purposes of the order and where a trustee extracts a promise from one beneficiary solely for the benefit of another.[66]

10–016 **When is influence "undue"?** A transaction will be set aside when it was procured by undue influence; not when it was procured by influence. This begs the obvious question, therefore, of when influence is "undue"? Is the concern to protect B from an inability to express his own free will, or to prevent A from improperly taking advantage of that inability, whether or not he benefits personally? One can certainly find statements which would suggest that it is the latter:

> "However great the influence which one person may be able to wield over another equity does not intervene unless that influence has been abused. Equity does not save people from the consequence of their own folly; it acts to save them from being victimised by other people."[67]

But this and similar statements which refer to the "unconscionable conduct" of A[68] are somewhat circular in that what is being said is no more than that equity will not intervene to protect against the exercise of influence, only the exercise of *undue* influence, or the abuse of influence. That still leaves the question of when influence is "undue", or when it is that the weaker party has been "victimised".

---

[62] *Progress Bulk Carriers Ltd v Tube City IMS LLC* [2012] EWHC 273 (Comm); [2012] 1 Lloyd's Rep. 501 at [25]; cf. *Ruttle Plant Hire v Secretary of State for the Environment and Rural Affairs* [2007] EWHC 2870 (TCC) at [85]; *Investec Bank (Channel Islands) Ltd v The Retail Group Plc* [2009] EWHC 476 (Ch) at [122]; *Holyoake v Candy* [2017] EWHC 3397 (Ch) at [403]. In *Kolmar Group AG v Traxpo Enterprises Pvt Ltd* [2010] 2 Lloyd's Rep. 653 at [118]–[121] damages were awarded for the tort of intimidation, but the same sum was also awarded by way of restitution, either on the grounds of duress, or failure of consideration.

[63] *Sheikh Tahnoon Bin Saeed Bin Shakhboot Al Nehayan v Kent* [2018] EWHC 333 (Comm); [2018] 1 C.L.C. 216 at [224] (emphasis added).

[64] Lewison, Chancery Bar Association Conference Lecture 2011.

[65] *Royal Bank of Scotland v Etridge (No.2)* [2001] UKHL 44; [2002] 2 A.C. 773 at [7].

[66] *Allcard v Skinner* (1887) L.R. 36 Ch D. 145; *Ellis v Barker* (1871) L.R. 7 Ch. App. 104; cf. *Bullock v Lloyds Bank* [1955] Ch. 317.

[67] *National Commercial Bank of Jamaica v Hew* [2003] UKPC 51 at [33], per Lord Millett.

[68] *Dunbar Bank v Nadeem* [1998] 3 All E.R. 876 at 883–884; *Royal Bank of Scotland v Etridge (No.2)* [2001] UKHL 44; [2002] 2 A.C. 773 at [8]–[10].

It has been said that it is not necessary to prove any misconduct by A,[69] and transactions have been set aside on the ground of undue influence when it is clear that A had been attempting to act in the best interests of B.[70] It is submitted therefore that *undue* influence is exercised by A whenever, through his influence, the transaction was not entered into as a result of B's own free will.[71] It is not necessary that the transaction should have been to B's disadvantage or one that calls for explanation,[72] but this will often be the case and the latter will have to be proved in order to raise a presumption that undue influence was exercised.[73] If the court finds that the transaction was not entered into as a result of B's own free will, A's conduct is always "improper" or "unconscionable" in the sense that he seeks to uphold a transaction entered in such circumstances, but what matters is the finding as to the exercise of B's free will. In this sense, it is probably most apt to say only that undue influence always has a "connotation of impropriety".[74] What is sufficient for a finding of undue influence is that B did not exercise his "*free*" will: "a finding of undue influence does not depend, as a necessary pre-requisite, upon a conclusion that … [B's] will and intention was completely overborne".[75]

**Causation.** In *Bank of Credit and Commerce International SA v Aboody*,[76] the Court of Appeal applied the "but-for" test of causation, i.e. the transaction would not be set aside, even where undue influence had actually been proved, if the evidence established "on balance of probabilities" that the victim of the influence would have entered into it in any event. The *Aboody* case has been overruled on other grounds,[77] and in *UCB Corporate Services v Williams*[78] the Court of Appeal rejected its earlier "but for" test as inconsistent with Lord Browne-Wilkinson's statement of principle in the *Pitt* case that the victim of undue influence is entitled to have the transaction set aside "as of right".[79] Once it is established that the victim's consent was vitiated, there is no further requirement to prove that, **10–017**

[69] *Jennings v Cairns* [2003] EWCA 1935; [2004] W.T.L.R. 361 at [34]–[35], [40]; *Macklin v Dowsett* [2004] EWCA Civ 904; (2004) 34 E.G. 68 at [10]; *Niersmans v Pesticcio* [2004] EWCA Civ 372; [2004] W.T.L.R. 699 at [20]; *Turkey v Awadh* [2005] EWCA Civ 382; [2005] 2 F.C.R. 7 at [11]; *Hart v Burbidge* [2013] EWHC 1628 (Ch); [2013] W.T.L.R. 1191 at [51]; affirmed [2014] EWCA Civ 992; [2014] W.T.L.R. 1361.

[70] e.g. *Cheese v Thomas* [1994] 1 W.L.R. 173.

[71] *Hart v Burbidge* [2013] EWHC 1628 (Ch); [2013] W.T.L.R. 1191 at [49]; affirmed [2014] EWCA Civ 992; [2014] W.T.L.R. 1361; Birks and Chin in Beatson and Friedmann (eds), *Good Faith and Fault in Contract Law* (1995); cf. Chen-Wishart 59 C.L.P. 231.

[72] *Thompson v Foy* [2009] EWHC 1076 (Ch); [2010] 1 P. & C.R. 16 at [99]; *Birmingham CC v Beech* [2014] EWCA Civ 830; [2014] H.L.R. 38 at [60].

[73] See para.10–021.

[74] *Royal Bank of Scotland v Etridge (No.2)* [2001] UKHL 44; [2002] 2 A.C. 773 at [32]; *Abbey National Bank Plc v Stringer* [2006] EWCA Civ 338 at [46].

[75] *Hewett v First Plus Financial Group Plc* [2010] EWCA Civ 312; [2010] 2 F.L.R. 177 at [25].

[76] [1990] 1 Q.B. 923.

[77] See para.10–021.

[78] [2002] EWCA Civ 555; [2003] 1 P. & C.R. 12.

[79] *CIBC Mortgages v Pitt* [1994] 1 A.C. 200 at 209.

"absent the equitable fraud", the victim would not have executed the transaction in question.[80] As explained by Briggs J in *Hewett v First Plus Financial Group Plc*[81]:

> "It has never been part of the proof of undue influence that, but for the relevant abuse of trust, the impugned transaction would not have been entered into. The right to set aside the transaction arises not because, on a but for causation analysis, it would otherwise have been avoided, but because the equitable wrong constituted by the abuse of confidence was part of the process by which the victim's consent to it was obtained."

The requirement that undue influence was "part of the process", rather than "a reason" or "present" in the claimant's mind, which may be sufficient for fraudulent misrepresentation,[82] or duress of the person,[83] may reflect the fact that a causal link put in such terms would be "odd … given the likelihood that the claimant is precisely unaware of the influence."[84] It has been suggested above that the "but for" test must be satisfied in all cases of misrepresentation and duress and the legal burden lies on the claimant.[85] If, however, fraudulent misrepresentation or duress to the person is proved by the claimant, the evidential burden which shifts to the defendant to prove that the claimant would have entered into the contract in any event may only be discharged on proof that it played no part at all in the claimant's decision.[86] A similar submission may be made in relation to undue influence and a distinction drawn between actual undue influence and presumed undue influence, on the basis that the former is regarded as a "species of fraud".[87]

10–018 **"Actual" undue influence and "presumed" undue influence.** The traditional distinction between "actual" undue influence and "presumed" undue influence is employed in this part, but it is potentially misleading. As will be seen below, any claimant seeking to set aside a transaction on the ground that it was procured by undue influence must prove his case, i.e. he must prove that undue influence was exercised. In cases of so-called presumed undue influence, the transaction will only be set aside if the court is satisfied on the "totality of the evidence"[88] that there was undue influence, albeit it may make that finding with the aid of a presumption. The real distinction therefore is between those cases where the exercise of undue influence is actually proved and those where it is presumed and cannot be rebutted.[89]

---

[80] *UCB Corporate Services v Williams* [2002] EWCA Civ 555; [2003] 1 P. & C.R. 12 at [91].
[81] [2010] EWCA Civ 312; [2010] 2 F.L.R. 177 at [84].
[82] See para.9–028.
[83] See para.10–005.
[84] Burrows, *A Restatement of the English Law of Contract* (2016), p.201.
[85] See paras 9–030, 10–005.
[86] See paras 9–030, 10–005.
[87] *CIBC Mortgages v Pitt* [1994] 1 A.C. 200 at 209; *UCB Corporate Services v Williams* [2002] EWCA Civ 555; [2003] 1 P. & C.R. 12 at [86].
[88] See para.10–031.
[89] *Royal Bank of Scotland v Etridge (No.2)* [2001] UKHL 44; [2002] 2 A.C. 773 at [92]; *Annulment Funding Co Ltd v Cowey* [2010] EWCA Civ 711; [2010] B.P.I.R. 1304 at [50].

### (a) Actual undue influence

There are "two strands" to the group of cases in which undue influence is actually proved.[90] In the first, one party induces the other to enter into the transaction by actual pressure which equity regards as improper but which was formerly thought not to amount to duress at common law because no element of violence to the person was involved.[91] For example, a promise to pay money could be set aside if obtained by a threat to prosecute the promisor,[92] or his close relative, or his spouse, for a criminal offence.[93] Such threats would now constitute duress, but may still be pleaded as actual undue influence.[94] In such cases, it is the improper threat or pressure which is key and there is no need to establish any particular relationship between the parties. Such a relationship is key to the second strand in which the party who claims relief on the ground of actual undue influence must show both that such influence existed and that it had been exercised,[95] i.e. that he had no "means of forming an independent judgment".[96] Cases in which the party seeking relief relies on actually proving undue influence in this sense, as opposed to its presumption, are relatively rare but, if proved, there is no further requirement, as there is for the presumption to arise, that the transaction must be shown to be to the manifest disadvantage of the party seeking to set it aside[97] or, as is now the case, that the transaction must be one that "calls for explanation"[98] by the other party. **10–019**

### (b) Presumed undue influence

The second group of cases in which equity gives relief for undue influence is that in which the relationship between the parties is such as to give rise to what has been called a "presumption of undue influence".[99] This phrase contains an unfortunate element of ambiguity: it can mean either that such influence is presumed to *exist* or that it is presumed to have been *exercised*. It might be better if use of the phrase were abandoned; but as there is little prospect of such a **10–020**

[90] *Libyan Investment Authority v Goldman Sachs International* [2016] EWHC 2530 (Ch) at [136].

[91] *Turnbull & Co v Duvall* [1902] A.C. 429 at 434; *Barclays Bank v O'Brien* [1994] 1 A.C. 180 at 191–192; *Avon Finance Co v Bridger* [1985] 2 All E.R. 281 at 285.

[92] Such a threat was formerly thought to be incapable of giving rise to duress at common law: *Flower v Sadler* (1882) 10 Q.B.D. 572.

[93] *Williams v Bayley* (1866) L.R. 1 H.L. 200; *Kaufman v Gerson* [1904] 1 K.B. 591; *Mutual Finance Ltd v Wetton* [1937] 2 K.B. 389.

[94] *Libyan Investment Authority v Goldman Sachs International* [2016] EWHC 2530 (Ch) at [136]–[137]; *Holyoake v Candy* [2017] EWHC 3397 (Ch) at [404]–[408]; cf. *Daniel v Drew* [2005] EWCA Civ 507; [2005] 2 F.C.R. 365 which is decided as a case of actual undue influence and in which the improper pressure, in "the rare and exceptional" circumstances of the case, was a lawful "threat" to institute civil proceedings.

[95] *Howes v Bishop* [1909] 2 K.B. 390; *Bank of Montreal v Stuart* [1911] A.C. 120 at 127.

[96] *Bank of Montreal v Stuart* [1911] A.C. 120 at 136.

[97] *CIBC Mortgages v Pitt* [1994] 1 A.C. 200; disapproving *Bank of Credit & Commerce International SA v Aboody* [1990] 1 Q.B. 923 on this point.

[98] See para.10–021.

[99] *Barclays Bank Plc v O'Brien* [1994] 1 A.C. 180 at 189; *Royal Bank of Scotland v Etridge (No.2)* [2001] UKHL 44; [2002] 2 A.C. 773 at [16].

development, we shall here continue to use it, drawing attention from time to time to its different shades of meaning. At this stage, it suffices to say that, where the presumption applies, it is not necessary for the party claiming relief actually to prove that the impugned transaction was procured by undue influence.

### (i) *The presumption of undue influence*

10–021 **Requirements.** To give rise to the "presumption of undue influence",[100] two basic facts must be established by the party claiming relief.[101] The first is the existence of a relationship between A and B by virtue of which B either in fact reposed trust and confidence in A or is taken as a matter of law to have done so. The kinds of relationship which are capable of producing these effects are discussed below.[102] The second basic fact relates to the nature of the impugned transaction. A former view was that B had to show that the transaction was to his "manifest disadvantage"[103] but this was later doubted[104] and in the *Etridge* case the use of such a concept was discouraged. Instead, the second requirement is that the transaction must be one which "calls for explanation",[105] or one which "is not readily explicable by the relationship between the parties."[106] This formulation differs from that in terms of "manifest disadvantage" since a substantial transaction may call for an explanation from A, even though B may benefit from it indirectly (so that the disadvantage, if any, to B would not be "manifest").[107] On the other hand, an ordinary (or moderate) Christmas or birthday gift from B to A would not (even where there was a relationship of trust and confidence between them) "call for explanation" and so could not be set aside for presumed undue influence.[108] These two requirements are sequential in that the transaction which calls for explanation must follow the establishment of the relationship. A party who enters into such a transaction, and in the course of that transaction reposes trust and confidence in the other party, does not benefit from the presumption of undue influence.[109]

10–022 **Effect and nature.** Once the basic facts of the presumption are established, then the presumed fact is that "the transaction can only have been procured by undue

---

[100] See at fn.199.
[101] *Royal Bank of Scotland v Etridge (No.2)* [2001] UKHL 44; [2002] 2 A.C. 773 at [13].
[102] See para.10–024.
[103] *National Westminster Bank Plc v Morgan* [1985] A.C. 686 at 706; cf. *Hart v O'Connor* [1985] A.C. 1000 at 1024.
[104] *CIBC Mortgages Plc v Pitt* [1994] 1 A.C. 200 at 209.
[105] *Royal Bank of Scotland v Etridge (No.2)* [2001] UKHL 44; [2002] 2 A.C. 773 at [14] (Lord Nicholls, with whose speech Lords Bingham and Clyde agreed). See *Turkey v Awadh* [2005] EWCA Civ 382; [2005] 2 F.C.R. 7 at [20]–[22], [220], preferring the requirement of Lord Scott that the transaction must be one that cannot be explained by ordinary motives.
[106] *Royal Bank of Scotland v Etridge (No.2)* [2001] UKHL 44; [2002] 2 A.C. 773 at [21].
[107] *Macklin v Dowsett* [2004] EWCA Civ 904; (2004) 34 E.G. 68 at [10].
[108] *Royal Bank of Scotland v Etridge (No.2)* [2001] UKHL 44; [2002] 2 A.C. 773 at [24], [156]; cf. at [104] (reasonable fee paid to solicitor). Small sums which, considered individually, may not call for explanation, may do so when taken in the aggregate: *Aldridge v Turner* [2004] EWHC 2768 (Ch).
[109] *Perwaz v Perwaz* [2018] UKUT 325 (TCC).

influence."[110] This presumption has been described as "a rebuttable evidential presumption of undue influence".[111] As the first of the phrases just quoted shows, the presumed fact is that such influence has been *exercised* (or that the trust and confidence has been abused). In this respect, the present presumption differs from another presumption, to be discussed below,[112] which merely establishes (or dispenses with the need to establish) that the first basic fact (a relationship of trust and confidence) *exists*. The statement that the presumption with which we are here concerned is "rebuttable" refers to the point that it can be displaced in one of the ways to be more fully discussed below,[113] e.g. that B took independent legal advice before entering into the transaction; or by other evidence that the transaction was the "expression of [B's] free will".[114] The meaning of the statement that the presumption is "evidential"[115] seems to be that, after proof by B of the basic facts giving rise to the presumption that the transaction was procured by undue influence, the onus shifts to A to prove that it was not so procured.[116]

**Relationships of trust and confidence.** These relationships have traditionally been divided into two categories which became known as "class 2A" and "class 2B" cases.[117] Some difficulty arises in determining whether this classification has survived after the *Etridge* case. It will be convenient first to describe the traditional categories and then to consider the effect on the classification of that case. It should be emphasised that this discussion is concerned with only *one* of the basic facts which must be established before it can be presumed that the transaction "can only have been procured by undue influence".[118] Even if the requisite relationship is established, this presumption will arise only if it is *also* shown that the impugned transaction is one "which calls for explanation".[119] **10–023**

**Relationships of presumed trust and confidence (class 2A).** Where one of the types of relationship to be listed below exists, it is settled by law or (what amounts to the same thing), "the law presumes, irrebuttably, that [A] had influence over [B]".[120] This presumption has been held to apply where the relationship between A and B is that of parent and child,[121] guardian and ward,[122] **10–024**

---

[110] *Royal Bank of Scotland v Etridge (No.2)* [2001] UKHL 44; [2002] 2 A.C. 773 at [14].
[111] *Royal Bank of Scotland v Etridge (No.2)* [2001] UKHL 44; [2002] 2 A.C. 773 at [16], [153], [194].
[112] See para.10–024.
[113] See para.10–030.
[114] *Royal Bank of Scotland v Etridge (No.2)* [2001] UKHL 44; [2002] 2 A.C. 773 at [7].
[115] See at fn.111.
[116] See *Royal Bank of Scotland v Etridge (No.2)* [2001] UKHL 44; [2002] 2 A.C. 773 at [158].
[117] This terminology goes back to *Bank of Credit & Commerce International SA v Aboody* [1990] 1 Q.B. 923 at 953 and was approved in *Barclays Bank Plc v O'Brien* [1994] 1 A.C. 180 at 189–190. "Class 1" (not relevant to the present discussion) comprises cases of *actual* undue influence (para.10–019).
[118] *Royal Bank of Scotland v Etridge (No.2)* [2001] UKHL 44; [2002] 2 A.C. 773 at [14].
[119] *Royal Bank of Scotland v Etridge (No.2)* [2001] UKHL 44; [2002] 2 A.C. 773.
[120] *Royal Bank of Scotland v Etridge (No.2)* [2001] UKHL 44; [2002] 2 A.C. 773 at [18]; cf. at [104].
[121] *Bullock v Lloyds Bank* [1955] Ch. 317; *Cocking v Pratt* (1749) 1 Ves. Sen. 400; cf. *Re T* [1993] Fam. 95.

religious adviser and disciple,[123] doctor and patient,[124] solicitor and client,[125] trustee and cestui que trust[126] and fiancé and fiancée.[127] The present presumption does not apply between husband and wife,[128] or between employer and employee.[129] Nor does it apply to all relationships which are fiduciary in the sense that they give rise to a duty of disclosure: thus it does not apply between agent and principal.[130] The presumption may apply even after the relationship has ceased if the influence continues, for example, between solicitor and ex-client;[131] and between parent and child for a "short" time[132] after the child has come of age, but not once the child is "emancipated" from parental control.[133] Even the marriage of a child does not invariably have this effect.[134]

10–025 **A presumption *of* influence only.** The present presumption must be "distinguished sharply"[135] from the "evidential presumption" described above.[136] In the special relationship (Class 2A) cases, there is an irrebuttable presumption *of* influence, i.e. that A "had influence over"[137] B. It is unnecessary for B to show that he actually reposed trust and confidence in A and, on the other, irrelevant for A to show that this was not the case.[138] The "evidential presumption" that undue influence was *exercised* is raised only if the transaction entered into by A and B was also one that "calls for explanation". An ordinary or moderate Christmas or birthday present can no more be set aside where it is made by a child to a parent or by a client to his solicitor than where it is made by a wife to her husband.[139] Thus the two presumptions will operate in the same case and the "evidential" presumption remains rebuttable (e.g. by evidence that B was independently

---

[122] *Hylton v Hylton* (1754) 2 Ves. Sen. 547; the de facto relation of guardian and ward suffices: *Archer v Hudson* (1846) 15 L.J. Ch. 211.

[123] *Allcard v Skinner* (1887) L.R. 36 Ch D. 145; cf. *Tufton v Sperni* [1952] 2 T.L.R. 516; *Roche v Sherrington* [1982] 1 W.L.R. 599 at 606.

[124] *Dent v Bennett* (1839) 4 My. & Cr. 269; cf. *Re CMG* [1970] Ch. 574; *Claughton v Price* [1997] E.G.C.S. 51.

[125] *Wright v Carter* [1903] 1 Ch. 27; cf. *Wintle v Nye* [1959] 1 W.L.R. 284.

[126] *Ellis v Barker* (1871) L.R. 7 Ch. App. 104; *Thomson v Eastwood* (1877) 2 App. Cas. 215.

[127] *Re Lloyds Bank Ltd* [1931] 1 Ch. 289; *Leeder v Stevens* [2005] EWCA Civ 50.

[128] *Bank of Montreal v Stuart* [1911] A.C. 120; *Mackenzie v Royal Bank of Canada* [1934] A.C. 468; *National Westminster Bank Plc v Morgan* [1985] A.C. 686 at 703; *Kings North Trust Ltd v Bell* [1986] 1 W.L.R. 119 at 127.

[129] *Mathew v Bobbins* (1980) 256 E.G. 603.

[130] *Re Coomber* [1911] 1 Ch. 723.

[131] *McMaster v Byrne* [1952] 1 All E.R. 1362; cf. *Longstaff v Birtles* [2002] EWCA Civ 1219; [2002] 1 W.L.R. 470 (a case, not of presumed undue influence, but of breach of fiduciary duty: see at [40]); *Allison v Clayhills* (1907) 97 L.T. 709 at 711.

[132] See *Re Pauling's Settlement Trusts* [1964] Ch. 303 at 337.

[133] *Bainbrigge v Browne* (1881) 18 Ch D. 188.

[134] *Lancashire Loans Ltd v Black* [1934] 1 K.B. 380.

[135] *Royal Bank of Scotland v Etridge (No.2)* [2001] UKHL 44; [2002] 2 A.C. 773 at [18].

[136] See para.10–022.

[137] *Royal Bank of Scotland v Etridge (No.2)* [2001] UKHL 44; [2002] 2 A.C. 773 at [18].

[138] It is only irrelevant to the question of whether there was a relationship of influence; evidence that A did not, in fact, have any influence over B may be relied upon to rebut the presumption that undue influence *was exercised*: para.10–030.

[139] *Royal Bank of Scotland v Etridge (No.2)* [2001] UKHL 44; [2002] 2 A.C. 773 at [24], [156]; cf. at [104].

advised) even where the relationship between A and B was such as to give rise to the "irrebuttable" presumption of influence.

**Relationships of actual confidence (class 2B).** In this group of cases, i.e. all those falling outside class 2A, the relationship between A and B must be one in which B has in fact reposed trust and confidence in A. The paradigm case is one in which B has reposed trust and confidence in A in relation to the management of B's *financial* affairs,[140] but more generally it is necessary for B to establish that A has acquired influence over B "in relation to some general aspect of (B's) affairs".[141] If B shows this, and that the transaction which B seeks to avoid was such as to call for explanation, then the rebuttable presumption will arise that the transaction was procured by undue influence.[142] 10–026

**Illustrations.** It follows from the nature of the present group of cases that the question in each such case will be whether the party seeking to set the transaction aside has reposed sufficient trust and confidence in the other, rather than whether the relationship between the parties belongs to a particular type.[143] For example, the relationship of banker and customer will not normally amount to one of trust and confidence in the sense which is required,[144] but it can do so in exceptional cases if the customer has placed himself entirely in the hands of the bank.[145] The flexible character of the present group of cases is illustrated by *Tate v Williamson*,[146] where the defendant became financial adviser to an extravagant Oxford undergraduate who sold him his estate for half its value and then drank himself to death at the age of 24. His executors successfully claimed that the sale should be set aside. Lord Chelmsford said: "The courts have always been careful not to fetter this jurisdiction by defining the exact limits of its exercise."[147] A more modern illustration of the principle is provided by *O'Sullivan v* 10–027

[140] *Royal Bank of Scotland v Etridge (No.2)* [2001] UKHL 44; [2002] 2 A.C. 773 at [14].

[141] *Morley v Elmaleh* [2009] EWHC 1196 (Ch) at [598]; *Hewett v First Plus Financial Group Plc* [2010] EWCA Civ 312; [2010] 2 F.L.R. 177 at [27]; cf. *Goldsworthy v Brickell* [1987] Ch. 378 at 404. It may be established, in part, by the execution of a power of attorney by B in favour of A: *Hackett v Crown Prosecution Service* [2011] EWHC 1170 (Admin) at [54].

[142] *Barclays Bank Plc v O'Brien* [1994] A.C. 180 at 189–190; *Royal Bank of Scotland v Etridge (No.2)* [2001] UKHL 44; [2002] 2 A.C. 773 at [14].

[143] Cited with approval in *Royal Bank of Scotland v Etridge (No.2)* [2001] UKHL 44; [2002] 2 A.C. 773 at [10]; cf. at [80] ("cannot be exhaustively classified").

[144] *National Westminster Bank Plc v Morgan* [1985] A.C. 686; *Bank of Baroda v Panessar* [1987] Ch. 335; *Libyan Investment Authority v Goldman Sachs International* [2016] EWHC 2530 (Ch); *Maxted v Investec Bank Plc* [2017] EWHC 1997 (Ch) at [25].

[145] *Lloyds Bank Ltd v Bundy* [1955] Q.B. 326, esp. at 342. The case was said in *National Westminster Bank Plc v Morgan* [1985] A.C. 686 at 698 to turn on its "very special facts"; cf. *Cornish v Midland Bank Plc* [1985] 3 All E.R. 513 at 518.

[146] (1866) L.R. 2 Ch. App. 55. For similar relationships between the aged and their advisors or companions, see *Inche Noriah v Shaik Allie bin Omar* [1929] A.C. 127; *Re Craig* [1971] Ch. 95; contrast *Re Brocklehurst* [1978] 1 Ch. 14.

[147] *Tate v Williamson* (1866) L.R. 2 Ch. App. 55 at 60; cf. *Tufton v Sperni* [1952] 2 T.L.R. 516; *National Westminster Bank Plc v Morgan* [1985] A.C. 686 at 708–709; *Goldsworthy v Brickell* [1987] Ch. 378; *Cheese v Thomas* [1994] W.L.R. 129.

*Management Agency & Music Ltd*[148] where the relationship between the claimant (then a young and unknown composer and performer of music) and his manager was held to be such as to give rise to a presumption of undue influence; and transactions which turned out to be unfair to the claimant when he later became a celebrity were accordingly set aside.

10–028 **Effects of the *Etridge* case.** In the *Etridge* case, the leading speech was given by Lord Nicholls and he did not make any express reference to the distinction between "class 2A" and "class 2B" cases. But he did distinguish between cases in which there is "[p]roof that [B] has placed trust and confidence in [A]"[149] and those in which B "need not prove he actually reposed trust and confidence in" A because their relationship is such that "the law presumes, irrebuttably, that [A] had influence over [B]",[150] e.g. where their relationship is that of parent and child. This distinction appears to resemble the substance (though not the nomenclature) of the distinction between class 2A and class 2B cases. Lord Hobhouse, on the other hand, said that "the so-called class 2B presumption ought not to be adopted"[151] while Lord Scott doubted "the utility of the class 2B classification".[152] The question arises how these statements[153] are to be reconciled with the distinction drawn by Lord Nicholls in the terms just quoted.

One possible answer is that if the distinction between class 2A and 2B is confined to the question of whether there is the necessary relationship of trust and confidence, it makes no sense to speak in terms of a class 2B *presumption*. By definition, relationships falling within class 2B are all those which do not fall within class 2A and in which it is necessary to *prove* that a relationship of trust and confidence existed. However, in the context in which they cast doubt on the utility of the class 2B presumption, it seems clear that Lords Hobhouse and Scott are referring to the presumption that undue influence has been *exercised*. It is submitted therefore that a preferable way of reconciling the apparent conflict of opinion is to have regard to the exact context in which it arose in the *Etridge* case.

10–029 **Surety spouses.** The appeals before the House of Lords in the *Etridge* case concerned a group of cases in which wives had provided security for their husbands' business debts, usually by means of a guarantee by the wife of those debts, supported by a charge on the matrimonial home owned either by the wife alone or by her and the husband jointly. On the principal debtor's default, the lender (usually a bank) would seek to enforce the security, typically by sale of the house. The question to what extent and in what circumstances such a third party is adversely affected by actual or presumed undue influence between husband

---

[148] [1985] Q.B. 428; cf. also *Mahoney v Purnell* [1996] 3 All E.R. 61; *Crédit Lyonnais Bank Nederland NV v Burch* [1997] 1 All E.R. 144 (employer and employee) (approved in *Royal Bank of Scotland v Etridge (No.2)* [2001] UKHL 44; [2002] 2 A.C. 773 at [83], [86]).

[149] *Royal Bank of Scotland v Etridge (No.2)* [2001] UKHL 44; [2002] 2 A.C. 773 at [14].

[150] *Royal Bank of Scotland v Etridge (No.2)* [2001] UKHL 44; [2002] 2 A.C. 773 at [18].

[151] *Royal Bank of Scotland v Etridge (No.2)* [2001] UKHL 44; [2002] 2 A.C. 773 at [107].

[152] *Royal Bank of Scotland v Etridge (No.2)* [2001] UKHL 44; [2002] 2 A.C. 773 at [161].

[153] Lord Clyde also questioned "the wisdom … of attempting to make classifications of cases of undue influence": *Royal Bank of Scotland v Etridge (No.2)* [2001] UKHL 44; [2002] 2 A.C. 773 at [92].

and wife will be discussed later in this chapter.[154] Our present concern is with the question to what extent the presumption of undue influence operates in such cases between husband and wife. This way of putting the question assumes that the interests of these parties are opposed to each other; but in practice this may well not be true in the present context. In a realistic sense, husband and wife in the situations under discussion may well make common cause against the bank since, if the wife's case of undue influence succeeds against the husband, then the bank may not be able to evict the couple from their home. There is little doubt that this aspect of such cases has influenced the development of the branch of the law.

It is against this background that Lord Nicholls observed that "in the ordinary course" a guarantee by a wife of her husband's business debts is not "to be regarded as a transaction which, failing proof to the contrary, is explicable only on the basis that it has been procured by the exercise of undue influence";[155] similarly, Lord Scott observed that undue influence is a "relatively unlikely" explanation of such a guarantee.[156] This may be because there is nothing out of the ordinary in the relationship between the husband and wife beyond the normal trust and confidence to be found between a "mutually loyal married couple",[157] or because the transaction is not one which "calls for an explanation",[158] such as, e.g. the guarantee of a loan for the sole and exclusive use of the husband in his personal capacity. In this context, the statements of Lord Hobhouse and Lord Scott,[159] rejecting, or doubting the utility of, the class 2B presumption are therefore, with respect, entirely appropriate (and are indeed reflected in the speech of Lord Nicholls[160]). In "spouse surety" cases, it would normally be inappropriate to apply the class 2B presumption; and the same is probably true of the closely analogous situation of parties living together in a quasi-marital relationship without being married.[161] But it is submitted that the same reasoning does not apply to other situations in which there is a relationship of trust and confidence, a transaction calling for explanation, and *no* explanation more plausible than that it was procured by undue influence, e.g. in cases such as *Tate v Williamson*.[162] In such cases, there is still scope for the presumption that the transaction was procured by undue influence, even though the relationship of the

---

[154] See para.10–041. One of the cases under appeal concerned a different kind of dispute, i.e. one between the wife and her solicitor.

[155] *Royal Bank of Scotland v Etridge (No.2)* [2001] UKHL 44; [2002] 2 A.C. 773 at [30].

[156] *Royal Bank of Scotland v Etridge (No.2)* [2001] UKHL 44; [2002] 2 A.C. 773 at [162].

[157] *Royal Bank of Scotland v Etridge (No.2)* [2001] UKHL 44; [2002] 2 A.C. 773 at [159]. See also Lord Scott's assessment of the facts in the *Harris* appeal, at [224]. cf. the appeal in *Barclays Bank v Coleman* in which it was found that the wife was "in a position of subservience and obedience to the wishes of her husband" (at [283]) and could therefore have set the transaction aside "against" her husband; her claim for relief against the bank whose loan to him she had guaranteed failed on grounds to be discussed later in this chapter: para.10–041.

[158] *Royal Bank of Scotland v Etridge (No.2)* [2001] UKHL 44; [2002] 2 A.C. 773 at [31].

[159] See fnn.151 and 152.

[160] *Royal Bank of Scotland v Etridge (No.2)* [2001] UKHL 44; [2002] 2 A.C. 773 at [30].

[161] cf. *Royal Bank of Scotland v Etridge (No.2)* [2001] UKHL 44; [2002] 2 A.C. 773 at [47].

[162] *Tate v Williamson* (1866) L.R. 2 Ch. App. 55; para.10–027 and other cases there cited.

parties is not one in which (in Lord Nicholls' words) "the law presumes, irrebuttably, that one party had influence over the other".[163]

### *(ii) Rebutting the presumption*

10–030 **The free exercise of independent will.** The presumption of undue influence is rebutted if the party benefiting from the transaction (A) shows that it was "the free exercise of independent will".[164] The most usual way of doing this is to show that the other party (B) had independent advice before entering into the transaction.[165] But the mere fact that independent advice was given will not of itself save the transaction.[166] The advice must be competent and based on knowledge of all the relevant facts.[167] It has been suggested that the independent adviser must also approve the transaction, and that his advice must be followed.[168] This may be necessary where the influence is particularly strong, or where a very large gift is made; but it is not necessary in every case.[169] There is indeed no invariable rule that independent advice is necessary to save the transaction;[170] but A would lack elementary prudence if he did not ensure that such advice was given.

10–031 **The totality of the evidence.** Although the provision of independent advice is the most usual way of rebutting the presumption of undue influence, it is clear from the above that it is not decisive in every case and the reality is that the "kind of evidence needed to rebut the presumption is entirely at large".[171] As it has been said, even where the requirements for the presumption have been met "when the principal participants have given oral evidence, the issue for the Court is whether on the totality of the evidence, including any appropriate inference, it finds that the transaction was in fact brought about by undue influence."[172] It is primarily for this reason that the distinction between actual and presumed undue influence

---

[163] *Royal Bank of Scotland v Etridge (No.2)* [2001] UKHL 44; [2002] 2 A.C. 773 at [18].

[164] *Inche Noriah v Shaik Allie bin Omar* [1929] A.C. 127 at 136; *Mahoney v Purnell* [1996] 3 All E.R. 61 at 85; *Royal Bank of Scotland v Etridge (No.2)* [2001] UKHL 44; [2002] 2 A.C. 773 at [7]; *Hammond v Osborn* [2002] EWCA Civ 865; [2002] W.T.L.R. 1125.

[165] *Allcard v Skinner* (1887) 36 Ch D. 145 at 190; *Bullock v Lloyds Bank* [1955] Ch. 317; *Claughton v Price* [1997] E.G.C.S. 51.

[166] Particularly stringent rules apply where a solicitor buys from or sells to his client: *Wright v Carter* [1903] 1 Ch. 27, or where a trustee buys from his cestui que trust: *Thomson v Eastwood* (1877) 2 App. Cas. 215.

[167] *Inche Noriah v Shaik Allie bin Omar* [1929] A.C. 127.

[168] *Powell v Powell* [1900] 1 Ch. 243 at 246; *Wright v Carter* [1903] 1 Ch. 27; *Crédit Lyonnais Bank Nederland v Burch* [1997] 1 All E.R. 144 at 155–156.

[169] *Re Coomber* [1911] 1 Ch. 723 at 730; *Banco Exterior Industrial SA v Thomas* [1997] 1 All E.R. 46.

[170] *Inche Noriah v Shaik Allie bin Omar* [1929] A.C. 127 at 135; *Re Brocklehurst* [1978] Ch. 14; *R. v HM Attorney General for England and Wales* [2003] UKPC 22 at [23].

[171] Lewison, Chancery Bar Association Conference Lecture 2011.

[172] *Royal Bank of Scotland Plc v Chandra* [2010] EWHC 105 (Ch); [2010] 1 Lloyd's Rep. 677 at [121]; *Hackett v Crown Prosecution Service* [2011] EWHC 1170 (Admin) at [72]–[74] advocating the need for special care where B is suffering from a mental impairment or a learning difficulty cf. *Royal Bank of Scotland v Etridge (No.2)* [2001] UKHL 44; [2002] 2 A.C. 773 at [219].

is misleading; they are not "alternatives to each other".[173] It follows that if the court finds as a fact that B was *not* the victim of actual undue influence,[174] then B cannot succeed on the ground of presumed undue influence; for the former finding rebuts the presumed fact.[175]

**Successive agreements.** A and B may enter into an initial agreement which is voidable for undue influence, but then replace it with a further agreement which is not, in itself, voidable. If the undue influence which procured the first agreement is still "operative", i.e. B is unaware that the first agreement could have been set aside, the "voidability" of the first agreement may be "transferred" to the second. Thus, in one case where a first mortgage granted by B was procured by the undue influence of A, B was entitled to set aside a second mortgage entered into to discharge the first, notwithstanding that the second mortgage itself was not procured by undue influence, on the basis that the second mortgage was granted before B became aware that she had a right to avoid the first.[176] By contrast, in another case B was not entitled to set aside a settlement agreement which had been entered into to terminate an earlier management agreement. The management agreement was found to have been procured by undue influence, but B had received independent advice before entering the settlement agreement which would have made him aware of the right to set aside the management agreement.[177] 10–032

## (c) Remedies

**Rescission.** The normal remedy in cases of undue influence is to set aside the impugned transaction.[178] The right to rescind for undue influence is barred on grounds similar to those which limit the right to rescind for misrepresentation.[179] 10–033

**Impossibility of restitution.** The party seeking rescission must restore benefits that he has obtained under the contract. He may be allowed to rescind in spite of the fact that he cannot make *precise* restitution, so long as equity can achieve a result that is "practically just".[180] The point is illustrated by *O'Sullivan v* 10–034

[173] *Royal Bank of Scotland v Etridge (No.2)* [2001] UKHL 44; [2002] 2 A.C. 773 at [291].

[174] There is no inconsistency in the court finding it to have been proved that B *was* the victim of undue influence, but relying in the alternative on the presumption: *Annulment Funding Co Ltd v Cowey* [2010] EWCA Civ 711; [2010] B.P.I.R. 1304 at [70].

[175] *Royal Bank of Scotland v Etridge (No.2)* [2001] UKHL 44; [2002] 2 A.C. 773 at [281]. In this regard, see Lewison, Chancery Bar Association Conference Lecture 2011 and his criticism of the following decisions: *Hammond v Osborn* [2002] EWCA Civ 865; [2002] W.T.L.R. 1125; *Jennings v Cairns* [2003] EWCA 1935; [2004] W.T.L.R. 361; *Niersmans v Pesticcio* [2004] EWCA Civ 372; [2004] W.T.L.R. 699; *Goodchild v Bradbury* [2006] EWCA Civ 1868; [2007] W.T.L.R. 463.

[176] *Yorkshire Bank Plc v Tinsley* [2004] EWCA Civ 816; [2004] 1 W.L.R. 2380; cf. *Davies v AIB Group UK Plc* [2012] EWHC 2178 (Ch); [2012] 2 P. & C.R. 19 at [119].

[177] *Wadlow v Samuel* [2007] EWCA Civ 155.

[178] It may be set aside in part, if severable: *Barclays Bank Plc v Caplan* [1998] 1 F.L.R. 532.

[179] See paras 9–113—9–131.

[180] *Erlanger v New Sombrero Phosphate Co* (1878) 3 App. Cas. 1218 at 1279; para.9–119; *Cheese v Thomas* [1994] 1 W.L.R. 129 (cf. *Dunbar Bank Plc v Nadeem* [1998] 3 All E.R. 876 (where the claim based on undue influence failed)).

*Management Agency & Music Ltd*[181] where the claimant sought to set aside for undue influence a number of management, sole agency, recording and publishing agreements and transfers of copyrights. On the one hand the defendants argued that rescission should not be allowed as they could no longer be restored to their pre-contract position in view of the work which they had done to promote the claimant's success; on the other hand the claimant argued that rescission for undue influence was (unlike rescission for misrepresentation) not subject to any requirement of restitution at all. The court rejected both arguments, holding that, even though precise restitution was not possible, rescission could be ordered so long as the court could do substantial justice. This could be done by upholding the claim for rescission while allowing the defendants a reasonable remuneration for their work on behalf of the claimant.[182]

The pursuit of practical justice may also require a sharing of loss, as well as the restoration of benefits received. In *Allcard v Skinner*[183] where the right to rescind a gift was lost through delay,[184] it was held that, in any event, the claimant would only have been entitled to recover so much of the gift as remained in the defendant's hands after some of it had been spent in accordance with the claimant's wishes.[185] Similarly, where the purchase of a house jointly by the claimant and defendant was set aside for undue influence after the value of the house had fallen, the claimant was not entitled to recover in full the sum he had invested, but only that sum which represented the same proportion as his contribution to the purchase price.[186] In neither case is the right to rescind lost, but the claimant is expected to bear some or all of a subsequent reduction in the value of the property in question.

10–035 **Affirmation and estoppel.** The right to rescind on the ground of undue influence may be lost by affirmation of the transaction, acquiescence, or estoppel,[187] but only after the influence (or the relationship giving rise to a presumption of influence) has ceased.[188] It has been held that affirmation is effective though made without independent advice and in ignorance of the right to have the transaction set aside.[189] It is submitted that the law on this point should (as in cases of misrepresentation and termination for breach) require the injured party to know, or to have obvious means of knowing, of the right to rescind.[190] Where a wife had, under her husband's undue influence, joined him in charging the matrimonial home to a bank and later affirmed the transaction as against the husband, it was held that she had also lost the secondary right of avoidance

---

[181] [1985] Q.B. 428; para.10–027.
[182] cf. para.9–119 for similar relief in cases of misrepresentation.
[183] (1887) 36 Ch D. 145.
[184] See para.10–036.
[185] *Allcard v Skinner* (1887) 36 Ch D. 145 at 164, 171, 180, 186.
[186] *Cheese v Thomas* [1994] W.L.R. 129; Chen-Wishart 110 L.Q.R. 173; *Smith v Cooper* [2010] EWCA Civ 722; [2010] 2 F.C.R. 551.
[187] *Goldsworthy v Brickell* [1987] Ch. 378 at 410–411.
[188] *Moxon v Payne* (1873) L.R. 8 Ch. App. 881 at 885.
[189] *Mitchell v Homfray* (1882) 8 Q.B.D. 587. See also: *Goldsworthy v Brickell* [1987] Ch. 378 at 412, 416.
[190] See para.9–125; para.18–097.

against the bank[191] which would, but for the affirmation, have been available to her under the rules stated later in this chapter.[192]

**Delay.** The victim of undue influence must "seek relief within a reasonable time after the removal of the influence under which the gift was made".[193] If with knowledge or obvious means of knowledge of his rights he fails to seek relief, he is assumed to have affirmed the transaction. **10–036**

**Third party rights.** The right to rescind may be lost by the intervention of third party rights. In one common type of case[194] this has given rise to a number of problems, so that this issue is discussed separately below. **10–037**

**Compensation.** Damages as such are not available for undue influence. Where, however, rescission is no longer possible, the court may make an award in the nature of damages giving the victim of the undue influence the difference between the amount for which he parted with the subject-matter and its fair value at the time of the transaction.[195] More broadly, it has been said that there is "no reason in principle why the court should not be able, in effect, to grant compensation to those injured by the exercise of undue influence".[196] Thus, in the case in which this was said, it was no longer possible to restore to an estate certain properties which had been sold as a result of undue influence, but the court ordered the defendants to make payments which represented their "economic value" to the claimant beneficiaries of the estate.[197] **10–038**

## (d) Third parties

Two types of cases call for discussion. In the first, A acquires property from B under a transaction procured, or presumed to have been procured, by undue influence; and A then transfers that property to C. In the second, A by undue influence, or in circumstances in which undue influence may be presumed, induces B to enter into a contract with C. The question in each case is to what extent C is adversely affected by the undue influence exerted, or presumed to have been exerted, by A on B. The principles which have emerged from cases concerned mainly with undue influence also apply where B's consent has been "vitiated" in other ways, e.g. misrepresentation,[198] or duress.[199] **10–039**

---

[191] *First National Bank Plc v Walker* [2001] 1 F.L.R. 505.

[192] See para.10–041.

[193] *Allcard v Skinner* (1887) 36 Ch D. 145 at 187.

[194] The second of those explained in para.10–039.

[195] *Mahoney v Purnell* [1996] 3 All E.R. 61; Birks [1997] R.L.R. 72.

[196] *Hart v Burbidge* [2013] EWHC 1628 (Ch); [2013] W.T.L.R. 1191 at [142]; affirmed [2014] EWCA Civ 992; [2014] W.T.L.R. 1361.

[197] *Hart v Burbidge* [2013] EWHC 1628 (Ch); [2013] W.T.L.R. 1191 at [141]; affirmed [2014] EWCA Civ 992; [2014] W.T.L.R. 1361.

[198] As in *Barclays Bank Plc v O'Brien* [1994] 1 A.C. 180; cf. *Annulment Funding Co Ltd v Cowey* [2010] EWCA Civ 711; [2010] B.P.I.R. 1304 at [64].

[199] *Halpern v Halpern* [2006] EWHC 603 (Comm); [2006] 2 Lloyd's Rep. 83 at [96]; appeal allowed in part [2007] EWCA Civ 291; [2008] Q.B. 195.

10–040 **Property acquired by undue influence transferred to third party.** In this type of case, B can set the transaction aside if C did not give value for the transfer from A or if he took it "with notice of the equity … or with notice of the circumstances from which the court infers the equity".[200] In this context, "notice" refers not only to actual knowledge of those circumstances but also to cases in which it is alleged that C ought to have known of them, or (in other words) where he had constructive notice of them. The "circumstances," notice of which will prejudicially affect C, are those that would, but for the transfer to him, have entitled B to relief against A on the ground of undue influence.[201] But B will not be entitled to set the transaction aside against C on this ground if C has in good faith (i.e. without notice, actual or constructive) and for value acquired an interest for value in the subject-matter. For example, in *O'Sullivan v Management Agency & Music Ltd*[202] relief was not available against a company which had acquired some of the claimant's copyrights and tapes in good faith and for value.

10–041 **Undue influence inducing contract with third party.** Our concern here is with the situation in which A is alleged to have induced B to deal directly with C. The most common (though not the only)[203] illustration of this situation is provided by a large group of cases in which a loan was made by C (a bank or building society) to A for the purposes of A's business[204] and B (usually A's wife) guaranteed the loan and provided security for it, e.g. by a charge on the matrimonial home owned by B or by A and B jointly. On A's default, the question is whether C was adversely affected by undue influence exerted or presumed to have been exerted by A on B (or by some other vitiating factor, such as misrepresentation, that would have operated between A and B, had the impugned transaction been between them).

10–042 **Whether third party "put on inquiry".** Before *Royal Bank of Scotland v Etridge (No.2)*, the answer to this question had been said to depend on whether C had "constructive notice"[205] of the circumstances that would (or would be presumed to have) vitiated the transaction between A and B.[206] In the *Etridge* case,[207] however, the House of Lords discouraged this use, in the present context, of the concept of "constructive notice" (which normally operates in the context of transfers of *property* by persons with a defective title).[208] Instead, the test is

---

[200] *Bainbrigge v Browne* (1881) 18 Ch D. 188 at 197.

[201] See paras 10–015—10–032.

[202] [1985] Q.B. 428 at 459–460; para.10–027.

[203] See *Naidoo v Naidu, The Times*, 1 November 2000.

[204] *Bank of Cyprus v Markou* [1999] 2 All E.R. 707; *Royal Bank of Scotland v Etridge (No.2)* [2001] UKHL 44; [2002] 2 A.C. 773 at [49].

[205] *Barclays Bank Plc v O'Brien* [1994] 1 A.C. 180 at 186.

[206] An alternative ground for allowing B to set the transaction aside was that C had constituted A as his agent for the purpose of concluding the transaction with B. But the reasoning has been described as "artificial" (*Barclays Bank Plc v O'Brien* [1994] 1 A.C. 180 at 195) and is now unlikely to be followed unless A had acted as C's agent "in a real sense": *CIBC Mortgages Plc v Pitt* [1994] 1 A.C. 200 at 211.

[207] *Royal Bank of Scotland v Etridge (No.2)* [2001] UKHL 44; [2002] 2 A.C. 773.

[208] *Royal Bank of Scotland v Etridge (No.2)* [2001] UKHL 44; [2002] 2 A.C. 773 at [39].

whether C, the bank, is "put on inquiry."[209] Even this is "strictly a misnomer"[210] since C is not bound to investigate the state of the relationship between A and B;[211] but the phrase is a convenient one to indicate that C must take reasonable steps to reduce the risk of B's entering into the transaction as a result of undue influence (or other similar vitiating factor) exerted by A on B.[212] The circumstances in which such steps must be taken go far beyond those in which the vitiating factor actually exists or is presumed to exist. Thus, "a bank is put on inquiry whenever a wife offers to stand surety for her husband's debts",[213] even though (as the discussion in an earlier part of this chapter shows) in many such cases the wife will not be able to show that the guarantee was actually procured by undue influence or to rely on the presumption that it was so procured.[214] The law as to when C is "put on inquiry" (or in other words required to take steps to protect B against the risk of B's consent having been improperly obtained) was extensively reviewed in the *Etridge* case, from which it appears that C's duty in this respect depends primarily on two factors.

**The nature of the impugned transaction.** The first factor which may put C on inquiry is the nature of the impugned transaction. Thus, C's duty will arise where B guarantees business debts incurred by A or by a company through which A runs his business.[215] But a bank is not "put on inquiry" where it makes a joint loan to a husband and wife (even if the loan is secured on their matrimonial home) "unless the bank is aware that the loan is being made for the husband's purposes, as distinct from their joint purposes."[216] The reason for the distinction is that a wife's guarantee of her husband's business debts is, on its face, disadvantageous to her (in the sense of her not deriving any direct benefit from it), while this is not true of a joint loan to her and her husband.[217] 10–043

**The relationship between the parties.** The second factor which may put C on inquiry is the relationship between A and B. In most of the reported cases, B was A's wife; but C's duty applies equally in the converse case where "the husband stands surety for his wife's debts"[218] and to "the case of unmarried couples, 10–044

[209] *Royal Bank of Scotland v Etridge (No.2)* [2001] UKHL 44; [2002] 2 A.C. 773 at [44].
[210] *Royal Bank of Scotland v Etridge (No.2)* [2001] UKHL 44; [2002] 2 A.C. 773.
[211] *Mortgage Agency Services Number Two Ltd v Chater* [2003] EWCA Civ 490; [2004] 1 P. & C.R. 4 at [67].
[212] *Royal Bank of Scotland v Etridge (No.2)* [2001] UKHL 44; [2002] 2 A.C. 773 at [41].
[213] *Royal Bank of Scotland v Etridge (No.2)* [2001] UKHL 44; [2002] 2 A.C. 773 at [44], [46]. The burden of proof is on B to show that C knew her to be A's wife living with him (or that there was an analogous relationship between them) and that the transaction was one calling for an explanation; it is then up to C to show that it took reasonable steps to ensure that B's consent was properly obtained: *Barclays Bank Plc v Boulter* [1999] 1 W.L.R. 1919.
[214] See para.10–029.
[215] *Royal Bank of Scotland v Etridge (No.2)* [2001] UKHL 44; [2002] 2 A.C. 773 at [48].
[216] *Royal Bank of Scotland v Etridge (No.2)* [2001] UKHL 44; [2002] 2 A.C. 773 at [48]; citing *CIBC Mortgages v Pitt* [1994] 1 A.C. 200; contrast *Goode Durrant Administration v Biddulph* [1995] F.C.R. 196; *Allied Irish Bank v Byrne* [1995] 2 F.L.R. 325.
[217] Nor of a joint loan to mother and son: *Mortgage Agency Services Number Two Ltd v Chater* [2003] EWCA Civ 490; [2004] 1 P. & C.R. 4.
[218] *Royal Bank of Scotland v Etridge (No.2)* [2001] UKHL 44; [2002] 2 A.C. 773 at [47].

whether heterosexual or homosexual".[219] It can apply even where the relationship is neither a marital nor a quasi-marital one but is one in which trust and confidence is in fact reposed by B in A.[220] According to a "wider principle" approved by Lord Nicholls in the *Etridge* case,[221] the bank's duty extends to all cases in which the relationship between the surety (B) and the principal debtor (A) is a non-commercial one.[222] The advantage of this formulation of the principle is that it promotes certainty in the sense that the creditor's duty to take steps to protect the surety against the risks described above will arise in all such suretyship cases and will not depend on any investigation by the bank of the actual state of the relationship between A and B. The principle would not, on the other hand, apply where the relationship between A and B was a commercial one, e.g. where they were associated companies or where A paid B a fee for acting as surety.[223]

10–045 **Steps to be taken by a third party put on inquiry.** The steps that C (the bank) is required to take in performance of its duty were also reviewed in the *Etridge* case. As the duty is no more than one to take reasonable care to protect B (the surety) against the risk of undue influence, C is not required itself to investigate the question whether B was in fact subjected to such influence.[224] Nor is it necessary[225] for C to arrange for one of its representatives to hold a personal meeting with B.[226] It suffices for C to communicate directly[227] with B to the effect that C will require a solicitor acting for B[228] (who may also act for A or C (or both of them)) in the transaction[229] to confirm to C in writing that the solicitor has explained to B the nature and effects of the documents to be signed by B, containing the transaction.[230] This explanation must be given in a face-to-face meeting between the solicitor and B, conducted in the absence of A.[231] The solicitor must also be supplied by C with the financial information that he needs for the purpose of this explanation.[232] If these steps are taken, C will normally be entitled to rely on the solicitor's confirmation that he has "advised the wife [B]

---

219 *Royal Bank of Scotland v Etridge (No.2)* [2001] UKHL 44; [2002] 2 A.C. 773 at [47]; *Barclays Bank Plc v O'Brien* [1994] A.C. 180 at 198; *Massey v Midland Bank Plc* [1995] 1 All E.R. 929 at 933.

220 e.g. *Avon Finance Co v Bridger* [1985] 2 All E.R. 281, approved in *Barclays Bank Plc v O'Brien* [1994] 1 A.C. 180; *Crédit Lyonnais Bank Nederland NV v Burch* [1997] 1 All E.R. 144.

221 *Royal Bank of Scotland v Etridge (No.2)* [2001] UKHL 44; [2002] 2 A.C. 773 at [82]; citing Birks in Rose (ed.), *Restitution and Banking Law* (1998), p.185.

222 *Royal Bank of Scotland v Etridge (No.2)* [2001] UKHL 44; [2002] 2 A.C. 773 at [87].

223 *Royal Bank of Scotland v Etridge (No.2)* [2001] UKHL 44; [2002] 2 A.C. 773 at [88].

224 *Royal Bank of Scotland v Etridge (No.2)* [2001] UKHL 44; [2002] 2 A.C. 773 at [53].

225 Though such a step may be sufficient if the required explanation and recommendation to seek independent legal advice are given: *Royal Bank of Scotland v Etridge (No.2)* [2001] UKHL 44; [2002] 2 A.C. 773 at [50].

226 *Royal Bank of Scotland v Etridge (No.2)* [2001] UKHL 44; [2002] 2 A.C. 773 at [55].

227 *Royal Bank of Scotland v Etridge (No.2)* [2001] UKHL 44; [2002] 2 A.C. 773 at [79].

228 See *National Westminster Bank Plc v Amin* [2002] UKHL 9; [2002] 1 F.L.R. 735, where it was not clear that this requirement had been satisfied.

229 *Royal Bank of Scotland v Etridge (No.2)* [2001] UKHL 44; [2002] 2 A.C. 773 at [74].

230 *Royal Bank of Scotland v Etridge (No.2)* [2001] UKHL 44; [2002] 2 A.C. 773 at [79].

231 *Royal Bank of Scotland v Etridge (No.2)* [2001] UKHL 44; [2002] 2 A.C. 773 at [76].

232 *Royal Bank of Scotland v Etridge (No.2)* [2001] UKHL 44; [2002] 2 A.C. 773 at [79].

appropriately".[233] The word "advised" here refers to the solicitor's duty to *explain* the transaction: it is no part of his duty "to veto the transaction"[234] merely because he thinks it is not in B's best interests.[235] If, indeed, it is "*glaringly* obvious that the wife (B) is being *grievously* wronged"[236] he should decline to act further; and it seems that, if he did not so decline, his confirmation would not protect C. But in cases falling outside this extreme range, C is not precluded from relying on the solicitor's confirmation merely because the solicitor is not satisfied that the transaction was one into which [B] "could sensibly be advised to enter",[237] nor even because the transaction was "one into which no competent solicitor could have advised the wife [B] to enter".[238] If C takes the required steps (outlined above), it will normally[239] be entitled to rely on the solicitor's confirmation that the solicitor has "advised the wife [B] appropriately."[240] If C fails to take the required steps, C runs the risk of not being able to enforce the transaction against B.[241] The above steps are designed to protect B against the *risk* of undue influence, or similar vitiating factors. The mere fact that they were not taken does not therefore provide grounds on which B will be entitled to set the transaction aside. B will be so entitled, even if C has not taken the required steps, only if B can also establish the requirements for setting aside the transaction as if it had been entered into with A.

## 3. UNCONSCIONABLE BARGAINS[242]

Equity can give relief against "unconscionable bargains"[243] in certain cases in which one party is in a position to exploit a particular weakness of the other. The burden of justifying such a transaction is on the former party.[244] The equitable **10–046**

[233] *Royal Bank of Scotland v Etridge (No.2)* [2001] UKHL 44; [2002] 2 A.C. 773 at [56]; *Barclays Bank Plc v Goff* [2001] EWCA Civ 635; [2001] 2 All E.R. (Comm) 847.
[234] *Royal Bank of Scotland v Etridge (No.2)* [2001] UKHL 44; [2002] 2 A.C. 773 at [61].
[235] *Royal Bank of Scotland v Etridge (No.2)* [2001] UKHL 44; [2002] 2 A.C. 773.
[236] *Royal Bank of Scotland v Etridge (No.2)* [2001] UKHL 44; [2002] 2 A.C. 773 at [62] (emphasis added).
[237] *Royal Bank of Scotland v Etridge (No.2)* [2001] UKHL 44; [2002] 2 A.C. 773 at [58]–[59].
[238] *Royal Bank of Scotland v Etridge (No.2)* [2001] UKHL 44; [2002] 2 A.C. 773 at [63].
[239] *Royal Bank of Scotland v Etridge (No.2)* [2001] UKHL 44; [2002] 2 A.C. 773 at [61]; but not if C knows that the solicitor "has not duly advised" B: *Royal Bank of Scotland v Etridge (No.2)* at [57]; cf. *National Westminster Bank Plc v Breeds* [2001] N.L.J. 170.
[240] *Royal Bank of Scotland v Etridge (No.2)* [2001] UKHL 44; [2002] 2 A.C. 773 at [56]; cf. at [292] where this requirement was held to have been complied with in *Barclays Bank Plc v Coleman*, one of the cases under consideration in the *Etridge* case.
[241] But only against B; if the property against which the loan is secured is jointly owned by A and B, the court may order its sale so as to realise A's share: *First National Bank Plc v Achampong* [2003] EWCA Civ 487; [2004] 1 F.C.R. 18.
[242] Capper 126 L.Q.R. 403.
[243] Not against *gifts*, though these can be set aside for undue influence: *Langton v Langton* [1995] F.L.R. 890.
[244] *Aylesford v Morris* (1873) L.R. 8 Ch. App. 484.

rule is based on unconscientious conduct by the stronger party:[245] relief will not be granted merely because the transaction is unfair[246] or improvident.[247] A fortiori, mere inadequacy of consideration is not a ground for relief where the parties have bargained on equal terms.[248] While the scope of this jurisdiction is uncertain, it has been invoked in the following broad categories of case.

10–047 **Catching bargains.** Equity can set aside or modify an agreement with an "expectant heir" made in anticipation of his expectations. The transaction need not amount to a sale of or charge on the expectation.[249] Thus equity can relieve against a post-obit bond, by which a debtor promises his creditor a certain sum if the debtor survives a named person and becomes entitled to a share in his estate.[250] Nor is the equitable jurisdiction confined to "heirs": relief can be given to a young man whose sole expectation of wealth is from his father, who is still alive.[251] A person who sold a reversionary interest could at one time obtain relief by proving only that the sale was at an undervalue. The law was changed by the Sales of Reversions Act 1867, now re-enacted in s.174 of the Law of Property Act 1925. This provides that no sale of a "reversionary interest" (which includes a mere expectancy) shall be opened or set aside merely on the ground of undervalue; but the section expressly preserves the jurisdiction of the court to set aside or modify unconscionable bargains. Undervalue remains "a material element in cases in which it is not the sole equitable ground for relief",[252] and may form the sole ground for relief if it is "so gross as to amount of itself to evidence of fraud".[253] Fraud is not here used in its common law sense[254] but means "an unconscientious use of the power arising out of" the relative positions of the parties.[255]

10–048 **Dealing with "poor and ignorant" persons** In *Evans v Llewellin*[256] a poor man became entitled to a share of an estate worth £1,700. He sold it for 200 guineas cash, and was later able to set the transaction aside as it was "improvidently obtained". A modern illustration of the principle may be provided by a case in which an employee of modest financial means guaranteed her employer's

---

245 *O'Rorke v Bolingbroke* (1877) 2 App. Cas. 814; *Multiservice Bookbinding Ltd v Marden* [1979] Ch 84 at 110; *Alec Lobb (Garages) Ltd v Total Oil (Great Britain) Ltd* [1985] 1 W.L.R. 173; *Portman Building Society v Dusangh* [2000] 2 All E.R. (Comm) 221; *Strydom v Vendside Ltd* [2009] EWHC 2130 (QB); [2009] Costs L.R. 886 at [36].

246 *Alec Lobb (Garages) Ltd v Total Oil (Great Britain) Ltd* [1985] 1 W.L.R. 173; *Hart v O'Connor* [1985] A.C. 1000; *Boustany v Pigott* (1995) 69 P. & C.R. 298. *Irvani v Irvani* [2000] 1 Lloyd's Rep. 412 at 425; *Nosworthy v Instinctif Partners Ltd*, EAT, 28 February 2019.

247 *Fineland Investments Ltd v Pritchard* [2011] EWHC 113 (Ch).

248 See *Collier v Brown* (1788) 1 Cox C.C. 428; *Western v Russell* (1814) 3 Ves. & B. 187.

249 *Aylesford v Morris* (1873) L.R. 8 Ch. App. 484.

250 See *Chesterfield v Janssen* (1750) 2 Ves. Sen. 125.

251 *Nevill v Snelling* (1880) 15 Ch D. 679.

252 *O'Rorke v Bolingbroke* (1877) 2 App. Cas. 814 at 833; *Portman Building Society v Dusangh* [2000] 2 All E.R. (Comm) 221 at 228 (transaction must be "manifestly disadvantageous").

253 *Fry v Lane* (1888) 40 Ch D. 312 at 321.

254 See para.9–039.

255 *Aylesford v Morris* (1873) L.R. 8 Ch. App. 484 at 491.

256 (1787) 1 Cox C.C. 333; mentioned with approval in *Fry v Lane* (1888) 40 Ch D. 312; *Clark v Malpas* (1862) 4 D.F. & J. 401; *Lloyds Bank Ltd v Bundy* [1975] Q.B. 326 at 337.

overdraft for up to £270,000. The transaction was described as "harsh and unconscionable"[257] and set aside; but the actual ground for the decision was that the relationship between employer and employee was such as to give rise to a presumption of undue influence. It seems that equity may, even in the absence of such influence, give such relief when unfair advantage is taken of a person who is poor, ignorant or weak-minded, or is for some other reason in need of special protection.[258] Specific performance may be refused on similar grounds.[259]

## 4. Statutory Protection

Reference has been made in Ch.7 to legislation which provides for administrative control of exemption clauses and of other unfair terms in consumer contracts.[260] It can also be argued that some legislation protects the consumer against a form of economic duress, such as the statutory provisions giving consumers a "cooling-off" period in certain cases. For example, a person who is induced to sign a regulated consumer credit agreement[261] at home is entitled to cancel it within such a period.[262] 10–049

### (a) Unfair credit relationships

Statutory powers to control credit agreements are now contained in the Consumer Credit Act 1974 (as amended by the Consumer Credit Act 2006). Under that Act, the court has wide powers in relation to an "unfair relationship".[263] It may exercise those powers where the relationship between the creditor and the debtor is unfair because of any of the following: any of the terms of the agreement or of any related agreement; the way in which the creditor has exercised or enforced any of his rights under the agreement or any related agreement; and any other thing done (or not done) by, or on behalf of,[264] the creditor (either before or after the making of the agreement or any related agreement).[265] In deciding whether to make a determination that a relationship is unfair, the court shall have regard to all matters it thinks relevant.[266] Earlier authorities which were concerned with whether an agreement amounted to an "extortionate credit bargain" regarded the requirements to be met as stringent, e.g. a bargain was not "extortionate" merely 10–050

[257] *Crédit Lyonnais Bank Nederland NV v Burch* [1997] 1 All E.R. 144 at 151.

[258] e.g. *Cresswell v Potter* [1978] 1 W.L.R 255n. (wife in course of divorce proceedings transferring her share in the matrimonial home to husband without getting independent advice and for inadequate consideration); cf. *Backhouse v Backhouse* [1978] 1 W.L.R. 243. Mere unfamiliarity with the English language is not a ground for relief: *Barclays Bank Plc v Schwartz*, *The Times*, 2 August 1995.

[259] e.g. *Falcke v Gray* (1859) 4 Drew. 651: see para.21–034.

[260] See para.7–131.

[261] See para.5–007.

[262] Consumer Credit Act 1974 ss.67–68; cf. Consumer Contracts (Information, Cancellation and Additional Charges) Regulations 2013 (2013/3134) reg.29.

[263] Consumer Credit Act 1974 s.140(A)–(C).

[264] Confined to "agency relationships and deemed agency relationships": *Plevin v Paragon Personal Finance Ltd* [2014] UKSC 61; [2014] 1 W.L.R. 4222 at [32].

[265] Consumer Credit Act 1974 s.140(A)(1).

[266] Consumer Credit Act 1974 s.140(A)(2).

because it was harsh or even unconscionable.[267] The amendments introduced by the 2006 Act represent a widening of the powers of the court.[268] That said, as Lord Sumption has observed in *Plevin v Paragon Personal Finance Ltd*[269]:

> "… the great majority of relationships between commercial lenders and private borrowers are probably characterised by large differences of financial knowledge and expertise. It is an inherently unequal relationship. But it cannot have been Parliament's intention that the generality of such relationships should be liable to be reopened for that reason alone."

In the *Plevin* case itself the Supreme Court held that a credit agreement amounted to an unfair relationship solely on the basis that the creditor had failed to disclose the very high commission it was to receive for having sold the debtor payment protection insurance.[270] In doing so, it overruled the narrow view which had been taken in an earlier decision of the Court of Appeal.[271]

### (b) Unfair commercial practices

**10–051** The Unfair Commercial Practices Directive[272] prohibits, among other things, aggressive commercial practices.[273] The Directive itself operates "without prejudice to contract law, and, in particular, the rules on the validity, formation and effect of a contract".[274] However, as a result of amendments[275] to the Consumer Protection from Unfair Trading Regulations 2008[276] (the 2008 Regulations) remedies are now provided, in certain circumstances,[277] to "consumers"[278] who have entered into a contract or made a payment to a "trader"[279] as a result of a "prohibited practice" amounting to "misleading action"[280] or "aggressive practice", the latter of which includes the use of "coercion" and "undue influence".[281] The requirement that a trader or someone for whom the trader is made responsible[282] must have engaged in a "commercial

---

[267] *Paragon Finance Plc v Nash* [2001] EWCA Civ 1466; [2002] 1 W.L.R. 685; *Paragon Finance Plc v Pender* [2005] EWCA Civ 760; [2005] 1 W.L.R. 3412.

[268] *Plevin v Paragon Personal Finance Ltd* [2014] UKSC 61; [2014] 1 W.L.R. 4222 at [7] (earlier provisions "set too high a bar"), [24].

[269] [2014] UKSC 61; [2014] 1 W.L.R. 4222 at [10].

[270] cf. *Nelmes v NRAM Plc* [2016] EWCA Civ 491; [2016] C.T.L.C. 106.

[271] *Harrison v Black Horse Ltd* [2011] EWCA Civ 1128; [2012] E.C.C. 7.

[272] Unfair Commercial Practices Directive 2005/29 [2005] O.J. L149/22; Twigg-Fleisner 121 L.Q.R. 386.

[273] Unfair Commercial Practices Directive art.8.

[274] Unfair Commercial Practices Directive art,3(2).

[275] Made by the Consumer Protection (Amendment) Regulations 2014 (SI 2014/870).

[276] SI 2008/1277. The amended 2008 Regulations apply to contracts entered into, or payments made, on or after 1 October 2014.

[277] 2008 Regulations reg.27A.

[278] As defined in reg.2(1) in a way which is very similar to the definition under the Consumer Rights Act 2015 s.2(3): para.7–091.

[279] As defined in reg.2(1) in a way which is very similar to the definition under the Consumer Rights Act 2015 s.2(3): para.7–090.

[280] Regulation 5. "Misleading action" is more akin to misrepresentation: see para.9–002.

[281] 2008 Regulations reg.7.

[282] 2008 Regulations reg.27A(4).

*practice*" does not necessarily rule out a single instance of aggressive conduct.[283] The prohibited practice must have been "a significant factor" in the consumer's decision to enter into the contract or make the payment.[284]

**Rights of redress.** The additional forms of redress potentially available to consumers include the right to "unwind" the contract[285] (which is very similar in process to rescission of the contract),[286] the right to a discount[287] and to claim damages.[288] The latter remedy not only includes "financial loss" other than "in respect of the difference between the market price of a product and the amount payable for it under a contract",[289] but also damages for "alarm, distress or physical inconvenience or discomfort" caused by the prohibited practice.[290] In both cases the loss must have been reasonably foreseeable at the time of the prohibited practice.[291] The consumer's right to damages is subject to the trader's defence of "reasonable precautions" and "due diligence".[292] 10–052

**Effect on existing law.** The law set out earlier in this chapter is unaffected by this development since nothing in the amendments introduced to the 2008 Regulations "affects the ability of a consumer to make a claim under a rule of law or equity, or under an enactment, in respect of conduct constituting a prohibited practice".[293] However, a consumer may not recover compensation under both the 2008 Regulations and another rule of law or equity or an enactment.[294] 10–053

## 5. INEQUALITY OF BARGAINING POWER[295]

A number of judicial statements give some support to the view that one party to a contract may be entitled to relief if the other has taken unfair advantage of the fact that there is a marked inequality of bargaining power between them. 10–054

**Restraint of trade.** One group of such statements is concerned with the special problem of the validity of covenants in restraint of trade.[296] This depends on whether the covenant is "reasonable", and the adequacy of consideration is taken into account in determining the issue of reasonableness.[297] The fairness of the 10–055

[283] *R v X Ltd* [2013] EWCA Crim 818; [2013] C.T.L.C. 145.
[284] 2008 Regulations reg.27A(6).
[285] 2008 Regulations regs 27E–27H.
[286] See para.10–013.
[287] 2008 Regulations reg.27I.
[288] 2008 Regulations reg.27J.
[289] 2008 Regulations reg.27J(1)(a),(3). See comment at para.9–003, text to fn.28.
[290] 2008 Regulations reg.27J(1)(b).
[291] 2008 Regulations reg.27J(4).
[292] 2008 Regulations reg.27J(5).
[293] 2008 Regulations reg.27(L)(1).
[294] 2008 Regulations reg.27(L)(2).
[295] Cartwright, *Unequal Bargaining*; Thal 8 O.J.L.S. 17.
[296] *A Schroeder Music Publishing Co v Macaulay* [1974] 1 W.L.R. 1308 at 1315; cf. *Clifford Davis Management v WEA Records* [1975] 1 W.L.R. 61; *Shell UK Ltd v Lostock Garage Ltd* [1976] 1 W.L.R. 1187 at 1197.
[297] See para.11–130.

bargain (which to some extent depends on the relative bargaining positions of the parties) is therefore relevant to the validity of the restraint; but the fact that it is taken into account for this purpose does not support a general principle of relief against harsh bargains on the ground of inequality of bargaining power.

10–056 **A general principle?** A general principle of inequality of bargaining power was stated (as an alternative ground of decision) by Lord Denning MR in *Lloyds Bank Ltd v Bundy*.[298] He referred to a number of rules (discussed earlier[299] in this chapter) under which relief was given against harsh or unfair contracts; and he derived from them the generalisation that:

> "… English law gives relief to one who, without independent advice, enters into a contract upon terms which are very unfair or transfers property for a consideration which is grossly inadequate, when his bargaining power is grievously impaired by reason of his own needs or desires, or by his own ignorance or infirmity, coupled with undue influence or pressures brought to bear on him by or for the benefit of the other".[300]

The other members of the Court of Appeal based their decision solely on the equitable doctrine of undue influence.[301] Thus, while expressing "some sympathy"[302] for Lord Denning's principle, they did not find it necessary to express a concluded opinion on it. It follows that the principle does not form the ground for the decision.[303] In a number of later cases, Lord Denning has nevertheless repeated his view that the law recognised a principle of "inequality of bargaining power".[304] The scope of the alleged principle seems to be very wide: it can apparently apply to such disparate transactions or terms as the contract in *Lloyds Bank Ltd v Bundy*,[305] the renegotiation of a contract,[306] the settlement of a tort claim,[307] and the inclusion of an exemption clause in a cleaning contract made in standard form.[308] No clear limit to the principle is stated except that a bargain will not be upset if it is "the result of the ordinary interplay of forces".[309]

10–057 **Rejection of the principle of inequality of bargaining power itself as a ground for relief.** Lord Denning's principle has little judicial support in England. On the contrary, in *Pao On v Lau Yiu Long*[310] the Privy Council, having held that

---

[298] [1975] Q.B. 326; para.10–027.
[299] See paras 10–015—10–048.
[300] *Lloyds Bank Ltd v Bundy* [1975] Q.B. 326 at 339; Beatson 1 O.J.L.S. 426.
[301] See para.10–027; cf. *Horry v Tate & Lyle Refineries Ltd* [1982] 2 Lloyd's Rep. 417 at 422.
[302] *Lloyds Bank Ltd v Bundy* [1975] Q.B. 326 at 347 (Sir Eric Sachs, with whom Cairns LJ agreed); cf. *Backhouse v Backhouse* [1978] 1 W.L.R. 243 at 251; *Crédit Lyonnais Bank Nederland NV v Burch* [1997] 1 All E.R. 144.
[303] *National Westminster Bank Ltd v Morgan* [1985] A.C. 686 at 708–709.
[304] *Arrale v Costain Civil Engineering Ltd* [1976] 1 Lloyd's Rep. 98 at 102; *Levison v Patent Steam Carpet Cleaning Co Ltd* [1978] Q.B. 69 at 78.
[305] *Lloyds Bank Ltd v Bundy* [1975] Q.B. 326; para.10–027.
[306] *D & C Builders v Rees* [1966] 2 Q.B. 617.
[307] *Arrale v Costain Civil Engineering Ltd* [1976] 1 Lloyd's Rep. 98.
[308] *Levison v Patent Steam Carpet Cleaning Co Ltd* [1978] Q.B. 69.
[309] *Lloyds Bank Ltd v Bundy* [1975] Q.B. 326 at 336.
[310] [1980] A.C. 614.

the contract was not voidable for duress,[311] also rejected the argument that it was invalid as having been procured by "an unfair use of a dominant bargaining position".[312] To treat this as a ground of invalidity distinct from duress would, in Lord Scarman's words, "be unhelpful because it would render the law uncertain".[313] In *National Westminster Bank Plc v Morgan* Lord Scarman again expressed similar views when questioning "whether there is any need in the modern law to erect a general principle of relief against inequality of bargaining power".[314] Legislation having dealt with a number of specific instances in which superior bargaining power might be abused,[315] he doubted "whether the courts should assume the burden of formulating further restrictions";[316] and the need for them to do so has also been reduced both by the widening of the scope of duress[317] and further legislative intervention.[318] Decisions of the lower courts have similarly rejected the argument that inequality of bargaining power is, of itself, a ground of invalidity;[319] and this is true even in the restraint of trade cases, in which the courts have traditionally taken the "fairness" of the bargain into account.[320]

---

311 See para.10–010.
312 *Pao On v Lau Yiu Long* [1980] A.C. 614 at 634.
313 *Pao On v Lau Yiu Long* [1980] A.C. 614 at 634.
314 *National Westminster Bank Ltd v Morgan* [1985] A.C. 686 at 708.
315 e.g. The Unfair Contract Terms Act 1977: see para.7–039 .
316 *National Westminster Bank Ltd v Morgan* [1985] A.C. 686 at 708; cf. *Lloyds Bank Ltd v Bundy* [1975] Q.B. 326 at 336.
317 See para.10–002.
318 See para.10–049.
319 *Horry v Tate & Lyle Refineries Ltd* [1982] 2 Lloyd's Rep. 417 at 422; *Alec Lobb (Garages) Ltd v Total Oil (Great Britain) Ltd* [1985] 1 W.L.R. 173; *CTN Cash & Carry Ltd v Gallaher Ltd* [1994] 4 All E.R. 714 at 717; *Times Travel (UK) Ltd v Pakistan International Airlines Corp* [2019] EWCA Civ 828; [2019] 3 W.L.R. 445 at [41].
320 *Alec Lobb (Garages) Ltd v Total Oil (Great Britain) Ltd* [1985] 1 W.L.R. 173, above, concerned restraint of trade.

---

CHAPTER 11

# ILLEGALITY

**11–001** The law may refuse to give full effect to a contract on the ground of illegality, i.e. because the contract involves the commission of a legal wrong or is in some other way contrary to public policy. The circumstances in which this is the case has been described as "notoriously knotty territory".[1] This reflects the fact that, beyond the obvious example of a contract which is itself expressly prohibited by statute, the extent to which a contract is "tainted by illegality"[2] will vary enormously from one case to another depending on, among other things, the purpose of the rule which has been infringed, the seriousness of the infringement, the centrality of the conduct in question to the contract and the relative culpability of the parties. Since, in such cases, the withholding of relief is justified on grounds of public policy, it is hardly surprising that it has proved difficult to formulate any general rule capable of ensuring an appropriate outcome in individual cases, other than by introducing so many qualifications or exceptions as to undermine the purpose of a rule in the first place; and even then it is very difficult to reconcile some of the cases. A majority of the Supreme Court has acknowledged that the deployment of a general rule, or rules, should be abandoned in favour of a more discretionary approach, based on a range of factors such as those outlined above.[3]

## 1. INTRODUCTION

**11–002** **The problem of classification.** English writers commonly divide the cases in which contracts are affected by illegality into a number of classes. One object of this classification is to make it possible to generalise about the *effects* of

[1] *ParkingEye Ltd v Somerfield Stores Ltd* [2012] EWCA Civ 1338; [2013] Q.B. 840 at [28].
[2] *Patel v Mirza* [2016] UKSC 42; [2017] A.C. 467 at [9], [109], [134].
[3] *Patel v Mirza* [2016] UKSC 42; [2017] A.C. 467. See paras 11–010, 11–108—11–109.

illegality; but it is doubtful whether any of the suggested classifications achieve this object to any considerable extent. Another object of classification is purely expository, and this does no harm so long as it is not actually misleading.

**Source of the rule infringed.** One classification is based on the source of the rule infringed. Thus it is sometimes said that a contract is more likely to be invalid for violation of a statute than for violation of a rule of common law. The distinction is appropriate where a statute expressly prohibits or invalidates a contract. But it is not decisive where the statute contains no such express prohibition and the illegality consists only in the method of making or performing the contract.[4] In *St John Shipping Corp v Joseph Rank Ltd*[5] a shipowner committed a statutory offence by overloading his ship while performing a number of contracts for the carriage of goods. Devlin J held that he was nonetheless entitled to freight, because the object of the statute was to prevent overloading and not to prohibit contracts. This object was to be achieved by imposing a fine, and not by subjecting the shipowner to the additional financial loss which would result from invalidating the contracts of carriage. It is submitted that this approach should not be confined to cases in which the offence is statutory.[6] It would have been just as appropriate, and would probably have led to the same result, had the shipowner been convicted of manslaughter committed in the course of the voyage. **11–003**

**Statutory invalidity.** Where a statute prohibits or regulates the making or performance of a contract, breach of the statute may amount to a crime, in which case the effects of its breach depend on the principles discussed in the first part of section 2 below.[7] Apart from these principles, the effect of a breach of a statute depends primarily on its express provisions, which may, for example, make the contract (or the offending term[8]) void,[9] voidable[10] or unenforceable;[11] or state that the breach is not to affect the validity of the contract.[12] The difficult cases are those in which the statute gives no clear lead, as is apparent from some of the examples discussed in the following paragraphs. **11–004**

**"Void" contracts held to be illegal.** Section 1 of the Life Assurance Act 1774 provides that "no insurance shall be made" by any person on the life of another, or on certain other risks, unless the assured has an interest in the subject-matter of the insurance. Contracts of insurance made in breach of this section are declared **11–005**

---

[4] See *Shaw v Groom* [1970] 2 Q.B. 540; *London & Harrogate Securities Ltd v Pitts* [1976] 1 W.L.R. 1063.

[5] [1957] 1 Q.B. 267; para.11–109.

[6] *Wetherell v Jones* (1832) 3 B. & Ad. 221 at 225–226; *Coral Leisure Group v Barnett* [1981] I.C.R. 503 at 509.

[7] See paras 11–011—11–031.

[8] e.g. Equality Act 2010 s.142(1).

[9] e.g. Matrimonial Causes Act 1973 s.34 (para.11–048).

[10] Companies Act 2006 s.213(2); *Re Ciro Citterio Menswear Plc* [2002] EWHC 662 (Ch); [2002] 2 All E.R. 717.

[11] Either in so many words (e.g. Equality Act 2010 s.142(1) or by saying that "no action shall be brought", or by use of similar expressions, e.g. Statute of Frauds 1677 s.4; para.5–015.

[12] e.g. Financial Services and Markets Act 2000 s.20(2)(b); Criminal Justice Act 1993 s.63(2).

to be "void" but have repeatedly been held illegal.[13] Similarly, s.1 of the Marine Insurance Act 1745 provided that "no assurance shall be made" on the terms that no further proof of interest than the policy should be required and declared that policies made in breach of the section were to be "void"; and again such policies were held illegal.[14] But when the section was replaced by s.4(1) of the Marine Insurance Act 1906, which simply made such policies void, it was held that they were no longer illegal.[15] The reason for this distinction seems to be that the older Acts first prohibited the contracts (though without penalty) and then declared them void, while the Act of 1906 contains no prohibition but only a declaration of nullity.

11–006 **Consequences of breach not specified.** A statute may prohibit the making of a contract without imposing a criminal penalty or specifying all the civil consequences of breach. Contracts which violated such a prohibition were held illegal[16] if such a consequence was, in the court's view, necessary to give effect to the purpose of the prohibition.[17]

11–007 **Formalities required by statute.** A statute may require some formalities to be observed in making a contract, or require some specific terms to be inserted into the contract, and again fail to specify the consequences of failure to comply with the requirement.[18] The question then is whether the statutory requirement is to be construed as being "directory only or obligatory".[19] Failure to comply with the statute makes the contract void if the requirement is obligatory, but not if it is only directory. In the case in which the distinction was drawn, statutory requirements as to the execution of a mortgage of a ship were held to be obligatory. Failure to comply with them accordingly invalidated the transaction though this effect of the failure was not specified in the legislation.[20] It seems that in applying the distinction the court will ask whether it is necessary, to promote the object of the statute, to hold that failure to comply with its requirements should invalidate transactions.[21] In the absence of any express provision in the statute concerned, a failure to comply with the formalities required does not make the contract illegal so as to trigger the effects discussed in Pt 3 of this chapter.

---

[13] *Hughes v Liverpool Victoria Legal Friendly Society* [1916] 2 K.B. 482; *Re London County Commercial Reinsurance Office* [1922] 2 Ch. 67. cf. *Fuji Finance Inc v Aetna Life Ins Co Ltd* [1997] Ch. 173.

[14] *Gedge v Royal Exchange Assurance* [1900] 2 Q.B. 214; *contra, Tasker v Scott* (1815) 6 Taunt. 234.

[15] *Re London County Commercial Reinsurance Office* [1922] 2 Ch. 67.

[16] *Sykes v Beadon* (1897) 11 Ch D. 170; disapproved in *Smith v Anderson* (1880) 15 Ch D. 247, but not on this point: *Shaw v Benson* (1883) 11 Q.B.D. 563; cf. *Greenberg v Cooperstein* [1926] Ch. 657. The prohibition with which these cases were concerned is repealed by the Regulatory Reform (Removal of 20 Member Limit in Partnerships, etc.) Order 2002 (SI 2002/3203).

[17] For conflicting views on the purpose of a statutory provision which failed to specify the civil consequences of a prohibition, see *Fuji Finance Ltd v Aetna Life Ins Co Ltd* [1997] Ch. 173; cf. para.11–081.

[18] See paras 5–007–5–011 for cases in which the statute does specify the effects of non-compliance.

[19] *Liverpool Borough Bank v Turner* (1860) 2 D.F. & J. 502 at 508.

[20] *Liverpool Borough Bank v Turner* (1860) 2 D.F. & J. 502 (actual decision reversed by Merchant Shipping Act 1894 s.57).

[21] cf. *St. John Shipping Corp v Joseph Rank Ltd* [1957] 1 Q.B. 267; para.11–003.

**Gaming and wagering, or "gambling" contracts.** Previously, a contract that fell into the category of a gaming or wagering contract was unenforceable because it was "null and void".[22] As a result of Pt 17 of the Gambling Act 2005 "the fact that a contract relates to gambling shall not prevent its enforcement".[23] This wording deliberately leaves open the possibility that such a contract may be unenforceable on some other ground,[24] including illegality.[25] The 2005 Act may itself be the source of such illegality, e.g. in the case of a gambling contract entered into pursuant to unlicensed commercial gambling.[26] The effect of the reforms contained in Pt 17 is that the "special" unenforceability of gambling contracts has been removed. Their unenforceability on grounds of illegality will turn on the principles to be considered in the rest of this chapter. 11–008

**The approach adopted in this chapter.** In Pt 2 of this chapter, for the purpose of exposition only, illegal contracts are divided into two groups, namely contracts involving the commission of a legal wrong and contracts otherwise contrary to public policy. The exact effects of illegality should ideally be discussed separately in relation to each type of contract, but such treatment would be inordinately long. An attempt will therefore be made in Pt 3 of this chapter to provide a general discussion of the effects of illegality. This approach can be justified on the ground that many of the relevant rules or considerations apply to all types of illegal contracts; but it is also often true that the effects vary with the type of illegality. Where this is the case, the general propositions in Pt 3 will be qualified accordingly. The classification of contracts which are contrary to public policy includes one particularly important type of contracts, those in restraint of trade. Because of the complexity of the law relating to such contracts, they will be discussed separately in Pt 4. Finally, a contract or a particular term may be illegal or contrary to public policy only in part and the question which arises is whether the offending part can be "severed", allowing for what remains of the contract or term to be enforced. This question of severance is dealt with in Pt 5. 11–009

**Patel v Mirza.** The decision of the Supreme Court in *Patel v Mirza*[27] is primarily concerned with the effects of illegality and is therefore considered in detail in Pt 3 of this chapter, but such is its significance that some awareness of it is helpful 11–010

[22] Gaming Act 1845 s.18.

[23] Gambling Act 2005 s.335(1). One consequence of the wording of s.335(1) is that the parties may expressly reassert the status of a gaming contract prior to the 2005 reforms by ensuring, through appropriate drafting, that there is no "contract" between them, save in honour only; cf. para.11–055. Nothing in the 2005 Act appears intended to affect Marine Insurance Act 1906 s.4 under which insurance without an insurable interest is void, but the technique used to achieve this is to deem it to be a "gaming or wagering contract" (s.4(2)).

[24] In addition to the grounds on which any other contract may be unenforceable, the Gambling Commission has the power, in certain cases, to make an order that any contract in relation to a bet is void: s.336. If such an order is made any money paid in relation to the bet must be repaid to the payor: s.336(2).

[25] 2005 Act s.335(2) states: "Subsection (1) is without prejudice to any rule of law preventing the enforcement of a contract on the grounds of unlawfulness (other than a rule relating specifically to gambling)."

[26] 2005 Act ss.33, 37.

[27] [2016] UKSC 42; [2017] A.C. 467; Grabiner 76 C.L.J. 168; Goudkamp 133 L.Q.R. 14; Strauss [2016] R.L.R. 145; Green and Bogg (eds), *Illegality after Patel v Mirza* (2018).

from the outset. A majority of the Court decided that the effect of illegality on the enforcement of a contract and other forms of relief should henceforward be decided not on the basis of any particular rule, or rules, but on the basis of a broad assessment of whether granting or denying relief would be most consistent with the public interest of ensuring the integrity of the legal system. That assessment is to be based primarily on a "trio of necessary considerations", namely "the underlying purpose of the prohibition which has been transgressed, … any other relevant public policies which may be rendered ineffective or less effective by denial of the claim, and keeping in mind the possibility of overkill unless the law is applied with a due sense of proportionality".[28] As Lord Toulson acknowledged, those considerations can be found in the case law[29] and they should be borne in mind as we embark on an analysis of some of the leading cases.

## 2. TYPES OF ILLEGALITY

### (a) Contracts involving the commission of a legal wrong

#### *(i) Contracts amounting to a legal wrong*

11–011 **Examples.** A contract is illegal[30] if the making of it is a legal wrong, e.g. if legislation prohibits the making of the contract.[31] At common law, a contract to "rig the market" by offering inflated prices for shares in a particular company is similarly illegal as it is a criminal conspiracy.[32] A contract to stifle a prosecution for treason is illegal as it amounts to compounding. It is also an offence for a person who knows that a "relevant offence" has been committed, and that he has information which may help to secure the conviction of the offender, to accept or agree to accept any consideration (other than the making good of the loss or injury caused by the offence) for not disclosing the information.[33] The making of some contracts is expressly made criminal by statute: it is, for example, an offence to agree to indemnify a surety in criminal proceedings against liability to forfeit a recognisance,[34] and to deal for payment in human material.[35] Such contracts are no doubt illegal, as is one which causes or permits a child or young person to gamble with the holder of an operating licence under the Gambling Act 2005.[36] And where the making or variation of a contract is prohibited by a court order, disobedience of the order amounts to contempt of court; and the prohibited contract, or variation, is illegal.[37]

---

[28] *Patel v Mirza* [2016] UKSC 42; [2017] A.C. 467 at [101].
[29] *Patel v Mirza* [2016] UKSC 42; [2017] A.C. 467 at [101].
[30] Except to the extent that a statute provides the contrary, e.g. Equality Act 2010 s.142(1).
[31] See *Mohamed v Alaga & Co* [2000] 1 W.L.R. 1815; *Hughes v Kingston upon Hull CC* [1999] Q.B. 1193.
[32] *Scott v Brown* [1892] 2 Q.B. 724; cf. *Harry Parker Ltd v Mason* [1940] 2 K.B. 590.
[33] Criminal Law Act 1967 s.5(1); "relevant offence" is defined by s.4(1A).
[34] Bail Act 1976 s.9.
[35] Human Tissue Act 2004 s.32.
[36] 2005 Act s.46.
[37] *Clarke v Chadburn* [1985] 1 W.L.R. 78.

**Champerty.** A contract by which one person agrees to finance another's litigation in return for a share in the proceeds, the former having no genuine or substantial interest in the outcome,[38] used to amount to the crime and tort of champerty; and accordingly the contract was illegal. Although criminal and tortious liability for champerty have been abolished,[39] a champertous agreement remains, as a general rule, illegal.[40] The agreement must amount to "wanton or officious intermeddling with the disputes of others", to which "must be added the notion of a division of the spoils."[41] The former requirement is a description of maintenance[42] so that champerty may be seen as a sub-species thereof. More recently, and in the light of the statutory developments which are described in the next paragraph, it has been acknowledged that there may be champerty without maintenance and that what is "in play" is the policy "against a person who is in a position to influence the outcome of litigation having an interest in that outcome."[43] 11–012

**Contingency or conditional fees.** At common law agreements between a client and his legal advisers in litigation for the payment of either a "contingency" or a "conditional" fee are champertous and illegal.[44] Conditional fee agreements are those which provide that the legal adviser is to be paid his fee if he wins the case but not if he loses it. With respect to such agreements, legislation now provides[45] that, in most cases,[46] an agreement in writing can validly be made[47] by which a client promises to pay a "conditional fee" to a person who provides him with advocacy or litigation services in legal proceedings.[48] The condition may be that the litigation ends in the client's favour; and the fee may be a "success fee", that is, one which provides that, in that event, the provider's fee is to be increased above the amount of the normal fee[49] by a percentage (not exceeding that specified by the Lord Chancellor).[50] Conditional fee agreements which are not in terms validated by this legislation are declared by it to be unenforceable,[51] and 11–013

---

[38] See paras 15–063—15–067.

[39] Criminal Law Act 1967 ss.13(1), 14(1).

[40] Criminal Law Act 1967 s.14(2); *Trendtex Trading Corp v Crédit Suisse* [1982] A.C. 679; *McFarlane v EE Caledonia (No.2)* [1995] 1 W.L.R. 366 at 372.

[41] *Giles v Thompson* [1994] 1 A.C. 142 at 164; citing *British Cash and Parcel Conveyors Ltd v Lamson Store Service Co Ltd* [1908] 1 K.B. 1006 at 1014.

[42] See para.15–060.

[43] *Sibthorpe v Southwark LBC* [2011] EWCA Civ 25; [2011] 1 W.L.R. 2111 at [54]; citing *R. (Factortame Ltd) v Secretary of State for Transport, Local Government and the Regions (No.8)* [2002] EWCA Civ 932; [2003] Q.B. 381 at [76].

[44] *Wallersteiner v Moir (No.2)* [1975] Q.B. 373; *Awwad v Geraghty & Co* [2001] Q.B. 570; *Westlaw Services Ltd v Boddy* [2010] EWCA Civ 929; [2011] P.N.L.R. 4; *Sibthorpe v Southwark L.B.C.* [2011] EWCA Civ 25; [2011] 1 W.L.R. 2111.

[45] Courts and Legal Services Act 1990 ss.58 and 58A.

[46] Criminal proceedings and most family proceedings are excluded by s.58A(1) of the 1990 Act.

[47] Courts and Legal Services Act 1990 s.58(3).

[48] These need not be court proceedings: Courts and Legal Services Act 1990 s.58A(4).

[49] Courts and Legal Services Act 1990 s.58(2)(a): i.e. the amount to which he would have been entitled if his right to payment had not been conditional on the success of the client's claim.

[50] Courts and Legal Services Act 1990 s.58(4)(c).

[51] Courts and Legal Services Act 1990 s.58(1).

are also illegal at common law,[52] though it has been suggested that it may be right "to step back and consider the matter afresh in the light of modern conditions."[53] This has led to the view that there is at least no requirement to *expand* the scope of champerty in this area, so that a conditional fee agreement which was otherwise lawful was not illegal because the legal advisers also provided an indemnity to their client against the costs which would have to be paid if the claim was unsuccessful.[54] It has not, as yet, led to the view that agreements which are champertous under the existing law should be regarded as lawful.[55] Thus, for example, contingency fee agreements under which the legal adviser is remunerated by a share in the amount recovered remain illegal. So far as agreements with parties who are not legal advisers are concerned, e.g. accountants[56] and surveyors,[57] the modern approach is to make an assessment on a case by case basis and only to regard as illegal those agreements which "would corrupt public justice".[58]

### *(ii) Contracts to commit a crime*

11–014 A contract for the deliberate commission of a crime is obviously illegal.[59] Such a contract would also amount to conspiracy. But many statutory crimes can be committed without criminal intent; and there are cases in which only one of the parties to a contract has any criminal intent. The exact effects of illegality on such contracts, where one or both parties act in good faith, will be considered later in this chapter.[60]

### *(iii) Contracts to commit a civil wrong*

11–015 **Deliberate commission of a civil wrong.** A contract is illegal where its object is the *deliberate* commission of a civil wrong. Thus contracts to assault[61] or defraud[62] a third party are illegal: and the same is true of a contract by an

---

[52] See the cases cited in fn.44.

[53] *Thai Trading Co v Taylor* [1998] Q.B. 785 at 790; *Kellar v Williams* [2004] UKPC 30 at [21]; *Factortame Ltd v Secretary of State for Transport, Local Government and the Regions (No.8)* [2002] EWCA Civ 932; [2003] Q.B. 381 at [32].

[54] *Sibthorpe v Southwark LBC* [2011] EWCA Civ 25; [2011] 1 W.L.R. 2111.

[55] *Sibthorpe v Southwark LBC* [2011] EWCA Civ 25; [2011] 1 W.L.R. 2111 at [54]. Any view to the contrary expressed in *Thai Trading Co v Taylor* [1998] Q.B. 785 is to be regarded as *per incuriam* and treated with caution: *Sibthorpe* at [24], [39]; The *Thai Trading* case was also doubted in *Westlaw Services Ltd v Boddy* [2010] EWCA Civ 929; [2011] P.N.L.R. 4.

[56] *Factortame Ltd v Secretary of State for Transport, Local Government and the Regions (No.8)* [2002] EWCA Civ 932; [2003] Q.B. 381, cf. *Giles v Thompson* [1994] 1 A.C. 142.

[57] *Picton Jones & Co v Arcadia Developments* [1989] 1 E.G.L.R. 43.

[58] *Sibthorpe v Southwark LBC* [2011] EWCA Civ 25; [2011] 1 W.L.R. 2111 at [35].

[59] e.g. *Bigos v Bousted* [1951] 1 All E.R. 92; cf. *Ashton v Turner* [1981] Q.B. 137; *Pitts v Hunt* [1991] 1 Q.B. 24. Ignorance of the law makes no difference: see *Belvoir Finance Co Ltd v Stapleton* [1971] 1 Q.B. 210.

[60] See paras 11–069–11–087.

[61] *Allen v Rescous* (1676) 2 Lev. 174.

[62] *Begbie v Phosphate Sewage Co Ltd* (1875) L.R. 10 Q.B. 491; cf. *Customs & Excise Commissioners v Oliver* [1980] 1 All E.R. 355; *Taylor v Bhail* [1995] C.L.C. 337.

insolvent debtor to pay one of his creditors in fraud of the others.[63] Where a contract involves the *unintentional* commission of a civil wrong two types of cases call for discussion.

**Unintentional commission of a civil wrong: one party innocent.** One party may know that the performance of the contract will involve the commission of a civil wrong, while the other is innocent. In *Clay v Yates*[64] the claimant agreed with the defendant to print a book with a dedication. He refused to print the dedication on discovering that it was libellous, but claimed the cost of printing the book. The defendant did not plead illegality but argued that the obligation to print the book with the dedication was "entire",[65] and that the claimant could not recover anything as he had performed only in part. In rejecting this argument, Pollock CB said that there was an implied undertaking to pay "for so much of the work *as is lawful*";[66] while Martin B said that the defendant was liable "to pay the [claimant] for that part *which he has performed*".[67] If the claimant had printed the dedication without knowing the facts which made it libellous, it seems that he could not have recovered his charges on Pollock CB's test but that he could have done so under Martin B's test; and it is submitted that the latter is the preferable view.[68] 11–016

**Unintentional commission of a civil wrong: both parties innocent.** If neither party knows that performance of the contract involves the commission of a civil wrong the contract is not illegal.[69] A contract for the sale of goods belonging to a third party may make buyer and seller liable to that third party in tort[70] even though they believed that the goods belonged to the seller; but such a contract has never been held illegal.[71] 11–017

### *(iv) Use of subject-matter for unlawful purpose*

A contract which is in itself lawful may be illegal if its subject-matter is to be used for an unlawful purpose. In *Langton v Hughes*[72] Spanish juice, isinglass and ginger were sold to a brewer who, as the seller knew, intended to put them into his beer. The contract was held to be illegal because an Act of 1802 made it an offence to use anything except malt and hops to flavour beer. Later cases suggest that this rule applies only if the seller to some extent "participates" in the illegal 11–018

---

[63] *Mallalieu v Hodgson* (1851) 16 Q.B. 689; cf. *Cadbury Schweppes Plc v Somji* [2001] 1 W.L.R. 615.

[64] (1856) 1 H. & N. 73.

[65] See para.17–031.

[66] *Clay v Yates* (1856) 1 H. & N. 73 at 79 (emphasis added).

[67] *Clay v Yates* (1856) 1 H. & N. 73 at 80.

[68] Williams 8 C.L.J. at 54; Martin B's view may be reconciled with *Frank W Clifford Ltd v Garth* [1956] 1 W.L.R. 570; para.11–161, on the ground that the builder in that case took a conscious risk of illegality; cf. *ZYX Music GmbH v King* [1995] 3 All E.R. 1 at 10.

[69] *Clarion Ltd v National Power Association* [2000] 1 W.L.R. 1888 at 1908.

[70] See para.22–019.

[71] Sale of Goods Act 1979 s.12 assumes that the contract is valid.

[72] (1813) 1 M. & S. 593; cf. *Gas Light & Coke Co v Turner* (1839) 6 Bing. N.C. 324.

purpose.[73] Where the line is to be drawn in any particular case is a question of fact and degree, but the more the subject-matter has been "tailored" for the unlawful purpose, the more readily can the inference of participation be made.[74]

### (v) *Unlawful method of performance*

11–019 **Breach of statute.** A contract which is lawful in itself may be performed in a way which involves one or both parties in criminal liability. It used to be thought that the contract was illegal[75] if its performance involved breach of a statute passed for the protection of the public; but that, if the statute was passed only for the protection of the revenue, the contract was not illegal.[76] But the distinction between these two types of statutes is by no means decisive.[77] Even where the object of the statute is to protect the public (or a section of it) a contract involving a breach of it is not invariably illegal. Thus a contract to grant (or to transfer) a lease is not illegal merely because the landlord has committed a statutory offence by receiving or demanding an illegal premium. The tenant can accordingly enforce the contract, though without having to pay the premium.[78] Similarly, a tenancy is not illegal merely because the landlord has committed a statutory offence by failing to give his tenant a rent-book. Here the illegality relates to a merely collateral matter, so that the contract can be enforced even by the offender: i.e. the landlord can sue for the rent.[79] On the other hand, a contract may be illegal although the statute which it violates was passed for the protection of the revenue.[80] The test for determining whether an otherwise lawful contract is illegal because its performance involved the breach of a statute is that laid down in *St John Shipping Corp v Joseph Rank Ltd*:[81] did the statute intend only to penalise *conduct* or also to prohibit *contracts*? Some statutes expressly solve this problem: a contract for the supply of goods is not, for example, to be void or

---

[73] *JM Allan (Merchandising) Ltd v Cloke* [1963] 2 Q.B. 340 at 348; cf. *Ashmore, Benson Pease & Co Ltd v AV Dawson Ltd* [1973] 1 W.L.R. 828, para.11–074.

[74] *Anglo Petroleum Ltd v TFB (Mortgages) Ltd* [2007] EWCA Civ 456; [2008] 1 B.C.L.C. 185 at [79].

[75] *Little v Poole* (1829) 9 B. & C. 192; *Brightman & Co v Tate* [1919] 1 K.B. 463.

[76] *Johnson v Hudson* (1805) 11 East 180; *Learoyd v Bracken* [1894] 1 Q.B. 114; cf. *Wetherell v Jones* (1832) 3 B. & Ad. 221.

[77] *Cope v Rowlands* (1836) 2 M. & W. 149 at 157.

[78] *Ailion v Spiekermann* [1976] Ch. 158; for the enforceability of the contract by an innocent third party (in spite of a formal defect making one of the parties liable to a fine) see *OTV Birwelco Ltd v Technical & General Guarantee Co Ltd* [2002] EWHC 2240 (TCC); [2002] 4 All E.R. 668 at [55].

[79] *Shaw v Groom* [1970] 2 Q.B. 504; cf. *London & Harrogate Securities Ltd v Pitts* [1976] 1 W.L.R. 1063; *P & B (Run Off) Ltd v Woolley* [2002] EWCA Civ 65; [2002] 1 All E.R. (Comm) 577.

[80] e.g. where the object of the contract is to evade or to delay the payment of income tax: *Napier v National Business Agency Ltd* [1951] 2 All E.R. 264; cf. *Miller v Karlinski* (1945) 62 T.L.R. 85; para.11–056.

[81] [1957] 1 Q.B. 267; para.11–003; *Crédit Lyonnais v PT Barnard & Associates* [1976] 1 Lloyd's Rep. 557; cf. *Curragh Investments Ltd v Cook* [1974] 1 W.L.R. 1559; *Mohammed v Alaga & Co* [2000] 1 W.L.R. 1815 at 1824, applying the same test to legislation which prohibited the *making* of a contract.

unenforceable merely because, in performing it, the seller has committed an offence under the Trade Descriptions Act 1968.[82]

**Licensing requirements.** A statute may subject contracts to a licensing or similar requirement, so that they can be lawfully performed only with the consent of some public body. Such a statute may expressly prohibit (and so render illegal) a contract made in breach of its provisions;[83] and even where the statute does not expressly prohibit the contract, it may do so by implication. Such an implication is most likely to arise where *both* parties are prohibited from making or performing the contract; but the implication may arise even where the statutory prohibition is directed at only one of the parties. At common law, this was the position where an insurer committed a statutory offence by engaging in certain types of insurance business without government authorisation;[84] by statute, such contracts are no longer illegal, but only unenforceable against the other party.[85] 11–020

A licensing or similar requirement may also apply merely to the performance of a particular contract (as opposed to the carrying on of a business), e.g. where a licence is required for the erection of a building or for the export or import of goods. Such a contract is not illegal if it is expressly or by implication made subject to the relevant consent.[86] It will be illegal only if it is performed without such licence or consent,[87] or if the parties intend to perform it even though no licence or consent is obtained.[88] A party may, however, guarantee that the licence will be obtained; if so, the undertaking can be enforced against him as a collateral contract, even though the main contract is illegal.[89] He may also be liable in damages for failing to perform an express or implied promise to make reasonable efforts to obtain the licence.[90]

**Subsequent commission of a civil wrong.** A contract which is initially lawful may become illegal if, in the course of performing it, the parties agree deliberately to commit a civil wrong, e.g. to defraud a third person who had undertaken to provide the finance necessary for its performance.[91] But a contract which is in itself lawful does not become illegal merely because in the course of performing it one party commits a fraud on the other,[92] or on a third party.[93] That 11–021

[82] Section 35; and see para.11–079. Such a legislative provision may also be implied: see *Currencies Direct Ltd v Ellis* [2002] EWCA Civ 779; [2002] 2 B.C.L.C. 482 (Companies Act 1985 s.341 (now Companies Act 2006 s.213(2)), by making a prohibited loan *voidable by the company*, by implication entitled company to enforce it).

[83] cf. *Re Mahmoud and Ispahani* [1921] 2 K.B. 716; para.11–078.

[84] *Bedford Ins Co Ltd v Instituto de Resseguros do Brazil* [1985] 1 Q.B. 966; *Phoenix General Ins Co of Greece v Halvanon Ins Co Ltd* [1988] Q.B. 216.

[85] Financial Services and Markets Act 2000 ss.26(1), 27(1A).

[86] *Michael Richards Properties Ltd v St Saviour's Parish* [1975] 3 All E.R. 416.

[87] e.g. *J Dennis & Co Ltd v Munn* [1949] 2 K.B. 327. For an exception, see *Ancienne Maison Marcel Bauche SA v Woodhouse Drake & Carey (Sugar) Ltd* [1982] 2 Lloyd's Rep. 516.

[88] e.g. *Bigos v Bousted* [1951] 1 All E.R. 92.

[89] *Peter Cassidy Seed Co Ltd v Osuustukkukauppa* [1957] 1 W.L.R. 273, as explained in *Walton (Grain and Shipping) Ltd v British Trading Co* [1959] 1 Lloyd's Rep. 223 at 236; cf. para.11–083. Both cases concerned foreign licensing requirements.

[90] See para.2–111; para.17–071.

[91] *Birkett v Acorn Business Machines Ltd* [1999] 2 All E.R. (Comm) 429.

[92] *Broaders v Kalkare Property Maintenance* [1990] I.R.L.R. 421.

fraud is, however, likely to be a repudiatory breach if perpetrated on the other party, so that the victim of the fraud will be entitled to terminate the contract and so to avoid further liability under it.[94]

### (vi) *Contracts to indemnify against liability for unlawful acts*

11–022 **Criminal liability.** A contract to indemnify a person against criminal liability is illegal if the crime is one which can only be, or in fact is, committed with guilty intent.[95] But the position is less clear where the crime is one of strict liability. In *Cointat v Myham & Sons*[96] the defendants sold to a butcher the carcass of a pig, which was unfit for food. The butcher innocently exposed it for sale and was consequently convicted and fined £20. It was held that he could recover this sum from the defendants; but the legality of their implied promise to indemnify him was not discussed. The case has been criticised on the ground that "punishment inflicted by a criminal court is personal to the offender" and is fixed "having regard to the personal responsibility of the offender in respect of the offence".[97] One object of imposing strict criminal liability is to make a person take care not to commit the offence; and this object might be defeated by allowing him to recover the fine from a third party. Nonetheless it seems that the courts will allow a person to recover an indemnity against criminal liability if they are satisfied that he is wholly innocent. For example, in *Osman v J Ralph Moss Ltd*[98] a motorist had been convicted of driving while uninsured. He was morally innocent, having been told by his insurance agent that he was properly insured, and it was held that his fine could be included in the damages recoverable from the agent for breach of contract.

11–023 **Guilty intent.** That the guilty intent of the person claiming an indemnity is to be taken into account is supported by a number of cases. In *Gray v Thames Trains Ltd*,[99] the claimant was convicted of manslaughter by diminished responsibility as a result of his suffering from a mental illness after an accident caused by the negligence of the defendant. The House of Lords was concerned not with a contract to indemnify the claimant, but with the question of whether the defendant's liability in negligence to the claimant extended to the losses incurred by him as a consequence of his criminal act.[100] A distinction was drawn between cases where the claimant seeks compensation for loss which flows from a

---

93 *ParkingEye Ltd v Somerfield Stores Ltd* [2012] EWCA Civ 1338; [2013] Q.B. 840.
94 See para.18–030 and following.
95 *Colburn v Patmore* (1834) 1 C.M. & R. 73; *Safeway Stores Ltd v Twigger* [2010] EWCA Civ 1472; [2011] 1 Lloyd's Rep. 462.
96 [1913] 2 K.B. 220; reversed on another ground [1914] W.N. 46.
97 *Askey v Golden Wine Co* (1948) 64 T.L.R. 379 at 380; cf. *R Leslie Ltd v Reliable Advertising, etc. Agency Ltd* [1915] 1 K.B. 652.
98 [1970] 1 Lloyd's Rep. 313; cf. *Griffin v UHY Hacker Young & Partners* [2010] EWHC 146 (Ch) (claim in tort).
99 [2009] UKHL 33; [2009] 1 A.C. 1339. See also earlier cases in tort: *Clunis v Camden and Islington Health Authority* [1998] Q.B. 978; *Vellino v Chief Constable of the Greater Manchester Police* [2001] EWCA Civ 1249; [2002] 1 W.L.R. 218.
100 Though one of the heads of loss was an indemnity against any claims made against him by the representatives of the deceased.

*sentence* imposed in consequence of his unlawful act[101] and those where he seeks compensation for loss which flows from the criminal act itself,[102] but in either instance in *Gray* the claimant was found guilty of an offence where mens rea was an essential element. In a later case[103] where the claimant sought damages from his accountant for failing to advise him that his conduct in winding up a company might lead to a fine and other consequential losses as a result of his conviction for what was a strict liability offence,[104] the claim was not struck out on the basis that "it could at least be argued that negligence [of the claimant] would not be sufficient to deprive a claimant guilty of some, at least, strict liability offences of a remedy against a defendant guilty of professional negligence."[105] It has also been said that, before the claimant can be prevented from claiming an indemnity there must have been "moral turpitude or moral reprehensibility involved in the relevant conduct".[106]

**Company acting through its agents.** The requirement of a guilty intent may be problematic where the claimant is a company which is said to have been guilty of illegality through the actions of its agents or its employees and it claims an indemnity either from a third party, or from the agents or employees themselves. The former case may be demonstrated by the facts of *Stone & Rolls Ltd v Moore Stephens*[107] where a company perpetrated frauds on a number of banks and then sought damages from the company's auditors for failing to detect the dishonest activities of the director responsible, S. The company was prevented from doing so on the basis of illegality, but a key feature of the case, as decided, was that the company was entirely owned, controlled and managed by S and, as his was the "directing mind and will" of the company, the liability of the company was direct and personal.[108] In subsequent cases, it has been said that this decision is of little 11–024

[101] cf. Lord Denning's emphasis on "punishment" in the passage quoted from *Askey v Golden Wine Co* (1948) 64 T.L.R. 379, fn.97.

[102] *Gray v Thames Trains Ltd* [2009] UKHL 33; [2009] 1 A.C. 1339 at [29]. The former ("narrower") instance is based on the "inconsistency" of requiring the law to compensate for damage imposed by the law as a matter of penal policy. The latter ("wider") instance is based on a broader policy which, in the context of the negligence claim in *Gray*, was described in terms similar to the "public conscience" test which is considered at para.11–072: "the wider rule has to be justified on the ground that it is offensive to public notions of the fair distribution of resources that a claimant should be compensated . . . for the consequences of his own criminal conduct", [2009] 1 A.C. 1339 at [51].

[103] *Griffin v UHY Hacker Young & Partners* [2010] EWHC 146 (Ch); [2010] P.N.L.R. 20.

[104] Of becoming a director of another company using a trade name of the liquidated company without obtaining leave of the court: Insolvency Act 1986 s.216(3).

[105] *Griffin v UHY Hacker Young and Partners* [2010] EWHC 146 (Ch); [2010] P.N.L.R. 20 at [60]; cf. *United Project Consultants Pte Ltd v Leong Kwok Ong* [2005] 4 S.L.R. 214.

[106] *Safeway Stores Ltd v Twigger* [2010] EWHC 11 (Comm) at [26] (reversed on appeal [2010] EWCA Civ 1472; [2011] 1 Lloyd's Rep. 462); cf. *Stone & Rolls Ltd v Moore Stephens* [2009] UKHL 39; [2009] 1 A.C. 1391 at [24].

[107] [2009] UKHL 39; [2009] 1 A.C. 1391; cf. *Berg, Sons & Co Ltd v Mervyn Hampton Adams* [2002] Lloyd's Rep. PN 41.

[108] This was the primary reasoning of Lord Walker and Lord Brown, but the other Law Lord in the majority, Lord Phillips, based his reasoning on the scope of the duty owed by the auditors, holding that it did not extend to the creditors of the company, who were not tainted by illegality. Lord Walker has subsequently described the facts in the *Stone & Rolls* case as "extreme and exceptional": *Moulin Global Eyecare Trading Ltd v Commissioner of Inland Revenue* [2014] HKCFA 22; (2014) 17 HKCFAR 218 at [133].

value as a precedent[109] and the question of attribution, in relation to a claim against a third party, depends very much on the context.[110] In *Singularis Holdings Ltd v Daiwa Capital Markets Europe Ltd*[111] the defendant was a stockbroker who was sued in negligence and for breach of a co-extensive contractual duty of care in failing to prevent fraudulent payments being made out of the claimant company's account by an officer of the company who was its sole shareholder. The defendant failed to prove that the claimant was a "one man company",[112] but in any event attribution was not appropriate in the context of the claim made against the defendant. In particular, the defendant was in breach of a very specific duty of care owed by banks (and those akin to banks like the defendant stockbroker) to account holders which is aimed at guarding against the fraudulent conduct of officers of the account-holder.[113] Vos LJ agreed with Rose J at first instance that "such an attribution would denude the duty of any value in cases where it is most needed."[114]

11–024 The case in which a company claims an indemnity from the guilty agents or employees themselves may be demonstrated by *Jetivia SA v Bilta (UK) Ltd*[115] where the company in question was rendered insolvent and left with a VAT liability as a result of fraud perpetrated by two directors. The Supreme Court held that where the claim is by a company against its own officers[116] (as opposed to a third party, such as the auditors in *Stone & Rolls*), the guilty intent of the officers is not attributed to the company, even in circumstances where one of the directors was also the sole shareholder, and for this reason the defence of illegality did not bar the company's claim.[117] This may be contrasted with the earlier decision in *Safeway Stores Ltd v Twigger*[118] where a company admitted its liability for breach of certain of the provisions of the Competition Act 1998 and the principal element of the loss it suffered as a result was the fine imposed. It sought to recover this loss from the former directors and employees who were, for the purpose of an application to strike out the claim, assumed to have been

---

109 *Jetivia SA v Bilta (UK) Ltd* [2015] UKSC 23; [2015] 2 W.L.R. 1168 at [30] (Lord Neuberger: "not in the interests of the future clarity of the law for it be to treated as authoritative or of assistance save (as to its particular facts)".

110 *Jetivia SA v Bilta (UK) Ltd* [2015] UKSC 23; [2015] 2 W.L.R. 1168 at [29] (Lord Neuberger), [48]–[50] (Lord Mance).

111 [2018] EWCA Civ 84; [2018] 1 W.L.R. 2777.

112 Defined by Vos LJ as "a company in which, whether there was one or more than one controller, there were no innocent directors or shareholders": [2018] EWCA Civ 84; [2018] 1 W.L.R. 2777 at [53].

113 The "*Quincecare* duty" after *Barclays Bank Plc v Quincecare Ltd* [1992] 4 All E.R. 363.

114 [2017] EWHC 257; [2017] 1 Lloyd's Rep. 226 at [184].

115 [2015] UKSC 23; [2015] 2 W.L.R. 1168; cf. *UBS AG v Kommunale Wasserwerke Leipzig GmbH* [2017] EWCA Civ 1567; [2017] 2 Lloyd's Rep. 621 (claim against a third party accessory); *Crown Prosecution Service v Aquila Advisory Ltd* [2019] EWCA Civ 588 at [25] (CPS in no better a position than the company's officers in seeking to enforce a confiscation order against the company).

116 The principal claim was made in tort for unlawful means conspiracy between the directors and two further parties based on breach of fiduciary duty by the directors and the dishonest assistance of the additional parties.

117 Lords Toulson and Hodge also held that, in any event, the defence of illegality did not apply where it would empty the duty of the directors of an insolvent company to act in the interests of creditors of the company (see Companies Act 2006 ss.172(3), 180(5)): [2015] UKSC 23; [2015] 2 W.L.R. 1168 at [130].

118 [2010] EWCA Civ 1472; [2011] 1 Lloyd's Rep. 462.

responsible for the infringements. The trial judge had refused to strike out the claim because it had not been shown that the company was "personally" at fault,[119] but it was said by Longmore LJ that it was simply not possible for the company to make such a submission when it had admitted its liability, albeit via the actions of its employees and agents, for an offence for which a penalty could be imposed under the 1998 Act only on the company and in circumstances where the infringement was committed "intentionally or negligently."[120] In *Jetivia SA v Bilta (UK) Ltd*, the decision in the *Safeway* case is explained as turning on the statutory scheme and "not authority for any proposition applying more generally".[121]

**Civil liability arising out of criminal acts.** Where an act amounts both to a crime and to a civil wrong, a promise to indemnify the wrongdoer against civil liability incurred as a result of the act is often illegal. For example, in *Gray v Barr*[122] a husband shot and killed his wife's lover in circumstances amounting in the view of the Court of Appeal to manslaughter (though in the criminal proceedings he had been acquitted). It was held that the husband could not recover under an insurance policy (even if it covered the occurrence) the damages which he had had to pay to the lover's estate. The decision was based on the public interest in deterring armed violence; but it does not follow that promises to indemnify against civil liability are necessarily invalid merely because the act giving rise to that liability also amounts to a crime. There are a number of situations in which they may be upheld. **11–025**

First, a promise to indemnify a person against civil liability can be enforced, even though the act giving rise to that liability is criminal, if the crime is one of strict liability or is in fact committed without mens rea. Thus in *Gray v Barr* the possibility was left open that a person who committed manslaughter in circumstances amounting to little more than an error of judgment might be able to recover an indemnity from his insurance company.[123] The view that such an indemnity is recoverable is supported by a dictum in a later case, according to which the test "is not the label which the law applies to the crime which has been committed, but the nature of the crime itself".[124] Similarly, if the butcher in *Cointat v Myham & Son*[125] had had to pay damages for breach of contract to a customer who was poisoned by the pork, he should have been able to claim an indemnity against this loss from the defendant.

---

[119] *Safeway Stores Ltd v Twigger* [2010] EWHC 11 (Comm) based on the decision of the House of Lords in *Stone & Rolls Ltd v Moore Stephens* [2009] UKHL 39; [2009] 1 A.C. 1391.
[120] Competition Act 1998 s.36(3); [2010] EWCA Civ 1472; [2011] 1 Lloyd's Rep. 462 at [18], [25], [37], [43].
[121] *Jetivia SA v Bilta (UK) Ltd* [2015] UKSC 23; [2015] 2 W.L.R. 1168 at [83] (Lord Sumption, with whom Lords Neuberger, Clarke and Carnwath concurred (at [31])); Lord Mance (at [52]) and Lords Toulson and Hodge (at [159]–[162]) doubted the correctness of the decision in the *Safeway* case itself.
[122] [1971] 2 Q.B. 554; cf. *Haseldine v Hosken* [1933] 1 K.B. 822.
[123] *Gray v Barr* [1971] 2 Q.B. 554 at 581; cf. *Gregory v Ford* [1951] 1 All E.R. 121 (employment contract).
[124] *R. v National Insurance Commissioner Ex p. Connor* [1981] Q.B. 758 at 765; cf. *Gray v Thames Trains Ltd* [2009] UKHL 33; [2009] 1 A.C. 1339; para.11–023.
[125] [1913] 2 K.B. 220; para.11–022.

The second situation arises in the law of motor insurance. In *Tinline v White Cross Insurance*[126] a motorist, who was insured against liability for "accidental personal injury" to third parties, killed a pedestrian by driving with criminal negligence, and was convicted of manslaughter. He successfully sued the insurers for the damages which he had had to pay to the deceased. The motorist has this right only where the crime is committed negligently—not where it is committed deliberately.[127] But even in the latter case the position of the innocent victim of the motorist's crime is protected by being given rights in certain circumstances against the insurer or against the Motor Insurers' Bureau.[128] The existence of such rights is obviously necessary to maintain the effectiveness of the scheme of compulsory motor insurance.

Thirdly, the principle stated in *Gray v Barr* applies only to contracts to indemnify the wrongdoer *himself* against civil liability arising out of criminal conduct. That conduct may also make the wrongdoer's *employer* civilly liable to the victim; and the employer can validly insure against such liability, even to the extent that the wrong gives rise to a claim against him for exemplary (or punitive) damages.[129]

Fourthly, there is nothing contrary to public policy in one party agreeing to provide funds to another to enable the latter to defend himself in civil proceedings arising out of a criminal event or to satisfy the judgment if the defence is unsuccessful;[130] nor in agreeing to provide funds to defend any criminal charge[131] (but not to meet the consequences of any unsuccessful defence unless the case falls within the exceptional circumstances discussed above).[132]

11–026 **Civil liability.** In *Les Laboratoires Servier v Apotex Inc*[133] the Supreme Court gave a clear statement of principle that mere civil liability, such as torts, breaches of contract, statutory and other civil wrongs, does not constitute the turpitude necessary for the defence of illegality. In that case, the defendant obtained an injunction against the claimant preventing its sale of a product in the UK in support of a claim for infringement of a European patent. When that claim failed, the defendant was liable for damages under a cross undertaking given as a condition of obtaining the injunction. The claimant was entitled to damages notwithstanding that the manufacture of the product in question in Canada amounted to a breach of the defendant's Canadian patent.[134] The public interest which underpins the defence of illegality was not engaged and the private interest of the defendant in the Canadian patent could be vindicated by an award of

[126] [1921] 3 K.B. 327; followed in *James v British General Ins Co Ltd* [1927] 2 K.B. 311; doubted in *Haseldine v Hosken* [1933] 1 K.B. 822 but approved in *Marles v Philip Trant & Sons Ltd* [1954] 1 Q.B. 29 at 40, and in *Gray v Barr* [1971] 2 Q.B. 544 at 568, 581.

[127] *Gardner v Moore* [1984] A.C. 548 at 560; *Pitts v Hunt* [1991] 1 Q.B. 24 at 30; *Charlton v Fisher* [2001] EWCA Civ 112; [2002] Q.B. 578.

[128] See para.14–143; *Hardy v MIB* [1964] 2 Q.B. 743; *Gardner v Moore* [1984] A.C. 548 at 560–561.

[129] *Lancashire CC v Municipal Mutual Ins Ltd* [1997] Q.B. 897.

[130] *Mulcaire v News Group Newspapers Ltd* [2011] EWHC 3469 (Ch); [2012] 2 W.L.R. 831.

[131] *Coulson v News Group Newspapers Ltd* [2012] EWCA Civ 1547; [2013] I.R.L.R. 116.

[132] See para.11–022.

[133] [2014] UKSC 55; [2014] 3 W.L.R. 1257.

[134] No injunction had been ordered in Canada.

damages by the Canadian courts.[135] However, Lord Sumption acknowledged that illegality is not confined to criminal acts and may extend to "quasi-criminal acts" which includes cases of dishonesty or corruption even in the context of purely civil disputes.[136]

It has been held that a contract to indemnify a person against civil liability may be illegal if the wrong is intentionally and knowingly committed,[137] e.g. a contract to indemnify a person against liability for deceit is illegal; but not where there is a bona fide dispute about such liability.[138] Similarly, a person who publishes what he knows to be a libel cannot recover an indemnity from the person who instigated the publication,[139] for the tendency of such an agreement might be to increase the circulation of the libel. On the other hand, a contract to keep a communication confidential, and to indemnify the maker against any liability resulting from its disclosure, has been held valid even where the communication contained a malicious libel[140] —apparently because the tendency of such an agreement is to restrict the circulation of the libel.

It is clear that a contract to indemnify a person against civil liability is perfectly valid if the liability was incurred innocently or negligently.[141] Indeed, in many such cases promises to indemnify, far from being illegal, are actually implied in law. The general principle is that where A at B's request does an act which is not "manifestly tortious", B must indemnify A for any liability incurred by A if the act turns out to be injurious to C.[142] The cases provide many illustrations of the validity of such express or implied promises to indemnify. Thus an agent can recover an indemnity from his principal if he is made liable in conversion for selling a third person's property on the principal's instructions.[143] An employer can insure himself against civil liability for the tort of his employee; and he may also be entitled to an indemnity against such liability from the employee under the contract of employment.[144] And where A holds property which is claimed by B and C, a promise by one of them to indemnify A against liability to the other if he delivers the property to the promisor is perfectly valid.[145]

---

135 *Les Laboratoires Servier v Apotex Inc* [2014] UKSC 55; [2014] 3 W.L.R. 1257 at [28].

136 *Les Laboratoires Servier v Apotex Inc* [2014] UKSC 55; [2014] 3 W.L.R. 1257 at [26]; cf. *Tchenguiz v Grant Thornton UK LLP* [2016] EWHC 3727 (Comm) at [45].

137 *Brown Jenkinson & Co Ltd v Percy Dalton (London) Ltd* [1957] 2 Q.B. 621.

138 *The Jag Ravi* [2011] EWCA Civ 180; [2012] 1 Lloyd's Rep. 637 at [50]–[52].

139 *WH Smith & Sons v Clinton* (1909) 99 L.T. 840.

140 *Weld-Blundell v Stephens* [1919] 1 K.B. 520; affirmed [1920] A.C. 956, but "[t]he difficulty about this case is that its ratio has never been clear": *Les Laboratoires Servier v Apotex Inc* [2014] UKSC 55; [2014] 3 W.L.R. 1257 at [26] (Lord Sumption); *Bradstreets British Ltd v Mitchell and Carpanayoti & Co Ltd* [1933] Ch. 190; contrast *Howard v Odham's Press Ltd* [1938] 1 K.B. 1. And see *Distillers Co Ltd v Times Newspapers Ltd* [1975] Q.B. 613.

141 *Betts v Gibbins* (1834) 2 A. & E. 57; cf. *Yeung v Hong Kong & Shanghai Banking Corp* [1981] A.C. 787.

142 *The Nogar Marin* [1988] 1 Lloyd's Rep. 412 at 417.

143 *Adamson v Jarvis* (1827) 4 Bing. 66; *Betts v Gibbins* (1834) 2 A. & E. 57.

144 *Lister v Romford Ice & Cold Storage Co Ltd* [1957] A.C. 555; para.6–072.

145 e.g. *Betts v Gibbins* (1834) 2 A. & E. 57.

### (vii) *Promises to pay money on the commission of an unlawful act*

11–027 A contract may be illegal if it provides for the payment of money to a person in the event of his doing an unlawful act, e.g. if A promises B £5 if B breaks the speed limit. A life insurance policy was never wholly illegal merely because it provided that the sum insured was to be paid even if the assured committed suicide (which was formerly a crime). It could clearly be enforced if he died in some other way. But in *Beresford v Royal Exchange Assurance*[146] it was, however, held that such a policy could not be enforced by the personal representatives of the assured if he did commit suicide; to allow a man, or his estate, to benefit from his own crime was said to be against public policy.[147] But if the assured assigned the policy and then committed suicide, the assignees were entitled to the policy moneys since it was they, and not the assured, who benefited from the crime.[148] It is hard to see the force of this distinction where, as in *Beresford*'s case, the assured was bankrupt, so that the only people who could benefit were his creditors. The actual decision can now be regarded as resting on the alternative ground that, under ordinary principles of insurance law, the assured cannot recover if he by his own deliberate act causes the event on which the insurance money is payable.[149]

### (viii) *Effect of changes in the law*

11–028 In relation to contracts which involve the commission of a legal wrong it is necessary to consider the effect of changes in the law, both on contracts in existence at the time of the change and on contracts made after the change.

11–029 **Conduct made unlawful.** The law may change so that previously lawful conduct becomes a legal wrong. The effect of such a change may be to frustrate existing contracts[150] and to make future contracts illegal. Whether it actually has this effect will depend on the principles stated in *St John Shipping Corp v Joseph Rank Ltd.*[151]

11–030 **Conduct made lawful: future contracts.** A second kind of change is one by which conduct previously amounting to a legal wrong ceases to be so; and prima facie the effect of such a change in the law is that future contracts involving such conduct will be valid. This would be the case where the conduct in question had been criminal under some regulatory statute (e.g. one requiring certain work to be

[146] [1938] A.C. 586; Goodhart 52 L.Q.R. 575.

[147] This principle applies even though the contract is not illegal: *Davitt v Titcumb* [1989] 3 All E.R. 417 (murderer not allowed to benefit indirectly from policy on joint lives of victim and himself); *Geismar v Sun Alliance* [1978] Q.B. 383 (insurer not liable to pay for loss of goods smuggled into this country; liability for loss of *other* goods covered by the policies seems not to have been disputed); contrast *Euro-Diam Ltd v Bathurst* [1990] Q.B. 1; para.11–107.

[148] *White v British Empire, etc. Assurance Co* (1868) L.R. 7 Eq. 394; *Charlton v Fisher* [2001] EWCA Civ 112; [2002] Q.B. 518 at [13].

[149] *Beresford v Royal Exchange Assurance* [1938] A.C. 586 at 595; *Reeves v Commissioner of Police of the Metropolis* [2000] 1 A.C. 360 at 388 (Lord Hobhouse, dissenting).

[150] See para.19–045.

[151] [1957] 1 Q.B. 267; para.11–003.

licensed) which was then repealed. But there are exceptions to this general rule. First, a statute abrogating a rule of law under which certain conduct was unlawful may expressly preserve a rule under which a contract involving such conduct was previously illegal: this is the position (in general)[152] with regard to champertous agreements.[153] Secondly, it is possible that, even after the conduct in question has ceased to be a legal wrong, a contract involving such conduct would still be contrary to public policy. But contracts should not generally be regarded as contrary to public policy merely because they involve conduct which was formerly criminal. Thus it is submitted that a contract to render services in connection with a lawful abortion is valid even though it would have been a contract to commit a crime before the Abortion Act 1967. Similarly it is submitted that the reasoning of *Beresford*'s case is obsolete now that suicide is no longer a crime.[154]

**Conduct made lawful: existing contracts.** The effect of this second kind of change in the law on contracts already in existence when the law was changed is more problematical. Changes in the law made after action is brought are generally disregarded[155] but there seems to be no authority on the effect of changes in the law between the making of the contract and the commencement of the action. One possible view is that the validity of the contract must be determined, once and for all, when it is made. But it is submitted that, so long as the act in question is lawful *when it is done*, no useful purpose is served by holding the contract invalid.[156] The statute may itself solve the problem by specifying whether, and if so to what extent, the change in the law has retrospective effect. **11–031**

### (b) Contracts contrary to public policy[157]

A contract which does not involve the commission of a legal wrong may be illegal because its tendency is to bring about a state of affairs of which the law disapproves on grounds of public policy. A contract is illegal for this reason only if its harmful tendency is clear, that is, if injury to the public is its probable and not merely its possible consequence.[158] Such contracts are often called "illegal",[159] but it is sometimes said that they are only "void" or "unenforceable"[160] to emphasise that no specific legal wrong is involved. So long as this **11–032**

---

[152] For an exception, see Courts and Legal Services Act 1990 ss.58 and 58A; para.11–013.

[153] Criminal Law Act 1967 s.14(2); para.11–012.

[154] Suicide Act 1961; cf. *Gray v Barr* [1971] 2 Q.B. 544 at 582. In practice, insurers may pay in such circumstances: see *Foskett v McKeown* [2001] 1 A.C. 102.

[155] *Hitchcock v Way* (1837) 6 A. & E. 943.

[156] cf. *Iranian Offshore Engineering & Construction Co v Dean Investment Holdings SA* [2019] EWHC 472 (Comm) at [198].

[157] Lloyd, *Public Policy*; Winfield 42 Harv. L.R. 76.

[158] *Fender v St John Mildmay* [1938] A.C. 1, 13; cf. [1979] Ch. 84 at 104.

[159] e.g. *McEllistrim's Case* [1919] A.C. 548 at 571; cf. Criminal Law Act 1967 s.14(2) ("contrary to public policy or otherwise illegal").

[160] e.g. *Bennett v Bennett* [1952] 1 K.B. 249 at 260; *Pau On v Lau Yiu Long* [1980] A.C. 614 at 634–635; *O'Sullivan v Management Agency & Music Ltd* [1985] Q.B. 428 at 447, 448, 469.

point is borne in mind, no harm is done by using the traditional terminology in which these contracts are "illegal".[161] Perhaps the most important type of contracts of which the law disapproves on grounds of public policy are those in restraint of trade. They are made the subject of separate consideration after first considering other examples.[162]

11–033 **Scope of the doctrine of public policy.** Public policy is a variable notion, depending on changing manners, morals and economic conditions. In theory, this flexibility of the doctrine of public policy could provide a judge with an excuse for invalidating any contract which he violently disliked. With this danger in mind, judges have sometimes criticised the doctrine of public policy. In 1824 Burroughs J described it as "a very unruly horse, and when once you get astride it you never know where it will carry you. It may lead you from the sound law".[163] And Lord Halsbury has denied that any court could "invent a new head of public policy".[164] On the other hand, the law does adapt itself to changes in economic and social conditions, as can be seen particularly from the development of the rules as to contracts in restraint of trade. This point has often been recognised judicially. Thus Lord Haldane has said: "What the law recognises as contrary to public policy turns out to vary greatly from time to time".[165] And Lord Denning has put a similar point of view: "With a good man in the saddle, the unruly horse can be kept in control. It can jump over obstacles".[166] The present attitude of the courts represents a compromise between the flexibility inherent in the notion of public policy and the need for certainty in commercial affairs.

11–034 **A general reluctance to extend.** In the interests of certainty the courts will in general refuse to apply the doctrine of public policy to contracts of a kind to which the doctrine has never been applied before. In *Printing & Numerical Registering Co v Sampson*,[167] for instance, an inventor assigned a patent to a company and also agreed to assign to the company any patent of a like nature thereafter to be acquired by him. He argued that this agreement was contrary to public policy as it tended to discourage inventors. In rejecting the argument, Jessel MR said: "You are not to extend arbitrarily those rules which say that a given contract is void as being against public policy".[168] One reason why the

---

[161] cf. *Mogul SS Co Ltd v McGregor Gow & Co* [1892] A.C. 25 at 46.

[162] See below, Pt 4.

[163] *Richardson v Mellish* (1824) 2 Bing. 229 at 252.

[164] *Janson v Driefontein Consolidated Mines Ltd* [1902] A.C. 484 at 491; cf. *Geismar v Sun Alliance & London Ins* [1978] Q.B. 383 at 389; *Deutsche Schachtbau-und Tiefbohrgesellschaft mbH v Ras Al Khaima National Oil Co* [1990] 1 A.C. 295 at 316 (reversed on other grounds [1990] 1 A.C. 295 at 329 and following).

[165] *Rodriguez v Speyer Bros* [1919] A.C. 59 at 79; cf. *Nordenfelt v Maxim Nordenfelt Guns & Ammunition Co* [1894] A.C. 535 at 553; *Gray v Barr* [1971] 2 Q.B. 554 at 582; *Thai Trading Co v Taylor* [1998] Q.B. 781 at 786 (as to which see para.11–013); *Kellar v Williams* [2004] UKPC 30; [2005] 4 Costs L.R. 559 at [21]; *XX v Whittington Hospital NHS Trust* [2018] EWCA Civ 2832; [2019] Med. L.R. 99 at [64].

[166] *Enderby Town FC Ltd v The Football Association Ltd* [1971] Ch. 591 at 606.

[167] (1875) L.R. 19 Eq. 462.

[168] *Printing & Numerical Registering Co v Sampson* (1875) L.R. 19 Eq. 462 at 465.

courts are less ready to apply the doctrine of public policy to new classes of contracts is that Parliament and its delegates have become more active in this field.[169]

**Novel applications.** In some cases judicial intervention may still as a last resort be desirable.[170] The courts may occasionally invalidate a contract even though it is of a kind to which the doctrine of public policy has not been applied before. Such novel applications of the doctrine of public policy are illustrated by decisions to the effect that a contract by which a trade journal promises not to comment on the affairs of a company is illegal as it may prevent the journal from exposing frauds perpetrated by the company;[171] that an attempt to contract out of certain statutory provisions governing the liquidation of companies is contrary to public policy;[172] and that the same is true of an attempt to deprive an agricultural tenant of security of tenure where he is entitled to it by statute.[173] There are also cases in which attempts to impeach agreements by reference to new heads of public policy have been rejected on the ground that the agreement in question did not in fact have any injurious tendency.[174] It may be possible to infer from this reasoning that, if such a tendency had been established, the attempt would not have failed merely because the alleged head of public policy was a novel one. **11–035**

**Disguised applications.** There are, finally, cases in which the courts may invalidate contracts or contractual provisions on what are essentially grounds of public policy without, as a general rule, making express reference to the doctrine of public policy, or to some established "head" of public policy. Some of the limitations on contractual capacity could be based on public policy: and indeed the former "incapacity"[175] of a barrister to make a contract with his client,[176] has been explained on this ground. At one time the invalidity of promises to pay extra wages to seamen who were already bound to serve[177] and of promises not to **11–036**

[169] See *D v NSPCC* [1978] A.C. 171 at 235; *Johnson v Moreton* [1980] A.C. 37 at 67; *Cheall v APEX* [1983] 2 A.C. 180 at 191; cf. *Multiservice Bookbinding Ltd v Marden* [1979] Ch. 84 (Swiss franc uplift clause in mortgage); *Nationwide BS v Registry of Friendly Societies* [1983] 1 W.L.R. 1226 (index-linked mortgage).

[170] cf. *Monkland v Jack Barclay Ltd* [1951] 2 K.B. 252 at 265; *ARB v IVF Hammersmith Ltd* [2017] EWHC 2438 (QB); [2018] 2 W.L.R. 1223 (breach of contract by a clinic when it allowed the claimant's sperm to be used for impregnation, but contrary to public policy to award damages representing the financial consequences of raising the child).

[171] *Neville v Dominion of Canada News Co Ltd* [1915] 3 K.B. 556; cf. *Initial Services Ltd v Putterill* [1968] 1 Q.B. 396 at 410; *Slater v Raw*, *The Times*, 15 October 1977.

[172] *British Eagle International Airlines Ltd v Cie Nationale Air France* [1975] 1 W.L.R. 758; *Folgate London Market Ltd v Chaucer Insurance Plc* [2011] EWCA Civ 328; [2011] B.C.C. 675; cf. *Belmont Park Investments Pty Ltd v BNY Corporate Trustee Services Ltd* [2011] UKSC 38; [2012] 1 A.C. 383.

[173] *Johnson v Moreton* [1980] A.C. 37; *Featherstone v Staples* [1986] 1 W.L.R. 861; *Gisborne v Burton* [1989] Q.B. 390. The statute in question did not specify the legal effects of attempts to "contract out" of its provisions.

[174] e.g. *Giles v Thompson* [1994] 1 A.C. 142 at 165.

[175] *Kennedy v Broun* (1863) 13 C.B. (N.S.) 667 at 736.

[176] *Rondel v Worsley* [1969] 1 A.C. 191 at 264. See now Courts and Legal Services Act 1990 s.61.

[177] *Harris v Watson* (1791) Peake 102; para.3–048.

enforce claims which were known to be invalid[178] was explained on grounds of public policy; though it is now more common to base these rules on lack of consideration.[179] The rule against the assignment of "mere rights of action"[180] was not usually discussed under the heading of public policy, though it might well be considered to belong there.[181] The same is true of the rules under which penalty clauses are invalid,[182] and of some of the common law rules which limit the operation of exemption clauses.[183] All these rules could be regarded as disguised extensions or applications of the doctrine of public policy.

11–037 **Categories.** What follows is discussion of contracts which, in the past, the courts have not enforced because they have been found to be contrary to public policy, organised into certain categories. It should be borne in mind that the scope of these categories has been, and will continue to be, affected by changes in prevailing attitudes and, in some cases, the very existence of a particular category may be called into question.[184]

### *(i) Agreements by married persons to marry*

11–038 An agreement to marry was formerly regarded as a contract, the breach of which gave rise to an action for damages. It was, however, thought to be against public policy to allow such actions to be brought on a promise by a married person to marry.[185] Actions for breach of promise of marriage were abolished by s.1 of the Law Reform (Miscellaneous Provisions) Act 1970, but s.2 of the Act provides that "where an agreement to marry is terminated" the formerly engaged couple is to be treated for the purpose of certain rights[186] in, and disputes about, property as if they had been married. Difficult problems with regard to rights in property can obviously arise when an ex-fiancée makes a claim under s.2 against a man who, when he promised to marry her, was already married to someone else. It has been held that a party to an agreement to marry which is later brought to an end can take the benefit of s.2 even though that party was already married and so before the Act could not have claimed damages for breach of the promise.[187] It seems, a fortiori, to follow that the other (unmarried) party to the dissolved engagement should also be entitled to rely on the section. In such a case care must, however,

---

[178] *Wade v Simeon* (1846) 2 C.B. 548 at 564 ("almost *contra bonos mores*"); *Edwards v Baugh* (1843) 11 M. & W. 641 at 646.

[179] *Stilk v Myrick* (1809) as reported in 2 Camp. 317; *Poteliakhoff v Teakle* [1938] 2 K.B. 816; paras 3–036, 3–048.

[180] See para.15–060.

[181] *Trendtex Trading Corp v Crédit Suisse* [1982] A.C. 679 at 694.

[182] See para.20–135 and following; *Robophone Facilities Ltd v Blank* [1966] 1 W.L.R. 1428 at 1446; *Azimut-Benetti SpA v Healey* [2010] EWHC 2234 (Comm); 132 Con L.R. 113 at [24].

[183] e.g. paras 7–033–7–038: see the reference to "public policy" in *HIH Casualty & General Ins v Chase Manhattan Bank* [2000] EWCA Civ 1250; [2001] 2 Lloyd's Rep. 483 at [103], reversed in part [2003] UKHL 6; [2003] 2 Lloyd's Rep. 61.

[184] See the former category of agreements between spouses for future separation (12th edn, para.11–103) which has been "swept away": para.11–049.

[185] *Spiers v Hunt* [1908] 1 K.B. 720; *Wilson v Carnley* [1908] 1 K.B. 729; *Fender v St John Mildmay* [1938] A.C. 1.

[186] Not all: *Mossop v Mossop* [1989] Fam. 77.

[187] *Shaw v Fitzgerald* [1992] 1 F.L.R. 357.

be taken to safeguard the rights of the other party to the marriage, e.g. where the property in question was a house in which a man had lived first with his wife and then with a fiancée from whom he had later parted.[188]

### (ii) *Agreements in contemplation of divorce*

At common law, an arrangement or agreement between parties to divorce proceedings (about such matters as the wife's maintenance) was invalid if it was made with a corrupt intention, e.g. if it amounted to a bribe to institute, or carry on, the proceedings,[189] or to a conspiracy to deceive the court. But it was valid if it was an honest attempt to minimise the difficulties which had arisen between the parties.[190] The law on this topic was formerly influenced by the rule that collusion was a bar to divorce; but the abolition of this rule "completely alters the public policy on this point",[191] so that an agreement is no longer invalid merely because it is collusive. **11–039**

### (iii) *Agreements inconsistent with parental responsibility*

At common law a father had the custody of his legitimate child and a contract by which he purported to assign that custody to any person was contrary to public policy as it was "repugnant entirely to his parental duty".[192] By statute,[193] both parents have "parental responsibility"[194] for their child if they were married to each other at the time of the child's birth; if they were not, the mother has parental responsibility.[195] In the latter case, the parents may enter into a "parental responsibility agreement" providing for the father to have parental responsibility for the child;[196] but freedom of contract in making such an agreement, and in bringing it to an end, is severely restricted so as to protect the interests of the child.[197] The effect of such an agreement seems to be that parental responsibility is vested in both parents: the mother does not lose such responsibility since "a person who has parental responsibility for a child may not surrender or transfer such responsibility to another".[198] This statutory provision resembles the common law principle stated above and seems to be based on similar grounds of **11–040**

[188] cf. Family Law Act 1996 s.33(1)(b)(i) permitting the court to make an order relating to a "matrimonial home" in favour of an "associated" person; persons are "associated" if "they have agreed to marry one another (whether or not that agreement has been terminated)" (s.62(3)(e)). The 1996 Act does not deal with the question whether the validity of the agreement is affected by the fact that one of the parties to it was married when it was made.

[189] *Hope v Hope* (1857) 8 D.M. & G. 731; *Churchward v Churchward* [1895] P. 7.

[190] *Scott v Scott* [1913] P. 52.

[191] *Sutton v Sutton* [1984] Ch. 184 at 194; cf. *N v N* [1992] 1 F.L.R. 266.

[192] *Vansittart v Vansittart* (1858) D. & J. 249 at 259; cf. Adoption and Children Act 2002 ss.92, 95, 96.

[193] Amendments have been introduced to the provisions which follow to deal with children born to same sex relationships and as a result of surrogacy arrangements: see, e.g. Children Act 1989 s.2(1A), (2A).

[194] As defined by Children Act 1989 s.3.

[195] Children Act 1989 s.2(1), (3); and see s.2(4), abolishing the former common law rule.

[196] Children Act 1989 s.4(1)(b).

[197] Children Act 1989 ss.4(1) and (3), 1(1).

[198] Children Act 1989 s.2(9).

public policy. The person with parental responsibility may "arrange for some or all of it to be met by one or more persons acting on his behalf".[199] In such a case the responsibility is not transferred but vicariously performed.[200]

### (iv) *Agreements in restraint of marriage*

11–041 A contract may be invalid on the ground that it unjustifiably restricts a person's freedom to marry. This is, for example, true of a promise by a widow to pay £100 if she remarries,[201] and of a promise not to marry anyone except a specified person (not amounting to a promise to marry that person).[202] It may be that such promises are valid if they are limited in duration or otherwise reasonable, e.g. if a limited restraint is imposed for the sake of a person's health or (conceivably) of his moral well-being.[203] It is also possible that a promise not to marry anyone except a member of a fairly large group (e.g. some religious denomination) might be valid.

The above cases concern actual promises not to marry, or to pay a sum of money on marriage. It seems that a contract is not invalid merely because it may in some other way deter one of the parties from marrying. Thus a promise to pay an allowance, or to permit a person to occupy a house, until the promisee's marriage, is valid.[204] Such promises may tend to discourage marriage, but they do not impose any contractual liability on a person as a result of marriage.[205]

### (v) *Marriage brokage contracts*[206]

11–042 A marriage brokage contract is one by which a person promises in return for a money consideration to procure the marriage of another. Until the eighteenth century such contracts were valid at common law, thus making it possible for servants of young heiresses to obtain payment for assisting their charges to elope with fortune-hunters.[207] Equity therefore prevented the enforcement of these contracts;[208] and this equitable principle is not restricted to contracts to procure a marriage between one of the contracting parties and a *particular* third person. Thus a contract by which a marriage bureau simply undertakes to make efforts to find a spouse for a client has been held invalid, because it involved "the introduction of the consideration of a money payment into that which should be free from any such taint".[209] The harmful tendencies of such contracts seem to be

[199] Children Act 1989 s.2(9); cf. also Child Support Act 1991 s.9, providing for the legal effects of certain maintenance agreements in favour of children.
[200] cf. para.17–007.
[201] *Baker v White* (1690) 2 Vern. 215; cf. *Hartley v Rice* (1808) 10 East 22.
[202] *Lowe v Peers* (1768) 2 Burr. 2225.
[203] cf. *Denny v Denny* [1919] 1 K.B. 583; para.11–061.
[204] *Gibson v Dickie* (1815) 3 M. & S. 463.
[205] Contrast the position in the restraint of trade cases, para.11–134.
[206] Powell 6 C.L.P. 254.
[207] e.g. *Goldsmith v Bruning* (1700) 1 Eq. Ca. Abr. 89, pl. 4.
[208] *Cole v Gibson* (1750) 1 Ves. Sen. 503 at 506.
[209] *Hermann v Charlesworth* [1905] 2 K.B. 123 at 130; para.11–089.

no greater than those of contracts between "computer dating" agencies and their clients; and it has not been suggested that such contracts are contrary to public policy.

### (vi) *Contracts promoting sexual immorality*

A contract may be illegal if its object is sexually immoral. The common law originally applied this principle to all cases in which a contract could be said to promote such an object. But a distinction is now drawn between contracts with purely meretricious purposes and those which are intended to regulate stable extra-marital relationships. Some of the examples of the former must now be regarded as extremely doubtful and the law may well have moved on, even if the courts have not yet had the opportunity to acknowledge this. **11–043**

**Meretricious purposes.** A promise by a man to pay a woman money if she will become his mistress is illegal.[210] A promise to pay money to a woman with whom the promisor had illicitly cohabited in the past is not contrary to public policy since it does not *promote* immorality. It is simply void because the consideration for it is past,[211] but it will be valid if made in a deed.[212] The validity of a promise in a deed made *during* cohabitation depends on its purpose. If it is simply a gift,[213] or voluntary bond, it is as valid as one given after cohabitation.[214] But if its object is to secure the continuance of cohabitation, it is illegal.[215] A bond given after cohabitation would also be invalid if it were merely given to secure the performance of a promise of payment made before cohabitation. **11–044**

A contract is also illegal if it indirectly promotes sexual immorality. Thus in *Pearce v Brooks*[216] a contract to hire out a brougham to a prostitute for the purposes of her profession was held to be illegal. The same would be true of a contract of employment by which the employee undertook to procure prostitutes for the employer's clients.[217] On the other hand, a contract to let a room to a prostitute who practises her profession elsewhere is valid "because persons of that description must have a place to lay their heads".[218]

In the cases on this subject "immorality" always means extra-marital sexual intercourse. A contract might promote some other form of activity that could be described as immoral and sexual. For example, a contract might be made to publish an indecent book whose publication did not amount to a crime. Such a

---

[210] *Benyon v Nettlefold* (1850) 3 Mac. & G. 94.

[211] *Beaumont v Reeve* (1846) 8 Q.B. 483.

[212] *Annadale v Harris* (1727) 2 P. Wms. 432; affirmed 1 Bro. P.C. 250; *Knye v Moore* (1822) 1 S. & S. 61.

[213] A promise to pay must also be distinguished from a completed gift: *Ayerst v Jenkins* (1873) L.R. 16 Eq. 275.

[214] *Gray v Mathias* (1800) 5 Ves. 286; *Hall v Palmer* (1844) 3 Hare 532.

[215] *The Lady Cox's Case* (1734) 3 P. Wms. 339; *Walker v Perkins* (1764) 3 Burr. 1568.

[216] (1866) L.R. 1 Ex. 213; cf. *Upfill v Wright* [1911] 1 K.B. 506, a case viewed with some scepticism in *Heglibiston Establishment v Heyman* (1977) 36 P. & C.R. 351.

[217] See *Coral Leisure Group v Barnett* [1981] I.C.R. 503 at 508; cf. *The Siben* [1996] 1 Lloyd's Rep. 35 at 62.

[218] *Appleton v Campbell* (1826) 2 C. & P. 347; cf. *Bowry v Bennett* (1808) 1 Camp. 348; *Lloyd v Johnson* (1798) 1 B. & P. 340.

contract might formerly have been regarded as invalid on account of its "grossly immoral" tendency;[219] "(b)ut at the present day the difficulty is to identify what sexual conduct is to be treated as grossly immoral"[220]—so that it is less likely that such a contract would now be struck down on this ground.

11–045 **Stable relationships.** The traditional common law approach to immoral contracts no longer applies to persons who live together in a common household as husband and wife without being married. It has for example been held that a licence under which such a couple occupied furnished accommodation was not contrary to public policy.[221] The law also recognises that legal effects can flow from agreements between such persons with respect to the house in which they live. Where the house is owned by one of them, the agreement can confer legally enforceable rights on the other, such as a contractual licence to remain there,[222] or a share in the value of the house in respect of the contribution made by the other to its acquisition, maintenance or improvement.[223] The opening of a bank account by one party to such a relationship with funds intended to belong to both jointly has been held (on proof of the appropriate intention) to amount to a declaration of trust in favour of the other.[224] And "when an illegitimate child has been born, there is certainly nothing contrary to public policy in the parents coming to an agreement which they intend to be binding in law, for the maintenance of the child and mother".[225]

These illustrations[226] show that the law now recognises that "unmarried cohabitation, whether heterosexual or homosexual, is widespread";[227] and they suggest that the old common law rule governing immoral contracts will in future be confined to meretricious relationships (of whatever sexual orientation). Where domestic arrangements between parties to the present group of stable relationships satisfy the requirement of contractual intention, they will no longer be struck down on grounds of public policy.[228]

### *(vii) Contracts interfering with the course of justice*

11–046 A contract may be illegal because the mere making of it amounts to a conspiracy to pervert the course of justice, e.g. where a person promises another money for

[219] cf. *Glyn v Weston Feature Film Co* [1916] 1 Ch. 261; approved in *Attorney General v Guardian Newspapers (No.2)* [1990] A.C. 109 at 262, 276; contrast *ZYX Music GmbH v King* [1995] 3 All E.R. 1 at 10; *A v B* [2000] E.M.L.R. 1007.

[220] *Stephens v Avery* [1988] Ch. 449 at 453.

[221] *Somma v Hazelhurst* [1979] 1 W.L.R. 1014 (disapproved on another point in *Street v Mountford* [1985] A.C. 809); cf. also *Watson v Lucas* [1980] 1 W.L.R. 1493.

[222] *Tanner v Tanner* [1975] 1 W.L.R. 1346; cf. *Fitzpatrick v Sterling Housing Association* [2001] 1 A.C. 27 (homosexual partner part of "family" for purposes of Rent Act 1977).

[223] *Eves v Eves* [1975] 1 W.L.R. 1338.

[224] *Paul v Constance* [1977] 1 W.L.R. 527.

[225] *Horrocks v Forray* [1976] 1 W.L.R. 230 at 239.

[226] cf. *Heglibiston Establishment v Heyman* (1977) 36 P. & C.R. 351.

[227] *Barclays Bank Plc v O'Brien* [1994] 1 A.C. 180 at 198; *Royal Bank of Scotland v Etridge (No.2)* [2001] UKHL 44; [2002] 2 A.C. 773 at [47].

[228] Devlin 39 M.L.R. 1 at 12; Dwyer 93 L.Q.R. 386.

giving false evidence on his behalf in criminal proceedings[229] or where two men agree to bribe a prosecution witness to withdraw a charge of rape.[230] A contract may also (even though it does not amount to a criminal conspiracy) be illegal if its object is to interfere with the course of justice. Before the distinction between felonies and misdemeanours was abolished, a contract to stifle a prosecution for a misdemeanour was not itself an offence but such contracts were often held illegal. Thus contracts to stifle prosecutions for perjury, riot, assault on a police officer, interfering with a public road, and obtaining by false pretences were held illegal.[231] But this rule was not applied where the misdemeanour was said to be of a "private" nature. Thus in *McGregor v McGregor*[232] it was held that a husband and wife who had taken out cross-summonses for assault against each other could validly compromise them in a separation agreement. It has similarly been held that a prosecution for trade mark offences could be compromised by agreement between the owner and the offender;[233] and it has been said that the same principle applies to criminal libel.[234]

These older cases must now be read in the light of the abolition of the distinction between felonies and misdemeanours and of the creation of the offence of concealing a "relevant offence".[235] A person does not, however, commit this offence if he withholds information which may lead to the conviction of the offender in consideration only of the making good of the loss or injury caused by the offence;[236] and it is doubtful whether an agreement to this effect should now be held illegal.[237] One view is that the agreement may still be illegal, even though it does not itself amount to an offence, for this was precisely the position under the old law where an agreement was made to stifle a prosecution for a misdemeanour. A second view is that, where the only consideration is the making good of the loss, no public interest is harmed by upholding the agreement; and this view can be supported by reference to the old cases concerning misdemeanours of a "private" nature. A third view is that the legality of an agreement to stifle a prosecution (not amounting to a conspiracy to pervert the course of justice or to the offence of concealing a relevant offence) should depend on the question whether it was in the public interest that the prosecution should be brought; and it is submitted that this is the best view.

The principle of public policy is not confined to contracts to stifle a prosecution: thus a contract to indemnify a surety in criminal proceedings is

---

[229] *R. v Andrews* [1973] Q.B. 422.

[230] *R. v Panayiotou* [1973] 3 All E.R. 112; cf. *R. v Ali* [1993] Crim.L.R. 396.

[231] *Collins v Blantern* (1767) 2 Wils. K.B. 341; *Keir v Leeman* (1846) 9 Q.B. 371; *Clubb v Huston* (1865) 18 C.B. (N.S.) 414 (embezzlement); cf. *Howard v Odham's Press Ltd* [1938] 1 K.B. 42 (contract not to disclose confession of fraud). Contracts to stifle a prosecution for a felony were sometimes held illegal on this ground (e.g. *Rawlings v Coal Consumers' Association* (1874) 43 L.J.M.C. 111; *Whitmore v Farley* (1881) 45 L.T. 99), but were also illegal as they formerly amounted to compounding.

[232] (1888) 21 Q.B.D. 424.

[233] *Fisher & Co v Apollinaris Co* (1875) L.R. 10 Ch. App. 297.

[234] *Fisher & Co v Apollinaris Co* (1875) L.R. 10 Ch. App. 297 at 303.

[235] Criminal Law Act 1967 ss.1, 5(1).

[236] Criminal Law Act 1967 s.5(1).

[237] Hudson 43 M.L.R. 532.

illegal.[238] Nor is the principle restricted to contracts affecting criminal proceedings. Thus agreements to obstruct bankruptcy proceedings[239] and corrupt agreements relating to matrimonial proceedings[240] are illegal. It has also been said that a contract by which a witness promised one party to a civil dispute not to give evidence for the other would be contrary to public policy.[241] On the other hand, it has been held not to be contrary to public policy for one party to an agreement to undertake that he would not oppose the other's application for planning applications and not give evidence in support of a compulsory purchase order relating to the land in question.[242] An ordinary civil claim can, of course, be validly compromised,[243] even though the facts giving rise to the claim also amount to a crime. But in such a case an agreement to abandon "any legal proceedings" may be illegal, as this phrase is wide enough to refer to possible civil *and* criminal proceedings.[244]

### *(viii) Contracts purporting to oust the jurisdiction of the courts*

**11–047** A contract is at common law contrary to public policy if it purports to deprive the courts of a jurisdiction which they would otherwise have. For example, a clause in an insurance policy which provides that the policy is in certain events to become "incontestable"[245] does not prevent the court from deciding whether the assured had any insurable interest.[246] Such agreements are contrary to public policy because they would, if valid, make it possible to evade or contravene many peremptory rules of law. It follows that they are invalid only so far as they purport to exclude the jurisdiction of the courts on a point of *law*. An agreement is not invalid to the extent that it gives a non-judicial body power to make final and binding decisions on questions of *fact*.[247] Such a provision does not, moreover, normally[248] rule out the possibility of a legal challenge to the decision on the ground of "unfairness, bad faith or perversity",[249] so that the provision does not wholly exclude the jurisdiction of the courts even on questions of fact. Whether a power conferred on the courts by statute is one which the parties are entitled to exclude depends upon the proper interpretation of the statute.[250] The

238 *Herman v Jeuchner* (1885) 15 Q.B.D. 561. It is now an offence to make such an agreement: Bail Act 1976 s.9.

239 *Elliott v Richardson* (1870) L.R. 5 C.P. 744; cf. *Kearley v Thomson* (1890) 24 Q.B.D. 742.

240 See para.11–039.

241 *Harmony Shipping Co SA v Saudi Europe Line Ltd* [1979] 1 W.L.R. 1380 at 1386.

242 *Fulham Football Club Ltd v Cabra Estates* (1992) 56 P. & C.R. 284.

243 *Australia & New Zealand Banking Group Ltd v Compagnie Noga d'Importation et d'Exportation SA* [2007] EWHC 293 (Comm); [2007] 1 Lloyd's Rep. 487 at [31].

244 *Lound v Grimwade* (1888) 39 Ch D. 605.

245 *Anctil v Manufacturers' Life Ins Co* [1899] A.C. 604.

246 But such clauses are effective to prevent the insurer from contesting certain matters of *fact*, e.g. that statements in the proposal form were true: cf. at fn.247.

247 *The Glacier Bay* [1996] 1 Lloyd's Rep. 370 and see fn.295.

248 For a common law exception, see at fn.296.

249 *The Glacier Bay* [1996] 1 Lloyd's Rep. 370 at 379; *Charles Stanley & Co Ltd v Adams* [2013] EWHC 2137 (QB) at [17].

250 *Aribisala v St James Homes (Grosvenor) Dock Ltd* [2007] EWHC 1694 (Ch); [2007] 37 E.G. 234 (contract to exclude s.49(2) Law of Property Act 1925 contrary to public policy).

rule against allowing parties by contract to oust the jurisdiction of the courts is further illustrated by the following cases.

**Agreements for maintenance.** One spouse may, as part of a separation agreement or in the course of matrimonial proceedings, promise to pay the other an allowance in return for a promise not to apply to the court for maintenance. In *Hyman v Hyman*[251] the House of Lords held that such an agreement did not prevent the other spouse from applying to the court for maintenance. The contract was illegal, since the "wife's right to future maintenance is a matter of public concern which she cannot barter away".[252] But this rule had one unfortunate result: if the first spouse failed to pay the promised allowance, the other could not sue for it, since a promise cannot be enforced if the sole or main consideration for it is illegal.[253] By statute, if the agreement is in writing, an action may be brought for the promised allowance, in spite of the fact that the promise not to apply to the court is void.[254] The court can also take the agreement into account when exercising its power to grant ancillary relief.[255] 11–048

**Nuptial agreements.** Ante- and post-nuptial agreements were at one time unenforceable because of the rule that agreements providing for *future* separation were contrary to public policy. That rule is now obsolete and has been "swept away".[256] Such agreements are still contrary to public policy to the extent that they oust the jurisdiction of the courts, but they may be taken into account by the courts in the exercise of their power under Pt II of the Matrimonial Causes Act 1973 to order ancillary relief when granting a decree of divorce, nullity, or judicial separation.[257] In this sense, at least as a matter of English law,[258] their enforceability is a "red herring" since "in ancillary relief proceedings the court is not bound to give effect to nuptial agreements, and is bound to have regard to them, whether or not they are contracts."[259] 11–049

---

[251] [1929] A.C. 601.

[252] *Hyman v Hyman* [1929] A.C. 601 at 629. But such an agreement is not contrary to public policy if it only ousts the jurisdiction of a foreign court: *Addison v Brown* [1954] 1 W.L.R. 779; nor if it is sanctioned by order of the court: *L v L* [1962] P. 101; *Minton v Minton* [1979] A.C. 594.

[253] *Bennett v Bennett* [1952] 1 K.B. 249; cf. *Sutton v Sutton* [1984] Ch. 184 (where *each* party promised not to invoke the jurisdiction of the court); and see para.11–158.

[254] Matrimonial Causes Act 1973 s.34. In *Sutton v Sutton* [1984] Ch. 184 the agreement was oral, so that s.34 did not apply. Under Child Support Act 1991 s.9 (as amended by Child Support Act 1995 s.18), similar rules apply to certain maintenance agreements in respect of children.

[255] *Edgar v Edgar* [1980] 1 W.L.R. 1410.

[256] *Radmacher v Granatino* [2010] UKSC 42; [2011] 1 A.C. 534 at [52].

[257] *Radmacher v Granatino* [2010] UKSC 42; [2011] 1 A.C. 534 at [52]; cf. *Z v Z* [2011] EWHC 2878 (Fam); [2012] 1 F.L.R. 1100; *V v V* [2011] EWHC 3230 (Fam); [2012] 1 F.LR. 1315.

[258] The fact that such agreements might be enforced in a foreign court which lacks jurisdiction under Pt II of the Matrimonial Causes Act 1973 led Lord Mance (*Radmacher v Granatino* [2010] UKSC 42; [2011] 1 A.C. 534 at [128]) to express no view on the binding nature of an ante-nuptial agreement and was one of the reasons for the dissenting speech of Baroness Hale.

[259] *Radmacher v Granatino* [2010] UKSC 42; [2011] 1 A.C. 534 at [62]. The decision of the Supreme Court that *ante*-nuptial agreements are not otherwise contrary to public policy and are enforceable is therefore "mercifully *obiter*" (Baroness Hale, at [138]). The Privy Council had earlier decided that *post*-nuptial agreements are not contrary to public policy in *MacLeod v MacLeod* [2008] UKPC 64; [2010] 1 A.C. 298.

11–050 **Arbitration clauses.** There is no doubt about the validity of such clauses if they merely provide that the parties are to resort to arbitration before going to court. In *Scott v Avery*[260] a clause of this kind was upheld as it did not purport to oust the jurisdiction of the court,[261] but simply to lay down at what stage the cause of action arose upon which that jurisdiction might be exercised. At common law such a clause did not prevent the courts from nevertheless determining the dispute, though the party who disregarded the clause and in breach of it brought an action was liable in damages.[262] The courts have, however, an inherent jurisdiction to stay an action brought in breach of an agreement to decide disputes in some way other than by bringing an action.[263] Moreover, the Arbitration Act 1996 provides that, where an arbitration agreement is in writing,[264] the court must stay an action brought in breach of the agreement[265] unless the agreement is "null and void, inoperative or incapable of being performed". Where the agreement is made between a party acting in the course of a business and a consumer, it does not bind the consumer if the amount claimed is less than £5,000;[266] but it binds the other party.

11–051 **Potential grounds of invalidity.** The fact that an arbitration clause excluded the jurisdiction of the court might at common law make the clause invalid on one of two grounds. First, such a clause was invalid to the extent that it purported to deprive the parties of the right to go to court to sue on a completed cause of action, or to exclude the power granted to the courts by statute to control the decisions of arbitrators on points of law.[267] This rule was justified by the argument that, if such a clause were valid, an arbitrator who decided a dispute on principles at variance with the general law would be subject to no control at all;[268] and this would be particularly undesirable if he made an award enforcing a wholly illegal agreement.[269] A substantially similar risk could arise where the clause, though not in terms restricting the parties' right to ask the court to control the arbitrator's decision, laid down standards which made such control nugatory. This is a second ground of invalidity at common law, so that "a clause which purported to free arbitrators to decide without regard to law and according, for example, to their own notions of what would be fair would not be a valid

[260] (1855) 5 H.L.C. 811; cf. *Atlantic Shipping & Trading Co Ltd v Louis Dreyfus & Co* [1922] 2 A.C. 250; *Persson v London County Buses* [1974] 1 W.L.R. 569.

[261] See *Halifax Financial Services v Intuitive Systems Ltd* [1999] 1 All E.R. (Comm) 303 at 310, where the clause in question was a "dispute resolution" clause which failed for lack of certainty: cf. para.2–103.

[262] *Doleman & Sons v Ossett Corp* [1912] 3 K.B. 257 at 267.

[263] *Channel Tunnel Group Ltd v Balfour Beatty Construction Ltd* [1993] A.C. 334; cf. *Cott UK Ltd v FE Barker Ltd* [1997] 3 All E.R. 540; and *T & N Ltd & Sun Alliance Plc* [2002] EWHC 2420 (Ch); [2002] C.L.C. 1342 where a stay was refused.

[264] For this requirement, see s.5(1).

[265] 1996 Act s.9(4); *Halki Shipping Corp v Sopex Oils Ltd* [1998] 1 W.L.R. 726; this rule cannot be excluded by contract: see s.4 and Sch.1.

[266] 1996 Act s.91; Unfair Arbitration Agreements (Specified Amounts) Order 1999 (SI 1999/2167).

[267] *Czarnikow v Roth Schmidt & Co* [1922] 2 K.B. 478.

[268] Clauses making an arbitrator's decision "final" do not have this effect: see *Ford v Clarkson's Holidays Ltd* [1971] 1 W.L.R. 1412; cf. *Jones v Sherwood Computer Services* [1992] 1 W.L.R. 227 ("final and conclusive" valuation reviewable for error of law).

[269] cf. *Soleimany v Soleimany* [1999] Q.B. 785 at 799. See now after fn.277.

types of claim.[293] An arbitration agreement stipulating that the arbitrators are to be drawn from members of a particular religious group is not contrary to rules against religious discrimination.[294]

**Construction of rules of associations.** A clause in the rules of an association such as a trade union may purport to give to the committee of the association exclusive jurisdiction to construe the rules. But, as the construction of the rules is a question of law, it has been held that any attempt to deprive the courts of their jurisdiction over it is invalid.[295] By contrast, the jurisdiction of the Visitor of a University to decide matters governed by the "internal laws" of the University is at common law[296] exclusive, so that his decisions on points of this kind cannot be challenged in the ordinary courts.[297] **11–054**

**Scope of the rule against ousting the jurisdiction of the courts.** Contracts purporting to exclude the jurisdiction of the courts must be distinguished from promises in honour only.[298] A provision that a promise "shall not be enforced in any court" makes the promise legally unenforceable, but does not purport to oust the jurisdiction of the court to say so. Similar reasoning applies to the compromise of a genuine dispute as to legal rights. Such a compromise may vary or supersede the legal rights of the parties; but it does not prevent the courts from determining what those rights are. It is therefore not contrary to public policy;[299] and this is true even though the public can be said to have some interest in the dispute, e.g. because it relates to the performance of duties under a charitable trust.[300] **11–055**

### *(ix) Contracts to deceive public authorities*

In *Alexander v Rayson*[301] a landlord let a service flat to the defendant for £1,200. Two documents were executed: in the first the defendant agreed to pay £450 for the flat and certain services; in the second she agreed to pay £750 for the same services, plus the use of a refrigerator. The landlord's object in splitting up the contract in this way was to defraud the rating authorities by showing them the **11–056**

[293] See, e.g. Employment Rights Act 1996 s.203; Equality Act 2010 s.144; *Clyde & Co LLP v van Winkelhof* [2011] EWHC 668 (QB); [2011] I.C.R. 467.

[294] *Jivraj v Hashwani* [2011] UKSC 40; [2011] 1 W.L.R. 1872.

[295] *Lee v Showmen's Guild of Great Britain* [1952] 2 Q.B. 329; cf. *Edwards v Aberayron Ins Society Ltd* (1876) 1 Q.B.D. 563; *Re Davstone Estate Ltd's Leases* [1969] 2 Ch. 378; *Edwards v SOGAT* [1971] Ch. 354. There is no objection to leaving questions of *fact* to the final determination of a private tribunal: *Brown v Overbury* (1856) 11 Exch. 715; *Cipriani v Burnett* [1933] A.C. 83. See also Trade Union and Labour Relations (Consolidation) Act 1992 s.63 (right of union members to go to court after six months).

[296] The jurisdiction of the Visitor is now drastically reduced: Higher Education Act 2004 ss.20, 46.

[297] *Thomas v University of Bradford* [1987] A.C. 795 (for subsequent proceedings before the Visitor, see *Thomas v University of Bradford* [1992] 1 All E.R. 964); *R. v Lord President of the Privy Council Ex p. Page* [1993] A.C. 682. Contrast *Clark v University of Lincolnshire and Humberside* [2000] 1 W.L.R. 1985.

[298] See para.4–010.

[299] See para.3–034. For compromise of a claim known by the claimant to be invalid, see para.3–036.

[300] *Bradshaw v University College of Wales* [1988] 1 W.L.R. 190.

[301] [1936] 1 K.B. 169; cf. *Chettiar v Chettiar* [1962] A.C. 294.

first document only. The contract was therefore held to be illegal. A contract by which an employee gets an expense allowance grossly in excess of the expenses he actually incurs is similarly illegal as a fraud on the Revenue.[302] But where the contract is in itself lawful and is merely the "setting for an act contrary to public policy"[303] it is not illegal if it is too remote from the intention to defraud.[304] Furthermore, the contract is illegal only if the scheme that it furthers is a fraudulent one. Thus it is perfectly lawful for a contract of employment to provide that the employee is to receive a specified amount "free of tax", so long as the employer accounts to the revenue authorities for the tax due.[305] And where a seller sent out a false invoice with the intention of merely postponing the payment of VAT, it was held that this did not turn an originally lawful sale into an illegal contract, it having been found as a fact that the seller had acted without dishonest intent.[306]

### *(x) Sale of offices and honours*

**11–057** Certain contracts for the sale of public offices were prohibited by statute[307] while others are illegal at common law.[308] Contracts of this kind are contrary to public policy because of their tendency to lead to corruption and inefficiency. Similarly, it was held in *Parkinson v College of Ambulance Ltd*[309] that a contract to procure a knighthood was illegal as it might lead to corruption and as it was "derogatory to the dignity of the Sovereign".[310] It is now an offence to make such a contract.[311] And a contract by a Member of Parliament to vote in accordance with the direction of some body outside Parliament is invalid.[312]

### *(xi) Lobbying and bribery*

**11–058** Similar problems about the potential to corrupt can arise from the practice of "lobbying" for government contracts. While in some cases the practice has been said to be "recognised and respectable",[313] it is in others contrary to public policy. This was, for example, held to be the case where the defendant promised large commissions to the claimant for using its influence to secure the renewal of contracts between the defendant and a foreign government. It was essential to the success of the scheme that the government should be kept in ignorance of the

---

302 *Miller v Karlinski* (1945) 62 T.L.R. 85; cf. *Hyland v JH Barker (North West)* [1985] I.C.R. 861; *Corby v Morrison* [1980] I.C.R. 564.

303 Furmston (1966) University of Toronto L.J. 267 at 287.

304 *21st Century Logistic Solutions Ltd v Madysen Ltd* [2004] EWHC 231 (QB); [2004] 2 Lloyd's Rep. 92.

305 See *Newland v Simmons & Willer (Hairdressers) Ltd* [1981] I.C.R. 521.

306 *Skilton v Sullivan*, *The Times*, 25 March 1994; see further para.11–074.

307 Sale of Offices Act 1551 (now repealed).

308 e.g. *Garforth v Fearon* (1787) 1 H.B.L. 327; *Law v Law* (1735) 3 P. Wms. 391; *Parsons v Thompson* (1790) 1 H.B. 322. cf. the rule against assignment of a public officer's salary: para.15–068.

309 [1925] 2 K.B. 1.

310 *Parkinson v College of Ambulance Ltd* [1925] 2 K.B. 1 at 14.

311 Honours (Prevention of Abuses) Act 1925.

312 *ASRS v Osborne* [1910] A.C. 87.

313 *Lemenda Trading Co Ltd v African Middle East Petroleum Co* [1988] Q.B. 448 at 458.

claimant's financial interest in the matter, while the claimant knew that the original contract provided that no commissions should be paid to third parties. The claim for the commission was therefore rejected on grounds of public policy.[314] There is no public policy requiring a court to refuse to enforce a contract which is procured by bribery, or which is preceded by a failed attempt at bribery,[315] but a contract obtained by bribery may be voidable and liable to be set aside.[316]

Under the Bribery Act 2010, it is now an offence to promise or give a financial or other advantage to a person if it is intended to induce that person, or another, to perform improperly a relevant function or activity, or if it is intended to reward that person, or another, for the improper performance of such a function or activity, or the person conferring the advantage knows or believes that the acceptance of it would itself constitute the improper performance of a relevant function or activity.[317] A relevant function or activity includes "any function of a public nature", as well as any activity connected with a business, any activity performed in the course of a person's employment, and any activity performed by or on behalf of a body of persons (whether corporate or unincorporate),[318] if the person performing it is either in a position of trust by virtue of its performance or is expected to perform it in good faith, or impartially.[319] A relevant function or activity is improperly performed if performance, or the failure to perform, is in breach of a "relevant expectation[320]", i.e. that it will be performed in good faith, impartially or in a manner consistent with the position of trust bestowed on the person in question.[321] Special provision is made for the bribery of foreign public officials.[322]

### (xii) *Trading with the enemy*

A contract made during a war to which this country is a party is illegal if it involves commercial intercourse with an enemy.[323] An enemy, for this purpose, is a person voluntarily resident or carrying on business in enemy-occupied territory.[324] Such contracts are illegal as they tend to aid the economy of the enemy country. A contract is not illegal if one of the parties to it is an "enemy" **11–059**

[314] *Lemenda Trading Co Ltd v African Middle East Petroleum Co* [1988] Q.B. 448 at 458. Contrast *Tekron Resources Ltd v Guinea Investment Co Ltd* [2003] EWHC 2577 (QB); [2004] 2 Lloyd's Rep. 26. See now the Bribery Act 2010 s.6.

[315] *National Iranian Oil Co v Crescent Petroleum Co International Ltd* [2016] EWHC 510 (Comm); [2016] 2 Lloyd's Rep. 146.

[316] See para.16–111.

[317] Bribery Act 2010 s.1. Under s.2 similar provisions deal with the offence of being bribed.

[318] Bribery Act 2010 s.3(2).

[319] Bribery Act 2010 s.3(3).

[320] i.e. "what a reasonable person in the United Kingdom would expect in relation to the performance of the type of function or activity concerned" (s.5(1)). Where the performance is not subject to the law of any part of the UK, any local custom or practice is to be disregarded unless it is permitted or required by the written law applicable to the country or territory concerned (s.5(2)).

[321] Bribery Act 2010 s.4.

[322] Bribery Act 2010 s.6.

[323] *Sovfracht (V/O) v Van Udens Scheepvaart en Agentuur Maatschappij (NV Gebr.)* [1943] A.C. 203.

[324] *Porter v Freudenberg* [1915] 1 K.B. 857.

but its performance involves no further commercial intercourse with the enemy[325] and it can be enforced if this does not benefit the enemy.[326] It is a statutory offence to trade or to attempt to trade with an enemy.[327]

### *(xiii) Contracts which involve doing an illegal act in a friendly foreign country*

**11–060** In the interests of good foreign relations, the courts will not enforce a contract which is lawful on its face if it is entered for a purpose which is unlawful under the law of a friendly foreign state.[328] For example, contracts[329] which had as their objective the smuggling of whisky into the US during the Prohibition period have been held unenforceable.[330] And in *Regazzoni v KC Sethia Ltd*[331] a contract was made for the export of Indian jute to Italy, with a view to re-export to South Africa. The House of Lords refused to enforce the contract as it contravened an Indian law prohibiting the export of goods produced in India to South Africa, and as it could be performed only by making false declarations in India.

### *(xiv) Contracts restricting personal liberty*

**11–061** A contract may be illegal if it so severely restricts the liberty of an individual as to reduce him to a quasi-servile condition. In *Horwood v Millar's Timber and Trading Co*[332] a clerk borrowed money from a moneylender and agreed that he would not without the lender's written consent leave his job, borrow money,

---

[325] *Tingley v Muller* [1917] 2 Ch. 144.

[326] *Rodriguez v Speyer Bros* [1919] A.C. 59.

[327] Trading with the Enemy Act 1939.

[328] Since the coming into force of the Rome I Regulation (593/2008), it seems that this rule must be accommodated within art.21 (formerly Rome Convention (Contracts (Applicable Law) Act 1990 s.2(1), Sch.1 art.16).

[329] All of the contracts which implement the unlawful "scheme" are unenforceable: *Beijing Jinalong Heaavy Industry Group v Golden Ocean Group Ltd* [2013] EWHC 1063 (Comm); [2013] 2 Lloyd's Rep. 61 at [40].

[330] *Foster v Driscoll* [1929] 1 K.B. 470; cf. *Mahonia Ltd v JP Morgan Chase Bank* [2003] EWHC 1927; [2003] 2 Lloyd's Rep. 911; *Soleimany v Soleimany* [1999] Q.B. 785 at 797; contrast *Libyan Arab Foreign Bank v Bankers Trust Co* [1989] Q.B. 728 at 744–745 (where there was no intention to do or procure an illegal act abroad); *Bangladesh Export & Import Co Ltd v Sucden Kerry SA* [1995] 2 Lloyd's Rep. 1 at 6 (where there was no obligation to do such an act); *Royal Boskalis Westminster NV v Mountain* [1997] 2 All E.R. 929; *Emeraldian Partnership Ltd v Wellmix Shipping Ltd* [2010] EWHC 1411 (Comm); [2011] 1 Lloyd's Rep. 301 at [175]–[179]; cf. *Ralli Bros v Compañia Naviera Sota y Aznar* [1920] 2 K.B. 287 (*supervening* illegality of payment and therefore probably best seen as a case of frustration).

[331] [1958] A.C. 301. Contrast *Fox v Henderson Investment Fund Ltd* [1999] 2 Lloyd's Rep. 303 (no illegality merely because acts to be done *in England* in performance of the contract would involve breach of an order made by a *foreign* court).

[332] [1917] 3 K.B. 305; cf. *Hepworth Manufacturing Co v Ryott* [1920] 1 Ch. 1; *Gaumont-British Picture Corp v Alexander* [1936] 2 All E.R. 1686. See also *Tailby v Official Receiver* (1888) 13 App. Cas. 533; *King v Michael Faraday & Partners Ltd* [1939] 2 K.B. 753; *Syrett v Egerton* [1957] 1 W.L.R. 1130. Under Human Rights Act 1998 s.1 and Sch.1 Pt I art.5, contractual restrictions on personal liberty of the kind described in the text above could be unlawful if imposed by a "public authority": see s.6. Such restrictions do not appear to fall within art.1 of Sch.1 Pt I.

dispose of his property or move house. The contract was held to be illegal as it unduly restricted the liberty of the borrower.

But a case has to be extreme to fall within this principle. In *Denny v Denny*[333] a father promised to pay his son's debts and to make him an allowance if the son did not become a bankrupt; became and remained a reformed character; gave up some named associates (who were swindlers); did not go within 80 miles of Piccadilly Circus without his father's previous consent; did not borrow money, or bet or directly or indirectly have any business or personal relations with any moneylenders, bookmakers or turf accountants or their servants. This contract was upheld even though, taken literally, it prevented the son from having personal relations with a bookmaker's clerk, who might be perfectly honest. The court was mainly influenced by the fact that the father had imposed the restrictions for the son's benefit, while the moneylender in *Horwood*'s case had acted from selfish motives.

## 3. EFFECTS OF ILLEGALITY

### (a) Introduction

**No plea of illegality necessary.** Where a contract is unenforceable by one or both parties, the court "may refuse to enforce it even if illegality is not pleaded or alleged".[334] The unenforceability of illegal contracts, and the barring of other forms of relief, rests on overriding grounds of public interest[335] and "the judge is required to take the point of his own motion even if the parties have not raised it".[336] **11–062**

**The consistency principle.** The difficulty facing the courts in determining the effects of illegality is due to the need to resolve a conflict of policies. As Bingham LJ put it in *Saunders v Edwards*: **11–063**

> "Where issues of illegality are raised, the courts have … to steer a middle course between two unacceptable positions. On the one hand it is unacceptable that any court of law should aid or lend its authority to a party seeking to pursue or enforce an object or agreement which the law prohibits. On the other hand, it is unacceptable that the court should, on the first indication of unlawfulness affecting any aspect of a transaction, draw up its skirts and refuse all assistance to the plaintiff, no matter how serious his loss nor how disproportionate his loss to the unlawfulness of his conduct."[337]

333 [1919] 1 K.B. 583; cf. *Upton v Henderson* (1912) 28 T.L.R. 398.

334 *Birkett v Acorn Business Machines Ltd* [1999] 2 All E.R. (Comm) 429 at 433; *Les Laboratoires Servier v Apotex Inc* [2014] UKSC 55; [2014] 3 W.L.R. 1257 at [23]. But facts giving rise to illegality must be pleaded where the contract is not ex facie illegal: *Bank of India v Transcontinental Merchants Ltd* [1982] 1 Lloyd's Rep. 427.

335 *Birkett v Acorn Business Machines Ltd* [1999] 2 All E.R. (Comm) 429 at 435; *Awwad v Geraghty & Co* [2001] Q.B. 570 at 596.

336 *Patel v Mirza* [2016] UKSC 42; [2017] A.C. 467 at [160] (Lord Neuberger); at [267] (Lord Sumption).

337 *Saunders v Edwards* [1987] 1 W.L.R. 1116 at 1134.

While it has been observed that "a generalised statement of the conceptual basis for the doctrine under which illegality may bar a civil claim has always proved elusive",[338] there is relatively widespread agreement, at least in recent decisions of the Supreme Court,[339] that the underlying principle which should dictate the "middle course" to which Bingham LJ refers is the principle of "consistency". For example, in *Patel v Mirza*[340] Lord Toulson referred to the "question whether allowing recovery for something which was illegal would produce inconsistency and disharmony in the law, and so cause damage to the integrity of the legal system",[341] while Lord Sumption referred to the "underlying principle … that for reasons of consistency the court will not give effect, at the suit of a person who committed an illegal act … , to a right derived from that act."[342] What divided the Supreme Court Justices in *Patel v Mirza* was how to determine whether this principle applies in any particular case. According to Lord Sumption, the test which "has usually been adopted"[343] is the "reliance test" and he advocated its retention,[344] whereas Lord Toulson and a majority of the Court[345] held that it should no longer be followed.[346] Instead, Lord Toulson advocated a broader policy-based approach under which the decision in any individual case depends on the weighing up of a "range of factors". This is now the applicable test.

11–064 **The structure of this section.** This part will begin by explaining in very broad outline the "reliance test" and the "range of factors test", as they are articulated in *Patel v Mirza*, before analysing some of the decisions of the courts. As in previous editions, that analysis is divided into actions for the enforcement of the contract and actions in restitution for the recovery of benefits bestowed under a contract which may be unenforceable because of illegality. This distinction is retained because, whichever test is applied, the considerations to be taken into account in these two categories are markedly different. In very simple terms, it is one thing for the courts to "undo" an illegal contract (restitution), and another to order its enforcement. It should be stated at the outset that, in many of the cases

[338] *Hounga v Allen* [2014] UKSC 47; [2014] 1 W.L.R. 2889 at [54] (Lord Hughes).
[339] In addition to *Patel v Mirza*, see *Stone and Rolls Ltd v Moore Stephens* [2009] UKHL 39; [2009] 1 A.C. 1391 at [128] (Lord Walker), [226] (Lord Mance); *Hounga v Allen* [2014] UKSC 47; [2014] 1 W.L.R. 2889 at [43] (Lord Wilson); *Les Laboratoires Servier v Apotex Inc* [2014] UKSC 55; [2015] A.C. 430 at [24] (Lord Sumption); *Jetivia SA v Bilta (UK) Ltd* [2015] UKSC 23; [2016] A.C. 1 at 172 (Lord Toulson and Lord Hodge).
[340] [2016] UKSC 42; [2017] A.C. 467.
[341] *Patel v Mirza* [2016] UKSC 42; [2017] A.C. 467 at [100]. It is only in this sense (inconsistency) that one should read Lord Toulson's reference to the "integrity *of the legal system*" (emphasis added); it is not about the integrity *of the court* and whether it is required to "sully its hands" which is, it is submitted, rightly rejected by Lord Sumption as a rationale for the illegality defence: [2016] UKSC 42; [2017] A.C. 467 at [228].
[342] *Patel v Mirza* [2016] UKSC 42; [2017] A.C. 467 at [233].
[343] *Patel v Mirza* [2016] UKSC 42; [2017] A.C. 467 at [233].
[344] As did Lords Clarke and Mance.
[345] Lady Hale and Lords Kerr, Wilson and Hodge agreed with Lord Toulson. Lord Kerr also gave a short speech of his own explaining his reasons for preferring the approach advocated by Lord Toulson; and Lord Neuberger, while agreeing with the reasoning of the minority on the correct approach to the reliance test, also concluded that Lord Toulson's approach "provided as reliable and helpful guidance as it is possible to give in this difficult field" (at [174]).
[346] *Patel v Mirza* [2016] UKSC 42; [2017] A.C. 467 at [110].

considered below, there is little or no overt consideration of the "reliance test" as such, or the alternative approach advocated by Lord Toulson, not least because it is only in recent cases that the latter approach has been openly articulated. It is possible that, in some of the cases which are discussed, a different result might now be reached under the range of factors test, but since Lord Toulson observed that the "trio of necessary considerations" which inform the range of factors test can already be found in the case law,[347] it is very likely that the same result would be reached. This part will finish with an assessment of which of the two tests offers the best "fit" with the decided cases and ensures the most coherent application of the principle of consistency.

**A preliminary point about Patel v Mirza.** The claim in *Patel v Mirza* was for restitution of sums paid under a contract which had been entered into for an illegal purpose, but which had been thwarted by the turn of events. It is in the context of that particular type of claim that further consideration is given to the case itself.[348] The Supreme Court was unanimous in its decision that restitution should be ordered, but differed in its reasons. While it dealt with a claim in unjust enrichment, it is nonetheless clear that the Supreme Court in *Patel v Mirza* also considered itself to be determining the correct approach to the effect of illegality on contractual claims,[349] and probably civil claims in general.[350] Indeed, it is no doubt because this was anticipated that the appeal was heard before a panel of nine Supreme Court Justices, rather than the more customary five. 11–065

**The reliance test.** The reliance test is implicit in Lord Mansfield's classic statement of principle in *Holman v Johnson*: "No court will lend its aid to a man who founds his cause of action upon an immoral or an illegal act."[351] This begs the question of when the claimant's action is "founded on" his illegal act. It is clear that it must be applied flexibly. As Lord Sumption explained in *Patel v Mirza*: 11–066

> "There is … nothing about the reliance test that limits its relevance to certain causes of action. But the test may apply in different ways, depending on what it is that the law regards as illegal. In a tort case or a property case it is generally enough to identify the illegal act and demonstrate the dependence of the cause of action upon the facts making it illegal. In a contract case, the position is less straightforward. A contract may be affected by illegality because terms lawful in themselves are intended to be performed in an illegal way or for an illegal purpose not apparent from the contract itself. This does not mean that contracts vitiated by this circumstance can be enforced simply by putting the case without reference to the illegal purpose or proposed mode of performance. It is enough to give rise to the defence that the claimant must rely on a contract which is in fact illegal, whether that is apparent from the terms or not."[352]

[347] *Patel v Mirza* [2016] UKSC 42; [2017] A.C. 467 at [101].
[348] See below, para.11–090.
[349] *Patel v Mirza* [2016] UKSC 42; [2017] A.C. 467 at [164]–[166] (Lord Neuberger).
[350] This submission was accepted by the Court of Appeal in *XX v Whittington Hospital NHS Trust* [2018] EWCA Civ 2832; [2019] Med. L.R. 99 at [67] (negligence claim).
[351] *Holman v Johnson* (1775) 1 Cowp. 341 at 343.
[352] *Patel v Mirza* [2016] UKSC 42; [2017] A.C. 467 at [235].

As will be seen below,[353] Lord Sumption considered that the main problem with the reliance test was the way it had been applied in *Tinsley v Milligan*.[354]

11–067 **Exceptions to the reliance test.** The reliance test is subject to a number of exceptions where relief may be granted even if the action is founded on an illegal act. They are described by Lord Sumption as the two main categories of case where the law regards the parties as not *in pari delicto*, i.e. not "legally on the same footing".[355] The first category is where the claimant's participation in the illegal act is treated as involuntary, e.g. because it has been brought about by the fraud of the defendant,[356] or the claimant has been made strictly liable for the illegal act of another.[357] The second category is where a defence of illegality would be inconsistent with the rule of law which makes the act illegal, e.g. where the statute infringed was intended to protect the claimant,[358] or was intended only to prohibit certain conduct and not to prohibit contracts.[359]

11–068 **The "range of factors" test.** What has been referred to as the "range of factors" test eschews any attempt to formulate a "master rule based on reliance"[360] (or indeed any other "rules"[361]), with exceptions, in favour of a broader approach. There is some debate in *Patel v Mirza* about whether this amounts to a "discretion",[362] a "structured approach",[363] or a "principled evaluation",[364] but it is put in the following terms by Lord Toulson:

> "The essential rationale of the illegality doctrine is that it would be contrary to the public interest to enforce a claim if to do so would be harmful to the integrity of the legal system (or, possibly, certain aspects of public morality, the boundaries of which have never been made entirely clear and which do not arise for consideration in this case). In assessing whether the public interest would be harmed in that way, it is necessary a) to consider the underlying purpose of the prohibition which has been transgressed and whether that purpose will be enhanced by denial of the claim, b) to consider any other relevant public policy on which the denial of the claim may have an impact and c) to consider whether denial of the claim would be a proportionate response to the illegality, bearing in mind that punishment is a matter for the criminal courts. Within that framework, various factors may be relevant, but it would be a mistake to suggest that the court is free to decide a case in an undisciplined way. The public interest is best served by a principled and transparent assessment of the considerations

---

353 See para.11–101.
354 [1994] 1 A.C. 340.
355 *Patel v Mirza* [2016] UKSC 42; [2017] A.C. 467 at [241].
356 See para.11–084.
357 See, e.g. *Osman v J Ralph Moss Ltd* [1970] 1 Lloyd's Rep. 313; para.11–022.
358 Lord Sumption cites as examples: *Kiriri Cotton Co Ltd v Dewani* [1960] A.C. 192, para.11–095; and *Hounga v Allen* [2014] UKSC 47; [2014] 1 W.L.R. 2889.
359 See e.g. *St John Shipping Corpn v Joseph Rank Ltd* [1957] 1 Q.B. 267; para.11–003.
360 *Patel v Mirza* [2016] UKSC 42; [2017] A.C. 467 at [84] (Lord Toulson), at [139] (Lord Kerr).
361 See *Patel v Mirza* [2016] UKSC 42; [2017] A.C. 467 at [85] and the consideration therein of a number of rules set out in Burrows, *Restatement of the English Law of Contract* (2016), p.225, based on the premise that the reliance test is essentially confined to the creation of property rights: see below, para.11–108.
362 That is certainly how it is seen by the minority and is the principal basis of their criticism: [2016] UKSC 42; [2017] A.C. 467 at [217] (Lord Clarke), [265] (Lord Sumption); see para.11–109.
363 *Patel v Mirza* [2016] UKSC 42; [2017] A.C. 467 at [175] (Lord Neuberger).
364 *Patel v Mirza* [2016] UKSC 42; [2017] A.C. 467 at [41] (Lord Toulson).

> identified, rather than by the application of a formal approach capable of producing results which may appear arbitrary, unjust or disproportionate."[365]

In deciding whether it would be disproportionate to refuse relief, various factors may be relevant, but Lord Toulson preferred not to "lay down a prescriptive or definitive list because of the infinite possible variety of cases".[366] He did, however, say that "[p]otentially relevant factors include the seriousness of the conduct, its centrality to the contract, whether it was intentional and whether there was marked disparity in the parties' respective culpability."[367]

## (b) Enforcement

A court will never "enforce" an illegal contract in the sense of ordering a party actually to do something that is unlawful or contrary to public policy.[368] But if A promises B £10 in return for B's promise to do such an act the court may sometimes award damages to A if B fails to do the act, or allow B to claim the £10 if he has actually done it. The law on this question is complex and not entirely satisfactory. 11–069

**An unenforceable contract may still be performed.** A contract affected by illegality is sometimes unenforceable by one party and sometimes unenforceable by both. Where it is "wholly unenforceable because it is contrary to English law, it may … accurately be said to be void as a contract, that is, not to be a contract at all";[369] or to be "illegal and void".[370] In the restraint of trade cases considered below, the illegality often affects only the term which imposes the restraint, and generally its effect is not to make the contract wholly void: it only makes *the stipulation in restraint of trade* unenforceable or "void"[371] in so far as it has not been performed.[372] It follows that, where one party voluntarily performs[373] another term of such a contract by paying money to the other, the payment cannot be recovered back from the payee; nor, if the contract is between more than two parties, can any other party to it prevent the payor from voluntarily making the payment to the payee.[374] But the payor must have *performed*, i.e. made the payment. It is not sufficient that the right to payment may have accrued before the 11–070

---

[365] *Patel v Mirza* [2016] UKSC 42; [2017] A.C. 467 at [120].

[366] *Patel v Mirza* [2016] UKSC 42; [2017] A.C. 467 at [107].

[367] *Patel v Mirza* [2016] UKSC 42; [2017] A.C. 467 at [107].

[368] e.g. to perform a contract if to do so would amount to a criminal offence: cf. paras 11–014, 11–019; cf. *Patel v Mirza* [2016] UKSC 42; [2017] A.C. 467 at [262] (Lord Sumption).

[369] *Mackender v Feldia* [1967] 2 Q.B. 590 at 601; cf. *Clarke v Chadburn* [1985] 1 W.L.R. 78 at 81 ("void for illegality").

[370] *Phoenix General Ins Co of Greece SA v Halvanon General Ins Co* [1988] Q.B. 216 at 249, 267, 268 (as to which see para.11–020); *Harbour Assurance (UK) Ltd v Kansa General International Ins* [1993] Q.B. 701 at 703, 724.

[371] *Rock Refrigeration Ltd v Jones* [1997] I.C.R. 938 at 948, 953.

[372] *Esso Petroleum Ltd v Harper's Garage (Stourport) Ltd* [1968] A.C. 269 at 297 ("a [contract in restraint of trade] is only unenforceable if a party chooses not to abide by it").

[373] See para.11–161.

[374] *Boddington v Lawton* [1994] I.C.R. 478.

payee "repudiates" the contract for restraint of trade.[375] In such circumstances, the payee is left with a claim for a quantum meruit for the services rendered.[376] A contract in restraint of trade would only be "wholly unenforceable" and "void" (in accordance with the statements quoted above) where the restraint formed the sole or principal subject-matter of the contract;[377] and it would also be appropriate to describe it as void where the law provided a third party with a remedy to prevent the parties to the contract from acting in accordance with it.[378]

### *(i) Position of guilty party*

11–071 **No enforcement by guilty party.** An illegal contract cannot usually be enforced by a guilty party. Thus a person who hired a hall to deliver blasphemous lectures could not sue for possession;[379] and a landlord who let premises with guilty intent could not sue for rent.[380] Nor can a guilty party enforce the contract indirectly.[381] Thus, the court will set aside or refuse to enforce an arbitration award enforcing an illegal contract,[382] and will not administer the funds of an illegal association.[383] Nor, where an illegal contract purports to release rights under an earlier valid contract, will a guilty party be allowed to rely on the illegal contract by way of defence to a claim to enforce those rights.[384]

11–072 **Difficult cases.** As noted above,[385] the defence of illegality vindicates the public interest; it exists, "not for the sake of the defendant, but because the courts will not lend their aid to such a (claimant)".[386] Thus, it applies even though the defendant shares the claimant's guilt and even though its effect may be to allow

375 *Proactive Sports Management Ltd v Rooney* [2011] EWCA Civ 1444; [2012] I.R.L.R. 241 at [115].

376 *Proactive Sports Management Ltd v Rooney* [2011] EWCA Civ 1444; [2012] I.R.L.R. 241 at [117]; para.11–106.

377 As in *Amoco Australia Pty v Rocca Bros Motor Engineering Pty Ltd* [1975] A.C. 561, where acts done under the agreement were accordingly annulled with retrospective effect: para.11–168.

378 See *Newport Association FC v Football Association of Wales Ltd* [1995] 2 All E.R. 87; para.11–141.

379 *Cowan v Milbourn* (1867) L.R. 2 Ex. 230.

380 cf. *Alexander v Rayson* [1936] 1 K.B. 169; *Edler v Auerbach* [1950] 1 K.B. 359.

381 *The Angel Bell* [1981] Q.B. 65 at 72–73.

382 *David Taylor & Sons Ltd v Barnett Trading Co* [1953] 1 W.L.R. 562; *Soleimany v Soleimany* [1999] Q.B. 785; and see at fn.291. But this principle does not apply to findings of *fact* on which the legality of the contract depend: *Binder v Alachouzos* [1972] 2 Q.B. 151; nor does an arbitrator necessarily lack jurisdiction to determine whether a contract is illegal: *Harbour Assurance (UK) Ltd v Kansa General International Ins Co Ltd* [1993] Q.B. 701; Arbitration Act 1996 s.30(1)(a); nor is he deprived of such jurisdiction merely because it is alleged that performance of an originally lawful contract subsequently became illegal: *Prodexport v ED & F Man Ltd* [1973] 1 Q.B. 389; *Soleimany v Soleimany* [1999] Q.B. 785 at 804.

383 *Sykes v Beadon* (1879) 11 Ch D. 170; *Shaw v Benson* (1883) 11 Q.B.D. 563. The court can order repayment of such funds to the members or contributors: *Barclay v Pearson* [1893] 2 Ch. 154; *Greenberg v Cooperstein* [1926] Ch. 657.

384 *Royal Boskalis Westminster NV v Mountain* [1997] 2 All E.R. 929 (Phillips LJ dissenting on this point).

385 See para.11–063.

386 *Holman v Johnson* (1775) 1 Cowp. 341 at 343; *Soleimany v Soleimany* [1999] Q.B. 785 at 800.

the defendant to keep a substantial benefit for nothing.[387] For example, where money has been lent under an illegal loan, a guilty lender cannot recover it from the borrower.[388] The defence is capable of producing harsh results,[389] particularly as a party may be "guilty" without being morally to blame.[390] For example, in *Howard v Shirlstar Container Transport Ltd*[391] the defendants, who owned two aircraft which had been detained in Nigeria after a *coup d'état*, promised to pay $25,000 to the claimant if he flew the aircraft out of that country. The claimant did fly the aircraft out of Nigeria and, in doing so, he committed breaches of Nigerian air traffic control regulations in order to make good his escape, after he had been warned that his life and that of his wireless operator (who was also his fiancée) would be in danger if they stayed in Nigeria. It was held that the claim to enforce the contract was not barred by illegality since "in the perilous and life-threatening circumstances … it would not amount to an affront to the public conscience to afford the (claimant) the relief he sought".[392] The test of an "affront to the public conscience"[393] was later rejected by the House of Lords[394] and *Howard v Shirlstar Container Transport Ltd* has been explained[395] instead as an illustration of the principle in *St John SS Corp v Joseph Rank Ltd*,[396] i.e. on the ground that the purpose of the legislation was not to invalidate contracts but only to prohibit conduct.[397] This puts it in the second of the exceptions to the reliance test referred to by Lord Sumption in *Patel v Mirza*,[398] whereas under the range of factors test it would seem to turn on the weight given not only to the purpose of the rules infringed, but also the circumstances in which the illegality arose, as well as considerations of proportionality.[399] It may be relevant that in *Howard v Shirlstar* there were no passengers on board the aircraft, and that it made its escape by flying low over the sea. A different view might have been taken if an aircraft with passengers on board had (in breach of air traffic regulations) been flown low over a densely populated area. To have allowed the pilot in such circumstances to enforce the contract might well have been thought to contravene the purpose of the legislation and to have justified the withholding of relief.

---

[387] This is of course subject to any claim in restitution: see para.11–088.

[388] *Boissevain v Weil* [1950] A.C. 372; *Spector v Ageda* [1973] Ch. 30; cf. *Shanshal v Al Kishtaini* [2001] EWCA Civ 264; [2001] 2 All E.R. (Comm) 601, also holding that his position is not affected by Human Rights Act 1998 Sch.1 Pt II.

[389] *Birkett v Acorn Business Machines Ltd* [1999] 2 All E.R. (Comm) 429 at 434.

[390] See para.11–074.

[391] [1990] 1 W.L.R. 1292.

[392] *Howard v Shirlstar Container Transport Ltd* [1990] 1 W.L.R. 1292 at 1301.

[393] See also *Euro-Diam Ltd v Bathurst* [1990] Q.B. 1 at 35; cf. (in the context of recovery of property obtained illegally) *Thackwell v Barclays Bank Plc* [1986] 1 All E.R. 676 at 687.

[394] *Tinsley v Milligan* [1994] 1 A.C. 340 at 358–361 and 363–364 (Lord Goff, who dissented in the result but with whose views on the present point all the other members of the House of Lords directly or indirectly expressed their agreement).

[395] *Tinsley v Milligan* [1994] 1 A.C. 340 at 360.

[396] *St John SS Corp v Joseph Rank Ltd* [1957] 1 Q.B. 267; para.11–019.

[397] cf. *Hill v Secretary of State for the Environment, Food and Rural Affairs* [2005] EWHC 696 (Ch); [2006] 1 B.C.L.C. 601.

[398] See para.11–067.

[399] See para.11–068.

11–073 **Other remedies.** While a guilty party may not be able to enforce *the contract*, it does not necessarily prevent him from recovering damages in tort where the other party's conduct constitutes, not merely a breach of the illegal contract, but also an independent tort.[400] This was the position in *Saunders v Edwards*,[401] where a contract had been made for the sale of a flat and the furniture in it; the purchasers had been induced to enter into the contract by the vendor's fraudulent misrepresentation that the premises included a roof-garden. The contract was also illegal[402] in that £5,000 of the agreed price of £45,000 was attributed to the furniture, which was worth no more than £1,000: this was apparently done at the suggestion of the purchasers, with a view to saving them the relatively small sum of £300 in stamp duty. Their claim for damages of over £7,000 for the vendor's deceit was nevertheless upheld. One reason for this result was that the purchasers were "not seeking to enforce the contract"[403] but only to claim damages in tort.[404] Another was that, in deciding whether to allow the tort claim, the court could, and should, have regard to the "relative moral culpability"[405] of the parties: the purchasers' fairly moderate tax evasion was outweighed by the vendor's more serious fraud. The former reason is consistent with the reliance test, whereas the latter is really only relevant under the range of factors test. Under either test a guilty party to an illegal contract will not necessarily be able to succeed merely by formulating his claim in tort. For example, in *Ashton v Turner*[406] one of two persons who had agreed (when drunk) to commit burglary together sued the other for injuries inflicted by the latter when negligently driving the get-away car. The action failed as it would have been obviously contrary to public policy to allow such a claim and can be explained on the basis that the claim in tort still relied on the illegal conduct of the parties, or that to withhold relief was the appropriate response when weighing up the relevant factors.

11–074 **Determining the "guilty" party.** There is some latitude in determining who is a "guilty" party where the illegality lies in the method of performance. For the present purpose, a party is not "guilty" merely because he performs a contract in an unlawful manner. Thus, the shipowner in *St John Shipping Corp v Joseph Rank Ltd*[407] succeeded in his claim for freight although he had overloaded his ship; but it was said that he could not have enforced the contract if he had at the

---

[400] For a similar principle governing claims for the recovery of money paid or property transferred under an illegal contract, see para.11–097; cf. *Hounga v Allen* [2014] UKSC 47; [2014] 1 W.L.R. 2889 (illegality of employment contract no bar to claim for racial discrimination); contrast *Vakante v Addey & Stanhope School* [2004] EWCA Civ 1065; [2005] I.C.R. 231.

[401] [1987] 1 W.L.R. 1116; cf. *The Siben* [1996] 1 Lloyd's Rep. 35 at 63; *Watts v Watts* [2014] W.T.L.R. 1781.

[402] On the principle of *Alexander v Rayson* [1936] 1 K.B. 169; para.11–056.

[403] *Saunders v Edwards* [1987] 1 W.L.R. 1116 at 1125.

[404] cf. the successful tort claim in *Edler v Auerbach* [1950] 1 K.B. 359.

[405] *Saunders v Edwards* [1987] 1 W.L.R. 1116 at 1127.

[406] [1981] Q.B. 137; cf. *Pitts v Hunt* [1991] 1 Q.B. 24; *Gala v Preston* (1991) 172 C.L.R. 243.

[407] [1957] 1 Q.B. 267; cf. *Shaw v Groom* [1970] 2 Q.B. 504; *Yango Pastoral Co Pty Ltd v First National Chicago Australia Ltd* (1978) 139 C.L.R. 410, as explained in *Phoenix General Ins Co of Greece SA v Halvanon General Ins Co Ltd* [1988] Q.B. 216 (as to which see para.11–020); *Euro-Diam Ltd v Bathurst* [1990] Q.B. 1.

time of contracting intended to overload his ship.[408] Similarly, a seller of fish succeeded in his claim for the price even though, after the contract was made, he committed an offence by sending a false invoice to the buyer with the intention of postponing the payment of VAT on the sale;[409] but it seems that his claim would have failed if at the time of the sale he had already formed the intention of issuing the false invoice. Where the intention that one party should do an unlawful (or immoral) act exists at the time of contracting, even the other party may be unable to sue on the contract. In *Ashmore, Benson, Pease & Co Ltd v AV Dawson Ltd*[410] a contract to carry two 25-ton loads was performed by using lorries which could not lawfully carry loads of more than 20 tons. This was known both to the carrier and to the owner of the goods, whose claim for damage done to them in the course of transit was rejected as he not only knew of the illegality but "participated" in it. "Participation" here means that he assented to a method of performance which he knew to be illegal,[411] and that he hoped to benefit from it by saving the extra expense of having the goods carried on different vehicles. The distinctions drawn in these cases are perhaps easier to explain under the range of factors test than under the reliance test.[412]

### *(ii) Position of innocent party*

**Party "innocent" because of ignorance or mistake of law.** In general, ignorance of the law or a mistake of law does not give a party the right to enforce a contract which is affected by illegality. In *Nash v Stevenson Transport Ltd*[413] A agreed to allow B to use goods vehicle licences taken out by A in his own name. This arrangement was made in good faith, but by statute it involved both parties in criminal liability. It was held that A could not sue for the money promised to him under the contract. In *Nash* the performance or enforcement of the contract *necessarily* involved a breach of the law. Where this is not the position, the effect of mistake of law is harder to determine. In *Waugh v Morris*[414] a ship was chartered to carry hay from a French port to London. The cargo was to be taken from the ship "alongside," and the master was orally instructed to deliver it to a wharf in Deptford Creek. This could not lawfully be done because, before the time of contracting, an order had, unknown to the parties, been made prohibiting 11–075

[408] *St John Shipping Corp v Joseph Rank Ltd* [1957] 1 Q.B. 267 at 283; cf. *Fielding & Platt Ltd v Najjar* [1969] 1 W.L.R. 357. Quaere whether in the *St John Shipping* case the test of intention would have been strictly subjective. If the shipowner had made a single contract for so much cargo that his ship would inevitably be overloaded, would the court have said that he "must have" intended at the time of contracting to break the law?

[409] *Skilton v Sullivan, The Times*, 25 March 1994.

[410] [1973] 1 W.L.R. 828; Hamson [1973] C.L.J. 199.

[411] *Hall v Woolston Hall Leisure Ltd* [2001] 1 W.L.R. 225 at 234 ("knowingly participated … "); *Wheeler v Quality Deep Ltd* [2004] EWCA Civ 1085; [2005] I.C.R. 265; cf. *Enfield Technical Services v Payne* [2008] EWCA Civ 393; [2008] I.R.L.R. 500 at [38]: "The requirement of knowing participation does not require that the employee should realise that what is being done is illegal, but it is necessary that he or she should know of the facts which make it illegal".

[412] In *Patel v Mirza* [2016] UKSC 42; [2017] A.C. 467 at [3]–[7] Lord Toulson refers to the difficulty of reconciling the *Joseph Rank* case and the *Ashmore Benson* case; cf. at [208] (Lord Mance).

[413] [1936] 2 K.B. 128; cf. *Corby v Morrison* [1980] I.C.R. 218; *Mohamed v Alaga & Co* [2000] 1 W.L.R. 1815 at 1820, 1824, 1827.

[414] (1873) L.R. 8 Q.B. 202; cf. *Hindley & Co Ltd v General Fibre Co Ltd* [1940] 2 K.B. 517.

the landing of hay from French ports in the UK. The hay was therefore trans-shipped and exported. It was held that the shipowner could sue on the charterparty as it could have been, and in fact had been, performed lawfully. Similarly, in *ParkingEye Ltd v Somerfield Stores Ltd*[415] the claimant was entitled to sue for the wrongful termination of a contract under which it collected fines from customers who exceeded the parking times in the defendant supermarket's car park notwithstanding that the third of four successive letters which the claimant sent out to recover the fines amounted to the tort of deceit. Unlike *Waugh v Morris*, the contract had been performed unlawfully in that the claimant had sent out some such letters but the Court of Appeal took into account that the contract was not a "one-off"; it was intended to last for 15 months, the illegality was not essential nor central to the performance of the contract, and it could and would have been performed lawfully if the defendant had drawn attention to the objectionable feature of the letter.

By contrast with the decision in *Waugh v Morris*, in *JM Allan (Merchandising) Ltd v Cloke*[416] a roulette wheel was let on hire for the purpose of enabling the hirer to play roulette royale at a country club. Both parties honestly thought that this game was lawful when it was not. It was held that the owner of the wheel could not sue for payment of the agreed hire. One reason for the decision was that the parties had a "common design to use the subject-matter for an unlawful purpose".[417] But it is equally true in *Waugh v Morris* that the parties had a common design to land the hay in Deptford, and that this was an unlawful purpose. Alternatively, there was in *Cloke*'s case an actual contract that the wheel should be used for playing roulette royale;[418] the position was as it would have been in *Waugh v Morris*, had the contract there been to *land* the hay at Deptford and not deliver it "alongside". It is, of course, possible that the hirer could, without committing a breach of contract, have used the wheel to play some other game; but this would not alter the fact that the owner had contracted to provide facilities for playing roulette royale. Thus, if one party cannot perform his obligations without committing or abetting a breach of the law he cannot enforce the contract even though he was "innocent" in the sense that he made a mistake of law. Lord Sumption's formulation of the reliance test for contracts, namely that "the claimant must rely on a contract which is *in fact* illegal",[419] might explain the cases referred to in this paragraph on the basis that a contract is only "in fact" illegal in the circumstances referred to in the previous sentence; whereas Lord Toulson referred to *Waugh v Morris* and *ParkingEye* as cases which illustrated the weight to be given to proportionality under the range of factors test.[420]

11–076 **Party "innocent" because of ignorance or mistake of fact.** A party may be innocent in the sense of being unaware of, or mistaken about, the *facts* which give rise to the illegality. The right of such a party to enforce the contract has been

[415] [2012] EWCA Civ 1138; [2013] Q.B. 840.
[416] [1963] 2 Q.B. 340.
[417] *JM Allan (Merchandising) Ltd v Cloke* [1963] 2 Q.B. 340 at 348.
[418] *JM Allan (Merchandising) Ltd v Cloke* [1963] 2 Q.B. 340 at 351.
[419] See text to fn.352 (emphasis added).
[420] *Patel v Mirza* [2016] UKSC 42; [2017] A.C. 467 at [68]–[71].

upheld in some cases but denied in others; even where it has been denied, other remedies may be available to the innocent party.

**Cases upholding the innocent party's claim.** A decision in favour of the innocent party is *Bloxsome v Williams*[421] where a person sold a horse on a Sunday and thereby committed an offence under the Sunday Observance Act 1677,[422] as he was a dealer. The buyer did not know that the seller was a dealer and recovered the money he had paid for the horse as damages for breach of warranty. *Bloxsome v Williams* was doubted in *Bedford Ins Co Ltd v Instituto de Resseguros do Brasil*,[423] where a company issued insurance policies in violation of a statutory prohibition against "the effecting and carrying out of [certain] contracts of insurance" without government authorisation. The policies were described as "illegal and void ab initio"; and it was said that the insured person, though innocent, acquired no rights under the policies "for it would be an offence for the insurer to pay him."[424] In the case of such contracts, this result has been reversed by statute,[425] and, even if the reasoning is sound as a matter of common law, it does not follow that *Bloxsome v Williams* was wrongly decided; for the buyer in that case was claiming, not delivery of the horse, but the return of his money. In upholding this claim, the court was not ordering the defendant to do an act prohibited by statute. This was also the position in *Archbolds (Freightage) Ltd v Spanglett Ltd*,[426] where the defendants contracted to carry the claimants' whisky in a van which was not licensed to carry goods belonging to third parties. In carrying the whisky in this van, the defendants committed a statutory offence. The whisky was stolen and the claimants, who did not know that the van was not properly licensed, recovered the value of the whisky as damages for breach of the contract. 11–077

**Cases rejecting the innocent party's claim.** The leading case in this group is *Re Mahmoud and Ispahani*,[427] where a contract was made to sell linseed oil at a time when it was (under delegated legislation) an offence to buy or sell such oil without licence. The seller had a licence to sell to other licensed dealers and was induced to enter into the contract by the buyer's fraudulent representation that he also had a licence. The buyer later refused to accept the oil, and it was held that the seller could not claim damages for non-acceptance, even if his lack of mens 11–078

[421] (1824) 3 B. & C. 232; cf. *Newland v Simons & Willer* [1981] I.C.R. 521. See also: *Clay v Yates* (1856) 1 H. & N. 73; para.11–016.

[422] Now repealed.

[423] [1985] Q.B. 966.

[424] *Bedford Ins Co Ltd v Instituto de Resseguros do Brasil* [1985] Q.B. 966 at 982; approved in *Phoenix General Ins Co of Greece SA v Halvanon Ins Co Ltd* [1988] Q.B. 216: see para.11–020; see also *Fuji Finance Inc v Aetna Life Ins Co Ltd* [1997] Ch. 173 (where conflicting views were expressed on the effects on contracts of the breach of a statute which did *not* amount to an offence); and *Parks v Esso Petroleum Co Ltd* [1999] 1 C.M.L.R. 445 (where on appeal it was held that there was no illegality: [2000] Eu. L.R. 25).

[425] See now Financial Services and Markets Act 2000 ss.26(1) and 32; para.11–020; para.11–080.

[426] [1961] 1 Q.B. 374. cf. *Fielding & Platt Ltd v Najjar* [1969] 1 W.L.R. 357.

[427] [1921] 2 K.B. 716; cf. *Yin v San* [1962] A.C. 304; Williams 8 C.L.J. 51; Buckley 38 M.L.R. 535; Treitel in Tapper (ed.), *Crime, Proof and Punishment: Essays in Memory of Sir Rupert Cross* (1981), pp.96–99.

rea would exonerate him from criminal liability. Similarly, it has been held that builders who did work in the bona fide but mistaken belief that the necessary licences had been obtained could not enforce the contracts under which the work was done.[428]

11–079 **Distinguishing the two groups of cases.** Various tests have been suggested for distinguishing between the cases in which the innocent party can, and those in which he cannot, enforce the contract. One is to say that the contract can be enforced by the innocent party so long as it is not ex facie illegal. But if the contract is ex facie illegal and one party is innocent his mistake is almost always one of law; and the mere fact that the contract is ex facie legal is certainly not enough to enable the innocent party to sue.[429] Another suggestion is that the innocent party can enforce the contract where it is illegal as performed but not where it is illegal as formed. But in *Bloxsome v Williams* the innocent party's claim was upheld even though the contract was illegal as formed. Moreover, in *Archbolds (Freightage) Ltd v S Spanglett Ltd* the Court of Appeal regarded it as irrelevant whether the contract was to carry the whisky in the particular van, and yet this fact would be crucial if enforceability depended on whether the contract was illegal as formed or as performed. A third suggestion is that the innocent party's claim will succeed in cases of common law but not of statutory illegality. But this again does not fit the cases: in *Bloxsome v Williams* and *Archbolds (Freightage) Ltd v S Spanglett Ltd* the innocent party succeeded although the illegality was statutory. It is, moreover, hard to see why the innocent party's rights should depend on the distinction between statutory and common law illegality.

11–080 **Express or implied statutory provision.** The distinction between statutory and common law illegality can, of course, be decisive where the illegality is statutory and the statute expressly or by implication specifies its effect on contracts. On the one hand, the statute may expressly provide that the validity of the contract is not to be affected. It is, for example, an offence under s.65(1) of the Road Traffic Act 1988 to supply certain vehicles which do not comply with specified safety requirements; and s.65(4) provides that "nothing in subsection (1) … shall affect the validity of any contract or any rights arising under or in relation to a contract".[430] On the other hand, the statute may expressly or impliedly provide that even an innocent party is not to be entitled to enforce the contract. This possibility was formerly illustrated by the cases, already mentioned,[431] in which insurance policies were issued in the course of a business carried on without government authorisation, thus making the insurers who had issued them guilty of a statutory offence; the general view was that such policies could not be enforced even by an insured person who was quite innocent of the illegality.[432]

[428] *J Dennis & Co Ltd v Munn* [1949] 2 K.B. 327; and see para.11–083.

[429] e.g. *Re Mahmoud and Ispahani* [1921] 2 K.B. 716.

[430] cf. Road Traffic Act 1988 s.75(7); Criminal Justice Act 1993 s.63(2), the effect of which appears to be to reverse this aspect of *Chase Manhattan Equities Ltd v Goodman* [1991] B.C.L.C. 897.

[431] viz. *Bedford Ins Co Ltd v Instituto de Resseguros do Brazil* [1985] Q.B. 966; and *Phoenix General Ins Co of Greece SA v Halvanon Ins Co Ltd* [1988] Q.B. 216; para.11–020.

[432] The statements to this effect were strictly obiter since in the *Bedford* case the action was by a *guilty* insurer against an innocent reinsurer while in the *Phoenix* case no offence had been committed.

This result was thought to follow from the wording of the statute, which was considered to have impliedly invalidated the contract by prohibiting the "carrying out" of the policies. But to deny a remedy to the innocent party certainly did not promote the policy of the statutory requirement,[433] which had been imposed on insurers for the protection of insured persons; and the law in cases of this kind has been changed by the Financial Services and Markets Act 2000. This lays down the general principle that, where A provides specified financial services to B without A's having the requisite authorisation, then the contract is unenforceable against (not by) B,[434] who is also entitled to the return of money paid or property transferred by him under it, and to compensation for loss suffered by him as a result of having parted with the money or property.[435] However, if A (no less than B) is innocent of the illegality, then the court may exceptionally allow the contract to be enforced and money or property transferred under it to be retained.[436] Similarly, under the Gambling Act 2005, it is an offence for the holder of an operating licence to permit a child or young person to gamble[437] and any contract will not be enforced in the sense that the licence holder may not give a prize to the child or young person.[438] Any money paid by the latter must, however, be repaid.[439]

**Test of the purpose of the statute, or the relevant rule of the common law.** **11–081**
Where the statute does not expressly or by implication specify the effects of the illegality on contracts, those effects are, it is submitted, to be determined primarily by reference to the purpose of the statute. This approach is suggested by Devlin LJ in *Archbolds (Freightage) Ltd v S Spanglett Ltd*, where he said:

> "I think that the purpose of this statute is sufficiently served by the penalties prescribed for the offender; the avoidance of the contract would cause grave inconvenience and injury to members of the public *without furthering the object of the statute*."[440]

Although Devlin LJ refers only to statutory illegality, it is submitted that the same approach would be appropriate where the illegality was due to a rule of common law:[441] the court has to consider how it would further the object of the relevant rule of law to invalidate the contract. Where the rule exists for the protection of a class of persons, its object will obviously not be promoted by rejecting a claim to

For cases following or approving the reasoning of these cases see *Re Cavalier Ins Co Ltd* [1989] 2 Lloyd's Rep. 430; *DR Ins Co v Seguros America Banamex* [1993] 1 Lloyd's Rep. 120.

433 From this point of view, the result in *Stewart v Oriental Fire & Marine Ins Co Ltd* [1985] 1 Q.B. 988 (giving the innocent party a remedy on the contract against the guilty party) was preferable to the reasoning of the authorities cited in fn.431; cf. Clarke [1987] L.M.C.L.Q. 201; *DR Ins Co Ltd v Central National Ins Co* [1996] 1 Lloyd's Rep. 74.

434 Financial Services and Markets Act 2000 ss.26(1), 27(1).

435 Financial Services and Markets Act 2000 ss.26(2), 27(2); if B elects not to perform or claims restitution he must in turn restore benefits received by him under the contract: s.28(7).

436 Financial Services and Markets Act 2000 s.28(3)–(6).

437 Gambling Act 2005 s.46.

438 Gambling Act 2005 s.83(1)(b).

439 See para.11–095.

440 *Archbolds (Freightage) Ltd v S Spanglett Ltd* [1961] 1 Q.B. 374 at 390 (emphasis added).

441 cf. *Hughes v Asset Managers Plc* [1995] 3 All E.R. 669 at 674.

enforce the contract made by an innocent member of that class.[442] In other cases, it is more difficult to strike a balance between the interests of the public (which the invalidating rule is meant to protect) and those of the innocent party. Of course, specific performance of a promise to do an act that is unlawful or against public policy will not be ordered. The questions are whether, if the guilty party has failed to perform such a promise, the innocent party should be entitled to damages; and whether, if the latter party has innocently done such an act, he should be entitled to enforce the guilty party's counter-promise (typically, one to pay the agreed sum).[443] In what way does it ever "further the object" of the invalidating rule to deny the innocent party such a remedy?

11–082 **Other remedies.** One possible answer to the question just posed is that the denial of a remedy may induce the innocent party to take greater care not to enter into an illegal transaction. Another is that a remedy should be refused whenever the contract is executory, since the availability of such a remedy might induce the other (guilty) party to perform. But where these arguments are sound, the innocent party should have no remedy at all, or at least no remedy as good as the action on the contract. In fact, the innocent party who cannot enforce the contract may have other remedies, and one of these seems to be no worse than an action on the contract. There are three such remedies.

11–083 **Collateral warranty.** First, the innocent party may be able to recover damages for breach of "collateral warranty". In *Strongman (1945) Ltd v Sincock*[444] the defendant employed a firm of builders to modernise his house. He promised to get the necessary licences (without which it was illegal to do the work), but he got licences for only part of the work and refused to pay for the rest on the ground that the contract to do it was illegal. The builders could not enforce the contract although they had acted in good faith. But they recovered damages (amounting to the value of the unlicensed work) for breach of the defendant's collateral undertaking to get the necessary licences. This is a useful device for doing justice to the innocent party, and in *Strongman (1945) Ltd v Sincock* little harm was done to the public interest. For in that case the defendant was an architect so that the builders were not careless[445] in failing to ask to see the licence. And the work had been completed, so that it would have been futile to deny a remedy on the ground that to grant it might induce the performance of an illegal act. But to allow the innocent party to sue on a "collateral warranty" in a case like *Re Mahmoud and Ispahani*[446] would be quite inconsistent with the rationale of the rule denying him a remedy on the contract. It would be mere sophistry to say: we will protect the public interest by denying a remedy on the contract, but we will also protect the innocent claimant by giving him as good a remedy on a collateral warranty. This remedy should be granted only where it will provide no incentive to do the illegal

442 See *Nash v Halifax Building Society* [1979] Ch. 584, so far as it relates to the enforcement of the security; cf. *Hughes v Asset Management Plc* [1995] 3 All E.R. 669 at 674, 675. The contract cannot of course be enforced *against* a member of the protected class: *Johnson v Moreton* [1980] A.C. 37.

443 It is assumed that the making of the payment is not prohibited.

444 [1955] 2 Q.B. 525.

445 *Strongman (1945) Ltd v Sincock* [1955] 2 Q.B. 525 at 536.

446 [1921] 2 K.B. 716; para.11–078.

act and where the innocent party was not careless. But if these conditions are satisfied there seems to be no reason why the innocent party should not be able to enforce on the contract itself. Alternatively, the innocent party could be given a restitutionary claim for the reasonable value of his services. This follows a fortiori from the suggestion (to be discussed later in this chapter)[447] that such a remedy may sometimes be available even to the guilty party.

**Misrepresentation.** Secondly, the innocent party may be able to recover damages in tort for misrepresentation. In *Shelley v Paddock*[448] the claimant was by the fraud of the defendant induced to enter into a contract to buy a house in Spain and to make payments under it which were illegal as they violated exchange control regulations. Since the claimant's breach of the law was innocent and resulted from the defendant's fraud, she was entitled to damages for that fraud. Even where the misrepresentation was *not* fraudulent, a person who had, as a result of it, innocently entered into an illegal contract might similarly be entitled to damages, either for negligence at common law[449] or under the Misrepresentation Act 1967; and he might also be able to rescind the contract. But these remedies could be less advantageous than an action on the contract as they would not give the innocent party damages for loss of his bargain.[450] **11–084**

**Restitution.** Thirdly, innocence may be material in an action for the recovery of money paid or property transferred under an illegal contract.[451] The object of the invalidating rule is less likely to be defeated by this remedy than by an award of damages for breach of contract since it amounts rather to an undoing[452] than to an enforcement[453] of the contract.[454] The remedy may, however, be less advantageous than any of those so far discussed, for under it the claimant can only get back what he gave: he cannot recover in respect of other losses incurred in reliance on the contract, or for loss of his bargain. **11–085**

### *(iii) De facto enforcement*

**Remedy for enforced performance.** A contract which is illegal may be enforced de facto in the sense that one party may secure compliance with its terms by using **11–086**

[447] See para.11–106.

[448] [1980] Q.B. 348; cf. *Burrows v Rhodes* [1899] 1 Q.B. 816; and *Saunders v Edwards* [1987] 1 W.L.R. 1116 (para.11–173), where even a "guilty" party recovered damages for a fraud unconnected with the illegality.

[449] *Mohammed v Alaga & Co* [2000] 1 W.L.R. 1815 at 1826.

[450] cf. para.9–073. In *Shelley v Paddock* [1980] Q.B. 348, above, the damages did not include any element of compensation for loss of the claimant's bargain: see [1979] Q.B. 120. In *Mohamed v Alaga & Co* [2000] 1 W.L.R. 1815 at 1826 Lord Bingham CJ said that he could not "conceive that the (claimant) could be regarded as recovering anything under this head [i.e. in tort] as damages which he would be debarred from recovering under the contract".

[451] cf. para.11–097.

[452] This was the outcome of *Bloxsome v Williams* (1824) 3 B. & C. 232 (para.11–077) where the buyer's claim was for "damages" but the amount that he recovered was the price paid by him.

[453] This was the nature of the claim unsuccessfully made by the seller in *Re Mahmoud and Ispahani* [1921] 2 K.B. 716 (para.11–078); if he had actually delivered the oil to the buyer he could no doubt have recovered it: para.11–097.

[454] See paras 11–088—11–106.

or threatening to use some form of economic pressure. Such measures may be taken in good faith, and the question then arises whether the party who is thus induced to perform a contract that was not binding on him has any remedy in respect of loss suffered in consequence. In *Shell UK Ltd v Lostock Garage Ltd*[455] a garage proprietor was in effect compelled to observe the terms of a solus agreement by the oil company's threats that, if other suppliers were to sell petrol to him, it would sue them for inducing a breach of the solus agreement. Lord Denning MR held that the solus agreement was unenforceable and that the garage proprietor was entitled to damages in respect of the loss he had suffered through being nevertheless compelled to observe it.[456] Ormrod LJ held that no such damages were available,[457] while Bridge LJ awarded them on the different ground that the oil company was in breach of an implied term of its contract with the garage proprietor.[458] Lord Denning held that no such term could be implied,[459] so that the damages awarded by him cannot have been for breach of contract. His award seems rather to have been based on the novel principle, that the de facto enforcement of an illegal contract can, if it causes loss, give rise to a claim for damages.

11–087 **Prevention of de facto enforcement.** The above discussion is based on the assumption that performance of the illegal contract has actually been secured. Before this has happened, the court may be able to intervene to prevent such performance, e.g. by an injunction to restrain a party from drawing on a letter of credit issued to secure payment under an illegal contract. Since the effect of such a remedy is to prevent illegality, it may be granted even to the guilty party.[460]

## (c) Restitution

11–088 A person who cannot enforce an illegal contract may instead claim restitution in respect of money paid, property transferred or services rendered by him under the contract.

11–089 **General rule.** In previous editions of this book, it was said that the general rule is that money paid or property transferred under an illegal contract cannot be recovered,[461] but that this was subject to a number of exceptions.[462] The general

455 [1977] 1 W.L.R. 1187.

456 *Shell UK Ltd v Lostock Garage Ltd* [1977] 1 W.L.R. 1187 at 1200; cf. under TFEU art.101, *Courage Ltd v Crehan* [2002] Q.B. 507 (European Court of Justice); *Crehan v Inntrepreneur Pub Co CPC* [2004] EWCA Civ 637; [2004] C.L.C. 803 CA (reversed on other grounds [2006] UKHL 38; [2006] 3 W.L.R. 148).

457 *Shell UK Ltd v Lostock Garage Ltd* [1977] 1 W.L.R. 1187 at 1200–1201.

458 *Shell UK Ltd v Lostock Garage Ltd* [1977] 1 W.L.R. 1187 at 1204.

459 See para.6–055; Ormrod L.J. agreed with Lord Denning on this point.

460 *Group Josi Re v Walbrook Ins Co Ltd* [1996] 1 W.L.R. 1152 at 1164, where the actual decision was that the performance of the contracts was saved from illegality by legislation of the kind described at para.11–080, after fn.433, so that no injunction was available.

461 Based on, for example, *Scott v Brown* [1892] 2 Q.B. 724; *Edler v Auerbach* [1950] 1 K.B. 359; cf. *Shaw v Shaw* [1965] 1 W.L.R. 537. See generally Grodecki 71 L.Q.R. 254; Higgins 25 M.L.R. 598; Rose in (Rose ed.), *Consensus ad Idem, Essays in the Law of Contract in Honour of Guenter Treitel*, p.202.

rule was not settled without a good deal of hesitation; and in particular equity at one time inclined to the opposite view.[463] It is the opposite view that now prevails. This is the most immediate consequence of the decision of the Supreme Court in *Patel v Mirza*.[464]

**Patel v Mirza.** In *Patel v Mirza*, A paid £620,000 to B in order that B could purchase and sell for a profit shares on the basis of inside information. This amounted to an offence under s.52 of the Criminal Justice Act 1993, but the agreement was never carried out because the inside information was not forthcoming. B refused to return the money to A. According to Lord Toulson, under the range of factors test of the majority it would be "rare" for a claim in unjust enrichment to fail: **11–090**

> "... a person who satisfies the ordinary requirements of a claim in unjust enrichment[465] will not prima facie be debarred from recovering money paid or property transferred by reason of the fact that the consideration which has failed was an unlawful consideration."[466]

He agreed with Gloster LJ in the Court of Appeal that the policy underlying the rule which made the contract between A and B illegal would not be stultified if A's claim for the return of the money was allowed; to forfeit the monies to B "would not be a just and proportionate response to the illegality".[467] Lord Sumption also agreed that the general rule is that money paid or property transferred under an illegal contract can be recovered,[468] but for him this was the consequence of the reliance test:

> "... the courts will not give effect to an illegal transaction or to a right derived from it. But restitution does not do that. It merely recognises the ineffectiveness of the transaction and gives effect to the ordinary legal consequences of that state of affairs. The effect is to put the parties in the position in which they would have been if they had never entered into the illegal transaction."[469]

---

[462] It was also said that it would be better if the law did not adopt a "general rule", but asked in relation to each type of illegality whether it was recovery or non-recovery that was the more likely to promote the purpose of the invalidating rule.

[463] *Morris v McCullock* (1763) Amb. 432; *Neville v Wilkinson* (1782) 1 Bro.C.C. 547 at 548; *Hermann v Charlesworth* [1905] 2 K.B. 123. The same view was sometimes taken at common law; e.g. *Munt v Stokes* (1792) 4 T.R. 561.

[464] [2016] UKSC 42; [2017] A.C. 467.

[465] The claim in unjust enrichment was made on the basis of a "failure of consideration" and this would suffice since no part of the contract was put into effect ([2013 EWHC 1892 at [12]), but Lord Toulson appears to envisage that it is the illegality of the contract which provides the basis for such a claim; cf. at [248] where Lord Sumption refers to a "general right to the restitution of money paid under an illegal contract", by analogy with other cases of ineffective contracts: see para.22–021. This is consistent with the view that full or partial performance should not prevent recovery: see para.11–093.

[466] *Patel v Mirza* [2016] UKSC 42; [2017] A.C. 467 at [116].

[467] *Patel v Mirza* [2016] UKSC 42; [2017] A.C. 467 at [115].

[468] cf. at [146] (Lord Neuberger); at [197] (Lord Mance).

[469] *Patel v Mirza* [2016] UKSC 42; [2017] A.C. 467 at [250]. He cited in support *Neville v Wilkinson*, fn.463; and *Smith v Bromley* (1760) 2 Doug 696n, 697: restitution of an illegal consideration was "necessary for the better support and maintenance of the law" (Lord Mansfield).

11–091 **Exceptions.** If the general rule is that restitution of benefit transferred under an illegal contract is available, that begs the question whether there are now any exceptions under which it is not available. There is very little room for an exception under the logic of the reliance test. Thus, for example, Lord Sumption thought that restitution was available regardless of the degree of illegality, including a contract to murder a third party;[470] an example with which Lord Neuberger agreed even on the basis of Lord Toulson's policy based approach.[471] As for Lord Toulson himself, he appeared to leave open the possibility[472] that there might be "cases where the contract may be of a nature too grossly immoral for the court to enter into any discussion of it: as where one man has paid money by way of hire to another to murder a third person."[473] Notwithstanding the example of a contract to murder a third party, Lord Neuberger did not rule out exceptions to a general rule of recovery and suggested two possibilities:[474] first, where one of the parties, especially the defendant, is in a class which is intended to be protected by any criminal legislation involved. Under the previous general rule, this was seen as an exception allowing recovery,[475] but the suggestion is that it may provide the basis for the defendant to retain a benefit transferred under an illegal contract;[476] secondly, where the defendant was unaware of the facts which gave rise to the illegality, especially if he had received the money and had altered his position so that it might be oppressive to expect him to repay it.[477] Again, "oppression" has previously been referred to as an exception which allowed for recovery,[478] but the suggestion is that it might result in no recovery, or only partial recovery.

11–092 **Indirect enforcement.** In *Patel v Mirza* Lord Sumption expressly acknowledged one possible exception to a general rule in favour of recovery which he described as "sound", but without expressing a concluded view. He was referring to cases in which an order for restitution "would be functionally indistinguishable from an order for enforcement", as in the case of recovery of an advance under an illegal loan,[479] where the "traditional view is that if the courts will not enforce an agreement it will not give the same financial relief under a different label."[480] However, Lord Neuberger thought that there was "nothing in that point" and "[if]

---

[470] *Patel v Mirza* [2016] UKSC 42; [2017] A.C. 467 at [254]. The example is used for illustrative purposes, but as Lord Sumption acknowledges, it is rather artificial since both parties would be exposed to confiscation orders under the Proceeds of Crime Act 2002.

[471] *Patel v Mirza* [2016] UKSC 42; [2017] A.C. 467 at [176].

[472] *Patel v Mirza* [2016] UKSC 42; [2017] A.C. 467 at [116].

[473] *Tappenden v Randall* (1801) 2 Bos & Pul 467 at 471 (Heath J, obiter).

[474] *Patel v Mirza* [2016] UKSC 42; [2017] A.C. 467 at [162].

[475] See para.11–095.

[476] But see the doubts expressed by Lord Mance: [2016] UKSC 42; [2017] A.C. 467 at [198]. Lord Neuberger's suggested use of this exception should not be confused with Lord Sumption's suggestion that it may provide an exception to the reliance test: para.11–067. Under the former, recovery would not be allowed even though the claim *is not* founded on an illegal act; under the latter, relief may be awarded even if the action *is* founded on an illegal act.

[477] Such circumstances may, of course, give rise to a defence of change of position.

[478] See para.11–096.

[479] See, e.g. *Boissevain v Weil* [1950] A.C. 327; para.11–072.

[480] *Patel v Mirza* [2016] UKSC 42; [2017] A.C. 467 at [255].

a particular outcome is correct, then the mere fact that the same outcome could have been arrived at on a wrong basis does not make it the wrong outcome."[481]

**Performance of the contract.** Those members of the Court who turned their attention to the issue did not consider that the general rule allowing recovery depended on whether the illegal contract had been performed, in full or in part. When discussing the example of a contract to murder a third person, Lord Sumption observed that, if the contract is carried out, the "rational response is the same", i.e. recovery of any payment made.[482] And Lord Neuberger considered that the reasons supporting the general rule of recovery in cases where the illegal activity had not occurred "apply for the same reasons to contracts where the contemplated illegal activity has been wholly or partly performed".[483] If, as a result, A has benefited this should be reflected in the claim for restitution. Thus, if in *Patel v Mirza* B had been able to purchase a few shares and had accounted to B for the sale of those shares in the sum of £10,000, A could have sued to recover the £620,000 he had paid, less the £10,000 which he had received.[484] According to Lord Sumption, "the rational rule … is that restitution is available for so long as mutual restitution of benefits remains possible".[485] This represents a departure from previous cases in which it had been said that recovery was only available if "the illegal purpose has [not] been wholly or partly performed", but this view was closely associated with the requirement that A must have repudiated the illegal purpose which is of little or no significance after *Patel v Mirza*.[486] 11–093

**Effect on existing case law.** As noted above,[487] benefits transferred under an illegal contract have previously been recovered and such instances were regarded as exceptions to a general rule barring recovery. Such instances are briefly considered in the paragraphs which follow,[488] but in many cases they must now be regarded as correctly decided on the basis of a general rule which allows recovery, justified by reference to the range of factors test. 11–094

**Class protecting statutes.** In a number of cases, recovery was allowed because the contract was made illegal by a statute passed for the protection of a class of persons, and the payor was a member of that class. For example, in *Kiriri Cotton Ltd v Dewani*,[489] a landlord had, by accepting an illegal premium from his tenant, committed an offence under a Rent Restriction Ordinance. The Privy Council held that the tenant could recover the premium because the statute was passed for the protection of tenants. The same decision would now be reached under the 11–095

481 *Patel v Mirza* [2016] UKSC 42; [2017] A.C. 467 at [171].
482 *Patel v Mirza* [2016] UKSC 42; [2017] A.C. 467 at [254].
483 *Patel v Mirza* [2016] UKSC 42; [2017] A.C. 467 at [168].
484 *Patel v Mirza* [2016] UKSC 42; [2017] A.C. 467 at [168].
485 *Patel v Mirza* [2016] UKSC 42; [2017] A.C. 467 at [253]; cf. [2016] UKSC 42; [2017] A.C. 467 at [198] ("I would not see any necessary objection to permitting rescission after part performance, by making, where possible, appropriate adjustments for benefits received." (Lord Mance)).
486 See para.11–099.
487 See para.11–089.
488 For more detailed consideration, readers are referred to the last edition.
489 [1960] A.C. 192; cf. *Nash v Halifax BS* [1979] Ch. 584, so far as it relates to the money lent; and see para.11–081.

general rule allowing recovery and there is certainly no countervailing policy reason against recovery; quite the contrary, as recovery is more likely to promote the purpose of the invalidating rule.

11–096 **Oppression.** A person could recover money paid or property transferred under an illegal contract if he was forced by the other party to enter into that contract. In *Atkinson v Denby*[490] an insolvent debtor offered to pay his creditors a dividend of 5s. in the £. All the creditors were willing to accept the dividend in full settlement of their claims, except the defendant, who said he would accept it only if the debtor first paid him £50. The debtor did so, but was later allowed to recover the £50 on the ground that he had been forced to agree to defraud the other creditors. Recovery would now be allowed under the general rule and, in policy terms, avoids the undesirable result of enabling one creditor to keep more than his fair share of the insolvent debtor's assets.

11–097 **Misrepresentation.** A person could recover money paid or property transferred under an illegal contract if he entered into the contract as a result of the other party's fraudulent misrepresentation that the contract was lawful,[491] but recovery would presumably now be possible under the general rule unless, for example, it would undermine the purpose of the invalidating rule. And it would also be available even if the misrepresentation was innocently made, whereas previously recovery was not possible in such a case.[492]

11–098 **Mistake.** A party who enters into a contract under a mistake of fact as to its legality can sometimes enforce the contract.[493] In such a situation he should be equally entitled to recover money paid or property transferred under the contract. Mistake could also be a ground for recovery of money or property even where it did not give the mistaken party the right to enforce the contract.[494] In *Oom v Bruce*[495] the claimant, as agent for the Russian owner of goods in Russia, took out a policy of insurance on the goods with the defendant. Neither party knew (or could have known) that Russia had declared war on this country before the contract was made. It was held that the claimant could get back his premium as he was not guilty of any fault or blame in entering into the illegal contract. Here again, recovery could now be explained on the basis of the general rule and no useful purpose would be served by preventing it.

11–099 **Repudiation of illegal purpose: *locus poenitentiae.***[496] As an exception to a general rule barring recovery, it was said that a person might be able to reclaim

---

490 (1862) 7 H. & N. 934; cf. *Smith v Cuff* (1817) 6 M. & S. 160; *Davies v London & Provincial Marine Ins Co* (1878) 8 Ch D. 469.

491 See, e.g. *Hughes v Liverpool Victoria Legal Friendly Society* [1916] 2 K.B. 482; cf. *Reynell v Sprye* (1852) 1 D.M. & G. 660.

492 *Harse v Pearl Life Assurance Co* [1904] 1 K.B. 558; cf. *Edler v Auerbach* [1950] 1 K.B. 359.

493 See para.11–076.

494 e.g. on facts such as those of *Re Mahmoud and Ispahani* [1921] 2 K.B. 716; fn.684.

495 (1810) 12 East 225; cf. *Edler v Auerbach* [1950] 1 K.B. 359 at 374–375, where mistake of the payor alone was said to be insufficient; sed quaere.

496 Beatson 91 L.Q.R. 313; Merkin 97 L.Q.R. 420.

money paid or property transferred under an illegal contract if he repudiated the illegal purpose in time.[497] This was the basis of the decision of the majority in the Court of Appeal in *Patel v Mirza*.[498] By giving a party this right, the law encouraged him to give up the illegal purpose. Whether on the basis of the reliance test, or the range of factors test, this reason for allowing recovery must now be regarded as almost entirely redundant after *Patel v Mirza*.[499] If the general rule is that recovery of benefits transferred under an illegal contract is allowed,[500] even if the contract has been fully or partly performed,[501] there is no relevance to the question of whether the claimant has repudiated the illegal purpose, unless perhaps it might be taken into account in cases where there are other factors in favour of non-recovery. Lord Sumption described the development of this ground for recovery as the law taking a "different" and "less satisfactory turn" to a general rule in favour of recovery.[502] And Lord Toulson found it "unnecessary to discuss the question of locus poenitentiae which troubled the courts below, as it has troubled other courts, because it assumed importance only because of a wrong approach to the issue whether Mr Patel was prima facie entitled to the recovery of his money."[503] The demise of *locus poenitentiae* is unlikely to be the subject of any mourning since it gave rise to "difficult and conflicting case law"[504] about how penitent the claimant needed to have been, and how penitent he had been. Some of the cases decided on this basis are briefly considered in light of the change of approach in *Patel v Mirza*.

In *Tribe v Tribe*[505] a father transferred shares in a company to his son in order to "safeguard his interests"[506] against claims for dilapidations by the lessors of shops of which the father was tenant and in which the company carried on business. The issue of dilapidations was later resolved without the share transfer having been shown to the lessors or to any other creditor. It was held that the father was entitled to the return of the shares since the illegal purpose had "not been carried into effect in any way".[507] After *Patel v Mirza* recovery would be allowed under the general rule unless perhaps this could be said to be a case where the remedy in restitution was functionally indistinguishable from enforcement of the contract (i.e. the return of the shares) and enforcement itself would not have been available.[508]

---

[497] *Hastelow v Jackson* (1828) 8 B. & C. 221 at 226; *Bone v Eckless* (1860) 5 H. & N. 925 at 928; *Taylor v Bowers* (1876) 1 Q.B.D. 291; *Kearley v Thomson* (1890) 24 Q.B.D. 742; *Hermann v Charlesworth* [1905] 2 K.B. 123; *Chettiar v Chettiar* [1962] A.C. 294; *Bigos v Bousted* [1951] 1 All E.R. 92; *Tribe v Tribe* [1996] Ch. 107 at 113.

[498] [2014] EWCA Civ 1047; [2015] 2 W.L.R. 405.

[499] cf. Lord Mance [2016] UKSC 42; [2017] A.C. 467 at [202], but he recasts *locus poenitentiae* to mean only that it must be possible to undo the transaction, even if performed.

[500] See para.11–089.

[501] See para.11–093.

[502] *Patel v Mirza* [2016] UKSC 42; [2017] A.C. 467 at [252]; cf. at [156] (Lord Neuberger).

[503] *Patel v Mirza* [2016] UKSC 42; [2017] A.C. 467 at [116].

[504] *Patel v Mirza* [2016] UKSC 42; [2017] A.C. 467 at [44].

[505] [1996] Ch. 107.

[506] *Tribe v Tribe* [1996] Ch. 107 at 113.

[507] *Tribe v Tribe* [1996] Ch. 107 at 121. For further problems which arose in this case because the relationship of transferor and transferee was that of father and son, see para.11–102.

[508] *Patel v Mirza* [2016] UKSC 42; [2017] A.C. 467 at [171] (Lord Neuberger); para.11–092.

It was said that the claimant "must withdraw voluntarily, and that it is not sufficient that he is forced to do so because his plan has been discovered".[509] For example, in *Bigos v Bousted*[510] a father provided security under an illegal contract to acquire foreign currency, in order to send his daughter to Italy as a cure for her recurrent attacks of pleurisy. He failed in his claim to recover the security after the other party had refused to perform. This was always an extremely doubtful decision[511] and, after *Patel v Mirza*, it seems certain that recovery would be allowed.[512]

11–100 **Recovery of property.** We have thus far considered examples of cases in which the courts were concerned with the recovery of money paid under an illegal contract. It is in relation to the recovery of property, or remedies for the protection of property, that the reliance test was most prominent. For example, in *Bowmakers Ltd v Barnet Instruments Ltd*[513] machine tools had been let out under hire-purchase agreements which were illegal[514] as they contravened war time maximum price and licensing regulations. The hirers failed to pay the instalments due under the agreements, sold some of the goods and kept the rest. The owners successfully claimed damages for the conversion of all the goods. They did not have to "found [their] claim on the illegal contract or … plead its illegality in order to support [their] claim",[515] but relied simply on their title.

11–101 **Tinsley v Milligan.** *Tinsley v Milligan*[516] is the leading case on the application of the reliance test, and its perceived shortcomings. The dispute in that case arose out of an agreement between the claimant and the defendant relating to a house in which they lived as lovers and which they jointly ran as a lodging house. The house had been purchased with money provided by both parties; and, although the parties accepted that the house was to be owned by them jointly, it was conveyed into the sole name of the claimant. This was done to enable the defendant to make false claims for social security benefits on the footing that she did not own her home; and such claims were in fact made. The parties later quarrelled and it was held that the defendant was entitled to an order for the sale of the house and to a declaration that it was owned by the parties in equal shares. The leading speech of the majority was given by Lord Browne-Wilkinson.[517] He held that title to property can pass under an unlawful transaction and the court

[509] *Tribe v Tribe* [1996] Ch. 107 at 135 (Millett LJ); cf. *Alexander v Rayson* [1936] 1 K.B. 169 at 190.
[510] [1951] 1 All E.R. 92.
[511] In *Tribe v Tribe* [1996] Ch. 107 at 135 Millett LJ expressed doubt whether *Bigos v Bousted* was not also a case of voluntary withdrawal where the scheme was "frustrated by the refusal of the other party to carry out his part".
[512] Lord Sumption described the decision in *Bigos v Bousted* as one of the decisions in which a moralistic approach to *locus poenitentiae* reached its high point: *Patel v Mirza* [2016] UKSC 42; [2017] A.C. 467 at [252].
[513] [1945] K.B. 65; Hamson 10 C.L.J. 249; Coote 35 M.L.R. 38; Stewart 1 J.C.L. 134.
[514] The owners had acquired the goods from one Smith under a contract which was also illegal; for this aspect of the case, see fn.539.
[515] *Bowmakers Ltd v Barnet Instruments Ltd* [1945] K.B. 65 at 71.
[516] [1994] 1 A.C. 340.
[517] Lord Goff, in the minority, held that if A puts property in the name of B intending to conceal A's interest for a fraudulent or illegal purpose, neither law nor equity will allow A to recover the property whether or not A's case could be advanced without reference to the underlying purpose. This was not

would not assist an owner to recover the property if he had to rely on his own illegality to prove his title. The defendant did not fall foul of the reliance test because she was entitled to a half share in the house by virtue of the presumption which normally arises in equity where one party transfers property to another, or provides money for the acquisition of property by another, that the property is held by the latter party (to the appropriate extent) on a resulting trust for the former party. It was this presumption of resulting trust which gave rise to the defendant's equitable title.[518] To establish that title, she had no need to impeach the transaction by relying on its illegality. It was, on the contrary, the claimant who sought to impeach the transaction by relying on its illegality in order to deprive it of its normal effect of giving the defendant an equitable title.

**Criticism.** The crucial factor in *Tinsley v Milligan* was that the defendant was able to rely on the presumption that property bought in part with her money was to that extent, or to the extent agreed upon by the parties, held in trust for her. That presumption could, of course, have been rebutted by proof that the defendant had intended to make a gift; and if the claimant had proved this, then the defendant's claim to a share in the property would have failed for it would then have been the defendant who would have relied on the illegality to defeat the gift.[519] In the case of certain relationships between the parties to the transaction, such an intention to make a gift is, moreover, presumed, thus reversing the normal presumption of resulting trust. This is, for example, the position where a father transfers property (or pays for property to be transferred) to his child: in such cases there is said to be a "presumption of advancement", or, in other words, a presumption that the transfer was intended as a gift to the child. It follows that, if the transfer in such a case is alleged to have been made for an illegal purpose, then the general rule will be that the father will not be able to claim the property by relying on his title; and that he will not be able to do so by impeaching the transfer by reference to the illegal purpose, for this would require him to rely on the illegality. This was the position in *Collier v Collier*[520] where a father granted a lease of property to his daughter to hold on trust for him in order to deceive creditors. His claim to beneficial title was rejected on the ground of illegality, because it was held that he needed to rely on the illegal purpose in order to rebut the presumption of advancement which arose in favour of the daughter. **11–102**

As was demonstrated by these cases, the difficulty with the reliance test was that it meant the outcome of a case depended on otherwise arbitrary differences in rules of evidence or pleading. Suppose, for example, that the lease in *Collier v Collier* had not been from father to daughter, but from daughter to father to enable the daughter to evade her creditors. There would then have been no

a result which he welcomed, but he rejected the introduction of a discretionary approach by the courts, based at that time on the test of "affronting the public conscience", and recommended an inquiry by the Law Commission.

[518] cf. *Silverwood v Silverwood* (1997) 74 P. & C.R. 9; *Mortgage Express v McDonnell* [2001] EWCA Civ 887; [2001] 2 All E.R. (Comm) 886 (equitable title acquired under earlier fraudulent transaction); *O'Kelly v Davies* [2014] EWCA Civ 1606; [2015] Fam. Law 383 (equitable title derived from a constructive trust based on the common intention of the parties).

[519] *Tribe v Tribe* [1996] Ch. 107 at 128–129.

[520] [2002] EWCA 1095; [2002] B.P.I.R. 1057; cf. *Chettiar v Chettiar* [1962] A.C. 294.

presumption of advancement but, on the contrary, a presumption of resulting trust; and it would seem to follow from the reasoning of *Tinsley v Milligan* that the daughter could have recovered on the strength of her equitable title. Such a conclusion would scarcely have promoted the purpose of the rule of law which was infringed in that case. Reasoning which is based on proprietary concepts no doubt has the advantage of predictability but its disadvantage in the present context is that it pays insufficient regard to the policy considerations with which the courts are normally concerned in working out the effects of illegality on contracts.[521]

11–103 **The effect of Patel v Mirza.** We have already noted that a majority of the Court in *Patel v Mirza* held that the "reliance rule as laid down in *Bowmakers* and *Tinsley v Milligan*" should no longer be followed.[522] It remains the case that, unless a statute provides otherwise, property can pass from A to B under an illegal contract,[523] but whether A will be entitled to recover depends upon the range of factors test and not on whether he has to rely on the illegal contract to make good his claim for recovery. This is to be welcomed in that it ensures that due prominence is given to the crucial question: whether to allow A to recover would tend to promote or to defeat the purpose of the rule of law which makes the contract illegal.[524] In *Patel v Mirza* Lord Toulson noted[525] that the court in the *Bowmakers* case ended its judgment by saying: "We are satisfied that no rule of law, and no considerations of public policy, compel the court to dismiss the plaintiffs' claim in the case before us, and to do so would be, in our opinion, a manifest injustice."[526] According to Lord Toulson, that conclusion, "rather than the answer to a procedural question, should have been the end of the illegality defence, since it is based on public policy".[527]

Under the approach of the majority in *Patel v Mirza*, the same result would be reached in a case like *Tinsley v Milligan*,[528] but it seems that a different result, i.e. recovery, would be reached in a case like *Collier v Collier*, unless perhaps this could be said to be a case where the remedy in restitution was functionally indistinguishable from enforcement of the contract (i.e. the return of the land) and enforcement itself would not have been available.[529] A different result in that case would also be reached even under the approach of the minority in *Patel v Mirza*, either on the basis that "reliance in order to restore the status quo is

[521] cf. in Australia, *Nelson v Nelson* (1995) 132 A.L.R. 132.
[522] *Patel v Mirza* [2016] UKSC 42; [2017] A.C. 467 at [110] (Lord Toulson).
[523] *Patel v Mirza* [2016] UKSC 42; [2017] A.C. 467 at [110]; *Singh v Ali* [1960] A.C. 167 at 176 (see para.11–105); *Sharma v Simposh Ltd* [2013] Ch. 23 at [27]–[44].
[524] Treitel in Tapper (ed.), *Essays in Memory of Sir Rupert Cross* (1981), pp.99–104.
[525] *Patel v Mirza* [2016] UKSC 42; [2017] A.C. 467 at [108].
[526] *Bowmakers Ltd v Barnet Instruments Ltd* [1945] K.B. 65 at 72.
[527] *Patel v Mirza* [2016] UKSC 42; [2017] A.C. 467 at [111].
[528] *Patel v Mirza* [2016] UKSC 42; [2017] A.C. 467 at [112] (Lord Toulson: "disproportionate to have prevented [Miss Milligan] from enforcing her equitable interest in the property"); cf. at [136] (Lord Kerr who thought *Tinsley v Milligan* was a case where the majority "*gave effect* to rather than unravelled the illegal agreement made between the parties", but that nonetheless recovery was the correct result); at [181] (Lord Neuberger).
[529] See above, para.11–092.

unobjectionable",[530] or because of a restatement of the reliance test. In relation to the latter Lord Sumption stated that the "true principle … depends on what facts the court must be satisfied about in order to find an intention giving rise to an equitable interest. It does not depend on how those facts are established". In both *Tinsley v Milligan* and *Collier v Collier* A was entitled to an equitable interest because there was no intention to make a gift: "[t]hat was all the court needed to be satisfied about."[531]

**Special cases?** It has been suggested that if the property transferred is such that it is unlawful to deal with it at all (e.g. an obscene book) it cannot be recovered.[532] There is also some support for the view that the price paid for such a book cannot be recovered by the buyer,[533] though this is scarcely the best way of discouraging the trade in such things. A further suggestion is that there is no right of recovery if the object of the contract is to enable one party to commit a serious crime,[534] e.g. if a dagger is loaned to commit murder. On the other hand, a person who undertakes the safe-keeping of a burglar's house-breaking tools is apparently bound to give them up to the burglar on demand.[535] In *Patel v Mirza*, Lord Toulson acknowledged that "[t]here may be circumstances in which a court will refuse to lend its assistance to an owner to enforce his title as, for example, where to do so would be to assist the claimant in a drug trafficking operation."[536] **11–104**

**Remedies available for the protection of money or property obtained under an illegal contract.** The mere fact that something has been obtained under an illegal contract does not deprive the recipient of the usual remedies for its recovery or protection.[537] Thus if goods are sold and delivered under an illegal contract, and the property in them has passed to the buyer, he can recover them or their value if they are later taken away from him by the seller.[538] Such remedies are also available against third parties,[539] and even (subject to statutory exceptions) against the police.[540] They may, moreover, be available to a buyer who has acquired the property in goods under an illegal sale, even though the **11–105**

[530] *Patel v Mirza* [2016] UKSC 42; [2017] A.C. 467 at [199] (Lord Mance).

[531] *Patel v Mirza* [2016] UKSC 42; [2017] A.C. 467 at [238].

[532] *Bowmakers Ltd v Barnet Instruments Ltd* [1945] K.B. 65 at 72; *Costello v Chief Constable of Derbyshire Constabulary* [2001] EWCA Civ 381; [2001] 1 W.L.R. 1437 at [33]. *Aliter* if the book is seditious? See *Elias v Pasmore* [1934] 2 K.B. 164 at 174.

[533] *The Siben* [1996] 1 Lloyd's Rep. 35, 62; para.9–120.

[534] cf. para.11–091.

[535] *R. v Lomas* (1913) 110 L.T. 239; as explained in *R. v Bullock* [1955] 1 W.L.R. 1.

[536] *Patel v Mirza* [2016] UKSC 42; [2017] A.C. 467 at [110].

[537] *Stoffel & Co v Grondona* [2018] EWCA Civ 2031; [2018] P.N.L.R. 36 at [33].

[538] *Singh v Ali* [1960] A.C. 167.

[539] See the discussion of *Bowmakers Ltd v Barnet Instruments Ltd* [1945] K.B. 65 in *Tinsley v Milligan* [1994] 1 A.C. 340 at 369: the owners succeeded in spite of the illegality not only of the hire-purchase agreements, but also of the contracts under which they had acquired the goods from their former owner. Contrast *Halley v Law Society* [2003] EWCA Civ 97 (no claim in equity to funds held by trustee where the funds had been obtained fraudulently).

[540] *Gordon v Chief Commr of Metropolitan Police* [1910] 2 K.B. 1080; *Porter v Chief Constable of Merseyside Police* [2000] Q.B. 427. Many statutes confer powers on the courts to make forfeiture, confiscation or similar orders. The complete discussion or even list of such provisions is beyond the scope of this book.

goods have never been in his possession. In *Belvoir Finance Co Ltd v Stapleton*,[541] Belgravia wanted to acquire cars from Francis, finance being provided by Belvoir. In relation to each car, two contracts were made: a sale by Francis to Belvoir and a letting on hire-purchase by Belvoir to Belgravia. All these contracts were illegal. Belvoir never acquired possession of the cars, which were delivered by Francis straight to Belgravia. It was held that Belgravia's assistant manager was liable to Belvoir for conversion of the cars, since the property in them had passed to Belvoir as soon as the contracts of sale between them and Francis were "executed".[542] The decision is, however, concerned only with the relative rights of the buyer and a third person. *The seller* had no further interest in the cars and was not in possession of them. The case therefore does not support the proposition that a buyer to whom property in goods has passed under an illegal contract can claim them, or damages for their conversion, *from a seller who has never delivered them at all*. Such a claim would not differ in substance from a claim for the delivery, or for damages for the non-delivery, of the goods under the illegal contract. Its success would thus defeat the object of the rule against the enforcement of such a contract.[543]

11–106 **Restitution in respect of services** Work done under an illegal contract may (no less than money paid or property transferred) give rise to a restitutionary claim, that is, to one for a reasonable remuneration on a quantum meruit basis. This possibility is illustrated by a case[544] in which the claimant had done work under a contract signed by him on behalf of a company. The contract was void because the company no longer existed;[545] and by trading in the name of a company which no longer existed the claimant had also committed an offence under s.34 of the Companies Act 1985 (now repealed). It was held that his claim was "maintainable on a quantum meruit though not under a supposed contract".[546] One possible reason for this result is that the policy of s.34 was not contravened by allowing such a claim.[547] Another is that (as in the cases allowing recovery of property before *Patel v Mirza*) the claimant did "not need to rely on any illegality to found a claim in that form".[548] The reason why he had no such need was that the contract was void for some *other* reason than the illegality, i.e. on account of the non-existence of the company. Where the *only* ground of invalidity is illegality, a guilty party who has done work under the contract may not have a quantum meruit claim if to allow such a claim would be inconsistent with the policy of the invalidating rule.[549] This explains why a solicitor who cannot

[541] [1971] 1 Q.B. 210; cf. *Kingsley v Sterling Industrial Securities Ltd* [1967] 2 Q.B. 747 at 783.

[542] *Belvoir Finance Co Ltd v Stapleton* [1971] 1 Q.B. 210 at 220.

[543] See para.11–081.

[544] *Cotronic (UK) Ltd v Dezonie (t/a Wendaland Builders Ltd)* [1991] B.C.L.C. 721.

[545] See para.16–083.

[546] *Cotronic (UK) Ltd v Dezonie (t/a Wendaland Builders Ltd)* [1991] B.C.L.C. 721 at 726.

[547] This is suggested by the reference in *Cotronic (UK) Ltd v Dezonie (t/a Wendaland Builders Ltd)* [1991] B.C.L.C. 721 at 726 to *Shaw v Groom* [1970] 2 Q.B. 504; para.11–003.

[548] *Cotronic (UK) Ltd v Dezonie (t/a Wendaland Builders Ltd)* [1991] B.C.L.C. 721 at 726; relying on the analogy of *Bowmakers Ltd v Barnet Instruments Ltd* [1945] K.B. 65; *AL Barnes Ltd v Time Talk (UK) Ltd* [2003] EWCA Civ 402; [2003] B.L.R. 331 at [14].

[549] e.g. in cases such as *Ashmore Benson Pease & Co Ltd v AV Dawson Ltd* [1973] 1 W.L.R. 828; para.11–074; cf. *Taylor v Bhail* (1995) 50 Con L.R. 70; contrast *AL Barnes Ltd v Time Talk (UK) Ltd*

enforce a conditional fee agreement, because it is illegal under the rules stated earlier in this chapter,[550] is also precluded from recovering the reasonable value of services rendered under it on a quantum meruit basis.[551] The same is not, however, necessarily true of a quantum meruit claim made against a guilty party by a party who is innocent of the illegality (in the sense of being unaware of the rule of law making the contract illegal) in respect of services not affected by the illegality. In *Mohamed v Alaga & Co*[552] the claimant agreed to introduce clients to solicitors who, in return, promised to pay him a share of the fees paid by those clients; he did not know that such an arrangement was prohibited[553] and that the fee-sharing contract was therefore illegal. It was held that he could neither enforce that contract nor bring a quantum meruit claim in respect of the work of introducing clients;[554] but that such a claim was available in respect of other services rendered by him in acting as interpreter between the clients in question and the solicitors.[555] In *Patel v Mirza* Lord Toulson affirmed this decision and rejected the view that it should be confined to "its own peculiar facts".[556]

## (d) Collateral transactions

Collateral transactions may be infected with the illegality of a principal contract if they help a person to perform an illegal contract, or if they would, if valid, make possible the indirect enforcement of an illegal contract.[557] Thus a loan of money is illegal if it is made to enable the borrower to make or to perform an illegal contract,[558] or to make an illegal payment,[559] or to pay a debt contracted under an illegal contract.[560] Similarly, a policy of insurance on an illegal venture is illegal;[561] a bond, bill of exchange or pledge given to secure an illegal debt is illegal;[562] and a bank is not liable on a letter of credit[563] to the extent that[564] the **11–107**

[2003] EWCA Civ 402; [2003] B.L.R. 331 (where the claim was for a contractual quantum meruit and *Taylor* was distinguished as applying to contracts illegal on their face or intended by the parties to be illegally performed).

550 See para.11–013.

551 *Awwad v Geraghty & Co* [2001] Q.B. 570 at 596.

552 [2000] 1 W.L.R. 1815.

553 By the Solicitors' Practice Rules, which have the force of law: *Swain v Law Society* [1983] A.C. 598 at 608.

554 *Mohamed v Alaga & Co* [2000] 1 W.L.R. 1815 at 1824–1825.

555 *Mohamed v Alaga & Co* [2000] 1 W.L.R. 1815 at 1825–1827; as explained in *Awwad v Geraghty & Co* [2001] Q.B. 570.

556 *Patel v Mirza* [2016] UKSC 42; [2017] A.C. 467 at [119]; cf. at [180] (Lord Neuberger).

557 But not simply where the legal contract happens to coincide with the illegal: *Sutton v Hutchinson* [2005] EWCA Civ 1773 (true loan repayable despite having been made to a prostitute whom the claimant also paid for her services).

558 *De Begnis v Armistead* (1833) 10 Bing. 107; *M'Kinnell v Robinson* (1838) 3 M. & W. 434.

559 *Cannan v Bryce* (1819) 3 B. & Ald. 179; as explained in *Spector v Ageda* [1973] Ch. 30.

560 *Spector v Ageda* [1973] Ch. 30.

561 *Toulmin v Anderson* (1808) 1 Taunt. 227.

562 *Fisher v Bridges* (1854) 3 E. & B. 642 (bond); *Clugas v Penaluna* (1791) 4 T.R. 466 (bill of exchange; as to the rights of a holder in due course, see below, para.15–046); *Taylor v Chester* (1869) L.R. 4 Q.B. 309 (pledge). Contrast *Sharif v Azad* [1967] 1 Q.B. 605; as explained in *Mansouri v Singh* [1986] 1 W.L.R. 1393.

563 See para.3–161.

underlying contract of sale is prohibited by statute.[565] But if it is the collateral transaction which is illegal, it does not follow that this illegality infects the otherwise lawful principal contract. Thus where an illegal security was in good faith taken to secure the performance of a legal agreement that agreement was not thereby invalidated.[566]

A contract is not necessarily illegal merely because one of the parties to it is also a party to an illegal contract which is remotely connected with the first. Thus a policy of marine insurance on a voyage is not illegal merely because the master has incurred statutory penalties through failing to make the service contracts with his crew in proper form;[567] a policy of insurance on goods is not illegal merely because, in the course of acquiring the goods, the insured had committed a violation of a foreign revenue law;[568] nor is a promise by one solicitor to pay another's charges in respect of a particular transaction illegal merely because the latter solicitor's client intended (without that solicitor's knowledge) to use the transaction in question as a vehicle of fraud.[569] In such cases, the first contract is illegal only if its object was to assist one of the parties in achieving the unlawful purpose under the second contract.[570]

## (e) Evaluation

11–108 **A rule-based approach.** In *Patel v Mirza* Lord Sumption appeared to favour not only a rule-based approach, but the application of one master rule in the form of the reliance test.[571] As he acknowledged, while this may work reasonably well in a property case (and in a tort case), at least after his reformulation of the test to avoid the potentially arbitrary consequences of *Tinsley v Milligan*,[572] in a contract case "the position is less straightforward."[573] His formulation that the claimant "must rely on a contract which is in fact illegal"[574] begs as many questions as it answers and is then subject to a number of exceptions which are somewhat open textured.[575] It may be possible to apply the reliance test alongside other rules which may be extrapolated from the cases, particularly on enforcement. Two suggestions are:

---

564 See para.11–161.

565 *The American Accord* [1983] 1 A.C. 168 (where the sale was not illegal but only unenforceable under the Bretton Woods Agreement Act 1945); *Group Josi Re v Walbrook Ins Co Ltd* [1996] 1 Lloyd's Rep. 345 at 363–364. A cheque given in pursuance of such a transaction is likewise unenforceable between the parties to the transaction: *Mansouri v Singh* [1986] 1 W.L.R. 1393.

566 *South Western Mineral Water Co Ltd v Ashmore* [1967] 1 W.L.R. 1110; cf. *Carney v Herbert* [1985] A.C. 301; para.11–168; cf. the position in relation to otherwise lawful contracts obtained by bribery; para.11–058.

567 *Redmond v Smith* (1844) 7 Man. & G. 457.

568 *Euro-Diam Ltd v Bathurst* [1990] Q.B. 1; the violation of the foreign law did not benefit the insured but only benefited his supplier; Clarke [1988] L.M.C.L.Q. 124; Tan 104 L.Q.R. 523; Tettenborn [1988] C.L.J. 338.

569 *Rooks Rider v Steel* [1994] 1 W.L.R. 818.

570 See *Re Trepca Mines Ltd* [1963] Ch. 199; A.L.G. 79 L.Q.R. 49; cf. [1974] 6 C.L. 266.

571 See para.11–066.

572 See para.11–103.

573 *Patel v Mirza* [2016] UKSC 42; [2017] A.C. 467 at [235].

574 *Patel v Mirza* [2016] UKSC 42; [2017] A.C. 467 at [235].

575 See para.11–067.

> "*Rule 1:* A contract which has as its purpose, or is intended to be performed in a manner that involves, conduct that is illegal (such as a crime) or contrary to public policy ... is unenforceable (b) by either party if both parties knew of that purpose or intention; or (b) by one party if only that party knew of that purpose or intention.
>
> *Rule 2*: If rule 1 is inapplicable because it is only the performance of a contract that involves conduct that is illegal or contrary to public policy, the contract is unenforceable by the party who performed in that objectionable way but is enforceable by the other party unless that party knew of, and participated in that objectionable performance."[576]

The difficulty, however, with any rule-based approach is that it is almost impossible to formulate a rule, or rules, which can cater for the "infinite possible variety of cases".[577] By way of just two examples: under Rule 1, there is no room to consider the proportionality of the defence in cases where the illegality may have been incidental and/or trivial and the consequences for the claim drastic, as for example in *ParkingEye Ltd v Somerfield Stores Ltd*;[578] a similar comment may be made in relation to Rule 2 and this may explain why it is contradicted by the outcome in cases like *St John Shipping Corp v Joseph Rank Ltd*.[579]

**Range of factors.** Perhaps the first criticism which may be made of the shift to a range of factors test in *Patel v Mirza* is that it amounts to judicial legislation but, as Lord Toulson observed, it is the "responsibility of the courts for dealing with defects in the common law".[580] It was also, to some extent, invited by the Law Commission which favoured a broader policy based approach. It concluded that the defence of illegality should not be made the subject of legislation on the basis that: 11–109

> "(t)he recent case law[581] shows that the courts have become more open in explaining the policy reasons behind the illegality defence. Therefore, in most areas of law, we think that the illegality defence should be left to developments in the common law".[582]

More importantly, the range of factors test is open to the criticism that it makes the law less certain. Lord Sumption had, for example, already criticised it as relegating the defence of illegality from a "rule of law" based on public policy to a "mere discretionary power" based on "the perceived balance of merits between the parties to any particular dispute",[583] a criticism which is repeated in *Patel v Mirza*.[584] Other judges have defended it against such criticism[585] and, if it does

576 Burrows, *Restatement of the English Law of Contract* (2016), p.225.
577 *Patel v Mirza* [2016] UKSC 42; [2017] A.C. 467 at [107] (Lord Toulson).
578 [2012] EWCA Civ 1138; [2013] Q.B. 840; para.11–075.
579 [1957] 1 Q.B. 267; para.11–019. Lord Sumption regarded this case as an example of his second exception to the reliance test: para.11–067.
580 *Patel v Mirza* [2016] UKSC 42; [2017] A.C. 467 at [114].
581 Specific reference is made to: *Gray v Thames Trains Ltd* [2009] UKHL 33; [2009] 1 A.C. 1339; *Stone & Rolls Ltd v Moore Stephens* [2009] UKHL 39; [2009] 1 A.C. 1391; *Nayyar v Denton Wilde Sapte* [2009] EWHC 3218 (QB); [2010] P.N.L.R. 15; and *Lincoln v CB Richard Ellis Hotels Ltd* [2009] EWHC 2344 (TCC); [2009] B.L.R. 591.
582 Law Com No.328, para.1.8.
583 *Les Laboratoires Servier v Apotex Inc* [2014] UKSC 55; [2014] 3 W.L.R. 1257 at [11].
584 *Patel v Mirza* [2016] UKSC 42; [2017] A.C. 467 at [192] (Lord Mance), [261] (Lord Sumption).
585 *ParkingEye Ltd v Somerfield Stores Ltd* [2012] EWCA Civ 1338; [2013] Q.B. 840 at [39] (Sir Robin Jacob); cf. *Patel v Mirza* [2016] UKSC 42; [2017] A.C. 467 at [123] (Lord Kerr), [175] (Lord Neuberger: "a structured approach"). Any consideration of the merits is not as "between the parties".

represent a different approach, the difference is one of emphasis given the open textured nature of the rule, or rules of law, and their exceptions. As Lord Sumption explained in *Patel v Mirza*:

> "The real issue … is whether the "range of factors" … are to be regarded (i) as part of the policy rationale of a legal rule and the various exceptions to that rule, or (ii) as matters to be taken into account by a judge deciding in each case whether to apply the legal rule at all."[586]

At the very least, this implies that the range of factors test is not intended to result in markedly different outcomes in individual cases. This is significant because Lord Sumption also referred to the reliance test as the "narrowest" available and his concern was that a more discretionary approach would "widen the application of the defence".[587] A widening of the defence is certainly not implied by the tenor of the speeches of Lord Toulson and Lord Kerr in *Patel v Mirza*. The charge of uncertainty might be addressed by emphasising what appears to be the most important of the "trio of necessary considerations" which should primarily be taken into account; namely "to consider the underlying purpose of the prohibition which has been transgressed and whether that purpose will be enhanced by denial of the claim".[588] This is the most significant factor for any legal system which aims to be consistent. It is noticeable that what seems to have particularly concerned Lord Sumption was the consideration of "proportionality" and questions such as "how illegal is illegality", with the risk of different answers from different judges.[589] But a version of this question has to be asked as part of the rule-based approach[590] and it is included as one of the trio of necessary considerations primarily to cater for those cases where the illegality is relatively minor and to allow the defence would be disproportionate, as in *ParkingEye Ltd v Somerfield Stores Ltd*.[591] Some emphasis might also be put on whether the claimant is attempting to "profit" from his illegal act.[592] This obviously begs the question of what is meant by "profit",[593] but it explains why the general rule is that an illegal contract will not be *enforced*,[594] while the general rule is that it may be *undone* via a claim in restitution.[595] Ultimately, some form of discretion seems inevitable and it is better that this is openly acknowledged by the courts, while endeavouring nonetheless to provide as much guidance as possible as to the

Since, by definition, A must have shown that he has a claim against B before the defence of illegality comes into play, what needs to be balanced is the private interest of A in allowing his claim against the public interest of consistency in the legal system.

586 *Patel v Mirza* [2016] UKSC 42; [2017] A.C. 467 at [261].

587 *Patel v Mirza* [2016] UKSC 42; [2017] A.C. 467 at [239].

588 *Patel v Mirza* [2016] UKSC 42; [2017] A.C. 467 at [101], [120] (Lord Toulson).

589 *Patel v Mirza* [2016] UKSC 42; [2017] A.C. 467 at [263].

590 See para.11–026; cf. *Les Laboratoires Servier v Apotex Inc* [2014] UKSC 55; [2014] 3 W.L.R. 1257 at [29] (Lord Sumption: "there may be exceptional cases where even criminal and quasi-criminal acts will not constitute turpitude for the purposes of the illegality defence").

591 [2012] EWCA Civ 1338; [2013] Q.B. 840; para.11–075.

592 cf. *Hall v Hebert* [1993] 2 S.C.R.159; *Hounga v Allen* 2014] UKSC 47; [2014] 1 W.L.R. 2889 at [44] (Lord Wilson); *Patel v Mirza* [2016] UKSC 42; [2017] A.C. 467 at [99] (Lord Toulson); [143] (Lord Kerr).

593 *Patel v Mirza* [2016] UKSC 42; [2017] A.C. 467 at [100] (Lord Toulson).

594 See para.11–069.

595 See para.11–089; *Patel v Mirza* [2016] UKSC 42; [2017] A.C. 467 at [115] (Lord Toulson: "Mr Patel is seeking to unwind the arrangement, not to profit from it"), [203] (Lord Mance).

outcome in future cases. As has been said by Lord Hoffmann, in the context of a tort case, the maxim ex turpi causa[596] "expresses not so much a principle as a policy" and that "policy is not based upon a single justification but on a group of reasons, which vary in different situations."[597]

**Illustrations of the new approach in practice.**[598] *Patel v Mirza* was concerned with a claim in unjust enrichment and the Supreme Court was unanimous in its decision that it should be allowed, regardless of the test applied.[599] For an illustration of the new test in practice where the claim was to enforce the contract, one might briefly consider *Harb v Aziz*.[600] A claimed that she was promised a significant sum of money and the transfer of two flats by B in exchange for agreeing to withdraw certain factual assertions about B's father which were damaging to his reputation. A's subsequent withdrawal by way of a statutory declaration meant that she committed the offence of perjury under s.5(a) of the Perjury Act 1911. The agreement was found to be unenforceable in any event either because of the lack of any intention to create legal relations, or because it was too uncertain, but had it overcome these obstacles, Arnold J held that A's claim would not have been barred by the defence of illegality. He invoked the "trio of necessary considerations" referred to by Lord Toulson in *Patel v Mirza* and held, as follows: (a) the purpose of s.5(a) of the 1911 Act is to ensure that statutory declarations are truthful and this is an important purpose; (b) the two relevant public policies which would be rendered less effective by denying A's claim were the general policy that contracts should be enforced (which will always, by definition, be relevant in a claim for enforcement) and the policy of favouring settlement out of court;[601] and (c) to allow the defence would be disproportionate, particularly as B was "nearly as culpable" as A because he demanded that A retract allegations which B knew A had sworn to be true in an earlier affidavit. 11–110

A further illustration is provided by *Stoffel & Co v Grondona*.[602] In that case B transferred the leasehold interest in a property to A who obtained a mortgage, ostensibly to fund the purchase but as part of a fraudulent conspiracy to obtain finance for B by misrepresentation. A's solicitors should have registered A's interest in the property and the mortgage and removed a charge in relation to B's previous mortgage, but in breach of their retainer failed to do so, allowing B to raise further finance, causing loss to A. At first instance, before *Patel v Mirza* had

596 *Ex turpi causa non oritur actio* (no action arises from a disgraceful cause).

597 *Gray v Thames Trains Ltd* [2009] UKHL 33; [2009] 1 A.C. 1339 at [30]; para.11–023.

598 In addition to the decisions referred to in the text, see also: *XX v Whittington Hospital NHS Trust* [2018] EWCA Civ 2832; [2019] Med. L.R. 99 (negligence claim); *Iranian Offshore Engineering & Construction Co v Dean Investment Holdings SA* [2019] EWHC 472 (Comm) at [189]–[198].

599 See also *Kliers v Schmerler* [2018] EWHC 1350 (Ch) where undoing the transactions entered into furthered the purpose of the rules infringed and the claimant's participation had been procured by undue influence.

600 [2018] EWHC 508 (Ch).

601 *Harb v Aziz* [2018] EWHC 508 (Ch) at [227] ("It would be very unfortunate if the enforcement of settlements could be prevented merely because one party had withdrawn an allegation it believed to be true. On the other hand, there are ways in which an allegation can be withdrawn without the party withdrawing it falsely swearing to its falsity.")

602 [2018] EWCA Civ 2031; [2018] P.N.L.R. 36.

been decided in the Supreme Court, the court allowed A's claim against the solicitors on the basis that she did not have to rely on the illegal contract between her and B to make good the claim against the solicitors; it was irrelevant how she acquired the interest which the solicitors had failed to register. After *Patel v Mirza*, that decision could no longer be based on *Tinsley v Milligan*, but it was upheld by the Court of Appeal under the range of factors test. As to the first of the "trio of necessary considerations", it was questionable that mortgage fraud was more likely to be deterred by denying the claim against the solicitors than by allowing it.[603] As to the second, there was a "a genuine public interest in ensuring that clients who use the services of solicitors are entitled to seek civil remedies for negligence [or] breach of contract … arising from a legitimate and lawful retainer which was entered into between them, in circumstances where the client was not seeking to profit[604] or gain from her mortgage fraud, but merely to ensure that that the chargee's security was adequately protected by registration."[605] As to the third, it would "be entirely disproportionate" to deny A's claim given a number of factors, including that A was not seeking to evade her obligations under the new mortgage and that her illegal conduct was "not central" to the contract of retainer with the solicitors.[606]

11–111 **Nature of an appeal.** One consequence of the shift to a range of factors test is that the prospects for a successful appeal may be more limited.[607] The appellate courts are slow to interfere with a discretionary decision[608] and this seems likely to be the approach taken in relation to the range of factors test. Thus, in *Singularis Holdings Ltd v Daiwa Capital Markets Europe Ltd*[609] Vos LJ adopted the following approach:

> "… an appellate court should not interfere merely because it would have taken a different view had it been undertaking the evaluation. The test involves balancing multiple policy considerations and applying a proportionality approach. Accordingly, an appellate court should only interfere if the first instance judge has proceeded on an erroneous legal basis, taken into account matters that were legally irrelevant, or failed to take into account matters that were legally relevant. That would be the approach in any other situation where proportionality was in issue on an appeal and should, therefore, be the case here."[610]

---

603 *Stoffel & Co v Grondona* [2018] EWCA Civ 2031; [2018] P.N.L.R. 36 at [37].

604 See text to fn.595. A had agreed with B to share any profits on the sale of the property, but it was no part of her claim against the solicitors to enforce that entitlement; she was seeking only the funds she would have been entitled to had her interest been registered to reduce or discharge the new mortgage.

605 *Stoffel & Co v Grondona* [2018] EWCA Civ 2031; [2018] P.N.L.R. 36 at [38].

606 *Stoffel & Co v Grondona* [2018] EWCA Civ 2031; [2018] P.N.L.R. 36 at [39].

607 Goudkamp 133 L.Q.R. 14.

608 See, e.g. *Jackson v Murray* [2015] UKSC 5; [2015] 2 All E.R. 805 at [28].

609 [2018] EWCA Civ 84; [2018] 1 W.L.R. 2777. The defence of illegality failed because the illegal conduct of a company agent was not attributed to the claimant company (para.11–024) but the judge at first instance applied the "*Patel v Mirza* test" on the assumption that it had been.

610 *Singularis Holdings Ltd v Daiwa Capital Markets Europe Ltd* [2018] EWCA Civ 84; [2018] 1 W.L.R. 2777 at [65].

## 4. CONTRACTS IN RESTRAINT OF TRADE[611]

### (a) Introduction

Contracts which prevent or regulate business competition were at one time regarded as invariably void;[612] and persons who made them were even threatened with imprisonment.[613] But it came to be recognised that this inflexible attitude might defeat its own ends. A master might be reluctant to employ and train apprentices if he could not to some extent restrain them from competing with him after the end of their apprenticeship. And a trader might be unable to sell the business he had built up if he could not bind himself not to compete with the purchaser. The courts therefore began to uphold contracts in restraint of trade, and in 1711 the subject was reviewed in *Mitchel v Reynolds*.[614] The effect of that case, as interpreted in later decisions, was that a restraint was prima facie valid if it was supported by adequate consideration and was not general, i.e. did not extend over the whole Kingdom. 11–112

**Summary of the present position.** Since then, the law has changed in three respects. First, restraints are no longer prima facie valid; they are prima facie void, but can be justified if they are reasonable and not contrary to the public interest.[615] Secondly, it is no longer essential that the consideration should be adequate,[616] "though … the quantum of consideration may enter into the question of the reasonableness of the agreement".[617] Thirdly, the rule that a restraint must not be general no longer applies. In *Nordenfelt v Maxim Nordenfelt Guns & Ammunition Co*[618] the owner of an armaments business sold it to a company and covenanted not to carry on such a business for 25 years except on behalf of the company. The covenant was held valid although it prevented competition anywhere in the world. 11–113

**Time for determining validity.** Most authorities support the view that the question whether a restraint is valid must be determined once and for all by reference to the circumstances in existence when the contract was made.[619] The view that a restraint which satisfies the tests of validity at that time may become invalid or unenforceable in the light of subsequent events[620] has been generally rejected as it would give rise to an unacceptable degree of uncertainty. 11–114

---

611 Heydon, *The Restraint of Trade Doctrine*, 4th edn (2018).

612 *Claygate v Batchelor* (1602) Owen 143.

613 *Dyer's Case* (1414) Y.B. 2 Hen. V, Pasch. pl. 26.

614 (1711) 1 P. Wms. 181.

615 See paras 11–125–11–130.

616 *Tallis v Tallis* (1853) 1 E. & B. 391.

617 [1894] A.C. 535 at 565; *Esso Petroleum Ltd v Harper's Garage (Stourport) Ltd* [1968] A.C. 269 at 318, 323; *Alec Lobb (Garages) Ltd v Total Oil (Great Britain) Ltd* [1985] 1 W.L.R. 173 at 179.

618 [1894] A.C. 535.

619 See, e.g. *Commercial Plastics Ltd v Vincent* [1965] 1 Q.B. 623 at 644 (citing earlier authorities); *A Schroeder Music Publishing Co Ltd v Macaulay* [1974] 1 W.L.R. 1308 at 1309; *Shell UK Ltd v Lostock Garage Ltd* [1976] 1 W.L.R. 1187 at 1203; *Proactive Sports Management Ltd v Rooney* [2011] EWCA Civ 1444; [2012] I.R.L.R. 241 at [149]: see para.11–145.

620 *Shell UK Ltd v Lostock Garage Ltd* [1976] W.L.R. 1187 at 1198.

11–115 **Categories.** Agreements which have been held to be within the doctrine of restraint of trade can be divided into a number of groups or categories which will be discussed below. We shall see that some agreements which are, or may be, within the doctrine do not fall readily within any of these categories; and that other agreements which can in a sense be said to restrain trade are not within the doctrine at all, and are therefore not subject to the conditions on which the validity of covenants in restraint of trade depends.[621]

11–116 **Competition law.** Our main concern is with the common law rules on this topic. As we will see, the common law relating to restrictive trading agreements[622] gives only limited protection to third parties who might be adversely affected by the willingness of the parties to such agreements to give effect to them. A more comprehensive attack on this problem has, since 1956,[623] been made by legislation. The relevant rules are now contained in the Competition Act 1998.[624] It is beyond the scope of this book to give an account of the 1998 Act or the EU law[625] which applies in this area.[626] The common law rules operate alongside the legislative prohibitions on anti-competitive practices, so that it is perfectly possible for an agreement to fall outside those prohibitions but nevertheless to be invalid for restraint of trade at common law. This is because the purpose of the two sets of rules is different: the legislative prohibitions are concerned with the effect of agreements (etc.) on the economy as a whole, while under the common law rules an agreement may be void by reason of its adverse effect merely on the party restrained by it.

## (b) Sale of a business and employment

11–117 In this group of cases, a covenant in restraint of trade is invalid unless three conditions are satisfied: there must be an interest meriting protection;[627] the restraint must be reasonable;[628] and it must not be contrary to the public interest.[629]

### *(i) Interest*

11–118 **Interest must arise from the relationship of the parties.** The interest meriting protection must arise from the relationship of the parties as buyer and seller or as employer and employee. In the absence of such a relationship, freedom from

621 See para.11–153.
622 See para.11–141.
623 When the first of the Restrictive Trade Practices Acts (now repealed) was passed.
624 Chapter I of Pt 1 prohibits a number of anti-competitive practices; Ch.II of Pt 1 prohibits the abuse of a "dominant position".
625 See, in particular, arts 101–102 of the Treaty on the Functioning of the European Union ("TFEU").
626 See, e.g. Bellamy and Child, *European Community Law of Competition*, 8th edn (2018).
627 See paras 11–118—11–124.
628 See paras 11–125—11–130.
629 See paras 11–131—11–133.

ordinary trade competition is not, of itself, an interest meriting protection.[630] Thus a bare promise to a shopkeeper not to open (or work for) a competing business would be void; such a promise is known as a covenant in gross. Normally the covenant must be contained in a contract of sale or employment, but this is not absolutely necessary. It is enough if the covenant is closely related to such a contract, e.g. if it is contained in a contract made (shortly after the termination of an employment contract) to settle outstanding differences.[631]

**Sale of a business.** Even in the absence of a covenant in restraint of trade, the purchaser of the goodwill of a business can restrain the vendor from canvassing the old customers of the business.[632] This rule would not prevent the vendor from competing in other ways (e.g. from dealing with his old customers if they spontaneously came to him); but the purchaser can validly stipulate against such competition by a covenant in restraint of trade. His right to do so is said to depend on his "proprietary interest" in the goodwill of the business which he has bought.[633] **11–119**

It follows that the purchaser is entitled to protection only in respect of the business which he has bought, and not in respect of some other business which he already carries on or may carry on in the future. If a company which owns shops in all parts of the country buys a village shop it can restrain the seller from competing in or near that village, but not at other places where it happens to carry on business.[634] Similarly, in the *Nordenfelt* case[635] the covenant restrained the seller from engaging not only in the manufacture of armaments but also "in any other business competing or liable to compete with that for the time being carried on by" the buyer. The latter part of the covenant was invalid. Its effect would be to restrain the seller from competing with the company if it started to make ploughshares; and he had sold no such business.[636] But a person who buys a business which is about to expand may be able to take a covenant against competition covering the area of the proposed expansion.[637] And the rule that the buyer can restrain the seller from competing only with the business formerly carried on by the seller is subject to a common-sense exception. A person who sells shares in a company which he controls may covenant not to compete in respect of the business carried on by *the company*. Such a covenant may be valid if it was in substance the seller who, through his control of the company, carried on the business:[638] and even a seller of a minority shareholding can validly covenant with the buyer not to use confidential information which relates to the

---

[630] cf. *Vancouver Malt & Sake Brewing Co v Vancouver Breweries Ltd* [1934] A.C. 181.
[631] *Stenhouse Australia Ltd v Phillips* [1974] A.C. 391.
[632] *Trego v Hunt* [1896] A.C. 7.
[633] There can be such an interest even though the goodwill is inalienable: see *Whitehill v Bradford* [1952] Ch. 236; *Kerr v Morris* [1987] Ch. 90; and even though the interest is not purely financial: cf. in an analogous context, *Young v Evans-Jones* [2001] EWCA Civ 732; [2001] 1 P. & C.R. 176.
[634] cf. *British Reinforced Concrete Engineering Co Ltd v Schelff* [1921] 2 Ch. 563.
[635] *Nordenfelt v Maxim Nordenfelt Guns & Ammunition Co* [1894] A.C. 535.
[636] cf. (between employer and employee) *Scully UK Ltd v Lee* [1998] I.R.L.R. 259.
[637] *Lamson Pneumatic Tube Co v Phillips* (1904) 91 L.T. 363; *TSC Europe (UK) Ltd v Massey* [1999] I.R.L.R. 22 at 27–28.
[638] *Connors Bros v Connors Ltd* [1940] 4 All E.R. 179; cf. *Kirby (Inspector of Taxes) v Thorn EMI* [1988] 1 W.L.R. 445 (covenant on sale by company of shares in its subsidiary).

business of the company.[639] If, however, the *business* carried on by a company (as opposed to the *shares* in it) is sold, it may be hard to frame a suitable covenant to protect the buyer from competition by associated companies.[640]

11–120 **Employment.**[641] Even in the absence of a covenant in restraint of trade, the law gives an employer some degree of protection against his employee. He can restrain the employee from: (i) using or disclosing trade secrets; (ii) using or disclosing confidential information falling short of a trade secret,[642] except where disclosure would be in the public interest;[643] and (iii) soliciting the employer's customers. The restriction on the use or disclosure of trade secrets applies at any time;[644] that on the solicitation of customers applies only to solicitation during the period of employment;[645] while that relating to confidential information occupies an intermediate position. It is normally limited to the employee's conduct during employment;[646] but it can extend beyond that period, e.g. where, on leaving his job, the employee takes away, copies or memorises lists of the employer's trade connections.[647] He can then be restrained from using such information for his own benefit (or for that of a third party) for so long as such use would give him (or the third party) an unfair competitive advantage over the employer.[648] A similar restriction may be imposed where the employee *sells* such information, as opposed to using it to earn his living.[649] Certain confidential information acquired by employees in the public service is also subject to a lifelong duty of confidentiality.[650] All these rights of the employer are once again said to constitute "proprietary interests" which the employer is entitled to protect

639 *Systems Reliability Holdings v Smith* [1990] I.R.L.R. 377.

640 See *Doyle v Olby (Ironmongers) Ltd* [1969] 2 Q.B. 158.

641 The following principles may also be applied, by analogy, to the restraint of an agent, against whom it has been said to be "unlikely" that he should have more onerous covenants upheld: *BCM Group Plc v Visualmark Ltd* [2006] EWHC 1831 (QB).

642 See at fn.647.

643 e.g. where the employer has been guilty of misconduct which ought to be disclosed: *Initial Services Ltd v Putterill* [1968] 1 Q.B. 396; cf. *Malone v Metropolitan Police Commissioner* [1979] Ch. 344 at 361–362; *British Steel Corp v Granada Television Ltd* [1981] A.C. 1096 at 1168, 1177, 1201; *Attorney General v Guardian Newspapers Ltd (No.2)* [1990] A.C. 109 at 268. Contrast *Distillers Co Ltd v Times Newspapers Ltd* [1976] Q.B. 613; *Schering Chemicals Ltd v Falkman Ltd* [1982] Q.B. 1; *Re Barlow Clowes Gilt Managers Ltd* [1992] Ch. 208.

644 *Printers & Finishers Ltd v Holloway* [1965] 1 W.L.R. 1; *Faccenda Chicken Ltd v Fowler* [1987] Ch. 117 at 136; *Berkeley Administration v McClelland* [1990] F.S.R. 565; cf. *Attorney General v Barker* [1990] 3 All E.R. 257; *Poly Lina Ltd v Finch* [1995] F.S.R. 751.

645 *Wessex Dairies Ltd v Smith* [1935] 2 K.B. 60; cf. *Wallace Bogan & Co v Cove* [1997] I.R.L.R. 453. If the solicitation occurs during employment it is irrelevant that the actual contract with the customers is made thereafter: *Sanders v Parry* [1967] 1 W.L.R. 753.

646 cf. *Murray v Yorkshire Food Managers Ltd* [1998] 1 W.L.R. 951.

647 *Faccenda Chicken Ltd v Fowler* [1987] Ch. 117 at 139; cf. *Johnson & Blay (Holdings) Ltd v Wolstenholme Rink Plc* [1989] F.S.R. 135; *Universal Thermosensors Ltd v Hibden* [1992] 1 W.L.R. 840 at 850.

648 *Roger Bullivant Ltd v Ellis* [1987] I.C.R. 464. The "springboard relief" provided by this decision is not confined to the misuse of confidential information: *UBS Wealth Management UK Ltd v Vestra Wealth LLP* [2008] EWHC 1974 (QB); [2008] I.R.L.R. 965.

649 *Faccenda Chicken Ltd v Fowler* [1987] Ch. 117 at 139.

650 *Attorney General v Guardian Newspapers (No.2)* [1990] A.C. 109 at 264, 284; *Lord Advocate v Scotsman Publications Ltd* [1990] 1 A.C. 812 at 821. Contrast *Attorney General v Blake* [1998] Ch. 439 at 454–455 where the information was no longer confidential and an injunction to restrain its use

by a covenant in restraint of trade; and such a covenant may (as in the cases between vendor and purchaser) afford somewhat greater protection[651] than that provided by law in the absence of a covenant. But the employer cannot justify a covenant in restraint of trade simply on the ground that the covenant would protect the business in which the employee has worked.

**Contrast with sale of business.** It will be seen from the above that the interest meriting protection is more narrowly defined between employer and employee than between buyer and seller,[652] and two reasons have been given for this distinction. First, buyer and seller may bargain on a more equal footing than employer and employee. The courts certainly attach importance to disparity of bargaining power in restraint of trade cases.[653] But this factor would scarcely be significant where the terms of employment were settled between an employer and a powerful trade union, or where the restraint was undertaken by a company director who, though technically an employee, was by no means in a weak bargaining position.[654] In such cases, it is better to fall back on the second justification for the distinction between the two types of contract. The buyer of a business pays for freedom from competition and would lose part of what he paid for if the seller began to compete with him.[655] An employer pays for his employee's services and would not be deprived of what he paid for if the employee competed with him after leaving his service. 11–121

**Limits to an employer's protectable interest.** Unlike the purchaser of a business, an employer cannot protect himself by a covenant in restraint of trade against his former employee's competition as such. He cannot restrain the employee from using his own skill even though that skill was learnt from the employer.[656] To establish that he has an interest meriting protection, the employer must show *either* that the employee has learnt the employer's trade secrets, *or* that he has acquired influence over the employer's clients or customers.[657] Trade secrets include secret formulae or processes, and certain other similar kinds of highly confidential information[658] (but not information which is merely confidential in the sense that the employee must not disclose it during 11–122

was said to be an unjustifiable restraint of trade; in the House of Lords, the defendant was held liable for breach of his *express* promise not to disclose the information: [2001] 1 A.C. 268; para.20–011.

651 See *Attorney General v Blake* [1998] Ch. 439.

652 *Mason v Provident Clothing & Supply Co* [1913] A.C. 724; *Bridge v Deacons* [1984] A.C. 705 at 713; *Systems Reliability Holdings v Smith* [1990] I.R.L.R. 377.

653 *A Schroeder Music Publishing Co Ltd v Macaulay* [1974] 1 W.L.R. 1308; *Clifford Davies Management v WEA Records Ltd* [1975] 1 W.L.R. 61; para.11–079.

654 "A managing director can look after himself": *M & S Drapers v Reynolds* [1957] 1 W.L.R. 9 at 19.

655 *Attwood v Lamont* [1920] 3 K.B. 571 at 590; cf. *Herbert Morris Ltd v Saxelby* [1916] 1 A.C. 688 at 701.

656 *Herbert Morris Ltd v Saxelby* [1916] 1 A.C. 688; cf. *Eastes v Russ* [1914] 1 Ch. 468; *Faccenda Chicken Ltd v Fowler* [1987] Ch. 117 at 137.

657 Where the employer is a holding company with no clients of its own, it may still have the necessary interest as a result of the business carried out by its subsidiaries: *Beckett Investment Management Group Ltd v Hall* [2007] EWCA Civ 613; [2007] I.C.R. 1539 at [23].

658 *Caribonum Co Ltd v Le Couch* (1913) 109 L.T. 587; cf. *The Littlewoods Organisation Ltd v Harris* [1977] 1 W.L.R. 1472. And see *Lansing Linde Ltd v Kerr* [1991] 1 W.L.R. 251 at 259, 268, 270; *Balston v Headline Filters* [1990] F.S.R. 385 at 417.

employment).[659] It used to be thought that "know-how" could not be protected[660] but now that such expertise has become a saleable commodity[661] it is likely that the courts will recognise it as an interest meriting protection.[662] In respect of clients or customers, the employer is entitled to protection only if the nature of the employment was such as to enable the employee to acquire influence over them,[663] e.g. where the employee was a solicitor's managing clerk,[664] or a hairdresser's assistant[665] but not where he was a factory worker who never came into contact with customers. If the employee comes into contact with some customers, the employer may be able to protect himself also in respect of some others.[666]

11–123 **Commercial interests.** The question whether there is any other interest which an employer can protect by a covenant in restraint of trade was raised in *Eastham v Newcastle United Football Club Ltd.*[667] The defendant club employed a professional footballer subject to the "retain and transfer" system.[668] Under that system, a player who was "retained"[669] by one club could not be employed by another; nor could he be transferred to another club without the consent of both clubs. The defendant club could not claim that this system protected either of the two traditional interests. But Wilberforce J said that "it would be wrong to pass straight to the conclusion that no … interest … exists".[670] He considered other possible interests, such as the danger that, but for the "retain and transfer" system, all the best players might go to the richest clubs. He found that such consequences would not in fact follow if the system were abandoned;[671] that there was thus no interest to be protected; and that the system was invalid. But his approach suggests that interests other than the traditional ones might be entitled to protection. A covenant by a film actor not to appear on the stage for three months, made with the object of furthering the success of a new film,[672] might be enforceable even though it did not protect either of the orthodox interests. Such new interests would differ from the traditional ones in that they would be protected *only* if there was a covenant, while the traditional ones are to some extent protected even if there is no covenant. For this reason the new interests may be called "commercial" rather than "proprietary" ones; and we shall see that

---

659 *Faccenda Chicken Ltd v Fowler* [1987] Ch. 117 at 136; *Brooks v Olyslager Oms (UK) Ltd* [1998] I.R.L.R. 590; *Intelsec Systems Ltd v Grech-Cini* [2000] 1 W.L.R. 1190.

660 *Herbert Morris Ltd v Saxelby* [1916] 1 A.C. 688; *Sir WC Leng & Co v Andrews* [1909] 1 Ch. 763 at 768.

661 Blanco White 15 Conv. 89; 26 Conv. 366.

662 cf. *Commercial Plastics Ltd v Vincent* [1965] 1 Q.B. 623 at 642.

663 *Faccenda Chicken Ltd v Fowler* [1987] Ch. 117 at 137.

664 *Fitch v Dewes* [1921] 2 A.C. 158; para.11–127.

665 *Marion White Ltd v Francis* [1972] 1 W.L.R. 1423.

666 *GW Plowman & Son Ltd v Ash* [1964] 1 W.L.R. 568; and see para.11–126.

667 [1964] Ch. 413; cf. *Greig v Insole* [1978] 1 W.L.R. 302.

668 See further at fn.775.

669 A player could be "retained" by giving him notice and paying him a reasonable wage (determined, in case of dispute, by the Football Association).

670 *Eastham v Newcastle United Football Club Ltd* [1964] Ch. 413.

671 Subsequent events would appear to have proved him wrong.

672 For this practice, see *Higgs v Olivier* [1951] Ch. 899; cf. *Vaughan-Neil v IRC* [1979] 1 W.L.R. 1283 (covenant by a barrister, on becoming an employee of a company, not to practise at the Bar).

in some categories of contracts in restraint of trade the law now recognises that such commercial interests may be protected by covenants.[673] It is possible that this recognition will help to modify the strict insistence on the need for a "proprietary" interest in cases between vendor and purchaser, and between employer and employee. The mere goodwill of a company, however, is not a legitimate interest capable of protection by a restriction on a former employee.[674]

**Other cases.** The distinction between vendor-purchaser and employer-employee covenants is by no means exhaustive. Thus a covenant by a retiring doctor or solicitor not to compete with his former partners does not fall precisely into either category;[675] but the courts do not subject it to the strict tests of validity that they apply to employer-employee covenants.[676] A covenant by a writer or composer not to dispose of his work except to a particular publisher may for present purposes be treated in the same way as an employer-employee covenant, even though there was never any contract of employment between the parties.[677] A person may sell his business to a company of which he then becomes managing director. It seems that a covenant by such a person not to compete should be treated in the same way as a vendor-purchaser covenant, whether it is contained in the sale agreement or in the service agreement[678] or in both.[679] Similarly, the restraints on an ex-franchisee are assessed in much the same ways as those on a vendor, in order to protect the goodwill of the business to be made available to the new franchisee.[680] 11–124

### *(ii) Reasonableness*

A restraint is valid only if it goes no further than is reasonably necessary for the protection of the covenantee's interest. Reasonableness is determined by looking at the relationship between that interest and the covenant.[681] 11–125

**Area covenants and solicitation covenants.** To be reasonable, the restraint need not be precisely co-terminous with the interest.[682] If there were such a requirement, there would be little point in taking a covenant, since a "proprietary 11–126

---

673 See paras 11–138, 11–147.

674 *Countrywide Assured Financial Services Ltd v Smart* [2004] EWHC 1214 (Ch).

675 *Bridge v Deacons* [1984] A.C. 705 at 714.

676 *Whitehill v Bradford* [1952] Ch. 236; *Espley v Williams* [1997] 1 E.G.L.R. 9; contra, *Jenkins v Reid* [1948] 1 All E.R. 471—but the defendant's covenant seems to have been "in gross".

677 See *A Schroeder Music Publishing Co Ltd v Macaulay* [1974] 1 W.L.R. 1308.

678 See *Silverman Ltd v Silverman, The Times*, 7 July 1969; cf. *Blake v Blake* (1967) 111 S.J. 715 (restraints imposed, on dissolution of a company, on its major shareholders: these were treated in the same way as vendor-purchaser covenants); *Allied Dunbar (Frank Weisinger) Ltd v Frank Weisinger* [1988] I.R.L.R. 60; *Alliance Property Group Plc v Prestwich* [1995] I.R.L.R. 25; *Dawnay Day & Co v D'Alphen* [1997] I.R.L.R. 442 (so far as it relates to the service agreement).

679 *T & C Europe (UK) Ltd v Massey* [1999] I.R.L.R. 22 at 26.

680 *Kall Kwik Printing (UK) Ltd v Rush* [1996] F.S.R. 114; *Dymond Plc v Reeve* [1999] F.S.R. 148 at 153; *Convenience Co Ltd v Roberts* [2001] F.S.R. 35; *Chipsaway International Ltd v Kerr* [2009] EWCA Civ 320; *PSG Franchising Ltd v Lydia Darby Ltd* [2012] EWHC 3707 (QB).

681 *Allied Dunbar (Frank Weisinger) Ltd v Frank Weisinger* [1988] I.R.L.R. 60 at 65.

682 cf. *Systems Reliability Holdings v Smith* [1990] I.R.L.R. 377 at 384; *Marshall v NM Financial Management Ltd* [1997] 1 W.L.R. 1527 at 1533.

interest" is (by definition) protected even in the absence of a covenant.[683] So long as the employer has trade secrets he can take a covenant which to some extent prevents the employee from using his own skill by restraining him from working in competition with the employer. And an employer who has a "proprietary" interest in his relations with clients or customers can restrain his employee from working in the *area* in which those clients or customers live, even though most of the inhabitants of the area have never dealt with the employer.[684] Such restraints may be necessary for the protection of the employer as the actual infringement of his proprietary interests could be very hard to establish: in particular it would, if the employee were allowed to work for a competitor, be hard to tell whether he was disclosing trade secrets.[685] The covenant may, moreover, be enforced even though the "proprietary interest" infringed is of little value to the employer. Thus a former employee can be restrained from dealing with a client who has decided to deal with the ex-employee, rather than with the employer, since it is precisely this type of competition "against which the covenant is designed to give protection".[686]

On the other hand, such "area covenants" may operate to some extent as pure restraints on competition; and in a number of cases[687] the courts have distinguished them from "solicitation covenants" (against soliciting the employer's old clients or customers). On the facts of those cases the courts have held or said that only "solicitation covenants" would be regarded as reasonable. The cases do not absolutely rule out the possibility that an "area covenant" may be valid between employer and employee;[688] but such a covenant will be void if it covers a much larger area than is needed for the protection of the employer's interest. Thus in *Mason v Provident Clothing & Supply Co Ltd*,[689] a canvasser who was employed to sell clothes in Islington covenanted not to enter into similar business within 25 miles of London. The covenant was held void because the area of the restraint was about 1,000 times as large as that in which the canvasser had been employed. It was said that the employer could have protected himself by a covenant restricted to the area in which the canvasser had worked. But if that area is very large and the employee has only dealt with a small number of customers within it, an area covenant will not,[690] though a solicitation covenant might,[691] be upheld.

---

683 See paras 11–119, 11–120.

684 *Fitch v Dewes* [1921] 2 A.C. 158; *Scorer v Seymour-Johns* [1966] 1 W.L.R. 1419; contrast *Fellowes v Fisher* [1976] Q.B. 122.

685 *Poly Lina Ltd v Finch* [1995] F.S.R. 751; *Thomas v Farr Plc* [2007] EWCA Civ 118; [2007] I.C.R. 932; cf. *Kall Kwik Printing (UK) Ltd v Rush* [1996] F.S.R. 114 (franchise agreement).

686 *John Michael Design Plc v Cooke* [1987] I.C.R. 445 at 446.

687 *SW Strange Ltd v Mann* [1965] 1 W.L.R. 629; *Gledhow Autoparts Ltd v Delaney* [1965] 1 W.L.R. 1366; *T Lucas & Co Ltd v Mitchell* [1974] Ch. 129; *Stenhouse Australia Ltd v Phillips* [1974] A.C. 391; *Dairy Crest Ltd v Pigott* [1989] I.C.R. 92; cf. *Bridge v Deacons* [1984] A.C. 705 (solicitation covenant in partnership agreement between solicitors upheld); *Hanover Ins Brokers v Schapiro* [1994] I.R.L.R. 82.

688 e.g. *Anscombe & Ringland v Butchoff* (1984) 134 N.L.J. 37.

689 [1913] A.C. 724; cf. *Empire Meat Co Ltd v Patrick* [1939] 2 All E.R. 85; *Office Angels Ltd v Rainer-Thomas* [1991] I.R.L.R. 214; for conflicting dicta in a borderline case, see *Lyne-Pirkis v Jones* [1969] 1 W.L.R. 1293.

690 *Marley Tile Co Ltd v Johnson* [1982] I.R.L.R. 75.

Between vendor and purchaser (and in analogous cases)[692] area covenants are commonly enforced; and a restraint may be reasonable even though it is *unlimited* as to area. In the *Nordenfelt* case[693] such a restraint was enforced against the vendor of an armaments business since that business extended over the whole world; and where an employer is entitled to protect trade secrets of a business which has no clear geographical limits, a covenant which is unlimited as to area may similarly be enforced against the employee.[694] A "solicitation covenant" in a contract of employment may likewise be enforced though it contains no express limitations as to area,[695] particularly if it is limited to customers with whom the employee came into contact in the course of his employment;[696] but such a limitation is not essential to the validity of the covenant.[697] A worldwide restraint against disclosing confidential information is unlikely to be upheld if the information in question relates only to business done by the employer in a limited geographical area (e.g. to customers in one country).[698]

**Duration of the restraint.** The question whether a restraint is invalid for excessive duration depends on the nature of the business to be protected.[699] If it is one to which customers or clients are likely to resort for a long time, a restraint for the lifetime of the covenantor may be valid. Thus in *Fitch v Dewes*[700] a lifelong restraint on a solicitor's managing clerk not to practise within seven miles of his principal's office was upheld. But in view of the distinction between "area" and "solicitation" covenants, it is unlikely that a *lifelong* restraint in an "area" covenant would now be regarded as valid.[701] A more lenient view was taken of a "solicitation" covenant for a *fixed period* in *Bridge v Deacons*:[702] the Privy Council there upheld a covenant by a partner in a firm of solicitors not to act as solicitor in Hong Kong for any client of the firm for five years after ceasing **11–127**

[691] *Gledhow Autoparts Ltd v Delaney* [1965] 1 W.L.R. 1366. Contrast *Office Angels Ltd v Rainer-Thomas* [1991] I.R.L.R. 214; and *Lapthorne v Eurofi Ltd* [2001] EWCA Civ 999; [2001] U.K.C.L.R. 999.

[692] e.g. *Kerr v Morris* [1987] Ch. 90; cf. *Kall Kwik Printing (UK) Ltd v Bell* [1994] F.S.R. 674 (franchisee); *Alliance Property Group Plc v Prestwich* [1996] I.R.L.R. 25.

[693] *Nordenfelt v Maxim Nordenfelt Guns and Ammunition Co* [1894] A.C. 535; cf. *Systems Reliability Holdings v Smith* [1990] I.R.L.R. 377 at 382; *Dawnay Day & Co v D'Alphen* [1997] I.R.L.R. 442. Contrast *Convenience Co Ltd v Roberts* [2001] F.S.R. 35.

[694] *Poly Lina Ltd v Finch* [1995] F.S.R. 751.

[695] *GW Plowman & Son Ltd v Ash* [1964] 1 W.L.R. 568; cf. *Morris Angel & Son Ltd v Hollande* [1993] I.C.R. 71.

[696] As in *Stenhouse Australia Ltd v Phillips* [1974] A.C. 391; contrast *Austin Knight (UK) v Hinds* [1994] F.S.R. 52 (covenant invalid as not so limited).

[697] *GW Plowman & Son Ltd v Ash* [1964] 1 W.L.R. 568.

[698] *Lansing Linde Ltd v Kerr* [1991] 1 W.L.R. 251 at 259.

[699] *Janes v Johal* [2006] EWHC 286 (Ch); [2006] I.C.R. 742 at [32]; *Beckett Investment Management Group Ltd v Hall* [2007] EWCA Civ 613; [2007] I.C.R. 1539 at [25]–[26] (12 months reasonable for a senior employee of a financial services company).

[700] [1921] 2 A.C. 158.

[701] See *Fellowes v Fisher* [1976] Q.B. 122.

[702] [1984] A.C. 705; the suggestion made ([1984] A.C. 705 at 717) that a covenant which is otherwise reasonable will not be struck down "solely because of its duration" is, with respect, hard to reconcile with *Esso Petroleum Co Ltd v Harper's Garage (Stourport) Ltd* [1968] A.C. 269 (para.11–144), so far as that case related to the 21-year tie; and with *Eastes v Russ* [1914] 1 Ch. 468.

to be a partner; and a one-year "area" covenant operating within a 10-mile radius has likewise been enforced against an assistant solicitor.[703] Where the business to be protected is of a more fluctuating nature, long restraints are unlikely to be upheld whether they are contained in "area" or in "solicitation" covenants.[704] A maximum duration of two years is prescribed by legislation in the case of a restraint on a "commercial agent".[705]

An employee's covenant not to disclose confidential information relating to the employer need not be limited as to time: such a covenant has, for example, been upheld where an employee of the Royal Household undertook that he would not either during or after service disclose information concerning any member of the Royal Family (and certain other persons) without written authority.[706] Such a limited restraint does not prevent the former employee from working for others, and is therefore not objectionable on grounds of public policy.

11–128 **Scope of restraint.** A restraint must not extend to an activity which is irrelevant to the interest to be protected. Thus a restraint in a tailor's service contract against working as a hatter is unreasonable.[707] Nor can an employer use his proprietary interest in trade secrets and confidential information to support a covenant restraining an employee from disclosing any information whatsoever "relating to the company [i.e. the employer] or its customers of which [the employee] becomes possessed while acting as sales director";[708] for much information of this kind will have nothing to do with the employer's proprietary interest.

11–129 **Construction.** So long as there is an interest meriting protection, some restraint can be validly imposed, but the draftsman may, by drawing the restraint too widely, wholly fail to achieve his purpose.[709] An attempt to evade this difficulty was made in *Davies v Davies*,[710] where the covenant simply restrained competition "so far as the law allows"; but this was held void for uncertainty.[711] The draftsman is therefore forced to use more precise language and this may impose an excessive restraint even though the parties may not have intended that meaning. The same principles are applied to the construction of a covenant in restraint of trade as are applied to the construction of any other written term,[712] but in choosing between two possible meanings:

---

[703] *Hollis & Co v Stocks* [2000] U.K.C.L.R. 685.

[704] e.g. *M & S Drapers v Reynolds* [1957] 1 W.L.R. 9; cf. *Eastes v Russ* [1914] 1 Ch. 468.

[705] See para.16–014; SI 1993/3053 reg.20(2).

[706] *Attorney General v Barker* [1990] 3 All E.R. 257.

[707] *Attwood v Lamont* [1920] 3 K.B. 571; cf. *Scully UK Ltd v Lee* [1998] I.R.L.R. 259.

[708] *Lawrence David v Ashton* [1989] I.C.R. 123; cf. *Intelsec Systems Ltd v Grech-Cini* [2000] 1 W.L.R. 1190.

[709] cf. para.11–166.

[710] (1887) 36 Ch D. 359.

[711] cf. *Days Medical Aids Ltd v Pihsiang Machinery Manufacturing Co Ltd* [2004] EWHC 44 (Comm); [2004] 1 All E.R. (Comm) 991.

[712] *Beckett Investment Management Group Ltd v Hall* [2007] EWCA Civ 613; [2007] I.C.R. 1539 at [11].

> "it is legitimate to adopt a construction which limits the clause to reasonable protection of a legitimate business interest, with the consequence that the clause will be valid and enforceable, and to reject a construction which would render the clause void."[713]

For example, in *Home Counties Dairies Ltd v Skilton*[714] a covenant in a milk roundsman's contract provided that he should not serve or sell "milk or dairy produce". It was argued that this would prevent him from serving cheese as a grocer's assistant, but the court refused to invalidate the covenant as the parties clearly did not intend it to bear this meaning.[715] This approach "should not be pushed too far":[716] the court cannot in the face of unambiguous language re-cast the parties' bargain[717] and nor can the apparent width of a restraint be cut down by an "artificially implied term."[718] In *Tillman v Egon Zehnder Ltd*,[719] Lord Wilson inclined to the view that before the "validity principle" can be invoked, the alternative construction under which the clause would be valid must be "realistic".[720]

**Consideration and bargaining power.** The law of restraint of trade has long recognised two principles: that adequacy of consideration is relevant to the validity of a restraint[721] and that the law has regard to the relative bargaining strengths of the parties.[722] This does not mean that a restraint is invalid merely because it was undertaken by the weaker party; for the transaction may be a perfectly fair one, having regard to the benefits obtained by that party under it.[723] It is only where the stronger party makes unconscionable use of his superior bargaining power that the resulting bargain may be struck down on account of its 11–130

713 *PSG Franchising Ltd v Lydia Darby Ltd* [2012] EWHC 3707 (QB) at [31]; *The Littlewoods Organisation Ltd v Harris* [1977] 1 W.L.R. 1472; (doubting *Commercial Plastics Ltd v Vincent* [1961] 1 Q.B. 623 on the issue of interpretation); *Turner v Commonwealth Minerals Ltd* [2000] I.R.L.R. 114 at [14]; *TFS Derivatives Ltd v Morgan* [2004] EWHC 2809; [2005] I.R.L.R. 246 at [44].

714 [1970] 1 W.L.R. 526. The court read into the contract the words "as a dairyman"; cf. *Clarke v Newland* [1991] 1 All E.R. 97 ("as a general medical practitioner"); and *Hollis & Co v Stocks* [2000] I.R.L.R. 712 ("as a solicitor").

715 cf. *GW Plowman Ltd v Ash* [1964] 1 W.L.R. 568; *Edwards v Worboys* [1984] A.C. 724n.; *Kynixa Ltd v Hynes* [2008] EWHC 1495 (QB) at [179]–[180] ("very little weight" to be given to "remote possibilities"); *Coppage v Safety Net Security Ltd* [2013] EWCA Civ 1176; [2013] I.R.L.R. 970 at [23]. A similar approach was adopted in *Rock Refrigeration Ltd v Jones* [1997] I.C.R. 938. The decision in *Lyne-Pirkis v Jones* [1969] 1 W.L.R. 1293 is open to doubt; cf. *Peyton v Mindham* [1972] 1 W.L.R. 8; *JA Mont (UK) Ltd v Mills* [1993] I.R.L.R. 172; *Advantage Business Systems Ltd v Hopley* [2007] EWHC (QB) 1783.

716 *PSG Franchising Ltd v Lydia Darby Ltd* [2012] EWHC 3707 (QB) at [31].

717 *Prophet Plc v Huggett* [2014] EWCA Civ 1013; [2014] I.R.L.R. at [797], where the effect of the drafting was to deprive the covenant of any restriction at all; *Harcus Sinclair LLP v Your Lawyers Ltd* [2019] EWCA Civ 335; [2019] 4 W.L.R. 81 at [58].

718 *Townends Group Ltd v Cobb* [2004] EWHC 3432 (Ch); *The Times*, 1 December 2004 at [53].

719 [2019] UKSC 32; [2019] 3 W.L.R. 245.

720 *Tillman v Egon Zehnder Ltd* [2019] UKSC 32; [2019] 3 W.L.R. 245 at [42].

721 See para.11–113.

722 See para.11–121.

723 *Alec Lobb (Garages) Ltd v Total Oil (Great Britain) Ltd* [1985] 1 W.L.R. 173; this case, and those cited in the next note, were concerned with the type of restraint discussed below, para.11–143 and following.

unfairness.[724] To this extent, the fairness of the bargain is a *necessary* condition of the validity of the restraint; but it is submitted that it is not a *sufficient* condition. It has indeed been said that a restraint cannot be unreasonable if the parties have freely agreed to it[725] or if it is to their mutual advantage. This is true in the sense that the agreement of the parties may determine how much the covenantee has bought, and hence how much he can protect. But once the interest has been defined, the restraint will be upheld only if it is necessary for the protection of that interest.[726] This will generally depend on the relation between the restraint and the interest.[727] A world-wide restraint in a contract for the sale of a village shop would not satisfy this test however much both parties wanted to enter into it and even if the buyer had paid a greatly enhanced price to secure the restraint. The same point can be made in relation to a partnership agreement. Thus in *Bridge v Deacons* one factor emphasised by the Privy Council was "the mutuality of the contract", by which the five-year restraint "applied equally to all partners".[728] But while this was relevant to the validity of a five-year solicitation covenant it would not, it is submitted, have justified a lifetime area covenant covering the whole of Hong Kong since that would have been wholly disproportionate to the interest recognised as meriting protection. The rule that the restraint must not go further than necessary for the protection of the recognised interest of the covenantee is one of public policy and accordingly cannot be excluded merely by the agreement of the parties.

### *(iii) Public interest*

11–131 **Employment.** In one sense, the requirement of reasonableness can be said to raise issues of public interest. But even if the restraint is "reasonable" in relation to the interest which the covenantee is entitled to protect, it may still be invalid if it is likely to prejudice the public. Many dicta state this rule,[729] but there is little direct authority to support it. In *Wyatt v Kreglinger & Fernau*[730] the employers of a wool broker promised to pay him a pension on his retirement provided that he

[724] *A Schroeder Music Publishing Co v Macaulay* [1974] 1 W.L.R. 1308 at 1315–1316 (where Lord Diplock did not distinguish between unfairness and unconscionability); *Clifford Davis Management Ltd v WEA Records Ltd* [1975] 1 W.L.R. 61. Quaere whether it is up to the stronger party to establish the fairness of the restraint or to the weaker party to establish its unfairness. The latter view perhaps derives some support from the comparison in *Barclays Bank Plc v Caplan* [1998] F.L.R. 532 at 546 of restraint of trade with undue influence cases: see para.10–015 and following.

[725] *NW Salt Co v Electrolytic Alkali Co Ltd* [1914] A.C. 461 at 471; *English Hop Growers Ltd v Dering* [1928] 2 K.B. 174 at 185. cf. *World Wide Fund for Nature v World Wrestling Federation* [2002] EWCA Civ 196; [2002] U.K.C.L.R. 388 at [42], as to which see further para.11–136.

[726] cf. *A Schroeder Music Publishing Co Ltd v Macaulay* at 1316 ("reasonably necessary for the protection of the legitimate interests of the promisee").

[727] See para.11–125; *Allied Dunbar (Frank Weisinger) Ltd v Frank Weisinger* [1988] I.R.L.R. 60 at 65.

[728] *Bridge v Deacons* [1984] A.C. 705 at 716.

[729] e.g. *Attorney-General for Australia v Adelaide SS Co* [1913] A.C. 781 at 796; *Herbert Morris Ltd v Saxelby* [1916] A.C. 688 at 700; *McEllistrim's Case* [1919] A.C. 548 at 562; *Bridge v Deacons* [1984] A.C. 705 at 713; *Harcus Sinclair LLP v Your Lawyers Ltd* [2019] EWCA Civ 335; [2019] 4 W.L.R. 81 at [88]; cf. *Kerr v Morris* [1987] Ch. 90, where the covenant was admitted to be reasonable in area and duration and public interest was discussed as a *separate* issue.

[730] [1933] 1 K.B. 793.

did not re-enter the wool trade and did nothing to their detriment (fair business competition excepted). Nine years later the Court of Appeal rejected his claim for arrears of pension. Three reasons can be found in the judgments: that the employers' promise to pay the pension was simply a gratuitous promise; that the stipulation against competition was void because it was unreasonable; and that the stipulation against competition was void because it was contrary to the public interest. The view that a restraint imposed on an elderly wool broker at the time of his retirement was likely to injure the public may be regarded with some scepticism, especially in view of the countervailing public interest of encouraging young recruits to the profession.[731] Reaction against it has gone so far that it has sometimes been said that public interest was not an independent ground of invalidity at all.[732] But *Wyatt*'s case was followed in a later similar case;[733] and it is arguable that a restraint on persons whose services are in short supply may be contrary to the public interest, even though it is reasonable in relation to the interest which the covenantee is entitled to protect.[734] This argument is not, it is submitted, inconsistent with cases holding that it was not contrary to the public interest to restrain a solicitor from acting for a particular client or group of clients *merely* because of the fiduciary relationship between solicitor and client.[735] For the present purpose, the decisive factor is not the nature of the services but the availability of alternative sources of supply: the public interest lies in their general availability and not in their being rendered by a particular individual. Thus a restraint on a former partner in a general medical practice would not be invalid merely because patients wished to continue to be treated by *that* partner,[736] but such restraint might be contrary to the public interest if there was a shortage of doctors in the area in question.

**Sale of business.** The principle of public interest may, equally, apply to covenants for the sale of a business. In the *Nordenfelt* case[737] it was said that, as the business sold was a foreign one, a restraint on the vendor would not injure "the public policy of this country"; and more recently the promotion of export sales has been mentioned as a head of public interest.[738] The principle of public interest has, moreover, become increasingly important in relation to other categories of contracts in restraint of trade;[739] and it now seems to be clear that it can be an independent ground of invalidity. 11–132

**Scope of "public interest".** In the common law relating to restraint of trade, the "public interest" refers to legally recognised interests, and in particular to the 11–133

[731] cf. *Bridge v Deacons* [1984] A.C. 705 at 718.
[732] *Routh v Jones* [1947] 1 All E.R. 179 at 182; cf. *Systems Holdings v Smith* [1990] I.R.L.R. 377 at 382; but at 384 reasonableness *and* public interest are stated as separate requirements of validity.
[733] *Bull v Pitney-Bowes Ltd* [1967] 1 W.L.R. 273; Koh 30 M.L.R. 587.
[734] cf. *Dranez Anstalt v Hayetz* [2002] EWCA Civ 1729; [2003] F.S.R. 32 at [25].
[735] *Edwards v Worboys* [1984] A.C. 724n.; *Bridge v Deacons* [1984] A.C. 705 at 720; disapproving contrary dicta in *Oswald Hickson Collier & Co v Carter-Ruck* [1984] A.C. 720n.
[736] *Kerr v Morris* [1987] Ch. 90; overruling *Hensman v Traill* (1980) 124 S.J. 776; cf. *Araci v Fallon* [2011] EWCA Civ 668; [2011] L.L.R. at [60].
[737] *Nordenfelt v Maxim Nordenfelt Guns & Ammunition Co* [1894] A.C. 535 at 550; cf. at 574.
[738] *Bull v Pitney-Bowes Ltd* [1967] 1 W.L.R. 273 at 276.
[739] See paras 11–143—11–152.

interest of the public that a person should not be subjected to unreasonable restrictions on his freedom to work or trade. An agreement is unlikely to be invalidated by a common law court because it is alleged to infringe some wider public interest, e.g. because it might lead to an improper allocation of economic resources, or prove inflationary. Such allegations often lack precision, and courts of law are not well equipped to evaluate them.[740]

### (iv) *No actual covenant against competition*

**11–134** The restraint of trade doctrine may apply where the terms of the contract provide a party with a financial incentive not to compete, even though he makes no actual promise not to do so: this was the position in *Wyatt v Kreglinger & Fernau* where the employee made no promise not to compete, but his right to his pension was conditional on his not doing so.[741] Similarly, in *Stenhouse Australia Ltd v Phillips*[742] the defendant undertook to pay to his former employers half the gross commission which he might receive in respect of business done with their clients. This was held to be in restraint of trade (though there was no covenant) since it was "in effect … likely to cause the employee to refuse business which otherwise he would take …".[743] On the other hand, in *Alder v Moore*[744] a professional footballer was paid £500 for "permanent total disability". He made a "declaration" not to play professional football again "and in the event of infringing this condition I will be subject to a penalty of £500". He did infringe the "condition" and a majority of the Court of Appeal held that he was liable to repay the £500. The sole question discussed was whether the stipulation to repay was a penalty;[745] and no reference was made to the restraint of trade doctrine. Prima facie, the stipulation appears to fall within that doctrine, though it may have been perfectly reasonable and not contrary to the public interest.

### (v) *Restraint operating during employment*

**11–135** In the employment cases so far discussed, the issue has been as to the validity of covenants operating *after* the end of the period of service.[746] Restrictions on competition *during* that period are normally valid,[747] and indeed may be implied

---

[740] *Texaco Ltd v Mulberry Filling Station Ltd* [1972] 1 W.L.R. 814 at 827, a case concerned with the type of restraint discussed at para.11–143 and following; contrast *Bull v Pitney-Bowes Ltd* [1967] 1 W.L.R. 273.

[741] *Wyatt v Kreglinger & Fernau* [1933] 1 K.B. 793 (Scrutton and Slesser LJJ; Greer LJ interpreted the correspondence to mean that there *was* a covenant not to complete); cf. *Sadler v Imperial Life Assurance of Canada* [1988] I.R.L.R. 388; *Marshall v NM Financial Management Ltd* [1997] 1 W.L.R. 1527 at 1533; *20:20 London Ltd v Riley* [2012] EWHC 1912 (Ch).

[742] [1974] A.C. 391.

[743] *Stenhouse Australia Ltd v Phillips* [1974] A.C. 391 at 402–403.

[744] [1961] 2 Q.B. 57.

[745] See para.20–135.

[746] The restraint of trade doctrine may apply to an option entitling the employer to *re-employ* the employee at some time in the future: *Leeds Rugby Ltd v Harris* [2005] EWHC 1591 (QB).

[747] *One Money Mail Ltd v RIA Financial Services* [2015] EWCA Civ 1084; cf. *GFI Group v Eaglestone*, *The Times*, 29 October 1993; *Crédit Suisse Asset Management Ltd v Armstrong* [1996] I.C.R. 882 covenant operating during "garden leave" (para.17–054) valid; but see at fn.750.

by law by virtue of the servant's duty of fidelity.[748] In such cases the restriction is generally reasonable, having regard to the interests of the employer, and does not cause any undue hardship to the employee, who will receive a wage or salary for the period in question. But the contract may be a long-term one, and the main purpose of the restraint may be, not to secure faithful service, but to protect the employer from competition by sterilising the employee's working capacity. In such a case the restraint may be invalid even though it operates only during the period in which the employee can be required to serve,[749] and even if it is valid, the court may refuse the remedy of an injunction to the employer.[750] An increasingly common form of restraint operating during employment is "gardening leave", where the employee is paid during a period of notice, but not required to work for the employer. It is established "as a matter of principle" that the existence of a garden leave clause can be taken into account in determining the validity of a post-termination restraint.[751] For example, if the restraints imposed during that period are valid, any additional *post-termination* restraint may be challenged on the basis that it could more reasonably have been achieved by extending the period of gardening leave.[752]

### (vi) *Establishing validity of restraint*

**Burden of proof.** The reasonableness of the restraint must be established by the person who seeks to enforce the contract; it is then up to the party resisting enforcement to establish that the restraint is contrary to the public interest.[753] Thus in the normal case, in which the covenantee sues to enforce the restraint, he must establish its reasonableness and the covenantor its tendency to injure the public. But where, as in *Wyatt v Kreglinger & Fernau*[754] the action is brought by the covenantor to enforce the promise for which the restraint constitutes the consideration, the roles are reversed: the person under the restraint must show that it is reasonable and the other party that it is contrary to the public interest. It has further been held that where a stipulation in restraint of trade is contained in an agreement for the settlement of a genuine dispute relating to intellectual 11–136

[748] See para.6–068. *Faccenda Chicken Ltd v Fowler* [1987] Ch. 117 at 135–136; cf. *Evening Standard Co Ltd v Henderson* [1987] I.C.R. 588; *Provident Financial Group Plc v Hayward* [1989] I.C.R. 160; *One Money Mail Ltd v RIA Financial Services* [2015] EWCA Civ 1084 at [8] (sole agency).

[749] *A Schroeder Music Publishing Co Ltd v Macaulay* [1974] 1 W.L.R. 1308; para.11–145; cf. *Clifford Davis Management Ltd v WEA Records* [1975] 1 W.L.R. 61. Contrast *Greig v Insole* [1978] 1 W.L.R. 302 at 326.

[750] *William Hill Organisation Ltd v Tucker* [1998] I.R.L.R. 313; *Symbian Ltd v Christenson* [2001] I.R.L.R. 37; para.21–068.

[751] *Crédit Suisse Asset Management Ltd v Armstrong* [1996] I.C.R. 882; *Tradition Financial Services Ltd v Gamberoni* [2017] EWHC 768 (QB); [2017] I.R.L.R. 698 at [112].

[752] See *TFS Derivatives Ltd v Morgan* [2004] EWHC 2809; [2005] I.R.L.R. 246, where Cox J declined to express any general view; cf. *Tradition Financial Services Ltd v Gamberoni* [2017] EWHC 768 (QB); [2017] I.R.L.R. 698 where a six-month restraint was reasonable, even if the employee was placed on garden leave for three months prior to termination, resulting in a nine-month absence from his work as a broker.

[753] See *Herbert Morris Ltd v Saxelby* [1916] A.C. 589 at 700, 706–707; *Attwood v Lamont* [1920] 3 K.B. 571 at 587–588; *Kores v Kolok Manufacturing Co Ltd* [1959] Ch. 108 at 120.

[754] [1933] 1 K.B. 793; para.11–131.

property rights, then it is not up to the party seeking to enforce the settlement to show that it is "reasonable".[755] The public policy against restraint of trade here appears to come into conflict with that in favour of bona fide compromises and the latter prevails so that it is up to the party resisting enforcement of the compromise to show that there was no genuine dispute or claim. It seems that "reasonableness" here refers to the genuineness of the underlying dispute;[756] and this is a different issue from the "reasonableness" which is a requirement of the validity of covenants in restraint of trade.[757] The questions of reasonableness and public interest are questions of law[758] so that it is strictly inaccurate to say that the party claiming enforcement has the *onus of proving* that the covenant is reasonable. What he must do is to prove the circumstances from which the court may conclude that the ratio between the restraint and the interest is reasonable.[759] The same principle applies to the question of public interest.

### (c) Restrictive trading and similar agreements

11–137 Agreements between suppliers of goods or services restricting competition between them are at common law[760] subject to the restraint of trade doctrine, so that they are prima facie void, but valid if reasonable and not contrary to the public interest. They also give rise to a number of special problems.

11–138 **The interest.** In *McEllistrim*'s *Case* Lord Birkenhead said that "in this class of case the covenantee is not entitled to be protected against competition *per se*".[761] But he evidently regarded "stability in their lists of customers"[762] as an interest which producers were entitled to protect; and it is not clear how this differs from protection against "competition per se". It seems that in this group of cases, as in another to be discussed below,[763] a "commercial" as opposed to a "proprietary" interest[764] may support a covenant.

11–139 **Conditions of validity.** The broad definition of the interest meriting protection by agreements of the present kind made it relatively easier to establish their validity than that of restraints between vendor and purchaser or between employer and employee. In *English Hop Growers v Dering*,[765] for example, the court upheld an agreement by which hop growers undertook to deliver their crops

---

755 *World Wide Fund for Nature v World Wrestling Foundation* [2002] EWCA Civ 196; [2002] U.K.C.L.R. 388 at [42].

756 cf. paras 3–037–3–038.

757 This difference may account for the fact that none of the authorities cited at fnn.753 and 754 is referred to in *World Wide Fund for Nature v World Wrestling Foundation* [2002] EWCA Civ 196; [2002] U.K.C.L.R. 388.

758 *Dowden & Pook Ltd v Pook* [1904] 1 K.B. 45.

759 *Herbert Morris Ltd v Saxelby* [1916] 1 A.C. 688 at 707 ("no question of onus either way").

760 Such agreements are also subject to legislative controls which regulate anti-competitive practices: see para.11–116.

761 *McEllistrim*'s *Case* [1919] A.C. 548 at 564.

762 *McEllistrim*'s *Case* [1919] A.C. 548 at 564.

763 i.e. at para.11–143.

764 See para.11–118.

765 [1928] 2 K.B. 174; cf. *NW Salt Co v Electrolytic Alkali Co Ltd* [1914] A.C. 461.

to a central selling agency in order to avoid cut-throat competition at a time when it was feared that there would be a glut of hops on the market. But even agreements of this kind were held invalid if they were plainly unreasonable or contrary to the public interest, e.g. where the effect of the agreement was to force one of the parties to close down his business altogether.[766]

**Hardship to a particular group.** An agreement may cause hardship to a particular group of persons, without being contrary to the interests of the public at large. In *Kores Manufacturing Co Ltd v Kolok Manufacturing Co Ltd*[767] two manufacturers of carbon paper and typewriter ribbons each agreed not to employ the others' former employees for five years after they had left their original employer. The Court of Appeal held that, although the parties were entitled to protect their trade secrets, the covenant was invalid, as it covered all employees, whether they knew trade secrets or not, and as it was of excessive duration. It was further argued that the parties were entitled to protect their labour supplies, but the court doubted whether "labour supplies" were an interest meriting protection. If they were, employers could, by contracting with each other, achieve what they could not do by contracting directly with the employees themselves. An undertaking by an employee not to work for another employer would be invalid for lack of a proper interest[768] if he knew no trade secrets and had no influence over customers. The same principle should apply where the restraint was contained in a contract between employers and indirectly prejudiced their employees' opportunities of finding work.[769] It seems that the court can take hardship to third parties into account and hold that it invalidates a contract of this kind by making it contrary to the public interest,[770] so that a covenant by which A promised B not to employ or to offer to employ B's employees would be invalid[771] (though one by which A merely promised "not to solicit or entice away" B's employees could be upheld since it would not preclude A from employing them if they came to him of their own accord).[772] 11–140

**Remedies of third parties.** Reasoning of the kind just considered can help a third party only where one of the parties to the agreement has challenged its validity. In practice, these restrictive agreements were rarely broken, because they were usually beneficial to the contracting parties, however much third parties might suffer from them; and at common law the contracting parties are at liberty to give 11–141

---

[766] cf. *Joseph Evans & Co v Heathcote* [1918] 1 K.B. 418; *McEllistrim's Case* [1919] A.C. 548; *Collins v Locke* (1879) 4 App. Cas. 674.

[767] [1959] Ch. 108; cf. *Mineral Water, etc. Trade Protection Society v Booth* (1887) 36 Ch D. 465; Sales 104 L.Q.R. 600.

[768] See para.11–122.

[769] See *TSC Europe (UK) Ltd v Massey* [1999] I.R.L.R. 22 at 29; cf. at fn.777.

[770] See *Esso Petroleum Ltd v Harper's Garage (Stourport) Ltd* [1968] A.C. 269 at 300, 319.

[771] *Hanover Ins Brokers v Shapiro* [1994] I.R.L.R. 82; *Dawnay Day & Co Ltd v D'Alphen* [1997] I.R.L.R. 442, so far as it relates to cl.12.1.2 of the service contract: see [1997] I.R.L.R. 285 at 296 (contrast *Alliance Paper Group Plc v Prestwich* [1996] I.R.L.R. 25, where the "no poaching" covenant referred only to *senior* employees).

[772] See the *Dawnay Day* case [1997] I.R.L.R. 442 at 448 (at fn.771) so far as it relates to cl.12.1.1. of the contract.

effect to the agreement.[773] If they did so, the third parties could not claim damages for conspiracy at common law;[774] and it used to be thought that they had no standing at all to challenge such agreements. But in *Eastham v Newcastle United Football Club Ltd*[775] a professional footballer sought a declaration that the "retain and transfer" system was invalid. The remedy was granted, not only against his club, but also against the Football Association and the Football League, with whom the claimant had never been in any contractual relationship; and it was said to be available "whether or not the (claimant) has a legal cause of action against the defendants".[776] The weakness of this remedy by way of declaration is that it has no coercive effect: it would not prevent the parties to the invalid agreement from continuing to act in accordance with it. The declaration could help the third party only by giving one of the contracting parties grounds for thinking that he could break the agreement with impunity if it suited him to do so.

Sometimes a third party may, even at common law, have a more effective remedy. There is some support for the view that a person can obtain an injunction against a professional association to restrain it from applying a rule under which he is excluded from membership, and so prevented from exercising the profession,[777] on grounds not relevant to his capacity to do so.[778] Whether such a remedy is available in cases of this kind to a claimant who has no "cause of action against the defendants"[779] is, however, open to doubt,[780] for normally an injunction will be granted only where there is such a cause of action.[781] In one case[782] it was held that this requirement was satisfied where football clubs claimed a declaration that a resolution passed by an association from which they had resigned was in restraint of trade. The mere availability of a declaration was said to be a "cause of action", so that an interlocutory injunction could be granted to the clubs to restrain the association from acting on the resolution until the action for a declaration came to trial. This conclusion is, however, hard to reconcile with that part of the reasoning of the *Eastham* case (quoted above)[783] which assumes that a declaration is available even though the claimant has *no* cause of action against the third party. The possibility of the third party's obtaining injunctive relief appears, in any event, to be restricted to cases in which

[773] *Boddington v Lawton* [1994] I.C.R. 478.

[774] *Mogul SS Co v McGregor, Gow & Co* [1892] A.C. 25 at 39, 42, 46, 51, 57, 58.

[775] [1964] Ch. 413; para.11–123; cf. *Greig v Insole* [1978] 1 W.L.R. 302; *Newport Association Football Club Ltd v Football Association of Wales Ltd* [1995] 2 All E.R. 87.

[776] *Eastham v Newcastle United Football Club Ltd* [1964] Ch. 413 at 426; cf. *R. v Jockey Club Ex p. RAM Racecourses Ltd* [1993] 2 All E.R. 225 at 243.

[777] The rule would not be contrary to public policy unless it had this effect: cf. *Cheall v APEX* [1983] 2 A.C. 180 at 191 (expulsion from a trade union).

[778] See *Nagle v Feilden* [1966] 2 Q.B. 633; A.L.G. 82 L.Q.R. 319. That case concerned discrimination now unlawful under the Equality Act 2010.

[779] See at fn.776.

[780] *R. v Disciplinary Committee of the Jockey Club Ex p. Aga Khan* [1993] 1 W.L.R. 909 at 933, where the applicant did have a cause of action in contract.

[781] See para.21–071.

[782] *Newport Association FC v Football Association of Wales Ltd* [1995] 2 All E.R. 87.

[783] At fn.776.

the right to work (or perhaps the right to trade)[784] is arbitrarily restricted by a contract between others. It seems unlikely that a buyer of goods or services could at common law get an injunction against a price-ring merely because it operated to his prejudice.

### (d) Trade unions and employers' associations

At common law the validity of the rules of a trade union depended nominally on the principles which governed other contracts in restraint of trade. But in practice there was at one time a strong judicial tendency to hold such rules illegal. The courts relied in particular on the fact that the rules of a trade union might require an employee to stop work against his will; and they were no doubt also influenced by the fear that they might be called on to enforce a strike by injunction. The common law position was changed by legislation as long ago as 1871;[785] and the matter is now dealt with by the Trade Union and Labour Relations (Consolidation) Act 1992. A detailed analysis of this complicated Act cannot be attempted in this book; but the main point is that under s.11 the purposes of a trade union[786] are not, by reason only of the fact that they are in restraint of trade, to be unlawful so as to make void or voidable any agreement; nor is any rule of a union to be unenforceable by reason only of its being in restraint of trade.[787] The Act contains similar provisions with regard to the purposes and rules of employers' associations,[788] which are to the same extent excepted from the scope of the restraint of trade doctrine.[789] But an agreement or rule of a trade union may still be invalid for some other reason. In particular, an employee (or person seeking employment) has a statutory right not to be excluded or expelled from a trade union[790] except in certain specified circumstances; and union rules which restrict membership are unenforceable unless they satisfy one or more of a number of criteria laid down by the legislation, e.g. they may validly restrict membership by reference to qualifications for the type of work in question.[791] 11–142

[784] It was this right which was at stake in *Newport Association FC v Football Association of Wales Ltd* [1995] 2 All E.R. 87.
[785] Trade Union Act 1871 s.3.
[786] As defined by s.1.
[787] The exact scope of s.11 depends on whether or not the union is a "special register body" as defined by s.117.
[788] As defined by s.122(1).
[789] Section 128: the exact scope of this section depends on whether the association is incorporated.
[790] Trade Union and Labour Relations (Consolidation) Act 1992 ss.174–177 (as substituted by Trade Union Reform and Employment Rights Act 1993 s.14); cf. also Equality Act 2010 s.57.
[791] 1992 Act s.174(3).

## (e) Exclusive dealing

### *(i) In general*

11–143 **Originally regarded as valid.** The original tendency of the common law was to regard exclusive dealing arrangements as valid. This attitude is illustrated by decisions upholding sole agency and exclusive service agreements,[792] agreements not to buy or sell goods except from or to a particular person,[793] and agreements not to use goods except with others made by the same manufacturer.[794] In other cases, the courts have upheld a contract by which the owner of a restaurant agreed to buy all the burgundy sold there from the claimants;[795] and a contract by a purchaser of garage premises to buy from the vendor all petrol used in the business carried on there.[796] Where the agreements were upheld, the rules relating to restraint of trade were in some cases simply not mentioned, while in others the rules were mentioned but the contracts were nevertheless held valid. In these cases, it was not always clear whether the contracts were valid because the restraint of trade doctrine did not apply to them at all or because its requirements were satisfied. The distinction is crucial because if the doctrine did not apply at all it would be unnecessary for the person seeking to enforce the agreement to establish its reasonableness.

11–144 **The effect of decisions on "solus agreements".** The older authorities must now be read subject to a line of cases concerned with the validity of "solus agreements" between oil companies and garage proprietors. These agreements were usually made when an oil company advanced money to help with the purchase or development of garage premises; in return, the garage proprietor would give three undertakings: a "tying covenant", to buy all petrol (and sometimes certain other products) from the oil company; a "compulsory trading covenant", to keep his garage open at all reasonable times for the sale of petrol; and a "continuity covenant", to extract similar undertakings from any person to whom he might sell the garage during the subsistence of the solus agreement. The leading *Esso* case[797] concerned solus agreements made in respect of two garages. One agreement was to last for about four and a half years, and the other for 21 years. The House of Lords held that the solus agreements were within the restraint of trade doctrine; that the four-and-a-half year agreement was valid; but that the 21-year agreement was invalid as it was unreasonable and contrary to the public interest. Undertakings with regard to solus petrol agreements were later given to the Government by oil companies in consequence of a report by the

[792] See *Esso Petroleum Co Ltd v Harper's Garage (Stourport) Ltd* [1968] A.C. 269 at 294, 307, 336.
[793] *Metropolitan Electric Supply Co v Ginder* [1901] 2 Ch. 799; *Monkland v Jack Barclay Ltd* [1951] 2 K.B. 252.
[794] *United Shoe Machinery Co of Canada v Brunet* [1909] A.C. 330, criticised in *Esso Petroleum Co Ltd v Harper's Garage (Stourport) Ltd* [1968] A.C. 269 at 297.
[795] *Bouchard Servais v Prince's Hall Restaurant Ltd* (1904) 20 T.L.R. 574; *Greenall's Management Ltd v Canavan, The Times*, 20 August 1997.
[796] *Foley v Classique Coaches* [1934] 2 K.B. 1.
[797] *Esso Petroleum Co Ltd v Harper's Garage (Stourport) Ltd* [1968] A.C. 269; Heydon 85 L.Q.R. 229; Koh [1967] C.L.J. 151; and see Whiteman 29 M.L.R. 507.

Monopolies Commission;[798] but the decision in the *Esso* case gives rise to a number of general problems which still require discussion.

### (ii) *Whether such agreements are within the restraint of trade doctrine*

In the *Esso* case Lord Pearce distinguished between "those contracts which are in restraint of trade and … those which merely regulate the normal commercial relations between the parties and which are therefore free from the doctrine".[799] He regarded solus agreements as falling within the former class, principally on the ground that the oil company gave no assurance that it would provide a supply of petrol at a reasonable price.[800] Lord Wilberforce said that contracts were not within the doctrine of restraint of trade if they were "such … as, under contemporary conditions, may be found to have passed into the accepted and normal currency of contractual or conveyancing relations".[801] The agreements in the *Esso* case were not of a kind which had in this way "passed into acceptance … ; the solus system is both too recent and too variable for this to be said".[802] However, Lord Wilberforce reserved the powers of the court to subject even "accepted" contracts to scrutiny in the light of changing social or economic conditions or of special features in individual transactions.[803] Later decisions have, in particular, made it clear that a contract is not taken out of the restraint of trade doctrine merely because it is in standard form and contains only terms which are usual in that type of transaction.[804] This factor may take contracts out of the restraint of trade doctrine if they have been freely negotiated,[805] but the position is different where there is great disparity of bargaining power and the terms are imposed by the stronger on the weaker party. In *A Schroeder Music Publishing Co v Macaulay*[806] it was accordingly held that a contract by which an unknown song-writer undertook to give his exclusive services to a publisher who made no promise to publish his work was subject to the doctrine. Lord Reid said: 11–145

> "Normally the doctrine of restraint of trade has no application to such restrictions: they require no justification. But if contractual restrictions appear to be unnecessary or to be reasonably capable of enforcement in an oppressive manner, then they must be justified before they can be enforced".[807]

---

[798] 1965, HC Paper No.264; further undertakings have been given subsequently.
[799] *Esso Petroleum Co Ltd v Harper's Garage (Stourport) Ltd* [1968] A.C. 269 at 327.
[800] *Esso Petroleum Co Ltd v Harper's Garage (Stourport) Ltd* [1968] A.C. 269 at 329.
[801] *Esso Petroleum Co Ltd v Harper's Garage (Stourport) Ltd* [1968] A.C. 269 at 332–333.
[802] *Esso Petroleum Co Ltd v Harper's Garage (Stourport) Ltd* [1968] A.C. 269 at 337.
[803] *Esso Petroleum Co Ltd v Harper's Garage (Stourport) Ltd* [1968] A.C. 269 at 333; *Watson v Prager* [1991] 1 W.L.R. 726 at 744.
[804] *Watson v Prager* [1991] 1 W.L.R. 726.
[805] *A Schroeder Music Publishing Co Ltd v Macaulay* [1974] 1 W.L.R. 1308 at 1314.
[806] [1974] 1 W.L.R. 1308; cf. *O'Sullivan v Management Agency & Music Ltd* [1985] Q.B. 428; *Watson v Prager* [1991] 1 W.L.R. 726.
[807] *A Schroeder Music Publishing Co Ltd v Macaulay* [1974] 1 W.L.R. 1308 at 1314; *Watson v Prager* [1991] 1 W.L.R. 726 at 747.

This may be the position even where the contract is made on terms settled by a professional association for the purpose of protecting the party subject to the restraint, and where both parties have no alternative but to make use of such terms.[808]

The tests proposed by Lords Pearce and Wilberforce in the *Esso* case, and by Lord Reid in the *Schroeder* case continue to recognise the possibility that some exclusive dealing and exclusive service agreements will not be subject to the doctrine of restraint of trade. Many of the earlier cases which support this view[809] were cited, and none was overruled, in the *Esso* case. At the same time, the tests are vague and leave much discretion to the courts in defining the scope of the doctrine in relation to such contracts. It seems probable that the doctrine will apply to contracts of this kind if they present any novel or unusual features,[810] or if they contain terms which are likely to operate harshly on a party of weak bargaining power. Thus, in *Proactive Sports Management Ltd v Rooney*[811] a young professional football player entered into an agreement to exploit his "image rights" which imposed very substantial restraints upon his freedom to exploit them other than through the defendant who was entitled to a commission of 20 per cent. In fact, the agreement was performed very profitably for both parties over a period of five years, but judged at the time of its execution there were several factors which indicated that it was "oppressive"; in particular, the unusual length of the agreement and the absence of any effective right of termination, the fact that the player was only 17 years old at the time of the agreement and the lack of any independent legal advice for him or his parents which "underscored" the inequality of bargaining power between the parties. Taken together, they took the agreement "out of the range of a normal commercial contract imposing restrictions on a contracting party's ability to carry on a business activity."[812]

### *(iii) Requirements of validity*

11–146 Where an exclusive dealing or service contract is subject to the doctrine of restraint of trade, the usual requirements must be satisfied before it can be enforced, though as has been noted some of the factors which are relevant at this stage may also be relevant to whether the doctrine is engaged at all.[813]

808 *Watson v Prager* [1991] 1 W.L.R. 726.
809 See para.11–143.
810 *Days Medical Aids Ltd v Pihsiang Machinery Manufacturing Co Ltd* [2004] EWHC 44 (Comm); [2004] 1 All E.R. (Comm) 991 at [224] (doctrine applied and restraint unreasonable if 10-year term also included right of perpetual renewal).
811 [2011] EWCA Civ 1444; [2012] I.R.L.R. 241.
812 *Proactive Sports Management Ltd v Rooney* [2011] EWCA Civ 1444; [2012] I.R.L.R. 241 at [99]. The Court rejected a submission that the doctrine did not apply because it did not restrict the claimant's primary trade, i.e. playing football; cf. *Tillman v Egon Zehnder Ltd* [2019] UKSC 32; [2019] 3 W.L.R. 245 at [30].
813 *Proactive Sports Management Ltd v Rooney* [2011] EWCA Civ 1444; [2012] I.R.L.R. 241 at [59], [147], [156], in which the defendant argued solely that the doctrine had no application and made no attempt to argue that the restrictions in question were reasonable.

**Interest.** We have distinguished elsewhere between "proprietary" and "commercial" interests;[814] and the *Esso* case shows that a "commercial" interest will suffice in the present group of cases. Lord Reid there said that the statement "that a person is not to be protected against mere competition" was "not ... very helpful in a case like the present"[815] and Lord Pearce, after expressing substantially the same view, seems to have regarded the oil company's "network of outlets"[816] as the interest which they sought to protect. Some difficulty arises from Lord Morris' description of the covenants as "naked covenants or covenants in gross";[817] but he obviously regarded this, not as a ground of invalidity[818] (for he upheld one of the covenants), but merely as a ground for subjecting the covenants to the doctrine of restraint of trade. **11–147**

**Reasonableness.** To satisfy the test of reasonableness, the party seeking to enforce the restrictions must show that they were "no more than what was reasonably required to protect his legitimate interest".[819] Here, as elsewhere,[820] relevant factors include the length of the restraint[821] and the adequacy of the consideration provided for it.[822] The reasonableness of the length of restraint may depend upon the type of contract concerned: **11–148**

> "A period of 912 years is not a long one in the context of a defence project using and developing cutting edge technology... A decade in the pop music business, by contrast, is a very long time indeed".[823]

We have seen that in the *Esso* case a four-and-a-half year tie was upheld and a 21-year one struck down.[824] But in a later case a 21-year tie in a solus agreement contained in a lease was upheld since the premises were already, before the lease, subject to a valid three-year tie, since the tenant had the right to break the lease after seven and 14 years, and since the landlord had paid the tenant £35,000 under a previous transaction leading to the execution of the lease.[825]

**Fairness.** The fairness of the contract is also a relevant factor, particularly where the restrictions are imposed on the weaker party to a relationship of unequal bargaining power. The point is well illustrated by agreements between musical performers and recording companies. In one case,[826] a long-term (though not exclusive) contract of this kind was made to settle differences which had arisen **11–149**

[814] See para.11–123.
[815] *Esso Petroleum Co Ltd v Harper's Garage (Stourport) Ltd* [1968] A.C. 269 at 301.
[816] *Esso Petroleum Co Ltd v Harper's Garage (Stourport) Ltd* [1968] A.C. 269 at 329.
[817] *Esso Petroleum Co Ltd v Harper's Garage (Stourport) Ltd* [1968] A.C. 269 at 309.
[818] cf. para.11–118.
[819] *A Schroeder Music Publishing Co Ltd v Macaulay* [1974] 1 W.L.R. 1308 at 1310.
[820] See paras 11–125–11–128.
[821] *Watson v Prager* [1991] 1 W.L.R. 726 at 748.
[822] *Societa Esplosivi Industriali SpA v Ordnance Technologies (UK) Ltd* [2004] EWHC 48 (Ch); [2004] 1 All E.R. (Comm) 619 at [145].
[823] *Societa Esplosivi Industriali SpA v Ordnance Technologies (UK) Ltd* [2004] EWHC 48 (Ch); [2004] 1 All E.R. (Comm) 619 at [146].
[824] See para.11–144.
[825] *Alec Lobb (Garages) Ltd v Total Oil (Great Britain) Ltd* [1985] 1 W.L.R. 173.
[826] *Panayiotou v Sony Music Entertainment (UK) Ltd*, *The Times*, 30 June 1994.

under an earlier contract between the parties; when the new contract was made, the performer's reputation was well established and he had the benefit of expert legal advice. In these circumstances, the new contract was regarded as reasonable in view of the benefits which the performer had received under it. By contrast, the restriction imposed on the composer in *A Schroeder Music Publishing Co Ltd v Macaulay*[827] was neither necessary nor fair. It extended over a period of five years, during which he had to submit all his compositions to the publishers, while they were under no obligation to promote his work and had to make no more than minimal payments if they failed to do so. The restriction was accordingly invalid as it went beyond the protection of the publishers' legitimate interests and operated harshly on the other party: "his work will be sterilised and he can earn nothing from his abilities as a composer".[828]

Terms may also be unfair because the party claiming the benefit of the restriction is under the contract put into a position where his interest conflicts with the duty that he owes to the other party. This was the position in *Watson v Prager*[829] where a professional boxer agreed to be "managed and directed exclusively" by the defendant, who was both a manager and a boxing promoter and who undertook to negotiate terms "as advantageous as possible" for the boxer; the agreement was for an initial period of three years, renewable for a further period of equal length. The main reason why the agreement was held to be contrary to public policy was that it was not fair to hold the boxer to an agreement of such long duration since under it the defendant's duty as manager was to negotiate the highest possible fees for the boxer, and this conflicted with his interest as promoter, since in that capacity he would have to meet the cost of these fees.

11–150 **Public interest.** Lord Reid in the *Schroeder* case based his decision partly on the ground that:

> "The public interest requires in the interests both of the public and of the individual that everyone should be free so far as practicable to earn a livelihood and give to the public the fruits of his particular abilities".[830]

The *Esso* case, too, is noteworthy for the stress placed on the element of public interest; indeed Lord Hodson based the invalidity of the 21-year agreement "on the public interest rather than on that of the parties".[831] Lord Pearce said that the ultimate ground for interference in all cases is public policy so that there is no real separation between "what is reasonable on grounds of public policy and what is reasonable as between the parties".[832] Lord Wilberforce appeared to take the same view but added that it is "important that the vitality of the second limb … of

[827] [1974] 1 W.L.R. 1308; para.11–145.
[828] *A Schroeder Music Publishing Co Ltd v Macaulay* [1974] 1 W.L.R. 1308 at 1314.
[829] [1991] 1 W.L.R. 726.
[830] *A Schroeder Music Publishing Co Ltd v Macaulay* [1974] 1 W.L.R. 1308 at 1313; Lord Diplock at 1315 seems to view this point with some scepticism.
[831] *Esso Petroleum Co Ltd v Harper's Garage (Stourport) Ltd* [1968] A.C. 269 at 321; cf. para.11–132. See also: *Proactive Sports Management Ltd v Rooney* [2011] EWCA Civ 1444; [2012] I.R.L.R. 241 at [145].
[832] *Esso Petroleum Co Ltd v Harper's Garage (Stourport) Ltd* [1968] A.C. 269 at 324.

the wider aspects of a single public policy rule should continue to be recognised".[833] These statements show that the courts would in these cases reject the once fashionable argument[834] that, if an agreement was shown to be reasonable between the parties, the public interest would also be satisfied.

### (f) Covenants affecting the use of land

**No restraint of trade if giving up no right?** Covenants affecting the use of land are commonly enforced although they no doubt restrain trade, e.g. by imposing restrictions on building, or on the carrying on of some particular business or trade, or by providing that the land shall be used for residential purposes only. In the *Esso* case a majority of the House of Lords explained these cases on the ground that: 11–151

> "A person buying or leasing land had no previous right to be there at all, let alone to trade there, and when he takes possession of that land subject to a negative restrictive covenant he gives up no right or freedom which he previously had".[835]

It has therefore been held that where a person enters into a solus agreement when he acquires land, and that agreement is a term of the conveyance by which the land is transferred, the doctrine of restraint of trade does not apply at all.[836] Nevertheless, it is submitted that the reasoning is hard to reconcile with the emphasis placed in the *Esso* case itself on the element of public interest;[837] for restrictions on the use of land may cause harm to the public where they are imposed at the time when the land is acquired, no less than where they are imposed later. Of course, generally speaking, the object of a restrictive covenant affecting land is to preserve amenities and not to restrain trade or to prevent competition; and in most cases such a covenant would in any event pass the test of reasonableness because it would affect only a small area. But sometimes covenants of this kind do expressly restrain the carrying on of a particular business on the land acquired;[838] and cases of this kind can be imagined in which the covenant would not be reasonable.

A person who owned a garage business on a 1,000-acre estate might sell all the land except for the garage and take a covenant that the purchaser would not carry on a garage business on any part of the land bought. Such a covenant could offend public policy just as much as a covenant not to compete within a given radius of the garage. Moreover, we may vary the example by supposing the original owner sells the garage but keeps the rest of the land, and covenants not to

---

[833] *Esso Petroleum Co Ltd v Harper's Garage (Stourport) Ltd* [1968] A.C. 269 at 341.

[834] See para.11–131.

[835] *Esso Petroleum Co Ltd v Harper's Garage (Stourport) Ltd* [1968] A.C. 269 at 298; cf. at 309, 316–317, 325.

[836] *Cleveland Petroleum Ltd v Dartstone Ltd* [1969] 1 W.L.R. 116; Korah 32 M.L.R. 323; fn.840. See also *Re Ravenseft Properties Ltd's Application* [1978] Q.B. 52 (where exceptions are envisaged at 67–68).

[837] See at fn.831; cf. *Peninsula Securities Ltd v Dunnes Stores (Bangor) Ltd* [2018] NICA 7 (Northern Ireland Court of Appeal).

[838] See, e.g. *Holloway Bros v Hill* [1902] 2 Ch. 612; *Newton Abbott Co-operative Society Ltd v Williamson & Treadgold Ltd* [1952] Ch. 286; cf. *Rother v Colchester Corp* [1969] 1 W.L.R. 720.

carry on a garage business on it. This covenant would, according to the reasoning of the *Esso* case, be subject to the doctrine of restraint of trade, for the landowner would be giving up a right which he previously had, to carry on a garage business on the land which he kept. It is hard to see why the doctrine of restraint of trade should not apply to the first as well as to the second of these hypothetical cases. Suppose, further that the owner of a garage sells or leases it to an oil company and then *leases it back* on terms that include a solus agreement. Here it would seem that he did have a "previous right to be there" so that the doctrine of restraint of trade would apply.[839] Attempts have, indeed, been made to evade this result by interposing a company controlled by the garage owner into such an agreement. Thus there is some support for the view that, if the land is leased from a garage owner and leased back to a company controlled by him, then the restraint of trade doctrine should not apply because *the company* had no "previous right to be there".[840] But the distinction between this situation and that in which the two leases are between the same parties can hardly be justified in terms of public policy. Accordingly, it has been held that the restraint of trade doctrine did apply where garage premises were owned by a company controlled by a mother and son, leased by that company to an oil company and then leased back to the mother and son personally.[841] It was said that the court should "pierce the corporate veil" and not give effect to such a "palpable device"[842] for evading the restraint of trade doctrine.

11–152 **Situations in which the restraint of trade doctrine applies to covenants affecting land.** In three further situations the restraint of trade doctrine applies to covenants affecting land. First, it applies where the covenant is given by A to B on the acquisition of land by A, not from B, but from a third party C, e.g. where (as in the *Esso* case itself) the oil company (B) takes the covenant as one of the terms of a loan to A to enable him to buy a garage from C.[843] Secondly, it applies where the owner of a garage mortgages his existing premises and the mortgage contains a solus agreement.[844] Thirdly, it applies where the restriction is imposed not in the conveyance itself but in a separate contemporaneous agreement: this was the position in *Foley v Classique Coaches*[845] where it was assumed that the doctrine did apply and this assumption seems to have been accepted in the *Esso*

[839] e.g. *Amoco Australia Pty Ltd v Rocca Bros Motor Engineering Co Pty Ltd* [1975] A.C. 561.

[840] *Cleveland Petroleum Ltd v Dartstone Ltd* [1969] 1 W.L.R. 116, where the claim to enforce the restraint was actually made against an assignee of the company's leasehold interest in the garage.

[841] *Alec Lobb (Garages) Ltd v Total Oil (Great Britain) Ltd* [1985] 1 W.L.R. 173 (where the restraint was held reasonable).

[842] *Alec Lobb (Garages) Ltd v Total Oil (Great Britain) Ltd* [1985] 1 W.L.R. 173.

[843] Heydon 85 L.Q.R. 229 at 233 argues that this makes the reasoning in the *Esso* case inconsistent with the decision: as A had "no previous right to be there", the restraint of trade doctrine should not have applied. But it is submitted that this part of the reasoning was intended only to apply where the agreement imposing the restriction was between the same parties as the disposition of the land; cf. also *Petrofina (Great Britain) Ltd v Martin* [1966] Ch. 146, where a solus agreement with an oil company on the purchase of a garage from a third party was also held invalid for restraint of trade.

[844] *Texaco Ltd v Mulberry Filling Station Ltd* [1972] 1 W.L.R. 814; semble the mortgage in the *Esso* case was similarly executed after the defendant company had acquired the Corner Garage (though it was executed in pursuance of an earlier agreement).

[845] [1934] 2 K.B. 1; para.11–143.

case.[846] But it is once again by no means clear why, if the doctrine of restraint of trade can apply in these cases, it should not apply to a restrictive covenant forming part of a conveyance between the parties to the covenant. Perhaps similar principles can be applied, if not at common law, then by virtue of s.84 of the Law of Property Act 1925.[847] That section gives the Lands Tribunal a statutory power in certain cases to discharge or modify restrictive covenants affecting land if they have become obsolete by reason of changes in the character of the neighbourhood or because their continued existence "would impede some reasonable user of the land for private or public purposes". This enactment is, in effect, a statutory extension of the doctrine of public policy to these covenants.[848]

### (g) Other agreements

**Categories "never closed".** In the past the courts were reluctant to apply the doctrine of restraint of trade to new classes of contracts. Thus at common law price-maintenance agreements are valid,[849] though some such agreements may be void under the rules which prohibit certain anti-competitive agreements.[850] So, too, at common law an agreement between two persons not to bid against each other at an auction is not illegal[851] but if at least one of them is a dealer they may be guilty of a statutory offence under the Auctions (Bidding Agreements) Act 1927.[852] This Act also provides that the contract can be set aside by the owner of the property auctioned; and, although it does not explicitly invalidate the agreement not to bid as between the parties to it, such invalidity probably follows at common law from the criminality of the agreement.[853] In these cases legislative intervention has been necessary to extend the scope of the doctrine of restraint of trade, but there are signs that the courts are prepared to resume a more creative role in this field. In the *Esso* case Lord Wilberforce said that no exhaustive tests could be stated for defining or identifying contracts in restraint of trade;[854] and that, although such contracts might "be listed, provisionally, in categories … the classification must remain fluid and the categories can never be closed".[855] Similarly, in *Tillman v Egon Zehnder Ltd* Lord Wilson said that "[b]ased as it is on public policy, the doctrine has regularly had to adjust to social change."[856] 11–153

[846] See *Esso Petroleum Co Ltd v Harper's Garage (Stourport) Ltd* [1968] A.C. 269 at 296, 311, 316, 327, 339.

[847] As amended by s.28 of Law of Property Act 1969.

[848] Under the section, the person seeking modification may be ordered to pay compensation. It is arguable that this practice should be extended to some other cases where a person seeks relief from a promise in restraint of trade for which he has received consideration.

[849] *Palmolive Co (of England) v Freedman* [1928] Ch. 264; cf. *Re Dott's Lease* [1920] 1 Ch. 281 (covenant to maintain price of tickets at the Garrick Theatre).

[850] See para.11–116.

[851] *Rawlings v General Trading Co Ltd* [1921] 1 K.B. 635; *Harrop v Thompson* [1975] 1 W.L.R. 545.

[852] As amended by Auctions (Bidding Agreement) Act 1969.

[853] See para.11–011.

[854] *Esso Petroleum Co Ltd v Harper's Garage (Stourport) Ltd* [1968] A.C. 269 at 332.

[855] *Esso Petroleum Co Ltd v Harper's Garage (Stourport) Ltd* [1968] A.C. 269 at 337; cf. *Petrofina (Great Britain) Ltd v Martin* [1966] Ch. 146 at 169.

[856] *Tillman v Egon Zehnder Ltd* [2019] UKSC 32; [2019] 3 W.L.R. 245 at [26].

11–154 **New departures.** Subsequent cases illustrate a number of new departures. It has, for example, been held that covenants in a joint venture agreement (not amounting to a partnership) were subject to the restraint of trade doctrine and so enforceable only to the extent to which they were reasonable, having regard to the covenantee's interest.[857] It seems that, where a dispute about intellectual property is settled, the doctrine can apply to terms of the settlement which restrict a party's right to make use of the property.[858] It also applies to the assignment of a patent which entitles the assignee to any improvements.[859] A further application of the doctrine is illustrated by *Pharmaceutical Society of Great Britain v Dickson*,[860] where the House of Lords held that a rule of the Society restricting the trading activities of chemists was invalid. One ground for the decision was that the rule was ultra vires;[861] but a majority of the House of Lords also held that it was invalid for restraint of trade.[862] The rule was held invalid on this ground even though it was no more than part of a professional code of ethics which was not legally binding (whether as a contract or otherwise). A fortiori, a rule of a professional association may be in restraint of trade if it *is* intended to have contractual force. It has, for example, been said that the rule of the International Tennis Federation by which its members are subject to disqualification for taking prohibited drugs is in restraint of trade, though reasonable and hence valid at common law.[863]

11–155 **Essential feature of contracts within the doctrine.** The doctrine of restraint of trade does not apply merely because a contract restricts a party's freedom to deal with its particular subject-matter, for every contract "necessarily limits the freedom to enter into another contract".[864] The essential feature of contracts within the doctrine is that of "fettering a person's freedom in the future to carry on his trade, business or profession".[865] Various further kinds of agreements or arrangements can be imagined which might have this effect, e.g. an agreement by A not to manufacture a certain product in competition with B;[866] an agreement on the sale of a ship not to operate her on certain routes; an agreement by a buyer not to export goods to a particular country[867]; or an agreement, on the lease of a hall for an exhibition, not to hold a similar exhibition there for six months.[868] It is not suggested that all or any of such agreements will be held invalid; but they may require justification under the doctrine of restraint of trade.

---

[857] *Dawnay Day & Co Ltd v D'Alphen* [1997] I.R.L.R. 422.
[858] *World Wide Fund for Nature v World Wrestling Federation* [2002] EWCA Civ 196; [2002] U.K.C.L.R. 388 at [40]–[42] (agreement held valid).
[859] *Buchanan v Alba Diagnostics Ltd* [2004] UKHL 5; [2004] R.P.C. 34 (agreement held valid).
[860] [1970] A.C. 403; Koh 31 M.L.R. 70.
[861] See para.12–065 and following.
[862] Contrast *R. v General Medical Council Ex p. Coleman* [1990] 1 All E.R. 489 (refusal to allow advertising of holistic medical practice held not to be open to challenge for restraint of trade as the refusal was authorised by statute).
[863] *Wilander and Novacek v Tobin & Jude* [1997] 2 Lloyd's Rep. 295 at 297.
[864] *Shearson Lehman Hutton Inc v Maclaine Watson & Co* [1989] 2 Lloyd's Rep. 570 at 615.
[865] *Shearson Lehman Hutton Inc v Maclaine Watson & Co* [1989] 2 Lloyd's Rep. 570 at 615.
[866] *International Pediatric Products Ltd v Cuddle-King Products Ltd* (1964) 46 D.L.R. (2d) 581.
[867] As in *National Panasonic (UK) Ltd v Commission of the European Communities* [1981] I.C.R. 51.
[868] cf. *Modern Exhibition Services v Cardiff Corp* (1965) 63 L.G.R. 316, where restraint of trade was not discussed.

## 5. SEVERANCE

Where a contract is illegal only in part, two problems can arise. The first is the problem of severance of consideration: can a promise be enforced if it is lawful in itself but is in part supported by illegal consideration? The second is the problem of severance of promises: can a promise be enforced if it is lawful in itself but is coupled with an illegal promise? 11–156

### (a) Severance of consideration

**Where illegal consideration is substantial.** A promise cannot be enforced if the whole or substantially the whole[869] of the consideration for it is illegal. In *Lound v Grimwade*[870] A, who had committed a fraud making him civilly and criminally liable, promised to pay B £3,000 in return for B's promise not to take "any legal proceedings" in respect of the fraud. B's claim for the £3,000 failed as a substantial part of the consideration for A's promise to pay it was B's own illegal promise to stifle a criminal prosecution.[871] 11–157

**Where illegal consideration is subsidiary.** On the other hand, a promise can be enforced if the main consideration for it is lawful, although it is also supported by a subsidiary illegal consideration.[872] For example, an employee who enters into too wide a contract in restraint of trade can recover his wages.[873] The main consideration for the employer's promise to pay is the employee's promise to serve, or the performance of it; his promise not to compete is only subsidiary. The position is similar where an employee as a term of his contract of service enters into a pension scheme which contains an invalid stipulation in restraint of trade. That stipulation forms only a subsidiary part of the consideration which the employee provides for the various promises made by the employer under the contract as a whole; and if the stipulation is invalid it can be severed, so that the pension will be payable although the stipulation is not complied with.[874] But if the sole consideration for the promise to pay the pension is an invalid stipulation in restraint of trade the employee cannot recover the pension. This was the position in *Wyatt v Kreglinger & Fernau*[875] where the promise was made on the 11–158

869 *Marshall v NM Financial Management Ltd* [1997] 1 W.L.R. 1527 at 1532.

870 (1888) 39 Ch D. 605; cf. *Walrond v Walrond* (1858) Johns. 18.

871 See para.11–046. For rejection on similar grounds of a claim to rescind a contract, see *The Siben* [1996] 1 Lloyd's Rep. 35 at 62.

872 See *Goodinson v Goodinson* [1954] 2 Q.B. 118 (the actual decision is obsolete: Matrimonial Causes Act 1973 s.34; para.11–048); cf. *Kearney v Whitehaven Colliery Co* [1893] 1 Q.B. 700; *Fielding & Platt Ltd v Najjar* [1969] 1 W.L.R. 357 at 362.

873 *McFarlane v Daniell* (1938) S.R. (N.S.W.) 337; approved in *Carney v Herbert* [1985] A.C. 301 at 311; cf. *Sadler v Imperial Life Assurance Co of Canada* [1988] I.R.L.R. 388; and *Marshall v NM Financial Management Ltd* [1997] 1 W.L.R. 1527 (similar principle applied to agent's claim for commission).

874 *Bull v Pitney-Bowes Ltd* [1967] 1 W.L.R. 273; semble the stipulation was not a mere condition but formed part of the consideration for the employer's promise since it was entered into at the employer's request: see para.3–010.

875 [1933] 1 K.B. 793; para.11–131.

lawful termination of the contract of service and the employee provided no consideration for the promise except his assent to, or performance of, the invalid stipulation in restraint of trade.

11–159 **Sale of business.** Similar principles apply where the vendor of a business enters into too wide a contract in restraint of trade. If the price is promised mainly for the business premises and stock-in-trade, the illegal promise not to compete is only a subsidiary part of the consideration for the promise to pay, so that the vendor can recover the price. But if the purpose of the transaction, viewed objectively,[876] was the elimination of a competitor, rather than the purchase of a business, it might be held that the vendor's promise not to compete formed a substantial part of the consideration for the purchaser's promise to pay; and that accordingly the vendor would not be entitled to the price.

11–160 **Primacy of fulfilling the policy of the invalidating rule.** The distinction so far drawn may, however, be displaced by the policy of the invalidating rule. In *Ailion v Spiekermann*[877] the vendor of a leasehold interest required the purchasers to pay an illegal premium. He thereby committed a statutory offence, but the purchasers (who were "unwilling victims")[878] committed none by promising to pay the premium. It was held that they could specifically enforce the vendor's obligations without having to pay the premium. They were able to do this, whether or not their promise to pay the premium constituted a substantial part of the consideration; for such enforcement by them was the most effective way of promoting the legislative policy against illegal premiums.

11–161 **Apportionment of promise to legal part of consideration.** In the cases so far discussed, the claimant has either failed or succeeded in full. The claimant in *Lound v Grimwade*[879] got nothing, though part of the consideration provided by him was lawful; while an employee who enters into too wide a restraint of trade can recover his entire wages, though the employer loses one of the advantages for which he bargained. It might be thought fairer to make the defendant liable in proportion to the legal part of the consideration. The objection to such a rule is that it would often be hard to apply as the court cannot easily tell what value the parties attributed to the legal and illegal parts of the consideration respectively. But it seems that where the legal and illegal parts can be precisely valued, the claimant can recover so much of the promised payment as can be attributed to the lawful part of the consideration. In *Frank W Clifford Ltd v Garth*[880] a builder agreed to do building work for the defendant on a "cost plus" basis, so that the total cost of the work could not be known in advance. The bill for the completed work came to £1,911. The defendant refused to pay anything because work costing more than £1,000 was illegal unless licensed, and no licence had been

876 *Triggs v Staines Urban DC* [1969] 1 Ch. 10; para.11–131.

877 [1979] Ch. 158.

878 *Ailion v Spiekermann* [1979] Ch. 158 at 165.

879 (1888) 39 Ch D. 605.

880 [1956] 1 W.L.R. 570; cf. *Ex p. Mather* (1797) 3 Ves. 373; *J Dennis & Co v Munn* [1949] 2 K.B. 327; *Blue Chip Trading v Helbawi* [2009] I.R.L.R. 128; and see *The American Accord* [1983] 1 A.C. 168.

obtained. But he was held liable to pay £1,000: his promise to pay was enforced to the extent to which it was supported by lawful consideration.[881] A person who has done work under a contract which is only partly illegal may also be awarded a reasonable sum in respect of the lawful part of the work.[882] Such an award is based on restitutionary principles and does not strictly speaking amount to partial enforcement *of the contract*, but in practical terms the outcome will often quite closely resemble such enforcement.[883]

### (b) Severance of promises

Where the promises of one party to a contract are partly lawful and partly illegal, the court may cut out the illegal promises and enforce the lawful ones alone. In *Tillman v Egon Zehnder Ltd*[884] the Supreme Court held that the court will do this only if three conditions are satisfied:[885] it must not be necessary to redraft the contract;[886] the remaining terms must continue to be supported by consideration;[887] and severance must not alter the whole nature of the covenant.[888] 11–162

**Whether the promise must be of such a kind as can be severed.** In addition to the conditions just outlined, it has been said that there can be no severance of a criminal or immoral promise.[889] But although this may be generally true, it seems that a criminal promise could be severed if it was made without guilty intent.[890] It has also been said that there can be no severance of a promise to trade with the enemy[891] or of a promise to defraud the Revenue.[892] Promises are most frequently severed in contracts in restraint of trade; and it has been assumed that 11–163

[881] It seems the builder would have recovered nothing if he had agreed to do the work without a licence, knowing from the start that it would cost over £1,000: *Frank W Clifford v Garth* [1956] 1 W.L.R. at 572; cf. para.11–074.

[882] *Mohamed v Alaga & Co* [1999] 3 All E.R. 699 at 707, 710; para.11–106.

[883] See para.11–092.

[884] [2019] UKSC 32; [2019] 3 W.L.R. 245.

[885] In approving these criteria Lord Wilson endorsed the decision in *Beckett Investment Management Group Ltd v Hall* [2007] EWCA Civ 613; [2007] I.C.R. 1539; and overruled the decision in *Attwood v Lamont* [1920] 3 K.B. 571 which is discussed below: para.11–167.

[886] See para.11–164.

[887] See para.11–165.

[888] See para.11–166.

[889] *Bennett v Bennett* [1951] 1 K.B. 249 at 254.

[890] As in the case of severance of consideration: cf. *Frank W Clifford Ltd v Garth* [1956] 1 W.L.R. 570 at 572.

[891] *Kuenigl v Donnersmarck* [1955] 1 Q.B. 515; cf. *Royal Boskalis Westminster NV v Mountain* [1999] Q.B. 674 at 693.

[892] *Miller v Karlinski* (1945) 62 T.L.R. 85; *Corby v Morrison* [1980] I.C.R. 564; the contrary was assumed in *Napier v National Business Agency* [1951] 2 All E.R. 265 but it was held that the contract was not severable as there was only one promise in substance; cf. *Lincoln v CB Richard Ellis Hotels Ltd* [2009] EWHC 2344 (TCC). In the case of long-term employment, the contract is wholly invalid during the period in respect of which the illegal payments are made, but not in respect of the rest of its duration; *Hyland v JH Barker (North-West) Ltd* [1985] I.C.R. 861.

promises excluding the jurisdiction of the courts can be severed.[893] The question whether other illegal promises can be severed at all is still an open one.

11–164 **Must not be necessary to redraft the contract: the "blue pencil" test.** Under this test, the court will sever only where this can be done by cutting words out of the contract (or by running a blue pencil through the offending words). The court will not redraft the contract by adding or rearranging words, or by substituting one word for another.[894] In *Mason v Provident Clothing & Supply Co Ltd*[895] the House of Lords refused to strike out of the contract the words "within 25 miles of London" and to substitute "in Islington"; to do so would be, not to sever, but to redraft the contract. The test does little to protect the party subject to the restraint since it can easily be satisfied by skilful draftsmanship, while on the other hand it may entirely prevent enforcement of a restraint drawn up by laymen where some degree of enforcement would be reasonable.[896] Nevertheless, it was approved by the Supreme Court in *Tillman v Egon Zehnder Ltd* as "an appropriate brake on the ability of employers to secure severance of an unreasonable restraint customarily devised by themselves."[897]

The courts will apply the blue pencil test with some latitude. In *T Lucas & Co Ltd v Mitchell*[898] a contract provided that a sales representative should not within a certain *area* "deal in any goods similar to" those allocated to him for sale; or "*solicit orders* for … any *such* goods". It was held that the area covenant was invalid while the solicitation covenant was valid; and that the area covenant could be severed. Strictly speaking, this left no point of reference for the word "such" in the solicitation covenant, but the deleted area covenant could be looked at to give the word meaning.

It used to be thought that promises could be severed merely because the "blue pencil" test was satisfied;[899] but this view no longer prevails. The test may restrict, but it does not determine, the scope of the doctrine of severance. Even if the legal and illegal promises are actually contained in separate documents,[900] the court will sever only if the other requirements are also satisfied.[901]

11–165 **The remaining terms must continue to be supported by consideration.** As is apparent from the discussion above,[902] and as confirmed by Lord Wilson in

---

[893] *Re Davstone Estate Ltd's Leases* [1969] 2 Ch. 378; but severance failed because the "blue pencil" test (below) was not satisfied; *Home Ins Co v Administratia Asigurarilor* [1983] 2 Lloyd's Rep. 674 at 677.

[894] And will not give effect to an express provision calling for the same: *Townends Group Ltd v Cobb* [2004] EWHC 3432 (Ch); *The Times*, 1 December 2004 at [60]. Contrast the court's statutory power to revise contracts: in the cases described at para.11–169.

[895] [1913] A.C. 724 (para.11–126).

[896] See *Commercial Plastics Ltd v Vincent* [1965] 1 Q.B. 623 at 647.

[897] *Tillman v Egon Zehnder Ltd* [2019] UKSC 32; [2019] 3 W.L.R. 245 at [85].

[898] [1974] Ch. 129.

[899] *Putsman v Taylor* [1927] 1 K.B. 637 at 640; the Court of Appeal held the covenant valid *in toto*, so that severance was not necessary: [1927] 1 K.B. 741.

[900] As in *Kenyon v Darwen Cotton Manufacturing Co Ltd* [1936] 2 K.B. 193.

[901] *British Reinforced Concrete Engineering Co Ltd v Schelff* [1921] 2 Ch. 563, a vendor and purchaser case in which *Attwood v Lamont* [1920] 3 K.B. 571 (now overruled (see para.11–167) was followed on this point.

[902] See para.11–158.

*Tillman v Egon Zehnder Ltd*,[903] this requirement can "usually be ignored" in the "usual post-employment situation" where it is the employer who is seeking severance, since he is "in no way proposing to diminish the consideration passing from himself under the contract such as is necessary to support the obligation which he seeks to enforce."[904] It may be more problematic where it is the employee who is seeking severance. The removal of the unreasonable obligation may raise the question of whether there is any remaining consideration to enforce the employer's promise of a post-employment benefit such as continued remuneration,[905] commission,[906] or a pension.[907]

**Severance must not alter the nature of the covenant.** The court will not sever if to do so alters the whole nature of the covenant.[908] This was described by Lord Wilson in *Tillman v Egon Zehnder Ltd* as the "crucial criterion" and he expressed it in the following terms: 11–166

> "… whether removal of the provision would not generate any major change in the overall effect of all the post-employment restraints in the contract. It is for the employer to establish that its removal would not do so. The focus is on the legal effect of the restraints, which will remain constant, not on their perhaps changing significance for the parties and in particular for the employee."

Application of this requirement, and of the other two requirements outlined above, can be illustrated by the *Tillman* case itself. In that case a senior employee of an executive recruitment company was subject to a restrictive covenant under which she agreed that she would not "directly or indirectly engage or be concerned or interested in any business carried on in competition with any of the businesses of the [c]ompany". The inclusion of "or interested" was unreasonable since it prevented her from holding even a minority shareholding in a competitor, but it could be severed: the words "or interested" could simply be removed without generating "any major change in the overall effect of the restraints"; and this was a case where the requirement of consideration could be "ignored".[909]

Similarly, in *Goldsoll v Goldman*[910] the seller of an imitation jewellery business in New Bond Street undertook that he would not for two years deal in real or imitation jewellery in the UK or certain named places abroad. The covenant was too wide in *area* as the seller had not traded abroad, and in respect of *subject-matter* as he had scarcely dealt in real jewellery. But it was held that the references to the foreign places and to real jewellery could be severed, and that the restraint on dealing in imitation jewellery in the UK could be enforced. The only question discussed by the court was whether the "blue pencil" test was

[903] [2019] UKSC 32; [2019] 3 W.L.R. 245.
[904] *Tillman v Egon Zehnder Ltd* [2019] UKSC 32; [2019] 3 W.L.R. 245 at [86].
[905] See, e.g. *Marshall v NM Financial Management Ltd* [1997] 1 W.L.R. 1527.
[906] See, e.g. *Sadler v Imperial Life Assurance of Canada* [1988] I.R.L.R. 388.
[907] See, e.g. *Wyatt v Kreglinger & Fernau* [1933] 1 K.B. 793, discussed at para.11–158.
[908] *Putsman v Taylor* [1927] 1 K.B. 637 at 646; cf. *Spector v Ageda* [1973] Ch. 30 at 45; *Royal Boskalis Westminster NV v Mountain* [1999] Q.B. 674 at 693. This requirement does not apply to an agreement partly invalid under the rules of competition law stated at para.11–116: *Barrett v Inntrepreneur Pub Co (GL) Ltd* [1999] E.G.C.S. 93.
[909] See text to fn.904.
[910] [1915] 1 Ch. 292.

satisfied; but it can be argued that the object of the original covenant was to protect the business which the buyer had bought; that the object of the covenant after severance remained the same; and that severance had thus not altered the nature of the original covenant.

11–167 **No requirement of two separate covenants, or that part to be severed must be "trivial or technical".** In *Attwood v Lamont*,[911] based in part on earlier dicta of Lord Moulton in *Mason v Provident Clothing & Supply Co Ltd*,[912] a majority of the Court of Appeal had suggested that severance of a covenant was available only where it was "not really a single covenant but [was] in effect a combination of several different covenants"[913] and that it should be confined to the "trivial and the technical".[914] This was said as part of a reluctance to sever post-employment restraints, but that view has since been deprecated,[915] and in *Tillman v Egon Zehnder Ltd*, while Lord Wilson acknowledged the need for a "cautious approach"[916] to severance in this context, these two additional requirements were rejected and the decision in *Attwood v Lamont* was overruled.[917] In the *Attwood* case the claimants had a general outfitters' business in Kidderminster which was divided into several departments, each of which was supervised by one of their employees. The head of each department undertook that he would not after leaving the claimants' service "be concerned in any of the following trades or businesses: that is to say, the trade or business of a tailor, dressmaker, general draper, milliner, hatter, haberdasher, gentlemen's, ladies' or children's outfitter" within 10 miles of Kidderminster. In an action to enforce this covenant against the head of the tailoring department, the claimants admitted that the covenant was too wide in point of subject-matter, but they argued that everything except the reference to tailoring should be severed, and that part alone enforced. This argument was rejected by Lord Sterndale MR on the basis that severance would have altered the whole nature of the covenant, which is retained as a requirement.[918] The decision of the Supreme Court in the *Tillman* case not only to reject the additional requirements referred to above, but to overrule the decision in *Attwood v Lamont* must be based on the view that it cannot be sustained on the basis of the requirements which remain, but nowhere is this explained in the speech of Lord Wilson.

11–168 **Whether other promises affected.** In the restraint of trade cases discussed above, the covenant not to compete formed part of a larger transaction; and the effect of holding that excessive parts of the restraint could not be severed was

[911] [1920] 3 K.B. 571.

[912] [1913] A.C. 724 at 745.

[913] *Attwood v Lamont* [1920] 3 K.B. 571 at 593.

[914] *Attwood v Lamont* [1920] 3 K.B. 571 at 594–595.

[915] *Commercial Plastics Ltd v Vincent* [1965] 1 Q.B. 623 at 647 (para.11–164); *T Lucas & Co Ltd v Mitchell* [1974] Ch. 129; *The Littlewoods Organisation Ltd v Harris* [1977] 1 W.L.R. 1472 (where no question of severance arose); *Business Seating (Renovations) Ltd v Broad* [1989] I.C.R. 729 at 734–735; *Dawnay Day & Co Ltd v D'Alphen* [1997] I.R.L.R. 285 at 296, 422; *Beckett Investment Management Group Ltd v Hall* [2007] EWCA Civ 613; [2007] I.C.R. 1539 at [38]–[39].

[916] *Tillman v Egon Zehnder Ltd* [2019] UKSC 32; [2019] 3 W.L.R. 245 at [66], [82].

[917] *Tillman v Egon Zehnder Ltd* [2019] UKSC 32; [2019] 3 W.L.R. 245 at [921].

[918] See para.11–166.

simply that *that covenant* was wholly void. *Other* promises or obligations of the covenantor under the contract as a whole may nevertheless be enforceable. For example, an employee who has entered into a wholly void covenant in restraint of trade may still be restrained from breaking his duty of fidelity.[919] And a person to whom money has been lent on terms which include an invalid covenant in restraint of trade is nevertheless liable to repay the loan and to pay interest.[920] In such cases, it can be said that the main purpose of the contract is to create the relationship of employer and employee or of lender and borrower; and the fact that the contract seeks to impose an invalid restraint on the employee or borrower does not vitiate the entire relationship.

On the other hand, where the main purpose of the contract is to impose the restraint, the invalidity of that restraint can lead to the nullity of the whole contract. In such cases, the issue is not whether one part of the restraint can be severed from another without altering the nature *of the covenant* in restraint of trade; it is, rather, whether the invalidity of the restraint has left *the contract as a whole* without subject-matter. Two cases which raise the latter question may be contrasted. Both were concerned with solus petrol agreements; in each case the garage proprietor had leased his garage to the oil company which had then leased it back by granting an underlease to the garage proprietor, the solus agreement being contained in the underlease.[921] In the *Amoco*[922] case, the underlease was at a nominal rent for a period just one day shorter than the original lease: in these circumstances it was held that the solus agreement "constituted the heart and soul of the underlease".[923] As the solus agreement was invalid, it followed that neither the underlease nor the original lease (which was part of the same arrangement) could remain in force. On the other hand, in the *Alec Lobb*[924] case the original lease was for a period of 51 years; the oil company had paid a premium of £35,000 (the fair market value) for it; the underlease was for only 21 years and yielded a rent of £2,250 per annum. The solus agreement was held valid;[925] but it was said that, even if it had been invalid, the lease and underlease would have remained in force since the transaction as a whole would not, merely because of the invalidity of that one term, have "so changed its character as not to be the sort of contract that the parties intended to enter into at all".[926] The contract would have remained one "for letting a petrol station ... at a rent which was not nominal. It was therefore the sort of contract which the parties intended to enter into".[927]

---

[919] See para.6–068; *Commercial Plastics Ltd v Vincent* [1965] 1 Q.B. 623; *Royal Boskalis Westminster NV v Mountain* [1999] Q.B. 674 at 693.

[920] cf. *Cleveland Petroleum Co v Trinity Garage (Bexleyheath)*, *The Times*, 8 September 1965.

[921] See para.11–144.

[922] *Amoco Australia Pty v Rocca Bros Motor Engineering Pty Ltd* [1975] A.C. 561.

[923] *Amoco Australia Pty v Rocca Bros Motor Engineering Pty Ltd* [1975] A.C. 561 at 578.

[924] *Alec Lobb (Garages) Ltd v Total Oil (Great Britain) Ltd* [1985] 1 W.L.R. 173; cf. *Amoco Australia Pty v Rocca Bros Motor Engineering Pty Ltd* [1975] A.C. 561 at 579.

[925] See para.11–148.

[926] *Alec Lobb (Garages) Ltd v Total Oil (Great Britain) Ltd* [1985] 1 W.L.R. 173 at 192; applying the test stated by Buckley LJ in *Chemidus Wavin Ltd v Société pour la Transformation et l'Exploitation des Resines Industrielles* [1978] 3 C.M.L.R. 514 at 520.

[927] *Alec Lobb (Garages) Ltd v Total Oil (Great Britain) Ltd* [1985] 1 W.L.R. 173 at 192. An alternative ground for the decision in the *Alec Lobb* case is suggested by the statement there made at

The principle just stated is not restricted to cases in which the source of illegality is restraint of trade. In *Carney v Herbert*[928] a contract was made for the sale of shares by instalments; the sellers asked for security for the payment of these instalments, and the form of security agreed on and given was illegal. It was held that the contract as a whole was not vitiated, so that the buyer remained liable for the price since the illegal security "did not go to the heart of the transaction".[929] The sellers had only wanted *some* security and the invalidity of the particular security given did not change the essential character of the contract as one for the sale of the shares.

## (c) Statutory severance

**11–169** Acts of Parliament which make specific terms in certain contracts unlawful sometimes contain provisions which give rise to a kind of statutory severance. Under the Equality Act 2010, for example, the court may make orders for offending terms to be "removed or modified".[930]

181 that "The tie provisions … were not *either* the sole consideration for the tie *or* the sole object of the transaction" (emphasis added). While the second alternative here stated is (with respect) plainly correct, the first is hard to follow: it seems to suggest that the tie could in part be consideration for itself.

928 [1985] A.C. 301; cf. para.11–107.

929 *Carney v Herbert* [1985] A.C. 301 at 316.

930 Equality Act 2010 s.143.

# CHAPTER 12

# CAPACITY



In this chapter we are concerned with the circumstances in which one party to a contract may be regarded, as a matter of law, as lacking the capacity to do so and the effect on the contract of any such incapacity. A party may lack capacity in order to protect the party in question, e.g. in the case of minors,[1] or to protect the interests of third parties, such as the shareholders of a company.[2] **12–001**

[1] See para.12–002.

[2] See para.12–065.

## 1. MINORS

12–002 In the law of contract, persons below the age of majority were formerly called infants; and this expression is used in many of the older cases which deal with their contractual capacity. They are now more generally called minors; and, as this term is used in modern legislation on the subject, it will also be used in this chapter. When the age of majority was reduced from 21 to 18,[3] the practical importance of the rules which determine the extent to which minors are bound by their contracts was greatly reduced. If the decided cases are any guide, many of the legal problems in this area have in the past concerned the contracts of persons between 18 and 21, whose contractual capacity is now normal. But the question whether persons under 18 are bound by contracts can still arise today, e.g. out of the contracts of young professional entertainers[4] or athletes,[5] or out of hire-purchase agreements or contracts of employment involving minors. Legal problems can also arise where a claim is made by the minor against the other party, either to enforce the contract or to reclaim money or property with which the minor has parted under it.

12–003 **General principles.** The law on this topic is based on two principles. The first, and more important, is that the law must protect the minor against his inexperience, which may enable an adult to take unfair advantage of him, or to induce him to enter into a contract which, though in itself fair, is simply improvident.[6] This principle is the basis of the general rule that a minor is not bound by his contracts. The second principle is that the law should not cause unnecessary hardship to adults who deal fairly with minors. Under this principle certain contracts with minors are valid; others are voidable in the sense that they bind the minor unless he repudiates; and a minor may be under some liability in tort and in restitution.

### (a) Valid contracts

#### *(i) Necessaries*

12–004 A contract for necessaries is binding "not for the benefit of the tradesman who may trust the infant, but for the benefit of the infant himself".[7] It is assumed, rightly or wrongly,[8] that the tradesman would not give credit to the minor unless the law imposed liability. In this connection it should be noted that parents are not liable on their child's contract unless the child acts as their agent;[9] and that in

[3] Family Law Reform Act 1969 s.1; s.9 provides that a person attains 18 "at the commencement of the [18th] anniversary of his birth."

[4] e.g. *Mills v IRC* [1975] A.C. 38 at 53.

[5] *Proform Sports Management Ltd v Proactive Sports Management Ltd* [2006] EWHC 2903 (Ch); [2007] Bus. L.R. 93.

[6] e.g. if the minor for a fair price agrees to buy something that he cannot afford.

[7] *Ryder v Wombwell* (1868) L.R. 4 Ex. 32 at 38; *Zouch v Parsons* (1763) 3 Burr. 1794.

[8] cf. para.12–008.

[9] *Blackburn v Mackey* (1823) 1 C. & P. 1; *Law v Wilkin* (1837) 6 A. & E. 718; *Mortimore v Wright* (1840) 6 M. & W. 482.

English law a minor's contract cannot be validated by the consent or authorisation of his parent or guardian. Necessaries include goods supplied and services rendered to a minor. He is bound by a contract for necessaries only if it is on the whole for his benefit: not if it contains harsh and onerous terms.[10] Nor is he bound by an indivisible contract comprising necessaries and non-necessaries.[11]

**Necessary goods.** Necessary goods are not confined to necessities: they include "such articles as are fit to maintain the particular person in the state, station and degree … in which he is".[12] In one case[13] a livery for a minor's servant was held to be a necessary; and in another[14] the court refused to disturb a verdict that rings, pins and a watch-chain supplied to the son of a rich man were necessaries. These "quaint examples of a bygone age"[15] are hardly cases in which liability was imposed "for the benefit of the infant himself".[16] The wide definition of necessaries was adopted rather for the protection of suppliers who reasonably gave credit to young men from wealthy families. 12–005

**Not "mere luxuries".** On the other hand, the definition of necessaries was limited so as to exclude "mere luxuries". These were distinguished from "luxurious articles of utility",[17] which could be necessaries. Since few articles are so luxurious that they cannot be used at all, the real question was whether it was reasonable for the minor, however rich, to be supplied with articles of the kind in question. Thus it was said that if the son of the richest man in the kingdom bought a racehorse, it could not be a necessary[18] but where an apprentice bought a racing bicycle (which was no more expensive than an ordinary one) it was held to be a necessary.[19] It is doubtful whether goods bought by a minor to be given away can normally be necessaries.[20] But an engagement ring bought to be given to the minor's fiancée, whom he later marries, can be a necessary.[21] 12–006

**A question of mixed law and fact.** Much difficulty was caused in the nineteenth century by the tendency of juries (consisting of 12 shopkeepers) to stretch the definition of necessaries beyond its legitimate limits. In one case "an Oxford jury held that champagne and wild ducks were necessaries to an infant undergraduate".[22] To counteract this tendency, the courts first distinguished between articles 12–007

---

[10] *Fawcett v Smethurst* (1914) 84 L.J.Ch. 473.

[11] *Stocks v Wilson* [1913] 2 K.B. 235.

[12] *Peters v Fleming* (1840) 6 M. & W. 42 at 46; *Bryant v Richardson* (1866) 14 L.T. 24 at 26.

[13] *Hands v Slaney* (1800) 8 T.R. 578. But a claim for the price of cockades for soldiers under the minor's command was disallowed.

[14] *Peters v Fleming* (1840) 6 M. & W. 42.

[15] *Allen v Bloomsbury Health Authority* [1993] 1 All E.R. 651 at 661.

[16] See para.12–004.

[17] *Chapple v Cooper* (1844) 13 M. & W. 252 at 258.

[18] *Wharton v Mackenzie* (1844) 5 Q.B. 606 at 612. Contrast *Barber v Vincent* (1680) Free. K.B. 581 (horse sold to a minor to carry him about his necessary business held a necessary).

[19] *Clyde Cycle Co v Hargreaves* (1898) 78 L.T. 296.

[20] *Ryder v Wombwell* (1868) L.R. 4 Ex. 32; *Hewlings v Graham* (1901) 84 L.T. 497.

[21] *Jenner v Walker* (1869) 19 L.T. 398.

[22] Parl.Deb., Vol.219, ser.3, col.1225 (1874).

which could, and those which could not, as a matter of law, be necessaries.[23] They held, secondly, that the question whether goods were necessaries was:

> "one of mixed law and fact; in so far as it is a question of fact it must be determined by the jury ... ; but there is in every case ... a preliminary question which is one of law, namely whether there is any evidence on which the jury could properly find the question for the party on whom the onus of proof lies".[24]

In *Ryder v Wombwell*[25] the son of a deceased baronet bought jewelled cufflinks for £12 10s. apiece and an antique goblet to give to a friend. The jury found that these articles were necessaries. But the court set the verdict aside as there was no evidence on which it could properly be based.

12–008 **Burden of proof.** The onus of proving that goods are necessaries lies on the supplier who must show both that the goods are capable of being necessaries and that they actually are necessaries. In *Nash v Inman*[26] a tailor sued a minor for the price of clothes, including 11 fancy waistcoats. The action failed because the tailor had not adduced any evidence fit to be left to the jury that the clothes were suitable to the condition in life of the minor, *and* that the minor was not already adequately supplied with clothes. The courts have put on the claimant the burden of proving the difficult negative proposition that the minor was not adequately supplied. As a general rule a person is only required to prove a negative if such proof depends on facts peculiarly within his own knowledge; here the proof required of the supplier depends on facts peculiarly within the knowledge of the minor. It was further held that the minor is not liable if he already had an adequate supply, even though the supplier did not know this.[27] Such a rule may help to protect minors; but it is difficult to reconcile with the view that minors are liable for necessaries because, if they were not, traders would not give them credit. For the rule makes it impossible for the supplier to tell, when the contract is made, whether the minor will indeed be bound by it.

12–009 **Necessary services.** Certain services rendered to a minor may be necessaries. These include education (whether liberal or vocational)[28] and medical and legal advice.[29] The provision of a funeral for her deceased husband has been held a necessary for his widow, who was a minor.[30] It seems that any service can be a necessary if it satisfies the tests already stated in relation to necessary goods.

12–010 **Are executory contracts for necessaries binding?**[31] It is disputed whether a minor is bound by an executory contract for necessary goods. Is he liable only if

[23] *Ryder v Wombwell* (1868) L.R. 4 Ex. 32.
[24] *Ryder v Wombwell* (1868) L.R. 4 Ex. 32 at 38.
[25] (1868) L.R. 4 Ex. 32 at 38; cf. *Wharton v Mackenzie* (1844) 5 Q.B. 606.
[26] [1908] 2 K.B. 1.
[27] *Foster v Redgrave* (1867) L.R. 4 Ex. 35n.; *Barnes v Toye* (1884) 13 Q.B.D. 410.
[28] *Walter v Everard* [1891] 2 Q.B. 369; *Roberts v Gray* [1913] 1 K.B. 520. For contracts to pay school fees, see *Practice Direction* [1980] 1 W.L.R. 1441; *Practice Direction* [1983] 1 W.L.R. 800; *Sherdley v Sherdley* [1988] A.C. 213 at 225.
[29] *Huggins v Wiseman* (1690) Carth. 110; *Helps v Clayton* (1864) 17 C.B. (N.S.) 553.
[30] *Chapple v Cooper* (1844) 13 M. & W. 252.
[31] Miles (1927) 43 L.Q.R. 389; Winfield (1942) 58 L.Q.R. 83.

the goods have actually been delivered, or also if he wrongfully repudiates before delivery? Three main arguments have been used to support the view that the minor is liable only if the goods have been delivered.

First, in *Nash v Inman* Fletcher Moulton LJ said that the minor was liable because he had been supplied, and not because he had contracted:

> "An infant, like a lunatic,[32] is incapable of making a contract … in the strict sense of the word: but if a man satisfies the need of the infant or lunatic by supplying to him necessaries, the law will imply an obligation to repay him for the services so rendered, and will enforce that obligation against the estate of the infant or lunatic".[33]

But Buckley LJ said that a contract for necessaries was "such as the infant, notwithstanding infancy, could make" and that "an infant had a limited capacity to contract".[34] And the analogy of the "lunatic" is, with respect, imperfect. Sometimes the reason why such a person is "incapable of making a contract" may be that he cannot consent; and if he is then supplied with necessaries there is not even the shadow of an agreement to accept and pay for the goods. This may also be true when necessaries are supplied to a very young child.[35] But it is not true when a young man of 17 orders clothes and promises to pay for them. He can and does consent: the only question is whether he ought as a matter of legal policy to be held to the agreement.

Secondly, the minor is liable only for a reasonable price, which may not be the same as the contract price. "That does not imply a consensual contract."[36] But the law often interferes with one or more of the terms of a transaction and this does not necessarily deprive it of its essential character as a contract.[37]

Thirdly, s.3(2) of the Sale of Goods Act 1979 provides that "Where necessaries are sold and delivered to a minor … he must pay a reasonable price for them". Section 3(3) then defines "'necessaries' in subsection (2) above" to mean "goods suitable to the condition in life of the minor … and to his actual requirements *at the time of sale and delivery*." The words here italicised may seem to suggest that goods cannot be necessaries unless they have actually been delivered. But the definition is of necessaries "in subsection (2) above", and that subsection deals only with necessaries sold and delivered. The definition does not apply to goods sold but not yet delivered.

Thus, the arguments in support of the view that the minor is not liable on an executory contract are inconclusive; and the contrary view is supported by *Roberts v Gray*.[38] The claimant, a famous billiards player, agreed to take a minor on a world billiards tour, and to pay for his board and lodging and travelling expenses. This was a contract for necessaries, mainly because its object was to teach the minor the profession of a billiards player. The minor repudiated the contract while it was still partly executory; and he was held liable in damages.

---

[32] Now called a person lacking mental capacity: see para.12–053 and following.

[33] *Nash v Inman* [1908] 2 K.B. 1 at 8; cf. *Re J* [1909] 1 Ch. 574.

[34] *Nash v Inman* [1908] 2 K.B. 1 at 12.

[35] See *Sherdley v Sherdley* [1988] A.C. 213 at 225; *R. v Oldham MBC Ex p. Garlick* [1993] A.C. 509 at 517.

[36] *Pontypridd Union v Drew* [1927] 1 K.B. 214 at 220.

[37] See para.1–007.

[38] [1913] 1 K.B. 520.

Hamilton LJ said: "I am unable to appreciate why a contract which is in itself binding … can cease to be binding merely because it is still executory".[39] It has been said that *Roberts v Gray* can be explained on the ground that contracts for education are more closely analogous to beneficial contracts of service[40] than to contracts for the supply of necessary goods.[41] But it is hard to see why any distinction should for this purpose be drawn between necessary goods and education; or between necessaries of either kind and beneficial contracts of service. The reasons for holding a minor liable, and for limiting his liability, are the same in all these cases. It is thought that the minor's overall position might be prejudiced if he could not bind himself, and also that liability should be imposed to protect the legitimate interests of the adult. These considerations have to be balanced against the need to protect the minor. If a balancing of all these factors justifies the view that the minor should be bound by an executory contract for education or of service, it is submitted that it can equally justify the view that he should be bound by an executory contract for the supply of necessary goods.

12–011 **Legislation affecting the maintenance of children.** The common law rules relating to liability for necessaries are not directly affected by legislation imposing on an absent parent the duty to maintain a child[42] or empowering courts to make orders against parents for financial relief in respect of children.[43] Such legislation may, however, indirectly affect a minor's contractual liabilities for necessaries, in the sense that if, as a result of its operation, the minor is already adequately supplied with the goods or services in question, they will not fall within the common law definition of necessaries.

12–012 **Loans for necessaries.** At common law a person who spends money in buying necessaries for a minor is entitled to recover it from the minor.[44] One who lends money to a minor to enable him to buy necessaries cannot recover it at law, but can in equity recover such part of the loan as was actually used by the minor to discharge his liability for necessaries supplied to him.[45] A promise in a mortgage deed to repay such a loan is ineffective since the minor is not bound by his deed.[46] The law leaves the lender for necessaries in a somewhat precarious position—perhaps because a loan of money can more easily be misapplied than an actual supply of necessaries.

---

39 *Roberts v Gray* [1913] 1 K.B. 520 at 530.

40 See paras 12–013–12–018.

41 *Cheshire, Fifoot and Furmston's Law of Contract*, 15th edn (2006), p.552.

42 Child Support Act 1991 s.1(1).

43 Children Act 1989 s.15.

44 *Ellis v Ellis* (1689) Comb. 482; *Earle v Peale* (1712) 10 Mod. 67.

45 *Marlow v Pitfeild* (1719) 1 P. Wms. 558; *Re National Permanent Benefit Building Society* (1869) L.R. 5 Ch. App. 309 at 313.

46 *Martin v Gale* (1876) 4 Ch D. 428.

## (ii) Service contracts

**Binding if for minor's benefit.** A minor[47] is bound by a service contract if it is on the whole for his benefit. He may be bound even though some of the terms of the contract are to his disadvantage. In *Clements v L & NW Ry*[48] a minor who was a railway porter agreed to join an insurance scheme, to which his employers contributed, and to give up any claim for personal injury under the Employers' Liability Act 1880. His rights under the scheme were in some ways more, and in other ways less, beneficial than those under the Act; and it was held that the contract was on the whole beneficial, so that the minor was bound by it. But a term which simply limits or excludes the liability of the employer without giving the minor any rights in return is unlikely to be upheld.[49] A minor is, a fortiori, not bound by a service contract which is on the whole harsh and oppressive to the minor.[50] **12–013**

**Whether contract is for minor's benefit.** In deciding whether a service contract is on the whole beneficial the court is entitled to look at surrounding circumstances. For example, a service contract with a minor may contain a covenant in restraint of trade. Such a covenant, if otherwise valid,[51] does not invalidate the contract if the minor could not have got similar work on any other terms.[52] But it would invalidate a service contract with a minor if it was of a kind that was not usually found in service contracts in that trade and locality.[53] These principles also apply to contracts connected with service contracts and determine the validity of contracts to carry minors to work,[54] of compromises of industrial injury claims,[55] and of agreements to dissolve service contracts.[56] **12–014**

**Professions.** The principles evolved in relation to service contracts also determine the validity of contracts under which a minor makes a living by the exercise of some profession, e.g. as an entertainer or author or athlete. In *Doyle v White City Stadium Ltd*[57] a professional boxer who was a minor made a contract to fight for £3,000, win, draw or lose, subject to the rules of the British Boxing Board of Control, under which a boxer who was disqualified forfeited his **12–015**

[47] Contracts of service with children are to some extent regulated by statute: see, e.g. Children and Young Persons Acts 1933 s.18; 1963 s.37.

[48] [1894] 2 Q.B. 482; *Slade v Metrodent* [1953] 2 Q.B. 112; *Mills v IRC* [1975] A.C. 38 at 53.

[49] *Olsen v Corry and Gravesend Aviation Ltd* [1936] 3 All E.R. 241. Even if valid at common law, the term may be ineffective by statute: see, e.g. Unfair Contracts Terms Act 1977 s.2 (paras 7–048, 7–052), and see Sch.1 para.4 ("except in favour of the employee"); cf. Consumer Rights Act 2015 ss.62, 65 (paras 7–098, 7–108).

[50] *De Francesco v Barnum* (1889) 43 Ch D. 165; (1890) 45 Ch D. 430.

[51] See para.11–112 and following. The fact that the employee was a minor may be relevant to the issue of the reasonableness of the covenant: see *Sir WC Leng & Co Ltd v Andrews* [1909] 1 Ch. 763 at 771–772.

[52] *Bromley v Smith* [1909] 2 K.B. 235; cf. *Leslie v Fitzpatrick* (1877) 3 Q.B.D. 229.

[53] *Sir WC Leng & Co Ltd v Andrews* [1909] 1 Ch. 763.

[54] *Flower v London and North Western Ry* [1894] 2 Q.B. 65.

[55] *Stephens v Dudbridge Ironworks Co* [1904] 2 K.B. 225.

[56] *Waterman v Fryer* [1922] 1 K.B. 499.

[57] [1935] 1 K.B. 110. cf. also *Lumley v Wagner* (1852) 1 D.M. & G. 604, where a famous soprano was under age, as appears from 5 De G. & Sm. 485.

"purse". The minor was disqualified for hitting below the belt and his claim for the £3,000 was dismissed. Although in the circumstances the rules operated against him, he was bound by them: they were, on the whole, for his benefit as a professional boxer since they encouraged clean fighting. This case was followed in *Chaplin v Leslie Frewin (Publishers) Ltd*[58] where a minor contracted to give a firm of publishers the exclusive right to publish his memoirs. The Court of Appeal unanimously held that this was the sort of contract which could bind the minor if it was on the whole for his benefit.[59] Applying this test Lord Denning MR thought that, having regard to the contents of the memoirs, the contract was not binding, as it was not for the minor's good "that he should exploit his discreditable conduct for money".[60] But Danckwerts and Winn LJJ took the more materialistic view that "the mud may cling but the profits will be secured": thus the contract was on the whole beneficial, and bound the minor as it enabled him to "make a start as an author".[61]

12–016 **Validity of "beneficial contract" limited to service or analogous contracts.** The rule that a minor is bound by "beneficial" contracts is restricted to service or analogous contracts.[62] There is no general principle that a minor is bound by a contract merely because it is for his benefit. For example, a minor would not be contractually liable to repay[63] a loan without interest. And it has long been settled that a minor is not bound by a trading contract. Thus, he is not liable for goods supplied to him for the purpose of trade, nor for damages if he fails to deliver goods which he has sold as a trader.[64] Nor can he be made bankrupt for trade debts.[65]

12–017 **Trading contracts.** It may be asked: why does the law distinguish between a minor who earns his living by the exercise of a profession and one who earns his living by trading? The traditional answer is that "the law will not suffer him to trade, which may be his undoing".[66] A minor who trades thereby necessarily risks his capital. If he exercises some profession or calling he may incur expense, but putting his capital at risk is not of the essence of the matter. Of course, there are difficult borderline cases. A minor who is a haulage contractor is a trader,[67] but probably one who was a racing driver would not be so regarded. Similarly, it is

---

[58] [1966] Ch. 71; the case was later compromised: *The Times*, 16 February 1966.

[59] The same rule seems to apply to a contract between an entertainer who is under age and his agent: see *Denmark Productions Ltd v Boscobel Productions Ltd* (1967) 111 S.J. 715; reversed on other grounds [1969] 1 Q.B. 699; paras 16–119, 21–011.

[60] *Chaplin v Leslie Frewin (Publishers) Ltd* [1966] Ch. 71 at 88.

[61] *Chaplin v Leslie Frewin (Publishers) Ltd* [1966] Ch. 71 at 88, 95.

[62] *Proform Sports Management Ltd v Proactive Sports Management Ltd* [2006] EWHC 2903 (Ch); [2007] Bus. L.R. 93 at [35].

[63] For liability to make restitution, see para.12–037 and following.

[64] *Mercantile Union Guarantee Corp Ltd v Ball* [1937] 2 K.B. 498; *Cowern v Nield* [1912] 2 K.B. 491; para.12–052.

[65] *Ex p. Jones* (1881) 18 Ch D. 109; but he can be made bankrupt in respect of tax liability incurred in the course of trade: *Re a Debtor* [1950] Ch. 282.

[66] *Whywall v Campion* (1738) 2 Stra. 1083.

[67] *Mercantile Union Guarantee Corp Ltd v Ball* [1937] 2 K.B. 498.

probable that a minor who was a house painter would, while one who was a portrait painter would not, be regarded as a trader. There is no precise definition of "trade" for this purpose.

**Apprenticeship.** Contracts of apprenticeship were governed by special rules. It was held in the seventeenth century that an apprentice who was under age was not liable in damages if, in breach of contract, he departed from service.[68] This rule was originally based on the fact that the master had other remedies such as having the minor ordered by a justice of the peace to return to work. These remedies no longer exist[69] and it seems that contracts of apprenticeship will now be governed by the normal rules.[70] A minor is not bound by an apprenticeship deed as such, but he is bound by it as a simple contract. Thus, he is liable to pay any premium which he has agreed to pay.[71] Similarly, a covenant in restraint of trade (if otherwise valid)[72] or an arbitration clause contained in the apprenticeship deed can be enforced against him so long as the deed is on the whole for his benefit.[73] 12–018

## (b) Voidable contracts

### *(i) Cases of voidable contracts*

In four cases a minor's contract is voidable: that is, it binds both parties but the minor can avoid liability by repudiating before majority or within a reasonable time thereafter. The other party cannot repudiate.[74] 12–019

**Contracts concerning land.** A lessee who is under age is liable for rent unless he repudiates.[75] A minor who agrees to purchase freehold land is similarly bound unless he repudiates.[76] It seems that the same principle applies where a minor lets or agrees to sell land.[77] Actual conveyances to and by minors give rise to special problems which are outside the scope of this book. 12–020

**Shares in companies.** A minor who agrees to subscribe for shares in a company, or buys shares which are not fully paid, is liable for calls unless he repudiates. A mere plea that he has not ratified the transaction does not relieve him from 12–021

---

[68] *Gylbert v Fletcher* (1630) Cro. Car. 179.
[69] Family Law Reform Act 1969 s.11.
[70] Under the Apprenticeships, Skills, Children and Learning Act 2009 "approved English apprenticeships" (s.A5) and "Welsh apprenticeships" (s.35) are treated as "contracts of service".
[71] *Walter v Everard* [1891] 2 Q.B. 369.
[72] See fn.50.
[73] *Gadd v Thompson* [1911] 1 K.B. 304; *Slade v Metrodent* [1953] 2 Q.B. 112.
[74] *Clayton v Ashdown* (1714) 2 Eq. Ca. Abr. 516.
[75] *Davies v Benyon-Harris* (1931) 47 T.L.R. 424.
[76] *Whittingham v Murdy* (1889) 60 L.T. 956; *Orakpo v Manson Investments Ltd* [1978] A.C. 95 at 106, 113.
[77] *Slator v Trimble* (1861) 14 Ir. C.L.R. 342.

liability.[78] If he repudiates he ceases to be liable and can have his name removed from the company's register.[79] If the minor buys shares from a previous owner and fails to repudiate liability for calls on them, *the company* cannot generally avoid the transaction and so make the transferor liable for the calls.[80] But if the company is being wound-up while the buyer is still a minor, the liquidator can exercise the minor's right of repudiation for him and so make the transferor again liable for calls.[81]

The cases on this subject all concern the relations between the minor and the company or between the company and the person who has transferred shares to a minor. There appears to be no authority on the effect between buyer and seller of a sale of shares by or to a minor. Suppose that a minor buys shares, fails to pay for them when due, and then repudiates after majority. If the contract is voidable this repudiation may be too late,[82] so that the minor will be liable to pay. But he would not be liable if the contract had never been binding on him at all.[83]

12–022 **Partnership.** A minor can become a partner and is to some extent bound by the partnership agreement. He cannot be sued during minority by persons who give credit to the firm,[84] or be made liable for its losses.[85] But he is liable if after majority he fails to put an end to the partnership.[86] And he is not entitled to any share in the profits or assets of the partnership until its liabilities have been discharged.[87]

12–023 **Marriage settlements.** It was once thought that a marriage settlement by a minor was binding to the extent to which it benefited him; but was otherwise not binding unless ratified after majority.[88] But the prevailing view is that such a settlement binds the minor unless he repudiates.[89]

---

[78] *North Western Ry v M'Michael* (1850) 5 Ex. 114 at 128; *Ebbett's Case* (1870) L.R. 5 Ch.App. 302. The rule applies to shares in all companies, however incorporated.

[79] *Dublin & Wicklow Ry v Black* (1852) 8 Exch 181; *Steinberg v Scala (Leeds) Ltd* [1923] 2 Ch. 452.

[80] *Lumsden's Case* (1868) L.R. 4 Ch. App. 31; *Gooch's Case* (1872) L.R. 8 Ch. App. 266.

[81] *Capper's Case* (1868) L.R. 3 Ch. App. 458; *Symon's Case* (1870) L.R. 5 Ch. App. 298.

[82] See para.12–025.

[83] i.e. if it fell within the general rule stated at para.12–028.

[84] *Goode v Harrison* (1821) 5 B. & Ald. 147 at 157; *Lovell & Christmas v Beauchamp* [1894] A.C. 607.

[85] *Goode v Harrison* (1821) 5 B. & Ald. 147 at 159.

[86] *Goode v Harrison* (1821) 5 B. & Ald. 147 at 159.

[87] *Lovell & Christmas v Beauchamp* [1894] A.C. 607 at 611. Semble, the rules stated in this paragraph would apply to the relations between persons who became members of a limited liability partnership (para.12–085) if one or more of them were a minor: ss.4 and 5 of the Limited Liability Partnerships Act 2000 contain no reference to minority. Since under s.1 of the Act such a partnership is a body corporate, a minor would not (any more than a person of full age) be liable on its contracts; but his liability to contribute to the assets of the partnership would seem to be governed by the principles stated at fn.78.

[88] See *Simson v Jones* (1831) 2 Russ & My. 365.

[89] *Duncan v Dixon* (1890) 44 Ch D. 211; *Edwards v Carter* [1893] A.C. 360; [1892] 2 Ch. 278.

### (ii) *Loans for voidable contracts*

**Rights of the lender.** A minor may borrow money to enable him to make a payment due from him under a voidable contract, and actually use the money borrowed to make the payment. The minor is not for this reason bound by the contract for the loan of the money;[90] but the lender has rights similar to those of a lender for necessaries.[91] In *Nottingham Permanent Benefit Building Society v Thurstan*[92] a minor borrowed money from a building society to buy land. She paid the money to the vendor and executed a mortgage to the society. The mortgage was void,[93] but the society was entitled to stand in the shoes of the vendor and to exercise the lien that he would have had over the property, if he had not been paid. 12–024

### (iii) *Rules relating to repudiation*

**Time of repudiation.** A voidable contract can be repudiated during minority, but such a repudiation can be withdrawn by the minor before, or within reasonable time of, majority.[94] If the minor repudiates during minority he need take no further steps to avoid liability on reaching full age.[95] If the minor does not repudiate during minority, he must do so within a reasonable time of reaching full age. This is so even though he did not know of his right to repudiate, and even though his obligation under the contract had not yet matured. Thus, a covenant by a minor in a marriage settlement to settle after-acquired property may not become operative for many years after the settlor comes of age. But it binds him unless he repudiates it within a reasonable time of majority. In *Edwards v Carter*[96] it was held that a settlement could not be repudiated nearly five years after the majority of the settlor, although he was for most of that time ignorant of his right to repudiate. 12–025

**Effects of repudiation.** Repudiation relieves the minor from liabilities which would, but for the repudiation, have accrued after its date. There are conflicting dicta[97] on the question whether liabilities which have already accrued are extinguished by repudiation. According to an Irish case repudiation has no retrospective effect;[98] thus a lessee who is under age is liable for rent which has become payable before repudiation. A minor cannot recover money paid under a voidable contract unless there has been a "total failure of consideration".[99] In 12–026

---

90 It falls within the general rule stated at para.12–028.

91 See para.12–012.

92 [1903] A.C. 6.

93 See at fn.46.

94 *North Western Ry v M'Michael* (1850) 5 Ex. 114 at 127; *Slator v Trimble* (1861) 14 Ir. C.L.R. 342.

95 *Newry and Enniskillen Ry v Combe* (1849) 3 Ex. 565 at 575.

96 [1893] A.C. 360.

97 *North Western Ry v M'Michael* (1850) 5 Ex. 114 at 125 (retrospective); *Keteley's Case* (1613) 1 Brownl. 120 (not retrospective); dicta in *Steinberg v Scala (Leeds) Ltd* [1923] 2 Ch. 452 at 463 can be cited on both sides.

98 *Blake v Concannon* (1870) I.R. 4 C.L. 323.

99 See para.22–003.

*Steinberg v Scala (Leeds) Ltd*,[100] a minor applied for shares in a company but repudiated after allotment. She thus avoided liability for future calls, but her claim for the return of money already paid was rejected as there was no total failure of consideration: she had got the very shares she bargained for. Property transferred under a marriage settlement would similarly be irrecoverable once the marriage had taken place. On the other hand, in *Corpe v Overton*[101] a minor agreed to enter into a partnership and paid a deposit of £100, to be forfeited if he failed to execute the partnership deed. No partnership deed was ever executed because the minor repudiated, and it was held that he could get his deposit back as there had been a total failure of consideration. An adult, too, can recover money if there has been a total failure of consideration; but a minor (unlike an adult) can do so even though the failure of consideration is due to his own act in repudiating the contract.

### *(iv) Why are these contracts voidable?*

12–027 **No satisfactory explanation.** In general, a minor is not bound by his contracts.[102] He need not repudiate to escape liability. There is no satisfactory explanation for the existence of this separate class of voidable contracts. It perhaps provides the clearest illustration of the dilemma in which the law sometimes finds itself when it tries at the same time to protect minors and not to cause undue hardship to adults who deal with them. But this dilemma exists in all cases of contracts with minors and scarcely justifies special treatment of the four classes of voidable contracts. They may be based on social and economic factors which have long since passed away.

## (c) Other contracts

12–028 **Minor not bound.** Contracts which are neither valid, nor voidable in the sense just discussed, do not bind the minor but have a number of legal effects.

12–029 **Other party bound.** Contracts in this group bind the other party.[103] However, the remedies available to the minor are somewhat restricted in that he cannot claim specific performance of the contract.[104]

12–030 **Ratification.** The minor as a general rule becomes liable on the contract if he ratifies it after reaching full age.[105] Ratification may be express, or implied from conduct: the latter possibility is illustrated by the case in which the former minor continues after majority to act on the contract in such a way as to show that he regards it as binding on himself.[106] Because contracts in this group became

---

[100] [1923] 2 Ch. 452.

[101] (1833) 10 Bing. 252; *Everett v Wilkins* (1874) 29 L.T. 846.

[102] See para.12–028.

[103] *Farnham v Atkins* (1670) 1 Sid. 446; *Bruce v Warwick* (1815) 6 Taunt. 118.

[104] *Flight v Boland* (1828) 4 Russ. 298; *Lumley v Ravenscroft* [1895] 1 Q.B. 683; para.21–047.

[105] See *Williams v Moor* (1843) 11 M. & W. 256.

[106] e.g. *Brown v Harper* (1893) 68 L.T. 488.

binding as a result of ratification, they were sometimes called "voidable". But this is misleading as "voidable" normally means binding unless repudiated, whereas these contracts do not bind the minor unless he ratifies.

**Executed contracts.** Once the minor has actually performed the contract he cannot recover money paid or property transferred by him under it merely on the ground that the contract did not bind him by reason of his minority.[107] He can recover such money or property only in the same circumstances in which this remedy is available to an adult, e.g. he can recover money paid under the contract if there has been a failure of consideration.[108] There is, indeed, some doubt as to the scope of the rule that property transferred in pursuance of contracts in this category cannot be recovered. In *Chaplin v Leslie Frewin (Publishers) Ltd*[109] a majority of the Court of Appeal accepted the view that the minor would not be able to recover the copyright which he had transferred under the contract even if (contrary to the view of that majority) the contract did not bind him.[110] Lord Denning MR, on the other hand, said that the rule, by which property could not be recovered, applied only to transfers by delivery and not to those which require a written document: it would be "absurd to hold that a contract to make a disposition is voidable and that the disposition is not".[111] But it is, with respect, hard to see why this is more absurd when the disposition has to be in writing than when it can, and does, take effect by delivery.[112] 12–031

**Passing of property to minor.** It was said by Lush J in *Stocks v Wilson*[113] that, where goods were delivered to a minor under a contract of sale, the property in them passed to him "by the delivery". The view that property can pass to a minor under a contract which does not bind him seems to be supported by s.3(1) of the Minors' Contracts Act 1987: this subsection[114] refers to "property acquired" by the minor under such a contract, and to the power of the court to order him to "transfer" such property.[115] The property, in the case put, seems to pass by delivery with intention to pass property. It may indeed be argued that the seller's intention to pass property is based on the assumption that the contract binds the minor and is nullified if this assumption is untrue, just as (in cases not involving minors) a seller's intention to pass property is nullified if the contract is void for 12–032

---

[107] *Wilson v Kearse* (1800) Peake Add. Cas. 196; *Ex p. Taylor* (1856) 8 D.M. & G. 254 at 256.

[108] See para.22–003.

[109] [1966] Ch. 71; para.12–015.

[110] This view was based "on the authorities cited to us" (at 94). But these were not strictly in point as the contract in one of them (*Steinberg v Scala (Leeds) Ltd* [1923] 2 Ch. 452) was truly voidable, while in the other two (*Valentini v Canali* (1889) 24 Q.B.D. 166; *Pearce v Brain* [1929] 2 K.B. 310) the contracts were "absolutely void" within s.1 of Infants Relief Act 1874 (repealed by Minors' Contracts Act 1987 s.1(a)). The majority's view is more appropriately supported by the authorities cited in fn.18. See the doubts expressed by Baroness Hale in *Fisher v Brooker* [2009] UKHL 41; [2009] 1 W.L.R. 1764 at [26].

[111] *Chaplin v Leslie Frewin (Publishers) Ltd* [1966] Ch. 71 at 90; cf. *G(A) v G(T)* [1970] 2 Q.B. 643 at 652.

[112] No such distinction is drawn where the contract is voidable for misrepresentation, para.9–093 and following.

[113] [1913] 2 K.B. 235 at 246; cf. *Watts v Seymour* [1967] 2 Q.B. 647.

[114] See para.12–038.

[115] See further paras 12–038–12–043.

mistake as to the identity of the buyer.[116] But delivery to the wrong person may well differ in legal effect from delivery for the wrong reason. In the first case there is no intention to pass the property to the person to whom the delivery is made; in the second there is such an intention, though possibly based on a mistaken assumption. Thus, it is submitted that delivery of the goods to the minor can pass property to him. The attraction of this view is that it enables the law to protect an innocent third party who later buys the goods from the minor. It is an open question whether property can pass to the minor without delivery,[117] simply by virtue of the contract. The question is of small practical importance since property is unlikely to pass in this way until the price has been paid;[118] and in that case the seller generally has no interest in claiming that he still has the property in the goods.

12–033 **Passing of property from minor.** Cases such as *Chaplin v Leslie Frewin (Publishers) Ltd*[119] show that property can pass *from* the minor under a contract which does not bind him.[120] The same principle would apply where the minor made a pledge to secure a debt incurred under such a contract. The person taking the pledge would normally be guilty of an offence,[121] but this does not affect the civil consequences of the transaction.[122] Thus it seems that a special property in the thing pledged would pass to the pledgee and that the minor could not get the thing back without paying off the loan. This conclusion may be disadvantageous to the minor, but the argument that property passes by delivery seems to apply as much where the delivery is made *by*, as where it is made *to*, the minor.

## (d) Liability in tort

12–034 **Cause of action arising out of non-binding contract.** The general rule is that minors are liable in tort in the same way as adults. One possible exception to this rule exists in the case of very young children. Our concern here, however, is with another exception, which exists where a cause of action in tort arises out of, or in connection with, a contract which does not bind the minor.

12–035 **Distinction between wrongful and forbidden conduct.** Conduct amounting to a breach of contract may also be a tort.[123] If a minor engages in such conduct and is sued in tort, he can sometimes set up the invalidity of the contract as a defence to the tort claim. He can do so where the tort consists of wrongfully doing an act

---

[116] *Shogun Finance v Hudson* [2003] UKHL 62; [2004] 1 A.C. 919; para.8–039.

[117] e.g. under Sale of Goods Act 1979 s.18 r.1.

[118] See *RV Ward Ltd v Bignall* [1967] 1 Q.B. 534 at 545.

[119] [1966] Ch. 71; para.12–015.

[120] Even Lord Denning accepted this view where the property was alleged to have passed by *delivery*: see at fn.111.

[121] Consumer Credit Act 1974 s.114(2).

[122] Consumer Credit Act 1974 s.170(1); quaere whether this excludes the rules stated at para.11–095. See also *Wilson v Robertsons (London) Ltd* [2006] EWCA Civ 1088; [2007] C.T.L.C. 84 (claim for conversion available alongside sanctions imposed for breach of the Act).

[123] See para.20–116.

authorised by the contract,[124] but not where it consists of doing an act forbidden by the contract.[125] The distinction between these two types of cases can be explained as the product of the law's two conflicting desires: to protect minors, but without causing unnecessary hardship to adults who deal with them.

**Tortious procurement of the contract.** The minor may be immune from liability in tort, not only where he commits a tort in breaking the invalid contract, but also where he commits a tort in procuring it. It was held in *R Leslie Ltd v Sheill*[126] that a minor could not be sued in deceit for inducing an adult to lend him money by fraudulent misrepresentations as to his age. Similarly, it was held in *Stocks v Wilson*[127] that a minor could not be sued in deceit for inducing an adult by such misrepresentations to sell and deliver goods to him. The practical effect of a judgment in tort in such cases would be to force the minor to repay the money lent or to pay the value of the goods obtained; and this would once again undermine the protection which the law gives to the minor by holding the contract invalid. 12–036

### (e) Liability in restitution

Before the Minors' Contracts Act 1987, a minor could be held liable to restore certain benefits received by him under a contract which did not bind him. Such liability was imposed in equity if the minor was guilty of fraud,[128] and (probably) in certain other cases at common law.[129] Section 3(1) of the 1987 Act now gives the court discretion to order the minor to transfer to the adult party any property acquired by the minor under such a contract, or any property representing it. Section 3(2) goes on to provide that nothing in s.3 "shall be taken to prejudice any other remedy available to the" adult party to the contract. Thus, in cases which fall outside s.3(1), or in which the court declines to exercise its discretion under that subsection, it remains open to the adult to seek restitution under the old rules of equity or common law. These therefore still call for discussion, even though generally claims for restitution are now likely to be made under s.3(1), since the conditions imposed by the subsection are less onerous than those imposed by the equitable or the common law rules. 12–037

#### *(i) Minors' Contracts Act 1987 s.3(1)*

**Scope.** This subsection deals with the case where a contract has been made with a minor and the contract "is unenforceable against [the minor] (or he repudiates it)[130] because he was a minor when the contract was made". In such a case the 12–038

[124] *Jennings v Rundall* (1799) 8 T.R. 335; cf. *Fawcett v Smethurst* (1914) 84 L.J.K.B. 473.
[125] *Burnard v Haggis* (1863) 14 C.B.(N.S.) 45; cf. *Ballett v Mingay* [1943] K.B. 281.
[126] [1914] 3 K.B. 607; *Johnson v Pye* (1665) 1 Sid. 258.
[127] [1913] 2 K.B. 235.
[128] See para.12–044.
[129] See para.12–049.
[130] This phrase refers to the "voidable" contracts discussed at paras 12–020–12–023.

court "may, if it is just and equitable to do so, require [the minor] to transfer to the [other party] any property acquired by the [minor] under the contract, or any property representing it".

12–039 **Restoration of property acquired.** The subsection would most obviously apply to a case like *Nash v Inman*:[131] the minor could be ordered to return the fancy waistcoats to the seller. Such an order could be made even though the minor was not guilty of fraud, which is essential to liability in equity;[132] and even though there would, in the case put, be no liability in restitution at common law.[133]

12–040 **No claim against the general assets of the minor.** Section 3(1) goes beyond the simple case just put, in that the court can order the minor to transfer either the "property acquired … under the contract" or "any property representing it". Thus, if the minor were to exchange the fancy waistcoats for a set of silver candlesticks, he could be ordered to transfer those to the seller of the fancy waistcoats. On the other hand, s.3(1) would not apply where the minor had dissipated the property acquired under the contract or its proceeds, e.g. where he had bought champagne and consumed it, or where he had sold property acquired under the contract for cash and had used the money to pay for a holiday. Section 3(1) only empowers the court to order the minor to transfer either the property acquired under the contract or property representing it: the court cannot order him to pay either the price or the reasonable value of what he has obtained out of his other assets. The underlying principle seems to be that the minor should not be enriched by retaining "property" obtained under the contract. But his general assets (other than that "property") are not to be diminished as a result of the exercise of the court's discretion under the section.

12–041 **Property representing the property acquired.** The discretion will present few problems where the "property acquired … under the contract" is still in the minor's possession; but difficulty can obviously arise where the discretion is invoked in respect of "property representing it". The case in which the minor simply exchanges the "property acquired" for something else will be relatively uncommon. More usually, he will sell the "property acquired" and use the money to buy something else; that other thing may have been paid for wholly or in part with the money obtained from the sale of the property originally acquired. Further problems can arise where that money is paid by the minor into a bank account which is in credit and from which money is then drawn out to pay for the substitute purchase. In such a case it may be very hard to tell whether that substitute is indeed "property representing" the property acquired under the original contract. Even greater difficulties could arise if the substitute had been bought under another contract which was unenforceable against the minor, and if

[131] [1908] 2 K.B. 1; para.12–008.

[132] See para.12–044.

[133] This is on the basis that English law does not recognise any common law restitutionary claim for the recovery of chattels (as distinct from money): see *Power v Wells* (1778) 2 Cowp. 818 and the only possible claim for chattels is in tort for wrongful interference with possession or with an immediate right to possession; and in the case put there would be no such claim as property in the goods would have passed to the minor.

only part of the price due under that contract had been paid by the minor; in such a case claims under s.3 for the transfer of the same thing might be made by two sellers.

**Meaning of "property."** A final difficulty is to determine what is meant by "property" in the section; and in particular whether "property" includes money.[134] The difficulty arises because the cases decided before the Act displayed a somewhat greater reluctance to make a minor "restore" a sum of money than to return goods obtained by him under the contract[135]—apparently because a judgment against him to pay a sum of money was more likely than one for the return of goods to present the appearance of indirectly enforcing the contract. But those cases do not rule out the possibility of making the minor restore money,[136] at least where he was guilty of fraud, and s.3(1) seems to be intended to extend such liability to cases in which there was no fraud.[137] Moreover, it appears from the legislative history of the Act that s.3(1) is intended to produce the result that "the minor can be compelled to hand over the proceeds if he has sold the property";[138] and, in the case of goods at least, the proceeds of a *sale*, by definition, consist of money.[139] This supports the view that the "property representing" the "property acquired" includes money; and if this is so, then it is submitted that the "property acquired" also includes money, since the word "property" must prima facie bear the same meaning in both the places in which it occurs in the subsection. Thus, it is submitted that where a minor buys goods under a contract which is unenforceable against him by reason of his minority, and then sells them, he can be ordered to transfer the money to the seller; while if the minor borrows money under such a contract, and uses it to buy goods, he can be ordered to transfer those goods to the lender. 12–042

**Discretion of the court.** Section 3(1) does not entitle the other party to the transfer of the property as of right: it only provides that the court "may, if it is just and equitable to do so," order the transfer. Of the factors which the court can take into account in exercising this discretion, two call for comment. The first is the difficulty, where the minor has disposed of the property acquired, of determining whether assets still owned by him are indeed "property representing" what he originally acquired. The process of "tracing" assets into their product can be complex; and the court may restrict the operation of s.3(1) to cases in which it is relatively clear that the property which the minor is ordered to restore does indeed represent that acquired under the contract. To extend the operation of the subsection beyond this point would increase the danger that an order to transfer property (especially in the form of money) would amount to indirect enforcement of the contract against the minor. The operation of the equitable doctrine of 12–043

[134] The Act contains no definition of property; contrast Theft Act 1968 s.4(1), expressly providing that "property" includes money.
[135] See *R Leslie Ltd v Sheill* [1914] 3 K.B. 607 (para.12–046); *Cowern v Nield* [1912] 2 K.B. 419 (para.12–052).
[136] See *Stocks v Wilson* [1913] 2 K.B. 235; para.12–047, and paras 12–049–12–052.
[137] See Law Com. No.134, para.4.21.
[138] See Law Com. No.134, para.4.21.
[139] Sale of Goods Act 1979 s.2(1) ("for a money consideration").

restitution in cases of the minor's fraud gave rise to a similar danger, and it was to avert this danger that the courts restricted the scope of that doctrine. The relevant equity cases are discussed below[140] (even though the equitable doctrine has lost much of its former practical importance) because it is submitted that they now provide guidance for the exercise of the statutory discretion. The second factor which the court might take into account is the fairness of the original contract: thus if the court regarded the price payable under the contract as too high it might order the minor to return the property unless he paid a reasonable price fixed by the court.[141] In failing to specify the circumstances and manner in which the discretion is to be exercised, the subsection no doubt gives rise to some uncertainty; but it avoids complexity. In context, the balance that it thus strikes seems to be satisfactory, since the rules which govern a minor's liability in restitution are not of a kind on which either party to the contract relies (or should be encouraged to rely) in conducting his business affairs.

### *(ii) Effects of fraud*

12–044 **Common law.** At common law, a minor cannot be made liable on a contract merely because he has committed a fraud on the other party in inducing him to enter into the contract.[142] The other party can at most rely on the fraud as a defence or as a ground of rescission.[143]

12–045 **Equity.** The common law rules just stated unduly favoured a class of minors that least deserved protection. Hence equity gave further relief against minors on the ground of fraud. For this purpose, it seems that fraud meant some misrepresentation by the minor as to his age, so that his mere failure to declare that he was under age did not amount to fraud;[144] nor was it fraud for him to keep, without paying, goods obtained by him under a contract which did not bind him.[145] Equitable relief on the ground of fraud took a number of forms.

---

140 See paras 12–045–12–048.

141 See the reference in Law Com. No.134 paras 4.21–6.10 of the Commission's earlier Working Paper No.81 on Minors' Contracts.

142 *Bartlett v Wells* (1862) 1 B. & S. 836; *Miller v Blankley* (1878) 38 L.T. 527; *Levene v Brougham* (1909) 25 T.L.R. 265.

143 e.g. *Lemprière v Lange* (1879) 12 Ch D. 675. No attempt seems to have been made in the cases to argue that the adult could, by rescinding the contract for fraud, avoid the minor's title *at law* (cf. para.9–094). Quaere whether the court could award damages in lieu of rescission against a minor under s.2(2) of Misrepresentation Act 1967 (para.9–066). To do this might amount to indirect enforcement of the contract in the sense discussed at para.12–047.

144 For the definition of fraud, see para.9–039. In equity a person could be guilty of fraud even though he had no "actual intention to cheat": *Nocton v Ashburton* [1914] A.C. 932 at 954; but in the present context a number of cases state the requirement of a misrepresentation as to age: *Stikeman v Dawson* (1847) 1 De G. & Sm. 90 at 103; *Ex p. Jones* (1881) 18 Ch D. 109 at 120; *Re Hodson* [1894] 2 Ch. 421 at 427.

145 This must have been assumed in *Nash v Inman* [1908] 2 K.B. 1; for the contrary view, see Atiyah 22 M.L.R. 273 at 275. Because of the Minors' Contracts Act 1987 s.3(1), the point no longer has any practical importance: see after fn.151.

**Restoration of benefits.** Our principal concern is with the power of equity to order the fraudulent minor to restore benefits obtained under the contract.[146] The remedy, being equitable, was presumably discretionary,[147] and in this respect it resembles the statutory remedy now available under s.3(1) of the Minors' Contracts Act 1987.[148] On the other hand, the statutory remedy is in two respects more favourable to the adult than the old equitable remedy. First, the statutory remedy is available even though the minor was not guilty of fraud. Secondly, there is no doubt that the statutory remedy extends to the proceeds of the thing obtained under the contract,[149] while it was disputed whether the equitable remedy was available in respect of such proceeds.[150] Thus although the equitable remedy is one of those expressly preserved by the 1987 Act,[151] there seems to be no reason why the other party should wish to resort to it. It follows that questions as to the exact scope and extent of the equitable remedy no longer have any practical importance. The cases concerned with such questions are now useful only as providing illustrations of the factors that the courts may take into account in deciding whether to exercise their statutory discretion to order the minor to transfer property acquired under the contract, or property representing it. 12–046

**Examples of the courts' discretion.** In *Stocks v Wilson*[152] a minor had obtained goods under a contract induced by fraud and had disposed of some of those goods. He was held liable to account[153] to the original seller for the proceeds of the goods. By contrast, in *R Leslie Ltd v Sheill*[154] a minor had by fraud obtained a loan of £400 and was held not liable in equity to restore the money. Lord Sumner said: 12–047

> "the money was paid over to be used as the defendant's own and he has so used it, and, I suppose, spent it. There is no question of tracing it, no possibility of restoring the very thing got by fraud, nothing but compulsion through a personal judgment to pay an equivalent sum out of his present or future resources …".[155]

The crucial point in *R Leslie Ltd v Sheill* was that there was no question of tracing the money, that is of showing that it, or some asset representing it, was still in the hands of the minor. If he had still got the £400 he could have been made to restore it in equity;[156] and if he had used the £400 to buy a car he could have been ordered to hand the car over to the lender.[157] An order to "transfer … property"

[146] e.g. *Clarke v Cobley* (1789) 2 Cox 173.
[147] cf. para.8–028 and see para.9–114 and following; paras 21–031, 21–059.
[148] See para.12–038.
[149] See the words "any property representing it" in s.3(1): para.12–041.
[150] See at fnn.152–159.
[151] 1987 Act s.3(2).
[152] [1913] 2 K.B. 235.
[153] *Stocks v Wilson* [1913] 2 K.B. 235 at 247—a passage criticised in *R Leslie Ltd v Sheill* [1914] 3 K.B. 607.
[154] [1914] 3 K.B. 607; see para.12–036.
[155] *R Leslie Ltd v Sheill* [1914] 3 K.B. 607 at 619.
[156] There would have been, in Lord Sumner's words ([1914] 3 K.B. 607 at 619), a "possibility of restoring the very thing got by fraud."
[157] It is assumed that the money lent could be "traced" into the car, within Lord Sumner's words ([1914] 3 K.B. 607 at 619).

could now be made in such circumstances under s.3(1) of the 1987 Act, even in the absence of fraud.[158] Conversely, in a case like *Stocks v Wilson* the minor could, under the subsection, be ordered to transfer the proceeds of sale if they could be identified as "property representing" the goods.[159] It is submitted that such an order could be made even if the minor had happened to resell the goods for the exact equivalent of the contract price. It is no objection to a claim for restitution that it leads to the same *measure* of recovery as an action on the contract. To order a minor to pay such an amount (or any amount) becomes objectionable only on account of the *nature* of the judgment: that is, if the judgment is, in Lord Sumner's words, "a personal judgment to pay an equivalent sum out of his present or future resources". The only type of order that can be made against the minor is one to *restore* the property acquired, or its proceeds, in equity, or to *transfer* it under s.3(1). He cannot be made liable to *pay* for the property acquired or to *account* for its proceeds by a personal judgment enforceable against his general assets. This point seems to have been overlooked in *Stocks v Wilson* where the court ordered the minor to *account for* the proceeds of sale without enquiring whether those proceeds were still in the hands of the minor.[160] The purpose of the equitable and statutory remedies is to ensure that the minor is not enriched as a result of the transaction which is not binding on him; but the remedy should not diminish such general resources as he had apart from the transaction. It follows that the remedies are limited by the value of the property in the hands of the minor at the time of judgment. If by then the minor has dissipated part of the property (or its proceeds) the remedy is available only in respect of the remainder.

12–048 **Other forms of relief.** Equity gives relief against fraudulent minors in a number of other ways. It has, for example, been held that a minor who obtained payment of a share in a trust fund by fraudulently pretending to be of age could not claim a second payment on reaching full age;[161] and that a minor remainderman who by fraud enabled the tenant for life to mortgage the estate could not, when the estate vested in him, deny the validity of the charge.[162] These cases do not call for extended discussion here as they are not directly connected with the law of contract. It has been further suggested that equity recognised a broad principle of relief: viz. that if a minor sued without offering to pay he would be guilty of "fraud" which would give the adult an equitable defence,[163] even (apparently) where, under the contract, payment from the minor was not due until after the adult's performance. But the authorities do not support such a broad definition of "fraud": on the contrary, they support the view that, even in equity, relief is

[158] See paras 12–038–12–041.
[159] See para.12–041.
[160] In *Westdeutsche Landesbank Girozentrale v Islington BC* [1996] A.C. 669 at 716 Lord Browne-Wilkinson refers with evident approval to *Stocks v Wilson* but treats it as a case in which the minor was "bound in equity to *restore*" property obtained by fraud.
[161] *Cory v Gertcken* (1816) 2 Madd. 40.
[162] *Watts v Cresswell* (1714) 2 Eq. Ca. Abr. 515.
[163] Atiyah 22 M.L.R. 273.

available to the other party only where the minor's "fraud" takes the form of a misrepresentation by him as to his age.[164]

### (iii) *Liability in restitution at common law*

In certain circumstances a minor who has obtained benefits at the expense of an adult may be liable to make restitution to the adult at common law. This remedy is available as of right, and it is expressly preserved by s.3(2) of the Minors' Contracts Act 1987. 12–049

**Waiver of tort.** It is illustrated by cases of so-called waiver of tort, in which the victim of a fraud (and of certain other torts) can claim restitution in respect of certain benefits obtained by the tortfeasor. Such an action lies against a minor if he would have been liable to the direct action in tort. Thus, it was available in *Bristow v Eastman*,[165] where an apprentice, while under age, had embezzled[166] his master's property. 12–050

**No circumvention of the minor's lack of capacity.** The courts will not allow a minor's lack of contractual capacity to be circumvented by means of a restitutionary action. In *R Leslie Ltd v Sheill* the lenders made an alternative claim that the minor was liable to repay the money lent as money had and received to their use. This claim also failed as "the cause of action is in substance *ex contractu* and is so directly connected with the contract of loan that the action would be an indirect way of enforcing that contract".[167] Here again the decisive objection is not that the measure of liability may be the same in a restitutionary action as in one for breach of contract: the crucial point is that, where the money had been spent, the only possible effect of the judgment in either kind of action would be to impose personal liability on the minor, enforceable against his assets generally.[168] 12–051

**Cowern v Nield.** Much difficulty is caused by *Cowern v Nield.*[169] A minor who was a trader sold hay and clover, and was paid in advance. He failed to deliver any hay, and the clover which he delivered was defective, so that the buyer justifiably rejected it. As the contract was a trading contract, the buyer's claim for damages failed; and his claim for the return of the money that he had paid was also rejected. The court took the view that such a claim could have succeeded if the minor had obtained the money by fraud, and therefore ordered a new trial on the issue of fraud. But this view is, with respect, open to doubt. A minor cannot be made liable in restitution if "the action would be an indirect way of enforcing [the invalid] contract".[170] If (contrary to the submission made above) this means 12–052

[164] See para.12–045.

[165] (1794) 1 Esp. 172. "Even this has been doubted": *R Leslie Ltd v Sheill* [1914] 3 K.B. 607 at 613 (Lord Sumner).

[166] Such conduct would now be an offence under Fraud Act 2006 s.4.

[167] *R Leslie Ltd v Sheill* [1914] 3 K.B. 607 at 621; cf. 613.

[168] cf. para.12–047.

[169] [1912] 2 K.B. 419.

[170] *R Leslie Ltd v Sheill* [1914] 3 K.B. 607 at 621.

that the judgment must not impose the same *measure* of liability as a judgment in action for breach of contract, then the action for the return of the price should have succeeded in *Cowern v Nield* irrespective of fraud. For the minor's duty under the contract was to deliver the goods, and the damages for their non-delivery might have been quite different from the price. But if (as seems more probable) indirect enforcement refers to the imposition of *personal* liability on the minor, the action should not have succeeded merely on proof of fraud. The minor should have been liable only to the extent that the money or its identifiable proceeds were still in his hands. Under s.3(1) of the Minors' Contracts Act 1987 the court could now order the minor to transfer such money, or property representing it, to the buyer, irrespective of fraud; but that remedy is discretionary, so that the buyer might prefer to pursue his restitutionary remedy at common law, as this is available as of right.

## 2. MENTAL INCAPACITY

12–053 The law relating to contracts with persons "who lack capacity" represents a compromise between two principles. The first is that such a person should not be liable on his contracts if he did not have the capacity to consent. The second is that it might cause hardship to one contracting party to allow the other to "stultify himself".[171]

12–054 **Lack of capacity.** For the purposes of the Mental Capacity Act 2005, a person "lacks capacity in relation to a matter if at the material time he is unable to make a decision for himself in relation to the matter because of an impairment of, or a disturbance in the functioning of, the mind or brain."[172] Section 3 goes on to state that a person is unable to make a decision for himself if he is:

> "unable (a) to understand the information relevant to the decision, (b) to retain that information, (c) to use or weigh that information as part of the process of making the decision, or (d) to communicate his decision (whether by talking, using sign language or any other means)".[173]

This is broadly consistent with the test applied by the courts at common law which has been to ask whether a person had an understanding of what "was going on and what was involved in the transaction involved".[174] Since it would seem to make little sense to have two broadly similar, but potentially different, tests in operation, it is submitted that the test laid down in the 2005 Act should be applied even in cases which are not governed by the Act, e.g. the enforceability of a

[171] *Beverley's Case* (1603) 4 Co. Rep. 123b.

[172] 2005 Act s.2(1).

[173] For other factors which should, and should not, be taken into account, see ss.2(2)–(4) and 3(2)–(4).

[174] Fridman 79 L.Q.R. 502, 518–519. See: *Manches v Trimborn* (1946) 115 L.J.K.B. 305; *In the Estate of Park* [1954] P. 112; *Gibbons v Wright* (1954) 91 C.L.R. 423; *Re Beaney* [1978] 1 W.L.R. 770; cf. *Fehily v Atkinson* [2016] EWHC 3069 (QB); [2017] Bus. L.R. 695 at [102] ("the capacity to absorb, retain, understand, process and weigh information about the key features and effects of the contract, and the alternatives to it, if explained in broad terms and simple language").

contract other than for necessaries.[175] A person who lacks capacity, whether under the common law test, or that stated in the 2005 Act, will be referred to in this part as M.

## (a) In general

**Contract generally valid.** A contract with M is valid, except in the two cases dealt with below. 12–055

### *(i) Incapacity known to other party*

If the other contracting party knows of M's incapacity, the contract is voidable at M's option.[176] The burden is on M to show that his incapacity prevented him from understanding the transaction,[177] and that the other party knew this. It seems that M becomes absolutely bound if he ratifies the contract after he is no longer suffering from the incapacity.[178] There is also some support for the view that the contract is binding so long as it was a fair one, even though the incapacity of M was known to the other party.[179] Where the other party does not know of M's incapacity, the contract is valid: it cannot be attacked merely on the ground that it was "unfair" in the sense that its terms were more favourable to the other party than they were to M.[180] The contract can be attacked on the ground of "unfairness" only (if at all) where the circumstances are such that M can rely, like a person of normal capacity, on the equitable rules relating to undue influence or unconscionable bargains.[181] 12–056

The requirement that the other party must have known of M's incapacity is attributed to the decision of the Court of Appeal in *Imperial Loan Co v Stone*,[182] but in *Dunhill v Burgin* it was cited by Baroness Hale in support of the proposition that a contract is voidable if the other party "knew *or ought to have known*" that M lacked capacity.[183] The *Imperial Loan* case does, however, appear to require actual knowledge,[184] as do other decisions.[185] Baroness Hale's comment was obiter dictum, but in *Dunhill v Burgin* itself it was held that a contract to compromise litigation made by M is voidable if, at the time of

---

175 See para.12–055 and following. In *Local Authority X v MM (an adult)* [2007] EWHC 2003 (Fam); [2009] 1 F.L.R. 443 at [79]–[80] it is said that the courts may adopt the new definition in cases not covered by the Act, if "appropriate"; cf. *Saulle v Nouvet* [2007] EWHC 2902 (QB); [2008] W.T.L.R. 729; *Kicks v Leigh* [2014] EWHC 3926 (Ch); [2015] 4 All E.R. 329.

176 *Molton v Camroux* (1849) 4 Ex. 17; *Imperial Loan Co v Stone* [1892] 1 Q.B. 599.

177 *Re K* [1988] Ch. 310.

178 *Birkin v Wing* (1890) 63 L.T. 80; *Manches v Trimborn* (1946) 115 L.J.K.B. 305.

179 *Dane v Kirkwall* (1838) 8 C. & P. 679.

180 *Hart v O'Connor* [1985] A.C. 1000; *Irvani v Irvani* [2000] 1 Lloyd's Rep. 412 at 420.

181 See para.10–015 and following.

182 [1892] 1 Q.B. 599.

183 *Dunhill v Burgin* [2014] UKSC 18; [2014] 1 W.L.R. 933 at [1] (emphasis added).

184 *Imperial Loan Co v Stone* [1892] 1 Q.B. 599 at 602.

185 cf. *Blankley v Central Manchester & Manchester Children's University Hospitals NHS Trust* [2014] EWHC 168 (QB) at [30]; affirmed [2015] EWCA Civ 18; [2015] 1 Costs L.R. 119.

entering into it, M did not have a "litigation friend",[186] whether or not the other party knows, or ought to have known, of M's incapacity.

### (ii) *Property and affairs subject to control of the court*

12–057 **Contract only binding on other party.** If M's property is subject to the control of the court,[187] an attempt by him to dispose of the property does not bind him, since, if it did bind him, it would interfere with the court's control over the property.[188] But the contract binds the other party.[189]

12–058 **Scope of the rule.** The rule that the contract does not bind M clearly applies to any contract which purports to dispose of M's property. But it is not clear whether the rule applies *only* to such contracts, or whether it extends to *all* contracts with those whose property is subject to the control of the court. On the one hand it can be argued that every contract creates a potential liability to pay money and thus interferes with the court's control over the property. On the other hand, there are some negative contracts which can be enforced by injunction against M's person which need not interfere with his property. There is no reason, in principle, why such contracts should not be enforced in this way. The question is largely academic as the court only exercises control over the property and affairs of M in cases of serious incapacity. The other party will generally know of such incapacity and his claim will fail on this ground.

## (b) Necessaries

12–059 Section 7 of the 2005 Act provides that: "If necessary goods or services[190] are supplied to a person who lacks capacity to contract for the supply, he must pay a reasonable price for them." For this purpose, "'necessary' means suitable to a person's condition in life and to his actual requirements at the time when the goods or services are supplied."[191]

12–060 **No effect on already binding contract.** If M would be bound by the contract under the rules stated above, his liability for necessaries is not affected by s.7. Thus, a person who supplies necessaries to M without knowing of his incapacity can enforce the contract:[192] he is not limited to an action for a reasonable price.

[186] i.e. someone permitted to act in proceedings on behalf of a litigant who lacks capacity under CPR 21.

[187] Under ss.15–19 and Pt 2 of the 2005 Act.

[188] *Re Walker* [1905] 1 Ch. 160; *Re Marshall* [1920] 1 Ch. 284.

[189] cf. *Baldwyn v Smith* [1900] 1 Ch. 588.

[190] Services were not covered by s.3(2) of the Sale of Goods Act 1979 (which is superseded by s.7 of the 2005 Act), but as illustrated in the case of minors, it was supplemented in this regard by the common law: para.12–013; cf. *Blankley v Central Manchester & Manchester Children's University Hospitals NHS Trust* [2014] EWHC 168 (QB) at [54]–[57]; affirmed [2015] EWCA Civ 18; [2015] 1 Costs L.R. 119, without consideration of this issue.

[191] 2005 Act s.7(2). See *Aster Healthcare Ltd v Shafi* [2014] EWHC 77; [2014] 3 All E.R. 283.

[192] *Baxter v Portsmouth* (1826) 5 B. & C. 170.

**Effect on non-binding contract.** If M would not be bound by the contract under the rules stated above, he is liable under s.7. Thus, a person who supplies necessaries to M knowing of his incapacity cannot enforce the contract: he can only recover a reasonable price. Section 3(2) of the Sale of Goods Act 1979, which s.7 replaces, had applied where necessaries were "sold and delivered" to M. Those words were scarcely appropriate where necessaries are simply supplied to a patient whose incapacity is so serious that he is incapable of rational thought; or where a patient in this condition is simply maintained at the expense of another person. In such cases the person who supplied or paid for the necessaries had a remedy at common law under the doctrine of agency of necessity[193] unless he acted gratuitously, without thought of recompense.[194] Since s.7 now refers simply to goods or services which are "supplied", it may be that the "supplier" will be entitled to a reasonable price; alternatively, the proper construction of the provision may be to confine it to the supply of necessaries under a purported contract for the supply which is found not to be binding, in which case the position will be unaltered. 12–061

**Loans.** A person who lends money to M knowing of his incapacity cannot enforce the contract, but can recover so much of the money as has actually been spent on necessaries.[195] 12–062

## 3. INTOXICATION

**Drink.** Extreme drunkenness is a defence to an action on a contract if it prevents the defendant from understanding the transaction, and if the claimant knows this.[196] The drunkard is liable if he ratifies the contract when he becomes sober.[197] He is also liable for necessaries.[198] 12–063

A defendant cannot rely at law on drunkenness which merely blurred his business sense: but such drunkenness is a ground on which equity may refuse to order specific performance.[199] Nor does a party's habitual drunkenness deprive him of contractual capacity[200] but it could be a ground for relief if the other party had taken over the position of guardian or adviser to the drunkard so as to give rise to a presumption of undue influence between them.[201]

---

193 *Brockwell v Bullock* (1889) 22 Q.B.D. 567; *Pontypridd Union v Drew* [1927] 1 K.B. 214 at 220; see also *Re Rhodes* (1889) 44 Ch D. 94; and para.16–046.
194 *Re Rhodes* (1889) 44 Ch D. 94.
195 *Re Beavan* [1912] 1 Ch. 196.
196 *Gore v Gibson* (1843) 13 M. & W. 623.
197 *Matthews v Baxter* (1873) L.R. 8 Ex. 132.
198 *Gore v Gibson* (1843) 13 M. & W. 623 at 626; Sale of Goods Act 1979 s.3(2).
199 See para.21–033.
200 *Irvani v Irvani* [2000] 1 Lloyd's Rep. 412 at 425.
201 *Irvani v Irvani* [2000] 1 Lloyd's Rep. 412 at 425; para.10–020 and following.

12–064 **Drugs.** The rules relating to drunkenness could perhaps be applied by analogy to the case of a person whose ability to understand the transaction was impaired by drugs.[202]

## 4. CORPORATIONS

### (a) Common law corporations

12–065 Corporations are created at common law by Royal Charter. The orthodox view is that a common law corporation has the same contractual capacity as a natural person of full age and capacity. Although this view is based only on dicta,[203] which have been doubted,[204] it is probably good law. Thus, a contract with such a corporation is binding although it is forbidden, or not authorised, by its charter. But if the corporation makes such a contract the Attorney General can take proceedings for the revocation of its charter; and any member of the corporation can restrain it by injunction from carrying on a forbidden activity which may lead to the revocation of its charter,[205] or claim a declaration that the activity is ultra vires.[206]

### (b) Statutory corporations

12–066 **Creation of statutory corporations.** Statutory corporations can be created in two ways: first, by complying with the formalities required by statute; and secondly, by special statute, passed to create the particular corporation in question. Since 1862, most trading companies have been created in the first of these two ways; the relevant Act in this regard is now the Companies Act 2006.

#### *(i) Companies created under the Companies Act 2006*

12–067 **The ultra vires doctrine.** The contractual capacity of a company created under the Companies Acts was formerly limited by the ultra vires doctrine, under which any act which was not authorised by the memorandum of association was void in law; and, being a nullity, it could not be ratified even by a unanimous vote of the company's shareholders.[207] It followed that the company was not liable on a contract which was not authorised by its memorandum. The primary purpose of the doctrine was to protect investors in the company by giving them some

---

[202] The mere fact that a person was a habitual drug addict does not suffice for this purpose: see *Irvani v Irvani* [2000] 1 Lloyd's Rep. 412 at 425.

[203] *British S Africa Co v De Beers Consolidated Mines* [1910] 1 Ch. 354 at 374; *Jenkin v Pharmaceutical Society* [1921] 1 Ch. 392 at 398; *Institution of Mechanical Engineers v Cane* [1961] A.C. 696 at 724; *Hazell v Hammersmith & Fulham LBC* [1992] 2 A.C. 1 at 39. The point is left open in *Crédit Suisse v Allerdale BC* [1997] Q.B. 306 at 336. For the possibility that the powers of a charter corporation may be restricted by special legislation, see para.12–074.

[204] e.g. Holdsworth, *A History of English Law*, Vol.9 (2010), pp.55–66.

[205] *Jenkin v Pharmaceutical Society* [1921] 1 Ch. 392.

[206] *Pharmaceutical Society of Great Britain v Dickson* [1970] A.C. 403.

[207] *Ashbury Ry Carriage & Iron Co v Riche* (1875) L.R. 7 H.L. 653.

assurance that the assets of the company would not be used in some wholly unexpected way. On the other hand, a person who made a contract with the company was liable to be prejudiced by the doctrine, since he was unlikely to have read the company's memorandum, or (if he had read it) to have understood it. The doctrine could also prejudice the company itself by preventing it from taking advantage of business opportunities which (perhaps as a result of a defect in drafting) fell technically outside its objects. The company could to some extent avoid this prejudice by altering its objects, but its power to make such alterations could be exercised only for seven specified purposes.[208] It could also draw its objects clause in very wide terms, enabling it to do almost any act which could be done by a company;[209] but such very widely drawn clauses tended to be restrictively interpreted by the courts,[210] since they made the protection which the ultra vires doctrine was intended to give to shareholders quite illusory.

**Reform.** The effects of the ultra vires doctrine, as described above, were the subject of much criticism and significant reforms were introduced by the Companies Act 1989, which have now been taken further by the Companies Act 2006. 12–068

**A company's constitution.** Under s.17 of the 2006 Act a company's constitution includes the articles of association, and any resolutions and agreements to which Ch.3 of Pt 3 of the Act applies. While this is intended to be a non-exhaustive[211] definition,[212] it does not include the memorandum of association which will no longer state the objects of the company and is now confined to a role in its formation.[213] Unless specifically restricted by its articles of association, the objects of a company are unrestricted.[214] In the absence of any such restrictions the ultra vires doctrine can have no application. Where any restrictions have been included in the articles of association, it is necessary to distinguish between the *capacity* of the company and the *powers* of the board of directors to bind it.[215] 12–069

**The company's capacity.** Under s.39(1) of the 2006 Act the validity of an act done by a company shall not be called into question on the ground of lack of 12–070

---

[208] Companies Act 1985 s.4 (original version, now repealed).

[209] *Cotman v Brougham* [1918] A.C. 514; *Brady v Brady* [1989] A.C. 755 at 772.

[210] e.g. *Rolled Steel (Holdings) Ltd v BSC* [1986] Ch. 246, drawing the distinction referred to at fn.215.

[211] Other documents will have constitutional relevance for certain purposes, e.g. the certificate of incorporation summarises key information pertaining to the company such as whether it is public or private: s.15.

[212] This definition applies throughout the 2006 Act unless the context requires a wider or more restricted meaning, e.g. s.257 expands the definition of a company's constitution for the purposes of Pt X: see para.12–071.

[213] Companies Act 2006 s.8. In the case of companies already in existence, provisions that are contained in the memorandum but are not of the kind now required by s.8 are to be treated as provisions of the company's articles: s.28, though the company in question may also alter its articles to this effect.

[214] Companies Act 2006 s.31(1).

[215] This is a distinction which was recognised in previous English case law: *Rolled Steel (Holdings) Ltd v BSC* [1986] Ch. 246.

capacity by reason of anything in the company's constitution.[216] The argument that a contract is void for lack of capacity if it is not authorised by the company's constitution is thus no longer available, either to the company or to the person dealing with the company.[217]

12–071 **The powers of the directors.** The directors of a company must act in accordance with the company's constitution[218] and only exercise powers for the purposes for which they are conferred.[219] But this duty may be breached and, where a contract is not authorised by the company's constitution, the mere fact that it cannot be called into question on the ground of lack of capacity will not enable a person who deals with the company to enforce it; for the making of such an unauthorised contract is necessarily beyond the powers of the directors. Further protection to such a person is therefore given by s.40 of the Act.[220] This provides that, "in favour of a person dealing with[221] a company in good faith, the power of the directors to bind the company, or authorise others to do so, is deemed to be free of any limitation under the company's constitution."[222] The person who deals with the company is not bound to enquire as to any limitation on the powers of the directors to bind the company or authorise others to do so.[223] He is presumed to have acted in good faith until the contrary is proved;[224] and he is not to be regarded as acting in bad faith "by reason *only* of his knowing that an act is beyond the powers of the directors under the company's constitution."[225] This provision allows for the possibility that it may be in the interests of the company to take advantage of a commercial opportunity by entering into a contract which is technically not authorised by its constitution. On the other hand, a person would presumably not be dealing with the company in good faith if the transaction in question was not only beyond the powers of the directors but also constituted a breach of their fiduciary duty to it, or was otherwise a collusive

[216] This rule is modified if the company is a charity, by s.42, under which such acts will be ultra vires unless the person dealing with the charity can satisfy one of the requirements set out.

[217] Companies Act 2006 s.39(1).

[218] For this purpose, the "company's constitution" is given a wider definition than in s.17 (para.12–069) and includes decisions taken in accordance with the company's articles, and other decisions taken by the members (or a class of them) if they are to be treated by virtue of any enactment or rule of law as decisions of the company: s.257.

[219] Companies Act 2006 s.171; Payne and Prentice [2005] L.M.C.L.Q. 447.

[220] The rules set out in s.40 are modified for transactions involving directors or their associates (see s.41), and companies that are charities (see s.42; fn.216).

[221] A person "deals with" a company if he is a party to any transaction or other act to which the company is a party (s.40(2)(a)), but this does not apply to "an internal arrangement with no diminution or increase in the assets or liabilities of the company": *EIC Services Ltd v Phipps* [2004] EWCA Civ 1069; [2005] 1 W.L.R. 1377 at [35] (s.40(1) (formerly, s.35A of the 1985 Act) not applicable to shareholder receiving bonus share issue).

[222] Companies Act 2006 s.40(1). For this purpose, "limitations on the directors' powers under the company's constitution" include limitations deriving from a resolution of the company or of any class of shareholders, or from any agreement between the members of the company or of any class of shareholders: s.40(3).

[223] Companies Act 2006 s.40(2)(b)(i). But if there are circumstances which should have "put him on enquiry" and he does not so enquire he may be found not to have dealt in good faith: *Wrexham Association Football Club Ltd v Crucialmove Ltd* [2006] EWCA Civ 237; [2007] B.C.C. 139 at [47].

[224] Companies Act 2006 s.40(2)(b)(ii).

[225] Companies Act 2006 s.40(2)(b)(iii) (emphasis added).

attempt on the part of the directors and the person dealing with the company to act in a way that was contrary to the interests of the company. In such a case the fact that a contract was not authorised by the company's constitution would not, indeed, make it open to challenge on the ground of lack of capacity; but by reason of the element of bad faith the contract would be unenforceable as it was beyond the directors' powers, and it would not be saved by s.40(1). Section 40(1) only operates "in favour of a person dealing with" the company. It therefore does not confer rights on the company. The company can however acquire such rights by ratifying the transaction.[226]

**Liability of the directors.** Persons who deal with the company are further protected by s.40(5) which provides that s.40 does not affect any liability incurred by the directors, or any other person, by reason of the directors' exceeding their powers. Where the company *is* liable by virtue of s.40(1), such liability is unlikely to be incurred by the directors;[227] though it is possible for a director to undertake additional personal liability under a collateral contract. Where the company is *not* liable because the person dealing with it did so in bad faith, a claim against the directors is unlikely to succeed: it would probably be dismissed by analogy with the rule that a contract to defraud a third party (i.e. the company) is illegal and void.[228] **12–072**

**Restraining acts outside the powers of the directors.** Members of the company are protected in that they can bring proceedings to restrain the doing of an act which is beyond the powers of the directors.[229] But no such proceedings lie "in respect of an act to be done in fulfilment of a legal obligation arising from a previous act of the company".[230] Presumably it follows that proceedings cannot be brought to restrain a company from performing a contract which a person dealing with the company could enforce against it under s.40(1). It seems that such a contract will, by virtue of that subsection, be deemed to be an "act of the company" even though the directors actually had no power to enter into it on the company's behalf. **12–073**

### *(ii) Corporations incorporated by special statute*

The ultra vires doctrine was originally established in relation to such corporations.[231] With respect to them, it is not affected by the reforms which have been described above,[232] though it has been mitigated with respect to certain contracts made by local authorities.[233] Before any of these reforms came into force, many of the rules which determine the scope and effects of the doctrine **12–074**

[226] *Grant v UK Switchback Ry* (1888) 40 Ch D. 135.
[227] e.g. the remedy for breach of warranty of authority (para.12–082) would not be available if the contract bound the company under s.40(1).
[228] See para.11–015.
[229] Companies Act 2006 s.40(4).
[230] Companies Act 2006 s.40(4).
[231] See *Eastern Counties Ry v Hawkes* (1855) 5 H.L.C. 331 at 347–348 (citing earlier cases).
[232] See para.12–069 and following; *Crédit Suisse v Allerdale BC* [1997] Q.B. 306.
[233] Local Government (Contracts) Act 1997.

were laid down in cases arising out of contracts with companies incorporated under the Companies Acts (or with local authorities). These cases are obsolete now that the common law doctrine no longer invalidates such contracts (or has been mitigated with respect to them). But the principles stated in them can still (where appropriate) apply to transactions with other corporations which are created, or whose capacity is limited, by special statute. For this reason, the following account is to some extent based on such cases.

12–075 **The ultra vires doctrine.** The contractual capacity of a corporation created by special statute continues, in general,[234] to be restricted by the ultra vires doctrine. The objects of such a corporation are set out in the statute by which it was created (or in rules made in pursuance of that statute). Any act done by or on behalf of the corporation which is not authorised by (or under) the incorporating statute is ultra vires and ineffective. It follows that an ultra vires contract made by such a corporation does not bind the corporation.[235] The corporation can also be restrained from doing ultra vires acts.[236] The same rules apply where the corporation has been created in some other way (e.g. by Royal Charter) but its capacity is nevertheless defined or limited by statute.[237]

12–076 **Whether transaction is ultra vires.**[238] The question whether a particular transaction falls within the powers of the corporation turns in the first place on the construction of the statute[239] by which it is incorporated, or which otherwise defines or limits its capacity. Particular difficulty can arise where the statute, after setting out the specific objects for which the corporation is created, goes on to confer a general power to do other acts which it is necessary or desirable for the company to do in order to achieve these objects. When the ultra vires doctrine applied to companies incorporated under the Companies Acts, the courts were faced with similar difficulties arising from analogous, broadly drafted, provisions in memoranda of association.[240] In deciding questions of this kind, they distinguished between the *objects* of a company and its *powers*. They went on to hold that, although powers could be exercised only for the purpose of the objects, their exercise for other purposes was not ultra vires but only beyond the powers of the directors; and that their exercise for other purposes could not confer rights on the other party to the transaction if he had notice of the fact that the powers

---

[234] For a statutory exception, see fn.233.

[235] An attempt to apply the reforms in ss.39 and 40 of the Companies Act 2006 (see para.12–069) by way of a "modification" of the common law where still applicable was rejected in *Crédit Suisse International v Stichting Vestia Groep* [2014] EWHC 3103 (Comm) at [256]–[259].

[236] e.g. *LCC v Attorney General* [1902] A.C. 165.

[237] e.g. *Hazell v Hammersmith and Fulham LBC* [1992] 2 A.C. 1.

[238] In *Crédit Suisse International v Stichting Vestia Groep* [2014] EWHC 3103 (Comm) at [186] Andrew Smith J held that the burden lies on the party seeking to enforce the contract to prove that the other party had capacity; contrast *Standard Chartered Bank v Ceylon Petroleum Corp* [2011] EWHC 1785 where Hamblen J proceeded on the basis that it is for the other party to prove its lack of capacity; affirmed [2012] EWCA Civ 1049. The latter appears correct.

[239] *Den Norske Creditbank v The Sarawak Economic Development Corp* [1988] 2 Lloyd's Rep. 616; *Standard Chartered Bank v Ceylon Petroleum Corp* [2012] EWCA Civ 1049.

[240] See fn.209.

had been so exercised.[241] It is arguable that the same distinction between objects and powers may apply where the officers of a corporation, whose capacity is defined by the incorporating statute, purport to exercise a general power (conferred by the statute) but do so for the purpose of achieving unauthorised objects: e.g. where they give a guarantee and it is alleged that the transaction in respect of which it is given is not an authorised object.[242] In the last resort, however, the question in cases of the present kind turns simply on the construction of the relevant legislation. Thus, where the corporation was empowered to do "anything … which in its opinion is calculated to facilitate the proper discharge of its functions or is incidental or conducive thereto," it was held that a guarantee given by the corporation could not be challenged on the ground that it was ultra vires.[243]

**Incidental objects.** Even in the absence of widely drafted provisions of the kind just discussed, a corporation can do acts which it is not expressly authorised to do, if they are fairly incidental to the objects for which it was established.[244] For example, in *Foster v London, Dover & Chatham Ry*[245] it was held that a railway company could validly grant short leases of the spaces under the arches of a viaduct, so long as those leases did not disable it from carrying on its railway business. But this rule does not enable the corporation to carry on activities substantially distinct from those authorised. A corporation authorised to run trams could not "incidentally" run buses.[246] **12–077**

**Contracts ex facie intra vires.** A contract which is on the face of it within the capacity of the corporation is not invalid merely because the corporation uses its proceeds for an ultra vires purpose, e.g. where an intra vires loan is spent on an ultra vires purpose.[247] But the corporation would not be bound by the contract if the lender knew that it intended to use the loan for such a purpose, or if he knew facts from which he could reasonably have deduced that the corporation had such an intention.[248] **12–078**

**Alternative remedies.** Where a transaction with a corporation is ultra vires, its invalidity can be a source of hardship to the other party: that party will, for example, have no remedy against the corporation if the corporation defaults on a **12–079**

[241] *Rolled Steel Products (Holdings) Ltd v BSC* [1986] Ch. 246; cf. at fn.215. See also *Introductions Ltd v National Provincial Bank Ltd* [1970] Ch. 199; Wedderburn 32 M.L.R. 563; 46 M.L.R. 204; Gregory 48 M.L.R. 109.

[242] *Crédit Suisse v Allerdale BC* [1997] Q.B. 306; *Crédit Suisse v Waltham Forest LBC* [1997] Q.B. 362; *Sutton LBC v Morgan Grenfell & Co* (1997) 29 H.L.R. 608; in all these cases, the guarantees were held void.

[243] *Den Norske Creditbank v The Sarawak Economic Development Corp* [1988] 2 Lloyd's Rep. 616 (where the incorporating legislation was a Malaysian Ordinance).

[244] *Ashbury Railway Carriage Co Ltd v Riche* (1875) L.R. 7 H.L. 653.

[245] [1895] 1 Q.B. 711; cf. *Charles Roberts & Co v British Railways Board* [1965] 1 W.L.R. 396.

[246] *LCC v Attorney General* [1902] A.C. 165; cf. *Hazell v Hammersmith & Fulham LBC* [1992] 2 A.C. 1 at 31 ("a power is not incidental merely because it is convenient or desirable or profitable"); *Mexico Infrastructure Finance LLC v Corporation of Hamilton* [2019] UKPC 2 at [42].

[247] *Re David Payne & Co Ltd* [1904] 2 Ch. 608.

[248] *Re Jon Beauforte Ltd* [1953] Ch. 131; cf. *Introductions Ltd v National Provincial Bank Ltd* [1970] Ch. 199.

transaction which has, by reason of market fluctuations, turned out to be disadvantageous to the corporation.[249] In theory, the other party can protect himself against this risk, before entering into the transaction, by reading the statute which defines or limits the corporation's powers. But in practice the other party is unlikely to take this step; and, even if he does take it, he runs the risk that his interpretation of the statute may, in legal proceedings on the contract, be held to have been erroneous. The law to some extent mitigates this hardship by making a number of alternative remedies available to the other party to the transaction.

12–080 **Subrogation.** An ultra vires lender can recover so much of his loan as is used by the company to pay debts incurred under intra vires contracts.[250]

12–081 **Return of money.** Money paid under an ultra vires contract is normally recoverable as money paid under a void contract.[251] This remedy is more fully discussed in Ch.22.[252]

12–082 **Remedy against officers.** A person who is induced to contract with a corporation by the false representation of a director that the contract is intra vires may be able to sue the director in tort for deceit or negligence,[253] or in contract for breach of implied warranty of authority.[254] The contractual action lies even though the representation was made innocently and in good faith.[255] It has been held that this remedy is not available if the misrepresentation is one of law;[256] though for reasons given in Ch.9 the present status of this restriction on the scope of the remedy is open to question.[257] The construction of the company's incorporating statute is a matter of law,[258] so that a director who represents that, on the true construction of the statute, a contract is intra vires, makes a representation of law. An ultra vires contractor may, finally, be able to show that the director is personally liable on the contract itself. Intention on the part of an agent to assume personal liability is readily inferred when the principal is non-existent.[259] Such an inference might also be drawn where the principal exists but lacks capacity to make the contract.

---

[249] e.g. *Hazell v Hammersmith and Fulham BC* [1992] 2 A.C. 1.

[250] *Blackburn BS v Cunliffe, Brooks & Co* (1882) 22 Ch D. 61; on appeal it was not necessary to decide this point: 9 App. Cas. 857.

[251] *Westdeutsche Landesbank Girozentrale v Islington LBC* [1996] A.C. 669; disagreeing with *Sinclair v Brougham* [1914] A.C. 398 so far as contra.

[252] See para.22–021.

[253] At common law, but not under s.2(1) of Misrepresentation Act 1967; see para.9–053 at fn.282.

[254] See para.16–089.

[255] *Firbank's Executors v Humphreys* (1886) 18 Q.B.D. 54; cf. *Weeks v Propert* (1873) L.R. 8 C.P. 427; *Cherry v Colonial Bank of Australia* (1869) L.R. 3 P.C. 24.

[256] See para.16–094.

[257] See para.9–020.

[258] *Rashdall v Ford* (1866) L.R. 2 Eq. 750; cf. *Beattie v Ebury* (1872) L.R. 7 Ch. App. 777; affirmed L.R. 7 H.L. 102.

[259] *Kelner v Baxter* (1866) L.R. 2 C.P. 174; para.16–055.

**Enforcement of another contract.** It is clear that a corporation cannot expand its own capacity by estoppel or contract.[260] We have seen in other contexts that a party cannot succeed on the basis of estoppel if that would subvert the policy which rendered the contract unenforceable[261] and the policy behind the doctrine of ultra vires is the protection of investors (in the case of corporations) and the public (in the case of local authorities). Similarly, if a corporation warrants in the contract that it has (or will not lack) capacity, the claim to enforce the warranty runs into the circular argument that it is only enforceable to the extent that the contract is enforceable and the contract is not enforceable if the corporation lacked capacity. But what if the representation upon which the estoppel is based, or the warranty, is set out in another contract which the corporation did have capacity to enter into? This was the position in *Crédit Suisse International v Stichting Vestia Groep*[262] in which a bank and a Dutch social housing association entered into a master agreement pursuant to which they executed a series of "swaps" transactions. Some of the swaps executed by the housing association were found to be ultra vires and unenforceable,[263] but in relation to them the bank was able to claim under the master agreement in which the housing association had "represented" and "warranted" that any swaps it might enter would, in effect, be intra vires (i.e. in compliance with its articles of association etc.). Andrew Smith J held that this allowed the bank to claim under the master agreement, and not under the unenforceable swaps themselves, on the basis either of contractual estoppel,[264] or for breach of warranty.[265] It is submitted, with great respect, that both conclusions are open to doubt. 12–083

While it is the case that "contractual estoppel" does not share some of the usual characteristics of estoppel (e.g. there is no requirement of reliance or unconscionability),[266] it is nonetheless a species of estoppel in that its effect is to bind the party to the facts, or the state of affairs, which have been agreed as a matter of contract (e.g. in the context of a claim for misrepresentation, that no representations have been made).[267] Accordingly, the effect of such an estoppel in the *Crédit Suisse* case appears to have been to make the ultra vires swaps enforceable on the basis that the housing association was bound by its representation that they were intra vires, contrary to the clear statement of principle with which this paragraph began. Andrew Smith J held otherwise on the basis that the bank's claim was that they were entitled "to enforce the Master Agreement *as if* the ultra vires contracts were valid",[268] but the claim being enforced was described as "*breach* of the compliance provision" of the master

---

[260] *York Corp v Henry Leetham & Sons* [1924] 1 Ch. 557 at 573; *Hazell v Hammersmith and Fulham LBC* [1992] 2 A.C. 1 at 36.

[261] See paras 5–012 and 5–028.

[262] [2014] EWHC 3103 (Comm).

[263] The capacity of the housing association was determined by Dutch law; the consequences of any lack of capacity were determined by English law as the law governing the transactions: *Haugesund Kommune v Depfa ACS Bank* [2010] EWCA Civ 579; [2012] Q.B. 549.

[264] *Crédit Suisse International v Stichting Vestia Groep* [2014] EWHC 3103 (Comm) at [319]–[320].

[265] *Crédit Suisse International v Stichting Vestia Groep* [2014] EWHC 3103 (Comm) at [322].

[266] See para.9–137.

[267] See para.9–137.

[268] *Crédit Suisse International v Stichting Vestia Groep* [2014] EWHC 3103 (Comm) at [319].

agreement.[269] As Andrew Smith J pointed out, for the purpose of contractual estoppel the representations made by the housing association in the compliance provisions could include representations applicable to the future, i.e. the housing association will have capacity at the time each swap is executed, but at that time they were still only representations *of fact* which prevented (estopped) the housing association from claiming that the swaps were ultra vires; as with estoppel generally,[270] they were not promissory obligations which gave rise to a claim for breach of the master agreement.[271]

No such difficulty arises with the alternative claim for breach of warranty, i.e. a promise that the swaps would be intra vires and, logically, the damages for such a breach are the amount to which the bank would have been entitled if the swaps were valid.[272] This produces a result which is the exact equivalent of the enforcement of the ultra vires swaps and raises the question of whether this is consistent with the principle that a corporation cannot expand its own capacity by contract. This aspect of Andrew Smith J's judgment proceeded on the basis that it was "not disputed" that the housing association had capacity to make the master agreement,[273] but if a corporation has no capacity to enter into an ultra vires contract does it have any more capacity to enter into a guarantee (i.e. the warranty) that the contract will be intra vires, or, to put it another way, should the policy which invalidates the ultra vires contract not also invalidate the guarantee (warranty)?[274] The position would be different if the guarantor was a third party, though even here the guarantee may be unenforceable on grounds of policy.[275]

12–084 **Enforcement by the corporation.**[276] The ultra vires doctrine normally operates so as to prevent a contract from being enforced *against* the corporation. The authorities provide no clear answer to the question whether the doctrine also precludes enforcement of the contract *by* the corporation. A similar problem used to arise where a contract with a corporation should have been, but was not, made under its common seal.[277] If such a contract was executory, the company could not enforce it because its own promise, being invalid, was no consideration for that of the other party;[278] but if the corporation actually performed its own invalid promise it thereby provided consideration and so became entitled to enforce the contract.[279] It can be argued that a similar distinction should be applied to ultra vires contracts; but it is submitted that the better approach is to ask whether the

[269] *Crédit Suisse International v Stichting Vestia Groep* [2014] EWHC 3103 (Comm) at [320].

[270] See para.3–090.

[271] If, alternatively, there is no estoppel at all in a "contractual estoppel", but merely a contractual promise (cf. McMeel [2011] L.M.C.L.Q. 185)—in this case not to assert that a swap is ultra vires—this is no different to the claim for breach of warranty which is analysed in the next paragraph.

[272] *Crédit Suisse International v Stichting Vestia Groep* [2014] EWHC 3103 (Comm) at [322].

[273] Quaere, if none of the swaps had been enforceable whether the master agreement was unenforceable in its own right for want of consideration; cf. *Spreadex Ltd v Cochrane* [2012] EWHC 2190 (Comm); [2012] Info T.L.R. 1; para.3–030, fn.140.

[274] cf. Unfair Contract Terms Act 1977 s.10; para.7–073.

[275] See para.13–012.

[276] Furmston 24 M.L.R. 215.

[277] This formal requirement was abolished by Corporate Bodies Contracts Act 1960.

[278] *Kidderminster Corp v Harwick* (1873) L.R. 9 Ex. 13; para.3–157.

[279] *Fishmongers' Co v Robertson* (1843) 5 Man. & G. 131.

object of the statutory limitation on the corporation's capacity would be subverted by allowing it to enforce the contract (rather than to ask whether the corporation had provided consideration). Where the corporation wishes to enforce the contract but has *not* yet performed its part, that object is likely to be subverted by allowing such enforcement, at least if enforcement by the corporation were (as would often be the case)[280] conditional on performance by it. In such cases the corporation would be encouraged to engage in ultra vires activity so as to satisfy the condition; and since it should not be given any incentive to engage in such activity, the contract should not be enforceable by it.[281] Where, on the other hand, the corporation *has* performed its part, this argument has no force: enforceability by the corporation could not encourage it to engage in future ultra vires activity since (at least in relation to the transaction in question)[282] the ultra vires activity has already taken place; and this reasoning gives some support to the view that a corporation which has performed its part of the contract should be able to enforce that contract. But it is submitted that this result should not necessarily follow and that a distinction should be drawn between cases in which the nature of the performance is such that it cannot, and those in which it is such that it can, be restored to the corporation.

The first possibility is illustrated by the case in which the corporation has rendered services under an ultra vires contract. In such a case, the object of the rule making the contract ultra vires is hardly likely to be defeated by allowing the corporation to sue for the agreed price of the services so that there is no strong argument against allowing it to enforce the contract; though the injustice of denying it such a remedy would at least be mitigated by allowing it to claim a reasonable remuneration in respect of services rendered by it under a void contract.[283]

The second possibility can be illustrated by supposing that the corporation has purported to sell an article which it was by its incorporating statute prohibited from selling,[284] and that it had actually delivered that article to the buyer. The object of the statute would, it is submitted, be more effectively promoted by allowing the corporation to sue for the return of the article than by allowing it to sue for the price, or for damages for non-acceptance of the subject-matter of the sale. This argument is supported by a group of cases in which moneys had been paid both by and to corporations under ultra vires contracts and it was held that the payments must be returned to the corporation where it was the payor[285] and by the corporation where it was the payee.[286] It must follow from these cases that

[280] See para.17–014; exceptions would be cases of independent promises (para.17–019) and of accepted anticipatory breach (paras 17–027, 17–092, 18–011).

[281] See *Pellatt's Case* (1867) L.R. 2 Ch. App. 527; *Triggs v Staines Urban DC* [1969] Ch. 10; *Bell Houses Ltd v City Wall Properties Ltd* [1966] 1 Q.B. 207 (reversed [1966] 2 Q.B. 656 on the ground that the contract was intra vires).

[282] *Bell Houses Ltd v City Wall Properties Ltd* [1966] 2 Q.B. 656 at 694.

[283] On the principle of *Craven-Ellis v Cannons Ltd* [1936] 2 K.B. 403; para.22–034.

[284] e.g. British Museum Act 1963 s.3(4).

[285] *South Tyneside MBC v Svenska International Plc* [1995] 1 All E.R. 545; *Kleinwort Benson Ltd v Lincoln CC* [1999] 2 A.C. 349 at 416.

[286] e.g. *Westdeutsche Landesbank Girozentrale v Islington LBC* [1996] A.C. 669; *Guinness Mahon & Co Ltd v Kensington & Chelsea Royal BC* [1999] Q.B. 215; *Kleinwort Benson Ltd v Lincoln CC* [1999] 2 A.C. 349; para.22–025.

the corporation could not have enforced the contracts by claiming the money or damages for failure to pay it; and emphatic statements in them that the contracts were "wholly void"[287] and "devoid of any legal contractual effects"[288] lend further support to the view that an ultra vires contract cannot be enforced by, any more than against, the corporation.

### *(iii) Limited liability partnerships*

12–085 **No ultra vires doctrine.** The Limited Liability Partnerships Act 2000 makes provision[289] for the incorporation of limited liability partnerships by registration of specified documents. Such a partnership is "a body corporate (with legal personality separate from its members)"[290] and "has unlimited capacity".[291] The ultra vires doctrine therefore does not apply to it.

[287] *Morgan Grenfell & Co Ltd v Welwyn Hatfield DC* [1995] 1 All E.R. 1 at 4.
[288] *Guinness Mahon & Co Ltd v Kensington & Chelsea Royal BC* [1999] Q.B. 215 at 284.
[289] Limited Liability Partnerships Act 2000 s.2.
[290] Limited Liability Partnerships Act 2000 s.1(2). The general law relating to other partnerships (which do not have legal personality separate from their members) does not apply to limited liability partnerships: Limited Liability Partnerships Act 2000 s.1(5).
[291] Limited Liability Partnerships Act 2000 s.1(3).

CHAPTER 13

# PLURALITY OF PARTIES



A promise may be made by or to more than one person. Such a promise must be distinguished from a multilateral contract.[1] If three persons agree to run a race subject to certain rules, there are three sides to the contract, but each side consists of only one person.[2] If two persons promise to pay a third £10, or if one person promises to pay £10 to two others, there may only be two sides to the contract, one consisting of two persons and the other of one person. This chapter is concerned with promises of this kind. 13–001

## 1. PLURALITY OF DEBTORS[3]

### (a) Definitions

**Independent promises.** If A and B *each separately* promise to pay C £10 this does not amount to one promise by several to one, but to two independent promises. Thus, C is entitled to £10 from A and a further £10 from B. This was, 13–002

---

[1] See para.2–077.
[2] cf. *Rockeagle Ltd v Alsop Wilkinson* [1992] Ch. 47 at 50 ("tripartite agreement").
[3] Williams, *Joint Obligations* (1997).

for example, the position where C granted licences to A and B under agreements providing for payment of a weekly sum by each of them,[4] and where a group of Lloyd's underwriters issued an insurance policy to an assured by which they bound themselves "each for his own part and not one for another".[5] There may be two such separate promises even where both are contained in the same document.[6]

13–003 **Joint or joint and several promises.** If A and B *together* promise to pay £10, the promise may be joint, or joint and several.[7] It is joint if A and B make only one promise binding both of them; it is joint and several if they make one promise binding both of them and if in addition each makes a separate promise binding him alone. A joint and several promise is distinguishable from two entirely separate promises in that it does not involve the promisors in cumulative liability. If A and B jointly and severally promise to pay C £10, C is not entitled to more than £10 in all. It is a question of interpretation whether a promise is joint, or joint and several.[8] A promise by two persons together is deemed to be joint, unless it is qualified in some way.[9] To make a promise joint and several, it is advisable to say expressly "we promise jointly and severally," or "we, and each of us, will pay". But this is not the only way of creating joint and several liability. In *Tippins v Coates*[10] three persons executed a bond by which they bound themselves "jointly and our respective heirs". This was held to be a joint and several promise, since that was evidently the intention of the parties: if it were held to be a joint bond, the *respective* heirs of the promisors would not be bound, but only the heir of the survivor.[11]

13–004 **Express provision by statute.** In some cases, the question of whether liability is joint, or joint and several, is expressly dealt with by statute. For example, s.9 of the Partnership Act 1890, provides that "every partner in a firm is liable jointly with the other partners … for all debts and obligations of the firm incurred while he is a partner". On the other hand, promissory notes made by a number of persons are deemed to be joint and several.[12]

---

[4] *Mikeover v Brady* [1989] 3 All E.R. 618.

[5] *Touche Ross & Co v Colin Baker* [1992] 2 Lloyd's Rep. 207 at 209.

[6] *Collins v Prosser* (1823) 1 B. & C. 682; *Gibson v Lupton* (1832) 9 Bing. 297; *Lee v Nixon* (1834) 1 A. & E. 201.

[7] In identifying the mutual obligations of the debtors, it is unlikely to make any difference whether their covenant was joint, joint and several or only several: *Stroude v Beazer Homes Ltd* [2005] EWHC 2686; (2005) 48 E.G. 223 (implied term that one landowner had right to enter land of another to fulfil concurrent obligation to construct bypass).

[8] *In re Rhinegold Publishing Ltd* [2012] EWHC 587 (Ch).

[9] *Levy v Sale* (1877) 37 L.T. 709; *White v Tyndall* (1888) 13 App. Cas. 263; *The Argo Hellas* [1984] 1 Lloyd's Rep. 296 at 300; *Katara Hospitality v Guez* [2018] EWHC 3063 (Comm) at [131].

[10] (1853) 18 Beav. 401.

[11] See para.13–009.

[12] Bills of Exchange Act 1882 s.85(2); see also Law of Property Act 1925 s.119; Landlord and Tenant (Covenants) Act 1995 s.13(1).

## (b) Differences between joint, and joint and several, promises

### (i) Parties to the action

**Action on a joint promise.** At common law, an action on a *joint* promise had to be brought against all the surviving joint debtors.[13] If this was not done the defendants could plead the non-joinder of their co-debtors in abatement. Although pleas in abatement no longer exist, it is still the general rule that the action must be brought against all the joint debtors.[14] But the court has discretion to allow the action to proceed against one joint debtor if the other is out of the jurisdiction, or cannot be traced.[15] If one joint debtor is bankrupt, the other or others may be sued without him.[16] 13–005

**Action on a joint and several promise.** An action on a *joint and several* promise could at common law be brought against one or all the co-debtors but not, it seems, against some (but not all). The creditor could either sue each debtor individually on his several promise or all on their joint promise; but he could not, by suing some, treat the contract as joint without also joining all the others.[17] It seems that in such a case the court now has discretion to order all the other joint and several debtors to be joined to the action since it may order the names of persons to be joined to an action if their presence is "desirable … so that the court can resolve all matters in dispute in the proceedings".[18] The court might order such joinder so that the amount of the debt may be conclusively established for the purpose of the contribution[19] between all the debtors. It seems that the onus is on the debtor who is sued to bring his co-debtors before the court as third parties, with a view to claiming contribution from them.[20] 13–006

### (ii) Judgment

**Judgment against one joint debtor.** If one *joint* debtor is sued alone and does not plead non-joinder of the others, judgment may be given against him alone. After the creditor had recovered such a judgment, it was formerly the rule that he could not take further proceedings against any of the other joint debtors (even though the judgment remained unsatisfied) because the original cause of action was merged in the judgment.[21] This rule was, however, likely to cause hardship to 13–007

[13] *Cabell v Vaughan* (1669) 1 Wms. Saund. 291; *Richards v Heather* (1817) 1 B. & Ald. 29.

[14] *Norbury, Natzio & Co Ltd v Griffiths* [1918] 2 K.B. 369; it is up to the defendant to take the point; *Wegg-Prosser v Evans* [1895] 1 Q.B. 108.

[15] *Wilson, Sons & Co Ltd v Balcarres Brook SS Co Ltd* [1893] 1 Q.B. 422; *Robinson v Geisel* [1894] 2 Q.B. 685.

[16] Insolvency Act 1986 s.345(4).

[17] *Cabell v Vaughan* (1669) 1 Wms. Saund. 291, n.4.

[18] CPR r.19.2(2)(a).

[19] See para.13–019.

[20] cf. *Wilson, Sons & Co Ltd v Balcarres Brook SS Co Ltd* [1893] 1 Q.B. 422 at 428 (where the contract was joint).

[21] *Kendall v Hamilton* (1879) 4 App. Cas. 504.

the creditor; and it has been abolished by statute,[22] so that a creditor is no longer precluded from suing one joint debtor merely because he has previously obtained a judgment against another. He is so precluded if the judgment has been satisfied.[23]

13–008 **Judgment against one joint and several debtor.** Where the contract is *joint and several*, judgment against one debtor was never regarded as a bar to proceedings against another.[24] Each is liable on his separate promise, as well as on the joint promise: hence there are several causes of action only some of which are merged in the first judgment.[25] A claim against joint and several debtors is barred only if one of them satisfies it, whether under a judgment or otherwise.

### (iii) *Survivorship*

13–009 **Common law.** At common law the liability of a *joint* debtor passed on his death to the surviving joint debtors.[26] The creditor therefore had no claim against the estate of the deceased, but only one against the surviving joint debtors. If they paid, they might be able to recover contribution from the estate of the deceased;[27] but the creditor himself had no direct right against the estate. On the death of the last surviving joint debtor, the creditor could recover the debt from his estate.[28]

On the death of a *joint and several* debtor his several (though not his joint) liability remained enforceable against his estate.[29]

13–010 **Equity.** The rule that joint liability passed to the surviving debtors might be convenient where the debtors were engaged in administering a trust, but it was highly inconvenient in commercial affairs. If only one of a number of joint debtors was solvent, and that one happened to die, the creditor would lose all substantial remedy. The difficulty was particularly acute in partnership cases. Equity therefore treated partnership debts as joint and several to this extent, that they could be enforced against the estate of a deceased partner.[30] This rule is confirmed by s.9 of the Partnership Act 1890.[31]

The equitable right to enforce a joint debt against the estate of a deceased joint contractor was applied mainly in partnership cases, but there is some authority for

---

[22] Civil Liability (Contribution) Act 1978 ss.3, 7(1). For a situation not covered by these provisions, see *The Argo Hellas* [1984] 1 Lloyd's Rep. 296 at 304. Section 3 also does not apply where a debt is discharged by an accord and satisfaction which is later embodied in a court order: *Morris v Molesworth* [1998] N.L.J. 1551; cf. CPR r.12.8 (default judgment): *Otkritie International Investment Management Ltd v Urumov* [2012] EWHC 890 (Comm).

[23] *Bryanston Finance Ltd v de Vries* [1975] 1 Q.B. 703 at 733, 739 (tort); *Jameson v CEGB* [2000] 1 A.C. 455 at 473 (tort); cf. *Vanden Recycling Ltd v Tumulty* [2015] EWHC 3616 (QB) (also tort).

[24] *Balgobin v South West Regional Health Authority* [2012] UKPC 11; [2013] 1 A.C. 582 at [21].

[25] *Blyth v Fladgate* [1891] 1 Ch. 337.

[26] *Cabell v Vaughan* (1669) 1 Wms. Saund. 291, n.4(f); *Godson v Good* (1816) 6 Taunt. 587 at 594.

[27] *Batard v Hawes* (1853) 2 E. & B. 287; para.13–017.

[28] *Calder v Rutherford* (1822) 3 Brod. & B. 302.

[29] *Read v Price* [1909] 1 K.B. 577.

[30] See *Kendall v Hamilton* (1879) 4 App. Cas. 504 at 517.

[31] But under this section separate debts of a deceased partner must be paid in priority to the partnership debts.

saying that it was not confined to such cases, nor even to cases involving mercantile transactions.[32] It is therefore arguable that, on the question of survivorship, there was, before the Judicature Act 1873, a conflict between common law and equity, so that equity now prevails.[33] It is also arguable that the principle of survivorship has been abolished by s.1(1) of the Law Reform (Miscellaneous Provisions) Act 1934, which provides that all causes of action subsisting against a person at the time of his death shall (with certain exceptions) survive against the estate. The object of this provision was to abolish the common law rule that actions *in tort* could not be brought against the estate of a deceased tortfeasor; but its words seem apt to abolish the rule that the liability of a joint debtor passed on his death to the surviving joint debtors (so that it could no longer be enforced against his estate).

### (c) Similarities between joint, and joint and several, promises

#### (i) *Defence of one*

**Whether defence of one is a defence for all.** If one of several co-debtors has a defence to the action, the question whether that defence also avails the others depends on its nature. If it goes to the root of the claim, and wholly destroys it, the other debtors can take advantage of it. Thus they can do so if one co-debtor can prove that the debt has been paid, or that the creditor is not entitled to payment because of his own breach of contract, or that a written contract is a forgery, or that the creditor was guilty of fraud.[34] But if the defence is personal to one co-debtor, e.g. that he was a minor or that he had been discharged as a result of bankruptcy proceedings, it does not avail the others as co-debtors.[35] 13–011

**Contracts of guarantee.** Special rules apply to contracts of guarantee, under which the guarantor generally undertakes joint and several liability with the principal debtor.[36] It has been held that the guarantor is not liable if the principal debt is illegal,[37] or if the principal debtor has been discharged as a result of the creditor's breach,[38] or if the principal debt is unenforceable under the rule against penalties.[39] A guarantor of a debt that was unenforceable under the Moneylenders Acts was not liable on the guarantee;[40] and the Consumer Credit Act 1974 (which repeals those Acts) lays down a similar rule in the case of a guarantee given in 13–012

---

[32] *Thorpe v Jackson* (1837) 2 Y. & C. Ex. 553.

[33] Judicature Act 1873 s.25(11); now Senior Courts Act 1981 s.49(1).

[34] *Porter v Harris* (1663) 1 Lev. 63; *Gardner v Walsh* (1855) 5 E. & B. 83; *Pirie v Richardson* [1927] 1 K.B. 448.

[35] *Burgess v Merrill* (1812) 4 Taunt. 468; *Lovell & Christmas v Beauchamp* [1894] A.C. 607; *Pirie v Richardson* [1927] 1 K.B. 448; cf. *Chaplin v Leslie Frewin (Publishers) Ltd* [1966] Ch. 71.

[36] e.g. *Anderson v Martindale* (1801) 1 East 497; *Read v Price* [1909] 1 K.B. 577.

[37] *Swan v Bank of Scotland* (1836) 10 Bli. (N.S.) 627; *Heald v O'Connor* [1971] 1 W.L.R. 497.

[38] *Unity Finance Ltd v Woodcock* [1963] 1 W.L.R. 455; explained on another ground in *Goulston Discount Co Ltd v Clark* [1967] 2 Q.B. 493.

[39] *Azimut-Benetti SpA v Healey* [2010] EWHC 2234 (Comm); 132 Con L.R. 113 (where the debt did not amount to a penalty).

[40] *Eldridge & Morris v Taylor* [1931] 2 K.B. 416; *Temperance Loan Fund Ltd v Rose* [1932] 2 K.B. 522.

respect of a regulated agreement.[41] These rules cannot be deduced from the general principles governing joint and several contracts, but appear to be based on considerations of policy.[42] It is obviously undesirable to allow a person who lends for an illegal purpose, or a lender who tries to evade the Consumer Credit Act, to recover his loan from any person whatsoever.

13–013 **Corporation debts.** On the other hand, a guarantee may be valid where the principal debtor is a corporation acting ultra vires. Whether it is actually valid depends on its interpretation: did the guarantor undertake to pay only what the corporation could lawfully be required to pay, or what it had in fact promised to pay?[43] Where the principal debt is incurred by a company incorporated under the Companies Act 2006, the validity of that debt can no longer (as a general rule) be called into question on the ground of lack of the company's capacity by reason of anything in its constitution;[44] it follows that the guarantee cannot be called into question on this ground. The position is the same where the principal debt arises out of a contract which is made by a person dealing with the company in good faith, but which is, under the company's constitution, beyond the power of the board of directors: in favour of the other contracting party, the power of the board is (as a general rule) deemed to be free from any limitation under the company's constitution,[45] so that the contract giving rise to the debt, and consequently also the guarantee, cannot be challenged on the ground that it was beyond the powers of the board. The general rule is that the principal contract will be invalid only if the other party to it dealt with the company in bad faith; and mere knowledge of the fact that the contract was beyond the powers of the directors is not sufficient to constitute bad faith.[46] It seems that some kind of dishonesty is required to constitute bad faith; and if the principal transaction is invalid on this ground, then it is submitted that the guarantee should also be invalid. This submission is based on an analogy with illegal contracts,[47] for the principal contract in our last example would be, or would come close to being, one to defraud the company.[48] The only other situations in which the principal contract is now likely to be invalid on the ground that it is ultra vires are: (i) those in which a statutory corporation is not incorporated under the Companies Act, so that the common law doctrine of ultra vires still applies to it;[49] and (ii) those in which, though the company is incorporated under the 2006 Act, the statutory modifications of the ultra vires doctrine, described above, exceptionally do not apply.[50] If in such

---

41 Consumer Credit Act 1974 s.113(1) and (2); see para.5–007 for the meaning of "regulated" agreement.

42 Mitchell 63 L.Q.R. 354.

43 *Yorks Ry & Wagon Co v Maclure* (1882) 21 Ch D. 309; *Garrard v James* [1925] Ch. 616; as explained in *Heald v O'Connor* [1971] 1 W.L.R. 497.

44 Companies Act 2006 s.39(1) (modified rules apply to companies which are charities: ss.39(2), 42); para.12–070.

45 Companies Act 2006 s.40(1) (modified rules apply to companies which are charities: ss.40(6), 42; and transactions with directors and their associates: ss.40(6), 41); para.12–071.

46 Companies Act 2006 s.40(2)(b)(iii).

47 See at fn.37.

48 cf. para.11–015.

49 See para.12–074; subject to the exceptions there stated relating to local authorities.

50 i.e. charities and transactions with directors or their associates; fnn.44, 45.

cases the creditor is induced to enter into the contract in reliance on a guarantee given by one of the corporation's directors or officers, it is submitted that the guarantor should be liable on the guarantee: there seems to be no ground of policy for allowing him to rely on the invalidity of the principal debt.[51]

**Minors' debts.** Similar policy considerations apply where the principal debtor is a minor: it would be wrong to allow the guarantor on this ground to escape from a liability deliberately undertaken since such a result would not be necessary for the protection of minors. It has therefore been provided by statute that the guarantee shall not be unenforceable against the guarantor merely because the principal obligation was unenforceable against the debtor because he was a minor when he incurred it.[52] 13–014

### *(ii) Release of one*

**Release of one debtor by the creditor is a release of all.** If the creditor releases one co-debtor, the release is available for the benefit of all the others since it wholly destroys the cause of action.[53] At first sight, the application of this rule to joint and several debtors looks illogical, since there are several causes of action against them; but it may be justified on the ground that it would make the release partly futile to hold that only one of the co-debtors was released. If the others could still be sued, they could claim contribution from the one who had been released, who would thus indirectly be made liable, notwithstanding the release.[54] But in spite of this argument, a covenant not to sue a single co-debtor releases him alone and does not release the other co-debtors.[55] 13–015

**Reservation of right to sue co-debtors.** It used to be thought that a release granted to one co-debtor released the others even though it reserved the creditor's rights against them.[56] But the courts originally evaded this rule by distinguishing between a release and a covenant not to sue. The former released all the co-debtors; the latter released only the debtor with whom it was made.[57] The distinction turned on the interpretation of the document and the present approach is to go directly to the question of interpretation without first distinguishing 13–016

---

[51] For the possibility that an enforceable "guarantee" might be given by the company itself, see the discussion in para.12–083.

[52] Minors' Contracts Act 1987 s.2 (reversing *Coutts & Co v Browne-Lecky* [1947] K.B. 104); and see s.4, amending Consumer Credit Act 1974 s.113(7).

[53] *Nicholson v Revill* (1836) 4 A. & E. 675; *Re WEA* [1901] 2 K.B. 642; *Morris v Molesworth* [1998] N.L.J. 1551. In tort, the rule applies where the liability is joint: *New Zealand Guardian Trust Ltd v Brooks* [1995] 1 W.L.R. 96; and where it is concurrent: *Jameson v CEGB* [2000] 1 A.C. 455.

[54] *Jenkins v Jenkins* [1928] 2 K.B. 501 at 508.

[55] See the authorities cited in fn.57.

[56] *Nicholson v Revill* (1836) 4 A. & E. 675 at 683.

[57] *Hutton v Eyre* (1815) 6 Taunt. 289; *Webb v Hewitt* (1857) 3 K. & J. 438; *Ex p. Good* (1876) 5 Ch D. 46. In *Duck v Mayeu* [1892] 2 Q.B. 511 and *Gardiner v Moore* [1969] 1 Q.B. 55 the same rule was applied in tort; the latter case also shows that reservation of the rights against one of the persons liable may be implied; cf. *Gladman Commercial Properties v Fisher Hargreaves Proctor* [2013] EWCA Civ 1466; [2014] P.N.L.R. 11; *Starlight Shipping Co v Allianz Marine and Aviation Versicherungs AG* [2014] EWHC 3068 (Comm); [2014] 2 Lloyd's Rep. 579 at [58].

between "release" and "covenant not to sue".[58] Accordingly, if the document releases one co-debtor but reserves the creditor's rights against the other or others, the courts will give effect to the intention of the parties as so expressed.[59] But a document which simply released one co-debtor without expressly or impliedly[60] reserving the creditor's rights against the others would still wholly extinguish those rights.[61]

13–017 **Release of one debtor by operation of law is no release of co-debtors.** The rules discussed above apply only to release by act of the parties. Where one co-debtor is released by operation of law (e.g. by an order of discharge in bankruptcy) the others are not released.[62] If the creditor appoints one co-debtor his executor, both the co-debtor and the others are released when probate is obtained. The reason for this rule is that "the debt is deemed to have been paid by the debtor [*qua* debtor] to himself as executor" and thus discharged.[63] In equity the executor is then deemed to have the amount of the debt in his hands as assets of the testator, and is thus accountable for it to the estate.[64]

13–018 **Release of one debtor under an independent promise.** Problems similar to those discussed above can arise where A and B are not joint, or joint and several, debtors but are persons who have entered into, and then broken, two entirely separate contracts with C.[65] The losses suffered by C in consequence of these breaches may be related, e.g. where A and B are associated companies and A's wrongful termination of an agency contract with C on the ground of C's alleged but unsubstantiated misconduct leads B wrongfully to terminate a similar (but not identical) contract, also with C.[66] An agreement by which C settles his claim against A may be expressed to release C's claim against A in respect of loss suffered by C by reason, not only of A's, but also of B's, wrongful termination of the contracts with C;[67] and the effect, if any, of this agreement on C's claim

---

[58] *Johnson v Davies* [1999] Ch. 117 at 127–128; following *Watts v Aldington, The Times*, 16 December 1993.

[59] *Johnson v Davies* [1999] Ch. 117; for earlier cases reaching the same conclusion, see *Price v Barker* (1855) 4 E. & B. 760; *Apley Estates Co v De Bernales* [1947] Ch. 217 (tort); cf. *Banco Santander SA v Bayfern Ltd* [2000] 1 All E.R. (Comm) 776 at 780 (release of one joint and several debtor by assignment of the creditor's right to that one). If payments made by the co-debtors who have been released extinguish the debt in full, there can be no surviving cause of action against any remaining co-debtor notwithstanding a reservation of rights against him: *Crooks v Newdigate Properties Ltd* [2009] EWCA Civ 283; [2009] C.P. Rep. 34.

[60] See *Gardiner v Moore* [1969] 1 Q.B. 55.

[61] cf. *Cutler v McPhail* [1962] 2 Q.B. 292; *Deanplan Ltd v Mahmoud* [1993] Ch. 151 (where the liability of successive assignees of a lease was cumulative).

[62] Insolvency Act 1986 s.281(7); *Re Garner's Motors Ltd* [1937] Ch. 594.

[63] *Jenkins v Jenkins* [1928] 2 K.B. 501 at 509; Administration of Estates Act 1925 s.21A, as inserted by Limitation (Amendment) Act 1980 s.10.

[64] *Jenkins v Jenkins* [1928] 2 K.B. 501 at 509; *Commissioner of Stamp Duties v Bone* [1977] A.C. 511.

[65] For the distinction between the two types of promises, see para.13–002.

[66] As in *Heaton v Axa Equity and Law Life Assurance Society Plc* [2002] UKHL 15; [2002] 2 A.C. 329.

[67] *Heaton v Axa Equity and Law Life Assurance Society Plc* [2002] UKHL 15; [2002] 2 A.C. 329, where A's (unsubstantiated) allegations of misconduct may also have influenced B.

against B depends on its interpretation.[68] If it meant that the sum paid in pursuance of it was intended to represent the full amount of C's loss, resulting from both breaches, then C, having been fully compensated for that loss by A, would have no further claim in respect of it against B.[69] But such an agreement to release A from liability for A's breach will not bar C's claim against B in respect of other causes of action (than B's breach of contract) which C may have against B or in respect of loss caused by B's breach to the extent to which that loss was attributable to B's (rather than to A's) breach.[70] The only effect of C's settlement with A on such a claim results from the principle that C cannot recover twice over the same loss: that is, C must give credit to B for sums paid by A under the settlement so far as they represent the loss suffered by C as a result of B's breach[71] for which A nevertheless accepted liability on the ground that this breach was a consequence of A's prior breach.

### *(iii) Contribution*

If one co-debtor, being liable to pay the entire debt,[72] has paid it in full, he is entitled to recover contribution from the others.[73] Prima facie, he is entitled to recover from each co-debtor the amount of the debt divided by the number of co-debtors. If one of the co-debtors has died, his estate is liable to contribute, even if he was a joint debtor. The general rule may be varied by the terms of the contract or by the bankruptcy of one co-debtor. **13–019**

**Terms of the contract.** The co-debtors can make any provision they like as to contribution. Where the co-debtors are principal debtor and surety, it is implied that the surety, if called on to pay, is entitled to be wholly indemnified by the principal debtor. Conversely, if the principal debtor pays the whole debt, he has no right of contribution against the surety. Several sureties for the same debt are prima facie entitled inter se to contribution in proportion to their number; but where one surety (A) promises to pay only if neither the debtor nor another surety (B) does so, and B pays on the debtor's default, then B will not be entitled to contribution from A.[74] **13–020**

---

68 *Heaton v Axa Equity and Law Life Assurance Society Plc* [2002] UKHL 15; [2002] 2 A.C. 329 at [8], [9], [27], [41].

69 *Heaton v Axa Equity and Law Life Assurance Society Plc* [2002] UKHL 15; [2002] 2 A.C. 329 at [8].

70 This was the outcome in the *Heaton* case.

71 In the *Heaton* case, C accepted the need to give credit for such sums (paid by A) in their claim against B and this concession was evidently regarded as correct by Lord Mackay: [2002] UKHL 15; [2002] 2 A.C. 329 at [47], with whose reasoning Lords Bingham, Steyn and Hutton agreed.

72 For this requirement, see *Legal & General Assurance Society v Drake Ins Co Ltd* [1992] Q.B. 887 where a debtor who was liable for only part of the debt, but had paid it in full, was held not to be entitled to contribution. Where a guarantee provided for payment on demand and one guarantor paid more than his share before any such demand had been made, he was nevertheless held entitled to contribution as the payment had not been made "officiously" and the making of the demand was said not to be a "condition precedent" of his liability: *Stimpson v Smith* [1999] 2 All E.R. 833.

73 e.g. *Davitt v Titcumb* [1990] Ch. 110 at 117.

74 *Scholefield Goodman & Sons Ltd v Zyngier* [1986] A.C. 562.

13–021 **Bankruptcy.** At common law, the rule that the amount of contribution was the amount of the debt divided by the number of co-debtors prevailed even though some of the co-debtors were insolvent.[75] Equity adopted the fairer rule that the amount of contribution was the amount of the debt divided by the number of sureties who were *solvent* when the right to contribution arose.[76] This equitable rule now prevails.[77]

## 2. PLURALITY OF CREDITORS

### (a) Definitions

13–022 **Independent promises.** If X promises to pay A and B £10, he may make two separate promises, under which A and B are entitled to £10 *each*, so that X's total liability is to pay £20. No special problems arise out of such promises. But if X makes only one promise to A and B, so that he is liable to pay only £10 in all, it becomes important to determine whether his promise to A and B is made to them jointly, or whether it is made to them severally.

13–023 **Joint or several.** At common law, the question whether a contract was made with two persons jointly or with them severally depended on the wording of the contract, and on the interests of the parties in enforcing it. If the contract was made with a number of persons "jointly" and their interests were joint, it was a joint contract;[78] if it was made with a number of persons severally, i.e. "with them and each of them" and their interests were several, it was a several contract.[79] If the contract was ambiguous, or did not state whether it was joint and several, then it was joint if the interests of the creditors were joint, and otherwise several.[80] The interests of the creditors were joint if each had the same interest in the performance of the contract, even though they had separate interests in the property affected. Hence a covenant to repair made with a number of lessors jointly was joint, though they did not hold the land jointly, but in common, so that their interests in it were several.[81] On the other hand, where land was sold by tenants in common and the purchaser promised to pay them the price in fixed proportions corresponding with their shares in the land, the promise was regarded as several.[82] The position was less clear where the contract was expressly joint

[75] *Lowe v Dixon* (1885) 16 Q.B.D. 455 at 458.
[76] *Hitchman v Stewart* (1855) 3 Drew. 271.
[77] *Lowe v Dixon* (1885) 16 Q.B.D. 455. The rules as to assessment of contribution laid down in Civil Liability (Contribution) Act 1978 s.2 do not alter this position: they apply to *damages* but not to *debts*; for this distinction, cf. para.21–001.
[78] cf. *Sorsbie v Park* (1843) 12 M. & W. 146 at 158.
[79] *James v Emery* (1818) 5 Price 529.
[80] e.g. *Anderson v Martindale* (1801) 1 East 487; *Palmer v Mallett* (1887) 36 Ch D. 411.
[81] *Bradburne v Botfield* (1845) 14 M. & W. 559; *Thompson v Hakewill* (1865) 19 C.B. (N.S.) 713. For the position between the tenants in common *inter se*, see *Beer v Beer* (1852) 12 C.B. 60.
[82] *James v Emery* (1818) 5 Price 529.

and the interests several, or conversely; but the prevailing view appears to be that the court would give effect to the intention of the parties, as expressed in the agreement.[83]

**Joint and several.** The common law did not originally recognise the possibility that a promise *to* a number of persons could be joint *and* several.[84] The possibility was, however, recognised in the late 19th century;[85] and the question is now of little importance as s.81 of the Law and Property Act 1925 provides that a covenant, and a contract made under seal[86] and a bond or obligation under seal made with two or more persons jointly, shall, if made after 1925, "be construed as being also made with each of them"[87] unless a contrary intention is expressed; where the instrument is executed by an individual, s.1 of the Law of Property (Miscellaneous Provisions) Act 1989 provides that it need no longer be sealed: execution as a deed in accordance with the requirements of that section is sufficient.[88] Such covenants, etc. are now prima facie joint and several.[89] Section 81 of the 1925 Act applies only to promises in deeds;[90] its object seems to have been to avoid in relation to such promises the common law rule that on the death of a joint creditor his rights passed by survivorship[91] to the other or others. In this respect, it resembles the rule under which a contract for the repayment of money lent by a number of lenders was presumed in equity to create a several right in each lender, even though under the common law rules the contract was joint.[92] The presumption could be rebutted, e.g. if the lenders were trustees;[93] here survivorship was administratively convenient, and created no substantive injustice. It seems that promises regarded as several under s.81 and under the equitable presumption will be so regarded not only for the purpose of limiting the doctrine of survivorship, but also for the other purposes to be discussed below. 13–024

[83] *Sorsbie v Park* (1843) 12 M. & W. 146 at 158; *Keightley v Watson* (1849) 3 Ex. 716; *Beer v Beer* (1852) 12 C.B. 60; for the earlier view that the interest of the parties was always decisive, see *Slingsby's Case* (1588) 5 Co. Rep. 18b.; *Withers v Bircham* (1824) 3 B. & C. 254 at 256; *Hopkinson v Lee* (1845) 6 Q.B. 964.

[84] *Slingsby's Case* (1588) 5 Co. Rep. 18b; *Anderson v Martindale* (1801) 1 East 487; *Bradburne v Botfield* (1854) 14 M. & W. 559 at 573; *Keightley v Watson* (1849) 3 Ex. 716 at 723 (criticising the rule).

[85] *Thompson v Hakewill* (1865) 19 C.B. (N.S.) 713 at 726; *Palmer v Mallett* (1887) 36 Ch D. 410 at 421.

[86] See now Law of Property (Miscellaneous Provisions) Act 1989 s.1(7).

[87] The section does not affect the law relating to joint *debtors*: *Johnson v Davies* [1999] Ch. 117 at 127.

[88] Law of Property (Miscellaneous Provisions) Act 1989 s.1(8) and Sch.1. And see para.3–172 for execution of deeds by corporations.

[89] See *Josselson v Borst* [1938] 1 K.B. 723; for a statutory exception, see Law of Property Act 1925 s.119 (covenants with several mortgagees deemed to be joint).

[90] The primary meaning of "covenant" is a promise by deed: see *Rank Xerox Ltd v Lane* (*Inspector of Taxes*) [1981] A.C. 629 at 639. It seems that in Law of Property Act 1925 s.81, "covenant" refers to a promise which would not be binding unless it were under seal, and "contract … under seal" to one which would be binding even if it were not sealed.

[91] See para.13–027.

[92] *Steeds v Steeds* (1889) 22 Q.B.D. 537.

[93] *Steeds v Steeds* (1889) 22 Q.B.D. 537 at 542.

## (b) Parties to the action

13–025 **Joint promise.** Where a promise is made to a number of persons *jointly*, all of them (if living) must be parties to the action.[94] If one joint creditor is unwilling to join, the one wishing to sue must offer him an indemnity as to costs; if he still refuses to join he can then be added as co-defendant.[95]

13–026 **Several promise.** Where a promise is made to two or more persons *severally* an action can be brought by one or more of them: it is not necessary to join them all.[96]

## (c) Survivorship

13–027 **Joint creditor.** On the death of a *joint* creditor, his rights pass to his surviving co-creditors.[97]

13–028 **Several creditor.** On the death of a *several* creditor, his rights pass, not to his co-creditors, but to his personal representatives.[98]

## (d) Defence against one

13–029 **Joint contract.** Where a contract is *joint*, a defence available against one creditor can be raised against the others if it goes to the root of the claim. For example, "when two persons are jointly insured and their interests are inseparably connected, so that a loss or gain necessarily affects them both, the misconduct of one is sufficient to contaminate the whole insurance".[99] It seems, although there is no authority precisely in point, that a defence available against one joint creditor does not avail against the other if it is purely personal to the first. Thus, if the debtor can plead ultra vires against one joint creditor,[100] he may remain liable to the others.

---

[94] *Jell v Douglas* (1821) 4 B. & Ald. 374; *Sorsbie v Park* (1843) 12 M. & W. 146; *Thompson v Hakewill* (1865) 19 C.B. (N.S.) 713.

[95] *Cullen v Knowles* [1898] 2 Q.B. 380; no such indemnity need be offered to one joint creditor who is guilty of a fraud on the other: *Johnson v Stephens & Carter Ltd* [1923] 2 K.B. 857. If a joint creditor is added as co-defendant without being offered such an indemnity, the only person who can object is that joint creditor, and not the debtor; *Burnside v Harrison Marks Productions Ltd* [1968] 1 W.L.R. 728.

[96] *James v Emery* (1818) 5 Price 529; *Keightley v Watson* (1849) 3 Ex. 716; *Palmer v Mallett* (1887) 36 Ch D. 411.

[97] *Anderson v Martindale* (1801) 1 East 497.

[98] *Withers v Bircham* (1824) 3 B. & C. 254.

[99] *P Samuel & Co v Dumas* [1924] A.C. 432 at 445; *Arab Bank Plc v Zurich Insurance Co* [1999] 1 Lloyd's Rep. 263 at 272.

[100] See para.12–074.

**Several contract.** Where a contract is *several*, a defence available against one creditor cannot be raised against the others. In *Hagedorn v Bazett*[101] an insurance of cargo covered goods some of which belonged to British subjects, some to neutrals and some to an alien enemy. It was held that the policy amounted to a number of separate policies, one with each owner, and was not wholly vitiated by the fact that one of the owners was an alien enemy. "There was no common or joint interest in the whole of the property insured subsisting in the different individuals, nor was there any fraud".[102] The reason why fraud would have vitiated the whole insurance is that the fraud referred to was that of the common agent of all the parties, and thus imputable to them all. It does not follow that the fraud of one several creditor is a defence against others to whom it cannot be imputed. Had the policy been joint (as it might have been if a single item jointly owned by the promisees had been its subject-matter), the fact that one of the owners was an alien enemy would have made it wholly illegal since it seems that this kind of illegal promise cannot be severed.[103] **13–030**

**Joint bank accounts.** Where a joint bank account is opened in the names of two persons, the amount standing to the credit of the account is owed to them jointly, so that neither of them can enforce the debt against the bank without joining the other.[104] But a promise by the bank to honour only instructions given by both account holders is made separately to each of them, so that, if the bank allows one of them to draw on the account without the knowledge or authority of the other, the latter can sue alone and recover damage from the bank for breach of this promise.[105] **13–031**

## (e) Release by one

**Joint creditor.** A release granted by one *joint* creditor discharges the debt. Unless this were so, the one who granted the release might be able, after the death of his co-creditor, to recover the debt in spite of his own release, under the rule of survivorship.[106] But if the release is given by one creditor in fraud of another, the latter can have it set aside.[107] **13–032**

**Several creditor.** A release granted by one of a number of creditors entitled *severally* (whether at law or in equity) releases only the share of the grantor.[108] **13–033**

---

[101] (1813) 2 M. & S. 100; *State of the Netherlands v Youell and Hayward* [1997] 2 Lloyd's Rep. 440; affirmed on other grounds [1998] 1 Lloyd's Rep. 236.
[102] *Hagedorn v Bazett* (1813) 2 M. & S. 100 at 105.
[103] See para.11–163.
[104] *Brewer v Westminster Bank Ltd* [1952] 2 T.L.R. 568 (as to which, see next note).
[105] *Catlin v Cyprus Finance Corp (London) Ltd* [1983] Q.B. 759; not following *Brewer v Westminster Bank Ltd* [1952] 2 T.L.R. 568 on this point.
[106] *Wallace v Kelsall* (1840) 7 M. & W. 264 at 274.
[107] *Jones v Herbert* (1817) 7 Taunt. 421.
[108] *Steeds v Steeds* (1889) 22 Q.B.D. 537.

### (f) Payment to one

13–034 **Joint creditor.** The general rule is that payment to one of two *joint* creditors discharges the debt.[109] But this rule may be varied by the contract, and such variation may be implied from a course of dealing. Thus where persons have a joint account with a bank, and the usual course of dealing is to make payments only with the authority of them all, a payment made to one without the authority of the others does not discharge the bank.[110] Even where payment to one discharges the debt, it does not discharge any security which may have been given for the debt except to the extent of the payee's beneficial interest in the debt.[111]

13–035 **Several creditor.** Payment to one of a number of *several* creditors clearly does not discharge the whole debt since each is separately entitled to his share.

### (g) Consideration moving from one[112]

13–036 **Joint promise.** Where a promise is made to A and B *jointly*, it can be enforced by both of them, even though the whole consideration was provided by A.[113] If this were not so, the promise could not be enforced at all; for, if A tried to sue alone, he would be defeated by the rule that all the promisees must be parties to the action.[114] It follows from the doctrine of survivorship[115] that B would be entitled to the entire benefit of the promise after A's death.

13–037 **Several promise.** None of the above reasoning applies where a promise is made to A and B *severally*. Hence each promisee must provide consideration for the separate promise made to him.

13–038 **Joint and several promise.** It is, however, uncertain which of the above rules applies to the intermediate case of a promise made to two persons *jointly and severally*.[116] In *McEvoy v Belfast Banking Co*,[117] a father (A) deposited £10,000 in a bank; the deposit receipt stated that the money had been received from him and his son (B) and that it was payable "to either or the survivor". Lord Atkin said obiter that the contract was not by the bank with A for the benefit of B[118] but "with A and B, and I think with them jointly and severally. A purports to make a

---

[109] *Husband v Davis* (1851) 10 C.B. 645; *Powell v Broadhurst* [1901] 2 Ch. 160 at 164; *Barrett v Universal Island Records Ltd* [2006] EWHC 1009 (Ch); [2006] E.M.L.R. 21 at [214].

[110] *Husband v Davis* (1851) 10 C.B. 645 at 650.

[111] *Powell v Broadhurst* [1901] 2 Ch. 160 at 166.

[112] Cullity 85 L.Q.R. 530; Winterton 47 Can. Bar Rev. 483; Coote [1978] C.L.J. 301.

[113] This proposition seems to have been accepted in *Coulls v Bagot's Executor and Trustee Co Ltd* [1967] A.L.R. 385; although the majority of the court held that no joint promise had in fact been made; para.14–046, fn.260.

[114] See para.13–025.

[115] See para.13–027.

[116] For this type of promise, see para.13–003.

[117] [1935] A.C. 24.

[118] On this view, B would not be a "third party" for the purposes of the discussion in Ch.14.

contract on behalf of B as well as himself, and the consideration supports such a contract."[119] Of course after A's death (which in *McEvoy*'s case had occurred), B would be entitled to enforce any joint promise under the doctrine of survivorship.[120] But it is harder to see how he could sue on any several promise, for this is ex hypothesi an independent promise, and on the facts stated no consideration for it moved from B.[121] Indeed, the more probable view of such facts is that the bank makes no promise to B but only has authority to pay him. Hence it is discharged by a payment to B, but is not liable to him.[122] The bank would not, however, be discharged by such payment if it was *not* authorised by its contract with A to pay B. This possibility is illustrated by *Thavorn v Bank of Credit & Commerce SA*,[123] where A opened a bank account in the name of her nephew B (who was under age), stipulating that only A should operate the account. It was held that B was a mere nominee and that the bank was not discharged by (or was liable in damages for) paying B at the sole request of B and without any instructions from A. As no promise to (or in favour of) B had been made by the bank, it follows that B could not have sued the bank on its promise to A.

---

[119] *McEvoy v Belfast Banking Co* [1935] A.C. 24 at 43.
[120] cf. *Aroso v Coutts & Co* [2002] 1 All E.R. 241, where the contract expressly so provided.
[121] S.J.B. 51 L.Q.R. 419.
[122] See *Coulls v Bagot's Executor and Trustee Co Ltd* [1967] A.L.R. 385; fn.113.
[123] [1985] 1 Lloyd's Rep. 259. The Contracts (Rights of Third Parties) Act 1999 (para.14–099) would not apply to such a case since it was not the intention of the contracting parties that B should be entitled to enforce the contract: see s.1(2) of the Act.

---



(1939) 1 O.R. 140.

See *Coulls v Bagot's Executor and Trustee Co Ltd* (1967) 119 C.L.R. 460, 478.

## CHAPTER 14

# THIRD PARTIES

## 1. INTRODUCTION

**14–001** Our concern in this chapter is with the extent to which persons can either enforce, or be bound by, contracts to which they are not parties. At common law, the doctrine of privity states first, that a contract cannot confer rights and secondly that it cannot impose liabilities, on anyone except a party to it. The second of these propositions is generally regarded as just and sensible and for that reason has generated far less controversy. It is not affected by the reform immediately referred to below. The limited exceptions or modifications to this aspect of privity are dealt with primarily at the end of this chapter,[1] although the extent to which an exemption clause may bind a non-party is deal with separately.[2]

**14–002** **Contracts (Rights of Third Parties) Act 1999.** The bulk of this chapter is concerned with the first aspect of privity, i.e. that a contract cannot confer rights on a non-party. It has been subjected to much criticism,[3] which culminated in a Report, issued by the Law Commission in 1996.[4] The recommendations of this Report have been implemented by the Contracts (Rights of Third Parties) Act 1999.[5] It is important at the outset to make a point about the nature of the reforms made by the 1999 Act, since this determines the present structure of the subject. A crucial passage in the Report states that:

> "it is important to emphasise that, while our proposed reform will give some third parties the right to enforce contracts, there will remain many contracts where a third party stands to benefit and yet will not have a right of enforceability. Our proposed statute carves out a general and wide-ranging exception to the third party rule, but it leaves that rule intact for cases not covered by the statute".[6]

The rights conferred on third parties by the 1999 Act therefore have the character of a new statutory exception[7] to the common law doctrine of privity; and the Act

---

[1] See para.14–147 and following.
[2] See paras 14–079–14–084.
[3] See para.14–015.
[4] Law Com. No.242.
[5] The Act does not precisely follow the Report in all respects, but the only major departure from the recommendations made is s.8 of the Act, subjecting the third party's rights to arbitration agreements, contrary to the views expressed in the Report, paras 14.14–14.19.
[6] Law Com. No.242, para.5.16; and see para.13.2.
[7] *Heaton v Axa Equity & Law Life Assurance Plc* [2002] UKHL 15; [2002] 2 A.C. 329 at [9]; cf. *Alfred McAlpine Construction Ltd v Panatown Ltd* [2001] 1 A.C. 518 at 535 (Lord Clyde), and at 575

is therefore treated as such an exception in this chapter, though because of its importance a separate section is devoted to it.[8]

14–003 **The limits of the 1999 reform.** The new exception created by the 1999 Act is limited in two ways. First, a number of situations which have in the past been perceived as giving rise to problems resulting from the doctrine of privity are simply outside the scope of the exception and so are not affected by the provisions of the 1999 Act at all: this is, for example, true of cases in which third parties who have suffered loss in consequence of the breach of a contract between others have sought a remedy in tort against the party in breach.[9] Secondly, the exception created by the 1999 Act is, in turn, under that Act subject to exceptions[10] to which the third party's new statutory rights do not extend; and the effect of this is that in some[11] of these cases the common law doctrine of privity continues to apply. The Act also does not affect any rights which the third party has apart from its provisions:[12] thus it does not deprive the third party of rights which he has because the case falls either outside the *scope* of the common law doctrine[13] or within one of the *exceptions* to it recognised either at common law, or in equity or under other legislation.[14]

The scope of the doctrine and these other exceptions therefore continue to call for discussion, particularly because the content of rights available apart from the 1999 Act in some ways differs from that of the rights available under it.[15] The Act also does not affect any rights of the promisee to enforce any term of the contract:[16] such questions as whether the promisee can recover damages in respect of the third party's loss will therefore continue to be governed by the rules which have been (and no doubt will further be) developed as a matter of common law.[17] There is finally the point that the 1999 Act does not apply to contracts made before the end of the period of six months beginning on the day on which it was passed and came into force,[18] except where a contract made within that period expressly provides that the Act is to apply to it.[19] It is still therefore possible, though increasingly unlikely, for the courts to be concerned with contracts subject to the rules of law established before the Act came into force. These rules will also, in a significant number of the situations described above, continue to apply even to contracts made after that date. They therefore still

---

(Lord Browne-Wilkinson). It is respectfully submitted that Lord Goff is not quite right when he refers to the "abolition" by the Act of the doctrine of privity: *Alfred McAlpine Construction Ltd v Panatown Ltd* [2001] 1 A.C. 518 at 544.

[8] See para.14–099 and following.

[9] For further discussion of this point, see para.14–050 and following.

[10] See s.6 of the Act, discussed at para.14–127.

[11] e.g. 1999 Act s.6(2) and (3); under some of the other exceptions, the third party will be able to get rights by another legal route, e.g. under those stated in s.6(1) and (5): see para.14–127.

[12] 1999 Act s.7(1), below paras 14–129–14–130; Law Com. No.242, para.12.12.

[13] See paras 14–049–14–059.

[14] See paras 14–085–14–098, 14–136–14–146.

[15] e.g. ss.2 and 3 of the 1999 Act do not apply where the third party has rights apart from the Act; paras 14–129–14–130.

[16] 1999 Act s.4; para.14–134.

[17] See para.14–025 and following.

[18] On 11 November 1999, when the Act received Royal Assent: see s.10(2).

[19] See 1999 Act s.10(3).

require discussion, even though a considerable number of the cases on which they are based would, if their facts occurred now, be decided differently (where they had denied the third party the right to enforce the contract) or be decided on different grounds (where they had given the third party such a right). The result of all these points is that the 1999 Act may have improved, but it has scarcely simplified, the law on this topic.[20]

## 2. THE COMMON LAW DOCTRINE[21]

14–004 **General rule.** The common law doctrine of privity means that a contract cannot, as a general rule, confer rights or impose obligations arising under it on any person except the parties to it. Two questions arise from this statement: who are the parties to the agreement, and has the claimant provided consideration for the promise which he is seeking to enforce?

### (a) Parties to the agreement

14–005 Normally, the parties to the agreement are the persons from whose communications with each other the agreement has resulted. There may, indeed, be factual difficulties in identifying these persons;[22] but such difficulties do not generally raise any questions of legal principle. Problems as to the legal analysis of clearly established facts can, however, arise in situations in which there is clearly an agreement, while it is doubtful exactly who the parties to it are, or in which there are several contracts which affect the same subject-matter and involve more than two parties. The rights of all the parties to such contracts arise independently of the Contracts (Rights of Third Parties) Act 1999, and are not limited by its provisions.[23]

#### *(i) Collateral contracts*[24]

14–006 **Illustrations.** A contract between two persons may be accompanied by a "collateral" contract between one of them and a third person relating to the same subject-matter. In *Shanklin Pier v Detel Products Ltd*,[25] the claimants employed contractors to paint a pier and instructed them for this purpose to buy and use paint made by the defendants. The instruction was given in reliance on a representation made by the defendants to the claimants that the paint would last for seven years. In fact, it lasted for only three months. The main contract for the

---

[20] Stevens 120 L.Q.R. 292.

[21] Wilson 11 Sydney L. Rev. 300; Flannigan 105 L.Q.R. 564; Kincaid [1989] C.L.J. 454; Andrews 8 *Legal Studies* 14.

[22] e.g. *The Zinnia* [1984] 2 Lloyd's Rep. 211; *Uddin v Ahmed* [2001] EWCA Civ 240; [2001] 3 F.C.R. 300; *The Starsin* [2003] UKHL 12; [2004] 1 A.C. 715 at [175].

[23] Contracts (Rights of Third Parties) Act 1999 s.7(1).

[24] Wedderburn [1959] C.L.J. 58.

[25] [1951] 2 K.B. 854; followed in *Wells (Merstham) Ltd v Buckland Sand & Silica Co Ltd* [1965] 2 Q.B. 170; cf. *Moody v Condor Ins Ltd* [2006] EWHC 100 (Ch); [2006] 1 W.L.R. 1847 at [39]; also para.16–088.

sale of the paint was between the contractors and the defendants, but it was held that there was also a collateral contract between the claimants and the defendants that the paint would last for seven years.[26]

The same reasoning can apply where a person buys goods from a dealer and is given a guarantee issued by the manufacturer. The main contract of sale is between the dealer and the customer, but it seems that the guarantee is a collateral contract between the manufacturer and the customer.[27] Special legislation applies to certain guarantees given to consumers in respect of goods sold or supplied to them. Where the requirements specified in this legislation are satisfied, such guarantees are to take effect as contractual obligations[28] whether or not the requirements of a collateral contract[29] are satisfied; but these requirements continue to apply to manufacturers' guarantees not covered by this legislation, e.g. where the person to whom the guarantee is given is not a "consumer".[30] A collateral contract may also arise in the context of building work between a developer and a nominated sub-contractor;[31] in the use of a cheque card or credit card for the purchase of goods between the supplier and the issuer of the card;[32] and in the context of employment between an agency worker and the party for whom work is carried out.[33]

The collateral contract device has also been used in the context of hire-purchase agreements. The customer may think of himself as "buying on hire-purchase" from the dealer on whose premises he selects the goods. Actually, the transaction may involve a sale of the goods by the dealer to a finance company which then hires them out to the customer and grants him an option to purchase them. Thus, the main contract of hire-purchase is between the customer and the finance company. A representation by the dealer as to the quality of the goods used not to bind the finance company,[34] but it could be enforced against the dealer as a collateral contract.[35] If the transaction is a regulated agreement within

---

[26] cf. *Fuji Seal Europe Ltd v Catalytic Combustion Corp* [2005] EWHC 1659; 102 Con L.R. 47 (no collateral contract between a parent company and a customer of one of its subsidiaries (though the parent was found liable in negligence: see para.14–050); it was an "important feature" of the *Shanklin Pier* case that the claimants and the contractors were "at arms' length": at [157]).

[27] cf. para.3–017.

[28] Consumer Rights Act 2015 s.30.

[29] i.e. those of consideration and contractual intention (paras 14–007, 14–008).

[30] e.g. on facts such as those of the *Shanklin Pier* case.

[31] *Holland Hannen & Cubitts (Northern) v Welsh Health Technical Services Ltd* (1987) 7 Con L.R. 14; cf. *Greater Nottingham Co-operative Soc Ltd v Cementation Ltd* [1989] Q.B. 71; for the sub-contractor's possible liability in tort, see para.14–054.

[32] *Re Charge Card Services* [1987] Ch. 150; affirmed [1989] Ch. 497; cf. *Customs & Excise Commissioners v Diners Club Ltd* [1989] 1 W.L.R. 1196; *First Sport Ltd v Barclays Bank Plc* [1993] 1 W.L.R. 1229. For the several contracts involved in a "loyalty card" scheme, see *Revenue and Customs Commissioners v Aimia Coalition Loyalty UK Ltd* [2013] UKSC 15; [2013] 1 All E.R. 719.

[33] *Brook Street Bureau Ltd v Dacas* [2004] EWCA Civ 217; [2004] I.C.R. 1437; *Cable & Wireless Plc v Muscat* [2006] EWCA Civ 220; [2006] I.C.R. 975; *Smith v Carillion (JM) Ltd* [2015] EWCA Civ 209; [2015] I.R.L.R. 467.

[34] *Campbell Discount Co Ltd v Gall* [1961] 1 Q.B. 431; reversed on other points in *Branwhite v Worcester Works Finance Ltd* [1969] 1 A.C. 552; and *United Dominions Trust Ltd v Western* [1976] Q.B. 513.

[35] *Brown v Sheen & Richmond Car Sales* [1950] 1 All E.R. 1102; *Andrews v Hopkinson* [1957] 1 Q.B. 229; cf. *Astley Industrial Trust Ltd v Grimley* [1963] 1 W.L.R. 584; as to damages, see *Yeoman Credit Ltd v Odgers* [1962] 1 W.L.R. 215.

the Consumer Credit Act 1974,[36] a dealer who conducts antecedent negotiations is deemed to do so as agent of the finance company as well as in his actual capacity.[37] His representations can therefore make the finance company liable under the main contract, while he himself may still be liable under a collateral contract.[38]

14–007 **Consideration.** To be enforceable as a collateral contract, a promise must be supported by consideration,[39] and in the cases so far discussed this requirement was clearly satisfied. In the *Shanklin Pier* case the consideration was the instruction given by the claimants to their contractors to buy the defendants' paint;[40] in the guarantee case it is the purchase by the customer of the goods from the dealer;[41] in the building sub-contractor case, it is similarly the nomination of the sub-contractor by the client; in the cheque or credit card case it is the supply of goods by the supplier to the customer and the discount allowed by the supplier to the issuer of the card;[42] and in the hire-purchase case it is the entering by the customer into a hire-purchase agreement with the finance company. A case in which the problem of consideration gives rise to more difficulty is *Charnock v Liverpool Corp*,[43] where a car was damaged and repaired under a contract between the owner's insurance company and a garage. It was held that there was also a collateral contract by which the garage promised the owner to do the repairs reasonably quickly. Although the owner did not pay or promise to pay the garage anything,[44] he had provided consideration by "leaving his car with the garage for repair".[45] This might not be a detriment to the owner, at least in the factual sense,[46] but it benefited the garage in giving it the opportunity of making a contract for the repair of the car with the insurance company; and this benefit constituted the consideration for the garage's promise to the owner.[47]

14–008 **Contractual intention.** In the present context, as in others,[48] a promise will not amount to a collateral contract if it was made without contractual intention. For

[36] See para.5–007.
[37] 1974 Act s.56(2); cf. also s.75, under which the finance company is liable for any breach of contract by the supplier, but entitled to an indemnity from him in respect of such liability.
[38] This follows from s.56(2), above.
[39] cf. *Brikom Investments Ltd v Carr* [1979] Q.B. 467 (para.3–065), where no third party problem arose.
[40] *Shanklin Pier v Detel Products Ltd* [1951] 2 K.B. 854 at 856.
[41] cf. (in a different context) *Penn v Bristol & West BS* [1997] 1 W.L.R. 1356 at 1363 ("entering into some transaction with a third party").
[42] *Customs & Excise Commissioners v Diners Club Ltd* [1989] 1 W.L.R. 1196.
[43] [1968] 1 W.L.R. 1498.
[44] cf. *Godfrey Davis Ltd v Culling and Hecht* [1962] 2 Lloyd's Rep. 349; *Brown & Davies v Galbraith* [1972] 1 W.L.R. 997.
[45] *Charnock v Liverpool Corp* [1968] 1 W.L.R. 1498 at 1505.
[46] See para.3–006.
[47] cf. para.3–050. For similar reasoning, see *International Petroleum Refining & Supply Sociedad v Caleb Brett & Son Ltd* [1980] 1 Lloyd's Rep. 569 at 594.
[48] See paras 4–015, 5–010, 6–038, 9–063.

example, in *Independent Broadcasting Authority v EMI Electronics*[49] EMI had contracted to erect a television mast for the IBA, on the terms that the actual work was to be done by a sub-contractor, who was not a party to the main contract. The sub-contractor wrote to the IBA, saying: "We are well satisfied that the structure will not oscillate dangerously". The mast having later collapsed, it was held that this letter did not have contractual force for want of intention to contract[50] (though the sub-contractor was held liable in negligence).

### *(ii) Agency*

Where an agent negotiates a contract with a third party on behalf of his principal, that contract will generally be between the principal and the third party.[51] But it is sometimes doubtful whether a person acted as agent or on his own behalf.[52] Thus where a husband booked tickets on a cross-Channel ferry for himself, his wife and children, there was said to be a "contract of carriage between the [wife] and the [carriers]",[53] presumably made by the husband as agent of the wife. Where a husband and wife lunched together at a restaurant, it was again held that there was a contract between the wife and the proprietor, though on the different ground that husband and wife each made a separate contract with the proprietor.[54] But if there were no such separate contracts and the host on such an occasion did not act as agent, it has been said that there would be a contract only between him and the restaurant proprietor.[55] Similar problems arise where an agent employs a sub-agent. In some such cases there is a direct contract between principal and sub-agent; while in others the sub-agent is in a contractual relationship only with the agent who employed him.[56] In these cases it is again clear that there is a contract, but doubtful who the parties to it are.[57] 14–009

### *(iii) Multilateral contracts*

**Clubs or other unincorporated associations.** When a person joins a club or other unincorporated association he may be in direct communication only with the secretary and be unaware of the identity of the other members. But his 14–010

[49] (1980) 14 Build. L.R. 1; cf. *Alicia Hosiery Ltd v Brown Shipley Ltd* [1970] 1 Q.B. 195; *Lambert v Lewis* [1982] A.C. 225; *Law Debenture Trust Corp v Ural Caspian Oil Corp Ltd* [1993] 1 W.L.R. 138 at 142.

[50] cf. also *Hannam v Bradford CC* [1970] 1 W.L.R. 937; *Construction Industry Training Board v Labour Force Ltd* [1970] 3 All E.R. 220.

[51] See para.16–063 and following.

[52] See paras 16–005–16–010; *P Samuel & Co Ltd v Dumas* [1923] 1 K.B. 593; [1924] A.C. 431. Similar problems commonly arise in relation to "forwarding agents": see, e.g. *Elektronska, etc. v Transped, etc.* [1986] 1 Lloyd's Rep. 49.

[53] *The Dragon* [1979] 1 Lloyd's Rep. 257 at 262; affirmed [1980] 2 Lloyd's Rep. 415; cf. *Bowerman v Association of British Travel Agents* [1995] N.L.J. 1815 (holiday booked for pupil by teacher).

[54] *Lockett v AM Charles Ltd* [1938] 4 All E.R. 170.

[55] *Jackson v Horizon Holidays Ltd* [1975] 1 W.L.R. 1468 at 1473 (where *Lockett v AM Charles Ltd* [1938] 4 All E.R. 170 was not cited).

[56] See para.16–114; contrast *Robbins v Fennell* (1847) 11 Q.B. 248 with *Collins v Brook* (1860) 5 H. & N. 700; cf. also *The Antama* [1982] 2 Lloyd's Rep. 112.

[57] *Henderson v Merrett Syndicates Ltd* [1995] 2 A.C. 145 at 202D–202G; *Grosvenor Casinos Ltd v National Bank of Abu Dhabi* [2008] EWHC 511 (Comm); [2008] 1 Lloyd's Rep. at [147]–[149].

contract of membership is likely to be with them,[58] and not with the secretary.[59] It has similarly been held that an insurance policy, which was expressed to be between the assured and a syndicate of underwriters at Lloyd's, nevertheless constituted a number of separate contracts between the assured and each member of the syndicate.[60]

14–011 **Competitions.** Problems of this kind can also arise where a number of persons agree to enter into a competition subject to rules laid down by the organising club. In *The Satanita*[61] it was held that the competitors in a regatta had contracted not only with the committee of the club but also with each other. But in *Ellesmere v Wallace*[62] it was held that persons who entered horses for races organised by the Jockey Club had contracted with the club, and not with each other.

### *(iv) Corporations*

14–012 **Companies.** Under the Companies Act 2006, the provisions of a company's constitution[63] bind the company and its members to the same extent as if there were covenants on the part of the company and of each member to observe those provisions.[64] This has been said to amount to a "statutory contract"[65] between each member and the company;[66] and also to one between the members inter se.[67] But they only have the latter effect between the members in their capacity as members;[68] a director is not liable or entitled under them in his capacity as director simply because he happens also to be a member.[69]

14–013 **Limited liability partnerships.** In the case of a limited liability partnership (which is a body corporate),[70] the mutual rights and liabilities of the members

---

[58] *Lee v Showmen's Guild* [1952] 2 Q.B. 329 at 341.

[59] *Gray v Pearson* (1870) L.R. 5 C.P. 568; *Evans v Hooper* (1875) 1 Q.B.D. 45; *Nutting v Baldwin* [1995] 1 W.L.R. 201. But where a club was *owned by a company* of which the club's members were shareholders, the rules of the club were held to constitute contracts between each member and the company, and not between the members inter se: *Peskin v Anderson* [2000] 2 B.C.L.C. 1.

[60] *Touche Ross & Co v Colin Bank* [1992] 2 Lloyd's Rep. 207 at 209–210.

[61] [1895] P. 248; affirmed sub nom. *Clarke v Dunraven* [1897] A.C. 59, where only Lord Herschell dealt with the point here discussed; cf. *White v Blackmore* [1972] 2 Q.B. 651 (where there was no contractual intention).

[62] [1929] 2 Ch. 1.

[63] As defined by the 2006 Act s.17.

[64] Companies Act 2006 s.33(1).

[65] *Soden v British Commonwealth Holdings* [1998] A.C. 298 at 323.

[66] *Hickman v Kent or Romney Marsh Sheepbreeders Association* [1915] 1 Ch. 881; cf. *Cumbrian Newspapers Group v Cumberland and Westmorland Herald Ltd* [1987] Ch. 1.

[67] *Rayfield v Hands* [1960] Ch. 1; *JH Rayner (Mincing Lane) Ltd v DTI* [1989] Ch. 72 at 190 (approved on this point [1990] 2 A.C. 418 at 515); cf. *Russell v Northern Bank Development Corp Ltd* [1992] B.C.L.C. 1016. But there is no contract between members on the one hand and third parties on the other: *Eley v Positive, etc., Assurance Co* (1876) 1 Ex. D. 88.

[68] For limitations on the scope of this contract, see *Soden v British and Commonwealth Holdings* [1998] A.C. 298. They are not affected by Contracts (Rights of Third Parties) Act 1999: see s.6(2), para.14–128.

[69] *Beattie v E & F Beattie Ltd* [1938] Ch. 708; *Rayfield v Hands* [1960] Ch. 1 is difficult to reconcile with this principle: L.C.B.G. 21 M.L.R. 401.

[70] See para.12–073.

inter se and between the members and the partnership are governed by agreement between the members or between them and the partnership;[71] or, in the absence of such agreement, by regulations made under the Act governing such partnerships.[72]

### (b) Party to the consideration

**Two distinct rules.** The common law rule that only a party to the agreement can enforce it will often lead to the same result as the rule that consideration must move from the promise;[73] but the two rules appear to be distinct. They require the claimant to show: (1) that the promise was made to him; *and* (2) that the consideration for it moved from him. The statement that consideration must move *from the promisee* simply assumes that the first requirement has been satisfied. If the rule were stated to be that consideration must move *from the party seeking to enforce the promise* it would clearly be distinct from the common law rule that only a party to the agreement can sue. A father might, for example, promise his daughter to pay £1,000 to anyone who married her. A man who married the daughter with knowledge of and in reliance on such a promise might provide consideration for it, but could not enforce it, as it was not addressed to him.[74] **14–014**

### (c) Reasons for the doctrine

There are two aspects of the common law doctrine of privity: no one except a party to a contract can acquire rights under it; and no one except a party can be subjected to liabilities under it. The reason for the second aspect of the doctrine is obvious: a person should not, as a general rule, have contractual obligations imposed on him without his consent. The first aspect of the doctrine is harder to explain; indeed, Steyn LJ has gone so far as to say that there is "no doctrinal, logical or policy reason"[75] for it. The rule that a third party cannot acquire rights under a contract can scarcely be justified by saying that a contract is, or gives rise, to a personal relationship, affecting only the parties to it; for this is rather a restatement of the rule than a reason for its existence. Nor is it satisfactory to say that it would be unjust to allow a person to sue on a contract on which he could not be sued;[76] for the law enforces unilateral contracts, to which the same argument applies.[77] A further possible reason is that, if third parties could enforce contracts made for their benefit, the rights of contracting parties to rescind or vary such contracts would be unduly hampered: this reasoning has certainly been influential in limiting the development of one of the judge-made exceptions to the **14–015**

[71] Limited Liability Partnership Act 2000 s.5(1)(a).

[72] Limited Liability Partnership Act 2000 s.5(1)(c).

[73] See *Price v Easton* (1833) B. & Ad. 433; *Tweddle v Atkinson* (1861) B. & S. 393.

[74] cf. *Uddin v Ahmed* [2001] EWCA Civ 204; [2001] 3 F.C.R. 300 at [20]. Support for the view that the two rules are distinct may be provided by the decision of the Privy Council in *Kepong Prospecting Ltd v Schmidt* [1968] A.C. 810.

[75] *Darlington BC v Wiltshier Northern Ltd* [1995] 1 W.L.R. 68 at 76.

[76] *Tweddle v Atkinson* (1861) 1 B. & S. 393 at 398.

[77] See paras 2–052–2–058, 3–160.

doctrine,[78] and also is reflected in the reform introduced by the 1999 Act.[79] Yet another possible reason is that the third party is often a mere donee. A system of law which does not give a right to enforce a gratuitous promise to the promisee may well be reluctant to give such a right to a gratuitous beneficiary who is not even a promisee. None of these reasons for the common law doctrine takes account of the inconvenience that can result from its practical operation. This factor accounts for the many exceptions to the doctrine which will be discussed later in this chapter.[80]

## (d) Development

14–016 **Early development.** In the early authorities, there was considerable conflict on the question whether a person could enforce a contract to which he was not a party.[81] A negative answer to this question was given in 1861 in *Tweddle v Atkinson*,[82] where A promised B to pay a marriage portion to B's son C on C's marriage to A's daughter. It was held that C could not enforce this promise against A. This case was generally considered to have established the common law doctrine,[83] which was approved by the House of Lords in 1915, when the principle that "only a person who is a party to the contract can sue on it" was said to be a "fundamental"[84] one in English law. This view was judicially doubted in a number of cases,[85] but in 1961 the House of Lords once again affirmed the existence of the doctrine,[86] and this view of the law has been accepted in many later cases.[87]

---

[78] See para.14–092.

[79] In s.2: para.14–113.

[80] See para.14–099 and following; see also paras 14–085–14–098.

[81] In *Crow v Rogers* (1724) 1 Str. 592; *Bourne v Mason* (1669) 1 Ventr. 6; and *Price v Easton* (1833) 4 B. & Ad. 433 the third party's claim failed; but it was upheld in *Thomas v* —— (1655) Sty. 461; *Dutton v Poole* (1678) 2 Lev. 210; affirmed T. Raym. 302; and approved in *Martyn v Hind* (1776) Cowp. 437 at 443; *Green v Horn* (1693) Comb. 219 (reversed (1694) 1 Salk. 197 on the ground that the third party must at least be mentioned in the deed); and *Marchington v Vernon* (1786) 1 B. & P. 101n.(c); E.J.P. 70 L.Q.R. 467; Scammel 8 C.L.P. 134–135; Palmer 33 Am. Jl. of Legal History 3; Ibbetson in Barton (ed.), *Towards a General Law of Contract* (1990), pp.67, 96–99; Palmer, *The Paths to Privity: the History of Third Party Beneficiaries in English Law* (2015); Andrews 69 Tulane L. Rev. 69.

[82] (1861) 1 B. & S. 393.

[83] *Gandy v Gandy* (1884) 30 Ch D. 57 at 69.

[84] *Dunlop Pneumatic Tyre Co Ltd v Selfridge & Co Ltd* [1915] A.C. 847 at 853; for a similar, earlier, statement, see *Keighley Maxsted & Co v Durant* [1901] A.C. 240 at 246.

[85] In *Smith and Snipes Hall Farm Ltd v River Douglas Catchment Board* [1949] 2 K.B. 500 at 519; *Pyrene Co Ltd v Scindia Steam Navigation Co Ltd* [1954] 2 Q.B. 402 at 426; *Rayfield v Hands* [1960] Ch. 1; cf. Andrews 8 Legal Studies 14; Flannigan 105 L.Q.R. 564.

[86] *Scruttons Ltd v Midland Silicones Ltd* [1962] A.C. 446; para.14–066; see also *Green v Russell* [1959] 2 Q.B. 226.

[87] *Rookes v Barnard* [1964] A.C. 1129 (para.14–060); *Hepburn v A Tomlinson (Hauliers) Ltd* [1966] A.C. 451; *The Eurymedon* [1975] A.C. 154 at 166; *The New York Star* [1981] 1 W.L.R. 138; *Woodar Investments & Development Ltd v Wimpey Construction UK Ltd* [1980] 1 W.L.R. 277; *Rhone v Stephens* [1994] 2 A.C. 310 at 321; *The Pioneer Container* [1994] 2 A.C. 324 at 335; *White v Jones* [1995] 2 A.C. 207 at 252, 266; *The Mahkutai* [1996] A.C. 650 at 658; *The Starsin* [2003] UKHL 12; [2003] 1 A.C. 715.

**Beswick v Beswick.** The leading modern case is *Beswick v Beswick*.[88] A coal merchant transferred his business to his nephew who made various promises in return. One of these was that he would, after the uncle's death, pay £5 per week to the uncle's widow. The uncle died and the widow became his administratrix. She brought an action to enforce the nephew's promise, suing both in her own right and as administratrix. The House of Lords held that the widow could enforce the nephew's promise in her capacity as administratrix of the promisee and that she was entitled to an order of specific performance against the nephew, obliging him to make the payments to her for her personal benefit. In the Court of Appeal Lord Denning MR had said that the widow could also sue in her own right at common law,[89] because the doctrine of privity was "at bottom … only a rule of procedure"[90] and could be overcome by simply joining the promisee as a party to the action. The House of Lords found it unnecessary to express a concluded view on this point. But the speeches all assume the correctness of the generally accepted view that a contract can at common law be enforced only by the parties to it;[91] though the House of Lords has on a number of occasions indicated its willingness to reconsider this position.[92] **14–017**

**Reform.** The difficulties of reaching satisfactory results in this area through purely judicial reconsideration are formidable:[93] they arise, particularly, in defining exactly what classes of third parties can acquire rights under the contract, and in determining how those rights are to be affected by attempts by the contracting parties to rescind the contract or to vary it, and by defences available between the contracting parties.[94] A satisfactory solution of such difficulties is more likely to be achieved by legislative reform,[95] such as that contained in the Contracts (Rights of Third Parties) Act 1999.[96] In a significant number of situations, however, third parties will not acquire rights by virtue of **14–018**

---

[88] [1965] 2 All E.R. 858; [1966] Ch. 538; [1968] A.C. 58; Goodhart 83 L.Q.R. 465; Fairest [1967] C.L.J. 149; Treitel 29 M.L.R. 657; 30 M.L.R. 687.

[89] For the effect of Law of Property Act 1925 s.56, see below, para.14–144.

[90] *Beswick v Beswick* [1966] Ch. 538 at 557.

[91] *Beswick v Beswick* [1968] A.C. 58 at 72, 81, 83, 92–93, 95.

[92] *Beswick v Beswick* [1968] A.C. 58 at 72; *Woodar Investment Development Ltd v Wimpey Construction UK Ltd* [1980] 1 W.L.R. 277 at 291, 297–298, 300; *Swain v Law Society* [1983] 1 A.C. 598 at 611; cf. *Trident Ins Co Ltd v McNiece Bros Pty Ltd* (1988) 165 C.L.R. 107; Edgell [1989] L.M.C.L.Q. 139.

[93] Kincaid 2 J.C.L. 160. For a different judicial approach in Canada, proceeding by means of the creation of an exception to the doctrine in the context of exemption clauses, see *London Drugs Ltd v Kuehne & Nagel International Ltd* [1992] 3 S.C.R. 299 (para.14–066); Waddams 109 L.Q.R. 349; Adams and Brownsword 56 M.L.R. 722. See also: *Fraser River Pile and Dredge Ltd v Can-Drive Services Ltd* [2000] 1 Lloyds Rep. 199 (Supreme Court of Canada).

[94] See the elaborate discussion of these problems in American law (which in principle recognises the rights of third-party beneficiaries) in *Corbin on Contracts* Chs 41–44. The effect of rescission or variation by the contracting parties gives rise to particular difficulties: cf. para.14–092.

[95] See Treitel 29 M.L.R. 657 at 665; Reynolds 105 L.Q.R. 1 at 3; contrast *Darlington BC v Wiltshier Northern Ltd* [1995] 1 W.L.R. 68 at 76, favouring judicial reform.

[96] See para.14–099 and following.

this Act;[97] and in many such situations the common law doctrine of privity will continue (at least for the time being)[98] to apply.

### (e) Promisee's remedies

14–019 Although at common law a third party cannot generally assert rights under a contract made for his benefit, the contract remains nevertheless binding between promisor and promisee. The fact that the contract was made for the benefit of a third party does, however, give rise to special problems so far as the promisee's remedies against the promisor are concerned. Actual performance of the contract may also lead to disputes between promisee and third party.

#### (i) *Specific performance*

14–020 The promisee may seek specific performance. If, as in *Beswick v Beswick*,[99] this remedy is granted, the third party will in fact receive the benefit contracted for. But the scope of the remedy of specific performance is limited in various ways; these limitations, and their applicability to cases involving third parties, are discussed in detail in Ch.21.[100]

#### (ii) *Injunction*

14–021 Where the promise is negative in nature, the promisee's most obvious remedy is an injunction to restrain the promisor's breach. This remedy would, for example, be available where A validly promised B not to compete with C.

14–022 **Promise not to sue third party.** One type of negative promise which gives rise to special difficulty is a promise by A to B *not to sue* C, e.g. for a debt owed by C to A. If, in breach of such a promise, A nevertheless did sue C, it would not be appropriate for B to start a second action for an injunction to restrain A from proceeding with the first action; for such a step would lead to undesirable multiplicity of legal proceedings.[101] B's remedy is to ask the court to exercise its discretion[102] to stay A's action against C. In *Gore v Van der Lann*[103] the Court of Appeal held that B could obtain a stay of A's action against C only if two conditions were satisfied: there must be a definite promise by A to B not to sue C, and B must have a sufficient interest[104] in the enforcement of A's promise. This last requirement would not be satisfied unless, as a result of A's breach, B were

---

[97] See paras 14–106, 14–126–14–128.

[98] The passing of the 1999 Act has probably reduced the pressure for judicial reform.

[99] [1968] A.C. 58; para.14–017.

[100] See paras 21–056–21–058.

[101] Senior Courts Act 1981 s.49(2).

[102] Senior Courts Act 1981 s.49(3).

[103] [1967] 2 Q.B. 31; Davies 1 *Legal Studies* 287; *European Asian Bank AG v Punjab and Sind Bank* [1982] 2 Lloyd's Rep. 356; *The Chevalier Roze* [1983] 2 Lloyd's Rep. 438; and see para.14–077.

[104] *The Elbe Maru* [1978] 1 Lloyd's Rep. 206 at 209–210l; *Deepak Fertilisers & Petrochemical Corp v ICI Chemicals & Polymers Ltd* [1999] 1 Lloyd's Rep. 378 at 401; *The Marielle Bolten* [2009] EWHC 2552 (Comm); [2010] 1 Lloyd's Rep. 648.

exposed to the risk of incurring legal liability to C, e.g. where B had *contracted with* C to procure his release from a debt or a liability to A, and would be put in breach of that contract by A's action against C.

*Snelling v John G Snelling Ltd*[105] goes even further in giving effect to a promise of this kind. Three brothers had lent money to a family company of which they were directors. They agreed that if one of them resigned he should "forfeit" any money due to him from the company. One of them did resign and sued the company for the amounts due to him. By way of defence the company relied on the agreement between the brothers, and, if matters had rested there, the defence would have failed as the company was not a party to the agreement.[106] But the other two brothers applied to be joined as defendants to the action, adopted the company's defence and counterclaimed for a declaration that the third brother's loan was forfeited. It was held that they were entitled to such a declaration by virtue of the contract between them and that brother.[107] Ormrod J further held that they could obtain a stay of the action against the company and that the most convenient way of disposing of the action against the company was to dismiss it. So far as the granting of the stay is concerned, the judgment is hard to reconcile with the requirement of a sufficient interest as defined in *Gore v Van der Lann*;[108] but it is submitted that Ormrod J's decision is consistent with the spirit of *Beswick v Beswick*.[109] If *the promisee* takes steps specifically to enforce the contract the court should, wherever possible, grant such remedy as is most appropriate for that purpose. Normally this will be an order of specific performance or an injunction. The fact that the latter remedy is not appropriate to enforce a promise not to sue should not deter the court from granting other remedies that serve substantially to enforce the promise. Such a remedy is, again, available only if it is sought *by the promisee*.[110] If the two brothers in the *Snelling* case had not applied to be joined to the action, the company could not have relied on the agreement between them and the third brother by way of defence.[111]

### *(iii) Restitution*

The promisee may claim restitution of the consideration provided by him. But part performance by the promisor[112] might defeat this remedy,[113] and it might also be unjust to restrict the promisee to such a claim, e.g. return of premiums could be a quite inadequate remedy where a policy of life insurance had been taken out for the benefit of a third party and had matured. 14–023

---

[105] [1973] Q.B. 87; Wilkie 36 M.L.R. 214.

[106] *Snelling v John G Snelling Ltd* [1973] Q.B. 87 at 95.

[107] *Snelling v John G Snelling Ltd* [1973] Q.B. 87 at 96.

[108] [1967] 2 Q.B. 31.

[109] [1968] A.C. 58; para.14–017.

[110] cf. *Heaton v Axa Equity and Law Life Assurance Society Plc* [2002] UKHL 15; [2002] 2 A.C. 329 at [9] ("is enforceable by B", i.e. the promisee. No such promise had been made: see para.13–018).

[111] *Snelling v John G Snelling Ltd* [1973] Q.B. 87 at 95.

[112] As in *Beswick v Beswick* [1968] A.C. 58.

[113] As there would be no "total failure of consideration"; and as termination for breach could probably not be allowed unless the third party was willing to restore any performance received: para.22–012. For the suggestion that *the third party* may have a claim in restitution, see para.14–061.

### (iv) *Action for the agreed sum*

14–024 The promisee may claim payment to himself of an agreed sum. It can be objected that to allow such a claim would force the promisor to do something which he never contracted to do, viz. to pay the promisee when he contracted to pay the third party; and one view is therefore that the promisee cannot sue for the agreed sum,[114] save in the exceptional circumstances to be described later in this chapter.[115] But the objection to allowing the promisee to claim payment to himself loses most of its force where the promisor would not in fact be prejudiced by having to pay the promisee rather than the third party (so long as such payment gave him a good discharge). In such a case, the contract may, on its true construction, be one to pay the third party or as the promisee shall direct,[116] so that it would not be inconsistent with its terms to allow the promisee to claim payment for himself. The promisee is a fortiori so entitled where the contract is one to pay him (the promisee) as nominee for the third party:[117] such a contract is not one for the benefit of a third party[118] in the sense of one purporting to give that party a right against the promisor.

### (v) *Damages*

14–025 **Damages in respect of promisee's loss.** The promisee may claim damages where he has suffered loss as a result of the promisor's failure to perform in favour of the third party.[119] But in *Beswick v Beswick* the majority of the House of Lords evidently thought that no such loss had been or would be suffered and that the damages recoverable by the estate for breach of the nephew's promise would be merely nominal.[120] Lord Upjohn explained that this would be the case because the promisee "died *without any assets* save and except the agreement which he hoped would keep him and then his widow for their lives".[121] It seems from this that damages might have been substantial if the promisee had had other assets—either because the widow might then have had a claim against those assets if the promise was not performed,[122] or because the promisee or his estate would in fact, even if not legally obliged to do so, have made some other, wholly voluntary, provision for the widow. The loss suffered by the promisee would be the cost of making an alternative provision, and there is some authority to support the view that damages for breach of contract may be recovered to compensate for

---

[114] See *Coulls v Bagot's Executor and Trustee Co Ltd* [1967] A.L.R. 385 at 409–411; cf. *Beswick v Beswick* [1968] A.C. at 88, 101 (dealing with the remedy of damages).

[115] See *Cleaver v Mutual Reserve Fund Life Association* [1892] 1 Q.B. 147; cf. para.14–093.

[116] *The Spiros C* [2000] 2 Lloyd's Rep. 319 at 331; para.14–046.

[117] *Turiddu* [1999] 2 Lloyd's Rep. 401 at 407.

[118] *Turiddu* [1999] 2 Lloyd's Rep. 401 at 407.

[119] *De Jongh Weill v Mean Fiddler Holdings* [2005] All E.R. (D.) 331.

[120] Lord Pearce thought that damages would be substantial: [1968] A.C. 58 at 88.

[121] *Beswick v Beswick* [1968] A.C. 58 at 102 (emphasis added).

[122] e.g. under Inheritance (Family Provision) Act 1938, now Inheritance (Provision for Family and Dependants) Act 1975.

such loss even though the provision is wholly voluntary.[123] A fortiori the promisee can recover substantial damages where he is under a legal obligation to make a payment to the third party and where this obligation would have been discharged if the promisor had paid in accordance with the contract. Where loss *is* in fact suffered by the promisee, substantial damages can be recovered even though the promisee is under a legal duty to pay those damages to a third party.[124]

**Damages in respect of third party's loss: general rule.** The starting point of the following discussion is the general principle that, in an action for damages, a claimant cannot recover more than the amount required to compensate him for *his* loss,[125] so that he cannot, in general, recover damages for breach of a contract made for the benefit of a third party in respect of loss suffered, not by the promisee, but by that third party.[126] This general principle was doubted by Lord Denning MR in *Jackson v Horizon Holidays Ltd*,[127] where the defendants contracted with the claimant to provide holiday accommodation for the claimant, his wife and their two three-year-old children.[128] The accommodation fell far short of the promised standard, and the claimant recovered damages, including £500 for "mental distress".[129] Lord Denning MR said that this sum would have been excessive compensation for the claimant's own distress.[130] He nevertheless upheld the award on the ground that the claimant had made a contract for the benefit both of himself and of his wife and children[131]; and that he could recover damages in respect of their loss as well as in respect of his own. But the authorities cited in support of this conclusion seem to contradict rather than to favour it. Moreover, in *Beswick v Beswick* the majority of the House of Lords said that the promisee's estate could have recovered no more than nominal damages as it had suffered no loss.[132] This is scarcely consistent with the view that the promisee under a contract for the benefit of a third party is, as a general rule, entitled to damages in respect of the third party's loss. James LJ in *Jackson*'s case seems to have regarded the £500 as compensation for the claimant's own distress.[133] No doubt this was increased by his witnessing the distress suffered by his wife and children, and if the promisee himself suffers loss he should not be 14–026

[123] *Admiralty Commissioners v SS Amerika* [1917] A.C. 38 at 61 (the actual decision was that payments voluntarily made to the victim of an alleged *tort* could not be recovered: on this point see also *Esso Petroleum Co Ltd v Hall Russell & Co Ltd* [1989] A.C. 643). See further para.14–030.

[124] *Chappell v Somers & Blake* [2003] EWHC 1644; [2004] Ch. 19; discussed at para.14–057.

[125] See para.20–004; cf. *White v Jones* [1995] 2 A.C. 207; para.14–057, where the damages recoverable by the estate of the other party to the contract would have been no more than nominal.

[126] *The Albazero* [1977] A.C. 774 at 846; *Linden Gardens Trust Ltd v Lenesta Sludge Disposals Ltd* [1994] 1 A.C. 85 at 114; *Alfred McAlpine Construction Co Ltd v Panatown Ltd* [2001] 1 A.C. 518; at fnn.168 and 169.

[127] [1975] 1 W.L.R. 1468; Yates 39 M.L.R. 202.

[128] It was assumed that the wife and children were not parties to the contract.

[129] *Jackson v Horizon Holidays Ltd* [1975] 1 W.L.R. 1468 at 1472.

[130] *Jackson v Horizon Holidays Ltd* [1975] 1 W.L.R. 1468 at 1474.

[131] *Jackson v Horizon Holidays Ltd* [1975] 1 W.L.R. 1468 at 1474; cf. *McCall v Abelesz* [1976] Q.B. 585 at 594.

[132] See para.14–025.

[133] *Jackson v Horizon Holidays Ltd* [1975] 1 W.L.R. 1468 at 1474.

prevented from recovering it in full merely because the contract was made partly for the benefit of third parties[134] who also suffered loss.

In *Woodar Investment Development Ltd v Wimpey Construction Co Ltd*[135] the House of Lords disapproved Lord Denning's approach to the question of damages in *Jackson*'s case, though the actual decision in the latter case was supported on the ground that the damages were awarded in respect of the claimant's own loss;[136] or alternatively on the ground that cases such as the booking of family holidays or ordering meals in restaurants[137] might "call for special treatment".[138] In the *Woodar* case itself a contract for the sale of land provided that, on completion, the purchaser should pay £850,000 to the vendor and also £150,000 to a third party. The vendor claimed damages on the footing that the purchaser had wrongfully repudiated the contract and the actual decision was that there had been no such repudiation,[139] so that the issue of damages did not arise. But the question of what damages would have been recoverable in the *Woodar* case itself if there had been a wrongful repudiation was there described as "one of great doubt and difficulty":[140] presumably it would turn on such factors as whether the vendor was under a legal obligation to ensure that the third party received the payment, or whether, on the purchaser's failure to make the payment, the vendor had himself made it, or procured it to be made, from other resources available to him.

14–027 **The problem of the "legal black hole".** The assumption underlying the *Woodar* case thus seems to be that, where a contract for the benefit of a third party has been broken, the promisee cannot generally recover damages in respect of a loss suffered only by the third party. But this position was there described as "most unsatisfactory"[141] and said to be in need of reconsideration, either by the legislature or by the House of Lords itself.[142] It is unsatisfactory because it can give rise to what has been called a "legal black hole";[143] that is, to a situation in which the promisor has committed a plain breach which has caused loss to the

---

[134] cf. *Radford v De Froberville* [1977] 1 W.L.R. 1262 (damages for failure to build a wall not reduced merely because claimant had entered into the contract, not only for his own benefit alone, but also for that of his tenants).

[135] [1980] 1 W.L.R. 277.

[136] *Woodar Investment Development Ltd v Wimpey Construction Co Ltd* [1980] 1 W.L.R. 277 at 283, 293, 297. Where a contract is made with a company and the breach causes loss to its subsidiary, damages may be recovered by the company since the value of its holding in the subsidiary will be reduced in consequence of the loss: *George Fischer (Great Britain) Ltd v Multi Construction Ltd* [1995] 1 B.C.L.C. 260.

[137] cf. *Lockett v AM Charles Ltd* [1938] 4 All E.R. 170, where agency reasoning was used in such a situation.

[138] *Woodar Investment Development Ltd v Wimpey Construction Co Ltd* [1980] 1 W.L.R. 277 at 283; cf. *Calabar Properties Ltd v Stitcher* [1984] 1 W.L.R. 287 at 290.

[139] See para.18–039.

[140] *Woodar Investment Development Ltd v Wimpey Construction Co Ltd* [1980] 1 W.L.R. 277 at 284. See also fn.244.

[141] *Woodar Investment Development Ltd v Wimpey Construction Co Ltd* [1980] 1 W.L.R. 277 at 291; cf. at 297–298, 300–301.

[142] cf. *Beswick v Beswick* [1968] A.C. 58 at 72.

[143] *Darlington BC v Wiltshier (Northern) Ltd* [1995] 1 W.L.R. 68 at 79; for the origins of this metaphor, see *Alfred McAlpine Construction Ltd v Panatown Ltd* [2001] A.C. 518 at 529.

third party whom the contracting parties intended to benefit but none to the promisee, and in which no other remedy[144] (than damages for the third party's loss) is available against the promisor.

**Damages in respect of third party's loss: exceptions.** Judicial awareness of the unsatisfactory results which can flow from the general rule that a promisee can recover damages only for his own loss has led to the creation of exceptions to that rule. For example, substantial damages for breach of contract can be recovered by a trustee even though the loss is suffered by the beneficiary of the trust;[145] by an agent even though the loss is suffered by his undisclosed principal;[146] by a local authority even though the loss is suffered (ultimately) by its inhabitants;[147] and by the shipper of goods for breach of the contract of carriage with the shipowner even though the loss is suffered by a person to whom he has sold the goods, and to whom the risk and property in them had passed, but who has not himself acquired any rights to sue the shipowner under the contract of carriage.[148] It will be convenient, for later reference, to refer to the last example just given as "the *Albazero* exception", after the leading modern case in which it is recognised.[149] In all these exceptional cases a person recovers substantial damages for breach of contract even though the breach caused loss, not to him, but to a third party. **14–028**

**The Linden Gardens case.** The list of exceptions just stated should not be regarded as closed and the possibility of extending them or of creating further exceptions is illustrated by a line of cases beginning with *Linden Gardens Trust v Lenesta Sludge Disposals Ltd*.[150] In that case, a building contract between parties described in it as employer and contractor provided for work to be done by the contractor by way of developing a site owned by the employer as shops, offices and flats. The site (but not the benefit of the contract) was later transferred by the employer to a third party, and it was assumed, for the purpose of the proceedings on a preliminary issue of law, that the third party had suffered financial loss as a result of having to remedy breaches of the building contract committed after the transfer. In an action for breach of the building contract brought by the employer, the contractor argued that no loss had been suffered by the employer as he was no longer owner of the land when the alleged breaches occurred, and that the **14–029**

---

144 e.g. by way of specific performance, as in *Beswick v Beswick* [1968] A.C. 58.

145 *Rolls Royce Power Engineering Plc v Ricardo Consulting Engineers Ltd* [2003] EWHC 2871 (TCC); [2004] 2 All E.R. (Comm) 129 at [116]; *Shell UK Ltd v Total UK Ltd* [2010] EWCA Civ 180; [2010] 3 W.L.R. 1192 at [144].

146 See, e.g. para.16–081.

147 cf. *St Albans' CC v International Computers Ltd* [1996] 4 All E.R. 481.

148 *Dunlop v Lambert* (1839) 2 Cl. & F. 626 at 627 (as to which see *Alfred McAlpine Construction Ltd v Panatown Ltd* [2001] 1 A.C. 518 at 523 and following); *The Sanix Ace* [1987] 1 Lloyd's Rep. 465; *The Chanda* [1989] 2 Lloyd's Rep. 494.

149 *The Albazero* [1977] A.C. 774, in which the rule in *Dunlop v Lambert* was recognised, but held inapplicable as the buyer had acquired his own contractual rights against the shipowner under s.1 of the Bills of Lading Act 1855 (now repealed and replaced by Carriage of Goods by Sea Act 1992); Weir [1977] C.L.J. 24. In the case of contracts to which the Carriage of Goods by Sea Act 1992 applies, a special statutory exception is created by s.2(4) of the Act to the general rule that a person can recover damages only in respect of his own loss.

150 [1994] 1 A.C. 85; Duncan Wallace 110 L.Q.R. 42.

employer was therefore entitled to no more than nominal damages. In the House of Lords, this argument was rejected, and the employer's claim upheld, on two distinct grounds.

14–030 **The "broader ground": promisee's loss.** Lord Griffiths upheld the employer's claim on what has become known as the "broader ground"[151] that the employer "ha[d] suffered financial loss because he ha[d] to spend money to give him the benefit of the bargain which the defendant had promised but failed to deliver".[152] He added that "the court will of course wish to be satisfied that the repairs have been or are likely to be carried out".[153] This approach is, it is submitted, consistent with the explanation given in *Beswick v Beswick*[154] of the fact that the damages there were regarded as no more than nominal: the court there could not be satisfied that the substitute provision for the widow was likely to be made, precisely because the promisee lacked the means to make it.[155] The essence of Lord Griffiths' reasoning is that the promisee recovers damages in respect of the loss which he himself has suffered in ensuring that the third party receives the intended benefit.

14–031 **The "narrower" ground: recovery of third party loss.** Although Lord Keith had "much sympathy"[156] with, and Lord Bridge was "much attracted by",[157] Lord Griffiths' reasoning, they (as well as Lord Ackner) preferred to base their decision on the narrower ground stated by Lord Browne-Wilkinson. This treats the loss as having been suffered by the third party rather than by the employer, but concludes that the employer could nevertheless recover substantial damages as the case fell within the rationale of the *Albazero* exception, referred to above.[158] The rationale of this exception is that, in the carriage of goods cases to which it applies, the shipper and carrier must have contemplated that property in the goods might be transferred to third parties after the contract had been made, and that the shipper must therefore be treated in law as having made the contract of carriage for the benefit of all persons who might after the time of contracting acquire interests in the goods.[159] This rationale applied equally to the facts of the *Linden Gardens* case since the contractor could foresee that parts of the new development were going to be "occupied and possibly purchased by third parties" so that "it could be foreseen that damage caused by a breach would cause loss to later owners".[160] The contractor could also foresee that a later owner would not have acquired rights under the building contract against the contractor since that contract expressly prohibited assignment by the employer without the contractor's written

[151] *Linden Gardens Trust Ltd v Lenesta Sludge Disposals Ltd* [1994] 1 A.C. 85 at 96–97 (Lord Griffiths); cf. *Alfred McAlpine Construction Ltd v Panatown Ltd* [2001] 1 A.C. 518, e.g. at 532.

[152] *Linden Gardens Trust Ltd v Lenesta Sludge Disposals Ltd* [1994] 1 A.C. 85 at 97.

[153] *Linden Gardens Trust Ltd v Lenesta Sludge Disposals Ltd* [1994] 1 A.C. 85 at 97.

[154] [1968] A.C. 58.

[155] *Beswick v Beswick* [1968] A.C. 58 at 102; para.14–025.

[156] *Linden Gardens Trust Ltd v Lenesta Sludge Disposals Ltd* [1994] 1 A.C. 85 at 95.

[157] *Linden Gardens Trust Ltd v Lenesta Sludge Disposals Ltd* [1994] 1 A.C. 85 at 96.

[158] See at fn.148.

[159] *The Albazero* [1977] A.C. 744 at 847; *HSBC Rail (UK) Ltd v Network Rail Infrastructure Ltd* [2005] EWCA Civ 1437; [2006] 1 W.L.R. 643 at [23].

[160] *Linden Gardens Trust Ltd v Lenesta Sludge Disposals Ltd* [1994] 1 A.C. 85 at 114.

consent, which had not been sought. The effect of the *Linden Gardens* case was thus to extend the *Albazero* exception to other contracts,[161] but it was consistent with two factors which had restricted the scope of that exception: namely that: (a) the loss or damage was caused to property which had been transferred by one of the contracting parties to the third party; and (b) the third party had not acquired any rights under the contract[162] and it was foreseeable (by reason of the prohibition against assignment) that he would not do so. The significance of these factors is further considered in the later cases discussed below.

**No transfer of the subject-matter to third party.** In *Darlington BC v Wiltshier Northern Ltd*[163] a local authority (the council) wished to develop land which it already owned. The building work was to be done by the defendant. The necessary finance was to be provided by a bank but this could not be done in the most obvious way, by a loan to the council from the bank, since such an arrangement would have violated government restrictions on local authority borrowing. The transaction was therefore cast in the form of two contracts: (1) a building contract in which the bank was the employer and the defendant the building contractor; and (2) a contract between the council and the bank, by which the bank undertook to procure the erection of the buildings on the site, to pay all sums due under the building contract and to assign to the council the benefit of any rights against the defendant to which the bank might be entitled at the time of the assignment. Clause 4(5) of this second contract provided that the bank was not to be liable to the council "for any incompleteness or defect in the building work"; and it was this provision which was the principal source of the difficulties in the case. The bank duly assigned its rights against the defendant to the council which claimed damages as such assignee from the defendant in respect of defects in the work. **14–032**

Since an assignee cannot recover more than the assignor could have done,[164] this raised the question of what the bank could have recovered. It was argued that it could have recovered no more than nominal damages since it had suffered no loss, having no interest in the land (or buildings) on which the work had been done and being protected by cl.4(5) from any liability to the council for defects in the work. But the Court of Appeal rejected this argument and held that the bank could have recovered substantial damages from the defendant in respect of the council's loss and that it was this right which had been assigned to the council.

---

[161] cf. *JP Morgan Chase Bank v Springwell Navigation Corp* [2005] EWHC 1044 (Comm) at [45] in which the exception is described simply as "*a contract* rule"; *Smithkline Beecham Plc v Apotex Europe Ltd* [2006] EWCA Civ 658; [2007] Ch. 71; *DRC Distribution Ltd v Ulva* [2007] EWHC 1716 (QB) at [68]–[75]; *Mirant Asia-Pacific (Hong Kong) Ltd v Ove Arup and Partners International Ltd* [2007] EWHC 918 (TCC); [2007] C.I.L.L. 2840 (fn.186); *Starlight Shipping Co v Allianz Marine and Aviation Versicherungs AG* [2014] EWHC 3068 (Comm); [2014] 2 Lloyd's Rep. 579 at [93]. The underlying concern "to see that justice is done between the parties" has also been reflected in the assessment of damages after assignment: *Offer-Hoar v Larkstore Ltd* [2006] EWCA Civ 1079; [2006] 1 W.L.R. 2926, para.15–045.

[162] cf. fn.148.

[163] [1995] 1 W.L.R. 68.

[164] See para.15–045, especially the discussion of *Offer-Hoar v Larkstore Ltd* [2006] EWCA Civ 1079; [2006] 1 W.L.R. 2926.

This amounted to an extension[165] of the *Linden Gardens* case to a situation in which there was no transfer of the property affected by the breach from the promisee to the third party. This extension was later approved by the House of Lords,[166] so that, at least in the context of defective performance of building contracts, such a transfer is no longer a necessary condition of the promisee's right to recover damages in respect of the third party's loss.

14–033 **Third party with independent contractual right against promisor.** In *Alfred McAlpine Construction Ltd v Panatown Ltd*[167] the facts resembled those of the *Darlington* case in that a building contract was again made, not between the building contractor and the company which owned the site (the owner), but between that contractor and another company (the employer) associated with the owners. The object of adopting this tripartite structure was to avoid VAT. On the same day on which this building contract was made, a separate contract (the "Duty of Care Deed") was made between the owner and the contractor. The obligations imposed on the contractor by this deed were not precisely co-terminous with those imposed on him by the building contract; and the deed did not, while the contract did, contain an arbitration clause. The employer alleged that the building work was seriously defective and in arbitration proceedings claimed damages from the contractor, who argued that the employer should recover no more than nominal damages since any loss resulting from the alleged defects in the work had been suffered, not by the employer (as the employer had never owned the property), but by the owner. The House of Lords, by a majority, upheld the contractor's argument and so rejected the employer's claim for substantial damages in respect of the owner's loss. It was accepted by the majority[168] and by one of the dissentients[169] that, as a general rule, a contracting party could not recover damages in respect of loss suffered, not by himself, but by a third party; and the question therefore arose whether the case could be brought within an exception to that general rule. This raised, in turn, the question whether either of the grounds for the decision in the *Linden Gardens* case[170] supported the employer's claim.

14–034 **The "narrower ground" in McAlpine v Panatown.** It will be recalled that the "narrower" ground for the decision in the *Linden Gardens* case was derived from the "*Albazero* exception" under which a shipper of goods can sometimes recover

---

[165] *Darlington BC v Wiltshier Northern Ltd* [1995] 1 W.L.R. 68 at 79 (Steyn LJ). Dillon LJ regarded the result in the *Darlington* case as a "direct application" of the *Linden Gardens* case: [1995] 1 W.L.R. 68 at 75. These two views may be reconciled if the facts are approached *as if* the property had first been owned by the bank and then transferred to the council. See also *John Harris Partnership v Groveworld Ltd* [1999] P.N.L.R. 697.

[166] *Alfred McAlpine Construction Ltd v Panatown Ltd* [2001] A.C. 518 at 531, 566 (Lords Clyde and Jauncey); at 545, 584 (Lords Goff and Millett (dissenting)).

[167] *Alfred McAlpine Construction Ltd v Panatown Ltd* [2001] 1 A.C. 518; Coote 117 L.Q.R. 81, McKendrick (2003) O.U.C.L.J. 145 (reversing (1998) 58 Con L.R. 58; Treitel 114 L.Q.R. 572).

[168] *Alfred McAlpine Construction Ltd v Panatown Ltd* [2001] 1 A.C. 518 at 522, 563, 575.

[169] Lord Millett: [2001] 1 A.C. 518 at 580–581; Lord Goff is more sceptical: at 538–539.

[170] *Linden Gardens Trust v Lenesta Sludge Disposals Ltd* [1994] 1 A.C. 85; para.14–029; referred to as the *St Martin* case throughout the speeches in the *Panatown* case.

damages in respect of a third party's loss.[171] That exception is, however, subject to the restriction that it does not apply where the third party had himself acquired contractual rights against the carrier, usually by transfer to the third party of a bill of lading.[172] In the *Panatown* case, the majority held (and the dissentients accepted) that the case fell within this restriction, so that the *Albazero* exception did not apply because the Duty of Care Deed gave the owner an independent contractual right against the contractor. This point was, moreover, decisive even though that right did not arise under a *building* contract, so that, in this respect the restriction was somewhat expanded: in the carriage by sea cases, the restriction normally[173] came into operation because the third party had acquired rights under a contract of *carriage*. Nevertheless it is respectfully submitted that this aspect of the *Panatown* case is consistent with the rationale of the restriction. In the carriage by sea cases, this could and did apply even though the *content* of the third party's contractual right against the carrier was not the same as that of the shipper's right;[174] and it was based on the reasoning that, where the third party had his own contractual rights against the carrier, the exception did not apply "because it was not needed".[175] It was not needed because, where the third party had his own contractual rights against the party in breach there was no risk of the "legal black hole" which had driven judges to create exceptions to the general rule that a contracting party can recover damages only in respect of his own loss.[176]

**The "broader ground" in McAlpine v Panatown.** The majority in the *Panatown* case further held that the existence of the third party's rights against the contractor under the Duty of Care Deed also precluded the employer from recovering damages under the "broader ground" given by Lord Griffiths in the *Linden Gardens* case. In view of the existence of those rights, the employer had no pecuniary interest in curing the defects in the contractor's work.[177] Hence he neither had suffered nor would suffer any loss of his own, in consequence of the contractor's breach,[178] and under the "broader ground" it is in respect of his *own* (not of the third party's) loss that the promisee recovers damages. This conclusion can, on the facts of the *Panatown* case, be supported for two further reasons. First, the creation or extension of exceptions to the general rule that a party can recover damages only in respect of his own loss is and should be driven and 14–035

[171] *The Albazero* [1977] A.C. 774; para.14–028.

[172] See fn.148.

[173] The restriction could also apply where the third party's contractual rights against the carrier were under an implied contract of the kind illustrated by *Brandt v Liverpool, etc. SN Co* [1924] 1 K.B. 575; see *The Albazero* [1977] A.C. 774 at 847.

[174] As in *The Albazero* [1977] A.C. 774.

[175] *Alfred McAlpine Construction Ltd v Panatown Ltd* [2001] 1 A.C. 518 at 575; *The Albazero* [1977] A.C. 774 at 847–848; cf. *Catlin Estates Ltd v Carter Jonas* [2005] EWHC 2315; [2006] P.N.L.R. 15 at [304] (*Albazero* exception not excluded unless the third party has a claim which can be brought "on the same conditions"; in that case, a potential claim under Defective Premises Act 1972 (not established) would not have prevented the application of the exception).

[176] *Darlington BC v Wiltshier Northern Ltd* [1995] 1 W.L.R. 68 at 79.

[177] *Alfred McAlpine Construction Ltd v Panatown Ltd* [2001] 1 A.C. 518 at 574 and 577 (Lords Jauncey and Browne-Wilkinson).

[178] cf. para.20–008.

limited by necessity:[179] that is, by the need to guard against the risk of "legal black holes" of the kind described above; and in the *Panatown* case there was no such risk.[180] Secondly, the decision gives effect to the "contractual scheme"[181] created by the parties; and this point, so far from being undermined by the fact that the contractor's obligations to the owner under the Duty of Care Deed were not precisely co-terminous with his obligations to the employer under the building contract, is reinforced by this fact. As the parties had taken the "plain and deliberate course"[182] of giving the owner a "distinct entitlement"[183] against the contractor in respect of defects in the work, and as this entitlement was to be governed by the terms of one contract (the Duty of Care Deed), it followed that there was no good practical reason for holding the contractor liable in respect of the same defects on the terms of another contract (the building contract) for substantial damages to the employer, to whom these defects had caused no loss of his own. The fact that the "general rule" has been the subject of frequent judicial disapproval no doubt gives rise to the temptation to continue the process of eroding it by creating new or extending existing exceptions to it. But that criticism has occurred mainly in cases in which the third party problem was an inescapable consequence of normal commercial factors such as those which existed in the *Linden Gardens* case. The pressure for eroding the general rule is much less strong where the third party problem is, so to speak, manufactured by the parties for an ulterior motive, such as government restrictions on borrowing, as in the *Darlington* case, or avoiding tax,[184] as in the *Panatown* case. In the view of the majority any such pressure was eliminated for the further reason that the third party had his own contractual remedy against the party in breach under a separate contract between these parties.

14–036 **Status of the "broader ground", or "performance interest".** The *Panatown* case is significant not only for the points it decides, but also for some of those which it leaves open. The first such point relates to the effect of the case on the status of Lord Griffiths' "broader ground" in the *Linden Gardens* case. This ground forms the basis of the two dissenting speeches[185] in the *Panatown* case, in which it is referred to as the "performance interest". It is not the subject of any adverse comment from the majority,[186] whose speeches do not rule out the possibility of its being applied in the, perhaps more common, situation in which the third party has *no* contractual rights of his own against the promisor in respect of loss suffered by him in consequence of the defective services rendered under the contract between promisor and promisee. It seems that, even in such a situation, the majority would deny the employer's right to recover substantial

---

[179] See the references given in fn.175.

[180] *Alfred McAlpine Construction Ltd v Panatown Ltd* [2001] 1 A.C. 518 at 574 (Lord Jauncey); cf. *Smithkline Beecham Plc v Apotex Europe Ltd* [2006] EWCA Civ 658; [2007] Ch. 71 at [94].

[181] *Alfred McAlpine Construction Ltd v Panatown Ltd* [2001] 1 A.C. 518 at 577 (Lord Browne-Wilkinson); and see 76 Con L.R. 224 at [38] ("made their contractual bed").

[182] *Alfred McAlpine Construction Ltd v Panatown Ltd* [2001] 1 A.C. 518 at 536 (Lord Clyde).

[183] *Alfred McAlpine Construction Ltd v Panatown Ltd* [2001] 1 A.C. 518 at 536 (Lord Clyde).

[184] For the contrary view, see Lord Goff, dissenting: [2001] 1 A.C. 518 at 556–557.

[185] Of Lords Goff and Millett.

[186] Lords Clyde, Jauncey and Browne-Wilkinson.

damages under the "performance interest" unless *either* the condition stated by Lord Griffiths is satisfied, i.e. "the repairs have been or are likely to be carried out",[187] or the employer has entered into a separate contract with the owner undertaking liability in respect of defects in the contractor's work.[188] Where neither of these requirements is satisfied, the result of allowing the promisee to recover the cost of repairs as damages for his own loss would be "unattractive" in that it would enable him to "put the money in his own pocket"[189] without carrying out or paying for repairs: the technique of requiring him to hold the damages for the third party applies, on the authorities,[190] only where damages are recovered (under one of the exceptions to the general rule) in respect of the third party's loss, not in respect of the promisee's own loss. It follows that the requirements stated above[191] do not apply where the promisee's claim can succeed on the "narrower ground": in this respect, that ground is, paradoxically, broader than the "broader ground", or "performance interest".

**Scope of the broader ground, or "performance interest".** If the "performance interest" is accepted for cases in which the third party has no contractual rights of his own against the promisor, then a further problem arises as to its scope. It need not be confined to building contracts, but it clearly does not apply merely because a third party has been adversely affected by a breach of contract.[192] The example given by Lord Griffiths in support of this ground is one in which loss is caused by reason of the *defective* performance of a contract to render *services*.[193] The case put by him[194] is that of a husband who contracts with a builder to have his wife's house repaired; if the builder does the work defectively the husband is (so long as the other requirements of the "broader ground" are satisfied) entitled (in the example) to substantial damages, i.e. to the cost of putting the defects right. Two questions then arise. The first is whether the rationale of the "broader ground" applies to cases in which the breach consists of a simple *failure* or *refusal* to perform. And the second is whether it applies where the obligation which is not performed is one to do something other than to render services. 14–037

The two questions come together in a case where, for a consideration provided or to be provided by B, a promise is made by A to B to pay a sum of money to C and A fails or refuses, wholly or in part to perform that promise. Those were, in substance, the facts of *Beswick v Beswick*[195] where the majority of the House of Lords took the view that the damages recoverable by the estate would be no more than nominal. That may not, indeed, amount to a direct rejection of the "broader

[187] *Linden Gardens Trust v Lenesta Sludge Disposals Ltd* [1994] 1 A.C. 85 at 97; see further at fn.230.

[188] No such separate contract was established in the *Panatown* case: see 76 Con L.R. 224 at [35].

[189] *Alfred McAlpine Construction Ltd v Panatown Ltd* [2001] 1 A.C. 518 at 571.

[190] See para.14–046.

[191] See at fnn.187 and 188.

[192] *Smithkline Beecham Plc v Apotex Europe Ltd* [2006] EWCA Civ 658; [2007] Ch. 71 at [95].

[193] Lord Millett's dissent is restricted to this situation: [2001] 1 A.C. 518 at 591; Lord Goff's dissent does not appear to be so restricted: [2001] 1 A.C. 518 at 545, 552–553; cf. *Rolls Royce Power Engineering Plc v Ricardo Consulting Engineers Ltd* [2003] EWHC 2871 (TCC); [2004] 2 All E.R. (Comm) 129 at [128].

[194] *Linden Gardens Trust v Lenesta Sludge Disposals Ltd* [1994] 1 A.C. 85 at 97.

[195] [1968] A.C. 58; para.14–017.

ground" in such cases. The reason given in *Beswick v Beswick* for the view that the promisee's damages would there have been merely nominal was that the estate had no assets out of which it could make the payments to C which A had promised, but failed, to make.[196] But it is not clear whether in substance that reasoning is inconsistent with the "broader ground"; for, if the cost to B of securing the benefit intended for C is to be defrayed *out of the damages*, then it should not matter that B cannot provide that benefit out of his *other* assets, at least so long as B is solvent. The views expressed in *Beswick v Beswick* on the question of damages recoverable by the estate should, it is submitted, now be read subject to the developments of the law as to damages in respect of a third party's loss in the later cases.

14–038 **The need to avoid the "legal black hole".** The most directly relevant of the later cases is the *Woodar* case[197] where it appears to be assumed that, as a general rule,[198] B cannot recover substantial damages from A for A's failure to perform his promise to B to pay a sum of money to C. This conclusion seems to be based on the assumptions that the loss is C's and that B cannot generally recover damages in respect of C's loss. It does not seem to preclude the possibility of B's recovering damages in respect of any loss which he himself might have suffered in consequence of A's breach, e.g. because B was under a contractual obligation to procure the payment to C or because B, acting reasonably, has made alternative provision for C.[199] Even in the absence of such factors, it is submitted that, in the light of the developments since the *Woodar* case,[200] the law should take account of the possibility that, unless A were held liable for substantial damages to B, then he might be under no substantial liability at all: in other words, that there would be a "legal black hole". In *Beswick v Beswick* and the *Panatown* case there were no such "black holes": in the former case, because of the availability of a satisfactory remedy for B against A by way of specific performance in favour of C;[201] in the latter because of the availability of a satisfactory remedy for C against A in damages under the separate contract between these parties.[202] If there is no such remedy and if the conditions in which B can (under the "broader ground") recover damages in respect of his *own* loss are not satisfied,[203] then the lack of any such remedy should, it is submitted, be a ground for allowing B to claim damages in respect of C's loss. The need to avoid the "black hole" should generate this remedy;[204] and, where B has suffered no loss himself, the result of

[196] *Beswick v Beswick* [1968] A.C. 58 at 102; para.14–025.

[197] *Woodar Investment Development Ltd v Wimpey Construction UK Ltd* [1980] 1 W.L.R. 277; para.14–026.

[198] i.e. unless B can show that A's breach caused loss *to* B *himself*.

[199] See para.14–027.

[200] i.e. in *Linden Gardens Trust v Lenesta Sludge Disposals Ltd* [1994] A.C. 85; *Darlington BC v Wiltshier Northern Ltd* [1995] 1 W.L.R. 68; and *Alfred McAlpine Construction Ltd v Panatown Ltd* [2001] 1 A.C. 518.

[201] See para.14–017.

[202] See para.14–034.

[203] See after fn.230.

[204] That the need to avoid the "black hole" should determine the scope of the narrower ground, and its relationship with the broader ground, is supported by the decision of the Court of Appeal in *Offer-Hoar v Larkstore Ltd* [2006] EWCA Civ 1079; [2006] 1 W.L.R. 2926 in the context of

allowing him to recover damages in respect of C's loss (rather than in respect of B's own loss) would also have the advantage of ensuring that these damages were to be held for C,[205] thus avoiding the "unattractive" result of allowing B to "put the money in his own pocket".[206]

**Is the narrower ground confined to the transfer of property?** One obstacle in the way of the suggestion just made is the perception that the narrower ground is confined to cases where the third party suffers loss as the intended transferee of property affected by the breach. This was said to rule it out in *Swynson Ltd v Lowick Rose LLP*, where B sought to recover damages on behalf of C for A's defective accounting report produced in fulfilment of A's contract with B.[207] It also seems to be the reason why it did not apply in *BV Nederlandse Industrie Van Eiproduktien v Rembrandt Enterprises Inc*[208] where A refused to accept and pay for goods under a contract with B, in circumstances where half the goods were to be supplied by (and therefore half the price and any resulting profit was due to) C.[209] In both cases, the broader ground also failed for a further reason which would also have ruled out the narrower ground, namely that the contract between A and B was not intended to benefit C. 14–039

**The contract must have been intended to benefit the third party.** In the *Swynson* case C was the owner of a corporate lender (B). B faced a loss on a loan which it had entered into on the basis of a defective accounting report provided by A. For a combination of commercial and fiscal reasons, C advanced a sum to the borrower which allowed it to repay the loan to B. B nevertheless still claimed recovery from A, either on the basis that repayment of the loan was a "collateral benefit" which should be left out of account,[210] or on the basis that B was entitled to recover under the broader ground. Lord Sumption stated that there was "much to be said" for the broader ground as a solution to the black hole problem, but it was not necessary to decide whether it applied in *Swynson* because it was no part of the contract between the accountants (A) and the lender (B) to benefit B's owner (C).[211] Lord Neuberger agreed, but also confined the broader ground to 14–040

assignment, which is discussed at para.15–045. According to Rix LJ (at [83]): "where a real loss has been caused by a real breach of contract, then there should if at all possible be a real remedy which directs recovery from the defendant towards the party which has suffered the loss."; cf. *Starlight Shipping Co v Allianz Marine and Aviation Versicherungs AG* [2014] EWHC 3068 (Comm); [2014] 2 Lloyd's Rep. 579 at [93].

205 See para.14–048.

206 *Alfred McAlpine Construction Ltd v Panatown Ltd* [2001] 1 A.C. 518 at 571.

207 *Swynson Ltd v Lowick Rose LLP* [2017] UKSC 32; [2018] A.C. 313 at [17] (Lord Sumption: "Since [C] did not suffer his loss in his capacity as the owner of property, only the broader principle of transferred loss could be relevant to his case", though he did refer earlier (at [15]) to the *Linden Gardens* case having extended the rationale of the *Albazero* exception "to contracts generally").

208 [2019] EWCA Civ 596; [2019] 3 W.L.R. 1113.

209 Given the reliance placed on the decision in the *Swynson* case, this is assumed to be the reason for counsel's concession that "the narrow ground simply did not apply on the facts": [2019] EWCA Civ 596; [2019] 3 W.L.R. 1113 at [69].

210 This argument failed: see para.20–111.

211 *Swynson Ltd v Lowick Rose LLP* [2017] UKSC 32; [2018] A.C. 313 at [17]. Lords Neuberger, Clarke and Hodge agreed with Lord Sumption, but Lord Neuberger also gave a short speech of his own with which Lord Clarke agreed and which is referred to in the text. Lord Mance thought that this

injury done to an asset or property which comes into the hands of C because in that way B and C suffer the same loss; in *Swynson*, C suffered a loss on the new loan he made to the borrower while B suffered a loss under the original loan.[212]

In the *Rembrandt Enterprises* case, B agreed to sell a large quantity of egg-based product to A and, after the contract had been entered into, arranged for half of the product to be supplied by C, another company in the same corporate group. A refused to accept the product and pay for it, but as C had no cause of action against A, B sought recovery of the entire loss of profit.[213] Coulson LJ saw "some force" in the argument that the broader ground does not apply to contracts for the sale of goods, but it is respectfully submitted that he was right to caution that it is "difficult to justify treating different types of contracts in a different way".[214] He held that it was unnecessary to decide the issue because the broader ground can only apply where "there was a common intention and/or a known object to benefit the third party or a class of persons to which the third party belonged".[215] That requirement was not met where A was unaware, at the time of the contract with B, of any arrangement between B and C. The care is perhaps an unusual one. The arrangement between B and C was, in one sense, a sub-contract for the supply of some of the product. On that basis, A's non-performance may have exposed B to a potential liability to C which B might have recovered from A, subject to remoteness.[216] But B had not pleaded its case on this basis and a late amendment to allow it to do so, based on a "settlement agreement" entered into by B and C, was rejected.[217] It having been rejected, this does appear to be a case where half the damages otherwise payable by A do indeed disappear into a black hole. Coulson LJ questioned whether that was the case, but then answered his own question in the following terms:

> " … it appears to have been agreed that [C] could look to [B] to recover its losses, which is what one would expect. This is not therefore a situation in which the party who has suffered the loss has no means of redress against anyone. On the other hand, I can see that, since [B] could not have recovered from [A] any sums paid out to [C], that could be said to establish the necessary black hole for these purposes."[218]

In such circumstances, it may be questioned whether it is necessary that A is aware that B intends to use a third party for some or all of the supply. This is not necessarily to fall into the trap of allowing recovery merely because a third party

---

was only relevant to, and ruled out, the narrower ground, but the broader ground did not assist B because it had no "performance interest" other than being indemnified in respect of the loss on the loan which had been satisfied by its repayment: [2017] UKSC 32; [2018] A.C. 313 at [54].

212 *Swynson Ltd v Lowick Rose LLP* [2017] UKSC 32; [2018] A.C. 313 at [107].

213 A claim for additional profit based on a re-negotiated price was dismissed on the basis that it was induced by a fraudulent misrepresentation: see para.9–030.

214 *BV Nederlandse Industrie Van Eiproduktien v Rembrandt Enterprises Inc* [2019] EWCA Civ 596; [2019] 3 W.L.R. 1113 at [78].

215 *BV Nederlandse Industrie Van Eiproduktien v Rembrandt Enterprises Inc* [2019] EWCA Civ 596; [2019] 3 W.L.R. 1113 at [73].

216 See para.20–119.

217 Since under the settlement agreement B was only obliged to account to C for so much of C's loss *as B recovered* that may just have begged the question of what B was entitled to recover.

218 *BV Nederlandse Industrie Van Eiproduktien v Rembrandt Enterprises Inc* [2019] EWCA Civ 596; [2019] 3 W.L.R. 1113 at [79].

has been adversely affected by a breach of contract,[219] since A must have been aware that *someone* would supply the product and expect to be paid for it[220] and A had consented to the supply by C when informed of the arrangement.[221]

**Non-performance.** Notwithstanding the decision in *Rembrandt Enterprises* (which was a case of failure to perform), it is submitted that the approach advocated in para.14–038 is also appropriate to the case where the contract between A and B is one for services for the benefit of C which A simply fails or refuses to perform, instead of performing them defectively, as in Lord Griffiths' example,[222] in which it seems to be assumed that B has paid for the work. Lord Griffiths does not discuss the case of total non-performance by A, presumably assuming that in such a case A would not have been paid.[223] If B then gets another builder to do the work and that other builder charges more than A would have done, B will (subject to questions of mitigation[224] and remoteness) be able to recover the difference as damages for his *own* loss. The position will be substantially the same where B has paid A in advance and A has done no part of the work: in that case B will be entitled to claim restitution of his payment[225] together with damages for his own loss in respect of any extra cost of employing a substitute builder.[226] So in none of these cases of total non-performance is there any "black hole" and hence no need to generate a new remedy at the suit of B in respect of C's loss. The most difficult case is that of an advance payment by B followed by *part* performance by A in circumstances in which B himself has suffered no loss, e.g. because B was under no obligation to C to secure completion of the performance that A was to render and has neither himself taken any steps to secure that completion nor is likely to do so.[227] In such a case of partial performance there might be considerable difficulty in holding A liable for partial restitution;[228] and if, in addition, the remedy of specific performance were not available (e.g. because the contract was one for personal services to be 14–041

[219] *Smithkline Beecham Plc v Apotex Europe Ltd* [2006] EWCA Civ 658; [2007] Ch. 71 at [95].

[220] The issue referred to by Lord Neuberger in the *Swynson* case (above, fn.212) may be encountered in that the loss incurred by C may be different to the loss incurred by B: C's loss depends on the price charged to B; B's loss depends on the price charged to A. The curious feature of the *Rembrandt Enterprise* case is that A accepted some product direct from C, prior to its breach, and invoiced C directly (it is assumed at the price agreed with B, though the report does not make this clear): [2019] EWCA Civ 596; [2019] 3 W.L.R. 1113 at [54]. Quaere why this was not a case of vicarious performance by C of B's obligation: see para.17–007.

[221] See fn.220; cf. *Glory Wealth Shipping Pte Ltd v Flame* [2016] EWHC 293 (Comm); [2016] 1 Lloyd's Rep. 571 where B arranged for the freight payable under a contract of affreightment with A to go through C, who was also to meet the expenses of fulfilling the contract. This was done to protect B's assets from being attached. B was still entitled to recover the loss of profit when A defaulted on the basis that it was entirely a matter for B what it chose to do with the freight to which it was entitled, including any disposal of it prior to receipt.

[222] See at fn.195.

[223] Performance of the work is in contracts of this kind prima facie a condition precedent of the right to be paid: para.17–015.

[224] e.g. damages on a "cost of cure" basis are not recoverable if the cost of cure is wholly disproportionate to the benefit to be derived from cure: para.20–044.

[225] There will be a "total failure of consideration": para.22–003.

[226] See para.20–039.

[227] As in *Beswick v Beswick* [1968] A.C. 58; para.14–017.

[228] The "failure of consideration" would be only "partial": see para.22–007.

rendered by A)[229] then there would be at least a partial "black hole" and this fact should (it is again submitted) be a ground for allowing B to recover substantial damages from A in respect of C's loss.

14–042 **Broader ground: use to which damages are put.** It will be recalled that, in his statement of the "broader ground" in the *Linden Gardens* case, Lord Griffiths said that the court would wish to be "satisfied that the repairs have been or are likely to be carried out".[230] In later cases, conflicting views have been expressed on the question whether this is an essential requirement for the operation of the "broader ground".

One view is that it is not, since (at least as a general rule)[231] a court in awarding damages is not concerned with the question of what the claimant intends to do with these damages[232]; that question is said to be relevant only to the issue of "reasonableness". This issue, however, arises, not for the purpose of determining the *existence* of a claim for substantial damages, but its *extent*: it may be relevant in determining whether damages in a two-party case are to be assessed on a difference in value or on a cost of cure basis,[233] or whether the claimant has failed to mitigate his loss;[234] but such questions arise only on the assumption that a claim for substantial damages does exist. A related argument in favour of the view that the claimant's intention with regard to the disposal of the damages is irrelevant is that he has been deprived by the defendant's breach of the benefit of his bargain, and this fact is, of itself, enough to support a claim for substantial damages.[235] This line of reasoning is, however, with respect, hard to reconcile with the principle that the victim of a breach has no claim to substantial damages if the breach has no adverse effect.[236] The assumption underlying this principle is that the mere failure to perform a contract does not suffice to sustain a claim for substantial damages: as Lord Clyde said in the *Panatown* case, "A breach of contract may cause a loss but is not in itself a loss in any meaningful sense".[237] In the cases here under consideration, the breach will have no adverse effect *on the claimant* (the promisee)[238] unless he has carried out or intends to carry out cure; and the argument that he has been deprived of his bargain cannot answer the question whether it must be shown that this deprivation has had an adverse effect *on him*: it merely pushes this question back one stage.

229 See paras 21–039—21–043.

230 *Linden Gardens Trust Ltd v Lenesta Sludge Disposal Ltd* [1994] 1 A.C. 85 at 97.

231 For a possible exception, see the discussion at para.20–046 of the question whether cost of cure is recoverable where cure is not undertaken.

232 See *Darlington BC v Wiltshier Northern Ltd* [1995] 1 W.L.R. 68 at 80; *Alfred McAlpine Construction Ltd v Panatown Ltd* [2001] 1 A.C. 518 at 556, 592 (Lords Goff and Millett, dissenting); *Ruxley Electronics and Construction Co v Forsyth* [1966] A.C. 344 at 357 and 359.

233 See para.20–042.

234 See para.20–104 and following.

235 See the references to *Darlington BC v Wiltshier Northern Ltd* [1995] 1 W.L.R. 68 and *Alfred McAlpine Construction Ltd v Panatown Ltd* [2001] 1 A.C. 518 in fn.232.

236 See para.20–008.

237 *Alfred McAlpine Construction Ltd v Panatown Ltd* [2001] 1 A.C. 518 at 534.

238 Our concern here is with adverse *financial* effect on the claimant. A claim for damages for "loss of amenity" will generally be one for loss suffered by the claimant, though in the family holiday cases (para.14–026) this loss may be increased by the claimant's witnessing the suffering of his family; cf. also para.20–093.

The alternative view is that damages in respect of the cost of curing the breach (and so of securing the intended benefit for the third party) can be recovered only if cure has been, or is likely to be, carried out. The main practical argument in favour of this view is that (as noted above) it would be "unattractive" to allow the promisee to recover the cost of cure as damages in respect of his own loss and then to "put the money in his own pocket".[239] It is respectfully submitted that this is the preferable view.[240] In a two-party case it is indeed generally[241] no concern of the court's what the claimant intends to do with the damages; but the rationale of this rule does not necessarily apply in a three-party case. The rationale in a two-party case is that the defendant has, by reason of the breach, inflicted injury, loss or damage on the person or property *of the claimant* (or has failed to improve, or to transfer, an asset belonging to, or to be vested in, the claimant) who should therefore be able to deal in whatever way he pleases with the damages awarded to him in substitution of the interest *of his own* of which he has been deprived by the breach. For example, in the case of a contract to repair the claimant's own house, he could, but for the breach, have sold the house at a price reflecting the value of the repairs, had they been properly carried out, and then have disposed of the proceeds of the sale in any way he pleased; and so he should be able to dispose in the same way of the damages due to him for failure to carry out the repairs. Obviously, this reasoning cannot apply where the house is owned, not by the claimant, but by a third party. There is also the further point that, although in Lord Griffith's example the claimant as a matter of legal principle recovers damages in respect of his *own* loss, as a practical matter the purpose of the award in such a case is to protect the interests of the third party. Where damages are awarded in respect of a third party's loss (under one of the exceptions to the general rule) the court requires the promisee to hold these damages for the third party.[242] No such machinery is available where the damages are awarded in respect of the promisee's own loss; but a practical way of ensuring that the damages are in fact destined for the benefit of the third party is to require the promisee to show (as a condition of his entitlement to substantial damages) that they will be so used.

**Relation to third party's right.** Even where, in one of the exceptional situations discussed above, the promisee can recover damages in respect of the third party's loss, no right to enforce the contract is conferred directly on the third party, whose only claim will be to the fruits of any action which the promisee may decide to bring.[243] The third party will have a direct right against the promisor 14–043

[239] *Alfred McAlpine Construction Ltd v Panatown Ltd* [2001] 1 A.C. 158 at 571.

[240] See *Riva Properties Ltd v Foster & Partners Ltd* [2017] EWHC 2574 (TCC); 175 Con L.R. 45 at [301] (B entitled to recover the sums that "will have to be expended"); cf. *Mirant Asia-Pacific (Hong Kong) Ltd v Ove Arup and Partners International Ltd* [2007] EWHC 918 (TCC); [2007] C.I.L.L. 2840, at [628] ("in principle" the claimant was entitled to recover damages for loss that may have been incurred by a sister company as a result of the breach of an engineering design contract on the basis that "*it* did not receive from the defendants the performance of the bargain which it contracted for". It is not entirely clear whether "it" refers to the claimant (broader ground) or the sister company (narrower ground)).

[241] See fn.232.

[242] See para.14–046.

[243] See para.14–046.

only under one of the exceptions to the doctrine of privity. On the facts of some[244] (though not of all)[245] of the cases discussed above, the third party would probably, if those facts recurred now, have such a right under the Contracts (Rights of Third Parties) Act 1999.[246] If the third party has such a right, then this very fact may restrict the number of situations in which the promisee can recover damages in respect of the third party's loss;[247] and it will probably reduce the pressure on the courts to extend the range of such situations.[248] Section 4 of the 1999 Act, however, preserves the promisee's rights under the contract.[249] The question of his right to recover damages in respect of the third party's loss will therefore continue to arise and to be of practical importance, e.g. where the promisor has a defence against the third party which is not available against the promisee.[250]

14–044 **Summary of the present position.** Despite a series of decisions at the highest level, there are still "a number of points open in this difficult area"[251] and an attempt to summarise the present position may be thought an invidious task. The most recent decision of the Supreme Court in the *Swynson* case stresses that both the narrower ground and the broader ground are confined to cases where it is part of the object of the contract between A and B to benefit C, but that begs the question of what is necessary to meet this requirement given that C need not have been expressly identified as a beneficiary, at least for the purpose of the narrower ground.[252] The same decision confines the narrower ground to cases where C suffers loss as the intended transferee of property affected by the breach,[253] but while that is the context of previously decided cases, it is submitted for the reasons given above that it should not necessarily be so confined and that what is more important is the aim of avoiding the "black hole" in which a loss caused by A's breach is not recoverable by B or C.[254] The scope of the broader ground remains the most uncertain aspect of this area of the law,[255] but provided the

[244] e.g. *Woodar Investments & Development Ltd v Wimpey Construction UK Ltd* [1980] 1 W.L.R. 277 (para.14–026); see Law Com. No.242, para.7.49.

[245] e.g. probably *Linden Gardens Trust v Lenesta Sludge Disposals Ltd* [1994] 1 A.C. 85 (para.14–029): see para.14–106.

[246] See para.14–099 and following. Subsections 1(1)(a) and (3) of the 1999 Act will make it possible to draw up contracts, on facts similar to those of *Linden Gardens Trust v Lenesta Sludge Disposals Ltd* [1994] 1 A.C. 85 (para.14–029) so as to confer a right of enforcement directly on the third party: see para.14–100.

[247] On the reasoning of *The Albazero* [1977] A.C. 774; para.14–028 and of *Alfred McAlpine Construction Ltd v Panatown Ltd* [2001] 1 A.C. 518; para.14–033.

[248] The "legal black hole" referred to in *Darlington BC v Wiltshier Northern Ltd* [1995] 1 W.L.R. 68 at 79 would be much reduced in significance.

[249] See para.14–134.

[250] 1999 Act s.3(4); para.14–124.

[251] *Swynson Ltd v Lowick Rose LLP* [2017] UKSC 32; [2018] A.C. 313 at [106] (Lord Neuberger); cf. *Helmsley Acceptances Ltd v Lambert Smith Hampton* [2010] EWCA Civ 356 at [13] ("a developing and difficult area of the law" (Longmore LJ).

[252] See para.14–031.

[253] See para.14–039.

[254] See para.14–038.

[255] See para.14–037.

narrower ground is not necessarily restricted to property cases, it should be confined to cases where B has or intends to make good the benefit of which C has been deprived by B's breach.[256]

### (vi) *Position between promisee and third party*

The promisor may be willing to perform, and may actually perform, in favour of the third party, e.g. by paying him the agreed sum. These possibilities give rise to further problems between the third party and the promisee. In discussing these problems we shall at this stage assume that the case does not fall within any of the exceptions to the doctrine of privity which will be considered later in this chapter.[257] **14–045**

**Promisor pays or is willing to pay.** The first problem arises where the promisor has actually paid the third party or is willing to pay him, and the promisee claims that the third party is not entitled to keep the money for his own benefit but must hold it on behalf of the promisee. Such a claim is not likely to be made by the promisee himself, as he wants to benefit the third party. But it might be made by the promisee's trustee in bankruptcy, or by his personal representative on death. In *Beswick v Beswick* the House of Lords held that the third party (the widow) was entitled to keep the money which the promisor (the nephew) was ordered to pay her, simply because it appeared that this was the intention of the contracting parties.[258] It seems that the position would be the same where payments were made willingly, i.e. without any order of the court.[259] Payments actually received by the third party can be claimed by the promisee only if, on the true construction of the contract, they were made to the third party as nominee for the promisee.[260] Where the money has not yet been paid, the promisor and the promisee can agree to rescind or vary the contract; and if they vary it so as to provide for payment to the promisee, the third party has no claim under the contract. But the question whether the promisee can unilaterally (i.e. without the consent of the promisor) demand that payment should be made to himself depends once again on the construction of the contract. If the contract can be construed as one to pay the third party "or as the promisee shall direct", then the promisee is entitled to demand payment to himself.[261] But the contract is not likely to be construed in this way where it is a matter of concern to the promisor that payment should be **14–046**

---

[256] See para.14–042.

[257] See para.14–084 and following.

[258] *Beswick v Beswick* [1968] A.C. 58 at 71, 96; on this point overruling *Re Engelbach's Estate* [1924] 2 Ch. 348 and doubting *Re Sinclair's Life Policy* [1938] Ch. 799.

[259] This appears from the treatment in *Beswick v Beswick* of *Re Engelbach's Estate* [1924] 2 Ch. 348, where the money had in fact been paid to the third party: see 93 L.J.Ch. 616 at 617.

[260] cf. *Coulls v Bagot's Executor and Trustee Co* [1967] A.L.R. 385 where the High Court of Australia held that there was no *promise* to pay the third party but only a *mandate* by the promisee authorising the promisor to pay the third party (so that such payment would discharge the promisor). This mandate was revocable and had been revoked by the promisee's death. See also: *Thavorn v Bank of Credit & Commerce SA* [1985] 1 Lloyd's Rep. 259; *The Turridu* [1999] 2 Lloyd's Rep. 401.

[261] *The Spiros C* [2000] 2 Lloyd's Rep. 319 at 331; *The Bulk Chile* [2013] EWCA Civ 184; [2013] 1 W.L.R. 3440 at [23]; cf. *Mitchell v Ede* (1840) 11 Ad. & El. 888; *The Lycaon* [1983] 2 Lloyd's Rep. 548.

made to the third party, e.g. because the third party is a close relative of the promisor and it matters to the promisor that the third party should be provided for.[262]

14–047 **Promisee refuses to sue.** The second problem arises where the promisee fails or refuses to take any action to enforce the promise. Lord Denning has suggested that, even at common law the third party could in such a case circumvent the doctrine of privity by suing the promisor and joining the promisee as co-defendant.[263] But in one of the cases where this was suggested Diplock and Salmon LJJ said that the action can (in cases not falling within any of the exceptions to the doctrine of privity)[264] be brought only by the promisee;[265] and it is submitted that this is the correct view. Lord Denning's view is inconsistent with the common law doctrine of privity which was recognised in *Beswick v Beswick* and in later cases.[266] It is also inconsistent with the reasoning of the cases on trusts of promises to be discussed below,[267] for if the third party could always sue by joining the promisee to the action, it would be pointless to insist that he must in addition show the existence of a trust.

14–048 **Promisee sues for damages or restitution.** The final problem arises where the promisee sues but claims some form of relief other than specific performance in favour of the third party, i.e. where he claims damages or recovery of the consideration provided by him. If such a claim succeeded, it would seem to lead to a judgment for payment to the promisee and not to the third party; and the question would arise whether the promisee could keep the payment for his own benefit or whether he would be bound to hold it for the third party. In tort, a person can sometimes recover damages for a loss suffered, not by himself, but by another, e.g. a husband may get damages for loss of earnings suffered by his wife in giving up her job to nurse him after an accident and such damages must then be held on trust for the other person.[268] Similarly, damages for breach of contract can in the exceptional situations discussed above be recovered in respect of loss suffered by another;[269] such damages must be held for that other person.[270] This may also be the position in the cases which call "for special treatment",[271] such as the booking of family holidays or ordering meals in restaurants; if, in such cases, the promisee can recover damages in respect of the third party's loss, it may be that those damages, when recovered, would be held by the promisee as money

262 As in *Re Stapleton-Bretherton* [1941] Ch. 482.
263 *Beswick v Beswick* [1966] Ch. 538 at 557; *Gurtner v Circuit* [1968] 2 Q.B. 587 at 596.
264 *Gurtner v Circuit* [1968] 2 Q.B. 587 at 599, 606.
265 See at fn.247.
266 See paras 14–016–14–017.
267 See paras 14–089–14–097.
268 *Hunt v Severs* [1994] 2 A.C. 350 at 363.
269 See paras 14–028–14–029.
270 *The Albazero* [1977] A.C. 774 at 845; *O'Sullivan v Williams* [1992] 3 All E.R. 385 at 387; discussing *The Winkfield* [1902] P. 42; *Linden Gardens Trust v Lenesta Sludge Disposals Ltd* [1994] 1 A.C. 85 (para.14–029); *John Harris Partnership v Groveland Ltd* [1999] P.N.L.R. 697; Carriage of Goods by Sea Act 1992 s.2(4).
271 *Woodar Investment Development Ltd v Wimpey Construction UK Ltd* [1980] 1 W.L.R. 277 at 283; para.14–026.

had and received for the use of the third party.[272] But apart from these exceptional or special cases there does not appear to be any similar possibility where the promisee claims damages for breach of a contract merely because the contract was made for the benefit of a third party. The general rule in such a case is that damages will be awarded only to compensate the promisee for his *own* loss;[273] and where that general rule applies, it does not seem that he can be under any obligation to pay those damages (or any part of them) over to the third party.[274]

## 3. SCOPE

### (a) General

The common law doctrine of privity means that a person cannot acquire rights or be subjected to liabilities *arising under* a contract to which he is not a party. It does not mean that a contract between A and B cannot affect the legal rights of C indirectly. For example, an agreement between A and B under which A accepts from B part payment of a debt owed by C to A in full settlement of that debt can benefit C by precluding A from suing C for the balance of the debt;[275] and a fortiori full performance by B of C's obligation to A can discharge that obligation.[276] Conversely, a building contract between A and B may benefit C by defining his rights, e.g. by specifying the time at which payment becomes due to C under a sub-contract between B and C for the execution of part of the work.[277] It is also possible for a contract between A and B to affect C adversely.[278] The circumstances in which this may happen are discussed in the last part of this chapter. In this part, we are concerned with the circumstances in which a contract between A and B may *benefit* C without C acquiring any right to enforce the contract itself, or relying on the remedies available to B.[279] 14–049

### (b) Liability in negligence to third parties

While the primary effect of a contract between A and B is to oblige them to perform their respective promises to each other, the contract may also impose on A a duty of care to C, the breach of which will enable C to sue A in tort for negligence. The contract may have this effect because it gives rise to a relationship in which A owes a duty of care to C, e.g. to the relationship of passenger (or cargo-owner) and carrier,[280] of occupier of premises and visitor,[281] 14–050

---

272 *Jackson v Horizon Holidays Ltd* [1975] 1 W.L.R. 1468 at 1473 (Lord Denning).

273 See para.14–036.

274 cf. *Coulls v Bagot's Executor and Trustee Co Ltd* [1967] A.L.R. 385 at 411.

275 *Hirachand Punamchand v Temple* [1911] 2 K.B. 330; para.3–110; cf. *Johnson v Davies* [1999] Ch. 117 at 130.

276 For the conditions to be satisfied for such discharge, see para.17–007 and following.

277 *Co-operative Wholesale Society Ltd v Birse Construction Ltd* (1997) 84 B.L.R. 58.

278 e.g. *The Glacier Bay* [1996] 1 Lloyd's Rep. 370; *Banque Financière de la Cité v Parc (Battersea) Ltd* [1999] 1 A.C. 221; cf. paras 14–079–14–084.

279 As discussed at paras 14–019 and following.

280 *Austin v GW Ry* (1867) L.R. 2 Q.B. 442; *The Antonis P Lemos* [1985] A.C. 711.

281 Occupiers' Liability Act 1957 s.3; Defective Premises Act 1972 ss.1(1)(b), 4.

or of bailor and sub-bailee,[282] or of building owner and sub-contractor.[283] In a number of cases, persons providing professional services, such as solicitors,[284] insurance brokers[285] and safety consultants,[286] have been held liable in tort to persons other than their immediate clients for negligence in the performance of contracts with those clients. Surveyors, valuers, accountants and auditors can similarly be liable for negligent misrepresentation to third parties: the basis, and limits, of such liability have been discussed in Ch.9.[287] Sometimes the provider of the services is liable in tort because his negligence in performing the contract with his client of itself causes loss to the third party, e.g. where a solicitor's negligence in failing to carry out his client's testamentary instructions causes an intended gift to a prospective beneficiary to fail.[288] Sometimes the defendant's negligence results in his making a misrepresentation to the third party and the loss is suffered by the latter in consequence of his acting in reliance on the representation, e.g. where a valuer (A) employed by B negligently makes a report on the structure of a house and the report is communicated to C and induces him to buy the house for more than its true value.[289]

14–051 **Policy factors.** As will be apparent from the paragraph above, one can point to a significant body of case law in which A's defective performance of his contract with B has led to a liability in negligence to C. Ever since the decision in *Donoghue v Stevenson*,[290] this has been largely uncontroversial where the loss suffered by C is some form of personal injury, or damage to C's property. The fact that A, the manufacturer of the ginger beer alleged to contain a decomposed snail, had supplied it under his contract with a distributor (B) did not amount to an automatic bar against liability in negligence when it was later consumed by Mrs Donoghue (C) and made her ill. But, as will be seen,[291] even in cases of personal injury or damage to C's property, the circumstances of the case may be such as to negate the existence of any duty of care and one of those circumstances may be the contract which existed between A and B. The courts are concerned, in particular, to ensure that a claim in tort does not have the effect of upsetting the contractual allocation of the risk of injury or damage which the parties, including C, may deliberately have put in place, and which privity operates to keep intact.

A further potential problem is that in a number of the cases in which C has sued A in negligence, he has done so for pure economic loss, i.e. financial loss which is not the consequence of injury to C, or damage to his property. For

[282] *Moukataff v BOAC* [1967] 1 Lloyd's Rep. 396; *Bart v BWIA* [1967] 1 Lloyd's Rep. 239.
[283] See para.14–054.
[284] See para.14–057.
[285] *Punjab National Bank v de Boinville* [1992] 1 W.L.R. 1138 at 1152; cf. *Henderson v Merrett Syndicates Ltd* [1995] 2 A.C. 145 (discussed at para.14–056); *BP v AON Ltd* [2006] EWHC 424; [2006] 1 C.L.C. 881.
[286] *Driver v William Willett (Contractors) Ltd* [1969] 1 All E.R. 655; cf. *Dove v Banham's Patent Locks Ltd* [1983] 1 W.L.R. 1436; Contrast *The Nicholas H* [1996] 1 A.C. 211; para.14–055.
[287] See paras 9–042–9–048.
[288] See para.14–057.
[289] e.g. *Smith v Eric S Bush* [1990] 1 A.C. 831; para.9–028; cf. *Niru Battery Manufacturing Co v Milestone Trading Ltd* [2003] EWCA Civ 1446; [2004] 1 Lloyd's Rep. 344.
[290] [1932] A.C. 562.
[291] See para.14–055.

example, where A sells defective goods to B who, in turn, sells them to C, C's claim may simply be for the reduction in the value of the goods and the loss caused by his inability to use them in their defective state. Such a claim may be made by C in an action for breach of contract *against B*. The purpose of a contract is the performance of B's promise and, as a general rule, the remedies for breach seek to put the promisee (C) into the same position *as if the contract had been performed*.[292] This type of claim is not normally available in the tort of negligence, where damages are awarded to put C into the position in which he was *before the tort was committed*, i.e. to ensure that C is no worse off; hence the usual requirement that C must point to some personal injury or damage to property other than that supplied.[293] In fact, this problem may be overstated.[294] In the example just given, the position C was in before A supplied defective goods was one in which he had the anticipated benefit of a valid performance from B; the "loss of opportunity" to C, caused by A's negligence, is one which has been recognised in other claims in tort.[295] For this reason, it is submitted that the first problem, namely interference with the parties' contractual allocation of the risk of loss, provides a securer basis for explaining the cases in which liability in negligence has been imposed on A for pure economic loss, and those in which it has not.

The examples considered thus far have been concerned with claims by C for losses caused by A's *defective performance* of his contract with B and not for any *failure to perform*. As a general rule, there is no action in negligence for a failure to act[296] and the same is true when A's failure constitutes a breach of his contract with B. A claim for failure to perform may be brought in contract, e.g. C may sue B in contract for any non-performance by B of a contract between C and B brought about by A's non-performance of his contract with B, but, as a general rule, C may not sue A in negligence. In some cases, however, the courts seem to have been able to overcome even this problem.[297]

For these various reasons, the general rule remains that A is not liable in negligence to C for pure economic loss caused by A's defective performance of his contract with B,[298] nor for any failure to perform. There are exceptions, but the limited nature of those exceptions and the restrictions imposed on the duty of care which A may owe to C are largely explained by the presence of some, or all, of the factors outlined above.

---

[292] See para.20–024.

[293] This also serves to put a limit on the claims which may be made against A so as to avoid the problem of "opening the floodgates".

[294] *White v Jones* [1995] 2 A.C. 207 at 269.

[295] e.g. *East v Maurer* [1991] 1 W.L.R. 461; see para.9–076.

[296] *Smith v Littlewoods Organisation Ltd* [1987] A.C. 241.

[297] See para.14–057.

[298] *Tate & Lyle Industries Ltd v GLC* [1983] 2 A.C. 509 at 530–531; cf. *Greater Nottingham Co-operative Soc Ltd v Cementation Piling & Foundation Ltd* [1989] Q.B. 71 at 94. The decision in *European Gas Turbines Ltd v MSAS Cargo International Ltd* [2001] C.L.C. 880 is at first sight hard to reconcile with the other authorities cited in this note, but may be explained as a case of "assumption of responsibility" by A (sub-contracting carrier) which was reasonably relied upon by C (cargo owner).

14–052 **General principles.** In claims for pure economic loss, and now more generally in the law of negligence,[299] two tests have emerged to determine when a duty of care may be owed by the defendant (A) to the claimant (C). The first is to ask whether A "assumed responsibility for what he said and did vis-à-vis [C], or is to be treated by the law as having done so".[300] The second may be referred to as the "threefold test": whether loss to C was a reasonably foreseeable consequence of what A did or failed to do; whether the relationship between the parties was sufficiently proximate; and whether in all the circumstances it is fair, just and reasonable to impose a duty of care on A towards C.[301] It seems that the first test of "assumption of responsibility" is to be regarded as a sufficient, but not a necessary, condition of liability: if it is satisfied, it is unnecessary to ask whether it would be fair, just and reasonable to impose liability; if not, further consideration is called for under the threefold test.[302]

As for the tests themselves, there is candid recognition that they are of doubtful utility.[303] It is clear from the dictum of Lord Bingham above[304] that the test of assumption of responsibility is applied objectively; it is not a case of what A intended but, "as in the case of contractual liability", what would reasonably be inferred from his conduct against the background of all the circumstances of the case.[305] A notable feature of the test of assumption of responsibility is that it requires the court to identify a relationship "equivalent to contract".[306] Furthermore, it has been said that one of its functions is to make up for the apparent shortcomings of the law of contract in cases where no claim is available because of the absence of consideration,[307] or because of the operation of the doctrine of privity.[308] Under the threefold test, it is the third element which will usually be determinative and which inevitably raises questions of fairness and policy.

While, therefore, in the cases which follow, decisions have been reached by applying one test or the other, of far greater relevance have been the circumstances of the case and the relationship between the parties in the context

[299] See, e.g. *The Nicholas H* [1996] A.C. 211; *Phelps v Hillingdon LBC* [2001] 2 A.C. 619; *Watson v British Boxing Board of Control Ltd* [2001] Q.B. 1134; cf. *Robinson v Chief Constable of West Yorkshire* [2018] UKSC 4; [2018] A.C. 736.

[300] *Customs and Excise Commissioners v Barclays Bank Plc* [2006] UKHL 28; [2007] 1 A.C. 181 at [4] (Lord Bingham).

[301] *Customs and Excise Commissioners v Barclays Bank Plc* [2006] UKHL 28; [2007] 1 A.C. 181 at [4]; cf. *Caparo Industries Plc v Dickman* [1990] 2 A.C. 605 at 617–618; *Murphy v Brentwood DC* [1991] 1 A.C. 398 at 480, 486.

[302] *Customs and Excise Commissioners v Barclays Bank Plc* [2006] UKHL 28; [2007] 1 A.C. 181 at [4], [35]; *Henderson v Merrett Syndicates Ltd* [1995] 2 A.C. 145 at 181.

[303] *Customs and Excise Commissioners v Barclays Bank Plc* [2006] UKHL 28; [2007] 1 A.C. 181 at [36]; *Caparo v Dickman* [1990] 2 A.C. 617 at 628; *Merrett v Babb* [2001] EWCA Civ 214; [2001] Q.B. 1174 at [41].

[304] See at fn.300.

[305] *Customs and Excise Commissioners v Barclays Bank Plc* [2006] UKHL 28; [2007] 1 A.C. 181 at [35] (Lord Hoffmann). There must however have been an element of voluntariness in the conduct of A upon which an assumption of responsibility can be established. Thus, in the *Customs and Excise* case no duty of care was owed by a bank served with a freezing order to the judgment creditor in whose favour the order had been granted.

[306] *Hedley Byrne & Co Ltd v Heller & Partners Ltd* [1964] A.C. 465 at 530.

[307] See para.3–171.

[308] *Williams v Natural Life Health Foods Ltd* [1998] 1 W.L.R. 830 at 837.

of their legal and factual situation, with particular emphasis on the three policy factors outlined above.[309] This is an area of the law which to some extent resists categorisation, but for present purposes the cases may be considered under the following broad and non-exhaustive headings. By so dividing the cases it is not suggested that the arguments of principle which are applied are confined to the particular type of case under consideration.

**Supply of goods.** We have already seen that where A sells goods to B, who in turn sells or supplies them to C, A owes a duty of care to C not to cause personal injury, or damage to property other than the goods supplied.[310] However, as a general rule, A owes no duty of care to avoid pure economic loss, including any loss which flows simply from the defect in the goods supplied.[311] In *Simaan General Contracting Co v Pilkington Glass Ltd (No.2)*[312] the defendants (A) had been nominated as suppliers of glass for incorporation in a building which was being erected by the claimants (C) as main contractors for a client in Abu Dhabi. The glass had been sold by A to a sub-contractor (B) engaged by C, so that there was no contract between C and A; the glass was perfectly sound but was not of the colour specified in the contract of sale or in the main building contract. In consequence of this shortcoming, C was not paid by the employer and so suffered financial loss; but it was held that A's breach of the contract with B did not give C any right of action in tort against A merely because that breach had caused C to suffer financial loss. 14–053

The distinction between recoverable property damage and irrecoverable economic loss is well illustrated by *Muirhead v Industrial Tank Specialities Ltd*[313] where C, who owned a lobster farm, had entered into a contract with B for the installation of pumps which failed because of a defect in their electric motors. There was no contract between C and the supplier of the motors (A) but C's claim against A succeeded in tort in respect of the physical damage caused by the failure (i.e. lobsters which had died); and in respect of "any financial loss suffered by (C) in consequence of that physical damage"[314] (i.e. any profits on the lost sale of the lobsters which had died). But a further claim "in respect of the whole economic loss suffered"[315] by C (i.e. for loss of the profits that he would have made from rearing further lobsters) was rejected: such damages might have been recoverable from B in contract but they could not be claimed from A, as supplier to B, in tort.

In *Henderson v Merrett Syndicates Ltd* Lord Goff observed that, in the type of case exemplified by the *Simaan* case, there is generally no assumption of responsibility by the supplier (A), "the parties having so structured their

[309] See para.14–051.

[310] See para.14–051, fn.290.

[311] *Aswan Engineering Establishment Co v Lupine Ltd* [1987] 1 W.L.R. 1; cf. *Bacardi-Martini Beverages Ltd v Thomas Hardy Packaging Ltd* [2002] EWCA Civ 549; [2002] 2 Lloyd's Rep. 379 at [18] (contaminated ingredient used in manufacturing making finished product useless).

[312] [1988] Q.B. 758.

[313] [1986] Q.B. 507.

[314] *Muirhead v Industrial Tank Specialities Ltd* [1986] Q.B. 507 at 533.

[315] *Muirhead v Industrial Tank Specialities Ltd*[1986] Q.B. 507 at 533.

relationship that it is inconsistent with any such assumption of responsibility."[316] For example, A may have supplied the goods to B with the benefit of certain exclusions or limitations of liability which are reflected in the price paid by B; B in turn may have sold to C either with no such exclusions or limitations, or with the benefit of different exclusions or limitations, which are reflected in the price paid by C. If C sues A in negligence for pure economic loss, he is able, in effect, to secure the benefit of a bargain which none of the parties had envisaged, i.e. between A and C. Since none of the exclusions and limitations for which A negotiated with B will ordinarily affect C's claim,[317] A will be left with the burden of a "contract" which is not reflected in the price received by him and C may enjoy the benefit of a "contract" for which he has not paid in full. It is principally for this reason that C is entitled to sue in negligence only where A's breach of his contract with B has caused damage to C himself or his property. The parties themselves may create a direct contractual relationship (e.g. in the form of a manufacturer's guarantee),[318] but it is not for the courts to create such a relationship.

14–054 **Building contracts.** Similarly, in *Henderson v Merrett Syndicates Ltd* Lord Goff was also of the opinion that a sub-contractor (A) working for a main contractor (B) will not generally be found to have assumed responsibility to a developer, or building owner (C).[319] It is certainly true that, as a general rule, A is under no liability for defects in the property constructed or economic loss flowing therefrom to anyone other than the main contractor (B),[320] or any other parties[321] with whom he is in a direct contractual relationship.[322] His liability in negligence is limited to personal injury or damage to "other" property.[323] Again, the principal reason is the effect that such liability would have on the parties' contractual allocation of risk. In the *D & F Estates* case,[324] a lessee (C) claimed damages in tort for the cost of remedying defects alleged to be due to the negligence of a building contractor (A) in the performance of a contract to which the lessee was not a party. A was held not liable in tort, even if he was negligent, since the defects had been discovered before they had caused any personal injury, or damage to other property belonging to C. To make A liable for the purely

[316] *Henderson v Merrett Syndicates Ltd* [1995] 2 A.C. 145 at 196; cf. *Simaan General Contracting Co v Pilkington Glass Ltd (No.2)* [1988] Q.B. 758 at 781 (Lord Bingham).

[317] cf. fn.349. For possible exceptions, see para.14–078 and para.14–081.

[318] See para.14–006.

[319] *Henderson v Merrett Syndicates Ltd* [1995] 2 A.C. 145 at 196.

[320] As a general rule, his liability for pure economic loss will be limited to breach of contract; it seems he owes no concurrent duty of care in tort *even to B*: *Robinson v PE Jones (Contractors) Ltd* [2011] EWCA Civ 9; [2011] 3 W.L.R. 815.

[321] See the discussion of collateral warranties, at fn.326.

[322] *D & F Estates Ltd v Church Commissioners for England* [1989] A.C. 177; *Department of the Environment v Thomas Bates & Son Ltd* [1991] 1 A.C. 499; *Murphy v Brentwood DC* [1991] 1 A.C. 398; cf. *Galliford Try Infrastructure Ltd v Mott Macdonald Ltd* [2008] EWHC 1570 (TCC); 120 Con L.R. 1.

[323] *Nitrigin Eirann Teoranta v Inco Alloys Ltd* [1992] 1 W.L.R. 498; *Targett v Torfaen BC* [1992] 3 All E.R. 27; *British Telecommunications Plc v James Thomson & Sons (Engineers) Ltd* [1999] 1 W.L.R. 9; *Bellefield Computer Services Ltd v E Turner & Sons* [2000] B.L.R. 97.

[324] *D & F Estates Ltd v Church Commissioners for England* [1989] A.C. 177; cf. *Department of the Environment v Thomas Bates & Son Ltd* [1991] 1 A.C. 499.

economic loss suffered by C in remedying the defect would "impose upon [A] for the benefit of those with whom he had no contractual relationship the obligation of one who warranted the quality of"[325] his work. That this now seems to be the accepted position is reflected in the practice of the parties concerned. In commercial developments, if the developer (or owner) (C) wishes to secure the benefit of a claim for pure economic loss against a party (A) with whom he is not already in a direct contractual relationship, he is expected to negotiate for it, usually in the form of a collateral warranty, and pay a price.[326] In the case of a residential purchase, which will often take place long after the building work, a collateral warranty from the builder (A) is unrealistic, but the purchaser (C) is expected to protect his interest[327] by obtaining a survey.[328]

In the context of building contracts, there is one notable exception to the general rule. In *Junior Books Ltd v Veitchi Co Ltd*[329] B was to build a factory for C under a contract which entitled C to nominate sub-contractors. C nominated A as flooring sub-contractor; B in consequence entered into a contract with A by which A undertook to lay the floor; but no contract came into existence between A and C.[330] The floor later cracked and, on the assumption that this was due to A's negligence in doing the work defectively, it was held that A was liable to C for the loss suffered by C in consequence of the fact that the work had to be done again, i.e. for defects in the floor itself. Later authorities have emphasised the exceptional nature of the circumstances of the *Junior Books* case. It has been said that those circumstances were "unique";[331] that the case "cannot now be regarded as a useful pointer to the development of the law"[332] or "as laying down any principle of general application in the law of tort";[333] and that the statement of principle in Lord Brandon's dissenting speech is to be preferred to that of the majority.[334] The authority of the case is further undermined by the fact that the reasoning of the majority is to a considerable extent based on earlier decisions[335] which (so far as they hold the defendants liable for economic loss) have since been overruled by the House of Lords.[336] In consequence of these developments,

325 *D & F Estates Ltd v Church Commissioners for England* [1989] A.C. 177 at 207; cf. at 211–212.

326 See, e.g. *Safeway Stores Ltd v Interserve Projects Ltd* [2005] EWHC 3085 (TCC); 105 Con L.R. 60 (C's claim against A limited to the extent of A's liability to B).

327 The incentive to protect his interest in this way is all the greater since his claim in contract against the vendor (B) may be of little value, subject as it is to the principle of caveat emptor.

328 Or by relying on a survey prepared for the lender from whom he borrows the funds to purchase the property: *Smith v Eric S Bush* [1990] 1 A.C. 831: see para.9–045.

329 [1983] 1 A.C. 520; Palmer and Murdoch 46 M.L.R. 213. See further Reynolds (1985) 11 N.Z.U.L.R. 215; Stapleton 104 L.Q.R. 213 and 389; Huxley 53 M.L.R. 361; Beyleveld and Brownsword 54 M.L.R. 48. The Contracts (Rights of Third Parties) Act 1999 probably does not apply on such facts: para.14–106.

330 Quaere whether a collateral contract might have been found to exist: see para.14–006.

331 *D & F Estates Ltd v Church Commissioners for England* [1989] A.C. 177 at 202; cf. *Van Oppen v Clerk to the Bedford Charity Trustees* [1989] 1 All E.R. 273 at 289; affirmed [1990] 1 W.L.R. 235; *Nitrigin Eirann Teoranta v Inco Alloys Ltd* [1992] 1 W.L.R. 498 at 504.

332 *Simaan General Contracting Co v Pilkington Glass Ltd (No.2)* [1988] Q.B. 758 at 784.

333 *D & F Estates Ltd v Church Commissioners for England* [1989] A.C. 177 at 202; cf. at 215.

334 *D & F Estates Ltd v Church Commissioners for England* [1989] A.C. 177 at 202, 215; cf. *Murphy v Brentwood DC* [1991] 2 A.C. 398 at 466, 469.

335 i.e. *Anns v Merton LBC* [1978] A.C. 728; *Dutton v Bognor Regis Urban DC* [1972] 1 Q.B. 373.

336 *Murphy v Brentwood DC* [1991] 2 A.C. 398.

the decision in the *Junior Books* case has been described as "discredited",[337] "virtually extinguished"[338] and "aberrant (and) heretical".[339]

14–055 **Carriage of goods by sea.** The rights and liabilities of carriers and cargo-owners are regulated by international Conventions which have the force of law and claims in negligence by cargo-owners which have attempted to bypass them have not met with success. In *The Aliakmon*[340] A, a carrier, had contracted with B for the carriage of a quantity of steel coils which B had sold to C. The coils were damaged, as a result of A's negligent breach of the contract of carriage, after the risk in them had passed to C under the contract of sale, but while B remained owner. C had no claim under the contract of carriage as he was not a party to it;[341] and the House of Lords held that he also had no cause of action against A in tort in respect of the loss which he had suffered as a result of remaining liable for the full price of the coils in spite of the fact that they had been damaged in transit. This conclusion was based on a long line of authority[342] which had established the "principle of law that, in order to enable a person to claim in negligence for loss caused to him by reason of loss or damage to property, he must have had either the legal ownership of or a possessory title to the property concerned at the time when the loss or damage occurred"[343] or, where the loss is caused by a continuing process, at the time when the cause of action in respect of it first accrued.[344] It is not enough for him "to have only had contractual rights in relation to such property"[345] when the loss or damage occurred.[346] The House of Lords refused to create an exception to this principle where (as in the present case) the contractual right which C had under his contract of sale with B was one to have property and possession of the goods transferred to him at a later date. The main reason for this refusal was that the contract of carriage between A and B was expressed to be subject to the Hague Rules[347] which gave A (as carrier) the benefit of certain immunities from, and limitations of, liability; and to have held A liable in tort to C would have produced the undesirable result of depriving A of

337 *Société Commerciale de Réassurance v ERAS International Ltd* [1992] 1 Lloyd's Rep. 570 at 599.
338 *The Volvox Hollandia (No.2)* [1993] 2 Lloyd's Rep. 315 at 322; *The Orjula* [1995] 2 Lloyd's Rep. 395 at 401.
339 *Robinson v PE Jones (Contractors) Ltd* [2011] EWCA Civ 9; [2011] 3 W.L.R. 815 at [92].
340 [1986] A.C. 785; Treitel [1986] L.M.C.L.Q. 294; Tettenborn [1987] J.B.L. 12; cf. *The Ciudad de Pasto* [1988] 1 W.L.R. 1145; *The Filiatra Legacy* [1991] 2 Lloyd's Rep. 337 at 339; *The Gudermes* [1993] 1 Lloyd's Rep. 311 at 326.
341 On the facts of *The Aliakmon* rights under the contract of carriage would now be transferred to C by virtue of the Carriage of Goods by Sea Act 1992 s.2: see *White v Jones* [1995] 2 A.C. 207 at 265.
342 *Cattle v Stockton Waterworks Co* (1875) L.R. 10 Q.B. 453; *The Wear Breeze* [1969] 1 Q.B. 219; *The Mineral Transporter* [1986] A.C. 1.
343 *The Aliakmon* [1986] A.C. 785 at 809.
344 *The Starsin* [2003] UKHL 12; [2004] 1 A.C. 715 at [40], [64], [90], [139].
345 *The Aliakmon* [1986] A.C 785 at 809.
346 Beneficial ownership will suffice if the legal owner is joined as a party to the action: *The Aliakmon* [1986] A.C. 785 at 812; *Shell UK Ltd v Total UK Ltd* [2010] EWCA Civ 180; [2010] 3 W.L.R. 1192 at [119]. A bailor may retain an immediate possessory interest in goods even after transferring his contractual rights to the bailee: *Scottish & Newcastle International Ltd v Othon Ghalanos Ltd* [2008] UKHL 11; [2008] 1 Lloyd's Rep. 462 at [46].
347 As set out in the Schedule to the Carriage of Goods by Sea Act 1924, now superseded in England by Carriage of Goods by Sea Act 1971 (the Hague-Visby Rules).

the protection of that contract,[348] since C (being a stranger to it) was no more bound by its terms than entitled to assert rights under it.[349]

Such is the concern to ensure that the internationally accepted regimes operating in this area should not be by-passed, a claim in negligence may fail even where C has suffered damage to goods in which he has the proprietary interest required by the decision in *The Aliakmon*. In *The Nicholas H*[350] a ship classification society (A) had, in breach of its contract with shipowners (B), advised them that their ship could proceed on her current voyage until the cargo which she was then carrying had been discharged. In the course of that voyage the ship sank, and it was held that the owners of the cargo (C) had no cause of action in tort against A in respect of the loss of their cargo. The main reason given by the House of Lords for this conclusion was that B was, as a result of the loss of the cargo, in breach of the contract of carriage with C; and that it was not fair, just and reasonable[351] to impose on A liability in tort to C since this would not be subject to the limitations of liability available to B under the international Conventions[352] which are intended to regulate liability. The effect of holding classification societies liable in tort to cargo-owners in this situation would be to deprive shipowners of the benefits of these Conventions since the societies would pass on their unlimited liability to shipowners; and this would be an undesirable conclusion,[353] particularly as loss suffered by cargo-owners in excess of the Convention limits was "readily insurable".[354]

**Financial services.** In the context of what may be referred to as financial services there is a notable exception to the general rule that A owes no duty of care where the negligent performance of services under a contract with B causes pure economic loss to a third party, C.[355] *Henderson v Merrett Syndicates Ltd*[356] involved claims in negligence by underwriting members at Lloyd's (C), known as Names, against managing agents (A) who were alleged to have been negligent in the conduct of the Names' underwriting affairs, leading to excessive losses. In **14–056**

[348] cf. para.14–082; *Simaan General Contracting Co v Pilkington Glass Ltd (No.2)* [1988] Q.B. 758 at 782–783.

[349] In the Court of Appeal ([1985] Q.B. 350 at 399) Robert Goff LJ proposed that any duty owed to C might be modified by the terms of the contract between A and B, but his theory of "transferred loss" was rejected by the House of Lords; cf. *White v Jones* [1995] 2 A.C. 207 at 268 where, as Lord Goff, he achieved something similar in his use of an "extended" assumption of responsibility; cf. Markesinis 103 L.Q.R. 354; para.14–084.

[350] [1996] A.C. 211; cf. *Reeman v Dept of Transport* [1997] 2 Lloyd's Rep. 648.

[351] Nor had there been an "assumption of responsibility" (para.14–052) since the cargo-owners were "not even aware of [the classification society's] examination of the ship": *The Nicholas H* [1996] A.C. 211 at 242.

[352] In *The Nicholas H* [1996] A.C. 211 the Convention in question related to tonnage limitations; effect was given to it by Merchant Shipping Act 1979 s.17 and Sch.4, now superseded by Merchant Shipping Act 1995 s.185 and Sch.7 Pt I. In *Perrett v Collins* [1998] 2 Lloyd's Rep. 255 no such policy reasons were held to exist for protecting an aircraft inspection society from liability for personal injury to a passenger; cf. *Watson v British Boxing Board of Control Ltd* [2001] Q.B. 1134.

[353] cf. at fnn.347 and 348.

[354] *The Nicholas H* [1996] A.C. 211 at 242.

[355] Many of the cases in the area of financial services have been concerned with liability for negligent misrepresentation and are considered earlier: see paras 9–042—9–048.

[356] [1995] 2 A.C. 145.

some cases, the managing agents were in a direct contractual relationship with the Names, but in others the Names dealt with members' agents (B), so that the underwriting was conducted by the managing agents as sub-agents. Unlike cases such as the *Simaan* case,[357] which was considered by analogy by Lord Goff, in the cases in *Henderson v Merrett* where a sub-agency was involved, the parties were not found to have "structured their relationship so as to exclude any duty of care owed."[358] Lord Goff emphasised that the situation in *Henderson v Merrett* was "most unusual".[359] One possible distinguishing feature is that the Names had "no choice",[360] or control, over the internal organisation of the agents involved which determined whether or not they were in a direct contractual relationship with the managing agents, as opposed to the *Simaan* case where the contractual structure was deliberately and consciously put in place by all of the parties involved. This may be a relevant factor but it is not necessarily determinative, such that, if it is absent, no duty of care is owed by A to C. Rather, the question with which the courts are concerned is whether the contractual structure, *and the circumstances in which it was put in place by the parties*, is inconsistent with the existence of a duty of care owed by A to C which cuts across that structure.

This is evident from a further exception to the general rule. In *Riyad Bank v Ahli United Bank (UK) Plc*[361] an investment fund (C) was set up by the Riyad bank, and an entity within the Riyad bank (B) acted as C's general adviser. The defendant (A), a Kuwaiti bank, provided advice on the investments under a contract with B, but had no contract with C; it was, in formal terms, a sub-adviser. C suffered losses as a result of A's negligent advice as to the value of the investments made. The contractual structure had been deliberately adopted by the parties, in contrast to *Henderson v Merrett*, but the background made it clear that this was not inconsistent with an assumption of responsibility by A to C. In reality, C was the creation of A which had operated similar funds in the past and it was A which acted as principal adviser. It had only been necessary to set up a separate fund and interpose B because of objections to the Riyad bank's customers investing in a Kuwaiti-administered fund and dealing with a Kuwaiti bank. In those circumstances, A was found to owe a duty of care to C.

14–057 **Disappointed beneficiaries.** The courts appear to have gone furthest in imposing a duty of care on A not to cause pure economic loss to C in a number of cases concerned principally with the failure of solicitors to fulfil their client (B)'s testamentary instructions in the drawing up of the will, or the administration of the estate. In *White v Jones*,[362] B had instructed his solicitor (A) to draw up a will

---

357 *Simaan General Contracting Co v Pilkington Glass Ltd* (*No.*2) [1988] Q.B. 758: see para.14–053.

358 *Henderson v Merrett Syndicates Ltd* [1995] 2 A.C. 145 at 195. The duty owed was based on the test of assumption of responsibility: see para.14–052.

359 *Henderson v Merrett Syndicates Ltd* [1995] 2 A.C. 145 at 195.

360 This was counsel for the defendant's argument in *Riyad Bank v Ahli United Bank (UK) Plc* [2006] EWCA Civ 780; [2006] 2 Lloyd's Rep. 292.

361 [2006] EWCA Civ 780; [2006] 2 Lloyd's Rep. 292; cf. *BP v AON Ltd* [2006] EWHC 424 (Comm); [2006] 1 C.L.C. 881 (liability of insurance sub-broker to insured).

362 [1995] 2 A.C. 207 (Lords Keith and Mustill dissenting), approving the result (though not the reasoning) in *Ross v Caunters* [1980] Ch. 287, where A's negligence took the form, not of simply failing to carry out B's instructions, but of carrying them out ineffectively; cf. *Esterhuizen v Allied Dunbar Assurance Plc* [1998] 2 F.L.R. 668 (similar liability of company offering will-making

containing bequests in favour of his daughters C and D, but A negligently and in breach of his contract with B had done nothing to carry out these instructions by the time of B's death. The House of Lords by a majority held that A was liable in tort to C and D, and that the damages to which they were entitled consisted of the amounts which they would have obtained under B's will, if A had duly carried out B's instructions. The case presented certain special features, namely that C had discussed B's testamentary intentions with A, and that the letter setting out B's wishes had been drafted by D's husband. The majority do not seem to restrict the principle of liability to such special circumstances[363] though they accept that there must be "boundaries to the availability of the remedy" which "will have to be worked out … as practical problems come before the courts".[364] It is, for example, an open question whether such a remedy would be available to a prospective beneficiary who had no previous connection with the testator or knowledge of his intentions; and it seems that the solicitor would not be liable for the amount of the intended benefit where it would have been reasonable for the beneficiary to have secured this benefit by taking proceedings against the estate for rectification of the will.[365]

Where the principle (whatever its precise scope) does apply, its effect is to put C into the position in which he would have been if the contract between A and B had been properly performed. One distinguishing feature of the cases in this category, compared to those considered above, is that there is no chain of contracts involved, i.e. a contract between A and B, and between B and C. C does not therefore have even the protection of a claim in contract against B for any breach by B brought about by A's defective performance of his contract with B. All that C has is the expectation that B wished to bestow the legacy upon him, and this cannot be fulfilled where, as in *White v Jones*, B has died. Where, however, a defect in the will is discovered when cure is still possible, the solicitor owes no duty to the beneficiary, since C can request B to execute a new will and it is entirely a matter for B whether he chooses to do so.[366] There are also the points that, if any duty is to be imposed on the solicitor to the disappointed beneficiary, the only realistic measure of damages is the value of the lost benefit; and that no more than nominal damages could be recovered from the solicitor by the client's estate, since it would have suffered no loss. The negligent solicitor would thus escape all substantial liability if he were not held liable to the disappointed beneficiary for the value of the lost benefit.

services); and, in Australia, *Hill v van Erp* (1997) 142 A.L.R. 687 (also a case of actual misfeasance by the solicitor); *Martin v Triggs Turner Bartons* [2009] EWHC 1920 (Ch); [2010] P.N.L.R. 3; *Feltham v Bouskell* [2013] EWHC 1952 (Ch); 152 Con L.R. 124. Contrast *Clark v Bruce Lance* [1988] 1 All E.R. 364 (solicitor acting for testator in a different transaction held to owe no duty to beneficiary).

363 *White v Jones* [1995] 2 A.C. 207 at 295.

364 *White v Jones* [1995] 2 A.C. 207 at 269. The alleged beneficiary's claim clearly cannot succeed without proof of the requisite testamentary intention in his favour: see *Gibbons v Nelsons* [2000] Lloyd's Rep. P.N. 603.

365 Contrast *Walker v Geo H Medlicott & Son* [1999] 1 W.L.R. 727, with *Horsfall v Hayward* [1999] 1 F.L.R. 1182.

366 *Hemmens v Wilson Browne* [1995] Ch. 223; cf. *Hughes v Richards* [2004] EWCA Civ 266; [2004] P.N.L.R. 35.

An important feature of *White v Jones* is that the estate had suffered no loss. Where it has done so as a result of the solicitor's negligence, a claim may be made by the estate[367] which will then be under a duty to account to the intended legatee for any damages received.[368] The result achieved is similar to that seen in the cases considered earlier where damages are recovered on behalf of a third party,[369] but the duty to account is here derived from the terms of the will. As a consequence, where any recovery by the estate will benefit not the intended legatee, but instead the person entitled under the will to the residuary estate, thus defeating the intention of the testatrix, a claim[370] may still be made by the intended legatee.[371]

14–058 **Disappointed beneficiaries: analogous cases.** The principle of the "disappointed beneficiary" cases has been extended to other situations. In *Gorham v British Telecommunications Plc*[372] an insurance company (A) sold a policy to a customer (B) who had made it clear to A that he was buying the policy to provide for his wife and dependent children (C) in the event of his predeceasing them. A negligently failed to advise B that C would have been better off if B had joined his employers' pension scheme; and it was held that A was liable to C for loss of benefits under the employers' scheme up to (but not beyond) the time when A had corrected its original advice. The principle of *White v Jones*[373] applied because (as in that case) B had not himself suffered any loss, so that, if C's claims had been rejected, then neither the persons who had suffered loss nor anyone else would have any claim for established negligence; and because the advice had been given "in a context in which the interests of [C] were fundamental to the transaction".[374] In both these respects, the case was closely analogous to that of a disappointed testamentary beneficiary.[375]

The "disappointed beneficiary" cases go further than any other group of negligence cases in encroaching on the common law doctrine of privity of contract.[376] Perhaps for this reason, they were described as "an unusual class of case" in *Goodwill v British Pregnancy Advisory Service*.[377] In that case, the defendant (A) had arranged for B to have a vasectomy and, after the operation

367 In contract and in tort.

368 *Chappell v Somers & Blake* [2003] EWHC 1644 (Ch); [2004] Ch. 19.

369 See para.14–031.

370 In tort alone.

371 *Carr-Glynn v Frearsons* [1998] 4 All E.R. 225. Whether the claim is brought by the estate, or the intended legatee, the court will seek to ensure there is no prospect of double recovery: *Corbett v Bond Pearce* [2001] EWCA Civ 531; [2001] 3 All E.R. 769; *Chappell v Somers & Blake* [2003] EWHC 1644 (Ch); [2004] Ch. 19 at [17]; cf. *Daniels v Thompson* [2004] EWCA Civ 307; [2004] P.N.L.R. 33.

372 [2000] 1 W.L.R. 2129.

373 [1995] 2 A.C. 207; para.14–057.

374 *Gorham v British Telecommunications Plc* [2000] 1 W.L.R. 2129 at 2142.

375 cf. the reference in *Dean v Allin & Watts* [2001] EWCA Civ 758; [2001] 2 Lloyd's Rep. 249 at [69] by Robert Walker LJ to the "very special problems" which had arisen in *White v Jones* and *Gorham*'s case, evidently not sharing the view of Lightman J in *Dean v Allin & Watts* at [40] that the decision there represented a further extension of the principle in *White v Jones*.

376 Liability is imposed in some cases for A's failure to perform, rather than his defective performance, and while liability is said to be based on the test of assumption of responsibility, there is no reliance by C, which had previously been thought to be a necessary element of that test.

377 [1996] 1 W.L.R. 1397 at 1403.

had been carried out, told B that it had been successful and that he no longer needed to use any other method of contraception. Some three years later, B formed a sexual relationship with C, to whom he communicated the information given to him by A relating to the vasectomy; C ceased to use any method of contraception after having consulted her own general practitioner who told her that there was only a minute chance of her becoming pregnant. The vasectomy having undergone a spontaneous reversal, C became pregnant by B and one reason given for holding that A was not liable to C in damages[378] was that a doctor performing a vasectomy could not realistically be described as having been employed to confer a benefit on his patient's future sexual partners. The case was also said to be unlike the "disappointed beneficiary" cases in that dismissal of the claim would not produce the "rank injustice"[379] that would arise in those cases if in them the only person with a claim against the negligent solicitor were the testator's estate, and that estate had suffered no loss. In a sterilisation case, a substantial remedy for negligence (if established) would normally be available to the patient him (or her) self.[380]

**Assessment.** The categories of case considered above are not exhaustive of the circumstances in which A may owe a duty of care to C arising from the performance of his contract with B.[381] Nothing is to be gained, however, by considering further examples since, in each case, the existence and scope of any duty will be determined by the courts' assessment of the policy factors outlined in para.14–051 and illustrated by the cases above. The point to be stressed, by way of conclusion, is that the majority of cases involve a chain of contracts which link A and C, but under which C is normally expected to rely on his claims against the party (B) with whom he has a contractual relationship within the chain. This, of course, is the very essence of privity. The difficulty for the courts is that "there cannot be a general proposition that, just because a chain exists, no responsibility ... is ever assumed to a non-contractual party. It all depends on the facts."[382] Where C is not at the end of a chain and does not have the benefit of a claim against B in contract, the courts have gone furthest and, in exceptional cases, have been prepared to impose liability in negligence in order to produce a just outcome.[383] 14–059

For the most part, where A is liable in negligence to C, such claims do not represent an exception to the doctrine of privity. In cases where C sues for

378 Damages are now limited to a conventional sum in such cases, in any event: *Rees v Darlington Memorial Hospital NHS Trust* [2003] UKHL 52; [2004] 1 A.C. 309.

379 *Goodwill v British Pregnancy Advisory Service* [1996] 1 W.L.R. 1397 at 1403.

380 But see now fn.378.

381 In addition to those considered above, and earlier in paras 9–042–9–048, see also: *Al Kandari v JR Brown & Co* [1988] Q.B. 665; *Dean v Allin & Watts* [2001] EWCA Civ 758; [2001] 2 Lloyd's Rep. 249 at [33]; *Riva Properties Ltd v Foster & Partners* [2017] EWHC 2574 (TCC); 175 Con L.R. 45 at [148] (no duty of care owed by architect (A) to third party (C) where A's contract with B allowed for direct warranties in favour of C but there had been no attempt made to use the contractual mechanism); cf. *BDW Trading Ltd v Integral Geotechnique (Wales) Ltd* [2018] EWHC 1915 (TCC); 179 Con L.R. 112 at [169].

382 *Riyad Bank v Ahli Bank (UK) Plc* [2006] EWCA Civ 780; [2006] 2 Lloyd's Rep. 292 at [32] (Longmore LJ).

383 See paras 14–057—14–058.

personal injury or damage to "other" property, any claim in negligence protects a different interest from that protected in contract.[384] Even in cases where A is liable to C in negligence for pure economic loss, there will normally be important differences in the claims which may be made by C, when compared to a claim for the direct enforcement of the contract between A and B. With the exception of the disappointed beneficiary cases, A is only liable in negligence if he has been guilty of defective performance of his contract with B, and not merely a failure to perform. C must also prove that such defective performance amounted to, or was the consequence of, negligence, whereas A's liability under his contract with B may be strict. Furthermore, in contract, B has a cause of action against A as soon as the breach occurs, but in tort C's cause of action accrues only when the resulting loss is suffered.[385]

### (c) Intimidation

**14–060** The tort of intimidation is committed where A induces B to act to the detriment of C by threatening B with some unlawful course of conduct. In *Rookes v Barnard*[386] the House of Lords decided that a threat by A to break his contract with B is for this purpose a threat to do an unlawful act. Such a threat may therefore entitle C to sue A for intimidation. It has been said that this view outflanks the common law doctrine of privity.[387] No doubt in such a case C bases his cause of action on the threat to break a contract to which he is not a party. But the doctrine of privity only prevents C from enforcing A's promise to B; and in cases of intimidation C is certainly not doing that. If A induces B to dismiss C by threatening to defame B, C may be able to sue A for intimidation, but not for defamation. So, if A induces B to dismiss C by threatening to break A's contract with B, C may be able to sue A for intimidation, but not for breach of contract. In such a case C is not trying to enforce A's promise to B: "his ground of action is quite different".[388] C's complaint is not that A has broken his promise to B but that he has coerced B into acting to C's detriment.[389] The House of Lords has therefore rejected the argument that the doctrine of privity would be outflanked by holding that the tort of intimidation could be committed by threatening to commit a breach of contract.[390]

---

[384] See para.14–051.

[385] *Dove v Banham's Safety Locks Ltd* [1983] 1 W.L.R. 1463; cf. *Bell v Peter Browne & Co* [1990] 2 Q.B. 495.

[386] [1964] A.C. 1129.

[387] Wedderburn 24 M.L.R. 572 at 577; in *Rookes v Barnard* the argument was accepted in the Court of Appeal: [1963] 1 Q.B. 623 at 695, but rejected by the House of Lords.

[388] *Rookes v Barnard* [1964] A.C. 1129 at 1168; cf. at 1208; if C were trying to enforce the contract, the damages might be quite different.

[389] *Rookes v Barnard* [1964] A.C. 1129 at 1208.

[390] *Rookes v Barnard* [1964] A.C. 1129 at 1168, 1200, 1208, 1235; Hamson [1961] C.L.J. 189; [1964] C.L.J. 159; Hoffmann 81 L.Q.R. 116 at 124–128. This proposition is not affected by the attempt to re-state the principles of the so-called economic torts in *OBG Ltd v Allan* [2007] UKHL 21; [2008] 1 A.C. 1 in which intimidation is described (at [7]) as a "variant" of the tort of causing loss by unlawful means.

## (d) Restitution?

**Benefit received from promisee.** It has been suggested in Australia that the third party may have a claim in restitution where the promisor has received payment (or some other performance) from the promisee and has then failed or refused to perform the promise in favour of the third party; and that the measure of recovery on such a claim is the amount promised.[391] The suggestion was made where premiums under a policy of liability insurance for the benefit of a third party had been paid by the promisee to the promisor (the insurance company) which had then refused to pay the third party. The promisor's liability in restitution was said to be based on his unjust enrichment, and to arise in spite of the fact that there was no correlative impoverishment of the third party. But while it is true that liability in restitution is not based on loss to the claimant, it is (in the case put) based on gain to the defendant and it is hard to see what justification there can be for wholly disregarding this *basis* of restitutionary liability in determining its *measure*. And the argument that, to hold the promisor liable to the third party was "not an abrogation of the doctrine of privity of contract",[392] merely because the liability was said to arise in restitution, is, it is submitted, inconsistent with the practical result of making the promisor so liable. In England, as a general rule, the promisor is not liable in tort where the practical effect of imposing such liability would be to abrogate the doctrine of privity;[393] and there seems to be no reason why the position should be different merely because the alleged basis of liability is restitution rather than tort. The suggestion that the promisor is liable in restitution to the third party for the amount promised, merely because the promisor has received performance from the promisee is also inconsistent with the reasoning of *Beswick v Beswick*,[394] where it was assumed that the third party had no common law right to sue the promisor in her own name, in spite of the fact that the promisor had received performance in full from the promisee. The view that claims of the kind here discussed fall outside the scope of the doctrine of privity of contract must therefore be regarded with scepticism. The argument based on restitution would in any event be of no avail to the third party where the promisor was willing to pay and the issue was merely whether it should pay the third party or the promisee:[395] in such cases the promisor would not be unjustly enriched so that there would be no basis for restitutionary liability. 14–061

**Benefit received from third party.** The above discussion is based on the assumption that the promisor would be unjustly enriched if he were allowed to retain a payment received *from the promisee* in spite of his failure to perform his promise to pay the third party. There is the further possibility that the promisor may have received a benefit *from a third party*, e.g. where A contracts to grant a development lease to B, a company controlled by C, and C incurs expense in 14–062

[391] *Trident Ins Co Ltd v McNiece Bros Pty Ltd* (1988) 165 C.L.R. 107 (Gaudron J); this view does not seem to be shared by any other member of the court; Soh 105 L.Q.R. 4.
[392] *Trident Ins Co Ltd v McNiece Bros Pty Ltd* (1988) 165 C.L.R. 107 at 177.
[393] *Balsamo v Medici* [1984] 1 W.L.R. 951, 959–960; cf. para.14–054, at fn.325.
[394] [1968] A.C. 58; para.14–017.
[395] See above, para.14–046; cf. such cases as *Re Schebsman* [1944] Ch. 83 (para.14–090); and *Re Sinclair's Life Policy* [1938] Ch. 799 (para.14–092).

improving A's land in anticipation of the development, which then fails to take place because of A's failure to perform his contract with B. In such a case, it is arguable that C may have a restitution claim against A.[396] To allow such a claim would not be inconsistent with the doctrine of privity since in such a case C's claim is not based on any promise made by A to B for the benefit of C; no such promise has been made. The basis and measure of any restitution claim which C may have against A is more closely analogous to cases in which restitution is granted in respect of benefits conferred under anticipated contracts which fail to come into existence.[397]

## 4. EXEMPTION CLAUSES AND THIRD PARTIES

**14–063** Where an exemption clause purports to affect a third party, two questions arise. Can the third party take the benefit of the clause? Can he be bound by it? For the purpose of this discussion, it will be assumed that the clause is valid under the rules stated in Ch.7.[398]

### (a) The benefit

#### *(i) Privity and exceptions*

**14–064** Originally, the courts held that a person could only take the benefit of an exemption clause in a contract which he did not make himself if one of the recognised exceptions to the doctrine of privity could be invoked in his favour, e.g. if the contract was made through an agent acting either for him or for the other party.[399] Such agency reasoning might sometimes be artificial, but it at any rate saved the face of the doctrine of privity. A further exception has been created by the Contracts (Rights of Third Parties) Act 1999, under which third parties are, if the requirements of the Act are satisfied,[400] entitled to the benefit of exemption clauses in contracts between others.[401] But some of the cases with which the following discussion is concerned are[402] or may[403] not be covered by that

---

[396] *Brennan v Brighton BC*, *The Times*, 15 May 1997, where B was a company which had been wound-up and so could no longer sue A for breach of the contract between them.

[397] See para.22–031.

[398] Many of the cases discussed in this section concern contracts for the international carriage of goods by sea and would not be affected by the Unfair Contract Terms Act 1977 or by the Consumer Rights Act 2015; paras 7–084, 7–120. Where this legislation does apply, some would now be differently decided, or decided on other grounds.

[399] *Hall v NE Ry* (1875) L.R. 10 Q.B. 437; cf. *Barrett v Great Northern Ry* (1904) 20 T.L.R. 175; *The Kirknes* [1957] P. 51.

[400] See especially s.1(1), (2) and (3); below, paras 14–099–14–110.

[401] Contracts (Rights of Third Parties) Act 1999 s.1(6).

[402] e.g. *Adler v Dickson* [1955] 1 Q.B. 158; *Scruttons Ltd v Midland Silicones Ltd* [1962] A.C. 446; see para.14–108.

[403] For the question whether *Elder Dempster & Co v Paterson Zochonis & Co* [1924] A.C. 522 would be covered by the 1999 Act, see fn.692.

legislation; and in others it may be to the third party's advantage to rely, not on the new statutory exception, but on a common law exception,[404] since this is not limited by the provisions of the Act.[405]

**Vicarious immunity rejected.** The principle of vicarious immunity, as a means of extending the benefit of an exemption clause to a non-party, was introduced by the decision of the House of Lords in *Elder Dempster & Co v Paterson, Zochonis & Co.*[406] B agreed to carry the claimant's palm-oil from West Africa to Hull and time-chartered a ship for this purpose. The contract of carriage was evidenced by a bill of lading, the parties to which were the claimants and B; this bill exempted "the shipowners, hereinafter called the company",[407] from liability for bad stowage. The oil was damaged by bad stowage and it was held that the shipowners were protected by the exemption clause, although there was no express contract directly made between them and the claimants. One possible ground for this decision was that B (the charterer) had acted as the shipowners' agent for the purpose of making a contract between them and the claimants.[408] The inference that B had so acted appears to have been based on the ground that the exemption clause expressly referred to, and purported to protect, the shipowners; and, although this fact would no longer of itself support such an inference,[409] the agency reasoning is consistent with the doctrine of privity in that it gives rise to a contract between the claimants and the shipowners. **14–065**

A second possible ground for the decision was that the act of the claimants in presenting the goods for carriage, followed by that of the captain in accepting them for this purpose on behalf of the shipowners,[410] gave rise to what Lord Sumner called a "bailment on terms"[411] between the claimants and the shipowners, that is, to one which incorporated the exemption clause by tacit reference.[412] "Bailment on terms" is, however, unfortunately an expression with more than one possible meaning. It has been judicially interpreted to refer *either* to a bailment into which terms were incorporated by virtue of an implied contract[413] arising from the conduct of the parties, *or* to a bailment operating

[404] Section 7(1) of the Act preserves the third party's right to rely on such an exception.

[405] e.g. by ss.2 or 3: paras 14–113–14–125.

[406] [1924] A.C. 522; *The Golden Lake* [1982] 2 Lloyd's Rep. 632; *The Forum Craftsman* [1985] 1 Lloyd's Rep. 291 (especially at 295); and in *The Kapetan Markos NL (No.2)* [1987] 2 Lloyd's Rep. 321 at 331.

[407] It was admitted that these words were apt to protect the shipowners: [1923] 1 K.B. 422.

[408] *Elder Dempster & Co Ltd v Paterson Zochonis & Co Ltd* [1924] A.C. 522 at 534 (first sentence).

[409] *Cosgrove v Horsfall* (1946) 62 T.L.R. 140; *Genys v Matthews* [1965] 3 All E.R. 24; *Gore v Van der Lann* [1967] 2 Q.B. 31; for the effect of Contracts (Rights of Third Parties) Act 1999, see para.14–100.

[410] The charter being a time charter, the captain remained the shipowners' employee and took possession of the goods on the shipowners' behalf: cf. the authorities cited in fn.878.

[411] *Elder Dempster & Co v Paterson, Zochonis & Co* [1924] A.C. 522 at 564.

[412] Lord Sumner's reference ([1924] A.C. 522 and 564) to "the known and contemplated form of bill of lading" suggests the analogy of incorporation by custom or usage: para.6–080.

[413] *Pyrene Co Ltd v Scindia Navigation Co Ltd* [1954] 2 Q.B. 402 at 406 (Devlin J); *Scruttons Ltd v Midland Silicones Ltd* [1959] 2 Q.B. 171 at 187 (Diplock J); cf. *Sandeman Coprimar SA v Transitos y Transportes Integrales* [2003] EWCA Civ 113; [2003] 2 Lloyd's Rep. 172 at [62], [63]; fn.532.

irrespective of contract.[414] On the former view, the requirement of privity would be satisfied, while on the latter there would be no need to satisfy it, bailment being a relationship which can come into existence without any contract.[415] The bailment reasoning is thus again consistent with the doctrine of privity.

A third possible reason for the decision in the *Elder*, *Dempster* case is the so-called principle of vicarious immunity: this states that, where a person employs an agent to perform a contract, that agent is entitled, in performing the contract, to any immunity from liability which the contract confers on the principal.[416] Under this principle, the shipowners were protected by the exemption clause because, in carrying out the carriage *operation*, they had acted as agents for B, even though the *contract* to perform that operation was between B and the claimants. This reasoning is inconsistent with the doctrine of privity in the sense that it would enable an agent to rely by way of defence on the terms of a contract to which he was not a party; and it was rejected by the House of Lords in *Scruttons Ltd v Midland Silicones Ltd*.[417]

14–066 **The Midland Silicones case.** In that case a drum of chemicals had been shipped under a contract between shipper and carrier evidenced by a bill of lading which limited the liability of "the carrier" to $500. After the rights and duties of the shipper under this contract had passed to the claimants by transfer of the bill of lading,[418] the drum was damaged by the negligence of a firm of stevedores who had been employed by the carrier to unload the ship. The House of Lords[419] held that the stevedores could not rely on the $500 limitation of liability as they were not parties to the contract of carriage; and that the principle of vicarious immunity was not the ratio decidendi of the *Elder Dempster* case.

Nor did any of the other reasons for that decision help the stevedores. It was not possible to infer that the carrier had intended to act as agent of the stevedores for the purpose of making a contract between them and the claimants so as to give the stevedores the benefit of the limitation clause in the bill of lading, for that term limited the liability only of *the carrier* and made no reference to the stevedores,[420] nor were there any circumstances extrinsic to the bill on which an inference of agency could be based.[421] Nor did any implied contract arise between the claimants and the stevedores since the claimants had not asked the

[414] *The Pioneer Container* [1994] 2 A.C. 324 at 335, 339–340 (Lord Goff: "notwithstanding the *absence of any contract*").

[415] See para.3–168.

[416] *Elder Dempster & Co v Paterson, Zochonis & Co* [1924] A.C. 522 at 534 (second sentence), approving the view of Scrutton LJ in the Court of Appeal [1923] 1 K.B. 420 at 441–442; cf. *Mersey Shipping & Transport Co v Rea* (1925) 21 Ll. L.R. 375 at 378.

[417] [1962] A.C. 446.

[418] See now Carriage of Goods by Sea Act 1992 ss.2 and 3; paras 15–009, 15–087.

[419] Lord Denning dissenting; his dissent was based, not on the ground that the stevedores were entitled to the *benefit* of the limitation provision in the contract of carriage, but on the ground that the cargo-owners were *bound* by a similar term (para.14–079) in the contract between carrier and stevedores: see [1962] A.C. 446 at 489.

[420] *Scruttons Ltd v Midland Silicones Ltd* [1962] A.C. 446 at 466; contrast *South Australia Management Corp v Sheahan* [1995] A.L.M. 3577.

[421] For such extrinsic circumstances, see, e.g. *The Kirknes* [1957] P. 51 at 66; *Raymond Burke Motors Ltd v Mersey Docks & Harbour Co* [1986] 1 Lloyd's Rep. 155; *Texas Instruments Ltd v Nason (Europe) Ltd* [1991] 1 Lloyd's Rep. 146 at 149.

stevedores to render any services that would normally be governed by contractual terms between them.[422] The claimants had merely applied to the carrier for delivery of the drum, which had been stored in a shed rented by the carrier from the port authority; and when the process of moving the drum from that shed into the lorry sent by the claimants to collect it was carried out through the instrumentality of the stevedores, the latter regarded this as no more than "the performance of their own obligations under the contract which they had made with"[423] the carrier. The implied contract argument thus failed for want of contractual intention.[424]

The stevedores were also unable to invoke the "bailment on terms" reasoning since, in the circumstances just described, they had not been entrusted with possession of the drum so as to become bailees of it.[425] Even if they had been such bailees (e.g. if the drum had been stored in a shed owned by them) it is far from clear that the mental element requisite for the incorporation of the limitation clause into the supposed bailment would have been satisfied. There would obviously be no requirement of *contractual* intention where the bailment was a non-contractual one, but it would appear that the *consent* of the claimants and of the stevedores was a necessary condition for the incorporation of the terms of the contract of carriage into the supposed bailment;[426] and though the stevedores may be assumed to have consented to a limitation clause which could operate only in their favour,[427] there would have been nothing to show that the claimants had consented, not only to the hypothetical sub-bailment, but also to the inclusion of that clause in the sub-bailment so as to protect the stevedores.[428]

**Criticism.** The reasoning of the *Midland Silicones* case may give the appearance of being merely a technical application of the doctrine of privity;[429] but the decision also reflects a conflict of policies. On one hand, there is the view that a "self-confessed tortfeasor" should not be allowed to "shelter behind a document that is no concern of his",[430] particularly where it is not clear that the injured party has agreed to the third party's having the benefit of the contractual 14–067

[422] The mere moving of the goods from a store to a waiting lorry would not by itself normally be governed by contractual terms. See also [1962] 1 Q.B. 102 at 136.
[423] *Scruttons Ltd v Midland Silicones Ltd* [1962] A.C. 446 at 496.
[424] See para.4–027.
[425] *Scruttons Ltd v Midland Silicones Ltd* [1962] A.C. 446 at 470; *The Starsin* [2003] UKHL 12; [2004] 1 A.C. 715 at [146]. Contrast *The Rigoletto* [2000] 2 Lloyd's Rep. 532 at 540 (goods in stevedores' possession for six days before loss).
[426] See *The Pioneer Container* [1994] 2 A.C. 324 at 339–340 where Lord Goff, in discussing the "bailment on terms" explanation of the *Elder Dempster* case refers in turn to the state of mind of the shipowners ("the terms upon which the shipowners implicitly received the goods") and of the shippers ("the shippers … [having] impliedly consented" to the terms of the sub-bailment); cf. his use of the phrase "impliedly agreed" in the *The Mahkutai* [1996] A.C. 650 at 661.
[427] The requirement of the third party's consent is nevertheless significant, particularly where the term alleged to be incorporated in the bailment is one that can operate against him, e.g. an exclusive jurisdiction clause which the third party wished to contest: see *The Forum Craftsman* [1984] 2 Lloyd's Rep. 102 at 107.
[428] *Scruttons Ltd v Midland Silicones Ltd* [1962] A.C. 446 at 474.
[429] *Scruttons Ltd v Midland Silicones Ltd* [1962] A.C. 446 at 463, 473 and 494.
[430] *Wilson v Darling Island Stevedoring Co* [1956] 1 Lloyd's Rep. 349 at 359; cf. *Adler v Dickson* [1955] 1 Q.B. 158 at 187.

exemptions from and limitations of liability. On the other hand, there is force in the argument that, if the third party were not protected, there would often be an "easy way round"[431] exemption and limitation clauses; it was this argument which was originally used to support the principle of vicarious immunity.[432] In rejecting that principle, the *Midland Silicones* case severely limited the effectiveness of such clauses. A person who suffered loss or injury as a result of a negligent breach of contract generally had a remedy against someone, if only against the workman who was negligent. In practice the employer would often feel morally obliged to pay the damages awarded against his employee,[433] and might be legally liable to do so.[434] Hence employers tried to protect their servants or agents by differently worded exemption clauses, and the cases to be discussed below make it clear that they can now do so by using appropriate words.

There is no objection to this on policy grounds where the clause is itself valid[435] and constitutes a legitimate device for allocating contractual risks and the burden of insurance. The Contracts (Rights of Third Parties) Act 1999 now provides a relatively simple drafting mechanism for giving third parties the benefit of exemption and limitation clauses;[436] and some statutes which limit the liability of carriers expressly extend these limitations to the carriers' servants or agents.[437] This position is generally regarded as acceptable.[438] The doctrine of privity was never a satisfactory instrument for controlling undesirable exemption clauses,[439] and should no longer be used for this purpose now that the ability of a contracting party to exclude or restrict liability by means of such clauses is directly controlled by legislation.[440] Direct control of exemption clauses between the contracting parties is clearly preferable to indirect evasion by means of a claim against a third party whom the words of the clause seek to protect.

### *(ii) Himalaya clauses*

**14–068** Since, on balance, policy considerations support the view that a third party should, in appropriate cases, be able to take advantage of an exemption clause, the remaining question is how this result may be achieved. The most obvious

[431] *Elder Dempster & Co v Paterson, Zochonis & Co* [1923] 1 K.B. 420 at 441, approved [1924] A.C. 522 at 534.

[432] The same argument continues to be used in support of that principle: see *London Drugs Ltd v Kuehne & Nagel International Ltd* [1992] 3 S.C.R. 299 at 499.

[433] In *Adler v Dickson* [1955] 1 Q.B. 158, the employers said that they would satisfy any judgment which might be given against their servants.

[434] i.e. under an express contract to indemnify the servant or agent. The influence of this on the interpretation of a release is evident in the decision of Flaux J in *Starlight Shipping Co v Allianz Marine and Aviation Versicherungs AG* [2014] EWHC 3068 (Comm); [2014] 2 Lloyd's Rep. 579 at [51].

[435] See *The Starsin* [2003] UKHL 12; [2003] 2 W.L.R. 711; para.14–074, where this requirement was not complied with.

[436] See ss.1(1)(a) and (b) and 6(5) ("tailpiece"); para.14–099 and following, especially 14–100, 14–127; *Precis (521) v William Mercer Ltd* [2005] EWCA Civ 114; [2005] P.N.L.R. 28.

[437] e.g. Carriage of Goods by Sea Act 1971 Sch. art.4*bis* (stevedores, being independent contractors rather than agents, would not be protected under this provision).

[438] See, in Canada: *London Drugs Ltd v Kuehne & Nagel International Ltd* [1992] 3 S.C.R. 299.

[439] cf. *Mason v Uxbridge Boat Centre* [1980] 2 Lloyd's Rep. 593 at 598.

[440] See para.7–039 and following.

possibility is by drafting the clause in such a way as to extend its protection to the third party; for the decision in the *Midland Silicones* case was partly based on the fact that the clause there did not refer to the stevedores at all, but only to the carrier. At common law it would not suffice simply to say that the third party was to be protected,[441] or that he was to be deemed to be a party to the contract.[442] But a much more elaborate clause (known as a "Himalaya" clause)[443] was considered in *The Eurymedon*,[444] where it was held to be capable of protecting the third party. Our present concern is with the common law rules relating to such clauses: the effect on them of the Contracts (Rights of Third Parties) Act 1999 is considered later in this chapter.[445]

**Nature and effect.** In *The Eurymedon* a contract was made between a shipper and a carrier for the carriage of machinery from England to New Zealand. The machinery was damaged by the stevedore while it was being unloaded; and the question was whether the stevedore was protected by a time limit on the bringing of a claim in the bill of lading issued by the carrier to the shipper as evidence of the contract. The relevant clause of the bill provided that no servant or agent (including independent contractor) of the carrier was to be liable for any act or default in the course of his employment; that every limitation applicable to the carrier should be available to such persons; that for the purpose of the clause the carrier should be deemed to be acting as agent or trustee for such persons; and that they should to this extent be or be deemed to be parties to the contract. All the members of the Privy Council agreed that such third persons could be protected by an appropriately drawn clause; and a majority held that the clause in question did protect the stevedore. Lord Wilberforce said that the bill of lading "brought into existence a bargain initially unilateral but capable of becoming mutual, between the shipper and the [stevedore], made through the carrier as agent. This became a full contract when the [stevedore] performed the services by discharging the goods".[446] At this stage, a new contract arose[447] between the shipper[448] and the stevedore, separate from or collateral to the main contract of carriage, to which the stevedore was not a party. 14–069

**Possible objections.** One objection to this analysis is that stevedores (unlike carriers) might not be aware of the terms of bills of lading under which goods 14–070

441 *Cosgrove v Horsfall* (1946) 62 T.L.R. 140; *Genys v Matthews* [1965] 3 All E.R. 24. Contrast *The Hellespont Ardent* [1997] 2 Lloyd's Rep. 547 at 579, 592.

442 cf. in another context, *Taddy v Sterious* [1904] 1 Ch. 354.

443 So named after the cruise ship in *Adler v Dickson* [1955] 1 Q.B. 155.

444 [1975] A.C. 154; Reynolds 90 L.Q.R. 301; Coote 37 M.L.R. 453; Palmer [1974] J.B.L. 101, 220; Davies and Palmer [1979] J.B.L. 337. And see para.14–080.

445 See para.14–100.

446 *The Eurymedon* [1975] A.C. 154 at 167–168. It has subsequently been suggested that the contract would be regarded as "nowadays bilateral": *The Mahkutai* [1996] A.C. 650 at 664; but this description should not be understood as meaning that the contract granting the third party the limitation of or exemption from liability imposes executory obligations on the third party: see *The Starsin* [2003] UKHL 12; [2003] 1 A.C. 715 at [34], [93], [152], [153] and [196], where the contract is described as "unilateral".

447 See at fn.467.

448 It was the cargo-owner who was ultimately bound by the time limit: see para.14–080.

were carried, so that these could not amount to offers to them which they could accept by performing the services. But it is by no means unknown for contracts to come into existence by a process which cannot be strictly analysed in terms of offer and acceptance.[449] The decision should therefore be evaluated, not in terms of such analysis, but by asking two questions: (1) was there any objection on grounds of policy to extending the protection of the clause to third parties such as the stevedores?; and (2) did that extension give effect to the intention of the parties? It has already been suggested[450] that the first question should be answered in the negative, and this must have been the view even of the dissentients in *The Eurymedon*, for they accepted that a third party could be protected by an appropriately-worded clause. The second question is harder to answer but it seems unlikely that the parties at the time of contracting made any conscious distinction between the shipper's rights against the carrier and against persons employed by the carrier in the performance of the contract of carriage; while it was no doubt the stevedore's intention to perform the work of unloading the goods only under the protective terms of the bill of lading. It is submitted that the majority's interpretation of an admittedly obscure clause did give effect to the intentions and commercial expectations of the parties; and that the decision is therefore to be welcomed.

14–071 **Agency requirements?** Some difficulty with regard to Himalaya clauses arises from a much-quoted passage in Lord Reid's speech in the *Midland Silicones* case. This states a number of requirements which must be satisfied before a third party, such as a stevedore, can at common law claim the protection of terms in the contract between shipper and carrier. Our present concern is with two of these requirements: first, the clause must make it clear that the carrier had contracted as agent of the stevedore for the purpose of securing the benefit of such terms for him; and secondly, the carrier must have had "authority from the stevedore to do so, or perhaps later ratification would suffice".[451]

The first of these requirements is a question of the interpretation of the relevant term[452] and is normally satisfied simply by a declaration of agency in the Himalaya clause; but the second refers to factors extrinsic to the contract in which that clause is contained. In *The Eurymedon*, the relevant extrinsic factor was the previous connection between carrier and stevedore (as associated companies); and the reasoning of the case leaves open the possibility that, in the absence of some such previous connection, the requirement of "authority from the stevedore" would not be satisfied.

In one case it was indeed held that the lack of any such connection made it impossible to regard the carrier as the stevedore's agent for the purpose of making a contract between him and the shipper (or the owner of the goods[453]), so

[449] See *The Satanita* [1895] P. 248; affirmed sub nom. *Clarke v Dunraven* [1897] A.C. 59; para.2–077.
[450] See para.14–066.
[451] *Scruttons Ltd v Midland Silicones Ltd* [1962] A.C. 446 at 474.
[452] *The Borvigilant* [2003] EWCA Civ 935; [2003] 2 Lloyd's Rep. 520 at [17]–[33].
[453] See fn.448.

that the stevedore was not protected by virtue of the Himalaya clause.[454] But in *The New York Star*[455] the Privy Council followed *The Eurymedon* in unanimously holding that stevedores (who were regularly employed and partly owned by the carriers) were protected by virtue of a similarly-worded clause. Lord Wilberforce said that stevedores would "normally and typically" be protected by such a clause and that "their Lordships would not encourage a search for fine distinctions which would diminish the general applicability, in the light of established commercial practice, of the principle".[456] In the later Privy Council case of *The Mahkutai* Lord Goff did, indeed, say that it was "inevitable that technical points of contract and agency law will continue to be invoked" and that counsel had acted "legitimately"[457] in raising such points. But he evidently did not regard the requirement of the third party's having authorised the carrier to act on his behalf as an obstacle to the enforceability of the Himalaya clause in that case, though reliance on it failed on grounds to be discussed below.[458] Similarly, in *The Pioneer Container* the actual decision was that a third party was protected by the terms of his *own* sub-bailment from the carrier, so that he did not have to rely on the Himalaya clause;[459] but it was also said that he could have relied on that clause.[460] In both these cases, *The Eurymedon* and *The New York Star* were discussed with evident approval and with no direct reference to or emphasis on the special circumstances[461] of those cases; nor was there evidence of extrinsic circumstances from which previous authorisation could be inferred in *The Pioneer Container* and *The Mahkutai*. Moreover, while there are no doubt good reasons for requiring such previous authorisation where the contract arising by virtue of the Himalaya clause can impose obligations on the third party, it is hard to see what practical grounds there are for such a requirement where the only effect of that contract can be to *benefit* that party (by excluding his liability) and where that contract cannot, by reason of its nature as a unilateral contract,[462] impose any obligations on him. And even where the common law requirement of previous authorisation is not satisfied, the stevedore or other third party will "in the majority of cases"[463] be able to ratify the carrier's act and so by virtue of the

[454] *The Suleyman Stalskiy* [1976] 2 Lloyd's Rep. 609; cf. *Southern Water Authority v Carey* [1985] 2 All E.R. 1077 at 1085.
[455] [1981] 1 W.L.R. 138; Reynolds 96 L.Q.R. 506; Coote [1981] C.L.J. 13; Rose 44 M.L.R. 336. The reasoning of *The Eurymedon* was also approved in *The Starsin* [2003] UKHL 12; [2003] 1 A.C. 715, though in that case the third party was, for the reason given at para.14–074, not protected by the clause.
[456] *The New York Star* [1981] 1 W.L.R. 138 at 144; cf. *The Borvigilant* [2003] EWCA Civ 935; [2003] 2 Lloyd's Rep. 520 at [57].
[457] *The Mahkutai* [1996] A.C. 650 at 664.
[458] See para.14–073.
[459] See para.14–081.
[460] *The Pioneer Container* [1994] 2 A.C. 324 at 344.
[461] i.e. to the fact that stevedores and carriers were associated companies; cf. *Godina v Patrick Operations Ltd* [1984] 2 Lloyd's Rep. 333; *The Zinnia* [1984] 2 Lloyd's Rep. 211 at 217.
[462] See at fn.446.
[463] *The Mahkutai* [1996] A.C. 650 at 664 (Lord Goff). The phrase "in the majority of cases" is not amplified. It could refer to the requirement in the law relating to ratification that the stevedoring company must have been in *existence* when the carrier purported to act as its agent by issuing the bill of lading containing the Himalaya clause: for this requirement see para.16–055.

Himalaya clause gain the protection of the exemptions from and limitations of liability available under the main contract of carriage to the carrier.

14–072 **Scope.** The scope of the Himalaya clause depends on its interpretation; and since typically such a clause is expressed to protect the third party only while he is engaged in the performance of the contract in which the clause is contained, he will not be protected by the clause in such terms, if he damages the goods before performance of that contract has begun[464] or after such performance has been completed.[465] At common law, the part of the typical Himalaya clause which purports to exclude or limit the third party's liability cannot *itself* produce the desired effect.[466] This can follow only from the separate contract[467] which arises or may arise from the agency provision of such a clause followed by the conduct of the third party and the injured party in relation to each other; the effect of this contract may be to extend to the third party the protection of, not only the Himalaya clause itself, but also *other* terms of the contract in which that clause is contained. Two further questions can therefore arise.

14–073 **Interpretation of the Himalaya clause.** The first is whether the provision which the third party seeks to invoke is covered by the wording of the Himalaya clause. This question arose in *The Mahkutai*[468] where such a clause in a bill of lading provided that sub-contracting carriers were to have the benefit of "all exceptions, limitations, provisions and liberties herein". It was held that these words did not entitle the sub-contractors to rely on an exclusive jurisdiction clause in the bill of lading, since they referred only to those provisions in it which benefited *one* of the parties to it, while the exclusive jurisdiction clause was a "mutual agreement" creating "mutual obligations".[469]

14–074 **Interpretation and validity of the provision covered by the Himalaya clause.** The second question is whether the terms of the clause, or of other provisions in the main contract to which it refers, do indeed protect the third party. The answer to this question depends on the rules relating to the interpretation and effectiveness of exemption clauses generally. These are discussed in Ch.7; here it is necessary only to make the point that the third party would not be protected by a clause which, on its true interpretation, would not apply in the events which have happened or cover the loss which has occurred, or by a clause which was legally invalid.[470] The latter possibility is illustrated by *The Starsin*,[471] where goods were damaged whilst being carried in a chartered ship under a bill of

[464] *Raymond Burke Motors Ltd v Mersey Docks & Harbour Co* [1986] 1 Lloyd's Rep. 155; cf. *The Rigoletto* [2000] 2 Lloyd's Rep. 532 at 545, 547.

[465] This is implicit in the reasoning of *The New York Star* [1981] 1 W.L.R. 138, where the actual decision was that at the relevant time such performance had *not* been completed.

[466] See at fn.447.

[467] *The Starsin* [2003] UKHC 12; [2003] 1 A.C. 715 at [59] (dissenting, but not on this point), [93].

[468] [1996] A.C. 650.

[469] *The Mahkutai* [1996] A.C. 650 at 666; followed on this point in *Bouygues Offshore SA v Caspian Shipping Co (No.2)* [1997] 2 Lloyd's Rep. 485 at 490.

[470] e.g. *Eisen and Metall AG v Ceres Stevedoring Co Ltd* [1977] 1 Lloyd's Rep. 665.

[471] [2003] UKHL 12; [2004] 1 A.C. 715.

lading constituting a contract between charterer and shipper.[472] The benefit of a Himalaya clause in the bill of lading was claimed by the shipowner who was not a party to the contract of carriage and who relied on words in the clause exempting him from "any liability whatsoever to the shipper" for loss resulting from acts done by the shipowner in the course of his employment by the carrier (i.e. in this case the charterer).[473] The clause also provided that the shipowner was (to the extent to which it protected him) to be deemed to be a party to the bill of lading contract;[474] and another term of that contract[475] incorporated into it an international Convention known as the Hague Rules. These rules specify certain obligations of a carrier of goods by sea, make available to him certain exemptions from and limitations of liability, and provide that any clause in the contract "lessening such liability otherwise than as provided in this Convention shall be null and void."[476] The House of Lords held[477] that this provision of the Rules invalidated the wide words of exclusion quoted above, so that the shipowner was not protected by them.

**Terms of any express contract will prevail.** The cases on the effect of a Himalaya clause assume that the third party seeking to invoke it is not in any contractual relationship with the claimant except for the collateral contract which may arise by virtue of such a clause. Where there is also an express contract between these parties on terms inconsistent with those of any such collateral contract, then the terms of that express contract will prevail, e.g. where a stevedore enters into an express contract with the cargo-owner making him liable to the cargo-owner for negligence but the bill of lading contains a Himalaya clause the effect of which would (if there were no such express contract) be to exonerate the stevedore from such liability.[478] 14–075

**Defect in the main contract.** In *The Eurymedon*[479] the Himalaya clause in the contract between shipper and carrier gave rise to a separate contract between shipper and stevedore collateral to the main contract of carriage.[480] This collateral contract has what may be called certain parasitic qualities so that it may fail to protect the third party, at least in certain cases, where the main contract suffers from some legal defect. Thus in a South African case,[481] in which the relations of 14–076

---

472 In this respect, the case resembles the *Elder Dempster* case [1924] A.C. 522; para.14–065.

473 cl.5(1) of the bill of lading, in the numbering given by Lord Bingham in *The Starsin* [2003] UKHL 12; [2004] 1 A.C. 715 at [20].

474 cl.5(3), in the same numbering.

475 cl.2: see *The Starsin* [2003] UKHL 12; [2004] 1 A.C. 715 at [31].

476 art.III.8: see now the Hague Visby Rules art.III.8, which have the force of law by virtue of Carriage of Goods by Sea Act 1971 s.1 and Sch.

477 Lord Steyn dissenting. Lord Hobhouse took the view that the contract between shipper and shipowner created by virtue of the Himalaya clause was a "contract of carriage within the Rules": see at [153], [156]; but this view is rejected by Lord Millett at [203] and does not seem to be adopted by Lord Bingham or Lord Hoffmann: Peel 120 L.Q.R. 11. See also: *The Marielle Bolten* [2009] EWHC 2552 (Comm); [2010] 1 Lloyd's Rep. 648 at [32]–[42].

478 *The Rigoletto* [2000] 2 Lloyd's Rep. 532.

479 [1975] A.C. 154.

480 See at fnn.447, 467.

481 *Bouygues Offshore v Ultisol Transport Contractors* [1996] 2 Lloyd's Rep. 153, Note.

the parties were governed by English law,[482] the main contract between A and B contained a Himalaya clause by virtue of which C was prima facie entitled to the benefits of the exemptions from liability which the main contract conferred on B. The main contract was rescinded by A on account of B's misrepresentations and it was held that the Himalaya clause did not entitle C to the protection of the exemption clauses in the main contract since "once those ... exemptions ... fall away on rescission of the [main contract], nothing remains to exempt [C]".[483] This was so even though the Himalaya clause had given rise to a "separate contract" between A and C, since under the terms of that contract C took only "the benefits of the same exemptions which the carrier [B] receives, no more and no less".[484]

It is an essential part of this reasoning that the effect of misrepresentation on a contract is to "wipe it out altogether"[485] with retrospective effect. The position would be the same where the main contract was void for mistake at common law. On the other hand, the reasoning would not apply where the main contract was terminated for B's breach, since this process brings the contract to an end only from the time of termination[486] and therefore does not deprive the guilty party of the protection of exemption and limitation clauses in respect of breaches occurring before such termination;[487] consequently, it would not deprive the third party of this benefit where he was otherwise entitled to it by virtue of a Himalaya clause. If the main contract were frustrated, the third party would likewise be deprived of its protection by virtue of such a clause only in respect of breaches of duty which had occurred after, and not in respect of those which had occurred before the frustrating event: this follows from the principle that frustration discharges the contract only from the time of the frustrating event.[488] The most difficult cases would be those in which the main contract was affected by illegality. The source of the difficulty is that the effects of illegality vary widely;[489] and that the illegality of the main contract does not necessarily affect the validity of a collateral contract.[490] The guiding principle, it is submitted, should be that the illegality which affects the main contract should deprive the third party of the protection of the collateral contract which arises by virtue of the Himalaya clause only where such a result would in some way promote the policy of the rule of law, the violation of which had given rise to the illegality. No doubt in applying this principle the court would have regard not only to the nature of the illegality but also to the third party's knowledge of or participation in the illegal purpose.[491]

---

[482] *Bouygues Offshore v Ultisol Transport Contractors* [1996] 2 Lloyd's Rep. 153 at 154, 155.

[483] *Bouygues Offshore v Ultisol Transport Contractors* [1996] 2 Lloyd's Rep. 153 at 165.

[484] *Bouygues Offshore v Ultisol Transport Contractors* [1996] 2 Lloyd's Rep. 153 at 165. For a similar restriction on the third party's right to rely on exemption clauses under Contracts (Rights of Third Parties) Act 1999, see s.3(6) of that Act (para.14–125).

[485] *The Kanchenjunga* [1990] 1 Lloyd's Rep. 391 at 398; para.9–097.

[486] See para.18–017.

[487] See para.7–027.

[488] See para.19–097.

[489] See paras 11–062–11–087.

[490] See para.11–107.

[491] cf. para.11–068.

### (iii) Other drafting devices

**Promise not to sue, etc.** The third party could also be protected by a form of words other than that used in *The Eurymedon*. For example, an exemption clause in a contract between A and B may contain an express promise by A to B not to sue C. Under the rules already considered, B can, even at common law, enforce that promise by getting a stay of any action by A against C,[492] e.g. if there is a contract between B and C under which B is bound to indemnify C against liability to third parties incurred in the performance of his duties under that contract.[493] Alternatively, the contract between A and B might provide that A should be liable to pay over to B any sum that A might recover from C.[494] 14–077

### (iv) Clauses defining duties

**Restricting any duty of care.** The preceding discussion is based on the assumptions that C is under a prima facie liability in tort to A and that C seeks to rely on a provision in a contract between A and B in order to exclude or restrict the liability. But it is arguable that the terms of that contract can be relevant at an earlier stage, namely in determining the extent of any duty of care owed to A by C. For example, work under a building contract between A and B may be done by a sub-contractor (C), who is a party to the sub-contract between himself and B, but not a party to B's main contract with A. If C does the work negligently and so causes harm to A (e.g. by damaging other property belonging to A),[495] then C may be liable in tort to A, and an exemption clause in the main contract between A and B will not, as such, at common law protect C. But in the *Junior Books* case, Lord Roskill suggested that a "relevant exclusion clause in the main contract" might "limit the duty of care"[496] of C and so indirectly provide him with a defence to a claim in tort by A.[497] This suggestion has been followed in a number of later cases in which exemption clauses in the main contract between A and B have been held to negative any duty of care which C might (but for such clauses) have owed to A.[498] It has, however, been held that not only must A have assented to the clause, but C must also have known about it, before commencing work.[499] 14–078

---

[492] *Snelling v John G Snelling Ltd* [1973] 1 Q.B. 87; para.14–022.

[493] See *Gore v Van der Lann* [1967] 2 Q.B. 31; para.14–022; *The Elbe Maru* [1978] 1 Lloyds's Rep. 206. For the purpose of enforcement of such a covenant, it suffices that C has a claim for such an indemnity which is not "obviously bad": *Deepak Fertilisers & Petrochemicals Corp v ICI Chemicals & Polymers Ltd* [1999] 1 Lloyd's Rep. 378 at 401. Contrast *The Chevalier Roze* [1983] 2 Lloyd's Rep. 438 (where the contract between A and B had been fully performed before A's cause of action against C arose, and so did not protect C).

[494] For further possible devices, see *Scruttons Ltd v Midland Silicones Ltd* [1962] A.C. 446 at 473 and Hamson [1959] C.L.J. 150.

[495] In this respect the facts of the example given in the text differ from those of the *Junior Books* case [1983] 1 A.C. 520 and so do not give rise to the difficulties occasioned by that case (see para.14–055).

[496] *Junior Books Ltd v Veitchi Co Ltd* [1983] 1 A.C. 520 at 546, applied in *Southern Water Authority v Carey* [1985] 2 All E.R. 1077 at 1086.

[497] In *The Aliakmon* [1986] A.C. 785 at 817 this suggestion was doubted by Lord Brandon, but his own view was later questioned in *Pacific Associates Inc v Baxter* [1990] 1 Q.B. 993 at 1022.

[498] *Southern Water Authority v Carey* [1985] 2 All E.R. 1077; *Norwich CC v Harvey* [1989] 1 W.L.R. 828; *Pacific Associates Inc v Baxter* [1990] 1 Q.B. 993; Adams and Brownsword [1990] J.B.L. 23.

[499] *Precis (521) v William Mercer Ltd* [2005] EWCA Civ 114; [2005] P.N.L.R. 28 at [25].

In such cases, C is protected, in spite of the absence of privity of contract,[500] because the clause "destroys the duty of [C] if duty there ever was".[501] It follows that the clause may be available not only to C, but also to any other person whose hypothetical duty is in this way affected. It may thus protect C's employees as well as C himself: in one case of this kind it was said that if C owed no duty "then neither can any of their employees have done so".[502] Whether a clause affects the duty of persons other than C depends simply on its interpretation and not on the doctrine of privity.

Lord Roskill's statement refers only to "a *relevant* exclusion clause": that is, to one which can "limit *the duty of care*". A clause which merely imposed a financial limit on the *amount recoverable* would not be of this kind since such a clause would come into operation only on the assumption that a duty was owed and had been broken.[503] Similarly, the clause must refer to the duty of the person relying on it: thus if a contract between a building owner and a contractor contained a provision restricting the duty of sub-contractors *nominated* by the owner, that provision would not protect *other* sub-contractors (who had not been so nominated).[504]

## (b) The burden

### (i) *General rule*

14–079 **Non-party to contract not bound by exemption clause.** The law starts with the principle that a person is not bound by an exemption clause in a contract to which he is not a party, unless one of the recognised exceptions to the doctrine of privity (such as agency) can be invoked against him.[505] In the *Midland Silicones* case[506] the contract between the carrier and the stevedore provided that the stevedore should have "such protection as is afforded by the terms of the bill of lading". The owners of the drum nonetheless recovered full damages from the stevedore. They were not bound by what was, in effect, a limitation clause in the contract between the stevedore and the carrier.[507] Similarly, in *The Aliakmon*[508] the buyers were not bound by exemption provisions in the contract of carriage since the only parties to that contract were the sellers and the shipowners.[509] The general rule may be unsatisfactory in practice, and is therefore subject to a number of exceptions.

500 *Norwich CC v Harvey* [1989] 1 W.L.R. 828 at 837.

501 *Pacific Associates Inc v Baxter* [1990] 1 Q.B. 993 at 1038.

502 *Norwich CC v Harvey* [1989] 1 W.L.R. 828 at 834.

503 cf. para.14–082.

504 *British Telecommunications Plc v James Thomson & Sons (Engineering) Ltd* [1999] 2 All E.R. 241.

505 *Delaurier v Wyllie* (1889) 17 R. (Ct. of Sess.) 167: cf. *The Kite* [1933] P. 164; *White v Warwick (John) & Co Ltd* [1953] 2 W.L.R. 1285 at 1294.

506 *Scruttons Ltd v Midland Silicones Ltd* [1962] A.C. 446; para.14–066.

507 *Scruttons Ltd v Midland Silicones Ltd* [1962] A.C. 446.

508 [1986] A.C. 785; para.14–056.

509 Paradoxically, it was the buyers who argued (unsuccessfully) that they *were* bound, their object being to establish that the undesirable consequence of depriving the shipowners of the benefit of those provisions (see para.14–056) would not follow if the shipowners were held liable to them in tort.

### (ii) *Exceptions*

**Agency or implied contract.** The first such exception is illustrated by *Pyrene Co Ltd v Scindia Navigation Co Ltd*,[510] where a fire tender which had been sold for export was to be shipped under a contract between buyer and carrier, which limited the latter's liability. The seller presented the tender for loading to the carrier who, in carrying out this operation, damaged the tender while it was still at the seller's risk. It was held that the seller was bound by the limitation clause. The decision was partly based on the doubts which had been expressed in earlier cases as to the existence of the doctrine of privity.[511] It can no longer be supported on this ground; nor is the seller's tort claim against the carrier in such a case adversely affected by the Contracts (Rights of Third Parties) Act 1999, since under this Act a person will not, in general, be *bound* by terms of a contract to which he is not a party. But the *Pyrene* case can still be justified either on the ground that the buyer was the seller's agent in making the contract with the carrier, at least so far as it concerned the seller;[512] or on the ground that an implied contract incorporating the limitation clause arose between seller and carrier when the tender was presented by the seller and accepted by the carrier for loading. The latter explanation is the one now generally accepted[513] though it is not entirely free from difficulty since the carrier may at this stage have intended merely to perform his contract of carriage with the buyer and so have lacked the contractual intention necessary for the creation of a new contract.[514] 14–080

Implied contract reasoning was also used in *The Eurymedon*,[515] to deal with the point that the action against the stevedore was brought, not by the shipper, but by the consignee (i.e the person to whom the machinery was to be delivered), who (it was assumed) was not a party to the contract of carriage contained or evidenced in the bill of lading.[516] It was held that the consignee was nevertheless bound by the exclusion clause in that contract since an implied contract arose[517] between stevedore and consignee, as a result of the consignee's "acceptance of [the bill of lading] and request for delivery of the goods thereunder";[518] and this implied contract incorporated the terms of the bill of lading (which protected the stevedore).[519] In the *Midland Silicones* case,[520] by contrast, there was no implied contract between the claimants and the stevedore incorporating the terms of the

---

[510] [1954] 2 Q.B. 402.

[511] *Pyrene Co Ltd v Scindia Navigation Co Ltd* [1954] 2 Q.B. 402 at 426; and see para.14–015.

[512] See *Pyrene Co Ltd v Scindia Navigation Co Ltd* [1954] 2 Q.B. 402 at 423–425; *The Kite* [1933] P. 164 at 181 ("limited authority").

[513] *Scruttons Ltd v Midland Silicones Ltd* [1962] A.C. 446 at 471; *The Kapetan Markos NL (No.2)* [1987] 2 Lloyd's Rep. 321 at 331; *The Captain Gregos (No.2)* [1990] 2 Lloyd's Rep. 395 (claim by B.P.).

[514] cf. para.4–027.

[515] [1975] A.C. 154.

[516] It was assumed that the consignee had not become a party to the contract under Bills of Lading Act 1855 s.1 since it was not clear that the requirements of the section had been satisfied. See now Carriage of Goods by Sea Act 1992 s.2; paras 15–009, 15–087.

[517] On the analogy of *Brandt v Liverpool, etc. SN Co Ltd* [1924] 1 K.B. 575.

[518] *The Eurymedon* [1975] A.C. 154 at 168.

[519] See para.14–069.

[520] *Scruttons Ltd v Midland Silicones Ltd* [1962] A.C. 446; para.14–066.

contract between the carrier and the stevedore. The case differs from *The Eurymedon* in that there the consignees had possession of the bill of lading and so knew, or at least had means of knowing, its terms, while in the *Midland Silicones* case there was nothing to indicate that the claimants knew anything about the contract between the carrier and the stevedore.[521] The implied contract argument may also fail on other grounds. In *The Aliakmon* the buyers had presented a bill of lading to which they were not parties, and took delivery of the goods; but no implied contract arose since they had done these acts purely as agents of the sellers.[522]

Where an injured party is bound by the exemption clause in a contract between two others by virtue of agency or implied contract reasoning, the legal basis for his being so bound is not in doubt: it is that he is brought into a contractual relationship with the party relying on the clause. There are, however, a number of further grounds on which the injured party may be bound by an exemption clause in a contract to which he is not a party in spite of the fact that he has not come into any contractual relationship with the person relying on the clause; and it is with these grounds that the following discussion is concerned.

14–081 **Bailment on terms.** One such ground is that the injured party is so bound by virtue of a bailment on terms. Earlier in this chapter, we saw that this concept could be invoked to enable a person to get the *benefit* of an exemption clause in a contract to which he was not a party.[523] Our present concern is with the use of the concept for the converse purpose of *binding* a person by such a clause in a contract between others. This possibility is illustrated by the case in which a customer sends goods to a cleaner or repairer and allows him to send the work out to a sub-contractor. If the sub-contract contains an exemption clause, the owner may be bound by it on the ground that he has "expressly or impliedly consented to the bailee making a sub-bailment containing those conditions, but not otherwise".[524] The same principle was applied in *The Pioneer Container*[525] where C had entered into a contract with B for the carriage of C's goods on terms which authorised B to sub-contract "on any terms". B did enter into a sub-contract with A (another carrier) on terms containing an exclusive jurisdiction clause and it was held that C was bound by this clause. Lord Goff said that the effect of the clause on C did "not depend for its efficacy either on the doctrine of privity of contract or on the doctrine of consideration";[526] in other words, C was bound by it

[521] *Scruttons Ltd v Midland Silicones Ltd* [1962] A.C. 446 at 467, 493.

[522] *The Aliakmon* [1986] A.C. 785 at 808; this fact was known to the carrier: see [1985] Q.B. 350 at 364.

[523] *Elder Dempster & Co v Paterson, Zochonis & Co* [1924] A.C. 522 at 564; para.14–065.

[524] *Morris v CW Martin & Sons Ltd* [1966] 1 Q.B. 716 at 729; cf. [1966] 1 Q.B. 716 at 741; *Port Swettenham Authority v TW Wu & Co* [1979] A.C. 580; Palmer [1988] L.M.C.L.Q. 466.

[525] [1994] 2 A.C. 324; *Johnson Matthey & Co v Constantine Terminals Ltd* [1976] 2 Lloyd's Rep. 215; *The Gudermes* [1993] 1 Lloyd's Rep. 311 at 328; *Sonicare International Ltd v EAFT Ltd* [1997] 2 Lloyd's Rep. 48; Coote [1977] C.L.J. 177; *East West Corp v DKBS 1912* [2003] EWCA Civ 83; [2003] Q.B. 1509 at [30], [69]; *The Starsin* [2003] UKHL 12; [2004] 1 A.C. 715 at [133]–[136]; *Scottish & Newcastle International Ltd v Othon Ghalanos Ltd* [2008] UKHL 11; [2008] 1 Lloyd's Rep. 462 at [47]; cf. *The Agia Skepi* [1992] 2 Lloyd's Rep. 467 at 472; *The Termagent* (1914) 1 Com. Cas. 239, where no consent to the sub-bailment had been given.

[526] *The Pioneer Container* [1994] 2 A.C. 324 at 339.

irrespective of contract.[527] He was bound under the law of bailment, because he had consented to the making of the sub-bailment by B to A and to the terms of that sub-bailment. C's consent to those terms was thus essential;[528] though no doubt the law will here (as elsewhere) apply an objective test, so that C may be bound by terms of the sub-bailment, even though he has not actually consented to them, if he has conducted himself in such a way as to induce A to believe that he has so consented.[529] The principle of such cases is, however, confined to situations in which there is a relationship of bailor and bailee (or sub-bailee) between the claimant and the defendant. In *The Aliakmon*, the exception did not apply as no such relationship there existed between the *buyers* and the shipowners: "The only bailment of the goods was one by the sellers to the shipowners".[530] Similarly, in the *Midland Silicones* case the present exception did not apply since, for the reasons given earlier in this chapter,[531] the stevedore was not a bailee of the drum.[532]

Where the present exception does apply, the head bailor, C, is bound by an exemption clause in the sub-bailment between the head bailee, B, and the sub-bailee, A, in spite of the fact that there is no contract between A and C. Some legal basis other than contract must therefore be found to explain this result. One view is that C is bound simply because he consented to the inclusion of the term in the contract between B and A.[533] But if this were the reason for the exception, then it would not be restricted, as on the authorities it is,[534] to cases of bailment. The reason for the restriction appears to be that (in cases of the present kind) C has consented, not only to the terms of the contract between B and A, but also to the creation of the very relationship of bailor and sub-bailee between C and A which is the sole source of the duty alleged to be owed by A to C and to have been broken.[535] It follows that the exception does not apply where C does not

---

527 C may be bound by reason *both* of a bailment on terms *and* of a contract between C and A made through the agency of B: see *Sandeman Coprimar SA v Transitos y Transportes Integrales SL* [2003] EWCA Civ 113; [2003] 2 Lloyd's Rep. 172 at [62], [63]. See also *East West Corp v DKBS 1912* [2003] EWCA Civ 83; [2003] Q.B. 1509 at [24], [69].

528 *The Pioneer Container* [1994] 2 A.C. 324 at 340–342, rejecting the view expressed by Donaldson J in *Johnson Matthey & Co v Constantine Terminals Ltd* [1976] 2 Lloyd's Rep. 215 at 221.

529 See Lord Goff's reference in *The Pioneer Container* [1994] 2 A.C. 324 at 342 to ostensible authority.

530 *The Aliakmon* [1986] A.C. 785 at 818; cf. *Swiss Bank Corp v Brink's-Mat Ltd* [1986] 2 Lloyd's Rep. 79 at 98; *The Captain Gregos (No.2)* [1990] 2 Lloyd's Rep. 395 (claim by PEAG), but the same case shows that a bailment incorporating the terms of the contract can arise by subsequent attornment of the carrier to the buyer (claim by B.P.). On the question whether a bailment relationship can arise between a carrier and a buyer of goods who is not an original party to the contract of carriage, see also *The Kapetan Markos NL (No.2)* [1987] 2 Lloyd's Rep. 321, where it was said at 332 that the existence of such a relationship was "not seriously disputed"; and *Sonicare International Ltd v EAFT* [1997] 2 Lloyd's Rep. 48 at 53.

531 See para.14–066.

532 *Scruttons Ltd v Midland Silicones Ltd* [1962] A.C. 446 at 470.

533 This appears to have been the view of Denning LJ in *Morris v CW Martin Ltd* [1966] 1 Q.B. 716 at 729 and in his dissenting speech in *Scruttons Ltd v Midland Silicones Ltd* [1962] A.C. 446 at 491.

534 See *Scruttons Ltd v Midland Silicones Ltd* [1962] A.C. 446 and the authorities cited in fn.524; and *The Mahkutai* [1996] A.C. 650 and fn.535.

535 See *The Pioneer Container* [1994] 2 A.C. 324 at 336; *The Starsin* [2003] UKHL 12; [2004] 1 A.C. 715 at [136]. The view that the exception may extend beyond cases of bailment derives some support from an obiter dictum in *Henderson v Merrett Syndicates Ltd* [1995] 2 A.C. 145 at 196; and is also

need to rely on the bailment to establish that A owed him a duty of care. This would be the position, not only where A was never a bailee of C's goods at all (as in the *Midland Silicones* case), but also where A was such a bailee and C's loss resulted, not from A's breach of his custodial duty as bailee, but from A's conduct causing damage to C's goods in breach of a duty which had arisen quite apart from the bailment, "simply by virtue of A's proximity to the goods".[536]

14–082 **Clauses defining duties.** A distinction must here (as elsewhere)[537] be drawn between exemption clauses and clauses which define a party's duty. Clauses of the latter kind can adversely affect a claimant even though they are contained in a contract to which he is not a party. Breach of that contract may amount also to breach of a duty of care owed to a third party, giving that third party a remedy in tort[538] and the terms of the contract can be relevant to the scope of that duty of care. For example, where work in pursuance of a building contract between C and B is done by A under a roofing sub-contract between B and A, the terms of the latter contract would clearly determine the type of work to be done by A.[539] If the sub-contract merely required A to tile the roof he would not be liable in tort to C on the ground that the main contract required the roof to be tiled and felted, or even on the ground that tiling and felting was standard practice for the type of building in question. It would not, in such a case, be "unfair"[540] to C to deprive him of a right in tort against A by a term in a contract over which C had no control; for C would not (even if B were authorised to sub-contract the work) be precluded from recovering damages for breach of contract from B if the work done by A was not in conformity with the contract between C and B.[541] Different reasoning would apply to a clause in the sub-contract which merely limited A's liability (e.g. to the cost of replacing defective tiles). Such a clause would not be relevant to the definition of A's duty to C in tort since it would not define what A had to do, but merely specify the legal consequences of failing to do it.[542] Hence such a clause would as a general rule[543] not bind C contractually, since he was not a party to the contract in which it was contained.

14–083 **Comparison with the 1999 Act.** Under the Contracts (Rights of Third Parties) Act 1999 a third party C is, in circumstances to be discussed later in this

---

supported by Toulson J in *Lukoil-Kalingradmorneft Plc v Tata Ltd* [1999] 1 Lloyd's Rep. 365 at 375; affirmed [1999] 2 Lloyd's Rep. 129, without reference to this point.

536 *The Kapetan Markos NL (No.2)* [1987] 2 Lloyd's Rep. 321 at 340; cf. *Johnson Matthey & Co v Constantine Terminals Ltd* [1976] 2 Lloyd's Rep. 215 at 222.

537 See paras 7–014, 14–078.

538 See paras 14–050—14–059.

539 *Junior Books Ltd v Veitchi Co Ltd* [1983] 1 A.C. 520 at 534; cf. *Simaan General Contracting Co v Pilkington Glass Ltd (No.2)* [1988] Q.B. 758 at 782–783.

540 *Junior Books Ltd v Veitchi Co Ltd* [1983] 1 A.C. 520 at 534, discussing a sale of goods example.

541 See para.17–012.

542 See *The Aliakmon* where the contract incorporated the Hague Rules which contained an intricate set of provisions, some of which defined duties while others provided immunities and limitations; taken together, these could not be "synthesised into a standard of care": [1985] Q.B. 350 at 368; approved [1986] A.C. 785 at 818; cf. *Twins Transport Ltd v Patrick Brocklehurst* (1983) 25 Build. L.R. 65.

543 But see the other exceptions already considered in this part.

chapter,[544] entitled to enforce a term in a contract between two others; but his right to do so is, in general, subject to defences which would have been available to the promisor A if the proceedings to enforce the term had been brought by the promisee B.[545] If, for example, a contract between A and B contained: (1) a promise by A to B to render some service to C; and (2) a term excluding or limiting A's liability for specified breaches, then, in an action by C under the 1999 Act to enforce the first of these terms, A would be entitled to rely on the second. In such a case, C's right, being derived from B's right, is subject to the restrictions which govern the latter right.[546] This statutory rule, however, applies only where C's claim against A is one to enforce a term of the contract between A and B under the 1999 Act. It does not apply where C's claim is not derived from that contract but arises independently of it and is made apart from the Act. This was the position in most of the cases with which the preceding discussion has been concerned. In them, the claim made by C against A was typically one in tort, and it was argued that C's right to sue A in tort was excluded or limited by the terms of a contract between A and B. That contract was not, in such cases, the basis of C's claim against A, but (at most) part of the history or chain of events giving rise to the circumstances in which A owed (or was alleged to owe) a duty of care to C. The 1999 Act expressly states that such common law claims are not to be affected by its provisions.[547]

**"Transferred loss".** A more controversial way in which a person might, at common law, be adversely affected by an exemption clause in a contract to which he is not a party has been said to arise under the so-called "principle of transferred loss".[548] The principle was, so far as English law is concerned, first stated by Robert Goff LJ (as he then was) in *The Aliakmon*. It is said to apply where A, in breach of a duty of care in tort, causes physical damage to B's property but can reasonably foresee that the loss will fall on C, e.g. because B has sold the property to C and the risk under that contract has passed to C. The effect of the doctrine is then said to be that "C will be entitled, *subject to the terms of any contract restricting A's liability to B*, to bring an action in tort against A in respect of such loss or damage to the extent to which it falls upon him".[549] In *The Aliakmon* itself[550] the effect of the principle, on the assumption that the damage was due to the negligence of A,[551] would, in Robert Goff LJ's view, have been that C would have acquired a tort claim against A, and that this claim would have been subject to any terms in the bill of lading contract between A and B which restricted or excluded A's liability to B under that contract. But when the case reached the House of Lords, Lord Brandon[552] described the principle as "not only 14–084

[544] See para.14–099 and following.

[545] 1999 Act s.3(2); para.14–122.

[546] cf. Law Com. No.242, para.10.24.

[547] 1999 Act s.7(1); para.14–129.

[548] *The Aliakmon* [1986] A.C. 785 at 820; *White v Jones* [1995] 2 A.C. 207 at 264; Unberath, *Transferred Loss: Claiming Third Party Loss in Contract Law* (2003).

[549] *The Aliakmon* [1985] Q.B. 350 at 399 (emphasis added).

[550] See para.14–055.

[551] In fact A was found to owe no duty of care to C: see para.14–055.

[552] With whom all the other members of the House agreed.

unsupported by authority, but ... on the contrary inconsistent with it"[553] and declared himself unwilling to introduce it into English law.

A more favourable view of the principle of transferred loss was taken by Lord Goff in *White v Jones*,[554] the "disappointed beneficiary" case discussed earlier in this chapter.[555] The actual decision in that case could not, indeed, be based on the principle since the solicitor's breach of duty had not caused any loss to his client;[556] but the analogy between cases covered by the principle and the facts of *White v Jones* was said to be "very close".[557] One point of resemblance between them is that, in Lord Goff's view, the solicitor's tort liability to an intended beneficiary would be "subject to any term of the contract between the solicitor and the testator which may exclude or restrict the solicitor's liability to the testator ... ".[558] The fact that there is no support in the speeches of other members of the majority in *White v Jones* for this restriction on the beneficiary's tort claim[559] may be explicable on the ground that the restriction would be based on terms of a contract to which the beneficiary was not a party, to which he had not consented and which he had not authorised; for the principle of transferred loss, as formulated above, does not contain any requirement that C should have consented to or authorised the exemption or limitation clauses in the contract between A and B. This position may be contrasted with the requirement of such consent which has been stated in a number of other contexts in which a person is or may be bound at common law by an exemption clause in a contract to which he is not a party: for example, in the sub-bailment cases discussed above.[560] If the principle of transferred loss were to be accepted in English law, and if rights of a third party arising under it could be excluded or restricted by the terms of a contract between others, further judicial consideration would have to be given to the question whether there should, for the purpose of binding the third party by such terms, be a requirement of his authorisation of or consent to them. One possible view is that the bailment and other cases, in which such a requirement seems now to be firmly established, should be followed by analogy in cases in which the third party's right (if any) arose under the principle of transferred loss. The alternative view is that in those other cases the third party has an independent tort claim, of which he should not be deprived by terms of a contract over which he had no control, while a third party who relied on the principle of transferred loss would assert what is, in effect, a derivative claim which, in its nature, should not be more extensive than the claim of the person from whom it is derived.

[553] *The Aliakmon* [1986] A.C. 785 at 820.

[554] [1995] 2 A.C. 207 at 264–265. In *Alfred McAlpine Construction Ltd v Panatown Ltd* [2001] 1 A.C. 518 at 529, the principle is referred to with apparent approval and, with some misgivings, by Lord Goff (dissenting) at 557, citing Unberath 115 L.Q.R. 535.

[555] See para.14–057.

[556] *White v Jones* [1995] 2 A.C. 207 at 265.

[557] *White v Jones* [1995] 2 A.C. 207 at 265.

[558] *White v Jones* [1995] 2 A.C. 207 at 268; cf. *Trusted v Clifford Chance* [2000] W.T.L.R. 1219.

[559] There is no reference to the point in the speech of Lord Browne-Wilkinson, while Lord Nolan at 294 left the point open.

[560] See especially *The Pioneer Container* [1994] 2 A.C. 324; cf. also Lord Goff's dictum in *Henderson v Merrett Syndicates Ltd* [1995] 2 A.C. 145 at 196; fn.535.

## 5. EXCEPTIONS

14–085 The doctrine of privity would, if inflexibly applied, give rise to considerable injustice and inconvenience. Many exceptions to it have therefore been developed by the courts and the legislature. The most important of these is the "general and wide ranging"[561] one which has been created by the Contracts (Rights of Third Parties) Act 1999. This Act preserves any right or remedy which the third party may have apart from its provisions.[562] The exceptions which were established before the Act came into force therefore still call for discussion, particularly because situations may arise in which it will be to the third parties' advantage to rely on one of these exceptions, rather than on the new one which has been created by the Act.[563]

### (a) Judge-made exceptions

#### *(i) Covenants concerning land*

14–086 Covenants in a lease can benefit or bind persons, other than the original parties to the lease, who later acquire an interest in the property or the reversion; a person may be able to enforce a covenant affecting land made by his predecessor in title, and one who acquires land with notice that it is burdened by a restrictive covenant may be bound by it although he was not a party to the covenant. Detailed discussion of these topics will be found in works on land law.[564]

#### *(ii) Agency*

14–087 Agency is the relationship which arises when one person (the principal) authorises another (the agent) to act on his behalf and the agent agrees to do so. One legal consequence of this relationship is that the principal acquires rights and incurs liabilities under contracts made by the agent on his behalf with third parties. It is sometimes said that this is only an apparent exception to the doctrine of privity, since in such cases the agent is only the instrument of the principal, who is the real contracting party.[565] This may be true where the agent acts within his actual authority. But it is only doubtfully true where the principal is liable under the doctrine of apparent authority although the agent's act is unauthorised, or where the principal ratifies.[566] And the principles of agency would seem to constitute a clear exception to the doctrine of privity where the agent acts without

---

561 Law Com. No.242, para.5.16.
562 s.7(1); this can apply not only to existing, but also to future, exceptions.
563 See para.14–003; paras 14–100, 14–129—14–131.
564 e.g. *Megarry and Wade: The Law of Real Property*, 9th edn (2019), Ch.31.
565 cf. *Pollock's Principles of Contract*, 13th edn (1950), p.163.
566 See paras 16–024–16–033, 16–049–16–061.

actual but within his "usual" authority,[567] where the principal is undisclosed,[568] and in certain cases of agency of necessity.[569] These matters are discussed in Ch.16.

### (iii) *Assignment*

14–088 Assignment is a process whereby a contractual right is transferred to someone other than the original creditor without the consent of the original debtor. It is a clear exception to the doctrine of privity and is discussed in Ch.15.

### (iv) *Trusts of promises*[570]

14–089 Equity developed a more general exception to the doctrine of privity by use of the concept of trust. A trust is an equitable obligation to hold property on behalf of another. It may be express or implied; and a person may be trustee not only of a physical thing or of a sum of money, but also of a *chose in action*,[571] such as a debt owed to him. In equity, a person could, moreover, be trustee of a promise to pay money, not to himself, but to a third party; and where such a trust was established, the third party could enforce the promise against the promisor.[572] This device was applied in a number of eighteenth- and nineteenth-century cases[573] and was even recognised by the common law courts, who sometimes allowed the promisee to recover more than he had lost on the ground that he was bound to hold the surplus for a third party.[574] It was approved by the House of Lords in *Les Affréteurs Réunis, SA v Leopold Walford (London) Ltd*,[575] where a broker (C) negotiated a charterparty by which the shipowner (A) promised the charterer (B) to pay the broker a commission. It was held that B was trustee of this promise for C, who could thus enforce it against A.[576] Many problems arise in determining the scope and effects of this trust device.

14–090 **Intention to create a trust.** A promisee will not be regarded as trustee for a third party unless he has the intention to create a trust.[577] Such an intention can be

---

[567] *Watteau v Fenwick* [1893] 1 Q.B. 346; paras 16–034–16–036.

[568] See paras 16–065–16–070.

[569] See paras 16–037–16–048.

[570] Corbin 46 L.Q.R. 12; Jaconelli [1998] Conv. 88.

[571] See para.15–002.

[572] *Tomlinson v Gill* (1756) Amb. 330. For the effectiveness of directions (not of a contractual nature) to executors in favour of a third party, see *Crowden v Aldridge* [1993] 1 W.L.R. 433.

[573] e.g. fn.572; *Lloyd's v Harper* (1880) 16 Ch D. 290.

[574] e.g. *Robertson v Wait* (1853) 8 Ex. 299; *Prudential Staff Union v Hall* [1947] K.B. 685.

[575] [1919] A.C. 801; *Atlas Shipping Agency (UK) Ltd v Suisse Atlantique Société d'Armement SA* [1995] 2 Lloyd's Rep. 188. Contrast *The Manifest Lipkowy* [1989] 2 Lloyd's Rep. 138, where an agreement for the sale of a ship provided for deduction of the broker's commission from the price, but seems to have contained no *promise* by the seller to pay the broker.

[576] Lord Finlay seems to have regarded the broker as a party to the contract.

[577] *Swain v Law Society* [1983] 1 A.C. 598 at 620; Feltham 98 L.Q.R. 17. For the purpose of the present discussion, it is assumed that formal requirements, such as that imposed by Law of Property Act 1925 s.53(1)(b), have been satisfied.

made clear by using the word "trust" or "trustee",[578] but a trust may be created without using any particular form of words, and where the word "trust" or "trustee" is not used, the question of intention gives rise to great difficulty. Two cases may be contrasted. In *Re Flavell*[579] a partner retired and the continuing partners promised him that they would, after his death, pay an annuity to his widow. It was held that there was a trust in favour of the widow. But in *Re Schebsman*[580] a company promised one of its employees on his retirement that it would, after his death, pay annuities to his widow for a specified period, or (if she should die within that period) to his daughter. It was held that there was no trust in favour of the widow or daughter.

Similarly, a life insurance policy expressed to be for the benefit of a third party has in some cases been held to create a trust in his favour,[581] but in others to confer no rights on him.[582] And in some cases concerning other types of insurance[583] the courts have held that a third party could take advantage of the policy under the trust device[584] while in others they have held that the third party had no rights because of the doctrine of privity.[585] These cases cannot be reconciled. They represent different stages of development and show that the courts became reluctant to apply the trust device because, once a trust was held to have been created, the parties to the contract lost their right to rescind or vary that contract by mutual consent.[586] The most that can be done is to try to extract from them a number of principles which will at any rate serve as guides to the solution of future problems.

**There must be an intention to benefit the third party.** If the promisee intends the promise to be for his own benefit, there will be no trust in favour of the third party.[587] The same result may follow if it is as consistent with the facts that the promisee took the promise for his own benefit as for that of a third party.[588] 14–091

[578] *Fletcher v Fletcher* (1844) 4 Hare 67; *Bowskill v Dawson* [1955] 1 Q.B. 13.

[579] (1883) 25 Ch D. 89; see further, cf. *Re Gordon* [1940] Ch. 851; *Drimmie v Davies* [1899] 1 I.R. 176.

[580] [1944] Ch. 83; see further, fn.599; cf. *Re Stapleton-Bretherton* [1941] Ch. 482. In *Beswick v Beswick* [1968] A.C. 58 (para.14–017) it was conceded that there was no trust.

[581] *Royal Exchange Assurance v Hope* [1928] Ch. 179; *Re Webb* [1941] Ch. 225; *Re Foster's Policy* [1966] 1 W.L.R. 222.

[582] *Re Burgess' Policy* (1915) 113 L.T. 443; *Re Sinclair's Life Policy* [1938] Ch. 799; *Re Engelbach's Estate* [1924] 2 Ch. 348.

[583] For statutory exceptions to the doctrine of privity in cases of insurance, see paras 14–137–14–143.

[584] *Williams v Baltic Ins Co* [1924] 2 K.B. 282; cf. *Waters v Monarch Assurance Co* (1856) 5 E. & B. 870 at 881. See also Deane J in *Trident General Ins Co Ltd v McNiece Bros Pty Ltd* (1988) 165 C.L.R. 107.

[585] *Vandepitte v Preferred Accident Ins Corp* [1933] A.C. 70; *Green v Russell* [1959] 2 Q.B. 226, cited with approval in *McCamley v Cammell Laird Shipbuilders* [1990] 1 W.L.R. 963 at 969.

[586] See para.14–015, para.14–092.

[587] See *West v Houghton* (1879) 4 C.P.D. 197; criticised in *Re Flavell* (1883) 25 Ch D. 89 at 98 and in *Lloyd's v Harper* (1880) 16 Ch D. 290 at 311.

[588] *Vandepitte v Preferred Accident Ins Corp* [1933] A.C. 70, where one relevant factor for denying that a motor insurance policy created a trust in favour of a person authorised to drive the insured's car was that the insured was himself liable for the torts of that person. Contrast *Williams v Baltic Ins Co* [1920] 2 K.B. 283; for the statutory position relating to such policies, see para.14–139.

Conversely, the fact that the promisee had *not* intended to take the promise for his own benefit can be relied on to support the argument that there was a trust in favour of the third party.[589]

14–092 **The intention to benefit the third party must be irrevocable.** It is now[590] settled that a contract will not normally[591] give rise to a trust in favour of a third party if, under the terms of the contract, the promisee is entitled to deprive the third party of the intended benefit by diverting it to himself. Thus in *Re Sinclair's Life Policy*[592] a policy of life insurance, taken out by the assured for the benefit of his godson, contained an option enabling the assured to surrender the policy for his own benefit.[593] This fact negatived the intention to create a trust. On the other hand, the existence of such a power to divert the benefit was held not to negative the intention to create the trust where the power was expressed to be exercisable only for a limited period and was not exercised within that period.[594] Nor will the existence of a trust necessarily be negatived where the contract names a group of beneficiaries but reserves to the promisee the power to alter the nature or destination of the benefit as between those beneficiaries.[595] And where a contract *by statute* creates a trust[596] a general provision in the contract entitling the promisee to divert the benefit to whom he pleases will not defeat the trust: on the contrary such power can be exercised only for the benefit of objects of the trust.[597] The court may conclude that there was no intention irrevocably to benefit the third party even though the contract contains no express provision entitling the promisee to divert the benefit away from the third party. It may do so on the ground that the contract would, if it were held to give rise to a trust, unduly limit the freedom of action of the parties or of one of them, e.g. by restricting the promisee's freedom of movement[598] or by depriving the parties to the contract of their rights to vary it by mutual consent.[599]

14–093 **Intention to benefit third party is not necessarily sufficient.** An intention to create a trust must be distinguished from an intention to make a gift.[600] There are also many cases in which the courts have refused to apply the trust device although the promisee clearly and without qualification intended to benefit the

---

589 *Lyus v Prowsa Developments Ltd* [1982] 1 W.L.R. 1044.

590 Contrast the earlier decisions in *Hill v Gomme* (1839) 5 My. & Cr. 250; *Page v Cox* (1852) 10 Hare 163.

591 For exceptions, see at fnn.594–597.

592 [1938] Ch. 799; criticised on another ground in *Beswick v Beswick* [1968] A.C. 58 at 96; fn.258.

593 A provision of this kind would not fall within Contracts (Rights of Third Parties) Act 1999 s.2 since this applies only to rescission or variation by *agreement*: see para.14–119.

594 *Re Foster's Policy* [1966] 1 W.L.R. 432.

595 *Re Webb* [1941] Ch. 225; *Re Flavell* (1883) 25 Ch D. 89.

596 See para.14–138.

597 *Re a Policy of the Equitable Life Assurance of the United States and Mitchell* (1911) 27 T.L.R. 213; *Re Fleetwood's Policy* [1926] Ch. 48.

598 e.g. *Re Burgess' Policy* (1915) 113 L.T. 443 (policy to become void if insured went "beyond the boundaries of Europe" without previously notifying insurers).

599 e.g. *Re Schebsman* [1944] Ch. 83 at 104 (parties "intended to keep alive their common law right consensually to vary the terms of the obligation").

600 See *Richards v Delbridge* (1874) L.R. 18 Eq.11.

third party.[601] It seems that the necessary intention to create a trust will readily be found where the contract for the benefit of the third party is made in performance of a previous contract between promisee and third party, e.g. where an employer promises to insure his employee against accident and then does so.[602] An intention to create a trust should, on principle, involve an intention on the part of the promisee to assume fiduciary responsibilities towards the third party.[603] But there is no clear definition of "fiduciary" for this purpose; and the courts did not at one time insist very strictly on proof of the intention to create a trust. The fact that they later came to do so is largely responsible for the present, more restricted, scope of the trust device.

**The effect of other exceptions on the creation of a trust.** The intention to create a trust may, finally, be negatived on the ground that a trust is not necessary to give rights to the third party because he is entitled to enforce the contract, even in the absence of a trust, under a statutory exception to the doctrine of privity.[604] **14–094**

**Effects of the trust.** The third party is entitled to sue the promisor for the money or property which the promisor had promised to pay or to transfer to him,[605] but only where that is consistent with the terms of the promise.[606] He must join the promisee as a party to the action[607] since if this were not done the promisor might be sued a second time by the promisee. As this rule as to joinder of parties exists for the benefit of the promisor, it can be waived by him. The third party is (as a general rule)[608] also beneficially entitled to any money paid or payable under the contract; the promisee has no right to such money.[609] After *Beswick v Beswick*[610] the third party can generally keep money paid to him even if there is no trust. **14–095**

There are exceptional cases in which the promisee may be entitled to the money even though there was a trust. In *Cleaver v Mutual Reserve Fund Life Association*[611] a husband insured his life for the benefit of his wife by a policy

601 *Re Engelbach's Estate* [1924] 2 Ch. 348 (overruled on another point in *Beswick v Beswick* [1968] A.C. 58); *Re Clay's Policy of Assurance* [1937] 2 All E.R. 548; *Re Stapleton-Bretherton* [1941] Ch. 482; *Green v Russell* [1959] 1 Q.B. 28; *Re Cook's Settlement Trusts* [1965] Ch. 902; cf. *Cleaver v Mutual Reserve Fund Life Association* [1892] 1 Q.B. 147 at 152.

602 See *Re Independent Air Travel Ltd*, *The Times*, 20 May 1961, where counsel, with the approval of the court, conceded this point.

603 See *Harmer v Armstrong* [1934] Ch. 65, where the fact that the promisee was the third party's agent, and so under a fiduciary duty (para.16–109), helped to establish the necessary intention.

604 *Swain v Law Society* [1983] 1 A.C. 598, especially at 621.

605 But where a trustee engages a professional adviser for the purpose of administering the trust, a claim for negligence against that adviser cannot be brought by the beneficiary since such a claim is not part of the trust property (though any damages recovered by the trustee would be): *Bradstock Trustee Services Ltd v Nabarro Nathanson* [1995] 1 W.L.R. 1405.

606 e.g. not where a prohibition on assignment also prohibits a declaration of trust; cf. *Barbados Trust Co Ltd v Bank of Zambia* [2007] EWCA Civ 148; [2007] 1 Lloyd's Rep. 495; para.15–050.

607 cf. *Performing Right Society Ltd v London Theatre of Varieties* [1924] A.C. 1; *Atlas Shipping Agency (UK) Ltd v Suisse Atlantique Société d'Armement* [1995] 2 Lloyd's Rep. 188 at 193; and para.15–007.

608 i.e. subject to the exception stated at fn.611.

609 *Re Flavell* (1883) 25 Ch D. 89; *Re Gordon* [1940] Ch. 851; cf. *Paul v Constance* [1977] 1 W.L.R. 52.

610 [1968] A.C. 58; see para.14–022.

611 [1892] 1 Q.B. 147.

which, by statute, created a trust in her favour.[612] The wife was convicted of murdering the husband and was therefore disqualified from enforcing the trust. It was held that the executors of the husband were entitled to the policy moneys. It can be argued that the promisor should not have been held liable to pay the promisee when its promise was one to pay the third party.[613] But it seems that the destination of the payments was a matter of indifference to the insurance company and that there was nothing to show that the company would (even if there had been no conviction) have been in any way prejudiced by paying the husband's executors rather than the wife.[614] The actual decision may also turn on the interpretation of the statute creating the trust.[615]

14–096 **Kinds of promises which can be held on trust.** The trust device has so far been applied only to promises to pay money or to transfer property.[616] It is sometimes suggested that it might be applied to other kinds of promises, e.g. that an employer might hold the benefit of an exemption clause on trust for his employee.[617] But the present judicial tendency is to restrict the scope of the trust device; and the suggestion has therefore been rejected on the ground that "the conception of a trust attaching to a benefit under an exclusion clause extends far beyond conventional limits".[618] Other techniques for making the benefit of such clauses available to third parties have been discussed earlier in this chapter.[619]

14–097 **Relation between trust device and privity.** The trust device has here been treated as an exception to the doctrine of privity,[620] of limited if uncertain scope. It has, however, been argued that where a third party was enabled by this device to enforce a contract made for his benefit there was, before the Judicature Act 1873, a conflict between the rules of equity and those of common law; that the rules of equity now prevail;[621] and that therefore the third party generally has a right of action.[622] But this view has not been accepted.[623] Even in equity the third party did not succeed merely because the contract was expressed to have been made for his benefit: he had to show, in addition, that a trust had been created in

[612] Married Women's Property Act 1882 s.11; para.14–138.

[613] Ames, *Lectures*, p.320; *Coulls v Bagot's Executor & Trustee Co Ltd* [1967] A.L.R. 385 at 410–411 (Windeyer J, dissenting).

[614] cf. para.14–025.

[615] See *Cleaver v Mutual Reserve Fund Life Association* [1892] 1 Q.B. 147 at 157.

[616] For a possible extension, see *Swain v Law Society* [1982] 1 A.C. 598, where a promise to provide indemnity insurance was evidently regarded as a possible subject-matter of a trust; though for the reason given at para.14–094 at fn.604 there was no intention to create a trust.

[617] See the clause in *The Eurymedon* [1975] A.C. 154; para.14–069.

[618] *Southern Water Authority v Carey* [1985] 2 All E.R. 1077 at 1083.

[619] See paras 14–065—14–078.

[620] *Barbados Trust Co Ltd v Bank of Zambia* [2007] EWCA Civ 148; [2007] 1 Lloyd's Rep. 495 at [99].

[621] Judicature Act 1873 s.25(11); now Senior Courts Act 1981 s.49(1).

[622] *Drimmie v Davies* [1899] 1 I.R. 176 at 182 (the actual decision was that specific performance could be obtained by the executors of the promisee); Corbin 46 L.Q.R. 12 at 36; cf. Langbein 105 Yale L.J. 625 at 646–647.

[623] *Re Schebsman* [1943] 1 Ch. 366 at 370; approved [1944] Ch. 83 at 104.

his favour.[624] And the argument that third parties were entitled to enforce contracts made for their benefit has been rejected in many cases after the Judicature Act 1873. Some of these were admittedly argued entirely on common law principles,[625] but in others the equitable argument was considered and rejected.[626]

#### (v) *Covenants in marriage settlements*

A covenant to settle after-acquired property contained in a marriage settlement can be enforced by all persons "within the marriage consideration", i.e. the spouses and issue of the marriage, but not by anyone else.[627] For example, it cannot be enforced by either spouse's next-of-kin, who are regarded as volunteers.[628] **14–098**

### (b) Contracts (Rights of Third Parties) Act 1999[629]

#### (i) *Third party's right of enforcement*

"A general and wide-ranging exception to"[630] the doctrine of privity is created by the Contracts (Rights of Third Parties) Act 1999, the central purpose of which is to enable a third party to acquire rights under a contract[631] if, and to the extent that, the parties to the contract so intend. Subsection 1(1) provides that a person who is not a party to the contract may in his own right enforce a term of the contract in the two situations to be described below. In discussing these situations and other provisions of the Act, it will be convenient, and consistent with earlier usage in this chapter, to refer to the person who makes the promise which the third party is claiming to enforce (the promisor) as A, to the person to whom that promise is made (the promisee) as B,[632] and to the third party as C. **14–099**

---

624 *Colyear v Mulgrave* (1836) 2 Keen 81; the actual decision has been criticised, but the principle remains unimpaired. See *Page v Cox* (1852) 10 Hare 163; *Kekewich v Manning* (1851) 1 D.M. & G. 176.

625 e.g. *Dunlop Pneumatic Tyre Co Ltd v Selfridge & Co Ltd* [1915] A.C. 847.

626 *Re Burgess' Policy* (1915) 113 L.T. 443; *Re Sinclair's Life Policy* [1938] Ch. 799; *Re Schebsman* [1944] Ch. 83; *Green v Russell* [1959] 1 Q.B. 28.

627 *Hill v Gomme* (1839) 5 My. & Cr. 250 at 254; *Re D'Angibau* (1880) 15 Ch D. 228 at 242; *Re Plumptre's Marriage Settlement* [1910] 1 Ch. 609 at 619. These cases, apart from constituting an exception to the doctrine of privity, are also hard to reconcile with the modern definition of consideration: para.3–021.

628 *Re Cook's Settlement Trusts* [1965] Ch. 902 at 915–918; Lee 85 L.Q.R. 213; Barton 91 L.Q.R. 326; Meagher and Lehane 92 L.Q.R. 427.

629 Andrews 60 C.L.J. 353; Burrows [2000] L.M.C.L.Q. 540; MacMillan 63 M.L.R. 721; Stevens 120 L.Q.R. 292; Beale in Burrows and Peel (eds), *Contract Formation and Parties* (2010).

630 Law Commission Report on *Privity of Contract: Contracts for the Benefit of Third Parties* (1996), Law Com. No.242.

631 In *Prudential Assurance Co Ltd v Ayres* [2007] EWHC 775 (Ch); [2007] 3 All ER 946, no argument was made that the Act did not apply to a supplemental *deed* (appeal allowed without consideration of the Act: [2008] EWCA Civ 52; [2008] 1 All E.R. 1266).

632 cf. the definitions of "promisor" and "promisee" in s.1(7) of the 1999 Act.

14–100 **Express intention: provision conferring third party right of enforcement.** Under subs.1(1)(a) of the 1999 Act, C can enforce a term of the contract if "the contract expressly provides that he may", e.g. where a contract contains a promise by A to B to pay £1,000 to C and also provides that C is to be entitled to enforce the term which contains this promise. If the contract contains such a provision, there is no further requirement (as there is under subs.1(1)(b), to be discussed below) that the promise must have been made for C's own benefit, e.g. he can enforce the term even though the payment is to be made to him as trustee for D.[633] Express provisions in contracts of the kind just described, to the effect that C is to be entitled to enforce the term containing the promise made by A to B, have hitherto been rare, presumably because under the doctrine of privity they would at common law have been ineffective.[634] Whether an express term has the effect of conferring on C the right to enforce a promise made to B is simply a matter of interpretation of the term in question. Thus, in one case a term entitling C "to enforce the terms of this Agreement" was found, in the context of the contract as a whole, only to entitle C to enforce the substantive right of holding A liable for breach of contract, but not the procedural right of proceeding by way of an adjudication.[635]

14–101 **Comparison with other exceptions.** Subsection 1(1)(a) of the 1999 Act provides a new drafting device to enable the contracting parties to give effect to their intention that C is to acquire an enforceable right against A. Apart from the Act, a similar result can be achieved by creating a trust of A's promise in favour of C[636] or by making him a joint promisee.[637] There is a procedural advantage in making use of the machinery of subs.1(1)(a) in that, if C sues under this provision, he will not (it seems) need to join B as a party to the action;[638] though the court could order B to be so joined where claims against A were made by both B and C, or where A relied against C on a defence available to A against B,[639] since in such cases B's presence before the court is likely to be "desirable ... so that the court can resolve all the matters in dispute in the proceedings".[640] If C does have a claim apart from the Act as the beneficiary of a trust of A's promise or as joint promisee, it may, in spite of the need to join B to the action, be in C's interest to pursue that claim since it would not be subject to other provisions of the Act which may restrict his rights under it, e.g. to those relating to the rescission or variation of the contract between A and B, or to defences available to A against B.[641]

---

633 Law Com. No.242, para.7.5.
634 As in *Tweddle v Atkinson* (1861) 1 B. & S. 393; para.14–016.
635 *Hurley Palmer Flatt Ltd v Barclays Bank Plc* [2014] EWHC 3042 (TCC); 155 Con L.R. 213.
636 See para.14–089.
637 See *McEvoy v Belfast Banking Co* [1935] A.C. 24; para.13–038.
638 This appears to follow from the words "in his own right" in subs.1(1); cf. Law Com. No.242, para.14.3.
639 Under s.3 of the 1999 Act: see para.14–121.
640 CPR r.19.2(2)(a); cf. para.13–006.
641 See ss.2 and 3 (paras 14–113—14–125) and s.7(1) of the Act (para.14–129). For the effect on one co-promisee of a defence available against, or of a release granted by, another, see paras 13–011–13–012.

**Examples.** Subsection 1(1)(a) is likely to apply to terms such as Himalaya clauses,[642] by which A promises B that exemptions from or limitations of liability contained in a contract between A and B shall be available for the benefit of C, who typically will be an employee, agent or sub-contractor employed by B for the purpose of performing some or all of B's obligations under the contract. This follows from subs.1(6) of the 1999 Act, by which references to C's "enforcing" a term which "excludes or limits liability"[643] are to be "construed as references to his availing himself of the exclusion or limitation". Words in the contract to the effect that C is to be protected by the exemption or limitation clause therefore amount in themselves to an express provision that C may enforce the clause;[644] no further words will be necessary. C's protection under the Act will, however, be based on a theory different from that which accounts for the effectiveness of Himalaya clauses at common law. The common law theory is that such clauses, and the conduct of the relevant parties, can give rise to a separate or collateral contract between A and C.[645] Under the Act, by contrast, C enforces a term of a contract to which he is *not* a party.[646] It follows that the agency requirements which exist at common law[647] are irrelevant for the purposes of the Act. On the other hand, under the Act C's right to "enforce" a Himalaya clause is subject to the provisions of the Act[648] while at common law the operation of such a clause is subject only to the common law rules discussed earlier in this chapter;[649] and if C wishes to rely on his common law rights, in preference to those under the Act, it is open to him to do so.[650] For these (among other[651]) reasons, what may be called the old law relating to Himalaya clauses retains a considerable degree of practical importance, so that it would not be safe to rely exclusively on the simpler forms of words that can protect third parties under the Act. 14–102

**Implied intention: term purporting to confer a benefit on third party.** Under subs.1(1)(b) of the 1999 Act, C may enforce a term of the contract if "the term purports to confer a benefit on him"; but his right to do so in such a case is subject to subs.1(2), by which C has no such right "if on a proper interpretation of the contract it appears that [A and B] did not intend the term to be enforceable by" C. These will probably be the most significant provisions of the 1999 Act and their interpretation is likely to give rise to a number of difficulties. It seems that a "benefit" within subs.1(1)(b) can include any performance due under the contract between A and B: thus it can include a payment of money, a transfer of property, or the rendering of a service; it can also (by virtue of subs.1(6)) include the benefit of an exemption or limitation clause. The term must, moreover, purport to 14–103

642 See para.14–068.

643 This phrase would not include *other* terms in the contract on which C might wish to rely, e.g. not choice of forum clauses: see Law Com. No.242, para.14.9; cf. at common law, *The Mahkutai* [1996] A.C. 650; para.14–073.

644 Law Com. No.242, para.7.10.

645 See para.14–069.

646 Section 1(1) ("a person who is not a party … ").

647 See para.14–071.

648 Section 1(1); see especially ss.2 and 3; paras 14–113–14–125.

649 See paras 14–076–14–078.

650 1999 Act s.7(1).

651 See fn.643.

*confer* the benefit on C, so that it is not enough for C to show that he would happen to benefit from its performance.[652] The question whether the term purports to confer a benefit on C is one of interpretation.[653] For example, a term requiring payment to be made by A to B by making payment into C's account might result in a benefit to C, e.g. by allowing him to deduct his commission before accounting to B, but the term itself does not purport to confer a benefit on C.[654] The benefit to C in such a case is merely an "incidental effect" of the term in the contract between A and B.[655] This must be distinguished from a term which purports to confer a benefit on B *and* C at the same time which will suffice for the purpose of s.1(1)(b).[656]

14–104 **Rebutting the presumption created under s.1(1)(b).** A further and different question of interpretation arises (with regard to the intention of A and B) under subs.1(2) (quoted above). It appears from the wording of this subsection that the burden of proof under it rests on A. If a term purports to confer a benefit on C, there is a rebuttable presumption that the term is intended by A and B to be enforceable by C.[657] To rebut the presumption, A must (in the words of subs.1(2)) show that "the parties" did not intend the term to be enforceable by C. This seems to mean that it is not enough for A to show that he did not so intend; he must show that neither he nor B had this intention. Nor is the presumption rebutted merely because in the contract A and B had reserved the right to rescind or vary the contract: this follows from the provisions with regard to such rescission or variation made in s.2 of the Act and discussed below.[658] A standard clause which states that *the agreement* is not "intended to benefit or be enforceable by" anyone other than the parties may be insufficient to rebut the presumption created by a particular *term* which contains an undertaking in favour of the third party personally.[659] As the question of intention put in subs.1(2) is there described as one of interpretation, it seems that the evidence which A will be allowed to adduce for this purpose will, in general, be limited by the rules which restrict the

---

[652] *Dolphin Maritime & Aviation Services Ltd v Sveriges Angfartygs Assurans Forening* [2009] EWHC 716 (Comm); [2009] 2 Lloyd's Rep. 123 at [74]; *San Evans Maritime Inc v Aigaion Insurance Co SA* [2014] EWHC 163 (Comm), [2014] 2 Lloyd's Rep. 265 at [39]; *Royal Bank of Scotland Plc v McCarthy* [2015] EWHC 3626 (QB) at [136]–[137]; cf. *Petrologic Capital SA v Banque Cantonale de Geneve* [2012] EWHC 453 (Comm); [2012] I.L. Pr. 20 at [54].

[653] *The Laemthong Glory (No.2)* [2005] EWCA Civ 519; [2005] 1 Lloyd's Rep. 688 esp. at [40]; *Prudential Assurance Co Ltd v Ayres* [2007] EWHC 775 (Ch); [2007] 3 All E.R. 946 at [28] (appeal allowed without consideration of the Act: [2008] EWCA Civ 52; [2008] 1 All E.R. 1266); cf. *The Jag Ravi* [2011] EWCA Civ 180; [2012] 1 Lloyd's Rep. 637.

[654] *Dolphin Maritime & Aviation Services Ltd v Sveriges Angfartygs Assurans Forening* [2009] EWHC 716 (Comm); [2009] 2 Lloyd's Rep. 123.

[655] *Dolphin Maritime & Aviation Services Ltd v Sveriges Angfartygs Assurans Forening* [2009] EWHC 716 (Comm); [2009] 2 Lloyd's Rep. 123 at [74].

[656] *Cavanagh v Sec of State for Work & Pensions* [2016] EWHC 1136 (QB); [2016] I.C.R. 826 at [73].

[657] Law Com. No.242, paras 7.5, 7.17; *Nisshin Shipping Co Ltd v Cleaves & Co Ltd* [2003] EWHC 2602 (Comm); [2004] 1 Lloyd's Rep. 38 at [23].

[658] See paras 14–113–14–120. If, of course, A and B have the right to vary the contract they may be able to do so to the prejudice of any right of enforcement in favour of C: *Dolphin Maritime & Aviation Services Ltd v Sveriges Angfartygs Assurans Forening* [2009] EWHC 716 (Comm); [2009] 2 Lloyd's Rep. 123 at [79].

[659] *Mentmore International Ltd v Abbey Healthcare (Festival) Ltd* [2010] EWCA Civ 761 at [33].

types of evidence admissible on other questions of interpretation, and what the courts must establish is the objective intention of the parties.[660]

**Effect of other exceptions.** It seems that it will not be sufficient to rebut the presumption created under s.1(1)(b) for A to point to another means by which the term might be enforced by, or on behalf of, C. In *Nisshin Shipping Co Ltd v Cleaves & Co Ltd*[661] a term for the payment of commission to a shipbroker was included in the charterparty which the broker had negotiated between the shipowners and the charterers. This is the normal practice and, in the past, a trust of the promise was found to have been created.[662] The existence of such a trust is unaffected by the Act,[663] but in the absence of any indication in the contract there was no evidence of the parties' intention that it should be the *only* means for enforcing the broker's right to payment.[664] Nor does the mere existence of a chain of contracts rebut the presumption that C is entitled to enforce a term direct against A, e.g. where A is under contract with B and B is under contract with C.[665] In some well-known situations, however, the commercial practice may be sufficient to rebut the presumption that C is entitled to enforce a term in a way which cuts across the legal framework customarily employed:[666] possible examples[667] are claims by a developer (C) against a sub-contractor (A) which attempt to bypass the developer's contract with the head-contractor (B),[668] and claims by a purchaser of goods (C) against a manufacturer (A) which attempt to bypass the purchaser's contract with the retailer (B).[669] **14–105**

**Illustrations.** There is not, as yet, a lot of case law on the application of the Act. It is helpful therefore to speculate how its provisions would apply to some of the leading cases in which the doctrine of privity was applied. In *Beswick v Beswick*,[670] for example, the contract no doubt purported to confer a benefit on C; but no finding of fact was made (because such a finding would have been irrelevant) as to the intention of A and B on the issue of legal enforceability by C. It is conceivable that A could succeed on this issue if, for example, he could show that A and B had, when the contract was made, instructed the solicitor who drafted it to do so in such a way as *not* to confer legally enforceable rights on **14–106**

[660] *Royal Bank of Scotland Plc v McCarthy* [2015] EWHC 3626 (QB) at [129]; see paras 6–029–6–033.

[661] [2003] EWHC 2602 (Comm); [2004] 1 Lloyd's Rep. 38.

[662] *Les Affréteurs Réunis, SA v Leopold Walford (London) Ltd* [1919] A.C. 801; para.14–089.

[663] 1999 Act s.7(1).

[664] *Nisshin Shipping Co Ltd v Cleaves & Co Ltd* [2003] EWHC 2602; [2004] 1 Lloyd's Rep. 38 at [31].

[665] *The Laemthong Glory (No.2)* [2005] EWCA Civ 519; [2005] 1 Lloyd's Rep. 688 at [53].

[666] In *Dolphin Maritime & Aviation Services Ltd v Sveriges Angfartygs Assurans Forening* [2009] EWHC 716 (Comm); [2009] 2 Lloyd's Rep. 123 *if* the term requiring payment to B to be made via C had raised the presumption created by s.1(1)(b) (see text to fn.654), it would have been rebutted; on a proper interpretation of the contract, it was (at [84]) "in the same category as that of A who agrees to pay B at B's bankers, C".

[667] Law Com. No.242, para.7.18.

[668] The expectation is probably still that the developer must negotiate for a direct right against the sub-contractor under a collateral warranty: see para.14–054.

[669] The purchaser may have a direct right under a manufacturer's guarantee; para.14–006.

[670] [1968] A.C. 58; para.14–017.

C.[671] On the facts (if they now recurred) of a number of other cases, the position under the 1999 Act would, it is submitted, be clearer.

In the "disappointed beneficiary" cases such as *White v Jones*[672] C would not get a right under the Act against A, the negligent solicitor, since the terms of the solicitor's retainer (even if they identified C)[673] would not purport to confer a benefit on C: the intended benefit was to come, not from A, but from B, the testator.[674]

It is similarly unlikely that cases such as the *Junior Books* case,[675] in which A is a sub-contractor employed by B to enable B to perform his contract with C, would be covered. Even if the sub-contract named C, the purpose of such a sub-contract would prima facie be to regulate the relations between A and B rather than to confer a benefit on C, and any presumption created by s.1(1)(b) would be rebutted by the legal framework adopted by the parties.[676]

Cases such as the *Linden Gardens* case[677] would likewise not be affected by s.1 of the Act, since the mere possibility that land on which work is done by a building contractor might be transferred to purchasers from the owner would not be sufficient to show that the term relating to the quality of the work purported to "confer a benefit" on such purchasers; nor would the contract, without more, adequately "identify"[678] such purchasers as third parties for the purpose of subs.1(1)(b).

Nor, in circumstances such as those in the *Panatown* case,[679] would the mere fact that the building contractor (A) knew that the property on which he was working in pursuance of his contract with B belonged to someone other than B suffice to show that a benefit was to be conferred on that other person (C): the answer to the question whether the work was being done for the benefit of C or of B would depend on the contractual relations between B and C, the details of which A might be wholly unaware.

In the "family holiday" cases[680] the outcome under the Act would depend on the nature of the transaction. If the person making the booking supplied the names of other members of the family when the contract was made, those other members would probably acquire rights under subs.1(1); but no such rights are likely to be acquired if a person simply rented a holiday cottage without giving any information as to the number or names of the persons with whom he proposed to share the accommodation. In many of the situations which have here been discussed, the question whether the contract purports to confer a benefit on C will be closely related to the question, to be discussed in the following paragraph, whether C is adequately "identified" in the contract between A and B.

---

671 The solicitor could certainly have drafted the contract so as to make it enforceable by C, e.g. by expressly making B trustee for C (para.14–090) or by making C a joint promisee with B (paras 13–036—13–038).

672 [1995] 2 A.C. 207; para.14–057.

673 See para.14–107.

674 Law Com. No.242, para.7.25.

675 [1983] 1 A.C. 520; para.14–054.

676 See para.14–104.

677 *Linden Gardens Trust Ltd v Lenesta Sludge Disposals Ltd* [1994] 1 A.C. 85; para.14–029.

678 Within subs.1(3), below.

679 *Alfred McAlpine Construction Ltd v Panatown Ltd* [2001] 1 A.C. 518; para.14–033.

680 See para.14–027.

**Identification of third party.** Under subs.1(3) of the 1999 Act, it is a requirement of C's right to enforce A's promise that C must have been "*expressly* identified" in the contract between A and B, either "by name, as a member of a class or as answering a particular description".[681] It follows from this requirement that C cannot rely for the purpose of subs.1(1) on the argument that the contract refers to him by implication,[682] but he can, it seems, establish the necessary express identification as a matter of interpretation.[683] So long as C is identified in accordance with these requirements, there is no need for C to be in existence when the contract was made, e.g. a promise in favour of an unborn child, a future spouse or an unformed company could be enforced by[684] such a third party when it came into existence. 14–107

**Relationship between subs.1(3) and subs.1(1) and (2).** The requirements of subs.1(3) are additional to those of subss.1(1) and (2), but very often the question of whether C has been identified will be closely related to the question of whether it was the parties' intention to entitle C to enforce a term of the contract. For example, on the facts of the *Midland Silicones*[685] case, C would not be able to enforce the limitation clause since the contract between A and B contained no express reference to C (whether by name, by description or as a member of a class). C would not therefore have been identified and this very fact would indicate that the contract did not purport to confer a benefit on him under subs.1(1)(b). Where a contract is contained in or evidenced by a bill of lading, it is now likely to contain a Himalaya clause,[686] which would be likely adequately to identify C and confer a right on him to "enforce"[687] the limitation clause under subs.1(1)(a).[688] 14–108

In *Chudley v Clydesdale Bank Plc*[689] the claimants (C) were investors in an offshore property development scheme set up by a company (B) which was found to have been run fraudulently and which went into liquidation. B and the defendant bank (A) had signed a letter of instruction ("LOI") which required A to open a segregated client account for the scheme and not to withdraw any funds from it before August 2010 except on receipt of a solicitor's undertaking that the

[681] *Prudential Assurance Co Ltd v Ayres* [2007] EWHC 775 (Ch); [2007] 3 All E.R. 946 ("any previous tenant"); *Crowson v HSBC Insurance Brokers Ltd* [2010] Lloyd's Rep. I.R. 441 at [12] (director of company).

[682] *Avraamides v Colwill* [2006] EWCA Civ 1533; [2006] N.P.C. 120 at [19].

[683] *Starlight Shipping Co v Allianz Marine and Aviation Versicherungs AG* [2014] EWHC 3068 (Comm); [2014] 2 Lloyd's Rep. 579 at [88] where the term "Underwriters" was interpreted to include the servants and agents of the underwriter which therefore identified a class of which C was a member; contrast *Avraamides v Colwill* [2006] EWCA Civ 1533; [2006] N.P.C. 120 at [19] where it is said that s.1(3) "simply does not allow a process of construction".

[684] A company which did not at the time of the contract exist could, on coming into existence, by virtue of subs.1(3) enforce a term made for its benefit (within subs.1(2)); but the rules relating to contracts made on behalf of such a company stated at para.16–083 would continue to govern the extent to which such a company could be *bound* by a contract made on its behalf: Law Com. No.242, paras 8.9–8.16.

[685] *Scruttons Ltd v Midland Silicones Ltd* [1962] A.C. 446; para.14–066.

[686] See para.14–068.

[687] See s.1(6); para.14–100.

[688] See para.14–100.

[689] [2019] EWCA Civ 344; [2019] 1 Lloyd's Rep. 333.

money would be repaid. In fact, C's investments were paid into a different account from which payments were made by A in 2009 at B's direction and without an undertaking. It was held that C could claim against A under the 1999 Act for breach of its obligation under the LOI.[690] The reference in the LOI to the opening of "a client account" in relation to the property development in question was enough both to identify C as a class (s.1(3)) *and* indicate that A's obligations in relation to the account "purported to confer a benefit" on C (s.1(1)(b)). While the requirements under s.1(1)(b) and 1(3) are cumulative and must both be met, they could be satisfied by the same term.[691]

The question whether C is identified in such a way as to give him an enforceable right may also raise a question of interpretation, e.g. where the words of the term are literally adequate to identify C but the term does not purport (or A and B do not intend) to confer a benefit on him.[692]

14–109 **No requirement of consideration moving from third party.** The 1999 Act does not impose any requirement that consideration for A's promise must move from C. It does not contain any express provision to this effect;[693] but the consequence follows from the fact that the Act gives C the right to enforce the term and is further supported by the general principle that C is not to be treated as a party to the contract between A and B.[694] Since the promise in contracts of the kind in question is made to B, the fact that C need not provide any consideration for it is not strictly an exception to the rule that consideration must move *from the promisee*, but it can be regarded as a quasi-exception to that rule in the sense that C is a person in whose favour a promise is made and who can enforce it even though he may be no more than a gratuitous beneficiary.

14–110 **Conditional benefit.** The 1999 Act does not affect the principle that C cannot be bound by a contract between A and B. However, the effect of subs.1(4) is that the term *benefiting* C can only be enforced "subject to and in accordance with any other relevant terms of the contract". In this sense, C may have to comply with the burden of certain terms as a condition to acquiring the benefit of others, but the burden cannot be imposed on him independently of the benefit to which it is attached, e.g. if A, under a contract with B, grants a right of way over his land to C subject to C keeping it in repair, A may withdraw the right of way if C fails to keep it in repair, but C cannot be sued for breach of the repairing obligation.[695]

14–111 **Remedies.** Where C has a right to enforce a term of the contract by virtue of subs.1(1) of the 1999 Act, he has this right in spite of the fact that he is not a party

[690] C was unaware of the LOI but this did not matter since their claim was not reliance based (in misrepresentation) but for breach of contract.

[691] *Chudley v Clydesdale Bank Plc* [2019] EWCA Civ 344; [2019] 1 Lloyd's Rep. 333 at [79].

[692] See the argument of counsel to this effect, which was rejected by the Court of Appeal, in *The Laemthong Glory (No.2)* [2005] EWCA Civ 519; [2005] 1 Lloyd's Rep. 688 at [37]–[48]. A similar argument might have been raised on the facts in *Elder Dempster & Co v Paterson Zochonis & Co* [1924] A.C. 522, para.14–065; cf. *Broughton v Capital Quality Ltd* [2008] EWHC 3457 (QB) at [27]–[28].

[693] Law Com. No.242, para.6.8, fn.8.

[694] See at fn.696.

[695] Law Com. No.242, para.10.26.

to the contract: the Act does not, in general, adopt the technique of transferring rights from B to C or of treating C as having acquired rights by means of the fiction that he has become a party to the contract.[696] It does, however, make use of such a fiction so far as C's *remedies* are concerned.[697] Subsection 1(5) provides that[698]:

> "For the purpose of exercising his right to enforce a term of the contract, there shall be available to the third party any remedy that would have been available to him in an action for breach of contract if he had been a party to the contract (and the rules relating to damages, injunctions, specific performance and other relief shall apply accordingly)".

It follows from this provision that C can invoke the same kinds of judicial remedies as would be available to B if no third party were involved, and that C can recover damages for "expectation" loss[699] even though the contract was made, not with him, but with B. It also follows that the same principles which would limit B's remedies in a two-party case apply to an action brought by C, e.g. the principles of remoteness[700] and mitigation[701] and those which restrict the availability of specific relief.[702] The application of these principles may, however, lead to different practical results where the action is brought by C from those which would follow from them in an action brought by B. For example, in an action brought by C, the test of remoteness would be whether it was C's (not B's) loss which A ought reasonably have contemplated; the principles of mitigation would require the court to ask what steps C (not B) ought reasonably have taken to mitigate his loss; and the question whether specific relief should be refused on account of the conduct of the claimant could receive one answer where the action was brought by C and another if it were brought by B.

**Arbitration agreements.** The contract containing the term which C seeks to enforce against A may also contain an arbitration clause amounting to a written arbitration agreement within the Arbitration Act 1996.[703] Section 8(1) of the 1999 Act provides that, if C seeks to enforce the former term against A, then C is to be treated as a party to the arbitration agreement.[704] It follows that, if C attempted to enforce that term *by action*, A could obtain a stay of that action under the 1996 **14–112**

[696] 1999 Act s.7(4). This refers only to other *legislation*, but the principle that C is not to be treated as a party to the contract appears also to apply for the purpose of rules of common law: see at fn.694.

[697] Also for a number of other purposes relating to defences available to A against C: see s.3(4) and (6); paras 14–121–14–125; and to arbitration provisions: see s.8; para.14–112.

[698] For the purposes of s.1(5), "remedy" does not extend to a form of dispute resolution such as adjudication: *Hurley Palmer Flatt Ltd v Barclays Bank Plc* [2014] EWHC 3042 (TCC); [2014] B.L.R. 713 at [50].

[699] See para.20–024.

[700] See para.20–119.

[701] See para.20–104.

[702] See para.21–019; and cf. para.21–001. Law Com. No.242, paras 3.32, 3.33.

[703] See para.11–052.

[704] 1999 Act s.8(1). Some difficulty is created in this regard by the wording "is subject to a term providing for" arbitration. If the arbitration agreement refers only to A and B, and not C, C will nonetheless be "subject to" it because he occupies a position equivalent to that of a statutory assignee: *Nisshin Shipping Co Ltd v Cleaves & Co Ltd* [2003] EWHC 2602; [2004] 1 Lloyd's Rep. 38 at [42].

Act and so secure compliance by C with the arbitration agreement.[705] The "enforcement" of a term includes taking the benefit of an exclusion clause by way of a defence,[706] but because its inclusion under s.8(1) could have the effect of compelling C to submit the question of its enforcement to arbitration in proceedings commenced by A rather than by C, very clear words are needed before the court will conclude that this was the intention of A and B.[707]

A contract between A and B may also provide that C is to be entitled to submit to arbitration some dispute between himself and A *other* than one concerning the enforcement by C against A of one of the other terms of the contract. Such an arbitration provision cannot compel C to resort to arbitration of (for example) a tort claim between himself and A.[708] But if the provision is a term which C is entitled to enforce under s.1 of the 1999 Act and is also a written arbitration agreement within the Arbitration Act 1996 and C *chooses* to submit the dispute with A to arbitration, then C is treated for the purpose of the 1996 Act as a party to the arbitration agreement so that the arbitration proceedings will be governed by that Act.[709]

### *(ii) Right to rescind or vary the contract*

14–113 Under the judge-made rules relating to contracts for the benefit of third parties, one objection to the creation of such rights has been that it would deprive the contracting parties of their right to rescind or vary the contract by mutual consent.[710] The 1999 Act deals with this problem by means of a compromise: it specifies the circumstances in which A and B prima facie lose this right, while it at the same time enables them so to draw up their contract so as to retain the right, or to change the prima facie rules laid down in the Act which specify when it is lost.

14–114 **General rule: C's consent required.** The general rule, stated in subs.2(1) of the 1999 Act, is that, once C has acquired the right to enforce a term of the contract between A and B "under section 1", then, if one of the circumstances to be described below has arisen, A and B may not, without C's consent, by agreement rescind or vary the contract, or vary it so as to "extinguish or alter" C's entitlement. Rescission calls for no further comment here; but with regard to variation it should be noted that A and B are, under the general rule, precluded

705 This is a further example of a "conditional benefit": see para.14–110.

706 1999 Act s.1(6). It is sufficient at the time of assessing *the claim* that there is an intimation that C will seek to rely on the exclusion clause as a defence: *Fortress Value Recovery Fund I LLC v Blue Skye Special Opportunities Fund LP* [2013] EWCA Civ 367; [2013] 1 W.L.R. 3466 at [34].

707 *Fortress Value Recovery Fund I LLC v Blue Skye Special Opportunities Fund LP* [2013] EWCA Civ 367; [2013] 1 W.L.R. 3466; where it was C who was seeking to enforce the arbitration agreement by seeking a stay; cf. *Hurley Palmer Flatt Ltd v Barclays Bank Plc* [2014] EWHC 3042 (TCC); 155 Con L.R. 213.

708 Since it would represent the imposition of a "pure burden" rather than the enforcement of a conditional benefit: para.14–110.

709 1999 Act s.8(2); *Sodzawiczny v Ruhan* [2018] EWHC 1908 (Comm); [2018] 2 Lloyd's Rep. 280 at [69]–[72].

710 This has been one reason for the restrictions on the scope of the equitable exception to the doctrine of privity by way of trust of the promise: para.14–091.

from varying the contract not only so as to *extinguish* but also *so as to alter* C's rights. An alteration may of course operate, not only to C's prejudice, but also to his advantage, e.g. where it purports to increase payments to be made to C under the term in question. Such a variation is unlikely to give rise to any problems between A and C, since C will presumably consent to it as soon as he hears of it. But the argument that C is entitled to enforce a term of a contract between A and B can also give rise to problems between one of these parties and outside interests, e.g. creditors of B in the event of B's insolvency.[711] Such persons may seek to invoke subs.2(1) where the variation increases C's rights but where, on the crucial date for the assertion of their rights, C has either not yet acquired any knowledge of the variation or has not yet made any communication to A or done any other act from which his assent to the variation can be inferred.

**Consent required where C has "assented" to the term.** The first of the circumstances in which A and B may not, without C's consent, agree to rescind the contract, or vary it in the ways described above, arises where C has communicated his assent to the term to A;[712] communication to B does not suffice for this purpose.[713] C must have communicated his assent before A and B purport to vary or rescind the contract.[714] The assent may be by words or conduct;[715] and if it is "sent" to A by post or other means, it is not regarded as communicated to him "until received by him".[716] In other words, the "posting" rule, as developed in cases of contract formation[717] does not apply in the present context. "Sent" here seems to refer to some act done by C in order to communicate *words* of assent to A. The rule relating to an assent "sent" to A by post or other means is negative in nature: it states that the assent is not communicated to A until received by him. It thus leaves open the question whether an assent which has been so sent can take effect before it has actually come to A's notice, e.g. where it has been delivered to his address but not yet been read by him. If the overriding requirement is one of communication, it may not be satisfied in such a case. The expression "sent" also does not seem to be appropriate to refer to an assent by *conduct*; but it seems that such an assent must come to A's notice: this seems to follow from the general requirement that C's assent must be "communicated"[718] to A. No formality (such as writing) is required even for an assent in words, so that an oral communication suffices. 14–115

**Consent required where C has relied on the term.** The right to rescind or vary the contract is also barred where A is aware of C's having relied on the term,[719] or 14–116

---

711 As, for example, in *Re Schebsman* [1944] Ch. 83; para.14–090.
712 1999 Act s.2(1)(a).
713 This follows from the words "to the promisor" in s.2(1)(a).
714 *Precis (521) v William Mercer Ltd* [2005] EWCA Civ 114; [2005] P.N.L.R. 28 at [30] (where the benefit to C is in the form of an exemption clause, there is no further requirement on C to communicate his assent before committing the acts in relation to which the contract between A and B excluded liability).
715 1999 Act s.2(2)(a).
716 1999 Act s.2(2)(b).
717 See para.2–031.
718 1999 Act s.2(1)(a).
719 1999 Act s.2(1)(b).

where A could reasonably have foreseen such reliance and it has actually taken place.[720] It would seem that, in such cases, C may be entitled, not merely to the promised performance, but also to damages in respect of his reliance loss, e.g. where he has travelled to the place specified in the contract for the receipt by him of the promised performance.[721] This follows from the rule laid down by the 1999 Act with respect to C's remedies;[722] it also follows from this rule that C could not claim under both heads to the extent to which such a combination of claims would result in double recovery or in his being placed in a better position than that in which he would have been if A had performed his promise in accordance with its original terms.

14–117 **Consequences of attempted rescission or variation without C's consent.** The general rule in subs.2(1) is that A and B "may not" by agreement rescind the contract, or vary it in the ways described above, without C's consent. The most obvious consequence of this provision is that a purported rescission or variation without C's consent is simply *ineffective*, so that C can, in spite of it, enforce the term in question *against A*. But such enforcement may, because of the rescission, become a practical impossibility (e.g. because A has in consequence of the rescission put it out of his power to perform); and it is arguable that the purported rescission is also *wrongful* so as to give C a remedy in damages *against B*, perhaps on the analogy of liability for wrongful interference with contractual rights.[723] This possibility could have practical significance in the event of A's insolvency.

14–118 **Contract conferring choices on promisee.** Subsection 2(1) of the 1999 Act deals with the situation in which C has become entitled to enforce a term of the contract "under section 1" and A and B then attempt by agreement to rescind or vary the contract. This situation must be distinguished from that in which A promises B to perform in favour of C *or as B shall direct*. If, in such a case, B directs A to perform in favour of D (or of B himself) the contract is not varied. On the contrary, it is performed in accordance with its original terms, under which B has a choice as to the person to whom performance is to be rendered. The case therefore does not fall within subs.2(1), so that the requirement of C's consent, as there stated, does not apply.[724] Another way of explaining this conclusion is to say that, in the case put, the mere making of the promise was not intended to confer an indefeasible right on C; for the fact that B had power to divert the benefit away from C would indicate that A and B did not at this stage intend[725] the term to be enforceable by C if B exercised that power. A term of the present kind might, however, also limit B's power to divert the benefit away from C, e.g. by providing that the power was to be exercisable only for a specified period. After the end of the period, C could no longer be deprived of the benefit of A's promise by the unilateral act of B since the consent of A and B would then as a

720 1999 Act s.2(1)(c).
721 cf. para.20–037.
722 1999 Act s.1(5); para.14–111.
723 See para.14–148.
724 cf. Law Com. No.242, para.10.30.
725 Within s.1(2).

matter of common law be necessary to vary the contract; and any *such* variation would then be subject to the requirement of C's consent under subs.2(1).

**Requirement of consent altered by contrary provision in the contract.** The general requirement of C's consent, imposed by subs.2(1), may be displaced by an express term of the contract. Two possibilities are envisaged. The first, stated in subpara.2(3)(a), is for such an express term to state that A and B may by agreement rescind or vary the contract without the consent of C. A and B can then rescind or vary the contract by agreement in spite of the fact that C has acquired a right under subs.1(1) and in spite of the fact that the circumstances specified in subs.2(1) have occurred: that is, even after communication of assent by C to A, or after reliance by C of which A is aware or which he could reasonably have been expected to foresee. It is not entirely clear whether it is enough for the express term to provide that A and B may by agreement rescind or vary the contract or whether it must go on to say in so many words that they may do so without the consent of C; but to be sure of achieving the desired result, A and B would be well advised to use the latter form of words. **14–119**

The second possibility, stated in subs.2(3)(b), is for the express term to provide that the consent of C is required in circumstances other than those specified in subs.2(1). For example, the term might provide that such consent was required only for a specified period or that it must be given in a specified form (e.g. by registered letter). Again, effect would be given to such provisions, so that in the first of our two examples C's consent would no longer be needed (even after the circumstances described in subs.2(1) had occurred) after the end of the period; and in the second it would be ineffective if not given in the specified form.

**Judicial discretion to dispense with consent.** Subsection 2(4) gives the court power, on the application of A and B, to dispense with the requirement of C's consent to a rescission or variation of the contract in two situations: (a) where C's consent cannot be obtained because "his whereabouts cannot reasonably be ascertained"; or (b) where he is mentally incapable of giving his consent.[726] On a similar principle, the court has under subs.2(5) the same power where it is alleged that C's consent is required because A could reasonably have foreseen that C would rely on the term[727] but it cannot reasonably be ascertained whether he has in fact relied on it. Where the court under these provisions dispenses with C's consent, it may order compensation to be paid to him;[728] such an order may presumably be made against either A or B or both of them. **14–120**

[726] The Mental Capacity Act 2005 sets out a test of mental incapacity "for the purposes of the Act" (i.e. the 2005 Act s.2(1)), and, as yet, no consequential amendment has been made to s.2(4)(b) of the 1999 Act; in the absence of any such amendment it is submitted, nonetheless, that the test in the 2005 Act should be applied: para.12–054.

[727] See s.2(1)(c).

[728] 1999 Act s.2(6).

### (iii) *Promisor's defences against third party*

14–121 Section 3 of the 1999 Act contains an elaborate set of provisions which specify matters on which A can rely by way of defence, set-off or counterclaim against C in an action by C for the enforcement, "in reliance on section 1",[729] of a term of the contract between A and B.

14–122 **General principle.** The starting principle, stated in subs.3(2), is that A can rely by way of defence or set-off on any matter that "arises from or in connection with the contract [between A and B] and is relevant to the term" and would have been available to A if the proceedings (to enforce the term) had been brought by B. Under this principle, A could, for example, rely against C on a valid exemption clause in the contract between A and B;[730] and on the fact that the contract was void for mistake or voidable for misrepresentation,[731] or that A's promise was unenforceable on grounds of public policy,[732] or that it had been frustrated or that A was justified in refusing to perform it on account of B's repudiatory breach.

14–123 **Contrary provision.** This general principle can, however, be excluded by a contrary provision in the contract: i.e. by a term in the contract between A and B that A is not to be entitled to rely on such matters against C;[733] though where the contract between A and B was wholly void such a term would appear to be of no more effect than the rest of the purported contract. The general principle can, conversely, be extended by an express term in the contract. Subsection 3(3) provides that A can (in addition to the matters referred to in subs.3(2)) rely by way of defence or set-off against C on any matter if "an express term of the contract provides for it to be available to him in proceedings brought by" C and it would have been so available to A in proceedings brought by B. Under this provision, A could rely against C on debts owed by B to A even though the debts arose out of other transactions, if the contract containing the term which C was seeking to enforce contained an express term that A was to be entitled to rely on those debts also against C.

14–124 **Defences against C only.** There is the further possibility that A may have defences or counterclaims against C which he would not have against B, e.g. where A had been induced to enter into the contract by C's misrepresentation, or where C was indebted to A under another transaction. Subsection 3(4) enables A to rely on such matters against C if they could have been so relied on if C had been a party to the contract; though this rule, like the general principle stated in subs.3(2), can be modified or excluded by an express term of the contract between A and B.[734]

---

[729] 1999 Act s.3(1).
[730] cf. Law Com. No.242, para.10.31.
[731] *Moody v Condor Ins Ltd* [2006] EWHC 100; [2006] 1 W.L.R. 1847 at [30].
[732] *The Jag Ravi* [2011] EWCA Civ 180; [2012] 1 Lloyd's Rep. 637 where this plea failed: see para.11–026, fn.138.
[733] 1999 Act s.3(5).
[734] 1999 Act s.3(5) applies to subs.3(4) as well as to subs.3(2).

**Reliance on exemption clauses.** A rule analogous to the general principle of subs.3(2) applies where the "enforcement" of the term by C takes the form of his availing himself of an exemption or limitation clause in his favour in the contract between A and B.[735] Subsection 3(6) provides that C cannot in this way "enforce" the term if he could not have done so, had he been a party to the contract. This restriction on C's right to enforce the term would, for example, apply if, by reason of the Unfair Contract Terms Act 1977[736] the clause had been invalid or if it had not satisfied the requirement of reasonableness imposed by that Act; or if C was guilty of a fraud on A and so could not have relied on the term (even though B might have been able to do so) by reason of the common law rule that an exemption clause does not protect a party from liability for his own fraud.[737] **14–125**

### *(iv) Exceptions to third party's entitlement*

A number of situations which prima facie fall within s.1 of the 1999 Act are excepted by s.6 from the operation of s.1. These exceptions fall into two groups. In cases which fall within the first group, C has, or can acquire, rights under the contract between A and B by virtue of some other rule of law; and the purpose of excepting these cases from the operation of s.1 is to preserve the conditions under which C's rights arise or may arise under those other rules of law. In cases which fall within the second group, by contrast, C has prima facie no rights under other rules of law; and the purpose of excepting these cases from the operation of s.1 is to preserve in them the general rule of common law by which C acquires no rights under the contract between A and B. Such cases, in other words, continue to be governed by the common law doctrine of privity, subject to any limitations on its scope and to any exceptions to it that may exist at common law or under other legislation. **14–126**

**Where C can acquire rights under some other rule of law.** The first of the above group of exceptions includes contracts on bills of exchange, promissory notes and other negotiable instruments[738]: third parties can acquire rights under such contracts under the rules relating to negotiability, discussed elsewhere in this book, and it is not the purpose of the 1999 Act to extend these rights.[739] It also includes contracts for the carriage of goods by sea which are governed by the Carriage of Goods by Sea Act 1992, and corresponding electronic transactions to which that Act may be applied by Order.[740] The carefully regulated scheme of the 1992 Act[741] for the acquisition of rights under such contracts by third parties (such as transferees of bills of lading) would be seriously disrupted if such third parties could acquire rights under the 1999 Act in circumstances in which no such **14–127**

[735] See s.1(6); para.14–100.
[736] See para.7–039 and following; Law Com. No.242, para.10.22; cf. Consumer Rights Act 2015: para.7–086 and following.
[737] See para.7–034.
[738] 1999 Act s.6(1).
[739] See para.15–046; Law Com. No.242, para.12.16.
[740] 1999 Act s.6(5).
[741] For details of this scheme, see *Carver on Bills of Lading*, 4th edn (2017), para.5–012 and following.

rights would be acquired under the 1992 Act. The same is (mutatis mutandis) true of contracts for the international carriage of goods by rail, road and air, which are governed by international Conventions having the force of law in the UK,[742] so that these contracts are likewise excepted from the operation of s.1 of the 1999 Act.[743]

The exception is, however, in turn, subject to a further exception: C is not precluded from taking the benefit of an exemption or limitation clause in a contract for the carriage of goods governed by the 1992 Act or by the international Conventions referred to above merely because such legislation applies to the contract.[744] Before the 1999 Act, C could in many cases take the benefit of an exemption or limitation clause in the contract of carriage, e.g. where that contract contained a Himalaya clause.[745] The legal reasoning on which this result was based was that a separate or collateral contract arose by virtue of such a clause between A and C.[746] Since C is a *party* to this contract, his right to "enforce" it does not depend (in the words of the present exception) on any "reliance on ... section" 1.[747] The effectiveness of Himalaya clauses would therefore not be directly affected by the present exception[748] to a *third party's* entitlement under s.1 to "enforce" an exemption or limitation clause. But one of the objects of the 1999 Act appears to have been to simplify the drafting of Himalaya clauses and to remove obstacles to their efficacy which might be encountered in establishing the separate contract between A and C;[749] and it is for this reason that the present exception to the operation of s.1 does not apply to exemption and limitation clauses in contracts of carriage which, for other purposes, fall within that exception.

14–128 **Where C acquires no rights.** The second of the groups of exceptions described above includes the contract which binds a company and its members on the terms of the company's constitution, by virtue of s.33 of the Companies Act 2006. The purpose of this exception is presumably to preserve the established limitations of the scope of this "statutory contract":[750] e.g. the rule that this contract confers no rights on a director of the company as such.[751] The second group also includes contracts of employment and certain analogous contracts to the extent that such a contract will not give the employer's customer any right under s.1 of the 1999 Act to enforce any term of the contract against the employee.[752]

---

742 See *Chitty on Contracts*, 33rd edn, Vol.II, Chs 35 and 36.
743 1999 Act ss.6(5)(b) and 8.
744 1999 Act s.6(5), "tailpiece".
745 See para.14–068.
746 See para.14–069.
747 Section 1(1) confers a right of enforcement only on a "person who is *not* a party" to the contract.
748 i.e. that contained in s.6(5) of the 1999 Act.
749 See paras 14–068–14–076; cf. Law Com. No.242, paras 2.35, 12.10.
750 *Soden v British & Commonwealth Holdings* [1998] A.C. 298 at 323.
751 See para.14–012.
752 1999 Act s.6(3) and (4).

### (v) *Third party's other rights unaffected*

**Rights or remedies available apart from the 1999 Act.** Subsection 7(1) of the 1999 Act provides that "Section 1 does not affect any right or remedy of a third party that exists or is available apart from this Act". It follows that C will continue, after the coming into force of the Act, to be able to enforce rights and to rely on defences arising under a contract between A and B, if before then he could have done so under exceptions to the doctrine of privity established at common law, in equity or under other legislation, or if he could have done so because the case fell outside the scope of the doctrine of privity of contract: these possibilities are discussed elsewhere in this chapter.[753] C will, for example, continue to be able to enforce a promise made by A to B if there is a trust of the promise in his favour;[754] he will be able to rely on Himalaya clauses and on other common law and statutory rules under which the benefit of an exemption clause in a contract between A and B is available to him;[755] and he will continue to be able to enforce collateral contracts between himself and A.[756] Indeed, in some such cases the person seeking to enforce the term is not truly a "third party" within the 1999 Act.[757] The whole point of the collateral contract device is to establish a direct contractual relationship between the parties that have here been called A and C; and the legal basis for the efficacy of Himalaya clauses is similarly that a contract of some kind comes into existence between A and C, though this is not the same as "the contract" (i.e. that between A and B) containing the term which C is seeking to enforce.[758] Subsection 7(1) also preserves any rights which C may have to sue A in tort in respect of loss suffered by C in consequence of A's breach of his contract with B; we have seen that in such cases C will often have no rights under the 1999 Act.[759] The subsection also leaves it open to the courts to develop new exceptions at common law to the doctrine of privity of contract.[760] 14–129

**Scope of the saving in subs.7(1).** Although subs.7(1) in terms states only that "Section 1" does not affect other rights and remedies available to C, it follows from the structure of the 1999 Act that many of its other provisions will likewise not apply where C's rights against A arise apart from the Act. Of particular significance are the points that the rules as to rescission and variation, contained in s.2, and the rules as to defences and related matters, contained in s.3, will not so apply, since s.2 applies only "where a third party has a right *under s.1* to 14–130

[753] See para.14–050 and following; para.14–136 and following.
[754] See para.14–089 and following, but this alone will not affect his right to enforce a term of the contract under the 1999 Act: *Nisshin Shipping Co Ltd v Cleaves & Co Ltd* [2003] EWHC 2602 (Comm); [2004] 1 Lloyd's Rep. 38; see para.14–105.
[755] See para.14–072 and following.
[756] See para.14–066 and following.
[757] 1999 Act s.1(1) ("not a party …").
[758] See para.14–072.
[759] See para.14–106.
[760] See at fn.793.

enforce a term of the contract"[761] and s.3 applies only "where, *in reliance on s.1*, proceedings for the enforcement of a term of a contract are brought by a third party".[762]

14–131 **The interaction of C's rights under, and apart from, the Act.** The structure resulting from the above distinctions is therefore a complex one. Four types of cases call for consideration.

The first is that in which C has rights under the 1999 Act but none at common law because the case falls within the scope of the doctrine of privity of contract but not within any of the judge-made or other legislative exceptions to it. Here C's rights and remedies are clearly subject to the provisions of the Act.

The second is the case in which C has no rights under the Act (either because the requirements of its s.1 are not satisfied or because one of the exceptions listed in its s.6 applies) but in which he does have rights apart from the Act, because the case falls either outside the scope of the doctrine of privity of contract or within one of the judge-made or other legislative exceptions to it. Here the rights and remedies to which C is entitled are clearly not subject to the provisions of the Act.[763]

The third is the case in which C has rights both under the Act and apart from it (because the case falls outside the scope of the doctrine of privity of contract or within one of the judge-made or other legislative exceptions to it). It would seem that in such a case C can choose between making his claim under the Act (and so subject to its provisions) and apart from the Act (and so not subject to its provisions).[764] If, for example, C has a cause of action against A in tort at common law, it may be to C's advantage to pursue that claim (rather than one which may also be prima facie available to him under s.1) since in making such a common law claim he would not, in general, be bound by an exemption clause in the contract between A and B, while he would be so bound if he made a claim under the Act.[765]

The fourth is the case in which C has no rights under the Act and none under the existing rules of common law or under other legislative exceptions to the doctrine of privity of contract. Here, C's only hope is to induce the court to create a new exception to the doctrine of privity or (in the Supreme Court) to reject that doctrine altogether. If C's claim were upheld on one of these grounds, it would plainly not be subject to the provisions of the 1999 Act.

761 1999 Act s.2(1).

762 1999 Act s.3(1). See *Moody v Condor Ins Ltd* [2006] EWHC 100 (Ch); [2006] 1 W.L.R. 1847 at [30].

763 *White v Jones* [1995] 2 A.C. 207 (para.14–057) illustrates this possibility.

764 *Nisshin Shipping Co Ltd v Cleaves & Co Ltd* [2003] EWHC 2602 (Comm); [2004] 1 Lloyd's Rep. 38.

765 1999 Act s.3(2); para.14–122.

### *(vi) Nature of the third party's rights*

14–132 Although the 1999 Act for a number of purposes[766] makes use of the fiction of treating C as if he were a party to the contract, it in general treats C's rights and defences as being sui generis. It does not, in other words, except for those purposes treat C as if he were or were deemed to be, or to have become, a party to the contract. In particular, the Act provides that C is not to be treated as a party to the contract between A and B for the purposes of other legislation.[767] For example, the references to a party or to the parties to a contract in the Law Reform (Frustrated Contracts) Act 1943[768] and in the Misrepresentation Act 1967[769] do not, under the Act, include references to C. The same is true of the Unfair Contract Terms Act 1977. The point can be illustrated by supposing that a contract was made between A and B on A's standard terms of business, that a term of this contract conferred a benefit on C, that this term was enforceable by C by virtue of s.1 of the Act, and that the contract contained a term excluding or restricting A's liability for defects in the performance rendered to C. The requirement of reasonableness under s.3 of the 1977 Act[770] would not apply in favour of C since he was not one of the parties to the contract between A and B, or a party who had dealt on A's standard terms: the requirement would apply only in favour of B.[771] The justification given by the Law Commission for this position is that to apply the 1977 Act in a three-party case would raise complex policy issues going beyond those involved in reforming the doctrine of privity.[772]

### *(vii) Effect on Unfair Contract Terms Act 1977 s.2*

14–133 The relationship between the 1999 Act and the Unfair Contract Terms Act 1977 gives rise to the further difficulty that, under s.2(1) of the 1977 Act,[773] contract terms may be void if they purport to exclude or restrict liability for death or personal injury resulting from negligence; and that under s.2(2)[774] contract terms may be subject to the requirement of reasonableness if they purport to exclude or restrict liability for negligence in respect of other loss. Negligence here can include the breach of a contractual duty of care,[775] so that a claim by C affected by s.2 of the 1977 Act could be brought either under the 1999 Act or in tort, apart from the Act. Where it is brought under the 1999 Act, a compromise solution is adopted for cases of the kind here under discussion, i.e. for those in which C sues

---

[766] See s.1(5), relating to C's remedies: para.14–111; s.3(4), relating to certain defences and s.3(6), relating to restrictions on the availability of exemption clauses: para.14–125; for a different technique, see s.7(3), relating to limitation of actions and s.8, relating to arbitration agreements (para.14–112).

[767] 1999 Act s.7(4). This provides that C is not to be so treated "by virtue of section 1(5) or 3(4) or 3(6)". No reference is made to s.8, by virtue of which C *is* treated as a party to an arbitration agreement for the purposes of Arbitration Act 1996: see para.14–112.

[768] See para.19–103 and following.

[769] See para.9–049 and following.

[770] See para.7–051.

[771] Law Com. No.242, para.13.10; for B's right of enforcement, see para.14–134.

[772] Law Com. No.242, para.13.10(vii) and (viii).

[773] See para.7–048.

[774] See para.7–052.

[775] Unfair Contract Terms Act 1977 s.1(1)(a).

A for breach of a duty of care arising out of a contract between A and B, and A seeks to rely on a term of that contract as excluding or restricting his liability for negligence.[776] Where C in consequence of the breach suffers death or personal injury, the strong policy considerations against contract terms excluding or restricting A's liability for such harm are to prevail, so that nothing in the 1999 Act will affect C's right to impugn the validity of a term excluding or restricting A's liability for such harm under s.2(1) of the 1977 Act.[777] But where C suffers other loss, the case is regarded as more closely analogous to the situation (described above) that can arise under s.3 of the 1977 Act. Subsection 7(2) of the 1999 Act therefore provides that s.2(2) of the 1977 Act is not to apply where A's alleged negligence consists of the breach of an obligation arising from a term of a contract (between A and B) and the claim by C is brought in reliance on s.1 of the 1999 Act. In such an action, therefore, a term in that contract excluding or restricting A's liability for loss other than death or personal injury is not subject to the requirement of reasonableness under the 1977 Act.[778]

### (viii) *Promisee's rights*

14–134 **In general.** At common law, the doctrine of privity of contract does not preclude the promisee from enforcing the contract[779] and this position is preserved by s.4 of the 1999 Act, by which "Section 1 does not affect any right of the promisee to enforce any term of the contract". The contract between A and B can thus be enforced by B even where the 1999 Act also gives C the right to enforce one of its terms against A. On A's failure to perform that term in favour of C, B can therefore make any claims for the agreed sum, for other specific relief or for damages that would have been available to him at common law apart from the Act. There is also nothing in the Act that affects B's right to restitution[780] against A in the event of the latter's non-performance of the term in favour of C, even though B's right to restitution would not normally be a "right of [B] to *enforce* a term of the contract" within s.4: it would have this character only where the contract provided for the return by A of the consideration provided by B to A in the event of A's failure to perform in favour of C. The 1999 Act also contains nothing to affect the common law rules which govern the relative rights of B and C where A has performed, or is willing to perform, in favour of C.[781]

14–135 **Provision against double liability.** At common law, A's failure to perform in favour of C may, in circumstances discussed earlier in this chapter,[782] give B a right to recover damages in respect of C's loss or in respect of expenses incurred

[776] See Law Com. No.242, para.13.12.
[777] Or under s.65 of the Consumer Rights Act 2015 which now applies to such a term in a consumer contract, or a consumer notice: Unfair Contract Terms Act 1977 s.2(4).
[778] Unfair Contract Terms Act 1977 s.2 no longer applies to a term in a consumer contract, or a consumer notice (see s.2(4) of the 1977 Act) but no amendment appears to have been made to apply s.7(2) of the 1999 Act to the equivalent provisions in the Consumer Rights Act 2015 (s.62).
[779] See para.14–020.
[780] See para.14–023.
[781] See para.14–045 and following.
[782] See para.14–028 and following.

by B in making good A's default, e.g. in completing A's unfinished, or in repairing A's defective, work. If, after B had recovered such damages, C were to make a claim against A under s.1 of the 1999 Act, there would be a risk of A's being made liable twice over for the same loss. Section 5 of the Act therefore directs the court in such circumstances "to reduce any award to [C] to such extent as it thinks appropriate to take account of the sum recovered by" B. Such a reduction would not prejudice C since, where damages had been recovered by B in respect of C's loss, these would have to be held by B for C;[783] and where B had incurred expense in curing A's breach, C's loss would be reduced in fact by his receipt of the intended benefit,[784] though by a route other than that envisaged by the contract. Section 5 of the Act applies only where B has recovered "a sum" (i.e. of money) in respect of C's loss or B's expense in making good A's default. Thus it will normally apply where B has recovered *damages*, though the possibility of its also applying where B has recovered *the agreed sum* or where he has made a successful claim for *restitution* does not appear to be excluded. It will not, however, apply where B has obtained an order for the specific performance of an obligation by A to render some performance to C other than the payment of money, or where B has obtained an injunction to enforce a negative promise made by A for the benefit of C. In such cases, C will obtain the performance due to him under the term made enforceable by him by virtue of s.1 and so will not have any right to damages for its non-performance. But C might, in addition to the receipt of the performance, claim damages from A, e.g. in respect of delay in rendering the performance. Such a claim is not, and should not be, affected by s.5 of the 1999 Act since its success would not make A liable twice over for the *same* loss.

## (c) Other statutory exceptions

A number of other exceptions to the doctrine of privity have been created by statute and continue to be available to the third party after the Contracts (Rights of Third Parties) Act 1999.[785] The most important of these are the following. **14–136**

### *(i) Insurance*

The doctrine of privity applies to contracts of insurance.[786] It was in practice much modified in this field by the trust device and by agency; but the inadequacy of these exceptions has led to the creation of further exceptions to the doctrine by statute. **14–137**

**Life insurance.** Section 11 of the Married Women's Property Act 1882 provides that where a husband insures his life for the benefit of his wife or children, or a **14–138**

[783] See para.14–048.
[784] cf. para.20–110.
[785] 1999 Act s.7(1).
[786] See *Boston Fruit Co v British & Foreign Marine Ins Co* [1906] A.C. 336; *Yangtsze Ins Association v Lukmanjee* [1918] A.C. 585. Contrast, in Australia, *Trident General Ins Co Ltd v McNiece Bros Pty Ltd* (1988) 165 C.L.R. 107 (para.14–017).

wife insures her life for the benefit of her husband or children,[787] the policy "shall create a trust in favour of the objects therein named". This provision also now applies to civil partnerships[788] and marriage between same sex couples.[789] It is a good provision so far as it goes, but it is subject to some odd limitations. It applies only where a person insures his or her own life, and not where the policy is on the life of the third party;[790] and it is restricted to policies for the benefit of spouses and children, so that it does not apply in favour of other dependants, such as informally adopted children.[791] These restrictions will not be affected by the 1999 Act;[792] but persons who have no rights under s.11 of the 1882 Act may, if the requirements of the 1999 Act are satisfied, acquire the more restricted[793] rights conferred on third parties by that Act. They may also have rights under the trust exception to the doctrine of privity.[794]

14–139 **Motor insurance.** A person driving a car with the owner's consent can take the benefit of the owner's insurance policy (provided the policy so allows) without having to prove that the owner intended to constitute himself trustee.[795]

14–140 **Fire insurance.** Where a house which is insured is destroyed by fire, "any person … interested" may require the insurance money to be laid out towards reinstating the house;[796] thus a tenant may claim under his landlord's insurance,[797] and a landlord under his tenant's insurance.

14–141 **Insurance by persons with limited interests.** A person may insure property for its full value although he has only a limited interest in it. He may then be able to recover its full value from the insurers but be liable to pay over to the other persons interested any sum exceeding his own loss.[798] A number of real or

---

787 Illegitimate children are included: Family Law Reform Act 1969 s.19(1).

788 Civil Partnership Act 2004 s.70.

789 Marriage (Same Sex Couples) Act 2013 s.11(3), Sch.3

790 *Re Engelbach's Estate* [1924] 2 Ch. 348; overruled on another point in *Beswick v Beswick* [1968] A.C. 58.

791 *Re Clay's Policy of Assurance* [1937] 2 All E.R. 548.

792 Law Com. No.242, para.12.27.

793 e.g. powers of rescission or variation under s.2 of the 1999 Act do not apply where a trust has arisen under s.11 of the 1882 Act; cf. para.14–132.

794 *Re Foster's Policy* [1966] 1 W.L.R. 222; para.14–090.

795 Road Traffic Act 1988 s.148(7), replacing Road Traffic Act 1930 s.36(4), discussed in *Tattersal v Drysdale* [1935] 2 K.B. 174; *Austin v Zurich, etc., Ins Co* [1944] 2 All E.R. 243 at 248.

796 Fires Prevention (Metropolis) Act 1774 s.83.

797 *Portavon Cinema Co Ltd v Price and Century Ins Co* [1939] 4 All E.R. 601; *Mark Rowlands Ltd v Berni Inns Ltd* [1986] Q.B. 211; *Lonsdale & Thompson Ltd v Black Arrow Group Plc* [1993] Ch. 361.

798 *Waters v Monarch Ins Co* (1856) 5 E. & B. 870; *Hepburn v Tomlinson (Hauliers) Ltd* [1966] A.C. 451; cf. *Petrofina (UK) Ltd v Magnaload Ltd* [1984] Q.B. 127 (head contractor insuring for the benefit of himself and sub-contractors); contrast *Stone Vickers Ltd v Appledore Ferguson Shipbuilders Ltd* [1992] 2 Lloyd's Rep. 578, where the main contractor had no authority or intention to contract on behalf of the sub-contractors; cf. *Colonia Versicherung AG v Amoco Oil Co* [1997] 1 Lloyd's Rep. 261 at 270–272; and see *Simon Container Machinery Ltd v Emba Machinery AB* [1998] 2 Lloyd's Rep. 428 at 437.

supposed limitations on this principle have been removed by statute.[799] Thus it has been provided that any person who has an interest in the subject-matter of a policy of marine insurance can insure "on behalf of and for the benefit of other persons interested as well as for his own benefit".[800] On a somewhat similar principle, where property is sold and suffers damage before the sale is completed, any insurance money to which the vendor is entitled in respect of the damage must be held by him for the purchaser, and be paid over to the purchaser on completion.[801]

**Solicitors' indemnity insurance.** Under s.37 of the Solicitors Act 1974, a scheme has been established by the Law Society for the compulsory insurance of solicitors against liability for professional negligence or breach of duty. The scheme takes the form of a contract between the Society and insurers whereby the insurers undertake, on being paid the appropriate premiums, to provide indemnity insurance to solicitors. It has been held that the scheme gives rise to reciprocal rights and duties between the insurers and solicitors.[802] This result follows "by virtue of public law, not the ordinary English private law of contract";[803] for in operating the scheme the Society acts, not in its private capacity as a professional association, but in its public capacity as a body, one of whose functions is to protect members of the public against loss which they may suffer from dealings with solicitors. 14–142

**Third parties' rights against insurers.** Our concern here is not with insurance contracts which purport to confer benefits on third parties, but with those which insure the policy-holder against liability to third parties. By statute[804] such a third party may in certain circumstances[805] enforce the rights of the insured under the policy by proceeding directly against the insurance company. In the case of victims of motor accidents, these rights are supplemented by an agreement originally made between the Motor Insurers' Bureau and the Minister of Transport.[806] This provides that the Bureau will pay any judgment (to the extent 14–143

799 The principle may be displaced by the wording of the policy: *Ramco (UK) Ltd v International Ins Co of Hanover* [2004] EWCA Civ 675; [2004] 2 Lloyd's Rep. 595; *Ramco Ltd v Weller Russell and Laws Insurance Brokers Ltd* [2008] EWHC 2202 (QB); [2009] Lloyd's Rep. I.R. at [12].

800 Marine Insurance Act 1906 s.14(2).

801 Law of Property Act 1925 s.47. In contracts for the sale of land, s.47 appears to be commonly excluded: see Law Com. No.191, para.3.2; cf. also Law of Property Act 1925 s.108 as to the application of insurance money where property is mortgaged.

802 *Swain v Law Society* [1983] 1 A.C. 598.

803 *Swain v Law Society* [1983] 1 A.C. 598 at 611.

804 See, e.g. Third Parties (Rights Against Insurers) Act 2010; on the question of when the 2010 Act applies, rather than the previous Third Party (Rights Against Insurers) Act 1930, see *Redman v Zurich Insurance Plc* [2017] EWHC 1919 (QB); [2018] 1 W.L.R. 280. See also: Road Traffic Act 1988 ss.151–153.

805 Under the Third Parties (Rights Against Insurers) Act 2010 rights are transferred on the "insolvency" of the insured, but the insured must qualify as a "relevant person" and this is defined to include circumstances which do not amount to insolvency as such (see the list in ss.4–7). The insured must be shown to have been liable to the third party, but this can be established in the proceedings brought by the third party against the insurer (ss.1(3), 2).

806 *Hardy v MIB* [1964] 2 Q.B. 745 at 770; *White v London Transport* [1971] 2 Q.B. 721 at 729; *White v White* [2001] UKHL 9; [2001] 1 W.L.R. 481.

to which it remains unsatisfied) "in respect of any liability which is required to be covered by a policy of insurance" under the statutory scheme of compulsory motor insurance. A person who is injured in a road accident cannot technically enforce the agreement as he is not a party to it. But the agreement may be specifically enforced by the Minister,[807] and, although "the foundations in jurisprudence" of the agreement "are better not questioned",[808] the Bureau's practice is not to rely on the doctrine of privity as a defence to claims by the injured parties themselves.[809]

### (ii) *Law of Property Act 1925 s.56*

14–144 **Common law background.** At common law a person could not take an immediate interest in property, or the benefit of any covenant, under an indenture purporting to be inter partes, unless he was named as a party to the indenture.[810] An indenture was a deed whose top was indented to match with a counterpart, as a precaution against fraud. It was said to be "inter partes" if it was expressed to be "between A of the first part, B of the second part … ", etc. The common law rule did not apply to deeds poll (deeds with a smooth top) or to indentures not inter partes.[811] In the case of such deeds the grantee never had to be named *as a party*; and it was eventually settled that he need not be named at all, so long as he was sufficiently designated.[812] Deeds no longer have to be indented for any purposes,[813] but the law still distinguishes between deeds inter partes and other deeds and the distinction seems to retain some practical significance.[814]

14–145 **Section 56.** The common law rule with regard to indentures inter partes was modified by s.5 of the Real Property Act 1845,[815] which was in turn replaced by s.56(1) of the Law of Property Act 1925, which provides:

> "A person may take an immediate or other interest in land or other property, or the benefit of any condition, right of entry, covenant or agreement over or respecting land or other property, although he may not be named as a party to the conveyance or other instrument".

---

[807] See *Gurtner v Circuit* [1968] 2 Q.B. 587.

[808] *Gardner v Moore* [1984] A.C. 548 at 556.

[809] *Persson v London County Buses* [1974] 1 W.L.R. 569; and see *Hardy v MIB* [1964] 2 Q.B. 745 at 757; *Randall v MIB* [1968] 1 W.L.R. 1900; for enforceability of the agreement by third parties, see also *Charlton v Fisher* [2001] EWCA Civ 112; [2002] Q.B. 578 at [25], [82].

[810] *Scudamore v Vandenstene* (1587) 2 CoInst. 673; *Southampton v Brown* (1827) 6 B. & C. 718.

[811] *Cooker v Child* (1673) 2 Lev. 74; *Chelsea & Waltham Green Building Society v Armstrong* [1951] Ch. 853; *Moody v Condor Ins Ltd* [2006] EWHC 100 (Ch); [2006] 1 W.L.R. 1847.

[812] *Sunderland Marine Ins Co v Kearney* (1851) 16 Q.B. 925; qualifying *Green v Horn* (1694) 1 Salk. 197. The old rule relating to indentures inter partes appears still to apply to deeds inter partes in cases falling outside s.56(1) of the Law of Property Act 1925; see *Beswick v Beswick* [1968] A.C. 58 at 104.

[813] Law of Property Act 1925 s.56(2).

[814] See fn.812; *Moody v Condor Ins Ltd* [2006] EWHC 100 (Ch); [2006] 1 W.L.R. 1847 (deed of guarantee of instalments due on the sale of a company held to amount to a deed poll and enforceable by the seller, though it was not a party to the deed).

[815] s.5 of the 1845 Act applied only to real property: *Beswick v Beswick* [1968] A.C. 58 at 87, 104, and, in the case of covenants, to those which ran with the land: *Forster v Elvet Colliery Co Ltd* [1908] 1 K.B. 629 (in the House of Lords, Lord Macnaghten reserved the point: *Dyson v Forster* [1909] A.C. 98 at 102); *Grant v Edmondson* [1931] 1 Ch. 1.

The 1925 Act further defines "property" to include "any thing in action".[816] In *Beswick v Beswick* Lord Denning MR and Danckwerts LJ held that a promise in writing by A to B to pay a sum of money to C would, by virtue of this definition of "property", be within s.56(1) and so give C a right to sue A.[817] In their view, s.56(1) was a "clear" provision to this effect, doing away with the doctrine of privity where the contract is written. But the words "although he may not be *named as a party*" are far from clear. They could refer to a number of things: to a party who is not named but only described; to a person who is named but not as a party; and to a person who is neither named nor a party[818] (e.g. where A promises B to pay a pension "to any of your employees who is injured at work"). The House of Lords in *Beswick v Beswick* rejected the view of Lord Denning MR and Danckwerts LJ, principally on the ground that the definition of "property" in the Act was stated to apply "unless the context otherwise requires". The context in s.56(1) did otherwise require, since s.56(1) was part of a consolidating Act and was designed to reproduce s.5 of the 1845 Act, which admittedly did not have the wide effect suggested for s.56(1).[819] There was, moreover, nothing in the legislative history of s.56(1) to support the view that the subsection was intended to abolish the doctrine of privity in relation to written contracts.[820]

**The scope of subs.56(1).** Section 56(1) therefore does not apply to a bare promise in writing by A to B to pay a sum of money to C; and the correctness of a number of previous decisions to this effect[821] is reaffirmed by *Beswick v Beswick*. But the question, to what other cases the subsection does apply, remains one of great difficulty. There is support in *Beswick v Beswick* for four limitations on its scope: namely, that it applies only (1) to real property;[822] (2) to covenants running with the land;[823] (3) to cases where the instrument is not merely for the benefit of the third party but purports to contain a grant to or covenant with him;[824] and (4) to deeds strictly inter partes.[825] But there is no clear majority in the speeches in favour of all, some or even one of these limitations, so that the scope of the subsection remains obscure. There appear to be only three reported cases in which s.56(1) has actually been applied. The first[826] is consistent with all four of the above limitations, the second[827] is consistent only with the last two 14–146

[816] 1925 Act s.205(1)(xx).

[817] *Beswick v Beswick* [1966] Ch. 538; see also *Smith and Snipes Hall Farm Ltd v River Douglas Catchment Board Ltd* [1949] 2 K.B. 500; and *Drive Yourself Hire Co (London) Ltd v Strutt* [1954] 1 Q.B. 250; criticised on this point by Wade [1954] C.L.J. 66.

[818] cf. the side-note to s.56: "Persons taking who are not parties."

[819] *Beswick v Beswick* [1968] A.C. 58 at 77, 81, 87.

[820] *Beswick v Beswick* [1968] A.C. 58 at 77, 81, 104; cf. Treitel 29 M.L.R. 657 at 661.

[821] *Re Sinclair's Life Policy* [1938] Ch. 799 (criticised on another ground in *Beswick v Beswick* [1968] A.C. 58 at 90); *Re Foster* [1938] 3 All E.R. 357; *Re Miller's Agreement* [1947] Ch. 615.

[822] See *Beswick v Beswick* [1968] A.C. 58 at 87 and 76; contrast 105. See also *Southern Water Authority v Carey* [1985] 2 All E.R. 1077 at 1083.

[823] *Beswick v Beswick* [1968] A.C. 58 at 87; contrast 77, 93, 105.

[824] *Beswick v Beswick* [1968] A.C. 58 at 94, 106; cf. 74–75 and 87.

[825] *Beswick v Beswick* [1968] A.C. 58 at 94, 106; cf. 76–77. See para.14–144.

[826] *Re Ecclesiastical Commissioners' Conveyance* [1936] Ch. 430; cf. *Re Windle* [1975] 1 W.L.R. 1628 at 1631 (not affected on this point by doubts expressed in *Re Kumar* [1993] 1 W.L.R. 224 at 235).

[827] *Stromdale and Ball Ltd v Burden* [1952] Ch. 223.

and it is not clear whether the third is consistent with any of them.[828] The third limitation was regarded as the operative one in both of the first two cases and also in a number of others in which the courts have refused to apply the subsection.[829] It seems probable that the subsection will be applied only where this limitation is satisfied. There is also much to be said on historical grounds for the fourth limitation, which is consistent with all the cases, though it does not form a ground of decision in any of them. The scope of s.56(1) is further limited by a rule which it was not necessary to consider in *Beswick v Beswick*, namely, that a person cannot take the benefit of a covenant under the subsection unless he, or his predecessor in title, was in existence[830] and identifiable in accordance with the terms of the instrument at the time when it was made.[831]

## 6. IMPOSING LIABILITY ON THIRD PARTIES

14–147 **General rule.** The general rule is that what may sometimes be referred to as the "burden" of the contract cannot be imposed on a third party: A and B cannot by a contract between them impose an obligation on C to perform duties arising under the contract. This aspect of the doctrine of privity is so obvious that it scarcely needs to be stated: if A and B agreed that C was to pay £100 to A, no one would suppose that this agreement could oblige C to make the payment. Similarly, as a general rule, A and B cannot by a contract between them seek to impose on C an exclusion clause. The circumstances under which C may nevertheless be bound by such a clause have been dealt with earlier.[832] We have also seen that the 1999 Act does not affect the general rule, but there are circumstances in which C may have to fulfil an obligation under the contract between A and B as a condition of enforcing a term against A.[833]

14–148 **Inducing breach of contract.** Although a contract primarily creates rights and duties enforceable by the contracting parties against each other, it also incidentally imposes on third parties the duty not to interfere with the contracting parties in performing the contract and if they do so they may be liable for the tort of inducing breach.[834] This is a form of "accessory" liability, i.e. C is an accessory to B's breach of the contract between A and B.[835] As such, C is liable

[828] *OTV Birwelco Ltd v Technical & General Guarantee Co Ltd* [2002] EWHC 2240 (TCC); [2002] 4 All E.R. 686 at [12]; the statement of facts leaves the point in doubt.

[829] See the cases cited in fn.821; *White v Bijou Mansions* [1937] Ch. 610; affirmed [1938] Ch. 351; *Lyus v Prowsa Developments Ltd* [1982] 1 W.L.R. 1044 at 1049; *Amsprop Trading Ltd v Harris Distribution Ltd* [1997] 1 W.L.R. 1025. This is a more stringent requirement than those contained in Contracts (Rights of Third Parties) Act 1999 s.1(1) and (2); paras 14–104—14–108.

[830] There is no such requirement under Contracts (Rights of Third Parties) Act 1999: see s.1(3); para.14–107.

[831] *Kelsey v Dodd* (1883) 52 L.J. Ch. 34; *Westhoughton Urban DC v Wigan Coal Co* [1919] 1 Ch. 159 (both these cases were decided under s.5 of Real Property Act 1845, but the position under s.56(1) of the 1925 Act seems to be the same); *White v Bijou Mansions*[1937] Ch. 610; affirmed [1938] Ch. 351.

[832] See para.14–079 and following.

[833] See para.14–110.

[834] *OBG Ltd v Allan* [2007] UKHL 21; [2008] 1 A.C. 1; cf. *Lumley v Gye* (1853) 2 E. & B. 216.

[835] It may be contrasted with the "primary" liability in the tort of causing loss by unlawful means, though the two torts might sometimes overlap on the same set of facts, e.g. where C uses unlawful

only if there has, in fact, been a breach of the contract between A and B[836] and C's acts "of encouragement, threat, persuasion and so forth [had] a sufficient causal connection with the breach by [B]."[837] C must have known that he was inducing a breach, where knowledge includes "turning a blind eye", i.e. a reckless indifference to whether there is a breach of contract, but not negligence.[838] C must also have intended to cause the breach as an end in itself or as the means to another end, but mere foresight of a breach as a possible consequence of his acts is not sufficient.[839]

**Contracts affecting property.** The tort of inducing breach may help to solve the problem which arises when C acquires property with notice of a contract concerning it, previously made between A and B. The problem is: to what extent is C restricted by the contract in the use which he is entitled to make of the property? Such contracts may be divided into four groups.[840] The first consists of contracts restricting the use or disposition of goods, e.g. contracts that goods shall be sold only in packets sealed by the manufacturer, or after a certain time has elapsed. The second group of contracts consists of those requiring the use of *particular* chattels for their performance, without creating any proprietary or possessory interest in those chattels; e.g. a contract to carry cargo in a particular ship. The third group consists of contracts for the hire of a chattel, and the fourth of options to purchase a chattel. These last two groups are now very common; a hire-purchase agreement is a contract for the hire of a chattel, coupled with an option to purchase it. **14–149**

**Protection against third parties in special cases.** In a number of special cases, the courts protect the rights arising under such contracts against third parties with notice of them, e.g. where an option to purchase a chattel is specifically enforceable, it may be enforced against third parties who acquire the chattel with notice of the option.[841] The same would be true where money was lent on the terms that the loan was to be repaid out of specific property. Since such an undertaking to repay is specifically enforceable, it would create a charge in equity **14–150**

means to cause loss to A and that loss is caused by B having breached a contract with A. C will, however, be liable to A for inducing breach where he meets the requirements for that tort, even if his actions do not constitute "unlawful means" or he did not intended to cause loss: *OBG Ltd v Allan* [2007] UKHL 21; [2008] 1 A.C. 1 at [21].

836 *OBG Ltd v Allan* [2007] UKHL 21; [2008] 1 A.C. 1 at [44], [178].

837 *OBG Ltd v Allan* [2007] UKHL 21; [2008] 1 A.C. 1 at [36].

838 *OBG Ltd v Allan* [2007] UKHL 21; [2008] 1 A.C. 1 at [40]; cf. *Emerald Construction Co Ltd v Lowthian* [1966] 1 W.L.R. 691, at 700–701; *Meretz Investments NV v ACP Ltd* [2007] EWCA Civ 1303; [2008] Ch. 244.

839 *OBG Ltd v Allan* [2007] UKHL 21; [2008] 1 A.C. 1 at [42]–[43]. The earlier decision of the Court of Appeal in *Miller v Bassey* [1994] E.M.L.R. 44 is disapproved in this regard.

840 See Chafee 41 H.L.R. 945; cf. Wade 44 L.Q.R. 51; Gardner 98 L.Q.R. 278; Tettenborn [1982] C.L.J. 58.

841 *Falcke v Gray* (1859) 4 Drew. 651, as explained in *Erskine Macdonald Ltd v Eyles* [1921] 1 Ch. 631 at 641.

over the property in favour of the lender, and this would prevail against a third party who later acquired an interest in it, unless he was a bona fide purchaser for value without notice.[842]

14–151 **General principle of protection against third parties rejected.** A more general principle was formulated in *De Mattos v Gibson*,[843] where Knight Bruce LJ said:

> "Reason and justice seem to prescribe that, at least as a general rule, where a man, by gift or purchase, acquires property from another, with knowledge of a previous contract, lawfully and for valuable consideration made … with a third person, to use and employ the property … in a specified manner, the acquirer shall not, to the material damage of the third person, in opposition to the contract and inconsistently with it, use and employ the property in a manner not allowable to the giver or seller".

This principle came to be associated with the rule in *Tulk v Moxhay*[844] under which third parties are bound by restrictive covenants concerning land. That rule was later confined to cases in which the claimant's interest in enforcing the covenant consisted in the ownership of land capable of being benefited by the covenant. This usually meant adjacent land;[845] and since adjacency is hardly a satisfactory criterion of interest in the case of things that can be moved, the tendency of these developments of the rule in *Tulk v Moxhay* was to undermine the suggested general principle.[846] Nevertheless, in *Lord Strathcona SS Co v Dominion Coal Co*[847] the Privy Council relied on that principle to hold that the time charterer of a ship had an interest in the ship which he could enforce against a purchaser of the ship with notice of the charterparty; the purchaser was also said to be "in the position of a constructive trustee, with obligations which a court of equity would not allow him to violate".[848] The decision provoked adverse criticism,[849] particularly because the land law analogies and the constructive trust reasoning on which it was based might lead to the third party's being made liable where he had only constructive notice of the earlier contract. Where that contract concerned the use or disposition of a chattel, such a conclusion was open to the objection that it might have the undesirable effect of introducing the doctrine of constructive notice into commercial affairs. When a similar problem arose in *Port Line Ltd v Ben Line Steamers Ltd*,[850] Diplock J therefore refused to follow the Privy Council's decision. Alternatively, he was prepared to distinguish it: the buyer of the ship in the *Port Line* case knew that she was under charter to the

[842] *Swiss Bank Corp v Lloyds Bank Ltd* [1982] A.C. 548 at 598, 613; the actual decision was that the contract of loan did *not* create an obligation to repay out of specific property so that there was no specifically enforceable agreement affecting it: see para.21–022, fn.103; cf. *MacJordan Construction Ltd v Brookmount Erostin* [1992] B.C.L.C. 350.

[843] (1858) 4 D. & J. 276 at 282.

[844] (1848) 2 Ph. 774.

[845] *LCC v Allen* [1914] 3 K.B. 642; the actual decision was reversed by statute, but the principle stated in the text remains unimpaired.

[846] See *Barker v Stickney* [1919] 1 K.B. 121 at 131; for criticism, see *Tito v Waddell* (*No.2*) [1977] Ch. 106 at 300.

[847] [1926] A.C. 108.

[848] *Lord Strathcona SS Co v Dominion Coal Co* [1926] A.C. 108 at 125.

[849] e.g. *Greenhalgh v Mallard* [1943] 2 All E.R. 234.

[850] [1958] Q.B. 146.

claimant, but he did not have actual notice of the precise extent of the claimant's rights under the charterparty.[851] Thus the *Port Line* case rejects the principle stated by Knight Bruce LJ so far as it relates to contracts concerning chattels; but it does not decide that a third party can always disregard such a contract. A number of possibilities must be considered.

**Limited remedy available.** Later authorities have restricted the principle stated in *De Mattos v Gibson*[852] by emphasising that the remedy there sought was simply an injunction to restrain the acquirer, C, from using the property inconsistently with the terms of the contract between A and B, known to C.[853] The principle therefore cannot impose any positive obligation on C to perform the terms of the contract between A and B. Thus where B acquired shares from A, promising to make payments to A on the occurrence of specific events, which later happened, it was held that that promise could not be enforced against C who later acquired the shares from B with knowledge of the contract between A and B, nor against D who acquired them from C with such knowledge.[854] An injunction on the principle of *De Mattos v Gibson* was not available against C or D as they were not proposing to act inconsistently with the contract between A and B: "they [were] merely proposing … to do nothing whatever".[855] **14–152**

**Third party's liability in tort.** A third party who acquires a chattel with knowledge[856] of a contract affecting it may, if his acquisition or use of the chattel is inconsistent with that contract, be liable in tort for inducing its breach.[857] Thus in *BMTA v Salvadori*[858] B bought a car and covenanted with A that he would not resell it for one year without first offering it to A. During the year, C bought the car from B with notice of the covenant, and was held liable to A for inducing a breach of the contract between A and B. It has been suggested that the decision of the Privy Council in the *Lord Strathcona* case[859] can be explained on the ground that the purchaser of the ship had committed this tort against the charterer.[860] The tort may be committed even though B was quite willing to break his contract with A. Thus it is immaterial whether B or C began the negotiations leading to the contract between them;[861] indeed, C's tort liability may arise precisely because he **14–153**

[851] Hence the buyer was not liable in tort: see fn.856.
[852] See at fn.843.
[853] *Swiss Bank Corp v Lloyds Bank Ltd* [1979] Ch. 581 at 574 (as to which see also at fn.860).
[854] *Law Debenture Trust Corp v Ural Caspian Oil Corp Ltd* [1993] 1 W.L.R. 138; Tettenborn [1993] C.L.J. 382; for a successful appeal on another point see [1995] Ch. 152; fn.866.
[855] *Law Debenture Trust Corp v Ural Caspian Oil Corp Ltd* [1993] 1 W.L.R. 138 at 146.
[856] As now defined after *OBG v Allan* [2007] UKHL 21; [2008] 1 A.C. 1: see fn.838. In *Port Line Ltd v Ben Line Steamers Ltd* [1958] Q.B. 146 (para.14–151) the defendant was not liable in tort as he honestly believed that the terms of the charterparty were such that it would not be breached.
[857] See para.14–148.
[858] [1949] Ch. 556; *Rickless v United Artists Corp* [1988] Q.B. 40 at 58–59; cf. *Law Debenture Corp v Ural Caspian Oil Corp Ltd* [1993] 1 W.L.R. 138, where the fifth defendant admitted liability on this ground; for a successful appeal on another point, see [1995] Ch. 152.
[859] *Lord Strathcona SS Co v Dominion Coal Co* [1926] A.C. 108.
[860] *Swiss Bank Corp v Lloyds Bank Ltd* [1979] Ch. 548 at 574; in the Court of Appeal it was conceded that there was "no substance" in the point in that case: see [1982] A.C. 584 at 598 and fn.874.
[861] *Sefton v Tophams Ltd* [1965] Ch. 1140 at 1161, 1167; reversed [1967] A.C. 50, without reference to this point.

has colluded with B in an effort to get rid of a restriction imposed in favour of A by the contract between A and B.[862] The merit of this approach is that it avoids the danger of importing the doctrine of constructive notice into this branch of the law. On the other hand, it is subject to two limitations.

First, the tort is not committed if the defendant's interference was not the cause of the claimant's loss. In the *Lord Strathcona* case,[863] the purchasers of the ship (who were the defendants in the Privy Council proceedings) mortgaged her, but were too poor to put her to sea. The mortgage gave the mortgagees the right to sell the ship, and it was held that they were entitled to sell her free from the charterer's rights, though they had notice of those rights. The cause of the failure to perform the charterparty was the shipowners' poverty, and not the mortgagees' sale of the ship.[864] Similarly, where breach of the contract has already been induced by C's acquisition of the property from B, there will be no tort liability for inducing breach of contract on D, who subsequently buys the property from C, even with knowledge of the contract between A and B, for D's conduct will not have played any part in inducing the original breach.[865] Nor is D in such a case liable for interference with the remedies arising out of the broken contract between A and B.[866]

Secondly, C's tort liability is based on intentional wrongdoing.[867] It follows that, if a defendant negligently damaged a ship which was subject to a time charterparty, he would not commit this tort against the charterer; nor would he be liable to the charterer in negligence for pecuniary loss, such as hire wasted or profits lost while the ship was, by reason of the damage, out of service.[868]

So far, in discussing the third party's liability for inducing a breach of contract, it has been assumed that C either knew, or that he did not know, of the contract between A and B. In the former situation, he could, but in the latter he could not, be liable for the tort.[869] There is also an intermediate situation, in which C at the time of his contract with B had no more than constructive notice of B's earlier contract with A, but then acquired actual knowledge of that contract before calling for (or receiving) performance of his own contract with B.[870] The question then arises whether, on such facts, C is liable to A for the tort of inducing a breach of the contract between A and B. That tort is subject to the defence of "justification",[871] which is certainly available to C where he had contracted with

---

862 *Esso Petroleum Co Ltd v Kingswood Motors (Addlestone) Ltd* [1974] Q.B. 142.

863 *Lord Strathcona SS Co v Dominion Coal Co* [1926] A.C. 108; para.14–151.

864 *The Lord Strathcona* [1925] P. 143; judgment in this case was given four months before judgment in the Privy Council proceedings so that the injunction issued by the Privy Council never took effect. *De Mattos v Gibson* suffered a similar fate: (1858) 4 D. & J. 276. Cf. *The Myrto* [1977] 2 Lloyd's Rep. 243; *Lyus v Prowsa Developments Ltd* [1982] 1 W.L.R. 1044 at 1049; *Anton Durbeck GmbH v Den Norske Bank ASA* [2005] EWHC 2497 (Comm); [2006] 1 Lloyd's Rep. 93 at [50]–[64].

865 *Law Debenture Trust Corp v Ural Caspian Oil Corp Ltd* [1993] 1 W.L.R. 138; and see next note.

866 *Law Debenture Trust Corp v Ural Caspian Oil Corp Ltd* [1995] Ch. 152; reversing the decision at first instance (above) on this point.

867 See para.14–148.

868 On the principle stated at para.14–055: *The Mineral Transporter* [1986] A.C. 1.

869 See para.14–148.

870 This was the position in *Swiss Bank Corp v Lloyds Bank Ltd* [1982] A.C. 584: see [1979] Ch. 548 at 568–569, and see fn.874.

871 *OBG Ltd v Allan* [2007] UKHL 21; [2008] 1 A.C. 1 at [193].

B *before* A had done so.[872] The defence is a flexible one,[873] and the principle on which it is based appears to be equally applicable where C's contract with B was made *after* A's but in ignorance of it. The exercise by C of rights thus acquired in good faith against B should not, it is submitted, make C liable for the tort to A.[874] Even in such a situation, however, C may be liable to A (under the rules relating to special cases stated above)[875] if A's contract with B is specifically enforceable. Where the specific enforceability of this contract gives rise to an equitable interest, this can be asserted against C even though he had, when he contracted with B, only constructive notice of B's contract with A. In such a case, the tort claim would be "of no value"[876] if, as has been submitted above, it arises only where C, when he contracted with B, had actual knowledge of A's rights; but it would equally be unnecessary to rely on it,[877] since A could succeed against C on the different ground that A's contract with B was specifically enforceable and therefore conferred an equitable interest on A.

**Protection of "possessory rights".** A final possibility relates to contracts under which possession of a chattel is, or is to be, transferred. The contracts in the *Strathcona* and *Port Line* cases were not of this kind: they were time charters, under which a shipowner undertakes to render services by the use of a particular ship, which remains in his possession.[878] Such charters must be contrasted with demise charters, which are contracts for the hire of a ship under which the shipowner does transfer, or undertake to transfer, possession of the ship to the charterer.[879] The nearest analogy in land law to a contract for the hire of a chattel is a lease,[880] and not a restrictive covenant. Hence the development of the doctrine of *Tulk v Moxhay*, discussed above,[881] need not affect cases concerning such contracts. One reason given by Diplock J for his decision in the *Port Line* case was that a time charterer had "no proprietary *or possessory* rights in the ship".[882] It can be inferred that a "possessory right" might have been protected. **14–154**

[872] *Smithies v National Association of Operative Plasterers* [1909] 1 K.B. 310 at 337; *Edwin Hill & Partners v First National Finance Corp Plc* [1989] 1 W.L.R. 225 at 230; *Meretz Investments NV v ACP Ltd* [2007] EWCA Civ 1303; [2008] Ch. 244 at [142]. For terms which may be imposed on C as a condition of obtaining relief against A, see *Guinness Peat Aviation (Belgium) NV v Hispania Lineas Aereas SA* [1992] 1 Lloyd's Rep. 190.

[873] *Glamorgan Coal Co v South Wales Miners' Federation* [1903] 2 K.B. 545 at 574–575.

[874] This was admitted in *Swiss Bank Corp v Lloyds Bank Ltd* [1979] Ch. 548 at 569–573; cf. *Anton Durbeck GmbH v Den Norske Bank ASA* [2005] EWHC 2497 (Comm); [2006] 1 Lloyd's Rep. 93.

[875] See para.14–150.

[876] *Swiss Bank Corp v Lloyds Bank Ltd* [1982] A.C. 584 at 598, where it was held, on construction, that the contract was *not* specifically enforceable; see para.21–022, fn.103.

[877] *Swiss Bank Corp v Lloyds Bank Ltd* [1982] A.C. 584 at 598.

[878] *The Lancaster* [1980] 2 Lloyd's Rep. 497 at 500; *The Scaptrade* [1983] A.C. 694 at 702; *The Nizuru* [1996] 2 Lloyd's Rep. 66 at 72; *The Starsin* [2003] UKHL 12; [2004] 1 A.C. 715 at [119].

[879] *Baumwoll Manufactur v Furness* [1893] A.C. 8; *The Giuseppe di Vittorio* [1998] 1 Lloyd's Rep. 136 at 156; *BP Operating Co Ltd v Chevron Transport (Scotland) Ltd* [2001] UKHL 50; [2003] A.C. 197 at [78], [79].

[880] cf. *Ashburn Anstalt v Arnold* [1989] Ch.1.

[881] See para.14–151.

[882] *Port Line Ltd v Ben Line Steamers Ltd* [1958] 2 Q.B. 146 at 166 (emphasis added).

Where the hirer of a chattel is in actual possession of it he should certainly be protected against a third party who acquires the chattel with notice of the hirer's interest.

It is less clear whether, in this context, the words "possessory rights" refer only to rights *of* possession, or extend also to rights *to* possession, i.e. whether a person who has a contractual right to the *future* possession of a chattel would similarly be protected against the third party. In *The Stena Nautica (No.2)*[883] B had demise-chartered his ship to A under a contract which also gave A an option to purchase her. Later, while B was in possession of the ship, he granted a second demise charter of her to C who had no knowledge of the earlier contract. A exercised his option to purchase and it was held that his only remedy was by way of damages against B: since A's option to purchase was not specifically enforceable,[884] he could not assert rights to the ship against C. The question whether A could assert a *right to future possession as demise charterer* against C did not, strictly speaking, arise since A was suing to enforce, not that right, but rather his right as a person who had exercised an option to purchase. But it seems from the reasoning of the Court of Appeal that A's right to possession as demise charterer would have been protected only if the contract under which the right arose was one in respect of which the court was willing to make an order of specific performance. The argument of commercial convenience which justifies the decision in the *Port Line* case[885] would seem to apply as much where a contract creates a right to the future possession of a chattel as where it creates the right to have some particular use made of the chattel. In each case the right is hard to discover and should not be enforced against a third party *without* actual knowledge of it; and adequate protection against a third party *with* such knowledge is provided by the rules relating to the tort of inducing a breach of contract.

[883] [1982] 2 Lloyd's Rep. 336.
[884] See para.21–026.
[885] See para.14–151.

# CHAPTER 15

# ASSIGNMENT[1]



[1] Smith & Leslie, *The Law of Assignment*, 3rd edn (2018); Tolhurst, *The Assignment of Contractual Rights*, 2nd edn (2016); Ying, *Guest on The Law of Assignment*, 3rd edn (2018).

**15–001** The benefit of a contract may be transferred to a third party by a process called assignment. This is a transaction between the person entitled to the benefit of the contract (called the creditor or assignor) and the third party (called the assignee) as a result of which the assignee becomes entitled to sue the person liable under the contract (called the debtor). The debtor is not a party to the transaction and his consent is not necessary for its validity.

## 1. AT COMMON LAW

**15–002** The common law refused to give effect to assignments of "choses in action", that is, of rights which could be asserted only by bringing an action and not by taking possession of a physical thing. The early lawyers found it hard to think of a transfer of something intangible like a contractual right.[2] Later the rule was based on the fear that assignments of choses in action might lead to maintenance,[3] that is, to "intermeddling in litigation in which the intermeddler has no concern."[4] Such conduct was formerly a crime and a tort.[5] Exceptionally, debts due to and by the Crown[6] and negotiable instruments[7] could be assigned at law. The common law also recognised that assignments were effective in equity: thus a promise by the assignee not to sue the debtor was good consideration for a promise by the debtor to pay the assignee.[8] And although an assignment did not at law entitle the assignee to sue the debtor, it might be binding as a contract between assignor and assignee, for breach of which the assignee could recover damages.[9] The common law did give effect to three kinds of transactions which to some extent did the work of assignment.

**15–003** **Novation.** Novation is a contract between debtor, creditor and a third party that the debt owed by the debtor shall henceforth be owed to the third party. This is not assignment because the consent of all three parties,[10] including that of the

[2] Pollock and Maitland, *The History of English Law*, Vol.II (1899), p.226.

[3] *Johnson v Collings* (1880) 1 East 98; *Liversidge v Broadbent* (1859) 4 H. & N. 603; *Fitzroy v Cave* [1905] 2 K.B. 364 at 372.

[4] *Neville v London Express Newspaper Ltd* [1919] A.C. 368 at 385.

[5] Criminal and tortious liability for maintenance and champerty (bargaining for a share in the proceeds of the litigation) were abolished by Criminal Law Act 1967 ss.13(1) and 14(1), but under s.14(2) this has (in general) no effect on the validity of contracts: see para.11–012. For possible effects on the validity of certain assignments, see para.15–060 and following.

[6] *Miles v Williams* (1714) 1 P. Wms. 249 at 259.

[7] *Ryall v Rowles* (1750) 1 Ves. Sen. 348; para.15–046.

[8] *Forth v Stanton* (1681) 1 Wms. Saund. 210; cf. *Moulsdale v Birchall* (1772) 2 W. Bl. 820.

[9] *Gerrard v Lewis* (1867) L.R. 2 C.P. 305.

[10] See *The Aktion* [1987] 1 Lloyd's Rep. 283 at 309.

debtor,[11] is necessary, and because the original debt is not, strictly, transferred. The third party's right against the debtor is based on the new contract between him and debtor,[12] the consideration for the debtor's promise typically taking the form of some benefit (such as a payment of money) provided by the third party to the original creditor.[13] As the "third party" is thus a party to the tripartite contract of novation, it follows that he would not acquire any rights under the Contracts (Rights of Third Parties) Act 1999.[14] At common law, the third party's claim under the novation would fail if no consideration moved from him for the debtor's promise to pay him.[15]

**Acknowledgment.**[16] If a creditor asks his debtor to pay a third party, and the debtor agrees to do so, and notifies the third party of his agreement, then the third party may be entitled to sue the debtor.[17] It was for long doubtful whether such a transaction had to be supported by consideration. In the second half of the nineteenth century, the following distinction was established: that consideration was, in general, necessary; but that it was not necessary where the debtor actually had in his hands (e.g. as banker) a fund belonging to the creditor.[18] But this distinction, which seems to have little merit, was disregarded in the later case of *Shamia v Joory*.[19] The defendant owed some £1,200 to his agent Youssuf, who asked him to pay £500 of this sum to the claimant, Youssuf's brother. The defendant agreed to do so and notified the claimant of this agreement. It was held that the claimant could sue the defendant for the £500, though no consideration moved from him. If this decision is right, acknowledgment is in one respect more advantageous than assignment, since certain types of assignment have to be supported by consideration.[20] On facts such as those of *Shamia v Joory*, it is probable that the defendant's promise to Youssuf to pay the £500 to the claimant could now be enforced by the claimant against the defendant by virtue of the **15–004**

[11] Such consent may be given in advance, in the initial contract with the creditor: *Habibsons Bank Ltd v Standard Chartered Bank (Hong Kong) Ltd* [2010] EWCA Civ 1335; [2011] Q.B. 943 at [22]; *Budana v Leeds Teaching Hospitals NHS Trust* [2017] EWCA Civ 1980; [2018] 1 W.L.R. 1965 at [68] Gloster LJ); quaere whether the agreement of the parties at the outset that both the benefits and burdens of the contract may be assigned should be effected by assignment (even in relation to burdens: see para.15–078) or novation: contrast the *Budana* case at [93] (Davis LJ).

[12] e.g. *Rasbora Ltd v JCL Marine Ltd* [1977] 1 Lloyd's Rep. 645.

[13] Consideration need not move to the promisor (the original debtor): para.3–024.

[14] Rights are conferred by virtue of this Act only on "a person who is not a party" to the contract (s.1(1)).

[15] *Tatlock v Harris* (1789) 3 T.R. 174 at 180; *Cuxon v Chadley* (1824) 3 B. & C. 591; *Wharton v Walker* (1825) 4 B. & C. 163.

[16] Davies 75 L.Q.R. 220; cf. Yates 41 Conv. 49.

[17] *Wilson v Coupland* (1821) 5 B. & Ald. 228; *Hamilton v Spottiswoode* (1842) 4 Ex. 200; *Griffin v Weatherby* (1868) L.R. 3 Q.B. 753.

[18] *Liversidge v Broadbent* (1859) 4 H. & N. 603 at 612.

[19] [1958] 1 Q.B. 448.

[20] See para.15–024 and following.

Contracts (Right of Third Parties) Act 1999[21]; and such a claim could succeed even though the claimant had not provided any consideration for that promise.[22]

15–005 **Power of attorney.** A creditor can give a third party a power of attorney, authorising him to sue for the debt in the creditor's name, without any liability to account to creditor. But this device had many disadvantages from the third party's point of view. The most important of these was that a power of attorney could generally be revoked by the creditor, and was often revoked automatically by his death.[23]

## 2. EQUITABLE ASSIGNMENTS

15–006 Equity regarded the common law's fear of maintenance as unrealistic[24] and took the view that choses in action were property[25] which ought, in the interest of commercial convenience, to be transferable, e.g. to provide security for a loan. Choses in action were therefore assignable in equity.[26] The phrase "choses in action" here refers to claims for the enforcement of a contract (e.g. for the sum due under it or for damages for its breach). These must be distinguished from *remedies* that are sometimes provided by law for purposes other than enforcement, e.g. where a person who has entered into a transaction as a result of misrepresentation or undue influence is entitled to rescind it. It has been held that this remedy is not itself a chose in action and therefore cannot be assigned; but it is possible for the person to whom the remedy is available to agree to account to another person for any financial benefit which he may derive from its exercise.[27] Where a chose in action is assigned, the machinery used for enforcing the assignment varied with the nature of the chose in action, which might be legal or equitable. A legal chose is one which could be sued for only in a common law court, e.g. a contract debt. An equitable chose is one which could be sued for only in the Court of Chancery, e.g. an interest in a trust fund.

15–007 **Legal choses.** There were four reasons why equity could not simply allow the assignee of a legal chose to sue the debtor in the Court of Chancery. First, equity did not in general enforce purely legal debts. Secondly, the debtor might suffer hardship if he were later sued for a second payment at common law by the original creditor (the assignor): he would have to take separate proceedings in Chancery to make good his defence. Thirdly, the assignor might retain some

[21] This would depend on whether: (a) the agreement between the defendant and Youssuf had contractual force; and (b) the requirements of s.1(1)(a) or (b) and (2) were satisfied: see paras 14–100–14–102.

[22] See para.14–109. Any such claim would not affect the claimant's common law rights as described in the text above: see 1999 Act s.7(1).

[23] See para.16–122.

[24] *Wright v Wright* (1750) 1 Ves. Sen. 409 at 411 ("very refined").

[25] cf. *Alloway v Phillips (Inspector of Taxes)* [1980] 1 W.L.R. 888 at 893.

[26] *Crouch v Martin* (1707) 2 Vern. 595; *Ryall v Rowles* (1750) 1 Ves. Sen. 348; *Ex p. South* (1818) 3 Swanst. 392.

[27] *Investors Compensation Scheme Ltd v West Bromwich BC* [1998] 1 W.L.R. 896; for contrary dicta, see para.15–065.

interest in the debt, e.g. he might assign only part of it: in such a case, it was desirable to have him (as well as the assignee) before the court, so that the relative rights of all the parties could be determined in a single action. Fourthly, the assignor might wish to dispute the validity of the assignment: this possibility again made it desirable to have him before the court at some stage.

These difficulties were solved by allowing the assignee to sue the debtor at common law in the name of the assignor. If the assignor refused to co-operate, equity could compel him to do so. In the resulting proceedings in Chancery, the rights of the assignor could be adequately safeguarded. Now that common law and equity are administered in the same courts, the first of the above two reasons for the original method of enforcing equitable assignments are of purely historical interest, but the third and fourth reasons may retain their force and sometimes make it important to have all the parties before the court.[28] But the action against the debtor need no longer be brought in the name of the assignor:[29] he is simply joined as co-claimant if he is willing to co-operate with the assignee, and as co-defendant if he is not,[30] i.e. if he wishes to dispute the validity of the assignment. The machinery of joining the assignor as a party to the action may, however, break down if the assignor has ceased to exist, e.g. because the assignor is a company which has been dissolved[31]; and as "a purely procedural requirement" it can be dispensed with by the court.[32] Where the assignor is a natural person and has died, it would seem to be possible for the assignee to sue, joining the assignor's legal personal representatives.

**Equitable choses.** The assignee of an equitable chose could in his own name sue the trustee in the Court of Chancery.[33] The chose being equitable, the trustee was not exposed to the danger of a subsequent action in a different (common law) court by the assignor. It was necessary to make the assignor a party to the proceedings only if he retained some interest in the subject-matter. If he wished to dispute the validity of the assignment, he could take separate proceedings for that purpose.[34] **15–008**

[28] *The Aiolos* [1983] 2 Lloyd's Rep. 25 at 33; cf. *Deposit Protection Board v Dalia* [1994] 2 A.C. 367 at 387, reversed on other grounds [1994] 2 A.C. 367 at 391. See generally, Tolhurst 118 L.Q.R. 98.

[29] *Weddell v J A Pearce & Major* [1988] Ch. 26 at 40.

[30] Conversely, if the assignor sues the debtor, the assignee must be joined as a party to the action: *Three Rivers DC v Bank of England* [1996] Q.B. 292; this is not a "mere procedural rule" but "a matter of substantive law in view of the insufficiency of the assignor's title": *National Westminster Bank Plc v Kapoor* [2011] EWCA Civ 1083; [2012] 1 All E.R. 1201 at [30].

[31] See *MH Smith (Plant Hire) Ltd v DL Mainwaring (T/A Onshore) Ltd* [1986] 2 Lloyd's Rep. 244, where subrogation (fn.252) was said at 246 in this respect to resemble equitable assignment.

[32] *National Westminster Bank Plc v Kapoor* [2011] EWCA Civ 1083; [2012] 1 All E.R. 1201 at [30]; *Mailbox (Birmingham) Ltd v Galliford Try Construction Ltd* [2017] EWHC 67 (TCC) at [50]; contrast fn.30.

[33] *Cator v Croydon Canal Co* (1841) 4 Y. & C. Ex. 405 at 593; *Donaldson v Donaldson* (1854) Kay 711.

[34] e.g. *Bridge v Bridge* (1852) 16 Beav. 315.

## 3. STATUTORY ASSIGNMENTS

15–009 Certain specific contracts, such as life and marine insurance policies and bills of lading, were made assignable by statute during the nineteenth century.[35] A more general provision was made by the Judicature Act 1873, which fused the courts of common law and equity, and so made obsolete some of the reasons for the original method for enforcing equitable assignments of legal choses. There was no longer any difficulty in allowing the assignee to sue in any Division of the High Court; and a debtor who was successfully sued by the assignee no longer had to take separate proceedings if he were sued again by the assignor: he could simply rely on his payment to the assignee as a defence in the second action. Thus it was no longer necessary to have the assignor before the court unless he retained an interest in the subject-matter[36] or wished to dispute the validity of the assignment.

15–010 **Law of Property Act 1925 s.136(1).** Section 136(1) of the Law of Property Act 1925 (re-enacting s.25(6) of the Judicature Act 1873), provides that an absolute assignment by writing under the hand of the assignor (not purporting to be by way of charge only) of any debt or other legal thing in action, of which express notice in writing has been given to the debtor or trustee, is effectual in law to pass the legal right to the debt or thing in action to the assignee. The effect of such an assignment is to enable the assignee to sue the debtor in his own name, and to sue alone, i.e. without joining the assignor as a party to the action. The subsection finally makes provision for enabling the assignor to dispute the validity of the assignment; if he does so, the debtor can drop out of the proceedings and leave the dispute to be fought out between assignor and assignee.

### (a) Absolute assignment

15–011 Under s.136(1), the assignee can sue alone only if the assignment is *absolute*; this requirement excludes cases in which the assignor retains an interest in the subject-matter so that it is still desirable to have him before the court. Absolute assignments are for this purpose contrasted with the following.

15–012 **Assignment by way of charge.** In *Durham Bros v Robertson*[37] a builder to whom £1,080 was due under a building contract borrowed money and assigned the £1,080 to the lender as security for the loan "until the money [lent] … be repaid." This was held to be an assignment by way of charge. The builder had not assigned the £1,080 absolutely to the lender; he had only charged that sum with the repayment of the money he had borrowed. But an assignment may be absolute

[35] e.g. Bills of Lading Act 1855 s.1 (now repealed and superseded by Carriage of Goods by Sea Act 1992); Policies of Assurance Act 1867 (life insurance); Marine Insurance Act 1868 (see now 1906 Act s.50(1)).

[36] *The Mount I* [2001] EWCA Civ 68; [2001] 1 Lloyd's Rep. 597 at [60].

[37] [1898] 1 Q.B. 765; cf. *Jones v Humphreys* [1902] 1 K.B. 10; *Mercantile Bank of London Ltd v Evans* [1899] 2 Q.B. 613; *Colonial Mutual General Ins Co v ANZ Banking Group (New Zealand)* [1995] 1 W.L.R. 1140 at 1144.

although it is made by way of mortgage, and does not transfer the subject-matter out-and-out. Thus in *Tancred v Delagoa Bay, etc. Ry*[38] a debt was assigned as security for a loan of money, with the proviso that, if the assignor repaid the loan, the debt should be reassigned to him. This was held to be an absolute assignment.

The distinction between these two cases can best be understood by taking the point of view of the debtor, and assuming that he wants to pay the debt. In *Tancred*'s case, he can find out from documents in his own possession whether he ought to pay the assignor or the assignee; for even if the debt is reassigned to the assignor, the debtor can safely pay the assignee until he gets notice of the reassignment.[39] But in *Durham Bros v Robertson* the debtor does not know whether to pay the assignee until it is settled whether the assignor still owes anything to the assignee. The debtor cannot find this out from documents in his own possession: he would have to investigate the state of accounts between the assignor and assignee. Similarly, if the assignee sued the debtor, the court could not determine whom the debtor should pay without investigating the state of accounts between assignor and assignee; and it cannot satisfactorily do this if the assignor is not before the court. For similar reasons, an assignment of a debt to a bank was held to be by way of charge only where it was expressed to be made as security for a loan from the bank and was to become operative only on the assignor's failing to perform his obligations under the original contract which had given rise to the debt or under the loan agreement with the bank.[40]

In *Bank of Liverpool v Holland*[41] a creditor assigned a debt of £285 to a bank "to hold the same absolutely. And it is hereby agreed and declared that the amount recoverable by these presents shall not at any time exceed" £150. This was held to be an absolute assignment of the whole debt, with the proviso that, if the bank recovered more than £150, it was to hold the excess on trust for the assignor. This part of the arrangement did not concern the debtor: he could get a good discharge by paying the bank at any time.

**Assignment of part of a debt.** An assignment of part of a debt (e.g. of £500 out of the £1,000 which X owes me; or of half of what X owes me) is not absolute.[42] In such a case a debtor who wants to pay may know perfectly well how much to pay to whom. But to hold such an assignment absolute might cause hardship to a debtor who wished to dispute the debt. If the assignment were absolute, the assignee would be able to sue alone. In this action, the debtor might be able to show that there was no debt. But he would have to prove this over again if he were later sued by the assignor for the balance of the alleged debt. And if the assignor split the debt up into a large number of small parts, the debtor might **15–013**

[38] (1889) 23 Q.B.D. 239; cf. *Hughes v Pump House Hotel Co Ltd* [1902] 2 K.B. 190; *The Cebu* [1983] Q.B. 1005 at 1016 (where nothing seems to have turned on the distinction between equitable and statutory assignments); *Bexhill UK Ltd v Razzaq* [2012] EWCA Civ 1376.

[39] See para.15–023.

[40] *The Halcyon the Great* [1984] 1 Lloyd's Rep. 283.

[41] (1926) 43 T.L.R. 29; cf. *Comfort v Betts* [1891] 1 Q.B. 737; *Fitzroy v Cave* [1905] 2 K.B. 364; *Ramsay v Hartley* [1977] 1 W.L.R. 686.

[42] *Forster v Baker* [1910] 2 K.B. 636; *Re Steel Wing Co* [1921] 1 Ch. 349; *Williams v Atlantic Assurance Co Ltd* [1933] 1 K.B. 81 at 100 (the actual decision seems to turn on Marine Insurance Act 1906 s.50(2)); *Deposit Protection Board v Dalia* [1994] 2 A.C. 367 at 392; *The Mount I* [2001] EWCA Civ 68; [2001] 1 Lloyd's Rep. 597 at [74].

have to defend many actions arising out of the same transaction. Hence it is necessary, for the protection of the debtor, to have all the interested parties before the court. For the same reason, an *assignor* of part of a debt cannot sue for the part he retains without joining the assignee as a party to the action.[43] This reasoning does not apply to an assignment of the *balance* of a debt. Suppose A owes B £100 and pays off £25 of the debt. An assignment of the remaining £75 would be absolute since it would be an assignment of B's entire remaining interest in the debt.[44] And where B assigns the debt for a sum which represents a percentage of the full debt potentially recoverable, the assignment is absolute since the assignee recovers in full, albeit it may then have to pay the agreed percentage to B.[45]

15–014 **Conditional assignment.** Section 136(1) of the Law of Property Act 1925 contrasts absolute assignments with assignments by way of charge; but some judgments also distinguish between absolute and conditional assignments.[46] Many assignments by way of charge are, in fact, assignments subject to the condition subsequent that they will cease to have effect when the assignor pays off the debt which he owes to the assignee. Assignments which are subject to some other condition (whether precedent or subsequent) should be treated in the same way.[47] Whatever the condition may be, the assignor retains a contingent interest in the debt, and is thus a desirable party to an action to recover it. Suppose that A assigns rent due under a lease "to my daughter until she marries". The assignment should not be absolute since it is desirable that A should be a party to an action brought by his daughter against the tenant for rent. If the daughter could sue alone, she might be able to prove that she was unmarried, and so entitled to the rent. But this would not prevent A, in a subsequent action against the tenant, from proving that the court in the first action had made a mistake in finding that the daughter was unmarried, so that the tenant would have to pay over again. What matters to the tenant is not whether the daughter is married but that the question should be decided, one way or the other, so as to bind both A and the daughter.[48]

## (b) Debt or other legal thing in action

15–015 A "debt" in s.136(1) is a sum certain due under contract or otherwise.[49] The phrase "other legal thing in action" has been broadly interpreted: it means any "debt or right which the common law looks on as not assignable by reason of its being a chose in action, but which a court of equity deals with as being

[43] *Walter & Sullivan Ltd v J Murphy & Sons Ltd* [1955] 2 Q.B. 584.
[44] e.g. *Harding v Harding* (1886) 17 Q.B.D. 442.
[45] *Casehub Ltd v Wolf Cola Ltd* [2017] EWHC 1169 (Ch) at [29]; cf. *JEB Recoveries LLP v Binstock* [2015] EWHC 1063 (Ch).
[46] e.g. *Durham Bros v Robertson* [1898] 1 Q.B. 765 at 773; cf. *The Balder London* [1980] 2 Lloyd's Rep. 489 at 495.
[47] e.g. *The Halcyon the Great* [1984] 1 Lloyd's Rep. 283; *Herkules Piling v Tilbury Construction* (1992) 61 Build. L.R. 107 at 117.
[48] cf. *The Aiolos* [1983] 2 Lloyd's Rep. 25 at 33.
[49] e.g. under statute: *Dawson v Great Northern & City Ry* [1905] 1 K.B. 260.

assignable".[50] The phrase includes equitable choses in action,[51] though this point is of little practical importance since an assignment of an equitable chose is no more effective under the statute than it is in equity. The phrase also includes a debt not yet due but accruing due,[52] and the benefit of an obligation to do something other than to pay money,[53] or of one to forbear from doing something.[54] It does not include choses in action which can be transferred *only*[55] by complying with some other statute; thus shares in a company cannot be assigned by statutory assignment under s.136, but only in the manner prescribed by the articles of association of the company.[56]

## 4. GENERAL REQUIREMENTS

### (a) Formalities

A statutory assignment must be "by writing under the hand of the assignor". An assignment which for some reason fails to take effect as a statutory assignment may still be a good equitable assignment. Thus although an oral assignment cannot take effect under the statute, it may be valid in equity.[57] The statute merely provides an alternative method of making assignments; it does not destroy the earlier method. A disposition of an equitable interest "must be in writing signed by the person disposing of the same or by his agent thereunto lawfully authorised".[58] This rule is mandatory: an oral assignment of an equitable chose is therefore void.[59] As a general rule, writing is not necessary for an equitable assignment of a legal chose in action. But a contract may provide that rights under it shall be assigned only by use of a specified form, such as writing.[60] An attempt to assign such rights without using the stipulated form is probably not effective as an assignment, though it may amount to a contract to assign.[61] For the protection of the assignor's creditors, provision has been made by various statutes **15–016**

[50] *Torkington v Magee* [1902] 2 K.B. 427 at 430 (actual decision reversed on another ground: [1903] 1 K.B. 644); cf. *King v Victoria Ins Co* [1896] A.C. 250 at 254; *Manchester Brewery v Coombs* [1901] 2 Ch. 608 at 619.

[51] *Re Pain* [1919] 1 Ch. 38 at 44.

[52] *Brice v Bannister* (1878) 3 Q.B.D. 569 at 574; *Walker v Bradford Old Bank* (1884) 12 Q.B.D. 511; *Re Green* [1979] 1 W.L.R. 1211 at 1219–1224. Contrast *Law v Coburn* [1972] 1 W.L.R. 1238, where the date on which the debt became due was crucial under the relevant legislation.

[53] *Torkington v Magee* [1902] 2 K.B. 427.

[54] *Jacoby v Whitmore* (1883) 49 L.T. 335.

[55] s.136 may apply to a policy of marine insurance though such a policy is also assignable under Marine Insurance Act 1906 s.50: see *The Mount I* [2001] EWCA Civ 68; [2001] 1 Lloyd's Rep. 597 at [74].

[56] Companies Act 2006 s.544(1).

[57] cf. para.15–035.

[58] Law of Property Act 1925 s.53(1)(c), formerly Statute of Frauds 1677 s.9. Unlike the Statute of Frauds s.53(1)(c) applies to all "dispositions", whether they are assignments or not. It does not apply to resulting, implied or constructive trusts: see s.53(2) and *Neville v Wilson* [1997] Ch. 144.

[59] *Oughtred v IRC* [1960] A.C. 206; cf. *Grey v IRC* [1960] A.C. 1.

[60] cf. *Sumitomo Mitsui Banking Corp Europe Ltd v Euler Hermes Europe SA (NV)* [2019] EWHC 2250 (Comm); [2019] B.L.R. 561, where a performance bond could only be assigned if the assignee confirmed its acceptance of the assignor's repayment obligation.

[61] cf. para.15–025.

for the registration of certain assignments. Section 344 of the Insolvency Act 1986, for example, requires general assignments of book debts (or any class of them) made by a person engaged in any business to be registered; if they are not registered they are void as against the trustee in bankruptcy to the extent specified in the section.

### (b) Intention to assign

15–017 Although assignments must sometimes be in writing, no particular form of words has to be used to effect an assignment. The document need not on its face purport to be an assignment.[62] As Lord Macnaghten said in *William Brandt's Sons & Co v Dunlop Rubber Co*[63]:

> "An equitable assignment does not always take that form. It may be addressed to the debtor. It may be couched in the language of command. It may be a courteous request. It may assume the form of mere permission. The language is immaterial if the meaning is plain. All that is necessary is that the debtor should be given to understand that the debt has been made over by the creditor to some third person."[64]

An assignment is not itself a contract between assignor and debtor: its legal nature is that of a direction amounting to the transfer of a right. It follows that an assignment does not confer rights on the assignee under the Contracts (Rights of Third Parties) Act 1999.[65]

15–018 **Assignment distinguished from mandate.** A creditor does not necessarily assign a debt by asking his debtor to pay a third party. The request may be intended only as a mandate (or instruction) to the debtor to pay the third party.[66] Such a mandate does not give the third party any rights against the debtor, and can be revoked by the creditor. Similarly, a person who draws a cheque on his bank in favour of a third person does not thereby assign part of his bank balance.[67] The bank is not liable to the third party, though if it fails to pay him it may be liable in damages to its own customer. The position is the same where the customer gives a standing order or direct debit instruction to his bank in favour of the third party.

---

[62] But an ineffective transfer (i.e. a novation, see para.15–003) may not suffice as an intention to assign: *Essar Steel Ltd v The Argo Fund* [2006] EWCA Civ 241; [2006] 2 Lloyd's Rep 134 at [63].

[63] [1905] A.C. 454.

[64] *William Brandt's Sons & Co v Dunlop Rubber Co* [1905] A.C. 454 at 462; cf. also *Spellman v Spellman* [1961] 1 W.L.R. 921; *Palmer v Carey* [1926] A.C. 703; *Colonial Mutual General Ins Co Ltd v ANZ Banking Group (New Zealand) Ltd* [1995] 1 W.L.R. 1140; *Coulter v Chief of Dorset Police* [2003] EWHC 3391 (Ch); [2004] 1 W.L.R. 1425; and see *Swiss Bank Corp v Lloyds Bank Ltd* [1982] A.C. 584 at 613; and *Kijowski v New Capital Properties* (1990) 15 Con L.R. 1 (where there was no assignment).

[65] See para.14–099 and following.

[66] *Ex p. Hall* (1878) 10 Ch D. 615; cf. *Re Williams* [1917] 1 Ch. 1; *Timpson's Executors v Yerbury* [1936] 1 K.B. 645; *Dalton v IRC* [1958] T.R. 45.

[67] Bills of Exchange Act 1882 s.53(1); *Schroeder v Central Bank of London Ltd* (1876) 34 L.T. 735; *Deposit Protection Board v Dalia* [1994] 2 A.C. 367 at 400.

### (c) Communication to assignee

An assignment has no effect unless it is communicated[68] to the assignee by the assignor, or by someone with his authority[69]; or unless it is made in pursuance of a prior agreement between assignor and assignee. The reason for the requirement is not immediately obvious since a person can have property transferred to him without his knowledge, subject to a right to repudiate the transfer when he becomes aware of it.[70] One possible reason for the requirement is that communication to the assignee is evidence of intention to assign[71]; but such an intention could equally well be proved by other evidence. Alternatively, communication to the assignee may be regarded as the equivalent of the delivery which is necessary to perfect a gift of a chattel made otherwise than by deed.[72] A final possible explanation of the requirement is that it is based on the nature of assignment as a transaction between assignor and assignee. 15–019

### (d) Notice to debtor

#### *(i) How to give notice*

Notice of an equitable assignment may be oral,[73] but if the chose assigned is equitable, oral notice will seldom be effective between successive assignees.[74] Notice of a statutory assignment under s.136 of the Law of Property Act 1925 must be in writing.[75] It need not be given by the assignor, nor at the time of the assignment: it may be given by the assignee and is effective so long as it is given before action is brought.[76] There must, however, be a *notice* of assignment given by assignor or assignee: it is not enough to show that the debtor came to know of the assignment in some other way, e.g. as a result of discovery in legal or arbitral proceedings.[77] No particular form of words is necessary[78]; but the notice must clearly and unconditionally[79] tell the debtor to pay a third party *as assignee*, and not merely as agent for the creditor.[80] A notice which incorrectly states the date of 15–020

[68] According to *Alexander v Steinhardt, Walker & Co* [1903] 2 K.B. 208 posting is sufficient communication, but that case was doubted in *Timpson's Executors v Yerbury* [1936] 1 K.B. 645 at 657.

[69] e.g. by the debtor: *Burn v Carvalho* (1839) 4 My. & Cr. 690.

[70] *Standing v Bowring* (1885) 31 Ch D. 282.

[71] See *Re Hamilton* (1921) 124 L.T. 737.

[72] See para.15–029.

[73] *Ex p. Agra Bank* (1868) L.R. 3 Ch. App. 555.

[74] See para.15–023.

[75] See para.15–016; there is no requirement of notice for an assignment under Marine Insurance Act 1906 s.50: *The Mount I* [2001] EWCA Civ 68; [2001] 1 Lloyd's Rep. 597.

[76] *Walker v Bradford Old Bank* (1884) 12 Q.B.D. 511; *Bateman v Hunt* [1904] 2 K.B. 530; *Re Westerton* [1919] 2 Ch. 104; *Holt v Heatherfield Trust Ltd* [1942] 2 K.B. 1.

[77] *Herkules Piling Ltd v Tilbury Construction Ltd* (1992) 61 Build. L.R. 107.

[78] *Smith v SS "Zigurds" Owners* [1934] A.C. 209.

[79] *The Balder London* [1980] 2 Lloyd's Rep. 489 at 495.

[80] *James Talcott Ltd v John Lewis & Co Ltd* [1940] 3 All E.R. 592.

the assignment or, it seems, the amount of the debt, is invalid.[81] But a notice which says nothing at all about these particulars appears to be valid, so long as it describes the debt with sufficient certainty. A notice is valid although it inaccurately states that another notice had been previously given.[82]

A notice sent through the post has been said to take effect when it is received by the debtor.[83] This is clearly right where a dispute arises between assignee and debtor, for it is unreasonable to make the debtor suffer for failing to act on a notice of which he is not yet aware. But where the dispute is between successive assignees, it is at least arguable that the first to post his notice should have priority over any other assignee who has not yet posted his notice (or otherwise communicated with the debtor) when the first notice was posted.[84]

### *(ii) Effects of notice*

15–021 **Between assignor and assignee.** The rights of these parties may depend on whether the assignment is statutory[85]; and it can only have this character if notice is given.[86] If no notice is given, the assignment may still be effective in equity.[87] Notice to the debtor is not necessary to perfect the rights of an equitable assignee against the assignor.[88]

15–022 **Between assignee and debtor.** Notice is, however, necessary to perfect the title of an equitable assignee against the debtor,[89] since without such notice the debtor is entitled to assume that he remains liable to his original creditor (the assignor) and that he will get a good discharge by paying the assignor.[90] Notice may[91] also turn the assignment into a statutory assignment, in which case the debtor is liable to be sued by the assignee alone: he can no longer insist that the assignor be made a party to the action. Where the assignment is statutory, the debtor ceases, as soon as notice has been given, to be liable to the assignor[92] and becomes liable to the assignee. It is submitted that the same is true, where an assignment of part of a

---

[81] *Stanley v English Fibres Industries Ltd* (1889) 68 L.J.Q.B. 839; *WF Harrison & Co Ltd v Burke* [1956] 1 W.L.R. 419; criticised by R.E.M. 72 L.Q.R. 321; and distinguished in *Nicoll v Promontoria (Ram 2) Ltd* [2019] EWHC 2410 (Ch); [2019] B.P.I.R. 1519 at [60] on the basis that the notice misstated the date of the *deed of assignment* and not the assignment); cf. *Mannai Investment Co Ltd v Eagle Star Life Assurance Co Ltd* [1997] A.C. 749.

[82] *Van Lynn Developments Ltd v Pelias Construction Ltd* [1969] 1 Q.B. 607.

[83] *Holt v Heatherfield Trust Ltd* [1942] 2 K.B. 1 at 6.

[84] *Holt v Heatherfield Trust Ltd* [1942] 2 K.B. 1 is not inconsistent with this suggestion since the order in which the two claimants communicated with the debtor is not stated in the report.

[85] See para.15–026.

[86] Law of Property Act 1925 s.136(1).

[87] *Holt v Heatherfield Trust Ltd* [1942] 2 K.B. 1.

[88] *Gorringe v Irwell India Rubber, etc. Works* (1886) 34 Ch D. 128; *Re Trytel* [1952] 2 T.L.R. 32; *General Nutrition Investment Co Ltd v Holland & Barrett International Ltd* [2017] EWHC 746 (Ch) at [35], [67].

[89] *Warner Bros Records Inc v Rollgreen Ltd* [1976] Q.B. 430; Kloss 39 Conv. (N.S.) 261; *Herkules Piling v Tilbury Construction* (1992) 61 Build. L.R. 107 at 119.

[90] See *Stocks v Dobson* (1853) 4 D.M. & G. 11.

[91] i.e. if the assignment is in writing and is "absolute" (paras 15–011–15–014).

[92] *Cottage Club Estates Ltd v Woodside Estates (Amersham) Ltd* [1928] 2 Q.B. 463 at 467; *The Halcyon the Great* [1984] 1 Lloyd's Rep. 283 at 289.

debt is valid in equity, to the extent of the amount assigned[93]; for it has been held that if the debtor in such a case ignores the notice and pays the assignor he is not discharged and will have to make a second payment to the assignee.[94] Nor, once notice of an equitable assignment had been given, could the assignor sue the debtor without joining the assignee[95]; and if he does join the assignee his claim will fail to the extent of the amount assigned.[96]

In *Warner Bros Records Inc v Rollgreen Ltd*, it is suggested that an equitable assignment of a legal chose in action gives the assignee rights only against the assignor but none against the debtor, so that where, as in that case, the assignee of an option to renew a contract for services had not given notice to the debtor, it could not exercise the option.[97] This suggestion may be true of an agreement to assign a chose in action in the future; but any historical support which may once have existed for it in the case of an actual present assignment seems to have been made obsolete by the developments outlined at paras 15–006–15–008. The suggestion seems, with respect, to be based on failure to distinguish between the substantive rights arising in equity out of assignments and the procedure for their enforcement.[98]

**Between successive assignees.** A chose in action may be successively assigned by an insolvent assignor to several persons for more than it is worth. It is then necessary to decide in what order the assignees are to be paid. The rule is that successive assignments taken in good faith rank in the order in which notice is given to the debtor. Thus a later assignee may gain priority over an earlier one by giving notice first.[99] Notice of the assignment of an equitable chose should be given in writing, since oral notice of an assignment of such a chose does not give priority over later assignees in good faith and for value.[100] **15–023**

[93] The contrary view was, indeed, taken by Simon Brown LJ in *Deposit Protection Board v Dalia* [1994] 2 A.C. 367 at 382, but in a dissenting judgment; actual decision reversed but on other grounds [1994] 2 A.C. 391.

[94] *Jones v Farrell* (1857) 1 D. & J. 208; *Brice v Bannister* (1878) 3 Q.B.D. 569 (where the assignment was equitable: see *Durham Bros v Robertson* [1898] 1 Q.B. 765 at 774); *Ex p. Nichols* (1883) 22 Ch D. 782 at 787.

[95] See para.15–013.

[96] *Deposit Protection Board v Dalia* [1994] 2 A.C. 367 at 386, 387; reversed on other grounds [1994] 2 A.C. 367 at 391.

[97] *Warner Bros Records Inc v Rollgreen Ltd* [1976] Q.B. 430 at 443, 445; cf. *General Nutrition Investment Co Ltd v Holland & Barrett International Ltd* [2017] EWHC 746 (Ch).

[98] See *Three Rivers DC v Bank of England* [1996] Q.B. 292 at 315; and [1996] Q.B. 292 at 312, describing the requirement of joinder of the assignor to the action as "procedural and not substantive"; cf. *First Abu Dhabi Bank PJSC v BP Oil International Ltd* [2018] EWCA Civ 14 at [37] (" … who is the claimant is a mere procedural matter. In equity, the equitable assignee is the owner and controller of the chose and is entitled to sue on the chose for its recovery in his own name.") Contrast Edelman and Elliott 131 L.Q.R. 228.

[99] *Dearle v Hall* (1828) 3 Russ. 1; cf. *Stocks v Dobson* (1853) 4 D.M. & G. 11; *Mutual Life Assurance Society v Langley* (1886) 32 Ch D. 460; *Pfeiffer Weinkellerei-Weineinkauf GmbH & Co v Arbuthnot Factors* [1988] 1 W.L.R. 150. See also Goode 92 L.Q.R. 554–559; Donaldson 93 L.Q.R. 324; Goode 93 L.Q.R.487.

[100] Law of Property Act 1925 s.137(3).

## 5. CONSIDERATION[101]

15–024 The question whether an assignment must be supported by consideration is one of great complexity. Two points must be made to clear the ground for the discussion. First, the dispute concerns only the relative rights of assignor and assignee. The debtor cannot refuse to pay the assignee on the ground that the assignment was gratuitous[102]; he is liable to pay the debt in any event and his only interest is to see that all possible claimants are before the court, so that he does not run the risk of having to pay twice over. So long as this possibility of prejudice to the debtor is removed by the joinder of all appropriate parties, it is only the assignor who can raise an issue as to the validity of the assignment on the ground that no consideration was given for it; indeed the only purpose of taking the point is to enable the assignor to claim payment of the debt for himself. In practice this most frequently happens if the assignor has died or become bankrupt: his representatives may, for the benefit of his estate or of his creditors, wish to challenge the validity of the assignment. Secondly, the discussion concerns all gratuitous assignments, even those made by deed or for a nominal consideration.[103] The fact that an assignment is so made may make an assignor who disputes it liable in damages for breach of contract,[104] or make an agreement to assign binding contractually. But it does not, of itself, make the assignment effective as a transfer of the debt.

### (a) Assignments of future property

15–025 An assignment is the transfer of an existing right. There can be no assignment of rights which do not yet exist or belong to the assignor. Such rights are sometimes called "future property". An attempt to assign future property may operate as an agreement to assign which must be supported by consideration if it is to be binding.[105]

Money payable in the future under an existing contract is not necessarily future property, and a disposition of the right to receive such money may be an assignment and not an agreement to assign.[106] If the contingency on which the

[101] Megarry 59 L.Q.R. 58; Hollond 59 L.Q.R. 129; Hall [1959] C.L.J. 99; Sheridan 33 Can. Bar Rev. 284.

[102] *Walker v Bradford Old Bank* (1884) 12 Q.B.D. 511; the question of consideration may also be relevant for revenue purposes, but the question in cases of this kind is always whether the assignor could have denied the validity of the assignment, as against the assignee, e.g. *Re Rose* [1952] Ch. 499; *Letts v IRC* [1957] 1 W.L.R. 201.

[103] *Kekewich v Manning* (1851) 1 D.M. & G. 176 (deed); *Dillon v Coppin* (1839) 4 My. & Cr. 647 (nominal consideration).

[104] *Gerrard v Lewis* (1867) L.R. 2 C.P. 305; *Cannon v Hartley* [1949] Ch. 213.

[105] *Tailby v Official Receiver* (1888) 13 App. Cas. 523; *Glegg v Bromley* [1912] 3 K.B. 474; *Cotton v Heyl* [1930] 1 Ch. 510; cf. *Meek v Kettlewell* (1843) 1 Ph. 342; *The Attika Hope* [1988] 1 Lloyd's Rep. 439 at 442 (where "or future chose" seems to be a misprint for "of a future chose"); *Wu Koon Tai v Wy Yau Loi* [1997] A.C. 179 at 189; *The Cebu (No.2)* [1993] Q.B. 1 (where it was not necessary to distinguish between an assignment and an agreement to assign); *The Mount I* [2001] EWCA Civ 68; [2001] 1 Lloyd's Rep. 597 at [80] ("for value"); *Smith v Smith* [2001] 1 W.L.R. 1937 at [11]; *Bexhill UK Ltd v Razzaq* [2012] EWCA Civ 1376.

[106] cf. *Performing Rights Society v Rowland* [1997] 3 All E.R. 336 at 348.

money is payable is within the control of the creditor, there is no difficulty in holding that the disposition is an assignment: thus a builder can assign instalments to become due to him under a building contract as the work progresses, for here the contingency on which the money will become due is simply his own performance.[107] If, however, the contingency is not within his control, the disposition is prima facie an agreement to assign: this would be the position where a person purported to assign future dividends in a company which was not under any obligation to him to declare any dividends.[108] But even where the rights of the assignor depend on a contingency outside his control, he may purport to assign *either* his present right to future income from a specified source *or* the future income itself. A disposition of the first kind may be regarded as an assignment[109] and a disposition of the second kind as an agreement to assign.[110] The question into which category it falls turns on the interpretation of the document purporting to effect the disposition.

### (b) Statutory assignments

A statutory assignment, whether of a legal or of an equitable chose in action, is effective although it is made without consideration.[111] The reasons for this rule are discussed below.[112] **15–026**

### (c) Equitable assignments

The effects of a "voluntary" equitable assignment (i.e. one which is not supported by consideration) must be discussed historically. **15–027**

#### *(i) Before the Judicature Act 1873*

**Procedural view.** There are two main views as to the position in equity before 1873. According to one view, the need for consideration depended on the procedure for enforcing the assignment. In *Re Westerton*[113] Sargant J gave the following reason for holding that a statutory assignment was effective without consideration: **15–028**

> "Apart from the Judicature Act … the want of consideration would have been fatal to [the assignee's] claim. Prior to the Judicature Act … a legal chose in action such as this debt could not be transferred at law, and the assignee of the debt could only have sued in the name of the assignor, and in the absence of consent … or of a binding contract by the assignor … the use

---

[107] e.g. *Hughes v Pump House Hotel Co Ltd* [1902] 2 K.B. 190.

[108] *Norman v Commissioner of Taxation* (1963) 109 C.L.R. 9.

[109] *Shepherd v Commissioner of Taxation* [1966] A.L.R. 969; *The Mount I* [2001] EWCA Civ 68; [2001] 1 Lloyd's Rep. 597 at [80].

[110] *Williams v Commissioner of Inland Revenue* [1965] N.Z.L.R. 395.

[111] *Harding v Harding* (1886) 17 Q.B.D. 442; *Re Westerton* [1919] 2 Ch. 104.

[112] See after fn.114 and at fn.127.

[113] [1919] 2 Ch. 104.

> of the assignor's name could only have been enforced by filing a bill in equity ... and equity would not have granted that relief unless the assignment had been for valuable consideration".[114]

Since a statutory assignee can now sue the debtor without the co-operation of the assignor, "there is no reason for continuing against the assignee those terms which were imposed by equity as a condition of granting relief".[115] In other words, consideration is necessary if the assignee needs the co-operation of the assignor to recover the debt, but is not necessary if the assignee does not need such co-operation. If this were true three things would follow.

First, consideration should not have been necessary in the rare cases in which the assignee could sue alone at law.[116] This assumption is to some extent supported by the rule that the voluntary transferee of a negotiable instrument could sue all the parties liable on it, except the transferor.[117] But this rule was based on commercial practice, and not on the fact that the transferee did not need the co-operation of the transferor. It is not clear whether assignments of debts due to and from the Crown had to be supported by consideration.

Secondly, consideration should not have been necessary for absolute assignments of equitable choses, since the assignee could sue without the co-operation of the assignor.[118] This assumption, too, is borne out by cases in which such assignments were upheld, though they were voluntary. But in most of these cases the fact that the assignee could sue alone is not even mentioned, let alone relied on.[119] The decisions were based on the view that the assignor had made a completed gift.[120] And in some cases voluntary assignments of equitable choses were held invalid as incomplete gifts[121]; these are hard to explain on the procedural view.

Thirdly, consideration should have been generally[122] necessary for the assignment of a legal chose, since the assignee could not sue the debtor without the co-operation of the assignor. Here the procedural view breaks down. Although some voluntary assignments of legal choses were held invalid, others were upheld.[123] The distinction between valid and invalid assignments was not based on procedural requirements. It depended on the question whether the assignor had made a completed gift.

---

[114] *Re Westerton* [1919] 2 Ch. 104 at 111.

[115] *Re Westerton* [1919] 2 Ch. 104 at 114.

[116] See para.15–002.

[117] *Easton v Pratchett* (1835) 1 Cr. M. & R. 798 at 808. There is no reference to consideration in Carriage of Goods by Sea Act 1992 s.2, which deals with the transfer of rights arising under a contract contained in or evidenced by a bill of lading.

[118] See para.15–008.

[119] Exceptionally, the argument is mentioned in *Ward v Audland* (1845) 8 Beav. 201 (the actual decision was doubted in *Kekewich v Manning* (1851) 1 D.M. & G. 176).

[120] *Kekewich v Manning* (1851) 1 D.M. & G. 176; *Bentley v Mackay* (1851) 15 Beav. 12; *Voyle v Hughes* (1854) 2 Sm. & G. 18; *Donaldson v Donaldson* (1854) Kay 711; *Nanney v Morgan* (1887) 37 Ch D. 346; *Re Way's Trust* (1864) 2 D.J. & S. 365.

[121] e.g. *Bridge v Bridge* (1852) 16 Beav. 315 (doubted but distinguished in *T Choithram International v Pagarani* [2001] 1 W.L.R. 1 at 12); *Beech v Keep* (1854) 18 Beav. 285.

[122] Except where the legal chose was, even before the Judicature Act, assignable by some special statute (para.15–009) or at common law (para.15–002).

[123] *Ex p. Pye* (1811) Ves. 140; *Fortescue v Barnett* (1834) 3 My. & K. 36; *Paterson v Murphy* (1853) 11 Hare 88; *Richardson v Richardson* (1867) L.R. 3 Eq. 686; *Re King* (1879) 14 Ch D. 179 (where the

**Completed gift view.** A person may enter into a contract to dispose of his property, or make a gift of it, or create a trust of the property in favour of another. Consideration (or a deed) is clearly necessary for the validity of a contract to dispose of property, including a contract to assign a chose in action. It is equally clear that consideration is not necessary for the validity of a trust of a chose in action.[124] All that is necessary is that the settlor should clearly have expressed his intention to create a trust. As in the case of trusts of promises for the benefit of a third party,[125] a mere intention to benefit is not enough: there must be an intention to create a trust. The settlor must intend to undertake a legally binding obligation to hold the subject-matter for the beneficiary, or to persuade someone else to undertake such an obligation.[126] **15–029**

Consideration is also unnecessary for the validity of a completed gift. Thus in *Harding v Harding*[127] a voluntary statutory assignment was held binding on the ground that it was a completed gift. In many cases, the law requires a gift to be made in a prescribed way, e.g. the gift of a chattel must be made by delivery with intention to pass the property, or by deed of gift.[128] If a purported gift of a chattel is not made in one of these two ways, it is incomplete or imperfect; and equity refuses to complete an imperfect gift by ordering the donor to make it in the proper legal manner.[129] In the same way, a voluntary assignment of a chose in action did not bind the assignor unless it was made in the manner, if any, required by law. In *Milroy v Lord*[130] the owner of shares in a company voluntarily assigned them by deed poll. This was held to be an imperfect gift since the legal title to the shares could not be transferred except by the execution of a proper instrument of transfer. Turner LJ said:

> "In order to render a voluntary settlement valid and effectual, the settlor must have done everything which, according to the nature of the property comprised in the settlement, was necessary to be done in order to transfer the property and render the settlement binding upon him."[131]

---

assignment was made before the Judicature Act); cf. *Re Patrick* [1891] 1 Ch. 82; and *Re Griffin* [1899] 1 Ch. 408, in which the provisions of the Judicature Act relating to assignment were not mentioned.

[124] *Ex p. Pye* (1811) Ves. 140; *Bentley v Mackay* (1851) 15 Beav. 12; *Paterson v Murphy* (1853) 11 Hare 88; *Richardson v Richardson* (1867) L.R. 3 Eq. 686; *Paul v Constance* [1977] 1 W.L.R. 527. A declaration of trust is not, strictly, an assignment: see *Grey v IRC* [1958] Ch. 690; affirmed on other grounds: [1960] A.C. 1; cf. *Barbados Trust Co Ltd v Bank of Zambia* [2007] EWCA Civ 148; [2007] 1 Lloyd's Rep. 495.

[125] See paras 14–089—14–090.

[126] *Bayley v Boulcott* (1828) 4 Russ. 345; *Smith v Warde* (1845) 15 Sim. 56; *Re Caplen's Estate* (1876) 45 L.J.Ch. 280.

[127] (1886) 17 Q.B.D. 442.

[128] *Re Breton's Estate* (1881) 17 Ch D. 416; *Cochrane v Moore* (1890) 25 Q.B.D. 57; *Re Cole* [1964] Ch. 175.

[129] *Ellison v Ellison* (1802) 6 Ves. 656 at 662. For a special exception in cases of so-called *donatio mortis causa* see *Sen v Headley* [1991] Ch. 425 (land); *Woodard v Woodard* [1995] 3 All E.R. 980 (chattel).

[130] (1862) 4 D.F. & J. 264; cf. *Antrobus v Smith* (1805) 12 Ves. 39; *Jones v Lock* (1865) L.R. 1 Ch. App. 25; *Richards v Delbridge* (1874) L.R. 18 Eq. 11; *Heartley v Nicholson* (1875) L.R. 19 Eq. 233; *Macedo v Stroud* [1922] 2 A.C. 330; *Re Wale* [1956] 1 W.L.R. 1346; *Pappadakis v Pappadakis* [2000] 1 W.L.R. 79; McKay 40 Conv. 139.

[131] *Milroy v Lord* (1862) 4 D.F. & J. 264 at 274.

The assignment thus failed as a gift but the assignees argued that it could still take effect as a declaration of trust. This argument, too, was rejected, as the donor had no intention to create a trust, but only an intention to make a gift.

15–030 **Mitigation of the rule in Milroy v Lord.** A gift is only incomplete under the rule in *Milroy v Lord* if something more has to be done *by the donor* to transfer the property. If the donor has done all that he needs to do to transfer the property, the gift is complete even though further steps to vest the property in the donee have to be taken by a third party,[132] or by the donee himself.[133] The rigour of the rule has, moreover, been mitigated in a number of ways. It has been held that, where the gift takes the form of a declaration of trust, the vesting of its subject-matter in *one* of a number of trustees suffices to complete the gift[134]; and that a gift of shares in a company may be completed by the execution of a proper instrument of transfer (coupled with evidence of intention that this was to take effect as a gift and with circumstances making it unconscionable for the donor to resile from the gift) even without delivery of the instrument of transfer to either the donee or to the company.[135] Where further steps to complete the gift are capable of being taken by the donee, the donor may constitute himself the agent for the donee to take those steps, e.g. by telling the donee that nothing more needs to be done by the donee to perfect the gift. Failure by the donor to take those steps will not then vitiate the gift if the donee has relied on the donor's statement so as to make it unconscionable for the donor to invoke that failure as a ground of invalidity.[136]

The rule in *Milroy v Lord* applied only to gifts which had, by law, to be made in a certain form. The only formal requirement for the assignment of an *equitable* chose was that it must be in writing.[137] Hence in *Kekewich v Manning*[138] a voluntary settlement in writing of an equitable interest in property was held binding on the settlor, since there was nothing more that he could have done to transfer the property. Again, in the absence of special rules, such as those governing the transfer of shares in companies, equity did not lay down any formal requirements for the transfer of *legal* choses. Thus in *Fortescue v Barnett*[139] a voluntary assignment by deed[140] of a life insurance policy[141] was held binding on the assignor, as there was nothing more that he could do to complete the transfer.

[132] *Re Rose* [1952] Ch. 499; following *Re Rose* [1949] Ch. 78; cf. *Mascall v Mascall* (1985) P. & C.R. 119 (transfer of a house); contrast *Re Fry* [1946] Ch. 312.

[133] cf. *Re Paradise Motor Co Ltd* [1968] 1 W.L.R. 1125 (defective execution by transferee did not invalidate gift of shares).

[134] *T Choithram International SA v Pagarani* [2001] 1 W.L.R. 1.

[135] *Pennington v Waine* [2002] EWCA Civ 227; [2002] 1 W.L.R. 2075; the execution of the instrument of transfer by donor is essential for this purpose: [2002] EWCA Civ 227 at [69].

[136] *Pennington v Waine* [2002] EWCA Civ 227; [2002] 1 W.L.R. 2075 at [67].

[137] See para.15–016; cf. *Chinn v Collins* [1981] A.C. 533 at 548.

[138] (1851) 1 D.M. & G. 176; cf. *Re Way's Trusts* (1864) 2 D.J. & S. 365; *Nanney v Morgan* (1887) 37 Ch D. 346, decided after the Judicature Act, but without reference to its provisions regarding assignments.

[139] (1834) 3 My. & K. 36; cf. *Edwards v Jones* (1836) 1 My. & Cr. 226; *Re King* (1879) 14 Ch D. 179; *Re Patrick* [1891] 1 Ch. 82.

[140] This would not cure the want of consideration for the present purpose: para.15–024.

[141] See para.15–009: for assignment of life insurance policies.

**Other forms of incomplete gift.** A gift may be imperfect for some reason other than failure to use the proper form. The donor may only have said that he would make a gift in the future, or subject to some condition which can only be satisfied by his doing some further act. Thus a gift "to my daughter when she marries a man of whom I approve" is imperfect until the donor gives his approval. 15–031

**Completed gift view to be preferred.** The "completed gift" view seems to be preferable to the "procedural" view in two respects. It is more consistent with the reasoning of the cases decided before the Judicature Act. And it explains why voluntary assignments of legal choses were sometimes upheld. 15–032

### *(ii) After the Judicature Act 1873*

An assignment may now fail to be statutory, and so take effect (if at all) in equity, for one of three reasons. 15–033

**No written notice.** An assignment which fails to be statutory merely because written notice has not yet been given to the debtor is effective although it is not supported by consideration.[142] The assignor has done all that need be done *by him* to transfer the property, as notice can be given by the assignee. It would be futile to insist that the assignee must give consideration, since he could evade the requirement by simply writing to the debtor and so making the assignment statutory. 15–034

**No writing.** An oral assignment of an equitable chose is void, quite apart from the question of consideration.[143] It is more doubtful whether a voluntary oral assignment of a legal chose can be valid as a gift. 15–035

One view is that consideration is not now necessary in cases of this kind because the assignee no longer needs the co-operation of the assignor to sue the debtor: if the assignor refuses to join as co-claimant, he can simply be joined as co-defendant. But this argument is based on the untenable "procedural" view of the old rules of equity and it would fail even if that view were sound. It can make no difference whether the assignor is joined as co-claimant or as co-defendant. The important point is that he is joined at all. He is joined, not out of respect for history, but "to allow him to dispute the assignment."[144] One reason for disputing it might be that it was voluntary. If the assignor disputed the assignment on this ground, the debtor would in practice leave the assignor and assignee to fight out the dispute in which the debtor would have no interest. Thus in substance the assignor would be the sole defendant.[145] To argue that he will lose simply because he has been made defendant is to assume the very point in issue.

Another view is that an oral voluntary assignment of a legal chose in action fails as an imperfect gift under the rule in *Milroy v Lord*.[146] On this view, the

---

[142] *Holt v Heatherfield Trust Ltd* [1942] 2 K.B. 1.
[143] See para.15–016.
[144] *Durham Bros v Robertson* [1898] 1 Q.B. 765 at 770.
[145] cf. para.15–007.
[146] (1862) 4 D.F. & J. 264; para.15–029.

proper way to transfer a debt is by making a statutory assignment. If the assignor does not put the assignment into writing, he has not done "everything which, according to the nature of the property … was necessary to be done [by him] to transfer the property". This view was adopted in the Australian case of *Olsson v Dyson*[147] where a voluntary oral assignment of a debt was accordingly held ineffective.

Under the first of the above views, all oral voluntary assignments of legal choses would be valid; under the second they would all be invalid. Neither of these conclusions can be accepted. The law may recognise two ways of making a gift of a chose in action, just as it recognises two ways of making a gift of a chattel.[148] Before the Judicature Act a gift of a chose in action could be made by equitable assignment and equity laid down no formal requirements for this purpose. The Act provided a second method of making such a gift, without necessarily affecting the first. Thus in *German v Yates*[149] a voluntary oral assignment of a debt was held binding on the personal representatives of the assignor. Lush J rejected the argument that the gift was imperfect, and said that the Judicature Act had not "destroyed equitable assignments or impaired their validity in any way".[150]

The true position seems to be that oral voluntary assignments of legal choses can be valid so long as they are perfect gifts. They are not imperfect *merely* for want of writing, but they may be imperfect for some other reason. In particular, there may be room for doubt whether an oral statement was a completed gift, rather than a promise to make a gift in the future.

15–036 **Not absolute.**[151] An assignment of part of a debt may be effective without consideration. This can be deduced from *Re McArdle.*[152] A testator left his estate in equal shares to his five children. The wife of one of them, at her own expense, made improvements to a farm belonging to the estate. Thereafter, the children wrote to the wife: "In consideration of your carrying out certain alterations … we … hereby agree that the executors shall repay you [£488] from the estate." This promise was supported only by past consideration[153] and was held to be ineffective because it purported to be a contract and not a gift. It was further said that, even if the letter could be construed as a gift, it was not perfect, because something more had to be done by the donors; the executors could not have paid the wife without referring back to the children to find out whether the work had been done to their satisfaction.[154] On this reasoning, the result would have been different if the letter had on its face been a gift and had involved no reference back to the children. A letter simply saying "We hereby agree that the executors shall pay you £488 out of the estate" would have been a valid equitable assignment.

---

[147] (1969) 120 C.L.R. 365.
[148] See para.15–029.
[149] (1915) 32 T.L.R. 52.
[150] *German v Yates* (1915) 32 T.L.R. 52 at 53.
[151] See paras 15–011–15–014.
[152] [1951] Ch. 669; Stone 14 M.L.R. 356.
[153] See para.3–017.
[154] For criticism of this reasoning, see R.E.M. 67 L.Q.R. 295.

The question whether an assignment by way of charge must be supported by consideration is not likely to arise. Such an assignment is almost always made to secure a debt, so that there will generally be consideration for it in the shape of the assignee's advancing money or promising not to sue or actually forbearing to sue.[155] Moreover, such an assignment is usually intended to operate as a disposition by way of contract, and cannot be construed as a gift merely because, for some technical reason, there is no consideration. Even if the assignment were intended to operate as a gift, the fact that the amount assigned would fluctuate from time to time as the assignor increased or decreased his indebtedness to the assignee would show that the gift was not perfect.

The validity of a voluntary conditional assignment depends on the nature of the condition. An assignment of rent due under a lease "to A until she marries" might well be a perfect gift, and so might an assignment "to A when she marries", unless it is construed as a promise to make a gift in the future. But a gift "to A when she marries a man of whom I approve"[156] would be imperfect as it could not take effect until some further act had been done by the donor.

## 6. Subject to Equities

An assignee takes "subject to equities",[157] i.e. subject to any defects in the assignor's title and subject to certain claims which the debtor has against the assignor. He takes subject to such defects and claims whether they arise at law or in equity, and whether or not he knew of their existence when he took his assignment.[158] And he cannot recover more than the assignor could have recovered. The object of these rules is to ensure that the debtor is not prejudiced by the assignment.[159] 15–037

### (a) Defects of title

An assignor cannot confer any title if he had none himself. Thus if a builder assigns money to become due to him under a building contract, and then fails to perform the contract so that the money never becomes due, the assignee takes nothing.[160] Similarly, the assignee of a contract which is affected by mistake or illegality generally[161] takes no greater rights than the assignor would have had. Defences available by the terms of the contract to the debtor against the assignor can similarly be raised against the assignee.[162] On the other hand payment of the 15–038

[155] See paras 3–034–3–042.

[156] It is assumed that this is a condition and not consideration (cf. para.3–011).

[157] *Ord v White* (1840) 3 Beav. 357; *Mangles v Dixon* (1852) 3 H.L.C. 702 at 731; Law of Property Act 1925 s.136(1).

[158] *Athenaeum Soc v Pooley* (1853) 3 D. & J. 294.

[159] cf. *Sinclair v British Telecommunications Plc* [2001] 1 W.L.R. 38 (action by assignee stayed till an order for costs against assignor on an earlier action on the same contract had been satisfied).

[160] *Tooth v Hallett* (1869) L.R. 4 Ch. App. 242.

[161] An assignee for value may be able to enforce a life insurance policy though the estate of the assured could not do so because he died by his own hand: para.11–027.

[162] *The League* [1984] 2 Lloyd's Rep. 259 (arbitration clause); *Glencore International AG v Metro Trading International Inc* [1999] 2 All E.R. (Comm) 899 at 917 (exclusive jurisdiction clause).

debt to the assignor is a defence against the assignee only if made before notice of the assignment was given to the debtor[163] and the same is presumably true of rescission of the contract assigned by subsequent agreement between debtor and assignor.

## (b) Claims by debtor against assignor

15–039 The debtor may have claims[164] against the assignor which he could set up, if he were sued by the assignor, to diminish or extinguish his liability. Whether he can rely on such claims against the assignee depends on the way in which they arose.

### *(i) Claims arising out of the contract assigned*

15–040 **Defence or set off.** If the debtor has claims *arising out of the contract assigned*, on which he could have relied by way of defence or set off against the assignor, he can also rely on those claims against the assignee, and he can do so whether the claims have arisen before or after notice of the assignment is given to him.[165] Thus if a builder assigns money due to him under a building contract, and then commits a breach of that contract, the debtor can set off against the assignee the amount of any damages which he could have recovered from the assignor.[166] If this amount exceeds the sum assigned, the assignee will not be entitled to anything; but he is not liable to the debtor for the excess[167] as he is not himself in breach of the contract. Nor, once the assignee has been paid, is he liable to return the payment merely because events later happen which make the assignor liable to return it to the debtor.[168]

15–041 **Rescission for misrepresentation.** If the debtor has been induced to enter into the contract by a misrepresentation on the part of the assignor, he can rely against the assignee on the right to rescind the contract on that ground[169]; but a further problem arises where that right has been lost. In *Stoddart v Union Trust Ltd*,[170] the defendants were induced by the fraud of one Price to buy a business from him. Price made an assignment of £800, part of the agreed price, and the assignees now claimed this sum from the defendants. Two defences were raised. First, the defendants counterclaimed for damages for Price's fraud, but such a

[163] See para.15–022. If payment is made before the assignment then there is, of course, nothing left to assign: *Ibrahim v Barclays Bank Plc* [2012] EWCA Civ 640; [2013] Ch. 400 at [67].

[164] For this purpose legal (as opposed to equitable) claims can be "equities": *Roxburghe v Cox* (1881) 17 Ch D. 520; *Glencore Grain Ltd v Agros Trading Co* [1999] 2 Lloyd's Rep. 410 at 420.

[165] *Graham v Johnson* (1869) L.R. 8 Eq. 36; *William Pickersgill & Sons Ltd v London & Provincial Marine, etc. Ins Co Ltd* [1912] 3 K.B. 614; *The Raven* [1980] 2 Lloyd's Rep. 266; contrast *The Dominique* [1987] 1 Lloyd's Rep. 239 at 251 (approved [1989] A.C. 1056 at 1109–1101), where the debtor's claim could not have been set up against the assignor and was therefore not available against the assignee.

[166] cf. *Govt of Newfoundland v Newfoundland Ry* (1888) 13 App. Cas. 199.

[167] *Young v Kitchin* (1878) 3 Ex. D. 127.

[168] *The Trident Beauty* [1994] 1 W.L.R. 161.

[169] See *Banco Santander SA v Bayfern Ltd* [2000] 1 All E.R. (Comm) 766.

[170] [1912] 1 K.B. 181; the decision is viewed with scepticism in *Banco Santander v Bayfern Ltd* [2000] 1 All E.R. (Comm) 766.

claim could not be made against the assignees, as they were not themselves guilty of fraud, nor responsible for the fraud of Price. Secondly, the defendants pleaded that by reason of Price's fraud they had suffered loss exceeding £800, so that no money was due from them. This defence would have succeeded against Price; but it failed against the assignees as the claim for damages did not "arise out of the contract in question at all"[171] but was "something *dehors* the contract".[172] The decision seems to lead to the regrettable result that a contract may be worth more in the hands of the assignee than in the hands of the assignor, and so to defeat the purpose of the rule that an assignee takes "subject to equities". No attempt was made by the defendants to rely simply on their right to rescind the contract. They had disposed of the subject-matter and seem to have assumed that they could not rescind as they were unable to make restitution.[173] But the victim of a criminal fraud can rely on it by way of defence without making restitution.[174] This defence would seem to be an "equity" and should have been available against the assignee.

### *(ii) Claims arising out of other transactions*

**Claims against assignor.** The debtor may have a claim against the assignor arising out of some transaction other than the contract assigned, e.g. a debtor may owe money under a building contract and in turn have a claim against the builder for the price of goods sold and delivered. Such a claim can only be set up against an assignee of the debt due under the building contract if it arose before notice of the assignment was given to the debtor.[175] If the claim arises later, the debtor is not prejudiced by being unable to raise it against the assignee. He knows that the assignor is no longer his creditor in respect of the debt assigned and cannot therefore expect to set off against it any claims which he may later acquire against the assignor. 15–042

**Claims against intermediate assignee.** Where a debt which has been assigned to one person is then assigned by him to another, the question may arise whether a claim or defence which the debtor has against the first assignee can be set up against the second assignee. Such a claim or defence should be available against the second assignee, if it arose after the first assignment,[176] but before notice of the second assignment had been given to the debtor. If the debtor *paid* the first assignee before the notice of the second assignment, he would clearly not have to 15–043

---

[171] *Stoddart v Union Trust Ltd* [1912] 1 K.B. 181 at 193.

[172] *Stoddart v Union Trust Ltd* [1912] 1 K.B. 181 at 194.

[173] See para.9–114 and following.

[174] See para.9–106.

[175] *Stephens v Venables* (1862) 30 Beav. 625; cf. *Watson v Mid Wales Ry* (1867) L.R. 2 C.P. 593; *Roxburghe v Cox* (1881) 17 Ch D. 520; *Business Computers Ltd v Anglo-African Leasing Ltd* [1977] 1 W.L.R. 578; *Bibby Factors Northwest Ltd v HFD Ltd* [2015] EWCA Civ 1908; [2016] 1 Lloyd's Rep. 517 at [32].

[176] Not if it arose before then, since in that case the debtor can have had no expectation of being able to set it up in diminution of the debt assigned: *The Raven* [1980] 2 Lloyd's Rep. 266.

make a second payment to the second assignee. The same rule should apply if the debtor supplied goods to the first assignee on the terms that the price was to be set off against the debt assigned.[177]

15–044 **Effect of provisions of the contract.** The rule that claims arising before notice of the assignment can be set-off against the assignee may be excluded by the express provisions of the contract creating the debt. Such provisions are often found in debentures issued by companies to secure loans, since the rule that an assignee takes subject to equities unduly restricts the transferability of such instruments.

### *(iii) Assignee cannot recover more than assignor*

15–045 The assignee cannot recover more from the debtor than the assignor could have done. In *Dawson v GN & City Ry*[178] a landowner had a statutory claim against a railway company for injuriously affecting his land. He sold the land and assigned the statutory claim to the buyer. It was held that the railway company's liability to the buyer must be measured by the loss which would have been suffered by the assignor and that any *extra* loss suffered by the buyer by reason of a trade carried on by him, but not by the assignor, must be disregarded.

An attempt to distort the rather limited purpose of this principle was made in *Technotrade Ltd v Larkstore Ltd*.[179] The defendant produced a soil inspection report for the assignor in connection with the development of a site which the assignor then sold to the assignee. During the course of development by the assignee, a landslip occurred, after which the assignor assigned the benefit of the soil report to the assignee. The defendant argued that the assignee was unable to recover for the loss caused by the landslip since the assignor had parted with the site for full value and, having suffered no loss as a result of any breach by the defendant, could not itself have recovered damages from the defendant. This argument was rejected by the Court of Appeal as contrary to "legal principle and good sense".[180] The principle that the assignee cannot recover more than the assignor is intended to ensure that the debtor is no worse off as a consequence of the assignment, as in the *Dawson* case; it is not intended to enable the debtor to

---

177 According to a dictum in *Re Milan Tramways Co* (1884) 25 Ch D. 587 at 593 an ultimate assignee takes "free from any equities which only attach on the intermediate assignee"; but this view could cause injustice to the debtor, and the actual decision can be explained on the ground that the intermediate assignee's liability to the debtor was not established until after the second assignment had been made (see at 637). The actual decision in the *Milan Tramways* case was approved in *Fryer v Ewart* [1902] A.C. 187 at 192.

178 [1905] 1 K.B. 260; cf. *Crooks v Newdigate Properties Ltd* [2009] EWCA Civ 283; [2009] C.P. Rep. 34.

179 [2006] EWCA Civ 1079; [2006] 1 W.L.R. 2926; cf. *Prescott v Dunwoody Sports Marketing* [2007] EWCA Civ 461; [2007] 1 W.L.R. 2343 at [33]–[39].

180 *Technotrade Ltd v Larkstore Ltd* [2006] EWCA Civ 1079; [2006] 1 W.L.R. 2926 at [44]. The decision reached by the Court of Appeal was said to be supported by decisions which have extended the recovery of damages for third party losses: *Linden Gardens Trust v Lenesta Sludge Disposals* [1994] A.C. 85; *Darlington BC v Wiltshier Northern Ltd* [1975] 1 W.L.R. 68; *Alfred McAlpine Construction Ltd v Panatown Ltd* [2001] 1 A.C. 518 (discussed at para.14–028 and following), the aim of which is to ensure "that where a real loss has been caused by a real breach of contract, then there should if at all possible be a real remedy which directs recovery from the defendant towards the party which has suffered the loss" ([2006] 1 W.L.R. 2926 at [83] (Rix LJ)).

rely on the fact of the assignment in order to escape all legal liability for his breach of contract.[181] In the context of what was the transfer of land with the benefit of an assignment, the Court of Appeal approved the following dictum of Staughton LJ: "the assignee can recover no more than the assignor could have recovered if there had been no assignment, *and if the building* (land) *had not been transferred to the assignee*".[182] More generally, the assignee recovers to the same extent that the assignor could have done on the hypothesis that there had been no assignment and the assignor had not disposed of the subject-matter of the contract.[183] On this basis, so far as assigning the benefit of a contract is concerned,[184] it makes no difference, for the purpose of the present rule,[185] whether the breach, or the loss, occurs before or after the transfer of the subject-matter, or the assignment.[186]

## 7. NEGOTIABLE INSTRUMENTS

Special rules apply to the assignment of certain written contracts, called negotiable instruments, such as bills of exchange, cheques and promissory notes. A bill of exchange is a written order made by one person (the drawer) requiring another (the drawee) to pay a sum of money either to, or to the order of, the drawer or a named third person, or simply to the bearer.[187] If the drawee accepts the bill, he becomes liable as acceptor of a bill. A cheque is a bill of exchange drawn on a banker payable on demand[188]; cheques are now usually deprived of negotiability by being crossed "a/c payee" or "a/c payee only".[189] A promissory note is an unconditional promise in writing to pay a person a sum of money.[190] The categories of negotiable instruments are not closed, so that instruments can still become negotiable by mercantile custom, i.e. by being regularly so treated by **15–046**

[181] *Technotrade Ltd v Larkstore Ltd* [2006] EWCA Civ 1079; [2006] 1 W.L.R. 2926 at [42].

[182] *Linden Gardens Trust v Lenesta Sludge Disposals* 57 B.L.R. 57 at 80–81 (emphasis added) (in the House of Lords, a prohibition against assignment was found to be valid (at fn.204) and the decision of the Court of Appeal was varied on other grounds: [1994] A.C. 85; see para.14–029).

[183] cf. *Landfast (Anglia) Ltd v Cameron Taylor One Ltd* [2008] EWHC 343 (TCC); 117 Con L.R. 53 at [29]; *Pegasus v Ernst & Young* [2012] EWHC 738 (Ch); [2012] P.N.L.R. 24.

[184] For the purpose of assigning a claim in tort, the damage must have occurred prior to any sale so as to constitute the chose in action the benefit of which is then assigned, as in *GUS Property Management Ltd v Littlewoods Mail Order Stores Ltd,* 1982 S.L.T. 583 (but claims in tort are generally non-assignable: see para.15–061).

[185] cf. para.15–065.

[186] In the *Technotrade* case, the breach occurred before the sale of the site and the loss occurred after the sale, but before the assignment; in *Linden Gardens Linden Gardens Trust v Lenesta Sludge Disposals,* 57 B.L.R. 57; [1994] A.C. 85 the breach and the loss (though not the financial cost of remedying it) both occurred before the sale and assignment. This difference was regarded as "not crucial": *Technotrade Ltd v Larkstore Ltd* [2006] EWCA Civ 1079; [2006] 1 W.L.R. 2926 at [75]. *Darlington BC v Wiltshier Northern Ltd* [1975] 1 W.L.R. 68 (see para.14–032) is the equivalent of a case where breach and loss occurred after the "sale" and assignment since the assignor never owned the site to be developed.

[187] Bills of Exchange Act 1882 s.3.

[188] Bills of Exchange Act 1882 s.73.

[189] Bills of Exchange Act 1882 s.81A, as inserted by Cheques Act 1992; *Esso Petroleum Ltd v Milton* [1997] 1 W.L.R. 938 at 946, 954.

[190] Bills of Exchange Act 1882 s.83(1). A promissory note must be distinguished from an IOU, which is only evidence of a debt.

businessmen.[191] The transfer of a negotiable instrument differs from the assignment of an ordinary chose in action in the following ways.

15–047 **Transfer by delivery.** A negotiable instrument is actually or potentially transferable by delivery. A bill of exchange payable to bearer can be transferred by simply handing it to the transferee. If a bill of exchange is payable to the order of A, he can transfer it by indorsing it, i.e. by signing his name on it, and then handing it to the transferee. Notice of the transfer need not be given to the person or persons liable on the instrument.

15–048 **Defects of title.** An ordinary assignee takes "subject to equities",[192] but negotiable instruments pass from hand to hand like cash, so that it is particularly important that those who deal with them should be able to rely on their apparent validity. The transferee of a negotiable instrument therefore takes it free from certain defects in the title of prior parties[193] and from defences available among them, if he is a "holder in due course".[194] Such a holder is a person in possession of the instrument who has in good faith given value for it, provided that it is complete and regular on its face, not overdue and that it has not, to his knowledge, been dishonoured.[195] Every holder is prima facie deemed to be a holder in due course[196] unless the instrument is affected by fraud, duress or illegality[197]; but even in such a case the holder can still enforce the instrument if he can prove that he in fact gave value for the instrument in good faith. The only cases in which his title is no better than that of the transferor are those in which a party's signature to the instrument is wholly void, i.e. for mistake or under statute.[198]

15–049 **Consideration.** The holder of a bill of exchange is deemed to be a holder for value if value[199] has at any time[200] been given for the bill. Thus he can enforce it against (for example) the acceptor even though he himself gave no consideration for it. This rule should be distinguished from the further rule that consideration is not necessary for the validity of a transfer of a negotiable instrument.[201] Suppose that A draws a bill of exchange on B who accepts it. If A transfers the bill to C, neither A nor B can deny the validity of the transfer on the ground that it was gratuitous. But B can escape liability by showing that his acceptance was

---

[191] *Crouch v Crédit Foncier of England Ltd* (1873) L.R. 8 Q.B. 374.

[192] See para.15–037.

[193] Bills of Exchange Act 1882 s.38(2).

[194] Bills of Exchange Act 1882 s.29. And see Consumer Credit Act 1974 s.125, for special provisions designed to prevent evasions of that Act.

[195] Bills of Exchange Act 1882 s.29(1).

[196] Bills of Exchange Act 1882 s.30(2).

[197] Bills of Exchange Act 1882 s.30(2).

[198] *Foster v Mackinnon* (1869) L.R. 4 C.P. 704.

[199] An antecedent debt or liability is sufficient by way of exception to the rule that consideration must not be past: Bills of Exchange Act 1882 s.27(1)(b); para.3–022.

[200] Bills of Exchange Act 1882 ss.30(2), 27(2).

[201] *Easton v Pratchett* (1835) 1 Cr. M. & R. 798 at 808. The transferee could not sue the transferor, but the transferor could not prevent the transferee from collecting the amount due from the other parties liable.

gratuitous, and that C gave no consideration for the transfer. Want of consideration may enable the acceptor to resist an action *on the bill*. But it does not entitle the transferor to deny the validity of the *transfer*.

## 8. RIGHTS WHICH ARE NOT ASSIGNABLE[202]

### (a) Contracts expressed to be not assignable[203]

**Prohibited assignment.** If a contract provides that the rights arising under it shall not be assigned, a purported assignment of such rights is not only a breach of that contract but is also ineffective, in the sense that it does not give the assignee any rights against the debtor.[204] For example, a hire-purchase agreement may provide that the rights of the hirer shall not be assignable; and if he nevertheless purports to assign them, the assignee cannot enforce them against the owner.[205] An assignment of the benefit of a contract which is expressed to be not assignable may be binding as a contract or as a declaration of trust between assignor and assignee.[206] Thus it has been held that a settlement of an insurance policy, expressed to be not assignable, could be enforced by the beneficiaries against the settlor.[207] The beneficiary may be able to enforce the contract against the debtor, albeit indirectly, by joining the trustee as a party to the action.[208] **15–050**

**Assignment prohibited without the consent of the debtor.** Where assignment is prohibited without the prior consent of the debtor and it is not sought, it is no answer to say that, if it had been sought, it could not have been unreasonably withheld.[209] Where the contract states that consent will be deemed to have been **15–051**

[202] Tettenborn [2007] L.M.C.L.Q. 392; Tettenborn in Burrows & Peel (eds), *Contract Formation and Parties* (2010); Turner [2008] L.M.C.L.Q. 306; Tolhurst and Carter [2014] C.L.J. 405.

[203] Goode [2009] L.M.C.L.Q. 300; Carter and Tolhurst [2014] C.L.J. 405; Bridge 132 L.Q.R. 47.

[204] *Helstan Securities Ltd v Hertfordshire CC* [1978] 3 All E.R. 262; Munday [1979] C.L.J. 50; *Linden Gardens Trust Ltd v Lenesta Sludge Disposals Ltd* [1994] 1 A.C. 85 (rejecting the argument that such a prohibition is contrary to public policy); cf. *Hendry v Chartsearch Ltd* [1998] C.L.C. 1382; see generally Goode 42 M.L.R. 453; Alcock [1983] C.L.J. 328. For the construction of clauses prohibiting assignment, see *Flood v Shand Construction Ltd* (1987) 81 B.L.R. 31.

[205] *United Dominion Trust Ltd v Parkway Motors* [1955] 1 W.L.R. 719 (disapproved as to the effect of such a provision on measure of damages in *Wickham Holdings Ltd v Brooke House Motors Ltd* [1967] 1 W.L.R. 295).

[206] *Barbados Trust Co Ltd v Bank of Zambia* [2007] EWCA Civ 148; [2007] 1 Lloyd's Rep. 495; *First Abu Dhabi Bank PJSC v BP Oil International Ltd* [2018] EWCA Civ 14 at [26]; Turner 134 L.Q.R. 532; cf. *Co-operative Group Ltd v Birse Developments Ltd* [2014] EWHC 530; [2014] B.L.R. 359.

[207] *Re Turcan* (1888) 40 Ch D. 5; cf. *Don King Productions Inc v Warren* [2000] Ch. 291; *Spellman v Spellman* [1961] 1 W.L.R. 921.

[208] *Barbados Trust Co Ltd v Bank of Zambia* [2007] EWCA Civ 148; [2007] 1 Lloyd's Rep. 495 at [47], [119]; contrast, [2007] 1 Lloyd's Rep. 495 at [139]; para.14–095 at fn.607; Smith 124 L.Q.R. 517; Turner (2004) 20 J.C.L. 97.

[209] *Hendry v Chartsearch Ltd* [1998] C.L.C. 1382 (Henry and Millett LJJ; Evans LJ preferred not to express a concluded view); cf. *CEP Holdings Ltd v Steni AS* [2009] EWHC 2447 (QB). In *Hendry* the contract stated expressly that consent was not to be unreasonably withheld. Where there is no qualification to the debtor's consent, it may be subject to the requirement that it shall be exercised in good faith and must not be withheld "arbitrarily" or "capriciously": *Lymington Marina Ltd v McNamara* [2007] EWCA Civ 151; [2007] N.P.C. 27 (see para.2–098, fn.493).

given within a certain period of the request, it only takes effect at the end of that period and any earlier assignment will be ineffective.[210]

15–052 **Statutory exception.** The validity of prohibitions against assignment can be commercially inconvenient, particularly in the context of the sale of multiple debts ("receivables") on a discounted basis ("factoring"). For this reason, s.1 of the Small Business, Employment and Enterprise Act 2015 authorises the making of regulations invalidating a "non-assignment of receivables term". Subject to certain exceptions,[211] the Act applies to a contract for goods, services or intangible assets (including intellectual property) if at least one of the parties has entered into it in connection with the carrying on of a business.[212] The regulations made may provide that any such term has no effect, or has no effect in relation to persons of a prescribed description, or has effect in relation to persons of a prescribed description only for such purposes as may be described.[213] Regulations have now been made which apply to contracts entered into on or after 31 December 2018[214] and under which "a term in a contract has no effect to the extent that it prohibits or imposes a condition, or other restriction, on the assignment of a receivable arising under that contract or any other contract between the same parties".[215] This regulation does not apply to a fairly extensive list of excluded contracts,[216] nor if at the time of the assignment the supplier is a large enterprise or a special purpose vehicle.[217]

## (b) Personal contracts

15–053 The benefit of a contract cannot be assigned if it is clear that the debtor is willing to perform only in favour of one particular creditor, and if it would be unjust to force him to perform in favour of another. In such cases it is sometimes said that the "personal" nature of the contract prevents assignment.

15–054 **Employment contracts.** An important application of this principle is that an employer cannot assign the benefit of his employee's promise to serve. It has been said that the right of the employee to choose whom he would serve "constituted the main difference between a servant and a serf".[218] But in the case of an employee of a company, this right of choice will often depend on distinctions which are somewhat technical. If *the shares* in the company are sold,

[210] *Barbados Trust Co Ltd v Bank of Zambia* [2007] EWCA Civ 148; [2007] 1 Lloyd's Rep. 495.
[211] The Act does not apply to an "excluded financial services contract" which includes a regulated agreement under the Consumer Credit Act 1974, if prescribed by the regulations: ss.1(3)–(5).
[212] Small Business, Employment and Enterprise Act 2015 s.1(3).
[213] Small Business, Employment and Enterprise Act 2015 s.1(1).
[214] Business Contract Terms (Assignment of Receivables) Regulations 2018 (SI 2018/1254); Day 135 L.Q.R. 205.
[215] 2018 Regulations reg.2(1).
[216] 2018 Regulations reg.4.
[217] 2018 Regulations reg.3.
[218] *Nokes v Doncaster Amalgamated Collieries Ltd* [1940] A.C. 1014 at 1026; cf. *Denham v Midland Employer's Mutual Assurance Soc Ltd* [1955] 2 Q.B. 437; *O'Brien (Inspector of Taxes) v Benson's Hosiery (Holdings) Ltd* [1980] A.C. 562 at 572; *Don King Productions Inc v Warren* [2000] Ch. 291.

and its directors are replaced by others in the course of a take-over bid, the employee is, it seems, bound to go on serving the company. In law he still has the same employer[219] but his right of choice is in such cases of more theoretical than real importance. If, on the other hand, the company sells its *business*, then at common law the effect of the sale is to terminate the contracts of employment.[220] This common law rule has in turn been modified by delegated legislation by which certain transfers of undertakings do not terminate the contracts of their employees. Each contract of employment is kept in being as if it had originally been made between the employee and the transferee of the undertaking.[221] It follows that the contract can be enforced by the transferee against the employee,[222] but the employee can avoid this consequence by giving notice to the transferor or to the transferee that he objects to becoming employed by the transferee:[223] hence his legal right to choose his employer is preserved.

**Contracts involving personal confidence.** The common law principle applies to all contracts involving personal confidence. Thus a publisher cannot assign the benefit of an author's contract to write a book if the author relied on the publisher's skill and judgment as a publisher.[224] And the holder of a motor insurance policy cannot assign it since the insurer relies on the holder's skill and record as a driver.[225] It may be that even the benefit of a builder's promise under a building contract cannot be assigned, since such contracts are "pregnant with disputes" so that the builder may intend to deal only "with the particular employer with whom he has chosen to enter into a contract."[226] However, these comments have to be seen in context. They were put forward as one of the reasons why the builder may wish to insert into the contract an express prohibition against assignment and the implication is that, in the absence of such a prohibition, the builder's promise is assignable. Thus, it has been held that the benefit to the employer of a lump sum building contract is assignable.[227] In general, while a contract between a solicitor and his client might be regarded as a personal contract from the point of view of both the solicitor and the client, the question is fact specific and depends on the individual retainer.[228] In *Budana v Leeds Teaching Hospitals NHS Trust*[229] the Court of Appeal held that, given the 15–055

[219] cf. *Re Mack Trucks (Britain) Ltd* [1967] 1 W.L.R. 780; *Griffiths v S of S for Social Services* [1974] Q.B. 468; *Nicholl v Cutts* 1985 P.C.C. 311 (service contracts not determined by appointment of receiver).

[220] *Re Foster Clark Ltd's Indenture Trusts* [1966] 1 W.L.R. 125.

[221] Transfer of Undertakings (Protection of Employment) Regulations 2006 (SI 2006/246) reg.4(1); cf. also Learning & Skills Act 2000 s.95.

[222] *Morris Angel & Son Ltd v Hollande* [1993] I.C.R. 71; cf. *Newns v British Airways* [1992] I.R.L.R. 575. For enforcement by the employee against the transferee, see para.15–086.

[223] Transfer of Undertakings (Protection of Employment) Regulations 2006 (SI 2006/246) reg.4(7); *Humphreys v Oxford University* [2000] I.C.R. 405.

[224] *Stevens v Benning* (1854) 1 K. & J. 168; 6 D.M. & G. 223; *Hole v Bradbury* (1879) 12 Ch D. 886; *Griffith v Tower Publishing* Co [1897] 1 Ch. 21.

[225] *Peters v GAFLAC* [1937] 4 All E.R. 628.

[226] *Linden Gardens Trust Ltd v Lenesta Sludge Disposals Ltd* [1994] 1 A.C. 85 at 105.

[227] *Charlotte Thirty Ltd and Bison Ltd v Croker Ltd* (1990) Con L.R. 46 QBD.

[228] *Budana v Leeds Teaching Hospitals NHS Trust* [2017] EWCA Civ 1980; [2018] 1 W.L.R. 1965 at [47].

[229] [2017] EWCA Civ 1980; [2018] 1 W.L.R. 1965.

circumstances in which most personal injury litigation is now conducted, a conditional fee agreement[230] between a solicitor and a client lacks the features of a personal contract and is therefore assignable,[231] but since the consent of the client is also crucial, the process by which it may be transferred from one solicitor to another is novation[232] and not assignment.[233]

15–056 **Sale of goods.** In some circumstances, the principle may apply to contracts for the sale of goods. In *Kemp v Baerselman*[234] a farmer agreed to supply to a baker all the eggs which the latter should need in his business for one year; and the baker agreed not to buy eggs elsewhere during that period. The baker sold his business to a large company, to whom he purported to assign the benefit of his contract with the farmer. It was held that the farmer was justified in refusing to supply eggs to the company. One reason for the decision was that the baker's promise to deal exclusively with the farmer could not be enforced against the company.[235] Thus if the farmer were compelled to supply eggs to the company he would be subject to all the burdens of the original contract, but would lose the privilege of exclusive trading for which he had originally bargained.

But the benefit of a long-term contract for the sale of goods can be assigned if it was expressly or impliedly made with the buyer *or his assigns*. In *Tolhurst v Associated Portland Cement Co*[236] Tolhurst agreed that he would for 50 years supply to Imperial so much chalk as it should require for the manufacture of cement on certain land which was described in the contract. Imperial sold its business to Associated (a much larger concern), to which it purported to assign the benefit of its contract with Tolhurst. It was held that Tolhurst was not justified in refusing to supply chalk to Associated, since the contract was impliedly made between the parties and their respective assigns. The fact that Associated was a larger concern than Imperial did not increase Tolhurst's burden, since the contract obliged him only to supply so much chalk as was needed on the land originally occupied by Imperial.

15–057 **Accrued right to a fixed sum of money.** It seems that the rule against the assignment of "personal" contracts does not apply where the creditor has an accrued right to a fixed sum of money. A person who is indebted to an indulgent

---

[230] See para.11–013.

[231] cf. *Plevin v Paragon Personal Finance Ltd* [2017] UKSC 23; [2017] 1 W.L.R. 1249 at [5] ("common ground that the CFA was in principle assignable").

[232] See para.15–003.

[233] In the *Budana* case, Davis LJ held that it was more consistent with the intention of the parties to give effect to the transfer of both the benefit and burdens of the agreement by assignment, even if that required an incremental extension to the concept of conditional benefit: see para.15–081.

[234] [1906] 2 K.B. 604; cf. *Cooper v Micklefield Coal & Lime Co Ltd* (1912) 107 L.T. 457.

[235] For the validity of such exclusive dealing arrangements, see paras 11–143–11–150. Where a lease contains such a covenant by the tenant (e.g. one to buy all the petrol that he needs for his business on the premises) it may "run with the land". If so, the principle in *Kemp v Baerselman* does not apply and the covenant is at common law enforceable against an assignee of the landlord's interest in the land by virtue of the rules referred to in para.14–086: *Clegg v Hands* (1890) 44 Ch D. 503; *Caerns Motor Services Ltd v Texaco Ltd* [1994] 1 W.L.R. 1249.

[236] [1903] A.C. 414; cf. *Shayler v Woolf* [1946] Ch. 320.

creditor cannot apparently complain if the creditor assigns the debt to the debtor's trade rival (who may make him bankrupt), or to a debt-collecting agency.[237]

**Benefit assignable by one party.** In cases of "personal contracts", one party may be able to assign the benefit of the contract while the other cannot do so. Thus in *Kemp v Baerselman*[238] the farmer could no doubt have assigned the benefit of the baker's promise to pay for the eggs. **15–058**

**Effect between assignor and assignee.** Where a purported assignment fails because of the "personal" nature of the debtor's obligation, the transaction may nevertheless take effect between assignor and assignee by way of contract between them or by way of trust.[239] **15–059**

## (c) Mere rights of action

**Maintenance and champerty.** Maintenance involves the "wanton and officious intermeddling with the disputes of others in which the [maintainer] has no interest whatever, and where the assistance he renders to the one or the other party is without justification or excuse."[240] Champerty involves maintenance with the "added[241] notion of a division of the spoils."[242] Equity in general[243] regarded the common law's fear that assignments would lead to maintenance as exaggerated. But where assignments in fact savoured of maintenance[244] or champerty,[245] equity refused to enforce them. The Criminal Law Act 1967 abolishes criminal and tortious liability for maintenance and champerty[246] but goes on to provide that this "shall not affect any rule of law as to the cases in which a contract is to be treated as contrary to public policy or otherwise illegal".[247] Although reference is made to "a contract", it seems that this saving is not confined to contracts to assign, but extends to assignment itself. The rule against the assignment of certain rights known as "mere rights of action" has therefore survived the 1967 Act.[248] But, partly as a result of the Act, and partly as **15–060**

---

[237] cf. *Fitzroy v Cave* [1905] 2 K.B. 364. But the "personality" of the creditor may be material to the debtor: see *Gordon v Street* [1899] 2 Q.B. 641.

[238] [1906] 2 K.B. 604; para.15–056.

[239] *Don King Productions Inc v Warren* [2000] Ch. 291; Tettenborn [1998] L.M.C.L.Q. 498; [1999] L.M.C.L.Q. 353; cf. at fn.207.

[240] *Giles v Thompson* [1994] 1 A.C. 142 at 164; citing *British Cash and Parcel Conveyors Ltd v Lamson Store Service Co Ltd* [1908] 1 K.B. 1006 at 1014. It is the lack of any interest which is the key: *Simpson v Norfolk & Norwich University Hospital NHS Trust* [2011] EWCA Civ 1149; [2012] Q.B. 640 at [22].

[241] In some contexts (see para.11–012) there may be champerty without maintenance: *Sibthorpe v Southwark LBC* [2011] EWCA Civ 25; [2011] 1 W.L.R. 2111 at [54].

[242] *Sibthorpe v Southwark LBC* [2011] EWCA Civ 25; [2011] 1 W.L.R. 2111 at [54].

[243] See para.15–006.

[244] *Rees v De Bernardy* [1896] 2 Ch. 437.

[245] *Laurent v Sale & Co* [1963] 1 W.L.R. 829; *Trendtex Trading Co v Crédit Suisse* [1982] A.C. 679 at 694–695; *Camdex International Ltd v Bank of Zambia* [1998] Q.B. 22 at 37.

[246] Criminal Law Act 1967 s.13(1) and (2).

[247] Criminal Law Act 1967 s.14(2).

[248] *Trendtex Trading Corp v Crédit Suisse* [1982] A.C. 679.

a result of the current "more liberal attitude"[249] towards maintenance and champerty, the courts have considerably restricted the scope of the rule.

### (i) *Claims in tort*

15–061 **Assignment generally ineffective.** A right of action in tort cannot generally be assigned.[250] A person who is defamed or assaulted cannot sell his right to sue the tortfeasor. He can, however, sue the tortfeasor and agree to assign any damages he may recover; this is unobjectionable as it does not give the assignee any right to interfere with the conduct of the action.[251] Exceptionally, a right of action in tort can be assigned to an insurance company which has compensated the victim of the tort[252] and by a trustee in bankruptcy or the liquidator of an insolvent company who is, by statute, entitled to sell all rights of action for the benefit of the bankrupt's or of the company's creditors.[253]

15–062 **Criticism.** The generality of the rule against assignment of claims in tort is open to criticism. Such claims may be brought to assert rights of property;[254] and it is hard to see why the assignment of a right of action in (for example) conversion is more likely to lead to maintenance than the assignment of a debt.[255] Some tort claims can be enforced by restitutionary actions,[256] and it is arguable that the assignment of these, at least, should be allowed.[257] A move away from a general rule against assignment may be detected in the approach of Moore-Bick LJ in *Simpson v Norfolk & Norwich University Hospital NHS Trust*:

---

[249] *Trendtex Trading Corp v Crédit Suisse* [1982] A.C. 679 at 702. cf. *Giles v Thompson* [1994] 1 A.C. 142; see para.11–013.

[250] *Defries v Milne* [1913] 1 Ch. 98.

[251] *Glegg v Bromley* [1912] 3 K.B. 474; *Trendtex Trading Corp v Crédit Suisse* [1982] A.C. 679 at 702.

[252] *King v Victoria Ins Co* [1896] A.C. 250; *Compania Colombiana de Seguros v Pacific Steam Navigation Co* [1965] 1 Q.B. 101. Even if there is no assignment, the insurer is entitled to be subrogated to the victim's rights against the tortfeasor: Mitchell and Watterson, *Subrogation: Law and Practice* (2007), para.10.40.

[253] *Norglen Ltd v Reeds Rains Prudential Ltd* [1999] 2 A.C. 1 at 11–12. But see *Ruttle Plant Ltd v Secretary of State for Environment, Food and Rural Affairs (No.3)* [2008] EWHC 238 (TCC); [2009] 1 All E.R. 448 where the liquidator purported to assign the fruits of the cause of action and the rights which he had to commence and conduct those proceedings. The latter are not assets of the company but powers conferred on the liquidator by statute and not therefore assignable, so that the purported assignment was champertous. The insolvent company could be joined as a party and continue the proceedings and it seems that the problem would not arise on an assignment of the bare cause of action since in that case "the liquidator is thereby exercising the power of sale granted to him and an intrinsic part of that sale is the right to commence or continue those proceedings": [2009] 1 All E.R. 448 at [44].

[254] *Dawson v Great Northern and City Ry* [1905] 1 K.B. 260; *Ellis v Torrington* [1920] 1 K.B. 399; *GUS Property Management Ltd v Littlewoods Mail Order Stores Ltd*, 1982 S.L.T. 583.

[255] In *Three Rivers DC v Bank of England (No.1)* [1996] Q.B. 292 no objection seems to have been raised to the assignment on the ground that its subject-matter was described at 305 as a claim "for a tortious wrong".

[256] i.e. in cases of so-called "waiver" of tort where the tort benefits the defendant, e.g. where he converts the claimant's property. See Burrows, *The Law of Restitution*, 3rd edn (2010), Ch.24.

[257] cf. *Re Berkeley Securities (Property) Ltd* [1980] 1 W.L.R. 1589 at 1611.

> "It is difficult to see why a claim for damage to property caused by negligence should not be regarded as a chose in action and capable of assignment and if that is so, I can see no reason in principle why a claim for damages for personal injury should not be regarded in the same way."[258]

In the *Simpson* case itself, S's husband died after contracting an infection in the defendant's hospital. S settled a claim against the defendant without any admission of liability and continued to feel that the hospital had failed to confront its shortcomings and implement proper infection control procedures. In order to allow her to press these concerns she took an assignment of another claim against the hospital by C who had contracted the same infection. The claim was assigned for a consideration of £1 and the amount of the claim was £15000. While the Court of Appeal did not regard a claim for damages for personal injuries caused by negligence as inherently incapable of assignment, it regarded this claim as unlawful and void on the grounds of maintenance and champerty. The changing perceptions of public interest[259] meant that it was "not possible to state in definitive terms what does and what does not constitute a sufficient interest to support the assignment of a cause of action in tort for personal injury", but however genuine or laudable S's concerns may have been, a "collateral interest of this kind" did not qualify.[260]

### *(ii) Liquidated claims*

**Assignment allowed whether or not liability of the debtor is denied.** A liquidated sum due under contract (e.g. for money lent, goods supplied, or services rendered) or otherwise[261] can be assigned in spite of the fact that the debtor denies liability. A debtor cannot destroy the assignability of a debt by refusing to pay it.[262] The same is true of a claim to restitution of a liquidated sum in the event that the contract is unenforceable.[263] Nor is it relevant that such an assignment is made or taken with an oblique motive. An assignment of a debt is not invalid merely because its object is to enable the assignee to make the debtor bankrupt;[264] a fortiori if it is to pursue collective action on the part of multiple assignors on the basis that it would not be cost effective for each individual assignor to bring a claim.[265] **15–063**

---

[258] *Simpson v Norfolk & Norwich University Hospital NHS Trust* [2011] EWCA Civ 1149; [2012] Q.B. 640 at [7].

[259] See para.11–013, fnn.53, 54.

[260] The earlier decision of *Holden v Thompson* [1907] 2 K.B. 489 was explained as an exception to the general law of maintenance "in respect of charitable support": *Simpson v Norfolk & Norwich University Hospital NHS Trust* [2011] EWCA Civ 1149; [2012] Q.B. 640 at [24].

[261] *Dawson v Great Northern and City Ry* [1905] 1 K.B. 260.

[262] *County Hotel & Wine Co v London and North Western Ry* [1918] 2 K.B. 251 at 258; *Camdex International Ltd v Bank of Zambia* [1998] Q.B. 22; *JEB Recoveries LLP v Binstock* [2015] EWHC 1063 (Ch) at [54].

[263] *Casehub Ltd v Wolf Cola Ltd* [2017] EWHC 1169 (Ch) at [25].

[264] *Fitzroy v Cave* [1905] 2 K.B. 364; *Camdex International Ltd v Bank of Zambia* [1998] Q.B. 22 at 32; for a different oblique motive, see *Deposit Protection Board v Dalia* [1994] 2 A.C. 367 and see at fn.274.

[265] *Casehub Ltd v Wolf Cola Ltd* [2017] EWHC 1169 (Ch) at [28].

### (iii) Unliquidated claims

15–064 **Assignment before breach.** If the benefit of a contract, e.g. to deliver goods, is assigned before breach, the assignee can claim damages for the seller's subsequent refusal to deliver the goods.

15–065 **Assignment after breach.** It is less clear whether the right to claim unliquidated damages for breach of contract can be assigned after the contract has already been broken. One view is that such a right is a "mere" right of action and cannot be assigned.[266] But this view causes difficulty where the contract provides for the payment of a fixed sum in the event of its breach. Such a provision may be: (i) invalid as a penalty, in which case no more than the actual loss is recoverable; or (ii) valid as a liquidated damages clause, in which case the fixed sum (no more and no less) is recoverable.[267] According to the present view, the assignment would be valid if the contractual provision were a liquidated damages clause, and invalid if the contractual provision were penal. But this distinction has no relevance to the tendency of the assignment to maintenance. Another view is that a right to claim unliquidated damages for breach of contract can, generally,[268] be assigned. But this view in turn gives rise to difficulty where the claim which has been assigned could be framed in contract or in tort.[269] The assignability of the right to damages can hardly depend on the way in which it is described, though as we have seen, the rule against assignment of claims in tort has been called into question.[270]

15–066 **Whether in fact assignment savours of maintenance or champerty.** As both the views so far discussed are unsatisfactory, the law has adopted the intermediate view that a right to unliquidated damages for breach of contract may be validly assigned, so long as the assignment does not in fact savour of maintenance or champerty. If, for example, the assignee has a *proprietary* interest in the subject-matter, the assignment is valid since maintenance is committed only where a person interferes in another's litigation without having a genuine or substantial interest[271] in the outcome. Thus a vendor of land can assign to the purchaser the right to claim damages for breaches of covenant committed by the vendor's tenants before the sale;[272] and a buyer of goods which turn out to be defective can assign his claim in respect of the defect to a sub-buyer to whom he has resold the goods.[273] Similarly, "a conveyance of land can include the right to

---

[266] *May v Lane* (1894) 64 L.J.Q.B. 236 at 237, 238.
[267] See paras 20–135 and following.
[268] In *County Hotel & Wine Co v London and North Western Ry* [1918] 2 K.B. 251 at 259, an exception is made for contracts which are "personal" in the sense discussed at paras 15–053–15–059.
[269] e.g. *Matthews v Kuwait Bechtel Corp* [1959] 2 Q.B. 57 at 77.
[270] See para.15–062.
[271] *Martell v Consett Iron Co Ltd* [1955] Ch. 363.
[272] *Williams v Protheroe* (1829) 5 Bing 309; *Defries v Milne* [1913] 1 Ch. 98; *Ellis v Torrington* [1920] 1 K.B. 399.
[273] *Total Liban SA v Vitol Energy SA* [2001] Q.B. 643.

set aside an earlier transaction relating to it".[274] And a person can assign the benefit of a specifically enforceable contract, though the assignee elects, or is forced, to claim damages.[275]

**Assignment valid if the assignee has a "genuine commercial interest".** Even where the assignee has no proprietary interest, the assignment may be valid if he has a "genuine commercial interest"[276] in the subject-matter of the action. In *Trendtex Trading Ltd v Crédit Suisse*[277] a bank had financed a sale of cement by one of its customers. It was held that the bank could validly have taken an assignment from the customer of his claim for damages for wrongful failure to pay for the cement.[278] But the assignment actually made was held to be champertous and invalid because it was expressed to have been taken for the purpose of enabling the bank to resell the customer's right of action to a third party, so that the profit resulting from its enforcement (which was considerable)[279] could be divided between the third party and the bank. The crucial fact was that the assignee contemplated a further sale of the right, as opposed to its enforcement by himself. If he intends to pursue the latter course, the assignment is not champertous merely because he expects to improve his position by taking the assignment: unless this were so, few assignments would be valid.[280] 15–067

### *(iv) Other assignments contrary to public policy*

**Wages or salary.** In English law, an assignment of wages or salary is generally valid,[281] so long as it does not deprive the employee of his sole means of support.[282] But a public officer cannot assign his salary.[283] This rule was originally based on two considerations of public policy. First, it was thought that a public officer must not be deprived of the means to maintain the dignity of his 15–068

[274] *Defries v Milne* [1913] 1 Ch. 98 at 110; citing *Dickinson v Burrell* (1866) L.R. 1 Eq. 337 (see especially at 342). The only point of these dicta is that such an assignment is not champertous. On the issue of the assignability of a right to rescind, they are hard to reconcile with *Investors Compensation Scheme Ltd v West Bromwich BC* [1998] W.L.R. 896 (para.15–006) where they were not cited.

[275] *Torkington v Magee* [1902] 2 K.B. 427; reversed on another ground: [1903] 1 K.B. 644.

[276] *Trendtex Trading Ltd v Crédit Suisse* [1982] A.C. 679 at 703; cf. *The Aiolos* [1983] 2 Lloyd's Rep. 25; *Brownton Ltd v Edward Moore Inbucon Ltd* [1985] 3 All E.R. 499 (where the same result could now be reached without assignment under Civil Liability (Contribution) Act 1978 ss.1(1), 2(1)); *The Kelo* [1985] 2 Lloyd's Rep. 85; *Weddell v J A Pearce & Major* [1988] Ch. 26 at 43; *Murray v Young & Co's Brewery Co* [1997] 1 Lloyd's Rep. 236; *Tharros Shipping Co v Den Norske Bank Plc* [1997] 1 Lloyd's Rep. 541; *Stocznia Gdanska v Latvian Shipping Co (No.2)* [1999] 3 All E.R. 822; *Massai Aviation Services v Attorney General of the Bahamas* [2007] UKPC 12.

[277] [1982] A.C. 679; Thornely [1982] C.L.J. 29.

[278] The claim was not against the buyer for the price but against a bank for damages for failing to honour a letter of credit: cf. para.20–067.

[279] The bank paid $800,000 for the claim and sold it for $1,100,000 to the third party who settled it for $8,000,000.

[280] *Brownton Ltd v Edward Moore Inbucon Ltd* [1985] 3 All E.R. 499 at 506, 509; cf. *Massai Aviation Services v Attorney General of the Bahamas* [2007] UKPC 12 (shareholders retained the benefit of a lawsuit by assigning it to a new company and sold existing business at a reduced price because it did not include the lawsuit).

[281] For a statutory exception, see Merchant Shipping Act 1995 s.34(1)(c).

[282] *King v Michael Faraday & Partners Ltd* [1939] 2 K.B. 753.

[283] *Methwold v Walbank* (1750) 2 Ves. Sen. 238; *Liverpool Corp v Wright* (1859) 28 L.J.Ch. 868.

office; but this argument now has little force, except, perhaps, in the case of ambassadors. Secondly, it was thought that public officers must have the means to pay damages for wrongs committed by them or by their order; but this is no longer important since the injured party can now sue the Crown.[284] It could perhaps be argued that to allow such assignments might lead to corruption. But this seems to be a remote contingency; and the argument proves too much. Officers who are paid out of local funds can assign their salaries,[285] but are presumably just as corruptible as officers paid out of national funds.

15–069 **Maintenance payments.** Maintenance and other similar payments to which a wife may become entitled as a result of matrimonial proceedings are inalienable, since to allow the wife to assign them might leave her destitute.[286]

15–070 **Statutory restrictions.** There are many other statutory restrictions on assignment, based on various considerations of public policy.[287]

15–071 **Oblique motive.** An assignment is not contrary to public policy merely because it was made and taken with an oblique motive, e.g. if its purpose was to enable the assignee to obtain legal aid when this would not have been available in an action brought by the assignor against the debtor.[288]

## 9. Assignment by Operation of Law

### (a) Death

15–072 **Rights generally pass to personal representatives.** On the death of a contracting party, his rights generally pass to his personal representatives, who can recover any sums due under the contract or damages for its breach. The representatives may sometimes recover less than the deceased would have done, and sometimes more. Thus, personal representatives cannot recover exemplary damages.[289] On the other hand, in *Otter v Church, Adams, Tatham & Co*[290] solicitors negligently advised a client that he had an absolute interest in property, when in fact he had an entailed interest. Had the mistake been discovered while the client was alive, he could have barred the entail, so that the solicitors would only have been liable for nominal damages. But the mistake was not discovered until after the client's death, with the result that the solicitors had to pay substantial damages as the entailed property was through their negligence lost to the client's estate.

---

[284] Under the Crown Proceedings Act 1947.

[285] *Re Mirams* [1891] 1 Q.B. 594.

[286] *Watkins v Watkins* [1896] P. 222.

[287] e.g. Police Pensions Act 1976 s.9; Pensions Act 1995 s.91.

[288] See *Norglen Ltd v Reeds Rains Prudential Ltd* [1999] 2 A.C. 1; cf. at fn.264.

[289] Law Reform (Miscellaneous Provisions) Act 1934 s.1(2)(a)(i), as amended by Administration of Justice Act 1982 s.4. Such damages are hardly ever (if at all) recoverable on a breach of contract: para.20–022.

[290] [1953] Ch. 280.

**Personal contracts.** Where at time of death the contract is still partly executory, the personal representatives are generally entitled to complete its performance and to claim the agreed remuneration. But they cannot do so if the contract is "personal" in the sense that one party places confidence in the skill, judgment or integrity of the other. Thus if either party to a contract of employment dies, his right to go on serving, or to be served (as the case may be), does not pass to his representatives: they can enforce only rights which had accrued before,[291] or which accrue on,[292] death. It is possible for one party, but not the other, to rely on such personal considerations. If a painter contracted to paint a house and died when the work was half-done, his representatives might not be entitled to finish the work and claim the contract price; but if the houseowner died, his representatives might well be able to demand further performance from the painter. 15–073

## (b) Bankruptcy

**Deemed assignment to trustee in bankruptcy.** When a person is adjudged bankrupt, things in action forming part of his estate at the commencement of the bankruptcy[293] are "deemed to have been assigned" to his trustee in bankruptcy.[294] Thus the trustee can recover debts due to the bankrupt and claim damages for breach of any contract with the bankrupt. Where the contract is executory, the trustee may be entitled to perform it and claim payment from the other party. 15–074

**Personal contracts.** Certain "personal" rights do not pass to the trustee. The word "personal" is here used in two senses. First: rights do not pass to the trustee if they are concerned with the person or personal affairs of the bankrupt. Thus a right to claim damages for injury to reputation does not pass,[295] nor does the benefit of a contract "to carry him [the bankrupt] in safety, [or] to cure his person of a wound or disease … ."[296] Such rights do not pass to the trustee, even though they have accrued before bankruptcy. The rule is based on the view that only the bankrupt's property is divisible between his creditors: they are not entitled to benefit from injuries to his person. The "property"[297] of the bankrupt that vests in his trustee[298] includes "things in action"[299] without qualification; it includes contractual rights even though the contract giving rise to them in terms prohibits their assignment.[300] But the definition has not changed the previous rules relating 15–075

291 *Stubbs v Holywell Ry* (1867) L.R. 2 Ex. 311.

292 e.g. death benefits payable under a contract of employment.

293 For after-acquired property, see Insolvency Act 1986 s.307.

294 Insolvency Act 1986 s.311.

295 *Wilson v United Counties Bank* [1920] A.C. 102.

296 *Beckham v Drake* (1849) 2 H.L.C. 579 at 627.

297 Insolvency Act 1986 s.283(1).

298 Insolvency Act 1986 s.306.

299 Insolvency Act 1986 s.436; *Re Landau* [1998] Ch. 223; *Performing Right Society v Rowland* [1997] 3 All E.R. 336 at 348.

300 See *Re Landau* [1998] Ch. 223; *Krasner v Dennison* [2001] Ch. 76; and see fn.304.

to "personal" rights of the kind just described.[301] The bankrupt may have a single cause of action giving rise to a right to damages in respect both of personal loss (such as pain and suffering resulting from personal injury) and economic loss (such as loss of earnings resulting from the same injury). The cause of action is then vested in his trustee but the trustee must account to the bankrupt for such part of the amount recovered as relates to the bankrupt's personal loss, and to earnings lost after the bankrupt's discharge.[302] The proceeds of insurance against permanent disability, on the other hand, do pass to the trustee since the purpose of such a policy is to protect the insured against economic loss by the payment of premiums which, had they not been used for this purpose, would have been available for the payment of his debts.[303] By statute, rights under certain pension schemes are excluded from the bankrupt's estate.[304]

Secondly, the benefit of an *executory* contract does not pass to the trustee if it was "personal" in the sense that the other contracting party relied on the skill and judgment of the bankrupt. In such a case the other party cannot be required to accept performance from the trustee or someone employed by him. Thus where a contract to build a house was "personal" in this sense, the trustee was not entitled to finish the house and then to demand payment.[305] But the trustee may employ the bankrupt to finish the work, and if the other party in this way gets precisely what he bargained for, the trustee can enforce the contract against him.[306]

15–076 **Income to which the bankrupt is from time to time entitled.** Special rules apply to payments in the nature of income to which the bankrupt is from time to time entitled.[307] Such entitlement may not vest in the trustee because the bankrupt's right to the payment may not arise until after the commencement of the bankruptcy,[308] typically where the income consists of the bankrupt's earnings after the date of the bankruptcy. In respect of such earnings,[309] the trustee may apply to the court for an "income payments order"[310] requiring either the bankrupt or the person from whom the payments are due[311] to pay to the trustee so much of the income as may be specified in the order. In deciding what part (if any) of the income is to be paid over to the trustee, the court takes account of "what appears … to be necessary for meeting the reasonable domestic needs of the bankrupt and his family":[312] an income payments order must not be made if its effect would be to reduce the income of the bankrupt below this level. These provisions are not based on the "personal" nature of the contract under which the

[301] *Heath v Tang* [1993] 1 W.L.R. 1421 at 1423; *Ord v Upton* [2000] Ch. 352 at 360; *Haigh v Aitken* [2001] Ch. 110 (bankrupt's personal correspondence not "property" for present purpose); *Cork v Rawlins* [2001] EWCA Civ 202; [2001] Ch. 792 at [21].
[302] *Ord v Upton* [2000] Ch. 352.
[303] *Cork v Rawlins* [2001] EWCA Civ 202; [2001] Ch. 792.
[304] Welfare Reform and Pensions Act 1999 s.11.
[305] *Knight v Burgess* (1864) 33 L.J. Ch. 727; cf. *Lucas v Moncrieff* (1905) 21 T.L.R. 683.
[306] *Oliphant v Wadling* (1875) 1 Q.B.D. 145; *Re Shine* [1892] 1 Q.B. 522.
[307] Insolvency Act 1986 s.310(7).
[308] Insolvency Act 1986 s.283(1)(a).
[309] See *Krasner v Dennison* [2001] Ch. 76 at [33] (on such facts see now at fn.288).
[310] Insolvency Act 1986 s.310(1).
[311] Insolvency Act 1986 s.310(3).
[312] Insolvency Act 1986 s.310(2).

income is earned (for *ex hypothesi* the bankrupt is himself still rendering the services) but on the need to allow the bankrupt to work to maintain himself and his family.[313]

**Priority.** A trustee in bankruptcy is in a less favourable position than an ordinary assignee in that he cannot gain priority over a previous assignee for value by being the first to give notice to the debtor.[314] 15–077

## 10. ASSIGNMENT DISTINGUISHED FROM TRANSFER OF LIABILITIES

**No assignment of liability.** Assignment is the transfer of a *right* without the consent of the debtor. The common law does not recognise the converse process of the transfer of a contractual *liability* without the consent of the creditor: "the burden of a contract can never be assigned without the consent of the other party to the contract … ."[315] If A has a contractual right against X, he cannot be deprived of that right merely because X and Y agree that X's duty under his contract with A is to be performed by Y and not by X.[316] The phrase "assignment of liabilities" is highly misleading and should be avoided. It is of course possible for Y to perform X's obligation. The question whether the creditor is bound to accept such vicarious performance (so as to discharge X) will be considered in Ch.17.[317] It is also possible, in the situations to be discussed below, for Y to become liable to perform the obligation originally undertaken by X; but in these situations there is generally[318] no true transfer of liability. 15–078

### (a) Novation

We have seen that it is possible by novation to substitute one creditor for another.[319] Similarly, one debtor may by novation be substituted for another. In *Miller's Case*[320] the claimant insured his life with the X Co, which was later amalgamated with the Y Co, which agreed to become liable on the policy if the claimant paid future premiums to it. The claimant did so, and it was held that he could enforce the policy against the Y Co. It has been suggested that a similar 15–079

---

[313] cf. *Re Roberts* [1900] 1 Q.B. 122, commenting on the position under earlier legislation.

[314] *Re Wallis* [1902] 1 K.B. 719. This rule does not seem to be affected by Insolvency Act 1986 s.311(4).

[315] *Linden Gardens Trust Ltd v Lenesta Sludge Disposals Ltd* [1994] 1 A.C. 85 at 103; *Don King Productions Inc v Warren* [1998] 1 All E.R. 609 at 631; affirmed [2000] Ch. 291; cf. *Société Commerciale de Réassurance v ERAS International Ltd* [1992] 1 Lloyd's Rep. 570 at 595–596; *Weldon v GRE Linked Life Assurance Ltd* [2000] 2 All E.R. (Comm) 914 at 922.

[316] For statutory exceptions to this principle, by which either party to a lease may be released from liabilities under it in consequence of the assignment of his interest, see Landlord and Tenant (Covenants) Act 1995 ss.5, 6.

[317] See paras 17–007–17–013.

[318] For what seems to be an exception, see para.15–087.

[319] See para.15–003.

[320] (1876) 3 Ch D. 391; cf. *Société Commerciale de Réassurance v ERAS International Ltd* [1992] 1 Lloyd's Rep. 570 at 596. Contrast *Re a Company (No.0032314 of 1992), Duckwari Plc v Offerventure Ltd* [1995] B.C.C. 89.

analysis may apply where a customer pays by credit card[321] for goods supplied by a retailer: the customer's liability to the retailer is discharged and a new liability to the retailer is undertaken by the company issuing the card.[322] Such arrangements are binding only if they are made with the appropriate contractual intention,[323] and if they are supported by consideration. Usually the creditor provides consideration for the new debtor's promise to pay him by agreeing to release the original debtor or to accept a discount;[324] and the original debtor provides consideration for the creditor's promise to release him by providing a new debtor.[325] The effect of novation is not, in strict theory, to *transfer* a liability, but to extinguish it and put a new one in its place.[326]

### (b) Benefit and burden

15–080 Generally, a person to whom the benefit of a contract is assigned makes no promise to perform the obligations of the assignor; and in the ordinary case such an assignee does not become liable under the contract. Suppose, for example, that a builder assigns to a bank moneys due or to become due under a building contract. The bank is under no liability to the builder's client for any breach of contract by the builder; the most that the client can do is to rely on the builder's breach in diminution or extinction of the bank's claim.[327]

15–081 **Conditional benefit.**[328] There are, however, exceptions, or apparent exceptions, to this general rule.[329] In particular, the discharge of a burden may be a condition of the enjoyment of the benefit, so that the burden can be said to be annexed to the benefit, or to the subject-matter of the contract. Where this is the case, a person (other than one of the original contracting parties) to whom the benefit is transferred must perform the burden, or at least forego the benefit if he fails to do so. If, for example, a right to extract minerals is subject to the duty to pay compensation if the surface of the land is let down, such compensation may have to be paid by the assignee of the mining right.[330] This exception, however, does

[321] See para.17–005.

[322] *Customs & Excise Commissioners v Diners Club Ltd* [1989] 1 W.L.R. 1196; citing *Re Charge Card Services* [1989] Ch. 497 at 513 ("quasi-novation").

[323] A requirement not satisfied in *Tito v Waddell (No.2)* [1977] Ch. 106: see at 287.

[324] *Customs & Excise Commissioners v Diners Club Ltd* [1988] 2 All E.R. 1016 at 1023; affirmed [1989] 1 W.L.R. 1196.

[325] See para.3–165.

[326] The substitution of a party to one particular obligation does not necessarily mean that the rest of a large and complex contract which contains other obligations has been terminated and replaced by an entirely new one: *Langston Group Corp v Cardiff City Football Club Ltd* [2008] EWHC 535 (Ch) at [42].

[327] See *Young v Kitchin* (1878) 3 Ex. D. 127; *The Trident Beauty* [1994] 1 W.L.R. 161 at 165, 170; Tettenborn [1993] C.L.J. 220; para.15–040.

[328] For discussion of the limits of this principle and whether it requires the parties to effect a novation rather than assignment, see the difference of opinion between Gloster LJ and Davis LJ in *Budana v Leeds Teaching Hospitals NHS Trust* [2017] EWCA Civ 1980; [2018] 1 W.L.R. 1965.

[329] For a statutory exception relating to covenants in leases, see Landlord and Tenant (Covenants) Act 1995 s.3.

[330] e.g. *Aspden v Seddon (No.2)* (1876) 1 Ex. D. 496; cf. *Chamber Colliery Co Ltd v Twyerould* (1893) [1915] 1 Ch. 268n; *Werderman v Société Générale d'Electricité* (1881) 19 Ch D. 246;

not apply if the burden, though imposed in the same instrument which creates the right, is not a condition of its exercise but an independent obligation undertaken by the original grantee of the right.[331]

**"Pure principle of benefit and burden".** But even the burden of such independent obligations may have to be performed by an assignee under a second, and broader, exception to the general rule. This has been called by Megarry VC the "pure principle of benefit and burden";[332] it is "distinct from the conditional benefit cases, and cases of burdens annexed to property."[333] In *Tito v Waddell (No.2)*[334] a company that was engaged in mining phosphates on a Pacific island had acquired land there under contracts obliging it to return any worked out land to its former owners and to replant it. The rights under these contracts were transferred to commissioners "subject to ... the covenants ... therein contained"; and the commissioners undertook to keep the company indemnified against claims by the landowners under the original contracts. Many years after the company had been wound-up, it was held that the commissioners were liable to the landowners for failing to perform the covenant to replant. Their liability was based on the "pure principle of benefit and burden".[335] **15–082**

That principle had been recognised in a number of earlier cases;[336] but its existence does give rise to the problem of how it is to be reconciled with the rule "that in general contractual burdens are not assignable, though contractual benefits are".[337] A person is certainly not subject to the burdens of a contract merely because he has taken benefits under it: it has, for example, been held that the equitable assignee of a licence to use a patent was not subject to the burdens imposed by the licence on the original licensee.[338] The "pure principle" is best regarded as a limited exception to this rule, restricted in scope by two factors. The first is that "the condition [which gives rise to the burden] must be relevant to the exercise of the right".[339] This limitation is illustrated by *Rhone v Stephens*[340]

---

*Schiffahrtsgesellschaft Detlev von Appen GmbH v Voest Alpine Intertrading* GmbH [1997] 2 Lloyd's Rep. 279 at 286, 291; *Jones v Link Financial Ltd* [2012] EWHC 2402 (QB); [2013] 1 W.L.R. 693 (legal assignee of a debt required to perform statutory duties under Consumer Credit Act 1974 in order to enforce the debt and therefore qualified as a "creditor" under the Act)).

[331] *Radstock Co-operative and Industrial Society v Norton-Radstock UDC* [1967] Ch. 1094; [1968] Ch. 605. For independent obligations, cf. para.17–019.

[332] *Tito v Waddell (No.2)* [1977] Ch. 106 at 302.

[333] *Tito v Waddell (No.2)* [1977] Ch. 106 at 302.

[334] [1977] Ch. 106 at 302.

[335] *Tito v Waddell (No.2)* [1977] Ch. 106 at 307; the original contracts between the company and the landowners had not made the benefits conditional on discharge of the burdens.

[336] *Elliston v Reacher* [1908] 2 Ch. 665 at 669 (in argument); *Halsall v Brizell* [1957] Ch. 169 at 182 (but the point was conceded—see 180—and not necessary for the decision); *ER Ives Investment Ltd v High* [1967] 2 Q.B. 379 at 394, 399, 400 (where estoppel was another ground of decision).

[337] *Tito v Waddell (No.2)* [1977] Ch. 106 at 291; cf. at 299; para.15–078.

[338] *Bagot Pneumatic Tyre Co v Clipper Pneumatic Tyre Co* [1902] 1 Ch. 146; cf. *Cox v Bishop* (1857) 8 D.M. & G. 815; *Barker v Stickney* [1919] 1 K.B. 121.

[339] *Rhone v Stephens* [1994] 2 A.C. 310 at 322; *Davies v Jones* [2009] EWCA Civ 1164; [2010] 5 E.G. 114 at [27]; "a matter of substance rather than form": *Wilkinson v Kerdene Ltd* [2013] EWCA Civ 44; [2013] 2 E.G.L.R. 163 at [27]; *Elwood v Goodman* [2013] EWCA Civ 1103; [2014] 2 W.L.R. 967 at [28].

[340] [1994] 2 A.C. 310; see also *Amsprop Trading Ltd v Harris Distribution Ltd* [1997] 1 W.L.R. 1025 at 1034–1035.

where the owner of a house covenanted to keep the common roof of the house and an adjoining cottage in repair and both properties were then sold. It was held that the "pure principle" did not entitle the purchaser of the cottage to enforce the repairing covenant against the purchaser of the house: the duty to repair the roof was not a "relevant" condition of the right to occupy the house as there was no necessary connection between them. The second factor which restricts the operation of the "pure principle" is the intention of the parties to the assignment.[341] An intention to subject the assignee of contractual rights to liabilities arising under the contract will not normally be inferred.[342] In particular, any such inference will be displaced where it is the assignor who has undertaken (in the contract between assignor and assignee) to discharge the burden;[343] where it is plainly the intention of both parties to the assignment that the assignee is *not* to be subject to the obligations imposed by the original contract on the assignor;[344] and where the assignment is of benefits acquired by the assignor under one instrument but the burden is imposed by another, recording a separate transaction.[345] Even where the "pure principle" does apply, its effect is not strictly to transfer a liability; for the assignor remains liable to the other contracting party.

## (c) Operation of law

15–083 In the following cases, a creditor may by operation of law be entitled to sue someone (other than the original debtor) who has not voluntarily undertaken such liability.

15–084 **Death.** Contractual liabilities pass to the personal representatives of a deceased person in the sense that they must apply his assets in discharging those liabilities. They are not personally liable, so that there is no true transfer of liability.

15–085 **Bankruptcy and insolvency.** Contractual liabilities of a bankrupt pass to his trustee in bankruptcy in the sense that the latter must distribute the bankrupt's assets among his creditors. Again there is no true transfer of liability as the trustee is not personally liable. He can also disclaim a contract which is wholly or partly executory if it is onerous or unprofitable, e.g. a lease at too high a rent.[346] Such disclaimer puts an end to the contract but does not relieve the bankrupt's estate from liability for breach of it.[347] An administrative receiver of a company may become liable on contracts by "adopting" them;[348] but this liability arises from a

[341] *Tito v Waddell (No.2)* [1977] Ch. 106 at 302; *Davies v Jones* [2009] EWCA Civ 1164; [2010] 5 E.G. 114.

[342] *Tito v Waddell (No.2)* [1977] Ch. 106 at 291; cf. at 299.

[343] *Tito v Waddell (No.2)* [1977] Ch. 106 at 302.

[344] *Law Debenture Trust Corp v Ural Caspian Oil Corp Ltd* [1993] 1 W.L.R. 138 at 146–147.

[345] *Law Debenture Trust Corp v Ural Caspian Oil Corp Ltd* [1993] 1 W.L.R. 138 at 146; *Davies v Jones* [2009] EWCA Civ 1164; [2010] 5 E.G. 114 at [27].

[346] Insolvency Act 1986 s.315; cf. Insolvency Act 1986 s.178. For exceptions, see Companies Act 1989 s.164.

[347] For the measure of such liability, see *Re Park Air Services Plc* [2000] 2 A.C. 172.

[348] Insolvency Act 1986 s.44; *Powdrill v Watson* [1995] 2 A.C. 394.

new contract taking effect on such adoption, rather than under a transfer of the company's liability, incurred before adoption, under the old contract.

**Employment.** Under legislation referred to earlier in this chapter,[349] not only the benefit but also the burden of a contract of employment may be transferred as a result of the transfer of the undertaking. The transferor thus ceases to be liable on the contract,[350] while liabilities under it are imposed on the transferee, though the employee can take steps to avoid being bound to serve the transferee.[351] In this sense, the consent of all three parties to the transfer is necessary; and, perhaps for this reason, the process has been described as a "statutory novation"[352] of the contract. **15–086**

**Carriage of goods by sea.** Under the Carriage of Goods by Sea Act 1992, a person may acquire rights under a contract for the carriage of goods by sea to which he was not an original party, e.g. by becoming the lawful holder of the bill of lading which contains or evidences the contract.[353] Such a person may also become subject to liabilities under the contract, e.g. if he takes or demands delivery of the goods.[354] But the original party to the contract of carriage remains liable under it, so that again there is no *transfer* of liability.[355] **15–087**

349 Transfer of Undertakings (Protection of Employment) Regulations 2006 (SI 2006/246) reg.4(1).
350 Transfer of Undertakings (Protection of Employment) Regulations 2006 (SI 2006/246) reg.4(2); *Wilson v St Helens BC* [1999] 2 A.C. 52 at 76, 83.
351 See at fn.223.
352 *Newns v British Airways* [1992] I.R.L.R. 575 at 577.
353 Carriage of Goods by Sea Act 1992 s.2(1)(a).
354 Carriage of Goods by Sea Act 1992 s.3(1)(a); see *The Berge Sisar* [2001] UKHL 17; [2002] 2 A.C. 205.
355 Carriage of Goods by Sea Act 1992 s.3(3).

# CHAPTER 16

# AGENCY[1]



[1] *Bowstead and Reynolds on Agency*, 21st edn (2017).

## 1. DEFINITION

16–001 Agency describes the relationship in which one person, called the agent, is authorised to act on behalf of another, called the principal. Its most important effect, for the purpose of this book, is that it enables the agent to make a contract between his principal and a third party.

### (a) Agreement

16–002 Generally, the relationship of principal and agent arises out of an agreement[2] and such agreement is often a contract. But agency may also arise out of an agreement which does not amount to a contract because one of the parties lacks contractual capacity[3] or because there is no consideration. Thus the committee of a club, though they act gratuitously, may be agents of the members.[4] In the cases referred to below there may be agency without agreement.

16–003 **Agency without agreement by operation of law.** The law may attribute an agent to a person, e.g. when a company is first formed, its original directors are its agents by operation of law.[5] Public corporations created by statute are sometimes regarded as agents of the Crown:[6] such agency arises simply by virtue of the incorporating statute. Moreover, by statute, one person, or the court, may have power to appoint an agent to act on behalf of another: thus a mortgagee can in certain circumstances appoint an agent of the mortgagor;[7] an administrative receiver appointed by debenture holders is deemed to be the agent of the company;[8] and a "deputy" may be appointed by the court to manage the affairs of a person lacking mental capacity by acting as that person's agent.[9] At common law, one person may be regarded as the agent of another, even against the latter's will, under the doctrine of agency of necessity.[10]

16–004 **Apparent and usual authority.** Under the doctrines of apparent and usual authority[11] a principal is liable on contracts made by his agent although he has not authorised the agent to make them.

---

[2] *Garnac Grain Co Inc v Faure & Fairclough Ltd* [1968] A.C. 1130 at 1137; Fridman 84 L.Q.R. 224.
[3] See para.16–013.
[4] cf. *Flemyng v Hector* (1836) 2 M. & W. 172.
[5] cf. Companies Act 2006 s.154. But English law does not regard the company as agent for its shareholders: *JH Rayner (Mincing Lane) Ltd v DTI* [1989] Ch. 72 at 188 (approved on this point [1990] 2 A.C. 418 at 515). See also Limited Liability Partnerships Act 2000 s.6(1): members of a limited liability partnership (which is a body corporate: s.1(2)) are agents of the partnership.
[6] e.g. *Bank voor Handel en Scheepvaart NV v Administrator of Hungarian Property* [1954] A.C. 584.
[7] Law of Property Act 1925 s.109; see *Medforth v Blake* [2000] Ch. 86.
[8] Insolvency Act 1986 s.44(1)(a); cf. s.8 Sch.B1.
[9] Mental Capacity Act 2005 s.19(6).
[10] See para.16–037 and following.
[11] See paras 16–024–16–036.

### (b) Intention to act on behalf of principal

An agent must intend to act on behalf of his principal.[12] This rule distinguishes agency from other analogous relationships, and is helpful in cases where it is clear that a person acted as agent, but not clear whose agent he was. **16–005**

**A question of fact.** Whether a person intends to act on behalf of another is a question of fact. Thus a person who agrees out of friendship to ferry another's car from one place to another can be regarded as the owner's agent,[13] so that his negligent driving may make the owner liable in tort; but a person who borrows another's car for his own purposes would not be so regarded.[14] Even where the owner is liable for the driver's torts, it does not follow that the driver is his agent for other purposes, such as pledging his credit for fuel or repairs. Where a person does intend to act on behalf of another, agency may arise although a contract between the parties declares that there is no such relationship.[15] Conversely, the mere fact that a person says he is an agent does not make him one if he intends to act on his own behalf and not on behalf of his alleged principal.[16] **16–006**

#### *(i) Agency distinguished from other relationships*

**Intermediate seller.** A retailer or distributor may describe himself as the "agent" of the manufacturer whose products he sells. This description is legally accurate if he negotiates a contract between manufacturer and customer, accounts to the manufacturer for the price paid by the customer, and is remunerated by a commission or salary paid by the manufacturer; it may be accurate even if he is remunerated by a "mark-up" on the price that he pays to the manufacturer.[17] But generally the retailer acts, not in this capacity,[18] but as a middleman who buys and resells on his own behalf. He is the manufacturer's "agent" only in a commercial, and not in the legal sense.[19] Thus if the goods are defective the customer can sue only the retailer, and not the manufacturer, on the contract of **16–007**

---

[12] For debate as to whether this refers to subjective intention, or intention objectively ascertained, see: *Magellan Spirit ApS v Vitol SA* [2016] EWHC 454 (Comm); [2016] 2 Lloyd's Rep. 1 (undisclosed principal); cf. *Sackville UK Property Select II (GP) No.1 Ltd v Robertson Taylor Insurance Brokers Ltd* [2018] EWHC 122 (Ch); [2018] L.Q.T.R. 22 at 46 (disclosed, but unnamed principal): see para.16–067.

[13] e.g. *Ormrod v Crosville Motor Services Ltd* [1953] 1 W.L.R. 1120; *Vandyke v Fender* [1970] 2 Q.B. 292.

[14] e.g. *Hewitt v Bonvin* [1940] 1 K.B. 188; *Morgans v Launchbury* [1973] A.C. 127.

[15] *McLaughlin v Gentles* (1919) 51 D.L.R. 383.

[16] *Kennedy v De Trafford* [1897] A.C. 180 at 188.

[17] cf. *Mercantile International Group Plc v Chuan Soon Huat International Group Ltd* [2002] EWCA Civ 288; [2002] 1 All E.R. (Comm) 788.

[18] cf. whether a person who is asked to procure goods for another is his agent or a seller to him: see *Kloeckner & Co AG v Gatoil Overseas Inc* [1990] 1 Lloyd's Rep. 177; cf. *The Coral Rose* [1991] 1 Lloyd's Rep. 563.

[19] cf. *AMB Imballaggi Plastici SRL v Pacflex Ltd* [1999] 2 All E.R. (Comm) 249.

sale. The manufacturer may be liable to the customer on a separate contract if he gives a guarantee;[20] he may also be liable in tort[21] if the customer suffers loss or injury because of a defect in the goods.

16–008 **Hire-purchase.** A dealer who negotiates a hire-purchase agreement between a customer and a finance company is considered at common law to act primarily on his own behalf.[22] But he may be the agent of the company for some purposes, e.g. to accept offers on the terms of the company's proposal form.[23] And under the Consumer Credit Act 1974 he may be treated as the agent of the company when he makes any representation in the course of negotiations as to the quality of the goods,[24] and when he receives notice from the customer that the agreement has been cancelled or rescinded, or that the customer's offer has been withdrawn.[25]

16–009 **Banker and customer.** The relation of banker and customer is primarily that of debtor and creditor but may for certain purposes be that of agent and principal, e.g. where a bank on the instructions of its customer makes a transfer of funds out of the customer's account.[26] Conversely, an ordinary agency agreement does not give rise to the relationship of banker and customer merely because funds belonging to or destined for the principal are held (and used to make payments under the agreement) by the agent.[27]

16–010 **Provision of services.** Persons who are engaged in the business or profession of supplying services may be described as "agents" in the commercial sense, without being agents in the legal sense: "To carry on the business of an 'agent' is not the same thing as saying that you are contracting as agent."[28] For example, where a "forwarding agent" is engaged to arrange for goods to be transported to a foreign destination, he may act as agent (in the legal sense) in making a contract between the exporter and a carrier;[29] but he may equally well act as principal in undertaking to get the goods to the specified destination.[30] Whether such persons act in the legal sense as agents depends on the responsibilities that they undertake in relation to the particular transaction.[31] An estate agent who is instructed to

[20] See paras 3–017, 4–007 (at fn.29), 14–006.

[21] For negligence at common law or under Consumer Protection Act 1987.

[22] *Mercantile Credit Co Ltd v Hamblin* [1965] 2 Q.B. 242 at 269; *Shogun Finance Ltd v Hudson* [2003] UKHL 62; [2004] 1 A.C. 919 at [51]; cf. the divided view of the House of Lords in *Branwhite v Worcester Works Finance Ltd* [1969] 1 A.C. 552.

[23] *Northgran Finance Ltd v Ashley* [1963] 1 Q.B. 476.

[24] Consumer Credit Act 1974 s.56(2); by s.56(3) a provision in a regulated agreement purporting to make the dealer the *customer's* agent is void.

[25] Consumer Credit Act 1974 ss.69(6), 102(1), 57(3). See also s.175 for the "agent's" duty to transmit such notices.

[26] *Barclays Bank Plc v Quincecare Ltd* [1992] 4 All E.R. 363.

[27] *Kingscroft Ins Co Ltd v HS Weaver (Underwriting) Agencies Ltd* [1993] 1 Lloyd's Rep. 187 at 191.

[28] *Elektronska etc. v Transped etc.* [1986] 1 Lloyd's Rep. 49 at 52.

[29] *Lukoil-Kalingradmorneft Plc v Tata Ltd* [1999] 2 Lloyd's Rep. 129 at 138.

[30] See *Jones v European General Express* (1920) 25 Com. Cas. 296; cf. *Poseidon Freight Forwarding Co Ltd* [1996] 2 Lloyd's Rep. 388 at 389.

[31] See, for example: *Leicestershire CC v Michael Faraday & Partners Ltd* [1941] 2 K.B. 205 at 216 (valuer); *Tudor v Hamid* [1988] 1 E.G.L.R. 251; contrast *Hastingwood Property Ltd v Sanders Bearman Anselm* [1991] Ch. 114 (solicitor); *Gibbon v Pease* [1905] 1 K.B. 810 (architect).

negotiate the sale of a house by private treaty has normally[32] no power to make a contract between his client and a prospective purchaser.[33] He may for certain purposes act on behalf of the client, e.g. for the purpose of making representations about the property:[34] and he also owes the client certain duties similar to those owed by an agent to his principal.[35] But "an estate agent, despite the style, is an independent person"[36] who for most purposes does not normally act in the legal sense as the vendor's agent. In particular, he does not so act when he receives a deposit from a person who has agreed, subject to contract, to buy the property.[37] So long as no contract of sale has been concluded, he must not pay the deposit over to his client. He holds the money in trust for the prospective purchaser,[38] and must return it to him on demand; but if he fails to do so the client is not liable for the deposit unless he had expressly authorised the estate agent to receive it on his behalf.[39]

### *(ii) Whose agent?*

It may be clear that a person is an agent, but doubtful whose agent he is.[40] Thus it has been held that a London agent employed by a country solicitor was the agent, not of the lay client, but of the country solicitor.[41] On the other hand counsel, though briefed by the solicitor, may be the client's agent.[42] **16–011**

**Agent for both principal and third party.** It is possible for a person to act as agent both for principal and third party (who is also therefore a principal). This will, of course, put the agent into a position of conflict of interest for which he will require the "informed consent" of both principals.[43] **16–012**

**Agent of another for some purposes.** In other cases the question is whether a person who is undoubtedly the agent of P may not also for some purposes be the agent of Q. Thus persons employed by an insurance company to solicit proposals for insurance are generally the company's agents,[44] but may become the agents of **16–013**

---

32 i.e. unless specifically so authorised, as seems to have been the case in *Spiro v Lintern* [1973] 1 W.L.R. 1002 at 1006.

33 *Wragg v Lovett* [1948] 2 All E.R. 968.

34 *Sorrell v Finch* [1977] A.C. 728 at 753.

35 e.g. *Regier v Campbell-Stuart* [1939] Ch. 766 (agent engaged to *find* a property for the client); cf. in the case of a commodity broker, *Brandeis (Brokers) Ltd v Black* [2001] 2 Lloyd's Rep. 359.

36 *Sorrell v Finch* [1977] A.C. 728 at 753.

37 *Sorrell v Finch* [1977] A.C. 728; *John McCann & Co v Pow* [1974] 1 W.L.R. 1643 at 1647; Reynolds 92 L.Q.R. 484.

38 Estate Agents Act 1979 s.13(1)(a).

39 *Ryan v Pilkington* [1959] 1 W.L.R. 403; as explained in *Sorrell v Finch* [1977] A.C. 728 at 750.

40 Where an agent is acting for two separate principals under two separate contracts, the question is which contract he has *performed*, see: *Albright & Wilson (UK) Ltd v Biachem Ltd* [2002] UKHL 37; [2002] 2 All E.R. (Comm) 753.

41 *Robbins v Fennell* (1847) 11 Q.B. 248.

42 *Grindell v Bass* [1920] 2 Ch. 487.

43 *UBS AG v Kommunale Wasserwerke Leipzig GmbH* [2014] EWHC 3615 (Comm) at [593] (for further proceedings, see [2017] EWCA Civ 1567; [2017] 2 Lloyd's Rep. 621); see para.16–110.

44 *Bawden v London Assurance* [1892] 2 Q.B. 534; *Stone v Reliance Mutual Ins Soc Ltd* [1972] 1 Lloyd's Rep. 469; Reynolds 88 L.Q.R. 462.

the proposer when helping him to complete the proposal form.[45] On the other hand insurance brokers are for most purposes agents of the insured persons and not of the insurers.[46] But they may be agents of the insurers for some purposes, such as the provision of interim insurance cover until the policy is issued.[47] The Consumer Insurance (Disclosure and Representations) Act 2012 sets out a number of rules, and factors to be taken into account, to determine whether the agent is taken to be the agent of the insurer or of the insured[48] in a consumer insurance contract.[49] Again, directors of a company are primarily the agents of the company, and not of the shareholders; but they may for some purposes become agents of the shareholders, e.g. for the purpose of negotiating a sale of their shares.[50]

### (c) Commercial agents

16–014 **Commercial Agents Regulations.** Our main concern in this chapter is with the common law principles of agency. Some of these are in effect restated, but others are modified, by regulations which give effect to an EC Council Directive[51] governing the relations between "commercial agents" and their principals.[52] The Regulations define "commercial agent" to mean "a self-employed intermediary who has continuing authority to negotiate the sale or purchase of goods on behalf of another person (the "principal"), or to negotiate and conclude the sale or purchase of goods on behalf of and in the name of the principal".[53] A detailed discussion of these Regulations is beyond the scope of this book,[54] but their effect on the rules here under discussion will be noted at appropriate points in this chapter.

## 2. CAPACITY

16–015 **Capacity to act as agent.** As agency is a consensual but not necessarily a contractual relationship,[55] any person who is capable of consenting can act as agent, although his contractual capacity may be limited, e.g. because he is a minor. But to say that a person of limited contractual capacity can act as agent does not mean that his agreement to do so gives rise to all the legal consequences that usually result from the relationship of principal and agent. It means that he can make a contract between his principal and a third party, but not that he

[45] *Biggar v Rock Life Assurance Co* [1902] 1 K.B. 516; *Newsholme v Road Transport Ins Co* [1929] 2 K.B. 356.
[46] *Anglo-African Merchants v Bayley* [1970] 1 Q.B. 311 at 322; *McNealy v Pennine Ins Co* [1978] 2 Lloyd's Rep. 18; For criticism, see *Roberts v Plaisted* [1989] 2 Lloyd's Rep. 341 at 345.
[47] *Stockton v Mason* [1978] 2 Lloyd's Rep. 430 (except in cases of marine insurance: cf. para.5–014).
[48] Consumer Insurance (Disclosure and Representations) Act 2012 s.9; Sch.2.
[49] As defined in s.1.
[50] *Briess v Woolley* [1954] A.C. 333.
[51] Directive 86/653.
[52] Commercial Agents (Council Directive) Regulations 1993 (SI 1993/3053), as amended.
[53] Regulation 2(1); for excepted cases, see reg.2(1)(i)–(iii) and (2).
[54] See *Bowstead & Reynolds on Agency,* 21st edn (2017), Ch.11.
[55] See paras 16–003—16–004.

acquires all the rights or is subject to all the liabilities of an agent towards his principal or the third party. The agent could not be made liable if to hold him liable would defeat the protection which the law means to give him by limiting his capacity. Thus he could not be made liable on the contract between principal and third party, even though the circumstances were such that an agent of full capacity would be so liable.[56] On the other hand, there is no reason to suppose that he would be denied the ordinary agent's right of indemnity[57] against his principal.

**Capacity to act as principal.** Capacity to act as principal is determined by the rules governing contractual capacity generally. Thus a minor cannot make himself liable for luxuries merely by employing an agent; but he can appoint an agent to make a contract which would have bound him if he had made it personally.[58] This rule again applies primarily to determine the reciprocal rights and liabilities of principal and third party. It might also protect the principal from liability to the agent. Thus a principal who was under age would not be liable to indemnify an agent employed to buy luxuries. But the rule would not necessarily protect the agent: thus an under-age principal might well have a remedy against the agent if the latter accepted a bribe[59] from the third party. 16–016

## 3. CREATION OF AGENCY

Agency may arise by express or implied agreement, or without agreement under the doctrines of apparent and usual authority, and where a person has authority of necessity. Finally, agency may arise ex post facto by ratification. 16–017

### (a) Agency by agreement

#### (i) *Express authority*

**No formality required.** An agent's authority is commonly conferred by express appointment. At common law, no formality is required.[60] Oral appointment suffices even where the agent is appointed to make a contract which has to be in writing, or evidenced in writing.[61] 16–018

**Scope of authority.** The extent of an agent's express authority depends on the interpretation of the words of the appointment.[62] If these are vague or ambiguous, 16–019

[56] See para.16–076 and following.
[57] See para.16–105.
[58] *G (A) v G (T)* [1970] 2 Q.B. 644 at 651–652; Webb 18 M.L.R. 861; R.E.M. 69 L.Q.R. 446.
[59] See para.16–111.
[60] For a statutory exception, see Law of Property Act 1925 s.53(1)(a).
[61] *Heard v Pilley* (1869) L.R. 4 Ch. 548; *McLaughlin v Duffill* [2008] EWCA Civ 1627; [2010] Ch. 1, distinguishing s.53(1)(a) and Law of Property Miscellaneous Provisions Act 1989 s.2.
[62] Where authority is conferred by a power of attorney, see the approach approved by Hamblen J in *Brown v Innovatorone* [2012] EWHC 1321 (Comm) at [807]–[809]; cf. *Katara Hospitality v Guez* [2018] EWHC 3063 (Comm) at [57].

the principal may be bound even though the agent, in good faith, interprets them in a sense not intended by the principal.[63] But in such cases the speed of modern communications will often make it reasonable for the agent to seek clarification of his instructions, and if he fails to do so he will not be able to rely on his own mistaken interpretation.[64] Where the agent's instructions are clear, it makes no difference that the principal acted under a mistake in giving them, e.g. if he instructed the agent to insure a ship for £3 million he is liable to indemnify the agent for the premium even though his actual intention was to insure her for only £2 million.[65]

16–020 **Effect of the agent's fraud or acting in his own interest.** It has been said that "an act of an agent within the scope of his actual or apparent authority does not cease to bind his principal merely because the agent was acting fraudulently and in furtherance of his own interests",[66] but this statement of the law should be limited to apparent authority, i.e. acting fraudulently or in furtherance of the agent's own interests will by its very nature nullify actual authority (both express and implied), but not apparent authority.[67]

### *(ii) Implied authority*

16–021 The authority to act as agent may be "inferred from the conduct of the parties and the circumstances of the case."[68] For this purpose, the conduct of the parties is assessed objectively but it is not necessary to meet the test of "necessity" laid down for implied terms since "implied authority depends on consent not contract."[69] It follows that an agency relationship will exist if the parties have agreed to what in law amounts to an agency relationship even if they have professed to disclaim it.[70] In one case it was held that the third party may be bound under the doctrine of contractual estoppel[71] by a term that an intermediary

---

[63] *Weigall v Runciman* (1916) 85 L.J.K.B. 1187; cf. *Ireland v Livingston* (1871) L.R. 5 H.L. 395; as explained in *Woodhouse AC Israel Cocoa Ltd SA v Nigerian Produce Marketing Co* [1972] A.C. 741 at 757, 771–772; *Crédit Agricole Indosuez v Muslim Commercial Bank Ltd* [2000] 1 Lloyd's Rep. 275 at 280.

[64] *European Asian Bank v Punjab & Sind Bank (No.2)* [1983] 1 W.L.R. 642 at 656.

[65] *The Tzelepi* [1991] 2 Lloyd's Rep. 265.

[66] *Macmillan Inc v Bishopsgate Trust (No.3)* [1995] 1 W.L.R. 978 at 984.

[67] *Hopkins v TL Dallas Group Ltd* [2004] EWHC 1379 (Ch.); [2005] 1 B.C.L.C. 543 at [89]; cf. *LNOC Ltd v Watford Association Football Club Ltd* [2013] EWHC 3615 (Comm) at [66] emphasising that, in the context of a company director's authority, the director does not exceed his authority if he honestly believes he is acting in the company's best interest.

[68] *Hely-Hutchinson v Brayhead Ltd* [1968] 1 Q.B. 549 at 583; *Branwhite v Worcester Works Finance Ltd* [1969] 1 A.C. 552 at 587; *Sino Channel Asia Ltd v Dana Shipping & Trading PTE Singapore* [2017] EWCA Civ 1703; [2018] 1 Lloyd's Rep. 17 at [36].

[69] *Targe Towing Ltd v Marine Blast Ltd* [2004] EWCA Civ 346; [2004] 1 Lloyd's Rep. 721 at [19]–[22]; cf. *Hudson Bay Apparel Brands Inc LLC v Umbro International Ltd* [2010] EWCA Civ 949; [2011] 1 B.C.L.C. 259 at [50].

[70] *Garnac Grain Co Inc v Faure & Fairclough Ltd* [1968] A.C. 1130 at 1137; *Branwhite v Worcester Works Finance Ltd* [1969] 1 A.C. 552 at 587.

[71] See para.9–137.

is not the agent of the principal, but there was no evidence to suggest that the relationship was that of principal and agent in any event.[72]

**Incidental acts.** An agent who is appointed for a particular purpose may have implied authority to do acts incidental to the execution of that authority. For example, a solicitor, or counsel engaged to conduct litigation, may have implied authority to compromise the suit,[73] and, "in a suitable and, no doubt, rare case" an agent may have authority to accept service.[74] On the other hand, an agent employed to sell a thing has generally no authority to receive payment for it.[75] The question whether he has authority to warrant its quality is one of fact, depending on the circumstances of each case.[76] **16–022**

**Customary authority.**[77] A principal who employs an agent to act for him in a particular market impliedly authorises the agent to act in accordance with the custom of that market.[78] He is bound by the custom even if he is not aware of it.[79] But the inference that the principal authorises the agent to act in accordance with the custom cannot be drawn if the custom is inconsistent with the instructions given by the principal to the agent, or with the very relationship of principal and agent. The custom is then said to be "unreasonable" and the principal is not bound by it unless he knows of it.[80] Thus in *Robinson v Mollett*[81] there was a custom in the tallow market by which an agent employed by several principals was allowed to buy in bulk to satisfy the needs of all. The custom was held unreasonable since its effect was to turn an agent into a seller. This was inconsistent with the relationship of principal and agent since an agent must buy for his principal as cheaply as he can, while a seller sells at the highest price he can get. But in *Scott v Godfrey*[82] a custom of the Stock Exchange permitting stockbrokers to buy enough shares for several principals from a single seller was held reasonable because all the parties intended that contracts should be made between the seller and the various buyers. **16–023**

---

[72] *Premium Credit Ltd v Primary Care Management Solutions Ltd* [2018] EWHC 3083 (Comm).
[73] *Waugh v HB Clifford & Sons* [1982] Ch. 374.
[74] *Sino Channel Asia Ltd v Dana Shipping & Trading PTE Singapore* [2017] EWCA Civ 1703; [2018] 1 Lloyd's Rep. 17 in which the arrangements between principal and agent were described (at [48]) as "remarkable", the principal taking an entirely "passive" role; cf. *Glencore Agriculture BV v Conqueror Holdings Ltd* [2017] EWHC 2893 (Comm); [2018] Lloyd's Rep. 233.
[75] *Butwick v Grant* [1924] 2 K.B. 483.
[76] Such authority was implied in *Alexander v Gibson* (1811) 2 Camp. 555; and *Baldry v Bates* (1885) 52 L.T. 620; contrast *Brady v Todd* (1861) 9 C.B. (N.S.) 592.
[77] cf. para.6–080, for the view that it is artificial to base such authority on actual agreement.
[78] *Graves v Legg* (1857) 2 H. & N. 210.
[79] *Pollock v Stables* (1848) 12 Q.B. 765; *Reynolds v Smith* (1893) 9 T.L.R. 494.
[80] e.g. *Perry v Barnett* (1885) 15 Q.B.D. 388 (custom to make contract without complying with statutory formalities and hence void); contrast *Seymour v Bridge* (1885) 14 Q.B.D. 460, where the principal knew of the custom.
[81] (1875) L.R. 7 H.L. 802; cf. *North & South Trust Co v Berkeley* [1971] 1 W.L.R. 471.
[82] [1901] 2 Q.B. 726.

## (b) Agency without agreement

### (i) Apparent authority

16–024 Where a person represents to a third party that he has authorised an agent to act on his behalf, he may, as against the third party, not be allowed to deny the truth of the representation, and be bound by the agent's act whether he in fact had authorised it or not.[83] The following conditions must be satisfied before apparent authority arises.

16–025 **Representation of authority.** This may be express[84] but it is more frequently implied, e.g. from a course of dealing,[85] or from placing the agent in such a position that it is reasonable for third parties to assume that he has the principal's authority to make a contract of the kind in question;[86] or from the known relationship of the parties, so that where a partner has retired he continues to be liable to those who deal with the firm and know that he had been a partner but not that he had retired;[87] and conversely the firm will be liable to such third parties on contracts made by him, ostensibly on its behalf.[88] In such cases, the apparent authority is said to be *general* in character since it extends generally to all transactions which a person, in the position in which the principal has placed the agent, is normally regarded as having authority to conclude.[89] Even where the agent has no such apparent authority by virtue of his position, he may have *specific* apparent authority to enter into a particular transaction; but since in such cases it is (ex hypothesi) clear to the third party that the agent does not *normally* have authority to conclude a transaction of that kind, the principal will be liable on the basis of specific apparent authority only if the third party can show that the principal expressly represented that the agent had authority to enter into the particular contract on his behalf.[90]

---

[83] *Summers v Solomon* (1857) 7 E. & B. 879; cf. *Pole v Leask* (1862) 33 L.J. Ch. 155; *The Unique Mariner* [1978] 1 Lloyd's Rep. 438; *Waugh v HB Clifford & Sons* [1982] Ch. 374; *First Sport Ltd v Barclays Bank Plc* [1993] 1 W.L.R. 1229. The following discussion deals only with the extent to which the principal can as a result of the representation be held liable on an unauthorised contract. It is not concerned with any other form of liability for misrepresentation.

[84] e.g. *Gurtner v Beaton* [1993] 2 Lloyd's Rep. 369.

[85] *PEC Ltd v Asia Golden Rice Co Ltd* [2014] EWHC 1583 (Comm) at [67] (representation "not readily" inferred from course of dealing); cf. *Slingsby v District Bank Ltd* [1932] 1 K.B. 544 at 566.

[86] *Panorama Developments (Guildford) Ltd v Fidelis Furnishing Fabrics Ltd* [1971] 2 Q.B. 711; *The Ocean Frost* [1986] A.C. 717 at 777; cf. *Strover v Harrington* [1988] Ch. 390 at 409–410; contrast *Cleveland Manufacturing Co v Muslim Commercial Bank Ltd* [1981] 2 Lloyd's Rep. 646.

[87] Partnership Act 1890 s.14(1); and cf. *Scarf v Jardine* (1882) 7 App. Cas. 345.

[88] cf. Limited Liability Partnerships Act 2000 s.6(3)(a).

[89] *The Ocean Frost* [1986] A.C. 717 at 777. The relevant "transactions" for which it is said that the agent has apparent authority may have to be quite specific: *Sea Emerald SA v Prominvestbank* [2008] EWHC 1979 (Comm) at [107], distinguishing between "guarantees" and the particular refund guarantee which the third party was seeking to enforce; cf. *PEC Ltd v Asia Golden Rice Co Ltd* [2014] EWHC 1583 (Comm) at [70].

[90] *The Ocean Frost* [1986] A.C. 717 where the third party's claim on this basis failed.

**Must the representation be one of fact?** The view that a representation of law does not give rise to apparent authority[91] predates the decision of the House of Lords in *Kleinwort Benson Ltd v Lincoln CC*[92] removing the bar preventing recovery of payments made under a mistake of law, and may therefore need to be reconsidered. Furthermore, it is a decision which it has been said "now permeates the law of contract",[93] so that a contract may be *void* for a mistake of law,[94] or (it seems) *rescinded* for a misrepresentation of law.[95] It may be, however, that the present rule is unaffected, since it is concerned with the *creation* of contractual rights. 16–026

**The representation must be that the "agent" is authorised to act as agent.** Apparent authority does not arise if a person is represented to be the *owner* of a business or other property. In such cases the representor may be bound under the doctrine of usual authority, or under some analogous doctrine.[96] But the scope of these doctrines is limited, and where they do not apply, the representee can fall back on the more general doctrine of apparent authority only if the representation is one of *agency*. 16–027

**The representation must be made by the principal.** Apparent authority can arise only out of a representation made by the principal: it cannot arise out of a representation made by some other person[97] or out of one made by the agent himself.[98] Of course, a principal may represent that the agent has authority to make further representations on the principal's behalf; and the principal may make such a representation by conduct, e.g. by placing the agent in a position in which he would normally have authority to enter into a transaction of the type in question[99] or to communicate what purports to be the principal's approval of it[100] (even though the principal's instructions had negatived the agent's *actual* authority to take such steps).[101] In such a case, the agent may by his own 16–028

91 *Chapleo v Brunswick PBBS* (1881) 6 Q.B.D. 696.
92 [1999] 2 A.C. 349.
93 *Brennan v Bolt Burdon* [2004] EWCA Civ 1017; [2005] Q.B. 303 at [10].
94 *Brennan v Bolt Burdon* [2004] EWCA Civ 1017; [2005] Q.B. 303; para.8–023.
95 See para.9–020.
96 See paras 16–0304–16–036.
97 *The Rhodian River* [1984] 1 Lloyd's Rep. 373; *First Sport Ltd v Barclays Bank Plc* [1993] 1 W.L.R. 1229 at 1240; cf. *Sea Emerald SA v Prominvestbank* [2008] EWHC 1979 (Comm) at [114].
98 *Attorney General for Ceylon v Silva* [1953] A.C. 461; *The Raffaella* [1985] 2 Lloyd's Rep. 36 at 43; *The Ocean Frost* [1986] A.C. 717 at 778; *Re Selectmove* [1995] 1 W.L.R. 474 at 478.
99 cf. *Pacific Carriers Ltd v BNP Paribas* (2004) 218 C.L.R. 451; Reynolds 121 L.Q.R. 55; *Sino Channel Asia Ltd v Dana Shipping & Trading PTE Singapore* [2017] EWCA Civ 1703; [2018] 1 Lloyd's Rep. 17 at [58].
100 *First Energy (UK) Ltd v Hungarian International Bank Ltd* [1993] 2 Lloyd's Rep. 195; cf. *Kelly v Fraser* [2012] UKPC 25; *PEC Ltd v Asia Golden Rice Co Ltd* [2014] EWHC 1583 (Comm) at [77].
101 *United Bank of Kuwait v Hamoud* [1988] 1 W.L.R. 1051.

representation enlarge an existing authority,[102] or confer authority on another agent,[103] but such a representation cannot create an apparent authority out of nothing.[104]

16–029 **The representation must be made to the third party.** The representation must be made to a third person or group of persons. The old notion of holding a person out as agent "to the world"[105] has long been discredited.[106] Nor can a representation made by principal to agent give rise to apparent authority.

16–030 **The third party must have relied on the representation.** The third party must have been induced by the representation to deal with the agent in the belief that the principal had authorised the agent to enter into the transaction.[107] Two consequences flow from this requirement. First, the representation must actually be known to the third party; and this requirement cannot be satisfied if the representation is contained in a document which has not actually come to his attention.[108] Secondly, the third party is not allowed to say that he relied on the representation if he knew that it was untrue,[109] or if he failed to make the inquiries that a resonable person would have made in order to verify that the agent had authority. The onus on the third party to make reasonable inquiries has been re-stated by the Privy Council[110] in the face of case law which had supported the view that the third party could rely on the appearance of authority unless his belief was dishonest or irrational.[111]

---

[102] *The Raffaella* [1985] 2 Lloyd's Rep. 36 at 43.

[103] *British Bank of the Middle East v Sun Life Assurance Co of Canada (UK) Ltd* [1983] 2 Lloyd's Rep. 9 at 17; *ING Re (UK) Ltd v R&V Versicherung AG* [2006] EWHC 1544 (Comm); [2007] 1 B.C.L.C. 108 at [100].

[104] *The Ocean Frost* [1986] A.C. 717 at 778; *United Bank of Kuwait v Hamoud* [1988] 1 W.L.R. 1051 at 1064 ("cannot hold himself out"); cf. *Hirst v Etherington* [1999] Lloyd's Rep. P.N. 938.

[105] *Whitehead v Tuckett* (1812) 15 East 400 at 411.

[106] *Dickinson v Valpy* (1829) 10 B. & C. 128 at 140.

[107] *Kooragang Investments Pty Ltd v Richardson & Wrench Ltd* [1982] A.C. 462; *Bedford Ins Co Ltd v Instituto de Ressaguros do Brasil* [1985] Q.B. 966; cf. *Nationwide BS v Lewis* [1998] Ch. 482; *Acute Property Developments Ltd v Apostolou* [2013] EWHC 200 (Ch) at [25].

[108] *The Ocean Frost* [1986] A.C. 717 at 778.

[109] See: *Hopkins v TL Dallas Group Ltd* [2004] EWHC 1379 (Ch); [2005] 1 B.C.L.C. 543 at [95]. If a third party knows that the contract is contrary to the commercial interests of the principal, it is "likely to be very difficult … to assert … that he believed the agent did have actual authority. Lack of such belief would be fatal to a claim that the agent had apparent authority": *Criterion Properties Plc v Stratford UK Properties LLC* [2004] UKHL 28; [2004] 1 W.L.R. 1846 at [31]; cf. *Lexi Holdings v Pannone & Partners* [2009] EWHC 2590 (Ch) at [99] where it is said that, beyond actual knowledge, nothing less than "Nelsonian knowledge" (wilful blindness) or "bad faith" will do; *Stavrinides v Bank of Cyprus Public Co Ltd* [2019] EWHC 1328 (Ch) at [103]; Limited Liability Partnerships Act 2000 s.6(2).

[110] *East Asia Co Ltd v PT Satria Tirtatama Energindo* [2019] UKPC 30; cf. *Jacobs v Morris* [1902] 1 Ch. 816; *Overbrooke Estates Ltd v Glencombe Properties Ltd* [1974] 1 W.L.R. 1335; Coote [1975] C.L.J. 17; cf. para.9–033.

[111] *Thanakharn Kasikorn Thai Chankat (Mahachon) v Akai Holdings Ltd* [2010] HKFCA 64; [2011] 1 H.K.L.C. 357 at [52]; *Gaydamak v Leviev* [2012] EWHC 1740 (Ch) at 249; *PEC Ltd v Asia Golden Rice Co Ltd* [2014] EWHC 1583 (Comm) at [73]; cf. *Quinn v CC Automative Group Ltd* [2010] EWCA Civ 1412; [2012] 2 All E.R. (Comm) 584 at [23], doubting the "room for any consideration of whether the third party was 'put on enquiry'"; quaere if the transaction is an "abnormal one": *Ukraine v Law Debenture Trust Corp Plc* [2018] EWCA Civ 2026; [2019] 2 W.L.R. 655 at [90] at [103]–[104].

**Company agents.** The requirements for apparent authority have given rise to particular difficulties in cases in which a third party dealt with a corporation through an agent who had no actual authority to enter into the transaction. In the case of a company incorporated under the Companies Acts, these difficulties arose largely because the authority of such an agent might be set out in, or limited by, the company's memorandum or articles of association; and the rule was that the third party had constructive notice of these documents.[112] Furthermore, this doctrine of constructive notice operated in favour of the company but not against it.[113] This state of the law could cause considerable hardship to third parties, and important changes were made which can now be found in the Companies Act 2006. 16–031

A provision which would have abolished the doctrine of constructive or deemed notice of the company's registered documents was never brought into force.[114] It may be that this was thought to be unnecessary because of a further provision under which "a person dealing with a company is not bound to enquire as to any limitation on the powers of the directors to bind the company or authorise others to do so."[115] The third party is thus not bound to inquire whether the directors actually had the power to authorise the agent, with whom he dealt, to enter into the transaction on behalf of the company. In addition, in favour of a person dealing in good faith with the company, the power of the board of directors to bind the company is "deemed to be free of any limitation under the company's constitution".[116] This provision has already been discussed;[117] here it is only necessary to repeat that a person does not act in bad faith merely because he knows that an act is beyond the powers of the directors under the company's constitution.[118] Liability under this provision may therefore arise even though the requirements of the doctrine of apparent authority are *not* satisfied because the third party knows of the limitation on the directors' authority.

The common law principles governing apparent authority can, however, still apply where the third party relies, not on the apparent *existence* of powers, but on their *exercise*. The point may be illustrated by supposing that the board of directors of a company has power under the company's constitution[119] to appoint a managing director, but that the person with whom the third party has dealt as such has not actually been appointed to the post. The third party cannot then rely simply on the fact that the board had power to make the appointment. But the third party's claim will be upheld if he can show that there has been a

[112] *Mahony v East Holyford Mining Co Ltd* (1875) L.R. 7 H.L. 869.

[113] See *Rama Corp v Proved Tin & General Investments Ltd* [1952] 2 Q.B. 147, discussing earlier authorities; for further discussion, see *Freeman & Lockyer v Buckhurst Properties (Mangal) Ltd* [1964] 2 Q.B. 480.

[114] Companies Act 1985 s.711A(1) (as inserted by Companies Act 1989 s.142); repealed by Companies Act 2006 s.1295, Sch.16. Under Limited Liability Partnerships Act 2000 s.6(3)(b) the apparent authority of a member of such a body can be terminated by giving notice that he has ceased to be a member to the Registrar of Companies.

[115] See now Companies Act 2006 s.40(2)(b)(i).

[116] Companies Act 2006 s.40(1).

[117] See para.12–071.

[118] Companies Act 2006 s.40(2)(b)(iii).

[119] For the definition of what constitutes the "company's constitution" for this purpose, see Companies Act 2006 ss.17, 257; para.12–071 at fn.218.

representation by the persons entitled to make the appointment, to the effect that it has in fact been made. Such a representation need not be express but may be implied from conduct, e.g. from the action of the board in allowing the person with whom the third party dealt to act as managing director. The company will then be bound by contracts made by him (even though he has not actually been appointed managing director) so long as those contracts are within the scope of the authority normally conferred on managing directors.[120] A company may also be bound by contracts made by its officers on the ground that they were impliedly authorised to make them; but here the liability is based on actual (implied) and not on apparent authority.[121]

16–032 **Forgeries by agent.** In two cases, company secretaries affixed the common seals of their companies to documents which they had forged. It was held that third parties who were taken in by the forgeries could not, against the companies, rely on them.[122] But in *Uxbridge PBS v Pickard*[123] a solicitor's clerk obtained money by way of mortgage on the strength of forged title deeds alleged to belong to a fictitious client. His principal was held liable. In the former cases, the secretaries had not been held out as having authority to execute the documents (respectively a power of attorney and a share transfer). In the latter case, the clerk had been held out as having authority to conclude mortgage transactions. Alternatively, the first two cases can be regarded as cases in which the agent had, in effect, forged the principal's signature. When this happens, the third party is induced to believe, not that the agent has his principal's authority, but that the signature is the act of the principal himself. Such a belief does not give rise to apparent authority.[124] The person whose signature is forged is, however, liable if he knew of the forgery and acquiesced in it.[125]

16–033 **Subsequent conduct of principal.** A person may be bound by a contract, even though the requirements of apparent authority are not satisfied, if he is precluded by his subsequent conduct from denying that the contract was made on his behalf. In *Spiro v Lintern*[126] a wife purported to enter into a contract for the sale of her husband's house. She had no actual authority to do so, nor had the husband before the transaction led the purchaser to believe that she was his agent for the purpose. But afterwards the husband met the purchaser, gave him the impression that there was a binding contract and allowed him to incur expenses in connection with the

---

[120] *Freeman & Lockyer v Buckhurst Properties (Mangal) Ltd* [1964] 2 Q.B. 480.

[121] *Hely-Hutchinson v Brayhead Ltd* [1968] 1 Q.B. 549 at 573; Nock 30 M.L.R. 705.

[122] *Bank of Ireland v Evan's Trustees* (1855) 5 H.L.C. 389; *Ruben v Great Fingall Consolidated* [1906] A.C. 439; cf. *Stavrinides v Bank of Cyprus Public Co Ltd* [2019] EWHC 1328 (Ch).

[123] [1939] 2 K.B. 248.

[124] cf. *Kooragang Investments Pty Ltd v Richardson & Wrench Ltd* [1982] A.C. 462.

[125] *Greenwood v Martins Bank Ltd* [1933] A.C. 51.

[126] [1973] 1 W.L.R. 1002; followed in *Worboys v Carter* [1987] 2 E.G.L.R. 1; cf. *Janred Properties Ltd v Ente Nazionale Italiano per il Turismo* [1989] 2 All E.R. 444; *Geniki Investments International Ltd v Ellis Stockbrokers Ltd* [2008] EWHC 549 (QB); [2008] 1 B.C.L.C. 662.

property. It was held that the husband was estopped[127] from denying his wife's authority to make the contract on his behalf.

### (ii) *Usual authority*

**Meaning.** The phrase "usual authority" is used in a number of senses and can be a source of confusion.[128] First, it may mean implied authority, and, in particular, incidental authority.[129] Secondly, it may refer to cases in which an agent has apparent authority because he has been placed by his principal in a situation in which he would have had incidental authority, if this had not been expressly negatived by instructions given to him by the principal (and not communicated to the third party).[130] But the phrase will here be used in a third sense, to refer to cases in which a principal is bound by his agent's contracts although there is no express, implied or apparent authority. This usage is based on *Watteau v Fenwick*,[131] where the owner of a public house was sued for the price of cigars bought without his authority by his manager for the purposes of the business. The manager had bought the cigars in his own name. Thus the seller could not rely on any appearance of authority since he believed, at the time of the contract, that the manager was contracting on his own behalf. But the defendant was nonetheless held liable. Wills J said: 16–034

> "The principal is liable for all the acts of the agent which are within the authority usually confided to an agent of that character, notwithstanding limitations, as between the principal and the agent, put upon that authority. It is said that this is only so where there has been a holding out of authority … But I do not think so."[132]

**Criticism.** The decision in *Watteau v Fenwick* has been criticised,[133] and has been more often distinguished than followed, but later courts which have thought it necessary to distinguish it must have regarded it as still good law.[134] There are, moreover, other cases in which a principal is bound by his agent's acts done outside the scope of his express, implied or apparent authority. Thus if a principal 16–035

[127] Detrimental reliance by the third party is necessary for this type of estoppel (para.9–190); while for the purposes of apparent authority, "the only detriment that has to be shown … is the entering into the contract": *The Tatra* [1990] 2 Lloyd's Rep. 51 at 59.

[128] *Ukraine v Law Debenture Trust Corp Plc* [2018] EWCA Civ 2026; [2019] 2 W.L.R. 655 at [90].

[129] See para.16–022.

[130] *The Raffaella* [1985] 2 Lloyd's Rep. 36 at 41; *First Energy (UK) Ltd v Hungarian International Bank Ltd* [1993] 2 Lloyd's Rep. 195 at 201.

[131] [1893] 1 Q.B. 346.

[132] *Watteau v Fenwick* [1893] 1 Q.B. 346 at 348–349; cf. *The Ocean Frost* [1986] A.C. 717 at 734; affirmed, *The Ocean Frost* [1986] A.C. 717 at 773, where there was no holding out for the different reason stated at para.16–028.

[133] See *Bowstead and Reynolds on Agency*, 21st edn (2017), para.8–077 ("most doubtful"); Montrose 17 Can. Bar Rev. 693; Hornby [1961] C.L.J. 239; *The Rhodian River* [1984] 1 Lloyd's Rep. 373 at 379.

[134] See *Johnston v Reading* (1893) 9 T.L.R. 200; *Lloyds Bank v Swiss Bankverein* (1912) 107 L.T. 309; 108 L.T. 143; *Jerome v Bentley & Co* [1952] 2 T.L.R. 58. Two Privy Council decisions can be said to be inconsistent with the principle of usual authority, in that they simply did not consider it as a possible basis of liability where the requirements of apparent authority were not satisfied: *Miles v McIlwraith* (1883) 8 App. Cas. 120; *Attorney General for Ceylon v Silva* [1953] A.C. 461; para.16–028 at fn.101.

gives his agent documents and authorises him to borrow a fixed sum on the security of them, he may be liable to a third party from whom the agent borrows more, even though the third party did not think that the agent had any authority to borrow.[135] Similarly, at common law a person was bound by an unauthorised sale of his goods by a factor, though the factor sold in his own name.[136] At common law, he was not bound by an unauthorised pledge, but under the Factors Act 1889, he is bound, if certain conditions are satisfied, by any disposition (though unauthorised) made by such an agent. These rules are, it is submitted, based on the same principle as *Watteau v Fenwick*. That principle seems to be more closely analogous to the doctrine of vicarious liability in tort (under which an employer may be liable even for forbidden acts if done by an employee in the course of employment)[137] than to the doctrine of apparent authority.

16–036 **Scope.** The extent of an agent's usual authority depends on the class of agent to which he belongs and on the common understanding of the trade concerning such agents. *Watteau v Fenwick* should from this point of view be contrasted with *Daun v Simmins*,[138] where it was held that the manager of a tied public house had no usual authority to order spirits from any person he chose. And where the agent does not belong to a well-known class of agents, but is simply appointed for an isolated transaction, the doctrine of usual authority does not apply. Thus in *Jerome v Bentley & Co*[139] a retired army officer to whom jewellery had been entrusted for sale was held not to have the usual authority which a mercantile agent would have had in the same circumstances.

A principal is liable under the doctrine of usual authority only if there is some dealing between the third party and the agent: the doctrine does not apply if the agent's involvement in the transaction has been concealed so that the third party thinks that he is dealing directly with the principal.[140] The contract must also be made in the course of the principal's business: in *Kinahan v Parry*[141] it was accordingly held that a hotel owner was not liable for whisky bought without his authority by his manager, since it was not proved that the manager had bought it for use in the hotel rather than for his personal use. Similarly, where the manager of a tied house bought beer from outside suppliers and resold it on the premises on his own account, it was said that his employers could not have been sued for the price of the beer.[142] A person is, a fortiori, not liable under the doctrine of usual authority if the business in the course of which the contract was made was not his business at all. Thus in *MacFisheries Ltd v Harrison*[143] the owner of a public house sold it as a going concern, but forgot to transfer the licence to the

[135] *Brocklesby v Temperance PBS* [1895] A.C. 173; *Fry v Smellie* [1912] 3 K.B. 282; cf. *Wishart v Credit & Mercantile Plc* [2015] EWCA Civ 655; [2015] 2 P. & C.R. 15 at [52]. For criticism of the reasoning of these cases, see *Bowstead and Reynolds on Agency*, 21st edn (2017), para.8–135.
[136] *Coles v NW Bank* (1875) L.R. 10 C.P. 354 at 362.
[137] *Limpus v LGOC* (1862) 1 H. & C. 526; *Rose v Plenty* [1976] 1 W.L.R. 141.
[138] (1879) 41 L.T. 783.
[139] [1952] 2 T.L.R. 58.
[140] *Kooragang Investments Pty Ltd v Richardson & Wrench Ltd* [1982] A.C. 462.
[141] [1911] 1 K.B. 459.
[142] *Attorney General's Reference (No.1 of 1985)* [1986] Q.B. 491 at 506.
[143] (1924) 93 L.J.K.B. 811.

buyer. He was not liable for food supplied to his successor for consumption on the premises, since the latter was carrying on the business entirely on his own behalf.

### *(iii) Authority of necessity*[144]

Under this heading, we shall first discuss a number of situations in which one person acts to protect some interest of another without any previous authorisation from that other person.[145] We shall then consider whether any useful purpose is served by attempting to bring all these, somewhat disparate, cases within the scope of a single doctrine. **16–037**

**Acceptance of a bill of exchange for the honour of the drawer.** When a bill is not accepted by the person on whom it is drawn, a stranger may, with the consent of the holder, accept the bill for the honour of the drawer. If the stranger has to pay on this acceptance, he becomes entitled to the rights of the holder to sue the drawer on the bill.[146] **16–038**

**Shipmasters.** Where it is necessary[147] to do so for the further prosecution of the voyage, the master of a ship has authority of necessity to borrow on the shipowner's credit, to hypothecate the ship, cargo and freight, or the cargo alone, to sell part of the cargo,[148] and to enter into a salvage agreement on behalf of the cargo-owner.[149] **16–039**

**Salvage.** A person who goes to the aid of a ship in distress at sea[150] and saves life or property is entitled to a reward the amount of which is (subject to certain limitations), at the discretion of the court. **16–040**

**Other cases.** The courts have been reluctant to extend the doctrine of agency of necessity, because it may deprive a person of his property, or subject him to an obligation, without his consent.[151] But the doctrine is not confined to the three situations described above. It extends to a number of other situations, in some (but not in all) of which the authority is based on some prior relationship between the parties.[152] **16–041**

---

144 Treitel 3 W.A.A.L. Rev. 1; Wade 19 Vanderbilt L. Rev. 1183; Birks 10 C.L.P. 110; Matthews [1981] C.L.J. 340.

145 In addition to the situations discussed in the text, see also: Mental Capacity Act 2005 ss.5–8; cf. para.12–059.

146 See Bills of Exchange Act 1882 ss.65–68.

147 See para.16–045.

148 See *Notara v Henderson* (1872) L.R. 7 Q.B. 225.

149 *The Winson* [1982] A.C. 939. But where the conditions stated at para.16–045, are not satisfied, the master has no *implied* authority to enter into such an agreement: *The Choko Star* [1990] 1 Lloyd's Rep. 516.

150 For this restriction, see *The Goring* [1988] A.C. 831.

151 *Falcke v Scottish Imperial Assurance Co* (1886) 34 Ch D. 234 at 248; *The Winson* [1982] A.C. 939 at 962.

152 *Re F* [1990] 2 A.C. 1 at 75; cf. *Crantrave Ltd v Lloyds Bank Plc* [2000] Q.B. 917 at 922–923, where there was no "necessity".

16–042 **Powers of sale.** It has been held that land carriers can have authority of necessity to sell.[153] At common law, the courts were reluctant to hold that a bailee with whom goods had been left for storage or repair was entitled to sell them merely because the owner had failed to collect them and could not be traced. By statute, the bailee is now entitled to sell in a number of situations if he has given notice to the bailor of his intention to sell or if he has failed to trace the bailor after having taken reasonable steps to do so.[154] This statutory power extends to cases in which there was, at common law, no authority of necessity to sell.[155] There may also be cases in which, though the statutory requirements are not satisfied, a sale can be justified under the common law doctrine of agency of necessity. For example, a buyer of goods may justifiably reject them on the ground that they are not in conformity with the contract of sale; and if the seller refuses to accept their return, the buyer may then have authority of necessity to sell them for the account of the seller.[156]

16–043 **Preservation of another's property.** A number of cases raise the question whether a person who preserves another's property has any claim against the owner. Two eighteenth-century cases decided that such a person has no lien on the property saved;[157] but it does not necessarily follow that he has no claim for reimbursement. In *Tetley v British Trade Corp*[158] an agent who, contrary to his principal's express instruction, removed goods from Batum to Constantinople (to save them from seizure by an invading army) recovered the expense of the removal from his principal. In *The Winson*[159] a salvor of goods from a stranded ship took them to a place of safety and (to prevent them from deteriorating) had them stored in a warehouse there. It was held that the owner was liable to the salvor for the cost of warehousing the goods.

16–044 **Improvement of another's property.** A person who improves another's property may do so in the mistaken but honest belief that it is his own. In such a case there is no agency of necessity since the improver's intention is to act on his own behalf, and not on behalf of the owner. If the subject-matter is goods and the owner sues the improver for wrongful interference, the improver is by statute entitled to an allowance (against the owner's claim) in respect of the improvements.[160] A similar rule existed at common law, and presumably applies in relation to property other than goods.[161] It is more doubtful whether the

[153] *Sims & Co v Midland Ry* [1913] 1 K.B. 103 at 112; *Springer v Great Western Ry* [1921] 1 K.B. 257 at 265, 267; cf. Carriage of Goods by Road Act 1965 Sch. arts 14(2), 16(3), for statutory provisions in case of international carriage.

[154] Torts (Interference with Goods) Act 1977 ss.12, 13 and Sch.1.

[155] e.g. *Munro v Wilmott* [1949] 1 K.B. 295.

[156] *Graanhandel T Vink BW v European Grain & Shipping Co* [1989] 2 Lloyd's Rep. 531 at 533 (where there was no such agency as the buyer had lost his right to reject); cf. *The Olib* [1991] 2 Lloyd's Rep. 108 at 114.

[157] *Binstead v Buck* (1776) 2 Wm.Bl. 1117; *Nicholson v Chapman* (1793) 2 H. Bl. 254.

[158] (1922) 10 Ll. L.R. at 678.

[159] [1982] A.C. 939; cf. *GN Ry v Swaffield* (1874) L.R. 9 Ex. 132; cf. *ENE Kos 1 Ltd v Petroleo Brasileiro SA Petrobras* [2012] UKSC 17; [2012] 2 A.C. 164.

[160] Torts (Interference with Goods) Act 1977 ss.6(1), 3(7).

[161] *Peruvian Guano Co v Dreyfus Bros* [1892] A.C. 166 at 176.

improver has an independent claim in respect of the improvements,[162] i.e. one that he can assert even though no action has been brought against him by the owner.

If the improver knows that he has no title to the property he may again have certain limited rights in respect of the improvements. In *Munro v Wilmott*[163] the claimant with the defendant's permission left his car in the defendant's yard. Some years later, the defendant wanted to have the car moved, and, after trying unsuccessfully to contact the claimant, spent some £85 on making the car saleable, and sold it. He was held liable for conversion, but the damages were reduced by £85 "not from the point of view of payment for what he has done, but in order to arrive at ... the true value of the property which the [claimant] had lost".[164] The case would now come within the statutory provisions authorising sales of uncollected goods,[165] so that the defendant would no longer be liable in conversion. Under the statutory provisions the bailee must account for the proceeds of sale to the bailor and is entitled to deduct items such as the costs of sale and sums due to him under the terms of the bailment;[166] but nothing is said about the value of improvements.[167] However, the bailee can apply to the court for an order authorising the sale "subject to such terms ... as may be specified in the order".[168] These could perhaps give him the right to make a deduction in respect of improvements. Even this possibility would not be open to the bailee if he did not sell the goods but simply returned them to the bailor. In such a case he could perhaps invoke the doctrine of agency of necessity.

**Conditions to be satisfied in cases of sale, preservation, or improvement.** In the cases just discussed,[169] the common law doctrine of agency of necessity will apply only if certain conditions are satisfied.[170] It must be impossible to communicate with the owner of the goods in time to get his instructions or impossible to obtain such instructions because the owner (though he can be reached) fails to give them;[171] the agent must act reasonably, in good faith and in the interests of the owner; and his acts must have been commercially necessary. 16–045

[162] For a suggestion that there is such a claim, see *Greenwood v Bennett* [1973] Q.B. 195 at 201 (but see at 203); Jones 93 L.Q.R. 273.
[163] [1949] 1 K.B. 295.
[164] *Munro v Wilmott* [1949] 1 K.B. 295 at 299.
[165] Torts (Interference with Goods) Act 1977 ss.12, 13 and Sch.1; Palmer [1987] L.M.C.L.Q. 43.
[166] Torts (Interference with Goods) Act 1977 s.12(5).
[167] Torts (Interference with Goods) Act 1977 s.6 would not apply as the defendant knew that he had no title to the car.
[168] Torts (Interference with Goods) Act 1977 s.13(1)(a).
[169] See paras 16–042—16–044.
[170] See *Springer v GW Ry* [1921] 1 K.B. 257; *Prager v Blatspiel, Stamp & Heacock Ltd* [1924] 1 K.B. 566. These principles also apply to a shipmaster's authority of necessity: para.16–039; cf. *The Winson* [1982] A.C. 939.
[171] *The Winson* [1982] A.C. 939 at 962; *The Olib* [1991] 2 Lloyd's Rep. 108 at 104; the possibility that the owner may fail to give the instructions shows that the difficulty of obtaining them is not invariably "overcome today by modern means of communication" (*Re F* [1990] 2 A.C. 1 at 75); cf. *The Choko Star* [1990] 1 Lloyd's Rep. 516 at 524); it may also be impracticable for a shipmaster to obtain instructions from *all* the cargo-owners.

For example, it is not "necessary" to sell goods merely because they are causing inconvenience,[172] for there may be a reasonable opportunity of storing them.[173]

16–046 **Preservation of life or health.** The doctrine of agency of necessity may apply where one person preserves the life or health of another. Thus it is the basis on which a person can sue for the value of necessaries supplied to a person lacking mental capacity.[174] A doctor who gives medical attention to an unconscious person might recover a fee on the same ground;[175] the case for allowing him to do so would be particularly strong where the doctor's acts are not merely lawful but are done in the performance of a legal duty to render the services in question.[176] A right to payment would of course be negatived if the circumstances were such that the services would not normally be paid for: this would be the position where emergency treatment is given under the National Health Service. Special statutory provisions entitle the doctor to a fee where he gives emergency treatment to the victim of a road accident[177] and require National Health Service charges to be paid to the Secretary of State in respect of treatment given by the Service to an "injured person" if a "compensation payment" is made (normally by an insurer) by or on behalf of a person who is, or is alleged to be, liable to any extent in respect of the injury, or in pursuance of a compensation scheme for motor accidents.[178]

16–047 **Scope and terminology.** It will be seen from the situations discussed above that "agency of necessity" can produce three quite different results. First, it may enable the agent to create a contract between the principal and a third party;[179] secondly it may entitle the agent to dispose of the principal's property;[180] and thirdly it may entitle the agent to recompense or reimbursement in respect of the efforts that he has made, or the expense that he has incurred, to protect the interests of the principal.[181] It has been suggested that the expression "agency of necessity" should no longer be used in its traditional broad sense, to refer to all these consequences, but that it should be used in a narrower sense, to refer only to cases in which the question is whether the agent has, by reason of the necessity, the power to create a contract between his principal and a third party.[182]

The purpose of this suggested departure from the traditional terminology is to make the point that the three consequences described above do not necessarily depend on the same requirements.[183] Thus a person who, to prevent another's goods from deteriorating, arranges for them to be stored in a warehouse, may

---

172 *Sachs v Miklos* [1948] 2 K.B. 23.

173 As in *Prager v Blatspiel, Stamp & Heacock Ltd* [1924] 1 K.B. 566. Semble the statutory power of sale referred to at para.16–042 would not extend to the facts of this case.

174 See paras 12–059–12–062.

175 *Cotnam v Wisdom* 83 Ark. 601; 104 S.W. 164 (1907); *Re Crisan's Estate* 102 N.W. 2d 907 (1961).

176 *Re F* [1990] 2 A.C. 1 at 55, where the issue was whether the treatment was *lawful*.

177 Road Traffic Act 1988 ss.158, 159.

178 Health and Social Care (Community Health and Standards) Act 2003 s.150.

179 e.g. at fn.149.

180 e.g. at fn.153.

181 e.g. at fnn.158–159.

182 *The Winson* [1982] A.C. 939 at 958.

183 *The Winson* [1982] A.C. 939 at 958.

have a claim against the owner for reimbursement of the charges that he has paid to the warehouseman. It does not follow from this that he also has the power to make a contract between the owner and the warehouseman, so that the warehouseman can sue the owner directly for his charges.[184] On the other hand, the fact that both consequences depend on necessity makes it at least likely that similar factors will often be relevant to each of them. Similarly, it is relevant for the purpose of both consequences to ask whether the agent acted in the interests of the owner or out of self-interest.[185]

Thus it is submitted that the question whether the label "agency of necessity" should be used in its traditional broad, or in a new narrow, sense is largely one of emphasis, or, as has been said, a "purely terminological"[186] one. It is part of the wider question as to the effects of non-consensual agency, to be discussed later in this chapter.[187] Such agency scarcely ever produces *all* of the effects of agency based on agreement, but it generally does produce *some* of those effects. This is true of all forms of non-consensual agency; and it is submitted that, so long as the relationships discussed under the present heading produce at least some of the consequences that normally flow from agency by agreement, it is not inappropriate to say that they give rise to "agency of necessity". **16–048**

## (c) Ratification

### *(i) What amounts to ratification*

**Express or implied.** Ratification may be express or implied. It can be implied if the principal by conduct unequivocally affirms the agent's acts, even though he purports to repudiate them.[188] It can, for example, be implied from a pleading which denies liability provided it relies on the contract in dispute.[189] Mere passive acquiescence does not of itself amount to ratification,[190] but it may, when combined with other circumstances, have this effect, e.g. where the principal knows that the third party believes him to have accepted the agent's act as having been authorised and takes no steps within a reasonable time to repudiate the transaction.[191] Where an arbitral tribunal is not properly constituted because service of the notice of arbitration is made on an agent without authority, the **16–049**

---

[184] *The Winson* [1982] A.C. 939 at 958.

[185] *The Winson* [1982] A.C. 939 at 962.

[186] *The Winson* [1982] A.C. 939 at 965; cf. *Re F* [1990] 2 A.C. 1 at 75 (using the expression to refer to the intervenor's right to reimbursement).

[187] See para.16–116.

[188] *Cornwall v Henson* (1750) 1 Ves. Sen. 509.

[189] *Rabiu v Marlbray Ltd* [2016] EWCA Civ 476; [2016] 1 W.L.R. 5147 at [59]–[67].

[190] *Moon v Towers* (1860) 8 C.B. (N.S.) 611; reversed on other grounds: (1860) 9 H.L.C. 78. Contrast the now doubtful case of *Waithman v Wakefield* (1807) 1 Camp. 120; and *Michael Elliott & Partners v UK Land* [1991] 1 E.G.L.R. 39.

[191] *Suncorp Ins & Finance v Milano Assicurazioni SpA* [1993] 2 Lloyd's Rep. 225 at 241; *Demco Investment & Commercial SA v Interamerican Life Assurance (International) Ltd* [2012] EWHC 2053 (Comm) at [106].

principal who has not participated in the arbitration proceedings cannot ratify the award by "mere silence and inaction".[192]

16–050 **Principal must have knowledge of the unauthorised act.** Ratification will not generally be implied from conduct unless the principal has full knowledge of the agent's unauthorised act.[193] Where the question of ratification arises in the context of a claim by the third party against the principal, as opposed to a claim by the principal against the agent for breach of authority, it may be sufficient that the principal has knowledge of what the agent has done, but not that the agent lacked the authority to do it.[194] But whatever the context, a principal may be held to have ratified if he indicates that he will support whatever the agent has done on his behalf, even though he does not know exactly what the agent has agreed to: in such a case the principal takes the risk of the agent's having exceeded his authority.[195]

16–051 **Need for a free choice.** An act will be regarded as ratification only if the principal had a free choice whether to do it or not. Merely taking back one's own property after a third party has, in reliance on unauthorised instructions, done work on it is not ratification.[196]

### *(ii) When ratification is possible*

16–052 **The agent must purport to act on behalf of the principal.** A principal can only ratify acts which the agent purported to do on his behalf.[197] The most important consequence of this rule is that if the agent purports to act on his own behalf the principal cannot ratify; or, in other words, that an undisclosed principal[198] cannot ratify. Thus in *Keighley, Maxsted & Co v Durant*[199] an agent bought corn at a price above that at which he had been instructed to buy. He intended to buy for his principal, but did not disclose this fact to the seller. The undisclosed principal purported to ratify the purchase, but later refused to accept delivery. It was held that the ratification was ineffective and that the principal was not liable. Lord Macnaghten said that "Civil obligations are not to be created by or founded upon

---

[192] *Sino Channel Asia Ltd v Dana Shipping & Trading PTE Singapore* [2016] EWHC 1118; [2016] 2 Lloyd's Rep. 97 at [60]; affirmed [2017] EWCA Civ 1703; [2018] 1 Lloyd's Rep. 17 at [65].

[193] *Lewis v Read* (1845) 13 M. & W. 834; *Sea Emerald SA v Prominvestbank* [2008] EWHC 1979 (Comm) at [102]. "Ignorance of the law" is no defence: *AMB Generali Holding AG v SEB Trygg Liv Holding Aktiebolag* [2005] EWCA Civ 1237; [2006] 1 W.L.R. 2276 at [43] ("a party cannot meet a claim of ratification by saying that if he had properly understood the effect of a legal document he would not have acted as he did").

[194] *ING Re (UK) Ltd v R&V Versicherung AG* [2006] EWHC 1544 (Comm); [2007] 1 B.C.L.C. 108 at [155]–[157].

[195] *Fitzmaurice v Bayley* (1856) 6 E. & B. 868; cf. *Haseler v Lemoyne* (1858) 5 C.B. (N.S.) 530; *Suncorp Ins & Finance v Milano Assicurazioni SpA* [1993] 2 Lloyd's Rep. 225 at 234.

[196] *Forman & Co Pty Ltd v The Liddesdale* [1900] A.C. 190.

[197] *Wilson v Tumman* (1843) 6 Man. & G. 236.

[198] For the definition of "undisclosed principal", see para.16–063.

[199] [1901] A.C. 240; cf. *The Astyanax* [1985] 2 Lloyd's Rep. 109; *Welsh Development Agency v Export Finance Co* [1992] B.C.L.C. 148; *Siu Yin Kwan v Eastern Ins* [1994] 2 A.C. 199 at 207.

undisclosed intentions."[200] It could be objected that this reasoning would destroy the whole law relating to undisclosed principals. But the decision is nonetheless intelligible, having regard to the common law doctrine of privity of contract. Ratification and the undisclosed principal are two important exceptions to that doctrine. To allow both exceptions to operate on the same set of facts would go far towards overthrowing the doctrine of privity altogether.

On the other hand, an unnamed principal[201] can ratify. Policies of marine insurance may be taken out "for and on behalf of any person interested"; and such persons can ratify although they are not named in the policy.[202]

The rule that the agent must *purport* to act on behalf of the principal does not mean that he must *intend* to do so. Thus the principal may ratify although the agent intended to defraud him.[203]

In *Brook v Hook*[204] an agent forged his principal's signature to a promissory note. The principal's later ratification was held to be ineffective. This case has given rise to a dispute on the question whether a forgery can ever be ratified. But it does not seem that this question arises in a case of this kind. If an agent forges his principal's signature he does not say "I am signing for my principal" but "this is my principal's signature". The principal cannot ratify because the agent did not purport to act on his behalf.[205] But if the principal stands by knowing that his agent will forge his signature he may be estopped from denying its genuineness.[206]

**Capacity: corporations.** At common law, a corporation cannot ratify the unauthorised act of its agent in entering into an ultra vires contract.[207] There are two reasons why, in general,[208] this rule no longer applies in relation to companies incorporated under the Companies Act 2006. First, the validity of an act done by such a company can no longer be called into question on the ground of lack of capacity by reason of anything in the company's constitution.[209] Secondly, in favour of a person dealing with the company in good faith, the power of the board of directors to bind the company, or to authorise others to do so, is deemed to be free of any limitation under the company's constitution.[210] **16–053**

---

200 *Keighley, Maxsted & Co v Durant* [1901] A.C. 240 at 247.

201 For the definition of "unnamed principal," see para.16–063.

202 *Hagedorn v Oliverson* (1814) 2 M. & S. 485. Quaere whether the requirement stated in *Watson v Swann* (1862) 11 C.B. (N.S.) 756 at 771, that the person seeking to ratify must be described at the time of the contract in such a way as to be ascertainable at that time is generally accepted: see *Boston Fruit Co v British & Foreign Marine Ins Co* [1906] A.C. 336 at 338–339 (a case apparently overlooked in *Southern Water Authority v Carey* [1985] 2 All E.R. 1077 at 1085).

203 *Re Tiedemann & Ledermann Frères* [1899] 2 Q.B. 66.

204 (1871) L.R. 6 Ex. 89.

205 *Imperial Bank of Canada v Begley* [1936] 2 All E.R. 367; *Demco Investment & Commercial SA v Interamerican Life Assurance (International) Ltd* [2012] EWHC 2053 (Comm) at [121]–[122].

206 *Greenwood v Martins Bank Ltd* [1933] A.C. 51.

207 *Ashbury Ry Carriage & Iron Co v Riche* (1875) L.R. 7 H.L. 653; *Mann v Edinburgh N Tramways* [1893] A.C. 69; *Rolled Steel Products (Holdings) Ltd v BSC* [1986] Ch. 246 at 304.

208 For exceptions, see fnn.209, 210.

209 Companies Act 2006 s.39(1) (modified rules apply to companies which are charities: ss.39(2), 42); para.12–070.

210 Companies Act 2006 s.40(1) (modified rules apply to companies which are charities: ss.40(6), 42; and transactions with directors and their associates: ss.40(6), 41); para.12–071.

Entering into a contract which is outside the company's objects constitutes a breach of duty by a director.[211] Section 239 of the 2006 Act permits ratification of a breach of duty by a director by ordinary resolution, but what is being ratified is the breach of duty and not the contract, as this is made binding by the operation of the provisions mentioned earlier.[212]

16–054 **Capacity: minors.** A person can become liable on a contract made by him while he was a minor if he "ratifies" it after reaching full age.[213] "Ratification" here seems to refer to confirmation by a person of a contract made by himself; but there seems to be no reason why a person should not be similarly liable on a ratification after full age of a contract made on his behalf, but without his authority, while he was a minor. There are, however, cases in which a person is not liable on a ratification in the sense of a confirmation of a contract made during minority by himself;[214] and it is submitted that he would equally not be liable if, after full age, he ratified a contract of this kind which had during his minority been made on his behalf but without his authority.[215]

16–055 **The principal must have been in existence when the act was done.** This rule can give rise to inconvenience when promoters contract on behalf of a projected company. It was held in *Kelner v Baxter*[216] that the company could not, after its formation, ratify the promoters' contracts, since it was not in existence when those contracts were made. One way of evading this rule is for the promoter to enter into a draft agreement providing that the company, when formed, shall enter into a similar agreement with the third party and that the liability of the promoter shall thereupon cease. But the draft agreement creates no binding contract between company and third party, so that each can, with the collusion of the promoter, deprive the other of the expected benefit of the contract. The position is somewhat better in equity. The company may be able to enforce the contract against the third party by showing that the promoter acted as trustee for it,[217] and the third party may be able to claim a reasonable remuneration out of any sum which the company has paid, or bound itself to pay, to the promoter for initial expenses.[218] But the third party has no such right if the company has neither made nor promised any payment to the promoter;[219] nor has he any claim against the company on a purely executory contract. By statute, a contract which purports

211 Companies Act 2006 s.171(a).

212 In the exceptional cases where the contract is not binding on the company, there is no provision in the 2006 Act for ratification *of the contract* (cf. s.41(6)); furthermore, s.239 does not affect "any rule of law as to acts that are incapable of being ratified by the company" (s.239(7)), which would suggest that the common law rule stated at the outset of this paragraph continues to apply in such cases.

213 See para.12–030.

214 A penal bond could not be ratified as it was considered to be wholly void: *Baylis v Dineley* (1815) 3 M. & S. 477.

215 On the principle that a nullity cannot be ratified: para.16–057.

216 (1866) L.R. 2 C.P. 174; cf. *Melhado v Porto Alegre Ry* (1874) L.R. 9 C.P. 503.

217 See para.14–089 and following.

218 *Touche v Metropolitan Ry* (1871) L.R. 6 Ch. App. 671; cf. *Re Hereford, etc., Engineering Co* (1876) 2 Ch D. 621 (where the third party lost his rights because of the promoter's fraud); *Re Empress Engineering Co* (1880) 16 Ch D. 125. *Spiller v Paris Skating Rink Co* (1878) 7 Ch D. 368 states the equitable principle too widely.

219 *Re Rotherham Alum & Chemical Co* (1883) 25 Ch D. 103.

to be made by or on behalf of a company before it is formed has effect (subject to contrary agreement) as a contract between the third party and the person purporting to act for the company or as agent for it.[220] But it is still impossible to create a direct contract between the company and the third party by ratification after incorporation. It would be better if the rule in *Kelner v Baxter* were wholly repealed by legislation.[221] We shall see that legislation to some extent solves the problems which arise out of pre-incorporation contracts; but it does so by techniques other than ratification.[222]

**The principal must ratify in time.** A contract cannot be ratified after the time fixed for its performance;[223] if no such time is fixed, it must be ratified within a reasonable time of the principal's acquiring notice of the unauthorised act.[224] Nor can a contract be ratified at a time when the principal could not validly have made it.[225] Thus it has been held that, where an agent, without authority, insures his principal's property, the latter cannot ratify the insurance after the destruction of the property,[226] since he could not at that time have insured it. But exceptionally a policy of marine insurance can be ratified after the destruction of the property insured[227] and it has been suggested that this rule should also be applied to other kinds of insurance.[228] 16–056

**A nullity cannot be ratified.**[229] Although ratification is not confined to lawful acts, an act which is simply void in law cannot be validated by ratification. Similarly, a principal cannot become liable if the unauthorised contract was prohibited by statute: "life cannot be given by ratification to prohibited transactions".[230] This is an additional reason for saying that a forgery cannot be ratified.[231] 16–057

### *(iii) Effect of ratification*

**Ratification relates back to time of unauthorised act.** The effect of ratification is to put principal, agent and third party into the position in which they would 16–058

[220] Companies Act 2006 s.51; para.16–083.

[221] Given that this opportunity was not taken in the Companies Act 2006 (s.51; fn.220 merely restates the rule previously set out in Companies Act 1985 s.36C), it must be thought an unlikely development in the near future. The Explanatory Notes to the 2006 Act (at para.141) suggest novation as a possible solution, which "may be express or implied": para.15–003.

[222] See paras 16–071, 16–075, 16–083.

[223] *Metropolitan Asylums Board v Kingham* (1890) 6 T.L.R. 217; *Dibbins v Dibbins* [1896] 2 Ch. 348.

[224] *Re Portuguese Consolidated Copper Mines* (1890) 45 Ch D. 16; cf. *Bedford Ins Co Ltd v Instituto de Ressaguros do Brasil* [1985] Q.B. 966 at 987 (and see para.11–020).

[225] cf. *Bird v Brown* (1850) 4 Ex. 786 at 789, quoted with approval by Dillon LJ in *Presentaciones Musicales SA v Secunda* [1994] Ch. 271; for another explanation of *Bird v Brown*, see fn.237.

[226] *Grover & Grover Ltd v Matthews* [1910] 2 K.B. 401.

[227] *Williams v N China Ins Co* (1876) 1 C.P.D. 757; Marine Insurance Act 1906 s.86.

[228] *NOW v DOL* [1993] 2 Lloyd's Rep. 582 at 607–608.

[229] For a discussion of this rule, see *Danish Mercantile Co v Beaumont* [1951] Ch. 680 (where the act was held not to be a nullity).

[230] *Bedford Ins Co Ltd v Instituto de Ressaguros do Brasil* [1985] Q.B. 966 at 986 (and see para.11–020).

[231] See para.16–052.

have been, if the agent's acts had been authorised from the start: his authority is said to relate back to the time of the unauthorised act. Thus in *Bolton Partners v Lambert*[232] an agent without authority purported to buy a house for his principal from the defendant, who later repudiated the contract. The principal then ratified. It was held that the defendant was bound by the contract. His repudiation was ineffective as the principal's ratification related back to the time of the agent's unauthorised purchase. The same rule applies where the agent does some act other than the making of a contract. Where, for example, he without authority, begins legal proceedings on behalf of his principal, the principal can ratify even after the expiry of the period of limitation.[233] For the purpose of the doctrine of relation back, it is assumed that the unauthorised act is not a nullity: if it were, ratification would be ineffective either because a nullity cannot be ratified or on the ground that, when it took place, the principal could not himself have validly or effectively done the act in question.[234]

16–059 **Contracts made subject to ratification.** The rule that ratification relates back does not apply where the agent contracts "subject to ratification": in such a case the third party can withdraw at any time before ratification.[235] Nor does the rule apply where before ratification the agent and the third party have cancelled the unauthorised transaction by mutual consent.[236]

16–060 **No retrospective effect where ratification would cause unfair prejudice to the third party.** It has been held that the retrospective effect of ratification will not be permitted to defeat a "vested property right". That may be true in the sense that it will not be allowed to deprive a stranger to the contract of a property right which had vested in him before ratification.[237] Beyond that, any interference with a property right should simply be seen as one example of a broader principle that ratification is not effective where to permit it would unfairly prejudice the third party.[238] In accordance with this principle, it has been held that ratification was effective to prevent time running for the purpose of limitation, even though it took place after the expiry of the relevant period,[239] and it was also effective to confer an immunity even though it took place after the casualty in relation to which the immunity was conferred.[240] By contrast, it has been held that

[232] (1888) 41 Ch D. 295; cf. *Maclean v Dunn* (1828) 4 Bing. 722; *Koenigsblatt v Sweet* [1923] 2 Ch. 314.
[233] *Presentaciones Musicales SA v Secunda* [1994] Ch. 271.
[234] *Presentaciones Musicales SA v Secunda* [1994] Ch. 271 at 280.
[235] *Watson v Davies* [1931] 1 Ch. 455; *Warehousing & Forwarding Co of East Africa Ltd v Jafferali & Sons Ltd* [1964] A.C. 1.
[236] *Walter v James* (1871) L.R. 6 Ex. 124; *Pacific & General Ins Co Ltd v Hazell* [1997] L.R.L.R. 65.
[237] *Bird v Brown* (1850) 4 Ex. 786, as explained in *Presentaciones Musicales SA v Secunda* [1994] Ch. 271 at 285; Tan Cheng Han 117 L.Q.R. 626.
[238] *Smith v Henniker-Major* [2002] EWCA Civ 762; [2003] Ch. 182 at [71], [73]; *The Borvigilant* [2003] EWCA Civ 935; [2003] 2 Lloyd's Rep. 520 at [70] and following; approving the principle to this effect in *Bowstead and Reynolds on Agency*, 18th edn (2006), art.19. In *The Borvigilant* Clarke LJ stressed (at [87]) that "in the vast majority of cases it would be unjust to the third party to give effect to a ratification if to do so would divest a vested property right."
[239] *Presentaciones Musicales SA v Secunda* [1994] Ch. 271; cf. *Nottinghamshire Health Care Trust v Prison Officers Association* [2003] I.C.R. 1192.
[240] *The Borvigilant* [2003] EWCA Civ 935; [2003] 2 Lloyd's Rep. 520.

ratification of the assignment of a cause of action three years after its execution was not effective in circumstances where the delay in bringing proceedings had caused unfair prejudice to the defendant.[241]

**Criticism.** The rule in *Bolton Partners v Lambert* has been criticised on the ground that it puts the third party at the mercy of the principal, who is free to ratify or not as he pleases.[242] But the hardship to the third party should not be exaggerated. If the principal does not ratify, the third party has his remedy against the agent for breach of implied warranty of authority.[243] If the principal does ratify, the third party will be liable to him; but since this is precisely what he expected, he cannot complain.[244] The only hardship is that the principal may be able to keep the third party waiting while he decides whether to ratify, but the recognition of the broad principle referred to in the last paragraph does much to address any real prejudice caused by such delay. In any event, the principal must ratify within a reasonable time; and the extent of such time is considerably abridged if the third party tells the principal that he wishes to withdraw from the contract.[245] Moreover, a principal cannot ratify after he has, by words or conduct, intimated to the third party that he does not intend to do so;[246] and such an intention could probably be inferred from his remaining silent for more than a comparatively short time after notice of the third party's intention to withdraw. Thus the third party need not be kept indefinitely in suspense. He can, in effect, say to the principal: ratify quickly or not at all. 16–061

## 4. EFFECTS OF AGENCY

When an agent makes a contract on behalf of his principal with a third party, the transaction can give rise to legal effects between principal and third party, between agent and third party, and between principal and agent. In discussing these effects, we shall first assume that the agency has arisen by consent, and then consider to what extent the same effects result from non-consensual agency. 16–062

### (a) Between principal and third party

#### (i) *Rights of principal against third party*

**Whether principal disclosed or undisclosed.** The rights of principal against third party depend in part on the distinction between disclosed and undisclosed principals. A *disclosed principal* is one of whose existence the third party is aware at the time of contracting. He is called a named principal if the third party also knew his name, and an unnamed principal if the third party did not know his 16–063

[241] *Smith v Henniker-Major* [2002] EWCA Civ 762; [2003] Ch. 182 (this aspect of the decision was obiter).
[242] Wambaugh 9 Harv. L.R. 60; and see *Fleming v Bank of New Zealand* [1900] A.C. 577.
[243] See paras 16–089–16–096.
[244] *The Borvigilant* [2003] EWCA Civ 935; [2003] 2 Lloyd's Rep. 520 at [88].
[245] *Re Portuguese Consolidated Copper Mines* (1890) 45 Ch D. 16.
[246] *McEvoy v Belfast Banking Co* [1935] A.C. 24.

name.[247] An *undisclosed principal* is one of whose existence the third party is unaware at the time of contracting. Where a person makes a contract "as agent" or "on behalf of my client" the principal will generally be disclosed. But such words may not make it clear that that person is acting as agent *in the legal sense*;[248] they may merely indicate that he is acting as agent in a commercial sense. If that is the position and the person described as "agent" actually has a principal in the legal sense, that principal may be undisclosed.[249]

16–064 **Disclosed principal.** The general rule is that a disclosed principal can enforce the contract against the third party.[250] The third party is not discharged by settling with the agent unless the principal by his conduct induced the third party to do so, or unless the agent had authority to receive payment.[251] The third party cannot set off against the principal any debt which the agent may owe to the third party;[252] and a custom enabling the agent to receive payment by such set-off is unreasonable.[253]

16–065 **Undisclosed principal.**[254] An undisclosed principal can also, in general, enforce the contract against the third party. Attempts have been made to reconcile this rule with the doctrine of privity. One view is that the contract is "in truth" made with the undisclosed principal,[255] but this is scarcely consistent with the rule that the agent is fully entitled and liable under the contract.[256] Other views recognise that the contract is between agent and third party but say that the principal can intervene because his contract with the agent entitles him to do so, or because he is a cestui que trust or a quasi-assignee.[257] But the better view seems to be that the undisclosed principal's right is not based on the theory that he has somehow acquired the agent's right. His right is an independent right,[258] established by way of exception to the common law doctrine of privity,[259] in the interests of commercial convenience.[260]

---

[247] Reynolds in Rose (ed.), *Consensus ad Idem, Essays in the Law of Contract in Honour of Guenter Treitel* (1996), p.77.

[248] See para.16–007 and following.

[249] See a difference of opinion on this point in *Teheran-Europe Co Ltd v ST Belton (Tractors) Ltd* [1968] 2 Q.B. 545 at 552, 556, 561.

[250] *Langton v Waite* (1868) L.R. 6 Eq. 165.

[251] *Yates v Freckleton* (1781) 2 Dougl. 623; *Linck, Moeller & Co v Jameson & Co* (1885) 2 T.L.R. 206; *Butwick v Grant* [1924] 2 K.B. 483.

[252] *Pratt v Willey* (1826) 2 C. & P. 350; *Cooke v Eshelby* (1887) 12 App. Cas. 271; unless the agent has authority to receive payment in this way: *Stewart v Aberdein* (1838) 4 M. & W. 211 at 228.

[253] *Pearson v Scott* (1878) 9 Ch D. 198.

[254] Tettenborn [1998] C.L.J. 274; Tan Cheng-Han 120 L.Q.R. 480.

[255] *Keighley Maxsted & Co v Durant* [1901] A.C. 240 at 261.

[256] See para.16–081.

[257] For discussions of the basis of the doctrine, see Ames, *Essays*, p.453; Seavey 29 Y.L.J. 859; Goodhart and Hamson 4 C.L.J. 320; Montrose 16 Can. Bar Rev. 757; Dowrick 17 M.L.R. 25; Higgins 28 M.L.R. 167; Reynolds in Rose (ed.), *Consensus ad Idem, Essays in the Law of Contract in Honour of Guenter Treitel* (1996), pp.89–90.

[258] *Pople v Evans* [1969] 2 Ch. 255; *The Havprins* [1983] 2 Lloyd's Rep. 356 at 362.

[259] *Welsh Development Agency v Export Finance Co Ltd* [1992] B.C.L.C. 148 at 182.

[260] *Siu Yin Kwan v Eastern Ins Co Ltd* [1994] 2 A.C. 199 at 207. The Contracts (Rights of Third Parties) Act 1999 does not confer any rights on the undisclosed principal because he is, by definition, not "expressly identified" within s.1(3) (para.14–107).

**Limitations on the right of undisclosed principal.** The undisclosed principal's right could prejudice a third party, who necessarily thought that he was dealing only with the agent. To avoid such prejudice, the undisclosed principal's right is limited in the following ways. **16–066**

**Principal's intervention must be consistent with the terms of the contract.** An undisclosed principal is not allowed to intervene where this would be inconsistent with the terms of the contract.[261] In *Aspen Underwriting Ltd v Credit Europe Bank NV*[262] the specification of particular parties implied that there was no scope for an undisclosed principal[263] and in *Magellan Spirit ApS v Vitol SA*[264] Leggatt J stated as follows: **16–067**

> "Where a contract is made by or on behalf of a named legal person and there is nothing in the terms of the contract or surrounding circumstances to indicate to the other contracting party that the named person is making the contract as an agent, then the presumption must be that the named person is contracting as a principal. That presumption is capable of being displaced; but in order to displace it, convincing proof is needed that the named party was – contrary to appearances - contracting on behalf of an undisclosed principal."[265]

In *Humble v Hunter*[266] a person signed a charterparty as "owner". This was held to mean that he and he alone was owner,[267] so that his undisclosed principal was not allowed to intervene. By contrast, in *F Drughorn Ltd v Rederiaktiebolaget Transatlantic*[268] the fact that an agent signed a charterparty as "charterer" did not exclude his undisclosed principal's right to enforce the contract; and in *Siu Yin Kwan v Eastern Ins Co Ltd*[269] the fact that the agent was described in an employer's liability policy as the employer did not exclude the right of the undisclosed principal (who was in fact the employer) to intervene. The apparent reluctance of the courts in some cases to hold that the right to intervene has been excluded by descriptive words in the contract may be explained on the basis that

[261] *Teheran-Europe v Belton* [1968] 2 Q.B. 545 at 552; *Aspen Underwriting Ltd v Credit Europe Bank NV* [2018] EWCA Civ 2590; [2019] 1 Lloyd's Rep. 221 at [48].

[262] [2018] EWCA Civ 2590; [2019] 1 Lloyd's Rep. 221.

[263] The inclusion of an entire agreement clause is further evidence which may exclude the right of the undisclosed principal, but is not determinative: *Kaefer Aislamientos SA de CV v AMS DRilling Mexico SA de CV* [2019] EWCA Civ 10; [2019] 1 W.L.R. 3514 at [113].

[264] [2016] EWHC 454 (Comm); [2016] 2 Lloyd's Rep. 1.

[265] *Magellan Spirit ApS v Vitol SA* [2016] EWHC 454 (Comm); [2016] 2 Lloyd's Rep. 1; cf. *Actegy Ltd v Société Logitique Nivelloise Spl* [2018] EWHC 2400 (Comm).

[266] (1842) 12 Q.B. 316; *Formby Bros v Formby* (1910) 102 L.T. 116; cf. *The Astyanax* [1985] 2 Lloyd's Rep. 109.

[267] For the interpretation in this context of phrases such as "disponent owner" or "operating owner", see *The Yanxilas* [1982] 2 Lloyd's Rep. 444. In the context of a bill of lading, "[ship]owner" can refer to the person with whom the shipper enters into the contract of carriage and so include a charterer: *The Stolt Loyalty* [1995] 1 Lloyd's Rep. 598.

[268] [1919] A.C. 203; *Danziger v Thompson* [1944] K.B. 654. Contrast *The Starsin* [2003] UKHL 12; [2004] 1 A.C. 715 at [84], [85].

[269] [1994] 2 A.C. 199; *Rolls Royce Power Engineering Plc v Ricardo Consulting Engineers Ltd* [2004] EWHC 2871; 98 Con L.R. 169; *Ferryways NV v Associated British Ports* [2008] EWHC 225; [2008] 1 Lloyd's Rep. 639.

it would tend to defeat the considerations of commercial convenience on which the doctrine of the undisclosed principal is based.[270]

16–068 **Personal considerations relating to the agent.** If the third party can show that he wanted to deal with the agent *and with no one else*, the undisclosed principal cannot intervene. This will, for example, be the position where the third party wished to contract only with the agent because the nature of the contract was such as to show that the third party relied on the agent's business reputation, or integrity;[271] or because the agent owed him money which was to be set off against the amount due from the third party under the contract which the principal sought to enforce.[272] But the third party will not be prejudiced by the undisclosed principal's right to intervene if (as may be the case in many commercial contexts) it is a matter of indifference to him whether his contract is with the agent or with the undisclosed principal.[273] This was held to be the position in the *Siu Yin Kwan*[274] case, where the Privy Council also rejected the argument that the undisclosed principal's right should be excluded merely because the contract was one of indemnity insurance. While in some such contracts the insurer may rely on personal considerations relating to the insured,[275] he had not done so here since the proposal form had given him all the information relating to the principal that was relevant to the risk.[276] Presumably, however, the principal could not have intervened if the insurer had proved that, in entering into the contract, he had in fact relied on personal considerations relating to the agent.

16–069 **Personal considerations relating to the principal.** A third party who has no particular reason for wanting to deal with the agent may nevertheless *not want to* deal with the principal. If the agent expressly says that he is not acting for the principal, the third party can avoid the contract for fraud.[277] If he makes no such misrepresentation, the law is less clear.

In *Nash v Dix*[278] a committee of Roman Catholics wanted to buy a Congregational chapel from the defendants and to turn it into a place of Roman Catholic worship. The defendants refused to deal with the committee as they disapproved of the proposed user. The committee then told the claimant that if he could buy the chapel from the defendants they would buy it from him for £100 more than he had paid for it. The defendants sold the chapel to the claimant but repudiated the contract on discovering that he intended to resell to the committee.

[270] *Siu Yin Kwan v Eastern Ins Co Ltd* [1994] 2 A.C. 199 at 210; cf. *Epps v Rothnie* [1945] K.B. 562 at 565, doubting *Humble v Hunter* (1842) 12 Q.B. 316; *Talbot Underwriting Ltd v Nausch Hogan & Mirray Inc* [2006] EWCA Civ 889; [2006] 2 Lloyd's Rep. 195 at [35]–[36].

[271] *Collins v Associated Greyhound Racecourses Ltd* [1930] Ch. 1 (underwriting contract).

[272] *Greer v Downs Supply Co* [1927] 2 K.B. 28; quaere whether this decision was necessary for the protection of the third party since an undisclosed principal can intervene only subject to the third party's right of set-off against the agent: para.16–070.

[273] *Siu Yin Kwan v Eastern Ins Co Ltd* [1994] 2 A.C. 199 at 210.

[274] *Siu Yin Kwan v Eastern Ins Co Ltd* [1994] 2 A.C. 199 at 210. The claim was by employees of the principal under the equivalent of Third Parties (Rights Against Insurers) Act 1930; para.14–143.

[275] cf. para.15–055 for restrictions on the assignment of such policies on this ground.

[276] *Siu Yin Kwan v Eastern Ins Co Ltd* [1994] 2 A.C. 199 at 208.

[277] *Archer v Stone* (1898) 78 L.T. 34; cf. *Berg v Sadler & Moore* [1937] 2 K.B. 158; para.9–106.

[278] (1898) 78 L.T. 445.

North J held that the defendants were bound: (1) because the claimant was not an agent, but simply a person who had bought for resale; and (2) because the claimant had not been guilty of any misrepresentation. It appears from the judgment that the claimant would have failed if he *had* been the agent of the committee.

In *Said v Butt*[279] the claimant wanted to go to the first night of a play, but knew that the proprietors of the theatre would not sell him a ticket as he had in the past strongly criticised their conduct. He therefore sent a friend to the box office to buy a ticket for him without disclosing his name, but he was later refused admission by the manager of the theatre. In an action against the manager for inducing a breach of contract, McCardie J held that there was no contract between the proprietors and the claimant: since the proprietors reserved the right to sell first-night tickets to specially selected persons, the "personality" of the other contracting party was a material element in the contract.

Both these cases were distinguished in *Dyster v Randall & Sons*.[280] The claimant wanted to buy land from the defendants, who, to his knowledge, would not deal with him as they distrusted him. He employed an agent to buy the land in the agent's own name, and then claimed that he was entitled to intervene as undisclosed principal. Lawrence J upheld the claim: he said that it would be futile to deny the claimant's right to sue since the agent could have assigned the benefit of the contract to him. But this reasoning does not satisfactorily distinguish *Said v Butt*: theatre tickets can (unless they expressly provide the contrary) be assigned no less than contracts to buy land. Again it was said that "personal" consideration entered into the two earlier cases but not into *Dyster v Randall & Sons*. While this may distinguish *Said v Butt*, it does not satisfactorily explain why the action in *Nash v Dix* would have failed if the claimant had been an agent; for it is hard to see why an objection based on religious grounds is more "personal" than one based on distrust.

It is submitted that an undisclosed principal should not be allowed to intervene if he knows that the third party does not want to deal with him. If the principal directly concealed his identity, the contract would be void for mistake, or voidable for fraud; and the principal should not be able to improve his position by simply employing an agent. The position is the same where the agent knows, or should know, that the third party wanted to contract *only* with him.[281]

**Other safeguards.** The rights of the undisclosed principal against the third party are subject to any defences which the third party has against the agent.[282] This rule is necessary for the protection of the third party, who thinks that he is dealing with the agent alone. Thus if the agent owes money to the third party, the debt can be set off by the third party against the principal, and if the third party pays the agent he can rely on the payment against the principal.[283] This rule does not apply where the third party has no belief that he is dealing with the agent alone. In 16–070

279 [1920] 3 K.B. 497.

280 [1926] Ch. 932; cf. *Smith v Wheatcroft* (1878) 9 Ch D. 223.

281 *Siu Yin Kwan v Eastern Ins Co Ltd* [1994] 2 A.C. 199 at 207.

282 *Browning v Provincial Ins Co of Canada* (1873) L.R. 5 P.C. 263 at 272.

283 *George v Clagett* (1797) 7 T.R. 359; *Mann v Forrester* (1814) 4 Camp. 60; *Montague v Forwood* [1893] 2 Q.B. 350; Derham [1986] C.L.J. 384.

*Cooke v Eshelby*[284] the third party had no belief one way or the other whether the person with whom he was dealing was principal or agent. He was in fact an agent. The third party was not allowed to set off against the principal a debt which the agent owed to the third party.

The principal may intend the agent to disclose his existence, but the agent may fail to do so because he wants to misappropriate the proceeds of the contract, or to induce the third party to accept the principal's property in discharge of a debt which the agent owes to the third party. In such cases the third party can only rely on his settlement with, or set-off against, the agent, in an action brought by the principal, if the latter has so conducted himself as to enable the agent to appear as principal in the transaction.[285]

16–071 **Non-existent principal.** At common law, a principal cannot become a party to a contract made on his or its behalf before the principal came into existence. This is, for example, the position where a contract purports to be made on behalf of a corporation before its incorporation: such a contract is a nullity because one party to it does not exist.[286] The Contracts (Rights of Third Parties) Act 1999, however, makes it possible so to draw up the contract as to make the corporation a third party beneficiary; it will then, in the circumstances specified in the Act,[287] be entitled to enforce the relevant terms of the contract.[288] The Act expressly provides that, for this purpose, the third party "need not be in existence when the contract is entered into."[289] Statutory provisions which deal with the contractual relations between the *agent* and the third party under pre-incorporation contracts are discussed later in this chapter.[290]

### *(ii) Liability of principal to third party*

16–072 **General rule.** The general rule is that a principal, whether disclosed or undisclosed, is liable to the third party.[291] The limitations on the right of an undisclosed principal to intervene exist mainly for the protection of the third party. Hence they do not necessarily apply where the third party sues the principal. But a person who is alleged to have contracted on behalf of another may, on the true interpretation of the contract, have contracted solely on his own behalf. In that case he alone is liable on the contract:[292] the reason why the other is not liable is not that he is an undisclosed principal whose liability is excluded, but that he is not a principal in the transaction at all.

284 (1887) 12 App. Cas. 271; Reynolds [1983] C.L.P. 119.
285 *Drakeford v Piercey* (1866) 14 L.T. 403.
286 See fn.344.
287 See especially s.1(1) and (2); paras 14–100–14–105.
288 Contracts (Rights of Third Parties) Act 1999 s.1(1).
289 Contracts (Rights of Third Parties) Act 1999 s.1(3).
290 See para.16–083.
291 See *Boyter v Thomson* [1995] 2 A.C. 629 at 632.
292 *JH Rayner (Mincing Lane) Ltd v DTI* [1989] Ch. 72 at 190–191, approved on this point [1990] 2 A.C. 418 at 515.

**Set-off.** The principal cannot set off against the third party any money owed to the principal by the agent.[293] If the principal gives the agent the money with which to pay the third party, but the agent fails to pay it over, the principal remains liable to the third party: he must seek out his creditor and see that he is paid.[294] The principal is discharged by payment to the agent only if such payment is made at the third party's request,[295] or if the third party looked to the agent for payment and so induced the principal to settle with the agent.[296] 16–073

**Undisclosed principal settling with agent.** In *Heald v Kenworthy*[297] it was assumed that an undisclosed principal is not (any more than one who is disclosed) discharged by settling with his agent. But in *Armstrong v Stokes*[298] the court said that this rule produced "intolerable hardship",[299] and refused to follow it. Thus it was held that an undisclosed principal who settled with his agent was not liable to make a second payment to the third party if the agent failed to pay over the money. Of course, it is hard for the principal to have to pay twice over; but it is equally hard for the third party not to be paid at all. It could be argued that the law should, in this situation, have no sympathy for the third party since he did not rely on the credit of a principal of whose existence he was unaware at the time of contracting. But this proves too much: whenever an undisclosed principal is sued the third party gets a windfall of this kind. Thus the case for applying a special rule to undisclosed principals in this context is weak. *Armstrong v Stokes* was doubted by the Court of Appeal in *Irvine v Watson*;[300] and it is submitted that an undisclosed principal who settles with his agent should remain liable to the third party. 16–074

**Contracts (Rights of Third Parties) Act 1999.** At common law, a contract purporting to be made with a non-existent principal, e.g. with a corporation before its incorporation, is a nullity[301] and so cannot impose liabilities, any more than it can confer rights, on the corporation. This position is not directly affected by the Contracts (Rights of Third Parties) Act 1999; for although a third party can by virtue of this Act acquire *rights* under a contract, the Act does not impose any *liabilities* on the third party.[302] However, the third party's right to enforce the term conferring a benefit on that party is "subject to … any other terms of the contract".[303] Thus it is possible to draw up a pre-incorporation contract so as to make the corporation's right of enforcement (once it has come into existence) subject to its discharging liabilities undertaken by its agents on its behalf. Even if this is not done, the corporation's right of enforcement under the Act is subject to 16–075

[293] *Waring v Favenck* (1807) 2 Camp. 85.
[294] *Irvine v Watson* (1880) 5 Q.B.D. 414.
[295] *Smyth v Anderson* (1849) 7 C.B. 21.
[296] See *Wyatt v Hertford* (1802) 3 East 147.
[297] (1855) 10 Ex. 739; Reynolds (1983) C.L.P. 119.
[298] (1872) L.R. 7 Q.B. 598.
[299] *Armstrong v Stokes* (1872) L.R. 7 Q.B. 598 at 610.
[300] (1880) 5 Q.B.D. 414.
[301] See at fn.344.
[302] See para.14–110.
[303] Contracts (Rights of Third Parties) Act 1999 s.1(4).

defences available against the promisee (i.e. in the present context, the agent).[304] The result is that the corporation cannot enforce rights under the contract unless it discharges the relevant liabilities. But if it chooses not to enforce the rights, then the liabilities cannot be enforced against it merely because it is named as a third party beneficiary in the contract. By statute, this problem is now in part resolved in the case of an agreement made before the incorporation of a limited liability partnership between the persons who subscribe their names to the incorporation document.[305] Such an agreement "may impose obligations"[306] on the partnership to take effect after its incorporation. But even this provision does not extend to agreements made with *other* persons before the incorporation of the partnership and purporting to impose liabilities on it.[307]

## (b) Between agent and third party

**16–076** Agent and third party may incur reciprocal rights and liabilities either under the contract which the agent makes on behalf of his principal, or under a collateral contract. The agent may also be liable for breach of implied warranty of authority and for other misrepresentation.

### *(i) Under the contract*

**16–077** **General rule.** The general rule is that an agent is neither liable under,[308] nor entitled to enforce,[309] a contract he makes on behalf of his principal. An agent may however enter into a contract on his own behalf as well as on behalf of the principal and so be liable or entitled under the contract. This possibility is illustrated by the following cases.

**16–078** **Agent contracting personally: liability of agent.** An agent is liable under the contract if he intended to undertake personal liability. Where the contract is in writing, the question whether he had this intention is one of interpretation.[310] An agent who is described in a written contract as a party to it and signs it without qualification is liable under it although the third party knew that he was acting as agent.[311] He may be liable even though such a contract also provides that it is

---

304 Contracts (Rights of Third Parties) Act 1999 s.3(2); cf. para.14–083, fn.546.

305 For the status of such a partnership as a body corporate, see Limited Liability Partnerships Act 2000 s.1(2).

306 Limited Liability Partnerships Act 2000 s.5(2).

307 The rule contained in Companies Act 2006 s.51 (para.16–055) applies to limited liability partnerships by virtue of Limited Liability Partnership (Application of Companies Act 2006) Regulations 2009 (SI 2009/1804) reg.7, but does not impose liabilities on the principal.

308 *Robins v Bridge* (1837) 3 M. & W. 114; *N & J Vlassopulos v Ney Shipping Ltd* [1977] 2 Lloyd's Rep. 478; *Boyter v Thomson* [1995] 2 A.C. 629 at 632.

309 *Lucas v Beale* (1851) 10 C.B. 739; *Fairlie v Fenton* (1870) L.R. 5 Ex. 169.

310 *Punjab National Bank v de Boinville* [1992] 1 W.L.R. 1138 at 1155; cf. *Ignazio Messina & Co v Polskie Linie Oceaniczne* [1995] 2 Lloyd's Rep. 566 at 571; *Internaut Shipping GmbH v Fercometal SARL* [2003] EWCA Civ 812; [2003] 2 Lloyd's Rep. 430; *Foxtons Ltd v Thesleff* [2005] EWCA Civ 514; (2005) 21 E.G. 140.

311 *Basma v Weekes* [1950] A.C. 441; cf. *Davies v Sweet* [1962] 2 Q.B. 300; *Sika Contracts v Gill* (1978) 9 Build. L.R. 11; *Kai Yung v Hong Kong & Shanghai Banking Corp* [1981] A.C. 787 at 795.

signed on behalf of a third person, for such a provision may merely be intended to mean that that person is to be a party to the contract and not that the agent is to be absolved from liability under it.[312] Conversely, an agent who is described as agent in the contract and signs as agent is not liable.[313] But an agent may be described as agent in the body of the contract and sign without qualification; or he may be described as a party in the body of the contract and sign as agent.[314] A distinction has been drawn in such cases between words which merely describe the agent's profession, and words of representation, which show that he is acting as agent. The former do not, while the latter do, exonerate him from liability. Thus the words "we, as solicitors, undertake … " were held in *Burrell v Jones*[315] to be merely descriptive; and even the words "as agent" when used in their commercial, rather than their legal, sense have been held to be descriptive.[316] The words "on behalf of" or "*per procurationem*" are generally representative. But no particular formula is conclusive; and where the description is equivocal the court will rely on other relevant circumstances in order to determine, on an objective basis, whether an undertaking of personal liability may be inferred.[317] An agent is no longer personally liable merely because he acts on behalf of a foreign principal.[318]

**Agent contracting personally: entitlement of agent.** Just as the agent may on the true interpretation of the contract, be liable, so he may be entitled.[319] The courts will, if possible, hold that "the existence of the liability on the one hand involves the existence of the correlative right on the other";[320] but words which indicate that the agent is not to be liable are not necessarily interpreted to mean that he is not to be entitled. Thus where an agent had contracted "on account of" his principal, it was held that the agent was not personally liable on the contract;[321] but where a policy of insurance described the assured as a bank "a/c [a named customer]" it was held to confer rights on the bank (the agent), the reference to the customer being merely intended to remind the bank which of its customers was concerned with the transaction in question.[322] It follows that the agent can be entitled without being liable or liable without being entitled, if that **16–079**

312 *The Sun Happiness* [1984] 1 Lloyd's Rep. 381.

313 *Mahony v Kekulé* (1854) 14 C.B. 390; *The Rialto (No.2)* [1998] 1 Lloyd's Rep. 322 at 328.

314 As in *Gadd v Houghton* (1876) 1 Ex. D. 357; *Universal Steam Navigation Co Ltd v James McKelvie & Co* [1923] A.C. 492 (in these cases the agents were held not liable); *The Maria D* [1992] 1 A.C. 21.

315 (1819) 3 B. & Ald. 47.

316 *Parker v Winlow* (1857) 7 E. & B. 942; cf. para.16–007.

317 *The Swan* [1968] 1 Lloyd's Rep. 5; Reynolds 85 L.Q.R. 92; Legh-Jones 32 M.L.R. 325; cf. *Tudor Marine Ltd v Tradax Export SA* [1976] 2 Lloyd's Rep. 135; *The Riza Sun* [1997] 2 Lloyd's Rep. 314; *British Energy Power & Trading Ltd v Credit Suisse* [2008] EWCA Civ 53; [2008] 1 Lloyd's Rep. 413; contrast *Astilleros Canarios SA v Cape Hatteras Shipping Co SA* [1982] 1 Lloyd's Rep. 518.

318 *Miller, Gibb & Co v Smith & Tyrer Ltd* [1917] 2 K.B. 141; Hudson 23 M.L.R. 695; 29 M.L.R. 353; 35 Can. Bar Rev. 336.

319 *Short v Spackman* (1831) 2 B. & Ad. 962; *HO Brandt & Co v HN Morris & Co Ltd* [1917] 2 K.B. 784; cf. *The Yanxilas* [1982] 2 Lloyd's Rep. 444; *Fraser v Thames Television* [1984] Q.B. 44; *Transcontinental Underwriting Agency SRL v Grand Union Ins Co Ltd* [1987] 2 Lloyd's Rep. 409.

320 *Repetto v Millar's Karri & Jarrah Forests Ltd* [1901] 2 K.B. 306 at 310.

321 *Gadd v Houghton* (1876) 1 Ex. D. 357.

322 *Punjab National Bank v de Boinville* [1992] 1 W.L.R. 1138.

is the true meaning of the contract. In the first of these situations, there may indeed be some difficulty in seeing what consideration has been provided by the agent so long as the contract remains wholly executory, but there would be no such difficulty where the agent has actually performed, e.g. by making a payment under the contract on behalf of the principal. In the second situation there is no similar difficulty even if the contract is still executory; the third party provides consideration for the agent's promise by undertaking liability towards the principal and it is immaterial that the consideration does not move to the agent: consideration must move from the promisee (the third party) but need not move to the promisor (the agent).[323]

16–080 **Trade usage or custom.** An agent may be personally liable or entitled if that is the usual course of business either between particular parties or in relation to a particular class of agents.[324] For example, "where one attorney does work for another, it is common practice for him to give credit to that other and not to the client".[325] A local or trade custom can have the same effect.[326]

16–081 **Undisclosed principal.** Where the principal is undisclosed the agent is both entitled and liable;[327] but this rule does not apply where the agent uses words of representation and the principal is only unnamed.[328] The agent's failure to name the principal may make it easy to infer that he intended to contract personally; but there is no general rule to that effect.[329]

16–082 **Agent in fact principal.** An agent may purport to act on behalf of a principal when he is in fact acting on his own behalf. If he purports to act for an unnamed principal, he can enforce the contract for his own benefit.[330] But if he purports to act for a named principal, he can enforce the contract only after giving due notice to the third party that he acted on his own behalf.[331] Even then the agent will not be allowed to enforce the contract if this would prejudice the third party.[332] These safeguards are necessary as the third party may have relied on the principal's

---

[323] See para.3–024.

[324] This may be the best explanation of the decision that a collecting bank acts as an "agent with an interest" and is entitled to sue the buyer under an irrevocable payment undertaking: *Raiffeisen Zentralbank Österreich Attorney General v China Marine Bunker (Petrochina) Co Ltd* [2006] EWHC 212 (Comm); [2006] All E.R. (D) 37 at [33].

[325] *Scrace v Whittington* (1823) 2 B. & C. 11. The above dictum makes the agent *exclusively* liable: cf. para.16–087.

[326] *Fleet v Murton* (1871) L.R. 7 Q.B. 126; cf. *Cory Brothers Shipping Ltd v Baldan Ltd* [1997] 2 Lloyd's Rep. 58 (forwarding agent acting for unnamed principal liable, by custom, for freight).

[327] *Sims v Bond* (1833) 5 B. & Ad. 389 at 393; *Siu Yin Kwan v Eastern Ins Co Ltd* [1994] 2 A.C. 199 at 207; *Boyter v Thomson* [1995] 2 A.C. 629 at 632.

[328] e.g. *Universal Steam Navigation Co v James McKelvie & Co* [1923] A.C. 492; *Benton v Campbell, Parker & Co Ltd* [1925] 2 K.B. 410.

[329] *N & J Vlassopulos v Ney Shipping Ltd* [1977] 2 Lloyd's Rep. 478; cf. *Pershore Produce (Fruit & Vegetables) Ltd v Reed* [2010] EWCA Civ 795.

[330] *Schmaltz v Avery* (1851) 16 Q.B. 655; *Harper & Co v Vigers Bros* [1909] 2 K.B. 549. This rule has been described as "doubtful": *Bowstead and Reynolds on Agency*, 21st edn (2017), para.9–096.

[331] *Bickerton v Burrell* (1816) 5 M. & S. 383; *aliter* if the other party knows that the "agent" is the real principal: *Rayner v Grote* (1846) 15 M. & W. 359.

[332] See *Fellowes v Gwydyr* (1829) 1 Russ. & M. 83.

solvency or other attributes when he made the contract. It follows that the agent cannot enforce the contract if he knew that, for some "personal" reason, the third party was unwilling to contract with him either at all, or on the same terms as those on which he was willing to contract with the principal.[333] If the claimant in *Said v Butt*[334] had gone in person to buy a ticket, pretending that it was not for him but for a friend, he could not later have said that his friend was in fact himself.

The present exception to the general rule, that an agent acquires no rights under the contract, is based on the assumptions that he has: (i) purported to contract as agent; and (ii) in fact contracted as principal. The exception therefore did not apply where a father conducted negotiations for the purchase of a house and the resulting contract was drawn up in the name of his son (who was a minor). It was held that the father could not enforce the contract since the contract did not say that he had entered into it on behalf of the son, or indeed mention the father's name at all.[335]

**Non-existent principal.** Where the alleged principal does not exist, it may be easy to infer that the agent intended to assume personal liability. At common law this inference was drawn in *Kelner v Baxter*[336] with the result that promoters were held personally liable on a contract made by them on behalf of a company which had not yet been formed. But such an inference is not necessarily drawn merely because the agent purports to act for a non-existent principal:[337] the question is one of intention in each case.[338] The agent was accordingly held not liable where the contract was with a non-existent company which was believed to form part of a group of companies, the third party's intention being merely to contract with a company within that group, and one such company having accepted responsibility under the contract.[339] Similarly, it is arguable that the agent should not be personally liable where, under the rules discussed earlier in this chapter,[340] the principal can be held liable under the contract in spite of not having been in existence when the contract was made. **16–083**

**Pre-incorporation contracts.** Section 51(1) of the Companies Act 2006 provides that "a contract that purports to be made … on behalf of a company[341] at a time when the company has not been formed has effect, subject to any agreement to the contrary,[342] as one made with the person purporting to act … as agent for" the **16–084**

---

[333] *The Remco* [1984] 2 Lloyd's Rep. 205.

[334] [1920] 3 K.B. 497; para.16–069.

[335] *Hector v Lyons* (1989) 58 P. & C.R. 156. No such point arose in *Shogun Finance Ltd v Hudson* [2003] UKHL 62; [2004] 1 A.C. 919 (para.8–041) where any attempt by the rogue to enforce the contract would have failed by reason of his fraud.

[336] (1886) L.R. 2 C.P. 174; cf. *Phonogram Ltd v Lane* [1982] Q.B. 938; Green 47 M.L.R. 671.

[337] *Holman v Pullin* (1884) Cab. & El. 254.

[338] *Black v Smallwood* [1966] A.L.R. 744; Baxt 30 M.L.R. 328; Lücke 3 Adelaide L. Rev. 102.

[339] *Coral (UK) Ltd v Rechtman* [1996] 1 Lloyd's Rep. 235.

[340] See at fn.306.

[341] i.e. one incorporated in the UK: *Rover International Ltd v Cannon Film Sales Ltd (No.3)* (1987) 3 B.C.C. 369, reversed in part on other grounds [1989] 1 W.L.R. 912. The same rule applies to limited liability partnerships: see fn.307.

[342] See *Royal Mail Estates Ltd v Maple Teesdale* [2015] EWHC 1890 (Ch); [2016] 1 W.L.R. 942.

company. Under this subsection, the agent can no longer escape liability merely on the ground that he entered into the contract "as agent";[343] it is up to him to establish that there was an "agreement to the contrary" exonerating him from liability. The subsection puzzlingly concludes with the words "and he [i.e. the agent, in our examples] is personally liable on the contract accordingly". It seems these words merely spell out *one* consequence of the previous words and do not limit their operation, i.e. the agent may be *entitled* as well as liable.

At common law, a distinction was drawn between the cases so far considered where the agent purported to *act on behalf* of the unformed company, and those in which he said that the contract *actually was that* of the company and purported to affix the company's signature. In the latter case it was held that the resulting transaction was a complete nullity,[344] and that the agent could not acquire any rights under it.[345] But the distinction between the two situations was criticised as highly technical[346] and one which businessmen were unlikely to appreciate. The provisions of s.51(1) of the Companies Act 2006 therefore extend also to "a contract which purports to be made by a company" before it is formed. Such a contract has effect (again subject to contrary agreement) "as one made with the person purporting to act for the company", e.g. by the officer purporting to affix the company's signature. The concluding words of the subsection again refer only to the *liability* of such a person, but it has been held that he is also *entitled* to enforce the contract, subject only to restrictions which may be imposed on his right to do so at common law,[347] e.g. on the ground that, for "personal" reasons of the kind described above, the third party was willing to contract only with the company, or unwilling to contract with the person purporting to act on its behalf.[348] But the subsection does not apply where the contract purports to have been made by a company which had once existed and later been dissolved before the time of the putative contract. That contract is then a nullity and cannot be enforced either by the person purporting to have acted for the company or by a new company formed after the date of contracting to carry on the business of the former company. The reason why such a case is not within s.51(1) is that the agent purported to act for the old company rather than on behalf of the new company before it was formed.[349]

343 *Phonogram Ltd v Lane* [1982] Q.B. 938 at 944; McMullen [1982] C.L.J. 47. Contrast *Badgerhill Properties v Cottrell* [1991] B.C.L.C. 805 (agent not liable merely because existing company's name was incorrectly stated in the contract).

344 *Rover International Ltd v Cannon Film Sales Ltd* (*No.3*) [1989] 1 W.L.R. 912—a position described in earlier proceedings in the same case as "a blot on English jurisprudence": [1987] 1 W.L.R. 670 at 679; cf. *Rolle Family & Co Ltd v Rolle* [2017] UKPC 35; [2018] A.C. 205.

345 *Newborne v Sensolid* (*Great Britain*) *Ltd* [1954] 1 Q.B. 45.

346 *Phonogram Ltd v Lane* [1982] Q.B. 938 at 944.

347 *Braymist Ltd v Wise Finance Co Ltd* [2002] EWCA Civ 127; [2002] Ch. 273 (applying s.36C(1) of the Companies Act 1985).

348 *Braymist Ltd v Wise Finance Co Ltd* [2002] EWCA Civ 127; [2002] Ch. 273 at [63], [83]. The *Braymist* case itself was not of this kind.

349 *Cotronic (UK) Ltd v Dezonie (t/a Wendaland Builders Ltd)* [1991] B.C.L.C. 721.

**Deeds.** At common law, an agent who executed a deed was personally liable on it even though the deed said that he had executed it on behalf of his principal.[350] It seems, however, that this rule has been reversed by statute.[351] **16–085**

**Statute.** An agent may be personally liable by statute, e.g. an administrative receiver appointed by debenture holders, who is deemed to be the agent of the company,[352] is nevertheless personally liable on a contract into which he enters in carrying out his functions, except in so far as the contract or legislation otherwise provides.[353] **16–086**

**Election.**[354] Where an agent is liable on the contract, one possible interpretation of the transaction is that he is solely liable, or, in other words, that the contract is simply between him and the third party and not between the third party and the principal at all.[355] Another possibility is that the agent and the principal are both liable under the contract.[356] This is certainly the position where the principal is undisclosed[357] and it may also be true where an agent incurs personal responsibility under a contract made on behalf of a disclosed principal.[358] **16–087**

Where both principal and agent are liable on the contract, the third party may lose his right to sue one of them on the ground that he has "elected" to hold the other liable. This doctrine is most commonly discussed in relation to cases involving undisclosed principals, though there is some authority for applying it in all cases in which both principal and agent are liable on the contract.[359] The reasons for the doctrine are obscure: it is hard to see why a principal should be released merely because the third party has "elected" to hold the agent liable. It might be more satisfactory to hold that the principal should be released only if he had relied on the third party's conduct in such a way that he would be prejudiced by being subsequently held liable, e.g. if the principal had adjusted his accounts with the agent in reliance on the third party's conduct.[360] Election to hold the principal liable may similarly be a ground for releasing the agent if it has led to action in reliance by the agent, e.g. to his giving up rights against the principal. Where there has been no action in reliance on the third party's conduct, the courts do not often apply the doctrine of election. What amounts to election is a question of fact; and in the decided cases the courts have been somewhat reluctant to find

---

[350] *Appleton v Binks* (1804) 5 East 148.

[351] Powers of Attorney Act 1971 s.7(1).

[352] Insolvency Act 1986 s.44(1)(a).

[353] Insolvency Act 1986 s.44(1)(b) as amended by Insolvency Act 1994 s.2; cf. *Powdrill v Watson* [1995] 2 A.C. 394 (personal liability on "adopted" contracts of employment); for his right of indemnity, see 1986 Act s.45.

[354] Reynolds 86 L.Q.R. 318.

[355] e.g. at fn.325; fn.359.

[356] See Reynolds 85 L.Q.R. 92.

[357] See paras 16–065, 16–081.

[358] See *The Swan* [1968] 1 Lloyd's Rep. 5 at 12; *Teheran-Europe Co v ST Belton (Tractors) Ltd* [1968] 2 Q.B. 545 at 558; *The Kurnia Dewi* [1997] 1 Lloyd's Rep. 553 at 559.

[359] *Debenham v Perkins* (1925) 113 L.T. 252 at 254. Other cases which have been cited to support the doctrine of election where the principal was disclosed may turn rather on the point that he was never liable under the contract at all because it was made solely with the agent, e.g. *Thomson v Davenport* (1829) 9 B. & C. 78; *Calder v Dobell* (1871) L.R. 6 C.P. 486.

[360] *Smethurst v Mitchell* (1859) 1 E. & E. 622; *Davison v Donaldson* (1882) 9 Q.B.D. 623.

an election. Merely sending a bill to one of two parties liable has been held not to be an election;[361] and even the commencement of legal proceedings, though strong evidence of election,[362] is not necessarily conclusive.[363] The mere obtaining of a judgment against principal or agent will no longer bar proceedings against the other;[364] though it might, presumably, still amount to an "election".

### (ii) *Under a collateral contract*

16–088 There may be a collateral contract between agent and third party, quite distinct from the main contract between principal and third party. Thus when goods are sold by auction, the auctioneer undertakes certain obligations towards the buyer,[365] but they are not co-extensive with those of the seller. The seller undertakes that he has the right to sell, but the auctioneer only undertakes to give the buyer possession[366] so that he is not liable for the seller's lack of title.[367] The collateral contract may confer rights, as well as impose liabilities, on the agent. Thus an auctioneer can sue the buyer for the price of the goods sold.[368] The liability of an auctioneer who refuses to knock goods down to the highest bidder at an auction sale without reserve[369] has also been explained on the ground of a "collateral agreement existing between the auctioneer and the bidder."[370]

### (iii) *Implied warranty of authority*

16–089 **Nature of liability.** An agent who purports to act for a principal, knowing that he has no authority to do so, is liable to the third party in deceit, even if he believed that the principal would ratify.[371] It was at one time thought that if the agent honestly believed that he had authority when in fact he had none, he was under no liability.[372] But it was settled in *Collen v Wright*[373] that the agent was in such circumstances liable for breach of an implied warranty that he had the authority which he purported to have. It makes no difference that the agent has acted in good faith and with due diligence.[374] The rule sometimes operates harshly on the

361 *Chesterton v Barone* [1987] 1 E.G.L.R. 15.

362 See *Scarf v Jardine* (1882) 7 App. Cas. 345.

363 *Curtis v Williamson* (1874) L.R. 10 Q.B. 57; *Clarkson Booker Ltd v Andjel* [1964] 2 Q.B. 775; cf. *The Scaplake* [1978] 2 Lloyd's Rep. 380; *Taylor v Van Dutch Marine Holdings Ltd* [2019] EWHC 1951 (Ch).

364 Civil Liability (Contribution) Act 1978 s.3.

365 *Woolfe v Horne* (1877) 2 Q.B.D. 355.

366 *Wood v Baxter* (1883) 49 L.T. 45.

367 *Benton v Campbell, Parker & Co* [1925] 2 K.B. 410.

368 *Coppin v Walker* (1816) 7 Taunt. 237; cf. *Wilson v Pike* [1949] 1 K.B. 176; *Chelmsford Auctions Ltd v Poole* [1973] Q.B. 542.

369 See paras 2–008, 3–164.

370 *Barry v Davies* [2000] 1 W.L.R. 1962 at 1968.

371 *Polhill v Walter* (1832) 3 B. & Ad. 114.

372 This was one basis of *Smout v Ilbery* (1842) 10 M. & W. 1; see also para.16–093.

373 (1857) 8 E. & B. 647; approved by the House of Lords in *Starkey v Bank of England* [1903] A.C. 114 and followed in *V/O Rasnoimport v Guthrie & Co Ltd* [1966] 1 Lloyd's Rep. 1; Reynolds 83 L.Q.R. 189.

374 *Yonge v Toynbee* [1910] 1 K.B. 215; see para.16–121, for survival of apparent authority in cases of the principal's insanity.

agent, and it might be more reasonable to imply a warranty that the agent should not negligently exceed his authority.[375] The agent's position has been alleviated by legislation, so that an agent who acts under a power of attorney incurs no liability if the power of attorney has without his knowledge been revoked.[376]

**No warranty of performance.** The agent does not impliedly[377] warrant that the contract which he makes between principal and third party will be performed, but only that he has authority to make it.[378] This has an important bearing on damages. If the third party could have obtained full satisfaction from the principal, had the contract been binding on him, the agent is liable to the same extent.[379] But if the principal is insolvent, the third party cannot recover more from the agent than he would have got from the principal, had the agent had authority; and this may be very little, or nothing, according to the degree of the principal's insolvency.[380] **16–090**

**Effect of implied warranty.** Normally, the effect of the warranty is to induce the third party to enter into a contract with the supposed principal. But liability may also be incurred if the third party acts in reliance on the warranty in some other way, e.g. where the agent falsely represents to a building society that he is authorised to act for a vendor of property and the society in consequence makes a loan to the purchaser.[381] **16–091**

**Restrictions on liability.** An agent is not, or may not be, liable for breach of implied warranty of authority in the following cases. **16–092**

**Want of authority known to third party.** The agent is not liable where the third party knew, or must be taken to have known, that the agent had no authority.[382] The agent may also not be liable where he and the third party had equal means of knowing that the agent had no authority; though the claim in the case[383] which **16–093**

[375] Negligence may lead to liability in damages at common law or under Misrepresentation Act 1967; but the measure of such damages could differ from that for breach of implied warranty of authority: cf. para.9–073 and following.

[376] Powers of Attorney Act 1971 s.5(1), which is also extended to apply to lasting powers of attorney (see para.16–129): Mental Capacity Act 2005 s.14(5).

[377] He may expressly do so as (for example) in *The Maria D* [1992] 1 A.C. 21.

[378] *Nelson v Nelson* [1997] 1 W.L.R. 233; *AMB Generali Holding AG v SEB Trygg Liv Holding Aktiebolag* [2005] EWCA Civ 1237; [2006] 1 W.L.R. 2276 at [63]; cf. *Knight Frank LLP v Du Haney* [2011] EWCA Civ 404; [2011] N.P.C. 40 (agent not liable where name of principal had been misrepresented but was capable of being established).

[379] cf. *Habton Farms v Nimmo* [2003] EWCA Civ 68; [2004] Q.B. 1.

[380] See para.20–100.

[381] *Penn v Bristol & West BS* [1997] 1 W.L.R. 1356.

[382] *Lilly, Wilson & Co v Smales, Eeles & Co* [1892] 1 Q.B. 456; *Halbot v Lens* [1901] 1 Ch. 344; cf. *Zoya Ltd v Ahmed* [2016] EWHC 2249 (Ch); [2016] 4 W.L.R. 174; *P&P Property Ltd v Owen White & Catlin LLP* [2018] Ch.273 (third party held not to have *relied* on the existence of authority). See Reynolds 134 L.Q.R. 511.

[383] *Smout v Ilberry* (1842) 10 M. & W. 1.

supports this view was actually one for goods sold and delivered, i.e. on the main contract of sale. Thus the case may not be authoritative on an agent's liability for breach of implied warranty.[384]

16–094 **Representation of law.** The traditional view (which is now open to doubt[385]) is that the agent is not liable where the representation is one of law.[386] Accordingly, it has been held that, since the interpretation of a document is a matter of law, an agent who misrepresents its meaning is not liable for breach of implied warranty. Thus if the director of a statutory corporation[387] which has, on the true interpretation of its incorporating statute, no borrowing powers, purports to borrow on its behalf, he is not liable for breach of implied warranty.[388] But if such a corporation has a limited power to borrow up to, say, £10 million, and the director purports to borrow on its behalf above that limit, he is liable for breach of implied warranty, for he has misrepresented a fact: namely, that the company has not yet borrowed £10 million.[389] If a loan is made to a company incorporated under the Companies Act 2006 by a lender dealing with the company in good faith, the contract of loan will normally be enforceable against the company even though the directors had, under the company's constitution, no power to enter into the contract.[390] The lender's claim for breach of warranty against the directors will therefore fail on the principle stated in the next paragraph. If the lender had *no* claim against the company because he had acted in bad faith, he would know that the loan was unauthorised. His claim for breach of warranty of authority would fail on the ground that he knew of the agent's want of authority.[391]

16–095 **Principal liable on main contract.** An agent who has no actual authority is probably not liable for breach of implied warranty if the principal is liable to the third party on the ground of apparent or usual authority. In *Rainbow v Howkins*[392] an auctioneer who had authority to sell a horse, subject to a reserve price, sold it without reserve. It was held that he was not liable for breach of implied warranty, as the buyer could have enforced the main contract against the seller on the ground that the auctioneer had apparent authority to sell without reserve.[393] Similarly, an agent would not be liable for breach of implied warranty if he did an unauthorised act which the principal later ratified.

---

384 See *Oliver v Bank of England* [1901] 1 Ch. 652 at 660.

385 See the discussion of *Kleinwort Benson Ltd v Lincoln CC* [1999] 2 A.C. 349, para.16–026.

386 *Saffron Walden, etc. BS v Rayner* (1880) 14 Ch D. 406.

387 Such corporations remain subject to the ultra vires doctrine: para.12–075.

388 *Rashdall v Ford* (1866) L.R. 2 Eq. 750.

389 *Cherry v Colonial Bank of Australasia* (1869) L.R. 3 P.C. 24; *Weeks v Propert* (1873) L.R. 8 C.P. 427.

390 Companies Act 2006 s.40(1); see para.12–069 for certain exceptions.

391 See at fn.382.

392 [1904] 2 K.B. 322; criticised in *McManus v Fortescue* [1907] 2 K.B. 1 at 6, but that case can be explained on the ground that the third party knew of the agent's want of authority.

393 cf. *Mitsui & Co Ltd v Marpo Industrial Ltd* [1974] 1 Lloyd's Rep. 386 at 393. Quaere whether this reasoning might have been applied in *Yonge v Toynbee* [1910] 1 K.B. 215; cf. fn.534.

**Crown agent.** An agent of the Crown is probably not liable for breach of implied warranty of authority. The assumption that such an agent impliedly warrants his authority is "utterly inconsistent with the facts".[394] In view of the enormous value of some government contracts, it would be extremely harsh to impose liability on a civil servant who in good faith and without negligence had misrepresented his authority. **16–096**

### (iv) *Other liability for misrepresentation*

The agent's liability for breach of warranty of authority arises where he misrepresents his authority; but he may also be liable to the third party in tort for other misrepresentations. This was, for example, held to be the case where an estate agent who had been engaged by the vendor of property negligently made misrepresentations about it to a prospective purchaser who, in reliance on those representations, entered into a contract with the vendor for the purchase of the property.[395] **16–097**

## (c) Between principal and agent

### (i) *Rights of agent*

**Whether commission is payable.** Whether an agent is entitled to any commission at all depends on the terms of the agreement between principal and agent. In *Taylor v Brewer*[396] an agent was to receive "such commission ... as should be deemed right" by the principal. It was held that he had no legal right to commission. But where the agency is a commercial relationship the courts are reluctant to send the agent away empty-handed.[397] Thus if the agreement merely provides that the *amount* of commission is to be left to the principal's discretion, and he refuses to fix the amount, he may be liable to pay a reasonable sum.[398] On the other hand, the director of a company may agree to work for it "for such remuneration as the other directors may determine" on the understanding that he will receive nothing until the company has "got on its feet". If this never happens, he cannot claim a reasonable remuneration for his work.[399] **16–098**

**When commission is earned.** Commission is payable only in respect of a transaction which the agent was employed to bring about. In *Toulmin v Millar*[400] the owner of a house employed an agent to find a tenant. The agent found a tenant, who later bought the house. His claim for commission on the sale failed, since he was only employed to let the house. The transaction must also be caused **16–099**

---

394 *Dunn v Macdonald* [1897] 1 Q.B. 555 at 558.
395 *McCullagh v Lane Fox & Partners Ltd* [1994] 1 E.G.L.R. 48.
396 (1813) 1 M. & S. 290.
397 See *Kofi Sunkersette Obu v A Strauss & Co Ltd* [1951] A.C. 243.
398 *Bryant v Flight* (1839) 5 M. & W. 114; *British Bank for Foreign Trade Ltd v Novinex Ltd* [1949] 1 K.B. 623; *Powell v Braun* [1954] 1 W.L.R. 401.
399 *Re Richmond Gate Property Co Ltd* [1965] 1 W.L.R. 335.
400 (1887) 12 App. Cas. 746; cf. *Millar v Radford* (1903) 19 T.L.R. 575; *Charania v Harbour Estates* [2009] EWCA Civ 1123; [2009] N.P.C. 119.

by the agent's efforts.[401] In *Tribe v Taylor*[402] a principal employed an agent to raise a loan of money. The lender later entered into partnership with the principal and on this occasion made a further loan. The agent's claim for commission on this second loan failed, since it was not brought about by his efforts.

Unless otherwise agreed,[403] the agent is not entitled to commission in respect of transactions which take place after the termination of the agency.[404] A contract may, however, provide that commission is *earned* when the agent secures the order (so that nothing more need be done by him to perfect his entitlement to it) but that it is only to *become payable* at some later stage, e.g. when the order is executed. In such a case the agent is entitled to commission on orders obtained before, though not executed till after, the termination of the agency.[405] Under the Regulations which apply to "commercial agents",[406] such an agent has somewhat more extensive rights in respect of transactions concluded after the termination of the agency[407] and in respect of transactions not brought about by his efforts but concluded in breach of an exclusive agency agreement.[408]

16–100 **More than one agent engaged.** A principal may engage more than one agent, e.g. where an owner instructs two estate agents to find a purchaser for his house. Commission will then be due to the agent whose efforts have brought about the sale;[409] and where the efforts of both have contributed to this result, each may[410] be entitled to commission.[411] Where two "commercial agents" appointed in succession claim commission on the same transaction, the first agent is not

[401] In the absence of any contrary provision, it is usually implied that the agent must have been "the effective cause" of the transaction; whether he is or not will depend on all the circumstances, including of course what is meant by the "transaction" (see, in relation to estate agents, para.16–101). See, e.g. *Foxtons Ltd v Bicknell* [2008] EWCA Civ 419; [2008] 24 E.G. 142 and the summary of the propositions to be derived from the decided cases set out at [20]; *County Homesearch Co (Thames and Chilterns) Ltd v Cowham* [2008] EWCA Civ 26; [2008] 1 W.L.R. 909; *Great Estates Group Ltd v Digby* [2011] EWCA Civ 1120; [2011] 3 E.G.L.R. 101; Contrast *Glentree Estates Ltd v Favermead Ltd* [2010] EWCA Civ 1473; [2011] 11 E.G. 104.

[402] (1876) 1 C.P.D. 505; cf. *Debenham, Tewson & Chinnocks Plc v Rimington* [1989] 2 E.G.L.R. 26 (where, however, the agents were awarded a reasonable remuneration for their efforts); *Harwood v Smith, The Times*, 8 December 1997; contrast *Nahun v Royal Holloway and Bedford New Colleges Ltd, The Times*, 19 November 1998.

[403] *Levy v Goldhill* [1917] 2 Ch. 297; cf. *Brian Cooper & Co v Fairview Estates (Investments) Ltd* [1987] 1 E.G.L.R. 18; *Barnard Marcus & Co v Ashraf* [1988] 1 E.G.L.R. 7; *Marshall v N M Financial Management Ltd* [1997] 1 W.L.R. 1527 (so far as it relates to the "renewal commission").

[404] *Crocker-Horlock v B Lang & Co Ltd* [1949] 1 All E.R. 526; *Bronester Ltd v Priddle* [1961] 1 W.L.R. 1294.

[405] *Sellers v London Counties Newspapers* [1951] 1 K.B. 784; *Explora Group Plc v Hesco Bastion Ltd* [2005] EWCA Civ 646.

[406] See para.16–014.

[407] SI 1993/3053 regs 7(1)(b), 8.

[408] SI 1993/3053 reg.7(2); at common law, the agent's remedy in such a case would be by way of damages: cf. *Alpha Trading Ltd v Dunshaw-Patten* [1981] Q.B. 290; para.16–104. For exclusive dealing agreements, see para.11–143 and following.

[409] *John D Wood & Co v Dantata* (1985) 275 E.G. 1278; *Chasen Rider v Hedges* [1993] 1 E.G.L.R. 47.

[410] Depending on the terms of the contract: see the authorities cited at fnn.415–423.

[411] *Lordgate Properties v Balcombe* (1985) 274 E.G. 493; *Anscombe & Ringland v Watson* [1991] 2 E.G.L.R. 28.

normally entitled to commission, but the court may, if it is equitable to do so, order the commission to be shared between the two agents.[412]

**Estate agents' commission: common law.**[413] The precise stage at which the agent becomes entitled to commission depends on the terms of the contract between principal and agent. This question has given rise to much litigation in cases concerning estate agents' commission,[414] but in the absence of any provision to the contrary it is payable on completion and made from the proceeds of sale.[415] In *Luxor (Eastbourne) Ltd v Cooper*[416] the landowner undertook to pay the estate agent his commission "on completion of sale". No sale took place because the owner refused to deal with the prospective purchaser introduced by the agent. It was held that the agent was not entitled to commission.[417] Again, a contract for the payment of commission on the agent's "introducing a person ready, willing and able to purchase" does not entitle him to commission if the prospective purchaser makes a conditional offer subject to contract and satisfactory survey; or if he makes an offer and withdraws it before the vendor accepts;[418] or if he signs a contract which cannot be completed because of a defect in the vendor's title;[419] or if, before the prospective purchaser is introduced, the owner has entered into a binding contract to sell the property to a purchaser introduced by another agent.[420] Nor does a promise to pay commission "in the event of your introducing … a person prepared to enter into a contract" entitle the agent to commission where the person introduced only agrees to sign a contract which is subject to conditions.[421] Even a contract for the payment of commission "in the event of securing for you an offer" does not entitle the agent to commission unless a firm, unconditional offer is made.[422] But where the contract was to pay commission as soon as "any person introduced by us enters 16–101

[412] SI 1993/3053 reg.9.

[413] In addition to the cases discussed in this para, see the authorities referred to above in fn.401.

[414] Gower 13 M.L.R. 490; Hardy-Ivamy (1951) C.L.P. 305.

[415] *Wells v Devani* [2019] UKSC 4; [2019] 2 W.L.R. 617.

[416] [1941] A.C. 108; *Foxtons Ltd v Thesleff* [2005] EWCA Civ 514; (2005) 21 E.G. 140.

[417] The award of a quantum meruit will be rare "in the face of the express provision for remuneration which the contract contains. This must necessarily exclude such a claim, unless it can (upon the facts of a particular case) be based upon a contract subsequent to the original contract, and arising from some conduct on the part of the principal", [1941] A.C. 108 at 125; *Adler v Ananhall Advisory & Consultancy Services Ltd* [2009] EWCA Civ 586; [2009] N.P.C. 80.

[418] *Dennis Reed Ltd v Goody* [1950] 2 K.B. 277; *Graham & Scott (Southgate) Ltd v Oxlade* [1950] 2 K.B. 257. Contrast *Christie Owen & Davies Ltd v Rapacioli* [1974] Q.B. 781 (where a vendor who withdrew after a firm offer had been made by the prospective purchaser was held liable for commission).

[419] *Dellafiora v Lester* [1962] 1 W.L.R. 1208; cf. *Blake & Co v Sohn* [1969] 1 W.L.R. 1412.

[420] *AA Dickinson & Co v O'Leary* (1979) 254 E.G. 731.

[421] *AL Wilkinson Ltd v Brown* [1966] 1 W.L.R. 1914.

[422] *Bennett, Walden & Co v Wood* [1950] 2 All E.R. 134; cf. *Christie, Owen & Davies Ltd v Stockton* [1953] 1 W.L.R. 1353.

into a legally binding contract to purchase" it was held that the agent was entitled when such a contract was made although the vendor later terminated it on account of the purchaser's breach.[423]

16–102 **Estate agents' commission: statutory provisions.** The common law on this topic is far from satisfactory. On the one hand it is hard for the estate agent, who may have gone to much trouble and expense in advertising[424] a house and securing offers, to be deprived of all reward through the caprice of his client. On the other hand it is hard for the client to have to pay commission where it is not his fault that no sale takes place: the common understanding is that the commission should come out of the proceeds of sale.[425] In this conflict of interests, the estate agents usually have the advantage of being able to submit a standard form of contract to the client, who may accept its terms without question. The courts have to some extent redressed the balance in favour of the client. They have (as the above cases show) construed stipulations for commission strictly against the agents,[426] or held them to be ineffective for uncertainty or for misrepresentation.[427] But it remains possible for commission to be payable even though there is no sale. It would perhaps be better if the question when an estate agent was entitled to commission ceased to be regarded purely as one of interpretation. Only legislation could now achieve this result; but the Estate Agents Act 1979 (which regulates the activities of estate agents) does not lay down any rules for this purpose. It merely requires the agent, before a client enters into an agency contract with him, to give the client particulars of the circumstances in which the commission will become due.[428] Nor are the estate agency cases affected by the Regulations which apply to "commercial agents" since these Regulations apply only to agents who have continuing authority and who negotiate sales or purchases of *goods*.[429] If an agent acts for purposes relating to his trade, business or profession and the client is a consumer, some terms might not be binding on the client under the Consumer Rights Act 2015,[430] e.g. if a term provided for payment of the full commission even if no sale took place. Even where the agent is not entitled to commission, he may have other rights against the client. He may be entitled to damages[431] where the sale goes off

[423] *Scheggia v Gradwell* [1963] 1 W.L.R. 1049; cf. *Midgeley Estates Ltd v Hand* [1952] 2 Q.B. 432; *Drewery & Drewery v Ware-Lane* [1960] 1 W.L.R. 1204; *aliter* if the contract goes off because of the agent's misrepresentation: *Peter Long & Partners v Burns* [1956] 1 W.L.R. 413.

[424] The agent can expressly stipulate for reimbursement of advertising expenses, as in *Bernard Thorpe & Partners v Flannery* (1977) 244 E.G. 129.

[425] *Wells v Devani* [2019] UKSC 4; [2019] 2 W.L.R. 617.

[426] See at fnn.415–423.

[427] See *Jaques v Lloyd D George & Partners* [1968] 1 W.L.R. 625.

[428] Section 18(2)(a); supplemented by Estate Agents (Provision of Information) Regulations 1991 (SI 1991/859). In *Foxtons Ltd v Bicknell* [2008] EWCA Civ 419; [2008] 24 E.G. 142 the estate agent's term for the payment of commission closely followed the prescribed provisions of the Regulations ("purchaser introduced by us") but this still raised a question of interpretation which was resolved in favour of the purchaser; cf. *Great Estates Group Ltd v Digby* [2011] EWCA Civ 1120; [2011] 3 E.G.L.R. 101 where the Court of Appeal was divided.

[429] See para.16–014.

[430] See para.7–086.

[431] Unless the contractual provision for commission is intended to be his *only* remedy, as in *Property Choice v Fronda* [1991] 2 E.G.L.R. 249.

as a result of the client's fault.[432] If the sale goes off as a result of the purchaser's default, and the purchaser's deposit is forfeited to the client, it has been suggested that the agent should be entitled to a quantum meruit out of the sum so forfeited.[433]

**Commercial Agents Regulations.** Under the Regulations which apply to "commercial agents", commission becomes due when the principal has executed the transaction or when he should have done so or when the third party has done so;[434] and it becomes due at the latest when the third party has executed the transaction or would have done so if the principal had duly executed his part of it.[435] Where "execution" fails, the Regulations give the agent the right to commission only if the failure is due to the principal's breach of his contract with the third party.[436] Except in this situation, the question whether the agent can become entitled to commission before "execution" of that contract is (under the Regulations, no less than at common law) one of interpretation of the agency agreement. 16–103

**Opportunity to earn commission.** If a principal employs an agent for a fixed period he is not, in general, bound to stay in business merely to enable the agent to earn his commission.[437] But if, on the true construction of the agency contract, the principal has undertaken to stay in business so as to enable the agent to earn his commission, then the principal is liable in damages if he fails to do so. This was the effect of the contract in *Turner v Goldsmith*,[438] where the principal employed the agent for five years to obtain orders for shirts "manufactured or sold" by the principal. It was held that he was not justified in putting an end to the agency agreement simply because the factory in which he manufactured shirts was burnt down. An agency agreement may, moreover, relate to a specific contract which is actually concluded between principal and third party. In such a 16–104

[432] *Dennis Reed Ltd v Goody* [1950] 2 K.B. 277 at 285; for this purpose the default must be wilful, and not merely inability to complete on account of a defect of title: *Blake & Co v Sohn* [1969] 1 W.L.R. 1412.

[433] *Boots v E Christopher & Co* [1952] 1 K.B. 89 at 99; cf. *Debenham Tewson & Chinnock Plc v Rimington* [1989] 2 E.G.L.R. 26. Contrast *The Manifest Lipkowy* [1989] 2 Lloyd's Rep. 138 (buyer's agent held to have no right to commission against defaulting seller).

[434] SI 1993/3053 reg.10(1); para.16–014.

[435] SI 1993/3053 reg.10(2). This rule cannot be excluded to the detriment of the agent: reg.10(4).

[436] SI 1993/3053 reg.10(2); this would seem to apply in a situation analogous to that in those estate agency cases in which completion was prevented by a defect in the vendor's title: at fn.419. The actual estate agency cases fall outside the scope of the 1993 Regulations for the reason stated at fn.429.

[437] *Rhodes v Forwood* (1876) 1 App. Cas. 256; cf. *L French & Co Ltd v Leeston Shipping Co Ltd* [1922] 1 A.C. 451; Burrows 31 M.L.R. 390. Contrast the position of "commercial agents" (para.16–014), SI 1993/3053 reg.17(7): *Page v Combined Shipping & Trading Co* [1997] 3 All E.R. 656.

[438] [1891] 1 Q.B. 544; cf. *Re Patent Floor Cloth Co* (1872) 26 L.T. 467; *Standard Life Healthcare Ltd v Gorman* [2009] EWCA Civ 1292; [2010] I.R.L.R. 233.

case, a term may be implied into the agency agreement that the principal will not break *that contract* so as to deprive the agent of his commission.[439]

A client who employs an estate agent to sell a house is, in general, under no liability if he sells it himself or through a second agent.[440] If the agent is appointed "sole agent" the client cannot sell through another agent, but he can still sell the house himself unless he gives the agent "the sole and exclusive right to sell".[441] A manufacturer's "sole agent" may simply be a buyer and not an agent at all.[442] The manufacturer's undertaking to sell all his output to such a "sole agent" would bind him not to dispose of any of it himself,[443] so long as it was not invalid for restraint of trade.[444]

16–105 **Agent's indemnity against liability.** A principal must indemnify his agent against all liabilities reasonably incurred or discharged by him in the execution of his authority.[445] This right of indemnity exists not only where the agent incurs contractual liability, but also where he incurs tortious liability, e.g. as a result of selling a third person's property under the instructions of his principal.[446] The agent is not entitled to any indemnity in respect of an obviously illegal transaction,[447] nor in respect of a liability due to his own breach of duty.[448] An agent may even be entitled to an indemnity in respect of payments which he was not legally obliged to make[449] so long as the payment, though not legally due, was made in the usual course of business, or possibly if it was made under a strong moral obligation.

16–106 **Agent's lien.** An agent is (unless otherwise agreed)[450] entitled to a lien on all property of the principal which has come into his possession in the course of the agency. Every agent has a *particular* lien: that is, he can hold the property until the principal satisfies all claims of the agent arising out of the agency. An agent may by custom or by special contract also have a *general* lien, entitling him to hold the property until the principal satisfies all claims of the agent, whether they have arisen out of the agency or not.

---

439 *Alpha Trading Ltd v Dunshaw-Patten* [1981] Q.B. 290; Carter 45 M.L.R. 220; cf. paras 2–107–2–110 and at fn.424; *George Moundreas & Co SA v Navimpex Centrala Navala* [1985] 2 Lloyd's Rep. 515; *Explora Group Plc v Hesco Bastion Ltd* [2005] EWCA Civ 646 at [86].

440 *Luxor (Eastbourne) Ltd v Cooper* [1941] A.C. 108.

441 *Bentall Horsley & Baldry v Vicary* [1931] 1 K.B. 253; *Hampton & Sons Ltd v George* [1939] 3 All. E.R. 627.

442 See para.16–007.

443 *WT Lamb & Sons v Goring Brick Co Ltd* [1932] 1 K.B. 710.

444 See para.11–143 and following.

445 *Thacker v Hardy* (1878) 4 Q.B.D. 685; *Reynolds v Smith* (1893) 9 T.L.R. 494; cf. Insolvency Act 1986 s.44(1)(c) and (3); contrast *Wilson v Avec Audio Visual Equipment Ltd* [1974] 1 Lloyd's Rep. 80 (payment made after termination of authority).

446 *Adamson v Jarvis* (1827) 4 Bing. 66.

447 *Thacker v Hardy* (1878) 4 Q.B.D. 685 at 687.

448 cf. *Lister v Romford Ice & Cold Storage Co Ltd* [1957] A.C. 555; para.6–072.

449 *Read v Anderson* (1884) 13 Q.B.D. 779; cf. *Adams v Morgan* [1924] 1 K.B. 751.

450 *Rolls Razor Ltd v Cox* [1967] 1 Q.B. 552.

### (ii) *Duties of agent*

**To carry out his instructions.** An agent who is appointed under a contract is obviously obliged to carry out any instructions which are binding on him. He may be liable for failing to do so even if the contract which he was instructed to make would not, if made, have been a binding one.[451] He will also be in breach if he acts in a way not authorised by the terms of his appointment.[452] An agent who acts gratuitously or under a unilateral contract[453] is not bound to do anything, but may be liable if he starts to perform and then leaves the task unfinished. **16–107**

**To act with due care and skill.** The degree of care and skill expected of an agent depends on the circumstances. A person who holds himself out as being skilled in some profession or trade[454] must show greater care and skill than one who merely offers to give what help he can as a friend. There is probably no rigid distinction between paid and gratuitous agents for this purpose. The fact that the agent is paid is taken into account, along with other circumstances, in determining the degree of the care and skill to be expected of him; but even a gratuitous agent may be liable in tort for acting negligently.[455] **16–108**

**Fiduciary duty.** Although the position of an agent in various respects differs from that of a trustee,[456] an agent does, because the principal places confidence in him, owe a fiduciary duty to the principal.[457] This duty is distinct from his duty to act with due care and skill: its breach "connotes disloyalty or infidelity" and not merely failure by the agent to do his "incompetent best".[458] Its most important consequences are dealt with in paras 16–110–16–113. **16–109**

**Conflict of interest and duty.** The agent must not put himself into a position where his interest and duty conflict.[459] He must not, for instance, sell his own goods to the principal when he is employed to buy: his interest as a seller would be to get the highest possible price, whereas his duty as agent is to buy at the **16–110**

---

[451] *Fraser v BN Furman (Productions) Ltd* [1967] 1 W.L.R. 898; *Dunbar v A & B Painters Ltd* [1986] 2 Lloyd's Rep. 38.

[452] *County Ltd v Girozentrale Securities* [1996] 3 All E.R. 834.

[453] See paras 2–052, 3–160, 3–171; *The Zephyr* [1985] 2 Lloyd's Rep. 529 at 538.

[454] See para.6–068.

[455] *Hedley Byrne & Co Ltd v Heller & Partners Ltd* [1964] A.C. 465 at 495, 510, 526–527, 530, 538; approving *Wilkinson v Coverdale* (1793) 1 Esp. 75; para.3–171.

[456] See, e.g. para.10–024; *Kingscroft Ins Co Ltd v HS Weaver (Underwriting) Ltd* [1993] 1 Lloyd's Rep. 187 at 191.

[457] *Attorney General of Hong Kong v Reid* [1994] 1 A.C. 324; at fn.469 and para.16–112.

[458] *Bristol & West BS v Mothew* [1998] Ch. 1 at 18; cf. *Coulthard v Disco Mix Club* [2000] 1 W.L.R. 707.

[459] *Lamb v Evans* [1893] 1 Ch. 218; cf. *Reading v Attorney General* [1951] A.C. 507. An agent's duty of loyalty may also require him to disclose his own wrongdoing to the principal: *Fassihi v Item Software Ltd* [2004] EWCA Civ 1244; [2004] I.R.L.R. 928 at [44]; cf. *G Attwood Holdings Ltd v Woodward* [2009] EWHC 1083 (Ch); *Brandeaux Advisers Ltd v Chadwick* [2010] EWHC 3241 (QB); [2011] I.R.L.R. 224 at [47]; *GHLM Trading Ltd v Maroo* [2012] EWHC 61 (Ch); [2012] 2 B.C.L.C 369 at [193] (*Fassihi* "a somewhat controversial decision").

lowest possible price.[460] Similarly, he must not, if employed to sell, buy the principal's property for himself.[461] Again, he must not subject himself to conflicting duties by acting as agent for both principal and third party,[462] unless he fully discloses the position to each of these persons.[463] Where the nature of the agent's business is such that he will normally act for more than one principal it is an implied term of the contract of agency that he should be free to do so, even though the interests of the various principals are likely to conflict. Thus an estate agent is entitled to accept instructions for the sale of properties from several principals, and where he does so he is both entitled and bound not to disclose confidential information received from any one of his clients to the other or others.[464] In cases where the agent is not known normally to act for multiple principals, he can only do so where all principals give their fully informed consent.[465]

A contract made in breach of this fiduciary duty is voidable at the option of the principal. The agent himself cannot avoid a transaction on the ground that it may conflict with his duties to his principal.[466]

16–111 **Bribes.**[467] The agent must not without the principal's consent[468] accept a commission from a third party. A secret commission is a "bribe" if the third party, at the time of paying it, knew that the payee was acting as agent for another: the payment is then regarded as "a gift accepted by a fiduciary as an inducement to betray his trust".[469] It is immaterial that the third party had no corrupt motive in

---

460 *Armstrong v Jackson* [1917] 2 K.B. 822; *Tetley v Shand* (1871) 25 L.T. 658; *Guiness Plc v Saunders* [1990] 2 A.C 663; cf. Companies Act 2006 ss.182–187.

461 *McPherson v Watt* (1877) 3 App. Cas. 254.

462 *Fullwood v Hurley* [1928] 1 K.B. 498 at 502; *Anglo-African Merchants v Bayley* [1970] 1 Q.B. 311 at 322–323; *North & South Trust Co v Berkeley* [1971] 1 W.L.R. 470.

463 See *Harrods Ltd v Lemon* [1931] 2 K.B. 157; and *Clark Boyce v Mouat* [1994] 1 A.C. 428 (where full disclosure was made); Estate Agents Act 1979 s.21 (imposing a statutory duty of disclosure on estate agents: the remedy is disqualification under s.3 of the Act).

464 *Kelly v Cooper* [1993] A.C. 205; contrast *Rossetti Marketing Ltd v Solutions Marketing Ltd* [2012] EWCA Civ 1021; [2013] Bus L.R. 543 at [24]–[25].

465 *Hurstanger Ltd v Wilson* [2007] EWCA Civ 299; [2007] 1 W.L.R. 2531 at [35]; *Rossetti Marketing Ltd v Solutions Marketing Ltd* [2012] EWCA Civ 1021; [2013] Bus L.R. 543 at [22]; *McWilliam v Norton Finance (UK) Ltd* [2015] EWCA Civ 186; [2015] 2 B.C.L.C. 730; cf. *Prince Jefri Bolkiah v KPMG* [1999] 2 A.C. 222; *Hilton v Barker Booth & Eastwood* [2005] UKHL 8; [2005] 1 W.L.R. 567; Getzler 122 L.Q.R. 1.

466 *Boulting v ACCT* [1963] 2 Q.B. 606.

467 Needham 95 L.Q.R. 536. For the potential criminal liability of the agent, see Bribery Act 2010 ss.1, 2 and of the principal for bribery committed by the agent, see ss.7, 8.

468 See *Anangel Atlas Compania Naviera SA v Ishikawajima-Harima Heavy Industries Co* [1990] 1 Lloyd's Rep. 167; *Medsted Associates Ltd v Canaccord Genuity Wealth (International) Ltd* [2019] EWCA Civ 83; [2019] 2 All E.R. 959.

469 *Attorney General of Hong Kong v Reid* [1994] 1 A.C. 324 at 330; *Allwood v Clifford* [2002] E.M.L.R. 3; cf. *UBS AG v Kommunale Wasserwerke Leipzig GmbH* [2017] EWCA Civ 1567; [2017] 2 Lloyd's Rep. 621 at [112].

making the payment,[470] but where it is made by an agent of the third party it must be shown that it was made within the scope of the agent's authority.[471]

**Effects of a bribe.** The promise or payment of a bribe has drastic effects. The agent can (even if he has been appointed for a fixed period) be summarily dismissed;[472] he loses his right to commission on the tainted transaction;[473] and he must account to the principal for any profit made, whether or not the principal has suffered loss.[474] The courts had not provided a consistent answer[475] to the question whether the principal also has a proprietary claim with the result that he will rank ahead of any unsecured creditors of the agent, can trace into other assets purchased with the funds in question, and can claim any increase in the value of the bribe or of its product. In *FHR European Ventures LLP v Cedar Capital Partners Plc*[476] the Supreme Court conceded that it was not possible to reconcile all of the earlier authorities but considered that, "taken as a whole",[477] they favoured the answer that the principal has a proprietary claim to any benefit received by the agent in breach of his fiduciary duty.[478] This was also said to have the merit of simplicity given the uncertain scope of any more restricted proprietary claim[479] and to be most consistent with the underlying policy of imposing the duty of utmost loyalty on the agent in the first place.[480] A number of previous decisions in which the law was said to have taken "a wrong turn" were overruled as a result.[481] **16–112**

---

[470] *Industries & General Mortgage Co v Lewis* [1949] 2 All E.R. 573; *Conway v Eze* [2018] EWHC 29 (Ch) at [127]; affirmed [2019] EWCA Civ 88.

[471] *UBS AG v Kommunale Wasserwerke Leipzig GmbH* [2014] EWHC 3615 (Comm) at [615] (for further proceedings, see [2017] EWCA Civ 1567; [2017] 2 Lloyd's Rep. 621).

[472] *Boston Deep Sea Fishing & Ice Co v Ansell* (1888) 39 Ch D. 339. For the effect of such dismissal on the agent's rights to salary (or recompense for work actually done), see paras 17–035—17–036.

[473] *Solomon v Pender* (1865) 3 H. & C. 639; *Andrews v Ramsay* [1903] 2 K.B. 635 (commission on other transactions remains payable if they are severable: *Nitedals Taenstickfabrik v Bruster* [1906] 2 Ch. 67) (doubted in *Imageview Management Ltd v Jack* [2009] EWCA Civ 63; [2009] 1 Lloyd's Rep. 436 and said to be limited to cases of "harmless collaterality"; see para.16–113).

[474] *Reading v Attorney General* [1951] A.C. 507; *Phipps v Boardman* [1967] 2 A.C. 46.

[475] And nor had academic commentators; see, inter alia, in addition to the commentary referred to in fnn.478 and 479, below: Hayton [2012] Co Law 161; Swadling (2012) *Trusts and Trustees* 985; Virgo 70 C.L.J. 502; Edelman 129 L.Q.R. 66; Watts 129 L.Q.R. 527; Etherton (2014) 2(1) *Birkbeck Law Review* 59.

[476] [2014] UKSC 45; [2015] A.C. 250.

[477] *FHR European Ventures LLP v Cedar Capital Partners Plc* [2014] UKSC 45; [2015] A.C. 250 at [46].

[478] cf. *Attorney General of Hong Kong v Reid* [1994] 1 A.C. 324; followed in *Daraydan Holdings Ltd v Solland International Ltd* [2004] EWHC 622 (Ch); [2005] Ch. 119; Millett [1993] Rest L.R. 7; 71 C.L.J. 583; Smith 72 C.L.J. 60.

[479] cf. *Sinclair Investments (UK) Ltd v Versailles Trade Finance Ltd* [2011] EWCA Civ 347; [2012] Ch. 453; Goode 127 L.Q.R. 493; Worthington 72 C.L.J. 720.

[480] *FHR European Ventures LLP v Cedar Capital Partners Plc* [2014] UKSC 45; [2015] A.C. 250 at [33].

[481] Most notably *Metropolitan Bank v Heiron* (1880) 5 Ex. D. 319; and *Lister v Stubbs* (1890) 45 Ch D. 1 and any subsequent decisions "at least in so far as they relied on or followed *Heiron* and *Lister*" (*FHR European Ventures LLP v Cedar Capital Partners Plc* [2014] UKSC 45; [2015] A.C. 250 at [50]): e.g. *Sinclair Investments (UK) Ltd v Versailles Trade Finance Ltd* [2011] EWCA Civ 347; [2012] Ch. 453, fn.479.

If the bribe has not yet been paid, the agent cannot recover it from the third party, but the principal can do so.[482] The principal can further set the tainted transaction aside and retain the bribe, if it has been paid over to him by the agent.[483] Whether or not it has been paid, the principal can, as an alternative to claiming the bribe,[484] claim damages from the agent and the third party for the loss suffered as a result of the bribery.[485] These claims are available even though the payment of the bribe did not induce the principal to enter into any contract with the third party.[486] If the principal was induced to enter into such a contract with the third party, that party is also liable to the principal for an account of the profits made by the third party from that contract, but only to the extent that these exceed the profits that he would have made if the contract had not been induced by bribery and provided that the third party has not already been required to pay such amounts to the principal by way of damages.[487]

16–113 **Secret profit.** Where the agent makes a secret profit in breach of his fiduciary duty in circumstances not amounting to a bribe, the third party is under no contractual or tortious liability. The agent can be summarily dismissed.[488] He may also be liable to account for the profit to the principal[489] and, in the case of a breach of fiduciary duty going beyond "harmless collaterality", forfeit any commission.[490]

16–114 **Performance of the agent's duties.** The general rule is that an agent cannot delegate the performance of his duties, unless the principal expressly or impliedly authorises him to appoint a sub-agent.[491] But an agent does not "delegate" by instructing his own employees to do various necessary acts in connection with the execution of his duty. An agent may have authority to appoint a sub-agent and to

[482] *Harrington v Victoria Graving Dock Co* (1878) 3 Q.B.D. 549; *Industries & General Mortgage Co v Lewis* [1949] 2 All E.R. 573.

[483] *Logicrose v Southend United FC* [1988] 1 W.L.R. 1256; Jones [1989] C.L.J. 22. If the contract has been entered and the agent is bribed in the course of its performance the principal may set it aside *in futuro* as from the moment of discovery; similarly if rescission is not available because of one of the bars (e.g. delay, third party rights, etc.). The remedy here is not rescission, but termination for repudiatory breach by the bribing party: *Tigris International NV v China Southern Airlines Co Ltd* [2014] EWCA Civ 1649 at [143].

[484] *T Mahesan S/O Thambiah v Malaysian Government Officers' Housing Society* [1979] A.C. 374; disapproving dicta in *Salford Corp v Lever* [1891] 1 Q.B. 168; Tettenborn 95 L.Q.R. 68; *Arab Monetary Fund v Hashim* [1993] 1 Lloyd's Rep. 543; *Island Records Ltd v Tring International Plc* [1996] 1 W.L.R. 1256 at 1257; *Fyffes Group Ltd v Templeman* [2000] 2 Lloyd's Rep. 643.

[485] *Salford Corp v Lever* [1891] 1 Q.B. 168.

[486] *Petrotrade Inc v Smith* [2000] 1 Lloyd's Rep. 486, where the "third party" had itself been appointed as agent but the bribes were paid by its employees to *another* of the principal's agents, i.e. to one of the latter's employees.

[487] *Fyffes Group Ltd v Templeman* [2000] 2 Lloyd's Rep. 643 at 672.

[488] *Neary v Dean of Westminster* [1999] I.R.L.R. 288; cf. *Novoship (UK) Ltd v Mikhaylyuk* [2014] EWCA Civ 908; [2015] Q.B. 499.

[489] See, e.g. *Parr v Keystone Healthcare Ltd* [2019] EWCA Civ 1246; [2019] 4 W.L.R. 99.

[490] *Imageview Management Ltd v Jack* [2009] EWCA Civ 63; [2009] 1 Lloyd's Rep. 436; Watts 129 L.Q.R. 369; Oram [2010] L.M.C.L.Q. 95; cf. *HPOR Servicos de Consultoria Ltda v Dryships Inc* [2018] EWHC 3451 (Comm); [2019] 1 Lloyd's Rep. 260; *Staechelin v ACLBDD Holdings Ltd* [2019] EWCA Civ 817; [2019] 3 All E.R. 429 at [93].

[491] e.g. *John McCann & Co v Pow* [1974] 1 W.L.R. 1643.

make a contract between the sub-agent and the principal.[492] He may, alternatively, have authority to delegate (in the sense that he commits no breach of duty by performing through another) but have no authority to make a contract between principal and sub-agent.[493] In such a case the agent remains contractually liable to the principal if the sub-agent performs defectively,[494] while the sub-agent is under no contractual duty to the principal.[495] The sub-agent may, however, be liable on other grounds, e.g. for breach of fiduciary duty[496] or in tort if he negligently causes damage to the principal's property.[497] But the sub-agent is not liable in tort merely because he has negligently paid over the proceeds of the principal's property to an impostor (so that the principal suffers financial loss);[498] for such liability would be in practice indistinguishable from contractual liability and so be inconsistent with the absence of a contractual relationship between principal and sub-agent. The contract between agent and sub-agent could also be drawn up in such a way as to confer rights on the principal under the Contracts (Rights of Third Parties) Act 1999.[499]

**Principal's indemnity.** It is an implied term in a contract of employment that the employee will indemnify the employer against any liability to third parties incurred by reason of the employee's negligence in doing what he was employed to do.[500] A contract of agency will generally give rise to a similar liability to indemnify the principal. 16–115

### (d) Effects of non-consensual agency

**Dependent upon the underlying policy.** It is a difficult and largely unsolved problem to what extent the effects of agency which have so far been discussed arise where the agency is not created by agreement between principal and agent, e.g. in cases of apparent and usual authority, and in cases of agency of necessity. 16–116

One effect of apparent or usual authority is to make the principal liable to the third party. But is the third party liable to the principal? When an agent acts within his apparent authority, the principal is liable because he is estopped from

492 *De Bussche v Alt* (1878) 8 Ch D. 286.

493 *New Zealand & Australian Land Co v Watson* (1881) 7 Q.B.D. 374; *Royal Products Ltd v Midland Bank Ltd* [1981] 2 Lloyd's Rep. 194 at 198; *Henderson v Merrett Syndicates Ltd* [1995] 2 A.C. 145 at 202; *Prentis Donegan & Partners v Leeds & Leeds Plc* [1998] 2 Lloyd's Rep. 326; Tettenborn 115 L.Q.R. 655.

494 *Powell & Thomas v Evan Jones & Co* [1905] 1 K.B. 11 apparently disapproved, but on another point, in *Attorney-General of Hong Kong v Reid* [1994] 1 A.C. 324 at 337.

495 *Calico Printers Association v Barclays Bank* (1931) 145 L.T. 51.

496 *Markel International Insurance Co Ltd v Surety Guarantee Consultants Ltd* [2008] EWHC 1135 (Comm).

497 *Meyerstein v Eastern Agency* (1885) 1 T.L.R. 595; cf. *Stewart v Reavell's Garage* [1952] 2 Q.B. 545.

498 *Balsamo v Medici* [1984] 1 W.L.R. 951; contrast *Henderson v Merrett Syndicates Ltd* [1995] 2 A.C. 145, where in a "most unusual" (at 195) situation a sub-agent was held liable in tort to the principal for negligently inflicted financial loss; see para.14–056. See also *Aiken v Stewart Wrightson Members Agency* [1995] 1 W.L.R. 1281.

499 See para.14–099 and following.

500 *Lister v Romford Ice & Cold Storage Co Ltd* [1957] A.C. 555; contrast *Harvey v RG O'Dell Ltd* [1958] 2 Q.B. 78.

denying the agent's authority; but no similar estoppel need arise against the third party. If the principal wants to enforce the contract, he will usually ratify. But there may be some reason why he cannot do so,[501] and, if this is the case, it is far from clear that he could sue the third party simply because the third party can sue him. An agent who does an unauthorised act which binds his principal is clearly not entitled to commission, but is probably subject to the usual liabilities if he accepts a bribe or makes a secret profit.[502] An agent of necessity often acquires rights of recompense or reimbursement against his principal, but it is less common for him to be able to create a contract between principal and third party. Thus it is impossible to make any general statement about the effects of non-consensual agency. The problems which may arise must be considered in the light of the considerations of policy which underlie each type of non-consensual agency.

## 5. TERMINATION

16–117 Agency as a contract is determined by any event which terminates a contract,[503] and also in certain special ways. After discussing these, we shall discuss the effects of termination and finally consider some cases of irrevocable agency.

### (a) Modes of termination

#### *(i) Consensual agency*

16–118 It will be convenient first to consider modes of termination at common law and then to deal with special rules applicable to "commercial agents".[504]

16–119 **Notice.** An agent's authority can be determined by giving him notice. Where the agency is contractual it may be for a fixed term or specify a period of notice. If no term or period of notice is specified, the contract is determinable on reasonable notice.[505] A notice given in breach of contract is, in general,[506] nonetheless *effective*. It determines the agent's actual authority[507] and the relationship of principal and agent. Thus the agent cannot restrain the breach by injunction or obtain a declaration that his dismissal was void or claim his agreed remuneration in respect of periods after the wrongful termination.[508] His normal remedies are

[501] See para.16–049 and following; e.g. it may be too late to ratify.

[502] *English v Dedham Vale Properties Ltd* [1978] 1 W.L.R. 93.

[503] e.g. by performance, termination for breach, or frustration.

[504] See para.16–014.

[505] *Martin-Baker Aircraft Co Ltd v Canadian Flight Equipment Ltd* [1955] 2 Q.B. 556; cf. *Re Spenborough UDC's Agreement* [1968] Ch. 139; *Richardson v Koefod* [1969] 1 W.L.R. 1812 at 1814.

[506] For exceptions, see para.21–041.

[507] i.e. the authority based on the wrongfully repudiated contract; as to apparent authority, usual authority and authority of necessity, see para.16–125.

[508] *Denmark Productions Ltd v Boscobel Productions Ltd* [1969] 1 Q.B. 699; *Roberts v Elwells Engineering Co Ltd* [1972] 2 Q.B. 586; *Gunton v Richmond upon Thames LBC* [1981] Ch. 448; *Delaney v Staples* [1992] 1 A.C. 687 at 692; para.21–011; Freedland 32 M.L.R. 314; Drake [1969] J.B.L. 113. Remuneration earned before the dismissal but payable thereafter could be claimed on the

by way of damages for wrongful dismissal and a declaration that the dismissal was wrongful.[509] He may also be able to restrain by injunction the breach of a negative stipulation in the agency contract,[510] such as an undertaking by the principal not to appoint another agent to conduct the business in question.[511]

**Inconsistent conduct.** It seems that agency can be determined without notice by conduct inconsistent with its continuance, e.g. if the principal sells the subject-matter of the agency.[512] Such conduct may again be a breach of contract but nevertheless puts an end to the agency. **16–120**

**Incapacity.** At common law,[513] agency is determined by the supervening incapacity of principal or agent if the incapacity is inconsistent with the consensual nature of agency. The principal's incapacity terminates agency even though the agent has no notice of it.[514] However, where the agent's authority arises from a contract, e.g. a solicitor's retainer, the supervening incapacity of the principal will terminate the agent's authority, but may not result in the termination of the underlying contract,[515] nor its frustration.[516] Alternative steps might then be taken to provide the solicitor with instructions on behalf of the principal,[517] unless and until the principal's capacity is restored.[518] **16–121**

**Death.** The death of principal or agent terminates agency, whether the survivor has notice or not.[519] Dissolution of a company has the same effect, and so has dissolution of a partnership, unless the contract is, on its true interpretation, with **16–122**

---

principle of *Sellers v London County Newspapers* [1951] 1 K.B. 784. Remuneration can also be claimed where the termination is lawful because it is authorised by a contractual provision for notice or payment in lieu: *Abrahams v Performing Right Society* [1995] I.C.R. 1028.

[509] As to damages, see *Denmark Productions Ltd v Boscobel Productions Ltd* [1969] 1 Q.B. 699; *Marsh v National Autistic Society* [1993] I.C.R. 453; and *Boyo v Lambeth LBC* [1994] I.C.R. 727; as to declaration, see *Taylor v NUS* [1967] 1 W.L.R. 532.

[510] See paras 21–064–21–067.

[511] *Decro-Wall International SA v Practitioners in Marketing Ltd* [1971] 1 W.L.R. 361.

[512] *EP Nelson & Co v Rolfe* [1950] 1 K.B. 139.

[513] For a statutory exception, see paras 16–128–16–129.

[514] *Yonge v Toynbee* [1910] 1 K.B. 215, but note that "[t]here is much to be said in favour of a fresh examination or reconsideration of the principle in *Yonge v Toynbee*": *Blankley v Central Manchester & Manchester Children's University Hospitals NHS Trust* [2015] EWCA Civ 18; [2015] 1 Costs L.R. 119 at [36]; cf. *Dunhill v Burgin* [2014] UKSC 18; [2014] 1 W.L.R. 933 at [31].

[515] See para.12–056.

[516] See para.19–016.

[517] e.g. by the appointment of a deputy: see para.16–003.

[518] *Blankley v Central Manchester & Manchester Children's University Hospitals NHS Trust* [2015] EWCA Civ 18; [2015] 1 Costs L.R. 119.

[519] *Campanari v Woodburn* (1854) 15 C.B. 400; *Pool v Pool* (1889) 58 L.J.P. 67; *Lodgepower Ltd v Taylor* [2004] EWCA Civ 1367; [2005] 1 E.G.L.R. 1.

the partners constituting the firm from time to time.[520] However, in such a case dissolution may be a repudiatory breach, justifying termination of the contract by the agent.[521]

16–123 **Bankruptcy.** The principal's bankruptcy terminates the agent's authority.[522] The bankruptcy of the agent terminates his authority if it makes him unfit to perform his duties.[523]

16–124 **Commercial agents.** The Regulations governing "commercial agents"[524] specify minimum periods of notice (depending on the duration of the agency contract) which must be given to terminate the agency contract.[525] The relevant rules appear to apply only to the relationship of the parties to that contract. They do not seem to apply to the agent's authority: in other words, the position under the Regulations appears to resemble the common law position that failure to give proper notice makes the termination wrongful, but not ineffective. Even where proper notice is given, the agent is entitled under the Regulations to compensation or to an indemnity in respect of the termination.[526] The object of this rule appears to be to provide the agent with a sort of redundancy or severance payment, reflecting the loss of the agency business, including whatever goodwill attaches to it.[527] The rights of compensation and indemnity can also apply where the agency contract is terminated by the death of the agent[528] or by notice given by himself on the ground of his age, illness or infirmity,[529] or on account of the principal's breach,[530] or by effluxion of time.[531] But the agent has no such rights where termination is justified by his own breach.[532]

---

520 *Salton v New Beeston Cycle Co* [1900] 1 Ch. 43. And see *Brace v Calder* [1895] 2 Q.B. 253; *Tunstall v Condon* [1980] I.C.R. 786; *Briggs v Oates* [1990] I.C.R. 473. Dissolution of a limited liability partnership incorporated under the Limited Liability Partnership Act 2000 (para.12–085) seems for the present purpose to have the same effect as dissolution of a company.

521 *Briggs v Oates* [1990] I.C.R. 473.

522 *Elliott v Turquand* (1881) 7 App. Cas. 79.

523 *McCall v Australian Meat Co Ltd* (1870) 19 W.R. 188.

524 See para.16–014.

525 SI 1993/3053 reg.15.

526 SI 1993/3053 reg.17. The choice of compensation or indemnity does not entitle the principal to impose on the agent whichever is the cheaper: *Shearman v Hunter Boot Ltd* [2014] EWHC 47 (QB); [2014] 1 C.L.C. 240.

527 *Lonsdale v Howard & Hallam* [2007] UKHL 32; [2007] 1 W.L.R. 2055; Saintier 128 L.Q.R. 31; *McQuillan v McCormick* [2010] EWHC 1112 (QB); [2011] E.C.C. 18; *Invicta UK Ltd v International Brands Ltd* [2013] EWHC 1564 (QB); [2013] E.C.C. 30; *Warren v Drukkerij Flach BV* [2014] EWCA Civ 993; [2015] 1 Lloyd's Rep 111.

528 SI 1993/3053 reg.17(8).

529 cf. *Abbott v Condici Ltd* [2005] 2 Lloyd's Rep. 450.

530 SI 1993/3053 reg.18(b).

531 *Tigana v Decoro Ltd* [2003] EWHC 23; [2003] Eu. L.R. 189.

532 SI 1993/3053 reg.18(a). Termination by notice will not preclude the application of reg.18(a) so as to prevent the agent from claiming compensation if it is "because of" a breach which would have justified termination for that reason: *Crane v Sky In-Home Service Ltd* [2007] EWHC 66 (Ch); [2007] 1 C.L.C. 389 at [90]–[91]; contrast *Cooper v Pure Fishing (UK) Ltd* [2004] EWCA Civ 375; [2004] 2 Lloyd's Rep. 518 where the agency terminated through effluxion of time and the principal chose not to renew; the agent was entitled to compensation even though the principal believed he had grounds to terminate for breach.

### (ii) *Non-consensual agency*

The events listed above terminate an agent's express or implied authority, but do not necessarily terminate apparent or usual authority, or authority of necessity. Notice to the agent obviously does not terminate apparent or usual authority: notice must be given to the third party to have this effect.[533] Again, a principal's insanity terminates his agent's actual authority; but a third party who goes on dealing with the agent without notice of the principal's insanity may be able to hold the principal liable on the ground that the agent still had apparent authority.[534] It is submitted that the position should be the same where (unknown to the third party) the agent's actual authority has been terminated by the principal's death.[535] Agency of necessity can sometimes be terminated by notice, e.g. a shipmaster's authority would be terminated, just as it could be prevented from arising, in this way. But notice would not terminate such authority where the need to encourage the agent to act was particularly strong.[536] **16–125**

## (b) Irrevocable agency

As a general rule the authority of an agent may be revoked by the principal even if it is agreed to be irrevocable; the revocation is effective to terminate the agent's authority, but gives rise to a claim for damages.[537] In the following cases agency is irrevocable in the sense that any attempt to revoke it is not merely a breach of contract but also ineffective. The agent's authority continues in spite of the attempt to revoke it. **16–126**

**Authority coupled with an interest.** The "main exception" to the general rule is the case where the agent has a relevant interest of his own in the exercise of his authority.[538] This exception only applies if the authority was intended for the protection of the interest.[539] It therefore cannot apply where the interest arises after the creation of the authority.[540] The agent's commercial interest in continuing to act in order to earn commission is not enough to make his authority irrevocable since such an interest does not exist independently of the agency,[541] but his interest in recovering a debt in respect of commission *already* earned may **16–127**

[533] *AMB Generali Holding AG v SEB Trygg Liv Holding Aktiebolag* [2005] EWCA Civ 1237; [2006] 1 W.L.R. 2276 at [30]–[32].
[534] *Drew v Nunn* (1879) 4 Q.B.D. 661; cf. *Yonge v Toynbee* [1910] 1 K.B. 215 where the court did not consider the possibility that the principal might have been held liable on the footing of apparent authority.
[535] As in *Blades v Free* (1829) 9 B. & C. 167, where apparent authority was not discussed.
[536] *GN Ry v Swaffield* (1874) L.R. 9 Ex. 142; para.16–043.
[537] *Bailey v Angove's Pty Ltd* [2016] UKSC 47; [2016] 1 W.L.R. 3179 at [6].
[538] *Bailey v Angove's Pty Ltd* [2016] UKSC 47; [2016] 1 W.L.R. 3179 at [7].
[539] *Frith v Frith* [1906] A.C. 254; *Bailey v Angove's Pty Ltd* [2016] UKSC 47; [2016] 1 W.L.R. 3179 at [8].
[540] *Smart v Sandars* (1848) 5 C.B. 895.
[541] *Bailey v Angove's Pty Ltd* [2016] UKSC 47; [2016] 1 W.L.R. 3179 at [9].

suffice. This was acknowledged by Lord Sumption in *Bailey v Angove's Pty Ltd*[542] where the agent could establish no such interest on the facts.

In *Carmichael's Case* [543] one Phillips promoted a company to buy a mine from him. Carmichael agreed to underwrite 1,000 shares in this company—i.e. to take up so many of these shares as could not be sold to the public—and authorised Phillips to apply for the shares on his behalf. This authority was held to be irrevocable; it was coupled with an "interest" because, if the shares were not taken up, Phillips would not get the purchase-money for the mine. In *Bailey v Angove's Pty Ltd*, this decision, and several others,[544] are described by Lord Sumption as "special cases in which the authority of an agent has been held to be irrecoverable on what appears to be a wider basis".[545] This appears to refer to his earlier comment that, in addition to agreement that the agent's authority shall be irrevocable, the interest of the agent must be "either a proprietary interest (for example a power of attorney given to enable the holder of an equitable interest to perfect it) or a liability (generally in debt) owed to him personally".[546]

16–128 **Powers of attorney.** At common law a power of attorney, even though coupled with an interest, was revoked by the death of the donor, i.e. of the principal.[547] This rule might cause hardship both to the agent and to a person who bought from him in ignorance of the principal's death. The Powers of Attorney Act 1971 therefore provides that a power of attorney which is expressed to be irrevocable and is given to secure a proprietary interest of, or the performance of an obligation owed to, the donee shall not be revoked by the donor without the consent of the donee, or by the donor's death, incapacity or bankruptcy, so long as the interest or obligation secured by it remains in being.[548] The Act also protects third parties who deal in good faith with the donee of a power which is expressed to be irrevocable and to be given by way of security. Such persons are entitled to assume (unless they know the contrary) that the power cannot be revoked except by the donor acting with the consent of the donee, and that it has not been revoked in this way.[549]

16–129 **Lasting powers of attorney.** Under the Mental Capacity Act 2005,[550] a lasting power of attorney is one under which the donee has authority to make decisions about the donor's personal welfare,[551] as well as his property or financial

[542] [2016] UKSC 47; [2016] 1 W.L.R. 3179 at [9].

[543] [1896] 2 Ch. 643; cf. *Walsh v Whitcomb* (1797) 2 Esp. 565; *Re Olympic Fire & General Reinsurance Co Ltd* [1920] 2 Ch. 341.

[544] *Van Praagh v Everidge* [1902] 2 Ch. 266; *Daly v Lime Street Underwriting Agencies* [1987] 2 F.T.L.R. 277; *Society of Lloyd's v Leighs* [1997] C.L.C. 759.

[545] *Bailey v Angove's Pty Ltd* [2016] UKSC 47; [2016] 1 W.L.R. 3179 at [9].

[546] *Bailey v Angove's Pty Ltd* [2016] UKSC 47; [2016] 1 W.L.R. 3179 at [7].

[547] *Watson v King* (1815) 4 Camp. 272.

[548] Powers of Attorney Act 1971 s.4.

[549] Powers of Attorney Act 1971 s.5(3); special protection is provided for transferees under stock exchange transactions by s.6.

[550] The Enduring Powers of Attorney Act 1985 is repealed, but existing enduring powers are unaffected: 2005 Act s.66, Sch.4.

[551] Such decisions are subject to the restrictions set out in s.11.

affairs.[552] It includes authority to make such decisions in circumstances where the donor no longer has capacity.[553] In addition to a number of other requirements laid down by the Act,[554] the donor must have reached the age of 18 and must have had capacity to execute the instrument creating the power of attorney. He may revoke a lasting power of attorney at any time when he has the capacity to do so[555] and it will also be revoked in the following circumstances if the donee is not replaced or, in the case of joint donees, there is no remaining donee:[556] disclaimer of the appointment by the donee;[557] the death or winding-up of the donee;[558] the dissolution or annulment of a marriage or civil partnership between the donor and the donee, unless the instrument provides otherwise;[559] and the lack of capacity of the donee. In addition, the bankruptcy of the donor or the donee will revoke the power in so far as it gives authority to deal with the donee's property and affairs, but not his personal welfare.[560] The operation of a lasting power of attorney is subject to the powers of the court laid down in the Act.[561]

---

[552] 2005 Act s.9(1).
[553] 2005 Act s.9(1).
[554] 2005 Act ss.9(2), 10, Sch.1.
[555] 2005 Act s.13(2).
[556] 2005 Act s.13(7).
[557] 2005 Act s.13(6)(a).
[558] 2005 Act s.13(6)(b).
[559] 2005 Act s.13(6)(c), (11).
[560] 2005 Act ss.13(3), (4), 6(b), (8), (9).
[561] See 2005 Act s.23.

CHAPTER 17

# PERFORMANCE AND BREACH[1]



[1] Andrews, Clarke, Tettenborn and Virgo, *Contractual Duties: Performance, Breach, Termination and Remedies*, 2nd edn (2017).

**17–001** A party who performs a contract in accordance with its terms is thereby discharged from his obligations under it. Such performance also normally entitles him to enforce the other party's undertakings. It is often possible to perform a contract vicariously, i.e. by procuring performance by a third party. In the vast majority of cases (but not all),[2] a failure to perform will amount to a breach of contract. The consequences of such a finding are dealt with in Chs 18 (termination for breach), 20 (damages) and 21 (specific remedies).

## 1. METHOD OF PERFORMANCE

**17–002** **When performance is due.** The general rule is that performance is due without demand: a debtor must seek his creditor.[3] This rule can be varied by contrary agreement, by mercantile usage or by other rules of law. The first possibility is illustrated by a contract which provides for payment to be made "on demand". The effect of these words is that the debtor is not bound to pay before the demand is made,[4] and that normally he must pay within a reasonable time of receiving the demand.[5] The second possibility is illustrated by the rule that the holder of a bill of exchange is not entitled to payment unless he first presents the bill for payment.[6] A demand or notice of default may also have to be given where the party from whom performance is claimed cannot, without notice, reasonably be expected to know that performance is due.[7] Thus "a landlord is not in breach of his covenant to repair [the demised premises][8] until he has been given notice of the want of repair and a reasonable time has elapsed in which repair could have been carried out."[9] The third possibility is illustrated by a legislative provision by which a tenant under a long lease of a dwelling is not liable to make payment of rent under the lease unless the landlord has given him a notice relating to the payment.[10]

---

[2] See para.17–059.

[3] *Walton v Mascall* (1844) 13 M. & W. 452; cf. *Carne v Debono* [1988] 1 W.L.R. 1107.

[4] *Esso Petroleum Co Ltd v Alstonbridge Properties Ltd* [1975] 1 W.L.R. 1474; *Libyan Arab Foreign Bank v Bankers Trust Co* [1989] Q.B. 728 at 748–749. The requirement of a "demand" may be waived: see *Stimpson v Smith* [1999] Ch. 340; para.13–019.

[5] *Bank of Baroda v Panessar* [1987] Ch. 335. If the debtor has made it clear that he cannot or will not pay, he will be in default as soon as the demand is made: *Sheppard & Cooper Ltd v TSB Bank* [1996] 2 All E.R. 654.

[6] Bills of Exchange Act 1882 ss.41(1)(a), 40(1).

[7] *Vyse v Wakefield* (1840) 6 M. &W. 442, 453; *Edwards v Kumarasamy* [2016] UKSC 40, [2016] A.C. 1334 at [29]–[38].

[8] *British Telecommunications Plc v Sun Life Assurance Society Plc* [1996] Ch. 69 at 74.

[9] *Calabar Properties Ltd v Stitcher* [1984] 1 W.L.R. 287 at 298.

[10] Commonhold and Leasehold Reform Act 2002 s.166.

**Time of the essence.** Stipulations as to time and, in particular, whether time is "of the essence" are principally relevant in the context of the injured party's right to terminate for breach and are dealt with in Ch.18.[11] **17–003**

**Tender of performance.** A tender of money is ineffective unless the money is actually produced, or unless production is dispensed with by the creditor.[12] Tender of part of a debt is a bad tender.[13] Conversely, tender of too large a sum, requiring change, is also a bad tender, as this might put an unreasonable burden on the creditor.[14] Tender of goods due under a contract of sale must be made at a reasonable hour. What is a reasonable hour is a question of fact.[15] Where a bad tender is rejected and is, within the time fixed for performance, followed by a good tender, the latter must generally be accepted.[16] But if the first tender entitles the injured party to terminate the contract, and he does so, he will not be bound to accept the second tender. **17–004**

**Payment by cheque or negotiable security.** There is a presumption that payment by cheque or negotiable[17] security operates only as conditional payment: that is, the payer is not discharged until the cheque or security is honoured.[18] During the currency of the security, the creditor impliedly undertakes not to sue on the original debt.[19] But the presumption of conditional payment can be rebutted by proof of contrary intention, i.e. by showing that the creditor had accepted the security unconditionally in payment of the debt.[20] The presumption that payment is merely conditional does not apply where a customer pays for goods or services by use of a debit or credit card. Use by the customer of such a card discharges his obligations under the contract with the supplier and makes the customer liable to reimburse the card issuing company in accordance with the contract between these two parties. If the company should fail to pay the supplier (e.g. because it has become insolvent) the supplier's sole remedy is against the **17–005**

---

[11] See para.18–111 and following.

[12] *Finch v Brook* (1834) 1 Bing. N.C. 253; *Farquharson v Pearl Ins Co Ltd* [1937] 3 All E.R. 124; *Marksans Pharma Ltd v Peter Beck & Partner VVW GmbH* [2015] EWHC 1608 (Comm).

[13] *Dixon v Clark* (1847) 5 C.B. 365.

[14] *Betterbee v Davis* (1811) 3 Camp. 70; *Robinson v Cook* (1815) 6 Taunt. 336.

[15] Sale of Goods Act 1979 s.29(5); cf. Consumer Rights Act 2015 s.28 (delivery of goods in a consumer contract).

[16] *Tetley v Shand* (1871) 25 L.T. 658; cf. *Borrowman Phillips & Co v Free & Hollis* (1878) 4 Q.B.D. 500; *Bremer Handelsgesellschaft mbH v J H Rayner & Co* [1979] 2 Lloyd's Rep. 216 at 224–229; *The Playa Larga* [1983] 2 Lloyd's Rep. 171 at 186; Apps [1994] L.M.C.L.Q. 525.

[17] Cheques are now rarely negotiable: para.15–046.

[18] Once it is honoured, payment is taken to have been made when the cheque was received: *Homes v Smith* [2000] Lloyd's Rep. Bank. 139.

[19] *Sayer v Wagstaff* (1844) 14 L.J.Ch. 116; *Re Romer & Haslam* [1893] 2 Q.B. 286; cf. *Maran Road Saw Mill v Austin Taylor & Co Ltd* [1975] 1 Lloyd's Rep. 156; and *EDF Man v Nigerian Sweets & Confectionery Co* [1977] 2 Lloyd's Rep. 50 (payment by letter of credit). Payment by direct debit has been treated as equivalent to payment by cheque, at least for the purpose of set-off: *Esso Petroleum Ltd v Milton* [1997] 1 W.L.R. 938. In *DPP v Turner* [1974] A.C. 357 at 367–368; and *Jameson v CEGB* [2000] 1 A.C. 455 at 478 it is suggested that giving a cheque amounts to payment but that the debt revives if the cheque is not met. However, in *Sayer v Wagstaff* (above) "payment" was held to have taken place when the promissory note was *paid*, not when it was *given*.

[20] *Sard v Rhodes* (1836) 1 M. & W. 153.

company.[21] He cannot claim the price from the customer; for to allow him to do so would make the customer liable to immediate full payment in cash for the goods or services supplied and so impose on him an obligation substantially more onerous than that to which he agreed when contracting with the supplier on the terms that payment was to be made by means of the card.

17–006 **Alternative performance.**[22] A contract may provide for performance in one of several ways without stating which party is to have the power of choosing between them. In *Reed v Kilburn Co-operative Society*[23] the claimant lent £50 to the defendants at 6 per cent per annum "for six or nine months". The period of the loan was held to depend on the choice of the borrower. One reason given was that "the alternative was put in for the benefit of the borrower".[24] On this view the result could vary with the state of the market: the alternative might be for the benefit of the borrower if interest rates were thought likely to rise and for that of the lender if they were thought likely to fall. But this is not the law: the choice is always the borrower's, unless the contract expressly provides the contrary. Another reason given was that "the option is in the party who is to do the first act; here the borrower is to do the first act by paying".[25] But this test would not satisfactorily solve all cases. Quain J during the argument said: "A lease for seven, fourteen, or twenty-one years, without saying at whose option, is at the option of the lessee."[26] Yet before one knows whose the option is, it is impossible to tell who is to do the first act, i.e. whether landlord or tenant must give notice of termination. No general rule is satisfactory where parties make such obscure contracts. It is a matter to be resolved by the interpretation of the contract, though the "natural meaning" is likely to be that it is for the promisor to choose.[27]

## 2. VICARIOUS PERFORMANCE

17–007 A contract may be performed by a third party on behalf of the debtor. The legal effects of such performance depend on whether it is made (or tendered) with or without the creditor's consent.

[21] *Re Charge Card Services Ltd* [1989] Ch. 497; cf. *Richardson v Worrall* [1985] S.T.C. 693 at 717, 720; *Customs & Excise Commissioners v Diners Club Ltd* [1989] 1 W.L.R. 1196 at 1205–1206 rejecting the argument that the debt is not extinguished but assigned to the card-issuing company.
[22] cf. para.19–056.
[23] (1875) L.R. 10 Q.B. 264; cf. *Price v Nixon* (1813) 5 Taunt. 338.
[24] *Reed v Kilburn Co-operative Society* (1875) L.R. 10 Q.B. 264 at 265.
[25] *Reed v Kilburn Co-operative Society* (1875) L.R. 10 Q.B. 264 at 265
[26] *Reed v Kilburn Co-operative Society* (1875) L.R. 10 Q.B. 264 at 265.
[27] *Mora Shipping Inc v Axa Corporate Solutions Assurance SA* [2005] EWCA Civ 1069; [2005] 2 Lloyd's Rep. 769 at [44].

### (a) With the creditor's consent

**Vicarious performance will generally discharge the contract.** If the creditor agrees to accept[28] performance by a third party, such performance can discharge the contract, even though it is not the same as that stipulated for in the contract. In *Hirachand Punamchand v Temple*[29] a debt was held to have been discharged when the creditor accepted a smaller sum from the debtor's father in full settlement. Payment by a third party will, however, discharge the debtor only if it was made by the third party on behalf of the debtor and with the intention of discharging him. These requirements are illustrated by a case[30] in which a company made an ex gratia payment to a person who had been defrauded by its secretary. The victim of the fraud was nevertheless entitled to claim the whole of his loss from the secretary, since the company's payment was not made on the secretary's behalf. Similarly, part-payment by one of two persons who are both liable for a debt will not discharge the other, since it will be presumed to have been made on account of his own and not of his co-debtor's liability.[31] It is an open question whether the debt is discharged if payment by a third party is made without the knowledge or consent of the debtor.[32] Some dicta support the view that the debt is discharged;[33] and this consequence clearly results if the debtor adopts or ratifies the payment.[34] But if, before he has done so, the transaction between creditor and third party is cancelled and the payment is returned to the third party, there is no discharge;[35] nor will the payment discharge the debt if the third party made it in the mistaken belief (however genuine)[36] that he was authorised by the debtor to pay the debt on his behalf.[37] It follows that, where a bank without its customer's authority or ratification pays the customer's debt, then the debt is not discharged; nor is the bank entitled to debit the customer's account with the amount of the payment.[38] The cases on this subject all concern the payment of debts; but presumably the same principles apply where a creditor agrees to accept vicarious performance of some other obligation.[39] **17–008**

---

[28] See *Customs & Excise Commissioners v National Westminster Bank Plc* [2002] EWHC 2204; [2003] 1 All E.R. (Comm) 327.

[29] [1911] 2 K.B. 330; para.3–110.

[30] *Re Rowe* [1904] 2 K.B. 483; *Pacific Associates Inc v Baxter* [1990] 1 Q.B. 993 at 1033–1034.

[31] *Jones v Broadhurst* (1850) 9 C.B. 173; *Cook v Lister* (1863) 13 C.B. (N.S.) 543 at 594; *Kemp v Balls* (1854) 10 Ex. 607.

[32] See generally Beatson, *The Use and Abuse of Unjust Enrichment* (1991), Ch.7.

[33] *Cook v Lister* (1863) 13 C.B. (N.S.) 543 at 594; contrast *Guardian Ocean Cargoes Ltd v Banco do Brasil SA* [1991] 2 Lloyd's Rep. 68 at 88; affirmed [1994] 2 Lloyd's Rep. 152. A theoretical objection might be based on the doctrine of privity but it is submitted that cases of the present kind fall outside the scope of that doctrine as properly understood: see para.14–049. For the possible application of Contracts (Rights of Third Parties) Act 1999 to cases of this kind, see para.3–110.

[34] See *Walter v James* (1871) L.R. 6 Ex. 124 at 127.

[35] This was the position in *Walter v James* (1871) L.R. 6 Ex. 124; cf. para.16–058.

[36] *Crantrave Ltd v Lloyds Bank Plc* [2000] Q.B. 917.

[37] *Barclays Bank Ltd v WJ Simms Son & Co (Southern) Ltd* [1980] Q.B. 677. Contrast *Lloyds Bank Plc v Independent Ins Ltd* [2000] Q.B. 110, where the payment was authorised.

[38] *Crantrave Ltd v Lloyds Bank Plc* [2000] Q.B. 917.

[39] *William Page & Co Ltd v BNP Paribas Securities Services Customer Bank Ltd* [2008] EWHC 3077; [2009] L & T.R. 8.

## (b) Without the creditor's consent

17–009 Even if not done with his consent, a creditor cannot object to vicarious performance if he is not prejudiced by the fact that the debtor does not perform personally. Thus a tradesman, to whom money is owed for goods, cannot object if the debtor procures full payment in cash to be made on his behalf by a third party. The same is often true of obligations to do something other than pay cash. Thus in *British Waggon Co v Lea & Co*[40] it was held that a contract to let out railway wagons and to keep them in repair for seven years could be vicariously performed: it did not matter to the hirer who kept the wagons in repair so long as the work was efficiently done by someone. But a creditor may be entitled to object to vicarious performance either on account of the nature of the contract or because of its terms.

17–010 **Nature of the contract.** When a contract is "personal" in the sense that one party relies on the skill and judgment of the other, the latter must perform personally. Thus duties under a contract of service cannot be vicariously performed;[41] an estate agent who has been instructed to find a purchaser for a house cannot perform vicariously, since he "holds a position of discretion and trust";[42] and a person who agrees to store another's goods must perform personally, since the owner of the goods relies on his skill and integrity.[43] It has been held that a shipowner must perform a charterparty personally in the sense that he cannot require the charterer to accept performance from a third party to whom the ship has been sold,[44] but in a later case where the parties had used a "cryptic expression" to describe the owners and the vessel which would perform the voyage, it was held that the owners were obliged to nominate a vessel to carry the charterers' cargo but without any contractual requirement that the nominated vessel possessed, vis-à-vis the owners, any particular contractual status or relationship.[45] There are cases in which even a contract for the sale of goods must be personally performed by the seller, e.g. if the goods are to be manufactured by the seller and the buyer has relied on the seller's skill as a manufacturer[46] or if the buyer has in some other way relied on the personal integrity of the seller.[47] It is very unlikely that the obligation to pay is one which cannot be performed vicariously since "the very essence of money is that it is a depersonalised medium of exchange".[48]

---

[40] (1880) 5 Q.B.D. 149; cf. *Phillips v Alhambra Palace Co* [1901] 1 Q.B. 59.

[41] *Robson v Drummond* (1831) 2 B. & Ad. 303 would seem an extreme example.

[42] *John McCann & Co v Pow* [1974] 1 W.L.R. 1643 at 1647; cf. para.16–114; *Southway Group v Wolff* (1991) 57 Build L.R. 33 (supervision by architect).

[43] *Edwards v Newland* [1950] 2 K.B. 534.

[44] *Fratelli Sorrentino v Buerger* [1915] 3 K.B. 367 at 370, but that case shows that the charterer cannot object if, notwithstanding the sale, the shipowner can still perform personally, i.e. if he retains the control and management of the ship during the chartered period or voyage; cf. *Humble v Hunter* (1842) 12 Q.B. 310; para.16–067.

[45] *The Glory Wealth* [2013] EWHC 3153 (Comm); [2014] 2 W.L.R. 1405.

[46] *Johnson v Raylton, Dixon & Co* (1881) 7 Q.B.D. 438.

[47] *Dr Jaeger's Sanitary Woollen System Co Ltd v Walker & Sons* (1897) 77 L.T. 180.

[48] *North v Brown* [2012] EWCA Civ 223 at [6], in which the trial judge's failure to distinguish between assignment and vicarious performance led him to the contrary conclusion.

**Terms of the contract.** It is obvious that a contract must be personally performed if it expressly so provides. A contract may also contain terms which impliedly rule out vicarious performance. In *Davies v Collins*[49] the defendant accepted a uniform for cleaning under a contract which provided: "Whilst every care is exercised in cleaning … garments, all orders are accepted at owners' risk." It was held that the defendant had broken the contract by sending the uniform to be cleaned by a sub-contractor (who had lost it); for the words "whilst every care is exercised in cleaning … "were inconsistent with the right to perform the cleaning operation vicariously. If, however, the uniform had been properly cleaned, and returned, by the sub-contractor, the owner would not have been prejudiced by the fact of vicarious performance, and it is submitted that he should have been liable to make at any rate some payment.[50] Lord Greene MR said that the clause did not preclude every kind of sub-contracting: the cleaner might have employed a sub-contractor to perform some purely ancillary service, such as returning the uniform to the customer. It is arguable that the clause precluded only vicarious performance of the duty to take care of the goods, and that, so long as that duty remained unbroken, the owner was liable to pay the cleaning charges. 17–011

### (c) Vicarious performance distinguished from assignment

**No transfer of liability.** The factors which determine whether a contract can be vicariously performed closely resemble those which determine whether the benefit of a "personal" contract is assignable.[51] For this reason, vicarious performance is sometimes called *assignment of liabilities*; but this is (as already noted) a concept which is not recognised by the common law.[52] Where vicarious performance is permitted no liability is *transferred*; the original debtor remains liable for the due performance of his obligations under the contract;[53] and the actual performer does not at common law become liable in contract to the creditor. In *Stewart v Reavell's Garage*[54] the owner of a 1929 Bentley motorcar took it to the defendants' garage to have the brakes relined. At the defendants' suggestion, the owner agreed that the work should be done by a sub-contractor, who did it so badly that the brakes failed, and the owner was injured. The defendants were clearly entitled to perform vicariously, as the owner had agreed to their doing so. But they were nonetheless held liable for the sub-contractor's defective workmanship: their liability was not transferred. Nor did the sub-contractor incur any contractual liability to the owner. He might have been liable to the owner in tort for doing the work negligently[55] but he would not have been liable to the owner in contract, had he failed to do the work at all. The 17–012

---

[49] [1945] 1 All E.R. 247; cf. *Kollerich & Cie SA v The State Trading Co of India* [1980] 2 Lloyd's Rep. 32.

[50] cf. para.17–043.

[51] See, e.g. *Don King Productions Inc v Warren* [2000] Ch. 291 at 335–336; paras 15–053–15–059.

[52] See para.15–078.

[53] *North v Brown* [2012] EWCA Civ 223 at [8].

[54] [1952] 2 Q.B. 545; cf. *Basildon DC v JE Lesser (Properties) Ltd* [1985] Q.B. 839; *Wong Mee Wan v Kwan Kin Travel Services Ltd* [1996] 1 W.L.R. 38.

[55] cf. *Learoyd Bros v Pope & Sons* [1966] 2 Lloyd's Rep. 142; *British Telecommunications Plc v James Thomson & Sons (Engineers) Ltd* [1999] 1 W.L.R. 9.

Contracts (Rights of Third Parties) Act 1999[56] makes it possible to draw up the sub-contract in such a way as to confer rights against the sub-contractor on the creditor; but even if this is done, the debtor will not be relieved from his liability to the creditor under the main contract.

17–013 **Contracts to arrange a service.** The above discussion is based on the assumption that a contract contains an undertaking by A to B for the provision of some service and that the contract permits A to delegate the performance of the service to C. It is, however, also possible for A's undertaking to be, not one that he will *render* the service, but one that he will *arrange* for it to be rendered by another person (C) as his agent.[57] In that case, A's duty is merely to exercise reasonable care and skill in selecting the agent;[58] and if he performs that duty he will not be liable to B for defects in C's performance. Such a case is not one of *vicarious* performance at all: A will have *personally* performed the only duty which the contract imposed on him.

## 3. ORDER OF PERFORMANCE

17–014 The order in which contracting parties must perform their respective obligations depends on the distinction between conditions precedent, concurrent conditions, and independent promises. Somewhat confusingly, English law also uses the expression "condition" in rules which deal with the *conformity* of one party's performance with that promised (as opposed to the *order* in which the two performances must be rendered). This usage, and the distinction between these two senses of "condition," are discussed in Ch.18.[59]

### (a) Condition precedent

17–015 Performance by one party, A, is a condition precedent to the liability of the other, B, when A has to perform before B's liability accrues. This will most obviously be the case if the contract expressly provides that A's act is to be done before B's.[60] Thus if A agrees to work for B at a weekly wage payable in arrear, B need not pay A until A has done a week's work.[61] Performance by A may also be a

---

[56] See para.14–099 and following.

[57] *Wong Mee Wan v Kwan Kin Travel Services* [1996] 1 W.L.R. 38, where the contract was not of this kind, and A was held liable for C's defective performance.

[58] *Wong Mee Wan v Kwan Kin Travel Services* [1996] 1 W.L.R. 38; *Raflatac Ltd v Eade* [1999] 1 Lloyd's Rep. 507 at 509. The same conclusion has been drawn where performance required specialist skills which A could not reasonably be expected to have: see *Investors in Industry Commercial Property Ltd v Bedfordshire CC* [1986] 1 All E.R. 787 at 807 (not reported on this point in [1986] Q.B. 1034).

[59] See para.18–043 and following.

[60] *Société Générale de Paris v Milders* (1883) 49 L.T. 55 at 59; cf. *Pioneer Concrete (UK) Ltd v National Employers Mutual, etc.* [1985] 2 All E.R. 395; *Kazakstan Wool Processors (Europe) Ltd v Nederlandsche Credietverzekering Maatschappij NV* [2000] C.L.C. 822.

[61] *Morton v Lamb* (1797) 7 T.R. 125; *Cresswell v Board of Inland Revenue* [1984] I.C.R. 508; *Miles v Wakefield MDC* [1987] A.C. 539 at 561, 574; *Wiluszynski v Tower Hamlets LBC* [1989] I.C.R. 493 at 498; see further para.17–045.

condition precedent to the liability of B even though the contract does not expressly state the order in which the two acts are to be done. In *Trans Trust SPRL v Danubian Trading Co*[62] A bought steel from B to be paid for by "cash against shipping documents from a confirmed credit to be opened by" an American company (to whom A had resold) in favour of B. A undertook that the credit would be opened "forthwith". Performance by A of his undertaking to procure the letter of credit was regarded as a condition precedent to the liability of B although the order in which their acts were to be done was not expressly laid down in the contract. A knew that B could not get supplies of steel unless the credit was made available. Hence the nature of the contract made it clear that A was to perform before B became liable.

**Condition precedent in the promissory sense.** In Ch.2 we distinguished between contingent and promissory conditions, and noted that "condition" was used to refer either to an event or to a term of a contract.[63] Our present concern is with conditions as events. In this sense, a contingent condition is an event which neither party undertakes to bring about and on which the existence of a contract, or the binding force of its principal obligations, depends. A promissory condition, on the other hand, refers to an event which one party is obliged by the contract to bring about. In the *Trans Trust* case, A argued that the opening of the credit was a condition of the former kind, so that A was not liable when his sub-buyer failed to open the credit. But the court rejected the argument and held A liable on the ground that the opening of the credit was not a condition precedent to the existence of the contract, but only a condition precedent to the liability of B. In other words, it was not a contingent, but a promissory condition. In its contingent sense, condition precedent is contrasted with condition subsequent. In its promissory sense (with which we are here concerned), condition precedent is contrasted with concurrent condition and independent promise: these concepts are discussed below. 17–016

**Whether condition precedent is contingent or promissory.** The distinction between a contingent and a promissory condition turns on the question whether the agreement purports to impose on A an obligation to bring about the stipulated event.[64] For example, in one case A undertook to erect buildings on B's land, and B undertook, when A had done so, to grant a lease of the land to A. This was held not to be a (contingently) "conditional contract", but a case in which performance by A was a (promissory) condition precedent to the liability of B.[65] The position is similar where A contracts to buy a house from B and to pay a deposit. As A promised to pay the deposit, that payment is not a contingent condition precedent 17–017

---

[62] [1952] 2 Q.B. 297. For a similar argument in a different context, see *Films Rover International v Cannon Film Sales Ltd* [1987] 1 W.L.R. 670 at 684; for further proceedings see [1989] 1 W.L.R. 912. Contrast *Clowes Development (UK) Ltd v Mulchinock* [1998] 1 W.L.R. 42.

[63] See para.2–104; cf. para.18–043.

[64] cf. *Albion Sugar Co Ltd v Williams Tankers Ltd* [1977] 2 Lloyd's Rep. 457 at 464; *The Fanti and the Padre Island* [1991] 2 A.C. 1 at 31; *UR Power GmbH v Kuok Oils and Grains Pte Ltd* [2009] EWHC 1940 (Comm); [2009] 2 Lloyd's Rep. 495 at [15].

[65] *Eastham v Leigh, London & Provincial Properties Ltd* [1971] 1 Ch. 871; cf. *Michaels v Harley House (Marylebone) Ltd* [1997] 1 W.L.R. 967.

to the existence of the contract[66] but a promissory condition precedent to the liability of B. If the deposit is not paid, B is, moreover, entitled to terminate the contract,[67] while A can be sued for the unpaid deposit, or for damages for failing to pay it.[68]

### (b) Concurrent condition

17–018 The two performances are said to be concurrent conditions when the parties undertake to perform concurrently (or simultaneously). In the case of a contract for the sale of goods, delivery and payment are concurrent conditions: this means that the buyer cannot claim delivery unless he is ready and willing to pay, and the seller cannot claim the price unless he is ready and willing to deliver.[69] This rule can be varied by contrary agreement: the seller may agree to give credit or the buyer to pay in advance. Similarly, under a charterparty, delivery of the goods by the shipowner and payment of the freight are (unless otherwise agreed[70]) concurrent conditions.[71]

### (c) Independent promises

17–019 If promises are "independent" each party can enforce the other's promise although he has not performed his own. The remedy of the party sued is not to withhold performance, but to make a counterclaim to enforce the promise of the party suing. A contract for the sale of land would now generally require conveyance and payment to take place concurrently. But a tenant's covenant to pay rent and a landlord's covenant to repair are still regarded as independent, so that the landlord is not entitled to refuse to perform his covenant to repair merely because the tenant is in arrears with his rent.[72] Similarly, where goods carried on a chartered ship are damaged as a result of the shipowner's breach of the charterparty, before the time fixed for payment of freight, the charterer must nevertheless make the payment when that time comes: his remedy is by way of a cross-action for damages.[73]

---

[66] *Michael Richards Properties Ltd v St Saviour's Parish* [1975] 3 All E.R. 416 at 420; *Millichamp v Jones* [1982] 1 W.L.R. 1422; *The Blankenstein* [1985] 1 W.L.R. 435. These authorities reject the contrary view stated in *Myton Ltd v Schwab-Morris* [1974] 1 W.L.R. 331 at 336.

[67] *Myton Ltd v Schwab-Morris* [1974] 1 W.L.R. 331 at 337; para.18–036.

[68] See paras 18–023, 20–176.

[69] Sale of Goods Act 1979 s.28; *Morton v Lamb* (1797) 7 T.R. 125; *The Aktor* [2008] EWHC 1330 (Comm); [2008] 2 Lloyd's Rep. 246 at [66].

[70] e.g. *The Karin Vatis* [1988] 2 Lloyd's Rep. 330.

[71] *Paynter v James* (1867) L.R. 2 C.P. 348 at 355; cf. *Stanton v Richardson* (1872) L.R. 7 C.P. 421 at 433; affirmed 45 L.J.Q.B. 78; *The Poseidon* [2001] 1 Lloyd's Rep. 697.

[72] *Taylor v Webb* [1937] 2 K.B. 283 at 290 (reversed, [1937] 2 K.B. 283 at 290, on another ground which was disapproved in *Regis Property Co Ltd v Dudley* [1959] A.C. 370); cf. *Johnstone v Milling* (1886) 16 Q.B.D. 460 at 468; *Tito v Waddell (No.2)* [1977] Ch. 106 at 290; *Yorbrook Investments Ltd v Batten* (1986) P. & C.R. 51.

[73] See paras 17–036, 18–043, fn.241; the rule applies even though the shipowner's breach was repudiatory: see *The Dominique* [1989] A.C. 1056 (not a case of damage but of delay).

### (d) Criteria for drawing the distinction

The distinction between conditions precedent, concurrent conditions and independent promises is easily illustrated by reference to stereotyped situations, such as the employment, sale of goods and tenancy cases referred to in the preceding discussion. In those cases, the distinction is governed by well-settled rules, though these can be excluded by express or implied[74] agreement. But more difficulty arises in drawing the distinction in cases of first impression which fall outside these stereotyped situations. For this purpose the courts have regard to certain policy considerations, though these can be displaced by evidence of the intention of the parties. 17–020

**Presumption in favour of concurrent conditions if simultaneous performance is possible.** The effect of holding promises to be independent is to expose each party to the risk of having to perform without any security for the performance of the other; the effect of holding performance by one party to be a condition precedent is to expose that party to the same risk. To reduce the first of these risks, the courts have long been reluctant to classify promises as independent[75] unless the intention of the parties to that effect was clear. Both risks would be eliminated if the two performances were held to be concurrent conditions; and for this reason the law should, in doubtful cases, favour such a classification whenever simultaneous performance by both parties is possible. In a contract between a commercial seller or supplier and a consumer, a term which makes the consumer's undertaking (e.g. to pay the agreed price or charge) independent of the due performance of the other party's obligations is prima facie unfair under the Consumer Rights Act 2015,[76] and if it is actually unfair it will not bind the consumer.[77] 17–021

**Where simultaneous performance is not possible.** Where simultaneous performance is not possible (as in the case of contracts to do work over a period of time) performance by one party must necessarily be a condition precedent to the liability of the other. Which party has to perform first depends on their relative bargaining power and on the court's view (right or wrong) as to which of them is more likely to default after the other has performed. These factors no doubt account for the general rule that work must precede pay.[78] The position of the person doing the work is in practice safeguarded by stipulating for interim payments, such as weekly or monthly remuneration under contracts of employment, or progress payments under building contracts. 17–022

**Simultaneous performance possible, but promises classified as independent.** Even where it is possible for the two performances to be rendered simultaneously, it does not follow that they should invariably be classified as concurrent conditions. It may be appropriate to classify a promise as independent where it is 17–023

---

[74] As in *Trans Trust SPRL v Danubian Trading Co* [1952] 2 Q.B. 297; para.17–015.
[75] See *Kingston v Preston* (1773) Lofft. 194; and *Jones v Barkley* (1781) 2 Dougl. 648 at 689.
[76] Consumer Rights Act 2015 Sch.1 para.18; see para.7–117.
[77] Consumer Rights Act 2015 s.62(1); see para.7–125.
[78] See para.17–015.

only of minor importance,[79] or where the circumstances show that this was the intention of the parties.[80] Promises may also be classified as independent because of their commercial setting. This possibility arises where goods are sold for export on "c.i.f." terms, that is, for an inclusive price covering their cost, insurance and freight. Under such a contract the seller must ship goods that are in conformity with the contract and tender certain shipping documents to the buyer, while the buyer must pay the price on tender of the documents. So long as the documents are in accordance with the contract, the buyer cannot refuse to pay against tender of those documents merely because the goods were not, when shipped, in conformity with the contract.[81] This is true even if the non-conformity of the goods is such that it would justify their rejection when the goods themselves (as opposed to the documents) later reach the buyer. The seller's undertaking with respect to the conformity of *the goods* can therefore be described as an independent promise in the sense that his failure to perform it does not prevent the buyer's duty to pay the price from arising on tender of *documents*. The buyer's remedies, in the case put, are to claim damages for the defects in the goods, or to reject them and reclaim the price if, on their arrival at the agreed destination, it turns out that they suffered, when they were shipped, from defects of a kind that justify their rejection.[82]

### (e) Effects of the distinction

17–024 **Whether failure to perform justifies termination of the contract.** In Ch.18 we will see that a failure to perform by one party (A) may entitle the other (B) to "terminate" the contract, in the sense that B is released from his obligation to perform. It follows from the nature of an independent promise that failure by A to perform such a promise does not justify termination by B. The position where A fails to perform a condition precedent or a concurrent condition is more complex: such a failure justifies B's refusal to perform for so long as the failure continues, but it does not, of itself, justify termination in the sense of an outright refusal by B to perform, or to accept further performance from A. If A, a buyer of goods, fails to perform the concurrent condition of paying or tendering the price when due, the seller, B, is prima facie justified in withholding delivery; but it does not follow that B is, merely on account of the failure, entitled to terminate the contract:[83] he may, for example, still be bound to deliver if A tenders the price on the day after that fixed by the contract. A's failure to perform will only justify termination if it is (in accordance with the principles to be discussed in Ch.18)[84] *either* sufficiently serious *or* such that it falls within one of the exceptions to the requirement of serious failure.

---

[79] *Huntoon Co v Kolynos (Inc)* [1930] 1 Ch. 528 at 558.

[80] *The Odenfeld* [1978] 2 Lloyd's Rep. 357.

[81] *Gill & Duffus SA v Berger & Co Inc* [1984] A.C. 382, more fully discussed in *Benjamin's Sale of Goods*, 10th edn (2018), paras 19–179—19–182.

[82] e.g. from defects amounting to a breach of condition: see para.18–043 and following.

[83] cf. Sale of Goods Act 1979 s.10(1); para.18–120.

[84] See paras 18–030—18–086.

### (f) Wrongful refusal to accept performance

#### (i) *Where injured party terminates the contract*

In general, A's failure to perform a condition precedent or a concurrent condition justifies a refusal by B to perform. But this rule is displaced if, before performance from A has become due, B has repudiated the contract by wrongfully refusing to accept performance (or indicating that he would do so) and A has terminated the contract on account of that repudiation.[85] The effect of this displacement may differ depending upon whether A's failure to perform was induced by B's repudiation. 17–025

**Where failure to perform induced by other party's repudiation.** Suppose that a contract for the sale of goods provides that the goods are to be manufactured by A to B's order. If, before anything has, or should have been, done by A, B wrongfully repudiates the contract (i.e. indicates that he will not accept the goods and pay for them),[86] A is entitled to terminate the contract. If he does so, two things follow: A need no longer manufacture the goods, and he can claim damages from B,[87] though he must account for the costs he would have incurred in manufacture in the calculation of those damages.[88] It would be pointless to require A to manufacture and tender the goods when the tender was virtually certain to be rejected. His inability to deliver the goods at the agreed time is not allowed to prejudice his rights against B as it was induced by B's wrongful repudiation; another way of putting the point is to say that B is estopped from relying on A's inability to perform.[89] A buyer is similarly not entitled to rely on the seller's failure to deliver where that failure was induced by the buyer's insistence on delivery at a place other than that specified by the contract.[90] 17–026

**Where failure to perform not induced by other party's repudiation.** In the situations just described, it has been assumed that A could have performed, and would have done so, if B had not repudiated. But sometimes A can recover damages even though he cannot show that he would, but for B's repudiation, have been able to perform his part. In *British and Beningtons Ltd v NW Cachar Tea Co Ltd*[91] A sold tea to B who, before delivery was due, without justification stated that they would refuse to accept it. It was held that A was entitled to damages even though he could not show that he could have delivered the tea at the agreed 17–027

---

[85] See, generally, Ch.18.

[86] See para.17–075.

[87] e.g. *Glencore Grain Rotterdam BV v LORICO* [1997] 2 Lloyd's Rep. 386, where a seller's refusal to load goods was justified by the buyer's refusal to operate the contractual payment mechanism unless unjustified demands by the buyer were met; cf. *Grant v Cigman* [1996] B.C.L.C. 24 (A's inability to perform induced by B's failure to co-operate). As to A's remedy in such cases, see *The Odenfeld* [1978] 2 Lloyd's Rep. 357; para.21–015.

[88] See para.20–006.

[89] *The Simona* [1989] A.C. 788 at 805–806.

[90] *Bulk Oil (Zug) AG v Sun International Ltd* [1984] 1 Lloyd's Rep. 531 at 546.

[91] [1923] A.C. 48; cf. *Cort v Ambergate Ry* (1851) 7 Q.B. 127; *Rightside Properties Ltd v Gray* [1975] Ch. 72 at 87; *Texaxo Ltd v Eurogolf Shipping Co Ltd* [1987] 2 Lloyd's Rep. 541.

time and place. B's wrongful refusal to accept was an anticipatory breach,[92] and, once this had been "accepted" by A so as to terminate the contract, later events affecting A's ability to perform did not deprive A of his right of action;[93] for, by terminating the contract, A had been liberated from his duty of further performance.[94] The position would have been different if, at the time of B's refusal to accept, A had himself already committed a repudiatory breach,[95] for such a breach would have justified B's refusal. It is therefore crucial to determine which party committed the first breach,[96] whether that breach was repudiatory, and whether it was accepted by the other party so as to terminate the contract.

These questions are easy enough to formulate but they can raise difficult issues of fact and law where each party to a commercial dispute in good faith believes that he is acting in accordance with the contract, and that the other is not. The issue is further complicated by two rules. The first is that A is not necessarily in breach merely because he makes a defective tender; for it may be open to him to cure the defect by making a second (and good) tender within the time allowed for performance.[97] The second is that B is not necessarily in breach merely because, at the time of his refusal to accept A's performance, he gives an inadequate reason for the refusal, or none at all; for if he actually had a lawful

[92] See paras 17–074–17–095.

[93] See para.17–092; *Braithwaite v Foreign Hardwood Co* [1905] 2 K.B. 543, as explained in *The Simona* [1989] A.C. 788 at 805.

[94] *Gill & Duffus SA v Berger & Co Inc* [1984] A.C. 382 at 390; cf. *MSC Mediterranean Shipping Co SA v BRE Metro Ltd* [1985] 2 Lloyd's Rep. 239 at 240; *Glencore Grain Rotterdam BV v LORICO* [1997] 2 Lloyd's Rep. 386 at 394–395; contrast *The Glory Wealth* [2013] EWHC 3153 (Comm); [2014] 2 W.L.R. 1405 which is discussed at para.17–030. In *North Sea Energy Holdings NV v Petroleum Authority of Thailand* [1997] 2 Lloyd's Rep. 418 at 432, the principle stated in the text above was held at first instance not to apply because the contract had become ineffective by reason of failure of a condition precedent, without default of the allegedly repudiating party, *before* acceptance of any repudiation by the other party; the decision was affirmed on appeal without further reference to the present point: [1999] 1 Lloyd's Rep. 483. Dawson 96 L.Q.R. 239 argues that *Universal Cargo Carriers Corp v Citati* [1957] 2 Q.B. 401 is inconsistent with the explanation of the *British and Beningtons* case given in the text above. But the claim in the *Citati* case was made *against* the party alleged to be unable to perform (the charterer) while in the *British and Beningtons* case it was made *by* that party. Moreover, in the *Citati* case the charterer was already in breach (actual and anticipatory) at the time of the shipowner's refusal to perform while in the *British and Beningtons* case the sellers were not in breach at the time of the buyer's refusal. The crucial issue in the *Citati* case was simply whether the charterer's breach was sufficiently serious to justify the shipowner's termination.

[95] i.e. one that satisfied the requirement of "substantial failure" (paras 18–032—18–034) or fell within an exception to that requirement (paras 18–043—18–086). In *Braithwaite v Foreign Hardwood Co* [1905] 2 K.B. 543 A had already shipped non-conforming goods before B's repudiation; but there are at least three possible reasons why this did not justify that repudiation: (1) A had not yet tendered the goods: *Taylor v Oakes Roncoroni & Co* (1922) 38 T.L.R. 349 at 351; affirmed (1922) 38 T.L.R. 349 at 517; (2) A still had the opportunity to cure the breach (at fn.97) and was induced by B's repudiation not to make use of it: cf. below, at fn.114; and (3) as the contract was on c.i.f. terms (see 74 L.J.K.B. 688 at 694) A's shipment of non-conforming goods was a breach only of an independent covenant and hence did not justify B's repudiation: para.17–023. See further *Benjamin's Sale of Goods*, 10th edn (2018), paras 19–184—19–188.

[96] *Glencore Grain Rotterdam BV v LORICO* [1997] 2 Lloyd's Rep. 386; cf. *The Energy Progress* [1993] 1 Lloyd's Rep. 355 at 358; *Aircraft Purchase Fleet Ltd v Compagnia Area Italiana SpA* [2018] EWHC 3315 (Comm).

[97] See para.17–004.

excuse he can (in general) rely on it later even though he did not state it, or even know of it, at the time of his refusal to accept performance.[98]

**Pre-termination non-repudiatory breach by injured party.** Before terminating the contract on account of B's repudiation, A may himself have committed a breach, but one which did not justify B's repudiation, e.g. a breach of an independent promise.[99] Termination by A does not affect his liability for that pre-termination breach;[100] so that the damages to which A is entitled on account of B's wrongful repudiation will be reduced by those for which he is liable in respect of his own pre-termination breach.[101] Those damages will prima facie be the amount by which A's breach reduces the value of his performance.[102] 17–028

### *(ii) Where injured party does not terminate the contract*

The reason for the rule that A may be entitled to damages for B's repudiation, without having to show that he could have performed, is that, when A accepts B's repudiation, he is liberated from his own duty to perform.[103] That reasoning obviously cannot apply where A does not accept the repudiation. In such a case, A continues to be bound by his own duties under the contract, so that his failure to perform these duties, even after B's repudiation, can (if not induced by B's repudiation)[104] amount to a breach by A. Such a breach will make A liable in damages,[105] and, if it is repudiatory,[106] it will also justify B's refusal to perform and so absolve B from liability in damages to A.[107] 17–029

Where A does not accept B's repudiation and then commits a breach which does *not* justify B's refusal to perform (e.g. because it is a breach of an independent promise),[108] A's breach will nevertheless be relevant to the damages to which A is entitled on account of B's repudiation. At the least, those damages will (as in the case where A has terminated) be reduced by the damages for which A is liable by reason of his own breach, e.g. by the amount by which the value of goods delivered by A is reduced by reason of a defect in them. There are, moreover, circumstances in which, if A has not terminated the contract, B can rely on A's breach so as to reduce still further the damages for which B is liable by reason of his repudiation. This possibility arises where A's breach, though not originally of such a kind as to justify B's repudiation, later acquires that character. Where goods are sold on c.i.f. terms, the buyer is not justified in refusing to pay

[98] See para.17–062.
[99] See para.17–019.
[100] See para.18–022.
[101] *Gill & Duffus SA v Berger & Co Inc* [1984] A.C. 382 at 390 (where a "certification clause" in the contract excluded such liability).
[102] See para.20–053.
[103] See para.17–027.
[104] See para.17–027.
[105] *Regent OHG Aisenstadt und Barig v Francesco of Jermyn Street* [1983] 3 All E.R. 327 at 335.
[106] In the sense described in fn.95.
[107] See *The Simona* [1989] A.C. 788, where A's failure was not a breach but justified cancellation under an express cancelling clause in the contract; Marston [1988] C.L.J. 340; Carter [1989] L.M.C.L.Q. 81.
[108] See para.17–019.

against *documents* merely because the *goods* were not, when shipped, in conformity with the contract; but such non-conformity may give him the right to reject the goods, a right that he will usually exercise when the goods arrive at the contractual destination and are actually delivered to him.[109] That stage is never reached if the seller terminates the contract on the buyer's wrongful refusal to pay against documents;[110] but if the seller does *not* terminate the contract, and the defect in the goods is such as to give the buyer the right to reject them on arrival, then the buyer will be able to argue that he would, even if he had duly paid against documents, have rejected the goods on arrival and so have become entitled to the return of the money that he ought to have paid at the earlier stage of tender of documents.[111] The effect of this argument is that the seller's damages will be merely nominal: he will have lost nothing but the worthless right to be paid a sum of money which he would (had it been paid) have later become liable to repay.[112] Such an argument is not, however, available to the buyer where it was still open to the seller to have cured his breach[113] and his failure to do so was induced by the buyer's wrongful repudiation.[114] If the seller's failure to cure was induced in this way, the buyer cannot rely on it in reduction of damages, any more than he can rely on the seller's original failure to perform (when so induced) on the issue of liability.[115]

### *(iii) Evaluation*

**17–030** The rule that A is entitled to terminate the contract and to recover damages where his own inability to perform is induced by B's repudiation is generally regarded as uncontroversial. But there is dispute about the merit of the rule that A has the same rights where he could not have performed even if B had not repudiated and where his inability to perform was not in any way induced by B's conduct. This aspect of the rule can be criticised by saying that B is made liable in damages for his failure to perform, or merely for saying that he will not perform, even though he may not thereby cause any prejudice to A. This was the view taken by Teare J in *The Glory Wealth*.[116] In that case a charterer, B, had repudiated a contract of affreightment by refusing to declare laycans.[117] The shipowner, A, accepted B's repudiation and terminated the contract. B submitted that A was not entitled to

[109] See para.17–023.

[110] As in *Gill & Duffus SA v Berger & Co Inc* [1984] A.C. 382.

[111] See *Henry Dean & Sons (Sydney) Ltd v O'Day Pty Ltd* (1929) 39 C.L.R. 330 at 340, so far as it relates to the *seller's* claim; the disapproval of that decision in *Gill & Duffus SA v Berger & Co Inc* [1984] A.C. 382 relates to the *buyer's* claim only; and in the *Gill & Duffus* case itself the House of Lords treated the seller's termination as crucial to the success of his claim.

[112] cf. *The Mihalis Angelos* [1971] 1 Q.B. 641; para.18–077. An alternative view is that the seller's damages are nominal only if the defect makes the goods worthless: see *Bunge Corp v Vegetable Vitamin Foods (Private) Ltd* [1985] 1 Lloyd's Rep. 613 at 620; but the buyer's case is not that *the goods* are worthless: it is that the seller's *right to have them accepted* is worthless because the buyer's option to reject them would certainly have been exercised.

[113] See at fn.97.

[114] This is one possible explanation of *Braithwaite v Foreign Hardwood Co* [1905] 2 K.B. 543; fn.96; cf. *Sheffield v Conran* (1987) 22 Con L.R. 108.

[115] cf. para.17–026.

[116] [2013] EWHC 3153 (Comm); [2014] 2 W.L.R. 1405.

[117] The dates upon which the vessel must be available for loading.

damages representing the difference between the contract rate and the market rate on the basis that subsequent events[118] had shown that A could not have provided the vessels required because of a deterioration in its financial position brought about by a precipitous collapse in freight rates. This submission was rejected by the arbitrators, but accepted by Teare J, though he found on the facts that A would have been able to perform.[119]

Teare J was particularly concerned that a rejection of B's submission would have run contrary to the "compensatory principle", i.e. that A should only be awarded damages to put him in the same position as if B had fulfilled its obligations. However, this resulted in the conclusion that it was for A, as claimant, to prove that he would have been able to perform.[120] In circumstances where B is guilty of a repudiation which A has accepted, this is a debatable proposition.[121] B can avoid any hardship by simply waiting till A's performance is due: if it is not forthcoming at that time it is A, not B, who will be liable in damages; and any hardship that the rule may cause to B if he repudiates before that time is mitigated by the qualifications on its scope that have been stated above.[122] Alternatively, B can try to justify his own failure to perform on the basis of an anticipatory breach by A.[123] It will be for B to prove that A could not have performed in the future to the standard required for an anticipatory breach,[124] and he should be required to do so as at the date of B's own failure to perform, i.e. without the benefit of relying on subsequent events.[125] For these reasons, it does not seem that the rule causes undue prejudice to B and nor is it an unjustified departure from the "compensatory principle". It can be justified on the ground that it promotes certainty by discouraging premature repudiation.

## 4. ENTIRE AND SEVERABLE OBLIGATIONS

### (a) Entire obligations

**Definition.** A contractual obligation is said to be "entire" when the contract requires it to be *completely* performed by one party (A) before the other (B) is to pay, or to render such other counter-performance as may have been agreed. 17–031

[118] The case is also therefore relevant to the question of whether the court should take into account events which are known to have happened after the date of acceptance of the repudiation: see para.20–087.

[119] Principally because A's obligation in this respect was one which could have been performed vicariously: see para.17–007.

[120] Having found that A would have been able to perform, the only alternative hypothesis which Teare J deals with is one in which it is "clear" that he would not have been able to perform. It is not clear what approach should be taken in circumstances falling between these two extremes.

[121] Peel 131 L.Q.R. 29; contrast Winterton [2014] L.M.C.L.Q 124; McLauchlan [2015] J.B.L. 530. And see para.20–087.

[122] i.e. at fnn.97–113.

[123] cf. *Acre 1127 Ltd v De Montfort Fine Art Ltd* [2011] EWCA Civ 87 at [51] (for further proceedings, see: [2011] EWCA Civ 130). This would not provide B with a defence to liability in a case like *Gill & Duffus SA v Berger & Co Inc* [1984] A.C. 382 where B's obligation to pay was an independent promise: see para.17–019.

[124] See paras 17–088–17–090.

[125] See para.20–089.

Complete performance by A is sometimes said to be a "condition precedent" to B's liability; but the cases are not necessarily concerned with disputes as to the *order* of performance.[126] Often the dispute arises because A's purported performance, though rendered in the stipulated order, is in some way incomplete or defective.

17–032 **No recovery for partial performance.** Where A fails to complete performance of an entire obligation, B is entitled to refuse to pay even though the deficiency in A's performance causes him little prejudice or none at all.[127] At common law A is not even generally entitled to any other recompense for the partial performance which he has rendered. In *Cutter v Powell*[128] a seaman agreed to serve on a ship bound from Jamaica for Liverpool; he was to be paid 30 guineas "ten days after the ship arrives at Liverpool … provided he proceeds, continues and does his duty … from hence to the port of Liverpool." On 2 August the ship sailed from Jamaica; she arrived at Liverpool on 9 October, but the seaman had died on 20 September. It was held that his administratrix could not recover for the work he had done before his death; for the contract meant that nothing was to be paid unless and until he had served for the whole voyage. At the ordinary rates of pay then prevailing, he would have earned only £8 for such a voyage. The higher rate of pay seems to have been intended to throw the risk of his completing the voyage on him. Lord Kenyon CJ said: "It was a kind of insurance".[129] The result was that the administratrix recovered neither the 30 guineas, nor a proportionate part of it, nor a reasonable sum for the six or seven weeks' service which the deceased had rendered. According to one case, the same rule applies even where a contract of employment is terminated by mutual consent.[130]

Similarly, where a contract for the carriage of goods by sea provides that freight is to become due on arrival of the goods at the agreed destination, the shipowner cannot recover either the stipulated freight, or freight pro rata, if he is compelled to abandon the voyage by perils of the sea and to discharge the cargo at an intermediate port.[131] The rule can be excluded by contrary provision in the contract, e.g. by one to the effect that freight is to be deemed to have been *earned* on loading.[132] In such a case, the shipowner can recover the freight even though

[126] cf. para.17–014.

[127] Where, however, the partial performance confers a benefit on him which he voluntarily accepts, he may be under an obligation to pay a reasonable sum for it: see para.17–041 and following.

[128] (1795) 6 T.R. 320; Stoljar 34 Can. Bar. Rev. 288; Dockray 117 L.Q.R. 626.

[129] *Cutter v Powell* (1795) 6 T.R. 320 at 324. Quaere whether it was really insurance against the death of members of the crew, or against their desertion. For possible effects of the Apportionment Act 1870 and of the Law Reform (Frustrated Contracts) Act 1943 in a case like *Cutter v Powell*, see paras 17–047, 19–112.

[130] *Lambourn v Cruden* (1841) 2 M. & G. 253.

[131] *Vlierboom v Chapman* (1844) 13 M. & W. 230; *St Enoch Shipping Co Ltd v Phosphate Mining Co* [1916] 2 K.B. 624; cf. *The Fort Kip* [1985] 2 Lloyd's Rep. 168. See, similarly, where the ship is abandoned at sea and later saved by third parties: *The Kathleen* (1874) L.R. 4 A. & E. 269; contrast *Bradley v H Newsom, Sons & Co* [1919] A.C. 16 (where there was no abandonment).

[132] *The Dominique* [1989] A.C. 1056; Crabtree [1989] L.M.C.L.Q. 289; *The Karin Vatis* [1988] 2 Lloyd's Rep. 330.

the contract provides that it is to be *paid* on or after unloading: that provision affects only the *time* of payment, not the creation of the obligation to pay.[133]

The same principle is again illustrated by *Sumpter v Hedges*[134] where a builder agreed to build two houses for the defendant on the latter's land for a lump sum of £565. When the houses were still unfinished the builder told the defendant that he had run out of money and could not finish the work; and the defendant later completed the houses himself. It was held that the builder could not recover the agreed sum; nor could he recover a reasonable remuneration for his work as there was no evidence of a "new contract" to pay such a sum.[135]

**Sale of goods.** As a general rule, a contract for the sale of goods is considered to impose an entire obligation with regard to the quantity contracted for.[136] If the seller fails to deliver the correct quantity the buyer is not bound to accept and pay (though if he does accept he must pay at the contract rate).[137] The rule applies where the seller delivers *more* than the quantity contracted for just as much as where he delivers less.[138] The rule is, however, subject to a number of qualifications. First, it can be varied by the provisions of the contract, e.g. by one calling for delivery of "about" the stipulated quantity, or for "five per cent more or less"[139] (though such a margin must not be exceeded).[140] Secondly, the rule does not permit rejection for a wholly trivial discrepancy, e.g. for an excess of 55lbs, in a contract calling for delivery of 4,950 tons of wheat.[141] Thirdly, the rule is subject to a statutory exception which applies where the buyer does *not* deal as a consumer: in such a case he may not reject the whole of the quantity actually delivered on account of a shortfall or excess which is "so slight that it would be unreasonable for him to do so".[142] It seems that a defect may be "slight" for the purpose of this exception even though it is not wholly trivial within the common law exception stated above. The statutory exception applies only where the discrepancy is slight *and* it would be unreasonable for the buyer to reject. Thus it does not apply merely because the discrepancy is "slight", for it may nevertheless be commercially reasonable for the buyer to reject;[143] nor, where the discrepancy is *not* "slight", does the exception apply merely because it would be unreasonable for the buyer to reject (e.g. where his sole motive for rejection was to escape from 17–033

[133] See the authorities cited in fn.132; contrast *The Lorna I* [1983] 1 Lloyd's Rep. 373 (where there was no stipulation as to when the freight was *earned*, but only one as to when it was to be *paid*).
[134] [1898] 1 Q.B. 673; cf. *Munro v Butt* (1858) 8 E. & B. 738; *Bolton v Mahadeva* [1972] 1 W.L.R. 1009.
[135] For this requirement, see para.17–042.
[136] See *Oxendale v Wetherell* (1829) 9 B. & C. 386–387; *Reuter v Sala* (1879) 4 C.P.D. 239; cf. *Cobec Brazilian Trading & Warehousing Corp v Alfred C Toepfer* [1983] 2 Lloyd's Rep. 386.
[137] Sale of Goods Act 1979 s.30(1); Consumer Rights Act 2015 s.25(1). Conversely, the buyer cannot insist on delivery of less than he agreed to accept: *Honck v Muller* (1881) 7 Q.B.D. 92.
[138] Sale of Goods Act 1979 s.30(2); Consumer Rights Act 2015 s.25(2).
[139] e.g. *Re Thornett and Fehr and Yuills* [1921] 1 K.B. 219; Sale of Goods Act 1979 s.30(5); cf. Consumer Rights Act 2015 s.25(8).
[140] *Tamvaco v Lucas* (1859) 1 E. & E. 581.
[141] *Shipton Anderson & Co v Weil Bros* [1912] 1 K.B. 574.
[142] Sale of Goods Act 1979 s.30(2A).
[143] e.g. because he has resold under a contract from which s.30(2A) is excluded: see at fn.145.

a bad bargain).[144] The uncertainty caused by the vagueness of the statutory exception is mitigated by the fact that the exception can be excluded by contrary agreement;[145] and it is submitted that it would be so excluded where the contract had expressly stipulated for a margin and that margin had been exceeded. Finally, the rule entitling the buyer to reject merely on account of quantitative defects does not apply where the contract provides for delivery by instalments, so that, where short delivery is made of one instalment the buyer is not entitled to refuse to accept either future deliveries, or even the instalment in question.[146]

17–034 **Complete performance justifiably prevented by other party.** The rule that a party cannot recover anything for partial performance of an entire obligation also applies where that party was willing to complete performance but was justifiably prevented from completing by the other party, e.g. where an employee is dismissed for misconduct.

## (b) Severable obligations

17–035 **Definition.** A contract imposes severable obligations if payment under it is due from time to time as performance of a specified part of the contract is rendered. This is the situation under contracts of employment, which typically provide for payment to be made at weekly or monthly intervals, even though the contract may be expressed to continue for longer periods. Similarly, in building contracts the rule in *Sumpter v Hedges*[147] is often excluded by provision for "progress payments", to be made at specified stages of completion of the work. The principle can be further illustrated by contrasting *Cutter v Powell*[148] with the case in which a seaman agrees to serve at a fixed rate *per month*; under such a contract, he can recover his pay for each completed month although he fails to complete the voyage for which he was engaged.[149] This would be so even though no money was actually to be *paid over* until the end of the voyage. On the same principle, a piece-rate worker does not forfeit wages already earned simply because it was agreed that nothing should actually be paid out to him till the end of each working week and he left or was lawfully dismissed before the end of the week.[150] Similarly, a contract for the sale of goods may be made severable by providing for delivery and payment in instalments. In all these cases, no more than the specified part of the performance need be rendered before the corresponding payment can be claimed. It is also true that, as a general rule, the specified part must be rendered in full. Thus an employee cannot at common

[144] As in *Cunliffe v Harrison* (1851) 6 Ex. 901; para.17–039, where the excess (of 50 per cent) was far from "slight".

[145] Sale of Goods Act 1989 s.30(5); cf. Consumer Rights Act 2015 s.25(8).

[146] *Regent OHG Aisenstadt und Barig v Francesco of Jermyn Street* [1981] 3 All E.R. 327: such a case is governed by s.31(2) of the Sale of Goods Act 1979. For the contrast between s.31(2) and s.30(1), see para.18–035, fn.180. Quaere whether s.30(1) should not apply to the short-delivered instalment itself. For consumer contracts, see the Consumer Rights Act 2015 s.26.

[147] [1898] 1 Q.B. 673; para.17–032.

[148] (1795) 6 T.R. 320; para.17–032.

[149] *Taylor v Laird* (1856) 25 L.J. Ex. 329; *Button v Thompson* (1869) L.R. 4 C.P. 330.

[150] *Warburton v Heyworth* (1880) 6 Q.B.D. 1.

law[151] recover his current pay if he is justifiably dismissed for misconduct during the period at the end of which he is to be paid.[152]

**Recovery for partial performance.** Where a contract imposes severable obligations, a party who has fully performed the specified part can recover the corresponding payment even though his failure to complete the whole of the promised performance is a breach of contract. In *Ritchie v Atkinson*[153] a shipowner agreed to carry a cargo at a stipulated rate *per ton*. He carried only part of the cargo, and was entitled to recover a corresponding proportion of the freight. But he was later held liable in damages for failing to carry the rest of the cargo.[154] There is a similar liability in damages where performance of one of the specified parts is completed but is defective because it in some way falls short of the performance promised. For example, an employee may serve for the full payment period but fail or refuse, in the course of that period, to carry out some task which he was contractually obliged to perform. The employer is then entitled to damages in respect of that failure or refusal even though he may be bound to pay the agreed remuneration.[155] Whether he is so bound, and what other remedies may be available to him, are matters to be discussed later in this chapter.[156] **17–036**

### (c) Distinction between entire and severable obligations

**Obligations, and not contracts, are entire or severable.** In discussions of the cases so far considered, it is sometimes said that the *contracts* are entire or severable. But this is misleading: what is entire or severable is a particular *obligation*[157] arising under the contract. The point is most easily illustrated by reference to contracts for the carriage of goods by sea. Suppose a shipowner agrees to carry 1,000 tons at a stated rate, due on delivery, for each ton carried to London. If he carries 1,000 tons to Southampton he is not entitled to any freight;[158] if he carries 750 tons to London he is prima facie entitled to three-quarters of the freight;[159] and if he carries 1,000 tons to London but the **17–037**

[151] For the position under the Apportionment Act 1870 s.2, see para.17–047.

[152] *Ridgway v Hungerford Market Co* (1835) 3 A. & E. 171; *Boston Deep Sea Fishing & Ice Co v Ansell* (1888) 39 Ch D. 339. Semble that he can recover remuneration which became due before dismissal though it was earned after a breach of duty justifying dismissal: *Healey v SA Française Rubastic* [1917] 1 K.B. 947; the employer's claim for damages in the form of the salary paid may be offset by the value of the work done: *Brandeaux Advisers Ltd v Chadwick* [2010] EWHC 3241 (QB); [2011] I.R.L.R. 224 at [56]. For the position where the employee is *not* dismissed see para.17–045.

[153] (1808) 10 East 295.

[154] *Ritchie v Atkinson* (1808) 10 East 295 at 530.

[155] *Sim v Rotherham Metropolitan BC* [1987] Ch. 216; *Miles v Wakefield Metropolitan DC* [1987] A.C. 539 (where the measure of damages was said to be, obiter, the wages for the "lost hours of work". Strictly speaking the measure of damages should be the loss suffered by the employer, which is not necessarily the same. cf. paras 20–042, 22–020).

[156] See paras 17–038, 17–045.

[157] cf. *Cobec Brazilian Trading & Warehousing Corp v Alfred C Toepfer* [1982] 1 Lloyd's Rep. 528 at 531 ("indivisible obligation"); affirmed [1983] 2 Lloyd's Rep. 386; *Baltic Shipping Co Ltd v Dillon* (1993) 176 C.L.R. 344 at 350.

[158] See para.17–032, para.17–044.

[159] *Ritchie v Atkinson* (1808) 10 East 295. If the contract provides for "lump sum" freight, the shipowner will, in such a situation, be entitled to the entire freight: *Merchant Shipping Co v Armitage*

goods arrive damaged, he will be entitled to full freight[160] unless the damage is so serious that the description under which the goods have been shipped ceases to apply to them, e.g. where cement solidifies as a result of being damaged by water.[161]

A building contract may provide for payments as the work progresses, subject to a "retention fund" to be paid over on completion. There is then a series of severable obligations to complete each stage as well as an entire obligation to complete the whole.[162] In *Sumpter v Hedges*[163] the builder's obligation was entire with respect to the quantity of work to be done; but his claim would not have been dismissed merely because he had failed in some other way to comply with the contract, e.g. by completing a week late[164] or (unless the contract had expressly made his right to payment subject to his doing the work strictly in accordance with the contract)[165] by completing the buildings with minor defects. In *Hoenig v Isaacs*[166] the claimant contracted to redecorate and furnish the defendant's flat for £750. There were minor defects in the furniture, which could have been made good for £55. The defendant argued that the claimant was entitled to no more than a reasonable remuneration for work done in accordance with the contract. But the court held that he was entitled to be paid at the full contract rate (less the cost of making the defects good), as he had substantially completed the work. The obligation of a seller of goods is, again, generally entire as to quantity, but if the correct quantity is delivered he may be able to enforce the contract in spite of the fact that the goods are defective in quality.[167] Of course failure to perform an obligation which is not entire may give the other party a right to terminate the contract on some other ground, e.g. that the failure is substantial;[168] but it does not release him from liability under the present rule.

17–038 **A question of construction.** In the cases so far discussed the distinction between entire and severable obligations is clearly settled either by the express terms of the contract or by commercial practice recognised by law. But there may be no

(1873) L.R. 9 Q.B. 99; *Thomas v Harrowing SS Co* [1915] A.C. 58. He will also be entitled to the whole freight if the contract provides for freight to be computed by reference to the quantity taken on board though it is only payable after discharge of the cargo: see *The Aries* [1977] 1 W.L.R. 185; *The Metula* [1978] 2 Lloyd's Rep. 5; unless the contract provides for a deduction to be made if the quantity delivered is less than that taken on board, as in *The Olympic Brilliance* [1982] 2 Lloyd's Rep. 205.

[160] *Dakin v Oxley* (1864) 15 C.B. (N.S.) 646; *The Brede* [1974] Q.B. 233 (no freight allowed in respect of a part of the goods that was *lost*: see [1972] 2 Lloyd's Rep. at 514, 519; but the Court of Appeal was concerned only with the part of the goods that was *damaged*: [1974] Q.B. at 245).

[161] *Duthie v Hilton* (1868) L.R. 4 C.P. 138; cf. *The Caspian Sea* [1980] 1 W.L.R. 48; *Dakin v Oxley* (1864) 15 C.B. (N.S.) 646 at 664; contrast *Britannia Distribution Co Ltd v Factor Pace Ltd* [1998] 2 Lloyd's Rep. 420 at 423.

[162] *Hoenig v Isaacs* [1952] 2 All E.R. 176 at 181.

[163] [1898] 1 Q.B. 673.

[164] *Sumpter v Hedges* [1898] 1 Q.B. 673 at 676.

[165] *Eshelby v Federated European Bank* [1932] 1 K.B. 423.

[166] [1952] 2 All E.R. 176; approving *Dakin & Co Ltd v Lee* [1916] 1 K.B. 566; which had been doubted in *Eshelby v Federated European Bank* [1932] 1 K.B. 423; *Williams v Roffey Bros & Nicholls (Contractors) Ltd* [1991] 1 Q.B. 1; fn.182.

[167] e.g. as in *The Hansa Nord* [1976] Q.B. 44; para.18–052, fn.317.

[168] See para.18–032.

rule of law on the point and the contract may be silent or self-contradictory, e.g. where A employs B to paint A's house for £1,000 but fails to say when it is to be paid; or where the contract provides for payment of "£200 per room payable on completion". In such cases the question whether a particular obligation is entire or severable is one of construction; and where a party agrees to do work under a contract, the courts are reluctant to construe the contract so as to require complete performance before any payment becomes due: "Contracts may be so made; but they require plain words to shew that such a bargain was really intended".[169] If the contract contains contradictory provisions the courts tend to give greater weight to those making the obligation to work a severable one. Thus, where a contract provided: (1) for payment at a fixed rate per month; but (2) that nothing was to be paid till performance was complete, the first clause prevailed over the second, i.e. the contract was construed as imposing severable obligations.[170] In one type of case this hostility towards entire obligations has been reinforced by statute: an agreement by a seaman to abandon his right to wages in case the ship is lost is void.[171]

**Sale of goods.** The reason why the courts are reluctant to construe obligations to do work as entire is that such a construction will often lead to the unjust enrichment of the party receiving the partial or defective performance.[172] There is no such reluctance in contracts for the sale of goods: we have seen that the buyer is not generally bound to accept a different quantity from that contracted for;[173] nor is he bound, unless the contract so provides,[174] to accept delivery in instalments.[175] This state of the law does not give rise to any danger of unjust enrichment: if a buyer of goods rejects delivery of the wrong quantity, the goods will be returned to the seller. But even in this type of case rejection may cause a different type of hardship to the seller, namely that of throwing back on him the risk of market fluctuations. In *Cunliffe v Harrison*[176] a seller of wine delivered more than the agreed quantity. It was held that the buyer was not bound to accept any part of the wine, "although it may be that the refusal to take the wine was not bona fide but grounded upon the fact that the wine had fallen in price".[177] 17–039

[169] *Button v Thompson* (1869) L.R. 4 C.P. 330 at 342; cf. *Roberts v Havelock* (1832) 3 B. & Ad. 404; *Davidson v Jones-Fenleigh* (1980) 124 S.J. 204; *Smales v Lea* [2011] EWCA Civ 1325; 140 Con L.R. 70 at [43].

[170] See *The Juliana* (1822) 2 Dods. 504.

[171] Merchant Shipping Act 1995 s.38(1) (reversing the common law rule that freight was the "mother of wages").

[172] See para.17–042.

[173] See para.17–033.

[174] On this question of construction, contrast *Reuter v Sala* (1879) 4 C.P.D. 239 with *Brandt v Lawrence* (1876) 1 Q.B.D. 344.

[175] Sale of Goods Act 1979 s.31(1). For consumer contracts, see the Consumer Rights Act 2015 s.26.

[176] (1851) 6 Ex. 901.

[177] *Cunliffe v Harrison* (1851) 6 Ex. 901 at 907; of course it is possible that the seller was not acting bona fide either but that he was trying to unload an excessive quantity on a falling market. For the potential application of the Sale of Goods Act 1979 s.30(2A), see para.17–033.

### (d) So-called doctrine of substantial performance[178]

17–040 Cases such as *Hoenig v Isaacs*[179] are sometimes explained on the ground that the claimant had "substantially" performed an "entire contract".[180] It is submitted that the explanation is unsatisfactory since it is based on the error that *contracts*, as opposed to particular *obligations*, can be entire.[181] The basis of *Hoenig v Isaacs* is that the builder, even if he was under an entire obligation as to the quantity of work to be done, was under no such obligation as to its quality.[182] Defects of quality therefore fell to be considered under the general requirement of substantial failure, and on the facts there was no such failure.[183] To say that an obligation is entire *means* that it must be completely performed before payment becomes due. Suppose a contract is made to carry goods from Melbourne to London and the freight is payable on delivery in London. If the goods are carried only to Southampton, the carrier may have "substantially" performed; but he is not entitled to the freight.[184] In relation to "entire" obligations, there is no scope for any doctrine of "substantial performance".[185]

### (e) Voluntary acceptance of benefit

17–041 Where a party terminates for breach of an entire obligation[186] but "voluntarily" accepts the partial or defective[187] performance he must make some payment for it. The present principle applies only if the benefit is accepted "voluntarily".[188] A person is not considered to accept a benefit "voluntarily" if he merely takes possession of his own property. Thus, a shipowner who discharges cargo at an intermediate port cannot recover freight pro rata merely because the cargo-owner has under protest taken possession of his own goods there.[189] In *Sumpter v*

[178] Beck 38 M.L.R. 413.
[179] [1952] 2 All E.R. 176; para.17–037.
[180] *Geipel v Smith* (1872) L.R. 7 Q.B. 404 at 411; cf. *Dakin v Lee* [1916] 1 K.B. 566 at 598; *Sim v Rotherham MBC* [1987] Ch. 216 at 253; *Williams v Roffey Bros & Nicholls (Contractors) Ltd* [1991] 1 Q.B. 1 at 8–10; no such view is in terms stated by the court in *Hoenig v Isaacs* [1952] 2 All E.R. 176.
[181] See para.17–037.
[182] *Williams v Roffey Bros & Nicholls (Contractors) Ltd* [1991] 1 Q.B. 1 (where a sub-contractor recovered instalments subject to a "small deduction for defective and *incomplete* items" ([1991] 1 Q.B. 1 at 17) purports to follow *Hoenig v Isaacs*, but that case was concerned only with defective, not with incomplete, items.
[183] Contrast *Lawson v Supasink* (1984) Tr. L. 37 (where qualitative defects in kitchen installations were sufficiently serious to justify termination).
[184] See para.17–032; cf. *Metcalfe v Britannia Ironworks* (1877) 2 Q.B.D. 423.
[185] Even when correctly understood, it has no application at all where the defendant is not in breach, e.g. where a builder has done less than the work anticipated in a fixed-price contract: *SWI Ltd v P & I Data Services Ltd* [2007] EWCA Civ 663; [2007] B.L.R. 430.
[186] In the absence of termination, the parties' rights and obligations continue to be governed by the contract, as opposed to the law of restitution, but see the employment cases discussed at para.17–045 where the contract had not been terminated.
[187] i.e. where the defect prevents complete performance of the obligation in question: see para.17–037; cf. *Bolton v Mahadeva* [1972] 1 W.L.R. 1009, para.17–042.
[188] *Christy v Row* (1808) 1 Taunt. 300; cf. *Lambourn v Cruden* (1841) 2 M. & G. 253 at 256.
[189] *Metcalfe v Britannia Ironworks Co* (1877) 2 Q.B.D. 423; cf. para.17–032.

*Hedges*[190] the builder's claim for the reasonable value of his work was dismissed on similar grounds. Such a claim would succeed only if a "new contract"[191] to pay a reasonable sum could be inferred. No such inference could be drawn from the mere fact that the defendant had reoccupied his own land with the partly completed buildings on it; he had no real "option whether he will take the benefit of the work done or not."[192] He did, however, "voluntarily" make use of certain loose materials left by the builder on the site and was held liable for the reasonable value of these materials.

**A concern to avoid unjust enrichment.** The object of the requirement of a "new contract" is, no doubt, to protect the party receiving the partial or defective performance, who may be prejudiced by having to pay pro rata or a reasonable sum. He may have suffered loss in consequence of the failure in performance, and, if the failure does not amount to a breach,[193] termination of the contract may be his only remedy.[194] Even if there has been a breach, the damages legally recoverable for it may fall short of the actual loss suffered. The victim may have stipulated for complete performance before payment precisely in order to protect himself against these risks. On the other hand, the failure in performance may not cause any loss at all,[195] or it may cause a loss worth much less than the value of the partial performance. In such cases the requirement of a "new contract" may lead to the unjust enrichment of the party by whom such performance has been received. Under the rule in *Sumpter v Hedges* a landowner may get nearly completed buildings for nothing. This did not actually happen in the leading case itself, in which considerable payments had been made to the builder on account of the work.[196] But in *Bolton v Mahadeva*[197] a builder recovered nothing for his defective performance of a contract to install a central heating system for £560, even though no part of this sum had been paid to him, the defects in his work cost only £170 to put right, and the house-owner's other damages were assessed at £15. Again, where a shipowner discharges goods at an intermediate port, the cargo-owner may get the benefit of having them carried a considerable distance for nothing. This possibility is strikingly illustrated by a case in which it was held that the cargo-owner was not bound to pay anything even though the failure to carry the goods to their destination apparently benefited him, the goods having been sold for *more* at the intermediate port than they were worth at the agreed 17–042

[190] [1898] 1 Q.B. 673; para.17–032.

[191] The language of a "new contract" may no longer be entirely apt given the rejection of "quasi-contract" as the basis of a common law restitutionary claim (*Westdeutsche Landesbank Girozentrale v Islington LBC* [1996] A.C. 669 at 710; *Cleveland Bridge UK Ltd v Multiplex Constructions UK Ltd* [2010] EWCA Civ 139 at [118]–[138]). It is retained either on the basis that it is confined to a "genuine" implied contract (*Chitty on Contracts*, 33rd edn (2018), para.21–036) or, as exemplifying the need in the present group of cases for a *voluntary* acceptance of the benefit.

[192] *Westdeutsche Landesbank Girozentrale v Islington LBC* [1996] A.C. 669 at 676.

[193] e.g. because it is the subject of some lawful excuse: see para.17–059.

[194] See, generally, Ch.18.

[195] See at fn.198.

[196] The value of the work done is stated to be "about £333" and the builder had received £219 (67 L.J.Q.B. 545) or £119 plus two horses worth £100 (46 W.R. 464).

[197] [1972] 1 W.L.R. 1009.

destination.[198] At the same time the requirement of a "new" contract may bear very harshly on the party conferring the benefit; and therefore the requirement that acceptance of the benefit must be "voluntary" so as to support the inference of a new contract is, or may be, modified in a number of situations.

17–043 **Sale of goods.** The clearest modification of the requirement of voluntary acceptance can be seen in cases in which a seller of goods delivers the wrong quantity, e.g. a quantity less than that contracted for. In such a case the buyer can generally reject the goods[199] but if he "accepts" them he "must pay for them at the contract rate."[200] This acceptance need not be "voluntary" in the full sense, for the buyer may do acts amounting to "acceptance" before he knows of the defect in delivery.[201]

17–044 **Deviation.** A second situation in which the requirement of "voluntary" acceptance may be modified arises where a carrier by sea deviates.[202] This gives the cargo-owner the right to terminate the contract;[203] but he may not exercise this right and may accept the goods after the carrier has carried them to their agreed destination. This acceptance of the goods is no more "voluntary" than taking possession of goods which have been discharged without their owner's consent at an intermediate port; but dicta in the House of Lords in *Hain SS Co Ltd v Tate & Lyle Ltd*[204] support the view that the shipowner may in such a case be entitled to a reasonable freight. This is not necessarily the same as the stipulated freight, so that the risk of any fall in freight rates would be on the carrier; but it seems most unlikely that he would be allowed to rely on the deviation to secure the benefit of any rise in freight rates.

17–045 **Contracts of employment.** A third modification of the requirement that acceptance of the benefit must be "voluntary" may exist where breaches of a contract of employment are committed in the course of an industrial dispute. Such a breach may take the form, not only of an outright refusal to work, but also of a refusal merely to carry out certain specified tasks. If (as will often be the case) the refusal amounts to a breach giving rise to the right to terminate,[205] the employer is at common law entitled to dismiss the employee. But he may not exercise that power and instead follow one of three other courses of action. First, he may voluntarily accept such services as the employee is willing to render. In that case, he can at the very least deduct from the employee's wages, by way of

---

[198] *Hopper v Burness* (1876) 1 C.P.D. 137; it was said that there was no hardship to the shipowner as "the proper remedy is by insurance of freight" (at 141).

[199] See para.17–033.

[200] Sale of Goods Act 1979 s.30(1); Consumer Rights Act 2015 s.25(1).

[201] See para.18–106.

[202] For deviation, see para.7–036.

[203] See para.7–036.

[204] (1936) 41 Com. Cas. 350 at 358, 367, doubting contrary dicta in the Court of Appeal 34 Com. Cas. 259 at 285; for the basis of liability, see *Carver on Bills of Lading*, 4th edn (2017), paras 9–036—9–059; cf. *Bornman v Tooke* (1808) 1 Camp. 376. Contrast *Pilbrow v Pearless De Rougement & Co* [1999] 3 All E.R. 355 at 360 (no claim for the reasonable value of the services rendered was made in that case).

[205] See para.17–073.

damages, any loss which he has suffered as a result of the breach.[206] Even if he has not suffered any loss, he can deduct from the employee's pay such part of the agreed wages as is attributable to the work which the employee has refused to perform:[207] that amount (at least) will not have been earned by reason of the employee's failure to perform a condition precedent.[208] Secondly, he may tell the employee that he declines to accept the services (falling short of those due under the contract) which the employee is prepared to render, and actually does render. In that event, the employee is not entitled to pay for any period during which no services are rendered;[209] nor is he entitled to any pay for rendering services falling short of those due, even if the employer has not physically prevented him from rendering them.[210] Thirdly, the employer may accept the services which the employee is prepared to render, and do so, not voluntarily, but "of necessity":[211] he may do this either because he has no practical choice (where he cannot in fact prevent the employee from gaining access to his place of work), or because he is required to accept the services offered in order to mitigate his loss.[212] In such a case there has been no "voluntary" acceptance of a benefit; but there is nevertheless some support for the view that the employer must pay a reasonable remuneration for the services actually rendered.[213] This view seems to be based on unjust enrichment rather than on a "new contract": the employer is liable because he has received a benefit, not because he has impliedly agreed to pay for it. The difficulty in accepting this view, however, arises precisely because in the case put the employer has *not* terminated the contract, so that prima facie the rights and duties of the parties continue to be governed by that contract.[214]

**Wrongful prevention of performance.** In the cases just discussed, the courts were concerned with the reasonable remuneration of the party in breach. If, in a contract under which one party (A) is not to be paid until he completes performance, A begins to perform but the other party (B) wrongfully refuses to let him complete, A can, no doubt, claim damages for breach of contract.[215] Alternatively, he can claim a quantum meruit for the work he has done. In *Planché v Colburn*[216] A agreed to write a book on costume and ancient armour which was to appear in serial form in B's periodical. B stopped publishing the periodical when A had written the greater part of the work, and it was held that A **17–046**

[206] *Sim v Rotherham Metropolitan BC* [1987] Ch. 216, where the action was not for the agreed wages; but for a declaration that the employer was not entitled to deduct damages: see *Miles v Wakefield Metropolitan DC* [1987] A.C. 539 at 574–575.

[207] *Miles v Wakefield Metropolitan DC* [1987] A.C. 539; the contrary assumption made in *Sim v Rotherham Metropolitan BC* [1987] Ch. 216 at 255) is no longer maintainable.

[208] See para.17–015.

[209] *Ticehurst & Thompson v British Telecommunications* [1992] I.C.R. 383.

[210] *Wiluszynski v Tower Hamlets LBC* [1989] I.C.R. 493; Mead 106 L.Q.R. 192; *Macpherson v Lambeth LBC* [1988] I.R.L.R. 470.

[211] *Miles v Wakefield Metropolitan DC* [1987] A.C. 539 at 553.

[212] *Miles v Wakefield Metropolitan DC* [1987] A.C. 539 at 561; cf. para.20–107.

[213] *Miles v Wakefield Metropolitan DC* [1987] A.C. 539 at 553 (Lord Brightman) and 561 (Lord Templeman). The point is left open by Lord Brandon (at 552) and Lord Oliver (at 576).

[214] *Miles v Wakefield Metropolitan DC* [1987] A.C. 539 at 552 (Lord Bridge), and cf. para.22–033.

[215] It is assumed here that A could have completed but for B's wrongful refusal, so that the problem discussed at paras 17–025–17–030, does not arise.

[216] (1831) 8 Bing. 14.

was entitled to a quantum meruit. No benefit appears to have been received by B which may suggest that this rule differs from those applicable when the claim is made by the party in breach.[217] Alternatively, it has been suggested[218] that the award in *Planché v Colburn* is better viewed as being the equivalent of damages and that for claims by the innocent party, just as much as for claims by the party in breach, it is necessary to establish that the defendant has been benefited.[219]

### (f) Apportionment Act 1870

17–047 Section 2 of the Apportionment Act 1870 provides that:

> "All rents, annuities, dividends and other periodical payments in the nature of income … shall … be considered as accruing from day to day, and shall be apportionable in respect of time accordingly."

By s.5 "annuities" includes "salaries and pensions"; and by s.7 the Act does not apply where it is "expressly stipulated that no apportionment shall take place."[220]

It seems that a "periodical" payment refers to a sum or sums payable under a contract at the end of a stipulated time, or at fixed intervals of time. A single lump sum payable for a specific piece of work would not be a periodical payment; and this is one reason why the Act would not apply to a case like *Cutter v Powell*.[221] Nor would the payment be periodical merely because the contract stipulated the time within which the piece of work was to be done: thus the Act would not apply to a case like *Sumpter v Hedges*[222] even though the contract in that case contained a completion date. A bonus, the payment and level of which is dependent upon an uncertain factor, such as the level of profits made by an employer does not qualify as a "salary", nor as a "periodical payment".[223]

In *Fassihi v Item Software (UK) Ltd*[224] the Court of Appeal held that the Act entitles a person whose salary is payable at the end of a stipulated period to recover on a proportionate basis if he works for only part of the period. This decision brought to an end a considerable period of uncertainty about the application of the Act to "part-earned" salary,[225] and it has been followed by the Supreme Court.[226] It did not entirely resolve a further question which is whether the Act can be invoked where the party in question is in breach of contract. This

[217] See paras 17–041–17–045.

[218] Burrows, *The Law of Restitution*, 3rd edn (2010), p.346.

[219] As appears to have been the case in *De Bernardy v Harding* (1853) 8 Exch. 822.

[220] *Hartley v King Edward VI College* [2017] UKSC 39; [2017] 1 W.L.R. 2110.

[221] (1795) 6 T.R. 320; apportionment would also on such facts be excluded by the express terms of the contract: see para.17–032.

[222] *Sumpter v Hedges* [1898] 1 Q.B. 673.

[223] *Vaught v Tel Sell UK Ltd* [2005] EWHC 2404 at [152].

[224] [2004] EWCA Civ 1244; [2004] I.R.L.R. 928.

[225] Earlier authorities providing implicit support for the application of the Act (see the cases to follow) were preferred to those seemingly against (see fn.228): *Moriarty v Regent's Garage Co* [1921] 1 K.B. 423 (reversed on procedural grounds: [1921] 2 K.B. 766, where the issue was left open); *Sim v Rotherham Metropolitan BC* [1987] Ch. 216 at 255; *Treacy v Corcorran* (1874) I.R. 8 C.L. 40. See also: *Thames Water Utilities v Reynolds* [1996] I.R.L.R. 186.

[226] *Hartley v King Edward VI College* [2017] UKSC 39; [2017] 1 W.L.R. 2110.

was, in fact, the situation in the *Fassihi* case, but while it was decided at first instance that the Act could be invoked where the employee was guilty of misconduct, this further issue was not the subject of any appeal. Nonetheless, Holman J felt that the issue "demands an answer" and observed that there was nothing in the Act to exclude its application. This interpretation of the Act is to be welcomed.[227] Earlier authorities which at least appeared to suggest that the Act cannot be invoked by a party in breach were considered by the Court of Appeal in relation to the question of "part-earned" salary and found not to stand as authority on the interpretation of the Act at all.[228]

### (g) Criticism

Notwithstanding the mitigations of the rule in *Sumpter v Hedges*,[229] a party who has failed to complete performance of an entire obligation may have no rights at all against the other party. This can plainly lead to the unjust enrichment of the latter party, and seems to go further than necessary for his protection.[230] He should normally be liable to make some payment for benefits received, though he should be entitled to a deduction in respect of any loss that he has suffered as result of the failure in performance.[231] **17–048**

## 5. BREACH

A breach of contract is committed when a party without lawful excuse fails or refuses to perform what is due from him under the contract, or performs defectively or incapacitates himself from performing. A breach of contract may entitle the injured party to claim damages, the agreed sum, specific performance or an injunction, in accordance with the principles discussed in Chs 20 and 21. In appropriate circumstances he may be entitled to more than one of these remedies, e.g. to an injunction and damages. Breach may also give the injured party the right to "terminate" the contract in the circumstances which are discussed in Ch.18.[232] An "anticipatory" breach may occur before performance is due and is considered separately below.[233] **17–049**

[227] Williams 57 L.Q.R. 381–383; cf. Matthews 2 *Legal Studies* 302 whose more restricted interpretation of the Act was rejected by the Court in the *Fassihi* case.

[228] *Boston Deep Sea Fishing and Ice Co v Ansell* (1888) 39 Ch D. 339; *McConnell's Claim* [1901] 1 Ch. 728; *Healey v SA Française Rubastic* [1917] 1 K.B. 947; *Miles v Wakefield Metropolitan DC* [1987] A.C. 539 at 570.

[229] See paras 17–041–17–047.

[230] Burrows, *The Law of Restitution*, 3rd edn (2010) at 356–358; *Cleveland Bridge UK Ltd v Multiplex Constructions UK Ltd* [2010] EWCA Civ 139 at [118]–[138].

[231] See Law Com. No.121; not to be implemented: Law Commission, *19th Annual Report*, para.2.11; Burrows 47 M.L.R. 76. See also McFarlane and Stevens 118 L.Q.R. 596.

[232] See para.18–032 and following.

[233] See para.17–074.

### (a) Failure or refusal to perform

17–050 Failure or refusal to perform a contractual promise when performance has fallen due is prima facie a breach. This point looks obvious enough, but it does raise a number of problems.

17–051 **Whether stipulation is a promise or a condition.** It must be determined whether the stipulation which has not been complied with is indeed a promise, or only a condition. In the standard case of a unilateral contract, where A promises B £100 if B will walk to York,[234] B has not promised to do anything: his walking to York is merely a condition[235] of A's liability. Hence B commits no breach if he does not start the walk, or if, having started, he fails to complete it. But the distinction between the two types of stipulations is sometimes hard to draw.[236] It is, for example, not clearly settled whether an estate agent who is engaged to find a buyer for a house makes any promise to do anything;[237] and it is also possible for a person to commit a breach by failing to complete performance of an act which he was not originally bound to do if, by beginning performance, he impliedly promised to complete it.[238]

17–052 **Whether performance has become due.** Obviously performance is not due before the stipulated time: a promise to pay £100 tomorrow is not broken by failing to pay today. But greater difficulty arises where the contract, or the liability of one party, is subject to a condition. Where the contract is subject to a *contingent* condition precedent,[239] failure to perform is not a breach if the condition has not occurred; nor does the principal obligation of either party become due if one of them fails to bring about the condition on which the binding force of that obligation depends. At most, that party may be liable for breach of some subsidiary duty, e.g. he is often under a duty not actively to prevent the occurrence of the condition; and he may be under a duty to make reasonable efforts to bring about its occurrence.[240] On the other hand, where the liability of A is subject to a *promissory* condition[241] to be performed by B, failure by B to perform that promise not only puts B in breach[242] of his principal obligation, but also prevents A's obligation to perform his counter-promise from becoming due.

17–053 **Whether party under any obligation.** A contract may contain a promise by one party, but fail to make it clear exactly what (if anything) has been promised in return by the other. In *Churchward v R.*[243] a contractor agreed with the Admiralty that he would for 11 years carry from Dover to Calais such mail as he should

---

[234] See para.2–052.
[235] i.e. in the contingent sense (para.2–105) as B makes no promise.
[236] cf. para.2–052; and see paras 18–084–18–086.
[237] See para.2–057.
[238] See para.2–052.
[239] See para.2–105.
[240] See paras 2–106–2–112.
[241] See paras 17–015–17–017.
[242] e.g. *Trans Trust SPRL v Danubian Trading Co* [1952] 2 Q.B. 297; para.17–015.
[243] (1865) L.R. 1 Q.B. 173; cf. *R. v Demers* [1900] A.C. 103.

from time to time be asked to carry by the Admiralty or the Postmaster-General. He was not given any mail to carry and claimed damages. One reason why his claim failed was that the agreement did not oblige the Admiralty to employ him: it only obliged him to carry mail if the Admiralty asked him to do so. The agreement thus resembled a tender by the contractor and amounted to no more than an offer, which might be accepted by the Admiralty from time to time.[244] A document which in terms imposes an obligation on only one party may, indeed, by implication also oblige the other to do something which is not expressly stated. Thus it was said in *Churchward v R.* that:

> "Where there is an engagement to manufacture some article [for a customer] a corresponding engagement on the other party is implied to take it, for otherwise it would be impossible that the party bestowing his services could claim any remuneration."[245]

Similarly, where a document is headed "contract of sale" and in terms only imposes an obligation on the seller to sell, the court might imply an obligation on the buyer to buy.[246] But no such implication will be made where the terms of the document or the surrounding circumstances negative any intention on the prospective buyer's part to give such an undertaking.[247]

**Specifying the obligation.** A contract may clearly oblige a party to do *something* but fail to specify exactly what. The question sometimes arises, for example, whether an employer is bound only to pay the agreed wages, or whether he must actually give the employee work. The traditional view is that generally the employer need only pay wages,[248] though this rule does not apply where one of the objects of the contract is to enable the employee to gain, or retain, a skill, or to keep his name before the public. Thus a person who employs a well-known actor must actually give him a part in the play for which he was engaged.[249] It has also been said that the law in some cases recognises a "right to work"[250] and that the question whether the contract gives rise to such a right depends on its express or implied terms.[251] If the employee needs to work to acquire or retain a skill or reputation, this fact is likely to support an implication that the employer must actually give him work. It does not follow that this duty can be specifically enforced;[252] but an employer who breaks a duty to provide work may be liable in damages on that account. 17–054

[244] cf. para.2–022.

[245] *Churchward v R.* (1865) L.R. 1 Q.B. 173 at 195; cf. *The Unique Mariner (No.2)* [1979] 1 Lloyd's Rep. 37 at 51–52.

[246] *Firstpost Homes Ltd v Johnson* [1995] 1 W.L.R. 1567 at 1574.

[247] *Firstpost Homes Ltd v Johnson* [1995] 1 W.L.R. 1567 at 1574.

[248] *Turner v Sawdon* [1901] 2 K.B. 653; cf. *Delaney v Staples* [1992] 1 A.C. 687 at 692 (discussing so called "garden leave"); *Marshall (Cambridge) Ltd v Hamblin* [1994] I.R.L.R. 260; *Abrahams v Performing Right Society* [1995] I.C.R. 1028.

[249] *Herbert Clayton & Jack Waller Ltd v Oliver* [1930] A.C. 209.

[250] *Langston v AUEW* [1974] 1 W.L.R. 185; cf. *Gunton v Richmond-upon-Thames LBC* [1981] Ch. 448 at 472. Even if the employer is not in breach by failing to provide work, he may be unable to restrain such an employee from working for others in breach of another term of the contract of employment: see *Provident Financial Group Plc v Hayward* [1989] I.C.R. 160; para.21–064.

[251] *William Hill Organisation Ltd v Tucker* [1998] I.R.L.R. 313.

[252] *Langston v AUEW (No.2)* [1974] I.C.R. 510; para.21–039.

17–055 **Failure to perform in substance.** There may be a breach if a party *in substance* refuses to perform, and paradoxically he may do this by insisting with too great literalness on the terms of the contract. "Working to rule" in order to disrupt the employer's business may therefore be a breach of a contract of employment.[253]

## (b) Defective performance

17–056 The phrase "defective performance" arguably contains an element of self-contradiction, in the sense that a person who promises to do one thing does not perform if he does another. Where the "defect" in performance is of a particularly serious kind, the acts done by the party in breach may indeed amount or lead to non-performance rather than defective performance, as in the case of the seller who promises beans but delivers peas.[254] But where the performance rendered is of the same kind as that promised, differing from it only in point of time, quantity or quality, it is reasonable to refer to it as defective performance.[255] It undoubtedly amounts to a breach; but the effects of such a breach often differ from those of a complete failure or refusal to perform.[256]

## (c) Incapacitating oneself

17–057 A person may break a contract by incapacitating himself from performing it. Thus a seller commits a breach of contract for the sale of a specific thing if he sells it to a third party;[257] and a shipowner commits a breach of a charterparty if he sells the ship to a third party "free from any … charter engagement".[258] But a person who is entitled to make a choice as to the method of performance does not incapacitate himself merely by declaring that he will perform in a way that is impossible. For example, a seller of generic goods does not put himself in breach merely by telling the buyer that he will make delivery from a source which does not exist.[259] He is normally entitled and bound to deliver from another source, and is in breach only if he fails or refuses to do so.

17–058 **Insolvency.** A person is not incapacitated from performing a contract under which he is obliged to pay money, merely because he is insolvent.[260] If the contract is profitable, his trustee in bankruptcy will probably wish to enforce it and provide funds to discharge his obligations under it. Insolvency incapacitates a contracting party only if no assets are set aside out of his estate for the

---

[253] *Secretary of State v ASLEF (No.2)* [1972] 2 Q.B. 455; contrast *Power Packing Casemakers Ltd v Faust* [1983] Q.B. 471 (ban on overtime not a breach).

[254] *Chanter v Hopkins* (1838) 4 M. & W. 399 at 404; *Pilbrow v Pearless De Rougemont & Co* [1999] 3 All E.R. 355.

[255] *The Stork* [1955] 2 Q.B. 68 at 76; *Leeds Shipping Co Ltd v Soc Française Bunge* [1958] 2 Lloyd's Rep. 124 at 145; *Pilbrow v Pearless De Rougemont & Co* [1999] 3 All E.R. 355 at 360.

[256] See para.18–032 and following, paras 22–001–22–020.

[257] *Bowdell v Parsons* (1808) 10 East 359; *Lovelock v Franklyn* (1846) 8 Q.B. 371.

[258] *Omnium D'Entreprises v Sutherland* [1919] 1 K.B. 618.

[259] *The Vladimir Ilich* [1975] 1 Lloyd's Rep. 322 at 329.

[260] *Re Agra Bank* (1867) L.R. 5 Eq. 160.

performance of the contract.[261] Where, after a contract has been made, one party to it is made bankrupt, the other party may apply to the court for an order discharging obligations under the contract; and the court may make such an order on such terms as to payment of damages by the bankrupt or by the other party as appear to the court to be equitable.[262]

### (d) Without lawful excuse

**Excused failure to perform: illustrations.** There is no breach when non-performance of a contract is justified by some lawful excuse. In one sense, such an excuse for non-performance exists where one party is entitled to refuse to perform because the other has failed to perform a promissory condition precedent or a concurrent condition. In such cases, performance of the former party's obligation has never become due. This topic has already been discussed;[263] our present concern is with cases in which *after* an obligation has accrued, an extraneous event occurs which interferes with its performance. The event may interfere so seriously with performance that both parties are discharged under the doctrine of frustration (to be discussed in Ch.19). But even where its effects are less drastic, it may still provide a party with an excuse for non-performance. Thus an employee who does not go to work because he is ill is not in breach,[264] even though the illness is not so serious as to frustrate the contract (so that performance must be resumed when the illness is over). Other extraneous circumstances may similarly justify refusal to perform, or to accept performance, at least in part. In one case it was, for example, held that the owner of a London café, who had engaged the claimants to give cabaret performances there, was justified in refusing to allow such performances to take place on the day on which King George V died, and on the following day, but not on the four days after that.[265] Again, if a farmer agrees to sell 500 tons of wheat to be grown on his farm and, through no fault of his, only 200 are produced, he is not liable for failing to produce the other 300 tons, though he will be liable in damages if he fails to deliver the 200 tons.[266] And a tenant is not in breach of a covenant to redevelop a site by a specified date if such redevelopment is prevented by an order listing a building on the site as of special architectural interest.[267] 17–059

**Excuse provided by express provision.** Excuses for non-performance may be provided by the contract itself, which may contain "exceptions" absolving a party from his duty to perform if he is prevented from doing so by specified circumstances, such as strikes or similar delays. Failure to perform, if brought 17–060

[261] *Ex p. Chalmers* (1873) L.R. 8 Ch. App. 289; cf. *Sale Continuation Ltd v Austin Taylor & Co* [1968] 2 Q.B. 849.

[262] Insolvency Act 1986 s.345(1) and (2).

[263] See paras 17–015–17–017.

[264] *Poussard v Spiers* (1875–76) L.R. 1 Q.B.D. 410 at 414; para.19–024; but contrast *Bettini v Gye* (1875–76) L.R. 1 Q.B.D. 183 at 189.

[265] *Minnevitch v Café de Paris (Londres) Ltd* [1936] 1 All E.R. 884.

[266] *Howell v Coupland* (1876) 1 Q.B.D. 258; *HR and S Sainsbury Ltd v Street* [1972] 1 W.L.R. 834; Goldberg 88 L.Q.R. 464.

[267] *John Lewis Properties v Viscount Chelsea* [1993] 2 E.G.L.R. 77.

about by such events, is not a breach at all. The function of the "exception" is not to exclude liability for an assumed breach but rather to define the scope of the contracting party's obligations.[268]

17–061 **Excuse must exist at the time performance is due.** A party relying on an excuse for non-performance must show that the excuse existed at the time of his refusal to perform: it is not enough for him to show that it arose or would (if the other party had not discharged the contract on account of the refusal) have arisen at some later time.[269] Suppose, for example, that a seller of wheat of a certain description is about to deliver wheat of a different description. The buyer cannot at this stage rely on the non-conformity as a ground for discharging the contract, for the seller is not actually in breach until he tenders non-conforming goods.[270] Once a defective tender has been made, the buyer is indeed entitled to reject it, but it still does not follow that he is entitled to terminate the contract; for if, within the time allowed for delivery, the seller can make a further good tender, the buyer is normally bound to accept it.[271]

17–062 **Whether excuse must be stated.** The general rule is that a refusal to perform by a party who has an excuse for non-performance is not a breach, even though he did not state the excuse, or even know of it, at the time of the refusal. Thus an employer can lawfully dismiss an employee who has committed a breach of duty justifying dismissal, though he did not at the time of the dismissal know of the breach, and though at that time he gave some other, insufficient, reason, or no reason at all.[272] Similarly a buyer can reject goods, if there has been a breach of condition, even though he did not know of the breach; and the rejection will not be wrongful merely because at the time he mistakenly alleged breach of some other condition.[273]

The rule may sometimes be justifiable on the ground that it prevents the party in breach from benefiting from the concealment of his own wrong. But it can also cause surprise and even hardship to the party in breach, and it has therefore been limited in a number of ways. A party cannot rely on an excuse which he did not specify at the time of his refusal to perform "if the point which was not taken is one which if taken could have been put right."[274] This might be the position if the

---

[268] *The Angelia* [1973] 1 W.L.R. 210; para.7–014; cf. para.19–081.

[269] *British & Beningtons Ltd v NW Cachar Tea Co* [1923] A.C. 48; para.17–027; cf. *The Siboen and the Sibotre* [1976] 1 Lloyd's Rep. 293.

[270] *Braithwaite v Foreign Hardwood Co Ltd* [1905] 2 K.B. 543; as explained in *Taylor v Oakes, Roncoroni & Co* (1922) 38 T.L.R. 349 at 351; and see para.17–027.

[271] See para.17–004.

[272] *Ridgway v Hungerford Market Co* (1835) 3 A. & E. 171; *Boston Deep Sea Fishing & Ice Co v Ansell* (1888) 39 Ch D. 339; *Cyril Leonard & Co v Simo Securities Trust Ltd* [1972] 1 W.L.R. 80; *Glencore Grain Rotterdam BV v LORICO* [1997] 2 Lloyd's Rep. 386 at 394; *Stocznia Gdanska SA v Latvian Shipping Co* [2002] EWCA Civ 889; [2002] 2 Lloyd's Rep 436 at [32]; *South Caribbean Trading Ltd v Trafigura Beheer BV* [2004] EWHC 2676 (Comm); [2005] 1 Lloyd's Rep. 128 at [133]–[134]; *Reinwood Ltd v L Brown & Sons Ltd* [2008] EWCA Civ 1090; 121 Con L.R. 1, para.18–013, fn.79.

[273] e.g. *Arcos Ltd v E A Ronaasen & Sons* [1933] A.C. 470.

[274] *Heisler v Anglo-Dal Ltd* [1954] 1 W.L.R. 1273 at 1278; *André & Cie v Cook Industries Inc* [1987] 2 Lloyd's Rep. 463; *Thai Maparn Trading Co Ltd v Louis Dreyfus Commodities Asia Pte Ltd* [2011] EWHC 2492 (Comm); [2011] 2 Lloyd's Rep. 274 at [24].

effect of a buyer's failure to state the ground which justified rejection was to deprive the seller of the opportunity of curing the defect and making a second good tender[275] within the time allowed for performance.[276] The case is even stronger if the buyer makes some groundless objection to the seller's tender and the seller incurs trouble or expense in investigating or seeking to cure that objection.[277] In such circumstances, an estoppel can arise, precluding the buyer from alleging the existence of another, sufficient, reason for his refusal to perform.

It has been said, obiter, that the general rule cannot apply where the unstated excuse is in the form of renunciation since "no amount of 'deemed knowledge' ... can remedy the complete absence of the essential ingredient of renunciation, namely communication to or knowledge of [the claimant] at the time of what are said to have been renunciatory words or conduct".[278] However, the claimant may have heard the words, or know of the conduct in question, but fail to appreciate their significance until they are later relied upon to excuse non-performance.

**The Panchaud Frères case.** One controversial case holds that a buyer who failed to specify a defect in existence at the time of rejection could not later rely on it, even though the defect was one which the seller could *not* have cured and even though the seller did not in any way change his position in consequence of the buyer's original failure to specify it. This is the *Panchaud Frères* case,[279] where maize was sold under a contract which provided for shipment to be made in "June/July". The goods were shipped in August and the buyers could have rejected them on this ground. But they paid against documents which would, if carefully examined, have revealed the fact of late shipment; and when the goods arrived the buyers rejected them for defects of quality. This was a bad ground as the goods were sound when shipped and the sellers were not responsible for their subsequent deterioration. The buyers claimed their money back, and, three years after their rejection of the goods, they relied for the first time on the fact of late shipment. Their claim failed, no doubt because the court was impressed by the possibly harsh consequences of allowing the buyers at such a late stage to rely on an originally unstated excuse for non-performance. To allow the buyers to do this would, it was said, be inconsistent with a "requirement of fair conduct."[280] But the vagueness of this requirement makes it virtually impossible to tell which cases will be governed by it and which by the general rule that a party can rely on an originally unstated excuse for non-performance.[281] Hence other attempts have been made to explain the *Panchaud Frères* case. One suggestion is that the case 17–063

[275] See para.17–004.

[276] Hence the present exception does not apply where that time has expired by the time of the refusal: see *Glencore Grain Rotterdam BV v LORICO* [1997] 2 Lloyd's Rep. 386 at 395, where it was the buyer who was guilty of the wrongful repudiation.

[277] cf. *The Lena* [1981] 1 Lloyd's Rep. 68 at 79; *The Eurometal* [1981] 1 Lloyd's Rep. 337 at 341.

[278] *The Ekha* [2009] EWHC 1530 (Comm); [2010] 1 Lloyd's Rep. 543 at [267]; affirmed, without reference to this point: [2010] EWCA Civ 691; 131 Con L.R. 9.

[279] *Panchaud Frères SA v Établissement General Grain Co* [1970] 1 Lloyd's Rep. 53.

[280] *Panchaud Frères SA v Établissement General Grain Co* [1970] 1 Lloyd's Rep. 53 at 59.

[281] Perhaps for this reason, the decision is treated with some reserve in *The Proodos C* [1980] 2 Lloyd's Rep. 390 at 392.

was one of waiver[282] (in the sense of election);[283] but this was rejected in the case itself on the ground that the buyers did not know of the late shipment when they accepted the documents.[284] Another view is that the buyers' conduct gave rise to an estoppel or equitable estoppel.[285] These doctrines, however, operate only if two requirements are satisfied: an unequivocal representation made by one party and reliance on it by the other.[286] In one later case[287] the argument based on estoppel accordingly failed on the ground that no such representation had been made; and in the *Panchaud Frères* case, even if the inference of a representation could be drawn from the buyers' acceptance of the documents, it is hard to see in what way the sellers had relied on that representation.[288] They certainly lost no chance of curing the defect in their tender, for when that tender was made such a cure was no longer possible. Probably the safest explanation of the case is that the buyers had lost their right to reject by "acceptance"[289] when they paid against documents which disclosed the fact of late shipment.[290] It follows that the buyers could have relied on the fact of late shipment if they had *rejected* the documents, even though they had, at the time of such rejection, given an inadequate reason, or none at all.[291]

17–064 **Unstated excuse operates as a shield, not as a sword.** While the rule stated herein has the effect of protecting the party who has an excuse for non-performance, it is not applied by deeming that party to have relied on the excuse at the time of its otherwise unlawful refusal to perform. For example, if the contract is terminated for the other party's repudiatory breach, the injured party may recover damages for "loss of bargain", i.e. loss resulting from the premature termination of the contract.[292] If, however, it is terminated on grounds which did not in fact justify termination, the rule under present consideration will operate to validate the termination on the basis of any later discovered repudiatory breach, but cannot alter the fact that it was terminated for reasons *other than the repudiatory breach which is found to have been committed*. On this basis damages will only be awarded up to the time of termination and not for

---

[282] *V Berg & Son Ltd v Vanden Avenne-Izegem PVBA* [1977] 1 Lloyd's Rep. 499 at 502–503; *Bremer Handelsgesellschaft mbH v C Mackprang Jr* [1979] 1 Lloyd's Rep. 221 at 225.

[283] See para.18–089.

[284] For the requirement of such knowledge, see para.18–100.

[285] This was the view of Lord Denning MR in the *Panchaud Frères* case itself: [1970] 1 Lloyd's Rep. 53 at 56; cf. *V Berg & Son Ltd v Vanden Avenne-Izegem PVBA* [1977] 1 Lloyd's Rep. 499 at 502–503; *The Manila* [1988] 3 All E.R. 843 at 852.

[286] See paras 9–190, 3–081—3–085.

[287] *Glencore Grain Rotterdam BV v LORICO* [1997] 2 Lloyd's Rep. 386.

[288] cf. *Raiffeisen Hauptgenossenschaft v Louis Dreyfuss & Co* [1981] 1 Lloyd's Rep. 345 at 352, where the *Panchaud Frères* case was held inapplicable precisely because the requirement of reliance was not satisfied.

[289] *BP Exploration Co (Libya) Ltd v Hunt* [1979] 1 W.L.R. 783 at 810–811; affirmed [1983] 2 A.C. 352, without reference to this point; *Glencore Grain Rotterdam BV v LORICO* [1997] 2 Lloyd's Rep. 386 at 396. For acceptance in the strict sense, see para.18–105.

[290] The defect in the goods must be apparent on the face of the documents and the only relevant documents for this purpose are the *shipping* documents, i.e. those the seller is obliged to tender in fulfilment of the contract: *The Manila* [1988] 3 All E.R. 843.

[291] cf. *V Berg & Son Ltd v Vanden Avenne-Izegem PVBA* [1977] 1 Lloyd's Rep. 499.

[292] See below, para.18–022.

"loss of bargain".[293] The rule "operates as a shield against a claim for damages on the basis of wrongful termination, not as a sword to claim damages (for the future) on the basis of justified termination".[294] Nonetheless, this does risk rewarding a party who has been guilty of repudiatory breach and of having successfully concealed it.

## (e) Standard of Duty[295]

### (i) *Strict liability*

**Non-performance.** Many contractual duties are strict.[296] The most obvious illustration of this principle is provided by the case of a buyer who cannot pay the price because his bank has failed or because his expectation of raising a loan has not been fulfilled, or because he is prevented by exchange control regulations from remitting money to the place where he has agreed to pay,[297] or because his supply of the currency in which he has agreed to pay has become exhausted and cannot be replenished.[298] In such cases, there is no doubt that he is liable:[299] inability to pay money, even if it occurs entirely without the fault of the party who was to make the payment, is not an excuse for failing to make the payment. The same principle of strict liability applies to the duty of a seller of generic goods to make delivery. It is no defence for him to say that he was prevented from making delivery because he was let down by his supplier,[300] or because no shipping space was available to get the goods to their agreed destination.[301] A charterparty similarly imposes a strict duty on the charterer to provide a cargo, so that inability to find one is no excuse.[302] In all these cases, the principle of strict liability may be modified by the terms of the contract (e.g. by a "force majeure" clause), but unless this is done liability is quite independent of fault. **17–065**

**Defective performance.** The principle of strict liability also applies to certain cases of defective performance. At common law, a carrier of goods by sea was **17–066**

[293] *Lonsdale Sports Ltd v Leofelis SA* [2012] EWCA Civ 985; for related proceedings, see [2012] EWCA Civ 1366.
[294] *Lonsdale Sports Ltd v Leofelis SA* [2012] EWCA Civ 985 at [33]. See para.18–073.
[295] Treitel in Bos and Brownlie (eds), *Liber Amicorum for Lord Wilberforce* (1987), p.185.
[296] *Raineri v Miles* [1981] A.C. 1050 at 1086.
[297] *Universal Corp v Five Ways Properties Ltd* [1979] 1 All E.R. 552.
[298] *Congimex SARL (Lisbon) v Continental Grain Export Corp (New York)* [1979] 2 Lloyd's Rep. 346.
[299] cf. *Francis v Cowcliffe* (1977) 33 P. & C.R. 368.
[300] *Barnett v Javeri & Co* [1916] 2 K.B. 390; *PJ van der Zijden Wildhandel v Tucker & Cross Ltd* [1975] 2 Lloyd's Rep. 240; cf. *The Al Tawfiq* [1984] 2 Lloyd's Rep. 598 (late delivery).
[301] *Lewis Emanuel & Son Ltd v Sammut* [1952] 2 Lloyd's Rep. 629.
[302] *The Aello* [1961] A.C. 135 (overruled on another point in *The Johanna Oldendorff* [1974] A.C. 479); *The Zuiho Maru* [1977] 2 Lloyd's Rep. 552; cf. *Hills v Sughrue* (1846) 15 M. & W. 252 (where it was the shipowner who undertook to find the cargo); *The World Navigator* [1991] 2 Lloyd's Rep. 23 at 30, 31 (time of loading); *The Athanasia Comninos* [1990] 1 Lloyd's Rep. 277 at 282; and *The Giannis K* [1998] A.C. 605 at 619, 624 (shipper's "warranty" that cargo is not dangerous); *Classic Maritime Inc v Limbungan Makmur SDN BHD* [2019] EWCA Civ 1102; [2019] 4 All E.R. 1145).

held to give an "absolute" warranty of seaworthiness:[303] it was not enough for him to show that he had taken reasonable care to make the ship seaworthy. In practice, sea carriers often contracted out of this strict liability; and in many cases the duty is now reduced by statute to one of due diligence.[304]

Liability is, again, strict where goods delivered under a contract of sale are defective, e.g. because they do not comply with the seller's undertakings as to quality.[305] It is no defence for the seller to show that he took all reasonable care to see that there were no defects,[306] or that he could not have discovered the defects because he was a retailer selling goods in packages sealed by the manufacturer.[307] The position appears to be the same where goods are supplied under a contract for the supply of goods other than one of sale, e.g. under one of hire or hire-purchase.[308]

A contractor who executes repairs or building work is also strictly liable for defects in components fitted by him. He is not exonerated by showing that the components were supplied by a reputable manufacturer and that the defects were latent so that they could not have been discovered by the exercise of reasonable care.[309] Contracts of this kind contain both a supply of goods, and a service, element. Strict liability with regard to the supply element can be justified on the ground that this is closely analogous to sale; and also on the ground that it is the first link in a chain of contractual liability which will stretch back to the manufacturer, on whom the liability should properly rest. The customer has no rights against the manufacturer in contract, as there is no contract between them;[310] and, by making the contractor strictly liable to the customer, the law gives the contractor an incentive to recoup the loss so incurred by claiming damages for breach of contract from the manufacturer from whom he had bought the components. The introduction of the manufacturer's strict "product liability"[311] directly to the customer weakens this argument for the contractor's strict liability in contract to the customer, but does not wholly deprive it of its force since "product liability" is subject to many important qualifications.[312] The "chain of liability" argument is also open to the objection that the chain may be

---

303 *Steel v State Line SS Co* (1877) 3 App. Cas. 72 at 86.

304 Carriage of Goods by Sea Act 1971 s.3.

305 e.g. with those implied under Sale of Goods Act 1979 s.14, or Consumer Rights Act 2015 ss.9–10.

306 *Frost v Aylesbury Dairy Co Ltd* [1905] 1 K.B. 608; cf. *Lockett v AM Charles Ltd* [1938] 4 All E.R. 170; *H Parsons (Livestock) Ltd v Uttley Ingham & Co Ltd* [1978] Q.B. 791 at 799–800.

307 *Daniels v White & Son* [1938] 4 All E.R. 258.

308 See Supply of Goods (Implied Terms) Act 1973 s.10; Supply of Goods and Services Act 1982 ss.4 and 9; Consumer Rights Act 2015 ss.3(2), 9–10; cf. *Wettern Electric Ltd v Welsh Development Agency* [1983] Q.B. 796 (strict liability for breach of implied undertaking in licence to occupy factory that premises are fit for occupier's purpose).

309 *GH Myers & Co v Brent Cross Service Co* [1934] 1 K.B. 46; *Young & Marten Ltd v McManus Childs Ltd* [1969] 1 A.C. 454; cf. *Hancock v Brazier* [1966] 1 W.L.R. 1317; *Barclays Bank Plc v Fairclough Builders Ltd* [1995] Q.B. 214; *The Zinnia* [1984] 2 Lloyd's Rep. 211 at 218 where the question of strict liability did not arise because of the finding that the repairer had not exercised reasonable care, in any event.

310 A direct contractual relationship may be created through the use of a manufacturer's guarantee: see para.14–006.

311 Consumer Protection Act 1987 Pt I.

312 e.g. those arising from the meaning given to "defect" by s.3 of the 1987 Act, the defences made available by s.4, and the definition of "damage" in s.5.

broken by a valid exemption clause. It has therefore been suggested that, if the manufacturer is willing to sell the components only on terms that exclude his liability, and this fact was known both to the contractor and to his customer, then the contractor would not be strictly liable to his customer for defects in those components.[313]

### *(ii) Liability based on fault*

**Supply of services.** Under the Supply of Goods and Services Act 1982, a person who supplies a service in the course of a business impliedly undertakes to "carry out the service with reasonable care and skill".[314] Such liability is clearly based on fault; but the Act also preserves "any rule of law which imposes on the supplier a stricter duty".[315] Hence the question whether the supplier's liability is strict or is based on fault will continue to depend on distinctions drawn at common law. 17–067

**Supply of services and components.** Where the contract is one for the supply of *services and components*, liability for defects in the components is (as we have just seen) generally strict;[316] but the contractor's liability with regard to other phases of his operation is often based on fault. For example, a car repairer's duty with regard to the safe-keeping of a customer's car is one of care only.[317] The standard of a building or repairing contractor's duty with regard to the actual carrying out of the work that he is employed to do is less clear. In one of the relevant cases,[318] a sharp distinction was drawn between the "supply of goods" and "service" elements of the contract, and it seems to have been accepted that, in respect of the "service" element, the contractor's duty was one of care only.[319] Similarly, a contract for the supply of goods may impose on the supplier a duty not only to supply the goods but also to service, or to repair defects in, them after they have been supplied. He will then be strictly liable in respect of defects in the goods when supplied, but his service or repair undertakings will impose duties of diligence only.[320] 17–068

---

[313] In *Young & Marten Ltd v McManus Childs Ltd* [1969] 1 A.C. 454 at 467; the suggestion is perhaps based on the fact that the building contract specified tiles which could be obtained only from a single manufacturer.

[314] Supply of Goods and Services Act 1982 s.13; *Wilson v Best Travel Ltd* [1993] 1 All E.R. 353. For consumer contracts, see the Consumer Rights Act 2015 s.49(1).

[315] Supply of Goods and Services Act 1982 s.16(3)(a).

[316] See para.17–066. Section 12(3)(a) of Supply of Goods and Services Act 1982 provides that such a contract is a contract for the supply of services for the purposes of the Act; but it does not specify the standard of liability. Under the Consumer Rights Act 2015 such a contract may amount to a "mixed contract" (s.1(4)) and subject to both Pt 2 (goods) and Part 4 (services) where applicable.

[317] See *Hollier v Rambler Motors (AMC) Ltd* [1972] 2 Q.B. 71; cf. *Alderslade v Hendon Laundry Ltd* [1945] 1 K.B. 189; *Smith v Eric S Bush* [1990] 1 A.C. 831 at 843.

[318] *Young & Marten Ltd v McManus Childs Ltd* [1969] 1 A.C. 454.

[319] *Young & Marten Ltd v McManus Childs Ltd* [1969] 1 A.C. 454 at 465; cf. *H Parsons (Livestock) Ltd v Uttley Ingham & Co Ltd* [1978] Q.B. 791 at 800; *The Raphael* [1981] 2 Lloyd's Rep. 659 at 665. See also *BP Exploration (Libya) Ltd v Hunt* [1979] 1 W.L.R. 783 at 796; affirmed [1983] 2 A.C. 352.

[320] *BHP Petroleum Ltd v British Steel Plc* [1999] 2 Lloyd's Rep. 583; affirmed [2000] 2 Lloyd's Rep. 277.

17–069 **Supply of services alone.** Where the contract is one for the supply of *services alone*, liability is, as noted,[321] often based on fault. Thus the general rule is that contracts under which services are rendered by professional persons (such as solicitors, architects, accountants or doctors) impose duties of care only.[322] In some at least of such cases, the person rendering the services obviously does not guarantee to produce a result: this is particularly clear in the case of the lawyer engaged to conduct litigation since one party must inevitably lose, and of the doctor since a person who provides medical treatment is not normally understood to guarantee its success.[323] All that such persons undertake is to perform the promised services with reasonable care and skill. The same is true of the architect to the extent that he undertakes to supervise the work of others, or the supply of materials by them: in performing this function he cannot be expected to do more than exercise a reasonable degree of professional care and skill. But the position is different where an architect commits an error, not of supervision, but of design: there is considerable support for the view that, where he designs a structure, he gives an "absolute warranty"[324] that it will be fit for his client's purposes. Similarly, a person who in the course of a profession or business undertakes to *design and supply* an article has been held strictly liable for defects in that article.[325] Some dicta, indeed, suggest that liability is strict *only* where the contract contains a "supply" as well as a "service" element;[326] but this limitation on the incidence of strict liability may, with respect, be doubted. In some of the relevant authorities no defect in the components or raw materials was alleged;[327] and where a defendant is thus held liable for defects in services alone it would be strange if the standard of that liability depended on the existence of another obligation (i.e. to supply materials) in respect of which he was not in breach.

---

321 See para.17–067.

322 e.g. *Clark v Kirby-Smith* [1964] Ch. 506 (solicitor); *Bagot v Stevens, Scanlan & Co Ltd* [1966] 1 Q.B. 197 (architect); *O'Connor v Kirby* [1972] 1 Q.B. 90 (insurance broker); *Perry v Sidney Phillips & Son* [1982] 1 All E.R. 1005 at 1010, varied [1982] 1 W.L.R. 1287 (surveyor); *Henderson v Merrett Syndicates Ltd* [1995] 2 A.C. 145 (underwriting agent).

323 See *Eyre v Measday* [1986] 1 All E.R. 488; and *Thake v Maurice* [1986] Q.B. 644. There may be a duty to warn of the risk of an unsuccessful outcome, in contract (*Thake v Maurice*), or in tort (*Goodwill v Pregnancy Advisory Service* [1996] 1 W.L.R. 1379); para.14–058.

324 *Greaves & Co (Contractors) Ltd v Baynham Meikle & Partners* [1975] 1 W.L.R. 1095 at 1101; *IBA v EMI (Electronics) Ltd* (1980) 14 Build. L.R. 1, especially at 47–48 (where the contract contained a supply of goods element but no defect in the goods was alleged); *CFW Architects v Cowlin Construction Ltd* [2006] EWHC 6 (TCC); 105 Con L.R. 116 at [46].

325 *Samuels v Davies* [1943] K.B. 526 (dentist supplying false teeth: here the "supply" element predominated and du Parq LJ regarded the contract as one of sale); *IBA v EMI (Electronics) Ltd* (1980) 14 Build. L.R. 1 (contract to design and erect a television mast).

326 *Basildon DC v J E Lesser Properties* [1985] 1 All E.R. 20 at 26 (not reported on this point in [1985] Q.B. 839); cf. *Cynat Properties Ltd v Landbuild (Investments & Property) Ltd* [1984] 3 All E.R. 513 at 523; *Wimpey Construction UK Ltd v DV Poole* [1984] 2 Lloyd's Rep. 499 at 514 (no undertaking by *designer* as to quality and *execution* of the work); *George Hawkins v Chrysler (UK)* (1986) 38 Build. L.R. 36 (where the contract contained no supply element).

327 There was no such allegation in the cases cited in fn.325.

### (iii) *Fault and excuses for non-performance*

Failure to perform is not a breach where a supervening event either discharges a contract under the doctrine of frustration[328] or provides a party with an excuse for non-performance.[329] An event has this effect only if it occurs without the fault of the party relying on it. In cases of frustration, this requirement is expressed by saying that frustration must not be "self-induced".[330] Similarly, a party generally[331] cannot rely as an excuse for non-performance on an event that is due to his fault, e.g. a farmer who agreed to sell a quantity of wheat to be grown on his land could not rely on the fact that less was produced if this was due to want of proper cultivation.[332] **17–070**

Excuses for non-performance may be provided by "exceptions" in the contract itself, and such provisions must be distinguished from exemption clauses. Where performance is prevented by an event specified in an "exception", there is no breach at all, while an exemption clause excludes or restricts liability once a breach has been established. One factor tending to put a provision into the category of "exceptions" is that the specified event was beyond the control of the party relying on the provision, and occurred without fault.[333] Here again fault is relevant in determining whether non-performance is excused or amounts to a breach.

### (iv) *Conditional contracts*

Where a contract is subject to a contingent condition,[334] two rules apply which to some extent make fault relevant to the issue of contractual liability. First, a party may be in breach if he deliberately prevents the occurrence of the condition.[335] Secondly, a party may be under some degree of duty to bring about the occurrence of the condition, e.g. where goods are sold "subject to" export or import licence. In such a case the duty of the party who is to obtain the licence is normally one of diligence only,[336] so that fault is again relevant to the question whether a breach of contract has been committed. **17–071**

---

[328] See Ch.19.

[329] See para.17–059.

[330] See para.19–089.

[331] Illness preventing performance of a contract of personal service may be an exception: cf. para.19–092.

[332] Lack of fault is mentioned, apparently as an essential ingredient of the excuse, in the cases discussed at para.17–059.

[333] *The Angelia* [1973] 1 W.L.R. 210 at 230; para.7–014; cf. *The Xantho* (1877) 2 App. Cas. 503; para.19–081.

[334] See paras 2–104—2–114.

[335] See para.2–109.

[336] See para.2–111.

### (f) Breach Distinguished From Lawful Termination

17–072 A contract may give a party the right lawfully to terminate it by notice. If that party says to the other that he no longer intends to perform, it may be hard to tell whether he has broken or lawfully terminated the contract. In *Bridge v Campbell Discount Co Ltd*[337] a hire-purchase agreement gave the hirer the right to terminate it by notice. He wrote to the owners:

> "Owing to unforeseen circumstances I am sorry but I will not be able to pay any more payments ... Will you please let me know when and where I will have to return the car. I am very sorry regarding this, but I have no alternative."

The House of Lords held (by a majority) that he had not terminated but broken the contract, apparently because that was his intention. "Why should the hirer apologise so humbly, twice, if *he thought* that he was merely exercising an option given to him by the agreement?"[338]

17–073 **Industrial action.** The analogous question has been raised whether a strike or other "industrial action" amounts to a breach of a contract of employment.[339] This depends in the first place on the exact form taken by the conduct in question. While "working to rule" may be a breach,[340] no breach is committed merely because employees who usually work overtime (without being under any contractual obligation to do so) refuse to continue the practice.[341] In the more common case of a refusal by employees to perform their contractual obligation to work, there is clearly a breach if the contract contains a "no strikes" clause.[342] The same is true if an employee stops work (whether in the course of a strike or not) without giving the notice required by the terms of the contract. If the contract does not contain a "no strikes" clause and if due notice of the strike has been given, one view is that the notice terminates the contract; but this is said[343] to be unrealistic since both parties would expect a return to work under the old contract (suitably modified) after the strike was over. A second view is that a strike notice operates as a lawful suspension of the contract, at least if the notice is no shorter than that required for lawful termination of the contract.[344] This view in turn gives rise to difficulties, particularly as the notion of "suspending" a contract is

---

337 [1962] A.C. 600; cf. *United Dominions Trust (Commercial) Ltd v Ennis* [1968] 1 Q.B. 54; *Marriott v Oxford & District Co-operative Society Ltd* [1970] Q.B. 186.

338 *Bridge v Campbell Discount Co Ltd* [1962] A.C. 600 at 615 (emphasis added); cf. at 674. Another (and probably most likely) reason for the decision is that it was in the hirer's interest to establish that he was in breach: see para.20–144.

339 Foster 34 M.L.R. 274.

340 See para.17–055.

341 *Tramp Shipping Corp v Greenwich Marine Inc* [1975] 1 W.L.R. 1042; cf. *Power Packing Casemakers v Faust* [1983] Q.B. 471.

342 As in *Rookes v Barnard* [1964] A.C. 1129.

343 By Donovan LJ in *Rookes v Barnard* [1963] 1 Q.B. 623 at 682. The statement was approved in the House of Lords by Lord Devlin: [1964] A.C. 1129 at 1204, though the decision of the Court of Appeal was reversed. See also Wedderburn 25 M.L.R. 258; 27 M.L.R. 268.

344 *Morgan v Fry* [1968] 2 Q.B. 710 at 728 (Lord Denning MR); cf. [1968] 2 Q.B. 710 at 733 (Davies LJ); O'Higgins [1968] C.L.J. 223. Trade Union and Labour Relations (Consolidation) Act 1992 s.234A requires at least seven days' notice to be given.

one with which English law is unfamiliar[345] and which the courts have not favoured.[346] The prevailing view, therefore, is[347] that generally a strike is a breach of contract and that it is, moreover, a "repudiatory breach",[348] i.e. one which at common law[349] entitles the employer to dismiss the employee. The employer's other remedies by way of damages and withholding pay have already been discussed.[350]

## 6. ANTICIPATORY BREACH[351]

### (a) The doctrine of anticipatory breach

An "anticipatory breach"[352] is said to occur when, before performance is due, a party either renounces the contract or disables himself from performing it.[353] **17–074**

**Renunciation.** Renunciation requires a "clear" and "absolute"[354] refusal to perform. This need not be a refusal to perform *at all*; it is sufficient that one party intends to act in a manner "substantially inconsistent with his obligation",[355] i.e. in a way which would amount to a substantial failure to perform which is the general requirement for the right to terminate for "actual" breach.[356] Nor does a renunciation need to be express; it can take the form of conduct indicating that the party is unwilling, even though he may be able, to perform. A renunciation may even be inferred from silence where it is a "speaking silence", e.g. the previous conduct of a party in refusing to perform another related contract may give rise to the inference that he will refuse to perform the contract in question. His silence or inactivity can then be a renunciation of that contract unless he takes **17–075**

[345] See *Daily Mirror Newspapers Ltd v Gardner* [1968] 2 Q.B. 762; *Gorse v Durham CC* [1971] 1 W.L.R. 775. A contract can only be "suspended" if it contains a provision to that effect, as, for example, in *Bird v British Celanese Ltd* [1945] K.B. 336. But see the effect of s.10(2) of the Insurance Act 2015: para.18–009.

[346] *Shell UK Ltd v Lostock Garage Ltd* [1976] 1 W.L.R. 1187.

[347] *Simmons v Hoover Ltd* [1977] Q.B. 284; Napier [1977] C.L.J. 34; cf. *Rookes v Barnard* [1963] 1 Q.B. 623 at 682 (Donovan LJ); *Chappell v Times Newspapers Ltd* [1975] 1 W.L.R. 482 at 502.

[348] *Miles v Wakefield Metropolitan DC* [1987] A.C. 539 at 562; *Wiluszynski v Tower Hamlets LBC* [1989] I.C.R. 493 at 503.

[349] By statute, the dismissal may be *unfair*, even where it is not *wrongful* at common law: see Employment Rights Act 1996 s.94.

[350] See para.17–045.

[351] Liu, *Anticipatory Breach* (2011).

[352] For criticism of this terminology, see *Bradley v H Newsom, Sons & Co* [1919] A.C. 16 at 53; *The Mihalis Angelos* [1971] 1 Q.B. 164 at 196. And see Dawson [1981] C.L.J. 83; Mustill, *Anticipatory Breach: Butterworth Lectures*, 1989–1990, p.1.

[353] *Universal Cargo Carriers Corp v Citati* [1957] 2 Q.B. 401 at 438; cf. *The Angelia* [1973] 1 W.L.R. 210; Tiplady 89 L.Q.R. 465.

[354] *The Hermosa* [1982] 1 Lloyd's Rep. 570 at 572; cf. *The Gregos* [1994] 1 W.L.R. 1465; *Jaks (UK) Ltd v Cera Investment Bank SA* [1998] 2 Lloyd's Rep. 89 at 93; *Eminence Property Developments v Heaney Ltd* [2010] EWCA Civ 1168; (2010) 43 E.G. 99 at [61].

[355] *Ross T Smyth & Co v TD Bailey, Son & Co* [1940] 3 All E.R. 60 at 72.

[356] See para.18–032.

positive steps to dispel that inference.[357] The conduct must indicate to the other party that the party alleged to have renounced the contract is about to commit a breach of it: an indication given to a third party of an intention to commit a breach at an unspecified time in the future has been held not to amount to a renunciation.[358]

17–076 **Disablement.** Disablement need not be "deliberate",[359] in the sense that there may be an anticipatory breach even though it was not the party's intention to disable himself from performing; but the disablement must be due to the party's "own act or default".[360] Such disablement is most clearly illustrated by cases in which a party does a positive act which is certain to prevent performance, such as disposing elsewhere of the specific thing[361] which forms the subject-matter of the contract.

17–077 **Omission as disablement.** Disablement may also take the form of an omission. For example, a contract may be made for the sale of goods for future delivery, to be manufactured by the seller, or to be acquired by him from a third party, and the seller may fail to take any steps to manufacture the goods or to acquire them from the supplier. The failure will then amount to his "own default" in the sense that he will have failed to do something that he was obliged by the contract to do in order to put himself into the position of being able to perform on the due date. But if a seller of goods to be acquired from a third party had duly contracted with that third party to acquire the goods, he would not be in anticipatory breach merely because it became highly unlikely that the third party would deliver them under his contract with the seller, so that the seller himself would, in turn, be unable to perform his contract with the buyer. A fortiori a seller is not in anticipatory breach merely because the buyer *fears* that the subject-matter of the sale, when delivered, will turn out to be defective.[362] Nor would a buyer be in anticipatory breach merely because, before the time fixed for payment, some external cause (such as exchange control, or the failure of a bank) made it virtually certain that he would be unable to pay on the due date. In the last three examples there is no disablement by the party's "own default": hence the prospective inability does not amount to an anticipatory breach,[363] even though it would, if it persisted up to the

---

[357] *Stocznia Gdanska SA v Latvian Shipping Co* [2002] EWCA Civ 889; [2002] 2 Lloyd's Rep 436 at [96].

[358] *Laughton and Hawley v BAPP Industrial Supplies* [1986] I.C.R. 245.

[359] *Universal Cargo Carriers Corp v Citati* [1957] 2 Q.B. 401 at 438; contrast *The Super Servant Two* [1989] 1 Lloyd's Rep. 149 at 155 ("deliberate or at least voluntary"); affirmed [1990] 1 Lloyd's Rep. 1.

[360] *Universal Cargo Carriers Corp v Citati* [1957] 2 Q.B. 401 at 441; or (as in that case) from the act or default of another person to whom he had delegated performance of his contractual duty.

[361] Where the subject matter is not specific the seller may be able to perform by supplying another thing of the contract description out of stock or from another source: *Texaco Ltd v Eurogulf Shipping Co Ltd* [1987] 2 Lloyd's Rep. 541; cf. *Alfred C Toepfer International GmbH v Itex Itagrani Export SA* [1993] 1 Lloyd's Rep. 360.

[362] *The Veracruz I* [1992] 1 Lloyd's Rep. 356; *The P* [1992] 1 Lloyd's Rep. 470.

[363] *FC Shepherd & Co Ltd v Jerrom* [1987] Q.B. 301 at 327–328.

time when performance was due, then amount to an actual breach.[364] Difficulties can obviously arise in deciding whether a prospective inability resulting from an omission is due to the party's "own default." The difficulty is illustrated by the very case in which this requirement is stated, *Universal Cargo Carriers Corp v Citati*.[365] In that case, a charterer was held to be in anticipatory breach of his obligation to provide a cargo, at the time fixed for loading, because of the prospective failure of a third party, with whom he had contracted for the supply of the goods, to deliver them within that time. This aspect of the case has been judicially described as "debatable";[366] it can perhaps be explained on the ground that the charterer had failed to ensure that his supply contract was effective for the purpose of the performance of his own obligations under the charterparty.

**Effect.** Where one party has committed an anticipatory breach, the other has a choice. He can try to keep the contract alive by continuing to press for performance,[367] in which case the anticipatory breach will have the same effects as an actual breach if it persists until the time when performance is due. Alternatively, he can "accept" the anticipatory breach, in which case his rights to damages and termination are governed by the special rules to be discussed below. **17–078**

## (b) Acceptance of the breach

An anticipatory breach can be accepted by bringing an action for damages; or by giving notice of intention to accept it to the party in breach. Conduct known to the party in breach will suffice even if no notice of it is given by the injured party.[368] Once the injured party has made it plain that he is treating the contract as at an end, he "does not need to *do* anything more".[369] Mere acquiescence or inactivity will often be equivocal and so fail to constitute an acceptance for this purpose.[370] But there is no absolute rule of law to this effect, e.g. the fact of the injured party's having failed, in response to the breach, to take the steps which he would normally have been expected to take in the further performance of the contract may unequivocally indicate his acceptance of the breach.[371] **17–079**

---

[364] This may be so even though the party in breach is in no way at fault, e.g. where his source of funds fails: see para.17–065.

[365] [1957] 2 Q.B. 401; and see para.17–090.

[366] *FC Shepherd & Co Ltd v Jerrom* [1987] Q.B. 301 at 323.

[367] *Michael v Hart & Co* [1902] 1 K.B. 482; *Harvela Investments Ltd v Royal Trust of Canada (CI) Ltd* [1986] A.C. 207 at 227.

[368] *Vitol SA v Norelf Ltd* [1996] A.C. 800, as to which see also fn.371.

[369] *Lefevre v White* [1990] 1 Lloyd's Rep. 569 at 574.

[370] *Cranleigh Precision Engineering Ltd v Bryant* [1965] 1 W.L.R. 1293; *State Trading Corp of India v M Golodetz Ltd* [1989] 2 Lloyd's Rep. 277 at 286; *Lefevre v White* [1990] 1 Lloyd's Rep. 569 at 574, 576–577.

[371] *Vitol SA v Norelf Ltd* [1996] A.C. 800. The case was treated in the lower courts as one of anticipatory breach, but, except in quotations from the judgments of those courts, no reference to this aspect of the case was made in the House of Lords.

17–080 **Complete and unequivocal acceptance.** The injured party's acceptance must be complete and unequivocal.[372] A party cannot accept an anticipatory breach of one term in a contract while treating the contract as still in existence for other purposes.[373]

## (c) Effects of accepting the breach

### *(i) Damages for anticipatory breach*

17–081 **Damages available at once.** The most striking feature of the doctrine of anticipatory breach is that acceptance of the breach entitles the victim to claim damages at once, before the time fixed for performance.[374] This rule was established in *Hochster v De la Tour*[375] where the defendant had agreed to employ the claimant as courier for three months from 1 June, and repudiated the contract on 11 May. The claimant was able to claim damages at once: he did not have to wait until 1 June before beginning his action. The main reason for the decision was that "if the claimant has no remedy for breach of contract unless he treats the contract as in force and acts upon it down to the 1st of June 1852, it follows that, till then, he must enter into no employment".[376] This reasoning has been justly criticised,[377] for the court could have held that the defendant's repudiation gave the claimant *the option to terminate* at once but did not *entitle him to damages* until 1 June: there is no necessary connection between these two consequences of the repudiation.

17–082 **Practical problems.** Where the interval between the anticipatory breach and the time fixed for performance is a long one, there are also practical objections to the rule in *Hochster v De la Tour*, and these are particularly strong where the trial takes place well before the time fixed for performance.[378] One such objection is that the rule may lead to a wrong quantification of damages. If a seller of goods to be delivered in three years' time is guilty of an anticipatory breach and the buyer claims damages at once, the quantification of those damages may depend on the market price at the time fixed for delivery;[379] but if the case is tried before that time the court can only guess what that price will be. Another objection to the rule is that it results in an acceleration of the defendant's obligation; he will have to pay damages now, even though under the contract he was not to perform until

[372] *Norwest Holst Group Administration Ltd v Harrison* [1985] I.C.R. 668; *Jaks (UK) Ltd v Cera Investment Bank Ltd* [1998] 2 Lloyd's Rep. 89 at 94.

[373] This was one reason for the decision in *Johnstone v Milling* (1886) 16 Q.B.D. 460.

[374] Some of the issues which can arise in the assessment of damages for anticipatory breach are considered at paras 20–081–20–087.

[375] (1853) 2 E. & B. 678.

[376] *Hochster v De la Tour* (1853) 2 E. & B. 678 at 689.

[377] Vold 41 Harv. L. Rev. 340 suggests that anticipatory breach might be regarded as a tort; cf. Weir [1964] C.L.J. 231; but see Hoffmann 81 L.Q.R. 116.

[378] Where it takes place *after* the time fixed for performance, the court may take into account events which are known to have happened and which, if relevant, reduce the value of the contract to the injured party: *The Golden Victory* [2007] UKHL 12; [2007] 2 A.C. 353; para.20–084.

[379] See para.20–076.

some future time.[380] Thus if a debtor repudiates liability to repay future instalments of a debt, the creditor can claim damages at once, even though the instalments, or some of them, are not payable until a future day. Of course, in assessing those damages the court will allow the debtor "a discount for accelerated payment".[381] Even more strikingly, the defendant will have to pay damages at once although at the time of the action his liability is still contingent and might never mature at all. Thus, damages have been recovered for anticipatory breach of a husband's promise to make a will leaving a life interest in property to his wife, although it was uncertain at the time of the action whether the wife would survive the husband.[382]

**Defence of the rule.** In spite of these objections, the rule in *Hochster v De la Tour* is well established[383] and at least two points can be made in its favour. First, the rule may help to minimise loss. In a case like *Hochster v De la Tour*, the injured party might in fact be more *likely* (whether or not he was *bound*) to keep himself ready to perform if he had no right to sue at once. The rule giving him that right provides at any rate some incentive for him to abandon the contract, and so to avoid this extra loss. Secondly, the rule may sometimes be necessary to protect the injured party, e.g. if he has paid in advance for a promise of future performance which is then repudiated. In such a case the injured party could be seriously prejudiced if he had no claim against the other party until the time fixed for performance had arrived; for, having made the advance payment, he might lack the means to procure a substitute contract. 17–083

### *(ii) Termination for anticipatory breach*

**General requirement of substantial failure.** An anticipatory breach, like an actual breach, can give rise to a right to terminate and that right arises immediately, i.e. before performance is due. Whether it does give rise to such a right depends on the factors discussed in Ch.18.[384] Generally, the right to terminate will arise only if the prospective effects of the anticipatory breach are such as to satisfy the requirement of substantial failure in performance.[385] Thus a charterer's advance announcement of a deliberate delay of one day in loading would not (any more than an actual delay of this kind)[386] justify termination. 17–084

[380] If the injured party affirms the contract and sues for specific performance, the court may give judgment in his favour at once, but the judgment will not order the defendant to perform until the time fixed for performance arrives: see *Hasham v Zenab* [1960] A.C. 316.

[381] *Lep Air Services Ltd v Rolloswin Investments Ltd* [1973] A.C. 331 at 356; *Re Park Air Services* [1999] 1 All E.R. 673 at 676.

[382] *Synge v Synge* [1894] 1 Q.B. 466.

[383] See *Lep Air Services Ltd v Rolloswin Investments Ltd* [1973] A.C. 331 at 356, 358; *Woodar Investments Development Ltd v Wimpey Construction UK Ltd* [1980] 1 W.L.R. 277 at 297; *Gunton v Richmond-upon-Thames LBC* [1981] Ch. 448 at 467; *The Hazelmoor* [1980] 2 Lloyd's Rep. 351.

[384] See paras 18–032—18–086.

[385] See paras 18–032—18–040.

[386] See para.18–038.

17–085 **Exceptions.** In relation to actual breach the requirement of substantial failure is subject to exceptions;[387] and the question arises whether the same exceptions apply to termination for anticipatory breach.

17–086 **Express provision.** There is one type of case in which a negative answer must clearly be given to this question, namely that in which the right to terminate exists by reason only of an express provision in the contract for determination.[388] For example, under such provisions in charterparties charterers cannot exercise their rights to cancel for late arrival of the ship, nor owners withdraw for non-payment of hire, merely because it has become certain that the ship *will not* arrive, or that the hire *will not* be paid in time: they are only entitled to terminate when the specified day has gone by without performance being rendered.[389] In *The Afovos* a shipowner gave notice (under such an express provision) of his intention to terminate on account of the charterer's failure to pay hire in time, but he did so while the charterer's breach was merely anticipatory; and Lord Diplock, in holding the purported termination to be wrongful, said: "it is to fundamental breaches alone that the doctrine of anticipatory breach is applicable".[390]

17–087 **Breach of condition.** The fact that the right to terminate for anticipatory breach does not apply to *one* exception does not support the conclusion that it cannot apply to *any* of them. In this regard, Lord Diplock's suggestion in *The Afovos*,[391] that there can be no right to terminate for an anticipatory breach of condition may, with respect, be doubted. In part, the question whether there can be such a right is one of terminology. Lord Diplock has elsewhere defined "conditions" as terms the breach of which gives rise to the right to terminate because the parties have so "agreed, whether by express words or by implication of law".[392] Under this definition, express provisions for determination on non-performance *are* "conditions"; but a term is often classified as a "condition" by statute or by judicial decision[393] even though the parties have not expressly agreed that *any* breach of it is to give rise to the right to terminate. This group of conditions is in practice the more important group of such terms:[394] and it is submitted that the right to terminate for anticipatory breach does extend to conditions of this kind.[395] Furthermore, if the parties have expressly agreed that a term is a condition and not merely that there is a right to terminate, it is submitted that this too confers a right to terminate which can be exercised on the basis of an

---

387 See paras 18–041—18–086.

388 See paras 18–067—18–083.

389 See para.18–077.

390 *The Afovos* [1983] 1 W.L.R. 195 at 203.

391 [1983] 1 W.L.R. 195 at 203.

392 *Photo Production Ltd v Securicor Transport Ltd* [1980] A.C. 827 at 849; cf. below, paras 18–043—18–046.

393 See paras 18–048—18–049.

394 See paras 18–048—18–049.

395 See *The Aktor* [2008] EWHC 1330 (Comm); [2008] 2 Lloyd's Rep. 246, where the analysis appears to be that the contract for sale of a vessel was validly terminated for an anticipatory breach of condition. The reference to the right of cancellation at [69] is not thought to cast doubt on the decision in *The Afovos*.

anticipatory breach. In one leading case[396] on anticipatory breach the court asked *first* whether the prospective breaches were breaches of condition and (having reached the conclusion that they were not)[397] proceeded *secondly* to the question whether they were sufficiently serious to justify termination for anticipatory breach.[398] The first enquiry would have been unnecessary if the doctrine of anticipatory breach could never apply to breaches of condition.

**Standard of proof as to prospective effect of breach.** In cases of anticipatory breach, the right to terminate may depend on the prospective effects of the breach. A question therefore arises as to what the injured party has to show to justify termination. Is it enough for him to show that, at the time of termination, he *reasonably believed* that the breach would, by the time fixed for performance, have acquired the character of a breach giving rise to the right to terminate? Or must he show that, at the time of termination, it was *already certain* that the breach was going to be of this kind? This depends on the form taken by the anticipatory breach, but the courts take a strict approach which is readily understandable. They are asked to grant relief on the basis that it is sufficiently clear that the other party would not have been able or willing to perform at the time when performance was due. As has been explained by Popplewell J: 17–088

> "anticipatory breaches are treated in the same way as actual breaches because they are bound to happen. In the case of self-induced impossibility, this means actual inevitability. In the case of renunciation, it means legal inevitability, in the sense that the innocent party is entitled to treat as inevitably going to happen that which the contract breaker clearly conveys by words or conduct that he intends will happen".[399]

**Renunciation.** The first form of anticipatory breach is by renunciation, i.e. by a "clear" and "absolute"[400] refusal to perform. This may be inferred from conduct where the party in breach has "acted in such a way as to lead a reasonable man to conclude that [he] did not intend to fulfil [his] part of the contract".[401] Whether conduct has this effect "is to be considered as at the time when it is treated as terminating the contract, in the light of the then existing circumstances".[402] The court therefore looks to the time of termination to determine whether the injured party reasonably took the view that the refusal was sufficiently clear and absolute to give him the right to terminate.[403] The assessment is an objective one,[404] but the motive of the party in breach is not irrelevant "if it reflects something of 17–089

[396] *Universal Cargo Carriers Corp v Citati* [1957] 2 Q.B. 401.
[397] See fnn.408, 409.
[398] See at fn.411.
[399] *Geden Operations Ltd v Dry Bulk Handy Holdings Inc* [2014] EWHC 885 (Comm); [2014] 2 Lloyd's Rep. 266 at [17].
[400] *The Hermosa* [1982] 1 Lloyd's Rep. 570 at 572.
[401] *The Hermosa* [1982] 1 Lloyd's Rep. 570 at 580.
[402] *The Hermosa* [1982] 1 Lloyd's Rep. 570 at 572.
[403] *The Hermosa* [1982] 1 Lloyd's Rep. 570 at 573; *Universal Cargo Carriers Corp v Citati* [1957] 2 Q.B. 401 at 439–440; *The Sanko Iris* [1987] 1 Lloyd's Rep. 487; Carter [1988] L.M.C.L.Q. 21; *Geden Operations Ltd v Dry Bulk Handy Holdings Inc* [2014] EWHC 885 (Comm); [2014] 2 Lloyd's Rep. 266.
[404] For the suggestion that the claimant must subjectively believe that the defendant has the intention not to perform, see *The Pro Victor* [2009] EWHC 2974 (Comm); [2010] 2 Lloyd's Rep. 158 at

which the innocent party was, or a reasonable person in his or her position would have been, aware and throws light on the way the alleged repudiatory act would be viewed as such by a reasonable person."[405]

17–090 **Prospective disability.** Where a party is alleged to have committed an anticipatory breach by disabling himself from performing, the question whether the other party is entitled to terminate will generally depend on the seriousness of the resulting failure in performance. That failure being wholly prospective, its seriousness is more than usually a matter of speculation;[406] but the injured party may nevertheless seek to terminate before the time fixed for performance. The problem arose in *Universal Cargo Carriers Corp v Citati*[407] where a charterparty obliged the charterer to provide a cargo of 6,000 tons of scrap iron, to load it at the rate of 1,000 tons a day, and to complete the loading by 21 July. He had failed to provide any cargo by 18 July and on that day the shipowners purported to terminate. The charterer's failure to provide a cargo was an actual breach, though not one which of itself justified termination.[408] It seems that the charterer was also in breach of his obligation to load, for if loading were to be completed at the rate of 1,000 tons a day by 21 July it ought to have begun before 18 July. However, perhaps because the obligation to complete loading still lay in the future, the breach was at least in part anticipatory;[409] and the question discussed[410] was whether this breach by the charterer, assuming it to be anticipatory, justified termination by the shipowners on 18 July. This depended on the seriousness of the breach: the shipowners had to show "that on July 18 the charterer was unable to load a cargo within such a time as would not have frustrated the venture".[411] It was not sufficient for them to show that on 18 July they had reasonable grounds for believing that such a frustrating delay would occur; they were justified in terminating only if they could prove that a delay of this kind would actually have occurred.[412]

This rule is likely to prove inconvenient in practice. It does not apply where the contract is alleged to be frustrated.[413] In one such case Scrutton J said that:

[91]–[97]; cf. *Vitol SA v Beta Renowable Group SA* [2017] EWHC 1734 (Comm); [2017] 2 Lloyd's Rep. 338 at [48]; *Phones 4U Ltd v EE Ltd* [2018] EWHC 49 (Comm); [2018] 1 Lloyd's Rep. 204 at [57]. See Liu [2010] L.M.C.L.Q. 359.

405 *Eminence Property Developments v Heaney Ltd* [2010] EWCA Civ 1168; (2010) 43 E.G. 99 at [63]; *Tullett Prebon Plc v BGC Brokers LP* [2011] EWCA Civ 131; [2011] I.R.L.R. 420 at [22]–[29].

406 *The Nema* [1982] A.C. 724 at 744 (Lord Diplock); 752 (Lord Roskill); *MSC Mediterranean Shipping Co SA v Cottonex Anstalt* [2016] EWCA Civ 789; [2016] 2 Lloyd's Rep. 494 at [25].

407 [1957] 2 Q.B. 401; *Re Simoco Digital UK Ltd* [2004] EWHC 209 (Ch); [2004] 1 B.C.L.C. 541 at [22]–[23].

408 *Universal Cargo Carriers Corp v Citati* [1957] 2 Q.B. 401 at 429. He was also in breach of his obligation to nominate a berth. Neither breach was one of condition: see at 429 and cf. para.18–052.

409 Devlin J at 429 discusses whether *this* breach (which was also not one of condition) was actual or anticipatory and concludes that "it must be one or the other".

410 *Universal Cargo Carriers Corp v Citati* [1957] 2 Q.B. 401 at 436.

411 *Universal Cargo Carriers Corp v Citati* [1957] 2 Q.B. 401 at 450.

412 *Universal Cargo Carriers Corp v Citati* [1957] 2 Q.B. 401 at 449. The point appears to have been conceded; cf. *Geden Operations Ltd v Dry Bulk Handy Holdings Inc* [2014] EWHC 885 (Comm); [2014] 2 Lloyd's Rep. 266 at [18].

413 See paras 19–054—19–055.

> "Commercial men must not be asked to wait till the end of a long delay to find out from what in fact happens whether they are bound by a contract or not; they must be entitled to act on reasonable commercial probabilities at the time when they are called upon to make up their minds."[414]

In the *Citati* case Devlin J held that this principle did not apply to "questions of breach of contract";[415] and he added that "An anticipatory breach must be proved in fact and not in supposition."[416] One can to some extent justify the distinction between the two types of cases. Frustration leads only to discharge of the contract, while anticipatory breach can lead both to termination and to liability in damages. It seems obviously unfair to hold one party (A) liable *in damages*, merely because the other (B) reasonably believed that A would be unable to perform, if it turns out that A is in fact able to perform at the appointed time. But it does not follow that B should not in these circumstances be entitled to terminate. On this point the reasoning of the *Citati* case is open to the same objection as that of *Hochster v De la Tour*:[417] it assumes that, in cases of anticipatory breach, the right to damages and the right to terminate necessarily arise at the same time. This is, however, no criticism of the actual decision in the *Citati* case, which appears to be consistent with the view here put forward; for the issue in the case was not whether the shipowners were liable for wrongful termination, but whether the charterer was liable in damages for an anticipatory breach of his obligation to load.

**Prospective effects of actual breach.** A reasonable belief that a substantial failure will occur is also sufficient to justify termination where there has at the time of termination been an actual breach which gives rise to uncertainty as to future performance. For example, where a ship is unseaworthy, "the charterer may rightly terminate … if the delay in remedying any breach is so long in fact, *or likely to be so long in reasonable anticipation*, that the commercial purpose of the contract would be frustrated".[418] In such a case the court need not fear that the shipowner will be held liable in damages merely because it was reasonably anticipated that he could not perform. His liability in damages is already established by reason of the actual breach; all that is in issue is the right of the injured party to terminate. *That right* should, it is submitted, depend on "reasonable anticipation" in cases of anticipatory, no less than of actual[419] breach. 17–091

**Consequences of termination.** Where the injured party is entitled to, and does, terminate for anticipatory breach, two results follow. First, he is released from 17–092

---

[414] *Embiricos v Sydney Reid & Co* [1914] 3 K.B. 45 at 54.

[415] *Universal Cargo Carriers Corp v Citati* [1957] 2 Q.B. 401 at 449.

[416] *Universal Cargo Carriers Corp v Citati* [1957] 2 Q.B. 401 at 450; Carter 47 M.L.R. 422; cf. *BV Oliehandel Jongkind v Coastal International Ltd* [1983] 2 Lloyd's Rep. 463 where the contract to some extent modified the English rule stated by Devlin J in the *Citati* case.

[417] (1853) 2 E. & B. 678 at 679; para.17–081.

[418] *Hongkong Fir Shipping Co Ltd v Kawasaki Kisen Kaisha Ltd* [1962] 2 Q.B. 26 at 57 (emphasis added); *Snia v Suzuki & Co* (1929) 29 Com. Cas. 284 (the *Citati* case itself may have been of this kind: see para.17–090); cf. *The Hermosa* [1982] 1 Lloyd's Rep. 570 at 580 (where a mere reasonable *suspicion*, as opposed to a reasonable *conclusion*, of future inability was held insufficient to justify termination).

[419] See para.18–036.

future obligations under the contract: this is so even though between acceptance of the anticipatory breach and the time fixed for performance the party in breach changes his mind and offers after all to perform.[420] Secondly, the injured party is no longer bound to perform in order to establish his right of action on the contract; indeed he need not even show that he could at the time fixed for performance have performed a condition precedent to the other party's liability or a concurrent condition, though the existence and extent of this rule is controversial.[421]

### (d) Effects of not accepting the breach

17–093 **Contract remains in force.** If the injured party does not accept the breach, he remains liable to perform,[422] and he retains the right to enforce the other party's primary obligations.[423] As a practical matter, he also keeps alive the possibility of securing actual performance of the contract without legal action.

17–094 **Whether affirmation irrevocable.** The fact that the injured party initially calls for performance does not prevent him from terminating the contract on account of a later *actual* breach;[424] but there is a conflict of judicial opinion on the question whether, after the injured party has affirmed the contract, he can then change his mind while the breach remains anticipatory and still continues at the time of the injured party's later termination. One view is that the injured party should not be allowed to change course in this way[425] since, if the guilty party has acted in reliance on the affirmation by making continued efforts to perform the contract, he will be prejudiced by that change of course.[426] But where no such prejudice is suffered,[427] it is hard to see why effect should not be given to the change of course in cases of anticipatory (as it is in cases of actual)[428] breach. Refusal to give it such effect could unduly prejudice the injured party. For one thing, such refusal could require that party to "engage in performance that is entirely pointless and wasteful"[429] while the other party's anticipatory breach continued. For another, the injured party's initial reaction to the anticipatory

[420] *Danube, etc. Ry v Xenos* (1863) 13 C.B. (N.S.) 825; cf. *Decro-Wall International SA v Practitioners in Marketing Ltd* [1971] 1 W.L.R. 361 at 382.

[421] See paras 17–025—17–030.

[422] See para.18–026.

[423] See para.18–026.

[424] *Stocznia Gdanska SA v Latvian Shipping Co* [1997] 2 Lloyd's Rep. 228 at 236; cf. paras 18–028—18–029.

[425] This was the point actually decided in *Stocznia Gdanska SA v Latvian Shipping Co* [1997] 2 Lloyd's Rep. 228; Treitel 114 L.Q.R. 22. The decision was later set aside by the House of Lords: [1998] 1 W.L.R. 574 at 594 but without final resolution of the point here under discussion.

[426] *Stocznia Gdanska SA v Latvian Shipping Co* [1997] 2 Lloyd's Rep. 228 at 235–236.

[427] No such prejudice could have been suffered in *Stocznia Gdanska SA v Latvian Shipping Co* [1997] 2 Lloyd's Rep. 228 since the injured party had originally served notices of termination; but as these were served *under* express provisions of the contract they formed (somewhat paradoxically) part of the process of affirmation.

[428] See paras 18–028–18–029.

[429] *Stocznia Gdanska SA v Latvian Shipping Co* [2001] 1 Lloyd's Rep. 537 at 565; affirmed [2002] EWCA Civ 889; [2002] 2 Lloyd's Rep. 436.

breach might well be to call on the guilty party to perform and this might be regarded as an affirmation of the contract. One way of protecting the injured party in such cases would be to hold that the demand did not of itself amount to an affirmation,[430] but this possibility might be ruled out on the facts, e.g. by the terms of the demand. In such cases the possible hardship to the guilty party has to be set against that to the injured party and it is submitted that, on balance, the preferable view[431] is that the injured party should not, as a general rule, be precluded by his initial affirmation from terminating the contract, even while the breach remains anticipatory, if after the affirmation the guilty party persists in his refusal. Any hardship which this view might cause to the guilty party would be removed by holding that there could be no such change of course where the original demand for performance induced the guilty party to continue, in response to the demand, to make efforts to perform the contract.

**Damages.** A party who does not accept the breach cannot at common law get damages before the time fixed for performance;[432] and meanwhile he runs the risk of losing his right of action altogether. This could, for example, happen if the contract created a contingent right and events occurred to defeat that right between the time of the anticipatory breach and that fixed for performance.[433] The injured party will similarly lose his rights in respect of the anticipatory breach if he does not accept it and if, before performance from the guilty party has become due, that party withdraws his repudiation,[434] or lawfully puts an end to the contract, e.g. under an express cancelling clause.[435] The position is the same if, before that time, the contract was discharged by operation of law under the doctrine of frustration;[436] it would, in such a case, make no difference if the repudiating party had been unable to perform even if the frustrating event had not occurred.[437] **17–095**

430 See *Yukong Line Ltd of Korea v Rendsburg Investments Co of Liberia* [1996] 2 Lloyd's Rep. 604; *Stocznia Gdanska SA v Latvian Shipping Co* [2001] 1 Lloyd's Rep. 537 at 563–564; affirmed on this ground [2002] EWCA Civ 889; [2002] 2 Lloyd's Rep. 436 at [87]–[92].

431 Expressed in *Stocznia Gdanska SA v Latvian Shipping Co* [2001] 1 Lloyd's Rep. 537; affirmed [2002] EWCA Civ 889; [2002] 2 Lloyd's Rep. 436, leaving the present point open at [97]–[100] but inclining towards the view stated in the text above.

432 For a possible statutory power to award damages in such a case, if the contract was of a kind that is specifically enforceable, see para.21–070.

433 e.g. if in *Synge v Synge* [1894] 1 Q.B. 466; para.17–082, the wife had died before the husband without accepting the breach.

434 *Norwest Holst Group Administration Ltd v Harrison* [1985] I.C.R. 668.

435 *The Simona* [1989] A.C. 788; cf. para.18–075.

436 *Avery v Bowden* (1855) 5 E. & B. 714; (1856) 6 E. & B. 953; cf. *The Playa Larga* [1983] 2 Lloyd's Rep. 171 at 186; for frustration, see Ch.19.

437 *Continental Grain Export Corp v STM Grain Ltd* [1979] 2 Lloyd's Rep. 460 at 470.

# CHAPTER 18

## TERMINATION FOR BREACH[1]



### 1. INTRODUCTION

**Terminology.** Termination in the present context is used to describe the remedy by which one party (the "injured party") is released from his obligation to perform because of the other party's defective or non-performance. It differs from other remedies such as damages, or specific performance, which seek to put the injured party into the position in which he would have been if the contract had been performed. It may, and often will, be used in combination with a claim for 18–001

[1] Devlin [1966] C.L.J. 192; Reynolds 79 L.Q.R. 534; Treitel 30 M.L.R. 139; Shea 42 M.L.R. 623; Beatson 97 L.Q.R. 389; Andrews, Clarke, Tettenborn and Virgo, *Contractual Duties: Performance, Breach, Termination and Remedies*, 2nd edn (2017) Stannard and Capper, *Termination for Breach of Contract* (2014); *Carter's Breach of Contract*, 2nd edn (2018).

damages, provided the failure to perform also amounts to a breach.[2] In some circumstances, the injured party may wish not only to be released from his own obligation to perform, but to "undo" the transaction by returning the defective performance and claiming back the consideration which he provided for it, e.g. he may return defective goods and sue for recovery of the price which he had paid for them.[3]

In earlier editions of this book "rescission" was the term used for the remedy with which this chapter is concerned, rather than "termination". No term seems ideally suited.[4] In the *Photo Production* case, Lord Diplock described the use of either "determination" or "rescission" as "misleading" unless it was borne in mind that such rescission did not deprive the injured party of his right to claim damages for breach.[5] The chief source of this possible confusion seems, however, to lie with the word "rescission"[6] and the contrast with rescission *for misrepresentation*, the effect of which is to deprive the injured party of his claim in damages *for breach*.[7] Therefore, while the courts and Parliament[8] may sometimes continue to use the term "rescission", "termination" is preferred here so as to distinguish clearly the remedy available specifically for breach.

18–002 **Interests of the injured party.** The interests of the injured party in seeking termination may be grouped under three heads. First, termination will be his only remedy where the failure in performance is not, in fact, a breach.[9] Secondly, termination may, even where the failure is a breach, lead to a result which is more favourable to the injured party in monetary terms than a claim for damages. This will be true where the contract would have been a bad bargain for the injured party even if it had been duly performed;[10] and also where the loss or injury which he suffers is one for which he might not recover damages in an action for breach of contract, e.g. if his loss (or part of it) is irrecoverable because itis too remote.[11] Thirdly, the injured party may, by terminating, get a quicker and more efficacious remedy. A buyer who has not yet paid for defective goods will often prefer to "terminate" (in the sense of rejecting the goods and refusing to pay) than

---

[2] In the vast majority of cases failure to perform will amount to a breach and that is the assumption made in this chapter, while acknowledging that in some cases there may be no breach because of a lawful excuse: see, e.g. *Poussard v Speirs & Pond* (1876) 1 Q.B.D. 410 at 414; para.18–036, fn.185. On lawful excuse generally, see para.17–059.

[3] This remedy is more fully discussed paras 22–002—22–020.

[4] It is also quite common to see the remedy discussed in this chapter described as "discharge by breach". "Discharge" may be appropriate to describe the effect of the remedy on the obligations of the parties, but is not ideal vis-à-vis the contract itself: "[T]he aggrieved party is *discharged* from his obligations and can *rescind* the contract": Devlin [1966] C.L.J. 192. Even the word "by" may not be thought entirely appropriate since it tends to suggest an automatic process rather than one which depends on the election of the injured party; para.18–005.

[5] *Photo Production Ltd v Securicor Transport Ltd* [1980] A.C. 827 at 851; para.18–022; cf. *Federal Commissioner of Taxation v Reliance Carpet Co Pty Ltd* (2008) 236 C.L.R. 342.

[6] *Photo Production Ltd v Securicor Transport Ltd* [1980] A.C. 827 at 844 (Lord Wilberforce); cf. an earlier criticism in *Heyman v Darwins Ltd* [1942] A.C. 356 at 399.

[7] See para.9–109.

[8] e.g. the Sale of Goods Act 1979 s.48(4).

[9] See fn.2.

[10] This is a constantly recurring problem: see para.17–039; paras 18–037, 18–050, 18–051.

[11] See para.20–119 and following.

to perform his side of the bargain and be left to pursue a claim for damages. By terminating he avoids the delays of litigation, and the risk that the seller's credit may fail.

**Interests of the defaulting party.** The party who fails to perform in accordance with the contract may have equally strong interests in resisting terminating. He may have incurred expenses in the course of performance, e.g. by paying commission on a sale or by transporting goods to a distant place; and these expenses will be thrown away if the contract is terminated. He may, in addition, have conferred benefits on the injured party who may be unjustly enriched by being allowed to terminate: termination of partly performed building contracts may, for example, produce this result.[12] And he may suffer hardship if the injured party is allowed to terminate on a falling market: he may be left with goods whose value has diminished by an amount far in excess of the loss which the defect in his performance would have caused to the injured party. **18–003**

**A complex and difficult area.** The law governing the right to terminate for breach is complex and difficult; and in this it reflects the difficulty of balancing or reconciling the conflicting interests of the parties in respectively seeking, and resisting, termination.[13] The courts have developed a number of rules and distinctions which prima facie determine the availability of termination as a remedy for breach. Further rules specify that the right to terminate, even where it is prima facie available, may be limited or barred by certain supervening factors. Before they are considered it is necessary to understand the nature and effect of termination. **18–004**

## 2. NATURE AND EFFECT OF TERMINATION

### (a) Nature

**No automatic termination.**[14] A breach which justifies termination (often referred to as a "repudiatory breach") does not automatically determine the contract.[15] It only gives the injured party the option either to terminate the contract or to affirm it and to claim further performance.[16] This is generally the **18–005**

[12] See para.17–042.
[13] Honnold 97 U. of Pa. L. Rev. 457.
[14] Carter 128 L.Q.R. 283.
[15] *Heyman v Darwins Ltd* [1942] A.C. 356 at 361; *Decro-Wall International SA v Practitioners in Marketing Ltd* [1971] 1 W.L.R. 361 at 368, 375, 381; *The Simona* [1989] A.C. 788 at 800; cf. the overruling in *Photo Production Ltd v Securicor Transport Ltd* [1980] A.C. 827 of *Harbutt's "Plasticine" Ltd v Wayne Tank & Pump Co Ltd* [1970] 1 Q.B. 447. See Thompson 41 M.L.R. 137, suggesting a possible reconsideration of the rule stated in the text.
[16] *Geys v Société Générale* [2012] UKSC 63; [2013] 1 A.C. 523; *MSC Mediterranean Shipping Co SA v Cottonex Anstalt* [2016] EWCA Civ 789; [2016] 2 Lloyd's Rep. 494 at [29]; *Budana v Leeds Teaching Hospitals NHS Trust* [2017] EWCA Civ 1980; [2018] 1 W.L.R. 1965 at [38].

case, even if the contract says that it is to become "void" on breach.[17] Normally such a stipulation is interpreted[18] restrictively so as to prevent one party from relying on his own breach of duty to the other party.[19] The reason for the rule that termination depends on the injured party's election is that the guilty party should not be allowed to rely on his own wrong so as to obtain a benefit under the contract,[20] or to excuse his own failure of further performance, or in some other way to prejudice the injured party's legal position under the contract.[21] Thus the guilty party is not allowed to take advantage of the breach by arguing that the original contract is discharged, so as to be entitled to a quantum meruit for work done by him,[22] or that he need pay only at the market rate (below that fixed by the contract) for services rendered to him.[23] Nor is he allowed to rely on the breach so as to prevent the injured party from enforcing provisions in the contract which are advantageous to that party and which may operate after the breach (such as a valid exclusive dealing clause);[24] or so as to deprive the injured party of the chance of claiming specific relief,[25] or of obtaining a lien on the guilty party's property.[26]

18–006 **Employment contracts.**[27] There was some support for the view that termination is automatic where an employee does not continue to work for the employer after a repudiatory breach,[28] e.g. because he has been wrongfully dismissed.[29] One argument in support of this view is that, where the employee is no longer working

---

[17] cf. *Davenport v R.* (1877) 3 App. Cas. 115; *New Zealand Shipping Co v Société des Ateliers, etc., de France* [1919] A.C. 1. Automatic termination results only if the event on which the contract is expressed to come to an end occurs without breach of duty, as in *Brown v Knowsley BC* [1986] I.R.L.R. 102.

[18] e.g. *Alghussein Establishment v Eton College* [1988] 1 W.L.R. 587; for the status of the rule as one of interpretation, capable of being excluded by contrary provision, see *Cheall v APEX* [1983] 2 A.C. 180 at 189; cf. *The Bonde* [1991] 1 Lloyd's Rep. 136 at 144; *BDW Trading Ltd v JM Rowe Investments Ltd* [2011] EWCA Civ 548 at [31].

[19] For the requirement that the duty must be owed to the other party, see *Thompson v ASDA-MFI Group Plc* [1988] Ch. 241; contrast *Cheall v APEX* [1983] 2 A.C. 180 (breach of duty to third party).

[20] See *Alghussein Establishment v Eton College* [1988] 1 W.L.R. 587.

[21] *Alghussein Establishment v Eton College* [1988] 1 W.L.R. 587; contrast *Cheall v APEX* [1983] 2 A.C. 180 (breach of agreement with third party).

[22] *Boston Deep Sea Fishing & Ice Co v Ansell* (1888) 39 Ch D. 339 at 364. The circumstances in which the injured party may terminate for breach and claim a quantum meruit are discussed at para.22–032; cf. para.17–046.

[23] Example based on *Timber Shipping Co SA v London & Overseas Freighters Ltd* [1972] A.C. 1 (where there was no breach).

[24] e.g. *Decro-Wall International v Practitioners in Marketing Ltd* [1971] 1 W.L.R. 361; cf. *Thomas Marshall (Exports) Ltd v Guinle* [1979] Ch. 227; *WPM Retail v Laing* [1978] I.C.R. 787 (employee preserving right to bonus after wrongful dismissal); *Lusograin Commercio Internacional de Cereas Ltda v Bunge AG* [1986] 2 Lloyd's Rep. 654 (seller's right to "carrying charges" (para.20–140) after repudiation by buyer). For exclusion of the rule by contrary agreement, see fn.18.

[25] See *Decro-Wall International SA v Practitioners in Marketing Ltd* [1971] 1 W.L.R. 361; *Evening Standard Co Ltd v Henderson* [1987] I.C.R. 588.

[26] *G Barker v Eynon* [1974] 1 W.L.R. 462.

[27] Ewing [1993] C.L.J. 405; Cabrelli and Zahn (2012) 41 I.L.J. 346.

[28] *Sanders v Ernest A Neale* [1974] I.C.R. 565; *Gannon v Firth* [1976] I.R.L.R. 415; cf. *Hare v Murphy Bros Ltd* [1974] I.C.R. 603; Thomson 38 M.L.R. 347; Napier [1975] C.L.J. 36.

[29] This is clearly not the position where he is able to continue to work: *Rigby v Ferodo Ltd* [1988] I.C.R. 29.

for the employer (in consequence of the repudiation), the employment *relationship* has plainly come to an end,[30] even against the wishes of the injured party. But it does not follow from this that the *contract* of employment is similarly terminated:[31] the argument that the repudiating party should not be allowed to rely on his own wrong to deprive the injured party of valuable rights under the contract has as much force where the contract is one of employment as it has in relation to other contracts.[32]

A further argument for the view that a contract of employment is automatically terminated by repudiatory breach is that, if the contract were not so terminated, a wrongfully dismissed employee would be entitled to sue for his wages until the time of his election to terminate; whereas it is settled that his remedy is in damages and not by action for the agreed wages.[33] But this argument fails to distinguish between the continued existence of the *contract*, and the *remedies* for its breach.[34] This point is by no means restricted to contracts of employment. Suppose, for example, that a buyer wrongfully repudiates an instalment contract for the sale of goods by refusing to accept further instalments. If the seller elects to treat the contract as remaining in existence, it does not follow that he can sue for *the price* of the undelivered instalments. His remedy is normally in damages, though the amount recoverable may depend on whether he elects to terminate.[35] Similarly, where a time charter is wrongfully repudiated by the charterer, the shipowner is not bound to accept the repudiation; but even if he elects to affirm his remedy may be in damages rather than for the agreed hire:[36] "It is ... the range of remedies which is limited, not the right to elect."[37] The same is true of contracts of employment: it does not follow from the continued existence of the *contract* that a wrongfully dismissed employee's *remedy* is by action for the agreed sum.[38] Thus it is submitted that the general rule applies to such contracts, i.e. that a repudiatory breach by either party does not lead to automatic termination, but only gives the injured party an option to terminate the contract.[39] This view was confirmed by a majority of the Supreme Court in *Geys v Société*

[30] *Micklefield v SAC Technology* [1990] 1 W.L.R. 1002 at 1006; *Delaney v Staples* [1992] 1 A.C. 687 at 692; *Wilson v St Helens BC* [1998] I.C.R. 1141 at 1152.

[31] *Gunton v Richmond-upon-Thames LBC* [1981] Ch. 448 at 474; followed, though with reluctance, in *Boyo v Lambeth LBC* [1995] I.C.R. 727; cf. para.15–054; *Micklefield v SAC Technology* [1990] 1 W.L.R. 1002; *Lister v Forth Dry Dock & Engineering Co Ltd* [1990] 1 A.C. 546 at 568. Conversely, the *relationship* may continue after the *contract* has come to an end: *Eastbourne BC v Foster* [2001] EWCA Civ 1091; [2002] I.C.R. 234.

[32] *Geys v Société Générale* [2012] UKSC 63; [2013] 1 A.C. 523 at [66].

[33] *Denmark Productions Ltd v Boscobel Productions Ltd* [1969] 1 Q.B. 699 at 726; *Gunton v Richmond-upon-Thames LBC* [1981] Ch. 448 at 474; *Marsh v National Autistic Society* [1993] I.C.R. 453; *Geys v Société Générale* [2012] UKSC 63; [2013] 1 A.C. 523 at [79]; cf. *Delaney v Staples* [1992] 1 A.C. 687 at 693; *Cerberus Software Ltd v Rowley* [2001] EWCA Civ 78; [2001] I.C.R. 376.

[34] See para.21–011, fn.34.

[35] See para.20–081.

[36] See para.21–015.

[37] *The Alaskan Trader (No.2)* [1983] 2 Lloyd's Rep. 645 at 651.

[38] e.g. *Silvey v Pendragon Plc* [2001] EWCA Civ 784; [2001] I.R.L.R. 685.

[39] *Simmons v Hoover Ltd* [1977] Q.B. 284; *Gunton v Richmond-upon-Thames LBC* [1981] 1 Ch. 448; *Burdett-Coutts v Hertfordshire CC* [1984] I.R.L.R. 91; *Evening Standard Co Ltd v Henderson* [1987] I.C.R. 586 at 593, 595; cf. also *Decro-Wall International SA v Practitioners in Marketing Ltd* [1971] 1 W.L.R. 361 at 369–370, 375–376, 380–381; the same assumption seems to underlie *Miles v Wakefield MDC* [1987] A.C. 539; para.18–026.

*Générale*[40] in which the practical issue was the date of termination for the purpose of calculating a severance payment due to the employee. The was held to be the date upon which the contact was validly terminated by the employer under an express provision for determination,[41] and not the date upon which the employer was guilty of a repudiatory breach in the form of an unlawful summary dismissal.

18–007 **An exception: further performance is "impossible"?** The principal reason why the injured party may elect to affirm the contract is in order to claim the remedy of an agreed sum (i.e. an action for the price), rather than damages.[42] In order to do so, it must be possible for him to complete his own performance and, even then, the courts may confine him to damages if he has no "legitimate interest" in doing so.[43] For example, an employee is usually only entitled to his wages if he performs the work required of him, but since the employer cannot be compelled to provide him with work, he is unable to satisfy the first requirement. Strictly speaking, as noted above, in such a case the court only denies the injured party the *remedy* to which he would normally be entitled and not his *right* to elect whether to affirm or terminate. This may "appear to be a distinction without a difference"[44] in that, in practice, the remedy of damages left to the injured party is consistent with the contract having been (automatically) terminated. But the distinction remains an important one in a case like *Geys v Société Générale* where the employee was not suing for his salary, but rather the severance payment.

In one type of case, however, it appears that the courts have acknowledged that termination may be automatic, or something even closer to it. In *MSC Mediterranean Shipping Co SA v Cottonex Anstalt*[45] the defendant shipper was allowed a certain amount of "free" time after the delivery of containers of cotton to unpack and return the containers to the carrier, after which they were required to pay demurrage[46] at a daily rate. The containers were delivered and the buyers, through their banks, paid for the cotton. This meant that the shipper had no title to the cotton and therefore no entitlement to deal with it, but the buyers refused to collect it. Furthermore, the custom authorities refused to allow the containers to be released without a court order which there was little or no prospect of obtaining. This state of affairs had existed for about two years by the time the carrier issued a claim form in April 2013 in which it claimed demurrage for the entire period and on a continuing basis. The Court of Appeal found that by

---

[40] [2012] UKSC 63; [2013] 1 A.C. 523 (Lord Sumption dissenting). Without suggesting that the decision was incorrect, it has been said to give rise to a number of "consequential conundrums": *Sunrise Brokers LLP v Rodgers* [2014] EWCA Civ 1373; [2015] I.C.R. 272 at [58], per Longmore LJ.

[41] In *Geys v Société Générale* [2012] UKSC 63; [2013] 1 A.C. 523, the employer was only able to rely on this method once it had fully complied with the procedure laid down: see para.18–077; cf. *Gisda Cyf v Barratt* [2010] UKSC 41; [2010] I.C.R. 1475 (effective date of termination for the purpose of claims under the Employment Rights Act 1996 s.97(1)).

[42] See para.21–001 and following.

[43] These two requirements are considered further at paras 21–009—21–017.

[44] *MSC Mediterranean Shipping Co SA v Cottonex Anstalt* [2016] EWCA Civ 789; [2016] 2 Lloyd's Rep. 494 at [40] (Moore-Bick LJ).

[45] [2016] EWCA Civ 789; [2016] 2 Lloyd's Rep. 494.

[46] A form of liquidated damages: see para.20–135.

February 2012, the shipper was in repudiatory breach on the basis that the commercial purpose of the venture had become frustrated,[47] but at no time had the carrier elected to terminate.

This was not a case where the carrier needed to complete its own performance since it had already done so by delivering the containers,[48] but had it been necessary to do so, the Court would have held that the carrier had no legitimate interest in continuing to insist on performance by the shipper. The accrued demurrage already exceeded by a considerable amount the value of the containers and replacement containers were readily available at the port. The carrier had no interest in keeping the contract alive other than to earn demurrage pending their return in the form of delivery. However, it was not necessary to decide the case on this basis because it "was not open to the carrier to affirm the contract".[49] According to Tomlinson LJ the *Geys* case was distinguishable in that it did not involve a contract which has "become repudiated because it is no longer capable of performance, as in the classic case of frustrating delay"[50]:

> "… the innocent party simply cannot treat the contract as subsisting because it is no longer capable of performance as agreed. There is no alternative to the conclusion that *the contract has come to an end*. The fact that the carrier continued to press for performance, in the shape both of redelivery of the containers and the payment of demurrage, is neither here nor there. Those were acts in vain, unrelated to an existing contract."[51]

It seems therefore that in a case of anticipatory breach by "impossibility"[52] the contract may have "come to an end", regardless of any election by the injured party.

**Insurance contracts: old law.** In the law of insurance "warranty" has been used in a sense similar to that now more usually given to "condition", i.e. to refer to a term, the breach of which justifies the injured party's refusal to perform.[53] But the exact legal effects of a breach of "warranty" in insurance law were not identical with those elsewhere given to a breach of "condition": in particular, there was no requirement in insurance law that an insurer who is the victim of a breach of "warranty" must take any steps to exercise his option to avoid liability. A statutory statement of this position was given in s.33(3) of the Marine Insurance Act 1906, which provided that "[a] warranty is a condition which must be exactly **18–008**

[47] The clearest indication of this was an offer by the carrier to sell the containers to the shipper which the shipper had rejected.
[48] *MSC Mediterranean Shipping Co SA v Cottonex Anstalt* [2016] EWCA Civ 789; [2016] 2 Lloyd's Rep. 494 at [33], [39].
[49] *MSC Mediterranean Shipping Co SA v Cottonex Anstalt* [2016] EWCA Civ 789; [2016] 2 Lloyd's Rep. 494 at [43] (Moore-Bick LJ).
[50] *MSC Mediterranean Shipping Co SA v Cottonex Anstalt* [2016] EWCA Civ 789; [2016] 2 Lloyd's Rep. 494 at [61].
[51] *MSC Mediterranean Shipping Co SA v Cottonex Anstalt* [2016] EWCA Civ 789; [2016] 2 Lloyd's Rep. 494 at [61] (emphasis added).
[52] *MSC Mediterranean Shipping Co SA v Cottonex Anstalt* [2016] EWCA Civ 789; [2016] 2 Lloyd's Rep. 494 at [43] (Moore-Bick LJ: "further performance became impossible"); see para.17–076.
[53] See para.18–043.

complied with, whether it be material to the risk or not. If it be not so complied with, then … the insurer is discharged from liability as from the date of the breach of warranty."

The effect of these words was considered in *The Good Luck*,[54] where a ship had been insured under a policy entitling the insurers to declare certain areas as prohibited and containing a "warranty" that the shipowner would comply with any such prohibition. The policy was assigned to a bank (to which the ship had been mortgaged) and the insurers undertook to notify the bank "promptly" if they "ceased to insure" the ship. Some months later the ship was struck by an Iraqi missile while trading in the Persian Gulf (which had been declared by the insurers to be a prohibited area) and became a constructive total loss. A claim on the policy having been rejected, it was held that the insurers were liable on their undertaking to the bank. They had "ceased to insure" the ship as soon as she had entered the prohibited area: this breach of "warranty" released the insurers automatically,[55] without any election on their part. This followed from the wording of s.33(3), by which the insurer "is discharged from liability as from the date of the breach of warranty". These words should be contrasted with those of the Sale of Goods Act 1979, giving a buyer, in cases of breach of condition, "a right to treat the contract as repudiated".[56]

18–009 **Changes introduced by the Insurance Act 2015.** Part 3 of the Insurance Act 2015 came into force on 12 August 2016[57] and significantly alters the law as described in the preceding paragraph.[58] Marine Insurance Act 1906 s.33(3) no longer states that the insurer is discharged from liability as from the date of the breach of warranty[59] and, more generally, any rule of law that breach of warranty in an insurance contract results in discharge of the insurer's liability is abolished.[60] But while s.33(3) continues to state that a warranty "is a condition which must be exactly complied with", the legal effects of a breach of "warranty" are still not made identical with those elsewhere given to a breach of "condition". Rather, for so long as a breach has occurred and has not been remedied,[61] the insurer's liability is only suspended, i.e. the insurer has no liability for anything which occurs, or which is attributable to something happening,[62] during this period.[63] The insurer remains liable in respect of losses occurring before the breach of warranty, or after it has been remedied, if capable of remedy.[64] The

---

54 [1992] 1 A.C. 233.

55 cf. *Hussain v Brown* [1996] 1 Lloyd's Rep. 627 at 630.

56 Sale of Goods Act 1979 s.11(3).

57 Sale of Goods Act 1979 s.23(2).

58 In addition to the change in the law discussed in the text, see also s.11 which limits the extent to which an insurer can exclude, limit or discharge its liability for non-compliance with any term of the contract (other than a term defining the risk as a whole) which would reduce the risk of loss of a particular kind, or at a particular location, or at a particular time.

59 Insurance Act 2015 s.10(7)(a).

60 Insurance Act 2015 s.10(1).

61 As to which, see s.10(5) and (6).

62 i.e. it is the relevant event which must have happened even if the loss is suffered after the breach has been remedied.

63 Insurance Act 2015 s.10(2).

64 Insurance Act 2015 s.10(4).

insurer's liability is not suspended if the warranty ceases to be applicable to the circumstances of the contract, or if compliance with it is rendered unlawful by any subsequent law, or if the insurer waives the breach.[65] Where it takes effect, the suspension of the insurer's liability is automatic.

**Restrictions on injured party's choice.** Although termination depends (except in the situations discussed above) on the election of the injured party, that party's option is to some extent curtailed by the rule that the damages to which he is entitled may be reduced if he fails to take reasonable steps to mitigate his loss.[66] This rule will sometimes put pressure on the injured party to terminate, for one common way of mitigating loss is to make a substitute contract; and the effect of doing this will often be to put it out of the injured party's power to perform the old contract. Where this is the case, the making of the substitute contract will involve the termination of the original one. Thus if a wrongfully dismissed employee mitigates his loss by taking another job[67] he will thereby be "taken to have accepted his wrongful dismissal as a repudiatory breach leading to a determination of the contract of service".[68] The same would be true where a seller, on the buyer's repudiation, disposed elsewhere of the subject-matter. In these cases the injured party is not under any legal obligation to make the substitute contract;[69] so that in this sense he remains free to choose between affirmation and termination. But his freedom of choice is limited in that, if he acts unreasonably in failing to make such a contract, he will suffer a reduction in the damages to which he is entitled by reason of breach of the original contract. **18–010**

Conversely, the mitigation rules may require the injured party to accept performance from the party in breach even though it is not in accordance with the contract, e.g. they may require a buyer to accept late delivery.[70] In such a case, the mitigation rules again do not, strictly speaking, restrict the injured party's right to terminate, but they do require him, having terminated, to enter into a new contract for late performance at the original price (subject to damages for delay).[71] The injured party does not commit any breach of duty by failing to enter into such a new contract, but his failure to do so will reduce the damages to which he is entitled for breach of the original contract. Hence his freedom of choice will, as a practical matter, be restricted, this time in the direction of putting him under pressure to accept performance, though subject to relatively minor modifications.

**Exercise of the option to terminate: an "unequivocal" intention.** The question whether the option to terminate has been exercised has been described as one of **18–011**

[65] Insurance Act 2015 s.10(3).

[66] See para.20–104.

[67] And he will usually be required to do so because the only remedy available is in damages and not for his salary: see para.18–087 above.

[68] *Gunton v Richmond-upon-Thames LBC* [1981] Ch. 448 at 468. The same result can follow where the employee continues to work for the employer "on an entirely different basis" from that of the repudiated contract: *Eastbourne BC v Foster* [2001] EWCA Civ 1091; [2002] I.C.R. 234.

[69] See para.20–104.

[70] *The Solholt* [1981] 2 Lloyd's Rep. 574; affirmed [1983] 1 Lloyd's Rep. 605.

[71] *The Solholt* [1983] 1 Lloyd's Rep. 605, criticising *Strutt v Whitnell* [1975] 1 W.L.R. 870 for failing to observe the distinction drawn in the text.

fact;[72] but this description assumes that a number of legal requirements have been satisfied. The prime requirement is that the behaviour of the injured party must unequivocally indicate his intention to exercise the option.[73] For example, a notice which purports to terminate the contract, but stipulates *unilaterally* that it shall continue to be performed on a without prejudice basis is not effective.[74] A notice of intended termination at a later date if certain conditions are not fulfilled is not effective unless the threatened termination is then implemented.[75]

18–012 **Silence and inactivity.** Normally mere "silence and inactivity"[76] will not suffice as evidence of an unequivocal intention to terminate, but there is no absolute rule to this effect. Thus in *Vitol SA v Norelf Ltd*[77] a contract for the sale of propane was wrongfully repudiated by the buyer and, after receiving the repudiation, the seller made no attempt to take any of the steps which he would have been expected to take for the purpose of performing the contract,[78] if he were treating it as still in force. The House of Lords held that an arbitrator's finding that the seller had accepted the repudiation was not wrong in law; for, even if the seller's reaction to the breach could be described as "inactivity", it was in the circumstances not equivocal since it clearly conveyed to the buyer that the seller was treating the contract as at an end.

18–013 **Whether notice of termination required.** The option to terminate will commonly be exercised by giving notice to this effect to the party in breach,[79] and sometimes such notice must be given, e.g. where the injured party seeks the return of property with which he has parted under the contract.[80] But there is plainly no such requirement where "inactivity" suffices for the exercise of the

[72] *Kish v Taylor* [1912] A.C. 604 at 617; *Agrokor AG v Tradigrain SA* [2000] 1 Lloyd's Rep. 497 at 500.

[73] *Sookraj v Samaroo* [2004] UKPC 50 at [17].

[74] *Leofelis SA v Lonsdale Sports Ltd* [2008] EWCA Civ 640; [2008] E.T.M.R. 63. After termination, the parties may *agree* to the continued performance of the contract on a without prejudice basis, which *may* avoid a finding of repudiation by the party serving the notice if it is later found to be invalid (cf. *Federal Commerce Navigation Co Ltd v Molena Alpha Inc* [1979] A.C. 757), or may serve to mitigate any loss if there is a finding of repudiation.

[75] *Standard Bank Plc v Agrinvest International Inc* [2010] EWCA Civ 1400; [2010] 2 C.L.C. 886. The wording of the relevant letter in that case ("we will close out … ") does not rule out an effective "conditional" termination without the need to take any additional steps.

[76] *State Trading Corp of India v M Golodetz Ltd* [1989] 2 Lloyd's Rep. 277 at 286; *Glencore Grain Rotterdam BV v LORICO* [1997] 2 Lloyd's Rep. 386 at 394. cf. para.17–089.

[77] [1996] A.C. 800.

[78] Such as tendering shipping documents as "a precondition to payment of the price": *Vitol SA v Norelf Ltd* [1996] A.C. 800 at 811. Contrast *Jaks (UK) Ltd v Cera Investment Bank SA* [1998] 2 Lloyd's Rep. 89 at 96 (failure to take steps to perform another contract with a third party not sufficient); *Vitol SA v Beta Renowable Group SA* [2017] EWHC 1734 (Comm); [2017] 2 Lloyd's Rep. 338.

[79] Notice to a third party may suffice where the defendant cannot be traced: *Bell Electric Ltd v Aweco Appliance Systems GmbH & Co KG* [2002] C.L.C. 1246 at [30]. A notice *of termination* is valid notwithstanding that it refers to a notice *of default* which is found to be invalid, in circumstances where it is possible to rely instead on an earlier valid notice of default: *Reinwood Ltd v L Brown & Sons Ltd* [2008] EWCA Civ 1090; 121 Con L.R. 1 (based on the general rule referred to in para.17–062).

[80] *Lakshmijit v Sherani* [1974] A.C. 605.

option; nor does notice seem to be necessary where the injured party has put it out of his power to perform the original contract by making a substitute contract to satisfy the mitigation requirement.[81] The option can also be exercised by the commencement of proceedings brought on the contract,[82] or in the pleading of a defence.[83] The mere issue of a claim form in which the claimant purports to terminate the contract is too unequivocal an act; acceptance of the defendant's repudiation occurs upon service (unless some other form of notice is given before then).[84]

18–014 **Termination and other remedies.** Obviously the injured party affirms the contract by claiming specific performance, though he may later terminate on the basis of the guilty party's continued failure to perform,[85] but a "decision not to pursue a remedy of specific performance does not commit the innocent party to accept a repudiatory or anticipatory breach."[86] There is no inconsistency between claiming damages for a prior breach, or for the breach in question, and exercising the option to terminate.[87] There are, moreover, cases in which the victim merely refuses to perform until the other party either cures his breach or (in the case of contracts calling for continuing performance) resumes performance in conformity with the contract. For example, an employer may refuse to pay wages, or to pay them in full, for so long as his employee refuses (in the course of "industrial action") to perform his duties under the contract of employment. Such a temporary refusal on the employer's part does not amount to an exercise by him of the option to terminate.[88]

18–015 **No partial termination.** If the injured party accepts further performance after breach, he may be held to have affirmed, so that he cannot later terminate the contract.[89] He must, moreover, terminate the contract as a whole, e.g. a tenant cannot remain on premises and ignore a particular term of the lease on the ground that the landlord had, in the past, failed to perform his obligations under that term.[90]

---

[81] *Gunton v Richmond-upon-Thames LBC* [1981] Ch. 448 at 468.

[82] *Downing v Al Tameer Establishment* [2002] EWCA Civ 721; [2002] C.L.C. 1291. It can be exercised even after beginning of the proceedings: *Tilcons Ltd v Land & Real Estate Investments Ltd* [1987] 1 W.L.R. 46.

[83] *Carter v Lifeplan Products Ltd* [2013] EWCA Civ 453 at [17].

[84] *Bell Electric Ltd v Aweco Appliance Systems GmbH & Co KG* [2002] C.L.C. 1246 at [28].

[85] See para.18–029.

[86] *Bear Stearns Bank Plc v Forum Global Equity Ltd* [2007] EWHC 1576 (Comm) at [127].

[87] *General Billposting Co Ltd v Atkinson* [1909] A.C. 118. Contrast *United Dominions Trust (Commercial) Ltd v Ennis* [1968] 1 Q.B. 54 at 65 (para.18–074).

[88] *Wiluszynski v Tower Hamlets LBC* [1989] I.C.R. 493; it is assumed that the breach justified termination. For the different question whether failure to perform a condition precedent of itself *entitles* the injured party to terminate, see para.17–024.

[89] cf. para.18–089 and following; an *unsatisfied demand* for performance does not have the same effect: para.18–028.

[90] *Total Oil Great Britain Ltd v Thompson Garages (Biggin Hill) Ltd* [1972] 1 Q.B. 318.

## (b) Effects of termination or affirmation

### (i) Termination

18–016 **Effect on obligations of the injured party.** After termination, the injured party is no longer bound to accept or pay for further performance.[91] He is also entitled to refuse to make payments which had not yet fallen due at the time of termination, e.g. because the other party's performance was incomplete or defective;[92] and he is released from other obligations which, under the contract, were to be performed in the future, e.g. a wrongfully dismissed employee is no longer bound by covenants in restraint of trade in his contract of employment.[93]

18–017 **Termination is prospective.** Termination does not operate retrospectively,[94] in the sense of liberating the injured party from his duty to perform obligations which had accrued before termination.[95] In this fundamental respect it differs from rescission which entitles the innocent party to treat the contract as never having come into existence.[96] For example, where freight under a charterparty is deemed earned on loading, the charterer remains liable to pay it even though he later justifiably terminates on account of the shipowner's repudiatory breach.[97] The injured party may also himself have been in breach at the time of the other party's repudiation, but not in such a way as to justify that repudiation.[98] In such a case, the injured party is, in spite of his own breach, entitled to terminate, but he remains liable in damages for the breach which he had himself committed before terminating.[99] The injured party also continues to be bound, after termination, by ancillary obligations of the kind to be described below,[100] and even by primary obligations where the contract expressly so provides.[101]

---

[91] *Photo Production Ltd v Securicor Transport Ltd* [1980] A.C. 827 at 849.

[92] e.g. para.17–032; *SCI (Sales Curve Interactive) v Titus SARL* [2001] EWCA Civ 591; [2001] 2 All E.R. (Comm) 416 at [28]–[33], [65].

[93] *General Billposting Co Ltd v Atkinson* [1909] A.C. 118; *Briggs v Oates* [1990] I.C.R. 473; cf. *Thompson v Corroon* (1993) 66 P. & C.R. 445; *Brown v Neon Management Services Ltd* [2018] EWHC 2137 (QB) at [170]–[174]. Contrast *Lawrence David Ltd v Ashton* [1991] 1 All E.R. 384 (where it was not clear that the employer was in repudiatory breach); and *Rock Refrigeration Ltd v Jones* [1997] I.C.R. 938 (Phillips LJ).

[94] *Hurst v Bryk* [2002] 1 A.C. 185.

[95] *The Bow Cedar* [2004] EWHC 2929; [2005] 1 Lloyd's Rep. 275 at [34]–[35].

[96] *Howard-Jones v Tate* [2011] EWCA Civ 1130; [2012] 2 All E.R. 369.

[97] *The Dominique* [1989] A.C. 1056; cf. *Hurst v Bryk* [2002] 1 A.C. 185 for the application of this principle to a partner's obligation to pay his share of the partnership liabilities incurred before, but falling due after, termination; the partnership itself cannot be dissolved by acceptance of a repudiatory breach; cf. *Mullins v Laughton* [2002] EWHC 2761 (Ch); [2003] Ch. 250; *Golstein v Bishop* [2014] EWCA Civ 10; [2014] Ch. 455; *Flanagan v Liontrust Investment Partners LLP* [2015] EWHC 2171 (Ch); [2016] 1 B.C.L.C. 177.

[98] e.g. where the injured party's own breach is a breach of an independent covenant (para.17–019); or one which is not sufficiently serious to justify termination (para.18–032 and following); or one which occurs simultaneously with the other party's breach, as in *State Trading Corp of India v M Golodetz* [1989] 2 Lloyd's Rep. 277 at 288.

[99] *Gill & Duffus SA v Berger & Co Inc* [1984] A.C. 382 at 390.

[100] See after fn.111.

[101] See at fn.109.

**Limited retrospective effect.** If, at the time of termination, the injured party has already performed, he may be entitled to recover that performance in some cases. For example, a buyer who justifiably rejects goods for breach of condition is normally entitled to the return of the price.[102] To this extent, termination has a retrospective effect. It is submitted that, where the injured party would thus be entitled, after he has terminated, to recover money paid before termination, he should also be relieved from liability to pay sums which had become due (but had not been paid) before termination; for it would make no practical sense to hold him liable in one action for a payment which he could then claim back in another.[103] **18–018**

**Effect on obligations of the party in breach.** For the purpose of stating the effects of termination on the obligations of the party in breach, it is necessary to distinguish between primary and secondary obligations. The primary obligation is one to render the actual performance promised; the secondary obligation is one to pay damages for failure to perform the primary obligation. **18–019**

**Effect on primary obligations.**[104] The effect of termination on the primary obligations of the party in breach is exactly the same as its effect on those of the injured party: normally the party in breach is released from primary obligations which had not yet fallen due at the time of termination,[105] but he remains liable to perform those which had already fallen due at that time,[106] except where a payment which he should have made before termination was one which he could, if he had so made it, have recovered, even on termination for his own breach,[107] e.g. where there has been a total failure of consideration.[108] These rules can be excluded by contrary provision in the contract or by other evidence of contrary intention.[109] Thus even a primary obligation which has not yet fallen due can **18–020**

[102] See para.22–012.

[103] cf. *McDonald v Denys Lascelles Ltd* (1933) 48 C.L.R. 457 (see para.20–176) where a claim against the party in breach failed on similar reasoning, which should a fortiori protect the *injured party*; and para.19–101.

[104] On the difficulty of applying the effects of termination for repudiatory breach on multi-party agreements where only one of the parties is guilty of breach see *Flanagan v Liontrust Investment Partners LLP* [2015] EWHC 2171 (Ch); [2016] 1 B.C.L.C. 177 at [240].

[105] cf. para.18–016. It follows that there can be no specific enforcement of those primary obligations: see *Walker v Standard Chartered Bank* [1992] B.C.L.C. 535.

[106] *Stocznia Gdanska SA v Latvian Shipping Co* [1998] 1 W.L.R. 574; cf. *Fielding & Platt Ltd v Najjar* [1969] 1 W.L.R. 357 at 361; *Lep Air Services v Rolloswin Investments Ltd* [1973] A.C. 331 at 354–355; *Photo Production Ltd v Securicor Transport Ltd* [1980] A.C. 827 at 844, 849; *Hyundai Heavy Industries Ltd v Papadopoulos* [1980] 1 W.L.R. 1129; para.20–176; *The Trident Beauty* [1994] 1 W.L.R. 161 at 164.

[107] *McDonald v Denys Lascelles Ltd* (1933) 48 C.L.R. 457.

[108] *Mirimskaya v Evans* [2007] EWHC 2073 (TCC); (2007) 114 Con L.R. 131.

[109] *Yasuda Fire & Marine Ins Co of Europe v Orion Marine Ins Underwriting Agency Ltd* [1995] 1 Lloyd's Rep. 525.

survive termination if the contract so provides,[110] while liability for one which had fallen due will not survive if the contract validly provides that termination is to be the sole remedy.[111]

18–021 **Ancillary obligations.** Primary obligations must be distinguished from ancillary ones, i.e. those imposed by provisions which deal not with the performance to be rendered, but with such matters as the resolution of disputes arising out of the contract,[112] or the inspection by one party of records to be kept by the other for the purpose of ascertaining what rights and duties have come into existence under the contract.[113] Normally, such ancillary obligations are intended to survive termination and are accordingly not released by it.[114]

18–022 **Secondary obligation to pay damages.** The important difference between the effects of termination on the obligations of the two parties is that the party in breach (unlike the injured party) comes, as a result of termination, under a secondary obligation to pay damages,[115] and that his liability in damages may relate both to breaches committed before termination and to losses suffered by the injured party as a result of the non-performance of future obligations brought about by termination.[116] Suppose, for example, that a hirer under a hire-purchase agreement fails to make the agreed payments in circumstances amounting to a wrongful repudiation and therefore gives the owner the right to terminate. If the owner does terminate, the hirer remains liable for instalments which had fallen due *before* termination, his primary obligation to pay these being unaffected;[117] but he is not liable for *subsequent* instalments, having been released by termination from his primary obligation to make these payments. On the other hand, the hirer is liable in damages for wrongful repudiation and these may include compensation for loss suffered by the owner after, and as a result of, the premature termination of the agreement, e.g. where he has to dispose of the goods elsewhere for less than the amount which would have been paid by the defaulting hirer if the agreement with him had run its full course. Damages for the

---

[110] *Harbinger UK Ltd v GE Information Services Ltd* [2000] 1 All E.R. (Comm) 166 (a case of lawful termination by notice; but there seems to be no reason why a similar express provision should not take effect after termination for breach).

[111] *Malcolm-Ellis (Liverpool) v American Electronics Laboratory* (1984) N.L.J. 500.

[112] *Heyman v Darwins Ltd* [1942] A.C. 356 (arbitration); *Connex South Eastern Ltd v MJ Building Services Group Plc* [2004] EWHC 1518 (TCC); [2004] B.L.R. 333 at [25]; affirmed [2005] EWCA Civ 193; [2005] 1 W.L.R. 3323, without consideration of this issue; cf. Arbitration Act 1996 s.7.

[113] *The Yasuda Fire & Marine Ins Co of Europe Ltd v Orion Marine Ins Underwriting Agency Ltd* [1995] 1 Lloyd's Rep. 525; cf. *Royal Petrol Trading Co UK v Total India PVT Ltd* [2018] EWHC 1272 (Comm).

[114] See the authorities cited in fnn.112 and 113.

[115] *RV Ward Ltd v Bignall* [1967] 1 Q.B. 534 at 548; *Lep Air Services Ltd v Rolloswin Investments Ltd* [1973] A.C. 331, especially at 350; *State Trading Corp of India v M Golodetz Ltd* [1989] 2 Lloyd's Rep. 277 at 286; Carter 1 J.C.L. 113 and 249.

[116] *R Leslie Shipping Co v Welstead* [1921] 3 K.B. 420; *Bridge v Campbell Discount Co Ltd* [1962] A.C. 600; *Hyundai Heavy Industries Ltd v Papadopoulos* [1980] 1 W.L.R. 1129 at 1141; *Photo Production Ltd v Securicor Transport Ltd* [1980] A.C. 827 at 849 ("anticipatory secondary obligation"); *Gill & Duffus SA v Berger Co Inc* [1984] A.C. 382 at 390.

[117] *Brooks v Beirnstein* [1909] 1 K.B. 98; *Chatterton v Maclean* [1951] 1 All E.R. 761; cf. *The Almare Seconda* [1981] 2 Lloyd's Rep. 443; and see para.20–176, fn.1070.

non-performance of future obligations brought about by termination are not available where the injured party terminates under an express contractual provision in circumstances which would not entitle him to terminate under the general law.[118]

**Claim for agreed sum.** For the purpose of these rules, it is important to distinguish between a claim for *damages* (which can be brought in respect of future losses) and a claim for an *agreed sum*[119] (which can be brought only in respect of sums that have become due at the time of termination). The distinction is sometimes overlooked because there is a tendency to describe any claim for money as one for damages, even when it is actually a claim for the enforcement of a primary obligation to pay an agreed sum. The point can be illustrated by taking the common case of a contract of sale which requires the buyer to pay a deposit and which is terminated by the seller after, and on account of, the buyer's breach in failing to pay that deposit. In such a case, the seller will be entitled to: (i) the deposit as an agreed sum due at the time of termination; and (ii) damages for the buyer's repudiatory breach,[120] e.g. for loss suffered because the seller can resell the property only for an amount which falls short of the contract price by more than the amount of the deposit. In such a case, it is not strictly accurate to say that the seller can "sue for damages *including* the amount of the unpaid deposit."[121] This statement is accurate only where the seller has terminated on account of some *other* breach by the buyer *before* the buyer's primary obligation to pay the deposit had accrued. This was the position in *The Blankenstein*,[122] where a contract for the sale of three ships provided for the signing of a formal memorandum and for the payment of a deposit of $236,500 on such signing. The seller terminated on account of the buyer's wrongful refusal to sign and resold the ships for $60,000 less than the original contract price. As the deposit was to be paid only on signing, the primary obligation to pay it never accrued. But it was held that the seller was entitled to $236,500 as damages for the buyer's repudiation in wrongfully refusing to sign the memorandum. The majority of the Court of Appeal rejected the argument that the seller's damages should be no more than $60,000; and their view seems, with respect, to be correct. At the time of termination, the seller had been deprived, by the buyer's breach, of his right to receive the full amount of the deposit. He thus became entitled to damages of a precisely ascertainable amount, and later events (i.e. the relatively favourable resale of the ships) should not be allowed to deprive him of that accrued right. Such events should be relevant to the assessment of damages only where, at the time of termination, it is *not* possible to put an exact value on the injured party's loss. 18–023

**No inconsistency in terminating for breach and claiming damages.** It follows from the preceding discussion that there is no inconsistency between terminating a contract for breach and at the same time claiming damages for that breach. 18–024

[118] Discussed further at para.18–068 and following.
[119] See para.21–001 and following.
[120] See para.18–022.
[121] *Millichamp v Jones* [1982] 1 W.L.R. 1422 at 1430.
[122] [1985] 1 W.L.R. 435; Carter 104 L.Q.R. 207.

Accordingly it has been held that damages can be recovered by a buyer who rejects goods because they are defective,[123] or delivered late;[124] by a wrongfully dismissed employee who has terminated so as to free himself from a covenant in restraint of trade;[125] by a vendor of land who has terminated because of the purchaser's failure to comply with a notice to complete[126]; and by a purchaser of land who has terminated on account of the vendor's breach.[127] Termination for breach differs in this respect from rescission for misrepresentation, the effect of which is to treat the contract as if it had never existed.[128]

18–025 **Insurance contracts.** The rules stated above assume that the injured party has, and has exercised, an option to terminate. We have seen that in the law of insurance an insurer may be discharged from liability automatically, without any such election on his part;[129] and where he is so discharged it does not follow that even the *primary* obligations of the other party are similarly discharged. Thus the assured can remain liable for premiums even though his breach of "warranty" has discharged the insurer.[130] There is nothing in the changes introduced by Pt 3 of the Insurance Act 2015 to indicate that this position is altered when the insurer's liability is suspended automatically.[131]

### (ii) *Affirmation or failure to terminate*

18–026 **Contract remains in force.** The injured party may positively affirm the contract,[132] or simply fail to exercise his option to terminate.[133] In either of these cases, the contract remains in force,[134] so that each party is bound to perform his primary obligations when that performance falls due.[135] It must, however, be recalled that, under the rules relating to the order of performance,[136] the effect of one party's breach may be to prevent performance of the other's obligations from falling due. For example, an employee may, in breach of contract, refuse to perform his duty to work and so give the employer a right to dismiss him.[137] The

---

[123] *Millar's Machinery Co Ltd v David Way & Son* (1935) 40 Com. Cas. 204; cf. Sale of Goods Act 1979 s.48(4) (right of seller).

[124] *The Al Tawfiq* [1984] 2 Lloyd's Rep. 598.

[125] *General Billposting Co Ltd v Atkinson* [1909] A.C. 118.

[126] *Buckland v Farmar & Moody* [1979] 1 W.L.R. 221; *Johnson v Agnew* [1980] A.C. 367.

[127] The contrary was held in *Horsler v Zorro* [1975] Ch. 302 but that decision was disapproved in *Buckland v Farmar & Moody* [1979] 1 W.L.R. 221, and overruled in *Johnson v Agnew* [1980] A.C. 367.

[128] See para.9–099 and cf. *Johnson v Agnew* [1980] A.C. 367 at 395, 398.

[129] See para.18–008.

[130] *The Good Luck* [1992] A.C. 233 at 263.

[131] See para.18–008.

[132] See para.18–089 and following.

[133] Mere inaction does not necessarily amount to such failure: see this situation discussed after fn.76.

[134] e.g. *Segap Garages Ltd v Gulf Oil (Great Britain) Ltd*, *The Times*, 24 October 1989; *BMBF (No.12) v Harland & Wolff Shipbuilding & Heavy Industries Ltd* [2001] EWCA Civ 862; [2001] 2 Lloyd's Rep. 227. These were cases of *actual* breach. The same rule applies in cases of *anticipatory* breach: para.17–093.

[135] For certain effects of the injured party's inability to perform, see para.17–026 and following.

[136] See para.17–014 and following.

[137] See para.18–038.

mere fact that the employer does not exercise that right does not lead to the result that the employer must continue to pay the agreed wages. On the contrary, he is under no such liability since performance of the employee's duty to work is a condition precedent of the employer's duty to pay.[138] The position is more complex where the employee's breach takes the form, not of an outright refusal to work, but of a refusal merely to perform specified tasks while continuing to perform the remaining duties of his employment. This situation has already been discussed;[139] the only point which needs to be made here is that, if the employer voluntarily accepts such partial performance, he must pay for it at the contract rate,[140] while the employee is liable in damages for loss caused by his breach.[141] It is in this sense that the obligations of both parties "remain in force".

**Remedies.** The statement just made relates only to the *obligations* of the parties, and not to the *remedies* for their enforcement. To say that a party remains bound under the contract to do or to abstain from doing some act does not mean that these obligations can be enforced by an order of specific performance or by an injunction; and similarly to say that a party remains bound to make certain payments does not mean that an action for the agreed sum can be brought against him.[142] The circumstances in which these remedies are available are discussed in Ch.21;[143] here it is necessary only to say that, in any of the cases just mentioned, the injured party's only remedy may be an action for damages. **18–027**

### *(iii) Change of course*

**Injured party pressing for performance before terminating.** Once the injured party has terminated, he cannot later affirm and demand performance: this follows from the rule that termination releases the defaulting party from his primary obligation to perform.[144] On the other hand, where the injured party's original reaction to the breach is to press for performance, he plainly does not release the guilty party from any obligation; nor does he, by demanding performance after breach,[145] necessarily waive his right to terminate, since such a demand is not of itself a "clear and unequivocal" representation[146] that that right **18–028**

---

[138] See para.17–015.

[139] See para.17–045.

[140] i.e. he can make a pro rata deduction in respect of the unperformed services: *Miles v Wakefield Metropolitan DC* [1987] A.C. 539.

[141] *Sim v Rotherham Metropolitan BC* [1987] Ch. 216.

[142] *Telephone Rentals v Burgess Salmon*, *The Independent*, 22 April 1987.

[143] See especially paras 21–001—21–017.

[144] See para.18–020; *Johnson v Agnew* [1980] A.C. 367 at 393; cf. *Meng Leong Developments Pte Ltd v Jip Hong Trading Co* [1985] A.C. 511. The position may be different where the party in breach denies the breach and maintains the continued existence of the contract: see *Systems Control Plc v Munro Corporate Plc* [1990] B.C.L.C. 659 at 666.

[145] Our concern here is with the injured party's reaction to an *actual* breach. For the position in cases of *anticipatory* breach, see para.17–093.

[146] See para.18–096, e.g. *Yukong Line Ltd of Korea v Rendsburg Investments Co of Liberia* [1996] 2 Lloyd's Rep. 604.

will not be exercised.[147] So long as there are no other circumstances from which such a representation can be inferred, the injured party can therefore still terminate if the other party does not comply with the demand for performance.[148]

18–029 **Order for specific performance and termination.** A special application of the rule just stated is to cases in which the injured party has actually obtained an order of specific performance. If the defendant fails to comply with the order, one possible course of action open to the injured party is to apply to the court for enforcement of the order. There was formerly some support for the view that this was the only remedy available to him, and that he could not, after having obtained an order of specific performance, then terminate and claim damages.[149] But this view was rejected by the House of Lords in *Johnson v Agnew*.[150] In that case, vendors of land were (as the purchaser knew) relying on the proceeds of the sale to pay off a mortgage on the land. The purchaser failed to complete, even after specific performance had been ordered against her, with the result that the land was sold by the mortgagee. The vendors were therefore no longer able to enforce the order of specific performance (since they could no longer convey the land) and it was held that they were entitled to damages, not only under the special statutory power to award damages in lieu of specific performance,[151] but also at common law.[152] The reasoning of *Johnson v Agnew* is not, moreover, restricted to the situation in which failure to comply with the order of specific performance has disabled the party who had obtained it from performing his side of the bargain. It is based on the general rules relating to the effects of repudiatory breach and therefore applies even where no such disability results. The right to damages is subject only to the qualification that, where an order of specific performance has not been complied with, the party who had obtained the order and now wishes to claim damages must apply to the court for the dissolution of the order "and ask the court to put an end to the contract".[153]

147 Even in cases where the injured party has affirmed the contract, he may still terminate if the guilty party commits a further breach, or persists in the initial breach: see para.18–094.

148 cf. *Tilcon Ltd v Land and Real Estate Investments Ltd* [1987] 1 All E.R. 615; *Safehaven Investments Inc v Springbok Ltd* (1995) 71 P. & C.R. 59 at [68]; *Stocznia Gdanska SA v Latvian Shipping Co* [2002] EWCA Civ 889; [2002] 2 Lloyd's Rep. 436 at [100].

149 See *Capital & Suburban Properties Ltd v Swycher* [1976] Ch. 319 and the authorities there cited; Dawson 93 L.Q.R. 232; Oakley [1977] C.L.J. 20.

150 [1980] A.C. 367; Alberry 91 L.Q.R. 337; Gummow 92 L.Q.R. 5; Dawson 39 M.L.R. 241; Hetherington 96 L.Q.R. 401; Jackson 97 L.Q.R. 26.

151 See para.21–070; such damages had been awarded in *Biggin v Minton* [1977] 1 W.L.R. 701.

152 *Singh v Nazeer* [1979] Ch. 474 is contrary, but that case followed *Capital & Suburban Properties v Swycher* [1976] Ch. 319, which is now disapproved: fn.149.

153 *Johnson v Agnew* [1980] A.C. 367 at 394; *GKN Distributors v Tyne Tees Fabrication* (1985) 50 P. & C.R. 403; *Hillel v Christoforides* (1991) 63 P. & C.R. 301.

## 3. Availability of the Right to Terminate

**Renunciation, impossibility and substantial failure to perform.** In the case of termination for actual breach, the general rule is that the party in default must have been guilty of a substantial failure to perform,[154] but this is subject to a number of exceptions.[155] As we have seen, a right to terminate may also arise on the basis of anticipatory breach for renunciation, or impossibility.[156] A party is guilty of renunciation where, by words or conduct, he has "clearly shown an intention to abandon and altogether refuse to perform the contract."[157] Impossibility refers to the situation where one party has by his "own act or default" disabled himself from performing.[158] In such cases the court will assess whether that which one party is refusing to do, or cannot now do, would have justified termination at the time when performance was due,[159] i.e. whether it would have amounted to a substantial failure to perform[160] (or, by way of exception, to a breach of condition).[161] In practice, termination may be justified on the basis of both anticipatory breach and actual breach: "A party may be in repudiatory breach as a result of breaches that he has committed or indicated that he will commit or a combination of the two".[162] 18–030

**Right to terminate distinguished from the order of performance.** We saw in Ch.17 that there is no right to terminate for breach of an independent promise.[163] In the case of "dependent" promises (whether condition precedent or concurrent condition), a breach justifies the injured party's refusal to perform for as long as the breach continues; but it does not, of itself, justify termination. It has the latter effect only where the failure is (in accordance with the principles to follow) either sufficiently serious to justify termination or such that it falls within one of the exceptions to the requirement of substantial failure.[164] 18–031

---

[154] See para.18–032. This may be traced back to the decision in *Boone v Eyre* (1777) 1 Hy. Bl. 273n.; 2 W. Bl. 1312, or, to be more accurate, the discussion of it in a number of later cases: *Duke of St Albans v Shore* (1789) 1 Hy. Bl. 270; *Glazebrook v Woodrow* (1799) 8 T.R. 366 at 374; *Ellen v Topp* (1851) 6 Ex. 424 at 442.

[155] See paras 18–043—18–086.

[156] See paras 17–075—17–076.

[157] *Eminence Property Developments v Heaney Ltd* [2010] EWCA Civ 1168; (2010) 43 E.G. 99 at [61]; see para.17–075.

[158] See para.17–076.

[159] *The Afovos* [1983] 1 W.L.R. 195 at 203; *Geden Operations Ltd v Dry Bulk Handy Holdings Inc* [2014] EWHC 885 (Comm); [2014] 2 Lloyd's Rep. 266 at [15].

[160] *Ross T Smyth & Co v TD Bailey, Son & Co* [1940] 3 All E.R. 60 at 72. This requirement will obviously be satisfied where one party refuses, or is unable, to perform at all.

[161] See para.18–043 and following; and paras 17–085—17–087.

[162] *Dalkia Utilities Services Plc v Celtech International Ltd* [2006] EWHC 63; [2006] 1 Lloyd's Rep. 599 at [133].

[163] See para.17–024.

[164] See para.17–025 and following.

## (a) General requirement of substantial failure

18–032 **When failure is substantial.** Whether a failure in performance is sufficiently serious to entitle the injured party to terminate gives rise to very great difficulty.[165] As with the test for frustration, with which an analogy is sometimes drawn,[166] the assessment involved is "multi-factorial".[167] The frequent references in the cases to breaches which "substantially" deprive a party of what he bargained for, or "go to the root" of a contract, or which "frustrate" his purpose in making the contract are not particularly helpful in analysing the law or in predicting the course of future decisions.[168] It is submitted that the courts, in applying the general requirement of substantial failure,[169] classify a failure in performance with an eye on the consequences: on the one hand, whether termination (as opposed to damages) is necessary to protect the injured party; on the other hand, the prejudice which termination will cause to the other party. If, on balancing these considerations, they conclude that the injured party should be allowed to terminate, they will classify the failure in performance as "substantial" in order to produce the desired result; and conversely.[170] An attempt will be made in the following pages to illustrate this approach. The decisions are for the most part soundly based on practical considerations; though it must be admitted that these do not always appear very clearly from the judgments. Whether a failure in performance is sufficiently serious is assessed at the time that the injured party purports to terminate the contract.[171]

18–033 **Unjust enrichment.** Where the requirement of substantial failure applies,[172] the courts are reluctant to allow a party to refuse to perform if he has received a benefit from the other party's partial or defective performance and cannot, or will not, restore that benefit.[173]

18–034 **Adequacy of damages.** Sometimes the main reason for allowing termination is that damages would not adequately compensate the injured party. In *Vigers v Cook*[174] an undertaker had contracted to make arrangements for the funeral of the defendant's son, but so negligently constructed the coffin that it could not be

---

165 *Rice v Great Yarmouth BC* [2003] T.C.L.R. 1. at [35].

166 *Grand China Logistics Holding (Group) Co Ltd v Spar Shipping* [2016] EWCA Civ 982; [2016] 2 Lloyd's Rep. 447 at [78]; Wilmot-Smith 134 L.Q.R. 307.

167 *Valilas v Januzaj* [2014] EWCA Civ 436; 154 Con L.R. 38 at [53]; *Grand China Logistics Holding (Group) Co Ltd v Spar Shipping* [2016] EWCA Civ 982; [2016] 2 Lloyd's Rep. 447 at [101].

168 *Ampurius Nu Homes Holdings Ltd v Telford Homes (Creekside) Ltd* [2013] EWCA Civ 577; [2013] 4 All E.R. 377 at [50]; cf. *Grand China Logistics Holding (Group) Co Ltd v Spar Shipping* [2016] EWCA Civ 982; [2016] 2 Lloyd's Rep. 447 at [76].

169 Different factors govern the exceptions discussed at para.18–043 and following.

170 *Decro-Wall International SA v Practitioners in Marketing Ltd* [1971] 1 W.L.R. 361 at 380.

171 *Ampurius Nu Homes Holdings Ltd v Telford Homes (Creekside) Ltd* [2013] EWCA Civ 577; [2013] 4 All E.R. 377 at [44].

172 In some cases, termination often does lead to unjust enrichment, e.g. where one party's refusal to pay is justified by the other's failure to perform an "entire" obligation; para.17–032.

173 This factor may explain, in part, the different outcomes in *Boone v Eyre* (1777) 1 Hy. Bl. 273n.; 2 W. Bl. 1312 and *Duke of St Albans v Shore* (1789) 1 Hy. Bl. 270; cf. *Cornwall v Henson* [1900] 2 Ch. 298.

174 [1919] 2 K.B. 475; cf. *Sinclair v Bowles* (1829) 9 B. & C. 92.

taken into the church where the funeral service was held. He was not entitled to recover any part of his charges as it was "an essential part of the funeral that the body should be taken into the church so that the service might be read in its presence".[175] The breach was one for which a money payment could not compensate.[176] But where the loss suffered in consequence of the breach can be valued with relative certainty, an award or allowance of the sum so assessed will be regarded as an adequate remedy, more suitable than termination.[177] For example, in one case the fact that a party was persistently late in making payments under a long-term contract was held not to be a ground of termination, since the other party suffered no prejudice except in having to pay a relatively small amount of interest on the outstanding sums, and this loss could easily have been recovered from the party in breach.[178]

**Ratio of failure to the performance undertaken.** The higher the ratio of the failure is to the performance undertaken, the more likely it is that the court will regard the failure as substantial. Thus where a buyer of oil deliverable in two instalments without justification refused to accept one of them (and added that he would not accept any other delivery) it was held that the seller was entitled to terminate.[179] On the other hand, in the *Maple Flock* case[180] a contract provided for delivery of 100 tons of rag flock in instalments of 1.5 tons at the rate of three instalments a week. The sixteenth instalment contained an excessive amount of chlorine and one reason why the court held that this breach did not entitle the buyers to terminate was that it related to a single instalment which bore only a small quantitative ratio to the contract as a whole.[181] Similarly, in the *Hongkong Fir* case,[182] a ship began service under a 24-month time charterparty. She was later found to be unseaworthy and to need extensive repairs which took altogether 20 weeks to complete. The charterers purported to terminate on a number of grounds,[183] one of which was that the delay caused by the unseaworthiness was such as to "frustrate" their purpose in entering into the contract. One reason why **18–035**

[175] *Vigers v Cook* [1919] 2 K.B. 475 at 479.

[176] Had the defendant claimed damages he would (at least as the law then stood) have recovered nothing for injury to his feelings: para.20–088 and following.

[177] cf. the rule that specific relief may be refused where the more appropriate remedy is in damages: para.21–019 and following.

[178] *Decro-Wall International SA v Practitioners in Marketing Ltd* [1971] 1 W.L.R. 361; cf. *Valilas v Januzaj* [2014] EWCA Civ 436; 154 Con L.R. 38; also para.18–117.

[179] *Warinco AG v Samor SpA* [1979] 1 Lloyd's Rep. 450.

[180] *Maple Flock Co Ltd v Universal Furniture Products (Wembley) Ltd* [1934] 1 K.B. 148; cf. *Simpson v Crippin* (1872) L.R. 8 Q.B. 14 (failure by buyer to take delivery). For such instalment contracts, the vague language of Sale of Goods Act 1979 s.31(2) gives virtually no guidance on the question when a breach justifies termination. Contrast the very rigid rule laid down by s.30(1) with respect to short delivery (modified, in the case of non-consumer sales, by s.30(2A)); para.17–033. The position would appear to be no clearer under s.26 of the Consumer Rights Act 2015.

[181] cf. *Financings Ltd v Baldock* [1963] 2 Q.B. 104; *The Seaflower* [2000] 2 Lloyd's Rep. 37 at 41 (in further proceedings ([2001] 1 Lloyd's Rep. 341) the term in question was held to be a condition: see para.18–043).

[182] *Hongkong Fir Shipping Co Ltd v Kawasaki Kisen Kaisha Ltd* [1962] 2 Q.B. 26.

[183] See also paras 18–033, 18–037, 18–052.

this argument was rejected was that the ship was still available, after the completion of repairs, for 17 out of the original 24 months of the charterparty.[184]

18–036 **Uncertainty as to future performance.** In the case of continuing contracts, calling for repeated acts of performance over a period of time, the courts are influenced by the need to remove the uncertainty which may result from failure to perform some of those acts.[185] In *Bradford v Williams*,[186] for example, the defendant's ship was chartered for one year from May to May; but in September the charterers wrongfully refused to provide a cargo. This refusal justified the defendant in putting an end to the contract as "no cross-action for damages would have fully compensated him".[187] In such a cross-action it might be alleged that he had failed to mitigate[188] by finding substitute employment for the ship. It would be hard for him to know for how long such employment should be sought, since, if the original charterparty had remained in force, the charterers might later have demanded further performance, and the shipowner would have been bound to have his ship available in response to such a demand. Again, the failure of a house-buyer to pay a deposit as required by the contract gives rise to uncertainty in depriving the vendor of an important safeguard against eventual default; and accordingly it justifies termination by the vendor.[189]

By way of contrast, further reference may be made to the *Hongkong Fir*[190] case, where it was said that, once major repairs were begun, there was no reasonable ground for believing that the ship would not be available for service within a fairly short and predictable time.[191] In the *Maple Flock* case[192] the court similarly stressed that the sellers' business was well conducted, that the source of the defect could easily be tracked down, and that the likelihood of its recurrence was small. Such likelihood has also been stressed where a seller has sought to terminate an instalment contract because of the buyer's refusal to pay in accordance with its terms.[193] Similarly, the insolvency of a buyer who has failed to pay may justify the seller's refusal to perform (at least in the sense that he need

---

184 *Hongkong Fir Shipping Co Ltd v Kawasaki Kisen Kaisha Ltd* [1962] 2 Q.B. 26 at 40, per Salmon J, whose judgment on this issue was simply approved by the Court of Appeal: see [1962] 2 Q.B. 26 at 61, 73.

185 The need to remove uncertainty as to future performance is one factor which helps to explain the distinction between *Poussard v Speirs & Pond* (1876) 1 Q.B.D. 410 and *Bettini v Gye* (1876) 1 Q.B.D. 183.

186 (1872) L.R. 7 Ex. 259; *The Sanko Iris* [1987] 1 Lloyd's Rep. 487.

187 *Bradford v Williams* (1872) L.R. 7 Ex. 259 at 269.

188 See para.20–104.

189 *Myton Ltd v Schwab-Morris* [1974] 1 W.L.R. 331; *The Blankenstein* [1985] 1 W.L.R. 435 at 446. In *Samarenko v Dawn Hill House Ltd* [2011] EWCA Civ 1445; [2013] Ch. 36 at [15] Lewison LJ expressed the view that Goulding J in the *Myton* case had "in effect characterised the payment of the deposit (including the time of payment) as a condition of the contract, any breach of which would amount to a repudiation"; para.18–127.

190 *Hongkong Fir Shipping Co Ltd v Kawasaki Kisen Kaisha Ltd* [1962] 2 Q.B. 26.

191 *Hongkong Fir Shipping Co Ltd v Kawasaki Kisen Kaisha Ltd* [1962] 2 Q.B. 26 at 40; cf. *The Hermosa* [1982] 1 Lloyd's Rep. 570, where it was held that a charterer was not entitled to terminate even though his "demand for reassurance" (at 580) was not met.

192 *Maple Flock Co Ltd v Universal Furniture Products (Wembley) Ltd* [1934] 1 K.B. 148.

193 Contrast *Withers v Reynolds* (1831) 2 B. & Ad. 882 with *Mersey Steel and Iron Co v Naylor Benzon and Co* (1884) 9 App. Cas. 434; and *Freeth v Burr* (1874) L.R. 9 C.P. 208; para.18–039.

no longer deliver *on credit*) if it is unlikely that the buyer or his trustee in bankruptcy will eventually be able to pay in accordance with the contract.[194] On the other hand, mere delay in payment will not of itself justify termination. In the *Decro-Wall* case[195] an English company had been appointed "sole concessionaires" for the sale in the UK of decorative tiles manufactured by a French company. The English company was persistently (though only slightly) late in making payments under the contract. One reason[196] why this did not justify termination by the French company was that the delays did not give it any reason to doubt that payment would be made as soon as the English company had disposed of the goods.

**Ulterior motives for termination.** It sometimes happens that a party's real motive for wishing to terminate is not that there has been some failure in performance, but that the contract was, or has because of market movements become, a bad bargain for him.[197] In such circumstances the courts will often (if the case is one to which the general requirement of substantial failure applies)[198] hold that the failure in performance is not sufficiently serious and so refuse to allow termination. The underlying policy has been stated by Roskill LJ: "Contracts are made to be performed and not to be avoided according to the whims of market fluctuation."[199] Such considerations may have influenced the decision in the *Hongkong Fir* case.[200] By the time the ship had been repaired, there had been a "catastrophic fall in the freight market"[201] to 13s. 6d. per ton, as against the 47s. per ton reserved in the charterparty.[202] In a 24-month charterparty the risk of such a fall in the freight market would normally be on the charterer; and the court was probably reluctant to allow him to throw it back on the shipowner by putting an end to the charterparty. It may also be relevant that the shipowner's breaches did not (so far as appears from the report) cause the charterer any loss at all.[203] But if a charterer can show that the owner's breach *was* a source of serious prejudice to him, he will not be prevented from terminating merely because there has been a steep fall in the freight market. This is particularly true if his conduct shows that his real motive for terminating was to avoid the prejudice caused by the breach, and not to escape from what has turned out to be a bad bargain.[204] 18–037

---

[194] *Bloomer v Bernstein* (1874) L.R. 9 C.P. 588; Insolvency Act 1986 s.345(1) and (2); *Leyland Daf Ltd v Automotive Products Plc, The Times*, 6 April 1993, affirmed *The Times*, 9 April 1993.

[195] *Decro-Wall International SA v Practitioners in Marketing Ltd* [1971] 1 W.L.R. 361.

[196] For another see para.18–034.

[197] cf. para.18–002.

[198] Where exceptions to the general requirement apply, refusal to perform has often been allowed even though the motive for it fairly clearly was to escape from a bad bargain, e.g. *Cunliffe v Harrison* (1851) 6 Exch. 901; para.17–039; *Arcos v Ronaasen* [1933] A.C. 470; para.18–050.

[199] *The Hansa Nord* [1976] Q.B. 44 at 71; cf. *Dakin v Oxley* (1864) 15 C.B. (N.S.) 647 at 667–668; *The Gregos* [1994] 1 W.L.R. 1465 at 1475.

[200] *Hongkong Fir Shipping Co Ltd v Kawasaki Kisen Kaisha Ltd* [1962] 2 Q.B. 26; para.18–035.

[201] *Hongkong Fir Shipping Co Ltd v Kawasaki Kisen Kaisha Ltd* [1962] 2 Q.B. 26 at 39.

[202] *Hongkong Fir Shipping Co Ltd v Kawasaki Kisen Kaisha Ltd* [1961] 2 All E.R. at 261.

[203] The shipowner's breaches can be said to have benefited the charterer by relieving him for 20 weeks from the obligation to pay the high rate of hire reserved by the charterparty, since, while the ship was under repair, she was "off hire".

[204] cf. *Federal Commerce Navigation Co Ltd v Molena Alpha Inc* [1979] A.C. 757.

18–038 **Deliberate breach.** A breach will not justify termination merely because it is deliberate.[205] The fact that the breach is deliberate may justify termination on the ground that it is evidence of "an intention no longer to be bound by the contract"[206] so far as any *future* performance is concerned, and so also amounts to an anticipatory breach in the form of renunciation.[207] But termination for the *actual* breach itself will depend on whether it was sufficiently serious,[208] whether or not it was committed deliberately.[209] For example, in the *Hongkong Fir* case[210] it was held that unseaworthiness is not of itself a ground on which a charterer is entitled to terminate a charterparty; it has this effect only if it produces a substantial failure in performance. But in the *Hongkong Fir* case it was also said that the charterer could have refused to accept the ship if the unseaworthiness had been discovered on or before her delivery and the shipowner had refused to comply with a request to put the matter right within the time allowed for delivery. Such refusal would have been evidence of the shipowner's intention no longer to be bound by the contract.[211] Conversely, the giving by time charterers of an order for a voyage which is illegitimate because the voyage cannot be completed within the period of the charter will not of itself entitle the owner to terminate,[212] but he will become entitled to do so if the charterers' "persistence in it … showed that they did not intend to perform the charter."[213] It should be stressed that where a breach is deliberate, or is persisted in, and this is taken as evidence of intention not to perform, the intention must go to a matter which is itself sufficiently serious to justify termination; in the *Hongkong Fir* case it would have been the delivery on time of a vessel in accordance with the charterparty, the time of delivery being regarded as a condition of the contract.[214] In some cases, it may not be that the party in breach has no intention of remedying the breach, but

[205] *Suisse Atlantique Société d'Armament SA v NV Rotterdamsche Kolen Centrale* [1967] 1 A.C. 361 at 435; cf. *Decro-Wall International SA v Practitioners in Marketing Ltd* [1971] 1 W.L.R. 361 at 369; and in the context of employment: *Gorse v Durham CC* [1971] 1 W.L.R. 775; *Miles v Wakefield MDC* [1987] A.C. 539 at 559–560.

[206] *Freeth v Burr* (1874) L.R. 9 C.P. 208 at 213; cf. *Bradley v H Newsom, Sons & Co* [1919] A.C. 16 at 52; *Suisse Atlantique Société d'Armament SA v NV Rotterdamsche Kolen Centrale* [1967] 1 A.C. 361 at 394, 429, 435; *The Product Star (No.2)* [1993] 1 Lloyd's Rep. 397 at 407; *Cantor Fitzgerald International v Callaghan* [1999] 2 All E.R. 411 at 420. Contrast *The Aktion* [1987] 1 Lloyd's Rep. 283.

[207] *Withers v Reynolds* (1831) 2 B. & Ad. 882; *Total Oil Great Britain Ltd v Thompson Garages (Biggin Hill) Ltd* [1972] 1 Q.B. 318 at 322; *Alan Auld Associates Ltd v Rick Pollard Associates* [2008] EWCA Civ 655; [2008] B.L.R. 419; contrast *Valilas v Januzaj* [2014] EWCA Civ 436; 154 Con L.R. 38.

[208] Or whether termination was available on the basis of one of the exceptions considered at para.18–041 and following.

[209] *Millar's Karri & Jarrah Co (1902) v Weddell, Turner & Co* (1909) 100 L.T. 128; cf. *Robert A Munro & Co Ltd v Meyer* [1930] 2 K.B. 312; *Federal Commerce and Navigation v Molena Alpha* [1979] A.C. 757. Similarly, for dishonest breach: *The Mercandian Continent* [2001] EWCA Civ 1275; [2001] 2 Lloyd's Rep. 563 at [35]; *Acre 1127 Ltd v De Montfort Fine Art Ltd* [2011] EWCA Civ 87 at [43]: "dishonesty will be material only if it is of itself destructive of a necessary relationship of trust or if it is of itself indicative of an intention no longer to be bound by the contract."

[210] *Hongkong Fir Shipping Co Ltd v Kawasaki Kisen Kaisha Ltd* [1962] 2 Q.B. 26.

[211] *Hongkong Fir Shipping Co Ltd v Kawasaki Kisen Kaisha Ltd* [1962] 2 Q.B. 26 at 56.

[212] See para.18–052.

[213] *The Gregos* [1994] 1 W.L.R. 1465 at 1476.

[214] *Hongkong Fir Shipping Co Ltd v Kawasaki Kisen Kaisha Ltd* [1962] 2 Q.B. 26 at 56 (Sellers LJ).

rather that "it *cannot* be remedied within such a time as not to frustrate the object of the (contract)" so that the injured party is entitled to terminate for this reason.[215]

**Honest mistaken belief.** The distinction between actual breach and anticipatory breach may also help to explain the circumstances when a party may rely on his honest, but mistaken, belief that the terms of the contract justified his refusal to perform so as to deny the injured party's right to terminate.[216] In the case of an actual breach which justifies termination, it is no defence that the party in breach was acting on the advice of his lawyers, or that he was under an honest misapprehension.[217] By contrast, in the case of termination for anticipatory breach by way of renunciation,[218] the honest mistake of the party in breach, and any legal advice he has received, may be relevant. In *Mersey Steel & Iron Co v Naylor Benzon & Co*[219] a buyer of steel under an instalment contract refused to pay for one instalment. The refusal to pay at the time due amounted to an actual breach, but this was not sufficiently serious to justify the seller in withholding delivery;[220] nor did it justify termination by the seller on the basis of renunciation since the buyer's refusal to pay on this occasion was not evidence of his intention no longer to be bound by the contract.[221] The buyer wished to fulfil the contract,[222] but had been advised, incorrectly, that it could not safely pay the instalment due without the sanction of a court order, the seller having been made the subject of a winding up petition. Similarly,[223] in *Woodar Investment Development Ltd v Wimpey Construction UK Ltd*[224] a purchaser of land purported 18–039

[215] *Stanton v Richardson* (1872) L.R. 7 C.P. 421 at 437 (Brett J); affirmed (1875) 45 L.J.C.P. 78. An important feature of the *Hongkong Fir* case (*ex hypothesi*) and *Stanton v Richardson* is that the charterer was entitled not to perform until the shipowner's breach had been remedied: in *Hongkong Fir* by not accepting delivery of an unseaworthy vessel and in *Stanton v Richardson* by not loading on an uncargoworthy vessel; cf. *Mantovani v Carapelli SpA* [1978] 2 Lloyd's Rep. 63 at 72; affirmed [1980] 1 Lloyd's Rep. 375.

[216] *Spettabile Consorzio Veneziano, etc. v Northern Ireland Shipbuilding Co Ltd* (1919) 121 L.T. 628 at 635; *James Shaffer Ltd v Findlay Durham & Brodie* [1953] 1 W.L.R. 106.

[217] *Federal Commerce and Navigation v Molena Alpha* [1978] Q.B. 927 at 929 (Lord Denning); affirmed [1979] A.C. 757; Carter [1979] C.L.J. 270; cf. *Dalkia Utilities Services Plc v Celtech International Ltd* [2006] EWHC 63; [2006] 1 Lloyd's Rep. 599 at [150]; *James Shaffer Ltd v Findlay Durham & Brodie* [1953] 1 W.L.R. 106.

[218] See para.17–075 and para.18–032.

[219] (1884) 9 App. Cas. 434; cf. *Payzu Ltd v Saunders* [1919] 2 K.B. 581; *Sweet & Maxwell Ltd v Universal News Ltd* [1964] 2 Q.B. 699; *Toepfer v Cremer* [1975] 2 Lloyd's Rep. 118; *Bunge GmbH v CCV Landbouwberlang* [1980] 1 Lloyd's Rep. 458.

[220] *Mersey Steel & Iron Co v Naylor Benzon & Co* (1884) 9 App. Cas. 434 at 439.

[221] cf. *Quest Advisors Ltd v McFeely* [2011] EWCA Civ 1517.

[222] Lord Blackburn refers (*Mersey Steel* 9 App. Cas. 434 at 443) to the fact that the market price of the steel bought "had risen above the contract price"; cf. paras 18–002, 18–037.

[223] Unlike the *Mersey Steel* case, in *Woodar v Wimpey*, below, the purchaser was guilty of no actual breach at all; the case turned entirely on whether it had evinced an intention not to perform when required to do so; cf. *Concord Trust v Law Debenture Trust Corp Plc* [2005] UKHL 27; [2005] 1 W.L.R. 1591; Peel 122 L.Q.R. 179.

[224] [1980] 1 W.L.R. 277; Carter [1980] C.L.J. 256; Nicol and Rawlings (1980) 43 M.L.R. 696; cf. *The Hazelmoor* [1980] 2 Lloyd's Rep. 351; *Gulf Agri Trade FZCO v Aston Agro Industrial AG* [2008] EWHC 1252 (Comm); [2008] 2 Lloyd's Rep. 376 at [44]; Contrast *Agrokor AG v Tradigrain* [2000] 1 Lloyd's Rep. 497 (unfounded assertion that performance was impossible said to amount to a repudiation).

to withdraw on a ground which, on the true construction of a somewhat obscure term in the contract, did not justify his withdrawal; but the House of Lords held that he had not repudiated, for he had acted in the bona fide belief that he was entitled to withdraw and had indicated throughout that he would perform if it should be decided that his interpretation of the contract was wrong.[225] The same principle can apply where a party makes a demand which goes beyond his rights, e.g. where a seller in good faith claims a price higher than that to which he is under the contract entitled,[226] or where a minor and obvious error is made in the calculation of the date for completion under a notice to complete.[227] By contrast, where a tug boat owner purported to exercise a right of cancellation in circumstances where it was plainly not available, the court rejected the submission that it was willing to continue to perform when it transpired that it was mistaken.[228]

18–040 **Other factors.** The factors influencing decisions as to the availability of termination by reason of the effects of a failure in performance cannot be exhaustively classified. Even where none of the factors discussed above is present, termination may nevertheless be justified. In *Aerial Advertising Co v Batchelor's Peas Ltd*,[229] for example, the claimants agreed to conduct an advertising campaign for the defendants. On Armistice Day 1937 one of the claimants' aeroplanes set out with a banner bearing the message "Eat Batchelor's Peas". Unfortunately, the aeroplane towed the banner over the main square of Salford, Lancashire, at the precise time when a large crowd was gathered there observing the two-minute silence. The effect of this breach of contract was described as "disastrous",[230] and it was held that the defendants were justified in refusing to accept further performance of the contract. Again, where a contract presupposes the continuation of a relationship involving personal confidence, it is possible for some isolated act of one party to destroy that confidence and so to justify termination by the other.[231] In some of the cases, termination was held to be justified because the nature or effects of the breach were regarded as

---

[225] Lord Salmon and Lord Russell of Killowen dissented. One of the factors which persuaded Lord Russell that Wimpey had been guilty of repudiation was its failure to take out a construction summons to test its interpretation of the contract. While this may be taken into account, it is respectfully submitted that, on the facts of the case as a whole, the view of the majority is to be preferred; cf. *Multiplex Constructions UK Ltd v Cleveland Bridge UK Ltd* [2006] EWHC 1341 (TCC); 107 Con L.R. 1.

[226] *Vaswani v Italian Motors (Sales and Services) Ltd* [1996] 1 W.L.R. 270; Peel [1996] L.M.C.L.Q. 309.

[227] *Eminence Property Developments v Heaney Ltd* [2010] EWCA Civ 1168; (2010) 43 E.G. 99; *Oates v Hooper* [2010] EWCA Civ 1346; (2010) 48 E.G. 85.

[228] *Regulus Ship Services PTE Ltd v Lundin Services BV* [2016] EWHC 2674 (Comm); [2016] 2 Lloyd's Rep. 612 at [114].

[229] [1938] 2 All E.R. 788.

[230] *Aerial Advertising Co v Batchelor's Peas Ltd* [1938] 2 All E.R. 788 at 792.

[231] See *Denmark Productions Ltd v Boscobel Productions Ltd* [1969] 1 Q.B. 699 (termination not justified on the facts; cf. *Bell v Lever Bros Ltd* [1932] A.C. 161 (original service agreement) (para.8–019).

sufficiently "serious" in ways that are hard to explain or even to articulate.[232] Such a vague notion has its dangers, but it cannot be altogether eliminated from a discussion of this branch of the law.

### (b) Exceptions to the requirement of substantial failure

The preceding discussion attempts to identify factors that influence decisions on the issue of substantial failure in performance; but it must be admitted that their practical operation is not easy to predict. In the interests of greater certainty, the law therefore recognises a number of exceptions[233] to the requirement of substantial failure. Inevitably, the resulting certainty has sometimes been achieved only at the expense of justice, so that these exceptions have attracted an increasing weight of criticism. **18–041**

**Entire obligations.** One "exception", in the form of the distinction between entire and severable obligations, has been dealt with earlier.[234] In the case of an entire obligation, it is not so much that the injured party is entitled to terminate the contract for incomplete performance, but rather that he is released from his own obligation to perform until the obligation of the other party is completed in full, whatever the degree of seriousness in the shortfall. If the other party's failure to perform amounts to a substantial failure, or falls within one of the exceptions which follow, the injured party may terminate and will be released from his own obligation to perform at any time. **18–042**

#### *(i) Conditions, warranties and intermediate terms*

**Statement of the distinction.** English law recognises a distinction between two classes of contractual terms: conditions and warranties. "Condition" is here used (in its promissory sense)[235] to refer to a contractual term the breach of which gives the injured party the right to terminate the contract. Of course he need not terminate but may instead affirm; and he can claim damages whether he affirms[236] or terminates.[237] A warranty, on the other hand, is a term "the breach of which gives rise to a claim for damages but not to a right … to treat the contract as repudiated,"[238] so that the injured party is not entitled to terminate merely[239] on account of such a breach.[240] The injured party can generally set up the **18–043**

[232] See *Bright v Ganas* (1936) 189 A. 427, where a servant forfeited all rights to pay for four-and-a-half years' service by writing a love-letter to his employer's wife.

[233] For a further special exception in the law of agency, see paras 16–109—16–113.

[234] See para.17–031 and following.

[235] See para.2–104.

[236] e.g. *Aruna Mills Ltd v Dhanrajmal Gobindram* [1968] 1 Q.B. 655.

[237] See, e.g. *Millar's Machinery Co Ltd v David Way & Son* (1935) 40 Com. Cas. 204; *New India Assurance Co Ltd v Yeo Beng Chow* [1972] 1 W.L.R. 786; cf. *General Billposting Co v Atkinson* [1909] A.C. 118; *Kwei Tek Chao v British Traders & Shippers Ltd* [1954] 2 Q.B. 459 at 473 (but see [1954] 2 Q.B. 459 at 477); and cf. para.18–022.

[238] Sale of Goods Act 1979 s.61(1) (definition of "warranty").

[239] See para.18–066.

[240] cf. *United Scientific Holdings Ltd v Burnley BC* [1978] A.C. 904 at 945; and see fn.339.

damages to which he is entitled by reason of a breach of warranty in diminution or extinction of the price[241] and if they are equal to, or exceed, the price he will not have to pay anything. Such an outcome may seem to resemble termination (in the sense of refusal to pay); but the process differs from termination in that it requires the injured party to prove both the breach and his loss, while termination requires him to prove no more than the breach. The distinction between conditions and warranties is not exhaustive and, in many cases, a term will be neither. Such terms are referred to as "innominate" or "intermediate" terms and the effect of any breach is determined by the general requirement of a substantial failure to perform. It is the classification of a term as a condition which represents an exception to the general requirement of substantial failure.

18–044 **Nature of the distinction.** In Ch.17 we saw that the phrases "condition precedent" and "concurrent condition" were used to make a point about the *order* of performance.[242] At this stage, the word "condition" is used to make a different point, namely, one about the *conformity* of the performance rendered with that promised. In the first of these two senses, the *performance* by one party may be a "condition precedent" to the liability of the other; in the second it is a *term* of the contract which is described as the "condition". It is perfectly possible for a party to comply with a condition in one of these senses but not in the other, e.g. a seller of goods by sample who has agreed to give credit may deliver the goods before being paid and so perform a "condition precedent", but if the goods turn out not to correspond with the sample he will be in breach of "condition".[243] The distinction was formerly obscured by use of the phrase "condition precedent" in cases concerned with conformity, rather than with order of performance:[244] thus "condition precedent" was used to refer both to a term of a contract and to an event, i.e. the prior or concurrent performance by one party before that of the other became due. The use of the same phrase in these two senses is, however, confusing since the effects of one party's failure to perform a "condition precedent" or a "concurrent condition" differ in two ways from those of breach of "condition" (as opposed to warranty). First, a failure of the former kind only justifies refusal by the injured party to perform for so long as the failure continues;[245] while breach of condition justifies termination in the sense of an outright refusal[246] to perform and to accept further performance from the party in breach. Secondly, the injured party's right to refuse to perform so long as a condition precedent or concurrent condition remains unperformed can be exercised without any previous election by the injured party (whose position is simply that his performance is not yet due);[247] while such an election is required

---

[241] Sale of Goods Act 1979 s.53(1)(a); cf. the right of a buyer under a consumer contract to a price reduction: Consumer Rights Act 2015 s.24.

[242] See para.17–014 and following.

[243] See para.18–049.

[244] e.g. *Glaholm v Hays* (1841) 2 Man. & G. 257 at 267; *Behn v Burness* (1863) 3 B. & S. 751 at 755: *Bentsen v Taylor* [1893] 2 Q.B. 274 at 281.

[245] See para.17–024.

[246] It is assumed that the time for "curing" any defect in performance, under the rule stated at para.17–027, at fn.97, has expired.

[247] See *The Good Luck* [1992] 1 A.C. 233 at 262.

for the purpose of the more drastic remedy of termination (in the sense of an outright refusal of the kind just described) for breach of condition.[248] Modern authority accordingly recognises the distinction between the two concepts[249] and tends[250] to use the phrase "condition" when discussing conformity, and "condition precedent" when discussing the order of performance. That usage is adopted in this chapter so that "condition precedent" is contrasted with "concurrent condition" and "independent promise";[251] while "condition" (without any qualifying adjective) is contrasted with "warranty" and "intermediate term".[252]

**Basis of the distinction.** The distinction between conditions and warranties was originally based on two factors. One was the intention of the parties, as expressed in the contract: hence the question into which category a stipulation fell was treated as one of construction.[253] But often the intention of the parties in this respect was not discoverable from the words used; and so the courts relied secondly on the general requirement of substantial failure in performance. If "performance of the stipulation [went] to the very root … of the contract",[254] then the stipulation was treated as a condition. The potentially serious effects of breach are still taken into account as evidence of the intention of the parties,[255] but whether a term is a condition or a warranty (or neither and therefore an "intermediate term"[256]) is "a pure question of interpretation".[257] If a contractual term[258] relates to "a substantial ingredient in the identity of the thing sold",[259] it may be classified as a condition, and its breach will entitle the victim to terminate, on the basis that it would be unjust to require him to accept and pay for something which differed in an important way from that for which he had contracted. A warranty, on the other hand, concerns some less important or subsidiary element of the contract. Its breach does not entitle the victim to terminate, on the basis that a minor breach can be adequately remedied by the payment of money. 18–045

[248] See para.18–043.

[249] e.g. *State Trading Corp of India v M Golodetz Ltd* [1989] 2 Lloyd's Rep. 277 at 284 treating "condition" and "condition precedent" as distinct concepts; Treitel 106 L.Q.R. 185.

[250] But not invariably: see, e.g. *The Aktion* [1989] 1 Lloyd's Rep. 283 at 285; *Soon Hua Seng Co Ltd v Glencore Grain Ltd* [1996] 1 Lloyd's Rep. 398 at 402; *Alfred McAlpine Plc v BAI (Run-off) Ltd* [2000] 1 Lloyd's Rep. 437 at 441, 444.

[251] See paras 17–018—17–019.

[252] See para.18–052.

[253] *Glaholm v Hays* (1841) 2 Man. & G. 257 at 266; Sale of Goods Act 1979 s.11(3); cf. *Tradax Export SA v European Grain & Shipping Co* [1983] 2 Lloyd's Rep. 100.

[254] *Glaholm v Hays* (1841) 2 Man. & G. 257 at 268; cf. *Bentsen v Taylor* [1893] 2 Q.B. 274 at 281.

[255] Thus the fact that the breach is *not* likely to cause serious prejudice can support the view that the term is not a condition: see *State Trading Corp of India v M Golodetz Ltd* [1989] 2 Lloyd's Rep. 277; para.18–056, fn.342.

[256] See para.18–052.

[257] *Grand China Logistics Holding (Group) Co Ltd v Spar Shipping* [2016] EWCA Civ 982; [2016] 2 Lloyd's Rep. 447 at [98]; cf. at [52]; *The Arctic* [2019] EWCA Civ 1161; [2019] 2 Lloyd's Rep. 603 at [40].

[258] *Harlingdon & Leinster Enterprises Ltd v Christopher Hull Fine Art Ltd* [1991] 1 Q.B. 564 at 586; para.9–062.

[259] *Couchman v Hill* [1947] K.B. 544 at 559.

In a number of cases decisions were based on the commercial importance of the term to the injured party, e.g. if a buyer said that he would not buy goods at all unless they had a certain quality, then this fact would tend to support the view that an undertaking with respect to that quality was a condition.[260] Where there was no such evidence of intention, the court might base its decision on its own view of the commercial importance of the term, but "insofar as commercial value judgments arise for consideration ... they form part of the *construction* and classification exercise".[261]

Some of the older authorities must be treated with caution, because in them the word "warranty" was sometimes used to refer to what would now be called a "condition".[262] But the cases do establish that there are certain terms the breach of which prima facie gives rise to a right to terminate and which are therefore "conditions" in the terminology now current. In *Behn v Burness*[263] a ship was described in a charterparty as "now in the port of Amsterdam" when in fact she was elsewhere. It was held that the charterer was entitled to terminate: the statement was a condition because of the commercial importance which charterers usually attach to such descriptive statements. Similarly, a statement that a ship will sail on a certain day has been treated as a condition in a charterparty.[264] The same is true of a statement in a charterparty that the ship is "expected ready to load" on or about a certain day.[265] The commercial importance of such a statement is, indeed, reduced by the rule that the shipowner will not be in breach merely because the ship is not ready on or about the day named. The term is broken only if the statement was made dishonestly or without reasonable grounds, so that it does not give the charterer any firm assurance as to the date of readiness. The classification of the statement as a condition can, however, be justified on the ground that a shipowner who has made such a statement dishonestly or without reasonable grounds is in a poor position to complain of any prejudice which he may suffer as a result of termination.[266]

18–046 **Breach of condition need not, in fact, amount to substantial failure to perform.** At one time the view was expressed that a term could be a condition *only* if "every breach ... [of it would] ... deprive the party not in breach of substantially the whole benefit which it was intended that he should obtain from

---

260 cf. *Bannerman v White* (1861) 10 C.B. (N.S.) 844; para.9–060.

261 *The Arctic* [2019] EWCA Civ 1161; [2019] 2 Lloyd's Rep. 603 at [40] (emphasis added).

262 e.g. in *Behn v Burness* (1863) 3 B. & S. 751 at 755: "a warranty, that is to say a condition ... ". A similar (though not identical) usage has survived in insurance law: see para.18–008.

263 (1863) 3 B. & S. 751; cf. *The New Prosper* [1991] 2 Lloyd's Rep. 93 (statement as to ship's ability to comply with load port regulations); *The Aegean Dolphin* [1992] 2 Lloyd's Rep. 178 (statement as to speed of cruise ship).

264 *Glaholm v Hays* (1841) 2 Man. & G. 257; cf. *Bentsen v Taylor* [1893] 2 Q.B. 274 (statement that ship "now sailed or about to sail" held to be a condition).

265 *The Mihalis Angelos* [1971] 1 Q.B. 164; Rogers 34 M.L.R. 190; Greig 89 L.Q.R. 93; cf. *The Mavro Vetranic* [1985] 1 Lloyd's Rep. 580 at 584 (estimated time of ship's arrival); *The Baleares* [1993] 1 Lloyd's Rep. 215 at 225.

266 *The Mihalis Angelos*, [1971] 1 Q.B. 164 at 205. The charterer could also rescind for misrepresentation: at 194.

the contract".[267] But this view was rejected by the House of Lords in *Bunge Corp v Tradax Export SA*, where Lord Roskill said that there were:

> "many cases ... where terms the breaches of which do not deprive the innocent party of substantially the whole benefit which he was intended to receive from the contract were nonetheless held to be conditions any breach of which entitled the innocent party to rescind".[268]

The statement that "conditions ... have the property that any breach of them is treated as going to the root of the contract"[269] must similarly be viewed with caution. It is accurate only in the sense that a breach of condition, like one going to the root of the contract, gives rise to a right to terminate; but that right arises, in the two cases, for different reasons. Where the breach *actually* "goes to the root of the contract", the right to terminate is intended to protect the injured party from serious prejudice; where the breach is one of condition, that right is intended to promote certainty, "without regard to the magnitude of the breach".[270] For this reason, breach of condition is here treated as an exception to, and not as an application of, the requirement of substantial failure in performance.

**Express classification by the parties.** As is apparent from the discussion in the preceeding paragraphs, while the potential seriousness of the consequences of any breach is a factor to be taken into account, the basis for determining whether a term is a condition rather than a warranty is the intention of the parties[271] which "depends on the contract and the context in question".[272] Thus, if a contract expressly says that a particular term is a condition,[273] or that performance of the term is "of the essence",[274] that term will generally be so regarded;[275] and the same may be true where the contract expressly states that termination will be available on breach of the term,[276] though it is important to distinguish between wording which converts a term into a condition and wording which only amounts to an express provision for determination, which is dealt with below.[277] 18–047

[267] *Hongkong Fir Shipping Co Ltd v Kawasaki Kisen Kaisha Ltd* [1962] 2 Q.B. 26 at 69, per Diplock LJ; cf. *United Scientific Holdings v Burnley BC* [1978] A.C. 904 at 928.

[268] *Bunge Corp v Tradax Export SA* [1981] 1 W.L.R. 711 at 724; cf. at 715–716, 718. On this point the House of Lords followed the reasoning of Megaw LJ in the Court of Appeal: see [1980] 1 Lloyd's Rep. 294 at 305. Lord Diplock himself took a similar view in *Photo Production Ltd v Securicor Transport Ltd* [1980] A.C. 827 at 849.

[269] *Lombard North Central Plc v Butterworth* [1987] Q.B. 527 at 535.

[270] *Lombard North Central Plc v Butterworth* [1987] Q.B. 527 at 535 (referring, apparently, to terms which are conditions by express classification of the parties).

[271] *Bunge Corp v Tradax Export SA* [1981] 1 W.L.R. 711 at 717.

[272] *Grand China Logistics Holding (Group) Co Ltd v Spar Shipping* [2016] EWCA Civ 982; [2016] 2 Lloyd's Rep. 447 at [48]; para.18–070.

[273] e.g. *Dawson's Ltd v Bonnin* [1922] 2 A.C. 413.

[274] See, e.g. *Lombard North Central Plc v Butterworth* [1987] Q.B. 527; para.18–069.

[275] *Personal Touch Financial Services Ltd v Simplysure Ltd* [2016] EWCA Civ 461; [2016] Bus. L.R. 1049 at [28].

[276] *Harling v Eddy* [1951] 2 K.B. 739; *George Hunt Cranes Ltd v Scottish Boiler & General Ins Ltd* [2001] EWCA Civ 1964; [2002] 1 All E.R. (Comm) 366.

[277] See para.18–067.

18–048 **Express classification not conclusive.** If a term can be broken in a way which will cause only trifling (if any) loss, the court may hold that such a breach will not justify termination even though the term is called a "condition" in the contract. In *Wickman Ltd v Schuler AG*[278] it was a "condition" of a four-year distributorship agreement that the distributor should visit six named customers once a week. The House of Lords held that the contract could not be terminated *merely* because this term had been broken. The parties could not have intended the agreement to mean that a failure to make only one out of an obligatory total of some 1,400 visits should have such drastic results. More probably they had used "condition" in a non-technical sense, to mean simply a term of the contract (as in the phrase "conditions of sale"). This view was supported by the fact that another clause in the contract conferred an express power of "determination" for any "material" breach. The exercise of such a power may not require the proof of a "serious" breach,[279] in the sense discussed earlier in this chapter, but it clearly implied the need for something more than the minor breach committed by the distributor. The decision in the *Schuler* case has subsequently been described as the "high-water mark" of the courts reluctance "to classify terms as … conditions".[280]

18–049 **Statutory classification.** In some cases the question whether a particular term is a condition or a warranty is determined by statute. The outstanding example of statutory classification is to be found in ss.12–15 of the Sale of Goods Act 1979, which lay down in some detail which of the implied terms in a contract for the sale of goods are conditions and which are warranties. A full discussion of these provisions will be found in works on the sale of goods; but it is interesting to note that most of them are implied *conditions* (thus favouring the buyer's right to reject);[281] and a few of them may be mentioned here to illustrate the distinction between conditions and warranties. It is an implied condition that goods sold by description shall correspond with the contractual description,[282] that goods sold by sample shall correspond with the sample,[283] and (in certain cases) that goods shall be of satisfactory quality and fit for a particular purpose.[284] The right to terminate for breach of these implied conditions is subject to a statutory restriction to be discussed later in this chapter.[285] There is an implied condition that the seller has the right to sell the goods,[286] but only an implied warranty that they are free from charges or incumbrances in favour of third parties.[287] To allow

---

278 [1974] A.C. 235; Baker [1973] C.L.J. 196; Brownsword 37 M.L.R. 104.
279 See the authorities referred to at fn.482.
280 *Heritage Oil & Gas Ltd v Tullow Uganda Ltd* [2014] EWCA Civ 1048; [2014] 2 C.L.C. 61 at [33].
281 This is also true of the similar terms implied in other contracts for the supply of goods: Supply of Goods (Implied Terms) Act 1973 ss.8–11; Supply of Goods and Services Act 1982 ss.2–5, 7–10.
282 Sale of Goods Act 1979 s.13.
283 Sale of Goods Act 1979 s.15.
284 Sale of Goods Act 1979 s.14.
285 See para.18–058.
286 Sale of Goods Act 1979 s.12(1); an *express* term to this effect is likewise a condition: *Barber v NSW Bank Ltd* [1996] 1 W.L.R. 641.
287 Sale of Goods Act 1979 s.12(2).

the seller to enforce the contract, when he had no right to sell, would generally[288] cause hardship to the buyer, as he would have to give the goods up to the true owner. But there is less hardship if the goods are subject to third party charges; these can simply be paid off so that the buyer can adequately and conveniently be compensated by damages. Subject to restrictions already discussed,[289] *quantitative* defects in the performance of a contract for the sale of goods justify termination even though they cause little or no prejudice to the buyer.[290]

Under the Consumer Rights Act 2015 corresponding provisions are "treated as included" in a consumer contract,[291] but are not described as conditions or warranties.[292] A buyer's right to reject the goods for breach of such terms[293] is dealt with as an express remedy which is made available in certain circumstances, rather than as a remedy which follows from the nature of the term which has been breached.[294] The remedy of "treating the contract as at an end"[295] is not available for breach of such terms, save in limited circumstances,[296] but is available for breach of any express term and the parties are free to classify an express term as a condition.[297]

**Technical applications of the distinction.** In some cases, termination is allowed simply because the term broken has previously been classified as a condition, either by statute or a previous decision of the courts. It is allowed even though there is no indication in the contract that the parties intended the remedy to be available, and even though the breach causes little prejudice, or none at all, to the injured party. Cases of this kind give rise to the question why the injured party should, in such circumstances, be entitled to terminate. **18–050**

Sometimes, this result is justified by an argument based on hypothetical hardship. Termination is allowed because the breach *might* have caused serious prejudice, irrespective of the question whether it *actually* did so.[298] In other cases, no attempt is made to justify the result even by reference to such hypothetical hardship. Thus in *Arcos Ltd v Ronaasen*[299] timber was bought for the purpose of making cement barrels and was described in the contract as half an inch thick. Most of the timber delivered was in fact 9/16 of an inch thick, but this did not in the least impair its usefulness for making cement barrels. It was held that the buyers were nevertheless entitled to reject for breach of the condition that the

---

[288] For an exception, see Sale of Goods Act 1979 s.12(3) (agreement to transfer only such title as seller or third party may have).

[289] See para.17–033.

[290] Sale of Goods Act 1979 s.30(1) and (2).

[291] As defined by s.1(1).

[292] Consumer Rights Act 2015 ss.9–17; see para.6–072.

[293] There are similar provisions for contracts for the sale or supply of digital content: Consumer Rights Act 2015 ss.34–41. For contracts for services, see Consumer Rights Act 2015 ss.49–52.

[294] See para.18–062.

[295] i.e. of "treating it as repudiated": Consumer Rights Act 2015 s.19(13).

[296] Consumer Rights Act 2015 s.19(12).

[297] Consumer Rights Act 2015 s.19(11). A term which is designated as a condition in favour of the trader may be challenged as an unfair term: see para.7–100 and following.

[298] *Re Moore & Co Ltd and Landauer Co* [1921] 2 K.B. 519 at 525.

[299] [1933] A.C. 470.

timber would correspond with its description.[300] It seems probable that their motive for wishing to do so was not that the timber did not comply with the description but that the market price of the timber had fallen. Similarly, goods may be sold on the terms that they will be (or have been) shipped within a particular month. Such a term is part of the description of the goods and if they are shipped by so much as a day before or after the stipulated period the buyer can reject.[301] He can do this even though the early or late shipment does not in the least affect the value of the goods or prejudice him in any way; and even though his motive for rejection is simply to escape from a bad bargain on a falling market.

Such decisions can perhaps be explained on the ground that they promote certainty. Once a term has been classified as a "condition", the injured party can safely terminate for breach of it, without having to consider the often difficult question whether the breach amounted to a "substantial" failure in performance. On the other hand, in some of the examples given above, the exercise of the right to terminate can occasion obvious hardship to the party in breach: it results in his having to bear a loss that was not caused by the breach at all, but by market movements. For this reason, there has been some judicial reaction against the authorities which give a wide scope to the right to terminate; and in contracts for the supply of goods that right has also been limited by legislation.

**18–051** **Restrictions of technical applications.** In *Reardon Smith Line Ltd v Hansen Tangen*[302] Lord Wilberforce[303] said that some of the authorities just discussed were "excessively technical and due for fresh examination in this House";[304] and that generally, where goods are sold by description, the court should "ask whether a particular item in a description constitutes a substantial ingredient in the identity of the thing sold, and only if it does … treat it as a condition".[305] However, he recognised a possible exception in the case of "unascertained future goods (e.g. commodities) as to which each detail of the description must be assumed to be vital".[306] Since such goods often pass rapidly through many hands, the argument of commercial certainty is in such cases particularly strong: it is important for each buyer to be able to tell at once whether some defect or misdescription justifies rejection.

The judicial reaction against the excessively technical use of the right to terminate is illustrated by *Reardon Smith Line Ltd v Hansen Tangen* itself. The case arose out of the sub-charter of a tanker then under construction and therefore not yet named. In the contract, she was accordingly described as "Yard No. 354 at Osaka … " (the name of the shipbuilder). She was built elsewhere, but by a

---

300 Then under Sale of Goods Act 1893 s.13.

301 *Bowes v Shand* (1877) 2 App. Cas. 455. The duty to tender conforming shipping documents (e.g. in performance of a c.i.f. contract) is similarly a condition: *The Hansa Nord* [1976] Q.B. 44 at 70; *Soon Hua Seng Co v Glencore Grain Ltd* [1996] 1 Lloyd's Rep. 398.

302 [1976] 1 W.L.R. 989; cf. *Sanko SS Co Ltd v Kano Trading Co Ltd* [1978] 1 Lloyd's Rep. 156.

303 With whom Lords Simon and Kilbrandon agreed.

304 *Reardon Smith Line Ltd v Hansen Tangen* [1976] 1 W.L.R. 989 at 998.

305 *Reardon Smith Line Ltd v Hansen Tangen* [1976] 1 W.L.R. 989 at 998.

306 *Reardon Smith Line Ltd v Hansen Tangen* [1976] 1 W.L.R. 989 at 998.

company under Osaka's control and in accordance with the physical specifications in the sub-charter. The tanker market fell and the sub-charterers sought to reject, but it was held that they were not entitled to do so. The phrase "Yard No. 354 at Osaka" was not part of the description but a mere substitute for a name: it was a means of identification, which, in the circumstances, had not failed. The effect of the case is to narrow the scope of an implied term which is undoubtedly a condition, i.e. the term requiring the goods to correspond with the contractual description.

**Intermediate or innominate terms.** The courts have reduced the number of terms which are to be classified as conditions by recognising that the distinction between conditions and warranties is not exhaustive. As Diplock LJ has said: **18–052**

> "There are many … contractual undertakings … which cannot be categorised as being 'conditions' or 'warranties' … Of such undertakings, all that can be predicated is that some breaches will and others will not give rise to an event which will deprive the party not in default of substantially the whole benefit which it was intended that he should obtain."[307]

These "intermediate or innominate terms"[308] differ from conditions, in that their breach does not of itself give rise to a right to terminate; and from warranties in that the injured party's remedy is not even prima facie restricted to damages. He can terminate for breach of an intermediate term only if the requirement of substantial failure is satisfied.[309] Thus it has been held that a shipowner's undertakings in a charterparty to provide a seaworthy ship[310] and to use reasonable despatch[311] are not conditions, so that the *mere* fact that they are not performed will not entitle the charterer to terminate. The same is true of the charterer's obligation to load within the time stipulated in the charterparty, so that the mere fact of delay will not justify termination by the shipowner.[312] Similarly, it has been held that a time-charterer's obligation to repair the ship before redelivery is not a condition, so that his failure to repair does not, of itself, justify the shipowner's refusal to accept redelivery;[313] and it is probable that his breach

---

307 *Hongkong Fir Shipping Co Ltd v Kawasaki Kisen Kaisha Ltd* [1962] 2 Q.B. 26 at 70.

308 *Bunge Corp v Tradax Export SA* [1981] 1 W.L.R. 711 at 714.

309 e.g. *Freeman v Taylor* (1831) 8 Bing. 124; cf. *The Antaios* [1985] A.C. 191 at 200; *Federal Commerce & Navigation v Molena Alpha* [1979] A.C. 757 esp. at 779. In insurance, breach by the insured of an intermediate term relating to a claim may entitle the insurer to reject that claim but not to avoid the whole policy: see *Alfred McAlpine Plc v BAI (Run-off) Ltd* [2000] 1 Lloyd's Rep. 437 at 444; followed in the *Mercandian Continent* [2001] EWCA Civ 1275; [2001] 2 Lloyd's Rep. 563; *Bankers Ins Co Ltd v South* [2003] EWHC 380; [2004] Lloyd's Rep. I.R. 1, but disapproved in *Friends Provident Life & Pensions Ltd v Sirius International Ins* [2005] EWCA Civ 601; [2005] 2 Lloyd's Rep. 517; see now the reforms dealt with in para.18–009.

310 *Hongkong Fir Shipping Co Ltd v Kawasaki Kisen Kaisha Ltd* [1962] 2 Q.B. 26; cf. *The Ymnos* [1982] 2 Lloyd's Rep. 574; *The Torenia* [1983] 2 Lloyd's Rep. 210 at 217.

311 *Clipsham v Vertue* (1843) 5 Q.B. 265; *MacAndrew v Chapple* (1886) L.R. 1 C.P. 643.

312 *Universal Cargo Carriers Corp v Citati* [1957] 2 Q.B. 401; *The Angelia* [1973] 1 W.L.R. 210.

313 *Attica Sea Carriers Corp v Ferrostaal Poseidon Bulk Reederei GmbH* [1976] 1 Lloyd's Rep. 250 at 253, 256.

ordering the ship to embark on a voyage which is illegitimate (because it cannot be completed within the period of the charter) will not of itself entitle the shipowner to terminate.[314]

Some terms implied by statute seem also to fall into the category of intermediate terms. This seems to be true of the terms implied by the Supply of Goods and Services Act 1982 into contracts for the supply of services, that the services will be carried out with due care and skill and in a reasonable time; for the Act describes them simply as "terms"[315] (as opposed to the "conditions" and "warranties" implied into contracts for the supply of goods by the same Act).[316] The category of intermediate terms is thus established and is of general application.[317] Its existence does, however, give rise to two further problems.

18–053 **Are there three categories of terms?** This is a largely terminological problem.[318] The general view is that there are three classes of contractual terms: conditions, the breach of which gives rise to a right to terminate;[319] warranties, the breach of which gives rise only to a right to damages; and intermediate terms, the breach of which gives rise to a right to terminate if the consequences of the breach amount to a substantial failure, but otherwise sounds only in damages. There is, however, support for the view that there are only two categories: conditions and other terms.[320] This view is based on the argument that the injured party may be entitled to terminate even for a breach of warranty, if the effect of the breach is sufficiently serious. There is considerable force in this argument.[321] If it is correct, a warranty may be said to resemble an intermediate term, in that the availability of termination as a remedy for breach of either type of term depends on the seriousness of the breach. Nevertheless, the weight of authority supports the continued existence of the threefold division of contractual terms.[322] It is respectfully submitted that this is the preferable view since the distinction between warranties and intermediate terms remains for practical purposes an important one. Even if, in extreme cases, termination is available for breach of warranty, there is at least a prima facie rule that the normal remedy for such a breach is by way of damages. In relation to intermediate terms, there is no such prima facie rule; so that (to put the matter at its lowest) there is a greater likelihood that termination will be available for breach of an intermediate term than for breach of warranty.

---

314 *The Gregos* [1994] 1 W.L.R. 1465 at 1476.

315 Supply of Goods and Services Act 1982 ss.13, 14.

316 Supply of Goods and Services Act 1982 ss.2–5 and 7–10. For consumer contracts, see the Consumer Rights Act 2015 s.54(6) and s.54(7)(f).

317 Any doubt whether the category of intermediate terms existed in relation to contracts for the sale of goods was removed by the decision in *The Hansa Nord* [1976] Q.B. 44; Reynolds 92 L.Q.R. 17; Weir [1976] C.L.J. 33; para.18–066.

318 *The Ymnos* [1982] 2 Lloyd's Rep. 574 at 583.

319 For statutory exceptions see para.18–058.

320 e.g. in *The Hansa Nord* [1976] Q.B. 44 at 60; cf. *Koompahtoo Local Aboriginal Land Council v Sanpine Pty Ltd* [2007] H.C.A. 61, 233 C.L.R. 115 at [109].

321 See para.18–038.

322 *Bunge Corp v Tradax Export SA* [1981] 1 W.L.R. 711 at 725; *Regent OHG Aisenstadt und Barig v Francesco of Jermyn Street* [1981] 3 All E.R. 327 at 334; *The Mercandian Continent* [2001] EWCA Civ 1275; [2001] 1 Lloyd's Rep. 563 at [13]; cf. Lord Diplock's division of stipulations as to time into three categories in *United Scientific Holdings Ltd v Burnley BC* [1978] A.C. 904 at 943.

**Scope of the category of intermediate terms.** Granted that the threefold classification of terms does exist, the question then arises into which category particular terms should be placed. In discussing this question we shall assume that the parties have not expressly classified the term in the contract itself; and that the court will generally apply a previous judicial classification of the term.[323] Our concern here is therefore with previously unclassified terms. Since judicial classification of a term as a warranty is rare,[324] the important issue is whether a previously unclassified term is to be classified as a condition or as an intermediate term. This issue is a difficult one because it gives rise to a conflict between two policies. 18–054

**Policy considerations.** The first of these policies is to restrict the right to terminate to cases in which the breach causes serious prejudice to the injured party, and so to prevent a party from terminating for ulterior motives (such as his wish "of escaping from an unwelcome bargain"),[325] or on grounds that have been criticised as "excessively technical."[326] This policy favours the classification of terms as intermediate. It is illustrated by the *Hongkong Fir*[327] case and by a number of later decisions.[328] It can be displaced by evidence of contrary intention,[329] but where there is no such evidence of the intention of the parties, the policy of "leaning in favour"[330] of classifying stipulations as intermediate terms can be said to promote the interests of justice by preventing the injured party from terminating on grounds that are technical or unmeritorious. 18–055

The second policy, by contrast, emphasises the requirement of commercial certainty; and it in turn favours the classification of terms as conditions. Such a classification makes it unnecessary to go into the difficult questions of fact and degree which arise in determining whether a breach is "serious and substantial."[331] And once a term has been classified as a condition, the breach of such a term will, in a future case, enable the injured party to know, as soon as the breach has been committed, that he is entitled to terminate: he will not need to show anything about its effects. These considerations prevailed in *Bunge Corp v Tradax Export SA*.[332] A contract for the sale of soya bean meal provided that the goods were to be delivered during June. Delivery was to begin on a day in that

---

[323] Occasionally the court may wish to reconsider such a classification: cf. Lord Wilberforce's suggestion in *Reardon-Smith Line Ltd v Hansen Tangen* [1976] 1 W.L.R. 989 at 998; para.18–051.

[324] For an example of such a classification, see *The Captain George K* [1970] 2 Lloyd's Rep. 21.

[325] *The Gregos* [1994] 1 W.L.R. 1465 at 1475.

[326] *Reardon-Smith Line Ltd v Hansen Tangen* [1976] 1 W.L.R. 989 at 998.

[327] *Hongkong Fir Shipping Co Ltd v Kawasaki Kisen Kaisha Ltd* [1962] 2 Q.B. 26; para.18–052.

[328] *The Hansa Nord* [1976] Q.B. 44; *Tradax Internacional SA v Goldschmidt SA* [1977] 2 Lloyd's Rep. 604; *Bremer Handelsgesellschaft mbH v Vanden Avenne-Izegem PVBA* [1978] 2 Lloyd's Rep. 109 at 113; *Federal Commerce & Navigation v Molena Alpha* [1979] A.C. 757.

[329] The fact that there was evidence of such intention appears to be the best ground for distinguishing *Tradax Internacional SA v Goldschmidt SA* [1977] 2 Lloyd's Rep. 604 from *Tradax Export SA v European Grain & Shipping Co* [1983] 2 Lloyd's Rep. 100: see also *The Zeus V* [2002] 2 Lloyd's Rep. 587. It is clearly not the law that a term is a condition unless there is an indication to the contrary: *RG Grain Trade LLP (UK) v Feed Factors International Ltd* [2011] EWHC1889 (Comm); [2011] 2 Lloyd's Rep. 433 at [42].

[330] *Tradax Internacional SA v Goldschmidt SA* [1977] 2 Lloyd's Rep. 604 at 612.

[331] *Tradax Internacional SA v Goldschmidt SA* [1977] 2 Lloyd's Rep. 604 at 612.

[332] *Bunge Corp v Tradax Export SA* [1981] 1 W.L.R. 711.

month to be chosen by the buyers and was to be made free on board on a ship provided by the buyers at a US Gulf port to be selected by the sellers. The contract went on to require the buyers to give at least 15 days' notice of the ship's readiness to load the goods. It was held that this term was a condition, so that the sellers were entitled to terminate on the ground that the notice reached them five days too late.[333] Two justifications for this classification were given. First, the sellers could not, as a practical matter, perform their own obligation of nominating a port until the buyers had given them notice of the ship's readiness to load;[334] but later cases show that, though this factor is relevant to the classification of the term,[335] it is not decisive, so that terms have been classified as conditions even where there was no such interdependence between the obligations of the parties.[336] The second, and more important, point was that the classification promoted certainty, for it enabled the sellers to tell, immediately on receipt of the notice of the ship's readiness to load, whether they were bound to deliver.

18–056 **Time clauses.**[337] Failure to adhere to similar timetables laid down by commodity contracts and charterparties has, in a number of other cases, likewise been held to amount to a breach of condition.[338] One explanation for this special treatment of time clauses is that "as to such a clause there is only one kind of breach possible, namely to be late";[339] while terms that have been classified as intermediate are typically such as might be broken in various ways, some trivial and some serious.[340] This is, for example, true of the shipowner's undertaking of seaworthiness in a charterparty; but it is equally true that delay may be trivial or serious; and the law does not always give the injured party the right to terminate for delay which is not serious: we have, for example, seen that a charterer is not in breach of condition merely because he has failed to load within the time stipulated in the charterparty.[341] Stipulations as to the time of performance can,

333 i.e. the required 15 days would have ended after the last date for shipment; contrast *Thai Maparn Trading Co Ltd v Louis Dreyfus Commodities Asia Pte Ltd* [2011] EWHC 2492 (Comm); [2011] 2 Lloyd's Rep. 274 where sellers could not justify their refusal to perform on the basis of short notice of the vessel's estimated time of arrival.

334 cf. *Gill & Duffus SA v Société pour l'Exportation des Sucres SA* [1986] 1 Lloyd's Rep. 322.

335 *Universal Bulk Carriers Ltd v Andre & Cie* [2001] EWCA Civ 588; [2001] 2 Lloyd's Rep. 65 at [40].

336 *The Mavro Vetranic* [1985] 1 Lloyd's Rep. 580 at 583; *The Nizuru* [1996] 2 Lloyd's Rep. 66 at 71; *The Seaflower* [2001] 1 Lloyd's Rep. 341.

337 See further, para.18–111 and following.

338 e.g. *Krohn & Co v Mitsui & Co Europe GmbH* [1978] 2 Lloyd's Rep. 419; *Toepfer v Lenersan-Poortman NV* [1980] 1 Lloyd's Rep. 143; cf. *Nichimen Corp v Gatoil Overseas Inc* [1987] 2 Lloyd's Rep. 46; *The Naxos* [1990] 1 W.L.R. 1337; *The Aktor* [2008] EWHC 1330 (Comm); [2008] 2 Lloyd's Rep. 246; Treitel [1991] L.M.C.L.Q. 147; for time stipulations in charterparties, see *The Nizuru* [1996] 2 Lloyd's Rep. 66 (distinguished in *Universal Bulk Carriers Ltd v Andre & Cie* [2001] EWCA Civ 588; [2001] 2 Lloyd's Rep. 65); and *The Seaflower* [2001] 1 Lloyd's Rep. 341. And see the authorities cited in fnn.334 and 336.

339 *Bunge Corp v Tradax Export SA* [1981] 1 W.L.R. 711 at 715.

340 *Bunge Corp v Tradax Export SA* [1981] 1 W.L.R. 711 at 715; cf. *The Ymnos* [1982] 2 Lloyd's Rep. 574 at 584.

341 See at fn.312; cf. Lord Wilberforce's statement that a charterer's deliberate delay in loading of only one day "can appropriately be sanctioned by damages": *Suisse Atlantique Société d'Armament SA v NV Rotterdamsche Kolen Centrale* [1967] 1 A.C. 361 at 423 (para.18–038).

however, be put into a separate category on the ground that breach by delay is particularly easy to establish: if the injured party has received no performance by the due day, there can be no doubt about the fact of delay; while qualitative breaches (such as unseaworthiness) can give rise to many disputed issues of fact. Delay is also of obvious commercial importance in dealings with commodities, which can fluctuate rapidly in value. It is this combination of the ease of establishing the breach without legal proceedings and of its likely commercial importance which accounts for the readiness of the courts to treat stipulations as to the time of performance in contracts for the sale of commodities as conditions, so that *any* breach of them will justify termination.

It follows from the above reasoning that a stipulation as to the time of performance will not invariably be treated as a condition.[342] It may, for example, not be so treated precisely because the context shows that its due performance is *not* of vital importance;[343] or because of the effect of other provisions;[344] or because to give the injured party the right to terminate for *any* breach of it would make the contract unworkable;[345] or because the contract provides that damages are to be the sole remedy for failure to comply with the stipulation;[346] or because failure by one party to perform the stipulation did not create any uncertainty as to the time at which the other party would have to perform;[347] or because the stipulation did not specify a *precise* time for performance, or enable that time to be precisely ascertained in the light of later events,[348] so that its classification as a condition would not promote certainty. Thus the House of Lords has held that a stipulation requiring a seller to give notice "without delay" of the occurrence of circumstances entitling him to invoke a prohibition of export clause was an intermediate term only.[349] In a later decision at first instance, on the other hand, a term in a contract of sale required the seller to give the buyer a notice appropriating goods to the contract "as soon as possible after vessel's sailing".[350] This term was held to be a condition and the earlier decision was distinguished on the ground that in it the House of Lords had been concerned with a stipulation

---

342 *Grand China Logistics Holding (Group) Co Ltd v Spar Shipping* [2016] EWCA Civ 982; [2016] 2 Lloyd's Rep. 447 at [56].

343 *State Trading Corp of India v M Golodetz Ltd* [1989] 2 Lloyd's Rep. 277 (where the stipulation was contained in one contract but related to a different contract between the same parties which was not to be performed for six months and was relatively unimportant in terms of money); *The Ballenita* [1992] 2 Lloyd's Rep. 445 at 464–465; *The Gregos* [1994] 1 W.L.R. 1465 at 1475.

344 *ERG Raffinerie Mediterranée SpA v Chevron USA Inc* [2007] EWCA Civ 494; [2007] 2 Lloyd's Rep. 542 (time of loading normally a condition in an fob contract, but not where laycan provision also included).

345 As in *The Honam Jade* [1991] 1 Lloyd's Rep. 39.

346 As in *The Aragon* [1991] 1 Lloyd's Rep. 61.

347 *Universal Bulk Carriers Ltd v Andre & Cie* [2001] EWCA Civ 588; [2001] 2 Lloyd's Rep. 65 at [40].

348 For terms enabling the time so to be ascertained, see *Toepfer v Lenersan-Poortman NV* [1980] 1 Lloyd's Rep. 143; *The Naxos* [1990] 1 W.L.R. 1337.

349 *Bremer Handelsgesellschaft mbH v Vanden Avenne-Izegem PVBA* [1978] 2 Lloyd's Rep. 109, so far as it relates to the notice under cl.21 of the contract; cf. *Tradax Export SA v Italgrani di Francesco Ambrosio* [1986] 1 Lloyd's Rep. 112 at 120; *Greene King Plc v Quisine Restaurants Ltd* [2012] EWCA Civ 698; [2012] 2 E.G.L.R. 64 (obligation of "reasonable endeavours" to give notice of arrears to guarantor not a condition).

350 *The Post Chaser* [1981] 2 Lloyd's Rep. 695.

governing the machinery of *termination*, while the later case was concerned with a stipulation governing the machinery of *performance*.[351] But the explanation is not entirely convincing[352] since an important question in relation to either kind of term is whether the breach of it entitles the injured party to treat the contract as at an end. The main justification for classifying the term as a condition is that this will significantly promote certainty by enabling the buyer to know exactly when delay on the seller's part in giving the notice will justify him (the buyer) in terminating the contract.[353] Vague expressions such as "without delay", or "as soon as possible" do not enable him to know this, and stipulations containing such words should not be classified as conditions[354] in the absence of express provisions to that effect,[355] or of other evidence that the parties clearly intended them to take effect as such.

18–057 **"Leaning in favour" of intermediate terms.** The foregoing discussion shows that there is considerable support both for the view that the court should "lean in favour"[356] of classifying contractual stipulations as intermediate terms, and for the view that commercial certainty sometimes requires their classification as conditions. The second of these views was applied in *Bunge Corp v Tradax Export SA*;[357] but the first was not rejected. On the contrary, Lord Wilberforce said that "the courts should not be too ready to interpret contractual clauses as conditions";[358] while Lord Roskill recognised "the modern approach of not being over-ready to construe terms as conditions unless the contract clearly requires the court to do so."[359] The effect of the decision is not to discard, but rather to qualify, that approach by emphasising the importance traditionally attached in certain commercial contracts to exact compliance with stipulations as to the time of performance.[360] Stipulations of this kind are now likely to be classified as conditions if they are sufficiently precise; and other terms may also be so classified if exact performance of them is regarded as commercially vital,[361] or if there is evidence either from the commercial setting or from the course of

[351] *The Post Chaser* [1981] 2 Lloyd's Rep. 695 at 700; cf. *McDougall v Aeromarine of Emsworth Ltd* [1958] 1 W.L.R. 1126 (duty to deliver within a *reasonable time*).
[352] For the difficulty of reconciling the two cases here under discussion, see *Concordia Trading BV v Richco International Ltd* [1991] 1 Lloyd's Rep. 475 at 481.
[353] See *Tradax Export SA v Italgrani di Francesco Ambrosio* [1986] 1 Lloyd's Rep. 112 at 120.
[354] *Alfred McAlpine Ltd v BAI (Run-off) Ltd* [2001] 1 Lloyd's Rep. 437; *The Beursgracht* [2001] EWCA Civ 2051; [2002] 1 Lloyd's Rep. 574 at [43], [44].
[355] As in *George Hunt Cranes Ltd v Scottish Boilers & General Ins Co Ltd* [2001] 2 Lloyd's Rep. 65 at [28].
[356] In addition to those referred to in fn.349, see *State Trading Corp of India v M Golodetz Ltd* [1989] 2 Lloyd's Rep. 277 at 283; *The Gregos* [1994] 1 W.L.R. 1465 at 1475; *Universal Bulk Carriers Ltd v Andre & Cie* [2001] 2 Lloyd's Rep. 65 at [28]; *The Arctic* [2019] EWCA Civ 1161; [2019] 2 Lloyd's Rep. 603 at [46].
[357] [1981] 1 W.L.R. 714; para.18–055.
[358] *Bunge Corp v Tradax Export SA* [1981] 1 W.L.R. 714 at 715.
[359] *Bunge Corp v Tradax Export SA* [1981] 1 W.L.R. 714 at 727; cf. also *Toepfer v Lenersan Poortman NV* [1980] 1 Lloyd's Rep. 143 at 147; *The Ymnos* [1982] 1 Lloyd's Rep. 574 at 583; *The Gregos* [1994] 1 W.L.R. 1465 at 1475.
[360] cf. *Bowes v Shand* (1877) 2 App. Cas. 455; para.18–050.
[361] *The Post Chaser* [1981] 2 Lloyd's Rep. 695 may be explicable on this ground: see at 700; or on the ground of concessions made in that case, see *British & Commonwealth Holdings Plc v Quadrex Holdings Inc* [1989] Q.B. 842 at 857. The arbitrators' finding as to the commercial importance of

negotiations that the parties intended them to have the force of conditions.[362] Where a term does not fall within any of these three categories, the judicial attitude continues to be one of not being "too ready" to classify it as a condition. Such other terms are therefore likely to be classified as intermediate, so that termination will be allowed only where the breach causes serious prejudice to the injured party: "the modern approach is that a term is innominate unless a contrary intention is made clear".[363]

**Statutory restriction on right to terminate for breach of condition.** As a result of amendments to the Sale of Goods Act 1979,[364] the right to reject the goods for breach of condition is restricted where the buyer does not deal as consumer.[365] Similar restrictions apply to other contracts for the supply of goods;[366] but for the sake of brevity the following discussion will deal only with cases of sale. Section 15A of the 1979 Act applies where the buyer would be entitled to reject by reason of a breach of condition implied into the contract as to correspondence with description or sample and as to quality.[367] It provides that if, in such cases, the seller can show[368] that the breach is "so slight that it would be unreasonable"[369] for the buyer to reject the goods, then the breach is "not to be treated as a breach of condition but may be treated as a breach of warranty".[370] When it is so treated, the buyer's remedy will be in damages. **18–058**

**Scope of s.15A Sale of Goods Act 1979.** This exception to the general common law rule that breach of condition automatically justifies termination is "not intended as a major alteration in the law".[371] Its scope is, in particular, limited in the following ways. First, it applies only to contracts for the supply of goods: the law relating to breach of condition in, for example, time or voyage charterparties,[372] is unaffected. Secondly, it applies only to breaches by the supplier: a case such as *Bunge Corp v Tradax Export SA*[373] would not be affected since the breach was committed by the buyer. Thirdly, it applies only to breach of **18–059**

compliance with the stipulation was a second ground for the decision in *The Naxos* [1990] 1 W.L.R. 1337; cf. *Petrotrade Inc v Stinnes Handel GmbH* [1995] 1 Lloyd's Rep. 142.

[362] e.g. *Tradax Export SA v European Grain & Shipping Co* [1983] 2 Lloyd's Rep. 100; *Bergerco USA v Vegoil Ltd* [1984] 1 Lloyd's Rep. 440. Any such evidence must be subject to the rule discussed in para.6–030.

[363] *Grand China Logistics Holding (Group) Co Ltd v Spar Shipping* [2016] EWCA Civ 982; [2016] 2 Lloyd's Rep. 447 at [93].

[364] By the Sale and Supply of Goods Act 1994.

[365] The rights of a buyer under a consumer contract are now regulated by the Consumer Rights Act 2015: see para.18–062.

[366] See Supply of Goods (Implied Terms) Act 1973 s.11A and Supply of Goods and Services Act 1982 s.5A, as inserted by Sale and Supply of Goods Act 1994 s.7(1) and Sch.2 paras 4 and 6.

[367] i.e. the terms implied by ss.13, 14 and 15 of the 1979 Act: para.18–049.

[368] Sale of Goods Act 1979 s.15A(3).

[369] Sale of Goods Act 1979 s.15A(1)(b).

[370] Sale of Goods Act 1979 s.15A(1).

[371] Law Com. No.160, para.4.21.

[372] See para.18–045.

[373] [1981] 1 W.L.R. 711; para.18–055.

certain *implied* terms: the right to reject for breach of an *express* condition[374] is not affected. Fourthly, it applies only to breach of the statutorily implied terms listed above.[375] It does not apply to any other terms which may be implied by statute,[376] nor to terms implied as a matter of common law. Fifthly, the exception is excluded where "a contrary intention appears in, or is to be implied from, the contract".[377] Such an implication may arise from the nature of the contract or from its commercial setting. It is, for example, envisaged that the exception will for this reason not apply to breaches of such time clauses in commercial contracts as have been classified as conditions[378] (though the wording of the new s.15A can scarcely be said to make this point clear). Sixthly, the exception does not apply where the buyer deals as consumer: such a buyer is not well placed to dispose of defective goods on the market, so that it is important to preserve his unqualified right to reject for breach of the statutorily implied conditions;[379] and this right has been further enhanced by the reforms discussed below.[380]

18–060 **Requirements of Sale of Goods Act 1979 s.15A.** Where a case falls within s.15A, two requirements must be satisfied before the buyer is deprived of his right to reject for breach of condition: the breach must be "slight" *and* it must be "unreasonable for [the buyer] to reject" the goods. The policy underlying these requirements is similar to that on which the development of the category of intermediate terms is based:[381] it is to prevent the buyer from rejecting on unmeritorious grounds (though his motives for rejection are said not to be relevant).[382] But it should not be thought that, where the section applies, it has the effect of turning the implied conditions to which it refers into intermediate terms. The section only precludes the buyer from rejecting where the breach is "slight"; and a breach which is too serious to be "slight" may nevertheless not be serious enough to deprive the buyer of substantially the whole benefit which it was intended that he should obtain from the contract.[383] Where the breach falls between these extremes, the buyer's right to reject for breach of condition is not affected by s.15A, even though a similar breach would not give him a right to reject for breach of an intermediate term. The question just when a breach is so slight as to make it unreasonable for the buyer to reject the goods remains to be settled by judicial decision; and the vagueness of s.15A on this point is a source of regrettable uncertainty. It is, for example, far from clear how a case such as *Arcos Ltd v Ronaasen*[384] would now be decided. The difference between half an inch and 9/16 of an inch is by no means obviously "slight" (at least as a

[374] As, for example, in *Bremer Handelsgesellschaft mbH v Vanden Avenne-Izegem PVBA* [1978] 2 Lloyd's Rep. 109 (so far as it relates to cl.22).
[375] See at fn.366.
[376] e.g. by Sale of Goods Act 1979 s.12(1) (such a breach might be "slight" if it affected only part of the goods sold).
[377] Sale of Goods Act 1979 s.15A(2).
[378] Law Com. No.160, para.4.24; e.g. *Bowes v Shand* (1877) 2 App. Cas. 455; para.18–050.
[379] See Law Com. No.160, Scot. Law Com. No.104, paras 4.09–4.15.
[380] See para.18–062.
[381] See para.18–052.
[382] Law Com. No.160, paras 4.18 and 4.19.
[383] See para.18–032.
[384] [1933] A.C. 470; para.18–050.

proportion); and if it were not slight the buyer would not be deprived of his right to reject merely because it was unreasonable for him to reject, or because his motive for rejection was to escape from what had turned out to be a bad bargain because of a fall in the market.[385]

**Criticism of Sale of Goods Act 1979 s.15.** Section 15A is, it is submitted, an unfortunate provision which manages to fall between two stools. On the one hand, the section undermines the certainty which classification of the implied terms in question as conditions was intended to provide. It is no answer to this argument to say that the limitation on the right to reject which the section imposes will not often apply: the point is that it is hard to predict when it will apply, so that a buyer's legal adviser will not be able to answer that question with certainty.[386] Nor is it an answer to say that the limitation can be excluded by implied agreement:[387] it is, again, impossible to predict with certainty when such an implication will be made. On the other hand, the section scarcely goes far enough to promote justice: for this purpose, the right to reject should be restricted to serious breaches and not merely excluded if the breach is slight. If a case like *Arcos Ltd v Ronaasen*[388] would not be affected by s.15A, the right to reject could still be exercised so as to cause injustice. Even if the section did cover all cases in which it would be unjust to allow the buyer to reject, it would be extraordinarily partial in its operation. Termination by a seller can lead to just as much injustice as rejection by the buyer; but the section does nothing to limit the exercise by a seller of a right to terminate. 18–061

**Buyer dealing as consumer.** As we have seen, in a consumer contract[389] for the sale of goods (and the supply of digital content), the buyer has the benefit of a number of terms which are "to be treated as included" in the contract, such as the goods must be of satisfactory quality, fit for purpose, comply with description or sample and so on.[390] Such terms are not described as conditions and, as a consequence, if they are breached there is no right to "terminate" the contract in the sense of "treating it as repudiated".[391] Instead, the buyer's remedies for breach of such terms, including any right to reject, are dealt with expressly by other provisions of the Consumer Rights Act 2015. In summary,[392] the consumer has a short term right to reject until the expiry of the time limits set out under s.22 of the 2015 Act.[393] The trader and the consumer may agree to extend the time 18–062

---

385 See at fn.382.

386 For a similar view in an analogous context, see *Union Eagle Ltd v Golden Achievement Ltd* [1997] A.C. 514 at 519; para.18–081.

387 *Union Eagle Ltd v Golden Achievement Ltd* [1997] A.C. 514 at 519.

388 [1933] A.C. 470; para.18-050.

389 As defined by s.1(1).

390 See para.6–072.

391 Consumer Rights Act 2015 s.19(12), (13).

392 For a detailed account of a consumer's remedies, see *Chitty on Contracts*, 33rd edn (2018), Ch.38.

393 The basic time limit is 30 days, but there are a number of requirements to be met before time begins to run (s.22(3)), the time may be shortened in the case of perishable goods (s.20(4)), and there are further provisions to deal with the consequence of the consumer having requested or agreed to the repair or replacement of the goods during the time allowed: s.22(6)–(8).

limit,[394] but an agreement under which the short term right to reject would be lost before the time limit passes is not binding on the consumer.[395] After the time limit for the short term right to reject expires,[396] the consumer may exercise the right to repair or replacement,[397] but will become entitled to either a price reduction,[398] or a final right to reject and obtain a refund[399] in the following circumstances:[400] (i) after one repair or replacement, the goods do not conform to the contract; (ii) both repair and replacement are impossible; or (iii) the consumer has required the trader to repair or replace the goods, but the trader is in breach of the requirement[401] to do so within a reasonable time and without significant inconvenience to the consumer.

18–063 **Other restrictions on termination for breach of condition.** The right to terminate for breach of condition may be limited in the following further ways.

18–064 **Term excluding the right to terminate.** The contract may contain a term purporting to exclude the right to terminate.[402] Such a clause is subject to the rules discussed in Ch.7, which limit the effectiveness of exemption clauses. It is submitted that, in applying the statutory tests of reasonableness[403] and fairness[404] to clauses excluding the right to terminate for breach of condition, the courts may be influenced by the likely effects of the breach (as viewed at the time of contracting), and so take into account the factors which determine whether a failure in performance is sufficiently "substantial" to give rise to a right to terminate. A similar point can be made with regard to the process of construction which is applied to exemption clauses in certain cases of particularly serious breach.[405]

18–065 **Misrepresentation Act 1967 s.2(2).** Where a person has been induced to enter into a contract by a false statement of *fact*, his right to rescind for misrepresentation is subject to the discretion of the court, under s.2(2) of the Misrepresentation Act 1967,[406] to declare the contract subsisting and to award damages in lieu of rescission. It is arguable that this discretion can be exercised

[394] 2015 Act s.22(1).

[395] 2015 Act s.22(2).

[396] One effect of the introduction of a short term right to reject which is subject to a time limit is that the rules for "acceptance" of goods are redundant and s.35 of the Sale of Goods Act 1979 (see para.18–106) no longer applies to a contract to which Ch.2 of Pt 1 of the 2015 Act applies: Sch.1 para.24.

[397] As determined in accordance with s.23.

[398] As determined in accordance with s.24(1)–(4).

[399] As determined in accordance with ss.20(9)–(19), 24(8)–(15) and 58(5) and (6).

[400] 2015 Act s.24(5).

[401] 2015 Act s.23(2)(a).

[402] e.g. a "non-rejection" or "non-cancellation" clause which bars the right to terminate without affecting the right to damages: *The Aegean Dolphin* [1992] 2 Lloyd's Rep. 178.

[403] A clause which excludes only the right to terminate is caught by the Unfair Contract Terms Act 1977 under s.13(1)(b): see para.7–043.

[404] Under Pt 2 of the Consumer Rights Act 2015: see para.7–100.

[405] See *J Aron & Co (Inc) v Comptoir Wegimont* [1921] 3 K.B. 435 for the application of these principles to non-rejection clauses.

[406] See para.9–066.

even where the misrepresentation which induced the contract is later incorporated in it as a condition. But the better view seems to be that the subsection applies only to the right to rescind a contract *for misrepresentation*, and that it has not affected the right to terminate for breach.[407]

**Termination for breach of warranty?** It has been suggested[408] that breach of warranty may justify termination where it leads (or amounts) to a substantial failure in performance. There is at first sight some difficulty in applying this suggestion to contracts for the sale of goods. The difficulty arises because "warranty" is defined in the Sale of Goods Act 1979 as an agreement "collateral to the main purpose of [the] contract, the breach of which gives rise to a claim for damages but not to a right to reject the goods … ".[409] On the other hand, it is arguable that the rule allowing termination for a "substantial" failure in performance is a rule of common law, preserved by s.62(2) of the Act "except in so far as … inconsistent with the express provisions of this Act". In *The Hansa Nord*[410] this subsection was invoked in support of the view that the statutory classification of terms into conditions and warranties was not exhaustive. It can similarly be used to support the view that the 1979 Act does not exhaustively state the effects of breach of warranty.[411] If in particular circumstances such a breach leads to a substantial failure in performance, the prima facie rule[412] that damages are the only remedy for breach of warranty should be displaced and termination should be allowed. **18–066**

### *(ii) Express provision for determination*

A contract may expressly provide that one party shall be entitled to terminate in circumstances which do not amount to a breach, or a failure to perform, e.g. where the contract provides that it may be terminated upon giving a specified period of notice,[413] or because the other party has gone into administration.[414] But such provisions can also confer a right to terminate for some specified failure to perform.[415] For example, a voyage charterparty may stipulate that the ship is expected to be ready to load at a named port on (or about) a specified date, and that if she fails to arrive there within (say) 10 days of that date the charterer shall be entitled to cancel; and a time charterparty may provide that the charterer shall be entitled to cancel if the ship becomes unavailable for service for more than a **18–067**

[407] See para.9–112.

[408] *Astley Industrial Trust Ltd v Grimley* [1963] 1 W.L.R. 584 at 599. The term broken in this example would now be a condition under Supply of Goods and Services Act 1982 s.9(4) if the party in breach acted in the course of a business.

[409] Sale of Goods Act 1979 s.61(1).

[410] [1976] Q.B. 44.

[411] *The Hansa Nord* [1976] Q.B. 44 at 83.

[412] See para.18–043.

[413] See, e.g. *Timeload Ltd v British Telecommunications Plc* [1995] E.M.L.R. 459.

[414] See, e.g. *Phones 4U v EE Ltd* [2018] EWHC 49 (Comm); [2018] 1 Lloyd's Rep. 204.

[415] The failure to perform will often, but need not necessarily, amount to a breach: see fn.2.

specified number of days.[416] The injured party's right to terminate is dictated by the terms of the provision. There is no requirement to establish a substantial failure to perform, unless this is what the express provision requires.[417]

18–068 **Effect: termination and damages.** We saw earlier that the effect of termination for a "repudiatory breach" is that both parties are released from their primary obligations to perform and the guilty party comes under a secondary obligation to pay damages.[418] So far as the guilty party's *primary* obligation to perform is concerned, the exercise of a right to terminate which has arisen under an express contractual provision has the same effect: in general, accrued obligations remain due, while future obligations (other than "ancillary" obligations)[419] are released.[420] But there is an important difference between the effects of termination under the general law for a repudiatory breach and termination under an express provision on the guilty party's *secondary* obligation to pay damages. Where the injured party terminates for a repudiatory breach, he can recover damages in respect of any loss suffered by reason of the premature determination of the contract, i.e. for "loss of bargain",[421] but he has (unless the contract otherwise provides)[422] no such right where he terminates for a non-repudiatory breach[423] under an express provision entitling him to do so.

Suppose, for example, that a hire-purchase agreement expressly provides that the owner can terminate for any failure by the hirer to pay an instalment. If the owner terminates for the hirer's failure to pay two out of 24 instalments, he can sue for the two unpaid instalments, but not for any further instalments which would have accrued later if he had not terminated the agreement.[424] Moreover, it was held in *Financings Ltd v Baldock*[425] that he cannot recover damages for "loss of bargain", i.e. the remaining sum due under the outstanding rentals, less any sums recovered in mitigation. In the case put, the hirer's only breach is his failure to pay the two instalments. He is not, in addition, guilty of a repudiation of the whole contract. This restriction on the right to damages can, it is submitted, be supported on the policy ground that it alleviates the sometimes harsh operation of express provisions which allow a party to terminate even for a minor breach.[426]

---

416 *The Span Terza (No.2)* [1984] 1 W.L.R. 27; such a clause avoids the difficulties that arose in *Hongkong Fir Shipping Co Ltd v Kawasaki Kisen Kaisha Ltd* [1962] 2 Q.B. 26; para.18–035. See also: *The Solholt* [1983] 1 Lloyd's Rep. 605; cf. *Bettini v Gye* (1876) 1 Q.B.D. 183 at 187.

417 See para.18–076.

418 See paras 18–016, 18–020, 18–022.

419 See para.18–021.

420 See at fnn.96–97; for exceptions, see at fnn.105, 106, 107, 114.

421 See at fn.120.

422 As in *The Solholt* [1981] 2 Lloyd's Rep. 574 at 579; affirmed [1983] 1 Lloyd's Rep. 605, without reference to this point.

423 Assuming there is a breach: see fn.415.

424 *Financings Ltd v Baldock* [1963] 2 Q.B. 104 at 110; *Brady v St Margaret's Trust* [1963] 2 Q.B. 494; *Charterhouse Credit Corp v Tolly* [1963] Q.B. 683; *UCB Leasing Ltd v Holtom* [1987] R.T.R. 362.

425 [1963] 2 Q.B. 104; *Amev-UDC Finance Ltd v Austin* (1986) 162 C.L.R. 170 (discussing earlier Australian cases); Goode 104 L.Q.R. 25; Beale 104 L.Q.R. 355; Opeskin 106 L.Q.R. 293.

426 Contrast Randall [2014] C.L.J. 113.

**Distinguishing termination under the general law for a "repudiatory breach" and under an express provision for determination.** The distinction between cases in which the right to terminate arises under the general law for a "repudiatory breach" and those in which it arises under an express provision may give rise to difficulty. The source of this difficulty is the willingness of the courts to regard any termination for a breach of condition as a "repudiatory breach" and, in that sense, the equivalent of a substantial failure to perform, even where the breach in question is a minor one.[427] Moreover, a term may be a condition on the sole ground that the parties have expressly classified it as such in their contract.[428] *Financings Ltd v Baldock*[429] may from this point of view be contrasted with *Lombard North Central Plc v Butterworth*,[430] where a contract of hire provided: (1) that the owner could terminate for any failure to pay instalments when due; and (2) that the time of payment was "of the essence" of the contract. It was held that the second of these provisions made the stipulation as to the time of payment a condition of the contract[431] so that its breach entitled the owners not only to terminate but also to damages for "loss of bargain". The decision was reached with evident reluctance[432] since there was no substantial distinction between the facts of this case and those of *Financings Ltd v Baldock*.[433] 18–069

The different result in these two cases can perhaps only be justified on the basis of the intention of the parties who may agree either that a breach only confers a right to terminate but no right to damages for "loss of bargain" (an express provision for determination), or that a breach confers the right to both (a condition). Given the significant difference in these two outcomes, the court will need to be satisfied that it was the intention of the parties that a term should be treated as a condition. This is another reason why, when it comes to terms which have not been expressly classified, the courts lean in favour of classification as an intermediate term;[434] and why, when it comes to terms which have been described as a "condition", the courts will enquire whether the parties did mean condition in the strict sense.[435] This did not assist the buyer in the *Lombard* case because it is so firmly established that "of the essence" is understood to classify the term in question as a condition. In a consumer contract, it may be possible to argue that such a term is unfair and not binding.[436]

[427] See para.18–043 and following; *SCI (Sales Curve Interactive) v Titus SARL* [2001] EWCA Civ 591; [2001] 2 All E.R. (Comm) 416 at [19]; *Stocznia Gdanska SA v Latvian Shipping Co (No.3)* [2002] EWCA Civ 889; [2002] 2 Lloyd's Rep. 436 at [76] (where there was, in fact, also an actual repudiation).

[428] See para.18–045.

[429] [1963] 2 Q.B. 104; para.18–061.

[430] [1987] Q.B. 527; Treitel [1987] L.M.C.L.Q. 143; Nicholson 1 J.C.L. 64; cf. also *The Afovos* [1983] 1 W.L.R. 195 at 203; *BNP Paribas v Wockhardt EU Operations (Swiss) AG* [2009] EWHC 3116 (Comm); 132 Con L.R. 177.

[431] See para.18–047.

[432] *Lombard North Central Plc v Butterworth* [1987] Q.B. 527 at 540, 546.

[433] See para.18–068; Carter 133 L.Q.R. 395; Carter, Courtney and Tolhurst [2018] C.L.J. 97.

[434] See para.18–057; and see the discussion of the *Spar Shipping* case in the next paragraph.

[435] See para.18–048.

[436] See para.7–100 and following.

18–070 **Condition or express provision for determination: withdrawal clauses.** The question of whether the parties' agreement amounts only to an express provision for determination, rather than an agreement that the underlying term is a condition, can be illustrated by reference to the right of a shipowner under a time charterparty to withdraw the vessel for late payment of hire. In *Grand China Logistics Holding (Group) Co Ltd v Spar Shipping*[437] the Court of Appeal resolved a degree of uncertainty over this issue by holding that it amounts to an express provision for determination.[438] This does not prevent the parties from agreeing that timely payment of hire is a condition, but the inclusion of a withdrawal clause alone does not have this effect. Indeed, its inclusion may be regarded as an indication that the parties did not intend that timely payment of hire is a condition since, if it is, the express right of withdrawal is superfluous.[439] There is nothing to prevent the parties from taking other steps to make clear their intention to treat timely payment as a condition, e.g. by using the term "condition", or making compliance "of the essence",[440] though, as we have seen, the former is not necessarily conclusive.[441] In a previous case, in addition to the right of withdrawal, the charterparty also contained an express provision entitling the shipowner to loss of bargain damages. This was said to make it clear "that the obligation to make punctual payment of hire is a condition or essential term",[442] but in *Financings Ltd v Baldock* a similar provision was unenforceable as a penalty, precisely because it amounted to an agreement for the award of damages to which the injured party was not entitled on the basis that the term breached was *not* a condition.[443]

In the *Spar Shipping* case, there was no dispute that the shipowner had the right to terminate because of the withdrawal clause; the issue was whether damages for loss of bargain were also available because of a fall in the market

---

[437] [2016] EWCA Civ 982; [2016] 2 Lloyd's Rep. 447.

[438] The Court of Appeal upheld the decision of Popplewell J [2015] EWHC 718 (Comm); [2015] 2 Lloyd's Rep. 407, in which he had declined to follow the decision of Flaux J in *The Astra* [2013] EWHC 865 (Comm); [2013] 2 Lloyd's Rep. 69 that payment of hire is a condition. For earlier conflicting dicta on the status of a withdrawal clause, see: *United Scientific Holdings v Burnley BC* [1978] A.C. 904 at 924 (Lord Diplock); *The Afovos* [1983] 1 W.L.R. 195 at 203 (Lord Diplock); *Stocznia Gdanska v Latvian Shipping Co* [2002] EWCA Civ 889; [2002] 2 Lloyd's Rep. 436 at [80] (Rix LJ); *The Georgios C* [1971] 1 Q.B. 488 (Donaldson J and Lord Denning MR) (overruled in *The Laconia* [1977] A.C. 850, but not in relation to the issue at hand); *The Brimnes* [1973] 1 W.L.R. 386 (Brandon J, where the decision that timely payment was not a condition was part of the ratio, but the issue was not "ventilated" on appeal: [1975] Q.B. 929); *The Kos* [2012] UKSC 17; [2012] 2 A.C. 164 at [7] (Lord Sumption).

[439] *Grand China Logistics Holding (Group) Co Ltd v Spar Shipping* [2016] EWCA Civ 982; [2016] 2 Lloyd's Rep. 447 at [45]–[47] (Gross LJ); cf. at [93] (Hamblen LJ).

[440] *Grand China Logistics Holding (Group) Co Ltd v Spar Shipping* [2016] EWCA Civ 982; [2016] 2 Lloyd's Rep. 447 at [55].

[441] See para.18–048.

[442] *The Astra* [2013] EWHC 865 (Comm); [2013] 2 Lloyd's Rep. 69 at [120]; cf. *BNP Paribas v Wockhardt EU Operations (Swiss) AG* [2009] EWHC 3116 (Comm); 132 Con L.R. 177 at [33]. This feature of the contract was not present in the *Spar Shipping* case; nonetheless Gross LJ still held that *The Astra* was wrongly decided on the question of whether timely payment of hire was a condition.

[443] *Financings Ltd v Baldock* [1963] 2 Q.B. 104 at 111.

after termination[444] and the prospect of this "disproportionate consequence" for what might be a trivial breach was another factor taken into account in requiring that the parties make clear their intention to treat a term as a condition.[445] In fact, the shipowner was still entitled to damages for loss of bargain. While timely payment is not a condition, it is an intermediate term and the charterer's defaults were sufficiently persistent that it was guilty of renunciation.[446]

**Relationship between express provision for determination and repudiatory breach.** The fact that a contract contains an express provision for determination upon breach does not necessarily exclude the right to terminate under the general law for a repudiatory breach. It is a question of construction[447] and the courts are unlikely to find that this was the intention of the parties in the absence of "clear words".[448] Nonetheless, the terms of an express provision may give guidance on whether a particular breach is to be treated as repudiatory.[449] Where an express provision only allows for termination if the breach reaches a certain level of seriousness, or makes it subject to a period of notice to remedy the breach, a breach falling below that level or without the opportunity to remedy is "unlikely" to amount to a repudiatory breach.[450] 18–071

**Whether contract terminated under the general law for a "repudiatory breach", or under an express provision for determination.**[451] If damages for "loss of bargain" are available for a repudiatory breach and such a breach has in fact been committed, does it matter that the injured party purports to terminate under an express provision for determination? Some earlier cases seem to proceed on the assumption that it does not[452] and, as we have seen,[453] no particular form is required for an acceptance of the other party's repudiation. In others, it is suggested that if the injured party terminates under an express provision it may be too late to accept the repudiatory breach in support of a claim for loss of bargain damages. 18–072

---

[444] More often, a shipowner will exercise the right of withdrawal, even if the breach is only very slight, because the market has risen and the vessel can be re-hired, sometimes to the same charterer, at a higher rate.

[445] *Grand China Logistics Holding (Group) Co Ltd v Spar Shipping* [2016] EWCA Civ 982; [2016] 2 Lloyd's Rep. 447 at [65].

[446] *Grand China Logistics Holding (Group) Co Ltd v Spar Shipping* [2016] EWCA Civ 982; [2016] 2 Lloyd's Rep. 447

[447] *Leslie Shipping v Welstead* [1921] 3 K.B. 420; *The Mihalis Angelos* [1971] 1 Q.B. 164.

[448] *Dalkia Utilities Services Plc v Celtech International Ltd* [2006] EWHC 63; [2006] 1 Lloyd's Rep. 599 at [21]; *Plantation Holdings (FZ) LLV v Dubai Islamic Bank PJSC* [2017] EWHC 520 (Comm) at [242].

[449] *Lockland Builders v Rickwood* (1995) 46 Con L.R. 92.

[450] *BSkyB Ltd v HP Enterprise Services UK Ltd* [2010] EWHC 86 (TCC); [2010] B.L.R. 267 at [1366]; cf. *Wickman Ltd v Schuler AG* and the discussion of the reasoning in that case, para.18–048.

[451] Liu [2011] L.M.C.L.Q. 4; Carter and Goh 26 J.C.L. 103; Peel [2013] L.M.C.L.Q. 519.

[452] *Yeoman Credit Ltd v Waragowski* [1961] 1 W.L.R. 1124; *Hyundai Heavy Industries Ltd v Pournaras* [1980] 1 W.L.R. 1129; *The Almare Seconda* [1981] 2 Lloyd's Rep. 433; *Lombard North Central Plc v Butterworth* [1987] Q.B. 527; *And So To Bed Ltd v Dixon* [2001] F.S.R. 47, said "not to stand" with the decision in *Lonsdale Sports Ltd v Leofelis SA* [2012] EWCA Civ 985: *Phones 4U v EE Ltd* [2018] EWHC 49 (Comm); [2018] 1 Lloyd's Rep. 204 at [95].

[453] See para.18–011.

18–073 **"Loss of bargain" damages irrecoverable on grounds of causation.** It is helpful to begin with a case in which the injured party purports to terminate the contract for repudiatory breach, but the court finds that the breach relied upon was not repudiatory, or a breach at all. As we have seen, the injured party may be able to rely on a further repudiatory breach which would have justified termination, so that the injured party is not himself guilty of a repudiatory breach by wrongful termination,[454] but can he also still bring a claim for "loss of bargain" damages? This was the situation in *Lonsdale Sports Ltd v Leofelis SA*[455] where the Court of Appeal held that they are not available. The injured party has to establish that the "loss of bargain" was caused by the repudiatory breach upon which he now relies, and cannot do so where it is caused by the erroneous decision to terminate on the strength of the breach which was alleged at the date of termination. As explained by Lloyd LJ, the principle which allows the injured party retrospectively to rely on a further breach "operates as a shield against a claim for damages on the basis of wrongful termination, not as a sword to claim damages (for the future) on the basis of justified termination".[456] By parity of reasoning, if the injured party cannot claim loss of bargain damages where he terminates for the "wrong" breach, he cannot do so where he terminates on grounds that do not amount to a breach at all. In *Phones 4U v EE Ltd*[457] the claimant gave notice of termination under an express provision on the basis that the defendant had gone into administration. Even assuming that the defendant had also been guilty of a repudiatory breach,[458] the claimant could not rely on this in support of a claim for loss of bargain damages. Based on the *Leofelis* case, Baker J held that "if a termination letter communicates clearly a decision to terminate only under an express contractual right to terminate that has arisen irrespective of any breach, then it cannot be said that the contract was terminated for breach and so a claim for damages for loss of bargain at common law cannot run."[459]

18–074 **"Loss of bargain" damages irrecoverable on grounds of "affirmation".** In the *Leofelis* case the injured party relied on the "wrong" breach and in the *Phones 4U* case the injured party did not rely upon a breach at all as the reason for terminating the contract. A further possibility is that the injured party relies, correctly, on the same repudiatory breach throughout, but does so initially on the basis that it allows him to terminate under an express provision for determination. Of such a situation, it has been said:

> "The fact that service of a contractual notice of termination is not inconsistent with the acceptance of a repudiation does not mean that in *all* cases such a notice amounts to such an acceptance. If the notice makes explicit reference to a particular contractual clause, and nothing else, that may, in context, show that the giver of the notice was not intending to accept

[454] See para.17–062.
[455] [2012] EWCA Civ 985.
[456] *Lonsdale Sports Ltd v Leofelis SA* [2012] EWCA Civ 985 at [33]; para.17–064.
[457] [2018] EWHC 49 (Comm); [2018] 1 Lloyd's Rep. 204.
[458] It was at least arguable for the purpose of the application for summary judgment before the court.
[459] *Phones 4U v EE Ltd* [2018] EWHC 49 (Comm); [2018] 1 Lloyd's Rep. 204 at [121]; cf. *Shell Egypt West Manzala GmbH v Dana Gas Egypt Ltd* [2010] EWHC 465 (Comm); *Cavenagh v William Evans Ltd* [2012] EWCA Civ 697; [2013] 1 W.L.R. 238.

> the repudiation and was only relying on the contractual clause; for instance if the claim made under the notice of termination is inconsistent with, and not simply less than, that which arises on acceptance of a repudiation."[460]

In practice, this appears to mean that if the injured party does no more than invoke the express provision for determination, but does so on the basis of what is in fact a repudiatory breach, he may also claim to have accepted the repudiatory breach and claim other consequences, such as "loss of bargain" damages.[461] He will not, however, be able to do so if he goes further and makes a claim which is "inconsistent" with such acceptance, e.g. where he claims payment of a "termination sum",[462] or makes a claim under a "minimum payment clause",[463] or claims under a refund guarantee which is confined to termination under the express provision.[464] In such a case, the objection to the recovery of "loss of bargain" is less one of causation (as in the cases considered above), but rather, and paradoxically, a question of affirmation which arises if the injured party is required to "elect" between "alternative rights which have different consequences".[465]

Even in a case where the injured party is put to his election because the differing modes of termination invoke inconsistent rights,[466] it may be possible to give notice that the contract is terminated for repudiatory breach, thereby ensuring that a claim for damages for "loss of bargain" may be brought if there

---

[460] *Dalkia Utilities Services Plc v Celtech International Ltd* [2006] EWHC 63 (Comm); [2006] 1 Lloyd's Rep. 599 at [144].

[461] *Stocznia Gdanska SA v Latvian Shipping Co* [2002] 2 Lloyd's Rep. 436; *Dalkia Utilities Services Plc v Celtech International Ltd* [2006] EWHC 63 (Comm); [2006] 1 Lloyd's Rep. 599 at [143]; *Force India Formula One v Etihad* [2010] EWCA Civ 1051 at [117]–[118]; *Gold Group Properties Ltd v BDW Trading Ltd* [2010] EWHC 1632 (TCC) at [110]; *Bolton MBC v Municipal Mutual Ins Ltd* [2006] EWCA Civ 50; [2006] 1 W.L.R. 1493; *Kris Motor Spares Ltd v Fox Williams LLP* [2009] EWHC 2813 (QB); [2009] 6 Costs L.R. 931 at [99]; *Parbulk II A/S v Heritage Maritime Ltd SA* [2011] EWHC 2917 (Comm); [2012] 1 Lloyd's Rep. 87 at [39]; cf. *Regulus Ship Services PTE Ltd v Lundin Services BV* [2016] EWHC 2674 (Comm); [2016] 2 Lloyd's Rep. 612 at [11] (defective notice of termination under an express provision not effective as acceptance of a repudiatory breach).

[462] *Dalkia Utilities Services Plc v Celtech International Ltd* [2006] EWHC 63 (Comm); [2006] 1 Lloyd's Rep. 599 at [144] where the dictum of Christopher Clarke J in this respect is obiter in that he found that there had been no repudiatory breach.

[463] *United Dominions Trust (Commercial) Ltd v Ennis* (1968) 1 Q.B. 54 at 65–66; cf. *UCB Leasing Ltd v Holtom* [1987] R.T.R. 362 at 368; *Laing Management Ltd v Aegon Ins Co (UK) Ltd* (1998) 86 Build. L.R. 70.

[464] This was the decision of Burton J at first instance in *Stocznia Gdynia SA v Gearbulk Holdings Ltd* [2008] EWHC 944 (Comm); [2008] 2 Lloyd's Rep. 202 but the Court of Appeal held that "loss of bargain" damages were available under the express provision in any event because it amounted to termination for breach of condition: [2009] EWCA Civ 75; [2010] Q.B. 27. It is only in this particular context that the following dictum of Moore-Bick LJ (at [20]) can be explained: "it is wrong to treat the right to terminate in accordance with the terms of the contract as different in substance from the right to treat the contract as discharged by reason of repudiation at common law." It is clear from the discussion in para.18–069 that they are different in substance, at least when it comes to any additional claim for damages; cf. *Imperial Chemical Industries Ltd v Merit Merrell Technology Ltd* [2017] EWHC 1763 (TCC); 173 Con L.R. 137 at [187]–[188].

[465] *Stocznia Gdynia SA v Gearbulk Holdings Ltd* [2009] EWCA Civ 75; [2010] Q.B. 27 at [44].

[466] Where the consequences of exercising the two rights are different, but not inconsistent, it is necessary to make it clear which right is being exercised, or that both rights are being exercised; otherwise there will not be the certainty required for an effective termination: *Newland Shipping & Forwarding Ltd v Toba Trading FZC* [2014] EWHC 661 (Comm).

was in fact a repudiatory breach, while taking the precaution of giving notice in the alternative that, if there was no repudiatory breach, the contract is terminated pursuant to the express provision.[467] It may in fact be necessary to do no more than ensure that the notice which is given is notice of termination for repudiatory breach. If that is challenged and it is later found that there was no repudiatory breach, it is the injured party who may have been guilty of wrongful termination, but he may at that point invoke the right to terminate under the express provision (assuming it is available) by reference to the principle discussed above that a refusal to perform by a party who has an excuse for non-performance is not a breach, even though he did not state the excuse, or even know of it, at the time of the refusal.[468] There is no reason to confine that principle to cases where the excuse is a (or another) repudiatory breach, but where the excuse is in the form of the right to terminate the contract under an express provision, it may be said that the injured party has failed to meet the requirement of strict compliance,[469] and the principle of unstated excuse is subject to a number of exceptions.[470] It is perhaps for this reason that a notice in the alternative may be the safer course of action.[471]

18–075 **Literal enforcement in general.** The purpose of an express provision for determination is to prevent disputes from arising as to the often difficult question whether the failure in performance is sufficiently serious to justify termination; and they take effect even though there is no substantial failure.[472] For example, under the type of withdrawal clause discussed in para.18-070, the shipowner can exercise his right of withdrawal immediately on the charterer's failure to pay;[473] and he can do this even though the charterer tenders payment very soon after it was due and the short delay in payment causes the shipowner little prejudice. Such clauses are literally enforced because, in cases of this kind, "certainty is of

[467] *Shell Egypt West Manzala GmbH v Dana Gas Egypt Ltd* [2010] EWHC 465 (Comm) at [34]. No such notice was given in the *Shell* case, but Tomlinson J could see "no reason" why it should not. It may run the risk that it is too equivocal to be effective as a notice of either mode of termination (cf. *Leofelis SA v Lonsdale Sports Ltd* [2008] EWCA Civ 680; *The Times*, 23 July 2008, para.18–011), or that it is invalid as an attempt to approbate and reprobate the contract at the same time: *Suisse Atlantique Société d'Armament SA v NV Rotterdamsche Kolen Centrale* [1967] 1 A.C. 361 at 398.

[468] See para.17–062.

[469] *Decro-Wall International SA v Practitioners in Marketing Ltd* [1971] 1 W.L.R. 361 at 371, 378, 382.

[470] See para.17–062.

[471] Whether an acceptance of repudiatory breach is given first, in the alternative, or on its own, if it is effective (i.e. there was a repudiatory breach and it has been accepted) the injured party may then be deprived of additional benefits, such as a refund guarantee, since the premise of the reasoning employed in some of the cases above is that it was necessary to invoke the express provision for determination to obtain those benefits.

[472] Such clauses are probably not within s.3(2)(b)(ii) of the Unfair Contract Terms Act 1977 for the reasons given at para.7–057, and because termination under such clauses terminates the primary obligations of *both* parties; cf. *The Super Servant Two* [1990] 1 Lloyd's Rep. 1 at 7, distinguishing between cancellation and exemption clauses.

[473] *The Brimnes* [1975] Q.B. 929; *The Laconia* [1977] A.C. 850; Rose 30 C.L.P. 213; cf. *The Chikuma* [1981] 1 W.L.R. 314; Mann 97 L.Q.R. 379–382.

primary importance";[474] while the charterer can mitigate the severity of the clause by insisting (if his bargaining position permits) on the inclusion of a so-called "anti-technicality" provision requiring notice of default and allowing a period of time to remedy it before withdrawal.[475]

Although the law normally gives literal effect to express provisions for determination, it does insist on compliance with three requirements: first, it must be shown that the term does, as a matter of construction, apply to the breach relied upon;[476] secondly, the party seeking to terminate must act strictly in accordance with the terms of the clause;[477] and thirdly, the party relying on the express provision must terminate without undue delay.[478]

**Does the express provision apply?** In *Rice v Great Yarmouth BC*[479] a term in a four-year maintenance contract allowed one party to terminate in the event of the other's breach of "*any* of its obligations under the contract", but the court held that the parties could not have intended that this was to apply, literally, to any breach. It was conceded that the clause did not allow termination for a "trivial" breach, but it is open to doubt whether the court was correct to conclude that the term added nothing to the general law such that the only breaches in fact covered were those which would have amounted to a repudiatory breach in any event, i.e. a substantial failure to perform.[480] This does not apply as "a general proposition" and, in a subsequent case, it was said that such wording "will generally be construed as permitting termination for significant or substantial breaches as opposed to trivial, insignificant or insubstantial ones".[481] The parties may attempt to avoid the difficulty encountered in the interpretation of "any" breach by expressly confining a provision for termination to certain types of breach, short of repudiatory breach, e.g. "material breach",[482] or a breach "not capable of remedy".[483] **18–076**

[474] *The Laconia* [1977] A.C. 850 at 878; *The Lutetian* [1982] 2 Lloyd's Rep. 140 at 159; cf. *The Chikuma* [1981] 1 W.L.R. 314 at 322; cf. in contracts for the sale of land: *Union Eagle Ltd v Golden Achievement Ltd* [1997] A.C. 514 at 519; cf. at 523; para.18–081.

[475] As in *The Libyaville* [1975] 1 Lloyd's Rep. 537; and in *Federal Commerce and Navigation Co Ltd v Molena Alpha Inc* [1979] A.C. 757; cf. *The Laconia* [1977] A.C. 850 at 878; *The Afovos* [1983] 1 W.L.R. 195; *Bespoke Couture Ltd v Artpower Ltd* [2006] EWCA Civ 1696 (notice of default not sufficient to effect termination which also required election of injured party).

[476] See para.18–076.

[477] See para.18–077.

[478] See para.18–078.

[479] [2003] T.C.L.R. 1.

[480] But see to similar effect: *The Antaios* [1985] A.C. 191; *Dominion Corporate Trustees Ltd v Debenhams Properties Ltd* [2010] EWHC 1193 (Ch); [2010] 23 E.G. 106 at [32].

[481] *Obrascon Huarte Lain SA v Attorney General for Gibraltar* [2014] EWHC 1028 (TCC); [2014] B.L.R. 484 at [324] where, in context, a "substantial" breach does not require a repudiatory breach (upheld, without consideration of this point: [2015] EWCA Civ 712; [2015] B.L.R. 521).

[482] *Glolite Ltd v Jasper Conran Ltd*, *The Times*, 28 January 1998; *Fortman Holdings v Modem Holdings* [2001] EWCA Civ 1235; *Dalkia Utilities Services Plc v Celtech International Ltd* [2006] EWHC 63; [2006] 1 Lloyd's Rep. 599.

[483] *Force India Formula One Team Ltd v Etihad Airways PJSC* [2010] EWCA Civ 1051; [2011] E.T.M.R. 10 at [100]–[110].

18–077 **Strict compliance.** A good example of this requirement is provided by a voyage charterparty which may provide that the charterer can cancel if the ship is not at the port of loading by 30 September. The charterer would not be entitled to cancel on 29 September, even though at that time the ship was so far away from the port that she could not possibly get there the next day.[484] Conversely, where a time charterparty gives the shipowner the right to give notice of withdrawal if hire is not paid on the due day, he is not entitled to exercise that right before the end of that day, even though the bank at which payment was to be made had already closed so that the charterer could not possibly have made the payment in accordance with the contract.[485] Similarly, the courts will normally require precise compliance with any procedure for effecting termination.[486]

18–078 **No undue delay.** In cases of non-payment of hire by a time charterer it has been said that the shipowner must exercise his right to withdraw the ship "within a reasonable time after default".[487] This rule is based either on waiver or on an implied term that the right to withdraw must be exercised within a reasonable time.[488]

18–079 **Relief against forfeiture.**[489] The willingness of the courts to give effect to express provisions for determination is, in the cases so far discussed, based on the assumption that the parties have bargained on more or less equal terms.[490] Where this is not the case, the law has developed restrictions on the right of a party to rely on an express provision for determination. This is the position where a lease entitles the landlord to forfeit if the tenant breaks *any* covenant; and where a regulated hire-purchase agreement[491] entitles the owner to terminate it if the hirer defaults in the payment of even a single instalment. In such cases the provision for determination would deprive a party who committed some quite minor breach of the benefit of a contract which he has for a long period performed satisfactorily; and the court may allow him a period of grace within which to make good his default.[492] Normally such "relief against forfeiture" only gives the party in breach extra time to perform;[493] but in "exceptional circumstances" relief may be granted on a basis which does not assume that the contract had applied

---

[484] *The Mihalis Angelos* [1971] 1 Q.B. 164; cf. *The Madeleine* [1967] 2 Lloyd's Rep. 224 at 243.
[485] *The Afovos* [1983] 1 W.L.R. 195; cf. *The Pamela* [1995] 2 Lloyd's Rep. 249.
[486] *Geys v Société Générale* [2012] UKSC 63; [2013] 1 A.C. 523; cf. *Ellis Tylin Ltd v Co-operative Retail Services Ltd* [1999] B.L.R. 205; *ED&F Man Commodity Advisers Ltd v Fluxo-Cane Overseas Ltd* [2010] EWHC 212 (Comm) at [58]; *Sucden Financial Ltd v Fluxo-Cane Overseas Ltd* [2010] EWHC 2133 (Comm); [2010] 2 C.L.C. 216 at [45].
[487] *The Laconia* [1977] A.C. 850 at 872; *The Scaptrade* [1981] 2 Lloyd's Rep. 425 at 430; affirmed [1983] 2 A.C. 699, without reference to this point; cf. *The Great Marine* [1990] 2 Lloyd's Rep. 245 at 249.
[488] *The Antaios* [1985] A.C. 191; cf. *Nichimen Corp v Gatoil Inc* [1987] 2 Lloyd's Rep. 46 at 54.
[489] Smith [2001] C.L.J. 178.
[490] See *The Scaptrade* [1983] Q.B. 529 at 539–540, approved [1983] 2 A.C. 699.
[491] See para.5–007.
[492] See Consumer Credit Act 1974 ss.88, 89; requiring formal notice of termination and giving the hirer at least 14 days to make good his default; and the rules relating to relief against forfeiture of leases: Law of Property Act 1925 s.146.
[493] See *Nutting v Baldwin* [1995] 1 W.L.R. 201 at 208.

continuously up to the time of relief,[494] and sometimes such relief is allowed even though the breach cannot be remedied at all. Thus, where a tenant had innocently broken a covenant against subletting it was held that the landlord could not enforce a forfeiture clause, as the breach had not prejudiced him in any way.[495] Further statutory restrictions apply to a landlord's right to forfeit certain long leases of dwelling-houses for non-payment by the tenant of rent or certain other charges.[496]

**Relief confined to proprietary or possessory rights.** In some of the time charterparty cases discussed above, it was suggested that relief against forfeiture should be granted to a charterer who failed to pay hire on time, and that the exercise by the shipowner of his right to withdraw the ship under a withdrawal clause should be restricted accordingly.[497] But the House of Lords rejected these suggestions[498] for two reasons. First, the courts should give effect to commercial agreements concluded (as time charters usually are) between parties who had bargained on equal terms. Secondly, the principle of relief against forfeiture was restricted to cases where the party in breach would, if the contract were literally enforced, be deprived of "proprietary or possessory rights",[499] while a time charter conferred only contractual rights, being merely a contract for services to be rendered by the shipowner.[500] **18–080**

The distinction between terms which deprive a party of "proprietary or possessory rights" and those which deprive him only of contractual rights can be a fine one. The point can be illustrated by contrasting two cases. In *Sport International Bussum BV v Inter-Footwear Ltd*[501] it was held that relief against forfeiture was not available where A granted B a licence to use certain trade-marks and the contract provided that the licence was to determine on B's default. But in *BICC Plc v Burndy Corp*[502] such relief was held to be available where an agreement by which certain patents were vested in A and B provided that, on B's default, he should assign his rights in the patents to A. No doubt the cases are technically distinguishable on the ground that the actual *assignment* of a patent involves a transfer of "property", while the *termination of a contractual licence* to use a trade mark does not. But from a commercial point of view a licence to use such forms of "intellectual property" often serves the same purpose

494 *Cukurova Finance International Ltd v Alfa Telecom Turkey Ltd* [2013] UKPC 20; [2016] A.C. 923 (relief granted from appropriation of shares charged by way of security and loan "revived" but accrual of interest was suspended for a period and the rate was confined to the contract rate, rather than the default rate); for further proceedings, see [2013] UKPC 25; [2013] 4 All E.R. 989.

495 *Scala House & District Property Co Ltd v Forbes* [1974] Q.B. 575; cf. *Akici v LR Butlin Ltd* [2005] EWCA Civ 1296; [2006] 1 W.L.R. 201.

496 Commonhold and Leasehold Reform Act 2002 ss.167–170.

497 *The Afovos* [1980] 2 Lloyd's Rep. 477 at 479; reversed on other grounds [1983] 1 W.L.R. 195; *The Tropwind* [1982] 1 Lloyd's Rep. 232 at 234.

498 *The Scaptrade* [1983] 2 A.C. 694 and see the authorities cited above, fn.474.

499 *The Scaptrade* [1983] 2 A.C. 694 at 702; cf. *SCI (Sales Curve Interactive) v Titus SARL* [2001] EWCA Civ 591; [2001] 2 All E.R. (Comm) 416 at [47].

500 *The Scaptrade* [1983] 2 A.C. 694 at 702; *Jones v Society of Lloyd's*, *The Times*, 2 February 2000.

501 [1984] 1 W.L.R. 776; Harpum 100 L.Q.R. 369.

502 [1985] Ch. 232.

as an actual transfer; and the practical effect of the clause in each case was to deprive the party in default of the right to make use of the "property".

In the charterparty cases both lines of the reasoning employed supported the conclusion that there should be no relief against forfeiture. But a contract of a "commercial" nature may confer "proprietary or possessory rights" on the party in breach. That will be sufficient to determine the *existence* of the court's jurisdiction to grant relief,[503] but the policy of giving effect to commercial contracts militates against its *exercise*. It is, with respect, open to question whether some of the decisions in which the courts have exercised their jurisdiction in favour of the party in breach of a commercial contract[504] are consistent with the emphasis on the requirements of commercial certainty in a number of House of Lords and Privy Council decisions concerned with express provisions for determination.[505] A more consistent approach can be seen in *The Jotunheim*[506] in which the possessory right conferred by a demise charterparty was sufficient to confer jurisdiction to grant relief, but it was not granted principally because of the need for certainty in the commercial context.

18–081 **Sale of land.** By virtue of the conclusion of a contract for the sale of land, the purchaser acquires an equitable interest in the land which might be considered sufficient, in the light of the cases considered above, to allow for relief in the event of late payment by the purchaser. In *Union Eagle Ltd v Golden Achievement Ltd*,[507] however, Lord Hoffmann confirmed that the courts are "unwilling to grant relief by way of specific performance against breach of an essential condition as to time."[508] At most, the purchaser may be able to obtain "restitutionary … relief against forfeiture" by securing the return of a penal deposit.[509] It is not entirely clear whether, in such cases, the courts have no jurisdiction to grant relief, or that they will very rarely exercise it. There is rather more support for the former interpretation.[510] Lord Hoffmann endorsed the principle that the courts *never* exercise the jurisdiction "where the parties have

---

503 Provided also that the right of forfeiture is to secure the payment of money or is security for the attainment of a specific result which can be achieved through the courts: *Shiloh Spinners Ltd v Harding* [1973] A.C. 691; *On Demand Information Plc v Michael Gerson (Finance) Plc* [2001] 1 W.L.R. 155 CA (this aspect of the decision was not challenged in the appeal to the House of Lords, fn.504); *Celestial Aviation Trading 71 Ltd v Paramount Airways Private Ltd* [2010] EWHC 185 (Comm); [2011] 1 Lloyd's Rep. 9. In *Cukurova Finance International Ltd v Alfa Telecom Turkey Ltd* [2013] UKPC 2; [2015] 2 W.L.R. 875 at [90] this is described as the "paradigm" case for relief.

504 In addition to *BICC Plc v Burndy Corp* [1985] Ch. 232, see: *Transag Haulage Ltd v Leyland DAF Finance Plc* [1994] 2 B.C.L.C. 88; *On Demand Information Plc v Michael Gerson (Finance) Plc* [2002] UKHL 13; [2003] 1 A.C. 368.

505 See *The Laconia* [1977] A.C. 850; *The Chikuma* [1981] 1 W.L.R. 314; *The Scaptrade* [1983] 2 A.C. 694; *Union Eagle Ltd v Golden Achievement Ltd* [1997] A.C. 514. Contrast *Cukurova Finance International Ltd v Alfa Telecom Turkey Ltd* [2013] UKPC 2; [2015] 2 W.L.R. 875, a case which involved "a combination of unusual features which are most unlikely to be repeated" (at [125]).

506 [2004] EWHC 671 (Comm); [2005] 1 Lloyd's Rep. 181; cf. *Celestial Aviation Trading 71 Ltd v Paramount Airways Private Ltd* [2010] EWHC 185 (Comm); [2011] 1 Lloyd's Rep. 9 at [122].

507 [1997] A.C. 514.

508 *Union Eagle Ltd v Golden Achievement Ltd* [1997] A.C. 514 at 520.

509 See para.20–147.

510 In *Samarenko v Dawn Hill House Ltd* [2011] EWCA Civ 1445; [2013] Ch. 36 at [11] the *Union Eagle* case is cited for the proposition that if time is of the essence "equity will not interfere".

expressly intimated in their agreement that it is not to apply by providing that time is to be the essence of their bargain."[511] He also stressed that the mere *existence* of the power to grant relief is sufficient to create the uncertainty to be avoided and held that the purpose of the express term is to "restore to the vendor his freedom to deal with the land as he pleases."[512] The mere *availability* of relief by way of specific performance would (while restitutionary relief would not) make it impossible for the vendor to know with certainty when that freedom had been restored. While Lord Hoffmann acknowledged the existence of cases where relief by way of specific performance had been granted,[513] they might be explained on the basis that, in the state of English law at the time they were decided, it would not have been easy to find a restitutionary remedy which provided adequate relief against forfeiture.[514]

**Consumer protection.** An express cancellation clause in a contract between a commercial seller or supplier and a consumer may also be open to challenge under the Consumer Rights Act 2015 on the ground that it is "unfair" to the consumer and hence not binding on him.[515] The list of prima facie invalid terms given in Pt 2 of the Act refers only to cancellation clauses in contracts "of indeterminate duration";[516] but as the list is "non-exhaustive", this restriction would not preclude the court from holding that a cancellation clause in a fixed-term contract was also unfair. **18–082**

**Unenforceability on other grounds.** It is arguable that in exceptional circumstances an "oppressive" cancellation clause may be open to attack at common law in accordance with the principles discussed in Ch.7, or at least restricted in its operation so that the power to cancel can be exercised only on reasonable grounds.[517] A provision entitling a party to refuse to make payments under a contract in default of exact performance by the other may also be unenforceable as a penalty.[518] **18–083**

### *(iii) Unilateral contracts and options*

**Contingent conditions: unilateral contracts.** A party may fail to perform some act which he has not promised to perform, but the performance of which is a **18–084**

[511] *Steedman v Drinkle* [1916] 1 A.C. 275 at 279. Where time is "of the essence", the contract may be terminated for breach of condition (see below, para.18–096), for which there is no jurisdiction to grant relief.

[512] *Union Eagle Ltd v Golden Achievement Ltd* [1997] A.C. 514 at 520; cf. the conditions laid down by *Shiloh Spinners Ltd v Harding* [1973] A.C. 691, fn.453.

[513] e.g. *In Re Dagenham (Thames) Dock Co Ex p. Hulse* (1872–73) L.R. 8 Ch. App. 1022 (the purchaser had been in possession of the land pending completion for five years, during which time it had constructed a dock at its own expense).

[514] *Union Eagle Ltd v Golden Achievement Ltd* [1997] A.C. 514 at 521.

[515] See para.7–125.

[516] Consumer Rights Act 2015 Sch.2 para.8.

[517] *Timeload Ltd v British Telecommunications Plc* [1995] E.M.L.R. 459 at 467; cf. *Hadley Design Associates v Westminster CC* [2003] EWHC 1617 (TCC); [2004] T.C.L.R. 1; contrast *Looney v Trafigura Beheer NV* [2011] EWHC 125 (Ch).

[518] See para.20–146.

contingent condition[519] of the other party's liability. Such a condition must be strictly complied with. The rule may be illustrated by the case of a unilateral contract.[520] If A promises B £100 if B walks from London to York, B must walk all the way to York before he is entitled to the £100.[521] The requirement of strict performance can be explained on the ground that A has no other remedy than to withhold performance. He cannot recover damages if B fails to complete the walk, since B has made no promise.

18–085 **Contingent conditions: bilateral contracts.** The distinction between promises and conditions can apply also in relation to particular terms in bilateral contracts and has, in relation to such terms, given rise to differences of judicial opinion.[522] The question in each case is whether the term, on its true construction, imposes an obligation on one of the parties to do an act (e.g. to give a specified notice to the other) or whether its effect is merely to make the performance of the act a prerequisite of the accrual of the other party's liability. The authorities give little guidance on this question of construction, but at least the effect of the resulting distinction is clear. If the term in question is construed as a condition, the party seeking to terminate need not show that the other's failure to comply with the term prejudiced him seriously or at all. Yet where a term is construed as a *promise* such prejudice must, as a general rule,[523] be shown by a party who seeks to terminate.

18–086 **Options.** The requirement that conditions which are not promises must be strictly complied with also applies to options to purchase. If the grantee fails to comply in any respect with a condition to which the exercise of the option is subject, he cannot enforce the option.[524] It makes no difference that the failure causes only insignificant prejudice, or none at all, to the grantor. Moreover, in the case of an option the rule applies even though the condition is the performance by the grantee of an obligation under another term of the agreement in which the option is contained. Thus in *West Country Cleaners* (*Falmouth*) *Ltd v Saly*[525] a lease gave a tenant an option to renew "providing all covenants herein contained have been duly observed and performed." The tenant had committed minor breaches of his covenant to paint the interior of his premises; and it was held that he was not

[519] See para.2–104.

[520] See para.2–052.

[521] It is assumed that A has not attempted to withdraw before B reaches York: see para.2–054.

[522] e.g. *Shires v Brock* (1977) 247 E.G. 127 where the disputed term appears to have been treated by Goff and Buckley LJJ at 131 and 133 as a contingent condition, but by Scarman LJ at 133 as a promise; cf. *United Dominion Trust Ltd v Eagle Aircraft Ltd* [1968] 1 W.L.R. 74, criticised by Atiyah 31 M.L.R. 332 but approved in *United Scientific Holdings Ltd v Burnley BC* [1978] A.C. 904 at 928, 945, 951.

[523] i.e. in cases falling within the general rule discussed at paras 18–030—18–039, as opposed to the exceptions discussed at paras 18–040—18–073.

[524] *Hare v Nicholl* [1966] 2 Q.B. 160; *Allardyce v Roebuck* [2004] EWHC 1538 (Ch); [2005] 1 W.L.R. 815 at [25]. The rule may be excluded by the terms of the option: see *Millichamp v Jones* [1982] 1 W.L.R. 1422.

[525] [1966] 1 W.L.R. 1485.

entitled to exercise the option, even though it did not appear that the landlord was seriously prejudiced by the breaches. This application of the rule has been explained on the ground that:

> "an option of this character is a privilege—a right which has always been treated by the law as requiring complete compliance with the terms and conditions upon which the option is to be exercised".[526]

The severity of the rule is, however, mitigated in a number of ways. Thus the rule does not apply where a tenant was at one time in breach but has cured that breach by the time of the exercise of the option, e.g. if by that time he has paid off rent which had at an earlier stage been overdue.[527] The rule may also be displaced by a strict construction of the term imposing the condition, leading to the conclusion that there has been no failure to comply with it.[528]

## 4. LIMITATIONS ON THE RIGHT TO TERMINATE

We have seen that the right to terminate may be excluded by the terms of the contract.[529] Our present concern is with cases in which a right to terminate has at one stage arisen but it is later lost or limited. Where there are several breaches, each giving rise to a right to terminate, the fact that one such right has been lost does not necessarily bar the other or others.[530] **18–087**

**A good faith limitation?** It has been suggested that the choice conferred on the injured party by the right to terminate should be equated to the exercise of contractual discretion seen in a number of cases[531] and therefore subject to an implied term that it must be exercised in good faith for the purpose for which it was conferred, and not arbitrarily, capriciously or irrationally.[532] The better view, it is submitted, is that the right to terminate is in the nature of an "absolute right"[533] which is not subject to the implied term in question. As Longmore LJ has commented: **18–088**

> "The right to terminate is no more an exercise of discretion, which is not to be exercised in an arbitrary or capricious (or perhaps unreasonable) manner, than the right to accept repudiatory conduct as a repudiation of a contract".[534]

---

[526] *West Country Cleaners (Falmouth) Ltd v Saly* [1966] 1 W.L.R. 1485 at 1486.
[527] *Bass Holdings Ltd v Morton Music Ltd* [1988] Ch. 493.
[528] *Little v Courage Ltd* (1995) 70 P. & C.R. 469.
[529] See para.18–064
[530] See *Kwei Tek Chao v British Traders & Shippers Ltd* [1954] 2 Q.B. 459.
[531] See para.6–078.
[532] *MSC Mediterranean Shipping Co SA v Cottonex Anstalt* [2015] EWHC 283 (Comm); [2015] 1 Lloyd's Rep. 359 at [98]; described as not "necessary" on appeal: [2016] EWCA Civ 789; [2016] 2 Lloyd's Rep. 494 at [45].
[533] This is the terminology of Jackson LJ in *Mid Essex Hospital Services NHS Trust v Compass Group UK & Ireland Ltd* [2013] EWCA Civ 200; [2013] B.L.R. 265 at [91]; para.6–078.
[534] *Lomas v JFB Firth Rixson Inc* [2012] EWCA Civ 419; [2012] 2 Lloyd's Rep. 548 at [46]; cf. *Monde Petroleum SA v Westernzagros Ltd* [2016] EWHC 1472; [2016] 2 Lloyd's Rep. 229; *Ilkerler*

### (a) Affirmation, waiver and estoppel

#### *(i) The different senses of waiver*

18–089 **Waiver in the sense of election: affirmation.** Waiver is used in a number of senses, of which two (or possibly three)[535] are relevant to the present discussion. First, a party who is entitled to terminate may indicate that he will nevertheless perform his part of the contract. He is then said to have waived his right to terminate, or to have elected[536] to affirm the contract. Such waiver in the sense of election is referred to hereafter as "affirmation".

18–090 **Examples.** In *Bentsen v Taylor*[537] a charterparty falsely described the ship as "now sailed or about to sail" from a specified port. This was a breach of condition[538] on account of which the charterer could have refused to load; but he said that he would nevertheless load, and then refused to do so. It was held that he was liable for failure to load as he had waived his right to terminate.[539] Conversely, in *The Kanchenjunga*[540] it was the charterer who was guilty of breach when he nominated a port which was unsafe because of the Gulf war between Iran and Iraq, but the shipowner nevertheless pressed him to load there, and then sailed away. It was held that the shipowner had waived the charterer's breach and that he would have been liable in damages, if he had not been protected from such liability by a "war clause" in the charterparty. On the same principle, a shipowner loses his right to put an end to a charterparty under an express term entitling him to withdraw the ship for late payment of hire if he accepts such a payment knowing that the time for making it has passed;[541] a landlord loses the right to forfeit a lease for breach of covenant by the tenant if, knowing of the breach, he makes a demand for rent; [542] and a buyer of goods may lose the right to reject for breach of *one* implied condition if he has agreed with

*Otomotiv Sanayai Ve Ticaret Anonim Sirketi v Perkins Engines Co Ltd* [2017] EWCA Civ 183; [2017] 4 W.L.R. 144 at [29]. Contrast *Bates v Post Office* [2019] EWHC 606 (QB) at [899]; Foxton [2017] L.M.C.L.Q. 360.

535 What are referred to below as "total waiver" and "waiver by estoppel" are both forms of equitable estoppel. For other senses of waiver, see para.3–066 and following.

536 *The Kanchenjunga* [1990] 1 Lloyd's Rep. 391 at 397–398.

537 [1893] 2 Q.B. 274.

538 See para.18–046.

539 *Bentsen v Taylor* [1893] 2 Q.B. 274 at 283, 285.

540 [1990] 1 Lloyd's Rep. 391.

541 *The Brimnes* [1975] Q.B. 929 at 954–956; *The Libyaville* [1975] 1 Lloyd's Rep. 537 at 554; cf. *Modern Transport Co Ltd v Duneric SS Co* [1917] 1 K.B. 370 (submission of question whether hire was due to arbitration held to be a waiver of the right to withdraw). But there is no waiver if the late payment is made into the owner's bank and rejected by him as soon as he learns of the payment: *The Laconia* [1977] A.C. 850; cf. *John Lewis Properties v Viscount Chelsea* [1993] 2 E.G.L.R. 77; and acceptance of an underpayment does not amount to waiver if there is still a reasonable possibility that the balance may be paid in time: *The Mihalios Xilas* [1979] 1 W.L.R. 1018.

542 *David Blackstone Ltd v Burnetts* [1973] 1 W.L.R. 1487; *Thomas v Ken Thomas Ltd* [2006] EWCA Civ 1504; [2007] 1 E.G. 94; *Greenwood Reversions Ltd v World Environment Foundation Ltd* [2008] EWCA Civ 47; [2008] H.L.R. 31 at [26]–[37]. Contrast *Re a Debtor (No.13A–10–1995)* [1995] 1 W.L.R. 1127 (no waiver where rent is demanded before or on the breach in question); cf. *Parbulk II A/S v Heritage Maritime Ltd SA* [2011] EWHC 2917 (Comm); [2012] 1 Lloyd's Rep. 87, doubting

the seller that he will reject *only* for a breach of a *different* implied condition.[543] The examples just given all depend on the innocent party having been put to an "immediate election"; if, under the contract, he acquires the right to terminate "at any time" after a specified event has occurred, his continued performance will not amount to affirmation because it is not inconsistent with his right to terminate at a later date, unless his conduct also indicates an intention to abandon *that right* in clear and unequivocal terms.[544]

**Affirmation bars only the right to terminate.** An important characteristic of affirmation is that it bars only the injured party's right to terminate: it does not deprive him of his right to damages for the breach. The shipowner in *The Kanchenjunga*, above, would have been entitled to damages if his ship had entered the port and suffered damage there as a result of the charterer's breach.[545] **18–091**

**Affirmation distinguished from estoppel.** Affirmation, as a type of waiver, must be distinguished from estoppel, or "waiver by estoppel". The latter may arise where the injured party has by his words or conduct led the party in breach to believe that the right to terminate will not be exercised and the party in breach has relied upon this representation.[546] **18–092**

**Affirmation distinguished from total waiver.** Another type of estoppel is "total waiver" where the injured party represents not only that he will not exercise the right to terminate, but that he will forgo performance altogether, including the right to damages,[547] i.e. he purports wholly to abandon rights under the contract.[548] Section 11(2) of the Sale of Goods Act 1979 provides that "where a contract of sale is subject to a condition to be fulfilled by the seller, the buyer may *waive* the condition, *or* may *elect* to treat the breach of condition as a breach of warranty and not as a ground for treating the contract as repudiated."[549] Here "waive" is used to refer to total waiver (i.e. an abandonment by the buyer of his rights to terminate *and* to claim damages); while "elect" refers to affirmation (or waiver in the sense of election, i.e. to the buyer's abandonment of the right to terminate, while keeping alive his right to damages). **18–093**

---

whether the principle in the landlord and tenant cases extends beyond *acceptance* of rent to *demand*; contrast *Force India Formula One Team Ltd v Aerolab SRL* [2013] EWCA Civ 780; [2013] R.P.C. 36 at [40].

[543] *SN Kurkjan (Commodity) Brokers Ltd v Marketing Exchange for Africa Ltd* [1986] 2 Lloyd's Rep. 614.

[544] *BDW Trading Ltd v JM Rowe Investments Ltd* [2011] EWCA Civ 548 where the right to terminate arose not on breach by the other party but upon the failure to fulfil a condition precedent. At first instance ([2010] EWHC 1987 (Ch) at [136]), Peter Smith J doubted whether this was a case "involving election at all"; cf. *Monde Petroleum SA v Westernzagros Ltd* [2016] EWHC 1472; [2016] 2 Lloyd's Rep. 229 at [289].

[545] *The Kanchenjunga* [1990] 1 Lloyd's Rep. 391 at 393, 397, 401.

[546] See para.18–104.

[547] *Ets Soules & Cie v International Trade Development Co Ltd* [1980] 1 Lloyd's Rep. 129 at 137–138; cf. *Banning v Wright* [1972] 1 W.L.R. 972; *The Happy Day* [2002] EWCA Civ 1068; [2002] 2 Lloyd's Rep. 487 at [64]–[65], [67].

[548] cf. *Tufton Associates Ltd v Dilmun Shipping* [1992] 1 Lloyd's Rep. 71, where the requirement of full performance of an entire obligation (para.17–031) was displaced by waiver.

[549] Emphasis added.

### (ii) *Effect*

18–094 **Revocability.** In principle, affirmation and estoppel have a different effect. Affirmation is irrevocable[550] and, in that sense, final; once the injured party's decision to affirm the contract has been communicated to the party in breach, he cannot later change his mind and terminate the contract. By contrast, we have already seen that estoppel only has a suspensory effect[551] so that the injured party might, upon giving reasonable notice, retract his waiver and terminate the contract. In practice, the difference in effect is less marked. Affirmation is only irrevocable in relation to the particular breach which gave rise to the right to terminate. The injured party may later terminate either on the basis that a further separate breach has occurred,[552] or that the other party has continued to persist in the same breach.[553] Whether a breach is a continuing one depends on all the circumstances.[554] Conversely, estoppel will have a permanent effect in cases where it would be inequitable to allow the injured party to retract his waiver.[555] This is perhaps most likely to occur in the context of waiver of breach because the injured party's failure to exercise the right to terminate may have deprived the other party of the opportunity to tender a substitute performance.[556]

### (iii) *Requirements*

18–095 **Summary.** Since affirmation and estoppel will often have the same effect in practice, the more important differences between them lie in the requirements to be met; in some cases both may be applicable, but in others it will only be possible to invoke one or the other. For both, there is the need for a clear and unequivocal representation.[557] For affirmation, there is also a requirement of knowledge of the right to terminate. This is not needed for estoppel, where there is an additional requirement of reliance, which is not needed for affirmation.

---

[550] *Hain SS Co Ltd v Tate & Lyle Ltd* (1936) 41 Com. Cas. 350 at 355; *Peyman v Lanjani* [1985] Ch. 457; *Yukong Line of Korea v Rendsburg Investments Co of Liberia* [1996] 2 Lloyd's Rep. 604 at 607.

[551] See para.3–086.

[552] *Yukong Line of Korea v Rendsburg Investments Co of Liberia* [1996] 2 Lloyd's Rep. 604 at 607. In *Bell Electric Ltd v Aweco Appliance Systems Gmbh & Co KG* [2002] C.L.C. 1246 at [37] it is said that a further breach can be regarded as repudiatory "when seen against" earlier breaches, even though those earlier breaches can no longer be relied upon themselves because of the injured party's affirmation; cf. *Parbulk II A/S v Heritage Maritime Ltd SA* [2011] EWHC 2917 (Comm); [2012] 1 Lloyd's Rep. 87 at [33]; *Kaur v Leeds Teaching Hospitals NHS Trust* [2018] EWCA Civ 978; [2019] I.C.R. 1 ("last straw doctrine").

[553] *Johnson v Agnew* [1908] A.C. 367; *Stocznia Gdanska SA v Latvian Shipping Co* [2002] EWCA Civ 889; [2002] 2 Lloyd's Rep. 436 at [94]–[100].

[554] *Automotive Latch Systems Ltd v Honeywell International Inc* [2008] EWHC 2171 (Comm) at [660]; cf. *White Rosebay Shipping SA v Hong Kong Chain Glory Shipping* [2013] EWHC 1355 (Comm); [2013] 2 Lloyd's Rep. 618 at [50]. On the distinction between a continuing breach and a breach already committed but which has continuing consequences, see *Plantation Holdings (FZ) LLV v Dubai Islamic Bank PJSC* [2017] EWHC 520 (Comm).

[555] See para.3–087.

[556] e.g. *Toepfer v Warinco AG* [1978] 2 Lloyd's Rep. 569 at 576.

[557] See para.18–096.

**"Clear and unequivocal" representation.** The operation of affirmation, estoppel and total waiver each depend on a "clear and unequivocal representation".[558] In relation to estoppel and total waiver, this requirement is discussed in Ch.3.[559] Affirmation also requires "an unequivocal act or statement"[560] by which the injured party clearly indicates that he intends, not to terminate, but to affirm, the contract. The reference to an "unequivocal act" shows that the injured party need not make an express statement of his intention to affirm: it is enough if he does some positive act from which that intention can be inferred. If the intention does not clearly appear from his words or conduct, there is no affirmation. This may be the position where the injured party accepts defective performance subject to an express reservation of his rights,[561] or against the background of a "no waiver" clause,[562] but since the question of whether he has elected to affirm is ultimately a question of fact, his conduct may imply the necessary intention notwithstanding such a reservation.[563] It has, similarly, been held that the right to terminate was not lost by affirmation where a vendor of land, after the purchaser should have performed, said that he would consider a request for an extension of time;[564] where a buyer to whom short delivery had been made called for a "full tender";[565] where a landlord, after the tenant had committed a breach of covenant, sent him a "negotiating document" designed to resolve the dispute;[566] where an employee continued, after the employer's breach, to accept wages for such time as was reasonably necessary for him to consider his position;[567] and where the injured party merely called on the guilty party to reconsider his position and to withdraw his repudiation.[568] An intention to affirm the contract cannot be inferred because the injured party has taken one of several alternative courses of action; the action taken must have been *inconsistent* with termination of the contract.[569] **18–096**

**Whether representation amounts to total waiver.** In the case of a representation by words it will be a matter of construction whether the innocent party represented that he would forego the right to terminate, or forego performance **18–097**

---

[558] *Peyman v Lanjani* [1985] Ch. 457 at 501; *The Kanchenjunga* [1990] 1 Lloyd's Rep. 391 at 399; *The Great Marine (No.1)* [1990] 2 Lloyd's Rep. 245 at 249.

[559] See para.3–081.

[560] *The Mihalios Xilas* [1979] 1 W.L.R. 1018 at 1024; cf. *Bremer Handelsgesellschaft mbH v Finagrain (etc.) SA* [1981] 2 Lloyd's Rep. 259 at 266.

[561] *Bremer Handelsgesellschaft mbH v Deutsche Conti Handelsgesellschaft mbH* [1983] 2 Lloyd's Rep. 45; cf. *Nova Petroleum International Establishment v Trican Trading Ltd* [1989] 1 Lloyd's Rep. 312. Where several grounds of termination exist and the reservation refers to only some of these, it will not preclude affirmation in respect of the others: *The Wise* [1989] 2 Lloyd's Rep. 451.

[562] *State Securities Plc v Initial Industry Ltd* [2004] All E.R. (D.) 317 (Jan) at [57].

[563] *Tele 2 International Card Co SA v Post Office Ltd* [2009] EWCA Civ 9; cf. *Sumitomo Mitsui Banking Corp Europe Ltd v Euler Hermes Europe SA (NV)* [2019] EWHC 2250 (Comm); [2019] B.L.R. 561 at [64].

[564] *Prosper Homes v Hambros Bank Executor & Trustee Co* (1979) 39 P. & C.R. 395.

[565] *Cobec Brazilian Trading & Warehousing Corp v Alfred C Toepfer* [1983] 2 Lloyd's Rep. 386.

[566] *Expert Clothing Services & Sales Ltd v Hillgate House Ltd* [1986] Ch. 340.

[567] *Bliss v SE Thames Regional Health Authority* [1987] I.C.R. 700.

[568] *Yukong Line of Korea v Rendsburg Investments Co of Liberia* [1996] 2 Lloyd's Rep. 604; for further proceedings, see *The Times*, 30 October 1997.

[569] *Bolton MBC v Municipal Mutual Ins Ltd* [2006] EWCA Civ 50; [2006] 1 W.L.R. 149; *Cook v MSHK Ltd* [2009] EWCA Civ 624; [2009] I.R.L.R. 838 at [56].

altogether, i.e. "total waiver".[570] In the case of representation by conduct, it will be a matter of what can reasonably be inferred from such conduct and in this case it is likely that, if any clear and unequivocal representation can be inferred *at all*, it will be a representation to forego performance altogether. Since a representation by words is most likely to be made in circumstances where the injured party *knows* of the right to terminate and so will amount to affirmation,[571] cases of estoppel will usually be based on conduct and will, for the reasons just stated, amount to a "total waiver", but a more limited estoppel in which the injured party is only estopped from exercising his right to terminate is also possible.

18–098 **Delay in exercising the right to terminate.** The right to terminate is not lost by mere failure to exercise it: such failure is not normally a sufficiently clear indication that the right will not be exercised;[572] and the injured party has a reasonable period of time in which to decide whether to accept a repudiation.[573] But where, as a matter of business, it is reasonable to expect the injured party to act promptly, unreasonable delay in exercising the right to terminate may give rise to the inference that the contract has been affirmed.[574]

18–099 **Curing the breach.** In the period when he "is making up his mind what to do" in the face of an anticipatory breach the injured party runs the risk that, while he may not have affirmed the contract, the guilty party may resume performance and thus end the right to terminate in that way.[575] It seems that this does not extend to an actual breach so that, once committed, it cannot be "cured" and thereby take away the injured party's option of termination or affirmation.[576] Thus, where an employee's reputation was damaged by the repudiatory breach of his employer, the later vindication of the employee in a report did not cure the breach and prevent him from terminating the contract.[577] All that the guilty party can do "is

---

[570] See para.18–093.

[571] See para.18–089.

[572] See *Allen v Robles* [1969] 1 W.L.R. 1193; cf. *Bremer Handelsgesellschaft mbH v Deutsche Conti Handelsgesellschaft mbH* [1983] 2 Lloyd's Rep. 45; *The Scaptrade* [1981] 2 Lloyd's Rep. 425 at 430; affirmed [1983] 2 A.C. 694, without reference to this point; *Cantor Fitzgerald International v Callaghan* [1999] 2 All E.R. 411 at 423.

[573] *Stocznia Gdanska SA v Latvian Shipping Co* [2002] EWCA Civ 889; [2002] 2 Lloyd's Rep. 436 at [87]; *White Rosebay Shipping SA v Hong Kong Chain Glory Shipping* [2013] EWHC 1355 (Comm); [2013] 2 Lloyd's Rep. 618 at [21].

[574] *The Scaptrade* [1981] 2 Lloyd's Rep. 425 at 430; *The Laconia* [1977] A.C. 850 at 872; *Stocznia Gdanska SA v Latvian Shipping Co* [2002] EWCA Civ 889; [2002] 2 Lloyd's Rep. 436 at [87]; *Force India Formula One Team Ltd v Etihad Airways PJSC* [2010] EWCA Civ 1051; [2011] E.T.M.R. 10 at [113], [122].

[575] *Stocznia Gdanska SA v Latvian Shipping Co* [2002] EWCA Civ 889; [2002] 2 Lloyd's Rep. 436 at [87].

[576] The parties may of course agree that the contract cannot be terminated until the party in default has been given a period of time to remedy the breach, if remediable.

[577] *Buckland v Bournemouth University Higher Education Corp* [2010] EWCA Civ 121; [2010] 3 W.L.R. 1664; cf. *Gebremariam v Ethiopian Airlines Enterprise* 4 February 2014, EAT; [2014] I.R.L.R. 354.

invite affirmation by making amends".[578] At first sight, this is not easy to reconcile with the view taken in a later case that[579]:

> "A breach of contract, although serious, may be capable of remedy. If it is remedied before the injured party purports to exercise a right of termination, then the fact that the breach has been remedied is an important factor to be taken into account. Likewise if there is delay in performance of an on-going obligation it may well be possible for the delay to be made up by faster performance."

In the case in question, however, while there had been actual breach in the form of delay which had already occurred up to the date of termination, the court was at this point primarily concerned with whether there had been a repudiatory breach based on the forward looking element of the uncertainty of future performance[580] and here the fact that the breach had been remedied, or the prospect of a cure, was a relevant consideration.[581]

**Knowledge: affirmation.**[582] At the very least, affirmation requires an "informed choice, made with knowledge of the facts giving rise to the right" to terminate.[583] **18–100** There is also some support for the view that the injured party must not only know *the facts giving rise to the right* to terminate, but must also know that he has *the right*.[584] In *Peyman v Lanjani*[585] the defendant had obtained a leasehold interest in a restaurant by means of a fraudulent impersonation, and later agreed to sell that interest. By reason of the fraud, the defendant's title was defective and the buyer, with knowledge of the fraud but not of the fact that it gave him the right to terminate, paid £10,000 and went into possession of the restaurant as the defendant's manager. It was held that the buyer had not lost the right to terminate; and one reason[586] for this conclusion was that he could not have elected to affirm the contract until he had become aware, not merely of the facts giving rise to the right to terminate, but of the existence of the right itself.[587]

---

578 *Buckland v Bournemouth University Higher Education Corp* [2010] EWCA Civ 121; [2010] 3 W.L.R. 1664 at [40].

579 *Ampurius Nu Homes Holdings Ltd v Telford Homes (Creekside) Ltd* [2013] EWCA Civ 577; [2013] 4 All E.R. 377 at [63].

580 See para.18–036.

581 cf. *Wuhan Ocean Economic & Technical Co-operation Ltd v Schiffarts-Gesellschaft "Hansa Murcia" mbH & Co KG* [2012] EWHC 3104 (Ch); [2013] 1 Lloyd's Rep. 273 and the discussion therein of a "remediable breach".

582 i.e. "actual knowledge or knowledge which a person deliberately refrains from acquiring": *Transcatalana de Commercio SA v Incrobasa Industrial e Commercio Brazileira SA* [1995] 1 Lloyd's Rep. 215 at 219.

583 *The Kanchenjunga* [1990] 1 Lloyd's Rep. 391 at 399; *Cobec Brazilian Trading & Warehousing Corp v Alfred C Toepfer* [1983] 2 Lloyd's Rep. 386 at 392; *The Happy Day* [2002] EWCA Civ 1068; [2002] 2 Lloyd's Rep. 487 at [68].

584 cf. Handley 122 L.Q.R. 82.

585 [1985] Ch. 457; applied in *Transcatalana de Commercio SA v Incrobasa Industrial e Commercio Brazileira SA* [1995] 1 Lloyd's Rep. 215, discussing both "waiver in the sense of election" (219) and estoppel (220); cf. in the context of misrepresentation, *Habib Bank Ltd v Tufail* [2006] EWCA Civ 374 at [20] ("undoubtedly the law that knowledge of the right to rescind is essential").

586 A second was that there had been no unequivocal representation: *Peyman v Lanjani* [1985] Ch. 457 at 501–502.

587 cf. *Yukong Line of Korea v Rendsburg Investments Corp* [1996] 2 Lloyd's Rep. 604 at 608, 609; *Donegal International Ltd v Zambia* [2007] EWHC 197 (Comm); [2007] 1 Lloyd's Rep. 397 at [467];

18–101 **Knowledge: estoppel.** In cases of estoppel, no knowledge of the existence of the right to terminate, nor of the facts giving rise to it, is necessary. Statements to the effect that a person can "waive" rights without being aware of their existence are best regarded as referring to waiver by estoppel,[588] which is based on action in reliance by the party *to* whom the representation is made rather than on the subjective[589] intention of the (allegedly affirming) party *by* whom it is made.

18–102 **Reliance: affirmation.** We saw in Ch.3 that waiver by estoppel operates only where the party to whom the representation was made has acted in reliance on that representation.[590] There is no such requirement for the operation of affirmation. The distinction is recognised in a number of cases,[591] though in some it is obscured by the use of "waiver" to describe the different processes involved in affirmation, estoppel and total waiver.[592]

18–103 **Reliance: total waiver.** In the case of total waiver, one explanation for the requirement of reliance is that the injured party makes a promise wholly to give up his right to some or all of the performance due to him under the contract. Prima facie, this cannot be any benefit to him or any detriment to the party in breach, so that the promise is unsupported by consideration.[593] Action in reliance on the promise is necessary as a substitute for, or alternative to, consideration so as to give at least some legal effect to the promise.[594] In the case of affirmation, the injured party has indicated that he is giving up only one of his remedies (i.e. termination) but not any of his other remedies (by way of enforced performance or damages). Even if such an indication can be said to amount to a promise not to terminate, the process has never been considered to give rise to any problems of consideration.[595] The injured party is not *necessarily* in a worse position if he elects, instead of terminating, to keep the contract in being and to claim damages. This *may* be more beneficial to him than termination; and this possibility is sufficient to satisfy the requirement of consideration.[596]

*Hudson Bay Apparel Brands LLC v Umbro International Ltd* [2010] EWCA Civ 949; [2011] 1 B.C.L.C. 259 at [60]; *BDW Trading Ltd v JM Rowe Investments Ltd* [2011] EWCA Civ 548 at [75]. In *The Kanchenjunga* [1990] 1 Lloyd's Rep. 391 at 398 it was not necessary to discuss the conflict on this point since the injured party knew of the facts giving rise to the right to rescind *and* of the existence of the right.

[588] See *Bremer Handelsgesellschaft mbH v C Mackprang Jr* [1979] 1 Lloyd's Rep. 221 at 230; contrast [1979] 1 Lloyd's Rep. 221 at 229.

[589] "Subjective" only in the requirement that the injured party must have the knowledge referred to; whether the necessary representation has been made is an objective legal concept: *Argo Systems FZE v Liberty Insurance Pte Ltd* [2011] EWCA Civ 1572; [2012] 1 Lloyd's Rep. 126 at [41].

[590] See para.3–083.

[591] *The Scaptrade* [1981] 2 Lloyd's Rep. 425 at 430; affirmed [1983] A.C. 694; *Peyman v Lanjani* [1985] Ch. 457 at 493, 500–501; *The Kanchenjunga* [1990] 1 Lloyd's Rep. 391 at 399; *The Happy Day* [2002] EWCA Civ 1068; [2002] 2 Lloyd's Rep. 487 at [67].

[592] e.g. *The Eurometal* [1981] 1 Lloyd's Rep. 337 at 341; cf. *Bremer Handelsgesellschaft mbH v Finagrain (etc.) SA* [1981] 2 Lloyd's Rep. 259 at 265.

[593] See paras 3–057—3–065.

[594] See paras 3–066—3–093.

[595] *The Kanchenjunga* [1990] 1 Lloyd's Rep. 391 at 398.

[596] cf. paras 3–063, 3–104—3–112.

**Reliance: estoppel short of total waiver.**[597] The requirement of reliance for estoppel short of total waiver might be explained on the basis that the representation is "different in character in the two cases" of affirmation and estoppel.[598] In the case of affirmation, the injured party is communicating his choice whether or not to exercise the right to terminate. In the case of estoppel, he is representing that he will not *in future* enforce his legal rights; his representation is therefore in the nature of a promise which requires some element of reliance for any legal consequences because it is not supported by consideration.[599] But it has been noted in the previous paragraph that an election to affirm can be viewed as a promise not to terminate, so that this explanation may appear somewhat formalistic. In addition, where the injured party has represented only that he will not exercise his right to terminate, he retains the benefit of the contract and his right to damages, so that he too *may* be better off than he would be if the contract was terminated, i.e. it may be possible to satisfy the requirement of consideration. A further and perhaps better explanation for the distinction between affirmation and estoppel, so far as reliance is concerned, lies in the role played in each of them by the requirement of knowledge. The injured party should only unknowingly lose his right to terminate[600] by virtue of estoppel if the other party has relied upon it to such an extent that it would be inequitable still to exercise it.[601] 18–104

## (b) Acceptance

**Part performance generally no bar.** The fact that the party in breach has partly performed the contract does not of itself bar the right to terminate. For example, express provisions for determination often operate after part performance of the contract.[602] That illustration concerns an *exception* to the requirement of serious failure in performance. In cases to which that requirement *applies*, the courts do sometimes take the fact of part performance into account so as to conclude that the failure is not sufficiently serious to give rise to a right to terminate at all.[603] But once the failure is found to be of the required degree of seriousness, the injured party will not lose the right to refuse to perform or to accept further performance[604] merely because the other party has partly performed the contract.[605] 18–105

---

[597] For the reasons explained above (see para.18–097), most cases of estoppel will, in practice, amount to total waiver.

[598] *The Kanchenjunga* [1990] 1 Lloyd's Rep. 391 at 399.

[599] *The Kanchenjunga* [1990] 1 Lloyd's Rep. 391 at 399.

[600] And then perhaps only temporarily if the estoppel has only suspensory effect: para.3–086.

[601] In cases of total waiver this provides an additional explanation to that advanced in the previous paragraph.

[602] e.g. para.18–067.

[603] e.g. in *Boone v Eyre* (1777) 1 Hy. Bl. 273n.

[604] For the effect of part performance on his right to recover money paid, or to return payments received, see Ch.22.

[605] See, e.g. *Aerial Advertising Co v Batchelor's Peas Ltd* [1938] 2 All E.R. 786; para.18–040.

18–106 **Sale of goods.** Although part performance does not usually bar the right to terminate, s.11(4) of the Sale of Goods Act 1979 provides that where a non-consumer buyer[606] has "accepted"[607] goods under a contract which is not severable[608] "the breach of a condition to be fulfilled by the seller can only be treated as a breach of warranty, and not as a ground for rejecting the goods and treating the contract as repudiated."[609] This rule differs from affirmation[610] in that it can apply even though the injured party has no knowledge of the breach.[611] A buyer of defective goods is, for example, deemed to have accepted them if he retains them after the lapse of a reasonable time without intimating to the seller that he has rejected them.[612] In determining what is, for this purpose, a reasonable time, the court will consider whether the buyer has had a reasonable *opportunity* of examining the goods;[613] but he may have accepted them, and so have lost the right to reject, even though he has not actually discovered the defect.[614] The general rule, then, is clear: "acceptance" bars the right to terminate the contract for breach of condition. But the rule is subject to the following qualifications.

18–107 **Partial aceptance.** A buyer of goods may have the right to reject all the goods even though only some of them are not in conformity with the contract. If he accepts some of the goods, he does not thereby lose his right to reject the rest.[615]

18–108 **Incorporated misrepresentation.** If a misrepresentation made before the contract is incorporated in the contract as a condition, the right to rescind the contract *for misrepresentation* survives and may be exercised in spite of the fact that the contract has been performed.[616] A buyer of goods might be able to exercise this right even though his right to terminate *for breach* was barred by "acceptance".[617] But the right to rescind for misrepresentation is subject to the court's discretion[618] to declare the contract subsisting and to award damages in lieu of rescission. It seems probable that the court will generally follow this

---

606 See s.11(4A). For consumer contracts, see para.18–062.

607 See para.9–131.

608 See para.17–035.

609 Where the goods have nonetheless been returned the seller may have waived the right to argue that they had been accepted, and be confined to a claim in damages for non-acceptance: *Whitecap Leisure Ltd v John H Rundle Ltd* [2008] EWCA Civ 429; [2008] 2 Lloyd's Rep. 216 at [48].

610 In this respect, it also differs from voluntary acceptance of a benefit: see para.17–041.

611 *The Kanchenjunga* [1990] 1 Lloyd's Rep. 391 at 398; *Transcatalana de Commercio SA v Incrobasa Industrial e Commercio Brazileira SA* [1995] 1 Lloyd's Rep. 215 at 220.

612 Sale of Goods Act 1979 s.35(4).

613 Sale of Goods Act 1979 s.35(5).

614 e.g. *Bernstein v Pamson Motors (Golders Green) Ltd* [1987] 2 All E.R. 220; Reynolds 104 L.Q.R. 16. It has been said that, in the light of amendments to s.35, the decision in *Bernstein* "does not represent the law now": *Clegg v Olle Andersson (T/A Nordic Marine)* [2003] EWCA Civ 320; [2003] 2 Lloyd's Rep. 32 at [63]; cf. *Jones v Gallagher* [2004] EWCA Civ 10; [2005] 1 Lloyd's Rep. 377; Bradgate 120 L.Q.R. 558; *Mitchell v BJ Marine* [2005] N.I.Q.B. 72; *Kingsway Hall Hotel Ltd v Red Sky IT (Hounslow) Ltd* [2010] EWHC 965 (TCC); [2010] Const L.J. 542. A more generous approach may now be taken, but what is a reasonable time remains a question of fact and a buyer may still lose the right to reject before he has discovered the defect.

615 Sale of Goods Act 1979 s.35A.

616 Misrepresentation Act 1967 s.1(a); para.9–145.

617 cf. para.9–131.

618 Misrepresentation Act 1967 s.2(2); para.9–066.

course where the right to terminate for breach has been lost by "acceptance", though there may be cases of hardship to a buyer in which the court would not wish to confine him to a remedy in damages.

## (c) Both parties in breach

**Non-simultaneous breaches.** Where both parties are alleged to have committed breaches, each of which is claimed to be a ground for termination, the first question to be considered is the order in which the alleged breaches have occurred. If A's breach occurred before B's, the normal position is that A's breach gives B a right to terminate, and, if B exercises that right, his subsequent failure to perform does not amount to a breach at all (even though it would have done so, if A had not committed the earlier breach).[619] If B has not exercised the right to terminate, A remains free to terminate for B's breach, provided the performance of the obligation which A has earlier breached was not a condition precedent to performance of the obligation which B is alleged to have breached.[620] In *DRC Distribution Ltd v Ulva*[621] A served a 30-day notice of termination on the basis of B's later breach but during that 30 day period B exercised its right to terminate with immediate effect. B's termination was valid, but any damages payable by A were confined to the period when the contract would have terminated in accordance with A's notice. 18–109

**Simultaneous breaches.** The normal rule where both parties simultaneously commit breaches, each of which, standing alone, would justify termination is that each party is entitled to terminate on account of the other's breach.[622] There is, however, some support for a different conclusion where the two breaches are interrelated in the sense that the second consists of failure to perform a duty to avoid the consequences of the first. This was said to be the position in a line of cases concerning agreements to submit claims to arbitration. Where a claimant had committed a breach of such an agreement by undue delay in prosecuting his claim after it had been brought, it was held to be the duty of the respondent to apply to the arbitrator for directions to put an end to that delay. It was said to follow that "both claimant and respondent were in breach of their contractual obligations to each other;[623] and neither can rely on the other's breach as giving him a right to treat the primary obligations of each to proceed with the reference as at an end".[624] This reasoning had the unfortunate practical consequence that an arbitration might be allowed to continue after so long a delay that a satisfactory 18–110

---

[619] See para.17–027.

[620] *State Trading Corp of India v M Golodetz Ltd* [1989] 2 Lloyd's Rep. 277 at 286. The position *may* be different in the context of employment contracts: see *Brandeaux Advisors UK Ltd v Chadwick* [2010] EWHC 2370 (QB) and the conflicting authorities referred to therein.

[621] [2007] EWHC 1716 (QB).

[622] *State Trading Corp of India v M Golodetz Ltd* [1989] 2 Lloyd's Rep. 277 at 286.

[623] cf. Arbitration Act 1996 s.40(2)(b), stating a more restricted duty.

[624] *Bremer Vulkan u Maschinenfabrik v South India Shipping Co* [1981] A.C. 909 at 987; this reasoning was affirmed, and the decision followed, in *The Hannah Blumenthal* [1983] 1 A.C. 854; cf. *The Matja Gubec* [1981] 1 Lloyd's Rep. 31; *The Frotanorte* [1996] 2 Lloyd's Rep. 461, referring to criticisms of the rule.

hearing was no longer possible. This problem has been discussed in Ch.2, where a number of common law and statutory solutions to it were considered.[625] The present point is that the reasoning just quoted is, with respect, open to question; for if both parties are in breach it is by no means clear why it should follow that neither can terminate; it is equally possible to conclude that each party has the option to do so. Now that the reasoning of the arbitration cases has been made largely obsolete by statute,[626] it should no longer be regarded as justifying an exception to the general rule that, where both parties are guilty of breaches justifying termination, each should be entitled to terminate the contract. The justification for that general rule is, it is submitted, that no good purpose is served by holding parties to a contract after each of them has committed a breach justifying its termination.[627]

## 5. STIPULATIONS AS TO TIME[628]

18–111 Failure to perform a stipulation as to time does not differ intrinsically from any other failure to perform; indeed a number of cases already discussed in this chapter concern stipulations of this kind. But the subject has a history and terminology of its own; and for this, perhaps not very satisfactory, reason it is usually discussed separately.

18–112 **No time stipulated.** Where no period of time is specified for performance which is to be rendered by one party,[629] a term is implied that it must take place within a reasonable time.[630] What is a reasonable time for this purpose is a "broad consideration" and is assessed by taking into account all of the circumstances, including the benefit of hindsight, i.e. it is not confined to what the parties contemplated at the time of the contract.[631]

18–113 **Payment on a specified day.** Where a contract provides that money is to be paid on, or by, a specified day, the debtor has the whole of that day to make the payment. The creditor cannot treat him as in default before the end of that day (i.e. before midnight) merely because the bank at which payment was, under the

[625] See paras 2–005, 2–048.

[626] Arbitration Act 1996 s.41.

[627] Unless, of course, they both elect to affirm the contract: see para.18–089 and following.

[628] Stannard, *Delay in the Performance of Contractual Obligations*, 2nd edn (2018). For the principles determining *when* performance is due, see para.17–014 and following.

[629] Joint acts of the parties are subject to an implied term that each will use reasonable diligence in performing his part: *Ford v Cotesworth* (1868) L.R. 4 Q.B. 127; (1870) L.R. 5 Q.B. 544.

[630] *Postlethwaite v Freeland* (1880) 5 App. Cas 599; *Hick v Raymond & Reid* [1893] A.C. 22; *Hulthen v Stewart & Co* [1903] A.C. 389; cf. *Orchard Developments (Holdings) Ltd v Reuter Ltd* [2009] EWCA Civ 6; [2009] 16 E.G. 140 at [30] (no room for implication without underlying obligation to act (in that case to acknowledge informal break notice)); Consumer Rights Act 2015 s.52.

[631] *Peregrine Systems Ltd v Steria Ltd* [2005] EWCA Civ 239; [2005] Info T.L.R. 294 at [15]; *Astea (UK) Ltd v Time Group Ltd* [2003] EWHC 725 (TCC) at [144]; cf. *Hick v Raymond & Reid* [1893] A.C. 22.

contract, to be made had already closed.[632] As a practical matter, the debtor therefore cannot be treated as in default until the day following that specified in the contract.

**Termination for breach of a time stipulation.** Certain stipulations as to time are said to be "of the essence" of a contract.[633] Any failure to perform such a stipulation justifies termination; it makes no difference that the failure is trivial and causes little or no prejudice to the injured party; in that sense, a time provision which is found to be "of the essence" amounts to a condition.[634] Where, on the other hand, a stipulation as to time is *not* of the essence, only a substantial or serious failure to comply with it will justify termination.[635] **18–114**

**General rule: breach of time stipulation must amount to a substantial failure to perform.** At common law, stipulations which specified[636] the time of performance were normally regarded as "of the essence".[637] Equity did not follow the common law rule but took the view that stipulations as to time were not generally "of the essence".[638] The equitable rule now prevails[639] and the general rule is that delay which amounts to a breach will justify termination only where it causes serious prejudice to the other party.[640] There may, of course, be a liability in damages.[641] **18–115**

**Exceptions where time is "of the essence".** A time stipulation will be regarded as "of the essence" if it is made so expressly by the parties, or by implication from the circumstances of the contract, or the nature of the subject-matter, i.e. it is a question of construction.[642] For these exceptions to apply, the stipulation must specify a date or time for performance: they cannot apply where a contract merely provides for performance "as soon as practicable."[643] **18–116**

---

632 *The Lutetian* [1982] 2 Lloyd's Rep. 140; *The Afovos* [1983] 1 W.L.R. 195.

633 See, paras 18–116—18–118.

634 In the sense in which that term is used above: para.18–048 and following.

635 See para.18–115.

636 cf. para.18–112.

637 *Parkin v Thorold* (1852) 16 Beav. 59 at 65; unless the contract, on its true construction, provided otherwise: *Rightside Properties Ltd v Gray* [1975] Ch. 72 at 89.

638 *Parkin v Thorold* (1852) 16 Beav. 59; cf. *Cole v Rose* [1978] 3 All E.R. 1121; *Graham v Pitkin* [1992] 1 W.L.R. 403.

639 Law of Property Act 1925 s.41. This section is not restricted to cases in which equity would have intervened before the Judicature Acts; it enables the courts also to take into account the subsequent development of equitable principles: *United Scientific Holdings Ltd v Burnley BC* [1978] A.C. 904 at 925, 957; Baker 93 L.Q.R. 529.

640 *United Scientific Holdings Ltd v Burnley BC* [1978] A.C. 904 at 942; *Peregrine Systems Ltd v Steria Ltd* [2005] EWCA Civ 239; [2005] Info T.L.R. 294 at [15]; *Shawton Engineering v DGP International Ltd* [2005] EWCA Civ 1359; [2006] B.L.R. 1 at [33]; cf. *Amherst v James Walker Goldsmith & Silversmith Ltd* [1983] Ch. 305; *Metrolands Investments Ltd v JH Dewhurst Ltd* [1986] 3 All E.R. 659.

641 *Raineri v Miles* [1981] A.C. 1050 (rejecting the view that the right to damages was restricted to cases of negligent or wilful default); Samuels 44 M.L.R. 100.

642 *Samarenko v Dawn Hill House Ltd* [2011] EWCA Civ 1445; [2013] Ch. 36 at [9].

643 *British & Commonwealth Holdings Plc v Quadrex Holdings Inc* [1989] Q.B. 842 (not followed, on another point, in *Behzadi v Shaftesbury Hotels Ltd* [1992] Ch. 1); *Videocon Global Ltd v Goldman Sachs International* [2016] EWCA Civ 130; [2016] 1 C.L.C. 528 at [64].

18–117 **Time "of the essence" by express agreement.** Time will obviously be of the essence if the contract expressly so provides.[644] The contract may provide that the stipulation as to time is a condition[645] and where time is expressed to be "of the essence" that is itself a form of words which the courts have accepted as sufficient to create a condition.[646] Alternatively, the contract may simply provide that in the event of one party's failure to perform within the stipulated time, the other is to be entitled to terminate,[647] without making the time stipulation into a condition.[648] In such cases, the contract may be terminated on the basis of the express provision, but the innocent party will not have the benefit of the consequences which may flow from terminating for breach of condition.[649]

18–118 **Time "of the essence" by implication.** In the absence of any express provision, the question of whether time is of the essence is often determined by rules of law which have classified certain commonly found stipulations as to time in certain types of contracts as either being, or not being, of the essence.

18–119 **Charterparties.** We have seen that in a charterparty failure by the shipowner to comply with a stipulation as to the time of sailing,[650] or as to the ship's expected readiness to load,[651] of itself justifies termination; while the charterer's failure to load within the agreed time only has this effect if the delay is so serious as to frustrate the purpose of the contract.[652]

18–120 **Sale of goods.** In a contract for the sale of goods a stipulation as to the time at which the seller is to deliver the goods is treated as of the essence of the contract;[653] while a stipulation as to the time at which the buyer is to pay for them is not normally so regarded (presumably because it is thought, rightly or wrongly, that late payment is unlikely to cause serious prejudice to the seller).[654] To the latter rule there are, however, many exceptions: it will, for example, be displaced if the goods are perishable;[655] or if there are other indications of the intention of

---

644 e.g. *Steedman v Drinkle* [1916] 1 A.C. 275; cf. *Country & Metropolitan Homes Surrey Ltd v Topclaim Ltd* [1996] Ch. 307 at 313.

645 i.e. in the sense discussed at para.18–043 and following; *The Scaptrade* [1983] 2 A.C. 694 at 703.

646 See, e.g. *Lombard North Central Plc v Butterworth* [1987] Q.B. 527; para.18–069.

647 e.g. para.18–067.

648 See, e.g. *Lombard North Central Plc v Butterworth* [1987] Q.B. 527 (cl.5); para.18–069.

649 e.g. the recovery of damages for "loss of bargain": see para.18–068.

650 *Glaholm v Hays* (1841) 2 Man. & G. 751; para.18–045.

651 *The Mihalis Angelos* [1971] 1 Q.B. 164; para.18–045.

652 *Universal Cargo Carriers Corp v Citati* [1957] 2 Q.B. 401; paras 17–090, 18–052.

653 *Hartley v Hymans* [1920] 3 K.B. 475 at 484; cf. *Aruna Mills Ltd v Dhanrajmal Gobindram* [1968] 1 Q.B. 655; *Toepfer v Lenersan Poortman NV* [1980] 1 Lloyd's Rep. 143 (time of tender of shipping documents). See also *Bowes v Shand* (1877) 2 App. Cas. 455 (where *early* shipment by the seller justified rejection; para.18–050).

654 *Martindale v Smith* (1841) 1 Q.B. 389; Sale of Goods Act 1979 s.10(1). For a similar rule as to the effect of delay in payment in a distributorship agreement, see *Decro-Wall International SA v Practitioners in Marketing Ltd* [1971] 1 W.L.R. 361; cf. *Figre Ltd v Mander* [1999] Lloyd's Rep. I.R. 193 (time of payment of reinsurance premium not of the essence).

655 See *Maclean v Dunn* (1828) 4 Bing. 722 at 728; *Ryan v Ridley & Co* (1902) 8 Com. Cas. 105; *RV Ward Ltd v Bignall* [1967] 1 Q.B. 534 at 550; Sale of Goods Act 1979 s.48(3).

the parties to treat the stipulation as of the essence.[656] The position is similar with regard to stipulations as to the time of taking delivery: failure by the buyer to comply with such a stipulation will not normally entitle the seller to terminate;[657] but it will have this effect if the goods are perishable,[658] or if the buyer undertakes to provide the ship on which the goods are to be loaded but fails to do so within the agreed time,[659] or if he fails within the time specified by the contract to notify the seller of the ship's readiness to load.[660]

**Sale of land.** In contracts for the sale of land, it has been held that time is of the essence in sales of short leaseholds[661] or reversionary interests;[662] since the former will depreciate and the latter appreciate rapidly with the passing of time. Time has also been held to be of the essence of a contract for the sale of a public house as a going concern;[663] of a contract for the sale of land which the buyer wanted to develop quickly for business purposes;[664] and, it seems, of a contract for the sale of a brickfield.[665] On the other hand, it has been held that time was not of the essence of a contract to sell 34 plots of land as and when each was built on.[666] This result may be justified on the ground that the completion date was "only a target."[667] **18–121**

**Deposits.** In contracts generally, the timely payment of a deposit is, in the ordinary case, of the essence.[668] **18–122**

**Highly speculative subject matter.** Time will also be regarded of the essence where the subject-matter of the contract is of a highly speculative nature.[669] **18–123**

**A general principle of classification?** Attempts have been made to formulate some general principle governing the legal classification of stipulations as to time. Thus it has been said, on the one hand, that "In modern English law time is **18–124**

---

656 e.g. where payment was to be by irrevocable letter of credit to be opened within a stipulated time: see *Bunge Corp v Tradax Export SA* [1981] 1 W.L.R. 711 at 725.
657 *Woolfe v Horne* (1877) 2 Q.B.D. 355 (rags).
658 *Sharp v Christmas* (1892) 8 T.L.R. 687 (potatoes).
659 *The Osterbek* [1973] 2 Lloyd's Rep. 86.
660 *Bunge Corp v Tradax Export SA* [1981] 1 W.L.R. 711; para.18–053.
661 *Hudson v Temple* (1860) 29 Beav. 536.
662 *Newman v Rogers* (1793) 4 Bro. C.C. 391; unless there is evidence of contrary intention: *Patrick v Milner* (1877) 2 C.P.D. 342.
663 *Coslake v Till* (1826) 1 Russ. 376; *Lock v Bell* [1931] 1 Ch. 35.
664 *Bernard v Williams* (1928) 44 T.L.R. 436; cf. *Hargreaves Transport Ltd v Lynch* [1969] 1 W.L.R. 215.
665 See *Harold Wood Brick Co Ltd v Ferris* [1935] 2 K.B. 198.
666 *Williams v Greatrex* [1957] 1 W.L.R. 31.
667 *Williams v Greatrex* [1957] 1 W.L.R. 31 at 35.
668 *Samarenko v Dawn Hill House Ltd* [2011] EWCA Civ 1445; [2013] Ch. 36, in which the decision in *Millichamp v Jones* [1982] 1 W.L.R. 1422 at 1431 (no termination for deposit paid late by "mere oversight") is regarded as suspect (at [20]). The *Samarenko* case was not itself an "ordinary case" in that the deposit was to be paid sometime *after* the contract had been entered into, but nonetheless timely payment was still found to be a condition.
669 See *Hare v Nicholl* [1966] 2 Q.B. 130.

*prima facie* not of the essence of the contract";[670] and, on the other hand, that "*Broadly speaking* time will be considered of the essence in mercantile contracts."[671] But the italicised words indicate the tentative nature of these generalisations; and (as a glance at the rules stated in the preceding paragraph shows) they are, with respect, of limited value.[672] The classification of stipulations as to time seems to be based on considerations of commercial convenience applicable in particular contexts, rather than on any general principle or presumption as to time being, or not being, of the essence.

18–125 **Conditional contracts.** The performance by one party of some stipulated act may be a condition precedent either to the existence of the contract or to the obligation of the other party.[673] Where the very existence of the contract depends on a condition to be performed by one of the parties, that condition must be performed within the time expressly or impliedly fixed by the contract.[674] If no time is expressly fixed, the condition must be performed by the date fixed for completion.[675] If no date is fixed for completion, it must be performed within a reasonable time.[676] The equitable principle that time is not of the essence of a contract does not apply in these cases, for until the condition is performed the whole existence of the contract remains in doubt. For the same reason, an option can be exercised only within the time laid down in the agreement by which it was granted.[677]

18–126 **Waiver.** The general principle that the right to terminate may be lost by affirmation[678] (or estoppel)[679] applies where time is of the essence of a contract.[680] Accordingly, the requirement of punctual performance may be waived by giving the party in breach a further period for performance after the expiry of the period specified in the contract. Such waiver only has the effect of substituting the extended time for the original time; it is "not an utter destruction

---

670 *United Scientific Holdings Ltd v Burnley BC* [1978] A.C. 904 at 940; *British and Commonwealth Holdings Plc v Quadrex Holdings Inc* [1989] Q.B. 842 at 857.

671 *Bunge Corp v Tradax Export SA* [1981] 1 W.L.R. 711 at 716.

672 cf. *Bunge Corp v Tradax Export SA* [1981] 1 W.L.R. 711 at 729; *The Peter Schmidt* [1998] 2 Lloyd's Rep. 1 at 7; *Peregrine Systems Ltd v Steria Ltd* [2005] EWCA Civ 239; [2005] Info T.L.R. 294 at [15].

673 See para.17–015.

674 cf. *Hare v Nicholl* [1966] 2 Q.B. 130.

675 *Re Sandwell Park Colliery Co* [1929] 1 Ch. 277; *Aberfoyle Plantations v Cheng* [1960] A.C. 115; aliter where the completion date is only a target date subject to the occurrence of the condition; *Hargreaves Transport Ltd v Lynch* [1969] 1 W.L.R. 215 at 220; and where the condition is subsequent (para.2–104) and time is expressly stated *not* to be of the essence, as in *29 Equities Ltd v Bank Leumi (UK) Ltd* [1986] 1 W.L.R. 1490.

676 *Re Longlands Farm* [1968] 3 All E.R. 522.

677 *Hare v Nicholl* [1966] 2 Q.B. 130; *United Dominions Trust (Commercial) Ltd v Eagle Aircraft Ltd* [1968] 1 W.L.R. 74; *United Scientific Holdings Ltd v Burnley BC* [1978] A.C. 904 at 936.

678 See para.18–089.

679 See paras 18–092—18–093.

680 In addition to waiver by the injured party, the court may grant equitable relief in cases of late payment, e.g. *Shiloh Spinners Ltd v Harding* [1973] A.C. 691 at 722. See, generally, para.18–079 and following.

of the essential character of time."[681] Moreover, the mere fact that the injured party has not accepted the guilty party's failure to perform as a repudiation does not amount to affirmation. The fact that the contract has not been terminated merely entitles the guilty party to "perform the contract according to its terms";[682] and this is no longer possible after the expiry of the stipulated time.

**Notice making time "of the essence".**[683] Where time is not of the essence under the contract, but there has been a delay and, therefore, a breach, the injured party may serve a notice on the guilty party requiring him to comply. The notice may be served as soon as the other party is in default.[684] It has been noted that such a notice is invariably described as one making time of the essence,[685] but this description is "not quite accurate".[686] Time is not made "of the essence" in the sense that the relevant stipulation is converted into a condition: "one party cannot vary the terms of the contract on his own".[687] What the injured party is entitled to do is stipulate a reasonable time within which the guilty party must comply. If the time stipulated is reasonable and the guilty party has failed to comply when it expires, the injured party is entitled to terminate.[688] In this sense, it resembles a condition of the contract in that, as soon as the guilty party is in default of the notice, the contract may be terminated. It is for this reason that it is, perhaps, permissible to refer to the notice as having made time of the essence. The reality is that the injured party has a right to terminate because the unreasonable delay of the guilty party amounts to a repudiation of the contract. The questions of whether the notice has stipulated a *reasonable* time, or the guilty party has been guilty of an *unreasonable* delay amounting to a repudiation of the contract amount to the same thing: 18–127

> "The result of non-compliance with the notice is that the party in default is guilty of unreasonable delay in complying with a non-essential time stipulation. The unreasonable delay amounts to a repudiation and this justifies rescission."[689]

---

[681] *Barclay v Messenger* (1874) 43 L.J. Ch. 449; *Nichimen Corp v Gatoil Overseas Inc* [1987] 2 Lloyd's Rep. 46.

[682] *Union Eagle Ltd v Golden Achievement Ltd* [1997] A.C. 514 at 518.

[683] Stannard 120 L.Q.R. 137; Carter, Courtney and Tolhurst [2017] C.L.J. 63.

[684] *Behzadi v Shaftesbury Hotels Ltd* [1992] Ch. 1, overruling *Smith v Hamilton* [1951] Ch. 174 and the requirement that there must have been an unreasonable delay before the notice can be served. Of course, where the contract is an "open" one, i.e. where no date for performance of the obligation is stipulated, it is only when there has been an unreasonable delay that there will have been a breach in the first place: *Shawton Engineering v DGP International Ltd* [2005] EWCA Civ 1359; [2006] B.L.R. 1 at [72].

[685] It is often so worded by the injured party.

[686] *Behzadi v Shaftesbury Hotels Ltd* [1992] Ch. 1 at 12, 24; *Sentinel International Ltd v Cordes* [2008] UKPC 60 at [41].

[687] *Behzadi v Shaftesbury Hotels Ltd* [1992] Ch. 1 at 12, 24. See, to similar effect: *Eshun v Moorgate Mercantile Credit Co Ltd* [1971] 1 W.L.R. 722 at 726; *Urban I (Blonk Street) Ltd v Ayres* [2013] EWCA Civ 816; [2014] 1 W.L.R. 756 at [44](6).

[688] Under Sale of Goods Act 1979 s.48(3) an unpaid seller of goods can give the buyer notice of his intention to resell the goods and may resell them if the buyer does not "within a reasonable time" pay or tender the price.

[689] *Louinder v Leis* 149 C.L.R. 509 at 526, per Mason J.

Some difficulty is created in this respect by the judgment in *Samarenko v Dawn Hill House Ltd*[690] in which Lewison LJ suggests that the effect of the notice depends on the nature of the term broken. If the term in question is an innominate term, then the position is as just outlined, i.e. it cannot be converted into a condition by a notice making time of the essence. If, however, the term in question is one which would have been regarded as a condition at common law the effect of the notice is to remove the intervention of equity so that the contract may be terminated upon expiry of the notice, though this is put on the basis of renunciation, rather than breach of condition.[691] This was said to be the position in *Samarenko* where Lewison LJ was concerned with the time for payment of a deposit in a contract for the sale of land. The difficulty lies in the fact that, after the fusion of equity and law, a time stipulation is either a condition ("of the essence") or it is not. Thus, in *Samarenko* the timely payment of the deposit was held to be a condition so that a notice making time of the essence was not, in fact, necessary.[692] If it had been necessary, it could only have been on the basis that timely payment was not a condition under the contract; in which case, it must have been an innominate term[693] and, as explained above, service of the notice and the expiry of the period set out therein could not of itself have the effect of turning it into a condition.[694] Even on the basis of Lewison LJ's analysis, the notice must stipulate a reasonable time for compliance,[695] and in a later case Sir Terence Etherton confirmed that, while failure to comply with the notice to complete may be some evidence, the intention to renounce must be determined in the light of the evidence as a whole.[696]

If service of a notice and the expiry of the period set out therein is not of itself sufficient to justify termination, it may be questioned whether anything is to be gained by the injured party in serving a notice, since he may simply wait until an unreasonable delay has occurred.[697] There are, at least, two possible benefits. First, the notice is intended, in the first instance, to encourage the party in default to perform and it may have this effect whether the time stipulated is reasonable or

---

690 [2011] EWCA Civ 1445; [2013] Ch. 36; Carter 129 L.Q.R. 149.

691 *Samarenko v Dawn Hill House Ltd* [2011] EWCA Civ 1445; [2013] Ch. 36 at [42] ("tantamount to a refusal to perform that obligation"); cf. the earlier judgment of Lewison J in *Multi Veste 226 BV v NI Summer Row Unitholder BV* [2011] EWHC 2026 (Ch); 139 Con L.R. 23 in which he concedes that he may have been "too prescriptive": *Samarenko* at [42].

692 As a result, Lewison LJ's comments on the effect of a notice making time of the essence are obiter.

693 It almost certainly was not a warranty: above, para.18–045. In *Samarenko* Lewison LJ is not prepared to go so far, [2011] EWCA Civ 1445; [2013] Ch. 36 at [39]: "the general acceptance of the tripartite classification of contract terms (conditions, warranties and innominate terms) may mean that some adaptation must be made to the traditional view of courts of equity that all time stipulations were viewed as conditions by the common law" (emphasis added).

694 The position is different if the parties have agreed at the outset that time is not of the essence unless a notice is served.

695 *Samarenko v Dawn Hill House Ltd* [2011] EWCA Civ 1445; [2013] Ch. 36 at [34].

696 *Urban I (Blonk Street) Ltd v Ayres* [2013] EWCA Civ 816; [2014] 1 W.L.R. 756 at [44](7).

697 This appears to have influenced the approach of Lewison in *Multi Veste 226 BV v NI Summer Row Unitholder BV* [2011] EWHC 2026 (Ch); 139 Con L.R. 23; fn.691.

not. Secondly, while the court will have to be persuaded that the time allowed was reasonable, the injured party is given the opportunity to convert that into something a little more precise.[698]

What is a reasonable time is a question of fact.[699] If one party has constantly pressed the other to complete, he can rely on this fact to shorten the amount of time which must be allowed by the notice.[700] Where the injured party elects to serve a notice immediately upon breach he must be "cautious" about the time allowed before he reserves the right to terminate. A notice, once given, binds *both* parties. Thus, if one of them gives notice to complete within a reasonable time, but is not ready to do so when the notice expires, the other can terminate.[701]

## 6. CRITICISM[702]

The law relating to termination for breach is hard to state; and parts of it are still harder to justify. Criticism can, in particular, be directed at some of the exceptions to the requirement that a failure in performance must be substantial if it is to justify termination. A number of judicial restrictions[703] on the scope of these exceptions may have improved the law; but it is arguable that two major defects remain. **18–128**

**Termination where no prejudice occurs.** The first is that a party may still be entitled to terminate though the breach does not prejudice him seriously or at all, e.g. where the breach is of a term previously classified as a "condition", or where a seller fails to deliver the correct quantity.[704] In such cases, the right to terminate can simply provide a party with an excuse for escaping from a bad bargain.[705] It would, it is submitted, be more satisfactory as a general principle to focus attention on the question whether damages were an adequate remedy for the breach; and to restrict exceptions to this general principle to cases in which the interests of commercial certainty require a clear recognition of the right to terminate for certain breaches, irrespective of their effects.[706] Some of the **18–129**

698 *Dalkia Utilities Services Plc v Celtech International Ltd* [2006] EWHC 63; [2006] 1 Lloyd's Rep. 599 at [131]. In this regard there may also be the benefit of a "margin of appreciation" in that the court may be persuaded to accept as "reasonable" a time-table which is not precisely the one which would they would otherwise have adopted.

699 *North Eastern Properties Ltd v Coleman* [2010] EWCA Civ 277; [2010] 1 W.L.R. 2715. A notice giving only seven days to deduce title was held in *Behzadi v Shaftesbury Hotels Ltd* [1992] Ch. 1 to be too short so that the purchaser was guilty of a wrongful repudiation by terminating the contract on the strength of the notice.

700 *Stickney v Keeble* [1915] A.C. 386.

701 *Quadrangle Development and Construction Co Ltd v Jenner* [1974] 1 W.L.R. 68; *Clarke Investments Ltd v Pacific Technologies* [2013] EWCA Civ 750; [2013] 2 P & C.R. 20.

702 Treitel 30 M.L.R. 139.

703 Especially *Wickman Ltd v Schuler AG* [1974] A.C. 235; *The Hansa Nord* [1976] Q.B. 44; and *Reardon-Smith Line Ltd v Hansen-Tangen* [1976] 1 W.L.R. 989.

704 See paras 18–043, 17–033.

705 e.g. in *Cunliffe v Harrison* (1851) 6 Ex. 901; *Arcos Ltd v Ronaasen* [1933] A.C. 470; paras 17–039, 18–050.

706 e.g. *Bunge Corp v Tradax Export SA* [1981] 1 W.L.R. 711 (para.18–055); cf. also *The Laconia* [1977] A.C. 850; *The Chikuma* [1981] 1 W.L.R. 314 (para.18–067).

legislative limitations on the right to terminate[707] may have mitigated the defect in the law under which that right can be exercised on unmeritorious or technical grounds. But they have failed wholly to remove that defect while they have, on the other hand, undermined the virtue of certainty precisely in those commercial cases in which exceptions to the requirement of substantial failure in performance are intended to promote that virtue.[708]

18–130 **The rule in Sumpter v Hedges.** The second main defect in the law is the rule in *Sumpter v Hedges*,[709] under which a party who has failed to complete performance may have no rights at all against the other party to the contract, following termination.[710]

[707] Sale of Goods Act 1979 ss.15A and 30(2A); and other legislation referred to fn.366.
[708] See para.18–061.
[709] [1898] 1 Q.B. 673; para.17–032.
[710] See paras 17–032, 17–048.

CHAPTER 19

# FRUSTRATION[1]



[1] Treitel, *Frustration and Force Majeure*, 3rd edn (2014); McKendrick (ed.), *Force Majeure and Frustration of Contract*, 2nd edn (1995).

19–001 Under the doctrine of frustration a contract may be discharged if after its formation events occur making its performance impossible or illegal, and in certain analogous situations. This chapter will consider first the development of the doctrine and then its applications and effects. In the light of the decided cases, it concludes with an assessment of the theoretical basis of frustration.

## 1. DEVELOPMENT

19–002 **The doctrine of absolute contracts.** At one time most contractual duties were regarded as absolute, in the sense that supervening events provided no excuse for non-performance. In *Paradine v Jane*[2] a tenant was sued for rent and pleaded that he had for about two years of his tenancy been dispossessed by act of the King's enemies. This plea was held bad:

> "When the party by his own contract creates a duty or charge upon himself, he is bound to make it good, if he may,[3] notwithstanding any accident by inevitable necessity, because he might have provided against it by his contract".[4]

This doctrine of absolute contracts works well enough (and continues to apply) where it would be reasonable, having regard to the nature of the contract or the circumstances in which it was made, to expect it to provide for the event.[5] But where this is not the case, the doctrine is no longer regarded as a satisfactory way of allocating the loss that is occasioned by supervening events.

19–003 **Origins of the doctrine of frustration.** The doctrine of absolute contracts probably never applied where a contract called for personal performance by a party who died or was permanently incapacitated;[6] and another early exception to it was recognised in cases of supervening illegality.[7] In *Taylor v Caldwell*[8] Blackburn J relied on the first of these exceptions, and on a number of others, as bases for formulating the general rule of discharge which has become known as

[2] (1647) Aleyn 26; Ibbetson in Rose (ed.) *Consensus ad Idem: Essays in the Law of Contract in Honour of Guenter Treitel* (1996), p.3.
[3] i.e. if performance has not become illegal: para.19–045.
[4] *Paradine v Jane* (1647) Aleyn 26 at 27.
[5] e.g. in *Lewis Emanuel & Son Ltd v Sammut* [1959] 2 Lloyd's Rep. 629 where the seller could reasonably have been expected to contract "subject to shipment", but did not do so.
[6] *Taylor v Caldwell* (1863) 3 B. & S. 826 at 836.
[7] *Brewster v Kitchell* (1691) 1 Salk. 198; *Atkinson v Ritchie* (1809) 10 East 530 at 534–535.
[8] (1863) 3 B. & S. 826.

the doctrine of frustration. The defendants in that case had contracted to hire out the Surrey Gardens and Music Hall "for the purpose of giving four grand concerts" on four designated days in the summer of 1861; the defendants were also to provide various side-shows and other entertainments in the gardens. The hirers agreed to pay £100 on the evening of each of the designated days and to provide "all the necessary artistes". Six days before the first concert was to have been given, the hall was destroyed by an accidental fire, so that "it became impossible to give the concerts".[9] It was held that the defendants were not liable in damages for the hirers' wasted advertising and other expenses. The contract had been discharged because, "the parties must from the beginning have known that it could not be fulfilled unless … some particular specified thing continued to exist", and in these circumstances it was "not to be construed as a positive contract, but as subject to an implied condition that the parties shall be excused in case, before breach, performance becomes impossible from the perishing of the thing without the fault of the contractor".[10]

**Extension.** After being established in *Taylor v Caldwell*, the doctrine of frustration entered into a period of growth. It was extended to cases in which performance became impossible otherwise than through the perishing of a specific thing; and even to cases where performance did not become impossible at all but the commercial object, or purpose, of the contract was frustrated. In *Krell v Henry*[11] the defendant hired a flat in Pall Mall for the days on which the processions planned for the coronation of King Edward VII were to take place. His object was to see the processions, though this was not expressly stated in the contract.[12] The contract was frustrated when the processions were postponed because of the illness of the King. Performance was not physically impossible: the defendant could have used and paid for the flat on the days in question. But frustration was not restricted to physical impossibility: it also applied: **19–004**

> "to cases where the event which renders the contract incapable of performance is the cessation or non-existence of an express condition or state of things, going to the root of the contract, and essential to its performance".[13]

**Limits.** It can fairly be said that the defendant in *Krell v Henry* would have suffered unacceptable hardship if he had been held to the contract in the altered circumstances. But the courts have refused to extend the doctrine beyond this point; for to do so might enable a party to claim relief merely because circumstances had changed so as to turn the contract, for him, into a very bad bargain. In the *British Movietonews* case[14] the House of Lords rejected the view **19–005**

---

[9] *Taylor v Caldwell* (1863) 3 B. & S. 826 at 830.
[10] *Taylor v Caldwell* (1863) 3 B. & S. 826 at 833.
[11] [1903] 2 K.B. 740. See further para.19–043.
[12] In this respect *Krell v Henry* is unique among the "coronation seat" cases: the contracts in all the other reported cases expressly refer to one or both of the two planned processions.
[13] *Krell v Henry* [1903] 2 K.B. 740 at 748.
[14] *British Movietonews Ltd v London and District Cinemas* [1952] A.C. 166.

that a mere "uncontemplated turn of events"[15] (in that case, the cessation of wartime conditions in which the contract had been made) was a ground of frustration. Lord Simon said:

> "The parties to an executory contract are often faced, in the course of carrying it out, with a turn of events which they did not at all anticipate—a wholly abnormal rise or fall in prices, a sudden depreciation of currency, an unexpected obstacle to the execution, or the like. Yet this does not in itself affect the bargain which they have made".[16]

Lord Roskill has similarly said that the doctrine of frustration was "not lightly to be invoked to relieve contracting parties of the normal consequences of imprudent commercial bargains".[17]

A less strict approach appears at first sight to have been taken by Lord Hailsham in *National Carriers Ltd v Panalpina (Northern) Ltd*, when he described the "proposition that the doctrine was not to be extended" as "untenable".[18] But the point of this observation was that the doctrine applied to contracts generally: thus suggestions that it did not apply to particular contracts, such as time charters, demise charters, and leases of land, have from time to time been rejected by the courts.[19] The actual decision in the *National Carriers* case was that events which temporarily prevented one of the parties from putting the subject-matter to its intended use were not sufficiently serious to frustrate the contract. In this respect, the case, so far from departing from, actually illustrates, the approach adopted in the *British Movietonews* case.

19–006 **A narrowing of the doctrine.** Since the *British Movietonews* case, there seems to have been some narrowing in the scope of the doctrine of frustration. Many factors account for this trend: the reluctance of the courts to allow a party to rely on the doctrine as an excuse for escaping from a bad bargain; the difficulty of drawing the line between cases of frustration and cases where liability for breach of contract is strict; the tendency of businessmen to "draft out" possible causes of frustration by making their own express provisions for obstacles to performance; and the practical difficulties to be discussed in the paragraph that follows.

This trend is illustrated by the fact that the Second World War gave rise to few[20] reported cases in which contracts were held to be frustrated otherwise than by supervening illegality.[21] The Suez crisis of 1956 produced only two reported English cases in which frustration was successfully pleaded. Both these cases

---

[15] *British Movietonews Ltd v London and District Cinemas* [1951] 1 K.B. at 201 (Denning LJ).

[16] *British Movietonews Ltd v London and District Cinemas* [1952] A.C. 166 at 185; cf. *Multiservice Bookbinding Ltd v Marden* [1979] Ch. 84 at 112–113.

[17] *The Nema* [1982] A.C. 724 at 752; cf. *Tsakiroglou & Co Ltd v Noblee Thorl GmbH* [1962] A.C. 93 at 115; *The Super Servant Two* [1990] 1 Lloyd's Rep. 1 at 8; *The Sea Angel* [2007] EWCA Civ 547; [2007] 2 Lloyd's Rep. 517 at [111].

[18] *National Carriers Ltd v Panalpina (Northern) Ltd* [1981] A.C. 675 at 689; cf. at 694, 712.

[19] *Bank Line Ltd v Arthur Capel & Co* [1919] A.C. 435 (time charters); *Blane Steamships Ltd v Minister of Transport* [1951] 2 K.B. 965 (demise charters); *National Carriers Ltd v Panalpina (Northern) Ltd* [1981] A.C. 675 (leases of land).

[20] There were some, e.g. *Morgan v Manser* [1948] 1 K.B. 184.

[21] *Fibrosa Spolka Ackcyjna v Fairbairn, Lawson Combe Barbour Ltd* [1943] A.C. 32; *Denny, Mott & Dickson v James B Fraser & Co Ltd* [1944] A.C. 265; and *Cricklewood Property Investment Trust Ltd v Leighton's Investment Trust Ltd* [1945] A.C. 221 were all cases of supervening illegality.

were later overruled.[22] When the Suez Canal was again closed in 1967, pleas of frustration met with no more success;[23] and the "energy crisis" resulting from further hostilities in the Middle East in 1973 did not lead to any reported cases in England in which frustration was even raised as a defence.[24] All this is not to say that the doctrine will not be applied where performance is actually prevented, as it was in a number of charterparty cases in which ships were trapped for long periods after the outbreak of hostilities between Iran and Iraq in 1980,[25] so that performance of the agreed services became impossible. In the Suez cases there was (with one exception)[26] no such prevention: performance merely became more onerous for the party alleging frustration. There is now a marked reluctance to apply the doctrine in such circumstances.

**Practical difficulties.** From a practical point of view, the doctrine of frustration gives rise to two related difficulties. The first is that it may scarcely be more satisfactory to hold that the contract is totally discharged than to hold that it remains in full force: often some compromise may be a more reasonable solution. Thus in some of the coronation seat cases the contracts provided that, if the procession were cancelled, the ticket-holder should be entitled to use the ticket on the day on which the procession eventually did take place.[27] Similarly, after 1956, contracts for the carriage or sale of goods began to specify which party was to bear any extra expense that might be incurred, should the Suez Canal again be closed.[28] In the absence of such express provisions, this kind of solution is not open to the courts: they have no power to *modify* contracts in the light of supervening events. **19–007**

The second difficulty is that the allocation of risks produced at common law by the doctrine of frustration is not always entirely satisfactory. In a case like *Taylor v Caldwell* it may be reasonable that neither party should be liable for loss of the benefit that the other expected to derive from performance, so that the one should not recover his loss of anticipated profits, nor the other the payments promised to him. But it does not follow that loss suffered by one party as a result of acting in reliance on the contract should equally lie where it falls. In *Taylor v Caldwell* the hirers' claim was not one for loss of profits, but only one for expenses thrown away in advertising and preparing for the concerts.[29] No doubt the defendants also incurred expenses on the side-shows and other facilities for

[22] *Carapanayoti & Co Ltd v ET Green Ltd* [1959] 1 Q.B. 131; overruled in *Tsakiroglou & Co v Noblee Thorl GmbH* [1962] A.C. 93; and *The Massalia* [1961] 2 Q.B. 278; overruled in *The Eugenia* [1964] 2 Q.B. 226.

[23] For the Suez cases, see para.19–032, below.

[24] cf. *Sky Petroleum Ltd v VIP Petroleum Ltd* [1974] 1 W.L.R. 576, where the only dispute was as to the injured party's remedy; no attempt was made to rely on frustration.

[25] *The Evia (No.2)* [1983] 1 A.C. 736; *The Agathon* [1982] 2 Lloyd's Rep. 211; *The Wenjiang (No.2)* [1983] 1 Lloyd's Rep. 400; *The Chrysalis* [1983] 1 Lloyd's Rep. 503.

[26] i.e. *The Eugenia* [1964] 2 Q.B. 226; but there the fact that the ship was trapped in the Canal did not lead to frustration as it was due to the charterer's prior breach of the contract: see para.19–090.

[27] For contracts containing such provisions, see *Clark v Lindsay* (1903) 19 T.L.R. 202; and *Victoria Seats Agency v Paget* (1902) 19 T.L.R. 16 (first contract).

[28] *Achille Lauro v Total Societa Italiana per Azioni* [1969] 2 Lloyd's Rep. 65; *DI Henry Ltd v Wilhelm G Clasen* [1973] 1 Lloyd's Rep. 159.

[29] *Taylor v Caldwell* (1863) 3 B. & S. at 827.

entertainment, which the contract obliged them to provide. It might be more satisfactory if such losses could be apportioned. At common law this was possible only where the contract expressly so provided, e.g. in one of the coronation cases the contract provided that, if the procession was cancelled, the ticket-holder was to get his money back, less a percentage to cover the other party's expenses.[30] A more general, but still limited, power of adjustment now exists by statute, but it does not cover all cases in which some form of apportionment would seem to be desirable.[31]

19–008 **A "multi-factorial" approach.** What follows in the next two parts of this chapter are illustrations of the doctrine of frustration in practice, in which, for the purpose of analysis, the relevance of particular factors will fall to be assessed. It is helpful to stress at the outset therefore that the application of the doctrine requires a "multi-factorial" approach.[32] As it has been put:[33]

> "Among the factors which have to be considered are the terms of the contract itself, its matrix or context, the parties' knowledge, expectations, assumptions and contemplations, in particular as to risk, as at the time of contract, at any rate so far as these can be ascribed mutually and objectively, and then the nature of the supervening event, and the parties' reasonable and objectively ascertainable calculations as to the possibilities of future performance in the new circumstances."

Thus, in the case from which this dictum is taken, a vessel used for a salvage operation was detained by the port authorities in the last few days of a 20-day charter. At the date when the contract was said to have been frustrated, it had been detained for five weeks with the prospect of at least a further four to six weeks of delay while legal proceedings for its release were pursued. Nonetheless, the charter was not frustrated because of other factors: the contractual risk of delay was on the charterers,[34] the detention was foreseeable[35] and the purpose for which the vessel had been chartered had been performed.[36]

[30] *Victoria Seats Agency v Paget* (1902) 19 T.L.R. 16 (second contract); cf. *Elliott v Crutchley* [1904] 1 K.B. 565; affirmed [1906] A.C. 7.

[31] See para.19–103 and following.

[32] *The Sea Angel* [2007] EWCA Civ 547; [2007] 2 Lloyd's Rep. 517 at [111]; cf. *The Mary Nour* [2008] EWCA Civ 856; [2008] 1 Lloyd's Rep. 179 at [14]; *Islamic Republic of Iran Shipping Lines v Steamship Mutual Underwriting Association (Bermuda) Ltd* [2010] EWHC 2661 (Comm); [2011] 1 Lloyd's Rep. 195.

[33] *The Sea Angel* [2007] EWCA Civ 547; [2007] 2 Lloyd's Rep. 517 at [111].

[34] Based both on the terms of the charterparty and the salvage agreement: [2007] EWCA Civ 547; [2007] 2 Lloyd's Rep. 517 at [119]; cf. *Bunge SA v Kyla Shipping Co Ltd* [2012] EWHC 3522 (Comm); [2013] 1 Lloyd's Rep. 565 at [79].

[35] See further para.19–085.

[36] The remaining obligation was the redelivery of the vessel. The parties were therefore disputing on which of them the financial consequences of the detention should fall.

## 2. APPLICATIONS

### (a) Impossibility

Supervening impossibility of performance is the most obvious ground of frustration. The various ways in which it can arise are discussed below; but it must be emphasised at the outset that such impossibility is by no means invariably a ground of discharge. We shall see that even the destruction of the subject-matter of a contract does not necessarily discharge it;[37] and where liability for breach of contract is strict,[38] a party may be liable for failing to do the impossible. For example, a seller who has undertaken to ship goods to his buyer may be liable for failing to do so, even though the failure was due to lack of shipping space caused by events entirely beyond his control.[39] By contrast, a shipowner may be excused from liability under a charterparty if, after the time of contracting, his ship is disabled by an explosion which is not proved to be due to his fault.[40] The distinction between the two situations is not easy to put into words. In neither of them is the party claiming excuse at fault, so that lack of fault is not sufficient (though it is necessary)[41] to discharge the contract. It could be said that lack of shipping space was a risk undertaken by the seller in our first example, while in the second the explosion was not within the contractual risk taken by the shipowner; but this seems to amount to a restatement of the distinction rather than to an explanation for it. Another way of expressing the distinction is that in the first case the seller *undertook* that shipping space would be available, while in the second the parties merely *assumed* that the particular ship would remain available; and that it is impossibility resulting from the failure of such a common assumption that leads to discharge. **19–009**

#### *(i) Destruction of a particular thing*

**Illustrations.** The clearest illustration of frustration by the destruction of a particular thing is *Taylor v Caldwell*[42] itself, where it was the subject-matter of the contract which was destroyed. An agreement for the sale of specific goods is similarly avoided if, without the fault of either party, the goods perish before the risk has passed to the buyer.[43] For the present purpose, destruction need not amount to total annihilation. In *Asfar & Co v Blundell*[44] a cargo of dates was sunk and so affected by water and sewage as to become "for business purposes **19–010**

---

[37] See the discussion of frustration and risk at para.19–013.
[38] See paras 17–065–17–066.
[39] *Lewis Emanuel & Sons Ltd v Sammut* [1959] 2 Lloyd's Rep. 629.
[40] *Joseph Constantine SS Line v Imperial Smelting Corp Ltd* [1942] A.C. 154; para.19–096.
[41] See para.19–090.
[42] (1863) 3 B. & S. 826; para.19–003.
[43] Sale of Goods Act 1979 s.7; for risk, see para.19–014.
[44] [1896] 1 Q.B. 123.

something else",[45] though it was still sold for £2,400. The cargo-owner's liability to pay freight was discharged as the merchantable character of the cargo had been destroyed.

19–011 **Destruction of only part of the subject-matter.** *Taylor v Caldwell* shows that a contract may be frustrated by the destruction of only part of the subject-matter. The contract related to "the Surrey Gardens and Music Hall" and was discharged though only the Hall was destroyed, while the gardens remained in use as a place of entertainment. The contract was frustrated because its main purpose (the giving of the concerts) had been defeated.[46] Partial destruction which does not defeat the main purpose of the contract will not frustrate it, though it may provide one party with an excuse for not performing in full[47] or give the other party the option to terminate.[48]

19–012 **Destruction of something essential for performance.** A contract may be frustrated where what is destroyed is not its subject-matter but something essential for its performance. For example, a contract to install machinery in a particular factory can be frustrated by the destruction of the *factory*,[49] even though its subject-matter is the *machinery*. The question whether something is essential for performance depends on the terms of the contract. Thus where an agency agreement related to goods to be "manufactured *or sold*" by the owner of a factory it was held that destruction of the factory did not frustrate the agreement.[50]

19–013 **The relevance of rules on risk of loss.** Even the destruction of the subject-matter of the contract will not necessarily frustrate it. In certain types of contracts, it will instead be governed by rules which determine when the "risk of loss" passes from one party to the other. Where these rules apply, the contract will not be frustrated by the destruction of the subject-matter, though it may be frustrated by other events (such as delay or illegality).[51] The effects of the risk rules are radically different from those of frustration. The difference can be summed up by saying that where the destruction leads to frustration it discharges all the contractual obligations of both parties, while where it is governed by the rules as to risk it discharges only some of the obligations of one party. At this stage,[52] two types of contracts will serve to illustrate the distinction.

---

45 *Asfar & Co v Blundell* [1896] 1 Q.B. 123 at 128; cf. *The Badagry* [1985] 1 Lloyd's Rep. 395 at 399. Contrast *Horn v Minister of Food* [1948] 2 All E.R. 1036.

46 cf. paras 19–021, 19–024, 19–032, 19–044, 19–061, 19–062.

47 See para.17–059.

48 See para.19–024.

49 *Appleby v Myers* (1867) L.R. 2 C.P. 651.

50 *Turner v Goldsmith* [1891] 1 Q.B. 544.

51 See paras 19–020, 19–048 19–065.

52 For the passing of risk and related problems in contracts for the sale of land, see paras 19–065—19–068.

**Risk in sale of goods.** Under a contract for the sale of goods, the general rule is that (unless otherwise agreed) risk passes with property.[53] Property may pass before delivery,[54] so that it is possible for the risk in goods to have passed to the buyer while they are still in the hands of the seller. If the goods are destroyed *after* the risk has passed, the contract is not frustrated: on the contrary, the statement that the risk has passed *means* that the buyer must still pay the price, while the seller is discharged from his duty to deliver. But the seller is not necessarily discharged from *all* his obligations: he may, for example, have expressly or impliedly undertaken to transfer the benefit of insurance on the goods to the buyer, and this obligation would survive their destruction.[55] If goods are destroyed *before* the risk has passed, the contract is frustrated if the goods are specific,[56] or if they are to be taken from a particular source and all the goods from that source are destroyed.[57] If, on the other hand, the sale is of unascertained goods by description, the contract is not frustrated merely because the particular goods which the seller intended to supply under the contract were destroyed before the risk had passed. On the contrary, to say that the risk has not passed in this situation means that the seller is bound to deliver other goods of the contract description; and if he does so the buyer must accept and pay. **19–014**

**Risk in building contracts.** Under a building contract, the risk of the work is (unless otherwise agreed) on the builder until the agreed work is completed. Thus a contract to build a house or a factory would not be frustrated by destruction of the buildings before completion. On the other hand, where a builder agrees to do work on an existing building, e.g. to install new machinery in a factory, a distinction must be drawn. If, before the work is finished, the *factory* is destroyed, the contract is frustrated;[58] but if only the *machinery* is destroyed there is no frustration and the builder will remain bound to complete the installation without extra charge.[59] **19–015**

## *(ii) Death or incapacity*

**Personal contracts.** Certain "personal" contracts, such as contracts of employment, or apprenticeship, are discharged by the death of either party.[60] Even a commercial contract may involve reliance by one party on the personal skill of the other;[61] in which case the death of that party (though not that of the other) can discharge the contract. The same rules apply where a party is permanently incapacitated from performing such a contract. Thus a contract to write a book **19–016**

---

[53] Sale of Goods Act 1979 s.20(1). Under a consumer contract (see para.7–042 above) risk does not pass until the goods come into the physical possession of the consumer: Consumer Rights Act 2015 s.29.

[54] e.g. under Sale of Goods Act 1979 s.18 r.1.

[55] e.g. *Manbré Saccharine Co Ltd v Corn Products Co Ltd* [1919] 1 K.B. 198.

[56] Sale of Goods Act 1979 s.7.

[57] See paras 19–025—19–026.

[58] *Appleby v Myers* (1867) L.R. 2 C.P. 651.

[59] *Appleby v Myers* (1867) L.R. 2 C.P. 651 at 660.

[60] cf. *Cutter v Powell* (1795) 6 T.R. 320; *Whincup v Hughes* (1871) L.R. 6 C.P. 78; para.17–032.

[61] cf. para.15–055.

would be frustrated by the supervening insanity of the author;[62] and a contract to render services would be frustrated if continued performance involved a serious risk to the health of the person who had agreed to render them.[63] A contract may likewise be frustrated where it is the capacity of a party to *receive* performance that is affected by the supervening event, e.g. where a person who had booked a course of dancing lessons was so seriously injured that he could no longer dance.[64] A contract may also be frustrated by the death or incapacity of a third party, e.g. a contract between A and B to paint a portrait of C could be frustrated if C died before work on the portrait had begun.

19–017 **Agency.** In the context of agency, the supervening incapacity of the principal will terminate the principal's authority,[65] but does not necessarily result in the frustration of any underlying contract by which such authority had been conferred on the agent, e.g. a contract of retainer with a solicitor. Depending on the terms of the retainer, alternative steps might be taken to provide the solicitor with instructions on behalf of the principal,[66] unless and until the principal's capacity is restored.[67]

### *(iii) Unavailability*

19–018 **In general.** A contract may be frustrated if its subject-matter, or a thing or person essential for the purpose of its performance, though not ceasing to exist or suffering permanent incapacity, becomes unavailable for that purpose. Thus charterparties have been frustrated where the ship was seized, detained[68] or requisitioned,[69] and where cargo was unavailable because of a strike at the port of loading.[70] A contract for the sale of goods has been frustrated where the goods were requisitioned.[71] A contract to operate and share in the profits of an oilfield has been frustrated where the interests of both parties were expropriated by the government of the country in which the oilfield was situated;[72] and contracts for personal services have been frustrated where one of the parties fell ill,[73] or was interned or conscripted.[74]

19–019 **Temporary unavailability.** A person or thing essential for performance may, as a result of the supervening event, be unavailable at the time fixed for performance,

---

[62] *Jackson v Union Marine Ins Co Ltd* (1874) L.R. 10 C.P. 125 at 145.
[63] *Condor v The Barron Knights Ltd* [1966] 1 W.L.R. 87.
[64] *Parker v Arthur Murray Inc* 295 N.E. 2d 487 (1973).
[65] See para.16–121.
[66] e.g. by the appointment of a deputy: see para.12–057, fn.187.
[67] *Blankley v Central Manchester & Manchester Children's University Hospitals NHS Trust* [2015] EWCA Civ 18; [2015] 1 Costs L.R. 119.
[68] e.g. in the Gulf War cases (para.19–006, para.19–055), and in *The Adelfa* [1988] 2 Lloyd's Rep. 466; cf. *The Sea Angel* [2007] EWCA Civ 547; [2007] 2 Lloyd's Rep. 517, para.19–008.
[69] e.g. *Bank Line Ltd v Arthur Capel & Co* [1919] A.C. 435.
[70] *The Nema* [1982] A.C. 724.
[71] e.g. *Re Shipton, Anderson & Co* [1915] 3 K.B. 676.
[72] *BP Exploration (Libya) Ltd v Hunt* [1983] 2 A.C. 352; para.19–111.
[73] e.g. *Hart v A R Marshall & Sons (Bulwell) Ltd* [1977] 1 W.L.R. 1067.
[74] e.g. *Morgan v Manser* [1948] 1 K.B. 184.

but become available later. Such temporary unavailability will most obviously frustrate the contract where it is clear from the terms or nature of the contract that it was to be performed only at, or within, the specified time, and that the time of performance was of the essence[75] of the contract. Thus a contract to play in a concert on a particular day is frustrated by the performer's illness on that day.[76] Temporary unavailability may also frustrate a contract even though no fixed date is expressly specified for performance and even though a time is fixed but is not of the essence. In such cases, the contract may be frustrated, not by the mere *fact*, but by the *length*, of the delay in performance.

**Delay frustrating purpose of contract.** This possibility is illustrated by *Jackson v Union Marine Ins Co*,[77] where a charterparty was made in November 1871 for the carriage of rails from Newport to San Francisco; it provided that the ship was to proceed to Newport with all possible despatch. On her way there she went aground in January 1872 and was not repaired until the following August. The contract was held to have been frustrated by the length of the delay, in consequence of which the voyage which the ship was capable of making was substantially different from that envisaged in the contract. It was as if a ship chartered "to go from Newport to St. Michael's … in time for the fruit season"[78] did not become available till after the season was over. Contracts in cases of this kind are frustrated because performance at the end of the delay is no longer of any use to the party to whom it was to be rendered, i.e. to the charterer. **19–020**

**Change in conditions.** In another group of cases, the contract is frustrated for the different reason that, after the delay, the performance to be rendered by one party would be significantly more onerous for that party. This possibility is illustrated by *Metropolitan Water Board v Dick, Kerr & Co*[79] where wartime restrictions imposed an indefinite delay on the performance of a contract to build a reservoir. It was held that the contract was frustrated since it was likely that there would be a total change in conditions by the time that the restrictions might be lifted. **19–021**

Even where delay does not increase the *costs* of the party whose performance is affected by it, that party may be prejudiced for the different reason that rates of pay for the service which he was to render have increased substantially between the time of contracting and the end of the delay. This sort of reasoning appears to explain *Bank Line Ltd v Arthur Capel & Co*,[80] where a ship was chartered for 12 months; it was contemplated, though not expressly provided, that the period would run from April 1915 to April 1916. She was requisitioned before delivery and the owners did not procure her release till September 1915. In an action by the charterer for damages for non-delivery, the House of Lords held the charterparty frustrated. The contract was, in substance if not in form, an April to April charter; and to hold the parties to a September to September charter would

[75] See para.18–111.

[76] *Robinson v Davison* (1871) L.R. 6 Ex. 269.

[77] (1874) L.R. 10 C.P. 125.

[78] *Jackson v Union Marine Ins Co* (1874) L.R. 10 C.P. 125 at 143.

[79] [1918] A.C. 119; cf. *Acetylene Co of GB v Canada Carbide Co* (1922) 8 Lloyd's Rep. 456.

[80] [1919] A.C. 435; cf. *Hirji Mulji v Cheong Yue SS Co Ltd* [1926] A.C. 497; *Autry v Republic Productions* 180 P.2d 888 (1947).

be to hold them to a contract which was "as a matter of business a totally different thing".[81] The reason for this view cannot have been that the delay prejudiced the charterers (for they were claiming performance). It seems rather to have been that the shipowners would have been prejudiced by the delay (if the contract had not been discharged) because freight rates had risen[82] so that by September they could have charged considerably more for their services than the amount payable under the original contract.[83]

19–022 **Delay and part performance.** In the cases so far considered, it was claimed that performance should be rendered *in full* when the temporary unavailability ceased. In other cases, involving long-term contracts, the claim was that *the balance* of the contract should then be performed. Obviously such a claim cannot succeed if the delay lasts, or is likely to last, for so long that *no* part of the agreed performance remains possible. Thus in *Countess of Warwick SS Co v Le Nickel SA*[84] the wartime requisition of a ship was held to frustrate a one-year charter which, at the time of the requisition, still had six months to run, because it was unlikely that the ship would be released in time to render any substantial services under the charter. For the same reason, charterparties were frustrated in a number of cases in which ships became unavailable for service as a result of being trapped for long periods in the course of the Gulf War between Iran and Iraq.[85]

If, on the other hand, performance for some balance of the contract period remains, or is likely to remain, possible, the outcome of claims for that balance depends on the proportion of the interruption, or likely interruption, to the contract period: the greater that proportion is, the more likely it is that the contract will be frustrated. Thus in *The Nema*[86] a charterparty for six or seven voyages to be made from April to December was frustrated when, after the first voyage, a long strike at the loading port made it impossible to accomplish more than a further two voyages within the contract period. By contrast, in *Tamplin SS Co Ltd v Anglo-Mexican Petroleum Co*[87] the wartime requisition of a ship in February 1915 did not frustrate a five-year charter which was not due to expire till December 1917: the majority of the House of Lords took the view that "there may be many months during which the ship will be available before the five years have expired".[88] The effect of such requisition must theoretically be determined at or near the time when it takes place.[89] In practice, the courts no doubt take later events into account, but the *Tamplin* case was decided before the end of the chartered period. Thus the House of Lords had to speculate as to the probable length of the requisition and indirectly as to the probable duration of the war. In

[81] *Bank Line Ltd v Arthur Capel & Co* [1919] A.C. 435 at 460.

[82] cf. *Modern Transport Co Ltd v Duneric SS Co* [1917] 1 K.B. 370 at 376.

[83] This appears from the fact that £31,000 would have been awarded to the charterers by way of damages if the contract had not been discharged: see *Bank Line Ltd v Arthur Capel & Co* [1919] A.C. 435 at 441.

[84] [1918] 1 K.B. 372.

[85] *The Evia (No.2)* [1983] A.C. 736; *The Agathon* [1982] 2 Lloyd's Rep. 211; *The Wenjiang (No.2)* [1983] 1 Lloyd's Rep. 400; *The Chrysalis* [1983] 1 Lloyd's Rep. 503.

[86] [1982] A.C. 724.

[87] [1916] 2 A.C. 397; cf. *Port Line v Ben Line Steamers Ltd* [1958] 2 Q.B. 146.

[88] *Tamplin SS Co Ltd v Anglo-Mexican Petroleum Co* [1916] 2 A.C. 397 at 405.

[89] See para.19–054.

the light of later events, the majority may have speculated wrongly. But this is no criticism of the decision, which has also been supported on another ground to be discussed later in this chapter.[90]

**Contracts involving personal service.** Events such as illness, conscription or internment may interfere temporarily with the performance of long-term contracts involving personal service. Here again one test of frustration is the proportion which the interruption, or likely interruption, bears to the period specified in the contract. In *Morgan v Manser*[91] a music hall artiste employed a manager for 10 years from 1938. He was conscripted in 1940 and demobilised in 1946. The contract was held to be frustrated since in 1940 it was likely that the artiste would remain in the Army for a very long time. On the other hand, in *Nordman v Rayner & Sturgess*[92] a long-term commission agency was not frustrated when the agent (an Alsatian with anti-German sympathies) was interned, since his internment was not likely to last long and in fact only lasted one month. 19–023

**Employment contracts.** A contract of employment may be frustrated by the illness of the employee. This is true, not only where the contract is a long-term one, but also where it provides for determination by relatively short periods of notice, since even such a contract is often intended to give rise to an enduring relationship.[93] But temporary illness will not of itself frustrate a contract of employment:[94] it will have this effect only where it is so serious as to put an end to the possibility of performance "in a business sense",[95] e.g. by making resumption within a reasonable time a practical impossibility.[96] Where the employee is unable to work because of a disability, it may be necessary to determine whether the employer is in breach of the obligation to make reasonable adjustments to allow for the disability before the doctrine of frustration applies.[97] An illness which is not serious enough to frustrate the contract may have a number of other legal effects. It may give the employee a *temporary* excuse for non-performance, and it may also give the employer an *option* to terminate.[98] Unless and until this option is exercised, the employee is prima facie entitled to 19–024

---

[90] See para.19–098.

[91] [1948] 1 K.B. 184 (where it is not clear what prejudice the artiste would have suffered by being held to the balance of the contract); cf. *Unger v Preston Corp* [1942] 1 All E.R. 200 (a case very near the line).

[92] (1916) 33 T.L.R. 87.

[93] *Notcutt v Universal Equipment Co (London) Ltd* [1986] 1 W.L.R. 641; cf. *R. (Verner) v Derby CC* [2003] EWHC 2708 (Admin); [2004] I.C.R. 535.

[94] *Marshall v Harland & Wolff Ltd* [1972] 1 W.L.R. 899; *Williams v Watson's Luxury Coaches* [1990] I.C.R. 536; cf. *Mount v Oldham Corp* [1973] Q.B. 309.

[95] *Jackson v Union Marine Ins Co Ltd* (1874) L.R. 10 C.P. 124 at 145.

[96] e.g. *Hart v A R Marshall & Sons (Bulwell) Ltd* [1977] 1 W.L.R. 1067; *Notcutt v Universal Equipment Co (London) Ltd* [1986] 1 W.L.R. 641; cf. *Gryf-Lowczowski v Hinchingbrooke Healthcare NHS Trust* [2005] EWHC 2407 (QB); [2006] I.C.R. 100 (contract of under-performing surgeon not frustrated because still a realistic possibility of "re-skilling").

[97] *Warner v Armfield Retail & Leisure Ltd* [2014] I.C.R. 239 EAT (no breach of the duty to make reasonable adjustments under the Equality Act 2010).

[98] See paras 17–059, 18–036.

wages during sickness.[99] This prima facie rule can be displaced by an express contrary provision, or by circumstances from which a contrary provision can be implied.[100]

### *(iv) Failure of a particular source*

19–025 A contract may be discharged where the subject-matter was to be obtained from a particular source which without the fault of either party becomes unavailable, e.g. where goods were to be taken from a particular crop which fails as a result of drought or disease; or where they are to be imported from a particular country and such import is prevented by war, natural disasters or prohibition of export. Such cases raise two questions: whether the failure frustrates the contract; and what is the position where the source only fails in part.

19–026 **Express reference to source.** Where the contract expressly provides that the goods are to be taken from the specified source, the contract is frustrated if that source fails. Thus in *Howell v Coupland*[101] a farmer sold 200 tons of potatoes to be grown on land specified in the contract. That crop largely[102] failed, and it was held that the contract was frustrated so that the farmer was not liable in damages for non-delivery. For this purpose it is assumed that the contract specifies an *exclusive* source of supply. Where it refers to several sources, the contract is not frustrated merely because one of them becomes unavailable.[103]

19–027 **Source intended by one party only.** Where the contract contains no reference to the source and only one of the parties intends to use that source, the failure of that source does not lead to frustration. Thus a contract for the sale of "Finland birch timber" was not frustrated merely because the seller expected to get supplies from Finland and could not do so because of the severing of trade routes after the outbreak of war in 1914. For all the buyer knew, delivery might have been made from stocks kept in England.[104] Nor is a contract frustrated merely because the seller is let down by his supplier.[105] This is so even where that supplier is the sole producer of goods of the contract description, so long, at least, as the buyer was unaware of this fact.[106] The same rule applies where a buyer's source of payment fails. Thus a contract is not frustrated merely because the buyer intends (unknown to the seller) to pay with money to be remitted from a foreign country and the remittance is prevented or delayed by changes in that country's exchange control

---

[99] *Marrison v Bell* [1939] 2 K.B. 187; *Mears v Safecar Securities Ltd* [1983] Q.B. 54 at 79; cf. Employment Rights Act 1996 s.64.

[100] *Mears v Safecar Securities Ltd* [1983] Q.B. 54.

[101] (1876) 1 Q.B.D. 258.

[102] Not entirely: for a discussion of this aspect of the case, see para.19–029.

[103] e.g. *Turner v Goldsmith* [1891] 1 Q.B. 544; cf. *The Super Servant Two* [1990] 1 Lloyd's Rep. 1; and see para.19–056.

[104] *Blackburn Bobbin Co Ltd v TW Allen Ltd* [1918] 2 K.B. 467.

[105] *The Mary Nour* [2008] EWCA Civ 856; [2008] 1 Lloyd's Rep. 179.

[106] *Intertradex SA v Lesieur Torteaux SARL* [1978] 2 Lloyd's Rep. 509.

regulations.[107] A fortiori, a contract is not frustrated merely because the buyer's supply of the currency in which payment was to be made has become exhausted.[108]

**Source intended by both parties.** The most difficult cases are those in which the contract makes no express reference to the source but *both* parties contemplate that it will be used. Such contracts are sometimes construed as containing an implied reference to the source;[109] but for this purpose it is not enough to show that the parties contemplated the source: they must have intended that that source (and no other), should be used.[110] There is little English authority on the question whether (in the absence of any evidence of such intention) the failure of a source which was merely contemplated by both parties will frustrate a contract. In one case, it was conceded that the partial failure of such a source released the seller in part.[111] The view that the total failure of a mutually contemplated source will frustrate the contract is sometimes said to be supported by *Re Badische Co*,[112] where a contract for the supply of chemicals was held to be frustrated by illegality on the outbreak of war in 1914 because both parties intended the goods to be obtained from Germany. But this was a special case: it would clearly be contrary to public policy to allow such a contract to subsist; and this would be so whether the parties had specified the source or merely contemplated that it should be used. The problems raised where the supervening event makes the contract illegal differ significantly from those which arise where it makes performance impossible;[113] and there is no clear English decision on the effect of failure of a mutually contemplated (but unspecified) source of supply. Where that source was contemplated by one party only, the courts have sometimes emphasised this fact in rejecting the defence of frustration;[114] and this may give some support to the view that the defence would succeed where the source was contemplated by both. On the other hand, in some such cases the commercial background may now be that it would be usual for the seller to protect himself against the contingency, e.g. by a prohibition of export clause. Where this is the position it is less likely that failure of even a mutually contemplated source would frustrate the contract. **19–028**

**Partial failure of source.** A contract for the sale of goods may specify the source from which the goods are to be taken, so that the total failure of that source would undoubtedly lead to frustration. Further problems can then arise if the source fails only in part. Such partial failure normally has three consequences. First, the seller is excused to the extent of the deficiency. This was the outcome in *Howell v Coupland*,[115] where the seller had delivered the small quantity actually produced, **19–029**

[107] *Universal Corp v Five Ways Properties Ltd* [1979] 1 All E.R. 552. For an analogous situation, see *Hole & Pugsley v Sumption* [2001] N.L.J. 1851.

[108] *Congimex SARL (Lisbon) v Continental Grain Export Corp (New York)* [1979] 2 Lloyd's Rep. 346 at 353; cf. *Janos Paczy v Haendler & Natermann GmbH* [1981] 1 Lloyd's Rep. 302.

[109] e.g. *Ockerby & Co Ltd v Murdock* (1916) 19 W.A.R. 1; affirmed (1916) 22 C.L.R. 420.

[110] See at fn.103.

[111] *Lipton Ltd v Ford* [1917] 2 K.B. 647.

[112] [1921] 2 Ch. 331.

[113] See para.19–045.

[114] *Blackburn Bobbin Co Ltd v TW Allen Ltd* [1918] 2 K.B. 467.

[115] (1876) 1 Q.B.D. 256; para.19–026.

and was held not to be liable for the rest of the quantity sold. Secondly, the seller is bound to deliver the quantity actually produced;[116] unless, perhaps, it is so small that it is uneconomical to harvest it.[117] Thirdly, the buyer is not generally bound to accept the quantity produced if it is less than that contracted for;[118] but as partial crop failures normally lead to a rise in prices this point is of little practical importance.

19–030 **Partial failure and multiple contracts.** Additional complications arise where a seller has made a number of contracts to deliver goods from a specified source, and that source fails in part. For example, a farmer who reasonably expects his land to yield 1,000 tons agrees to sell 200 tons to each of five customers, and as a result of partial crop failure only 600 tons are produced; or a seller of goods to be taken from a foreign source similarly agrees to sell 200 tons to each of five customers, and, as a result of export restrictions, cannot obtain more than 600 tons. If total failure of the source would have frustrated the contracts,[119] what difference does it make that the failure was only partial?

One possible view is that it makes no difference, so that all the contracts are frustrated because the seller cannot perform them all in full. But this is unlikely to be accepted because it would enable the seller to keep the available goods and so to make a windfall profit from the rising prices likely to result from the shortage.[120]

A second possibility is to say that none of the contracts is frustrated: if the seller delivered 200 tons to each of three buyers, his inability to deliver to the other two would be due to his voluntary act or "election" and would therefore be incapable of frustrating his contracts with these two.[121] This view derives some support from an analogous case;[122] but it will be submitted later in this chapter that there is no true "election" where, after the supervening event, the seller's only choice is whether to perform one contract rather than another.[123] The argument that discharge is due to the seller's "election" could also be met by imposing legal restrictions on his choice.

This possibility leads to the third view, that some of the contracts are discharged. If this view were interpreted to mean that the seller must deliver to such buyers as were designated by law (e.g. by reference to the order in which

---

[116] *HR and S Sainsbury Ltd v Street* [1972] 1 W.L.R. 834; para.17–059.

[117] The contrary seems to have been held in *International Paper Co v Rockefeller* 146 N.Y.S. 371 (1914); sed quaere: such a case could be regarded as being, in substance, one of total failure of the source.

[118] Sale of Goods Act 1979 s.30(1). For qualifications of the buyer's right to reject, see para.17–033.

[119] See *Bremer Handelsgesellschaft mbH v Continental Grain Co* [1983] 1 Lloyd's Rep. 269, where this requirement was not satisfied.

[120] The view that all the contracts are frustrated may at first sight seem to be supported by *Tennants (Lancashire) Ltd v CS Wilson & Co Ltd* [1917] A.C. 495; but the only point actually decided was that no single buyer was entitled to delivery *in full*; and the seller was a middleman who would himself have had to pay the higher prices and so could not have profited from frustration.

[121] See paras 19–093—19–095.

[122] *The Super Servant Two* [1990] 1 Lloyd's Rep. 1; para.19–095.

[123] See para.19–095.

their contracts were made or to the standard of reasonableness) it would not be open to the objection that the seller's failure to deliver to the other buyers resulted from his "election".

A fourth view adopts the principle of pro rata division, so that in our examples the contracts would not be frustrated, but each buyer would receive 120 tons.[124] The difficulty with this view is that, under it, the contracts would be modified, rather than discharged;[125] and at common law the doctrine of frustration appears to be capable only of leading to a total discharge of the contract.[126] The principle of pro rata division does, however, have considerable support in cases in which the seller has relied on the partial failure of the source as discharging him, not under the common law doctrine of frustration, but under an express provision of the contract, such as a force majeure or prohibition of export clause. In such cases, there is support for two versions of the pro rata principle. One states negatively that no buyer is entitled to delivery in full;[127] the other states affirmatively that each buyer is entitled to his pro rata share, so that he would be entitled to damages if he received no delivery at all.[128] But there is also support for the view that, if the seller allocates all his supplies to earlier buyers, he is not liable if he delivers nothing to later ones.[129]

Probably, the overriding test is whether the seller acted reasonably in allocating the available supplies. In applying this test, the court can have regard to circumstances other than the order in which the contracts were made, e.g. to the fact that the available quantity was "too small to be sensibly apportioned among relevant purchasers".[130] Pro rata division is, of course, possible only where the subject-matter is physically divisible. Suppose that a farmer sold to each of five buyers "a calf to be born to my herd", expecting that at least five calves would be so born, and that (for reasons beyond his control) only three calves were born. In such a case, pro rata division would not work,[131] and it is submitted that, if the farmer delivered to the earliest three buyers, his contracts with the later two should be frustrated.[132]

---

[124] cf. in the US U.C.C. s.2–615(b). The rule there stated, that the seller can take into account "regular customers not … under contract", does not seem to represent English law: see *Pancommerce SA v Veecheema BV* [1983] 2 Lloyd's Rep. 304. Much less are the English courts likely to accept the further rule stated in s.2–615(b) that the seller can take into account "his own requirements for further manufacture": this seems inconsistent with *Maritime National Fish Ltd v Ocean Trawlers Ltd* [1935] A.C. 524; para.19–094; see generally Hudson 31 M.L.R. 535.

[125] *The Super Servant Two* [1989] 1 Lloyd's Rep. 148 at 158; affirmed [1990] 1 Lloyd's Rep. 1.

[126] See para.19–007; para.19–094.

[127] *Bremer Handelsgesellschaft mbH v Vanden Avenne-Izegem P v BA* [1978] 2 Lloyd's Rep. 109 at 115, 128, 131 (where the exact method of division is left open); cf. *Tennants (Lancashire) Ltd v CS Wilson & Co Ltd* [1917] A.C. 495 at 511–512.

[128] *Bremer Handelsgesellschaft mbH v C Mackprang Jr* [1979] 1 Lloyd's Rep. 221 at 224; the point is left open in *Continental Grain Export Corp v STM Grain Ltd* [1979] 2 Lloyd's Rep. 460 at 472.

[129] *Intertradex SA v Lesieur Torteaux SARL* [1978] 2 Lloyd's Rep. 509; cf. *Continental Grain Export Corp v STM Grain Ltd* [1979] 2 Lloyd's Rep. 460 at 473; *The Marine Star* [1993] 1 Lloyd's Rep. 329 at 332–333; and (in another context) *Cox v Bankside* [1995] 2 Lloyd's Rep. 434.

[130] *Bremer Handelsgesellschaft mbH v Continental Grain Co* [1983] 1 Lloyd's Rep. 269 at 293, citing *Westfalische Genossenschaft GmbH v Seabright Ltd* unreported, per Robert Goff J.

[131] See I Kings 3: 25.

[132] *The Super Servant Two* [1990] 1 Lloyd's Rep. 1 is distinguishable on the ground that the defendant claimed discharge in respect of the *earlier* contract: see para.19–095.

### (v) *Method of performance impossible*

19–031 **In general.** A contract may be discharged if it provides for a method of performance which becomes impossible. In *Nickoll & Knight v Ashton Edridge & Co*[133] a contract was made for the sale of cottonseed "to be shipped per steamship *Orlando* from Alexandria during … January". The *Orlando* later went aground in the Baltic so that she could not get to Alexandria in January. It was held that the contract was frustrated since, in the view of the majority of the Court of Appeal, it was to be construed as providing for performance *only* in the stipulated manner. If the stipulated method had not been regarded as exclusive, the seller might have been obliged to perform in a different way, e.g. by shipping the goods on a different ship or at a later time.[134] Whether he would actually have been obliged to do this would then have depended on whether the substituted method of performance differed fundamentally from that originally undertaken. This appears from the Suez cases to be discussed below.

19–032 **The Suez cases.** These cases arose because an agreed or contemplated method of performance became impossible when the Suez Canal was closed as a result of hostilities in the Middle East in 1956 and again in 1967. The first question was whether the parties had actually stipulated for the particular method of performance, or had only expected that it would probably be used. In *Tsakiroglou & Co Ltd v Noblee Thorl GmbH*[135] a contract was made for the sale of Sudanese groundnuts at an inclusive price to cover the cost of the goods, insurance and carriage to Hamburg. When the contract was made both parties expected that shipment would be via Suez, but the contract did not so provide. It was held that the contract was not frustrated by the closure of the Suez Canal, so that the seller ought to have shipped the goods via the Cape of Good Hope. Although this would have taken two and a half times as long as shipment via Suez and would have doubled the cost of carriage, the difference between the two methods of performance was not sufficiently fundamental to frustrate the contract.[136] If the difference had been of this kind, it seems that the contract could have been frustrated even though the method of performance was not specified in the contract but only contemplated by both parties.[137]

Where, on the other hand, there is no such fundamental difference, the contract may stand even if it does provide for performance by the method which becomes

---

[133] [1901] 2 K.B. 126; cf. *Maine Spinning Co v Sutcliffe & Co* (1918) 87 L.J.K.B. 382.

[134] cf. in the US, *Meyer v Sullivan* 181 P. 847 (1919); U.C.C. s.2–614(1). This rule prevents the seller from making a profit out of frustration on a rising market: cf. para.19–098.

[135] [1962] A.C. 93.

[136] Shortly after the end of the shipment period, the market price of the goods had risen by £18 15s per ton above the contract price, while the cost of shipment via the Cape was only £7 10s per ton more than the cost of shipment via Suez.

[137] cf. in another context, *Florida Power & Light Co v Westinghouse Electric Corp* 826 F.2d 239 (1987), where the contemplated method of performing an obligation to remove irradiated fuel from a nuclear power station was *by reprocessing* and when this became impossible the obligation could be performed only *by storing* the fuel. The difference between these modes was held to be sufficiently fundamental to discharge the obligation since reprocessing would have yielded a profit to the contractor of some $18 million while storing the fuel would have imposed costs on him in the region of $80 million.

impossible. Thus it was suggested in the *Tsakiroglou* case[138] that the contract there would not have been frustrated even if it *had* provided for shipment via Suez. The same view is supported by a number of cases in which shipowners argued that voyage charters were frustrated because of the extra length and expense of the voyage via the Cape of Good Hope. In some of these cases the contracts expressly referred to Suez;[139] and even where there was no such reference it was no doubt an implied term that the ship should go via the Suez Canal as that was the usual and customary route when the contract was made. Nevertheless the contracts were not frustrated,[140] so that the shipowners were bound to carry the goods at no extra charge by the longer, available, route. The difference between the two routes was not sufficiently fundamental, even though in one case[141] the voyage actually accomplished was twice as long as that originally contracted for and in another added nearly a third to the shipowner's anticipated costs.[142] The same principle can, on the other hand, favour the shipowner where the charterparty provides for payment by reference to the time taken to accomplish the voyage. In one such case[143] the charterer pleaded frustration but the plea was rejected: once again the court took the view that the voyage via the Cape was not fundamentally different from that via Suez, though exceeding it in length by about a third. To provide an illustration of frustration resulting from the closure of the Canal it is necessary to put a more extreme case, such as that of a contract to carry perishable goods from Port Sudan to Alexandria.

### *(vi) Impossibility and impracticability*

**Impracticability distinguished from impossibility.** The doctrine of frustration originated in cases where performance was said to have become "impossible". That is, in itself, something of a relative term. What is "impossible" depends partly on the current state of technology,[144] and partly on the amount of trouble and expense to which one is prepared to go to achieve it. It has been said that even *Taylor v Caldwell* was not a case of literal impossibility since "by the expenditure of huge sums of money" the music hall could probably have been rebuilt "in time for the scheduled concerts";[145] but no reasonable businessman would have been expected to incur such expenditure. For this reason the trend in the US has been to abandon the very words "impossible" and "impossibility" and to use instead the terms "impracticable" and "impracticability".[146] This seems, 19–033

[138] *Tsakiroglou & Co Ltd v Noblee Thorl GmbH* [1962] A.C. 93 at 112; cf. *Congimex Companhia Geral, etc. v Tradax Export SA* [1981] 2 Lloyd's Rep. 687 at 692; affirmed [1983] 1 Lloyd's Rep. 250.

[139] e.g. *The Captain George K* [1970] 2 Lloyd's Rep. 21; *The Washington Trader* [1972] 1 Lloyd's Rep. 463; 453 F.2d 939.

[140] See, the authorities cited in fn.139; and *Glidden v Hellenic Lines Ltd* 275 F. 2d. 253 (1960); *Transatlantic Finance Corp v USA* 363 F.2d 312 (1966).

[141] *The Captain George K* [1970] 2 Lloyd's Rep. 21.

[142] *The Washington Trader* [1972] 1 Lloyd's Rep. 463.

[143] *The Eugenia* [1964] 2 Q.B. 226.

[144] See, e.g. the illustration of "absolute" impossibility given in *Corbin on Contracts* (1962), para.1325: "No-one can go to the moon".

[145] Fuller & Eisenberg, *Basic Contract Law*, 3rd edn (1972), p.801.

[146] U.C.C. s.2–615; Restatement 2d, *Contracts*, para.261.

moreover, to be intended to widen the scope of the doctrine of discharge by supervening events.[147] "Impracticability" includes "extreme and unreasonable difficulty, expense, injury or loss"[148] to one of the parties. Examples include "A severe shortage of raw materials or of supplies due to war, embargo, local crop failure, unforeseen shutdown of major sources of supply or the like, which … causes a marked increase in cost … ".[149] The caveat is entered that "Increased cost alone does not excuse performance … "[150] but it is suggested that a price increase "well beyond the normal range"[151] could lead to discharge. In England, dicta to the effect that a contract may be discharged if its performance becomes "impracticable" are occasionally found in the cases.[152] But the weight of English authority rejects this view. Thus it has been said in the House of Lords that "a wholly abnormal rise or fall in prices"[153] would not affect the bargain; and that:

> "The argument that a man can be excused from performance of his contract when it becomes 'commercially' impossible seems to me a dangerous contention which ought not to be admitted unless the parties have plainly contracted to that effect".[154]

19–034 **Impracticability not generally sufficient.** A number of cases illustrate the view that "impracticability" is not generally sufficient to frustrate a contract in English law. In *Davis Contractors Ltd v Fareham Urban DC*[155] contractors agreed to build 78 houses for a local authority in eight months for £94,000. Because of labour shortages, the work took 22 months and cost the contractors £115,000. They claimed that the contract had been frustrated and that they were therefore entitled to extra remuneration on a quantum meruit basis.[156] But the House of Lords rejected the claim as the events which caused the delays were within the ordinary range of commercial probability and had not brought about a fundamental change of circumstances. Lord Radcliffe said:

---

[147] *Neal-Cooper Grain Co v Texas Gulf Sulphur Co*, 508 F.2d 283 at 293 (1974) ("less stringent test of impracticability"); cf. *Nora Springs Co-operative Co v Brandau* 247 N.W.2d 744 at 748 (1976).

[148] Restatement, *Contracts*, §454; Restatement 2d, *Contracts*, §261, Comment d.

[149] Restatement, *Contracts*, §454; Restatement 2d, *Contracts*, §261, Comment d; U.C.C. s.2–615, Comment 4.

[150] U.C.C. s.2–615, Comment 4.

[151] Restatement 2d, *Contracts*, §261, Comment d.

[152] e.g. *Horlock v Beal* [1916] A.C. 486 at 492; *Nile Co for the Export of Agricultural Crops v H & J M Bennett (Commodities) Ltd* [1986] 1 Lloyd's Rep. 555 at 581; cf. *The Badagry* [1985] 1 Lloyd's Rep. 395 at 399. See further Beatson in Rose (ed.), *Consensus ad Idem, Essays in the Law of Contract in Honour of Guenter Treitel* (1996), p.123.

[153] *British Movietonews Ltd v London and District Cinemas* [1952] A.C. 166 at 185.

[154] *Tennants (Lancashire) Ltd v CS Wilson & Co Ltd* [1917] A.C. 495 at 510 (where the sellers were excused by the express terms of the contract); cf. *Shearson Lehman Hutton Inc v Maclaine Watson & Co Ltd* [1989] 2 Lloyd's Rep. 570 at 508 (commodity contract not frustrated by closure of market); and see the cases discussed in the next paragraph.

[155] [1956] A.C. 696.

[156] See para.22–027.

> "It is not hardship or inconvenience or material loss itself which calls the principle of frustration into play. There must be as well such a change in the significance of the obligation that the thing undertaken would, if performed, be a different thing from that contracted for".[157]

The Suez cases[158] similarly reject the argument that the greater expense caused to the party prejudiced by the closure of the Canal was a ground of frustration. In the words of Lord Simonds, "an increase of expense is not a ground of frustration".[159] Extreme cost increases might, however, be relevant where all that a party was bound to do was to take reasonable steps to produce a specified result. For example, in *Brauer & Co (Great Britain) Ltd v James Clark (Brush Materials) Ltd* it was said that a seller would not be liable for failure to get an export licence if the cost of getting it were 100 times the contract price;[160] the seller's duty in that case would have been limited to one to take reasonable steps even if the contract had not been expressly "subject to export licence".[161] Where performance would, in view of changed circumstances, cause not merely extra expense but acute personal hardship to one party, it has been said that "equitable relief may ... be refused because of an unforeseen change of circumstances not amounting to legal frustration".[162] But in such cases the contract is not discharged: the defendant remains liable in damages even though specific performance is refused on the ground of severe hardship.[163]

**Possible exceptions.** Four types of cases to be discussed below may at first sight seem to give some support to the view that a contract can be frustrated by "impracticability". But it will be submitted that these cases are all explicable on other grounds and that they do not support the view that impracticability (in the sense of great financial or commercial hardship to one of the parties) is of itself sufficient to discharge a contract in English law. **19–035**

**Impracticability combined with impossibility or illegality.** First, there are the cases in which discharge is based, not on impracticability alone, but on this factor when it is combined with impossibility or illegality. One group of such cases is that already discussed,[164] in which long delays in performance resulted from wartime restrictions, and it was held that performance need not be resumed in the totally altered conditions which prevailed when those restrictions were removed. **19–036**

---

[157] *Davis Contractors Ltd v Fareham Urban DC* [1956] A.C. 696 at 729; cf. *Multiservice Bookbinding Ltd v Marden* [1979] Ch. 84 at 113; *Chaucer Estates v Fairclough Homes* [1991] E.G.C.S. 65.

[158] See para.19–032.

[159] *Tsakiroglou & Co v Noblee Thorl GmbH* [1962] A.C. 93 at 115; cf. *Exportelisa SA v Guiseppe Figli Soc Coll* [1978] 1 Lloyd's Rep. 433; *Finland Steamship Co Ltd v Felixstowe Dock Ry Co* [1980] 2 Lloyd's Rep. 287; *The Mercedes Envoy* [1995] 2 Lloyd's Rep. 559.

[160] *Brauer & Co (Great Britain) Ltd v James Clark (Brush Materials) Ltd* [1952] 2 All E.R. 497 at 501.

[161] See para.2–111.

[162] *Patel v Ali* [1984] Ch. 283 at 288.

[163] See para.21–032. In *Patel v Ali* [1984] Ch. 283 the defendant was required to pay £10,000 into court as a condition of the discharge of the order of specific performance against her.

[164] *Metropolitan Water Board v Dick Kerr & Co* [1918] A.C. 119; *Acetylene Co of GB v Canada Carbide Co* (1922) 8 Lloyd's Rep. 456; para.19–021; cf. *Florida Power & Light Co v Westinghouse Electric Corp* 826 F.2d 239 (1987): fn.137.

It could be said that performance at the later time was "impracticable"; but this was only one factor leading to discharge, the other being that, for a considerable period, the wartime conditions made performance actually impossible. Similar reasoning can apply where a supervening change in the law makes it illegal to perform a contract to render a service unless (for example) additional safety precautions are taken by the party who is to render it. The extra expense to be incurred by that party in taking those precautions may then be regarded as a kind of "impracticability", leading to discharge;[165] but this result will, more significantly, be based on the special considerations of public policy on which discharge is based in cases of supervening illegality:[166] in other words, it does not follow that the contract would be discharged if the same amount of extra expense were occasioned simply by commercial factors, without any element of supervening illegality.

19–037 **Express contractual provision.** Secondly, there are cases in which contracts were discharged, not under the general doctrine of frustration, but under express contractual provisions (such as force majeure or prohibition of export clauses) which excuse one party, or both, if a specified event prevents performance. Such clauses do not protect a party merely because supervening events make performance more difficult or more expensive for him;[167] nor do they normally protect him where he can perform in alternative ways and only one of them becomes impossible, e.g. a seller who cannot obtain the goods that he had undertaken to deliver from the source intended by him (e.g. because of being let down by his supplier or because of an export embargo) must obtain them from other sources that remain available.[168] But this rule is subject to an exception which applies where it would be unreasonable to require the seller to perform in this way, because attempts to do so by him, and by other sellers similarly situated, would drive prices up to "unheard of levels".[169] In one case of this kind, it was said that the seller need not make such an attempt where to require him to do so would be "impracticable and commercially unsuitable".[170] These cases are, however, concerned, not with discharge under the general doctrine of frustration, but with discharge under express contractual provisions for supervening

---

[165] It seems to have been so regarded in *William Cory v LCC* [1951] 1 K.B. 8; affirmed [1951] 2 K.B. 476. Similar considerations may in part account for the American decision in *Florida Power & Light Co v Westinghouse Electric Corp* 826 F.2d 239 (1987).

[166] See para.19–045.

[167] See, e.g. *Brauer & Co (Great Britain) Ltd v James Clark (Brush Materials) Ltd* [1952] 2 All E.R. 497; *B & S Contracts & Designs Ltd v Victor Green Publications Ltd* [1984] I.C.R. 419; *Thames Valley Power Ltd v Total Gas & Power Ltd* [2005] EWHC 2208; [2006] 1 Lloyd's Rep. 441; *Tandrin Aviation Holdings Ltd v Aero Toy Store LLC* [2010] EWHC 40 (Comm); [2010] 2 Lloyd's Rep. 668.

[168] e.g. *PJ van der Zijden Wildhandel NV v Tucker & Cross Ltd* [1975] 2 Lloyd's Rep. 240; *Agrokar AG v Tradigrain SA* [2000] 1 Lloyd's Rep. 497. For the possibility of excluding this rule by the terms of the clause, see *The Morning Watch* [1996] 2 Lloyd's Rep. 383.

[169] *Tradax Export SA v André & Cie* [1976] 1 Lloyd's Rep. 416 at 423; cf. *André & Cie SA v Tradax Export SA* [1983] 1 Lloyd's Rep. 254; *Cook Industries v Tradax Export SA* [1983] 1 Lloyd's Rep. 327 at 344; affirmed [1985] 2 Lloyd's Rep. 454, without reference to this point.

[170] *Bremer Handelsgesellschaft mbH v Vanden Avenne-Izegem PV BA* [1978] 2 Lloyd's Rep. 109 at 115; cf. *Owners of Steamship Matheos v Louis Dreyfus* [1925] A.C. 654 at 666 ("commercially impracticable").

events.[171] Such a provision often operates in circumstances falling short of frustration under the general law.[172] Thus the fact that it may, on its true construction, cover "impracticability" does not support the view that the same circumstances would frustrate a contract which contained no such provision.

**Contracts of indefinite duration.** Thirdly, it is arguable that impracticability may be a ground of discharge where the contract is one of indefinite duration. In *Staffordshire Area Health Authority v South Staffordshire Waterworks Co*[173] a hospital had in 1919 contracted to give up to a waterworks company its right to take water from a well, and the company had in return promised "at all times hereafter" to supply water to the hospital at a fixed price specified in the contract. In 1975 the cost to the company of making the supply had risen to over 18 times that fixed price and the company gave seven months' notice to terminate the agreement. It was held that this notice was effective. Lord Denning MR regarded the contract as frustrated by the change of circumstances which had occurred between 1919 and 1975. But this view is, with respect, open to question, as it was based on the very passage of his own judgment in the *British Movietonews* case which had there been disapproved by the House of Lords.[174] The preferable reason for the decision in the *Staffordshire* case is therefore that of the majority, who held that the agreement was, on its true construction, intended to be of indefinite (and not of perpetual) duration:[175] hence the case fell within the general principle under which, in commercial agreements of indefinite duration, a term is often implied entitling either party to terminate by reasonable notice.[176] It follows from this reasoning that the decision would have gone the other way if the agreement had been for a fixed term, e.g. for 10 years. The agreement could then not have been terminated by notice before the end of the 10 years, nor would an increase in the suppliers' costs during that period have been a ground of frustration. This view is supported by later authority[177] and seems also to be correct in principle: if parties enter into a fixed term fixed price contract they must be taken thereby to have allocated the risks of market fluctuations. If the **19–038**

[171] The same is true of *Ford & Sons (Oldham) Ltd v Henry Leetham & Sons Ltd* (1915) 21 Com. Cas. 55, which is nevertheless cited in support of the general principle of discharge by "impracticability" in U.C.C. s.2–615, Comment 4.

[172] See para.19–079. For the significance of the distinction between discharge by frustration and under an express term, cf. also *The Super Servant Two* [1989] 1 Lloyd's Rep. 148 at 149; [1990] 1 Lloyd's Rep. 1 at 8.

[173] [1978] 1 W.L.R. 1387; Rose 96 L.Q.R. 177.

[174] *British Movietonews Ltd v London and District Cinemas* [1952] A.C. 166 at 185; para.19–005.

[175] "At all times hereafter" was (obviously) not to be taken literally, but meant "at all times hereafter during the subsistence of the agreement." The majority view was followed in *Tower Hamlets LBC v British Gas Corp*, *The Times*, 23 March 1982, affirmed *The Times*, 14 December 1983, and approved in *Watford DC v Watford Rural DC* (1988) 86 L.G.R. 524 at 529.

[176] cf. para.16–119; contrast *Watford DC v Watford Rural DC* (1988) 86 L.G.R. 524, where it was held that no such term could be implied in an agreement to contribute variable amounts towards the maintenance of cemeteries; *Islwyn BC v Newport BC* (1994) 6 Admin. L.R. 386. For exclusion of an implied term permitting termination on reasonable notice by other words in the contract, see also *Harbinger UK Ltd v GE Information Services Ltd* [2000] 1 All E.R. (Comm) 166; *Servicepower Asia Pacific Pty Ltd v Servicepower Business Solutions Ltd* [2009] EWHC 179 (Ch); [2010] 1 All E.R. 238 (Comm).

[177] *Kirklees MBC v Yorks Woollen District Transport Co* (1978) 77 L.G.R. 448.

parties are not prepared to accept these risks (or to accept them in full) they can adopt the now common practice of providing in the contract itself for flexible pricing.[178]

19–039 **The Playa Larga.** The three situations so far discussed should be distinguished from a fourth which arose in *The Playa Larga*.[179] Sugar had been sold by a Cuban state trading organisation to a buyer controlled by a state trading organisation in Chile. When the contract was made, Cuba and Chile were both ruled by Marxist governments; but before deliveries under the contract had been completed, the Marxist Government in Chile was overthrown; diplomatic relations between the two countries were severed; and there was a complete breakdown of commercial relations between them. It was held that the contract was frustrated even though its performance had not become impossible in any of the senses discussed in this chapter. The decision was, however, based, not on extreme hardship to the seller, but on the fact that, in the altered conditions, there was no possibility of the implementation of the contract on either side;[180] and the court concluded that, in these conditions, the contract was no longer intended to be binding. A breakdown of diplomatic and commercial relations between governments would not normally be a ground of discharge; but in *The Playa Larga* it had this effect because both contracting parties were controlled by the governments in question.

19–040 **Inflation.** In the cases so far discussed, increases in the cost of performing a particular contract have made that contract unprofitable to one party. A similar situation may arise where the general process of inflation reduces in real terms the benefit which that party expected to obtain under the contract. In the *British Movietonews* case "a sudden depreciation of currency" is listed as one of the uncontemplated turns of events which do *not* frustrate a contract.[181] The passage continues to make the general point that a contract would cease to bind if a "fundamentally different situation" were to emerge. This may refer back to the illustrations, previously given in the passage, of events (such as currency fluctuations) which are stated *not* to frustrate a contract; but more probably the reference is to *other* (i.e. to frustrating) events. Again, in *Wates Ltd v GLC*[182] a building contract to some extent protected the builder against inflation, by means of a price-escalation clause; and it was said that the fact that "inflation increased not [at] a trot or at a canter but at a gallop … was not so radical a difference from the inflation contemplated and provided for as to frustrate the contract".[183] Thus the English authorities do not support the view that inflation is a ground of frustration, though the possibility that extreme (as opposed to merely severe)

[178] See *Superior Overseas Development Corp v British Gas Corp* [1982] 1 Lloyd's Rep. 262; *Wates v GLC* (1983) 25 Build L.R. 1 (at fn.182); *Watford DC v Watford Rural DC* (1988) 86 L.G.R. 524 at 548; *Queensland Electricity Generating Board v New Hope Collieries Pty Ltd* [1989] 1 Lloyd's Rep. 205.

[179] [1983] 2 Lloyd's Rep. 171.

[180] *The Playa Larga* [1983] 2 Lloyd's Rep. 171 at 188.

[181] *British Movietonews Ltd v London and District Cinemas* [1952] A.C. 166 at 185.

[182] (1983) 25 Build. L.R. 1.

[183] *Wates Ltd v GLC* (1983) 25 Build. L.R. 1 at 34.

inflation may be capable of frustrating a contract cannot be wholly ruled out.[184] It is again open to a party who fears that he will be prejudiced by inflation to guard against this risk by an express term, e.g. by providing (if his bargaining position permits) for "index-linked" payments.[185]

**Currency fluctuations.** A debtor whose obligations are defined by reference to a foreign currency cannot avoid liability to pay in full merely because the pound sterling has fallen in value in relation to that currency by an unexpectedly large amount.[186] 19–041

## (b) Frustration of purpose

**Definition.** Frustration of purpose is, in a sense, the converse of impracticability. The two ideas resemble each other in that neither is concerned with cases in which performance has become impossible. Impracticability is normally said to arise when a *supplier* of goods, services or other facilities alleges that supervening events have made performance of his own promise so much more burdensome to him that he should no longer be bound to render it. The argument of frustration of purpose, on the other hand, is normally put forward by the *recipient* of the goods, services or facilities:[187] it is that supervening events have so greatly reduced the value to him of the other party's performance that he should no longer be bound to accept it and to pay the agreed price. 19–042

**The coronation cases.** Such an argument succeeded in some of the cases which arose out of the postponement of the coronation of King Edward VII. We have seen that in *Krell v Henry*[188] the effect of the postponement was to discharge a contract for the hire of a flat overlooking the route of the proposed processions. The obvious danger of such a rule is that it can all too easily be invoked by a party for whom a contract has simply become a very bad bargain. *Krell v Henry* has therefore attracted much criticism;[189] but the decision can be justified[190] on the ground that the contract was, on its true construction, not merely one for the hire of the flat, but one to provide facilities for viewing the coronation 19–043

[184] cf. Lord Roskill's reference in *National Carriers Ltd v Panalpina Northern Ltd* [1981] A.C. 675 at 712 to "inflation" as one of the "circumstances in which the doctrine [of frustration] has been invoked, sometimes with success, *sometimes without*".

[185] See *Nationwide BS v Registry of Friendly Societies* [1983] 1 W.L.R. 1226.

[186] *Multiservice Bookbinding Ltd v Marden* [1979] Ch. 84.

[187] Occasionally, the normal positions are reversed so that a buyer relies on impracticability where the cost to him of taking delivery has risen sharply (as in *Mineral Park Land Co v Howard* 156 P. 458 (1916)) or a seller relies on frustration of purpose where supervening events affect his ability to realise the financial instruments by which payment is to be made (as in *Re Comptoir Commercial Anversois and Power Sons & Co* [1920] 1 K.B. 868).

[188] [1903] 2 K.B. 740 (para.19–004).

[189] *Blackburn Bobbin Co Ltd v T W Allen & Sons Ltd* [1918] 1 K.B. 540 at 542; affirmed [1918] 2 K.B. 467); cf. *Maritime National Fish Ltd v Ocean Trawlers Ltd* [1935] A.C. 524 at 528; *Scanlan's New Neon Ltd v Toohey's Ltd* (1943) 67 C.L.R. 169 at 191–194.

[190] See *Codelfa Construction Pty Ltd v State Rail Authority of NSW* (1982) 149 C.L.R. 337 at 358.

processions.[191] The actual decision may be contrasted with an example given in one of the judgments: a contract to take a cab to Epsom on Derby day "at a suitable enhanced price"[192] would not be frustrated if the Derby were cancelled. Here the contract was evidently regarded as one to get the passenger to Epsom—not as one to get him to the Derby. Similar reasoning distinguishes *Krell v Henry* from *Herne Bay Steam Boat Co v Hutton*,[193] another of the coronation cases. A pleasure boat was hired "for the purpose of viewing the naval review and for a day's cruise round the fleet". The review, which formed part of the proposed coronation celebrations, was cancelled when the King fell ill, but the contract was not frustrated. It was construed simply as a contract for the hire of a boat; and it could still be performed although one of the motives of the hirer[194]—to carry passengers at high prices to see the review—was defeated.

19–044 **Limited application.** Although the actual decision in *Krell v Henry* appears to be justifiable on the grounds stated above, the case has scarcely ever been followed in England. Normally, a contract is not frustrated merely because supervening events have prevented one party from putting the subject-matter to the use intended by him, even though that use was also contemplated by the other.[195] Thus a contract by which a gas company agreed with a local authority to "provide, maintain and light" street lamps was not frustrated when wartime black-out regulations prohibited the lighting of such lamps,[196] since performance of the maintenance obligation ("which cannot be regarded as … trivial")[197] remained possible. Similarly, a contract for the sale of goods is not frustrated merely because the buyer's purpose to export the goods from, or to import them into, a particular country is defeated by export or import restrictions.[198] In *Canary Wharf (BP4) T1 Ltd v European Medicines Agency*[199] the EMA submitted that a 25 year lease for premises in Canary Wharf was frustrated on the basis that the purpose of the lease was to provide the EU headquarters for the Agency and this purpose would be thwarted by the UK's withdrawal from the EU ("Brexit"[200]). While Marcus Smith J agreed that the "common purpose" of a contract is not

[191] cf. *The Great Peace* [2002] EWCA Civ 1407; [2003] Q.B. 679 at [66] (contract for "a room with a view").

[192] *Krell v Henry* [1903] 2 K.B. 740 at 750.

[193] [1903] 2 K.B. 683.

[194] For the requirement that the purpose of *both* parties must be frustrated, see *The Siboen and the Sibotre* [1976] 1 Lloyd's Rep. 293.

[195] *North Shore Ventures Ltd v Anstead Holdings Inc* [2010] EWHC 1485 (Ch); [2010] 2 Lloyd's Rep. 265 (use to which part of loan could be put partially restricted).

[196] *Leiston Gas Co v Leiston-cum-Sizewell Urban DC* [1916] 2 K.B. 428; on the interpretation of express contractual provisions for such events, see *Williams v Mercer* [1940] 3 All E.R. 293 and contrast *Egham & Staines Electricity Co Ltd v Egham Urban DC* [1944] 1 All E.R. 107.

[197] *Leiston Gas Co v Leiston-cum-Sizewell Urban DC* [1916] 2 K.B. 428 at 433.

[198] e.g. *D McMaster & Co v Cox McEwen & Co* 1921 S.C. (HL) 1; *Congimex SARL (Lisbon) v Continental Grain Export Corp (New York)* [1979] 2 Lloyd's Rep. 346; *Bangladesh Export Import Co Ltd v Sucden Kerry SA* [1995] 2 Lloyd's Rep. 1.

[199] [2019] EWHC 335 (Ch); 183 Con L.R. 167.

[200] See above, para.1–013. As it was not yet clear that this was going to happen and in what circumstances, the court dealt with the submission on the hypothesis that the UK simply left the EU without any deal, on the basis that, if this did not result in frustration, withdrawal with any sort of deal was not likely to do so.

simply a matter of reciting the individual terms and conditions and involves "something much more elemental"[201] and also acknowledged that the premises had been adapted to some extent to serve as the Agency's headquarters,[202] he held that this did not "come close to a case of frustration of common purpose".[203] A material consideration in this respect was the provisions in the lease regarding alienation by the EMA. They may not have been as flexible as the EMA would have preferred, but they allowed the court to conclude that it got "what it bargained for".[204] Perhaps the most striking illustration of the reluctance of the courts to apply the principle of frustration of purpose is provided by the *Amalgamated Investment & Property*[205] case, where it was held that a contract for the purchase of property for redevelopment was not frustrated when the buildings on the land were listed as being of special architectural or historic interest, so that redevelopment became more difficult or impossible and the property lost most of its value.[206]

Such cases show that "the frustrated expectations and intentions of one party to a contract do not necessarily, or indeed usually, lead to the frustration of that contract".[207] They make it difficult to establish the defence of frustration of purpose; but they do not make it impossible. In *Denny, Mott & Dickson v James B Fraser & Co Ltd*[208] an agreement for the lease of a timber yard was made for the purpose of enabling the parties to carry out a contract between them for the sale of timber. When performance of the contract of sale was prohibited by wartime regulations, the House of Lords held that the agreement for the lease of the yard was also frustrated. The actual decision may to some extent rest on special policy considerations applicable to cases of supervening illegality; but other situations can be imagined in which the principle of frustration of purpose might also apply. For example, if premises were leased as a warehouse and supervening events made their use as such impossible for the whole period of the lease, it seems that the contract might be frustrated.[209] In such a case, the contract would be discharged, even though performance had not become impossible, because the supervening event had destroyed "some basic, though tacit assumption on which the parties had contracted".[210]

---

201 *Canary Wharf (BP4) T1 Ltd v European Medicines Agency* [2019] EWHC 335 (Ch); 183 Con L.R. 167 at [29].

202 *Canary Wharf (BP4) T1 Ltd v European Medicines Agency* [2019] EWHC 335 (Ch); 183 Con L.R. 167 at [58]–[61].

203 *Canary Wharf (BP4) T1 Ltd v European Medicines Agency* [2019] EWHC 335 (Ch); 183 Con L.R. 167 at [247].

204 *Canary Wharf (BP4) T1 Ltd v European Medicines Agency* [2019] EWHC 335 (Ch); 183 Con L.R. 167 at [248].

205 *Amalgamated Investment & Property Co Ltd v John Walker & Son Ltd* [1977] 1 W.L.R. 164.

206 The listing was said to have reduced the value of the property to £200,000—against a contract price of £1,710,000.

207 *Congimex Companhia Geral, etc., SARL v Tradax Export SA* [1983] 1 Lloyd's Rep. 250 at 253.

208 [1944] A.C. 265.

209 This seems to be assumed in *National Carriers Ltd v Panalpina (Northern) Ltd* [1981] A.C. 675 (paras 19–060–19–064), where the temporary nature of the interruption was stressed in rejecting the plea of frustration.

210 *Sir Lindsay Parkinson Ltd v Commissioners of Works* [1949] 2 K.B. 632 at 665.

## (c) Illegality

19–045 A contract may be discharged by a supervening prohibition if the prohibition would have made the contract illegal, had it been in force when the contract was made.[211]

19–046 **Public interest considerations.** The object of the doctrine of frustration in cases of supervening impossibility or of frustration of purpose is to provide a satisfactory method of allocating or distributing the loss caused by the supervening event. Where, however, a contract is affected by supervening illegality, the court has to take into account, not only the relative interests of the parties, but also the interests of the public in seeing that the law is observed;[212] and this public interest may sometimes outweigh the importance of achieving a fair distribution of loss. For this reason supervening illegality is a ground of discharge distinct from supervening impossibility, and is to some extent governed by special rules.

19–047 **Illegality under foreign law.** This book deals only with discharge by supervening illegality which arises under English law. The justification for discharge where the illegality arises under foreign law (e.g. under a foreign prohibition of export or import) is somewhat different.[213] In the *Canary Wharf* case discussed above,[214] in addition to frustration of purpose, the EMA argued that the lease was frustrated by supervening illegality on the basis that, under EU law, it no longer had the capacity either to pay the rent due under the lease at all, or to occupy the premises or alienate them to any other EU institution following the UK's withdrawal. Marcus Smith J rejected this submission on the basis that performance had not become illegal,[215] but if he was wrong about that, frustration was not available either because, in the case of supervening (as opposed to initial[216]) capacity, the courts do not have regard to the foreign law of incorporation or domicile of the relevant party,[217] or because any supervening incapacity was "self-induced".[218]

### *(i) Illustrations*

19–048 **Trading with the enemy.** The public interest considerations just mentioned are particularly strong where a contract becomes illegal as a result of the wartime

[211] See para.11–029.

[212] cf. para.11–063.

[213] *Benjamin's Sale of Goods*, 10th edn (2017), para.18–387

[214] See para.19–044.

[215] *Canary Wharf (BP4) T1 Ltd v European Medicines Agency* [2019] EWHC 335 (Ch); 183 Con L.R. 167 at [160].

[216] See para.12–083, fn.263.

[217] *Canary Wharf (BP4) T1 Ltd v European Medicines Agency* [2019] EWHC 335 (Ch); 183 Con L.R. 167 at [189].

[218] *Canary Wharf (BP4) T1 Ltd v European Medicines Agency* [2019] EWHC 335 (Ch); 183 Con L.R. 167 at [208]; see para.19–089.

prohibition against trading with the enemy. In the leading *Fibrosa* case[219] a contract for the sale of machinery to be shipped to Gdynia was frustrated when that port was occupied by the enemy during the Second World War. Although it might have been physically possible to get the goods to the destination,[220] the contract was discharged because of the strong public interest in ensuring that no aid should be given to the enemy economy in time of war. The same principle applies where goods are to be imported from an enemy country: the contract is frustrated even though the enemy source is not specified in the contract but only contemplated by the parties.[221] The public interest principle is so strong in these cases that frustration by or as a result of the prohibition cannot be excluded even by an express provision in the contract.[222]

**Other prohibitions.** The cases provide many illustrations of frustration by supervening prohibitions other than that against trading with the enemy. In the *Denny, Mott*[223] case, for example, a contract for the sale of timber was frustrated by a wartime prohibition against dealing in goods of the contract description. Contracts can similarly be frustrated by prohibition of export or import, or by restrictions on the movement of capital.[224] Such prohibitions will not frustrate the contract if they can be overcome by a licence and no attempt has made to obtain one, unless it can be shown that no licence could have been obtained in any event.[225] In these cases the public interest in seeing that the prohibition is observed is less strong than in the trading with the enemy cases; and they differ from the trading with the enemy cases in two further ways. First, frustration results only if it is an actual term of the contract that the subsequently prohibited act is to be done. Thus a contract for the sale of goods may be frustrated by prohibition of export if it provides that the goods are to be exported,[226] but not merely because the buyer intended to export them, even though the seller knew this.[227] Secondly, frustration can be excluded by express contractual provisions. Thus provisions suspending performance in the event of prohibition of export are valid[228] since, so far from contravening the policy of the prohibition, they assume **19–049**

[219] *Fibrosa Spolka Ackcyjna v Fairbairn, Lawson Combe Barbour Ltd* [1943] A.C. 32.

[220] The mere outbreak of war does not frustrate a contract: see *The Chrysalis* [1983] 1 W.L.R. 1469 (where the war was one to which the UK was not a party, so that no question of trading with the enemy could arise). The suggestion in *Stocznia Gdanska SA v Latvian Shipping Co* [1998] 1 W.L.R. 574 at 600 that in the *Fibrosa* case "the outbreak of war frustrated the contract" is, with respect, open to question: it was not the outbreak of war, but the enemy occupation of the port of destination, which was the ground of frustration.

[221] *Re Badische Co* [1921] 2 Ch. 331; para.19–028.

[222] *Ertel Bieber & Co v Rio Tinto Co Ltd* [1918] A.C. 260; para.19–084.

[223] *Denny, Mott & Dickson v James B Fraser & Co Ltd* [1944] A.C. 265; para.19–044; cf. *Marsh v Glanvill* [1917] 2 K.B. 87 at 91.

[224] See *Libyan Arab Foreign Bank v Bankers Trust Co* [1989] Q.B. 728 at 749, though in that case there was no frustration: [1989] Q.B. 728 at 771–772; cf. *Wahda Bank v Arab Bank Plc, The Times*, 23 December 1992; for further proceedings in this case, see [1996] 1 Lloyd's Rep. 470.

[225] *Dalmia Dairy Industries Ltd v National Bank of Pakistan* [1978] 2 Lloyd's Rep. 223 at 253.

[226] As in *Andrew Millar & Co v Taylor & Co Ltd* [1916] 1 K.B. 402 (see at 403, 417); but in that case the plea of frustration failed as the embargo was not permanent: as to this point see para.19–054, fn.251.

[227] See para.19–044.

[228] See para.19–079.

that it will be observed. Similar provisions in trading with the enemy cases are contrary to the public interest since they involve continuing relations with an enemy subject, and so may indirectly support the enemy economy.

### (ii) *Supervening and antecedent prohibition*

19–050 **No frustration for an antecedent prohibition.** Under the rules stated above, frustration may result from a supervening prohibition, i.e. from one imposed by a law made after the contract was made.[229] If, at the time of contracting, the prohibition is already in force, the case is one of antecedent prohibition. This may make the contract void ab initio for illegality,[230] but it will not bring about frustration.

19–051 **An intermediate situation: consent of public authority withheld.** There is an intermediate situation in which at the time of contracting a law is in force under which the contract can be lawfully performed only with the consent of a public authority, e.g. if a licence to build, or to export or import goods, is obtained. Such a licence may be sought but refused *after* the contract is made; and it is then possible to regard the refusal as a supervening event which frustrates the contract.[231] But it is submitted that generally there will be no frustration in cases of this kind. The cases fall into three groups.

In the first, the parties intend to perform, or actually perform, without the required licence. In such cases, the contract is not frustrated but illegal ab initio.[232]

In the second, the parties intend to perform only if the required licence is obtained. Here the principal obligations under the contract are subject to the condition precedent that the licence will be obtained; and normally one of the parties (e.g. a seller of goods for export) will be under a duty to take reasonable steps to obtain the licence.[233] If he takes such steps but the licence is nevertheless refused, he is not liable in damages;[234] but the reason is not that he is prevented from performing (and so discharged) but that he *has* performed by doing all that was required of him. Equally, the buyer is not liable, but again the reason is not that his liability is discharged: it is that he never became liable because the seller was unable to deliver and so failed to perform a condition precedent to, or a concurrent condition of, the buyer's duty to accept and pay.[235] Thus, although

[229] For the present purpose, a prohibition is supervening if it was imposed after the contract even though the state of affairs on which it is based already existed when the contract was made, as in *Gamerco SA v ICM/Fair Warning (Agency) Ltd* [1995] 1 W.L.R. 1226, where a stadium in which a "rock concert" was to be given suffered *before* the contract was made from an undiscovered structural defect and use of the stadium for giving the concert was prohibited when the defect was discovered *after* the contract was made.

[230] See paras 11–019—11–020.

[231] This is a possible interpretation of a dictum in *AV Pound & Co Ltd v MW Hardy Inc* [1956] A.C. 588 at 604 that "further performance of the contract was excused"; for another interpretation, see fn.236.

[232] See para.11–014.

[233] See para.2–111.

[234] *Benjamin's Sale of Goods* 10th edn (2017), para.18–376.

[235] See paras 17–015—17–018.

neither party is liable, the contract is not frustrated.[236] The question whether the contract is frustrated, or whether the parties escape liability on other grounds, is of more than academic interest: if there is no frustration the Law Reform (Frustrated Contracts) Act 1943[237] does not apply. An alternative possibility, in cases of this kind, is that the seller has undertaken absolutely to obtain a licence.[238] "Clear words" are required to impose such an absolute duty, especially where the law prohibiting performance is passed after the time of contracting.[239] If the seller fails, he is liable in damages; and to avoid conflict with the rules as to illegal contracts it has been said that the seller's liability is based on a collateral contract that he will secure the licence.[240]

In the third group of cases the licensing requirement is in existence at the time of the contract and the parties intend to perform only if a licence is obtained; but afterwards there is a change in government policy with regard to the issue of such licences. If such a change leads to the refusal of licences which previously had been issued as a matter of course,[241] it is possible that the change of policy may be regarded as a supervening event which is capable of frustrating the contract.[242]

### *(iii) Partial and temporary illegality*

**Whether contract frustrated.** Whether partial or temporary illegality frustrates the contract depends (as in cases of partial impossibility)[243] on whether it defeats the main purpose of the contract. Thus in the *Denny, Mott* case[244] a long-term agreement for the sale of timber provided that "to enable the aforesaid agreement to be carried out" the buyer should let a timber yard to the seller. When dealings in timber under the agreement were prohibited, it was held that the whole contract was frustrated, since its main object, namely trading in timber, had become illegal. Hence the seller could not enforce the part of it that related to the letting **19–052**

---

[236] This is an alternative, and preferable, interpretation of the dictum in *AV Pound & Co Ltd v MW Hardy Inc*, cited at fn.231; the issue of frustration was specifically left open in that case. cf. *Benjamin's Sale of Goods,* 10th edn (2017), paras 18–377.

[237] See para.19–103 and following.

[238] *Peter Cassidy Seed Co Ltd v Osuustukkukaupa Ltd* [1957] 1 W.L.R. 273; *Pagnan Spa v Tradax Ocean Transport SA* [1987] 3 All E.R. 565; cf. *Congimex Companhia Geral, etc., SARL v Tradax Export SA* [1983] 1 Lloyd's Rep. 250.

[239] *The Playa Larga* [1983] 2 Lloyd's Rep. 171 at 191.

[240] *Walton (Grain and Shipping) Ltd v British Italian Trading Co* [1959] 1 Lloyd's Rep. 223 at 226; *Johnson Matthey Bankers Ltd v State Trading Co of India* [1984] 1 Lloyd's Rep. 427 at 434.

[241] cf. the example given in *C Czarnikow Ltd v Centrala Handlu Zagranicznego "Rolimpex"* [1979] A.C. 351 at 372 (dog and television licences); *Johnson Matthey Bankers Ltd v State Trading Corp of India* [1984] 1 Lloyd's Rep. 427 at 429; contrast *Atisa SA v Aztec AG* [1983] 2 Lloyd's Rep. 579 (where the foreign government simply broke its contract to supply the seller).

[242] This was assumed in *Maritime National Fish Ltd v Ocean Trawlers Ltd* [1935] A.C. 524 (where the plea of frustration failed for reasons discussed at para.19–094); cf. also *Walton (Grain and Shipping) Ltd v British Trading Co* [1959] 1 Lloyd's Rep. 223 at 236 (where the seller was excused by a force majeure clause); *Congimex SARL (Lisbon) v Continental Grain Export Corp (New York)* [1979] 2 Lloyd's Rep. 386; *Nile Co for the Export of Agricultural Produce v H & JM Bennett (Commodities) Ltd* [1986] 1 Lloyd's Rep. 555 at 581–582.

[243] See para.19–011.

[244] *Denny, Mott & Dickson v James B Fraser & Co Ltd* [1944] A.C. 265; cf. *Nile Co for the Export of Agricultural Crops v H & JM Bennett (Commodities) Ltd* [1986] 1 Lloyd's Rep. 555 at 581 (foreign government imposing change on method of payment).

of the yard. But in *Cricklewood Property Investment Trust Ltd v Leighton's Investment Trust Ltd*[245] temporary wartime restrictions on building did not frustrate a 99-year building lease; for the illegality did not destroy the main object of the lease as there would probably be ample time for building after the wartime restrictions were removed.

19–053 **Whether non-performance excused.** The second question is whether illegality which does not frustrate the contract but affects only some subsidiary obligation excuses non-performance of that obligation. On principle it should have this effect. For example, a charterparty might provide that a ship should call at 10 ports. If one of them became an enemy port, the shipowner could hardly be made liable for failing to call there, even if it were physically possible for him to do so.[246] Where temporary illegality does not discharge the contract,[247] it has similarly been held to provide an excuse for non-performance for so long as the prohibition lasted.[248] But in *Eyre v Johnson*[249] a tenant was held liable in damages for breach of his covenant to repair even though wartime regulations made it illegal for him to do the work. The better view, however, is that the tenant ought not to be held liable for refusing to do an act which subsequent legislation has made illegal. Though the lease as a whole is not frustrated, the illegality should provide the tenant with an excuse for non-performance of the part that has become illegal.[250]

## (d) Prospective frustration

19–054 **General rule: frustration assessed at time of event.** A claim that a contract has been discharged may be made before there actually *has* been any (or any sufficiently serious) interference with performance, on the ground that supervening events have made it highly probable that there *will* be such interference. The general rule is that the effect of those events must then be determined, not by waiting to see how they actually affect performance, but by reference to the time when they occur. The point is well illustrated by *Embiricos v Sydney Reid & Co*[251] where a Greek ship had been chartered for a voyage involving passage of the Dardanelles. On the outbreak of war between Greece and Turkey, it was held

---

[245] [1945] A.C. 221; cf. *Islamic Republic of Iran Shipping Lines v Steamship Mutual Underwriting Association (Bermuda) Ltd* [2010] EWHC 2661 (Comm); [2011] 1 Lloyd's Rep. 195 (order preventing continuation of insurance cover allowed for temporary continuation of limited cover which was held still to be in force when the relevant insured event occurred).

[246] cf. *Hindley & Co Ltd v General Fibre Co Ltd* [1940] 2 K.B. 517.

[247] As in *Cricklewood Property Investment Trust Ltd v Leighton's Investment Trust Ltd* [1945] A.C. 221, at fn.245.

[248] *Libyan Arab Foreign Bank v Bankers Trust Co* [1989] Q.B. 728 at 772 ("suspended but not discharged"); cf. *John Lewis Properties v Viscount Chelsea* [1993] 2 E.G.L.R. 77 (where it was not necessary to distinguish between impossibility and illegality).

[249] [1946] K.B. 481.

[250] *Cricklewood Property Investment Trust Ltd v Leighton's Investment Trust Ltd* [1945] A.C. 221 at 233, 244; *Sturcke v S W Edwards Ltd* (1971) 23 P. & C.R. 185 at 190; cf. *Brewster v Kitchell* (1691) 1 Salk. 198 ("the statute repeals the covenant"); *Grimsdick v Sweetman* [1909] 2 K.B. 740.

[251] [1914] 3 K.B. 45; so far as contra, *Andrew Millar v Taylor & Co Ltd* [1916] 1 K.B. 402 is criticised in *Watts, Watts & Co Ltd v Mitsui & Co Ltd* [1917] 2 A.C. 227 at 245.

that the charterer was justified in treating the contract as frustrated, even though later the Turkish authorities unexpectedly announced that Greek ships were to be allowed through the straits during an "escape period" which would have made performance of the contract voyage possible. Similarly, where requisition interferes with performance of a charterparty, the question whether it frustrates the contract is to be determined by reference to the time of requisition.[252] The reason for the rule is that rights should not be left indefinitely in suspense.[253]

**Qualifications to the general rule.** The general rule is based on the assumption that the event is of such a kind that a reasonable view of its probable effect on the contract can be taken as soon as it occurs. Where this cannot be done, because the event is one which may equally well cause slight or serious interference with performance, the rule is necessarily subject to some qualification. This is, for example, the position where a strike of dockworkers interferes with performance of a charterparty.[254] The contract is not frustrated at once, as soon as the strike begins. It is "necessary to wait upon events"[255]—not, indeed, until the strike is over,[256] but until it has gone on for so long that a reasonable person would conclude that it was likely to interfere fundamentally with performance. This test determines not only the question whether the contract is frustrated, but also the date of frustration. The point arose in a number of cases in which ships which had been time-chartered were detained in the Shatt al Arab in the course of the Gulf War between Iran and Iraq.[257] That war is generally regarded as having begun on 22 September 1980; but at that time commercial opinion was that the war would soon be brought to an end and that foreign vessels would be speedily released. Later events falsified these forecasts and there was no doubt that the length of the detention which occurred was sufficient to frustrate the charterparties. But it was held that the contracts could be frustrated before the detention had *actually* gone on for this length of time, and that they were frustrated as soon as "a sensible prognosis of the commercial probabilities"[258] could be made that the delay *would* continue for so long as to prevent the resumption of substantial services under the charterparties.[259] Similarly, where an employee suffered from a heart attack, his 19–055

[252] *Bank Line Ltd v Arthur Capel & Co* [1919] A.C. 435; cf. also *National Carriers Ltd v Panalpina (Northern) Ltd* [1981] A.C. 675 at 706; *Wong Lai Ying v Chinachem Investment Co* (1979) 13 Build. L.R. 81.

[253] *Bank Line Ltd v Arthur Capel & Co* [1919] A.C. 435 at 454; cf. *Embiricos v Sydney Reid & Co* [1914] 3 K.B. 45 at 54, quoted in para.17–090, at fn.414; *Total Gas Marketing Ltd v Arco British Ltd* [1998] 2 Lloyd's Rep. 209 at 222.

[254] As in *The Nema* [1982] A.C. 724.

[255] *The Nema* [1982] A.C. 724 at 753.

[256] *The Nema* [1982] A.C. 724 at 753 ("businessmen must not be required to await events too long"); cf. *Chakki v United Yeast Ltd* [1982] I.C.R. 140.

[257] *The Evia (No.2)* [1983] 1 A.C. 736; *The Wenjiang (No.2)* [1983] 1 Lloyd's Rep. 400; *The Chrysalis* [1983] 1 W.L.R. 1469.

[258] *The Evia (No.2)* [1982] 1 Lloyd's Rep. 334 at 346; affirmed [1983] 1 A.C. 736; *The Wenjiang (No.2)* [1983] 1 Lloyd's Rep. 400 at 408; cf. *The Adelfa* [1988] 2 Lloyd's Rep. 466 (delay in unloading due to arrest of ship).

[259] Commercial arbitrators had fixed the date of frustration as 4 October 1980 in *The Evia (No.2)* [1982] 1 Lloyd's Rep. 334, and as 24 November 1980 in *The Wenjiang (No.2)*[1983] 1 Lloyd's Rep.

contract of employment was not discharged at once, but only when the effects of his heart attack could be assessed and "both sides accepted that … [he] was not going to work again".[260]

## (e) Alternative obligations

19–056 **General rule: no frustration if alternative performance possible.** A contract is said to impose an alternative obligation when it gives a party the right to choose between two or more specified performances (e.g. to deliver X or Y) or between two or more specified ways of rendering performance (e.g. to deliver X on any day in October).[261] The power of selection between the alternatives may be given to either party, e.g. a contract providing for goods to be delivered during a specified month, or at a range of ports, may give the power to choose the date or place of delivery or shipment to either seller[262] or buyer.[263] The general rule is that if a supervening event makes one of such alternative performances impossible or illegal, the contract is not discharged so long as another remains possible and lawful.[264] For example, if a contract is to deliver goods at X or Y, delivery must be made at X if delivery at Y has become impossible; if shipment is to be made from X or Y, shipment must be made from X if shipment from Y has become impossible.[265] The general rule, and the qualifications of it to be discussed below, apply not only where the contract is alleged to have been frustrated, but also where a party relies on the supervening event as providing him with an excuse under an express term of the contract, such as a force majeure clause.[266]

19–057 **Exceptions.** The general rule can be excluded by an express provision in the contract, e.g. by a strike clause which on its true construction excuses a seller if the port from which he intended to ship becomes strikebound, even though shipment from other ports within the contractual range remains possible.[267] Nor does the general rule apply where the contract calls for performance X and gives the party who is to render it a liberty to substitute Y, e.g. where a charterparty names ship X as its subject-matter but entitles the shipowner to substitute another ship. Under such a contract, X is due unless the liberty to substitute another ship

400 and in *The Chrysalis* [1983] 1 W.L.R. 1469. The courts expressed no opinion of their own as to the dates of frustration, merely holding that the arbitrators had applied the correct principle of law in fixing those dates.

[260] *Notcutt v Universal Equipment Co (London) Ltd* [1986] 1 W.L.R. 641 at 644.

[261] e.g. *Ross T Smyth & Co (Liverpool) v WN Lindsay (Leith)* [1953] 1 W.L.R. 1280 at 1283.

[262] *Ross T Smyth & Co (Liverpool) v WN Lindsay (Leith)* [1953] 1 W.L.R. 1280 at 1283.

[263] e.g. *David T Boyd & Co Ltd v Louis Louca* [1973] 1 Lloyd's Rep. 209 (where no issue of discharge arose).

[264] *Barkworth v Young* (1856) 1 Drew. 1 at 25; *Reardon Smith Line Ltd v Ministry of Agriculture Fisheries and Food* [1963] A.C. 691 at 730; cf. *The Super Servant Two* [1989] 1 Lloyd's Rep. 148 at 157; affirmed [1990] 1 Lloyd's Rep. 1; for further difficulties arising from this case, see para.19–095.

[265] *The Furness Bridge* [1977] 2 Lloyd's Rep. 367; cf. *Warinco AG v Fritz Mauthner* [1978] 1 Lloyd's Rep. 151; *The Safeer* [1994] 1 Lloyd's Rep. 637 at 642.

[266] See para.19–037; cf. *Warinco AG v Fritz Mauthner* [1978] 1 Lloyd's Rep. 151.

[267] *Sociedad Iberica de Molturacion SA v Tradax Export SA* [1978] 2 Lloyd's Rep. 545.

(Y) is exercised,[268] while in the case of a true alternative obligation one cannot at the time of contracting tell whether X or Y is due. Hence, in the case of a liberty to substitute, the destruction of X before Y had been substituted, or the destruction of Y after the substitution had been made, would discharge the contract.[269] The distinction is further illustrated by contrasting a case in which a charterparty required the charterer to load a cargo of wheat, and gave him an "option" of instead loading rye,[270] with one in which a charterparty required the charterer to load a cargo of wheat or rye.[271] A contract of the first kind is sometimes said to confer a "contractual option" while one of the second kind is said to give rise to a "performance option".[272] Whatever terminology may be used to express the distinction, its effect (in the context of frustration) is clear. Supervening impossibility of loading wheat will discharge the contract in the first case (if the option to load rye has not been exercised when it became impossible to load wheat);[273] but it will not have this effect in the second case even if the charterer has indicated that he intends to load wheat.[274]

**Alternative obligation distinguished from contingent obligation.** An alternative obligation must also be distinguished from a contingent obligation, i.e. from one to do X but, if X is not done, to do Y.[275] Under such a contract, the primary obligation is to do X[276] and Y becomes due only if X is not performed and without any notice of election on the debtor's part.[277] Clearly the obligation to do X is not affected if it becomes impossible to do Y. Whether supervening impossibility of doing X is a ground of discharge depends on the construction of the contract: the contract would be discharged if it meant that Y was to become due if the debtor in *breach of contract* failed to do X, but not if it meant that Y was to become due if *for any reason* X was not done. **19–058**

[268] *The Marine Star* [1993] 1 Lloyd's Rep. 329; *The Fjord Wind* [1999] 1 Lloyd's Rep. 307 at 328; affirmed [2000] 2 Lloyd's Rep. 191.
[269] See *The Badagry* [1985] 1 Lloyd's Rep. 395.
[270] *Reardon Smith Line Ltd v Ministry of Agriculture Fisheries and Food* [1963] A.C. 691.
[271] *Brightman & Co v Bunge y Born Limitada Sociedad* [1924] 2 K.B. 619; affirmed on another ground [1925] A.C. 799.
[272] *The Didymi and the Leon* [1984] 1 Lloyd's Rep. 583 at 587, per Sir John Donaldson MR. A contractual term may also impose an *obligation* on one party to notify the other as to the way in, or time at, which performance is to be required. Such a term is distinct from one merely giving the former party an *option*: see *Universal Bulk Carriers Ltd v André & Cie* [2001] EWCA Civ 588; [2001] 2 Lloyd's Rep. 65 at [17].
[273] This follows from the reasoning of *Reardon Smith Line Ltd v Ministry of Agriculture Fisheries and Food* [1963] A.C. 691.
[274] *Brightman & Co v Bunge y Born Limitada Sociedad* [1924] 2 K.B. 619 at 637; cf. at 630.
[275] See *Deverill v Burnell* (1873) L.R. 8 C.P. 475.
[276] In this respect it differs from a "performance option" (at fn.272).
[277] In this respect it differs from a "contractual option" (at fn.272).

## (f) Events affecting only one party's performance

19–059 **Both parties are discharged.** In *Taylor v Caldwell*[278] the court was directly concerned only with the liability of the defendants, the performance of whose obligation to supply the music hall was made impossible by the fire. Yet the court clearly regarded the hirers as also having been discharged,[279] even though their principal obligation (to pay the agreed hire) had in no way become impossible. This is a common situation: in a typical bilateral contract one party undertakes to perform some act or abstention, while the other undertakes to pay for it. Supervening impossibility normally affects only the former undertaking (though illegality may affect either or both).[280] This fact was at one time thought to support the view that a time charter could not be frustrated by the unavailability of the ship: "if the shipowner's object is to receive the chartered hire … he does not care how much the charterer's adventures are frustrated, so long as he is able to pay".[281] But the argument was rejected on the ground that the "common object"[282] of the parties was frustrated; for even the owner's object "is not only to get hire but to afford services".[283] The "common object" in all these cases is the *exchange* of the services or facilities to be provided by one party for the payment to be made by the other. The same reasoning applies to cases of frustration of purpose. In *Krell v Henry*[284] the common object of the parties was the provision of facilities for seeing the coronation processions: this was what one party intended to sell and the other to buy. It made no difference that the one expected to benefit by receiving a sum of money and the other by seeing the processions. Hence both parties are discharged even though the supervening event affects only the performance of one.

## (g) Special factors affecting land

### *(i) Leases*

19–060 **Frustration does apply to a lease of land.** It was formerly thought that a lease of land could not be frustrated[285] because, in giving the tenant the right to exclusive possession for the specified time, it created a legal estate in the land. This estate was regarded as the subject-matter of the contract and survived even if later events prevented the tenant from making any use of the premises. But the commercial reality is that, generally, the tenant bargains for use and occupation

---

[278] (1863) 3 B. & S. 826; para.19–003.
[279] *Taylor v Caldwell* (1863) 3 B. & S. 826 at 840 ("both parties are excused").
[280] cf. *Libyan Arab Foreign Bank v Bankers Trust Co* [1989] Q.B. 728 at 749, recognising that "an obligation to pay money can be frustrated" by illegality.
[281] *Bank Line Ltd v Arthur Capel & Co* [1919] A.C. 435 at 452.
[282] *Hirji Mulji v Cheong Yue SS Co Ltd* [1926] A.C. 497 at 507; contrast *Scanlan's New Neon v Toohey's Ltd* (1943) 67 C.L.R. 169 at 196–197.
[283] *Bank Line Ltd v Arthur Capel & Co Ltd* [1919] A.C. 435 at 453.
[284] [1903] 2 K.B. 740; paras 19–004, 19–043.
[285] See the authorities cited in fnn.293–298.

and not simply for a legal estate; and in *National Carriers Ltd v Panalpina* (*Northern*) *Ltd*[286] the House of Lords held that the doctrine of frustration could apply to leases of land.

**Frustration a rare event.** In the *National Carriers* case the House of Lords emphasised that the frustration of a lease will be a very rare event.[287] One reason for this is that a lease for a long period of years is in the nature of a long-term speculation. Such a transaction is hard to frustrate since the parties must contemplate that circumstances may change radically during its currency, and so to a large extent take the risk of supervening events.[288] Nor would interruption of enjoyment which was likely to last for only a few years frustrate a lease for a long term, such as 99 years, since the ratio of the interruption to the whole would be too small.[289] Even the physical destruction of the premises would not usually frustrate since it would normally be covered by express provisions[290] in the lease, such as covenants to repair and to keep the premises insured. A further reason why frustration of leases is uncommon is that to hold a long-term lease frustrated by the destruction of the buildings on the land could, paradoxically, operate to the prejudice of *tenants*, especially in a period of rising land values. Frustration operates automatically,[291] so that its effect, in the case put, would be to deprive the tenant of a valuable site long before the end of the agreed term. 19–061

For these reasons, the House of Lords in the *National Carriers*[292] case did not disapprove any of the earlier decisions to the extent that they held that the leases in question *were not* frustrated.[293] In those cases it had been held that the leases were not discharged by the destruction of the premises by enemy action;[294] by the requisitioning of the premises;[295] by wartime legislation which prevented the tenant from residing on the premises[296] or from developing the land;[297] or by the death of the tenant of furnished rooms.[298] In the *National Carriers* case itself a tenant claimed that a 10-year lease of a warehouse had been frustrated when, four-and-a-half years before the end of the term, the only access road to the premises had been closed by the local authority and had remained closed for 20

---

[286] [1981] A.C. 675.
[287] *National Carriers Ltd v Panalpina* (*Northern*) *Ltd* [1981] A.C. 675 at 692, 697.
[288] cf. para.19–072.
[289] cf. para.19–022.
[290] cf. para.19–073.
[291] See para.19–097.
[292] *National Carriers Ltd v Panalpina* (*Northern*) *Ltd* [1981] A.C. 675.
[293] Though see *National Carriers Ltd v Panalpina* (*Northern*) *Ltd* [1981] A.C. 675 at 715; *Matthey v Curling* [1922] 2 A.C. 180 was described as "a singularly harsh decision from the tenant's point of view."
[294] *Redmond v Dainton* [1920] 2 K.B. 256; *Denman v Brise* [1949] 1 K.B. 22; *Cusack-Smith v London Corp* [1956] 1 W.L.R. 1368.
[295] *Whitehall Court Ltd v Ettlinger* [1920] 1 K.B. 680; *Matthey v Curling* [1922] 2 A.C. 180; *Swift v Macbean* [1942] 1 K.B. 375.
[296] *London & Northern Estates Ltd v Schlesinger* [1916] 1 K.B. 20.
[297] *Cricklewood Property and Investment Trust Ltd v Leighton's Investment Trust Ltd* [1945] A.C. 221.
[298] *Youngmin v Heath* [1974] 1 W.L.R. 135.

months. The claim was rejected on the ground that the interruption was not sufficiently serious to bring about frustration.[299]

19–062 **Short-term leases.** The doctrine of frustration is most likely to apply where the lease is a short-term one for a particular purpose, e.g. where a holiday cottage which has been rented for a month is burnt down without the fault of either party. Similarly, the contracts in cases like *Taylor v Caldwell*[300] and *Krell v Henry*[301] could be frustrated, even if the transactions were expressed as leases and not (as they actually were) as licences.[302] A lease could also be frustrated if "some vast convulsion of nature swallowed up the property altogether, or buried it in the depths of the sea"; or if, in the case of a building lease, "legislation were subsequently passed which permanently prohibited private building in the area or dedicated it as an open space for ever".[303]

19–063 **Agreement for a lease.** The doctrine of frustration can apply to an agreement for a lease, no less than to an executed lease.[304]

19–064 **Excuse for non-performance.** Even where the lease is not frustrated, supervening events can nevertheless provide a party with an excuse for not performing a particular obligation imposed by the lease. In *Baily v De Crespigny*[305] a landlord covenanted that neither he nor his assigns would permit building on a paddock adjoining the land let. The paddock was then compulsorily acquired by a railway company, which built a station on it. It was held that the landlord was not liable in damages for breach of his covenant, first because on the true construction of the covenant "assigns" did not include assigns by compulsion of law, and secondly because it was impossible for him to secure performance of the covenant.[306] Similarly, a tenant who covenanted to build would not be liable in damages if wartime conditions or legislation made building impossible or illegal.[307]

---

[299] cf. para.19–005.

[300] (1863) 3 B. & S. 826; para.19–003.

[301] [1903] 2 K.B. 740; paras 19–004, 19–043.

[302] *Tay Salmon Fisheries Co v Speedie* 1929 S.C. 593 (lease of a salmon fishery held to be frustrated when construction of a nearby bombing range prevented the tenant from using the fishery).

[303] *Cricklewood Property and Investment Trust Ltd v Leighton's Investment Trust Ltd* [1945] A.C. 221 at 229; cf. at 245.

[304] *Denny, Mott & Dickson v James B Fraser & Co Ltd* [1944] A.C. 265 (a decision not confined to Scots Law: see *National Carriers Ltd v Panalpina (Northern) Ltd* [1981] A.C. 675 at 704); *Rom Securities Ltd v Rogers (Holdings) Ltd* (1968) 205 E.G. 427; cf. *Property Discount Corp Ltd v Lyon Group Ltd* [1981] 1 W.L.R. 300 at 305.

[305] (1869) L.R. 4 Q.B. 180.

[306] The actual decision seems to be very unjust. The landlord presumably got compensation from the railway company and was able to keep this for himself though the tenant's interests were prejudiced by the erection of the station.

[307] *Cricklewood Property and Investment Trust Ltd v Leighton's Investment Trust Ltd* [1945] A.C. 221 at 233; *Eyre v Johnson* [1946] K.B. 481, contra, is doubted at para.19–053.

### *(ii) Sale of land*

**General rule as to risk.** The doctrine of frustration applies to contracts for the sale of land,[308] but its operation in relation to such contracts is restricted by the rule that under such a contract risk of loss passes[309] (unless otherwise agreed) as soon as the contract is made. It follows that the contract is not frustrated if the house or buildings on the land (for the sake of which it was bought) are destroyed or seriously damaged between contract and completion.[310] 19–065

**Express contractual provision.** The rule just mentioned promotes certainty by making it unnecessary to ask whether partial destruction is sufficiently serious to bring about frustration. On the other hand, it can cause hardship to the purchaser by making him bear the risk of losses occurring before he has possession and hence before he can take steps to safeguard the property. This hardship can be mitigated by the fact that the purchaser has the benefit of the vendor's insurance;[311] but as he cannot be sure of the adequacy of this insurance he would normally need to take out his own insurance as soon as contracts were exchanged. This position could lead to double insurance and hence to a windfall for insurers. The parties can, however, agree to provisions which deal expressly with the passing of risk and the obligation to insure. 19–066

**Sale of land with buildings to be constructed.** The rule that risk passes on contract applies where the land is sold with buildings already on it. Where a developer sells land with a house *to be built* on it, the risk *of the work* remains (unless otherwise agreed) on the vendor until the work is completed, in accordance with the rules applicable to building contracts.[312] Hence destruction of the partly completed building does not frustrate the contract and the vendor must do the work again at no extra cost. But the contract may be frustrated on other grounds. Thus where a landslip not only destroyed a partly completed block of flats, but also delayed the construction work for two-and-a-half years, it was held that a contract for the sale of one of the flats was frustrated *by the delay*; for in the interval market conditions had changed to such an extent as to make performance at the end of the delay radically different from that originally undertaken.[313] 19–067

**The effect of a compulsory purchase order.** Specific performance of a contract for the sale of land can be ordered against the purchaser even though, after contract, a compulsory purchase order is made in respect of the land.[314] The 19–068

308 This is assumed in *Amalgamated Investment and Property Co Ltd v John Walker & Co Ltd* [1977] 1 W.L.R. 164, where, for reasons stated at para.19–044, the contract was not frustrated.

309 See para.19–013.

310 *Paine v Meller* (1801) 6 Ves. 349; *E Johnson & Co (Barbados) Ltd v NSR Ltd* [1997] A.C. 400 at 406.

311 Law of Property Act 1925 s.47 (para.14–141, at fn.801).

312 See para.19–015.

313 *Wong Lai Ying v Chinachem Investment Co* (1979) 13 Build. L.R. 81.

314 *Hillingdon Estates Co v Stonefield Estate Co* [1952] Ch. 627. The mere making of such an order does not affect ownership of the land.

contract is not frustrated because the risk of compulsory acquisition is on the purchaser from the time of the contract;[315] and because the court's order will result in the conveyance of the land to him, against payment of the price, so that he will in due course get the compensation payable by the acquiring authority. Where, in pursuance of the compulsory acquisition order, the land is taken over by the acquiring authority *after* completion has become due, but before the hearing, the court will not order *specific* performance, since it cannot order the vendor to convey, but the contract is not frustrated, so that the purchaser's failure to complete on the due day is a breach for which he is liable in damages.[316] The position is different where the land is sold with vacant possession and is actually requisitioned *before* completion is due. In such a case it has been held, not only that the vendor cannot specifically enforce the contract[317] (since he cannot perform his obligation to give possession on the due date), but also that the purchaser can get back his deposit.[318] It must follow from this reasoning that the purchaser will not be liable in damages.

### (h) A question of fact or law?

19–069 The question whether frustration is a matter of fact or law used to be important in determining the respective functions of judge and jury. Trial by jury is now rare in civil cases; but the question whether frustration is a matter of fact or law is still important in determining whether a court can control an arbitrator's finding. Such a finding is generally conclusive on matters of fact,[319] but does not bind the court when determining appeals from arbitrators on points of law.

19–070 **A question of law, or of mixed law and fact.** The point is illustrated by the Suez cases where such questions as the greater length and cost of a voyage round the Cape of Good Hope and its physical effect on the ship or the goods were clearly questions of fact. In the *Tsakiroglou* case[320] the arbitrator found, in general terms, that performance of the contract by shipping via the Cape was "not commercially or fundamentally different from" performance by shipping via Suez. The House of Lords agreed with this finding, but added that it did not bind the court as the question whether the difference was fundamental was one of law,[321] or one of mixed law and fact.[322]

19–071 **Limits of review by the courts.** It does not follow from the description of the issue of frustration as one of law that the court will substitute its own view for

[315] See para.19–065.
[316] *E Johnson Co (Barbados) Ltd v NSR Ltd* [1997] A.C. 400.
[317] *Cook v Taylor* [1942] Ch. 349.
[318] *James Macara Ltd v Barclays Bank Ltd* [1945] K.B. 148.
[319] See, e.g. *Universal Petroleum Co Ltd v Handels und Transport Gesellschaft mbH* [1987] 1 Lloyd's Rep. 517.
[320] *Tsakiroglou & Co v Noblee Thorl GmbH* [1962] A.C. 93.
[321] cf. *Re Comptoir Commercial Anversois and John Power Sons & Co* [1920] 1 K.B. 868; *The Captain George K* [1970] 2 Lloyd's Rep. 21; *The Wenjiang (No.2)* [1983] 1 Lloyd's Rep. 400 at 402.
[322] *Tsakiroglou & Co v Noblee Thorl GmbH* [1962] A.C. 93 at 116 and 123; *The Chrysalis* [1983] 1 W.L.R. 1469 at 1475.

that taken by an arbitrator merely because it disagrees with his conclusion. It will do so only if the arbitrator has applied the wrong legal test or, while purporting to apply the correct test, has reached a conclusion which no reasonable person would have reached on the primary facts as found.[323] That said, the issue of frustration arises in "a wide range of different factual circumstances" ranging from those which call for "the evaluation of a range of factors which a commercial tribunal is particularly well equipped to undertake" to those which call for "the application of established principles to a clearly defined event rendering performance impossible".[324] In the case of the latter, the court must accept the findings of fact made by the arbitrators, but need not "be unduly inhibited by the arbitrators' conclusion that the facts they have found are sufficient to satisfy the legal test for frustration".[325]

## 3. LIMITATIONS

Even if an event occurs which would normally frustrate a contract under the rules so far considered, the doctrine of frustration may be excluded if the contract provides for the event; if the event was foreseen or foreseeable; or if it was due to the "fault" of one of the parties. **19–072**

### (a) Contractual provision for the event

In this part, our principal concern is with cases where the contract would otherwise be frustrated, but this is expressly, or impliedly excluded by a provision of the contract.[326] We shall, however, also consider the converse situation where the parties may agree that the contract shall be treated *as if* it is frustrated in circumstances where this would not be the case under the general law.[327] **19–073**

#### *(i) In general*

**Express exclusion of frustration.** The object of the doctrine of frustration is to find a satisfactory way of allocating the risk of supervening events. There is, however, nothing to prevent the parties from making their own provisions for this purpose. Thus they can expressly provide that the risk of supervening events shall be borne by one of them and not by the other[328] or they can apportion it or deal with it in various other ways.[329] Such provisions exclude frustration;[330] and the **19–074**

---

323 *The Nema* [1982] A.C. 724 (disapproving on this point *The Angelia* [1973] 1 W.L.R. 210); *The Wenjiang (No.2)* [1983] 1 Lloyd's Rep. 400; *The Chrysalis* [1983] 1 W.L.R. 1469 at 1475; *The Safeer* [1994] 1 Lloyd's Rep. 637.

324 *The Mary Nour* [2008] EWCA Civ 856; [2008] 2 Lloyd's Rep. 526 at [11]. *The Nema* [1982] A.C. 724 is cited as a prime example of the former category; *The Mary Nour* itself (see para.19–027 fn.105) is regarded as an example of the latter.

325 *The Mary Nour* [2008] EWCA Civ 856; [2008] 2 Lloyd's Rep. 526 at [11].

326 See paras 19–074—19–078.

327 See paras 19–079—19–082.

328 *Budgett v Binnington & Co* [1891] 1 Q.B. 35 at 41; *Thiis v Byers* (1876) 1 Q.B.D. 244.

329 e.g. by provisions of the type mentioned at para.19–006, or by provisions for flexible pricing (para.19–038); as in *Wates Ltd v GLC* (1983) 25 Build. L.R. 1.

same is true of an express term which, though it does not precisely cover the supervening event, shows that the parties had contemplated it and allocated the risk of its occurrence.[331]

19–075 **Implied exclusion of frustration.** A provision that excludes frustration may also be implied, e.g. where the nature of the contract makes it clear that the parties intended the risk of supervening events to lie where it falls. In *Larrinaga & Co v Société Franco-Américaine des Phosphates de Médulla*[332] a contract was made in 1913 for the carriage of six cargoes of phosphates between March 1918 and November 1920. After the end of the First World War, the carriers argued that the contract was frustrated because of the altered shipping conditions then prevailing. The argument was rejected by the House of Lords. A contract of this kind, not to be performed for many years, was essentially speculative,[333] since each party had consciously taken the risk that conditions might alter. An implied agreement to exclude frustration may also be based on other characteristics of a transaction. In *The Maira (No.2)* agents had undertaken to manage a ship which was subsequently lost. It was held that this did not frustrate the management contract since the parties could hardly have intended "that the managers should be entitled to wash their hands of all duties concerning the vessel as soon as [it] was lost";[334] they would be expected to attend to such matters as the repatriation of the crew and the settlement of claims arising out of the loss.[335] Similarly, in *Bunge SA v Kyla Shipping Co Ltd*[336] the cost of repairing a chartered vessel exceeded its value once repaired, but the owners could not rely on this as frustrating the charterparty on the grounds of "commercial impossibility" because they had provided a continuing warranty that they would maintain insurance at a level which exceeded the cost of the repairs. According to Flaux J the effect of the warranty was that "the contract allocates to the owner the risk that if a casualty occurs, the vessel requires repair, where the cost of repair is within the insured value".[337] It is finally possible for legislation to provide for the implication of a term which excludes frustration.[338]

330 *Joseph Constantine SS Line Ltd v Imperial Smelting Corp Ltd* [1942] A.C. 154 at 163; *The Safeer* [1994] 1 Lloyd's Rep. 637.

331 *Bangladesh Export Import Co Ltd v Sucden Kerry SA* [1995] 2 Lloyd's Rep. 1; cf. *Select Commodities Ltd v Valdo SA* [2006] EWHC 1137 (Comm); [2007] 1 Lloyd's Rep. 1 (liberty clause in charterparty not found to exclude doctrine of frustration).

332 (1923) 92 L.J.K.B. 455.

333 cf. para.1–003.

334 *The Maira (No.2)* [1985] 1 Lloyd's Rep. 300 at 311; affirmed on other grounds [1986] 2 Lloyd's Rep. 12.

335 cf. *Armchair Answercall Ltd v People In Mind Ltd* [2016] EWCA Civ 1039 (contract for the management of a franchise business not frustrated when the franchisees terminated their franchise agreements).

336 [2012] EWHC 3522 (Comm); [2013] 1 Lloyd's Rep. 565.

337 *Bunge SA v Kyla Shipping Co Ltd* [2012] EWHC 3522 (Comm); [2013] 1 Lloyd's Rep. 565 at [79].

338 See Package Travel, Package Holidays and Package Tours Regulations 1992 (SI 1992/2388) reg.10(1).

### (ii) *Qualifications*

**Trading with the enemy.** A contract may be frustrated by supervening illegality on the ground that it involves trading with the enemy; and such frustration is not excluded by a contrary provision in the contract. In *Ertel Bieber & Co v Rio Tinto Co Ltd*[339] an English company contracted to deliver copper ore to a German company from 1911 to 1919. It was held that the contract was wholly frustrated on the outbreak of war in 1914 even though it provided that, in the event of war, certain obligations should only be suspended; for to give effect to this provision would, for reasons stated earlier in this chapter, be contrary to public policy.[340] The rule is based on the particular strength of the policy against giving aid to the economy of an enemy in time of war. It does not apply to express provisions which deal with other kinds of supervening illegality, such as prohibition of export. If, for example, a contract provides for a payment to be made in the event of such a prohibition,[341] or for suspension of the contract, followed by its termination if the prohibition is not lifted by the end of a specified period,[342] frustration is effectively excluded. Clauses of this kind are not contrary to public policy[343] since they assume that the prohibition is going to be observed, and since the continuation of the contractual relationship in cases of this kind does not have any tendency to subvert the purpose of the prohibition. 19–076

**Provisions narrowly construed.** A clause may be literally wide enough to cover the event, but be held on its true construction not to have this effect. In *Metropolitan Water Board v Dick, Kerr & Co*[344] contractors agreed in July 1914 to construct a reservoir in six years; in the event of delays "however occasioned", they were to be given an extension of time. In February 1916, the contractors were required by a Government Order to stop work, and to sell their plant. It was held that the contract was frustrated although the events which had happened were literally within the delay clause. That clause was meant to apply to temporary difficulties, such as labour shortages, bad weather, or failure of supplies. It did not: 19–077

> "cover the case in which the interruption is of such a character and duration that it vitally and fundamentally changes the conditions of the contract, and could not possibly have been in the contemplation of the parties to the contract when it was made".[345]

---

339 [1918] A.C. 260; such clauses may also be narrowly construed, so as not to refer to war between the countries to which the contracting parties belong: *Re Badische Co Ltd* [1921] 2 Ch. 331 at 379; cf. *Fibrosa Spolka Ackcyjna v Fairbairn, Lawson Combe Barbour Ltd* [1943] A.C. 32.

340 *Ertel Bieber & Co v Rio Tinto Co Ltd* [1918] A.C. 260 at 286; para.19–048.

341 e.g. *Johnson Matthey Bankers Ltd v State Trading Corp of India* [1984] 1 Lloyd's Rep. 427.

342 e.g. in *Tsakiroglou & Co v Noblee Thorl GmbH* [1962] A.C. 93 at 95.

343 *Johnson Matthey Bankers Ltd v State Trading Corp of India* [1984] 1 Lloyd's Rep. 427 at 434.

344 [1918] A.C. 119; *The Penelope* [1928] P. 180 (approved, though with some reservations, in *The Nema* [1982] A.C. 724 at 754); cf. *Fibrosa Spolka Ackcyjna v Fairbairn, Lawson Combe Barbour Ltd* [1943] A.C. 32 at 40; *C Czarnikow Ltd v Centrala Handlu Zagranicznego Rolimpex* [1979] A.C. 351; *Wong Lai Ying v Chinachem Investment Co* (1979) 13 Build. L.R. 81; *The Playa Larga* [1983] 2 Lloyd's Rep. 171 at 189; *Notcutt v Universal Equipment Co (London) Ltd* [1986] 1 W.L.R. 641 at 647; *FC Shepherd & Co Ltd v Jerrom* [1987] Q.B. 301.

345 *Metropolitan Water Board v Dick, Kerr & Co* [1918] A.C. 119 at 126.

A fortiori, an express provision in a contract for *some* events which might otherwise frustrate it does not exclude the possibility of frustration by *other* events.[346]

19–078 **Incomplete provision.** A clause may make some provision for the event which happens, but fail to make complete provision for it. In *Bank Line Ltd v Arthur Capel & Co*[347] a shipowner was sued for damages for failing to deliver a ship due under a charterparty. He pleaded that the contract was frustrated by the requisition of the ship. The charterer argued that frustration was excluded by two clauses giving him, but not the owner, the option to cancel if the ship was commandeered by the Government or if she was not delivered by 30 April 1915. But the House of Lords held that the charterparty was frustrated. Lord Sumner said that a contract could not be frustrated by a contingency for which it made "full and complete"[348] provision; but he added:

> "A contingency may be provided for, but not in such terms as to show that the provision is meant to be all the provision for it. A contingency may be provided for, but in such a way as shows that it is provided for only for the purpose of dealing with one of its effects and not with all".[349]

Requisition or delay might frustrate the charterparty, but would not necessarily have this effect, e.g. if performance were only delayed by one week. The cancelling clauses entitled the charterer to cancel even if the contract was *not* frustrated. He could *escape* liability in that event. It did not follow that the shipowner should *remain* liable if requisition or delay did amount to frustration.

This principle is further illustrated by *Jackson v Union Marine Ins Co*[350] where a charterparty provided that the ship should proceed with all possible dispatch (dangers and accidents of navigation excepted) to Newport. On the way there she was so badly damaged that she was not ready for service for eight months. The charterparty was held to be frustrated in spite of the provision excepting dangers and accidents of navigation. One possible explanation is that these words were not intended to cover so long a delay as had actually occurred.[351] But the reason given by the court was that the words of the exception "excuse the shipowner, but give him no right".[352] A delay caused by dangers and accidents of navigation might (but for the exception) have amounted either to a breach or to a frustrating event. The effect of the exception was to prevent the delay from constituting a breach. It did not deal with the effect of such delay as a possible frustrating event, and thus did not rule out frustration. To say that the

---

346 *Intertradex SA v Lesieur-Torteaux SARL* [1978] 2 Lloyd's Rep. 509 at 515.

347 [1919] A.C. 435; cf. *BP Exploration (Libya) Ltd v Hunt* [1979] 1 W.L.R. 783 at 830; affirmed [1983] 2 A.C. 352; *The Evia* [1982] 1 Lloyd's Rep. 334; affirmed [1983] 1 A.C. 736 at 767.

348 *Bank Line Ltd v Arthur Capel & Co* [1919] A.C. 435 at 455.

349 *Bank Line Ltd v Arthur Capel & Co* [1919] A.C. 435 at 456.

350 (1874) L.R. 10 C.P. 125.

351 *Sir Lindsay Parkinson & Co Ltd v Commissioners of Works* [1949] 2 K.B. 632 at 665.

352 *Jackson v Union Marine Ins Co* (1874) L.R. 10 C.P. 125 at 144; cf. *Blane Steamships Ltd v Minister of Transport* [1951] 2 K.B. 965, where the words of the charterparty excused the charterer but were held to give him no rights.

shipowner is not liable for a delay does not lead necessarily to the conclusion that he can enforce the contract in spite of the delay.

### *(iii) Provision for non-frustrating events*

**Force majeure clauses.** In its practical operation, the doctrine of frustration can give rise to two problems. It can be a source of *uncertainty* because it is often hard to tell whether the effect of supervening events on the contract is indeed sufficiently serious to discharge it. And it can be a source of *hardship* because, as a result of its narrow scope, a party may remain bound by a contract in spite of the fact that supervening events have made it substantially more burdensome or less beneficial than he could reasonably have expected. To avoid these difficulties, the contract may include a "force majeure" clause which provides for discharge on the occurrence of specified events usually described as being "beyond the control" of the parties, or of one of them. The concept of something beyond a person's control sets a "comparatively high hurdle"[353] and a force majeure clause is normally construed so as to protect the party relying on it only if he has taken all reasonable steps to avoid the operation of the event, or to mitigate its results.[354] 19–079

**A question of construction.** A "force majeure" provision may take effect whether or not the event is such as to frustrate the contract under the general law. It may either give one of the parties the option to cancel the contract,[355] or provide for its automatic determination.[356] A clause of the latter kind has been described as a "contractual frustration clause".[357] The point of this description is, however, simply that the *effect* of the clause resembles that of frustration, in giving rise to automatic discharge.[358] The question *whether* the clause operates in the events which have happened depends simply on its construction[359] and not on the tests of frustration developed by the general law. If the clause does come into operation, the contract is discharged under one of its express terms and not under the general doctrine of frustration.[360] As a consequence, the Law Reform (Frustrated Contracts) Act 1943 will not apply.[361] 19–080

---

353 *Great Elephant Corp v Trafigura Beheer BV* [2013] EWCA Civ 905; [2014] 1 Lloyd's Rep. 1 at [25].

354 *Channel Island Ferries Ltd v Sealink UK Ltd* [1988] 1 Lloyd's Rep. 323; *The Kriti Rex* [1996] 2 Lloyd's Rep. 171 at 196; contrast (on the point of construction) *The Marine Star (No.2)* [1996] 2 Lloyd's Rep. 383.

355 e.g. *Bank Line Ltd v Arthur Capel & Co* [1919] A.C. 435.

356 e.g. in *Tsakiroglou & Co v Noblee Thorl GmbH* [1962] A.C. 93 at 95.

357 *Bremer Handelsgesellschaft mbH v Vanden Avenne-Izegem PVBA* [1978] 2 Lloyd's Rep. 109 at 112.

358 See para.19–097.

359 See, e.g. *Hoecheong Products Ltd v Cargill Hong Kong Ltd* [1995] 1 Lloyd's Rep. 584; *The Kriti Rex* [1996] 2 Lloyd's Rep. 171. As an exceptions clause it may have to be construed *contra proferentem* (see para.7–009): *Great Elephant Corp v Trafigura Beheer BV* [2013] EWCA Civ 905; [2014] 1 Lloyd's Rep. 1 at [25].

360 *Agrokor AG v Tradigrain SA* [2000] 1 Lloyd's Rep. 497 at 504.

361 See para.19-103.

19–081 **"Contractual frustration clause", or "exceptions clause"?** A "contractual frustration clause" under which the contract is discharged should be distinguished from what is sometimes referred to as an "exceptions clause" under which the contract is not discharged, but the parties may be relieved from liability in certain specified events, often also described as being beyond their control. One potential significance of this distinction[362] is that a party may be able to rely on the former without having to prove that, but for the event in question, he would have been able to perform. In *Classic Maritime Inc v Limbungan Makmur SDN BHD*[363] a charterer claimed that it was not in breach of a contract of affreightment for the carriage of iron ore pellets when it failed to supply the cargo for five shipments after a dam burst stopping production at the mine from which the iron ore was sourced. It relied on a clause under which it was not "responsible for … failure to supply" resulting from floods or accidents at the mine or any other causes beyond its control. It was unable to do so because it would not have been able to perform in any event, if the mine had not stopped production. This was contrasted with an earlier case in which the clause relied on stated that: "in case of prohibition of export … preventing fulfilment, this contract or any unfulfilled portion thereof so affected shall be cancelled".[364] In that case it was held that it was not necessary for the party relying on it to prove that it would have been able to perform in the absence of any prohibition. According to Males LJ:

> "… where the effect of a clause is to discharge the parties from an obligation to perform in the future, as distinct from to relieve them from liability to pay damages for a past breach, that may well have at least a bearing on the nature of the causative effect on a party's performance which an event is required to have. In such a case, both parties need to know at once when the event occurs whether they are under any continuing obligation. There is, therefore, much to be said for a simple and straightforward causation requirement (an embargo which makes it impossible for any goods to be shipped) without requiring investigation of matters known only to one party, such as whether it was able and willing to perform if the event had not occurred. Such a consideration has much less force after the event, when the time for performance is over and the only question is whether a party is liable to pay damages."[365]

19–082 **Statutory control.** Force majeure clauses are probably not subject to the Unfair Contract Terms Act 1977 since they are clauses which define the parties' duties rather than exemption clauses.[366] In the case of a consumer contract, a term operating only in circumstances beyond the control of the party relying on it would not normally be unfair under the Consumer Rights Act 2015.[367]

[362] It is ultimately a question of construction which is not necessarily pre-determined by the characterisation of the clause: *Classic Maritime Inc v Limbungan Makmur SDN BHD* [2019] EWCA Civ 1102; [2019] 4 All E.R. 1102 at [32].

[363] [2019] EWCA Civ 1102; [2019] 4 All E.R. 1145.

[364] *Bremer Handelsgesellschaft mbH v Vanden Avenne-Izegem PVBA* [1978] 2 Lloyd's Rep. 109.

[365] *Classic Maritime Inc v Limbungan Makmur SDN BHD* [2019] EWCA Civ 1102; [2019] 4 All E.R. 1145 at [57].

[366] See para.7–057.

[367] Consumer Rights Act 2015 Sch.2 para.8 ("except where there are serious grounds … ").

## (b) Foreseen and foreseeable events[368]

### (i) In general

**No frustration for foreseen or foreseeable events.** Where the parties can at the time of contracting foresee the risk that a supervening event may interfere with performance, the normal inference is that their contract was made with reference to that risk. If, for example, the event would make performance more expensive for one party, he is likely to increase his charges; if, on the other hand, it would frustrate the other's purpose, he is likely to reduce the amount that he is willing to pay. Having thus allocated the risk by their contract, or having had the opportunity to do so,[369] the parties should not be discharged if the event indeed occurs;[370] the loss caused by the event should lie where it falls. As Vaughan Williams LJ has said, "The test [of frustration] seems to be whether the event which causes the impossibility was or might have been anticipated … ".[371] Many other dicta similarly support the view that a contract cannot be frustrated by foreseen or foreseeable events,[372] though it is probably more accurate to say that foreseeability is just "a factor to be taken into account".[373] **19–083**

### (ii) Qualifications

**Trading with the enemy.** A contract may be frustrated by supervening illegality resulting from the wartime prohibition against trading with the enemy, in spite of the fact that the war was a foreseeable event. Even an express provision against frustration does not save the contract in such a case;[374] and the policy considerations which justify this rule apply just as strongly where the event was or should have been foreseen. Thus contracts made in the summer of 1939 could be frustrated as a result of the outbreak of war with Germany in September although this event was foreseeable. **19–084**

**Degree and extent of foreseeability.** The inference that the parties contracted with reference to the event (and so took the risk of its occurrence) can be drawn only if the event was either actually foreseen or if the degree of foreseeability was **19–085**

---

[368] Hall 4 *Legal Studies* 300.

[369] *Walton Harvey Ltd v Walker & Homfrays Ltd* [1931] 1 Ch. 274 at 282 ("They could have provided against [the] risk, but they did not").

[370] See *Comptoir Commercial Anversois v Power, Son & Co* [1920] 1 K.B. 868 at 895, 901.

[371] *Krell v Henry* [1903] 2 K.B. 740 at 752.

[372] *Tamplin SS Co Ltd v Anglo-Mexican Petroleum Co* [1916] 2 A.C. 397 at 424; *Bank Line Ltd v Arthur Capel & Co* [1919] A.C. 435 at 458; *Cricklewood Property Investment Trust Ltd v Leighton's Investment Trust Ltd* [1945] A.C. 221 at 228; *Davis Contractors Ltd v Fareham Urban DC* [1956] A.C. 696 at 731; *Denmark Productions Ltd v Boscobel Productions Ltd* [1969] 1 Q.B. 699 at 725; *The Hannah Blumenthal* [1983] 1 A.C. 854 at 909; *Gamerco SA v ICM (Fair Warning) Agency Ltd* [1995] 1 W.L.R. 1226 at 1231.

[373] *Canary Wharf (BP4) T1 Ltd v European Medicines Agency* [2019] EWHC 335 (Ch); 183 Con L.R. 167 at [211].

[374] See para.19–048.

a high one.[375] It is not sufficient for the low degree of foreseeability which constitutes the test of remoteness in tort[376] to be satisfied. In this sense, it was no doubt "foreseeable" that King Edward VII (who was 60 years old at the time) might fall ill on the day fixed for his coronation.[377] To support the inference of risk-assumption, the event must be one which any person of ordinary intelligence would regard as likely to occur. Moreover, the event or its consequences must be foreseeable in some detail. It is not sufficient that *a* delay or *some* interference with performance can be foreseen if *the* delay or interference which occurs is wholly different in extent. We have seen that this distinction restricts the scope of express provisions for a supervening event;[378] and there is no reason why it should not equally apply in relation to events alleged to have been foreseeable or foreseen. Where the "relevant" risk is foreseeable, it is unnecessary to draw distinctions between what are no more than "variants on a theme".[379] Thus, in *The Sea Angel*,[380] the relevant risk was the unreasonable detention by the port authorities of a vessel used for a salvage operation where there was a risk of pollution; it did not matter whether that detention was for the purpose of ensuring the continuation of the salvage operation, or, as was the case, to secure a claim against a third party responsible for the pollution.

**19–086** **WJ Tatem Ltd v Gamboa.** It is submitted that the points made above as to the degree and extent of foreseeability may provide the best explanation for cases in which it was said that a contract could be frustrated by foreseen or foreseeable events. One such case is *WJ Tatem Ltd v Gamboa*.[381] During the Spanish Civil War, the defendant, as agent for the Republicans, chartered a ship for 30 days from 1 July "for the evacuation of civil population from North Spain". Hire was to be paid at the rate of £250 per day "until her redelivery to the owners", but was to cease if the ship was "missing". On 14 July the ship was seized by the Nationalists, who kept her until 7 September, so that she was not redelivered to the owners till 11 September. The charterers had paid hire in advance up to 31 July, but the owners claimed further hire from 1 August to 11 September. Goddard J rejected the claim on the ground that the charterparty was frustrated. The actual decision can be justified on the ground that it was *not* foreseeable that the ship would be detained "not only for the period of her charter but for a long period thereafter".[382] But Goddard J added that the contract would have been frustrated even if that risk had been foreseen:

---

[375] *The Sea Angel* [2007] EWCA Civ 547; [2007] 2 Lloyd's Rep. 517 at [104], [127] where the submissions were described as "over-refined": "the less that an event … is foreseeable, the more likely it is to be a factor which, depending on other factors in the case, may lead to frustration".

[376] See para.20–133.

[377] cf. the express provisions made in some of the contracts for the possibility of postponement, e.g. *Victoria Seats Agency v Paget* (1902) 19 T.L.R. 16. According to D.N.B., 2d Supp. p.591, "A few days before the date appointed for the great ceremony rumours of the King's ill-health gained currency and were denied."

[378] See para.19–049.

[379] *The Sea Angel* [2007] EWCA Civ 547; [2007] 2 Lloyd's Rep. 517 at [128].

[380] [2007] EWCA Civ 547; [2007] 2 Lloyd's Rep. 517 at [128].

[381] [1939] 1 K.B. 132.

[382] *WJ Tatem Ltd v Gamboa* [1939] 1 K.B. 132 at 135.

> "If the true foundation of the doctrine [of frustration] is that once the subject-matter of the contract is destroyed or the existence of a certain state of facts has come to an end, the contract is at an end, that result follows whether or not the event causing it was contemplated by the parties".[383]

But it is submitted that a contract is not necessarily at an end if the existence of a certain state of facts has come to an end; for the parties may have been engaged in a deliberate speculation on this point.[384] A similar objection applies to the suggestion that an event can frustrate a contract, even though it "was or ought to have been foreseen", if it was "outside the scope of the contract on its true construction".[385] It is submitted that it would be wrong first to construe the contract and *then* to have regard to the fact that the event was foreseen; for that fact must be of crucial importance in determining "the scope of the contract", i.e. whether the parties took the risk of the occurrence of the event.[386] Where they actually foresaw the event, the more natural inference is that each of them took that risk unless the contract expressly protected him. In *WJ Tatem Ltd v Gamboa* the contract did not expressly protect the defendant from liability if the ship were seized and detained. The inference that he accepted the risk of these events (to the extent to which they were foreseen)[387] is strengthened by the fact that the contract did expressly protect him against another foreseen risk, namely, that the ship might be lost; in that event his liability to pay hire was to cease.[388]

**The Eugenia.** Another case in which it was said that a contract could be frustrated by foreseen or foreseeable events is *The Eugenia*.[389] In September 1956, the defendants wished to charter the owners' ship to carry iron goods from Russian Black Sea ports to India. At that time "mercantile men realised that there was a risk that the Suez Canal might be closed"[390] because of the Suez crisis. The agents of the parties appreciated this risk and each made a suggestion for dealing with it.[391] But when the charterparty was concluded on 19 September, nothing was expressly said about the risk of closure. The reason may be that before 16 November "mercantile men would not have formed any conclusion as to whether the obstructions in the Canal were other than temporary".[392] The actual decision was that the contract was not frustrated by the closure of the Canal on 31 October, resulting in the detention of the ship: the charterers could not rely on the 19–087

[383] *WJ Tatem Ltd v Gamboa* [1939] 1 K.B. 132 at 138; cf. *The Captain George K* [1970] 2 Lloyd's Rep. 21 at 31.

[384] cf. paras 1–003, 19–074.

[385] *Nile Co for the Export of Agriculture Crops v H & JM Bennett (Commodities) Ltd* [1986] 1 Lloyd's Rep. 555 at 582.

[386] *The Sea Angel* [2006] EWHC 1713 (Comm); [2006] 2 C.L.C. 600 at [84iv]; affirmed on appeal [2007] EWCA Civ 547; [2007] 2 Lloyd's Rep. 517; *Canary Wharf (BP4) T1 Ltd v European Medicines Agency* [2019] EWHC 335 (Ch); 183 Con L.R. 167 at [211].

[387] See at fn.382.

[388] The shipowners may have found it easier to insure against loss than against detention and have distinguished for this reason between the effect of the two events.

[389] [1964] 2 Q.B. 226.

[390] *The Eugenia* [1963] 2 Lloyd's Rep. 155 at 159. The facts are more fully stated in this report.

[391] *The Eugenia* [1963] 2 Lloyd's Rep. 155 at 159.

[392] *The Eugenia* [1963] 2 Lloyd's Rep. 155 at 162.

detention as it was due to their prior breach of contract and thus "self-induced";[393] nor on the extra length of the voyage as the difference between a voyage via the Canal and one via the Cape was not sufficiently fundamental.[394] But Lord Denning MR also seemed to reject the further argument that frustration might have been excluded on the ground that at the time of contracting the closure of the Canal was foreseeable. He said:

> "It has often been said that the doctrine of frustration only applies where the new situation is 'unforeseen' or 'unexpected' or 'uncontemplated' as if that were an essential feature. But it is not so. The only thing that is essential is that [the parties] should have made no provision for it in the contract".[395]

But these remarks are obiter and it is respectfully submitted that this aspect of the decision can be explained on other grounds. At the time of contracting, the risk of the Canal's being closed for a *very considerable time* was not foreseen; nor was it foreseeable on the high standard of foreseeability[396] required to exclude frustration. To the extent that the parties did foresee the risk, they seem to have allocated it by the terms of the charterparty. This provided that the voyage was to be paid for by the time it took,[397] so indicating an intention to throw the risk of delay on the charterers. There seems to be no reason why the court should, by applying the doctrine of frustration to foreseen events, reverse such an allocation of risks deliberately made by the contracting parties.

19–088 **Contrary intention.** The inference that the parties have assumed the risk of foreseen (or readily foreseeable) events is only a prima facie one and can be excluded by evidence of contrary intention. The parties may foresee an event and intend, if it occurs, "to leave the lawyers to sort it out";[398] or they may actually provide that if the event occurs they will then determine how it is to affect the contract.[399] If the lawyers cannot "sort it out" or if the parties cannot reach agreement, the contract may then be frustrated even though the event was foreseen. Similar reasoning explains *Bank Line Ltd v Arthur Capel Ltd*[400] where a charterparty was frustrated although the parties foresaw that the ship might be requisitioned and actually made some provision for this event. But it is by no means clear that the parties foresaw a requisition of such long duration as would frustrate the contract. Even if they did foresee this, the very fact that they had made *some* provision for the event complicated the issue. The contract entitled the charterer to cancel on requisition (so that the risk of the event was clearly not meant to be on him); but it made no reference to the effect of requisition on the liability of the owner. One could infer from this silence that the parties had decided to throw the risk of requisition on him, or that they had not thought about

[393] See para.19–090.
[394] See para.19–031.
[395] *The Eugenia* [1964] 2 Q.B. 226 at 239.
[396] See para.19–085.
[397] The contract was in the form of a "time charter trip" which has become common: see *The Cebu* [1983] 1 Lloyd's Rep. 302 at 305.
[398] *The Eugenia* [1964] 2 Q.B. 226 at 234.
[399] *Autry v Republic Productions* 180 P.2d 888 (1947).
[400] [1919] A.C. 435; para.19–078.

its effect on his liability at all. If the latter inference is correct, the contract could be frustrated although requisition was foreseen, and the House of Lords so held. The normal inference that parties take the risk of foreseen events was displaced by the special terms of the contract.

## (c) Self-induced frustration

19–089 A party cannot rely on "self-induced frustration",[401] that is, on frustration due to his own conduct or to the conduct of those for whom he is responsible. Thus, where cargo receivers failed to discharge a cargo from a chartered vessel, the charterers were unable to rely on this as a frustrating event since they were under a non-delegable duty to ensure that discharge was completed within a certain time and the receivers were their agents for this purpose. The charterers therefore remained liable to pay demurrage.[402] Frustration is not self-induced where the cause of the delay is the act of a third party for whom the defendant is not responsible,[403] nor merely because one of the parties is an enterprise controlled by a State which has by some legislative or executive act prevented performance of the contract or made it illegal.[404]

### *(i) Events brought about by one party's conduct*

19–090 **No frustration as a consequence of breach.** The doctrine of frustration obviously does not protect a party whose own breach of contract actually is, or brings about, the frustrating event. Nor does it protect him if the breach is only one of the factors leading to frustration. Thus, a charterer who in breach of contract orders a ship into a war-zone, so that she is detained, cannot rely on the detention as a ground of frustration.[405] Similarly, unseaworthiness amounting to a breach of contract may cause delays in the prosecution of the voyage; and if war intervenes, so that the voyage cannot be completed, the carrier will be liable in damages;[406] such cases show that even an omission (i.e. failure to make the ship seaworthy) can sometimes exclude frustration.[407] The doctrine likewise does not apply where the circumstances alleged to have brought it into operation result partly from the breach of one party and partly from that of the other, e.g. where both breaches contribute to an allegedly frustrating delay.[408]

---

401 *Bank Line Ltd v Arthur Capel & Co* [1919] A.C. 435 at 452; *Sudbrook Trading Estate Ltd v Eggleton* [1983] 1 A.C. 444 at 497; Swanton 2 J.C.L. 699.

402 *The Andra* [2012] EWHC 1984 (Comm); [2012] 2 Lloyd's Rep. 587.

403 *The Adelfa* [1988] 2 Lloyd's Rep. 466 at 471.

404 *C Czarnikow Ltd v Centrala Handlu Zagrancicznego "Rolimpex"* [1979] A.C. 351 at 372; *The Playa Larga* [1983] 2 Lloyd's Rep. 171 at 192.

405 *The Eugenia* [1964] 2 Q.B. 226; *The Lucille* [1984] 1 Lloyd's Rep. 244; cf. *Mertens v Home Freeholds Co* [1921] 2 K.B. 526.

406 See *Monarch SS Co v A/B Karlshamns Oljefabriker* [1949] A.C. 196. The breach must have a causal connection with the frustrating event: *The Silver Sky* [1981] 2 Lloyd's Rep. 95 at 98.

407 cf. *Amalgamated Investment & Property Co Ltd v John Walker & Sons Ltd* [1977] 1 W.L.R. 164 (failure to take any steps to obtain planning permission).

408 *The Hannah Blumenthal* [1983] 1 A.C. 854; rejecting suggestions in *The Splendid Sun* [1981] Q.B. 694 at 703; *The Argonaut* [1982] 2 Lloyd's Rep. 214 at 221; and *The Kehera* [1983] 1 Lloyd's Rep. 29 that there could be frustration "by mutual default". In *The Hannah Blumenthal* the plea of

19–091 **Deliberate acts not amounting to a breach.** Where the allegedly frustrating event results from one party's deliberate act, that party cannot rely on it as a ground of frustration, even though the act is not in itself a breach of the contract;[409] but the other party may be able to rely on it for this purpose. Thus where an employee has been prevented from performing the agreed work because he has been imprisoned for a criminal offence, the employer can rely on this circumstance as a ground of frustration, so as to defeat a claim by the employee for unfair dismissal; and he can do this even though the offence had no connection with the employment, so that its mere commission did not amount to a breach of the contract.[410] Whether the imprisonment actually frustrates the contract depends on such circumstances as the length of the sentence and the nature of the employment.[411] But an attempt by the employee to set up the imprisonment as a ground of frustration, in an action against him by the employer on the contract, would fail[412] on the ground that the employee could not rely on self-induced frustration.

### *(ii) Negligence*

19–092 **No frustration as a consequence of negligence.** Lord Simon has put the case of a prima donna who failed to perform a contract because she had lost her voice through carelessly catching cold. He seemed to incline to the view that she could rely on frustration so long as the incapacity "was not deliberately induced in order to get out of the engagement".[413] This result can perhaps be justified by the difficulty of foreseeing the effect of conduct on one's health. But it is submitted that generally negligence should exclude frustration, e.g. the plea should have failed in *Taylor v Caldwell*[414] if the fire had been due to the negligence of the defendants, for in such a case it would be unjust to make the other party bear the loss. Similarly, a shipowner cannot rely on the loss of his ship as a ground of frustration of a contract to carry goods in her if the loss is due to his negligence.[415] These examples show that "negligence" in this context is not restricted to "breach of an actionable legal duty": it includes "an event which the party relying on it had means and opportunity to prevent but nevertheless caused or permitted to come about".[416] In one case, frustration was ruled out on the basis that the event relied on was, at least in part, the result of the acts of the party

---

frustration failed on the further ground that the delay did not produce a radically different state of affairs; cf. on this point, *Stockport MBC v O'Reilly* [1983] 2 Lloyd's Rep. 70.

409 *Denmark Production Ltd v Boscobel Productions Ltd* [1969] 1 Q.B. 699; *Black Clawson International Ltd v Papierwerke Waldhof-Aschaffenburg AG* [1981] 2 Lloyd's Rep. 446 at 457.

410 *Harrington v Kent CC* [1980] I.R.L.R. 353; *FC Shepherd & Co Ltd v Jerrom* [1987] Q.B. 301; contra, *Norris v Southampton CC* [1982] I.C.R. 177.

411 *Chakki v United Yeast Ltd* [1982] I.C.R. 140; and *FC Shepherd & Co Ltd v Jerrom*[1987] Q.B. 301.

412 cf. *Sumnall v Statt* (1984) 49 P. & C.R. 367 (imprisonment of tenant no excuse for failing to perform covenant to "reside constantly" at farmhouse).

413 *Joseph Constantine SS Co v Imperial Smelting Corp Ltd* [1942] A.C. 154 at 166–167.

414 (1863) 3 B. & S. 826. Lack of "fault" is mentioned in the passage at 833 quoted at para.19–003.

415 See *The Super Servant Two* [1990] 1 Lloyd's Rep. 1.

416 *The Super Servant Two* [1990] 1 Lloyd's Rep. 1 at 10; cf. *North Shore Ventures Ltd v Anstead Holdings Inc* [2010] EWHC 1485 (Ch); [2010] 2 Lloyd's Rep. 265 at [316].

relying on it, "whether or not they can be said to amount to 'fault'",[417] though this comment was made largely in the context of a submission that the event in question was foreseeable.[418]

### (iii) *Choosing between several contracts*

Where a party has entered into a number of contracts, supervening events may deprive him of the power of performing them all, without depriving him of the power of performing one or some of them. He may then claim that one or more of the contracts are frustrated because the supervening event was one for which he was not responsible; but in two cases such claims have failed. **19–093**

**Maritime National Fish v Ocean Trawlers.** The first of those cases is *Maritime National Fish Ltd v Ocean Trawlers Ltd*,[419] where the defendants operated a fleet of five trawlers for fishing with otter trawls. Three of the trawlers were owned by the defendants through their subsidiaries,[420] while two, of which one was the *St Cuthbert*, were chartered from other owners. The use of otter trawls without licence was illegal, and because of a change in government policy[421] the defendants secured only three out of the five licences for which they had applied. Having allocated two of these to two of their own trawlers and one to the other chartered trawler,[422] they argued that the charter of the *St Cuthbert* had been frustrated. The argument was rejected by the Canadian courts on the ground that the defendants had taken the risk of not getting licences for all five trawlers, the licensing requirement being known both to them and to the owners of the *St Cuthbert* at the time of contracting. The Privy Council, though not dissenting from this view, preferred to base its decision on the ground that frustration was self-induced: "it was the act and election of [the defendants] which prevented the *St Cuthbert* from being licensed for fishing with an otter trawl".[423] On the facts, there clearly was such an election, for the defendants could have allocated one of the three licences to the *St Cuthbert* rather than to one of their own trawlers. But suppose that the defendants had operated only the two chartered trawlers, had obtained only one licence, and that the licensing requirement had been introduced after both charterparties were concluded. The question would then have arisen whether their choice to allocate their only licence to one of the trawlers would have been an "election", so as to exclude the doctrine of frustration in relation to the charter of the other. **19–094**

[417] cf. *Canary Wharf (BP4) T1 Ltd v European Medicines Agency* [2019] EWHC 335 (Ch); 183 Con L.R. 167 at [206] ("whether frustration is self-induced does not turn on technical questions of duty of care or fault").

[418] *Armchair Answercall Ltd v People In Mind Ltd* [2016] EWCA Civ 1039 at [47].

[419] [1935] A.C. 524.

[420] See [1934] 1 D.L.R. 621 at 623; [1934] 4 D.L.R. 288 at 299.

[421] See para.19–051.

[422] See the references in fn.420.

[423] *Maritime National Fish Ltd v Ocean Trawlers Ltd* [1935] A.C. 524 at 529.

19–095 **The Super Servant Two.** An affirmative answer to a similar question was given in *The Super Servant Two*,[424] where a contract was made to carry the claimants' drilling rig in one of two ships, the *Super Servant One* or the *Super Servant Two*, at the carrier's option. The *Super Servant Two* was lost and the carrier claimed that the contract was frustrated by this event because the *Super Servant One* was the subject of another fixture and hence not available for the purposes of performing the carrier's contract with the claimants. The argument was rejected on the ground that the carrier's decision to use the *Super Servant One* for the purpose of performing the other contract amounted to an "election" by him, thus precluding his reliance on the loss of the *Super Servant Two* as a ground of frustration, even if that loss was in no way due to his fault. Three grounds for the decision appear from the judgments but it is submitted with great respect that none of them is wholly convincing.

First, it was said that the *Maritime National Fish* case had established that a party could not rely on frustration where his failure or inability was due to his "election"; and that the court in *The Super Servant Two* should follow that decision.[425] It is, however, submitted that the two cases are readily distinguishable: in the *Maritime National Fish* case it was possible for the charterer to perform *all* the contracts which he had made with the owners of the other trawlers, even though only three licences had been allocated to him; while in *The Super Servant Two* it was no longer possible, after the loss of the ship, for the carrier to perform all the contracts which he had made to carry drilling rigs during the period in question.

Secondly, it was said that, if the carrier were given the choice which of the contracts he would perform, frustration of the other or others could come about only as a result of the exercise of that choice, and such a position would be inconsistent with the rule that frustration occurs automatically, *without* any election by either party.[426] Again, it is submitted that this line of reasoning is not conclusive since the rule that frustration operates automatically is subject to qualification precisely in cases of allegedly self-induced frustration: [427]we have seen, for example, that the imprisonment of an employee is a circumstance on which the employer, but not the employee, can rely as a ground of discharge,[428] so that discharge cannot in such cases be described as automatic. Even where the rule that frustration operates automatically does apply, we shall see that this rule forms one of the least attractive aspects of the doctrine of frustration,[429] so that it is one which should not be extended. Moreover, the element of "election" could be eliminated if the question which of the contracts was to be discharged were left to be determined, not by the free choice of the promisor, but by a rule of law, e.g. by a rule to the effect that the various contracts should for this purpose rank

---

424 [1990] 1 Lloyd's Rep. 1; affirming [1989] 1 Lloyd's Rep. 148; McKendrick [1990] L.M.C.L.Q. 153.

425 *The Super Servant Two* [1990] 1 Lloyd's Rep. 1 at 10, 13 (rejecting the contrary submission made in earlier editions of this book).

426 *The Super Servant Two* [1990] 1 Lloyd's Rep. 1 at 9, 14.

427 See para.19–098.

428 *Shepherd & Co Ltd v Jerrom* [1987] Q.B. 301; discussed at para.19–091.

429 See paras 19–097–19–098.

in the order in which they were made.[430] It may, from this point of view, be relevant that, in *The Super Servant Two*, some of the contracts which the carrier chose to perform (by the use of his other ship during the relevant period) had not been made "at any rate finally"[431] until *after* the contract with the claimants, and that, even after the loss of the *Super Servant Two*, the carrier had continued to negotiate for extra fees to be paid under one of those contracts, "before finally allocating the *Super Servant One* to the performance of these contracts".[432]

The third reason given for the decision is that "It is within the promisor's own control how many contracts he enters into and the risk should be his".[433] But this point seems to undermine the whole basis of the doctrine of frustration: it has just as much force where the promisor enters into a single contract as where he enters into two or more, with different contracting parties. This, indeed, is the fundamental objection to the reasoning of *The Super Servant Two*, and it is submitted that the rationale of the doctrine should lead to discharge of some of the contracts where the supervening event (which makes it impossible to perform them all) occurs without the fault of the party claiming discharge.[434] Consistency with the reasoning of the *Maritime National Fish* case could be preserved by holding that *which* contracts were to be discharged should depend, not on the election of the party who can no longer perform, but on a rule of law. On this view, the actual decision in *The Super Servant Two* could be justified by reference to the order in which the various contracts with the carrier were made.

### *(iv) Burden of proof*

**Burden on party alleging self-inducement.** The onus of proving that frustration is self-induced is on the party who alleges that this is the case. In *Joseph Constantine SS Line v Imperial Smelting Corp Ltd*[435] a ship was disabled by an explosion so that her owners were prevented from performing their obligations under a charterparty. The charterers' claim for damages was rejected: the House of Lords held that the shipowners were discharged by frustration without having to disprove fault and in spite of the fact that the cause of the explosion was never explained. A possible objection to the rule is that the charterers were much less likely than the owners to be able to show how the explosion occurred. This reasoning does, indeed, prevail in one group of cases: a person to whom goods have been bailed, and who seeks to rely on their destruction as a ground of frustration of the contract of bailment, must show that the destruction was not due to any breach of his duty as a bailee.[436] But, this special situation excepted, the rule as to burden of proof laid down in the *Joseph Constantine* case can be 19–096

430 cf. para.19–030.
431 *The Super Servant Two* [1990] 1 Lloyd's Rep. 1 at 9.
432 *The Super Servant Two* [1990] 1 Lloyd's Rep. 1 at 13.
433 *The Super Servant Two* [1989] 1 Lloyd's Rep. 148 at 158 (at first instance); the reasoning of this judgment was approved on appeal in [1990] 1 Lloyd's Rep. 1.
434 cf. *Bremer Handelsgesellschaft mbH v Continental Grain Co* [1983] 1 Lloyd's Rep. 269 at 292–293; the treatment of the 92 tonnes in *Bremer Handelsgesellschaft mbH v Vanden Avenne-Izegem PVBA* [1978] 2 Lloyd's Rep. 109 at 115; and see para.19–030.
435 [1942] A.C. 154; Stone 60 L.Q.R. 262. A contrary dictum in *FC Shepherd & Co Ltd v Jerrom* [1987] Q.B. 301 at 319 seems to have been made per incuriam.
436 *The Torrenia* [1983] 2 Lloyd's Rep. 210 at 216.

defended on the ground that, more often than not, catastrophic events which prevent performance do occur without the fault of either party. To impose the burden of disproving fault on the party relying on frustration is therefore less likely than the converse rule to lead to the right result in the majority of cases.

## 4. EFFECTS OF FRUSTRATION

### (a) In general

19–097 **Contract automatically terminated at time of frustrating event.** Frustration terminates a contract automatically at the time of the frustrating event.[437] The court may therefore hold that the contract was frustrated even though the parties for some time after the event went on behaving as if the contract still existed.[438] "Whatever the consequences of the frustration may be upon the conduct of the parties, its legal effect does not depend on their opinions, or even knowledge, as to the event".[439] Accordingly, "what the parties may say or do" has been described as "only evidence, and not necessarily weighty evidence, of the view to be taken of the event by informed and experienced minds".[440] This does not mean that the courts disregard the views of the parties as to the effect of the event: thus in one case Lord Sumner said: "Both [parties] thought its result was to terminate their contractual relations … and as they must have known more about it than I do there is no reason why I should not think so too".[441] The true position is that "the parties' beliefs are not determinative, but nor are they irrelevant".[442]

19–098 **No requirement of election.** As frustration operates automatically, it is generally thought to terminate the contract without any election by either party: in this respect it differs from breach, which enables the victim to choose whether to treat the contract as discharged.[443] It follows that frustration can be invoked by either party, and not only by the party likely to be adversely affected by the frustrating event. Suppose, for example, that a ship under charter is requisitioned so that the charterer does not receive the promised performance (i.e. the services of the ship). Frustration may, paradoxically, be claimed by the shipowner, even though

---

[437] *Hirji Mulji v Cheong Yue SS Co Ltd* [1926] A.C. 497 at 505; *BP Exploration (Libya) Ltd v Hunt* [1979] 1 W.L.R. 783 at 809; affirmed [1983] 2 A.C. 352; *The Super Servant Two* [1990] 1 Lloyd's Rep. 1 at 8, 9, 14.

[438] cf. *The Agathon* [1982] 2 Lloyd's Rep. 211 at 213; *GF Sharp & Co v McMillan* [1998] I.R.L.R. 632.

[439] *Hirji Mulji v Cheong Yue SS Co Ltd* [1926] A.C. 497 at 509; cf. *Morgan v Manser* [1948] 1 K.B. 184 at 191.

[440] *Hirji Mulji v Cheong Yue SS Co Ltd* [1926] A.C. 497; cf. *Armchair Answercall Ltd v People In Mind Ltd* [2016] EWCA Civ 1039 at [51] ("a pointer to whether the event was in truth a frustrating one").

[441] *Bank Line Ltd v Arthur Capel & Co* [1919] A.C. 435 at 460. See also *Black Clawson International Ltd v Papierwerke Waldhof-Aschaffenburg AG* [1981] 2 Lloyd's Rep. 446 at 457 where the fact that a party had "affirmed the contract" was said to exclude frustration.

[442] *The Wenjiang (No.2)* [1983] 2 Lloyd's Rep. 400 at 408.

[443] *FC Shepherd Ltd v Jerrom* [1987] Q.B. 301 at 327; see para.18–005; McKendrick in Dyson, Goudkamp and Wilmot-Smith (eds), *Defences in Contract* (2017).

the charterer is perfectly willing to pay the agreed hire;[444] for if the compensation paid by the Government for the requisition exceeds that hire, the shipowner will actually profit from frustration. The courts are understandably reluctant to allow the doctrine of frustration to be used in this way. Thus the rejection of the plea of frustration in the *Tamplin*[445] case has been explained precisely on the ground that the House of Lords saw no good reason why the shipowner should be allowed to make a profit of the kind just described.[446] It seems that the seller in the *Tsakiroglou*[447] case would have made a similar profit if his plea of frustration had been upheld, for the market price of the goods had risen by more than the extra cost of carriage via the Cape of Good Hope; and this fact may have had some influence on the decision that the contract remained in force. But in other cases the rule of automatic termination has, no doubt, enabled a party to profit from frustration.[448]

**Criticism.** It is doubtful whether automatic termination is necessary, and it might be better if frustration only gave an option to terminate to any party who is prejudiced by the supervening event in the sense of not receiving the now impossible performance (or, in cases of frustration of purpose, of not being able to use the subject-matter for its intended purpose). There is, indeed, some support for this view in the cases relating to self-induced frustration. Where an event is brought about by the deliberate act of one party (not amounting in itself to a breach), that party cannot rely on it as frustrating the contract; but the other party may be able so to rely on it. This is, for example, the position where an employee is imprisoned for a criminal offence and so unable to perform his part of a contract of employment. The employer can invoke frustration in such circumstances;[449] but the employee cannot do so since a party cannot rely on self-induced frustration.[450] **19–099**

## (b) Problems of adjustment[451]

The common law starts with the principle that frustration discharges the parties only from duties of "future performance".[452] Rights accrued before frustration therefore remain enforceable while those which would, but for the frustrating **19–100**

[444] e.g. *Bank Line Ltd v Arthur Capel & Co* [1919] A.C. 435.
[445] *Tamplin SS Co Ltd v Anglo-Mexican Petroleum Co* [1916] 2 A.C. 397; para.19–022.
[446] *Metropolitan Water Board v Dick Kerr & Co* [1918] A.C. 119 at 129; cf. also *Port Line Ltd v Ben Line Steamers Ltd* [1958] 2 Q.B. 146.
[447] *Tsakiroglou & Co v Noblee Thorl GmbH* [1962] A.C. 93; para.19–032, fn.136.
[448] A striking illustration is *The Isle of Mull* 278 F. 131 (1921); cf. also *Nickoll & Knight v Ashton Edridge & Co* [1901] 2 K.B. 126 (para.19–031) where the market price of the goods rose above the contract price so that the seller seems to have made a profit out of frustration.
[449] *FC Shepherd & Co v Jerrom* [1987] Q.B. 301; para.19–091.
[450] *FC Shepherd & Co v Jerrom* [1987] Q.B. 301.
[451] Williams, *The Law Reform (Frustrated Contracts) Act 1943*; Stewart and Carter [1992] C.L.J. 66.
[452] *Joseph Constantine SS Line v Imperial Smelting Corp Ltd* [1942] A.C. 154 at 187; cf. *The Super Servant Two* [1990] 1 Lloyd's Rep. 1 at 18 ("further liability").

event, have accrued after the time of discharge do not become due. These rules sometimes caused hardship which has been mitigated both by common law developments and by statute.

### (i) Rights accrued before frustration

19–101 **Common law.** The rule that rights which had accrued before frustration remain enforceable can be illustrated by supposing that in *Taylor v Caldwell*[453] the fire had occurred after the first, but before the second, of the four specified days. The rest of the contract would then have been discharged, while each party would have remained liable for any failure to perform obligations which had fallen due on the first day. The application of this principle could lead to injustice where one party's performance under the contract had become due before the frustrating event while that of the other was only to be rendered thereafter; for in such a case the former party would have still to perform, without getting what he had bargained for in return. For example, in *Chandler v Webster*[454] a contract for the hire of a room overlooking the proposed route of King Edward VII's coronation processions provided for payment of £141 15s. in advance: this was due, and £100 of it had been paid, before the day on which the processions were cancelled. The hirer was held liable to pay the remaining £41 15s. as the payment had fallen due before the contract was frustrated; while his claim to recover back the £100 already paid on the ground of "total failure of consideration"[455] was rejected:[456] it was thought that the failure of consideration was not total as frustration released the parties only from further performance, and did not make the contract void ab initio. This aspect of *Chandler v Webster* was overruled in the *Fibrosa* case.[457] An English company had agreed to sell machinery to a Polish company for £4,800, of which £1,600 was to be paid in advance. When £1,000 had been paid, the contract was frustrated by the German occupation of Gdynia after the outbreak of war in 1939. The House of Lords held that the Polish company could recover the £1,000 since the consideration for the payment had wholly failed: no part of the machinery had been delivered. Liability to pay the outstanding £600 must likewise have been discharged, for it would have been futile to require the buyer to make a payment which he would then immediately have been entitled to recover.[458]

19–102 **Defects in the common law.** This common law solution was defective in two ways. First, it applied only where the consideration had *wholly* failed.[459] In

453 (1863) 3 B. & S. 826; para.19–003.

454 [1904] 1 K.B. 493; cf. Buckland 46 Harv. L. Rev. 1281.

455 See para.22–003.

456 cf. *Blakeley v Muller & Co* [1903] 2 K.B. 760n. (referred to in *The Great Peace* [2002] EWCA Civ 1407; [2003] Q.B. 679 at [65], [76] under its alternative name of *Hobson v Pattenden & Co*); *Civil Service Co-operative Society v General Steam Navigation Co* [1903] 2 K.B. 756.

457 *Fibrosa Spolka Akcyjna v Fairbairn, Lawson, Combe, Barbour Ltd* [1943] A.C. 32; para.19–048. This point seems to have been overlooked in *Re Goldcorp Exchange Ltd* [1995] A.C. 74 at 103.

458 cf. in another context, *McDonald v Denys Lascelles Ltd* (1933) 48 C.L.R. 457; para.18–017; *Fibrosa Spolka Akcyjna v Fairbairn, Lawson, Combe, Barbour Ltd* [1943] A.C. 32 at 53.

459 cf. paras 22–003—22–004.

*Whincup v Hughes*[460] a father apprenticed his son to a watchmaker for six years at a premium of £25. After one year the watchmaker died. The father could not recover any part of the premium as the failure of consideration was only partial. Secondly, to allow the payor to recover the whole of his advance payment might in turn cause injustice to the payee, who might (and in the *Fibrosa* case did) use the advance payment to finance the initial stages of the contract. If, in consequence of frustration, that expenditure was wasted, the resulting loss would fall entirely on the payee.

**Law Reform (Frustrated Contracts) Act 1943 s.1(2).** To remedy the defects just described, s.1(2) of the Law Reform (Frustrated Contracts) Act 1943 lays down three rules. **19–103**

**Sums due before the frustrating event cease to be payable.** All sums payable under the contract before the time of discharge cease to be payable on frustration: thus in *Chandler v Webster* the claim for the unpaid £41 15s. would now fail. **19–104**

**Sums actually paid are prima facie recoverable.** All sums actually paid in pursuance of the contract before the time of discharge are recoverable from the payee "as money received by him to the use of the" payor. As the subsection does not refer to "total failure of consideration", this statutory right arises even where the failure is only partial, for example, in such cases as *Whincup v Hughes*. **19–105**

**The payee may retain or recover a sum on account of expenses.** If the party to whom sums were paid or payable in pursuance of the contract has before the time of discharge incurred expenses in or for the purpose of the performance of the contract, the court may allow him to retain or recover the whole or any part of the sums so paid or payable; but the court cannot allow him to retain or recover more than the actual amount of his expenses. The burden of proving that qualifying expenses were incurred falls on the payee.[461] The court can make an award in respect of expenses under s.1(2) only if the contract contains a stipulation for pre-payment; a party who incurs expenses without asking for a pre-payment, or who incurs greater expenses than the amount of the pre-payment, does so at his own risk.[462] **19–106**

**Amount retained or recovered by the payee at the discretion of the court.** The court is not bound to make any award in respect of expenses and has discretion as to the amount of the award. This discretion is subject to two upper limits: the award must not exceed either the amount of the expenses incurred, or the amount of the stipulated prepayment.[463] No doubt in exercising its discretion **19–107**

[460] (1871) L.R. 6 C.P. 78.

[461] *Gamerco SA v ICM/Fair Warning (Agency) Ltd* [1995] 1 W.L.R. 1226 at 1235; *DVB Bank SE v Shere Shipping Co Ltd* [2013] EWHC 2321 (Ch) at [62].

[462] An award in respect of expenses can be made under s.1(2) only where a *sum of money* was paid or payable to the party who has incurred expenses. Where that party has received a "payment in kind" a similar result may be reached under s.1(3)(a): para.19–110.

[463] Proceeds of insurance payable to the claimant by reason of the frustrating events must be disregarded: s.1(5).

the court will be influenced by the degree to which the expenses have been made useless by the frustrating event. If machinery made for one customer can easily be sold to another, very little will be awarded; if it cannot be disposed of except as scrap, the court is likely to make a substantial award. Even in such a case, however, the court will not necessarily award the maximum amount available under the Act. Suppose that in the *Fibrosa* case the seller had received a prepayment of £1,600 and had incurred expenses of exactly that amount. Under the common law rule he would have had to pay back the whole £1,600, and this was unjust because it left him to bear the entire loss of the wasted expenditure. If, under the Act, the court were to allow him to retain the whole £1,600, this could be equally unjust as it would leave the buyer to bear the whole of that loss. In the exercise of its discretion under s.1(2) the court could split the loss (instead of merely shifting it from one party to the other) in such proportions as it thought just.[464]

19–108 **Expenses incurred by the payor.** In exercising its discretion under s.1(2), the court can also take account of the fact that expenses have been incurred by the *payor*. This was the position in *Gamerco SA v ICM/Fair Warning (Agency) Ltd*,[465] where the promoter of a concert had made an advance payment to the performers and the contract was then frustrated. Exercising a "broad discretion",[466] the court allowed the promoter to recover the payment in full, without any deduction in respect of expenses incurred by the performers for the purpose of the performance of the contract.[467] It did so on the grounds that the promoter had also incurred expenses which not only exceeded the pre-payment[468] but also amounted to about nine times those incurred by the performers,[469] and that each set of expenses had been wholly wasted.

### *(ii) Rights not yet accrued*

19–109 **Common law** At common law, rights not yet accrued at the time of frustration are unenforceable.[470] If a builder agrees to build a house for £100,000 payable on completion he cannot recover the £100,000 if the contract is frustrated before completion. This rule is perfectly reasonable: it would be unjust to make the building-owner pay the full price for an unfinished house. But, further, at common law the builder could not recover anything at all for partial performance before frustration. He could not recover a quantum meruit as payment for doing part of the work would be inconsistent with the express agreement for payment on completion. Thus, in *Appleby v Myers*[471] engineering contractors agreed "to make and erect the whole of the machinery" in the defendant's factory "and to

[464] s.1(2) refers to "the whole *or any part* of the sums so paid or payable."
[465] [1995] 1 W.L.R. 1226.
[466] *Gamerco SA v ICM/Fair Warning (Agency) Ltd* [1995] 1 W.L.R. 1226 at 1236.
[467] s.1(5), above, also required the court to disregard the fact that both parties had insured against cancellation and received payments under those policies.
[468] The promoter's expenses exceeded $450,000; the prepayment amounted to $412,500.
[469] The performers' expenses appear to have been about $50,000.
[470] *The M Vatan* [1987] 2 Lloyd's Rep. 416 at 426.
[471] (1867) L.R. 2 C.P. 651; cf. *Cutter v Powell* (1795) 6 T.R. 320, para.17–032.

keep the whole in order for two years from the date of completion". After part of the machinery had been erected, an accidental fire destroyed the factory with such of the machinery as was already in it, and frustrated the contract. It was held that the contractors could recover nothing for the machinery which they had erected. The general view is that this result is unsatisfactory[472] and that the builder should get something for his work.

**Law Reform (Frustrated Contracts) Act 1943 s.1(3).** The common law rule stated above was modified by s.1(3) of the Law Reform (Frustrated Contracts) Act 1943, which provides that: 19–110

> "Where any party to the contract has, by reason of anything done by any other party thereto in, or for the purpose of, the performance of the contract, obtained a valuable benefit (other than a payment of money to which [s.1(2)] applies) before the time of discharge, there shall be recoverable from him by the said other party such sum (if any), not exceeding the value of the said benefit to the party obtaining it, as the court considers just, having regard to all the circumstances of the case"[473]

and in particular to: (a) the amount of any expenses incurred by the benefited party before the time of discharge; and (b) "the effect, in relation to the said benefit, of the circumstances giving rise to the frustration of the contract". Thus if A agrees to decorate B's house for £2,500 payable on completion but dies after decorating half the house, A's estate may recover something.

**Measure of recovery.** The measure of recovery under s.1(3) was the main issue in *BP (Exploration) Libya Ltd v Hunt*.[474] The case arose out of an elaborate agreement between BP and Mr Hunt for the exploitation of an oil concession in Libya belonging to Mr Hunt. BP were to do all the work of exploration and to provide the necessary finance; they were also to make certain "farm-in" payments in cash and oil. In return, they were to get a half share in the concession; and, as soon as the field began to produce oil, they were to receive "reimbursement oil" (to be taken out of Mr Hunt's share) until they had recouped 125 per cent of their initial expenditure. A large oil field was discovered and oil began to flow from it in 1967; but in 1971 the contract between BP and Mr Hunt was frustrated when their interests in the concession were expropriated by Libyan decrees. At this time, BP had received only about one-third of the "reimbursement oil" to which they were entitled in respect of their initial expenditure; and they brought a claim under s.1(3) of the 1943 Act. The claim was allowed by Robert Goff J, whose decision was (subject to relatively minor modifications)[475] upheld by the Court of Appeal and the House of Lords. 19–111

---

[472] cf. paras 17–041—17–042 for criticism of the rule that nothing can be recovered for partial performance of an entire obligation. One practical justification for that rule in cases of *breach* may be that it puts pressure to perform on the party in breach, but that argument cannot apply where performance is prevented by an event for which neither party is responsible.

[473] But not to the proceeds of insurance payable to the claimant by reason of the frustrating event: s.1(5).

[474] [1979] 1 W.L.R. 783; affirmed [1981] 1 W.L.R. 236; [1983] 2 A.C. 352; Baker [1979] C.L.J. 266.

[475] Recovery of a "farm-in" payment of $2 million in *cash* had been allowed under s.1(3) when it plainly should have been allowed under s.1(2): see [1981] 1 W.L.R. 236 at 240; [1983] 2 A.C. 352 at 370.

The learned judge held that, in considering a claim under s.1(3), the court must proceed in two stages: it must first identify and value the benefit obtained, and then assess the just sum (not exceeding the value of the benefit) which it was proper to award. At the first stage, he held that "benefit", on the true construction of s.1(3), referred, not to the cost of performance incurred by the claimant, but to the end product received by the other party. In the case before him, that end product was the enhancement of the value of Mr Hunt's share in the concession resulting from BP's work; but because s.1(3)(b) required the court to have regard to "the effect, in relation to the said benefit, of the circumstances giving rise to … frustration", the value of that benefit had to be reduced to take account of the expropriation. In view of this fact, the total benefit obtained by Mr Hunt was the net amount of oil he had received from the concession, plus the compensation paid to him by the Libyan Government. Of this total, half was attributed to BP's efforts and half to Mr Hunt's original ownership of the concession. The value of this benefit was quantified at some $85 million. In assessing the "just sum" to be awarded, however, Robert Goff J adopted a criterion which he had rejected in valuing the benefit, viz. the cost to BP of the work to the extent that it was done for Mr Hunt. To this was added the value of the "farm in" oil[476] and the resulting total was then reduced by the amount of the reimbursement oil already received by BP. On this basis, the just sum was some $34.67 million[477] and, as the valuable benefit exceeded this amount, BP recovered the just sum in full.

19–112 **Definition of "valuable benefit".** It follows from the definition of valuable benefit as an "end product" that s.1(3) will not apply merely because the claimant has incurred trouble and expense for the purpose of the performance of the contract.[478] On the other hand, there can be a valuable benefit within s.1(3) even though no physical thing has been transferred by the claimant to the defendant. Thus in *BP Exploration (Libya) Ltd v Hunt* the services rendered by BP to Mr Hunt constituted at least part of the benefit. In the case of a contract to paint a house, there would similarly be a valuable benefit if the contract was frustrated by illegality after half the work had been done.[479] In such cases the improvement to the defendant's property can be said to be an "end product"; but there are other contexts in which the definition of "valuable benefit" as an "end product" would be inappropriate, e.g. where the contract was one for the hire of a chattel. Such a contract is not intended to leave any "end product" in the hands of the hirer, who can nevertheless be said to have benefited if he has had the use of the chattel for part of the agreed period before the contract is frustrated. It would be unfortunate

[476] This value seems also to be relevant to the identification of the benefit.
[477] *BP (Exploration) Libya Ltd v Hunt* [1981] 1 W.L.R. 236 at 241.
[478] This was precisely the position in *Taylor v Caldwell* (1863) 3 B. & S. 826: see para.19–003. For the court's power to allow the *recipient* of the benefit to deduct expenses, see para.19–114.
[479] Illustration given by Lord Simon LC when introducing s.1(3): HL Deb., col.139 (29 June 1943).

if s.1(3) were held to be inapplicable in such a case merely because of the definition of valuable benefit adopted in the different context of *BP Exploration (Libya) Ltd v Hunt*.[480]

**Destruction of the benefit.** The machinery of the Act worked satisfactorily in *BP (Exploration) Libya Ltd v Hunt* because the valuable benefit, even when reduced in the light of the frustrating event, exceeded the just sum. But the position would have been different if the expropriation had occurred immediately before oil had begun to flow and if no compensation for expropriation had been paid. On the reasoning of the judgment, there would then have been no valuable benefit (beyond the "farm-in" oil); for that reasoning has regard to "the circumstances giving rise to the frustration" within s.1(3)(b) in *valuing the benefit* rather than in *assessing the just sum*. The same reasoning is adopted in an example which closely resembles *Appleby v Myers*[481]: 19–113

> "Suppose that a contract for work on a building is frustrated by a fire which destroys the building and which therefore destroys a substantial amount of the work already done by the [claimant]. Although *it might be thought just* to award the [claimant] a sum assessed on a *quantum meruit* basis, the effect of s.1(3)(b) will be to reduce the award to nil …".[482]

If this is right, *Appleby v Myers* would not be affected by the Act; but in view of the evident reluctance with which the learned judge reached this conclusion it is submitted that an alternative interpretation of s.1(3) is to be preferred. This would make the destruction of the benefit relevant, not to the identification of the benefit, but to the assessment of the just sum. Two points seem to support such an interpretation. First, s.1(3) applies where a valuable benefit has been obtained *before* the time of discharge: thus to identify the benefit in a case like *Appleby v Myers* the court must look at the facts as they were before, and not after, the fire. The partly completed installation would at least prima facie be a benefit, since completion of the installation would be likely to cost less after part of the work had been done. Secondly, there is the structure of the subsection. This begins by setting out the circumstances in which the court has power to make an award (i.e. when a valuable benefit has been obtained) and then provides guidelines for the exercise of that power. The guideline contained in s.1(3)(b) is introduced by the words "such sum as the court thinks just having regard to … "; and these words seem to link the guideline to the *exercise* rather than to the *existence* of the court's discretion. This interpretation cannot cause any injustice, for if the court thinks that very little or nothing should be awarded it can exercise its discretion to that effect; and for this purpose the court can take the destruction of the benefit into account so as to split the loss in such proportions as the court thinks just. But if such destruction necessarily led to the conclusion that no valuable benefit had been obtained before frustration, the court would have no discretion to award

---

480 s.1(3) should therefore apply on facts such as those in *Cutter v Powell* (1795) 6 T.R. 320; para.17–032 unless the contract was literally one of insurance: see para.17–032 and para.19–119. The "just sum" should not be based on the exceptionally high rate of pay contracted for, but on current market rates (see para.17–032).

481 (1867) L.R. 2 C.P. 651; para.19–109.

482 *BP (Exploration) Libya Ltd v Hunt* [1979] 1 W.L.R. 783 at 801 (emphasis added).

anything at all. It would be a pity if this useful discretion were restricted in a way that is neither clearly required by the words of the subsection nor necessary to promote justice.

19–114 **Relationship between s.1(2) and (3).** The power to make an award in respect of a valuable benefit under s.1(3) is, in theory, additional to the power to make an award in respect of expenses under s.1(2). Thus if a party who has incurred expenses has also both conferred a valuable benefit and received (or stipulated for) a pre-payment he can claim under both subsections. But any amount awarded in respect of expenses will be taken into account in deciding how much should be awarded in respect of valuable benefit, and vice versa.[483] If the party who has incurred expenses has *received* a valuable benefit other than money (e.g. a "pre-payment" in kind) he cannot make any claim in respect of expenses under s.1(2) as that subsection only applies where a *sum of money* is paid or payable. But the court can reach much the same result under s.1(3), for it can take the expenses into account in deciding how much the recipient of the valuable benefit should pay for it.[484]

### *(iii) Casus omissus?*

19–115 **Pre-frustration payments in kind.** Under s.1(2), sums of money payable before frustration cease to be payable on frustration. The subsection is restricted to *payments of money*. Section 1(3), by contrast, provides for restitution claims in respect of *other benefits*, e.g. where A renders services or transfers property to B before frustration. But nothing in s.1(3) in terms releases A where before frustration he ought to have performed an obligation to do something other than to pay cash, has failed to do so, and would, if he had performed, have been entitled to make a claim for restitution under s.1(3). Thus if A has promised to make an advance payment *in cash* and has failed before frustration to do so, he is released by s.1(2); but if the stipulated payment had been *in kind* he would not be released by anything in s.1(2) or s.1(3). Nor can he, in the latter case, neutralise his liability by making a claim under s.1(3), for B has not "by reason of anything done [by A] obtained a valuable benefit … *before* the time of discharge". On the contrary, B has failed to obtain an expected benefit by reason of something not done by A. B may *after* the time of discharge obtain a benefit by suing A, but this does not bring the case within s.1(3) as the benefit is obtained too late. Nor would it help A to argue that before the time of discharge B had a valuable benefit, namely, his right to sue A, for this benefit would not have been obtained "by reason of anything done [by A] in or for the purpose of the performance of the contract". It is hard to believe that these consequences were intended. The failure of the Act in these circumstances to provide for the release of obligations other than those to pay money seems to be a *casus omissus*.

---

483 See s.1(3)(a).

484 See s.1(3)(a).

### (iv) *Special cases*

**Severability.** A contract may provide for one party to make payments from time to time in response to specified parts of the other's performance. The common law rule was that, if the contract was frustrated, such payments as were due at the time of frustration could be recovered. In *Stubbs v Holywell Ry*[485] a consulting engineer was appointed for 15 months for £500 payable in five equal quarterly instalments. After two quarters he died. His administrator successfully claimed the £200 due to him at the date of his death. But he could have recovered nothing more had the deceased worked for another two months in the next quarter. Under the 1943 Act he can do so. Section 2(4) provides that if parts of a contract which have been wholly performed can properly be severed from the remainder, they are to be treated as separate contracts; and that the provisions of s.1 (discussed above) shall apply to the remainder of the contract. 19–116

Section 2(4) also affects the rights of a person to recover money paid under such a contract. At common law money could be recovered if paid for some severable part of the consideration which had wholly failed, even though the consideration for the whole payment had not failed.[486] If in *Stubbs v Holywell Ry* the whole £500 had been paid in advance, £200 could have been recovered as no work at all was done by the deceased in the last two quarters; but nothing could have been recovered in respect of the third quarter, if the deceased had done so much as a week's work in it. Now money paid in respect of the third quarter could be recovered, but the personal representative could claim under s.1(3) in respect of the work done by the deceased in that week. An obligation may also be severable by statute under the provisions of the Apportionment Act 1870.[487]

**Contrary agreement.** The common law rule that money is recoverable on the ground of total failure of consideration can be excluded by contrary agreement: the money may be paid out-and-out, with the intention that the payee shall keep it in any event.[488] The provisions of the Act can similarly be excluded by contrary agreement;[489] whether a term has this effect depends on its construction. In *BP* 19–117

[485] (1867) L.R. 2 Ex. 311.

[486] See *Tyrie v Fletcher* (1777) 2 Cowp. 666 at 668; Marine Insurance Act 1906 s.84(2) (divisible insurance policies); para.22–010. Section 84 of the 1906 Act must now be read subject to the Consumer Insurance (Disclosure and Representations) Act 2012 Sch.1: see Pt 4.

[487] See para.17–047.

[488] *Fibrosa Spolka Akcyjna v Fairbairn, Lawson, Combe, Barbour Ltd* [1943] A.C. 32 at 43, 77. The common law rule could still apply, e.g. to contracts excluded from the operation of the Act by s.2(5)(c): para.19–118 and following.

[489] Section 2(3). Contract terms *excluding the common law rule* stated at fn.488, would not be subject to the requirement of reasonableness under Unfair Contract Terms Act 1977 s.3(2)(b)(ii) (para.7–057) since in the case of a frustrated contract there would be *no* "contractual obligation" to perform. They might, however, be subject to the requirement of fairness under the Consumer Rights Act 2015 (para.7–100 and following): see Sch.2 Pt.1 para.18. Contract terms *excluding the 1943 Act* would not be subject to Unfair Contract Terms Act 1977, being "authorised" by s.2(3) of the 1943 Act and so excepted from the 1977 Act by virtue of s.29(1)(a) of that Act (para.7–084); but they could be subject to the Consumer Rights Act 2015, for although that Act does not apply to "mandatory statutory... provisions" (s.73(1)(a)) the provisions of the 1943 Act are (by reasons of s.2(3)) not "mandatory". The fact that s.2(3) permitted the parties to exclude the provisions of the 1943 Act would, however, be relevant to the question whether a term to this effect was "unfair" for the purposes of the 2015 Act.

*Exploration (Libya) Ltd v Hunt*[490] the contract provided that the defendant was not to be personally liable to repay any advances and that BP's rights were to be exercisable only against the defendant's share of the oil. This provision did not exclude the Act as, on its true construction, it was not intended to deal with the risk of expropriation but with the different risk that no oil might be found.

### (v) *Contracts excluded from the 1943 Act*

19–118 **Voyage charterparties and other contracts for the carriage of goods by sea.**[491] The 1943 Act does not apply to voyage charterparties and other contracts for the carriage of goods by sea. The object of this exception is to preserve two rules which are well established and known in the trade: first, that freight which has become due or been paid before frustration remains due and (if paid) cannot be recovered, even though the cargo is lost;[492] and, secondly, that a person who contracts to carry goods by sea to a specified port cannot recover freight pro rata, even if he is forced by events outside his control to discharge them at an intermediate port.[493]

19–119 **Contracts of insurance.** The 1943 Act does not apply to contracts of insurance.[494] This exception preserves the rule that there can, in general, be no apportionment of premiums under an insurance policy once the risk has begun to run. The essence of a contract of insurance is that "the contract is for the whole entire risk, and no part of the consideration shall be returned".[495] Thus if a ship is insured but lost in some way not covered by the policy after part of the period of insurance has run, no part of the premium can be recovered. This is obviously in accordance with the intention of the parties, for such a contract is essentially speculative. Had the ship been lost by one of the perils insured against on the first day, the insurer would have had to bear the whole loss. Conversely, he can keep the whole premium if the ship is lost by a peril that is not covered by the policy at any time during the period of insurance.

19–120 **Contracts to which s.7 of the Sale of Goods Act 1979 applies.** Section 2(5)(c) provides that the 1943 Act shall not apply to two types of contracts for the sale of goods. First, it does not apply to "any contract to which s.7 of the Sale of Goods Act 1979 … applies". Under s.7 of that Act, an agreement to sell specific goods is

---

490 [1983] 2 A.C. 352.

491 Section 2(5)(a) provides that the Act shall not apply "to any charterparty, except a time charterparty or a charterparty by way of demise, or to any contract (other than a charterparty) for the carriage of goods by sea." These words make it clear that the Act does not apply to voyage charterparties, but leave open the question whether it applies to a "time charter trip" (fn.397). The answer may depend on the degree of particularity with which the contract describes the voyage.

492 *Byrne v Schiller* (1871) L.R. 6 Ex. 319; unless the contract provides the contrary, as in *The Oliva* [1972] 1 Lloyd's Rep. 458; contrast *The Lorna I* [1983] 1 Lloyd's Rep. 373 where, on the true construction of the contract, freight was not to become due till after the frustrating event. Freight may be *earned* before it is *payable*: para.17–032.

493 *St Enoch Shipping Co Ltd v Phosphate Mining Co* [1916] 2 K.B. 625; para.17–032.

494 1943 Act s.2(5)(b).

495 *Tyrie v Fletcher* (1777) 2 Cowp. 666 at 668. For a contractual provision displacing the normal rule, see *The M Vatan* [1987] 2 Lloyd's Rep. 416.

avoided if the goods perish without any fault on the part of the seller or buyer before the risk[496] has passed to the buyer. That is, the buyer is not liable for the price and neither party is liable in damages. The same result would normally follow from the common law rules of frustration, since the destruction of specific goods would frustrate the contract. The cases in which the 1943 Act would (if it were not excluded by s.2(5)(c)) make a difference are those in which there has been an advance payment or part-delivery.

If the buyer pays in advance but does not get any of the goods, he can recover his payment on the ground of total failure of consideration.[497] The exclusion of the Act does not affect this right, but it does prevent the seller from setting off any expenses which he may have incurred, e.g. in putting the goods into a deliverable state.

Part-delivery followed by frustration raises two problems. First, a buyer of a specific parcel of goods may have paid the whole price in advance and received only part-delivery. He probably cannot recover any part of the payment at common law as the failure of consideration is not total.[498] Nor can he rely on the 1943 Act, as that is excluded. Secondly, a seller may have delivered part of the goods and been paid nothing. As the 1943 Act is excluded, he cannot rely on it to recover anything in respect of the valuable benefit obtained by the buyer. He may be able to recover something at common law if a new contract can be implied from the buyer's keeping the goods after frustration. But it would be hard to imply such a contract if the buyer no longer had the goods, e.g. because he had used or resold them before frustration.

**Where specific goods have perished.** The 1943 Act secondly does not apply to "any other contract for the sale, or the sale and delivery, of specific goods, where the contract is frustrated by reason of the fact that the goods have perished". These words seem to refer to a case which would not fall within s.7 of the Sale of Goods Act 1979, because the risk has passed to the buyer. It is difficult to imagine how in such a case the contract could be frustrated by the perishing of the goods. Perhaps the point of excepting such a case from the 1943 Act is to make it clear that the buyer is liable for the whole price and that there is no power to order restitution or to apportion expenses. 19–121

**Scope of s.2(5)(c).** Section 2(5)(c) can produce some entirely capricious distinctions. The 1943 Act is excluded only where the goods are specific. Suppose that a farmer agrees to sell 200 tons out of a crop to be grown on his land, and the crop is destroyed by events for which he is not responsible.[499] As the goods are not specific,[500] the 1943 Act is not excluded and the farmer can set off his expenses of cultivating the crop against any advance payment made by the buyer. But if an agreement were made to sell an identified parcel of 200 tons after the crop had been lifted, the goods would be specific so that the 1943 Act would 19–122

[496] See para.19–013.
[497] *Logan v Le Mesurier* (1846) 6 Moo. P.C. 116.
[498] It is assumed that the value of the part undelivered is not readily apportionable to the whole: see para.22–010.
[499] See *Howell v Coupland* (1876) 1 Q.B.D. 258; para.19–026.
[500] s.61(1) of Sale of Goods Act 1979; *Re Wait* [1927] 1 Ch. 606 at 631.

be excluded. Hence if the agreement in such a case had provided that the farmer was to put the goods into sacks, and if the goods had been destroyed before this operation had been completed, the farmer would have to return the whole of any advance payment made by the buyer,[501] and have no right to deduct any part of the expenses of packaging. The 1943 Act is also excluded only where the cause of frustration is the perishing of the goods. Thus the Act applies where the contract is frustrated by illegality or requisition.

The reason for these distinctions is far from clear; and one might ask why contracts for the sale of goods were singled out for separate treatment at all. As a matter of abstract justice, there seems to be no reason why the powers of restitution and apportionment provided by the Act should apply to a contract to build a house but not a contract to supply a specific piece of machinery. The main reason for not applying the Act to contracts for the sale of goods is that in such contracts certainty is more important than justice; and the certainty which the rules as to the passing of risk is meant to provide would be disrupted if their effects could be modified by the exercise of the discretionary powers conferred on the courts by the 1943 Act. But on this view contracts for the sale of goods should have been wholly excluded from the operation of the 1943 Act. Their partial exclusion does not satisfy the requirements of either certainty or justice.

## 5. JURISTIC BASIS[502]

### (a) Theories of frustration

**19–123** Much discussion is to be found in the cases as to the so-called theoretical or juristic basis of the doctrine of frustration. The first puzzle is why judges have devoted so much attention to this question. Perhaps the reason is that they have felt the need to justify in some way their departure from the doctrine of absolute contracts. The second puzzle is to know exactly what the discussion is about. Two questions have become, perhaps inevitably, intertwined: *why* are contracts frustrated, and *when*? Thus in *Davis Contractors Ltd v Fareham Urban DC* Lord Radcliffe said that "frustration occurs *whenever*" the changed circumstances make performance "radically different from that which was undertaken."[503] This seems to deal with the second question; but it has also been regarded as providing an answer to the first.[504] Discussions of the juristic basis of the doctrine of frustration attempt sometimes to justify the doctrine, and sometimes to evolve some general formula for describing the conditions in which it operates. The main theories of frustration found in the cases are as follows.

---

[501] Under the rule in *Fibrosa Spolka Akcyjna v Fairbairn, Lawson, Combe, Barbour Ltd* [1943] A.C. 32; para.19–101.

[502] McNair 56 L.Q.R. 173; Treitel, *Frustration and Force Majeure*, 3rd edn (2014), paras 16–006–16–017.

[503] *Davis Contractors Ltd v Fareham Urban DC* [1956] A.C. 696 at 729.

[504] e.g. in *National Carriers Ltd v Panalpina (Northern) Ltd* [1981] A.C. 675 at 688, 717; see para.19–128.

**Implied term.** The first theory is that the contract is discharged because it impliedly provides that in the events which have happened it shall cease to bind. This theory is put forward by Lord Loreburn in the *Tamplin* case. "No court has absolving power"[505] but the court will not regard an obligation as absolute if the parties themselves did not intend it to be absolute. If they "must have made their bargain on the footing that a particular thing or state of things would continue to exist … a term to that effect will be implied".[506] **19–124**

In a purely subjective sense this theory is clearly untenable. The implication would have to arise at the time of contracting and at that time the parties are unlikely to have any view as to the effects on the contract of the supervening event; and after the event has occurred, the parties might well have no *common* view as to its effects, e.g. one party might well take the view that it should, and the other that it should not, discharge the contract. Even if the parties could reach some agreement on the point, they would probably not agree to total, unconditional discharge. As Lord Wright has said, "they would almost certainly on the one side or the other have sought to introduce reservations or qualifications or compensations".[507] In fact, Lord Loreburn did not put forward a purely subjective version of the implied term theory. He said: "From the nature of the contract it cannot be supposed that the parties *as reasonable men* intended it to be binding on them under such altered conditions … ".[508]

The fact that the implied term theory did not seek to give effect to the subjective intention of the parties may explain why it fell out of favour,[509] but as has been noted earlier,[510] the implication of terms in general[511] is an objective process and it is very closely related to, if not the same as, the equally objective process of the "construction" of the contract which may provide the most satisfactory explanation for the doctrine of frustration.[512]

---

505 *Tamplin SS Co Ltd v Anglo-Mexican Petroleum Co* [1916] 2 A.C. 397 at 404.

506 *Tamplin SS Co Ltd v Anglo-Mexican Petroleum Co* [1916] 2 A.C. 397 at 403.

507 *Denny, Mott & Dickson v James B Fraser & Co Ltd* [1944] A.C. 265 at 275; cf. *Shell UK Ltd v Lostock Garage Ltd* [1976] 1 W.L.R. 1187 at 1196: *Atisa SA v Aztec AG* [1983] 2 Lloyd's Rep. 579 at 586 (implied term theory "now rejected"); *FC Shepherd & Co Ltd v Jerrom* [1987] Q.B. 301 at 322; *The Super Servant Two* [1989] 1 Lloyd's Rep. 145 at 154; affirmed [1990] 1 Lloyd's Rep. 1; *The Great Peace* [2002] EWCA Civ 1407; [2003] Q.B. 679 at [73] ("not realistic"); cf. Trakman 46 M.L.R. 39. For a possible power of the court to introduce "reservations", etc. by means of an implied term while holding the contract *not* frustrated, see *The Maira (No.2)* [1985] 1 Lloyd's Rep. 300 at 311; affirmed on other grounds [1986] 2 Lloyd's Rep. 12.

508 *Tamplin SS Co Ltd v Anglo-Mexican Petroleum Co* [1916] 2 A.C. 397 at 404; cf. *Davis Contractors Ltd v Fareham Urban DC* [1956] A.C. 696 at 728, per Lord Reid: "By this time it might seem that the parties themselves have become so far disembodied spirits that their actual persons should be allowed to rest in peace. In their place there rises the figure of the fair and reasonable man. And the spokesman of the fair and reasonable man, who represents after all no more than the anthropomorphic conception of justice, is and must be the court itself".

509 See fn.507.

510 See para.6–054.

511 i.e. terms implied *in fact*.

512 See para.19–127. There is an obvious analogy here with the doctrine of common mistake where there is a role for the "construction" of the contract, but the courts have rejected the implied term theory as the best explanation for when a contract is void for mistake: see paras 8–002—8–007. The analogy between frustration and mistake is considered further below: para.19–131.

19–125 **Just solution.** Lord Sumner once described the doctrine of frustration as "a device by which the rules as to absolute contracts are reconciled with a special exception which justice demands".[513] Lord Wright in the *Denny, Mott* case, found "the theory of the basis of the rule"[514] in this statement; he added that the doctrine of frustration did not depend on the possibility of implying a term, but was "a substantive and particular rule which the common law has evolved".[515] And in the *Constantine* case he said: "The court is exercising powers, when it decides that a contract is frustrated, in order to achieve a result which is just and reasonable".[516] This "just solution" theory does not purport to explain why the courts sometimes abandon the doctrine of absolute contracts: it simply says that they do so. The theory should not, moreover, be interpreted to mean that the courts can do what they think just whenever a change of circumstances causes hardship to one party: it does not supersede the strict rules which determine the scope of the doctrine of frustration,[517] though the "dictates of justice" are the "ultimate rationale of the doctrine".[518] Nor does it determine the type of relief which can be given. When a contract is frustrated, both parties are at common law discharged, though the "just solution" might be an apportionment of loss.

19–126 **Foundation of the contract.** This theory was stated by Lord Haldane in the *Tamplin* case:

> "When people enter into a contract which is dependent for the possibility of performance on the continued availability of a specific thing, and that availability comes to an end by reason of circumstances beyond the control of the parties, the contract is *prima facie* regarded as dissolved. ... Although the words of the stipulation may be such that the mere letter would describe what has occurred, the occurrence itself may yet be of a character and extent so sweeping that the foundation of what the parties are deemed to have had in contemplation has disappeared, and the contract itself has vanished with that foundation".[519]

In *WJ Tatem Ltd v Gamboa*[520] Goddard J regarded this as "the surest ground on which to rest the doctrine of frustration". At first sight this theory has the merit of simplicity as it does not involve speculation as to the intention of the parties. It is particularly appropriate where performance depends on the continued availability of a specific thing. But in other cases the metaphor "foundation" is unhelpful. How can one tell whether passage through the Suez Canal is the "foundation" of a charterparty? What is the "foundation" of a contract in which the parties take a deliberate risk as to the continued availability of a specific thing or existence of some state of affairs? Such questions can, in the last resort, only be resolved by

513 *Hirji Mulji v Cheong Yue SS Co Ltd* [1926] A.C. 497 at 510.

514 *Denny, Mott & Dickson v James B Fraser & Co Ltd* [1944] A.C. 265 at 275.

515 *Denny, Mott & Dickson v James B Fraser & Co Ltd* [1944] A.C. 265 at 274.

516 *Joseph Constantine SS Line Ltd v Imperial Smelting Corp Ltd* [1942] A.C. 154 at 186; cf. *National Carriers Ltd v Panalpina (Northern) Ltd* [1981] A.C. 675 at 696; *The Super Servant Two* [1990] 1 Lloyd's Rep. 1 at 8.

517 See paras 19–005, 19–034; *The Sea Angel* [2007] EWCA Civ 547; [2007] 2 Lloyd's Rep. 517 at [113].

518 *The Sea Angel* [2007] EWCA Civ 547; [2007] 2 Lloyd's Rep. 517 at [132].

519 *Tamplin SS Co Ltd v Anglo-Mexican Petroleum Co* [1916] 2 A.C. 397 at 406. Lord Haldane's was a dissenting speech.

520 [1939] 1 K.B. 132 at 137.

construing the contract. If this is so, there is no real difference between the "foundation" theory and the "implied term" theory in its objective sense. Indeed, exponents of one sometimes use the language of the other. Thus, in the *Tamplin* case Lord Loreburn, after stating the implied term theory, said that the court "can infer from the nature of the contract and the surrounding circumstances that a condition which is not expressed was a foundation on which the parties contracted".[521]

**Construction of the contract.** All the theories so far stated depend in the last resort on the construction of the contract: to this extent, they "shade into one another".[522] After stating the implied term theory, Lord Loreburn proposed, as the ultimate test: "what, in fact, is the true meaning of the contract?"[523] Similarly, in *Taylor v Caldwell*, Blackburn J said: **19–127**

> "the contract is not to be *construed* as a positive contract, but as subject to an *implied condition* that the parties shall be excused in case, before breach, performance becomes impossible. ..."[524]

Construing the contract and implying a term are in these cases only alternative ways of describing the same process. Similarly, the "foundation" theory raises a question of construction whenever it is at all doubtful what the "foundation" of the contract is. And Lord Wright, in the course of stating the "just solution" theory, said:

> "What happens is that the contract is held on its true construction not to apply at all from the time when the frustrating circumstances supervene".[525]

It seems that this is the most satisfactory explanation of the doctrine of frustration.[526]

**"Radically different" theory.** In *Canary Wharf (BP4) T1 Ltd v European Medicines Agency*[527] Marcus Smith J suggested that there is a "material difference" between what is referred to as the "construction of the contract" theory and the "performance is radically different" theory, the latter derived from **19–128**

---

521 *Tamplin SS Co Ltd v Anglo-Mexican Petroleum Co* [1916] 2 A.C. 397 at 404.
522 *National Carriers Ltd v Panalpina (Northern) Ltd* [1981] A.C. 675 at 693.
523 *Tamplin SS Co Ltd v Anglo-Mexican Petroleum Co* [1916] A.C. 397 at 404. There are obvious echoes here of the question proposed by Lord Hoffmann in *Attorney General of Belize v Belize Telecom Ltd* [2009] UKPC 10; [2009] 1 W.L.R. 1988 at [21] to determine whether a term should be implied in fact: "is that what the instrument, read as a whole against the relevant background, would reasonably be understood to mean?"; see para.6–051.
524 *Taylor v Caldwell* (1863) 3 B. & S. 826 at 833 (emphasis added).
525 *Denny, Mott & Dickson v James B Fraser & Co Ltd* [1944] A.C. 265 at 274; cf. *The Eugenia* [1964] 2 Q.B. 226 at 239; *The Siboen and the Sibotre* [1976] 1 Lloyd's Rep. 293 at 235.
526 *Bunge SA v Kyla Shipping Co Ltd* [2012] EWHC 3522 (Comm); [2013] 1 Lloyd's Rep. 565 at [70].
527 [2019] EWHC 335 (Ch); 183 Con L.R. 167.

the test formulated by Lord Radcliffe and referred to above.[528] The difference is said to be that the construction theory "resolves all" whereas the "radically different" theory "recognises the importance of the true construction of the contract, but also recognises that even construction has its limits when faced with extreme and unforeseeable supervening events".[529] This is, with respect, open to question. The construction theory is no more or less than an exercise in the allocation of risk[530] which admits of two broad outcomes: either the risk of an event is found to have been allocated to one or other of the parties, in which case its consequences are determined by the contract (and, if one party is prevented from performing, it is liable for breach); or it is allocated to neither of the parties and the contract is frustrated. The latter is the outcome when performance, in light of events which may have been "extreme and unforeseeable", is "radically different from that *which was undertaken*".[531] The conclusion that performance is radically different is determined *by* the construction of the contract ("that which was undertaken"); it is not a recognition of its *limits*.[532]

19–129 **Failure of consideration.** This theory is sometimes used to explain why *both* parties are discharged in the situation (discussed earlier in this chapter)[533] in which the supervening event makes the performance of only *one* party impossible. Thus destruction of a specific thing may make performance of the *supplier's* obligation impossible; but it has no such effect on the *recipient's* obligation to pay, and it can be said that the latter is discharged by failure of consideration, i.e. because he does not receive the performance for which he bargained. In England, however, these cases are explained on the ground that the "common object" of the parties is frustrated.[534] Moreover, in so far as the present theory suggests that the failure of consideration must be total[535] it is plainly wrong since frustration can occur in cases of partial destruction or after part performance; and the theory has for this reason been rejected in the House of Lords.[536]

---

528 See text to fn.503. This may be a further example of the confusion referred to above between *why* a contract is frustrated and *when* it is frustrated: At one point, Marcus Smith J refers to the construction *theory* and the radically different *test*: [2019] EWHC 335 (Ch); 183 Con L.R. 167 at [26].

529 *Canary Wharf (BP4) T1 Ltd v European Medicines Agency* [2019] EWHC 335 (Ch); 183 Con L.R. 167 at [26].

530 And for this reason, it does not seem correct to suggest that Rix LJ's "multi-factorial approach" in *The Sea Angel* [2007] EWCA Civ 547; [2007] 2 Lloyd's Rep. 517 at [111], with its focus on "risk" (para.19–008) encapsulates "the difference between the construction theory of frustration and the 'radically different' theory of frustration": *Canary Wharf (BP4) T1 Ltd v European Medicines Agency* [2019] EWHC 335 (Ch); 183 Con L.R. 167 at [33].

531 *Davis Contractors Ltd v Fareham Urban DC* [1956] A.C. 696 at 729 (emphasis added).

532 It seems that Marcus Smith J's perception of a difference between the two "theories" may turn on a narrow conception of "construction" which equates it with the interpretation of a written contract: see, for example, the citation of Lord Hoffmann's "restatement" of the principles of interpretation at [28] (see also fn.52 at [36]); and the reference to "common purpose" as "something *beyond* the true construction of the contract": at [244) (emphasis in original).

533 See para.19–059.

534 *Hirji Mulji v Cheong Yue SS Co Ltd* [1926] A.C. 497 at 510; para.19–059.

535 For total failure of consideration, see para.19–102; para.22–003.

536 *National Carriers Ltd v Panalpina (Northern) Ltd* [1981] A.C. 675 at 687, 702.

## (b) Practical importance

It is sometimes asked whether the above theoretical discussion has any practical importance. It seems to have none.[537] A number of possibilities must be discussed. 19–130

We have seen that in *WJ Tatem Ltd v Gamboa* Goddard J said that the contract would be frustrated although the parties foresaw that the ship would be seized and detained. He even said: "If the foundation of the contract goes, it goes whether or not the parties have made a provision for it".[538] These statements could only be made by an adherent of the "foundation" theory. But the first has been doubted earlier in this chapter,[539] while the second was qualified later in the judgment: "*Unless the contrary intention is made plain*, the law imposes this doctrine of frustration".[540]

In the *Davis Contractors* case, Lord Reid said that no review was possible of the arbitrator's decision on the "foundation" theory, as the question whether the "foundation" had disappeared was one of fact; while such review was possible on the "implied term" or "construction" theories, as implication and construction were questions of law.[541] But a question of law would be involved even on the "foundation" theory if the process of establishing the "foundation" is itself a question of construction. And after the *Tsakiroglou* case[542] it is difficult to argue that the right to review an arbitrator's decision is restricted by any particular theory.

In the same case, Lord Reid also said that there might be a further practical difference between the "implied term" and "construction" theories. On the latter theory:

> "there is no need to consider what the parties thought or how they or reasonable men in their shoes would have dealt with the new situation if they had foreseen it. The question is whether the contract which they did make is, on its true construction, wide enough to apply to the new situation: if not, then it is at an end".[543]

But in construing the contract the court does not disregard the intention of the parties. The court may not have to ask: what would the parties have said, had they thought of the frustrating event? But it does have to ask: in what circumstances did the parties intend the contract to operate? In answering this question, the court no doubt applies an objective test;[544] but it is only after the question has been answered that the intention of the parties becomes irrelevant: that is, it is not necessary to go on and ask whether they would have agreed to discharge or to

---

537 This seems to be the view of Lords Wilberforce and Roskill in *National Carriers Ltd v Panalpina (Northern) Ltd* [1981] A.C. 675 at 693, 717; cf. Lord Hailsham at 687. Contrast *Canary Wharf (BP4) T1 Ltd v European Medicines Agency* [2019] EWHC 335 (Ch); 183 Con L.R. 167 at [26], discussed at para.19–128.

538 *WJ Tatem Ltd v Gamboa* [1939] 1 K.B. 132 at 138.

539 See para.19–086.

540 *WJ Tatem Ltd v Gamboa* [1939] 1 K.B. 132 at 139 (emphasis added).

541 *Davis Contractors Ltd v Fareham Urban DC* [1956] A.C. 696 at 720.

542 *Tsakiroglou & Co v Noblee Thorl GmbH* [1962] A.C. 93; see generally para.19–069.

543 *Davis Contractors Ltd v Fareham Urban DC* [1956] A.C. 696 at 721.

544 cf. paras 1–002, 2–002.

some compromise. But this question does not arise under the implied term theory either, as frustration at common law always results in total discharge of the contract.

### (c) Frustration and mistake

19–131 Frustration is sometimes compared with common mistake[545] because the supposed subject-matter of the contract does not exist or is fundamentally different from the subject-matter as it was believed to be. Thus in *Krell v Henry*[546] a contract for the hire of a room overlooking the route of the coronation processions was frustrated when the processions were *later* cancelled; in *Griffith v Brymer*[547] a similar contract was held void for mistake when the processions had *already* been cancelled before the contract was made.

19–132 **Different juristic concepts.** This analogy is interesting and sometimes helpful; but it should not be pressed too far. Mistake and frustration are "different juristic concepts",[548] the one relating to the formation and the other to the discharge of contracts. Their factual bases are different in that mistake requires the parties to entertain an *affirmative belief* in the existence of the subject-matter, or of a state of affairs, when it in fact no longer exists. In cases of frustration, the parties often have no affirmative belief as to the event: they need not *believe* that it *will not* occur. Moreover, events which frustrate a contract would not necessarily make it void for mistake if, unknown to the parties, they had already happened when the contract was made.[549] Again, parties may validly agree on a contractual term "requiring one of them to do the impossible",[550] e.g. on a term requiring a seller of goods to deliver them from a named ship at a specified port which the ship was incapable of entering. The seller would then be liable for failing to deliver in accordance with that term; but he could be discharged if *after* the time of contracting an event happened which made it impossible for the ship to get into the port, e.g. "if a sudden storm had silted up the harbour"[551] there. The law seems to be less ready to hold a contract void for mistake than discharged by

545 See para.8–002 and following; *Associated Japanese Bank (International) Ltd v Crédit du Nord SA* [1989] 1 W.L.R. 255 at 264 ("related areas"); *William Sindall Plc v Cambridgeshire CC* [1994] 1 W.L.R. 1016 at 1039). See also the reference to *Krell v Henry* [1903] 2 K.B. 740 in *Bell v Lever Bros Ltd* [1932] A.C. 161 at 226 and the words "whether as to existing or future facts": [1932] A.C. 161 at 226–227; and the reliance on frustration cases in the mistake case of *The Great Peace* [2002] EWCA Civ 1407; [2003] Q.B. 679 at [61]–[76].

546 [1903] 2 K.B. 740; para.19–043.

547 (1903) 19 T.L.R. 434; para.8–003.

548 *Joseph Constantine SS Line Ltd v Imperial Smelting Corp Ltd* [1942] A.C. 154 at 186; cf. *Bell v Lever Bros Ltd* [1932] A.C. 161 at 237; *Fibrosa Spolka Akcyjna v Fairbairn, Lawson, Combe, Barbour Ltd* [1943] A.C. 32 at 77.

549 The view that the test for common mistake is stricter than that of frustration appears to be supported by *The Great Peace* [2002] EWCA Civ 1407; [2003] Q.B. 679 at [83] (test of frustration "may not be adequate in the context of mistake"). Hence the analogy between the two doctrines drawn in that case in the passages referred to at fn.545 is, at best, imperfect.

550 *The Epaphus* [1987] 2 Lloyd's Rep. 215 at 218; *The New Prosper* [1991] 2 Lloyd's Rep. 93 at 99.

551 *The Epaphus* [1987] 2 Lloyd's Rep. 215 at 220; cf. *Bell v Lever Bros Ltd* [1932] A.C. 161 at 218, per Lord Atkin, approving the formulation by counsel (Sir John Simon KC).

frustration, perhaps because it is, in general, easier to be sure of present facts than to foresee future events,[552] or because a contracting party is more likely, on the true construction of the contract, to have undertaken responsibility for an existing, than for an unexpected future, state of affairs.[553]

**Distinct legal effects.** The legal effects of the two doctrines are also distinct. At common law, mistake makes a contract void ab initio, while frustration discharges it only from the time of the frustrating event.[554] In equity, indeed, the courts at one time claimed a power to set contracts aside for certain kinds of mistake which did not make them void at law.[555] But the Court of Appeal has held that there is no such power,[556] and even if this view were to be rejected by the Supreme Court and the equitable jurisdiction were again to be recognised, its operation would still differ from that of frustration in two ways. First, the equitable power in cases of mistake was regarded as discretionary while frustration discharges a contract automatically, by operation of law, without any scope for judicial discretion; frustration moreover results in total discharge, while the equitable jurisdiction was to set the contract aside on terms.[557] It is, finally, clear from the wording[558] of the Law Reform (Frustrated Contracts) Act 1943 that the powers of adjustment conferred by that Act apply only to discharge by supervening (and not to invalidity on the ground of antecedent) events.[559] **19–133**

552 cf. *McAlpine Humberoak Ltd v McDermott International* (1992) 58 Build. L.R. 1.
553 *The Great Peace* [2002] EWCA Civ 1407; [2003] Q.B. 679 at [85].
554 See paras 8–001, 19–097.
555 See para.8–028.
556 *The Great Peace* [2002] EWCA Civ 1407; [2003] Q.B. 679.
557 See paras 8–028, 19–097.
558 s.1(1) ("where a contract ... *has become* impossible of performance or *been* otherwise frustrated").
559 *The Great Peace* [2002] EWCA Civ 1407; [2003] Q.B. 679 at [161].

CHAPTER 20

# DAMAGES[1]



[1] Burrows, *Remedies for Torts and Breach of Contract*, 4th edn (2019).

**20–001** **Damages and other remedies.** A breach of contract is a civil wrong. To break a contract can also occasionally be a criminal offence,[2] but in most cases it will involve only civil liability. Our sole concern in this chapter will be with the remedy of damages. In Ch.21 we will consider claims for specific relief (the action for an agreed sum, specific performance and injunctions). A person who has performed his part of the contract but has not received the agreed counter-performance may also claim back his performance or its reasonable value. These restitutionary remedies are not confined to cases of breach of contract and are considered separately in Ch.22.

**20–002** **Damages are available as of right.** A claim for damages is one for compensation in money for the fact that the claimant has not received the performance for which he bargained. It is always available, as of right, when a contract has been broken. It should, from this point of view, be contrasted with claims for specific relief and for restitution, which are either subject to the discretion of the court or only available if certain conditions (to be discussed in the following chapters) are satisfied. An action for damages can succeed even though the victim has not suffered any loss: in that event, it will result in an award of nominal damages. The effect of such an award may simply be to establish what the rights and liabilities of the parties under a contract are, though for this purpose the action for a declaration now provides a more convenient remedy. Generally the victim will claim damages for a substantial loss; and our concern is with the law governing the award of such damages.

**20–003** **A pragmatic subject.** It has been said that the assessment of damages in contract (and tort) is "a pragmatic subject … (which) does not lend itself to hard-and-fast rules"[3] and, in a similar vein, that "with so many disputes about damages, the

[2] e.g. Protection from Eviction Act 1977 s.1; cf. National Minimum Wage Act 1998 s.31.

[3] *Takaro Properties Ltd v Rowling* (1986) 1 N.Z.L.R. 22 at 69; cf. *Johnson v Agnew* [1980] A.C. 367 at 400–401.

issue is primarily one of fact."[4] This may be a reflection of the fact that, traditionally, the assessment of damages was seen as a matter for the good sense of the jury.[5] Even today, the courts sometimes revert to the language of "common sense" to explain their decisions,[6] but this is not an area devoid of rules and principles and it is by reference to them that this chapter has been organised. We shall consider, first, the general principles which govern awards of damages;[7] secondly, the way in which damages are assessed or quantified;[8] thirdly, the recovery of damages for non-pecuniary loss;[9] fourthly, certain rules limiting the damages which can be recovered;[10] and finally, contractual provisions purporting to establish in advance the amount that can be recovered (or retained) by the injured party.[11]

## 1. GENERAL PRINCIPLES

### (a) Damages are compensatory

#### *(i) Loss to claimant the criterion*

**General rule.** As a general rule,[12] damages are based on loss to the claimant[13] and not on gain to the defendant.[14] In a Scottish case,[15] a financier broke a contract to invest £15,000 in the business of a timber merchant and instead invested the same sum in a distillery. It was held that the timber merchant's damages were based on the loss to his business and not on the much larger profits which the financier had derived from the distillery. The same principle applies where a person who has agreed to sell goods for future delivery for £x fails to deliver because he has disposed elsewhere of the goods for £x + 100. If the buyer can in fact get goods of the same description for £x or less at the time fixed for delivery, he will have suffered no loss and will get no (substantial) damages: it is irrelevant that the seller has, in a sense, made a profit of £100 out of the breach.[16] **20–004**

[4] *Hussey v Eeels* [1990] 2 Q.B. 227 at 241; para.20–111.
[5] See, e.g. *Chaplin v Hicks* [1911] 2 K.B. 786 at 792–793, 796; para.20–062.
[6] *Galoo Ltd v Bright Grahame Murray* [1994] 1 W.L.R. 1360 at 1374–1375; para.20–100; *The Fanis* [1994] 1 Lloyd's Rep. 633 at 636–637.
[7] See paras 20–004–20–039.
[8] See paras 20–040–20–087.
[9] See paras 20–088–20–098.
[10] See paras 20–099–20–134.
[11] See paras 20–135–20–177.
[12] For possible exceptions, see paras 20–009—20–022.
[13] For exceptional cases in which the claimant can recover damages in respect of a third party's loss see para.14–025 and following.
[14] *Tito v Waddell (No.2)* [1977] Ch. 106 at 332; *The Solholt* [1983] 1 Lloyd's Rep. 605 at 608; Jones 99 L.Q.R. 443, Friedmann 80 Col. L. Rev. 504; Farnsworth 94 Yale L.J. 1339; Birks [1987] L.M.C.L.Q. 421; Friedmann 104 L.Q.R. 383; Birks 1990–1991 *Butterworth Lectures* 55; cf. Stoljar 2 J.C.L. 1; Edelman *Gain Based Damages*.
[15] *Teacher v Calder* (1889) 1 F. (H.L.) 39; cf. *The Siboen and the Sibotre* [1976] 1 Lloyd's Rep. 293 at 337; *The Sine Nomine* [2002] 1 Lloyd's Rep. 805 (arbitration award).
[16] *Acmé Mills v Johnson* 133 S.W. 784 (1911); cf. *The Solholt* [1983] 1 Lloyd's Rep. 605.

It also follows from the general rule that damages are not awarded merely on the ground that the defendant has by the breach saved himself expense.

### *(ii) What constitutes loss?*

20–005 **The meaning of "loss".**[17] Perhaps as a result of the pragmatic fact-based approach referred to above,[18] the law of damages for breach of contract lacks a clear conceptual basis of what constitutes "loss". This has left room for a number of theories: for example, that a more fundamental distinction should be drawn between what may be referred to as "direct" loss, i.e. the non-receipt of the performance bargained for, and "consequential loss", i.e. the subsequent adverse consequences of such non-receipt,[19] leading to the view that damages for the former should be awarded either as a "substitute" for the right infringed,[20] or as the cost of performance.[21] The principal practical effect of such theories is that damages, when awarded as a substitute for the right infringed, or as the cost of performance are not subject to the principles of mitigation or remoteness.[22] These theories, and others,[23] have led to a shift in terminology: traditionally, the claimant was said to be entitled to the protection of his "expectation interest", but increasingly reference is made to the "performance interest". The courts have not gone as far as is advocated by some, but recent developments have shown a willingness to expand the concept of loss beyond the more obvious forms of financial loss which are prevalent in the earlier cases in which the rules and principles for the recovery of damages were formulated.[24] Thus, we have already seen a willingness to embrace the concept of the "performance interest" in claims for losses suffered by a third party,[25] and in this chapter it is perhaps most evident in the award of damages for breach of contracts for services,[26] in the greater recognition of damages to compensate for disappointment, or loss of enjoyment,[27] and in the wider availability in exceptional cases of damages awarded by reference to gains made by the defendant.[28]

20–006 **Overall position taken into account.** In determining whether the victim has suffered loss for which damages should be awarded, his overall position is taken

---

[17] Scott [2007] L.M.C.L.Q. 465.

[18] See para.20–003.

[19] See para.20–028.

[20] Stevens in Neyers, Bronaugh and Pitel (eds), *Exploring Contract Law* (2009).

[21] Edelman (2010) 4 *Journal of Equity* 122.

[22] The rule of remoteness probably does not apply to direct loss in any event (*Re National Coffee Palace Co* (1883) 24 Ch D. 367 at 372); alternatively, it does apply but such loss always arises in "the ordinary course of things" and is not therefore too remote: see para.20–120.

[23] See, inter alia, Friedmann 111 L.Q.R. 628; Coote [1997] C.L.J. 537; Duncan Wallace 115 L.Q.R. 394; cf. Campbell and Harris 22 J. of L. Studies 208; Campbell [2003] J. Bus. L. 131.

[24] "The law recognises that a party to a contract may have an interest in performance which is not readily measurable in terms of money": *Attorney General v Blake* [2001] 1 A.C. 268 at 282 per Lord Nicholls.

[25] See paras 14–025—14–044.

[26] See para.20–049.

[27] See para.20–093.

[28] See para.20–009 and following.

into account.[29] Relevant factors include any benefits which he may have obtained under the broken contract, and his release from obligations under it. If, for example, a buyer has not yet paid and is released from his obligation to do so by the seller's wrongful failure to deliver, his loss will prima facie be the value of the goods less the price; and if he has agreed to pay no more than the goods are worth he may have suffered no loss at all.

The court will similarly take the claimant's overall position into account in determining the basis on which damages are to be assessed: it will not generally order the defendant to pay an amount which will actually make the claimant's position better than it would have been if the contract had been performed.[30] The principle is illustrated by *Philips v Ward*[31] where a surveyor in breach of contract failed to draw his client's attention to the fact that the roof timbers of a house, which the latter was about to buy, were rotten. It was held that the client was not entitled to damages based on the cost of making the defects good. Such an award would put him into a better position than that in which he would have been if the contract had not been broken; for it would enable him to have a new roof with new timbers, which would be less expensive to maintain than an old roof with sound timbers. Hence the client was entitled to recover only the difference between the price that he paid and the value of the house when he bought it;[32] or the difference between the price actually paid and that which would have been paid if the surveyor had made his report with due care.[33]

**Qualifications.** The principle that the claimant's overall position should not be made better than it would have been, if the contract had not been broken, is subject to a number of qualifications.[34] First, it is not inflexibly applied where costs are actually incurred by the claimant in remedying the breach.[35] In *Harbutt's "Plasticine" Ltd v Wayne Tank & Pump Co Ltd*[36] the claimant's factory was burnt down as a result of the defendant's breach of contract. It was held that the claimant could recover the cost of rebuilding the factory without making any allowance for the fact that he would then have a new (and therefore more valuable) factory. The case can be explained on the ground that the claimant had no reasonable alternative but to rebuild, or that he did so in order to mitigate his loss.[37] Secondly, the principle was modified where a client had suffered loss in **20–007**

[29] e.g. *The Baleares* [1990] 2 Lloyd's Rep. 130 (and see [1991] 2 All E.R. 110); cf. para.20–110.

[30] e.g. see para.20–031 (reliance); *Demarco v Perkins* [2006] EWCA Civ 188; [2006] P.N.L.R. 27 at [73].

[31] [1956] 1 W.L.R. 471.

[32] See *Perry v Sidney Phillips & Son* [1982] 1 W.L.R. 1297 at 1305, 1306; Burrows 47 M.L.R. 357; *Watts v Morrow* [1991] 1 W.L.R. 1421; *Gardner v Marsh & Parsons* [1997] 1 W.L.R. 489. Where the client pays *more* than the valuation, such excess may be irrecoverable: see *Lucas v Ogden* [1988] 2 E.G.L.R. 176.

[33] *Perry v Sidney Phillips & Son* [1982] 1 W.L.R. 1297 at 1302.

[34] In addition to the qualifications referred to, see also the discussion at para.17–030 and para.20–087 (effect of claimant's inability to perform).

[35] See further para.20–044.

[36] [1970] 1 Q.B. 447, followed on this point in *Bacon v Cooper Metals Ltd* [1982] 1 All E.R. 397, and *Haysman v Mrs Rogers Films Ltd* [2008] EWHC 2494 (QB); cf. *Re-Source America International Ltd v Platt Site Services Ltd* [2005] EWCA Civ 97; [2005] 2 Lloyd's Rep. 50 (full replacement cost reduced by savings made on refurbishment).

[37] See para.20–108.

consequence of bad investment advice given by the defendant and had, before suffering the loss, spent some of the income produced by the investments on living expenses. This expenditure yielded no permanent benefit to the client and did not have to be brought into account since the very object of the contract was to produce an increased income for the client, so that it was foreseeable that he might spend that income, or part of it, in a way that left no product of permanent benefit to him.[38] Thirdly, the principle in *Philips v Ward* does not require the court to take into account benefits derived by the claimant under some contract with the defendant, other than the one which has been broken. Thus if the claimant makes two contracts with the defendant, any profit made by the claimant in consequence of the performance of one of those contracts will not have to be brought into account in assessing his damages in respect of the breach of the other.[39]

### *(iii) Breach having no adverse effect*

20–008 A further consequence of the compensatory principle is that the claimant cannot recover substantial damages if the breach has not adversely affected his position;[40] for "damages are designed to compensate for an established loss and not to provide a gratuitous benefit to the aggrieved party".[41] Another way of putting the point is that "A breach of contract may cause a loss but is not itself a loss in any meaningful sense".[42] This aspect of the principle is most readily illustrated by the case in which a seller of goods wrongfully fails to deliver on a falling market. If the buyer has not paid and if, at the time fixed for delivery, he can buy substitute goods more cheaply elsewhere, the breach will prima facie have had no adverse effect on him, so that he will not be entitled to substantial damages. Similarly, a shipowner cannot get substantial damages for breach of the charterer's obligation to load if he finds alternative and more profitable employment for the ship.[43] Nor can a buyer recover substantial damages merely because the seller delivers goods which are not of the contract description if they are in fact no less valuable than goods which are of the contract description.[44] These are all instances where the claimant has suffered no loss at all. He similarly cannot recover in respect of a loss which he does suffer if he would have suffered the same loss, even if there had been no breach. This situation is discussed later in this chapter.[45]

[38] *R. v Investors Compensation Scheme Ex p. Bowden* [1995] Q.B. 107; reversed on other grounds [1996] A.C. 261.

[39] *Brown v KMR Services Ltd* [1995] 4 All E.R. 598 at 640.

[40] See, e.g. *Ford v White* [1964] 1 W.L.R. 885.

[41] *Ruxley Electronics and Construction Co Ltd v Forsyth* [1996] A.C. 344 at 357.

[42] *Alfred McAlpine Construction Ltd v Panatown Ltd* [2001] 1 A.C. 518 at 534.

[43] *Staniforth v Lyall* (1830) 7 Bing. 169.

[44] *Taylor v Bank of Athens* (1922) 27 Com. Cas. 142.

[45] See para.20–100.

### (iv) *Damages based on the gain made by the defendant*[46]

We have seen above that, as a general rule, damages for breach of contract are based on loss to the claimant and not on gain to the defendant. There is one clear exception to that general rule where the claimant is awarded an account of the profits made by the defendant as a consequence of the breach.[47] In a number of other cases, the claimant has been awarded damages which have sometimes been calculated, at least in part, by reference to the profits made by the defendant, but such "negotiating damages" are regarded as compensation for loss, albeit of an unconventional kind, and they are dealt with separately below.[48] **20–009**

**Account of profits.** In some situations, there is no doubt that a contract breaker must hand over to the injured party any gain resulting from the breach. If, for example, the subject-matter of a sale is land, the vendor is, after the conclusion of the contract, considered to hold the land as trustee for the purchaser; and if the vendor wrongfully resells the land to a third party, the purchaser is entitled to the proceeds of that sale, even though they may exceed his loss.[49] An account of profits may be ordered against a person who wrongfully uses another's trade secrets or confidential information;[50] and this remedy may also be available where the wrongful use amounts to a breach of a contract of employment,[51] or a confidentiality agreement.[52] Where a breach of contract amounts also to breach of a fiduciary obligation, damages may similarly be based on the defendant's profit.[53] For example, an agent who commits a breach of his fiduciary duty by taking a bribe, or by selling his own property to a principal, when he has been employed to buy for him, is liable to account for any profit made in this way.[54] **20–010**

**Attorney General v Blake.** The wider availability of an account of profits for breach of contract was recognised by the House of Lords in *Attorney General v Blake*.[55] While employed as a member of the security services, Blake passed secret information to agents of the Soviet Union, in breach not only of the terms of his employment but also of the Official Secrets Act 1911; he was convicted of offences under that Act and sentenced to 42 years' imprisonment. He escaped from prison and fled to Moscow where, over 20 years later, he entered into an agreement with an English publisher for the publication of his autobiography. **20–011**

---

[46] Edelman, *Gain Based Damages*; Cunnington 71 M.L.R. 559.
[47] See para.20–010.
[48] See para.20–014.
[49] See *Lake v Bayliss* [1974] 1 W.L.R. 1073.
[50] *Peter Pan Mfg Corp v Corsets Silhouette Ltd* [1964] 1 W.L.R. 96; *Attorney General v Guardian Newspapers (No.2)* [1990] A.C. 109 at 262, 288; cf. Law Com. No.110, paras 4.86 and 6.114(2)(b).
[51] cf. *Printers & Finishers Ltd v Holloway* [1965] 1 W.L.R. 1.
[52] *Pell Frischmann Engineering Ltd v Bow Valley Iran Ltd* [2009] UKPC 45; [2010] B.L.R. 73; *Vercoe v Rutland Fund Management Ltd* [2010] EWHC 424 (Ch). In both cases, the claim for breach of contract was confined to "negotiating damages" (see para.20–014).
[53] *Mathew v TM Sutton Ltd* [1994] 1 W.L.R. 1455; *Tang Man Sit v Capacious Investments Ltd* [1996] A.C. 514 (where the claimant elected to claim damages for breach of trust rather than an account of profits); cf. *Nottingham University v Fishel* [2000] I.C.R. 1462 at 1489.
[54] See para.16–113.
[55] [2001] 1 A.C. 268.

Although the information in the book was no longer confidential[56] at the time of the delivery of his manuscript and of the publication of the book, its disclosure amounted to both a further offence under the 1911 Act and a further breach of Blake's contract with the Crown. This breach, however, caused no material loss to the Crown in respect of which compensatory damages could have been recovered and, after publication, the remedy by way of injunction, which could have been sought before then, was no longer available; nor could the case be brought within any of the situations in which an account of profits had hitherto been awarded.[57] The House of Lords nevertheless held, by a majority, that where (as in *Blake*'s case) damages were not a "sufficient"[58] remedy, the court should "exceptionally" be able to "grant the discretionary remedy of requiring a defendant to account to the [claimant] for benefits derived from his breach of contract".[59] This development was based on the analogy of the discretionary remedies by way of specific relief in equity, which are available also where damages are not an adequate (or the most appropriate)[60] remedy for breach.

20–012 **Scope of the discretionary account of profits.** Two questions arise in relation to the discretion to award an account of profits for breach of contract: when does it *exist* and when will it be *exercised*? In relation to the equitable remedies by way of specific relief, the uncertainty that could arise from their discretionary nature is much reduced by the accumulation of case law which not only indicates which types of contracts can (and which cannot) be specifically enforced[61] but also lists factors to be taken into account in determining when the discretion to order specific relief will be exercised:[62] the overriding principle is that this discretion is "to be governed so far as possible by fixed rules and principles".[63] In relation to the discretion created by *Blake*'s case, there can be no guidance on when it exists since that discretion applies to breaches of contract generally; and with regard to its exercise, Lord Nicholls said that "no fixed rules can be prescribed".[64] He was prepared only to give the "general guide" that this depends on "whether the [claimant] had a legitimate interest in preventing the defendant's profit-making activity";[65] but this formula does little to reduce the resulting uncertainty. Some further guidance of a negative nature is, however, provided. An account of profits is not to be available *merely because* the defendant is guilty of either "skimped performance"[66] (the difference in value between what was and what should have been provided being the normal measure of damages in such a case),[67] or of breach of a negative obligation "by doing the very thing he has promised not to

56 So that the case did not fall directly within the exception (to the general rule that damages are compensatory) referred to, at fn.50.
57 See para.20–010.
58 *Attorney General v Blake* [2001] 1 A.C. 268 at 285.
59 *Attorney General v Blake* [2001] 1 A.C. 268 at 284–285.
60 See para.21–030.
61 See paras 21–039—21–052.
62 See para.21–018 and following.
63 See para.21–031.
64 *Attorney General v Blake* [2001] 1 A.C. 268 at 285.
65 *Attorney General v Blake* [2001] 1 A.C. 268 at 285.
66 *Attorney General v Blake* [2001] 1 A.C. 268.
67 *Attorney General v Blake* [2001] 1 A.C. 268. See para.20–049.

do";[68] nor merely because the breach was "cynical and deliberate", or "enabled the defendant to enter into a more profitable contract elsewhere";[69] nor merely because, by entering into such a contract "the defendant put it out of his power to perform his contract with the [claimant]".[70] But as no positive indications are given as to when the discretion to order an account of profits *will* be exercised, the creation of that discretion remains a source of uncertainty.[71]

**An exceptional remedy.** With regard to this uncertainty, a number of points can, however, be made in relation to *Blake*'s case. First, the facts of that case can fairly be described as not merely exceptional, but as extreme; and it is hard to take issue with the outcome. Secondly, on such facts there would normally be other ways (not available on the special facts) of stripping the wrongdoer of his profits, e.g. by a confiscation order[72] if Blake had at the relevant time been amenable to the jurisdiction of the English criminal courts, or by an injunction if that remedy had been sought in time. Thirdly, in the factual context the argument in favour of certainty lacks its usual force. Certainty in rules of contract law is intended to enable parties to *rely* on such rules in regulating their conduct; and there is little plausibility and even less merit in the argument that, in deciding to break his contract with the Crown, Blake relied (or should have been encouraged to rely) on the rule that damages were compensatory. But although these points may justify the actual decision in *Blake*'s case, they cannot entirely dispel the concern caused by the ill-defined discretionary exception to the compensatory principle that was there created. Lord Hobhouse, in his dissent, referred to the "disruptive"[73] consequences that could follow from attempts "to extend the decision of the present exceptional case to commercial situations so as to introduce restitutionary rights beyond those presently recognised by the law of restitution".[74] Such consequences could, for example, follow where a party to a commercial contract decided to commit a breach of it with a view to making a profit even after he has compensated the other party for his loss. It is hard to see why in such a case the law should "confer a windfall on the injured party"[75] by awarding such profits to him in excess of his loss or, a fortiori, why it should make such an award where he has suffered no loss at all. It seems from the terms of Lord Nicholls' speech that the discretion created in *Blake*'s case is not intended to extend to cases of this kind.[76] 20–013

---

[68] *Attorney General v Blake* [2001] 1 A.C. 268 at 286.

[69] *Attorney General v Blake* [2001] 1 A.C. 268 at 286; cf. Birks [1987] L.M.C.L.Q. 421.

[70] *Attorney General v Blake* [2001] 1 A.C. 268 at 286.

[71] cf. Beatson 118 L.Q.R. 377. In *Morris-Garner v One Step (Support) Ltd* [2018] UKSC 20; [2019] A.C. 649 Lord Reed confirmed that an account of profits for breach of contract is only exceptionally available and commented (at [82]) that the "soundness" of the decision in *Blake's* case was not in issue in the appeal before the Court (as to which, see below). That comment in itself perhaps signals some doubt.

[72] See para.11–105.

[73] *Attorney General v Blake* [2001] 1 A.C. 268 at 299.

[74] *Attorney General v Blake* [2001] 1 A.C. 268 at 299.

[75] *Surrey CC v Bredero Homes Ltd* [1993] 1 W.L.R. 1361 at 1370.

[76] See at fn.69; cf. *Luxe Holding Ltd v Midland Resources Holding Ltd* [2010] EWHC 1908 (Ch) at [53].

The exceptional nature of *Blake*'s case is borne out by the decision of the Court of Appeal in *Experience Hendrix LLC v PPX Enterprises Inc*,[77] where the defendant, in breach of an earlier settlement with the claimant, granted licences to others to market certain musical recordings. There, a claim for an account of profits was rejected[78] on the basis of three "obvious" distinctions from *Blake*'s case,[79] namely: that there was no parallel with the special interest of the state in maintaining national security and the integrity of its secret service; the fact that the notoriety which accounted for the level of Blake's royalty-earning capacity derived from his prior breaches of secrecy; or the close analogy between Blake's position and that of a fiduciary. On the other hand, and this is indicative of the uncertainty in this area, not all of these factors need to be present. In *Esso Petroleum v Niad*[80] an account of profits was ordered as a remedy for breach of a contractual scheme under which Esso provided financial support to the defendant, in exchange for him agreeing to keep the price at which petrol was sold from his garage at a certain level (the "Pricewatch" scheme). The defendant received the financial support, but did not lower the price as required. Damages were regarded as an inadequate remedy, since it was impossible for Esso to attribute any lost sales of petrol to breach of the scheme by one dealer, but it was equally impossible to assess the claimant's loss in the *Experience Hendrix* case, and the most that could be said of the *Niad* case, when compared to the distinguishing features of *Blake*'s case, is that Esso had a "special interest" in maintaining the integrity of the Pricewatch scheme. One possible explanation for the different outcome in the two cases may be that, while the claimant's loss in the *Experience Hendrix* case was impossible to quantify in normal terms, damages were not an inadequate remedy because they were available in the form of "negotiating damages" which are considered below.[81] But such an award might, and possibly should, have been made in the *Niad* case.

An attempt at "a more principled examination of the circumstances" in which the courts will award an account of profits was made by Sales J in *Vercoe v Rutland Fund Management Ltd*.[82] At a "high level of generality" the question is what is a just response to the wrong in question.[83] In this enquiry, there is a role for what has been referred to above as the "performance interest"[84] and in cases where the claimant's "interest in full performance is recognised as being particularly strong" (e.g. the infringement of proprietary rights, or a right of a kind where it would never be reasonable to expect that it could be bought out for some reasonable fee (such as the promise to keep state secrets in *Blake*'s case[85]),

---

[77] [2003] EWCA Civ 323; [2003] E.M.L.R. 515 at [56].

[78] The defendant was ordered to pay "negotiating damages": see para.20–015.

[79] *Experience Hendrix LLC v PPX Enterprises Inc* [2003] EWCA Civ 323; [2003] E.M.L.R. 515 at [37].

[80] [2001] All E.R. (D) 324.

[81] See para.20–014.

[82] [2010] EWHC 424 (Ch).

[83] *Vercoe v Rutland Fund Management Ltd* [2010] EWHC 424 (Ch) at [339]; *Attorney General v Blake* [2001] 1 A.C. 268 at 284H.

[84] Seepara.20–005.

[85] In *Morris-Garner v One Step (Support) Ltd* [2018] UKSC 20; [2019] A.C. 649 at [111] Lord Sumption analysed *Blake's* case as one in which the claimant had an "interest extending beyond financial reparation".

or the breach of a fiduciary duty) an account of profits may be the appropriate remedy. Where however "one is not dealing with infringement of a right which is clearly proprietary in nature … and there is nothing exceptional to indicate that the defendant should never have been entitled to adopt a commercial approach in deciding how to behave in relation to that right, the appropriate remedy is likely to be an award of damages assessed by reference to a reasonable buy out fee rather than an account of profits."[86] It is to the concept of a "reasonable buy out fee" that we turn next.

### *(v) Negotiating damages*

In *Pell Frischmann Engineering Ltd v Bow Valley Iran Ltd* Lord Walker referred to an award of damages for breach of contract on the basis of "a [hypothetical] negotiation between a willing buyer (the contract-breaker) and a willing seller (the party claiming damages) in which the subject matter of the negotiation is the release of the relevant contractual obligation", and in relation to which "both parties are to be assumed to act reasonably".[87] In *Morris-Garner v One Step (Support) Ltd*[88] the Supreme Court expressed a preference for the term "negotiating damages" to describe such an award[89] and that is the terminology adopted in the discussion which follows. It is helpful to begin with two examples of this award before addressing two questions. First, what is the nature of such damages; in particular, are they intended to compensate for the claimant's loss? Secondly, what are the circumstances in which such damages may be awarded? **20–014**

**Examples.** In *Wrotham Park Estate Co v Parkside Homes Ltd*[90] a developer had acquired land subject to a restrictive covenant which had been imposed for the benefit of an adjoining estate. In breach of the covenant, the developer built houses on the land. This did not diminish the value of the estate, but its owners nevertheless recovered substantial damages for the breach, amounting to 5 per cent of the additional profit made by the defendant. This percentage was said to represent "such sum of money as might reasonably have been demanded by the [claimants] from [the defendant] as a quid pro quo for releasing the covenant".[91] **20–015**

[86] *Vercoe v Rutland Fund Management Ltd* [2010] EWHC 424 (Ch) at [341]; cf. *Jones v Ricoh UK Ltd* [2010] EWHC 1743 (Ch); [2010] U.K.C.L.R. 1335 at [89]–[91]; *Luxe Holding Ltd v Midland Resources Holding Ltd* [2010] EWHC 1908 (Ch) at [55].

[87] *Pell Frischmann Engineering Ltd v Bow Valley Iran Ltd* [2009] UKPC 45; [2010] B.L.R. 73 at [49].

[88] [2018] UKSC 20; [2019] A.C. 649; Peel [2019] J.C.L. 216; Burrows 134 L.Q.R. 515.

[89] In preference to "*Wrotham Park* damages", after the decision in *Wrotham Park Estate Co v Parkside Homes Ltd* [1974] 1 W.L.R. 798 which is considered below.

[90] [1974] 1 W.L.R. 798; cf. *Amec Developments Ltd v Jury's Hotel Management (UK) Ltd* (2000) 82 P. & C.R. 286; *Lane v O'Brien Homes* [2004] EWHC 303 (QB); Sharpe and Waddams 1 O.J.L.S. 290. In *Surrey CC v Bredero Homes Ltd* [1993] 1 W.L.R. 1361 the Court of Appeal declined to award any damages in a very similar case. The decision is not easy to reconcile with the *Wrotham Park* case and it has been said that "so far as the *Bredero Homes Ltd* decision is inconsistent with the approach adopted in the *Wrotham Park* case, the latter is to be preferred": *Attorney General v Blake* [2001] 1 A.C. 268 at 283.

[91] *Wrotham Park Estate Co v Parkside Homes Ltd* [1974] 1 W.L.R. 798 at 815; cf. *Lunn Poly Ltd v Liverpool & Lancashire Properties Ltd* (2006) 25 E.G. 210 at [25].

Similarly, in the *Experience Hendrix* case, above,[92] the defendant was ordered to pay the sum that might reasonably have been charged and paid between willing parties for the release of the restriction imposed on the commercial exploitation of the recordings in question by the terms of the settlement agreement.[93]

20–016 **Compensation or restitution?** The concept of "a quid pro quo for releasing the covenant" which is referred to in the *Wrotham Park* case is equally consistent with a compensatory or a restitutionary analysis. The claimant is either compensated for the loss of the opportunity to bargain for a sum to release the defendant from his contractual obligation,[94] or the defendant is required to restore the gain made by his breach in the form of the opportunity to generate profit, or avoid the expense of fulfilling his obligation.[95] It is openly acknowledged that, in many cases, the claimant would not have been prepared to grant a release at any price[96] so there cannot, in any real sense, have been a "loss" of the opportunity to bargain for a release fee.[97] This artificiality has led to the view that a restitutionary analysis is to be preferred,[98] but while this has some judicial support,[99] the prevailing view is that negotiating damages should be regarded as compensation for the claimant's loss,[100] albeit "not loss of a conventional kind".[101]

Whichever analysis is preferred, the award of negotiating damages is not to be confused with an account of profits. While in both the *Wrotham Park* case and the *Experience Hendrix* case, the sum arrived at was expressed as a small percentage of the profit made by the defendant by exploiting the breach, this is explained on the basis that it may be "reasonable for the court to look at the eventual outcome and to consider whether or not that is a useful guide to what the parties would have thought at the time of their hypothetical bargain",[102] e.g. a reasonable release fee may have been negotiated on the basis of a proportion of the *anticipated* profits. But because the hypothetical bargain is, as a general rule,

---

[92] See at fn.77.

[93] cf. *World Wide Fund for Nature v World Wrestling Federation Entertainment Inc* [2007] EWCA Civ 286; [2008] 1 W.L.R. 445 where the claim was struck out as an abuse of process.

[94] Sharpe and Waddams (1982) 2 O.J.L.S. 290; Stoljar (1989) 2 J.C.L. 1.

[95] Edelman, *Gain-Based Damages* (2002), Ch.3.

[96] See, e.g. the *Wrotham Park* case: "the plaintiffs, rightly conscious of their obligations towards existing residents, would clearly not have granted any relaxation", [1974] 1 W.L.R. 798 at 815.

[97] *Experience Hendrix LLC v PPX Enterprises Inc* [2003] EWCA Civ 323; [2003] E.M.L.R. 515 at [45]; cf. *Douglas v Hello! Ltd (No.3)* [2005] EWCA Civ 595; [2006] Q.B. 125 at [246].

[98] Rotherham [2008] L.M.C.L.Q. 25; Burrows in Saidov and Cunnington (eds), *Contract Damages: Domestic and International Perspectives* (2008).

[99] *Surrey CC v Bredero Homes Ltd* [1993] 1 W.L.R. 1361 at 1369–1370; *Marathon Asset Management LLP v Seddon* [2017] EWHC 300 (Comm); [2017] I.C.R. 791.

[100] *Jaggard v Sawyer* [1995] 1 W.L.R. 269; *Attorney General v Blake* [2001] 1 A.C. 268 at 281; *Lane v O'Brien Homes* [2004] EWHC 303 (QB); *World Wide Fund for Nature v World Wrestling Federation Entertainment Inc* [2007] EWCA Civ 286; [2008] 1 W.L.R. 445 at [59]; *Force India Formula One Team Ltd v 1 Malaysia Racing Team Sdn Bhd* [2012] EWHC 616 (Ch) at [386]; *Abbar v Saudi Economic and Development Co (Sedco) Real Estate Ltd* [2013] EWHC 1414 (Ch) at [224]; cf. *Eaton Mansions (Westminster ) Ltd v Stinger Compania de Inversion SA* [2013] EWCA Civ 1308; [2014] H.L.R. 4 at [20]–[21] (a case of trespass).

[101] *Morris-Garner v One Step (Support) Ltd* [2018] UKSC 20; [2019] A.C. 649 at [30], [95].

[102] *Pell Frischmann Engineering Ltd v Bow Valley Iran Ltd* [2009] UKPC 45; [2010] B.L.R. 73 at [51].

negotiated at the date of breach and is based on the "opportunity value" of the breach, it may result in the award of a sum in excess of the profits subsequently made by the defendant. This was the outcome in *Pell Frischmann Engineering Ltd v Bow Valley Iran Ltd*[103] where the defendant, in breach of a confidentiality agreement with the claimant, entered into a contract with X which was meant to be entered into by way of a joint venture with the claimant. The profits made by the defendant were found to be in the region of $1–1.8 million. Nonetheless, the Privy Council awarded damages of $2.5 million on the basis that, as negotiating damages "*are meant to be compensatory*, and are normally to be assessed or valued at the date of breach, principle and consistency indicate that post-valuation events are normally irrelevant".[104] In *Morris-Garner v One Step (Support) Ltd* the Supreme Court rejected a view[105] that negotiating damages and an account of profits are "similar remedies (partial and total disgorgement of profits, respectively), at different points along a sliding scale, calibrated according to the degree of disapproval with which the court regards the defendant's conduct".[106] It did so on the basis that this contributed to the view, also rejected, that negotiating damages are awarded on a discretionary basis whenever necessary to produce a "just response".[107] That, however, begs the question of when negotiating damages are available, if at all, for breach of contract.

**Unconventional loss, or unconventional assessment?** In the *One Step* case a distinction was recognised by the Court between two different circumstances in which negotiating damages may be awarded. In the first, they represent damages awarded for conventional loss, but assessed on an unconventional basis. In the second, they represent damages awarded for an unconventional loss. 20–017

**Unconventional assessment.** In cases where the claimant has suffered some form of conventional pecuniary loss, but it is very difficult, or even impossible, to establish, negotiating damages may be awarded on the basis that they are simply an "evidential technique for estimating what the claimant can reasonably be supposed to have lost".[108] The notional release fee acts as a "surrogate for the loss of profits arising from the breach".[109] As explained by Lord Sumption: 20–018

[103] [2009] UKPC 45; [2010] B.L.R. 73.
[104] *Lunn Poly Ltd v Liverpool & Lancashire Properties Ltd* (2006) 25 E.G. 210 at [29] (Neuberger LJ) approved in *Pell Frischmann* [2009] UKPC 45; [2010] B.L.R. 73 at [50] (emphasis added).
[105] Seen, for example, in *Experience Hendrix LLC v PPX Enterprises Inc* [2003] EWCA Civ 323; [2003] E.M.L.R. 515 at [36]–[37], [44]
[106] *Morris-Garner v One Step (Support) Ltd* [2018] UKSC 20; [2019] A.C. 649 at [81], [90] (Lord Reed); cf. at [114] (Lord Sumption).
[107] *Morris-Garner v One Step (Support) Ltd* [2018] UKSC 20; [2019] A.C. 649 at [97].
[108] *Morris-Garner v One Step (Support) Ltd* [2018] UKSC 20; [2019] A.C. 649 at [106].
[109] *Morris-Garner v One Step (Support) Ltd* [2018] UKSC 20; [2019] A.C. 649 at [115]; cf. the award of "reliance damages", para.20–031.

> "the claimant, acting reasonably, has no reason to demand more than he anticipates he will lose by non-performance, and the defendant, acting reasonably, has no reason to share with the claimant any benefit which the latter may expect to derive from some especially profitable use attributable to his own skill or effort."[110]

It is a far from perfect technique since what the parties are notionally valuing is "not the actual performance as it turns out to be, but the prospects as seen at the time of the breach."[111] But as will be seen below,[112] the courts will, where necessary, allow for a degree of "speculation"[113] in the assessment of damages and, in this sense, the award of negotiating damages to compensate for conventional pecuniary loss is just an example of what has been referred to as "sound imagination and the practice of the broad axe".[114] For Lord Sumption, this was the explanation for the award of negotiating damages in the *Experience Hendrix* case and other "straightforward cases of breach of contract"[115] and Lord Reed, whose speech represents the majority in the *One Step* case, also acknowledged that evidence "led in relation to a hypothetical release fee" may be taken into account in the assessment of conventional pecuniary loss.[116]

The availability of negotiating damages as an evidential technique for assessing conventional pecuniary loss obviously depends on the court's willingness to accept that there is a distinction between cases where there is *no loss* and cases where the court is satisfied that such loss has been incurred, but it is difficult or impossible to establish how much has been lost.[117] Thus, in relation to the *Experience Hendrix* case, Lord Sumption highlighted the submission of the claimant that he "had no evidence and ... did not imagine that he could ever possibly get any evidence to show or quantify any financial loss"[118] and observed that this "was not an admission that there were no losses. It is clear that what the claimant was saying was that there were, but that it was impossible to establish how much it had lost".[119] Similarly, in relation to the *One Step* case itself, in which the defendant breached restrictive covenants intended to protect the goodwill of the business sold to the claimant, Lord Sumption noted that it was "practically inconceivable" that the claimant had not suffered "significant losses" and the "law would be failing in its economic purpose if it confined [the claimant] to the fraction of the business lost which was capable of being

---

110 *Morris-Garner v One Step (Support) Ltd* [2018] UKSC 20; [2019] A.C. 649 at [115].

111 *Morris-Garner v One Step (Support) Ltd* [2018] UKSC 20; [2019] A.C. 649 at [115].

112 See para.20–062.

113 *Simpson v The London and North Western Railway Co* (1876) 1 Q.B.D. 274 at 277 (Cockburn CJ).

114 *Watson, Laidlaw & Co Ltd v Pott, Cassels & Williamson* 1914 S.C. (HL) 18 at 29–30.

115 *Morris-Garner v One Step (Support) Ltd* [2018] UKSC 20; [2019] A.C. 649 at [121]. Lord Sumption included in this category the decisions in *Pell Frischmann Engineering Ltd v Bow Valley Iran Ltd* [2009] UKPC 45; [2010] B.L.R. 73; and *Vercoe v Rutland Fund Management Ltd* [2010] EWHC 424 (Ch).

116 *Morris-Garner v One Step (Support) Ltd* [2018] UKSC 20; [2019] A.C. 649 at [100].

117 "Where the claimant's interest in the performance of a contract is purely economic, and he cannot establish that any economic loss has resulted from its breach, the normal inference is that he has not suffered any loss": *Morris-Garner v One Step (Support) Ltd* [2018] UKSC 20; [2019] A.C. 649 at [95] (Lord Reed).

118 *Experience Hendrix LLC v PPX Enterprises Inc* [2003] EWCA Civ 323; [2003] E.M.L.R. 515 at [14].

119 *Morris-Garner v One Step (Support) Ltd* [2018] UKSC 20; [2019] A.C. 649 at [122].

demonstrated with the necessary degree of confidence".[120] These two cases may be contrasted with a contract for the sale of goods where there is an available market and, upon the buyer's breach in refusing to accept the goods, the seller is able to sell them in the market at the contract price and at no additional cost. In such a case, there is *no loss* and damages would be nominal,[121] whether assessed on a conventional basis, or as negotiating damages.[122]

**Unconventional loss.** As will be seen below, the courts have acknowledged that a contracting party may have an interest in performance which extends beyond a pecuniary interest and which may result in the award of damages.[123] Nevertheless, in order to arrive at an award of damages, the court has to ascribe an economic value to the contractual right which has been breached. As Lord Reed acknowledged in the *One Step* case, "the imaginary negotiation is merely a tool for arriving at that value",[124] so that it is once again being used as a "technique of assessment", but this time in relation to non-pecuniary, or unconventional loss, and "the real question is as to the circumstances in which that value constitutes the measure of the claimant's loss".[125] After the *One Step* case, it appears that there are two such circumstances:[126] where the contractual right amounts to an "asset";[127] and where damages are awarded in lieu of specific relief.[128] 20–019

**Contractual rights considered as "assets".** According to Lord Reed in the *One Step* case[129]: 20–020

> "Negotiating damages can be awarded for breach of contract where the loss suffered by the claimant is appropriately measured by reference to the economic value of the right which has been breached, considered as an asset. That may be the position where the breach of contract results in the loss of a valuable asset created or protected by the right which was infringed. The rationale is that the claimant has in substance been deprived of a valuable asset, and his loss can therefore be measured by determining the economic value of the right in question, considered as an asset. The defendant has taken something for nothing, for which the claimant was entitled to require payment."

This formulation is intended to draw an analogy with other causes of action in which the defendant has been ordered to pay a "fee", in addition to, or regardless of, any conventional pecuniary loss, for depriving the claimant of an "asset": for

[120] *Morris-Garner v One Step (Support) Ltd* [2018] UKSC 20; [2019] A.C. 649 at [122].
[121] See para.20–008.
[122] Strictly speaking, negotiating damages on the evidential basis are *available* in such a case and, indeed, in all cases of breach of contract, but where it is possible to provide that there is *no loss*, the release fee is zero.
[123] See para.20–088.
[124] *Morris-Garner v One Step (Support) Ltd* [2018] UKSC 20; [2019] A.C. 649 at [91].
[125] *Morris-Garner v One Step (Support) Ltd* [2018] UKSC 20; [2019] A.C. 649 at [91].
[126] In any other circumstances, it appears that negotiating damages are only available on the basis they are a technique for assessing conventional pecuniary loss: see [2018] UKSC 20; [2019] A.C. 649 at [94].
[127] See para.20–020.
[128] See para.20–021.
[129] *Morris-Garner v One Step (Support) Ltd* [2018] UKSC 20; [2019] A.C. 649 at [95].

example, the award of a "user rent" for trespassing on the claimant's land;[130] or of "user damages" for tortious interference with the claimant's chattels;[131] or of a notional royalty for infringing the claimant's intellectual property rights;[132] or of negotiating damages for breach of confidence.[133] The difficulty with this formulation, as Lord Reed himself acknowledges, is that "there is a sense in which any contractual right can be described as an asset, or indeed as property" and his answer to this objection that the contractual right must be of a "such a kind that its breach can result in an identifiable loss equivalent to the economic value of the right, considered as an asset, even in the absence of any pecuniary losses which are measurable in the ordinary way"[134] is rather circular.[135] What he goes on to say is that this is true of "some contractual rights … but by no means of all". For example, it is said to be true of a contractual right "to control the use of land, intellectual property or confidential information".[136] The first example covers the *Wrotham Park* case, though that decision may also be explained on another ground,[137] while the right to control the use of intellectual property covers the *Experience Hendrix* case where the defendant owned the copyright in the recordings in question but had conferred a contractual right on the claimant to control their exploitation. Lord Reed describes the decision (if not the reasoning) of the Court of Appeal in that case as one which "can be supported on an orthodox basis".[138] By contrast, the *One Step* case was an example of a contractual right which does not amount to an "asset" in that "the breach of a non-compete obligation may cause the claimant to suffer pecuniary loss resulting from the wrongful competition, such as a loss of profits and goodwill, which is measurable by conventional means, but in the absence of such loss, it is difficult to see how there could be any other loss."[139]

The comparison between the *Experience Hendrix* case and the *One Step* case is instructive. In the former, the claimant acquired contractual rights to control the use which the defendant made of its copyright in the recordings which were licensed in breach of contract. In the latter, the claimant acquired contractual rights to control the use which the defendant made of any competing business she might seek to establish. In both cases the contractual rights were intended to protect the goodwill in the claimant's own business.[140] If *Experience Hendrix* is a case in which a release fee might reasonably have been charged irrespective of any financial loss, it is not immediately apparent why the same may not be said of

---

130 See, e.g. *Whitwham v Westminster Brymbo Coal and Coke Co* [1896] 2 Ch. 538.

131 See, e.g. *Strand Electric & Engineering Co Ltd v Brisford Entertainments Ltd* [1952] 2 Q.B. 246.

132 See, e.g. *Watson, Laidlaw & Co Ltd v Pott, Cassels & Williamson* [1914] S.C. (HL) 18.

133 See, e.g. *Force India Formula One Team Ltd v 1 Malaysia Racing Team Sdn Bhd* [2012] EWHC 616 (Ch); [2012] R.P.C. 29.

134 *Morris-Garner v One Step (Support) Ltd* [2018] UKSC 20; [2019] A.C. 649 at [93].

135 Though the same circularity exists in the property cases referred to above, as is acknowledged by Lord Nicholls in *Attorney General v Blake* [2001] 1 A.C. at 281: "A property right has value to the extent only that the court will enforce it or award damages for its infringement".

136 *Morris-Garner v One Step (Support) Ltd* [2018] UKSC 20; [2019] A.C. 649 at [93].

137 See para.20–021.

138 *Morris-Garner v One Step (Support) Ltd* [2018] UKSC 20; [2019] A.C. 649 at [89].

139 *Morris-Garner v One Step (Support) Ltd* [2018] UKSC 20; [2019] A.C. 649 at [93].

140 In *Experience Hendrix* the claimant owned the copyright in more valuable recordings by the same artist and the restrictions agreed to by the defendant were intended to prevent the risk of damage to the market by the release of the defendant's inferior recordings.

the *One Step* case. There is, with respect, much to be said for Lord Sumption's view that in *both* cases damages should have been confined to conventional pecuniary loss, but that such damages might be assessed on the "negotiated" basis.[141] There is *a* distinction which might be drawn between the two cases. In the *Experience Hendrix* case the defendant's property over which the claimant enjoyed a right of control was intellectual property, whereas in *One Step* the defendant's "property" was her otherwise unfettered right to run her business as she wished. It is not clear that this provides a compelling reason for treating the two cases differently,[142] but the suggestion appears to be that the claimant must be able to point to the infringement of some form of derivative proprietary right.[143]

**Damages in lieu of specific relief.** As will be seen in the next chapter, damages may be awarded in lieu of specific relief[144] and in the *One Step* case Lord Reed acknowledged that one "possible method" of quantifying such damages is "on the basis of the economic value of the right which the court has declined to enforce, and which it has consequently rendered worthless."[145] The valuation of that right "can be arrived at by reference to the amount which the claimant might reasonably have demanded as a quid pro quo for the relaxation of the obligation in question".[146] The fact that the language of a "quid pro quo for relaxation" echoes the language used by Brightman J in the *Wrotham Park* case[147] is not accidental, since Lord Reed regards this as the best explanation of that decision, and others.[148] This is also not free from difficulty. It is the case that damages awarded in lieu of an injunction can be forward looking whereas damages at common law are only available for a cause of action which is complete[149] and it may seem particularly appropriate to contemplate the award of a fee which releases the defendant from the relevant obligation in the future. But the basis of the award is nonetheless the infringement, or potential infringement, of the obligation in question. For example, in the *Experience Hendrix* case, the claimant sought, and was awarded, an injunction to restrain any further breach and damages in relation to the licences which had already been granted. If the court had chosen to exercise its discretion and award damages in lieu of the injunction 20–021

[141] See para.20–018. Lord Sumption himself does not entirely rule out the award of negotiating damages for breach of contract beyond their role as an evidential technique of assessing conventional pecuniary loss, given his acknowledgement that they may be awarded "where the claimant has an interest in the observance of his rights which extends beyond financial reparation": [2018] UKSC 20; [2019] A.C. 649 at [109].

[142] cf. *Turf Club Emporium Pte Ltd v Yeo Boong Hua* [2018] SGCA 44 at [281].

[143] cf. Day [2018] R.L.R. 60; Quaere the decision in *Burrows Investments Ltd v Ward Homes Ltd* [2017] EWCA Civ 1577; [2018] 1 P. & C.R. 13 at [61] ("The benefit of the contractual restriction was a potentially valuable piece of property in its own right"); cf. *Lloyd v Google LLC* [2019] EWCA Civ 1599 at [68].

[144] See para.21–070.

[145] *Morris-Garner v One Step (Support) Ltd* [2018] UKSC 20; [2019] A.C. 649 at [95].

[146] *Morris-Garner v One Step (Support) Ltd* [2018] UKSC 20; [2019] A.C. 649 at [95]; cf. at [112]–[114] (Lord Sumption).

[147] See para.20–015.

[148] See, e.g. *Bracewell v Appleby* [1975] Ch. 408; *Jaggard v Sawyer* [1995] 1 W.L.R. 269.

[149] *Jaggard v Sawyer* [1995] 1 W.L.R. 269 at 284 (Millett LJ).

sought,[150] such damages would simply have reflected the more extensive infringement which would be committed by the defendant. As it was, the court was only required to assess the "buy-out" value for a more limited infringement, or more restricted release.[151] If the availability of injunctive relief does provide a further and separate basis upon which negotiating damages might be awarded, it is not helpful that important questions are left open in the *One Step* case, such as whether the court must have an application for an injunction before it,[152] or what it means to say that an injunction is "in principle available".[153]

### *(vi) Punitive damages*

20–022 **General rule: no punitive damages.** Punitive (or exemplary) damages can be awarded in certain tort cases.[154] The purpose of such damages is not to compensate the claimant, nor even to strip the defendant of his profit, but to express the court's disapproval of the defendant's conduct, e.g. where he has deliberately committed a wrong (such as defamation) with a view to profit.[155]

As a general rule, punitive damages cannot be awarded in a purely contractual action,[156] since the object of such an action is not to punish the defendant but to compensate the claimant.[157] Punitive damages are not available even though the breach was committed deliberately and with a view to profit. If the court is particularly outraged by the defendant's conduct, it can sometimes achieve much the same result by awarding damages for injury to the claimant's feelings.[158] In theory, such damages are meant to compensate the claimant for mental suffering, rather than to punish the defendant. But in practice the distinction is often hard to draw and—from the defendant's point of view—to perceive.[159] However, where

---

150 Highly unlikely on the facts of that case: see para.21–059.

151 cf. *Eaton Mansions (Westminster ) Ltd v Stinger Compania de Inversion SA* [2013] EWCA Civ 1308; [2014] H.L.R. 4 (a case of trespass).

152 *Morris-Garner v One Step (Support) Ltd* [2018] UKSC 20; [2019] A.C. 649 at [45] (Lord Reed).

153 *Morris-Garner v One Step (Support) Ltd* [2018] UKSC 20; [2019] A.C. 649 at [113] (Lord Sumption); cf. *Pell Frischmann Engineering Ltd v Bow Valley Iran Ltd*; [2009] UKPC 45; [2010] B.L.R. 73 at [48] ("not necessary … that there should have been any prospect on the facts, of [an injunction] being granted" (Lord Walker)). See also: *Jaggard v Sawyer* [1995] 1 W.L.R. 269 at 285; *Attorney General v Blake* [2001] 1 A.C. 268 at 282; *World Wide Fund for Nature v World Wrestling Federation Entertainment Inc* [2007] EWCA Civ 286; [2008] 1 W.L.R. 445 at [54]; Smith (1995) 24 Can B.L.J. 121.

154 See Lord Devlin's speech in *Rookes v Barnard* [1964] A.C. 1129; cf. *Kuddus v Chief Constable of the Leicestershire Constabulary* [2001] UKHL 29; [2002] 2 A.C. 122; *Borders (UK) Ltd v Metropolitan Police Commissioner* [2005] EWCA Civ 197; [2005] Po. L.R. 1.

155 *Cassell & Co Ltd v Broome* [1972] A.C. 1027.

156 *Perera v Vandiyar* [1953] 1 W.L.R. 672; *Reed v Madon* [1989] Ch. 408; *Johnson v Unisys Ltd* [2001] UKHL 13; [2003] 1 A.C. 518 at [15] (Lord Steyn, dissenting on the main issue in that case and see fn.158). Law Com. No.247 (1997), para.6.3.19 recommends no change to the general rule.

157 *Calabar Properties Ltd v Stitcher* [1984] 1 W.L.R. 287 at 297; *Ruxley Electronics and Construction Ltd v Forsyth* [1996] A.C. 344 at 352, 365, 373.

158 See para.20–088 and following; cf. the suggestion in *McCall v Abelesz* [1976] Q.B. 585 at 594 that damages for injury to feelings could now be awarded in a case like *Perera v Vandiyar* [1953] 1 W.L.R. 672; Law Com. No.247, para.6.1.2, preferring the phrase "damages for mental distress" to "aggravated damages" in cases of this kind.

159 See, e.g. *Chelini v Nieri* 196 P.2d 915 (1948) where damages of $10,000 for injury to feelings were awarded for breach of contract against a Californian embalmer.

the claimant has a cause of action both in tort and for breach of contract, he may be able to recover punitive damages by framing the claim in tort. For example, a landlord who unlawfully evicts his tenant is guilty both of a breach of contract and of a trespass; and punitive damages have been awarded in such a case.[160] Another type of case in which a defendant seeks to profit from a deliberate wrong which is both a breach of contract and a tort is that in which he gives a fraudulent warranty as to the subject-matter of a contract of sale. In the US, punitive damages have been awarded in such a case;[161] but in England conflicting views have been expressed on the question whether such damages can be awarded in an action based on fraud even if the action is brought in tort.[162] It can be argued, on the one hand, that the tort of deceit is generally one from which the defendant seeks to profit, so that it falls into the category of wrongs for which punitive damages are available;[163] and, on the other, that deceit generally involves the wrongdoer in criminal liability and that he should not suffer double punishment by being in addition ordered to pay punitive damages.[164]

### (b) Compensation for what?

The principle that, as a general rule, damages are compensatory gives rise to the question: for what is it that the victim of a breach of contract is entitled to be compensated? This question calls for an analysis of the various types of losses for which the victim of a breach of contract can recover damages;[165] and it also gives rise to certain related problems. **20–023**

#### *(i) Loss of bargain*

**Contract and tort damages contrasted.** The object of damages for breach of contract is to put the victim "so far as money can do it … in the same situation … as if the contract had been performed".[166] It has become fashionable to refer to this as the "compensatory principle". In other words, the victim is entitled to be compensated for the loss of his bargain, so that his expectations arising out of, or created by, the contract are protected. This protection of the victim's expectations must be contrasted with the principle on which damages are awarded in tort: the **20–024**

160 *Drane v Evangelou* [1978] 1 W.L.R. 455; cf. *Guppys (Bridport) v Brookling* (1984) 269 E.G. 846 (nuisance and landlord's breach of covenant to repair); *Millington v Duffy* (1984) 17 H.L.R. 232.
161 *Grandi v Le Sage* 399 P.2d 285 (1965).
162 *Mafo v Adams* [1970] 1 Q.B. 548; *Cassell & Co Ltd v Broome* [1972] A.C. 1027 at 1076, 1131; *Smith Kline & French Laboratories Ltd v Long* [1989] 1 W.L.R. 1; *Kuddus v Chief Constable of the Leicestershire Constabulary* [2001] UKHL 29; [2002] 2 A.C. 122 at [43]; cf. at [84] (point left open).
163 It is arguable that punitive damages for fraudulent warranties are no longer necessary in view of the recognition in *Attorney General v Blake* [2001] 1 A.C. 268 (para.20–011) of the possibility of awarding an account of profits in certain cases in breach of contract; see *Kuddus v Chief Constable of the Leicestershire Constabulary* [2001] UKHL 29; [2002] 2 A.C. 122 at [109]; but in breach of contract cases the latter remedy is exceptional and discretionary.
164 *Archer v Brown* [1985] Q.B. 401 at 418–423.
165 Fuller and Perdue 46 Yale L.J. 52, 373; cf. Burrows 99 L.Q.R. 217; Owen 4 O.J.L.S. 393.
166 *Robinson v Harman* (1848) 1 Ex. 850 at 855; *The Golden Victory* [2007] UKHL 12; [2007] 2 A.C. 353 at [9]; *Bunge SA v Nidera BV* [2015] UKSC 43; [2015] 2 Lloyd's Rep. 469 at [14], [85]; *Morris-Garner v One Step (Support) Ltd* [2018] UKSC 20; [2019] A.C. 649 at [34].

purpose of such damages is to put the victim into the position in which he would have been if the tort had not been committed.[167] Of course, in many tort actions the victim can recover damages for loss of expectations, e.g. for loss of expected earnings suffered as a result of personal injury, or for loss of expected profits suffered as a result of damage to a profit-earning thing. But these expectations exist quite independently of the tortious conduct which impairs them:[168] it is the nature of most torts to destroy or impair expectations of this kind, rather than to create new ones.

Tortious misrepresentation does, indeed, create new expectations, but the purpose of damages even for that tort is to put the victim into the position in which he would have been, if the misrepresentation had not been made, and not to protect his expectations by putting him into the position in which he would have been, if the representation had been true.[169] Such damages may be awarded in respect of losses which the victim could have avoided if the misrepresentation had not been made, and here again there is a sense in which the victim will recover damages for "loss of a chance",[170] but it is the chance of avoiding loss rather than that of making a profit for which he will be compensated. He may even be compensated for loss of profit if the tort impairs expectations which exist independently of it.[171] In a contractual action, on the other hand, damages are recoverable as a matter of course for loss of the expectations created *by the very contract for breach of which the action is brought*. That is why damages of this kind are the distinctive feature of a contractual action.

20–025 **What was the bargain: scope of duty broken.** It follows from the principle of compensating the victim for loss of his bargain that the first and crucial question is to determine exactly what had been bargained for, or, in other words, the exact scope of the duty breached by the defendant. This was the question discussed in *South Australia Asset Management Corp v York Montague Ltd*[172] (the *SAAMCO* case). Loans of money had been made on the security of properties which had been valued by the defendants who had been engaged by the lender to make these valuations. In breach of their duty to carry out the valuations with due care, the defendants had overvalued the properties, which then also fell in value, in line with the general weakness in the property market. On the borrowers' default, the lenders realised the securities but recovered less than the amounts that they had lent. The House of Lords held that the valuers were liable for loss suffered by the lenders to the extent of the overvaluation but not for any loss beyond this amount. The point can be illustrated by supposing that a sum of £8 million had been lent on the security of a property valued at £10 million but actually worth only £6 million and that, on the borrower's default, the property (having fallen in value after the loan) yielded no more than £1.5 million. In such a case, the valuers

---

[167] cf. para.1–011.

[168] This is also true in the "disappointed beneficiary" cases such as *White v Jones* [1995] 2 A.C. 207; para.14–057.

[169] See para.9–073.

[170] *John W Pryke v Gibbs Hartley Cooper Ltd* [1991] 1 Lloyd's Rep. 602 at 621.

[171] See para.9–076.

[172] [1997] A.C. 191; for subsequent proceedings, see *Nykredit Bank v Edward Erdman Group* [1997] 1 W.L.R. 1627; Peel in Burrows and Peel (eds), *Commercial Remedies* (2003).

would be liable, not for the £6.5 million lost by the lender, but only to the extent of the £4 million by which they had overvalued the security. This follows from the principle applied in *SAAMCO*[173] that a wrongdoer is liable only for "those consequences which are attributable to that which made the act wrongful":[174] and in the case of a breach of contract the definition of what "made the act wrongful" necessarily depends on the way in which the contractual duty is defined.

In the *SAAMCO* case, the duty was merely one to *provide information* (as to the value of the security) on which it was then up to the lenders to decide upon their course of action;[175] and the valuer was held liable for no more than the adverse consequences of his failure to take reasonable care as to the accuracy of that information. Such a duty was distinguished by Lord Hoffmann[176] from a duty to *advise* a client as to a course of action, i.e. "a duty to consider all relevant matters and not only specific matters in the decision" and to be "responsible for guiding the whole decision making process".[177] A defendant who commits a breach of a duty of this kind (by failing to take reasonable care in giving the advice) will be liable for all foreseeable loss suffered in consequence of the client's taking the advice. Liability in such a case could therefore extend to loss suffered by reason of a fall in the market value of the subject-matter acquired in reliance on the advice.[178] The distinction follows from the way in which the defendant's duty is defined; it "has nothing to do with questions of causation[179] or any limit or 'cap' imposed upon damages which would otherwise be recoverable".[180] Those limits cut down liability for losses for which a defendant is prima facie responsible;[181] our present concern is with the extent of his duty and hence of his prima facie responsibility.

**Scope of duty and remoteness.** The distinction just drawn between limiting damages and defining a duty can give rise to difficulty, particularly in relation to liability in tort for negligence. Here the rule that a defendant is not liable for unforeseeable loss has been explained on the ground that such loss is too remote; but it can equally well be explained on the ground that the defendant is under no 20–026

[173] A possible exception, applicable where the wrong is a misrepresentation which is, or is to be treated as being, fraudulent is recognised ([1997] A.C. 191 at 215) and discussed at para.9–076.
[174] *South Australia Asset Management Corp v York Montague Ltd* [1997] A.C. 191 at 213.
[175] *South Australia Asset Management Corp v York Montague Ltd* [1997] A.C. 191 at 214.
[176] *South Australia Asset Management Corp v York Montague Ltd* [1997] A.C. 191 at 214; all the other members of the House of Lords agreed with Lord Hoffmann's speech; *Nykredit Bank v Edward Erdman Group* [1997] 1 W.L.R. 1627 at 1638; cf. *Bristol & West BS v Mothew* [1998] Ch. 1 at 11; *Haugesund Kommune v Depfa ACS Bank* [2011] EWCA Civ 33; [2011] 3 All E.R. 655.
[177] *BPE v Hughes-Holland* [2017] UKSC 21; [2018] A.C. 599 at [40]; cf. *Manchester B. Soc v Grant Thornton UK LLP* [2019] EWCA Civ 40; [2019] 1 W.L.R. 4610 at [54].
[178] cf. *Intervention Board for Agriculture Products v Leidis* [2000] Lloyd's Rep. P.N. 144.
[179] In this respect the case differs from those discussed at paras 9–083–9–086 and para.20–055 where the question of recoverability of damages in respect of falls in market value depended on factors other than the definition of the defendant's duty.
[180] *Nykredit Bank v Edward Erdman Group* [1997] 1 W.L.R. 1627 at 1638; *Platform Home Loans Ltd v Oyston Shipways Ltd* [2000] 2 A.C. 190 at 208, 213; though the same case may raise an issue both as to the definition of the duty and as to a "cap" on damages, as in *Bank of Credit & Commerce (Overseas) Ltd v Price Waterhouse (No.3)*, *The Times*, 2 April 1998.
[181] See para.20–099 and following.

duty not to cause unforeseeable loss.[182] In the present group of cases, however, the two issues are clearly distinct: the "scope of the duty" depends on the true meaning of the contract (which clearly imposes *some* duty) while the test of remoteness depends on what consequences the valuer could have contemplated as likely to result from failure to make the valuation with due care.[183] If that test were applied, the valuer would be liable for the market loss; the effect of the "scope of duty" test is that in the "information" (as opposed to the "advice") cases he is under no prima facie liability for that loss because he has undertaken no duty with regard to the desirability or prudence of the transaction.[184]

20–027 **"Advice" and "information".** Considerable difficulty can arise in distinguishing, for the present purpose, between "advice" and "information".[185] This difficulty arises, in the first place, from the ambiguity of the word "advise": this may be used to mean either "advise that … " or "advise to … ". In the former sense, its primary meaning is "to provide information" while in the latter sense it is "to recommend a course of action … ". The duty to provide what is commonly called legal "advice" may, for example, be no more than one to provide information, e.g. as to the capacity of a party to contract,[186] or to the existence of restrictions on the use of land. The giving of such information does not involve any recommendation as to the commercial prudence of proceeding with a transaction, e.g. as to the creditworthiness of the other party,[187] or whether to make a loan on the security of the land in question.[188] The second source of the difficulty lies in the fact that a person who expressly undertakes to give information may, by performing that duty, also impliedly give advice.[189] If, for example, A says to B "the girders of this bridge are sound", that statement may well, in the context, mean "you can safely cross", and so amount to advice as well as to information. Similarly, in the *Aneco* case[190] brokers had wrongly told a client that reinsurance against the risk which the client was about to underwrite was available in the market. Their duty was held to be one to "advise on the

182 See Lord Hobhouse's discussion in *Platform Home Loans Ltd v Oyston Shipways Ltd* [2000] 2 A.C. 190; [1999] 1 All E.R. 835 at 847 of *The Wagon Mound* [1961] A.C. 388; cf. *Aneco Reinsurance Underwriting Ltd v Johnson & Higgins Ltd* [2001] UKHL 51; [2002] 1 Lloyd's Rep. 157 at [10]–[12].

183 See para.20–119. This is an important difference between the "scope of duty" question said to arise in *SAAMCO* and the "scope of duty" question said to arise in *The Achilleas* [2008] UKHL 48; [2009] 1 A.C. 61 where the issue was remoteness; para.20–131, fn.820.

184 cf. Lord Hobhouse's statement in *Platform Home Loans Ltd v Oyston Shipways Ltd* [2000] 2 A.C. 190 at 848 that the "development" in the *SAAMCO* case (fn.172) was to apply the "scope of duty" reasoning to "*quantification* of damages" as opposed to "kinds or categories of damage".

185 *Thomson v Christie Manson & Woods Ltd* [2005] EWCA Civ 555; [2005] P.N.L.R. 38 at [129]. Referred to as "category 1" and "category 2" cases in *Haugesund Kommune v Depfa ACS Bank* [2011] EWCA Civ 33; [2011] 3 All E.R. 655.

186 *Haugesund Kommune v Depfa ACS Bank* [2011] EWCA Civ 33; [2011] 3 All E.R. 655.

187 *Haugesund Kommune v Depfa ACS Bank* [2011] EWCA Civ 33; [2011] 3 All E.R. 655 at [74].

188 See *Lloyds Bank Plc v Crosse & Crosse* [2001] EWCA Civ 366; [2001] P.N.L.R. 34; *Dent v Davis Blank Furniss* [2001] Lloyd's Rep. P.N. 534.

189 See *Aneco Reinsurance Underwriting Ltd v Johnson & Higgins Ltd* [2001] UKHL 51; [2002] 1 Lloyd's Rep. 157 at [1], [17], [32]; Lord Millett's dissent on the facts is to be preferred: Peel in Burrows and Peel (eds), *Commercial Remedies* (2003).

190 *Aneco Reinsurance Underwriting Ltd v Johnson & Higgins Ltd* [2001] UKHL 51; [2002] 1 Lloyd's Rep. 157. Contrast *Haugesund Kommune v Depfa ACS Bank* [2011] EWCA Civ 33; 134 Con L.R. 51.

availability of reinsurance cover in the market, without which the transaction would not have gone ahead"[191] and they were therefore liable for the full loss suffered by the client as a result of having entered into that transaction. Despite subsequent attempts to clarify the distinction between "information" and "advice", the courts have not found it easy to apply.[192] Nevertheless, it has been affirmed by the Supreme Court in *BPE v Hughes-Holland*[193] in which Lord Sumption posed the question for the court in the following terms:

> "… what damages are recoverable in a case where (i) but for the negligence of a professional adviser his client would not have embarked on some course of action, but (ii) part or all of the loss which he suffered by doing so arose from risks which it was no part of the adviser's duty to protect his client against."[194]

In this sense, the scope of the defendant's duty is, ultimately, a question of construction and "information" or "advice" should probably be seen as little more than labels to be applied once that construction exercise is complete.

**Types of expectation: "direct" loss and "consequential" loss.** The above discussion is concerned only with one type of expectation, namely that of receiving the promised performance. A contract can, however, give rise to two quite separate expectations: that of receiving the promised performance and that of being able to put it to some particular use. For example, a buyer of goods (such as machinery or raw materials) may expect not only to receive the goods but also to use them for manufacturing purposes. If the seller fails to deliver, the buyer is entitled to damages based on the value of the goods that he should have received ("direct loss") and also to damages for loss of profits ("consequential loss")[195] suffered as a result of not receiving the promised delivery. **20–028**

### *(ii) Reliance loss*

In some cases, the claimant has sought to recover not his loss of bargain, or "expectation loss", but the expenditure which is said to have been wasted as a consequence of the defendant's breach, i.e. his "reliance loss". Sometimes, the expenses are of a kind which the claimant *must* incur if he is to perform his part of the contract, e.g. a contract for the sale of goods may provide that the seller is to deliver the goods at the buyer's premises; and if the buyer wrongfully refuses to accept them when they are tendered there, the seller can recover the expenses of delivery as an element of reliance loss. But sometimes wasted expenses may be recoverable as reliance loss even though the claimant was *not*, under the **20–029**

---

[191] *Aneco Reinsurance Underwriting Ltd v Johnson & Higgins Ltd* [2001] UKHL 51; [2002] 1 Lloyd's Rep. 157 at [1].

[192] See, e.g. *Bristol and West Building Society v Fancy & Jackson* [1997] 4 All E.R. 582 (Ch) which was overruled in part; and *Portman Building Society v Bevan Ashford* [2000] 1 E.G.L.R. 81 which was overruled in full in *BPE v Hughes-Holland* [2017] UKSC 21; [2018] A.C. 599.

[193] [2017] UKSC 21; [2018] A.C. 599.

[194] *BPE v Hughes-Holland* [2017] UKSC 21; [2018] A.C. 599 at [1].

[195] Provided that these are not too remote: para.20–119 and following.

contract, actually obliged to incur them. For example, in *McRae v Commonwealth Disposals Commission*,[196] the defendants were held liable under a contract for the salvage of a wrecked tanker for breach of an implied warranty that the tanker could be found lying in a specified position;[197] and the claimants recovered, inter alia, the £3,000 which it had cost them to send out an expedition to look for the tanker.

20–030 **Pre-contractual expenditure.** In the examples above, the reliance loss is incurred after the contract was made; but even expenditure incurred before then may be recoverable. In *Anglia Television Ltd v Reed*[198] the defendant broke his contract to take a leading part in the claimants' television play: and he was held liable for £2,750 spent by the claimants on the production before they had entered into the contract with him. Although the claimants had not incurred this expenditure in reliance on their contract with the defendant, it could be said that they had relied on that contract in allowing the expenditure to be wasted: in other words, in forbearing to look for another leading actor to take the part until it was too late. The pre-contract expenditure in such cases is recoverable because it leads to a loss which, after breach, can no longer be avoided.[199] Pre-contract expenditure may also be recoverable if it was incurred in reliance on an *agreement* before that agreement had become a legally binding *contract*. In *Lloyd v Stanbury*[200] a person who had contracted to sell land was accordingly held liable for certain expenses incurred by the purchaser in reliance on the agreement while it was still subject to contract.[201]

20–031 **Limit on recovery.** While the claimant has the option of claiming damages for his reliance loss,[202] this is only on the basis that such loss is presumed to represent his expectation loss, i.e. if the contract had been performed, the claimant would, at least, have recouped his expenditure.[203] The claimant is not entitled to claim his reliance loss in order to escape from what was a bad bargain. For example, in *McRae*'s case the claimants should not have been awarded the *whole* of their reliance loss of £3,000 if the tanker, had it existed, would have been worth only £2,000. In such a case the claimant would have lost £1,000, even if there had been no breach; and the court will not shift that loss to the defendant

---

[196] (1951) 84 C.L.R. 377, especially at 411.
[197] See para.8–004.
[198] [1972] 1 Q.B. 60; A.L.G. 88 L.Q.R. 168; Ogus 35 M.L.R. 423; Clarke [1972] C.L.J. 22.
[199] *CCC Films (London) Ltd v Impact Quadrant Films Ltd* [1985] Q.B. 16; Owen [1985] C.L.J. 24; Burrows 100 L.Q.R. 27.
[200] [1971] 1 W.L.R. 535.
[201] See para.2–090.
[202] *Cullinane v British "Rema" Mfg Co* [1954] 1 Q.B. 292 at 303; *Anglia Television Ltd v Reed* [1972] 1 Q.B. 60 at 63–64; *CCC Films (London) Ltd v Impact Quadrant Films Ltd* [1985] Q.B. 16 at 32; cf. *Lloyd v Stanbury* [1971] 1 W.L.R. 535 at 547.
[203] *The Mamola Challenger* [2010] EWHC 2026 (Comm); [2011] 1 Lloyd's Rep. 47, rejecting the view that reliance damages are based on a quite different principle of putting the claimant in the same position as if the contract had not been made: Treitel 108 L.Q.R. 229; cf. Tettenborn [2011] L.M.C.L.Q. 1; McLauchlan 127 L.Q.R. 23.

by allowing the claimant to recover the whole of his wasted expenditure.[204] It also follows that where the claimant has suffered no expectation loss because such loss has been mitigated in full, he is not entitled to damages on the basis of his reliance loss.[205] The burden of proof on this issue is on the defendant:[206] in other words, it is not up to the claimant to show that his venture would have been profitable but up to the defendant to show that it would have been unprofitable,[207] or that his expectation loss has been fully mitigated.[208]

As much of the relevant information on this issue may be more readily available to the claimant than to the defendant, the defendant may find this burden a hard one to discharge. It may be justified on the basis that it is only because of the defendant's breach that the claimant is prevented from putting to the test whether or not he would have recouped his expenditure.[209] On this basis, it has been held that the shift in the burden of proof does *not* apply where the defendant is sued for breach of a contractual duty of care and the claimant's expectation loss is the loss of the chance that an acquisition would have been made if the defendant had taken care[210] (as opposed to the loss of bargain involved where the claimant has been deprived of the contracted for subject-matter of the contract, such as goods, or a warranted performance or outcome). In such a case, the claimant is confined to his expectation loss and there is said to be nothing unfair in requiring him to prove that he lost a substantial chance and the extent of that chance, as would normally be the case.[211]

### *(iii) Restitution*[212]

A claim for restitution is not strictly one for "damages"[213] since its purpose is not to compensate the claimant for a loss, but to deprive the defendant of a benefit. The simplest case of restitution arises where a seller has been paid in advance and then fails to deliver. He is bound to restore the price and the effect of this is to put *both parties* into the position in which they would have been if the contract had *not been made*. A restitution claim obviously differs from a loss of bargain claim, which is meant to put the claimant into the position in which he would have been **20–032**

[204] See *C & P Haulage v Middleton* [1983] 1 W.L.R. 1461; cf. *CCC Films (London) Ltd v Impact Quadrant Films* [1985] Q.B. 16 at 38; *PJ Spillings Ltd v Bonus Flooring Ltd* [2008] EWHC 1516 (QB); *Grange v Quinn* [2013] EWCA Civ 24; [2013] 1 P & C.R. 18, in which Jackson LJ's reliance on the earlier decision in *Sampson v Floyd* [1989] 33 E.G. 41 appears not to take into account that the claim made in that case was, in effect, a claim for "reliance loss" and therefore subject to the limit referred to in the text.

[205] *The Mamola Challenger* [2010] EWHC 2026 (Comm); [2011] 1 Lloyd's Rep. 47.

[206] *Yam Seng Pte Ltd v International Trade Corp Ltd* [2013] EWHC 111 (QB); [2013] 1 Lloyd's Rep. 526 at [187].

[207] *CCC Films (London) Ltd v Impact Quadrant Films* [1985] Q.B. 16; cf. *L. Albert & Son v Armstrong Rubber Co* (1948) 178 Fed. Rep.182; *Commonwealth of Australia v Amann Aviation Pty Ltd* (1991) 66 A.L.J.R. 123; Treitel 108 L.Q.R. 226.

[208] *The Mamola Challenger* [2010] EWHC 2026 (Comm); [2011] 1 Lloyd's Rep. 47.

[209] *Parker v SJ Berwin & Co* [2008] EWHC 3017 (Comm); [2009] P.N.L.R. 17 at [77].

[210] See para.20–062.

[211] *Parker v SJ Berwin & Co* [2008] EWHC 3017 (Comm); [2009] P.N.L.R. 17.

[212] See further, Ch.22.

[213] *Portman BS v Hamlyn Taylor Neck* [1998] 4 All E.R. 202 at 205.

if the contract had been performed. It also differs from a claim for reliance loss since that will leave the defendant in a worse position if he is unable to discharge the burden of proving that the contract would have been unprofitable.[214] In practice there is considerable overlap between reliance and restitution. Performance by the claimant is a form of reliance which often benefits the defendant; and the requirement in restitution claims that the defendant must have "benefited" from that performance is a somewhat elastic one.[215] There may also be an overlap between loss of bargain and restitution where the amount paid by the injured party is the only evidence of the value of what he ought to have received; and in such a case that amount, or an "appropriate proportion"[216] of it will be the prima facie measure of the expectation loss which he suffers as a result of the defendant's failure to perform, or to perform in full.

### *(iv) Relationship between loss of bargain, reliance loss and restitution*

20–033 **Claimant's choice.** Where more than one type of claim is available the choice between them (if it has to be made) is the claimant's, who cannot be forced by the defendant to make one of the available claims rather than another. Suppose that a seller has been paid in advance and then fails to deliver. The buyer can choose between claiming the return of his money (restitution) and the value of the goods at the time fixed for delivery (loss of bargain). Obviously he will take the former course if he has made a bad bargain and the latter if he has made a good bargain. If the seller could force him to choose restitution, the buyer could easily be deprived of the benefit of a good bargain.

20–034 **Remedy awarded may be limited to reliance or restitution.** The claim for loss of bargain damages is, in principle, always available. But to make good such a claim the injured party must prove the value of his expectations. If he cannot do so with reasonable certainty, he may be limited to his reliance and restitution claims. The point may be illustrated by further reference to *McRae v Commonwealth Disposals Commission*[217] where the claimants sought damages for loss of their bargain, alleging that the value of the supposed tanker and its contents (for which they had paid £285) would have been £300,000. This basis for quantifying damages was dismissed as "manifestly absurd";[218] and the claimants recovered their payment of £285 (restitution) plus the £3,000 spent on their fruitless salvage expedition (reliance loss).

20–035 **Limits on restitution.** At the other extreme, the claimant's right to claim restitution is limited, in particular by the rule that he can (in general) recover money paid under the contract only if there has been a *total* failure of consideration. This rule will be discussed in Ch.22;[219] but a point to be emphasised here is that, if restitution is available, it is no objection to such a

---

[214] See para.20–030.

[215] See especially para.22–033.

[216] *Peninsular & Orient SN Co v Youell* [1997] 2 Lloyd's Rep. 136 at 141; para.22–010.

[217] (1951) 84 C.L.R. 377.

[218] *McRae v Commonwealth Disposals Commission* (1951) 84 C.L.R. 377 at 411.

[219] See paras 22–003—22–020.

claim that it will leave the claimant better off than he would have been, if the contract had been performed. Indeed, this will be the result of a successful restitution claim whenever the claimant has made a bad bargain, e.g. by paying more for goods than they are worth. There is an obvious contrast here with reliance loss where the claimant is not able to escape from a bad bargain (if proved by the defendant).[220] The reason for this result is that the defendant would otherwise be enriched; and there is no such enrichment merely because a claimant's reliance loss exceeds the value of his bargain.

**Suing in the alternative for loss of bargain and reliance loss.** It follows from the principles which govern the award of damages for reliance loss[221] that the sort of case in which such a claim is most likely to be pursued is one in which the claimant cannot prove the value of his expectation had the contract been performed.[222] Where he can do so and it exceeds his expenditure he will claim damages for his expectation loss in the normal way. This raises the question whether the claimant can sue for his expectation loss and his reliance loss in the alternative. Dicta in some cases suggest not[223] and that the claimant must elect between the two, but since reliance loss is not in fact an entirely separate basis of assessment to, but rather a presumption of, expectation loss, there is no election needed in the strict sense and it seems that he may therefore sue for them in the alternative.[224] It is nonetheless a slightly curious form of pleading which would require the defendant to prove that the claimant would not at least have recouped his expenditure (or to prove the extent to which he would have failed to do so) while leaving the claimant free, in the first instance, to attempt to prove that he might have gained more than that.[225] 20–036

**Whether claims can be combined.** There is sometimes said to be an inconsistency between combining the various types of claim so far discussed. The courts have not accepted this kind of reasoning and have, in appropriate cases, allowed the claims to be combined. In one case[226] machinery was bought, paid for and installed. The buyer rejected the machinery because it was not in accordance with the contract; and he recovered the price (restitution), installation expenses (reliance loss) and his *net* loss of profits resulting from the breach (loss of bargain). 20–037

---

220 See para.20–030.

221 See para.20–030.

222 This is no doubt why reliance loss was claimed in *Anglia Television Ltd v Reed* [1972] 1 Q.B. 60. But see *Parker v SJ Berwin & Co* [2008] EWHC 3017 (Comm); [2009] P.N.L.R. 17; para.20–030, text to fn.211.

223 *Filobake Ltd v Rondo* Ltd [2005] EWCA Civ 563 at [64]; *Anglia Television Ltd v Reed* [1972] 1 Q.B. 60 at 63–64.

224 *The Mamola Challenger* [2010] EWHC 2026 (Comm); [2011] 1 Lloyd's Rep. 47 at [55]; *Commonwealth of Australia v Amann Aviation Pty Ltd* (1992) 66 A.L.J.R. 123 at [35] (Mason CJ and Dawson J); cf. at [17] (Brennan J).

225 In *Parker v SJ Berwin & Co* [2008] EWHC 3017 (Comm); [2009] P.N.L.R. 17 at [80] it is described as "a recipe for confusion and uncertainty".

226 *Millar's Machinery Co Ltd v David Way & Son* (1935) 40 Com. Cas. 204; cf. *Naughton v O'Callaghan* [1990] 3 All E.R. 191 at 198.

20–038 **Principle against double recovery.** The true principle is not that there is any logical objection to combining the various types of claim, but that the claimant cannot combine them so as to recover more than once for the same loss.[227] Suppose that a buyer has paid in advance for goods which are not delivered. He obviously cannot recover both his payment (restitution) and the full value of the goods at the time fixed for delivery (loss of bargain).[228]

The principle against double recovery also applies where a claimant seeks both reliance loss and damages for the loss of his bargain. If the claimant in *McRae*'s[229] case had been able to establish the value of the hypothetical tanker, he should clearly not have been entitled to that amount *and* to the £3,285, for he would have had to spend the latter amount to acquire the former. Similarly, in *Cullinane v British "Rema" Manufacturing Co Ltd*[230] the defendants sold a clay pulverising machine, warranting that it could process clay at 6 tons per hour. The buyer claimed damages for breach of this warranty under two heads: first, the capital cost of the machine and its installation and, secondly, loss of profits. It was held that the buyer could not recover under both of these heads as "a claim for loss of profits could only be founded upon the footing that the capital expenditure had been incurred".[231] To allow the buyer to recover the capital expenditure and also his *full* profit would give him damages twice over for the same loss. It was, however, not established that the profits which would have been derived from the machine over the whole of its useful "life" would have *exceeded* its capital cost. If this had been proved the buyer could, according to a decision of the High Court of Australia, have recovered: (a) the capital cost of the machinery less its actual value; plus (b) the excess of the estimated profits over the sum calculated under (a).[232] This alone would put the buyer into as good a financial position as if the contract had been performed.

### (v) *Incidental loss*

20–039 The victim of a breach of contract can often recover loss which does not fit easily into the categories so far discussed. He may incur expenses after a breach has come to his attention, such as the administrative costs of buying a substitute,[233] or of sending back defective goods, or of wasted staff time.[234] Such expenses are hardly incurred in reliance *on the contract*; and they will in this chapter be called "incidental" loss.

---

227 *Peninsular & Orient SN Co v Youell* [1997] 2 Lloyd's Rep. 136 at 141.

228 cf. *The Unique Mariner* [1979] 1 Lloyd's Rep. 37 at 53; *Tang Man Sit v Capacious Investment Ltd* [1996] A.C. 514; *Baltic Shipping Co v Dillon* (1993) 176 C.L.R. 344 at 345.

229 *McRae v Commonwealth Disposals Commission* (1951) 84 C.L.R. 377; *Salvage Association v CAP Financial Services* [1995] F.S.R. 654 at 683.

230 [1954] 1 Q.B. 292; Macleod [1970] J.B.L. 19; Stoljar 91 L.Q.R. 68; cf. *JP Morgan Chase Bank v Springwell Navigation Corp* [2006] EWCA Civ 161; [2006] P.N.L.R. 28; *4Eng Ltd v Harper* [2008] EWHC 915 (Ch); [2009] Ch. 91 at [49]–[51].

231 *Cullinane v British "Rema" Manufacturing Co Ltd* [1954] 1 Q.B. 292 at 302.

232 *TC Industrial Plant Pty Ltd v Robert's (Queensland) Ltd* [1964] A.L.R. 1083.

233 See, e.g. *Robert Stewart & Sons Ltd v Carapanayoti* [1962] 1 W.L.R. 34.

234 The claimant must show that the relevant breach of contract caused "some significant disruption to the business; in other words that staff have been significantly diverted from their usual activities": *Standard Chartered Bank v Pakistan Shipping Corp* [2001] EWCA Civ 55; *Verizon UK Ltd v Swiftnet*

## 2. QUANTIFICATION

**Difficulty of assessment is no bar to recovery.** Damages always consist of a sum of money, so that the loss has to be quantified in terms of money. This process is variously referred to as "quantifying" or "measuring" or "assessing" damages. It gives rise to a number of problems, but at the outset it should be stated that difficulty of assessment is no bar to recovery. As acknowledged by Cockburn CJ in *Simpson v The London and North Western Railway Co*: 20–040

> "As to the supposed impossibility of ascertaining the damages, I think there is no such impossibility; to some extent, no doubt, they must be matter of speculation, but that is no reason for not awarding any damages at all."[235]

### (a) The bases of assessment

#### *(i) Reliance and restitution*

Relatively little difficulty arises where the injured party claims reliance loss or restitution. In the first case, the basis of assessment is the cost to him of his action in reliance on the contract; and in the second it is generally[236] the benefit obtained by the defendant under the contract. These assessments are particularly straightforward where the claimant has expended or the defendant received a sum of money. Where the reliance loss or the benefit to be "restored" consists of goods or services, a reasonable value must be placed on them. This may give rise to practical difficulties, but there is no doubt about the principle on which such assessment proceeds. 20–041

#### *(ii) Loss of bargain*

**"Difference in value" and "cost of cure".**[237] Where the injured party claims to be put into "the same situation … as if the contract had been performed",[238] there are two distinct bases of assessment: "difference in value" and "cost of cure". The distinction between these two bases is strikingly illustrated by an American case[239] in which a coal company took a mining lease of farmland, covenanting to restore the land to its original state at the end of the lease. The cost of doing the work would have been $29,000, but the result of not doing it was to reduce the 20–042

---

*Ltd* [2008] EWHC 551 (Comm) at [56]. When proven, the employment costs are awarded on the basis that employees of a commercial business are taken to generate revenue which is at least equal to the cost of employing them: see *Aerospace Publishing v Thames Water* [2007] EWCA Civ 3 [2007] Bus L.R. 726; cf. *Azzurri Communications Ltd v International Telecommunications Equipment Ltd* [2013] EWPCC 17; *Fluor v Shanghai Zhenhua Heavy Industry Co Ltd* [2018] EWHC 490 (TCC).

235 *Simpson v The London and North Western Railway Co* (1876) 1 Q.B.D. 274 at 277; cf. *Wemyss v Karim* [2016] EWCA Civ 27 at [49].

236 Not always, see, e.g. *Planché v Colburn* (1831) 8 Bing. 14 (para.17–046), where there is no evidence that the defendant benefited at all.

237 Rowan 76 C.L.J. 616.

238 *Robinson v Harman* (1848) 1 Ex. 850 at 855.

239 *Peevyhouse v Garland Coal Co* 382 P.2d 109 (1962); cf. *Attica Sea Carriers Corp v Ferrostaal Poseidon Bulk Reederei GmbH* [1976] 1 Lloyd's Rep. 250.

value of the land by only $300. Damages for the company's failure to do the work were assessed at the latter sum. In English law damages for breach of a tenant's covenant to repair are by statute assessed on a "difference in value" basis.[240] Apart from such statutory provisions, the law starts with certain prima facie assumptions for choosing between the two bases;[241] but these assumptions can be displaced. The point can be illustrated principally by reference to contracts for the supply of goods and for the execution of building work, before considering the difficulties which may arise in relation to contracts for services.

20–043 **Supply of goods.** Where a seller delivers goods which are not of the contract quality, the damages are prima facie assessed on a difference in value basis, so that the buyer can recover "the difference between the value of the goods … and the value they would have had"[242] if they had been in accordance with the contract. But the rule is only a prima facie one and if the defect in the goods is cured at a reasonable cost there is little doubt that the cost of such cure can be awarded. This is the position in analogous hire-purchase cases[243] and there seems to be no reason for not applying the same rule to sales.[244] Even the cost of an attempted cure which fails—such as veterinary fees spent on a sick animal which nevertheless dies—can be recovered.[245]

20–044 **Building work.** A defendant who is in breach of an obligation to do building work is prima facie liable on a "cost of cure" basis: i.e. he must pay for the cost of putting the defects right or of completing the work.[246] This, again, is only a prima facie rule, which can be displaced where the cost of putting the defect right would be out of all proportion to the advantage which cure would confer on the injured party.[247] This would, for example, be the position where components not in accordance with the contractual specifications had been built into a structure which would have to be substantially demolished to effect a cure;[248] where the cost of cure was greater than the value of the whole building;[249] or where execution of the promised building work would confer no economic benefit at all

[240] Landlord and Tenant Act 1927 s.18; *Culworth Estates Ltd v Society of Licensed Victuallers* (1991) 62 P. & C.R. 211. But in the absence of evidence as to difference in value, cost of repairs is a "starting point": *Drummond v SU Stores* (1980) 258 E.G. 1293 at 1294; cf. fn.211.

[241] *Watts v Morrow* [1991] 1 W.L.R. 1421 at 1441.

[242] Sale of Goods Act 1979 s.53(3); para.20–053; *The Athenian Harmony* [1998] 2 Lloyd's Rep. 410 at 419.

[243] e.g. *Charterhouse Credit Co Ltd v Tolly* [1963] 2 Q.B. 683 at 711–712.

[244] *Jacovides v Constantinou, The Times*, 27 October 1986 (a sale of land case where damages were awarded for misrepresentation apparently having contractual effect). In *Keeley v Guy McDonald* (1984) 134 N.L.J. 522 the *cost of repairing* an unmerchantable car was awarded *as the difference in value* between the car as it was and as it would have been if it had been merchantable.

[245] *Harling v Eddy* [1951] 2 Q.B. 739.

[246] *Mertens v Home Freeholds* [1921] 2 K.B. 526; *Hoenig v Isaacs* [1952] 1 T.L.R. 1360; cf. *Radford v de Froberville* [1977] 1 W.L.R. 1262 (breach of covenant to build a boundary wall); *Calabar Properties Ltd v Stitcher* [1984] 1 W.L.R. 287.

[247] *Ruxley Electronics and Construction Co Ltd v Forsyth* [1996] A.C. 344; *Birse Construction Ltd v Eastern Telegraph Co Ltd* [2004] EWHC 2512 (TCC); (2004) 47 E.G. 164; Contrast *Tabcorp Holdings Ltd v Bowen Investments Pty Ltd* [2009] H.C.A. 8; 236 C.L.R. 272.

[248] e.g. *Jacob & Youngs v Kent* 129 N.E. 889 (1921).

[249] cf. *Morris v Redland Bricks Ltd* [1970] A.C. 652.

on the claimant.[250] In such cases, difference in value (if any)[251] would form the normal basis of assessment.[252] This basis of assessment is, in turn, liable to be displaced by further circumstances. There is some support in the authorities for the view that the claimant can recover damages on the higher cost of cure basis if he can show *either* that he has in fact incurred that cost *or* that he will incur it by getting the work done.[253] He is, however, required to act reasonably to mitigate his loss,[254] and it is submitted that he would have failed to do so if he had insisted on cure even though its cost was wholly disproportionate to the resulting benefit to him. Where this is the position, he should recover only on a difference in value basis.[255] For this purpose, the disproportion would have to be a clear one, since the mitigation rules only require the injured party to act reasonably. Cost of cure which is actually incurred or going to be incurred may therefore be recoverable where the effect of cure on the value of property is speculative;[256] and where the cost of cure, though not resulting in any improvement to the property, is not excessive in relation to the initial value of the property.

**Surveys.** Damages against a surveyor who fails to draw his client's attention to defects in a house which the client buys in reliance on the surveyor's report are prima facie based on difference in value and not on cost of cure.[257] The reason for this rule is that the surveyor gives no warranty as to the condition of the house: he undertakes only to conduct the survey with reasonable care and skill.[258] The rule may be displaced by special circumstances, e.g. cost of cure may be recoverable if cure is undertaken in a reasonable effort to mitigate loss;[259] and the client may also be able to recover costs reasonably incurred in extricating himself from the transaction.[260] 20–045

**Where cure is not undertaken.** Where the claimant is prima facie entitled to damages based on cost of cure, the further question arises whether he can recover this amount (where it exceeds difference in value) even though he does not 20–046

[250] *James v Hutton* [1950] 1 K.B. 9 (where performance of the defendant's promise to restore a shop front to its pre-contract appearance would not have affected its value).

[251] There being no such difference in *James v Hutton* [1950] 1 K.B. 9, above, the damages were held to be nominal; cf. *Sunrock Aircraft Corp Ltd v Scandinavian Airlines Systems Denmark-Norway-Sweden* [2007] EWCA Civ 882; [2007] 2 Lloyd's Rep. 612.

[252] See *Jacob & Youngs v Kent* 129 N.E. 889 (1921); *The Rozel* [1994] 2 Lloyd's Rep. 160 (breach of charterer's undertaking to repair a ship); *GW Atkins Ltd v Scott* (1996) 46 Con L.R. 14.

[253] *Tito v Waddell (No.2)* [1977] Ch. 106 at 332, 335; *Radford v De Froberville* [1977] 1 W.L.R. 1262. For the position in tort, see *Ward v Cannock Chase DC* [1986] Ch. 546; Contrast *Wigsell v School for Indigent Blind* (1882) 8 Q.B.D. 357 (difference in value); and, see Harris, Ogus and Phillips 95 L.Q.R. 581. For the possible relevance of this factor to a claim for damages in respect of a *third party's* loss, see paras 14–030, 14–042.

[254] See para.20–104 and following.

[255] cf. e.g. *Darbishire v Warran* [1963] 1 W.L.R. 1067; *The Maersk Colombo* [2001] EWCA Civ 717; [2001] 2 Lloyd's Rep. 275 at [32] (also a tort case).

[256] *Sunshine Exploration Ltd v Dolly Varden Mines Ltd* (1969) 8 D.L.R. (3d) 441.

[257] See para.20–006.

[258] *Watts v Morrow* [1991] 1 W.L.R. 1421 at 1439.

[259] *Cross v David Martin & Mortimer* [1989] 1 E.G.L.R. 154.

[260] *County Personnel (Employment Agency) Ltd v Alan R Pulver & Co* [1987] 1 W.L.R. 916 (negligent solicitor); contrast *Fulham Leisure Holdings Ltd v Nicholson Graham & Jones* [2006] EWHC 2017 (Ch); [2006] 2 All E.R. 599 at [284] where costs incurred went beyond "extrication".

undertake cure, or propose to do so. There is, at least apparently, some conflict in the authorities on this point. The starting principle is that the cost of cure can be recovered in such cases since, in general, the court is not concerned with the use which the claimant makes of his damages.[261] But this principle is subject to significant qualifications. First, the fact that the injured party has decided not to effect cure is relevant to the issue whether it would have been reasonable for him to do so; if not, cost of cure will be irrecoverable under the mitigation rules already discussed.[262] Secondly, the conduct of the injured party after the breach may affect the basis of assessment, e.g. if he has disposed of the defective or damaged subject-matter without effecting cure, the court is likely to conclude that what he has lost is difference in value rather than cost of cure.[263] In such cases, therefore, difference in value will be the more appropriate basis of assessment.

20–047 **Both bases may lead to same result.** The two bases of assessment will not invariably lead to diverging results. For example, in *Dean v Ainley*[264] a vendor of land broke her contractual undertaking to seal a patio so as to prevent water from leaking into a cellar. The purchaser recovered the cost of doing the promised work, and this sum was variously described as the "cost of the works",[265] or as the extent to which the property was "clearly less valuable"[266] as a result of the vendor's failure to perform her undertaking. Where the only reliable evidence of difference in value is cost of cure,[267] the two methods of assessment will lead to the same practical result.

Sometimes the process of assessment can with equal plausibility be described as being based on difference in value or cost of cure. This is the position where a buyer is entitled to the difference between the contract and the market price of goods which the seller has failed to deliver.[268] It makes no difference whether such damages are described as the cost of curing the seller's breach or as the difference in value between what the buyer has received (i.e. nothing) and what he should have received (i.e. the goods). The buyer is, moreover, entitled to such damages whether or not he has actually made the substitute purchase.[269]

20–048 **Other bases of assessment.** The "difference in value" and "cost of cure" bases are not the only possible ones on which loss of bargain damages may be assessed. The point is well illustrated by *Ruxley Electronics and Construction Ltd v*

---

[261] *Ruxley Electronics and Construction Co Ltd v Forsyth* [1996] A.C. 344 at 359; cf. at 372; and see the cases discussed at para.20–048 in which damages are based on market prices.

[262] *Ruxley Electronics and Construction Co Ltd v Forsyth* [1996] A.C. 344; for this aspect of mitigation, see para.20–044.

[263] *Calabar Properties Ltd v Stitcher* [1984] 1 W.L.R. 297 at 229; cf. *Hole & Hole (Sayers Common) Ltd v Harrisons Ltd* [1973] 1 Lloyd's Rep. 345; *Leppard v Excess Ins Co Ltd* [1979] 1 W.L.R. 512; *Charterhouse Credit Ltd v Tolly* [1963] 2 Q.B. 683; *GW Atkins Ltd v Scott* (1996) 46 Con L.R. 14.

[264] [1987] 1 W.L.R. 1729; cf. *Watts v Morrow* [1991] 1 W.L.R. 1421 at 1435; *The Rozel* [1994] 2 Lloyd's Rep. 160 at 167.

[265] *Dean v Ainley* [1987] 1 W.L.R. 1729 at 1736.

[266] *Dean v Ainley* [1987] 1 W.L.R. 1729 at 1738.

[267] e.g. *Steward v Rapley (t/a Rapley Flatt & Co)* [1989] 1 E.G.L.R. 159.

[268] Sale of Goods Act 1979 s.51(3); at fn.293.

[269] cf. *Shearson Lehman Hutton Inc v Maclaine Watson & Co (No.2)* [1990] 1 Lloyd's Rep. 441 at 443 (seller's damages).

*Forsyth*,[270] where a builder had contracted to build a swimming pool in his customer's garden. The contract required the pool to have a maximum depth of 7ft 6in but the pool actually built had a maximum depth of only 6ft 9in. This breach of the contract did not significantly affect the value of the pool; nor, since the pool remained, in spite of the breach, perfectly safe and serviceable, would the cost of rebuilding it to the stipulated depth have been reasonably incurred, being wholly disproportionate to the benefit to be obtained by carrying out these operations. However, the trial judge had awarded the customer £2,500 for "loss of amenity" and this award was allowed to stand by the House of Lords,[271] even though it was recognised that in most building contract cases no such damages are available to the customer.[272] This aspect of the case is perhaps best explained on the ground that, in contracts for "home improvements",[273] damages can include compensation for the customer's "disappointed expectations"[274] arising from the contractor's failure to provide the degree of comfort or enjoyment which, to the contractor's knowledge, it was the customer's object to obtain.[275] In this sense, it may be said that damages were in fact awarded for "difference in value", but in their assessment the court was not confined to objective market value in relation to the pool itself.

**Services.** In the *Ruxley* case, the conclusion that there was no difference in value is the result of focusing on the end product of the builder's services, i.e. the pool. This may also explain the outcome in another case[276] where the defendant contracted with the claimant to provide a firefighting service and was paid the full contract price. At the end of the contract the claimant discovered that the defendant had not provided the stipulated number of firemen or horses, or the promised length of hosepipe, but it had not failed to put out any fires in consequence. The court ruled that the claimant had not proved it had suffered any loss and was unable to recover more than nominal damages. But it is clear that in some cases damages may be awarded by reference to the difference in value in the provision of the services themselves, particularly where there is no longer any opportunity for cure,[277] e.g. in the case of the sub-standard holiday,[278] or ruined wedding photographs.[279] Indeed, it is "obvious that in the ordinary way a party who contracts and pays for a superior service or superior goods and receives a 20–049

[270] [1996] A.C. 344; Coote [1997] C.L.J. 537.

[271] *Ruxley Electronics and Construction Ltd v Forsyth* [1996] A.C. 344 at 359; cf. Lord Lloyd's scepticism at 374 as to the amount of the award.

[272] *Ruxley Electronics and Construction Ltd v Forsyth* [1996] A.C. 344 at 374 (Lord Lloyd).

[273] See para.20–093, fn.566, 567.

[274] *Ruxley Electronics and Construction Ltd v Forsyth* [1996] A.C. 344 at 374.

[275] *Ruxley v Forsyth* [1996] A.C. 344 at 360–361, per Lord Mustill.

[276] *City of New Orleans v Firemen's Charitable Association* (1891) 9 So. 486.

[277] In accordance with the general rule (para.20–046), it is no bar to the award of such damages that the claimant has not sought to cure the breach: *Guido van der Garde BV v Force India Formula One Ltd* [2010] EWHC 2373 (QB) at [485], but a failure to do so may be relevant to any question of mitigation.

[278] *Jarvis v Swan Tours Ltd* [1973] Q.B. 233; *Milner v Carnival Plc* [2010] EWCA Civ 389; [2010] 3 All E.R. 701.

[279] *Diesen v Samson* 1971 S.L.T. (Sh. Ct.) 49.

substantially inferior service or inferior goods has suffered loss,"[280] and the "obvious measure" of that loss is the diminution in the value of the promised services.[281]

The real difficulty in such cases is how to determine the difference in value. This cannot be done by an apportionment of the price as such since that would amount to restitution and undermine the requirement that there must have been a total failure of consideration,[282] though it must be acknowledged that that requirement has been criticised[283] and it has been suggested that a refund of the difference in price would not amount to "a straining of principle in cases where the defendant provided inferior and cheaper services than those contracted for".[284] The difference in price between the performance contacted for and that provided may be accepted as *evidence* of the difference in value and, in the absence of any other evidence, may well produce a result not very different to a partial, or full refund.[285] It is on this basis that damages have been awarded for the difference in value between the holiday provided to the claimant and that which had been promised,[286] for failing to provide the claimant with a certain number of kilometres of driving in a formula one test car;[287] and, in the context of the interpretation and effect of an exclusion clause, to determine that the claimant was still left with a claim for the difference in value between the air-conditioned office promised and that provided.[288]

## (b) Actual and market values

20–050 Where damages are based on difference in value (or on the cost of a substitute) they may be assessed by reference either to actual or to market values. There is said to be a "market" for goods if they can be freely bought or sold at a price fixed by supply and demand,[289] but it has also been said that the court "is entitled

[280] *White Arrow Express Ltd v Lamey's Distribution Ltd* [1995] C.L.C. 1251 at 1254.

[281] *Regus (UK) Ltd v Epcot Solutions Ltd* [2008] EWCA Civ 361; [2009] 1 All E.R. (Comm) 586 at [30]; cf. the right to a "reduction in price of an appropriate amount" which is made available to a consumer under the Consumer Rights Act 2015 s.56.

[282] *White Arrow Express Ltd v Lamey's Distribution Ltd* [1995] C.L.C. 1251, where the claim for *damages* failed because it was put on that basis.

[283] See para.22–003.

[284] *Attorney General v Blake* [2001] 1 A.C. 268 at 286C (Lord Nicholls referred to a "similar approach" to a refund in the difference in price which would occur with supply of goods; by "similar" he may have been referring to the evidential role of the price, as discussed in the text); cf. *Experience Hendrix LLC v PPX Enterprises Inc* [2003] EWCA Civ 323; [2003] E.M.L.R. 515 at [28].

[285] *White Arrow Express Ltd v Lamey's Distribution Ltd* [1995] C.L.C. 1251 at 1256; *Milner v Carnival Plc* [2010] EWCA Civ 389; [2010] 3 All E.R. 701 at [46]; *Guido van der Garde BV v Force India Formula One Ltd* [2010] EWHC 2373 (QB) at [433], [487]; para.22–020; cf. *PlayUp Interactive Equipment (UK) Pty Ltd v Givemefootball Ltd* [2011] EWHC 1980 (Comm); [2011] Info T.L.R. 289 at [268]–[275].

[286] *Jarvis v Swan Tours Ltd* [1973] Q.B. 233; *Milner v Carnival Plc* [2010] EWCA Civ 389; [2010] 3 All E.R. 701; on the distinction between the damages awarded in such cases for difference in value and those awarded for "mental distress", see para.20–095.

[287] *Guido van der Garde BV v Force India Formula One Ltd* [2010] EWHC 2373 (QB).

[288] *Regus (UK) Ltd v Epcot Solutions Ltd* [2008] EWCA Civ 361; [2009] 1 All E.R. (Comm) 586.

[289] *Dunkirk Colliery Co v Lever* (1878) 9 Ch D. 20; *W L Thompson Ltd v Robinson (Gunmakers) Ltd* [1955] Ch. 177; *Charter v Sullivan* [1957] 2 Q.B. 117. A "black" market may be taken into account:

to infer the existence of a market from any sufficient evidence relevant to that issue."[290] Where there is a market, the loss is prima facie quantified by reference to it; but other factors may also have to be taken into account. Where there is no market, the loss must be quantified in some other, and sometimes more speculative, way.[291]

### (i) Where there is a market

**Non-delivery.** If a seller of goods fails to deliver, the buyer can go into the market and buy substitute goods at the prevailing price and will be expected to do so under his duty to mitigate if, for example, he requires the goods for a further sale, or use.[292] Thus his damages will prima facie be based on the amount (if any) by which the market price exceeds the contract price.[293] It is irrelevant that the seller has disposed of the goods to a third party for *less* than the market price.[294] Similarly, where breach by a carrier results in a failure of the goods to reach the agreed destination, the injured party's damages are based on the market value of the goods at that destination when they should have been delivered there.[295] **20–051**

The principle of assessment by reference to the market price normally applies even though the injured party has resold an equivalent quantity of goods at a different price, in the expectation of receiving those due under the contract. Such a sub-sale does not reduce the damages if it is made below the market price[296] for the buyer is nevertheless "entitled to recover the expense of putting himself into the position of having those goods [i.e. those which the seller has failed to deliver], and this he can do by going into the market and purchasing them at the market price".[297] So long as the sub-sale was not of the identical goods bought under the main contract,[298] the buyer might have been able to supply his sub-buyer from some other source before the market rose. He could then have resold the goods bought from the defendant to a third party and made a further

*Mouatt v Betts Motors Ltd* [1959] A.C. 71; but not a "monopoly market" fixed by a government: *The Texaco Melbourne* [1992] 2 Lloyd's Rep. 303 at 312; reversed on other grounds [1994] 1 Lloyd's Rep. 473.

290 *Bulkhaul Ltd v Rhodia Organique Fine Ltd* [2008] EWCA Civ 1452; [2009] 1 Lloyd's Rep. 353 at [29].

291 cf. *Luxmoore-May v Messenger May Baverstock* [1990] 1 W.L.R. 1009 at 1027.

292 See para.20–106.

293 Sale of Goods Act 1979 s.51(3); cf. *The Elena D'Amico* [1980] 1 Lloyd's Rep. 75 (failure to provide a ship under charterparty); *Murray v Lloyd* [1989] 1 W.L.R. 1060 (market cost of substitute accommodation awarded against negligent solicitor).

294 cf. *Barry v Davies* [2000] 1 W.L.R. 1962 (s.51(3) applied by analogy to auctioneer's wrongful refusal to knock goods down to the highest bidder (paras 2–008, 3–164)).

295 *Rodocanachi Sons & Co v Milburn Bros* (1876) 18 Q.B.D. 67; *The Texaco Melbourne* [1994] 1 Lloyd's Rep. 473 at 479; cf. *Watts, Watts & Co v Mitsui & Co Ltd* [1917] A.C. 227. Expenses saved by the shipper, such as the freight that he would have had to pay if the goods had duly arrived and (in case of failure to ship) insurance premiums are deducted from the amount recoverable on the principle of taking the claimant's overall position into account (para.20–006).

296 *Williams Bros v ET Agius Ltd* [1914] A.C. 510; cf. *Rodocanachi, Sons & Co v Milburn Bros* (1886) 18 Q.B.D. 67; *Brading v F McNeill & Co Ltd* [1946] Ch. 145; *Oxus Gold Plc v Templeton Insurance Ltd* [2007] EWHC 770 (Comm).

297 *Williams Bros v ET Agius Ltd* [1914] A.C. 510 at 531.

298 cf. *Euro-Asian Oil SA v Credit Suisse AG* [2018] EWCA Civ 1720; [2019] 1 Lloyd's Rep. 444 at [73].

profit. Conversely the sub-sale will not increase the damages if it was made above the market price, even if the seller knew that the buyer intended to resell.[299] In such a case the buyer's extra loss has not been caused by the seller's breach, but by the buyer's failure to go into the market to buy a substitute to satisfy his sub-buyer.[300] Once again, however, the position would be different if the sub-sale had been "of the self-same thing";[301] for in that case the buyer would not have been able to satisfy his sub-buyer with substitute goods. Consequently, he would have lost his profit on the sub-sale and could have recovered that loss, so long as it was not too remote.[302]

20–052 **Late delivery.** Where delay in delivery is a ground of rejection, and the right to reject is exercised, damages are assessed in the same way as for non-delivery.[303] But where late delivery is accepted, damages are assessed on a different basis, the contract price being irrelevant. The buyer's complaint in such a case is not that he has to go into the market to buy a substitute for more than he had originally agreed to pay. It is that he has got the goods at a time that was less advantageous to him than the delivery time fixed by the contract. If he intended, on receipt of the goods, to resell them in the market, he will accordingly have lost the amount by which their market value when they were delivered to him was less than their market value when they should have been delivered; and this amount will be recoverable provided that the chance of resale is not too remote a contingency.[304]

It is, however, disputed whether a buyer's damages will be reduced if he has resold the goods for *more* than the market price at the time of actual delivery. In *Wertheim v Chicoutimi Pulp Co*[305] wood pulp was sold for delivery in September/November but not delivered till the following June. The market price per ton was 70s. at the time fixed for delivery and 42s. 6d. at the time of actual delivery. Prima facie the buyers' loss was therefore 27s. 6d. per ton. But they had resold the pulp at 65s. per ton and were able to pass it on to their sub-buyers at that price. The Privy Council held that the sellers could rely on the sub-sale to reduce the damages to 5s. per ton. To allow the buyers to recover 27s. 6d. would, it was said, enable them to make a profit out of the breach. But this is hard to fit with the principles normally governing the assessment of damages.[306] Two possibilities exist in cases of this kind. First, the buyer has resold the very goods comprised in the main contract.[307] If so he has admittedly not lost 27s. 6d. per ton but it is difficult to see that he has lost anything at all; he would not have been

---

[299] *Kwei Tek Chao v British Traders & Shippers Ltd* [1954] 2 Q.B. 459 at 489.

[300] cf. para.20–104; *Mobil North Sea Ltd v PJ Pipe & Valve Co* [2001] EWCA Civ 741; [2001] 1 All E.R. (Comm) 289 at [30]. The burden of proof on the issue whether the injured party ought to have mitigated is on the party in breach: see *Standard Chartered Bank v Pakistan National Shipping Co (No.3)* [2001] EWCA Civ 55; [2001] 1 All E.R. (Comm) 822 at [41].

[301] *Williams Bros v ET Agius Ltd* [1914] A.C. 510 at 523; cf. *Seven Seas Properties Ltd v Al-Essa* [1988] 1 W.L.R. 1272.

[302] See para.20–119 and following; *Re R & H Hall Ltd and WH Pim Jr* (1928) 139 L.T. 50, where the contract itself expressly provided for resale; *The Honam Jade* [1991] 1 Lloyd's Rep. 38.

[303] e.g. *The Almare Seconda* [1981] 2 Lloyd's Rep. 433; cf. para.18–111.

[304] See para.20–122.

[305] [1911] A.C. 301.

[306] *Slater v Hoyle & Smith* [1920] 2 K.B. 11 at 23.

[307] cf. *Williams Bros v ET Agius Ltd* [1914] A.C. 510 at 530.

free to sell the pulp in the market at 70s. per ton as he was bound to deliver it to his sub-buyer. Secondly, the buyer has resold an equivalent quantity. If so the sub-sale should be disregarded. Had the pulp been delivered in September/November it could have *then* been sold to a third party, and the sub-buyer could still have been satisfied with an equivalent quantity bought in June at 42s. 6d. per ton. It is improbable that the buyer would have kept the pulp throughout this period on a falling market. On the other hand, if (in view of the delay) the buyer "had bought other goods and used them for the sub-contract he would have been left with the goods delivered at the time when the market price was 42s. 6d. instead of when it was 70s.".[308] Nor is it right to say that the buyer would make a profit *out of the breach* of contract if he were awarded 27s. 6d. a ton. He would make a profit *out of the advantageous sub-sale*.

**Defective delivery: in general.** Where defective goods are delivered, and are not (or can no longer be) rejected, the buyer's loss is prima facie the difference between the actual value of the goods that he has received and the value that they would have had if they had been in accordance with the contract.[309] As in cases of late delivery, the difference between the contract and the market price is not relevant:[310] the buyer's complaint is not that he will have to buy an equivalent elsewhere, but that he has got something of lower value than that which he should have received. A sub-sale is again ignored;[311] unless it is of the very goods comprised in the original contract.[312] **20–053**

**Bence Graphics.** A case of defective delivery which gives rise to much difficulty is *Bence Graphics International Ltd v Fasson UK Ltd*.[313] Vinyl film had been sold for use in the buyers' business of manufacturing decals which their customers attached to containers used in the carriage of goods. It was a term of the contract of sale that the decals were to have a "life" of five years; and this term was broken so that the film delivered was "worthless".[314] The defect being not immediately apparent, the buyers used the film for making decals; these were in turn defective, so that the buyers were faced with many complaints from their customers, though only with one relatively minor[315] claim; this was settled by the buyers who were compensated in this respect by the sellers. At first instance, the buyers recovered the whole of the price that they had paid since the film delivered had no value and since there was no evidence, other than the price, of the value which it would have had, if it had been in conformity with the contract. On appeal it was held by a majority that the sellers were liable for no more than **20–054**

---

308 *Slater v Hoyle & Smith* [1920] 2 K.B. 11 at 23–24.

309 Sale of Goods Act 1979 s.53(3); cf. *Vinmar International Ltd v Theresa Navigation SA* [2001] 1 Lloyd's Rep. 1 at [56] (goods damaged as a result of a *carrier's* breach).

310 cf. *Commercial Fibres (Ireland) Ltd v Zabiada* [1975] 1 Lloyd's Rep. 27.

311 *Slater v Hoyle & Smith* [1920] 2 K.B. 11.

312 As in *Champanhac Ltd v Waller Ltd* [1948] 2 All E.R. 724; cf. *Louis Dreyfus Trading Ltd v Reliance Trading Ltd* [2004] EWHC 525 (Comm); [2004] 2 Lloyd's Rep. 243.

313 [1998] Q.B. 87; Treitel 113 L.Q.R. 188; Bridge 132 L.Q.R. 405.

314 *Bence Graphics International Ltd v Fasson UK Ltd* [1998] Q.B. 87 at 108, where it is also said that the sellers "always accepted" this.

315 Relating to 349 out of over 100,000 decals produced.

the price of a small quantity of film which the buyers had returned,[316] plus the amount of the buyers' liability to the ultimate users of the decals; any loss in excess of this amount was regarded as too remote.[317]

It may, with respect, be doubted whether the case gave rise to any issue of remoteness. If a seller contracts to deliver an ounce of gold for £210 (its market value) and instead delivers an ounce of base metal worth only £5, there is no doubt that he is liable for £205; and this liability is not subject to any test of remoteness.[318] That test would apply only if he had suffered some *further* loss as a result (for example) of his use of the subject-matter; but no such claim was in issue in the *Bence Graphics* case.[319] A pure "difference in value" claim could, indeed, sometimes be resisted on the ground that the buyer had not lost that difference because he had passed the subject-matter on to a sub-buyer for a price which took no account of the defect. But this would be the position only where the sub-sale was of the very goods comprised in the contract and could be performed only by delivery of those goods.[320] In such a case the goods in the buyer's hands would be worth the amount for which he had resold them; but where the sub-sale is not of those very goods, the buyer does suffer the "difference in value" loss since he could have used *other* goods to satisfy his sub-buyer and would then have been left with the goods bought under the broken contract. If he succeeds in disposing of those goods under an advantageous sub-sale, then it should be "immaterial that by some good fortune with which the [sellers] have nothing to do he has been able to recoup himself what he paid for those goods".[321] This was the position in the *Bence Graphics* case, where the buyers were under no obligation to their customers to use the material supplied by the sellers.[322] From this point of view, the decision is open to the same criticisms as those which have been discussed above in relation to *Wertheim*'s case.[323] It is respectfully submitted that the buyers' claim in the *Bence Graphics* case should have been upheld[324] and that any "windfall" which they might in this way have obtained would have been obtained by the grace of those of their customers who had made no claims against them. There seems to be no reason why this indulgence should benefit the sellers who in breach of contract had delivered goods which they admitted to be worthless and who had received a price based on the warranted quality of those goods.

20–055 **Defective delivery and loss due to a fall in the market.** Where the market value of the goods has fallen between the making of the contract and the defective delivery, the buyer will normally wish to reject; for in this way he will be able to avoid the loss resulting, not from the breach, but from the fall in the market. If,

---

316 Worth £22,000; £564,328 had been paid for the whole amount supplied.

317 This follows from the reliance by the majority on the rule in *Hadley v Baxendale* (1854) 9 Ex. 341 (para.20–120) and Sale of Goods Act 1979 s.53(2), which is thought to embody that rule.

318 See fn.22.

319 It would have arisen if the buyers' customers had made unexpectedly large claims against them.

320 See at fn.312.

321 *Slater v Hoyle & Smith* [1920] 2 K.B. 11 at 18.

322 See Morland J at first instance, unreported 14 December 1994, Transcript, p.10.

323 *Wertheim v Chicoutimi Pulp Co* [1911] A.C. 301; para.20–052.

324 Subject only to a deduction in respect of the claim referred to in fn.316.

however, he has lost the right to reject, his only remedy will be in damages, and those damages are prima facie recoverable only in respect of the defect, and not in respect of the fall in the market. In one case,[325] a contract for the sale of beans stipulated for shipment by the end of August but the seller delivered a September shipment. By the time of breach the market value of the beans had fallen some £2,000 below the contract price, so that the buyer would certainly have rejected if he had known of the defect in time. But he had "accepted"[326] the goods and it was held that the damages to which he was entitled were no more than nominal as there was no difference between the market value of an August and a September shipment and as the fall in the value of the goods since the time of contracting was not a loss which had resulted[327] from the seller's breach. There may, however, in cases of this kind, be a defect, not only in the goods, but also in the documents which the seller is obliged by the contract to tender[328] and the buyer may have accepted the documents without knowing of the defects in them,[329] paid the price, and so have been deprived (whether as a matter of law or of business)[330] of the chance to reject the goods.[331] In such a case the buyer can get damages on the footing that the defect in the documents was the cause of his losing the chance to reject the goods on a falling market; and he can do so even though the fact that the goods are not of the contract description has in no way affected their value.[332] For this reason it has been said that there is "little merit"[333] in such a claim; and it is available only where there is a defect both in the documents and in the goods, each giving rise to an independent right to reject.[334]

**Defective delivery: consumer sales.** Where non-conforming goods are delivered to a buyer who deals as consumer, the buyer has in certain circumstances the right to require the seller to reduce the price "by an appropriate amount".[335] This concept of a price reduction is taken from the civil law, where the price of non-conforming goods is reduced in the proportion which the actual value of the goods bears to the value which they would have had, if they had been in 20–056

---

[325] *Taylor v Bank of Athens* (1922) 27 Com. Cas. 142.
[326] See para.18–106.
[327] Within Sale of Goods Act 1979 s.53(2).
[328] Especially under c.i.f. contracts, as to which see para.17–029.
[329] For the significance of this point, see *Vargas Pena v Peter Cremer GmbH* [1987] 1 Lloyd's Rep. 392.
[330] This was the position in *Kwei Tek Chao v British Traders & Shippers Ltd* [1954] 2 Q.B. 459.
[331] It is probably more accurate to say that what has been lost by the buyer is the chance to reject *the documents* and *by so doing* reject the goods at an earlier stage.
[332] *James Finlay & Co Ltd v NV Kwik Hoo Tong HM* [1929] 1 K.B. 400; *Kwei Tek Chao v British Traders & Shippers Ltd* [1954] 2 Q.B. 459; *The Kastellon* [1978] 2 Lloyd's Rep. 203. Contrast *Vargas Pena v Peter Cremer GmbH* [1987] 1 Lloyd's Rep. 394 where such damages were not available to a buyer who knew of the defect *in the documents* when he accepted them.
[333] *The Kastellon* [1978] 2 Lloyd's Rep. 203 at 207 (where the seller was not to blame for the defect in the documents).
[334] *Procter & Gamble Philippine Manufacturing Corp v Kurt A Becher* [1988] 2 Lloyd's Rep. 21; Treitel [1988] L.M.C.L.Q. 457.
[335] Consumer Rights Act 2015 s.56(1).

conformity with the contract.[336] Such a reduction is not the same as the "difference in value" measure discussed above:[337] the civil law price reduction would yield *more* than that measure if the buyer had agreed to pay more than the value of the goods if they had been in conformity with the contract, and *less* if the buyer had agreed to pay less than that value. It remains to be seen whether the English courts will, in interpreting the phrase "an appropriate amount", apply the civil law principle of proportionate price reduction.

20–057 **Refusal to accept and pay.** If a buyer of goods refuses to accept and pay for goods sold to him, the seller can go into the market and sell the goods at the prevailing price. He will then prima facie lose the amount (if any) by which the contract price exceeds the market price;[338] and it is normally[339] irrelevant that the seller has actually resold for a different price.[340] If the market price exceeds the contract price, the seller generally suffers no loss. But this is not always true. The contract may provide for an advance payment without which the seller himself cannot get the goods. If the buyer fails to make this payment, the seller suffers loss even though the market price has risen above the contract price: he loses a good bargain because he is not in a position to take advantage of a rising market. Subject to the rules of remoteness,[341] the buyer will be liable for such a loss.[342] The market may also be relevant where the buyer's breach takes the form of *delay* in taking delivery. If the contract provides that the price is to depend on the market price at the time of taking delivery, and that price falls between the time when delivery should have been, and when it was, taken, the seller will be entitled to damages in respect of that difference.[343]

### (ii) *Where there is no market*

20–058 **Failure to deliver.** If a seller or carrier fails to deliver goods which cannot be replaced by buying in the market, the court must assess the loss as best it can:[344] relevant factors include the cost of the goods and of their carriage, and a reasonable profit.[345] Where the goods have actually been resold, the resale price

---

[336] Vienna Convention on Contracts for the International Sale of Goods art.50 lays down the same formula.

[337] i.e. in Sale of Goods Act 1979 s.53(3); para.20–053.

[338] Sale of Goods Act 1979 s.50(3). For administrative expenses, see para.20–039.

[339] i.e. subject to the qualifications stated above (in the converse case of breach by the seller), at fnn.300–301.

[340] *Campbell Mostyn Provisions Ltd v Barnett Trading Co* [1954] 1 Lloyd's Rep. 65; *Texaco Ltd v Eurogulf Shipping Co Ltd* [1987] 2 Lloyd's Rep. 541 at 546; cf. *Jamal v Moolla Dawood Son & Co* [1916] 1 A.C. 175 (shares).

[341] See para.20–119 and following.

[342] cf. *Trans Trust SPRL v Danubian Trading Co Ltd* [1952] 2 Q.B. 297.

[343] cf. *Addax Ltd v Arcadia Petroleum Ltd* [2000] 1 Lloyd's Rep. 493.

[344] *Air Studios (Lyndhurst) Ltd v Lombard North Central Plc* [2012] EWHC 3162 (QB); [2013] 1 Lloyd's Rep. 63 at [99]; cf. *Bulkhaul Ltd v Rhodia Organique Fine Ltd* [2008] EWCA Civ 1452; [2009] 1 Lloyd's Rep. 353 at [29]: the court "is entitled to infer the value of goods from any sufficient relevant evidence of value."

[345] *O'Hanlan v GW Ry* (1865) 6 B. & S. 484; *Schulze v GE Ry* (1887) 19 Q.B.D. 30; *The Texaco Melbourne* [1994] 1 Lloyd's Rep. 473 at 479; cf. *The Pegase* [1981] 1 Lloyd's Rep. 175 at 183 (late delivery); *Shearson Lehman Hutton Inc v Maclaine Watson & Co (No.2)* [1990] 1 Lloyd's Rep. 441 at

is evidence of their value, but not conclusive evidence. The weight of the evidence will depend on such factors as the interval between the wrong and the resale and the extent of fluctuations in the market price of other similar goods.[346] When the court takes the latter factor into account, it may be said to have regard to a substitute market; and a similar process is sometimes adopted where there is no market at the place where delivery should have been made, but there is a market for goods of the kind in question elsewhere. It may be reasonable for the injured party to resort to that other market,[347] and damages may then be based on the cost of doing so at the time of breach.[348]

Where goods are bought for use, the cost of acquiring a substitute is in principle the correct measure. In one case this was assessed as the scrap value of the goods, and this assessment, though described in the Court of Appeal as "surprising"[349] was held not to be incorrect in principle. At first sight, the scrap value might seem to be an inappropriate measure where goods were, to the seller's knowledge, bought for use, since it can hardly represent the cost of acquiring a substitute. But the case can perhaps be explained on the ground that the goods in question were a spare part which was not immediately needed by the buyer and might never have been needed by him. In these circumstances the purchase of a substitute by the buyer might have been an unreasonable augmentation of his loss[350] which would be irrecoverable under the mitigation rules.[351]

**Failure to accept and pay.** If there is no market, the seller's damages for non-acceptance would prima facie be quantified by reference to the actual proceeds of a substitute sale,[352] so long as that transaction was in all the circumstances a reasonable one.[353] As in the case of failure to deliver, the substitute transaction would be evidence of the value of the goods at the time of breach only if it was concluded at, or close to, that time. If the seller did not resell, the value of the goods left on his hands would have to be assessed according to the general criteria stated above;[354] and his damages would prima facie be the amount (if any) by which the contract price exceeded that value. **20–059**

443; cf. *Quorum A/S v Schramm* [2002] 2 Lloyd's Rep. 72 at [100] and following (assessment of reduction in value of work of art as a result of fire damage).

346 Contrast *France v Gaudet* (1871) L.R. 6 Q.B. 196 and *Stroud v Austin & Co* (1883) Cab. & El. 119 with *The Arpad* [1934] P. 189 and *The Athenian Harmony* [1998] 2 Lloyd's Rep. 410 at 416.

347 See *Lesters Leather & Skin Co Ltd v Home Overseas Brokers Ltd* (1949) 82 Lloyd's Rep. 203 at 205.

348 So that loss due to currency fluctuations *after* that time will not be taken into account: see *The Texaco Melbourne* [1994] 1 Lloyd's Rep. 473.

349 *The Alecos M* [1991] 1 Lloyd's Rep. 120 at 125; Treitel 107 L.Q.R. 364.

350 *Ruxley Electronics and Construction Co Ltd v Forsyth* [1996] A.C. 344 at 321–372.

351 See para.20–104.

352 *Janred Properties Ltd v Ente Nazionale per il Turismo* [1989] 2 All E.R. 444; cf. *The Noel Bay* [1989] 1 Lloyd's Rep. 361 (damages for charterer's repudiation based on substitute voyage).

353 *Aercap Partners 1 Ltd v Avia Asset Management AB* [2010] EWHC 2431 (Comm); [2010] 2 C.L.C. 578.

354 At fn.345.

### *(iii) Other loss*

20–060 **Loss of profits, etc. by buyer.** The market and other related rules just stated do not form the limit of recovery. They deal only with the problem of valuing one element of the claimant's loss, namely his expectation of getting either the goods or the price. In addition, the claimant may be able to recover damages for loss of profits. Suppose that a seller has wrongfully failed to deliver goods which the buyer has sub-sold at a profit. Even if the resale price is *not* good evidence of value,[355] it may nevertheless be taken into consideration in assessing the buyer's damages for loss of profits. Under the rules of remoteness, however, the seller is liable for loss of resale profit only[356] if he knew or could have contemplated[357] that the goods were required for resale,[358] and even then he is not liable for loss of an extraordinary profit unless he is notified of the possibility that such a profit may accrue.[359] If, on the other hand, there is no market and the resale price *is* good evidence of the value of the goods the seller's liability is based on the amount of it, quite irrespective of his state of knowledge.[360] Where the seller is in breach by reason of a defect in the goods, the buyer may similarly (and subject to the rules of remoteness) be able to recover from the seller damages which he has paid, or for which he has become liable, to his sub-buyer in respect of the defect.[361]

20–061 **Loss of profits, etc. by seller.** The possibility of claiming additional damages for loss of profits also exists where a buyer wrongfully refuses to accept and pay for goods. Here the seller may expect both to get the price and to make a profit; and he may lose the profit even though he manages to resell the goods for exactly the same (or even a higher) price to another buyer. The point may be illustrated by cases in which car-dealers have claimed damages for loss of profits from customers who had agreed to buy cars and then in breach of contract refused to accept them. Three situations can be distinguished.[362] First, the sale is of a new car and the supply of cars of the contract description at the dealer's disposal exceeds the demand. Here the dealer's claim will succeed;[363] for he would, if the original customer had not defaulted, have been able to make a sale both to him

---

355 e.g. because the interval between the breach and the resale was too long, as in *The Arpad* [1934] P. 189.

356 *Schulze v GE Ry* (1887) 19 Q.B.D. 30.

357 See para.20–119 and following.

358 *Borries v Hutchinson* (1865) 18 C.B. (N.S.) 445; *Patrick v Russo-British Grain Export Co Ltd* [1927] 2 K.B. 535; *Household Machines v Cosmos Exporters Ltd* [1947] 1 K.B. 217; *J Leavey & Co Ltd v GH Hirst & Co Ltd* [1944] K.B. 24.

359 See para.20–128.

360 See fn.22.

361 *Total Liban SA v Vitol Energy SA* [2001] Q.B. 643.

362 For the burden of proof in such cases, see: *Sony Computer Entertainment UK Ltd v Cinram Logistics* [2008] EWCA Civ 955; [2009] Bus L.R. 529.

363 *WL Thompson Ltd v Robinson (Gunmakers) Ltd* [1955] Ch. 177; cf. *Re Vic Mill* [1913] 1 Ch. 465. For the application of similar principles to contracts other than sale, see *Inter-Office Telephones Ltd v Robert Freeman & Co Ltd* [1958] 1 Q.B. 190; *Robophone Facilities Ltd v Blank* [1966] 1 W.L.R. 1428.

and to the second customer: hence he would have made two profits,[364] one of which has been lost. Secondly, the sale is of a new car and the demand for cars of the contract description exceeds the supply available to the dealer. Here his claim will fail;[365] for the number of sales that he can make depends on the number of cars that he can get and not on the number of customers that he can find. Hence the default of the original customer does not reduce the number of profits that he can earn. Thirdly, the sale is of a second-hand car. In *Lazenby Garages Ltd v Wright*,[366] it was held that a second-hand BMW car was a "unique" object; and as the car was resold for more than the original price to a second customer, the original customer (who had refused to take it) was not liable for loss of profit. No such loss had been suffered in respect of the car in question; and the possibility that the dealer might have sold a different car to the second customer was dismissed as too remote.[367] Whether it is too remote perhaps depends on the type of car concerned. If the car had been of a kind more commonly sold after use as a "fleet" car, the dealer's chance of selling another (virtually identical) car to a second customer might have been regarded as sufficiently great to satisfy the test of remoteness. Even where the original customer is not liable for loss of profits, any expense of negotiating the second sale can presumably be recovered from him as "incidental" loss.[368]

### (c) Speculative damages

**Loss of chance.**[369] A contracting party can recover damages if he can show that the breach has caused him to lose the chance of gaining benefit. So long as the contingencies on which that chance depends are not wholly within the control of the party in breach,[370] the injured party can recover damages for loss of such a chance. He need not show that it was certain that he would have got the benefit if the contract had been performed; it is sufficient for the claimant to show that he had a real or substantial chance rather than a speculative one.[371] Thus damages can be recovered for loss of the chance of taking part in a beauty contest,[372] or of obtaining future orders from an established customer,[373] or of earning tips,[374] or **20–062**

[364] cf. *Jebson v E & W India Dock Co* (1875) L.R. 10 C.P. 300.
[365] *Charter v Sullivan* [1957] 2 Q.B. 117.
[366] [1976] 1 W.L.R. 459.
[367] See para.20–119 and following.
[368] See para.20–039.
[369] Poole [2007] L.M.C.L.Q. 63.
[370] See para.20–074. In *Commonwealth of Australia v Amann Aviation Pty Ltd* (1992) 66 A.L.J.R. 123, loss of profits on future contracts which the defendants would probably have awarded to the injured party (without being bound to do so) were taken into account in assessing damages. The claim was *for reliance loss* and the lost chance was taken into account for the purpose of the rule that such loss is recoverable only to the extent to which it will not leave the injured party better off than he would have been, if the contract had been performed: para.20–030.
[371] *Allied Maples Group Ltd v Simmons & Simmons* [1995] 1 W.L.R. 1602 at 1614; *Normans Bay v Coudert Bros* [2004] EWCA Civ 215 (more than "of no real value at all").
[372] *Chaplin v Hicks* [1911] 2 K.B. 786; cf. *Watson v Ambergate, etc. Ry* (1851) 15 Jur. 448. Contrast *McClory v Post Office* [1992] I.C.R. 758; Reece 59 M.L.R. 188.
[373] *Jackson v Royal Bank of Scotland Plc* [2005] UKHL 3; [2005] 1 W.L.R. 377; discussed para.20–127.

of obtaining pension benefits which depend on the exercise of discretion by a government department;[375] or of appealing against an arbitration award;;[376] or of avoiding or successfully contesting a criminal prosecution;[377] or of negotiating terms which could have protected the claimant from liabilities to a third party.[378] Where the chance also depends on what the claimant would have done if there had been no breach of contract, this must be proved on the balance of probability.[379] The injured party may, as a result of the breach, save the cost of getting the chance. That cost must then be deducted from the damages for loss of the chance, so that no such damages will be recoverable if the cost saved is equal to or greater than the value of the chance.[380]

20–063 **The loss of chance approach, where applicable, is mandatory.** In this area, it has been said that there is a distinction between two different types of "loss of chance claim".[381] In the first, the very thing which the claimant has lost is a "chance", or an opportunity to obtain something else, as in the example of taking part in a beauty contest. In the second, it is not so much that the claimant has lost a valuable right, but rather the opportunity of gaining a benefit which depends on a third party acting in a particular way, as in the example of not being in a position to negotiate terms which could have protected the claimant from liabilities to a third party. Whether such a distinction really exists,[382] or matters, once a claim is identified as a "loss of chance" of either type, damages must be assessed on a loss of chance basis.[383] This will benefit the claimant in those cases where the chance is assessed as "real or substantial", but less than 50 per cent, as he will still recover in proportion to the chance proved, e.g. in the beauty contest case, the claimant recovered a figure which represented between 13 per cent and 22 per cent of the financial benefit of winning the contest.[384] It will benefit the defendant where the chance exceeds 50 per cent since the claimant cannot in such a case claim that he has proved his loss on the balance of probability and therefore recover in full.[385]

To some extent, all claims for damages for breach of contract depend on the contingency of what would or might have happened if there had been no breach, but it is only in the two types of case referred to above that a "loss of chance"

---

374 *Manubens v Leon* [1919] 1 K.B. 208.

375 *Scally v Southern Health and Social Services Board* [1992] 1 A.C. 294.

376 *Corfield v Bosher& Co* [1992] 1 E.G.L.R. 163.

377 *Acton v Graham Pearce & Co* [1997] 3 All E.R. 909.

378 *Allied Maples Group Ltd v Simmons & Simmons* [1995] 1 W.L.R. 1602; cf. *Harrison v Bloom Camillin (No.2)* [2000] Lloyd's Rep. P.N. 89.

379 *Allied Maples Group Ltd v Simmons & Simmons* [1995] 1 W.L.R. 1602; *Wellesley Partners LLP v Withers LLP* [2015] EWCA Civ 1146; [2016] Ch. 529 at [100].

380 *Sapwell v Bass* [1910] 2 K.B. 486, as explained in *Chaplin v Hicks* [1911] 2 K.B. 786 at 796; *Demarco v Perkins* [2006] EWCA Civ 188; [2006] P.N.L.R. at [70].

381 *Vasiliou v Hajigeorgiou* [2010] EWCA Civ 1475 (Patten LJ); *Wellesley Partners LLP v Withers LLP* [2015] EWCA Civ 1146; [2016] Ch. 529.

382 It would seem that *Chaplin v Hicks* could be analysed on either basis.

383 *Assetco Plc v Grant Thornton UK LLP* [2019] EWHC 150 (Comm); [2019] Bus L.R. 2291.

384 Damages were assessed by the jury at £100. The winners were awarded contracts which paid between £450 and £750 over three years.

385 See, e.g. *Wellesley Partners LLP v Withers LLP* [2015] EWCA Civ 1146; [2016] Ch. 529 (60 per cent chance).

approach is taken. For example, they can be distinguished from a case where what is claimed is the loss of the opportunity to trade generally and the claimant seeks recovery of the profits he would have made. The claimant will need to prove on the balance of probability that he would have traded profitably and, if he does so, the court will seek to "quantify the loss".[386] At this stage, an element of "chance" may still be in play, as in the example of a restaurant which is prevented from trading, where the extent of the loss depends on the actions of multiple third parties in the form of potential customers.[387] Nevertheless, in such a case the court simply does its best to assess the loss[388] and since that will have involved an assessment of all the chances involved in trading, even if not in such terms, it is not appropriate to further discount the figure which is reached by the court.[389]

**Quantification of loss on a loss of chance basis.** The quantification of damages in such cases is necessarily speculative. It depends on the value of the expected benefit and the likelihood of the claimant's actually getting it.[390] The chance of winning a beauty contest is obviously worth less than the full prize. In deciding how much the chance is worth the court will consider two key factors. First, the number of contingencies on which it depends: "the more contingencies, the lower the value of the chance."[391] If the claim turns on the hypothetical and independent acts of two or more third parties, it is necessary to multiply the chances of each of them acting in a way which would have benefited the claimant, e.g. if there are two chances each of 50 per cent, the claimant will recover a lost chance of 25 per cent.[392] Where the various contingencies are not independent of each other, the court has to assess the overall chance "in the round".[393] Secondly, the likelihood of their being satisfied in the claimant's favour: the greater this likelihood, the higher the value of the chance.[394] Where the chance is assessed as "certain" no discount will be applied.[395] **20–064**

386 *Parabola Investments Ltd v Browallia Cal Ltd* [2010] EWCA Civ 486; [2010] 3 W.L.R. 1266 at [22]–[24].

387 See, e.g. *Vasiliou v Hajigeorgiou* [2010] EWCA Civ 1475.

388 cf. *Guido van der Garde BV v Force India Formula One Ltd* [2010] EWHC 2373 (QB) where the award of a round figure for the lost chance of a profitable career as a formula one racing driver was the result of a "broad brush" approach based on the "totality of the evidence" (at [412]).

389 *Vasiliou v Hajigeorgiou* [2010] EWCA Civ 1475 at [28].

390 *Salford CC v Torkington* [2004] EWCA Civ 1646; (2004) 51 E.G. 89 at [54] (where damages were, in fact, ordered on a different basis).

391 *Hall v Meyrick* [1957] 2 Q.B. 455 at 471 (actual decision reversed on another ground, [1957] 2 Q.B. 455 at 474); *Ministry of Defence v Wheeler* [1998] 1 All E.R. 790; cf. *Moda International Brands Ltd v Gateley LLP* [2019] EWHC 1326 (QB); [2019] P.N.L.R. 27

392 See, e.g. *Assetco Plc v Grant Thornton UK LLP* [2019] EWHC 150 (Comm); [2019] Bus L.R. 2291.

393 See, e,g. *Harding Homes (East Street) Ltd v Bircham Dyson Bell* [2015] EWHC 3329 (Ch) at [42].

394 e.g. *Dickinson v Jones Alexander & Co* [1993] 2 F.L.R. 521; cf. *Allied Maples Group Ltd v Simmons & Simmons* [1999] 1 W.L.R. 1602 at 1622–1623; *Maden v Clifford Coppock & Carter* [2004] EWCA Civ 1037; [2005] 2 All E.R. 43 (80 per cent chance of settlement at a certain level); *Football League Ltd v Edge Ellison* [2006] EWHC 1462 (Ch); [2007] P.N.L.R. 2 at [286].

395 *Nicholas Prestige Homes v Neal* [2010] EWCA Civ 1552 at [33]; *Assetco Plc v Grant Thornton UK LLP* [2019] EWHC 150 (Comm); [2019] Bus L.R. 2291.

## (d) Interest

20–065 **Common law.** In earlier editions, the extent to which loss of interest might be awarded as damages was assessed in the section of this chapter dealing with "methods of limiting damages". That reflected the general rule of the common law that interest could not be recovered as damages for failure to pay a debt when due.[396] To this anomalous rule, the House of Lords had created an anomalous exception,[397] but neither now requires any detailed consideration,[398] thanks to the almost total abolition of the rule by the House of Lords in *Sempra Metals Ltd v Commissioners of Inland Revenue*.[399] What survives is that loss of interest will not be awarded as general damages; such loss must be proved,[400] but, if proved (including proof of the loss of compound interest[401]), it is subject only to the same limits as any other claim for damages, e.g. mitigation and remoteness.[402]

20–066 **Obligations other than to pay money.** In the paragraph above, the recovery of loss of interest has been discussed in the context of the defendant's failure to pay a debt. That may be the most obvious context in which such a claim may arise, but their Lordships in the *Sempra Metals* case also referred more generally to claims for breach of contract: "the court has a common law jurisdiction to award interest, simple and compound, as damages on claims for non-payment of debts as well as on *other claims for breach of contract* and in tort."[403] Thus, if a seller fails to deliver goods, the buyer's normal remedy in damages is the difference between the market price and the contract price, but where there has been a period during which the buyer has had to bear a higher market price, he may also

---

[396] *London, Chatham & Dover Ry v South Eastern Ry* [1893] A.C. 429; *La Pintada* [1985] A.C. 104; Mann 101 L.Q.R. 30.

[397] i.e. that damages could be awarded if the loss of interest was proved as special damages falling within the "second limb" of the test of remoteness laid down in *Hadley v Baxendale* (1854) 9 Exch. 341 at 354 (para.20–120): *La Pintada* [1985] A.C. 104; *The Lips* [1988] A.C. 395 at 423, 429. The self-evident anomaly is that the more obvious the claim for loss of interest the less likely it could be recovered. One consequence of the rejection of the rule, and therefore the need for the exception, is that the earlier decision of the Court of Appeal in *Wadsworth v Lydall* [1981] 1 W.L.R. 598 may no longer be forced into the second limb when it seems more likely to have been a first limb case: *Sempra Metals Ltd v Commissioners of Inland Revenue* [2007] UKHL 34; [2008] 1 A.C. 561 at [215] (Lord Mance).

[398] For the detail, see the 12th edition, paras 20–113–20–120.

[399] [2007] UKHL 34; [2008] 1 A.C. 561; Mitchell 71 M.L.R. 290. The *Sempra Metals* case itself was concerned with claims in restitution and for breach of statutory duty, so that the views on the contract rule are, strictly speaking, obiter dictum. The decision that interest could be recovered as restitution for unjust enrichment was overruled in *Prudential Assurance Co Ltd v HMRC* [2018] UKSC 39; [2018] 3 W.L.R. 652.

[400] *JSC BTA Bank v Ablyazov* [2013] EWHC 867 (Comm) where the claimant's actual loss of interest was not even pleaded. Contrast *Equitas Ltd v Walsham Brothers & Co Ltd* [2013] EWHC 3264 (Comm); [2014] P.N.L.R. 8.

[401] The claims before the House of Lords proceeded on the basis of conventional rates and periods (for the purpose of compounding). On the degree of particularity of proof needed in general, see Lord Nicholls at [126]–[127].

[402] *Sempra Metals Ltd v Commissioners of Inland Revenue* [2007] UKHL 34; [2008] 1 A.C. 561 at [16]–[17], [94], [100], [132].

[403] *Sempra Metals Ltd v Commissioners of Inland Revenue* [2007] UKHL 34; [2008] 1 A.C. 561 at [100] (Lord Nicholls, emphasis added); cf. at [132] (Lord Scott).

be entitled to an award of interest.[404] And claims may be made in other cases where the consequence of the defendant's breach is to have put the claimant to expense or deprived him of the receipt of money.[405]

**Other claims for the loss of the use of money.** This part is entitled "interest" because that is the most obvious form in which a loss may be incurred by one party who does not receive, or is deprived of, money as a consequence of the other party's breach of contract. But as Lord Nicholls states in the *Sempra Metals* case, "the loss flowing from the late payment may take some other form."[406] The common law rule precluding recovery was said to apply only to claims *for interest* as damages for late payment of money.[407] Subject to limits on recovery such as mitigation and remoteness, damages other than for loss of interest can be recovered from a banker who wrongfully repudiates liability, or delays in making payments due under a letter of credit,[408] or who wrongfully fails to honour a customer's cheque;[409] from a buyer of goods who fails to provide a confirmed credit in accordance with the terms of the contract of sale;[410] from a person who breaks a contract to subscribe for debentures in a company or who fails to pay calls on shares;[411] from a hire-purchaser or instalment buyer whose wrongful failure to pay instalments amounts to a repudiation of the contract;[412] and probably from any person who breaks a contract to lend or advance money. **20–067**

**Late Payments of Commercial Debts (Interest) Act 1998.** Two modifications of the former common law rule against recovery of interest have been made by legislation. The first is the right to "statutory interest" which arises under the Late Payments of Commercial Debts (Interest) Act 1998. The Act applies only to contracts for the supply of goods and services where each party is acting in the course of a business.[413] Its central provision is that it is an implied term of a **20–068**

[404] *Panchaud Frères v Pagnan Fratelli* [1974] 1 Lloyd's Rep. 394 at 411.

[405] See, e.g. in the context of services: *Nykreditbank v Edward Erdman Group* [1997] 1 W.L.R. 1627; and in the context of the sale of land: *Bushwall Properties v Vortex Properties* [1975] 1 W.L.R. 1649, reversed on another ground: [1976] 1 W.L.R 591.

[406] *Sempra Metals Ltd v Commissioners of Inland Revenue* [2007] UKHL 34; [2008] 1 A.C. 561 at [95].

[407] *The Lips* [1988] A.C. 395 at 424; cf. *IM Properties Plc v Cape & Dalgleish* [1999] Q.B. 297 at 307 (where no such claim was made).

[408] *Prehn v Royal Bank of Liverpool* (1870) L.R. 5 Ex. 92; *Urquhart Lindsay & Co v Eastern Bank Ltd* [1922] 1 K.B. 318; *Ozalid Group (Export) Ltd v African Continental Bank Ltd* [1979] 2 Lloyd's Rep. 231.

[409] *Rolin v Steward* (1854) 14 C.B. 595.

[410] *Trans Trust SPRL v Danubian Trading Co Ltd* [1952] 2 Q.B. 297; *Urquhart Lindsay & Co v Eastern Bank Ltd* [1922] 1 K.B. 318 at 323; para.17–015.

[411] *Wallis Chlorine Syndicate Ltd v American Alkali Co Ltd* (1901) 17 T.L.R. 565.

[412] *Yeoman Credit Ltd v Waragowski* [1961] 1 W.L.R. 1124 at 1128; *Overstone Ltd v Shipway* [1962] 1 W.L.R. 117; cf. para.18–022.

[413] 1998 Act s.2(1); for definition of "business", see s.2(7); for definition of "goods and services", see s.2(2) and (3); contracts of service and apprenticeship are excluded by s.2(4).

contract to which it applies that "statutory interest"[414] will be payable on any "qualifying debt"[415] created by the contract (i.e. broadly, on the price payable under the contract).[416]

The date from which interest begins to run is determined by provisions of no little complexity and depends on whether the parties have agreed a date for payment or not.[417] Since statutory interest is available by virtue of an implied term, the supplier is in principle entitled to it as of right; but where by reason of his conduct the interests of justice so require, the court can remit such interest wholly or in part.[418] The parties remain free, in general, to make their own contractual provisions with regard to interest and the Act does not place any restrictions on their power to do so after the debt has been created.[419] But their right to contract out of the Act before that time[420] is restricted in that contract terms are, to the extent to which they purport to exclude or restrict the right to statutory interest or to vary it, void unless they provide for a "substantial remedy" for late payment of the debt.[421] Moreover, no reliance can be placed on any contract term purporting to postpone the time at which a qualifying debt would otherwise be created unless that term satisfies the requirement of reasonableness under the Unfair Contract Terms Act 1977;[422] this provision applies whether the contract in which the term is contained was the contract creating the debt or one made before or after that contract.[423]

The scope of the Act is restricted in that it applies only to contracts in which *each* party acts in the course of a business and only to contracts for the supply of "goods" and "services".[424] The latter expression may cover financial services, but consumer credit agreements and contracts intended to operate by way of mortgage, pledge, charge or other security are specifically excepted from the provisions of the Act.[425] A person who is entitled to statutory interest under the 1998 Act is, in addition, entitled to a relatively modest fixed sum,[426] intended to compensate him for the cost incurred by reason of the delay in payment.

---

414 The current rate of statutory interest is 8 per cent above the Bank of England's official dealing rate: Late Payment of Commercial Debts (Rate of Interest) (No.3) Order 2002 (SI 2002/1675).

415 The Act does not apply to a claim for unliquidated damages for breach of contract: *Board of Trustees of National Museums & Galleries on Merseyside v AEW Architects & Designers* [2013] EWHC 3025 (TCC).

416 1998 Act s.1(1) and (2); "qualifying debt" is defined in s.3; for the treatment of obligations to make an "advance payment", see s.11. For the approach to be taken when the sum payable is in dispute, see: *Ruttle Plant Hire Ltd v Sec of State for Environment, Food & Rural Affairs* [2009] EWCA Civ 97; [2009] B.L.R. 301.

417 1998 Act s.4.

418 1998 Act s.5. See *Banham Marshalls Services Unlimited v Lincolnshire CC* [2007] EWHC 402 (QB) at [67]–[73].

419 1998 Act ss.7(2) and 8(5).

420 1998 Act s.7(2).

421 1998 Act s.8(1), (3) (4); for the definition of "substantial remedy", see s.9.

422 1998 Act s.14, bringing such a term within Unfair Contract Terms Act 1977 s.3(2)(b) even where it is *not* contained in "written standard terms": see para.7–054.

423 This follows from the reference in s.14(3) to the definition of "contract term" in s.10(1).

424 1998 Act s.2(1).

425 1998 Act s.2(5).

426 1998 Act s.5A.

**Senior Courts Act 1981 section 35A.** The second modification of the former common law rule is now contained in s.35A of the Senior Courts Act 1981. This gives the courts a discretionary power to award interest when giving judgment for a debt or damages;[427] and where proceedings are brought for recovery of a debt and the defendant pays the debt before judgment.[428] The court in exercising this discretion will look at the overall position of the injured party in consequence of the breach. Thus, if he retains the income of property sold till payment, the court will not award him interest on the price, since this would amount to allowing double recovery.[429] Unlike the right to "statutory interest" under the 1998 Act, the discretion to award interest under the 1981 Act applies to all contracts; but it is subject to a number of limitations. If the contract has been terminated by the injured party before payment under it from the party in breach has become due, no action for *debt* will be available to the injured party;[430] and in such a case the statutory discretion to award interest will be exercisable only in relation to the *damages* to which that party is entitled.[431] This restriction (which appears to apply also to the right to "statutory interest" under the 1998 Act)[432] is a significant one: the damages suffered on a purchaser's default in completing a contract for the sale of a house are prima facie the difference between the contract price and the proceeds of resale,[433] a much smaller sum than the contract price. The statutory discretion to award interest under the 1981 Act does not, moreover, extend to the case where an overdue debt is paid *before* any proceedings for recovery of the debt have begun.[434] 20–069

**The relationship between the common law and statute.** It will be clear from the limits to the scope of the courts' power to award interest under the statutory regimes that there will be cases where an award of loss of interest may only be made at common law. But in many cases, it may be possible to make an award under either the common law, or statute, or both.[435] This possibility does not conflict with the legislation. Section 35(A) of the 1981 Act expressly states that it is not an exhaustive code and does not displace the jurisdiction of the courts themselves to award interest,[436] and a debt does not carry interest under a term implied by the 1998 Act if, or to the extent that, a right to demand interest on it 20–070

[427] 1998 Act s.35(A)(1); cf. County Courts Act 1984 s.69. Once judgment has been entered, interest accrues on the "judgment debt" at the present rate of 8 per cent: Judgments Act 1838 s.17(1).

[428] 1998 Act s.35A(3).

[429] *Janred Properties Ltd v Ente Nazionale Italiano per il Turismo* [1989] 2 All E.R. 444 at 456.

[430] See para.18–020.

[431] *Janred Properties Ltd v Ente Nazionale Italiano per il Turismo* [1989] 2 All E.R. 444.

[432] Since in the case put there can be no "qualifying *debt*" within ss.1(1) and 3 of the 1998 Act; and see fn.416.

[433] See para.20–059.

[434] As in *The World Symphony* [1991] 2 Lloyd's Rep. 251; affirmed [1992] 2 Lloyd's Rep. 115, without reference to the point; cf. *IM Properties Plc v Dalgleish* [1999] Q.B. 297 (same principle applied to damages). There is no such restriction on the right to "statutory interest" under the 1998 Act.

[435] It may be assumed that the courts will exercise the powers available to them in a way which will avoid double recovery; cf. *Fletcher v Tayleur* (1855) 17 C.B. 21 at 29; *Jacques v Millar* (1877) 6 Ch D. 153; *Trafigura Beheer BV v Mediterranean Shipping Co SA* [2007] EWCA Civ 794; [2007] 2 Lloyd's Rep. 622 at [42].

[436] 1998 Act s.35(A)(4).

which exists by virtue of any rule of law is exercised.[437] Furthermore, s.35(A) is concerned with interest on debts and damages and "says nothing about the principles to be applied by a court when assessing the amount of damages for which it gives judgment."[438] For a claimant, the principal advantage of the common law is that the courts may award compound interest, but such loss must be proved. Under the statutory provisions described above only an award of simple interest is available, but it can be made without proof that any loss of interest has been suffered. It is perhaps for these reasons that it has been observed that, in practice, especially where the period over which interest is sought is short or where the claimant does not have to borrow money to replace the debt, simple interest under s.35A of the 1981 Act is likely to be the more convenient remedy.[439]

## (e) Taxation

20–071 **The rule in Gourley's case.** The value of the claimant's loss may be affected by the incidence of taxation. In *BTC v Gourley*[440] a person was injured by the negligence of the defendant's servants, and claimed damages for loss of earnings. It was estimated that, but for the accident, the injured party would have earned £37,000. Had he actually earned this sum, it would have been taxed and £6,000 would have been left to him. But had he been awarded damages of £37,000 he could have kept the whole amount, since damages for loss of earnings resulting from personal injury are not taxable. The House of Lords held that the proper measure of damages was £6,000, that being the amount of the injured party's actual loss. *Gourley*'s case was an action in tort, but the same principle can apply where the liability is contractual, e.g. in assessing damages for wrongful dismissal.[441]

The reason for the rule is that the injured party ought not to make a profit out of the wrong by getting tax-free damages to compensate for loss of a benefit which would have been taxable. The rule applies only if two conditions are satisfied. First, the damages must be compensation for loss of a taxable income or gain, and not simply for loss of a capital asset. The rule would, therefore, probably not apply if a buyer of goods claimed the amount by which their market value exceeded the contract price. These damages are meant to compensate him for failure to obtain a capital asset (out of which he might make a profit or a loss).[442] Secondly, the damages themselves must not be taxable in the hands of

[437] 1998 Act s.3(3).

[438] *Sempra Metals Ltd v Commissioners of Inland Revenue* [2007] UKHL 34; [2008] 1 A.C. 561 at [99] (Lord Nicholls).

[439] *Sempra Metals Ltd v Commissioners of Inland Revenue* [2007] UKHL 34; [2008] 1 A.C. 561 at [17] (Lord Hope).

[440] [1956] A.C. 185; Jolowicz [1959] C.L.J. 85; Hall 73 L.Q.R. 212; Bishop and Kay 103 L.Q.R. 211.

[441] *Beach v Reed Corrugated Cases Ltd* [1956] 1 W.L.R. 807; *Re Houghton Main Colliery* [1956] 1 W.L.R. 1219; *Phipps v Orthodox Unit Trusts Ltd* [1958] 1 Q.B. 314.

[442] cf. *Spencer v MacMillan's Trustees* 1958 S.C. 300; *Lim Foo Yong Ltd v Collector of Land Revenue* [1963] 1 W.L.R. 295. But if goods are *sold* by a trader, damages for non-acceptance are taxable as receipts of his trade and so not subject to reduction in respect of tax: *Deeny v Gooda Walker Ltd (No.2)* [1996] 1 W.L.R. 426 at 432.

the victim of the breach.[443] Damages for wrongful dismissal are taxable to the extent that they exceed £30,000.[444] Hence such damages must be reduced by reference to the claimant's income-tax liability where his loss of income is less than £30,000;[445] where it is more, the court will assess his net loss and then award such sum as, after tax on the sum so assessed, would be equal to that loss.[446]

**Criticism.** The rule in *Gourley*'s case has been much criticised. It is said to involve a paradox: for revenue purposes damages for loss of earnings are treated as compensation for loss of a capital asset, since otherwise they would be taxable; while in assessing damages they are treated as compensation for loss of income, since otherwise the claimant's tax liability would be irrelevant.[447] A possible solution of this paradox is to say that the damages compensate the claimant for loss of *earning capacity*, which is a capital asset whose value depends on (amongst other things) the incidence of taxation.[448] Other criticisms are concerned with the practical effects of the rule. It is said that the rule enables the defendant to take advantage of wholly extraneous circumstances (e.g. that the claimant has a large private income); that it makes the assessment of damages highly speculative; and that the rule may make it cheaper to break a contract than to perform it. But similar criticisms could be made of other rules relating to damages, which have so far remained immune from them. Thus a seller can sometimes take advantage of an extraneous event, such as a sub-sale made by the buyer, in reducing damages for non-delivery;[449] speculative damages are by no means uncommon;[450] and it may sometimes be cheaper to break a contract than to perform it, e.g. where damages are assessed on a difference in value basis amounting only to a small fraction of the cost of performance.[451] The rule in *Gourley*'s case has therefore survived the criticisms which have been levelled against it; and it can be supported[452] on the ground that it gives effect to the principle that damages are meant only to compensate the claimant for his actual loss. **20–072**

**Tax savings.** A breach of contract may actually *reduce* the victim's tax liability. The amount of the reduction is then deducted from the damages for the breach, on the principle that the benefit of having to pay less tax in fact mitigates the victim's loss.[453] **20–073**

---

443 *Diamond v Campbell-Jones* [1961] Ch. 22; *Raja's Commercial College v Gian Singh & Co Ltd* [1977] A.C. 312; *Deeny v Gooda Walker Ltd (No.2)* [1996] 1 W.L.R. 426.

444 Income Tax (Earnings and Pensions) Act 2003 ss.401–404.

445 *Parsons v BNM Laboratories Ltd* [1964] 1 Q.B. 95.

446 *Bold v Brough, Nicholson & Hall Ltd* [1964] 1 W.L.R. 201; *Shove v Downs Surgical Plc* [1984] I.C.R. 582; Lee 47 M.L.R. 471.

447 Jolowicz [1959] C.L.J. 85.

448 Tucker [1959] C.L.J. 185. Damages for personal injury are not taxable as capital gains: Taxation of Chargeable Gains Act 1992 s.51(2).

449 See para.20–052.

450 See para.20–062.

451 See para.20–042.

452 See Law Reform Committee, 7th Report (1958), Cmnd.501.

453 *Levison v Farin* [1978] 2 All E.R. 1149; paras 20–120–20–111.

### (f) Alternative modes of performance

20–074 **General rule of "minimum performance".** Where a contract entitles the party in breach to perform in alternative ways, damages are, as a general rule,[454] said to be assessed on the assumption that he would have performed in the way that is least burdensome to himself and least beneficial to the other party.[455] For example, if a voyage charterparty gives the charterer the power to choose between a number of different ports of discharge, damages for his failure to load will be assessed on the assumption that he would have chosen the most distant port and so have reduced the shipowner's profit.[456] Similarly, where a supplier of goods has an option as to the exact quantity to be delivered, damages for non-delivery will be based on the assumption that he would have delivered the smallest permissible quantity.[457] The alternative relied upon must, however, constitute a valid performance and may be limited to a mode of performance which could in all the circumstances be regarded as reasonable.[458] Furthermore, performance which is "least burdensome" to the party in breach is not limited strictly to what was the *minimum* level of performance under the contract.[459] It is not to be assumed that he would have acted uncommercially.[460] As Diplock LJ has stated: to "cut off his nose to spite his face … would not be the mode of performing the contract which is 'the least burdensome to the defendant'".[461] Once this is taken into account, it is somewhat misleading, and not particularly helpful, to seek to establish the "least burdensome" performance, or to resort to what is sometimes referred to as the "minimum obligation rule".[462] The court is simply concerned to establish what it considers is most likely to have happened if the defendant had not breached the contract.[463]

---

[454] The rule may be excluded by express contrary stipulation: *Bremer HandelsgesellschaftmbH v Bunge Corp* [1982] 1 Lloyd's Rep. 108; affirmed [1983] 1 Lloyd's Rep. 476, without reference to this point.

[455] *Abrahams v Herbert Reiach Ltd* [1922] 1 K.B. 477; *Withers v General Theatre Corp* [1933] 2 K.B. 536; *The Rijn* [1981] 2 Lloyd's Rep. 267. The rule applies only where the obligation of the defendant is truly alternative: see *Deverill v Burnell* (1873) L.R. 8 C.P. 475.

[456] *Kaye SN Co Ltd v W & R Barnett Ltd* (1932) 48 T.L.R. 400; cf. *The World Navigator* [1991] 2 Lloyd's Rep. 23 at 33.

[457] *Re Thornett & Fehr and Yuills Ltd* [1921] 1 K.B. 219; where the contract does not clearly specify the supplier's options, these will have to be determined by the court as a matter of construction, as in *Paula Lee Ltd v Robert Zehil Ltd* [1983] 2 All E.R. 390.

[458] *Paula Lee Ltd v Robert Zehil Ltd* [1983] 2 All E.R. 390; *Mulvenna v Royal Bank of Scotland* [2003] EWCA Civ 1112; [2004] C.P. Rep. 8.

[459] *Durham Tees Valley Airport Ltd v Bmibaby Ltd* [2010] EWCA Civ 485; [2011] 1 Lloyd's Rep. 68 at [69]; *Jones v Ricoh UK Ltd* [2010] EWHC 1743 (Ch); [2010] U.K.C.L.R. 1335 at [75].

[460] *Durham Tees Valley Airport Ltd v Bmibaby Ltd* [2010] EWCA Civ 485; [2011] 1 Lloyd's Rep. 68 at [69]; *Jones v Ricoh UK Ltd* [2010] EWHC 1743 (Ch); [2010] U.K.C.L.R. 1335 at [79].

[461] *Lavarack v Woods of Colchester Ltd* [1967] 1 Q.B. 278 at 294.

[462] It has been noted that it is not easy to reconcile all of the dicta in the cases dealing with this principle: *Durham Tees Valley Airport Ltd v Bmibaby Ltd* [2010] EWCA Civ 485; [2011] 1 Lloyd's Rep. 68 at [95].

[463] *Durham Tees Valley Airport Ltd v Bmibaby Ltd* [2010] EWCA Civ 485; [2011] 1 Lloyd's Rep. 68 at [79]; *Dhanani v Crasnianski* [2011] EWHC 926 (Comm); [2011] 2 All E.R. (Comm) 799 at [110]; *Jet2.Com Ltd v SC Compania Nationala de Transporturi Aeriene Romane Tarom SA* [2014] EWCA Civ 87 at [51]; *Gul Bottlers (PVT) Ltd v Nichols Plc* [2014] EWHC 2173 (Comm) at [33]; McLauchlan [2019] L.M.C.L.Q. 75.

**Qualifications.** The "general rule" just stated is subject to a number of qualifications. A contract of sale may, for example, give the seller an option as to the time of delivery by allowing him to deliver at any time chosen by him in a stated month. In such a case, damages for non-delivery will prima facie be assessed by reference to the market price at the end of the period. They will not be assessed by reference to the time during it when the market was lowest;[464] for such a rule would give rise to too much uncertainty. Moreover, the party who has the option may declare before breach that he will exercise it in a particular way. Damages will then be assessed on that basis[465] if the effect of the declaration is to bind him contractually to perform in the specified way.[466] 20–075

### (g) Time for assessment[467]

#### (i) *Time of breach*

**The relevance of mitigation.** The starting principle is, or is generally assumed to be, that damages are assessed by reference to the time of breach. For example, where a buyer of goods fails to accept and pay for them (or a seller fails to deliver) the damages are prima facie the difference between the contract price and the market price "at the time or times when the goods ought to have been accepted [or delivered], or (if no time was fixed for acceptance [or delivery]) at the time of the refusal to accept [or deliver]".[468] The same principle of assessment by reference to the time of breach has been applied where a vendor of land wrongfully refused to convey.[469] 20–076

The theory behind the principle is that any loss suffered by reason of market movements after the time of breach is not caused by the breach, but rather by the injured party's failure to mitigate[470] by making a substitute contract. Since under the mitigation rules the claimant need only act reasonably, it follows that the principle is applied with some latitude. In *C Sharpe & Co Ltd v Nosawa*[471] a contract for the sale of peas required the seller to deliver on "about July 21" but no delivery was made. Goods of the precise contract quality were not available in the market. It was held that the buyers had "a reasonable time to consider their

[464] cf. *Harlow & Jones Ltd v Panex (International) Ltd* [1967] 2 Lloyd's Rep. 509; *Phoebus D Kyprianou Co v WH Pim Jr* [1977] 2 Lloyd's Rep. 570 (buyer's breach).

[465] See *The Delian Spirit* [1972] 1 Q.B. 103 at 111–112; *Shipping Co of India Ltd v Naviera Letasa SA* [1976] 1 Lloyd's Rep. 132; *Toprak Mahsulleri Ofisi v Finagrain Cie Commerciale* [1979] 2 Lloyd's Rep. 98.

[466] Contrast *The Rijn* [1981] 2 Lloyd's Rep. 267 at 270 (where the declaration was not of this kind).

[467] Dyson and Kramer 130 L.Q.R. 259.

[468] Sale of Goods Act 1979 ss.50(3), 51(3); cf. *Jamal v Moolla Dawood Sons & Co* [1916] 1 A.C. 175; *The "Ile aux Moines"* [1974] 1 Lloyd's Rep. 262; *Philips v Ward* [1956] 1 W.L.R. 471 at 474, 475, 478; *The Texaco Melbourne* [1994] 1 Lloyd's Rep. 473 at 476; and see fn.348.

[469] *Diamond v Campbell-Jones* [1961] Ch. 22 at 36; *Janred Properties Ltd v Ente Nazionale Italiano per il Turismo* [1989] 2 All E.R. 444 at 457.

[470] See para.20–105.

[471] [1917] 2 K.B. 814; cf. *The Good Friend* [1984] 2 Lloyd's Rep. 586 at 596; *Shearson Lehman Hutton Inc v Maclaine Watson & Co (No.2)* [1990] 2 Lloyd's Rep. 441 at 447.

position";[472] and accordingly the damages were assessed by reference to the market price of similar goods at the end of July.[473] And in *Hooper v Oates*[474] when a buyer failed to complete the purchase of a house, the sellers only decided to retain it after first taking reasonable, but unsuccessful, steps to find a substitute buyer. They were entitled to the difference between the contract price and the market value of the house at the time when they decided to retain it, and not at the date of breach.

The principle of assessment by reference to the time of breach is based on two assumptions: that the injured party knows of the breach as soon as it is committed, and that he can at that time take steps to mitigate the loss which is likely to flow from it. Where the facts falsify these assumptions, the courts will depart from the principle, and assess the damages by reference to "such other date as may be appropriate in the circumstances".[475] In particular they will have regard to the time when the breach was, or could have been discovered; and to the question whether it was possible or reasonable for the injured party to make a substitute contract immediately on such discovery.

### *(ii) Time of discovery of breach*

**20–077** The injured party may not have known of the breach when it was committed and may have been unable, acting with reasonable diligence, to discover it at that time. The damages will then prima facie[476] be assessed by reference (at the earliest)[477] to the time when that party, so acting, could have made the discovery. For example, a seller may first "appropriate" goods to the contract by indicating which particular goods he intends to deliver under a contract for the sale of unascertained goods, and then deliver them. If those goods are not in conformity with the contract, the seller will be in breach at the time of appropriation, but the damages are prima facie assessed by reference to the later time of *delivery*.[478] Where goods are sent to the buyer in sealed packages, the damages may be assessed by reference to the even later time, at which it is reasonable to expect the

---

[472] *C Sharpe & Co Ltd v Nosawa* [1917] 2 K.B. 814 at 821; cf. *Techno Land Improvements Ltd v British Leyland (UK) Ltd* (1979) 252 E.G. 805 at 809; *The Playa Larga* [1983] 2 Lloyd's Rep. 171 at 181.

[473] For similar reasons of convenience, the contract itself may provide for assessment by reference to a date other than that of breach: see, e.g. *Bremer HandelsgesellschaftmbH v Vanden Avenne-Izegem PVBA* [1978] 2 Lloyd's Rep. 109 at 117; *Lusograin Comercio Internacional de Cereas Ltda v Bunge AG* [1986] 2 Lloyd's Rep. 654 at 658.

[474] [2013] EWCA Civ 91; [2014] Ch. 287.

[475] *Johnson v Agnew* [1980] A.C. 367 at 401; *County Personnel (Employment Agency) Ltd v Pulver* [1987] 1 W.L.R. 916; *South Australia Asset Management Corp v York Montague Ltd* [1997] A.C. 191 at 221; quaere, whether time of breach was the appropriate time in *Mahoney v Purnell* [1996] 3 All E.R. 61 at 95–96; cf. *Habton Farms v Nimmo* [2003] EWCA Civ 68; [2004] Q.B. 1.

[476] The rule will not apply to the extent that delay in discovering the breach had no adverse effect on the injured party's position: cf. para.20–008 and see *Re Bell's Indenture* [1980] 1 W.L.R. 1217 (a case of breach of trust).

[477] For assessment by reference to later times, see paras 20–078–20–079.

[478] Sale of Goods Act 1979 s.53(3).

packages to be opened and their contents examined.[479] Similarly, where a builder does defective work and damages are based on cost of cure, they will normally be assessed by reference to the time when the customer, acting with reasonable diligence, could have discovered the defect.[480] Delay in discovering the defect may affect not only the time but also the very basis of assessment; for if at the time of discovery the cost of cure is disproportionately high in relation to the value of a sound building, or if cure has become as a practical matter impossible, the court will award damages on a difference in value basis.[481]

### *(iii) Possibility of acting on knowledge of breach*

Even if the injured party knows of the breach, it may be impossible for him to act on that knowledge by making a substitute contract so as to reduce the loss. For example, a buyer might wrongfully refuse to pay for goods after they had been despatched to him, and it might be impossible for the seller to resell them until they had reached their destination. In such a case the damages would be assessed by reference to the time at which the seller could reasonably resell, and not to the time of the buyer's refusal to pay.[482] **20–078**

The impossibility of acting on knowledge of the breach may also be due to the fact that the buyer lacks the means to buy a substitute on a rising market. In *Wroth v Tyler*[483] the defendant had contracted to sell his house for £6,000. The sale was to be completed in October 1971, when the value of the house had risen to £7,500; but in July 1971 the defendant had wrongfully repudiated the contract. The buyers started proceedings for specific performance and damages; judgment was given in January 1973, when the house was worth £11,500. It was held that specific performance should not be ordered;[484] that damages should be awarded in lieu[485] and that these should be assessed by reference to the value of the house at the time, not of breach, but of judgment,[486] i.e. not at £1,500 but at £5,500. Since the buyers had (as the defendant knew)[487] no financial resources beyond the £6,000 they had raised to buy the house, they could not act on their knowledge of the breach by making a substitute purchase on a rapidly rising market.

---

479 *Van den Hurk v R Martens & Co Ltd* [1920] 1 K.B. 850; cf. *The Hansa Nord* [1976] Q.B. 44 (damages assessed by reference to time of *arrival*, though breach occurred on *shipment*); cf. paras 9–083—9–086 for similar principles governing damages in tort for misrepresentation.

480 *East Ham BC v Bernard Sunley Ltd* [1966] A.C. 406; subsequent increases in cost may be taken into account if it is reasonable to delay the work: see (in tort) *Dodd Properties (Kent) Ltd v Canterbury CC* [1980] 1 W.L.R. 433; Duncan Wallace 96 L.Q.R. 101, 98 L.Q.R. 406; Waddams 97 L.Q.R. 445, 1 O.J.L.S. 134.

481 *Applegate v Moss* [1971] 1 Q.B. 406; *King v Victor Parsons Ltd* [1972] 1 W.L.R. 801.

482 cf. *Shearson Lehman Hutton Inc v Maclaine Watson & Co Ltd* [1989] 2 Lloyd's Rep. 570 at 647 (dealings suspended at time of alleged breach).

483 [1974] Ch. 30; for further discussion see at fn.452 and para.21–063; cf. *Hulbert v Avens* [2003] EWHC 76 (Ch).

484 See para.21–032.

485 See para.21–072.

486 For the possibility of assessment by reference to an even later time, see *Grant v Dawkins* [1973] 1 W.L.R. 1406.

487 *Wroth v Tyler* [1974] Ch. 30 at 57; but for this fact, the loss might (at least in part) have been too remote: para.20–124.

### (iv) *Reasonableness of acting on knowledge of breach*

**20–079** Even where it is possible for the injured party to make a substitute contract on discovering the breach, it may not be reasonable to expect him to do so because at that time there is still a reasonable probability that the defendant will make good his default. In such cases damages are prima facie assessed by reference to the time when that probability ceased to exist.[488] Thus if a seller of goods, after the delivery date has gone by, assures the buyer that he will deliver, but then declares his final inability to perform, the damages will be assessed by reference to the market at the date of that declaration.[489] Again, the injured party may continue to press for performance after the agreed time, but finally elect to terminate on account of the breach: in such a case damages are assessed by reference to the date of termination.[490] A similar principle applies where the injured party brings an action for specific performance: thus a further explanation of the decision in *Wroth v Tyler*[491] is that the buyers could not be expected to make a substitute contract so long as their claim for specific performance was being maintained.[492] The same is true where an order of specific performance has actually been made but is not complied with, so that the injured party is eventually driven to abandon his attempt to enforce performance and to seek his remedy in damages: these are then assessed "as at the date when … the contract is lost".[493]

### (v) *Late performance*

**20–080** If the party in default performs late and the other party suffers loss by reason of the delay, the damages for that loss will be assessed by reference to the date when performance actually was (and not by reference to the date when it should have been) rendered.[494]

### (vi) *Damages for anticipatory breach*

**20–081** **Breach not accepted.** The victim of an anticipatory breach can either continue to press for performance, or "accept" the breach.[495] If the injured party does not accept the breach, the principles (discussed above) as to the time for assessment apply. Assuming that subsequent events have not deprived the injured party of his

---

[488] *Radford v De Froberville* [1977] 1 W.L.R. 1262; *Johnson Matthey Bankers Ltd v State Trading Corp of India* [1984] 1 Lloyd's Rep. 427 at 437–438; cf. *Habton Farms v Nimmo* [2003] EWCA Civ 68; [2004] Q.B. 1.

[489] *Barnett v Javeri & Co* [1916] 2 K.B. 390.

[490] *Toprak Mahsulleri Ofisi v Finagrain Cie Commerciale* [1979] 2 Lloyd's Rep. 98; *The Aktion* [1987] 1 Lloyd's Rep. 283; cf. *Carpobego-Abastecimento de Combustiveis SA v Amci Export Corp* [2006] EWHC 72 (Comm); [2006] 1 Lloyd's Rep. 736.

[491] [1974] Ch. 30; para.20–078.

[492] *Radford v De Froberville* [1977] 1 W.L.R. 1262 at 1285–1286; *Domb v Isoz* [1980] Ch. 548 at 559; *Meng Leong Development Pty Ltd v Jip Hong Trading Co Pte Ltd* [1985] A.C. 511.

[493] *Johnson v Agnew* [1980] A.C. 367 at 401; cf. *Suleman v Shahsavari* [1988] 1 W.L.R. 1181; *Johnson & Co (Barbados) Ltd v NSR Ltd* [1997] A.C. 400 at 411–412.

[494] *Ozalid Group (Export) Ltd v African Continental Bank Ltd* [1979] 2 Lloyd's Rep. 231.

[495] See para.17–079; *Garnac Grain Co Inc v Faure & Fairclough Ltd* [1968] A.C. 1130 at 1140.

right to damages,[496] the general rule is that those damages will be assessed by reference to the time when the contract ought to have been performed[497] and not by reference to the time of the earlier anticipatory breach. The injured party is under no obligation to "accept" the breach.[498] It follows that if the market moves so as to increase his loss between the time of the anticipatory breach and the time fixed for performance, he is entitled to damages assessed by reference to the latter time.[499]

**Breach accepted.** Where the injured party does accept the breach, he can start his action before the time fixed for performance; but the principle of assessment by reference to that time applies even in this type of case.[500] If the action comes to trial before the time fixed for performance, the damages will therefore necessarily be speculative, as they will be based on forecasts or guesses as to future market movements.[501] But where the injured party accepts the breach, the principle of assessment by reference to the time fixed for performance is subject to an important qualification: his damages will be reduced if, after accepting the breach, he fails to take reasonable steps to mitigate his loss.[502] Under this rule, the injured party may, and if there is a market generally will, be required to make a substitute contract; and his damages will be assessed by reference to the time when that contract should have been made. This will usually be the time of acceptance of the breach[503] (or such reasonable time thereafter as may be allowed under the rules stated above).[504] If it is disputed whether a substitute contract could indeed have been made, the burden of proving that the injured party could have made such a contract lies on the party in breach. If that burden is not discharged, the damages will prima facie be assessed by reference to the time fixed for performance.[505] 20–082

**Effect of probable events after acceptance of the breach.** Under the rules just stated, market movements after acceptance of an anticipatory breach may be relevant to the assessment of damages; but it is further possible for the right to damages, or the extent of recovery, to depend on events (other than such a breach) that occur, or will probably occur, between acceptance of the breach and the time fixed for performance. This possibility is illustrated by cases in which charterparties gave charterers a right to cancel if the ship was not ready to load at a named port by a specified date, and the charterers then committed anticipatory breaches by purporting to cancel before that date. In *The Mihalis Angelos*[506] it 20–083

---

[496] See para.17–095 and para.20–083.
[497] *Tai Hing Cotton Mill Ltd v Kamsing Knitting Factory* [1979] A.C. 91.
[498] See para.18–005.
[499] *Tredegar Iron & Coal Co Ltd v Hawthorn Bros & Co* (1902) 18 T.L.R. 716.
[500] *Roper v Johnson* (1873) L.R. 8 C.P. 167; *Melachrino v Nickoll & Knight* [1920] 1 K.B. 693 at 699.
[501] As in *Roper v Johnson* (1873) L.R. 8 C.P. 167.
[502] See para.20–105.
[503] *Roth & Co v Taysen Townsend & Co* (1895) 1 Com. Cas. 240; (1896) 12 T.L.R. 211.
[504] See *C Sharpe & Co Ltd v Nosawa* [1917] 2 K.B. 814; paras 20–077—20–079; *Kaines (UK) Ltd v Oesterreichische Warenhandelsgesellschaft Autowaren, etc* [1993] 2 Lloyd's Rep. 1.
[505] *Roper v Johnson* (1873) L.R. 8 C.P. 167.
[506] [1971] 1 Q.B. 164; George [1971] J.B.L. 109.

was said that the owner's damages for such a wrongful[507] cancellation would (even if he had so accepted it) have been merely nominal, since in that case it was already clear at the time of cancellation that the ship could not possibly have reached the port of loading by the specified date. Hence the charterer could have relied on the point that he would have been entitled lawfully to cancel on the ship's late arrival; and as it was found that he would certainly have exercised that right, the contract was of no value to the shipowner.[508]

20–084 **Events known to have happened by the time of the hearing.** In *The Mihalis Angelos*[509] it was said by Megaw LJ that damages should be assessed as "at the date of acceptance of the breach" and that they may be reduced if the relevant events were "inevitable", or "pre-destined" to happen.[510] Lord Denning MR referred more generally to the need to "take into account all contingencies which might have reduced … the loss",[511] but both approaches adhere to the date of acceptance of the breach and seek to assess, as at that date, the likelihood that certain events *might have happened* in the future and the effect this would have on the loss suffered by the injured party as a consequence of the breach. But what is the position if certain events which would not have been anticipated at the date of acceptance of the breach *have happened* in the time between acceptance and the date of the hearing in which damages are to be assessed, and it is clear that they would have affected the performance of the contract had it not been terminated? This was the position in *The Golden Victory*.[512] There, the shipowners accepted the charterer's repudiation on 17 December 2001, when the charterparty was not due to end until 6 December 2005. On 20 March 2003, prior to the original award of the arbitrator, the Second Gulf War began, and the charterer argued that damages should not be awarded for the period beyond that date since it would have exercised its right to cancel under a War Clause. By a majority,[513] the House of Lords agreed, on the basis that to award damages for the period after 20 March 2003 "would be inconsistent with the overriding compensatory principle on which awards of contractual damages ought to be based."[514]

507 The actual decision was that the cancellation was justified by the shipowner's breach of condition: para.18–045; cf. *Walkinshaw v Diniz* [2002] 2 Lloyd's Rep. 165.

508 *The Mihalis Angelos* [1971] 1 Q.B. 164 at 209–210; cf. at 196, 202–203; *The Noel Bay* [1989] 1 Lloyd's Rep. 361 at 365; *The World Navigator* [1991] 2 Lloyd's Rep. 23 at 32; *North Sea Energy Holding NV v Petroleum Authority of Thailand* [1999] 1 Lloyd's Rep. 483 at 496.

509 [1971] 1 Q.B. 164 at 210.

510 cf. *North Sea Energy Holding NV v Petroleum Authority of Thailand* [1999] 1 Lloyd's Rep. 483 at 495.

511 *The Mihalis Angelos* [1971] 1 Q.B. 164 at 196; cf. *The Seaflower* [2000] 2 Lloyd's Rep. 37 where Lord Denning's formulation was preferred to that of Megaw LJ but, nevertheless, it was found that the relevant event was "inevitable". See, further, the discussion at fn.521.

512 [2007] UKHL 12; [2007] 2 A.C. 353; Morgan [2007] C.L.J. 263; Reynolds [2008] H.K.L.J. 333; Mustill 124 L.Q.R. 569; Stevens in Neyers, Bronaugh and Pitel (eds), *Exploring Contract Law* (2009); Carter and Peden 24 J.C.L. 145; Coote 123 L.Q.R. 503; Treitel 123 L.Q.R. 9, commenting on the decision of the Court of Appeal ([2005] EWCA Civ 1190; [2005] 2 Lloyd's Rep. 747), which was upheld in the House of Lords; cf. *Tele 2 International Card Co SA v Post Office Ltd* [2009] EWCA Civ 9 at [74]–[75].

513 Lord Scott, Lord Carswell and Lord Brown; Lord Bingham and Lord Walker dissented.

514 *The Golden Victory* [2007] UKHL 12; [2007] 2 A.C. 353 at [35].

It may be said that this is not an exception to the general rule that damages are assessed at the date of acceptance of the breach. Damages are still assessed as at that date,[515] but since the assessment depends upon a contingency, e.g. in *The Golden Victory* the likely remaining length of the charterparty, it makes no sense for the courts to confine themselves to what was a matter of guess or estimate on the date in question if it is now known ("the *Bwllfa* principle").[516] If not, strictly speaking, an exception, this is nonetheless an approach which makes the date of the hearing a determinative factor in the assessment of damages[517] and the uncertainty which this leads to was one of the reasons for the dissenting views of Lord Bingham[518] and Lord Walker.[519]

**The scope of "the Bwllfa principle".** In *The Golden Victory*, by the time of the hearing before the arbitrators the Second Gulf War had begun and the finding was that the charterers would have cancelled under the War Clause, i.e. the requirement that subsequent events must have been "inevitable, or "pre-destined to happen", referred to in *The Mihalis Angelos* had been met.[520] If the War had not begun and it was still only a possibility, it appears that the arbitrators would have had to make an assessment at the date of the hearing of the stage which events had reached. Where events have moved on in a way which would appear to have reduced the loss suffered by the claimant by the time of the hearing, but they remain unpredictable and could move again in a way which would restore or even increase that loss, it is very debatable whether the courts should do anything other than assess damages as at the date of acceptance of the breach and on the basis of what was known as at that date.[521] If the war had not started by the time of the hearing in *The Golden Victory* but it had appeared inevitable, it might nonetheless have been averted. By contrast, in *The Mihalis Angelos*, it was quite impossible for the vessel to arrive in time. 20–085

**Nature of the damages to be assessed.** What may also be relevant to the scope of the *Bwllfa* principle is the nature of the damages to be assessed. The *Bwllfa* case itself was not concerned with damages for breach of contract, but with the 20–086

[515] *Seatbooker Sales Ltd v Southend United Football Club* [2008] EWHC 157 (QB) at [119].
[516] After *Bwllfa and Merthyr Dare Steam Collieries (1891) Ltd v Pontypridd Waterworks Co* [1903] A.C. 426 which was relied upon by the majority.
[517] The party in breach may be discouraged from entering quickly into a settlement in the hope that events transpire which will reduce the damages payable; in *The Golden Victory* Lord Carswell acknowledged this risk, but felt that courts and arbitrators have the ability to prevent such abuse if application is made to them to proceed with dispatch: [2007] UKHL 12; [2007] 2 A.C. 353 at [67].
[518] *The Golden Victory* [2007] UKHL 12; [2007] 2 A.C. 353 at [35].
[519] Lord Walker described the point about the War Clause as one which was not in either party's mind at the date of breach, but which took on "a life of its own as the litigation has been prolonged": [2007] UKHL 12; [2007] 2 A.C. 353 at [42].
[520] See para.20–084.
[521] Even as at that date there appears to be a difference of opinion in *The Golden Victory*. According to Lord Brown (at [77]) this meant no more than that the prospect of war was "less than 50%" but this still represented a contingency which would have to be taken into account even if damages were assessed on the basis of what was known at the date of acceptance of the breach. It is debatable whether Lord Brown is right to conclude (at [76]) that Lord Bingham and Lord Walker accepted this as a matter of principle since they only went so far as to approve the test in *The Mihalis Angelos* that one takes account of the "inevitable".

award of statutory compensation payable under a notice preventing a coal mine from mining a seam. The House of Lords emphasised that compensation was payable for the loss of the use of the coal mine and "not the price on a transaction of sale".[522] Similarly, in *The Golden Victory* damages were being assessed for the loss to be suffered over a period, i.e. the charter term (subject to the "suspensive condition" of the War Clause),[523] and not the loss of the sale of the vessel with the benefit of the charterparty.[524] This may be contrasted with the damages which fell to be assessed in *Ageas (UK) Ltd v Kwik-fit (GB) Ltd*.[525] The claimant purchased a business from the defendant and was entitled to damages for breach of a warranty as to the level of bad debt, calculated as the difference between the value of the business had the warranty been fulfilled and its actual value on the basis of the accurate figures for bad debt. It was held that this assessment was to be made at the date of breach (being the date of acquisition) and should not take into account the fact that the level of bad debt had proved, after acquisition of the business, to be better than anticipated. Even if there had been no breach, this better than expected performance in relation to bad debt would have inured to the benefit of the claimant and to take it into account in the assessment of damages would have failed to enforce the bargain entered into by the parties. As Popplewell J stated:[526]

> "... it is important to keep firmly in mind any contractual allocation of risk made by the parties. Party autonomy dictates that an award of damages should not confound the allocation of risk inherent in the parties' bargain. It is not therefore sufficient merely that there is a future contingency which plays a part in the assessment. It is necessary to examine whether the eventuation of that contingency represents a risk which has been allocated by the parties as one which should fall on one or other of them. If the benefit or detriment of the contingency eventuating is a risk which has been allocated to the buyer, it is not appropriate to deprive him of any benefit which in fact ensues: it is inherent in the bargain that the buyer should receive such benefit."[527]

It is important to stress that this does not mean that the *Bwllfa* principle can never apply to a "one-off sale", as illustrated by the decision of the Supreme Court in *Bunge SA v Nidera BV*.[528] In that case the seller was guilty of an anticipatory breach by prematurely invoking a right to cancel based on a prohibition of export. The buyer accepted the breach, terminated the contract and sued for damages being the difference between the contract price and the market price at the date of default, i.e. when C accepted the breach and terminated. This claim was made

---

[522] *Bwllfa and Merthyr Dare Steam Collieries (1891) Ltd v Pontypridd Waterworks Co* [1903] A.C. 426 at 432 (Lord Robertson), at 431 (Lord MacNaghten); cf. *Joiner v George* [2002] EWCA Civ 160; [2003] B.C.C. 298 at [69] (*Bwllfa* decision of "no assistance"); *Gorne v Scales* [2006] EWCA Civ 311.

[523] *The Golden Victory* [2007] UKHL 12; [2007] 2 A.C. 353 at [82].

[524] Lord Bingham (at [22]) appears to refer to an available market *for the sale of the vessel* (as opposed to its re-letting), but Lord Scott (at [37]) stated that "it was accepted in argument before your Lordships that the owners' charterparty rights would not, in practice, have been marketable for a capital sum".

[525] [2014] EWHC 2178 (QB); [2014] Bus. L.R. 1348.

[526] *Ageas (UK) Ltd v Kwik-fit (GB) Ltd* [2014] EWHC 2178 (QB); [2014] Bus. L.R. 1348 at [38].

[527] cf. *Hut Group Ltd v Nobahar-Cookson* [2014] EWHC 382 (QB) at [184] ("Hindsight cannot be used to confound the allocation of risk under the bargain").

[528] [2015] UKSC 43; [2015] 2 Lloyd's Rep. 469; Carter 132 L.Q.R. 1.

under a "default clause" which had been incorporated in the contract. The seller was able to invoke *The Golden Victory* to argue that, at the time when delivery was due, the prohibition against export was still in place so that it would have been entitled to cancel in any event and the buyer had not suffered any loss as a result. The Supreme Court agreed that this was the position under the common law and confirmed that *The Golden Victory* is not excluded from application to a "one-off sale".[529] As Lord Sumption explained, the difference between the contract price and the market price may have "crystallised" at the date of default, but that still left the contingency of whether the seller would be obliged to deliver when delivery fell due and subsequent events showed that he was free of that obligation in circumstances which did not amount to breach, in the same way that the charterer was under no obligation to perform in *The Golden Victory* after the date when the Gulf War started.

**The effect of any prospective breach by the claimant.** An important feature of *The Mihalis Angelos* is that a cancelling clause gives the charterer an "independent option" to cancel if the ship is not ready to load by the specified date: it does "not impose any contractual obligation on the owners to commence loading by the cancelling date".[530] In other words, the right to cancel under such a clause is exercisable on the occurrence or non-occurrence of an *event*, and does not depend on any *breach* by the shipowner. The same is true of *The Golden Victory* and the charterer's right to cancel under the War Clause. It is submitted that the reasoning of these cases would not apply (so as to reduce damages to a nominal amount) where the charterer's case was that he would have been entitled to terminate on account of the shipowner's *future breach*; for once the shipowner had accepted the charterer's earlier repudiation and so terminated the contract for that anticipatory breach,[531] the shipowner would be relieved of any further obligation to perform, so that his failure to perform on the due day could no longer be a breach.[532] **20–087**

[529] That raised the question of whether the common law position was excluded by the terms of the default clause. The Supreme Court held that it was not.

[530] *The Simona* [1989] A.C. 788 at 795.

[531] *Gill & Duffus SA v Berger & Co Inc* [1984] A.C. 382 at 391; para.17–027. After this case, apparently contrary dicta in *Regent OHG Aisestadt und Barig v Francecso of Jermyn Street* [1981] 3 All E.R. 327; and *Bremer HandelsgesellschaftmbH v JH Rayner& Co* [1979] 2 Lloyd's Rep. 216 at 224, 229 can no longer be supported.

[532] This submission is rejected by Teare J in *The Glory Wealth* [2013] EWHC 3153 (Comm); [2014] 2 W.L.R. 1405 and is discussed in greater detail at para.17–030.

## 3. NON-PECUNIARY LOSSES

### (a) Mental distress[533]

#### (i) General principle

20–088 **No recovery for injured feelings.** In a contractual action,[534] the right to recover damages for injured feelings is restricted by the decision of the House of Lords in *Addis v Gramophone Co Ltd*,[535] where a company wrongfully dismissed its manager in a way that was "harsh and humiliating".[536] He recovered damages for loss of salary and commission, but not for the injury to his feelings caused by the manner of his dismissal. One possible justification for the rule is that such injury is not within the contemplation of the parties and is thus too remote; but an employer considering the effects of *such* a dismissal could surely contemplate injury to the employee's feelings.[537] More probably the rule results from a failure to distinguish between punitive (or exemplary) damages (which are not generally available in a contractual action) and damages for injured feelings (which are meant to compensate the claimant for a loss, though it is not a pecuniary one).[538]

20–089 **Claims for dismissal.** Whatever may be the basis of the rule in the *Addis* case, it continues to restrict the damages recoverable in a common law action for *wrongful* dismissal.[539] Such damages normally consist of the amount which the employee would have earned during the period of notice which the employer was legally obliged to give to bring the contract lawfully to an end. By statute, further compensation may be recoverable for *unfair* dismissal even where such notice is given; and the relevant legislation[540] subjects awards of such compensation to specified financial limits. In *Johnson v Unisys Ltd*,[541] an employee who had recovered the maximum amount available under this legislation (then some £11,600) sought to recover further damages (of some £400,000) at common law. He claimed that the manner of his dismissal constituted a separate breach of contract in the form of a breach of the implied term that the employer would not, without reasonable and proper cause, conduct itself in a manner calculated and

---

[533] Jackson 26 I.C.L.Q. 502; Enonchong 16 O.J.L.S. 617.

[534] The same conduct may amount both to a breach of contract and to a tort; and where this is the case the claimant can sometimes recover damages for distress by suing in tort even though such damages would not be available in an action for breach of contract: see, e.g. *Sampson v Floyd* [1989] 2 E.G.L.R. 49 as explained in *Branchett v Beany* [1992] 3 All E.R. 910 at 918.

[535] [1909] A.C. 488.

[536] *Addis v Gramophone Co Ltd* [1909] A.C. 488 at 493.

[537] cf. *Watts v Morrow* [1991] 1 W.L.R. 1421 at 1445.

[538] See para.20–022 and *Johnson v Unisys Ltd* [2001] UKHL 13; [2003] 1 A.C. 518 at [15] (Lord Steyn, dissenting on the main issue in that case).

[539] *Shove v Downs Surgical Plc* [1984] I.C.R. 532. The rule is viewed with scepticism, even in the context of wrongful dismissal, in *Johnson v Gore Wood* [2002] 2 A.C. 1 at 50 (Lord Cooke, dissenting on this point). Under the proposals in Law Com. No.247 (1997), para.6.1(2), damages for mental distress to reflect the conduct of the defendant would be available in contractual actions.

[540] Employment Rights Act 1996 Pt X.

[541] [2001] UKHL13; [2003] 1 A.C. 518.

likely to destroy or seriously damage the relationship of trust and confidence.[542] This was said to have caused him to suffer a mental breakdown and consequent loss of earnings. The House of Lords rejected the claim on the ground that it would be wrong to allow the financial limit laid down by the statutory scheme for compensation for unfair dismissal to be evaded by giving the dismissed employee a "parallel remedy[543] [at common law] which is subject to no such limit".[544] In *Johnson v Unisys Ltd* the parallel remedy was sought on the basis of breach of an implied term, but the same reasoning has also ruled out a claim based on breach of an express term of the contract dealing with the disciplinary procedure which an employer was alleged not to have followed and which led to dismissal.[545] In *Eastwood v Magnox Electric Plc*[546] the House of Lords subsequently held that the "*Johnson* exclusion area" is confined to claims arising *from dismissal*. If, before dismissal, the employee has already acquired a cause of action for breach of contract, that cause of action remains unimpaired by any subsequent dismissal.[547]

**Other claims.** It seems that, in cases *not* governed by any such statutory scheme, **20–090**
the House of Lords (now Supreme Court) would be prepared to review the principle in *Addis v Gramophone Co Ltd*.[548] This is an important point because that case, though strictly an authority only on damages for wrongful dismissal, has also been regarded as the basis of the wider principle that damages for injured feelings cannot, in general, be recovered in a contractual action.[549] That general principle has been applied so as to preclude the recovery of damages by a company director in respect of mental distress and anxiety suffered by him as a

---

542 *Malik v BCCI* [1998] A.C. 20; discussed para.20–097.

543 As well as the financial limit, compensation may not be awarded at all *by way of unfair dismissal* for non-pecuniary loss, including injured feelings: *Dunnachie v Kingston-upon-Hull CC* [2004] UKHL 36; [2005] 1 A.C. 226. On this basis the common law does not merely offer a "parallel" remedy. It has also been doubted whether the statutory award extends to financial loss caused by psychiatric illness: *Eastwood v Magnox Electric Plc* [2004] UKHL 35; [2005] 1 A.C. 503 at [42].

544 *Johnson v Unisys Ltd* [2001] UKHL 13; [2003] 1 A.C. 518 at [56], [57]; cf. at [2], [80] (Lord Steyn dissenting on this point).

545 *Edwards v Chesterfield Royal Hospital NHS Foundation Trust* [2011] UKSC 58; [2012] 2 A.C. 22.

546 [2004] UKHL 35; [2005] 1 A.C. 503; cf. *Monk v Cann Hall Primary School* [2013] EWCA Civ 826; [2013] I.R.L.R. 732.

547 As in *Johnson v Unisys Ltd*, the claims in the *Eastwood* case were for psychiatric illness and consequent loss of earnings, and outside the "*Johnson* exclusion area" the principle laid down in the *Addis* case is confined to claims for injured feelings: *Gogay v Hertfordshire CC* [2000] I.R.L.R. 703 at [68] (psychiatric illness); contrast *Bliss v SE Thames Regional Health Authority* [1987] I.C.R. 700 (injured feelings). The complex, and potentially unsatisfactory, interrelation between the common law and statute created by the decisions in *Johnson, Dunnachie* (fn.543) and *Eastwood* is said to merit the "urgent attention of the Government and the legislature": *Dunnachie v Kingston-upon-Hull CC* [2004] UKHL 36; [2005] 1 A.C. 503 at [33] (Lord Nicholls).

548 See, in *Johnson v Unisys Ltd*, apart from criticism of the *Addis* case in Lord Steyn's dissenting speech, the views of Lord Nicholls, [2001] UKHL 13; [2003] 1 A.C. 518 at [2]; and Lord Hoffmann at [43].

549 *Watts v Morrow* [1991] 1 W.L.R. 1421 at 1444; *Johnson v Unisys Ltd* [2001] UKHL 13; [2003] 1 A.C. 518 at [69]; *Farley v Skinner* [2001] UKHL 49; [2002] 2 A.C. 732 at [16], [34], [47], [54].

result of alleged breaches of duty by a firm of solicitors engaged by him and the company to carry through the purchase of development land by the company.[550]

### *(ii) Exceptions*

20–091 **Pain and suffering, and recognised psychiatric illness.** Damages can be recovered for pain and suffering for a breach of contract which causes personal injury.[551] Such an award takes account of the claimant's mental anguish and to this extent includes damages for injured feelings.[552] Moreover, it seems that personal injury can include physical or recognised psychiatric illness resulting from injury to feelings and that damages for such illness can be recovered,[553] so long as not too remote.[554]

20–092 **Mental distress consequent on physical inconvenience.** Damages can be recovered for physical inconvenience caused by the defendant's breach of contract,[555] and such damages now also extend to any mental suffering "directly related to that inconvenience".[556] Thus, in *Watts v Morrow*,[557] where the defendant omitted certain defects from the survey report upon which the claimants relied in purchasing a house, damages were awarded for the physical inconvenience and directly related mental distress of living in the house while it was being repaired.

20–093 **Loss of enjoyment, or amenity.** Damages for distress or vexation can be awarded in a group of cases in which at least one of the "major and important"[558] objects of the contract was to provide enjoyment, security, comfort or sentimental benefits. Such awards have, for example, been made against a travel agent who broke his contract to provide a couple with accommodation for their honeymoon;[559] against a package-tour operator who provided accommodation

---

[550] *Johnson v Gore Wood & Co* [2002] 2 A.C. 1; cf. *Groom v Crocker* [1939] 1 K.B. 194; *Hobbs v London and SW Ry Co* (1875) L.R. 10 Q.B. 111 at 122.

[551] e.g. *Godley v Perry* [1960] 1 W.L.R. 9.

[552] See *H West & Sons Ltd v Shephard* [1964] A.C. 326.

[553] e.g. *Cook v Swinfen* [1967] 1 W.L.R. 457; *Esso Petroleum Co Ltd v Mardon* [1976] Q.B. 801 at 822; *Attia v British Gas Plc* [1988] Q.B. 304 (where it is not clear whether the claim was in contract or in tort); *Gogay v Hertfordshire CC* [2000] I.R.L.R. 703.

[554] *Wiseman v Virgin Atlantic Airways* Ltd [2006] EWHC 1566 (QB) at [21]. In the employment context, remoteness would depend on the employer's knowledge of the employee's mental state (and so of the likelihood of his suffering mental illness in consequence of the breach) at the time of *contracting*, not at that of *breach*: see at fn.754. This point accounts for rejection of the claim in *Johnson v Unisys Ltd* [2001] UKHL 13; [2003] 1 A.C. 518 by Lord Steyn on the ground of remoteness; the same view is taken by Lord Millett at [70].

[555] *Bailey v Bullock* (1950) 66 T.L.R. (Pt. 2) 791; *Mafo v Adams* [1970] 1 Q.B. 548.

[556] *Watts v Morrow* [1991] 1 W.L.R. 1421 at 1445; cf. *McCall v Abelesz* [1976] Q.B. 585 at 594; *Perry v Sidney Phillips & Son* [1982] 1 W.L.R. 1287; *Patel v Hooper & Jackson* [1999] 1 W.L.R. 1792; *English Churches Housing Group v Shine* [2004] EWCA Civ 434; [2005] L & T.R. 7.

[557] [1991] 1 W.L.R. 1421 at 1445.

[558] *Farley v Skinner* [2001] UKHL 49; [2002] 2 A.C. 737 at [24].

[559] *Cook v Spanish Holiday Tours Ltd, The Times*, 6 February 1960.

falling short of the standard promised and so spoilt his client's holiday;[560] against a carrier for breach of a contract to convey guests to a wedding;[561] against a photographer for breach of a contract to take wedding photographs;[562] against a solicitor who failed to take necessary steps in non-molestation proceedings, so that the molestation of his client continued,[563] or who failed, negligently, to obtain custody of the claimant's children;[564] and against a cemetery for breach of a contract to grant exclusive burial rights.[565]

The award of damages for "loss of amenity" where a contract to build a swimming pool for the customer's personal use was broken by building the pool to less than the stipulated depth[566] can be explained on the same ground; and this explanation also accounts for the view that an architect who designs a house for his client's personal occupation is liable for failing to incorporate in the design agreed features, such as an impressive entrance hall and wide staircase, thus depriving the client of the pleasure which he expected to derive from these features.[567]

The distinction between cases in which damages are awarded on the present ground and those in which they are awarded for physical inconvenience (under the second exception, discussed above) is sometimes hard to draw.[568] The point is illustrated by *Farley v Skinner*[569] where the claimant had, before buying a house as his retirement home, engaged a surveyor whom he had specifically instructed to report on the question whether the house would be affected by aircraft noise. The surveyor in breach of contract carelessly failed to provide accurate information on this point and the purchaser recovered damages in respect of the adverse effect which such noise had on the peace and tranquillity of the property, even though the price paid for it by him did not exceed its market value. The main ground for the decision is that one important (though not the sole) object of the contract was to provide "pleasure, relaxation and peace of mind";[570] but there is also support in the speeches for the view that the award could have been supported on the ground that the claimant had suffered physical inconvenience

---

560 *Jarvis v Swan Tours Ltd* [1973] Q.B. 233; cf. *Jackson v Horizon Holidays Ltd* [1975] 1 W.L.R. 1468; *Wings Ltd v Ellis* [1985] A.C. 272 at 287; *Baltic Shipping Co v Dillon* (1993) 176 C.L.R. 144; *Milner v Carnival Plc* [2010] EWCA Civ 389; [2010] 3 All E.R. 701.

561 *Chandle v East African Airways Corp* [1964] E.A. 78.

562 *Diesen v Samson* 1971 S.L.T. (Sh. Ct.) 49.

563 *Heywood v Wellers* [1976] Q.B. 446; cf. *Dickinson v Jones Alexander & Co* [1993] 2 F.L.R. 521; contrast *Hartle v Laceys* [1997] C.L.Y. 3839 (solicitor employed for conveyancing purposes).

564 *Hamilton Jones v David & Snape* [2003] EWHC 3147 (Ch); [2004] 1 W.L.R. 924.

565 *Reed v Madon* [1989] Ch. 408.

566 *Ruxley Electronics Ltd v Forsyth* [1996] A.C. 344 (para.20–048) described in *Johnson v Gore Wood Co* [2002] 2 A.C. 1 at 37 as an "unusual case" but applied in *Farley v Skinner* [2001] UKHL 49; [2002] 2 A.C. 732 where the damages in the *Ruxley* case were said at [21] to have been awarded for "disappointment".

567 This follows from the overruling of *Knott v Bolton* (1995) 45 Con L.R. 127 in *Farley v Skinner* [2001] UKHL 49; [2002] 2 A.C. 732.

568 Either ground sufficed in *Haysman v Mrs Rogers Films Ltd* [2008] EWHC 2494 (QB).

569 [2001] UKHL 49; [2002] 2 A.C. 732.

570 *Farley v Skinner* [2001] UKHL 49; [2002] 2 A.C. 732 at [24].

(and not merely distress or vexation) in having to put up with the unexpected level of noise.[571] On either ground "awards in this area should be restrained and modest."[572]

20–094 **Borderline cases.** The question whether one of the main objects of the contract is to provide "pleasure, relaxation and peace of mind" can give rise to difficulty in borderline cases. Thus in one case damages for distress were awarded against the seller of a new car which broke down and would not restart, so that the buyer suffered "a totally spoilt day comprising nothing but vexation",[573] while in another it was held that no such damages were available for breach of a contract to repair a car.[574] Again, in *Farley v Skinner* it was said that the case was "not 'an ordinary surveyor's contract'"[575] and considerable emphasis was placed on the fact that the contract had specifically referred to aircraft noise. It seems that, but for this fact the surveyor would have been liable only for pecuniary consequences and inconvenience resulting from physical defects in the property itself, as opposed to the vexation caused by adverse environmental factors.[576]

20–095 **Nature of claims for non-pecuniary loss.** Where damages are recoverable for "disappointment" resulting from failure to perform an obligation to provide enjoyment, security or peace of mind, it is sometimes said that the basis of such recovery is that the claimant was "deprived of the contractual benefit to which he was entitled".[577] Such language is entirely appropriate in the context of awards which compensate the claimant in respect of a loss which he has in fact suffered, though the loss is non-pecuniary in nature. But phrases such as that quoted above could, if taken out of that context, be read as supporting the view that the mere fact of breach of contract, even though no loss of any kind had flowed from it, gave rise to a claim for substantial damages; and this view would be inconsistent with a number of the rules or principles on which such claims are based. One such principle is that damages for breach of contract cannot be recovered *merely* in respect of the "anxiety" or "disappointment" that may be caused by the breach.[578] Another, discussed earlier in this chapter, is that damages cannot be recovered in respect of a breach which has no adverse effect.[579] In none of these cases are damages recoverable *merely* because the injured party has not received

---

[571] *Farley v Skinner* [2001] UKHL 49; [2002] 2 A.C. 732 at [30], [38], [54], [105].

[572] *Farley v Skinner* [2001] UKHL 49; [2002] 2 A.C. 732 at [28]; cf. *Eiles v Southwark L.B.C.* [2006] EWHC 1411 (TCC); *Iggleden v Fairview New Homes (Shooters Hill) Ltd* [2007] EWHC 1573 (TCC); *Haysman v Mrs Rogers Films Ltd* [2008] EWHC 2494 (QB); *Milner v Carnival Plc* [2010] EWCA Civ 389; [2010] 3 All E.R. 701.

[573] *Bernstein v Pamson Motors (Golders Green) Ltd* [1987] 2 All E.R. 220 at 231; cf. *Jackson v Chrysler Acceptances Ltd* [1978] R.T.R. 474 (defects in car bought for touring holiday).

[574] *Alexander v Rolls Royce Motors Ltd* [1996] R.T.R. 95.

[575] *Farley v Skinner* [2001] UKHL 49; [2002] 2 A.C. 732 at [42]; referring to *Watts v Morrow* [1991] 1 W.L.R. 1421 at 1442.

[576] See especially *Farley v Skinner* [2001] UKHL 49; [2002] 2 A.C. 732 at [44], [54]–[57].

[577] *Farley v Skinner* [2001] UKHL 49; [2002] 2 A.C. 732 at [106]; cf. at [86].

[578] *Hayes v Dodd* [1990] 2 All E.R. 815; *Firsteel Cold Rolled Products v Anaco Precision Products*, *The Times*, 21 November 1994; *R. v Investors Compensation Scheme Ex p. Bowden* [1994] 1 W.L.R. 17; reversed on other grounds [1995] Q.B. 107, in turn reversed without reference to the present point [1996] A.C. 261.

[579] See para.20–008.

the benefit of the promised performance; and it is submitted that they support the view that "damages should not be awarded, unless perhaps nominally, for the fact of a breach of contract as distinct from the consequences of breach".[580] Of course the adverse consequences need not be of a *financial* kind, as is shown by the many exceptions to the general rule that damages for breach of contract cannot be recovered for injured feelings; but these cases do not negative the requirement that some adverse consequence to the claimant (other than mere "anxiety" or "disappointment") must flow from the breach in order to sustain an award of substantial damages.

Where damages are awarded for non-pecuniary loss, there may be the risk of duplication of any damages awarded for pecuniary loss. Thus, in the case of a sub-standard holiday,[581] it has been said that it is necessary to distinguish "the difference between what the supplier contracted to provide and what was actually provided", which is a pecuniary loss, and "how the client felt about the diminution in the service supplied" which is relevant to an award for non-pecuniary loss in the form of mental distress.[582] It might be said there should be no award for the latter if the claimant has been compensated in full for the former since he has received the equivalent of the holiday, in monetary terms. But the whole point is that the claimant who books a holiday does not want performance in purely monetary terms so that he still has an additional and further loss in the form of his mental distress.[583] This may nonetheless explain why awards under this head should be relatively modest.

### (b) Loss of reputation

**No recovery for loss of reputation itself.** In *Addis v Gramophone Co Ltd*[584] it was held by the House of Lords that no damages could be awarded for any loss of reputation caused to the claimant by the manner of his dismissal, and the wider principle that damages cannot be awarded for loss of reputation itself has not seriously been questioned in the courts.[585] **20–096**

**Financial loss consequent upon loss of reputation.** In the *Addis* case[586] it was further held that, in an action for wrongful dismissal, the employee could not recover damages for the loss that he might suffer because the dismissal made it **20–097**

[580] *Farley v Skinner* [2001] UKHL 49; [2002] 2 A.C. 732 at [40] (Lord Clyde). For the application of the same principle to cases where the breach causes loss to a third party but none (beyond the bare fact of breach) to the promisee, see *Alfred McAlpine Construction Ltd v Panatown Ltd* [2001] 1 A.C. 518 at 534 (Lord Clyde); para.14–042, at fn.287.

[581] *Milner v Carnival Plc* [2010] EWCA Civ 389; [2010] 3 All E.R. 701 in which a clear distinction was drawn between four different heads of loss: (i) diminution in value; (ii) consequential pecuniary loss (e.g. out of pocket expenses); (iii) physical inconvenience and discomfort; and (iv) mental distress.

[582] *Milner v Carnival Plc* [2010] EWCA Civ 389; [2010] 3 All E.R. 701 at [43].

[583] The award of the diminution in value compensates for direct loss; mental distress is a form of consequential loss, which is consistent with the application to non-pecuniary losses of the limit of remoteness: fn.554.

[584] [1909] A.C. 488; para.20–088.

[585] *Groom v Crocker* [1939] 1 K.B. 194.

[586] *Addis v Gramophone Co Ltd* [1909] A.C. 488.

more difficult for him to get another job. But the view that damages in such an action cannot be recovered for loss of employment prospects, or for injury to reputation, was hard to justify.[587] In *Malik v BCCI*[588] the House of Lords held that such "stigma damages" were in principle recoverable by former employees of a bank which had collapsed in consequence of corruption and dishonesty in which the employees had not been involved. The employees' claim ultimately failed as they were unable to establish that the stigma was the cause of the rejection of any job applications which had been made by them, or that any future applications had a sufficiently real chance of success to justify an award for damages for loss of a chance, or that, if such a chance existed, the stigma was the cause of its loss.[589] The damages which they could have recovered if they had been able to establish any of these points would have been in respect of financial loss, and not of injury to feelings. In addition, they would have been recoverable, not for wrongful dismissal,[590] but for breach of the employer's implied undertaking not without reasonable cause to conduct itself so as to destroy the relationship of trust and confidence between itself and its employees.[591] According to a further distinction drawn in *Malik*'s case, the employee can recover such damages where the effect of the breach is "positively to damage" his job prospects, but not where its effect is merely a "failure to improve them".[592] It is, however, respectfully submitted that the possibility of the employer's being held liable for loss of the latter kind should not be ruled out, particularly where the employment involves training or similar features intended to enhance the employee's prospects. It was, for example, established even before *Malik*'s case that an apprentice who was wrongfully dismissed before the end of his period of training was entitled to damages for diminution of his future prospects since "the very object of an apprenticeship agreement is to enable the apprentice to fit himself to get better employment".[593]

20–098 **Non-employment cases.** There are many other situations in which damages can be awarded for financial loss consequent upon injury to reputation resulting from a breach of contract. First, a trader can recover damages for injury to his business reputation, e.g. if his reputation suffers because his wholesaler supplies him with defective goods;[594] on the same principle a travel agent can recover damages for loss of "goodwill" from a shipowner who breaks his contract to supply accommodation for passengers on a pleasure cruise.[595] A similar rule applies

[587] *Johnson v Unisys Ltd* [2001] UKHL 13; [2003] 1 A.C. 518 at [70] ("may no longer be law").
[588] [1998] A.C. 20.
[589] *BCCI v Ali (No.2)* [2002] EWCA Civ 82; [2002] I.C.R. 1258.
[590] Where the claim is for loss of reputation caused by dismissal, recovery is ruled out by the reasoning of the House of Lords in *Johnson v Unisys Ltd* [2001] UKHL 13; [2003] 1 A.C. 518 (though not itself involving loss of reputation): para.20–089. This has, in turn, been qualified by the decision in *Eastwood v Magnox Electric Plc* [2004] UKHL 35; [2005] 1 A.C. 503 (also not involving loss of reputation): fn.547.
[591] See para.6–067.
[592] *Malik v BCCI* [1998] A.C. 20 at 37.
[593] *Dunk v George Waller & Sons Ltd* [1970] 2 Q.B. 163; cf. the award of damages for loss of a chance in *Guido van der Garde BV v Force India Formula One Ltd* [2010] EWHC 2373 (QB).
[594] *Cointat v Myham & Son* [1913] 2 K.B. 220.
[595] *Anglo-Continental Holidays Ltd v Typaldos Lines (London) Ltd* [1967] 2 Lloyd's Rep. 61.

where a bank wrongfully dishonours its customer's cheque. It has long been settled that, if the customer is a trader, he can recover general damages for the resulting injury to his business reputation.[596] A person who was not a trader was formerly thought to be entitled to no more than a nominal amount unless he proved special damages, i.e. particular items of loss resulting from the bank's breach.[597] But this view no longer prevails now that "the credit rating of individuals is as important for their personal transactions … as it is for those who are engaged in trade".[598] Hence such persons can also now recover general damages in respect of injury to what may be called their financial reputation[599] resulting from the wrongful dishonour of a cheque.[600] Secondly, an actor or author can recover damages for "loss of publicity", that is, for loss of the chance to enhance his reputation,[601] and also for injury to his existing reputation.[602] Thirdly, a person who is wrongfully expelled from a trade union can recover damages for the resulting loss of employment opportunities.[603] Finally, it has been suggested that a claimant should be entitled to damages for injury to reputation where the contract "had as its purpose, or one of its purposes, the protection of the claimant against the sort of damage suffered".[604] Thus damages of this kind were said to be recoverable for breach of a contract not to broadcast a programme concerning the activities of the claimants until after the publication of a report concerning those activities.[605]

## 4. METHODS OF LIMITING DAMAGES

To compensate the injured party fully for all loss that can, in some sense, be said to flow from a breach of contract would often lead to undesirable results. Such complete protection of the injured party's interests would either deter the other party from entering into the contract at all, or lead to an undue raising of charges. The law has therefore developed a number of rules for the purpose of limiting damages for breach of contract. **20–099**

[596] *Rolin v Steward* (1854) 14 C.B. 595 at 605; *Wilson v United Counties Bank Ltd* [1920] A.C. 102 at 112.

[597] *Gibbons v Westminster Bank* [1939] 2 K.B. 882.

[598] *Kpohraror v Woolwich Building Society* [1996] 4 All E.R. 119 at 124. The claimant in this case was a trader, so that it was not strictly necessary to decide the present point.

[599] Not for "loss of reputation *simpliciter*": *Kpohraror v Woolwich Building Society* [1996] 4 All E.R. 119 at 125. The phrase "financial reputation" is used in the text to avoid the awkwardness of referring to the "business reputation" of someone who is not in business.

[600] *Kpohraror v Woolwich Building Society* [1996] 4 All E.R. 119 at 124.

[601] *Herbert Clayton & Jack Waller Ltd v Oliver* [1930] A.C. 209; *Joseph v National Magazine Co Ltd* [1959] Ch. 14.

[602] *Malik v BCCI* [1998] A.C. 20, overruling *Withers v General Theatre Corp Ltd* [1933] 2 K.B. 536.

[603] *Edwards v SOGAT* [1971] Ch. 354 at 378–379.

[604] *Cambridge Nutrition Ltd v BBC* [1990] 3 All E.R. 523 at 540.

[605] *Cambridge Nutrition Ltd v BBC* [1990] 3 All E.R. 523 at 540; cf. *McLeish v Amoo-Guttfried & Co*, *The Times*, 13 October 1993.

### (a) Causation

20–100 Our present concern is with cases in which there is a breach, followed by a state of affairs clearly disadvantageous to the claimant, but the defendant argues that the breach did not bring about that state of affairs. For example, a shipowner may be technically in breach of contract because his ship was not equipped with a proper medicine chest; but if the ship later foundered in a storm, the owners of goods on board could not claim that the breach was the cause of their loss.[606] Another reason why loss may be held not to have been caused by the breach is that it would have been suffered even if the breach had not been committed. This was, for example, the position where solicitors acting for a mortgage lender committed a breach of contract and a breach of trust by parting with the lender's money before they should have done so; and the lender later suffered loss, not because the money had been paid over too soon, but because the security turned out to be inadequate. It was held that the solicitors were not liable for this loss since the lender had got exactly the charge it had bargained for, and since it would have suffered exactly the same loss, even if the solicitors' breach had not been committed.[607]

In the examples just considered, the defendant is not liable for a loss which is not caused by the breach at all as a matter of "factual" causation. In other cases, even though the loss would not have occurred as matter of fact "but for" the breach, damages are not awarded because the breach is found not to have been a "legal cause" of the loss, or because there has been a break in the "chain of causation". Such decisions go beyond a question of fact and are reached on grounds of legal policy. For example, the mere fact that a company continues to trade in consequence of its auditor's breach of duty in auditing its accounts does not make the auditor liable for losses incurred in the course of such trading: the auditor's breach is, as a matter of "common sense",[608] not an effective cause of the loss.[609]

20–101 **Concurrent causes.** A claimant may recover damages although the breach is not the *sole* cause of the loss. As Devlin J has said: "If a breach of contract is one of two causes, both co-operating and both of equal efficacy, … it is sufficient to carry a judgment for damages".[610] One such situation is dealt with below: the

---

606 See *Monarch SS Co v Karlshamns Oljefabriker (A/B)* [1949] A.C. 196 at 226.

607 *Target Holdings Ltd v Redferns* [1996] A.C. 421; cf. *Banque Keyser Ullman SA v Skandia (UK) Ins Co Ltd* [1991] 2 A.C. 249; *AIB Group (UK) Plc v Mark Redler & Co Plc* [2014] UKSC 58; [2014] 3 W.L.R. 1367; also *Sykes v Midland Bank Executor & Trustee Co Ltd* [1971] 1 Q.B. 113; A.L.G. 87 L.Q.R. 10; *County Natwest v Pinsent & Co* [1994] 3 Bank. L.R. 4; and *Swindle v Harrison* [1997] 4 All E.R. 705 (where damages were awarded for breach of fiduciary duty); *Freeguard v Rogers* [1999] 1 W.L.R. 375.

608 *Galoo v Bright Grahame Murray* [1994] 1 W.L.R. 1360 at 1375.

609 *Galoo v Bright Grahame Murray* [1994] 1 W.L.R. 1360; cf. *Bank of Credit & Commerce International (Overseas) Ltd v Price Waterhouse (No.3)*, *The Times*, 2 April 1998; *Equitable Life Assurance Society v Ernst & Young* [2003] EWCA Civ 1114; [2003] 2 B.C.L.C. 603.

610 *Heskell v Continental Express Ltd* [1950] 1 All E.R. 1033 at 1048; disapproved on another point in *Hedley Byrne & Co Ltd v Heller & Partners Ltd* [1964] A.C. 465 at 532; cf. *Vinmar International Ltd v Theresa Navigation SA* [2001] 2 Lloyd's Rep. 1 at [43]; *Supershield Ltd v Siemens Building Technologies FE Ltd* [2010] EWCA Civ 7; [2010] 1 Lloyd's Rep. 349.

victim of a breach of contract can recover damages for a loss caused partly by the breach and partly by his own lack of means (so long as the loss is not too remote).[611] Again, unseaworthiness is hardly ever the sole cause of a maritime loss: the shipowner is liable though ordinary sea perils have co-operated with unseaworthiness to produce the loss.[612] But he would not be liable if the unseaworthiness led to a delay and the ship then ran into a typhoon as such a catastrophe may occur anywhere[613] and as the delay would not be causally "of equal efficacy" with the typhoon. Nor is the party in breach liable for a loss in fact wholly caused by an extraneous supervening event, even though, if that event had not occurred, the same loss, or part of it, would have been caused by the breach.[614] Further problems of mitigation and contributory negligence, which arise where the concurrent cause is the victim's own conduct, are discussed below.[615]

**Intervening acts of the claimant.** The chain of causation which leads from the breach is only broken by an intervening act of the claimant when it can be shown[616] that the "true" cause of the loss is the conduct of the claimant.[617] As seen above,[618] it will not normally be sufficient to show that the breach and the claimant's subsequent conduct are concurrent causes.[619] The more unreasonable the conduct of the claimant, the more likely that the chain of causation will have been broken; conduct which amounts to recklessness is likely to be sufficient, but there is no rule of law that only this will do.[620] In assessing the reasonableness of his conduct, the state of knowledge of the claimant is an important factor. In *Lambert v Lewis*[621] the defendant supplied a defective towing hitch which led to an accident for which the claimant was held liable to a third party. The defendant was not liable to indemnify the claimant because the claimant had become aware, or ought to have been aware,[622] that the coupling mechanism in the hitch was damaged and he had failed to have it repaired or ascertain whether it was safe to use. By contrast, in *Borealis AB v Geogas Trading SA*[623] the defendant supplied **20–102**

611 See para.20–134.
612 *Smith, Hogg & Co Ltd v Black Sea Ins Co Ltd* [1940] A.C. 997.
613 *Monarch SS Co v Karlshamns Oljefabriker (A/B)* [1949] A.C. 196 at 215.
614 *Beoco Ltd v Alfa Laval Co Ltd* [1995] Q.B. 137.
615 See paras 20–104, 20–112.
616 There is an evidential burden on the defendant, but the legal burden of proving his loss remains on the claimant: *Borealis AB v Geogas Trading SA* [2010] EWHC 2789 (Comm); [2011] 1 Lloyd's Rep. 482 at [43].
617 *Borealis AB v Geogas Trading SA* [2010] EWHC 2789 (Comm); [2011] 1 Lloyd's Rep. 482 at [44]; *Barings Plc v Coopers & Lybrand* [2003] EWHC 1319 (Ch) at [838].
618 See para.20–101.
619 *County Ltd v Girozentrale* [1996] 3 All E.R. 834 at 849, 857, 858.
620 *County Ltd v Girozentrale* [1996] 3 All E.R. 834 at 857; *Lambert v Lewis* [1982] A.C. 225 at 252; *Borealis AB v Geogas Trading SA* [2010] EWHC 2789 (Comm); [2011] 1 Lloyd's Rep. 482 at [45].
621 [1982] A.C. 225; cf. *Schering Agrochemicals Ltd v Resibel NV SA* unreported 26 November 1992 CA.
622 It was "staring him in the face": *Borealis AB v Geogas Trading SA* [2010] EWHC 2789 (Comm); [2011] 1 Lloyd's Rep. 482 at [103].
623 [2010] EWHC 2789 (Comm); [2011] 1 Lloyd's Rep. 482; cf. *County Ltd v Girozentrale* [1996] 3 All E.R. 834; *Flanagan v Greenbanks Ltd* [2013] EWCA Civ 1702; 151 Con L.R. 98; *Stacey v Autosleeper Group Ltd* [2014] EWCA Civ 1551.

butane feedstock contaminated with fluorides which produced hydrochloric acid and led to extensive damage to the claimant's plant and equipment. A test of the feedstock shortly after discharge indicated a low pH reading, but the claimant took no further action. There had been no experience that low pH was harmful to the plant or equipment and it did not indicate what type of acid might be present; the claimant did not know and could not reasonably have been expected to know of the kind of acid introduced into the system by the breach of contract. Although the claimant's conduct fell below "best practice", it was not sufficiently unreasonable to break the chain of causation.

20–103 **Intervening acts of third party.** Where loss results partly from the breach and partly from the act of a third party, the party in breach is nevertheless liable for the loss if (but only if)[624] the third party's act was "foreseeable" on the standard of probability which governs remoteness in contract.[625] Thus a person who in breach of contract recommends a dishonest stockbroker is liable for loss caused by the broker's dishonesty;[626] and a house-painter who in breach of contract leaves his client's house unlocked is liable for the value of goods taken from it by thieves.[627] These cases show that, although remoteness and causation are "quite different concepts" (so that a loss may be too remote even though it is clearly caused by the breach)[628] nevertheless "some of the relevant considerations are the same".[629]

In *Weld-Blundell v Stephens*[630] a client employed an accountant to investigate the affairs of a company and wrote him a letter defaming two of the company's directors. The accountant's partner negligently dropped the letter in the company's office, where it was picked up by the manager and shown to the two directors. They recovered heavy damages for libel from the client who, in turn, claimed this amount from the accountant as damages for breach of contract. The House of Lords gave two reasons for dismissing the claim. First, the client's liability for defamation *existed* quite apart from the breach of contract, which simply brought that liability to the directors' attention.[631] Secondly, the loss was not caused by the breach, but by the act of the manager in showing the letter to the directors, and this act was *not* one which the defendant could have foreseen. The view that the manager's act was not foreseeable may be regarded with some scepticism, particularly as the jury found that it was the defendant's duty to keep the letter secret. But it forms one basis of *Weld-Blundell v Stephens*. The case

---

[624] *The Silver Sky* [1981] 2 Lloyd's Rep. 95.

[625] See para.20–119 and following; *Monarch SS Co v Karlshamns Oljefabriker (A/B)* [1949] A.C. 196; *British Racing Drivers' Club v Hextall Erskine & Co* [1996] 3 All E.R. 667.

[626] *De la Bere v Pearson Ltd* [1908] 1 K.B. 280; cf. *T v Surrey CC* [1994] 4 All E.R. 577 (child-minder); *Sasea Finance Ltd v KPMG* [2000] 1 All E.R. 676 (auditor failing to warn company of senior executives' fraud); cf. *Stone & Rolls Ltd v Moore Stephens* [2009] UKHL 39; [2009] 1 A.C. 1391, para.11–024.

[627] *Stansbie v Troman* [1948] 2 K.B. 48; cf. *Marshall v Rubypoint Ltd* [1997] E.G.C.S. 12.

[628] As in *Bates v Barrow Ltd* [1995] 1 Lloyd's Rep. 680.

[629] *The Yanxilas (No.2)* [1984] 1 Lloyd's Rep. 676 at 682; *The Eurus* [1998] 1 Lloyd's Rep. 351 at 362.

[630] [1920] A.C. 956.

[631] cf. *Clark v Kirby-Smith* [1964] Ch. 506.

does not support the proposition that a party who breaks a contract can escape liability for loss caused partly by his breach and partly by a *foreseeable* intervening act.

## (b) Mitigation

Two ideas are usually discussed under this heading. The first is that the claimant cannot recover damages for a loss that he ought to have avoided. He is said to be under a "*duty to* mitigate". This expression will be used here even though it is open to the objection that breach of the "duty" gives rise to no legal liability[632] but only reduces the amount that the claimant can recover. The second idea is that the claimant has to give credit for certain benefits accruing to him in consequence of the breach. Here it can be said that his loss is *in fact* mitigated. In both cases, the operative principle is causation; the claimant cannot recover for loss which was *caused* by his unreasonable failure to mitigate and must account for any benefit which was *caused* by the breach and not some independent event.[633] **20–104**

### (i) *The duty to mitigate*

There are two aspects to the duty to mitigate: first, the claimant must take reasonable steps to minimise his loss; and secondly he must forbear from taking unreasonable steps that increase his loss.[634] The duty will normally arise only when the claimant has become aware of the breach[635] and not merely because he was careless in failing to discover it; but such carelessness might be relevant for other purposes, e.g. in making the loss (or part of it) too remote or in reducing the amount recoverable on the ground of contributory negligence.[636] These techniques would normally lead to much the same result as the principles of mitigation; but it is submitted that there is no compelling reason for holding that those principles can never apply where the claimant had, but failed to take, clear opportunities of discovering the breach, e.g. where a buyer is warned of the need to test the goods but fails to do so. **20–105**

**Failure to minimise loss.**[637] If the claimant fails to take reasonable steps to minimise his loss, he cannot recover anything in respect of loss due to that failure. Commonly, he is required to make a substitute contract. For example, where a seller of goods fails to deliver, the buyer must go into the market[638] at the **20–106**

---

[632] *The Solholt* [1983] 1 Lloyd's Rep. 605 at 608; Lomnicka 99 L.Q.R. 495; *The Alecos M* [1991] 1 Lloyd's Rep. 120 at 124.

[633] In making this observation, I acknowledge the insights provided by supervising the thesis of Dr Andrew Summers: Summers, *Mitigation in the Law of Damages* (2020).

[634] For the burden of proof on this issue, see para.21–015, at fn.62.

[635] *The Superhulls Cover Case (No.2)* [1990] 2 Lloyd's Rep. 431 at 461.

[636] *The Superhulls Cover Case (No.2)* [1990] 2 Lloyd's Rep. 431 at 462; para.20–112.

[637] Bridge 105 L.Q.R. 398.

[638] If there are several markets, a transaction in any market that it was reasonable for the injured party to use can form the basis of assessment: *Gebruder Metelmann GmbH & Co KG v NBR (London) Ltd* [1984] 1 Lloyd's Rep. 614, a case of buyer's breach.

relevant time[639] to buy substitute goods. If he fails to do so he cannot recover any further loss that he may suffer because the market continues to rise or because he is deprived of the opportunity of making a profit out of the use or resale of the goods.[640] Conversely, a seller of shares who kept them after the buyer's breach could not recover any further loss that he might suffer as a result of a later fall in the market.[641] The injured party is, however, required to mitigate in this way only if the new transaction would be a true substitute for the old one. Where, for example, a customer wrongfully repudiates a contract for the provision of services at a time when the injured party has spare capacity, then the possibility of that party's making another contract with a new customer will not be taken into account: such a new contract will not be a true substitute for the broken contract since the injured party would, but for the breach, have been able to perform both contracts.[642]

Where the breach has induced the injured party not to claim sums due to him from third parties, the mitigation rules may require him to assert these claims.[643] But this is subject to the overriding rule that he need only take such steps as are reasonable: he therefore does not need to take steps which would involve him in complicated litigation,[644] or which would ruin his commercial reputation,[645] or which would involve him in unreasonable expense or inconvenience.[646]

20–107 **Accepting substitute performance from party in breach.** Sometimes the injured party will be required to mitigate by accepting from the party in breach a performance which differs in some way from that originally bargained for. Thus, where a charterer fails to load the agreed cargo, the shipowner may be bound to mitigate by accepting the charterer's reasonable offer of alternative cargo, even at a lower rate;[647] where a seller agrees to give credit and then refuses to deliver except for cash, the buyer may be bound to mitigate by accepting such delivery instead of buying against the seller on a rising market;[648] and where a seller cannot deliver at the agreed time the buyer may be required to mitigate by

639 See para.20–076 and following.

640 *Hussey v Eels* [1990] 2 Q.B. 227 at 233 ("deemed mitigation"); cf. *The Marine Star (No.2)* [1994] 2 Lloyd's Rep. 629 at 635 (reversed on another ground [1996] 2 Lloyd's Rep. 383); *The Elena D'Amico* [1980] 1 Lloyd's Rep. 75 at 79 (charterparty); and see para.20–051.

641 *Jamal v Moolla Dawood Sons & Co* [1916] 1 A.C. 175 at 179; cf. *Bristol & West BS v Fancy & Jackson* [1997] 4 All E.R. 582 at 623 (delay in realising security).

642 *Western Web Offset Printers Ltd v Independent Media Ltd*, *The Times*, 10 October 1995; cf. para.20–061.

643 *St Albans City & District Council v International Computers Ltd* [1996] 4 All E.R. 481 (the £484,000 claim).

644 *Pilkington v Wood* [1953] Ch. 770; *The Ines* [1995] 2 Lloyd's Rep. 144 at 159; *Markel International Insurance Co Ltd v Surety Guarantee Consultants Ltd* [2008] EWHC 3087 (Comm); cf. *The Greek Fighter* [2006] EWHC 1729 (Comm); [2006] 2 C.L.C. 497 at [340] and following.

645 *James Finlay & Co Ltd v NV Kwik Hoo Tong HM* [1929] 1 K.B. 400; cf. *London & South of England Building Society v Stone* [1983] 1 W.L.R. 1242 (building society not required to enforce borrower's *personal* covenant).

646 *The Griparion* [1994] 1 Lloyd's Rep. 533; *Hussey v Eels* [1990] 2 Q.B. 227; *Zodiac Maritime Agencies Ltd v Fortescue Metals Group Ltd* [2010] EWHC 903 (Comm); [2011] 2 Lloyd's Rep. 360 at [65].

647 *Harries v Edmonds* (1845) 1 Car. & K. 686.

648 *Payzu Ltd v Saunders* [1919] 2 K.B. 581; contrast *Harlow & Jones Ltd v Panex International Ltd* [1967] 2 Lloyd's Rep. 509 at 530 (claimant "not bound to nurse the interests of the contract breaker").

accepting late delivery.[649] In these cases, any loss suffered by the injured party by reason of the difference between the performance rendered and that originally bargained for can easily and adequately be allowed for in damages. He is not required to mitigate by accepting an offer of modified performance which purports to extinguish his right to such damages.[650] Nor is the injured party bound to mitigate by accepting an offer of modified performance if the offer is unclear,[651] or if it is not made in good faith and is nothing more than a "litigation stratagem",[652] or if the modification causes him substantial prejudice, e.g. a buyer of goods need not mitigate by accepting the seller's tender of goods of a lower quality than contracted for, even with an allowance for the inferiority.[653] On a somewhat similar principle, an employee who has been wrongfully dismissed need not accept an offer of re-employment involving a reduction in status,[654] or a lower grade of work;[655] nor need he accept the former employer's offer to take him back, even on the original terms, if the wrongful dismissal occurred in circumstances of personal humiliation, e.g. on a charge of misconduct made before others.[656]

**Unreasonably augmenting loss.** If the claimant acts unreasonably in attempting to mitigate, he cannot recover further loss which he suffers as a result.[657] Thus in general he should not, for example, spend more on curing a defect in performance than the subject-matter without the defect would be worth;[658] nor should he continue to incur expense for the purpose of tendering performance after the other party has clearly indicated that he will refuse to accept it. But these are only general rules: the crucial question in each case is whether the claimant has acted reasonably.[659] The point is strikingly illustrated by *Banco de Portugal v Waterlow & Sons Ltd.*[660] The defendants had contracted to print banknotes for the Bank of Portugal, and in breach of contract delivered a large number of these to a criminal, who put them into circulation in Portugal. On discovering this, the Bank withdrew the issue and undertook to exchange all the notes in question for others. The defendants argued that they were liable only for the cost of printing the **20–108**

---

[649] *The Solholt* [1983] 1 Lloyd's Rep. 605.

[650] *Shindler v Northern Raincoat Co Ltd* [1960] 1 W.L.R. 1038; *Velmore Estates v Roseberry Homes Ltd* [2005] EWHC 3061; cf. *Strutt v Whitnell* [1975] 1 W.L.R. 870 (said in *The Solholt* [1983] 1 Lloyd's Rep. 605 at 609 to turn "on its own special facts").

[651] *Manton Hire and Sales Ltd v Ash Manor Chees Co Ltd* [2013] EWCA Civ 548.

[652] *Gul Bottlers (PVT) Ltd v Nichols Plc* [2014] EWHC 2173 (Comm) at [26].

[653] *Heaven & Kesterton Ltd v Et François Albiac & Cie* [1956] 2 Lloyd's Rep. 316 at 321.

[654] *Yetton v Eastwood Froy Ltd* [1967] 1 W.L.R. 104.

[655] cf. *Edwards v SOGAT* [1971] 1 Ch. 354.

[656] *Payzu Ltd v Saunders* [1919] 2 K.B. 581 at 589; in the absence of such circumstances it was held in *Brace v Calder* [1895] 2 K.B. 253 that an offer of re-employment should have been accepted.

[657] *The Borag* [1981] 1 W.L.R. 274; *Seven Seas Properties Ltd v Al-Essa* [1988] 1 W.L.R. 1272 at 1276 (the reasoning of the case is obsolete on its facts in view of Law of Property (Miscellaneous Provisions) Act 1989 s.3).

[658] cf. para.20–042; *Darbishire v Warran* [1963] 1 W.L.R. 1067—a tort case; *Grant v Dawkins* [1973] 1 W.L.R. 1406; for an exception see *O'Grady v Westminster Scaffolding Ltd* [1962] 2 Lloyd's Rep. 238—another tort case.

[659] *LSREF III Wight Ltd v Gateley LLP* [2016] EWCA Civ 359; [2016] P.N.L.R. 21.

[660] [1932] A.C. 452.

notes: any further loss was due to the Bank's own act.[661] But the House of Lords, by a majority, held the defendants liable for the full face value of the notes as the conduct of the Bank was reasonable, having regard to its commercial obligations towards the public.[662] A similar result was reached where a manufacturer of soft drinks had been supplied with contaminated ingredients. It was held that, in withdrawing and destroying products containing the ingredient, the manufacturer had acted reasonably to protect its reputation, even though the contamination posed only a negligible risk to health; and that the supplier of the ingredient was liable for the manufacturer's wasted costs.[663]

On the same principle, the claimant may be able to recover amounts paid in reasonable settlement of a liability to a third party incurred in consequence of the breach.[664] Conversely, if the claimant decides to resist a claim brought against him by a third party as a result[665] of the breach, he may be able to recover legal expenses incurred in the proceedings between him and the third party. Thus a buyer can recover from the seller costs reasonably incurred in defending an action brought against him by a sub-buyer on account of a defect for which the seller is liable.[666] Similarly a person who sues an agent for breach of implied warranty of authority can recover costs thrown away in a previous action brought against the principal on the assumption that the agent had the authority he claimed to have.[667] But the costs must be reasonably incurred: the claimant cannot recover them if he persists in litigating when it is clear that he has no chance of success.[668]

20–109 **Recovery of reasonably incurred further loss.** It is possible for steps taken in performance of the duty to mitigate to be reasonable, but actually to increase the loss.[669] For example, a buyer who accepts a seller's anticipatory breach is bound to mitigate by buying a substitute in the market at the time of acceptance. If, when he makes the substitute purchase, the market price exceeds the contract price, he can recover the excess. This is so even though by the time fixed for

---

661 Portuguese currency was not convertible into gold; the bank had a monopoly of issuing notes as legal tender; and, although the amount of notes it could issue was limited by law, the limit had not been reached.

662 cf. at fn.645; and see *Buildings and Civil Engineering Holidays Scheme Management Ltd v Post Office* [1966] 1 Q.B. 247 (where the claim was not in contract).

663 *Britvic Soft Drinks Ltd v Messer UK Ltd* [2002] 1 Lloyd's Rep. 20 at [114]; affirmed [2002] EWCA Civ 548; [2002] 2 All E.R. (Comm) 321, without reference to this point.

664 *Biggin & Co Ltd v Permanite Ltd* [1951] 2 K.B. 314; *Bulk Oil (Zug) AG v Sun International Ltd* [1984] 1 Lloyd's Rep. 531 at 544; *Royal Brompton NHS Trust v Hammond* [1999] N.L.J. 89; contrast *Anglian Water Services Ltd v Crawshaw Robbins & Co* [2001] B.L.R. 173 (where loss of this kind was too remote).

665 See *The Antaios* [1981] 2 Lloyd's Rep. 284 at 299.

666 *Hammond & Co v Bussey* (1887) 20 Q.B.D. 79; *Lloyds & Scottish Finance Ltd v Modern Cars & Caravans (Kingston) Ltd* [1966] 1 Q.B. 764; *Bowmaker (Commercial) Ltd v Day* [1965] 1 W.L.R. 1396; cf. *The Saragasso* [1994] 1 Lloyd's Rep. 412.

667 *Hughes v Graeme* (1864) 33 L.J.Q.B. 335; *Godwin v Francis* (1870) L.R. 5 C.P. 295.

668 *Pow v Davies* (1861) 1 B. & S. 220; *Baxendale v London, Chatham & Dover Ry* (1874) L.R. 10 Ex. 38.

669 *Choil Trading SA v Sahara Energy Resources Ltd* [2010] EWHC 374 (Comm).

delivery the market price has fallen below the contract price so that the buyer, if he had not performed the duty to mitigate, would have suffered no loss at all.[670]

### *(ii) Mitigation in fact*

**Benefits accrued as a result of breach.** Loss is sometimes said to be "mitigated" where some benefit in fact accrues[671] to the claimant as a result of the breach. If, for example, he is released from his own obligation to perform, this fact is taken into account in deciding how much, if anything, he has lost.[672] Or he may benefit from performing his duty to mitigate, e.g. by finding a job comparable to that from which he was wrongfully dismissed.[673] Here again his earnings in the other job will be taken into account in assessing his damages for wrongful dismissal.[674] The principle underlying such cases is that the purpose of an award of damages is "to compensate [the claimant] for his loss, not to enrich him".[675] 20–110

There is a further group of cases in which the claimant benefits from doing something that he was *not required* to do in performance of his duty to mitigate, e.g. a wrongfully dismissed employee may take a job involving a reduction in status. His actual earnings in that job are taken into account in assessing damages, even though it was a job that he was not required to take in performance of his duty to mitigate.[676] But some benefits of this kind are not taken into account; and the distinction between the two kinds of benefit is illustrated by *Lavarack v Woods of Colchester Ltd*.[677] The claimant was wrongfully dismissed from his employment with the defendants and so freed from a provision in his contract with them that he should not, without their written consent, be engaged or interested in any other concern (except as a holder of investments quoted on a stock exchange). After his dismissal, he: (1) took employment with the X Co at a lower salary than he had earned with the defendants; (2) acquired half the shares in the X Co; and (3) invested money in shares in the Y Co. The value of the shares in both companies having risen, it was held that the increase in the value of the X Co shares, but not that of the Y Co shares, must be taken into account in

---

[670] *Melachrino v Nickoll & Knight* [1920] 1 K.B. 693 at 697.

[671] e.g. *Platt v London Underground Ltd*, *The Times*, 13 March 2001. "Benefit" here includes avoided loss: *The Kriti Rex* [1996] 2 Lloyd's Rep. 171 at 203.

[672] See para.20–006. See also *Levison v Farin* [1978] 2 All E.R. 1149; *C & P Haulage v Middleton* [1983] 1 W.L.R. 1461.

[673] cf. *Evans Marshall & Co v Bertola* [1976] 2 Lloyd's Rep. 17.

[674] e.g. *Cerberus Software Ltd v Rowley* [2001] EWCA Civ 74; [2001] I.C.R. 376; unless the contract otherwise provides, as in *Gregory v Wallace* [1998] I.R.L.R. 387. For the position in cases of unfair dismissal (which generally does not involve any breach of contract) see Employment Rights Act 1996 s.123(4).

[675] *Longden v British Coal Corp* [1998] A.C. 653 at 662; cf. in tort, *Dimond v Lovell* [2002] 1 A.C. 384.

[676] See para.20–107; see *Edwards v SOGAT* [1971] Ch. 354; *S of S for Employment v Wilson* [1978] 1 W.L.R. 568; cf. *The Concordia C* [1985] 2 Lloyd's Rep. 55; *Dalwood Marine Co v Nordana Line AS* [2009] EWHC 3394 (Comm); [2010] 2 Lloyd's Rep. 315.

[677] [1967] 1 Q.B. 278.

reducing the claimant's damages. The former was regarded as a disguised remuneration, while the latter was "not a direct result of his dismissal" but a "collateral benefit".[678]

The decision to leave out of account a rise in the value of the Y Co shares can be tested by asking whether the claimant could have recovered additional damages if they had fallen in value. Clearly, it would seem wrong to increase the damages payable by the defendant employer, notwithstanding that the opportunity to purchase the Y Co shares only arose as a consequence of the breach; the claimant took a risk for his own account which amounted to a break in the chain of causation. Similarly, where a shipowner took the opportunity to sell a vessel when the charterer terminated a charterparty with two years to run, at the end of which the market price of the vessel was much lower. The court did not take into account the "gain" from having sold the vessel earlier since that was an independent commercial decision of the shipowner which it could have taken at any time and not necessarily at the end of the charterparty.[679]

20–111 **Whether benefit is "collateral".** Whether a benefit is "collateral" or a "direct result" of the breach is a question of causation which is not always easy to resolve.[680] As Lord Sumption has stated:

> "It is difficult to identify a single principle underlying every case … [but] … [b]roadly speaking, collateral benefits are those whose receipt arose independently of the circumstances giving rise to the loss."[681]

It follows from this requirement that damages will not be reduced by reason of any insurance taken out by the injured party against the consequences of the breach[682] (unless the contract provides that the injured party's sole remedy is to be against the insurer);[683] or by reason of the fact that the victim is compensated for the loss under some other contract with a third party,[684] or that gratuitous benefits have been conferred on the victim in respect of the loss by a third

---

678 *Lavarack v Woods of Colchester Ltd* [1967] 1 Q.B. 278 at 290; cf. *Aruna Mills Ltd v Dhanrajmal Gobindram* [1968] 1 Q.B. 655 at 669; *Mobil North Sea Ltd v PJ Pipe & Valve Co* [2001] EWCA Civ 741; [2001] 2 All E.R. (Comm) 289.

679 *The New Flamenco* [2017] UKSC 43; [2017] 1 W.L.R. 2581; cf. *Thai Airways International Public Co Ltd v KI Holdings Co Ltd* [2015] EWHC 1250 (Comm); [2015] 1 C.L.C. 765.

680 It has been said to require a "common sense overall judgment on the sufficiency of the causal nexus between breach and profit or loss", *The Fanis* [1994] 1 Lloyd's Rep. 633 at 637.

681 *Lowick Rose LLP v Swynson Ltd* [2017] UKSC 32; [2018] A.C. 313 at [11].

682 cf. *Bradburn v Great Western Ry* (1874) L.R. 10 Ex. 1; *The Yasin* [1979] 2 Lloyd's Rep. 45; *Brown v KMR Services* [1994] 4 All E.R. 385 at 399 (varied on other grounds [1995] 4 All E.R. 598). Other techniques for avoiding double recovery in such cases are illustrated by *Arab Bank Plc v John D Wood* [2000] 1 W.L.R. 857; and *Amec Civil Engineering Ltd v Cheshire CC* [1999] B.L.R. 303.

683 *Mark Rowlands Ltd v Berni Inns Ltd* [1986] Q.B. 211; *Bristol & West BS v May, May & Merrimans (No.2)* [1998] 1 W.L.R. 306.

684 *Gardner v Marsh Parsons* [1997] 1 W.L.R. 489. For a possible qualification of this principle where a settlement agreement between one of two wrongdoers and the victim on its true construction covers the loss resulting from both breaches, see the discussion at para.13–018 of *Heaton v Axa Equity and Law Life Assurance Society Plc* [2002] UKHL 15; [2002] 2 A.C. 329, where the agreement was held to release the other wrongdoer.

party[685] who was under no legal obligation to act in this way.[686] An attempt to extend the well-established categories of insurance and benevolent third party payments was rejected by the Supreme Court in *Lowick Rose v Swynson Ltd*.[687] In that case the claimant sought damages for loss incurred under loans entered into as a consequence of the defendant's negligence, but the loans were, in fact, repaid because of a loan made by the claimant's owner to the borrowers. An analogy with the category of benevolent third party payments would have been appropriate if the claimant's owner had made a payment to the claimant, but a payment to the borrower to enable the loans to be repaid "could not possibly be regarded as collateral".[688] It "discharged the very liability whose existence represented [the claimant's] loss"[689] and the fact that this was achieved through money borrowed from the claimant's owner "was no more relevant than it would have been if it had been borrowed from a bank or obtained from some other unconnected party".[690]

A more difficult case is provided by *British Westinghouse Co v Underground Electric Rys Co of London*.[691] A agreed to supply B with turbines of a stated efficiency but supplied less efficient ones, which used more coal. B accepted and used them, reserving his right to claim damages. After some years, and before A's turbines were worn out, B replaced them with others. These were so much more efficient than A's would have been, even had they been in accordance with the contract, that, over the whole period during which A's turbines might have been expected to last, B actually used less coal than he would have done with turbines of the efficiency stated in the contract. The House of Lords held that B was under no duty to mitigate by buying new turbines.[692] But as he had bought the new turbines in consequence of A's breach, the financial advantage he gained by using them had to be set off against the cost of buying them. As B's savings in coal exceeded that cost, he recovered nothing in respect of it. This was so even though it could be argued that the benefit thus obtained by B was only in part the result of the breach; for the turbines originally contracted for had become obsolete so that a reasonable businessman would have replaced them even if they had been in accordance with the contract.[693] On the other hand, B had also, *before* replacing the turbines, suffered loss because the cost of operating them was greater than it

[685] Not where the benefit is conferred by the party in breach: *Williams v BOC Gases Ltd* [2000] I.C.R. 1181; cf. (in tort), *Hunt v Severs* [1994] 2 A.C. 350.

[686] *Merrett v Capitol Indemnity Corp* [1991] 1 Lloyd's Rep. 169; *Linklaters Business Services v Sir Robert McAlpine Ltd* [2010] EWHC 2931 (TCC); 133 Con L.R. 211 at [159]–[163].

[687] [2017] UKSC 32; [2018] A.C. 313; cf. *Tiuta International Ltd v De Villiers Surveyors Ltd* [2017] UKSC 77; [2017] 1 W.L.R. 4627.

[688] The rather unusual, and costly, conduct of the owner was explained by fiscal considerations and the fact that he wished to remove the bad loans from the claimant's books.

[689] *Lowick Rose LLP v Swynson Ltd* [2017] UKSC 32; [2018] A.C. 313 at [13].

[690] *Lowick Rose LLP v Swynson Ltd* [2017] UKSC 32; [2018] A.C. 313 at [12].

[691] [1912] A.C. 673; cf. *Erie County Natural Gas Co v Carroll* [1911] A.C. 105; *Levison v Farin* [1978] 2 All E.R. 1149; *Merrett v Capitol Indemnity Corp* [1991] 1 Lloyd's Rep. 169.

[692] In this respect the case differs from *Bellingham v Dhillon* [1973] Q.B. 304 (a tort case purporting to follow the *British Westinghouse* case and approved in *Dimond v Lovell* [2002] 1 A.C. 384).

[693] *British Westinghouse Co v Underground Electric Rys Co of London* [1912] A.C. 675 at 691.

would have been if they had been in accordance with the contract. This loss was not diminished as a result of the purchase of the new turbines and was accordingly recoverable.[694]

A case in which a benefit was plainly found to be collateral is provided by *Hussey v Eels*.[695] The claimants had been induced to buy a house as their home by a misrepresentation[696] that there had been no subsidence. More than two years later, they decided to demolish the house and resold the site for one-and-a-half times the price which they had paid, having obtained planning permission for two dwellings on the site. On the assumption that this resale yielded a profit[697] to the claimants, it was held that this was not to be taken into account: the wrong which had caused their loss had not also caused the gain as the resale was "not … part of a continuous transaction of which the purchase … was the inception".[698]

### (c) Contributory negligence

20–112 Where the injured party fails to perform the "duty" to mitigate, his damages are reduced because it can be said that he is at fault in failing to avoid loss. He may also be at fault in the sense of actually helping to bring about the loss or the event causing it.[699] In the law of tort, such conduct may lead to a defence of "contributory negligence". At common law, it in some cases totally barred the injured party's claim, while in others it was completely ignored, so that he recovered in full. The Law Reform (Contributory Negligence) Act 1945 now provides that, where a person suffers damage as a result partly of his own "fault" and partly of the "fault" of another person, his claim is not to be defeated, but his damages are to be reduced in proportion to his degree of responsibility.

20–113 **The Law Reform (Contributory Negligence) Act 1945.** Whether the 1945 Act applies in cases of breach of contract depends on the interpretation of "fault" in the Act which is defined as "negligence, breach of statutory duty, or other act or omission which gives rise to liability in tort or would, apart from this Act, give rise to the defence of contributory negligence". It has been argued that this includes *all* negligence, whether contractual[700] or tortious, and all *other* acts

[694] *British Westinghouse Co v Underground Electric Rys Co of London* [1912] A.C. 675 at 688.
[695] [1990] 2 Q.B. 227; cf. *Quilter v Hodson Developments Ltd* [2016] EWCA Civ 1125; [2017] P.N.L.R. 7. Contrast: *Bacciottini v Gotelee & Goldsmith* [2016] EWCA Civ 170; [2016] 4 W.L.R. 98.
[696] Not incorporated in the contract, so that the cause of action was in tort; but the judgment is based on earlier decisions in contract cases; cf. *Komercni Banka AS v Stone & Rolls Ltd* [2002] EWHC 2263 (Comm); [2003] 1 Lloyd's Rep. 383 at [167] (fraud).
[697] This depended on the cost of comparable accommodation at the time of the resale, as "The [claimants] were not property speculators but residents": *Hussey v Eels* [1990] 2 Q.B. 227 at 233.
[698] *Hussey v Eels* [1990] 2 Q.B. 227 at 241; cf. *Needler Financial Services v Taber* [2002] 3 All E.R. 501; *Primavera v Allied Dunbar Assurance Plc* [2002] EWCA Civ 1327; [2003] P.N.L.R. 12.
[699] See para.20–102.
[700] See at fnn.703 and 706–708.

giving rise to liability in tort.[701] But the word "other" supports the view that negligence is here used in its tortious sense.[702]

It does not, however, follow from this interpretation of "fault" that the Act can never apply to cases of breach of contract. Two further distinctions must be drawn. The first is between breaches of contract that are, and those that are not, negligent. Here the phrase "negligent breach of contract" refers to situations in which liability arises for breach of a contractual duty of care[703]—not to cases in which liability for breach of contract is strict,[704] but the breach happens to have been committed negligently.[705] The second distinction is between breaches of contract which amount also to torts and those which do not. The content of a contractual duty of care is often the same as that of the duty of care which the law of tort would impose, even if there were no contract between the parties; and in such cases the same careless conduct prima facie gives rise to liability both for breach of contract and in tort.[706] For example, the liability of many professional persons for breach of the duties of care that they owe to their clients arises both in contract and tort.[707] The same is true of duties arising out of a number of other contractual relationships, such as those between carrier and passenger, employer and employee, bailor and bailee, or occupier of premises and visitor.[708] The breach will not, however, amount to a tort where the imposition of a tortious duty would be "so inconsistent with the applicable contract that … the parties must be taken to have agreed that the tortious remedy is to be limited or excluded".[709] This possibility is illustrated by a case[710] in which a building subcontractor had entered into a direct contract with the building owner (and not merely into one

---

[701] Williams, *Joint Torts and Contributory Negligence* (1951), para.59.

[702] *Forsikringsaktieselskapet Vesta v Butcher* [1989] A.C. 852 CA; affirmed [1989] A.C. 880, without reference to this point; Newman 53 M.L.R. 201; cf. (in another statutory context) *Société Commerciale de Réassurance v ERAS International Ltd* [1992] 1 Lloyd's Rep. 570.

[703] *Quinn v Burch Bros (Builders) Ltd* [1966] 2 Q.B. 370 at 378–379 (affirmed on other grounds; ibid. at 381).

[704] cf. paras 17–065–17–066.

[705] *Quinn v Burch Bros (Builders) Ltd* [1966] 2 Q.B. 370 at 378–379.

[706] *Henderson v Merrett Syndicates Ltd* [1995] 2 A.C. 145 at 193.

[707] *Esso Petroleum Co Ltd v Mardon* [1976] Q.B. 801 at 819; *Arenson v Arenson* [1977] A.C. 405 at 420–421; *ForsikringsaktieselskapetVesta v Butcher* [1989] A.C. 852 at 860; affirmed on other grounds [1989] A.C. 880; *Henderson v Merrett Syndicates Ltd* [1995] 2 A.C. 145; *South Australia Asset Management Corp v York Montague Ltd* [1997] A.C. 191 at 211; *Nykreditbank v Edward Erdman Group* [1997] 1 W.L.R. 1327 at 1368.

[708] *Bagot v Stevens, Scanlan & Co Ltd* [1966] 1 Q.B. 197 at 204–205; cf. *Matthews v Kuwait Bechtel Corp* [1959] 2 Q.B. 57; *Sayers v Harlow UDC* [1958] 1 W.L.R. 623; *Johnson v Coventry Churchill International Ltd* [1992] 3 All E.R. 14 at 22–23; *The Angelic Grace* [1995] 1 Lloyd's Rep. 87 at 91; *Spring v Guardian Ins Plc* [1995] 2 A.C. 296 at 320; cf. at 340. But where the same facts are alleged to give rise to a claim in contract and in tort, the injured party cannot, after failing in contract, succeed by simply reclassifying his claim as one in tort: *Tai Hing Cotton Mill Ltd v Liu Chong Hing Bank* [1986] A.C. 80 at 107; *The Maira (No.3)* [1990] 1 A.C. 637 at 650 (reversed on other grounds 1990] 1 A.C. 637 at 672 and following); *Reid v Rush and Tompkins Group Plc* [1990] 1 W.L.R. 212.

[709] *Henderson v Merrett Syndicates Ltd* [1995] 2 A.C. 145 at 194.

[710] *Greater Nottingham Co-operative Society Ltd v Cementation Piling & Foundation Ltd* [1989] Q.B. 71; cf. *Tai Hing Cotton Mill Ltd v Liu Chong, Hing Bank* [1986] A.C. 80 at 107; *Johnstone v Bloomsbury Health Authority* [1992] Q.B. 333; *Scally v Southern Health & Social Services Board* [1992] 1 A.C. 294 at 303; *Aiken v Stewart Wrightson Members Agency Ltd* [1995] 1 W.L.R. 1281; *Robinson v PE Jones (Contractors) Ltd* [2011] EWCA Civ 9; [2011] 3 W.L.R. 815.

with the main contractor).[711] The court inferred from the nature of this arrangement that the parties had intended the relationship between owner and sub-contractor to be governed by the contract alone, so that the sub-contractor was not liable to the owner in tort. It follows from these distinctions that three categories of cases must be considered in discussing the application of the 1945 Act to cases involving breach of contract.[712]

20–114 **Breach of strict contractual duty alone.** The first category is where the defendant commits a breach of a strict contractual duty; and the claimant is careless. The Act does not apply: A's conduct, not being an act or omission giving rise to liability in tort falls outside the definition of "fault".[713] Hence at common law the result will depend on which party's conduct caused the loss.[714]

20–115 **Breach of contractual duty of care alone.** In the second category of case, the defendant commits a breach of a contractual duty of care; his conduct does not also amount to a tort, because the relations of the parties are intended to be governed by the contract alone;[715] and the claimant is also careless. Following the decision of the House of Lords in *Henderson v Merrett Syndicates Ltd*,[716] the circumstances in which the defendant is not also liable in tort are likely to be very limited, but for cases falling within this category, the Act does not apply;[717] the defendant's conduct may have been contractually negligent, but for the purpose of the Act it does not amount to "negligence ... or other act or omission which gives rise to liability in tort."

20–116 **Breach of contractual duty of care also amounting to a tort.** In the third category of case, the defendant commits a breach of a contractual duty of care; his conduct also amounts to a tort; and the claimant is also careless. The Act can apply to such a situation, e.g. where the claimant is injured partly through his own carelessness and partly through circumstances amounting both to a breach of contract by the defendant and to a breach of his duties as an occupier of

[711] cf. para.14–055.

[712] *Forsikringsaktieselskapet Vesta v Butcher* [1986] 2 All E.R. 488 at 508; affirmed [1989] A.C. 852, without reference to this point.

[713] *Basildon DC v JE Lesser Properties* [1985] Q.B. 839 (as explained in *Forsikringsaktieselskapet Vesta v Butcher* [1989] A.C. 852 at 865; affirmed [1989] A.C. 880, without reference to this point); *The Good Luck* [1990] 1 Q.B. 818 at 904 (reversed on other grounds [1992] 1 A.C. 233); *Barclays Bank Plc v Fairclough Building Ltd* [1995] Q.B. 214; *Hi-Lite Electrical Ltd v Wolseley (UK) Ltd* [2011] EWHC 2153 (TCC); [2011] B.L.R. 629 at [234].

[714] See para.20–100. See also *Young v Purdy* [1996] 2 F.L.R. 795; *Schering Agrochemicals Ltd v Resibel NV SA* unreported 26 November 1992; Burrows 109 L.Q.R. 175.

[715] See fnn.709 and 710.

[716] [1995] 2 A.C. 145.

[717] *Forsikringsaktieselskapet Vesta v Butcher* [1989] A.C. 852 at 866; affirmed [1989] A.C. 880, without reference to this point; *Raflatac v Eade* [1999] 1 Lloyd's Rep. 506. The Law Commission recommended that in cases of this kind the claimant's damages should be reduced on account of his contributory negligence, except where the contract expressly or by implication excludes this defence: Law Com. No.219 (1993), paras 4.7–15, 23–25. This may be the effect, in practice, of the decision in *Henderson v Merrett Syndicates Ltd* [1995] 2 A.C. 145, as a consequence of which very few cases will fall in the second category, rather than the third; para.20–116.

dangerous premises;[718] or where loss is caused partly by the negligent services of the defendant, amounting both to a breach of contract and to a tort against his client, and partly by that client's own carelessness,[719] e.g. where a mortgage lender suffers loss partly because of the negligence of a valuer engaged by him in overvaluing the security and partly because of the lender's own imprudent lending policy.[720] There was formerly some support for the view that, even in cases in this category, the Act applied only where the claim was framed in tort.[721] But this view has been rightly rejected[722] as it is not supported by the definition of "fault" in the Act, and as it would be unsatisfactory in enabling an injured party to evade the Act by simply suing in contract where he also had a claim in tort. On the other hand the Act would not apply where, though both contracting parties were careless, the court took the view that the loss was entirely caused by the carelessness of one, e.g. that of the client,[723] or that of his professional adviser.[724]

**Wrong committed by injured party.** In the three situations so far discussed, the defendant is guilty of a breach of contract and the claimant's conduct is careless; but that conduct does not amount to a legal wrong against the defendant. Where the loss to each party results in part from a breach of contract committed by one of them (A) against the other (B) and in part by an independent legal wrong committed by B against A, then the losses may be apportioned[725] (quite apart from the Act) on the ground that they resulted from two independent actionable wrongs. Each party can then recover in respect of his own loss to the extent that it was caused by the other's wrongful act. This was, for example, held to be the case where goods belonging to the tenant of part of a warehouse, and the **20–117**

[718] *Sayers v Harlow Urban DC* [1958] 1 W.L.R. 623; cf. *Targett v Torfaen BC* [1992] 3 All E.R. 27.

[719] *Forsikringsaktieselskapet Vesta v Butcher* [1989] A.C. 852; affirmed [1989] A.C. 880, without reference to this point (not followed in Australia: *Astley v Austrust Ltd* [1999] Lloyd's Rep. P.N. 758); *The Superhulls Cover Case (No.2)* [1990] 2 Lloyd's Rep. 431; cf. *Barclays Bank Plc v Fairclough Building Ltd (No.2)* [1995] I.R.L.R. 605; *Bristol & West BS v Fancy & Jackson* [1997] 4 All E.R. 582 at 625; *Sumitomo Bank Ltd v Banque Bruxelles Lambert SA* [1997] 1 Lloyd's Rep. 487; *Trebor Bassett Holdings Ltd v ADT Fire and Security Plc* [2012] EWCA Civ 1158; [2012] B.L.R. 441.

[720] *Platform Home Loans v Oyston Shipways Ltd* [2000] 2 A.C. 190. The reduction of damages on account of the claimant's contributory negligence is in such cases calculated on the loss actually suffered (the "basic loss") and not on the lower amount for which the defendant is responsible under the "scope of duty" test (para.20–025).

[721] *Sole v WJ Hallt* [1973] Q.B. 574; *The Shinjitsu Maru (No.5)* [1985] 1 W.L.R. 1270; cf. *Basildon DC v JE Lesser (Properties) Ltd* [1985] Q.B. 839 at 849 (as to which see fn.712); Andrews [1986] C.L.J. 8; Burrows 101 L.Q.R. 161; Spowart-Taylor 49 M.L.R. 102.

[722] *Forsikringsaktieselskapet Vesta v Butcher* [1989] A.C. 852 (where at 875 in the Court of Appeal, Neill LJ acknowledged the error of his former contrary view in *The Shinjitsu Maru (No.5)* [1985] 1 W.L.R. 1270).

[723] *O'Connor v BD Kirby & Co* [1972] 1 Q.B. 90; cf. *Quinn v Burch Bros (Builders) Ltd* [1966] 2 Q.B. 370; *County Ltd v Girozentrale Securities* [1996] 3 All E.R. 834.

[724] *UCB Corporate Services Ltd v Clyde & Co* [2000] 2 All E.R. (Comm) 256 at 265.

[725] It is an open question whether there can be such apportionment where B's loss is caused partly by A's legal wrong against B and partly by conduct by B amounting to a legal wrong against a third party (C): see *Standard Chartered Bank v Pakistan National Shipping Co (No.2)* [2000] 1 Lloyd's Rep. 218 at 230, 236 (reversed on another point [2002] UKHL 43; [2003] 1 A.C. 959), where the wrongs committed by A against B and by B against C amounted, not to breach of contract, but to the tort of deceit.

warehouse itself, were damaged as a result partly of the tenant's breach of covenant to repair and partly of omissions of the landlord giving rise to liability in tort. Each party was held liable for the other's loss to the extent that it had been caused by his own wrong.[726] The position would have been the same if the wrongs of both parties had been breaches of contract, e.g. if the tenant had undertaken to do internal and the landlord external repairs and the damage had been due to the failure of both to perform their respective undertakings. But the present line of reasoning cannot apply where only one party (the defendant) was guilty of a legal wrong, while the conduct of the claimant which is alleged to have contributed to his loss did not amount to such a wrong.[727]

20–118 **Where no wrong is committed by the defendant.** All the situations so far discussed must be distinguished from those in which the defendant's contractual undertaking is to compensate the claimant for a loss not brought about by any act or omission on the part of the defendant at all, e.g. where a bank issues travellers' cheques to a customer and promises to compensate him for their face value in the event of his losing them. If the loss is due to the customer's failure to guard against loss, the bank may, if the contract so provides,[728] escape liability for the loss; but such cases raise no issues of contributory negligence as no wrong, leading to the loss, is committed by the bank.

### (d) Remoteness

20–119 Even in cases where a loss is found to have been caused to the claimant as a consequence of the defendant's breach, and there is no basis for limiting it on grounds of mitigation or contributory negligence, some or all of that loss will not be recovered as damages if it is found to be too remote. In *The Achilleas*[729] the House of Lords revisited and, in the case of some of their lordships, "reformulated" the test of remoteness.[730] Since that reformulation appears to have been accepted, and implemented, by the lower courts subsequently, it may seem appropriate to begin with *The Achilleas*. Nevertheless it remains helpful to begin with an assessment of the law as it was understood prior to *The Achilleas*. The principal reason for this is that the reformulated approach is said to be confined to the exceptional case:[731] "cases of departure from the ordinary foreseeability rule

---

726 *Tenant Radiant Heat Ltd v Warrington Development Corp* [1988] 1 E.G.L.R. 41; distinguished from contributory negligence cases in *The Good Luck* [1990] 1 Q.B. 818 at 904 (reversed on other grounds [1992] 1 A.C. 233); applied in *W Lamb Ltd v J Jarvis & Sons Plc* [1999] 60 Con L.R. 1.

727 *Raflatac Ltd v Eade* [1999] 1 Lloyd's Rep. 507 at 510, where the defendant's wrong was also said at 511 to have been the "dominant cause" of the loss.

728 *Braithwaite v Thomas Cook Travellers Cheques Ltd* [1989] Q.B. 553; contrast *El Awadi v Bank of Credit and Commerce International SA* [1990] 1 Q.B. 606.

729 [2008] UKHL 48; [2009] 1 A.C. 61.

730 It may bemore accurate to describe the approach taken by some of their lordships in *The Achilleas* as a "rationalisation" of the rule of remoteness: *Supershield Ltd v Siemens Building Technologies FE Ltd* [2010] EWCA Civ 7; [2010] 1 Lloyd's Rep. 349 at [43]: para.20–132.

731 *The Sylvia* [2010] EWHC 542 (Comm); [2010] 2 Lloyd's Rep. 81 at [41]. Whether it is correct to think in terms of a general approach and exceptions or "departures" is open to debate: see para.20–132.

based on individual circumstances will be unusual."[732] Nonetheless, in order at the outset to give some sense of the debate which has been provoked by *The Achilleas*, it can be stated by reference to two questions: is the defendant liable for all types of loss which were, or ought to have been, within his reasonable contemplation at the time the contract was made (the "ordinary foreseeability rule"), or is the defendant held liable for all types of loss for which he is taken to have "assumed responsibility" in entering into the contract (the "reformulated" approach)? It is the "ordinary foreseeability" rule with which we will begin. Its development can be traced primarily by reference to three leading cases. An assessment will then be made of the impact of *The Achilleas* before attempting to draw some conclusions about the current approach of the courts to remoteness.

**Hadley v Baxendale.** The general rule on remoteness was formulated in *Hadley v Baxendale*.[733] A shaft in the claimants' mill broke and had to be sent to the makers at Greenwich to serve as a pattern for the production of a new one. The defendants agreed to carry the shaft to Greenwich but, as a result of their breach of contract, its delivery was delayed so that there was a stoppage of several days at the mill. The claimants claimed damages of £300 in respect of their loss of profits during this period. At the trial the case was left generally to the jury, who returned a verdict of £50 for the claimants. The defendants successfully applied for a new trial on the ground of misdirection. Alderson B stated the principles in accordance with which the jury should have been directed: **20–120**

> "The damages … should be such as may fairly and reasonably be considered either arising naturally, i.e. according to the usual course of things, from such breach of contract itself, or such as may reasonably be supposed to have been in the contemplation of both parties at the time they made the contract as the probable result of the breach".[734]

Here the stoppage was not the "natural" consequence of the delay: it could not have been contemplated by a carrier that delay in delivering the shaft would keep the mill idle: "In the great multitude of cases of millers sending off broken shafts to third persons by a carrier under ordinary circumstances, such consequences would not, in all probability, have occurred".[735] The claimants might have had a spare shaft[736] or been able to get one.[737] Nor could the stoppage, though it was no doubt anticipated by the *claimants*, have been contemplated by *both* parties at the time of contracting as the probable result of breach. The defendants were not told that any delay by them would keep the mill idle. If they had been told this, they might have attempted to limit their liability "and of this advantage it would be very unjust to deprive them".[738]

---

[732] *The Achilleas* [2008] UKHL 48; [2009] 1 A.C. 61 at [11] (Lord Hoffmann).

[733] (1854) 9 Ex. 341; Simpson 91 L.Q.R. 272; Danzig 4 *Journal of Legal Studies* 249; Pugsley 126 N.L.J. 420; Barton 7 O.J.L.S. 40.

[734] *Hadley v Baxendale* (1854) 9 Ex. 341 at 354.

[735] *Hadley v Baxendale* (1854) 9 Ex. 341 at 356.

[736] *Hadley v Baxendale* (1854) 9 Ex. 341 at 356.

[737] *Hadley v Baxendale* 23 L.J. Ex. at 180.

[738] *Hadley v Baxendale* (1854) 9 Ex. 341 at 355.

20–121 **The Victoria Laundry case.** These principles were developed in *Victoria Laundry (Windsor) Ltd v Newman Industries Ltd.*[739] The defendants sold a boiler to buyers who, as the defendants knew, wanted it for immediate use in their laundry business. The boiler was delivered some five months after the agreed date, so that the buyers suffered loss of profits. Asquith LJ said that the test of remoteness was whether the loss was "reasonably foreseeable as liable to result from the breach".[740] This depended on the state of the defendant's knowledge. Every defendant had imputed to him knowledge of what happens in the ordinary course of things. He might also have actual knowledge of special circumstances, which would enable a reasonable man to foresee extraordinary loss. Here the defendants knew that the buyers wanted the boiler for immediate use in their business: they were thus liable for loss of profits that would ordinarily result from such use. But they were not liable for loss of exceptionally lucrative government contracts, which the buyers would have been able to make if they had received the boiler in time: the defendants knew nothing of these contracts and could not reasonably have foreseen such loss.[741] The same reasoning would apply in the converse case of a buyer's breach, so that the seller could not recover damages in respect of his loss of profit to the extent that this was exceptionally large by reason of his having secured a supply of the goods in question at an unusually low price.[742]

20–122 **The Heron II.** The judgment in the *Victoria Laundry* case, and in particular the phrase "reasonably foreseeable as liable to result" gave rise to the view that the same test of "reasonable foreseeability" that governs remoteness in tort applies also in contract.[743] But this view was rejected by the House of Lords in *The Heron II.*[744] In that case a ship was chartered to carry sugar from Constanza to Basrah. At the time of contracting, the charterer intended to sell the sugar as soon as it reached Basrah. The shipowner did not actually know this; but he did know that there was a market for sugar at Basrah, and "if he had thought about the matter he must have realised that at least it was not unlikely that the sugar would be sold in the market at market price on arrival".[745] The shipowner in breach of contract deviated and reached Basrah nine days late. During these nine days the market price of sugar at Basrah fell; and it was held that the charterer was entitled to damages for the loss suffered by reason of the fall in the market. The House of Lords rejected the view that the test of remoteness in contract was "reasonable foreseeability", at least if this phrase referred to the very low degree of probability required to satisfy the test of remoteness in tort.[746] Lord Reid said that

[739] [1949] 2 K.B. 528.

[740] *Victoria Laundry (Windsor) Ltd v Newman Industries Ltd* [1949] 2 K.B. 528 at 539.

[741] cf. *Kpohraror v Woolwich BS* [1996] 4 All E.R. 119; *The Mass Glory* [2002] EWHC 27 (Comm); [2002] 2 Lloyd's Rep. 245.

[742] See *North Sea Energy Holdings NV v Petroleum Authority of Thailand* [1997] 2 Lloyd's Rep. 418 at 438; affirmed [1999] 1 Lloyd's Rep. 483.

[743] On the appropriate test of remoteness where the claimant has overlapping claims in contract and tort, see para.20–133.

[744] [1969] 1 A.C. 350; Pickering 31 M.L.R. 203.

[745] *The Heron II* [1969] 1 A.C. 350 at 382.

[746] *The Heron II* [1969] 1 A.C. 350 at 385, 411, 425; cf. at 413; Cartwright [1996] C.L.J. 488.

the *Victoria Laundry* case was wrong in laying down this test for contract.[747] But when Asquith LJ there referred to "loss reasonably foreseeable *as liable to result*"[748] he may have had a higher degree of probability in mind; and in this sense his judgment was approved by the other members of the House of Lords. Various expressions are used in *The Heron II* to describe the degree of probability required to satisfy the test of remoteness in contract. There must be a "serious possibility"[749] or a "real danger"[750] or a "very substantial"[751] probability of loss; it must be "not unlikely"[752] or "easily foreseeable"[753] that loss will occur. The result of the decision is that a higher degree of probability is required to satisfy the test of remoteness in contract than in tort. When used in contract cases, the word "foreseeability" refers to this higher degree of probability.

**Deduction by the standard of the reasonable person.** The test of remoteness to emerge from these cases is whether the loss resulting from the breach was within the reasonable contemplation of the parties at the time they entered into the contract.[754] What the defendant should have deduced from the facts known to him[755] is generally judged by the standard of the reasonable person. Thus, in *Hadley v Baxendale*, in the absence of any knowledge of the special circumstances, the defendants could not reasonably have deduced that their delay would keep the mill idle, as the millers might have had a spare shaft.[756] In the *Victoria Laundry* case, by contrast, it would have been mere fantasy to suppose that the buyers kept a spare boiler. **20–123**

In deciding what the defendant should reasonably have deduced from the facts known to him, the court can take into account the commercial capacity in which he contracted: "as reasonable businessmen each must be taken to understand the ordinary practices and exigencies of the other's trade or business".[757] Thus, a supplier of electricity to a building contractor cannot be expected to foresee the full consequences of a power failure on a complex construction project on which the contractor is engaged.[758] Similarly, in *Hadley v Baxendale* the defendants were general carriers and less well able to foresee the effects of delay than the defendants in the *Victoria Laundry* case, who were qualified engineers and knew

---

[747] *The Heron II* [1969] 1 A.C. 350 at 389.

[748] A phrase also used in *Farley v Skinner* [2001] UKHL 49; [2002] 2 A.C. 732 at [84].

[749] *The Heron II* [1969] 1 A.C. 350 at 414–415; *Malik v BCCI* [1998] A.C. 20 at 37.

[750] *The Heron II* [1969] 1 A.C. 350 at 425; cf. *Bates v Barrow* [1995] 1 Lloyd's Rep. 680 at 691; *The Kriti Rex* [1996] 2 Lloyd's Rep. 171 at 173.

[751] *The Heron II* [1969] 1 A.C. 350 at 388.

[752] *The Heron II* [1969] 1 A.C. 350 at 383; cf. *The Rio Claro* [1987] 2 Lloyd's Rep. 173; *The Achilleas* [2008] UKHL 48; [2009] 1 A.C. 61.

[753] *The Heron II* [1969] 1 A.C. 350 at 383.

[754] And not at the date of breach: *Jackson v Royal Bank of Scotland Plc* [2005] UKHL 3; [2005] 1 W.L.R. 377 at [36].

[755] i.e. save for his commercial capacity (see below), no allowance is made for his individual characteristics.

[756] cf. *Gee v Lancs. & Yorks. Ry* (1860) H. & N. 211 (carrier ignorant that manufacturer had no stocks of raw material); *The Pegase* [1981] 1 Lloyd's Rep. 175.

[757] *Monarch SS Co v Karlshamns Oljefabriker (A/B)* [1949] A.C. 196 at 224; cf. *The Arpad* [1934] P. 189 and Scrutton LJ's reference (at 201) to "business knowledge"; *The Achilleas* [2008] UKHL 48; [2009] 1 A.C. 61 at [67].

[758] *Balfour Beatty Construction (Scotland) v Scottish Power* 1994 S.L.T. 807 HL.

more than the uninstructed layman of the purposes for which boilers of the kind in question were likely to be used.[759] But even a carrier can be made liable for loss of the chance of making profits on resale[760] and for loss of profits suffered by a manufacturer through non-delivery of raw materials known to be wanted for manufacturing purposes.[761] Similarly, a carrier who specialises in a particular trade may have imputed to him "a greater knowledge of the relevant market than might have been appropriate in different circumstances",[762] and so be liable for loss suffered by the other contracting party in consequence of movements in that market.

20–124 **What must be "contemplated"?** In tort cases, it is said that the defendant is liable if he could have foreseen the type or kind of loss suffered, even though he could not have foreseen its extent or the precise manner of its happening[763] and it is clear that the same is now true in contract.[764] As in tort, this is open to the criticism that it allows the courts discretion[765] in the way they divide the claimant's loss into different types, and this can lead to uncertainty. Thus, in *Brown v KMR Services Ltd*[766] a member of Lloyd's recovered "underwriting losses"[767] from his agent as damages for breach of contract committed by the agent in pursuing a "high risk" strategy.[768] The *type* of loss was foreseeable even if its extent was not, due to a series of accidents and events in the relevant period. In the *Victoria Laundry*[769] case by contrast, it seems that the finding that profits lost on the government contracts were too remote must be explained on the basis that they represented a different *type* of lost profits, or the profits lost on a different *type* of contract, to those which a reasonable person would ordinarily have expected of a laundry business.[770]

---

[759] *Victoria Laundry (Windsor) Ltd v Newman Industries Ltd* [1949] 2 K.B. 528 at 540; cf. *The Achilleas* [2008] UKHL 48; [2009] 1 A.C. 61 at [67].
[760] e.g. *The Heron II* [1969] 1 A.C. 350; *Panalpina International Transport Ltd v Densil Underwear Ltd* [1981] 1 Lloyd's Rep. 187.
[761] *Montevideo Gas Co v Clan Line Steamers Ltd* (1921) 37 T.L.R. 866; *The Pegase* [1981] 1 Lloyd's Rep. 175; cf. *The Ocean Dynamic* [1982] 2 Lloyd's Rep. 88.
[762] *The Baleares* [1993] 1 Lloyd's Rep. 215 at 227.
[763] e.g. *Smith v Leech Brain & Co Ltd* [1962] 2 Q.B. 405 at 415; cf. *Muirhead v Industrial Tank Specialities Ltd* [1986] Q.B. 507 at 532.
[764] *Wroth v Tyler* [1974] Ch. 30 at 61; para.20–078; *GKN Centrax Gears Ltd v Matbro Ltd* [1976] 2 Lloyd's Rep. 555 at 568; *H Parsons (Livestock) Ltd v Uttley Ingham & Co Ltd* [1978] Q.B. 791; para.20–132; *Brown v KMR Services Ltd* [1995] 4 All E.R. 598 at 621; *North Sea Energy Holdings NV v Petroleum Authority of Thailand* [1997] 2 Lloyd's Rep. 418 at 438; affirmed [1999] 1 Lloyd's Rep. 483; *Wellesley Partners LLP v Withers LLP* [2015] EWCA Civ 1146; [2016] Ch. 529.
[765] Seemingly openly acknowledged by Stuart-Smith LJ in *Brown v KMR Services Ltd* [1995] 4 All E.R. 598 at 621.
[766] [1995] 4 All E.R. 598.
[767] This was Stuart-Smith's categorisation of the type of loss involved.
[768] This was Hobhouse LJ's categorisation of the type of loss involved (Peter Gibson LJ agreeing with him).
[769] *Victoria Laundry (Windsor) Ltd v Newman Industries Ltd* [1949] 2 K.B. 528; para.20–121; cf. also *The Forum Craftsman* [1991] 1 Lloyd's Rep. 81 at 85–86.
[770] *Brown v KMR Services Ltd* [1995] 4 All E.R. 598 at 621 (Stuart-Smith LJ who accepted that "difficulty in practice may arise in categorisation of loss into types or kinds, especially where financial loss is involved").

20–125 **Recovery of loss not in fact suffered.** A defendant is not normally liable for a loss which is likely to occur in the ordinary course of things if it is not in fact suffered;[771] nor for a loss which is suffered if it is too remote. But these rules are qualified where the claimant actually suffers a loss which is too remote, while the defendant could have anticipated that he would have suffered another, smaller, loss. In *Cory v Thames Ironworks Co*[772] the defendants agreed to sell the hull of a floating boom derrick, but delivered it six months late. The defendants expected the buyers to use the hull as a coal store, and, if it had been so used, the buyers would, as a result of the delay, have lost £420. But, unknown to the defendants, the buyers intended to use the hull for a revolutionary method of transferring coal from colliers to barges, and lost profits of £4,000. The buyers admitted that they could not recover £4,000 and claimed £420. The court held the defendants liable for the latter sum, rejecting their argument that, as the £420 represented a loss not actually suffered, they were not liable even to this extent. There was "no hardship or injustice"[773] in making the sellers liable for the smaller sum when the buyers had lost a larger amount.[774] It is more doubtful whether damages can be recovered if the loss actually suffered is different "in kind" from that which would have occurred in the ordinary course of things. Suppose A sells poisonous cattle-food to B,[775] who eats it himself in the course of an unforeseeable nutritional experiment, and dies. Can his executor sue A for the loss of a cow?

20–126 **Not solely a test of foresight.** Even before the decision in *The Achilleas* it was clear that the test of remoteness is not solely a test of foresight, but in this regard it did seem that a distinction had to be drawn between loss occurring in the "usual course of things" ("first limb" losses) and loss occurring as a result of special circumstances ("second limb" losses).[776]

20–127 **"First limb": loss occurring in the "usual course of things".** On this ground it has, for example,[777] been held that a person who agrees to supply or repair an obviously profit-earning thing is liable for loss of profits resulting from delay;[778] that a seller of poisonous cattle-food is liable for loss of the cattle to which it is fed;[779] that a merchant who sells defective seed to a farmer is liable for loss of the

---

771 *Sunley (B) & Co Ltd v Cunard White Star Ltd* [1940] 1 K.B. 740; *North Sea Energy Holdings NV v Petroleum Authority of Thailand* [1999] 1 Lloyd's Rep. 483.

772 (1868) L.R. 3 Q.B. 181.

773 *Cory v Thames Ironworks Co* (1868) L.R. 3 Q.B. 181 at 190.

774 *Building & Civil Engineering Holidays Scheme Management Ltd v Post Office* [1966] 1 Q.B. 247 at 261; the recovery of "ordinary" profits in *Victoria Laundry (Windsor) Ltd v Newman Industries Ltd* [1949] 2 K.B. 528 (para.20–121) illustrates the same point.

775 See text to fn.779.

776 The boundary between the two has been described as "hazy": *Sempra Metals Ltd v Commissioners of Inland Revenue* [2007] UKHL 34; [2008] 1 A.C. 561 at [215].

777 For further examples, see *The Almare Seconda* [1981] 2 Lloyd's Rep. 433; *The Good Luck* [1992] 1 A.C. 233; *The Kriti Rex* [1996] 2 Lloyd's Rep. 171 at 192; *Mason v Burningham* [1949] 2 K.B. 545; cf. *Bunny v Hopkinson* (1859) 27 Beav. 565.

778 *Fletcher v Tayleur* (1855) 17 C.B. 21; *Wilson v General Iron Screw Colliery Co Ltd* (1887) 47 L.J.Q.B. 239; cf. *Mira v Aylmer Square Investments Ltd* [1990] 1 E.G.L.R. 45.

779 *Pinnock Bros v Lewis & Peat Ltd* [1923] 1 K.B. 690; *Ashington Piggeries Ltd v Christopher Hill Ltd* [1972] A.C. 441; cf. *Cointat v Myham & Son* [1913] 2 K.B. 220; para.11–022.

expected crop;[780] and that a supplier of defective components to a manufacturer is liable for loss of business suffered by the latter when customers, dissatisfied with the end-product, do not place repeat orders.[781] Where a loss is identified as occurring in the usual course of things, it appeared that there was no basis, so far as remoteness is concerned, for imposing any further limit to its recovery.[782] It is assumed that the defendant had the opportunity to seek to limit his liability for any "first limb" loss and it is not for the courts to impose a limit which was not bargained for. Thus, in *Jackson v Royal Bank of Scotland Plc*[783] the defendant bank mistakenly disclosed information[784] which led to a loss of future business for the claimant. The Court of Appeal had limited the defendant's liability for such loss to one year of business on the basis of remoteness. This was criticised by the House of Lords as tantamount to the sort of limit upon liability which the defendant might have included in the contract with the claimant, but had not done so.[785] The only limit on the period of liability was the time at which the loss of future business became too speculative to be recovered at all,[786] which was found by the trial judge to be four years.

20–128 **"Second limb": knowledge of special circumstances.** In *Hadley v Baxendale* it was suggested that the defendants might have been liable for the mill owners' loss of profits if they had known,[787] at the time of contracting, that their delay would keep the mill idle. But mere knowledge of special circumstances is not sufficient.[788] Something more must be shown; and attempts were made in later cases to define that additional requirement. In one case, Blackburn J said that "in order that the notice [of special circumstances] may have any effect, it must be given under such circumstances as that an *actual contract* arises on the part of the defendant to bear the exceptional loss".[789] But it is clear that there need be no *express* contract to bear the exceptional loss.[790] Liability for loss caused by known special circumstances can perhaps be based on an "implied undertaking

[780] *George Mitchell (Chesterhall) Ltd v Finney Lock Seeds Ltd* [1983] 2 A.C. 803; and see para.20–038.

[781] *GKN Centrax Gears Ltd v Matbro Ltd* [1976] 2 Lloyd's Rep. 555.

[782] This no longer appears to be the case after *The Achilleas* [2008] UKHL 48; [2009] 1 A.C. 61: see para.20–130.

[783] [2005] UKHL 3; [2005] 1 W.L.R. 377.

[784] This amounted to breach of an obligation of confidence under a letter of credit provided to the claimant by the bank.

[785] *Jackson v Royal Bank of Scotland Plc* [2005] UKHL 3; [2005] 1 W.L.R. 377 at [37].

[786] In accordance with the principles discussed at para.20–062.

[787] Although Alderson B referred to communication of special circumstances "*by the (claimants)* to the defendants", this is not essential: it is sufficient that the defendant knows of the special circumstances and that the claimant knows that the defendant is aware of them without the need for that knowledge to have been acquired *from the claimant*: *Robophone Facilities Ltd v Blank* [1966] 1 W.L.R. 1428 at 1448; *The Achilleas* [2008] UKHL 48; [2009] 1 A.C. 61 at [68]–[69]; cf. *The Heron II* [1969] 1 A.C. 350 at 385, 411.

[788] e.g. *Mulvenna v Royal Bank of Scotland* [2003] EWCA Civ 1112; [2004] C.P. Rep. 8 at [26].

[789] *Horne v Midland Ry* (1873) L.R. 8 C.P. 131 at 141 (where this requirement was not satisfied); contrast *Laceys Footwear (Wholesale) Ltd v Bowler International* [1997] 2 Lloyd's Rep. 369 at 377 (loss of *ordinary* profits within contemplation of parties).

[790] *Robophone Facilities Ltd v Blank* [1966] 1 W.L.R. 1428 at 1448; cf. *The Heron II* [1969] 1 A.C. 350 at 422; *The Pegase* [1981] 1 Lloyd's Rep. 175 at 182; *Panalpina International Transport Ltd v Densil Underwear Ltd* [1981] 1 Lloyd's Rep. 187.

… to bear it",[791] but the reference seems to be to an undertaking implied in law (and not in fact), and so to mean that the defendant is liable for the exceptional loss, irrespective of any actual agreement to bear it.

*Simpson v L & NW Ry*[792] illustrates the circumstances in which such liability can arise. The defendants had contracted to carry samples of cattle-food from an agricultural show at Bedford to another at Newcastle. They had an agent on the showground at Bedford specifically to attract such custom; the goods were marked "must be at Newcastle by Monday certain" but no express reference was made in the contract of carriage to the Newcastle show. The samples failed to arrive "by Monday" and did not reach Newcastle until after the show there was over. It was held that the defendants were liable for loss of the profits which the owner of the samples would have made, had the samples reached Newcastle in time. This should be contrasted with an example given in a nineteenth-century case: a barrister going to Calcutta, where he had briefs awaiting him, could not sue the carriers for getting him there late, even if they knew why he was going to Calcutta.[793] The distinction between the cases lies in the nature of the two contracts. In the first, the contract was in substance one to carry samples to the Newcastle show—not simply to Newcastle. In the second the contract was one to carry the barrister to Calcutta—not to the Calcutta law sittings. Liability depends on "some knowledge *and acceptance* by one party of the *purpose and intention* of the other in entering the contract".[794]

**Partial knowledge.** The party in breach may know only some of the circumstances which lead to loss. He may then be liable for so much of that loss as he could have anticipated on the basis of the facts known to him, but not for further loss which results from other circumstances of which he was unaware.[795] In such cases, there is no rigid separation between the two limbs of the test in *Hadley v Baxendale*[796] and the defendant's liability increases with his degree of knowledge. Thus, one reason why some loss of profits was recovered in the *Victoria Laundry* case, but none in *Hadley v Baxendale*, was that in the former the defendants knew that the boiler was wanted for immediate use, while in the latter case they did not know that want of the shaft would keep the mill idle. In *The Heron II* the defendants' knowledge that there was a sugar market at Basrah sufficed to make them liable for loss due to market movements there. Similarly, **20–129**

[791] *Robophone Facilities Ltd v Blank* [1966] 1 W.L.R. 1428 at 1448.

[792] (1876) 1 Q.B.D. 274; *Jameson v Midland Ry* (1884) 50 L.T. 426.

[793] *BC Saw-Mill Co Ltd v Nettleship* (1868) L.R. 3 C.P. 499 at 510; cf. *Panalpina International Transport Ltd v Densil Underwear Ltd* [1981] 1 Lloyd's Rep.187, where a carrier knew that goods were wanted for the Christmas trade but delivered them too late.

[794] *Weld-Blundell v Stephens* [1920] A.C. 956 at 980 (emphasis added); contrast *GKN Centrax Gears Ltd v Matbro Ltd* [1976] 2 Lloyd's Rep. 555 at 580.

[795] *Borries v Hutchinson* (1865) 18 C.B. (N.S.) 445; cf. *International Minerals & Chemicals Corp v Karl O Helm AG* [1986] 1 Lloyd's Rep. 81 at 102 (exchange loss recoverable as damages for late payment in a currency known not to be "the currency of [the seller]"). See also: *Cottrill v Steyning & Littlehampton Building Society* [1966] 1 W.L.R. 753; cf. *G & K Ladenbau (UK) Ltd v Crawley & de Reya* [1978] 1 W.L.R. 266; *Seven Seas Properties Ltd v Al-Essa* [1988] 1 W.L.R. 1272. Contrast, *Diamond v Campbell-Jones* [1961] Ch. 22; cf. *Seven Seas Properties Ltd v Al Essa (No.2)* [1993] 1 W.L.R. 1083; *Strategic Property Ltd v O'Se* [2009] EWHC 3512 (Ch).

[796] *Kpohraror v Woolwich Building Society* [1996] 4 All E.R. 119 at 128; *Hotel Services Ltd v Hilton International (UK) Ltd* [2000] 1 All E.R. (Comm) 750 at 755.

delay in the arrival of a chartered ship at a loading port may cause loss to a charterer who intended to *buy* a cargo there, if the market rises during the period of the delay: the shipowner's liability in respect of such loss will depend on the degree of his knowledge of the market and of the charterer's arrangements in relation to the buying of the cargo.[797] And where a bank wrongfully dishonoured a customer's cheque, it was held liable to the customer for injury to his business reputation since it knew him to be a trader, but not for the further loss suffered by the customer when the particular transaction in respect of which the cheque had been drawn, and further business opportunities, were lost, since these were circumstances of which the bank neither was, nor could have been, aware on the basis of the facts known to it.[798]

20–130 **The Achilleas.** It is against the background of the understanding of the test of remoteness set out above that we can consider the impact of the decision of the House of Lords in *The Achilleas*.[799] The defendant charterers redelivered a vessel to the claimant owners nine days late. As a consequence, the claimants were forced to accept the cancellation of a follow on fixture which they had negotiated at a rate of $39,500 per day and enter into a new fixture at $31,500 per day. The defendants accepted that they were liable for the "overrun period", i.e. the difference between the charter rate which the defendants would continue to pay and the market rate for the nine days of delay, but argued that the losses flowing from the cancellation of the follow on fixture were too remote. This submission was rejected by a majority of the arbitrators, and at first instance,[800] and in the Court of Appeal.[801] An appeal was allowed unanimously by the House of Lords, but as a result of two different approaches.

Lord Rodger and Baroness Hale found that the loss had not been reasonably contemplated and was, therefore, too remote. An obvious difficulty with this apparently orthodox application of the test of remoteness is that the application of the same test before the arbitrators and in the lower courts produced the opposite result. This is not altogether surprising given that the defendant conceded that it was "not unlikely" that the late redelivery of the vessel would result in the loss of a follow on fixture, i.e. the loss was one which would occur in the usual course of things.[802] It seems that the conclusion reached by Lord Rodger and Baroness Hale can only be explained by a different conception of the relevant "loss". Lord Rodger referred to it as the financial consequences of the loss of the fixture which had occurred "only because of the extremely volatile market conditions which produced both the owners' initial (particularly lucrative) transaction … and the

[797] Contrast *The Rio Claro* [1987] 2 Lloyd's Rep. 173 with *The Baleares* [1993] 1 Lloyd's Rep. 215. See also *The Eurus* [1998] 1 Lloyd's Rep. 351.

[798] *Kpohraror v Woolwich Building Society* [1996] 4 All E.R. 119.

[799] [2008] UKHL 48; [2009] 1 A.C. 61; Peel 125 L.Q.R. 6; Kramer 125 L.Q.R. 408; Wee [2010] L.M.C.L.Q. 150; Hoffmann 14 Edinburgh L.R. 47; Coote 26 J.C.L. 211; Stiggelbout [2012] L.M.C.L.Q. 97.

[800] *The Achilleas* [2006] EWHC 3030 (Comm); [2007] 1 Lloyd's Rep. 19. In the 12th edn of this book, the decision of Christopher Clarke J was cited as a straightforward example of loss occurring in the usual course of things.

[801] *The Achilleas* [2007] EWCA Civ 901; [2007] 2 Lloyd's Rep. 555.

[802] See text to fn.752.

subsequent pressure on the owners to accept a lower rate for that fixture."[803] This appears to fall into error in requiring reasonable contemplation of the extent of the loss and not the type,[804] and to be inconsistent with earlier dicta that fluctuations in the market are only relevant if they are due to "any unusual or unpredictable factor".[805]

Lord Hoffmann and Lord Hope adopted a different approach in which they gave greater emphasis to what they identified as the underlying basis of remoteness. This basis is that the defendant is only liable for loss which it was the intention of the parties that he should bear, i.e. loss for which he has "assumed responsibility", or which falls within the scope of his duty.[806] As in other areas,[807] the intention of the parties must be objectively ascertained. In most cases it will be determined solely by the test of whether the loss was one which was, or should have been, reasonably contemplated, but in some cases other factors may lead to the conclusion that the parties did not intend that the defendant should be held liable even for a loss that was reasonably contemplated. *The Achilleas* was regarded as such a case. According to both Lord Hoffmann and Lord Hope, one factor was the unpredictable or unquantifiable nature of the loss over which the defendants had no control, i.e. the length and terms of the follow on charter.[808] An additional factor for Lord Hoffmann was market expectation, i.e. the understanding of the shipping industry that the liability of the charterer was confined to the overrun period.[809]

**Remoteness as "assumption of responsibility".** At the outset, it should be stressed that the approach advocated by Lord Hoffmann and Lord Hope does not represent a fundamental departure from the previous understanding of the test of remoteness. First, it has been seen above that, at least in some cases, the test is not merely one of foresight and that "something more" may be required; furthermore, the "something more" has been articulated as some sense that the defendant has accepted the risk of the loss.[810] Secondly, the technique of seeking to find an answer in the proper construction of the contract is used elsewhere, e.g. 20–131

[803] *The Achilleas* [2008] UKHL 48; [2009] 1 A.C. 61 at [60].

[804] See para.20–124.

[805] *The Heron II* [1969] 1 A.C. 350 at 394, 417. The charter market is ordinarily volatile and Lord Rodger does not appear to suggest that it was *particularly* volatile or distorted by an unusual or unpredictable factor at the relevant time. In *Pindell Ltd v AirAsia Berhad* [2010] EWHC 2516 (Comm); [2012] 2 C.L.C. 1 at [88] Tomlinson J considered it to be "axiomatic" that losses due to "extremely volatile market conditions" are too remote, but he was dealing with the unprecedented economic crisis in 2008 whereas the events in *The Achilleas* took place in 2004; and he subsequently resiled from this view (as Tomlinson LJ) in *John Grimes Partnership Ltd v Gubbins* [2013] EWCA Civ 37; [2013] B.L.R. 126 at [34].

[806] *The Achilleas* [2008] UKHL 48; [2009] 1 A.C. 61 at [9], [12], [23] (Lord Hoffmann); at [31] (Lord Hope); Kramer in Cohen and McKendick (eds), *Comparative Remedies for Breach of Contract* (2005); Hoffmann 14 Edinburgh L.R. 47.

[807] See paras 6–042, 6–054.

[808] *The Achilleas* [2008] UKHL 48; [2009] 1 A.C. 61 at [24], [34].

[809] *The Achilleas* [2008] UKHL 48; [2009] 1 A.C. 61 at [7], [23].

[810] See, e.g. *BC Saw-Mill Co Ltd v Nettleship* (1868) L.R. 3 C.P. 499 at 510 and in *The Achilleas* itself in the lower courts: [2006] EWHC 3030 (Comm); [2007] 1 Lloyd's Rep. 19 at [65]; [2007] EWCA Civ 901; [2007] 2 Lloyd's Rep. 555 at [115]. See also Lord Hoffmann's explanation that the

in determining whether a contract is void for common mistake,[811] or discharged by frustration.[812] Thirdly, if remoteness is not ultimately determined by the intention of the parties, the only alternative is to recognise that it is an external rule based on keeping liability within reasonable limits; the distinction between liability based on the intention of the parties, objectively ascertained, and liability based on an externally imposed standard of reasonableness is a fine one.[813]

Nonetheless, the approach advocated by Lord Hoffmann and Lord Hope does appear to go further than the courts have gone before. The requirement of "something more" than the requisite degree of foresight of the loss had been confined to losses occurring only as a result of special circumstances ("second limb"),[814] whereas *The Achilleas* was concerned with loss which occurred in the usual course of things[815] ("first limb").[816] In relation to the latter, it had previously been understood that there is no further limit to recovery so far as remoteness is concerned.[817] The technique of looking to the proper construction of the contract has been shown to have its limits and has led to the rejection of the implied term theory (i.e. that the answer is to be found by reference to the intention of the parties) to explain when a contract is void for mistake,[818] or is discharged for frustration.[819] There is certainly *a role* for the technique in relation to damages in that the secondary obligation to pay compensation is shaped by the primary obligation which has been breached. It is first necessary to know the scope of the defendant's primary obligation before one can ask what sum would put the claimant in the same position as if the defendant had fulfilled that primary obligation, and the scope of that primary obligation is a question of construction. But in *The Achilleas* the primary obligation of the defendant was not in doubt;[820] it was to have returned the vessel before the last date for redelivery and to press

dividing of loss into different types (para.20–124) "reflects what would reasonably have been regarded by the contracting party as significant for the purposes of the risk he was undertaking": [2008] UKHL 48; [2009] 1 A.C. 61 at [22].

[811] See para.8–003.

[812] See para.19–127.

[813] *Mulvenna v Royal Bank of Scotland* [2003] EWCA Civ 1112 at [33] (Evans LJ: "the chain of consequences is cut off as a matter of law, *either* because it is regarded as unreasonable to impose liability for that consequence of the breach, *or* because the scope of the duty is limited so as to exclude it." (Emphasis added.))

[814] See para.20–128.

[815] This is on the basis of the rejection of Lord Rodger's conception of the relevant loss: para.20–130.

[816] It is respectfully submitted that Beatson LJ is not correct when he describes it as "a case about the second limb of *Hadley v Baxendale*": *SC Confectia SA v Miss Mania Wholesale Ltd* [2014] EWCA Civ 1484 at [26].

[817] See para.20–127.

[818] See para.8–002.

[819] See para.19–124.

[820] This is an important difference between *The Achilleas* and *South Australia Asset Management Corp v York Montague Ltd* [1997] A.C. 191 *(SAAMCO)*, from which Lord Hoffmann draws support for his approach to remoteness. As explained at para.20–025, in *SAAMCO* the defendant valuer was not liable for all loss flowing from the loan entered into by the claimant lender since it did not fall within the scope of his duty (i.e. his primary obligation) to advise generally on the commercial wisdom of the loan; his duty was only to provide information and his liability was limited to the extent to which that information was incorrect.

into action a search for the intention of the parties, albeit objectively ascertained, so as to determine directly the scope of the secondary obligation seems to border on a fiction.[821]

The sense that Lord Hoffmann and Lord Hope may have gone further than before and, as a result, rendered the law less certain is reinforced by the decision which was reached in *The Achilleas* itself. If the courts are now invited to find that a loss may be too remote even though it occurred in the usual course of things, one would expect that result only to be reached in very exceptional circumstances. Lord Hoffmann referred to the understanding of the shipping industry that the charterer's liability is confined to the overrun period, but, as Rix LJ demonstrated in the Court of Appeal, this issue had not previously been directly before the courts and, when seen in context, there is rather less in the way of indirect support for this view than has been supposed.[822] Both Lord Hoffmann and Lord Hope referred to the unpredictable and unquantifiable nature of the loss, but again, as Rix LJ noted, the follow on fixture entered into was an entirely usual one whereas "an unusual contract is likely to be outside the 'usual course of things' which is the essential focus of the remoteness rule".[823] In this regard, there is a certain irony in that the usual loss which was actually suffered in *The Achilleas* is held to be too remote because of a hypothetical unusual loss which was not in fact suffered, whereas a usual but hypothetical loss was recovered in the *Victoria Laundry* case after ruling out the unusual loss which was in fact suffered (the loss on the government contracts).[824] This would suggest that the claimants in *The Achilleas* should have been entitled to recover for the loss of what was the usual fixture in that case and this would have represented the limit of recovery in any future cases where the owner had entered into an "unusual" fixture. Finally, Lord Hoffmann referred to the control which the owner enjoyed to prevent the loss in the form of his right to refuse to undertake the last voyage if it was bound to overrun and put the follow on fixture at risk.[825] That form of "control" is confined to the particular circumstances of the case before the House of Lords. In most cases, it is not the claimant who will be able to control whether a loss can be avoided; it is the defendant who can control his liability for that loss by the insertion of an appropriately drafted limit on his liability. In one sense, the result reached in *The Achilleas* appears to do what the House of Lords had previously said should not be done,[826] by introducing a limit upon liability which the defendant might have included in the contract with the claimant, but had not done so.[827]

---

[821] Robertson (2008) 28 L.S. 172; cf. Tettenborn (2007) 23 J.C.L. 120. One consequence of regarding remoteness as a matter of construction is that it involves a question of law: *The Achilleas* [2008] UKHL 48; [2009] 1 A.C. 61 at [25]; the question of whether the type of loss was foreseeable remains a question of fact: *Monarch Steamship Co Ltd v Karlshamns Oljefabriker (A/B)* [1949] A.C. 196.

[822] *The Achilleas* [2007] EWCA Civ 901; [2007] 2 Lloyd's Rep. 555 at [30] and following discussing, inter alia, dicta in *The Dione* [1975] 1 Lloyd's Rep. 115 at 117–118; *The Johnny* [1977] 2 Lloyd's Rep. 1 at 2; *The Peonia* [1991] 1 Lloyd's Rep. 100 at 118; *The Gregos* [1995] 1 Lloyd's Rep. 1 at 10.

[823] *The Gregos* [1995] 1 Lloyd's Rep. 1 at [112].

[824] See para.20–125, and fn.774.

[825] *The Achilleas* [2008] UKHL 48; [2009] 1 A.C. 61 at [23].

[826] *Jackson v Royal Bank of Scotland Plc* [2005] UKHL 3; [2005] 1 W.L.R. 377; para.20–127.

[827] See para.20–127.

20–132 **Current approach.** The reformulated approach to the test of remoteness in *The Achilleas* is attributed to Lord Hoffmann and Lord Hope whereas Lord Rodger and Baroness Hale appeared to apply the orthodox test, albeit in a way which is open to some doubt.[828] The precise ratio of the decision therefore turns on the interpretation of the speech of Lord Walker.[829] He concluded that he would allow the appeal for the reasons given by Lord Rodger *and* Lord Hoffmann and Lord Hope, but it could be argued that he does not go quite as far as the latter in his recognition that the underlying idea of remoteness is "what was the common basis on which the parties were contracting?"[830] Without considering it necessary to establish the *ratio* of the decision in *The Achilleas*, the reformulated approach appears to have been accepted by the Court of Appeal in *Supershield Ltd v Siemens Building Technologies FE Ltd*.[831] In that case, Toulson LJ referred to *Hadley v Baxendale* as the "standard rule",[832] but recognised that "there may be cases where the court, on examining the contract and the commercial background, decides that the standard approach would not reflect the expectation or intention reasonably to be imputed to the parties".[833] Furthermore, taken to its logical conclusion this approach may have an "inclusionary effect" (in contrast to the "exclusionary effect" in *The Achilleas*) in that the loss may be found to be within the scope of the defendant's duty even if it would not have occurred in the usual course of things (and, it seems, was not the result of special circumstances made known to the defendant).[834]

Similarly, in *The Sylvia*[835] Hamblen J referred to the decision in *The Achilleas* as resulting in "an amalgam of the orthodox and the broader approach".[836] He considered that it would only be in "unusual" cases that it would be necessary "specifically to address the issue of assumption of responsibility".[837] In that case, the defendant shipowner was in breach of a charterparty by delivering the vessel

[828] See para.20–130.

[829] Or possibly not: in *The Amer Energy* [2009] 1 Lloyd's Rep. 293 Flaux J regarded Lord Hoffmann alone as being in the minority in laying down a new test of remoteness; cf. *The Sylvia* [2010] EWHC 542 (Comm); [2010] 2 Lloyd's Rep. 81 at [39]–[40] in which Hamblen J considered "the *rationale* of assumption of responsibility to have had the support of the majority" (emphasis added); *Classic Maritime v Lion Diversified Holdings* [2009] EWHC 1142 (Comm); [2010] 1 Lloyd's Rep. 59; *Pindell Ltd v AirAsia Berhad* [2010] EWHC 2516 (Comm); [2012] 2 C.L.C. 1.

[830] *The Achilleas* [2008] UKHL 48; [2009] 1 A.C. 61 at [69]; there is a role for this even in the orthodox test: see para.20–128.

[831] [2010] EWCA Civ 7; [2010] 1 Lloyd's Rep. 349.

[832] *Supershield Ltd v Siemens Building Technologies FE Ltd* [2010] EWCA Civ 7; [2010] 1 Lloyd's Rep. 349 at [43].

[833] *Supershield Ltd v Siemens Building Technologies FE Ltd* [2010] EWCA Civ 7; [2010] 1 Lloyd's Rep. 349 at [43].

[834] *Supershield Ltd v Siemens Building Technologies FE Ltd* [2010] EWCA Civ 7; [2010] 1 Lloyd's Rep. 349 at [43]. This may be logical but one imagines that such an outcome will be rare. It was unnecessary for Toulson LJ to have to go that far in that the issue which he had to resolve was the reasonableness of a settlement of liability entered into by the claimant, including the points it had or had not taken viz. remoteness: at [45].

[835] [2010] EWHC 542 (Comm); [2010] 2 Lloyd's Rep. 81; cf. *The Great Creation* [2014] EWHC 3978 (Comm); [2015] 1 Lloyd's Rep. 315.

[836] *The Sylvia* [2010] EWHC 542 (Comm); [2010] 2 Lloyd's Rep. 81 at [40].

[837] *The Sylvia* [2010] EWHC 542 (Comm); [2010] 2 Lloyd's Rep. 81 at [41]; cf. *John Grimes Partnership Ltd v Gubbins* [2013] EWCA Civ 37; [2013] B.L.R. 126; *Saipol SA v Inerco Trade SA* [2014] EWHC 2211 (Comm); [2015] 1 Lloyd's Rep. 26 at [17].

late and was sued by the charterer for the loss of a sub-charter. This was not an "unusual" case in that, unlike *The Achilleas*, there was no relevant understanding of the industry that this was a loss for which the owner would not be held liable and the loss was not "unquantifiable, unpredictable, uncontrollable or disproportionate"[838] since, by definition, the length of the sub-charter could be no longer than the charterparty. But although the test in *Hadley v Baxendale* is described as the "standard rule" or the "orthodox approach" from which the courts should only depart in "unusual cases", the effect of this approach is that, in reality, the test of "assumption of responsibility" is *applied* in all cases. It is only in non-standard, or "unusual", cases that it will produce a different *result* to the test in *Hadley v Baxendale*. Even if the broader, or reformulated, approach is no more than a rationalisation of the test of remoteness, it is the very fact that it was applied in *The Achilleas* to loss which occurred in the usual course of things, and in circumstances that do not appear to have been particularly exceptional,[839] that may have rendered the law less certain.

**Contract and tort.** It has been noted above that the test for remoteness in contract is not the same as the test for remoteness in tort; in particular that a higher degree of foreseeability is needed in contract. It differs because, as Lord Reid said in *The Heron II*, a contracting party: 20–133

> "who wishes to protect himself against a risk which to the other party would appear to be unusual, ... can direct the other party's attention to it before the contract is made. In tort, however, there is no opportunity for the injured party to protect himself in that way ...".[840]

While the observation about a claim in tort will often be true and, when it is, a test for remoteness which is easier for the claimant to fulfil may be justified, there are cases in which the claimant has the same opportunity to protect against "unusual" risk even in a tort claim. This is most obviously so in a case of "concurrent liability" where the claimant can sue the defendant either for breach of a contractual duty of care or a common law duty of care. In *Wellesley Partners LLP v Withers LLP*[841] the Court of Appeal held[842] that, in such a case, it is the contract remoteness test which should be applied even to the tort claim.[843] That decision was concerned with a claim for pure economic loss, but there is some support, albeit tentative, that the same test should also be applied in a claim for damage to property.[844] Since the underlying justification for applying the contract remoteness test to the tort claim is the opportunity to warn of unusual risk, it is

---

838 *The Sylvia* [2010] EWHC 542 (Comm); [2010] 2 Lloyd's Rep. 81 at [73].

839 See para.20–131.

840 *The Heron II* [1969] 1 A.C. 350 at 385–386, cited in *H Parsons (Livestock) Ltd v Uttley Ingham & Co Ltd* [1978] Q.B. 791 at 806.

841 [2015] EWCA Civ 1146; [2016] Ch. 529.

842 For earlier, if indirect support for this view, see: *H Parsons (Livestock) Ltd v Uttley Ingham & Co Ltd* [1978] Q.B. 791; *Brown v KMR Services Ltd* [1995] 4 All E.R. 598; *Rubenstein v HSBC Bank Plc* [2012] EWCA Civ 1184; [2012] 2 C.L.C. 747.

843 In what was a claim primarily for "loss of chance" (see para.20–062), the Court found that the more stringent remoteness test was satisfied in any event.

844 *H Parsons (Livestock) Ltd v Uttley Ingham & Co Ltd* [1978] Q.B. 791 at 807 (Scarman LJ). In the same case, Lord Denning MR held that it is the type of harm which is determinative, not the cause of action, but that view has not prevailed.

arguable that it should be applied to any tort claim where this opportunity was available, even if the parties did not enter into a contract so that it is not a case of "concurrent liability". Roth J "inclined" to this view in the *Wellesley* case.[845]

20–134 **Extra loss due to claimant's lack of means.** A claimant may suffer extra loss because his financial position is such that he cannot avoid the adverse consequences of the breach. Damages can be recovered for such loss if the defendant knew of the claimant's lack of means and if the extra loss resulting from it "was such as might reasonably be expected to be in the contemplation of the parties as likely to flow from a breach of the obligation undertaken".[846]

## 5. LIQUIDATED DAMAGES

20–135 A contract may contain a term which provides for the payment of a fixed sum on breach, or some other form of agreed remedy, such as withholding a payment which is otherwise due to the defaulting party,[847] or requiring that party to transfer property for a pre-determined sum.[848] The aim of the term is to liquidate the damages which are due from the party in breach without the need to conduct an assessment of the loss which would be recoverable as damages at law; hence the term, "liquidated damages". The obvious advantage of such clauses is that they avoid the uncertainty involved in the assessment of damages at law which is evident from the discussion in this chapter. If enforceable, the further benefit of a liquidated sum is that the claimant may be able to proceed by way of summary judgment and dispense with the need for a full trial. However, a liquidated damages clause, or other form of agreed remedy, is not enforceable if it amounts to a "penalty"[849] and, in some circumstances, the court may also grant equitable relief.[850]

### (a) The rule against penalties

20–136 **An anomalous rule.** While its origins lie in equity's intervention in the enforcement of a penal bond,[851] the rule against penalties has evolved into a common law rule.[852] In very broad outline, it applies to terms which respond to, and are intended to deal with the consequences of, a prior breach of the contract. Such terms are not enforceable if they are "extravagant or unconscionable". The

---

[845] [2015] EWCA Civ 1146; [2016] Ch. 529 at [163].

[846] *Muhammed Issa el Sheik Ahmed v Ali* [1947] A.C. 414, as explained in *Monarch SS Co v Karlshamns Oljefabriker (A/B)* [1949] A.C. 196 at 224; cf. *Trans Trust SPRL v Danubian Trading Co Ltd* [1952] 2 Q.B. 297; *Wroth v Tyler* [1974] Ch. 30; *Perry v Sidney Phillips & Son* [1982] 1 W.L.R. 1297; contrast *Pilkington v Wood* [1953] Ch. 770 (where defendant did not know of claimant's overdraft); cf. in tort, *Lagden v O'Connor* [2003] UKHL 64; [2004] 1 A.C. 1067.

[847] See para.20–146.

[848] See para.20–151.

[849] See paras 20–136—20–171.

[850] See paras 20–172—20–177.

[851] See Loyd (1915) 29 *Harvard Law Review* 117; Williston, *A Treatise on the Law of Contracts* (1957), vol. 3, para.792.

[852] Simpson 82 L.Q.R. 392.

detail of the *scope* of the rule and the *test* for a penalty are dealt with below, but based on this broad outline for the moment, the question with which to start is why such a rule should exist, or be thought necessary? As we have seen earlier in this book, the courts may police the process by which a contract has been agreed, so as to ensure that the parties have given valid consent to its terms (see, e.g. the law relating to misrepresentation,[853] duress,[854] undue influence,[855] etc.), but this applies to any term, including a liquidated damages clause. The substantive control of contract terms is largely confined to statute, in particular for the protection of consumers,[856] but no statutory control applies to liquidated damages in a contract between two commercial parties.[857] Some common law rules apply to particular terms even in commercial contracts and apply substantive control over their enforceability on grounds of public policy, e.g. the doctrine of restraint of trade where there is also the need to take into account considerations of the "public interest".[858] While the rule against penalties is also regarded as a rule of, or based on, public policy,[859] it is not self-evident what is the underlying policy which justifies singling out a liquidated damages clause, particularly as to do so conflicts with the principle of freedom of contract.[860] This no doubt explains why Diplock LJ declared that he could "make no attempt, where so many others have failed, to rationalise this common law rule."[861]

**Cavendish v Makdessi.** The anomalous nature of the rule against penalties was acknowledged by the Supreme Court in *Cavendish Square Holding BV v El Makdessi*.[862] Lord Neuberger and Lord Sumption referred to it as "an ancient, haphazardly constructed edifice which has not weathered well"[863] and doubted whether "the courts would have invented the rule today if their predecessors had not done so three centuries ago."[864] Nevertheless, the Court rejected a submission that the rule should be abrogated, in part because it "is not only a long-standing principle of English law, but is common to almost all major systems of law."[865] It also expressed a concern for small businesses who might fall outside the statutory **20–137**

[853] See Ch.9.
[854] See paras 10–002—10–014.
[855] See paras 10–015—10–045.
[856] See, e.g. the Consumer Rights Act 2015, para.7–100 and following.
[857] The Unfair Contract Terms Act 1977 does not extend to liquidated damages: see para.7–044.
[858] See para.11–112 and following.
[859] *Robophone Facilities Ltd v Blank* [1966] 1 W.L.R. 1428 at 1446; *Azimut-Benetti SpA v Healey* [2010] EWHC 2234 (Comm); [2011] 1 Lloyd's Rep. 473 at [24]; *Cavendish Square Holding BV v El Makdessi* [2015] UKSC 67; [2016] A.C. 1172 at [243].
[860] *Cavendish Square Holding BV v El Makdessi* [2013] EWCA Civ 1539; [2013] 2 C.L.C. 968 at [44] ("blatant interference").
[861] *Robophone Facilities Ltd v Blank* [1966] 1 W.L.R. 1428 at 1446.
[862] [2015] UKSC 67; [2016] A.C. 1172; Conte 132 L.Q.R. 382; Morgan [2016] C.L.J. 11; Day [2016] J.B.L. 115; Summers [2017] L.M.C.L.Q. 95. The appeal in the *Makdessi* case was heard at the same time as an appeal in *ParkingEye Ltd v Beavis*. Hereafter, save where specific reference is made to the *ParkingEye* appeal, the decision of the Supreme Court in the conjoined appeal is referred to as the "*Makdessi* case".
[863] *Cavendish Square Holding BV v El Makdessi* [2015] UKSC 67; [2016] A.C. 1172 at [3].
[864] *Cavendish Square Holding BV v El Makdessi* [2015] UKSC 67; [2016] A.C. 1172 at [36].
[865] *Cavendish Square Holding BV v El Makdessi* [2015] UKSC 67; [2016] A.C. 1172 at [37]. The Court also highlighted that the Law Commission had not recommended abolition: English Law Commission Working Paper No 61; Scottish Law Commission Report No 171.

regulation referred to above,[866] but that is an argument in favour of a more general power of review for the protection of such parties and does not explain why it should be confined to liquidated damages clauses. According to Lord Neuberger and Lord Sumption, any anomalies in the operation of the rule were "better addressed" by "a realistic appraisal of the substance of contractual provisions operating upon breach, and by taking a more principled approach to the interests that may properly be protected by the terms of the parties' agreement".[867] It is clear that the intention of the Court was to narrow the circumstances in which a liquidated damages clause, or other forms of agreed remedy, may amount to an unenforceable penalty.[868] As far as the scope of the rule is concerned, the Court confirmed that it is confined to a term in the nature of a "secondary obligation".[869] The test applicable to such a term is whether it "imposes a detriment on the contract-breaker out of all proportion to any legitimate interest of the innocent party in the enforcement of the primary obligation", such that it would be "extravagant" or "unconscionable" to enforce it.[870] It is to the detail of this which we now turn.

### *(i) Scope*

20–138 There are two aspects to the scope of the rule against penalties. First, what is the nature of *the term* to which the rule applies. Secondly, does it matter what *remedy* is provided, e.g. payment of a fixed sum, the withholding of a payment otherwise due, the forced transfer of property, or the forfeiting of sums already paid? Examples of each of these types of remedy are dealt with below after considering the requirement that the term must be in the nature of a secondary obligation.

20–139 **The rule is confined to secondary obligations.** In the *Makdessi* case, the Supreme Court confirmed that the rule against penalties is confined to secondary obligations, i.e. a term which provides a remedy for the breach of a primary obligation. It does not apply to primary obligations themselves. Thus, if A agrees to pay £100 for goods which are worth £1, the rule has no application to his primary obligation to pay the price. If, however, A agrees to pay £1 for the same goods, but also agrees to pay £100 in damages if he fails to pay the price when due, the rule applies to the secondary obligation to pay liquidated damages for breach of the primary obligation to pay the price. This aspect of the rule may be further illustrated by a case like *Alder v Moore*[871] in which a professional footballer received £500 from an insurance company in respect of an injury which was thought to have disabled him permanently and undertook to repay the

---

[866] *Cavendish Square Holding BV v El Makdessi* [2015] UKSC 67; [2016] A.C. 1172 at [38].
[867] *Cavendish Square Holding BV v El Makdessi* [2015] UKSC 67; [2016] A.C. 1172 at [39].
[868] While this is to be welcomed, the continued existence of the rule, even in attenuated form, undermines the certainty of outcome which a liquidated damage clause is intended to achieve; cf. *Union Eagle Ltd v Golden Achievement Ltd* [1997] A.C. 514, discussed at para.18–081.
[869] See para.20–139. While the members of the Court differed over the question whether the relevant terms in the *Makdessi* case amounted to "secondary obligations", they were unanimous in their agreement that the scope of the rule was so limited.
[870] See para.20–154.
[871] [1961] 2 Q.B. 57; 77 L.Q.R. 300; Goff 24 M.L.R. 637.

money in the event of his again playing professional football. He committed no breach when he did play again, as he had made no promise not to do so, and the rule against penalties did not therefore apply to his primary obligation to repay the £500. Nor does it apply to a "bad leaver" provision under which an employee may be required to transfer shares or forego other entitlements if he leaves employment in circumstances which do not amount to a breach on his part.[872]

**Why is the rule confined to secondary obligations?** It is not immediately apparent why the courts should have a power to review the secondary obligation to pay £100 in the second example above, but no power to review the primary obligation to pay £100 in the first example. This is one apparent anomaly of the rule against penalties. If the answer in the first example is that a power of review would be contrary to the principle of freedom of contract, why is that not also the answer in the second example? In the *Makdessi* case, Lord Mance observed that: "in most cases parties know and reflect in their contracts a real distinction, legal and psychological, between what, on the one hand, a party can permissibly do and what, on the other hand, constitutes a breach and may attract a liability to damages for the breach".[873] It is not clear what exactly is meant by the reference to a "psychological" distinction, but it may refer to the fact that a secondary obligation is, by its very nature, a contingent obligation which a contracting party may not be required to perform. Thus, in the first example there is no contingency in A's obligation to pay the price of £100; he can expect to have to perform and this may explain why freedom of contract is applied without qualification, save in cases where A's consent has been vitiated in some way. In the second example, the obligation he can expect to perform is the obligation to pay the price of £1; his obligation to pay £100, which may bear no relation to the damages he would otherwise be required to pay, is a contingent one and he may have agreed to it on the basis that he (optimistically) assumed that he would not be required to perform it. The contingent nature of a secondary obligation may also be used to explain the special controls for the enforcement of exclusion clauses,[874] but if this is relied upon to justify the scope of the rule against penalties, it leads to a further anomaly in the ease with which it can be evaded through the drafting device of using contingent primary obligations.[875] For example, a "take or pay" clause is subject to the rule against penalties if the buyer is *obliged* to order a minimum quantity and fails to do so,[876] but it may be possible to impose the obligation to *pay* for a minimum quantity without imposing an obligation to order that quantity.[877] Again, a contract for the sale of goods may give the buyer the option 20–140

[872] See, e.g. *Richards v IP Solutions Group Ltd* [2016] EWHC 1835 (QB); [2017] I.R.L.R. 133; *Nosworthy v Instinctif Partners Ltd*, EAT, 28 February 2019; cf. *Signia Wealth Ltd v Vector Trustees Ltd* [2018] EWHC 1040 (Ch).

[873] *Cavendish Square Holding BV v El Makdessi* [2015] UKSC 67; [2016] A.C. 1172 at [130].

[874] *Bank of Credit and Commerce International SA v Ali* [2001] UKHL 8; [2002] 1 A.C. 251 at [66] ("taking with one hand what had been given with the other … " (Lord Hoffmann)); see para.7–009.

[875] A similar problem exists with exclusion clauses: see para.7–045; Coote, *Exception Clauses* (1964).

[876] *M&J Polymers Ltd v Imerys Minerals Ltd* [2008] EWHC 344 (Comm); [2008] 1 Lloyd's Rep. 541 (where the clause was not found to amount to a penalty in any event).

[877] e.g. where the seller agrees to supply as much of the product as the buyer *may* order from time to time, but the buyer agrees to pay a sum which equates to the minimum order; cf. *Associated British*

of postponing the date on which he is to take delivery, on payment of a "carrying charge". Such a provision is not a penalty since the permitted delay is not a breach and the extra charge is the price which the buyer pays for exercising the option conferred on him by the contract.[878]

20–141 **Contingent primary obligations.** The anomaly exposed by the examples at the end of the last paragraph raises two questions. First, should the rule be extended so that it applies to contingent primary obligations, at least in some circumstances? Secondly, if the rule is confined to secondary obligations, should the nature of the term be solely a matter of drafting? In relation to the first question, in *Andrews v ANZ Banking Group Ltd*[879] the High Court of Australia returned to the equitable origins of the rule against penalties to conclude that it is not confined to sanctions which are imposed upon a breach by the payor.[880] This may prevent the rule from being avoided by the skilled draftsman, but it invites the further problem of how to limit it if it is not predicated on a breach by the payor. The High Court held that the rule only applies to a "collateral stipulation" which is invoked upon the failure of a "primary stipulation" (which need not amount to a breach) and not to an "alternative stipulation". This is not an easy distinction to draw,[881] but may be illustrated by the facts of the *Andrews* case itself which involved the charges levied by banks against their customers in circumstances where, broadly speaking, they had exceeded their borrowing limits.[882] When the cases were remitted to the lower courts, it was held that many of the fees were, in fact, "alternative stipulations", i.e. the price payable for an alternative service and not, therefore, subject to the rule.[883]

A submission that the scope of the rule should be similarly so extended in English law was rejected by the Supreme Court in the *Makdessi* case for several reasons:[884] the reasoning in *Andrews* was not "consistent with the equitable rule as it developed historically"; if there is a distinct and wider equitable rule, "it

*Ports v Ferryways NV* [2008] EWHC 1265 (Comm); [2008] 2 Lloyd's Rep. 353; affirmed [2009] EWCA Civ 189; [2009] 1 Lloyd's Rep. without reference to this point; *E-Nik Ltd v Secretary of State for Communities and Local Government* [2012] EWHC 3027 (Comm); [2013] 2 All E.R. (Comm) 868.

[878] *Thomas P Gonzalez Corp v FR Waring (International) Pty Ltd* [1980] 2 Lloyd's Rep. 160; *Lusograin Commercio Internacional de Cereas Ltda v Bunge AG* [1986] 2 Lloyd's Rep. 654; *The Bonde* [1991] 1 Lloyd's Rep. 136 at 145. Demurrage clauses in charterparties (para.7–013) assume that the detention of the ship is a breach and provide for the payment of liquidated damages: *The Lips* [1988] A.C. 395; contrast *The Paragon* [2009] EWCA Civ 555; [2009] 2 Lloyd's Rep. 688 (clause adjusting hire to the market rate not construed as the price for the option of late redelivery); cf. *Jones v Society of Lloyd's*, *The Times*, 2 February 2000 (revival of original debt on debtor's failure to perform settlement agreement).

[879] [2012] HCA 30; (2012) 290 C.L.R. 595.

[880] The almost entirely historical reasoning has been criticised: Carter, Courtenay, Peden, Stewart and Tolhurst (2013) 30 J.C.L. 99; contrast Davies & Turner [2013] C.L.J. 20.

[881] Peel 129 L.Q.R. 152.

[882] cf. *The Office of Fair Trading v Abbey National Plc* [2008] EWHC 875 (Comm); [2008] 2 All E.R. (Comm) 625 where the rule against penalties was found not to apply because there was no breach by a customer in exceeding the limits; a decision from which there was no appeal: see para.7–105, fn.525.

[883] *Paciocco v ANZ Banking Group Ltd* [2015] FCAFC 50. The Full Federal Court held that a late payment fee was subject to the rule, but overturned the decision below that it amounted to a penalty.

[884] *Cavendish Square Holding BV v El Makdessi* [2015] UKSC 67; [2016] A.C. 1172 at [42].

appears to have left no trace in the authorities since the fusion of law and equity"; it is difficult to apply in a case where there is no breach of contract:[885] and the decision does not address "the major legal and commercial implications of transforming a rule for controlling remedies for breach of contract into a jurisdiction to review the content of the substantive obligations which the parties have agreed", given that "modern contracts contain a very great variety of contingent obligations". The difficulty with this last point of course is that, as a justification for retaining the current limit on the scope of the rule, it is entirely circular. That limit having been retained, the second question arises of how to determine if a clause amounts to a secondary obligation.

**A question of substance and not form.** It has long been recognised that the rule against penalties can be circumvented by careful drafting. This is evident from some of the cases already considered above,[886] but it is helpful to begin with a simple example: if B promises to complete a building by 1 January for A at a price of £10m, but also promises that for each week that completion is late, he will pay A the sum of £100k, the rule against penalties may be applied to the latter promise because it amounts to a secondary obligation triggered by the breach of the promise to complete by 1 January; if, however, B promises only to construct the building for a price which depends upon the date of completion, e.g. £1m if completed by 1 January, £9.9m if completed by 8 January, and so on, the rule against penalties does not apply because B is only ever required to perform the primary obligation to construct the building. And yet, in both cases, B has agreed to forfeit £100k per week on a contingent basis, i.e. depending on the date of completion. In the *Makdessi* case, Lord Hodge observed that "where it is clear that the parties have so circumvented the rule and that the substance of the contractual arrangement is the imposition of punishment for breach of contract,[887] the concept of a disguised penalty may enable a court to intervene".[888] Similarly, Lord Neuberger and Lord Sumption observed that the classification of terms for the purpose of the penalty rule depends on the substance of the term and not on its form.[889] 20–142

In the second example of the building contract above, the question which arises is whether the rule against penalties might apply even if there is no breach, but the question may arise in reverse. A significant feature of the decision in the

[885] According to the High Court, a potential penalty is any clause which is "in the nature of a security for and *in terrorem* of the satisfaction of the primary stipulation" and by "security" is meant a provision to secure "compensation ... for the prejudice suffered by the failure of the primary stipulation". But if there is no prior duty which has been breached "it is difficult to see where compensation comes into it": *Cavendish Square Holding BV v El Makdessi* [2015] UKSC 67; [2016] A.C. 1172 at [42].

[886] See para.20–140.

[887] The implication of asking if the clause is in substance a punishment is that the test for a penalty assumes a role in determining the scope of the rule in the first place: Summers [2017] L.M.C.L.Q. 95.

[888] *Cavendish Square Holding BV v El Makdessi* [2015] UKSC 67; [2016] A.C. 1172 at [258]; cf. *Interfoto Picture Library Ltd v Stiletto Visual Programmes Ltd* [1989] Q.B. 433 at 445–446 ("disguised penalty").

[889] *Cavendish Square Holding BV v El Makdessi* [2015] UKSC 67; [2016] A.C. 1172 at [15].

*Makdessi* case was the finding of at least three of their Lordships[890] that the terms in question did *not* amount to secondary obligations, notwithstanding the fact that both were invoked as a consequence of a prior breach of contract. In that case, the defendant sold a business to the claimant by way of the sale of shares representing a controlling interest, at a price which included a very significant premium for goodwill. Part of the price was guaranteed, but the balance was payable in instalments which depended on the future performance of the business. Under the share purchase agreement, if the defendant became a "Defaulting Shareholder" he was no longer entitled to the last two instalments of the price which would otherwise be due (cl.5.1) and the claimant could exercise an option for the purchase of his remaining shareholding at a price calculated by net asset value (cl.5.6), i.e. excluding any premium for goodwill. The defendant breached certain restrictive covenants in connection with his participation in other businesses and his soliciting of clients of the business sold which made him a "Defaulting Shareholder". The claimant sought to enforce both clauses. The estimate of the sums on which the defendant would lose out were inevitably a matter of speculation and dispute, but it was acknowledged that it could be up to c.$45m under cl.5.1 and up to c.$67m under cl.5.6.

According to Lord Neuberger and Lord Sumption (with whom Lord Carnwath agreed), cl.5.1 was "in reality a price adjustment clause",[891] i.e. it was not a secondary obligation. A similar analysis was applied to cl.5.6 which is dealt with below.[892] In substance, the parties had agreed to the sale and purchase of the shares on one of two bases, either with the goodwill intact or without; the former at the full price, the latter at a reduced price. The one reason to doubt this analysis is that the event which determined upon which of the two bases the sale would be completed amounted to a breach of the restrictive covenants, but the involvement of a breach, in context, was regarded as incidental.[893] This finding avoided the obvious difficulty which the Court of Appeal faced in its decision to apply the rule and find that the clause was a penalty; namely that, had compliance with the

---

[890] It is put this way on the basis that there is a degree of ambiguity in the speech of Lord Mance (who, for example, concluded that the effect was "to revise the basic price calculation for the shares": at [181]).

[891] *Cavendish Square Holding BV v El Makdessi* [2015] UKSC 67; [2016] A.C. 1172 at [74].

[892] See para.20–151.

[893] cf. *Euro London Appointments Ltd v Claessens International Ltd* [2006] EWCA Civ 385; [2006] 2 Lloyd's Rep. 437. A similar analysis may be applied to "default interest" provisions in loan agreements which *prospectively* adjust the rate payable by a borrower in default by way of a revaluation of the credit-risk for the lender: *Lordsvale Finance v Bank of Zambia* [1996] Q.B. 752; cf. *Hayfin Opal Luxco 3 Sarl v Windermere VII CMBS Plc* [2016] EWHC 782 (Ch); [2018] 1 B.C.L.C. 118 at [136]. See also the following where the rule was applied and the default rate was held to be a penalty: *Jeancharm Ltd v Barnet Football Club Ltd* [2003] EWCA Civ 58; 92 Con L.R. 26 (260 per cent p.a.); *First Personnel Services Ltd v Halfords Ltd* [2016] EWHC 3220 (Ch) (rate in excess of that payable under the Late Payment of Commercial Debts (Interest) Act 1998 (see para.20–068). In the following cases, the default rate was held not to be a penalty: *Taiwan Scot Co Ltd v The Masters Golf Co Ltd* [2009] EWCA Civ 685 at [17] (15 per cent p.a.); *North Shore Ventures Ltd v Anstead Holdings Inc* [2010] EWHC 1485 (Ch); [2010] 2 Lloyd's Rep. 265 (5 per cent increase with monthly compounding); *ZCCM Investments Holdings Plc v Konkola Copper Mines Plc* [2017] EWHC 3288 (Comm) (LIBOR plus 10 per cent p.a.); *Holyoake v Candy* [2017] EWHC 3397 (Ch) at [486] (no penalty in charging interest on default on a sum already including interest); *Cargill International Trading Pte Ltd v Uttam Galva Steels Ltd* [2019] EWHC 476 (Comm) (one month LIBOR plus 12 per cent).

restrictive covenants not been made the subject of any obligation on the part of the defendant, but had instead been made a condition precedent to his entitlement to the further payments, the rule would not have been engaged because there would have been no breach involved at all. Under the approach advocated by Lord Neuberger and Lord Sumption, for the rule against penalties to apply it is necessary not only for a breach to have been committed, but for the clause in question to have been intended to provide a remedial response to the breach.[894]

As Lord Neuberger and Lord Sumption acknowledged, "price adjustment clauses are open to abuse, and if cl.5.1 were a disguised punishment for the Sellers' breach, it would make no difference that it was expressed as part of the formula for determining the consideration. But before a court can reach that conclusion, it must have some reason to do so."[895] This brings us back to the point with which this paragraph began; namely, how the court determines whether a clause amounts to a secondary obligation, if it is not solely a question of drafting. This is not free from difficulty which perhaps explains why the Supreme Court was split on the question whether to treat cl.5.1 as a secondary obligation, and why it seems that in no case have the courts yet actually decided that a clause drafted as a primary obligation is subject to the rule against penalties in the absence of a breach. It is ultimately a question of construction.[896] In *Vivienne Westwood Ltd v Conduit Street Development Ltd*[897] the parties entered into a lease, accompanied by a side letter, the effect of which was to reduce the rent reserved under the lease. A further term stated that this arrangement could be terminated if the lessee breached any of the terms of the side letter or the lease, in which case the side letter was to be treated as if it "never existed". The lessor argued that the rule against penalties did not apply on the basis that the lessee was at all times under an obligation to pay the rent under the lease and the side letter conferred a "conditional collateral right" entitling the lessee to a discounted rent. The court rejected this submission and held that, "in substance", the true bargain concluded by the parties was that the lessee was obliged to pay the lower rent under the side letter. It was not comparable to a discount for prompt payment. When the lessee committed a breach, as it had some six years into the lease, it therefore came under the secondary obligation to pay the increased rent and the rule against penalties applied.[898]

**Payment on an event triggered by a breach.** It seems that the rule against penalties does not apply where the liability to pay arises, not on the breach itself, but only on an event triggered by the breach. This is the position where a lease provides that, on a tenant's failure to perform his covenant to repair, the landlord 20–143

[894] The breach of the restrictive covenants provided only the "occasion" for the operation of cl.5.1; it was "in no sense a secondary provision": [2015] UKSC 67; [2016] A.C. 1172 at [74].

[895] *Cavendish Square Holding BV v El Makdessi* [2015] UKSC 67; [2016] A.C. 1172 at [77].

[896] There may be some overlap with the test for a penalty, in that if, on the hypothesis that the rule applies, the term would be a penalty, that may pre-dispose the court to find that the rule does, in fact, apply. This may explain why, in the *Makdessi* case, having decided that cl.5.1 was a primary obligation, Lord Neuberger and Lord Sumption nonetheless went on to discuss whether the claimant had a "legitimate interest" to protect which was only relevant *if the test for a penalty applied*: see para.20–154.

[897] [2017] EWHC 350 (Ch); [2017] L. & T.R. 23.

[898] The term was held to be a penalty: see para.20–160.

is entitled to execute the repairs and to recover the cost of so doing from the tenant. A claim for that amount is not a claim for damages but one for the agreed sum,[899] and is not subject to the rule against penalties.[900] A stipulation is, similarly, not subject to the rule against penalties if it provides for the payment of a sum of money on breach of another contract with a third party. In one case A had contracted to build a refinery for B; C had undertaken responsibilities as guarantor for the financing of the project; and A had promised C that, in the event of a breach of A's contract with B, A would pay to C sums equivalent to those which C would have to pay under the guarantee. It was held that the latter stipulation was not a penalty as it "provided for payment of money on a specified event other than a breach of a contractual duty owed by the contemplated payor to the contemplated payee".[901] Similar reasoning seems to apply to performance bonds by which C promises to pay a sum of money to B if A fails to perform his contract with B. Such a promise is independent of the contract between A and B[902] and can be enforced by B against C even if the sum payable exceeds B's true loss; where that is subsequently shown to be the case, however, B must account for any overpayment.[903] Where, however, a clause in a contract between A and B is unenforceable against A because it amounts to a penalty, it is equally unenforceable against C, as guarantor of A's obligations.[904]

20–144 **Payment triggered by several events, not all of which amount to a breach.** It is less clear whether a clause in a contract can be penal if it provides for a payment on several events, one of which is a breach of that contract, while another is not. The problem has arisen under so-called minimum payment clauses in hire-purchase agreements. Such a clause may provide that on premature determination of the agreement the hirer shall bring his payments under it up to a specified proportion of the hire-purchase price (or the whole of it), sometimes described as being "by way of agreed compensation for depreciation". It then specifies the events on which the agreement may be determined. The owner is usually given the right to determine if the hirer commits a breach of the agreement, and in certain other events.[905] The hirer also often has a right to return the goods on bringing his payments up to the specified amount. If the agreement is in fact determined on the ground of the hirer's breach, the rule against penalties

---

[899] See para.21–001.

[900] *Jervis v Harris* [1996] Ch. 195 at 203; cf. *UK Housing Alliance (North West) Ltd v Francis* [2010] EWCA Civ 117; [2010] 3 All E.R. 519 at [10]; Conte 126 L.Q.R. 529.

[901] *Export Credits Guarantee Department v Universal Oil Products Co* [1983] 1 W.L.R. 399 at 402; cf. *Euro London Appointments Ltd v Claessens International Ltd* [2006] EWCA Civ 385; [2006] 2 Lloyd's Rep. 437; *Cadogan Petroleum Holdings Ltd v Global Process Systems LLC* [2013] EWHC 214 (Comm); *Berg v Blackburn Rovers Football Club* [2013] EWHC 1070 (Ch); [2013] I.R.L.R. 537; [2013] 2 Lloyd's Rep. 26; *Edgeworth Capital (Luxembourg) Sarl v Ramblas Investments BV* [2016] EWCA Civ 412.

[902] *Edward Owen Engineering Ltd v Barclays Bank International* [1978] Q.B. 159.

[903] Usually to A who will have procured and paid for the bond: *Cargill International SA v Bangladesh Sugar & Food Industries Corp* [1998] 1 W.L.R. 461; *Comdel Commodities Ltd v Siporex Trade SA* [1997] 1 Lloyd's Rep. 424 at 431; *Tradigrain v State Trading Corp of India* [2005] EWHC 2206 (Comm); [2006] 1 Lloyd's Rep. 216.

[904] *Azimut-Benetti SpA v Healey* [2010] EWHC 2234 (Comm); [2011] 1 Lloyd's Rep. 473.

[905] e.g. the hirer's bankruptcy.

applies.[906] If the agreement is determined on some ground other than the hirer's breach, e.g. because the hirer exercises his right to return the goods, the rule does not apply.[907] This compromise is unsatisfactory; for under it a hirer who wishes to return the goods may be better off if he simply defaults than he would be if he exercised his lawful right to determine the agreement.[908] The hirer's statutory right to determine on payment of one-half of the hire-purchase price and the power of the courts to order payment of a smaller sum under the Consumer Credit Act 1974,[909] if it will adequately compensate the owner, means that this unsatisfactory outcome can at least be avoided for a "regulated agreement".[910]

**What types of remedy are covered?** It is clear that the rule against penalties applies to what was referred to in the *Makdessi* case as a "straightforward damages clause",[911] i.e. a clause requiring the payment of a fixed sum. Examples of such clauses are dealt with below when considering the test for a penalty. Beyond this paradigmatic example, the position is less clear cut.[912] **20–145**

**Withholding payment.** The effect of cl.5.1 in the *Makdessi* case was to disentitle the defendant from receiving the last two instalments of the price due for the shares sold. Those of their Lordships who regarded it as a secondary obligation saw no difficulty in subjecting it to the rule against penalties[913] and while Lord Neuberger and Lord Sumption held that it amounted to a primary obligation, they were prepared to assume that the rule applied to such a remedy.[914] There seems to be no compelling reason to distinguish between a clause which calls for payment *from* the party in breach and a clause which withholds a payment due *to* the party in breach.[915] However, because the rule is confined to secondary obligations, it only applies to the withholding of a payment which has otherwise accrued; it does not apply where performance is a condition precedent to payment (unless this is regarded, in substance, as a disguised penalty).[916] Effect has been given to **20–146**

---

906 *Cooden Engineering Co Ltd v Stanford* [1953] 1 Q.B. 86; *Lamdon Trust Ltd v Hurrell* [1955] 1 W.L.R. 391; cf. *Anglo-Auto Finance Co Ltd v James* [1963] 1 W.L.R. 1042; *United Dominions Trust (Commercial) Ltd v Ennis* [1968] 1 Q.B. 54.

907 *Associated Distributors Ltd v Hall* [1938] 2 K.B. 83; *Re Apex Supply Co Ltd* [1942] Ch. 108; *Campbell Discount Co Ltd v Bridge* [1961] 1 Q.B. 445; reversed on other grounds [1962] A.C. 600, where the House of Lords was equally divided on the point discussed in the text.

908 cf. Law Commission Working Paper No.61, para.22.

909 Consumer Credit Act 1974 s.100(1) and (3).

910 See para.5–007.

911 *Cavendish Square Holding BV v El Makdessi* [2015] UKSC 67; [2016] A.C. 1172 at [32].

912 For the prospect of an agreed remedy by way of specific relief, see para.21–031.

913 *Cavendish Square Holding BV v El Makdessi* [2015] UKSC 67; [2016] A.C. 1172 at [154]–[156] (Lord Mance); at [226] (Lord Hodge).

914 *Cavendish Square Holding BV v El Makdessi* [2015] UKSC 67; [2016] A.C. 1172 at [73].

915 See also *Gilbert-Ash (Northern) Ltd v Modern Engineering (Bristol) Ltd* [1974] A.C. 689 at 698, 703, 711, 723. The authoritative status of this decision was questioned by Bingham LJ in *The Fanti and the Padre Island (No.2)* [1989] 1 Lloyd's Rep. 239 at 255, but in the same case the majority held that a clause providing for retrospective cesser of cover where a member of a P & I club failed, in breach of contract, to pay a call by the club was a penalty; *General Trading Company (Holdings) Ltd v Richmond Corp Ltd* [2008] EWHC 1479 (Comm); [2008] 2 Lloyd's Rep. 475.

916 cf. *Lehman Brothers Special Financing Inc v Carlton Communications Ltd* [2011] EWHC 718 (Ch) at [47]; *Imam-Sadeqe v Bluebay Asset Management (Services) Ltd* [2012] EWHC 3511 (Comm); [2013] I.R.L.R. 344 at [221] ("There is a distinction between contingent rights and accrued rights").

such provisions[917] without any reference to the law as to penalties. Somewhat similar reasoning was used where the rules of an association which had been formed for the enforcement of legal claims by its members provided that members who defaulted in the payment of subscriptions should not share in the proceeds of such claims. Their argument that this provision was a penalty was rejected on the ground that it was "an essential part of the pooling arrangement".[918]

20–147 **Deposits.**[919] A deposit is a sum of money paid as "a guarantee that the contract shall be performed".[920] At common law, it is generally irrecoverable[921] unless the contract otherwise provides,[922] including, if necessary, by a process of implication.[923] While a deposit is payable before, and not after breach, its function is similar to a liquidated damages clause and the rule against penalties can therefore apply to deposits.[924] In the *Workers Trust* case,[925] for example, a contract for the sale of land provided for the payment by the purchaser of a deposit of 25 per cent of the price and for forfeiture of that deposit in the event of the purchaser's default. After the purchaser had paid the deposit and then failed to complete on the due day, the vendor terminated the contract and purported to forfeit the deposit; but the Privy Council held that the deposit was penal and that it must be paid back to the purchaser.[926]

20–148 **Sale of land.** There is a well-established exception to the general rule that a penal deposit must be paid back. In contracts for the sale of land, it is the normal practice for the purchaser to pay a deposit of 10 per cent of the price and for the contract to provide for forfeiture of that deposit in the event of the purchaser's

---

[917] e.g. *Eshelby v Federated European Bank* [1932] 1 K.B. 423; para.17–037.

[918] *Nutting v Baldwin* [1995] 1 W.L.R. 201; cf. *SCI (Sales Curve Interactive) v Titus SARL* [2001] EWCA Civ 591; [2001] 2 All E.R. (Comm) 416 at [66].

[919] Beatson 97 L.Q.R. 389; Beatson, *The Use and Abuse of Unjust Enrichment: Essays on the Law of Restitution* (1991), Ch.3; Milner 42 M.L.R. 508; Harpum [1984] C.L.J. 134.

[920] *Howe v Smith* (1884) 27 Ch D. 89 at 95; cf. *Public Works Commissioners v Hills* [1906] A.C. 368 (so far as it relates to the retention fund); *The Selene G* [1981] 2 Lloyd's Rep. 180 at 185.

[921] *Howe v Smith* (1884) 27 Ch D. 89; *Harrison v Holland* [1921] 3 K.B. 297; [1922] 1 K.B. 211; *Union Eagle Ltd v Golden Achievement Ltd* [1997] A.C. 514 at 518; *Omar v El Wakil* [2001] EWCA Civ 1090; [2002] P. & C.R. 3 at [36].

[922] *Palmer v Temple* (1839) 9 A. & E. 508. A *pre-contract* deposit is recoverable if the negotiations fail to lead to the conclusion of the contemplated contract: *Chillingworth v Esche* [1924] 1 Ch. 97; *Guardian Ocean Cargoes Ltd v Banco do Brazil* [1991] 2 Lloyd's Rep. 68; *idem (No.3)* [1992] 2 Lloyd's Rep. 193.

[923] *JSD Corporation Pte Ltd v Al Waha Capital PJSC* [2009] EWHC 3376 (Ch) where a deposit said to be non-refundable in all circumstances was held only to be non-refundable for the buyer's "default".

[924] *Cavendish Square Holding BV v El Makdessi* [2015] UKSC 67; [2016] A.C. 1172 at [16]. Contrast *Cadogan Petroleum Holdings Ltd v Global Process Systems LLC* [2013] EWHC 214 (Comm); [2013] 2 Lloyd's Rep. 26 at [34].

[925] *Workers Trust and Merchant Bank Ltd v Dojap Investments Ltd* [1993] A.C. 573; Harpum [1993] C.L.J. 389; cf. *Public Works Commissioners v Hills* [1906] A.C. 368; *Starside Properties Ltd v Mustapha* [1974] 1 W.L.R. 816 at 819; *Jobson v Johnson* [1989] 1 W.L.R. 1026 at 1036, 1041.

[926] Contrast *Pye v British Automobile Commercial Syndicate Ltd* [1906] 1 K.B. 425 where the deposit was found to be reasonable in relation to the loss likely to be suffered and was therefore forfeited; cf. *Starside Properties Ltd v Mustapha* [1974] 1 W.L.R. 816 at 819.

default. It is generally agreed that such a provision is valid even though it does not, and does not purport to, bear any relation to the vendor's loss. In the *Workers Trust* case, the Privy Council described the exception as anomalous,[927] but nevertheless recognised its existence.

**Law of Property Act 1925 s.49(2).** This subsection gives the court power "if it thinks fit" to order the return of a deposit paid under a contract for the sale of land.[928] An earlier and narrow view that the subsection applied only when the vendor could not, for some reason, have obtained specific performance[929] has given way to a broader view that the discretion conferred by it is to be exercised "where justice requires it".[930] This is to be welcomed; but unfortunately the cases give no clear indication of the circumstances in which the courts will exercise their discretion under the subsection. That discretion is no longer needed where the deposit is penal in effect, now that the *Workers Trust* case has held such a deposit to be recoverable at common law. This development may have reduced the need to invoke the statutory discretion and may in part account for the recently expressed view that it will be exercised in favour of a defaulting purchaser only in "exceptional circumstances".[931] Just when circumstances are, for this purpose, exceptional remains obscure; but the requirement is evidently not satisfied merely by the fact that the deposit substantially exceeds the normal 10 per cent of the price[932] or by the fact that the vendor has not established that the breach has caused him any loss.[933] 20–149

**Prepayments.** A contract of sale may provide for payment of the price in instalments and add that, on default in payment of any one instalment, those already paid shall be forfeited. It has been held that "retention of instalments which have been paid under contract so as to become the absolute property of the 20–150

---

[927] *Workers Trust and Merchant Bank Ltd v Dojap Investments Ltd* [1993] A.C. 573 at 578; cf. at 580 ("without logic").

[928] It cannot be excluded by the agreement of the parties: *Aribisala v St James Homes (Grosvenor) Dock Ltd* [2007] EWHC 1694 (Ch); [2007] 37 E.G. 234.

[929] See *James Macara v Barclays Bank Ltd* [1944] 2 All E.R. 31 at 32; affirmed [1945] K.B. 148. See also *Michael Richards Properties Ltd v St Saviour's Parish* [1975] 3 All E.R. 416; *Zieme v Gregory* [1963] V.R. 214.

[930] *Universal Corp v Five Ways Properties Ltd* [1979] 1 All E.R. 552 at 555; Oakley [1980] C.L.J. 24; *Schindler v Pigault* (1975) 30 P. & C.R. 328 at 336.

[931] *Omar v El-Wakil* [2001] EWCA Civ 1090 at [37]; [2002] P. & C.R. 3; *Midill (97PL) Ltd v Park Lane Estates Ltd* [2008] EWCA Civ 1227; [2009] 1 W.L.R. 2460.

[932] *Omar v El-Wakil* [2001] EWCA Civ 1090 at [36]; the deposit was about 31 per cent of the price, but it was not argued that it was penal: at [31]. Perhaps for this reason, no reference was made to the *Workers Trust* case [1993] A.C. 573; para.20–147.

[933] *Omar v El-Wakil* [2001] EWCA Civ 1090 at [37]; *Aribisala v St James Homes (Grosvenor) Dock Ltd* [2008] EWHC 456 (Ch); [2009] 1 W.L.R. 1089; *Midill (97PL) Ltd v Park Lane Estates Ltd* [2008] EWCA Civ 1227; [2009] 1 W.L.R. 2460.

vendor does not fall within the penalty rule", but is subject to the court's jurisdiction to grant relief against forfeiture.[934] This jurisdiction is considered below.[935]

20–151 **Transfer of property.** We saw above that, in the *Makdessi* case, a further consequence of the defendant breaching the restrictive covenants and becoming a "Defaulting Shareholder" was that the claimant could exercise an option for the purchase of the defendant's remaining shareholding at a price calculated by net asset value (cl.5.6), i.e. excluding any premium for goodwill. Lord Neuberger and Lord Scarman held that cl.5.6 was intended to sever the connection between the claimant and the defendant, in light of his conduct, and to do so at a price which reflected the fact that the claimant would no longer have the benefit of the goodwill associated with his loyalty and service. It therefore belonged "among the parties' primary obligations, even if the occasion for its operation is a breach of contract".[936] By contrast, Lord Hodge regarded it as a secondary obligation, but could see "no reason in principle why the rule against penalties should not extend to clauses that require the contract-breaker to transfer property to the innocent party on breach",[937] and this is supported by earlier authority.[938] There is equally no reason why the rule should not extend to other forms of "payment in kind".

### *(ii) Test*

20–152 **A question of construction.**[939] The question whether a clause is penal depends on its construction and on the surrounding circumstances at the time of contracting, or at the time of any material variation to the contract;[940] not at the time of breach.[941] In answering this question, little or no weight should be attached to the fact that the clause is described in the contract as a "penalty", or as "liquidated damages".[942] Clauses in identical terms may be held penal or not, according to the subject-matter of the contracts and to the circumstances in which the contracts were made.[943]

---

934 *Else (1982) Ltd v Parkland Holdings Ltd* [1994] 1 B.C.L.C. 130 at 146, citing *Stockloser v Johnson* [1954] 1 Q.B. 476 in support, which is discussed below; cf. *Cadogan Petroleum Holdings Ltd v Global Process Systems LLC* [2013] EWHC 214 (Comm); [2013] 2 Lloyd's Rep. 26.

935 See para.20–172.

936 *Cavendish Square Holding BV v El Makdessi* [2015] UKSC 67; [2016] A.C. 1172 at [83].

937 *Cavendish Square Holding BV v El Makdessi* [2015] UKSC 67; [2016] A.C. 1172 at [230].

938 *Jobson v Johnson* [1989] 1 W.L.R. 1026.

939 Dawson [2016] L.M.C.L.Q. 207.

940 *Unaoil Ltd v Leighton Offshore Pte Ltd* [2014] EWHC 2965 (Comm); 156 Con L.R. 24.

941 *Dunlop Pneumatic Tyre Co Ltd v New Garage & Motor Co Ltd* [1915] A.C. 79 at 87; *Philips Hong Kong v Attorney General of Hong Kong* (1993) 61 Build. L.R. 41.

942 *Kemble v Farren* (1829) 6 Bing. 141 ("liquidated damages" held penalty); *Elphinstone v Monkland Iron & Coal Co Ltd* (1886) 11 App. Cas. 332 ("penalty" held liquidated damages); cf. *Pagnan & Fratelli v Coprosol SA* [1981] 1 Lloyd's Rep. 283; *GPP Big Field LLP v Solar EPC Solutions SL* [2018] EWHC 2866 (Comm); *Triple Point Technology Inc v PTT Public Co Ltd* [2019] EWCA Civ 230; [2019] 1 W.L.R. 3549.

943 Contrast *Phonographic Equipment* (1958) *Ltd v Muslu* [1961] 1 W.L.R. 1379 with *Lombank Ltd v Excell* [1964] 1 Q.B. 415.

**Punishment is prohibited; not deterrence.** A clause was said to be penal if it provided for "a payment of money stipulated as *in terrorem* of the offending party",[944] or, as it had been put more recently, if the contractual function of the clause was "deterrent rather than compensatory".[945] In the *Makdessi* case, the concept of deterrence was rejected by the Supreme Court as a guide to whether a clause is a penalty: 20–153

> "To describe [a clause] as a deterrent (or, to use the Latin equivalent, *in terrorem*) does not add anything.[946] A deterrent provision in a contract is simply one species of provision designed to influence the conduct of the party potentially affected. It is no different in this respect from a contractual inducement. Neither is it inherently penal or contrary to the policy of the law."[947]

**The "true test".** We saw above that the Supreme Court in the *Makdessi* case held that the test for a penalty is: 20–154

> "whether the impugned provision is a secondary obligation which imposes a detriment on the contract-breaker out of all proportion to any legitimate interest of the innocent party in the enforcement of the primary obligation."[948]

Lord Neuberger and Lord Sumption described this as the "true test", the intention behind this description being to move on from a test under which it was only necessary to ask whether the "detriment" agreed by the parties was a "genuine pre-estimate of loss". The relevant question is whether the contractual provision "is penal, not whether it is a pre-estimate of loss".[949]

**Legitimate interest of the innocent party.** The concept of a "legitimate interest" referred to as part of the "true test" has also been referred to in the context of judicial remedies such as the action for the agreed sum,[950] specific performance,[951] and an account of profits.[952] In the present context, it seems clear that it is a reference to what has been referred to as the "performance interest". This is evident from the words of Lord Neuberger and Lord Sumption which immediately follow their formulation of the "true test": "The innocent party can have no proper interest in simply punishing the defaulter. His interest is in performance or in some appropriate alternative to performance."[953] Put simply, an agreed remedy which goes beyond what the courts will acknowledge as the limit of the innocent party's performance (legitimate) interest is penal and unenforceable. 20–155

[944] *Dunlop Pneumatic Tyre Co Ltd v New Garage & Motor Co Ltd* [1915] A.C. 79 at 86.
[945] *Lordsvale Finance Ltd v Bank of Zambia* [1996] Q.B. 752 at 762G.
[946] Cf. *Campbell Discount Co Ltd v Bridge* [1962] A.C. 600 at 622.
[947] *Cavendish Square Holding BV v El Makdessi* [2015] UKSC 67; [2016] A.C. 1172 at [31].
[948] *Cavendish Square Holding BV v El Makdessi* [2015] UKSC 67; [2016] A.C. 1172 at [32]; cf. at [152] (Lord Mance), [255] (Lord Hodge).
[949] *Cavendish Square Holding BV v El Makdessi* [2015] UKSC 67; [2016] A.C. 1172 at [31].
[950] See para.21–013.
[951] See para.21–109.
[952] See para.20–011.
[953] *Cavendish Square Holding BV v El Makdessi* [2015] UKSC 67; [2016] A.C. 1172 at [32]; Rowan [2019] C.L.J. 148.

20–156 **"Out of all proportion"; "extravagant" and "unconscionable".** Lord Neuberger and Lord Sumption's formulation of the test for a penalty is to ask whether the agreed remedy is "out of all proportion" to the performance interest of the innocent party, whereas for Lord Mance[954] and Lord Hodge[955] it is to ask whether the remedy is "extravagant", "exorbitant", or "unconscionable" when regard is had to the "innocent party's interest in performance of the contract". It is clear that these are just different ways of putting the question whether the agreed remedy goes beyond what the courts acknowledge as the limit of the innocent party's performance interest. Lord Neuberger and Lord Sumption referred to the innocent party's interest "in performance, or *in some appropriate alternative to performance*" and the appropriate alternative, in the absence of any agreed remedy, is the judicial remedy which would be ordered by the courts, usually in the form of damages and intended as compensation for the innocent party's loss. What the reference to "out of all proportion", "exorbitant" etc., allows for is some degree of latitude, or what has been referred to as a "generous margin" in the parties' agreement on the appropriate level of compensation,[956] but not a fundamental departure from the underlying compensatory aim.[957]

20–157 **Actual loss and recoverable loss.** In determining the limits of the "generous margin" afforded to the parties, it may be helpful to draw a distinction between "actual loss" and "recoverable loss". "Actual loss" refers to all loss in fact caused by the defaulting party's breach of contract, whether or not it would be recovered as damages at law. "Recoverable loss" refers to all loss which is proved to have been caused by the defaulting party's breach and which is not ruled out as damages because of other limitations on recovery, such as mitigation and remoteness. Without suggesting that it may be possible to reconcile all of the decisions of the courts, it is submitted that, as a general guide, the parties are permitted to agree a remedy which allows them to contract around some of the uncertainty in their recoverable loss, but not beyond what the courts will regard as the limit of their actual loss (or performance interest). This is illustrated below by considering some of the leading cases in the context of the uncertainty surrounding mitigation, remoteness and proof of loss. This last category is the most difficult and it is in this context that it will be necessary to consider whether, and to what extent, the *Makdessi* case introduces a "broader approach".

20–158 **Mitigation uncertainty.** In *Murray v Leisureplay Plc*[958] no penalty was found to have been created by a clause which entitled a director to the payment of 12 months' gross salary and pension contributions for unlawful termination of his service contract. Arden LJ observed that a contractual provision is not a penalty simply because it may result in "overpayment", i.e. a sum greater than the legally recoverable damages, because "(t)he parties are allowed a generous margin".[959]

---

954 *Cavendish Square Holding BV v El Makdessi* [2015] UKSC 67; [2016] A.C. 1172 at [152].
955 *Cavendish Square Holding BV v El Makdessi* [2015] UKSC 67; [2016] A.C. 1172 at [255].
956 See text to fn.959.
957 However, see the discussion of the "broader approach" advocated in the *Makdessi* case below, para.20–161.
958 [2005] EWCA Civ 963; [2005] I.R.L.R. 946.
959 *Murray v Leisureplay Plc* [2005] EWCA Civ 963; [2005] I.R.L.R. 946 at [43].

The judge had found that the clause was a penalty because it failed to take any account of the requirement of mitigation which would have applied to an assessment of damages. Buxton LJ did not regard this as decisive on the basis that it would have been difficult to say with confidence at the time of entering into the contract what might happen to the director were he to be dismissed and "such a clause would directly invite disputes about the reasonableness of [the director's] behaviour after termination, of the kind that clauses stipulating the amount of compensation are precisely designed to avoid."[960] In sum, the parties were allowed some margin to contract around the *uncertainty* associated with mitigation. This might be contrasted with a case in which any question of mitigation would be clear and straightforward even at the time of the contract. For example, in a contract for the sale of goods where there is an available market, the normal measure of damages for breach by either the seller or the buyer is the difference between the contract price and the market price. This simply reflects the fact that, upon breach, either party is expected to mitigate by selling the goods,[961] or buying a substitute,[962] at the market price. If the parties to such a contract agreed in advance a liquidated sum to deal with breach, it seems very likely, in contrast to *Murray v Leisureplay,* that it would be regarded as a penalty to the extent that it failed to take account of the requirement of mitigation.[963]

It has been said that "where there is a liquidated damage clause which is valid … there is no room for arguments on mitigation of damages".[964] That is correct in the sense that, *if* the clause is valid, the claimant is simply entitled to the agreed sum without limitation, but the question of mitigation and its effect on the level of recoverable loss if the claimant had sued for damages may be relevant to the prior question of validity.[965] On this basis, it would be very odd if, having already taken mitigation into account, there was still "room for arguments on mitigation".

**Remoteness uncertainty.** In *Robophone Facilities Ltd v Blank* Diplock LJ dealt with the potential effect of remoteness on a liquidated damages clause in the following terms: 20–159

> "If the contract contained an express undertaking by the defendant to be responsible for all *actual loss* to the plaintiff occasioned by the defendant's breach, whatever that loss might turn out to be, it would not affect the defendant's liability for the loss actually sustained by the plaintiff that the defendant did not know of the special circumstances which were likely to cause any enhancement of the plaintiff's loss. And so if at the time of the contract the plaintiff informs the defendant that his loss in the event of a particular breach is likely to be £X by describing this sum as liquidated damages in the terms of his offer to contract, and the defendant expressly undertakes to pay £X to the plaintiff in the event of such breach, the

[960] [2005] EWCA Civ 963; [2005] I.R.L.R. 946 at [115].

[961] Sale of Goods Act 1979 s.50(3); see para.20–057.

[962] Sale of Goods Act 1979 s.51(3); see para.20–051.

[963] One imagines that such a provision would be very unusual, if used at all; more likely is a provision which attempts, by agreement, to "crystallise" the damages recoverable as the difference between the contract price and the market price: see, for example, Clause 20 of GAFTA 49: *Bunge SA v Nidera BV* [2015] UKSC 43; [2015] 2 Lloyd's Rep. 469.

[964] *Abrahams v Performing Right Society Ltd* [1995] I.C.R. 1028 at 1041.

[965] *MSC Mediterranean Shipping Co SA v Cottonex Anstalt* [2015] EWHC 283 (Comm) at [113]; cf. *Lansat Shipping Co Ltd v Glencore Grain BV* [2009] EWCA Civ 855; [2009] 2 Lloyd's Rep. 688.

clause which contains the stipulation is not a "penalty clause" unless £X is not a genuine and reasonable estimate by the plaintiff of the loss which he will in fact be likely to obtain."[966]

What appears to be said is that a reasonable estimate of the "actual loss" occasioned by the breach represents the limit of what may be recoverable by the injured party, but such sum is recoverable notwithstanding the fact that, *in the absence of the agreed sum*, the full extent of the claimant's actual loss might not be recoverable on grounds of remoteness.[967]

20–160 **Proof of loss uncertainty.** The suggested distinction between an agreement which amounts to a "generous margin" in determining the remedy intended to protect the performance interest and an agreement which goes beyond what could conceivably be awarded as a remedy by the courts is perhaps most difficult in the type of case where uncertainty lies not in the application of limitations like mitigation or remoteness, but in simply proving the actual loss occasioned by the breach. The leading example is *Dunlop Pneumatic Tyre Co Ltd v New Garage & Motor Co Ltd*[968] which was also the leading case on the rule against penalties prior to the *Makdessi* case. The parties entered into a contract for the supply of tyres, covers and tubes which contained a clause providing for the payment of £5 for every tyre, cover or tube sold in breach of any provision of the agreement. The supplier claimed liquidated damages under this clause when the purchaser sold on a tyre cover in breach of a resale price maintenance clause.[969] The *Dunlop* case had become most well-known for Lord Dunedin's formulation of a number of tests "which may prove helpful"[970] in determining whether a clause is a penalty. The decision that the clause in that case was not a penalty rested heavily on the last of these tests, namely that "[i]t is no obstacle to the sum stipulated being a genuine pre-estimate of damage that the consequences of breach are such as to make precise pre-estimation an impossibility. On the contrary, that is just the situation when pre-estimated damage was the true bargain between the parties".[971]

As explained by Lord Neuberger and Lord Sumption in the *Makdessi* case, it seems clear that the decision in the *Dunlop* case was heavily influenced by Lord Atkinson's reasoning. He emphasised the importance to Dunlop of the protection of their brand, reputation and goodwill, and their authorised distribution network. The provisions in the contract, including the resale price maintenance clause,

966 *Robophone Facilities Ltd v Blank* [1966] 1 W.L.R. 1428 at 1448 (emphasis added).

967 While Diplock LJ concludes that the injured party's actual loss would be recoverable notwithstanding that the requirements of the remoteness test have *not been met*, the way that test is rationalised by Lord Hoffmann in *The Achilleas* [2008] UKHL 48; [2009] 1 A.C. 61 and the Court of Appeal in *Supershield Ltd v Siemens Building Technologies FE Ltd* [2010] EWCA Civ 7; [2010] 1 Lloyd's Rep. 349 (namely that remoteness is determined by whether the defendant assumed responsibility for the type of loss incurred regardless of foresight or contemplation by the defendant; see para.20–131) provides an alternative analysis under which it is because of the agreed remedy that the test of remoteness *has been met*. In this respect, the finding of a penalty by Blair J in *The Paragon* [2009] EWHC 551 (Comm); [2009] 1 Lloyd's Rep. 658 at [22] is open to doubt (affirmed [2009] EWCA Civ 555; [2009] 2 Lloyd's Rep. 688 without explicit reference to this point, but see at [36]).

968 [1915] A.C. 79.

969 This would now be unlawful but was a legitimate restriction of competition at the time.

970 *Dunlop Pneumatic Tyre Co Ltd v New Garage & Motor Co Ltd* [1915] A.C. 79 at 87.

971 *Dunlop Pneumatic Tyre Co Ltd v New Garage & Motor Co Ltd* [1915] A.C. 79 at 87–88.

were intended to "prevent the disorganisation of their trading system and *the consequent injury* to their trade in many directions".[972] In that context, "they had an obvious interest to prevent … undercutting" and it was "impossible to say that *that interest* was incommensurate with the sum agreed to be paid".[973] In other words, while the cumulative effect of each individual breach damaged Dunlop's trading system and therefore its goodwill, the uncertainty, not to say impossibility, of attributing actual loss to each and every breach, if Dunlop was confined to a claim for damages, justified the payment of a fixed sum per breach which was not out of all proportion to Dunlop's performance interest, i.e. what the court acknowledged Dunlop may have actually lost.

The decision in *Dunlop* may be contrasted with the decision in the *Westwood* case which was considered earlier.[974] The clause under which the rent payable under the lease replaced that due under the side letter with retrospective effect[975] was a penalty because the lessor could "not establish that it had a greater interest in seeing [the lessee] perform all its obligations promptly than would be compensated by interest, damages and costs otherwise recoverable for a breach of covenant."[976] The conclusion appears to be that there was no reason to believe that damages would not adequately protect the lessor's performance interest in the form of any actual loss which it may have incurred; unlike *Dunlop*, this was not a case of an uncertain actual loss for which the lessor was simply being afforded a "generous margin".[977]

**A broader approach?** In the *Makdessi* case Lord Neuberger and Lord Sumption observed that, in the case of a "straightforward damages clause", the performance interest of the innocent party "will rarely extend beyond compensation for the breach, and we therefore expect that Lord Dunedin's four tests [in the *Dunlop* case[978]] would usually be perfectly adequate to determine its validity".[979] Those tests must therefore be regarded as having some continued utility and they were summarised as follows:[980] 20–161

> "(a) that the provision would be penal if 'the sum stipulated for is extravagant and unconscionable in amount in comparison with the greatest loss that could conceivably be

[972] *Dunlop Pneumatic Tyre Co Ltd v New Garage & Motor Co Ltd* [1915] A.C. 79 at 91–92 (emphasis added).

[973] *Dunlop Pneumatic Tyre Co Ltd v New Garage & Motor Co Ltd* [1915] A.C. 79 at 91–92 (emphasis added).

[974] See para.20–142.

[975] The court held that it would have been possible to sever the words which led to this effect so that the reversion to the market rent would only apply prospectively. The judge would still have found that this amounted to a penalty, but acknowledged that it would not have been so clear cut.

[976] *Vivienne Westwood Ltd v Conduit Street Development Ltd* [2017] EWHC 350 (Ch); [2017] L. & T.R. 23 at [52]. Contrast *Re SHB Realisations Ltd* [2018] EWHC 402 (Ch); [2018] 2 B.C.L.C. 654 at [37]–[38].

[977] This conclusion is, however, open to challenge. For example, it seems to be based on an assessment carried out at *the time of the breach* which was relatively minor, whereas the test for a penalty is applied at the date of the contract: see para.20–152. It may be supported on the ground that the increased rent was payable *in addition* to any damages recoverable.

[978] *Dunlop Pneumatic Tyre Co Ltd v New Garage & Motor Co Ltd* [1915] A.C. 79 at 87–88.

[979] *Cavendish Square Holding BV v El Makdessi* [2015] UKSC 67; [2016] A.C. 1172 at [32].

[980] *Cavendish Square Holding BV v El Makdessi* [2015] UKSC 67; [2016] A.C. 1172 at [21].

> proved to have followed from the breach';[981] (b) that the provision would be penal if the breach consisted only in the non-payment of money and it provided for the payment of a larger sum;[982] (c) that there was 'a presumption (but no more)' that it would be penal if it was payable in a number of events of varying gravity;[983] and (d) that it would not be treated as penal by reason only of the impossibility of precisely pre-estimating the true loss."

As we have already seen, the two clauses in question in the *Makdessi* case were not "straightforward damages clause" and in relation to such clauses, it is said that a "broader test",[984] or "broader approach",[985] is needed. It is, however, debatable whether the *test* is now broader given the obvious similarity between the "true test"[986] and the first of the tests formulated by Lord Dunedin, above. If the courts are now adopting a broader *approach*, that is really being applied to what they are prepared to recognise as the "performance interest", in relation to which the parties are afforded a generous margin in seeking to protect it by an agreed remedy. This may be illustrated by further consideration of the decision in the *Makdessi* case, as well as the decision in the conjoined appeal in *ParkingEye Ltd v Beavis*.

In the *Makdessi* case we have already seen that at least three of their Lordships held that cl.5.1 was a primary obligation in the form of a price adjustment clause, but all of their Lordships agreed that it was intended to protect the claimant's interest in the goodwill for which it had paid. What was lost by any breach of the restrictive covenants was the value of that goodwill. If regarded as a secondary obligation, which it was by Lord Hodge, in remedial terms what cl.5.1 was

---

981 See the example given in *Clydebank Engineering Co v Don Jose Ramos Isquierdo y Castaneda* [1905] A.C. 6 at 10.

982 To the extent that this "test" relied on the fact that the only amount recoverable, as damages for failure to pay money when due, was interest, and then only when available by statute or by special agreement (*Dunlop Pneumatic Tyre Co Ltd v New Garage & Motor Co Ltd* [1915] A.C. 79 at 87), it must now be of doubtful utility: see para.20–065. It does not apply merely because a contract under which a sum of money is payable in instalments provides that, on default of any payment, the whole balance is to become immediately due, i.e. an "acceleration clause": *Protector Loan Co v Grice* (1879–80) L.R. 5 Q.B.D. 592; *Wallingford v Mutual Society* (1880) 5 App. Cas. 685; cf. *Wadham Stringer Finance Ltd v Meany* [1981] 1 W.L.R. 39; *Sport International Bussum BV v Inter-Footwear Ltd* [1984] 1 W.L.R. 776 at 793; *White & Carter (Councils) Ltd v McGregor* [1962] A.C. 413, where it was conceded that the acceleration clause was valid; *Edgeworth Capital (Luxembourg) Sarl v Ramblas Investments BV* [2016] EWCA Civ 412; *ZCCM Investments Holdings Plc v Konkola Copper Mines Plc* [2017] EWHC 3288 (Comm); *Holyoake v Candy* [2017] EWHC 3397 (Ch) at [486]. A stipulation for accelerated payment of a loan *plus interest* for the *whole* contractual period was said to be penal in *The Angelic Star* [1988] 1 Lloyd's Rep. 122 at 125; applied in *County Leasing Ltd v East* [2007] EWHC 2907 (QB).

983 See, e.g. *Kemble v Farren* (1829) 6 Bing. 141; *Willson v Love* [1896] 1 Q.B. 626; *Ariston SRL v Charly Records Ltd*, *Financial Times*, 21 March 1990; cf. *Webster v Bosanquet* [1912] A.C. 394; *Philips Hong Kong v Attorney General of Hong Kong* (1993) 61 Build. L.R. 41. For continued reliance on this "test" post-*Makdessi*, see *Vivienne Westwood Ltd v Conduit Street Development Ltd* [2017] EWHC 350 (Ch); [2017] L. & T.R. 23 at [65].

984 *Cavendish Square Holding BV v El Makdessi* [2015] UKSC 67; [2016] A.C. 1172 at [25] (Lord Neuberger and Lord Sumption).

985 *Cavendish Square Holding BV v El Makdessi* [2015] UKSC 67; [2016] A.C. 1172 at [225] (Lord Hodge); cf. *Cine Bes Filmcilik ve Yapimcilik v United International Pictures* [2003] EWCA Civ 1669; [2004] 1 C.L.C. 401; *Murray v Leisureplay Plc* [2005] EWCA Civ 963; [2005] I.R.L.R. 946 at [113]; *General Trading Company (Holdings) Ltd v Richmond Corp Ltd* [2008] EWHC 1479 (Comm); [2008] 2 Lloyd's Rep. 475 at [133].

986 See para.20–154.

addressing was "the disloyalty of a seller who was prepared in any way to attack the company's goodwill".[987] As acknowledged by Lord Sumption in the *One Step* case, where the issue was the availability of negotiating damages,[988] it is notoriously difficult to value loss of goodwill: "the economic effect of the breaches is inherently incapable of being precisely estimated, and may be incapable of even imprecise measurement".[989] But as we have seen when considering the *Dunlop* case,[990] this is precisely when the parties are afforded a generous margin, provided the remedy stipulated for is not "extravagant and unconscionable in amount in comparison with the greatest loss that could conceivably be proved to have followed from the breach."[991] Thus, having decided that cl.5.1 was a secondary obligation, Lord Hodge concluded that it was "harsh", but not "exorbitant".[992]

There are passages in the speeches of their Lordships in the *Makdessi* case which suggest that the "broader approach" goes even further than allowing for a generous margin in the protection of the performance interest, conceived of in terms of "loss". We have seen that Lord Neuberger and Lord Sumption acknowledged an interest which extends "beyond compensation".[993] Similarly, Lord Mance observed that: "commercial interests may justify the imposition upon a breach of contract of a financial burden which cannot either be related directly to loss caused by the breach or justified by reference to the impossibility of assessing such loss."[994] The difficulty with divorcing the test for a penalty from any conception of what the claimant may have lost is that it is not obvious what is being compared when asking if the agreed remedy is "out of all proportion" or "exorbitant"; nor why the test should only be applied to clauses responding to a breach. What one is left with is what Lord Hodge described as a "value judgment".[995]

That may be the only basis upon which one can explain the *ParkingEye* case which concerned a fine of £85 imposed on a motorist who exceeded the limit of two hours free parking in a retail centre car park operated by the defendant, but owned by a third party. The decision of the Court was that the rule against penalties applied to the charge, but that it was not a penalty.[996] One difficulty with this conclusion is that the defendant suffered no financial loss if the claimant breached the obligation to vacate the space within two hours; indeed, its business model required some motorists to breach this obligation in order to provide the income stream which allowed it to cover the costs of operating the car park and make a profit from its services. Lord Neuberger and Lord Sumption concluded

---

987 *Cavendish Square Holding BV v El Makdessi* [2015] UKSC 67; [2016] A.C. 1172 at [275].

988 See para.20–018.

989 *Morris-Garner v One Step (Support) Ltd* [2018] UKSC 20; [2019] A.C. 649 at [105].

990 See para.20–160.

991 See text to fn.981.

992 *Cavendish Square Holding BV v El Makdessi* [2015] UKSC 67; [2016] A.C. 1172 at [282]. He came to the same conclusion about cl.5.6.

993 See text to fn.979.

994 *Cavendish Square Holding BV v El Makdessi* [2015] UKSC 67; [2016] A.C. 1172 at [145].

995 *Cavendish Square Holding BV v El Makdessi* [2015] UKSC 67; [2016] A.C. 1172 at [249], [259], [287].

996 Nor was it held to be an unfair term under the statutory regulations available for the protection of consumers (Lord Toulson dissenting): see para.7–110; and para.20–171.

that the defendant had a "legitimate interest … which extended beyond the recovery of any loss",[997] but it may be more accurate to say that it had an interest which extended beyond any *pecuniary* loss. In this regard, they referred to the interest of the third-party landowner who received a fee from the defendant for the right to operate the scheme and the interest of the retailers and their customers in ensuring a reasonable turnover of parking spaces, and rejected the submission that such third party interest was irrelevant.[998] This is, however, an approach to the relevant performance interest which appears to go beyond any previous case.[999] For example, in both the *Dunlop* case and the *Makdessi* case, it was possible to identify a "loss" but one which "does not admit of precise proof or calculation".[1000] But what loss of any sort was caused to the defendant by the breach in *ParkingEye*? The decision that the charge did not amount to a penalty can, it seems, only be explained on the basis of the court's willingness to recognise new forms of performance interest, as much as anything to uphold the parties' agreement.[1001] On this basis the real significance of the case may lie not in what it decided in relation to the test for a penalty, but in its recognition of new forms of non-pecuniary loss which might legitimately be regarded as the subject of judicial remedy.[1002]

20–162 **Nature of the contract.** In the *Makdessi* case Lord Neuberger and Lord Sumption observed that, while the modern rule against penalties is substantive, not procedural, and does not normally depend for its operation on a finding that one party has taken unfair advantage of another, "the circumstances in which the contract was made are not entirely irrelevant. In a negotiated contract between properly advised parties of comparable bargaining power, the strong initial presumption must be that the parties themselves are the best judges of what is legitimate in a provision dealing with the consequences of breach".[1003] In some cases, it may also be relevant to take account of "market expectations".[1004]

---

[997] *Cavendish Square Holding BV v El Makdessi* [2015] UKSC 67; [2016] A.C. 1172 at [99].

[998] *Cavendish Square Holding BV v El Makdessi* [2015] UKSC 67; [2016] A.C. 1172 at [99].

[999] As far as any third-party interest is concerned, while there are circumstances in which a contracting party may recover a third party's loss, it is far from clear that those circumstances were present in the *ParkingEye* case. There is no obvious analogy to the decision in *Beswick v Beswick* [1968] A.C. 58, para.21–024, where it was the order of the court which protected the third party and the circumstances of the case do not appear to fit the requirements for recovery of third party loss discussed at para.14–026 and following.

[1000] *Clydebank Engineering and Shipbuilding Co v Don Jose Ramos Yzquierdo y Castaneda* [1905] A.C. 6 at 20 (Lord Robertson).

[1001] It may have been preferable to find that the rule against penalties did not apply on the basis that the charge was not payable on breach, but represented the price payable for parking in excess of two hours. That would avoid the obvious difficulties associated with a breach from which a party is intended to gain, but the Court concluded that, "on reflection", it was not the correct analysis: *Cavendish Square Holding BV v El Makdessi* [2015] UKSC 67; [2016] A.C. 1172 at [94].

[1002] cf. Rowan [2019] C.L.J. 148 at [170]–[171].

[1003] *Cavendish Square Holding BV v El Makdessi* [2015] UKSC 67; [2016] A.C. 1172 at [35]. See the comment of Lord Mance to similar effect at [152]; cf. *Alfred McAlpine Capital Projects Ltd v Tilebox Ltd* [2005] EWHC 281 (TCC); [2005] Build. L.R. 271 at [48]; cf. *Philips Hong Kong v Attorney General of Hong Kong* (1993) 61 Build. L.R. 41 at 59–60; *ZCCM Investments Holdings Plc v Konkola Copper Mines Plc* [2017] EWHC 3288 (Comm) at [33].

[1004] *Murray v Leisureplay Plc* [2005] EWCA Civ 963; [2005] I.R.L.R. 946 at [70].

**Nature of the breach.** The nature of the breach committed may be relevant to the question of whether the sum stipulated is penal. Where the defendant is guilty of a non-repudiatory breach and the contract is terminated under an express provision, he is only liable in damages for the loss which flows from any breach committed prior to termination.[1005] A clause which stipulates for a sum which includes the loss flowing from the premature determination of the contract (the "loss of bargain") is likely therefore to be penal.[1006] Where, however, the defendant is guilty of a repudiatory breach (e.g. breach of a "condition")[1007] the defendant would be liable in damages for loss of bargain and the same clause is therefore unlikely to be penal.[1008] **20–163**

**The finding of a penalty is rare.** In addition to the decisions already considered above, other recent examples of a "broader approach" have led to the conclusion that the following do not amount to a penalty: the payment of 50 per cent of net salary and 50 per cent of the agreed signing fee by a finance broker for failing to honour his employment contract;[1009] the writing off of 90 per cent of the consideration for the purchase of shares where the seller failed to procure a loan guarantee;[1010] and payment on the customer's default of 20 per cent of the purchase price for the construction of a yacht.[1011] Even before the decision in the *Makdessi* case, a finding of a penalty was rare.[1012] **20–164**

**Liquidated sum intended to be below the estimated loss.** A clause may be intended to provide for payment of a sum below the estimated loss. Such a clause is not invalid as a penalty. In *Cellulose Acetate Silk Co Ltd v Widnes Foundry (1925) Ltd*[1013] a contract for the construction of an acetone recovery plant provided that if completion was delayed the contractors were to pay "by way of penalty £20 per working week". The plant was completed 30 weeks late, during which period the owners suffered losses of £5,850. It was held that they could recover £600 only. Both parties must have known that the actual loss would exceed £20 per week, so that one object of the clause was to limit the contractors' liability. But it was not a pure limitation clause, for the contractors would still have had to pay £20 per week even if the owners had lost less. For this reason, **20–165**

[1005] See para.18–068.

[1006] *Financings Ltd v Baldock* [1963] 2 Q.B. 104.

[1007] See para.18–043.

[1008] *Lombard North Central Plc v Butterworth* [1987] Q.B. 527; *BNP Paribas v Wockhardt EU Operations (Swiss) AG* [2009] EWHC 3116 (Comm); 132 Con L.R. 177; *Office of Fair Trading v Ashbourne Management Services Ltd* [2011] EWHC 1237 (Ch); [2011] E.C.C. 31 at [207].

[1009] *Tullett Prebon Group Ltd v El-Hajjali* [2008] EWHC 1924 (QB); [2008] I.R.L.R. 760.

[1010] *General Trading Company (Holdings) Ltd v Richmond Corporation Ltd* [2008] EWHC 1479 (Comm); [2008] 2 Lloyd's Rep. 475: see fn.918.

[1011] *Azimut-Benetti SpA v Healey* [2010] EWHC 2234 (Comm); [2011] 1 Lloyd's Rep. 473.

[1012] See the comment of Jackson J in *Alfred McAlpine Capital Projects Ltd v Tilebox Ltd* [2005] EWHC 281 (TCC); [2005] Build. L.R. 271 at [48].

[1013] [1933] A.C. 20.

liquidated damages clauses are probably not subject to the Unfair Contract Terms Act 1977,[1014] though they may in certain circumstances be subject to the Consumer Rights Act 2015.[1015]

### *(iii) Effect*

20–166 **If the clause is a valid liquidated damages clause.** The claimant can enforce a valid liquidated damages clause notwithstanding that he may recover more than he would have been able to recover as damages. That may still leave the question of whether liquidated damages have accrued, and whether the claimant may be entitled to recover additional damages.

20–167 **Whether liquidated damages have accrued.** This question is most likely to arise in circumstances where the contract has been terminated and a second contractor has been employed to complete the work required. As we saw earlier,[1016] termination has no effect on any "accrued rights". Whether the right to liquidated damages has accrued is simply a question of construction, but the cases support three possible outcomes. First, liquidated damages accrue until the date of completion.[1017] Given that this subjects the defaulting party to the payment of liquidated damages when he no longer has responsibility for the date of completion and depends on the parties having agreed that this is an obligation which is intended to apply even after termination, it is an outcome which should only be countenanced in cases of the clearest language to that effect in the clause in question.[1018] Secondly, liquidated damages accrue until the date of termination and the claimant may also have a claim for damages at large to cover any additional costs of completion by the second contractor.[1019] Thirdly, liquidated damages only accrue in relation to work which has been completed by the date of termination.[1020]

20–168 **Whether additional damages may be recovered.** This is also a question of construction. For example, if the parties agree that liquidated damages are payable for any delay, do they intend such damages to be the sole remedy for all of the consequences of delay? In *Aktieselskabet Reidar v Arcos Ltd*[1021] the charterers of a vessel exceeded the time allowed for loading and were subject to demurrage as liquidated damages for the excess period. However, a further consequence of the delay was that the time passed when the vessel could carry a

---

[1014] See para.7–044.
[1015] See para.20–171.
[1016] See para.18–017.
[1017] See, e.g. *Hall v Van Der Heiden (No 2)* [2010] EWHC 586 (TCC); *GPP Big Field LLP v Solar EPC Solutions SL* [2018] EWHC 2866 (Comm).
[1018] See the doubts expressed in *Triple Point Technology Inc v PTT Public Co Ltd* [2019] EWCA Civ 230; [2019] 1 W.L.R. 3549 at [108].
[1019] See, e.g. *Greenore Port Ltd v Technical & General Guarantee Co Ltd* [2006] EWHC 3119 (TCC); *Shaw v MFP Foundations and Pilings Ltd* [2010] EWHC 1839 (TCC).
[1020] *British Glanzstoff Manufacturing Co v General Accident, Fire and Life Assurance Co* [1913] A.C. 143; *Triple Point Technology Inc v PTT Public Co Ltd* [2019] EWCA Civ 230; [2019] 1 W.L.R. 3549.
[1021] [1927] 1 K.B. 352.

summer cargo and the shipowner was only able to carry a smaller winter cargo, leading to lost freight. The shipowner was entitled to recover the lost freight as additional unliquidated damages. According to Atkin LJ, "[t]he provisions as to demurrage quantify the damages, not for the complete breach, but only such damages as arise from the detention of the vessel."[1022]

Whether additional unliquidated damages may be recovered also arose in the *Makdessi* case.[1023] The defendant's breach of the restrictive covenants amounted to a breach of his fiduciary duty to the company which had been purchased by the claimant and for whom he remained a director. That claim was in fact settled by the company for $500,000.[1024] According to Lord Neuberger and Lord Sumption this did not matter because, having decided that cl.5.1 was a "price adjustment clause", "it was not concerned with the measure of compensation for the breach".[1025] As they pointed out: "The real question is whether any damages have been suffered on account of the breach in circumstances where the price has been adjusted downwards on account of the same breach".[1026] This acknowledges that the whole purpose of the adjustment was to capture the loss, or reduction in value, of the goodwill.[1027]

**If the clause is a penalty.** A clause which is a penalty is not enforceable and the innocent party is left to his ordinary remedies at law. In the *Makdessi* case, the decision of the Court of Appeal in *Jobson v Johnson* that a penalty might be enforceable on a "scaled down" basis, i.e. only to the extent of any actual loss suffered by the claimant was said to be "wrong in principle"[1028] and only consistent with the doctrine of relief against forfeiture which is considered below.[1029] 20–169

**Effect of penalty where stipulated sum less than actual loss.** The clause may be a penalty even though the stipulated sum falls short of the claimant's loss. This apparently paradoxical situation may arise because changing conditions have made an originally extravagant sum inadequate. The question then arises whether the clause is nevertheless effective to limit the defendant's liability to the amount of the penalty. According to one view, the clause is effective for this purpose; for 20–170

[1022] *Aktieselskabet Reidar v Arcos Ltd* [1927] 1 K.B. 352 at 363; cf. *Chandris v Isbrandtsen-Moller* [1951] 1 K.B. 240 at 248–255; *The Bonde* [1991] 1 Lloyd's Rep. 136, 139–142; *GPP Big Field LLP v Solar EPC Solutions SL* [2018] EWHC 2866 (Comm) at [241]–[243].

[1023] See para.20–142.

[1024] Any claim of their own by the claimant would have been irrecoverable as "reflective loss", at least for as long as the defendant remained a director: *Cavendish Square Holding BV v El Makdessi* [2015] UKSC 67; [2016] A.C. 1172 at [76], [180].

[1025] *Cavendish Square Holding BV v El Makdessi* [2015] UKSC 67; [2016] A.C. 1172 at [76].

[1026] *Cavendish Square Holding BV v El Makdessi* [2015] UKSC 67; [2016] A.C. 1172 at [76].

[1027] Though not dealt with explicitly by those of their Lordships who regarded cl.5.1 as a secondary obligation, it seems that the loss flowing from the particular breaches of the restrictive covenant was seen as separate to the loss caused more broadly to the goodwill of the business acquired: see para.20–161.

[1028] *Cavendish Square Holding BV v El Makdessi* [2015] UKSC 67; [2016] A.C. 1172 at [87]; cf. at [283] (Lord Hodge).

[1029] See para.20–172.

penalty clauses are struck down to prevent oppression[1030] and the party in breach cannot be oppressed by the clause when it actually works in his favour. But this view can cut across the general principle that the validity of the clause should be determined once for all by reference to the time of contracting;[1031] for under it a term which was originally invalid as a penalty could become valid as a limitation clause simply by reason of a change of circumstances. Hence in *Wall v Rederiaktiebolaget Lugudde*[1032] it was held that a shipowner could disregard a penalty clause in a charterparty and recover his actual loss, which exceeded the amount of the penalty. In the *Cellulose Acetate* case[1033] the question whether a penalty clause could always be disregarded in this way was left open as it is possible for a clause on its true construction to be both a penalty and a limitation clause. But this is an implausible construction of a clause which provides for payment of a fixed sum irrespective of proof of loss; and it seems that generally such a clause would be disregarded under the rule in *Wall*'s case.

### *(iv) Consumer Rights Act 2015*[1034]

**20–171** An illustration given in the Consumer Rights Act 2015 of a term which may be regarded as unfair[1035] and therefore not binding on the consumer, is one requiring "a consumer who fails to fulfil his obligations under the contract to pay a disproportionately high sum in compensation".[1036] Such a term is likely also to be invalid as a penalty at common law, so that normally the common law rules and the 2015 Act would lead to the same result.[1037] There are, however, significant differences between these two sets of rules. On the one hand, the scope of the common law rules is perfectly general, while that of the 2015 Act is limited in that it applies only to terms in contracts between a "trader"[1038] and a "consumer",[1039] in that even within these categories certain types of contract are excepted, and in that certain terms are excepted even in contracts within the scope of the Act.[1040] On the other hand, the scope of the Act is wider than that of the common law rules in that it may (at least in some cases) apply to sums payable otherwise than on breach. For example, the list of terms which may be unfair also includes "a term which has the object or effect of requiring that, where the

1030 *Elsley v JG Collins Ins Agencies* (1978) 3 D.L.R. (3d) 1; cf. *Philips Hong Kong v Attorney General of Hong Kong* (1993) 61 Build. L.R. 41; Hudson 101 L.Q.R. 480.
1031 See para.20–152.
1032 [1915] 3 K.B. 66 (not cited in *Elsley v JG Collins Ins Agencies* (1978) 3 D.L.R. (3d) 1); cf. *Dingwall v Burnett* 1912 S.C. 1097; *W & J Investments Ltd v Bunting* [1984] 1 N.S.W.R. 331.
1033 See fn.1013.
1034 See generally, para.7–086 and following.
1035 Consumer Rights Act 2015 s.63(1).
1036 Consumer Rights Act 2015 Sch.2 para.1(6).
1037 *ParkingEye Ltd v Beavis* [2015] UKSC 67; [2016] A.C. 1172; (term neither a penalty, para.20–161; nor unfair, para.7–110)). But see: *Munkenbeck & Marshall v Harold* [2005] EWHC 356 (TCC) (term unfair under the previous Regulations, but not a penalty).
1038 See para.7–090.
1039 See para.7–091.
1040 See paras 7–119—7–120.

consumer decides not to conclude or perform the contract, the consumer must pay the trader a disproportionately high sum in compensation or for services which have not been supplied."[1041]

### (b) Relief against forfeiture

**Relationship with the rule against penalties.** The doctrine of relief against forfeiture has already been considered in the context of termination under an express provision of the contract.[1042] While the scope of this equitable doctrine was not directly in issue before the Supreme Court in the *Makdessi* case, a number of their Lordships considered its relationship with the rule against penalties. Lord Mance held that it was both "logical and correct in principle" that the enforcement of a clause may be subject to both, so that a clause which is not unenforceable as a penalty may nonetheless be subject to the granting of relief;[1043] and a number of cases proceed on that basis.[1044] A key difference between the two doctrines is that a clause is assessed to determine if it is penal at the time of the contract, whereas the case for relief against forfeiture is determined at the time of enforcement.[1045] 20–172

**Forfeiture of instalments.** A contract of sale may provide for payment of the price in instalments and add that, on default in payment of any one instalment, those already paid shall be forfeited. We saw above that the rule against penalties does not apply to such "prepayments",[1046] but equity can sometimes grant certain kinds of relief against forfeiture to the purchaser if he is able and willing to perform after the agreed time,[1047] particularly where enforcement of the forfeiture provision would cause him some prejudice (such as the loss of the value of improvements he had made to the land) beyond merely depriving him of the benefit of his bargain;[1048] that is, it might be able to extend the time for 20–173

[1041] Consumer Rights Act 2015 Sch.2 para.1(5).
[1042] See para.18–079.
[1043] *Cavendish Square Holding BV v El Makdessi* [2015] UKSC 67; [2016] A.C. 1172 at [160]; cf. at [18] (Lord Neuberger and Lord Sumption); at [227] (Lord Hodge).
[1044] See, e.g. *BICC plc v Burndy Corp* [1985] Ch. 232; *Jobson v Johnson* [1989] 1 W.L.R. 1026.
[1045] *Cavendish Square Holding BV v El Makdessi* [2015] UKSC 67; [2016] A.C. 1172 at [227]; *Cadogan Petroleum Holdings Ltd v Global Process Systems LLC* [2013] EWHC 214 (Comm); [2013] 2 Lloyd's Rep. 26.
[1046] See para.20–150.
[1047] See *Jobson v Johnson* [1989] 1 W.L.R. 1026, where the defendant failed to comply with this requirement; and *Goker v NWS Bank Plc* [1990] C.C.L.R. 34, where relief was denied to a persistent defaulter.
[1048] *Union Eagle Ltd v Golden Achievement Ltd* [1997] A.C. 514 at 520; para.18–081.

payment,[1049] or order repayment of the forfeited instalments if the purchaser was able and willing to perform, but the vendor was for some reason justified in refusing to accept late performance.[1050]

20–174 **Relief against forfeiture where purchaser not able and willing to perform.**[1051] It is more doubtful whether equity could order the repayment of forfeited instalments to a purchaser who was *not* able and willing to perform. In *Mussen v Van Diemen's Land Co*[1052] land was sold for £321,000 payable in instalments and the contract provided that the vendor was to have the right to terminate, and to forfeit any money paid, in the event of the purchaser's default. Such default occurred after the purchaser had paid £40,200.[1053] His claim for the return of the money was rejected as it was not "unconscionable on the part of the vendor, who has contracted to part with his land on agreed terms, to enforce the contract … ".[1054] This case left open the possibility of ordering repayment when it *was* unconscionable for the vendor to keep the money. In *Stockloser v Johnson*[1055] quarrying machinery was sold under a contract which provided for payment in instalments, and, in the event of the buyer's default, for forfeiture of instalments paid. The buyer failed to keep up the agreed payments and the actual decision was that he was not entitled to the return of the forfeited instalments as, in the circumstances, it was not unconscionable for the seller to keep them after terminating the contract: the buyer had speculated on the success of the quarry, and lost. But Somervell and Denning LJJ said that repayment could have been ordered if the mere act of keeping the money had been unconscionable.[1056] Romer LJ, on the other hand, said that repayment could be ordered only if the vendor was guilty of fraud, sharp practice or other unconscionable conduct; and that there was "nothing inequitable *per se* in a vendor, whose conduct is not open to criticism in other respects, insisting on his contractual right to retain instalments of purchase-money already paid".[1057]

[1049] *Re Dagenham (Thames) Dock Co* (1873) L.R. 8 Ch. App. 1022; and *Kilmer v BC Orchard Lands Ltd* [1913] A.C. 319, as explained in *Union Eagle Ltd v Golden Achievement Ltd* [1997] A.C. 514 at 521; *Starside Properties Ltd v Mustapha* [1974] 1 W.L.R. 816; cf. *Millichamp v Jones* [1982] 1 W.L.R. 1422 (time for payment of deposit extended); Lang 100 L.Q.R. 427.

[1050] *Steedman v Drinkle* [1916] 1 A.C. 275, as explained in *Mussen v Van Diemen's Land Co* [1938] Ch. 253; but see *Stockloser v Johnson* [1954] 1 Q.B. 476.

[1051] In addition to the restrictions dealt with below, it is said that the jurisdiction to grant relief is confined to cases depriving a party of proprietary or possessory rights, and not purely contractual rights: *UK Housing Alliance (North West) Ltd v Francis* [2010] EWCA Civ 117; [2010] 3 All E.R. 519; Conte 126 L.Q.R. 529. This requirement, which applies to the forfeiture of the contract itself by way of termination, has been criticised (para.18–080) and there is no mention of its requirement in *Stockloser v Johnson* suggesting that it is not in fact required where relief is sought against the forfeiture of instalments as a consequence of termination: Conte 126 L.Q.R. 529; Smith 60 C.L.J. 178; cf. *Liberty Life Assurance Co v Sheikh, The Times*, 25 June 1985, CA; *Cavendish Square Holding BV v El Makdessi* [2015] UKSC 67; [2016] A.C. 1172 at [17].

[1052] [1938] Ch. 253.

[1053] Land equal in value to other payments had been conveyed to him.

[1054] *Mussen v Van Diemen's Land Co* [1938] Ch. 253 at 262.

[1055] [1954] 1 Q.B. 476; Diamond 19 M.L.R. 498; Price 20 M.L.R. 620.

[1056] *Stockloser v Johnson* [1954] 1 Q.B. 476 at 483, 485, 489–490.

[1057] *Stockloser v Johnson* [1954] 1 Q.B. 476 at 501; cf. *Kazakstan Wool Processors (Europe) Ltd v Nederlandsche Credietverzekering Maatschappij NV* [2000] C.L.C. 822.

Later dicta, as well as a decision at first instance,[1058] support Romer LJ's view, which is based on the principle that the law should not interfere with contracts freely made. But this principle is discarded in the law as to penalties, and in particular in the law relating to penal deposits. In the *Workers Trust* case,[1059] discussed above,[1060] the Privy Council left open the question whether relief against forfeiture of instalments should be given to a purchaser who has been let into possession. This fact may, indeed, affect the amount of the vendor's loss; but subject to this practical consideration, it is submitted that, since forfeiture provisions often resemble penalties in their purpose and effect,[1061] their validity should depend on the tests that differentiate penalties from liquidated damages clauses.[1062] On this basis, the court should have power to grant relief where, on these tests, the forfeiture provision is penal in nature.[1063] In the cases discussed above, such relief would take the form of ordering repayment of the forfeited instalments; but *Jobson v Johnson*[1064] illustrates the possible availability of other forms of relief. In that case a contract for the sale of shares to be paid for by instalments provided that, if the buyer defaulted, he should retransfer the shares for £40,000. It was admitted that this clause was penal in effect;[1065] and, on the buyer's default, it was held that the seller was entitled to an order for *either* the sale of the shares and the payment out of the proceeds of sale of the unpaid instalments, *or* the transfer of the shares so long as their value did not exceed the unpaid instalments by more than £40,000. This amounted to putting the seller into the same position as that in which he would have been if the penal element of the clause had been struck out: in this respect it resembled the legal consequence of a penalty clause in the normal sense of that expression.[1066]

**Contracts for services.** The foregoing discussion is concerned with contracts of sale, in which, as a result of the buyer's default, the contract is terminated and the subject-matter remains the property of, or is restored to, the seller. The position is different where the contract is one for services to be rendered over a period of **20–175**

---

[1058] *Galbraith v Mitchenall Estates Ltd* [1965] 2 Q.B. 473, citing dicta from *Campbell Discount Co Ltd v Bridge* [1961] 1 Q.B. 445 (reversed on other grounds [1962] A.C. 600); cf. *Else (1982) v Parkland Holdings* [1994] B.C.L.C. 130; *Amble Assets LLP v Longbenton Foods Ltd* [2011] EWHC 3774 (Ch); [2012] 1 All E.R. (Comm) 764.

[1059] *Workers Trust and Merchant Bank Ltd v Dojap Investments Ltd* [1993] A.C. 573 at 581–582, discussing *Stockloser v Johnson*.

[1060] See para.20–147.

[1061] *Jobson v Johnson* [1989] 1 W.L.R. 1026 at 1041.

[1062] This submission is based solely on consistency of approach. Such consistency might preferably be achieved by abolishing the rule against penalties and following Romer LJ's view for both agreed damages and forfeiture of payments already made.

[1063] cf. *Stockloser v Johnson* [1954] 1 Q.B. 476 at 491; Law Commission Working Paper No.61, paras 65, 66. Contrast *Cadogan Petroleum Holdings Ltd v Global Process Systems LLC* [2013] EWHC 214 (Comm); [2013] 2 Lloyd's Rep. 26 at [34].

[1064] [1989] 1 W.L.R. 1026; Harpum [1989] C.L.J. 370.

[1065] See para.20–151.

[1066] See para.20–169. In *Cavendish Square Holding BV v El Makdessi* [2015] UKSC 67; [2016] A.C. 1172 at [87] this decision was described as "entirely orthodox if it is treated as a forfeiture case, but … wrong in principle if it is treated as a penalty case". The purchaser had been required to invoke the rule against penalties because his counterclaim for relief was struck out for failing to comply with undertakings to the court.

time in return for payments to be made at stated intervals. If the recipient of the services fails to keep up the payments and the contract is terminated on that ground, he will not be able to recover back payments made before termination, at least if they "represent the agreed rate of hire [for the services] and not a penny more".[1067] In such a case the reasoning even of the majority in *Stockloser v Johnson* cannot apply as the payor will have received (and be unable to restore) pro rata what he bargained for in exchange for his payments.[1068] The position might be different if those payments contained a heavy element of "front loading".

20–176 **Failure to pay.** The preceding discussion of deposits and part-payments deals with the situation in which a payment has been made and the contract is *then* broken by the payor. The main issue in such cases is whether the payor can get back the payment that he has made. But the breach may also consist in failing to make the payment; and if the injured party terminates the contract on account of this breach,[1069] the question arises whether the payment can be sued for by the prospective payee. The view that it can be sued for is supported by the principle that termination does not retrospectively release the party in breach from accrued obligations;[1070] and, after some conflict of judicial opinion, this view has prevailed where the money was to have been paid as a *deposit*[1071] which, if it had been duly paid, could not have been claimed back by the payor.[1072] But acceptance of the same view in the case of a *part-payment* might lead to the absurdity that the prospective payee could sue for the money because it was due before breach, while the payor could then sue for its return because a part-payment can be recovered by the payor.[1073] Hence in cases involving contracts for the sale of land the position is that a part-payment which was due but remained unpaid at the time of termination cannot be sued for by the prospective payee.[1074] It is submitted that the same reasoning should apply even to a claim for an unpaid deposit where the case is one of those exceptional ones in which the deposit would, if paid, have been recoverable by the payor, either at

---

1067 *The Scaptrade* [1983] 2 A.C. 694 at 703; cf. para.20–177.

1068 See para.22–010.

1069 See paras 17–017, 18–036.

1070 See para.18–018.

1071 *Hinton v Sparkes* (1868) L.R. 3 C.P. 161; *Dewar v Mintoft* [1912] 2 K.B. 373; *Millichamp v Jones* [1982] 1 W.L.R. 1422 at 1428, 1430; Carter 99 L.Q.R. 503; *The Blankenstein* [1985] 1 W.L.R. 435 at 451, disapproving *Lowe v Hope* [1970] 1 Ch. 94, where the court may have been reluctant to enforce what it regarded as in substance a penalty. For a possible way of giving effect to that reluctance, see fn.1076; cf. *The MV Griffon* [2013] EWCA Civ 1567; [2014] 1 Lloyd's Rep. 471.

1072 See para.20–147.

1073 *Mayson v Clouet* [1924] A.C. 980.

1074 *McDonald v Denys Lascelles Ltd* (1933) 48 C.L.R. 457, cited with approval in *Johnson v Agnew* [1980] A.C. 367 at 396 and in *Hyundai Heavy Industries Ltd v Papadopoulos* [1980] 1 W.L.R. 1129 at 1141.

common law[1075] or under s.49(2) of the Law of Property Act 1925;[1076] and that a claim by the prospective payee for the payment of such a deposit should therefore be rejected.[1077]

In the cases just considered, the outcome can be justified on the ground that the seller will, as a result of termination, keep or get back the land, which constituted the entire consideration for the promised part-payment.[1078] Hence if liability to make the payments is discharged, each party will be left in, or restored to, his pre-contract position (though the buyer will be liable in damages). This is also true where a part-payment is to be made *in advance*, for work to be done in the future, i.e. after the part-payment had become due. In *Rover International Ltd v Cannon Films Ltd (No.3)*[1079] it was accordingly held that a payment in respect of services to be rendered in the future under an agreement for the distribution of films on television could not be sued for by the prospective payee, even though the payment had fallen due (but none of the services had been rendered) before termination. But the position was different where part-payments under shipbuilding contracts became due from time to time (as the work progressed) and the builder terminated for the other party's failure to make one of the payments when due.[1080] It was held that the builder was entitled to sue for that part-payment since the consideration, for which the part-payment was to be made, was not merely the delivery of the finished product, but also the builder's work. So far as the work which he had done was concerned, he could not be restored to his pre-contract position: hence it was proper to uphold his claim for a part-payment due before termination. For the same reason, instalments due under a hire-purchase agreement before termination can be sued for after termination:[1081] their legal character is that of payment for the hire of the subject-matter, and the benefit of possession during each period for which such a payment was due is one that cannot be restored by the hirer to the owner. It is submitted that this reasoning should also apply where the part-payment has actually been made before termination, and that, accordingly, the prima facie rule by which part-payments can be recovered back by the payor[1082] should be restricted to cases in which, as a result of termination, each party can be restored to his pre-contract position.

**Consumer Rights Act 2015.** An illustration given in the 2015 Act[1083] of a term which is regarded as unfair[1084] is one: **20–177**

1075 See para.20–147.
1076 See para.20–149.
1077 In a case like *Lowe v Hope* [1970] 1 Ch. 94 a court could justify its refusal to allow the prospective payee's claim on the ground that it would have ordered the return of the deposit (if paid) under s.49(2) of the 1925 Act.
1078 See para.22–003.
1079 [1989] 1 W.L.R. 912; Beatson 105 L.Q.R. 179; Andrews [1990] C.L.J. 15.
1080 *Hyundai Shipbuilding and Heavy Industries Co Ltd v Pournaras* [1978] 2 Lloyd's Rep. 502; *Hyundai Heavy Industries Ltd v Papadopoulos* [1980] 1 W.L.R. 1129 (Lords Russell and Keith *dubitante* on this point); *Stocznia Gdanska SA v Latvian Shipping Co* [1998] 1 W.L.R. 574.
1081 See para.18–022.
1082 See at fn.1073.
1083 See generally, para.7–086 and following.
1084 2015 Act s.63(1).

> "permitting the trader to retain sums paid by the consumer where the consumer decides not to conclude or perform the contract, without providing for the consumer to receive compensation of an equivalent amount from the seller or supplier where the latter is the party cancelling the contract".[1085]

This illustration is based on the civil law institution (which has no counterparty in the common law) by which a contract can, in effect, be dissolved on forfeiture of a deposit or on the return by the payee of double the amount.[1086] Thus forfeiture provisions of the kind discussed above do not correspond precisely with the illustration just quoted; but this fact would not prevent the court from holding that such a provision was unfair.[1087] It seems to follow not only that the seller or supplier could not sue for the payment, but also that he would have to return the payment, if it had been made.[1088] This may be important in practice since the 2015 Act can apply to contracts for the sale of land,[1089] and it is with such contracts that many of the English cases on deposits and part-payments are concerned. However, the 2015 Act applies only to contract terms or consumer notices[1090] and not to rights of forfeiture conferred by law. Once a payment is classified as a deposit, it can be forfeited even in the absence of a contract term to that effect; and in such a case there would appear to be no relevant term or notice on which the 2015 Act can operate. The mere description of the payment as a "deposit" would not suffice for this purpose since the question whether a payment has the legal characteristics of a deposit or of a part-payment is one of substance; the use of a particular word or phrase is clearly not decisive.[1091]

---

[1085] 2015 Act Sch.2 para.1(4).

[1086] Treitel, *Remedies for Breach of Contract: A Comparative Account* (1988), para.182.

[1087] The list of illustrations in Sch.2 is "non-exhaustive": s.63(1).

[1088] s.62(1) merely makes the term "not binding on the consumer" but the word "retain" in Sch.2 para.1(d) suggests the availability to the consumer of a remedy for the recovery of the payment.

[1089] See para.7–089.

[1090] See 2015 Act s.61.

[1091] If it were, the law as to part payments could be evaded by simply calling them deposits.

## CHAPTER 21

# SPECIFIC REMEDIES



## 1. ACTION FOR AN AGREED SUM

### (a) Distinguished from damages

**Nature of relief.** A contract commonly provides for the payment by one party of an agreed sum in exchange for some performance by the other. Goods are sold for a fixed price; work is done for an agreed remuneration, and so forth. An action for this price or other agreed remuneration is, in its nature, quite different from an action for damages.[1] It is a claim for the *specific* enforcement of the defendant's primary obligation to perform what he has promised;[2] though, as it is simply an action for money, it is not subject to those restrictions which equity imposes on the remedies of specific performance and injunction,[3] on the ground that it would be undesirable actually to force the defendant to perform certain acts (e.g. to render personal service) or that it would be difficult to secure compliance with the court's order. Obviously, these factors have no weight where the claim is simply one for a sum of money. Of the reasons given for refusing specific performance, **21–001**

[1] cf. *Re Park Air Services* [1999] 1 All E.R. 673 at 682–683. The distinction is sometimes obscured by the fact that damages may be *equal to* the agreed sum, as in *The Blankenstein* [1985] 1 W.L.R. 435: para.18–023.

[2] See para.18–020.

[3] See paras 21–031—21–055, 21–059—21–069.

only one calls for discussion in relation to an action for the agreed sum: this is the possibility that damages may be an "adequate" remedy.[4]

21–002 **Practical effects.** The action for the agreed sum differs from a claim for damages not only in its nature, but also in its practical effects. The claimant in an action for the agreed sum recovers that sum—neither more nor less; no questions of quantification nor of remoteness can arise.[5] It is irrelevant in an action for the price of goods to ask how much they are worth or how much they cost the seller. The argument that the claimant should have mitigated can, however, arise in an action for the agreed sum.[6] If successful, it will lead to the conclusion that the action is not available at all—not to recovery of a reduced price. Where the agreed sum is not paid and the claimant also suffers additional loss, he may be entitled to bring *both* the action for the agreed sum *and* an action for damages.[7]

21–003 **Insurance.** Where A (an insurer) promises B (the insured) to pay to B any damages for which B may become liable to C, B's claim against A for the amount of such damages has been described as being itself a claim for damages,[8] so that the action against the insurer is not one to enforce his primary obligation.[9] But in the case put A's only promise is to repay B the damages for which B is liable to C; hence A's primary obligation is to make that payment; and an action to recover it is, it is submitted, one for the specific enforcement of A's promise. It is an action for an agreed sum, in the sense of a sum determined by reference to the agreement, rather than one calculated by reference to the consequences of breach.[10]

21–004 **Contractual indemnities.** A may agree to indemnify B against any "loss" incurred on the occasion of certain specified events, one of which may include a breach of the contract between them *by A*. This may leave room for the submission that a claim under the indemnity is an action for the agreed sum, and not an action for damages, so that the principles of mitigation and remoteness are inapplicable.[11] The better view, it is submitted, is that while the claim may not be

[4] See paras 21–019—21–030; *Attica Sea Carriers Corp v Ferrostaal Poseidon Bulk Reederei GmbH (The Puerto Buitrago)* [1976] Lloyd's Rep. 250.

[5] *Jervis v Harris* [1996] Ch. 195 at 202; cf. *Malla v Gurung* unreported 16 December 2014 CA.

[6] See para.21–015.

[7] *Overstone Ltd v Shipway* [1962] 1 W.L.R. 117; cf. *The Halcyon Skies* [1977] Q.B. 14; *Lawlor v Gray* [1984] 3 All E.R. 345; and see paras 20–065–20–070.

[8] See *Chandris v Argo Ins Co Ltd* [1963] 2 Lloyd's Rep. 65; cf. *The Fanti and Padre Island* [1991] 2 A.C. 1, 35; *Hong Kong Borneo Services Ltd v Pilcher* [1992] 2 Lloyd's Rep. 593 at 597; *The Kyriaki* [1993] 1 Lloyd's Rep. 137 at 150.

[9] *Phoenix General Ins Co of Greece SA v Halvanon Ins Co Ltd* [1988] Q.B. 216 at 233 (reversed on other grounds [1988] Q.B. 216 at 248 and following).

[10] cf. *Jervis v Harris* [1996] Ch. 195, where a lease provided that, on a tenant's breach of his covenant to repair, the landlord could himself execute the repairs and recover the costs of so doing from the tenant. It was held that the landlord's claim to recover these costs "sounds in debt, not damages" (at 202). The action was one for an agreed sum even though that sum was not ascertained when the contract was made: it was enough for it to be ascertained when payment became due. This reasoning is, with respect, preferable to that of the insurance cases referred to above.

[11] As noted in *Jervis v Harris* [1996] Ch. 195, above, it is enough that the sum to be paid can be ascertained when payment is due.

one for damages, the extent of the recovery by B depends upon the construction of the term under which the "indemnity" is provided.[12] Furthermore, it has been said that a claim under a contractual indemnity which is triggered by a breach by A of his contract with B is presumed to cover no more than the sum which could have been recovered in an action for damages unless the parties have indicated clearly an intention to provide a "full" indemnity going beyond the obligation to indemnify which is itself the basis of a claim for damages.[13]

## (b) Availability of the action

### *(i) Duty to pay the agreed sum*

Obviously an action for the agreed sum cannot be brought if the duty to pay it has not arisen. Whether it has arisen depends primarily on the terms of the contract.[14] Suppose that a contract of employment provides that the employee is to be paid wages after working for a month and that he is wrongfully dismissed after a week. He cannot sue for his wages but only for damages for wrongful dismissal.[15] On the other hand, in *Mount v Oldham Corp*[16] a local authority wrongfully withdrew boys from a school without giving the customary one term's notice. It was held that the headmaster was entitled to bring an action for the term's fees as it was an implied term of the contract that these should be paid in advance. **21–005**

### *(ii) Rules of law*

The *action* for the agreed sum is not available merely because the *duty* to pay it has arisen. The contract specifies the *duties* of the parties, but the law determines their *remedies*. This is generally recognised when specific performance is sought,[17] and it is also true of the action for the agreed sum. **21–006**

**Sale of Goods.** The distinction[18] appears clearly in the Sale of Goods Act 1979. The *duty* to pay the price arises when the seller is ready and willing to deliver the goods (unless, of course, the sale is on credit or stipulates for an advance payment).[19] But s.49 of the Act provides that the *action* for the price is available to the seller if either the property in the goods has passed[20] to the buyer or the **21–007**

[12] *The Eurus* [1996] 2 Lloyd's Rep. 408; affirmed [1998] 1 Lloyd's Rep. 351; *Codemasters Software Co Ltd v Automobile Club de L'Ouest* [2009] EWHC 2361 (Ch); [2010] F.S.R. 12 at [20]–[21]; *Pindell Ltd v AirAsia Berhad* [2010] EWHC 2516 (Comm); [2012] 2 C.L.C. 1 at [94]; *The Kos* [2012] UKSC 17; [2012] 2 A.C. 164 at [12].

[13] *The Eurus* [1996] 2 Lloyd's Rep. 408 at 432; [1998] 1 Lloyd's Rep. 351 at 358; *Parbulk AS v Kristen Marine SA* [2010] EWHC 900 (Comm); [2011] 1 Lloyd's Rep. 220 at [25]–[26].

[14] *Doherty v Fannigan Holdings Ltd* [2018] EWCA Civ 1615; [2018] 2 B.C.L.C. 623 at [31].

[15] See paras 17–015, 18–006.

[16] [1973] Q.B. 309; cf. *Denman v Winstanley* (1887) 4 T.L.R. 127.

[17] See para.21–031.

[18] The distinction drawn in the text is sometimes overlooked, e.g. in *Huyton SA v Peter Cremer GmbH* [1999] 1 Lloyd's Rep. 620 at 630 and 642.

[19] Sale of Goods Act 1979 ss.27, 28.

[20] Sale of Goods Act 1979 s.49(1).

price is payable "on a day certain[21] irrespective of delivery[22]". In *Stein Forbes & Co Ltd v County Tailoring Co Ltd*[23] a contract for the sale of sheepskins provided for payment in cash "against documents on arrival of steamer". This provision did not name a "day certain"; and the buyer's wrongful refusal to pay on tender of documents prevented the property in the goods from passing to him. It was held that the seller could not claim the price, but only damages. The effect (and probable purpose) of this restriction on the seller's action for the price is to encourage him to dispose of the goods elsewhere and so to mitigate his loss.

The *Stein Forbes* case should be contrasted with *Workman Clark & Co v Lloyd Brasileno*[24] where a contract for the construction and sale of a boat provided for payments in instalments, the first of which was to become due when the keel was laid; and property was not to pass until this payment had been made. After the keel had been laid, the builder successfully sued for the first instalment. The case is hard to reconcile with the wording of s.49; but it nevertheless accurately reflects the underlying policy. At the stage which the work had reached it must have been hard for the builder to mitigate his loss by finding another customer for a boat built to the defendant's order—much harder, probably, than it was for the seller in the *Stein Forbes* case to resell the sheepskins.

21–008 **Does s.49 of the 1979 Act represent a "complete code"?** The decisions in *Stein Forbes* and *Workman Clark* are discussed above on the basis that no action for the price can be brought independently of s.49 of the 1979 Act and this was the view of the Court of Appeal in *Caterpillar (NI) Ltd v John Holt & Co (Liverpool) Ltd*.[25] However, in an obiter dictum in *The Res Cogitans*[26] Lord Mance rejected this view and concluded that there should be "some room for claims for the price in other circumstances than those covered by section 49".[27] While he said that the "precise limits of such circumstances" must be left for determination when they arise, he would have made the action available in *The Res Cogitans*. In that case bunkers were supplied subject to a retention of title clause under which property did not pass until payment of the price, but during the period of credit they were both at the buyer's risk as regards damage and destruction and the buyer was permitted to consume them in the operation of its vessel.[28]

---

[21] i.e. a particular date, such as 1 April, or "within 30 days of the date of the invoice": *Caterpillar (NI) Ltd v John Holt & Co (Liverpool) Ltd* [2013] EWCA Civ 1232; [2014] 1 W.L.R. 2365.

[22] Sale of Goods Act 1979 s.49(2) (not applicable where payment dependent upon delivery: *Otis Vehicle Rentals Ltd v Cicely Commercials Ltd* [2002] EWCA Civ 1064; [2002] All E.R. (D.) 203 (Jul)).

[23] (1916) 115 L.T. 215; cf. *Tradax Internacional SA v Goldschmidt SA* [1977] 2 Lloyd's Rep. 604; *Regent OHG Aisenstadt und Barig v Francesco of Jermyn Street* [1981] 3 All E.R. 327.

[24] [1908] 1 K.B. 968; this report differs in some significant respects from those in 77 L.J.K.B. 953; 99 L.T. 481; and 11 Asp. M.L.C. 126.

[25] [2013] EWCA Civ 1232; [2014] 1 W.L.R. 2365.

[26] [2016] UKSC 23; [2016] A.C. 1034. Lord Mance's comments are *obiter* because of the finding that the contract in the case was not a contract of *sale*.

[27] *The Res Cogitans* [2016] UKSC 23; [2016] A.C. 1034 at [53].

[28] *The Res Cogitans* [2016] UKSC 23; [2016] A.C. 1034 at [53]. See also Lord Mance's approval of the availability of the action for the price in the circumstances present in earlier cases: *Castle v Playford* (1872) L.R. 7 Ex. 98; *Martineau v Kitching* (1872) LR 7 Q.B. 436.

### (iii) *Conduct of the injured party*

**If injured party elects to terminate.** If, on wrongful repudiation of a contract, the injured party elects to terminate,[29] he cannot sue for any sum which, under the contract, was to accrue to him only after the date of termination.[30] He can claim damages for wrongful repudiation, and in assessing these the court may take into account any sums which he should have received under the broken contract. For example, if a hire-purchase agreement is wrongfully repudiated by the hirer and terminated by the owner, the owner cannot sue for instalments which were to accrue after the date of termination. But his damages may be based on the difference between the amount which the repudiating hirer was to have paid and the benefits obtained by the owner as a result of termination, e.g. in regaining possession of the goods.[31] 21–009

**If injured party elects to affirm the contract.** Where the injured party elects to keep the contract alive,[32] he can bring the action for the agreed sum if, at the time of repudiation, he has already done all that is required to make the action available. If he has not yet done all that is required, the action will depend on additional factors. 21–010

**Where the co-operation of the guilty party is needed.** No action for the agreed sum is available where it is impossible for the injured party to do the further required acts without the co-operation of the guilty party, who refuses to give it and who cannot be compelled to act by the court.[33] For example, if a singer wrongfully repudiates his contract with his agent, the latter cannot continue performance without the co-operation of the former; and the agent's only claim is for damages;[34] and where work is to be done by A on the land or goods of B, who wrongfully refuses to allow A to have access to or possession of the property, then A cannot do the work without some co-operation from B and so his only remedy is an action for damages.[35] A could only do the work without B's co-operation if he already had possession of the goods or if he could get them without B's co-operation (e.g. from a warehouseman who had been effectively directed to deliver them to A).[36] 21–011

[29] See Ch.18.
[30] See paras 18–017—18–019.
[31] See para.18–022.
[32] Assuming he still has this option: see *MSC Mediterranean Shipping Co SA v Cottonex Anstalt* [2016] EWCA Civ 789; [2016] 2 Lloyd's Rep. 494, discussed at para.18–007.
[33] *White & Carter (Councils) Ltd v McGregor* [1962] A.C. 413 at 429; cf. *Ministry of Sound (Ireland) Ltd v World Online Ltd* [2003] EWHC 2178 (Ch); [2003] 2 All E.R. (Comm) 823 (sum due on a "day certain" and not dependent on the performance of the injured party; the action for the price was therefore available notwithstanding the need for co-operation for any further performance, but subject to a "defence" of failure of consideration); contrast *Motortrak Ltd v FCA Australia Pty Ltd* [2018] EWHC 990 (Comm) at [106].
[34] *Denmark Productions Ltd v Boscobel Productions Ltd* [1969] 1 Q.B. 699; cf. *Roberts v Ellwells Engineering Ltd* [1972] Q.B. 586; para.16–119.
[35] *Hounslow LBC v Twickenham Garden & Builders Ltd* [1971] Ch. 233 at 252–254; cf. *Attica Sea Carriers Corp v Ferrostaal Poseidon Bulk Reederei GmbH* [1976] 1 Lloyd's Rep. 250 at 256.
[36] e.g. *George Barker Transport Ltd v Eynon* [1974] 1 W.L.R. 462 at 468.

21–012 **Where no co-operation of the guilty party is required.** It is disputed whether the action for the agreed sum is available to the injured party where, at the time of repudiation, that party has not yet done all that was required of him to make the action available,[37] but where he can, and does, continue performance without the co-operation of the other party. In *White & Carter (Councils) Ltd v McGregor*[38] the appellants agreed to advertise the respondents' garage business for three years on plates attached to litterbins. Payment was to be at the rate of 2s. per week per plate, plus 5s. per annum towards the cost of each plate. The respondents repudiated the contract on the very day on which it was made but the appellants nevertheless prepared the plates, displayed them, and claimed the full amount due under the contract. A majority of the House of Lords upheld the claim. The main reason given was that repudiation did not, of itself, bring a contract to an end. It only gave the injured party an option to terminate the contract; and if he chose instead to affirm, the contract remained "in full effect".[39] But this reasoning does not, of itself, lead to any conclusion as to the *particular remedy* available to the injured party. This appears from the cases in which the injured party *cannot* perform without the co-operation of the other party. Even here, repudiation does not of itself bring the contract to an end;[40] but the injured party's only remedy is an action for damages.[41]

21–013 **Whether the injured party has a "legitimate interest" in recovering the agreed sum.** The problem in cases of the kind seen in *McGregor*'s case is whether an award of the agreed sum is, on the one hand, necessary to protect the injured party, and, on the other, likely to cause undue hardship to the party in breach. In some cases it may make no difference to the injured party whether he: (1) incurs the expense of performance and recovers the agreed sum; or (2) saves that expense by not performing and recovers the difference between it and the agreed sum by way of damages. If this is the position, damages are a perfectly adequate remedy. But there are other situations in which the injured party would be prejudiced by discontinuing performance and claiming damages, e.g. where this leads to injury to his reputation, for which damages (so far as recoverable at all)[42] could not be accurately assessed;[43] where the injured party has entered into commitments with third parties which he must honour as a matter of business;[44]

---

[37] The reference to the injured party not yet having done all that is required of him appears to have been misunderstood, or misinterpreted, in counsel's submissions in *Reichman v Beveridge* [2006] EWCA Civ 1659; [2007] 1 P. & C.R. 20 at [29]; it is not literally a question of whether the injured party has anything *to do*, but whether or not he has *performed* in full so as to be entitled to the price. Thus, in the *Reichman* case, the landlord had granted the lease so that there was no more for him to do, but he had not performed in full in the sense of allowing the lease to run to the end of its term.

[38] [1962] A.C. 413; Goodhart 78 L.Q.R. 263; Nienaber [1962] C.L.J. 213; Liu 74 M.L.R. 171.

[39] *White & Carter (Councils) Ltd v McGregor* [1962] A.C. 413 at 427.

[40] See para.18–005.

[41] See the authorities cited in fn.34; cf. *The Alaskan Trader* [1983] 2 Lloyd's Rep. 645 at 651 (quoted at para.18–006).

[42] See para.20–096; cf. *The Odenfeld* [1978] 2 Lloyd's Rep. 357 (damages very hard to assess).

[43] See Lord Reid's example of an expert asked to prepare a report: *White & Carter (Councils) Ltd v McGregor* [1962] A.C. 413 at 431.

[44] See *Anglo-African Shipping Co of New York Inc v Mortner* [1962] 1 Lloyd's Rep. 81 at 94; affirmed on other grounds [1962] 1 Lloyd's Rep. 610; *The Odenfeld* [1978] 2 Lloyd's Rep. 357; para.21–015.

where part of the loss which the injured party would actually suffer is legally irrecoverable because it is too remote;[45] or where it is unclear that damages could be recovered at all.[46] It is only in cases of this kind that the rule in *McGregor*'s case will be applied, for Lord Reid there said that, if the injured party has "no substantial or legitimate interest"[47] in completing performance, his only remedy will be in damages. "Legitimate interest" here has been said to mean that "the innocent party must have reasonable grounds for keeping the contract open, bearing in mind also the interests of the wrongdoer",[48] but it has also been said to require that the innocent party must be guilty of conduct which is "wholly unreasonable",[49] or "perverse".[50] The burden is on the party in breach to show that the innocent party has no legitimate interest in performing the contract rather than claiming damages.[51]

**Arguments against recovery of the agreed sum.** If the conditions referred to in *McGregor*'s case are satisfied, it is hard to see why the injured party should not be entitled to complete his performance and claim the agreed sum. Three contrary arguments must, however, be considered. 21–014

**Mitigation.** The first, and most important, argument is that the injured party should mitigate his loss. It has been said, in reply, that mitigation is relevant only to a claim for damages and not to a claim for an agreed sum;[52] and in many cases this is no doubt true. A seller of goods who claims damages for non-acceptance may be under a duty to mitigate by reselling the goods; but once he has acquired the right to sue for the price[53] there seems to be no suggestion that he must mitigate even though he can easily resell and even though he is in a much better position than the buyer to do so. But even if this rule always[54] applies in cases involving sale of goods, it does not follow that it must necessarily apply to cases 21–015

[45] See para.20–119 and following.

[46] *Reichman v Beveridge* [2006] EWCA Civ 1659; [2007] 1 P. & C.R. 20 (landlord entitled to maintain lease and recover the rent because it is unclear whether damages for loss of future rent can be recovered after the landlord has taken back possession of the premises following a tenant's default; cf. *Walls v Atcheson* (1826) 3 Bing. 462 (damages not recoverable); the 2000 Blundell Lectures (delivered by Lord Millett and Sir David Neuberger).

[47] *White & Carter (Councils) Ltd v McGregor* [1962] A.C. 413 at 431; *The Alaskan Trader* [1983] 2 Lloyd's Rep. at 651; the legitimate "interest" may be in acquiring a security in the subject-matter: *George Barker Transport Ltd v Eynon* [1974] 1 W.L.R. 462.

[48] *Stocznia Gdanska SA v Latvian Shipping Co* [1996] 2 Lloyd's Rep. 132 at 139; reversed on another ground [1998] 1 W.L.R. 574.

[49] *Reichman v Beveridge* [2006] EWCA Civ 1659; [2007] 1 P. & C.R. 20; [2007] 1 P. & C.R. 20 at [41]; *MSC Mediterranean Shipping Co SA v Cottonex Anstalt* [2016] EWCA Civ 789; [2016] 2 Lloyd's Rep. 494 at [43], in which Moore-Bick LJ (at [45]) described as neither "necessary" nor "desirable" the suggestion of the court at first instance that this question should be informed by the concept of a duty of good faith.

[50] *The Aquafaith* [2012] EWHC 1077 (Comm); [2012] 2 Lloyd's Rep. 61 at [44].

[51] *The Dynamic* [2003] 2 Lloyd's Rep. 693; *The Aquafaith* [2012] EWHC 1077 (Comm); [2012] 2 Lloyd's Rep. 61 at [42].

[52] Scott [1962] C.L.J. 12.

[53] See para.21–002.

[54] If the seller is "bound to do something to [specific] goods for the purpose of putting them into a deliverable state, the property does not pass until the thing is done and the buyer has notice that it has been done": Sale of Goods Act 1979 s.18, r.2. Thus before the seller does the required act the action

involving other kinds of contracts. In particular, it is submitted that the policy of the mitigation rules (which is to prevent needless waste) should make those rules applicable, even in an action for the agreed sum, where at the time of repudiation the claimant has not yet done all that is required of him to make that action available. This submission is supported by the *Attica Sea Carriers*[55] case, where a demise charterparty imposed continuing obligations on both parties. The charterer undertook to execute certain repairs before redelivery of the ship and to pay the agreed hire till then; and for the present purpose it was assumed[56] that the contract did not require the owner to accept redelivery until the repairs had been done. On the charterer's refusal to do the repairs, it was nevertheless held that the owner's remedy was not an action for the agreed hire. As the cost of the repairs far exceeded the value of the ship when repaired,[57] the owner had no "legitimate interest" in insisting on continued performance. Hence the mitigation rules required him to accept redelivery of the unrepaired ship and to seek his remedy in damages.

It does not follow that, in cases of this kind, the mitigation rules will always require the injured party to take such a course, since they require him only to act reasonably.[58] In *The Odenfeld*[59] a time charterer wrongfully repudiated the charterparty by refusing to pay the agreed hire. It was held that the shipowners were not bound at once to accept the repudiation and seek their remedy in damages, but that they could sue for the agreed hire until they finally did accept the repudiation. They had acted reasonably in requiring continued performance since the ship remained available for service,[60] and since they had entered into an obligation to third parties (to whom they had assigned hire due under the charterparty) to keep the contract in existence.

The argument that the appellants should have mitigated by discontinuing performance was no doubt open to the respondents in *McGregor*'s case; but it is submitted that the result in that case was consistent with the mitigation rules. There are, as will be recollected,[61] two such rules. The first is that the appellants should have minimised loss by re-letting the advertising space. But the burden of proving that they could indeed have done this was on the respondents[62] and does

for the price is not generally available: s.49(1). It is sometimes assumed that, if the buyer repudiates at this stage, the seller can nevertheless do the act and sue for the price, but there is no actual decision to this effect.

[55] *Attica Sea Carriers Corp v Ferrostaal Poseidon Bulk Reederei GmbH* [1976] 1 Lloyd's Rep. 250; Kerr 41 M.L.R. 1 at 20–21; cf. *The Alaskan Trader* [1983] 2 Lloyd's Rep. 645 where a shipowner had no legitimate interest in spending more money than the ship was worth on repairing her so as to keep her available for service; Carter and Marston [1985] C.L.J. 18.

[56] The assumption was in fact regarded as ill-founded: para.18–052.

[57] cf. paras 20–042, 20–108.

[58] See para.20–105.

[59] [1978] 2 Lloyd's Rep. 357.

[60] *The Odenfeld* [1978] 2 Lloyd's Rep. 357 at 374; the owners could perform without the charterer's co-operation by simply (in the absence of orders) laying up the ship; cf. *The Aquafaith* [2012] EWHC 1077 (Comm); [2012] 2 Lloyd's Rep. 61 at [37]; contrast, on this point, *The Alaskan Trader* [1983] 2 Lloyd's Rep. 645 at 652.

[61] See paras 20–105—20–108.

[62] *Roper v Johnson* (1873) L.R. 8 C.P. 187; *Regent OHG Aisenstadt und Barig v Francesco of Jermyn Street* [1981] 3 All E.R. 327 at 332; *The Kriti Rex* [1996] 2 Lloyd's Rep. 171 at 199; (in these cases, the claims were for damages, but there is no reason to suppose that a different rule as to burden of

not seem to have been discharged.[63] The argument required proof that the demand for space exceeded the appellants' available supply[64] and no evidence seems to have been directed to this issue. The second rule is that the appellants should not have augmented loss by spending money on the preparation of the plates. This has to be considered on the assumption that the space could not have been re-let, or that it was doubtful whether it could have been re-let. As a matter of strict law, the appellants could (on this assumption) have abandoned the contract and recovered the difference between the agreed rental and any expenses thus saved by way of damages.[65] Hence it could be said that the expense of preparing the plates should not have been incurred as it did not benefit anyone. But the mitigation rules do not require the injured party to act in accordance with the strict law. They only require him to act reasonably;[66] and if there was no possibility of re-letting the space, or only a doubtful one, it seems that the appellants did act reasonably in incurring the expense necessary to substantiate their claim for the agreed sum.

**Indirect specific performance.** The second argument against *McGregor*'s case is that the award of the agreed sum amounted to indirect specific performance,[67] but it does not seem that any of the reasons for refusing direct specific performance of such a contract applied in the circumstances of the case. Possible reasons for such refusal are that enforcement of the decree would require "constant supervision"; that there was no "mutuality";[68] and that the contract involved "personal" service.[69] But the first two reasons do not apply where the contract has been fully performed by one party and the only outstanding liability of the other is to pay cash.[70] Nor does the third reason seem to apply (even if one makes the doubtful assumption that the services were "personal") where one party has been able to perform *without any co-operation from the other*.[71] **21–016**

proof would apply in an action for the agreed sum); and see *Sony Computer Entertainment UK Ltd v Cinram Logistics* [2008] EWCA Civ 955; [2009] Bus L.R. 529. The burden will be particularly difficult to discharge where the defendant could himself have carried out the "act of mitigation", but failed to do so: *Reichman v Beveridge* [2006] EWCA Civ 1659; [2007] 1 P. & C.R. 20 (tenant in default could have found an assignee and asked the landlord not to refuse his consent without reasonable grounds: Landlord and Tenant Act 1988 s.1(3)(a)).

[63] Lord Morton in *White & Carter (Councils) Ltd v McGregor* [1962] A.C. 413 at 432, says that the appellants "made no effort" to re-let the space. But there is nothing to show whether efforts to re-let would have succeeded; cf. *Reichman v Beveridge* [2006] EWCA Civ 1659; [2007] 1 P. & C.R. 20 at [15]; Rodger 93 L.Q.R. 168.

[64] Unless this were so, the appellants would be under no duty to re-let the space originally let to the respondents: they would be entitled to let *other* space to other customers, cf. para.20–061.

[65] cf. *British and Beningtons Ltd v NW Cachar Tea Co Ltd* [1923] A.C. 48; para.17–027.

[66] See para.20–105.

[67] *White & Carter (Councils) Ltd v McGregor* [1962] A.C. 413 at 433.

[68] *Ministry of Sound (Ireland) Ltd v World Online Ltd* [2003] EWHC 2178 (Ch); [2003] 2 All E.R. (Comm) 823 at [68].

[69] See paras 21–039–21–046, 21–054–21–055.

[70] See paras 21–044, 21–054—21–055. The contract in *McGregor*'s case was to display the advertisements for three years from November 1957 and the action was commenced in October 1958, the claim being brought under an acceleration clause. In view of this clause nothing turned on the fact that performance had not been completed when the action was brought: see *White & Carter (Councils) Ltd v McGregor* [1962] A.C. 413 at 426–427.

[71] *White & Carter (Councils) Ltd v McGregor* [1962] A.C. 413 at 429.

21–017 **Hardship.** A third argument against *McGregor*'s case is that it is hard on the party in breach to have to pay for a performance which he does not want. But the injured party will not be entitled to the agreed sum if he has no "substantial or legitimate interest"[72] in completing performance; and even if he has such an interest, his action for the agreed sum may still fail if he ought to have mitigated by discontinuing performance. When these qualifications are borne in mind, it is submitted that the rule in *McGregor*'s case represents a reasonable compromise between the interests of the two contracting parties.

## 2. SPECIFIC RELIEF IN EQUITY[73]

### (a) Specific performance[74]

21–018 The common law did not specifically enforce contractual obligations except those to pay money. Specific enforcement of other contractual obligations was available only in equity. It was (and is) subject to many restrictions. These are based partly on the drastic character of the remedy,[75] which leads (more readily than an award of damages or of the agreed sum) to attachment of the defendant's person.[76] But this is an important factor only where the contract calls for "personal" performance, i.e. for acts to be done by the defendant himself. Where the contract is not of this kind, it can be specifically enforced without personal constraint, e.g. by sequestration,[77] or by the execution of a formal document by an officer of the court.[78] Other reasons for restricting specific enforcement are that this form of relief may be unnecessary, undesirable or impracticable on various grounds to be considered in the discussion that follows. In a number of later authorities, some of these reasons are no longer regarded as entirely convincing,[79] so that these cases support some expansion in the scope of the remedy.[80] The decision of the House of Lords in *Co-operative Ins Society Ltd v Argyll Stores Ltd*[81] suggests, however, some degree of return to a more restrictive view, though with modern justifications.

---

[72] *White & Carter (Councils) Ltd v McGregor* [1962] A.C. 413 at 431.

[73] Spry, *Equitable Remedies*, 9th edn (2013); Sharpe, *Injunctions and Specific Performance*, 4th edn (2012).

[74] Fry, *A Treatise on the Specific Performance of Contracts*, 6th edn (1921); Jones and Goodhart, *Specific Performance*, 2nd edn (2006).

[75] cf. *Co-operative Ins Society Ltd v Argyll Stores (Holdings) Ltd* [1998] A.C. 1 at 12.

[76] cf. *Enfield LBC v Mahoney* [1983] 1 W.L.R. 749, where even imprisonment failed to induce compliance with an order for specific restitution.

[77] *Miliangos v George Frank (Textiles) Ltd* [1976] A.C. 443 at 494, 497.

[78] *The Messianiki Tolmi* [1983] 2 A.C. 787.

[79] e.g. paras 21–031, 21–039—21–046.

[80] A trend forecast by Fry LJ in his work on *Specific Performance* (1921), para.47; cf. Burrows 4 *Legal Studies* 102.

[81] *Co-operative Ins Society Ltd v Argyll Stores Ltd* [1998] A.C. 1; para.21–046.

### (i) Granted where damages not "adequate"

The traditional view is that specific performance will not be ordered where damages are an "adequate" remedy.[82] The burden is on the claimant to show that damages are not an adequate remedy.[83] In *Cavendish Square Holding EV v Makdessi* Lord Neuberger stated that "the minimum condition for an order of specific performance is that the innocent party should have a legitimate interest extending beyond pecuniary compensation for the breach",[84] but this is just an alternative way of putting the traditional requirement, i.e. if the claimant's interest cannot *adequately* be protected by the award of pecuniary compensation, then specific performance may be awarded.[85] 21–019

**Availability of satisfactory equivalent.** Damages are most obviously an adequate remedy where the claimant can get a satisfactory equivalent of what he contracted for from some other source. For this reason specific performance is not generally ordered of contracts for the sale of commodities, or of shares, which are readily available in the market.[86] In such cases the claimant can buy in the market and is adequately compensated by recovering the difference between the contract and the market price by way of damages. Indeed, he is required to make the substitute purchase in order to mitigate his loss.[87] If he fails to do so, he cannot recover damages for extra loss suffered because the market has risen after the date when the substitute contract should have been made. To award him specific performance in such a case would, in substance, conflict with the principles of mitigation[88] as well as being oppressive to the defendant.[89] Similar reasoning seems to underlie the rule that a contract to lend money cannot be specifically enforced by either party:[90] it is assumed that damages can easily be assessed by reference to current rates of interest. 21–020

---

[82] *Co-operative Ins Society Ltd v Argyll Stores Ltd* [1998] A.C. 1 at 11; *Bankers Trust Co v PT Jakarta International Hotels & Development* [1999] 1 Lloyd's Rep. 910 at 911.

[83] *The Stena Nautica (No.2)* [1982] 2 Lloyd's Rep. 336 at 348.

[84] *Cavendish Square Holding EV v Makdessi* [2015] UKSC 67; [2016] A.C. 1172 at [30]; cf. *Zinc Cobham 1 Ltd v Adda Hotels* [2018] EWHC 1025 (Ch); [2018] L. & T.R. 36 at [48].

[85] See Lord Neuberger's reference to the "paradigm case" which is dealt with in para.21–021.

[86] *Cud v Rutter* (1719) 1 P.Wms. 570; *Re Schwabacher* (1908) 98 L.T. 127 at 128; cf. *Fothergill v Rowland* (1873) L.R. 17 Eq. 137; *Garden Cottage Foods Ltd v Milk Marketing Board* [1984] A.C. 130; *aliter* if the shares are not readily available: *Langen & Wind Ltd v Bell* [1972] Ch. 685; *Jobson v Johnson* [1989] 1 W.L.R. 1026; *Pena v Dale* [2003] EWHC 1065; [2004] 2 B.C.L.C. 508 at [135]; *Watson v Watchfinder.co.uk Ltd* [2017] EWHC 1275 (Comm); [2017] Bus L.R. 1309, or if the contract is for the sale of shares giving a controlling interest in the company: *Harvela Investments Ltd v Royal Trust C of Canada (CI) Ltd* [1986] A.C. 207.

[87] See para.20–105.

[88] See *Buxton v Lister* (1746) 3 Atk. 383 at 384.

[89] See *Re Schwabacher* (1908) 98 L.T. 127, where shares rose in value after breach. In such a case the defendant could be given the option of transferring the shares or paying the difference between contract and market price on the day fixed for performance, as in *Colt v Nettervill* (1725) 2 P. Wms. 301. See also *Whiteley Ltd v Hilt* [1918] 2 K.B. 808; *MEPC v Christian Edwards* [1978] Ch. 281 at 293; affirmed on other grounds [1981] A.C. 205); *Chinn v Hochstrasser* [1979] Ch. 447 (reversed on other grounds [1981] A.C. 533).

[90] *Rogers v Challis* (1859) 27 Beav. 175 (suit by lender); *Sichel v Mosenthal* (1862) 30 Beav. 371 (suit by borrower: decision based on lack of mutuality (para.21–054) rather than adequacy of damages); cf. *Larios v Bonnany y Gurety* (1873) L.R. 5 C.P. 346. By statute the court can specifically

21–021 **No satisfactory equivalent available.** Damages will not be regarded as an adequate remedy where the claimant cannot obtain a satisfactory substitute. The law takes the view that a buyer of land or of a house (however ordinary) is not adequately compensated by damages,[91] and that he can therefore get an order of specific performance.[92] Even a contractual licence to occupy land, though creating no interest in the land,[93] may be specifically enforced.[94] A vendor of land, too, can get specific performance, though his only claim is for money.[95] One reason for this rule is that it is just to allow the remedy *to* him as it is available *against* him. Another is that damages will not adequately compensate him for not getting the whole price, as he may not easily be able to find another purchaser.[96] But the rule seems to apply though the land is readily saleable to a third party; and it has even been applied where after contract but before completion a compulsory purchase order was made in respect of the land.[97] Yet in such a case damages (consisting of the amount by which the contract price exceeded the compensation payable on compulsory acquisition) would normally be an adequate remedy.

21–022 **Damages hard to quantify.** A second factor which is relevant (though not decisive)[98] in considering the adequacy of damages is the difficulty of assessing and recovering them.[99] This is one reason why specific performance has been ordered of contracts to sell (or to pay) annuities,[100] and of a sale of debts proved in bankruptcy,[101] the value of such rights being uncertain. Similarly, a contract to execute a mortgage in consideration of money lent at, or before, the time of the contract can be specifically enforced,[102] since the value of obtaining security for a

---

enforce a contract to take debentures in a company, that is, to make a secured loan to the company: Companies Act 2006 s.740; reversing *South African Territories Ltd v Wallington* [1898] A.C. 309. A contract to subscribe for shares in a company is also specifically enforceable: *Odessa Tramways Co v Mendel* (1878) 8 Ch D. 235; *Sri Lanka Omnibus Co v Perera* [1952] A.C. 76.

[91] *Cavendish Square Holding EV v Makdessi* [2015] UKSC 67; [2016] A.C. 1172 at [30].

[92] Unless he elects to claim damages, as in *Meng Leong Developments Pte Ltd v Jip Hong Trading Co Pte Ltd* [1985] A.C. 511.

[93] See *Ashburn Anstalt v Arnold* [1989] Ch. 1; overruled on another point in *Prudential Assurance Co Ltd v London Residuary Body* [1992] 2 A.C. 386.

[94] *Verrall v Great Yarmouth BC* [1981] Q.B. 202.

[95] e.g. *Walker v Eastern Counties Ry* (1848) 6 Hare 594; *Miliangos v George Frank (Textiles) Ltd* [1976] A.C. 443 at 496; cf. *Amec Properties v Planning & Research Systems* [1992] 1 E.G.L.R. 70.

[96] *Lewis v Lord Lechmere* (1722) 10 Mod. 503.

[97] *Hillingdon Estate Co v Stonefield Estates Ltd* [1952] Ch. 627. The contract is not frustrated by the making of the order: para.19–068; but after title to the land has vested in the acquiring authority by virtue of the compulsory purchase, the vendor's remedy is in damages and not by way of specific performance: *E Johnson & Co (Barbados) v NSR Ltd* [1997] A.C. 400.

[98] *Société des Industries Métallurgiques SA v Bronx Engineering Co Ltd* [1975] 1 Lloyd's Rep. 465.

[99] *Thames Valley Power Ltd v Total Gas and Power Ltd* [2005] EWHC 2208 (Comm); [2006] 1 Lloyd's Rep. 441 at [64]; *Araci v Fallon* [2011] EWCA Civ 668; [2011] L.L.R. 440 at [46]; *The Bremen Max* [2008] EWHC 2755 (Comm); [2009] 1 Lloyd's Rep. 81.

[100] *Ball v Coggs* (1710) 1 Bro. P.C. 140; *Kenney v Wexham* (1822) 6 Madd. 355; *Beswick v Beswick* [1968] A.C. 58; see, however, Fry, *A Treatise on the Specific Performance of Contracts* (1921), para.65; *Crampton v Varna Ry* (1872) L.R. 7 Ch. App. 562.

[101] *Adderley v Dixon* (1824) 1 C. & S. 607.

[102] *Ashton v Corrigan* (1871) L.R. 13 Eq. 76; *Swiss Bank Corp v Lloyds Bank Ltd* [1982] A.C. 584 at 595; affirmed [1982] A.C. 584 at 610.

debt cannot be precisely quantified. The same is true of the right to have a loan repaid out of specific property; and a term in a contract of loan conferring such a right is therefore specifically enforceable.[103] Even where there is no such difficulty in *quantifying* the loss, damages may be an inadequate remedy because the claimant's loss is difficult to prove,[104] or because certain items of loss[105] may not be legally recoverable,[106] or because damages may be delayed for too long and put the claimant at risk of insolvency,[107] or quite simply because the defendant may not be "good for the money".[108]

**Limitation clauses and liquidated damages.** Is it possible for the claimant to meet the requirement that damages are not an adequate remedy on the basis that he would not recover his actual loss as a result of an exclusion or limitation of liability, or a liquidated damages clause to which the claimant had agreed? In two cases where the claimant sought an interim injunction rather than specific performance, the Court of Appeal has held that he can. In *Bath & North East Somerset DC v Mowlem Plc*[109] the Court held that, despite the inclusion of a liquidated damages clause in a building contract, the claimant was entitled to rely on the probable higher level of the actual loss that it would suffer to justify the award of an injunction allowing another builder access to the site. Mance LJ distinguished between a "claim to recover damages" where the parties' agreement is conclusive and "a claim for an injunction which is designed to avoid ... any cause for a claim to such damages" where it is not.[110] The latter description may equally be applied to a claim for specific performance. This decision was followed in *AB v CD*[111] to justify the award of an injunction restraining the termination of a licence pending an arbitration to resolve the claims between the licensor and licensee, on the basis that the actual loss suffered by the licensee if it was to prevail might fall within clauses which purported to exclude or to limit the 21–023

---

[103] *Swiss Bank Corp v Lloyds Bank Ltd* [1979] Ch. 548; reversed [1982] A.C. 584, but on the ground that the contract did not on its true construction contain any such term; cf. *Kingscroft Ins Co Ltd v HS Weaver (Underwriting) Agencies Ltd* [1993] 1 Lloyd's Rep. 187 at 193; *Napier and Ettrick v Hunter* [1993] 1 A.C. 713 at 952.

[104] *Decro-Wall International SA v Practitioners in Marketing Ltd* [1971] 1 W.L.R. 361; *Hollis v Stocks* [2000] U.K.C.L.R. 685.

[105] *Hill v CA Parsons Ltd* [1972] 1 Ch. 305; *Evans Marshall & Co Ltd v Bertola SA* [1973] 1 W.L.R. 349 (injury to employment prospects and reputation; formerly, but no longer, regarded as irrecoverable: see para.20–097).

[106] cf. *PJS v News Group Newspapers* [2016] UKSC 26; [2016] A.C. 1081 at [43]; *Kent Community Health NHS Foundation Trust v NHS Swale Clinical Commissioning Group* [2016] EWHC 1393 (TCC) at [15] (privacy and reputation).

[107] *Thames Valley Power Ltd v Total Gas and Power Ltd* [2005] EWHC 2208 (Comm); [2006] 1 Lloyd's Rep. 441 at [64].

[108] *Evans Marshall & Co Ltd v Bertola SA* [1973] 1 W.L.R. 349 at 380; cf. *The Oakworth* [1975] 1 Lloyd's Rep. 581 at 583; *Themehelp Ltd v West* [1996] Q.B. 84; *Kall-Kwik Printing (UK) v Bell* [1994] F.S.R. 674; *Taylor v Birmingham CC* [2017] EWHC 2576 (QB).

[109] [2004] EWCA Civ 115; [2004] B.L.R. 153.

[110] *Bath and North East Somerset DC v Mowlem Plc* [2004] EWCA Civ 115; [2004] B.L.R. 153 at [15].

[111] [2014] EWCA Civ 229; [2015] 1 W.L.R. 771; cf. *SDI Retail Services Ltd v Rangers Football Club* [2018] EWHC 2772 (Comm) at [60].

liability of the licensor. The fact that the parties have agreed the level of damages may be taken into account in the *exercise* of the courts' discretion to grant relief, but does not preclude its *existence*.[112]

21–024 **Damages nominal.** In *Beswick v Beswick*[113] specific performance was ordered of a contract to pay an annuity to a third party. A majority[114] of the House of Lords took the view that damages were an inadequate remedy because they would be purely nominal, the promisee or his estate having suffered no loss. The point here seems to be, not that the promisee would be inadequately compensated, but that the defendant would be unjustly enriched (if damages were the sole remedy) by being allowed to retain the entire benefit of the promisee's performance while performing only a small part of his own promise.

21–025 **Sale of goods.** Section 52 of the Sale of Goods Act 1979[115] gives the court discretion to order specific performance in an action for breach of a contract to deliver "specific or ascertained" goods.[116] Although the section deals only with cases in which this remedy is sought by the buyer, the court also has power to order specific performance at the suit of the seller.[117]

21–026 **Whether goods must be "unique".** Section 52 is based on an earlier enactment, which had been passed to broaden the scope of the remedy.[118] This seemed to have been restricted to cases in which the buyer could not get a satisfactory substitute because the goods were "unique". Heirlooms, great works of art and rare antiques are regarded as "unique" for this purpose;[119] and it seems that the courts go some way towards recognising a concept of "commercial uniqueness". Thus they may order specific performance of a contract to supply a ship,[120] or machinery or other industrial plant which cannot readily be obtained elsewhere.[121] Another special factor which may induce the court to order specific performance of a contract for the sale of goods is that the goods form the contents

---

[112] *AB v CD* [2014] EWCA Civ 229; [2015] 1 W.L.R. 771 at [30].

[113] [1968] A.C. 58; para.14–017; paras 21–057—21–058.

[114] For Lord Pearce's view, see fn.310.

[115] Not applicable to consumer contracts, but see the remedies available to a consumer under the Consumer Rights Act 2015 s.19.

[116] "Specific" primarily means "identified and agreed on at the time a contract of sale is made": s.61(1). "Ascertained" is not defined in the Act but seems to mean "identified in accordance with the agreement after the time a contract of sale is made": *Re Wait* [1927] 1 Ch. 606 at 630; or identified in any other way: *Thames Sack & Bag Co Ltd v Knowles* (1918) 88 L.J.K.B. 585 at 588.

[117] *The Messiniaki Tolmi* [1982] Q.B. 1248, affirmed [1983] 2 A.C. 787, without reference to this point. The practical effect of ordering specific performance at the suit of the seller is to enable him to get an order for the payment of the price in a case falling outside Sale of Goods Act 1979 s.49 (para.21–007).

[118] s.2 of the Mercantile Law Amendment Act 1856; Treitel [1966] J.B.L. 211.

[119] *Pusey v Pusey* (1684) 1 Vern. 273; *Lowther v Lowther* (1806) 3 Ves. 95; *Falcke v Gray* (1859) 4 Drew. 651 at 658.

[120] *The Laconia* [1977] A.C. 850 at 874.

[121] See *Nutbrown v Thornton* (1804) 10 Ves. 159; *Behnke v Bede Shipping Co* [1927] 1 K.B. 649; *The Star Gazer* [1985] 1 Lloyd's Rep. 370; cf. *Lingen v Simpson* (1824) 1 S. & S. 600 (pattern books); *Land Rover Group Ltd v UPF (UK) Ltd* [2002] EWHC 3183; [2003] 2 B.C.L.C. 222. Contrast *Société des Industries Métallurgiques SA v Bronx Engineering Co Ltd* [1975] 1 Lloyd's Rep. 465 (machinery available from another source); *The Stena Nautica (No.2)* [1982] 2 Lloyd's Rep. 336.

of a house which is being sold by the same seller to the same buyer, either by the same contract or by a separate contemporaneous one.[122] The court is particularly ready to order specific performance in such a case if removal of the goods would damage the land, but the remedy is not limited to such circumstances.[123]

Section 52 does not restrict the discretion to order specific performance to cases in which the goods are "unique"; but the courts nevertheless at one time took the view that the discretion should be sparingly exercised.[124] One reason for this view is that the specific enforceability of a contract for the sale of goods might give the buyer an equitable interest in the goods;[125] and this could adversely affect third parties who had only constructive (but no actual) notice of that interest, e.g. it could give the buyer priority over not only unsecured but also secured creditors if he had paid for the goods and the seller had then become insolvent.[126] But a restrictive view of the scope of specific performance has been taken even where this factor of insolvency was not present. For example, in *Cohen v Roche*[127] the court refused specific performance to a buyer of a set of Hepplewhite chairs, saying they were "ordinary articles of commerce and of no special value or interest".[128] It is hard to see what legitimate interest of the seller was protected by the court's refusal to grant specific performance in this case; nor is the notion that damages are necessarily an adequate remedy for breach of a contract to sell goods unless they are "unique" an easy one to defend. The buyer may not in fact be able to get a substitute; his loss may be hard to assess; and part of it may be irrecoverable (e.g. because it is too remote).

**Goods in bulk.** Section 52 refers only to goods which are "specific or ascertained".[129] The section therefore does not apply where the goods are purely generic (e.g. where the sale is of "1,000 tons of wheat"). Where the goods form an undifferentiated part of an identified bulk, a distinction must be drawn between two types of cases. The first consists of cases in which the part sold is expressed as a *fraction or percentage* of the bulk, e.g. half the cotton shipped on the *Peerless*. Such a contract is one for the sale of specific goods so long as the bulk was identified and agreed on when the contract was made;[130] and the court therefore has discretion to order specific performance of it under s.52 of the 1979 Act. The second consists of cases in which the part sold is expressed as a **21–027**

---

[122] *Record v Bell* [1991] 1 W.L.R. 853 at 862.
[123] *Record v Bell* [1991] 1 W.L.R. 853 at 862.
[124] A little-noticed exception is *Rawlings v General Trading Co* [1921] 1 K.B. 635.
[125] For the view that specific enforceability does not necessarily give rise to an equitable interest, see *Tailby v Official Receiver* (1888) 13 App. Cas. 523 at 548; *Re London Wine Co (Shippers)* [1986] P.C.C. 121 at 149; cf. also *Leigh & Sillivan Ltd v Aliakmon Shipping Co (The Aliakmon)* [1986] A.C. 785 at 812–813.
[126] Insolvency of the defendant is not a ground for refusing specific performance where the remedy is normally available as a matter of course: *Amec Properties v Planning Research and Systems* [1992] 1 E.G.L.R. 70.
[127] [1927] 1 K.B. 169.
[128] *Cohen v Roche* [1927] 1 K.B. 169 at 181. Contrast *Phillips v Lamdin* [1949] 2 K.B. 33 (Adam-style door).
[129] See fn.116.
[130] Sale of Goods Act 1979 s.61(1).

*specified quantity* of unascertained goods to be taken from an identified bulk,[131] e.g. 5,000 bales out of the cargo of cotton shipped or to be shipped on the *Peerless*, on which 10,000 bales are shipped in bulk. In such a case[132] the buyer can become owner in common of the goods to the extent that he had paid for them[133] and so he would have less need[134] to seek specific performance to secure priority over other creditors in the event of the seller's insolvency. He would, however, acquire such ownership, not because the goods were specific or ascertained, but in spite of the fact they remained unascertained.[135] Cases of this kind are therefore not covered by the words of s.52, under which the court has discretion to order specific performance of a contract for the delivery of "specific or ascertained" goods.

21–028 **Where goods are not "specific or ascertained".** It is an open question whether the court may not in appropriate circumstances have discretion to order a seller specifically to perform his undertaking to deliver goods even in cases which fall outside s.52. The section does not in terms say that specific performance can be ordered *only* where the goods are "specific or ascertained"; and it is arguable that the remedy should be available, even where the goods are not of this kind, if to grant it would give effect to the general principle governing its scope. This might, for example, be the position where a contract was made to supply a manufacturer with goods urgently needed by him for the purpose of his business. Damages might be an inadequate remedy in such a case, for they "would be a poor consolation if the failure of supplies forces a trader to lay off staff and disappoint his customers (whose affections may be transferred to others) and ultimately forces him towards insolvency ... ".[136]

The view that specific performance could be ordered on such grounds[137] seemed at one time to have been abandoned;[138] but later cases give it fresh support. During a steel strike in 1980 a manufacturer sought an order for the specific delivery of a quantity of steel belonging to him against a rail carrier who (in fear of strike action) refused to allow it to be moved. The court made the order because, during the strike, "steel [was] available only with great difficulty".[139] It is submitted that, in such circumstances, specific performance should similarly be

---

131 As in *Re Wait* [1927] 1 Ch. 606.

132 Sale of Goods Act 1979 s.20A(1).

133 Sale of Goods Act 1979 s.20A(2).

134 The buyer's property acquired by virtue of s.20A(2) would not necessarily prevail against a competing interest such as that of a bank to which documents of title representing the goods had been pledged, as in *Re Wait* [1927] 1 Ch. 606; and where it did not so prevail the court would be unlikely to order specific performance to disturb this state of affairs.

135 Sale of Goods Act 1979 s.20A(1) refers to the goods (in a case of the present kind) as "a specified quantity of *unascertained* goods."

136 *Howard E Perry & Co v British Railways Board* [1980] 1 W.L.R. 1375 at 1383.

137 *Taylor v Neville* unreported, cited with approval in *Buxton v Lister* (1746) 3 Atk. 383 and in *Adderley v Dixon* (1824) 1 S. & S. 607.

138 See *Fothergill v Rowland* (1873) L.R. 17 Eq. 137; *Pollard v Clayton* (1885) 1 K. & J. 462; *Dominion Coal Co v Dominion Iron & Steel Co* [1909] A.C. 293. Contrast *Donnell v Bennett* (1883) 23 Ch D. 835.

139 *Howard E Perry & Co v British Railways Board* [1980] 1 W.L.R. 1375 at 1383.

available to a buyer. This view is supported by a case[140] in which, during the "energy crisis" in 1973, an interim injunction was granted to stop an oil company from cutting off supplies of petrol to a garage, since alternative supplies were not available. As the goods were not "specific or ascertained", the case gives some support to the view that an obligation to deliver goods may be specifically enforced in a case falling outside s.52.[141]

**Defective goods: rights of consumers.** The concept of specific performance in s.52 is that of a remedy for *non-delivery* of goods; but there is the further possibility that specific relief may be sought in respect of *defective delivery*, i.e. delivery of goods which are not in conformity with the contract. This possibility is recognised by the Consumer Rights Act 2015 under which a buyer who deals as a consumer and to whom goods are sold by a commercial seller (a "trader") may, if the goods are not in conformity with the contract, require the seller to repair or replace them.[142] The remedy of specific performance is made available to enforce the seller's duty to comply with such a requirement;[143] and this extension of the remedy is, it is submitted, consistent with the principles governing specific relief in English law. Damages are unlikely to be the most appropriate remedy for a consumer who has bought (for example) an appliance which malfunctions; while hardship to the seller is avoided by a number of restrictions on the remedies described above. Thus repair or replacement cannot be ordered if either remedy is impossible,[144] or disproportionate in comparison to the other remedies available.[145] Specific performance can also be refused where another of the new remedies (such as price reduction) is "appropriate",[146] i.e. more appropriate than specific relief. 21–029

**Appropriateness of the remedy.** The extension of specific relief (in the cases discussed above)[147] to situations not within s.52, as well as its legislative extension to certain cases of defective delivery in consumer contracts, represents a more satisfactory approach to the scope of the remedy than that of the older authorities according to which the remedy was available to a buyer of goods which were "unique" or in a similar category.[148] A more liberal view of the scope of the remedy is also reflected in dicta to the effect that the availability of specific performance depends on the *appropriateness* of that remedy in the circumstances 21–030

[140] *Sky Petroleum Ltd v VIP Petroleum Ltd* [1974] 1 W.L.R. 576; cf. *Total Oil (Great Britain) Ltd v Thompson Garage (Biggin Hill) Ltd* [1972] 1 Q.B. 318 at 324; *Redler Grain Silos Ltd v BICC Ltd* [1982] 1 Lloyd's Rep. 435; *Thames Valley Power Ltd v Total Gas and Power Ltd* [2005] EWHC 2208 (Comm); [2006] 1 Lloyd's Rep. 441.

[141] This possibility was doubted in *Re London Wine Co (Shippers)* [1986] P.C.C. 121 at 149.

[142] Consumer Rights Act 2015 ss.19(3)–(4), 23. The 2015 Act provides similar remedies where goods are supplied to a consumer under a contract other than one of sale (s.3) and also where what is supplied is "digital content": ss.42(2), 43. The consumer also has a right to require repeat performance of a service which does not conform to the contract: ss.54(3), 55.

[143] Consumer Rights Act 2015 s.58(2).

[144] Consumer Rights Act 2015 s.23(3)(a); cf. para.21–039.

[145] Consumer Rights Act 2015 s.23(3)(b); cf. para.21–032.

[146] Consumer Rights Act 2015 s.58(3) and (4).

[147] See at fnn.133–140.

[148] See paras 21–025—21–027, especially at fnn.119–112.

of each case.[149] The question is not whether damages are an "adequate" remedy, but whether specific performance will "do more perfect and complete justice than an award of damages".[150] The point was well put in a case concerned with the analogous question whether an injunction should be granted:

> "The standard question …, are damages an adequate remedy? might perhaps, in the light of the authorities in recent years, be rewritten: is it just in all circumstances that the [claimant] should be confined to his remedy in damages …?"[151]

A similar approach has been adopted to the analogous question whether specific performance can be ordered where the action for the agreed sum is also available. At one time a negative answer was given to this question, apparently because the common law remedy was an "adequate" one.[152] The current view, however, is that specific performance can be ordered in such a case if it is, in the circumstances, the most appropriate remedy.[153]

### *(ii) Discretion*

21–031 Specific performance is a discretionary remedy: the court is not bound to grant it merely because the contract is valid at law and cannot be impeached on some specific equitable ground such as misrepresentation or undue influence.[154] The discretion is, however, "not an arbitrary … discretion, but one to be governed as far as possible by fixed rules and principles".[155] The court will, in particular, have regard to the grounds to be discussed below. Its discretion to refuse specific performance on such grounds cannot be excluded by the terms of the contract.[156]

21–032 **Severe hardship.** Specific performance can be refused on the ground of severe hardship to the defendant,[157] e.g. where the cost of performance to the defendant is wholly out of proportion to the benefit which performance will confer on the claimant.[158] The court is also "slow" to order specific performance against a person who can put himself into a position to perform only by taking legal proceedings against a third party, especially where the outcome of such

[149] *Beswick v Beswick* [1968] A.C. 58 at 88, 90–91, 102; cf. *Coulls v Bagot's Executor & Trustee Co Ltd* [1967] A.L.R. 385 at 412.

[150] *Tito v Waddell (No.2)* [1977] Ch. 106 at 322; *Rainbow Estates Ltd v Tokenhold* [1999] Ch. 64 at 72–73.

[151] *Evans Marshall & Co Ltd v Bertola SA* [1973] 1 W.L.R. 349 at 379.

[152] e.g. *Crampton v Varna Ry* (1872) L.R. 7 Ch. App. 562 at 567 ("a money contract not enforceable in this court").

[153] e.g. *Beswick v Beswick* [1968] A.C. 58.

[154] *Stickney v Keeble* [1915] A.C. 386 at 419.

[155] *Lamare v Dixon* (1873) L.R. 6 H.L. 414 at 423; *Co-operative Ins Society Ltd v Argyll Stores (Holdings) Ltd* [1998] A.C. 1 at 16.

[156] *Quadrant Visual Communications Ltd v Hutchison Telephone (UK)* [1993] B.C.L.C. 442.

[157] *Denne v Light* (1857) 8 D.M. & G. 774; cf. *Wedgwood v Adams* (1843) 6 Beav. 600; *Sullivan v Henderson* [1973] 1 W.L.R. 333; *Jaggard v Sawyer* [1995] 1 W.L.R. 269 (injunction); *Insurance Co v Lloyd's Syndicate* [1995] 1 Lloyd's Rep. 273 at 276 (injunction).

[158] *Tito v Waddell (No.2)* [1977] Ch. 106 at 326; cf. *Morris v Redland Bricks Ltd* [1970] A.C. 652.

proceedings is in doubt.[159] Severe hardship may be a ground for refusing specific performance even though it results from circumstances which arise after the conclusion of the contract, which affect the person of the defendant rather than the subject-matter of the contract, and for which the claimant is in no way responsible. For example, in *Patel v Ali*[160] specific performance of a contract for the sale of a house was refused after a four-year delay (for which neither party was responsible), the vendor's circumstances having during this time changed disastrously as a result of her husband's bankruptcy and of an illness which had left her disabled. On the other hand, "mere pecuniary difficulties" would "afford no excuse".[161] Thus the purchaser of a house will not be denied specific performance merely because the vendor, on a rising market, finds it difficult to acquire alternative accommodation with the proceeds of the sale.[162] Nor will specific performance be refused merely because compliance with the order exposes the defendant to the risk of a strike by his employees.[163]

**Contract obtained by unfair means.** The court may refuse specific performance of a contract which has been obtained by means that are unfair, even though they do not amount to grounds on which the contract can be invalidated. Thus in *Walters v Morgan*[164] the defendant agreed to grant the claimant a mining lease over land which the defendant had only just bought. Specific performance was refused because the defendant was "surprised and was induced to sign the agreement in ignorance of the value of his property".[165] But specific performance will not be refused merely because the claimant fails to disclose circumstances which affect the value of the property or the defendant's willingness to contract with him.[166] Something more must be shown, e.g. that the claimant has taken unfair advantage of his superior knowledge: in *Walters v Morgan* the court relied on the fact that the claimant had produced a draft lease during the negotiations, and had hurried the defendant into signing it before he could discover the true value of the property. On the same principle specific performance may be refused if the claimant has taken advantage of the defendant's drunkenness, though it was not so extreme as to invalidate the contract at law.[167] The claimant's failure to disclose his own breach of the contract, reducing the value of the subject-matter,[168] has also been held to be a ground for refusing specific performance, even though the non-disclosure was not a ground for setting the contract aside at law.[169] 21–033

159 *Wroth v Tyler* [1974] Ch. 30, where an additional ground for refusing specific performance was that the proceedings would have to be between the defendant and his wife thus tending to split up the family; cf. *Watts v Spence* [1976] Ch. 165 at 173.

160 [1984] Ch. 283.

161 *Patel v Ali* [1984] Ch. 283 at 288; cf. *Francis v Cowcliffe* (1977) 33 P. & C.R. 368.

162 *Mountford v Scott* [1975] Ch. 258; cf. *Easton v Brown* [1981] 3 All E.R. 278.

163 See *Howard E Perry v British Railways Board* [1980] 1 W.L.R. 1375.

164 (1861) 3 D.F. & J. 718; cf. *Heath v Heath* [2009] EWHC 1908 (Ch); [2010] 1 F.L.R. 610 at [26].

165 *Walters v Morgan* (1861) 3 D.F. & J. 718 at 723.

166 cf. paras 9–152, 9–154, 16–068—16–069.

167 *Malins v Freeman* (1837) 2 Keen 25 at 34; para.12–063.

168 *Quadrant Visual Communications v Hutchison Telephone (UK)* [1993] B.C.L.C. 442.

169 See para.9–180.

21–034 **Inadequacy of consideration.** The authorities on inadequacy of consideration as a ground for refusing specific performance are not easy to reconcile. On the one hand *mere* inadequacy of consideration is not a ground for refusing specific performance.[170] On the other hand the statement that inadequacy of consideration is not a ground for refusing specific performance unless it is "such as shocks the conscience and amounts in itself to conclusive and decisive evidence of fraud"[171] is probably too narrow, even when allowance is made for the possibility that fraud may have had a wider meaning in equity than at law. The best view seems to be that specific performance may be refused where inadequacy of consideration is coupled with some other factor, not necessarily amounting to fraud or other invalidating cause at law, e.g. mistake that is operative only in equity,[172] surprise[173] or unfair advantage taken by the claimant of his superior knowledge or bargaining position.[174]

21–035 **Conduct of the claimant.** "The conduct of the party applying for relief is always an important element for consideration".[175] Thus specific performance can be refused if the claimant fails to perform a promise which induced the defendant to enter into the contract, but which is neither binding contractually, nor (because it relates to the future) operative as a misrepresentation.[176] A similar view may be taken where the claimant has made a misrepresentation but the right to rescind for that misrepresentation has been lost. If the right has been lost by reason of the defendant's affirmation of the contract,[177] he will not be allowed to rely on the misrepresentation as a defence to specific performance since he in turn would be guilty of "unconscionable inconsistency in conduct"[178] in seeking, after *affirmation*, to invoke the misrepresentation for this purpose. But his conduct would not be open to such criticism where the right to rescind had been lost by impossibility of *restitution* arising otherwise than from the defendant's conduct.[179] Hence in a case of this kind the misrepresentation, though no longer a ground for rescission, could be relied on as a defence to the equitable remedy of specific performance.[180] The remedy may similarly be refused if the claimant has acted unfairly in performing the contract, though he has not broken any promise. Specific enforcement of a solus agreement[181] has accordingly been denied to a

---

[170] *Collier v Brown* (1788) 1 Cox C.C. 428; *Western v Russell* (1814) 3 V. & B. 187; *Haywood v Cope* (1858) 25 Beav. 140.
[171] *Coles v Trecothick* (1804) 9 Ves. 234 at 246.
[172] *Webster v Cecil* (1861) 30 Beav. 62; see para.8–060.
[173] See at fn.165; cf. *Mortlock v Buller* (1804) 10 Ves. 292.
[174] *Falcke v Gray* (1859) 4 Drew. 651.
[175] *Lamare v Dixon* (1873) L.R. 6 H.L. 414 at 423; cf. *Chappell v The Times Newspapers Ltd* [1975] 1 W.L.R. 482; *Wilton Group v Abrams* [1990] B.C.C. 310 at 317 ("commercially disreputable" agreement).
[176] *Lamare v Dixon* (1873) L.R. 6 H.L. 414; and see also para.9–016.
[177] See para.9–125.
[178] *Geest Plc v Fyffes Plc* [1999] 1 All E.R. (Comm) 672 at 694.
[179] See paras 9–114—9–123.
[180] *Geest Plc v Fyffes Plc* [1999] 1 All E.R. (Comm) 672.
[181] See para.11–144.

petrol company on the ground that it had given discounts to other garages, making it impossible for the defendant garage to trade on the terms of the agreement except at a loss.[182]

**Sale of land.** An action could formerly be brought on a contract for the sale of land against a party who had provided written evidence of it by one who had not.[183] It had, however, been held that specific performance would not be granted to a purchaser of land if he refused to perform a stipulation to which he had agreed, but which could not be enforced against him for want of written evidence.[184] A contract for the sale of land must now be made (and not merely evidenced) in writing, and the writing must incorporate all the terms on which the parties have expressly agreed.[185] Hence if the stipulation in question was such a term, but was not contained in the documents, specific performance would now be refused on the different ground that no contract had come into existence. An alternative possibility is that the stipulation might have been intended to take effect as a collateral contract.[186] In that event, the main contract would be valid but the reasoning of the cases referred to above might still lead the court to refuse specific performance to the purchaser if it considered that the vendor would not be adequately protected, after being ordered to perform, by his claim for damages for breach of the collateral contract.[187] **21–036**

**Impossibility.** Specific performance will not be ordered against a person who has agreed to sell land which he does not own and cannot compel the owner to convey to him,[188] or to the claimant,[189] "because the court does not compel a person to do what is impossible".[190] The position is the same where a person has agreed to assign a lease and the landlord withholds his consent, without which the assignment cannot lawfully be effected.[191] Impossibility of enforcing an order of specific performance (e.g. because the defendant is not, and has no assets, within the jurisdiction) may also be a reason for refusing to make such an order.[192] **21–037**

**Other factors.** The factors so far discussed operate negatively, as grounds for refusing specific performance. Others may operate positively, as grounds for awarding the remedy. Thus specific performance has been ordered of a contract **21–038**

---

[182] *Shell UK Ltd v Lostock Garage Ltd* [1976] 1 W.L.R. 1187.
[183] Law of Property Act 1925 s.40, now repealed by Law of Property (Miscellaneous Provisions) Act 1989 ss.1(8) and 4 and Sch.2; and see para.5–009.
[184] See *Martin v Pycroft* (1852) 2 D.M. & G. 785 at 795; *Scott v Bradley* [1971] Ch. 850.
[185] Law of Property (Miscellaneous Provisions) Act 1989 s.2(1); para.5–009.
[186] See para.5–009.
[187] i.e. on the principle of "mutuality" as now understood: paras 21–054—21–055.
[188] See *Castle v Wilkinson* (1870) L.R. 5 Ch. App. 534; *Watts v Spence* [1976] Ch. 165; cf. *Elliot & Elliot (Builders) Ltd v Pierson* [1948] Ch. 453. Contrast *Clark v Lucas Solicitors LLP* [2009] EWHC 1952 (Ch); [2009] 46 E.G. 144 at [57]–[58].
[189] *Jones v Lipman* [1962] 1 W.L.R. 832; *Coles v Samuel Smith Old Brewery Tadcaster* [2007] EWCA Civ 1461; [2008] 2 E.G.L.R. 159.
[190] *Forrer v Nash* (1865) 35 Beav. 167 at 171.
[191] *Wilmott v Barber* (1880) 15 Ch D. 96; *Warmington v Miller* [1973] Q.B. 877; cf. *Sullivan v Henderson* [1973] 1 W.L.R. 333. Contrast *Rose v Stravrou* [2000] L. & T.R. 133 (where the remedy sought was not specific performance but a declaration).
[192] *The Sea Hawk* [1986] 1 W.L.R. 657 at 665.

to grant a licence to use a hall for a political meeting, and one reason for making the order was that it would promote freedom of speech and assembly.[193] The courts have been divided on the extent to which the "public interest" more generally should be taken into account in ordering specific performance or granting an injunction.[194]

### (iii) *Contracts not specifically enforceable*

21–039 **Contracts involving personal service.** It has long been settled that equity will not, as a general rule, enforce a contract of personal service.[195] Specific enforcement against the employee is thought to interfere unduly with his personal liberty; it is this ground of policy which accounts for the rule, so that "questions of the adequacy of damages are irrelevant to this issue".[196]

21–040 **Statutes.** Legislative force is given to this principle by s.236 of the Trade Union and Labour Relations (Consolidation) Act 1992 which provides that no court shall compel an employee to do any work by ordering specific performance of a contract of employment or by restraining the breach of such a contract by injunction.[197] Conversely, an employer could not be forced to employ: it was thought to be difficult or undesirable to enforce the continuance of a "personal" relationship between unwilling parties. This principle is reflected in the provisions of the Employment Rights Act 1996,[198] as to the remedies for "unfair" dismissal (which is not normally a breach of contract at all). Under the Act, a tribunal may order the reinstatement or re-engagement of the employee; but if such an order is not complied with, the employer can, in the last resort, only be made to pay compensation.[199] In practice, reinstatement is "effected in only a tiny proportion of ... cases"[200] so that it is compensation which is the employee's "primary remedy".[201] The remedy for infringement of the statutory right of a person not to be excluded or expelled from a trade union is likewise by way of

---

[193] *Verrall v Great Yarmouth BC* [1981] Q.B. 202; cf. *Ashworth v Royal National Theatre* [2014] EWHC 1176 (QB); [2014] 4 All E.R. 238 (Human Rights Act 1998 s.12 (freedom of expression) applied in support of a decision not to order specific performance or grant a mandatory injunction.

[194] *British Airways v Unite the Union* [2009] EWHC 3541 (QB); [2010] I.R.L.R. 423 at [83]; contrast *Araci v Fallon* [2011] EWCA Civ 668; [2011] L.L.R. 440 at [59]–[60]; and in tort: *Coventry v Lawrence* [2014] UKSC 13; [2014] 2 W.L.R. 433.

[195] *Johnson v Shrewsbury and Birmingham Ry* (1853) 3 D.M. & G. 358; cf. *Taylor v NUS* [1967] 1 W.L.R. 532; *Chappell v Times Newspapers Ltd* [1975] 1 W.L.R. 482 (injunction); *The Scaptrade* [1983] 2 A.C. 694 at 700–701 (para.21–043); *Wishart v National Association of Citizens Advice Bureaux* [1990] I.C.R. 794; *Geys v Société Générale* [2012] UKSC 63; [2013] 1 A.C. 523 at [77].

[196] *Young v Robson Rhodes* [1999] 3 All E.R. 524 at 534.

[197] Injunctions in respect of industrial action may lie against the *organisers* of such action, e.g. under Trade Union and Labour Relations (Consolidation) Act 1992 ss.226 or 235A, but not against *individual employees*.

[198] Employment Rights Act 1996 Pt X.

[199] Employment Rights Act 1996 ss.113–117. Under ss.129(9) and 130 of the 1996 Act, orders may be made for the continuation of the contract, but these do not give rise to the remedy of specific performance.

[200] *Johnson v Unisys Ltd* [2001] UKHL 13; [2003] 1 A.C. 518 at [78] (Lord Millett).

[201] *Johnson v Unisys Ltd* [2001] UKHL 13; [2003] 1 A.C. 518 at [23] (Lord Steyn).

declaration and compensation.[202] Where an employee is dismissed in breach of contract, his normal remedy is a claim for damages or a declaration that the dismissal was *wrongful*: not specific enforcement,[203] or a declaration that the dismissal was *invalid*.[204] The statutory right to return to work[205] after maternity, parental or paternity leave appears likewise not to be specifically enforceable.[206]

**Exceptions.** The arguments usually advanced in support of the equitable principle are no longer wholly convincing.[207] It is subject to a growing list of exceptions.[208] A person who is dismissed from a public office in breach of the terms of his appointment may be entitled to reinstatement;[209] and the Visitor of a University has power to order the reinstatement of a wrongfully dismissed lecturer (even when such a remedy would not be available in the ordinary courts),[210] such a dismissal being, if it amounts to a violation of the University's Statutes, not merely wrongful but also invalid.[211] The continuance or creation of a "personal" relationship may also be enforced where an injunction is granted against expulsion from a social club,[212] or against the refusal of a professional association to admit a person to membership.[213] By way of contrast, it has been held that specific relief was not available against a fee-paying school to reinstate a pupil who had been excluded for alleged misconduct, since the "breakdown of trust" had made it undesirable to require the parties "to co-exist in a pastoral and educational relationship".[214] 21–041

**Modern employment.** More generally, the modern relationship of employer and employee is often much less personal than the old relationship of master and 21–042

[202] Trade Union and Labour Relations (Consolidation) Act 1992 s.176.

[203] See para.16–119, fn.509; para.21–063, fn.341.

[204] *Francis v Kuala Lumpur Councillors* [1962] 1 W.L.R. 1411; *Vidyodaya University Council v Silva* [1965] 1 W.L.R. 77; *Gunton v Richmond-upon-Thames LBC* [1981] Ch. 448; *Marsh v National Autistic Society* [1993] I.C.R. 453.

[205] Employment Rights Act 1996 Pt VIII, and see Employment Act 2002 s.7; Maternity and Parental Leave Regulations 1999 (SI 1999/3312) reg.18.

[206] The Regulations cited in fn.205 do not specify civil remedies for infringement of the right.

[207] See Clark 32 M.L.R. 532.

[208] Under the Consumer Rights Act 2015, the consumer has a right to require repeat performance of a service which does not conform to the contract: ss.54(3), 55.

[209] *Ridge v Baldwin* [1964] A.C. 40; Ganz 30 M.L.R. 288; *Chief Constable of the North Wales Police v Evans* [1982] 1 W.L.R. 1155; *Jones v Lee* (1979) 78 L.G.R. 213. The line between ordinary and public employment is by no means clear-cut: see criticisms of *Vidyodaya University Council v Silva* [1965] 1 W.L.R. 77 in *Malloch v Aberdeen Corp* [1971] 1 W.L.R. 1578 at 1595.

[210] *Thomas v University of Bradford* [1987] A.C. 795 at 824; for subsequent proceedings, see *Thomas v University of Bradford* [1992] 1 All E.R. 964.

[211] *Pearce v University of Aston (No.2)* [1991] 2 All E.R. 469.

[212] *Young v Ladies Imperial Club Ltd* [1920] 2 K.B. 522.

[213] cf. *Nagle v Feilden* [1966] 2 Q.B. 633; doubted in *R. v Disciplinary Committee of the Jockey Club Ex p. Aga Khan* [1993] 1 W.L.R. 909 at 933. In the context of charitable associations, see *Royal Society for the Prevention of Cruelty to Animals v Attorney General* [2002] 1 W.L.R. 448 (society required to invite persons about to be excluded to give reasons why they should be admitted). See also Equality Act 2010 s.101.

[214] *R. v Incorporated Froebel Educational Institute Ex p. L* [1999] E.L.R. 488 at 493; cf. *A v Lord Grey's School* [2004] EWCA Civ 382; [2004] Q.B. 1231 (request for reinstatement at state school denied, but damages awarded for breach of Human Rights Act 1998 Sch.1 Pt II art.2).

servant was believed to be; and there are signs that the courts are prepared to re-examine or qualify the old equitable principles in the light of this development.[215] Industrial conditions may in fact force an employer to retain an employee whom he would prefer to dismiss or to dismiss one whom he is perfectly willing to retain. For example, in *Hill v CA Parsons Ltd*[216] employers were forced by union pressure to dismiss an employee. The dismissal amounted to a breach of contract and the court issued an injunction to restrain the breach, thus in effect reinstating the employee. As the employers and the employee were perfectly willing to maintain their relationship, the decision does not seem to violate the spirit of the general equitable principle against the specific enforcement of employment contracts. An injunction to restrain dismissal can also be issued in respect of a period during which no services are to be rendered under the contract. Thus where an employee had been suspended on full pay while disciplinary proceedings against him were in progress, it was held that the employers could be restrained from dismissing him before the disciplinary proceedings had run their full course.[217]

21–043 **Scope of "personal service".** The equitable principle applies to all contracts involving personal service even though they are not strictly contracts of service. Thus an agreement to allow an auctioneer to sell a collection of works of art cannot be specifically enforced[218] by either party, though specific enforcement would hardly be an undue interference with personal liberty, even in a suit against the auctioneer. Again, an agreement to enter into a partnership will not be specifically enforced as "it is impossible to make persons who will not concur carry on a business jointly, for their common advantage".[219] The court can, however, order the execution of a formal partnership agreement, and leave the parties to their remedies on the agreement.[220] Similarly, the court can order the execution of a service contract even though that contract, when made, may not be specifically enforceable.[221] And where there is no need for any continuing personal relationship, specific performance may be awarded, e.g. an option to acquire a minority shareholding in a company.[222]

---

215 See *CH Giles & Co Ltd v Morris* [1972] 1 W.L.R. 307; cf. *Geys v Société Générale* [2012] UKSC 63; [2013] 1 A.C. 523 at [77].

216 [1972] Ch. 305; Hepple [1972] C.L.J. 47; cf. *Irani v Southampton, etc. Health Authority* [1985] I.C.R. 590; *Powell v Brent LBC* [1988] I.C.R. 176; *Hughes v Southwark LBC* [1988] I.R.L.R. 55; *Jones v Gwent CC* [1992] I.R.L.R. 521 at 526; *Grady v Prison Service* [2003] EWCA Civ 527; [2003] I.C.R. 753 at [22].

217 *Robb v Hammersmith and Fulham BC* [1991] I.C.R. 514; cf. *Gryf-Lowczowski v Hinchingbrooke Healthcare NHS Trust* [2005] EWHC 2407 (QB); [2006] I.C.R. 100; *Lauffer v Barking, Havering and Redbridge University Hospitals NHS Trust* [2009] EWHC 2360 (QB); [2010] Med L.R. 68.

218 *Chinnock v Sainsbury* (1861) 30 L.J. Ch. 409; cf. *Mortimer v Beckett* [1920] 1 Ch. 571; *Young v Robson Rhodes* [1999] 3 All E.R. 524.

219 *England v Curling* (1844) 8 Beav. 129 at 137; cf. *Internet Trading Clubs Ltd v Freeserve (Investments) Ltd* [2001] E.B.L.R. 142 at [3]; *Burrows and Burrows v Sharp* (1991) 23 H.L.R. 82 (house sharing arrangement where the basis of liability was proprietary estoppel (contrast *Stallion v Albert Stallion Holdings Ltd* [2009] EWHC 1950 (Ch); [2010] 2 F.L.R. 78).

220 *England v Curling* (1844) 8 Beav. 129.

221 *CH Giles & Co Ltd v Morris* [1972] 1 W.L.R. 307; cf. *Posner v Scott-Lewis* [1987] Ch. 25.

222 *Pena v Dale* [2003] EWHC 1065; [2004] 2 B.C.L.C. 508.

The equitable principle here under discussion applies only where the services are of a personal nature. There is no general rule against the specific enforcement of a contract merely because one party undertakes to provide services[223] under it. Thus specific performance can be ordered of a contract to publish a piece of music[224] and sometimes of contracts to build.[225] It has been suggested that a time charterparty cannot be specifically enforced against the shipowner because it is a contract for services;[226] but the services that the shipowner undertakes under such a contract will often be no more personal than those to be rendered by a builder under a building contract.[227]

**Contracts requiring constant supervision.** Specific performance will not be ordered of continuous contractual duties, the proper performance of which might require constant supervision by the court.[228] In *Ryan v Mutual Tontine Association*[229] the lease of a service flat gave the tenant the right to the services of a porter who was to be "constantly in attendance". Specific enforcement of this right was refused on the ground that it would have required "that constant superintendence by the court, which the court in such cases has always declined to give".[230] For the same reason the courts have refused specifically to enforce an undertaking to cultivate a farm in a particular manner;[231] a contract to keep a shop open;[232] a contract to keep an airfield in operation;[233] a contract to deliver goods in instalments;[234] and obligations to operate railway signals[235] and to provide engine power.[236] It has also been held on this basis that a voyage charterparty cannot be specifically enforced against the shipowner.[237] 21–044

[223] e.g. *Posner v Scott-Lewis* [1987] Ch. 25 (see at fn.242); *Ferrara Quay Ltd v Carillion Construction Ltd* [2009] B.L.R. 367.
[224] *Barrow v Chappell & Co* (1951), now reported in [1976] R.P.C. 355, and cited in *Joseph v National Magazine Co Ltd* [1959] Ch. 14; contrast *Malcolm v Chancellor Masters and Scholars of the University of Oxford, The Times*, 19 December 1990. For further related proceedings, see [2002] EWHC 10 (Ch); [2002] E.L.R. 277.
[225] See para.21–049.
[226] *The Scaptrade* [1983] 2 A.C. 694 at 700–701; cf. *Lauritzencool AB v Lady Navigation Inc* [2005] EWCA Civ 579; [2005] 1 W.L.R. 3686 at [12] where Mance LJ accepts "for present purposes" the generality of Lord Diplock's statement in *The Scaptrade*; para.21–066.
[227] Denial of specific performance in the case of time charters is best explained on other grounds. See at fn.237.
[228] The principle does not apply to continuous obligations to pay money: thus an agreement to pay an annuity can be specifically enforced (para.21–022).
[229] [1893] 1 Ch. 116.
[230] *Ryan v Mutual Tontine Association* [1893] 1 Ch. 116 at 123.
[231] *Rayner v Stone* (1762) 2 Eden 128; *Phipps v Jackson* (1887) 56 L.J.Ch. 350.
[232] *Braddon Towers Ltd v International Stores Ltd* [1987] 1 E.G.L.R. 209 (decided in 1959); *Co-operative Ins Society Ltd v Argyll Stores (Holdings) Ltd* [1998] A.C. 1; see at fn.243.
[233] *Dowty Boulton Paul Ltd v Wolverhampton Corp* [1971] 1 W.L.R. 204; for later proceedings see [1973] Ch. 94.
[234] *Dominion Coal Co v Dominion Iron & Steel Co* [1900] A.C. 293; but see para.21–027.
[235] *Powell Duffryn Steam Coal Co v Taff Vale Ry* (1874) L.R. 9 Ch. 331.
[236] *Blackett v Bates* (1865) L.R. 1 Ch. 177.
[237] *De Mattos v Gibson* (1858) 4 D. & J. 276 (voyage charter). The view expressed in *The Scaptrade* [1983] 2 A.C. 694 at 700–701, that a time charter is not specifically enforceable, is perhaps best explained on the ground that such enforcement would require too much supervision.

21–045 **Limits to the difficulty of constant supervision.** The difficulty of supervision should not be exaggerated.[238] In most cases the mere existence of the court's order will suffice to deter a deliberate breach. No practical difficulty seems to have arisen in the cases in which the courts have specifically enforced contracts to do building work.[239] If the defendant were recalcitrant, the court could appoint an expert as its officer to supervise performance. This is no more "difficult" than appointing a person to run the business of a bankrupt or to manage the property of a person lacking mental capacity. The court has appointed a receiver to run a mine in a rescission action;[240] the same thing could be done in an action for specific performance. Alternatively, the claimant could be empowered to appoint a person to act as agent of the defendant to supervise the enforcement of the order: this would not be radically different from the statutory power of a mortgagee to appoint a receiver to act as agent of the mortgagor.[241] Where the acts to be done under the contract are not to be done by the defendant personally, the court can order him simply to enter into a contract to procure those acts to be done. From this point of view, *Ryan v Mutual Tontine Association* may be contrasted with the later case of *Posner v Scott-Lewis*[242] where the lessor of a block of luxury flats covenanted, so far as lay in his power, to employ a resident porter to perform a number of specified tasks. It was held that the covenant was specifically enforceable in the sense that the lessor could be ordered to appoint a resident porter for the performance of the specified services.

21–046 **Co-operative Insurance Society v Argyll Stores.** This balancing of arguments for and against ordering specific performance in cases of this kind is well illustrated by *Co-operative Ins Society Ltd v Argyll Stores (Holdings) Ltd*,[243] where a 31-year lease of premises for use as a food supermarket in a shopping centre contained a covenant by the tenant to keep the premises "open for retail trade during the usual hours of business". Some six years after the commencement of the lease, the supermarket was running at a loss and the tenant ceased trading there. The main reason given by the House of Lords for refusing to order specific performance was the difficulty of supervising the enforcement of the order since the question whether it was being complied with might require frequent reference to the court. For this purpose, Lord Hoffmann distinguished between orders (such as that sought here) "to carry on an activity" and orders "to achieve a result".[244] In the latter case, "the court ... only has to examine the

---

[238] See, e.g. *Sparks v Biden* [2017] EWHC 1994 (Ch) at [67] (specific enforcement of implied term to market and sell new dwellings within a reasonable time of completion).

[239] See para.21–049; cf. *Storer v GW Ry* (1842) 2 Y. & C.C.C. 48 (specific performance ordered of an agreement "for ever ... to maintain one neat archway"); *Kennard v Cory Bros & Co* [1922] 2 Ch. 1 (mandatory injunction ordering defendant to keep a drain open); *Rainbow Estates Ltd v Tokenhold Ltd* [1999] Ch. 64.

[240] *Gibbs v David* (1870) L.R. 20 Eq. 373.

[241] Law of Property Act 1925 s.101; cf. Insolvency Act 1986 s.44.

[242] [1987] Ch. 25.

[243] [1998] A.C. 1.

[244] cf. *Vertex Data Science Ltd v Powergen Retail Ltd* [2006] EWHC 1340; [2006] 2 Lloyd's Rep. 591 at [46] (injunction); *BDW Trading Ltd v JM Rowe Investments Ltd* [2010] EWHC 1987 (Ch) at [163]; affirmed [2011] EWCA Civ 548 without reference to this point.

finished work"[245] so that compliance with the order could be judged ex post facto: it was on this ground that the cases in which building contracts had been specifically enforced[246] were to be explained. Difficulty of supervision was, however, not the sole ground for the decision. Lord Hoffmann referred also to a number of other factors, such as the "heavy-handed nature of the enforcement mechanism"[247] by proceedings for contempt; the injustice of compelling the tenant to carry on business at a loss which might well exceed the loss which the landlord would be likely to suffer if the covenant were broken; and the fact that it was not "in the public interest for the courts to require someone to carry on business at a loss if there is any plausible alternative by which the other party can be given compensation",[248] i.e. by way of damages. Reliance on such factors suggests that, if the court attaches sufficient importance to the claimant's interest in specific enforcement, it will not be deterred from granting such relief merely on the ground that it will require constant supervision.[249] The outcome in each case will depend on the "cumulative effect"[250] of this factor together with any others which favour[251] or (as in the *Co-operative Insurance* case) militate against specific relief.[252]

**Contracts which are too vague.** An agreement may be so vague that it cannot be enforced at all, even by an action for damages.[253] But although an agreement is definite enough to be enforced in some form of legal proceeding, it may still be too vague to be enforced specifically.[254] Thus specific performance has been refused of a contract to publish an article as to the wording of which the parties disagreed.[255] In such a case the court would find it difficult or impossible to state in its order exactly what the defendant was to do; and precision is essential[256] since failure to comply with the court's order may lead to attachment for contempt. An agreement is not, however, too vague to be specifically enforced **21–047**

---

[245] *Co-operative Ins Society Ltd v Argyll Stores (Holdings) Ltd* [1998] A.C. 1 at 13.
[246] See para.21–049.
[247] *Co-operative Ins Society Ltd v Argyll Stores (Holdings) Ltd* [1998] A.C. 1 at 12.
[248] *Co-operative Ins Society Ltd v Argyll Stores (Holdings) Ltd* [1998] A.C. 1 at 15.
[249] cf. *Alfa Finance Holdings AD v Quarzwerke GmbH* [2015] EWHC 243 (Ch).
[250] *Co-operative Ins Society Ltd v Argyll Stores (Holdings) Ltd* [1998] A.C. 1 at 16.
[251] *Luganda v Service Hotels* [1969] 2 Ch. 209 (mandatory injunction ordering defendants to allow a protected tenant, who had been wrongfully locked out of a room in a residental hotel, to resume his residence in the hotel); cf. *Films Rover International Ltd v Cannon Films Sales Ltd* [1987] 1 W.L.R. 670 at 682 (for further proceedings, see [1989] 1 W.L.R. 912); *Sutton Housing Trust v Lawrence* (1987) 19 H.L.R. 520.
[252] *Shiloh Spinners Ltd v Harding* [1973] A.C. 691 at 724; cf. *Co-operative Ins Society Ltd v Argyll Stores (Holdings) Ltd* [1998] A.C. 1 at 14 interpreting the remarks made in *Shiloh Spinners* as relating to relief against forfeiture rather than to the availability of specific performance and doubting their interpretation in *Tito v Waddell (No.2)* [1977] Ch. 106 at 322.
[253] See para.2–080; *Waring & Gillow v Thompson* (1912) 29 T.L.R. 154.
[254] *Tito v Waddell* (*No.2*) [1977] Ch. 106 at 322–323.
[255] *Joseph v National Magazine Co Ltd* [1959] Ch. 14; cf. *Slater v Raw*, *The Times*, 15 October 1977.
[256] cf. *Lock International Plc v Beswick* [1989] 1 W.L.R. 1268; *Lawrence David Ltd v Ashton* [1989] I.C.R. 123 at 132.

merely because it is expressed to be subject to such amendments as may reasonably be required by one (or by either) party.[257]

21–048 **Sale of goodwill.** The difficulty of precisely formulating the court's order was at one time thought to prevent the specific enforcement of contracts for the sale of goodwill alone (without business premises): it was considered impossible for the court in its decree to state precisely what the vendor was to do.[258] But in *Beswick v Beswick* it was said that such a contract could be specifically enforced.[259] The older, contrary, authorities were not cited; and it seems that they have been made obsolete by the growing legal and commercial precision of the concept of goodwill.[260]

21–049 **Building contracts.** The general rule is that a contract to erect a building cannot be specifically enforced.[261] There seem to be three reasons for this rule. First, damages may be an adequate remedy if the building owner can engage another builder to do the work. Secondly, the contract may be too vague if it fails to describe the building with sufficient certainty. Thirdly, specific enforcement of the contract may require more supervision than the court is willing to give. But where the first two reasons do not apply, the third has not been allowed to prevail. Specific performance of a contract to erect or repair buildings can therefore be ordered if: (i) the work is precisely defined with sufficient certainty; (ii) damages will not adequately compensate the claimant; and (iii) the defendant is in possession of the land on which the building is to be done,[262] since in that case the claimant cannot get the work done by employing another builder.

21–050 **Contracts specifically enforceable in part only.** In *Ryan v Mutual Tontine Association*[263] the court refused specifically to enforce a landlord's undertaking to have a porter "constantly in attendance"; and it seems unlikely that the court would, even now, order the landlord to enter into a contract with a porter *on such terms* (though it could make an order of a similar nature where the lease *specified*

[257] *Sweet & Maxwell Ltd v Universal News Services Ltd* [1964] 2 Q.B. 699; *Alpenstow Ltd v Regalian Properties Plc* [1985] 1 W.L.R. 721.
[258] See, e.g. *Bozon v Farlow* (1816) 1 Mer. 459 at 472; cf. *Darbey v Whitaker* (1857) 4 Drew. 134 at 139.
[259] *Beswick v Beswick* [1968] A.C. 58 at 89, 97.
[260] *Trego v Hunt* [1896] A.C. 7.
[261] *Flint v Brandon* (1808) 3 Ves. 159; and see *Wolverhampton Corp v Emmons* [1901] 1 Q.B. 515; cf. *Gyllenhammar Partners International v Sour Brodogradevna Industria* [1989] 2 Lloyd's Rep. 403 at 422 (contract to build a ship).
[262] *Wolverhampton Corp v Emmons* [1901] 1 Q.B. 515 at 525; as modified by *Carpenters Estates Ltd v Davies* [1940] Ch. 160; cf. *Jeune v Queens Cross Properties Ltd* [1974] Ch. 97; *Calabar Properties Ltd v Stitcher* [1984] 1 W.L.R. 287; Landlord and Tenant Act 1985 s.17; *Barrett v Lounova* [1990] 1 Q.B. 348; *Rainbow Estates Ltd v Tokenhold Ltd* [1999] Ch. 64 at 69, 75; *Blue Manchester Ltd v North West Ground Rents Ltd* [2019] EWHC 142 (TCC); 182 Con L.R. 59; and see *Channel Tunnel Group Ltd v Balfour Beatty Construction Ltd* [1993] A.C. 334, where the House of Lords took the view that it had jurisdiction to restrain a building contractor by injunction from stopping work, but refused such relief as a matter of discretion. For the converse question, whether a builder can, in effect, compel the owner to allow him to complete the work, contrast *Hounslow LBC v Twickenham Garden & Builders Ltd* [1971] Ch. 233 with *Mayfield Holdings v Moana Reef* [1973] 1 N.Z.L.R. 309.
[263] [1893] 1 Ch. 116; para.21–044.

*the tasks* to be done by the porter).[264] A further claim that the landlord should be ordered simply to appoint a porter was also rejected on the ground that "when the court cannot grant specific performance of the contract as a whole, it will not interfere to compel specific performance of part of a contract".[265] This does not mean that the court cannot order specific performance of one individual obligation out of a number imposed by a contract:[266] it means only that it will not make such an order in relation to one such obligation if it cannot so enforce the rest of the contract.[267] Even in this restricted sense, the rule is by no means an absolute one. Thus where a monetary adjustment can be made in respect of the unperformable part the court may order specific performance with compensation.[268]

**Terminable and conditional contracts.** If the party against whom specific performance is sought is entitled to terminate the contract, the order will be refused as the defendant could render it nugatory by exercising his power to terminate.[269] This principle applies whether the contract is terminable under its express terms[270] or on account of the conduct of the party seeking specific performance.[271] On a somewhat similar principle, an obligation which is subject to a condition precedent not within the control of the party seeking the remedy will not be specifically enforced before the condition has occurred;[272] here too the making of the order could turn out to be nugatory if the condition were not satisfied. The occurrence of the condition will remove this obstacle to specific performance.[273] 21–051

**Promises without consideration.** On the principle that equity will not aid a volunteer,[274] specific performance will not be ordered of a gratuitous promise 21–052

[264] As in *Posner v Scott-Lewis* [1988] Ch. 25 (para.21–045).
[265] *Ryan v Mutual Tontine Association* [1893] 1 Ch. 116 at 123.
[266] See *Odessa Tramways Co v Mendel* (1878) 8 Ch D. 235, where such an order was made.
[267] *Rainbow Estates Ltd v Tokenhold Ltd* [1999] Ch. 64 at 65–67; *Odessa Tramways Co v Mendel* (1878) 8 Ch D. 235 (where contract is severable, specific performance of each part can be separately ordered; cf. *Internet Trading Clubs Ltd v Freeserve (Investments) Ltd* [2001] E.B.L.R. 142 at [30]).
[268] See para.18–034.
[269] It perhaps goes without saying that specific performance is not available where the contract *has been* terminated: *Hampshire CC v Supportways Social Services Ltd* [2006] EWCA Civ 1035; [2006] B.L.G.R. 836; *Clarke Investments Ltd v Pacific Technologies* [2013] EWCA Civ 750; [2013] 2 P. & C.R. 20.
[270] e.g. *Sheffield Gas Co v Harrison* (1853) 17 Beav. 294; but cf. *Allhusen v Borries* (1867) 15 W.R. 739.
[271] *Gregory v Wilson* (1851) 9 Hare 683.
[272] *Chattey v Farndale Holdings Inc* [1997] 1 E.G.L.R. 153.
[273] cf. *Wu Koon Tai v Wu Yau Loi* [1997] A.C. 179 at 189.
[274] See para.3–016.

even though it is binding at law because it is made by deed or supported by nominal consideration,[275] so that damages or the agreed sum can be recovered by the promisee.[276]

Under the Contracts (Rights of Third Parties) Act 1999, promises for the benefit of a third party are (if the statutory requirements are satisfied) enforceable not only by the promisee, but also by the third party,[277] who has the right of enforcement even though he has not provided any consideration for the promise.[278] The third party, moreover, has available to him any remedy, including specific performance, that "would have been available to him in an action for breach of the contract if he had been a party to the contract".[279] Nothing in the Act, however, affects the principle that equity will not aid a volunteer. Hence it is clear that if, between promisor and promisee, the contract is binding at law only because it is contained in a deed or supported by no more than nominal consideration (moving from the promisee), then equity will not order specific performance at the suit of the third party, any more than it will do so at the suit of the promisee. It is less clear what the position would be in the more usual case in which substantial consideration is provided by the promisee but none is provided by the third party. One possible view is that, since the third party is in such a case a volunteer, specific performance will not be ordered in his favour. But this would make the reference to specific performance in the Act, as one of the remedies available to the third party, largely nugatory. The courts may, therefore, prefer to take the view that the equitable principle applies only to gratuitous promises and that specific performance can be ordered at the suit of the third party, even though he has not provided any consideration for the promise, so long as substantial consideration for it has been provided by the promisee.

21–053 **Options and gifts.** The principle that equity will not aid a volunteer does not apply where an option to buy land is granted by deed but without consideration, or for only a nominal consideration. Such an option is for the present purpose regarded as an offer coupled with a legally binding promise not to revoke[280]; and it may therefore be exercised in spite of an attempt to revoke it. The resulting contract of sale can then be specifically enforced[281]—always assuming that it is

---

[275] See *Re Parkin* [1892] 3 Ch. 510; *Cannon v Hartley* [1949] Ch. 213. Contrast *Gurtner v Circuit* [1968] 2 Q.B. 587 at 596 where an agreement by deed between the Minister and the Motor Insurer's Bureau was said to be specifically enforceable by the Minister. The fact that no consideration moved from him was not mentioned by the court; cf. para.14–143.

[276] *Fletcher v Fletcher* (1844) 4 Hare 67 at 74.

[277] See para.14–099 and following.

[278] See para.14–109.

[279] s.1(5) of the 1999 Act. See para.21–058.

[280] For the nature of an option, see para.3–162, fn.858.

[281] *Mountford v Scott* [1975] Ch. 258.

supported by substantial consideration. The equitable principle likewise does not affect the validity of a *completed gift*:[282] it is concerned with the enforceability of gratuitous *promises*.[283]

### (iv) *Mutuality of remedy*

The court will sometimes refuse to order specific performance at the suit of one party if it cannot order it at the suit of the other. Thus a party who undertakes to render personal services or to perform continuous duties cannot get specific performance as the remedy is not available against him;[284] and for the same reason a minor cannot get specific performance.[285] Such cases were explained on the ground that the remedy of specific performance must be mutual. **21–054**

**Mutuality only required at time of hearing.** It has been said that the requirement of mutuality has to be satisfied at the time when the contract was made.[286] There are, however, many cases in which specific performance can be obtained by a party even though it could not at the time of contracting have been ordered against him. Thus, if A agrees to grant a lease of land to B, who agrees to build on it, B cannot normally be forced to build; but if he actually does build he can get specific performance of A's promise to grant the lease.[287] Specific performance cannot be ordered against a person who sells land which he does not own[288] but if he becomes owner before the purchaser repudiates[289] he can get specific performance.[290] Conversely a vendor with defective title may be ordered to convey for a reduced price although he could not himself have obtained specific performance.[291] It seems that a person of full age can get specific performance of a voidable contract made during minority even though he could have elected to repudiate the contract.[292] And a victim of fraudulent or innocent misrepresentation can get specific performance although he may be entitled to rescind the contract so that it could not be enforced against him.[293] **21–055**

---

[282] Where a promise unsupported by consideration is made to a trustee for the benefit of a third party, it has been held that the trustee ought not to enforce the promise at law against the promisor (*Re Pryce* [1917] 1 Ch. 234; *Re Kay* [1939] Ch. 239), unless the promise can be regarded as constituting a trust which is "already perfect": *Fletcher v Fletcher* (1844) 4 Hare 67 at 74.

[283] *T Choithram International SA v Pagarani* [2001] 1 W.L.R. 1; *Pennington v Waine* [2002] EWCA Civ 227; [2002] 1 W.L.R. 2075.

[284] *Ogden v Fossick* (1862) D. F. & J. 426; *Blackett v Bates* (1865) L.R. 1 Ch. App. 117; cf. *Page One Records Ltd v Britton* [1968] 1 W.L.R. 157 (injunction). A dictum in *Warren v Mendy* [1989] 1 W.L.R. 853 at 866 rejects the requirement of mutuality even in this situation (but specific enforcement was refused for reasons discussed in para.21–064).

[285] *Flight v Bolland* (1828) 4 Russ. 298; *Lumley v Ravenscroft* [1895] 1 Q.B. 683.

[286] Fry, *A Treatise on the Specific Performance of Contracts* (1921), paras 460, 830.

[287] *Wilkinson v Clements* (1872) L.R. 8 Ch. App. 96.

[288] See para.21–037.

[289] *Halkett v Dudley* [1907] 1 Ch. 590 at 596; *Cleadon Trust v Davies* [1940] 1 Ch. 940.

[290] *Hoggart v Scott* (1830) 1 Russ. & My. 293; *Wylson v Dunn* (1887) 34 Ch D. 569.

[291] *Mortlock v Buller* (1804) 10 Ves. 292 at 315; *Wilson v Wilson* (1857) 3 Jur. (N.S.) 810.

[292] *Clayton v Ashdown* (1714) 9 Vin. Abr. 393 (G.4) 1.

[293] See para.9–099 and following.

Such cases show that the requirement of mutuality does not have to be satisfied at the time of contracting; the crucial time is that of the hearing.[294] The rule was reformulated by Buckley LJ in *Price v Strange*: the court:

> "will not compel a defendant to perform his obligations specifically if it cannot at the same time ensure that any unperformed obligations of the [claimant] will be specifically performed, unless perhaps damages would be an adequate remedy for any default on the [claimant's] part".[295]

The defendant in that case had promised to grant an underlease to the claimant who had in return undertaken to execute certain internal and external repairs. It was admitted that the claimant's undertakings were not specifically enforceable; and it seems clear that he could not have obtained specific performance of the promise to grant the underlease before any of the repairs had been done. For in that case the only remedy available to the defendant for default on the claimant's part might have been in damages, and this might have been inadequate,[296] especially if the claimant was of doubtful solvency. But in fact the claimant had done the internal repairs and was wrongfully prevented from doing the external ones by the defendant, who later had these done at her own expense. As by the time of the hearing all the repairs had been completed, specific enforcement of the defendant's promise to grant the underlease would not expose her to the risk of having no remedy except damages in the event of the claimant's default; and specific performance was ordered on the terms that the claimant make an allowance in respect of the repairs done by the defendant. The principle that mutuality is judged by reference to the time of the hearing similarly accounts for the rule that a person who has been induced to enter into a contract by misrepresentation can specifically enforce it against the other; for by seeking this remedy he affirms the contract[297] and so gives the court power to hold him to it. The court has no such power when specific performance is claimed on behalf of a minor: "the act of filing the bill by his next friend cannot bind him".[298]

### (v) *Specific performance and third parties*

**21–056** Where A promises B to render some performance in favour of C, two problems can arise. The first is whether B can specifically enforce the promise against A; the second is whether C can do so.

---

[294] cf. *E Johnson & Co (Barbados) Ltd v NSR Ltd* [1997] A.C. 400 at 410–411.

[295] *Price v Strange* [1978] Ch. 337 at 367–368; adopting Ames 3 Col. L. Rev. 1; cf. *Lyus v Prowsa Developments Ltd* [1982] 1 W.L.R. 1044 at 1053; *Rainbow Estates Ltd v Tokenhold Ltd* [1999] Ch. 64 at 69, 76. See also *Sutton v Sutton* [1984] Ch. 184 where the argument of lack of mutuality was rejected because one of the claimant's promises had been performed, even though another was not binding. Specific performance was refused on grounds of public policy: para.11–048.

[296] cf. *National Provincial BS v British Waterways Board* [1992] E.G.C.S. 149. If the claimant can be ordered to give additional, satisfactory security, he can obtain an order of specific performance even though he has not yet performed and is not ordered immediately to do so: *Langen & Wind Ltd v Bell* [1972] Ch. 685.

[297] See para.9–125.

[298] *Flight v Bolland* (1828) 4 Russ. 298 at 307.

**Claim by promisee.** In *Beswick v Beswick*[299] A promised B to pay an annuity to C in consideration of B's transferring the goodwill of his business to A. It was held that, although the promise did not give C any right of action, it could be specifically enforced by B's personal representative[300] against A; with the result that A was ordered to make the promised payments to C. Under the Contracts (Rights of Third Parties) Act 1999,[301] C is in many such cases entitled in his own right to enforce against A the term in the contract containing the promise in favour of C; and where C takes this course, the need for B to seek specific performance in favour of C will be much reduced. But it will not be altogether eliminated since there may still be situations in which C will not have any such right against A because the legislative requirements for its acquisition have not been satisfied.[302] The Act also expressly preserves B's right to enforce any term of the contract against A even where C has acquired a right of enforcement against A.[303] The scope of B's remedy by way of specific performance therefore still calls for discussion. **21–057**

In holding that this remedy was available to B, the House of Lords in *Beswick v Beswick* stressed three points: that B's remedy at law was inadequate as the damages which he could recover would be purely nominal;[304] that A had received the entire consideration for his promise as the business had been transferred to him;[305] and that the contract could have been specifically enforced by A, if B had failed to perform his promise to transfer the business.[306] It is also relevant to the issue of specific enforceability that A's promise, being one to pay an annuity, was of a kind which would have been specifically enforceable if it had been made to B for his own benefit;[307] and that, if the promise had been in these terms, none of the grounds for refusing specific performance which have been discussed in this chapter would have applied.

It does not, however, follow from *Beswick v Beswick* that specific performance in favour of a third party will be granted to the promisee *only* if the circumstances are such that the remedy would have been available in a two-party case. Thus it seems that specific performance could be ordered of a promise to pay a single lump sum to a third party,[308] though in a two-party case such an obligation would more appropriately be enforceable by a common law action for the agreed sum.[309] Again, it seems that specific performance in favour of a third party would not be excluded merely because substantial damages, constituting an "adequate"

[299] [1968] A.C. 58; para.14–017.
[300] Who happened to be C.
[301] See para.14–099 and following.
[302] e.g. because the requirements of subss.1(1) and (2) are not satisfied; see para.14–106 for the question whether they would be satisfied on the facts of *Beswick v Beswick*.
[303] s.4 of the 1999 Act.
[304] *Beswick v Beswick* [1968] A.C. 58 at 73, 81, 83, 102. Nor did B have any other more satisfactory remedy at law, e.g. he could not have sued for the amount to be paid to C, or for the return of the goodwill (paras 14–023—14–024). For the question of whether B could recover damages in respect of C's loss, see para.14–037.
[305] *Beswick v Beswick* [1968] A.C. 58 at 83, 89, 97, 102; cf. para.21–024.
[306] *Beswick v Beswick* [1968] A.C. 58 at 89, 97.
[307] See para.21–024.
[308] As in *Gurtner v Circuit* [1968] 2 Q.B. 587 (as to which see fn.275).
[309] See para.21–021.

remedy, were available to the promisee. As Lord Pearce[310] said in *Beswick v Beswick*, such damages "would be a less appropriate remedy since the parties to the agreement were intending an annuity … ; and a lump sum of damages does not accord with this".[311] On the other hand specific performance will obviously not be ordered in favour of B where A contracts with B to render personal services to C, for the policy of the rule against the specific enforcement of service contracts applies no less where the services are to be rendered to a third party than where they are to be rendered to the promisee. Again, A may contract with B to pay C £10,000 immediately in return for B's promise to serve A for one year. If A repudiates before B has performed the service, B's claim for specific performance in favour of C should probably be refused on the ground that the grant of the remedy would offend the mutuality requirement:[312] A would have no security for the performance of B's promise to serve except a common law action for damages.

The above examples show that specific performance should not be granted to the promisee merely because the contract provides for performance in favour of a third party, nor refused merely because it would not have been ordered had there been no third party in the case. As a general principle, it is submitted that specific performance in favour of a third party should prima facie be available to the promisee when it is the *most appropriate* remedy for the enforcement of the contract. But it should be open to the defendant to resist specific enforcement by showing that this remedy would lead to one of the undesirable results against which the established limitations on the scope of the remedy are meant to provide protection.

21–058 **Claim by third party.** Under the Contracts (Rights of Third Parties) Act 1999, C is in many cases entitled in his own right to enforce against A the term in the contract between A and B containing A's promise in favour of C.[313] The Act expressly lists specific performance as one of the remedies available to C where it would have been available to him "if he had been a party to the contract"; and it states that the rules relating to specific performance "shall apply accordingly".[314] Some such rules will apply to a claim by C in the same way as they apply to one by B, e.g. if A's promise is one to render personal service to C, it will not be specifically enforceable at the suit of either B or C. Other rules will obviously apply with some modification,[315] e.g. if A promises B to pay a lump sum to C, then the most appropriate remedy for B might be specific performance in equity, while for C it would be a common law action for the agreed sum. The application to claims by C of the limitations on the scope of specific performance will need to be worked out on a case-by-case basis in the light of the policies which have given rise to these limitations in two-party cases.

---

310 Who thought that the damages in *Beswick v Beswick* would be substantial: [1968] A.C. 58 at 88.
311 *Beswick v Beswick* [1968] A.C. 58 at 88; cf. at 102 and the citation at 90–91 with approval of a dictum of Windeyer J in *Coulls v Bagot's Executor & Trustee Co Ltd* [1967] A.L.R. 385 at 412.
312 See paras 21–054—21–055.
313 See para.14–099 and following.
314 s.1(5) of the 1999 Act.
315 See the discussion in para.21–052.

## (b) Injunction

### (i) General

**Prohibitory injunctions.** Where a contract is negative in nature, or contains a negative stipulation, breach of it may be restrained by injunction. In such cases, an injunction is normally granted as a matter of course; though, since it is an equitable (and thus in principle a discretionary) remedy, it may be refused on the ground that its award would cause such "particular hardship"[316] to the defendant as to be oppressive to him.[317] An injunction would not be "oppressive" merely because observance of the contract was burdensome to the defendant[318] or because its breach would cause little or no prejudice to the claimant;[319] for in deciding whether to restrain breach of a negative stipulation, the court is not normally concerned with "the balance of convenience or inconvenience".[320] This rule, however, applies only to a *prohibitory* injunction restraining a defendant from *future* breaches. **21–059**

**Mandatory injunctions.** Where the breach lies entirely in the past (e.g. where the defendant has fenced land that he had covenanted to leave open), the claimant may seek a *mandatory* injunction, ordering the breach to be undone. Such an order *is* subject to a "balance of convenience"[321] test and may therefore be refused if the prejudice suffered by the defendant in having to restore the original position heavily outweighs the advantage that will be derived from such restoration by the claimant.[322] In applying the "balance of convenience" test, the court will also take the nature of the breach into account. Thus where the defendant in breach of a restrictive covenant erected a building so as to block the claimant's sea view, a mandatory injunction was granted as the breach had been committed deliberately, with full knowledge of the claimant's rights, and as damages would not be an adequate remedy.[323] **21–060**

[316] *Insurance Co v Lloyd's Syndicate* [1995] 1 Lloyd's Rep. 273 at 276 (where there was no such hardship); cf. para.21–032.
[317] See para.21–061.
[318] cf. para.21–032.
[319] *Kemp v Sober* (1851) 1 Sim. (N.S.) 517; *Tipping v Eckersley* (1855) 2 K. & J. 264; *Marco Productions Ltd v Pagola* [1945] K.B. 111; *Hollis & Co v Stocks* [2000] U.K.C.L.R. 685.
[320] *Doherty v Allman* (1878) 3 App. Cas. 709 at 720; cf. *Warner Bros Pictures Inc v Nelson* [1937] 1 K.B. 209 at 217; *Araci v Fallon* [2011] EWCA Civ 668; [2011] L.L.R. 440.
[321] This phrase is not used in quite the same sense in which it is used when an interim injunction is sought (para.21–061): *SDI Retail Services Ltd v Rangers Football Club* [2018] EWHC 2772 (Comm) at [50].
[322] *Sharp v Harrison* [1922] 1 Ch. 502; *Shepherd Homes Ltd v Sandham* [1971] Ch. 340; for subsequent proceedings, see [1971] 1 W.L.R. 1062; *Sutton Housing Trust v Lawrence* (1988) 55 P. & C.R. 320 (mandatory and prohibitory injunction); *Reed v Madon* [1989] Ch. 408.
[323] *Wakeham v Wood* (1982) 43 P. & C.R. 40; *Chelsea v Muscut* [1990] 2 E.G.L.R. 48; cf. *Mortimer v Bailey* [2004] EWCA Civ 1514; [2005] 2 E.G. 102; *QBE Management Services (UK) Ltd v Dymoke* [2012] EWHC 80 (QB); [2012] I.R.L.R. 458.

21–061 **Interim injunctions.** A "balance of convenience" test also applies to interim injunctions,[324] (except where there is "a plain and uncontested breach of a clear covenant not to do a particular thing").[325] If, for example, the grant of an interim injunction would amount in substance to a final resolution of the dispute between the parties, the court will, in considering a claim for interim relief, take into account the likelihood of the claimant's success at the eventual trial.[326] The court can also take into account the financial prejudice which would be likely to be suffered either by the claimant if the injunction were refused,[327] or by the defendant if it were granted,[328] and if at the trial the dispute were resolved in that party's favour. An award of damages to that party might then be an "inadequate" remedy for reasons discussed earlier in this chapter, e.g. because there was an appreciable risk of the other party's not being able to pay the amount of the award[329] or because of the application of a limitation on liability, or a liquidated damages clause.[330]

21–062 **Oppression.** We shall see later in this chapter that the court has power, by statute, to award damages in lieu of specific performance or injunction.[331] This power is likely to be exercised if the injury to the claimant is small, if it can readily be estimated in money, if compensation in money would adequately compensate the claimant, and if the grant of an injunction would be oppressive to the defendant.[332] These conditions were satisfied, and an injunction was refused, in *Jaggard v Sawyer*,[333] where the defendants had built a house on land which could be reached only by committing a breach of covenant and a trespass against neighbouring house-owners, including the claimant. An injunction restraining such access would have rendered the new house "landlocked and incapable of beneficial ownership";[334] and this would have been oppressive as the defendants had acted "openly and in good faith",[335] and not "in blatant … disregard of the

---

[324] *Texaco Ltd v Mulberry Filling Station Ltd* [1972] 1 W.L.R. 814; *Evans Marshall & Co v Bertola* [1973] 1 W.L.R. 349; *Clifford Davis Management Ltd v WEA Records Ltd* [1975] 1 W.L.R. 61; *Evening Standard Co Ltd v Henderson* [1987] I.C.R. 588; *Channel Tunnel Group Ltd v Balfour Beatty Construction Ltd* [1993] A.C. 334. For the general principles governing such injunctions, see *American Cyanamid Co v Ethicon* [1975] A.C. 396; *Fellowes v Fisher* [1976] Q.B. 122; *Lawrence David Ltd v Ashton* [1989] I.C.R. 123.

[325] *Hampstead and Suburban Properties Ltd v Diomedous* [1969] 1 Ch. 248 at 259; cf. *Attorney General v Barker* [1990] 3 All E.R. 257; *Araci v Fallon* [2011] EWCA Civ 668; [2011] L.L.R. 440.

[326] *Cambridge Nutrition Ltd v BBC* [1990] 3 All E.R. 523; *Lansing Linde Ltd v Kerr* [1991] 1 W.L.R. 251 at 258; *Imutran v Uncaged Campaigns Ltd* [2001] 2 All E.R. 385.

[327] *Themehelp Ltd v West* [1996] Q.B. 84, doubted on another point in *Group Josi Re v Walbrook Ins Co Ltd* [1996] 1 W.L.R. 1152 at 1162; cf. *British Airways v Unite the Union* [2009] EWHC 3541 (QB); [2010] I.R.L.R. 423.

[328] *Cambridge Nutrition Ltd v BBC* [1990] 3 All E.R. 523; *PI International Ltd v Llewellyn* [2005] EWHC 407 (QB); [2005] U.K.C.L.R. 530.

[329] See at fn.108.

[330] See para.21–022.

[331] See para.21–070.

[332] *Shelfer v City of London Electric Lighting Co* [1895] 1 Ch. 287 at 322–323; *Rogers v Humphrey* [2017] EWHC 3681 (QB). But see now *Coventry v Lawrence* [2014] UKSC 13; [2014] 2 W.L.R. 433, especially at [161], [171].

[333] [1995] 1 W.L.R. 269.

[334] *Jaggard v Sawyer* [1995] 1 W.L.R. 269 at 288.

[335] *Jaggard v Sawyer* [1995] 1 W.L.R. 269 at 289.

[claimant's] rights"[336] in building the house. The test is once again[337] one of oppression rather than one of balance of convenience: if the claimant had sought interlocutory relief before the house had been built, she "would almost certainly have obtained it".[338]

### *(ii) No indirect specific performance*

21–063 An injunction will not be granted if its effect is directly or indirectly to compel the defendant to do acts which he could not have been ordered to do by an order of specific performance. Thus an employee cannot be restrained from committing a breach of his positive obligation to work, for that would amount to specific enforcement of a contract of service.[339] Nor can an employer generally[340] be restrained from dismissing his employee in breach of contract.[341]

21–064 **Contracts of personal service** A contract of employment may contain negative promises which can be enforced by injunction without indirectly compelling the employee to work, or the employer to employ.[342] Covenants in restraint of trade contained in such contracts are commonly enforced by injunction: this does not compel the employee to work for the employer, as such covenants generally begin to operate after the period of service is over. But some negative stipulations are expressed to operate during that period. These may be enforceable by injunction if the injunction merely provides an inducement to perform the positive obligation, but not if it in effect compels the employee to do the agreed work. Thus in *Lumley v Wagner*[343] Mlle Wagner undertook that for three months she would sing at Mr Lumley's theatre in Drury Lane on two nights a week and that during those three months she would not use her talents at any other theatre without Mr Lumley's written consent. She then agreed, for a larger payment, to sing for Mr Gye at Covent Garden, and to abandon her agreement with Mr Lumley. Mr Lumley was granted an injunction to restrain her from singing for Mr Gye. By contrast, a promise by an employee not to work in *any capacity* except for the employer[344] cannot be enforced by injunction since the effect of the injunction would be "to drive the defendant either to starvation or to specific performance of the positive covenants"[345] to work.

---

[336] *Jaggard v Sawyer* [1995] 1 W.L.R. 269 at 283.

[337] cf. after fn.317.

[338] *Jaggard v Sawyer* [1995] 1 W.L.R. 269 at 289; cf. at 283.

[339] *Whitwood Chemical Co v Hardman* [1891] 2 Ch. 416; cf. para.21–039.

[340] For an exception to the general rule, see *Hill v CA Parsons & Co Ltd* [1972] 1 Ch. 305; para.21–042.

[341] *Chappell v Times Newspapers Ltd* [1975] 1 W.L.R. 482; Hepple [1975] C.L.J. 212; cf. *City & Hackney Health Authority v NUPE* [1985] I.R.L.R. 252; *Alexander v Standard Telephone and Cables Ltd* [1990] I.C.R. 291.

[342] cf. *Evans Marshall & Co Ltd v Bertola SA* [1973] 1 W.L.R. 349.

[343] (1852) 1 D.M. & G. 604.

[344] *Ehrman v Bartholomew* [1898] 1 Ch. 671.

[345] *Warner Bros Pictures Inc v Nelson* [1937] 1 K.B. 209 at 216.

21–065 **Criticism of Lumley v Wagner.** The decision in *Lumley v Wagner* has been much criticised,[346] particularly in relation to contracts of employment. An injunction may put so much economic pressure on the employee as in effect to force him to perform the positive part of the contract. In *Warner Bros Pictures Inc v Nelson*[347] a film actress agreed to act for the claimants for a period of time during which she undertook not to act for anyone else without the claimants' written consent. She was restrained by injunction from breaking this undertaking; and it was said that this would not force her to act for the claimants as she could earn a living by doing other work. But it might be quite unreasonable to expect her to do this; and more recent cases support the view that an injunction should not be granted except where it leaves the employee with some other *reasonable* means of earning a living. This issue has often arisen where professional entertainers or athletes have entered into long-term exclusive contracts with managers, in whom they then lost confidence. It has been held that the managers could not obtain injunctions either against their clients,[348] or against third parties with whom those clients had entered into substitute management contracts,[349] if the effect of the injunction would "as a practical matter"[350] be to force the clients to make use of the services of the original manager; and this would commonly be the case in such contracts given the necessity of maintaining the skill or talent of such persons through their continued display.[351]

An injunction, in cases of this kind, will always put *some* pressure on the defendant to perform his positive obligation to render the agreed services; and the view that this factor is, of itself, a ground for refusing to grant the injunction[352] is, with respect, hard to reconcile with the reasoning of *Lumley v Wagner*.[353] The crucial question, in these cases, is whether the injunction would put *undue* pressure on an employee to perform his positive obligation to work; and this question can give rise to difficult issues of fact and degree: "What is required is a realistic evaluation of whether the pressures operating on the employee in the particular case are in truth liable to compel him to return to work for the employer".[354] In one case[355] a newspaper reporter undertook during the term of his contract not to work for others; the contract provided for termination by 12

[346] Stevens 6 Cornell L.Q. 235; Ashley 6 Col. L. Rev. 82; Clark 17 Col. L. Rev. 687; and see fn.349.

[347] [1937] 1 K.B. 209.

[348] *Page One Records Ltd v Britton* [1968] 1 W.L.R. 157.

[349] *Warren v Mendy* [1989] 1 W.L.R. 853; citing criticism of *Warner Bros Pictures Inc v Nelson* [1937] 1 K.B. 209 in *Nichols Advance Vehicle Systems Inc v De Angelis* unreported 1979; McLean [1990] C.L.J. 15.

[350] *Page One Records Ltd v Britton* [1968] 1 W.L.R. 157 at 166. *Lumley v Wagner* was distinguished at 165 on the ground that Mr Lumley had no obligation except to pay money; but in fact he also made certain promises which were negative in substance, e.g. that certain parts were to "belong exclusively" to Mlle Wagner.

[351] *Warren v Mendy* [1989] 1 W.L.R. 853 at 857.

[352] *Young v Robson Rhodes* [1999] 3 All E.R. 524 at 534 ("to coerce the defendants …").

[353] *Lumley v Wagner* was cited by counsel, but not referred to in the judgment, in *Young v Robson Rhodes* [1999] 3 All E.R. 524. It seems that the defendant in the former case was not in fact "coerced" into performing her positive obligation to sing at the claimant's theatre: see Waddams 117 L.Q.R. 431 at 440. The two cases may be distinguishable on the ground that there was no express negative covenant in *Young v Robson Rhodes*.

[354] *Sunrise Brokers LLP v Rodgers* [2014] EWCA Civ 1373; [2015] I.C.R. 272 at [32].

[355] *Evening Standard Co Ltd v Henderson* [1987] I.C.R. 588.

months' notice. The reporter gave only two months' notice of termination, and it was held that he could be restrained by injunction from breach of the negative stipulation. This was said not to subject him to undue pressure since the employers had undertaken to go on paying him, to allow him to go on working for them for the rest of the contract period, and not to claim damages if he should choose simply to draw his pay without doing such work. But the position might have been different if the employers had merely undertaken to go on paying him, without allowing him to work. In such cases, the court can balance the employee's interest in continuing to work (so as to maintain his skill and reputation) against any prejudice likely to be suffered by the employer if the employee works for a third party; and, where the remedy is discretionary,[356] the court may refuse to grant the injunction if it is satisfied that breach of the negative stipulation will not seriously prejudice the employer.[357] A fortiori, such relief will be denied to the employer where his refusal to allow the employee to work amounts to a breach of the contract of employment on the employer's part.[358]

**Other services.** An injunction to restrain the breach by an employee of a stipulation in a contract of employment will be issued only if the contract contains an *express* negative promise.[359] The remedy has been restricted in this way because, as has been seen,[360] an injunction may put so much economic pressure on the employee as in effect to force him to perform his positive obligation to work; and this is traditionally regarded as undesirable.[361] But where the defendant's obligation is not one to render personal services, there is less objection to an injunction which puts pressure on him to perform his positive undertaking, even though that undertaking may not be specifically enforceable; and in cases of this kind the courts have implied negative stipulations and restrained their breach by injunction. For example, it has been suggested that a time charterparty cannot be specifically enforced against the shipowner and, on this basis,[362] an injunction will not be granted which is "juristically indistinguishable" from an order for specific performance, e.g. an injunction restraining the shipowner from exercising his right of withdrawal.[363] It is, however, no objection to the grant of injunctive relief that it would "as a matter of practical reality"[364] compel the shipowner to perform, e.g. an injunction restraining him from using a 21–066

[356] See at fn.322; cf. *Delaney v Staples* [1992] 1 A.C. 687 at 692–693; and *William Hill Organisation Ltd v Tucker* [1998] I.R.L.R. 313, discussing so-called "garden leave"; see also *JM Finn & Co Ltd v Holliday* [2013] EWHC 3450 (QB); [2014] I.R.L.R. 102.

[357] *Provident Financial Group Plc v Hayward* [1989] I.C.R. 160; cf. *SG & R Valuation Co v Boudrais* [2008] EWHC 1340 (QB); [2008] I.R.L.R. 770.

[358] *William Hill Organisation Ltd v Tucker* [1998] I.R.L.R. 313; para.17–054.

[359] *Mortimer v Beckett* [1920] 1 Ch. 571; but breaches of negative obligations *imposed by law* can be restrained by injunction even though there is no express negative stipulation, e.g. *Hivac v Park Royal Scientific Instruments* [1946] Ch. 169.

[360] See para.21–064.

[361] See para.21–039.

[362] The precise reason for this is a matter of debate, and open to challenge: see para.21–043 and fn.237.

[363] *The Scaptrade* [1983] 2 A.C. 694 at 701.

[364] *Lauritzencool AB v Lady Navigation Inc* [2005] EWCA Civ 579; [2005] 1 W.L.R. 3686 at [12].

ship under charter inconsistently with the charterparty.[365] Similarly, the practical effect of injunctive relief has not prevented the courts from restraining breach of a promise to give a "first refusal" to purchase land[366] and breaches of various exclusive dealing agreements,[367] or of agreements to submit disputes to arbitration,[368] or to the English courts.[369] Furthermore, in such commercial agreements not involving any element of personal service, injunctive relief is not precluded by the fact that the parties will be compelled, in practice, to perform a contract which requires some degree of mutual co-operation or confidence,[370] though this is a factor which the courts will take into account.[371]

21–067 **The need for an implied and limited negative stipulation.** In the above cases, a negative stipulation, though not express, can readily be implied. The position would be different where the vagueness of the positive part of the contract made it impossible to say precisely what the defendant had undertaken *not* to do;[372] and also in other cases where an injunction would be "juristically indistinguishable" from an order for specific performance,[373] i.e. where the only negative stipulation which could be implied was one that would embrace the whole positive obligation. For example, if a contract were made for the sale of unascertained generic goods (such as "100 tons of coal") an injunction "not to break the contract" or "not to withhold delivery" would be indistinguishable from an order of specific performance,[374] and would not normally[375] be granted. And the implication of a narrower negative stipulation (e.g. not to sell to anyone else) would not fairly arise from the contract.

[365] *Lauritzencool AB v Lady Navigation Inc* [2005] EWCA Civ 579; [2005] 1 W.L.R. 3686; in which *Warren v Mendy* [1989] 1 W.L.R. 853 was distinguished (at [24]) on the basis that it was a contract of *personal* service, or a particular sub-category thereof involving special skills, or talent: see above, at fn.351. See also: *Sevin v Deslandes* (1860) 30 L.J. (Ch.) 457; *The Georgios C* [1971] 1 Q.B. 488; *The Oakworth* [1975] 1 Lloyd's Rep. 581.

[366] *Manchester Ship Canal v Manchester Racecourse Co* [1901] 2 Ch. 37.

[367] *Metropolitan Electric Supply Co v Ginder* [1901] 2 Ch. 799; *Decro-Wall International SA v Practitioners in Marketing Ltd* [1971] 1 W.L.R. 361; *Evans Marshall & Co v Bertola SA* [1973] 1 W.L.R. 349; *SAB Miller Africa v Esat African Breweries* [2009] EWHC 2140 (Comm); [2010] 1 Lloyd's Rep. 392. Contrast *Fothergill v Rowland* (1873) L.R. 17 Eq. 132. As to the validity of exclusive dealing agreements, see paras 11–143—11–150.

[368] e.g. *The Angelic Grace* [1995] 1 Lloyd's Rep. 87.

[369] e.g. *Sohio Supply Co v Gatoil (USA) Inc* [1989] 1 Lloyd's Rep. 588.

[370] *Evans Marshall & Co v Bertola SA* [1973] 1 W.L.R. 349 at 379; *Lauritzencool AB v Lady Navigation Inc* [2005] EWCA Civ 579; [2005] 1 W.L.R. 3686 at [33].

[371] *Ericsson AB v EADS Defence and Security Systems Ltd* [2009] EWHC 2598 (TCC); [2010] B.L.R. 131 at [47].

[372] *Bower v Bantam Investments Ltd* [1972] 1 W.L.R. 1120.

[373] See fn.363.

[374] cf. Fry, *A Treatise on the Specific Performance of Contracts* (1921), para.857; *Whitwood Chemical Co v Hardman* [1891] 2 Ch. 416 at 426. The granting in *Wake v Renault (UK) Ltd*, *The Times*, 1 August 1996 of an injunction "not to terminate" a distributorship agreement for some years is, with respect, open to question as it amounted to specific enforcement of an obligation of which specific performance would not normally be ordered since such an order would require "constant supervision" (para.21–044).

[375] For exceptions, see paras 21–026—21–028.

**Restraint of trade.** A further danger of the rule in *Lumley v Wagner*[376] is that the injunction may help to stifle competition. It is arguable that this was the purpose of the negative stipulation, and the effect of the injunction, in the leading case itself; for it might have been physically possible for Mlle Wagner to sing at Drury Lane for two nights a week and to sing elsewhere on other nights. Yet the question whether the contract was invalid for restraint of trade was not discussed at all. It used to be thought that this question arose only where the relevant contractual provisions came into effect *after* the period of employment. A possible reason for this view is that, where the period of employment is fairly short (as in *Lumley v Wagner*), the negative stipulation is reasonable (and therefore valid)[377] because of its limited duration.[378] But this reasoning loses much of its force where the employer has options to extend the term of service, sometimes for very long periods[379] or where long periods of notice have to be given to terminate the contract.[380] The present position is that stipulations which operate during employment (no less than those which operate thereafter) can sometimes have their validity tested under the restraint of trade doctrine;[381] but even where their *validity* is not subject to these tests, the *remedy* of injunction is likely to be granted only where these tests are satisfied.[382] If this were not so, the law as to restraint of trade could, to a considerable extent, be evaded by simply giving the employer options to extend the period of service or by requiring long periods of notice for the termination of the contract.[383] A converse suggestion may also be made. Even where a covenant in restraint of trade takes effect after the period of service and is valid, it may be appropriate not to enforce it *by injunction* (but only by action for damages) if the injunction would leave the employee with no other reasonable means of making a living: the grant of an injunction in such circumstances might well be regarded as oppressive.[384] 21–068

**Severance.** A negative stipulation which is too widely expressed may be severed and enforced in part. Severance is not here governed by the rules which govern 21–069

[376] (1852) 1 D.M. & G. 604; para.21–064.

[377] See paras 11–127, 11–135.

[378] Though in *Lumley v Wagner* it was unlimited as to area; cf. *Evening Standard v Henderson* [1987] I.C.R. 588.

[379] As in *Warner Bros Pictures Inc v Nelson* [1937] 1 K.B. 209; cf. the contract in *Riley v Coglan* [1967] 1 W.L.R. 1300, where a rugby league player agreed to serve his club "for the remainder of his football career … if the club should so long require." Contrast *Eastham v Newcastle United FC Ltd* [1964] Ch. 413, where the argument that the contract gave the employers a series of options was rejected.

[380] e.g. in cases of "garden leave" (para.17–054).

[381] *Esso Petroleum Ltd v Harper's Garage (Stourport) Ltd* [1968] A.C. 269 at 294, 328–329; discussing *Young v Timmins* (1831) 1 Cr. & J. 331; *A Schroeder Music Publishing Co Ltd v Macaulay* [1974] 1 W.L.R. 1308.

[382] *William Hill Organisation Ltd v Tucker* [1998] I.R.L.R. 313; *Symbian Ltd v Christensen* [2001] I.R.L.R. 77 at [52].

[383] It is no answer to an attack on the validity of the clause to say that the employee may get paid since: (a) he will not be entitled to any payment if he refuses to work for the employer, unless the contract expressly so provides; and (b) the mere fact that he gets paid does not oust the principles of restraint of trade: cf. *Wyatt v Kreglinger and Fernau* [1933] 1 K.B. 793. If the covenant is valid, the fact that the employee goes on working and gets paid is relevant to the employer's *remedy*: at fn.355 and at fn.356.

[384] cf. para.21–062.

severance of promises in illegal contracts:[385] the question is not (as it is in the restraint of trade cases) whether severance alters the nature of the contract, but simply whether an injunction to enforce such part of the negative stipulation as the claimant specifies amounts to indirect specific performance. Thus in *Warner Bros Pictures Inc v Nelson*[386] the actress undertook, not only that she would not *act* for third parties, but also that she would not "*engage in any other occupation*" without the employers' written consent. She could clearly not be restrained from breach of the latter undertaking as this would force her to choose between idleness and performance of her obligation to work. But as the injunction sought was only one to restrain her from acting for third parties the objection that the whole of her undertaking could not be enforced by injunction was "removed by the restricted form in which the injunction is sought".[387] Of course if the negative stipulation, though operating during employment, is as a whole invalid for restraint of trade, the question of severance will be determined by the principles governing severance of illegal promises in illegal contracts.

### (c) Damages and specific performance or injunction[388]

21–070 **Damages in lieu of specific performance or injunction.** Power to award damages in addition to or "in substitution for ... specific performance" was conferred on the Court of Chancery by s.2 of the Chancery Amendment Act 1858 (also known as Lord Cairns' Act). That power is now vested in the High Court by s.50 of the Senior Courts Act 1981. Under s.49 of the same Act, common law damages can also be awarded where specific performance or an injunction is claimed, even though the case is not one in which specific relief could have been ordered and, as a consequence, it is normally unnecessary to resort to the special power to award damages in lieu of these remedies. But it may sometimes be to the claimant's advantage to invoke that power where he has no completed cause of action at law, and its exercise has also given rise to certain special problems with regard to the assessment of damages.

21–071 **No completed cause of action at law.** Damages may be awarded in lieu of specific performance or injunction even though there is no completed cause of action at law. For example, a court can issue an injunction in respect of a threatened tort which has not yet been committed; and damages can be awarded in lieu of such an injunction.[389] A similar possibility exists where an anticipatory breach of contract has been committed and *not* been accepted. In such a case, an

[385] See paras 11–162—11–168.

[386] [1937] 1 K.B. 209; para.21–065.

[387] *Warner Bros Pictures Inc v Nelson* [1937] 1 K.B. 209 at 219; see para.21–065 for the question whether an injunction in even these limited terms should be granted; cf. *William Robinson & Co Ltd v Heuer* [1898] 2 Ch. 451; *Symbian Ltd v Christensen* [2001] I.R.L.R. 77. Where the contract is illegal, e.g. for restraint of trade, the objection that a non-severable restraint is too wide cannot be met by claiming part-enforcement: contrast *Warner Bros Pictures Inc v Nelson* with *Gledhow Autoparts Ltd v Delaney* [1965] 1 W.L.R. 1366.

[388] Jolowicz [1975] C.L.J. 224; Pettit [1977] C.L.J. 369; [1978] C.L.J. 51.

[389] *Leeds Industrial Co-operative Society Ltd v Slack* [1924] A.C. 851.

order for specific performance may be made at once;[390] and damages can be awarded in lieu under the Act even though there was (when the proceedings were commenced) no right to damages at common law.[391] However, a party is not in anticipatory breach of contract merely because the other fears that he will commit a breach of it; and where there is neither a present breach nor a wrongful repudiation, an injunction is not available against the former party,[392] so that there can be no award of damages in lieu. Again, an injunction is sometimes available against a refusal to contract; and it may be that damages can be awarded in lieu even though the refusal gives rise to no cause of action at common law.[393] An injunction may also be available to a third party where a contract between two others is in restraint of trade;[394] and in such cases it is arguable that damages may be awarded in lieu even though the third party has no cause of action for breach of contract against the parties to the contract in question.

**Assessment of damages.** There was formerly some support for the view that the assessment of damages might be more favourable to the claimant under Lord Cairns' Act than at common law, particularly where the value of the subject-matter had risen between the time of breach and the time of judgment. It was assumed that, at common law, damages were necessarily based on the difference between the contract price and the value of the subject-matter *at the time of breach*. In *Wroth v Tyler*[395] one reason given for nevertheless assessing the damages by reference to the *time of judgment*[396] was that they were awarded, not at common law, but under the Act, "in substitution for … specific performance". Such damages must, it was said, "constitute a true substitute for specific performance",[397] and give "as nearly as may be what specific performance would have given".[398] But even at common law the aim of damages is to put the claimant "in the same position … *as if* the contract had been *performed*";[399] and it is hard to see any difference in principle between the two phrases "as if … performed" and "in substitution for … specific performance". Both state the same general objective; neither is followed through to its logical conclusion. The judgment in *Wroth v Tyler* itself seems to recognise the possibility that part of the claimant's loss would have been irrecoverable if it had been too remote;[400] and the mitigation rules can also reduce the amount **21–072**

[390] *Hasham v Zenab* [1960] A.C. 316 (but the order will be for performance on the due day).
[391] cf. *Oakacre Ltd v Claire Cleaners (Holdings) Ltd* [1982] Ch. 197.
[392] *The Veracruz I* [1992] 1 Lloyd's Rep. 356; *The P* [1992] 1 Lloyd's Rep. 470; cf. *Zucker v Tyndall Holdings Plc* [1992] 1 W.L.R. 1127; *Mercantile Group (Europe) AG v Aiyela* [1994] Q.B. 366 at 375.
[393] See para.1–008; *Garden Cottage Foods Ltd v Milk Marketing Board* [1984] A.C. 130 (where the right to damages was said at 141 to be based on breach of statutory duty); where the refusal is wrongful by statute, the right to damages will often be regulated by that statute, e.g. Equality Act 2010 Pt 9.
[394] See para.11–141.
[395] [1974] Ch. 30; para.20–078; and see *Grant v Dawkins* [1973] 1 W.L.R. 1406; Pettit, 90 L.Q.R. 297.
[396] See para.20–078.
[397] *Wroth v Tyler* [1974] Ch. 30 at 58.
[398] *Wroth v Tyler* [1974] Ch. 30 at 59.
[399] *Robinson v Harman* (1848) 1 Ex. 850 at 855; para.20–024.
[400] *Wroth v Tyler* [1974] Ch. 30 at 61.

recoverable as damages in lieu of specific performance.[401] In *Johnson v Agnew*[402] the House of Lords accordingly expressed the view that the assessment of damages was governed by the same principles whether the damages were awarded at common law or in lieu of specific performance.[403] Even at common law, damages are not invariably assessed by reference to the date of breach. This method of assessment is adopted where it would have been reasonable for the claimant, at that date, to have mitigated his loss, e.g. by making a substitute contract; but if, for some reason, this is not the case, the damages will be assessed by reference to some other date.[404] In *Wroth v Tyler* the claimants were not at the time of breach in a position to make a substitute contract; and, so far as the assessment of damages is concerned, the decision must now be explained on that ground.[405]

21–073 **Damages and specific performance or injunction.** Damages may be awarded in addition to specific performance, or an injunction.[406] For example, where a vendor is in breach because his title is subject to an encumbrance, the purchaser can get specific performance ordering the vendor to convey what title he has, plus damages based on the cost of discharging the encumbrance.[407] The court may also award damages for delay in completion in addition to specific performance.[408]

---

[401] See *Radford v De Froberville* [1977] 1 W.L.R. 1262 at 1286; *Malhotra v Choudhury* [1980] Ch. 52; the point was, in effect, conceded in *Grant v Dawkins* [1973] 1 W.L.R. 1406.

[402] [1980] A.C. 367 at 400. This decision also makes it hard to accept the suggestion that damages under the Act can, as a general rule, be based on the defendant's gain (rather than, as at common law, on the claimant's loss): see *Surrey CC v Bredero Homes Ltd* [1993] 1 W.L.R. 1361; *Jaggard v Sawyer* [1995] 1 W.L.R. 269. For *other* grounds for basing an award on the defendant's gain and for criticism of the *Bredero* case, see para.20–015.

[403] But see the doubts expressed about the scope of this statement of principle in *Morris-Garner v One Step (Support) Ltd* [2018] UKSC 20; [2019] A.C. 649 at [47] (Lord Reed).

[404] *Johnson v Agnew* [1980] A.C. at 401; para.20–076 and following.

[405] See para.20–078.

[406] *Experience Hendrix LLC v PPX Enterprise Inc* [2003] EWCA Civ 323; [2003] E.M.L.R. 515.

[407] *Grant v Dawkins* [1973] 1 W.L.R. 1406.

[408] *Ford-Hunt v Ragbhir Singh* [1973] 1 W.L.R. 738; cf. *Oakacre Ltd v Claire Cleaners (Holdings) Ltd* [1982] Ch. 197 (damages for delay in substitution for specific performance). For damages for delay see *Raineri v Miles* [1981] A.C. 1050; para.18–116.

## CHAPTER 22

# RESTITUTION[1]



A party who has wholly or in part performed his side of the contract and has not received the agreed counter-performance may sometimes be entitled to restitution in respect of his own performance. Where this consists of a payment of money, the payor will simply seek to get it back; where it consists of some other benefit he will claim recompense in respect of it. At the outset, it is important to stress that this chapter is not concerned with any aspect of the law of contract as such; it is concerned with a cause of action which may arise when a contract has "failed". Before any claim for restitution may be allowed on this basis,[2] it must usually first be established that the payments made, or work done, never were, or are no longer, regulated by a contractual obligation,[3] i.e. the contract is void, or incomplete, or unenforceable, or it has been discharged for frustration, or terminated for breach. **22–001**

## 1. RECOVERY OF MONEY PAID

An action lies, in the cases to be discussed below, to recover money paid under a contract or purported contract. **22–002**

[1] Burrows, *The Law of Restitution*, 3rd edn (2010), Chs 14, 15; *Chitty on Contracts*, 33rd edn, Ch.29.

[2] Claims in restitution may be made *on other bases* where there is a subsisting contract between the parties, e.g. a claim based on a payment mistakenly thought to be due under the contract.

[3] *Goodman v Pocock* (1850) 15 Q.B. 576; *Thomas v Brown* (1876) 1 Q.B.D. 714; *Kwei Tek Chao v British Traders & Shippers Ltd* [1954] 2 Q.B. 459: *Re Richmond Gate Property Co Ltd* [1965] 1 W.L.R. 335; *The Trident Beauty* [1994] 1 WLR 161 at 166: "it is always recognised that serious difficulties arise if the law seeks to expand the law of restitution to redistribute risks for which provision has been made under an applicable contract"; *Costello v MacDonald* [2011] EWCA Civ 930; [2012] Q.B. 244. For apparent exceptions to this requirement, see *Miles v Wakefield DC* [1987] A.C. 539 (discussed at para.22–033); Tang Hang Wu 23 J.C.L. 201; *Barnes v Eastenders Group* [2014] UKSC 26; [2015] A.C. 1: text to fn.16; cf. *Roxborough v Rothmans of Pall Mall Australia Ltd* [2001] H.C.A. 68.

## (a) Failure of consideration[4]

22–003 **"Total failure of consideration".** A contracting party can recover money paid under a contract if there is a "total failure of consideration", i.e. if no part of the performance for which he bargained has been rendered.[5] In the *Fibrosa*[6] case, for example, a buyer of goods recovered an advance payment when frustration had prevented the delivery of any part of the goods. Lord Simon explained the meaning of "consideration" in this context:

> "In the law relating to the formation of contract, the promise to do a thing may often be the consideration, but when one is considering the law of failure of consideration and of the quasi-contractual right to recover money on that ground it is, generally speaking, not the promise which is referred to but the performance of the promise".[7]

22–004 **Failure of the promise rather than the performance.** Performance of the promise is only "generally speaking" the relevant failure[8] because a party may bargain for the promise itself. Thus a person who insures against the destruction of a thing by fire bargains for the insurer's promise. If the thing is then destroyed by water the insured person cannot recover his premium: there is no total failure of consideration as he still had the benefit of the insurer's promise for some time.[9] He could recover his premium only if the insurer had never been at risk, e.g. if the thing had been destroyed the day before the policy had begun to run.[10]

22–005 **Promises made by a third party.** It is also possible for A to buy the benefit of a promise made to B by C, e.g. where B contracts to assign[11] to A a debt owed by C to B. The actual assignment of the debt by B to A is then the *performance* of B's promise, even though the result of that performance is to confer on A a legal right to the performance of another promise, i.e. of that made by C to B. In such a case there would be a total failure of consideration if the contract between B and C were void in law, so that nothing was transferred from B to A; but this defect was said to have been cured where, as a result of a subsequent novation, A "got the substance of what they were paying for, a valid and enforceable contract

[4] Stoljar 75 L.Q.R. 53; Birks in Rose (ed.), *Consensus ad Idem, Essays in the Law of Contract in Honour of Guenter Treitel* (1996), p.179.

[5] *Stocznia Gdanska SA v Latvian Shipping Co* [1998] 1 W.L.R. 574 at 587, 600; para.20–176 (the test is whether performance has been *rendered*, not whether it has been *received*); *Argylae UAE Ltd v Par-La-Ville Hotel & Residences Ltd* [2018] EWCA Civ 1762 at [44].

[6] *Fibrosa Spolka Ackcyjna v Fairbairn Lawson Combe Barbour Ltd* [1943] A.C. 32; paras 19–048, 19–101.

[7] *Fibrosa Spolka Ackcyjna v Fairbairn Lawson Combe Barbour Ltd* [1943] A.C. 32 at 48; cf. *Rover International Ltd v Cannon Films Ltd (No.3)* [1989] 1 W.L.R. 912 at 923; *Goss v Chilcott* [1996] A.C. 788 at 797. The point seems to have been overlooked in *Re Goldcorp Exchange Ltd* [1995] 1 A.C. 74 at 103: see para.19–101, fn.457.

[8] cf. Lord Goff (dissenting) in *Westdeutsche Landesbank Girozentrale v Islington LBC* [1996] A.C. 669 at 683 ("need not be so narrowly confined").

[9] cf. *Tyrie v Fletcher* (1777) 2 Cowp. 666.

[10] cf. *Stevenson v Snow* (1761) 3 Burr. 1237; and see Marine Insurance Act 1906 s.84 which must now be read subject to the Consumer Insurance (Disclosure and Representations) Act 2012 Sch.1 and the Insurance Act 2015 Sch.1.

[11] See Ch.15.

with" C, so that "there was no failure of consideration at all".[12] It will be recalled that novation is a transaction involving all three parties,[13] so that B contributed to the end result that A became legally entitled to the benefit of C's promise. If this state of affairs had come about as a result of an independent subsequent transaction involving only A and C, then it would not have cured the defect in B's original performance or prevented the failure of consideration from being total.

**Non-promissory failure of consideration.** Although the dictum of Lord Simon, above, is expressed in terms of the performance of the *promise*, a claim may be made for the failure of a non-promissory state of affairs (or "basis"[14]) on which the agreement was premised. This was acknowledged in a claim for the value of services where a receiver had managed certain properties in the expectation of both parties,[15] which failed, that he would be remunerated by way of a lien over the property concerned.[16] **22–006**

**Must there have been a "total" failure of consideration?**[17] In the above cases, there is either a total failure of consideration or no failure at all. There is also an intermediate situation in which there has been a *partial* failure; and in such cases, the traditional view, or general rule, is that there is no right to recover back a proportionate part of the money paid.[18] If, for example, A employed B for a lump sum paid in advance to paint A's house, and B abandoned the job before it was finished, A could not recover any part of the payment. **22–007**

**Consistency with the law of damages.** One reason for the requirement of a total failure is that, in the example just given, A already has his remedy in damages. This is generally governed by the compensatory principle[19] under which A can recover no more than his loss; and to allow him to claim restitution in respect of *any* breach would cut across this principle, particularly where he had made a bad bargain by paying B more than B's performance was worth. If B had simply done nothing after receiving the advance payment, A's right to recover the payment could be justified on the ground that B would be unjustly enriched if he were allowed to keep money paid to him "for nothing but a broken promise".[20] But this **22–008**

[12] *Kleinwort Benson Ltd v South Tyneside MBC* [1994] 4 All E.R. 972 at 989.

[13] See para.15–003. In the present case, all three parties were involved: see *Kleinwort Benson Ltd v South Tyneside MBC* [1994] 4 All E.R. 972 at 989.

[14] There is support for a change of terminology to "failure of basis": *Goff & Jones: The Law of Unjust Enrichment*, 9th edn (2016), Ch.12.

[15] This seems to explain why, despite the continued validity of the contract, the risk of not being remunerated because of the unenforceability of the lien was not found to have been allocated to the receiver: *Barnes v Eastenders Group* [2014] UKSC 26; [2015] A.C. 1 at [115].

[16] *Barnes v Eastenders Group* [2014] UKSC 26; [2015] A.C. 1.

[17] Wilmot-Smith [2013] C.L.J. 414.

[18] *Whincup v Hughes* (1871) L.R. 6 C.P. 78; the actual decision is no longer law: above, para.19–102; *Salvage Association v CAP Financial Services* [1995] F.S.R. 654 at 682; *Baltic Shipping Co v Dillon* (1993) 176 C.L.R. 344 (no return of part of the price paid for aborted holiday cruise; though the price may be relevant in assessing *damages: Peninsular & Orient SN Co v Youell* [1997] 2 Lloyd's Rep. 136; and see para.22–020); cf. *Guido van der Garde BV v Force India Formula One Ltd* [2010] EWHC 2373 (QB) at [323].

[19] See para.20–004.

[20] Palmer 20 Ohio State L.J. 264, 267; para.20–004.

reasoning loses much of its force where B has performed in part,[21] particularly where only a small part remains unperformed.

22–009 **The difficulty of apportionment.** A second reason for the general rule is that it may not be easy for the law to apportion the amount of work actually done by B to the whole in respect of which the payment was made; and where this is the case the amount of restitution that he should be required to make is correspondingly hard to assess.

22–010 **Recovery for partial failure of consideration.** There are cases in which neither of the above justifications for the general rule applies; and in such cases recovery of money has been allowed even though the failure of consideration is only partial. Thus where apportionment of the unperformed part is in fact easy, the law will allow partial recovery, e.g. a buyer of 100 tons could get back half his money if only 50 tons were delivered.[22] Apportionment is also easy where the promise which is performed only in part is one by a borrower to pay money, whether by way of interest or of repayment of capital, under a contract for the loan of money. Normally the lender's action in such a case will be one for the recovery of the agreed sum, but where this is for some reason not available,[23] the fact that some payments have been made by the borrower will not deprive the lender of a restitutionary remedy based on failure of consideration.[24] Indeed, the very fact that *no* contractual remedy is available to the promisee will make the court anxious to allow restitution since in such cases this is the *only* way in which unjust enrichment of the promisor can be avoided.[25] This point is also reflected in the statutory provision by which money paid in advance under a contract which is later frustrated can be recovered even though the failure of consideration is only partial.[26] Any difficulty of making an apportionment is again outweighed by the fact that restitution is the payor's only possible remedy, since frustration provides the payee with a defence to any claim for damages. Partial failure of consideration can also give rise to a right to the return of advance payments where the contract in terms confers such a right.[27] The requirement that the failure must be "total" is, finally, attenuated in the cases, to be discussed below,[28] in which restitution of money has been allowed in spite of the fact that benefits other than those contracted for had been received by the payor; though in some of

[21] For the position where only a very small part has been performed, see para.22–013.
[22] *Whincup v Hughes* (1871) L.R. 6 C.P. 78 at 81; cf. *Ebrahim Dawood Ltd v Heath Ltd* [1961] 2 Lloyd's Rep. 512; *Clough Mill Ltd v Martin* [1985] 1 W.L.R. 111 at 117–118.
[23] See fnn.24 and 25 for examples.
[24] *Goss v Chilcott* [1996] A.C. 788, where the borrowers had been discharged from their contractual liability by an alteration of the repayment dates in a mortgage made on behalf of the lender.
[25] Hence perhaps the reference in *Kleinwort Benson Ltd v Glasgow CC* [1999] 1 A.C. 153 at 171 to "failure of consideration" (omitting "total") in the context of a claim for the recovery of money paid under a void contract.
[26] See para.19–103 and following.
[27] *The Trident Beauty* [1994] 1 W.L.R. 161 at 164–165.
[28] See paras 22–014—22–019.

those cases the grant of the restitutionary remedy is open to criticism precisely on the ground that it has led to the payor's being overcompensated.[29]

**The current position.** The above discussion shows that the requirement of a "total" failure of consideration is now much qualified.[30] These qualifications support the view that it should be restricted to those cases in which the reasons for it, stated above, still have force. It should, in other words, no longer apply where the payor has *no* remedy, or no satisfactory remedy, for breach (e.g. by way of action for damages[31]) in respect of the part left unperformed by the payee, or where there is in fact no difficulty in apportioning that part to the whole in respect of which the payor's advance payment had been made. **22–011**

**Returnable benefits.** A party who has received only partial or defective performance may, on that ground, be entitled to terminate the contract.[32] If he does terminate, and restores what he has received under the contract, he brings about a total failure of consideration and can therefore recover any money that he has paid. For example, a buyer who has paid in advance for goods may find, on delivery, that they suffer from a defect amounting to a breach of condition, or that they are not of the agreed quantity. In that case, he can generally reject the goods and get his money back.[33] Normally, he must restore the goods, but this requirement does not apply where his inability to restore them is due to the very defect which has given rise to the right to reject, e.g. if the goods were so defective that they disintegrated; or if they were taken away from the buyer because the seller had no title to them.[34] The position seems to be the same where restoration of the subject-matter is made impossible by some external cause for which neither party was responsible.[35] **22–012**

**Non-returnable benefits.** Where, on the other hand, the partial or defective performance is of such a nature that it cannot be returned, the mere fact that it has been rendered prevents the failure of consideration from being total, e.g. where work to be done under a lump sum building contract has been paid for in advance, but is left unfinished or is done defectively. In such cases, the client's remedy is in damages: he would be entitled to the return of his payment only if the builder's breach were so serious that the work was wholly useless to the **22–013**

---

[29] *Butterworth v Kingsway Motors Ltd* [1954] 1 W.L.R. 1286; and *Barber v NSW Bank Ltd* [1996] 1 W.L.R. 641; paras 22–016, 22–017.

[30] *Barnes v Eastenders Group* [2014] UKSC 26; [2015] A.C. 1 at [114] (Lord Toulson: "There is a lively academic debate whether it is an accurate statement of law today that failure of consideration cannot found a claim in restitution or unjust enrichment unless the failure is total"); the point was not argued in the case.

[31] Or, in the case of a loan of money, by way of action for the agreed sum.

[32] See Ch.18.

[33] e.g. *Bragg v Villanova* (1923) 40 T.L.R. 154; *Baldry v Marshall* [1925] 1 Q.B. 260. Contrast *Linz v Electric Wire Co of Palestine* [1948] A.C. 371 (where a buyer of shares forming part of an invalid issue had sold, and was therefore unable to restore, them; in some cases, the claimant may be entitled to return *other* identical shares: *Smith New Court Securities Ltd v Scrimgeour Vickers (Asset Management) Ltd* [1997] A.C. 254 at 262).

[34] e.g. *Rowland v Divall* [1923] 2 K.B. 500.

[35] e.g. *Head v Tattersall* (1871) L.R. 7 Ex. 7.

client.[36] Similarly, an employee may commit breaches of duty justifying his dismissal; but if he is not dismissed and is paid his salary or wages, the employer will not, on subsequently discovering the breaches of duty, be able to recover the payments[37]: his remedy is in damages.

Even if the subject-matter of the contract is returned (or if its return is not required under the rules stated above) the injured party may still have derived some benefit from it, e.g. by using or occupying it. Use for the sole purpose of testing is disregarded and so does not impair the right of the injured party to get his money back.[38] But any further use or occupation may prevent the failure of consideration from being total. In *Hunt v Silk*[39] an agreement for a lease provided that possession was to be given immediately; that certain repairs were to be done by the landlord; that the lease was to be executed within 10 days; and that, on execution of the lease, the tenant was to pay £10. The tenant went into possession and paid the £10 before the execution of the lease, but the landlord failed to do the repairs, or to execute the lease within 10 days. After a few more days, the tenant vacated the premises and claimed the return of his £10. The claim was rejected,[40] and the case has generally been taken to lay down the strict rule that, if a party has received any part of the benefit that he contracted for,[41] there is no total failure of consideration. The rule is open to the objection that it may bar a claim for the recovery of money even though the benefit received is only slight or technical.[42] On the other hand, the actual decision in *Hunt v Silk* does not seem to be unreasonable; for there is nothing in the reported facts to suggest that the tenant did not have a perfectly adequate remedy in damages.

**22–014** **Benefits other than those bargained for.** It does not follow from *Hunt v Silk* that the receipt of *any* benefit by the injured party will bar his right to get his money back. If the benefit received was *different in kind* from that bargained for,[43] there may be a total failure of consideration even though the benefit cannot be returned in specie, e.g. where a computer is delivered without the software needed to make it work,[44] or where it is made useless by the supplier's deliberately activating a disabling device.[45] This idea has made it possible to

[36] *Heywood v Wellers* [1976] Q.B. 446 at 458; cf. *Gartell & Son v Yeovil Town Football & Athletic Club Ltd* [2016] EWCA Civ 62; [2016] B.L.R. 206 at [32].

[37] *Horcal v Gatland* [1984] I.R.L.R. 288. For the employer's right to withhold pay, see para.17–045.

[38] e.g. *Baldry v Marshall* [1925] 1 Q.B. 260.

[39] (1804) 5 East 449.

[40] Contrast *Wright v Colls* (1848) 8 C.B. 149, where the premium was paid specifically for execution of the lease and was held recoverable when the landlord failed to execute it.

[41] cf. *Thorpe v Fasey* [1949] Ch. 649.

[42] A kind of statutory modification of the rule in *Hunt v Silk* is contained in the Consumer Rights Act 2015 s.24(8).

[43] For this concept, contrast *Wilkinson v Lloyd* (1845) 7 Q.B. 27 with *Stray v Russell* (1859) 1 E. & E. 889 at 916; cf. also *Pilbrow v Pearless De Rougement & Co* [1999] 3 All E.R. 355 where the victim of the breach made no restitution claim; and the question whether such a claim might be available was left open at 361; and see para.22–023 for the view (there doubted) that there is a "total failure of consideration" for payments made under a void contract; and *Lipkin Gorman v Karpnale Ltd* [1991] 2 A.C. 548; para.3–032.

[44] *South West Water Services Ltd v International Computers Ltd* [1999] B.L.R. 420.

[45] *Rubicon Computer Systems Ltd v United Paints Ltd* (2000) 2 T.C.L.R. 453.

temper the rigidity of the rule in *Hunt v Silk*, but it has led to rules and distinctions which have in turn attracted criticism.

**Rowland v Divall.** In *Rowland v Divall*[46] the claimant, who was a car dealer, bought a car from the defendant for £334, repainted it and resold it to a customer for £400. Subsequently the car was seized by the police as it had (unknown to any of the above parties) been stolen. The claimant thereupon repaid his customer the £400 and sued the defendant for the return of the £334. Meanwhile the original owner of the car had been compensated by his insurance company, who "took over the car themselves and then sold it to the (claimant) for £260".[47] The defendant took the position that his liability was limited to this sum and paid it into court.[48] But the Court of Appeal held that there had been a total failure of consideration, so that the claimant could recover back his payment of £334. He had not "received any portion of what he agreed to buy ... He did not get what he paid for—namely a car to which he would have title".[49] As the claimant was a dealer, this seems (with respect) to be a reasonable view: he did not want to use, but to resell, the car. For this purpose he needed a marketable title and not mere possession, which was wrongful against the owner. Moreover, the fact that he did not get title caused him serious prejudice beyond having to buy the car a second time; for it resulted in his losing a presumably profitable resale.[50] **22–015**

**Butterworth v Kingsway Motors.** The same rule has, however, also been applied in the absence of such circumstances. In *Butterworth v Kingsway Motors Ltd*[51] a car owned by a finance company was let out on hire-purchase to a hirer who wrongfully sold it before she had paid all the instalments. It passed through a number of hands until it was sold for £1,275 by the defendant to a buyer, both of whom acted in good faith. Nearly a year later, the finance company notified the buyer that the car was theirs and asked for its return. Alternatively, they offered to allow the buyer to acquire title for £175, this being all that remained due under the hire-purchase agreement as the hirer had kept up her payments under it. Meanwhile, however, second-hand car prices had fallen, so that the car was worth only £800. Two days after hearing from the finance company, the buyer claimed the return of the £1,275. After another eight days, the original hirer paid off the £175 and acquired a good title which could at that stage have been passed to the buyer. In these circumstances, the court rightly described the buyer's claim as "somewhat lacking in merits"[52]—but nevertheless allowed it in full. The decision represents a regrettable extension of *Rowland v Divall*. It is hardly realistic to say that the buyer did not get any part of what he bargained for: he bought the car for use and did use it for nearly a year. Moreover, any prejudice to the buyer from the defendant's lack of title was removed when the amount outstanding under the hire-purchase agreement was paid off. **22–016**

---

[46] [1923] 2 K.B. 500.
[47] This fact is stated in the report of the case in 129 L.T. 757.
[48] See again 129 L.T. 757.
[49] *Rowland v Divall* [1923] 2 K.B. 500 at 504.
[50] The eventual fate of the car is not known; cf. para.20–061.
[51] [1954] 1 W.L.R. 1286.
[52] *Butterworth v Kingsway Motors Ltd* [1954] 1 W.L.R. 1286 at 1291.

22–017 **Barber v NSW Bank.** The same result was again reached in *Barber v NSW Bank Plc*,[53] where the buyer entered into a conditional sale agreement with the defendants relating to a car which was (unknown to either party) the subject of an earlier finance agreement and to which the defendant therefore had no title. The buyer became aware of this fact when he attempted, some 20 months after entering into the agreement to resell the car; and after a further three months he terminated the agreement and successfully claimed the return of all the payments he had made under it. Although he had had the use of the car for nearly two years "without let or hinderance",[54] it was said to be "not inequitable in all the circumstances"[55] for him to recover his payments in full. This result was based "on the established authorities"[56] which appear to have included *Rowland v Divall* and *Butterworth v Kingsway Motors*, both of which were cited to the court though neither was referred to in the judgment.[57] It is, with respect, unfortunate that no attempt was made by the Court of Appeal in the *Barber* case to distinguish the former or to evaluate the latter decision. The car had been bought for use (though the breach came to light when the buyer attempted to resell it); and as the buyer had used the car for some 23 months it is hard to accept that he received no part of the benefit for which he had bargained. The court may have attached some weight to the fact that the defendants had become aware of the earlier finance agreement some six months before the buyer terminated[58] and they had made no attempt to settle the third party's claim during that interval.[59] It is, however, not easy to see how even this fact could be said to have deprived the buyer of the whole of what he had bargained for, particularly as he had used the car for more than 16 months before the defendants had acquired any knowledge of the earlier agreement[60] and so had any opportunity of settling the true owner's claim.

22–018 **Other cases.** A line of hire-purchase cases is open to similar criticisms. According to these, there is a total failure of consideration if the person letting a car out has no title, so that he cannot give the hirer a valid option to purchase.[61] But once a valid option has been conferred, there is no total failure because the hirer is for some reason prevented from exercising it;[62] or because the car suffers from defects which are so serious that it cannot, for practical purposes, be used at all.[63] It seems unrealistic to say that a hirer who actually uses the car for a

[53] [1996] 1 W.L.R. 641.
[54] *Barber v NSW Bank Plc* [1996] 1 W.L.R. 641 at 647.
[55] *Barber v NSW Bank Plc* [1996] 1 W.L.R. 641 at 647.
[56] *Barber v NSW Bank Plc* [1996] 1 W.L.R. 641 at 647.
[57] The court relied principally on the authorities cited in fn.61, though it accepted, at 646, that it was not bound by these cases.
[58] The defendants became aware of the third party's claim on 12 February 1991; the buyer terminated on 16 August 1991.
[59] They settled it on 2 September 1991.
[60] i.e. from 10 October 1989, when the car was supplied to the buyer, til 12 February 1991.
[61] See *Karflex Ltd v Poole* [1933] 2 K.B. 251; *Warman v Southern Counties Car Finance Corp Ltd* [1959] 2 K.B. 576 (where the point arose on a counterclaim against the hirer).
[62] *Kelly v Lombard Banking Co* [1959] 1 W.L.R. 41; cf. *CCC Films (London) Ltd v Impact Quadrant Films* [1985] Q.B. 16 at 28.
[63] *Yeoman Credit Ltd v Apps* [1962] 2 Q.B. 508.

substantial period is wholly deprived of what he bargained for merely because there was no valid option, while one who cannot use the car at all because of a physical defect is not so deprived.

**Criticism.** The view that the buyer in *Rowland v Divall* itself did not get *the* benefit for which he bargained is (as has been suggested above) a perfectly reasonable one. But the decision has nevertheless been criticised on the ground that the buyer recovered the *whole* of the price even though he and his sub-buyer had had the use of the car for some months. One way of meeting this criticism would be to reduce the buyer's claim for the return of the price by giving the seller the right to an allowance in respect of the benefit obtained by the buyer from his use of the subject-matter.[64] But this suggestion in turn gives rise to the problem of valuing that benefit. It would clearly be unfair to the buyer to assess it at a "reasonable rental value" since a person who is buying or hire-purchasing a car would not want to incur the cost of hiring one. An alternative possibility would be to value the buyer's benefit at the amount by which the cost of replacing the goods when the buyer was deprived of them was less than the contract price.[65] **22–019**

A further problem arises in cases of this kind because the true owner may have a claim in tort against either the buyer[66] or the seller[67] or both; he may be entitled not only to the return of the property or its value, but also its reasonable rental value.[68] If the owner has already claimed the rental value from the buyer, it seems clear that the seller should restore the *whole* price;[69] for if the buyer also had to give credit to the seller for the use of the goods, he would be required to pay twice over for the same benefit. Similar considerations apply where the true owner has not yet made his claim: if the buyer had to give credit to the seller he could later be sued for a similar sum by the owner. He might be able to claim that second payment back from the seller as damages; but by then the seller may have disappeared or the right to sue him may be barred by lapse of time. Of course the true owner may choose not to assert his claim for rental value; and in that case the buyer would no doubt be enriched by having had the use of the subject-matter and nevertheless being allowed to get back the whole price from the seller. But the enrichment would be at the expense of the *owner* and not at the expense of the seller, who accordingly should not have a claim in respect of it.[70] In view of the buyer's possible liability to the true owner, the buyer should only have to make an allowance to the seller for the benefit of the use of the goods if the claim of the true owner has first been satisfied.[71]

---

64 The Law Commissions (Law Com. No.160, Scot. Law Com. No.104, para.6.5) concluded that this subject is too complex for legislative reform; cf. *Salt v Stratstone Specialist Ltd* [2015] EWCA Civ 745; [2015] 2 C.L.C. 206 where an allowance was made in a claim for rescission based on misrepresentation: para.9–119.

65 Law Commission Working Paper 65, para.73.

66 *Hilberry v Hatton* (1864) 2 H. & C. 822.

67 *Martindale v Smith* (1841) 1 Q.B. 389.

68 *Strand Electric & Engineering Co Ltd v Brisford Entertainments Ltd* [1952] 2 K.B. 246.

69 As in *Newsome v Graham* (1829) 10 B. & C. 234 (where the subject-matter was an interest in land). cf. *Hizzett v Hargreaves* [1987] C.L.Y. 1164.

70 See *Warman v Southern Counties Car Finance Corp Ltd* [1959] 2 K.B. 576 at 582–583.

71 Law Commission Working Paper No.65, paras 68–70.

22–020 **Relation to damages.** In a number of cases it has been held or said that a claimant may be able to get back money paid under a contract *as damages* for the defendant's breach. For example, in one case a cow had been sold warranted healthy, but in fact she suffered from a disease from which she died; and the buyer recovered the price as one item of damages for breach of warranty.[72] Payments made under hire-purchase agreements by hirers have likewise been recovered by them as damages where the goods were so defective that they were completely useless or rightfully rejected by the hirers.[73] Similar relief has been given to buyers and hire purchasers of stolen goods who elected to claim damages;[74] and to tenants who left premises which had been leased to them in consequence of abusive conduct on the part of their landlord, amounting to breach of his covenant for quiet enjoyment.[75] Strictly speaking, the injured party's damages in such cases should be the *value of the subject-matter* at the relevant date,[76] and not *the price* as such. The cases can perhaps be explained on the ground that in them the price was the best, and indeed the only, evidence of value. It is also possible for the price paid under one contract to be recoverable as reliance loss by way of damages for breach of a second contract between the same parties.[77]

In an action for damages the injured party can often recover more than the money he has paid to the defendant. For example, if in consequence of a breach he is deprived of goods, he may be able to recover, not only what he has paid for them, but also money spent on them[78] or loss of profits (subject to the normal limitations on damages, such as remoteness and mitigation). On the other hand, when the injured party claims damages, benefits obtained by him under the contract are, in principle, taken into account;[79] and he will also recover less than the price if he has paid more for the subject-matter than it was worth, or than it would cost to replace. A claim for damages is also subject to practical difficulties, such as quantification and remoteness, which do not arise on a claim for the recovery of money. The question which action should be brought, where both are available,[80] requires a careful weighing of all these factors. It should certainly not be assumed that the action for the recovery of money is necessarily the better remedy.

---

72 *Harling v Eddy* [1951] 2 K.B. 739; cf. *George Wills & Sons Ltd v Thomas Brown & Sons* (1922) 12 Lloyd's Rep. 292, where no discussion as to damages is reported.

73 *Charterhouse Credit Co Ltd v Tolly* [1963] 2 Q.B. 683; *Farnworth Finance Facilities Ltd v Attryde* [1970] 1 W.L.R. 1053; *Doobay v Mohabeer* [1967] 2 A.C. 278.

74 *Mason v Burningham* [1949] 2 K.B. 545; *Warman v Southern Counties Car Finance Corp Ltd* [1949] 2 K.B. 576.

75 *Sampson v Floyd* [1989] 2 E.G.L.R. 49.

76 See paras 20–024 and 20–050 and following; *Greenwood v Bennett* [1973] Q.B. 195 at 201 ("the value of the car as he sold it to them"); *The Rio Sun* [1985] 1 Lloyd's Rep. 351 at 368 ("the value of the oil … on the date when [the buyers] received it"; cf. in case of failure to render services, *Miles v Wakefield MDC* [1987] A.C. 539 at 568; para.17–036, fn.155; *White Arrow Express Ltd v Lamey's Distribution Ltd* [1995] C.L.C. 1251; para.20–049; *Peninsular & Orient SN Co v Youell* [1997] 2 Lloyd's Rep. 136 at 141).

77 *CCC Films (London) Ltd v Impact Quadrant Films Ltd* [1985] Q.B. 16.

78 See the authorities cited in fnn.72 and 74.

79 See para.20–110.

80 See para.20–033.

### (b) Money paid under a void contract

**In general.** The law starts with the assumption that money paid under a void contract can be recovered.[81] Thus in *Bell v Lever Bros Ltd*[82] it was clearly assumed that the money paid by the claimants under the compensation agreements could have been recovered, had those agreements been void for mistake.[83] Where a hire-purchase agreement was wholly void for mistake it was accordingly held that the hirer could recover his deposit; and it does not seem that he was under any liability to pay for the use of the subject-matter of the agreement, which had been in his possession for over three months.[84] Where a contract was void because one of the parties was a company not yet in existence when the contract was made,[85] it was similarly held that instalments paid under it could be recovered by the payor.[86] The same rule has been applied where money was paid under an ultra vires contract[87] and where money was paid under a contract which was void by statute.[88] 22–021

**Basis of the rule allowing recovery.** The general rule that money paid under a void contract can be recovered is clearly established; but there has been some difference of opinion as to its legal basis. This has arisen in cases[89] involving "interest rate swap" contracts under which A (a bank) had made lump sum payments to B (a local authority) which had in turn made some or all of the payments to A which were expressed under the contracts to be due from B to A. The contracts were found to be ultra vires and void[90] because B had no legal power to enter into them and it was argued that A's claim for the recovery of the balance of its payments[91] was barred *either* on the ground that B had made some of the stipulated counter-payments, so that the failure of consideration for A's payments was no more than partial *or* on the ground that the contracts had been fully performed on both sides, so that there had been no failure of consideration at all. For the reasons to be discussed below, however, these arguments were 22–022

[81] e.g. *Re London County Commercial Reinsurance Office* [1922] 2 Ch. 67; cf. *Colesworthy v Collmain Services* [1993] C.C.L.R. 4; aliter if the contract or relevant term is only unenforceable: *Boddington v Lawton* [1994] I.C.R. 478.

[82] [1932] A.C. 161; Landon 51 L.Q.R. 650; Taylor 52 L.Q.R. 27; Landon 52 L.Q.R. 478; Hamson 53 L.Q.R. 118.

[83] See para.8–018.

[84] *Branwhite v Worcester Works Finance Ltd* [1969] 1 A.C. 552 where no claim of this kind was made by the finance company.

[85] See para.16–083.

[86] *Rover International Ltd v Cannon Films Ltd (No.3)* [1989] 1 W.L.R. 912; Birks 2 J.C.L. 227.

[87] *Westdeutsche Landesbank Girozentrale v Islington LBC* [1994] 1 W.L.R. 938.

[88] See the discussion in *Westdeutsche Landesbank Girozentrale v Islington LBC* at first instance and in the Court of Appeal [1994] 4 All E.R. 890 at 921–924; [1994] 1 W.L.R. 938 at 946, 952 of the cases on contracts made void by Grants of Life Annuities Act 1777 (17 Geo. 3 c.26) s.1. This is presumably the "annuity bill" to which Sir Peter Teazle refers in Sheridan's *The School for Scandal*, III.1 (first produced in 1777).

[89] See especially *Westdeutsche Landesbank Girozentrale v Islington LBC* [1994] 4 All E.R. 890; [1994] 1 W.L.R. 938; [1996] A.C. 669 (reversing the decision below on the issue of compound interest only); Birks 32 U.W.A.L.R. 195; Burrows [1995] R.L.R. 15.

[90] See *Hazell v Hammersmith & Fulham LBC* [1992] A.C. 1.

[91] i.e. the amount by which A's payments exceeded B's.

rejected, so that A's claim was upheld in spite of partial performance by B or even full performance by both parties of the void promises.

22–023 **Lack of consideration or failure of consideration?** One reason for allowing A's claim was that the principle on which money paid under a void contract is recoverable differs from that of recovery for "total failure of consideration" under a valid contract. Where the contract is void, the right to recover money paid under it is based, not on failure to perform a contractual obligation (since under a void contract there can be no duty to perform),[92] but on the ground that there is "no legal justification"[93] or "no consideration"[94] for the payment. A second, alternative, reason for upholding A's claim was that there *had* (in the interest rate swap cases) been a total failure of consideration. There are, in turn, two versions of this view. One is that all payments made in pursuance of a void contract are "necessarily made for a consideration which has totally failed".[95] But if there is *necessarily* such a total failure of consideration whenever the contract is void, then there is no *separate* requirement of total failure of consideration: recovery is allowed simply because the contract is void. The other version is that there is a total failure of consideration because A had bargained for B's "*obligation* … to make counter-payments"[96] and the benefit of B's having *in fact* made such payments was different in kind from the benefit for which A had bargained.[97] Again this will be true in all cases in which payments are made under void contracts, so that on this view, too, there is no *separate* requirement of total failure of consideration.[98]

22–024 **Practical considerations.** There are practical grounds for not applying the "total failure of consideration" requirement to claims for the recovery of payments under void contracts. Where the contract is *valid*, a party who is denied the right to recover payments because he has received partial performance will normally have a claim for damages in respect of the part left unperformed. Where, on the other hand, the contract is *void*, denial of restitution of money paid on the ground that the payee has partly performed his void promise, would leave the payor

[92] cf. *Guiness Mahon & Co Ltd v Kensington & Chelsea RLBC* [1999] Q.B. 215 at 236.

[93] *Westdeutsche Landesbank Girozentrale v Islington LBC* [1994] 1 W.L.R. 938 at 953; cf. [1994] 4 All E.R. 890 at 929 ("not contractual payments at all"); *Kleinwort Benson Ltd v Birmingham CC* [1997] Q.B. 380 at 394 ("no justification for the retention of the money").

[94] *South Tyneside MBC v Svenska International Plc* [1995] 1 All E.R. 545 at 577; cf. *Westdeutsche Landesbank Girozentrale v Islington LBC* [1994] 4 All E.R. 890 at 924 ("absence of consideration"); *Kleinwort Benson Ltd v Birmingham CC* [1997] Q.B. 380 at 386–387.

[95] *Guiness Mahon & Co Ltd v Kensington & Chelsea RLBC* [1999] Q.B. 215 at 230.

[96] *Westdeutsche Landesbank Girozentrale v Islington LBC* [1996] A.C. 669 at 711 (emphasis added) approving the reasoning of the Court of Appeal [1994] 1 W.L.R. 938 at 943, per Dillon LJ; Leggatt LJ, [1994] 1 W.L.R. 938 at 951–953 is more equivocal as to the basis of recovery; cf. *Kleinwort Benson Ltd v Glasgow CC* [1999] 1 A.C. 153 at 167, 171.

[97] In this respect these cases can be said to resemble *Rowland v Divall* [1923] 2 K.B. 500; para.22–015.

[98] cf. *Haugesund Kommune v Depfa ACS Bank* [2010] EWCA Civ 579; [2011] 1 All E.R. 190 at [62] where Aikens LJ referred to the distinction between "total failure of consideration" or "absence of consideration" as "a question of which is the more apt terminology; it does not have any legal significance". But see para.22–024.

without any remedy in respect of the unperformed part.[99] In the interest rate swap cases, there is the further point that there was no difficulty in apportioning the partial performance by B to the total performance for which A had bargained, so that one rationale of the requirement that the failure must be total did not exist and the cases could be brought within the exception to that requirement which exists in cases where apportionment is easily achieved.[100] Moreover, where the partial or total performance which has taken place consists simply of payments and counter-payments of money under a void contract, there is no difficulty in restoring each party to its pre-contract position and hence no injustice is likely to result from allowing recovery of the balance. It follows from this reasoning that the right to recover might be barred where supervening events do make such mutual restoration impossible.[101] The interest rate swap cases also do not directly touch the problem which would arise where the performance rendered by one party to a void contract is of such a nature that it cannot literally be restored, e.g. where A had paid a sum of money in advance to B in return for B's promise to render services and after some of the services had been rendered it was discovered that B had no power to enter into the contract so that it was ultra vires and void. It is submitted that in such a case A should be entitled to recover its payment on the ground that the contract was void; but that this right should be subject to B's right to retain so much of that payment as B could have recovered by way of quantum meruit for work done under a void contract.[102]

**Mistake.** Where money is paid under a void contract, the payment will often be made in the mistaken belief that the contract was valid. Such a mistake was not formerly a ground on which the payor was entitled to the return of his money since the mistake was one of law and it had been held that there was no right to recover money paid under a mistake of law (as opposed to one of fact). The authorities which had supported this view[103] were, however, overruled by the House of Lords in *Kleinwort Benson Ltd v Lincoln CC*,[104] where moneys had been paid by a bank to local authorities under interest rate swap contracts which were believed to be valid but which were actually void.[105] It was held that the bank was entitled to recover the moneys on the ground that they had been paid under a mistake of law.[106] It was further held that this right was not barred by the fact that the contract had been fully performed by both parties. The cases which supported the latter proposition where the claim was based, not on mistake, but **22–025**

99 cf. para.22–008.

100 See para.22–010.

101 See *Kleinwort Benson Ltd v South Tyneside MBC* [1994] 4 All E.R. 972.

102 See para.22–034.

103 *Bilbie v Lumley* (1802) 2 East 469; *Brisbane v Dacres* (1813) 5 Taunt. 143; *Kelly v Solari* (1841) 9 M. & W. 54.

104 [1999] 2 A.C. 349; *Nurdin & Peacock Plc v DB Ramsden & Co Ltd* [1999] 1 All E.R. 941.

105 See at fn.90.

106 The claimant may choose to recover either on the basis that the contract is void, or for mistake of law: *Deutsche Morgan Grenfell Group Plc v IRC* [2006] UKHL 49; [2007] 1 A.C. 558. The potential benefit of the latter is the more extensive limitation period applied under the Limitation Act 1980 s.32(1); cf. *Test Claimants in the Franked Investment Income (FII) Group Litigation v Her Majesty's Commissioners for Customs & Excise* [2012] UKSC 19; [2012] 2 A.C. 337.

simply on the fact that the contract was void[107] were referred to with approval, thus further supporting the view that money paid under a void contract is recoverable by the payor even though the circumstances are not such as would have given rise, if the contract had been valid, to a total failure of consideration. The reason for this conclusion was that the policy of the rule making the contract void might be defeated if full or partial performance of the contract were a bar to recovery, e.g. if a local authority were precluded by such a bar from recovering ultra vires payments made in the mistaken belief that they were intra vires and hence legally due.[108]

22–026 **Special cases.** The rule that money paid under a void contract is recoverable is no more than a general one,[109] which may be displaced by the policy considerations underlying the rule of law which makes the contract void. It may, for example, be displaced under the rules (discussed earlier in this book) relating to illegal contracts[110] and minors' contracts.[111]

## 2. RECOVERY OF NON-MONEY BENEFITS[112]

22–027 Here we are concerned with cases in which a party claims a reasonable recompense for some benefit (other than a payment of money) conferred by him under contract or a purported contract: quantum meruit where the benefit is in the form of services and quantum valebat if in the form of goods supplied. Many such cases have already been discussed elsewhere in this book and are mentioned here only for the sake of completeness. In those cases where there is a contract between the parties,[113] there may be an express provision for remuneration on specified events[114] and, where that is the case, the general rule is that the court cannot award any other remuneration on those events, nor can it award any remuneration if they do not occur.[115] To allow quantum meruit claims in such cases would contradict the agreement reached by the parties, and the courts will do this only if there are special circumstances justifying such interference.

22–028 **Valuation of the benefit.** In cases where the court orders the restitution of a non-money benefit and its valuation is not determined by the contract, an award is made for the market value of the benefit provided. This is an objective assessment,[116] but any agreement between the parties as to remuneration for the

[107] e.g. *Westdeutsche Landesbank Girozentrale v Islington LBC* [1994] 4 All E.R. 890; [1994] 1 W.L.R. 938; [1996] A.C. 669; *Guiness Mahon & Co Ltd v Kensington & Chelsea RLBC* [1999] Q.B. 215.

[108] *Kleinwort Benson Ltd v Glasgow CC* [1999] 2 A.C. 349 at 387, 415–416; cf. para.12–084.

[109] *Guiness Mahon & Co Ltd v Kensington & Chelsea RLBC* [1999] Q.B. 215 at 231.

[110] See para.11–092.

[111] See paras 12–037—12–043, 12–049—12–052.

[112] Birks (1974) C.L.P. 13; Jones (1977) 93 L.Q.R. 273.

[113] See paras 22–032, 22–033.

[114] e.g. payment only upon completed performance of an entire obligation: see para.22–033.

[115] *Wiluszynski v Tower Hamlets LBC* [1989] I.C.R. 493.

[116] And often a matter of expert evidence: *MacInnes v Gross* [2017] EWHC 46 (QB) at [184]; *Wright v Rowland* [2017] EWHC 2478 (Comm) at [86]; *AMP Advisory & Management Partners AG v Force India Formula One Team Ltd* [2019] EWHC 2426 (Comm).

benefit in question may be taken as evidence of objective market value.[117] The personal circumstances of the defendant are taken into account if they would have been taken into account by the market, e.g. where the buying power of a particular type of defendant would enable it to acquire services at a lower price than "ordinary" market value.[118] In exceptional circumstances, the market value may be decreased (but not increased)[119] on the basis of the defendant's own personal preferences (so-called "subjective devaluation").[120]

**Recovery based on failure of consideration.** The basis for recovery in these cases is also, as with many of the cases on recovery of money, failure of consideration. Nonetheless, for ease of exposition, and because they may raise slightly different issues, the cases below are analysed by reference to the principal basis on which the contract "failed", e.g. whether the anticipated contract never materialised, whether it was unenforceable, and so on. Precisely because the basis for recovery is failure of consideration, these categories are not exhaustive.[121] **22–029**

**Contracts not providing for remuneration.** A party can claim a sum for work done or a price for goods delivered under a contract which does not expressly provide how much he is to be paid, or which makes some, but not a full, provision for payment.[122] This will be the case where the whole agreement is implied from conduct,[123] or where it is simply silent as to the rate of payment. Sometimes it may be clear from the terms of the agreement, or from the circumstances in which it was made, that the claimant was not intended to have any legal right to be paid at all.[124] But if he was intended to have such a right the court will award a reasonable sum. Thus if a contract for the sale of goods does not fix the price, the buyer must pay a reasonable price;[125] and if a contract for services does not fix the remuneration, a reasonable sum must be paid.[126] In such cases, the claim is based on the enforcement of a payment obligation under the contract and the task of the court is to determine the intention of parties in this regard. This may be contrasted with cases where there is no concluded contract, where the court is required to determine the objective market value of any benefit **22–030**

[117] *MacInnes v Gross* [2017] EWHC 46 (QB) at [166].

[118] *Benedetti v Sawiris* [2013] UKSC 50; [2013] 3 W.L.R. 351.

[119] e.g. the courts will ignore a higher offer made in negotiations for a settlement: *Benedetti v Sawiris* [2013] UKSC 50; [2013] 3 W.L.R. 351.

[120] *Benedetti v Sawiris* [2013] UKSC 50; [2013] 3 W.L.R. 351; Mitchell [2013] L.M.C.L.Q. 436; cf. *Harrison v Madejski and Coys of Kensington* [2014] EWCA Civ 361.

[121] For a recent example of a case which does not readily fall into any of the categories which follow, see *Barnes v Eastenders Group* [2014] UKSC 26; [2015] A.C. 1; para.22–006.

[122] *Sir Lindsay Parkinson & Co Ltd v Commissioners of Works* [1949] 2 K.B. 632; cf. *Steven v Bromley & Son* [1919] 2 K.B. 722; *The Gregos* [1985] 2 Lloyd's Rep. 347; *The Saronikos* [1986] 2 Lloyd's Rep. 277; *Cooke v Hopper* [2012] EWCA Civ 175.

[123] See paras 2–004, 2–018; *Paynter v Williams* (1833) 1 C. & M. 810; cf. *The Batis* [1990] 1 Lloyd's Rep. 345; *The Kurnia Dewi* [1997] 1 Lloyd's Rep. 553.

[124] See paras 4–024, 16–098.

[125] Sale of Goods Act 1979 s.8(2).

[126] Supply of Goods and Services Act 1982 s.15(1); cf. at common law *Way v Latilla* [1937] 3 All E.R. 759; *Berezovsky v Edmiston & Co Ltd* [2011] EWCA Civ 431; [2011] 1 C.L.C. 922.

received.[127] It has been said that "the exercise of ascertaining what objectively [the parties] would have contemplated was a reasonable amount, is a very different exercise from that which is required of the court in the context of a restitutionary quantum meruit claim".[128] But since market value is the price which a reasonable recipient in the position of the defendant would have paid,[129] and an implied term (as to price) is also reached on an objective basis, i.e. what the parties, *as reasonable persons*, would have agreed,[130] the difference in practice may not be that great.

22–031 **No concluded contract.**[131] Work may be done and a quantum meruit awarded to the party who has done the work where the parties believe that there is a contract but this is not the case because there was never a clear acceptance of an offer.[132] Such an award may also be made where work is done, under an agreement which lacks contractual force for want of contractual intention,[133] in anticipation of a formal contract which fails to materialise for want of execution of the requisite formal document;[134] and where one party does work at the request of the other during negotiations which are expected to lead to a contract between them but are broken off before its conclusion.[135] But no such award will be made where the party doing the work takes the risk that the negotiations may fail. This was held to be the position where one party to an agreement "subject to contract"[136] incurred expenses without any request from, and without benefitting, the other but solely for the purpose of securing (and then of performing) the contract.[137]

22–032 **Contract terminated for breach: claim by innocent party.** Termination for breach operates prospectively and does not affect obligations and rights which accrued prior to termination;[138] if, at that time, the claimant has performed his

[127] See para.22–031.

[128] *Energy Venture Partners Ltd v Malabu Oil & Gas Ltd* [2013] EWHC 2118 (Comm) at [283]; cf. *Benedetti v Sawiris* [2013] UKSC 50; [2013] 3 W.L.R. 351 at [9].

[129] See text to fn.117.

[130] See para.6–054.

[131] Barker 19 J.C.L. 105; Edelman in Burrows and Peel (eds), *Contract Formation and Parties* (2010).

[132] *Peter Lind & Co Ltd v Mersey Docks & Harbour Board* [1972] 2 Lloyd's Rep. 234; para.2–020.

[133] *Galliard Homes Ltd v Jarvis Interiors Ltd* [2000] C.L.C. 411; *AMP Advisory & Management Partners AG v Force India Formula One Team Ltd* [2019] EWHC 2426 (Comm).

[134] *Galliard Homes Ltd v Jarvis Interiors Ltd* [2000] C.L.C. 411. This was accepted by both parties (though doubted by Evans LJ); *Rotam Agrochemical Co Ltd v GAT Microencapsulation* GmbH [2018] EWHC 2765 (Comm).

[135] *William Lacey (Hounslow) Ltd v Davis* [1957] 1 W.L.R. 932; *BSC v Cleveland Bridge & Engineering Co Ltd* [1984] 1 All E.R. 504; Ball 99 L.Q.R. 572; *Marston Construction Co v Kigass* (1990) 15 Con L.R. 116; Key 111 L.Q.R. 576; *Countrywide Communications Ltd v ICL Pathway Ltd* [2000] C.L.C. 324; *Cobbe v Yeoman's Row Management Ltd* [2008] UKHL 55; [2008] 1 W.L.R. 1752; *Whittle Movers Ltd v Hollywood Express Ltd* [2009] EWCA Civ 1189; [2009] 2 C.L.C. 771; Davies 126 L.Q.R. 175; *Killen v Horseworld Ltd* [2011] EWHC 1600 (QB).

[136] See para.2–096.

[137] *Regalian Properties Plc v London Dockland Development Corp* [1995] 1 W.L.R. 212, where *Marston Construction Co v Kigass* (1990) 15 Con L.R. 116 was at 229 described as a "surprising decision"; cf. *Blue Haven Enterprises Ltd v Tully* [2006] UKPC 17; *MSM Consulting Ltd v Tanzania* [2009] EWHC 121 (QB); 123 Con L.R. 154 at [171](d).

[138] See para.18–017.

part of the contract by carrying out work,[139] he will be confined to his action on the contract, e.g. in debt, or in damages.[140] Where he has been prevented from completing performance of an obligation he can claim a quantum meruit at the contract rate[141] for work done, even though the unperformed obligation is entire.[142] The party in breach cannot complain of having to pay in circumstances other than those provided for by the contract.

**Contract terminated for breach: claim by party in breach.** In Ch.17 we saw that, in general, a person who failed to complete performance of an entire obligation could not recover anything;[143] but that this rule was subject to a number of exceptions.[144] Under some of these, there is a right to payment of the contract price or at the contract rate. Under others, there is a right to a quantum meruit (or reasonable remuneration), e.g. where a benefit conferred by partial performance of services is "voluntarily" accepted by the other party. **22–033**

In a number of further exceptional cases, a reasonable sum is, or may be, payable for services rendered by the party in breach even though the services differ from, or fall short of, those bargained for, there has been no "voluntary" acceptance of them by the injured party, and the contract remains in force. For example, it has been said that a carrier by sea who deviates but carries the goods to the agreed destination can recover a reasonable freight;[145] and conflicting views have been expressed on the question whether an employer who "of necessity" accepts services falling short of those bargained for is liable to his employee for a quantum meruit.[146] Such exceptional cases are controversial precisely because they reveal a conflict between two policies. One is that the court should not unjustifiably contradict a subsisting contract by awarding a reasonable sum for services falling short of those promised; the other is that the court should not allow the injured party to have the benefit of those services for nothing, since this would lead to his being unjustly enriched. The exact scope and rationale of the present group of exceptional cases must therefore remain very much in doubt.

---

[139] For payments which have been made, termination may be given a retrospective effect: see para.22–012.

[140] *Taylor v Motability Finance* Ltd [2004] EWHC 2619 (Comm) at [25]; *Howes Percival v Page* [2013] EWHC 4104 (Ch); *Elek v Bar-Tur* [2013] EWHC 207 (Ch); [2013] 2 E.G.L.R 159.

[141] *Taylor v Motability Finance* Ltd [2004] EWHC 2619 (Comm) at [26]; *Elek v Bar-Tur* [2013] EWHC 207 (Ch); [2013] 2 E.G.L.R 159; cf. *Lusty v Finsbury Securities* (1991) 58 Build. L.R. 66; *Kehoe v Borough of Rutherford* 27 A 912 (1893); *Vedatech Corp v Crystal Decisions (UK) Ltd* [2002] EWHC 818 at [76]–[79]. There is support for the award of the actual value of the work without reference to the contract price: *Lodder v Slowey* [1904] A.C. 442; *Boomer v Muir* 24 P.2d. 570 (1933) but it seems absurd that the injured party should recover more for partial, than he could recover for full, performance; and the application of the contract rate may be justified as an example of "subjective devaluation": see text to fn.120; cf. *Mann v Paterson Constructions Pty Ltd* [2019] HCA 32. Where one party, after the other's breach, does *extra* work, the reasonable sum recoverable for the work may exceed the damages recoverable for the breach: *The Batis* [1990] 1 Lloyd's Rep. 345.

[142] See para.17–046.

[143] See paras 17–031—17–034.

[144] See paras 17–041—17–045.

[145] *Hain SS Co Td v Tate & Lyle Ltd* (1936) 41 Com. Cas. 350 at 358, 367; para.17–044, fn.204.

[146] *Miles v Wakefield Metropolitan DC* [1987] A.C. 539 at 552–553, 561; para.17–045; cf. *Wiluszynski v Tower Hamlets LBC* [1989] I.C.R. 493.

22–034 **Contract void.** In *Craven-Ellis v Canons Ltd*[147] the claimant worked for the defendant company as managing director. His service agreement with the company was void as neither he nor those who appointed him held the necessary qualification shares.[148] Thus he could not recover his agreed pay.[149] But the Court of Appeal held that he was entitled to a quantum meruit. The position is the same where a contract with a company is void because the company was not yet in existence or had been dissolved[150] when the contract was made.[151] A similar principle may apply where goods have been supplied under a contract of sale which is void for a mistake as to the identity of the buyer.[152]

Where the express contract is a nullity, the argument that the court must not interfere with the bargain between the parties loses much of its force.[153] It does not seem that liability in these cases is based on an agreement which can be implied from voluntary acceptance by the defendant of the claimant's services,[154] for the parties usually think that they are acting under an existing valid contract.[155] In *Craven-Ellis v Canons Ltd* Greer LJ said that the liability to pay a quantum meruit "is an inference which a rule of law imposes on the parties where work has been done or goods have been delivered under what purports to be a binding contract but is not so in fact".[156]

The principle just stated may, however, be displaced by countervailing policy considerations. In *Guinness Plc v Saunders*[157] a company director did work for the company in the course of negotiations for a take-over bid which was being made by the company. The agreement under which the work was done was void because those who purported to make it on behalf of the company had no authority to do so.[158] It was held that the director was not entitled to quantum meruit since the terms of the agreement (by which his remuneration increased with the amount paid by the company) gave rise to a conflict between his own financial interest and his fiduciary duty to the company as one of its directors.

22–035 **Contract frustrated.** Work done under a contract *before* it is frustrated does not give rise to any quantum meruit claim at common law, though a claim in respect of a valuable benefit conferred by such work can be made under the Law Reform (Frustrated Contracts) Act 1943.[159] But if work is done under the contract *after* frustration, it may be possible to claim a quantum meruit on the principle of

---

[147] [1936] 2 K.B. 403; Denning 55 L.Q.R. 54.

[148] See now Companies Act 2006 ss.40, 41; para.12–071.

[149] cf. *Re Bodega Co* [1904] 1 Ch. 276: if he is paid his contractual remuneration he must pay it back.

[150] See para.16–083.

[151] *Rover International Ltd v Cannon Films Ltd* (*No.3*) [1989] 1 W.L.R. 912; *Cotronic (UK) Ltd v Dezonie* [1991] B.C.L.C. 721; para.16–083.

[152] e.g. on the facts of *Boulton v Jones* (1857) 27 L.J. Ex. 117; for the exact nature of the appropriate remedy in such a situation, see para.8–049.

[153] *Rover International Ltd v Cannon Films Ltd (No.3)* [1989] 1 W.L.R. 912 at 927.

[154] Contra, Denning 55 L.Q.R. 54.

[155] And, for the same reason that the contract was void in the first place, there was no one qualified to "accept" the benefit; the company is viewed as having obtained the "incontrovertible benefit" of the director's services: Birks 24 C.L.P. 110.

[156] *Craven-Ellis v Canons Ltd* [1936] 2 K.B. 403 at 410.

[157] [1990] 2 A.C. 663; Beatson and Prentice 106 L.Q.R. 365.

[158] See now Companies Act 2006 ss.40, 41; para.12–071.

[159] Law Reform (Frustrated Contracts) Act 1943 s.1(3); para.19–110.

*Craven-Ellis v Canons Ltd.* The argument that the court must not interfere with the express contract is here met by the fact that the contract has no longer any legal force. A contract for the carriage of goods may be frustrated because the method of performance becomes impossible. The carrier may nonetheless get the goods to their destination in some other way. So long as he acts reasonably in doing so, he can claim a quantum meruit. It is irrelevant that a new contract cannot be implied from the mere fact that the cargo-owner accepts the cargo at its destination.[160]

**Contract unenforceable.** Work done under a contract which is unenforceable, e.g. for want of formality,[161] or because it is in restraint of trade,[162] may give rise to a quantum meruit provided such payment does not undermine the policy of the rule which rendered the contract unenforceable.[163] **22–036**

**Incapacity.** Where necessaries are sold and delivered to a minor, he need only pay a reasonable price for them, although he may have agreed to pay more.[164] There are obvious reasons of policy for interfering with the agreement in such a case. There would be no such reasons where the minor had agreed to pay less than a reasonable price. **22–037**

---

[160] *The Massalia* [1961] 2 Q.B. 278; overruled in *The Eugenia* [1964] 2 Q.B. 226, but not on this point.

[161] *Scarisbrick v Pattison* (1869) 20 L.T. 175; cf. *Pulbrook v Lawes* (1876) 1 Q.B.D. 284; *Deglman v Guaranty Trust Co of Canada and Constantineau* [1954] 3 D.L.R. 785; *Pavey & Matthews Ltd v Paul* (1987) 69 A.L.J.R. 577.

[162] *Proactive Sports Management Ltd v Rooney* [2011] EWCA Civ 1444; [2012] I.R.L.R. 241.

[163] *Pavey & Matthews Ltd v Paul* (1986) 162 C.L.R. 221 at 584–585; Beatson 104 L.Q.R. 13; cf. *Dimond v Lovell* [2002] 1 A.C. 384 at 398; *Langsam v Beachcroft LLP* [2011] EWHC 1451 (Ch); [2011] 3 Costs L.O. 380 at [253].

[164] See para.12–010; the same is also sometimes true where necessaries are sold and delivered to a person incapacitated by other factors, such as mental illness, drink or drugs: paras 12–053—12–064.

# INDEX

LEGAL TAXONOMY
FROM SWEET & MAXWELL

This index has been prepared using Sweet & Maxwell's Legal Taxonomy. Main index entries conform to keywords provided by the Legal Taxonomy except where references to specific documents or non-standard terms (denoted by quotation marks) have been included. These keywords provide a means of identifying similar concepts in other Sweet & Maxwell publications and online services to which keywords from the Legal Taxonomy have been applied. Readers may find some minor differences between terms used in the text and those which appear in the index. Suggestions to *sweetandmaxwell.taxonomy@tr.com*.

**All references are to paragraph number**